A

TOPOGRAPHICAL DICTIONARY

OF

ENGLAND,

IN FOUR VOLUMES

A TOPOGRAPHICAL DICTIONARY OF ENGLAND

By Samuel Lewis

VOLUME III

CLEARFIELD

Originally published, London, 1831
Reprinted, four volumes in two, 1996, by
Genealogical Publishing Co , Inc
Baltimore, Maryland

Reprinted in the original four-volume format, 2018, by
Genealogical Publishing Company for
Clearfield Company
Baltimore, Maryland

ISBN Volume III 9780806358697
Set ISBN 9780806315089

A

TOPOGRAPHICAL DICTIONARY

OF

ENGLAND,

COMPRISING THE

SEVERAL COUNTIES, CITIES, BOROUGHS, CORPORATE AND MARKET TOWNS,
PARISHES, CHAPELRIES, AND TOWNSHIPS,
AND THE ISLANDS OF GUERNSEY, JERSEY, AND MAN,

WITH

HISTORICAL AND STATISTICAL DESCRIPTIONS;

ILLUSTRATED BY

MAPS OF THE DIFFERENT COUNTIES AND ISLANDS,

AND EMBELLISHED WITH

ENGRAVINGS OF THE ARMS OF THE CITIES, BISHOPRICKS, UNIVERSITIES, COLLEGES, CORPORATE TOWNS,
AND BOROUGHS, AND OF THE SEALS OF THE SEVERAL MUNICIPAL CORPORATIONS

BY SAMUEL LEWIS.

IN FOUR VOLUMES

VOL III

— — ◆ ——

LONDON
PUBLISHED BY S LEWIS AND CO, 87, ALDERSGATE-STREET
M DCCC XXXI

A

TOPOGRAPHICAL DICTIONARY

OF

ENGLAND.

LACEBY, a parish in the wapentake of BRADLEY-HAVERSTOE, parts of LINDSEY, county of LINCOLN, 4½ miles (W S. W) from Great Grimsby, containing 523 inhabitants The living is a rectory, in the archdeaconry and diocese of Lincoln, rated in the king's books at £12 0 10 John Fardell, Esq was patron in 1819 The church is dedicated to St Margaret There is a place of worship for Wesleyan Methodists Sarah Stamford, in 1720, erected a school-house, and endowed it with land producing a comfortable maintenance for a master, who instructs the children belonging to the several parishes of Laceby, Bradley, and Barnoldby

LACK-DENNIS, a township in that part of the parish of GREAT BUDWORTH which is in the hundred of NORTHWICH, county palatine of CHESTER, 3¾ miles (E S E) from Northwich, containing 44 inhabitants

LACKFORD, a parish in the hundred of THIN-GOE, county of SUFFOLK, 5⅓ miles (N W by N) from Bury-St. Edmund s, containing 163 inhabitants The living is a rectory, in the archdeaconry of Sudbury, and diocese of Norwich, rated in the king's books at £19 10 5 Sir Charles E Kent, Bart was patron in 1807 The church is dedicated to St Lawrence The navigable river Lark runs on the northern side of this parish, and is there crossed by a bridge.

LACKINGTON (WHITE), a parish in the hundred of ABDICK and BULSTONE, county of SOMERSET, 1½ mile (E N E) from Ilminster, containing 242 inhabitants. The living is a discharged vicarage, in the archdeaconry of Taunton, and diocese of Bath and Wells, rated in the king's books at £7 10, endowed with £200 private benefaction, and £200 royal bounty, and in the patronage of the Prebendary of White Lackington in the Cathedral Church of Wells The church, dedicated to St Mary, has two small transepts and an embattled western tower

LACON, a township in that part of the parish of WEM which is in the Whitchurch division of the hundred of BRADFORD (North), county of SALOP, containing 45 inhabitants

LADBROOKE, a parish in the Southam division of the hundred of KNIGHTLOW, county of WARWICK, 1¼ mile (S) from Southam, containing 251 inhabitants.

The living is a rectory, in the archdeaconry of Coventry, and diocese of Lichfield and Coventry, rated in the king s books at £13 10, and in the patronage of Charles Palmer, Esq The church is dedicated to All Saints

LADOCK, a parish in the eastern division of the hundred of POWDER, county of CORNWALL, 4¼ miles (N W) from Grampound, containing 806 inhabitants The living is a rectory, in the archdeaconry of Cornwall, and diocese of Exeter, rated in the king's books at £18 Lord and Lady Grenville were patrons in 1814. The church is dedicated to St Ladoca. There is a place of worship for Wesleyan Methodists The small village of Pessick, in this parish, is remarkable for the picturesque beauty of its situation The Rev John Elliott, in 1763, left £5 a year for teaching children

LAINDON, a parish in the hundred of BARSTABLE, county of ESSEX, 3½ miles (S by E) from Billericay, containing, with the chapelry of Basildon, 544 inhabitants The living is a rectory, in the archdeaconry of Essex and Herts, concurrently with the Commissary of Essex and Herts, and in the jurisdiction of the Consistorial Court of the Bishop of London, rated in the king s books at £35 6 8., and in the patronage of the Bishop of London. The church is dedicated to St Nicholas

LAINSON, a parish in the hundred of MANS-BRIDGE, Fawley division of the county of SOUTH-AMPTON, 3 miles (N W) from Winchester The population is returned with the parish of Sparsholt The living is a discharged rectory, in the archdeaconry and diocese of Winchester, rated in the king's books at £2 13 4, and endowed with £600 royal bounty The Rt Hon. W H Freemantle and his Lady were patrons in 1826

LAITH-KIRK, a chapelry in the parish of ROMALD-KIRK, western division of the wapentake of GILLING, North riding of the county of YORK, 9 miles (N W) from Barnard-Castle The population is returned with the parish

LAKE, a tything in the parish of WILSFORD, hundred of UNDERDITCH, county of WILTS, 2½ miles (S W) from Amesbury The population is returned with the parish

B

LAKENHAM, county of NORFOLK.—See NORWICH

LAKENHEATH, a parish in the hundred of LACKFORD, county of SUFFOLK, 5¾ miles (N) from Mildenhall, containing 1042 inhabitants   The living is a discharged vicarage, with Undley, in the archdeaconry of Sudbury, and diocese of Norwich, rated in the king's books at £4 18 11½, endowed with £200 private benefaction, £200 royal bounty, and £400 parliamentary grant, and in the patronage of the Dean and Chapter of Ely   The church is dedicated to St Mary   There are places of worship for Huntingtonians and Wesleyan Methodists   The navigable Little Ouse runs on the north of the parish

LALEHAM, a parish in the hundred of SPELTHORNE, county of MIDDLESEX, 2 miles (S S E) from Staines, containing 499 inhabitants   The living is a perpetual curacy, annexed to the vicarage of Staines, in the archdeaconry of Middlesex, and diocese of London   The church is dedicated to All Saints

LAMARSH, a parish in the hundred of HINCKFORD, county of ESSEX, 7¼ miles (N E by E) from Halstead, containing 331 inhabitants   The living is a rectory, in the jurisdiction of the Commissary of Essex and Herts, concurrently with the Consistorial Court of the Bishop of London, rated in the king's books at £12 0 2½   Henry Sperling, Esq was patron in 1803   The church is dedicated to the Holy Innocents   The navigable river Stour runs on the eastern side of the parish

LAMBCROFT, a hamlet in the parish of KELSTERN, Wold division of the hundred of LOUTH-ESKE, parts of LINDSEY, county of LINCOLN, containing 31 inhabitants

LAMBERHURST, a parish partly in the hundred of BRENCHLEY and HORSEMONDEN, lathe of AYLESFORD, county of KENT, but chiefly in the hundred of LOXFIELD-PELHAM, rape of PEVENSEY, county of SUSSEX, 15 miles (S W by S.) from Maidstone, containing 1325 inhabitants   The living is a vicarage, in the archdeaconry and diocese of Rochester, rated in the king's books at £12 10 5, and in the patronage of the Dean and Chapter of Rochester   The church is dedicated to St. Mary   Here is a place of worship for Baptists   There were formerly very extensive ironworks in this parish, the ore having been obtained in the neighbourhood the balustrades of St. Paul's cathedral were cast at these works   Dame Elizabeth Hanby, in 1712, bequeathed a rent-charge of £6, for the instruction of children

LAMBETH, a parish in the eastern division of the hundred of BRIXTON, county of SURREY, separated from Westminster by the river Thames, comprising the hamlets of Brixton, Kennington, Stockwell, Vauxhall, a part of Norwood, and the extra-parochial liberty of Lambeth palace, and containing 57,638 inhabitants, according to the census of 1821, since which period the population has nearly doubled.   The name of this place, in the earliest records written Lambehith, and in Domesday book Lanchei, is variously written by the ancient historians, and, according to Camden, denotes a muddy station, or harbour, by other antiquaries it is supposed to have been originally Lamb's Hithe, and to have denoted a haven belonging to some ancient proprietor of that name   Canute, on his invasion of London, in 1026, is said to have cut a trench through

this parish, in order to convey his fleet to the west of London bridge, of which Maitland, in his History of London, affirms that he discovered evident traces , but the origin of these trenches is by other historians attributed, with greater probability, to a temporary diversion of the course of the river, for the erection of London bridge   At the end of Kennington-lane there were, till very lately, the remains of a horn-work, forming part of the lines of communication made, by order of parliament, round the metropolis, for its greater security during the parliamentary war   The manor of Lambeth was given by Goda, sister of Edward the Confessor, to the see of Rochester, one of whose bishops, Gilbert de Glanville, finding the buildings of his see greatly dilapidated, erected at Lambeth, in 1197, a mansion for himself and his successors, exchanged for other lands with Hubert Walter, Archbishop of Canterbury, became the archiepiscopal residence   Archbishop Boniface having obtained from Pope Urban IV the grant of a fourth part of the offerings at Becket's shrine, and permission to rebuild his house at Lambeth, laid the foundation of the present palace, which has been at various times enlarged and improved by his successors   Many of the metropolitan councils were held in the chapel of the palace while it belonged to the see of Rochester, in 1100, Archbishop Anselm convened an assembly to take into consideration the propriety of the marriage of Henry I with Maud, daughter of the King of Scotland, who had taken the veil, though not the vows, as a nun   After the exchange, a council was held here by Archbishop Peckham, at which a subsidy of one-fifteenth was granted by the clergy for three years , and, in 1282, the same prelate convoked a synod, at which all the bishops of the realm assisted, to deliberate upon the state of the church of England, of which complaints had been made at Rome to the Bishop of Hereford.   In 1381, the followers of Wat Tyler, after having barbarously put Archbishop Sudbury to death, attacked the palace, burnt the furniture and books, and destroyed all the registers and public papers   Henry VII was, for some days previous to his coronation, sumptuously entertained in the palace by Archbishop Bourchier ; and Catherine of Arragon, on her first arrival in England, remained there with her attendants for some days prior to her marriage   The palace was completely furnished by Queen Mary, for the reception of Cardinal Pole, whom she occasionally visited during his primacy , and Queen Elizabeth, during the time of Archbishops Parker and Whitgift, was a frequent guest at Lambeth, where she sometimes remained for several days.   Prior to the Reformation, the archbishops had a prison in the palace, for the confinement of offenders against the ecclesiastical laws, and Elizabeth frequently made it a place of liberal confinement, for persons who had fallen under her displeasure , to this place she committed the Catholic bishops, Tunstall and Thirlby , the Earl of Essex, previously to his being sent to the Tower, the Earl of Southampton, Lord Stourton, Henry Howard, brother of the Duke of Norfolk, and various other persons   In 1641, Archbishop Laud was attacked by a puritanical mob of five hundred persons, who assailed the palace at midnight , but having received intimation of their design, he had so fortified it as to preclude their doing further injury than breaking the windows

After the impeachment of Archbishop Laud, an ordinance was issued by the House of Commons, for removing the arms from Lambeth palace, which was carried into effect by Captain Royden, at the head of two hundred infantry and a troop of horse, and in the November following, Captain Brown entered to take possession of the palace for the parliament It was afterwards converted into a prison by the House of Commons, and among the prisoners confined there, were the Earls of Chesterfield and Derby, Sir Thomas Armstrong, who was afterwards executed at Kennington for having taken part in Monmouth s rebellion, Sir George Bunkley, and some others The palace being afterwards put up for sale, was purchased by Thomas Scot and Matthew Hardy, the former of whom, secretary to Cromwell, sat in judgment at the trial of Charles I, and was afterwards hanged as a regicide at Charing-Cross After the Restoration, Lambeth palace again reverted to its rightful owners, and became the residence of the archbishops During the riots occasioned by the assembling of the Protestant Association in 1780, under an impression that Archbishop Cornwallis was a favourer of the Roman Catholics, several hundreds of the mob, which had collected in St. George's Fields, proceeded to Lambeth, and raising the cry of No Popery, knocked loudly at the gate of the palace, but failing to obtain admission, withdrew, threatening to return in the evening, in the mean time the archbishop, with his family, retired to the house of Lord Hilsborough, in the county of Kent, and a detachment of the military being sent for the defence of the palace, it escaped further violence The palace has at various times afforded an asylum to learned foreigners, whom the intolerant spirit of their own countrymen had compelled to abandon their native land, among these were the early reformers, Martyr and Bucer, the learned Anthonio de Dominis, Archbishop of Spalatro, and numerous others This venerable pile of building, now undergoing a very extensive repair, and to which considerable additions are being made, is situated on the southern bank of the river Thames, and exhibits in its architecture the styles of various ages The principal entrance, through an arched gateway, flanked by two square embattled towers of brick, leads into the outer court, on the right hand of which is the great hall, rebuilt after the civil war by Archbishop Juxon, and since converted into a library it is a lofty structure of brick, strengthened with buttresses, and ornamented with cornices and quoins of stone, the interior is lighted by ranges of lofty windows, and by a double lanthern turret rising from the roof, which is finely arched, and richly ornamented with carved oak, in the windows are some heraldic devices in stained glass, and over the fire-places, at each end, are the arms, richly emblazoned, of Archbishop Bancroft, the founder of the library, and of Archbishop Secker, by whom it was augmented. Beyond the library is the chapel, which is by far the most ancient part of the building it is in the earliest style of English architecture, lighted on the sides by triple lancet-shaped windows, and by an east window of five lights The ancient painted glass, containing a series of subjects from the Old and the New Testament, the repairing of which was, on his trial, imputed as a crime to Archbishop Laud, was afterwards destroyed by the parliamentarian commissioners the roof, which is flat and divided into compartments, is embellished with the arms of that pre-

late A massive oak screen, richly carved, separates a portion of the western extremity from that part of the chapel which is fitted up for divine service Underneath the chapel is a spacious crypt, the roof of which is finely groined, and to the west of it is the Lollards tower, a lofty square embattled structure of stone, similar to that of the chapel, and formerly used as a prison The guard-room has been taken down, and is at present being rebuilt for a banquet hall, it is of Portland-stone, and in the later style of English architecture the original oak roof, of similar character to that of the library, has been carefully preserved, and will form a prominent and interesting feature in the new edifice From the first court, a handsome archway on the right leads into the area in which the additional buildings are being erected, these form a fine range, also in the later style of English architecture, decorated with turrets, and containing the state apartments, lodging-rooms, and the various offices requisite for the household establishment, in this part of the building are several windows of fine proportion, and some oriel windows of elegant design. The gardens and park, comprising thirteen acres, are tastefully laid out, and through the latter is a pleasant carriage road to the palace Carlisle house, formerly the residence of the Bishops of Rochester, and at that time called " La Place," was given by Henry VIII to Aldridge, Bishop of Carlisle, and, after having been for many years occupied as a private academy, it has almost disappeared in the recent improvements of the parish, and only some portions of the outer walls are remaining

Lambeth, originally a detached village, is now in fact united with Southwark, and may be considered as forming a suburb of the metropolis The great road from London to Portsmouth leads through the parish, by Vauxhall, and a new road, leading from Waterloo bridge to Newington, communicates with the preceding, and with other roads diverging into the counties of Kent, Sussex, and Hampshire There are two establishments for supplying Thames water to this district, the Lambeth water works, situated in Belvidere road, and the South London water-works, at Vauxhall bridge Lambeth was formerly celebrated for its medicinal well, of which the memorial is preserved in the name of a public house called the Fountain, and for its numerous places of public amusement, the principal of which were Cuper s gardens, and Spring gardens, now Vauxhall, the former, belonging to the Earl of Arundel, and constituting part of the gardens of Arundel house, were, by Mr Cuper, the earl s gardener, converted into a place of entertainment, consisting of music and fire-works, and upon the demolition of that mansion, in order to form a new street, became the depository of many of the Arundelian marbles brought from Italy by that nobleman, and, from their mutilated and imperfect state, deemed unworthy of a place in that splendid collection Among them were several beautiful, though imperfect, specimens of sculpture, of which, the best were purchased for the decoration of their seats, by several persons of distinction. The latter, as a fashionable place of public entertainment, has continued, under the highest patronage, to flourish with increasing splendour and additional attractions, the beauty of the scenery, the brilliancy of the illuminations, the rich and varied display of fireworks, the efficiency and talent of the orchestra, the gay assemblage of fashionable company, and the excellence of the numerous arrangements provided for their accommodation, have given to this scene of splendid gaiety an irresistible claim to the public patronage In this parish are also Astley's amphitheatre, near Westminster Bridge, and the Coburg theatre, in the Waterloo-road Lambeth, extending for a considerable way on the banks of the river, and connected with the opposite shore by Waterloo, Westminster, and Vauxhall bridges, is admirably situated for the carrying on of extensive works of every kind, and, in addition to what may be considered as the general trade of the place, there are, on the largest scale, lime, coal, and timber wharfs, iron and other foundries, saw-mills, manufactories for axle-trees, carriages, patent buoys, floorcloth, Morocco and Spanish leather, pins, varnish, saltpetre, soap, whiting, and patent shot (of which the lofty towers form conspicuous objects on the bank of the river), potteries of stone and earthenware, glass works, distilleries, ale and beer breweries, vitriol and other chemical works, vinegar works, and various others there is also a very extensive establishment for making steam-engines and almost every other kind of machinery, on the largest scale, conducted by Mr Maudesley, besides artificial stone works, and numerous other establishments of various kinds A weekly market, and a fair for fifteen days, granted in the reign of John, have long been discontinued The parish is within the jurisdiction of a court of requests held in the borough of Southwark, for the recovery of debts under £5, and within the limits of the New Police establishment.

The living is a rectory, in the archdeaconry of Surrey, and diocese of Winchester, rated in the king's books at £32 15 7½, and in the patronage of the Archbishop of Canterbury The church, dedicated to St. Mary, adjoining the palace, and rebuilt in the latter part of the fourteenth century, is a spacious structure in the early and decorated styles of English architecture, with some later insertions, and having a square embattled tower of freestone, with an octagonal turret at one of the angles The interior comprises the chapels of the Howard and Leigh families, subsequently erected, and contains numerous ancient and interesting records in one of the windows of the nave is the figure of a pedlar with his dog, painted in glass, supposed to be the rebus of a person named *Chapman*, who is thought to have given a piece of land to the parish, which is called Pedlar s Acre, formerly producing two shillings and sixpence per annum, now more than £200 Among the interments are those of Archbishops Bancroft, Secker, Tenison, Hutton, and Cornwallis, of Tunstall, Bishop of Durham, Thirlby, Bishop of Ely, and other distinguished prelates, several of the Howards, and other illustrious families, together with a curious monument of Col Robert Scot, and one of Elias Ashmole, who presented to the University of Oxford the museum which is distinguished by his name Among the numerous tombs in the church-yard are those of William Faden, the original printer of the Public Ledger, and John Tradescant, the original collector of the Ashmolean Museum The burial-ground in High-street was consecrated in 1705 Four new district churches have been erected in this parish by aid of the parliamentary commissioners, who granted one moiety of the cost, and a loan of the other

moiety to be repaid by a rate on the inhabitants, all of them were completed in 1824 St John s, in the Waterloo road, containing two thousand and thirty-two sittings, of which eight hundred and fifty-one are free, and built at an expense of £15,911 16 7, is a handsome structure in the Grecian style of architecture, with a tower of two stages, of which the upper is surmounted by a neat spire, terminating in a ball and cross, and having a fine portico of six columns of the Doric order supporting an entablature and triangular pediment. St Mark s at Kennington, St Matthew's at Brixton-Causeway, and St Luke s at Norwood, are described in the accounts of these places the livings are all district incumbencies, in the patronage of the Rector of Lambeth St Mary s chapel, at Lambeth Butts, erected in 1828, also by grant from the parliamentary commissioners, at an expense of £7634 10 4, and containing one thousand nine hundred and sixty sittings, of which one thousand three hundred and forty-seven are free, is a neat edifice in the later style of English architecture, with a campanile turret surmounted by a spire it is a chapel of ease to the rectory, as is also the chapel at Stockwell St Mark's, Kennington lane, St Matthew s, Denmark Hill, and the chapel at South Lambeth, are proprietary Episcopal chapels There are places of worship for Baptists, Independents, Wesleyan and Welch Methodists, and Swedenborgians

A parochial school for boys was established by subscription, in the early part of the last century, and is supported by the same means, together with a fund of nearly £1200 in the three per cents the school-room has been neatly rebuilt, on ground belonging to the see of Canterbury, and let by the archbishop, at a peppercorn rent there are about four hundred scholars in this institution, of whom, from thirty to forty are clothed annually, and several apprenticed. A parochial school for girls was established in 1780 it is supported by subscriptions, from the savings of which, and some donations, it has realised a fund of £400 in the three per cents there are two hundred girls in the school, of whom, forty are clothed Archbishop Tenison, in 1715, founded a school which he endowed with a house and land, for the clothing and instruction of twelve girls, the endowment, augmented with subsequent benefactions, produces about £350 per annum the school-room has been rebuilt upon an extensive scale, and the number of girls (each of whom, on producing a certificate of good conduct during a service of three years, receives a small gratuity,) has been increased Richard Lawrence, in 1661, gave two houses, with ground attached to them, in trust, for the clothing and instruction of twenty children of Lambeth Marsh, in one of which the school was formerly held, but becoming dilapidated, it was removed to a neat and commodious building, erected, in 1808, in the York road, by subscription, in which the children, for whose benefit the original endowment, producing £100 per annum, is appropriated, are instructed, in common with the children of the parish St John s school, in the Waterloo road, was rebuilt by subscription, at an expense of £2200, to which his late Majesty George IV gave £100 The Eldon school, on the road to Wandsworth, was instituted, in 1830, for the instruction of the children of the parishes of Lambeth, Battersea, and Clapham, in the National religion, and for the training of young men to act as teachers on the National system, the children, on leaving school, are placed out apprentices the building, which is in the later style of English architecture, was erected in commemoration of Lord Chancellor Eldon, at the sole expense of Charles Francis, Esq, by whom the school is supported　The Licensed Victuallers' school, in Kennington-lane in this parish, was established for the maintenance, clothing, and education, of children of deceased and indigent members of that society　the buildings are neat and commodious, and the regulations, both of the house and the school, in which there are at present eighty-nine boys, and eighty-nine girls, are well adapted to secure the important objects for which it was established　The asylum for female orphans, and for the reception of deserted females, the settlement of whose parents cannot be found, was first instituted in 1758, and incorporated in 1800　it is under the patronage of Her Royal Highness the Duchess of Cambridge, and the direction of a general committee (of which His Royal Highness the Duke of Cambridge is president), and of a ladies' committee　there are one hundred and forty children in the school, who are maintained, clothed, and taught reading, writing, and arithmetic, they are also instructed in plain needle-work, and in household business of every kind requisite to qualify them for being useful servants at fourteen years of age they are apprenticed for seven years, as servants in respectable families, and, on the completion of that term, receive from the institution a gratuity of £5 5, and a testimonial of good conduct　The buildings occupy three sides of a quadrangle, in the central range is a handsome chapel, with a portico of Corinthian columns supporting an entablature and triangular pediment, surmounted by a cupola, in which divine service is performed every Sunday, in the morning and evening, two morning preachers and one evening preacher are appointed by the general court, and also a chaplain, who reads the prayers, and instructs the children in their religious duties　The general lying-in hospital, for the reception of patients from all parts of the kingdom, and for the delivery of out-patients at their own habitations in the metropolis and its environs, was instituted in 1765, and incorporated in 1830　it was formerly in the Westminster bridge road, near Marsh gate, from which situation it has been recently removed to York road, where a neat square building of white brick, ornamented with stone, with a handsome receding portico of the Ionic order, has been erected the institution is under the patronage of Her Royal Highness the Duchess of Kent, and the direction of a committee, of which Earl Grosvenor is president　The Royal Universal Infirmary for children, in the Waterloo road, was originally established at St Andrew's hill, Doctors' Commons, in 1816, and is supported by donations and subscriptions　it administers relief in all diseases of children, from the time of the birth till fourteen years of age, being open in cases of emergency to all first applications for admission, without recommendation, and is under the patronage of His Majesty　The Benevolent Society of St Patrick, instituted in 1784, for the relief of the distressed Irish families in London and its environs, and for the education of their children, is under the patronage of His Majesty　a handsome and capacious building was erected for this purpose in Upper Stamford-street, in 1820, at an expense of £8000, com-

prising two school-rooms, with a house for the master and the mistress, committee rooms, and other offices The society has a fund of £25,000, and is liberally supported by annual subscription　there are four hundred and forty children in the schools, who are clothed and instructed, and, on their leaving the institution, are placed out apprentices, or to service in respectable families　Sir Noel Caron, in 1623, gave a rent-charge of £28 on his mansion at South Lambeth, for the maintenance of an almshouse which he had erected in the parish, for the support of seven aged widows, to each of whom he allowed £4 per annum, which has been augmented by an appropriation of a part of large sums of money bequeathed by Thomas, Earl Thanet, for charitable uses, by his administratrix, the Dowager Countess Gower　Almshouses have also been erected in Coldharbour lane, by the Company of Parish Clerks, for eight widows of members of that fraternity, and there are numerous and extensive charitable bequests for distribution among the poor

LAMBLEY, a parish in the western division of TINDALE ward, county of NORTHUMBERLAND, comprising the townships of Ash-Holm and Lambley, and containing 261 inhabitants, of which number, 139 are in the township of Lambley, 6½ miles (S W by S) from Haltwhistle　The living is a donative, in the patronage of R L Allgood, Esq　The church has been recently repaired by subscription　The South Tyne runs through the parish　Here are very productive mines of fine coal　An abbey of Benedictine nuns, in honour of St Patrick, was founded here, in the reign of John, by the king, or by Adam de Tindale, which, at the dissolution, had a revenue of £5 15 8　in 1296 this monastery was burned, and the neighbourhood laid waste, by the Scots　On Castle hill, the site of an old fortress, are vestiges of a deep moat, and lower down the river have been discovered some large coffins of oak, black as jet

LAMBLEY, a parish in the southern division of the wapentake of THURGARTON, county of NOTTINGHAM, 5¼ miles (N E) from Nottingham, containing 690 inhabitants　The living is a rectory, in the archdeaconry of Nottingham, and diocese of York, rated in the king's books at £10 16 3, and in the patronage of the Rev A D Flamstead　The church is dedicated to the Holy Trinity

LAMBOURN, a parish in the hundred of LAMBOURN, county of BERKS, comprising the market town of Chipping-Lambourn, and the tythings of Blagrave with Hadley, Eastbury with Bockhampton, and Upper Lambourn, and containing 2299 inhabitants, of which number, 1096 are in the town of Chipping-Lambourn, 5 miles (N) from Hungerford, and 68 (W) from London This place formed part of the dower of Ealswitha, Queen of Alfred the Great, and continued in royal demesne under Edward the Confessor, after the Conquest it was given to the baronial family of Fitzwarren, at whose instance a market and three fairs were granted to it by Henry III　The town is pleasantly situated in a hilly district, near the source of a small rivulet of the same name, and which has the peculiar property that, during the summer months it has a full stream, which, decreasing about October, for a few of the winter months, sometimes leaves the channel perfectly dry　The streets are neither paved nor lighted, the inhabitants are supplied with water from wells in the centre of the

.town is an ancient cross, consisting of a tall pillar, approached by a circular ascent of steps, and surmounted by an ornamented capital, supposed to have been originally the figure of a sphynx, but now nearly obliterated The market is on Friday, fairs are held on May 12th, October 14th, and December 4th, chiefly for cattle

The living is a vicarage, in the archdeaconry of Berks, and diocese of Salisbury, rated in the king s books at £10 11 10½ , and in the patronage of the Dean of St Paul s The church, which is dedicated to St Michael, is an ancient and handsome cruciform structure, in the early style of English architecture, with a square embattled tower rising from the intersection, and containing a peal of eight bells , in the interior are two chantry chapels, in one of which the inmates of the adjoining almshouses assemble every morning for prayers, kneeling around the tomb of the founder, Mr John Isbury, who died in 1372 There is a place of worship for Wesleyan Methodists Here are two free schools, one erected in 1735, by Organ Hippisley, Esq , and endowed with a small rent-charge for teaching eight boys to read and write a Sunday school has been united to this institution in which from sixty to one hundred children are taught to read, and for this an additional stipend is raised by subscription. Another school was founded , in 1792, by John Serjent, and endowed with a messuage and rent-charge of £11, for the education of twenty-five children , the master and children to be appointed by the vicar and churchwardens of the parish On the north side of the church is an hospital, founded, in 1502, by the son of the above-mentioned John Isbury, for ten poor men, who are nominated by the Warden and Fellows of New College, Oxford.

LAMBOURN (UPPER), a tything in the parish and hundred of LAMBOURN, county of BERKS, 1½ mile (N W) from Lambourn, containing 354 inhabitants

LAMBOURNE, a parish in the hundred of ONGAR, county of ESSEX, 5 miles (S by E) from Epping, containing 729 inhabitants The living is a rectory, in the archeaconry of Essex, and diocese of London, rated in the king s books at £14, and in the patronage of the Master and Fellows of Corpus Christi College, Cambridge. The church, dedicated to St. Mary and All Saints, contains a monument to the memory of Thomas Winniffe, Bishop of Lincoln in the seventeenth century Spencer, the warlike Bishop of Norwich, who put down Ket s rebellion, lived here , the square intrenchment called Bishop s Moat, each side of which extends two hundred yards, encompassed his residence, and still remains

LAMBRIGG, a township in that part of the parish of KENDAL which is in KENDAL ward, county of WESTMORLAND, 6¼ miles (E N E) from Kendal, containing 164 inhabitants A vein of copper-ore was formerly worked here, but proving unproductive, from the great quantity of water in the mine, it has long since been abandoned

LAMBROOK (EAST), a parish in the eastern division of the hundred of KINGSBURY, county of SOMERSET, 6¼ miles (S by E) from Langport The population is returned with the parish of Kingsbury-Episcopi The living is a discharged rectory, in the peculiar jurisdiction of the Chancellor in the Cathedral Church of Wells, rated in the king s books at £6 6 8, endowed with £400 private benefaction, and £400 royal bounty, and in the patronage of the Dean and Chapter of Wells

The church is dedicated to St. James There is a place of worship for Independents

LAMBROOK (WEST), a tything in the parish of KINGSBURY-EPISCOPI, eastern division of the hundred of KINGSBURY, county of SOMERSET, 6¼ miles (S) from Langport The population is returned with the parish

LAMBTON, a township in that part of the parish of CHESTER le STREET which is in the northern division of EASINGTON ward, county palatine of DURHAM, 8 miles (N N E) from Durham, containing 293 inhabitants Harraton hall, the ancient seat of the D Arcys, stood on the side of Lambton castle, which is situated in a beautiful park five miles in circuit, and intersected by the river Wear Just within the entrance is the site of an ancient chapel , and near it Worm hill, of which tradition says that it was anciently occupied by a formidable serpent, which was cut to pieces by some hero of the Lambton family, cased in armour set with razors for the purpose Two brine springs, from which salt is made, issue from the bottoms of two coal pits in the neighbourhood.

LAMERTON, a parish forming, with the parish of Sydenham-Damerel, a distinct portion of the hundred of LIFTON, being surrounded by that of Tavistock, county of DEVON, 2½ miles (N W) from Tavistock, containing 1069 inhabitants The living is a vicarage, in the archdeaconry of Totness, and diocese of Exeter rated in the king s books at £13 2 1 The Rev H H Tremayne was patron in 1816 The church, dedicated to St Peter, formerly belonged to Tavistock abbey it contains an interesting monument to Thomas Tremayne and his wife, with their eight sons and eight daughters Collacombe, an old mansion built in the reign of Elizabeth, and since converted into a farm-house, has a large transome window containing three thousand two hundred panes of glass. Here is a charity school supported by subscription

LAMESLEY, a chapelry in that part of the parish of CHESTER le STREET which is in the middle division of CHESTER ward, county palatine of DURHAM, 3½ miles (S) from Gateshead, containing 1720 inhabitants The living is a perpetual curacy, in the archdeaconry and diocese of Durham, endowed with £600 private benefaction, and £2100 parliamentary grant, and in the patronage of Lord Ravensworth The chapel, which is of ancient foundation, was rebuilt in 1759 There are extensive mines of coal, several quarries of stone for grindstones, and some beds of iron-stone, in the parish A free school was built in 1814, and is supported by Lord Ravensworth, for the instruction of twenty-five boys Lady Ravensworth allows an annual stipend for the education of girls

LAMMAS, a parish in the southern division of the hundred of ERPINGHAM, county of NORFOLK, 3 miles (N W by N) from Coltishall, containing, with the parish of Little Hautboys, 284 inhabitants The living is a discharged rectory, united to that of Little Hautboys, in the archdeaconry and diocese of Norwich, endowed with £200 private benefaction, and £200 royal bounty The church, dedicated to St Andrew, contains, in the north window, some specimens of ancient stained glass

LAMONBY, a township in the parish of SKELTON, LEATH ward, county of CUMBERLAND, 8¼ miles (N W by W) from Penrith, containing 274 inhabitants Here is a quarry of firestone.

LAMORRAN, a parish in the western division of the hundred of POWDER, county of CORNWALL, 4 miles (S W by W) from Tregoney, containing 93 inhabitants The living is a rectory, in the archdeaconry of Cornwall, and diocese of Exeter, rated in the king's books at £6 The Earl of Falmouth was patron in 1803 The church is dedicated to St Moren The parish is bounded on the south by the navigable river Fal

LAMPLUGH, a parish in ALLERDALE ward above Darwent, county of CUMBERLAND, 8 miles (E N E) from Whitehaven, comprising the townships of Ketton-Quarter, Lamplugh, Murton, or Moor Town, and Winder, and containing 661 inhabitants The living is a rectory, in the archdeaconry of Richmond, and diocese of Chester, rated in the king's books at £10 4 7 The Trustees of E Copeley, Esq were patrons in 1817 The church is dedicated to St. Michael. The parish is bounded on the east by Loweswater and Crummockwater, and two branches of the river Marron have their source here. There are extensive quarries of limestone, and some of freestone, and near the ancient hall is a mineral spring, the water of which is powerfully astringent. Richard Briscoe, Esq , in 1747, gave a rent-charge of £12, partly to the poor, and partly for the instruction of twelve children

LAMPORT, a parish in the hundred of ORLINGBURY, county of NORTHAMPTON, 8¼ miles (N) from Northampton, containing, with the hamlet of Hanging-Houghton, 233 inhabitants The living is a rectory, in the archdeaconry of Northampton, and diocese of Peterborough, rated in the king's books at £48 2 6 , and in the patronage of Sir J Isham, Bart The church is dedicated to All Saints At Faxton, in this parish, is a chapel of ease There is a school endowed by Sir Edmund Isham, Bart., who, in 1762, gave £1500 for this purpose and for the benefit of the poor

LAMYATT, a parish in the hundred of WHITESTONE, county of SOMERSET, 2¼ miles (W by N) from Bruton, containing 243 inhabitants The living is a rectory in the archdeaconry of Wells, and diocese of Bath and Wells, rated in the king's books at £12 4 2 The Rev George Ridout was patron in 1825 The church is dedicated to St. Mary and St John.

LANCASHIRE, a maritime county, and a county palatine, situated on the western coast, and bounded on the north by the counties of Cumberland and Westmorland, on the east by that of York, on the south by that of Chester, and on the west by the Irish sea it extends from 53° 23′ to 54° 24′ (N Lat.), and from 2° 18′ to 3° 7′ (W Lon.), and contains one million one hundred and seventy-one thousand eight hundred and forty statute acres, or one thousand eight hundred and thirty-one square miles. The population, in 1821, amounted to 1,052,859, being an increase, during the ten preceding years, of 224,549 The name of this county is a contraction of Lancaster-shire Its early British inhabitants were the Setantii, a tribe of the Brigantes Under the Roman dominion it was included in the province called Maxima Cæsariensis, and contained eight stations belonging to that people, besides being traversed by four great military roads, which severally led through this county, from Carlisle to Kinderton in Cheshire , from Overborough to Slack, or Almondbury, in Yorkshire , from the Neb of the Nese, on the right bank of the Ribble, eastward, and across Fulwood-moor,

to Ribchester , and from the ford of the Mersey, near Warrington, through Barton, Eccles, and Manchester, to Ilkley The Britons, under their renowned King Arthur, fought several great battles with the Saxons on the banks of the river Douglas, in this county, which was, however, at last conquered, about the year 559, by the Saxon chieftain, Ella, and formed part of the kingdom of Deira, over which that prince reigned From this period until the fifteenth century, we find little remarkable on record relative to Lancashire It shared in the general devastation of the northern part of England committed by the Conqueror, and, in 1323, it suffered from an invasion of the Scots, under Robert Bruce, who partly burned the town of Preston The year 1363, also, is remarkable in the Lancashire annals, as that in which the county was erected into a palatinate by Edward III , in favour of his fourth son, John of Gaunt, Duke of Lancaster In the wars between the rival houses of York and Lancaster this county was not the scene of any important event, except that, after the defeat of the Lancastrian party in the battle of Hexham, Henry VI was concealed for a year at Waddington hall, where he was at length discovered and taken, and was conveyed to London In the reign of Henry VII the impostor, Lambert Simnel, with a body of Irish partisans, and two thousand Germans, who had been sent to his assistance by Margaret, widow of Charles the Bold, Duke of Burgundy, landed at the Pile of Foudrey, in the bay of Morecambe, in this county, and thence proceeded to Coventry In the reign of Henry VIII , when the " Pilgrims of Grace," as the rebels of the north were called, were making their way southward, the malcontents of Lancashire took up arms, but were speedily subdued by the Earl of Shrewsbury, aided by the Earl of Derby During the great civil war in the reign of Charles I., no county was more frequently the scene of action than this In the commission of array issued by the king, James, Lord Strange, was appointed lord-lieutenant of the counties of Lancashire and Cheshire that nobleman soon after had a severe skirmish with the inhabitants of Manchester, for a magazine which they had formed , and shortly after another skirmish ensued at the same town, with some partisans of the parliament His lordship then mustered the county in three different places,—on the heaths by Bury , on the moor at Ormskirk , and on the moor at Preston , at each of which not less than twenty thousand men were assembled. Lord Molyneux also raised a regiment in the royal cause in this county , but many of the other most influential men were actively engaged in the parliamentarian interest. The forces thus raised soon dispersed, but Lord Strange, who immediately after, by the decease of his father, became Earl of Derby, having been commanded by the king to secure the town of Manchester, raised some troops at his own expense, and commenced the siege of that town on the 26th of September, 1642, at the head of four thousand three hundred men, but raised it at the end of the week following, in obedience to the commands of the king, whom he proceeded to join without delay Early in 1643, Sir Thomas Fairfax repaired from Yorkshire to Manchester, and there established his head-quarters. On the 10th of February, Sir John Seaton, Major-General of the parliamentarian forces, marched at the head of a body of troops from Manchester to Preston, which was then garrisoned by the king's troops, and attacked that town with such vigour, that it was taken after a combat of two hours, and soon after Lancaster was secured by the parliamentarian forces, with but little resistance. Sir John Seaton then marched to Wigan, where the Earl of Derby was strongly intrenched, and taking that place after a gallant resistance, compelled the earl to retreat to Blackburn. From Wigan the victorious forces proceeded to Warrington, which they obtained possession of after a short but resolutely-sustained siege. The united forces of the Earl of Derby and Lord Molyneux retook the town of Lancaster on the 10th of March, and three days after, their lordships advanced to Preston, which they carried by assault; but Lord Molyneux being obliged to join the king at Oxford, the Earl of Derby, with his forces, was compelled immediately to retreat to his own mansion of Latham house, which he had fortified. Early in the year 1644 commenced the memorable siege of that mansion, which was attacked by the parliamentarian forces under Sir Thomas Fairfax, and defended for three months by a strong garrison, inspirited by the heroic conduct of Charlotte Tremouille, Countess of Derby, until relieved by Prince Rupert, who pursued the parliamentarian army to Bolton. Here, the prince being joined by the Earl of Derby from the Isle of Man, Bolton was taken in a second furious assault, led by the earl at the head of two hundred chosen Lancashire men, when Colonel Rigby, the commander, and a number of his troops, succeeded in escaping from the town, and crossed the Yorkshire hills to Bradford. The prince forthwith advanced to Liverpool, which surrendered after a vigorous siege of about three weeks. He then hastened to York, but having been totally defeated, with the other generals of the royal party, at the decisive battle of Marston moor, he drew off the wreck of his army into Lancashire, where the strong holds he had so recently captured were speedily re-taken. In the summer of 1645, Latham house was again besieged by the parliamentarian forces, under the command of General Egerton, and, after a gallant defence by Colonel Rawsthorn, the garrison was at length compelled to yield to superior numbers. In the year 1648, the north of England being invaded by the Scottish army, under the Duke of Hamilton, and by another body of men which had been raised on the borders, under General Langdale, acting in concert and on behalf of the royal cause, Cromwell was ordered by the parliament to march into Lancashire to resist their further progress. These orders were promptly obeyed, and having joined the Lancashire forces which had been assembled under the command of Colonel Ashton, he advanced to Preston, where, on the evening of the 17th of July, he was met by the opposing army, which had in the mean time been joined by an Irish force under General Monroe. An action immediately ensued, in which, after a sanguinary conflict of four hours' duration in the fields, the Duke of Hamilton's troops began to give way, and were charged through the streets of Preston at the point of the bayonet, but beyond the town they made a stand for the night in this battle, Cromwell himself states that the enemy lost one thousand men killed, and four thousand prisoners. In the night of the 18th the duke retreated with the remainder of his army to Wigan, and the next day to Warrington, but, being still pursued, his troops made a resolute stand at a pass near Wenwick, which

they maintained for many hours, being at last overcome by the courage and discipline of the troops under Cromwell, when about one thousand men were killed, and two thousand made prisoners; the remainder were pursued to the town of Warrington, where they passed the bridge, and where General Bailey, to whom the Duke of Hamilton had confided the command of this division of his army, was compelled to surrender himself and all his officers and soldiers prisoners of war. by this capitulation, four thousand prisoners, with their arms, fell into the hands of the victors, and the infantry of the Scottish army was totally ruined: the remainder ultimately dispersed. The issue of this campaign compelled Sir Thomas Tyldesley, a zealous supporter of the royal cause, to abandon the siege of Lancaster castle, in which he was at that time engaged. King Charles II, with his Scottish forces, marched through this county, in 1651, on his route to Worcester; and the Earl of Derby, having collected at Preston all the strength he was able, consisting of about six hundred men, was proceeding to Worcester by way of Wigan, when he was opposed in Wigan lane by a considerable force under Colonel Lilburne, and his troops were totally routed the earl himself escaped with numerous wounds, but shortly afterwards fell into the hands of the enemy, and was beheaded at Bolton. In this year also Lancashire suffered much from pestilence. William III, on his way to Ireland, prior to the celebrated battle of the Boyne, passed through the southern part of Lancashire, and embarked at Liverpool, June 14th, 1690. In 1715, a body of the Scottish insurgents on behalf of the Pretender entered this county from the north, and having passed through Kirkby-Lonsdale and Lancaster, arrived at Preston on the 9th of November, their whole force amounting to one thousand six hundred men, and here, after some skirmishes of minor importance, they finally surrendered to the king's forces. In 1745, the army of the Young Pretender passed through Lancashire, in its progress southward, being joined in its route by small numbers of Lancashire men, and again, in its precipitate retreat, it traversed the county in the contrary direction.

Lancashire lies within the diocese of Chester, and province of York, being included partly in the archdeaconry of Chester, and partly in that of Richmond, and contains the deaneries of Blackburn, Leyland, Manchester, and Warrington, comprised in the archdeaconry of Chester, and those of Amounderness, Furness, Kendal, and Lonsdale, in the archdeaconry of Richmond. in these are sixty-six parishes, of which twenty-six are rectories, twenty-seven vicarages, and the remainder, with the exception of three rectorial churches in the parish of Manchester, perpetual curacies: there is also a very great number of chapels of ease throughout the county, particularly in the densely-inhabited manufacturing district. For civil purposes it is divided into the six hundreds of Amounderness, Blackburn (Higher and Lower), Leyland, Lonsdale (North and South of the Sands), Salford, and West Derby. It contains the borough, market, and sea-port towns of Lancaster and Liverpool, the borough and market towns of Clitheroe, Preston, and Wigan, the borough of Newton, the market of which has been discontinued, the market and sea-port towns of Poulton in the Fylde and Ulverstone, and the market towns of Ashton-under-Line, Blackburn, Bolton,

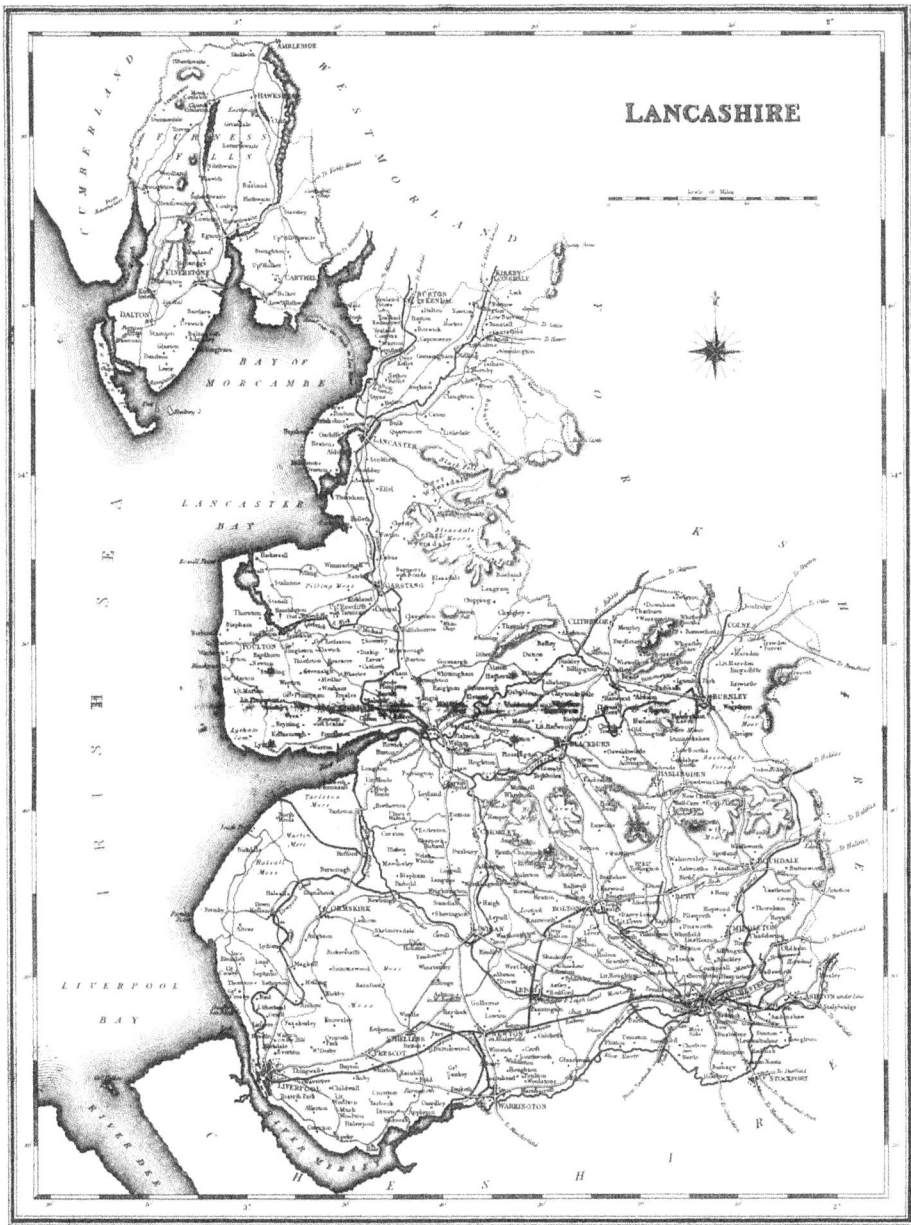

LANCASHIRE

Scale of Miles

CUMBERLAND

WESTMORLAND

IRISH SEA

BAY OF MORCAMBE

LANCASTER BAY

LANCASTER

AMBLESIDE

HAWKSHEAD

FURNESS FELLS

ULVERSTONE

DALTON

CARTMEL

KIRKBY LONSDALE

BURTON IN KENDAL

GARSTANG

POULTON

CLITHEROE

COLNE

BURNLEY

HASLINGDEN

ROCHDALE

BURY

MIDDLETON

BOLTON

CHORLEY

ORMSKIRK

WIGAN

LIVERPOOL BAY

LIVERPOOL

PRESCOT

ST HELENS

WARRINGTON

STOCKPORT

RIVER DEE

CHESHIRE

Burnley, Bury, Cartmel, Chorley, Colne, Dalton, Garstang, Hawkeshead, Haslingden, Hornbv, Kirkham, Manchester, Middleton, Oldham, Ormskirk, Prescot, Rochdale, Todmorden, and Warrington Two knights are returned for the shire, and two representatives for each of the boroughs This county is included in the northern circuit the assizes are held at Lancaster, where are also held the quarter sessions for the hundred of Lonsdale, on the Tuesdays in the first whole week after Epiphany, Easter Sunday, the festival of St Thomas à Becket, and October 11th, at Preston, for the hundreds of Amounderness, Blackburn, and Leyland, on the Thursdays following the days above named, at Salford, for the hundred of Salford, on the Mondays following, and at Kirkdale near Liverpool, for the hundred of West Derby, on the Monday fortnight after they commence at Salford The court of Annual General Sessions is holden at Preston, on the Thursday next after the feast of St John the Baptist, and afterwards by various adjournments until the multifarious causes within the peculiar cognizance of this court are determined The county gaol is at Lancaster, and there is a county house of correction at Manchester, another at Kirkdale, and a third at Preston there are one hundred acting magistrates The rates raised in the county for the year ending March 25th, 1827, amounted to £545,737 3, the expenditure to £539,388 6, of which £347,911 18 was applied to the relief of the poor

Prior to and under the Norman dynasty, Lancashire was probably distinguished as an Honour, and was of the superior order of seigniories The Honour of Lancaster was given by William the Conqueror to Roger de Poictou, who in turn bestowed various parts of it upon his followers In the interval between the first division of property among the Normans and the general survey, the lands between the Ribble and the Mersey were forfeited to the crown by the defection of that nobleman, and are consequently mentioned in that record as the property of the king The Honour of Lancaster was, however, restored to Roger de Poictou by William Rufus, in whose reign he again forfeited it by rebellion, and this princely inheritance was given to Stephen, Count of Blois, and afterwards King of England Stephen, on ascending the throne, bestowed it on his son, William de Blois, Earl of Mortaigne and Boulogne, and, on the death of this nobleman, Richard I gave it to his brother John, afterwards King of England At a subsequent period, Ranulph, fourth earl of Chester, possessed all the land between the Ribble and the Mersey, together with all the other territories which had been held by Roger de Poictou. Henry III made his youngest son, Edmund Crouchback, Earl of Lancaster, and gave him the Honour and estates His son Thomas, Earl of Lancaster, was beheaded at Pontefract, March 22nd, 1322, for his distinguished share in the insurrection to displace the De Spensers, the favourites of Edward III, but this sentence was afterwards reversed by parliament, and his title and estates devolved upon his brother Henry, who left an only son, on whom Edward III conferred the title of Duke of Lancaster These possessions afterwards descended to John of Gaunt, who married Blanche, daughter and co-heiress of the Duke of Lancaster just mentioned, and the title was revived in his favour Edward III also advanced the county of Lancaster to the dignity of a palatinate by a royal

patent expressed in these terms "We have granted for ourselves and our heirs to our son (John) that he shall have, during life, within the county of Lancaster, his court of Chancery, and writs to be issued out under his seal belonging to the office of Chancellor, his justices both for holding the pleas of the crown, and for all other pleas relating to common law, and the cognizance thereof, and all executions by his writs and officers within the same, and all other liberties and royalties relating to the county palatine as freely and fully as the Earl of Chester is known to enjoy them within the county of Chester,' &c This prince was succeeded in his estates by the celebrated Henry of Bolingbroke, afterwards King Henry IV of England, from whom the duchy of Lancaster descended to his son Henry V, and from that monarch to his son Henry VI But when the latter was attainted, in the first year of Edward IV, this duchy was declared by parliament to be forfeited to the crown, and an act was passed vesting the whole in Edward IV and his heirs for ever In the reign of Henry VII, however, another act was passed, vesting it in that monarch and his heirs for ever, since which time, the kings of England have always been Dukes of Lancaster The estates of the duchy were greatly increased by Henry VIII, at the time of the dissolution of religious houses, as well as by the act of Edward VI for the dissolution of colleges and chantries, and by a charter of Philip and Mary, granted in pursuance of an act of parliament, but the necessities of various succeeding monarchs compelled them to raise money on these estates, by means of long leases, grants in fee, &c, and the revenue arising from them is still much curtailed by the leases with which they are encumbered In the first year of the Commonwealth, a commission was appointed for the sale of the crown and duchy lands, the transaction of which was cancelled at the Restoration

The county palatine and the duchy of Lancaster, with regard to extent, are quite distinct, for there are various estates forming part of the duchy in twenty five other counties in England Belonging to the duchy also is a considerable share of ecclesiastical patronage, as also the appointment of sheriffs for the county palatine The peculiar jurisdiction and proceedings in the courts of law in the county palatine of Lancaster are the result of those privileges granted to its former dukes, who had, in fact, sovereign authority within the limits of their dominion, for, besides the privileges already mentioned, they had power to pardon treasons, murders, and felonies, and all offences were said to be committed against their peace, sword, and dignity, and not, as now, "against the peace of our Lord the King, his crown and dignity By the 27th of Henry VIII, however, which abridged the privileges of the counties palatine, it was enacted that all writs and processes should be made in the name of the king, but should be tested, or witnessed, in the name of the owner of the franchise All writs, therefore, must be under the seal of the respective franchises, and the judges who sit in this county palatine have a special commission from the duchy of Lancaster, and not the ordinary commission under the Great Seal of England The court of Chancery of the duchy has cognizance of matters of an equitable nature, whether they relate to the county palatine, or to the duchy, and of all questions of

revenue and council affecting the ducal possessions
It is also a court of appeal from the Chancery of the
county palatine , and, being held at the duchy office in
Westminster, all its proceedings are dated before His
Majesty " at his palace at Westminster," and not, as
other royal acts, at the residence of the monarch for the
time being. The principal officers of the ducal court
are, the chancellor, the attorney general, the king's
serjeant, the king's counsel, the receiver general, the
two auditors, the clerk of the council and registrar,
the deputy registrar and secretary, and two clerks
in court   The court of Chancery of the county palatine is an original and independent court, as ancient
as the 50th of Edward III   the office is at Preston, and
the court sits at least four times in the year, namely,
once at each assize at Lancaster, and once at Preston
in the interval of each assize   The general practice of
the court is similar to that of the High Court of Chancery,
with which and the court of Exchequer it has concurrent
jurisdiction in all matters of equity, its cognizance of
which depends on the person or lands of the defendant
being amenable to the process of this court , but its
jurisdiction is exclusive of all other courts of equity
when both the subject of the suit and the residences
of the parties litigant are within the county   An
appeal from the chancery of Lancashire lies to the
duchy chamber at Westminster, and from that to the
king in parliament   Although the bills are addressed
to the chancellor of the duchy, the vice-chancellor of
the county palatine is the judge of the court   the
chancellor of the duchy, assisted by two judges in commission for the county palatine, sits to hear causes at
Westminster   All original writs within the county
palatine issue from the Chancery of Lancashire and
writs from the courts of Westminster are directed to
the chancellor of the duchy, who makes out his mandate
to the sheriff of the county to execute and return them
into the chancery ; and the chancellor and vice-chancellor are authorised by act of parliament to appoint
commissioners for the purpose of taking special bail, or
affidavits, in any of the courts within the county palatine   The officers of this court are, the chancellor
of the duchy, the vice-chancellor, the registrar, ex-
aminer, and first clerk ; the five cursitors and clerks in
court, who are the attornies, the seal-keeper , and the
messenger   The court of Common Pleas for the county
palatine is an original superior court of record at
common law, having jurisdiction over all real actions
for lands, and in all actions against corporations
within the county, as well as over all personal actions
where the defendant resides in Lancashire, although the
cause of action may have arisen elsewhere : its returns
are on the first Wednesday in every month   The court
is held at Lancaster every assize, before two judges
of the courts at Westminster who have chosen the
northern circuit, and who are commissioned half-yearly,
one as the " Chief Justice, the other as " one of the
justices of the Common Pleas at Lancaster '   The patent
of the judges from the Common Pleas also appoints one
of the judges " Chief Justice," and the other " one of
the justices of all manner of pleas within the county
palatine ; " and under this, the causes sent by mittimus
from the courts at Westminster are tried at bar, as
well as all pleas of the crown   This court is of great
advantage to the commercial county of Lancaster, as

well because its process for arrests extends to all parts
of the county, and may be had without the delay of
sending to London, as on account of the celerity and
excellence of its practice   a great majority of the cases
now tried at Lancaster are brought in this court   The
general official business of the court of Common Pleas
is transacted by the prothonotary's deputy   the office
of prothonotary is a patent office in the gift of the
crown, in right of the duchy of Lancaster   The court
of King's Bench and the court of Common Pleas at
Westminster have concurrent jurisdiction with the court
of Common Pleas for the county palatine of Lancaster
in almost all cases   The cases in which the jurisdiction
of these courts is excluded, and that of the Common
Pleas of Lancaster must be adopted, are chiefly pleas of
lands within the county, actions against corporations
existing in Lancashire, or suits in which a defendant residing there is to be arrested for less than £20   All
writs out of the courts at Westminster, except those of
Habeas Corpus and Mittimus, are directed to the chancellor, and not to the sheriff in the first instance ; and,
where execution of them must be done by the sheriff,
the chancellor issues his mandate to that officer, and, on
receiving his return, certifies in his own name to the
court above, that the writ has been duly executed , and
if the chancellor return that he commanded the sheriff
and has received from him no answer, the court above
will rule the sheriff to return the mandate   There is
only one franchise in the county having the execution
of writs by its own officer, viz , the liberty of Furness,
to the bailiff of which the sheriff directs his precepts,
and receives from him the requisite returns   There are
an attorney-general and two king's counsel for the palatinate   The duchy of Lancaster had its star chamber,
until that court was dissolved in the 16th of Charles I
   The form of this county is very irregular , for, besides the deviousness of its boundaries on the land side,
its coast is indented by numerous bays and æstuaries ,
the principal of which are, the æstuary of the river
Mersey to the south of the county, that of the Ribble,
the expanse of the bay of Morecambe, into which open
the æstuaries of the Ken and the Leven , and the
æstuary of the Dudden, lying west of the northernmost
part of the county   On the north-west portion of
Lancashire is the island of Walney, a long strip of land
separated from the tract called Low Furness by a narrow channel of the sea.   Various other small islands
lie scattered within the vicinity of this, and eastward of
the southern part of it, the largest being that of Old
Barrow, near which are Ramsey island and the island
of Dova Haw , and at the entrance of Pile harbour
is that on which Foudrey castle stands, and which forms
a triangle with Roe island, Sheep island, and Foulney
island.   Lancashire is naturally divided into two grand
districts,—the high, mountainous, heathy tract of the
northern and eastern parts, and the low, level tract
which spreads out to the south and west , the line of
division between which may be drawn in a sinuous
course, below the first rising grounds of the high heathy
tracts, from the south-eastern limit of the county, by
the towns of Oldham, Rochdale, Bury, Bolton, Chorley,
Preston, Garstang, Lancaster, and Kellet, nearly to
Burton, on the northern boundary   The two portions
of high craggy land situated in that part of the county
which lies furthest to the north-west may also be sepa-

rated from the more level tracts, by a line passing from the boundary of the county just below Yealand, by Warton, Lindreth, Silverdale, and Allithwaite, to Newland, Ulverstone, and the line that forms the division between High and Low Furness, passing above Dalton, by Kirkby-Ireleth, to Dudden Sands For the clearer description of the surface and of the various soils of these two districts, it will be necessary to make the following subdivisions, viz the hilly and high heathy division, the steep fell, or High Furness, division, the elevated craggy limestone division, the valley-land division, the Mersey, or southern, division, the Ribble and Fylde division, the Lune and flat limestone division, the Low Furness division, and the moss, or peaty, division The first of these comprises different mountainous ridges which rise in succession from the south-eastern boundary of the county towards the town of Rochdale, and terminate in the high rocky tract above Leek, extending in breadth from the great line of division already marked out to the confines of Yorkshire Throughout the whole of this extent the land is almost invariably of the high moory freestone kind, and generally produces a coarse black heath, excepting only where the vales intervene The second division comprises the whole of those high rocky tracts called fells, situated north of the sands (the extensive flat tracts of the bay of Morecambe, which are always dry at low water, and separate the northern division of the hundred of Lonsdale from the rest of the county), extending, in one direction, from the towns of Ulverstone and Dalton to the river Brathy, and in the other, from the river Dudden to the river Winster at Bowland bridge. This tract is moory in different places, but the heath where it occurs is weak in its growth the rock is in general of the blue, or whin stone kind The third, or craggy limestone division, is of much smaller extent, the principal part of it lying chiefly in the north-western part of the county, and extending from a little above Warton and Yealand to the point where it joins the sea-coast at Silverdale there are small tracts in the Furness districts, and at the two Kellets, as well as at Chipping and Clitheroe towards the eastern limits of the county The fourth division includes the various vallies formed by the hills that constitute the two first divisions some of these are of very considerable extent, others very narrow, the more extensive vallies being those which border on the larger and less impetuous rivers the aggregate quantity of this kind of land is very considerable, and generally of excellent quality The Mersey division comprises a fertile and level tract of land, and extends from the northern bank of the Mersey to the southern border of the Ribble, in one direction, and from the sea-coast to considerably above the town of Oldham, in the other The sixth division is of less extent than the preceding, but little inferior in fertility, and stretches from the northern bank of the Ribble to the southern border of the Lune, and from Lytham and Bispham to near Inglewhite The seventh division is of small size, commencing at Sunderland point, at the mouth of the Lune, and running northward, in a narrow tract along the sea-coast, as far as the before-mentioned high, craggy, lime stone ridge, by Warton and Yealand to the east of this rises the ridge of high moory ground above Kellet The eighth division comprises a small portion of land on

the northern side of the sands, generally called Low Furness it extends from a little above Ulverstone and Dalton to the extreme southern point at Rampside, being bounded on both sides by the sea, and includes the several small islands that lie to the south The ninth and last division includes the different peaty and boggy tracts called *mosses* they are found in both of the grand natural divisions of the county, but they are by much the most extensive in the flat district, the two largest being Chat-moss near Worsley, in the southern part of the county, and Pilling-moss, much farther north in some situations these mossy tracts have undergone great improvement, but in others they remain nearly in their original state The lands of the first four of these divisions are chiefly in pasture, the more high and mountainous parts being for sheep, the declivities and vales for cattle and sheep The next four divisions are under various systems of cultivation, but grass land mostly prevails, especially in the vicinities of the towns and villages The improved boggy tracts generally become excellent land for either grass or grain Besides the districts above described, there are various tracts of sandy marsh land, lying on the borders of the sea-coast, which are liable to occasional inundations by the tide, and the principal of which are situated towards the northern extremity of the county, being those near Lancaster, the tract below Warton, the æstuaries of the Leven and Dudden, and the marsh lands about Walney island

The air of Lancashire, though everywhere pure and salubrious, is much more cold and piercing in the elevated mountainous tracts of the north and east, than in the vallies formed by them, and in the lower districts which shelve to the south and west, where it is generally mild and genial Great vicissitudes of heat and cold are felt in the vicinity of the large mosses, in consequence of the evaporation of the moisture which is there so long retained In the most northern part of Lancashire, the breezes that come directly from the Irish sea, and those that have crossed the mountains of Cumberland, in the spring and summer months, are frequently cold and chilling A greater quantity of rain falls in this county than in most others of the kingdom The seed time and harvest in the districts contiguous to the mountains of the north and east are later than in the southern and south-western tracts.

The principal soils are loams of various kinds, clay, sand, and peat-earth the substrata on which these rest are chiefly freestone, whin-stone, or limestone rocks, fossil coal, marl, gravel, and sand The greater part of the high ranges of hills in the eastern and northern parts of the county, their declivities more especially, are overrun with the heath plant, which rarely exists, except where there is a soil of peaty matter, which in these tracts is sometimes of considerable depth where these peaty materials are mixed with earthy particles they form a good friable mould, which constitutes the higher parts of the high ridges and of the lower elevations In some situations this peat-earth is mixed with a sort of blue clay, having a marly substratum the depth of these soils is from six or seven inches to several feet Lancaster and Scotforth moors have most of the stiff clayey substance in the composition of their soils, which are generally of smaller depth The soils of the moors north of the sands are generally much thinner than those to the south but of a better quality Compared with the tracts just mentioned, the deep moss and peat lands are of very small extent they are met with both in the hollows of the high mountain ridges and on the declivities of the hills, as well as in the extended plains below, but those in the latter situation are the deepest and of the greatest extent they consist of two beds, the upper of which is generally in thin lamina of a brownish colour, and very open and spongy in its texture , the lower bed is a kind of hard, compact, black vegetable earth, generally having below it clay or marl occasionally mixed with fine white sand rocky strata are also sometimes found below the peaty matter On the banks of the numerous streams is much rich valley land provincially called *holme*, the quality of which varies much according to situation and other circumstances The largest and most fertile of these vales are those of the Ribble the Lune, and the Wyer, the soil being a rich loam, varying in depth from one foot to upwards of four, the ordinary depth being about two feet The soil of such valley tracts as have hardly any stream through them is inferior in quality to those just mentioned, always bearing affinity to the soils of the adjacent rising grounds these vallies form the richest pastures and meadows of the county A tract of rich loam occupies the whole space between the Mersey and the Ribble and between the sea-coast and the eastern hilly tract the prevailing colours of the loam are yellow, red, brown, and black , some of them have almost the tenacity of clay, while others are light and sandy , and all of them are fertile, excepting only the peaty loams The greater part of this district is under grass and the remainder devoted to tillage Clayey loam of different qualities forms the soil of the tract which stretches from the northern bank of the Ribble to the southern border of the Lune, and extends in breadth from the sea-coast to the foot of the mountainous range on the eastern side of the county the lower part of this constitutes the rich tract of corn land commonly called the Fylde Almost the whole extent of land from below Stalmine by Preesall, to Pilling hall, having Pilling-moss on one side and the sea on the other, has an alluvial soil intermixed in different parts with white sand and peat-earth About one-third of this whole tract is under tillage the rest is chiefly appropriated to the dairy In the northern part of the county are tracts of dry loam and limestone soils, which are separated from each other by the æstuaries of the Ken and the Leven, and by the bay of Morecambe one extent reaches from the northern bank of the Lune and its æstuary to that part of the boundary of the county which runs from Herring Syke, by the crag at Dalton and Leighton Beck, to beyond Yealand, spreading between the sea-coast and the hilly moors another tract extends from the point of seacoast near Rampside to above the towns of Dalton and Ulverstone, being bounded by the sea on both sides , this latter tract is called Low Furness, and includes the islands of Walney, Old Barrow, &c , at its southern extremity A small portion of this kind of land extends from Allithwaite to beyond Flookborough, and is bounded on one side by the sea, and on the other by the high craggy ground there is also a small tract on the eastern side of the county, stretching from below the town of Clitheroe, in a northerly direction to the boundary of the county, and from the banks of the Ribble to

Pendle hill The surface of these limestone soils is throughout very uneven, the rocks frequently projecting above it , but they nevertheless comprise many fertile tracts of land the soil in higher situations is frequently thin, but very friable , in the flatter districts it is of considerable depth The island of Walney contains some good land of a strong quality, resting on a clay or on a sandy bottom in the central part of the island the soil is a clayey loam, sometimes blended with sand towards the north it is at some places mixed with peat earth at each end of the island the land is sandy The soil of Old Barrow island is a fine turnip loam, of tolerable depth The small island of Foulney is chiefly marshy alluvial land, under grass

It has been computed that a little more than one fourth of the land of this county is under tillage the principal tracts of arable land lie towards its western border, including those of the Fylde, the banks of the Lune, and Low Furness most of these are excellent wheat lands , but on the eastern side of the county the grain chiefly cultivated is oats, great quantities being also grown in all the corn districts The principal object with most of the farmers in the western part of the county is to obtain crops of potatoes and wheat, with the intervention of as few other crops as possible The crops most cultivated are wheat, barley, oats, beans, and potatoes The general average produce of wheat is estimated at about twenty-five bushels per statute acre , that of barley at about thirty-five bushels There is a greater proportion of oats than of any other grain grown in this county, a great quantity of oaten bread being consumed by the population of the northern and eastern parts of it the produce is about forty-five bushels per acre The produce of beans varies much, according to the quality and fitness of the soils Great attention is paid to the cultivation of potatoes, which are extensively grown in all parts of the county, the crop succeeding extremely well on the various kinds of loam, and on the drier peaty soils the usual produce is from three hundred to three hundred and fifty bushels per acre Onions are grown to a considerable extent in the neighbourhood of Middleton, Stretford, and other places near Warrington Very fine crops of clover are cultivated in this county, the seed being generally sown with wheat Rye, peas, tares, common turnips, Swedish turnips, cabbages, carrots and lucerne, are also cultivated, but none of them to such an extent as the crops abovementioned. By far the greater part of the county is under grass, immense quantities of hay being requisite for the supply of the horses and cows belonging to the inhabitants of the towns a great extent of grass land is also occupied as bleaching grounds This kind of land may be distinguished into the rich hay meadows, the fine feeding and dairy grounds, and the coarse pastures and elevated sheep tracts The meadow lands are chiefly the valley tracts on the banks of the numerous streams of the county, the richest being those which lie low and are frequently flooded The richer pastures are usually employed in feeding, or for the dairy, generally the latter when near large towns the best feeding pastures are considered to be those on the borders of the Lune and the Ribble There are also rich pastures on the banks of different streams in various parts of the county, as well as some near Liverpool There are some small tracts of excellent marsh land at different places on the sea-coast In the greater part of the county, and more especially in the eastern and northern parts of it, are large tracts of pasture land of inferior quality and unimproved condition upon these much young stock is reared and kept In the vicinity of the large towns and villages numerous and extensive dairies are kept, for supplying them with milk In the eastern parts of the county are many small dairy farms, but the most extensive dairy pastures are those on the strong soil north of the Ribble, the produce of which is principally cheese and those in different parts of the Fylde To the north of the Lune are some small dairy pastures, which produce excellent butter and a small quantity of cheese North of Lancaster sands are large dairy pastures furnishing both cheese and butter of excellent quality these are found in different parts of Low Furness, and also around Hawkeshead, and at different places in the northernmost portion of the county There are many extensive, mountainous, and moory tracts of land in the northern and eastern parts, provincially called *fells*, which support vast numbers of sheep through most of the year These sheep are frequently thus pastured in common, being brought down into the enclosed pastures only for a short time in the depth of winter Besides the common manures, the lands derive considerable benefit from the use of marl as a manure this substance is very generally met with, and is more valuable in proportion to the quantity of calcareous matter it may contain Sea-sand and muscles are also esteemed of great value in some situations, as well as peat-earth, and a particularly fat, unctuous kind of clay, which is dug close to the sea-shore in some places The breed of cattle, commonly called "Lancashire long-horns,' though in much request in the midland counties, is not very frequently met with in Lancashire the cows do not afford so much milk as some other breeds, but the cream is generally richer, and in greater quantity Where feeding is the object in view, this and the small Scotch breed are kept, but where much milk is wanted, the short-horned or Holderness cows, the Suffolk poll cows, the Yorkshire red sort, and sometimes the improved Derbyshire breed, are kept the long-horned breed are, however, found on the best dairy farms of the middle and northern parts of the county In Lancashire cattle are seldom white, but when they are, the long-horned breed is mostly employed In most parts of the county the farmers rear the greater part of their stock The larger grass farms near populous towns supply them with milk, the smaller farms with butter, cheese being made in the more remote parts of the county In several places cheese of excellent quality is made, equal in many respects to that of Cheshire the cows commonly kept for this purpose are of the long-horned or native breed, each cow produces from two to three hundred weight of cheese annually Several long-horned and Scotch cattle are fattened in the pastures, though but few cattle of any sort are fed in stalls during the winter The only breed of sheep peculiar to the county are those on the crags near Warton and Silverdale, of which tract they are natives they are of good size, have small horns, and white spotted faces, and are much esteemed for the flavour of their flesh, their proneness to fatten, and the fineness of their wool Few sheep are

found in the southern part of the county, but in the northern many are bred and kept upon the mountains and the moors these sheep are an inferior sort, being of the heath and of the Welch breed, with coarse wool They are turned on the hills early in the spring, and remain there until November, when they are brought down into the enclosed pastures at three or four years old they are usually sorted, and sold off for fattening in the pastures of the lowlands In this manner are also managed numerous large flocks, which are kept on the mountainous tracts of the eastern parts of the county, as well as others on the mountainous lands north of Lancaster sands upon Furness fells it is reckoned that not less than fifty thousand sheep are kept during the summer months, some becoming quite fat, and affording meat of the finest quality In this county sheep are never folded with the view of improving the land The new Leicester, and the South Down breed of sheep, have been introduced into Lancashire, and found to succeed in most parts of it Of hogs there is a middle sized white sort, with slouched ears, which is peculiar to this county, and is frequently met with in the district north of Lancaster, but there is no prevailing breed, the main supply being obtained from dealers, who bring them from Berkshire, Shropshire, Cheshire, and Yorkshire, as also from Wales and Ireland In almost every part of Lancashire are bred good horses of various kinds those in most request are strong team horses, stout, compact saddle horses, and a light mid dle-sized breed for mail-coach and post horses Near all the towns of magnitude are lands of considerable extent applied to the raising of vegetables and fruit the horticultural fields in the neighbourhood of Liverpool more especially, are very extensive, for besides the supply of the town, great quantities of vegetables are required for the shipping, quantities of dried herbs are carried out to Africa, and onions also are exported There are pretty good orchards in different parts of the county, the chief difficulty in raising the trees is that of protecting them from the violence of the western and southwestern winds The soil of the older orchards is often under grass, but that of the younger plantations is generally cultivated with either the spade or the plough Various agricultural societies have been established in different parts of the county The Manchester Agricultural Society was instituted in the year 1767, its views being at first confined to the hundred of Salford, but they have since been extended to a district of about thirty miles round it, comprehending the northern and central parts of the county of Chester its meetings are held twice in each year, one time at Manchester, the other at Altrincham in Cheshire Some time after this, another society of the same kind was established in the south-western part of the county, and, from the name of the hundred in which it is situated, it is denominated the West Derby Agricultural Society A similar institution has been formed in the eastern part of the county, which holds its half-yearly meetings at Whalley, and is called the Whalley Agricultural Society Northward of all these, Lancaster has for some time had its agricultural society, and one was established at Ulverstone, in the year 1805, called the North Lonsdale Agricultural Society

The waste lands consist either of moors and mountain land, or of the boggy tracts called mosses, and of marshes, they are of considerable extent, though of late years different commons have been enclosed, and some of the mosses have long been under tillage The quantity of waste mountain land is computed at about sixty-two thousand acres, and that of the mosses and marshes at about thirty-six thousand acres, of which twenty thousand are contained in the mosses, and the remainder in the marshes, which latter are chiefly found on the western coast The two most extensive tracts of improved moss-land are Trafford-moss, which is now for the most part converted into grass land, and Chat-moss, the draining of which is of later date The tracts which formerly constituted the Forest of Myerscough, Fulwood, Bleasdale, Wyersdale, and Quernmoor, situated in the more northern parts of the county, in the hundreds of Amounderness and Lonsdale, are the property of the King, as Duke of Lancaster The three first of these lie along the side of the great road from Preston to Lancaster Myerscough Forest is wholly enclosed, but those of Fulwood and Bleasdale still have large tracts of un-enclosed ground, more especially where they approach the high ridges of the eastern part of the county The Forest of Wyersdale now forms the township of that name, which lies along the elevated tract on the York-shire boundary it is divided into twelve different por-tions, which still retain the ancient name of vaccaries, or cow-pastures, four of these divisions are wholly en-closed, but the rest have all of them out-pastures, which are high mountainous commons and fells, frequently of great extent The Quernmoor Forest tract is situated further north, and is much smaller than that of Wyers dale, but contains several vaccaries the whole of it is now enclosed These two last-mentioned forests have separate courts, which are held half-yearly by the master forester

In this county there are many stone fences dry stone walls are frequently found in the north and north-eastern parts, dashed walls, and walls built with mor-tar, are most commonly seen in the northernmost part only, sod walls are met with in several places on the borders of the sea. The woods of the county are chief-ly in the more central parts, about Garstang, on the banks of the Wyer, the Ribble, the Lune, and some other rivers, and in the parks of several of the nobility and gentry The principal coppice woods are in the northern parts of the county, the land on which they grow being chiefly steep and rocky, and unfit for any other purpose their main produce is hoop-wood, charcoal, props for the coal mines, and oak-bark Various plantations have been made in different parts of the county, and, amongst other trees, of the alder, which is in great request in the manufacturing districts, where it is used to make cotton yarn on to dry, the wood acquiring a fine polish by use, and not splintering from exposure to the wea-ther the bark of this is made use of in dyeing

The freestone substrata are of three kinds, yellow, white, and red, and are found in almost every district of the county The blue rocky substratum prevails most in the elevated tracts of the liberty of Furness, and the division of Cartmel, north of the sands The lime stone substrata, which are much dispersed, are mostly white in the north-western part of the county, but near the eastern boundary they are often of a dark brown or black colour The limestone and freestone substrata

are often intermingled in a remarkable manner Coal is too deep from the surface to form the basis of soils, except in some places towards the eastern boundary of the county, where it approaches very near the surface Clay and marl, both separate and mingled, frequently form the subsoils of the flat tracts, and are met with at the depth of from five or six inches to several feet Gravel and sand in flat situations, and the latter on elevated ground also, are sometimes found to constitute the subsoil The chief mineral productions are coal, copper, lead, and iron The strata of coal seem to lie for the most part in three distinct parallel ranges, running across the county from south-west to north-east the first begins near Worsley, and takes its course north of Manchester, by Bury and Rochdale, to the eastern boundary of the county above Todmorden, the next, which is the most extensive tract, commences below Prescot, and passes south of Blackburn, by Colne, to the Yorkshire boundary, which it crosses, and the third, which is by far the smallest, begins above Lancaster, in the township of Quernmoor, and extends by Caton, Far-leton, Tatham, and Winnington, to the borders of York-shire These strata lie in some places at a very great depth, while in others they approach very near the sur-face, their thickness and quality also vary greatly, even in the different shafts of the same colliery coal of a black, compact, marbly appearance, called cannel coal, is found chiefly at Haigh, near Wigan. Numerous coal pits are sunk in various parts of the tracts above men-tioned, most of the large collieries having steam-engines of great power Though coal is the ordinary fuel, yet, in the vicinity of the mosses, peat and coal are burned together The principal tract in which copper is found in any considerable quantity is among the rugged barren mountains in the northernmost part of the High Furness district, approaching the borders of Cumberland Here are only two mines, Conistone and Muckle Gill, the former being the older The ore obtained from both mines is of the yellow sort, and but poor in metal after the ore obtained at Muckle Gill has been cleaned, sorted, and broken, it is forwarded to Cheadle in Staffordshire, there to be smelted and manufactured into wire, and sheets for coppering the bottoms of ships Lead-ore is chiefly found in the northern and eastern parts of the county, but it is no where obtained in great quantities The Anglezark mine has been worked for a long time the ore is of the common blue lead kind. The only part of the county where iron is found in sufficient quantity to be worked is in the liberty of Fur-ness, on the north side of Lancaster sands the principal mines are Lindal Moor and Cross Gates. The ore raised at Lindal Moor is generally either sent to the furnace at Newland, or to Old Barrow, to be shipped for Wales, the Carron works, and other places, that obtained at Cross Gates mine is chiefly conveyed to the neigh-bourhood of Broughton, where are extensive smelting works The county produces abundance of slates, flag-stones, limestone, and freestone, for the purposes of building. The blue slate quarries are very numerous, but are chiefly in the rocky mountainous tracts of the northern parts of High Furness slate of a lighter colour and very inferior quality is raised at different places in the county, south of the sands, and at the same places flag-stones are likewise obtained Quarries of freestone are wrought in most parts of the county, south of the sands the best sort of stones for sharpening scythes is found and prepared at Rainford Tracts of limestone, generally of small extent, exist in different parts of the county, both north and south of the sands, in which numerous quarries are worked

The pre-eminence of the manufactures of Lancashire over those of the other districts in England where the inhabitants are similarly engaged, has long been known and acknowledged These manufactures are various, but that of cotton in its different branches is by far the most important, and is one of the most extensive in the world. Manchester is its grand centre, and from that town it has extended over the adjoining and more northern parts of Lancashire, as well as into the adjacent counties on the east and south Soon after the year 1328, about which time the emigrant clothiers from Flanders were dispersed over England, Manchester became famous for the manufacture of a species of woollen goods, called "Manchester cottons" In the reign of Henry VIII this county had made some further progress in manufactures and commerce and at the period of the national disturbances, in the reign of Charles I., the manufactures of linen and cotton, as well as of woollen, were carried on here Until the year 1760, the sale of cotton goods had been almost entirely for home consumption, but about that period, considerable markets for this species of goods were opened on the continents of Europe and America, and the consequent urgent demand encouraged great and valuable improvements in the machinery employed These improvements, the successfully-attained object of which was to lessen the requisite quantity of manual labour, on their first introduction, gave rise to great tumults, the inhabitants of the manufacturing districts destroying the machines, in consequence of the groundless fear that they should otherwise be thrown out of employment One of the most recent inventions of this kind is the power-loom A factory of steam looms was first erected in this district at Manchester in 1806, with two others at Stockport, and a fourth at West Houghton, since which period they have been erected throughout the manufacturing district generally In each of these mills every process, from the picking of the raw cotton to its conversion into cloth, is performed, and on a scale of such magnitude that in a single factory is done as much work as would, in the last age, have engaged an entire district The steam looms are chiefly employed in the production of printing cloth and shirting; but they also weave thicksets, fancy cords, dimities, cambrics, and quiltings, besides silks, worsted, and woollen broad cloths Inkles, tapes, and checks, with woollens, flannels, baizes, and linens, all rank among the manufactures of this county, and have each their proper seat. The silk trade, which had formerly flourished to a considerable extent, but fell into decay in consequence of the rapid growth of the cotton business, has of late revived, and is now carried on with increased activity The spinning and manufacture of cotton prevail at Manchester, Oldham, Colne, Burnley, Haslingden, Preston, Accrington, Bury, Middleton, Ashton, Bolton, Chorley, Blackburn, Heap, Stayley, Wigan, Eccles, Bacup, Chowbent, Rochdale, &c, calico-printing and bleaching at Manchester, Blackburn, Bolton, Bury, Accrington, and Chorley, muslins at Manchester, Bolton, Chorley, and Preston, and fustians

at Manchester, Oldham, Bury, Bolton, Warrington, and Heap The manufacture of woollen goods is extensively carried on at Manchester, Bury, Bacup Newchurch, Rochdale, and Heap flannels are made at Manchester, Rochdale, and Haslingden There are several hat manufactories at Manchester, Oldham, Rochdale, Denton, Bolton, Audenshaw, Howley Hill, Colne, and Wigan Paper is made at Manchester, Bolton, Blackburn, Farnworth, Ashton, and Warrington. Lancaster, the county town, possesses comparatively but little of the above manufactures, its chief trade being in the manufacture and exportation of mahogany furniture and upholstery In the town of Warrington are large manufactories for pins, glass, and other articles, but the principal employment is in the making of sail-cloth At Ulverstone, as well as at Caton, are manufactories for the working of flax, and at the former town some checks are manufactured There are many iron works and nail manufactories in different parts of the county the principal works of this kind are those for smelting iron-ore, in that portion of the county which lies north of Lancaster sands In this part of the county also, on the banks of the Leven, are powder-mills Glass and earthenware establishments are very numerous, the largest being at St Helen's and Warrington, and in the south-western part of the county, watches, watch movements, and watch tools, are made to a considerable extent and in great perfection In these various branches of manufacture is employed an immense number of persons it is supposed that not less than one hundred and fifty thousand individuals are engaged in the cotton trade alone in Lancashire, the economy of labour produced by machinery at the same time being, in some of its branches, the spinning more especially, so great, that one man and four children will spin as much yarn as was spun by six hundred women and girls fifty years ago Immense quantities of cotton yarn are exported for the supply of the manufactures of France, Germany, and Switzerland

The commerce of Lancashire, like its manufactures and in conjunction with them, has risen with unexampled rapidity, and attained an importance unequalled by that of any other county, Middlesex alone excepted Besides the great port of Liverpool, there are the minor ones of Lancaster, Ulverstone, and Preston, which have each a coasting trade, though very little foreign commerce Great part of the foreign commerce of Lancashire, of which Liverpool is the grand medium, consists in the exportation of the manufactures of the county, together with the woollens and cutlery of Yorkshire, the produce of the salt-mines of Cheshire, the earthenware of Staffordshire, and the hardware of Warwickshire, which are poured into this great western emporium, and thence forwarded to America and the West Indies, Africa and the East Indies, and to the continent of Europe, exclusively of the vast trade with Ireland The imports consist of cotton, sugar, tobacco, rice, corn, timber, and a variety of other commodities, the productions of every civilized country and of all climates The canal system of inland navigation, which in this county is peculiarly extensive, and to which may be added the important ranges of newly formed rail-roads, facilitate and expedite this immense traffic in an astonishing degree

The rivers and streams of Lancashire are very numerous the Mersey, the Ribble, and the Lune, or Loyne, are its largest rivers, and next to these in magnitude are the Irwell, the Douglas, the Wyer, the Leven, the Crake, and the Dudden, all of which to some extent are navigable The Mersey constitutes the southern boundary of this county, separating it from Cheshire, and is formed by the small rivers Tame, Etherow and Goyt, which respectively rise in the counties of York, Chester, and Derby, and unite at Stockport, from which town the Mersey takes a winding south-westerly course, and below Warrington spreads into a channel of considerable breadth, the greater part of which is dry at low water, but it is suddenly contracted by the projecting point of land opposite Runcorn, below which it again expands, and having been augmented by various streams, forms a large æstuary, which opens into the Irish sea, in a north westerly direction a little below Liverpool, being much narrower opposite that town than it is some miles further inland The tide flows up this river as far as the vicinity of Warrington, where it is stopped by a weir In pursuance of an act of parliament obtained in the year 1720, for making navigable the rivers Mersey and Irwell, in that part of their course lying between Liverpool and Manchester, this river, by the aid of an artificial cut from the south of Warrington to some distance above that town, pursuant to an act obtained in 1720, is made navigable for barges of from sixty to seventy tons burden, as far as the mouth of the Irwell, which latter river in like manner is rendered navigable up to Manchester the Mersey yields salmon, smelts, and soles, besides a great variety of other fish The Ribble rises in the moors above Craven in Yorkshire, and having formed the boundary between that county and Lancashire for a few miles in the vicinity of Clitheroe, it enters the county, and intersects it from east to west, passing by Ribchester and Preston, below which latter town it soon expands into a broad æstuary which joins the Irish sea The tide flows up this river as high as Preston, near to which place it is navigable for vessels of small burden Salmon of delicious flavour frequent this river, and the fishery extends as high as Brockholes The Lune, or Loyne, has its rise in the mountainous tracts of Westmorland, and entering this county a little below the bridge at Kirkby-Lonsdale, pursues a south-westerly course to Lancaster, and some distance lower widens into a broad æstuary, and finally joins the Irish sea at Sunderland point This river is navigable for small vessels to Lancaster, but ships of great burden can pass no higher than Glasson point like the other navigable rivers of Lancashire, it affords a plentiful supply of salmon The Irwell is formed by several small streams which rise in the hilly tracts to the south of Haslingden, and runs in an irregular southerly course by Bury to Manchester, where it becomes navigable from this town it takes a south-westerly course, and falls into the Mersey a little below Flixton flowing through the most populous districts of the county, this river affords great advantage to the different manufactories situated on its banks The Douglas rises on the moors of Anglezark, to the north of Rivington Pike, and taking a southerly course to Wigan, runs from that town in a north-westerly direction, and falls into the æstuary of he Ribble at Hesketh Bank In the year 1727 this river was made navigable from the Ribble as high as Wigan, under the provisions of an act passed in 1719

by means of this work the northern parts of Lancashire and Westmorland are supplied with coal from this district, which receives limestone and slate from those parts in return the navigation has been improved at a later date by the substitution, in a part of its course, of an artificial cut for the natural channel of the river The Wyer has its source in the hills on the eastern border of the county, and flows in a south-westerly direction to Lower Garstang, where it takes a more westerly course, by Garstang Church Town, to Poulton, in the neighbourhood of which town it fast increases in breadth, and, turning towards the north, expands into a spacious bason called Wyer Water, which is terminated by a narrow passage through which the river flows into the Irish sea The Wyer is navigable for small vessels up to Poulton upon its banks are various factories, and the scenery of the valley through which it flows is in many places bold and romantic The Leven is the rapid river which flows out of the lake of Winandermere, through the township of Haverthwaite, into a large æstuary opening into the bay of Morecambe The Crake flows from the southern extremity of Conistone lake into the æstuary of the Leven, near Penny-bridge The Dudden, which, through almost the whole of its course, forms the boundary between this county and Cumberland, has its source among the small lakes, provincially called tarns, above Seathwaite, in the hilly tracts of High Furness, and, flowing southward, forms a large bay to the south-west of Broughton The mouth of the Ken, from Westmorland, which opens into the bay of Morecambe, isolates the northern division of the hundred of Lonsdale from the rest of the county The smaller streams are numberless, those most worthy of mention are the Alt, the East Calder, the West Calder, the torrent of Leck-beck, which falls into the Lune, and the Winster, which for some miles forms the boundary between that portion of the county which lies north of the sands and Westmorland In the northernmost portion of the county are different sheets of water of these Conistone lake, sometimes called Thurston water, is situated in the northern part of the High Furness district, between two ranges of rocky mountainous land, and extends in length six or seven miles from north to south, the breadth varying from half a mile to three-quarters its greatest depth is stated to be about forty fathoms its principal fish are char, trout, and perch, and of all an abundance Only a small contracted portion of the magnificent lake of Winandermere is contained in this county, but that piece of water bounds it on the east for the distance of eight or ten miles Esthwaite water is situated to the east of Hawkeshead, and is about a mile and a half in length, and somewhat less than half a mile in breadth, being contracted in the middle by a projection from each side its fish are pike, trout, eels, and perch Hareswater, which is of no great extent, lies northward of Leighton-moss its fish are pike and eels During the winter, Marten mere, near Ormskirk, is a large sheet of water, but in summer it becomes nearly dry In the northern parts of the county are different smaller lakes, commonly called tarns The springs which break forth from the more elevated grounds of the county are very numerous some are medicinal, as at Cartmel, Flookborough, Wigan, and other places. The artificial inland navigation of this county is very extensive, and it was here that the canal navigation of modern times first took its rise The first attempts of this kind were in rendering navigable the streams which run through these manufacturing and commercial districts, and after the deepening of the rivers before mentioned, an act was passed, in 1755, for making Sankey brook navigable, and in 1761 another act was obtained, which provided for the extension of the same line the present navigation is called the Sankey canal, and runs entirely separate from the brook, except at one spot about two miles below Sankey bridge, where it crosses it on a level at the distance of about nine miles and a quarter from its termination in the Mersey, it divides into three branches, and from the Mersey to the extremity of the longest of these the distance is eleven miles and three quarters, with a fall of about sixty feet this canal is of great benefit to the collieries and the various manufactories near it, in the vicinity of the populous town of St Helen s

The magnificent plans which have rendered the name of the Duke of Bridgewater so celebrated in the history of canal navigation, began to unfold themselves in 1758 and 1759, an act having passed in the former year enabling that nobleman to form a canal from Worsley to Salford, and also to Hollin-ferry on the Irwell, and another in the latter year permitting him to deviate from that course, and carry his canal from Worsley across the river Irwell to Manchester The formation of this canal was the work of that eminent self-taught engineer, James Brindley at its upper extremity at Worsley it passes through a tunnel of almost half a mile in length, partly arched with brick, and partly formed by the solid rock, whence it has been extended in various directions to the distance of thirty miles As it was a main object to keep this canal as much on the level as possible, the embankments and aqueducts in its course are numerous, but of the latter, that by far the most remarkable is at Barton, by which it passes over the navigable river Irwell, and which consists of three massive stone arches, of which the central arch is sixty-three feet wide, and thirty-eight feet high above the surface of the water, admitting the largest barges which navigate the Irwell to go through with masts and sails standing, and affording the curious and interesting spectacle of one vessel sailing over the top of another But before this first design was completed, the Duke of Bridgewater conceived the plan of extending his canal, by a branch which, running through part of Cheshire, in a line parallel with the river Mersey, should at length terminate in that river, below the limits of its artificial navigation. An act of parliament was accordingly obtained for the formation of this canal, which was completed in the five years following, and extends from Longford bridge, in the township of Stretford, to the river Mersey at Runcorn-gap, a distance of more than twenty-nine miles it is carried over the Mersey by an aqueduct similar to that over the Irwell, but lower, as the river is not there navigable In consequence of the formation of this canal, the rates of carriage between Liverpool and Manchester were reduced, at least one-half. Under the sanction of an act passed in 1795, a branch has been cut from the Duke of Bridgewater's canal at Worsley to Leigh The act for the formation of the Leeds and Liverpool canal, one of the greatest works of the kind in the kingdom, was obtained in 1770,

and the work was commenced the same year From its highest level in the basin of Foulridge, near Colne, the fall on the Lancashire side is four hundred and thirty-three feet four inches, and from this head it passes, in a south-westerly direction, by the towns of Burnley and Blackburn, and having crossed the river Douglas makes a large circuit round Ormskirk, at last reaching the Mersey, at the lower part of the town of Liverpool A branch from this canal to Wigan is upwards of seven miles and a half in length, with a fall of thirty-six feet, and when first completed, which was with great expedition, afforded to Liverpool a new and plentiful supply of coal, and caused a considerable exportation of that commodity from the port Under the authority of acts of parliament passed at various periods, different alterations and improvements have been made in this canal by the company to which it belongs, and one of these, passed in 1794, gave them the power of navigating a part of the then newly-formed Lancaster canal in pursuance of an act obtained in 1819, a navigable cut, six miles in length, was made, from the canal near Wigan to the Duke of Bridgewater s canal at Leigh The whole length of the Leeds and Liverpool canal (including the portion of the Lancaster canal navigated by the Leeds and Liverpool Company, the length of which is nearly eleven miles) is one hundred and twenty-seven miles and twelve chains the distance from Liverpool to its junction with the Lancaster canal is seventy-nine miles and twenty-six chains

In 1791, an act was passed for the formation of a canal which should connect the towns of Manchester, Bolton, and Bury this commences at the Irwell, on the western side of Manchester, and passes in a northerly course nearly parallel with that river, which it crosses at Clifton, and again at Little Lever, at which latter place there is a branch to Bolton, and another to Bury its total length is fifteen miles and one furlong, with a rise of one hundred and eighty-seven feet The district through which this canal passes abounds in coal and other mineral productions, besides which, its inhabitants are engaged in manufactures, and consequently the traffic with Manchester and its vicinity, by means of it, is very great. A cut thirteen miles in length, called the Haslingden Extension, passing by Haslingden, unites this with the Leeds and Liverpool canal, between Blackburn and Burnley, about four miles from the former town the act for the formation of this extension was obtained in 1793 In 1792 an act was passed, sanctioning the formation of a canal from Manchester to Ashton under Line and the vicinity of Oldham it commences on the east side of Manchester, crosses the Medlock, passes Fairfield, and terminates at Ashton under Line, there being at Fairfield a branch to the New Mill, near Oldham, from which there is a cut to Park colliery The whole length of this canal is eleven miles, with a rise of one hundred and fifty-two feet coal, lime, limestone, and manure, are its chief objects of traffic there is a branch from this canal to Stockport An act was passed in 1794, authorising the opening of a line of navigation from the Duke of Bridgewater s canal at Manchester to the Calder navigation at Sowerby bridge, near Halifax, and this, being completed, is called the Rochdale canal Commencing on the south-west side of Manchester, it leaves that town at its north-eastern extremity, and pursues its course to Failsworth, whence, turning directly north, it proceeds through the tract of coal country about Fox-Denton, Chadderton, Middleton, and Hopwood, at a short distance to the east of Rochdale, to which town a small branch diverges having passed Littleborough, it gains its summit level about Deanhead, whence it proceeds to Todmorden, at which place it turns north-east to Hebden bridge, and then inclines somewhat to the south-east, until it reaches the Calder navigation at Sowerby bridge, its whole length, from one extremity to the other, being thirty-nine miles and a half, exclusively of two short collateral branches of about a mile and a quarter from its summit level it falls two hundred and seventy-five feet on the Halifax side, and four hundred and thirty eight feet seven inches on the Manchester side great reservoirs have been made in the hilly country, near different parts of the course of this canal, sufficient to supply it abundantly with water The Huddersfield canal, the act for cutting which passed in 1794, has its western extremity at the Ashton under Line canal, and its eastern at Sir John Ramsden s canal to the Calder its general direction is north-east, and from Ashton it has its course parallel with the Tame (the windings of which river it frequently crosses), to Stayley-Bridge, and enters Yorkshire in the manufacturing district of Saddleworth the extreme length of this canal is nineteen miles and three quarters, and its fall, from the head level on the Ashton side, is three hundred and thirty-four feet eight inches The Kendal and Lancaster canal, for the formation of which an act of parliament was obtained in 1792, commences at Kendal, having a feeder from a rivulet about a mile beyond that town, and proceeding directly southward, enters Lancashire near Burton at Berwick, a little farther south it sinks to its mid level, which it preserves for upwards of forty-two miles, making a very circuitous course, and in some places approaching within a very short distance of the sea-beach a little above Lancaster it crosses the Lune by a magnificent aqueduct, and afterwards passes eastward and southward of that town at Garstang it crosses the Wyre, and having made a bend westward, by which it is brought within two miles of Kirkham, it next passes the western side of Preston, and crosses the Ribble, then, ascending through a series of locks, it joins the Leeds and Liverpool canal, and reaches its highest level, on which it proceeds a little to the eastward of Chorley, across the Douglas, and through Haigh, and bending to the east of Wigan, arrives at its termination at West Houghton, after a course of upwards of seventy-five miles and a half the fall from Kendal to the mid-level is sixty five feet, and the rise thence on the southern side two hundred and twenty-two feet A collateral cut in the neighbourhood of Chorley is nearly three miles long, another near Berwick, nearly two miles and a half, and a third, of about four miles in length, communicates with the dock at Glasson, near the mouth of the Lune The principal objects of this canal are to make an interchange of produce between the coal and the limestone countries, and to form a communication between the port of Lancaster and the interior parts to the north and south The Ulverstone canal is a short cut, about a mile and a half in length, from that town to the navigable channel of the river Leven.

The railways of this county also hold an important place among its facilities of commercial communication.

The most remarkable of these is the Liverpool and Manchester railway, constructed pursuant to an act passed in 1826, and designed to be opened for passengers in August, and for the conveyance of goods, &c, in September, 1830 It commences at the Company's yard in Wapping, Liverpool, by means of a tunnel, which is accessible by an excavation twenty-two feet deep, and forty-six wide, affording space sufficient for four lines of railway, with intervening pillars supporting the beams and flooring of the warehouses built over the excavation, under which the wagons pass to be loaded or unloaded, by means of trap-doors communicating with the upper stories wagons laden with coal or lime pass under the warehouses to the wharfs at the Wapping end of the station. Proceeding along the tunnel, this level line of railway curves to the right, till it reaches the bottom of the inclined plane, which is perfectly straight, and one thousand nine hundred and eighty yards long, with a uniform rise of three quarters of an inch in a yard, making the whole rise, from Wapping to the mouth of the tunnel at Edge-hill, one hundred and twenty-three feet The tunnel is twenty-two feet wide, and sixteen feet high, the sides rising perpendicularly to the height of five feet, and is surmounted by a semicircular arch of eleven feet radius it is cut through various strata of red rock, blue shale, and clay, but principally through rock of almost every degree of hardness the space, from its roof to the surface of the ground, varies from five feet to seventy through out its entire length, it is lighted with gas, and the sides and roof are white-washed At the upper end is a spacious and noble area, forty feet below the surface of the ground, excavated in the solid rock, and surmounted on all sides by embattled walls, from which a small tunnel, two hundred and ninety yards in length, fifteen feet wide, and twelve feet high, lighted also with gas, returns parallel with the large one, but inclining upwards in the opposite direction, and terminating at the Company's premises in Crown-street, on the eastern side of the town, this being the principal station for the railway coaches, and the depôt for coal for supplying the upper part of the town. Advancing eastward from the two tunnels, the road passes under a Moorish archway, intended to connect the two engine-houses, and forming the grand entrance to the Liverpool stations, whence it emerges into the open air, and proceeds to a little beyond Wavertree-lane, where it passes through a deep excavation, and under several massive arches, thrown across to form the necessary communication between the roads and farms on each side Beyond this, about half a mile north-west of the village of Wavertree, is the great rocky excavation through Olive Mount, seventy feet below the surface of the ground, and a little further is the great Raby embankment, formed of the materials dug out of the mount this embankment extends across the valley for about two miles, varying in height from fifteen feet to forty-five, and in breadth at the base from sixty to one hundred and thirty-five feet After leaving it, the line crosses the Hayton turnpike-road, and proceeds, in a slightly-curved direction, to the bottom of the inclined plane at Whiston this plane forms a straight line a mile and a half long, with a rise only of one yard in ninety-six, which, however, causes a perceptible decrease in the velocity of the carriage, but at its termination there is a portion of the road, nearly two miles in length, exactly level. About half a mile from the summit of the inclined plane, the railway passes under a substantial stone bridge on the line of the Liverpool and Manchester turnpike-road, at an angle of 34° this bridge is a curious and beautiful structure, on the diagonal principle, the span of the arch is fifty-four feet, while that of the railway, from wall to wall, is only thirty, each face of the arch extends diagonally forty-five feet beyond the square It was in the vicinity of this bridge that the trial of the locomotive engines, which contended for a premium of £500, took place in October, 1829 Passing over the summit level at Rainhill, the road reaches the Sutton inclined plane, which, descending in an opposite direction, is equal, in extent and inclination, to the Whiston plane, the summit level being eighty-two feet above the base of each It then crosses Par Moss, the foundation of the road along the principal part of it being composed of a deposit of clay and stone, twenty-five feet deep, dug out of the Sutton inclined plane Continuing its course, the railway is carried over the valley of the Sankey, with its canal at the bottom, by a noble viaduct of nine arches, each fifty feet in the span, built principally of brick faced with stone, at an expense of upwards of £45,000 the height, from the top of the parapets to the water in the canal, is seventy feet, and the width of the railway twenty-five The approach to this structure is along a stupendous embankment, formed chiefly of clay dug out of the high lands on the borders of the valley Approaching the borough of Newton, the railway crosses a narrow valley, by a short but lofty embankment, and a bridge of four arches, each fifty feet span A few miles beyond is the great Kenyon excavation, from which about eight hundred thousand cubic yards of clay were dug, part of which was applied in forming an embankment to the east and west of the excavation, the remainder being deposited in spoil banks on the adjacent lands Having crossed Bury-lane, and the small river Glazebrook, the road enters upon Chat Moss, a barren waste, comprising an area of about twelve square miles, which it crosses by means of an embankment consisting of about two hundred and seventy thousand cubic yards of moss earth, in the formation of which, about six hundred and seventy-seven thousand cubic yards of raw moss were used, the bottom is composed of clay and sand the expense of carrying the railway over this moss was £27,719 11 10 Beyond Chat Moss it traverses the Barton embankment, crossing the low lands for about a mile, between the moss and the Worsley canal, over which it is carried by a neat stone bridge, thence it proceeds to Manchester, passing through the town of Salford It is carried over the river Irwell, by a handsome stone bridge of two arches, each sixty-five feet in the span, and thirty feet high from the central summit to the surface of the water, and then over a series of arches to the Company's station, in Water-street, and the Liverpool-road. This railway is thirty-one miles in length, and the expense of its completion, including the cost of machinery and carriages, will amount to upwards of £800,000 there are sixty-three bridges, besides sundry culverts and foot-bridges, along the line There is a railway from Bolton to Leigh, and thence to the Liverpool and Manchester railway, communicating with the latter at Kenyon, by two branches A rail-

way from Wigan to Newton, with an extended line from Newton to Warrington, crossing the great railway, is in progress, as is also a line of railway from St Helen's to Runcorn Gap There is an extent of iron-railway from West Houghton, by Bulmer bridge, to Preston, upon which coal and other articles are conveyed to the Lancaster canal, at the last-mentioned town Nearly all the more extensive coal-works have similar roads on a smaller scale, and various manufacturing establishments are likewise provided with them

The great road from London to Carlisle enters the county from Knutsford in Cheshire, and passing through Warrington, Newton, Wigan, Standish, Preston, Lancaster, and Bolton, quits it for Burton in Westmorland The great road from London to Manchester and Preston enters the county from Stockport in Cheshire, and passes through Manchester, Bolton in the Moors, and Chorley The road from London to Halifax and Clitheroe enters Lancashire from Halifax in Yorkshire, and passes through Burnley The road from London to Manchester and Clitheroe branches off from the Preston road at Manchester, and passes through Bury and Haslingden The extent of public roads in Lancashire is very great those in the coal-tracts about Manchester, Bolton, and Wigan, are all paved Lancashire has, of late years, become celebrated for the many fine bathing stations along its coast, viz, Liverpool, Blackpool, Bootle, Lytham, South-port, &c, which are resorted to during summer by many thousands

Eight Roman stations according to Whitaker, were established within the limits of this county during the administration of Julius Agricola in Britain, viz, Ad Alaunam and Bremetonacæ, in the north, which are conjectured to have been at Lancaster and Overborough, respectively, Portus Sistuntiorum, in the west, Rerigonium and Coccium, about the centre, the latter supposed to have been at Blackrod, or Ribchester, Colonea, on the east, supposed to have been at Colne and Veratinum and Mancunium on the south, the latter having been at Manchester From this last station several Roman roads diverged, viz, one south-easterly, towards Stockport, another south-westerly, into Cheshire, by Stretford, a third north-westerly, to Blackrod, from which, near Pendleton, a vicinal way branched off to Warrington, a fourth ran to Coccium, or Ribchester, and thence to Bremetonacæ, or Overborough, a fifth was carried north-east, towards Halifax, and a sixth more easterly, towards Almondbury in Yorkshire The principal Roman remains discovered in this county have been found at Lancaster, Overborough, Colne, Ribchester, Warrington, and Manchester, the sites of the Roman stations Of ancient churches the most remarkable are the Collegiate Church of Manchester, and Cartmel church The number of religious houses before the Reformation was twenty-one, including three hospitals in different places, and the college at Manchester the principal remains of conventual buildings are those of the abbeys of Whalley, Cockersand, and Furness, especially the latter, which are very extensive Of ancient castles the principal remains are those at Clitheroe, Dalton, Gleaston, Greenhalgh, Hornby, and Lancaster, of which the last is the most remarkable, and entire, being now used as the county gaol Of ancient domestic architecture, there are numerous remains throughout the county, of which, Hulme hall, on the banks of the Irwell, near Manchester, the ancient residence of the Prestwich family, and Speake hall, on the banks of the Mersey, near Liverpool, the ancient residence of the Norris family, are the most curious and perfect specimens, though now fast falling to decay, and among the more distinguished modern seats are, Knowsley hall, the seat of the Earl of Derby, Ashton hall, of the Duke of Hamilton, and Heaton house, of the Earl of Wilton The most remarkable ancient earthworks are at Aldingham, Overborough, and Brierscliffe

Arms.

LANCASTER, a parish comprising the borough, port, and market town of Lancaster, having separate jurisdiction, the chapelries of Caton, Gressingham, Overton, Poulton, and Over Wyersdale, and the townships of Aldcliffe, Ashton with Stodday, Bare, Bulk, Heaton with Oxcliffe, Middleton, Quernmoor, Scotforth, Skerton, Thurnham, and Torrisholme, in the hundred of LONSDALE, south of the sands, and the chapelries of Bleasdale, and Stalmine with Stanall, and the townships of Fulwood, Myerscough, and Preesall with Hackersall, in the hundred of AMOUNDERNESS, county palatine of LANCASTER, and containing 19,372 inhabitants, of which number, 10,144 are in the borough of Lancaster, 240 miles (N N W) from London This place is supposed to have been the *Ad Alaunam* of the Romans, and the discovery of coins, urns, fragments of earthenware, calcined bones, votive altars, sepulchral lamps, and other Roman antiquities, confirms the probability of its having been occupied as a station by that people After the departure of the Romans from Britain, it was destroyed by an incursion of the Picts and Scots, and continued in a state of desolation till the time of the Saxons, by whom it was restored, and, from its situation as a fortress near the river Lune, called *Lun ceastre*, from which its present name is deduced In the seventh century, according to the same author, it had risen to such importance as to be made the capital of the county, an honour which it still retains, but it suffered so much injury during the Danish incursions, that in the Norman survey it is noticed only as a vill, or berewic, included in the manor of Halton At the time of the Conquest it was given by William I to Roger de Poictou, who is supposed to have enlarged and adapted for his baronial residence, the ancient castle, of which the western tower is erroneously said to have been built by Adrian, in 124, and that facing the town, by the father of Constantine the Great, in 305 the beautiful gateway tower was erected by John, Earl of Morton and Lancaster, who, after his accession to the throne, gave audience to the French ambassadors, and received the homage of Alexander, King of Scotland (whom he had subdued), in this castle John of Gaunt, the fourth son of Edward III, having succeeded to the title of his father-in-law, Henry Plantagenet, Duke of Lancaster, erected that tower in the castle which has obtained the name of John of Gaunt's chair On the accession of this prince to the dukedom, in 1376, the county was constituted a palatinate Separate courts for this independent jurisdiction are still opened at Lancaster, but they adjourn

to Preston, and business is chiefly transacted there and in the duchy court at Westminster In 1322 and 1369, the town was burnt and plundered by the Scots, and in the wars of the houses of York and Lancaster it was nearly depopulated, in consequence of the resolute adherence of the inhabitants to the cause of the Lancastrians During the parliamentary war it suffered severely, and, in 1698, an accidental fire destroyed a considerable portion of the town, which also, in the rebellion of 1745, participated in the agitations that disturbed the peace of the kingdom

The town is pleasantly situated on the acclivities of an eminence crowned with the stately towers of the castle, and on the southern bank of the river Lune, over which a handsome stone bridge of five elliptical arches has been erected, at an expense of £12,000, connecting the town with the township of Skerton, about half a mile to the east of an ancient bridge now in ruins, which had been built over the narrower part of the river, near St George's quay With the exception of a few which are spacious, the streets are generally narrow, but considerable improvement in the general appearance of the town has been made, under the provisions of an act of parliament obtained, in 1784, for erecting the bridge, and more is still in progress, under an act obtained, in 1824, for cleansing, watching, lighting, and paving the town the houses, built of freestone found in the neighbourhood, and covered with slate, are in general of handsome appearance, in various parts of the town are some noble mansions, and in the environs, which abound with varied and interesting scenery, are several elegant villas The theatre is occasionally opened, and assemblies are held in a suite of rooms well adapted to the purpose the public baths are conveniently arranged, and provided with every requisite accommodation a book society, called the Amicable, which was instituted in 1769, has accumulated a library of four thousand volumes, and a mechanics library was opened in 1824 A society for promoting the fine arts, by the purchase of paintings by the most eminent living artists, was established in 1820, and is well supported

The port is subject to much inconvenience from the difficulty of the navigation of the Lune, arising from the accumulation of sand in its channel, and an elevation in its bed, called Scaleford, probably the remains of a Roman ford across the river, which renders it inaccessible to vessels of large burden, in consequence of which, a dock was constructed, in 1787, at Glasson, nearly five miles down the river, capable of sheltering twenty-five merchantmen, which discharge their cargoes by lighters at St George's quay, on which a custom-house, a neat edifice with an Ionic portico, was erected, in 1764 The foreign trade is chiefly with America and the West Indies, the exports are mahogany furniture of every description, sadlery, shoes, woollen, linen, and cotton goods, soap, candles, and provisions, the imports are sugar, coffee, rum, cotton, mahogany and dye woods Lancaster carries on also a very considerable coasting trade twenty-eight British ships entered inwards from foreign ports, and twelve cleared outwards, in 1826, and the number of vessels belonging to the port, in 1829, was fifty one, averaging a burden of one hundred and thirteen tons there is a considerable salmon fishery on the river Lune, which also abounds with trout The principal manufactures are mahogany furniture and upholstery, for exportation, cordage, sail-cloth, and cotton goods, for which last there are three factories in the town, in two of which two hundred power-looms are employed · cotton and worsted yarn are also spun to a considerable extent there are two yards for boat-building, and formerly vessels of considerable burden were built here The Lancaster canal, constructed in pursuance of an act of parliament passed in 1792, opens a communication with the mining district, and supplies the neighbourhood with coal and other necessaries, but the want of a more extended line of internal navigation operates unfavourably to the increase of the trade, and the scarcity of fuel to the extension of the manufactures, of the town About a mile to the north-east, the canal is carried over the river Lune, by an aqueduct of stone, consisting of five semicircular arches, each seventy feet in the span, erected, at an expense of £48,000, under the direction of Mr Rennie The market days are Wednesday and Saturday the fairs, which are chiefly for cattle, cloth, cheese, and pedlary, and which continue for three days each, are, May 1st, July 5th, and October 10th, which last is the principal cheese fair in the county

Lancaster was first incorporated by charter, in the 4th year of the reign of Richard I, of John, Earl of Morton, afterwards King John, who granted and confirmed to the burgesses all the liberties he had before granted to those of Bristol, and Edward III confirmed and extended those privileges, allowing the mayor and bailiffs the privilege of having the pleas and sessions held here, to the exclusion of every other place in the county The government, under the charter of George III, granted in 1819 is vested in a mayor, recorder two bailiffs, seven aldermen, twelve capital burgesses and twelve common council men, assisted by a town clerk, two serjeants at mace, and subordinate officers The mayor, who acts as coroner for the borough, and the bailiff of the brethren, are elected annually on the Thursday after October 18th, by the aldermen and capital burgesses, from their own bodies, and the bailiff of the commons, by the free burgesses, from the common council-men The freedom is obtained by birth, or servitude, all the sons of freemen being entitled to it on payment of a small fee to the mayor, bailiffs, and commonalty Among the privileges may be reckoned an interest in the tract of ground called Lancaster Marsh, consisting of two hundred and ten acres, enclosed in 1795, the rents of which are divided amongst eighty of the oldest freemen, or their widows The mayor is a justice of the peace for the county, and he and the aldermen are justices of the peace within the borough, holding quarterly courts of session for all offences not capital, also a court of pleas every week, for the recovery of debts to any amount A court for the hundred of Lonsdale is also held here, on the first Wednesday in every month, for the recovery of debts under 40s The town hall is a neat building, erected, in 1781, at an expense of £1300, and containing a court-room and apartments for the trans-

Corporate Seal.

action of the public business of the corporation it is embellished with full length portraits of the Rt Hon William Pitt, and Admiral Lord Nelson, painted by Mr Lonsdale, a native of the town, and presented by him to the corporation The borough prison is a small edifice, for the temporary confinement of prisoners, who are subsequently sent to Lancaster castle The borough first exercised the elective franchise in the 23rd of Edward I., and continued to make returns till the 1st of Edward II, it afterwards intermitted till the reign of Edward VI, since which time it has regularly returned two members to parliament the right of election is vested in the freemen generally, of whom there are about three thousand the mayor and bailiffs are the returning officers The court of pleas for the county palatine is held twice in the year, before the judges of the northern circuit, and the assizes and general quarter sessions for the county are also held in this town, where also, as being the county town, the election of knights of the shire takes place The remains of the ancient castle are used as the county gaol, and additional buildings have been erected, upon a very extensive scale, at an expense exceeding £140,000 The entrance, through a gateway of beautiful design, over which is a statue of John of Gaunt, Duke of Lancaster, is flanked by octagonal towers and leads into a spacious court-yard enclosed with embattled walls and strengthened with towers, opposite to the entrance is the ancient square keep, a building of prodigious strength, to the north of which are the shire-hall and courts with the room for the grand jury, and other apartments the hall is of a semicircular form, and elegantly and commodiously arranged for the business of the assizes the nisi prius court, in which are full-length portraits of Colonel Stanley and Mr Blackburn, presented by the late Sir Robert Peel, Bart, exhibits some architectural beauty, and in the crown court is an equestrian portrait of King George III, painted by Northcote, and presented to the county by James Ackers, Esq, while high sheriff The common gaol comprises seventeen divisions for the classification of prisoners, seventy-three workrooms, thirty-two day-rooms, and twelve airing yards, there are two tread mills employed in pumping water and turning power looms, a considerable portion of their earnings is paid to the prisoners on their discharge The castle hill and terrace afford a fine promenade, commanding extensive views of the surrounding scenery, which is most richly diversified

The living is a vicarage, in the archdeaconry of Richmond, and diocese of Chester, rated in the king's books at £41, and in the patronage of Oliver Marton, Esq The church, dedicated to St Mary, and to which the privilege of sanctuary was anciently attached, was originally erected by Roger de Poictou, who founded a Benedictine priory here, as a cell to the abbey of St Martin de Seez in Normandy, which, on the suppression of Alien priories, was by Henry V annexed to the abbey of Sion in Middlesex the present edifice is in the later style of English architecture, and contains some fine specimens of skreen-work and carvings in oak, which are thought to have been brought from Cockersand abbey, on its dissolution The registry for this division of the archdeaconry is kept in this church, in which also the Commissary's court was formerly held Among the monuments is one by Roubiliac to the memory of William Stratford, L.L D , and in the church-yard is the shaft of a Danish cross, embellished with sculpture, and bearing an inscription in Runic characters St John s chapel was built by subscription, in 1755 the living is a perpetual curacy, endowed with £400 private benefaction, £400 royal bounty, and £800 parliamentary grant, and in the patronage of the Vicar of Lancaster St Ann s chapel was erected, in 1796, at the sole expense of the Rev Robert Houseman the patronage of the living, a perpetual curacy endowed with £800 royal bounty, will revert to the vicar in the course of fifty years after the date of its erection There are places of worship for Baptists, the Society of Friends, Independents, Primitive and Wesleyan Methodists, and Presbyterians, and a Roman Catholic chapel The free grammar school is of uncertain origin it existed prior to 1615, at which time Rundall Carter, of London, bequeathed £10 per annum as a salary for an usher , and it appears to have been generally supported by the corporation, by whom it was most probably founded, and who have the nomination of the head master there are about sixty scholars attending it, who pay a certain quarterage, and of whom a few receive classical instruction the salaries of the masters are paid by the corporation The Blue-coat charity school, established by subscription in 1770, has been incorporated with the National school for boys, for which a spacious stone building was erected, in 1817, by subscription, at an expense of £1100, and which in that year was endowed by Mr Matthew Pyper, one of the Society of Friends, with £2000 Navy five per cent annuities there are in this school three hundred and forty boys, of whom a certain number is clothed. A National school for girls with a house for the mistress, was built, in 1820, by subscription there are one hundred and twenty girls in the school, who are instructed in reading, writing, and household work, to qualify them for domestic service A charity school, established in 1772, in which sixty girls are taught to read, write, knit, sew, and spin, is supported partly by subscription, and partly by the earnings of the children, a fourth part of which is given to them A school, in which are eighty children, was established in 1820, and is sup ported by the Roman Catholics of the town , and there are Sunday schools in connexion with the established church and the several dissenting congregations Gardyner s almshouses, founded in 1485, consisting of four tenements adjoining the vicarage-house, are appropriated to four aged men, between whom the sum of £6 11 8 , in quarterly payments, is divided by the corporation Penny s almshouses, consisting of twelve tenements, with a chapel forming three sides of a quadrangle, the area of which is laid out in gardens for the almspeople, was founded, by a bequest from William Penny, Esq , in 1715, and endowed with lands producing about £340 per annum, for twelve aged men or women, who are appointed by the corporation, and receive each £3 6 8 per quarter, a suit of clothes, and other allowances from the same fund a chaplain receives a small stipend, for reading prayers to the almspeople, and some apprentice fees are given with poor children Eight almshouses were founded, in 1781, by Mrs Anne Gillison, who endowed them with land and money producing about £40 per annum, for eight unmarried women, to each of whom £4 and a gown are given annually There are numerous charitable bequests for distribution,

among which the most considerable is that of William Heysham, M P , who, in 1725, bequeathed an estate producing £256 per annum, in trust to the corporation, for the benefit of eight poor men resident within the borough , and there are several for the relief of prisoners for debt confined in Lancaster castle The county lunatic asylum, on Lancaster moor, was established in 1816, and is conducted under the superintendence of a committee of visiting magistrates, of whom the Rt Hon Lord Stanley is president the establishment comprise a physician, surgeon, superintendent, matron house-steward, treasurer, and chaplain The premises comprise a spacious quadrangular building of stone, with a handsome portico of the Doric order, and, with the gardens and grounds, occupy five acres of land the buildings contain hot and cold baths, with every accommodation requisite for the patients, and under the long covered galleries afford opportunities of exercise in bad weather , and the grounds furnish every kind of amusement that may contribute to the health and recreation of the patients there are about one hundred and forty males, and about one hundred and twenty females, in this asylum, who are individually treated with a due regard to their several degrees and species of malady , and a chapel has been erected, in which many of those whose state of mind renders them susceptible of its influence, derive the consolation of religion A dispensary for supplying the sick poor with medicine was instituted in 1781 , and connected with it is a house of recovery for persons labouring under contagious diseases The reigning sovereign enjoys the title of Duke of Lancaster

LANCAUT, a chapelry in the parish of TIDENHAM, hundred of WESTBURY, though locally in that of Blidesloe, county of GLOUCESTER, 2 miles (N) from Chepstow The population is returned with the parish The chapel, which is dedicated to St James, is under the rector of Wollastone, in the archdeaconry of Hereford, and diocese of Gloucester

LANCHESTER, a parish comprising the chapelries of Ebchester, Esh, Medomsley, and Satley, and the townships of Benfield-side, Burnop with Hamsteels, Butsfield, Collierly, Conside with Knitsley, Billingside, Greencroft, Heelyfield, Holmside, Ivestone, Kyo, Lanchester, and Langley, in the western division of CHESTER ward, and the township of Comsay, in the north-western division of DARLINGTON ward, county palatine of DURHAM, and containing 4979 inhabitants, of which number, 659 are in the township of Lanchester, 8 miles (N W by W) from Durham The living is a perpetual curacy, in the archdeaconry and diocese of Durham, endowed with £1040 private benefaction, £200 royal bounty, and £900 parliamentary grant, and in the patronage of the Bishop of Durham The church, dedicated to All Saints, is a venerable structure in the early style of English architecture, surmounted by a square tower of hewn stone, adorned with battlements and flying buttresses in the interior are several sculptured decorations, interesting monuments, and portions of stained glass It was made collegiate, for a dean and seven prebendaries, by Bishop Anthony Beke, about 1283, and valued, at the dissolution, at £49 3 4 , and in the Lincoln taxation at £90 13 4 , per annum the dean s house occupied a plot of ground surrounded by a fosse, a little northward from the church , but there are no vestiges, excepting six carved oak seats under an arch in the northern wall of the chancel, and a *piscina* on the southern side of the altar There is a place of worship for Wesleyan Methodists A free school was established by subscription, in 1748, and is endowed with £10 per annum, the bequest of George Clavering, Esq , of Green-croft At Cornsey, in this parish, almshouses for the maintenance of six poor men and six poor women, with a master and a mistress, were founded, by the late W Russel, Esq , of Brancepeth castle, and endowed with a rent-charge Petty sessions are held here once a fort-night, and a court for the recovery of debts under 40s twice a year The new turnpike road from Durham to Shotley bridge, made under an act of parliament ob-tained in 1810, passes through the vale in this parish Lanchester occupies the site of a principal Roman sta-tion, though its identity has been disputed by antiquaries Camden, Gale, and Hunter, call it *Longovicum*, Horsley, *Glambanta* or *Glanoventa* (considered the most perfect Roman station in the kingdom), whilst modern writers regard it as *Epiacum* the period of its origin is uncer-tain, but its restoration is ascribed to the Emperor Gordian it stood on the line of the Watling-street, and was successively garrisoned by a portion of the twen-tieth legion, the *Varduli*, and the *Ligones* The station occupied an eminence half a mile westward from the village , the rampart, enclosing a cultivated area of eight acres, is in most parts quite perfect numerous coins, altars, monuments, and other relics, have been disco-vered at different periods , several of which are pre-served in the library at Durham

LANCING, a parish in the hundred of BRIGHTFORD, rape of BRAMBER, county of SUSSEX, 2 miles (E N E) from Worthing, containing 590 inhabitants The living is a discharged vicarage, in the archdeaconry and diocese of Chichester, rated in the king's books at £6 9 4 , and in the patronage of the Bishop of Lincoln The church has lately received an addition of one hundred and fourteen sittings, of which seventy are free, the In-corporated Society for the enlargement of churches and chapels having granted £30 towards defraying the ex-pense The parish is bounded on the east by the river Adur and Shoreham harbour, and on the south by the English channel

LANDBEACH, a parish in the hundred of NORTH-STOW, county of CAMBRIDGE, 5 miles (N N E) from Cambridge, containing 371 inhabitants The living is a rectory, in the archdeaconry and diocese of Ely, rated in the king's books at £10 1 3 , and in the patronage of the Master and Fellows of Corpus Christi College, Cambridge The church is dedicated to All Saints

LANDCROSS, a parish in the hundred of SHEB-BEAR, county of DEVON, 2½ miles (S by E) from Bide-ford, containing 83 inhabitants The living is a dis-charged rectory, in the archdeaconry of Barnstaple, and diocese of Exeter, rated in the king s books at £5 4 9½ , endowed with £600 royal bounty, and in the patronage of Lord Rolle The church is dedicated to the Holy Trinity General Monk, afterwards Duke of Albermale, was born here in 1608

LANDEWEDNACK, a parish in the hundred of KERRIER, county of CORNWALL, 10½ miles (S S E) from Helston, containing 387 inhabitants The living is a discharged rectory, in the archdeaconry of Cornwall, and diocese of Exeter, rated in the king s books at

£11 16 10½ , and in the patronage of Vivian Robinson, Esq The church, dedicated to St Lanty, has a curious ancient font There is a place of worship for Wesleyan Methodists In this parish is the Lizard Point, the southernmost point of land in Great Britain, whence ships leaving the channel date their departure, and upon which are two lighthouses and a signal station About a mile from it is Kynan s Cove, one of the most remarkable curiosities on the coast it is formed of vast projecting rocks overhanging the sea, so as to resemble in one part of it an arched grotto The Soap rocks, three miles distant, yield the celebrated steatite, formerly in great request among the manufacturers of china

LANDFORD, a parish in the hundred of FRUST FIELD, county of WILTS, 10 miles (S E) from Salis bury, containing 213 inhabitants The living is a rec-tory, in the archdeaconry and diocese of Salisbury, rated in the king's books at £4 3 9 T Bolton, Esq was patron in 1800 The church is dedicated to St Andrew

LANDGUARD-FORT, in the parish of FELIXSTOW, hundred of COLNEIS, county of SUFFOLK, 12 miles (S E by S) from Ipswich, and 1½ mile (E S E) from Harwich, which see Here is a chapel for the garrison

LANDICAN, a township in the parish of WOOD-CHURCH, lower division of the hundred of WIRRALL, county palatine of CHESTER, 5¾ miles (N) from Great Neston, containing 53 inhabitants

LANDKEY, a parish in the southern division of the hundred of MOLTON, county of DEVON, 2¼ miles (E S E) from Barnstaple, containing 683 inhabitants The liv-ing is a perpetual curacy, annexed to that of Swim-bridge, in the peculiar jurisdiction of the Consistorial Court of the Bishop of Exeter, endowed with £200 royal bounty, and £1600 parliamentary grant The church is dedicated to the Holy Trinity At Herford in this parish, was anciently a chapel Here is a place of worship for Wesleyan Methodists

LANDMOTH, a joint township with Catto, in that part of the parish of LEAK which is in the wapentake of ALLERTONSHIRE, North riding of the county of YORK, 4 miles (E by S) from North Allerton, contain ing 59 inhabitants

LANDRAKE, a parish in the southern division of EAST hundred, county of CORNWALL, 4 miles (W N W) from Saltash, containing, with the parish of St Erney, 841 inhabitants The living is a discharged vicarage, with the curacy of St Erney, in the peculiar jurisdic-tion of the Consistorial Court of the Bishop of Exeter, rated in the king's books at £18 12 4 The Countess of Mount-Edgecombe was patroness in 1802 The church, dedicated to St Peter, is remarkable for the loftiness of its tower, which is a picturesque object for miles around The parish is bounded on the east by Lynher river, where it is crossed by a bridge Here are fairs for cattle on July 19th and August 24th A cha-rity school was founded, in 1703, by Sir Robert Jef-frey, Knt , who endowed it with lands now producing about £40 per annum There are five almshouses, with a small endowment in land

LANDULPH, a parish in the southern division of EAST hundred, county of CORNWALL, 5 miles (N) from Saltash, containing 579 inhabitants The living is a rectory, in the archdeaconry of Cornwall, and diocese of Exeter, rated in the king s books at £20 3 6½ ,

and in the patronage of the King, as Prince of Wales
The church, dedicated to St Dilpe, contains an inscription, giving an account of the pedigree of Theodore Paleologus, a lineal descendant of the last Christian emperors of Greece, who died in 1636, and whose remains were interred here The navigable river Tamer runs on the east and south of the parish

LANDWADE, a parish in the hundred of STAPLOE,
county of CAMBRIDGE, 4 miles (N N W) from Newmarket, containing 20 inhabitants The living is a perpetual curacy, annexed to the vicarage of Exning, in the archdeaconry of Sudbury, and diocese of Norwich. The church is dedicated to St Nicholas The remains of the ancient manor-house exhibit a specimen of the domestic architecture of the sixteenth century

LANEAST, a parish in the northern division of East hundred, county of CORNWALL, 7 miles (W) from Launceston, containing 229 inhabitants The living is a perpetual curacy, in the archdeaconry of Cornwall, and diocese of Exeter, endowed with £400 private benefaction, and £800 royal bounty W T Baron, Esq was patron in 1826 The church is dedicated to St Gulwel

LANE-END, a market town and chapelry in the parish of STOKE upon TRENT, northern division of the hundred of PIREHILL, county of STAFFORD, 4 miles (E S E) from Newcastle under Lyne, containing, with Longton, 7100 inhabitants This place, which is situated at the southern extremity of the district called "The Potteries," and on the road between Newcastle and Uttoxeter, has risen to opulence and importance within a few years, in consequence of the flourishing state of the earthenware and china manufacture The population is rapidly increasing, and among the indications of modern improvement may be mentioned the establishment of a mechanics institute The Trent and Mersey canal passes about two miles westward from the town, and through it runs a small stream, on which are several mills for grinding flints The market is held on Saturday for provisions, of which the supply is very abundant, and there are fairs for woollen cloth, hardware, and pedlary, on February 14th, May 29th, July 22nd, and November 1st The living is a perpetual curacy, in the archdeaconry of Stafford, and diocese of Lichfield and Coventry, endowed with land for the erection of a parsonage-house, £1000 private benefaction, £600 royal bounty, and £1500 parliamentary grant, and in the patronage of certain Trustees The chapel, which is a brick edifice, rebuilt about 1795, has recently received an addition of five hundred sittings, of which four hundred and fifty are free, the Incorporated Society for the enlargement of churches and chapels having granted £800 towards defraying the expense. In 1827 an act of parliament was obtained, authorising a sale of all tithes and rectorial dues belonging to the rectory of Stoke upon Trent, and which contained powers for further endowing and converting the chapelry of Lane End into a distinct rectory A new church is now being erected by the parliamentary commissioners appointed for the building of additional churches There are places of worship for Baptists, Independents, Calvinistic and Wesleyan Methodists, and Methodists of the New Connexion, and a chapel for Roman Catholics A charity school was founded in 1760, and endowed by John Bourne, Esq , the master having a salary of £15

per annum, and a rent free residence, for which he instructs about forty children of both sexes There is also a National school

LANEHAM, a parish within the liberty of SOUTHWELL and SCROOBY, though locally in the South-clay division of the wapentake of Bassetlaw, county of NOTTINGHAM, 6¾ miles (N E by E) from Tuxford, containing 347 inhabitants The living is a discharged vicarage, in the peculiar jurisdiction and patronage of the Dean and Chapter of York, rated in the king s books at £5 3 4 , and endowed with £400 royal bounty The church is dedicated to St. Peter The river Trent runs through the parish

LANERCOST-ABBEY, a parish in ESKDALE ward,
county of CUMBERLAND, 2½ miles (N E) from Brampton, comprising the townships of Askerton, Banks, Burtholme, Kingwater, and Waterhead, and containing 1512 inhabitants The living is a perpetual curacy, in the archdeaconry and diocese of Carlisle, endowed with £200 royal bounty, and £1400 parliamentary grant, and in the patronage of the Earl of Carlisle The church, dedicated to St Mary Magdalene, is part of the ancient abbey, and is principally in the early style of English architecture, with portions in the Norman In this parish, which was crossed by the great Roman wall of Julius Agricola, was the station of the Cohors Prima Ælia Dacorum, called Amboglana, the site of which is an extensive plain terminating in a precipitous descent to the river Irthing the dimensions of the castrum are one hundred and twenty yards north and south, by eighty east and west some altars have been found here, dedicated to Jupiter Optimus Maximus, as also dedications to Mars and Cocis, with various monumental and other inscriptions, though almost effaced by time a fragment of the ancient wall, ten feet in height, and five yards in length, is yet standing at Harehill On the north bank of the river Irthing are the very interesting ruins of an Augustine priory, dedicated to St Mary Magdalene, founded in 1169, by Robert de Vallibus, lord of Gilsland and endowed by himself and others with a revenue valued at the dissolution at £79 19 it was frequently visited by Edward I , and partly destroyed by conflagration in 1296 , in 1311, Robert Bruce, with his army, lay here for three days The ruins comprise vestiges of the conventual church, cloisters, refectory, and other buildings, the nave has been fitted up as the parish church , the dilapidated walls, which exhibit numerous specimens of architecture in the early style, are covered with ivy, ash, and other plants the western gateway consists of a circular arch, richly decorated and supported by pilasters, and is surmounted by a statue of Mary Magdalene, the tutelar saint of the abbey In a part of the ancient cemetery which has been converted into gardens, several stone coffins and monuments lie among the trees Within this parish, and about seven miles from Lanercost is Gilsland spa, the waters of which are sulphuretted chalybeate the scenery is beautiful and romantic, and there is every requisite accommodation for visitors, with billiard-tables, music-rooms, libraries, &c The spring, anciently called Holy Well, acquired its present name about the year 1770

LANGAR, a parish in the northern division of the wapentake of BINGHAM, county of NOTTINGHAM, 10½ miles (E S E) from Nottingham, containing, with Barnstone, 287 inhabitants The living is a rectory, in the archdeaconry of Nottingham, and diocese of York, rated in the king's books at £10 7 11 The Rev W Bowerbank was patron in 1825 The church, dedicated to St Andrew, is a large cruciform edifice, with a richly ornamented tower in it are several monuments of the Lords Scroope, one of which, in memory of Lord Scroope, who died in 1609, and his lady, is remarkably elegant it contains also a handsome monument to the memory of that distinguished officer Admiral Earl Howe, who died August 5th, 1799, and was buried here On an elevation near the village is the site of his lordship's once magnificent residence, which has been very much curtailed

LANGBAR, a joint township with Nesfield, in that part of the parish of Ilkley which is in the upper division of the wapentake of Claro, West riding of the county of York, $8\frac{1}{4}$ miles (E) from Skipton The population is returned with Nesfield There is a place of worship for Wesleyan Methodists

LANGCLIFFE, a township in the parish of Bentham, western division of the wapentake of Staincliffe and Ewcross, West riding of the county of York, $1\frac{1}{4}$ mile (N) from Settle, containing 420 inhabitants Here are cotton and paper manufactories

LANGDALE, a chapelry, comprising Great and Little Langdale, in the parish of Grasmere, Kendal ward, county of Westmorland, $3\frac{1}{4}$ miles (S E by S) from Orton, containing 317 inhabitants The living is a perpetual curacy, in the archdeaconry of Richmond, and diocese of Chester, endowed with £800 royal bounty, and in the patronage of the Rector of Grasmere The chapel is situated at Great Langdale, and another once stood at a place now called Chapel-Mire, in Little Langdale On a hill called Wrevnose are placed three stones, denominated shire-stones, and marking the point at which the counties of Cumberland, Westmorland, and Lancaster, meet and terminate Fine blue slate, much of which is sent to London and other parts, is obtained in the mountains on each side of the river Brathy, the loftiest pike of these, called Harrison Stickle, rises two thousand four hundred feet above the level of the sea Within the chapelry is Elter-water, near which is a gunpowder-mill, there are also several smaller lakes, and the two beautiful waterfalls, Colwith Force and Skelwith Force. A school was erected, in 1824, by the Gunpowder Company, in consideration of ground granted to them for the establishment of their manufactory

LANGDON (EAST), a parish in the hundred of Cornilo, lathe of St Augustine, county of Kent, $3\frac{3}{4}$ miles (N N E) from Dovor, containing 347 inhabitants The living is a discharged rectory, in the archdeaconry and diocese of Canterbury, rated in the king's books at £7 The Earl of Guildford was patron in 1788 The church is dedicated to St Augustine A fair for toys and pedlary is held on Old May-day Here is a workhouse for lodging the poor of this and some of the neighbouring parishes, in which several of them are employed in spinning and weaving linen, sacking, &c

LANGDON (WEST), a parish in the hundred of Bewsborough, lathe of St Augustine, county of Kent, $3\frac{1}{2}$ miles (N) from Dovor, containing 86 inhabitants The living is a rectory not in charge, in the archdeaconry and diocese of Canterbury, endowed with £200 royal bounty, and in the patronage of the Archbishop of Canterbury The church, which was dedicated to St Mary, is in ruins An abbey for White canons, dedicated to the Blessed Virgin Mary and St Thomas the Martyr, was founded here, in 1192, by William de Auberville, which at the dissolution had a revenue estimated at £56 6

LANGDON-HILLS, a parish in the hundred of Barstable, county of Essex, $2\frac{1}{2}$ miles (N by E) from Horndon on the Hill, containing 205 inhabitants The living is a discharged rectory, in the archdeaconry of Essex, and diocese of London, rated in the king's books at £10 3 9, and in the patronage of the Dean and Chapter of St Paul's, London The church is dedicated to St Mary and All Saints From the summit of this range of hills, the loftiest in this part of the county, are some extremely fine and extensive prospects, especially towards the south, south east, and south-west, of the metropolis, the whole river and vale of the Thames below London, and the hills and coast of Kent, as far as the Medway, being visible in clear weather

LANGENHOE, a parish in the hundred of Winstree, county of Essex, $5\frac{1}{4}$ miles (S by E) from Colchester, containing 131 inhabitants The living is a rectory, in the archdeaconry of Colchester, and diocese of London, rated in the king's books at £14 13 4 Earl Waldegrave was patron in 1809 The church is dedicated to St Andrew The parish is bounded on the east by the navigable river Colne

LANGFIELD, a township in the parish of Halifax, wapentake of Morley, West riding of the county of York, $11\frac{3}{4}$ miles (W by S) from Halifax, containing 2069 inhabitants On Stoodley Pike, a lofty eminence in this township, a column has been raised, commemorative of the great military achievements of the Duke of Wellington

LANGFORD, a parish in the hundred of Biggleswade, county of Bedford, $2\frac{1}{4}$ miles (S) from Biggleswade, containing 631 inhabitants The living is a discharged vicarage, in the archdeaconry of Bedford, and diocese of Lincoln, rated in the king's books at £8, endowed with £400 royal bounty, and in the patronage of the Crown The church is dedicated to St Andrew

LANGFORD, a parish comprising the tything of Little Farringdon, in the hundred of Farringdon, county of Berks, and the township of Grafton, and the hamlet of Radcutt, in the hundred of Bampton, county of Oxford, $3\frac{1}{2}$ miles (N E by E) from Lechlade, and containing 638 inhabitants The living is a vicarage, in the peculiar jurisdiction of the Prebendary of Langford Ecclesia in the Cathedral Church of Lincoln, rated in the king's books at £21 19 $4\frac{1}{2}$ The Rev John W Peters was patron in 1825 The church, dedicated to St Mary, has lately received an addition of two hundred and two sittings, of which one hundred and thirty-nine are free, the Incorporated Society for the enlargement of churches and chapels having granted £80 towards defraying the expense. It is said that the boundary line of the two counties divides the church and churchyard

LANGFORD, a parish in the hundred of Thurstable, county of Essex, 2 miles (N by W) from Maldon, containing 251 inhabitants. The living is a rectory, in the archdeaconry of Colchester, and diocese of London, rated in the king's books at £10 4 $9\frac{1}{2}$ Mrs Westcomb was patroness in 1813 The church is dedicated to St Giles The Chelmer and Blackwater navigation bounds the parish on the south

LANGFORD, a parish in the southern division of the hundred of GREENHOE, county of NORFOLK, 6¼ miles (W S W) from Watton, containing 29 inhabitants The living is a discharged rectory, with that of Ickborough, not rated in the king's books, in the archdeaconry of Norfolk, and diocese of Norwich Alexander Baring, Esq was patron in 1824 The church, dedicated to St Andrew, is an ancient building of flint, with a square western embattled tower, it contains several memorials of the Methwolds and Garrards, formerly lords of the place

LANGFORD, a parish in the northern division of the wapentake of NEWARK, county of NOTTINGHAM, 3¾ miles (N N E) from Newark, containing 147 inhabitants The living is a perpetual curacy, in the archdeaconry of Nottingham, and diocese of York, endowed with £600 royal bounty, and £200 parliamentary grant, and in the patronage of the Master and Fellows of Trinity College, Cambridge The church is dedicated to St Bartholomew The Fosse-road crosses the parish, and the river Trent bounds it on the west

LANGFORD (LITTLE), a parish in the hundred of BRANCH and DOLE, county of WILTS, 5¼ miles (N W) from Wilton, containing 32 inhabitants The living is a rectory, in the archdeaconry and diocese of Salisbury, rated in the king's books at £7 13 4, and in the patronage of the Earl of Pembroke The church is dedicated to St Nicholas

LANGFORD (STEEPLE), a parish in the hundred of BRANCH and DOLE, county of WILTS, 5¾ miles (N W) from Wilton, containing 557 inhabitants The living is a rectory, in the archdeaconry and diocese of Salisbury, rated in the king's books at £34 0 7½, and in the patronage of the President and Fellows of Corpus Christi College, Oxford. The church is dedicated to All Saints

LANGFORD BUDVILLE, a parish in the hundred of MILVERTON, county of SOMERSET, 3 miles (N W by W) from Wellington, containing 564 inhabitants The living is a perpetual curacy, annexed to the vicarage of Milverton, and in the peculiar jurisdiction of the Archdeacon of Taunton. The church is dedicated to St James

LANGHALE, a parish in the hundred of LODDON, county of NORFOLK, 6 miles (N N W) from Bungay The living is a rectory, with that of Kirstead, not rated in the king's books, in the archdeaconry of Norfolk, and diocese of Norwich.

LANGHAM, a parish in the Colchester division of the hundred of LEXDEN, county of ESSEX, 1¾ mile (W by N) from Dedham, containing 725 inhabitants The living is a rectory, in the archdeaconry of Colchester, and diocese of London, rated in the king's books at £17 11 0½, and in the patronage of the Chancellor of the duchy of Lancaster The church is dedicated to St. Mary There is a place of worship for Baptists The navigable river Stour runs on the north of the parish There is a small endowment for the instruction of children.

LANGHAM, a parish in the soke of OAKHAM, county of RUTLAND, 2 miles (N W) from Oakham, containing 571 inhabitants. The living is a perpetual curacy, annexed to the vicarage of Oakham, in the archdeaconry of Northampton, and diocese of Peterborough The chapel is dedicated to St Peter and St Paul

LANGHAM, a parish in the hundred of BLACKBOURN, county of SUFFOLK, 3¼ miles (E by S) from Ixworth, containing 268 inhabitants The living is a rectory, in the archdeaconry of Suffolk, and diocese of Norwich, rated in the king's books at £5 16 10½, and in the patronage of the Crown The church is dedicated to St. Mary

LANGHAM (GREAT), a parish in the hundred of HOLT, county of NORFOLK, 4 miles (W S W) from Cley, containing 324 inhabitants The living is a discharged vicarage, in the archdeaconry and diocese of Norwich, rated in the king's books at £4 10 2, and in the patronage of the Bishop of Norwich The church is dedicated to St Andrew

LANGHAM (LITTLE), a parish in the hundred of HOLT, county of NORFOLK, 3 miles (S W by W) from Cley The living is a vicarage, united to the rectory of Cockthorpe, Glandford, and Blakeney, in the archdeaconry and diocese of Norwich, rated in the king's books at £3 6 8 The church is dedicated to St Mary

LANGLEY, a chapelry in the parish of HAMPSTEAD-NORRIS, hundred of FAIRCROSS, county of BERKS, 3½ miles (S) from East Ilsey The population is returned with the parish The chapel has long since been desecrated

LANGLEY, a township in that part of the parish of LANCHESTER which is in the western division of CHESTER ward, county palatine of DURHAM, 5½ miles (N W) from Durham, containing 97 inhabitants On the bank of the river Browney are the ruins of an ancient mansion, part of which has been converted into a farm-house.

LANGLEY, a parish in the hundred of CLAVERING, county of ESSEX, 7¾ miles (W S W) from Saffron-Walden, containing 320 inhabitants The living is a perpetual curacy, annexed to the vicarage of Clavering, in the archdeaconry of Colchester, and diocese of London The church is dedicated to St John the Evangelist There is a place of worship for Baptists

LANGLEY, a parish in the hundred of EYHORNE, lathe of AYLESFORD, county of KENT, 4 miles (S E) from Maidstone, containing 263 inhabitants The living is a rectory, in the archdeaconry and diocese of Canterbury, rated in the king's books at £6 19 9½ Mrs Bouverie was patroness in 1789 The church is dedicated to St Mary There is a place of worship for Wesleyan Methodists

LANGLEY, a parish in the hundred of LODDON, county of NORFOLK, 7½ miles (S S W) from Acle, containing 349 inhabitants The living is a perpetual curacy, in the archdeaconry of Norfolk, and diocese of Norwich, endowed with £600 royal bounty Sir T B Proctor, Bart was patron in 1817 The church is dedicated to St Michael An abbey of Premonstratensian canons, in honour of the Blessed Virgin Mary, was founded and endowed, in 1198, by Robert Fitz-Roger Helke, the revenue of which, at the dissolution, was valued at £128 19 9 Its site is now called the Grange, and near it, in a fine park well stocked with deer, is Langley house, a handsome structure, having a quadrangular turret rising from each of its four angles

LANGLEY, a chapelry in the parish of SHIPTON under WHICHWOOD, hundred of CHADLINGTON, county of OxFORD, 5 miles (N E) from Burford, containing 63 inhabitants

LANGLEY, a chapelry in the parish of Acton-Burnell, hundred of Condover, county of Salop, 6½ miles (W) from Much Wenlock   The population is returned with the township of Ruckley

LANGLEY, a hamlet in the parish of Claverdon, Henley division of the hundred of Barlichway, county of Warwick, 4½ miles (S E bv E) from Henley in Arden, containing 192 inhabitants

LANGLEY, a tything in the parish of Kington St Michael, northern division of the hundred of Damerham, county of Wilts, 2¼ miles (N) from Chippenham, containing 504 inhabitants

LANGLEY (ABBOT'S), a parish in the hundred of Cashio, or liberty of St Alban s, county of Hertford, 1¾ mile (E by S) from King s Langley, containing 1733 inhabitants   The living is a discharged vicarage, in the archdeaconry of St Alban s, and diocese of London rated in the king s books at £15, endowed with £200 private benefaction, and £200 royal bounty   Sir J Filmer, Bart was patron in 1821   The church, dedicated to St Lawrence, is partly Norman, and partly in the later style of English architecture, it has a square tower surmounted by a short spire, and contains some handsome monuments, and other sepulchral memorials   The Grand Junction canal passes through the parish Nicholas de Breakspear, who first instructed the Norwegians in Christianity, and the only Englishman ever raised to the popedom, was born in this parish, though the place from which he took his name is situated in the adjoining parish of St Michael   he assumed the title of Adrian IV, and was poisoned in 1159, in the fifth year of his pontificate, by a citizen of Rome, whose son he refused to consecrate bishop

LANGLEY (KING S), a parish in the hundred of Dacorum, county of Hertford, 19 miles (W S W) from Hertford, containing 1242 inhabitants The living is a vicarage, in the archdeaconry of Huntingdon, and diocese of Lincoln, rated in the king s books at £8, and in the patronage of the Bishop of Ely   The church, dedicated to All Saints, is built of flint and stone, with a square embattled tower surmounted by a short spire, and is remarkable as containing the tomb of Edmund de Langley, fifth son of Edward III, and Duke of York, who was born at an ancient royal palace here, he died in 1402, and was buried in the church of the priory, from which, at the dissolution, his tomb was removed to the parish church   it has lately received an addition of two hundred and seventy-seven sittings, of which two hundred and fifty-seven are free, the Incorporated Society for the enlargement of churches and chapels having granted £200 towards defraying the expense   A priory, or house for friars preachers, founded here by Roger, son of Robert Helle, or Helke, but afterwards enlarged and more liberally endowed by the munificence of the kings Edward I, II, III, and IV, possessed, in the 26th of Henry VIII, a revenue of £150 14 8   Queen Mary restored it for a prioress and nuns, but it was totally suppressed in the 1st of Elizabeth   A large paper manufactory here affords employment to about fifty persons   The Grand Junction canal passes through the parish, in excavating which a human skeleton and jaw bones, of gigantic size, were found in 1820, and an ancient sword and a spear in 1822

LANGLEY (KIRK), a parish in the hundred of Morleston and Litchurch, county of Derby, 4¾ miles (W N W) from Derby, containing, with the township of Meynell-Langley, 552 inhabitants   The living is a rectory, in the archdeaconry of Derby, and diocese of Lichfield and Coventry, rated in the king s books at £12 2 1, and in the patronage of Godfrey Meynell, Esq   The church, dedicated to St Michael, was nearly destroyed by the violent tempest which happened in 1545   Courts leet and baron are annually held here   A school house was erected, by subscription, in 1750, and endowed, in 1752, by the Rev John Bailey, then rector, with land now let at £12 a year, and again, in 1768, with a rent-charge of £5 per annum, for the instruction of twelve children   A Sunday school has also been established by the rector

LANGLEY (MEYNELL), a township in the parish of Kirk-Langley, hundred of Morleston and Litchurch, county of Derby   The population is returned with the parish

LANGLEY-BURREL, a parish in the hundred of Chippenham, county of Wilts, 1¾ mile (N by E) from Chippenham, containing 428 inhabitants   The living is a rectory, in the archdeaconry of Wilts, and diocese of Salisbury, rated in the king's books at £12 7 3½   R Ashe, Esq was patron in 1807   The church is dedicated to St Peter

LANGLEY-DALE, a joint township with Shotton, in the parish of Staindrop, south-western division of Darlington ward, county palatine of Durham, 4½ miles (N) from Barnard Castle, containing, with Shotton, 198 inhabitants   There is a place of worship for Wesleyan Methodists   The smelt works established here yield weekly upwards of three thousand stone of lead, and four thousand ounces of silver   Here is an ancient tower, formerly an out-post belonging to Raby castle

LANGLEY-MARISH, a parish in the hundred of Stoke, county of Buckingham, comprising a portion of the market town of Colnbrook, and containing 1616 inhabitants   The living is a perpetual curacy, annexed to the vicarage of Wyrardisbury, in the archdeaconry of Buckingham, and diocese of Lincoln   The church, formerly a chapel of ease to the vicarage of Wyrardisbury, is dedicated to St Mary, and was erected at the expense of the Kedermisters, of whom, Sir John Kedermister left for public use a small library, consisting of works chiefly on divinity, it is deposited in the church, the place being separated from the rest of the building by an ancient screen   He also founded, in 1649, almshouses for six poor persons, and Henry Seymour erected others for four inmates, in support of which, Captain Henry Seymour, in 1733, bequeathed £200 to purchase lands   the inmates receive about two shillings and sixpence each per week   There are two places of worship for dissenters, one of which belongs to the Independents   Courts leet and baron are annually held here

LANGLEY-PRIORY, an extra parochial liberty, in the western division of the hundred of Goscote, county of Leicester, containing 13 inhabitants   A priory of Benedictine nuns, in honour of the Blessed Virgin Mary, was founded, in the beginning of the reign of Henry II, by William Pantulf, and Burgia his wife, the revenue of which, at the dissolution, was estimated at £34 6 2

LANGO, a chapelry in the parish and lower division of the hundred of Blackburn, county palatine of Lan-

CASTER, 5¼ miles (S W by S) from Clitheroe The population is returned with the parish The living is a perpetual curacy, in the archdeaconry and diocese of Chester, endowed with £ 200 private benefaction, £ 600 royal bounty, and £ 600 parliamentary grant, and in the patronage of the Vicar of Blackburn Here, in 798, Duke Wada fought an unsuccessful battle against Ardulph, King of Northumberland

Corporate Seal.

LANGPORT - EAST-OVER, a market town and parish, having separate jurisdiction, though locally in the hundred of Pitney, county of SOMERSET, 4½ miles (W S W) from Somerton, and 130 (W S W) from London, on the great western road, containing 1004 inhabitants This place is of great antiquity, and is supposed to have derived its name from the Saxon words *long*, extended, and *port*, a town, from the length of its principal street in the Norman survey it is called *Lanporth*. It was a royal burgh in the time of William the Conqueror, and contained thirty-four resident burgesses In the civil war between Charles I and the parliament, Langport, being considered a commanding station, was well garrisoned, and alternately in the possession of the royal and of the parliamentary forces In July 1644, the former were compelled to abandon the place, from the result of an engagement here, in which three hundred men were killed, and one thousand four hundred made prisoners The town is situated on the river Parret, which is navigable for barges, near its junction with the Yeo and the Ile at the western entrance a very ancient bridge of ten arches crosses the river, and there are nine other bridges, which are repaired from the funds of the corporation At the eastern approach, on the ancient lines of fortification, is an arch thrown over the road, which supports a building called the "Hanging Chapel," formerly devoted to religious uses, and, during Monmouth s rebellion, having been the place of execution, but now occupied as a private residence The principal part of the town is on an eminence, and commands some pleasing and extensive views , but that part near the river lying low is subject to frequent inundations since 1800, the general appearance of the whole has been much improved, by the erection of many new houses, and the inhabitants are supplied with excellent water from an adjacent well. A considerable traffic in coal, culm, iron, timber, salt, corn, &c , is carried on with London, Bristol, and various other places, and several boats, of from eight to fourteen tons burden, are constantly employed between this town and Bridgwater The market is on Saturday fairs are held on the Monday before Lent, the second Wednesday in August, the last Monday but one in September, and the last Monday in November, for cattle The government of the town is vested, by a renewed charter of James I., in the year 1617, in a corporation consisting of twelve chief burgesses, including a portreeve, justice, two bailiffs, assisted by a recorder, town clerk, serjeant at mace, and other officers The portreeve and bailiffs are elected from the body corporate, annually on the 1st of Novem-

ber, and the recorder, town clerk, and serjeant at mace, as vacancies occur The portreeve, justice, and recorder, are justices of the peace the portreeve is coroner for the borough and clerk of the market, and his predecessor is justice The corporation are empowered to hold a court of record before the portreeve, recorder, and bailiffs, every Tuesday, for pleas not exceeding the value of 40s The town-hall, which is a neat edifice, was erected about 1733 This borough sent members to parliament in the reign of Edward I , but the privilege was not subsequently exercised The living is a discharged vicarage, with that of Huish-Episcopi, in the peculiar jurisdiction and patronage of the Archdeacon of Wells, as Prebendary of Huish *cum* Brent in the Cathedral Church of Wells The church, dedicated to All Saints, is an ancient structure in the early style of English architecture , in the eastern window, amongst other representations in ancient stained glass, are those of the twelve Apostles the church has recently undergone new internal arrangement and decoration There is a place of worship for Independents The free grammar school was founded, about the year 1675, by Thomas Gillett, for all boys residing in the town the present income is £70 per annum, and the average number of scholars about thirty A National school, for children belonging to the parishes of Langport and Huish, was erected in 1827, and is supported by voluntary contributions Two poor persons of this parish are eligible to almshouses founded at Somerton, in this county, by Sir Edward Hext, in 1626 An hospital for lepers, dedicated to St Mary Magdalene, stood here previously to 1310

LANGRICK-VILLE, a chapelry in the soke of HORNCASTLE, parts of LINDSEY, county of LINCOLN, containing 195 inhabitants Langrick-Ville was, with six other districts, created a township, by act of parliament, in 1812, on the occasion of a very extensive drainage of about fourteen thousand acres of Wildmore, and the eastern and western fens, and is not dependent on any parish A chapel has been erected here, and was consecrated in 1818

LANGRIDGE, a parish in the hundred of BATH-FORUM, county of SOMERSET, 4 miles (N by W) from Bath, containing 103 inhabitants The living is a discharged rectory, in the archdeaconry of Bath, and diocese of Bath and Wells, rated in the king's books at £5 19 4½ , and in the patronage of William Blathwayt, Esq In rebuilding the rectory-house, a few years since, several stone coffins and sculls, and a silver mounted battle-axe, were discovered At one of the extremities of the parish is Lansdown hill, where a bloody, though indecisive, battle was fought between the royal and parliamentarian armies in 1643

LANGRIGG, a joint township with Mealrigg, in that part of the parish of BROOMFIELD which is in ALLERDALE ward below Derwent, county of CUMBERLAND, 7 miles (W S W) from Wigton, containing, with Mealrigg, 194 inhabitants

LANGRISH, a tything in the parish and hundred of EAST MEON, Alton (South) division of the county of SOUTHAMPTON The population is returned with the parish Langrish is within the jurisdiction of the Cheney Court held at Winchester every Thursday, for the recovery of debts to any amount

LANGSETT, a township in the parish of PENISTONE,

wapentake of STAINCROSS, West riding of the county of YORK, 5½ miles (S W by W) from Penistone, containing 325 inhabitants

LANGSTONE, a parish in the lower division of the hundred of CALDICOTT, county of MONMOUTH, 4¼ miles (E by N) from Newport, containing, with the hamlet of Llandeber, 171 inhabitants The living is a discharged rectory, in the archdeaconry and diocese of Llandaff, rated in the king s books at £4 1 0½, endowed with £200 royal bounty, and in the patronage of the Rev Charles Gore

LANGTHORNE, a township in that part of the parish of BEDALE which is in the wapentake of HALLIKELD, North riding of the county of YORK, 3¾ miles (N W by N) from Bedale, containing 135 inhabitants

LANGTHORP, a township in the parish of KIRBY on the MOOR, wapentake of HALLIKELD, North riding of the county of YORK, 1 mile (N W) from Boroughbridge, containing 143 inhabitants

LANGTHWAITE, a joint township with Tilts, in that part of the parish of DONCASTER which is in the northern division of the wapentake of STRAFFORTH and TICKHILL, West riding of the county of YORK, containing 21 inhabitants

LANGTOFT, a parish in the wapentake of NESS, parts of KESTEVEN, county of LINCOLN, 2 miles (N N W) from Market-Deeping, containing, with certain extra-parochial liberties in the Fens, 485 inhabitants The living is a discharged vicarage, in the archdeaconry and diocese of Lincoln, rated in the king s books at £5 5 7½, and in the patronage of Sir Gilbert Heathcote, Bart The church is dedicated to St Michael

LANGTOFT, a parish in the wapentake of DICKERING, East riding of the county of YORK, comprising the townships of Cotton and Langtoft, and containing 432 inhabitants, of which number, 416 are in the township of Langtoft, which is partly within the liberty of ST PETER of YORK, 6½ miles (N by W) from Great Driffield The living is a discharged vicarage, in the peculiar jurisdiction and patronage of the Prebendary of Langtoft in the Cathedral Church of York, rated in the king s books at £8 The church is dedicated to St Peter There is a place of worship for Wesleyan Methodists

LANGTON, a township in that part of the parish of GAINFORD which is in the south-western division of DARLINGTON ward, county palatine of DURHAM, 8¾ miles (E by N) from Barnard-Castle, containing 90 inhabitants

LANGTON, a parish in the southern division of the wapentake of GARTREE, parts of LINDSEY, county of LINCOLN, 1¼ mile (W by S) from Horncastle, containing 100 inhabitants The living is a discharged rectory, in the archdeaconry and diocese of Lincoln, rated in the king s books at £7 19 4½, endowed with £200 royal bounty, and in the patronage of the Bishop of Lincoln The church is dedicated to St Margaret

LANGTON, a parish in the hundred of HILL, parts of LINDSEY, county of LINCOLN, 3¾ miles (N by W) from Spilsby, containing 167 inhabitants The living is a rectory, in the archdeaconry and diocese of Lincoln, rated in the king s books at £10 12 3½ B Langton, Esq was patron in 1800 The church is dedicated to St Peter

LANGTON, a parish in the eastern division of the wapentake of WRAGGOE, parts of LINDSEY, county of LINCOLN, 1¼ mile (E S E) from Wragby, containing 193 inhabitants The living is a discharged vicarage, in the archdeaconry and diocese of Lincoln, rated in the king s books at £4 13 4, endowed with certain lands in reversion, private benefaction, and £200 royal bounty Earl Manvers was patron in 1802 The church is dedicated to St Giles

LANGTON, a joint township with Bongate, in the parish of APPLEBY ST MICHAEL, East ward, county of WESTMORLAND, 1½ mile (E) from Appleby, with which the population is returned Langton, or Long Town, was once a populous place, but was almost destroyed by the Scots, in the reign of Edward II At Kirkbergh there was anciently a church

LANGTON, a parish in the wapentake of BUCKROSE, East riding of the county of YORK, comprising the townships of Kennythorpe and Langton, and containing 363 inhabitants, of which number, 280 are in the township of Langton, 3½ miles (S S E) from New Malton The living is a rectory, in the archdeaconry of the East riding, and diocese of York, rated in the king s books at £17 4 7, and in the patronage of the Crown The church is dedicated to St Andrew

LANGTON (CHURCH), a parish in the hundred of GARTREE, county of LEICESTER, 4 miles (N by W) from Market-Harborough, comprising the chapelries of Thorp-Langton, Tur-Langton, and West Langton, and the township of East Langton, and containing 932 inhabitants The living is a rectory, in the archdeaconry of Leicester, and diocese of Lincoln, rated in the king s books at £48 13 4 The Rev William Hanbury was patron in 1817 The church is dedicated to St Peter The Rev William Hanbury, remarkable for his benevolent projects, and for his extensive and industrious cultivation of trees and plants, indigenous and exotic, was for many years rector of this parish, and died here in 1778

LANGTON (EAST), a township in the parish of CHURCH-LANGTON, hundred of GARTREE, county of LEICESTER, 3½ miles (N) from Market-Harborough, containing 309 inhabitants Thomas Staveley, an antiquary and church historian, was born here in 1626

LANGTON (GREAT), a parish in the eastern division of the wapentake of GILLING, North riding of the county of YORK, comprising the townships of Great Langton, and Little Langton, and containing 202 inhabitants, of which number, 116 are in the township of Great Langton, 5½ miles (W N W) from North Allerton The living is a discharged rectory, in the archdeaconry of Richmond, and diocese of Chester, rated in the king s books at £6 10 10 The Duke of Leeds was patron in 1792 The church is a small fabric without aisles or tower, it stands in a retired situation about half a mile from the village The river Swale runs through the parish

LANGTON (HERRING), a parish in the hundred of UGGSCOMBE, Dorchester division of the county of DORSET, 8½ miles (S W) from Dorchester, containing 152 inhabitants The living is a discharged rectory, in the archdeaconry of Dorset, and diocese of Bristol, rated in the king s books at £7 2 11, endowed with £200 royal bounty, and in the alternate patronage of the King, as Duke of Cornwall, and William Sparks, Esq This parish suffered much from an inundation of the sea in November 1824 It is bounded on the south-west by West Fleet, which separates it from that remarkable tongue of land termed the Chesil Bank Beds of shells abound here to a considerable depth, so that in many parts there is no soil

LANGTON (LITTLE), a township in the parish of Great Langton, eastern division of the wapentake of Gilling, North riding of the county of York, 4½ miles (W by N) from North Allerton, containing 86 inhabitants

LANGTON (THORP), a chapelry in the parish of Church-Langton, hundred of Gartree, county of Leicester, 3¾ miles (N by E) from Market-Harborough, containing 215 inhabitants

LANGTON (TUR), a chapelry in the parish of Church Langton, hundred of Gartree, county of Leicester, 5¼ miles (N by W) from Market-Harborough, containing 318 inhabitants

LANGTON (WEST), a chapelry in the parish of Church-Langton, hundred of Gartree, county of Leicester, 3¾ miles (N by W) from Market-Harborough, containing 90 inhabitants Walter de Langton, Lord High Treasurer of England, a favourite of Edward I, was born here in 1296

LANGTON-LONG-BLANDFORD, a parish in the hundred of Pimperne, Blandford (North) division of the county of Dorset, ¾ of a mile (E S E) from Blandford-Forum, containing 160 inhabitants The living is a rectory, in the archdeaconry of Dorset, and diocese of Bristol, rated in the kings books at £13 10, and in the patronage of John Ridout, Esq The church, dedicated to All Saints, is an ancient fabric, and had formerly a chantry, in honour of St Mary and St Thomas An hospital for lepers also existed here in the reign of Edward I The navigable river Stour runs through the parish

LANGTON-MATRAVERS, a parish in the hundred of Rowbarrow, Blandford (South) division of the county of Dorset, 4 miles (S E) from Corfe-Castle, containing 628 inhabitants The living is a rectory, in the archdeaconry of Dorset, and diocese of Bristol, rated in the kings books at £14 8 9 The Rev John Dampier was patron in 1808 The church, dedicated to St George, is an ancient building with an embattled tower, and has lately received an addition of three hundred free sittings, the Incorporated Society for the enlargement of churches and chapels having granted £200 towards defraying the expense It had formerly a chantry for the use of the small priory of St Leonard at Wilcheswode, which was founded before the time of Edward III There is a remarkable oblong tumulus within the parish on the south is the English channel

LANGTREE, a parish in the hundred of Shebbear, county of Devon, 3¾ miles (S W) from Great Torrington, containing 778 inhabitants The living is a rectory, in the archdeaconry of Barnstaple, and diocese of Exeter, rated in the kings books at £29 1 3, and in the patronage of Lord Rolle There was formerly a chapel at Cross Hill in this parish

LANGTREE, a joint township with Standish, in the parish of Standish, hundred of Leyland, county palatine of Lancaster, 4 miles (N W by N) from Wigan The population is returned with Standish

LANGWATHBY, a chapelry in the parish of Edenhall, Leath ward, county of Cumberland, 4¾ miles

(N E by E) from Penrith, containing 250 inhabitants The living is a perpetual curacy, united to the vicarage of Edenhall, in the archdeaconry and diocese of Carlisle The chapel, dedicated to St Peter, was erected by subscription in 1718, on the site of a more ancient edifice This chapelry is separated from the parish by the river Eden, over which is a bridge of three arches, built in 1686

LANGWITH, a parish in the hundred of Scarsdale, county of Derby, 6 miles (N by W) from Mansfield, containing 153 inhabitants The living is a discharged rectory, in the archdeaconry of Derby, and diocese of Lichfield and Coventry, rated in the kings books at £4 0 2½, and in the patronage of the Duke of Devonshire The church is dedicated to St Helen

LANGWITH, a township in the parish of Cuckney, Hatfield division of the wapentake of Bassetlaw, county of Nottingham, 7¼ miles (S S W) from Mansfield, containing 378 inhabitants

LANGWITH, a township in that part of the parish of Whel drake which is within the liberty of St Peter of York, though locally in the wapentake of Ouze and Derwent, East riding of the county of York, 5 miles (S E by E) from York, containing 39 inhabitants

LANHYDROCK, a parish in the hundred of Pyder, county of Cornwall, 2¾ miles (S by E) from Bodmin, containing 251 inhabitants The living is a perpetual curacy, in the archdeaconry of Cornwall, and diocese of Exeter, and in the patronage of G Hunt, Esq The church, dedicated to St Hydrock, though small, is an elegant fabric, with an embattled tower overgrown with ivy, a few years since it underwent a thorough repair, the ancient style of the building being preserved entire Lanhydrock house, which is approached from the river Fowey by a fine avenue of trees about a mile in length, was garrisoned for the parliament in the civil war, and surrendered to the royalists under Sir Richard Grenville, in August 1644 it is an embattled structure of granite, forming three sides of a quadrangle, in the style that prevailed in the early part of the seventeenth century, but of late years, through neglect, it has been going gradually to decay

LANIVET, a parish in the hundred of Pyder, county of Cornwall, 2½ miles (S W) from Bodmin, containing 803 inhabitants The living is a rectory, in the archdeaconry of Cornwall, and diocese of Exeter, rated in the kings books at £24 The Rev William Phillipps was patron in 1817 There is a place of worship for Wesleyan Methodists About a quarter of a mile from the church are considerable remains of a Benedictine monastery, called St Bene t s, and supposed to have been a nunnery subordinate to some foreign house There are certain lands, part of its former possessions, in this and other parishes, producing an income of about £110 per annum, vested in twelve feoffees, for the maintenance of poor persons in an ancient almshouse, with a charity school under the same roof, the master of which has a salary of £8, and a rent-free residence

LANLIVERY, a parish in the eastern division of the hundred of Powder, county of Cornwall, 1½ mile (W by S) from Lostwithiel, containing 1318 inhabitants The living is a vicarage, in the archdeaconry of Cornwall, and diocese of Exeter, rated in the kings books at £13 6 8 The Rev William Hocker was patron in

1915 The church is dedicated to St Brevita There is a place of worship for Wesleyan Methodists

LANOVER, in the county of MONMOUTH — See LLANOVER, and the same with regard to the other places in that county, having the prefix LLAN

LANREATH, a parish in WEST hundred, county of CORNWALL, 6 miles (W N W) from West Looe, containing 629 inhabitants The living is a rectory, in the archdeaconry of Cornwall, and diocese of Exeter, rated in the king's books at £32, and in the patronage of John Buller, Esq The church is dedicated to St. Marnarch Herod's Foot river, and the lakes Ball Water and Trebant Water, are in this parish Fairs for cattle are held on Whit-Tuesday, November 18th, and the third Tuesday after Shrovetide A charity school, founded in 1711, possesses a small endowment

LANSALLOES, a parish in WEST hundred, county of CORNWALL, 6 miles (W by S) from West Looe, containing 880 inhabitants The living is a rectory, in the archdeaconry of Cornwall, and diocese of Exeter, rated in the king's books at £18, and in the patronage of the Rev W Rawlings The church is dedicated to St Alwys The parish is bounded on the south by Lantivet bay

LANTEGLOS, a parish in the hundred of LES NEWTH, county of CORNWALL, 1½ mile (W S W) from Camelford, containing with the borough of Camelford, 1256 inhabitants The living is a rectory, with the perpetual curacy of Advent, in the archdeaconry of Cornwall, and diocese of Exeter, rated in the king's books at £34 11 3, and in the patronage of the King, as Prince of Wales The church is dedicated to St. Lanty The river Camel runs through the parish Here is an endowed school

LANTEGLOS, a parish in WEST hundred, county of CORNWALL, 2 miles (E) from Fowey, containing 973 inhabitants The living is a vicarage, in the archdeaconry of Cornwall, and diocese of Exeter, rated in the king's books at £14 7 1, and in the patronage of Lord Grenville The church is dedicated to St Lanty This parish is separated from the town of Fowey by the river and harbour of the same name, for the defence of which there is an old castle corresponding with one on the opposite shore it includes the fishing village of Polruan, which had anciently a market and a fair, and appears to have been a place of some importance, having furnished one ship and sixty mariners to the fleet before Calais in the reign of Edward III On the brow of a hill rising behind the village are the remains of an ancient chapel, which was dedicated to St Saviour, still serving as a noted land-mark Wheal Howell, a copper mine lately discovered, is in operation The Barton, a manor-house in this parish, having been garrisoned for the parliament, sustained much injury in the civil war, in August 1644, and ultimately surrendered to Sir Richard Grenville, who placed in it a garrison for Charles I, that monarch having narrowly escaped being shot here, whilst inspecting the harbour from a fine promenade in the grounds

LANTON, a township in the parish of KIRK-NEW-TON, western division of GLENDALE ward, county of NORTHUMBERLAND, 5 miles (N W by W) from Wooler, containing 69 inhabitants It is bounded on the south by the Glen river

LAPFORD, a parish in the hundred of NORTH TAWTON with WINKLEY, county of DEVON, 5¼ miles (S E) from Chulmleigh, containing 674 inhabitants The living is a rectory, in the archdeaconry of Barnstaple, and diocese of Exeter, rated in the king's books at £15 1 10½, and in the patronage of the Rev W Radford The church is dedicated to St Thomas à Becket

LAPLEY, a parish in the western division of the hundred of CUTTLESTONE, county of STAFFORD, 3¾ miles (W by S) from Penkridge, containing, with the township of Wheaton-Aston, 916 inhabitants The living is a discharged vicarage, in the archdeaconry of Stafford, and diocese of Lichfield and Coventry, rated in the king's books at £5 12 3½ John Swinfen, Esq was patron in 1800 The church is dedicated to All Saints In 1669, Joan Scutt gave £10 per annum for the instruction of poor children Here was anciently a priory of Black monks, subordinate to the abbey of St Remigius at Rheims

LAPWORTH, a parish in the Warwick division of the hundred of KINGTON, county of WARWICK, 3¼ miles (N N E) from Henley in Arden, containing, with a portion of the hamlet of Kingswood, 622 inhabitants The living is a rectory, in the archdeaconry and diocese of Worcester, rated in the king's books at £9 9 7, and in the patronage of the Warden and Fellows of Merton College, Oxford The church, dedicated to St Mary, contains specimens of the early, decorated, and later styles of English architecture the tower and spire are on the north side of the north aisle There is a place of worship for Independents Two schools for boys and girls were erected and are supported by the proceeds of divers united benefactions, amounting to £412 5 3 per annum, which is applied to various benevolent purposes, as severally indicated on a tablet in the church, about sixty boys and from twenty to thirty girls are instructed The Stratford on Avon canal passes through this parish

LARBRICK, a joint township with Little Eccleston, in the parish of KIRKHAM, hundred of AMOUNDERNESS, county palatine of LANCASTER, 4¼ miles (E N E) from Poulton, containing 224 inhabitants There is a chalybeate spring in this township

LARK-STOKE, a hamlet in that part of the parish of ILMINGTON which is in the upper division of the hundred of KIFTSGATE, county of GLOUCESTER, 4 miles (N E) from Chipping-Campden, containing 5 inhabitants

LARKTON, a township in the parish of MALPAS, higher division of the hundred of BROXTON, county palatine of CHESTER, 8½ miles (N by W) from Whitchurch, containing 60 inhabitants

LARLING, a parish in the hundred of SHROPHAM, county of NORFOLK, 2 miles (N W by N) from East Harling, containing 171 inhabitants The living is a rectory, in the archdeaconry of Norfolk, and diocese of Norwich, rated in the king's books at £10 0 2½, and in the patronage of N W Ridley Colborne, Esq The church, which is dedicated to St Ethelbert, presents a very fine specimen of early Norman architecture in the arch of the south porch

LARTINGTON, a township in the parish of ROM-ALD-KIRK, western division of the wapentake of GILLING, North riding of the county of YORK, 3 miles

(W N W) from Barnard-Castle, containing 243 inhabitants Here was formerly a chantry chapel, and attached to Lartington hall, the seat of Henry Witham, Esq , lord of the manor, is a very handsome Roman Catholic chapel, containing a painting of a crucifix, by Le Brun, which is considered so good an imitation of sculpture as to deceive the best judges A school was endowed, in 1686, by a benefaction of £60 from John Parken, and one of £40 from Francis Appleby, the income is £20 per annum eight children are educated

LARTON, a joint township with Newton, in the parish of WEST KIRBY, lower division of the hundred of WIRRALL, county palatine of CHESTER, 8 miles (N N W) from Great Neston, containing, with Newton, 48 inhabitants

LASBOROUGH, a parish in the hundred of LONG-TREE, county of GLOUCESTER, 4¾ miles (W by N) from Tetbury The population is returned with Weston-Birt The living is a discharged rectory, in the archdeaconry and diocese of Gloucester, rated in the king s books at £7 12 5 , and endowed with £200 royal bounty Edward Estcourt, Esq was patron in 1804

LASHAM, a parish in the hundred of ODIHAM, Basingstoke division of the county of SOUTHAMPTON, 4 miles (N W by W) from Alton, containing 188 inhabitants The living is a rectory, in the archdeaconry and diocese of Winchester, rated in the king s books at £6 18 9 , and in the patronage of G P Jervoise, Esq The church is dedicated to St Mary

LASKILL-PASTURE, a township in the parish of HELMSLEY, wapentake of RYEDALE, North riding of the county of YORK, 6 miles (N W by N) from Helmsley, containing 91 inhabitants

LASSINGTON, a parish in the lower division of the hundred of DUDSTONE and KING s BARTON, county of GLOUCESTER, 3¼ miles (N W) from Gloucester, containing 52 inhabitants The living is a discharged rectory, in the archdeaconry and diocese of Gloucester, rated in the king s books at £6 10 , and in the patronage of SIR B W Guise, Bart , and the Bishop of Gloucester, the former having two presentations, and the latter one The Herefordshire and Gloucestershire canal runs parallel with the river Leadon, which bounds this parish on the north and east, and falls into the western branch of the Severn near the ancient camp, where both rivers are crossed by the same bridge , here also the canal is crossed by a branch of the Severn, and joins the main branch at Gloucester The petrifaction called Astroites, or Star-stone, is met with in a hill in this neighbourhood

LASTINGHAM, a parish in the wapentake of RYE-DALE, North riding of the county of YORK, comprising the chapelry of Rosedale-West-Side, and the townships of Appleton le Moors, Farndale-East-Side, Farn dale High-Quarter, Hutton le Hole, Lastingham, and Spaunton, and containing 1834 inhabitants, of which number, 225 are in the township of Lastingham, 7 miles (N W) from Pickering The living is a discharged vicarage, in the archdeaconry of Cleveland, and diocese of York, rated in the king s books at £17 7 6 , and in the patronage of the Crown The church is dedicated to St. Mary A Benedictine monastery was founded here in honour of the Virgin Mary, about 648, by Cedd, Bishop of the East Saxons, of which the present church is probably the only vestige ,

underneath the choir is a vaulted crypt, the massive cylindrical columns and sculptured arches of which exhibit fine specimens of Norman architecture , the east end is circular, and at the west is a low tower , part of the church is in the Norman, and part in a later, style

LATCHFORD, a chapelry in the parish of GRAP-PENHALL, hundred of BUCKLOW, county palatine of CHESTER, 1½ mile (S E) from Warrington, containing 1252 inhabitants The living is a perpetual curacy, in the archdeaconry and diocese of Chester, endowed with £400 private benefaction, £1000 royal bounty, and £1400 parliamentary grant, and in the patronage of the Rector of Grappenhall The church, dedicated to St James, has lately received an addition of seven hundred and eighty seven sittings, of which four hundred are free, the Incorporated Society for the enlargement of churches and chapels having contributed £400 towards defraying the expense The Duke of Bridgewater s, the Mersey, and the Irwell, canals pass through this parish A cot ton manufactory has been recently established here Latchford had anciently two weekly markets and two annual fairs, granted in the fourteenth century

LATCHFORD, a hamlet in the parish of GREAT HASELEY, hundred of EWELME, county of OXFORD, 2½ miles (W) from Tetsworth The population is returned with the parish

LATCHINGDON, a parish in the hundred of DENGIE, county of ESSEX, 5½ miles (N W by W) from Burnham, containing 414 inhabitants The living is a rectory, in the peculiar jurisdiction and patronage of the Archbishop of Canterbury, rated in the king s books at £37 The church is dedicated to St Michael This parish extends across the hundred of Dengie, from Latchington creek and Blackwater river on the north, to the navigable river Crouch, on the south

LATHBURY, a parish in the hundred of NEWPORT, county of BUCKINGHAM, ¾ of a mile (N) from Newport-Pagnell, containing 164 inhabitants The living is a perpetual curacy, in the archdeaconry of Buckingham, and diocese of Lincoln, rated in the king s books at £5 6 8 , endowed with £200 private benefaction, and £200 royal bounty, and in the patronage of the Dean and Canons of Christ Church, Oxford The church is dedicated to All Saints A free grammar school was founded and endowed with £12 per annum, in the reign of Elizabeth, by Anthony Cave the right of appointing the master was vested in the Dean and Canons of Christ Church college he likewise gave two exhibitions, of £6 each, for the scholars the endowment has been lost, and the school-room was taken down in 1698 The learned Dr Chelsam, celebrated for his defence of Christianity, against Gibbon, held this living The parish is nearly surrounded by the river Ouse an ancient monastery formerly occupied the site of the present manor-house

LATHOM, a township in the parish of ORMSKIRK, hundred of WEST DERBY, county palatine of LANCAS-TER, 3¾ miles (N E by E) from Ormskirk, containing 2997 inhabitants The free grammar school at New-burgh, in this township, was erected, in 1714, by the Rev Thomas Crane, who endowed it with an estate at Dalton, to which Richard Okell, the schoolmaster, in 1761, added another, producing, together with an additional bequest of about £9 per annum, by Jonathan

Lucas, in 1793, a total income of £52 per annum there are one hundred scholars, of which number, forty poor children of Latham and Newburgh are instructed gratuitously At Latham park is an ancient almshouse consisting of several tenements, with a chapel There is a domestic chapel connected with the mansion of Lord Skelmersdale, by whom the officiating minister is appointed, his lordship has lately ornamented the chapel, at an expense of £1200, and has likewise erected a school-room, in which the children are educated at his own charge Lathom house, once "the chief seat of the Stanleys, was originally built by the De Lathoms, during the great civil war it sustained repeated sieges from the parliamentary forces, its owner, the Earl of Derbv, being one of the most staunch supporters of the royal cause On the 28th of February, 1644, it was besieged by General Sir Thomas Fairfax, with a force of three thousand troops, but was most gallantly defended by the Countess of Derby, with only a small band of three hundred men, who, in several destructive sallies, slew five hundred of the enemy, wounded one hundred and forty, and repeatedly destroyed their works on the 26th of May, the assailants were obliged to raise the siege, on the arrival of the royalists under Prince Rupert In the following year it was again besieged, by General Egerton, at the head of four thousand men, to whom, after an obstinate defence, it was surrendered, for want of ammunition, when it was plundered and the fortifications destroyed the fine seat of the Wilbraham family now stands on its site A market and a fair, to be held at this place, were granted to Robert de Lathom, in the 32nd of Edward I Here is a saline chalybeate spring, which also contains some portion of natron

LATTIMERS, a chapelry in the parish of CHESHAM, hundred of BURNHAM, county of BUCKINGHAM, 3¼ miles (S E by E) from Chesham, with which the population is returned

LATTON, a parish in the hundred of HARLOW, county of ESSEX, 1½ mile (W S W) from Harlow, containing 378 inhabitants The living is a vicarage, in the jurisdiction of the Commissary of Essex and Herts, concurrently with the Consistorial Court of the Bishop of London, rated in the king's books at £7 M Burgoyne, Esq was patron in 1820 The church is dedicated to St John the Baptist. Here was a priory of Black canons, founded in the fourteenth century, and dedicated to St John the Baptist some remains of the conventual buildings have been converted into a barn, they contain specimens in the decorated style

LATTON, a parish in the hundred of HIGHWORTH, CRICKLADE, and STAPLE, county of WILTS, 1½ mile (N W by N.) from Cricklade, containing 315 inhabitants The living is a vicarage, with which that of Eisey is annexed, in the archdeaconry of Wilts, and diocese of Salisbury, rated in the king's books at £9 3 4, and in the patronage of the Earl of St. Germans The church is dedicated to St John the Baptist A tesselated pavement was discovered here in 1670

LAUGHTON, a parish in the hundred of GARTREE, county of LEICESTER, 5¼ miles (W by N) from Market-Harborough, containing 173 inhabitants The living is a rectory, in the archdeaconry of Leicester, and diocese of Lincoln, rated in the king's books at £10 10 5, and in the patronage of the Rev Mr Humfrey The

Vol. III

church is dedicated to St Luke The Grand Union canal passes along the southern boundary of this parish

LAUGHTON, a parish in the wapentake of AVELAND, parts of KESTEVEN, county of LINCOLN, 1¾ mile (S by E) from Falkingham, containing 76 inhabitants The living is a vicarage, united with the rectory of Falkingham, in the archdeaconry and diocese of Lincoln The church has long been in ruins

LAUGHTON, a parish in the wapentake of CORRINGHAM, parts of LINDSEY, county of LINCOLN, comprising the township of Laughton, and the hamlet of Wildsworth, and containing 422 inhabitants, of which number, 319 are in the township of Laughton, 6 miles (N E by N) from Gainsborough The living is a vicarage, in the archdeaconry of Stow, and diocese of Lincoln, rated in the king s books at £12 The Marchioness of Hertford was patroness in 1820 The church is dedicated to All Saints There is a place of worship for Wesleyan Methodists

LAUGHTON, a hamlet in the parish of KETTLETHORPE, wapentake of WELL, parts of LINDSEY, county of LINCOLN, 10¼ miles (W N W) from Lincoln The population is returned with the parish

LAUGHTON, a parish in the hundred of SHIPLAKE, rape of PEVENSEY, county of SUSSEX, 6½ miles (E by N) from Lewes, containing 731 inhabitants The living is a discharged vicarage, in the archdeaconry of Lewes, and diocese of Chichester, rated in the king s books at £9 11 3, and endowed with £200 royal bounty The Earl of Chichester was patron in 1801 The church is principally in the early style of English architecture, with insertions of a later date

LAUGHTON en le MORTHEN, a parish partly within the liberty of St PETER of YORK, East riding, and partly in the southern division of the wapentake of STRAFFORTH and TICKHILL, West riding, of the county of YORK, comprising the chapelry of Letwell, and the townships of Gilden-Wells, Laughton en le Morthen, Throapham, and Woodsetts, and containing 1055 inhabitants, of which number, 652 are in the township of Laughton en le Morthen, 7½ miles (S W by W) from Tickhill. The living is a discharged vicarage, rated in the king's books at £6 13 4, endowed with £1400 parliamentary grant, and in the peculiar jurisdiction and patronage of the Chancellor in the Cathedral Church of York The church, dedicated to All Saints, is a fine specimen of the early English style the tower and spire are visible at the distance of sixty miles the height to the weathercock is one hundred and ninety-five feet There is a place of worship for Independents The free school is endowed with a dwelling-house, garden, and land, together with a rent-charge of £2 Ten poor children are educated gratuitously five children are also instructed for £5 per annum, the bequest of William Beckwith, in 1816

LAUNCELLS, a parish in the hundred of STRATTON, county of CORNWALL, 1 mile (E S E) from Stratton, containing 891 inhabitants The living is a vicarage, in the archdeaconry of Cornwall, and diocese of Exeter, rated in the king's books at £10 10 10 L W Buck, Esq was patron in 1825 The church is dedicated to St Andrew The Bude and Holsworthy canal passes through this parish, from west to east. There is an almshouse for four poor persons Here was a cell to the abbey of Hertland in Derbyshire

F

LAUNCESTON, a borough, market town, and parish, possessing separate jurisdiction, though locally in the northern division of East hundred, county of CORNWALL, 20½ miles (N E by E) from Bodmin, and 213 (W S W) from London, containing, exclusively of those portions of the borough which extend beyond

Seal and Arms.

the limits of the parish, 2193 inhabitants The ancient name of Launceston was *Dunheved*, the swelling hill it was also called *Lan-stephadon*, or Church Stephen Town Its present name seems to be a contraction of *Lan-cester-ton*, or Church Castle Town, the word *Llan* signifying a church in the British language The manor and honour of Launceston, which had a very extensive jurisdiction, belonged from time immemorial to the Earls of Cornwall, who had their chief seat at Launceston castle it was given by William the Conqueror to his half brother, Robert, Earl of Montaigne, whom he made Earl of Cornwall The church of the parish of St Stephen, now the borough of Newport, adjoining to Launceston, and considered as part of it, was made collegiate, before the Conquest, for Secular canons King Henry I gave this college to the church of Exeter Reginald, Earl of Cornwall, was a great benefactor to the college of St Stephen, and used all his influence with King Stephen to remove the bishop s see from Devonshire to Cornwall, and constitute this the cathedral church but it was successfully opposed by William Warlewast Bishop of Exeter, who, being then resident at Lawhitton, on his first triennial visitation, suppressed the college of Secular canons, and in its stead founded a priory of Augustine monks, in the parish of St Thomas, about half-way between St Stephen s and the castle The castle of Launceston passed with the earldom, and when Cornwall was erected into a duchy, was annexed to it by act of parliament Hubert de Burgh, who had large possessions in Cornwall, was made governor of the castle, and sheriff for the county, by King John From its strong position, and its situation at the entrance into the county, this castle was an important post during the parliamentary war It was at first in the hands of the parliament, and under the governorship of Sir Richard Buller, who, on the approach of Sir Ralph Hopton with the king s forces, quitted the town and fled In 1643, Sir Ralph was attacked by Major-General Chudleigh, without success In August, 1644, the place was surrendered to the earl of Essex, but fell into the hands of the royalists again after the capitulation of the earl s army In 1645, the Prince of Wales sojourned for some time in Launceston. In November of the same year the town was fortified, by Sir Richard Grenville, who, being at variance with Lord Goring, another of the king s generals, caused proclamation to be made in all the churches of Cornwall, that if any of Lord Goring s forces should come into Cornwall, the bells should ring, and the people rise to drive them out Shortly after, Sir Richard Grenville, having refused to take the chief command of the infantry under Lord Hopton, as generalissimo, was committed to the prison

of Launceston, Colonel Basset being then the governor who, in March, 1646, surrendered the place to Sir Thomas Fairfax In the time of the Commonwealth, the castle and park, being put up to sale by the government, were purchased by Robert Bennet, Esq, but on the Restoration, they reverted to the crown

The town is pleasantly situated near the western bank of the Tamar, on a steep ascent, at the foot of which is the little river Attery, on the summit of a hill is a high conical rocky mount, partly natural, and partly artificial, upon which the keep of the ancient castle, with a Norman gateway and part of the outer walls, is still standing some portions of the old town wall, and the north and south gates, one of which is on the Exeter road, also remain There are a few good houses, but the streets are in general narrow and badly paved, the inhabitants are well supplied with water, which is brought by pipes from Dunheved Green on the north side of the church is a pleasant promenade, shaded by an avenue of trees, and commanding a fine prospect over the adjacent country Assemblies are held at the White Hart inn during the assizes there are two book clubs, and a small subscription library About two years since, a library and philosophical institution, with a good apparatus, was established here, and is supported by subscription lectures are given during the winter at the grammar school, which is also occasionally used for concerts, plays, &c An extensive manufacture of serges was formerly carried on, but it has for several years been on the decline A branch of the Bude canal has recently been brought within four miles of the town, and promises materially to improve the general trade, fuel has already been reduced in price The markets are on Thursday for butchers meat, and on Saturday for corn and provisions of all sorts fairs are held on Whit-Monday, July 5th, November 17th, and December 6th, for cattle, and on the first Thursday in March, and the third Thursday in April, for cattle of all sorts, free of toll there are likewise three cattle fairs in the parish of St Stephen, on May 12th, July 31st, and September 25th.

Launceston was constituted a free borough in the reign of Henry III, by Richard, Earl of Cornwall, who granted various privileges to the burgesses, and a piece of ground on which to build their guildhall, to be held of him and his heirs by the annual tender of a pound of pepper the borough extends as far as Poulston bridge, on the Tamar, and into the parish of Lawhitton The charter of incorporation was granted by Queen Mary, in 1555 the municipal body consists of a mayor, eight aldermen, a recorder, and freemen, in all about seventeen persons The mayor is elected by the freemen, from two persons nominated by the aldermen, the aldermen are chosen by the freemen from their own body, and the freemen are elected by the whole corporation the mayor, the late mayor, the senior alderman, and the deputy recorder, are justices of the peace, and two general sessions of the peace are held within a month after Easter and a month after Michaelmas, when prisoners accused of petty offences are tried, more serious offences are reserved for the assizes A court of pleas, for the recovery of debts to an unlimited amount, is held every Monday, before the mayor, three aldermen, and the recorder Besides the parish of St Mary Magdalene, Launceston, the borough comprises the extra-parochial district of St Thomas-street, and portions of the parishes of Lawhitton and South Petherwin Petty sessions for the northern division of East hundred are held here, on the first Tuesday in every month The assizes for the county, formerly held wholly in this town, have, for more than half a century, been held here alternately with Bodmin, on which occasion only the county gaol at Launceston is now used The south gate, repaired about three years since, is used as the town prison This borough first returned members to parliament in the 23rd of Edward I the right of election is in the corporation, and the mayor is the returning officer the influence of the Duke of Northumberland is predominant

The living is a perpetual curacy, in the archdeaconry of Cornwall, and diocese of Exeter, endowed with £12 10 per annum private benefaction, and £400 royal bounty, and in the patronage of the Mayor and Corporation The church, formerly the chapel of St Mary Magdalene, was made parochial in the early part of the sixteenth century it is in the later style of English architecture, built with square blocks of granite, and covered with a profusion of grotesque ornaments the tower, which stands at the west end, is constructed of different materials, and is apparently of much greater antiquity There are places of worship for Independents and Wesleyan Methodists The grammar school was founded by Queen Elizabeth, and endowed with £16 per annum, chargeable on the estates of the duchy of Cornwall, to which an augmentation of £10 per annum was made, in 1685, by George Baron, Esq , whose descendants have the right of nominating ten free scholars , but the school has been discontinued for some years Two charity schools are supported by voluntary contributions Here was formerly an hospital for lepers, dedicated to St Leonard , the income, arising from certain fields which belonged to it, and amounting to about £25 per annum, is vested in the corporation for charitable uses Launceston gives the title of viscount to the reigning sovereign

LAUNCESTON TARRANT, county of Dorset — See TARRANT (LAUNCESTON)

LAUND BOOTH (NEW), a joint township with Reedly-Hallows and Filly-Close, in that part of the parish of WHALLEY which is in the higher division of the hundred of BLACKBURN, county palatine of LANCASTER, 2 miles (N) from Burnley, containing, with Reedly-Hallows and Filly-Close, 422 inhabitants

LAUND-BOOTH (OLD), a township in that part of the parish of MITTON which is in the higher division of the hundred of BLACKBURN, county palatine of LANCASTER, 3 miles (N) from Burnley, containing 390 inhabitants

LAUNDE, an extra-parochial liberty, in the eastern division of the hundred of GOSCOTE, county of LEICESTER, 6¼ miles (W N W) from Uppingham, containing 36 inhabitants A priory was founded here, in the reign of Henry I , by Richard Basset, and Maud his wife, for Black canons of the order of St Augustine, the revenue of which, at the dissolution, was valued at £510 16 5 the chapel and burial-ground are still preserved

LAUNTON, a parish in the hundred of PLOUGHLEY, county of OXFORD, 1¾ mile (E) from Bicester, containing 553 inhabitants The living is a rectory, in the archdeaconry and diocese of Oxford, rated in the king s

books at £11 9 4½ , and in the patronage of the Bishop of London The church is dedicated to St Mary

LAVANT, a parish comprising East and West Lavant, in the hundred of ALDWICK, though locally in that of Box and Stockbridge, rape of CHICHESTER, county of SUSSEX, 2½ miles (N) from Chichester, and containing 364 inhabitants. The living is a rectory, in the peculiar jurisdiction of the Archbishop of Canterbury, for the deanery of Pagham, the court for which is held in the parish of All Saints, Chichester , it is rated in the king s books at £20 18 1½ , and in the patronage of Lord Willoughby de Broke The church is dedicated to St Mary This parish has the privilege of sending four children to the charity school, founded by the Countess of Derby, at Boxgrove

LAVANT (MID), a parish in the hundred of WEST BOURN and SINCLETON, rape of CHICHESTER, county of SUSSEX, 2¾ miles (N by W) from Chichester, containing 243 inhabitants The living is a perpetual curacy, in the archdeaconry and diocese of Chichester, endowed with £600 royal bounty, and £200 parliamentary grant. L G Dorien, Esq was patron in 1814

LAVENDON, a parish in the hundred of NEWPORT, county of BUCKINGHAM, 2¾ miles (N E) from Olney, containing 613 inhabitants The living is a discharged vicarage, with the perpetual curacy of Cold Brayfield, in the archdeaconry of Buckingham, and diocese of Lincoln, rated in the king s books at £6 Sir G Noel, Bart was patron in 1817 The church is dedicated to St Mary An abbey of Premonstratensian canons was ounded, in the reign of Henry II , by John de Bidun, and dedicated to St John the Baptist, the revenue of which, at the dissolution, was valued at £79 13 8 Here was formerly a market on Tuesday, granted to Paulmus Peyore, in 1248, but now disused a fair is held on the Tuesday before Easter

LAVENHAM, a market town and parish in the hundred of BABERGH, county of SUFFOLK, situated on the river Brett, 18½ miles (W by N) from Ipswich, and 61 (N E) from London, containing 1898 inhabitants The town, which is remarkably healthy, occupies the declivities of two hills rising gradually from the river, and consists of several small streets, which are neither paved nor lighted , the houses are in general of mean appearance , the inhabitants are well supplied with water The manufacture of blue cloth formerly flourished here, under the direction of several guilds, each of which had its separate hall , but at present wool-combing and spinning, and these on a small scale, are the only trades carried on The market, now almost disused, is on Tuesday the market place is a spacious area, containing a stone cross Fairs are held for horses and cattle on Shrove-Tuesday, and October 11th, 12th, and 13th, for toys Lavenham was formerly governed by six capital burgesses, who held their office for life, assisted by inferior officers, but their authority has long since ceased, and the rector, who is a magistrate, possesses considerable authority in the town Courts leet and baron are held at the will of the lord of the manor The county magistrates hold their meetings at Lavenham , and there is a bridewell, which is also partly used as a work-house

The living is a rectory, in the archdeaconry of Sudbury, and diocese of Norwich, rated in the king s books at £20 2 11 , and in the patronage of the Master and

Fellows of Caius College, Cambridge The church, which is dedicated to St Peter, was rebuilt, in the reign of Henry VI, partly by the De Veres, Earls of Oxford, who formerly resided here, and partly by Mr Thomas Spring, a rich clothier, whose armorial bearings are jointly displayed in many parts of the building It is an eminently beautiful structure, in the later style of English architecture, with a lofty clerestory, enriched battlements, and a fine square tower the entrance is by a porch, supposed to have been erected by John, the fourteenth Earl of Oxford, and enriched with most elaborate embellishments the ceiling of the church is covered with exquisite tracery, and the pews of the Earl of Oxford, and the Spring family, are beautiful models of the most highly-finished carving in the latest English style In the church is a curious mural monument to Allaine Dister, a wealthy clothier of this town, and another of alabaster and marble to the Rev Mr Copinger There are places of worship for Independents and Wesleyan Methodists The free school was founded, in 1647, by Richard Peacock, Esq, with an endowment of £5 per annum, augmented, in 1699, by Edward Colman, Esq, with £16 per annum, a dwelling-house and garden for the master have been added by subscription there are at present only five boys on the foundation Two National schools for boys and girls are supported by the proceeds of a bequest of £2000 three per cent consols, by Henry Steward, in 1806, the income is £53 17 6 per annum There are thirty almshouses, the maintenance of them being chargeable on the old town lands, which produce an income of £186 per annum, being partly distributed among the necessitous poor, who enjoy the benefit of some other benefactions The Rev George Ruggle, author of a Latin comedy entitled Ignoramus, and other dramatic pieces, was born at Lavenham, in 1575

LAVER (HIGH), a parish in the hundred of ONGAR, county of ESSEX, 4 miles (N N W) from Chipping-Ongar, containing 464 inhabitants The living is a rectory, in the archdeaconry of Essex, and diocese of London, rated in the king's books at £14 1 8, and in the patronage of the Rev Philip Budworth The church is dedicated to All Saints Here is a National school The celebrated John Locke resided at the mansion house of Otes in this parish, during the last two years of his life he died in October 1704, and was interred on the south side of the church-yard over his remains is a black marble tomb, enclosed within iron rails, and on the wall of the church is his epitaph in Latin, composed by himself

LAVER (LITTLE), a parish in the hundred of ONGAR, county of ESSEX, 5 miles (N) from Chipping-Ongar, containing 107 inhabitants The living is a rectory, in the archdeaconry of Essex, and diocese of London, rated in the king's books at £15 10 5 Robert Palmer, Esq was patron in 1824 The church is dedicated to St Mary

LAVER MAGDALEN, a parish in the hundred of ONGAR, county of ESSEX, 5¼ miles (N W by N) from Chipping-Ongar, containing 236 inhabitants The living is a rectory, in the archdeaconry of Essex, and diocese of London, rated in the king's books at £16 12 1 The Rev J W Burford, D D was patron in 1794. The church is dedicated to St Mary Magdalene

LAVERSTOCK, a parish comprising the hamlet of

Ford in the hundred of ALDERBURY, and the tything of Milford in that of UNDERDITCH, county of WILTS, 1 mile (N E) from Salisbury, and containing 904 inhabitants The living is a perpetual curacy, in the archdeaconry and diocese of Salisbury, and in the patronage of the Vicars Choral of the Cathedral Church of Salisbury The church is dedicated to St Andrew. Here is a celebrated establishment for lunatics, under the superintendence of Dr Finch

LAVERSTOKE, a parish in the hundred of OVERTON, Kingsclere division of the county of SOUTHAMPTON, 2¾ miles (E N E) from Whitchurch, containing 101 inhabitants The living is a rectory, in the archdeaconry and diocese of Winchester, rated in the king's books at £8 10, and in the patronage of William Portal, Esq The church is dedicated to St Mary The river Test runs through the parish Laverstoke is within the jurisdiction of the Cheyney Court held at Winchester every Thursday, for the recovery of debts to any amount

LAVERTON, a hamlet in the parish of BUCKLAND, lower division of the hundred of KIFTSGATE, county of GLOUCESTER The population is returned with the parish

LAVERTON, a parish in the hundred of FROME, county of SOMERSET, 3½ miles (N) from Frome, containing 189 inhabitants The living is a discharged rectory, in the archdeaconry of Wells, and diocese of Bath and Wells, rated in the king's books at £6 18 6½, and in the patronage of the Bishop of Bath and Wells. The church is dedicated to St Mary There is a place of worship for Baptists

LAVERTON, a township in the parish of KIRKBY MALZEARD, lower division of the wapentake of CLARO, West riding of the county of YORK, 6¼ miles (W by N) from Ripon, containing 430 inhabitants.

LAVINGTON, otherwise LINTON, a parish in the wapentake of BELTISLOE, parts of KESTEVEN, county of LINCOLN, 6 miles (N N E) from Corby, comprising the township of Osgodby, and the hamlets of Hanby and Keisby, and containing 330 inhabitants The living is a rectory, in the archdeaconry and diocese of Lincoln, rated in the king's books at £14 7 1 Sir G Heathcote, Bart was patron in 1824 The church is dedicated to St. Peter

LAVINGTON (EAST or MARKET), a parish in the hundred of SWANBOROUGH, county of WILTS, comprising the market town of East Lavington, and the tything of Easterton, and containing 1438 inhabitants, of which number, 1061 are in the town of East Lavington, 6 miles (S) from Devizes, and 90 (W by S) from London The town is situated in a fertile valley, on the base of the chalk hills which form the northern boundary of Salisbury plain, and consists principally of one street the trade is chiefly in corn and malt. The market is on Wednesday, and a fair is held on the 10th of August A court baron for the manor is held twice a year The living is a vicarage, in the archdeaconry and diocese of Salisbury, rated in the king's books at £14. 2 6, and in the patronage of the Dean and Canons of Christ Church, Oxford The church, dedicated to St Mary, stands on a lofty eminence, hence the popular name of Steeple-Lavington given to the town There are two places of worship for Independents Here is a free school for the education of thirty-six children The learned and laborious antiquary, Dr Thomas Tanner, Bishop of St. Asaph, and author of the "Notitia Monastica," was born here, in 1674, his father having been vicar of the parish, and at his death, in 1733, he bequeathed £200 for the benefit of the poor

LAVINGTON (WEST), a parish in the hundred of POTTERNE and CANNINGS, county of WILTS, 1½ mile (8 W by S) from Lavington, containing, with the tything of Littleton-Pannell, 1123 inhabitants The living is a vicarage, in the archdeaconry and diocese of Salisbury, rated in the king's books at £11 16 3, and in the patronage of the Bishop of Salisbury The church is dedicated to All Saints A free school was liberally endowed with land, in 1542, by William Dauntsey There are three almshouses for as many poor women

LAWFORD, a parish in the hundred of TENDRING, county of ESSEX, 1½ mile (W) from Manningtree, containing 688 inhabitants The living is a rectory, in the archdeaconry of Colchester, and diocese of London, rated in the king's books at £15, and in the patronage of the Master and Fellows of St. John's College, Cambridge. The church, dedicated to St Mary, has recently received an addition of one hundred and sixty sittings, of which, one hundred and ten are free, the Incorporated Society for the enlargement of churches having contributed £100 In 1723, John Leach bequeathed a rent-charge of £22 4., for teaching ten poor children, and clothing ten poor persons not receiving parochial relief The navigable river Stour runs on the south of this parish

LAWFORD (CHURCH), a parish in the Rugby division of the hundred of KNIGHTLOW, county of WARWICK, 4 miles (W N W) from Rugby, containing 355 inhabitants The living is a rectory, in the archdeaconry of Coventry, and diocese of Lichfield and Coventry, rated in the king's books at £11 15 5, and in the patronage of Lord Montagu The church is dedicated to St Peter

LAWFORD (LITTLE) a hamlet in the parish of NEWBOLD upon Avon, Rugby division of the hundred of KNIGHTLOW, county of WARWICK, 4 miles (W) from Rugby, containing 27 inhabitants

LAWFORD (LONG), a hamlet in the parish of NEWBOLD upon Avon, Rugby division of the hundred of KNIGHTLOW, county of WARWICK, 2½ miles (W N W) from Rugby, containing 474 inhabitants

LAWHITTON, a parish in the northern division of EAST hundred, county of CORNWALL, 2¼ miles (S E by E) from Launceston, containing 435 inhabitants. The living is a rectory, in the archdeaconry of Cornwall, and diocese of Exeter, rated in the king's books at £19 6 8., and in the peculiar jurisdiction and patronage of the Bishop of Exeter The church is dedicated to St Michael This place had anciently a market and a fair, granted to one of the bishops of Exeter A small portion of this parish is included within the borough of Launceston.

LAWKLAND, a township in the parish of CLAPHAM, western division of the wapentake of STAINCLIFFE and EWCROSS, West riding of the county of YORK, 4 miles (N W by W.) from Settle, containing 351 inhabitants Eldroth chapel, in this township, formerly a chapel of ease, is now used as a school-room for teaching poor children, for which purpose there is an endowment in land and money, producing about £13 a year

LAWLING, a chapelry in the parish of LATCHING-

DON, hundred of DENGIE, county of ESSEX, 5¼ miles (N W) from Burnham The population is returned with the parish

LAWRENCE (ST), a parish in the hundred of DENGIE, county of ESSEX, 3 miles (S W by W) from Bradwell near the Sea, containing 229 inhabitants The living is a rectory, in the archdeaconry of Essex, and diocese of London, rated in the king's books at £18 6 8, and in the patronage of the Crown The Blackwater river is navigable on the north of this parish

LAWRENCE (ST), a parish in the hundred of RINGSLOW, or ISLE of THANET, lathe of ST AUGUSTINE, county of KENT, ¾ of a mile (W) from Ramsgate, containing 1601 inhabitants The living is a vicarage, in the archdeaconry and diocese of Canterbury, rated in the king's books at £7, and in the patronage of the Archbishop of Canterbury Pegwell bay, on the south of this parish, abounds with a delicious fish called Prill

LAWRENCE (ST), a chapelry in the parish of PRESTON, hundred of AMOUNDERNESS, county palatine of LANCASTER, 5½ miles (W N W) from Preston The population is returned with the parish.

LAWRENCE (ST), a parish in the liberty of EAST MEDINA, Isle of Wight division of the county of SOUTHAMPTON, 8¼ miles (S S E) from Newport, containing 96 inhabitants. The living is a discharged rectory, in the archdeaconry and diocese of Winchester, rated in the king's books at £4, endowed with £200 private benefaction, and £200 royal bounty, and in the patronage of Lord Yarborough The church is only twenty feet long and twelve wide the greater part of the parish consists of a slip of land extending about a mile and a half along the sea-shore, and forming part of the romantic tract called Undercliff

LAWRENCE (ST) ILKETSHALL, county of SUFFOLK—See ILKETSHALL (ST LAWRENCE)

LAWSHALL, a parish in the hundred of BABERGH, county of SUFFOLK, 7½ miles (S by E) from Bury-St Edmund s, containing 837 inhabitants The living is a rectory, in the archdeaconry of Sudbury, and diocese of Norwich, rated in the king's books at £20 2 8½ N Lee Acton, Esq was patron in 1810 The church is dedicated to All Saints The poor children of the Sunday school are partly clothed by means of various charitable bequests

LAWTON (CHURCH), a parish in the hundred of NORTHWICH, county palatine of CHESTER, 6 miles (S E) from Sandbach, containing 512 inhabitants The living is a discharged rectory, in the archdeaconry and diocese of Chester, rated in the king's books at £9 2 7, and in the patronage of —— Lawton, Esq The church, dedicated to All Saints, has a Norman south door There is a place of worship for Wesleyan Methodists Here is a small fund for the instruction of poor children The Trent and Mersey canal is joined here by the Macclesfield canal, and passes through the parish, upon its banks are coal wharfs, a small quantity of coal being raised in the parish the Old Lawton salt works are on the border of this parish and Asbury

LAXFIELD, a parish in the hundred of HOXNE, county of SUFFOLK, 6 miles (N by E) from Framlingham, containing 1158 inhabitants The living is a discharged vicarage, with that of Cratfield, in the archdeaconry of Suffolk, and diocese of Norwich, rated in the king s books at £9 13 4, and in the patronage of Lord Huntingfield. The church is dedicated to All Saints There is a place of worship for Baptists A free school was founded, in 1718, by John Smith, who endowed it with the proceeds of his manor and other estates the income is £170 per annum twenty boys are instructed and four apprenticed yearly and partly clothed A sum of £5 per annum is paid to a schoolmistress for teaching twelve poor girls to read and work, and a similar sum is assigned in aid of the Sunday school it is in contemplation to extend these schools, in consequence of the increased value of the endowment A free school was founded, under the will of Ann Ward, in 1721, who devised £30 for that and other charitable purposes £20 per annum is paid to a schoolmaster, who instructs ten poor children, and £10 is paid to the schoolmistress under Smith s charity, for teaching ten girls

LAXTON, a parish in the hundred of CORBY, county of NORTHAMPTON, 7¼ miles (N E by E) from Rockingham, containing 190 inhabitants The living is a perpetual curacy, in the archdeaconry of Northampton, and diocese of Peterborough, and in the patronage of Lord Carbery The church is dedicated to All Saints

LAXTON, or LEXINGTON, a parish in the Southclay division of the wapentake of BASSETLAW, county of NOTTINGHAM, 2¾ miles (S S W) from Tuxford, containing, with Moorhouse, 615 inhabitants The living is a discharged vicarage, in the archdeaconry of Nottingham, and diocese of York, rated in the king s books at £11, and in the patronage of Earl Manvers The church is dedicated to St Michael Forty shillings per annum, being the interest of £40, the bequest of a person unknown, is applied towards the education of children

LAXTON, a chapelry in the parish of HOWDEN, wapentake of HOWDENSHIRE, East riding of the county of YORK, 3½ miles (S E by E) from Howden, containing 268 inhabitants. The living is a perpetual curacy, in the jurisdiction of the peculiar court of Howdenshire, endowed with £1000 royal bounty, and in the patronage of the Vicar of Howden There is a place of worship for Wesleyan Methodists

LAYCOCK, a parish in the hundred of CHIPPENHAM, county of WILTS, 3¾ miles (S) from Chippenham, containing 1682 inhabitants The living is a vicarage, in the archdeaconry of Wilts, and diocese of Salisbury, rated in the king s books at £8 4 2 W H F Talbott, Esq was patron in 1814 The church is dedicated to St Cyriack There is a place of worship for Independents An abbey of nuns, of the order of St Augustine, was founded here, in 1232, by Ela, Countess Dowager of Salisbury it was dedicated to the Virgin Mary and St Bernard, and at the dissolution its revenue was valued at £203 12 3 The remains of the conventual buildings have been fitted up as a private residence belonging to a branch of the family of Talbot in a room, in which records are kept, is an original copy of the great charter of Henry III, deposited here by Ela, Countess of Salisbury, at the time when, during her widowhood, she held the shrievalty of the county of Wilts, being, as its endorsement imports, a copy of the principal charter sent to her in that capacity, for the use of the knights and military tenants of Wiltshire A weekly market and an annual fair were granted to this abbey, but the former has been disused fairs

are held on July 1st and December 21st In the centre of one of the streets of the village is an ancient stone cross

LAYER de la HAY, a parish in the hundred of WINSTREE, county of ESSEX, 4¼ miles (S W by S) from Colchester, containing 603 inhabitants The living is a perpetual curacy, in the archdeaconry of Colchester, and diocese of London, endowed with £600 private benefaction, and £600 royal bounty John Bawtree, Esq was patron in 1826

LAYER BRETON, a parish in the hundred of WINSTREE, county of ESSEX, 6¼ miles (S W by S) from Colchester, containing 259 inhabitants The living is a rectory, in the archdeaconry of Colchester, and diocese of London, rated in the king s books at £7 The Rev J F Benwell was patron in 1819 There is a place of worship for Independents

LAYER-MARNEY, a parish in the hundred of WINSTREE, county of ESSEX, 7 miles (S W) from Colchester, containing 246 inhabitants The living is a rectory, in the archdeaconry of Colchester, and diocese of London, rated in the king s books at £15 3 4 Matthew Corsellis, Esq was patron in 1828 The church, dedicated to St Mary, is principally in the later style of English architecture, and contains several fine ancient monuments of the Marney family In 1500, Sir Henry Marney erected Layer Marney hall, one of the earliest brick mansions in the kingdom part of the south side, and the great entrance tower, which is very lofty, are yet standing In an ancient brick edifice, about fifty yards from the church, William de Marney, in 1330, founded a college, for a warden and two chaplains

LAYHAM, a parish in the hundred of COSFORD, county of SUFFOLK, 1½ mile (S by E) from Hadleigh, containing 595 inhabitants The living is a rectory, in the archdeaconry of Sudbury, and diocese of Norwich, rated in the king s books at £16 0 7½, and in the patronage of the Master and Fellows of St John s College, Cambridge The church is dedicated to St Andrew

LAYSTERS, a parish in the hundred of WOFPHY, county of HEREFORD, 4 miles (S S W) from Tenbury, containing 227 inhabitants The living is a perpetual curacy, in the archdeaconry of Salop, and diocese of Hereford, endowed with £500 private benefaction, and £400 royal bounty, and in the patronage of the Rev Thomas Elton Miller The church is dedicated to St Andrew An ancient ecclesiastical establishment was connected with the priory of Shene in Surrey there are still some vestiges of the buildings on a farm called the Cinders, being partially surrounded by a moat

LAYSTHORPE, a joint township with East Newton, in the parish of STONEGRAVE, wapentake of RYEDALE, North riding of the county of YORK, 3½ miles (S S E) from Helmsley The population is returned with East Newton

LAYSTON, a parish in the hundred of EDWINSTREE, county of HERTFORD, ¾ of a mile (N N E) from Buntingford, containing 1014 inhabitants The living is a vicarage, with the perpetual curacy of Buntingford, in the archdeaconry of Middlesex, and diocese of London, rated in the king s books at £14 16 2, and in the patronage of William Butt, Esq The church, dedicated to St Bartholomew, is situated in the fields, about half a mile eastward from the town of Buntingford, in the centre of the site of the ancient village of Layston, which has totally disappeared it is used only for the solemnization of marriages, the parishioners resorting to the chapel at Buntingford, on account of its greater convenience There are two small endowments, one by Esdras Bland in 1668, and the other by Lady Jane Barkham in 1653, for the instruction of poor children. (See Buntingford)

LAYTHAM, a township in the parish of AUGHTON, Holme-Beacon division of the wapentake of HARTHILL, East riding of the county of YORK, 8 miles (N) from Howden, containing 125 inhabitants

LAYTON, a joint township with Warbrick, in the parish of BISPHAM, hundred of AMOUNDERNESS, county palatine of LANCASTER, 2½ miles (S W) from Poulton, containing with Warbrick, 749 inhabitants

LAYTON (EAST), a township in that part of the parish of STANWICK, ST JOHN, which is in the western division of the wapentake of GILLING, North riding of the county of YORK, 6 miles (E S.E) from Greta Bridge, containing 137 inhabitants

LAYTON (WEST), a township in the parish of HUTTON-MAGNUM, western division of the wapentake of GILLING, North riding of the county of YORK, 4¾ miles (S E by E) from Greta Bridge, containing 69 inhabitants

LAZONBY, a parish in LEATH ward, county of CUMBERLAND, comprising the chapelry of Plumpton-Wall, and the township of Lazonby, and containing 801 inhabitants, of which number, 533 are in the township of Lazonby, 1 mile (S W) from Kirk-Oswald The living is a vicarage, in the archdeaconry and diocese of Carlisle, rated in the king's books at £13 1 3, and in the patronage of the Bishop of Carlisle The church is dedicated to St Nicholas The river Eden bounds this parish on the east, and the Petterill on the west In Baron wood is a lofty rock, wherein is an artificial cave, called Giant's Chamber, or Sampson's cave The great Roman road passes from north to south, and another intersects the parish in a direction towards Salkeld bridge Here is a good freestone quarry, and one producing stone for mill-stones At Castle Rigg are the ruins of a moated building, and upon the fell, urns, containing bones and ashes, were discovered, some years ago There are several cairns on the commons

LEA, a township in that part of the parish of BACKFORD which is in the higher division of the hundred of WIRRALL, county palatine of CHESTER, 4 miles (N N W) from Chester, containing 87 inhabitants

LEA, a township in the parish of WYBUNBURY, hundred of NANTWICH, county palatine of CHESTER, containing 71 inhabitants The Ellesmere, or Wyrral, canal passes through this parish

LEA, county of DERBY —See DETHWICK-LEA

LEA, a parish partly in the hundred of ST BRIAVELLS, county of GLOUCESTER, and partly in the hundred of GREYTREE, county of HEREFORD, 4½ miles (F S E) from Ross, containing 180 inhabitants The living is a perpetual curacy, in the archdeaconry of Gloucester, and diocese of Hereford, endowed with £200 private benefaction, and £600 royal bounty, and in the patronage of the President and Fellows of St John's College, Oxford The church is dedicated to St John

LEA, a joint township with Ashton, Ingol, and Cottam, in the parish of PRESTON, hundred of AMOUNDERNESS, county palatine of LANCASTER, 3½ miles (W by N) from Preston, containing 658 inhabitants A school was erected and endowed with a rent-charge on an estate, in 1784, by Samuel Neeld, the income is £90 per annum, and there are fifteen scholars

LEA, a parish in the wapentake of CORRINGHAM, parts of LINDSEY, county of LINCOLN, 2¼ miles (S S E) from Gainsborough, containing 199 inhabitants The living is a rectory, in the archdeaconry of Stow, and diocese of Lincoln, rated in the king's books at £9 4 2, and in the patronage of the Rev Sir C J Anderson, Bart The church is dedicated to St Helen Here are some fish ponds and a moat, the remains of an ancient religious house Gypsum is found under the marl in this parish A Cistercian nunnery was founded, in 1180, at Hevening, in this parish, by Reyner Evermue, it was dedicated to the Blessed Virgin Mary, and at the dissolution had a revenue of £58 13 4

LEA, a parish in the hundred of MALMESBURY, county of WILTS, 1¾ mile (E S E) from Malmesbury, containing, with the township of Cleverton, 371 inhabitants The living is a perpetual curacy, annexed to the rectory of Allcannings, n the archdeaconry of Wilts, and diocese of Salisbury

LEA-BAILEY, a tything in the parish of NEWLAND, hundred of ST BRIAVELLS, county of GLOUCESTER, 4½ miles (S E) from Ross, containing 93 inhabitants

LEA-HALL, a hamlet in that part of the parish of BRADBORNE which is in the hundred of WIRKSWORTH, county of DERBY, 4½ miles (N N E) from Ashbourn, containing 23 inhabitants

LEA-MARSTON, a parish in the Atherstone division of the hundred of HEMLINGFORD, county of WARWICK, 4 miles (N) from Coleshill, containing 284 inhabitants The living is a perpetual curacy, in the archdeaconry of Coventry, and diocese of Lichfield and Coventry, endowed with £200 private benefaction, and £400 royal bounty C B Adderley, Esq was patron in 1817 The church is dedicated to St John the Baptist

LEA-NEWBOLD, a township in that part of the parish of ST OSWALD, CHESTER, which is in the lower division of the hundred of BROXTON, county palatine of CHESTER, 6 miles (S S E) from Chester, containing 61 inhabitants

LEACH, a joint township with Marlston, in that part of the parish of ST MARY, CHESTER, which is in the lower division of the hundred of BROXTON, county palatine of CHESTER, 2¼ miles (S W) from Chester The population is returned with Marlston

LEACROFT, a joint township with Hednesford, in the parish of CANNOCK, eastern division of the hundred of CUTTLESTONE, county of STAFFORD, 6 miles (S F by E) from Penkridge The population is returned with Hednesford Here is a considerable manufactory for edge tools, and coal is raised in this part of the parish

LEADENHAM, a parish in the wapentake of LOVEDEN, parts of KESTEVEN, county of LINCOLN, 9 miles (N W by W) from Sleaford, containing 574 inhabitants The living is a rectory, in the archdeaconry and diocese of Lincoln, rated in the king's books at £29 12 8½ The Rev Thomas Brown was patron in 1822 The church, dedicated to St Swithin, is partly in the decorated, and partly in the later English, style, and has a tower and spire of elegant proportions. The petty sessions for the division are held here

LEAD-HALL, a township in that part of the parish of RYTHER which is in the upper division of the wapentake of BARKSTONE-ASH, West riding of the county of YORK, 5 miles (S S W) from Tadcaster, containing 50 inhabitants

LEADON (HIGH), a hamlet in that part of the parish of RUDFORD which is in the lower division of the hundred of DUDSTONE and KING'S BARTON, county of GLOUCESTER, 5 miles (E. S E) from Newent, containing 92 inhabitants

LEAFIELD, a chapelry in the parish of SHIPTON under WHICHWOOD, hundred of CHADLINGTON, county of OXFORD, 5½ miles (N W by N) from Witney, containing 553 inhabitants. The living is a perpetual curacy, in the archdeaconry and diocese of Oxford, endowed with £800 royal bounty, and £1200 parliamentary grant. The chapel, founded in the reign of Elizabeth, by Sir Henry Upton, and dedicated to St Michael, has lately received an addition of two hundred and eighty sittings, of which, two hundred and fifty are free, the Incorporated Society for the enlargement of churches and chapels having contributed £250 towards defraying the expense

LEAGRAM, a joint township with Bowland, in that part of the parish of WHALLEY which is in the lower division of the hundred of BLACKBURN, county palatine of LANCASTER, 9 miles (W N W) from Clitheroe, containing, with Bowland, 370 inhabitants

LEAK, a parish comprising the townships of Borrowby, Crosby, Knayton with Brawith, Landmoth with Catto and Leak, in the wapentake of ALLERTONSHIRE, the chapelry of Nether-Silton, and the township of Gueldable, in the wapentake of BIRDFORTH, North riding of the county of YORK, and containing 1083 inhabitants, of which number, 11 are in the township of Leak, 6 miles (N) from Thirsk. The living is a vicarage, in the peculiar jurisdiction and patronage of the Bishop of Durham, rated in the king's books at £16 The church is dedicated to St Mary. There is a small sum for the instruction of poor children. Leak was once a large town, but was destroyed about the time of the Conquest the church and a farm-house alone remain in the township

LEAKE, a parish in the wapentake of SKIRBECK, parts of HOLLAND, county of LINCOLN, 7¼ miles (N E) from Boston, containing 1417 inhabitants. The living is a discharged vicarage, in the archdeaconry and diocese of Lincoln, rated in the king's books at £13 6 8, endowed with £200 royal bounty, and in the patronage of the Governors of Oakham school. The church is dedicated to St. Mary. There is a place of worship for Wesleyan Methodists. The Rev Thomas Allenson, in 1555, bequeathed land for the support of a school, and for the maintenance of five poor people of the parish

LEAKE (EAST), a parish in the southern division of the wapentake of RUSHCLIFFE, county of NOTTINGHAM, 4¼ miles (E.) from Kegworth, containing 783 inhabitants. The living is a rectory, with that of West Leake, not rated in the king's books, in the archdeaconry of Nottingham, and diocese of York. The church, dedicated to St. Mary, exhibits a fine specimen of the later style of English architecture. There are places of worship for Baptists and Wesleyan Methodists. A free school was founded and endowed with lands, about 1731, by John Blay, citizen of London, and a native of this place the income is about £48 per annum forty boys are instructed. He likewise bequeathed £10 to every farmer, and £5 to every cottager, in the village Many of the inhabitants are employed in frame-work knitting. This parish is in the honour of Tutbury, duchy of Lancaster, and within the jurisdiction of a court of pleas held at Tutbury every third Tuesday, for the recovery of debts under 40s

LEAKE (WEST), a parish in the southern division of the wapentake of RUSHCLIFFE, county of NOTTINGHAM, 2¾ miles (E) from Kegworth, containing 211 inhabitants. The living is a rectory, with which that of East Leake is united, in the archdeaconry of Nottingham, and diocese of York, rated in the king's books at £25 4 7, and in the patronage of the Marquis of Hastings

LEAMINGTON-HASTINGS, a parish in the Southam division of the hundred of KNIGHTLOW, county of WARWICK, 4½ miles (N. N E) from Southam, containing 444 inhabitants. The living is a vicarage, in the archdeaconry of Coventry, and diocese of Lichfield and Coventry, rated in the king's books at £20. The Rev. H W Sitwell was patron in 1822. The church is dedicated to All Saints. About thirty poor children are educated by a schoolmaster, who receives £25 per annum, chargeable on the parish land. In the reign of James I an hospital for the maintenance of eight poor persons of this parish was founded, and endowed by Humphrey Davis. An almshouse also was founded and endowed, in 1687, for two poor persons, by means of a bequest from Dorothy, widow of Sir Charles Wheeler, Bart. The Warwick and Napton canal passes through this parish, on the southern side

LEAMINGTON-PRIORS, a parish and fashionable watering-place, in the Kenilworth division of the hundred of KNIGHTLOW, county of WARWICK, 2½ miles (E) from Warwick, and 90 (N W) from London, containing 2183 inhabitants. This place derives its name from the river Leam, on which it is situated, and from its having originally belonged to the priory of Kenilworth. From an obscure hamlet consisting only of a few cottages it has, within the last twenty years, from the celebrity of its mineral springs, risen with unprecedented rapidity into a large and populous town, which, for the spaciousness of its streets, the elegance of its houses, and the beauty and interest of the surrounding scenery, is not excelled by any watering-place in the kingdom. It is visited during the season by numerous families of distinction, and by invalids who frequent it for the benefit of the waters, and, from the salubrity of the air, and the mildness of its temperature, it has become the permanent residence of a number of respectable families, who have erected handsome dwelling-houses in various parts of the town and its immediate vicinity. So rapid has been its increase that it has, within the short space of twenty years, quadrupled its population, which upon a moderate computation must have been more than doubled since the last census. The town is situated in a fine open vale, sheltered from the severity of the winds by gentle acclivities richly clothed with wood, and surrounded by a fertile and highly-cultivated tract of country, abounding with objects of historical interest, and with scenes of impressive beauty The river Leam, over which is a handsome stone bridge connecting the old with the new town, and the river Avon, wind through the adjoining meadows, enlivening the landscape, and in the distance are seen the stately towers of Warwick castle and church, rising above the intervening groves, and presenting themselves in various points of view with increasing beauty and effect The mineral springs are of three kinds, sulphureous, saline, and chalybeate the water of the sulphureous spring, according to the analysis of Dr Loudon, a resident physician, contains sulphuric acid, chlorine, soda, lime, and magnesia, the gases are oxygen, azote, carbonic acid, and sulphuretted hydrogen The saline water contains chlorine, lime, sulphuric acid, magnesia, silica, peroxide of iron, and soda, the gases are oxygen, azote, and carbonic acid. The chalybeate water contains chlorine, sulphuric acid, lime, magnesia, sodium, silica, and peroxide of iron, the gases are oxygen, azote, and carbonic acid, the saline and chalybeate waters differing chiefly in the proportions of their respective ingredients There is a constant and plentiful supply of the mineral waters for drinking and for bathing, and the varieties of the several springs comprehend the respective properties and rival the efficacy of the Cheltenham, Harrogate, and Tunbridge waters

The spring first discovered here, and now called the Old Well, is described by Camden, Speed, and Dugdale, its water was analysed in 1688, and it has recently been enclosed by Lord Aylesford, who has erected a neat pump-room over it, containing a marble font, from which a pipe is conducted on the outside of the building, for the use of the poor The second spring was discovered in 1784, by Mr Abbots, who erected six warm baths, a cold bath, and shower baths, with dressing-rooms adjoining, since that time, numerous establishments have been fitted up in various parts of the town, all similarly conducted, of which the principal are the Royal Spa, a handsome stone building with a fine colonnade of the Doric order, extending the whole length of the front, and having an entrance near each end leading respectively to the gentlemen s and ladies baths, and into the pump-room, which is in the centre This establishment contains fifteen hot, cold, and shower baths, of which two are provided with cranes for lowering and raising invalids in a chair the baths are furnished with dressing-rooms and every requisite accommodation, the pump-room, eighty five feet long, thirty-six wide, and of proportionate height, is lighted by a range of upper windows, the walls are ornamented with Doric pilasters supporting a handsome entablature at one end of the room is the pump, with two pipes, one of sulphureous, the other of saline, water, and at the other end is an orchestra, in which a well-selected band performs during the hours of attendance this elegant building, which forms one of the principal ornaments of the town, is situated on the banks of the river Leam, between the old and the new town, the grounds are tastefully laid out in lawns, shrubberies, and walks, affording a fine promenade, and, during the hours of walking, an excellent band is in attendance The Imperial Fount and marble baths in Clemens-street contain a complete arrangement of twelve hot, cold, sulphureous, vapour, fumigating, and shower baths, with jets d eau

for topical application, and a pump of sulphureous, saline, and chalybeate water, with every requisite accommodation and attendance Wise's baths, at the corner of Bath-street, Robbins bath, near the bridge, Smith s original baths, in Bath-street, and various similar establishments, are all arranged with due care, and attended with every regard to the accommodation of the persons frequenting them In proportion to the number and rank of the visitors are the hotels and lodging-houses provided for their accommodation. Among the numerous establishments of the kind, the most conspicuous are, the Regent's and Copps hotels the former is an extensive and elegant range of building in the new town, splendidly fitted up as a family hotel and public boarding-house, it has stabling for upwards of one hundred horses, with proportionate standings for carriage Nearly adjoining the hotel is a private lodging house belonging to the proprietor, a beautiful structure in the later English style of architecture, containing several spacious rooms, and a suite of offices, in every respect adapted for the residence of a family of distinction, with gardens and pleasure grounds tastefully laid out Copps, or the Royal hotel, in the High-street, formerly consisting of several houses, has been partly rebuilt, and now forms a splendid establishment, having a very handsome façade in the Grecian style of architecture, with an elegant portico of the Corinthian order the accommodations, in every respect, are adapted to the reception of families of the highest rank, and the domestic regulations are calculated to promote the comfort of its numerous guests it has accommodation for ninety horses, and carriages in proportion The Bedford hotel, in Union Parade, the Blenheim hotel, in Clemens-street, and numerous others on a smaller scale, are all under excellent regulation, and there are numerous private boarding and lodging-houses of every grade, suited to the taste, condition, and requirements of the various classes of visitors

The town is well paved, and lighted with gas under the direction of commissioners appointed under an act of parliament obtained for that purpose, and amply supplied with water, the streets are spacious, and intersect each other at right angles, the houses are handsomely built, and fronted with Roman cement, and many of them display elegant specimens of Grecian and other kinds of architecture The public library and reading-rooms, in Bath-street, constitute a handsome structure, with a colonnade of six Ionic pillars, supporting an entablature and pediment, and resting upon a piazza, which forms the entrance, the reading-room is forty feet long, and thirty six feet wide, with a circular end, separated from the principal area by two Ionic pillars, and two pilasters of green porphyry, and opening by folding doors into a pleasant lawn, in which are a fountain, and a small orchestra, contiguous to the principal reading-room is one smaller, which is generally used in the winter season Above the reading-rooms and library is a spacious and elegant assembly-room, eighty feet long, and forty feet wide, chastely ornamented, and lighted by three magnificent chandeliers suspended from the ceiling, at one end of the room is a noble mirror of plate glass, twelve feet high, and eight feet wide, the card and refreshment rooms are equally splendid, and the whole suite is admirably adapted for either for public or private meetings The upper assembly-rooms, in the Union Parade, comprise a ball-room ninety-six feet in length, forty-five feet in width, and twenty-six feet high, lighted by a range of seven windows on one side the walls are ornamented by a row of pilasters of the Ionic order, and the ceiling is divided into compartments, from which are suspended three elegant chandeliers, attached to the assembly-room are card and refreshment rooms, of uniform character subscription assemblies take place here every fortnight during the winter, and every week during the summer the Philharmonic concerts are held here four nights during the summer season The buildings, which were erected in 1812, comprise also a news-room and a billiard-room Bisset s museum and picture gallery is a place of general resort it contains a collection of British and foreign birds, beasts, fishes, and insects, the arms, dresses, and musical and war-like instruments, of barbarous nations, and an extensive collection of pictures The theatre, a small building neatly fitted up, is open three times in the week during the season, and the races which take place at Warwick, in the spring, from the patronage of the resident gentry, may be almost considered as belonging to this place, the ladies of Leamington contribute fifty guineas to the sweepstakes at these races, and the gentlemen, the Leamington cup, of fifty guineas value Ranelagh gardens, occupying ten acres, and neatly laid out in walks and shrubberies, form a pleasing promenade, a botanical collection is now in progress, and hot-houses and green-houses have been erected on an extensive scale The market is on Wednesday, and is abundantly supplied with provisions of every kind The Warwick and Knapton canal, passing through the town, supplies the inhabitants, at a moderate price, with coal from the pits in the neighbourhood of Birmingham

The living is a discharged vicarage, in the archdeaconry of Coventry and diocese of Lichfield and Coventry rated in the king s books at £6 10, and in the patronage of the Rev Henry Wise The church, dedicated to All Saints, is an ancient structure in the decorated style of English architecture, with a tower surmounted by a spire, it has been considerably enlarged, and has undergone many recent alterations An episcopal chapel in the upper town was erected after the design, and at the expense, of the Rev R Downes, the pre sent vicar, and has been licensed, but not consecrated the building is professedly after the Norman model, and in some respects the details of that style have been partially imitated the interior is darkened by the adoption of the massive round column, and the deep-toned painting of the glass in the windows, and the exterior forms a solitary and a striking deviation from the good taste which prevails generally in the architectural features of the town. There are places of worship for Independents and Wesleyan Methodists, and a Roman Catholic chapel, a small, but handsome edifice, having, in a niche over the entrance, a whole-length figure of St. Peter, with a key in his right hand, finely sculptured The National school is a neat and commodious building, having, on the ground-floor, a school-room for boys, and above it one of equal dimensions for girls, together with apartments for the master and the mistress Baths have been erected for the gratui-tous use of the poor, and there are various bequests for charitable purposes

LEAP, a tything in the parish of Exbury, in that part of the hundred of Bishop s Waltham which is in the New Forest (East) division of the county of Southampton, 11¼ miles (E by N) from Lymington The population is returned with the parish The village, being nearly opposite to Cowes, is the common place of embarkation for the Isle of Wight from this part of Hampshire

LEARCHILD, a township in the parish of Edling-ham, northern division of Coquetdale ward, county of Northumberland, 6½ miles (W S W) from Aln-wick, containing 30 inhabitants

LEASINGHAM (NORTH), or ROXHOLME, a parish in the wapentake of Flaxwell, parts of Kesteven, county of Lincoln, 2¾ miles (N by W) from Sleaford, containing 87 inhabitants The living is a rectory, united, in 1726, to the rectory of South Leasingham, in the archdeaconry and diocese of Lincoln, rated in the king s books at £10 15 5 The church, which was dedicated to St John the Baptist, has been demolished.

LEASINGHAM (SOUTH), a parish in the wapentake of Flaxwell, parts of Kesteven, county of Lincoln, 2 miles (N N W) from Sleaford, containing 259 inhabitants The living is a rectory, to which that of North Leasingham was united in 1726, in the archdeaconry and diocese of Lincoln, rated in the king s books at £13 2 8½ Sir J H Thorold, Bart was patron in 1786 The church is dedicated to St Andrew

LEATHERHEAD, a parish (formerly a market town) in the second division of the hundred of Copthorne, county of Surrey, 12 miles (E N E) from Guildford, and 18 (S W by S) from London, containing 1478 inhabitants This place, anciently called Leddrede, is pleasantly situated on the bank of the river Mole, over which there is a bridge of fourteen arches, built of brick The vale through which this stream flows, in its course to Reigate, is bounded on each side by a range of steep eminences, on the declivities of which are numerous elegant seats, and fine parks and plantations, and the scenery in the neighbourhood is highly picturesque and beautiful The trade of the town is inconsiderable, and the market is disused, but a fair is held on the 10th of October, in a field to the north of the town, chiefly for the sale of horses and pigs The living is a discharged vicarage, in the archdeaconry of Surrey, and diocese of Winchester, rated in the king s books at £14 6 0½, endowed with £200 private benefaction, and £200 royal bounty, and in the patronage of the Dean and Chapter of Rochester The church, dedicated to St Mary and St Nicholas, is a cruciform structure, said to have been founded by Edward I the nave and aisles are of the early English style, the chancel of the decorated, and the tower and north transept of the later English, the east window is ornamented with stained glass within is a fine screen, and a painting of the "Last Supper" There is a place of worship for Independents A free school for ten boys is endowed with £15 per annum, principally from a bequest of John Lucas, who, in 1796, left £400 South Sea annuities, for the support of this charity Several other benefactions have been made for distribution among the poor

LEATHLEY, a parish in the upper division of the wapentake of Claro, West riding of the county of

YORK, comprising the townships of Castley and Leathley, and containing 422 inhabitants, of which number, 312 are in the township of Leathley, 2½ miles (N E by E) from Otley The living is a rectory, in the archdeaconry and diocese of York, rated in the king s books at £7 2 8½, and in the patronage of the Crown A free school was founded and endowed with a rent-charge of £12, in 1769, by Anne Hitch, all children who apply are admitted

LEAVELAND, a parish in the hundred of FAVERS-HAM, lathe of SCRAY, county of KENT, 4 miles (S by W) from Faversham, containing 69 inhabitants The living is a discharged rectory, with that of Badlesmere, in the archdeaconry and diocese of Canterbury, rated in the king s books at £4, and in the patronage of Lord Sondes The church is dedicated to St Lawrence

LEAVENING, a township in the parish of ACKLAM, partly in the wapentake of BUCKROSE, and partly within the liberty of ST PETER of YORK, East riding of the county of YORK, 6¼ miles (S) from New Malton, containing 294 inhabitants There is a place of worship for Wesleyan Methodists

LEAVINGTON (CASTLE), a township in the parish of KIRK-LEAVINGTON, western division of the liberty of LANGBAURGH, North riding of the county of YORK, 2¾ miles (S E by E) from Yarm, containing 44 inhabitants Here was anciently a castle but the eminence on which it stood, called Castle hill, is the only remaining vestige of its existence

LEAVINGTON (KIRK), a parish in the western division of the liberty of LANGBAURGH, North riding of the county of YORK, comprising the townships of Castle-Leavington, Kirk-Leavington, Pickton, and Low Worsall, and containing 637 inhabitants, of which number, 282 are in the township of Kirk-Leavington, 2¼ miles (S S E) from Yarm The living is a perpetual curacy, in the archdeaconry of Cleveland, and diocese of York, endowed with £200 royal bounty, and £1400 parliamentary grant, and in the patronage of the Archbishop of York The church, dedicated to St Martin, is a small ancient structure

LEBTHORPE, a hamlet in the parish of NORTH WITHAM, wapentake of BEITISLOE, parts of KESTEVEN, county of LINCOLN, 3 miles (S E by S) from Colsterworth, containing 35 inhabitants

LECHLADE, or LEACHLADE, a market town and parish in the hundred of BRICHTWELLS BARROW, county of GLOUCESTER, 28 miles (S E) from Gloucester, and 75 (W by N) from London, containing, with Limhill, 1154 inhabitants The name of this place is derived from the little river Leche, and the Saxon word ladean, to empty, this stream rises near North-Leach, and falls into the Thames below St John s bridge, in this parish In Domesday-book the manor is reckoned among the possessions of Henry de Ferrars, who had an eel-fishery here The town is situated on the margin of the Thames, near its confluence with the Leche, on the road from Cirencester to London it is neatly built, and consists principally of one long and wide street, not regularly paved nor lighted, but the inhabitants are sufficiently supplied with water from wells Its commerce depends chiefly on the transit of commodities, particularly Wiltshire and Gloucester cheese, brought hither in wagons for conveyance to the metropolis by the Thames, that river becoming navigable at this place,

and here the canal terminates which unites this river and the Severn The market, for which a grant was obtained by Richard, Earl of Cornwall, brother of Henry III is held on Tuesday, but almost disused the fairs are, August 5th and 10th for cattle and toys, and September 9th for cattle and cheese, which last is much frequented A constable and a tythingman are appointed at a triennial court leet held by the lord of the manor

The living is a vicarage, in the archdeaconry and diocese of Gloucester, rated in the king s books at £12 13 4 and in the patronage of the Rev J Leigh Bennett The church, which is dedicated to St Lawrence, is a handsome structure in the later style of English architecture, built about the middle of the fifteenth century, at the joint expense of the vicar, the inmates of Lechlade priory, and the inhabitants of the parish , the spire is remarkable for its symmetrical beauty, and the pulpit is of sculptured stone There is a place of worship for Baptists In 1787, Thomas Oatridge bequeathed £100 stock in the three per cent consols , to the Sunday school in this parish, and £3 per annum is accordingly paid to it by the minister In a meadow near St John s bridge formerly stood a priory of Black canons, dedicated to St John the Baptist, which was founded by Richard, Earl of Cornwall, in the reign of Henry III , the revenue of which, on its suppression in 1743, was applied to the foundation of a chantry in the parish church There was also an hospital on or near the bridge, founded by Peter Fitz-Herbert, about the time of Henry III Towards the end of the last century, a subterraneous structure was discovered in a meadow in the vicinity, with brick pillars and Mosaic pavement, supposed to have been a Roman bath, from which circumstance it has been conjectured that this was a Roman town, to which a vicinal road extended from Cirencester Thomas Coxeter, an eminent antiquary, was born here in 1689

LECK, a chapelry in the parish of TUNSTALL, hundred of LONSDAIE, south of the sands, county palatine of LANCASTER, 2½ miles (S E by E) from Kirkby-Lonsdale, containing 284 inhabitants The living is a perpetual curacy, in the archdeaconry of Richmond, and diocese of Chester, endowed with £200 private benefaction, £600 royal bounty, and £300 parliamentary grant, and in the patronage of the Rector of Tunstall

LECKBY, a joint township with Cundall, in the parish of CUNDALL, wapentake of HALLIKELD, North riding of the county of YORK, 6 miles (N by E) from Boroughbridge The population is returned with Cundall

LECKFORD, a parish in the hundred of KING S SOMBOURN, Andover division of the county of SOUTHAMPTON, 1¾ mile (N N E) from Stockbridge, containing 200 inhabitants The living is a discharged vicarage, in the archdeaconry and diocese of Winchester, rated in the king s books at £8 16 10½, and in the patronage of the Prebendary of Leckford in the Cathedral Church of Winchester the prebend, or sinecure rectory, rated in the king s books at £9, is in the patronage of the President and Fellows of St John s College, Oxford The church is dedicated to St Nicholas The Andover canal passes close to the village

LECKHAMPSTEAD, a chapelry in the parish of CHIEVELEY, hundred of FAIRCROSS, county of BERKS,

5¼ miles (S W) from East Ilsley, containing 358 inhabitants

LECKHAMPSTEAD, a parish in the hundred and county of BUCKINGHAM, 3½ miles (N E by N) from Buckingham, containing 519 inhabitants The living is a rectory, in the archdeaconry of Buckingham, and diocese of Lincoln, rated in the king s books at £15 13 4, and in the patronage of John Beauclerk, Esq The church, dedicated to St Mary, contains an octagonal font, ornamented with representations of the Crucifixion, St Catherine, &c, rudely executed in basso relievo There is an endowment of £15 per annum for a free school This parish is divided into Church-end, North-end, and Lymes'-end within its limits there is a chalybeate spring

LECKHAMPTON, a parish in the hundred of CHELTENHAM, county of GLOUCESTER, 2 miles (S by W) from Cheltenham, containing 318 inhabitants The living is a rectory, in the archdeaconry and diocese of Gloucester, rated in the king s books at £18 13 4, and in the patronage of C N Trye, Esq The church is dedicated to St Peter A branch of the Gloucester and Cheltenham railway passes through this parish to the Crippets on the south

LECKONFIELD, a parish in the Hunsley-Beacon division of the wapentake of HARTHILL, East riding of the county of YORK, 3 miles (N N W) from Beverley, containing 302 inhabitants The living is a discharged vicarage, in the archdeaconry of the East riding, and diocese of York, rated in the king's books at £8, endowed with £200 private benefaction, and £600 royal bounty, and in the patronage of the Earl of Egremont Here was anciently a castle belonging to the Earls of Northumberland

LEDBURN, a hamlet in the parish of MENTMORE, hundred of COTTESLOE, county of BUCKINGHAM, 3 miles (S W by S) from Leighton-Buzzard, containing 165 inhabitants

LEDBURY, a parish in the hundred of RADLOW, county of HEREFORD, comprising the market town of Ledbury, and the township of Parkhold, and containing 3476 inhabitants, of which number, 3421 are in the town of Ledbury, 15 miles (E by S) from Hereford, and 120 (W N W) from London. This place derives its name from the Leden, which intersects the parish from north to south. The town, which stands at the eastern angle of the county, and at the southern extremity of the Malvern hills, is situated on a declivity, and consists of three principal streets, which run north and south, and are intersected by smaller ones at right angles, they are lighted, and partially paved, and the inhabitants are well supplied with water in the more ancient parts of the town the houses are composed of timber and brick, with projecting stories, the modern houses are of red brick, presenting a respectable appearance The manufacture of silk and broad cloth was carried on here to a considerable extent during the reigns of Elizabeth and James I, but at present the principal business consists in the manufacture of ropes, lines, and sacking, and there are also malt-houses and tan-yards Hops are cultivated, and cider and perry made, in the neighbourhood, and, in productive seasons, a great quantity of the former liquor is sent to all parts of the kingdom There are some quarries of excellent limestone, and others of grey marble The Hereford and Gloucester

canal, projected some years since, extends only from Gloucester to this town at present, having been left unfinished. The market is on Tuesday, for poultry, butter, and pedlary, and fairs are held on the Monday after Fe bruary 1st, Monday before Easter, May 12th, June 22nd, October 2nd, and the Monday before December 21st, for cattle, pigs, &c The market-house is an ancient edifice of timber and brick, supported on sixteen strong oak pillars The parish is divided into five parts, the borough, Wall Hills, Ledon and Haffield, Wellington, and Mitchell and Netherton, the last four of these form the Foreign of the manor for which courts leet and baron are held annually, when the constables for the town are chosen the borough is called the Denizen, and has likewise a court leet and baron annually Petty sessions for the hundred are held here every Wednesday. Ledbury sent members to two parliaments in the reign of Edward I, but surrendered the elective franchise subsequently, on the plea of poverty

The living is a vicarage, in the archdeaconry and diocese of Hereford, rated in the king s books at £14 12 6 the rectory is divided into the two portions of Overhall and Netherhall the Bishop of Hereford appoints the portionists, who present to the vicarage alternately The church, dedicated to St Michael, is a spacious and handsome structure, exhibiting some fine specimens of Norman architecture, particularly the door in the centre of the west front, and the chancel, on the north side of which is a chapel, dedicated to St Catherine, of decorated character the north porch is in the early style of English architecture, as is also the tower, which is detached from the church, and is surmounted by a finely-proportioned spire, about sixty feet in height, which in 1811, was struck by lightning, but sustained little injury Over the altar is a painting of the Lord s Supper, copied from an original by Rubens, and at the east end of the north aisle, a new window, recently made, is ornamented with the figures of Faith, Hope, and Charity, in stained glass, the expense of which was £500 the church has recently undergone internal repairs and decorations, the cost of which was defrayed by voluntary contributions there are several interesting monuments The Baptists, Independents, and Wesleyan Methodists have each a place of worship There are two endowed schools, with residences for the master and the mistress one for boys, who are taught to read and write, and another for girls, who are taught to read and work, at another school, said to have been founded at the dissolution of a chantry attached to the church, four boys are taught writing and arithmetic gratuitously, and there are other boys who pay £1 16 per annum the master receives a stipend annually from the Exchequer, and occupies the building rent free, formerly the masters of this school were clergymen, but within the last thirty years they have been laymen, and are chosen at a vestry meeting The hospital of St Catherine was founded, in the thirteenth century, by Hugh Foliot, Bishop of Hereford, and endowed for six widowers and four widows the revenue was valued at the dissolution at £32 7 11, but it was refounded by Elizabeth, in 1580, for a master, seven poor widowers, and three widows the Dean and Chapter of Hereford are the trustees The increase of funds enabled the trustees to erect a new hospital, in 1822, from a design by Mr Smirke, intended to comprise twenty-four dwellings, for as many brethren, twelve only of which have been hitherto completed, at an expense of £5888 each inmate receives six shillings per week, and a quarterly payment of £1 2, with other advantages The senior canon of Hereford cathedral, as master, has a good dwelling-house and a large garden near the hospital, where he is required to reside two months in the year, to his annual stipend is added a farm of seventy acres, and forty acres of coppice wood, and he has the appointment of the brethren and the sisters Morning service is performed in a chapel adjoining the hospital, four days in the week, by the chaplain, who, in addition to his salary, has the incumbency of one of the livings in the patronage of the Dean and Chapter There are several almshouses for poor persons, and a dispensary was established in 1824 At Well Hills, about a mile from the town, is a camp, supposed to have been originally British, though subsequently occupied as a Roman station, containing an area of about thirty acres, a smaller camp at Haffield was probably used as a temporary position Within this parish is also a part of the famous Beacon camp, considered by some antiquaries as one of the fortresses constructed by Caractacus, when this part of Britain was invaded by the Romans under Ostorius Scapula At Ledbury died Jacob Tonson, an eminent bookseller, and the subject of a satirical triplet by Dryden, whose epitaph, published in the Gentleman's Magazine for February 1736, was closely copied by Dr Benjamin Franklin, for his own tombstone, and has been often recorded in print.

LEDSHAM, a township in the parish of NESTON, higher division of the hundred of WIRRALL, county palatine of CHESTER, 6¼ miles (N W by N) from Chester, containing 74 inhabitants

LEDSHAM, a parish in the upper division of the wapentake of BARKSTONE-ASH, West riding of the county of YORK, comprising the townships of Fairburn, Ledsham, and Ledstone, and containing 881 inhabitants, of which number, 212 are in the township of Ledsham, 4½ miles (N W by N) from Ferry-Bridge The living is a discharged vicarage, in the archdeaconry and diocese of York, rated in the king s books at £7 4 2, endowed with £200 private benefaction, and £200 royal bounty Mrs Wheler was patroness in 1826 The church, dedicated to All Saints, contains a splendid monument to the memory of Lady Elizabeth Hastings, her figure is placed in a reclining posture, and those of Lady Frances and Lady Ann, her sisters, are placed on pedestals by its side the inscription is in Latin. Lady Elizabeth Hastings, in 1738, founded and endowed a school for twenty orphan girls, and another for twenty boys, all of whom are supplied with books

LEDSTONE, a township in the parish of LEDSHAM, upper division of the wapentake of BARKSTONE-ASH, West riding of the county of YORK, 5 miles (N W) from Ferry-Bridge, containing 243 inhabitants

LEDWELL, a hamlet in the parish of SANDFORD, hundred of WOOTTON, county of OXFORD, 4½ miles (N E) from Neat Enstone The population is returned with the parish Here was formerly a chapel, dedicated to St Mary Magdalene A fine sand, used in the manufacture of glass, is found in the vicinity

LEE, a parish in the hundred of AYLESBURY, county of BUCKINGHAM, 2½ miles (N) from Great Missenden, containing 198 inhabitants The living is a perpetual

curacy, in the archdeaconry of Buckingham, and diocese of Lincoln, endowed with £8 per annum and £200 private benefaction, £800 royal bounty, and in the patronage of Henry Deering, Esq The church, dedicated to St John the Baptist, was formerly a chapel of ease to the rectory of Weston-Turville

LEE, a parish in the hundred of BLACKHEATH, lathe of SUTTON at HONE, county of KENT, 7 miles (S E by E) from London, containing 737 inhabitants The living is a rectory, in the archdeaconry and diocese of Rochester, rated in the king s books at £3 11 8, and in the patronage of the Crown The church, dedicated to St Margaret, which stands on an eminence near Blackheath, is built of flint and stone, and has a neat cemetery containing several handsome monuments, the most conspicuous of which are those of the great astronomer, Edmund Halley, the celebrated comedian, William Parsons, the amiable Lady Dacre, and Sir Samuel Fludyer, Bart., who, as lord mayor of London in 1761, gave a sumptuous banquet to George III and his royal consort Christopher Boone, in 1683, founded and endowed an almshouse for six poor persons, with a chapel attached, and a school for twelve poor children, the endowment, which is vested in the company of Merchant Taylors in London, consists of certain lands and houses producing an income of about £71 per annum This parish has the right of sending one boy to the school at Blackheath founded by Mr Colfe

LEE (EAST, or CHAPEL), a liberty in the parish of EAST TILBURY, hundred of BARSTABLE, county of ESSEX, containing 10 inhabitants

LEE (ST JOHN), a parish in the southern division of TINDALE ward, county of NORTHUMBERLAND, 1½ mile (N N E) from Hexham, comprising the chapelries of Bingfield and Wall, and the townships of West Acomb, Anick, Anick Grange, Cocklaw, Fallowfield, Hallington, Portgate, and Sandhoe, and containing 1952 inhabitants The living is a perpetual curacy, in the peculiar jurisdiction of the Archbishop of York for the Peculiar Court of Hexhamshire, endowed with £200 private benefaction, £400 royal bounty, and £600 parliamentary grant, and in the patronage of T R Beaumont, Esq The church, dedicated to St John of Beverley, and situated on a fine eminence on the northern side of the river Tyne, was anciently noted for an annual procession made to it by the monks of Hexham There are mines of coal and lead in the parish

LEE-BOTWOOD, a parish in the hundred of CONDOVER, county of SALOP, 4 miles (N N E) from Church-Stretton, containing 204 inhabitants The living is a perpetual curacy, united to that of Longnor, in the archdeaconry of Salop, and diocese of Lichfield and Coventry, endowed with £200 private benefaction, and £600 royal bounty, and in the patronage of Archdeacon Corbett The church, dedicated to St. Mary, once belonged to the abbey of Haughmond. Coal and lime stone are obtained in the parish, through which runs a small brook called the Rae

LEE-BROCKHURST, a parish in the Whitchurch division of the hundred of BRADFORD (North), county of SALOP, 2¼ miles (S E by E) from Wem, containing 162 inhabitants The living is a perpetual curacy, in the archdeaconry of Salop, and diocese of Lichfield and Coventry, endowed with £800 royal bounty, and £200 parliamentary grant, and in the patronage of—Clayton, Esq   The church is dedicated to St Peter

LEE-WARD, a township in the parish of ROTH-BURY, western division of COQUETDALE ward, county of NORTHUMBERLAND, 3½ miles (S S E) from Rothbury, containing 93 inhabitants

LEEMAILING, a township in the parish of BEL-LINGHAM, north-western division of TINDALE ward, county of NORTHUMBERLAND, 1 mile (W N W) from Bellingham, containing 285 inhabitants   There is a neat domestic chapel at Hesleyside, the seat of William John Charlton Esq   The township is bounded on the north by the North Tyne river

LEEDS, a parish in the hundred of EYHORNE, lathe of AYLESFORD, county of KENT, 5 miles (E by S) from Maidstone containing 515 inhabitants   The living is a perpetual curacy, to which that of Broomfield is united, in the archdeaconry and diocese of Canterbury, endowed with £200 private benefaction, and £200 royal bounty, and in the patronage of the Archbishop of Canterbury The church, dedicated to St Nicholas, has at the west end a remarkably low square tower   Leeds is said to have derived its name from Ledian, counsellor to Ethelbert II, who built here a fortress in 978   Subsequently, in 1119, a priory of Black canons, in honour of St Mary and St Nicholas, was founded by Robert de Crepito Corde, alias Creveceur, or Croucheart, Knt, the revenue of which, at the dissolution, was £362 7 7   The abbey church was equal in magnitude and beauty to a cathedral, and the monastic buildings, considerable remains of which still exist, were of correspondent size and grandeur   Leeds castle, the residence of the family of Fairfax, is one of the most stately in the kingdom   it is seated in a beautiful park   is surrounded by a moat and approached by a stone bridge of two arches   the buildings, which are entirely of stone, are ranged round a spacious quadrangle, and though they exhibit the architecture of different periods, the structure as a whole produces a most striking and noble effect   It has two ancient gateways, a grand hall, and a magnificent suite of state apartments   there are also the remains of the inner vallum, of the keep, and of various other detached parts, said to have been erected by the Creveceurs, its ancient owners, by William of Wykeham, and by Henry VIII   George III and his royal consort were entertained here with great splendour in their excursion to Coxheath Camp, in 1779   Courts leet and baron are held annually, at which three officers, termed Borsholders, are appointed

Seal and Arms.

LEEDS, a parish and liberty, in the West riding of the county of YORK, comprising the market town of Leeds, which has a separate jurisdiction, though locally in the wapentake of Skyrack, the chapelries of Armley, Beeston, Bramley, Chapel-Allerton, Farnley, Headingley with Burley, Holbeck, Hunslet or Hunfleet, and Wortley, and the township of Potter-Newton, and containing 83,796 inhabitants, of which number, 48,603 are in the town of Leeds, 25 miles (S W by W) from York, and 191 (N N W) from

London   From what source this place, anciently called *Loidis*, derives its name, has not been ascertained It was made a royal vill after the destruction of the ancient *Cambodunum* by Cadwallo, a British prince, and Penda, King of Mercia, over the last of whom, on his subsequent invasion of Northumberland, in 655, Osweo, King of Bernicia, obtained a signal victory in the immediate vicinity of the town   During the reign of William the Conqueror, Ilbert de Lacy is supposed to have erected a castle here, which was besieged by King Stephen, on his route towards Scotland, and in which Richard II, after his deposition, was for some time confined, previously to his removal to Pontefract   but there are no vestiges of it, nor can the site, which is stated to have been on Mill hill, be distinguished by any traces of its previous existence   During the civil war in the reign of Charles I, many skirmishes between the contending parties took place in the neighbourhood, and that monarch resided for some time in the town, in a mansion supposed to have been the first in that part of the kingdom that was built of brick, and, from the colour of that material, called the Red Hall

The town, which is more celebrated as the principal seat of the woollen manufacture, than either for its antiquity or for its historical importance, is pleasantly situated on the summit and acclivities of an eminence rising gradually from the northern bank of the river Aire, over which are two substantial bridges of freestone, one consisting of five arches, and the other, about a mile to the west   erected in 1817, from a design by Rennie, at an expense of £7000, and called Wellington bridge, consisting of one beautiful arch, one hundred feet in span   to the east of the latter a suspension bridge is now being constructed, the expense of which is estimated at £4500   The streets in the more ancient parts of the town are inconveniently narrow, but in other parts spacious and commodious   many improvements have been effected under the provisions of acts of parliament obtained in 1809 and 1815, under which also the town is well paved, lighted with oil and coal gas by companies who have extensive works in York street and Park-street, and supplied with excellent water forced from the Aire by an engine into three capacious reservoirs, from which, after undergoing a process of purification, it is distributed to the houses of the inhabitants   The houses are in general neatly built of brick, and roofed with white slate, and in various parts of the town are some elegant mansions and handsome ranges of modern buildings, among which latter is Park-place, in front of which the ground is tastefully laid out in shrubberies and walks   the environs afford much beautiful scenery, and are embellished with numerous seats and elegant villas   There is an establishment of hackney coaches in the town   The Literary and Philosophical Society, consisting of sixty proprietary, and one hundred ordinary, members, was established in 1820, meetings are held on the first and third Fridays in every month, from November till May, for the discussion of literary and philosophical subjects   The hall appropriated to this purpose is a handsome stone building, erected, by Mr Chantrell, in the Grecian style of architecture, and comprises a lecture-room, library, and museum   A museum of natural curiosities was also established by Mr Calvert, in 1827 The Northern Society, for the encouragement of the fine arts, and under the patronage of the King, has a handsome gallery adjoining the music-hall , and a horticultural society, established in 1820, holds its meetings in the town   There are several public subscription libraries, of which the principal are, the old library, in Commercial-street, the new library, in Albion-street, consisting of one hundred proprietary members, whose shares are £7 7 each, and an annual subscription of £1 5 , the parochial library, containing works on Theology, for the use of the resident clergy of the establishment , the Methodists and the Eclectic libraries   The commercial buildings, a handsome edifice of stone, with a noble circular portico, comprising a news-room, hotel, and commercial offices, were erected in 1826, and are equally an accommodation and an ornament to the town   The mechanics institution, to which a useful library is attached, was established in 1825   The theatre, a neat building erected, in 1771, by Mr Tate Wilkinson, is opened, during the months of May and June, by the York company   subscription concerts take place every fortnight during the season, at the music-hall in Albion-street , and assemblies are held every alternate week during the winter, in a handsome suite of rooms over the White Cloth hall   The public baths, in Wellington-road, a handsome range of buildings erected, in 1820, by the same architect, and in the same style, as the philosophical hall, are commodiously arranged, and comprise hot, cold, shower, and vapour baths, with others artificially prepared, and possessing the properties and temperature of the Matlock and Buxton waters   The Masonic hall is a neat edifice in Stein s buildings, Briggate , and a bazaar, on the principle of those in the metropolis, was established in 1826, for which a neat building has been erected, which is well calculated for the exhibition and sale of fancy articles   The cavalry barracks, near the north road, form a very extensive and complete establishment, occupying eleven acres of ground , the buildings, which are handsome, and contain every requisite accommodation, were erected at an expense of £28,000

To the extent and variety of the manufactures carried on in this town and its neighbourhood, particularly the manufacture of woollen cloth, which has within the last few years been brought to a very high state of perfection, may, in a great degree, be attributed the prosperity of the West riding of the county   Formerly only the coarser kinds of cloth were made here, but, since the introduction of machinery, and more especially under the improvements made in the manufacture by Mr Hirst, a native of this town, the Yorkshire cloths, which were always regarded as inferior, have been made to equal, if not to surpass, those of the western counties of England, in fineness of texture, and brilliance and permanence of colour , and superfine black and blue cloths, made from wool carefully selected, have been sold for £5 per yard   Many very extensive factories have been established, in some of which the whole process, from the first breaking of the wool to the completion of the cloth for the consumer, is performed by machinery worked by steam   The principal branches of manufacture at present are, superfine broad and coarse narrow cloth, ladies pelisse cloth and shawls, stuffs of various kinds, Scotch camblets, blankets, and carpets   Several large factories have been established in the town and neighbourhood, for the spinning of flax, and a great

quantity of worsted goods, the manufacture of which has been progressively increasing, is sent hence to every part of the kingdom   The cotton manufacture has extended in some degree from Lancashire to this town, and at present affords employment to a small proportion of the labouring class   In the immediate vicinity are large manufactories for crown and flint glass and glass bottles , an extensive pottery, the reputation of which procures for its wares a large demand in every part of the united kingdom , several large iron foundries, and an extensive manufactory for steam-engines, inferior to few in the country   In the parish is dug clay for making fire-proof bricks, also another kind for tobacco-pipes   The neighbourhood abounds with mines of coal   on the banks of the Aire are numerous mills for grinding corn, rape-seed, dye-wood, and for fulling cloth, and several turning, carding, and spinning establishments   In addition to the staple trade and manufactures, Leeds carries on an extensive trade in tobacco, for the preparation of which from the leaf, several mills have been erected   The river Aire, which passes through the southern part of the town, affords a navigable communication with the Humber , and the Leeds and Liverpool canal, constructed in 1776, which joins the Aire, opens a direct line of navigation extending to Hull, Liverpool, and the principal towns in the kingdom   The cloth-halls are spacious buildings for the sale of cloth in an unfinished state   they occupy quad rangular areas divided into rows, on each side of which are stands for the manufacturers , the hall for dyed cloths contains one thousand eight hundred of these stands, and that for white cloths about the same number   the former was erected in 1758, and the latter in 1775   The market is announced by the ringing of a bell, and in the course of an hour, for which it continues open, purchases to the amount of many thousand pounds are effected, with the utmost regularity and in perfect silence, by the merchants who attend them, and under whose directions, or by persons accustomed to that business, the cloths are dressed and finished for the use of the consumer   The number of pieces of cloth manufactured in the West riding, from the year 1772 to 1781 inclusive, was two millions nine thousand nine hundred and seventy-two and a half, and from 1812 to 1821, the number was four millions five hundred and twenty one thousand seven hundred and forty-two   The market-days are Tuesday and Saturday, the former for corn and general merchandise, and the latter for woollen goods and provisions   The corn market is held in the corn exchange, in Briggate-street, a handsome stone building, having in the front a statue of Queen Anne sculptured in white marble   the market for cattle and hav is in Vicar-lane   the market for butchers meat is held in various parts of the town, of which the most central are Fleet-street, Cheapside, the South market, and Butchers -row , the wholesale market for carcasses is held in Leadenhall, a spacious area considerably below the ground, by which means it is pre served from the heat of summer and the frosts of winter, to this market is attached a spacious slaughter-house, also underground   the fish market is held at the Old Cross, in Fish-street , and the fruit, vegetable, poultry, and pig markets, are held in various parts of the town, and, like all the others, are abundantly supplied   The fairs are on July 10th and 11th for horses, and November 8th and 9th for cattle, and a fair for the sale of leather is held quarterly in the South market-place

The government of the town, by charter of incorporation granted in the reign of Charles I, and extended and renewed by Charles II, is vested in a mayor, recorder, twelve aldermen, and twenty-four common council men, assisted by a town clerk and subordinate officers. The mayor is appointed from among the aldermen, who in general succeed to that office in rotation. The common council-men fill up vacancies in their own body, and appoint a chief constable, deputy constable, and constables for the ten districts into which the town is divided. The mayor and aldermen are justices of the peace within the borough, and among the privileges enjoyed by the freemen is exemption from serving on juries out of the parish any inhabitant is eligible to offices under the corporation, and any person becoming an inhabitant is free to exercise his trade without restriction. The corporation hold quarterly courts of session for the borough, in January, April, July, and October, at which the mayor and recorder preside, for all offences not capital. the mayor sits daily for the examination of delinquents, and some of the aldermen attend every Tuesday and Friday at the court-house for the determination of police affairs. The town is within the jurisdiction of a court of record for the recovery of debts to any amount, and within that of a court baron for the recovery of debts not exceeding £5, for the Honour of Pontefract, the latter of these courts is occasionally held at Leeds. The Michaelmas quarter sessions for the West riding are held here, by adjournment from Knaresborough, and also the petty sessions for the wapentake of Skyrack. A relic of feudal servitude subsists in the custom which obliges all the inhabitants of Leeds, except those whose houses stand within the manor of Whitkirk (formerly belonging to the Knights Templars), to have their corn ground at the King's mills, which are held under a lease from the crown. The court-house, erected in 1813, is an elegant edifice of stone, with a handsome portico of the Corinthian order in the centre, on each side of which the façade is decorated with panels enriched with emblematical sculpture. the principal entrance, from Park-row, leads into a spacious vestibule, on one side of which is the Rotation office, and on the other the rooms appropriated to the magistrates of the West riding, communicating with the sessions-hall, which is commodiously arranged, above the vestibule are the grand jury room, and other requisite apartments. Behind the court-house is the prison for the town, containing thirteen cells, intended only for the confinement of prisoners prior to their trial, when, if found guilty, they are sent either to the house of correction at Wakefield, or to York castle. Leeds never enjoyed the privilege of parliamentary representation, except during the Protectorate of Cromwell, when one member was returned for this borough to the parliament of 1654. On the disfranchisement of Grampound, in 1821, a bill passed the House of Commons, for the transfer of the elective franchise to Leeds, but it was re-modelled in its progress through the upper house, and the town yet remains unrepresented

The living is a vicarage, in the archdeaconry and diocese of York, rated in the king's books at £38 0 2¼,

and in the patronage of twenty-five trustees. The parish church, dedicated to St Peter, is an ancient and venerable cruciform structure, with a square embattled tower rising from the centre, and decorated with pinnacles, and, though plain, retains considerable portions of its ancient Norman character, the roof is painted in fresco, and the interior contains several interesting monuments, marriages are solemnized at this church exclusively. Thoresby, author of the "*Ducatus Leodiensis*," who was a native of Leeds, is interred in it, but there is no monument to his memory. The church of St James, formerly a chapel belonging to those in the late Countess of Huntingdon's Connexion, is a neat octangular edifice of stone. the living is a perpetual curacy, in the patronage of the Vicar, and the Mayor and Corporation. St John's church was founded in 1634, and endowed with £80 per annum, and £10 per annum for repairs, by John Harrison, Esq, a native of the town, whose remains are therein deposited, under a monument of black marble. the living is a perpetual curacy, in the patronage of the Vicar, and the Mayor and Corporation. The church dedicated to St Paul is a neat stone building, the living is a perpetual curacy, endowed with £200 private benefaction, and £300 parliamentary grant, and in the patronage of the Vicar. Trinity church, erected in 1721, is a handsome structure in the Roman Doric style of architecture, with a tower surmounted by a spire. the living is a perpetual curacy, in the joint patronage of the Vicar, the Recorder and the Minister of St John's. The church on Quarry hill, dedicated to St Mary, and containing one thousand two hundred and seven sittings, of which eight hundred and one are free, was erected, in 1824, by a grant from the parliamentary commissioners, at an expense of £10,951 15 4. it is a handsome edifice in the later style of English architecture, with a square embattled tower. Christchurch, in Meadow-lane, containing one thousand two hundred and forty-nine sittings, of which eight hundred are free, was erected, also in 1824, by a grant of £10,456 13 from the same funds, and differs from St Mary's only in having angular pinnacles and no tower. The church at Woodhouse, dedicated to St Mark, was erected, in 1825, by grant from the parliamentary commissioners, at an expense of £9003, and contains one thousand two hundred sittings, of which eight hundred are free, the architecture is similar to that of St. Mary's. the livings are all perpetual curacies, in the patronage of the Vicar. There are upwards of twenty places of worship for Arians, Baptists, the Society of Friends, Independents, Wesleyan, Primitive, and other Methodists, Female Revivalists, Swedenborgians, and Unitarians, also a Roman Catholic chapel. The free grammar school was originally founded, in 1552, by William Sheafield, priest, who endowed it with several portions of land, on condition that the inhabitants should erect a school-house, which was subsequently built at the cost of John Harrison, Esq, in 1624, and enlarged, in 1692, by Godfrey Lawson, mayor, and in 1780 a house for the master was erected by the trustees. The original endowment, augmented by subsequent benefactions, produces an income of more than £1600 per annum. the establishment consists of a head-master, second master, and an assistant, whose salaries are respectively £500, £250, and £60. the school is free to all boys of the parish, for instruction in the classics and mathematics it is entitled to send a candidate for one of Lady Elizabeth Hastings' exhibitions at Queen s College Oxford , and it is also, in turn with the schools of Heversham and Halifax, entitled to one of three scholarships o £ 20 per ann. each, and tenable till the holders take the degree of M A , founded by the Rev Thomas Milner, in Magdalene College, and, in failure of a candidate from the school at Normanton, to one of two scholarships founded, by Mr Frieston, at Emanuel College, Cambridge A charity school, in which eighty girls are clothed and instructed, is supported by a portion of the produce of lands appropriated to charitable uses, amounting annually to nearly £400 , and a very neat and commodious building was erected for its use, in 1815, at the expense of £1000 A National school, also a neat building, erected in 1812, in which three hundred and twenty boys, and one hundred and eighty girls, are taught, a Lancasterian school, in which one thousand children are instructed, and a similar school for girls, are all supported by subscription there are also, in connexion with the established church and the various dissenting congregations, not less than forty Sunday schools in various parts of the town Harrison s hospital, comprising originally thirty almshouses, to which twelve more have been added, were founded, in 1653, by John Harrison, Esq , who endowed them with mills and tenements producing about £80 per annum the endowment has been augmented by Mrs Catherine Parker, Mr Joseph Midgley, Arthur Ikin, Esq , and others, and the buildings, occupying a large quadrangular area, afford an asylum to sixty-four aged women, who receive an allowance of £10 per annum each, paid quarterly Almshouses for ten aged widows were founded by Mrs Mary Potter, in 1729, and endowed by her with £2000, to which was added £400 by Mrs Barbara Chantrill, from the produce of which sums, together with other benefactions, each of the inmates receives an allowance of £12 12 per annum Eight houses were left by Josias Jenkinson Esq , in 1643, for the reception of sixteen aged persons, but no funds having been appropriated to keep them in repair, they became dilapidated, and have been since entirely rebuilt the rents of a farm bequeathed by the same Mr Jenkinson, for distribution among the poor, have been appropriated as an endowment to these houses, the tenants of which receive an annual allowance of £5 Under the superintendence of the governors of the workhouse are schools of industry, in which the children of the poor are taught to prepare the different wools for the loom, by an intimate intermixture of the various colours, in order to produce uniformity of pattern in the mixed cloths The general infirmary, founded in 1771, is a neat and commodious edifice, in an open and healthy situation it is liberally supported by subscription, and is well regulated under the superintendence of a president and a committee, and attended by three physicians, three surgeons, an apothecary, and an assistant. The house of recovery, in Vicarlane, was built by subscription in 1802, and has been found very efficacious in arresting the progress of contagion A dispensary for curing diseases of the eye was established in 1821, and is principally supported by members of the medical profession, by whom it is gratuitously attended The general dispensary, and a lying-in hospital, were both established in 1824 The

Strangers' Friend Society, for the visitation and relief of the distressed of all denominations , and the Guardian Society, for reclaiming females who have deviated from the path of virtue, are supported by subscription , and there are various other charitable institutions and bequests for the wants of the inhabitants of this large and populous manufacturing district Mrs Rachael Dixon bequeathed certain houses and premises in trust to the vicar of Leeds and the minister of St John s, the rents of which are to be equally distributed among three widows of clergymen of the established church In the neighbourhood are several chalybeate and other mineral springs that of Holbeck is like the sulphureous water of Harrogate, but more slightly impregnated , and it is so much esteemed, that it is brought daily to Leeds for sale On the declivity of Quarry hill are vestiges of a Roman camp, the trenches of which are covered with buildings, and Roman coins and other relics of antiquity have been discovered in the neighbourhood In Briggate street are some remains of the chantry of St Mary Magdalene, founded, in 1470, by the Rev William Evers, vicar of the parish , and on a sequestered spot on the banks of the Aire, about three miles from the town, are the picturesque ruins of Kirkstall priory, founded, in 1152, for monks of the Cistercian order, the revenue of which, at the dissolution, was £512 13 4 the remains, exhibiting a mixture of the Norman and early English styles of architecture, occupy a quadrangular area, four hundred and fifty feet in length, and three hundred and forty in breadth, and form one of the most interesting specimens of monastic grandeur in the kingdom Dr Berkenhout, author of several works on Chemistry, Natural History, and other subjects , Dr James Scot, author of three of the Seatonian prize-poems, and a writer in the Public Advertiser, under the signature Anti-Sejanus, and Benjamin Wilson, F R.S , a landscape painter of respectable talent, were natives of this town Leeds gives the title of duke to the family of Osborne

LEEK, a parish comprising the market town of Leek, the chapelries of Endon, Onecote, and Rushton-Spencer, and the townships of Bradnop, Longdon, Heaton, Leek Frith, Rushton James, Stanley, and Tittisworth in the northern, and the township of Rudyard with Caudery in the southern, division of the hundred of Totmonslow, county of Stafford, 23 miles (N N E) from Stafford, and 154 (N W by N) from London, and containing 4292 inhabitants This place is of great antiquity, and has been styled "The Capital of the Moorlands , subsequently to the Conquest the manor became the property of the Earls of Chester, one of whom obtained for the town the grant of a market from King John, and was eventually given to the monks of the abbey Dieu la Croix, in this parish In 1745, the troops of the Pretender marched through Leek on the 3d of December, in their advance to Derby, and returned on the 7th of the same month The town is pleasantly situated on an eminence on the main road from London to Manchester , the streets are well paved, and lighted with gas under an act of parliament obtained in 1824 , and the inhabitants are supplied with water by means of pipes, from a spring about one mile distant The curious phenomenon of a double sunset occurs here at a certain time of the year, owing to the relative position of a rocky mountain westward from the town The principal source of business is in the manufacture of ribands and various articles in silk a considerable quantity of cheese is made in the neighbourhood , and some valuable mines of coal, lead, and copper, in the adjacent hills, some of which were worked before the year 1680, afford employment to several individuals The Caldon branch of the Trent and Mersey canal passes within half a mile of the town, and near it runs the river Churnet The market is on Wednesday , and fairs, chiefly for cattle, are held on the Wednesday in Easter week, May 18th, on Whit-Monday, July 3rd and 28th, the Wednesday after the 10th of October, and November 13th Courts leet and baron are held by the lord of the manor, at which a constable is appointed , and the petty sessions for the northern division of the hundred are held here

The living is a discharged vicarage, in the archdeaconry of Stafford, and diocese of Lichfield and Coventry, rated in the king s books at £7 9 1½ , endowed with £ 200 private benefaction, £200 royal bounty, and £ 600 parliamentary grant, and in the patronage of the Earl of Macclesfield The church, dedicated to St Edward the Confessor, is a very ancient structure in the early style of English architecture , it has a tower with eight pinnacles, and stands on an eminence which commands a very extensive prospect There are places of worship for the Society of Friends, Independents, and Wesleyan Methodists that belonging to the Methodists is very large, and in connexion with it is a Sunday school, in which upwards of one thousand one hundred children are instructed A school-house was erected, at the expense of the Earl of Macclesfield, in the beginning of the last century, for a free grammar school, but it has no endowment, except from a benefaction by the Rev George Roades, who, in 1712, bequeathed property which was invested in the three per cents , and produces £9 13 10 per annum, which sum is paid to the master for teaching English to six poor boys of this parish Eight almshouses for single women not under sixty years of age were founded and endowed by Elizabeth Ash, in 1676, with a rent-charge of £ 40 per annum Additional benefactions to this charity make the total income £78 3 6 per annum Very munificent donations have been made from time to time in aid of the poor of this parish, and the sum of £290 arising from them is annually distributed in food, clothing, and other necessaries, including small sums of money The remains of Dieu la Croix abbey (now corrupted to Dieulacres), which was founded by Ranulph de Blundeville, Earl of Chester, in 1214, in honour of St Mary and St. Benedict, for Cistercian monks, and valued, at the dissolution, at £ 243 3 6 per annum, are here Thomas Parker, first Earl of Macclesfield, who became Lord High Chancellor, and President to the Royal Society, was born, in 1666, at Leek, where his father practised as an attorney

LEEK FRITH, a township in that part of the parish of LEEK which is in the northern division of the hundred of TOTMONSLOW, county of STAFFORD, 5 miles (N by W) from Leek, containing 806 inhabitants

LEEK-WOOTTON, a parish in the Kenilworth division of the hundred of KNIGHTLOW, county of WARWICK, 2¼ miles (S) from Kenilworth, containing 436 inhabitants The living is a vicarage, in the archdeaconry of Coventry, and diocese of Lichfield and Coventry, rated in the king's books at £5 12 1 Chandos

Leigh, Esq was patron in 1824 The church is dedicated to All Saints Daniel Winter, in 1776, bequeathed £10 per annum towards the support of a school, for which sum, together with others raised by contributions, and the free use of a house for his residence, the master teaches all poor children of the parish who apply

LEEMING, a chapelry in the parish of BURNESTON, wapentake of HALLIKELD, North riding of the county of YORK, 2½ miles (E N E) from Bedale, containing, with Exelby and Newton, 562 inhabitants The living is a perpetual curacy, in the archdeaconry of Richmond, and diocese of Chester, endowed with £1000 royal bounty, and £1000 parliamentary grant, and in the patronage of the Vicar of Burneston The church is dedicated to St John the Baptist The petty sessions for the division are held at the Oak Tree Inn, Leeming Lane The ancient Herman-street, which extends northward to Inverness, passes through this chapelry

LEES, a hamlet in the parish of DALBURY, hundred of APPLETREE, county of DERBY, 6¼ miles (W by N) from Derby The population is returned with the parish

LEES, a chapelry in the parish of ASHTON under LINE, hundred of SALFORD, county palatine of LANCASTER, 1½ mile (E) from Oldham The population is returned with the parish The living is a perpetual curacy, in the archdeaconry and diocese of Chester, and in the patronage of the Rector of Ashton under Line The turnpike-road from Oldham to Huddersfield passes through the village, near which is a chalybeate spring, called Lees Spa

LEESE, a township in that part of the parish of SANDBACH which is in the hundred of NORTHWICH, county palatine of CHESTER, 2½ miles (N E) from Middlewich, containing 135 inhabitants

LEESTHORPE, a hamlet in the parish of PICKWELL, hundred of GARTREE, though locally in that of Guthlaxton, county of LEICESTER, 4¼ miles (S E by S) from Melton-Mowbray The population is returned with the parish

LEFTWICH, a township in the parish of DAVENHAM, hundred of NORTHWICH, county palatine of CHESTER, 1 mile (S) from Northwich, containing 1192 inhabitants A charity school here is supported by annual donations, averaging about £13

LEGBOURN, a parish in the Marsh division of the hundred of CALCEWORTH, though locally in that of Louth-Eske, parts of LINDSEY, county of LINCOLN, 3 miles (S E by E) from Louth, containing 412 inhabitants The living is a perpetual curacy, in the archdeaconry and diocese of Lincoln, endowed with £200 private benefaction, £200 royal bounty, and £300 parliamentary grant The Rev R Powley was patron in 1800 The church is dedicated to All Saints There is a place of worship for Wesleyan Methodists A priory of Cistercian nuns, in honour of the Virgin Mary, was founded here before the reign of John, by Robert Fitz-Gilbert at the dissolution, its revenue, was £57 13 5

LEGSBY, a parish in the western division of the wapentake of WRAGGOE, parts of LINDSEY, county of LINCOLN, 3½ miles (S E) from Market-Raisen, containing 231 inhabitants The living is a discharged vicarage, in the archdeaconry and diocese of Lincoln, rated in the king's books at £6 4 2 Sir H Nelthorpe, Bart was patron in 1819 The church is dedicated to St Thomas the Apostle

Seal and Arms.

LEICESTER, a borough, market, and county town, having separate jurisdiction, in the county of LEICESTER, 97 miles (N N W) from London, containing, with the extra-parochial liberties of Black Friars and White Friars, and with the chapelry of Knightlow, in the hundred of GUTHLAXTON, and Bishop's Fee, in the hundred of GARTREE (both in the parish of St Margaret), and with the extra-parochial district called New Works, and a portion of the parish of St Mary, called the South Fields, both in the hundred of GUTHLAXTON, 30,508 inhabitants, according to the census of 1821, between which period and the year 1800, the population had nearly doubled, and, since 1821, it has increased to nearly 40,000 Leicester, which had flourished from remote antiquity as the principal town of the Coritani, was, upon the conquest of Britain by the Romans, made one of their stipendiary cities, and is clearly identified with the *Ratæ* of Antoninus, and the *Ratiscorion* of Richard of Cirencester That it was a Roman station of considerable importance is evident from the remains of a Roman temple, supposed to have been dedicated to Janus, and from numerous tesselated pavements and other relics of Roman antiquity which have been discovered in the vicinity By the Saxons it was, from its situation on the river Lear, now the Soar, called *Legerceastre*, of which its present name is simply a contraction Under the Heptarchy, this place belonged to the kingdom of Mercia, and it was for a short time the see of a bishop, whose successors removed to Dorchester, and finally to Lincoln. In 874, the Danes, having overrun this part of the kingdom, seized upon Leicester, which they constituted one of the five great cities of their empire in Britain, and retained, till Ethelfleda, daughter of Alfred, and widow of Ethelred, Earl of Mercia, who, after her husband's death, continued to govern the province, rescued it from their possession, after a successful encounter, in which the Danes were defeated with considerable slaughter At the time of the Norman Conquest, the castle, which had been nearly destroyed in the Danish wars, was rebuilt, and entrusted to Hugo de Grentemaisnel, on whom William bestowed the greater part of the town, but in the disputed succession to the throne, after the death of William, Hugo, embracing the cause of Robert, Duke of Normandy, in opposition to William Rufus, the castle was demolished by the partisans of the latter, and remained for some time in ruins In the reign of Henry I, Robert de Mellent being created Earl of Leicester, repaired, enlarged, and fortified the castle, which he made his baronial residence, but his son, Robert le Bossu, having taken part in the rebellion of the young Prince Henry against his father, Henry II, Leicester was besieged by the king's forces under Richard de Lucy, and, after an obstinate battle, in which the earl was taken prisoner, fell into the hands of the king The king's forces having entered the town, set fire to it in several places, razed the walls, and destroyed the fortifications, and having ultimately reduced the castle, which held out for a considerable time,

demolished it entirely The earl afterwards recovering his liberty, joined the Crusaders, and on his return from Palestine founded, in expiation of his rebellious conduct, the monastery of St Mary de Pratis, near the town, in which, having assumed the habit of a monk, he spent the remainder of his life A royal mint, which was established at Leicester in the reign of Athelstan, and situated near the North bridge, was maintained here till the commencement of this reign In the reign of John, Robert Fitz-Parnel, Earl of Leicester, obtained from that monarch a charter of incorporation and many privileges, which were afterwards extended and confirmed by Henry III, at the solicitation of Simon de Montfort, then Earl of Leicester, who, rebelling against his sovereign, and engaging in the baronial wars of that reign, was slain at the battle of Evesham After the death of Montfort, Henry III conferred the earldom of Leicester on his second son, Edmund, Earl of Lancaster, whose grandson Henry made this place his principal residence, and under him and his two immediate successors, the castle was restored to its former strength and magnificence After the accession of the house of Lancaster to the throne, Leicester was frequently visited by the sovereigns of that family A parliament was held here by Henry V, in 1414, and another by the Dukes of Bedford and Gloucester, during the minority of Henry VI, in 1425 In the conflict between the houses of York and Lancaster, the castle is supposed to have suffered severely, and in the reign of Richard III it had become so dilapidated, that when that monarch was at Leicester, a few evenings prior to the battle of Bosworth Field, he preferred to sleep at the Blue Boar inn, in the town the bedstead upon which he slept is now in the possession of 1 Babington, Esq, of Rothley Temple During the parliamentary war the town suffered materially, it was taken by storm by the royal army, in May 1645, but was retaken by the parliamentary forces under Fairfax, in June following, soon after which, orders were issued by the parliament to pull down what remained of the castle, and to dispose of the materials The remains are intermixed with the various buildings that have been erected on the site, the most conspicuous portion of them is a beautiful arched gateway tower, called the magazine, from its having been purchased by the county as a depôt for the ammunition of the trained bands, in 1682

The town is pleasantly situated nearly in the centre of the county, and on the banks of the river Soar, over which are four bridges, named respectively, North, West, Braunston, and Bow bridge, the first, a handsome structure erected in 1792, the others, ancient buildings which have been recently repaired the principal street, extending from south to north, is upwards of a mile in length, and there are many other spacious streets, the houses, which, within the last half century, have been much improved, are chiefly built of brick, and roofed with slate, the town is paved and watched by subscription, lighted with gas by a company incorporated in 1821, and supplied with water from a public conduit in the market-place, and from wells in various parts of the town A promenade, called the New Walk, which extends nearly three-quarters of a mile in length, in a south-eastern direction from the town, was formed about the year 1785, the ground was given by the corporation, and laid out by subscription it affords, in many parts, some pleasing views of the town, and of the hills of Charnwood Forest, which abound in beautiful scenery The town library, established by the corporation in 1632, consists chiefly of Theological works The theatre, a neat building, is opened in September, and assemblies are held, during the winter, in a suite of rooms in a building originally erected for an hotel, and purchased by the county for the accommodation also of the judges of the assize, and for the meetings of the county magistrates the ball-room, seventy-five feet long, and thirty-three feet wide, is elegantly painted by Remagle, and lighted on assembly nights by eight splendid lustres, and branches held by statues, after designs by Bacon A musical festival first took place here in 1827, which, from the patronage it received, will be triennially repeated Races are held in September, on the south-east side of the town, where a grand stand has been erected, and every means adopted for the improvement of the course, and on the north-east side of the town is an extensive enclosed cricket-ground An agricultural society, which has been established for many years, holds its meetings here annually in October The staple manufacture of the town, that of worsted and cotton hosiery, has been established for more than two centuries the number of frames in the town and neighbouring villages is about seven thousand, and the number of persons employed in the frame-work knitting, worsted spinning, wool combing and dyeing, is about twelve thousand In addition to the manufacture of hose, of which a great quantity is exported, there are manufacturers of lace, cotton thread, ropes and twine, stocking-frames, needles, and pipes, and several woolstaplers Situated on the great northern road, Leicester has every facility of land carriage to London, Manchester, Nottingham, Derby, and other towns, and, in 1791, an act of parliament was obtained for opening a communication with the Loughborough canal, and through that with the various lines of navigation connected with the Trent, the effect of which has been to introduce the coal of Derbyshire by the cheaper conveyance of water carriage The act also contained provisions for making an additional line of navigation from Loughborough to the Leicestershire collieries in Charnwood Forest, and although the expense of cutting the canal was incurred, it has never been brought into use In the parliamentary session of 1830, an act was obtained for constructing a rail-road, in a direct line, from Leicester to Swannington, a district abounding with coal The market, which is on Saturday, is particularly celebrated for the quality of the butchers' meat the fairs, principally for horses, cattle, sheep, and cheese, are on January 4th, March 2nd, the Saturday before Easter, May 12th, which lasts for three days, June 1st, July 5th, August 1st, September 13th, October 10th (for three days), November 2nd, and December 8th

The government, by charter of King John, confirmed and extended by succeeding sovereigns, and renewed, with all former privileges and immunities, in the 41st of Elizabeth, is vested in a mayor, recorder, high steward, bailiff, twenty-four aldermen, and forty-eight common council-men, assisted by a town clerk and subordinate officers The mayor and bailiff are annually elected in September, by the whole corporation, from among the aldermen, the mayor, recorder and the four aldermen

who have last past the chair, are justices of the peace for the borough and liberties, over the latter of which only the county magistrates have a concurrent jurisdiction The freedom is inherited by all the sons of a freeman, and acquired by servitude, by purchase, or by gift among the privileges are, exemption from toll in all the fairs of England, and the liberty of depasturing cattle in the Abbey meadows and other grounds The corporation hold quarterly courts of session for offences not capital, and a court of record, for the recovery of debts to any amount, is held by prescription, confirmed by charters of Elizabeth and James I, before the mayor, recorder, and aldermen, or any three of them, including the mayor, and there is also an officer called the steward, who issues all writs, manages the business, and presides in the absence of the recorder, he is appointed pursuant to the charter, as also is a bailiff, whose duties resemble those of a county sheriff The elective franchise was first exercised in the 23rd of Edward I, since which time the borough has returned two members to parliament the right of election is vested in the freemen generally not receiving alms, whether resident or not, and in the resident householders paying scot and lot, together about six thousand in number the mayor and bailiff are the returning officers. This being the county town, the election of knights of the shire, and the assizes and quarter sessions for the county, are held in it The guildhall is a neat and commodious building, containing, among other portraits with which the interior is decorated, one of Sir Thomas White, lord mayor of London, and founder of St John's College, Oxford The hall of the ancient castle has been fitted up for holding the assizes and sessions for the county, and, from the ample space which it affords, the courts are so arranged as not to interfere with each other The borough gaol contains two wards for male, and one for female, felons, and one ward for debtors, and, on the completion of the new county gaol, it will be converted into a house of correction The old common gaol for the county, now the town gaol, contains four divisions, one work-room, four day-rooms, and four airing-yards, for the classification of prisoners A new gaol and house of correction for the county has been built at the south end of the town, comprising eight distinct wards, ranged round the governor's house in the centre (in the upper part of which is the chapel, communicating by bridges with the upper stories of the several wards), with work-rooms, day-rooms, and airing-yards, an infirmary, and other offices, the whole enclosed within a stone wall, forming on the entrance side a handsome castellated façade in the ancient style of English architecture

The borough comprises the parishes of All Saints, St Leonard, St. Martin, and St Nicholas, and parts of the parishes of St Margaret and St. Mary, all, excepting St. Margaret's, which is within the peculiar jurisdiction of the Prebendary of that parish in the Cathedral Church of Lincoln, in the archdeaconry of Leicester, and diocese of Lincoln The living of All Saints' is a discharged vicarage, with those of St. Clement, St. Michael, and St Peter united, the churches of which are demolished, rated together in the king's books at £6 13 5, (St. Clement s and St Michael's being not in charge,) endowed with £400 royal bounty, and £1400 parliamentary grant, and in the patronage of the Crown the church is an ancient structure in the early style of English architecture, with a tower on the north side of the north aisle, the chancel is modern, but in various parts of the church are some fine old portions intermixed with later insertions, the interior contains an early English font of curious device, and some fine carving in wood The living of St Leonard s is a vicarage, endowed with £200 royal bounty, and united with that of St Margaret, being rated together in the king s books at £23 8. 6½, and in the patronage of the Prebendary of St Margaret's in the Cathedral Church of Lincoln the church of St Leonard was demolished during the parliamentary war, in 1645, that of St Margaret, erected about 1444, is a beautiful structure, combining portions in the early, decorated, and later styles of English architecture, with a tower of the later style, of which character are also the chancel and the clerestory of the nave the interior contains some wooden stalls and seats richly carved, and among the monuments is an alabaster tomb of Bishop Penny, previously abbot of the neighbouring monastery of St Mary de Pratis in the church-yard is the tomb of Andrew, Lord Rollo, decorated with military trophies The living of St Martin s is a discharged vicarage, rated in the king s books at £6 13 4, endowed with £400 royal bounty, and in the patronage of the Crown the church is a venerable cruciform structure, partly in the early, and partly in the later, style of English architecture, with a tower rising from the centre, and supported on four semicircular arches, opening into the nave, chancel, and transepts, the lower part of which is in the Norman style of architecture, surmounted by a spire of later date the interior was despoiled of its ornaments by the parliamentary troops, who converted it into barracks during their occupation of the town, but it has been restored with due regard to its ancient character, the chancel, which is in the later style, is decorated with three stone stalls under the south-east window, and it has a noble organ, built by Snetzler, and a fine painting of the Ascension, by Francesco Vanni, presented by Sir William Skeffington, Bart The archdeacon of Leicester holds his court in the south aisle, and the Bishop of Lincoln confirms in the chancel, of this church, at which the judges of assize attend divine service The living of St Mary's is a discharged vicarage, rated in the king s books at £8, endowed with £600 royal bounty, and £1600 parliamentary grant, and in the patronage of the Crown the church is an ancient structure, combining the Norman, and the early style of English, architecture, with later insertions the tower, which is surmounted by a lofty spire, is situated at the west end of the south aisle, and detached from the nave the spire was erected in 1783, at the expense of £300, in the place of a former spire, destroyed by lightning On the south side of the chancel are three fine Norman stalls, with double shafts and enriched mouldings, and on the south side of the south aisle are three early English stalls, highly ornamented the font is of curious and beautiful design, and the oak roofs, which are exquisitely carved, are in some parts in tolerable preservation The living of St. Nicholas' is a discharged vicarage, rated in the king's books at £3 11 3, endowed with £800 royal bounty, and £1000 parliamentary grant, and in the patronage of the Crown the church is in the early style of Norman architecture, with a tower between the nave and the chancel, and is said to have been built with the materials

of a Roman temple, of which a considerable fragment still remains in a wall adjoining the church yard The society for the enlargement of churches and chapels have granted £1500 in aid of a subscription among the inhabitants for rebuilding this church A very handsome district church, dedicated to St.George, and containing one thousand eight hundred sittings, of which nine hundred and ninety-nine are free, was erected in the parish of St Margaret, by grant from the parliamentary commissioners, in 1826, at an expense of £14,964 4 8, it is a handsome edifice in the later style of English architecture, with a tower surmounted by a spire the living is a perpetual curacy, in the patronage of the Vicar of St Margaret s There are seven places of worship for Baptists, one for the Society of Friends, one for Huntingtonians, three for Independents, one for Wesleyan Methodists, two for Primitive Methodists, one for Unitarians, and a Roman Catholic chapel the last is a handsome edifice in the ancient style of English architecture, and the Wesleyan meeting house is very spacious

The free grammar school is supposed to have been originally founded by Thomas Wigston, a prebendary of the collegiate church of St. Mary de Pratis, it was refounded, and a new school house erected, by the corporation in 1575, and is partly supported from the funds of Wigston hospital, and partly by the corporation, who appoint the master, it is open to all the sons of burgesses, for classical and commercial instruction there are two exhibitions of £6 per annum to Lincoln College, Oxford, founded by Mr Thomas Hayne, at the disposal of the corporation, for boys of this school, or, in failure of such, for boys of Melton-Mowbray school, an annuity of £4 per annum to be paid to two poor boys so long as they should continue in the school, and an exhibition of £6 per annum to Oxford or Cambridge, tenable for five years, founded by Henry, Earl of Huntingdon these exhibitions, not having been claimed for many years, are accumulating, and will be added by the corporation to funds with which they intend to found exhibitions of sufficient value to excite competition The Green-coat school was founded, in 1782, by Gabriel Newton, alderman, for the clothing and education of thirty-five boys the school was rebuilt in 1808, and the funds having increased, the number of scholars has also been increased to eighty, each of whom, after remaining three years in the school, receives an apprentice fee of £5 St Mary s charity school, for clothing and instructing eighty boys and forty girls, was established in 1785, and a schoolhouse built by subscription, at an expense of £600 St Martin s school was built, in 1791, at an expense of £950, and is supported by subscription, there are one hundred and fifty boys and eighty-four girls instructed and partly clothed in this institution A National school-room was erected, in 1814, by subscription, aided by a grant of £300 from the National Society, on a site bestowed by the Crown, as connected with the duchy of Lancaster, in this school from four hundred to five hundred children are taught on the National plan, and in St Margaret s school, erected in 1807, seventy-three boys and forty-one girls are instructed on the same plan, and annually clothed The Old Trinity hospital was founded, in 1330, by Henry, Earl of Leicester and Lancaster, who endowed it originally for fifty infirm and aged men, and five women to attend on them in 1354 the foundation was greatly augmented by his son, Henry, Duke of Lancaster, who converted the original establishment into a college, called the New Work, or *Collegium Novi Operis*, and it was further extended by John of Gaunt, son-in-law of Duke Henry The whole establishment consisted of a dean, twelve secular canons, twelve vicars, three clerks, six choristers, fifty poor men, fifty poor women, ten nurses, and other attendants, at the dissolution, its revenue was £800, and the corporation, having purchased the site, refounded on it the hospital for poor widows there are at present in this establishment about ninety men and women, who receive each three shillings and eightpence per week, and are nominated by the chancellor of the duchy of Lancaster, or, on his failing to appoint within three months, the vacancies are filled up by the corporation some of the men belonging to this hospital, clothed in ancient armour, attend in the procession at the proclamation of the fairs An hospital for a master, confrater, twelve aged men, and twelve aged women, all unmarried, was founded, and dedicated to St Ursula, in the latter part of the fifteenth century, by William Wigston, merchant-stapler, and mayor of Leicester the master, who has a salary of £160 per annum, and the confrater, who has £70 per annum, are appointed by the chancellor of the duchy of Lancaster, and appoint the hospitallers, who receive four shillings and tenpence per week, with an allowance of coal and candles The hospital of St John the Baptist, founded, in 1235, for a master, brethren, and sisters, was given by Queen Elizabeth to the corporation, who converted it into a hall for wool, but, in the reign of James I, they endowed it with £17 per annum, and placed in it six poor widows, among whom that sum is distributed An hospital for four aged widows, who receive four shillings per week, was founded, in 1703, by Mr Bent, alderman of this borough, and, in 1710, an hospital was founded by Mr Matthew Simson, who endowed it for six aged widows, each of whom receives £3 per annum, and five hundred weight of coal these premises were rebuilt by the trustees in 1807 The late John Johnson, Esq erected, in 1792, five neat dwellinghouses, which he called the *Consanguinitarium*, and intended as a residence for five of his needy relatives, assigning for the support of the establishment an income of more than £60 per annum The female asylum, in the New Works, was established, in 1800, by the exertions of the late Rev Thomas Robinson, for the maintenance, clothing, and instructing in household business, of sixteen poor orphan girls, who are admitted at the age of thirteen, and remain for three years in the institution, when they are placed out as servants in respectable families The infirmary, at the southern extremity of the town, was erected in 1771, and is supported by subscription the building, which is plain, consists of a centre and two wings, and contains accommodation for eighty-four patients, who are admitted without distinction from every part of the country attached to it is a house of recovery from fever, or other contagious diseases, added in 1818 Adjoining the infirmary is the lunatic asylum, towards the erection and support of which, Mrs Topp bequeathed £1000, and Mrs Ann Wigley £200 Sir Thomas White also bequeathed £10,000 in trust to the corporation, to be lent for nine years, without interest, in sums of £50,

which have been subsequently enlarged, to the freemen of Leicester, and other towns in the county, and there are charitable bequests, amounting to more than £800 per annum, at the disposal of the corporation, for distribution among the poor, included in which is the produce of a grant, by Charles I, of forty acres of land in the forest of Leicester

Among the monastic establishments anciently existing here, was a collegiate church, founded long before the Conquest, within the precincts of the castle, which was, with the city and the castle, destroyed in the wars during the reign of the Conqueror, and refounded, in 1107, by Robert de Mellent, Earl of Leicester the greater portion of its revenue was transferred to the abbey of St Mary de Pratis, but it continued, under the designation of St Mary the Less, till the dissolution, when the remaining part of it was valued at £24 13 11 the remains are only part of the crypt, still discernible in the cellar of a house erected on its site The abbey of St Mary de Pratis was founded, in 1143, by Robert le Bossu, Earl of Leicester, for Black canons, and dedicated to St Mary, in which that earl ended his days it became possessed of great wealth, and was frequently visited by several of the kings of England, and other illustrious personages, among whom was Cardinal Wolsey, who, lodging there on his route to London, after his disgrace, died within its walls, and was buried in the church at the dissolution its revenue was £1062 0 4¾ the remains consist chiefly of the outer walls, on which is an inscription curiously worked in bricks of different colours In the north part of the town was an hospital for lepers, founded, in the reign of Richard I, by William, son of Robert Blanchmains, Earl of Leicester In the north-western part was a convent of Franciscan or Grey friars, founded, in 1265, by Simon de Montfort, in the church of which was interred the body of Richard III, after his death at the battle of Bosworth Field in an island in the Soar was a house of Black friars, founded in the reign of Henry III, and dedicated to St. Clement, by one of the Earls of Leicester, and here was also a priory for canons Regular of the order of St Augustine, dedicated to St Catherine, which remained till the dissolution. Of the Roman relics here, the most curious are, a tessellated pavement, found in a cellar nearly opposite the town prison, in 1675, and a milliary, or Roman mile-stone, discovered, in 1771, on the side of the Fosse-road leading to New Works, and about two miles from the town This stone, which has given rise to much archaiological research, was removed to the town by the corporation, and is placed in Belgrave Gate, on a square pedestal, with a column above it, surmounted by a cross, and, from the inscription on it (often published), it appears to have been erected in the reign of the Emperor Hadrian, and is said to be the oldest that has been discovered in this country About a quarter of a mile south of the infirmary are the ancient artificial embankments, called the Rawdykes, supposed also to be of Roman origin, and among smaller remains are an abundance of coins, of which it is supposed that a complete series might have been formed from Nero to Valentinian. Dr Richard Farmer, the learned author of an essay on the learning and genius of Shakspeare, was a native of this town Leicester gives the inferior title of earl to Marquis Townshend.

LEICESTER-ABBEY, an extra parochial liberty, in the western division of the hundred of Goscote, county of Leicester, 1 mile (N) from Leicester, containing 15 inhabitants An abbey of Black canons, in honour of the Assumption of the Blessed Virgin Mary, was founded here, in 1143, by Robert Bossu, Earl of Leicester, the revenue of which, at the dissolution, was estimated at £ 1002 0 4, and the site granted by Edward VI to the Marquis of Northampton There are slight remains of the conventual buildings, the most remarkable portion of which is an outer wall, exhibiting on its face an inscription wrought in bricks of different colours

LEICESTER- FOREST, an extra-parochial liberty, in the hundred of Sparkenhoe, county of Leicester, containing 71 inhabitants

LEICESTERSHIRE, an inland county, bounded on the north-west by that of Derby, on the north by that of Nottingham, on the east by those of Lincoln and Rutland, on the south by that of Northampton, and on the south-west by that of Warwick it lies between 52° 23′ and 52° 58′ (N Lat), and between 41′ and 1° 38′ (W Lon), and includes eight hundred and four square miles, or five hundred and fourteen thousand, five hundred and sixty statute acres The population, according to the census of 1821, was 174,571 Leicestershire, so called from the name of its principal town, formed part of the territory of the Coritani, and, subsequently, of the Roman division of Britain named *Flavia Cæsariensis* Under the Anglo-Saxons it was a central portion of the powerful kingdom of Mercia. It suffered most severely from the incursions of the Danes, who, landing on the eastern coast, laid waste the whole county as far as Leicester, which town, having finally fallen into their possession, became, on their peaceable establishment in this part of the kingdom, one of their five principal cities in England The first remarkable historical occurrence in this county, subsequently to the Norman Conquest, was the destruction in 1173, of the town of Leicester in consequence of its being the chief place of refuge, after their defeat at Bury, of the adherents of Prince Henry, in his rebellion against his father, Henry II In 1217, in the reign of Henry III, the castle of Mount-Sorrel, being garrisoned by Saher de Quincy, Earl of Winchester, for Louis the Dauphin, was taken by the forces of the young king, under Ranulph de Blundeville, Earl of Chester, and razed to the ground In the general demolition of the baronial castles which took place at a later period of the same reign, when the royal cause was triumphant, the fortresses in Leicestershire appear to have been unsparingly levelled with the ground, owing probably, in a great measure, to the very prominent part taken on the side of the barons by the celebrated Simon de Montfort, Earl of Leicester, and consequently by his dependents and retainers It was in this county, by his preaching at Lutterworth, of which parish he was rector, that the doctrines of Wickliffe were first openly promulgated, towards the close of the fourteenth century, and at Leicester, in April 1414, was held the parliament which granted a subsidy of three hundred thousand marks to Henry V, to enable him to assert his title to the crown of France, and which ordained death to the maintainers of the doctrines of Wickliffe, and to the readers of the Scrip-

tures in English In 1485, this county was the scene of the memorable conflict of Bosworth Field, the last of thirteen pitched battles between the partisans of the houses of York and Lancaster, when, upon the defeat and death of Richard III, the Earl of Richmond was crowned upon the field, as Henry VII In 1644, at the period when this county, amongst others, took a decided part against Charles I, in the great contest between him and the parliament, on this same celebrated spot a skirmish took place, on the 1st of July, between the royalists and a detachment of Lord Grey s horse, under Captain Babington, when the former were defeated In 1645, the parliamentarian forces sustained two defeats within the limits of the county, from Sir Marmaduke Langdale, one between Harborough and Leicester, in which the former lost one hundred men killed and two hundred and fifty prisoners, the other near Melton-Mowbray, under Colonel Rossiter, when they lost a hundred and seventy killed It was on the 31st of May, in the same year, that Leicester was stormed and taken by Charles I and Prince Rupert

Leicestershire is included in the diocese of Lincoln, and province of Canterbury, and forms an archdeaconry comprising the six deaneries of Akelev, Framland, Gartree, Goscote, Guthlaxton, and Sparkenhoe, and two hundred and thirteen parishes, of which one hundred and thirteen are rectories, eighty-two vicarages, and eighteen perpetual curacies For civil purposes it is divided into the hundreds of Framland, Gartree, Goscote (East and West), Guthlaxton, and Sparkenhoe, in which are the borough and market town of Leicester, and the market towns of Ashby de la Zouch, Market-Bosworth, Market-Harborough, Hinckley, Loughborough, Lutterworth, Melton Mowbray, and Mount-Sorrel Two knights are returned for the shire, and two representatives for the borough of Leicester the county members are elected at Leicester This county is included in the midland circuit the assizes are held at Leicester, as also are the quarter sessions, on January 11th, April 19th, July 19th, and October 18th The county gaol is at Leicester there are fifty-two acting magistrates The rates raised in the county for the year ending March 25th, 1827, amounted to £138,182 15, the expenditure to £138,904 7, of which £117,962 2 was applied to the relief of the poor

The general surface of the county consists of innumerable gently-rising hills, with few precipitous declivities, so that almost the whole is available for cultivation The margins of the rivers and brooks are natural grass land, and the uplands partly arable and partly under grass The modern enclosures are almost entirely devoid of trees, but the fences of the more ancient abound with timber The highest grounds are, some of the summits of the Charnwood Forest hills, which consist of barren rocks, projecting abruptly above the surface, and composed of a kind of granite the elevation of these peaks is not more than eight or nine hundred feet above the level of the sea, and is consequently within a temperate region of the atmosphere, yet the views from them are some of the most extensive and beautiful in the kingdom Bardon hill, in particular, an isolated eminence, and the loftiest of the whole, is celebrated for the astonishingly expansive prospects which it commands, from this point the eye may range over the whole midland district of England, Lincoln cathedral, the Dunstable hills, the Malvern hills, the Sugar Loaf in South Wales, the Wrekin, and other mountains in Shropshire and North Wales, and the Peak of Derbyshire, being all visible from it The elevation of the meadows on the margins of the rivers is from one to two hundred feet above the level of the sea, and the climate of the whole county is mild and temperate

The soils are divisible into three classes 1 Clay loam, having a considerable degree of tenacity, and being generally of a good depth, which latter circumstance, together with its friability and porous quality, is the chief cause of its fertility this is unfit for turnips, but makes good corn and excellent grass land. 2 Sandy, or gravelly loam, which is more loose and friable than the last, generally of a good depth, adapted to the cultivation of turnips, and of every kind of grain, and excellent for grass, either natural or artificial 3 The peaty meadow soil, which has been formed from the decomposition of vegetable matter, and the sediment brought down by the streams from the uplands this is particularly adapted to grass, whether hay or pasture, but to grass only The best soil is generally upon the hills, and the worst and coldest in the vallies The soil of Charnwood Forest is for the most part a moist greyish-coloured loam, in want of drainage and improvement, and indeed the general characteristic of the upland soil of Leicestershire is a greyish or brownish friable loam, of greater or less depth, upon a substratum of clay, marl, gravel, or rock, the strongest and most tenacious is to be found in the vale of Belvoir About two hundred and forty thousand acres of land in this county are under occasional tillage The average produce of wheat is estimated at three quarters and a half, or twenty-eight bushels per acre, that of barley at rather less than five quarters the last-mentioned is the favourite grain crop of the Leicestershire farmer, and a greater breadth of land is sown with it than with any other corn Oats are grown to a great extent, on account of the number of horses bred and kept in the county, the average is about five quarters per acre Peas are not extensively cultivated Beans were formerly reckoned a staple growth, but their cultivation is now much less general Rye is chiefly grown as early spring pasture for sheep, and vetches, though not extensively, as green food for horses Common and Swedish turnips are cultivated to a great extent, being sown upon all soils that are not too strong and heavy Cabbages are extensively cultivated, as are also carrots and potatoes cole-seed or rape, red and white clover, trefoil, and ray-grass, are frequently sown About half the enclosed land of the county consists of permanent grass The natural meadows on the banks of the rivers and brooks are very numerous and extensive, and frequently of excellent quality The pastures are for the most part grazed by a mixed stock of sheep, and of cattle In various parts of the county are numerous good dairies, which produce large quantities of cheese Stilton cheese, the richest and highest-priced thick cheese produced in Great Britain, is made in most of the villages about Melton Mowbray, it obtained its name from the first maker of it, resident at Wymondham, near Melton-Mowbray, having supplied an inn at Stilton, where it first became generally known and esteemed This county has long been distinguished for the judgment and perseverance which persons of abi-

lity and consideration resident in it have displayed in improving every species of live stock, and bringing them to a high degree of perfection among these, the late Robert Bakewell, Esq, of Dishley farm, near Loughborough, who died in 1795, stood pre-eminent The breed of cattle now prevailing in Leicestershire is the long-horned, which is of handsome form, and greatly esteemed for the purpose of feeding, and there has been, besides, from time immemorial, and still continues to be, an influx of cattle to be fattened for the butcher, from Ireland, Wales, Scotland, Shropshire, Staffordshire, Herefordshire, Northumberland, and Lancashire. In the neighbourhoods of Hinckley, Bosworth, Appleby, and Snarestone, are many respectable dairies of long-horned cows, as well as in that part of the county bordering on Derbyshire and the Trent, and in the vale of Belvoir, but in this latter district the cows are in part of the short-horned Holderness breed the stock of dairy cows is kept up chiefly by rearing in the county The Leicestershire cattle, when full grown and fat, weigh, on an average, the cows from eight to ten score per quarter, the oxen from ten to fifteen score the prevailing colour is red, or brindled, with streaks of white along the back and belly The present stock of sheep consists of three varieties,—the Old Leicester, the New Leicester, and the Forest sheep The Old Leicester sheep are supposed to be an improvement of the old stock of the common fields, by intermixture with the Lincolnshire breed and by better keeping they are large and heavy, with much wool, but large in bone, rather coarse in the pelt, and take a considerable time to fatten The New Leicester breed was formed chiefly by Mr Bakewell the offals of these sheep are small, and their profitable parts large, their backs being broad and straight, their breasts full, their heads small, the flesh fine grained and well flavoured, and the wool fine of its kind, they are also capable of being fattened in a short time, on a small proportion of food, and to a great weight in proportion to their apparent size The Forest sheep are for the most part confined to Charnwood, and they are all clothed with a coarse combing wool Folding of sheep is hardly ever practised, except in the very few remaining common fields The improvement of hogs has been attended to with the same care and success as that of other live stock Leicestershire seems to have been always famous for a useful and beautiful breed of black horses, and from time immemorial more have been produced in the county than are required for its use Many blood horses are also bred in this county, asses are used in many parts for carrying burdens, and have been lately introduced as farmers stock, mules have long been in use here Charnwood Forest is situated in the northern part of the county, though some miles from the border, and is wholly devoid of timber, and almost of underwood its general face is, however, bold and romantic, having a great variety of hills, generally terminating in bare and rugged rocks, which have a very picturesque appearance to a considerable distance, and in all directions the substance of these rocks is a soft primeval stone of the vitreous kind, and is conveyed to a considerable distance in every direction, for the purpose of mending the roads this extensive tract, comprising from fifteen to sixteen thousand acres, has lately been enclosed. The Leicestershire and Rut-

LEICESTERSHIRE.

DERBYSHIRE

NOTTINGHAMSHIRE

LINCOLNSHIRE

RUTLANDSHIRE

NORTHAMPTONSHIRE

WARWICKSHIRE

CHARNWOOD

landshire Agricultural Society holds its annual meetings at Leicester another agricultural society meets at Oakham in Rutlandshire, and at Melton-Mowbray, alternately This county has long enjoyed pre-eminence in the annals of hunting Melton-Mowbray is the residence of a large number of the nobility and gentry during the season , many houses being let furnished for their accommodation, and in the town there is stabling for several hundred horses

The mineral products of Leicestershire are iron-stone, lead, coal, slate, limestone, and freestone Iron-stone is plentifully found upon Ashby Wolds, and has been smelted and cast into pigs and utensils for various purposes, at the works by the side of the Ashby canal the stone is found at from five to eight yards from the surface, mixed with twice its own quantity of a kind of blue marl rubbish A rich lead-ore is found in the fissures of the limestone obtained at Staunton-Harold, and is smelted There are coal mines at Cole-Orton, at the Lount, and Ashby Wolds the works at the two former places are ancient , those at the latter were established, about the commencement of the present century, by the late Marquis of Hastings, at a great expense, the coal being raised from a depth of nearly two hundred yards , the stratum is nine feet in thickness and of good quality At Swithland, to the east of Charnwood Forest, are raised large quantities of rather thick and heavy slate, which, however, is firm and durable, and is much used for roofing houses, and some of the thicker blocks for grave-stones and the purposes of building The Bredon limestone quarries are excavated in an isolated rock of considerable extent, which has a slight covering of earth there are lime-works very similarly situated at Cloud hill in the same neighbourhood At Barrow upon Soar is dug the stone from which is burned the famous Barrow lime, which is in such high request, more especially as a cement in the construction of works under water, it being carried for that purpose to a very great distance lime from these kilns was used in constructing the pier at Ramsgate, when other mortar had failed Between the stratum of stone and the surface are three or four yards of waste, the expense of removing which increases the price of the lime in the fissures of this limestone rock are found many curious fossil petrifactions Freestone exists in most parts of the county, as does also clay suitable for brick. The red granite from the rocks at Mount Sorrel furnishes a valuable material for Macadamizing the· roads

The principal manufactures are, woollen yarn, worsted, and stockings, which afford employment to many persons not only in Leicester, Hinckley, and other towns, but also in the principal villages throughout most parts of the county indeed the number of persons employed in trade here is to those employed in agriculture nearly as seven to four, and of these a very large proportion is employed in the manufacture of wool into stockings, principally at Leicester, Hinckley, and Loughborough, both for the London market and exportation At Loughborough, Hinckley, and Ashby, many hats are manufactured The manufacture of machine lace has been established here of late years, and is carried on to a considerable extent, principally in the towns and neighbourhoods of Loughborough, Leicester, and Ashby At Leicester and Loughborough are several malt-kilns A large quan-

tity of raw wool is sent into Yorkshire Several persons are engaged in the making of malt at Leicester and Loughborough Cheese is a considerable article of exportation, it being computed that not less than one thousand five hundred tons are annually conveyed down the Trent, for the use of the metropolis and the navy Numerous cattle, fattened in this county, are sold for London, Birmingham, and the populous parts of Staffordshire large quantities of sheep, bred here, are also fattened and sold to be forwarded to London or Birmingham , and others, not fully fattened, are sold to the farmers of the adjacent counties

The most important river in Leicestershire is the Soar which rises between Hinckley and Lutterworth, and flows northward by the towns of Leicester, Mount-Sorrel, and Loughborough, receiving the waters of numerous smaller streams, the principal of which is the Wreke passing near Dishley, during the latter part of its course, it forms the boundary between this county and Nottinghamshire for a distance of upwards of five miles, and at last falls into the Trent, near Sawley in Derbyshire This river, with the aid of different artificial cuts, has been made navigable from the Trent up to several miles above Leicester, a distance of upwards of twenty miles The small river Wreke rises in the eastern part of the county, and passing by Melton-Mowbray, falls into the Soar above Mount-Sorrel The river Trent bounds this county for the distance of between five and six miles at its north-western extremity, separating it from Derbyshire The river Avon, for some distance near its source, forms the boundary between the southernmost point of Leicestershire and Northamptonshire , and these counties, further to the east, are separated by the Welland, which rises near Market-Harborough, by which town it passes, and quits the county near Rockingham The little river Anker rises in the western part of the county, which it soon quits for Warwickshire, as does also the Swift, which flows by Lutterworth. The Ashby canal was first designed to communicate with the navigable channel of the Trent, below Burton, and with that view was constructed so as to be capable of floating barges of sixty tons burden, but the money which had been subscribed, amounting to £180,000, having been expended, the line from Ashby to the Trent, on which are a tunnel and several locks, was abandoned, and railways substituted upon the high grounds This canal is navigable from Ashby Wolds to the Coventry canal, in which it terminates, being near thirty miles in length, and cut on a level, without any lockage , it is navigated by boats of from twenty to twenty-four tons burden, being such only as can float on the Coventry canal , on Ashby Wolds is a reservoir that supplies it with water The line of the Leicester navigation is down the valley of the Soar, to the Trent, being sometimes along the channel of the Soar, and at others carried from it, by means of locks, into a new channel it is upwards of twenty miles in length, and is made so as to admit of being navigated by the Trent barges There is a collateral branch to Loughborough, which is continued over a portion of Charnwood Forest, partly by canal and partly by railway, to Cole-Orton colliery and the Cloud-hill limeworks this continuation, however, is now out of use, by reason of the coal from Derbyshire being obtained at a cheaper rate at the Leicester and Loughborough markets than that which was brought along this line The Melton canal is carried from the Leicester Soar navigation, along the valley of the Wreke, to Melton-Mowbray, whence it has been continued to Oakham The Grantham canal, from the Trent below Nottingham to Grantham, passes through the north-easternmost portion of this county, and is of great advantage to the vale of Belvoir, where there is a large reservoir for its supply The Union canal, from the navigable channel of the Soar, near Leicester, was designed to pass by way of Harborough, and join the Nene at Northampton, and also to communicate with the Grand Junction canal its progress towards completion was however arrested by untoward circumstances The iron railways attached to the Ashby canal extend about twelve miles from that navigation, by the town of Ashby, to the Lount colliery, Cole-Orton, Ticknall, and the Cloud hill lime-works On these railways, the construction of which cost £30,000, are various embankments, and deep cuttings, for the purpose of preserving the level, or an uniform ascent or descent, besides a tunnel of about a quarter of a mile long Pursuant to an act of parliament, obtained in 1830, a rail road is about to be commenced, extending in a direct line from Leicester to Swannington, &c

The great road from London to Manchester enters this county, from Northamptonshire, about eighty-three miles from London, at the bridge on the Welland, and passing through Market-Harborough, Mount-Sorrel, and Loughborough, quits the county for Derbyshire at Cavendish bridge, on the Trent The great road from London to Nottingham, Sheffield, and Leeds, branches off from the former at Loughborough, and quits the county for Nottinghamshire at the distance of about five miles from that town The Leeds mail road from London enters the county from Rutlandshire, about two miles south of Burton Lazars, and passes through Melton-Mowbray to Nether Broughton, between which and Over Broughton it enters Nottinghamshire

The ancient Watling-street first touches Leicestershire at Dove bridge, on the Avon, whence it proceeds in a north-easterly direction to the Anker, near Mancetter, not far from Atherstone, where it wholly quits the county for Warwickshire, after having formed the south-western boundary of Leicestershire for a distance of upwards of twenty miles The Fosse-road, from Lincolnshire, enters this county near the Roman station *Vernometum*, whence it proceeds by Segg s hill, over Thrussington Wolds, across the Wreke near Syston, and through Thurmaston to Leicester, whence it is continued over King Richard's bridge, having passed which, it turns to the left, over the second branch of the Soar, to the Narborough turnpike-road, along which it continues to the fourth milestone , then leaving it and the town and church of Narborough on the left, it continues to High Cross on the Watling-street The *Via Devana*, from Colchester to Chester, enters this county near Cottingham, and, crossing the Welland, passes Medbourne, near Slanston Mill, whence it is continued between the two Strettons to Leicester, where it joins the Fosse, which, however, it soon leaves to proceed to Grooby, whence it is carried by Ashby to Burton upon Trent The Fosse-way may be distinctly traced, more particularly on the eastern side of the county, and near the village of Narborough The *Via Devana* is visible on the hill

between the parishes of Cranoe and Glooston, and in different other parts of its course. Another ancient road, which the Rev T Leman, in his account of the Roman roads and stations in Leicestershire, calls the "Salt-Way," and considers of British origin, entered this county from Lincolnshire, in its way to the great saltworks at Droitwich after passing by Croxton, on the north-eastern border of the county, it continued to Segg s hill, and crossing the Fosse, proceeded to Barrow, its course being afterwards seen in some places in Charnwood Forest The Roman stations within the limits of this county were, *Ratæ*, or *Ratiscorion*, at Leicester , *Vernometum*, on the northern border, supposed to have been at Burrough hill, or near Willoughby, and *Benonæ*, near High Cross, besides which there was the celebrated one of *Manduessedum*, now Mancetter, situated on the Watling-street, on the borders of this county and Warwickshire The principal remains of Roman buildings have been found at Leicester , other miscellaneous Roman remains have been discovered at Rothley, Wanlip, Harborough, Burrough, and Calthorpe The most remarkable ancient churches are, St Mary s, Leicester, and those of Bottesford, Hinckley, and Melton-Mowbray, to which class of antiquities may be added, the chapel of Market-Harborough The religious houses, considered with regard to the dimensions of the county, were very numerous , including three colleges, six hospitals, three preceptories of the Knights Hospitallers, and one Alien priory, they amounted to thirty one the remains of monastic buildings are few and small , the principal are those of the abbey of St Mary de Pratis, near Leicester, those of Ulvescroft priory, and those of Grace Dieu nunnery This county comprises but few remains of ancient castles there are the picturesque ruins of the castellated mansion of Ashby, the most ancient portions of which are of the reign of Edward IV , and of Kirby castle Among the numerous elegant seats which adorn the county the most magnificent are, Belvoir castle, the seat of the Duke of Rutland, and Donnington park, that of the Marquis of Hastings There are medicinal springs at Ashby de la Zouch, Burton-Lazars Dalby on the Wolds, Gumley, Neville-Holt, Leicester, and Sapcote the baths at the first of these places constitute a fine Doric edifice, erected within the last six years the water is strongly impregnated with muriate of soda, containing, by ten or twelve degrees, more salt than sea water, and serviceable in rheumatic complaints

LEIGH, a tything in the parish of WIMBORNE-MINSTER, hundred of BADBURY, Shaston (East) division of the county of DORSET, 1 mile (E) from Wimborne-Minster, containing 358 inhabitants There was anciently a chapel here

LEIGH, a chapelry in the parish and hundred of YETMINSTER, Sherborne division of the county of DORSET, 6½ miles (S by W) from Sherborne, containing 343 inhabitants

LEIGH, a parish and sea port in the hundred of ROCHFORD, county of ESSEX, 17½ miles (S E by S) from Chelmsford, containing 905 inhabitants The living is a rectory, in the archdeaconry of Essex, and diocese of London, rated in the king s books at £15, and in the patronage of the Bishop of London The church is dedicated to St Clement There is a place of worship for Wesleyan Methodists This parish borders upon the Thames, and includes an island called Leigh

Marsh, with the east end of Canvey island, and the famous oyster creek there   In a hollow near the Thames is a small custom-house   About the year 1765, a quantity of Roman coins was discovered, on the fall of a cliff after heavy rain

LEIGH, a parish comprising the hamlet of Evington, in the lower division of the hundred of WESTMINSTER, but chiefly in the lower division of the hundred of DEERHURST, county of GLOUCESTER, 5½ miles (N N E) from Gloucester, and containing 340 inhabitants   The living is a discharged vicarage, in the jurisdiction of the peculiar court of Deerhurst, within which, however, no ecclesiastical authority is exercised, the parishes being virtually in the archdeaconry and diocese of Gloucester, it is rated in the king s books at £7 16 3, and in the patronage of the Crown   The church is dedicated to St James   The navigable river Severn and the Coombe Hill canal pass through the parish

LEIGH, a parish partly in the hundred of SOMERDEN, but chiefly in that of CODSHEATH, lathe of SUTTON at HONE, county of KENT, 3¾ miles (W) from Tunbridge, containing 876 inhabitants   The living is a vicarage, in the archdeaconry and diocese of Rochester, rated in the king s books at £9 18 9   The Rev Nathaniel May was patron in 1811   The church, dedicated to St Mary, contains some ancient monuments, and considerable remains of richly-stained glass   it had formerly a chantry, which was suppressed by Edward VI   The river Medway bounds the parish on the south, and there are mineral springs possessing properties similar to the water of Tunbridge Wells   A fair for pedlary is held on July 25th

LEIGH, a parish in the hundred of WEST DERBY, county palatine of LANCASTER, containing 18,372 inhabitants, and comprising the chapelries of Astley and Atherton, and the townships of Bedford, Tyldesley, Pennington, and West Leigh, the two latter including the market town of Leigh, 46 miles (S S E) from Lancaster, and 197 (N W) from London, the population of the town of Leigh being included in the return for the respective townships   The name of this place is pure Saxon, and synonimous with the English word Lea, a field or pasture   The manufacture of cambric-muslins and fustians is carried on, that of the former being the more considerable, and the general trade of the place has much improved of late years, chiefly in consequence of advantages derived from a branch of the Duke of Bridgewater's canal, which here forms a junction with the Leeds and Liverpool canal   Packet-boats, for passengers from Liverpool to Manchester, pass by this place every day   Coal and limestone are found in the parish, the latter, when burnt, is used in making a very excellent cement, which is impervious to water   The market is on Saturday, and fairs are held on the 24th and 25th of April, and on the 7th and 8th of December, for cattle, pigs, pedlary, &c   A court baron for the manor of Pennington, and a court for the manor of West Leigh, are held here annually by their respective lords, as are also the petty sessions for the Warrington division of the hundred of West Derby   The living is a discharged vicarage, in the archdeaconry and diocese of Chester, rated in the king s books at £9, endowed with £200 private benefaction, and £200 royal bounty, and in the patronage of Lord Lilford

The church, dedicated to St Mary, is an ancient stone edifice, consisting of a nave, chancel, and two side aisles, terminating in sepulchral chapels   There are places of worship for Independents, Wesleyan Methodists, Swedenborgians, and Roman Catholics   The free grammar school is of uncertain foundation, but was endowed, in 1655, by Piers Rancars, with a rent-charge of £5, in 1681, by Richard Bradshaw, with £6 per annum, which, with subsequent grants, produce an annual income of £25   there are seven free scholars, and the master has a dwelling-house rent-free   Upwards of one thousand children receive instruction in the various Sunday schools in this town   Several sums have been given, by charitable individuals, for distribution among the poor   The manufactures of Lancashire are eminently indebted to the ingenuity of Thomas Highs, a reed maker at this place, who, in 1764, constructed the first spinning-jenny, and, in 1767, invented the water-frame, which was afterwards improved and extensively introduced by Sir Richard Arkwright

LEIGH, a tything in the parish of PITMINSTER hundred of TAUNTON and TAUNTON-DEAN, county of SOMERSET, 4 miles (S S W) from Taunton   The population is returned with the parish   There is a place of worship for Wesleyan Methodists

LEIGH, a parish in the southern division of the hundred of TOTMONSLOW, county of STAFFORD, 5¾ miles (W N W) from Uttoxeter, containing, with the township of Field, 1019 inhabitants   The living is a rectory, in the archdeaconry of Stafford, and diocese of Lichfield and Coventry, rated in the king s books at £14 0 5, and in the patronage of Lord Bagot   The church, dedicated to All Saints, is an ancient cruciform structure   Stephen Spencer, in 1620, gave land now producing an annual income of £66, for the maintenance of a schoolmaster, who instructs about fifty-five free children

LEIGH, a parish in the first division of the hundred of REIGATE, county of SURREY, 3½ miles (S W) from Reigate, containing 453 inhabitants   The living is a rectory, in the archdeaconry of Surrey, and diocese of Winchester, rated in the king s books at £15 10 5, endowed with £1200 private benefaction, £200 royal bounty, and £1500 parliamentary grant, and in the patronage of R C Dendy, Esq   The church is dedicated to St Bartholomew

LEIGH, a chapelry in the parish of ASHTON-KEYNES, hundred of HIGHWORTH, CRICKLADE, and STAPLE, county of WILTS, 3¼ miles (W by S) from Cricklade, containing 263 inhabitants

LEIGH, a parish in the lower division of the hundred of PERSHORE, county of WORCESTER, 5 miles (W by S) from Worcester, containing, with the whole of the chapelry of Bransford, which is partly in the parish of Powick, 1810 inhabitants   The living is a rectory, in the archdeaconry and diocese of Worcester, rated in the king s books at £13 9 4½, and in the patronage of Earl Somers   The church is dedicated to St Edburgh

LEIGH (ABBOT'S), a parish in the hundred of PORTBURY, county of SOMERSET, 3¼ miles (W N W) from Bristol, containing 317 inhabitants   The living is a perpetual curacy, annexed to the vicarage of Bedminster, in the archdeaconry of Bath, and diocese of Bath and Wells   The church is dedicated to the Holy Trinity   This place formerly belonged to the abbot of St Augustine in Bristol, from which circumstance it derived its prefix After the battle of Worcester, Charles II was concealed in the old manor-house, which has since been replaced by an elegant mansion, called Leigh Court, commanding fine views of the Bristol channel, Gloucestershire, and the Welch hills

LEIGH (HIGH), a chapelry in that part of the parish of ROSTHERN which is in the hundred of BUCKLOW, county palatine of CHESTER, 5 miles (N W) from Knutsford, containing 854 inhabitants The living is a perpetual curacy, in the archdeaconry and diocese of Chester, endowed with £1000 private benefaction, and £3300 parliamentary grant Egerton Leigh, Esq was patron in 1826 A school-house was built, at the expense of the inhabitants, in 1717, for the use of poor children of the parish

LEIGH (LITTLE), a chapelry in that part of the parish of GREAT BUDWORTH which is in the hundred of BUCKLOW, county palatine of CHESTER, 3½ miles (N W by W) from Northwich, containing 359 inhabitants The living is a perpetual curacy, in the archdeaconry and diocese of Chester, endowed with £200 private benefaction, and £800 royal bounty, and in the patronage of the Vicar of Great Budworth The chapel is an ancient building, repaired in 1664 by the inhabitants, with the assistance of a small sum from the parishioners at large Here is a place of worship for Baptists There are some trifling donations for the education of children The Grand Trunk canal passes in the vicinity

LEIGH upon MENDIP, a parish in the hundred of MELLS and LEIGH, county of SOMERSET, 5½ miles (W) from Frome, containing 666 inhabitants The living is a perpetual curacy, annexed to the rectory of Mells, in the archdeaconry of Wells, and diocese of Bath and Wells The church is dedicated to St Giles

LEIGH de la MERE, a parish in the hundred of CHIPPENHAM, county of WILTS, 4¾ miles (N N W) from Chippenham, containing 125 inhabitants The living is a rectory, in the archdeaconry of Wilts, and diocese of Salisbury, rated in the king's books at £8 H C Vince, Esq was patron in 1786 The church is dedicated to St. Margaret. At this place Alfred encamped on the night before his attack upon the Danes at Edindon, and on Clay hill, in the neighbourhood, is a circular double-intrenched camp, to which the Danes fled, and there withstood a siege of fourteen days Near a field, called Courtfield, is a garden surrounded by a moat, supposed to be the site of a palace of one of the Saxon kings.

LEIGH (NORTH), a parish in the hundred of COLYTON, county of DEVON, 3¾ miles (W N W) from Colyton, containing 214 inhabitants The living is a rectory, in the archdeaconry and diocese of Exeter, rated in the king s books at £10 9 7 James Jenkins, Esq was patron in 1797 A small Sunday school has been endowed by the Rev Mr How

LEIGH (NORTH), a parish in the hundred of WOOTTON, county of OXFORD, 3¼ miles (N E by N) from Witney, containing 592 inhabitants The living is a discharged vicarage, in the archdeaconry and diocese of Oxford, rated in the king s books at £9 2, and in the patronage of the Crown The church is dedicated to St Mary There is a place of worship for Wesleyan Methodists Ann Perrott, in 1788, bequeathed a small sum for the education of seven children

LEIGH (SOUTH), a parish in the hundred of COLYTON, county of DEVON, 2¾ miles (W by S) from Colyton, containing 327 inhabitants The living is a rectory, in the archdeaconry and diocese of Exeter, rated in the king s books at £11 8 9 Charles Gorden, Esq was patron in 1825 The church is dedicated to St Lawrence The Rev James How, in 1816, gave £200 stock towards the support of a Sunday school, the dividends arising from which are applied to that purpose.

LEIGH (SOUTH), a chapelry in the parish of STANTON-HARCOURT, hundred of WOOTTON, county of OXFORD, 2¾ miles (E S E) from Witney, containing 316 inhabitants The chapel is dedicated to St James

LEIGH (WEST), a parish in the hundred of FREMINGTON, county of DEVON, 2½ miles (N E by N) from Bideford, containing 452 inhabitants The living is a discharged vicarage, in the archdeaconry of Barnstaple, and diocese of Exeter, rated in the king s books at £8 2 1, and in the patronage of the Dean and Chapter of Exeter

LEIGH-WOOLEY, a tything in the parish of GREAT BRADFORD, hundred of BRADFORD, county of WILTS, containing 1569 inhabitants

LEIGHLAND, a chapelry in the parish of OLD CLEEVE, hundred of WILLITON and FREEMANNERS, county of SOMERSET, 5 miles (S W by S) from Watchet. The population is returned with the parish The living is a perpetual curacy, in the archdeaconry of Taunton, and diocese of Bath and Wells, endowed with £200 private benefaction, £600 royal bounty, and £200 parliamentary grant, and in the patronage of the Vicar of Old Cleeve. The church is dedicated to St Giles

LEIGHS (GREAT), a parish partly in the hundred of CHELMSFORD, but chiefly in that of WITHAM, county of ESSEX, 5½ miles (S S W) from Braintree, containing, with the hamlet of Chatley, 667 inhabitants The living is a rectory, in the archdeaconry of Essex, and diocese of London, rated in the king's books at £25 7 1, and in the patronage of the Rector and Fellows of Lincoln College, Oxford. The church, dedicated to St Mary, has at the west end an ancient circular tower of flint and stone

LEIGHS (LITTLE), a parish in the hundred of CHELMSFORD, county of ESSEX, 5¼ miles (S W by S) from Braintree, containing 160 inhabitants The living is a rectory, in the archdeaconry of Essex, and diocese of London, rated in the king's books at £9 Lord and Lady Olmins were patrons in 1795 The church is dedicated to St John the Evangelist A priory of Black canons, in honour of the Blessed Virgin Mary and St John the Evangelist, was founded here, in the reign of Henry III, the revenue of which, at the dissolution, was estimated at £141 14 8 the gate-house, which still remains, is in the later style of English architecture

LEIGHTERTON, a chapelry in the parish of BOXWELL, upper division of the hundred of GRUMBALD'S ASH, county of GLOUCESTER, 4½ miles (W S W) from Tetbury The population is returned with the parish

LEIGHTON, a township in the parish and hundred of NANTWICH, county palatine of CHESTER, 3¾ miles (N E by N) from Nantwich, containing 270 inhabitants

LEIGHTON, a township in the parish of NESTON,

higher division of the hundred of WIRRALL, county palatine of CHESTER, 1 mile (N E) from Parkgate, containing 404 inhabitants

LEIGHTON, a parish in the hundred of LEIGHTONSTONE, county of HUNTINGDON, 5½ miles (N by E) from Kimbolton, containing 446 inhabitants The living is a discharged vicarage, in the peculiar jurisdiction and patronage of the Prebendary of Leighton in the Cathedral Church of Lincoln, rated in the king s books at £7 The church is dedicated to St. Mary

LEIGHTON, a parish in the Wellington division of the hundred of BRADFORD (South), county of SALOP, 5¼ miles (N by W) from Much Wenlock, containing 375 inhabitants The living is a discharged vicarage, in the archdeaconry of Salop, and diocese of Lichfield and Coventry, rated in the king's books at £7 12 6, endowed with £200 private benefaction, and £200 royal bounty Miss Maddocks was patroness in 1816 The church is dedicated to St. Mary

LEIGHTON-BUZZARD, a parish in the hundred of MANSHEAD, county of BEDFORD, comprising the market town of Leighton-Buzzard, and the chapelries of Billington, Eggington, Heath with Reach, and Standbridge, and containing 4421 inhabitants, of which number, 2749 are in the town of Leighton-Buzzard, 20 miles (W S W) from Bedford, and 42 (N W) from London The adjunct to the name is either derived from *Bosard*, the name of a family in the county, who were knights of the shire in the reign of Edward III, or from *Beau desert*, the prevailing opinion being in favour of the latter It is believed to be the *Lygean burgh* of the Saxon Chronicle, which was taken from the ancient Britons in 571, by Cuthwulph, the brother of Ceawlin, King of Wessex The town is situated on the eastern bank of the river Ouse, and consists of one wide street branching off to the right and left at its upper extremity, and neither paved nor lighted, the inhabitants are supplied with water from wells Near the markethouse is an ancient and elegant cross of pentagonal form, and in the later style of English architecture, the entire height, from the base to the top of the vane, is thirty-eight feet the upper story is divided into five niches, each of which contains a statue, the most perfect of which are a bishop, Christ and the Virgin, and St. John the Evangelist this structure, said to have been erected more than five hundred years, was repaired, in 1650, by means of a rate of fourpence levied upon each of the inhabitants

A considerable trade is carried on in timber, iron, lime, brick, corn, &c, and several females are employed in making lace and straw plat. The Grand Junction canal, which passes near the town, and is navigable for vessels of eighty tons, affords the means of communication with the northern counties The market, which is one of the oldest in the county, is on Tuesday, and is amply supplied with cattle, corn (which is toll-free), lace, straw-plat, &c Fairs are held, February 5th, the second Tuesday in April, Whit-Tuesday, July 26th, October 24th, and the second Tuesday in December, the first of these is remarkable for an extensive sale of horses The town is under the jurisdiction of the county magistrates, who meet on the market day, in a room over the market-house Courts leet and baron are held at Whitsuntide and Michaelmas, by the lessee of the manor, under the Dean and Canons of Windsor The living is a vicarage, in the peculiar jurisdiction and

patronage of the Prebendary of Leighton-Buzzard in the Cathedral Church of Lincoln, rated in the king s books at £15 The church, which is dedicated to All Saints, was formerly collegiate it is a large cruciform structure, principally in the early style of English architecture, with various additions and insertions of a later character, and has north, south, and west porches, together with a fine massive tower, surmounted by an octagonal stone spire, rising from the intersection the western door is a curious specimen of iron-work within the church are several ancient monuments, and a portion of good screen-work There are places of worship for Baptists, the Society of Friends, and Wesleyan Methodists A Lancasterian school, for an unlimited number of children of both sexes, is supported by voluntary contributions In 1704, the Hon Charles Leigh bequeathed a rent-charge of £10 for the education of ten poor boys this benefaction has been long discontinued; but instead of it a commodious brick building was erected, in 1790, at the expense of the Hon Mrs Leigh, for the use of a Sunday school, to which she also gave an annual donation of £20, the charity being further supported by subscription In 1630, almshouses for eight poor women were founded and endowed by Edward Wilkes, Esq, and an additional endowment was bequeathed by Matthew Wilkes, Esq, in 1692 the estates belonging to this charity produce about £200 per annum, from which the alms-women receive weekly stipends of four shillings each, besides money for firing and clothing, and the surplus is bestowed in premiums to poor children, on beginning their apprenticeship, or going to service In the time of Henry II there was an Alien priory at Grovebury, in this parish, subordinate to the abbey of Fontevralt in Normandy, also a house of Cistercian monks, a cell to Woburn abbey About half a mile from the town are the remains of an extensive circular camp, supposed to be of Roman origin.

LEINTHALL (EARLS), a chapelry in that part of the parish of AYMESTREY which is in the hundred of WIGMORE, county of HEREFORD, 7 miles (S W) from Ludlow The population is returned with the parish The living is a perpetual curacy, in the archdeaconry and diocese of Hereford, endowed with £600 royal bounty, and in the patronage of the Vicar of Aymestrey The church is dedicated to St Andrew A charity school here is endowed with about £9 a year, and a house and garden for the master There is also an almshouse

LEINTHALL-STARKES, a parish in the hundred of WIGMORE, county of HEREFORD, 6 miles (S W by W) from Ludlow, containing 131 inhabitants The living is a perpetual curacy, in the archdeaconry and diocese of Hereford, endowed with £1000 royal bounty, and £200 parliamentary grant, and in the patronage of the Bishop of Hereford The church is dedicated to St Mary Magdalene

LEINTWARDINE, a parish in the hundred of WIGMORE, county of HEREFORD, comprising the townships of Adforton, Brakes, Grange, Heath with Jay, Kinton, Leintwardine, Letton, Marlow, Newton, Payton, Walford, and Whitton with Trippleton, and containing 1277 inhabitants, of which number, 346 are in the township of Leintwardine, 9 miles (W by S) from Ludlow The living is a discharged vicarage, in the archdeaconry of Salop, and diocese of Hereford, rated in the king's books at £7 15 8, endowed with £200 private benefaction, and

£200 royal bounty, and in the patronage of the Rev D Winslow The church, dedicated to St Peter and St Paul, is a large structure, once famous for a profusion of stained glass, of which the windows still display some beautiful fragments, representing crowns, lions, fleurs de lis, the arms of Mortimer, &c Leintwardine is situated near the confluence of the Teme and the Clun, and from the quantity of fine fish, particularly graylings, with which these rivers abound, is much resorted to as a fishing-place There are quarries of limestone in the parish a fair is held on the 4th of April The Rt Hon Robert Harley, afterwards Earl of Oxford and Mortimer, founded, in the reign of Anne, a free school, and endowed it with land now producing an annual income of about £45 The ancient forest of Mocktree, which has been long disafforested, is in this parish

LEIRE, a parish in the hundred of GUTHLAXTON, county of LEICESTER, 4 miles (N N W) from Lutterworth, containing 435 inhabitants The living is a rectory, in the archdeaconry of Leicester, and diocese of Lincoln, rated in the king s books at £9 14 9½, and in the patronage of the Countess de Grey The church is dedicated to St Peter A school room has been erected by a subscription entered into by the parishioners, to celebrate the peace in 1814 it is a good brick building, covered with slate, and capable of accommodating seventy children Leire is in the honour of Tutbury, duchy of Lancaster, and within the jurisdiction of a court of pleas held at Tutbury every third Tuesday, for the recovery of debts under 40s

LEISTON, a parish in the hundred of BLYTHING, county of SUFFOLK, 4 miles (E by S) from Saxmundham, containing, with the hamlet of Sizewell, 954 inhabitants The living is a perpetual curacy in the archdeaconry of Suffolk, and diocese of Norwich, and in the alternate patronage of the Governors of Christ s Hospital, and the Master and Wardens of the Haberdashers Company, London The church is dedicated to St Margaret. An abbey of Premonstratensian canons, in honour of the Virgin Mary, was built and endowed by Ranulph de Glanvill, in 1182, the revenue of which, at the dissolution, was valued at £181 17 1

LELANT (UNY), a parish in the hundred of PENWITH, county of CORNWALL, 3 miles (S E) from St Ives, containing 1271 inhabitants The living is a vicarage, with the perpetual curacy of St Ives, in the archdeaconry of Cornwall, and diocese of Exeter, rated in the king s books at £22 11 10½, and in the patronage of the Bishop of Exeter The church, dedicated to St Ewny, is surrounded by banks of sand There are two places of worship for Wesleyan Methodists The parish is bounded on the north by St. Ives bay, and on the east by Hayle harbour and the river of that name, which is crossed by a bridge A considerable quantity of granite is raised here, and there are several tin mines in the neighbourhood, the principal of which are Wheal Reath and Wheal Speed A fair for cattle is held on August 15th

LELLEY, a township in the parish of PRESTON, middle division of the wapentake of HOLDERNESS, East riding of the county of YORK, 8 miles (E N E) from Kingston upon Hull, containing 119 inhabitants

LEMINGTON (LOWER), a parish in the upper division of the hundred of TEWKESBURY, though locally in the upper division of that of Westminster, county of GLOUCESTER, 2 miles (N E by N) from Moreton in the Marsh, containing 67 inhabitants The living is a perpetual curacy, in the archdeaconry and diocese of Gloucester, endowed with £200 private benefaction, and £600 royal bounty, and in the patronage of Lord Redesdale The ancient Fosse-way passes through this place, which seems to have been a Roman station, from the coins frequently discovered here

LEMMINGTON, a township in the parish of EDLINGHAM, northern division of COQUETDALE ward, county of NORTHUMBERLAND, 4¾ miles (W S W) from Alnwick, containing, with Battle-Bridge and Lemmington-Mills, 123 inhabitants

LENBOROUGH, a hamlet in the parish, hundred, and county of BUCKINGHAM, 2 miles (S) from Buckingham, containing 75 inhabitants

LENCH (ATCH), a hamlet in that part of the parish of CHURCH-LENCH which is in the lower division of the hundred of BLACKENHURST, county of WORCESTER, 5½ miles (N) from Evesham, containing 63 inhabitants

LENCH (CHURCH), a parish comprising the hamlets of Atch-Lench and Sheriff's Lench, in the lower division of the hundred of BLACKENHURST, and partly in the upper division of the hundred of HALFSHIRE, county of WORCESTER, 5¾ miles (N by W) from Evesham, and containing 342 inhabitants The living is a rectory, in the archdeaconry and diocese of Worcester, rated in the king s books at £9 11 10½, and in the patronage of the Crown There is a place of worship for Baptists

LENCH (ROUSE), a parish in the middle division of the hundred of OSWALDSLOW, county of WORCESTER, 7 miles (S W by W) from Alcester, containing 258 inhabitants The living is a rectory, in the archdeaconry and diocese of Worcester, rated in the king s books at £9 0 5, and in the patronage of Sir W E R Boughton, Bart The church is dedicated to St Peter

LENCH (SHERIFF'S), a hamlet in that part of the parish of CHURCH-LENCH which is in the lower division of the hundred of BLACKENHURST, county of WORCESTER, 4½ miles (N by W) from Evesham, containing 76 inhabitants

LENCH WICK, a chapelry in the parish of NORTON, lower division of the hundred of BLACKENHURST, county of WORCESTER, 2¼ miles (N) from Evesham The population is returned with the parish The chapel, which was dedicated to St Michael, has been demolished.

LENHAM, a parish in the hundred of EYHORNE, lathe of AYLESFORD, county of KENT, 10 miles (E by S) from Maidstone, containing 1959 inhabitants The living is a vicarage, in the archdeaconry and diocese of Canterbury, rated in the king s books at £13 15 2½ T F Best, Esq was patron in 1827 The church, dedicated to St Mary, is a handsome structure, having at the west end a tower steeple, containing a good set of chimes, in it are sixteen elegant stalls, a stone confessional, and other relics of antiquity There is a place of worship for Independents Lenham possesses a charter for a weekly market, but it has been long disused Fairs are held on June 6th and October 23rd, for horses and cattle John Foord, in 1766, founded a free school for ten poor boys, and endowed it with £300, which produces an income of about £12 per annum

LENTON, a parish in the southern division of the wapentake of BROXTOW, county of NOTTINGHAM, 1 mile (W S W) from Nottingham, containing 1240 inhabitants The living is a discharged vicarage, in the archdeaconry of Nottingham, and diocese of York, rated in the king's books at £9 2 5½, endowed with £400 royal bounty, and £200 parliamentary grant, and in the patronage of the Crown. The church is dedicated to the Holy Trinity The village of Lenton has recently increased in importance, several new streets, and many elegant mansions having been erected, and manufactories for lace and extensive bleaching-works established The Nottingham canal passes through the parish A fair for cattle, sheep, and hogs, is held on St Martin s day, and another on the Wednesday in Whitsun-week. The Peverel court, for the recovery of debts not exceeding £50, the jurisdiction of which extends over parts of the counties of Derby, Nottingham, and Stafford, is held here every Tuesday the charter for holding this court was granted by William the Conqueror to his son, William Peverel, and confirmed by others subsequently granted by Charles II and Anne the officers constituting the court are, a steward, deputy steward, and judge, prothonotary, and capital bailiff Here is a prison for debtors, of which the bailiff is gaoler There are some remains of a Cluniac priory, founded, in the reign of Henry I, by William Peverel, in honour of the Holy Trinity, it was subject to the great foreign abbey of Cluny, but, on the suppression of other Alien priories, the monks here procured it to be made denizen, and thus it survived till the general dissolution, when its revenue was estimated at £417 19 9 Here was also a house of Carmelite friars, and, in the church-yard, an hospital dedicated to St Anthony

LEOMINSTER, a parish in the hundred of WOI PHY, county of HEREFORD, comprising the borough of Leominster, having separate jurisdiction, the chapelry of Ivington, and the township of Broadward, and containing 4646 inhabitants, of which number, 3651 are in the borough of Leominster, 13½ miles (N) from Hereford, and 137 (W N W) from London

Seal and Arms.

This place, according to Leland, partly derives its name from a minster, or monastery, founded here by Merwald, King of West Mercia, about 660, and that Saxon prince is said to have had a castle, or palace, about half a mile eastward of the town A fortress was standing on the same spot in 1055, when it was seized by the Welch chieftains, and fortified At the time of the Norman survey, the manor, with its appurtenances, was assigned by Edward the Confessor to his queen, Editha in the reign of William Rufus, the fortifications were strengthened, to secure it against the incursions of the Welch in the reign of John, the town, priory, and church, were plundered and burned by William de Braose, Lord of Brecknock in the time of Henry IV it was in the possession of Owen Glyndwr, after he had defeated the Earl of March In the next century, the inhabitants of the town took a decisive part in the establishment of Mary on the throne, for which service she granted their first charter of incorporation, about the year 1554 The monastery founded by Merewald having been destroyed by the Danes, a college of prebendaries, and, subsequently, an abbey of nuns, were established here, but these institutions were destroyed previously to the time of Edward I, who endowed the abbey of Reading with the monastery of Leominster, to which it afterwards became a cell its revenue, at the dissolution, was £660 16 8

The town is situated in a rich and fertile valley, on the banks of the river Lugg, which bounds it to the north and east, the Kenwater and Pinsley, two smaller streams, passing through the town itself, and three other rivulets within half a mile the streets are indifferently paved and lighted, but considerable improvements are in contemplation several of the houses are in the ancient style of timber and brick, the beams being painted black, and ornamented with grotesque carvings, and the inhabitants are well supplied with water from springs A neat stone bridge has been lately erected across the Kenwater, at the estimated expense of £500, towards which, £100 was given by Lord Hotham, one of the representatives of the borough, and the remainder by the corporation There are, a public reading-room, or subscription library, and a theatre recently erected Near the town is a good race-course, where races are held about the end of August. An agricultural society holds its meetings here The manufactures chiefly consist of gloves and flannel the wool produced in the neighbourhood is proverbially excellent, and the cider and hops are held in high estimation. The market is on Friday, and fairs are held on February 13th, the Tuesday after Mid-Lent Sunday, May 2nd, July 10th, September 4th, and November 8th, to each of which is attached a court of pie-powder there is also a great market on the Friday after the 11th of December A neat market-house, for the sale of grain, was erected in 1803 The charter of incorporation received from Queen Mary was confirmed and extended by subsequent sovereigns, the last was by Charles II, in 1665, under which the corporation consists of a bailiff, chief steward, recorder, and twenty-four capital burgesses, with a chamberlain, town clerk, two serjeants at mace, and other officers the bailiff, the late bailiff, the recorder, and two aldermen elected annually by the corporation, are justices of the peace A court of record is held every Monday, before the bailiff, or two of the burgesses, for the reco very of debts to the amount of £100 within the borough, quarter sessions for the borough are held in January, April, July, and October, and petty sessions for the lower division of the hundred of Wolphy, are held here there is also a court leet annually This borough has sent two members to parliament since the 23rd of Edward I the right of election is vested in the bailiff, capital burgesses, and other inhabitants paying scot and lot the number of voters is about seven hundred, and the bailiff is the returning officer The town-hall, or butter-cross, is a singular building of timber and brick, supported by curiously-carved pillars of oak, it was built in 1633 A new gaol was erected in 1750

The living is a discharged vicarage, in the archdeaconry and diocese of Hereford, rated in the king s books at £10 3 8, endowed with £200 private benefaction, and £200 royal bounty, and in the patronage of the Crown The church, dedicated to St Peter and St Paul, is a spacious and irregular structure, exhibiting specimens of every style of Norman and English architecture the tower stands at the north-west angle, and with other parts of the western front, is of Norman character at the base, in the pointed style above, and embattled at the top the western doorway, which is extremely beautiful, is ornamented with pillars and receding arched mouldings, the windows are in the decorated and later English styles the massive pillars in the north aisle, supporting round arches surmounted by Norman arcades, are particularly curious The south side, which is modern, is appropriated to the performance of divine service the expense of its erection amounted to upwards of £16,000 the altar-piece is a painting of the Last Supper, from Rubens The length of the church within is one hundred and twenty-five feet, and its breadth one hundred and twenty-four feet There are places of worship for Baptists, the Society of Friends, Moravians, and Unitarians The free grammar school was founded by Queen Mary, and the master, who must be a member of one of the Universities, receives £20 per annum from the corporation There is a National school, for children of both sexes An almshouse for four poor widows was founded and endowed by Hester Clark, in 1735, the inmates of which receive £5 per annum each A spring has lately been discovered at the west end of the town, the water of which is impregnated with carbonate of soda, lime, and magnesia, and sulphate of lime, with sulphuretted hydrogen and iron, in minute proportions This place confers the title of baron upon the Earl of Pomfret, who styles himself Baron Lempster, that having been the ancient name of the town

LEOMINSTER, a parish in the hundred of POLING, rape of ARUNDEL, county of SUSSEX, 2 miles (S S E) from Arundel, containing, with the tything of Warningcamp, 675 inhabitants The living is a vicarage, annexed to that of Arundel, in the archdeaconry and diocese of Chichester, rated in the king's books at £9 1 3, and in the patronage of Eton College, on the nomination of the Bishop of Chichester The river Arun bounds the parish on the west A priory of Benedictine nuns, a cell to the nunnery of Almanesche in Normandy, was founded here by Roger de Montgomery, Earl of Arundel, in the time of William the Conqueror, and dedicated to St. Mary Magdalene, after the suppression of Alien houses, its possessions were granted by Henry VI to Eton College At Pynham, in this parish, was a priory of Black canons, founded by Adeliza, second wife of Henry I., and dedicated to St Bartholomew at its suppression, in the 17th of Henry VIII , its revenue, valued at £43, was given to Cardinal Wolsey, towards the endowment of his intended colleges

LEONARD (ST), a chapelry in the parish of ASTON-CLINTON, hundred of AYLESBURY, county of BUCKINGHAM, 3 miles (E by S) from Wendover, containing 185 inhabitants

LEONARD (ST), a parish in the hundred of WONFORD, county of DEVON, ½ a mile (S E) from Exeter, containing 206 inhabitants The living is a discharged rectory, in the archdeaconry and diocese of Exeter, rated in the king's books at £4 19 4½, endowed with

£200 private benefaction, and £200 royal bounty, and in the patronage of Sir Thomas Baring, Bart. In the churchyard there was formerly a hermitage, in which several females successively secluded themselves as anchorites The mansion called Mount Radford, erected in the sixteenth century, was garrisoned during the parliamentary war

LEONARD (ST), SHOREDITCH, county of MIDDLESEX.—See SHOREDITCH

LEPPINGTON, a chapelry in the parish of SCRAYINGHAM, wapentake of BUCKROSE, East riding of the county of YORK, 8 miles (S. by W) from New Malton, containing 129 inhabitants The living is a perpetual curacy, endowed with an estate vested in ten trustees, who appoint the minister The chapel was originally a chantry chapel belonging to the abbey of Missenden.

LEPTON, a township in the parish of KIRK-HEATON, upper division of the wapentake of AGBRIGG, West riding of the county of YORK, 4 miles (E by S) from Huddersfield, containing 2729 inhabitants A considerable quantity of woollen cloth, and some fancy goods, are manufactured here Richard Beaumont, Esq , in 1703, left £10 for apprenticing poor children

LESBURY, a parish comprising the townships of Alemouth, and Lesbury with Hawkhill, in the southern division of BAMBROUGH ward, and the townships of Bilton and Wooden, in the eastern division of COQUETDALE ward, county of NORTHUMBERLAND, and containing 982 inhabitants, of which number, 576 are in the joint township of Lesbury with Hawkhill, 4 miles (E by S) from Alnwick. The living is a discharged vicarage, in the archdeaconry of Northumberland, and diocese of Durham, rated in the king's books at £8 2 10 , and in the patronage of the Crown The church is dedicated to St Mary The river Alne is here crossed by a bridge, and discharges itself into the North sea at Alnmouth, where a great quantity of grain is shipped for London, and other markets A schoolroom and a house for the master have been given by the Duke of Northumberland, Mr Henry Strother having, in 1718, bequeathed a piece of land, now producing about £10 10 a year, for teaching poor children.

LESKEARD, county of CORNWALL — See LISKEARD

LESNEWTH, a parish in the hundred of LESNEWTH, county of CORNWALL, 5¼ miles (N by E) from Camelford, containing 123 inhabitants The living is a discharged rectory, in the archdeaconry of Cornwall, and diocese of Exeter, rated in the king's books at £8, and in the patronage of —— Glynn, Esq The church is dedicated to St Knet

LESSINGHAM, a parish in the hundred of HAPPING, county of NORFOLK, 7¼ miles (E by S) from North Walsham, containing 195 inhabitants The living is a discharged rectory, with that of Hempstead, in the archdeaconry of Norfolk, and diocese of Norwich, rated in the king's books at £6 The church is dedicated to All Saints Here is a small endowment for a school, bequeathed by Jonathan Challenor, in 1727 An Alien priory, subordinate to that of Okeburn in Wiltshire, the chief of all the houses in England belonging to the abbey of Bec in Normandy, was founded here in the time of William Rufus, and, at the suppression, was given to Eton College, but afterwards to King's College, Cambridge

LESSNESS, a chapelry in the parish of ERITH, hundred of LESSNESS, lathe of SUTTON at HONE, county of KENT, 2¼ miles (N N W) from Crayford   The population is returned with the parish   An abbey for Black canons, in honour of St Mary and St Thomas the Martyr, was founded here, in 1178, by Richard de Lucy, Chief Justice of England, and sometime regent of the kingdom, who assumed the habit, and shortly after died in this house, its revenue, at the dissolution, was estimated at £186 9, and the site was granted to Cardinal Wolsey, towards the endowment of his colleges   There is a place of worship for Baptists on Lessness heath

LETCHWORTH, a parish in the hundred of BROADWATER, county of HERTFORD, 2½ miles (N E by E) from Hitchin, containing 76 inhabitants   The living is a rectory, in the archdeaconry of Huntingdon, and diocese of Lincoln, rated in the king s books at £11 1 10½, and in the patronage of John Williamson, Esq

LETCOMB-BASSETT, a parish in the hundred of KINTBURY-EAGLE, county of BERKS, 3 miles (S W by S) from Wantage, containing 280 inhabitants   The living is a rectory, in the archdeaconry of Berks, and diocese of Salisbury, rated in the king s books at £15 0 2½, and in the patronage of the President and Fellows of Corpus Christi College, Oxford   The church is dedicated to All Saints   There is a place of worship for Wesleyan Methodists   The ancient Ikineld-street crosses the Vale of White Horse, in this parish   Dean Swift, during his residence at the rectory in 1714, wrote his pamphlet entitled "Free Thoughts on the Present State of Affairs,' but it was not printed till 1741

LETCOMB-REGIS, a parish in the hundred of KINTBURY-EAGLE, county of BERKS, 2 miles (S W by W) from Wantage, comprising the chapelries of East Challow and West Challow, and containing 800 inhabitants   The living is a discharged vicarage, in the archdeaconry of Berks, and diocese of Salisbury, rated in the king s books at £10 13 7, endowed with £300 private benefaction, and £200 royal bounty, and in the patronage of the Dean and Chapter of Winchester   The church is dedicated to St Andrew   Here is a school, endowed, in 1730, by George Fettiplace, with £8 per annum, for teaching twenty poor children to read   On the summit of the chalk hills to the south of the village is a very large quadrangular intrenchment, called Letcombe Castle, with single earth-works, about a mile north of which the Roman Ikineld-street crosses the Vale of White Horse   A branch of the river Ock, and the Wilts and Berks canal, also run through the parish

LETHERINGHAM, a parish in the hundred of LOES, county of SUFFOLK, 3 miles (N W) from Wickham-Market, containing 175 inhabitants   The living is a perpetual curacy, in the archdeaconry of Suffolk, and diocese of Norwich, endowed with £200 private benefaction, and £1200 royal bounty, and in the patronage of Mrs Sarah Reynolds   The church is dedicated to St Mary   The river Deben runs through the parish   Here was a small priory of Black canons, a cell to the monastery of St Peter in Ipswich   it was dedicated to the Blessed Virgin, and at the dissolution had a revenue of £26. 18 5   The remains have been converted into a farm-house

LETHERINGSETT, a parish in the hundred of

HOLT, county of NORFOLK, 1½ mile (W by N) from Holt, containing 251 inhabitants   The living is a discharged rectory, in the archdeaconry and diocese of Norwich, rated in the king s books at £12   Mrs Burrell and another were patrons in 1826   The church is dedicated to St Andrew   The river Glarvin runs through the village, and there is a brewery on its banks

LETTON, a parish comprising the township of Letton in the hundred of STRETFORD, and the township of Hurstley in the hundred of WOLPHY, county of HEREFORD, and containing 163 inhabitants, of which number, 95 are in the township of Letton, 6¾ miles (S W by W) from Weobly   The living is a rectory, in the archdeaconry and diocese of Hereford, rated in the king s books at £6 15 7½, and in the patronage of the Representatives of John Freeman, Esq   The church is dedicated to St. Peter

LETTON, a township in the parish of LEINTWARDINE, hundred of WIGMORE, county of HEREFORD, 5¾ miles (E S E) from Knighton, containing, with the townships of Newton and Walford, 208 inhabitants

LETTON, a parish in the hundred of MITFORD, county of NORFOLK, 5¼ miles (S by W) from East Dereham, containing 127 inhabitants   The living is a rectory, with that of Cranworth, in the archdeaconry of Norfolk, and diocese of Norwich, rated in the king s books at £7 14 7   The church is dedicated to All Saints

LETWELL, a chapelry in the parish of LAUGHTON en le MORTHEN, partly within the liberty of ST PETER of YORK, and partly in the southern division of the wapentake of STRAFFORTH and TICKHILL, West riding of the county of YORK, 5½ miles (S W by S) from Tickhill, containing 135 inhabitants   The living is a perpetual curacy, endowed with £1200 royal bounty, and in the peculiar jurisdiction and patronage of the Chancellor of the Cathedral Church of York   The church is dedicated to St Peter

LEVAN (ST), a parish in the hundred of PENWITH, county of CORNWALL, 9 miles (S W) from Penzance, containing 490 inhabitants   The living is a perpetual curacy, in the peculiar jurisdiction and patronage of the Rector of St Burian   Overhanging the sea, at the western extremity of the parish, are the celebrated rocks, or lofty piles of granite, called Castle Treryn, on the pointed summit of one of which the remarkable block, termed the Logan, or Rocking Stone, supposed to weigh about ninety tons, is so nicely balanced, as to be moved to and fro by a single individual   In 1820, though considered almost the greatest curiosity in Cornwall, some sailors dislodged this immense mass, and precipitated it into the abyss below, but this mischievous act exciting a general feeling of indignation throughout the country, steps were shortly afterwards successfully taken to replace it in its old position. There are a well, called St Levan's, and an ancient oratory in the parish

LEVEN, a parish comprising the townships of Hempholme and Leven, in the northern division of the wapentake of HOLDERNESS, East riding of the county of YORK, and containing 751 inhabitants, of which number, 658 are in the township of Leven, 7 miles (N E) from Beverley   The living is a rectory, in the archdeaconry and diocese of York, rated in the king s books at £16 13 4.   Sir William Pennyman, Bart was patron in 1815 The church is dedicated to St Faith There are places of worship for Independents and Wesleyan Methodists

LEVENS, a chapelry partly in the parish of HEVERSHAM, and partly in that of KENDAL, KENDAL ward, county of WESTMORLAND, 5½ miles (S S W) from Kendal, containing, with Beathwaite-Green, Sizergh-Fell side, and part of Brigsteer, 765 inhabitants A handsome chapel, with a low tower surmounted by an octagonal spire, was erected, in 1828, at an expense of £2000, defrayed by the Hon Fulk Greville Howard, who also built the parsonage-house, he appoints the minister, and allows him an annual stipend of £200 A school for forty poor girls was established, in 1810, by Lady Howard, who pays for their education, and partly clothes them Another school was erected, in 1825, by Colonel Howard, and is supported at his expense it is conducted on the Madras system, and is attended by about one hundred and forty children On the eastern bank of the river Kent, which is crossed by a bridge on the Kendal road, is Levens hall, the venerable mansion of the Howards, embosomed in a fine park, and crowned with towers, which, overtopping the highest trees, command extensive prospects on every side the entrance hall contains various relics of ancient armour One of the apartments is hung with splendid gobeline tapestry, and most of the other rooms are decorated with oak wainscoting exquisitely carved, and costly hangings of the richest colours In the park are the ruins of an ancient circular edifice, called Kirkstead, said to have been a Roman temple dedicated to Diana There is also a petrifying spring, termed the Dropping Well Levens Force is a celebrated waterfall of the river Kent An iron manufactory was established in the neighbourhood about the year 1750

LEVER (DARCY), a chapelry in the parish of BOLTON, hundred of SALFORD, county palatine of LANCASTER, 2½ miles (E by S) from Great Bolton, containing 956 inhabitants Coal is obtained here There is an aqueduct of three arches across the Irwell at this place

LEVER (GREAT), a township in the parish of MIDDLETON, hundred of SALFORD, county palatine of LANCASTER, 1½ mile (S) from Great Bolton, containing 631 inhabitants

LEVER (LITTLE) a chapelry in the parish of BOLTON le MOORS, hundred of SALFORD, county palatine of LANCASTER, 2¼ miles (E S E) from Great Bolton, containing 1854 inhabitants The living is a perpetual curacy, in the archdeaconry and diocese of Chester, endowed with £200 private benefaction, £800 royal bounty, and £1300 parliamentary grant, and in the patronage of the Vicar of Bolton The chapel is dedicated to St Matthew the Evangelist There is a place of worship for Wesleyan Methodists A school and a dwelling-house were erected, by subscription, in 1736, which are held by the schoolmaster, in consideration of his teaching six children free Coal is obtained here Lever hall, an ancient building within the chapelry, was formerly occupied by Bishop Bridgeman

LEVERINGTON, a parish in the hundred of WISBEACH, Isle of ELY, county of CAMBRIDGE, 2 miles (N W) from Wisbeach, containing, with the chapelry of Parson-Drove, 1523 inhabitants The living is a rectory, in the peculiar jurisdiction and patronage of the Bishop

of Ely, rated in the king's books at £25 0 7½ The church is dedicated to St Leonard and St John the Baptist There is a school for teaching poor children, endowed with £20 per annum, paid out of the produce of lands supposed to have belonged to the hospital of St John the Baptist, which existed here before the Reformation At Fitton, in this parish, there was, in 1389, a chantry chapel, dedicated to St Mary

LEVERSDALE, a township in the parish of IRTHINGTON, ESKDALE ward, county of CUMBERLAND, 7 miles (N E) from Carlisle, containing 450 inhabitants

LEVERTON, a parish in the wapentake of SKIRBECK, parts of HOLLAND, county of LINCOLN, 5¾ miles (N E by E) from Boston, containing 544 inhabitants The living is a discharged rectory, in the archdeaconry and diocese of Lincoln, rated in the king's books at £16 6, endowed with £200 private benefaction, and in the patronage of the Crown The church is dedicated to St Helen There is a place of worship for Wesleyan Methodists

LEVERTON, a tything in the parish of CHILTON-FOLIATT, hundred of KINWARDSTONE, county of WILTS, though locally in the hundred of Kintbury-Eagle, county of Berks, 1 mile (N) from Hungerford The population is returned with the parish

LEVERTON (NORTH), a parish in the North-clay division of the wapentake of BASSETLAW, county of NOTTINGHAM, 5½ miles (E by N) from East Retford, containing 300 inhabitants The living is a discharged vicarage, in the peculiar jurisdiction and patronage of the Prebendary of North Leverton in the Collegiate Church of Southwell, rated in the king's books at £5, and endowed with £200 royal bounty The church is dedicated to St Martin There is a place of worship for Wesleyan Methodists The river Trent, separating the counties of Nottingham and Lincoln, passes by the parish

LEVERTON (SOUTH), a parish in the North-clay division of the wapentake of BASSETLAW, county of NOTTINGHAM, 5¼ miles (E) from East Retford, containing, with the chapelry of Cottam, 374 inhabitants The living is a vicarage, in the archdeaconry of Nottingham, and diocese of York, rated in the king's books at £6 13 4, and in the patronage of the Dean of Lincoln The church is dedicated to All Saints There is a place of worship for Wesleyan Methodists The river Trent runs through the parish A free grammar school was founded, in 1691, by John Simpson, Esq, and endowed with a rent-charge of £20, and a house and garden for the master

LEVESDON, a hamlet in the parish of WATFORD, partly in the hundred of CASHIO, or liberty of St ALBAN's, and partly in the hundred of DACORUM, county of HERTFORD, 3 miles (N) from Watford, containing 404 inhabitants

LEVINGTON, a parish in the hundred of COLNEIS, county of SUFFOLK, 5¼ miles (S E) from Ipswich, containing 205 inhabitants The living is a discharged rectory, with that of Nacton, in the archdeaconry of Suffolk, and diocese of Norwich, rated in the king's books at £6 1 8 The church is dedicated to St Peter The navigable river Orwell runs along the southern boundary of the parish

LEVISHAM, a parish in PICKERING lythe, North riding of the county of YORK, 5½ miles (N N E) from

Pickering, containing 152 inhabitants The living is a discharged rectory, in the archdeaconry of Cleveland, and diocese of York, rated in the king's books at £7 8 1½ Mrs Skelton was patroness in 1818 John Poad, in 1783, devised an estate, after certain deductions, for the education of six poor children of this parish, and six of Lockton the income is £12 per annum

LEW, a hamlet in the parish of WITNEY, hundred of BAMPTON, county of OXFORD, 3¾ miles (S W) from Witney, containing 266 inhabitants

LEW (NORTH), a parish in the hundred of BLACK TORRINGTON, county of DEVON, 4 miles (S W by S) from Hatherleigh, containing 868 inhabitants The living is a rectory, in the archdeaconry of Totness, and diocese of Exeter, rated in the king's books at £27 8 9, and in the patronage of the Crown The church is dedicated to St Thomas à Becket At Redcliffe, within this parish, are the remains of an ancient chapel, and near it a quarry of excellent freestone

LEWANNICK, a parish in the northern division of EAST hundred, county of CORNWALL, 5 miles (S W by W) from Launceston, containing 623 inhabitants The living is a vicarage, in the archdeaconry of Cornwall, and diocese of Exeter, rated in the king's books at £7 18 9, and in the patronage of the Crown The church is dedicated to St Martin There is a place of worship for Wesleyan Methodists

LEWES, a borough and market town, chiefly in the hundred and rape of LEWES, county of SUSSEX, of which it is the chief town, 7 miles (N E by E) from Brighton, 38 (E by N) from Chichester, and 50 (S by E) from London, containing, with the parishes of St Thomas in the Cliffe and St John the Baptist Southover, the former in the hundred of RINGMER, and the latter in the hundred of SWANBOROUGH, 7083 inhabitants The most probable of the various etymologies assigned to Lewes, and which are respectively deduced from the Britons, Romans, and Saxons, seems to be that alluding to its peculiar situation, *Leau-Esc* (or *Lew-ys*, as it is engraved on the town seal), *Leau* meaning an arm, and *Isc*, or *Isca*, water, i e the arm (of land) in the water The remote origin of this town is proved by its being surrounded by earthworks, tumuli, &c, and the discovery of coins and other antiquities renders it probable that it was a Roman station, though the precise name appears uncertain It was very early a demesne of the crown, having appertained to the South Saxon kings, next to those of Wessex, and afterwards to the Saxon and Danish monarchs of all England During the Danish ravages, from the close of the eighth to the beginning of the eleventh century, Lewes was rendered, both by nature and art, the most eligible place of refuge for the inhabitants of the adjacent country In the reign of Athelstan it was so considerable, as to be allowed by that sovereign two mint-masters, and was then the chief town and market of half the shire A merchants' guild was established here so early as the reign of Edward the Confessor, on whose death

Seal and Arms.

the barony of Lewes devolved on Earl Harold, and was, on his defeat at Hastings, bestowed by William the Conqueror on his son-in-law, William de Warren, Earl of Surrey, who made it his chief residence, and rebuilt the castle, which is said to have been originally founded by Alfred the Great Henry III and his brother Richard, Earl of Cornwall, were confined in this fortress, after being taken prisoners in the great battle fought between the king and the barons under Simon Montfort, Earl of Leicester, in 1264, on an eminence adjoining the town A treaty, or convention, was subsequently concluded between the king and the insurgent barons which is distinguished in history by the appellation of the "Mise of Lewes"

The principal part of the town occupies a declivity on the western bank of the river Ouse, over which is a stone bridge of one arch, built in 1727, the former wooden bridge having been swept away by a flood, this river, being navigable from the sea to the distance of a few miles above the town, commands the trade of the surrounding district It is extensive and well built, and contains some good streets and many handsome houses, it is well paved, and lighted with gas, pursuant to an act of parliament obtained in 1806, under the direction of commissioners, and supplied with water for ordinary purposes by pumps or draw wells On the west side of the town is Southover, and on the east side of the river, under a lofty and impending chalk cliff, from which it receives its name, is the town of Cliff, the site of which is supposed to have been anciently covered by the sea About the year 1821, considerable improvement was made in the White Hill road, which passes through a valley near the town, by lowering the hill on each side, and filling up the valley with the materials, thus forming a causeway between thirty and forty feet high The environs extend to the South-Downs, a chain of chalk hills, rising like an amphitheatre to the mean elevation of about five hundred feet, and covered with the fine rich herbage which gives to the South-Down mutton its admired flavour There is a small theatre in West street The race-course is one of the finest four-mile courses in the kingdom, and has a commodious stand, erected in 1772 the races take place annually in March and August, the former, called Hunters' races, were established in 1828 , A book society was established in 1785, and now possesses several thousand volumes, many of them scarce works, and there is a Literary Society, consisting of about one hundred members, with a president, two vice presidents, a secretary, and an inspector, and a librarian they hold quarterly meetings, at which subscribers are balloted for, and are admitted on paying £6 6, and £1 5 annually A mechanics' institute was established in 1825 the building adjoins the theatre, and contains a reading-room, committee-room, and other apartments the society has a library of about seven hundred volumes, and a respectable philosophical apparatus The head office for stamps and legacy duties for the eastern district of Sussex, is at Lewes, and also the bishop's registrar-office for marriage licenses, probates of wills, letters of administration, &c, within the archdeaconry of Lewes The trade of the town, which was anciently very extensive in wool, at present consists principally of various kinds of grain and malt, and almost every species of the ordinary articles of consumption the latter are

imported at Newhaven, about seven miles off, and sent up the Ouse for the supply of the neighbouring parts There is also a paper manufactory Daily markets for provisions are established by act of parliament , that for corn is held every Tuesday, and for live stock every Tuesday fortnight the present market-house was completed in 1793, on a more convenient site There are five fairs , viz , May 8th, for cattle and pedlary, July 26th, for wool, Whit-Tuesday, for cattle, and September 21st, and October 2nd, for sheep, the number of which brought for sale at each of these fairs exceeds fifty thousand   A shew of fat cattle, takes place annually about Christmas   License was granted, in the 11th of Henry IV , for a market to be held at Cliff, on Wednesday, which has nearly fallen into disuse , and the fairs formerly held there, with the exception of a small fair for pedlary, are now held at Lewes

Lewes is a borough by prescription, having formerly had a separate shrievalty, but not incorporated   its principal officers are two constables and two headboroughs, who are chosen annually, by a jury of burgesses, at the court leet of the lord of the manor, which was anciently a regality, with separate jurisdiction extending to capital offences , but the town is now under the jurisdiction of the county magistrates   The summer and winter assizes for the county are held here, as are also the general quarter sessions for the eastern division of the county, which comprises the three rapes of Lewes, Pevensey, and Hastings   there are likewise adjourned annual sessions for the county at large   It has a sheriff's court for the recovery of debts under 40s , the jurisdiction of which extends over the three eastern rapes, but which has no power of imprisonment on non payment   The borough sends two members to parliament, who are elected by the inhabitant householders paying scot and lot, in number from six hundred to seven hundred   the constables are the returning officers   In 1812, a commodious and handsome assize hall was erected for the eastern district of the county, the expense of which, including the purchase of the ground and other property, was £15,500   it is eighty feet in length, and seventy-six in breadth, and comprises an extensive entrance-hall with record-rooms, a room for the petty sessions, two courts of judicature, civil and criminal, and a room for the judges and magistrates above these is a spacious and elegant room for the grand jury (which is occasionally used as a county ballroom), also a council-chamber and other apartments   In 1793, the house of correction for the eastern district was built, on Mr Howard's plan, to which a southern wing was added in 1817   it is well adapted to its purpose and contains a chapel and an infirmary , the southern wing is occupied by male, and the northern by female, prisoners   The prison contains seventy cells, each being nine feet by seven, of which fourteen are solitary   each division has five classes   There are two tread-mills for male prisoners , the females are employed in needle-work, &c   A constable and headborough for the adjoining parish of Cliff are chosen annually at the court leet of the Duke of Dorset

There were anciently eleven parish churches within the borough, but these nave been reduced to four   In the 37th of Henry VIII , the parishes of St Andrew, St Mary in Foro, St Martin, and St Michael, were united, and now form the parish of St Michael, the living of

which is a discharged rectory, with the rectory of St Andrew annexed, rated together in the king's books at £17 5 10 , endowed with £600 royal bounty, and £1000 parliamentary grant, and in the patronage of the Crown   The church, which was partially rebuilt and modernised in 1755, retains some portions of good later English architecture   it contains, among other mural monuments, a splendid one to the memory of Sir Nicholas Pelham, Knt , and Anne, his wife   St Anne's consists of the united parishes of St Peter within, and St Mary West-out, (the latter being without the borough boundaries, the line of demarcation passing through the chancel of the church of St Mary,) and that part of the parish which is westward of the borough, being within the hundred of Swanborough   Although the parochial church is dedicated to St. Anne, the parish, in all law proceedings, is denominated St Peter's and St Mary's West-out   The living is a discharged rectory, rated for both in the king's books at £19 13 6½ , and in the patronage of the Crown.   The church is ancient, being partly of Norman, and partly of early English, architecture   it contains a curious font   St John's under the Castle is a rectory, to which that of St Mary Magdalene was annexed in 1539, rated in the king's books at £3 11 3 , and in the patronage of the Rev Peter Crofts   Various parts of the church are of great antiquity, the nave resembling the Norman architecture of the castle, near which it stands, other portions of the structure are modern   in the churchyard are the remains of a monument ascribed to Magnus, son of Harold II , with an inscription chiefly in Anglo-Saxon characters   This parish extends beyond the boundaries of the borough, into the hundred of Swanborough, and is intersected by a part of the parish of Hamsey   The living of All Saints is a discharged rectory, rated in the king's books at £7, endowed with £400 private benefaction, £600 royal bounty, and £1200 parliamentary grant, and in the patronage of Charles Goring, Esq   The church, with the exception of the steeple, which is of later English character, was begun in 1805, on the union of the parishes of the Holy Trinity, St Peter the Less, and St Nicholas   All the preceding parishes are in the archdeaconry of Lewes, and diocese of Chichester   The precinct of the castle is extra-parochial, and is not rateable within the borough, nor subject to any ecclesiastical jurisdiction.   There are places of worship for the Society of Friends, Independents, Wesleyan Methodists, and Unitarians

The parishes of St Thomas in the Cliff, and St John, Southover, although without the limits of the borough, may be considered as forming part of the town of Lewes   The living of St Thomas's is a discharged rectory, in the peculiar jurisdiction and patronage of the Archbishop of Canterbury, rated in the king's books at £5 12 6 , endowed with £200 private benefaction, £200 royal bounty, and £800 parliamentary grant   The church, dedicated to St Thomas à Becket, contains a fine altar-piece, also an organ of superior workmanship, formerly in the chapel of the Duke of Chandos   Baptists, Independents, and Huntingtonians, have each a place of worship in this parish   William Huntington, the founder of the last sect, was interred here   The living of the parish of St John, Southover, is a discharged rectory, in the archdeaconry of

Lewes, and diocese of Chichester, rated in the king's books at £6 12, endowed with £600 royal bounty, and £800 parliamentary grant, and in the patronage of the Crown The church, dedicated to St John the Baptist, is a spacious edifice in 1698 the old steeple fell down, and the present square tower was begun in 1714, but the progress of its erection having ceased for some years, it was not completed before 1738 In ancient records Southover is called a borough, having enjoyed a separate jurisdiction The manor was an appendage of the monastery, on the dissolution of which it came into the possession of the crown, and was given to Cromwell after his attainder it again reverted to the crown, and was granted by Henry VIII to his divorced queen, Anne of Cleves, who, according to tradition, took up her residence here, in a very ancient building situated on the south side of the street There is a place of worship in Southover for General Baptists

The free grammar school was founded originally at Southover, by Agnes Morley, in 1512, who endowed it with a rent-charge of £20, vested in trustees, together with a house and garden, for a master and an usher this endowment was subsequently increased by various legacies, particularly that of Mrs Mary Jenkins, in 1709, who left a house, gardens, and appurtenances for the master, and the sum of £1533 16 1 for providing instruction for whatever number of boys the trustees should think fit, the present number being twelve the school was removed into St Anne s parish in 1714 Belonging to the borough is an exhibition to either University for four years, left by the Rev George Steere, "to a poor scholar, the son of parents residing in or near Lewes," the annual value of which is about £35 the scholar is chosen by the constables and four of the most respectable inhabitants in succession Sir John Evelyn, author of "Sylva, and John Pell, the celebrated mathematician, were educated here There is also a school for boys and girls, supported by voluntary subscriptions, and schools for infants of both sexes are supported in like manner A bank for savings was established in 1816

There are many interesting antiquities in and near Lewes The *Castra*, or earth works, still remaining on the summits of the Downs, may be reckoned amongst those of most remote date, but of what precise period it is difficult to determine tumuli are also scattered in various parts, in which have been found skeletons, urns, ashes, amber beads, and occasionally warlike instruments The numerous Roman coins found round the town, even of late years, form nearly a regular series from Tiberius to Constantine, Constans, and Magnentius , and a Roman ford has been discovered at Glynde The castle is supposed to have been originally erected by Alfred, about the year 890, and rebuilt by William de Warren. It is distinguished from every other in the kingdom by having an artificial mound of earth raised at each extremity of the base court the ruins of the keep are still visible at the western mound, and other traces at the eastern, which probably corresponded , the western keep was evidently of a quadrangular form, with an hexagonal tower, narrowing from the base to the summit, and was probably the prison The gateway is supposed to have been built at two periods, by the first and eighth earls of Warren and Surrey , it has an inner arch of Anglo-Norman masonry, of the thirteenth cen-

tury, and was defended by two machicolated towers and two portcullises In 1774, the site and ruins of the castle were leased to Mr Thomas Friend, and are now possessed by Thomas Read Kemp, Esq , by whom the keep has been repaired Of the once extensive priory of St Pancras, founded in 1072, and said to have covered an area of forty acres, but a very small portion remains it was the first and chief of the Cluniac monasteries established in England, and at the dissolution possessed a revenue of £1091 9 6 The eastern part of the church is faced with Caen stone ; on the left is a gothic window, in tolerable repair, although scarcely a trace of the ornamental carving is left The gate-house, the arch of which is supported by clustered columns of Sussex marble, is in better preservation than any other part of this dilapidated pile, and, being nearly overgrown with ivy and weeds, presents a highly romantic appearance A portion of the walls of St. Nicholas' hospital is still standing, and also part of the exterior walls of an hospital dedicated to St James, which has been converted into a barn Here was also a monastery of Grey friars, of which there are no vestiges, the site being occupied by a private dwelling-house The town walls were erected during the residence of the Earls of Warren and Surrey, and may still be accurately traced a great part of the western portion is standing, and vestiges of all the other parts are visible Among the distinguished natives of Lewes may be mentioned Richard Russel, Esq , F R S , M D , who, by his writings on the efficacy of the sea water at Brighton, laid the foundation of the subsequent prosperity of that fashionable bathing-place Thomas Paine, the notorious deistical writer, resided for some time at Lewes, in the capacity of an exciseman A great variety of mineral substances, vegetable fossils, and organic remains, has been found in the chalk formation of the vicinity There are several mineral springs within a few miles of the borough, which it is in contemplation to bring into use for medicinal purposes

LEWISHAM, a parish in the hundred of BLACKHEATH, lathe of SUTTON at HONE, county of KENT, 6½ miles (S E) from London, on the road to Tunbridge and Hastings, containing 8185 inhabitants The name is a slight corruption of the Saxon *Lewesham*, or, "the dwelling among the meadows,' and anciently written *Levesham* The village, which is situated on the river Ravensbourn, extends about a mile along the Tunbridge road, and consists principally of one street, which is neither paved nor lighted , the inhabitants are supplied with water from a stream rising at the upper end of the village, and flowing through it The Surrey canal passes through the parish. The county magistrates hold a weekly session here on Mondays , and the parish is within the jurisdiction of the court of requests at Greenwich, for the recovery of debts not exceeding £5, to which the vestry here sends twelve commissioners The living is a vicarage, in the archdeaconry and diocese of Rochester, rated in the king s books at £23 19 2 , and in the patronage of the Earl of Dartmouth The church dedicated to St Mary, was rebuilt in 1774, and is a handsome edifice with a square tower at the west end a portico on the south side is supported on four Corinthian columns, and the altar is placed in a circular recess. There are episcopal chapels at Blackheath, Southend, and Sydenham, the last was formerly a meeting-house for Presbyterians, of which, Dr John Williams, author of the Greek Concordance, was many years minister There are places of worship for Independents and Wesleyan Methodists The Rev Abraham Colfe, in 1656, devised in trust to the Leathersellers Company certain estates for the foundation of two schools, one for the classical instruction of thirty-one sons of the laity in the several parishes in the hundred, and one son of each incumbent in this and the hundred of Chiselhurst, the other for the education of thirty-one boys of Lewisham, in reading, writing, and arithmetic A classical master is appointed by the Company, who superintends the tuition of the thirty-one boys in English, under his usher the master receives about £40 per annum, and resides in the school house (which is situated on Blackheath) rent-free, having also the privilege of taking boarders According to the commissioners report in 1818, the total income of the estates was £342 15 6, out of which the Company pay £50 per annum to six almswomen, agreeably to the will of the donor A school for girls was instituted in 1699, to which Dr George Stanhope, Dean of Canterbury, bequeathed £150, and Mrs Stanhope £50, which sums, with subsequent benefactions, produce a salary for the mistress of £20 per annum Here was formerly a Benedictine priory, a cell to the abbey of St. Peter at Ghent it was suppressed in the time of Henry V, and the site granted to the prior and convent of Shene. Dr Stanhope, who distinguished himself as a theological writer, was presented to this vicarage in 1689, and was buried here in 1728 Lewisham confers the inferior title of viscount on the Earl of Dartmouth

LEWKNOR, a parish partly in the hundred of Desborough, county of Bucks, but chiefly in the hundred of Lewknor, county of Oxford, 3½ miles (S S E) from Tetsworth, containing, with the chapelries of Postcombe, Ashamstead, and Uphill, 691 inhabitants The living is a discharged vicarage, in the archdeaconry and diocese of Oxford, rated in the king s books at £11 17, and in the patronage of the Warden and Fellows of All Souls College, Oxford The church is dedicated to St. Margaret

LEWSTON, an extra-parochial liberty, in the hundred of Sherborne, Sherborne division of the county of Dorset, 4 miles (S) from Sherborne, containing 8 inhabitants

LEWTRENCHARD, a parish in the hundred of Lifton, county of Devon, 8½ miles (E by N) from Launceston, containing 344 inhabitants The living is a rectory, in the archdeaconry of Totness, and diocese of Exeter, rated in the king's books at £9 13 9 W B Gould, Esq was patron in 1786 The church is dedicated to St Peter

LEXDEN, a parish in the liberties of the town of Colchester, county of Essex, 1½ mile (W) from Colchester, containing 932 inhabitants The living is a rectory, in the jurisdiction of the Commissary of Essex and Herts, concurrently with the Consistorial Court of the Bishop of London, rated in the king s books at £12 — Papillon, Esq was patron in 1804 The church, dedicated to St Leonard, has lately received an addition of three hundred and fifty free sittings, the Incorporated Society for the enlargement of churches and chapels having granted £500 towards defraying the expense

LEXHAM (EAST), a parish in the hundred of Launditch, county of Norfolk, 6½ miles (N N E) from Swaffham, containing 186 inhabitants The living is a discharged rectory, united with that of Litcham in 1742, in the archdeaconry and diocese of Norwich, rated in the king s books at £8 6 The church is dedicated to St Andrew

LEXHAM (WEST), a parish in the hundred of Launditch, county of Norfolk, 5¾ miles (N by E) from Swaffham, containing 92 inhabitants The living is a discharged rectory, in the archdeaconry and diocese of Norwich, rated in the king s books at £5 11 8, and in the patronage of Lord Wodehouse The church is dedicated to St Nicholas

LEY (UPPER), a township in that part of the parish of Aymestrey which is in the hundred of Stretford, county of Hereford The population is returned with the parish

LEYBOURN, a market town in the parish of Wensley, western division of the wapentake of Hang, North riding of the county of York, 46 miles (N W by W) from York, and 236 (N N W) from London, containing 810 inhabitants This town is pleasantly situated in a fertile and picturesque district, adjacent to it, along a continued ridge of rocks, is Leyburn Sparol one of the finest natural terraces in the kingdom It is well built, and consists principally of an oblong square, which forms the market-place The mineral productions in the vicinity are lead, coal, and lime The market is on Friday fairs are held on the second Fridays in February, May, October, and December, and are noted for large sales of cattle There are places of worship for Independents and Wesleyan Methodists, also a Roman Catholic chapel A school is supported by voluntary contributions, and various benefactions have been made for apprenticing poor children, and other charitable purposes

LEYBOURNE, a parish in the hundred of Larkfield, lathe of Aylesford, county of Kent, 5 miles (N W by W) from Maidstone, containing 300 inhabitants The living is a rectory, in the archdeaconry and diocese of Rochester, rated in the king s books at £17 13 4 Sir Henry Hawley, Bart was patron in 1798 The church is dedicated to St Peter and St. Paul The Rev Edward Holme, in 1775, conveyed to trustees a school-room and a dwelling house, in this parish, with the interest of £1000 four per cent. consols, for the education of fifty poor children Here are considerable remains of an ancient castle, consisting of a gateway, flanked by circular towers, various arches, walls, &c, and traces of the moat by which it was surrounded part of the ruins has long been converted into a dwelling-house

LEYLAND, a parish in the hundred of Leyland, county palatine of Lancaster, comprising the chapelries of Euxton, Heapey, Hoghton, and Whittle le Woods, and the townships of Clayton le Woods, Cuerden, Leyland, Wheelton, and Withnell, and containing 12,959 inhabitants, of which number, 3173 are in the township of Leyland, 4½ miles (N W) from Chorley The living is a vicarage, in the archdeaconry and diocese of Chester, rated in the king s books at £11, and in the patronage of Thomas James Baldwin, Esq The church, dedicated to St Andrew, like Westminster and many other ancient halls, was originally erected without a single pillar, it was rebuilt and enlarged in 1817, and contains several marble monuments adjoining the chancel is an ancient chapel belonging to the Faringtons, beneath which is the burial vault of that family A place of worship for Wesleyan Methodists was erected in 1814 The petty sessions for the division are held here once in five weeks, on Monday A considerable manufacture of cotton is carried on in the parish Near the churchyard a free grammar school was founded by Queen Elizabeth, with an endowment of £3 18 per annum, in aid of which the Rev Thomas Armetriding, in 1718, bequeathed £250, in support of the master and an usher, the annual income, with subsequent benefactions, amounts to about £27, for which thirty children are taught to read only Another school was erected, in 1785, by the late Mr Balshaw, and endowed by him with lands now producing an annual income of £180, in which one hundred and ten boys and seventy girls are instructed on the National system, and are gratuitously supplied with books, stationery, &c There is also a small endowment left by the late Samuel Crook, Esq , for the education of children An almshouse for six poor persons was founded, in 1607, by William Farington, Esq , and further endowed, in 1665, by John Osbaldeston, Esq , the inmates of which receive each about £2 per annum, in money and fuel A savings bank was established in 1821 There are at Shawe hall, the seat of William Farington, Esq , a choice museum of natural curiosities, and a collection of valuable paintings, some of which were found in the ruins of Herculaneum

LEYSDOWN, a parish in the liberty of the ISLE of SHEPPY, lathe of SCRAY, county of KENT, 7¾ miles (E by S) from Queenborough, containing 132 inhabitants The living is a discharged vicarage, in the archdeaconry and diocese of Canterbury, rated in the king s books at £10 10 , and in the patronage of the Archbishop of Canterbury The church, dedicated to St Clement, is a neat modern edifice, erected near the site of a more ancient and spacious one, the ruins of which are still visible

LEYTON (LOW), a parish in the hundred of BECONTREE, county of ESSEX, 6 miles (N E) from London, containing, with the chapelry of Leytonstone, 3374 inhabitants This place derives its name, which appears to be a contraction of Lee town, from its situation on the river Lee it is supposed by Camden and others to be the site of the ancient Durolitum, but whether or not, it is evident that here was a Roman station various pavements, foundations of buildings, coins both consular and imperial, and other Roman antiquities having been repeatedly discovered, particularly near the manor-house At a place called Ruckholt are vestiges of an old intrenchment, now nearly covered with trees The village is situated on a gentle ascent, rising gradually from the western bank of the river Lee, and continuing to the Forest of Waltham, eastward of which is the hamlet of Leytonstone, now so populous as to comprise nearly one half of the inhabitants of the whole parish , the single street of which it consists extending nearly from the forest to Stratford, in the direct road from Epping to London, and lighted with gas here are several good houses, and some large mansions The living of Low Leyton is a discharged vicarage, in the jurisdiction of the Commissary of London, concurrently with the Consistorial Court of the Bishop, rated in the king s books at £7 12 , and in the patronage of J Pardoe, Esq The church, which is dedicated to St Mary, is a plain brick edifice, with a tower at the west end it was repaired and enlarged in the seventeenth century, and again in 1822 the chancel contains some elegant monuments of the family of Hickes, with marble effigies, and of that of Sir Robert Beachcroft, lord mayor of London in 1721, and a liberal benefactor to Christ s and St Thomas s hospitals , also one of Mr John Wood, who travelled over several parts of Europe, Asia, Africa, and America there is likewise one to the memory of the antiquary and biographer the Rev John Strype, who was vicar of Leyton, from 1669, till his death, which took place in 1737, at the great age of ninety-four , he rebuilt the vicarage-house, and was a liberal contributor to the church and parish A chapel of ease was erected at Leytonstone, in 1750, by subscription Within the parish are places of worship for Independents and Wesleyan Methodists In 1697, Robert Ozler bequeathed £300 for the erection, and a rent-charge of £12 for the endowment, of a free school, for a certain number of children of Leyton and Walthamstow the school was built here, and the present number of boys is fourteen There are National schools for boys, in connexion with schools of Industry for girls at Low Leyton and Leytonstone Almshouses for eight poor widows were founded, in 1653, by John Smith, who endowed them with £20 per annum, to which, in 1747, Charles and John Phillips added the respective rent-charges of £12 and £6, for their further support they were repaired in 1789, at the expense of William Bosanquet, Esq In addition to the antiquities above mentioned, an arched gateway, ten feet in height, and six feet wide, ornamented with mouldings, was discovered near the manor-house, several years ago , and numerous urns have also been dug up near Ruckholt in the year 1783, whilst some workmen were employed in digging a channel at the Temple Mills, in this parish, a stone coffin, in which were various pieces of armour, was discovered. The celebrated Sir Thomas Rowe, or Roe, ambassador to the great Mogul in the reign of Charles I , was a native of Leyton , and Lady Margaret Brian, governess to Edward VI , and the princesses Mary and Elizabeth, resided here in 1551 Edward Rowe Mores, Esq , a distinguished antiquary of the last century, long lived in a house of singular construction, built by himself, in this parish, now called Etloe place

LEZANT, a parish in the northern division of EAST hundred, county of CORNWALL, 4½ miles (S by E) from Launceston, containing 853 inhabitants The living is a rectory, in the archdeaconry of Cornwall, and diocese of Exeter, rated in the king s books at £32, and in the peculiar jurisdiction and patronage of the Bishop of Exeter The church is dedicated to St Breock At Trecarrel in this parish are the remains of an ancient chapel

LEZIATE, a parish in the Lynn division of the hundred of FREEBRIDGE, county of NORFOLK, 5 miles (E) from Lynn-Regis, containing 123 inhabitants The living is a rectory, not in charge, with that of Ashwicken, in the archdeaconry and diocese of Norwich

LIBBERSTON, a township in that part of the parish of FILEY which is in PICKERING lythe, North riding of the county of YORK, 4 miles (N) from Hunmanby, containing 143 inhabitants

Arms.

LICHFIELD, a city and county of itself, under the designation of the city and county of the city of Lichfield, though locally in the county of Stafford, 16½ miles (S E by E) from Stafford, and 118 (N W by N) from London, containing 6075 inhabitants This place, called by Bede *Licidfeld*, and by Ingulphus and Henry of Huntingdon *Lichfeld*, both implying the field of the dead, is supposed to have derived its name from the traditionary martyrdom of more than one thousand Christians, who are said to have been massacred here in the reign of the Emperor Dioclesian an allusion to this event appears in the heraldic bearings of the city, and a spot within its precincts, in which they are said to have been interred, still retains the appellation of the Christian field. During the Octarchy, it appears to have been distinguished by the Kings of Mercia, of whom Piada, son-in-law of Osweo, King of Northumbria, having been converted by the preaching of Cedd, a hermit, who had a cell near the site of St Chad s church, is said to have erected the first Christian church here in honour of that recluse, who had been assiduous in his efforts to convert the Mercians to Christianity, and afterwards became their bishop In the reign of Offa, this see not only obtained the precedence of all the Mercian bishopricks, but, through the interest of Offa with Pope Adrian, was made the archiepiscopal see, and invested with the greater part of the jurisdiction of Canterbury, Eadulph was made Archbishop of Lichfield in 789, and had for his suffragans the Bishops of Worcester, Hereford, Leicester, Sidnacester, Elmham, and Dunwich, but, in 803, Leo succeeding to the pontificate, restored the primacy to Canterbury, and Eadulph, stripped of his supremacy, died in 812 At the time of the Conquest, Lichfield, notwithstanding the distinction which it enjoyed under the Saxon kings, was but an inconsiderable place, and in 1075, when the council decreed that episcopal sees should no longer remain in obscure towns, Peter, Bishop of *Licedfeld*, transferred his see to Chester, where it continued till it was removed by his successor, Robert de Limsey, to Coventry, whence it was, in 1148, restored to Lichfield, by Roger de Clinton, who began the church and fortified the castle, of which latter there is not the slightest vestige At what time, or by whom, the castle was originally built, has not been clearly ascertained, but it is, upon very good authority, asserted that Richard II, after his deposition from the throne, was detained here as a prisoner, on his route to the Tower of London During the parliamentary war, Lichfield embraced the royal cause, and Charles I, after the battle of Naseby, slept for one night in the cathedral close, which, in 1643, Sir Richard Dyot, with some of the principal gentlemen of the county, under the command of the Earl of Chesterfield, fortified against the parliamentarian forces by which the town was besieged, under Lord Brooke and Sir John Gell, the former of whom, having stationed himself in the porch of an adjoining house, was shot, by a member of the Dyott family, from the battlements of the cathedral the attack being continued by Sir John Gell, the garrison surrendered on honourable terms, and the parliamentarians retired, leaving a body of troops to defend this post, who, in the following month, were repulsed by Prince Rupert, who marched hither after the reduction of Birmingham, the royalists retained possession of the town till its final surrender to the parliament During these conflicts the cathedral suffered material injury, its rich sculptures were destroyed, it was converted into stables by the parliamentarian troops, and, in 1651, it was set on fire, and, by order of parliament, stripped of its lead, and left to neglect and decay

The city is built in a pleasant and fertile vale, within two miles of the Roman station *Etocetum*, and about the same distance from Offlow Mount, another station at Swinfen The houses in the principal streets are handsome and well built, the streets in general are well paved, and the town is lighted with oil, and amply supplied with water, and is characterised by a prevailing appearance of cleanliness and respectability In the environs, which abound in varied scenery, are numerous handsome seats and elegant villas A permanent library, established within the last twenty years, is liberally supported by subscription a small theatre, in which Mrs Siddons made her first appearance after her marriage, is opened during the races, and occasionally at other times an amateur concert, called the Cecilian Society, has been established nearly a century The races take place in March and September, the former are principally supported by the members of the Anson Hunt, and at the latter a king s plate of one hundred guineas is run for on the first day, the course is on the road to Tamworth, about two miles from the city Lichfield is not a place of much trade there are an extensive carpet factory, and a small manufactory for spinning cotton thread The Birmingham canal passes within a quarter of a mile of the city, and within the distance of a mile and a half joins the Wyrley and Essington canal. The market is on Friday and the fairs are, January 10th, Shrove-Tuesday, and Ash Wednesday, for cattle, sheep, bacon, and cheese, and the first Tuesday in November for geese and cheese the market-house is a light and commodious building of stone, occupying the site of the ancient market-cross

Corporate Seal.

The city received a charter of incorporation from Edward VI, which was confirmed and extended by Mary and Elizabeth, the former of whom erected it, with a district of sixteen miles in circuit, into a county of itself, in 1623, the charter was renewed by James I, and confirmed with additional privileges by Charles II the government is vested in two bailiffs and twenty-one brethren (one of whom is town clerk and coroner), a recorder, steward, and sheriff, assisted by a sword bearer, two serjeants at mace, and subordinate officers The bailiffs are appointed on St James day, the senior bailiff is selected by the Bishop of the diocese, from two nominated by the corporation who themselves appoint the junior bailiff the recorder, steward, and town clerk, are appointed by the corporation, subject to the approval of the king, and by their charter, any of the citizens, not being one of the bailiffs or twenty-one brethren, is chosen sheriff by the corporation, who have power to fine him at their discretion for refusing to serve the office   two chief constables are chosen by a jury of burgage tenants, at their court leet, held on St George's day, and several petty constables at the great portmote court, held on the 22nd of July   The bailiffs, the late bailiffs, the recorder, and the steward, are justices of the peace within the city and county of the city, but their jurisdiction does not extend over the Close of the cathedral, which possesses exclusive privileges, and is under the sole jurisdiction of the Dean and Chapter   The freedom of the city is inherited only by the eldest sons of freemen, and acquired by purchase, or servitude in one of the trading companies, of which there are seven, viz, the Curriers, Smiths, Saddlers, Bakers, Dyers, Taylors, and Butchers   The corporation hold assizes for the city and county of the city, as occasion may require, for the trial of capital offenders, quarterly courts of session, and a petty session every week, they hold also a court of record weekly, for the recovery of debts to any amount above 40s, and a sheriff's court is held every month, for the recovery of debts under that amount   The guildhall is a neat edifice of stone, ornamented with a pediment in front, in the tympanum of which are the city arms the hall is spacious, and well adapted to the purposes of the several courts, and behind it are apartments in which the public business of the corporation is transacted, underneath is the common gaol for the city, containing rooms and cells for the confinement of debtors and felons   The city first exercised the elective franchise in the 33rd of Edward I, and continued to make regular returns till the 27th of Edward III, from which period it ceased till the time of its incorporation by Edward VI, who restored that privilege, and since then it has returned two members to parliament the right of election is vested in the bailiffs, magistrates, burgage tenants, freeholders to the amount of forty shillings per annum, and freemen enrolled and paying scot and lot, in all about eleven hundred   the sheriff is the returning officer   An annual fête, called the Court of Array, takes place on Whit-Monday in the guildhall, whence it is immediately adjourned to an eminence called Greenhill, in the parish of St Michael, where a temporary bower is erected for the occasion   it was formerly given by the corporation, but is continued by voluntary contributions   Upon this occasion, the city officers, attended by a large concourse of the inhabitants, with music and banners, after visiting the different wards of the city, adjourn to the guildhall, where they are treated with wine and refreshments   they then proceed to the market-place, where the town clerk delivers an oration, exhorting them to " perform their duty to the king and to their fellow citizens, and to pursue the paths of industry and virtue"   This ceremony is supposed by some to have been instituted by King Osory, to commemorate a victory obtained by him over Penda, but others, with more probability, ascribe it to an act passed in the reign of Henry II, and confirmed in succeeding reigns, ordaining that the high constables in each town should frequently inspect the arms of the inhabitants within their franchise

Arms of the Bishoprick.

Lichfield, jointly with Coventry, is an episcopal see, and since the demolition of the abbey and conventual buildings at Coventry, has become the sole seat of the diocese   the jurisdiction of the see extends over the counties of Derby and Stafford, and a considerable part of the counties of Warwick and Salop   The ecclesiastical establishment consists of a bishop, dean, precentor, chancellor, treasurer, the four archdeacons of Coventry, Stafford, Salop, and Derby, twenty seven prebendaries, five priest vicars seven lay clerks, eight choristers, and other officers, at the dissolution the revenue was £795 17 6   The cathedral, which had been reduced during the parliamentary war to a state of extreme dilapidation, was restored, by Dr Hacket, on his preferment to the united sees of Lichfield and Coventry, in 1661, to its original state of splendour and magnificence   various improvements have subsequently been made, and the choir has been greatly enlarged, under the superintendence of Mr Wyatt, by the removal of the screen in front of the lady chapel, the expediency of which alteration is very questionable, with regard to its influence on the proportion of its several parts   The prevailing character of the edifice is that of the early English, approaching very nearly to the decorated style of English architecture   the west front is magnificently rich, and the spires of the western towers, each one hundred and eighty three feet in height, are in beautiful combination with the lofty central spire, which is two hundred and fifty-eight feet high   the east end is hexagonal, and the whole exterior is highly ornamented in various parts with statuary and sculpture of exquisite design and elaborate execution   the interior presents various styles, with several later insertions   the transepts display considerable portions in the Norman character, and the choir, which deviates from the line of the nave, is in the decorated style of English architecture, it is richly ornamented, and lighted with windows of beautiful tracery   the bishop's throne, and the prebendal stalls, are fine specimens of tabernacle work   St Mary's chapel, built by Bishop Langton, is an edifice of elegant design, it is lighted with nine lofty windows, of which, the three at the east end are more rich in their tracery, and are ornamented with stained glass brought by Sir Brooke Boothby from the dissolved abbey of Herckenrode, in the bishoprick of Leige, in the central window on one side is a painting of the Resurrection, by Eggington, from a design by Sir Joshua Reynolds   in this chapel was the rich shrine of St Chad, which was demolished at the dissolution The whole length of the cathedral, from west to east, is four hundred and eleven feet, and the breadth, along the transepts, one hundred and fifty-three feet   Among the monuments which escaped the ravages of the parliamentary troops are, those of Bishops Hacket, Langton, and Pattishul   There is a monument to Doctor Samuel Johnson, a bust of Garrick, a mutilated statue of Captain Stanley, and a monument of exquisite beauty by Chantrey, to the memory of the infant children of Mrs Robinson   this monument, which is considered as a masterpiece of sculpture, is unrivalled for beauty of design, intensity of feeling, and force of expression. A passage from the north aisle leads to the chapter house, a decagonal building of great beauty, of which the finely-vaulted roof is supported on a clustered central column. Above it is the library, instituted by Dean Heywood, in which are the gospels of St Chad, an Alcoran taken at the siege of Buda, and a folio edition of Chaucer, richly illuminated. The bishop's palace, on the north-east side of the Close, is a spacious edifice.

The city comprises the parishes of St Mary, part of which is in the southern division of the hundred of Pirehill, St Chad, part of which is in the northern division of the hundred of Offlow, and St Michael, part of which is in the northern, and part in the southern, division of the hundred of Offlow, and the liberty of the Cathedral Close, which is extra-parochial, all in the peculiar jurisdiction of the Dean and Chapter of Lichfield. The living of St Mary's is a discharged vicarage, rated in the king's books at £10, and in the patronage of the Dean and Chapter of Lichfield: the church is a modern edifice, erected on the site of an ancient structure described by Leland as "right beautiful." The living of St Chad's is a perpetual curacy, endowed with £200 private benefaction, £200 royal bounty, and £1200 parliamentary grant, and in the patronage of the Vicar of St Mary's. The church, by far the oldest in Lichfield, was rebuilt, on the site of an ancient church erected by Bishop Headda, in honour of St Chad, and near his hermitage. The living of St Michael's is also a perpetual curacy, endowed with £200 private benefaction, £400 royal bounty, and £1200 parliamentary grant, and in the patronage of the Vicar of St. Mary's: the church, a plain edifice in the later style of English architecture, is situated on an eminence called Green-hill, it contains a tablet, with an inscription by Dr Johnson, to the memory of his parents. the church yard comprises from six to seven acres, and is the principal cemetery of the city. There are places of worship for Independents, Wesleyan Methodists, and Kilhamites, and a Roman Catholic chapel.

The free grammar school appears, from a small endowment payable out of the Exchequer, to have been founded by Edward VI: its annual income arises from the said grant from the Exchequer, a small sum paid out of the revenue of St John's hospital, a contribution from the feoffees of the Conduit Lands, and a stipend paid by the corporation: the present master of St John's hospital, the Rev Mr Chancellor Law, subscribes £75 annually towards the salary of the second master. The school house was erected, in 1692, at the joint expense of the corporation and the feoffees of the Conduit Lands, there are only six free scholars on the foundation, each of whom receives an annuity of £1 6 8., granted by Dean Walker to six scholars of the former school, in St John's hospital, now transferred to this school, the other scholars pay £2 2 per quarter to the head master, who has also a house rent-free and the privilege of taking boarders, and those who attend the lower school pay £1 1 per quarter to the second master. An English free school was founded, in 1677, by Mr Thomas Minors, who endowed it with a messuage for the school-house, and rents amounting to about £30 per annum. Andrew Newton, Esq, in 1801, bequeathed in aid of this charity the reversion of the dividends on

£3333 6 8 three per cent consols, after the decease of the then legatee Humphrey Torrick, Esq, in 1652, bequeathed a messuage, the rental of which, amounting to £9 per annum, is appropriated to the instruction of five poor boys, and in the parish of St. Michael's are donations of houses and land, producing £129 per annum, for the support of a schoolmaster and chaplain, and for other charitable uses. there are also a National and a British school for boys, supported by subscription.

St John's hospital was founded, in the reign of Henry III, by one of the bishops of the diocese, and, in 1252, Radulph de Lacock, canon of Lichfield, endowed it with lands at Elmhurst and Stitchbrook, for the maintenance of a priest, and the support of the poor and infirm in this hospital, which was visited by the Bishops of Lichfield for many years, but fell into neglect and decay, from which it was retrieved by Bishop Smyth, who was translated to the see in the reign of Henry VII: that prelate rebuilt the premises in 1495, and formed the statutes by which it is at present governed. The establishment consists of a master, or warden, in priest's orders (appointed by the Bishop of Lichfield and Coventry), a schoolmaster, also in priest's orders, an usher, and chaplain (appointed by the warden), thirteen almsmen, (who have each three shillings and sixpence per week, with other advantages), and a matron: the revenue is about £350, of which after paying the annual expenses, which amount on an average to about £200, the remainder is paid to the master: the premises comprise thirteen almshouses, apartments for the master and other officers, and a chapel. the school formerly attached to the hospital has been superseded by the free grammar school. An hospital for women was originally founded, in 1424, by Bishop Hayworth, and endowed, in 1504, by Thomas Milley, one of the canons residentiary, with tenements and lands producing, together with subsequent benefactions, an income of about £370, for the maintenance of fifteen aged women, who receive each a weekly allowance of seven shillings and sixpence, including a benefaction by Mr John Fecknam. the inmates are appointed by the trustees, and it is in contemplation to add a number of out-pensioners to the charity, the funds having accumulated, from the excess of the income above the annual expenditure. A dispensary, supported by subscription, was established in 1829. The Conduit Lands, producing an income of about £580, were devised to trustees, in 1546, by Henry Beane, master of the guild of St Mary, for the repair of the conduits and water courses of the city. There are numerous donations and bequests, amounting to more than £1000 per annum, for distribution among the poor.

Among the monastic establishments was a convent of Grey friars, founded in 1229, by Alexander, Bishop of Lichfield, it was burnt down in 1291, and being rebuilt, subsisted till the dissolution: the remains are now let on lease, and the rents appropriated to charitable uses. Several relics of antiquity are preserved in Mr Green's museum, among which is the wooden lintel of a doorway, pierced by a ball which killed Lord Brooke, the parliamentary officer, during the siege of the cathedral. There is a chalybeate spring, and some fine specimens of agate, in a state of decomposition, are found in the vicinity, where a fine sort of clay for pottery is also met with. Elias Ashmole, the antiquary, and founder of the Ashmolean museum at Oxford, Dr George Smalridge, and Dr Thomas Newton, both distinguished as theological writers, and the celebrated Dr Samuel Johnson, were natives of this place and among the residents were, Garrick, Dr Darwin, author of "the Botanic Garden," and his ingenious biographer, Miss Seward

LIDBROOK, a hamlet in the parish of ENGLISH-BICKNOR, hundred of ST BRIAVELLS, county of GLOUCESTER There is a place of worship for Baptists Iron and tin works furnish employment to about one hundred and twenty individuals they are said to be the first that were established in the kingdom Coal is brought from the Forest of Dean, by means of a railroad constructed from the Wye to the Severn

LIDDIARD-MILLICENT, a parish in the hundred of HIGHWORTH, CRICKLADE, and STAPLE, county of WILTS, 3 miles (N N E) from Wootton Basset, containing 391 inhabitants The living is a rectory, in the archdeaconry of Wilts, and diocese of Salisbury, rated in the king s books at £17 4 4½ S W Warneford, Esq was patron in 1809 The church is dedicated to All Saints

LIDDIARD-TREGOOZE, a parish in the hundred of KINGSBRIDGE, county of WILTS, 4 miles (W by N) from Swindon, containing 717 inhabitants The living is a rectory, in the archdeaconry of Wilts, and diocese of Salisbury, rated in the king s books at £10 5 5 G Watson Taylor, Esq was patron in 1780 The church is dedicated to All Saints

LIDDINGTON, a parish in the hundred of WRANDIKE, county of RUTLAND, 2½ miles (S by E) from Uppingham, containing 594 inhabitants The living is a discharged vicarage, in the peculiar jurisdiction of the Prebendary of Liddington in the Cathedral Church of Lincoln, rated in the king s books at £8 2, and in the patronage of the Dean and Chapter of Lincoln The church is dedicated to St. Andrew At Caldecott, in this parish, is a chapel of ease There is a place of worship for Wesleyan Methodists In 1721, Mary Parnham bequeathed £200 to be laid out in land, desiring the rental to be applied in educating five poor children of this parish, and five of Lavington, the proportion of income to each school is £9 16 10 per annum A palace, formerly belonging to the Bishops of Lincoln, a fine structure in the early style of English architecture, and consisting of a large hall with painted windows, has been converted into an hospital for a warden, twelve brethren, and two nurses, which charity was founded, in 1600, by Sir Thomas Cecil, Knt, Lord Burghley, and called Jesus Hospital

LIDDINGTON, a parish in the hundred of KINGSBRIDGE, county of WILTS, 4 miles (E S E) from Swindon, containing 409 inhabitants The living is a discharged vicarage, in the archdeaconry of Wilts, and diocese of Salisbury, rated in the king s books at £17, endowed with £200 private benefaction, and £200 royal bounty, and in the patronage of the Rector the rectory is a sinecure, rated in the king's books at £14, and in the patronage of the Duke of Marlborough The church is dedicated to All Saints On Beacon hill, in this parish, was a large circular work, called Liddington Castle

LIDGATE, a parish in the hundred of RISBRIDGE, county of SUFFOLK, 6¾ miles (S E by E) from Newmarket, containing 389 inhabitants The living is a

rectory, in the archdeaconry of Sudbury, and diocese of Norwich, rated in the king s books at £15 10 5, and in the patronage of the Duke of Rutland The church is dedicated to St Mary Here was an ancient castle, called King John s Castle, of unknown origin Lydgate the poet, who was also a monk of Bury, was born here

LIDLINGTON, or LITLINGTON, a parish in the hundred of REDBORNESTOKE, county of BEDFORD, 3½ miles (W by N) from Ampthill, containing 739 inhabitants The living is a discharged vicarage, in the archdeaconry of Bedford, and diocese of Lincoln, rated in the king s books at £11, endowed with £600 royal bounty, and £1200 parliamentary grant, and in the patronage of the Duke of Bedford The church, dedicated to All Saints, contains an ancient tomb, with a brass effigy in armour of one of the Goldingtons, who possessed the manor of Goldington, in this parish, in the fifteenth century There is a place of worship for Wesleyan Methodists

LIDNEY, or LYDNEY, a market town and parish in the hundred of BLIDESLOE, county of GLOUCESTER, 19 miles (S W by W) from Gloucester, and 123 (W by N) from London, containing, with the chapelry of Aylburton, 1393 inhabitants, of which number, 1040 are in the town of Lidney This place is thought by some to have been the Roman station Abona, which, however, is very doubtful In Lidney park are the remains of a Roman villa, and two Roman camps, the largest of which is of an oblong form, about eight hundred and thirty feet in length, and three hundred and seventy in breadth, surrounded by a single ditch, except at the east end, where it is double near the western border of this intrenchment is a Roman bath, still tolerably perfect in other parts are traces of ancient buildings, and fragments of tesselated pavements, urns, and statues, have been found, also coins of Adrian and Antoninus, and a silver one of Galba An old mansion, called Whitecross, was erected by Sir William Winter, Vice Admiral of England in the reign of Elizabeth, and it was fortified and garrisoned during the civil war in the reign of Charles I, by Sir John Winter, a distinguished royalist officer, who defended his house against repeated attacks of detachments from the parliamentary forces stationed at Gloucester The parish is bounded on the eastern side by the river Severn a rail-road from the Severn to the Wye runs parallel with a canal from Lidney dock to the wharf, whence the former passes northward, intersects the town, and continues its course through the parish. Veins of coal have been found here, forming part of the great coal field in the Forest of Dean, but none are now worked to any extent The market is on Wednesday fairs are held on the 4th of May and the 8th of November The living is a vicarage, with the perpetual curacies of St. Briavell s and Huelsfield, in the archdeaconry of Hereford, and diocese of Gloucester, rated in the king's books at £24 6 8, and in the patronage of the Dean and Chapter of Hereford The church is dedicated to St Mary Some small benefactions have been made for distribution among the poor There are some chalybeate springs in the parish

LIDSING, or LIDGEN a vill in the parish of GILLINGHAM, hundred of CHATHAM and GILLINGHAM, lathe of AYLESFORD, county of KENT, 4 miles (S S E) from Chatham, containing 42 inhabitants

LIDSTONE, a hamlet in the parish of CHURCH-ENSTONE, hundred of CHADLINGTON, county of Ox-FORD, 1½ mile (W N W) from Neat Enstone, containing 146 inhabitants

LIFTON, a parish in the hundred of LIFTON, county of DEVON, 4 miles (E by N) from Launceston, containing 1214 inhabitants The living is a rectory, in the archdeaconry of Totness, and diocese of Exeter, rated in the king s books at £31 2 11 , and in the patronage of Harris Arundel, Esq The church is dedicated to St Mary Two schools are supported by voluntary contributions there are mines of manganese in this parish The rivers Tonkay and Lyd flow in the vicinity Cattle fairs are held on the 2nd of February, on Holy Thursday, and October 28th There is a medicinal spring near Lifton bridge

LIGHTCLIFFE, a chapelry in the parish of HALIFAX, wapentake of MORLEY, West riding of the county of YORK, 3¼ miles (E) from Halifax, with which the population is returned The living is a perpetual curacy, in the archdeaconry and diocese of York, endowed with £600 private benefaction, and £800 royal bounty, and in the patronage of the Vicar of Halifax There is a place of worship for Independents

LIGHTGRAVE, or LEEGRAVE, a hamlet in the parish of LUTON, hundred of FLITT, county of BEDFORD, 3 miles (N W by W) from Luton, containing 282 inhabitants

LIGHTHORNE, a parish in the Kington division of the hundred of KINGTON, county of WARWICK, 4 miles (N by E) from Kington, containing 316 inhabitants The living is a rectory, in the archdeaconry and diocese of Worcester, rated in the king's books at £14 17 3¼ Lord Willoughby de Broke was patron in 1787 The church is dedicated to St. Lawrence

LILBOURN, a parish in the hundred of GUILSBOROUGH, county of NORTHAMPTON, 4 miles (E S E) from Rugby, containing 264 inhabitants The living is a discharged vicarage, in the archdeaconry of Northampton, and diocese of Peterborough, rated in the king s books at £6, and in the patronage of the Crown The church is dedicated to All Saints There is a place of worship for Wesleyan Methodists. The village is situated on the line of the ancient Watling-street, and is supposed to have been the Tripontium of the Romans vestiges of an ancient castle are still visible At Roundhill, about half a mile from the town, bones and skulls have been found , tradition states it to have been the scene of an engagement between the Danes and the Saxons The river Avon passes on the east of the parish

LILBURN (EAST), a township in the parish of EGLINGHAM, northern division of COQUETDALE ward, county of NORTHUMBERLAND, 4½ miles (S E by E) from Wooler, containing 97 inhabitants In 1768, on the removal of a heap of stones, superstitiously believed to have been raised by the devil, and called "the Apronful of stones,' the base and fragments of a cross, with four rows of steps, were discovered beneath

LILBURN (WEST), a township in the parish of EGLINGHAM, northern division of COQUETDALE ward, county of NORTHUMBERLAND, 3½ miles (S E by E) from Wooler, containing 171 inhabitants At the west end of the village there are some remains of an ancient mansion and tower, likewise of a chapel of ease

LILFORD, a parish in the hundred of HUXLOE, though locally in that of Polebrook, county of NORTHAMPTON, 3 miles (S by W) from Oundle, containing, with Wigsthorpe, 130 inhabitants The living is a vicarage, with the rectory of Thorpe-Achurch, in the archdeaconry of Northampton, and diocese of Peterborough, rated in the king s books at £7 12 3½ , and in the patronage of Lord Lilford The church is dedicated to St Peter Lilford confers the title of baron on the family of Powys

LILLESHALL, a parish in the Newport division of the hundred of BRADFORD (South), county of SALOP, 3 miles (S S W) from Newport, containing 3143 inhabitants The living is a discharged vicarage, in the archdeaconry of Salop, and diocese of Lichfield and Coventry, rated in the king s books at £6 17 11 , endowed with £200 private benefaction, and £200 royal bounty, and in the patronage of the Marquis of Stafford The church is dedicated to St Michael About 1145, an abbey, for regular canons of the order of St Augustine, was founded here at the dissolution the revenue was valued at £327 10 A branch of the Donnington Wood, or Marquis of Stafford s, canal terminates in the northern part of this parish

LILLEY, a parish in the hundred of HITCHIN and PIRTON, county of HERTFORD, 5 miles (W S W) from Hitchin, containing 427 inhabitants The living is a rectory, in the archdeaconry of Huntingdon, and diocese of Lincoln, rated in the king s books at £19 8 9 , and in the patronage of the Master and Fellows of St John s College, Cambridge The church is dedicated to St Peter

LILLIFFEE, a hamlet in the parish of HEDSOR, hundred of DESBOROUGH, county of BUCKINGHAM 3½ miles (E by S) from Great Marlow The population is returned with the parish

LILLINGS-AMBO, a township in the parish of SHERIFF-HUTTON, wapentake of BULMER, North riding of the county of YORK, 9½ miles (N N E) from York, containing 208 inhabitants

LILLINGSTONE-DAYRELL, a parish in the hundred and county of BUCKINGHAM, 4½ miles (N) from Buckingham, containing 127 inhabitants The living is a rectory, in the archdeaconry of Buckingham, and diocese of Lincoln, rated in the king's books at £7 9 7 , and in the patronage of Richard Dayrell, Esq , whose ancestors have been patrons upwards of five hundred years, and have resided here for eighteen generations The church is dedicated to St Nicholas

LILLINGSTONE-LOVELL, a parish in the hundred of PLOUGHLEY, county of OXFORD, though locally in the hundred and county of Buckingham, 4¾ miles (N by E) from Buckingham, containing 160 inhabitants The living is a rectory, in the archdeaconry and diocese of Oxford, rated in the king's books at £8 9 4½ , and in the patronage of the Crown The church is dedicated to St Mary

LILLINGTON, a parish in the hundred of SHERBORNE, Sherborne division of the county of DORSET, 3½ miles (S by W) from Sherborne, containing 185 inhabitants The living is a discharged rectory, in the peculiar jurisdiction of the Dean of Salisbury, rated in the king's books at £10 12 3½ Mr and Mrs Gordon were patrons in 1798 The church is dedicated to St. Martin

LILLINGTON, a parish in the Kenilworth division of the hundred of KNIGHTLOW, county of WARWICK, 2½ miles (N E by E) from Warwick, containing 226 inhabitants   The living is a discharged vicarage, in the archdeaconry of Coventry, and diocese of Lichfield and Coventry, rated in the king's books at £5 13 4   Matthew Wise, Esq was patron in 1795   The church is dedicated to St Mary Magdalene

LILLISDON, a tything in the parish and hundred of NORTH CURRY, county of SOMERSET, 5 miles (E by S) from Taunton   The population is returned with the parish

LILLY, a hamlet in the parish of CATMERE, hundred of COMPTON, county of BERKS, 5 miles (W by S) from East Ilsley   The population is returned with the parish

LILSTOCK, a parish in the hundred of WILLITON and FREEMANNERS, county of SOMERSET, 11¼ miles (N W) from Bridg water, containing 71 inhabitants   The living is a perpetual curacy, annexed to the vicarage of Stoke-Gursey, in the archdeaconry of Taunton, and diocese of Bath and Wells   The church is dedicated to St Andrew   This parish is bounded on the north by Bridg-water bay, in the Bristol channel

LIMBER (MAGNA), a parish in the eastern division of the wapentake of YARBOROUGH, parts of LINDSEY, county of LINCOLN, 5¼ miles (N by E) from Caistor, containing 421 inhabitants   The living is a discharged vicarage, in the archdeaconry and diocese of Lincoln, rated in the king's books at £9 18 4 , and in the patronage of the Crown   The church, which is dedicated to St. Peter, was given, in the time of Henry II , by Richard de Humet, constable of Normandy, to the Cistercian abbey of Aulnay, or Aveny, in Normandy, the abbot and convent of which established a cell here , this cell, at the suppression of Alien priories, was sold to the Carthusians of St Anne, near Coventry   There is a place of worship for Wesleyan Methodists

LIMBER (PARVA), a hamlet in the parish of BROCKLESBY, eastern division of the wapentake of YARBOROUGH, parts of LINDSEY, county of LINCOLN, 7 miles (N) from Caistor   The population is returned with the parish

LIMBURY, a hamlet in the parish of LUTON, hundred of FLITT, county of BEDFORD, 2½ miles (N W by N) from Luton, containing, with Biscott, 276 inhabitants

LIMEHOUSE, a parish in the Tower division of the hundred of OSSULSTONE, county of MIDDLESEX, 2 miles (E by S) from London, containing 9805 inhabitants   This place, which is situated on the north bank of the Thames, was formerly a hamlet belonging to Stepney, from which parish it was separated in 1730   It consists principally of a number of narrow streets and irregular buildings, diverging from the principal thoroughfare   There are several respectable houses , and among the numerous shops, warehouses, and manufactories, are some spacious and well-built structures, though many of the buildings are of an inferior description.   The streets are partly paved, and are lighted with gas   There are several rope-walks, the principal of which was established by the late Captain Huddart, F R S , who, about twenty-five years since, obtained a patent for a machine for twisting ropes for cables of the largest dimensions   it is worked by a steam-engine of

thirty-horse power   the number of persons employed during the late war was nearly three hundred, now about one hundred and fifty   The proprietors have likewise a machine for making flat rope   the walks, four hundred yards in length, are sheltered from the weather, and are lighted with gas made on the premises   In connexion with the above are a manufactory for sail cloth, and an extensive bleaching ground   the yarn is washed in a reservoir supplied by the waste water from the steam-engine   Here is also a very extensive establishment for the manufacture of patent chain cables, anchors, and various kinds of iron-work   Ship-blocks are made here, and there is a variety of other trades connected with the shipping   Ship-building is carried on extensively at Limehouse Hole   At the eastern extremity of the parish, are the West India Docks, which extend across the river to Blackwall   The northern dock, for unloading ships, covers thirty acres, and is capable of accommodating three hundred West Indiamen , the southern is for loading outward bound vessels   it covers twenty-four acres, and will admit two hundred ships   The former was opened in 1802, and the latter in 1805   they have extensive ranges of building, in which foreign goods are deposited previous to the payment of the duty   A canal from the river Lea, called the New Cut, crosses this parish and joins the Thames, superseding the circuitous navigation round the Isle of Dogs   The Regent's canal likewise passes through the parish, on the line of which, just before its junction with the Thames, is a basin, capable of admitting vessels of from two to three hundred tons burden   On the south side of the Commercial road is a tram-road, from the West India Docks to Whitechapel, constructed, at an expense of nearly £20,000

The living is a rectory not in charge, within the jurisdiction of the Commissary of London, concurrently with the Consistorial Court of the Bishop, and in the patronage of the Principal and Fellows of Brasenose College, Oxford   The church, dedicated to St Anne, is a massive structure, with two angular turrets at the east end, and a square tower at the west end, erected after a design by Nicholas Hawksmoor, one of the pupils of Sir Christopher Wren   it is one of the fifty churches erected pursuant to an act passed in the reign of Queen Anne   A place of worship for Wesleyan Methodists is now being erected   A charity school for boys was established by subscription about the middle of the last century, and Limehouse having been constituted a distinct parish, the school, in 1737, was united with one for the hamlets of Poplar and Blackwall, situated at Poplar, and again separated from it in 1607   In 1779, a school for girls was established by subscription, and in 1806 a school house was erected   in 1811 the two schools were united   The endowment belonging to this establishment consists of £1300 three per cent stock, producing £39 per annum , £10 10 per annum from a bequest by Captain Lovelace , £10 per annum from the Ironmongers Company , £130 per annum arising from landed property, and about £400 per annum, from subscriptions, contributions, &c   About three hundred and fifty boys, and one hundred and fifty girls, are now educated, on the National plan, of whom fifty of each sex are clothed   the master has a salary of £80, and the mistress and her assistant £70, per annum, the former two having each a house rent and tax free, and allowance for coal The charity is under the superintendence of a committee of the subscribers

LIMINGTON, a parish in the hundred of STONE, county of SOMERSET, 1¼ mile (E S E) from Ilchester, containing, with the tything of Draycott, 268 inhabitants The living is a rectory, in the archdeaconry of Wells, and diocese of Bath and Wells, rated in the king s books at £21 6 5½, and in the patronage of the Warden and Fellows of Wadham College, Oxford The church, dedicated to St Mary, contains the effigy of Sir Richard Gyverney, founder of a chantry here, and others of the family, but the figures are much mutilated On a pew in the chancel is the cipher of Cardinal Wolsey, who was sometime rector of this parish

LIMPENHOE, a parish in the hundred of BLOFIELD, county of NORFOLK, 5¼ miles (S) from Acle, containing 142 inhabitants The living is a discharged vicarage, with the rectory of Southwood, in the archdeaconry and diocese of Norwich, rated in the king s books at £6 13 4 The Rev John Love was patron in 1803 The church is dedicated to St. Botolph

LIMPSFIELD, a parish in the first division of the hundred of TANDRIDGE, county of SURREY, 4 miles (E N E) from Godstone, containing 918 inhabitants The living is a rectory, in the archdeaconry of Surrey, and diocese of Winchester, rated in the king's books at £20 0 5 Mr and Mrs Gower were patrons in 1806 The church is dedicated to St Peter

LINACRE, a township in the parish of WALTON on the HILL, hundred of WEST DERBY, county palatine of LANCASTER, 3¾ miles (N by W) from Liverpool The population is returned with the chapelry of Bootle

LINBRIGGS, a township in the parish of ALLENTON, western division of COQUETDALE ward, county of NORTHUMBERLAND, 11 miles (W by N) from Rothbury, containing 70 inhabitants The river Coquet, near where the Ridlee bourne empties itself into it, is crossed by a bridge several fine brooks run through the glens in this neighbourhood, and terminate in the river

LINBY, a parish in the northern division of the wapentake of BROXTOW, county of NOTTINGHAM, 7¾ miles (N N W) from Nottingham, containing 439 inhabitants The living is a discharged rectory, in the archdeaconry of Nottingham, and diocese of York, rated in the king's books at £4 9 9½, and in the patronage of Andrew Montague, Esq The church is dedicated to St Michael. This parish is bounded on the east by the small river Seen

LINCH, a parish in the hundred of EASEBOURNE, rape of CHICHESTER, county of SUSSEX, 5 miles (N N W) from Midhurst, containing 77 inhabitants The living is a discharged rectory, in the archdeaconry and diocese of Chichester, rated in the king s books at £3 12 8½, endowed with £200 private benefaction, and £500 parliamentary grant, and in the patronage of Mr and Mrs Poyntz

LINCHMERE, a parish in the hundred of EASEBOURNE, rape of CHICHESTER, county of SUSSEX, 7½ miles (N by W) from Midhurst, containing 282 inhabitants The living is a perpetual curacy, in the archdeaconry and diocese of Chichester, endowed with £10 per annum and £200 private benefaction, £600 royal bounty, and £300 parliamentary grant James Baker, Esq was patron in 1814

LINCOLN, a city and county of itself, locally in the county of Lincoln, of which it is the chief town, 132 miles (N by W) from London, containing, with the parishes of Bracebridge, Branston, Canwick, and Waddington, which constitute the liberties of the city, and exclusively of the parishes of St Mary Magdalene and St Paul in the Bail, and part of the parish of St Margaret in the Close, which are in the wapentake of Lawress, 10,367 inhabitants This place was founded by the ancient Britons, on the summit of a hill near the river Lindis, now the Witham, from which it derived its name, and has been distinguished, from the most remote period of British history, as a city of considerable importance After the invasion of Britain by the Romans, that people made it one of their principal stations in this part of the island, and established here a colony, which, in reference to the ancient British name of the place, they called *Lindum Colonia*, to which, through all the variations and contractions in its orthography by the Saxons, Danes, and Normans, the present appellation, Lincoln, may be distinctly traced The Roman city was in the form of a parallelogram, four hundred and thirty yards in length, and four hundred in breadth, defended by strong walls, and intersected at right angles by two streets, at the extremities of which were four gates, of which the northern, now called Newport gate, partly remaining, forms one of the most interesting relics of Roman architecture in the kingdom it consisted of three arch-ways the central arch is sixteen feet in span, and twenty-two and a half in height above the ground, and is formed of large rough stones apparently laid without mortar, one of the lateral arches is built up, and the other open. To the south-west of the gate is a considerable angular fragment of a Roman building, supposed to have been the mint, and there are various portions of the original fortifications, besides the remains of a bath and a sudatorium

After the departure of the Romans from Britain, Lincoln was made the capital of the kingdom of Mercia by the Saxons, in opposing whom, Vortimer, who had greatly signalized himself, was slain, and interred here During the repeated encounters which had previously taken place, the city had suffered great injury, and, for the security of its new inhabitants, it was substantially repaired, that part without the gate of Newport, which had been originally occupied by the Britons, was entirely rebuilt, and fortified with walls and a moat In 786, the Danes took the city by assault, but it was retaken by the Saxons, and during these conflicts, which were resumed with extreme obstinacy, the northern suburb was completely destroyed At length, on the subjugation of the Danes by Alfred the Great, tranquillity was restored, but under his successors the invaders renewed their attacks, and ultimately, in the partition of the kingdom between the contending parties, Lincoln, with the rest of the kingdom of Mercia, came into the possession of Canute At the time of the Conquest, a castle was erected here by William the Conqueror, which occupied nearly

Arms.

one-fourth part of the Roman city, and to make room for the erection of which, not less than two hundred and forty mansions were taken down In Domesday-book the city is stated to have contained fifty two parishes , and it became the residence of a succession of monarchs, who contributed greatly to adorn it with a variety of splendid buildings, the numerous vestiges of which, in various parts of the town, convey but a faint idea of its former grandeur and importance In 1140, the castle was surprised by the forces of a party in the interest of the Empress Matilda, and subsequently besieged by Stephen, aided by the inhabitants , but the Earl of Gloucester coming to its assistance with a powerful army, Stephen was made prisoner , and being afterwards exchanged for the earl, who was subsequently captured, he regained his liberty, and after his restoration to the throne, celebrated the festival of Christmas here, in 1144 Henry II , on the death of Stephen, after being crowned King of England in London, underwent the ceremony of coronation a second time at Wigford, a little to the south of this city John, in the 3d year of his reign, received here the homage of David, King of Scotland, and, during his struggle with the barons, the inhabitants remained steadily attached to his cause, and withstood the attempts of the opposing army for a considerable time , but the city was taken at last by Gilbert de Gaunt, afterwards created Earl of Lincoln The castle was retaken by a party of royalists, after having been defended for nearly twelve months, but falling again into the hands of the barons, John, while marching to attack it, with a powerful army, lost all his carriages in crossing the washes After the death of this monarch, his son, Henry III , assisted by the inhabitants of Lincoln, who adhered firmly to the royal cause, continued the war with the barons, who, assisted by Louis, the Dauphin of France, laid siege to the city, but were vigorously repulsed by the inhabitants , many, endeavouring to escape, were drowned in the river Witham, and several others were taken prisoners The castle, after remaining for a considerable length of time in the possession of the Crown, came into that of the celebrated John of Gaunt, who made it his summer residence, and is said to have erected a palace here Edward I held parliaments in Lincoln, in 1301 and 1305 , Edward II in 1316, and the year following, and Edward III in the first of his reign it was also visited by Henry VI , who held his court in the bishop's palace , and Henry VII , after the battle of Bosworth Field, spent three days here, where he made a splendid procession, and offered up public thanksgiving for his victory over Richard III

During the parliamentary war, the inhabitants embraced the royal cause, and the city was alternately in the possession of the contending parties, from both of whom it sustained considerable injury, more especially in its ecclesiastical edifices, which, during their occupation of the city, were converted into barracks, by the soldiers of Cromwell's army Among the disastrous events which have befallen Lincoln may be recorded the great storm in 701, which occasioned the destruction of one hundred and twenty houses, and many public buildings In 1110, an accidental fire nearly consumed the whole city , and in 1185 it was greatly damaged by an earthquake It may also be mentioned that,

on the 27th of July, 1255, eighteen Jews were executed, for the alleged crime of crucifying a child, and many more were murdered by the enraged mob

The city is pleasantly situated on the summit and declivities of an eminence rising from the river Witham, the suburbs extending for a considerable distance along the vale to the north and south in the upper part the streets are narrow, and the buildings, with the exception of those connected with the cathedral, are of somewhat mean appearance , the lower part consists principally of one spacious street, and, under an act of parliament recently obtained, many judicious alterations and improvements have been effected It is paved, and lighted with gas, by a special act, and is supplied with water from three public conduits, of which that near St Mary's church, Wigford, is an elegant building in the later style of English architecture, decorated with a pierced parapet , and that near the High Bridge is ornamented with a handsome obelisk, erected in 1763 The air has been rendered more salubrious by the draining of the fens, a large tract of ground on both sides of the river, consisting of one hundred thousand acres, for which an act of parliament was obtained in 1762 The city library, established in 1812 , the new permanent library , and St Martin's parochial library, established in 1822 , and the medical library, instituted in 1825, are well supported , and there are two newsrooms and several book societies in the town The theatre is opened annually in September, October, and November , and assemblies are held in the city and county assembly-rooms The races take place in September, a handsome stand has been recently erected on the course In various parts of the town are the remains of the numerous monastic and other establishments which formerly flourished here , of these, the remains of John of Gaunt's palace are distinguished by a beautiful oriel window of fine composition, and a building, said to have been the stables belonging to the palace, has a finely-enriched Norman arch, with some interesting details of early English architecture of the castle, which occupied the south-eastern angle of the Roman city, very little remains, except part of the outer walls, which were seven feet thick, and the gateway tower , the site has been appropriated to the erection of the county gaol and other buildings

At the time of the Norman survey Lincoln was distinguished for its commercial importance, and Edward III granted a charter to the weavers, prohibiting the exercise of that trade within twelve leagues of the city, but this decree, in 1351, was abolished by another, called the statute of cloths, and in the following year, on the removal of the staple of wool from Flanders, it was established in this town, to which was also granted the staple of lead and leather From the time of Edward III till the commencement of the eighteenth century the trade of the town declined there are now no manufactures, and the trade is principally in corn and wool. The Fosse dyke, a Roman work of considerable importance to the interests of Lincoln, by means of which a communication was obtained with the river Trent, and which Henry I cleared out and deepened, had again become innavigable, from the accumulation of sand in its channel, and, in 1741, a lease of two-thirds of it was granted, for nine hundred and ninety-nine years, at a rent of £ 50 per annum, and of the remaining third, for ninety-nine years, at £25 per annum, by the corporation, to Mr Ellison of Thorne, by whose spirited exertions this canal was cleared from its obstructions and re-opened in 1745 it was subsequently widened and made deeper in 1826, and at present forms a line of communication, twelve miles in length, from the Witham to the Trent, completing the navigation from Boston and the eastern coast to the Humber, the Ouse, and to the several canals in the counties of Derby, Nottingham, Stafford, and York The market, on Friday, is held for corn in a spacious square, called Corn Hill, in the parish of St Mary, for butter and poultry, in a neat building near the church of St. Peter at Arches, erected in 1736, for butchers meat, in a building erected by the corporation in 1774, adjoining Butchery-lane, and divided into convenient shambles, for fish, at the High bridge, and for cattle, in the Beast-square, on the south of the city gaol The Spring markets are on the Thursday before the fifth Sunday in Lent, and every alternate Thursday till the April fair (which commences on the third Tuesday in that month, and continues four days), the Friday in Easter week, July 5th, the Wednesday, Thursday, and Friday after Sept 12th, October 6th, and November 28th, a market for fat cattle is held every other Wednesday, and there are statutes for hiring servants, on the 1st, 2nd, and 3rd Fridays after old May-day

Lincoln has, from an early period, enjoyed many privileges by prescription, and was formerly governed by a portreeve under the charter granted by Charles I, in 1628 by which the government is vested in a mayor, twelve aldermen, two sheriffs, four coroners, twenty-six common council-men, and four chamberlains, assisted by a recorder, town

Corporate Seal.

clerk, steward of the borough-mote courts, sword bearer, mace bearer, and subordinate officers The city, with a district of twenty miles around it, was erected into a county in the 3d of George I, under the designation of the City and County of the City of Lincoln The mayor is annually elected on the 14th of September, when the senior alderman, who has not previously served, is usually appointed to that office one of the sheriffs is appointed by the mayor, and the other is chosen by the corporation, from those who have filled the office of chamberlain the chamberlains are appointed by the mayor from among the freemen, at a court leet on the Monday after the festival of St Michael, and are liable to fine or imprisonment for refusing to serve The mayor, and the aldermen who have passed the chair, are justices of the peace for the city and county of the city The freedom of the city is inherited by all the sons of a freeman, or acquired by servitude, purchase, or gift of the corporation, among the privileges is that of depasturing a greater number of cattle on the common lands than a non-freeman The justices for the city hold quarterly courts of session, for all offences not capital, a court of petty sessions weekly, for the city and liberties, and a court of record every alternate week, at which the sheriffs preside, for the recovery of debts to any amount,

but which has nearly fallen into disuse A court of requests is held by commissioners appointed by an act passed in the 24th of George II, for the recovery of debts under 40s. The guildhall is an ancient embattled structure, rebuilt in the reign of Richard II the south front consists of a fine arched gateway, flanked with two round towers in a niche in the eastern tower is a statue of the angel Gabriel holding a scroll, and in a corresponding niche in front of the western tower is a statue of the Virgin Mary treading on a serpent, above the gateway, and in front of the towers, are the city arms and others, finely sculptured The sessions-house for the city is a neat brick edifice, erected in the New road, in 1809, and behind it is the city gaol and house of correction, containing six day-rooms, six airing yards, in one of which is a tread-wheel, and three solitary cells, the whole adapted to the classification of prisoners, and surrounded by a lofty brick wall The assizes for the county are held in the new county hall, an elegant structure erected, in 1823, after a design by Smirke, at an expense of £40,000, and the petty sessions for the parts of Kesteven are held here, on the first Friday in every month, at the Rein Deer inn those for the parts of Lindsey are held every Friday, at the Judges' lodgings, an elegant mansion erected on the Castle hill, at the expense of the county, for the accommodation of the judges of assize The county gaol stands on the south side of the area enclosed within the castle walls it is a spacious structure of brick, containing, in addition to the keeper's house and apartments for the confinement of debtors, twelve day-rooms, and eight airing yards the privilege of walking in the castle grounds is occasionally allowed to prisoners whose health may require that indulgence, and the airing yard, appropriated to the use of the debtors, comprehends an area of more than two acres the buildings are constructed on the plan of Mr Howard, and are in every respect well adapted to the classification of prisoners, and capable of being enlarged to an almost indefinite extent The city first exercised the elective franchise in the 49th of Henry III, since which time it has continued to return two members to parliament the right of election is vested in the freemen generally, whether resident or not, of whom more than one thousand two hundred polled at the last contested election sheriffs are the returning officers

Arms of the Bishoprick.

Lincoln was first erected into a see in the reign of William Rufus, when, in pursuance of the decree of a synod held at London, for the removal of all episcopal sees to fortified places, Remigius, Bishop of Dorchester, fixed upon this city as the seat of that diocese, and purchased lands for the erection of a church, an episcopal palace, and other requisite buildings having built the church, Remigius died previously to its consecration, and his successor, Robert Bloet, completed his design, beautified the cathedral, and increased the number of prebends The diocese, which was originally very extensive, was, in the reign of Henry II, curtailed by the separation of a part, to form that of Ely, and, in the reign of Henry VIII, it was still further diminished, by the separation of those districts which constitute the sees of Oxford and Peterborough It is still one of the most extensive and valuable in the kingdom, and comprehends six archdeaconries, fifty-seven deaneries, and one thousand three hundred and eighty parishes, and at the Reformation its revenue was £2065 12 6 The ecclesiastical establishment consists of a bishop, dean, precentor, chancellor, subdean, six archdeacons, fifty-two prebendaries, four vicars, eight vicars choral, organist, seven poor clerks, eight choristers, seven Burghurst chaunters, &c The cathedral, dedicated to the Virgin Mary, is situated on the summit of the hill, near the castle, and, from its commanding station, forms a conspicuous and magnificent object, of which the stately towers are seen from a distance of twenty miles, in almost every direction the original buildings, soon after their completion by Bishop Bloet, were greatly injured by an accidental fire, and repaired by his successor Bishop Alexander, who, to prevent the recurrence of a similar calamity, covered the aisles with a vaulted roof of stone, the pressure of which being too great for the strength of the walls, St Hugh, a subsequent bishop, rebuilt the church in the reign of Henry II, upon a plan then newly introduced, and greatly enlarged it by taking down the east end, and re-building it upon a more extensive scale, and it has been subsequently embellished and increased by various succeeding bishops The prevailing character of this noble building is the early style of English architecture, of a peculiarly rich kind, intermixed occasionally with the decorated and later styles, the form is that of a double cross the west front is partly in the Norman style, intermixed with the richest character of the early English the doorways are richly moulded and decorated with sculpture and statuary, over the central entrance are statues of several of the kings of England, and above is a noble window, highly enriched with tracery the western towers are of the Norman character in the lower stages and of the early English in the upper, they are one hundred and eighty feet high, and at each angle of the tower are octagonal turrets, crowned with pinnacles A lofty and magnificent tower rises from the intersection of the nave and the principal transepts, to the height of two hundred and seventy feet, formerly surmounted by a spire, which, in 1547, fell down, and greatly damaged the roof there were also spires on the western towers, which were taken down in 1807 The length of the building is five hundred and twenty five feet, the breadth, measuring along the principal transepts, two hundred and twenty-two feet, and along the eastern transepts, one hundred and seventy feet The nave, of which the roof, as well as those of the aisles, is finely vaulted, and supported on piers of peculiar richness, and arches of graceful form, is spacious and lighted by a range of clerestory windows at the end of the north transept is a fine circular window of the early English character, and at the extremity of the south transept is one of the most beautiful specimens of a decorated circular window now extant The choir, which is separated from the nave by an elaborately-carved stone screen, is remarkably rich in its decorations, and beautiful in its style, the east window, of eight lights, is a fine composition of flowing tracery, of the decorated character, and over the altar is a good painting of the

Annunciation, by the Rev W Peters, R A the piers and arches which support the roof are in the richest character of the early English style, and the bishops throne and the prebendal stalls are beautiful specimens of tabernacle-work, highly enriched The Lady chapel, and some smaller chapels adjoining it, are peculiarly elegant, and in various parts of this magnificent structure are features of uncommon interest and impressive beauty Among the numerous monuments are some of exquisite design, under an arch to the south of the Lady chapel, and in the south aisle, are those of Bishops Russell and Longland, whose effigies are finely sculptured in the north-west tower is the celebrated bell, called Tom of Lincoln, the weight of which is nearly five tons, and the tone peculiarly fine Prior to the Reformation the cathedral was distinguished for its immense wealth, and the sumptuous costliness of its decorations Henry VIII is said to have taken from its treasury two thousand six hundred and twenty-one ounces of pure gold, and four thousand two hundred and eighty five ounces of silver, exclusively of two gorgeous shrines, one of St Hugh, of gold, the other of St John de Alderby, of massive silver, and numerous pearls and precious stones of the most costly description Three sides of the cloisters are yet remaining in their original state, and exhibit a fine specimen of the decorated style, and on the fourth side is the library of later erection, containing an extensive collection of books, and some curious Roman antiquities in the centre of the quadrangle, and at some depth below the surface, a beautiful tesselated pavement was discovered a few years since, over which a covering has been placed, to protect it from injury On the east side of the cloisters is a passage leading to the chapter-house, an elegant building in the form of a decagon, of which the finely-vaulted roof is supported on a single pillar in the centre There are some remains of the episcopal palace, and of the conventual buildings connected with this extensive establishment, which, in grandeur, beauty, and antiquity holds a prominent rank among the ecclesiastical edifices in the kingdom

Lincoln formerly contained fifty-two parish churches, of which number, thirty-four were destroyed prior to the time of Edward VI it comprises at present the parishes of St Benedict, St. Botolph, St John Newport, St Margaret in the Close (part of which is in the wapentake of Lawress), St. Mark, St. Martin, St Mary le Wigford, St Mary Magdalene in the Bail and Close, (part of which is in the wapentake of Lawress), St Michael on the Mount, St Nicholas Newport, St Paul in the Bail, St Peter at Arches, St. Peter in East-gate, St Peter at Gowts, and St Swithin, and the parishes of All Saints Bracebridge, All Saints Branston, All Saints Canwick, and St Michael, Waddington, which are within the county of the city, all of them being within the archdeaconry and diocese of Lincoln. The living of St Benedict's is a perpetual curacy, endowed with £800 royal bounty, and £1200 parliamentary grant, and in the patronage of the Prebendary of North Kelsey in the Cathedral Church the church is an ancient building retaining some portions of Norman architecture The living of St Botolph s is a perpetual curacy, endowed with £400 private benefaction, and £400 royal bounty, and in the patronage of the Prebendary of St Botolph s in the Cathedral Church The living of St. John s Newport is a vicarage not in charge, endowed with £400 royal bounty, and in the patronage of the Prebendary of Dunholme in the Cathedral Church the church has been demolished The living of St Margaret s in the Close is a perpetual curacy, united with that of St Peters' in Eastgate, endowed with £600 royal bounty, and in the alternate patronage of the Precentor and the Prebendary of Haydor in the Cathedral Church the church was taken down in 1778, and soon afterwards rebuilt The living of St Mark s is a perpetual curacy, endowed with £800 royal bounty, and in the patronage of the Precentor of the Cathedral Church The living of St. Martin s is a discharged vicarage, rated in the king s books at £4 13 4, endowed with £8 per annum private benefaction, £600 royal bounty, and £200 parliamentary grant, and in the patronage of the Prebendary of St Martin s in the Cathedral Church The living of St Mary s Wigford is a discharged vicarage, rated in the king s books at £5 3 9, and in the patronage of the Prebendary of Gretton in the Cathedral Church the church retains considerable portions of its ancient Norman character The living of St. Mary Magdalene s in the Bail and Close is a discharged rectory, rated in the king s books at £5, endowed with £200 royal bounty, and £1400 parliamentary grant, and in the patronage of the Dean and Chapter The living of St Michael s on the Mount is a perpetual curacy, endowed with £1000 royal bounty, and £800 parliamentary grant, and in the patronage of the Precentor of the Cathedral Church the church is of comparatively modern erection The living of St Nicholas Newport is a vicarage not in charge, in the patronage of the Dean and Chapter the church has been demolished The living of St Paul s in the Bail is a discharged rectory, rated in the king s books at £2 5 10, endowed with £600 royal bounty, and £200 parliamentary grant, and in the patronage of the Archdeacon of Lincoln The living of St Peter s at Arches is a discharged rectory, rated in the king s books at £5 12 8½, endowed with £200 parliamentary grant, and in the patronage of the Crown the church has been elegantly rebuilt as the corporation church, and is fitted up in an appropriate style The living of St Peter s in Eastgate is a perpetual curacy, united with that of St Margaret s in the Close in 1778, endowed with £400 royal bounty, and in the alternate patronage of the Precentor and the Prebendary of Haydor in the Cathedral Church the church has been rebuilt The living of St Peter s at Gowts is a perpetual curacy, endowed with £600 royal bounty, and £1000 parliamentary grant, and in the patronage of the Precentor of the Cathedral Church the church is an old edifice, and has considerable vestiges of its ancient Norman character The living of St Swithin s is a perpetual curacy, endowed with £800 royal bounty, and £200 parliamentary grant, and in the patronage of the Precentor of the Cathedral Church the church is of late erection There are places of worship for general and particular Baptists, the Society of Friends, the late Countess of Huntingdon s Connexion, Independents, Wesleyan Methodists, and Unitarians, and a Roman Catholic chapel

The free grammar school was founded, in 1567, by Robert Monson, Esq a school, formerly supported by the Dean and Chapter, in the Cathedral Close, has been united with it, and is supported jointly by the Dean

and Chapter, who appoint the head master, and pay two-thirds of his salary, and by the corporation, who pay the remainder, and the salary of the usher, each amounting to £50 per annum there are about twenty-five boys, who are taught gratuitously in this school the premises form a part of the old Franciscan priory, which was fitted up for that use in 1583, by the founder of the school The Blue coat school was founded, in 1602, by Richard Smith, M D, who endowed it with the manor and some lands at Potter-Hanwarth, for the maintenance, education, and clothing of twelve poor boys, which number, in consequence of the improvement in the funds, the governors have augmented to fifty, who are admitted from the age of seven till eight, and after remaining in the school until fourteen years of age, are apprenticed, with a premium of £16, and two suits of clothes each the governors consist of the mayor, a gentleman resident in the city, another resident in the Close, the junior residentiary canon of the Cathedral Church, the senior alderman, the recorder, and the town clerk The Jersey school was founded, in 1693, and endowed with £700, bequeathed by Henry Stone, of Skellingthorp, Esq, for maintaining a master to teach children to spin jerseys, and afterwards to employ and pay them for their work, but the introduction of machinery has diminished the value of this institution A free school in the Bail was endowed with lands producing £12 per annum, by Mr Wilkinson, for the instruction of twelve poor boys, and placed under the direction of the Governors of the Blue coat school The National school, established in 1813, and supported by subscription, affords instruction to three hundred boys and two hundred girls, to whom articles of clothing are distributed at Christmas The county hospital, a spacious and handsome brick building, erected in 1769, and supported by voluntary subscription, has been productive of much benefit to the city and its neighbourhood it is under the direction of a committee, and is attended by three physicians and four surgeons the average expenditure is about £1300 per annum The general dispensary was established in 1826, and is supported by subscription the poor who require attendance at their own houses, are visited by the house surgeon, and by the dispensing apothecary, who supplies them with medicines The lunatic asylum is a spacious handsome edifice, two hundred and sixty feet in length, and having a portico of the Ionic order in the centre, erected in 1820, from a design by Mr Ingleman, at an expense of £15,000, and containing apartments for fifty patients, with warm and cold baths, and every requisite accommodation the building and the grounds occupy three acres and a half the establishment is under the direction of a president vice-president, and a committee of governors, who are chosen from the principal subscribers it is open to patients of every class, who are expected to contribute towards the expense in proportion to their ability The lying in hospital was instituted in 1805, and is supported by subscription The Dorcas Society is also supported by subscription, and has been found to contribute material assistance in supplying the poor with articles of clothing There are various other establishments, and numerous charitable benefactions for the relief of the poor, among which may be noticed a bequest by John Smith, Esq, of lands now producing

£600 per annum, a legacy by Lady Margaret Thorold of Marlston, in 1731, of £1500 South Sea annuities, for the purchase of lands now producing £60 per annum, the great tithes of Glenham, bequeathed by T Sutton, Esq, founder of the Charter-house, London, and various others

Among the numerous monastic establishments which anciently existed here were, a nunnery founded prior to the erection of the cathedral, the site of which is occupied by the Dean s house, an hospital for lepers, near the city, founded by Remigius, first bishop of Lincoln, or, according to other authorities, by Henry I, of which, in the reign of Edward III, the revenue was £30, a priory of Gilbertine canons, founded by Robert, second bishop of Lincoln, and dedicated to St Catherine, of which, at the dissolution, the revenue was £270 1 3, a priory of Benedictine monks, dedicated to St Mary Magdalene, and a cell to the abbey at York, founded prior to the reign of Henry II, of which the remains, now called Monks house, about half a mile to the east of the city, consist of the walls of several apartments and a small chapel, a house of Franciscan friars, the foundation of which is uncertain, houses of Carmelite and Augustine friars, the former founded in 1269, and the latter in 1291 within the Close was founded, in 1355, by Sir Nicholas de Cantelupe, a college of priests to officiate at the altar of St Nicholas, in the cathedral, besides various others, of several of which, traces may be distinctly perceived in various parts of the city and its environs The Jews house is an ancient edifice of curious design, and belonged to Belaset de Wallingford, a jewess, who was hanged in the reign of Edward I, for clipping the coin Near Brayford water are some vestiges of a fort called Lucy Tower, between which and the castle was a subterranean communication, and in the city is a chalybeate spring of considerable strength Lincoln gives the inferior title of earl to the Duke of Newcastle

LINCOLNSHIRE, a maritime county, bounded on the north by the broad æstuary of the Humber, on the east by the German ocean, and by the wide arm of it called the Wash, on the south by the counties of Cambridge, Northampton, and Rutland, and on the west by those of Leicester, Nottingham, and York it extends from 52° 38′ to 53° 44 (N Lat), and from 18′ (E Lon) to 1° 3′ (W Lon), and contains two thousand seven hundred and forty-eight square miles, or, one million seven hundred and fifty-eight thousand seven hundred and twenty acres The population, in 1821, amounted to 283,058 This portion of the territory of the Coritani was included, on the Roman division of Britain, in the province called Britannia Prima, and, from the Roman remains still existing here, it is evident that those conquerors not only considered this district of great importance, in the state in which they found it, but also made some considerable efforts towards that removal of its natural disadvantages which in latter ages have been prosecuted with such signal success Of the Anglo-Saxon kingdom of Mercia this shire formed an important part, its northern portion, the division of Lindsey, having been wrested from that kingdom by Edwin of Northumbria Christianity seems to have been first introduced into Lincolnshire, soon after the conversion of that sovereign, by the Romish missionary, Paulinus We are told by Bede, that Paulinus,

after converting the Northumbrians, came into the northern part of the kingdom of Mercia, that he converted Blecca, then Governor of Lincoln, and baptized many people of this district in the river Trent. The see of Sidnacester, which is known to have comprised the district or province of Lindsey, (although the site of Sidnacester itself, which appears to have been somewhere in that district, is a subject of controversy among antiquaries,) was established in 678, and continued until the latter part of the eleventh century, when St Remigius, the nineteenth bishop, transferred the see to Lincoln In 827, at Castor in this county, Egbert, King of Wessex, defeated Wiglaf, King of Mercia, who fled to Croyland, where he was concealed for three months, when, by the mediation of its abbot, Siward, he was restored to his kingdom, on paying homage and becoming tributary to Egbert This part of the English territory was particularly exposed, by its locality, to the incursions and ravages of the Danes, so that their sanguinary fury was wreaked upon it with especial frequency and violence Early in the year 870, having landed at Humberston, in Lindsey, they destroyed the ancient and famous monastery of Bardney, and, after wasting all the country around it with fire and sword, they came, about Michaelmas, into Kesteven, which they devastated in like manner At that time Algar, Earl of Mercia, and his two seneschals, or lieutenants, Wibert and Leofric, assembled all the youth of the parts of Holland, with a body of two hundred men belonging to Croyland abbey, and about three hundred more from Deeping, Langtoft, and Boston they were also joined by Morkar, Lord of Brunne, with his numerous retainers, and by the sheriff of Lincoln, with the Lincolnshire forces, five hundred in number, and the whole being mustered together in Kesteven, on St Maurice s day, gave the Pagans battle, and routed them with great slaughter, and the death of three of their kings, pursuing them to their camp, where finding a very obstinate resistance, night at length parted the combatants, and the earl drew back his army The Danes were joined in the night by other princes of their nation, who had distributed themselves over the neighbouring country for the purpose of plunder, and in the morning, the English, notwithstanding their inferior forces, again engaged them, and, by keeping themselves in a compact body, maintained the conflict the whole day, until, deceived in the evening by a feigned flight of the enemy, they quitted their ranks, when the Danes, turning upon them, made dreadful slaughter The Christian combatants were thus nearly annihilated, a few youths of Gedney and Sutton alone escaping to Croyland abbey, whereupon the monks immediately employed themselves in secreting and sending away their relics and other things valuable, but the barbarians, after burning the villages on their way, soon reached the monastery, made a general massacre of its inhabitants, and committed the whole monastic buildings to the flames next day they marched, with an immense spoil of cattle, &c, to Medeshamsted, now Peterborough In 873 the Danes wintered at Torksey, and were there visited by Burhred, King of Mercia, who purchased from them a short peace On the tranquil settlement of these invaders in this part of England, Lincoln and Stamford were two of the five principal towns which they occupied, and from them they were

M 2

not expelled until the year 941, in the reign of Edmund the Elder

From this period until the Norman Conquest the transactions of the episcopal church and see of Lincoln form the principal subjects of historical narrative. In the war between Stephen and the Empress Matilda, Lincoln and its vicinity were the scene of some of the most interesting events, that city having been twice besieged by the king, who captured it on the first occasion, but on the second, the siege being raised by the arrival of the Earl of Gloucester and his army, the king, after fighting with desperate valour, was made prisoner. In 1174, the Isle of Axholme, being at that period surrounded by water, and consequently a position of considerable strength, Roger de Mowbray, Constable of England, one of the adherents of Prince Henry in his rebellion against his father, Henry II, maintained himself there until compelled to surrender by the Lincolnshire men, who razed his castle. The year 1216 is memorable for King John's disastrous march into Lincolnshire, when, after losing all his baggage in the washes, and narrowly escaping with his life, he first rested at Swineshead abbey, whence, being attacked by dysentery, he was removed in a litter to Sleaford and thence to Newark, where he died. On the 4th of June in the following year, the associated barons under Gilbert de Gaunt, Earl of Lincoln, and the French under the Count of Perche, were defeated at Lincoln, by the Earl of Pembroke, regent for the young king, Henry III, when the French commander and most of his men were slain, and the principal barons and four hundred knights made prisoners. At a later period of the same reign, the Isle of Axholme afforded a retreat to many of the disaffected nobles, after the battle of Evesham. In 1536, at Barlings, commenced an insurrection of the Lincolnshire men, in consequence of the suppression of some religious houses; the insurgents were headed by Dr Mackerel, abbot of Barlings, under the assumed name of Captain Cobler; but, on receiving the king's promise of pardon, they dispersed, and Mackerel was taken and hanged at Tyburn.

This county was the theatre of some considerable military transactions in the last general civil war. In the year 1643, by an ordinance of both houses, it was added to the Eastern Association. On March 22nd of the same year, Grantham and its garrison were captured for the king, by Col Charles Cavendish; and shortly afterwards, near that town, twenty-four troops of royalist cavalry were defeated by Oliver Cromwell, at the head of his own regiment. On May 11th, at Ancaster, the parliamentarians, under the younger Hotham, were defeated by Col Cavendish. On the 30th of July, Gainsborough was taken by the parliament's forces, under Lord Willoughby of Parham, and its governor, the Earl of Kingston, made prisoner, who, in his passage down the Humber to Hull, was, in a mistake, shot by the royalists soon afterwards; near Gainsborough, the royalists were defeated by Cromwell, and their commander, General Cavendish, slain; and on October 11th of the same year, at Horncastle, Lord Widrington, at the head of a detachment of the Marquis of Newcastle's army, was defeated, five hundred royalists slain, and eight hundred taken prisoners, by the Earl of Manchester, who, on May 6th, 1644, stormed Lincoln, and captured its governor, Col Francis Fane, with about eight hundred men.

This county is included in the diocese of Lincoln, and province of Canterbury, and forms the two archdeaconries of Lincoln and Stow, the former, comprising the deaneries of Aswardhurn cum Lafford, Aveland, Beltisloe, Bolingbroke, Candleshoe, Calceworth, Gartree, Grantham, Graffo, Grimsby, Hill, Holland, Horncastle, Lincoln, Longobovey, Lovedon, Louth-Eske, Ness, Stamford, Walshcroft, Wraggoe, and Yarborough; and the latter, the deanries of Aslacoe, Corringham, Lawress, and Manley. The number of parishes is six hundred and nine, of which, three hundred and five are rectories, two hundred and forty-four vicarages, and the remainder perpetual curacies. Lincolnshire consists of three grand divisions; namely, Lindsey, which is much the largest, including nearly one-half of the county, and extending from the German ocean to the borders of Nottinghamshire, and from the river Witham to the Humber; Kesteven, which forms the south-western portion of the county; and Holland, the south-eastern. The division of Lindsey comprises, exclusively of the city of Lincoln, the hundreds, or wapentakes of Aslacoe (East and West), Bradley-Haverstoe, (Marsh and Wold divisions), Candleshoe (Marsh and Wold divisions), Corringham, Gartree (North and South), Hill, Lawress, Louth Eske (Marsh and Wold divisions), Ludborough, Manley (East, North, and West), Walshcroft (North and South), Well, Wraggoe (East and West), and Yarborough (East, North, and South), and the sokes of Bolingbroke (East and West), and Horncastle: that of Kesteven, exclusively of the town and soke of Grantham, and the town of Stamford, comprises the wapentakes of Aswardhurn, Aveland, Beltisloe, Boothby-Graffo (High and Low), Flaxwell, Langoe (First and Second divisions), Loveden, Ness, and Winnibriggs and Threo; and that of Holland, exclusively of the town of Boston, the wapentakes of Elloe, Kirton, and Skirbeck. The county contains the city of Lincoln, the borough and market towns of Boston, Grantham, Grimsby, and Stamford, and the market towns of Alford, Barton upon Humber, Bolingbroke, Bourne, Caistor, Donington, Epworth, Falkingham, Gainsborough, Glandford-Bridge, Holbeach, Horncastle, Kirton, Louth, Market-Deeping, Market-Rasen, Sleaford, Spalding, Spilsby, Long Sutton, Swineshead, Tattershall, Wainfleet, and Wragby. Two knights are returned for the shire, two citizens for the city of Lincoln, and two burgesses for each of the boroughs. Lincolnshire is within the Midland circuit; the assizes are held at Lincoln, where is the county gaol; quarter sessions are held at Boston, for the parts of Holland, at Bourne and Falkingham, for the parts of Kesteven, and at Kirton, Louth, and Spilsby, for the parts of Lindsey; there are one hundred and ten acting magistrates. The houses of correction are at Bourne and Falkingham, for the parts of Kesteven, at Kirton, Louth, and Spilsby, for the parts of Lindsey, at Spalding, for the parts of Holland, with the exception of the wapentakes of Kirton and Skirbeck, the house of correction for which is at Skirbeck. The rates raised in the county, for the year ending March 25th, 1827, amounted to £214,750, the expenditure to £214,368 7, of which £167,987 12 was applied to the relief of the poor.

The discriminative features of Lincolnshire are strongly marked by nature; these consist of the lowland tracts, comprising about seven hundred and se-

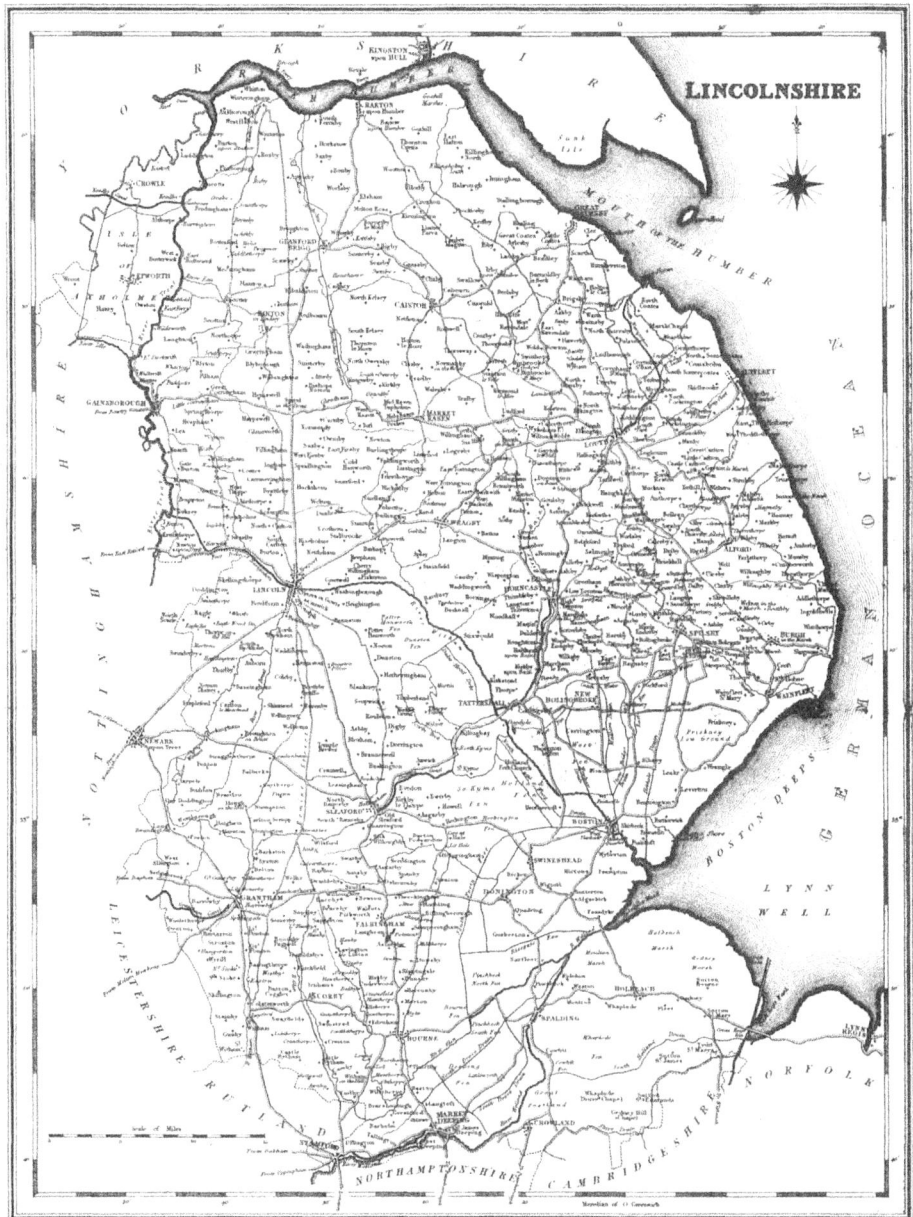

LINCOLNSHIRE

Drawn by R. Creighton. DRAWN & ENGRAVED FOR LEWIS' TOPOGRAPHICAL DICTIONARY. Engraved by J. & C. Walker.

venty-six thousand nine hundred and sixty acres, the heaths, extending to a great distance both north and south of Lincoln, the breadth of which, however, is not very great, and containing one hundred and eighteen thousand four hundred acres, and the Wolds in the north-eastern part of the county, which extend in length from Spilsby to the immediate vicinity of the Humber, and include about two hundred and thirty-four thousand eight hundred and eighty acres   Contiguous to the sea, in the southern part, spreads an immense extent of low land, much of which was once marsh land, but is now become, by means of the exertions made during a period of almost two hundred years, one of the richest tracts in the kingdom   it is a region of fertility, without beauty, in a climate which is not salubrious to the human constitution   Advancing northward, along the sea-shore, this tract becomes narrower, but is, however, continued to the Humber, on the margin of which it contracts to a mere stripe of marsh land, separated by the cliffs, which rise near the mouth of the Trent, from a nearly similar tract occupying all that part of the county lying on the left side of that great river   The heaths to the north and south of Lincoln, and the Wolds, are calcareous ranges of hills, commanding many fine views over the lower tracts   The remaining large portion of the county has no distinguishing feature, nor is it, on the whole, remarkable for superior fertility, yet from different situations in it are obtained beautiful and extensive views over the richer adjoining districts, more especially about Belton, and the cliff towns to the south of Lincoln, from the Cliff road to the north of that city, and in the vicinities of Gainsborough, Knaith, and Burton   The whole line of the Humber is included in the view from the higher Wolds, the surface of which is very uneven, in the neighbourhood of Louth, and more especially at Tathwell   there are also some very beautiful scenes in the neighbourhood of Thurgandy and Stainton

The climate has been greatly improved in salubrity by the drainage of the vast tracts of marshes, as a proof of which, upon the completion of the great Witham drainage, agues have been much less prevalent than before   The ague was formerly a common malady upon the margins of the Trent and Humber, but it disappeared in a great measure at the time of the draining of Wallin fen in Yorkshire   Along the whole coast the land is greatly exposed to the keen north-east winds, and in the months of March, April, and May, equally ungenial easterly winds are severely felt in the neighbourhood of Barton   this latter district also, at the time of the equinoxes, experiences extremely violent westerly winds, in consequence of which, the trunks of the trees are usually inclined towards the sea   The soils, besides other varieties in different situations and under various circumstances, include clay, sand, loam, chalk, and peat, which are all found in extensive districts   nearly all the variations extend in length from north to south   The heath, a high tract of land now enclosed   and from which the streams flow both eastward towards the ocean, and westward towards the Trent, has a soil of a good sandy loam, intermixed with a very small portion of clay, it is excellent turnip and barley land, and rests on a bed of limestone, its usual depth being from nine to eighteen inches. This high ground declines suddenly towards the west, the soil, on the declivity and for some distance into the lower tract, continuing much the same, at the first

line of villages, which extends in the same direction as the soil, from north to south, it is a rich loam, affording good pasturage   Beyond this is a tract of strong clay, which is harsh, stubborn, and unprofitable, very difficult to convert into good permanent grass, and next to this lies the immediate line of the Trent, which, like the borders of most rivers that pass through a flat country, has a soil of very rich warp loam of various descriptions   Returning to the heath hill, eastward of it, the country slopes gradually into a vale of soils too various for description, but not generally good   Half-way across this, towards the Wolds, is a narrow tract of good rising ground, extending in an irregular line, on which the villages are built, the whole district between the heath and the Wolds forming first the narrow ridge on which the villages are built, then the Ancholme flat, beyond which comes the ridge of pasture land, and lastly a bad flat moor, which is immediately succeeded by the Wolds   Between Gainsborough and Newark in Nottinghamshire, for the distance of twenty-five miles along the western border of this county, the whole is sand, with a flat marshy tract next the river Trent, which, however, is sometimes extremely narrow   eastward of this sand, which is good and in tillage, is a tract of cold wet clay, that becomes rich and makes excellent bean land, in the vicinity of Claypole, though much of it is subject to floods   A considerable tract about Grimsthorpe, Tromestead, Edenham, Swayfield, Bytham, Witham, &c, consists of sand, creech, and clay, the first being of a whitish, or light red, colour, the creech loam, the best arable land of the three, and the clay for the most part wet and poor   At Scott-Willoughby, Osbournby, and the neighbourhood of Falkingham, are three soils, viz, strong clay on a bottom resembling mortar, a wet creech loam, and rich hazel loam   from Belton to Normanton extends a remarkably rich tract of reddish-coloured land   The soil of the Isle of Axholme, lying to the west of the Trent, is among the finest in England, and comprises black sandy loams, warp land, brown sands, and rich soapy and tenacious loam   the understratum, in many places, is an imperfect plaster stone   In that corner of the county included between the Trent and the Humber are sand, cold clay, and various loams, the substratum of the whole being limestone at different depths   Barton Field, a tract containing six thousand acres, is a good dry turnip loam, upon chalk at various depths, fit for all ordinary crops   The soil of the great tract of the Wolds is a sandy loam on a chalk understratum, the quality of which greatly varies, from a poor sand to rich, deep, and fertile loams, that produce excellent crops of barley and wheat, and some even of beans   Between the eastern boundary of the Wolds and the sea is a tract divided into the Marsh and the Middle Marsh, the former consisting of a rich salt marsh, the soil of which is a fertile adhesive marine clay, and a very rich loam, while the latter is a line of strong land, the soil much resembling that of the marsh called "the Clays, extending from Beelsby towards Grimsby, and consisting of a strong brown loam much superior to real clay   To the west of Caistor is a barren moor, for some miles in extent, which consists of a peaty sand on a poor reddish sand stone. The soil of the wapentake of Skirbeck is very various   in that part near Boston, and some others, the surface is a rich loam resting upon a bed of clay, underneath which is found generally, at a certain level, the silt, which is a porous sea-sand, deposited many ages ago, and, when a surface soil, becomes hardened by the rain, but is not fertile near the sea is a thin surface of this resting upon clay, and near the fens a very stiff blue clay, the grass upon which is almost always mown the richest pastures are upon a black mould or mass of vegetable particles A large tract of sandy soil prevails from Spilsby to Revesby, and wholly, or partly, includes a great number of parishes The fen lands consist of a heavy deep sandy loam, which makes very rich breeding pastures for sheep, but not feeding pastures some also consist of a rich, soapy, blue clay, and others of black peat, which is formed of decayed vegetable substances, and, when drained, are considered to be the best for the purposes of tillage The whole of the south-eastern portion of the county, extending along the coast from near Wisbeach, northward, to Frieston beyond Boston, is of peat of great depth and extreme richness the understratum at Boston, when reached in boring, was found to consist of blue marl, the colour of Westmorland slate, and one hundred and fifty yards deep, with intervals of only a few inches There is a fen below Bourne and Morton, which joins the great tract to the Isle of Ely, and to Boston

The extreme flatness of the Lincolnshire coast, together with the slight fall and consequent sluggishness of the lower part of the course of the rivers, which terminate in æstuaries at its two extremities, have occasioned the formation, in remote ages, of a very large tract of marshes, occupying the whole eastern side of the present county, and forming upwards of a third of its superficies The extent of these fens, and the practicability of reclaiming some portion of them from their natural state of unproductiveness and insalubrity, seem to have attracted the attention of the Roman possessors of Britain, to whom is attributed the construction of the large drain called the Car-Dyke, signifying the fen dike, which extends from the river Witham, near Lincoln, to the river Welland, on the southern side of the county, the object and the use of which have been to receive the waters from the high grounds, which intersect that part of the county, running on the western side of the dyke, and so prevent them from inundating the low grounds immediately contiguous to it, on the east. The Old Sea Bank, as it is commonly called, which, though now running parallel with the shore at a considerable distance from the sea, has anciently protected the district of South Holland from inundation, is also considered to be a Roman work Of the tracts thus brought into cultivation, Deeping fen, on the banks of the Welland, appears to have received the earliest attention, for, at the beginning of Edward the Confessor s reign, a road was made across it, by Egebric, Bishop of Durham, and in the reign of William the Conqueror, Richard de Rulos, that monarch's chamberlain, enclosed this part of the fen country, from the chapel of St. Guthlake (now Market-Deeping) to the Car-Dyke, and beyond to Cleilake, near Cranmore, excluding the river Welland by a strong and extensive bank of earth As property became subdivided, greater attention was paid to the improvement of the soil, and various presentments were made, and grants obtained, for scouring the rivers, and draining off the superfluous waters The great trench, called the

Foss-Dyke, extending about seven miles from the great marsh near Lincoln, to the river Trent, in the vicinity of Torksey, was made, or materially altered, by Henry I, in 1121, as a general drain for the adjacent level, and also for the purpose of bringing up vessels from the Trent to Lincoln The cleansing of the channel of the Ancholme, with the like double object, first took place about the 18th of Edward I, and in succeeding reigns various statutes were enacted, for the more effectual drainage of this part of the county The Isle of Axholme was formerly one continued fen, owing to the silt, or sea-sand, washed up the channel of the Trent by the tides in the Humber, which, obstructing the waters of the Don and the Idle, forced them back over the circumjacent lands, so that their central parts, being the highest, formed a real island, the district still retaining the name of one, though no longer insular About the reign of Edward I, however, the draining of this tract appears to have commenced, and subsequently various commissions were granted for rendering it more effectual

In the beginning of the reign of Charles I., that important work was commenced, which embraced not only the marshes of Axholme, but all the adjacent fens, called Dikesmersh and Hatfield Chase, in the county of York These belonging chiefly to the crown, Charles II, under the Great Seal of England, contracted with Cornelius Vermuyden, Esq, of the city of London, by articles dated the 24th of May, in the second year of his reign, that the latter should, at his own charge, drain the lands specified, in consideration of which, he and his heirs for ever, should hold of the king one-third of the surrounding grounds, on the completion of the work, a corporation was to be formed of such persons as Vermuyden, or his heirs, should nominate, to make acts and ordinances for their preservation This great work was accordingly begun, and proceeded so successfully, that, at an expense of about £55,825, it was finished, within five years, the waters, which had usually overflowed the whole level, having been conveyed into the river Trent, through Snow sewer and Althorpe river, by a sluice, which excluded the flow of the tide, and discharged the drained water at every ebb It is traditionally affirmed, that large vessels could formerly sail up the river Witham, from Boston to Lincoln, which report seems to be corroborated by the fragments of vessels that have frequently been found near its channel at present, however, this river is navigable only for barges, and its current is so slow, that it does not clear away the accumulating mud The first notice of the inundations and other inconveniences arising from the obstruction of its waters, appears in the sixth year of Edward III, when commissioners were appointed for surveying it, between Lincoln and Beckingham other parts of the river were in like manner surveyed in subsequent reigns, and various regulations made for keeping its waters within due bounds, and conducting the land floods speedily to the sea In the reign of Henry VII., however, more effectual measures for the same purpose were found necessary, the most important of which was the construction of Boston sluice, to execute which a Flemish engineer, named Hake, was brought over and employed for defraying the expense, a rate was levied upon the lands lying in the contiguous wapentakes. To the north-east of the Witham, extending from that river nearly to Wainfleet, a distance of about twenty miles, lie large fenny tracts, called Wildmore fen, West fen, and East fen. Upon a writ of *Ad quod damnum*, issued in the 41st of Elizabeth, concerning the draining of these, it appears, that in East fen five thousand acres were under water, half of which was then considered drainable, and that the commons and severalties on the borders of the same fen contained about three thousand four hundred acres, the whole of which was surrounded and in the sixth of Charles I, at a session of sewers, held at Boston, it was decreed that the outfall at Wainfleet haven should be deepened and enlarged, and all other necessary works done for draining the said lands each person receiving benefit was to pay ten shillings to the undertakers. Down to the latter part of the last century however, notwithstanding the repeated exertions made in this branch of agricultural improvement, the success had scarcely been answerable to the amount of labour and expense employed, but since then, other undertakings of the same kind have been carried on with increased skill and spirit, and with far greater success. Deeping fen, which extends for nearly the whole of the eleven miles between Market-Deeping and Spalding, was drained towards the close of the last century it comprises about fifteen thousand acres, two-thirds of which is taxable under commissioners. Alnwick fen, containing one thousand and ninety-seven acres, and Holland fen, twenty-two thousand acres, have also been drained the very existence of the latter tract, as firm land, depends upon the security of its banks. In that long reach of fen extending from Lincoln to Tattershall a vast improvement has been made, by embanking and draining, the first act for which purpose was obtained in 1787, or 1788, and between twenty and thirty square miles of country have been enclosed and cultivated in consequence.

In the northern part of the county, the important drainage of the Ancholme Level was completed, in the latter part of the last century, by carrying the drain in a straight line through the low lands, of which those taxed to the drainage amount to seventeen thousand one hundred and ninety-seven acres, and are now chiefly pasture and meadow. The drainage of the Isle of Axholme, too, is one of very great importance. Since the year 1630, ten thousand acres have been secured from the sea, by means of embankment, in the parish of Long Sutton, and a new tract has been taken in, according to act of parliament, at Winteringham. At Humberston is a large piece of land fenced in from the sea by means of a low bank, and great tracts of valuable land yet remain to be secured from the sea, about North Somercoates, and other places on that part of the coast the distance between high water mark and low water mark is there as much as two miles. In the reparation of the banks that secure the marsh land from the sea, the towns next the coast, called Frontage towns, defray the expense, but in case of such a breach as renders a new bank necessary, the expense is assessed, according to the highest tides ever known, by level, over all the country below such level of high water, under the direction of the commissioners of sewers, the distance from the sea subject to taxation for drainage will, therefore, vary according to the level of the country. An act of parliament was obtained, in 1792, for embanking and draining certain salt marshes

and low lands in Spalding, Moulton, Whaplode, Holbeach, and Gedney, containing in all five thousand three hundred and thirty nine acres. South Holland, grossly estimated at one hundred thousand acres, has long been an object of embankment, of the banks that have been formed upon this tract, at various periods, the Old Sea-dyke bank is unquestionably Roman the New Sea-dyke bank, which is two miles nearer to the sea than the old one, still remains, but it is unknown when, or by whom, it was made. In taking the levels for making the new drain, it was found that the surface, on advancing to the Roman bank from the land, suddenly rose six feet, and continued on that level towards the sea, such being the depth of warp, or silt, deposited by the sea, since that bank had been made. In 1792, the act was obtained for the formation of the new embankment, a work of profit to the public, as well as to the proprietors.

In 1794, an act was passed for improving the outfall of the river Welland, and for better draining the low grounds, and discharging their waters into the sea, which object was to be effected by cutting an immense canal, from the reservoir below Spalding, capable of conducting the whole waters of the river Welland into the Witham, below Boston. About the year 1799, it was estimated that the total amount of land in Lincolnshire, which, at various periods, had been made available by drainage, was not less than one hundred and fifty thousand acres. Since that calculation was made, acts of parliament, for the better drainage of East, West, and Wildmore fens, amounting to upwards of thirty thousand acres, were passed in the 41st and 43rd years of the reign of George III the expenses amounted to about £400,000, and the value of the land recovered to about £2,000,000 the drainage was complete, and the land under cultivation, so early as the year 1808. In the fens of Lincolnshire, the *soak* is often spoken of, by which expression is meant the subterraneous water found at various depths, usually at only a very few feet below the surface this rises and sinks according to the season, and is supposed, from its saline quality, to be the sea-water filtered through a stratum of silt, which, more especially in Holland fen, seems to be very general, and at no great depth from the surface. It has also been remarked of this district, that, although retaining its ancient name of fen, it is now, on the whole, more in danger of suffering from want of water in summer, than from a superabundance of it in winter, for, in case of drought, the great drains become very shallow, and the water retained in the earth passes off, in a great measure, through the filtering stratum of silt, so that it is necessary to dig deep, in that season, to obtain water for the cattle.

On the arable lands no particular rotation of crops is observed, as they vary still more than the soils, in the fens, however, they always commence the course with paring and burning. Rape is very extensively cultivated in almost every part of the county, more especially in the fens and low lands its chief application is for feeding sheep. The woad grown is upon the deep rich loams and frequently in the saline maritime levels, grass land, upon the soil of which this plant is found to flourish best, is very commonly broken up for its cultivation the crop is regularly gathered twice, and in favourable seasons a third is wholly or partially collected, this third crop is of an inferior kind, when properly prepared, it is shipped chiefly into Yorkshire and Lancashire The artificial grasses mostly cultivated are, red clover and white, tre foil, lucerne and sainfoin, with various kinds of hay-seeds Many onions are cultivated in the Isle of Axholme The rich grazing lands of Lincolnshire are its distinguishing feature, in an agricultural point of view they are to be found on a rich loamy clay, sometimes very stiff, but of uncommon fertility The quantity is extremely great, the finest being in the vicinities of Boston, Algarkirk, Fosdyke, Sutterton, Kirton, Frampton, Wyberton, and Skirbeck, and these during the summer will feed a bullock and a half, besides four sheep, per acre, and two sheep per acre during the winter The marsh pastures, which lie between the Wolds and the sea, are for the most part of excellent quality, the best are used for feeding, those of inferior quality for breeding and keeping stock in common order Hanworth, to the north of Lincoln, is principally grass land, and there is a fine tract of second-rate pasture land, lying in the vale, between the heath and the Wolds The marsh grass lands on the Trent produce from a ton to a ton and a half of hay per acre on the hilly Wolds are some valuable pas tures About two thirds of the wapentake of Skirbeck is under grass, part of which is mown the best pasture is chiefly stocked with shearling wethers, bought in the spring, which, having yielded two fleeces, are sold the next year, and with cattle, during the summer, which are sold in the autumn the second best is grazed by young beasts and sheep, and a few breeding sheep, the worst is chiefly mown The marshes near the sea-shore, from Wrangle northward to Sutton, are separated from the higher part of the county by the fens, and the parishes situated on the clays From Tealby, on the edge of the Wolds, to Wragby, is a constant succession of grass lands, with hardly any tillage, and from Semperingham down to Deeping is a line of rich grazing land, two or three miles broad One of the most powerful of ma nures known in this county is the fish called Stickle back, it is extremely abundant in the east and west fens, and also comes from the sea into Boston haven Lime, and white, blue, and red marl are also used, and to these may be added a singular practice which subsists on the Wolds, of manuring by spreading dry straw on the land and then burning it there The water of the tides that run up the Trent, Ouse, Don, and other rivers that fall into the Humber, is muddy to an excess, and the peculiar custom of *warping*, which is very extensively followed, is by letting in the tide over the level lands on their banks, at high water, to deposit the muddy particles it contains, provincially called *warp*, and then permitting the water to run off again as the tide falls, for which purpose canals are made, joining the river, and having sluices at their mouths, which may be opened or shut at pleasure Around the fields to be warped, to prevent the water flowing over contiguous lands, are raised banks of from three or four, to six or seven feet high, according to circumstances one-eighth of an inch, on an average, is deposited by each tide that is let in upon the land

The live stock of this county are very numerous the two principal breeds of cattle are the Lincolnshire short-horned, and the Leicestershire long-horned, the former of which seems to be most generally preferred In the vicinity of Falkingham is found a dun-

coloured breed, said to have been originally brought from the Isle of Alderney there are also a few cattle of the several breeds of Devon, Teeswater, Holderness, Durham, and Alderney, and crosses between the long-horned and the short-horned breeds, between that of Devonshire and that of Lincolnshire, and between the Lincoln and the long horned Craven There are no dairies except for private use and the supply of the neighbouring markets with butter, the chief objects of the agriculturists being breeding and feeding About Normanby, Burton, &c, great numbers of cattle are bred but few are fed here, as they are generally sold to the graziers in the marshes Oxen are very frequently worked, more especially on the Wolds, and in the tract of country extending from Barton, by Grimsby, to Louth The two principal breeds of sheep are, the native Lincoln and the Leicester, the latter of which has become very general it is computed that there are usually not less than two million four hundred thousand sheep in the county The hogs common in Holland fen, about Boston, and its vicinity, are of inferior mongrel sorts, which, however, have been latterly improved Many thousand acres are occupied as rabbit-warrens in different parts of the county, the rabbits being of the silver and common grey kinds, with some black and some white ones Great quantities of geese are still kept in the low fenny tracts, though not to the same extent as formerly A considerable number of horses is bred in this county in Holland fen the number of breeding mares is very great, and about Normanby, Burton, &c, are bred from mares universally black, many saddle and coach horses, some of which are sold at Howden in Yorkshire, and the rest at the celebrated Horncastle fair Numerous cart-horses are bred in the marshes about Saltfleet On the Wolds some of the finest blood horses in the kingdom are bred, and greater attention is paid to them here even than in Yorkshire, or Durham A society, called the Lincolnshire Agricultural Society, was established at Falkingham, in 1796, being the earliest of the kind in the county

Very little of any kind of manufacture is carried on about Normanby and Burton, however, a good deal of flax is spun and woven into linen the woollen manufacture is conducted on a very small scale at Boston At the port of Gainsborough, besides the ship-building, which is an important branch of business, a considerable quantity of rope and coarse hemp sacking is made In Holland fen the women spin flax, and about Falkingham they spin flax and hemp

The principal rivers are the Trent, the Welland, the Witham, and the Ancholme The Trent first touches Lincolnshire at North Clifford, from which place to Stockwith, a few miles below Gainsborough, it forms its western boundary, separating it from the county of Nottingham at this latter point it begins to form the eastern border of the Isle of Axholme, which it separates from the rest of the county, until it has received the waters of the Don, opposite Aldborough, soon after which it joins with the Ouse to form the great æstuary of the Humber It is navigable as high as Gainsborough for merchant vessels of considerable burden, and for barges in all the rest of its course on the border of this county The Welland first reaches the county near Stamford, forming its southern boundary, and separating it from Northamptonshire, it flows by that town to Market Deeping, where it enters the fens, and between that place and Crowland wholly enters Lincolnshire, and divides into two branches, one of which proceeds south by east to Wisbeach, apparently in the natural course of the stream, while the other continues its sluggish course through an artificial channel to Spalding below which town, having been enlarged by the waters of the Glen, it empties itself into Foss-dyke wash, to the south of Boston The Witham, the whole course of which river is in this county, rises near South Witham, about ten miles north of Stamford, whence it proceeds due north to Grantham, below which, having run some distance in a westerly direction, it again assumes a northerly course, through a wide sandy valley, to Lincoln hence it flows in an easterly direction to Grubhill, where it turns to the south east, and passing near Tattershall, proceeds to Boston, below which town it falls into the ocean at Boston Deeps from Boston upwards towards Lincoln much of the present channel of this river is artificial, having been made for the purpose of improving the navigation, and better draining the contiguous fens The Ancholme is a small river, which, rising in the Wolds near Market Rasen, takes a northerly course, by Glandford-Bridge, to the Humber, from which it has been rendered navigable as high as Bishop-Bridge The large bay, or æstuary, called the Wash, into which the rivers passing through the immense tracts of fen land in the south eastern portion of the county are disembogued, is for the most part extremely shallow, and full of shifting sands

An artificial navigation has been cut along the course of the Witham, from Boston to Lincoln, whence it is continued by the Foss-dyke canal to the Trent the act for the formation of this navigation was obtained in 1788, in which year also it was completed, to the great benefit of Lincoln, and of the whole country through which it passes A canal from the river Witham, at Sleaford, to Boston, was completed in 1796 The Grantham canal extends from that town, through the north-easternmost part of Leicestershire, to the Trent, near Holm-Pierrepoint it was completed in 1796, is thirty-three miles in length, and cost £100,000 it passes near some fine beds of plaster, and lime, in large quantities, is brought along it from Crich in Derbyshire The Ancholme cut, which drains the Ancholme level, is navigable from Bishop Bridge to the Humber, at Ferraby sluice A navigable canal has also been formed, extending from Horncastle to the river Witham, at Dog-dyke, near Tattershall, and another from Louth to the sea, at Tetney

The great road from London to Edinburgh, after crossing the south-western corner of this county, for the space of about two miles, at Stamford, re-enters it about ten miles beyond that town, and, passing through Grantham, finally quits it for Nottinghamshire at Shire Bridge, about four miles south of Newark The great road from London to Hull enters at Market-Deeping, and runs the whole length of the county, passing through Bourne, Falkingham, Sleaford, Lincoln, and Glandford-Bridge, to Barton, where is the great ferry across the Humber to Hull the road from London to Grimsby branches off from the Hull and Lincoln road just within the northern verge of Northamptonshire, and, entering this county at St James', Deeping, passes through Spalding, Boston, Spilsby, and Louth

The Roman stations within the county were, Ad Abum, supposed to have been at Winterton, Aquis, at Aukborough, Bannovallum, at Horncastle, or Ludford, Causennæ, at Ancaster, or Great Ponton, Crococolana, at Brough, Iindum, at Lincoln, and Vainona, at Wainfleet The principal ancient roads are as follows the British Ermin-street, afterwards adopted by the Romans, first enters the county to the west of Stamford, then running by Great Casterton, in Rutlandshire, it proceeds by Ancaster and Lincoln to near the banks of the Humber A branch of this road diverges from it about five miles north of Lincoln, and crosses the Trent, near Littleborough, proceeding in a north-westerly direction to Doncaster Another branch left the Ermin-street, about six miles north of Stamford, and ran by Stainby, Denton, and Bottesford, towards Ad Pontem in its way to Southwell and Bawtry The Fosse way, beginning on the coast, not far from Ludborough, is visible from Ludford to Lincoln, and forward to Brough, and beyond that place in its course towards Newark The British road, called the Salt-way, branched from the Ermin street, near Ponton, and ran by Denton into Leicestershire There are remains of other British trackways, particularly of one running from Horncastle towards Caistor and the Humber The Car-Dyke already mentioned, and believed to have been of Roman construction, extends from the river Welland, on the southern side of the county, to the river Witham, near Lincoln, being sixty feet wide, with a broad flat bank on each side It has also been mentioned that the innermost of the great embankments of South Holland, called the Old Sea Bank, was also constructed by the Romans Remains of Roman buildings, and various miscellaneous relics of that people, have been found on the sites of the different stations above-mentioned Some of minor importance have also been discovered at Scampton, Torksey, Stow, Gainsborough, Caistor, Well, Gedney Hill, Whaplode, Pinchbeck, Sleaford, Little Ponton, and Denton

The ecclesiastical edifices in the division of Lindsey, excepting the cathedral of Lincoln, are inferior to those in the other parts of the county, they are of various periods, from the reign of Edward III, down to that of Henry VII The division of Kesteven abounds with churches, both magnificent in plan and rich in decoration, the greater portion of them having lofty central spires Those of Sleaford, Leasingham, Heckington, Threckingham, Horbling, and Grantham, with St Mary's, St John s, and All Saints, in Stamford, are particularly deserving of notice, as excellent specimens of ancient English architecture, and, from their height, form prominent objects from various distant points in the county The date of the churches in this division, excepting those of Sempringham, and St Leonard (Stamford), is in few instances earlier than the thirteenth century, and scarcely any of them having been rebuilt, few will be found of a more recent date than the reign of Henry VII It is principally, however, in the division of Holland that Lincolnshire exhibits superior excellence in ecclesiastical architecture among the numerous fine edifices of this kind which adorn this naturally unpicturesque district, may be specified the churches of Boston, Gosberton, Pinchbeck, Holbeach, Gedney, Spalding, Long Sutton, and Crowland, of these, the five first afford excellent specimens of the architecture of the fourteenth century This division has few churches of a later date than the reign of Edward III the stone of which they are built is invariably found to be of an excellent and durable quality some of them are cruciform, many have spires like those in Kesteven, and the rest have an embattled tower at the west end At the period when most of them were erected, the parts of Holland being one extensive fen, it was necessary to make artificial foundations, which was done so skilfully that few of the churches have swerved from their perpendicular Specimens of Anglo-Saxon, or early Norman, architecture are to be found in parts of the churches of Stow, Clee, Crowle, Washingborough, Fiskerton, St Peter at Gowts (Lincoln), and a few others The religious houses were particularly numerous, amounting to no fewer than one hundred and eight, in which number are included five Alien priories, five houses of the Knights Templars, five colleges, and fourteen hospitals The principal remains of monastic buildings are those of the abbeys of Bardney, Barlings, Crowland, and Swineshead, of Sempringham priory, and of Thornton college The most remarkable ancient castellated buildings which remain, either wholly or in part, are the castles of Tattershall, Torksey, Lincoln, and Falkingham, there are similar remains at Horncastle, Caistor, Somerton, Stamford, Scrivelsby, Bolingbroke, Pinchbeck, and Pilham, to which may be added Moor, Kyme, and Hussey towers of the castles of Bourne and Sleaford only the earthworks now exist There are ancient encampments near Brocklesby, Hibalston, Broughton, Roxby, Winterton Cliffs, Aukborough, Yarborough, South Ormsby, Burwell, Stamford, Gainsborough, Winteringham, Humington, Ingoldsby, Castle Carlton, Burgh Brough, and Barrow In the low districts of this county the water is almost every where brackish In the parishes of Tetney, Fulstow, and that vicinity, are some blow-wells, being flowing pits of clear water, about thirty feet in depth, the discharge of which is very powerful there is one of these wells at Bourne, the water of which turns a mill at a very short distance from its source at Louth is a spring which always runs in summer but never in winter The division of Lindsey gives the title of earl to the family of Bertie, and the division of Holland that of baron to the family of Fox

LINDALE, a chapelry in the parish of CARTMEL, hundred of LONSDALE, north of the sands, county palatine of LANCASTER, 3 miles (N E by E) from Cartmel The population is returned with the parish The living is a perpetual curacy, in the archdeaconry of Richmond, and diocese of Chester, endowed with £400 private benefaction, and £400 royal bounty, and in the patronage of Lord G H Cavendish

LINDETH, a joint township with Warton, in the parish of WARTON, hundred of LONSDALE, south of the sands, county palatine of LANCASTER, 4¾ miles (W S W) from Burton in Kendal The population is returned with Warton

LINDFIELD, a parish in the hundred of BURLEYARCHES, or BURARCHES, rape of PEVENSEY, county of SUSSEX, 3¾ miles (E by N) from Cuckfield, containing 1410 inhabitants The living is a perpetual curacy, in the peculiar jurisdiction and patronage of the Archbishop of Canterbury The church, which is dedicated to St John the Baptist, is in the decorated and later

styles of English architecture There is a place of worship for Independents A school of industry was founded, by William Allen, Esq, of London, for the instruction of children of both sexes in the art of agriculture, and various trades the building is of clay covered with cement, so as to give it the appearance of stone Fairs are held on April 1st and May 12th, for sheep and cattle, and on the 5th of August for lambs The river Ouse is navigable for barges to this place

LINDLEY, a hamlet in the parish of HIGHAM on the HILL, hundred of SPARKENHOE, county of LEICESTER, 5¼ miles (W by N) from Hinckley The population is returned with the parish Here are the ruins of an ancient chapel Mr William Burton, the Leicestershire antiquary and historian, and his brother Robert, author of the Anatomy of Melancholy, were natives of this place, the former born in 1575, and the latter in 1576

LINDLEY, a chapelry in the parish of HUDDERSFIELD, upper division of the wapentake of AGBRIGG, West riding of the county of YORK, 3 miles (N W by W) from Huddersfield, containing 2040 inhabitants A new church, or chapel, has recently been erected in this chapelry by the parliamentary commissioners, capable of accommodating eight hundred and sixtyseven persons, four hundred and fifty of the sittings are free the estimated expense was £2615 There is a place of worship for Wesleyan Methodists Lindley school was rebuilt by subscription in 1817 the site was given, in 1706, by Thomas Thornhill, Esq, and in 1767, Samuel Haigh devised £100 to trustees, the interest of which is paid to the master, who teaches about sixty scholars on moderate terms A considerable woollen manufacture is carried on here.

LINDLEY, a township in that part of the parish of OTLEY which is in the upper division of the wapentake of CLARO, West riding of the county of YORK, 3¾ miles (N E by N) from Otley, containing 178 inhabitants

LINDON, a hamlet in the parish of ROCK, lower division of the hundred of DODDINGTREE, county of WORCESTER The population is returned with the parish

LINDRICK, an extra-parochial liberty, in the lower division of the wapentake of CLARO, West riding of the county of YORK, 2¾ miles (W by S) from Ripon, containing 62 inhabitants

LINDRIDGE, a parish comprising the chapelries of Knighton upon Teme and Pensax, and the hamlet of Newnham, in the lower division of the hundred of OSWALDSLOW, though locally in the upper division of that of Doddingtree, county of WORCESTER, 5½ miles (E) from Tenbury, containing 1735 inhabitants The living is a vicarage, in the archdeaconry of Salop, and diocese of Hereford, rated in the king's books at £26 12 11, and in the patronage of the Dean and Chapter of Worcester The church is dedicated to All Saints A court leet is held annually The river Teme runs through the parish

LINDSELL, a parish in the hundred of DUNMOW, county of ESSEX, 4 miles (S E by S) from Thaxted, containing 353 inhabitants The living is a discharged vicarage, in the archdeaconry of Middlesex, and diocese of London, rated in the king's books at £8 The Earl of Guilford was patron in 1821

LINDSEY, a parish in the hundred of COSFORD, county of SUFFOLK, 4 miles (W N W) from Hadleigh, containing 232 inhabitants The living is a perpetual curacy, in the archdeaconry of Sudbury, and diocese of Norwich, and in the patronage of the Provost and Fellows of King s College, Cambridge The church is dedicated to St Peter This place was formerly celebrated for the manufacture of an article which has received the name of "Linsey Woolsey ' On a farm, called the Chapel farm, are the remains of an old chapel, now used as a barn, and on the same estate there is a Danish encampment

LINEHAM, a parish in the hundred of KINGS-BRIDGE, county of WILTS, 4¼ miles (S W) from Wootton-Basset, containing 910 inhabitants The living is a perpetual curacy, in the archdeaconry of Wilts, and diocese of Salisbury, endowed with £1400 parliamentary grant H Long, Esq was patron in 1815 The church is dedicated to St Michael Ralph Broome, in 1715, bequeathed £450, the income to be applied in teaching thirty children In the vicinity is a farm-house, which occupies the site of Bradenstoke priory, founded, about 1142, by Walter de Evreux, on de Saresbiæ, for Augustine monks, and dedicated to the Blessed Virgin

LINESIDE, a township in the parish of ARTHURET, ESKDALE ward, county of CUMBERLAND, 3 miles (E S E) from Longtown, containing 210 inhabitants This township lies at the confluence of the Esk and Line rivers, and is intersected by the Hallburn rivulet

LINFORD (GREAT), a parish in the hundred of NEWPORT, county of BUCKINGHAM, 1¾ mile (W S W) from Newport-Pagnell, containing 408 inhabitants The living is a rectory, in the archdeaconry of Buckingham, and diocese of Lincoln, rated in the king s books at £20 0 2½ Lord Bagot and others were patrons in 1786 The church is dedicated to St Andrew, the porch of the north door has a groined roof, with foliage in the centre In 1702, Sir William Pritchard bequeathed a rent-charge of £24 in support of an almshouse for six poor persons, likewise another of £10 for the instruction of children Lady Pritchard subsequently bequeathed a sum of money for apprenticing poor boys, and clothing the inmates of the almshouse Dr Richard Sandy, otherwise Napier, presented to this rectory in 1589, was held in superstitious reverence for his skill in the sciences of physic and astrology, and is said to have died in the posture of prayer, at a very advanced age

LINFORD (LITTLE), a parish in the hundred of NEWPORT, county of BUCKINGHAM, 2¼ miles (W by N) from Newport-Pagnell, containing 73 inhabitants The living is a perpetual curacy, in the archdeaconry of Buckingham, and diocese of Lincoln, endowed with £200 private benefaction, and £600 royal bounty The Rev P Knapp was patron in 1815 The church, dedicated to St. Leonard, was formerly a chapel of ease to the vicarage of Newport-Pagnell the inhabitants bury at Haversham

LING, a parish in the hundred of ANDERSFIELD, though locally in that of Taunton and Taunton-Dean, county of SOMERSET, 6¼ miles (S S E) from Bridgwater, containing, with part of the hamlet of Borough-bridge, 335 inhabitants The living is a discharged vicarage, in the archdeaconry of Taunton, and diocese of

Bath and Wells, rated in the king's books at £10 8 4 endowed with £600 private benefaction, £400 royal bounty, and £300 parliamentary grant Hill Dawes, Esq was patron in 1806 The church is dedicated to St Bartholomew Between the hamlet of Borough-bridge, part of which is in this parish, and the parish church, is the isle of Athelney, an elevation whereon is Alfred's monument, having been the noted retreat of that Saxon monarch during one of the Danish invasions Here, about 888, Alfred founded a Benedictine abbey, and dedicated it to Our Saviour and St Peter, the revenue of which, at the dissolution, amounted to £209 0 3¼ many architectural remains, bones, and other ancient relics, have been dug up on the site of the conventual buildings, which appear to have been both extensive and magnificent The navigable river Parret runs on the north-east, and the Tone on the south-east, of the parish, over which latter river is a bridge

LINGARTHS a township in the parish of ALMOND-BURY, upper division of the wapentake of AGBRIGG, West riding of the county of YORK, 5¼ miles (S.W by W) from Huddersfield, containing 809 inhabitants

LINGEN, a parish in the hundred of WIGMORE, county of HEREFORD, 4 miles (E N E) from Presteigne, containing 284 inhabitants The living is a perpetual curacy, in the archdeaconry and diocese of Hereford, endowed with £1000 royal bounty, and in the patronage of the Rev Thomas Wynn. The church is dedicated to St Michael

LINGFIELD, a parish in the first division of the hundred of TANDRIDGE, county of SURREY, 6 miles (S S E) from Godstone, containing 1684 inhabitants The living is a perpetual curacy, in the archdeaconry of Surrey, and diocese of Winchester, endowed with £1000 parliamentary grant Robert Ladbrooke, Esq was patron in 1819 The church is dedicated to St Peter and St Paul Here is a place of worship for Baptists A small sum is paid by the parish annually for the instruction of children. A collegiate church was founded here by Reginald, Lord Cobham in the reign of Henry VI, and dedicated to St Peter at the dissolution the revenue was valued at £79 15 10

LINGWOOD, a parish in the hundred of BLOFIELD, county of NORFOLK, 2¾ miles (W S W) from Acle, containing 292 inhabitants The living is a perpetual curacy, in the archdeaconry and diocese of Norwich, endowed with £1000 royal bounty The Rev E Goddard was patron in 1816 The church is dedicated to St Peter

LINKENHOLT, a parish in the hundred of PAS-TROW, Kingsclere division of the county of SOUTHAMP-TON, 7¾ miles (S E) from Great Bedwin, containing 73 inhabitants The living is a rectory, in the archdeaconry and diocese of Winchester, rated in the king s books at £7 0 5 Mrs Worgan was patroness in 1801 The church is dedicated to St Peter

LINKINHORNE, a parish in the northern division of EAST hundred, county of CORNWALL, 4 miles (N W) from Callington, containing 1080 inhabitants The living is a vicarage, in the archdeaconry of Cornwall, and diocese of Exeter, rated in the king's books at £13 Miss Hewish was patroness in 1780 The church is dedicated to St Mellor A free school for all the children of the parish was founded and endowed with the interest of £705, by Charles Roberts; two-

N 2

thirds of this sum are paid to the schoolmaster, and the remainder to a schoolmistress On Caernadon, or Carraton, downs, in this parish, Charles I drew up his forces, in 1644, the day after he had entered Cornwall, and here he was joined by Prince Maurice Here are the remarkable rocks called the Cheese wring and the Hurlers , as also Sharp Tor, from which is a very fine view

LINLEY, a parish within the liberty of the borough of WENLOCK, county of SALOI, 4¼ miles (N W by N) from Bridgenorth, containing 96 inhabitants The living is a rectory not in charge, united to that of Broseley, in the archdeaconry of Salop, and diocese of Hereford The church is dedicated to St Nicholas

LINMOU1H, a township in the parish of WOODHORN, eastern division of MORPETH ward, county of NORTHUMBERLAND, 7¼ miles (E N E) from Morpeth, containing 22 inhabitants This township derives its name from being situated near the river Line, at its confluence with the ocean in 1822, a spermaceti whale, sixty one feet in length, and thirty-seven feet four inches in circumference, came on shore at the mouth of the river, and was harpooned , it produced nine tons and one hundred and fifty-eight gallons of oil, which was claimed by the Admiralty as a droit of the crown

LINOP, a joint township with Ingram and Greenside hill, in the parish of INGRAM, northern division of COQUETDALE ward, county of NORTHUMBERLAND, 8¼ miles (S S W) from Wooler, containing, with Ingram and Greenside-hill, 74 inhabitants In this township is Linop Spout, a cataract, the precipice of which is forty-eight feet, and the basin seven feet in diameter, and fifteen feet in depth , it has also the appellation of Roughting Linn About three miles to the north-west are the Cardlaw cairns, some sepulchral monuments of the earliest inhabitants of the island. In the vicinity are foundations of an ancient British town, the area measuring two hundred and forty feet on the north side, and three hundred and two on the west A British road passes near this place, in its course to Langley ford

LINSHEELES, a township in the parish of HALLYSTONE, western division of COQUETDALF ward, county of NORTHUMBERLAND, 11¼ miles (W by N) from Rothbury, containing 97 inhabitants

LINSLADE, a parish in the hundred of COTTESLOE, county of BUCKINGHAM, 2 miles (N by W) from Leighton-Buzzard, containing 370 inhabitants The living is a perpetual curacy, in the archdeaconry of Buckingham, and diocese of Lincoln, endowed with £800 royal bounty, and in the patronage of A Corbett, Esq The church is dedicated to St Mary In the thirteenth century this place was noted for the resort of pilgrims, and frequent processions, to a holy well here, until they were prohibited, in 1299, by Oliver Sutton, Bishop of Lincoln, who cited the vicar to appear in his court, for having encouraged these pilgrimages to his own emolument A market on Thursday, and a fair, to be held for eight days at Lady-day, were granted, in 1251, to William de Beauchamp

LINSTEAD, a parish in the hundred of TEYNHAM, lathe of SCRAY, county of KENT, 3¼ miles (S E) from Sittingbourne, containing 890 inhabitants. The living is a vicarage, in the archdeaconry and diocese of Canterbury, rated in the king's books at £8 3 11½, and

in the patronage of the Archdeacon of Canterbury The church, dedicated to St Peter and St Paul, has lately received an addition of one hundred and fifty free sittings, the Incorporated Society for the enlargement of churches and chapels having granted £15 towards defraying the expense A fair for horses and cattle is held at Green street, in this parish, on May 12th Bartholomew Fowle, the last prior of St Mary Overie, was a native of this place, and received from it the additional name of Linstead

LINS FEAD (MAGNA), a parish in the hundred of BLYIHING, county of SUFFOIK, 4¾ miles (W by S) from Halesworth, containing 103 inhabitants The living is a perpetual curacy, in the archdeaconry of Suffolk, and diocese of Norwich, endowed with £600 royal bounty, and in the patronage of Lord Huntingfield The church is dedicated to St Peter

LINSTEAD (PARVA, or LOWER), a parish in the hundred of BLYIHING, county of SUFFOIK, 3¼ miles (W) from Halesworth, containing 164 inhabitants The living is a perpetual curacy, in the archdeaconry of Suffolk, and diocese of Norwich, endowed with £600 royal bounty, and £200 parliamentary grant, and in the patronage of Lord Huntingfield The church is dedicated to St Margaret

LINSTOCK, a township in that part of the parish of STANWIX which is in ESKDALE ward, county of CUMBERLAND, 2½ miles (N E by E) from Carlisle, containing 231 inhabitants Here was anciently a castle, which, till 1229, was the only palace of the bishops of Carlisle , about 1293, Bishop Halton entertained Johannes Romanus, Archbishop of York, in it, with a suite of three hundred persons, during his visitation , and in 1307, Edward I kept his court here for six days this edifice was repaired and modernised in 1768 , the ancient square tower is still remaining A little north-eastward of Linstock is Drawdykes castle, originally built with the materials of the Roman wall, which crossed its site, and partially rebuilt in the seventeenth century, by John Aglionby, Esq , recorder of Carlisle, who placed on the battlements three Roman stone busts which yet remain this ancient seat is now used as a farm-house , the Drawdykes estate is toll-free of the city of Carlisle

LINTHORP, a township in the parish of MIDDLESBOROUGH, western division of the liberty of LANGBAURGH, North riding of the county of YORK, 3½ miles (E by S) from Stockton upon Tees, containing 196 inhabitants

LINTHWAITE, a chapelry in the parish of ALMONDBURY, upper division of the wapentake of AGBRIGG, West riding of the county of YORK, 4 miles (S W by W) from Huddersfield, containing 2127 inhabitants There is a place of worship for Wesleyan Methodists Here is a considerable woollen manufacture

LINTON, a market town and parish, in the hundred of CHILFORD, county of CAMBRIDGE, 10½ miles (S E by E) from Cambridge, and 48 (N by E.) from London, containing 1519 inhabitants This town, which is situated on the high road from Cambridge to Colchester, is very indifferently built , the streets are neither lighted nor paved, but the inhabitants are well supplied with water from springs The market, granted in 1245, to William de Lay, is on Thursday , and there is a fair on July 30th, for sheep A court leet is held occasionally by the lord of the manor The living is a discharged vicarage, in the archdeaconry and diocese of Ely, rated in the king s books at £10 13 4 , and in the patronage of the Master and Fellows of Pembroke Hall, Cambridge The church, dedicated to St Mary, has a fine embattled tower , in the interior are several monuments, especially one of marble, erected by Peter Standley, Esq , to the memory of his sister There are places of worship for the Society of Friends and Independents An Alien priory, subordinate to the abbey of St Jacutus de Tusula in Britanny, was founded in the time of Henry III , at the suppression its revenue was valued at £23 8 10 , and it was granted by Henry VI to Pembroke Hall, Cambridge At Barham, in this parish, a priory of Crouched friars, a cell to the monastery of Welnetham in Suffolk, was established in the reign of Edward I the hall, chapel, and cloisters of the convent are still remaining, and form part of the mansion called Barham hall Several Roman coins have been dug up in this parish

LINTON, a township in the parish of CHURCH-GRESLEY, hundred of REPTON and GRESLEY, county of DERBY, 5½ miles (S S E) from Burton upon Trent, containing 241 inhabitants There is a place of worship for Wesleyan Methodists Linton is in the honour of Tutbury, duchy of Lancaster, and within the jurisdiction of a court of pleas held at Tutbury every Tuesday, for the recovery of debts under 40s

LINTON, a parish including the sea-port of Linmouth, in the hundred of SHERWILL, county of DEVON, 14 miles (E by N) from Ilfracombe, containing 632 inhabitants This parish, which is situated on the most northerly point of the Devonshire coast, comprises two manors, the lords of which had the power of inflicting capital punishment in the time of Edward I The village of Linton is situated on an eminence westward of an opening towards the Bristol channel, and is separated from the adjoining parish by the river Lyn, over which is a bridge of one arch Within a short distance to the east, by the sea side, near the junction of the East and West Lyn rivers, is Linmouth, formerly a fishing town of some consequence, but now possessing only about a dozen fishing-boats Turbot, soles, cod, herrings, and oysters, are still caught upon the coast, and shipped to Bristol and elsewhere several sloops, of from fifty to one hundred tons , are employed in the coasting trade , limestone, coal, and culm, are the principal articles of importation bark and grain the chief exports Here is a small pier, erected by the lord of the manor, which has afforded shelter to vessels of two hundred tons burden Both at Linton and Linmouth there are numerous lodging-houses for the accommodation of visitors , and in the neighbourhood are some elegant private residences Here is a plentiful supply of excellent water , and the river Lyn abounds with trout The lord of the manor holds a court leet and baron at Linton, soon after Easter, when a portreeve, tything-man, and ale-taster are appointed

The living is a perpetual curacy, with that of Countisbury, in the archdeaconry of Barnstaple, and diocese of Exeter, and in the patronage of the Archdeacon The church is dedicated to St Mary , and the prospect from the churchyard, embracing the rocky coast, the Bristol channel, and the Welch mountains, is singularly grand and beautiful There is a place of worship for Independents The scenery in this parish is of an Alpine character, and comprises every variety of form and colouring , the views are extensive, being terminated in the distant horizon by the shores of South Wales About a mile westward of Linton is the Valley of Rocks, presenting a forcible contrast to the general views the bed of this valley is about three quarters of a mile in length, but not above one hundred yards in width The acclivities on each side exhibit huge masses of fixed and detached rocks , and at the western extremity of the valley, which is terminated by a cove, or inlet, there is an isolated mass of great magnitude, somewhat in the form of a cone, partly intercepting the view of the chan nel The chain of rocks forming the northern side of the valley fronts the sea, and along this stupendous declivity is a path on the same level with the bed of the valley, leading from its north-west extremity to the village of Linton

LINTON, a hamlet in that part of the parish of CHURCHAM which is in the lower division of the hundred of DUDSTONE and KING S BARTON, county of GLOUCESTER, 1¾ mile (W by N) from Gloucester, containing, with Higham and Over, 252 inhabitants

LINTON, a township in the parish of BROMYARD, hundred of BROXASH, county of HERFFORD, 3 miles (S E) from Bromyard, containing 565 inhabitants A court leet was formerly held here, but has been discontinued for some time

LINTON, a parish in the hundred of GREYTREE, county of HEREFORD, 5 miles (E by N) from Ross, containing 630 inhabitants The living is a vicarage, in the archdeaconry and diocese of Hereford, rated in the king s books at £8 10 , and in the patronage of the Representatives of J Matthews, Esq The church is dedicated to St Mary There is a place of worship for Baptists A court leet is held once in three years

LINTON, a parish in the hundred of MAIDSTONE, lathe of AYLESFORD, county of KENT, 4 miles (S) from Maidstone, containing, with Crockhurst, 686 inhabitants The living is a vicarage, in the archdeaconry and diocese of Canterbury, rated in the king s books at £7 13 4 , and in the patronage of Earl Cornwallis The church is dedicated to St Nicholas In 1813, John Bowles bequeathed £200, the interest to be applied for the instruction of four children the income is £10 17 11 , which is paid to a schoolmistress, who instructs sixteen children in reading and sewing This village is situated near the great range of hills which bounds the Weald on the north About half a mile from it is Coxheath, an extensive plain, well watered and highly salubrious, on which have been several large encampments , in the year 1778 fifteen thousand men encamped on this heath

LINTON, a hamlet in the parish of WINTRINGHAM, wapentake of BUCKROSE, East riding of the county of YORK, 7½ miles (E) from New Malton The population is returned with the township of Wintringham

LINTON, a township in the parish of SPOFFORTH, upper division of the wapentake of CLARO, West riding of the county of YORK, 1¾ mile (W by S) from Wetherby, containing 167 inhabitants There is a place of worship for Wesleyan Methodists

LINTON, a parish in the eastern division of the wapentake of STAINCLIFFE and EWCROSS, West riding of the county of YORK comprising the townships of Grassington, Hebden, Linton, and Threshfield, and containing 1910 inhabitants, of which number, 313 are in the township of Linton, 9 miles (N) from Skipton The living is a rectory, in the archdeaconry and diocese of York, in medieties, each rated in the king's books at £16, and in the patronage of the Crown The church, dedicated to St. Michael, contains two reading-desks, the duty being peformed alternately by the two portionists, between whom the tithes of the parish are equally divided, each having also a parsonage-house The free school was founded and endowed with a rent-charge by the Rev Matthew Hewitt, £20 per annum is paid to the master, and £10 to the usher there are four exhibitions, of £12 per annum each, to St John's College, Cambridge, and the school is open to all applicants, for instruction in Latin and English grammar In 1721, Richard Fountain devised a rent-charge to trustees, among other charitable purposes, for apprenticing four boys annually, and for the foundation and support of an almshouse for six poor persons, each of whom receive £10 annually there are at present six poor widows

LINTON (WEST), or LEVINGTON, a township in the parish of KIRK-LINTON, or KIRK-LEVINGTON, ESKDALE ward, county of CUMBERLAND, 3 miles (S) from Longtown, containing 623 inhabitants

LINTON upon OUZE, a township in the parish of NEWTON upon OUZE, wapentake of BULMER, North riding of the county of YORK, 9 miles (S S W) from Easingwould, containing 268 inhabitants There is a place of worship for Roman Catholics, also a school with a small endowment

LINTZ-GREEN, a township in the parish of CHESTER le STREET, middle division of CHESTER ward, county palatine of DURHAM, 8 miles (8 W by W) from Gateshead, containing, with part of Tanfield colliery, 714 inhabitants

LINWOOD, a parish in the southern division of the wapentake of WALSHCROFT, parts of LINDSEY, county of LINCOLN, 2½ miles (S by E) from Market-Rasen, containing 138 inhabitants The living is a rectory, in the archdeaconry and diocese of Lincoln, rated in the king's books at £16 4 2, and in the patronage of A Wallis, Esq The church is dedicated to St Cornelius

LINWOOD, an extra-parochial liberty, in the northern division of the hundred of NEW FOREST, New Forest (East) division of the county of SOUTHAMPTON The population is returned with Godshill and Wood Green

LIPHOOK, a hamlet in the parish of BRAMSHOTT, hundred of ALTON, Alton (North) division of the county of SOUTHAMPTON, 4½ miles (W) from Haslemere. The population is returned with the parish

LIPWOOD, a township in the parish of WARDEN, north-western division of TINDALE ward, county of NORTHUMBERLAND, 7¾ miles (W) from Hexham, containing 526 inhabitants Grindon Lake, is situated in this township

LISCARD, a township in the parish of WALLAZEY, lower division of the hundred of WIRRALL, county palatine of CHESTER, 12 miles (N by E) from Great Neston, containing 345 inhabitants

LISCOMBE, a hamlet in the parish of SOULBURY,

hundred of COTTESLOE, county of BUCKINGHAM, 3 miles (W by N) from Leighton Buzzard The population is returned with the parish

LISKEARD, a borough, market town, and parish, having separate jurisdiction, though locally in West hundred county of CORNWALL, 18 miles (S S W) from Launceston, and 225 (W S W) from London, containing 3519 inhabitants, of which number, 2423 are in the borough The ancient name of this place was Lis Kerrett, derived probably from two

Seal and Arms.

Cornish words signifying "a fortified place ' It was formerly amongst the possessions of the Earls of Cornwall, and was, by act of parliament, annexed to the duchy, in the reign of Edward III the castle was occasionally the residence of Richard, Earl of Cornwall, King of the Romans In 1643, during the civil war, a battle was fought near this place, between the royalists, under Sir Ralph Hopton, and the parliamentary forces, in which the latter were defeated, and the royalist army marched into Liskeard the same night The king, on his entrance into Cornwall in 1644, halted here on the 2nd of August, and remained in the town until the 7th Liskeard is one of the most ancient and considerable towns in the county part of the town, which is irregularly built, is situated on rocky eminences, and the rest in a plain below the streets are well paved, but not lighted, the inhabitants are supplied with excellent water, and the air is considered very salubrious The river Looe runs through the parish The tanning of leather is carried on to a limited extent considerable facility for water carriage has been afforded by the canal from Liskeard to Looe, a distance of six miles, which has been recently completed, and terminates about one mile west of the town, where there is a paper mill This is one of the four coinage or stannary towns, but no coinage had taken place for some time, till within the last two years, when it was revived A handsome markethouse for poultry, fish, and vegetables, was erected, in 1822, at the expense of the corporation the butchers shambles are beneath the town-hall The market, on Saturday, is abundantly supplied with provisions of all kinds, a great part of which is purchased for the market at Devonport there are likewise great annual markets, on Shrove-Tuesday, the day after Palm-Sunday, and the Monday after St 'Nicholas' day Large cattle fairs are held on Holy Thursday, Aug 15th, Sep 21st, and Oct 2nd Liskeard was made a free borough, in 1240, by Richard, Earl of Cornwall, who conferred on the burgesses similar privileges to those enjoyed by the burgesses of Launceston and Helston, the date of the original charter of incorporation is unknown By the existing confirmatory charter of Elizabeth, granted in 1580, the corporation consists of a mayor, recorder, eight capital burgesses, and an indefinite number of freemen, with four constables, two serjeants at mace, and other officers the mayor is annually chosen from among the capital burgesses, by the freemen, and the freemen and burgesses fill up vacancies in their respective bodies The mayor and recorder are justices of the peace within the borough, the county magistrates having occasionally concurrent jurisdiction Sessions are held within a month of Easter, and on the first Tuesday after the 18th of Oct , also a court of pleas, every three weeks, for the recovery of debts to any amount, at which the mayor and capital burgesses, assisted by the recorder, preside Petty sessions for the east division of the hundred of West are also held, on the first Tuesday in every month This borough first sent representatives to parliament in the 23d of Edward I the right of election is vested in the mayor, capital burgesses, and an indefinite number of freemen chosen by them, at present amounting to forty-four the mayor is the returning officer the influence of the Earl of St Germans is predominant The town-hall, which is supported by granite columns, was erected, about 1707, at the expense of — Dolben, Esq , one of the representatives of the borough

The living is a vicarage, in the archdeaconry of Cornwall, and diocese of Exeter, rated in the king s books at £18 13 11½ The Rev Dr Gwynne was patron in 1821 The church, which is dedicated to St Martin, stands on an eminence at the eastern entrance into the town it is spacious and handsome, being built of fine large slate stone, and has a low embattled tower, which was erected in 1627 a tenement, called Lanseaton, now let at £50 per annum, is vested in the churchwardens for the repairs of the church There are places of worship for the Society of Friends, Independents, and Wesleyan Methodists A grammar school is supported by the Earl of St Germans, who allows a salary of £100 per annum to the master A free school for poor children, in which ten girls are now taught, was founded by the trustees of a donation by the Rev St John Eliot, who died in 1760, and endowed by them with £5 per annum a school for one hundred boys was opened about fifteen years ago, on Dr Bell's plan , and another for fifty girls, both supported by subscription In 1714, John Buller gave £18 per annum, for teaching and clothing poor boys , and there are other small benefactions for teaching children There are some vestiges of the ancient castle , and a great part of the conventual buildings belonging to the nunnery of Poor Clares, founded here, and endowed by Richard, Earl of Cornwall, yet remain it is called "The Great Place, and has been converted into dwelling-houses, the chapel is now a bakehouse About the year 1400, here was an hospital for lepers, dedicated to St Mary Magdalene

LISSETT, a chapelry in the parish of BEEFORD, northern division of the wapentake of HOLDERNESS, East riding of the county of YORK, 7½ miles (S S W) from Bridlington, containing 95 inhabitants The chapel is dedicated to St James

LISSINGTON, a parish in the western division of the wapentake of WRAGGOE, parts of LINDSEY, county of LINCOLN, 4¼ miles (S) from Market-Rasen, containing 183 inhabitants The living is a rectory, in the archdeaconry and diocese of Lincoln, rated in the king s books at £12 17 6 , and in the patronage of the Dean and Chapter of York The church, which is dedicated to St John the Baptist, has some portions in Norman, and others in the early style of English, architecture There is a place of worship for Wesleyan Methodists

LISTON, a parish in the hundred of HINCKFORD, county of ESSEX, 2¾ miles (N N W) from Sudbury,

containing 73 inhabitants The living is a rectory, within the jurisdiction of the Commissary of Essex and Herts, concurrently with the Consistorial Court of the Bishop of London, rated in the king s books at £12 W H Campbell, Esq was patron in 1800 The church is in the later style of English architecture

LITCHAM, a parish (formerly a market town) in the hundred of LAUNDITCH, county of NORFOLK, 7¼ miles (N E by N) from Swaffham, containing 586 inhabitants The market has been discontinued , but a fair for toys is held November 1st The county magistrates hold a session here once in six weeks , and a court leet is held annually in October, by the lord of the manor The living is a discharged rectory, with which that of East Lexham was united in 1742, in the archdeaconry and diocese of Norwich, rated in the king s books at £9 2 6 , and in the patronage of Lord Wodehouse The church is an ancient structure, dedicated to St Andrew, and built of flint and stone at the west end is a square embattled tower of brick, with freestone quoins , and there is an ancient carved oak screen A National school is supported by subscription An hospital, founded and endowed by Mr John Haloot, comprises tenements for two poor persons, who receive a small weekly allowance, chargeable on land in the adjoining parish of Beeston Here was anciently an hermitage, which has been converted into a farm house

LITCHBOROUGH, a parish in the hundred of FAWSLEY, county of NORTHAMPTON, 5½ miles (N W) from Towcester, containing 393 inhabitants The living is a rectory, in the archdeaconry of Northampton, and diocese of Peterborough, rated in the king's books at £16 9 7 , and in the patronage of the Rev W A Taylor The church is dedicated to St Martin A schoolmaster receives £25 per annum from Lady Katherine Leveson s charity, for educating all the poor children of the parish that are sent to him Litchborough was one of the four British garrisoned towns taken by the Saxons in 571

LITCHFIELD, a parish in the hundred of KINGSCLERE, Kingsclere division of the county of SOUTH AMPTON, 4 miles (N) from Whitchurch, containing 85 inhabitants The living is a rectory, in the archdeaconry and diocese of Winchester, rated in the king's books at £12 19 7 Sir R Kingsmill, Bart was patron in 1814 The church is dedicated to St James

LITCHURCH, a hamlet in that part of the parish of ST PETER, DERBY, which is in the hundred of MORLESTON and LITCHURCH, county of DERBY, 1½ mile (S E) from Derby, containing 93 inhabitants

LITHERLAND, a township in the parish of SEPHTON, hundred of WEST DERBY, county palatine of LANCASTER, 4¾ miles (N by W) from Liverpool, containing 501 inhabitants

LITHEWELL, or LUDWELL, a chapelry in the parish of DAWLISH, hundred of EXMINSTER, county of DEVON, ¾ of a mile (S by W) from Chudleigh The chapel is in ruins

LITTLEBOROUGH, a chapelry in that part of the parish of ROCHDALE which is in the hundred of SALFORD, county palatine of LANCASTER, 3¾ miles (N E by E) from Rochdale, with which the population is returned. The living is a perpetual curacy, in the archdeaconry and diocese of Chester, endowed with £600 private benefaction, £800 royal bounty, and £1300 parliamentary grant, and in the patronage of the Vicar of Rochdale The chapel, dedicated to St James, was licensed for mass by the abbey and convent of Whalley, in 1476 it was rebuilt about 1815, in the early style of English architecture, and has received an addition of four hundred and one sittings, of which three hundred are free, the Incorporated Society for the enlargement of churches and chapels having granted £300 towards defraying the expense There is a place of worship for Wesleyan Methodists Here was a small Roman station, and several antiquities have been found in the vicinity the Roman road from Manchester to York skirts the village

LITTLEBOROUGH, a parish in the North-clay division of the wapentake of BASSETLAW, county of NOTTINGHAM, 8½ miles (E by N) from East Retford, containing 64 inhabitants The living is a perpetual curacy, in the archdeaconry of Nottingham, and diocese of York, endowed with £1200 royal bounty J Hewett, Esq was patron in 1820 Here was the Roman station *Segelocum*, or *Agelocum*, and numerous Roman remains have been found The river Trent is here crossed by a ferry, which has existed ever since the Roman era in Britain.

LITTLEBOURN, a parish in the hundred of DOWNHAMFORD, lathe of ST AUGUSTINE, county of KENT, 4¼ miles (E) from Canterbury, containing 698 inhabitants The living is a vicarage, in the archdeaconry and diocese of Canterbury, rated in the king's books at £8, and in the patronage of the Dean and Chapter of Canterbury The church is dedicated to St Vincent A fair is held on the 5th of July A branch of the river Stour, on which are two corn-mills, passes by the village

LITTLEBURY, a parish in the hundred of UTTLESFORD, county of ESSEX, 2 miles (W N W) from Saffron-Walden, containing 766 inhabitants The living is a discharged vicarage, in the jurisdiction of the Commissary of Essex and Herts, concurrently with the Consistorial Court of the Bishop of London, rated in the king s books at £10 2 1, and in the patronage of the Rector the rectory is a sinecure, rated in the king s books at £26 13 4, and in the patronage of the Bishop of Ely The church, which is dedicated to the Holy Trinity, stands within the area of an ancient encampment On Chapel green was formerly a chapel of ease In 1585, Dame Jane Bradbury bequeathed land and houses for the instruction of all children born in the parish

LITTLECOT, a chapelry in the parish of CHILTON-FOLIATT, hundred of KINWARDSTONE, county of WILTS, 3 miles (W by N) from Hungerford The population is returned with the parish A curious tesselated pavement, the largest ever found in England, was discovered in Littlecot park, in 1730, but, unfortunately, soon destroyed it was forty one feet by twenty-eight in dimensions, and is supposed to have been the floor of a temple, from the two parts, the *Templum* and the *Sacrarium*, into which it was divisible It was decorated with various devices in the centre was a figure of Apollo with his harp, surrounded by four female figures, to represent the four seasons, with appropriate accompaniments an accurate drawing was made of it by Mr William George, steward to Edward Popham, Esq, who discovered it, and his widow worked a beautiful carpet, on a reduced scale, from which it was finally engraved, at the expense of the Antiquarian Society Pickedfield, formerly part of Littlecot domain, was purchased by government, in 1803, for the purpose of establishing a depôt for the interior of the county it includes about forty acres of ground, on which were erected three magazines, capable of containing near eleven thousand barrels of gunpowder, also a mixing-house for the powder, storehouses, apartments for the labourers employed upon the establishment, barracks for a military detachment, and houses for a store-keeper and clerk of the cheque At Knyghton, a small hamlet on the north bank of the Kennet, near Littlecot park, is an ancient encampment

LITTLECOTE, a hamlet in the parish of STEWKLEY, hundred of COTTESLOE, county of BUCKINGHAM, 5½ miles (S E by E) from Winslow The chapel, now in ruins, was a chapel of ease to Stewkley

LITTLEDALE, a chapelry in that part of the parish of LANCASTER, which is in the hundred of LONSDALE, south of the sands, county palatine of LANCASTER, 5¼ miles (E by N) from Lancaster, with which the population is returned The living is a perpetual curacy, in the archdeaconry of Richmond, and diocese of Chester, endowed with £200 private benefaction, and £600 royal bounty, and in the patronage of the Vicar of Lancaster The chapel was consecrated in 1755, and dedicated to St Anne under Caton

LITTLEHAM, a parish in the hundred of EAST BUDLEIGH, county of DEVON, 1½ mile (E) from Exmouth, containing, with the chapelry of Exmouth, 2841 inhabitants The living is a discharged vicarage, in the peculiar jurisdiction and patronage of the Dean and Chapter of Exeter, rated in the king s books at £15 12 6, endowed with £200 private bene-faction, and £300 parliamentary grant The church is dedicated to the Holy Trinity There is a place of worship for Wesleyan Methodists In 1717, Henry Peardon gave £80, the interest to be applied in the instruction of poor children, two small additions have since been made to this endowment by Sir John Elwill, Bart and Henry Peardon

LITTLEHAM, a parish in the hundred of SHEB-BEAR, county of DEVON, 2 miles (S S W) from Bideford, containing 367 inhabitants The living is a rectory, in the peculiar jurisdiction of the Dean and Chapter of Exeter, rated in the king's books at £14 16 10½ G Anthony and P Tapp, Esqrs were patrons in 1828 The church is dedicated to St Swithin

LITTLEMOOR, a liberty in the parish of ST MARY the VIRGIN, partly within the liberties of the CITY of OXFORD, and partly in the hundred of BULLINGTON, county of OXFORD, 2½ miles (S E by S) from Oxford, containing 354 inhabitants Here was formerly a chapel, now in ruins A priory of Benedictine nuns, founded here about the reign of Henry II, and dedicated to St Mary and St Nicholas, was suppressed by the papal bull given to Cardinal Wolsey, in 1524, and subsequently became part of the endowment of King s College, Oxford, until the time of the general dissolution at its suppression the revenue was valued at £33 6 8

LITTLE-OVER, a chapelry in the parish of MICKLE-OVER, hundred of MORLESTON and LITCHURCH, county of DERBY, 2 miles (S W by S) from Derby, containing 379 inhabitants

LITTLEPORT, a parish in the hundred and Isle of ELY, county of CAMBRIDGE, 5¼ miles (N by E) from

Ely, containing 2364 inhabitants The living is a vicarage, in the peculiar jurisdiction and patronage of the Bishop of Ely, rated in the king s books at £8. The church is dedicated to St George Here is a place of worship for Wesleyan Methodists

LITTLETHORPE, a hamlet in the parish of Cosby, hundred of Guthlaxton, county of Leicester, 6 miles (S W by S) from Leicester The population is returned with the parish

LITTLETON, a township in the parish of Christleton, lower division of the hundred of Broxton, county palatine of Chester, 2½ miles (E) from Chester, containing 43 inhabitants.

LITTLETON, partly in the parish of Blandford, St Mary, and partly in that of Langton, county of Dorset, 1½ mile (S E by S) from Blandford-Forum, once an independent parish, now only a single house and farm The living was a rectory, not rated in the king s books The last rector was inducted Jan 10, 1427

LITTLETON, a parish in the hundred of Spelthorne, county of Middlesex, 3½ miles (S E) from Staines, containing 149 inhabitants The living is a rectory, in the archdeaconry of Middlesex, and diocese of London, rated in the king s books at £14, and in the patronage of Thomas Wood, Esq The church is dedicated to St Mary Magdalene A free school is endowed with the interest of £355 1 2 stock, in the South Sea annuities, the amount of several benefactions, and the schoolmistress receives £20 per annum, for which all children who apply are instructed in reading, writing, arithmetic, and needle-work

LITTLETON, a parish in the hundred of Buddlesgate, Fawley division of the county of Southampton, 3 miles (N W by N) from Winchester, containing 108 inhabitants The living is a perpetual curacy, in the peculiar jurisdiction of the incumbent, endowed with £800 private benefaction, and £600 royal bounty, and in the patronage of the Dean and Chapter of Winchester The church is dedicated to St Mary Magdalene Littleton is within the jurisdiction of the Cheyney Court held at Winchester every Thursday, for the recovery of debts to any amount.

LITTLETON, a chapelry in the parish of Steeple-Ashton, hundred of Whorwelsdown, county of Wilts, 3½ miles (E N E) from Trowbridge, containing 68 inhabitants This place is sometimes, although improperly, called Little Hinton.

LITTLETON (HIGH), a parish in the hundred of Chewton, county of Somerset, 9½ miles (S W by W) from Bath, containing, with Hallabrow, 864 inhabitants The living is a discharged vicarage, in the archdeaconry of Bath, and diocese of Bath and Wells, rated in the king s books at £7 7 8½, endowed with £200 private benefaction, £400 royal bounty, and £1400 parliamentary grant, Mr W B Barter and Mrs Barter were patrons in 1804 The church, dedicated to the Holy Trinity, has been enlarged with one hundred and forty-four additional sittings, of which ninety are free, the Incorporated Society for enlarging churches and chapels having contributed £80 towards defraying the expense There is a place of worship for Wesleyan Methodists The substratum of the soil of this and the neighbouring parishes is coal, which is worked to a considerable extent

LITTLETON (MIDDLE), a township in the parish of North Littleton, upper division of the hundred

Vol. III.

of Blackenhurst, county of Worcester, 4½ miles (N E by E) from Evesham The population is returned with the parish

LITTLETON (NORTH), a parish in the upper division of the hundred of Blackenhurst, county of Worcester, 5 miles (N E) from Evesham, containing, with the township of Middle Littleton, 342 inhabitants The living is a perpetual curacy, united to that of South Littleton, in the archdeaconry and diocese of Worcester, rated in the king s books at £6 13 9 The church is dedicated to St Nicholas

LITTLETON upon SEVERN, a parish in the lower division of the hundred of Langley, and Swinehead, county of Gloucester, 2 miles (W) from Thornbury, containing 133 inhabitants The living is a discharged rectory, in the jurisdiction of the Consistorial Court of the Bishop of Bristol, rated in the king s books at £11 4 9½ Sir H C Lippincott, Bart was patron in 1810 The navigable river Severn runs on the western side of this parish

LITTLETON (SOUTH), a parish in the upper division of the hundred of Blakenhurst, county of Worcester, 3½ miles (N E by E) from Evesham, containing 204 inhabitants The living is a perpetual curacy, with that of North Littleton, in the archdeaconry and diocese of Worcester, rated in the king's books at £4 1 10½, and in the patronage of the Dean and Canons of Christ Church, Oxford. The church is dedicated to St. Mary and St Nicholas

LITTLETON (WEST), a chapelry in the parish of Tormarton, lower division of the hundred of Grumbald's Ash, county of Gloucester, 2¼ miles (N) from Marshfield, containing 109 inhabitants

LITTLETON DREW, a parish in the hundred of Chippenham, county of Wilts, 8 miles (N W) from Chippenham, containing 155 inhabitants The living is a discharged rectory, in the archdeaconry of Wilts, and diocese of Salisbury, rated in the king s books at £9 6 9, and in the patronage of the Bishop of Salisbury The church is dedicated to All Saints Near this village is a large barrow, with three stones of a fallen cromlech upon it, of large dimensions

LITTLETON-PANNELL, a tything in the parish of West Lavington, hundred of Potterne and Cannings, county of Wilts, 1½ mile (W) from East Lavington, containing 497 inhabitants This village was anciently the lordship of the Paganells, one of whom obtained for it the privilege of a market, in the reign of Edward II

LITTLEWORTH, an extra-parochial liberty, in the middle division of the hundred of Dudstone and King's Barton, county of Gloucester, and adjacent to the city of Gloucester, containing 237 inhabitants There is a place of worship for Wesleyan Methodists

LITTLINGTON, a parish in the hundred of Armingford, county of Cambridge, 3½ miles (W N W) from Royston, containing 505 inhabitants The living is a discharged vicarage, in the archdeaconry and diocese of Ely, rated in the king's books at £5 13 7, endowed with £400 private benefaction, £400 royal bounty, and £300 parliamentary grant, and in the patronage of the Master and Fellows of Clare Hall, Cambridge. The church, which is dedicated to St Catherine, is principally in the early, with some insertions in the later style of English architecture A Roman cemetery has been discovered in

*

O

this parish, whence many cinerary urns and other ancient vessels have been obtained several Saxon coins, principally of the reign of Burghred, have also been found.

LITTLINGTON, a parish in the hundred of LONG-BRIDGE, rape of PEVENSEY, county of SUSSEX, 4 miles (N by E) from Sleaford, containing 133 inhabitants The living is a discharged rectory, in the archdeaconry of Lewes, and diocese of Chichester, rated in the king s books at £12 13 6., and in the patronage of F F F Beane, Esq This parish is bounded on the west by Cuckmere river, the village being seated on its eastern bank

LITTON, a hamlet in the parish of TIDESWELL, hundred of HIGH PEAK, county of DERBY, ¾ of a mile (E S E) from Tidswell, containing 710 inhabitants The celebrated non-conformist divine, William Bagshaw, commonly called the Apostle of the Peak, was born here in 1628

LITTON, a parish in the hundred of WELLS-FORUM, county of SOMERSET, 6¼ miles (N N E) from Wells, containing 378 inhabitants The living is a discharged rectory, in the archdeaconry of Wells, and diocese of Bath and Wells, rated in the king s books at £8 12 8, endowed with £200 private benefaction, and £200 royal bounty, and in the patronage of the Prebendary of Litton in the Cathedral Church of Wells The church is dedicated to St Peter

LITTON, a township in that part of the parish of ARNCLIFFE which is in the western division of the wapentake of STAINCLIFFE and EWCROSS, West riding of the county of YORK, 11 miles (N E) from Settle, containing 102 inhabitants

LITTON-CHENEY, a parish in the hundred of UGGSCOMBE, Dorchester division of the county of DORSET, 6¼ miles (E S E) from Bridport, containing 424 inhabitants The living is a rectory, in the archdeaconry of Dorset, and diocese of Bristol, rated in the king's books at £33 7 8½, and in the patronage of the Rev James Cox, D D The church, which is dedicated to St Mary, is in the later style of English architecture, .and has a fine tower with battlements and pinnacles In 1690, Robert Thormer bequeathed £25 per annum for the maintenance of a free school, and part of £75 per annum for apprenticing poor children of the parish of Litton, the towns of Dorchester and Southampton, and the city of Salisbury In 1771, Thomas Hollis added £5 per annum for a schoolmaster s residence

LIVEDEN, county of NORTHAMPTON—See ALDWINKLE (ST PETER'S)

LIVERMERE (GREAT), a parish in the hundred of THEDWESTRY, county of SUFFOLK, 5¾ miles (N N E) from Bury-St Edmund s, containing 251 inhabitants The living is a rectory, with which that of Little Livermere is united, in the archdeaconry of Sudbury, and diocese of Norwich, rated in the king s books at £15 8 11½, and in the patronage of N L Acton, Esq The church is dedicated to St Peter

LIVERMERE (LITTLE), a parish in the hundred of BLACKBOURN, county of SUFFOLK, 6¼ miles (N N E) from Bury-St Edmund s containing 187 inhabitants The living is a discharged rectory, united to that of Great Livermere, in the archdeaconry of Sudbury, and diocese of Norwich, rated in the king s books at £6 12 11 The church is dedicated to St Peter

LIVERPOOL, an eminent sea-port, borough, and market town, having separate jurisdiction, though locally in the hundred of West Derby, county palatine of LANCASTER, 53 miles (S by W) from Lancaster, and 205 (N W by N) from London, containing 118,972 inhabitants, according to the census of 1821, since which period the population is

Arms.

computed to have increased to upwards of 140,000 This town, which within the last century has, by a progressive increase in extent, population, and commercial importance, obtained the first rank after the metropolis, is supposed to be noticed in Domesday book under the name *Esmedune*, or *Smedune* In other ancient records its various appellations are, *Litherpul*, *Lyrpul*, &c , signifying probably, in the ancient dialect of the county, the lower pool , though some have deduced its etymology from a pool frequented by an aquatic fowl, called a " Liver,' or from a sea-weed of that name , and others from its having belonged to a family of the name of Lever, whose antiquity is not sufficiently established to justify that conclusion Soon after the Conquest, William granted all that part of the county which was situated between the rivers Mersey and Ribble to Roger of Pioctiers, who, according to Camden, built a castle here, about the year 1089 , to which circumstance may probably be attributed the origin of the town The castle, which consisted of six circular towers, connected by embattled walls, and surrounded by a moat, commanded the harbour, and continued till the close of the parliamentary war, when it was demolished by order of the parliament. The remains were subsequently granted by Queen Anne to the corporation, but were finally removed in 1715, and the church of St George was erected on the site For a considerable length of time after the Conquest, Liverpool was but a small fishing-town , till, in 1172, its favourable situation, and the convenience of its port, attracted the notice of Henry II , who made it the place of rendezvous and embarkation of his troops for the conquest of Ireland, and in the following year is stated to have granted the inhabitants a charter, but this is doubtful, as such charter cannot be found among the records in the Tower the first charter was probably granted by King John, although two charters of Henry I are mentioned in the corporation records It now became the chief station for the embarkation of troops, and for the exportation of military stores, for the service of Ireland , and the consequent intercourse which was here maintained between the two countries appears to have laid the foundation of its subsequent commercial importance Henry III , in 1229, confirmed the preceding charter, made the town a free borough, instituted a guild merchant, and granted additional privileges By these charters, and the advantage of its local situation, it began to improve its resources, and in a short time had established a considerable trade with Ireland, and with several parts of the coast An old tower, which formerly stood in Water street, appears to have been built by a descendant of Edmund, Earl of Lancaster, third son of

Henry III, who, in the reign of Edward III, was created Duke of Lancaster, and, being ordered by that monarch to keep a strict guard on the coast of Lancashire, was permitted to embattle his house, which subsequently became the occasional residence of the Stanleys, Earls of Derby after having been converted successively into a suite of assembly-rooms and a prison, it was taken down in 1819, and warehouses were erected on its site Little is known of the state of the town from the fourteenth to the sixteenth century Leland describes it as a paved town, which, as a good haven, was much frequented by Irish merchants, and as supplying Manchester with yarn imported from Ireland From this time till the reign of Elizabeth it appears to have declined, but from what cause cannot be ascertained, in 1571, the inhabitants petitioned the queen to be relieved from a subsidy imposed on them, and in their petition described it as "Her Majesty s poor decayed town of Liverpool" In 1630, when writs were issued by Charles I, for the levying of ship-money, the town was rated only at £26, while Bristol was rated at £1000

The early history of Liverpool is not distinguished by any important events During the civil war in the reign of Charles I, the town was defended for the parliamentarians by Colonel Moore, against Prince Rupert, by whom it was besieged, and to whom, after an obstinate resistance, it was surrendered, June 26th, 1644, but was soon after retaken by the parliament In the reign of William III, that monarch embarked with all his train at this port for Ireland, previously to the battle of the Boyne During the rebellion in 1745, Liverpool raised several regiments to oppose the Pretender, and within twelve months after the war with France broke out, in 1778, one hundred and twenty privateers, carrying in the aggregate one thousand nine hundred and eighty six guns, and eight thousand seven hundred and fifty-four seamen, were equipped here The most important feature in the history of this place, is the extraordinary rapidity with which it has risen into a degree of splendour and importance without example in the history of any commercial country among the causes which have produced its elevation to a rank but partially inferior to that of the metropolis are, its situation on the shore of a noble river, which expands into a wide æstuary, its proximity to the Irish coast, its central position with respect to the united kingdom, its intimate connexion with the principal manufacturing districts, and with every part of the kingdom, by numerous rivers, canals, and rail-roads, and the persevering industry and enterprising spirit of its inhabitants The port is, by some, considered to have been anciently a member of the port of Chester, although it is not de scribed as such in any of the charters either of Chester or Liverpool it was assuredly, as is evedent from records belonging to the corporation, an independent port so early as the year 1335 In the sixteeenth century an attempt was made to prove it a creek within the limits of the port of Chester, which, however, was set aside by an order from the Board of Customs in London The commerce of the port may be divided into three distinct branches of these, the first and most important is its trade with Ireland, which appears to have been established, or greatly promoted, by the settlement here of several mercantile families from that country, about the middle of the sixteenth century, at which

time there were only fifteen vessels, of the aggregate burden of two hundred and fifty-nine tons, belonging to the port The principal imports are, linen, cattle, and provisions of every kind in the year ending June, 1829, forty-nine thousand six hundred and seventy four head of cattle, six thousand seven hundred and eighty-six calves, one hundred and twenty-five thousand one hun dred and ninety-seven sheep, and one hundred and fifty five thousand three hundred and nineteen pigs, were imported from Ireland The principal exports are, British manufactured goods, salt, coal, and general mer chandise the quantity of rock and white salt brought to this port, in 1829, from the mines in Cheshire, by the river Weaver, was three hundred and ninety thousand tons, of which sixty thousand were shipped to Ireland The number of vessels which entered in wards from Ireland, in the year 1829, was two thousand seven hundred and eighty-four, and of those which cleared outwards for that port, two thousand one hun dred and twenty-four

The second principal branch of the trade of this port is that with the United States of America, of which it engrosses more than three-fourths of the whole commerce of the kingdom of this, the chief article is cotton wool, which may be considered as forming the staple trade of the town, and from this port, Manchester and the cotton manufacturing districts are supplied with the raw material the sales of cotton, which upon an average exceed fourteen thousand bales per week, are negociated by brokers, of whom there is a considerable number This branch of commerce is subject to con siderable fluctuation, but, from returns made to parlia ment, it appears that the quantity of cotton imported into Liverpool from all parts of the world, of which by far the greater portion was from the United States, is nearly nine times as much as is imported into London, and more than six times the aggregate quantity brought to all the ports in the kingdom, London included The number of bales imported into England, in 1791, was sixty-eight thousand four hundred and four in 1823, five hundred and eighty thousand two hundred and fifty-five, and in 1829, seven hundred and forty-one thousand eight hundred and sixty three, of which last, six hundred and forty-one thousand three hundred and seventy-three bales were imported into Liverpool alone In 1764, one hundred and eighty-eight vessels entered inwards, and one hundred and forty-one cleared outwards, in the trade with North America, which has greatly increased since the termination of the war in 1783 In 1829, about eight hundred vessels entered inwards, and eight hundred and sixty-four cleared outwards, at this port, which enjoys great facility and frequency of intercourse with the principal sea-ports of the United States, by regular lines of packets, of which those for New York sail on the 1st, 8th, 16th, and 24th, of the month on this line are sixteen fine vessels, elegantly fitted up with every ac commodation for passengers, and which perform the voy age generally in twenty-three days and a half, though oc casionally it has been done in fifteen days The union line of packets, also to New York, sail on the 5th and 20th of the month The Philadelphia packets sail from Liverpool on the 8th and 21st of the month, and those for Boston sail always monthly, and sometimes twice in the month

The next in importance is the trade which Liverpool carries on with the West Indies, which had its commencement about the middle of the seventeenth century, and which was previously shared between London and Bristol, Liverpool, however, has successfully rivalled the latter of these ports, and secured to itself a very considerable portion of the trade the quantity of British plantation sugar imported in 1829, was forty-three thousand seven hundred hogsheads and tierces, of rum, eleven thousand six hundred and fifty puncheons, of tobacco, four thousand nine hundred and sixty-four hogsheads, and of coffee, including also that brought from the East Indies and the Brazils, eight thousand and eighty casks, and five thousand two hundred barrels and bags Liverpool was extensively concerned in the slave trade, in which, previously to its abolition, nearly one-fourth part of the vessels belonging to the port was employed In 1829, thirty-six vessels entered inwards from the ports of Africa, and fifty-seven cleared outwards In the same year, the number of vessels which entered inwards from the West Indies was one hundred and ninety-five, and of those which cleared outwards, two hundred and thirty-two In 1814 this port was, by an order in council dated December 17th, declared a fit and proper depôt for the custody of goods, wares, and merchandise, imported from every port and place within the limits of the East India Company's Charter, and in 1819 thirty-eight vessels entered inwards from the East Indes, but this branch of its trade has since declined, probably from the decreased value of East Indian produce, as the number of vessels that entered from the East Indies, in 1829, was thirty-three, and of those that cleared outwards, thirty five the principal imports are, cotton, indigo, hides, ginger, pepper, and sugar Liverpool carries on also a considerable trade with the principal ports in the Mediterranean and Levant seas, from which it imports wine, fruits, lemon and lime juice, olive and other oils, barilla, and brimstone, and from these ports one hundred and seventy vessels entered inwards, and one hundred and ninety cleared outwards, in 1829 Cotton was first imported here from Egypt in 1823, and twenty-two thousand four hundred and fifty-six bales were landed in 1829 The trade in ashes, tallow, and timber, has of late considerably increased, seventeen thousand four hundred casks of tallow were imported in 1829, when the number of ships entered inwards from the Baltic was ninety-five, and the number cleared outwards, one hundred and seventy Considerable trade is also carried on in timber with the British Colonies in North America from which, in 1829, two hundred and sixty six cargoes, of the aggregate value of £256,422, were imported, and ninety five cargoes, valued at £94,564, were also imported from the Baltic A limited intercourse is maintained with New South Wales and South Shetland, and in that with the Isle of Man, the imports from which are grain, herrings, and wool, one hundred and thirty vessels are employed The coasting-trade is very important, the number of arrivals in 1829 was not less than four thousand two hundred and fifty The fisheries do not appear ever to have been very extensive, in 1764, three ships were engaged in the Greenland whale fishery which number had increased, in 1788, to twenty-one, but from that time the trade began to decline, and has now ceased to exist, and the home fishery has diminished materially The exports are principally the manufactured articles of the neighbouring districts

In 1829, one thousand four hundred and eighty-five British, and eight hundred and ten foreign, vessels engaged in foreign trade entered inwards, and one thousand seven hundred British, and nine hundred foreign, vessels cleared outwards, and, including coasting vessels, the whole number which entered the port, in the year ending the 24th of June, 1830, was eleven thousand two hundred and fourteen, of which, the aggregate burden was one million four hundred and eleven thousand nine hundred and sixty-four tons, and the amount of duties paid at the custom-house was £3,123,758 8 10, and £166,550 11 11, at the dock office The number of vessels belonging to the port, in 1828, was seven hundred and fifty-nine, averaging a burden of one hundred and ninety nine tons each In addition to the regular packets for America there are packets for Rio Janeiro, Naples, Genoa, Leghorn, Smyrna, Constantinople, Lisbon, and Oporto There are thirty-six steam-packets established between this port and Ireland, two to the Isle of Man, seven to Scotland, six to Wales, one to Carlisle, one to Whitehaven, one to Lancaster besides which there are sixteen to the different ferries on the Mersey

The harbour is capacious and secure at the entrance of the river is the Black Rock lighthouse, erected on a point of rock on the western coast, which is covered at quarter flood, the water at high spring tides rising twenty feet above the surface of the rock this lighthouse was built at the expense of the corporation, from a design by Mr John Foster it is seventy five feet high from its foundation to the lantern, and thirty-five feet in diameter immediately below the base, and fifteen and a half at the cornice the lower part, to the height of twenty eight feet and a half, is solid, from which a spiral staircase leads to the store-room and the apartments of the three keepers, above these is the lantern, at a medium height of sixty feet above the level of the sea, in which is a light of thirty argand lamps, with reflectors, in a triangular frame, revolving once in three minutes, and presenting, successively, two lights of a natural colour and one of brilliant red, which attain their full lustre every successive minute, and in hazy weather a bell is constantly ringing to prevent accidents this building, which is of limestone brought from Beaumaris, was completed, and the light first exhibited, on the 1st of March, 1830 A floating light has also been placed eleven miles seaward from the mouth of the river, by the trustees of the docks, and pilot boats stationed there are constantly on the look out A telegraph has been established, by means of which communications have been interchanged between this town and Holyhead in the short space of three minutes, the signal stations extend along the coast, at intervals of eight miles distance from each other The limits of the port (as fixed by the commissioners appointed under a commission issued in the 10th of George I, in their certificate to the Exchequer, dated November 28th, 1723,) extend "from the Red Stones in Hollyake, at the point of Wirrall, southerly to the foot of the river called Ribble water, in a direct line northerly, and so upon the south side of the said river to Hesketh bank easterly, and to the rivers Asland and Douglas there, and so all along the sea-coasts of Meols and Formby, unto the river Mersey, and all over the rivers Mersey, Irwell, and Weaver

For the security of the shipping in the port, and for the greater facility of loading and unloading merchandise, an immense range of docks and warehouses, extending nearly two miles along the eastern bank of the river, has been constructed, on a scale of unparalleled magnificence, and forming one of those characteristics of commercial greatness in which this town is unrivalled The docks are of three kinds, the wet docks, the dry docks, and the graving docks the wet docks are chiefly for ships of great burden, employed in the foreign trade, and which float in them at all states of the tide, the water being retained by gates the dry docks, so called because they are left dry when the tide is out, are chiefly appropriated to coasting vessels, and the graving docks, which admit or exclude the water at pleasure, are adapted to the repair of ships, during which they are kept dry, and when completed are floated out by admitting the tide The Old dock, which was the first of the kind constructed in England, and for making which an act of parliament was obtained in 1708, is not now in use, its site having been appropriated to the erection of a new custom-house, and other offices connected with the trade of the port The Dry dock, which is about to be converted into a wet dock, was constructed under the authority of an act passed in the 11th of George II, and is chiefly occupied by sloops from the North coast, which import corn, provisions, and slate, and convey back the produce of the West Indies, the Mediterranean, Portugal, and the Baltic it has a quay five hundred yards in length, and has communication with three graving docks it has been considerably enlarged, and many of the buildings surrounding it have been taken down, with the view of obtaining more quay room The Salthouse dock, so named from some salt works formerly contiguous to it, was constructed about the same time as the Dry dock, the upper part of it is chiefly for ships that are laid up, and the lower part for vessels in the Levant, Irish, and coasting trades the quay is seven hundred and fifty-nine yards in extent, and is provided with convenient warehouses, with arcades for foot passengers on the east side, and extensive sheds on the west side between this dock and the river are some shipbuilders' yards, which the corporation intend to convert into docks for the craft employed in the inland trade George s dock was constructed, in the 2d of George III, at an expense of £21,000 it was originally two hundred and forty-six yards in length, and one hundred yards in breadth, with a quay of seven hundred yards in extent, but it has been enlarged, and the quay is now one thousand and one yards in length on the east side is a range of extensive warehouses, in front of which is an arcade for foot passengers, and on the west side are sheds for protecting the merchandise from the weather at the north and south ends of the dock are handsome cast-iron bridges, and a parade is continued westward for a considerable distance into the river this dock has a communication with the two preceding docks, and also with the Prince s dock, by basins, which

Seal of the Trustees of the Docks.

preclude the necessity of returning into the river The King's dock, constructed in the 25th of George III, is two hundred and seventy yards in length, and ninety-six in breadth, and is appropriated to vessels from Virginia and other parts, laden with tobacco, which article is exclusively landed here the new tobacco warehouses extend the whole length of the quay, on the west side, and are five hundred and seventy-five feet in length, and two hundred and thirty-nine in depth, the old warehouses, on the opposite side, which were appropriated to that purpose, have been converted into sheds for the security of merchandise ships from the Baltic, freighted with timber and naval stores, discharge their cargoes on the quay, across the entrance is a handsome swivel bridge of cast iron this dock has a communication on the south with a dry dock and two graving docks The Queen s dock, constructed at the same time, is four hundred and seventy yards long, and two hundred and twenty-seven and a half in breadth, with a spacious quay, and is chiefly occupied by vessels freighted with timber, and by those employed in the Dutch and Baltic trades at the south end it communicates with a basin of considerable extent, called the Brunswick half tide dock, which is also connected with the Brunswick dry basin on the south of the half-tide dock, a new dock of larger dimensions than any of the preceding, for vessels laden with timber, is in progress, to be called the Brunswick dock, with a basin to the south of it, and patent slips for the repairing of vessels, which will probably terminate the range of docks at the southern extremity The Prince s dock, constructed under an act passed in the 51st of George III, was opened with great pomp on the day of the coronation of His late Majesty George IV it is five hundred yards in length, and one hundred and six in breadth at the north end is a spacious basin belonging to it, and at the south end it communicates with the basin of George s dock at the north end is a handsome dwelling-house for the dockmaster, with suitable offices, and at the south end is a house, in which the master of George s dock at present resides the quays are spacious, and there are sheds for the protection of goods from the weather along the west side, near the river, is a beautiful marine parade, seven hundred and fifty yards long, and eleven wide, defended by a stone parapet wall, from which is a delightful view of the river and the shipping it is much frequented as a promenade, and at convenient intervals are three flights of steps leading down to the river, where boats are in constant attendance. To the north of the basin belonging to this dock, four spacious wet docks, and a large graving dock, which latter is to be fitted up with patent slips, are at present in a state of rapid progress, and, when completed, will probably terminate the range of docks on the north side of the town The Duke s dock, between Salthouse and the King's docks, is a small dock belonging to the trustees of the late Duke of Bridgewater, for the use of his flats, with commodious warehouses The several carriers by water have also convenient basins on the river, for the use of their barges, with quays for loading and unloading their goods, and the Mersey and Irwell Navigation Company have a small dock, called the Manchester dock, for the flats employed in that extensive trade, and for the transport to this town of the productions of Cheshire and the adjoining counties The whole range of the docks, when the northern and southern additions are completed, will be two miles and eight hundred and twenty yards in length, and spacious as they are, they are still considered inadequate to the increasing commerce of the port, and measures are in contemplation for their further extension The sums expended in the formation of these docks amount to more than two millions and a half sterling for clearing them from the accumulation of silt brought in by the tide, a dredging machine, worked by a steam-engine of ten-horse power, is in constant operation, by which fifty tons per hour are raised into barges, and deposited where it may be washed away by the current of the river The internal management of each dock is entrusted to a master resident on the spot, and the government of the whole establishment is vested, by an act of parliament obtained in 1825, in a committee of twenty one members, including a chairman and deputy chairman, who meet at least once every week, and oftener, when circumstances require it the committee consists of thirteen trustees nominated by the common council, and eight merchants, or ship-owners, chosen by the payers of rates or dues to the amount of £10, within one year prior to the election, and who are resident within eight miles of Liverpool

The new custom-house, which is now being erected on the site of the Old dock, at the joint expense of government and the corporation and under the superintendence of Mr John Foster, will be a superb and beautiful edifice in the Grecian style of architecture the probable cost, originally estimated at £175,000, will not be much less than £300 000, of which sum, £150,000 has been contributed by government According to the approved plan now in progress, the buildings will be four hundred and fifty-four feet in length, and two hundred and twenty-four in depth, with three principal fronts, of which the north presents, in the central and receding part, a noble portico of eight Ionic columns, the shafts of which are five feet in diameter, and forty six feet high, supporting an entablature with a triangular pediment having the royal arms in the tympanum in the centre will be a finely-groined archway, intended as a thoroughfare for foot passengers to the streets at the south end of the building, and having on each side an entrance into the central part of the edifice the entrance to the projecting wings will be through a loggia of two columns of similar dimensions and character the east and west fronts have each a portico in the centre, of similar elevation as the portico of the north front, and the faces of the building, on each side of the portico, are decorated with pilasters supporting a cornice and entablature from the centre of the building rises a noble dome, forty-six feet in diameter, of which the tambour is surrounded by Ionic pillars supporting an entablature surmounted by a balustrade The exterior, from every point of view, presents an object of beautiful magnificence, unrivalled by any public building of the kind the interior, in addition to ample accommodation for the business of the customs and excise, will contain the stamp and post offices, and the requisite offices connected with the docks the long room, for the custom house department, one hundred and forty-six feet in length, seventy feet in breadth, and forty feet high, will

be accessible from the lower part of the building, by two double staircases of ample dimensions under the building will be an extensive range of vaults for the reception of wines and spirits in bond The old custom-house, in which the business has hitherto been transacted, is of brick, ornamented with stone, convenient only from its central situation, but destitute of any architectural importance the present excise office consists of two private houses converted to that use Adjoining the dock office, which is near the custom-house, is a building appropriated to the business of the dock police, and the present post office is a small building, which cannot be noticed among the buildings of the town

The exchange buildings, erected by the late Mr John Foster, at an expense of £110,848, subscribed in shares of £100 each, were completed in 1806 they occupy three sides of a quadrangular area, one hundred and ninety seven feet long, and one hundred and seventy-eight in breadth, the north front of the town hall forming the fourth side the façades of the east and west sides, which are uniform, consist of a rustic basement story, forming an arched piazza, surmounted by a range of Corinthian columns, supporting a cornice and balustrade the south side of the quadrangle differs from the others, principally in the projection of its centre, which has a handsome portico of four duplicated columns, supporting an entablature, above which are four finely-sculptured figures of Portland stone, representing the four elements, and corresponding with similar figures on the front of the town-hall, which forms the other side The three sides of the quadrangle have a piazza fifteen feet in width, and in the centre of the area is a monument to the memory of Lord Nelson, erected by subscription, at an expense of £9000, and placed on a circular pedestal of marble, round the base of which are four figures of captives, emblematical of the four principal victories gained by that admiral, in the spaces between these figures are representations, in basso relievo, of some of his naval exploits, and on the pedestal is the figure of the admiral, receiving on his sword a fourth naval crown from Victory, while, at the same moment, a figure of Death appears rising from behind the drapery of the fallen standards of the vanquished enemy The entrances into the area are at the angles of the quadrangle, and from Old Hall-street is an additional entrance through three arches in the basement story, divided into avenues by duplicated columns of the Grecian Doric, with groined roofs richly ornamented the façade of this entrance from the street is a noble design of the Doric order, and the end fronts of the east and west ranges of the quadrangle, facing the town-hall, are handsome specimens of the Corinthian In the east wing is a news-room, ninety four feet long and fifty-two feet wide, above which is a spacious room for the use of the underwriters the central and west wings contain numerous counting-houses and offices, and behind them are extensive warehouses

The manufactures of the town are principally such as are connected with the port and the shipping, the promotion of its commerce, and the supply of the inhabitants there are several sugar-refineries upon a very large scale, extensive potteries, glass-houses, breweries, tanneries, salt and copperas works, iron and brass foundries, foundries for cannon, anchors, chain cables, the several parts of machinery connected with steam-engines, and various others manufactories for steam-engines, steam-boilers, and machinery of all kinds, guns, small arms, nails, files, ropes, sails, cordage, watches, tobacco, snuff, and soap, there are numerous corn-mills, and others for grinding mustard, colours, and dye-woods the manufacture of soap exceeds that of any place in England, the amount of duty paid for the year ending January 5th, 1830, being £316,942 16 1¾, and those of tobacco and snuff are very extensive the number of watches made annually, on an average, amount to ten thousand four hundred, a number greater than that of any town, except London Numerous shipwrights are constantly employed in repairing the vessels in the docks, and ship-building is carried on to a considerable extent, thirty-three vessels were built at this port in 1826, and several ships of war have been launched from the dock yards, among which were three of fifty and one of forty-four guns, together with several frigates The building of steam-packets, and the manufacture of engines and boilers for their use, have been greatly increasing within the last few years at Liverpool, which in this respect appears to take the lead of all other ports The trade of the town is greatly facilitated by an extensive line of inland navigation in every direction, by which it is connected with the manufacturing districts and the principal towns in the kingdom No less than five water conveyances fall into the Mersey, viz the Mersey and Irwell navigation, the late Duke of Bridgewater's canal, the Sankey canal, the Chester and Ellesmere canal and the Weaver navigation the first communicates with Manchester and with Bolton and Bury by a canal to those towns The Duke of Bridgewater s communicates also with Manchester, and, by the Rochdale canal, with Hull and the southern parts of Yorkshire, and, by means of the Grand Trunk canal, with almost every other canal or inland navigation to the south of Lancashire The Sankey canal has a communication with the extensive coal-mines at St Helen's and its neighbourhood The Chester and Elles mere canal, now being united to the Birmingham canal in Worcestershire, will open a communication with all the southern parts of England, and with the mining districts of North and South Wales The Weaver is the great medium of conveyance for the produce of the salt mines at Northwich and its neighbourhood In addition to these is the Leeds and Liverpool canal, communicating, by the Lancaster canal, with all the north part of Lancashire, by means of a cut lately made to the Duke of Bridgewater s canal, with Manchester, and, as the same imports, with Leeds, and consequently with the principal manufacturing towns in Yorkshire A rail-road from Manchester is also now being finished, which by means of a tunnel running under this town, from east to west, will deliver goods or passengers, by steam-engines propelled at the rate of from fifteen to thirty miles an hour, almost at the sides of the docks, without the inconvenience of passing through any part of the town for a more detailed account of this stupendous work, see the article on LANCASHIRE Other rail-roads are in progress in the vicinity, and one to Birmingham, and thence to London, has been projected

The town is beautifully situated on the east bank of the river Mersey, along which it extends for more than three miles on the west side are the immense ranges of docks, wharfs, and warehouses, in the neighbourhood of which the streets are narrow, and the houses of inferior appearance to those of more recent erection on the east side, to which it extends for upwards of a mile, are spacious streets, squares, and crescents, modern houses, built chiefly of brick and roofed with slate, of which many are elegant mansions The town is well paved, and brilliantly lighted with gas, by two companies, one established in 1818, for the supply of coal gas, and the other for the preparation of oil gas, in 1823 The inhabitants and the shipping in the docks are supplied with water from the springs at Bootle, about four miles distant, by the company of the Bootle water-works, and from springs in or contiguous to the town, by the company of the Liverpool and Harrington water-works The air is highly salubrious, and the convenience of sea-bathing is afforded by the construction of baths of every description, erected by the corporation, and furnished with every accommodation, by private establishments of a similar nature, by a floating-bath, and by numerous machines Steam-boats are constantly sailing to and from the ferries on the Cheshire shore, and every facility of aquatic excursions may be obtained by packets and pleasure boats, which are in constant attendance The docks afford delightful promenades, commanding extensive views of the river and of the shipping the public buildings, which are highly beautiful, give an air of grandeur to the town, and its numerous sources of refined amusement and social intercourse render it, independently of its mercantile attractions, a desirable place of residence The environs are pleasant abounding with interesting scenery, and with numerous handsome seats and beautiful villas The village of Everton, one mile north-east of the town, is the retreat of many of the opulent merchants from its elevated situation, it commands extensive and interesting views, and displays considerable architectural interest.

The public subscription libraries are numerous and well selected The Athenæum, a neat building of stone, erected, in 1799, at an expense of £4000, by a proprietary of five hundred members, whose annual subscription is £2 12 6, contains a news-room, and a library comprising fourteen thousand volumes adjoining the library are a committee-room and apartments for the librarian The Lyceum, a handsome edifice of the Ionic order, was erected by public subscription, in 1802, at an expense of £11,000 it contains a well-selected library of thirty thousand volumes, conveniently arranged in a circular room forty-five feet in diameter, tastefully decorated with busts, and lighted by a spacious dome, a coffee-room, sixty-eight feet in length, forty eight feet wide, and thirty one feet high, with an elegant coved ceiling, and a lecture and committee room the institution is under the direction of a president, vice-president, and a committee of twenty-four members, there are eight hundred subscribers to the library, and six hundred to the coffee-room The Union news-room, a substantial and neat building, was erected by public subscription, in 1800, at an expense of £6000 it contains a spacious coffee-room, with two recesses at the end, ornamented with Ionic pillars over the entrance to the bar is a painting, by Fuseli, emblematical of the union, and on the parapet above the entrance are the union arms, finely sculptured The exchange news-room, which occupies the lower story of the east wing of that splendid edifice, is ninety-four feet in length and fifty-two feet wide the ceiling, which is richly panelled, is divided into three arched compartments, by a double range of sixteen Ionic pillars, twenty feet high, forming an elegant colonnade in the centre of the room the side walls are decorated with sixteen pilasters of the same order, between which are spacious arched windows the whole of the interior preserves a character of striking beauty There are also a medical and a law library, supported by the members of those professions The royal institution, a spacious and handsome edifice, the purchase and adaptation of which to its purpose, cost £14,000, raised in shares of £100, consists of a centre and two wings, extending one hundred and forty-six feet in front, and containing on the ground-floor a reading-room for the subscribers, a lecture-room fifty feet in length and thirty feet wide, a committee room, and classical and mathematical school-rooms, and on the first floor, a large room for the Liverpool Literary and Philosophical Society, a library, a museum, a spacious exhibition-room for the members of the Liverpool academy of painting, an exhibition-room for casts from the Elgin and Egina marbles, a drawing school-room, and a committee room on the roof is an observatory, and behind the principal building are a laboratory and a theatre for chemical and philosophical experiments This institution was formed, in 1814, for the advancement of literature, science, and the arts, and the members were incorporated by royal charter, in 1822 the society appoints professors, who lecture on chemistry, anatomy, physiology, botany, and astronomy, and masters for teaching the classics, mathematics, English composition, the modern languages, and drawing A school of arts was established, in 1825, for the gratuitous instruction of the artisans of the town, in the principles of chemistry and mechanics, on which subjects lectures are delivered at the rooms in Slater street, by professors of the royal institution The Botanic gardens, near Edge hill, occupy about four acres of ground, enclosed within a stone wall, having a handsome entrance lodge, and containing apartments for the superintendent and others connected with the management the collection of plants is extensive and affords not only a practical illustration of the lectures delivered on that subject at the Royal Institution, but an interesting and pleasing recreation, strangers are admitted by a note from any of the proprietors the conservatory, two hundred and forty feet in length, is an elegant and highly ornamental structure The museum, in Church-street, consists of two apartments, in one of which a collection of natural productions is tastefully displayed, and in the other is a variety of ancient armour and warlike weapons and instruments

The new baths, on the west side of George s dock, form a neat range of stone building, two hundred and thirty-nine feet in length and eighty-seven in depth, on each side of the entrance, which is in the centre, is a colonnade of eighteen pillars, affording a sheltered walk, and in front of the building is a good promenade on the margin of the river The gentlemen s baths are on the north side the principal bath is forty-five feet long and twenty-seven wide, and the entrance from the dressing-rooms is under a projecting roof

supported on pillars, a handsome saloon, lighted by a dome, leads to the warm baths, which are well arranged, and provided with every accommodation the ladies baths, on the south side, are similarly arranged The theatre, on the east side of Williamson square, was built in 1772 it is a neat edifice of brick, with a circular stone front, ornamented with the king s arms, and with emblematical figures in bas relief the season commences in May, and closes in December The amphitheatre, in Great Charlotte-street, is a spacious and handsome building of brick, coated with stucco it is open, during the winter, for the performance of equestrian exercises, feats of agility, and pantomimes The circus, in Springfield-street, is used for similar exhibitions The Wellington rooms were built by public subscription, in 1815, in the centre of the front, which is of stone, is a lofty circular portico of the Corinthian order, from which two doors open into an octangular vestibule, twenty-five feet in diameter, beyond which is an ante-room, from which doors on the right and left lead into the card and supper rooms, and in the centre into the ball-room, eighty feet in length and thirty-seven feet wide, and splendidly decorated, the whole forming a suite of rooms admirably adapted to the uses for which they were erected The music-hall is a plain brick building, with a portico, in which subscription concerts are held during the winter months The diorama is a plain and substantial edifice, erected, at a considerable expense, by the Messrs Daguerre, members of the Legion of Honour, who are the inventors of that exhibition The rotunda is a handsome circular building of brick, elegantly fitted up for the exhibition of panoramic views, but now used as a billiard-room by a select number of subscribers At the entrance into the town from London is an equestrian statue of George III, the first stone of which was laid in Great George square, by the mayor and corporation, attended by the different trade associations, on the 25th of October, 1809, being the day on which His Majesty completed the fiftieth year of his reign, but since removed to its present site it is of bronze, and a copy of that of the Emperor Marcus Aurelius, at Rome the expense, amounting to nearly £4000, was raised by subscription. The races take place in July, and continue four days the course, at Aintree, about six miles to the north north-east of the town, is a mile and a half in length, and is enclosed by railing, with a straight run in of nearly one thousand one hundred yards, there is also an interior course, or training-ground stabling for fifty horses have been built at the upper end, with rooms over them for the grooms six common stands have also been built capable of accommodating six thousand persons The grand stand was erected in 1829 it is four stories in height, the ground floor, beneath which are spacious cellars, contains entrance halls and vestibules, from which two spacious staircases lead to the principal rooms on the first floor, and to the various rooms for refreshment and for promenade during the intervals of the running, the principal of these, overlooking the race ground, is ninety-one feet in length, twenty-two feet wide, and seventeen feet high, with circular ends, and lighted by fifteen windows in front is a balcony extending the whole length of the front and round the ends of the building, and at the back of the principal room are two withdrawing-rooms, each twenty-eight feet long and seventeen feet wide, one for gentlemen, and the other for ladies, above are two similar rooms, and the leads, commanding a view of the whole course, and a most beautiful and extensive prospect of the surrounding country, are capable of accommodating two thousand persons

The chartered market days are Wednesday and Saturday, but there are markets for provisions every day in the week except Sunday the market days for corn are Tuesday and Saturday, from ten in the morning till one o clock, the market being held in the corn exchange, a neat building, with an entrance in the centre into the lower area, and the basement story ornamented with Doric columns, supporting a cornice and entablature Numerous market places have been formed, and buildings erected, for the accommodation of persons attending them, of these, the principal is St John s market-place, nearly in the centre of the town, begun in August 1820, and completed in February, 1822, by the corporation, at an expense of £35,000 the building is of brick, with entrances and cornices of stone, it is one hundred and eighty-three yards in length, and forty-five yards wide, lighted with one hundred and thirty-six windows, and thoroughly ventilated there are eight spacious entrances, and the interior is divided longitudinally into five avenues, by four ranges of handsome cast-iron pillars, one hundred and sixteen in number, which support the roof St James s market-house, for the accommodation of the south part of the town and of Harrington, has been lately erected, and a similar building is in progress in Scotland road, for the convenience of the residents in Everton and Kirkdale In addition to these are the old fish market in James street, and open market places in Cleveland square, Islington, and Pownall-square, the cattle and hay markets, in Lime-street, and the pig market, in Great Howard-street The fairs are, July 25th and November 11th ten days prior to each fair, a hand is displayed in front of the town-hall, and remains there for ten days after the conclusion, during which time, every person entering or leaving the town on business connected with the fairs, is free from arrest for debt on borough process within the ancient liberties of the town

Liverpool, though a borough by prescription, received its first charter of incorporation from King John under this charter, confirmed and extended by many succeeding monarchs, and modified by William III, George II, III, and IV, the government is vested in a mayor, recorder, two bailiffs, an indefinite number of aldermen, a town clerk, and

Corporate Seal.

others, composing a common council of forty-one, assisted by subordinate officers The mayor is chosen annually on St. Luke s day from among the common council, by the burgesses generally, the recorder and town clerk are chosen by the common council, the senior bailiff is appointed by the mayor, and the junior bailiff by the burgesses, and such of the common council as have served the office of mayor become aldermen The mayor and aldermen are justices of the peace within the borough, and the mayor, by charter of William III, is also justice of the peace for the county, and, by charter of George IV, the junior alderman and the two bailiffs are coroners The freedom of borough is inherited by birth, and acquired by servitude or gift, among the privileges is the freedom of the city of Bristol, and of Waterford and Wexford, in Ireland, the resident burgesses of which places are reciprocally free of Liverpool, with the exception only of the right to vote at elections The corporation hold quarterly courts of session for all offences not capital, which are also held every Monday by adjournment, and a court of record, by prescription, for the recovery of debts to any amount, every Thursday a court of requests is held every Monday and Wednesday, under an act passed in the 25th of George II, by commissioners appointed by the corporation, for the recovery of debts not exceeding 40s A regular system of dock police has been established by act of parliament, and some of the borough magistrates attend daily at the dock office, for determining causes connected with that department, and the mayor or some of the magistrates attend daily at the sessions-house, for the transaction of public business The estates belonging to the corporation may be estimated at the value of £2,500,000, producing an income varying from £100,000 to £110,000 per annum, a considerable proportion of which is expended in the improvement of the port, and in the embellishment of the town, the gross sum laid out from 1786 to 1828, in widening the streets, and in other improvements within the liberties, was £602,554, and in building churches, charity schools, market-houses, and other public buildings, £465,000, making a total of £1,067,554, and an average expenditure of £25,417 per annum, for forty-two years The borough first exercised the elective franchise in the 23rd of Edward I, but made no other return till the reign of Edward VI, since which time it has continued to send two members to parliament the right of election is vested in the freemen generally not receiving alms, of whom the number is about five thousand the mayor and bailiffs are the returning officers

The town-hall, built in 1749, and of which the ground-floor was originally designed for an exchange, occupies an elevated situation at the north end of Castle-street, the whole of the interior was destroyed by fire in 1795, and has been since restored, upon a more improved plan, at an expense of £110,000 it is a stately and magnificent structure, in the Grecian style of architecture, with four elegant fronts, of which the north forms one side of the Exchange buildings, and the south, which is the principal, forms the grand entrance, a rustic basement surrounds the whole building, from which rise handsome ranges of Corinthian pillars, supporting an entablature and cornice, between the pillars are tablets, in which the emblems of commerce are finely sculptured in bas relief the principal front has a noble portico of Corinthian columns, supporting a triangular pediment in the central part, which has a bold projection the east and west fronts, which are uniform, have in the projecting central part a handsome portico of Corinthian columns, supporting triangular pediments, from the centre of the building rises a splendid and stately dome, supported on a range of lofty columns of the Corinthian order, grouped at the quoins

and surmounted by triangular pediments, round the tambour of the dome is an open gallery, commanding an extensive panoramic view, and the summit is crowned by a colossal figure of Britannia. The interior of this noble building contains on the ground floor a council-room, apartments for the mayor, committee-rooms, and offices for the town clerk, treasurer, and other officers of the corporation The grand staircase leads into a spacious saloon splendidly furnished, and ornamented with full-length portraits of George III, by Sir Thomas Lawrence, of His late Majesty George IV, when Prince of Wales, by Hopner, of the late Duke of York, by Phillips, and a portrait by Sir M A Shee of His present Majesty, William IV the saloon opens on the east and west sides into two magnificently-furnished drawing-rooms, thirty-two feet in length and twenty-seven feet wide, and on the north and east sides, into two spacious ball-rooms, superbly decorated, and lighted by three chandeliers of richly cut glass of great beauty, and of unusual magnitude the larger of these rooms is eighty-nine feet in length, forty-one feet wide, and forty feet high, the smaller is sixty one feet in length, twenty-eight feet wide, and twenty-six feet high, the ceilings are coved, and ornamented with highly enriched panels, the walls are decorated with pilasters of Scagliola marble, and the furniture is sumptuously elegant On the west of the saloon is the banquet-room, fifty feet in length, thirty feet wide and twenty-five feet high, the walls are ornamented with pilasters of variegated Scagliola marble, with capitals of the Corinthian order, the arched ceiling is richly panelled in compartments, and the whole is fitted up in a style of the most costly magnificence The refectory, adjoining the smaller ball-room thirty-six feet in length and twenty-one feet wide and lighted from the ceiling, is in a style of proportionate elegance The interior of the dome, as seen from the grand staircase, is strikingly beautiful, the entire height from the pavement is one hundred and six feet, and the ornaments are characterised by a due regard to purity of style and chasteness of embellishment the whole suite of rooms, for convenience of arrangement, and for splendour of decoration, are in perfect harmony with the general character of the building, which, for the magnitude of its dimensions, and the beauty of its architecture, is, perhaps, unparalleled by any edifice of the kind in Europe

The borough sessions house, near the west wing of the Exchange buildings, is a neat plain structure in the Grecian style of architecture it is one hundred and seventy four feet in length, and varies from fifty to eighty feet in depth, at the north front are two entrances, from which a winding staircase leads into a saloon, the ceiling of which is supported by four handsome Ionic columns the saloon opens into the sessions hall, sixty one feet in length, and thirty-nine feet wide, handsomely fitted up for the business of the sessions, the bar, communicating with some cells below to which there is an underground passage from the prison, occupies the centre of the hall, and a gradual flight of steps ascending from it affords accommodation to spectators the ceiling, in which are two domes, from which the hall is lighted, is handsomely panelled, and the walls are decorated with twelve pilasters supporting an enriched cornice at the other extremity of the building is another court of similar style, but of smaller dimensions,

in which the petty sessions and daily examinations are held there are also rooms for the magistrates, jurors, and persons connected with the court, and on the ground-floor are cells for prisoners awaiting their trial The borough gaol consists of six wings, of which three were let to the county as a temporary house of correction, till the new house of correction at Kirkdale should be completed three of these are now appropriated to the confinement of debtors, and three to that of offenders against the dock acts, and of prisoners for trial at the borough sessions it is capable of containing from five to six hundred prisoners, but is not well adapted for classification The house of correction at Kirkdale, recently erected, is of a circular form, with two large wings, and is capable of receiving eight hundred prisoners, for the classification of whom there are twenty-two wards the governor s house occupies the north front, and in the centre of the area are the chapel and the schools it contains a tread-mill with ten wheels, of which three are worked by females The sessious-house for the hundred of West Derby forms the south front of the house of correction, and is handsomely built of stone, with a portico of six lofty Ionic pillars, the sessions are held in a handsome room seventy feet long and forty-two feet wide, to which are attached apartments for the magistrates, barristers, and witnesses the petty sessions for the hundred are held every alternate Friday, in a smaller room in this building, which was completed in 1821, at an expense of £80,000 the average number of prisoners confined here is about five hundred and fifty, who are employed in various pursuits of profitable labour, and receive a portion of their earnings on their discharge A refuge for female prisoners, discharged in a destitute state has been established in the town, under the auspices of which, many have been restored to stations of usefulness and respectability in society

Liverpool was formerly a chapelry in the parish of Walton, from which it was separated in 1699, and constituted a distinct parish and a rectory, to be "called and esteemed a mediety, that is to say equal betwixt the two rectors that shall preach at the new church (St Peter s) and the parochial chapel (St Nicholas) ' it is in the archdeaconry and diocese of Chester Since the period of its separation from Walton, many new churches have been erected, and it has of late, by act of parliament, been divided into twenty-two districts, for ecclesiastical purposes the original, and the only church prior to 1699, was that of St Nicholas, the time of its foundation is not known, but, in 1361, a license was obtained from the Bishop of Lichfield, to bury in the churchyard during the plague, which then raged in the town the body of the church was rebuilt in 1774, and, in 1810, the spire and the upper part of the tower fell upon the roof, a few minutes before the hour of service, and killed several persons who had assembled in the church, and were entering at the time a new tower, in the later style of English architecture, has been erected, surmounted by a lantern, from a design by the late Mr Harrison, of Chester there were anciently four chantries in this church, but few monuments of antiquity are now remaining St Peter s church is a plain edifice, with a low square tower surmounted by an octagonal turret crowned with pinnacles the interior contains some good specimens of carving in oak, and on the south side of the chancel is a costly marble monument to the memory of Foster Cunliffe, merchant the rectory, or mediety of Liverpool is not in charge, and is in the patronage of the Mayor and Council The following churches, the livings of which are perpetual curacies, are also under the patronage of the Mayor and Council St George s, erected, in 1732, on the site of the ancient castle, and recently rebuilt, under the superintendence of Mr John Foster, the prevailing character is the Doric, and, in the elevation of the steeple, that style has been blended with the Ionic and the Corinthian the Mayor and Council usually attend divine service at this church The church, dedicated to St Thomas, built under the authority of an act passed in the 21st of George II, and consecrated in 1750, is a handsome edifice in the Grecian style of architecture, with a tower formerly surmounted by a very lofty spire, which was taken down, in consequence of the damage it sustained from a storm, in 1822 the interior is neatly fitted up, and the exterior walls are ornamented with duplicated columns of the Corinthian order, supporting a cornice surmounted by a balustrade St Paul s church, erected at the expense of the inhabitants in 1769, is a handsome edifice in the Grecian style of architecture, with a dome rising from the centre, and porticoes of the Ionic order, forming the principal entrances the Ionic character prevails throughout the building St Anne s, erected under an act passed in the 36th of George III, at the expense of two gentlemen of the town, is a neat building of brick, in the early style of English architecture, with a square brick tower crowned with pinnacles the east window is of painted glass St John s church, erected, in 1784, under an act passed in the 2nd of George III, is a neat structure, with a square embattled tower crowned with pinnacles St Michael s, erected under an act passed in the 54th of George III, and amended by a subsequent act in the 4th of George IV, is an elegant structure in the Grecian style of architecture, with a lofty steeple of two receding turrets surmounted by a neat spire it has a noble and boldly projecting portico of six lofty Corinthian columns, supporting a triangular pediment at the east end are four Corinthian columns supporting an entablature and cornice, which is continued round the building the interior contains one thousand three hundred and six sittings, of which five hundred and twenty are free the whole expense of its erection was £45,267 10 6, of which sum £10,267 10 6 was paid by the corporation St Luke s, recently erected at the expense of the corporation, after a design by Mr Foster, is an elegant structure in the later style of English architecture, with a square embattled tower, having turrets at the angles, which rise considerably above the battlements the walls are strengthened by richly-empanelled buttresses crowned with pinnacles in the lower stages, and carried up above the roof of the chancel, forming a series of highly-ornamented turrets The interior is richly decorated, and the chancel, which is after the model of the Beauchamp chapel at Warwick, is a beautiful specimen of the decorated style the windows, which are lofty and in fine proportion, are elegantly enriched with tracery, and the whole edifice is highly creditable to the taste and skill of the architect The church of St Martin s in the Fields, containing one thousand nine hundred and ten sittings, of which eight hundred and twenty-eight are free, was erected, in 1828,

by grant from the parliamentary commissioners, at an expense of £20,037 3 8 it is a handsome structure in the later style of English architecture, having a square embattled tower with angular turrets, surmounted by an octagonal spire, the whole rising to the height of one hundred and ninety-eight feet the chancel, of which the roof is finely groined, is separated from the nave by a lofty and richly-moulded arch, and the whole structure forms a striking ornament at the entrance into the town from the Ormskirk road the living, a perpetual curacy, is, under certain regulations, vested by an act passed in the 10th of George IV in the corporation

The following churches will, at the expiration of sundry terms, be also in the patronage of the Mayor and Council the church dedicated to the Holy Trinity, erected, by private subscription, under an act passed in the 32nd of George III, in 1792, is a neat edifice of stone, with a tower the living is a perpetual curacy now in the patronage of the Rev R Formby Christ Church, erected under an act of parliament passed in the 40th of George III, is an elegant building of brick ornamented with stone, and having a light and handsome cupola and dome the interior is well arranged, the chancel is lighted by a large Venetian window, and contains a marble tablet to the memory of John Houghton, Esq, by whom the church was built, at an expense of £21,000, and by whom it was endowed with £105 per annum, as a stipend for the minister the living is a perpetual curacy, now in the patronage of Edward Gibbon, Esq The church, dedicated to St Mark, erected under an act passed in the 56th of George III, at an expense of £18,000, raised by subscription, is a plain edifice of brick, with a square tower crowned with a balustrade, and ornamented with vases at the angles the interior is well arranged, and contains one thousand seven hundred and fourteen sittings, of which three hundred are free the living is a perpetual curacy, the patronage of which was vested in five Trustees, of whom John Whitley, Esq is the only survivor St Andrew s church, erected, in 1815, by John Gladstone, Esq, at an expense of £12,000, is a neat edifice, with a turret surmounted by a dome supported on eight columns it contains one thousand six hundred and fifty sittings, of which four hundred are free the living is a perpetual curacy, now in the patronage of John Gladstone, Esq The church dedicated to St Philip, erected under an act passed in the 1st of George IV, by John Cragge Esq, at an expense of £12,000, is a neat edifice in the later style of English architecture it contains one thousand sittings, of which one hundred and fifty are free the living is a perpetual curacy, now in the patronage of John Cragge, Esq St David s church is a neat edifice, erected for the accommodation of the Welch residing in the town the service of the church of England is regularly performed in the Welch language the living is a perpetual curacy, at present in the patronage of Trustees St Catherine s church, in Abercromby-square, erected by subscription at an expense of £10,000, is not yet completed, it is calculated to contain one thousand two hundred sittings the entrance is through a portico of six handsome Ionic columns, the interior is lighted by a dome in the centre, supported by Corinthian columns St Bride s church, now being erected by subscription, at an estimated expense of £5000, will contain one thousand three hun dred sittings, of which one hundred and twenty are to be free it will be in the Grecian style of architecture, with a handsome portico of six Ionic columns The two following will, in a short period, be under the patronage of the Rectors St Stephen s church, originally built for a congregation of Protestant Dissenters, but purchased and fitted up for the established religion, is a plain building with a small turret surmounted by a cupola the living is a perpetual curacy, now in the patronage of William Spurstow Miller, Esq St Matthew s was also purchased from a congregation of Dissenters the living is a perpetual curacy, now in the patronage of J T Holloway, Esq St Mary s, the church for the school for the indigent blind, with which it communicates by a subterraneous passage, was erected by subscription, after a design by Mr Foster, in 1818 it is an elegant structure in the Grecian style of architecture, with a noble portico of six massive columns of the Doric order, supporting an enriched entablature and triangular pediment, an exact copy of the portico of the temple dedicated to Jupiter Panhellenius, in the island of Egina the interior is beautifully arranged, and contains a splendid monument to the late Pudsey Dawson, Esq one half of the pews is reserved for strangers, whose contributions are received for the benefit of the charity the living is a perpetual curacy, in the patronage of five Trustees, of whom the mayor and the two senior aldermen are three There is also an episcopal chapel, dedicated to All Saints In George s dock is a floating chapel connected with the established church In addition to the churchyards are two public cemeteries the one near Edge hill is spacious, and contains a small chapel of brick, in the ancient style of English architecture, in which the funeral service is performed, the other, which is called St James cemetery, is a large tract of ground excavated as a quarry for stone used in the building of the docks, and converted into a depository for the dead, at an expense of £21,000 it contains forty-four thousand square yards, enclosed by a stone wall and handsome iron palisades, having four stately entrances the interior is intersected by roads wide enough to admit a carriage, which lead to catacombs excavated in the rock the oratory, or chapel, in which the funeral service is performed, is an elegant edifice in the Grecian style of architecture, and of the Doric order, forty six feet in length, and twenty-nine wide, at the west end is a noble portico of six massive columns supporting a rich entablature, which is carried round the building, and surmounted by a triangular pediment it was built after a design by Mr Foster, and forms an elegant specimen of purity of style, and of tasteful embellishment near it is a house for the officiating minister, a handsome edifice of stone, and at the south end of the cemetery is the porter s lodge St James church, nearly adjoining the cemetery, and from which it takes its name, is in the parish of Walton There are five places of worship for Baptists, three for Welch Calvinists, one for the Society of Friends, four for Independents, one for Welch Independents, five for Wesleyan Methodists, one for Welch Methodists, and one for those of the New Connexion, one for Sandemanians, one for Swedenborgians, and two for Unitarians two Scottish kirks, and two chapels for Seceders, five Roman Catholic chapels, and a syna-

gogue Of these, several are handsome buildings, among which may be noticed the Scottish kirk in Rodney - street, dedicated to St Andrew, and built after a design by Mr Foster, with a receding portico of the Ionic order, and a handsome balustrade, and having, at each end of the front, a turret surmounted by a dome, the Roman Catholic chapel on Copperas hill, in the early style of English architecture, strengthened on the sides by buttresses crowned with crocketed pinnacles, and the Synagogue, an elegant structure, with a handsome Ionic portico, and in every respect decorated in a style characteristic of the opulence of that portion of the inhabitants In the Salthouse dock is a floating chapel, under the management of a society of Dissenters, called the Bethel Union

The Blue-coat hospital, established in 1709, for the clothing and instruction of poor children, was, in 1714, extended also to their entire maintenance, and the present substantial building, occupying three sides of a quadrangle, was erected for that purpose by subscription the endowment arises from a bequest by William Clayton, Esq, of £1000, a bequest by the Cleveland family of premises which sold for £1706 13 9, and donations by the late Mr John Horrocks, amounting to £3022, its support being further provided for by subscription two hundred and fifty boys, and one hundred girls, are clothed, maintained, and educated, in this ancient and truly valuable institution Numerous other schools for the education of the children of the poor, in various parts of the town, are supported by subscription Two were erected and are supported by the corporation, one in Park-lane, founded in 1825, at an expense of more than £12,000, in which four hundred boys and three hundred girls are instructed, and the other at Bevington hill, in which an equal number of each sex is taught they are both handsome buildings of stone The Moorfields day and Sunday school, in which two hundred boys and one hundred and twenty girls are educated, is supported by subscription A school in Hunter-street was erected in 1792, by Mr Stephen Waterworth, and endowed by Frances Waterworth, his sister, with £4000, in which one hundred and sixty boys from any part of the country are instructed in reading, writing, and arithmetic, and one hundred and ten girls in reading, writing, knitting, and sewing St James school, built in 1802, by Mr Moses Benson, is supported by subscription, and two hundred boys and one hundred girls are educated in it St Matthew s day and Sunday school affords the means of instruction to one hundred and twenty boys and one hundred and thirty girls St Andrew s school was erected by John Gladstone, Esq, who endowed it with rents from St Andrew s church, for the instruction of one hundred and forty boys and one hundred and thirty girls The Welch Charitable Society, instituted in 1804, and under the patronage of His Majesty, has a school in Russell-street, in which three hundred and twenty boys and ninety girls, children of Welch parents residing in and near the town, are clothed, instructed, and apprenticed St Mark s school, in which one hundred and fifty boys and one hundred girls are educated, and the Harrington school, in which one hundred and fifty boys and one hundred and twenty girls are taught, are supported by subscription, besides various others connected with the established church Among those supported by the dissenting congregations are, the Manesty-lane school , the school of the Society of Friends, in Duncan-street, London-road, comprising two spacious buildings, in which two hundred boys and two hundred girls are taught on the Lancasterian plan , the Caledonian school, in Oldham-street, instituted in 1809, for the instruction of one hundred and sixty-six boys and ninety-seven girls, children of Scottish parents The Brunswick school, in which one hundred and forty boys and one hundred girls are taught , the Leeds-street school, in which are two hundred boys and one hundred and fifty girls , and the Jordan-street school, a large and commodious building, in which three hundred and ten boys and one hundred and sixty girls are educated, and instructed in some useful art, are supported by the Wesleyan Methodists The Mount Pleasant school, in which seventy-two boys and sixty girls are instructed, is supported by the Unitarians The school of the Benevolent Society of St Patrick, in Pleasant-street, instituted in 1807, is supported by subscription, and two hundred and sixty-four boys and one hundred and forty-eight girls, children of Irish parents, are clothed, instructed, and apprenticed The Bethesda school, in which are one hundred and ninety boys and one hundred girls, is supported by the congregation of Bethesda chapel in Duncan-street , and there are various other similar institutions, together with several infant schools recently established, in different parts of the town, which are liberally supported, and judiciously conducted

The school for the indigent blind was established in 1791, and the present spacious buildings were erected by subscription in 1808 they consist of a substantial dwelling-house for the conductor , behind which is a spacious range of building for the residence and employment of the inmates, for whose accommodation, and as a means of increasing the funds for their support, the handsome church already noticed has been erected, the pupils are instructed in various branches of learning, upon Dr Bell s plan, and are taught spinning, the art of making baskets, sacks, list-shoes, twine, packthread, worsted rugs, the weaving of linen, sacking, stair carpeting, and various other trades, by which they may obtain a livelihood they are also instructed in music, with a view to qualify them as organists and teachers and in stringing and tuning musical instruments the present number of pupils is one hundred and twenty, to whose health and moral improvement the greatest attention is paid the amount of goods manufactured and sold at the school is from £1500 to £2000 per annum An institution for the instruction of the deaf and dumb was established in 1825 the school room in Wood-street is well adapted to the accommodation of fifty pupils, of whom such as can afford it pay an adequate remuneration, and the rest are instructed gratuitously, adjoining the school is a respectable boarding-house, in which the pupils are received on suitable terms, the school is open to visitors every week, and a public examination of the pupils is held quarterly Many children of the poor are also instructed in various branches of trade in the house of industry, established in 1772, and said to be the largest of the kind in the kingdom , it is appropriated generally to the reception, maintenance, and employ-

ment of the poor to the east of the building is a house of recovery from fever, a spacious stone building, occupying an elevated situation, and in every respect well adapted to the purpose it is under the direction of the overseers of the poor, and was opened for the reception of patients in 1806 A school of industry for females, established in 1809, is under the direction of a committee of ladies there are one hundred females in the school, who are instructed in reading, writing, and arithmetic, and in knitting, spinning, and plain work a fund arising from the contribution of one half-penny per week by each scholar is appropriated to the payment of two guineas to each on her marriage, and an annuity of two guineas on attaining the age of fifty five years The female penitentiary was established in 1809, and a handsome brick building has been erected by subscription, for the reception of destitute and abandoned females, of whom, since its establishment, many have been reclaimed to virtue and to habits of industry, and restored to their families, or placed in stations of usefulness to society

The infirmary was originally instituted in 1749, but the building being found inadequate to the object, the present spacious and handsome edifice of stone was erected, by public subscription, in 1824 it consists of a centre and two receding wings, extending two hundred and four feet in length the front, in the centre of which is a noble portico of six massive columns of the Ionic order, supporting a frieze and boldly projecting cornice, with corresponding pilasters at each extremity, is one hundred and eight feet in depth, and the wings are twenty-six feet deep the building comprises three lofty stories, having one hundred and thirty-eight windows in front, and the whole, from the chaste elegance of its design, produces a pleasing grandeur of effect The ground-floor contains all the domestic offices , on the first floor is a suite of twenty rooms, for the committees, officers of the institution, and for the accommodation of the household , and one long room, which is fitted up as a ward for the reception of casualty patients the second and third stories are appropriated to the use of the patients, of whom the number in the house is two hundred and twenty, and two hundred and thirty-four beds are made up This institution is an excellent school of medicine and surgery, and is gratuitously attended by the medical professors of the town and neighbourhood the annual expenditure exceeds £5000, and it is open unlimitedly to all who may need its aid There are two public dispensaries, supported by subscription , the North, situated in Marybone, and for which a very handsome building is now being erected in Vauxhall road , and the South dispensary, in Upper Parliament-street they are liberally supported, and are each under the direction of a president, two auditors, three physicians, three surgeons, and an apothecary, who acts as secretary there were formerly three, but the central dispensary, in Church-street, has lately been taken down The institution for curing diseases of the eye, in Basnet-street, and a similar institution in Slater-street, are supported by public subscription , and, in 1825, an establishment for curing diseases of the ear was opened in Duke-street, and is liberally supported The lunatic asylum, near St John s church, originally founded in 1792, was found inadequate to the accommodation of the patients, and a new building was erected, in 1830, after a design by Mr Foster the basement story is fitted up with every convenience for the use of the establishment, and the building, which is two stories high, is divided into wards for the classification of the patients to each ward is an adjoining ground for exercise, in addition to which, a considerable portion of ground is laid out in walks and pleasure grounds, for the use of convalescent patients the asylum is capable of accommodating sixty general patients, exclusively of several suites of apartments for the reception of private patients, who are admitted on terms adapted to their circumstances, and accommodated in a manner corresponding with their rank A ladies charity, for the relief of poor married women lying-in at their own houses, was instituted in 1796, and is under the superintendence of a patroness, president, vice-president, and a committee of six ladies and seven gentlemen it is supported by subscription, aided by the proceeds of an annual ball its general expenditure exceeds £1000 per annum, and the charity, since its establishment, has afforded relief to nearly fifty thousand individuals A marine humane society was established, in 1823, for the encouragement of boatmen and fishermen to adventure for the relief of vessels in distress in the river and upon the coast, by the distribution of suitable rewards for their success in rescuing the lives of the crew it has, since its formation, been productive of great benefit The strangers friend society originated with the Wesleyan Methodists, and is open, without distinction of religious denomination, to all objects of distress it was established in 1789, and has afforded material assistance in the clothing and relief of numerous indigent and friendless strangers The marine society was instituted for the relief of reduced or aged masters of vessels, and for the support of their widows and children The seamen s hospital was established, in 1752, for the maintenance of decayed seamen, their widows, and children it is conducted on the plan of the Trinity-house, and is supported by a permanent fund of £33,000, the amount of unclaimed prize money, and by a contribution of sixpence per month from the wages of every seaman belonging to the port there are seven hundred individuals who receive monthly pensions from the funds An hospital for the relief of sick and wounded American seamen was opened in 1820, and is supported entirely by the American government, and a military hospital, for the relief of any regiment either quartered at or marching through the town, has accommodation for forty invalids, and is supported at the expense of Government The Liverpool merchant society consists of two hundred and seventy-four members, associated for the relief of widows of its decayed members, to twenty of whom it pays an annuity of £20

There are numerous provident and benefit societies, and the Liverpool charitable society administers relief to the poor at their own houses The society for ameliorating the condition and increasing the comforts of the poor is under the direction of a committee of twenty-one members, who have established a savings bank in Bold-street, a handsome building with a rustic basement story, from which rise four Doric columns supporting an enriched entablature and triangular pediment, with an ornamented architrave The Diocesan Society, for the relief of the widows and orphan children of the clergy, has been established for several years, and has been productive of considerable benefit The charitable institution house, a commodious building, was erected at the joint expense of John Gladstone, James Cropper, and Samuel Hope, Esqrs, for the gratuitous accommodation of the several committees of the various charitable institutions in the town the lower part of the building is used as a depositary by the Liverpool Auxiliary Bible Society, and attached to it is a record office, in which are kept the reports of all charitable institutions

Among the distinguished natives of the town may be noticed, Jeremiah Horrox, an eminent astronomer, who was born at Toxteth park in 1619 George Stubbs, a celebrated painter of animals, and author of a work on comparative anatomy, and of a series of drawings and engravings illustrative of the anatomy of the horse, born in 1724, William Sadler, who invented the method of applying copper-plate prints to the embellishment of earthenware, Edward Rushton, born in 1756, and John Deare, an eminent sculptor, born in 1760 Matthew Dobson, M D, F R S, and his wife, both respectable authors Dr William Enfield, Dr John Bostock the celebrated Mrs Hemans, and William Roscoe, Esq, author of the Life of Leo X, and of Memoirs of the family of Lorenzo de Medici, and the Rev Legh Richmond, author of the Dairyman s Daughter, were residents in this town Liverpool gives the title of earl to the family of Jenkinson

LIVERSEDGE, a chapelry in the parish of BIRSTALL, wapentake of MORLEY, West riding of the county of YORK, 6½ miles (N E) from Huddersfield, containing 4259 inhabitants The living is a perpetual curacy, in the archdeaconry and diocese of York, endowed with £2200 parliamentary grant The Rev H Roberson was patron in 1812 The chapel dedicated to Christ, has lately received an addition of three hundred and fifty free sittings, the Incorporated Society for the enlargement of churches and chapels having granted £350 towards defraying the expense The High Town school was erected by subscription among the inhabitants, and in 1722, Josias Farrer devised a rent-charge of £8, for the instruction of sixteen poor children, and in 1723, Edward Beaumont bequeathed £100, the interest to be applied in teaching six others of this township the annual income is £14, for which twenty-two free scholars are educated at a National school established here in 1821 During the disturbances in the manufacturing districts, and the prevalence of the Luddite system, in 1812, a mill belonging to Mr William Cartwright, at Rawfolds in this township, became the object of hostile attack, but was vigorously defended by its proprietor, when two of the assailants were killed, and several wounded, none of the efforts at demolition, however, proved successful, and, in admiration of the bravery of Mr Cartwright on the occasion, a public subscription, amounting to upwards of £3000, was made, and presented to that gentleman

LIVERTON, a chapelry in the parish of EASINGTON, eastern division of the liberty of LANGBAURGH, North riding of the county of YORK, 7½ miles (E by N) from Guilsbrough, containing 251 inhabitants.

LIVESEY, a township in the parish of BLACKBURN, lower division of the hundred of BLACKBURN, county palatine of LANCASTER, 3¼ miles (S W) from Blackburn, containing 1664 inhabitants

LLANARTH, a parish partly in the lower division

of the hundred of ABERGAVENNY, but chiefly in the lower division of the hundred of RAGLAND, county of MONMOUTH, 3¼ miles (N W) from Ragland, containing, with the chapelry of Clytha, 686 inhabitants The living is a discharged vicarage, in the archdeaconry and diocese of Llandaff, rated in the king s books at £10 3 4, and in the patronage of the Prebendary of Llanarth in the Cathedral Church of Llandaff The church is dedicated to St Teilaw

LLANBADOCK, a parish in the lower division of the hundred of USK, county of MONMOUTH, 1 mile (W S W) from Usk, containing 369 inhabitants The living is a perpetual curacy, in the archdeaconry and diocese of Llandaff, rated in the king's books at £5 8 9, endowed with £600 royal bounty, and £200 parliamentary grant, and in the patronage of the Marquis of Bute The church is dedicated to St Madocus

LLANBEDER, a chapelry in the parish of LANGSTONE, lower division of the hundred of CALDICOTT, county of MONMOUTH, 3¾ miles (E) from Caerleon, containing 46 inhabitants The chapel, now in ruins, was dedicated to St Peter

LLANCILLO, a parish in the hundred of EWYASLACY, county of HEREFORD, 14½ miles (S W) from Hereford, containing 89 inhabitants The living is a perpetual curacy, in the archdeaconry of Brecon, and diocese of St David, endowed with £200 private benefaction, and £400 royal bounty, and in the patronage of the Rev John Morris The church is dedicated to St Peter

LLANDEGVETH, a parish in the lower division of the hundred of USK, county of MONMOUTH, 3½ miles (N E) from Caerleon, containing 126 inhabitants The living is a discharged rectory, in the archdeaconry and diocese of Llandaff, rated in the king s books at £4 4 9½, and in the patronage of Vivian Robinson, Esq The church is dedicated to St Thomas

LLANDENNY, a parish in the lower division of the hundred of RAGLAND, county of MONMOUTH, 4 miles (N E) from Usk, containing 351 inhabitants The living is a discharged vicarage, annexed to that of Ragland, in the archdeaconry and diocese of Llandaff, rated in the king s books at £5 15 5, and endowed with £1000 royal bounty The church is dedicated to St. John

LLANDEVAND, a chapelry in the parish of LLANMARTIN, lower division of the hundred of CALDICOTT, county of MONMOUTH The population is returned with the parish The living is a perpetual curacy, in the archdeaconry and diocese of Llandaff, endowed with £800 royal bounty, and in the patronage of the Prebendary of Warthacwm in the Cathedral Church of Llandaff The chapel is in a state of dilapidation

LLANDEVENNY, a hamlet in the parish of ST BRIDE, NETHERWENT, lower division of the hundred of CALDICOTT, county of MONMOUTH, containing 53 inhabitants

LLANDINABO, a parish in the upper division of the hundred of WORMELOW, county of HEREFORD, 6½ miles (N W) from Ross, containing 52 inhabitants The living is a discharged rectory, in the archdeaconry and diocese of Hereford, rated in the king s books at £2 18 6½, endowed with £200 royal bounty, and in the patronage of Kedgwyn Hoskins, Esq The church is dedicated to St Dinebo

LLANDOGO, a parish in the upper division of the hundred of RAGLAND, county of MONMOUTH, 7¼ miles (S S E) from Monmouth, containing 612 inhabitants The living is a perpetual curacy, in the archdeaconry and diocese of Llandaff, endowed with £600 royal bounty, and £1400 parliamentary grant, and in the patronage of the Prebendary of Caire in the Cathedral Church of Llandaff The church is dedicated to St Dochoe There is a place of worship for Baptists

LLANELLEN, a parish in the upper division of the hundred of ABERGAVENNY, county of MONMOUTH, 2½ miles (S) from Abergavenny, containing 293 inhabitants The living is a discharged vicarage, in the archdeaconry and diocese of Llandaff, rated in the king s books at £8 10 7, and in the patronage of Charles Kemeys Tynte, Esq The church is dedicated to St Helen

LLANFOIST, a parish in the upper division of the hundred of ABERGAVENNY, county of MONMOUTH, 1½ mile (S W by W) from Abergavenny, containing 535 inhabitants The living is a rectory, in the archdeaconry and diocese of Llandaff, rated in the king s books at £7 4 4½, and in the patronage of the Earl of Abergavenny The church is dedicated to St Faith

LLANGARRAN, a parish in the lower division of the hundred of WORMELOW, county of HEREFORD, 5 miles (W S W) from Ross, containing 1016 inhabitants The living is a perpetual curacy, with the vicarage of Lugwardine, in the archdeaconry and diocese of Hereford The living is dedicated to St Deinst

LLANGATTOCK, a parish in the lower division of the hundred of USK, county of MONMOUTH, containing, with the market town of Caerleon, 1360 inhabitants The living is a discharged vicarage, in the archdeaconry and diocese of Llandaff, rated in the king s books at £8 1 5½, endowed with £250 private benefaction, and £200 royal bounty, and in the patronage of the Chapter of Llandaff The church is dedicated to St Cadocus

LLANGATTOCK nigh USK a parish in the upper division of the hundred of ABERGAVENNY, county of MONMOUTH, 3¼ miles (S S E) from Abergavenny, containing 160 inhabitants The living is a rectory, in the archdeaconry and diocese of Llandaff, rated in the king s books at £11 7 3½, and in the patronage of the Earl of Abergavenny The church is dedicated to St Cadocus

LLANGATTOCK LLINGOED, a parish in the lower division of the hundred of ABERGAVENNY, county of MONMOUTH, 6 miles (N E) from Abergavenny, containing 192 inhabitants The living is a discharged vicarage, in the archdeaconry and diocese of Llandaff, rated in the king s books at £5 6 5½, and in the patronage of the Crown The church is dedicated to St Cadocus

LLANGATTOCK-VIBON AVEL, a parish in the lower division of the hundred of SKENFRETH, county of MONMOUTH, 6 miles (N W) from Monmouth, containing 514 inhabitants The living is a discharged vicarage, in the archdeaconry and diocese of Llandaff, rated in the king s books at £6 18 11½ Thomas Philips, Esq was patron in 1818 The church is dedicated to St Cadocus

LLANGEVIEW, a parish in the upper division of the hundred of USK, county of MONMOUTH, 1 mile (E) from Usk, containing 173 inhabitants The living is a perpetual curacy, in the archdeaconry and diocese of Llandaff, endowed with £600 royal bounty, and £200 parliamentary grant, and in the patronage of Sir H Williams, Bart The church is dedicated to St David

LLANGIBBY, a parish in the lower division of the hundred of Usk, county of Monmouth, 2¼ miles (S by W) from Usk, containing 494 inhabitants The living is a rectory, in the archdeaconry and diocese of Llandaff, rated in the king s books at £19 10 10, and in the patronage of W A Williams, Esq The church is dedicated to St Cuby There is a place of worship for Independents The petty sessions for the division are held here and at Panteague alternately

LLANGOVEN, a parish in the upper division of the hundred of Ragland, county of Monmouth, 3¼ miles (E S E) from Ragland, containing 137 inhabitants The living is a perpetual curacy, with that of Pen-y Clawdd, in the archdeaconry and diocese of Llandaff, rated in the king s books at £3 7 1, endowed with £800 royal bounty, and in the patronage of the Chapter of Llandaff The church is dedicated to St Goven

LLANGUA, a parish in the upper division of the hundred of Skenfreth, county of Monmouth, 11 miles (N E by N) from Abergavenny, containing 74 inhabitants The living is a discharged rectory, annexed to that of Grosmont, in the archdeaconry and diocese of Llandaff, rated in the king s books at £2 15 10, endowed with £200 private benefaction, and £400 royal bounty J Scudamore, Esq was patron in 1908 The church is dedicated to St. James

LLANGWYM, a parish comprising the higher and lower divisions, in the upper division of the hundred of Usk, county of Monmouth, 3½ miles (E) from Usk, containing 337 inhabitants, of which number, 41 are in the higher, and 296 in the lower, division The living is a discharged vicarage, in the archdeaconry and diocese of Llandaff, rated in the king's books at £4 16 8, endowed with £200 private benefaction, and £200 royal bounty, and in the patronage of the Prebendary of Llangwym in the Cathedral Church of Llandaff The church is dedicated to St Hierom

LLANHENNOCK, a parish in the lower division of the hundred of Usk, county of Monmouth, 1¾ mile (N E by N) from Caerleon, containing 145 inhabitants The living is a perpetual curacy, in the archdeaconry and diocese of Llandaff, endowed with £600 royal bounty, and in the patronage of the Chapter of Llandaff The church is dedicated to St John the Baptist

LLANHILETH, a parish in the upper division of the hundred of Abergavenny, county of Monmouth, 11 miles (W by N) from Usk, containing 438 inhabitants The living is a discharged rectory, in the archdeaconry and diocese of Llandaff, rated in the king s books at £7 15 7½, endowed with £800 royal bounty, and in the patronage of the Earl of Abergavenny. The church is dedicated to St Iltyd Coal is obtained in the parish

LLANISHEN, a parish in the upper division of the hundred of Ragland, county of Monmouth, 8 miles (S S W) from Monmouth, containing 255 inhabitants The living is a perpetual curacy, in the archdeaconry and diocese of Llandaff, endowed with £800 royal bounty The Duke of Beaufort was patron in 1807 The church is dedicated to St Denis There is a place of worship for Wesleyan Methodists

LLANITHOG, an extra parochial liberty, in the

upper division of the hundred of Wormelow, county of Hereford, containing 23 inhabitants

LLANLLOWELL, a parish in the upper division of the hundred of Usk, county of Monmouth, 1½ mile (S E) from Usk, containing 63 inhabitants The living is a discharged rectory, in the archdeaconry and diocese of Llandaff, rated in the king s books at £2 13 1½, and endowed with £600 royal bounty The Rev John Saunders was patron in 1798

LLANMARTIN, a parish in the lower division of the hundred of Caldicott, county of Monmouth, 3¾ miles (E S E) from Caerleon, containing, with the chapelry of Llandevand, 161 inhabitants The living is a discharged rectory, with that of Willcrick, in the archdeaconry and diocese of Llandaff, rated in the king s books at £4 6 10½ Sir R Salusbury, Bart was patron in 1814 The church is dedicated to St Martin

LLANOVER, a parish comprising the higher and lower divisions, in the upper division of the hundred of Abergavenny, county of Monmouth, 3½ miles (S by E) from Abergavenny, and containing 2145 inhabitants, of which number, 1863 are in the higher, and 282 in the lower, division The living is a discharged vicarage, with the perpetual curacies of Mamhilad and Trevethin united, in the archdeaconry and diocese of Llandaff, rated in the king's books at £15 3 6½, and in the patronage of the Chapter of Llandaff Here are iron-works, which have lately been much extended, and an iron railway passes in the vicinity

LLANROTHALL, a parish in the lower division of the hundred of Wormelow, county of Hereford, 5 miles (N N W) from Monmouth, containing 118 inhabitants The living is a discharged vicarage, in the archdeaconry and diocese of Hereford, rated in the king s books at £3 15 5, and in the patronage of Joseph Price, Esq A college was founded here early in the sixth century, by St Dubricius, Archbishop of Caerleon, and King of Ergin, of which some assert that it contained one hundred students, while others state the number at one thousand Extensive foundations of buildings may be traced on an eminence rising from the western bank of the Wye.

LLANSAINTFREAD, a parish in the upper division of the hundred of Abergavenny, county of Monmouth, 3¾ miles (S E) from Abergavenny, containing 28 inhabitants The living is a discharged rectory, in the archdeaconry and diocese of Llandaff, rated in the king's books at £2 13 11½, endowed with £200 private benefaction, £400 royal bounty, and in the patronage of William Jones, Esq The church is dedicated to St Bride The rivers Tannat and Verniew form a junction near the village

LLANSOY, a parish in the upper division of the hundred of Ragland, county of Monmouth, 4¼ miles (E N E) from Usk, containing 139 inhabitants The living is a discharged rectory, in the archdeaconry and diocese of Llandaff, rated in the king s books at £6 10 10, and in the patronage of the Duke of Beaufort

LLANTHEWY RYTHERCH, a parish in the lower division of the hundred of Abergavenny, county of Monmouth, 4 miles (E) from Abergavenny, containing 317 inhabitants The living is a discharged vicarage, in the archdeaconry and diocese of Llandaff, rated in the king s books at £7 15 5 , and in the patronage of the Crown   The church is dedicated to St David

LLANTHEWY-SKIRRID, a parish in the lower division of the hundred of ABERGAVENNY, county of MONMOUTH, 4 miles (N E by E) from Abergavenny, containing 84 inhabitants   The living is a rectory, in the archdeaconry and diocese of Llandaff, rated in the king s books at £7 10 2½   John Wilmot, Esq was patron in 1799   The church is dedicated to St David

LLANTHEWY-VACH, a parish in the lower division of the hundred of USK, county of MONMOUTH, 3½ miles (S W) from Usk, containing 172 inhabitants   The living is a perpetual curacy, in the archdeaconry and diocese of Llandaff, endowed with £1000 royal bounty, and in the patronage of the Principal and Fellows of Jesus College, Oxford

LLANTHONY, an extra-parochial liberty, in the middle division of the hundred of DUDSTONE and KING s BARTON, adjacent to the city, and in the county, of GLOUCESTER   A priory, dedicated to the Blessed Virgin Mary and St John the Baptist, was founded here, in 1136, by Milo, Earl of Hereford, for Black canons, refugees from Llanthony abbey in Monmouthshire, to which it was at first a cell, but afterwards became the superior, and had, at the dissolution, a revenue of £748 19 11

LLANTHONY-ABBEY, a chapelry in the upper division of the parish of CWMYOY, lower division of the hundred of ABERGAVENNY, county of MONMOUTH, 10 miles (N by W) from Abergavenny   The population is returned with the parish   Here was formerly a priory of Black canons, for an account of which see Cwmyoy

LLANTILLIO-GROSSENNY, a parish in the upper division of the hundred of SKENFRETH, county of MONMOUTH, 7¼ miles (W N W) from Monmouth, containing 710 inhabitants   The living is a vicarage, in the archdeaconry and diocese of Llandaff, rated in the king s books at £10 10 5 , and in the patronage of the Chapter of Llandaff   The church, dedicated to St Teilaw, is a handsome structure of stone, with a tower surmounted by a lofty spire, and standing on part of the site of an ancient intrenchment   There is a considerable endowment, arising from bequests by James and John Powell, in 1645, for educating and apprenticing children   On the crest of an eminence, about one mile and a half from the village, are the stately ruins of White castle, encompassed by a deep moat, forming an irregular oval two hundred and eighty six yards in circuit

LLANTILLIO-PERTHOLEY, a parish in the lower division of the hundred of ABERGAVENNY, county of MONMOUTH, 1¾ mile (N N E) from Abergavenny, comprising the Citra and Ultra divisions, and containing 726 inhabitants, of which number, 339 are in the Citra, and 387 in the Ultra, division   The living is a discharged vicarage, in the archdeaconry and diocese of Llandaff, rated in the king s books at £8 3 9 , and in the patronage of the Chapter of Llandaff   The church is dedicated to St Teilaw

LLANTRISSENT, a parish in the upper division of the hundred of USK, county of MONMOUTH, 2½ miles (S by E.) from Usk, containing 271 inhabitants   The living is a discharged vicarage, in the archdeaconry and diocese of Llandaff, rated in the king s books at £6 8 9 , and endowed with £200 royal bounty   The Rev John

Saunders was patron in 1798   The church is dedicated to St Peter, St Paul, and St John.

LLANVACHES, a parish in the lower division of the hundred of CALDICOTT, county of MONMOUTH, 6 miles (E) from Caerleon, containing 247 inhabitants   The living is a discharged rectory, in the archdeaconry and diocese of Llandaff, rated in the king s books at £10   Sir Charles Morgan, Bart. was patron in 1810   There is a place of worship for Independents

LLANVAIR-DISCOED, a parish in the upper division of the hundred of CALDICOTT, county of MONMOUTH, 6½ miles (W by S) from Chepstow, containing, with the hamlet of Dinham, 211 inhabitants   The living is a perpetual curacy, in the archdeaconry and diocese of Llandaff, endowed with £600 royal bounty, £200 parliamentary grant, and in the patronage of the Chapter of Llandaff   The church is dedicated to St Mary

LLANVAIR-KILGIDIN, a parish in the upper division of the hundred of ABERGAVENNY, county of MONMOUTH, 5¾ miles (N by W) from Usk, containing 226 inhabitants   The living is a rectory, in the archdeaconry and diocese of Llandaff, rated in the king's books at £5 1 10½   Sir C Morgan, Bart was patron in 1813   The church is dedicated to St Mary

LLANVAIR WATERDINE, a parish in the hundred of PURSLOW, county of SALOP, 4½ miles (N W) from Knighton, containing 477 inhabitants   The living is a perpetual curacy, in the archdeaconry of Salop, and diocese of Hereford, endowed with £200 private benefaction, and £600 royal bounty, and in the patronage of the Earl of Powis   The church, dedicated to St Mary, is a mean building without a steeple   Before 1593 this was a chapelry within the parish of Clun   The river Teme separates the parish from Radnorshire

LLANVANAIR, a chapelry in the hundred of ABERCAVENNY, county of MONMOUTH, 9 miles (N W) from Monmouth   The living is a perpetual curacy, in the archdeaconry and diocese of Llandaff, endowed with £200 private benefaction, and £200 royal bounty

LLANVAPLEY, a parish in the lower division of the hundred of ABERGAVENNY, county of MONMOUTH, 4 miles (E) from Abergavenny, containing 112 inhabitants   The living is a rectory, in the archdeaconry and diocese of Llandaff, rated in the king's books at £10 5 2½., and in the patronage of the Earl of Abergavenny   The church is dedicated to St Mapley   There is a place of worship for Independents

LLANVETHERINE, a parish in the lower division of the hundred of ABERGAVENNY, county of MONMOUTH, 5 miles (N E by E) from Abergavenny, containing 212 inhabitants   The living is a rectory, in the archdeaconry and diocese of Llandaff, rated in the king s books at £14 17 8½   The Earl of Abergavenny was patron in 1785   The church is dedicated to St James the Elder

LLANVEYNOE, a chapelry in the parish of CLODOCK, hundred of EWYASLACY, county of HEREFORD, 17 miles (W S W) from Hereford, containing 323 inhabitants

LLANVIHANGEL near ROGGIET, a parish in the lower division of the hundred of CALDICOTT, county of MONMOUTH, 8 miles (S W by W) from Chepstow, containing 45 inhabitants   The living is a discharged rectory, in the archdeaconry and diocese of Llandaff, rated in the king s books at £6 9 4½ , and endowed with £400 royal bounty   Sir C Morgan, Bart was patron in 1812 The church is dedicated to St Michael

LLANVIHANGEL near USK, a parish in the upper division of the hundred of ABERGAVENNY, county of MONMOUTH, 6½ miles (N N W) from Usk, containing 99 inhabitants The living is a discharged rectory, in the archdeaconry and diocese of Llandaff, rated in the king s books at £3 8 9, and in the patronage of Sir Samuel Fludyer, Bart. The church is dedicated to St Michael

LLANVIHANGEL-CRUCORNEY, a parish comprising the hamlet of Penbiddle in the upper division of the hundred of SKENFRETH, but chiefly in the lower division of the hundred of ABERGAVENNY, county of MONMOUTH, 5 miles (N by E) from Abergavenny, and containing 366 inhabitants The living is a discharged vicarage, in the archdeaconry and diocese of Llandaff, rated in the king s books at £5 19 7, and in the patronage of the King, as Prince of Wales The church is dedicated to St Michael

LLANVIHANGEL-LLANTARNAM a parish in the lower division of the hundred of USK, county of MONMOUTH, 2 miles (N W by W) from Caerleon, containing 565 inhabitants The living is a perpetual curacy, in the archdeaconry and diocese of Llandaff, endowed with £800 royal bounty, and £200 parliamentary grant, and in the patronage of Thomas Bluett, Esq The church is dedicated to St Michael Here was a Cistercian abbey, the revenue of which was valued at the dissolution at £71 3 2

LLANVIHANGEL PONT-Y MOILE, a parish in the lower division of the hundred of USK, county of MONMOUTH, 5 miles (N by N) from Usk, containing 158 inhabitants The living is a perpetual curacy, in the archdeaconry and diocese of Llandaff, endowed with £300 private benefaction, £600 royal bounty, and £500 parliamentary grant, and in the patronage of Capel Hanbury Leigh, Lsq The church is dedicated to St Michael

LLANVIHANGEL TOR-Y-MYNYDD, a parish in the upper division of the hundred of RAGLAND, county of MONMOUTH, 6½ miles (E by N) from Usk, containing 213 inhabitants The living is a discharged rectory, in the archdeaconry and diocese of Llandaff, rated in the king s books at £2 15 5, endowed with £200 royal bounty, and in the patronage of the Archdeacon of Llandaff

LLANVIHANGEL-YSTERN LLEWERN, a parish partly in the lower division of the hundred of RAGLAND, and partly in the upper division of the hundred of SKENFRETH, county of MONMOUTH, 5½ miles (W by N) from Monmouth, containing 133 inhabitants The living is a rectory, in the archdeaconry and diocese of Llandaff, rated in the king s books at £9 8 4 The Earl of Abergavenny was patron in 1800 The church is dedicated to St Michael

LLANVRECHVA, a parish comprising the lower and upper divisions, in the lower division of the hundred of USK, county of MONMOUTH, 2 miles (N) from Caerleon, containing 973 inhabitants, of which number 662 are in the lower, and 311 in the upper division The living is a perpetual curacy, in the archdeaconry and diocese of Llandaff, endowed with £400 private benefaction, £800 royal bounty, and £1200 parliamentary grant, and in the patronage of the Chapter of Llandaff

LLANWARNE, a parish in the upper division of the hundred of WORMELOW, county of HEREFORD, 7 miles (N W by W) from Ross, containing 324 inhabitants The living is a rectory, in the archdeaconry and diocese of Hereford, rated in the king s books at £15, and in the patronage of the Governors of Guy s Hospital The church is dedicated to St John the Baptist

LLANWENARTH, a parish comprising Llanwenarth-Citra, in the lower, and Llanwenarth-Ultra, in the upper, division of the hundred of ABERGAVENNY, county of MONMOUTH, 2¼ miles (N W by W) from Abergavenny, and containing 2001 inhabitants, of which number, 188 are in the Citra, and 1813 in the Ultra, division The living is a rectory, in the archdeaconry and diocese of Llandaff, rated in the king s books at £26 6 3 The Earl of Abergavenny was patron in 1780 The church is dedicated to St Peter There is a place of worship for Baptists At Carn-y-Derris, in this parish, coal and iron works have been lately established

LLANWERN, a parish in the lower division of the hundred of CALDICOTT, county of MONMOUTH, 3¼ miles (S E) from Caerleon, containing 27 inhabitants The living is a discharged rectory, in the archdeaconry and diocese of Llandaff, rated in the king s books at £4 0 10, endowed with £400 royal bounty, and in the patronage of Sir Thomas Salusbury, Bart The church is dedicated to St Mary

LLANYBLODWELL a parish in the hundred of OSWESTRY, county of SALOP, 6 miles (S W by S) from Oswestry, containing 850 inhabitants The living is a discharged rectory, with the curacy of Moreton, in the archdeaconry and diocese of St Asaph, rated in the king s books at £7 12 1, and in the patronage of the Bishop of St Asaph The church, dedicated to St Michael, is a plain structure, with a small wooden turret rising from the roof of the west end, it contains some handsome monuments to the Bridgeman and Godolphin families Attached to the building is a school-room, and a dwelling house for the master, built and endowed by Mr Matthews, of Blodwell hall, for the education of poor children, and to which the late Rev Dr Donne was a great benefactor The small river Tannat flows through the parish, and Offa s Dyke bounds it on the east Here are quarries of limestone, and several lime-kilns, affording employment to most of the poor inhabitants of the neighbourhood, copper and lead ore also abound, though no regular mines of either seem to have been wrought since the time of the Romans, of whose works there are still considerable traces in this and the adjoining parishes In the township of Llynclys, a name derived from Llyn, a lake, and Lys, a palace, is a lake of extraordinary depth, of which it is vulgarly believed and affirmed, that when the water is clear and unruffled, towers and other parts of a large structure are plainly discernible at the bottom

LLANYMYNECH, a parish in the hundred of OSWESTRY, county of SALOP, 6 miles (S by W) from Oswestry, containing, with the townships of Llwyntlanan and Treprenal, 454 inhabitants The living is a rectory, in the archdeaconry and diocese of Llandaff, rated in the king's books at £12 13 4, and in the patronage of the Bishop of St Asaph The church is dedicated to St. Agatha Limestone of the finest quality abounds in the parish, and there are kilns for burning it Copper and lead ore are also found in the neighbourhood, but though no mines are now in operation, the "Ogof," a Welch word for cave, is evidently the mouth of an ancient mine, near which are vestiges of a Roman encampment The Llanymynech canal passes through the parish

LLOYNDU, a hamlet in that part of the parish of ABERGAVENNY which is in the lower division of the hundred of ABERGAVENNY, county of MONMOUTH, containing 121 inhabitants

LLWYNTLANAN a township in the parish of LLANYMYNECH, hundred of OSWESTRY, county of SALOP, 5¾ miles (8 by W) from Oswestry The population is returned with the parish

LOAD, a chapelry in the parish and hundred of MARTOCK, county of SOMERSET, 4½ miles (S S W) from Somerton The living is a perpetual curacy annexed to the vicarage of Martock, in the archdeaconry of Wells, and diocese of Bath and Wells, endowed with £200 private benefaction, and £400 royal bounty The chapel is dedicated to St Mary Magdalene The navigable river Yeo, or Ivel, is here crossed by a bridge

LOAN-END, a township in the parish of NORHAM otherwise Norhamshire, county palatine of DURHAM, though locally to the northward of Northumberland, 4½ miles (W S W) from Berwick upon Tweed, containing 143 inhabitants

LOBB, a hamlet in the parish of GREAT HASELEY, hundred of EWELME, county of OXFORD The population is returned with the parish

LOCKERIDGE, a township in the parish of OVERTON, hundred of SELKLEY, county of WILTS, 3 miles (W S W) from Marlborough The population is returned with the parish

LOCKERLEY, a parish in the hundred of THORNGATE, Andover division of the county of SOUTHAMPTON, 6 miles (N W) from Romsey, containing 504 inhabitants The living is a perpetual curacy, united to the rectory of Mottisfont, in the archdeaconry and diocese of Winchester The church is dedicated to St John There is a place of worship for Baptists The Salisbury and Southampton canal passes through the parish Sarah Rolle, in 1700, gave certain land, directing the income to be applied in clothing, maintaining, and educating all poor children of Lockerley, East Tytherley, Mounds-rure, and Stebbington

LOCKHAY, or LOCKO, a chapelry in the parish of SPONDON, hundred of APPLETREE, though locally in the hundred of Morleston and Litchurch, county of DERBY, 4½ miles (E N E) from Derby The population is returned with the parish Here was an hospital of the order of St Lazarus of Jerusalem, dedicated to St Mary Magdalene, and subordinate to a house in France in the reign of Edward III it was seized by the Crown, and given to the Society of King s Hall, Cambridge

LOCKING, a parish in the hundred of WINTERSTOKE, county of SOMERSET, 6¼ miles (N W) from Axbridge, containing 198 inhabitants The living is a discharged vicarage, in the archdeaconry of Wells, and diocese of Bath and Wells, rated in the king's books at £5 6 10½, endowed with £200 private benefaction, and £200 royal bounty The church, dedicated to St Augustine, is a modern structure, built principally at the expense of the Society of Merchant Adventurers

of Bristol, who are trustees of Colston charity in Bristol and, as such, patrons of this benefice

LOCKINGE (EAST and WEST), a parish in the hundred of WANTAGE, county of BERKS, 3¼ miles (S E) from Wantage, containing, with the tythings of Betterton and West Ginge, 342 inhabitants The living is a rectory, in the archdeaconry of Berks, and diocese of Salisbury, rated in the king s books at £31 10 , and annexed to the Wardenship of All Souls' College, Oxford, since 1764, by act of parliament The church is dedicated to All Saints

LOCKINGTON, a parish in the western division of the hundred of GOSCOTE, county of LEICESTER, 7½ miles (N W by N) from Loughborough, containing, with the township of Hemington, 627 inhabitants The living is a discharged vicarage, in the archdeaconry of Leicester, and diocese of Lincoln, rated in the king s books at £6 7 3¼, endowed with £200 private benefaction, and £200 royal bounty, and in the patronage of the Trustees of the late Rev P Story The living is dedicated to St Nicholas The navigable river Trent flows along the northern, and the Soar along the eastern, boundary of this parish, at the north-east angle of which they form a junction

LOCKINGTON, a parish in the Bainton-Beacon division of the wapentake of HARTHILL, East riding of the county of YORK, containing 426 inhabitants, 6½ miles (N N W) from Beverley it comprises part of the township of Aike, and part of that of Lockington, the remaining part being in the parish of Kilnwick The living is a rectory, in the archdeaconry and diocese of York, rated in the king s books at £20 The Rev Francis Lundy was patron in 1817 The church is dedicated to St Mary There is a place of worship for Wesleyan Methodists

LOCKTON, a township in the parish of MIDDLETON, PICKERING lythe, North riding of the county of YORK, 5 miles (N E by N) from Pickering, containing 324 inhabitants There is a place of worship for Wesleyan Methodists

LOCKWOOD, a chapelry in the parish of ALMONDBURY, upper division of the wapentake of AGBRICG, West riding of the county of YORK, 1½ mile (S W) from Huddersfield, containing 1881 inhabitants A handsome chapel has recently been erected by the parliamentary commissioners, containing nearly one thousand sittings, four hundred of which are free There is a place of worship for Baptists

LODDINGTON, a parish in the eastern division of the hundred of GOSCOTE, county of LEICESTER, 7¼ miles (N by W) from Uppingham, containing, with the liberty of Whatborough, 166 inhabitants The living is a perpetual curacy, in the archdeaconry of Leicester, and diocese of Lincoln, and in the patronage of Charles Morris, Esq The church is dedicated to St Michael

LODDINGTON, a parish in the hundred of ROTHWELI, county of NORTHAMPTON, 1¾ mile (S) from Rothwell, containing 214 inhabitants The living is a rectory, in the archdeaconry of Northampton, and diocese of Peterborough, rated in the king s books at £10 4 4½, and in the patronage of the Crown The church is dedicated to St Andrew There is a trifling rent-charge, the bequest of Sarah Wykes, in 1705, for teaching eight poor children

LODDISWELL, a parish in the hundred of STAN-

BOROUGH, county of DEVON, 3 miles (N N W) from Kingsbridge, containing 762 inhabitants The living is a vicarage, in the archdeaconry of Totness, and diocese of Exeter, rated in the king s books at £26 0 2½ Francis Freke Gunston, Esq was patron in 1824 The church is dedicated to St Michael In 1728, R Phillips bequeathed a house and lands for the benefit of the poor of this parish, the produce of which is annually distributed over the tomb of the testator Blackadon camp, an ancient military post, is in this neighbourhood

LODDON, a market town and parish in the hundred of LODDON, county of NORFOLK, 10 miles (S E) from Norwich, and 113 (N E) from London, containing 1038 inhabitants This place is situated on the banks of an inconsiderable stream, which flows from the neighbourhood of Howe into the Yare at Yardley cross, on the direct thoroughfare from Norwich to Beccles the streets are neither lighted nor paved, but the inhabitants are well supplied with water malting is carried on to a small extent The market is on Tuesday fairs are held on Easter-Monday, and on the 25th of November for horses, and a statute fair for hiring servants is held a fortnight before Michaelmas day The county magistrates hold their meetings monthly at this place A court baron is held at the will of the lord of the manor The living is a vicarage, in the archdeaconry of Norfolk, and diocese of Norwich, and in the patronage of the Bishop of Ely The church, dedicated to the Holy Trinity, was erected at the expense of Sir James Hobart, Chief Justice of the Court of Common Pleas in the reign of Henry VII It is a fine fabric of stone, surmounted by an elegant tower, in the later style of English architecture in the chancel is a marble altar-tomb of the Hobart family, with heraldic symbols and other devices, and another tomb for Dyonis Williamson, with a recumbent statue There is a place of worship for Wesleyan Methodists A National school has been established for children of both sexes, in which about one hundred are educated. A farm was left by the Hobarts for repairing the church.

LODSWORTH, a chapelry in the parish and hundred of EASEBOURNE, rape of CHICHESTER, county of SUSSEX, 3½ miles (W by N) from Petworth, containing 513 inhabitants The living is a perpetual curacy, in the archdeaconry and diocese of Chichester, endowed with £200 private benefaction, £200 royal bounty, and £500 parliamentary grant W S Poyntz, Esq was patron in 1808 The Rother, or Arundel, navigation is crossed by a bridge in this parish

LOFTHOUSE, a township in the parish of ROTHWELL, lower division of the wapentake of AGBRIGG, West riding of the county of YORK, 3 miles (N) from Wakefield The population is returned with the township of Carlton

LOFTHOUSE, a parish in the eastern division of the liberty of LANGBAURGH, North riding of the county of YORK, 8½ miles (E N E) from Guilsbrough, containing, with the hamlet of Wapley, 1178 inhabitants The living is a rectory, in the archdeaconry of Cleveland, and diocese of York, rated in the king s books at £10 11 0½, and in the patronage of the Crown The church is dedicated to St Leonard There is a place of worship for Wesleyan Methodists The vicinity abounds with stone and alum rocks, the latter being worked to a considerable extent A customary market is held on Thursday At Handale, or Greendale, in this parish, a priory of Benedictine nuns was founded, in 1133, by William de Percy, the third baron of that name, and dedicated to the Virgin Mary, at the dissolution the revenue was valued at £20 7 8

LOFTSOME, a joint township with Wressel, in the parish of WRESSEL, Holme-Beacon division of the wapentake of HARTHILL, East riding of the county of YORK, 3½ miles (W N W) from Howden. The population is returned with Wressel This township lies near the Derwent, over which is a wooden bridge, so constructed as to admit the passage of vessels

LOGASTON, a township in that part of the parish of ALMELEY which is in the hundred of WOLPHY, county of HEREFORD The population is returned with the parish

LOLWORTH, a parish in the hundred of NORTHSTOW, county of CAMBRIDGE, 6¼ miles (N W by W) from Cambridge, containing 111 inhabitants The living is a rectory, in the archdeaconry and diocese of Ely, rated in the king s books at £6 2 3½ Sir H Hawley, Bart., and P Orchard, Esq, were patrons in 1786 The church is dedicated to All Saints An extensive destruction of houses and corn, by lightning, occurred here in 1393

LONDESBOROUGH, a parish in the Holme Beacon division of the wapentake of HARTHILL, East riding of the county of YORK, 3 miles (N) from Market-Weighton, containing, with the hamlet of East Thorpe, 244 inhabitants The living is a rectory, in the archdeaconry and diocese of York, rated in the king s books at £16, and in the patronage of the Duke of Devonshire The church is dedicated to All Saints An hospital for twelve poor persons, being aged bachelors, widowers, or widows, was founded here by the first Earl and Countess of Burlington it is now in the patronage of the Duke of Devonshire Londesborough was, for several generations, the seat of the Clifford family, and in the village, park, and gardens, several Roman coins, and repositories of the dead, have been discovered, on which account, Dr Drake, considers it to have been the Roman station *Delgovitia* The Roman road from Brough is continued in a line to Londesborough park

Arms.

LONDON, the me
tropolis of the United Kingdom,the seat of Government,
and the principal port of the
empire, forming a city and
county of itself, is situated
on the northern bank of the
Thames, about sixty miles
from its mouth, in 51° 31′
(N Lat), and 5′ (W Lon)
from the meridian of Greenwich observatory, 395 miles
(S) from Edinburgh, and
338 (S E) from Dublin, and contains, including some
of the adjoining parishes, 1,225,694 inhabitants, according to the census of 1821, of this number, 56,874
are in the city of London Within the Walls, 69,260 in
the city of London Without the Walls (not including
any part of the borough of Southwark, in which there
are 84,098 inhabitants), and 182,085 in the city and liberties of Westminster the increase of population during the twenty years preceding the last census was
360,849, and since that period it has been augmenting
with greater celerity

The earliest notice that we find of London, which
is now the most important, if not the most extensive,
city in the world, is in Julius Cæsar s account of his two
exploratory expeditions from Gaul to Britain, styled
his Commentaries Its situation identifies it with the
Civitas Trinobantum, or city of the Trinobantes, by
which people it was probably selected on account of its
peculiarly fine situation on the north, it was protected
by an eminence, a forest, and a morass, on the west, by
the deep ravine called the Fleet, on the east, by another
ravine, since called Wal-brook, and on the south was
the Thames, connected with extensive marshes, shel
tered by the Kent and Surrey hills, thus combining, with other advantages, all the natural defences
that could be desired by an uncivilized people At
a very early period of its history it was considered peculiarly eligible as a seat of commerce, the proximity
to the sea being sufficient to afford the full advantage
of the tide, at the same time that the distance was
great enough to furnish a perfect security against any
sudden atack from the naval force of an enemy The
name *Londinium* is, according to the most prevailing
opinion, a Latinization of the British compound *I yn-
din*, the town on the lake, the vast æstuary formed by
the Thames here, at that time, being a peculiarity at-
taching to no other British town, whilst *Lun-dun*, the
town in the grove, and *Llhong-din*, the city of ships,
the next two most probable etymons, are liable to in-
superable objections, the former name expressing a feature said by Cæsar to have been common to all British
towns, which he describes as fortified woods, and the
latter being inapplicable before the place became known
as a naval station The Saxons called this city *Lunden-
ceaster*, which affix, as well as those of *wick*, and *byrg*
or *byrig*, occasionally used by them in place of it, appears to have been dropped at the time of the Norman
Conquest.

The earliest event recorded of London is its destruction by Boadicea, Queen of the Iceni, in the reign
of Nero, in the year 60 Its progress since the time
of Cæsar had been so rapid, that Tacitus describes it,
at this period, as "the chief residence of merchants,
and the great mart of trade, though not then dignified, like *Camalodunum* (Maldon, or Colchester), and
Verulamium (St Alban s), with the name of a colony,
nor, as it appears, fortified in the Roman manner A
few years afterwards, the Romans made it a permanent
station, subject to the authority of their own laws It is
agreed to have been surrounded by a wall in the fourth
century, and, according to Dr Stukeley, the Roman city
occupied an oblong square, extending in length from
Ludgate to Wal-brook, and in breadth, from Maiden lane,
Lad-lane, and Cateaton street, to the Thames This
space was between the river *Fleta*, on the west, and the
stream called Wal brook, on the east, and comprised
about one fifth of the area subsequently surrounded by
a wall the height of which, when perfect, was twenty-
two feet, throughout its whole circuit it commenced
at the Palatine tower, proceeded in a straight line along
the eminence of Ludgate-hill, as far as Newgate, and
was then suddenly carried eastward, to a spot a little
beyond Aldersgate, running thence straight in a nor
therly direction, almost as far as Cripplegate, from which
spot it returned, in a direct easterly course, as far as
Bishopsgate, where a large remnant of the wall, called
"London Wall," remained standing until the late removal of Bethlehem hospital From Bishopsgate the
wall assumed a gentle curvature to the Tower over the
site of which it originally passed, and probably finished
in a castellum at this, as it did at the western extremity
Another wall skirted the river, and ran the whole
length of Thames-street Strong towers and bastions,
of Roman masonry, to the number of fifteen, increased
the strength of these fortifications, to which, in after
times, was added a broad deep ditch, and at Barbican
stood the Specula, or Watch-tower, so named Four gates
afforded entrance from the great military roads which
then intersected South Britain the *Prætorian* way, improved from the British Watling-street, passed under
one of those gates, at the spot where Aldersgate formerly stood, whence it proceeded along that street
to Billingsgate, and thence continued, on the opposite
bank of the Thames, to its southern termination at
Dovor The Ermin street led from a *trajectus*, or
ferry, which crossed from Stony-street, Southwark, to
Dowgate, and passing by Bishopsgate, pursued the course
of the present road northwards, to *Ad Fines* (Braugh-
ing) Another road passed through Newgate, by Holborn and Oxford-street, to *Ad Pontes* (Staines), from
which there was a branch road, in a north-easterly direction, by Portpool-lane, Clerkenwell, Old-street, and
Hackney, to *Duroleiton*, the modern Layton in Essex
Bishopsgate, Moorgate, Ludgate, &c, were added as
new roads were formed Temple-bar is modern, not
having been built until after the great fire, in 1670
Roman antiquities, consisting of foundations of houses,
temples, walls, and streets, tesselated pavements, sepulchral monuments, urns, glasses, coins, articles of dress,
and numerous other remains of the same period, have
been discovered on the site of the present metropolis
The London stone, in Cannon-street, is considered, by
most antiquaries, as part of a Roman milliary, and the

central point from which the great Roman roads diverged

London continued to improve under the Romans, and had greatly increased in importance before the year 211, when we find it recorded as "a great and wealthy city, illustrious for the vast number of merchants who resorted to it, for its widely-extended commerce, and for the abundance of every species of commodity it could supply' Antoninus, at this period, makes seven of his fifteen *itinera* terminate here, and its early importance is further evinced by its having been a *municipium*, or free city, and the residence of the Vicars of Britain, under the Roman Emperors In the year 359, no less than eight hundred vessels are said to have been employed in the exportation from London of corn alone, and its commerce is stated to have increased proportionally, until the end of the fourth century On the abandonment of Britain by the Romans, a new and fierce race succeeded to their dominion The warlike Saxons, under their leaders Hengist and Horsa, landed, in 448, at *Upwines fleet* (the present Ebbs-fiete), in the Isle of Thanet The Britons, however, remained masters of London at least nine years after that event, for, being defeated in 457, at *Creccanford*, now Crayford, they evacuated Kent, and fled to the capital. On Hengist's death, in 498, having then been for some time in the possession of the Saxons, it was retaken by Ambrosius, and retained by the Britons during a considerable part of the following century In the year 604, London seems to have recovered from the ravages of the invaders, so that Bede terms it "a princely mart town,' and its chief magistrate was called *portgrave*, or *portreeve*

London was the chief town of the Saxon kingdom of Essex, and, on the conversion of the East Saxons to Christianity, it became an episcopal see Sabert was the first Christian king of Essex, and his maternal uncle, Ethelbert, King of Kent, founded here, about the commencement of the seventh century, a church, dedicated to St Paul, of which Mellitus was consecrated the first bishop In the years 764, 788, and 801, the capital suffered severely from fires, as it did also in 849, on an invasion of the Danes, who entered the Thames with two hundred and fifty ships, plundered and burnt the city, and massacred the inhabitants In a similar attempt with an increased naval force, two years afterwards, they were completely defeated by Ethelwulph and his son Ethelbald, yet London suffered more from these two invasions than it had ever done before Under Egbert, London, though not the seat of government, was advancing fast in importance, a wittenagemote having been held in 833, to consult on the means of repelling the Danes Alfred restored this city, and constituted London *the* CAPITAL *of all England*, but had the mortification, in 893, to see it almost entirely reduced to ashes by an accidental fire, which raged with the more uncontrollable fury as the houses were, at that time, almost wholly built of wood It was a second time rebuilt, and, for its better government, divided by Alfred into wards and precincts, that monarch also instituted the office of sheriff in London, as in other parts of the kingdom In 925, King Athelstan had a royal palace here, and appointed eight mints for the coinage of money The city increased in importance during the succeeding reigns, until the year 1015, when

Canute the Dane, with his fleet, sailed up the Thames and besieged it, but he was repulsed, and after having blockaded it and made several unsuccessful attempts, a compromise was agreed upon between the two kings, Edmund Ironside and Canute, whereby London was conceded to the latter The comparative opulence of the city, at this time, is indicated by its having paid a seventh part of the tax levied on the whole nation by that monarch, the total amount of which was £72,000 In a wittenagemote at Oxford, to determine the succession after the death of Canute, we find the "pilots of London summoned thereto, meaning its magistrates, or leading men Edward the Confessor granted to London the court of *Hustings*, and by his charter, in which the city is called *Tray-novant*, gave it pre-eminence over all his cities he moreover confirmed its right of manumission of slaves who had resided there a year and a day, from which is thought to be derived the custom of calling the city "The King's Free Chamber

On the successful invasion of England by William the Norman, the magistrates of London, in conjunction with the prelates and nobility, invited him to accept the title of king, and he was crowned at Westminster In return, that prince granted to the city two charters, confirming the whole of the privileges it had enjoyed under the Saxon kings, and adding several others The government of London, at this time, appears to have been vested in the bishop and a portreeve In the year 1077, another fire having destroyed a great part of the city, with St Paul's cathedral, Maurice, Bishop of London, laid the foundation of a new church, on a more extended scale than the former That part of the city which had been destroyed by the last-mentioned fire was soon rebuilt more magnificently than before, and the White Tower, now forming part of the Tower of London, was erected by William I, in 1078 Domesday-book contains no notice of London at this time owing, it is supposed, to a separate survey having been made of it, which is now lost, but mentions, as part of the suburbs, a vineyard in Holborn, in the possession of the crown, and ten acres of land, near Bishopsgate, belonging to the Dean and Chapter of St. Paul's the latter is the present manor of Norton-Falgate, and both are now situated within the limits of the metropolis In 1090, a tremendous hurricane overthrew about six hundred houses, with several churches, and damaged the Tower of London This fortress was repaired by William Rufus, and strengthened by additional works the same king, in 1097, founded Westminster hall Henry I, as a reward for the ready submission of the men of London to his usurped authority, granted to the city the first charter in which its privileges were circumstantially detailed, amongst them were the perpetual shrievalty of Middlesex, which enabled the citizens to unite the power of the two shrievalties of the city of London and of the county of Middlesex, in freemen of their own nomination. The standard of weights and measures was granted to them about the same time, and, by the same king's charter, it was further stipulated, that the city of London should have all its ancient privileges, as well by land as by water In the first year of the reign of Stephen, another fire, beginning near London stone, consumed all the houses eastward to Aldgate, and westward to St Paul's, together with

London bridge, which was then of wood this occasioned, in 1192, an order to the mayor and aldermen, that "all houses thereafter erected in the city, or liberties thereof, should be built of stone, with party walls of the same, and covered either with slate or tiles, to prevent the recurrence of fires, which had been occasioned by the houses having been built of wood, and thatched with straw, or reeds, but this order does not appear to have been extensively carried into effect

Of the state of London at this early period, an admirable picture is afforded in the description by Fitz-Stephen, a contemporary monk, wherein he informs us that the city was strongly walled and fortified, that it abounded in churches, convents, and public buildings, carried on an extensive commerce with distant parts of the world, and had a large disposable military force It was supplied with water from numerous wells, among which were Clerkenwell, Clement s well, Holywell, and others Moorfields was a great lake, the *Magna Nora* of the Conqueror all the suburbs are described as being filled with the gardens and summer-houses of the citizens, and watered with streams of pure water, which turned the numerous mills employed in grinding corn for the subsistence of the inhabitants The chief improvement during the reign of Henry II was the foundation, in 1176, of a new London bridge, of stone, which was completed in 1209 The year 1189 is memorable in the metropolitan annals for the cruel massacre of the Jews, which took place at the coronation of Richard I In the year 1210, King John empowered "the barons of London,' as they are styled, to choose their mayor annually, or continue him from year to year at pleasure, but in 1252 a by-law was made, ordaining that no one should be mayor longer than one year In 1212 occurred a tremendous fire, wherein, according to Stowe, as many as three thousand persons perished. In 1214, the Town ditch, surrounding the city walls, was commenced, and, after several hundred persons had been employed upon it for upwards of two years, was completed in 1218 In 1215, the citizens taking part with the barons against King John, opened their gates to Louis the Dauphin and his army In the same year happened a great fire, which began in Southwark, and extended to London bridge, where it destroyed three thousand persons, who were prevented from escape by another fire breaking out at the Middlesex end of the bridge

The increase of the metropolis in buildings, from the reign of Henry I to the period last named, had kept pace with the extension of its municipal privileges. In this interval, of little more than a century, twelve large monasteries were founded in London and its suburbs, including the magnificent establishments of the Knights Templars and the Knights Hospitallers, the superb priory of the Holy Trinity, in Aldgate, whose prior was an alderman of London, and others of nearly equal magnitude Several additional gates had also been erected, in consequence of the formation of new roads, as well as magnificent mansions built by the wealthy citizens, such as Gerard's Hall, Basing Hall, the Ledyn Porch, &c., and various parochial churches rebuilt on a grander and more substantial scale In consequence of the extensive foundations above mentioned, and the increased number of private houses, in the reign of Henry III., the supply of water furnished from

Old-bourne (Holborn), Wal-brook, and Ley-bourne, was found insufficient, and a new supply was obtained from the springs in the village of Tyburn, and, in 1285, a conduit in Cheapside was first supplied with this water, by leaden pipes The fee-farm of Queen hythe had, previously to this period, been purchased from Richard, Earl of Cornwall, by the corporation, subject to an annual quit rent of £50, thus affording additional facilities for the increased commerce of the metropolis In 1258, a dreadful famine was experienced in London, in consequence of the high price of corn, and twenty thousand persons are said to have died of hunger In 1262, a considerable part of West-cheap was reduced to ashes by a fire wilfully caused by some unknown incendiaries In 1266, the Earl of Gloucester, in rebellion against Henry III, entered the city with an army, and built bulwarks, cut trenches, &c

In 1296, in the reign of Edward I, the wards of London, first formed by Alfred, but uncertain as to their number, were extended to twenty-four, with each a presiding alderman, and common council-men appointed to be chosen annually, as at present, for the several precincts a common seal was also granted to the city In 1320, a fish-market was first established In 1325, the Bishop of Exeter, high treasurer to Richard II, and custos of the city, on the king's departure from London to the West of England, was seized by the citizens, and beheaded at the Cross in Cheapside they afterwards seized the constable of the Tower, and took possession of that fortress Edward III, who began his reign on the 25th of January, 1327, granted that the mayor should be one of the judges of Oyer and Terminer, or gaol delivery of Newgate, that the citizens should not be compelled to go to war out of the city, and, moreover, that the liberties and franchises of the city should not, after this time, on any pretext, be taken into the king s hands he also granted that the mayor should be the only escheator within the city In 1338, the serjeants of the mayor and sheriffs of London were empowered to bear maces of silver gilt, with the king s arms engraven on them, and in 1340, tolls were imposed for paving the streets In 1348 occurred a great plague, and in the course of the same year, Sir Walter Manny founded the Charter House, near Smithfield, with Pardon churchyard adjoining, to be a place of burial for such as died of it In 1354, the aldermen of London, having been hitherto changed yearly, it was ordained that they should not be removed without some special cause In 1356, the opulence of the citizens was strikingly displayed by Henry Piccard, the mayor, feasting at one entertainment the Kings of England, France, Cyprus, and Scotland, with other great personages In 1380 occurred Wat Tyler s rebellion, when William Walworth, mayor, was knighted in the field, together with several aldermen, for their gallant behaviour on the occasion, and the dagger is said to have been added to the city arms on account of Walworth having killed, with that weapon, the rebel Tyler, in Smithfield. In 1406, London was afflicted with another great plague, which swept away upwards of thirty thousand people In 1410, Stocks market-house was erected, on the site of the present mansion-house In 1416, Sir Henry Barton, mayor, ordained that lanterns, with lights, should be hung out on winter evenings, between Hallowtide and Candlemas, and in the following year this custom was general In 1417, a new guildhall was built on the site of the present edifice, in lieu of a mean cottage, formerly occupied as such, in Aldermanbury, and in 1419 Leadenhall was erected, as a public granary The supply of water being found insufficient, in 1443, pipes were laid from Paddington A few years afterwards the city ditch was cleansed, and the walls repaired In 1449, the Kentish rebel, Jack Cade, made his entry into London

About the year 1460 occurs the earliest notice of the use of brick in the buildings of London this material was first made in Moorfields, and afterwards gradually superseded wood, and became generally used in erecting dwelling-houses New conduits, and cisterns for water, were also constructed In 1469, the Tower of London being delivered to the mayor and his brethren, the aldermen, they set at liberty King Henry VI, who was confined there Under Richard III and Henry VII various additions were made to the royal palace at Westminster, and the latter monarch, besides founding his magnificent chapel at the abbey adjoining, also rebuilt Baynard s castle, in Thames street In the thirteenth year of his reign, several gardens in Finsbury were destroyed, and formed into a field for archers, whence the origin of the present Artillery Company During this reign also the river Fleet was made navigable, Houndsditch was arched over, and many less works of utility, or ornament, completed Henry VIII continued the improvements of the metropolis, and during his reign the police was better regulated, many nuisances were removed, the streets and avenues were mended and paved, and various regulations were carried into effect for supplying the metropolis with provisions sufficient to answer the demands of its increasing population The greatest alteration made in the aspect of the city, during this reign, was effected by the dissolution of religious houses, of which there had been upwards of twenty, founded between the reign of Edward I and the period of the dissolution, besides those before mentioned this event took place in the year 1535, and rendered London entirely a commercial city The religious establishments, usually occupying large plots of ground, now gave way to the erection of schools, hospitals, manufactories, noblemen s mansions, and other edifices There were fifty-four larger monasteries in London at the dissolution, exclusively of minor establishments Two royal palaces, St James and Bridewell, were among the splendid buildings erected by Henry VIII, and to the same monarch is to be attributed a considerable part of the buildings in New Palace Yard, Westminster, and at Whitehall, particularly the cock-pit, and the fine gateway by Holbein, which formerly stood at the latter palace, as also the laying out of St James' park Until the Reformation, the government of Westminster had been vested solely in its abbot, but, in the settlement of that great revolution, it was placed, first in the hands of a bishop, and subsequently in those of the Dean of Westminster, in whom it still, in some degree, continues Near this period, notwithstanding there had been a recent revival of commerce, and that the metropolis had been enlarged, it is stated that there were not above four merchant vessels exceeding one hundred and twenty tons' burden in the river Thames, and afterwards it is observed, in a letter from a London merchant to Sir William Cecil, that

there was "not a city in Europe, having the occupying that London had, that was so slenderly provided with ships yet a spirit of enterprise was then very general among our merchants The events which chiefly characterise the reign of Edward VI, as regards London, are, the conversion of Bridewell palace into an hospital, the refounding of that of St Thomas, and the completion of Christ s and St Bartholomew s hospitals, which had been begun by his father, all which establishments still remain, and will hereafter be described By an act, in the seventh year of this king's reign, for the general regulation of taverns and public-houses, it was directed, that there should be only *forty* in the city and liberties of London, and *three* in Westminster In this reign also Southwark was annexed to London, and constituted a twenty-sixth ward, under the name of "Bridge ward Without

The commencement of Elizabeth's reign was distinguished by the building of the Royal Exchange, and various other works of public utility In the year 1580, from the great increase of the city, that queen prohibited the erection of any new buildings within three miles of the city gates, and ordained that only one family should inhabit each house Another proclamation, in 1583, commanded that no new building should be erected within three miles of London and Westminster, that one dwelling-house should not be converted into two or more, and that the commons within three miles of London should not be enclosed At this period, notwithstanding the danger that was anticipated by increasing the size of the metropolis, it appears, from contemporary plans, that the greater part of London was contained within the walls, and even in those narrow limits there were numerous gardens, upon the sites of which have since been formed lanes courts, and alleys In the whole of the space now constituting the parishes of St Margaret, Westminster, St Martin in the Fields, St Paul, Covent Garden, St Anne, Soho, St Giles in the Fields, St George, Bloomsbury, and even including the extensive parish of St Mary le bone, there were not at that time two thousand houses All the north side of the city, continuing through Clerkenwell, as far as Shoreditch church, was very thinly scattered with dwellings, the whole of Spitalfields, Goodman s fields, Bethnalgreen, and Stepney and Limehouse fields, were, what their names import, open spaces of ground, having here and there groups of cottages and gardens and on the Surrey side of the river, with the exception of the borough of Southwark, Bermondsey, and part of Lambeth parish next to the Thames, the entire space was devoid of houses In 1594, the Thames water was first conveyed into houses, by means of an engine of a pyramidical form, erected at Broken wharf, to which succeeded the "London-bridge Water-Works,' and, in 1613, that great public benefit, the New River, which was projected and executed by Sir Hugh Myddelton, was brought to its head at Clerkenwell, from Amwell in Hertfordshire In 1616, the sides of the principal streets, which had before been laid with pebbles, were paved with broad stones and flags

Building continued to advance after the death of Elizabeth, and we find that most part of Spitalfields and about three hundred and twenty acres to the south and south-east of it, were then covered with houses James I, alarmed at this rapid growth of the metropolis, issued his proclamation, in 1618, against the erection of new buildings   The suburbs, notwithstanding, had greatly increased in 1640, especially to the westward, in the parishes of St. Giles in the Fields, and St Paul, Covent Garden   In 1643, Cheapside cross was demolished, by the authority of the common council, as a relic of superstition, thus increasing unintentionally the width and accommodation of that great central thoroughfare   Another attempt was made, during the Protectorate, in 1656, to prevent the enlargement of the metropolis, for which purpose, all houses built since the year 1620, within ten miles of it, were taxed, and fines were imposed on those who raised new buildings within that distance   About 1661, a great many streets, on the site of St James parish, were built, or finished, particularly St James street, Pall-Mall, and Piccadilly, other streets were ordered to be widened, and candles, or lights in lanterns, were to be hung out by the occupier of every house fronting the street, between Michaelmas and Lady-day, from nightfall until nine o clock, when it was presumed that people retired to bed   The dreadful plague, in 1665, put a temporary stop to the increase of the metropolis   This infection was generally thought to have been brought from Holland, about the close of the year 1664, and made its appearance in the neighbourhood of Drury-lane   sixty-eight thousand five hundred and ninety-six persons are calculated to have perished in the course of the year 1665, during which, London was so far deserted by its inhabitants, that grass grew in the principal streets

"The great fire of London, the most terrible conflagration that the metropolis ever suffered, succeeded "the Plague year," as it is emphatically styled   it broke out on Sunday, the 2nd of September, 1666, at the house of a baker in Pudding-lane, Thames-street   The houses being then for the most part of wood, with projecting stories, the uppermost of which, from the narrowness of the streets, almost met each other, and a strong easterly wind blowing at the time, the fire spread rapidly and continued raging until Thursday, when it was nearly extinguished, having destroyed thirteen thousand two hundred houses, and eighty nine churches, exclusively of the venerable Cathedral of St Paul, the greater part of the corporation halls, London bridge, and other public edifices, covering a plot of four hundred and thirty-six acres of ground with ruins   The value of the property involved in this destruction was calculated at upwards of £10,000,000   To perpetuate the remembrance of this melancholy event, "The Monument, on Fish street-hill, was erected, by order of parliament   it was commenced in 1671, and finished in 1677, from a design by Sir Christopher Wren, and is composed wholly of Portland stone   The column, rising from a pedestal forty feet high, and twenty-eight square at the base, is two hundred and two feet in height from the pavement, it is fluted, and of the Doric order   within is a staircase of black marble, leading to the summit   Above the capital of the column is a balcony of iron, encompassing a meta thirty-two feet high, supporting a blazing urn of brass gilt   On three sides of the pedestal are inscriptions, and on the fourth an emblematical representation, commemorative of the object of its erection   In rebuilding the city, many improvements were effected   the streets, which were before so

narrow that, according to Sir William Davenant s facetious remark, "they seemed to have been contrived in the days of wheelbarrows, were widened, many conduits and other obstructions were removed, and the buildings in general were constructed on a more substantial and regular plan.   An increased number of houses, amounting to nearly four thousand, was added, by building on the sites of the gardens belonging to the halls and merchants residences, and although the noble plans of Wren and Evelyn, for rebuilding the metropolis, were rejected, it arose, on the whole, with increased splendour   In 1670, an act was passed for widening the streets, and for restoring the navigation of the Fleet ditch   An order in council, issued in 1674, prohibited the building of new houses   Many houses in Southwark having been destroyed by an extensive fire, in 1676, an act was passed for rebuilding them of brick, instead of wood

In 1685, the population in Spitalfields and St Giles was much increased by the settlement of French Protestant manufacturers, who had left their native country in consequence of the revocation of the edict of Nantes, and the same year, the western suburbs increasing, two new parishes were formed, namely, those of St Anne, Soho, and St. James, both which were previously parts of the parish of St Martin in the Fields   In 1689, the district called the Seven Dials was built on a spot called Cock and Pye Fields   In consequence of the great increase of the commerce and shipping of London, the suburbs to the east of the Tower were become so populous in 1694, that a new parish was constituted, by the name of St John, Wapping   Soho-square and Golden-square were built at the close of this century   At this time, also, that useful institution called the Penny Post had its origin, a proof of the enlargement of the capital, and the number of hackney coaches, which, in Cromwell s time had been limited to three hundred, had increased to nine hundred, exclusively of two hundred sedan chairs   A few years afterwards, in the reign of Queen Anne, fifty new churches were erected in the metropolis and its vicinity   In 1722, the Chelsea Water-Works Company was established, for supplying the city of Westminster and the western suburbs with water   In a few years afterwards, Hanover-square, Cavendish-square, and the streets adjacent, Bedford row, Red-Lion-square, Hatton Garden, &c, were built   The streets from Leicester-square and St Martin s-lane to the Haymarket and Soho, and thence nearly to Knightsbridge, were finished in the reign of George II   In 1729, the north side of Oxford-street was partly built, and many streets near it were completed.   In 1730, the hamlet of Spitalfields became so populous, in consequence of the prosperity of the silk manufacture, as to make it necessary to form it into a distinct parish, which received the name of Christ Church   About the same period the parishes of St George in the East, St Anne, Limehouse, and St Matthew, Bethnal-green, were separated from Stepney, and the parish of St Luke was formed out of that of St Giles, in Farringdon ward Without

The improvements in the construction of the buildings, and in the local regulations of the metropolis, during the period last described, and principally in the reign of George III, were as follows   About the year 1760, most of the city gates were taken down   In

1762, an act was passed to remove the shop-signs, which, projecting from almost every house into the middle of the street, materially obstructed the light and air , and at the same time the water-spouts, which projected in like manner, were taken down by this act also, the names of the streets were ordered to be affixed at the corners of each In the building of dwelling-houses great improvement, both as regarded safety and uniformity of appearance, was effected, by the Building Act In 1768, commissioners were appointed by act of parliament for paving, cleansing, lighting, and watching the streets, and for regulating the stands of hackney coaches In 1774, an act was passed for placing fire cocks in the water pipes, with conspicuous notices of their distances and situations, and for keeping fire-engines and ladders in every parish About 1795, in pursuance of an act of parliament authorising a lottery for the purpose, called "The City Lottery, Snowhill, and the western side of Temple bar, were materially widened and improved During this period also, several new companies were established for supplying the metropolis with water, and subsequently for lighting the streets, shops, &c , with gas

London is eminently fortunate in being situated on rising ground, and on a river of ample extent, which, flowing through the town, is agitated twice in twenty-four hours, by a tide which ascends fifteen miles above it The mean breadth of the Thames here is about four hundred yards, and is crossed by five magnificent stone bridges, besides a sixth of cast-iron the river, by its winding in this part of its course, greatly contributes, not only to the embellishment, but to the healthful ventilation, of the metropolis Occupying a gentle slope on the north side of the river, which extends from east to west in a kind of amphitheatre, together with a level tract on the southern bank, it is surrounded on every side, for nearly twenty miles, by thickly-scattered villages and seats The streets are regularly paved, having a central carriage way, and a foot-path on each side , the pavement of the former is composed of small square blocks of Scotch granite, and the latter is laid with large flags some of the wider streets in the western part of the metropolis are Macadamized The foot-paths are in general broad, particularly those of the principal thoroughfares, and have a regular curb-stone, raised some inches above the carriage way, which latter has a slight convexity in the middle, to allow the water to pass off into channels on each side Underneath are large vaulted sewers, communicating with every house by smaller ones, and with every street by convenient openings and gratings, to carry off to the river all impurities that can be conveyed in that manner All mud and rubbish accumulating on the surface of the streets are taken away by scavengers employed for that purpose Nearly all the streets and principal shops are lighted with gas, supplied by several incorporated companies Almost the whole of the houses, those of ancient date excepted, are constructed of brick , the more modern and larger edifices being built of stone, or stuccoed to resemble it Excellent water is plentifully conveyed from the Thames and the New River reservoirs to almost every house , spring water is obtained from pumps, erected in various parts of the town

Strictly speaking, London is still confined within its ancient bounds, and the limits of the corporate jurisdiction of the city, but as a continuity of buildings has connected it with Westminster, Southwark, and all the neighbouring villages and hamlets, the name is, in common usage, given to them all collectively, their respective proper names being no more than sub-divisions of one great metropolis In this general view, therefore, London may be said to consist of several divisions, viz

" The City, properly so called, comprehends the most ancient and central part of London, and is almost exclusively occupied by shops, warehouses, and public offices devoted to business The East End of the Town includes Wapping, Shadwell, Ratcliffe highway,&c ,extending from Tower hill, eastward, to the East India Docks , the inhabitants of this large district being in general connected with the shipping interests, and consisting of ship-wrights, ship-owners, and captains of vessels, merchants, sailors, shop keepers, and others, who are supported by the business of the port This division of London has, within the last thirty years, assumed an importance unknown to preceding ages, and vast commercial docks and warehouses have been here constructed The West End is the most modern and elegant part of London it is inhabited by the nobility and gentry, and is the seat of Government and of the Court, as well as the centre of fashion , and consists principally of handsome squares and streets it may be said to extend westward from the meridian of Charing Cross Southwark, which lies on the south bank of the Thames, comprehends five parishes, connected with others by extensive ranges of houses Its population chiefly consists of merchants, traders, and manufacturers It had formerly only one main street, called the Borough High street, extending from London bridge towards Newington, but the increase of buildings has since added numerous others, stretching in various directions, and has formed it into a town, several miles in extent

That part of the metropolis lying on the north-west, and which may be considered as the latest enlargement, and the most elegant, as well as the most systematic in its arrangement of squares and streets, comprehends an immense mass of new buildings between Holborn and Somers-town, and in the parishes of St Mary le-bone and Paddington. Besides which, the villages of Chelsea, Knightsbridge, Paddington, Camden-town, Pentonville, Islington, Mile End, Limehouse, Rotherhithe, Bermondsey, Newington, Camberwell, Lambeth, &c , united, from the contiguity of their buildings, may be considered as appendages to this immense capital Thus regarded, the extent of London, from west to east, along the banks of the Thames, or, from the upper end of Knightsbridge to the lower end of Poplar, is seven miles and a half, and its breadth from north to south, or from Islington to Kennington, is about five miles and a half , its circumference is full thirty miles, hence it may be fairly estimated, that the buildings of this metropolis cover at least twenty square miles, extending in length seven miles This space contains between eight thousand and nine thousand streets and smaller avenues, more than seventy squares, and one hundred and seventy thousand houses, besides an immense number of public buildings The town, in the direction of east and west, is traversed by two principal ranges of streets, which may be termed the great southern and northern lines, forming a communication from one end to the other The most southern of them, for the greater part of its course, runs within a quarter of a mile of the Thames it commences at Knightsbridge, and is continued, under successive names, to the Tower, and thence by Ratcliffe-highway to the extremity of Shadwell The northern line commences on the west at Tyburn, and is continued to Whitechapel, and Mile-End, and thence may be said to extend as far as Stratford-le-Bow, a course of nearly eight miles The streets running north and south, which connect the above-mentioned lines, are comparatively short, as are also those from the southern line to the river Those from the northern line to the New-road are longer, but, with the exception of Tottenham-Court-road, and its continuation to Camden-town, St John's street, to the extremity of Islington, and Bishopsgate street, Shoreditch, and some others, are all of moderate length The longest single street in the metropolis is Oxford-street, the length of which is two thousand three hundred yards , the Commercial-road, extending from the back of Whitechapel church to the East India Docks, is more than double that length, but its buildings are not yet entirely continuous Portland-place is the widest street in London, and at the same time the most magnificent the one which ranks next to it, for breadth and the varied elegance of its buildings, is the newly-formed Regent-street, as continued from Portland-place, by the Quadrant and Waterloo-place, to St James Park.

The environs are greatly enhanced in beauty by a chain of hills to the north of the town, forming a second amphitheatre, entirely enclosing the first, of which Hampstead, Highgate, and Muswell hills, are the most prominent features On the east and west are extensive plains, stretching twenty miles, in each direction, along the banks of the Thames, and forming a most fertile, populous, and interesting valley, those which lie eastward of the town feeding numerous herds of cattle, and those westward being chiefly employed in the production of vegetables for the supply of the London market. That part of the metropolis which is situated south of the Thames occupies a flat surface, bounded by a landscape beautifully varied from west to east by the heights of Richmond, Wimbledon, Epsom, Norwood, and Blackheath, and terminating in the horizon with Leith hill, Box hill, the Reigate hills, the Wrotham hills, and Shooter's hill On every side the approaches are spacious and kept in admirable order, and, like the town, lighted at night with gas, and well watched and patrolled Country houses of opulent merchants and tradesmen, or the mansions of the nobility, standing detached and surrounded by plantations, or arranged together in successive handsome rows, are every where to be seen, either on the sides, or in the vicinity, of these roads, together with numerous villages, some of which imitate the commercial activity of the metropolis

The increase of London since the commencement of the present century has exceeded, if possible, that of the last in celerity and extent. It is visible on all sides, but perhaps more especially so on the western and northern, where the buildings in the parishes of Paddington, St. Mary-le-bone, Bloomsbury, and St Pancras, have been amazingly extended, by the formation of an incredible number of new streets, squares, and places, for the most part after elegant designs In the same quarter of the town also, the Regent s park has been laid

out, and surrounded with stately ranges of brick buildings, stuccoed so as to resemble stone A great number of excellent residences has been lately completed on the space behind Gower street, formerly called the Long Fields, and these again are adjoined eastward by the new church of St Pancras, and the elegant streets in its neighbourhood, together with a continued mass of building, extending along the south side of the New-road, and the City-road, as far as Old-street On the Southwark side of the Thames is Newington, with the streets adjacent to it, connecting Camberwell with Southwark , while Kennington, Brixton, Clapham, and Battersea-fields, have numerous, extensive, and continually-increasing, ranges of building Proceeding along the outskirts, towards the east, we perceive the village of Islington to have joined London on one side, St Pancras on the other, and to have stretched itself over the White Conduit fields (formerly celebrated amongst our early places of amusement) to the hamlet of Holloway, and through that link to Highgate and Hornsey In the parishes of Shoreditch, Hackney, Stratford-le Bow, &c , the extent of buildings has every where immensely increased , and at the direct eastern extremity of London are the East and West India, the London, and the St Katherine s, docks On viewing the surface of the parishes of Rotherhithe, Bermondsey, Walworth, Newington, Camberwell, and Lambeth, on the south side of London, much ground is yet occupied as fields or gardens , these parishes may be said, however, to form an immense connected town in many places, and are again joined to Deptford and Greenwich, to the east, and Peckham, Stockwell, Clapham, Battersea, &c , to the south and south-west. As evidence of the great extent of building mentioned, it is conjectured that, within the last fifty years, sixty thousand houses, at least, have been erected in London and its neighbourhood , and that these afford habitations for nearly three hundred thousand additional persons

The improvements at the west end of the town include the widening of the Strand, &c , the new and elegant buildings on the site of Carlton House and gardens, the laying-out of St James' Park, and various alterations and buildings in the interior, and at the entrances to Hyde Park , the immense mass of new streets and mansions on the north side of Pimlico, and various additions to the buildings of the Regent s Park and its neighbourhood, as well as on the intermediate space connecting Westminster with St Mary-le-bone, formed by the fine line of Regent-street, and the various branch streets and places leading from it. The *Strand Improvements* extend to the whole neighbourhood, between the King s mews and St Martin's lane, and beyond to the north boundary of Chandos-street, reaching westward to the Strand, and having its eastern termination beyond the late Exeter Change To correspond with the beautiful edifices of the Union Club-house, and the College of Physicians at Pall-Mall (East), there is to be an elegant opposite range of buildings, consisting of a row of public offices, a range of a new metropolitan police station, instead of the present inconvenient one at Bow-street, and which will extend in a line with St Martin s church the cemetery of the latter will be railed in, and adjoined by the vicarage-house and parochial schools, and the whole, with the noble portico of St. Martin s church, will be thrown open from Pall-Mall the north side, where was the Royal Riding house, is to be occupied by a new National Gallery and Royal Academy, and the south side of this quadrangle to lay open to Charing Cross The grand line of street is to be from West to East, by Pall Mall, passing the front of the National Gallery, and is to enter the Strand facing Hungerford-street, the Strand being widened as far as the New church, to a road-way of sixty feet Another wide carriage way is to run from the new line of street into Leicester-square, through Hemming s row, and there is to be a second communication between Castle-court and Bedford-street, as well as a fine new street continued over the site of the late English Opera house, in a line with Waterloo-place and bridge, to meet Great Charlotte-street, Bloomsbury The open spaces of ground contiguous to St Martin s church, &c, will be formed into squares It is calculated that nearly two millions of money are necessary to carry these several improvements into effect The alterations on the site of Carlton House and gardens consist in the erection of a corresponding side, or completion of the square begun by Waterloo-place, and will form a commodious communication between Regent-street and St James Park

The latest improvements in building, in the vicinity of Whitehall, include the entire renovation of the front of Whitehall chapel, and Mr Soane s erection opposite for the Council office, Board of Trade, &c the latter exhibits a long row of stone columns, with an enriched entablature and parapet, possessing considerable elegance, but justly found fault with as being too low, and wanting a balancing end on the north, for which there is no space but by destroying the fine line of street of Whitehall Richmond-terrace is an elegant row of first rate mansions, built on the site of the late Richmond House Belgrave-square and Wilton-crescent, erected on that part of Chelsea called the Five Fields, are both exceedingly elegant the former contains four symmetrical rows of first rate houses, with spacious isolated villas at the angles, the whole being partly stuccoed and partly of stone, ornamented in the Corinthian order Before the houses in the crescent, which are also first-rate in size and appearance, there is a handsome plantation, communicating right and left with the square a foot and carriage road have been completed from Knightsbridge to the King s road, for the convenience of the occupants of these new buildings, which are mostly inhabited by the nobility and gentry Eaton-square, of an oblong form, adjoins the preceding, and contains buildings of nearly equal splendour, together with a new, spacious, and handsome church at its east end Of these improvements, effected at the expense of Earl Grosvenor, Belgrave square alone is reckoned to have cost half a million of money

To particularise the public buildings included in the above-mentioned improvements would far exceed the limits of this article, but their number and consequence may be inferred from the circumstance that no less than fifty new churches have been erected, by the commissioners appointed under the late act of parliament, all having districts allotted to them, many of which already contain a vast and daily increasing population So numerous are the improvements constantly being projected and carried into effect, that scarcely a month passes in which there is not brought

forward some plan of elegant embellishment, of public or private utility, or of civil or commercial advantage In size, population, and wealth, in the extent, grandeur, and number of its religious edifices, its public establishments, its charitable institutions, its commercial docks, and its bridges, in the elegance of its squares, and the commodiousness of its habitations, the superiority of the English metropolis over that of every other country is manifest.

ROYAL PALACES AND HOUSES OF PARLIAMENT

St James is the only royal palace in the metropolis now in a habitable state It is an ancient building, and though, from the irregularity of its parts, its appearance is not imposing, yet, from its great extent, and the number of fine apartments it comprises, it is said to be the best adapted for royal parade of any in Europe Carlton House, the splendid residence of his late Majesty George IV, when Prince of Wales, has been recently demolished for the purpose of effecting the "Park Improvements, and on the site of Buckingham House, the palace of the late Queen Charlotte, a new royal residence is now being erected, by Mr Nash, to be called St George s palace this is of great extent, and, when completed, will consist of a centre and large wings projecting from it at right angles, forming, with the principal entrance, which is a detached marble gateway of great cost and splendour, a spacious and magnificent quadrangle. The Lords' and Commons' houses of parliament occupy parts of the old palace of Westminster, which, though possessing a certain degree of splendour, are chiefly venerable for their age and the purposes to which they are appropriated The House of Lords is a large oblong room, formerly the Court of Requests, and was fitted up for its present purpose on the union with Ireland, when the fine tapestry of the old House of Lords, representing the defeat of the Spanish Armada, was removed hither, and the apartment was otherwise handsomely and appropriately decorated at the upper end of the room is the throne, which has been renovated in a style of great magnificence a new entrance has lately been added, with a superb staircase and gallery by Mr Soane The House of Commons was originally the chapel of St Stephen, out of which it has been formed chiefly by raising a floor above the pavement, and adding an inner roof, considerably below the ancient one On removing the wainscot, when this room was lately enlarged, great part of the ancient decorations were discovered they are of extreme beauty, but were again closed up In its present state the House of Commons is a large plain apartment, of which the Speaker s chair, with its appendages, forms the chief decoration around it are galleries, supported by slender iron columns with gilt capitals, into one of which, namely, that at the lower end, over the bar of the house, strangers are admitted to hear the debates The house is wainscoted to the ceiling, and the benches for the members rise in regular gradation behind each other

THE PARKS, SQUARES, &c

St James Park, so called from the palace of the same name, contains about two hundred acres, the central part being laid out in a pleasing manner, and varied with water, shrubberies, and intersecting gravel walks, and the sides adorned with several avenues of stately trees The eastern extremity of the park is occupied by the Horse Guards, the Treasury, and other government offices, which have a noble appearance, the ground plot of the entire park is an oblong, and nearly two miles in circuit The King s foot guards, with a fine band of music, parade every day, between ten and eleven o clock, opposite the park front of the Horse Guards The Green Park is a triangular piece of ground, lying south of the western part of Piccadilly, and adjoining St James Park and the gardens of Buckingham House On the north side of it is a large basin, with a promenade round it, near which is the Ranger s house, embowered in a fine plantation, which adds greatly to the beauty of the prospect Hyde Park, which extends from the western extremity of the metropolis to the walls of Kensington Gardens, contains about four hundred acres It is a spot of great rural beauty, the drives round it forming one of the chief amusements of the gay and fashionable The Serpentine river, which adorns the lower part of it, is a large bending sheet of water Near the Piccadilly corner of Hyde Park stands a colossal bronze statue fo Achilles, erected in honour of the Duke of Wellington, on a pedestal of granite The entrances to this park have been greatly improved within the last few years at the Piccadilly entrance a handsome screen of the Ionic order, consisting of three arches, united by an open colonnade, with two side arches, has been erected, facing it is a new and magnificent arched gateway, (in imitation of the arch of Severus at Rome, the architecture from the temple of Jupiter Stator, in the same city,) leading into the gardens belonging to the King s palace in St James Park Kensington Gardens are beautiful and extensive pleasure grounds attached to the palace at Kensington, and were formerly part of Hyde Park they are open to all well-dressed people, and the promenade in them forms one of the most delightful and fashionable amusements of the metropolis during the months of summer The Regent s Park is a newly-formed park, on the site of what was formerly Mary-le-bone fields, containing about four hundred and fifty acres For the magnificence of the buildings by which it is surrounded, and the picturesque style in which it is laid out, this park indisputably excels the others, and it will do so in a still greater degree as the trees with which it is planted approach maturity

The residences of the nobility, though formerly scattered all over the town, and more especially along the banks of the Thames, from the Temple to Whitehall, have long been removed, almost exclusively to the western portion of it The largest and most elegant of them are, Apsley House, the residence of the Duke of Wellington, Devonshire House, the residence of the Duke of Devonshire, and Burlington House, that of Lord Cavendish, all in Piccadilly Cleveland House, the Marquis of Stafford s, Earl Spencer's, St James' Place, Lord Grenville s, in the Green Park, Marlborough House, Pall-Mall, the residence of Prince Leopold, Northumberland House, Charing-Cross, that of the Duke of Northumberland, the Marquis of Lansdowne s, in Berkeley-square, Chesterfield House, the Earl of Chesterfield's, in May Fair, and Uxbridge House, Burlington-gardens, that of the Marquis of Anglesey Great numbers of the nobility and gentry, who have not separate detached mansions like those above mentioned,

have spacious and, in many instances, superb residences in the grand squares The principal of these are, Grosvenor, Portman, Berkeley, St James, Hanover, Manchester, Cavendish, Bedford, Russell, Bloomsbury, Montagu, Bryanston, and Leicester Squares, and Lincoln s-Inn-Fields, all which contain large and elegant houses They may be noticed, according to their respective architectural merits, in the following order

Grosvenor Square has a finely-planted area of six acres, surrounded by magnificent houses It derives its name from having been erected at the expense of Sir Richard Grosvenor, Bart, and constitutes part of the present Earl Grosvenor s immense estates in this vicinity In the centre is a fine gilt equestrian statue of George I, placed there in 1726 Portman Square, finished in 1784, ranks next to the preceding Its planted area is laid out with great taste and richness, and the houses are of the first order of domestic architecture Montagu House, which stands beyond the north-west angle, forms an elegant addition to the whole, and is remarkable for having been the residence of the literary and talented Mrs Montagu Russell Square is likewise surrounded by elegant buildings, and has in the centre a perfect miniature landscape garden, laid out with every regard to taste and variety It is adorned with a finely executed statue of the late Duke of Bedford, in bronze, by Westmacott, Jun Fitzroy Square, if finished in accordance with the two sides already built, would, from the elegance of its buildings and the materials of which they are constructed, probably form the most elegant square in the metropolis The houses are fronted with stone, and are in the best taste of those excellent architects the Adams s Cavendish, Bedford, and Manchester Squares, are all surrounded by buildings of a uniform and handsome appearance, the residences of persons of the higher ranks, each comprising a beautiful planted area. In the first, which was planned so long ago as 1715, is a gilt equestrian statue of the conqueror at Culloden, William, Duke of Cumberland St James Square is small, but inhabited by some of the principal nobility At Norfolk House, in this square, George III was born. In the centre is a fine equestrian bronze statue of King William III Bloomsbury Square is chiefly remarkable for the fine statue of that distinguished statesman, Charles James Fox, which is of colossal size, and of bronze The figure is in a sitting posture, in the habit of a Roman senator, and is placed on the north side, facing an elegant street, which leads up to the statue of the Duke, of Bedford, in Russell-square Berkeley Square has on its south side the noble mansion of Lansdowne House, half enveloped in fine gardens and plantations Leicester Square contains a gilt equestrian statue of George I, and formerly possessed a degree of fashionable attraction which it has now lost, having at that time included Leicester and Saville Houses, the former having been the residence of Frederick, Prince of Wales, father of George III and the latter, that of the celebrated Sir George Saville The largest of the squares near this quarter of the town is Lincoln s-Inn-Square, commonly called Lincoln s-Inn-Fields The whole of its western side is composed of the masterly erections of Inigo Jones, amongst which is the fine mansion formerly called Lindsey, and afterwards Ancaster House On the eastern side is seen the beautiful range of law chambers called Stone Buildings, which overlooks the gardens of Lincoln s Inn

On the south side is Surgeons Hall, a handsome new erection , and on the north side the elegant house of Mr Soane, the architect This square was once inhabited by the first nobility, at the time that Newcastle House, one of the largest mansions which it comprises, was the residence of the Duke of Newcastle, Prime Minister to George II The centre of the square contains the most spacious and finely planted area of any square in the metropolis

Queen-square, Holborn , Golden-square, Piccadilly, Red Lion-square , Soho-square and in the north-eastern part of the town, Finsbury-square, Finsbury-circus, and numerous others, though not in the very first style of architecture, are all spacious and ornamental It may be observed, that the squares west of Tottenham-Court-road are chiefly occupied by the nobility and gentry , whilst those east of that line are for the most part the residence of merchants and professional men

Portland Place was, some years ago, almost the only street that, in point of width, length, and the uniform grandeur and elegance of its buildings, would have been worthy of especial notice. But the construction of the new line of street extending northwards from the site of Carlton House, under the names of Waterloo Place, the Quadrant, and Regent-street, and communicating with Portland place by means of Langham-place, forms a new era in our domestic architecture , and for vast length, width, and uniform elegance, this immense range of buildings, as a whole, is not exceeded by any in Europe Carlton-terrace, now being built on the site of Carlton House, promises, when completed, to vie in elegance with the noble avenue last named , and eastward of the fine street called Pall-Mall, an opening has been formed, to obtain a vista for the noble portico of St Martin's church Beyond this church, on the north side of the Strand, from the site of Exeter Change, lately demolished, westward, the Strand improvements are in progress, which will give to the whole neighbourhood a character of magnificence that it did not before in any degree possess Nor is there a doubt that the example which has been set in the western and northern parts of the town, and in various parts of the city, will soon be followed in other neighbourhoods, and give, at no distant date, an entire new face of beauty to the principal streets and thoroughfares of the metropolis

THEATRES AND PLACES OF AMUSEMENT.

The King s Theatre, or Italian Opera-House. This magnificent theatre, situated at the bottom of the Haymarket, on the western side, is appropriated exclusively to the performance of Italian operas, and ballets, in both which some of the most eminent vocal and instrumental performers and dancers in Europe are engaged, at very high salaries. The original edifice was burnt down in 1790, soon after which it was rebuilt, though externally it was not completed till 1818, after a design by Mr Nash It is built of brick cased with stucco, and is surrounded by a colonnade supported on cast-iron pillars of the Doric order the front is decorated with figures in bas relief, representing the origin and progress of music, executed in 1821 The interior consists of a stage sixty feet long and eighty broad , five tiers of boxes, all of them either private property, or

rented for the season, and affording accommodation to about nine hundred persons , a spacious pit and a gallery, with room in each for eight hundred spectators , a grand concert-room, ninety five feet long, forty-six broad, and thirty-five high, with dressing and other apartments, entrances, staircases, &c , rendering it nearly equal in magnitude to the celebrated theatre of La Scala, at Milan the fronts of the boxes are embellished, in compartments, with various emblematical designs, and the ceiling is adorned with a painting of the Nine Muses The season usually commences in January, and continues until August, operas being constantly performed on Tuesdays and Saturdays, and of late, towards the close of the season, on Thursdays, during that period.

Drury-lane Theatre, situated in Brydges-street, had its origin in a cock-pit, which was converted into a place of theatrical entertainment, and pulled down and rebuilt, under the name of the Phoenix, in the reign of James I A patent for dramatic performances having been granted by Charles II to Killigrew, a new theatre was erected on the site of the present structure, and the actors having belonged to the king s household, their successors at this house have ever since been styled " His Majesty s Servants " This theatre was burnt in 1671, and rebuilt by Sir Christopher Wren, but was displaced, in 1793, by a much larger one, from a design by Holland, which, however, was burnt down in 1809 and the present edifice erected, in 1811, under the superintendence of Mr B Wyatt the exterior is very plain the front is of the Doric order, and the portico, supporting a statue of Shakspeare, was added in 1820 a new colonnade, along the side extending from Brydges-street to Drury-lane, is in contemplation the building is the property of a number of shareholders The interior of the house, which was rebuilt in 1822, is on a scale of great splendour the grand entrance is through a spacious hall, supported by columns of the Doric order, leading to a rotunda, from which staircases ascend to the boxes there are three tiers of boxes, besides others on each side of the lower gallery, and some on a level with the pit, affording together room for one thousand eight hundred and twenty-eight spectators the pit, over the centre of which hangs an elegant chandelier of cut glass, with gas-burners, is capable of accommodating eight hundred persons, the lower gallery six hundred and seventy-five, and the upper gallery three hundred and eight, making a total of three thousand six hundred and eleven persons The stage, in front, is forty-three feet in width, and thirty-eight in height , and the height of the house, from the floor of the pit to the ceiling, is fifty feet and a half The grand saloon is a handsome room, circular at each end, and about eighty-six feet in length

Covent-Garden Theatre, situated in Bow street, was established by Sir W D Avenant, who received a patent in 1662, under which successive companies acted at the theatre in Lincoln s-Inn-Fields, until the erection of the original theatre in Covent Garden in 1733, which was burnt down in 1808, the present magnificent structure having been opened Sept 18th, 1809 It stands in an isolated situation, and is nearly of a square form, being built, from a design by Mr Smirke, Jun., in the Doric order, in imitation of the Temple of Minerva, situated in the Acropolis at Athens, at an expense of £150,000 In the centre of the principal front is a lofty portico of four large fluted baseless columns, elevated on a noble flight of steps, and supporting an enriched entablature and triangular pediment, on the tympanum of which are statues of Tragedy and Comedy by Flaxman on each side of the portico is a basso relievo, representing the ancient and the modern drama The entrance to the boxes is by a grand staircase adorned with Ionic columns, having Grecian lamps suspended between them, leading to an ante-room in which is a statue of Shakspeare, by Rossi, and from which a small flight of steps leads to the lobby forming the entrance to the boxes there are three tiers of boxes, a spacious pit, and lower and upper galleries over the centre of the pit hangs a magnificent chandelier of cut glass The house, it is computed, will afford accommodation to upwards of three thousand persons, and the receipts, in one night, may amount, at the highest calculation, to more than £900

The Haymarket Theatre, situated in the Haymarket, was erected originally in 1702 The present edifice was opened in 1821, having been built from a design by Mr Nash in front is a portico of six Corinthian columns, supporting a pediment, above which are nine circular windows, connected by sculptured ornaments The interior contains two tiers of boxes, and a row of boxes on each side of the pit, with two galleries, and is much smaller than any of the above-mentioned theatres, but exceedingly neat and compact within It is licensed for the performance of regular dramas during the summer, at which period only it is open. The other minor establishments, most of which are summer theatres, are, the *English Opera-House*, or *Lyceum*, in the Strand, opened June 15th, 1816, and lately considerably damaged by fire, which has afforded an opportunity of carrying into effect the long-projected improvement of forming a new road in the line of the Waterloo bridge road, to the vicinity of Bedford-square, the *Adelphi Theatre*, also situated in the Strand, and formerly called the " *Sans Pareil*,' the *Royal Circus*, or *Surrey Theatre*, in Blackfriars -road, originally used for equestrian performances, destroyed by fire in 1805, and rebuilt in a superior style, since which it has been appropriated to the performance of melo-dramas, ballets, &c , the *Royal Coburg Theatre*, in the Waterloo-road, first opened in 1818, *Sadler s Wells*, in St John s street road, so called from some wells anciently situated there, and from the name of a person who, in 1683, first opened a theatre in that neighbourhood the present edifice was erected in 1765, since which the interior has been rebuilt the space beneath the stage is filled with water, affording the proprietors the means of introducing aquatic exhibitions, which have imparted a peculiar character to the performances at this house *Astley s*, or the *Royal Amphitheatre*, opened, about 1767, as a riding-school, and converted into a regular theatre in 1780, is eminently distinguished for equestrian exhibitions it was burnt down in 1794 and again in 1803, having been since rebuilt in a neat and commodious manner *The Olympic Theatre*, in Wych-street, was built in 1806 the boxes afford room for three hundred and forty persons, the pit six hundred, and the gallery three hundred and twenty *The West London Theatre*, in Tottenham-street, was formerly called the Regency Theatre, and has of late been occupied, during the winter, by a company of French comedians

Vauxhall Gardens, now the only place of amusement of the kind adjoining the metropolis, are situated at Lambeth They were formerly little more than tea gardens, enlivened with instrumental music, but their rural beauty and easy access rendered them so great a place of resort, that the proprietor was encouraged to speculate on public patronage, and by a series of attractions introduced from time to time, at length enabled Vauxhall to rank among the finest gardens of the kind in Europe The entertainments commence after night-fall, and thirty thousand lamps are employed to illuminate the gardens on evenings of extraordinary splendour, contributing, with the aid of music, both vocal and instrumental, dramatic representations, fire-works, and other entertainments, to attract large companies in the summer months, during which only they are open

Among the higher class of amusements are the nobility s balls, held at Willis rooms, King-street, St James', commonly called Almack s, from the name of their former proprietor , where also, and at Hanover-square rooms, concerts take place oratorios and selections of miscellaneous music are performed at Drurylane and Covent-Garden theatres, on Wednesday and Friday evenings during Lent, and at other periods , the present age being distinguished, above all others in England, for the patronage bestowed upon the art of music There are various other miscellaneous public performances, but they are so multifarious and changeable, as to preclude a particular description

COMMERCE

The commerce of London has three principal branches 1st. The port of London, with the foreign trade and domestic wholesale business, 2ndly, the manufactures, and, lastly, the retail trade In 1268, the half-year s customs, for foreign merchandise in the city of London, amounted only to £75 6 10 In 1331, they amounted to £8000 In 1354, the duty on goods imported was ony £580 6 8, and on exports, £81,624 1 1 In 1590, they yielded £50,000 a year In 1641 just before the commencement of the civil war, the customs brought in £500,000 a year, the effect of a long series of peaceful days From the year 1671 to 1688 they were, on an average, £555,752 In 1709, they were raised to £2,319,320, and in the year ending April 1799, they amounted to £3,711,126 The astonishing increase in the extent of commercial intercourse in later years may be inferred from the following brief statement The average number of British ships and vessels of various kinds, in the Thames and docks, is estimated at thirteen thousand four hundred and forty-four, of which, the barges and other small craft, employed in lading and unlading, are not fewer than between three and four thousand two thousand eight hundred and eighty-eight barges and other craft are engaged in the inland trade , besides which, there are three thousand wherries, or small boats, for passengers About eight thousand watermen are employed in navigating the wherries and craft, four thousand labourers in lading and unlading ships, and twelve thousand revenue officers are constantly doing duty on the river In regard to tonnage, the East India Company s ships alone carry more burden, by many thousand tons, than all the vessels in London did a century ago The value of merchandise annually received and discharged in this port, is computed at between £60,000,000 and £70,000,000 sterling From accounts printed by order of the House of Commons, it appears that, in 1798, previous to docks being constructed in the port of London, the value of imports and exports was £30,290,000 In 1806, after the docks were formed, the value increased to £36,527,000 In 1819, it increased to £46,935,000, and in 1825 it amounted to £96,936,000, being an increase of sixty six millions and a half as compared with 1798 The number of coasters which entered the port in 1814 was fifteen thousand one hundred and thirty-nine, in 1821, eighteen thousand nine hundred and fifteen, being an increase in seven years of three thousand seven hundred and seventy-six ships The number of ships moored in the river, during 1804, after the West India docks were opened, was seven thousand three hundred and twenty-seven, and in 1823, when five docks, and three wet dock canals were opened and fully employed, notwithstanding the extended accommodation, thirteen thousand one hundred and twelve, being an increase of six thousand ships, in addition to which, about one thousand nine hundred voyages by steam-boats annually now obstructs the navigation above Greenwich From official returns of the Customs it appears that, in 1825, an increase of upwards of six hundred sail took place in the number of vessels which arrived in the port of London from foreign parts, since then, and till the present time, it has still kept rapidly increasing The number of vessels which entered inwards from foreign ports, in 1826, was three thousand four hundred and ninety-five British, and one thousand five hundred and eighty-six foreign, and the number cleared outwards, two thousand one hundred and forty nine British, and one thousand four hundred and eighty-six foreign The scene of this immense traffick occupies a space more than four miles in length, reaching from London bridge to Deptford, and from four hundred to five hundred yards in average breadth, which may be described as consisting of four divisions, three of them called the Upper, Middle, and Lower pools, and the fourth comprising the space between Limehouse and Deptford The present annual value of the custom and excise duties may be rated at somewhat more than £6,000,000 sterling It is, besides, calculated that above forty thousand wagons and other carriages, including their repeated journeys, arrive and depart, laden in both instances, with articles of domestic, colonial, or foreign merchandise, occasioning a transit, including cattle and provisions sent for the consumption of the inhabitants, of more than £50,000,000 worth of goods to and from the inland markets, making altogether a sum of £120,000,000 worth of property annually moving to and from the metropolis

London has long been celebrated for its manufactures, as well as its commerce So early as the reign of Henry I, the English goldsmiths had become so eminent for working the precious metals, as to be frequently employed by foreign princes, and the perfection of various other manufactures at this period appears both from history and antique remains The manufacturers of London had, in that reign, become so numerous as to be formed into fraternities, or companies, some of which are now disused, some have declined, as the Cappers, Bowyers, Fletchers, &c, and others still flourish, and are much increased in the number of their mem-

bers, in the extent of their property and patronage, and in general importance In 1556, a manufactory for the finer sorts of glass was established in Crutched Friars, and flint glass, not exceeded by that of Venice, was made at the same time at the Savoy About five years after, the manufacture of knit stockings was introduced, in consequence of the ingenuity of William Rider, an apprentice on London bridge, who, happening to see a pair from Mantua, at the house of an Italian, made another pair exactly similar to them, which he presented to William, Earl of Pembroke The manufacture of knives was shortly after begun by Thomas Matthews of Fleet bridge, and has since eclipsed that manufacture at Sheffield, where it was much earlier established Silk wove stockings were first made from the invention of Lee, a student at Oxford, in the reign of Elizabeth, which reign forms so splendid an era in the commercial and trading history of the metropolis Coaches were introduced in 1564, and in less than twenty years they became an extensive article of manufacture In the following year, the manufacture of pins was begun, and soon after that of needles The making of "earthen furnaces, earthen fire-pots, and earthen ovens transportable, began about the 16th year of Elizabeth, an Englishman of the name of Dyer having brought the art from Spain, and in 1579, the same individual being sent to Persia, at the expense of the city of London, brought home the art of dyeing and weaving carpets In 1577, pocket-watches were imported from Nuremberg, in Germany, and the manufacture of them almost immediately commenced In the reign of Charles I, saltpetre was made in such quantities as not only to supply the whole of England, but the greater part of the Continent The manufacture of silk, as well as of various articles of plate, had also become extensive The printing of calicoes commenced in 1676, and about the same time, weaving-looms were brought from Holland The other articles of manufacture, introduced or practised in the metropolis about the same time, are too numerous to particularise

The silk manufactory, which, under its different modifications, now affords employment to so many thousands, was first established at Spitalfields, by the expelled French Protestants, after the revocation of the edict of Nantes, in 1685 Since that period the productions of London have greatly increased, both in extent and value, in articles of elegance and utility, such as cutlery, jewellery, gold and silver ornaments, japan ware, cut glass, cabinet work, &c, as well as commodities requiring a great mart for their consumption, export, or sale, as porter, English wines, vinegar, refined sugar, soap, &c In short, the manufactures of London, as well as its commerce, are vast and flourishing, many of the goods manufactured here surpassing in quality those of any other part of the country In the silk trade alone fifty thousand persons are employed, and in most of the light manufactures the number is proportionably great For the more scientific manufactures, such as those of machinery, optical and mathematical instruments, &c, London has always been celebrated Ship-building is carried on to a great extent, and during the late war a considerable number of frigates was built for the government by private individuals, and with greater rapidity than they could be completed in the Royal Dock yards

The Commercial Docks, Canals, &c

Intimately connected with the commerce of the metropolis is the establishment of enclosed docks, which have yielded the most decided service to the revenue and trade of the country The former insecurity of property in the river, and the daring plunder committed on it, led to the formation of them

The West India Docks which were the first constructed, are situated on what may be called the isthmus of that peninsular part of the environs of London named the Isle of Dogs, and communicate with the Thames at Limehouse on the west, and at Blackwall on the east These docks were commenced on the 12th of June, 1800, and finished in August, 1802, occupying with the ground attached to them, an area of two hundred and four acres The import dock is two thousand six hundred feet long, five hundred and ten broad, and twenty nine feet deep , the export dock is of the same dimensions, except in breadth Both docks are enclosed by walls five feet thick, and surrounded by a series of very lofty and extensive warehouses they are stated to have cost £12,000,000 The proprietors are an incorporated body, under the title of the West India Dock Company In the vicinity is a school, established by the Company, for instructing apprentices in the West India navigation, whilst the vessels are in dock Parallel with the docks is a canal, which cost between £300,000 and £400,000, to enable merchant vessels of any burden to avoid the circuitous navigation round the Isle of Dogs *The East India Docks*, commenced in 1804, and completed in 1806, are lower down the river, but at no great distance from the former, and, like them, consist of an import and an export dock, the former about one thousand four hundred feet long, and five hundred and sixty wide , and the latter seven hundred and eighty feet long, and five hundred and twenty wide , the depth of each is thirty feet , and the space which they occupy is twenty-eight acres a basin was added to the export dock in 1817 The largest dock is capable of containing at one time, twenty-eight Indiamen, with double that number of smaller vessels The goods from both these docks are conveyed to town by a recently formed rail way running parallel with the Commercial road The establishment of the East and West India Docks, which afford employment to many thousand individuals, has occasioned in their immediate vicinity a very numerous resident population

The London Dock—This is also an extensive dock, situated between Ratcliffe highway and the Thames , it covers twenty acres of ground, and belongs to a Company whose capital is £12,000,000 It is capable of containing two hundred sail of merchantmen, and is not appropriated to any particular branch of commerce It was opened February 1st, 1805, and is surrounded, like the former, with immense warehouses, beneath which are capacious cellars another branch dock was opened in 1827 or 1828 *St Katherine's Docks* were commenced in 1825, and completed in 1829, by the merchants, shipowners, and traders of London, for securing additional accommodation to the great increase of shipping in the port, and a reduction in the rates and charges These docks receive annually about one thousand four hundred merchant vessels, besides craft for loading and discharging , and afford an improved mode of ingress and egress which no other docks in the kingdom possess, as vessels drawing twenty

feet of water may be locked from two to three hours after high water, and small vessels and lighters at all periods of the tide , the total outlay attending the construction of these docks (including the purchase of considerable property, capable of returning its price on re-sale) amounted to £1,827,113 The warehousing, bonding, and quay room, are nearly equal to the London Docks , and from an improved construction of the warehouses, which are within a few feet of the docks and basin, a considerable saving is effected in the expense of labour These docks are also enclosed with walls, and are entitled to all the privileges of the warehousing system, and of legal quays, preventing goods lodged there, on exportation, from being chargeable with the duties on deficiencies The *Bermondsey Collier Dock* is calculated to relieve the river from an obstruction to navigation by the number of small craft, which, in course of time, must otherwise have prevented ships with general cargoes approaching convenient places of discharge near the Custom House, and which had been serious matter of complaint for many years

Notwithstanding the greater part of the interior of the kingdom being intersected with canals, the inland navigation to the metropolis is at present confined, owing, it is supposed, in a great measure, to the policy which prohibits the carriage of coal by that conveyance, and which would be the grand inducement to undertakings of this nature The *Paddington canal*, which was the first, was not opened till July 10th, 1800 It leads from Paddington, and unites with the Grand Junction canal, whence the two are frequently mentioned by the joint name of the Grand Junction and Paddington canal From the basin at Paddington, it extends nearly one hundred miles, to the Oxford canal at Branston, in Northamptonshire, by which it is connected with the Coventry and Birmingham canal, the Grand Trunk canal, &c , thus forming a regular line of water conveyance from London into Lancashire and Yorkshire , another branch of the Grand Junction enters the Thames at Brentford The *Regent's canal* connects the Paddington Grand Junction, and other canals west of London, with the Thames on the east, or mercantile side of the city, and, skirting the northern suburbs, has occasioned a vast influx of trade, with its accompanying warehouses, wharfs, &c , at Paddington, Battle-bridge, the City-road, and other places , it was opened August 1st, 1820 it branches out of the Grand Junction at Paddington, and, passing by a tunnel under Maida hill, continues through the Regent's park and St Pancras parish to Islington, when it passes through a tunnel about three quarters of a mile long, immediately under the village and the bed of the New River, to the grand basin in the City-road, and proceeds on by Hoxton, Hackney, and Mile-End, to Limehouse, uniting all the principal canals in the kingdom with the Thames The whole length of this canal is nine miles, and within that space are comprised twelve locks and thirty-seven bridges the former are so admirably constructed, that a large barge can pass through each in three minutes and a half , they are capable of admitting barges twenty three feet long and fourteen wide this canal cost upwards of half a million of money, and was seven years in construction it was executed under the superintendence of Mr Nash On the Surrey side of the river is the *Grand Surrey canal*, which passes through the south-eastern suburbs, from Camberwell to the Thames at the lower extremity of Rotherhithe

PUBLIC BUILDINGS DEVOTED TO COMMERCE

The *Royal Exchange* is situated on the northern side of Cornhill The entire building occupies an area two hundred and three feet long, and one hundred and seventy-one broad, and its erection cost £80,000 The original Royal Exchange, at first named Britain s Bourse, was founded, in 1566, by Sir Thomas Gresham, an eminent merchant of London, nearly on the spot where the ancient Tun prison stood, the merchants before that time having had no suitable place in which to assemble, and having been in consequence compelled to meet in the open air The building erected by Sir Thomas was of brick and stone, with a lofty tower and vane, somewhat similar to the present, but much infe rior in grandeur this was destroyed by the great fire in 1666, and the present building of Portland stone was erected, in the reign of Charles II, from the designs of an architect named Jerman Its form is quadrangular, the interior being surrounded by piazzas, divided into walks, bearing the names of different countries, the merchants connected with which generally assembling at those particular spots Above the piazza is an entablature, with sculptures of the armorial bearings of the city companies, and other appropriate ornaments, and over these are twenty-four niches, nineteen of which are occupied by statues of the English sovereigns, from Edward I down to George III, Edward II, Richard II, Henry IV, and Richard III, being excluded, the statue of George III, occupying the twentieth niche, having been taken down for renovation, was restored in September, 1830 Sir Thomas Gresham's effigy, and that of Sir John Barnard, occupy niches within the piazza, the former at the north western, and the latter at the south-western, angle The open area is ornamentally paved with Turkey stone, and is adorned in the centre with a statue in white marble of Charles II, under whose auspices the Exchange was rebuilt The principal front, next Cornhill, is very noble, extending two hundred and ten feet in length, with a stately piazza, a lofty central gateway, which opens into the area, and ornamented with statues, bas-reliefs, and other embellishments, a newly-erected triple stoned tower rises above the gateway, with a circular peristyle, or colonnade, of eight Corinthian columns, surrounded with an entablature and dome surmounted by a lofty vane and gilt grasshopper, the crest of the founder The north front next Threadneedle-street has also a piazza, and a gateway in the centre, corresponding with the one opposite The galleries over the four sides of the building were originally divided into two hundred shops, but they are now occupied by the Royal Exchange Assurance and other offices, and, till their removal to the London Institution, the Gresham Lecture-rooms, also Lloyd s coffee-house, which is celebrated as a place of meeting for underwriters and insurance brokers they comprise two separate suites of extensive rooms, one of which is public, and the other exclusively appropriated to subscribers, who pay a premium of twenty-five pounds upon admission, and four guineas annually, these sums forming a fund for the general purposes of the establishment, which has agents for the protection of the commercial interests of its subscribers all over the world

Bank of England—The business of this great national corporation was originally transacted at Grocers Hall, Poultry In the year 1732, the first stone of a more splendid edifice comprising the central part of the present building was laid, on the site of the house and garden of Sir John Houblon, the first governor The eastern wing was completed about the year 1786, by the late Sir Robert Taylor, the north front, and the side towards Princes-street, were added from designs by Mr Soane in 1825, when considerable alterations and improvements were made throughout the whole of the interior The whole building forms an immense edifice, chiefly of stone The principal entrance is opposite Bank buildings, the front, consists of a centre of the modern Ionic order, and two extensive wings, ornamented with a colonnade The interior comprises numerous apartments appropriated to different branches of the establishment, amongst which are, the Rotunda, a large circular apartment, principally used by the stockbrokers for transacting business in the public funds, the hall, in which the bank notes are issued and exchanged, the chief cashier s office, a noble apartment, in imitation of the Temple of the Sun and Moon, at Rome, and the three per cents warrant-office, an oblong room, with a vaulted ceiling supported by decorated piers, and having a handsome dome resting on caryatides in the centre, the whole being constructed without timber, and various other offices too numerous to particularise the entire buildings are included in an area of irregular quadrangular form, the exterior wall of which measures three hundred and sixty-five feet in front, or on the southern side, four hundred and forty feet on the western side, four hundred and ten feet on the northern side, and two hundred and forty-five feet on the eastern side This area comprises, together with the various buildings and offices, eight open courts there are also underground apartments stored with bullion, coin, &c

The Stock Exchange stands in Capel-court, opposite the eastern entrance to the Bank It was completed in 1804, from a design by Mr James Peacock The business transacted here relates solely to the purchase and sale of stock in the public funds, Exchequer bills, India bonds, and other securities, an additional building having subsequently been erected for the transfer of foreign stock On the east side of the great room is a recess with an elevated desk, for the use of the commissioners for the redemption of the national debt, who make their purchases four times a week viz, on Monday, Wednesday, Thursday, and Friday, at the hour of twelve precisely No person can transact business but those who are balloted for annually by a committee, who, on being chosen, subscribe ten guineas each the number of Jew brokers is limited to twelve, who, before they are entitled to admission, must purchase a ticket of the lord mayor, which, on a vacancy occurring, is sold to him who will give the greatest sum, it being a perquisite of the lord mayor s for the time being the tickets generally producing from £1200 to £1500 each

The South Sea House, or, House of the South Sea Company, first incorporated in 1711, for the purpose of an exclusive trade to the south seas, is a substantial and handsome building of brick, ornamented with Portland stone the entrance is by a gateway, with a noble front, leading into a court having a piazza, formed by

Doric columns   The interior is grand and commodious, the court-room being particularly lofty, spacious, and elegant   The concerns of this company are managed by a governor, sub-governor, and twelve directors, annually elected

East India House —The present East India House, situated on the south side of Leadenhall street, comprises the principal offices of the East India Company, where their courts are held, and all official and general business transacted, and, as a public structure, it ranks among the most magnificent in the city   In consequence of the important additions to the old building erected in 1726, made under the superintendence of Mr Jupp, and consisting of the centre and the west wing, with other important parts, adjoining Leadenhall street, the whole may now be considered as almost a new edifice   The front, which is of stone, is about two hundred feet long   in the centre is a lofty portico of six fluted Ionic columns, the frieze of which is sculptured with antique ornaments, and above is a pediment, containing a group of figures in alto relievo by Bacon, emblematical of the commerce of the company   On the apex of the pediment is a figure of Britannia, and at the angles are figures emblematic of Europe and Asia   The wings have arched basement windows, with square windows above, and are surmounted by a handsome balustrade   The back, and part of the western side, of the building, are wholly enclosed by houses   The interior consists of a great number of apartments and offices, several of the former being of large dimensions and noble architecture   Those particularly worthy of observation, are the grand court room, the new sale-room, the old sale-room, the rooms for the committee of correspondence, the library, and the museum, all of them embellished either with emblematical designs and paintings illustrative of commerce, statues and portraits of distinguished individuals who have been connected with the company, or with India generally, views of Indian scenery or architectural ornaments   The library contains a fine collection of Indian and Chinese manuscripts, together with every book that has been published respecting Asia   The museum, which adjoins it, contains models of Indian and Gentoo idols, the library of the late Tippoo Saib, with his armour, and other trophies taken from that sovereign at Seringapatam, and abounds with Indian curiosities of every description   Connected with the business of the East India House are the extensive warehouses of the company, situated in New-street, Bishopsgate, Fenchurch-street, Crutched-Friars, and various other parts of London   The men employed are embodied into three regiments of Infantry, called "The Royal East India Volunteers," of which the superior clerks and officers in the company s service form the staff   In these warehouses teas, indigo, silks, china, crape, and other imported goods are deposited   The great height of these buildings, forming entire streets within themselves, with the multitude of windows, and of cranes for drawing up goods, combine to give an imposing idea of the commerce of this most important establishment

Custom House — The Custom House, or place where all the king s duties are collected on goods imported to, or exported from, London, stands on the north bank of the river, at a small distance to the westward of the Tower, having been removed to its present situation since the destruction of the former edifice by fire in 1814   it was begun in 1815, from a design by Mr David Laing, and occupies an immense extent of ground, reaching from Billingsgate eastward nearly to the site of the former Custom House   It is four hundred and eighty-nine feet long, by one hundred and seven feet wide, the whole cost of the erection being £167,050   The south front, next the river, is of Portland stone   the central compartment, which com prises the Long-room only, was at first quite plain, but this part of the building having lately sunk from some defect in the foundation, it has been rebuilt in a more ornamented style, having a noble colonnade standing on a projecting basement, and surmounted by an open gallery with balustrades   the façade of each of the wings is enriched also with a colonnade of six Ionic columns to correspond   The interior contains an immense number of apartments and offices appropriated to the vast extent of business carried on in them   the principal is the Long-room already mentioned, which is of astonishing extent, its length being one hundred and ninety feet, its breadth sixty-six feet, and the height about fifty-five feet   Beneath this immense edifice are equally extensive vaults and store cellars   Attached to the establishment are about six hundred and fifty clerks and officers, besides one thousand tide-waiters and servants

The Corn Exchange, instituted as a mart for the disposal of all kinds of grain through the medium of corn-factors, until very lately consisted only of a handsome brick building, on the east side of Mark-lane, but the vast increase of business requiring additional space, a new and commodious edifice of stone, was erected in 1828, adjoining the former   The principal façade consists of a centre and two wings, with a portico of six fluted Grecian Doric columns, supporting an entablature wreathed with chaplets of wheat-ears, and a cornice charged with lions heads, the whole being surmounted by a blocking-course   over the centre is a large pedestal crowned with a cornice, above which are the royal arms sculptured in stone, with ploughs and other emblems of agriculture   The roof rests on entablatures supported by twelve columns, their capitals being composed of wheat-sheaves   The market is held on Monday, Wednesday, and Friday, the first being the principal day

The Coal Exchange is situated in Thames-street, and comprises a spacious rotunda, with convenient divisions for the business of the coal merchants and dealers   It forms a small square, surrounded by an open arcade, and has a handsome front

The Excise Office, in Broad-street, is a spacious and noble building, erected in 1763, to which the business of the excise, established in 1643, and at first carried on in the Old Jewry, was transferred   In this office the town business of the excise is transacted, by nine commissioners, having under them numerous clerks and officers   It consists of two ranges of building, one of stone, the other of brick, separated from each other by a large yard   From the centre of each of these ranges, passages and staircases lead to the apartments of the commissioners and clerks

The Commercial Hall, situated in Mincing-lane, is an elegant structure, erected by subscription in 1811, for the sale of the various kinds of colonial produce.   The front is of Portland stone, ornamented with six attached

Ionic columns rising from the lower story, and supporting an entablature, between them are five emblematic devices, executed by Bubb, representing Britannia, Husbandry, Science, Commerce, and Navigation The interior, which is of considerable extent, contains five public sale-rooms, a large coffee-room, several shew rooms, and numerous counting houses let to various merchants.

The Auction Mart, Bartholomew-lane, was opened in 1810, principally for the sale of landed property by public auction it is constructed of Portland stone, and, though not very large, is unsurpassed in the metropolis for airiness, lightness, and gracefulness of design The internal arrangements, too, are all upon a plan which unites elegance with utility Previously to the erection of this edifice, the principal sales took place at Garraway s Coffee-house, in Change alley, where a great part of the business is still transacted At the Mart, particulars of all sales are preserved for the sake of public reference, as are also all charters and legislative enactments regarding canals, rail-roads, bridges, &c

Trinity House, Tower Hill — This corporation was originally established at Deptford, under the title of "The Master, Wardens, and Assistants of the Guild or Fraternity of the most Glorious and Undivided Trinity, and of St Clement, in the parish of Deptford Strand, in the county of Kent It was incorporated by Henry VIII, in the year 1516, at a period when the English navy began to assume an ascendancy, as a sort of guardian of the shipping, military and commercial, being for that purpose endowed with extensive powers, which it still exercises The members examine those children in Christ s Hospital, intended for the sea service, and the masters of king s ships, appoint pilots for the Thames, and settle the rate of pilotage, erect lighthouses and land-marks, grant licenses to poor seamen not free of the city, to navigate on the Thames, besides transacting a variety of other business connected with that river, and maritime affairs generally The originator of this establishment was Sir Thomas Spert, comptroller of the navy, and commander of the Harry Grace de Dieu The house which the company afterwards occupied in Water-lane, near the Custom House, being found inconvenient, the present structure was completed from a design by Mr Wyatt, in 1795 It is built of stone, in the purest style of Grecian architecture, within are several handsome apartments, and, having the advantage of a rising ground for its site, and a fine area in front, it deservedly ranks among the finest buildings of the metropolis

Post-Office The necessity for the removal of this establishment from its former confined situation in Lombard-street having long been urgent, an act was passed in 1815, for the erection of a new post-office, which was completed in 1829, from a design by Mr Smirke, a great portion of the interval having been consumed in the purchase and removal of the houses which were crowded upon its site This building is an isolated massive structure of large dimensions, composed of Portland stone, being about three hundred and eighty-nine feet long, one hundred and thirty broad, and sixty-four high, standing in an enclosed area of irregular figure, at the junction of the street called St Martin s-le-Grand with Newgate-street, a central and convenient situation The old buildings on the north

have been taken down as far as St Anne's lane, and it is presumed, that at least an equal area will be cleared on the south, by removing the few houses which still remain, and obstruct the approach from Cheapside The façade towards St Martin's le-Grand is the only one in which there is any architectural display, and this is confined to three porticos of the Ionic order, one at each end consisting of four columns, and one in the centre of six, the latter being surmounted by a pediment, on the frieze over the columns is the inscription, *Georgio Quarto Rege, MDCCCXXIX* Under the central portico, by an ascent of several steps, is the entrance to the grand public hall of the establishment, which extends through the building into Foster-lane, being eighty feet long, by about sixty feet wide, and divided by Ionic columns, into a centre and two aisles the centre rises to the height of about fifty-three feet, and admits of a dwarf, or attic pilastrade over the principal order, the intervals of which are glazed for the admission of light. In the northern aisle are the Inland, American, Ship-letter, and Newspaper offices, and at the eastern end is a staircase leading to the Letter-bill, Dead, Mis-sent, and Returned, letter offices In the southern are the Foreign and Two-penny post departments, the Offices of the Receiver-General and Accountant, and the entrance to the Assistant-Secretary s official residence North of the centre, and in the eastern front, is the entrance, or vestibule, where the bags are received from the mails Communicating with the vestibule is the Inland office, eighty-eight feet long, fifty six wide, and twenty-eight high, and adjoining it is that of the letter carriers, one hundred and three feet long, thirty-five wide, and thirty-three high The West India letters have an office appropriated expressly to them, on the eastern side Near which are the Comptroller's and Mail coach offices The communication between the apartments in the northern and southern divisions of the building is by a subterraneous passage beneath the Great Hall, in which the letters from one department to another are conveyed by machinery, invented by Mr Barrow The Inland office may be regulated to any temperature by a warm air apparatus, designed and fixed by Mr Sylvester On the first floor are the Board-room, the Secretary's rooms, and the Secretary s clerks office, the Solicitor s office, and those for the Letter-bill, Dead, Mis-sent, and Returned, letters On the second and third stories are lodging-rooms for the clerks of the foreign office, it being necessary, from the uncertainty of the time of arrival of the mails, that they should be always on the spot On the basement, which is vaulted, and therefore fire-proof, are the mail guards' room and armoury, the servants offices, the apparatus for warming the patent gasometer by the Messrs Crossleys, large enough to register four thousand cubic feet of gas per hour, and a "governor," by Mr Clegg, for regulating the supply of gas to nearly a thousand argand burners the gas is supplied by the City of London Gas Company The business is very extensive and complicated The building is divided into — The Inland Office, in which, according to a return for January, 1829, there are one hundred and thirteen clerks and other persons ordinarily in attendance at the morning duty, and one hundred and nineteen at the evening duty, the Returned Letter Office, in which there are an inspector and nine clerks, the Foreign Office, in which there are a comptroller and deputy, and six-teen clerks and sorters, including the West India office, the Letter-Bill Office, in which there are a superin-tendent and seven clerks, the Bye-Letter Office, in which there are an accountant and four clerks, besides the offices of the Receiver-General, the Accountant-General, the Surveyor and Superintendent of Mail coaches, and the Secretary, in which there are nearly fifty persons, making a total of nearly three hundred and fifty per-sons engaged in this important establishment.

The business of the Two-penny Post, which applies exclusively to London and its immediate vicinity, forms, only a branch of the General Post-Office The prin-cipal office being in Gerrard St. Soho The returns of the Commissioners of Revenue Enquiry afford a re-markable proof of the convenience of this mode of conveying letters through the metropolis and its vicinity, by exhibiting the great extent of business which is thus transacted. From them it appears that the average number of letters passing daily through the Two-penny Post-Office, taking May as the period when the returns are prepared, is forty thousand This account includes soldiers and sailors letters and newspapers, as well as those letters which are either delivered to, or from, the General Post-Office by the Two-penny Post There are six collections and deliveries of letters in town daily, Sundays excepted, and there are two dispatches *from*, and three deliveries *at*, most places in the country within the limits of this office Besides the principal office, there are scattered through the town and its environs about fifty receiving-houses for the General Post-Office, and upwards of one hundred for the Two-penny Post

FAIRS AND MARKETS

London has at present only one fair, well known by the name of Bartholomew fair, which, though anciently famous for the sale of cloth and other commodities, is now resorted to merely for amusement it was granted by Henry II to the prior and convent of St Bartholo-mew, and its opening is proclaimed by the lord mayor in civic state, on the 3rd of September, after which it continues three more days, a court of pie powder being held during the time The markets, held in different parts of the metropolis, amount to sixteen flesh mar-kets, and twenty-five for corn, hay, vegetables, &c Smithfield is the grand mart for the sale of live stock, which takes place on Mondays and Thursdays, on which latter day there is also one for horses upwards of one hundred thousand bullocks, and eight hundred thousand sheep, are, on an average, annually sold here Newgate, Leadenhall, and Whitechapel markets, are the principal wholesale markets for butchers' meat, and the two former for poultry, Leadenhall and the Borough markets are the only skin markets within the bills of mortality and at both Leadenhall and Newgate markets are sold pigs and poultry, killed in the country, with fresh butter, eggs, &c, to an immense amount Covent Garden market is celebrated for its early and abundant supply of fruit, vegetables, herbs, and flowers Farringdon market (formerly Fleet market), Spitalfields market, the Borough market, and Finsbury market, at least the three former, are noted for supplying an abundance of the commoner vegetables and fruit, and Farringdon, Newport, and Clare, markets for home killed butchers

meat The only market in London, exclusively for the sale of fish, is that of Billingsgate, but it is in contem-plation to establish another on the site of Hungerford market, Strand Billingsgate is principally supplied by fishing-boats and smacks from various parts, and partly with fresh fish by land carriage There are various less extensive markets for the sale of butchers meat, &c The incommodious and mean buildings which crowded the large area of Covent Garden have all been re-moved, and a new and handsome market-place com-pleted at the cost of the Duke of Bedford, who is the sole proprietor It consists of three principal ranges of building, extending in length from east to west, the external fronts of the northernmost and southern most ranges of which, as well as the west end of the centre one, being adorned with a colonnade of the Tus-can order, supporting a neat balustrade, and having a wide gateway in the centre Down the middle of the central range is a handsome arcade, having shops on each side, the western extremity of which is im-mediately opposite to the front of St Paul s church, the eastern to the end of Russell street The eastern end of these three ranges are connected by a terrace supported upon rows of baseless Tuscan columns, of single blocks of granite, like those of the colonnades, forming a pleasant promenade among flowers and plants tastefully arranged for sale One flight of steps leads up to this terrace from the end of each of the two outer ranges of building, and two from that of the centre one A great part of the space between the central and the northern ranges is roofed. The whole of the en-closed area is paved with flag stones, and it is sur-rounded by a spacious carriage way

The corporation of the city of London were autho rised, by an act of parliament passed in 1814, to re-move the old Fleet market, and to erect a new one The execution of this public improvement was confided to a committee, who obtained a new site, cleared away the houses upon it, erected suitable buildings and at length completed the numerous other necessary arrange ments, so as to enable the corporation to open the new market for business on November 20th, 1829 It forms a handsome and elevated quadrangle of two hun-dred and thirty two feet by one hundred and fifty, standing on a surface of one acre and a half The pur-chase of houses, &c, is stated to have cost £200,000, the building of the market-house, including paviours accounts, &c, £80,000 The avenue, under which are the shops of the dealers, and which extends round three sides of the market-place, is twenty five feet high, to what are technically called the tie-beams, with ven-tilators ranged at equal distances In the centre of the roof of the principal avenue are placed a turret and clock, the latter illuminated at night with gas The chief entrance is by two principal gates, for wagons, &c, in Stone-cutter street, which has been made double its former width, and there are two smaller ones for foot-passengers eighteen large gas lamps are placed in the centre of the market-place Eatables only are permitted to be bought and sold in this market The old mar-ket-place having been entirely removed, and the street repaved, it forms a fine line in connexion with Bridge-street, and Great Surrey street, being in the whole con-siderably more than a mile in length, and it is in con-templation to continue the line of road to Islington

MUNICIPALITY AND LEGAL JURISDICTION

CITY —The City of London, properly so called, consists of that part anciently *within the walls*, together with that termed *the Liberties*, which immediately surround them the liberties are encompassed by an irregular line, called *the line of separation*, which is the boundary line between them and the county of Middlesex Their superficial extent does not exceed three hundred acres, their boundaries are marked by *the Bars*, which formerly consisted of posts and chains, but are now marked by lofty stone obelisks, bearing the city arms, which may be seen eastward, in Whitechapel, the Minories, and Bishopsgate street, northward, in Goswell-street, at the end of Fan-alley, and in St John s-street, and westward, at Middle-row, Holborn, while at the western end of Fleet street, the boundary is the stone-gateway called Temple Bar

The grand division of the city is into twenty-five wards, exclusively of Bridge ward Without The number of wards, which in 1285 has been stated to have been twenty-four, was, by the division of Farringdon ward into two wards in the 17th of Richard II, augmented to twenty five, and when, in 1550, the liberties of the borough of Southwark were granted to the city, they were constituted a twenty-sixth ward, by the name of Bridge ward Without, and this number has continued ever since Of these wards, exclusively of the last-mentioned, thirteen are on the east, and twelve on the west, side of Walbrook Their names are as follows —Aldersgate (Within and Without), Aldgate, Bassishaw, Billingsgate, Bishopsgate (Within and Without), Bread-street, Bridge (Within), Broad-street, Candlewick, Castle-Baynard, Cheap, Coleman-street, Cordwainers Cornhill, Cripplegate (Within and Without), Dowgate, Farringdon (Within), Farringdon (Without), Langbourn, Lime-street, Portsoken, Queen-hythe, Tower-street, Vintry, Walbrook the wards are subdivided into several precincts, each of which returns one common council-man, the total number of precincts being two hundred and thirty-six

Aldersgate ward derived its name from the city gate, called Aldersgate, which has been thought by some antiquaries to have taken that denomination from being the oldest gate, by others from the alder-trees which anciently grew in the marshy soil in that neighbourhood It comprises two divisions and adjoins Cripplegate and Farringdon wards, has eight precincts (four in each division), and includes, among its principal thoroughfares, Aldersgate-street, Foster-lane, Noble-street, Little Britain, and the liberty of St Martin's-le-Grand it has an alderman, two deputies (one within the gates, and the other without), eight common council-men, and inferior officers

Aldgate ward is denominated from the gate of the same name Its precincts are seven, and its principal streets, Aldgate and the eastern parts of Leadenhall and Fenchurch streets it is under the superintendence of an alderman, a deputy, six common council-men, including the deputy, and inferior officers

Bassishaw ward the smallest in the city, contains only two precincts, and consists principally of one large street, called Basinghall street, the name of which is a corruption of *Basings-haugh*, or hall, a large mansion here, formerly belonging to the family of the Basings

it has an alderman, a deputy, four common council-men, and inferior officers

Billingsgate ward, situated on the side of the Thames, is divided into twelve precincts, and is governed by an alderman, ten common council-men, and inferior officers

Bishopsgate ward took its name from the gate which stood almost in the centre of it, between the ends of Camomile-street and Wormwood-street, dividing it into two divisions Within and Without It has nine precincts, five within, and four without, the gate The principal streets are Bishopsgate-street and part of Fenchurch street The buildings in this ward are among the most ancient in the metropolis, the great fire of 1666 not having extended far in this direction, and not at all to that part of the ward situated without the gate It has an alderman, two deputies (one within the gate, the other without), six common council-men, and inferior officers

Bread-street ward is situated nearly in the centre of the city, between the ward of Farringdon Within, and Cordwainers', Queen hythe, and Castle-Baynard wards It takes its name from the bread market formerly held on the present site of Bread-street, the bakers anciently not being allowed to sell bread in their shops or houses, but only in the open market The number of precincts is twelve, and the principal thoroughfares are Watling-street, with the streets in the same line to Old Fish-street, part of the south side of Cheapside, and several of the cross streets between the two it has an alderman, a deputy, twelve common council-men, and inferior officers

Bridge ward Within, so named from its contiguity to London bridge, (which, at the time it had houses upon it, formed three of its precincts,) is divided into fourteen precincts, the principal streets being Fish-street-hill, part of Gracechurch-street, Upper and Lower Thames-street, and Eastcheap it has an alderman, a deputy, and fifteen common council-men, including the deputy, with inferior officers

Bridge ward Without, although so long annexed to London, was never entirely incorporated with it, and is wholly unrepresented in the common council Its civil government is administered by a steward and a bailiff, appointed by the court of the lord mayor and aldermen. The Surrey magistrates, notwithstanding the royal grants to the city, retain the power of appointing constables, and licensing victuallers, and exercise other powers of justices of the peace for the county within the limits of the ward. This ward includes nearly the whole of the borough of Southwark, and extends to Newington on the south, almost as far as Lambeth westward, and to Rotherhithe on the east, having the Thames on its northern side The principal streets are, the Borough High-street, which is continued southward by St Margaret's hill and Blackman-street, Kent-street, the new Dover road, Tooley-street, and Union-street there are, besides, numerous others, several of which are of considerable length; and the great thoroughfares are inhabited by respectable and wealthy tradesmen The alderman who nominally governs this ward has the title of "Father of the City' Whenever a vacancy occurs in the aldermanry it is customary for the lord mayor and aldermen to appoint to it the senior alderman, this nominal office being regarded as an honourable sinecure, which relieves him from the fatigues of office That portion of the borough of Southwark situated without the city jurisdiction, or borough liberty, is called the Clink liberty, and is under the jurisdiction of the Bishop of Winchester, who appoints a steward and a bailiff for its government

Broad street ward is so denominated from a street in it which obtained the name of Broad street from being, before the fire, one of the widest within the walls its precincts are ten, and include within their limits Old Broad-street, Threadneedle-street, Bartholomew-lane, Throgmorton-street, Great and Little Winchester-streets, Austin-Friars, and part of Leadenhall-street the inhabitants elect an alderman, a deputy, and nine common council-men, with inferior officers

Candlewick ward, which took its name from Candle-wick (now Cannon) street, formerly much occupied by wax and tallow chandlers, is a small ward divided in-to seven precincts, the principal streets of which are, Great Eastcheap, and the west end of Cannon-street it has an alderman, a deputy, seven common council-men, and inferior officers

Castle-Baynard ward takes its name from the an-cient castle which stood on the site of the present Carron wharf, and was originally built by William Baynard, a soldier of fortune, who accompanied the Norman William in his invasion of England. It after-wards passed into the hands of the Fitz-Walters, who make a prominent figure in the early history of London, and who possessed, by virtue of this castellanship, the honour of being hereditary standard bearers to the city The soke, or liberty, anciently attached to this castle, forms the present ward, which is divided into ten pre-cincts, the principal streets being, the west end of Upper Thames-street, St Peter s-hill, St Bene t s-hill, Sermon and Carter lanes, Paul s chain, part of St Paul s churchyard, and the east sides of Creed, Ave-Maria, and Warwick lanes it has an alderman, ten common council-men, and inferior officers

Cheap ward, situated in the centre of the city, takes its name from the Saxon word *Chepe,* signifying a mar-ket, the present Cheapside having been anciently called "West Chepe, to distinguish it from another market called "East Chepe Before the street called Wal brook, which intersects this ward, was covered in, barges were towed up it from the Thames, as far as Bucklersbury It is divided into nine precincts, the east end of Cheapside, the Poultry, parts of Queen-street, Pancras, Ironmonger, Lawrence, and Bow lanes, King-street, and the north side of Cateaton-street, with Honey-lane market, from the principal thoroughfares of this ward, which is under the government of an alder-man, twelve common council-men, and inferior officers The standard, or cross, in Chepe, is familiar to the readers of civic history as the ancient place of execu-tion within the city

Coleman-street ward is so called from Coleman-street, the principal street in it, and supposed to de-rive its name from a family of the name of Coleman, who he buried in St Margaret s church, Lothbury, who might have been the builders, owners, or principal inha-bitants of that part of the city It contains six pre-cincts, and is governed by an alderman, a deputy, six common council men, and inferior officers

Cordwainer s ward derives its name from Cord-

wainers'-street, now Bow-lane, which was formerly a great mart for curriers, shoemakers, and others working in leather It has eight precincts, the principal streets being Watling-street, Bow lane, and Queen-street, and the inhabitants elect an alderman, nine common coun-cil men, and inferior officers

Cornhill ward is named from the principal street in it, which was anciently the great city market for corn, the precincts are four The extent of this ward is small, the principal thoroughfare being Cornhill, which is a spacious street of large well-built houses, and part of the great central thoroughfare through the city it has an alderman, a deputy, and six common council-men, including the deputy, with inferior officers

Cripplegate ward took its name from the city gate, called Cripplegate, comprises two divisions, Cripplegate Within, and Cripplegate Without, the walls It ad-joins Cheap, Bassishaw, and Coleman-street wards, and contains thirteen precincts, including, amongst its prin-cipal streets, Fore-street, White, and Red Cross streets, part of Jewin street, and Barbican, and has an alder-man, and (Within the walls) eight common council-men, and (Without the walls) four common council men, with inferior officers

Dowgate ward, supposed by some antiquaries to take its name from *dwyr-gate,* meaning, in the ancient British language, Water gate, which is by Stowe sup-posed to have been the *trajectus,* or ferry across the Thames, in the line of the Watling-street, has eight precincts This ward extends from Martin's-lane on the east, to Cloak-lane on the west, and from Cannon-street on the north, to the Thames on the south, nearly in the form of a square, within which space are con-tained Dowgate-hill and Dowgate dock, the Steel-yard, St Lawrence-Pountney-hill, Duckfoot-lane, Suffolk lane, Bush-lane, Chequer-yard, and Cloak lane it has an alderman, eight common council-men, and inferior officers

Farringdon wards (Within and Without) were origin-ally but one ward, the aldermanry of which was pur-chased by a family of that name It was divided into two wards in the 17th of Richard II Farringdon ward Within comprehends that part of the city which lay immediately within the walls, on the western side Far-ringdon ward Without includes all that part which lay without the walls, to the westward, as far as Tem-ple Bar the former contains seventeen precincts, the latter sixteen, and the two wards include a consi-derable number of the principal thoroughfares of the town viz, Ludgate-hill, Fleet street, part of Cheap-side, St Paul s churchyard, Hatton Garden, Skinner and Newgate streets, and West Smithfield, besides the whole of Black and White Friars, St. Paul s cathedral, Christ s hospital, and numerous other buildings, impor-tant places, and objects Farringdon ward Within, re-turns an alderman, a deputy, and eight common council men, and Farringdon ward Without, an alderman, three deputies, and sixteen common council men, inferior officers are appointed for each ward respectively

Langbourn ward takes its name from a brook that formerly ran from Fenchurch-street to the Thames, the stream spread so much near the head of the spring, that the neighbourhood received from it the name of "Fenny about ' and this circumstance is still perpetu-ated in the name of Fenchurch street It is divided into

*

twelve precincts the principal streets are, Fenchurch-street and Leadenhall-street an alderman, a deputy, ten common council-men, and inferior officers, are appointed for its government

Lime-street ward is said to have received its name from the making and selling of lime here, or, according to others, from lime trees having been anciently planted on the spot Though small, this ward includes parts of several parishes it has four precincts, and its principal streets are, Lime-street and a part of Leadenhall-street an alderman, a deputy, and four common council-men, including the deputy, with inferior officers, are appointed

Portsoken ward takes its name from being situated without the wall, or gate, of the city, the word *portsoken* signifying the franchise *ad Portam* It anciently included a considerable part of the Tower liberties it is divided into five precincts, the principal streets within which are Whitechapel (as far as the bars), part of Aldgate High-street, the Minories, and Houndsditch, it has an alderman, deputy, five common council-men, including the deputy, and inferior officers

Queen hythe ward takes its name from the harbour of Queen-hythe, which was formerly a principal place of loading and unloading goods, and was so called because the customs payable there were assigned by King John to his queen Eleanor, and to the queens of England who should succeed her, for their private use The ground, for a considerable space around the harbour, formed a soke, which was governed by the queen s bailiffs In the time of Henry III, however, it came into the hands of Richard, Earl of Cornwall, who conveyed it, in return for an annuity, to the Mayor and Corporation of London. It lies between Dowgate and Castle-Baynard wards, on the banks of the Thames, it has six precincts, and its principal street is part of Upper Thames-street the inhabitants appoint an alderman, six common council-men, and inferior officers

Tower ward is the first in the eastern part of the city within the walls, and takes its name from its vicinity to the Tower The precincts are twelve, and its principal streets are, Tower-street and a part of Thames-street the inhabitants elect an alderman, twelve common council-men, and subordinate officers

Vintry ward comprises a space on the northern bank of the Thames, where the merchants of Bourdeaux formerly bonded and sold their wines This spot was at the south end of Three Cranes-lane, so called from the cranes with which the wine was landed, and at the north-eastern corner of this lane, in Thames-street, opposite to College-hill, anciently stood a spacious and stately edifice, called the Vintry, from its being appropriated to the stowage of wine It is divided into nine precincts, the principal streets being part of Upper Thames-street, part of Queen-street, Great St Thomas the Apostle, Garlick-hill, and College-hill it has an alderman, nine common council-men, and inferior officers

Walbrook ward was so called from the brook which intersected the city wall at Dowgate, and flowed into the Thames, it has seven precincts, the principal streets and lanes in which are, Walbrook, Bucklersbury, Budge-row, Dowgate-hill, Cannon-street, Bearbinder-lane, St Swithin's-lane, and the west end of Lombard-street the inhabitants elect an alderman, eight common council-men, and officers

Corporate Seal.

Obverse.   Reverse.

The entire civil government of London is vested, by successive charters of the English sovereigns, in its own corporation, or body of citizens, confirmed, for the last time, by a charter passed in the 23rd of George II As then settled, the corporation consists of the lord mayor, two sheriffs for London and Middlesex conjointly, twenty-six aldermen, the common council-men of the several wards, and the livery, assisted by a recorder, chamberlain, common serjeant, comptroller, city remembrancer, town clerk, and various other officers

The *Lord Mayor* is elected annually on the 29th of September the livery in Guildhall, or common assembly, choose two aldermen by shew of hands, who are presented to a court called the Court of Lord Mayor and Aldermen, by whom one of the aldermen so chosen (usually the senior) is declared lord mayor elect, and on the 9th of November following he enters on his office He is supreme magistrate of the city his title, since the reign of Edward III, has been "The Rt Hon The Lord Mayor ' It is necessary that the nominee shall be free of one of the great city companies, shall have served the office of sheriff, and be alderman at the time of election The prerogatives are of great extent and importance as the immediate representative of the Sovereign, the lord mayor takes precedence of every other subject within the limits of the city, and, in the event of the monarch s decease, becomes the first officer in the realm, takes his seat at the privy council board, and signs before all other subjects in the kingdom As civil governor of the city, no act of the corporation is valid without the concurrence of the lord mayor According to a custom of nearly three hundred years standing, he sits every morning at the mansion-house, to hear and determine causes of offence within the jurisdiction of the city He is perpetual coroner and escheator for London, the Liberties, and Southwark, chief justice in all commissions for trial of felony and gaol delivery, and judge of all courts of wardmote for the election of aldermen. In other respects, his ordinary authority extends all over the city, and to part of the suburbs, and, as conservator of the Thames, it extends eastward on the river as far as Yardale, or Yantlet, and the mouth of the river Medway, and westward to Colne ditch, above Staines' bridge, and he is perpetual commissioner in all affairs relating to the river Lea To the lord mayor also belongs the ancient court of Hustings, which preserves the laws, rights, franchises, and customs, of the city He acts as chief butler at all coronations, receiving a golden cup and ewer for his fee, and is first commissioner of the lieutenancy, being invested with powers similar to those possessed by the lord-lieutenant of a county

The *Aldermen* are chosen for life, by the free house holders of every ward, that of Bridge Without excepted, to which the aldermen themselves elect   The lord mayor presides at the election of an alderman, and, if a poll be demanded, it terminates in three days   Those aldermen who have filled the civic chair are justices of the *quorum* , and all the other aldermen are justices of the peace within the city   They are subordinate governors of their respective wards, under the jurisdiction of the lord mayor, and they exercise an extensive power within their own districts   They hold courts of ward-mote, for the election of common council men and other ward officers, the regulation of the business of the ward, the removal of obstructions, &c , and, in the discharge of these duties, each alderman is assisted by one or two deputies, who are annually selected by himself from among the common council-men of his own ward   the aldermen are officially addressed by the title of "Your Worship"

The *Common Council men* represent the inhabitants of their respective wards   Their office is annual, and their number, which formerly varied, is at present fixed, according to the number of the city precincts, at two hundred and thirty-six, for the whole of the wards   They are chosen by the inhabitant householders, in the same manner as the aldermen, with this difference, that the lord mayor presides at the election of an alderman, and the alderman at the election of a common councilman   The election for each ward takes place on St. Thomas day, the alderman deciding on disputed votes, and declaring the return

The representatives of the wards, with the lord mayor and aldermen, constitute what is called the court of *Common Council*, or Three City Estates   The powers of this court are extensive   It has the entire disposal of the funds of the corporation, makes such by-laws as it thinks necessary for the regulation of its concerns and possesses the right of nomination to several of the subordinate city offices , and, in addressing it by petition or otherwise it has the style of "Honourable   The court debates in a spacious and elegant chamber attached to the guildhall, the lord mayor officially habited and attended, with the city regalia before him, occupying a state chair on an elevated platform at one end, below whom sit the aldermen also in their official costume   The sittings of the court are usually public, but it has the power, though rarely exercised, of excluding strangers   The common council cannot assemble without a summons from the lord mayor, and then for one sitting only , but it is his duty to call a meeting whenever it is demanded by requisition, and the law compels him to assemble the court a certain number of times during his mayoralty   The common council annually elect six aldermen and twelve common council-men, as a committee for letting the city lands, and this committee generally meets at the guildhall, on Wednesdays , it also appoints another committee of four aldermen, and eight common council-men, for transacting the affairs of Gresham college, who usually meet at Mercers' hall, according to the appointment of the lord mayor, who is always one of their number   Besides the appointment of these and several other committees, they, by virtue of a royal grant, annually choose a governor, deputy, and assistants, for the management of the city lands in Ireland   In short,

the civil administration, in all its branches, within the jurisdiction of the corporation (which in all cases embraces the city, and part of the borough of Southwark, and in some extends beyond), is exercised by the corporation, or its officers

The *Sheriffs* of London and Middlesex, who are, strictly speaking, officers of the king, are chosen by such citizens as are of the livery, out of their own number in the guildhall, upon Midsummer-day, but are not sworn into office until Michaelmas-day, when each sheriff enters into a bond of £1000 to the corporation to serve it faithfully , after which, they proceed in state to Westminster, to be accepted on behalf of the king, by the barons of the Exchequer   The mode of nominating the sheriff is, for the lord mayor to drink in succession to fourteen respectable citizens, two of whom are elected, and who are obliged to serve, according to a by-law made in 1748, under a penalty of £600, to be forfeited to the city, and £13 6 8 to the officers of the city prisons, unless the person chosen will swear that he is not worth £15,000   Of this £600, one hundred pounds is given to him who first agrees to fill the office   In the election of a sheriff, the opinion of the livery in common hall is not decisive, and if a poll be demanded, it continues open for seven days   The lord mayor cannot properly nominate a commoner as sheriff, if there be an alderman who has not served that office, though it is frequently done , but if the citizen drank to pays the fine, he is excepted from being again nominated for three years, unless within that term he becomes an alderman   No alderman can be exempted for more than one year after a previous payment, without the consent of the common council   The jurisdiction of the two sheriffs is, to a considerable extent, perfectly separate , but if either die, the other cannot act until a new one be chosen , for there must be two sheriffs for London, which, by charter, is both a city and a county, though they make but one jointly for the county of Middlesex   By grant of Edward IV , in 1473, the sheriffs are appointed to have sixteen serjeants, and every serjeant his yeoman , also a secondary, six clerks, a clerk of the papers, four under-clerks, and two under-sheriffs   In serving writs of process, where the king is a party, the sheriffs may break open doors, or untile houses, to gain admittance, if entrance be denied , but not upon private process, except upon outlawry after judgment

Of the officers associated with the corporation in the city government, the principal is the *Recorder*, who is appointed by the lord mayor and aldermen for life, with a salary of £2500 per annum   He must be a grave and learned lawyer, and as such, usually acts as judge at the Old Bailey, and other courts   he takes precedence in councils and courts before all aldermen who have not filled the office of mayor   The *Chamberlain, Common Serjeant*, and *Town Clerk*, are officers ranking next to the recorder, and have respectively duties to perform of great importance, as have also the *City Comptroller*, and *City Remembrancer*   There are various other inferior city officers.

Common-Halls, which are assemblies of the livery, are convenable on requisition of several of its members to the lord mayor, who presides, and are only called on extraordinary occasions   The *Livery*, about twelve hundred in number, and who return four members to parliament, are composed of the respective livery-men of the city companies, of which there are ninety-one The first twelve that stand on the list are called the Chief, or Twelve Great Companies, *viz*, Mercers, Grocers, Drapers, Fishmongers, Goldsmiths, Skinners, Merchant-Taylors, Haberdashers, Salters, Ironmongers, Vintners, and Clothworkers, and are sometimes styled "The Honourable The less important ones have the title of " Worshipful ' Nearly fifty of the companies have halls, some of which are remarkable as buildings, and others for their curiosities and paintings, most of them have " clerks, or solicitors, with offices on the premises, who have the custody of the Company's records, and transact its legal business Several of these Companies attend the lord mayor on his inauguration, in their livery gowns, with banners, streamers, music, &c, and on the water, conveyed in elegant state barges, concluding the ceremonies of the procession with splendid dinners at their respective halls The freedom of the city is obtained by apprenticeship to a freeman, by redemption, fine, or ransom, and by gift of the corporation to be a liveryman, however, it is necessary to be free of one of the incorporated companies

The *Guildhall*, or common hall of the corporation of London, where all their courts, meetings, and festivals are held, is situated at the upper end of King-street, Cheapside, and comprises numerous buildings and apartments It was originally erected by subscription, in 1411, prior to which period the corporation meetings (as before stated) were held in a small structure in Aldermanbury This edifice, having been greatly damaged by the fire in 1666, the present pile was formed from such parts as remained, excepting the new front facing King-street, which, with several additions and repairs, was completed in 1789 The hall is a very noble room, being one hundred and fifty-three feet long, forty-five broad, and fifty-five feet high the ceiling, since the fire, has been made flat and panelled Two magnificent windows of stained glass diffuse over the whole a strong but mellowed light in the eastern window, which is at the upper end of the hall, are emblazoned the arms of England, and in the western those of the corporation of London The sides of the hall are decorated with blank Gothic arches and panelling, besides large marble monuments erected to the memory of the Earl of Chatham, his son, the late Rt. Hon William Pitt, Admiral Lord Nelson, and the spirited lord mayor, William Beckford The magnitude and grandeur of the hall may be estimated from the fact that it is capable of holding six or seven thousand persons, and actually accommodated that number at the great feast given to the allied sovereigns in 1814 The giants in guildhall are two immense figures, carved in wood, supposed to represent an ancient Briton and a Saxon Of the apartments in the rear of the hall, appropriated to the use of the corporation, the principal is the council-chamber, a large room, the ceiling of which forms a dome, with a sky-light in its centre In this room the lord mayor, aldermen, and common council, hold their courts, or city parliaments It is decorated with a collection of paintings, most of which were presented to the city of London by the public-spirited Alderman Boydell, and at the upper end, immediately behind the chair of the lord mayor, upon a pedestal of white marble, stands a statue of George III The chamberlain's apartment is elegantly decorated with framed and glazed copies, richly and beautifully illuminated on vellum, of the numerous votes of thanks from

the corporation, to the heroes who signalized themselves in the late wars The court of Aldermen hold their meetings in the Old Council Chamber, the ceiling of which is highly decorated Over the entrance in the front of the hall a library of works relative to the history of London and the counties immediately adjoining, has been recently formed, and is already of considerable extent. The courts of King's Bench, Common Pleas, and Commissioners of Bankrupts, formerly situated at the back of the hall, now occupy the site of the ancient guildhall, chapel, and Blackwell hall, and near the same spot is the Court of Requests, the Irish Chamber, and other offices of the corporation, forming a mass of convenient though not very elegant buildings

Mansion House This building was finished in 1753, at an expense of £42,638 18 8, as a residence for the chief magistrate, who before had no suitable dwelling in which to exercise the duties and maintain the state and dignity of his office. It stands on the site of the Stocks market, at the western end of Lombard-street, and in the most central part of the city, and is a spacious and stately edifice, constructed entirely of Portland stone, but of rather ponderous aspect In front is a fine portico, composed of six large fluted Corinthian columns, which rise from a massive rustic basement, and are surmounted by a pediment, the tympanum of which exhibits a good piece of sculpture by Taylor, emblematic of the dignity and opulence of the city of London, and the various virtues by which they have been established and maintained In the centre of the basement story, under the portico, is the gateway leading to the kitchens and offices, and a double flight of steps leads over this story to the grand entrance beneath the portico A stone balustrade encloses these steps and is continued along the whole length of the front The body of the building presents two tiers of lofty windows, and over these, and above the portico, is an attic story surmounted by a balustrade, the cornices are rich and deep, and supported by Corinthian pilasters These parts, in themselves elegant and complete, have been universally allowed to be deformed by a supplementary piece of building (formerly two) raised on the top contrary to the architect's wish, to give a loftier ceiling to a ball-room, and from which he has derived unmerited censure The interior is arranged with taste and judgment, possessing, amongst other state apartments, a magnificent banquet-room, called "The Egyptian Hall, ninety feet long, the whole width of the mansion, and sixty feet broad, with a lofty and richly-ornamented concave roof, a ball-room, a withdrawing-room, and a state chamber, containing a magnificent state bed

COURTS OF LAW, &C

The Lord Mayor's Court is held in the King's Bench, Guildhall, by the lord mayor, recorder, and aldermen, for actions of debt and trespass, for appeals from inferior courts, and for foreign attachments, giving decisions in all cases whatsoever, in fourteen days, at an expense not exceeding thirty shillings The Court of Hustings is the ancient and supreme court of the city, for pleas of land, and common pleas The sheriffs hold courts of record, every Wednesday and Friday, for actions entered at Giltspur-street Compter, and on Thursday and Saturday for actions entered at the Poultry Compter, which are for debt, trespasses, accounts, covenant-breaking, attachments, and sequestrations, to any amount. The sheriffs, or their deputies, may sit with the judges of these courts upon trials, if they please The Court of Requests and of Conscience formerly took cognizance of no cause above 40s, but now extends to all debts under £5 the process is by summons, and if the party do not appear, the commissioners have power, after judgment is obtained, to apprehend and commit the commissioners examine the witnesses on oath, and according to their own judgment pronounce a verdict, from which there is no appeal The Court of Lord Mayor and Aldermen appoints monthly such aldermen and commoners for commissioners as they think fit, and these, or any three of them, compose a court, held on Wednesday and Saturday, from 12 till 2 o clock, in the new court room near guildhall The other city courts are— The Chamberlain s Court, held every day, to determine differences between masters and apprentices, and to admit such persons as are duly qualified to the freedom of the city The Court of Orphans, held before the lord mayor and aldermen, as guardians of the children of deceased freemen under twenty-one years of age The Pie Powder Court, held only during the continuance of Bartholomew fair A Court of Conservancy, held by the lord mayor and aldermen four times a year, as before stated A Court of Petty Session, for small offences, held daily at the Mansion House in the forenoon, by the lord mayor and one alderman, and daily at guildhall, by two aldermen in rotation The Coroner s Court, to enquire into the causes of sudden death, and the Court of the Tower of London, held within the verge of the city, by a steward, appointed by the Constable of the Tower, by whom are tried actions of debt, trespass, and covenants

The exercise of its own military government is one of the peculiar privileges possessed by the city of London from the earliest times, its forces formerly consisted of what were termed the trained bands, but now of two regiments of militia, raised, according to an act of parliament passed in 1794, by ballot, and consisting of two thousand two hundred men The officers are appointed by the commissioners of the king s lieutenancy for the city of London, of whom the lord mayor is the principal, and one regiment may, in certain cases, be placed by the king under any of his general officers, and marched to any place not exceeding twelve miles from the capital, or to the nearest encampment, the other being, at all such times, to remain in the city

With regard to the general civil government of London, it must be observed, that the suburbs in Middlesex are under the jurisdiction of the justices of the peace for the county, as part of the county The county hall for Middlesex is on Clerkenwell-green, and at the sessions there, great part of the civil government of the suburbs in Middlesex is exercised At the sessions-house in the Old Bailey, four general sessions of Oyer and Terminer are held, and four others by adjournment, (so that there are eight sessions every year,) for crime committed in London, or the county of Middlesex Over this court one of the twelve judges, the lord mayor, the aldermen who have passed the civic chair, and the recorder, or common serjeant, preside Both the sheriffs officially attend the juries are composed of citizens, for offences committed in the city, and of house-keepers in Middlesex, for those committed in the county the grand jury sits at the sessions-house on Clerkenwell-green

The government of Westminster, until the Reformation, was arbitrary under the abbot and monks, then under a bishop, dean and chapter, and subsequently, by an act passed in the 27th of Elizabeth, the civil government was placed in the hands of the laity, the dean being, at the same time, empowered to nominate the chief officers the principal magistrates are, a high steward, usually a nobleman, the office being generally held for life, a high bailiff, chosen by the high steward, also for life, and who has the chief management of parliamentary elections for Westminster, as well as the control of all the other bailiffs he summons juries, and in the courts leet sits next to the deputy steward To him all fines and forfeitures belong, which renders the situation very lucrative, and occasions a considerable sum to be given for it Besides these, there are sixteen burgesses and their assistants, whose functions in all respects resemble those of the aldermen's deputies of the city of London, each having his proper ward under his jurisdiction, and from these are elected two head burgesses, one for the city, and the other for the liberties, who in the court leet rank next to the high bailiff There is also a high constable, who is chosen by the court leet, and to whom all the other constables are subordinate The four principal courts for the city and liberties of Westminster are, the Court of the Duchy of Lancaster, held in Somerset-place, the Court of Quarter Sessions of the peace, held by the justices for the city and liberties, four times a year, at the guildhall, Westminster, St. Martin s-le-Grand Court and the Westminster Court, or court-leet The three first are courts of record, the duchy court being for all matters of law and equity relating to the duchy of Lancaster, that of quarter sessions, for all trespasses, petty larcenies, and other minor offences committed in Westminster and its liberties, that of St. Martin s-le Grand, for the trial of all personal actions appertaining to that particular liberty, and the court leet, which is held by the Dean of Westminster, or his deputy, for choosing parochial officers, preventing and removing nuisances, &c The city and liberties of Westminster return two members to parliament, who are elected by the inhabitant householders, the high bailiff being the returning officer

Southwark was governed by its own bailiffs until 1327, but the city suffering great inconvenience from the number of malefactors that escaped thither from the jurisdiction of the city magistrates, the mayor of London was then, by charter, constituted bailiff of Southwark, and empowered to govern it by his deputy Edward VI granted the "Borough, or Town of Southwark to the city of London, for a pecuniary consideration, and afterwards, for a further consideration of the same kind, it was made a twenty-sixth ward to the city, by the name of Bridge ward Without. It became, in consequence, subject to the lord mayor, who has under him a steward and a bailiff, the former of whom holds a court of record every Monday at St Margaret s hill, for debts, damages, and trespasses Here is also a court of record for the Clink liberty, held near Bankside, in Southwark, by the Bishop of Winchester s steward, for actions of debt, trespass, &c, within that liberty, The Borough returns two members to parliament, who are chosen by the inhabitant householders, and returned by the high bailiff

For the Suburbs there are three principal courts, viz,

the Sheriffs' Court for the county of Middlesex, for actions of debt, trespass, assault, &c , East Smithfield Court, which is a court leet and a court baron held for that liberty, to inquire into nuisances, &c in the court baron pleas are held to the amount of 40s General and Quarter Sessions of the peace, for the liberty of the Tower of London, are held by the justices of that liberty, eight times a year, for petty larcenies, trespasses, felonies, misdemeanours, &c A Court of Requests is held for the Tower Hamlets, for the recovery of debts under 40s

In the metropolis are also held the four great law courts of the kingdom, viz , The King's Bench, Common Pleas, Exchequer, and High Court of Chancery The two first are held alternately at Westminster hall and at Guildhall in the city, the Exchequer court at Westminster hall only, and the Court of Chancery alternately at Westminster hall and Lincoln's Inn, where causes are heard by the chancellor or vice-chancellor There is also the Rolls Court, held by the Master of the Rolls in the Rolls chapel, Chancery lane Civil and ecclesiastical causes are tried at Doctors Commons, at which place are also held the Courts of Admiralty The ecclesiastical courts are, The Court of Arches, for appeals from inferior ecclesiastical courts in the province of Canterbury, of which the Court of Peculiars here is a branch , the Prerogative Court, for causes relative to wills and administrations , the Faculty Court, empowered to grant dispensations to marry, &c , and the Court of Delegates, for ecclesiastical affairs

London also contains, besides the courts already described, the following The Palace Court, or Marshalsea, held formerly at the Old Court-house in the Borough, but now in Scotland-yard, opposite the Admiralty it has jurisdiction of all civil suits within twelve miles of Whitehall, the city of London excepted, and takes cognizance of debts to any amount above 40s , but all actions for debts above £20 may be removed into any of the superior courts The High Court of Admiralty, Doctors Commons, which takes cognizance of all maritime pleas, criminal and civil, the latter being determined according to the civil law, the plaintiff giving security to prosecute, and, if cast, to pay what is adjudged , but the former, being tried by special commission, at the sessions-house in the Old Bailey, by a judge and jury, a judge of the common law assists A Court for the relief of Insolvent Debtors, instituted a few years since, by act of parliament, for the purpose of releasing debtors in England and Wales, who have been imprisoned and apply by petition to be liberated, upon surrendering their effects to their creditors the commissioners, who preside as judges, hold their sittings at a newly erected court-house, in Portugal-street, Lincoln's Inn Fields Courts of Request for the summary recovery of debts not exceeding 40s are situated in various parts of the town there is one in Vine-street, Piccadilly , one in Kingsgate-street, Holborn, another in Trinity street, near Stones-end, Borough , one in Osbourne-street, Whitechapel , one in Castle-street, Leicester-square , and one in Bowling-Green-lane, Southwark

PRISONS, AND POLICE OF THE METROPOLIS

The prisons for criminals are, Newgate, Cold-bath-fields, the Penitentiary at Millbank, New Prison (Clerkenwell), Tothill-fields bridewell, and the gaol for the county of Surrey, Southwark The prisons for debtors are, Giltspur-street Compter, Debtors prison (White Cross-street), the King's Bench, the Fleet, the Marshalsea, and the Borough Compter Of these the majority are extensive, and, in several instances, though gloomy, not inelegant piles of building Newgate, the general criminal prison for the city of London and the county of Middlesex, may be particularly mentioned as being such It is of stone, divided within into several court-yards, and possesses a handsome uniform front towards the west, consisting of two wings, with the governor s house forming the centre Criminals are executed on a temporary scaffold fixed in front of this prison

The city of London, as already stated, is under the control of its own magistracy, consisting of the lord mayor and aldermen, &c , the marshalmen, beadles, and constables, amount to three hundred and nineteen , and the watchmen and patrols to eight hundred and three : in the Tower hamlets, including the eastern part of the town, are two hundred and eighteen constables, and two hundred and eight watchmen and patrols , and in the liberty of the Tower of London are seventeen constables, and fourteen watchmen and patrols for all the parts of the metropolis out of this jurisdiction stipendiary magistrates are appointed , four at Bow-street, with a jurisdiction long established, and twenty-four by virtue of a statute called the "Police Act,' the latter having eight different offices assigned to them, namely, one in each of the following situations Bow-street, Great Marlborough-street, Hatton Garden, Worship-street, Shoreditch Lambeth-street, Whitechapel, High-street, Marylebone, Queen s square, Westminster, and Union-street, Southwark Besides these, there is the Thames Police Office, Wapping, established under a separate act of parliament, and almost wholly confined to the investigation of offences either committed on the river Thames, or connected with maritime affairs Bow street office is the most celebrated, being the chief, or head, of the London police, and wholly under the direction of the Secretary of State for the Home Department This office has a principal, and three subordinate, magistrates, all of them in the commission of the peace for the counties of Middlesex, Surrey, Kent, and Essex to it are attached three clerks and eight officers, with their attendants

By the new police act the whole of the metropolis, exclusively of that part immediately denominated "the City and Liberties, is consolidated into one district, called "The Metropolitan Police district, and is not intended to interfere in any way with the police before noticed, but has been established with a view to the better security of the persons and property of the inhabitants, and to supersede the inefficient local police, previously existing in the several parishes within the district, which has been formed into seventeen divisions, comprising the whole of the metropolis, and extends eastward to Stratford, Poplar, and Greenwich , southward to Streatham, Tooting, and Wandsworth , westward to Acton, Ealing, and Brentford , and northward to Hampstead, Islington, Newington, and Hackney Each of the divisions is under the charge of a superior officer, named a superintendent of police, who is considered responsible for the activity and good conduct of the men acting within his division the total amount of force is three thousand and three hundred They are divided into four classes ,—the superintendent above-mentioned, with a salary of £200 per annum , the inspector, at a salary of £100 per annum, the police serjeant, paid at the rate of £1 2 6, and the ordinary police constable, at 19s, per week each division has one superintendent, six inspectors, and twenty-two serjeants, except the letter K division, which has thirty-two serjeants the men are provided with a plain blue uniform Two magistrates, or commissioners, with salaries of £800 per annum each, control, with the approbation of the secretary of state, the whole metropolitan police force, for which a new police office has been established at Westminster, and they have the power, not only of regulating all matters respecting arms, accoutrements, &c, but of discharging any person who acts improperly, besides whom there is a general receiver, or treasurer, with a salary of £700 per annum All appointments to the higher stations in the police are confined to those men who have distinguished themselves by good conduct in the lower ranks, they must be of vigorous constitution, not above thirty-five years old (excepting such as have served in the army), nor under five feet seven inches in height, and as the amount of pay is deemed sufficient for a comfortable livelihood, they are required to devote their whole time to the service, without exhausting themselves by other labour The annual expense of the establishment, which is defrayed by rates chargeable on the several parishes and places where they act, is about £200,000

INNS OF COURT, and COURTS OF JUDICATURE

The London Inns of Court were originally like colleges in a university, but confined to the study of the law Though their origin cannot be exactly ascertained, they may be presumed to have owed their rise to the establishment of the courts of justice at Westminster, by Henry III, which, collecting in their neighbourhood the whole body of common lawyers, or practitioners, in those courts, they began to form themselves into a society (supposed at Thaives Inn, Holborn,) in a collegiate manner, hence their place of residence was denominated an Inn (Hostell), or House of Court, and the king, in 1244, forbade the teaching of law in schools set up in the city, as had been accustomed, and restricted its study to these inns Their increase, as well as division into Inns of Court and Inns of Chancery, is not recognized till the reign of Edward III, when their students are called apprentices of the law (from the Fr Apprendre), and the Inns of Court became appropriated solely to the study of the common law, as were the latter to such clerks as studied the forming of writs and other process in chancery Till late in the seventeenth century, the students of the various inns were exercised before the principals in sham pleadings, called mootings, and many antiquated customs were retained, as well as occasionally splendid ceremonies exhibited At present these inns have become mere residences, not for lawyers only, but any persons who choose to hire chambers in them, and the law-student, before being called to the bar, is now only obliged to be entered of one of these places, and dine in the common hall a certain number of terms, after which, should his admission not be objected to by the members, an occurrence that rarely happens, he is legally qualified to plead and conduct causes The Inns of Court are not incorporated, consequently the masters, principals, benchers, &c, by whom they are governed, can make no by laws, nor possess

estates, &c, yet they have certain orders which, by consent and prescription, have obtained the force of laws the societies are entirely supported by sums paid for admissions and for chambers, and from the benchers, or seniors, in whom the government is vested, a treasurer is usually chosen to manage these funds, the other members may be divided into outer barristers, inner barristers, and students

The principal Inns of Court are four —The Inner Temple, Middle Temple, Lincoln s Inn, and Gray s Inn the Inns of Chancery are seven, viz, Clifford s Inn, Lyon s Inn, Clement s Inn, and New Inn, belonging to the two Temples, Furnival's Inn, belonging to Lincoln s Inn, and Staples Inn, and Bernard s Inn, belonging to Gray's Inn Thavies Inn, Scroop s Inn, Chester Inn, or Strand Inn, as well as Johnson s Inn, and some others in the city, have long been disused Of the two Serjeant s Inns, in Fleet-street and Chancery-lane, the latter only is appropriated as chambers for the Serjeants at law, who removed thither from Symond s Inn, which is falling to decay, and merely tenanted as chambers by any one who chooses to rent them Serjeant s Inn, Fleet-street, consists now of private residences

THE TEMPLE is so called from its original inhabitants, the Knights Templars, who, on quitting their old house in Southampton-buildings, Holborn, in the reign of Henry II, built a house in Fleet-street, thence called the New Temple, which occupied all the ground from White Friars to Essex-street On their suppression by Edward II, the Temple, after two or three intermediate grants from the Crown, was, by Edward III, given to the monastery of St John of Jerusalem, the prior and convent of which afterwards demised it to the lawyers, supposed to have emigrated here from Thavies Inn, at a yearly rent of £10, a sum for which they still enjoy from the Crown the whole of this splendid property The Temple is at present divided between the two societies—the Inner and Middle Templers, each consisting of benchers, barristers and students, the government being vested in the benchers In term-time the members dine in the hall of the society, which is called keeping commons, to dine a fortnight in each term, is deemed keeping the term, and twelve of those terms qualify a student, after being called to the bar, to plead and manage causes in the courts each society has also a treasurer, sub-treasurer, steward, chief butler, three under-butlers, upper and under cook, and various other officers and servants The Temple Church is the chief architectural attraction belonging to these societies, though each has also a fine large hall, and an extensive library, as well as beautiful gardens the garden of the Inner Temple affords a remarkably fine summer promenade The houses are generally large plain brick edifices, divided into sets of chambers, most of which are spacious apartments

Lincoln's Inn occupies, with its gardens and squares, a very extensive plot of ground on the western side of Chancery-lane It has a fine ancient brick gateway opening from Chancery-lane, built by Sir Thomas Lovel in the reign of Henry VII, a hall erected by the same person, wherein the Lord Chancellor holds his sittings, and a chapel built by Inigo Jones, in the English style of architecture The buildings occupy four large squares, exclusively of the avenues to them, &c, and the garden affords a most agreeable promenade

Gray s Inn is chiefly remarkable for its large and beautiful garden The buildings consist principally of two quadrangles, separated by a hall and chapel, and two handsome ranges of building recently erected, called Verulam and Raymond buildings the chambers and regulations of both these last inns are similar to those of the Temple Most of the other inns consist of double courts, surrounded by large brick buildings divided into chambers all of them have halls, and several have good libraries and gardens The finest, in point of architecture, is Furnival s Inn, situated in Holborn, which has been lately rebuilt in an excellent style, and forms a large and beautiful pile of buildings

The four great courts of Judicature are, the High Court of Chancery, the Court of Exchequer, the Court of King s Bench, and the Court of Common Pleas, held in Westminster Hall The rooms in which the business of these courts is transacted are situated on the western side of the great hall, and have been elegantly fitted up by Mr Soane This was the great hall of the ancient palace of Westminster, and is celebrated as the scene of many important events in English history the first hall was founded by William Rufus, but the present edifice was for the most part erected by Richard II The grand entrance is flanked by large square embattled towers, richly ornamented with canopies, once containing statues, in rows above each other Westminster Hall is considered to be the largest apartment in Europe unsupported by pillars, being two hundred and seventy feet long, seventy-four broad, and ninety high the floor is of stone , and the side walls and ends are pierced with elegant windows, the latter being of vast magnitude and highly-elaborate workmanship The roof has always excited particular admiration, it is of chesnut, forming an immense arch, supported by carved angels bearing shields of the founder s arms Parliaments were anciently held in this hall, and it was the court of justice in which the sovereign presided in person The coronation feasts have been held here for many ages past, and it is also occasionally used for the trial of peers, or other persons impeached by the commons

GOVERNMENT OFFICES and other PUBLIC BUILDINGS

The offices more immediately connected with the affairs of government occupy a grand line of buildings, stretching entirely across the eastern extremity of St James Park, from Spring Gardens to Downing-street The most northern is the Admiralty, next is the War Office, or Horse Guards , then the Treasury , lastly, the offices of the three Secretaries of State

The War Office, or Horse Guards, derives its latter appellation from the circumstance of that branch of the military mounting guard here It is a noble, though rather heavy building, erected by Ware, at an expense of more than £30,000 A handsome portal leads through it from St James Park into Parliament-street Here, in a variety of apartments, is transacted all business relative to the British army *The Admiralty* and *Treasury* are both fine buildings , the former, originally called Wallingford House, and facing Parliament - street, has a beautiful screen by Adams, which, with its spacious portico, renders it on the whole a commanding pile the Lords of the Admiralty have here their offices, together with spacious

private apartments on the top of the building is a semaphore telegraph, which communicates orders, by signal, to the principal parts of the kingdom. The Treasury is an extensive pile of buildings, partly formed out of the remains of Whitehall palace the principal front, which is of stone, looks into St James Park, that next Parliament-street has been rebuilt in a splendid style by Mr Soane. Besides the Board of Treasury, this edifice contains a variety of offices, amongst which is the Council Chamber The buildings of the other government offices situated in the immediate vicinity of the above, and which consist of the offices of the Secretaries of State, the Board of Control for the affairs of India, the offices of the Crown Lands, and of the Board of Works, &c , have nothing in them particularly worthy of notice

Somerset House, the most noble collection of the Government offices in London, derives its name from being built on the site of the magnificent palace erected by the Protector Somerset, in the reign of Edward VI After being for several ages occasionally inhabited by the queens of England, it was rebuilt, as it now stands, under the superintendence of Sir William Chambers, in 1775 It comprises the Navy Office, Navy Pay Office, Salt Office, Stamp Office, the Offices of the Auditor of the Exchequer, those of the Chancellors of the duchies of Cornwall and Lancaster, the Hawkers' and Pedlars' Office, Stage-coach Office, Legacy-duty Office, and the whole revenue establishment of the Tax Offices all these are situated in the quadrangle which forms the main body of the pile The beautiful front next the Strand has been munificently devoted to the use of the Royal Society, the Society of Antiquaries, and the Royal Academy of Arts Somerset House occupies a space of about eight hundred feet in width, and five hundred in depth , and for magnitude, as well as architectural merit, ranks among the foremost of the public buildings in London The magnificent Strand front, the extensive quadrangular court, the yet grander front next the Thames, with its terrace, one of the finest in the world, all combine, with the numerous spacious apartments and offices it contains, to excite admiration The buildings of the King's College, just founded, under the patronage of His late Majesty, for the purpose of giving instruction to youth in the metropolis, are to form the eastern wing of the south front of this edifice, which, without it, was incomplete this design is actively being carried into execution

Tower of London "The Tower," as it is familiarly called, stands on the northern bank of the Thames, and consists of a large pile of building, the irregularity of which arises from its having been erected and enlarged by various sovereigns, at distant periods of time it served the purpose of a fortified palace to many of the early monarchs of England Tradition ascribes the origin of this fortress to Julius Cæsar, but the earliest authentic account of it is, that William the Conqueror, having no great reliance on the fidelity of his new subjects of London, on fixing his residence in the metropolis, built a strong hold to overawe them, on part of the present site of the Tower In 1078, he appointed Gundulph, Bishop of Rochester, a skilful architect, to superintend the building of a larger fort, being the same, though repaired or rebuilt by some of his successors, which is now called the White Tower It is situated in the centre of the fortress, and is a square building with four watch-towers, one of which is used as an observatory this part of the building contains, besides a small armoury for the sea service, an ancient Norman chapel, dedicated to St John, in which the kings and queens who resided here performed their devotions it is of an oblong form, circular at the east end, and supported by short round pillars in this place the ancient records of the kingdom are now kept in presses in 1082, William Rufus laid the foundations of a castle southward and near to the river, which was finished by his successor, Henry I beneath it were two gates, one called Traitor s gate, through which state prisoners were conveyed to their cells, the other bearing the name of the Bloody gate Henry III added a strong gate and bulwark to the west entrance, repaired and *whitened* the square tower, which probably gave it the name it still retains, and extended the fortress by a mud wall, which was superseded by one of brick by Edward IV, who built within this enclosure the present Lions' tower Charles II and the succeeding sovereigns down to His late Majesty George IV, have made various additions and alterations within the area enclosed by the ancient fortifications the exterior walls of the tower now include an area of twelve acres and five roods The exterior circuit of the ditch, which entirely surrounds it, is three thousand one hundred and fifty-six feet it is separated from the Thames by a broad quay, behind which is a platform for mounting sixty-one pieces of cannon, which are brought out and fired on all occasions of public rejoicing The principal entrance is by three successive gates on the western side, two of which are outside the ditch, the second gate, on entering, leads to a stone bridge thrown across the ditch, and the third, which is the strongest, stands at the inner end of the bridge this is guarded by soldiers, and when these gates are opened in the morning, the formalities of a garrison are observed The interior, which forms a parish within itself, but subject to the visitation of the Bishop of London, contains several streets, and a variety of buildings, including the Tower parish church, or Royal Free Chapel of St Peter *ad Vincula*, the White Tower, the Ordnance Office, the Record Office, the Jewel Office, the Horse Armoury, the Grand Storehouse, the new or small Armoury, houses belonging to the officers of the Tower, barracks for the garrison, and two sutling-houses, commonly used by the officers of the garrison Several of the public buildings just mentioned are of great interest, and others contain numerous curiosities well worthy of inspection, particularly the Horse Armoury, the small Armoury, the room where the spoils of the Spanish Armada are kept, the Menagerie, and the Jewel Office, in which are kept the crowns and other regalia, used at coronations. The government is entrusted to a Constable, who is generally a person of high rank under his command are a lieutenant and a deputy-lieutenant, the latter being called the governor, with several other subordinate officers, besides forty wardens, who bear the same rich antique uniform worn by the corps at its formation by Henry VII the Tower is garrisoned by His Majesty s household troops

The Mint, originally situated within the limits of the Tower, and the business of which was afterwards for some time carried on at Soho, near Birmingham,

now stands at the north-eastern corner of Tower Hill, on the site of the old Victualling-Office It is a noble building, from a design by Mr Smirke, Jun, having an extensive stone front, it consists of a ground floor and two stories above, the whole surmounted by a handsome balustrade The wings are ornamented with pilasters, and in the centre are several demi-columns, over which is a pediment bearing the arms of England over the porch is a gallery with balustrades, &c, of the Doric order This extensive establishment contains steam-engines, and all the numerous mechanical works for facilitating the operations of the coinage

BRIDGES

The bridges which unite the southern with the northern part of the metropolis are remarkable for their architecture, magnitude and solidity

London Bridge, the most ancient of them all, was the only bridge connecting the Middlesex and Surrey shores of the capital until the eighteenth century, and may be regarded as the limit which separates the sea and river navigation of the Thames It was founded in 1176, and originally supported a street of houses, with a chapel, entrance gate-ways, &c, which remained, with various alterations, until the year 1756, when it was cleared of the whole of its buildings, thoroughly repaired, and surmounted, as at present, by an open balustrade and lamps In consequence of the inconvenience and danger to the navigation of the Thames by this bridge, it was determined to erect a new one

The New London Bridge was begun March 15th, 1824, under the superintendence of Mr Rennie, the architect, and, according to contract, was to be finished, for the sum of £506,000, in six years from that period, which sum was not to include the formation of approaches, nor the expense of removing the old bridge The work is now nearly completed, and will be entirely finished early in the year 1831 it is built of granite, the number of its noble arches is five, and, when completed, the sides will be guarded by plain balustrades. The approaches at both ends are to be carried over arches, and will communicate with spacious streets, that next the Borough, from exposing to the view the whole of St Saviour s church, will, in particular, give to the southern approach a novel and wonderful dignity

Southwark Bridge is a magnificent structure of cast-iron, with stone piers and abutments, forming a communication from the central part of the city to Bankside, Southwark, and thence to the roads leading into Kent and Surrey it was designed by Mr Rennie, and consists of three arches the centre arch rises twenty-four feet, with a span of two hundred and forty feet, the span of each of the side arches being two hundred and ten feet the whole was completed in March, 1819, at an expense, including the approaches, of £800,000, being one of the most stupendous works of the kind ever formed of such materials Many of the solid castings weigh ten tons each, and the total weight of the iron employed is about five thousand seven hundred and eighty tons The abutments are of solid masonry, laid in radiating courses, with large blocks of Bramly-fall and Whitby stones The work was commenced on the 23rd of September, 1814, and the bridge was opened in April, 1819

Blackfriars' Bridge was named, at the time of its foundation, "Pitt's bridge," as a testimony of the respect entertained by the citizens of London for the character and talents of that eminent statesman, William Pitt, the first Earl of Chatham, whose name was accordingly inscribed on a plate laid under the foundation stone The act of parliament empowered the corporation to raise £ 30,000 per annum, until the sum should amount to £ 160,000 The first stone was laid by the Lord Mayor, Sir Thomas Chitty, on the 31st of October, 1760, and in the course of 1770 the work was completed, its construction having occupied nearly eleven years the architect was Mr Robert Mylne The expense amounted only to £ 160,000, and was defrayed by a toll for several years The bridge has nine elliptical arches the span of the centre arch is one hundred feet, those on each side decreasing gradually towards the shores, being respectively ninety-eight, ninety-three, eighty-three, and seventy feet wide, leaving a clear water way of seven hundred and eighty-eight feet Each side of the bridge is guarded by an open stone balustrade, sufficiently low to allow to foot passengers a distinct prospect of the river Over each pier there is a square recess, supported by double Ionic pillars and pilasters, which have a very light and ornamental effect at each end of the bridge are two handsome flights of stone steps to the river

Waterloo Bridge crosses the Thames from a little to the west of Somerset House to the opposite shore of Lambeth Marsh, uniting the Strand with the newly-formed line, or street, which extends to the Obelisk in St George s Fields, and is regarded as one of the greatest magnificence Of an extent larger than that of any of the other bridges over the Thames, it affords a fine level passage across the river, and, from the beauty and simplicity of the design, and its stability, it is calculated to remain a monument of architectural skill down to remote ages The original projector was Mr George Dodd, but, in consequence of a misunderstanding between him and the company, the execution of the work devolved on Mr Rennie, who furnished two designs for the bridge, one having seven arches, and the other nine, the latter being adopted the work was commenced in 1811, and completed in 1817 The bridge consists of nine elliptical arches, each of one hundred and twenty feet span, and thirty five feet elevation it is forty-two feet broad, being of the same width as Blackfriars bridge, and its length is one thousand two hundred and forty-two feet, being nineteen feet longer, within the abutments, than Westminster bridge. The arches and piers are built of large blocks of granite, the latter being twenty feet thick, and surmounted by Tuscan columns, which support square recesses above Upon the entire work, including the approaches, a sum greatly exceeding £ 1,000,000 sterling was expended

Westminster Bridge was built between the years 1739 and 1750, and cost £ 389,500 It is one thousand two hundred and twenty-three feet long, and forty-four wide, having on each side of the carriage way a foot pavement, and it consists of thirteen large and two small semicircular arches, with fourteen intermediate piers and abutments on its top are twenty-eight semi-octagonal recesses, twelve of which are covered by demi-cupolas Under the arches is a free channel for the water, of eight hundred and seventy feet The two middle piers contain each three thousand solid feet, or two hundred tons of Portland stone The centre arch is seventy-six feet wide, the others diminish in width by four feet

equally on each side, and the two smaller ones close in shore are each about twenty-five feet wide The whole edifice is of stone, and rests upon a gravel bed, the piers having been sunk for that purpose to from five to fourteen feet under the bed of the river At the period of its erection this bridge was esteemed one of the noblest structures of the kind in the world its architect was M Labylie, an ingenious native of Switzerland although not a century old, like that of Blackfriars, it exhibits evident marks of decay, from the decomposition of the stone of which it is constructed

Vauxhall Bridge communicating with a new road across Tothill-fields, to Eaton-street, Pimlico, and Grosvenor-place, was commenced in the year 1813, and in August 1816 the bridge was completed and opened to the public the architect was Mr J Walker Although in magnitude and grandeur of proportions this bridge does not equal any one of the preceding, yet it merits praise for beauty and elegance It is light and elegant, consisting of nine arches of cast-iron, each of seventy-eight feet span, having between eleven and twelve feet rise, and resting on rusticated stone piers laid with Roman cement The breadth of the roadway is thirty-six feet, and the whole length of the bridge is eight hundred and nine feet the cost was above £ 300,000 This bridge, as well as Southwark and Waterloo bridges, was erected by an incorporated company of share holders, who are authorised to levy a toll, that on foot passengers, being one penny each

A bill has been recently brought into parliament for building a seventh bridge across the Thames at London, from the Horse-ferry road to Lambeth stairs, to be called the Royal Clarence bridge

THAMES TUNNEL

The idea of forming a subway under the bed of the Thames, to connect Rotherhithe with the opposite shore at Old Gravel lane, Wapping, was revived by Mr Brunel, in 1824, a similar attempt having been made in 1809, upon a much smaller scale, and, though the project was then relinquished, yet the miners having extended their operations to within one hundred and thirty feet of the opposite shore, was thought sufficient encouragement for the present undertaking, accordingly, the sum of £ 200,000 was raised by transferable shares of £ 50 each, and the work was begun in March, 1825 Mr Brunel s plan was, by means of frame-work, to excavate daily only such a space as could be immediately supported by brick arching, and a very considerable progress was made, with great promise of ultimate success, during several months in the end, however, a similar accident to that which occasioned the abandonment of the former undertaking, but much more fatal in its effects, caused Mr Brunel's attempt, like his predecessor s, to be suspended, and the excavation, after a great expenditure of money, and the loss of several lives, is for the present discontinued The tunnel, if completed, was to have consisted of two arcades, lighted by gas, forming distinct ways for going and returning, and each containing a roadway and footway, the form of the arcades was to be cylindrical, about fifteen feet high, by twelve at their base, the two ways, with a separation wall of four feet, making twenty-eight feet breadth, the whole mass of masonry extending in breadth and height thirty seven feet by twenty-two

ECCLESIASTICAL JURISDICTION

Arms of the Bishoprick.

At what precise period London was constituted the head of a diocese, is uncertain, but it is evident that it acquired this distinction not long after the introduction of Christianity into Britain It appears to have been at first an archbishoprick, but after the metropolitical power was transferred to Canterbury, in consequence of the conversion to Christianity of Ethelbert, King of Kent, by Augustine, London sunk into a bishoprick, and Mellitus was made the first bishop, in 604 The diocese was co-extensive with the ancient kingdom of the East Saxons, comprehending the counties of Middlesex and Essex, and part of Hertfordshire, to which have been added the British plantations in America. Though locally in the province of Canterbury, it is exempt from the visitation of the Archbishop, and the Bishop of London enjoys precedence over all the other bishops, ranking in dignity next to the Archbishop of York The ecclesiastical establishment is composed of a bishop, dean, precentor, chancellor, treasurer, five archdeacons, thirty prebendaries (three of whom are residentiary, and, with the dean, constitute the chapter), twelve petty or minor canons, six vicars choral, a sub dean, and inferior officers The twelve petty canons were incorporated a body politic, in 1399, by letters patent of Richard II they are governed by a warden, chosen from among themselves, and have a common seal

PARISHES IN LONDON, WESTMINSTER, SOUTHWARK, &c

Parishes marked thus * are within the jurisdiction of the Archdeacon of London, and those marked thus † are subject to the Commissary of London, for granting probates of wills and letters of administration; the Bishop of London exercising concurrent jurisdiction over all Parishes marked thus ‡ are within the peculiar jurisdiction of the Archbishop of Canterbury, and those marked thus § in that of the Dean and Chapter of St Paul's

CITY OF LONDON WITHIN THE WALLS

PARISH	LIVING	Val in the King's Books £ s d	PATRONS	Population
† St Alban, Wood-street	Rectory	16 8 11½	The Dean and Chapter of St. Paul s and Eton-college, alternately	631
† Allhallows, Barking	Vicarage	36 13 4	The Crown	1664
‡ Allhallows, Bread-street	Rectory	37 13 9	The Archbishop of Canterbury	320
* Allhallows the Great	Rectory	41 18 1½	The Archbishop of Canterbury	526
† Allhallows, Honey-lane	Rectory	19 3 9	The Archbishop of Canterbury for two turns, and the Grocers' Company for one	137
* Allhallows the Less	Rectory		United with that of Allhallows the Great	98
‡ Allhallows, Lombard-street	Rectory	22 6 8	The Dean and Chapter of Canterbury	580
† Allhallows Staining	Perpetual Curacy		The Grocers Company	577
* Allhallows on the Wall and St Augustine consolidated	Rectory	8 16 8	The Crown	1677
* St Alphage	Rectory	8 0 0	The Bishop of London	1206
† St Andrew Hubbard	Rectory	16 0 0	The Duke of Northumberland and the Parishioners, alternately	287
† St. Andrew Undershaft, with St. Mary Axe	Rectory	25 11 3	The Bishop of London	1161
* St. Andrew by the Wardrobe	Rectory	17 10 0	The Crown and the Parishioners, alternately	690
* St. Anne and St Agnes	Rectory	8 0 0	The Bishop of London and the Dean and Chapter of St Paul's, alternately	561
† St Antholin	Rectory	20 2 8½	The Crown and the Dean and Chapter of St Paul's, alternately	365
† St Anne, Blackfriars	Rectory		United with that of St Andrew by the Wardrobe	2938
* St. Augustine, Watling street	Rectory	19 16 0½	The Dean and Chapter of St. Paul's	307
* St Bartholomew by the Royal Exchange	Rectory	18 1 8	The Crown	339
† St Bene't Fink	Perpetual Curacy		The Dean and Canons of Windsor	511
† St Bene't Gracechurch	Rectory	18 1 3	The Dean and Chapter of St Paul's and the Dean and Chapter of Canterbury, alternately	290
† St. Bene t, Paul s Wharf	Rectory	13 19 4½	The Dean and Chapter of St Paul s	352
† St Bene t Sherehog	Rectory	8 13 4	United with that of St Stephen, Walbrook	142
† St Botolph, Billingsgate	Rectory	23 16 0½	The Crown and the Dean and Chapter of St Paul s, alternately	191

PARISH.	LIVING	Value in the King's Books. £ s. d.	PATRONS	Population.
* Christchurch ..	Vicarage	26 13 4	The Governors of St Bartholomew's Hospital and the Dean and Chapter of Westminster, alternately	2737
† St Christopher le Stocks	Rectory	14 0 0	United with that of St Margaret, Lothbury	84
† St Clement, Eastcheap	Rectory	13 2 1	The Bishop of London and the Dean and Chapter of St. Paul's, alternately .	273
‡ St Dionis Backchurch ..	Rectory	25 0 0	The Dean and Chapter of Canterbury	791
‡ St Dunstan in the East	Rectory	60 7 11	The Archbishop of Canterbury	1155
† St. Edmund the King	Rectory	21 14 2	The Crown and the Archbishop of Canterbury, alternately	442
* St Ethelburga	Rectory	11 12 6	The Bishop of London	704
9 St Faith the Virgin	Rectory	23 17 1	United with that of St Augustine, Watling-street	999
† St. Gabriel, Fenchurch	Rectory	12 0 0	United with that of St Margaret Pattens	343
† St George, Botolph-lane	Rectory	8 0 0	United with that of St Botolph, Billingsgate	215
§ St Gregory by St. Paul's	Rectory		Dean and Chapter of St. Paul's	1468
6 St Helen, Bishopsgate .	Vicarage		Dean and Chapter of St Paul's	696
† St. James, Duke's place	Perpetual Curacy		The Lord Mayor and Aldermen	732
† St James Garlick Hythe	Rectory	17 14 7	The Bishop of London	473
* St John Baptist	Rectory	15 18 9	United with that of St. Antholin	417
‡ St John Evangelist	Rectory	15 19 7	United with that of Allhallows, Bread-street	86
* St John Zachary	Rectory	11 2 1	United with that of St Anne and St. Agnes	322
* St Katherine, Coleman	Rectory	5 6 8	The Bishop of London	712
† St Katherine Creechurch	Vicarage		The Master and Fellows of Magdalene College, Cambridge	1814
† St Lawrence, Jewry	Vicarage	18 0 5	The Master and Fellows of Balliol College, Oxford, and the Dean and Chapter of St Paul's, alternately	702
† St. Lawrence Pounteney	Perpetual Curacy		United with the Rectory of St Mary, Abchurch	352
‡ St Leonard, Eastcheap	Rectory	20 10 0	United with that of St. Bene't, Gracechurch	307
† St Leonard, Foster-lane	Rectory	26 13 4	United with the Vicarage of Christchurch	377
* St. Magnus	Rectory	69 5 5	The Bishop of London	227
† St Margaret, New Fish-street	Rectory	31 11 8	United with that of St. Magnus	344
* St Margaret, Lothbury	Rectory	13 6 8	The Bishop of London	331
* St Margaret Moses	Rectory	12 4 4½	United with that of St Mildred, Bread-street	149
† St Margaret Pattens	Rectory	10 0 0	The Crown, the Lord Mayor and Aldermen, and the Lord Mayor and Common Council, alternately	185
† St Martin, Ironmonger lane	Rectory	12 7 6	United with the Vicarage of St. Olave, Old Jewry	132
* St. Martin, Ludgate	Rectory	33 17 8½	The Bishop of London	1200
† St. Martin Orgars	Rectory	19 16 3	United with that of St. Clement, Eastcheap	350
† St Martin Outwich	Rectory	13 9 9½	The Merchant Taylors' Company	252
† St. Martin, Vintry	Rectory	18 13 4	United with that of St. Michael Royal	205
* St Mary, Abchurch	Rectory	20 2 6	The Master and Fellows of Corpus Christi College, Cambridge	505
† St Mary, Aldermanbury	Perpetual Curacy		The Parishioners	883
‡ St Mary, Aldermary	Rectory	41 0 0	The Archbishop of Canterbury and the Dean and Chapter of St Paul's, alternately	429
‡ St Mary le Bow	Rectory	33 12 3½	United with those of Allhallows, Honey lane, and St Pancras	368
‡ St Mary Bothaw	Rectory	10 10 0	United with that of St. Swithin	225
* St Mary Colechurch	Rectory		United with that of St Mildred, Poultry	275
St Mary at Hill	Rectory	36 13 4	United with that of St. Andrew Hubbard	818
* St. Mary Magdalene, Old Fish st	Rectory	19 5 0	United with that of St Gregory, by St Paul's	721
+ St. Mary Magdalene, Milk-street	Rectory	19 17 6	United with the Vicarage of St. Lawrence Jewry	300
⁴ St. Mary Mounthaw	Rectory	6 10 0	United with that of St Mary Somerset	358
* St. Mary Somerset	Rectory	10 10 0	The Bishops of London and Hereford, alternately	270
* St. Mary Staining	Rectory	5 6 8	United with that of St. Michael, Wood street	221
† St. Mary Woolchurch Haw	Rectory	18 13 4	United with that of St. Mary Woolnoth	206
* St Mary Woolnoth	Rectory	25 0 0	The King and J Thornton, Esq., alternately	511
† St. Matthew, Friday street	Rectory	21 7 3½	The Bishop of London and the Duke of Buccleuch, alternately	228

PARISH	LIVING	Value in the King's Books £ s d	PATRONS.	Populatio
* St Michael, Bassishaw	Rectory	17 0 0	The Dean and Chapter of St. Paul's	714
† St Michael, Cornhill	Rectory	35 1 8	The Drapers' Company	492
‡ St Michael, Crooked Lane	Rectory	26 8 4	The Archbishop of Canterbury	576
* St Michael, Queen-hythe	Rectory	16 0 0	The Dean and Chapter of St Paul's and the Dean and Chapter of Canterbury, alternately	716
* St Michael le Quern	Rectory	21 10 5	United with that of St Vedast	252
‡ St Michael Pater noster Royal	Rectory	7 0 0	The Archbishop of Canterbury and the Bishop of Worcester, alternately	181
† St Michael, Wood street	Rectory	18 13 4	The Crown and the Parishioners, alternately	433
† St Mildred, Bread street	Rectory	16 6 8	The King and another, alternately	329
† St. Mildred, Poultry	Rectory	18 13 4	The Crown and the Mercers' Company, alternately	271
† St. Nicholas Acons	Rectory	13 0 0	United with that of St Edmund the King	180
† St Nicholas Cole Abbey	Rectory	18 13 4	The Crown and the Dean and Chapter of St Paul's, alternately	228
† St Nicholas Olave	Rectory	7 19 7	United with that of St. Nicholas Cole Abbey	350
* St. Olave, Hart-street	Rectory, consolidated with that of St Nicholas at the Shambles	17 14 2 23 7 6	The Parishioners	1012
† St Olave, Old Jewry	Vicarage	10 18 6½	The Crown	239
* St Olave, Silver-street	Rectory	7 7 11	United with that of St. Alban, Wood street	1135
‡ St Pancras, Soper-lane	Rectory	13 6 3	United with those of Allhallows, Honey lane, and St Mary le Bow	190
* St Peter, Cornhill	Rectory	39 5 7½	The Lord Mayor, Aldermen and Common Council	731
† St Peter near Paul's Wharf	Rectory	9 4 2	United with that of St. Bene't	346
† St. Peter le Poor	Rectory	5 16 8	The Dean and Chapter of St. Paul's	576
* St Peter, Westcheap	Rectory	26 7 9	United with that of St Matthew, Friday-street	266
† St. Stephen, Coleman-street	Vicarage	11 0 0	The Parishioners	3062
* St Stephen, Walbrook	Rectory	17 13 9	The Crown and the Grocers Company, alternately	273
† St Swithin, London-stone	Rectory	15 17 11	The Dean and Chapter of Canterbury and the Rev H G Watkins, alternately	
* St. Thomas Apostle	Rectory	12 0 0	United with that of St Mary Aldermary	365
* Trinity the Less	Rectory	8 7 6	United with that of St. Michael, Queen-hythe	502
‡ St Vedast Foster	Rectory	33 5 10	The Archbishop of Canterbury and the Dean and Chapter of St Paul's, alternately	398

CITY OF LONDON WITHOUT THE WALLS

PARISH	LIVING	Value in the King's Books £ s d.	PATRONS	Population
* St Andrew, Holborn	Rectory	18 0 0	The Duke of Buccleuch	6234 a
* St. Bartholomew the Great	Rectory	8 0 0	W Phillips, Esq	2931
* St Bartholomew the Less	Vicarage	13 6 8	The Governors of St Bartholomew's Hospital	823 b
* St. Botolph, without Aldersgate	Perpetual Curacy		The Dean and Chapter of Westminster	4003 c
* St. Botolph, Aldgate	Perpetual Curacy		R. Kynaston, Esq	9067 d
† St Botolph, without Bishopsgate	Rectory	20 0 0	The Bishop of London	10,140
† St. Bride	Vicarage	16 0 0	The Dean and Chapter of Westminster	7288
† St Dunstan in the West	Vicarage	26 4 9½	The Society for purchasing Livings	3549
§ St Giles, without Cripplegate	Vicarage	32 5 0	The Dean and Chapter of St Paul's	13,038 e
† St Sepulchre	Vicarage	20 0 0	The President and Fellows of St John's College, Oxford	8271 f
* Trinity in the Minories	Perpetual Curacy		The Crown	680

a The parish of St Andrew Holborn within the city includes the extra-parochial liberty of Barnard's Inn but the largest part of the parish is in the Holborn division of the hundred of Ossulstone the population of which is returned with the parish of St George the Martyr

b The return from the parish of St Bartholomew the Less includes four hundred and seventy one patients in St Bartholomew's hospital

c The entire parish of St Botolph, without Aldersgate, contains 5361 inhabitants, of which number, 1338 are in the liberty of Glasshouse Yard, in the Finsbury division of the hundred of Ossulstone

d The parish of St Botolph Aldgate is partly within the walls of the city

e The debtors in Whitecross street prison are included in the population of the parish of St Giles, Cripplegate

f The parish of St Sepulchre containing 13,011 inhabitants extends into the Finsbury division of the hundred of Ossulstone, county of Middlesex

U 2

PARISHES ADJACENT TO THE CITY OF LONDON,

the three former being in the Holborn division, and the two latter in the Tower division, of the hundred of Ossulstone, county of Middlesex

PARISH	LIVINGS	Value in the King's Books £ s d	PATRONS	Population
* St George the Martyr, and St. Andrew above Bars	Rectory		The Duke of Buccleuch	a
† St George, Bloomsbury	Rectory		The Crown	b
† St Giles in the Fields	Rectory		The Crown	b
† St. George in the East	Rectory		The Principal and Fellows of Brasenose College, Oxford	32,528
* St. John Baptist, Savoy	Perpetual Curacy		The Crown	222
St Peter ad Vincula, Tower	Rectory	18 13 4	The Crown	463

a The parish of St. George the Martyr includes the return for that part of the parish of St Andrew, Holborn, which is in the Holborn division of the hundred of Ossulstone, and the number of inhabitants is 25,402, besides which, the liberties of Saffron Hill, Hatton Garden, and Ely Rents, contain 9902 inhabitants, making the whole number, in the united parishes 41,728

b The parishes of St George, Bloomsbury, and St. Giles in the Fields united contain 51,793 inhabitants

CITY AND LIBERTY OF WESTMINSTER

The parishes marked thus * are subject to the Archdeacon of Middlesex, with whom the Bishop of London exercises concurrent jurisdiction and those marked thus † are within the royal peculiar jurisdiction of the Dean and Chapter of Westminster

PARISH	LIVING	Value in the King's Book £ s d	PATRONS	Population.
St Anne, Soho	Rectory		The Bishop of London	15,215
* St Clement Danes	Rectory	52 7 1	The Marquis of Exeter	10,753 a
St George, Hanover-square	Rectory		The Bishop of London	46,384
* St James, Piccadilly	Rectory		The Bishop of London	33,819
† St John Milbank	Rectory		The Dean and Chapter of Westminster	16 835 b
† St. Margaret	Rectory		The Dean and Chapter of Westminster	22,387
* St Martin in the Fields	Vicarage	12 0 0	The Bishop of London	28,252
* St Mary le Strand	Rectory	13 8 4	The Crown	1784 c
St. Mary le Savoy	Perpetual Curacy		The Chancellor of the Duchy of Lancaster	
* St Paul, Covent Garden	Rectory		The Duke of Bedford	5834

a The entire parish of St. Clement Danes, containing 14,763 inhabitants, extends into the Holborn division of the hundred of Ossulstone, and includes Clement's Inn and New Inn.

b The Milbank Penitentiary in which were seven hundred and thirteen persons is included in the parish of St John

c The entire parish of St. Mary le Strand, containing 2273 inhabitants, includes the precinct of the duchy of Lancaster, in the Holborn division of the hundred of Ossulstone

BOROUGH OF SOUTHWARK

The following parishes are within the jurisdiction of the Consistory Court of the Commissary of the Bishop of Winchester, as regards granting letters of administration, and within that of the Archdeacon of Surrey for granting probates of wills.

PARISHES	LIVINGS.	Value in th King's Books. £ s. d.	PATRONS.	Population
Christchurch	Rectory		The Trustees of Mr Marshall's Charities	13,339 a
St George the Martyr	Rectory	18 13 9	The Crown	36,368 b
St. John, Horsleydown	Rectory		The Crown	9163
St Olave	Rectory	68 4 9½	The Crown	8420 c
St. Saviour	Perpetual Curacy		The Parishioners	16,808
St. Thomas	Donative		The Governors of St Thomas' Hospital	1807 d

a Christchurch was formerly a part of St. Saviour's parish, but the inhabitants have lost, through disuse, the right to vote at elections for the borough. The parish extends into the East division of the hundred of Brixton but the entire population is given above

b The population of the parish of St. George includes five hundred and fifteen persons in the King's Bench prison ninety-nine in the Marshalsea prison two hundred and forty-three in the Deaf and Dumb Asylum one hundred and eighty in the Philanthropic Reform, ninety-six in the School for the Indigent Blind, sixty-seven in the Freemasons' school, eighty three in the Magdalene Hospital, and two hundred and forty-seven in Bethlehem Hospital

c St Olave's parish extends into the city of London.   *d* The return from St. Thomas' parish includes the inmates of St. Thomas and Guy's Hospitals

There are likewise numerous extra parochial liberties, namely, in the City of London Without the Walls, Barnard's Inn, the population of which is returned with St Andrew, Holborn, Bridewell Hospital and Precinct, containing, according to the last census, 443 inhabitants, Clifford s Inn, 101, Furnival's Inn, 100, Gray s Inn, 208, Lincoln s Inn, 268, Serjeant s Inn, Chancery-lane, 31, Serjeant s Inn, Fleet-street, 94, Staple Inn, 41, White Friars Precinct, 1247, Inner Temple, 405, Middle Temple, 298 adjacent to the City of London, Old Artillery Ground Liberty, containing 1487 inhabitants, Charter house, 144, Ely-place, 268, Norton-Falgate Liberty, 1896, Rolls Liberty, 2737, Old Tower Without (Precinct), 205, East Smithfield Liberty, 6429 in the City and Liberty of Westminster, the Close of the Collegiate Church of St Peter, containing 181 inhabitants, and the Verge of the palaces of St James and Whitehall, 641

St Paul s Cathedral is the chief ecclesiastical edifice of London and of the empire, and the masterpiece of its architect, Sir Christopher Wren This magnificent structure stands on the highest and most central spot of ground in the city, nearly covering the site of the ancient cathedral built by Bishop Maurice, which was destroyed by the fire of 1666 It is the cathedral of the diocese of London, the deanery of which is now held with the see of Llandaff, together with a spacious house in Doctors Commons The commission for building a new cathedral is dated in 1673, the interval between the fire and that period having been employed in endeavouring to repair the old fabric, which was at length found impracticable The first stone of the present structure, which was built from the third design of the architect, was laid June 21st, 1675, the walls of the choir and side aisles were finished in ten years, together with the semicircular porticoes on the north and south sides, and the last stone was laid on the top of the lantern in 1710, in the lifetime of the architect, by his son Christopher This stupendous edifice, of which only a general description can here be attempted, is wholly constructed of the best Portland stone, in the form of a Latin cross, the extreme length of which is five hundred and fourteen feet, and its breadth two hundred and sixteen The interior consists of a nave, choir, side aisles, transept, side chapels, &c From the intersection of the cross rises a stately cupola, universally admired for its grandeur and elegant proportions, being two hundred and fifteen feet in altitude, and measuring one hundred and forty-five in diameter, and four hundred and thirty feet in circumference From the top of this springs a lantern, adorned with large Corinthian pillars, surrounded at its base by a gallery, and terminating at the top in a superb gilt ball and cross the height, from the floor of the church to the summit of the cross, is four hundred and four feet, and the circumference of the entire fabric is two thousand two hundred and ninety-two feet A dwarf stone wall, supporting a massy balustrade of cast-iron, surrounds the churchyard, separating it from a spacious carriage and foot way, on the west, south, and east sides, and from a wide foot pavement on the north The principal architectural features of the exterior are two grand semicircular porticoes at the north and south ends of the transept, the magnificent western entrance, with its campanile turrets, and the cupola, or dome

The northern and southern porticoes consist each of a semi-cupola, supported by six fluted Corinthian columns, of four feet diameter, with semicircular flights of black marble steps The great western entrance is composed of a double story of twelve lofty Corinthian columns below, and eight of the Composite order above, supporting a grand enriched pediment crowned with a colossal figure of St Paul, and other statues the whole stands upon an elevated base, the ascent to which is by a flight of twenty-two square black marble steps, running the entire length of the portico The enriched pediment represents the Conversion of St Paul At the extremities of this western elevation are elegant campaniles, or steeples of two stories, of light pierced workmanship, terminating in domes formed by curves of contrary flexure, like bells, and ornamented at the top with gilt pine-apples At the eastern extremity is a circular projection, forming within a recess for the communion table The walls are of rustic work, and strengthened and ornamented by two ranges of coupled pilasters, one above the other, the lower being Corinthian, and the upper Composite Both the northern and southern sides have an air of uncommon elegance, having also richly-decorated windows and niches, scrolls, fruitage, and other suitable enrichments The cupola, which is the most distinguishing feature of the pile, towers in majestic proportion above the rest of the structure it is ornamented with thirty-two columns below, and a range of attic antæ above, the exterior circuit of which is flanked by a noble balustrade The interior is of correspondent beauty, being, like the exterior, constructed in the purest style of classical architecture It has lately been improved by the introduction of monuments and statues of British heroes, and other illustrious dead, which, being composed of the finest marbles, and generally of good design, add greatly to the rich appearance of this part of the cathedral. The interior of the grand cupola was painted by Sir James Thornhill, the designs being illustrative of some of the most remarkable occurrences in the life of St Paul The entire pavement, up to the altar, is of marble, chiefly consisting of square slabs, alternately black and white the floor round the communion table is of the same kinds of marble, mingled with porphyry The communion table is ornamented with four noble fluted pilasters, painted and veined with gold, in imitation of *lapis lazuli* The organ gallery is supported by eight Corinthian columns of blue and white marble, of exquisite beauty The stalls in the choir are beautifully carved by the celebrated Gibbons, and the other ornaments are of equal workmanship There is a chapel, where divine service is performed every day, Sundays excepted, and opposite is the consistory, each of them having a magnificent screen of carved wainscot of the Corinthian order In the crypt beneath the church, and immediately under the centre of the great dome, is the tomb of Admiral Lord Nelson. The building was erected at the national expense, and cost a million and a half of money The iron balustrade surrounding the churchyard, which, with its seven iron gates, weighs two hundred tons, cost £11,202 0 6 The extent of the ground plot occupied by the edifice is two acres and sixteen perches in the area of the west front is placed a statue of Queen Anne

The parochial churches may, for the most part, be

divided into two classes,—those built by Sir Christopher Wren, or his pupils, since the great fire, and those which escaped that calamity Of the former, the following most deserve notice St Mary s-le-Bow, in Cheapside, and St Bride s, in Fleet-street, are allowed to possess the most elegant steeples of any in London The first is a most successful endeavour to perpetuate the origin of its additional name of De Arcubus, or Le Bow, which arose, not only from the body being erected on *arches*, or a Norman crypt (which still remains), but from having a steeple, or lantern, resting on bows This singularity is retained in the present structure, the spire of which is partly supported by flying buttresses, Corinthian columns, and an elegant circular gallery, terminating in a lofty spire, the whole being a masterly display of the five orders The steeple of St Bride s is of a totally different form, but equally beautiful it consists of a series of elegant stories, diminishing in exact proportion as they ascend, and which, with the spire, originally reached the altitude of two hundred and thirty-four feet, but it was obliged lately to be reduced, on account of its having been damaged by lightning Other churches which are remarkable for fine or lofty steeples are St Antholin s Watling-street, St Dunstan s in the East, St Magnus, London-bridge, Christ Church, Newgate street and St Vedast s, Foster-lane St Stephen s, Walbrook, deserves the next mention to St Paul s, on account of the unrivalled beauty of its interior It was erected in place of the old church built in 1420, and burnt down in the great fire The plan of this structure is original, yet simple, the elevation surprising, yet chaste and beautiful It is a small church, in the form of a cross, being eighty seven feet ten inches in length and sixty four feet ten inches in breadth The dome, springing from the intersection, is supported by eight arches, rising from as many Corinthian columns, so disposed as to give the whole an effect of great lightness and spaciousness Over the altar is a fine painting, by West, of the Stoning of St Stephen

The above-named churches are amongst the finest of the fifty built by Sir Christopher Wren after the conflagration of 1666 The following claim notice either from their architectural character, or historical interest St Michael s, Wood street This church is of the Ionic order, and was erected in 1669 The original tower has of late years been replaced by a clumsy spire So early as the year ₋359, the church was liberally endowed, and Stow asserts that the head of James IV of Scotland was buried here, after the battle of Flodden Field St Mary s, Aldermanbury, having a large western tower with angular pinnacles, occupies the site of an old church refounded by Alderman Keeble, in the fifteenth century Judge Jeffreys was buried in this church St Mary s at Hill, Lower Thames-street, was only partially destroyed by the great fire This church is remarkable for containing some old and curious records, extracts from which have been published it has a plain square brick tower St Vedast s, Foster-lane, besides its stone spire before-mentioned, which is very handsome and of exact symmetry, possesses an altar-piece of singular elegance The railing before it is peculiarly rich, and the border that surrounds the *nimbus*, or glory, is composed for the most part of three cherubim, half immersed in clouds, and six winged infants,

in the highest possible relief, one sounding two trumpets, and the others bearing palm branches, the carving being either from the chisel of Gibbons, or some successful rival of that great artist St Sepulchre s, Snow hill, is a spacious stone structure, modernized from the remains of the former church built in 1440, and which escaped the great fire It has a fine groined porch, or entrance, and a lofty square tower with tall angular pinnacles, which, together with the interior, show that it must, before its modernization, have been a noble edifice of English architecture St Mary s Woolnoth, Lombard-street, is a fine specimen of the Tuscan order, erected by Nicholas Hawksmoor, a pupil of Sir Christopher Wren The whole exterior is of stone, the northern elevation being decorated with large semicircular rusticated arches, and the western end having a double tower with composite columns, a balustrade, and other ornaments The interior is a fine specimen of the most exquisite proportion, as well as of chaste decoration St Michael s, Cornhill, has a beautiful tower, which renders it one of the most conspicuous ornaments of the city It is surmounted by four fine fluted turrets, and is admirably light and elegant, and the various orders of architecture are harmoniously combined There is a monument to the memory of Fabian, the Chronicler, who was an alderman of London St Lawrence s, Jewry, was rebuilt in 1677 It is a neat edifice the interior has lately been rendered very elegant, and contains a monument of Archbishop Tillotson St Peter s, Cornhill, according to an inscribed brass plate in it, was the first Christian church erected in Britain, being said to have been built by King Lucius, so early as the year 79 The present structure is plain but neat it has a steeple of red brick, with a lofty spire terminating in a large key, the emblem of the patron saint St Bene t s, Paul s Wharf, was built in 1181, and rebuilt in 1682 Inigo Jones is said to have been buried in this church, but there is no record of the circumstance St Swithin s, Cannon-street, a small but elegant church, with a tower and spire, was built in 1680, on the site of one of very ancient foundation This church attracts notice from the famous " London stone being placed in front of it Christ Church, Newgate-street, is a spacious and elegant stone church, having a lofty tower, and is much frequented on account of the singing by the scholars of Christ s hospital, who attend divine service in it, and whose combined voices, from their great number, produce an extraordinary effect Previously to the dissolution of monasteries, this was the site of the Grey friars church which was three hundred feet long, and decorated with noble monuments the portion here edified was the choir of the ancient structure St Alban s, Wood-street, is a handsome stone edifice, with a lofty turretted tower, the interior being in good proportion, and containing a richly-ornamented altar-piece, and a pulpit finely carved The Saxon king, Athelstan, is said to have had a palace adjoining this church, and his name, somewhat corrupted and abridged, is thought to be preserved in Addle-street, formerly called King Adel-street, running by the side of it St Margaret s Pattens, Rood-lane, was rebuilt in 1667 The carving of the altar-piece is by the celebrated Grinlin Gibbons St Michael s, Crooked-lane, rebuilt in 1688 Sir William Walworth, who killed the rebel Wat Tyler, was buried in this ancient church, where he founded a college of Priests St *Michael s, College-hill*, is celebrated as the burial-place of the famous lord mayor, Richard Whittington, who here founded a college The ceiling, which is finely coved, is said to be the largest church ceiling in London unsupported by a single column The tower is surmounted by a singularly beautiful turret, decorated with Corinthian columns the altar-piece has carving by Grinlin Gibbons

Some of the city churches which escaped the great fire are of very considerable architectural merit, and most of them contain a number of curious and interesting monuments, they are as follows —

St *Andrew s Undershaft, Leadenhall street*, obtained its adjunct from a May-pole, or shaft, having formerly been set up every year on the first of May, which was higher than the church steeple The style of architecture is the later English, having been rebuilt in 1522, at the expense of William Fitz-William, the founder of the noble house of Wentworth The interior is decorated with great taste, the ceiling is adorned with angels, and the compartments over the pillar which support it painted in imitation of basso relievo The eastern window is richly ornamented with stained glass, in five compartments, representing the sovereigns Edward VI, Queen Elizabeth, James I, Charles I, and Charles II The pulpit is a fine specimen of carving The most remarkable monument is that of John Stowe, the London historian, who is represented sitting at study *St Helen s, Bishopsgate-street* Dr Stukeley affirms that this church is built on the site of one which existed in the time of the Roman dominion in Britain, and was dedicated to the Empress Helena The present fabric was the conventual church of an adjoining priory of Benedictine nuns, part of which was appropriated to the use of the parishioners It is chiefly remarkable for a number of ancient and curious monuments. St *James', Duke s Place*, was built in the reign of James I, on the site of the priory of the Holy Trinity, at Aldgate, from the materials of the conventual buildings St *Bartholomew s the Less*, and St *Bartholomew s the Great*, were both conventual churches, and are situated near Smithfield The former, which belonged to the hospital of St. Bartholomew, has been altered and modernized so much, that it retains no ancient feature worthy of description St Bartholomew's the Great is a fine specimen, and the only one remaining in London, of the massive Norman architecture, the nave being supported by ponderous low round columns the present church is only the choir of that of the priory Both churches were founded by Rayhere, said to have been minstrel, or jester, to Henry I, who has a tomb, with his effigy, in the structure last mentioned. St *Giles, Cripplegate*, was erected in 1546, on the site of the ancient church, built by Alfune, the first master of St Bartholomew s hospital, in 1090, and burnt down in the year 1545 it is a light well-proportioned structure Speed the historian, and Fox the martyrologist, were buried here Oliver Cromwell, afterwards Protector, was married in this church

The ecclesiastical structures without the city exhibit as great a variety in their age and construction as those within its limits. They may be divided into three classes, the churches of ancient erection, those erected in the reign of Queen Anne and her successors,

and the newly-built churches of His late Majesty s reign

The churches of the first class are, *in the City and Liberties of Westminster*, the abbey church of St Peter, St Margaret's, St John s the Baptist, in the Savoy, and the Temple church *In Southwark* St Saviour s church, and in *other parts of the town and suburbs*, St Pancras and Stepney churches, to which, as next in age, though different in style, may be added St James, Westminster, and St Anne s, Soho The principal churches built in the reign of Anne and her successors, George I, George II, and George III, are, St Martin s, St George s, Hanover-square, St Giles in the Fields, St George s, Bloomsbury, St Mary s le Strand, St Clement Dane s, St Paul s, Covent Garden, and St John s the Evangelist, Milbank, all situated in Westminster, or its Liberties, St Olave s, St George s, St Thomas, St Mary s, and Bermondsey and Christ churches, situated in Southwark, and on the northern and eastern sides of the metropolis, the churches of Bishopsgate, Spitalfields, Shoreditch, Old-street, St James, and St John Clerkenwell, Aldgate, Whitechapel, Bethnal Green, Limehouse, St George in the East, Shadwell, and Wapping The more modern churches, scattered through various parts of the metropolis and its suburbs, will be noticed hereafter

London contains no churches of the Anglo-Saxon period, excepting small portions of Westminster abbey church, concealed from view in consequence of their subterranean situation Of the Anglo Norman style, St Bartholomew s the Great, and the chapel at the White Tower, two of the finest specimens in the city, have been noticed Those religious edifices in the Anglo-Norman style, and of later English architecture, most deserving of notice in Westminster, Southwark, and the suburbs, are the following —

WESTMINSTER ABBEY, or, more properly, the collegiate church of St Peter at Westminster, is ascribed to Sebert, King of the East Saxons The neighbourhood by degrees became peopled, partly from this circumstance, and partly from the erection of a palace near it, which induced the chief nobility to erect town houses in its vicinity Edward the Confessor rebuilt the church in 1065, and by Pope Nicholas II it was appointed the place of inauguration for the kings of England On the general suppression of religious houses, Henry VIII, converted the Benedictine abbey attached to this church into a college of Secular canons, under the government of a dean, and afterwards appointed a bishop, making it the head of a diocese, comprising the entire county of Middlesex, except Fulham, which was retained by the Bishop of London, but this establishment was, a few years afterwards, dissolved by Edward VI, who restored the college, which was again changed by Queen Mary into an abbey Elizabeth put an end to that institution in 1560, and founded the present establishment, which is a college, consisting of a dean and twelve Secular canons, or prebendaries, to which she attached a school for forty scholars, called the Queen s Scholars, to be educated in the liberal sciences, preparatory to their removal to the University Private scholars are also admitted, and some of the most illustrious characters in the kingdom have received their education here To this establishment belong choristers, singing men, an organist, and twelve almsmen. It is imagined that a school was annexed to the abbey so long ago as the time of Edward the Confessor The present church was built by Henry III and his successors, and completed by the last abbot, with the exception of the two towers at the western entrance, which are the work of Sir Christopher Wren, and the northern doorway, called " the beautiful gate," which was erected at the expense of the unfortunate Bishop Atterbury Its length is three hundred and sixty feet, the breadth of the nave seventy-two feet, and the length of the transept one hundred and ninety-five feet. Some late improvements have exposed this venerable structure to the view, by pulling down the houses on its northern side, and forming a square before it, neatly planted with low shrubs On entering the western door, the whole body of the church presents itself at one view, terminated at the further end by the fine painted window over the portico of Henry the Seventh s chapel, and is highly impressive from its loftiness, lightness, and symmetry The nave is separated from the choir by a screen , the choir, in the form of a semi-octagon, was formerly surrounded by eight chapels, but there are now only seven, that which was then the central chapel at present forming the porch of that of Henry VII The roofs of the nave and transept are supported by two rows of arches, one above the other, resting on beautiful lofty clustered columns of Purbeck marble Corresponding with the central range of pillars are demi-pillars in the side walls, which, as they rise, spring into semi-arches, and meet others opposite in acute angles , by which means the roof is thrown into a variety of segments of arches, decorated with ornamental carvings The side aisles receive light from a middle range of windows, which, with the four large ones at the ends of the nave and the transept, give light to the whole of the main building The great western window is splendidly painted, representing figures of the patriarchs Moses and Aaron, the arms of Edward the Confessor, those of Westminster, and other devices The choir, one of the most beautiful in Europe, is terminated towards the east by the ancient high altar, beyond which, at a small distance, is seen the magnificent shrine of Edward the Confessor, rising from the centre of the chapel which bears his name The pavement before the altar-table is a splendid specimen of ancient Mosaic work, and one side of the enclosure is formed by the venerable tombs and effigies of Aymer de Valence, Ed ward Crouchback, the monuments of King Sebert, Anne of Cleves, &c The choir is enclosed on the northern and southern sides by handsome stalls, the floor being paved with black and white marble, and the roof ornamented with white tiles, divided into compartments, which are bordered with gilt carved work The ceremony of the coronation of the kings and queens of England is performed in this part of the abbey The best executed monuments are the productions of Roubilliac, Rysbrach, Flaxman, Westmacott, and Bacon In the southern extremity of the transept are monuments to the memory of many of the most eminent British poets, whence this spot has received the name of Poets Corner , and here are to be found, amongst others, the names and memorials of Chaucer, Spencer, Shakspeare, Ben Johnson, Milton, Dryden, Butler, Thomson, Gay, Goldsmith, Addison, Samuel Johnson, &c , together with the tombs of Handel and Garrick In the southern aisle the most remarkable monuments are those of Dr Watts, W

Hargrave, Esq , and Captain James Cornwall At the western end of the abbey are those of Sir Godfrey Kneller, Dr Mead, Sir Charles Wager, the Earl of Chatham, &c On the northern side of the entrance into the choir is the monument of Sir Isaac Newton, and near it is that of Earl Stanhope Near the great gates, and opposite the tomb of the Earl of Chatham, lie the remains, about twelve feet from each other, of the two great political rivals, Charles James Fox, and William Pitt , the monument of the latter is over the western entrance. Lord Mansfield's monument is erected under one of the lofty arches at the northern end of the transept

Around the choir are eight chapels, dedicated respectively to St Benedict, St Nicholas, St Paul, St Erasmus, St John the Baptist, St John the Evangelist, St Michael, and St Andrew, and in them is a variety of tombs, erected to the memory of distinguished persons the three last-named chapels have been converted into a single one Besides these are two other chapels deserving particular mention, viz , the chapel of Edward the Confessor, and Henry the Seventh s chapel

Edward the Confessor's Chapel stands immediately behind the altar of the church, upon an elevated floor, leading to which there is a flight of steps It is remarkable for containing the shrine of its patron saint, King Edward the Confessor, and the tombs of several of the ancient English monarchs, from which circumstance it has been denominated "the Chapel of the Kings The saint s shrine, erected pursuant to the orders of Henry III , by Peter Cavalini, stands in the centre, and was curiously ornamented with Mosaic work of coloured stones, with gilding and other ornaments, but only some fragments now remain Of the regal monuments around, that of Henry III is distinguished by large panels of polished porphyry, enclosed with Mosaic work of scarlet and gold, and that monarch s effigy of brass gilt, the size of life The remains of Edward I are contained in a plain coffin of grey marble The tomb of Edward III has his statue of brass gilt, and is surrounded by statues of his children, and others There is a tomb erected to the memory of Richard II and his queen, Anne of Bohemia, with their effigies Editha, consort of the Confessor , Eleanor, the affectionate wife of Edward I , the heroic Philippa, consort of Edward III , have tombs with their effigies, the former of brass gilt, and the latter of alabaster The tomb of Henry V is enclosed in a beautiful chantry chapel The coronation chairs, and the stone brought from Scone by Edward I , the sword and shield of King Edward III , the saddle and helmet used by Henry V at the battle of Agincourt , and various models of churches, by Sir Christopher Wren, are shewn among the curiosities here Along the frieze of the screen of this chapel are fourteen legendary sculptures, relating to the history of Edward the Confessor, which were executed in the reign of Henry III , and which are well worthy the attention of the antiquary

Henry the Seventh s Chapel, universally admitted to be one of the richest specimens of later English architecture in the kingdom, adjoins the eastern extremity of the abbey It was erected as a mausoleum for himself and his family by the king whose name it bears, on the site of a smaller chapel, dedicated, like the present, to the Virgin Mary, and cost £14,000, a sum estimated to have been equal to a quarter of a million of our present currency The exterior of this edifice is remarkable for richness and variety, which are greatly increased by fourteen buttresses, with crocketed turrets, projecting from the several angles of the building, and are beautifully ornamented with canopies, niches, and other decorations these buttresses add strength as well as beauty to the edifice, being connected with the upper part of the walls of the nave by pointed arches The interior, lighted by a double range of windows of magnificent dimensions and elegant workmanship, consists of a nave and two small aisles, and is entered by a flight of black marble steps, under a noble arch, that leads to a pair of large wrought brazen gates, thickly plated with gold, each panel being adorned with a rose and portcullis, alternately The nave is ninety-nine feet long, sixty-six broad, and fifty-four high, and terminates at the eastern end in a curve, having five deep recesses, entered by open arches The lofty stone ceiling, with its innumerable ornaments, excites the highest admiration Numerous oratories, canopies, and other embellishments, adorn the sides and ends of this chapel In the centre stands the altar-tomb of Henry VII, executed by Torregiano, in basaltic stone, ornamented with the royal effigy, and surrounded by a magnificent screen of the same material, the whole of which is said to have cost £10,000 Queen Mary, Queen Elizabeth, Mary Queen of Scots, Margaret of Richmond, several of the Brunswick family, and numerous other royal and distinguished persons, have been interred within the walls of this celebrated chapel

St Margaret's church, an elegant specimen of the architecture of the period of Edward IV, stands near the northern entrance of the abbey, and is remarkable for its beautiful eastern window of painted glass, representing the Crucifixion, which was presented by the magistrates of Dort, in Holland, to Henry VII, and intended for his chapel, then erecting, but he dying before it was finished, after passing through the hands of various owners, it was at last purchased for its present situation for the sum of £420 A board in this church is inscribed to the memory of the great Sir Walter Raleigh, who was beheaded in 1618, in Palace-yard adjoining The members of the House of Commons attend divine service in this church on particular occasions The Temple Church, dedicated to St Mary, deserves especial notice for its antiquity and peculiar architecture It is supposed to have been first erected in the year 1185, and to have been afterwards partially or wholly, rebuilt by the Knights Templars, in the year 1244 The form of the most ancient portion of the edifice is a peristyle, having six massive pillars, with fillets on the shafts, and Norman capitals This portion, which forms the vestibule of the present church, contains the tombs of eleven Knights Templars The main body of the edifice is of more modern English architecture, consisting of a nave, with two aisles, and a transept, divided by elegant clustered columns, supporting a fine arched roof Selden, Plowden, Lord Thurlow, and the eminent physician, Dr Mead, lie interred in this church The Norman arch, forming the entrance to the church, is much admired for the richness of its mouldings St John's the Baptist, now almost the only remnant of the ancient palace of the Savoy,

in the Strand, (which was built in 1245, and converted into an hospital in 1509, when the present church appears to have been erected), has a beautiful roof, divided into panels, on which numerous religious and heraldic devices are carved, and contains several ancient monuments of the Willoughby, Howard, and Compton families it was very tastefully repaired in 1820 St Saviour's, Southwark, formerly collegiate, is the most spacious parochial church in the metropolis, and one of the finest specimens of ancient architecture It has a nave and aisles, with a choir and transept, Lady chapel, &c Part of it appears to be of the period of Henry II, or III, and the remainder of that of Henry IV, in whose reign it was partly rebuilt Twenty-six pillars, in two rows, support the roof of this interesting edifice, and the chancel, and galleries in the walls of the choir, are adorned with arches, in a similar manner to Westminster abbey The tower, which is supported on four very strong pillars, is one hundred and fifty feet high, to the top of the large angular pinnacles, and contains a ring of twelve fine-toned bells During the progress of considerable embellishment and repairs, in the month of July, 1830, the remains of Dr Lancelot Andrews, Bishop of Winchester, who died Sept 21st, 1626, were discovered, in a state of great preservation, in a leaden coffin, walled up with brick, within his monument in Bishops chapel, a subterraneous passage leading from the church was also exposed to view soon afterwards Gower, one of the ancient English poets, has a small monument in this church, and several other eminent men lie interred here The churchwardens of St Saviour's, with others of the parish officers, form a corporate body, by charter of Henry VIII, granted at the dissolution of the college, or priory of Augustine canons here, when the inhabitants purchased the conventual church, and made it parochial St James', and St Anne's, Soho, are only remarkable, the former for containing a beautiful marble font, sculptured by Grinlin Gibbons, and the latter for being the burial-place of Theodore, King of Corsica, who lies in the churchyard, beneath a gravestone inscribed with some affecting lines from the pen of the late Lord Orford

Although Sir Christopher Wren was the architect principally employed in rebuilding the churches after the great fire of London, yet the erection of a few in different parts of the metropolis was confided to his contemporaries There were also several good churches built in the succeeding reigns, by other architects, and the following, as the most interesting of these, are entitled to a brief notice

St Martin's in the Fields has been invariably admired for its portico, which is the finest of any church in London, and the entire edifice is entitled to a comparison with the best works of Sir Christopher Wren It was erected between the years 1721 and 1726, from a design by James Gibbs, and unites the light and picturesque beauty of the modern temple with the sober grandeur and solidity of Grecian architecture The opening so long desired, for obtaining a proper view of this fine portico, has lately been made St George's, Hanover-square, is also remarkable for a very fine portico of the Corinthian order, consisting of six columns, with an entablature and pediment the steeple is an excellent piece of architecture Over the altar-piece is a tolerably good painting of the Last

Supper, attributed to Sir James Thornhill St Mary s-
le-Strand, though sometimes censured for its affected
display of the five orders of architecture, and otherwise
too lavish ornament, is a handsome edifice, erected by
Gibbs in 1717, just after his return from Italy The
western entrance is by a flight of semicircular steps,
which leads to a similarly-shaped portico of the Ionic
order, surmounted by a dome Two ranges of columns,
the lower Ionic, the upper Corinthian, run round the
body of the church, with pilasters of the same orders
at the corners, and in the intercolumniations are, in the
lower range, niches, and in the upper, windows, both
tastefully ornamented St Clement s Danes has a fine
lofty steeple by Gibbs, but the body of the church is said
to have been designed by Sir Christopher Wren It is
built of stone, with two tiers of windows, the lower
plain, the upper ornamented The western entrance
consists of a portico on each side of the steeple, having
domes supported by Ionic columns St Paul s, Covent
Garden, was originally erected by Inigo Jones, at the
expense of the Earl of Bedford On the 17th of September, 1795, this church was burnt down, but it was
rebuilt in imitation of the original edifice It has a
noble massive portico of the Tuscan order, and the
interior is of great neatness and simplicity Butler, the
author of Hudibras, and Dr Walcot, better known under
the assumed name of Peter Pindar, lie buried in the
churchyard St Giles in the Fields, erected from a design
by Mr Henry Flightcroft, is constructed entirely of
stone, in a simple yet elegant style, having a lofty handsome steeple, and was finished in 1734, at an expense of
£10,000 The entrance gateway has a fine sculptured
entablature, representing the Day of Judgment St
George s, Bloomsbury, was erected by Mr Nicholas
Hawksmoor, and finished in 1731 It is a singular,
and not very harmonious, compound of the Tuscan and
Corinthian orders, constructed entirely of stone, with
a good portico in front, and a pyramidical steeple,
grotesquely ornamented St John s the Evangelist, Milbank This church, designed by Sir John Vanbrugh,
is remarkable for having four steeples, one at each
corner, which give it rather a whimsical appearance ,
several of its details are, however, beautiful
The churches erected since the commencement of
the present century are numerous, and some of them
eminent specimens of architectural display, particularly
St Pancras , Marylebone, All Souls , Langham place ,
St Luke s, Chelsea, &c There are in various parts of
the metropolis, about four hundred and fifty places of
worship, of which nearly two hundred belong to the
establishment there are forty-seven for Baptists, six
for the Society of Friends, upwards of one hundred for
Independents, thirty-two for Wesleyan Methodists, four
for Swedenborgians, six for Unitarians, four for Welch
Calvinists, and numerous others for different classes of
Protestant dissenters There are also nine chapels in
connexion with the church of Scotland, fourteen Roman
Catholic chapels, seven synagogues, and eighteen Foreign
Protestant churches and chapels

COLLEGES, SCHOOLS, AND ESTABLISHMENTS FOR
INSTRUCTION AND STUDY OF VARIOUS KINDS

London contains two colleges, forty-five free schools
with perpetual endowments, seventeen schools for poor
and deserted children, and upwards of two hundred

parochial schools, in which the children are both clothed
and educated there are also numerous National and
Lancasterian schools, upwards of five hundred Sunday
schools, and about four thousand private schools in and
near the metropolis
King s College was so named from its having been
founded under the immediate patronage of his late Majesty, George IV , who presented the proprietors with
the site, on the condition that the college should be
completed in conformity to the design of Somerset
House Considerable progress has been made towards
the erection of the buildings, which, when finished, will
form the eastern wing of that noble pile, of which it
has hitherto been deficient, and will, by corresponding
with the other parts of the building, render it complete
The estimated expense, as given by the architect, Mr
Smirke, is £140,000, exclusively of £17,000 for the
purchase and removal of houses next the Strand, to
make room for the principal front, and £10,000 for furniture , making, with other additional items, £170,000,
besides the cost of furnishing the library and museum
The design of the institution is to afford to the youth
of the metropolis a course of instruction similar to
that pursued at the Universities of Oxford and Cambridge The principal, with a competent number of
professors, will be appointed by a council, consisting of
the Archbishops of Canterbury and York, the Lord
Chancellor, Lord Chief Justice of the Court of King s
Bench, Secretary of State for the Home Department,
Speaker of the House of Commons, Deans of St Paul
and Westminster, and the Lord Mayor by this body
all the fundamental regulations, respecting the discipline and course of education are to be approved The
Archbishop of Canterbury is appointed perpetual visitor
The funds for the erection and support of the institution
have been raised by donations, and by shares of £100
each, the dividends on which are not to exceed four
per cent , the surplus to be applied exclusively to
the benefit of the college
The London University was established with a view to
afford a liberal education principally to students who are
excluded from Oxford and Cambridge by the statutes of
religious conformity the students are not admitted
until they are able to perform certain exercises, and
are divided into three classes, according to the different
departments of literature in which they are engaged
The institution is governed by a council of twenty-four,
six of whom are chosen annually , these appoint a
warden and professors, each of whom receives a fixed
stipend, until the fees paid by the students constitute a
sufficient support, and are entitled to superannuated
allowances the University year excludes only the
months of August, September, and October The funds
of the institution are to be not less than £150,000, nor
more than £300,000 each proprietor has the right of
appointing one pupil, and receives four per cent on every
£100 share The building, the first stone of which was
laid on the 30th of April, 1827, by his Royal Highness
the Duke of Sussex, the contract for its completion being
£107,000, occupies, with its appendages, seven acres of
ground, near the New road, purchased for £90,000
that portion already built is entirely constructed of stone,
and the whole will, when completed, consist of a central portico of ten Corinthian columns, with enriched entablature and pediment, and two wings projecting at

right angles, with tetrastyle porticoes to correspond over the whole, springing from the vestibule, is an elevated dome, surmounted by a Grecian temple of eight pillars, and there are smaller corresponding domes to the wings two other wings of equal length extend from the back of the central part, and there are other connecting buildings the theatres, lecture rooms, and apartments of the interior, are all of elegant architecture, and commodiously adapted to their respective purposes

Westminster School, founded, in 1560, by Queen Elizabeth, for forty scholars, who receive an education preparatory for the University, besides whom are educated, as private scholars, many of the sons of the nobility and gentry the school is situated within the precincts of Westminster Abbey Eight boys are elected annually on the foundation and four more, called "Bishop's boys," who wear gowns of a different colour from those of the "King's scholars, are appointed by the Dean, on the establishment by Dr Williams, Bishop of Lincoln, in 1628, who directed an annual pecuniary allowance to be made to each, which is withheld until the boys are entered at St John's College, Cambridge, when the Dean and Chapter add so much as will make up £20 a year for four years The bishop also endowed four scholarships in the same college, for boys of this school, preference being given to those on his own foundation, each of the value of £20 per annum, for four years The other University advantages are, eight studentships and scholarships at Corpus Christi and Trinity Colleges, Cambridge, the former of the value of from £50 to £60 per annum, the latter £25, three scholarships at St John's College, Cambridge, founded by Sir Robert Wood, Knt, in 1659, a second nomination to three more at Corpus Christi College, of the annual value of £20 each, founded by Archbishop Parker, in 1569, and a rent charge of £90, assigned by Dr Triplett, in 1668, towards the support of four boys from this school at the University

The *Charter-house*, which comprises an hospital as well as a school, is so named from the word *Chartreuse*, the site having been occupied by a convent of Carthusian monks It was built and endowed, in the reign of James I, by Mr Thomas Sutton, a merchant of great opulence and liberality the purchase and completion of the buildings cost upwards of £20,000 The establishment of this noble seminary consists of a master, a preacher, two schoolmasters, and forty poor scholars, who are supported free of every expense The boys, presented by the Governors in rotation, are instructed in classical learning, and wear an academical dress, resembling that worn by the scholars of Eton and Westminster The hospital is for eighty decayed gentlemen, who have been merchants, or military officers, each of whom is allowed £14 a year, besides a gown, provisions, fuel, and two handsome apartments they dine in a common hall, and attend prayers daily in the chapel The buildings occupy the whole site of the ancient monastery, which, with its gardens and grounds, was of great extent, and several portions of the ancient monastic edifice, still remaining, present a very antique and venerable appearance From the revenue of the institution, twenty-nine exhibitioners, at either of the Universities, are allowed £80 per annum for the first four years, and, if they graduate re-

gularly, £100 per annum for the next four years It has also ten exhibitions at Christ Church, Pembroke, Worcester, and University, Colleges, Oxford, founded by Dame Elizabeth Holford, in 1720, its governors have the patronage of nine ecclesiastical benefices

St Paul's School, at the east end of St Paul's churchyard, was founded in 1509, by the celebrated Dr Colet, Dean of St Paul's, for the free education of one hundred and fifty-three boys, by a master, an usher, and a chaplain, under the direction of the Mercers Company, who are perpetual trustees, and on the appointment of the master of the company, as senior surveyor of the school The revenue of the school is upwards of £5000 in addition to which the Company are in the receipt of £1000 annually, on an average, arising from £18,834 15 three per cent reduced annuities, and the produce of tithes in the county of Northumberland, bequeathed by Viscount Campden, about 1685, for the endowment of exhibitions at Trinity College, Cambridge, in behalf of this school, for which nine exhibitioners are allowed £100 per annum each for five years There are also, an unlimited number of exhibitions, of the value of £50 a year each, tenable for seven years, at either University, one, of £30 a year, at Corpus Christi College, Cambridge, founded by John Stock, Esq, in 1781, tenable for seven years, five at Trinity College, Cambridge, of £10 per annum each, founded by Mr Perry, four scholarships at Corpus Christi College, founded, in 1766, by George Sykes, Esq and two exhibitions of £10 per annum each, jointly with the free grammar school at Dorchester, at St John's College, Cambridge, founded by Dr Gower, for clergymen's sons the school has also an interest in Sir Robert Wood's scholarships, in default of candidates from the schools at Canterbury and Westminster The school apartments were rebuilt in 1824, entirely of stone, in an elegant style, and with several enlargements, particularly a fine arcade for the recreation of the boys

Merchant Taylors School, founded in 1561, by Sir Thomas White, and liberally endowed by him and other members of the company, is conducted by a principal, and three under-masters, who teach the classics, and two writing-masters, recently appointed, for whom a room has been lately constructed out of some smaller apartments, previously occupied by the junior masters the number of boys is limited to two hundred and fifty, who are presented by the members of the court, each member exercising the privilege in rotation on admission the boys pay £5 2 each, and £2 2 per quarter, with some other trifling charges one half of the admission fees is set apart for founding exhibitions at the Universities It has thirty seven fellowships at St John's College, Oxford, six scholarships at Pembroke College, Cambridge, of the value of £40 a year each, tenable for seven years, founded by the Rev C Parkyn, six civil law fellowships of £50 per annum each, at St John's College, Oxford, two exhibitions, of £50 per annum each, one at St John's College, Oxford, and the other at Pembroke College, Cambridge, founded by Dr Stuart five Divinity scholarships, of £4 8 each, founded by Walter Fish, four of £4 per annum each, founded by John Vernon, in 1615, and one scholarship of £4 per annum, founded by John Wooller, all at St John's College, Oxford, and an exhibition, of uncertain value, to

X o

either University, arising from the amount of donations by individuals educated at this school there are also a by-fellowship and two scholarships at Catherine Hall, Cambridge, founded by Thomas Holwey, for boys from Eton, or Merchant Taylor's school, and it has an interest in Sir Robert Wood's scholarships, in default of boys from Canterbury and Westminster schools By a recent arrangement the boys in the two upper forms are taught mathematics no boy can derive any advantage from the foundation if he enters higher than the third form The buildings of the establishment, situated on the east side of Suffolk-lane, Cannon-street, consist of the school, apartments for the usher, a house for the head master, a library, and a chapel

Christ's Hospital, Newgate-street, founded by Edward VI , in 1552, on the site of a dissolved monastery of Grey friars, is the noble and celebrated establishment commonly denominated the Blue-coat school, from the costume of the children supported and educated there This institution, famed for its antiquity, extent, and high character, occupies the site of the Grey friars monastery, the buildings of which, having gone to decay, have just been magnificently re-edified in the original style. Upon this foundation there are generally from one thousand to fourteen hundred boys, who are clothed, boarded, and educated The lord mayor and corporation of London are governors and directors, *ex officio*, and there are other governors, amounting in all to about three hundred and fifty, who must be donors of £400 and upwards The New Hall, from a design by Mr John Shawe, is one of the grandest and most imposing modern attempts at later English architecture It stands on the site of the little cloisters of the monastery, measuring more than one hundred and eighty feet in length, and of proportionate height and width The structure is of stone, and the style, agreeing with the date of the charity, has been copied from the hall of Hampton Court palace, from which noble model, however, it differs in many respects, but yet in strict accordance with the style adopted. The staircases, and a fine cloister beneath, correspond, and concur, with the interior of the hall itself, to render this one of the most magnificent banqueting-rooms in England. There is an establishment at Hertford, to which the younger boys are generally sent preparatory to their entering on the foundation in London The revenue of the hospital, arising from landed and funded property, purchased with the donations of numerous private individuals, amounts to about £45,000 There are six exhibitions at Pembroke College, Cambridge, each of the value of £90 for the first four years, and £50 for the last three years, each scholar receiving £50 for an outfit, an exhibition of £70, with the same outfit, at any college in Oxford, every seventh year, two scholarships of £40 per annum each, at Pembroke College, Cambridge, founded by Mr Sergeant Moses, six of £10 per annum each, three at Emanuel College, and three at Christ College, Cambridge, founded by John Brown, in 1662, and two exhibitions of £12 per annum, at Emanuel College, founded by Emanuel Richards, the holders of which receive also an extra allowance

The edifices in which many of the other schools are held are handsome, and the establishments extensive

HOSPITALS, AND OTHER CHARITABLE INSTITUTIONS

London contains thirty hospitals, for the sick and diseased one hundred and seven almshouses, for the maintenance of the aged , eighteen asylums for the support of indigent persons of various other descriptions, numerous dispensaries for gratuitously supplying the poor with medicine and medical aid at their own dwellings, and in each parish a workhouse, for maintaining its own poor Exclusively of this ample list, the Livery Companies alone distribute above £75,000 annually in charities, and there is a multitude of institutions for the relief of the distressed, of a less public and prominent nature than those above specified The aggregate amount of the sums annually expended in public charities in London is estimated at little less than one million sterling The hospitals were chiefly founded by the munificence of private individuals, some of them being endowed with permanent revenues, and others supported by annual or occasional voluntary subscriptions The almshouses were built and endowed either by individuals or by the incorporated companies Many of the hospitals are buildings of immense extent and imposing architecture, and their internal regulations are worthy of their magnitude and importance The medical assistance is the best the profession can supply , the attendance ample, and the rooms and wards, bedding, &c , clean and wholesome The almshouses and other institutions for the support of the aged and indigent exhibit not merely an appearance, but the real possession, of competence and ease The hospitals and other institutions for the benefit of the sick, diseased, maimed, and afflicted, are as follows

St Bartholomew's Hospital was incorporated in the last year of the reign of Henry VIII , having formerly belonged to the priory of St Bartholomew, in Smithfield, founded, in 1102, by one Rayhere, said to have been jester to King Henry I The present edifice was constructed by Gibbs, in 1729, and consists of four magnificent piles of stone building, forming the four equal sides of a quadrangle, and connected by stone gateways The establishment is provided with three physicians, three surgeons, three assistant surgeons, an apothecary, and chaplain, with numerous nurses and attendants Persons injured by accident are received into this hospital at all hours , those afflicted with disease are only admitted on petition It administers relief upon an average to between ten and twelve thousand persons annually *St Thomas' Hospital*, of ancient monastic foundation, but refounded by Edward VI , stands in High street, Southwark It was rebuilt in 1693, in three beautiful squares, to which the governors, in 1732, added a fourth magnificent pile of building at their own expense. It is now composed of four quadrangular courts, comprising numerous wards, and having a chapel, and parochial church Belonging to the establishment are also hot and cold baths, a surgery, a theatre for the delivery of lectures, capable of accommodating three hundred persons, and a dispensary The annual expenditure is about £10,000, and the number of persons relieved nearly the same as at St Bartholomew's Hospital. Both are under the control of the lord mayor and aldermen *Guy's Hospital* stands at a small distance from St Thomas , and receives its name from its founder Thomas Guy, Esq , citizen of London, who expended £18,793 on its erection during his lifetime, and endowed it with the immense sum of £220,000 at his death The building consists of a centre and two wings, with a separate edifice in the rear, for lunatic patients It includes thirteen large wards, a hall and chapel, a theatre for lectures, a laboratory, a museum of anatomical preparations, and a library It also contains above four hundred beds, and affords relief to two thousand out-patients yearly, possessing an establishment of three physicians, three surgeons, and an apothecary, besides numerous attendants the funds of this hospital have lately been augmented by a very considerable benefaction, so as to have caused the intention of greatly enlarging its dimensions The *London Hospital,* in White-chapel-road, was first established in 1740, and the present building was erected in 1759 The patients relieved are, sick and wounded seamen, and other persons connected with the river and maritime affairs, their number amounts annually to many thousands This institution has an accumulating fund, under the management of twenty one guardians, chosen once in three years, intended to secure a provision for its permanent support The building is extremely large, possessing an extensive front towards the road The *Middlesex Hospital,* situated in Charles-street, Oxford-street, was built in 1745, for the reception of sick and lame patients, the relief of lying-in married women and of out patients, and the admission at all hours of persons wounded by accidents in 1792, an addition was made to it by a beneficent individual for affording relief to persons afflicted with cancers, who, if they choose, may remain in the hospital for life it is capable of receiving three hundred patients The *Westminster Hospital,* James street, Westminster, was founded in 1719, "for the relief of the sick and needy from all parts ' The building is neat and extensive, and the medical assistance ample The *New Bethlehem Lunatic Hospital,* Lambeth, is on a scale of real magnificence, the grand front being five hundred and eighty feet in length, and resembling rather a palace than an erection for the purposes of charity This establishment was founded by Henry VIII, and was removed from its old situation in Moorfields, in 1812 The building is of brick, and comprises a centre and two wings, the former being surmounted by a dome, and decorated with an Ionic portico of six columns, supporting the arms of the United Kingdom, and was completed at an expense of about £100,000, from a design by Mr Lewis It is capable of receiving four hundred and sixty patients, who are under the superintendence of a steward, apothecary, matron, keepers, &c, the whole being subject to the government of the lord mayor and aldermen The annual income of the hospital is about £18,000 *St Luke's Hospital,* also for lunatics, established by voluntary contributions, on account of the inadequacy of the last-mentioned establishment "for the relief of all indigent lunatics, is a noble building, situated in Old-street, having a front four hundred and ninety-three feet long, remarkable for simple grandeur Its interior arrangement constitutes a perfect model for similar charities, the number of patients is limited to three hundred The original building was erected, in 1732, on the north side of Upper Moorfields, the present was commenced in 1751, but not completed till 1786, at an expense of £55,000 *Bridewell Hospital*

occupies the site of Bridewell palace, near Fleet-street, before the fire of London, it consisted of several quadrangles, and is still of great extent This establishment was founded by Edward VI, for the relief of distress, and the punishment of vagrants, to which latter purpose it is still partly applied, being at present used as a house of correction for dissolute persons, and idle apprentices, committed by the chamberlain of the city, and for the temporary maintenance of distressed vagrants till they can be passed to their places of settlement it is under the government of the mayor and corporation

Besides these principal hospitals, there are several others of considerable magnitude, such as St George s hospital, Hyde Park Corner, now being rebuilt, the Lock hospital, Grosvenor-place, the Small-Pox hospital, Gray's Inn-lane, the hospitals for Spanish, Portuguese, Dutch, and German Jews, Mile-End-road, the hospital for aged French Protestants, St Luke s, the Fever hospital, Battle-bridge, &c The Lying-in hospitals are numerous, and receive upwards of five thousand poor women annually The principal are, The British, The City of London, The Queen s, Westminster, Middlesex, and Brownlow-street hospitals, all which are spacious buildings, and some of them, particularly the City of London and the Westminster hospitals, are of very handsome construction The subordinate institutions of this class furnish attendance to females at their own houses, and are situated in different parts of the town The Dispensaries, for affording medical relief in cases of sickness, accident, &c, amount in London, as has been stated, to upwards of twenty, exclusively of the various establishments for vaccine inoculation

The principal miscellaneous charitable establishments are, the Foundling hospital, Guildford-street, founded originally for the reception and maintenance of exposed and deserted children, and open for the reception of illegitimate children of females of good character, whose future prospects are not likely to be affected by a temporary dereliction of the path of virtue, the Magdalen hospital, Blackfriars-road, the London Female Penitentiary, Pentonville, and the Metropolitan Asylum, Hackney, for the relief and reformation of repentant prostitutes, the Asylum for Female Orphans, Westminster-road, the Marine Society, for fitting out indigent, distressed, and even depraved boys, for the naval service, the Asylum for the Indigent Blind, St. George s Fields, and that for the Deaf and Dumb, Kent-road, the Philanthropic Society, St George s Fields, for the children of convicted criminals, the Refuge for the Destitute, Hackney-road, the Royal Humane Society, for recovering persons from apparent death by drowning, &c, the National Vaccine Society, for the extermination of the small pox, by means of vaccination, the Samaritan Society, for the relief of patients discharged cured from the London hospital, the Society of Schoolmasters, for the benefit of the necessitous orphans and widows of that useful class of men, the Society for the relief and discharge of persons imprisoned for small debts, Craven-street, Strand, the Scottish hospital, for relieving distressed natives of Scotland, Crane-court, Fleet-street, the Benevolent Society of St Patrick, having, in regard to the natives of Ireland, the same objects as the Scottish Corporation, the Caledonian Asylum, for supporting and educating the children of soldiers, sailors, marines, &c, natives of Scotland, or born of indigent Scottish parents resident in London, the Society of Ancient Britons, Gray's-Inn-lane, for maintaining, instructing, clothing, and apprenticing children of Welch parents, born in and near London, the National Benevolent Institution, Freemasons hall, for the relief of distressed persons in the middle ranks of life, of any country or persuasion, the Corporation for the relief of poor widows and children of clergymen, being an extremely well-supported establishment, under the especial patronage of the established church, the anniversary meetings of which are held in St Paul s Cathedral, in the second week in May, when a grand musical festival is given for the "benefit of the sons of the Clergy, the African Institution, Westminster library, Jermyn-street, the Society for the relief of distressed foreigners, the London Maritime Institution, the Society for the relief of the widows and orphans of medical men in and near London, the Artists Benevolent Fund, and the Artists Joint Stock Fund the Sheriffs Fund, Raine's Charity, St George s in the East, the Literary Fund Society, Lincoln s Inn Fields, the Royal Society of Musicians, the Choral Fund, and the New Musical Fund, the Philological Society, King-street (West), Bryanston square, the Female Friendly Society, &c The Infirmaries are, the Sea bathing Infirmary, Tower street, the Royal Infirmary for disorders of the eye, Nassau street, the London Infirmary, for similar complaints, Finsbury, the New Rupture Society, Great Russell-street, and the City of London Truss Society, at the City Dispensary, Grocers -hall-court The Infirmary for the diseases of the spine, Upper St Martin's-lane Among the buildings of the above institutions which are worthy of notice, for their magnitude or architectural merit, may be particularised those of the Foundling hospital, the Magdalen, the Asylum for Female Orphans, the Deaf and Dumb Asylum, the Caledonian Asylum, and the Welch Society, Gray's-Inn-lane There are also numerous Religious Societies, of which the following are the principal The British and Foreign, The Naval and Military, and the Merchant Seamen s, Bible Societies, The Church of England, The London, the Wesleyan Methodist, The Baptist, and The Moravian, Missionary Societies, The Prayer Book and Homily Society, The London Hibernian, and The Irish Evangelical, Societies, The Society for promoting Christianity in Foreign parts, The Religious Tract Society, The Home Missionary, and the Christian Instruction, Societies, The Societies for promoting Christianity among the Jews, and for the conversion of Negro Slaves, The Society for the support and encouragement of Sunday schools, throughout the British dominions, and The National Society, for the education of the poor in the principles of the Established Church in England and Wales

LIBRARIES

London possesses a great number of public libraries, independently of those attached to different charitable foundations

The British Museum —This national repository, as well of antiquities and curiosities as of books and manuscripts, was established, by act of parliament, in 1753 Its originator was Sir Hans Sloane, who bequeathed his museum to the nation, on condition that parliament should pay £20,000 to his executors, and provide a house for its reception This was accomplished, by means of £85,000 raised by lottery for the purpose, and other collections being added, the whole were deposited in the noble mansion formerly belonging to the Duke of Montague, in Great Russell-street, Bloomsbury, which had been purchased for the purpose To the Sloanean museum parliament have added, at various times, the Cottonian library, given by Sir R Cotton to the public, and removed from Cotton house, Westminster Major Edwards library, the Harleian library, Dr Burney s rare and classical library, and the Lansdowne manuscripts various literary men and others have also increased the treasures of this establishment by donations and legacies George II gave the whole of the important library of printed books and manuscripts which had been gradually collected by the kings of England, from Henry VII to William III George III gave a large and valuable assortment of pamphlets, published between the years 1640 and 1660, and Garrick bequeathed to the Museum his collection of old plays Some of the principal private donations are, Dr Birch s library, left by will, together with £522 18 per annum in the funds for ever, a select library of classical works, by Thomas Tyrwhitt, Esq, a similar bequest by Sir William Musgrave, and a magnificent collection of printed books and prints by the late Rev M Cracherode The most recent, and one of the most important donations, is that of the magnificent library collected by George III, and presented to the trustees of this great national repository by His late Majesty, George IV, for the reception of which, an extensive and elegant gallery has been recently added to the buildings of the Museum Numerous other libraries, and valuable collections of pieces of ancient sculpture, curiosities, &c, have been added, by gift or purchase, rendering the British Museum, at the present time, in books, manuscripts, sculpture, antiquities, and the curiosities of art and nature, one of the richest in Europe The whole of the building, which is decaying in many parts, it has been proposed to re-edify, from the elegant designs of Mr Smirke The parts finished in the rebuilding of it consist of the splendid pile for the reception of the library given by the late king it has a front looking towards Bedford-square, faced with stone, and the projections in the centre are ornamented with four half columns of the Ionic order, fluted, and a pilaster at each end, of the same order, which support a pediment, the cornice, &c, of wrought stone, being placed at the top of the wall along the whole of this side The entrance is at the end of Montague-place The first and right-hand apartment is of very great length, extending to the projection in the centre of the building, where it is ornamented on each side with two superb Corinthian columns, having shafts and bases of highly-polished marble, with beautiful capitals of variegated marble it is adjoined by a second apartment of nearly equal dimensions, and two smaller rooms beyond The whole of this noble suite of apartments are very lofty, of equal height, and have an enriched cornice and frieze, with ceilings of the most magnificent description, they are supported with iron, which renders the building fireproof, and which is itself further supported by very strong iron girders, placed at intervals across the walls All the rooms are lighted on both sides with windows of equal dimensions, extending the entire length of the building, and the walls which separate the apartments are decorated at the angles with double-faced pilasters of polished marble, the upper suite of rooms, stone staircase, entrance-hall, and other portions on this side, as well as the whole of its exterior, is of correspondent grandeur The immense number, and splendid binding, of the works in the royal collection, in the principal library, amounting to sixty thousand volumes, many of them most costly and exquisite, are in harmony with the fitting-up of the apartment in which they are placed, and, with the books in the other apartments, form a collection of nearly one hundred and seventy thousand printed volumes, and twenty thousand volumes of manuscripts

The London Institution was formed in the autumn of 1805, by the exertions of a few public spirited individuals, as a public library for the more especial use of the city, and a charter of incorporation was obtained in January, 1807 The temporary house fixed upon for this purpose, until a suitable building could be erected, was, in the first place, the old mansion of Sir Robert Clayton, in the Old Jewry, and subsequently a house in King s Arms Yard, Coleman street In 1815, the present elegant building, which has the advantage of a peculiarly fine situation, in Finsbury-circus, was constructed, partly from the funds of the society, and partly from the voluntary contributions of such of its members as were friendly to the measure the first stone was laid by the lord mayor (S Birch, Esq), accompanied by the civic state officers, and the proprietors, and the edifice was completed and opened in 1819 The building is of stone, and has a beautiful front, the length of which is one hundred and forty feet The centre is adorned with a handsome portico, consisting of four Tuscan pillars, supporting an equal number of the Corinthian order on an upper story, the whole being surmounted by a pediment An entrance-hall of great elegance, decorated with columns and pilasters, leads by a grand double stone staircase to the library, a fine apartment ninety seven feet long, forty-two broad, and twenty-eight high, elegantly fitted up, with stone galleries running round the whole upper part, and containing a very extensive collection of books in recesses, being particularly rich in works relating to English history and Topography Besides committee rooms, reading rooms, and every other requisite convenience, there is an elegant theatre for the delivery of lectures The acquisition of a fine library, the diffusion of knowledge by means of lectures and experiments, and the providing for the subscribers a reading-room, furnished with the best English and foreign period cals, are the principal objects of this institution To accomplish these, nearly one thousand gentlemen and merchants subscribed seventy-five guineas each, and selected a committee who framed the laws by which the institution is governed this committee, consisting of twenty six members, is chosen annually, and the whole direction is vested in them

The Red Cross street Library was founded for Protestant dissenting ministers by Dr Williams, about the year 1716, and, in consequence of gifts and purchases since that time, it now contains about twenty thousand volumes The books are for the most part on Theological subjects, and admission may be procured by application to the librarian on any day in the week, except Saturday

Sion College, London Wall, is both a charitable and a literary institution The building was origin ally an hospital for blind paupers, and, after passing through various hands, was purchased for the purpose of erecting Sion college, for the use of the London clergy, who were incorporated by Charles I The purchase was made in consequence of the will of Dr Thomas White, vicar of St Dunstan's in the West, who left £3000 for the purpose The library was the gift of the Rev John Simpson, rector of St Olave s, Hart street, one of Dr White s executors, but it was afterwards considerably increased, both before and after the fire of London, which destroyed a great number of the books It now consists of a very extensive collection, like the former, chiefly Theological all rectors and vicars within the city are fellows of this college

LITERARY, PHILOSOPHICAL, AND OTHER LEARNED AND SCIENTIFIC INSTITUTIONS, &c

The number of these is very great, and is daily increasing The first in consequence and antiquity are the Royal Society, and the Antiquarian Society, the meetings of both which are held at Somerset House, and next in order are the Society for the Encouragement of Arts, Manufactures, and Commerce, situated in John street, Adelphi, the Royal Institution of Great Britain, Albemarle-street, the London Institution, already described, the Russell Institution, Great Coram street, the Mechanics Institution, Southampton-buildings, the City of London Literary and Scientific Institution, Aldersgate street, and the Westminster Literary and Scientific Institution, Leicester-square all these possess fine libraries, and the buildings in which they are held generally merit observation The names of the other principal institutions are, the British Mineralogical, and Entomological Societies, the Philosophical Society of London, the Astronomical Society, Lincoln s Inn-Fields, the City Philosophical Society, the Mathematical Society, Spitalfields, the Horticultural Society, the Linnæan Society, the Geological Society, Gresham College, &c The Medical and Surgical Institutions consist of the College of Physicians, removed from the fine building by Sir Christopher Wren, in Warwick-lane, to Pall-Mall (East), the Surgeons' College, Lincoln s-Inn-square, the Apothecaries Company and Hall, Blackfriars, the Medical Society, Bolt-court, Fleet-street, and the Medical and Chirurgical Society, in Lincoln s-Inn-Fields The principal Theatres of Anatomy and for Medical lectures are, Dr Bell s theatre in Great Windmill street, and those of the several hospitals, and in different other places numerous miscellaneous lectures are delivered on various branches of medical science

The Public Exhibitions of Paintings are those of the Royal Academy, Somerset House, the Gallery of the British Institution, Pall Mall, the Society of Painters in Water Colours, Pall-Mall (East), the Society of British Artists, Suffolk-street, the National Gallery, Pall-Mall, the various Panoramas, &c Of these, *The National Gallery* was begun by the purchase by government of the Angerstein collection of pictures, sub sequently to which were purchased some of the finest paintings of Correggio, A Carrachi, Murillo, Titian, &c, and twenty additional paintings were presented by Sir George Beaumont, including a beautiful landscape by Rubens The new building, from a design by Nash, was determined on by the late king and the proper authorities, in July 1828 it is to be called the New National Gallery and Royal Academy, and to be erected on the site of the present riding-house, in the King's Mews, having a front towards Charing Cross, three hundred yards in length, with a beautiful Corinthian portico and centre dome, a small one on each wing, and a still smaller on each of the principal extremities Being intended to have an elevation about twice the height of the first-rate houses already erected, it will form a very grand and noble line, extended, in a direction from Pall-Mall (East), nearly across to St Martin's church The space immediately in front will be occupied by the New Royal Academy, which is intended to represent an extensive Grecian temple, having at the exit and entrance a long flight of steps, and standing at right angles with the National Gallery

Zoological Society and its Gardens The gardens of this society, in the Regent s Park, are delightfully laid out in walks, interspersed with pheasantries and aviaries, sheds and enclosures, &c , for the preservation and rearing of the animals belonging to the society, brought from all parts of the globe Besides the museum, which contains six hundred species of mammalia, four thousand birds, one thousand reptiles and fishes, one thousand testucea and crustacea, and thirty thousand insects, the vivarium contains upwards of four hundred and thirty living quadrupeds and birds, the whole of which are accommodated in buildings and places calculated to afford them the opportunity of enjoying every approximation, consistent with a captive state to their natural habits , such as the bears pit, the lama house, beaver dam, kangaroo hut, and aviaries for hawks, owls, small birds, &c The society has lately received a valuable addition to its rapidly increasing collection from His present Majesty, who has munificently presented the collection of birds and beasts made by the late King, George IV , and so interesting and attractive has the establishment been found, that, in the short period of seven months, the gardens and museum are stated to have been visited by upwards of one hundred and thirty thousand persons

The Coliseum is a large building in the Regent s Park, bearing a considerable resemblance to the Pantheon at Rome, and was originally intended only for the exhibition of an immense panoramic picture of London, taken from the very summit of St Paul s Cathedral by Mr Horner, who projected the design of the building as at present finished, however, there is a variety of additional departments, such is a conservatory filled with a great variety of foreign and choice plants and shrubs , an aviary, grottos, waterfalls, *jets d eau*, a library, a reading-room, a refectory, and various other sources of amusement or recreation The work altogether is novel and unique in its kind, and nearly £70,000 has been expended in its execution

ANTIQUITIES

The antiquities of London, for the most part destroyed with the city in 1666, but, till within the last sixty or seventy years, still numerous, have of late through the extension of commercial enterprise, and the progress of modern improvement, externally almost disappeared The monasteries, forming the first class, amounted to nearly fifty, the names, situations, founders, dates, and orders of which were as follows

—*Convents of Monks* St Peter's, Westminster, founded by Sebert, in 605, for Benedictines , St Saviour's, Bermondsey, by Ailwin Child, in 1082, for Cluniacs , St Mary s of the Graces, or Eastminster abbey, Tower hill, by Edward III , in 1359, for Cistercians , the Chartreuse, or Charter-house, near Smithfield, by Sir Walter Manny, Knt , in 1371, for Carthusians *Nunneries* St Mary s, Clerkenwell, by Jordan Brisset and Wife, in 1100, for Benedictines , St John s the Baptist, Holywell, Shoreditch, by Richard I , in 1189, (refounded by Sir Thomas Lovel, Knt , in 1510,) for Benedictines , St Helen's, Bishopsgate-street, by William Basing, in 1212, for Benedictines , and St Clare s, or Nuns Minoresses, Minories, by Blanch, Queen of Navarre, in 1293 *Friaries* Franciscan, Newgate-street, by John Ewin, Mercer, in 1225 , Carmelite, Fleet-street, by Sir Richard Grey, in 1241 , Dominican, by Hubert de Bourgh, in 1242, in Holborn, and refounded at I udgate, by Archbishop Kilwarby, in 1279 , Augustine, Throgmorton street, by Humphrey Bohun, in 1253 , and Crouched or Crutched, Hart-street, Tower hill, by Ralph Hosier and Richard Laberne, in 1298 *Colleges* St Mary Overey s, or St Saviour s, Southwark, by Marv Overey, in 1000, for Augustine canons , St Martin s-le-Grand, by Ingelric and Girard, in 1056, for Augustine canons , Holy Trinity, Aldgate, by Queen Maud, in 1108 , London College, Guildhall, by Peter Fanlone, Adam Francis, and Henry Frowick, in 1299 , Corpus Christi, St Lawrence , Poultney-lane, by Sir John de Poultney, in 1346, St Michael s, Crooked-lane, by Sir William Walworth, in 1380, the Holy Ghost and St Mary's, College-hill, Thames-street, by Sir Richard Whittington, Knt , in 1418 , and Jesus s College, St Paul s Cathedral *Hospitals* St John s of Jerusalem, Smithfield, by Jordan Brisset and Wife, in 1100, St Giles' in the Fields, Bloomsbury, by Queen Matilda, in 1102, for lepers , St Bartholomew s Smithfield, by one Rayhere, in 1102 , St Thomas of Acon, Cheapside, by Thomas Fitz-Theobald de Heily and Wife, in 1170 , St Mary s Spital, Norton Falgate, by Walter Brune and Wife, in 1179, for Canons Regular , Knights Templars, Holborn, and afterwards Fleet street, in 1185, refounded in 1245 , St Mary s Bethlehem, Bishopsgate-street, by Simon Fitz-Mary, in 1246 , Elsinge Spital, London Wall, by William Elsinge, in 1329 , St Thomas', Southwark, St James , Pall-Mall, and the Savoy, for lepers and infirm *Priory* St Bartholomew s, Smithfield, by Rayhere, in 1102, for canons Regular of the order of St Augustine *Domus Conversorum* Rolls Chapel, Chancery-lane, by Henry III , in 1233, for Converted Jews *Guilds*, or *Fraternities of Priests*, &c Allhallows Barking, Tower street , Leadenhall, Leadenhall - street , St Peter s, Cornhill , St Augustine s, Papey, Camomile-street , Holy Trinity, Aldersgate-street, &c There were also in London the five cells, or hermitages, of St Catherine, Wapping , St James in the Wall, Cripplegate , St Mary Rouncival, Charing Cross, the hermitage of St James, opposite, and Our Lady of Pien, Westminster Of the above, the following only exhibit any external remains —Westminster abbey, independently of its fine church and cloisters, still retains its beautiful chapter-house, the shell of the great hall, the abbot s residence (now the deanery), and to which is attached the ancient kitchen, and the celebrated Jerusalem chamber, the abbey close, with numerous old buildings, and the exterior walls of its spacious gardens The remains of Bermondsey abbey, consisting of a few fragments of walls, and the side of the east gate leading into Grange-walk. The Charter-house still retains its original gateway in Charter-house-square, several of the monks' cells, now blocked up, part of the exterior wall surrounding the convent and gardens, and other inferior parts incorporated in walls and passages, &c Clerkenwell nunnery has a few square yards of ancient stone wall next Corporation-row "The Nonnes Ques," at St. Helen's, still exists, with the original nuns seats of oak, and the ancient grating, through which they could see divine service performed from the vaulted crypts beneath the hall of the nunnery Of the nunnery in the Minories very considerable remains were discovered after a fire there in 1797, and there still exists a portion of the south, or street, front of the abbey mansion, behind the houses in the Minories, besides much of its reverse front, now modernised into Haydon House Black friars' has diminished to a solitary piece of dingy stone wall, standing at the top of a passage in Glo'ster court, St. Andrew's Hill Of the White friars' there are only a few fragments of wall behind the houses in Bouverie-street, partly incorporated with the buildings of the Bolt and Tun Inn The vestiges of the Grey friars consist of the great cloisters and Whittington's library, both about to be demolished, as have other parts, for continuing the present improvements there Augustine friars has the fine nave of its church now occupied as a Dutch place of worship Of Crutched friars there only remain Sir John Milbourne s almshouses, which adjoined the east end of the friary church, they have a curious tablet of the Virgin Mary, encircled by angels The remains of St Mary Overey', which will speedily give way to the approaches to the new London bridge, consist, besides the fine conventual church, of a considerable length of ancient stone vaulting, supporting a chapel, or hall, and various detached parts, in doors, archways, &c, in Montague close Part of the vaulting of Corpus Christi College remains between St. Lawrence Poultney churchyard and Suffolk-lane Large remains of St Martin s le-Grand college chapel were discovered in digging the foundations of the New Post-office, the whole of which, as well as every other vestige of this very ancient institution, are now annihilated The priory, or college of the Holy Trinity, Aldgate, retains part of the south aisle of its Norman church, in a passage leading from Duke s place to St James' churchyard The priory of St Bartholomew the Great has the whole choir of its Norman church converted into the present church, its east cloister, the shell of its dining-hall, with fine vaults beneath, and various smaller parts the fratry, galleries, prior s house, and various other remains, were destroyed by fire, in May, 1830 Of the Temple, there remain the very beautiful church, with its circular vestibule, and the tombs of the ancient cross-legged knights, part of the cloisters entering into it, and some ancient Norman arch-work incorporated in the walls of the Inner Temple Society s kitchen The Hospital of St John of Jerusalem retains its large and well-known gateway from St. John's-lane, the choir of the conventual church converted to the present parish church of St John (and beneath which is the fine original crypt), with part of the chapels of the south aisle, and some smaller remains St Mary s Spital has the abutment of its principal gateway still standing at the corner of White Lion-street Elsinge Spital has part of its entrance porch and steeple incorporated in the present parish church of St. Alphage In St James' palace may still be discerned many parts of the ancient hospital The Savoy church is that of its ancient hospital Of the *Domus Conversorum* there still remains the ancient chapel, called the Rolls chapel and the hall of the Holy Trinity, Aldersgate, now Trinity chapel, is all that exists of the smaller monastic foundations

Amongst the remaining metropolitan antiquities, which are too reduced in number to render a classification necessary, may be enumerated several large fragments of the walls of London, at the back of Fore-street, in Cripplegate churchyard, at the back of the houses in Falcon-square, beneath the houses next Aldersgate, and in St Botolph s churchyard there, at the back of the Old Bailey, at the Cock in the Corner, Ludgate, and at the back of George Alley, next Tower hill the last, which is by far the largest, oldest, and most perfect portion, is intermixed with an abundance of Roman brick There are some crypts, or stone arched cellars, anciently belonging to religious structures, or mansions one of the finest specimens of the former was the priory of Lewes chapel, Tooley-street, just demolished for the approach to the New London bridge, there are also remains of another subterranean chapel, or church, beneath the house at the north-east corner of Leadenhall-street the most remarkable crypts belonging to ancient mansions are the vaults beneath Gerrard's hall, Basing-lane, and at Crosby House, Bishopsgate-street the great hall, with much of the superstructure, of the latter princely residence is also standing, and may rank as the finest specimen of domestic architecture in London The churches which, either wholly or in part, exhibit fine specimens of ancient building, and were not conventual, are, Bow church, Cheapside, which still retains its fine Norman crypt, and St Sepulchre s, which latter boasts a beautiful groined avenue from Snow-hill there are also various ancient parts, or incorporations, deserving notice in the churches of St. Olave, Hart-street, St Giles, Cripplegate, St Andrew, Undershaft, &c Of the ancient military architectural remains in various parts of the Tower of London, a brief account has already been given, besides which, there were, until destroyed very recently, vestiges of camps and fortified earthworks at Highbury, near White-Conduit-house and Battle-bridge, and at the descent from Gray s Inn-lane, the Fleet ditch, &c The remains of Roman roads connected with the metropolis are nearly obliterated, but may be still imperfectly traced by the diligent investigator, particularly in the old bridle way of Hugbush-lane, and in the continuation of Eald street, through Shoreditch churchyard, by Bethnal Green, &c The most celebrated remnant of antiquity, of all which appertains to London, however, is the supposed Roman milliary, in Cannon-street, denominated London stone, which, whether of Roman or British origin, was undoubtedly once of considerable magnitude, and is the first and oldest of our metropolitan antiquities Of the result of numerous excavations, at various times, in the discovery of Roman tesselated pavements, altars, coins, &c, mention has been made under their proper heads

Among the numerous distinguished individuals born in the metropolis may be enumerated the following —

Ingulphus, Abbot of Croyland, an English historian, who lived at the time of the Norman Conquest, Thomas à Becket, Archbishop of Canterbury, Matthew of Westminster, a Monkish historian of the fourteenth century, Geoffrey Chaucer, the first great English poet, born in 1328, Dr John Colet, the founder of St Paul s school, born in 1466, Sir Thomas More, author of a political romance, entitled "Utopia," Lord Chancellor under Henry VIII, in whose reign he was beheaded for denying the king s supremacy, born in 1480, John Leland, the English antiquary, John Stow, author of the "Survey of London," born in1525, William Camden, author of the "Britannia, born in 1551, Edmund Spenser, author of the "Fairy Queen," born about 1553, Francis Bacon, Lord Verulam, the father of modern philosophy, born in 1561, Edward Alleyn, a celebrated actor, the founder of Dulwich College, born in 1566, Inigo Jones, the reviver of a taste for classical architecture in England, born in 1572, Dr John Donne, a distinguished poet and divine, born in 1573, Ben Jonson, the dramatist, poet laureate in the reign of James I, born in 1574, John Milton, the author of "Paradise Lost," who was Latin Secretary to Oliver Cromwell, born in 1608, Algernon Sidney, a republican writer, executed on account of the Rye house plot in 1683, born about 1617, Abraham Cowley, the poet, born in 1618, Sir William Temple, eminent as a statesman and public writer, born in 1629, Dr Isaac Barrow, a celebrated divine and mathematician, born in 1630, Dr Edmund Halley, celebrated as a mathematician and an astronomer, born in 1656, Daniel Defoe, the author of "Robinson Crusoe, born in 1660, Anthony Ashley Cooper, Earl of Shaftesbury, a distinguished writer on morals and metaphysics, born in 1671, Colley Cibber, a dramatic writer and actor, poet laureate to George I, born in 1671, Sir John Vanbrugh, an eminent architect and dramatist, born about 1672, Alexander Pope, the poet, born in 1688, George Lillo, a goldsmith, who wrote "George Barnwell, and other popular dramas, born in 1693, Philip Dormer Stanhope, Earl of Chesterfield, distinguished as a statesman and a cultivator of polite literature, born in 1694, William Hogarth, the painter, born in 1698, Dr John Jortin, a learned theological writer, born in 1698, Dr Philip Doddridge, an eminent dissenting divine and scripture commentator, born in 1702, John Dollond, the inventor of an achromatic telescope, born in 1706, Dr Thomas Augustine Arne, a distinguished musician, born in 1710, Richard Glover, author of "Leonidas, and other poems, born in 1712, James Stuart, author of the "Antiquities of Athens," born in 1713, Thomas Gray, author of the "Elegy written in a Country Churchyard," and other works, born in 1716, Sir William Blackstone, author of "Commentaries on the Laws of England, born in 1723, John Wilkes, author of the "North Briton, born in 1726, Charles Churchill, the celebrated satirist, born in 1731, Richard Gough, F A S, the editor of Camden's "Britannia," born in 1735, Dr Samuel Horsley, a celebrated theological writer, born about 1737, Arthur Young, secretary to the Board of Agriculture, born in 1741, William Mitford, author of a valuable "History of Greece, and other works, born in 1744, Sir William Jones, a celebrated Orientalist and juridical writer, born in 1746, The Hon Anne Seymour Damer, born in 1748, Capel Lofft, a poet and miscellaneous writer, born in 1751,

Dr John Milner, a learned Catholic prelate, born in 1752, Sir Samuel Romilly, distinguished as a lawyer and a statesman, born in 1757, George Morland, the painter, born in 1764, The Right Hon George Canning, born in 1770, and George Noel Byron, Lord Byron, the author of "Childe Harold," and other poems, born in 1788

LONDON-COLNEY, a chapelry in the parishes of St Peter and St Albans, hundred of Cashio, or liberty of St Albans, county of Hertford, 3 miles (S E) from St Albans This place derives its name from its situation on the road to London, which crosses the river Colne here, over which there is a substantial brick bridge of seven arches The living is a perpetual curacy, in the archdeaconry of St. Albans, and diocese of London The chapel is a neat modern edifice, dedicated to St Peter, erected for the use of the inhabitants of the parishes of St Peter, Shenley, and Ridge, by subscription amounting to £2700, including a grant of £400 from the parliamentary commissioners for the erection of churches it contains about seven hundred sittings, one-half of which are free The site was given by the Earl of Hardwicke, who at the same time settled £40 per annum towards the support of the minister

LONDONTHORPE, a parish in the soke of Grantham, parts of Kesteven, county of Lincoln, 3½ miles (E N E) from Grantham, containing 195 inhabitants The living is a vicarage not in charge, with those of North Grantham and Great Gonerby, in the archdeaconry and diocese of Lincoln The church is dedicated to St John the Baptist.

LONGBOROUGH, a parish in the upper division of the hundred of Kiftsgate, county of Gloucester, 3 miles (N by W) from Stow on the Wold, containing, with the hamlet of Bankfee, 526 inhabitants The living is a discharged vicarage, with the rectory of Seasoncote united, in the archdeaconry and diocese of Gloucester, rated in the king s books at £5 15, and in the patronage of Chandos Leigh, Esq, and Sir Charles Cockerell, Bart, the former having two presentations, and the latter one. The church, dedicated to St James, has lately received an addition of one hundred and ninety sittings, of which one hundred and seventy-two are free, and towards defraying the expense of which the Incorporated Society for the enlargement of churches and chapels contributed £90 The source of the river Evenlode is in this parish, and the Fosse-way passes through it

LONGBURGH, a township in the parish of Burgh upon the Sands, ward and county of Cumberland, 6¼ miles (W N W) from Carlisle, containing 154 inhabitants

LONGCOT, a chapelry in the parish and hundred of Shrivenham, county of Berks, 3½ miles (S by W) from Great Farringdon, containing 419 inhabitants

LONGDON, a chapelry in the parish of Pontesbury, hundred of Ford, county of Salop, 5 miles (S W by S) from Shrewsbury, containing 387 inhabitants The living is a perpetual curacy, united with the rectory of Pontesbury, in the archdeaconry of Salop, diocese of Hereford, endowed with £400 royal bounty, and £200 parliamentary grant. The chapel is dedicated to St Ruthen.

LONGDON, a parish in the southern division of the hundred of Offlow, county of Stafford, 4 miles

(N W by N) from Lichfield, containing 1115 inhabitants The living is a vicarage, in the peculiar jurisdiction of the Prebendary of Longdon in the Cathedral Church of Lichfield, rated in the king s books at £5 5 , and in the patronage of the Prebendary, but, after his demise, in that of the Bishop of Lichfield and Coventry The church, dedicated to St James, has lately received an addition of one hundred sittings, of which sixty-four are free, the Incorporated Society for the enlargement of churches and chapels having contributed £30 towards defraying the expense There is a place of worship for Independents Several small bequests have been made for the instruction of children St Mary s almshouses, founded by Mrs Jane Cotton, are ten in number, nine of which are inhabited by poor women, each of whom receives three shillings and sixpence weekly , the tenth is occupied by a schoolmistress, who instructs twelve girls and five boys A court leet is held twice a year by the lord of the manor Indications of coal are observable here, but none has been raised The Trent and Mersey canal passes about two miles northward of the church At Castle Ring, a point in the Marquis of Anglesey s park at Beaudesert, are the remains of a British encampment. The Society of Friends have a very ancient burial-ground at Gentle Shaw, in this parish

LONGDON, a township in that part of the parish of LEEK which is in the northern division of the hundred of TOTMONSLOW, county of STAFFORD, 1¾ mile (W by S) from Leek, containing 350 inhabitants

LONGDON, a parish in the lower division of the hundred of PERSHORE, county of WORCESTER, 3 miles (S S W) from Upton upon Severn, containing 640 inhabitants The living is a vicarage, with the perpetual curacies of Castle Morton and Chaseley, in the archdeaconry and diocese of Worcester, rated in the king s books at £14 17 3½ , and in the patronage of the Dean and Chapter of Westminster The church, dedicated to St Mary, is surmounted by a tower of brick A free school was founded, about 1660, and endowed with land by Giles Godwin, Esq , for the instruction of children belonging to this parish , the master receives £28 per annum, for which he instructs about forty children in reading, writing, and arithmetic A court leet is held annually, for Longdon, Castlemeston, and Chaseley

LONGDON upon TERNE, a parish in the Newport division of the hundred of BRADFORD (South), county of SALOP, 3½ miles (N W by N) from Wellington, containing 95 inhabitants The living is a perpetual curacy, with the rectory of Pontesbury, in the peculiar jurisdiction of the Manorial Court of Longdon upon Terne The church is dedicated to St Bartholomew The Shrewsbury canal passes through this parish and village, and is here crossed by the river Terne

LONGFIELD, a parish in the hundred of AXTON, DARTFORD, and WILMINGTON, lathe of SUTTON at HONE, county of KENT, 5½ miles (S E) from Dartford, containing 113 inhabitants The living is a discharged rectory, in the archdeaconry and diocese of Rochester, rated in the king s books at £5 17 6 , and endowed with £400 private benefaction, and £400 royal bounty, and in the patronage of the Bishop of Rochester The church, dedicated to St. Mary Magdalene, contains the remains of the beneficent Archdeacon Plume, founder of the Plumean Professorship at Cambridge.

LONGFLEET, a tything in the parish of CANFORD-MAGNA, hundred of COGDEAN, Shaston (East) division of the county of DORSET, 1 mile (N N E) from Poole, containing 810 inhabitants

LONGFORD, a parish in the hundred of APPLETREE, county of DERBY, comprising the townships of Alkmonton, Hollington, and Longford, the liberty of Hungry Bentley, and the hamlet of Rodsley, and containing 1264 inhabitants, of which number, 573 are in the township of Longford, 6½ miles (S by E) from Ashbourn The living is a discharged vicarage, in the archdeaconry of Derby, and diocese of Lichfield and Coventry, rated in the king s books at £3 8 9 , and in the patronage of Thomas William Coke, Esq The church, dedicated to St Chad, has some portions in the Norman style of architecture, and three stone stalls in the chancel In 1688, Dame Catherine Coke bequeathed land for the education and apprenticing of poor children the income is £20 per annum , twenty poor boys are instructed by a master, and other children by a schoolmistress In 1687, Sir Robert Coke, Bart , founded an almshouse for six poor men or women, and endowed it with £55 per annum, £10 of which is paid to the vicar, whose duty it is to read prayers to the almspeople The foundations of some ancient religious house may be traced at Alkmonton

LONGFORD, a hamlet in those parts of the parishes of ST CATHERINE and ST MARY de LODE, GLOUCESTER, which are in the upper division of the hundred of DUDSTONE and KING S BARTON, county of GLOUCESTER, 1¼ mile (N E by N) from Gloucester, containing 215 inhabitants

LONGFORD, a parish in the Newport division of the hundred of BRADFORD (South), county of SALOP, 1¼ mile (W by S) from Newport, containing 234 inhabitants The living is a rectory, in the archdeaconry of Salop, and diocese of Lichfield and Coventry, rated in the king's books at £6 2 8½ R Leeke, Esq was patron in 1825 The church is dedicated to St Mary

LONGHAM, a parish in the hundred of LAUNDITCH, county of NORFOLK, 4 miles (N W by W) from East Dereham, containing 298 inhabitants The living is a perpetual curacy, in the archdeaconry and diocese of Norwich, endowed with £1000 royal bounty, and in the patronage of T W Coke, Esq The church is dedicated to St. Peter

LONGHOPE, a parish in the duchy of LANCASTER, county of GLOUCESTER, 5 miles (S W by S) from Newent, containing 790 inhabitants, of which number, 503 are in Lower, and 287 in Upper, Longhope. The living is a discharged vicarage, in the archdeaconry and diocese of Gloucester, rated in the king s books at £9 7 11½ , and in the patronage of the Rev John Probyn The church is dedicated to All Saints There is a place of worship for Wesleyan Methodists Courts leet and baron are held annually An annuity of £5 was given by Mr Thomas Nourse, for apprenticing one poor boy May hill, in this parish, forms a land-mark from the Bristol channel, it is planted with a clump of fir-trees on the summit, and is visible at a considerable distance from all parts of the adjacent country

LONGNEY, a parish in the upper division of the hundred of WHITSTONE, county of GLOUCESTER, 6¼ miles (S W by W) from Gloucester, containing 443 inhabitants The living is a discharged vicarage, in the archdeaconry and diocese of Gloucester, rated in the king's books at £12 1 8, and in the patronage of the Crown The church is dedicated to St Lawrence The navigable river Severn runs on the west of this parish

LONGNOR, a parish in the hundred of CONDOVER, county of SALOP, 8 miles (S) from Shrewsbury, containing 222 inhabitants The living is a perpetual curacy, in the archdeaconry of Salop, and diocese of Lichfield and Coventry, endowed with £200 private benefaction, £600 royal bounty, and £200 parliamentary grant, and in the patronage of Archdeacon Corbett. The church was a free chapel belonging to the abbey of Haughmond, and purchased of the vendees of the crown soon after the dissolution of the abbey, by the then proprietor of Longnor hall A school is endowed with the interest of £200, the bequest of Sir Richard Corbett, Bart, and there is a Sunday school, at which about sixty children attend This is the birthplace of the Rev Samuel Lee, Professor of Arabic in the University of Cambridge, an eminent self-taught linguist

LONGNOR, a market town and chapelry in the parish of ALLSTONEFIELD, northern division of the hundred of TOTMONSLOW, county of STAFFORD, 10 miles (N E) from Leek, and 162 (N N W) from London, containing 460 inhabitants This town is situated in the most northern part of the county, near the source of the river Manifold, and here a small canal terminates, which commences in the parish of Sheen, where it joins the Manifold The market is on Tuesday fairs are held on the Tuesday before Old Candlemas, Easter-Tuesday, May 4th and 17th, Whit-Tuesday, August 5th, Tuesday before Old Michaelmas, and November 12th. The living is a perpetual curacy, in the archdeaconry of Stafford, and diocese of Lichfield and Coventry, endowed with a rent-charge of £7 10, private benefaction, £600 royal bounty, and £1200 parliamentary grant, and in the patronage of the Vicar of Allstonefield The chapel, which is dedicated to St Giles, is a neat edifice of stone, with a lofty pinnacled-tower in the cemetery is a tombstone to the memory of W Billinge, who, after a long military career, died in the year 1791, at the age of one hundred and twelve years There is a place of worship for Wesleyan Methodists A small school, founded by subscription, is endowed with about £7 per annum, the proceeds of bequests made, in 1794, by John Robinson and Moses Charlesworth

LONGPARISH, a parish in the hundred of WHERWELL, Andover division of the county of SOUTHAMPTON, 3¼ miles (S. W) from Whitchurch, containing 693 inhabitants The living is a discharged vicarage, in the archdeaconry and diocese of Winchester, rated in the king s books at £8, endowed with £200 private benefaction, and £300 parliamentary grant, and in the patronage of the Rev H Woodcock, D D the church is dedicated to St Nicholas There is a place of worship for Baptists The river Test runs through the parish A trifling rent-charge, the gift of Thomas Baker, in 1696, is applied in teaching poor children

LONGPORT, commonly styled a borough in the parish of ST PAUL, CANTERBURY, but partly in the hundred of WESTGATE, lathe of ST AUGUSTINE, county of KENT, contiguous to the eastern side of the city of Canterbury, containing 684 inhabitants

LONGPORT, a manufacturing district within the parish and township of BURSLEM, northern division of the hundred of PIREHILL, county of STAFFORD This place was formerly called Longbridge, from a number of stepping-stones, forming a causeway across the meadows, but after the construction of the Trent canal, a branch of which passes through the district, its name was changed to Longport On the banks of the canal are several wharfs there are likewise some very considerable manufactories for earthenware and china, and a glass-house The Wesleyan Methodists have a place of worship here

LONGRIDGE, a township in the parish of NORHAM, otherwise Norhamshire, county palatine of DURHAM, though locally to the northward of Northumberland, 4 miles (S W) from Berwick upon Tweed, containing 81 inhabitants

LONGRIDGE, a chapelry in that part of the parish of RIBCHESTER which is in the lower division of the hundred of BLACKBURN, county palatine of LANCASTER, 7¼ miles (N E) from Preston The population is returned with the parish The living is a perpetual curacy, in the archdeaconry of Richmond, and diocese of Chester, endowed with £600 private benefaction, and £600 royal bounty Sir H Hoghton, Bart was patron in 1780 A festival, or guild, is held on St Lawrence's day, and there are fairs on March 16th, April 16th, the Monday preceding Holy Thursday, and November 5th, for cattle, pedlary, &c Here was an ancient hospital for a master and brethren, dedicated to the Virgin Mary and our Saviour

LONGSHAWS, a township in the parish of LONGHORSLEY, western division of MORPETH ward, county of NORTHUMBERLAND, 5½ miles (W N W) from Morpeth, containing 38 inhabitants Here are some remains of a very ancient edifice called the Launches

LONGSTOCK, a parish in the hundred of KING's SOMBOURN, Andover division of the county of SOUTHAMPTON, 1½ mile (N) from Stockbridge, containing 397 inhabitants The living is a discharged vicarage, in the archdeaconry and diocese of Winchester, rated in the king s books at £10 15, and in the patronage of Sir Charles Mill, Bart. The church is dedicated to St Mary

LONGSTONE (GREAT), a chapelry in the parish-o, BAKEWELL, hundred of HIGH PEAK, county of DERBY, 3 miles (N N W) from Bakewell, containing, with Holme, 442 inhabitants The living is a perpetual curacy, in the peculiar jurisdiction of the Dean and Chapter of Lichfield, and in the patronage of the Vicar of Bakewell The chapel, which is dedicated to St. Giles, contains several monuments belonging to the family of Eyres, Earls of Newburgh The chapelry is in the honour of Tutbury, duchy of Lancaster, and within the jurisdiction of a court of pleas held at Tutbury every third Tuesday, for the recovery of debts under 40s The commissioners for enclosing lands granted to trustees an allotment of waste land of about fourteen acres, for the support of a schoolmaster, which lets for £9 13 per annum, this sum, with £5 per annum, the bequest of William Wright in 1656, and an annual contribution of £5 from the Duke of Devonshire, is paid to the master for teaching twenty-five poor children gratuitously the school-room was built by subscription, and there is a house and garden for the master

LONGSTONE (LITTLE,) a hamlet in the parish of BAKEWELL, hundred of HIGH PEAK, county of DERBY, 3½ miles (N W by N) from Bakewell, containing 145 inhabitants

LONGTHORPE, a chapelry in that part of the parish of ST JOHN the BAPTIST, PETERBOROUGH, which is within the liberty of PETERBOROUGH, county of NORTHAMPTON, 2 miles (W) from Peterborough, containing 240 inhabitants The chapel is dedicated to St. John the Baptist

LONGTON, a chapelry in the parish of PENWORTHAM, hundred of LEYLAND, county palatine of LANCASTER, 5 miles (S W by W) from Preston, containing 1719 inhabitants The living is a perpetual curacy, in the archdeaconry and diocese of Chester, endowed with £850 private benefaction, £400 royal bounty, and £600 parliamentary grant J Rawstorne, Esq was patron in 1820 There is a place of worship for Wesleyan Methodists The free school was founded and endowed, in 1793, by Robert Moss, with a bequest of £400, for the instruction of the children of the inhabitants the present school-room was built by subscription in 1817, the income is £27 per annum, all the children of the chapelry who apply are taught gratuitously

LONGTON, a township in the parish of STOKE upon TRENT, northern division of the hundred of PIREHILL, county of STAFFORD, 4 miles (S E by E) from Newcastle under Line The population is returned with Lane-End.

LONGTOWN, a market town in the parish of ARTHURET, ESKDALE ward, county of CUMBERLAND, 8½ miles (N by W) from Carlisle, and 309 (N N W) from London, containing 1812 inhabitants This is a small town on the south bank of the river Eske, over which is a stone bridge, near the junction of that river with the Liddel The situation is pleasant and healthy, the houses are neatly built, and the streets are spacious, but not regularly paved nor lighted the inhabitants are supplied with water from wells Many of the lower class are employed in weaving for the manufacturers at Carlisle The market, originally held on Thursday, is almost disused, except for provisions, but there is another on Monday, principally for bacon and butter a fair is held on the Thursday before Whit Sunday, for horses, and there are statute fairs on the Thursday in Whitsun-week, and the Thursday in Martinmas, for hiring servants The county magistrates hold a meeting here on the last Thursday in every month Courts leet and baron are held at Easter and Michaelmas, at the former the constables are appointed There is a place of worship for Presbyterians In 1754, Lady Widdrington gave a rent-charge of £40, for the support of charity schools in the parishes of Arthuret and Kirk-Andrews, of which, £8 per annum is paid to a schoolmaster at Longtown, and a school for the instruction of an unlimited number of children is supported by Sir James R. G Graham, Bart. This place is eminently indebted to the liberality and public spirit of the late Dr Graham, who was mainly instrumental in raising it from the state of a poor village to its present improved condition.

LONGTOWN, a chapelry in the parish of CLODOCK, hundred of EWYASLACY, county of HEREFORD, 17 miles (S W by W) from Hereford, containing 842 inhabitants The living is a perpetual curacy, in the

archdeaconry of Brecon, and diocese of St David's, endowed with £400 private benefaction, and £200 royal bounty The Rev James Rogers was patron in 1816 The chapel is dedicated to St. Peter Courts baron for the parish and hundred are held here annually Lewis Gilbert, Esq bequeathed £4 per annum for the instruction of children There are some few vestiges of a castle, and to the eastward is an eminence called Money Farthing hill, probably from coins having been found there

LONGWOOD, a chapelry in the parish of HUDDERSFIELD, upper division of the wapentake of AGBRIGG, West riding of the county of YORK, 2¼ miles (W) from Huddersfield, containing 1942 inhabitants The living is a perpetual curacy, in the archdeaconry and diocese of York, endowed with £800 royal bounty, and £2400 parliamentary grant, and in the patronage of the Vicar of Huddersfield. A free school was founded and endowed with lands, in 1731, by William Walker, for the education of forty children of both sexes, to be elected from Longwood, Golcar, and Milnes Bridge the annual income is £97 11, and the master occupies the school-house, garden, and croft

LONGWORTH, a parish comprising the chapelry of Charney in the hundred of GANFIELD, and the hamlet of Draycot-Moore in the hundred of OCK, county of BERKS, 7 miles (N E by E) from Great Farringdon, and containing 974 inhabitants The living is a rectory, in the archdeaconry of Berks, and diocese of Salisbury, rated in the king's books at £27 1 10½, and in the patronage of the Principal and Fellows of Jesus College, Oxford The church is dedicated to St Mary There is a small sum for the instruction of children, the bequest of John Carter, by means of which eight boys and girls are taught to read and write This parish is entitled to send five boys to the school at Kingston-Bagpuze A National school has been lately established here. The ancient intrenchment called Cherbury Camp is in a detached part of the parish it is of an oval form, surrounded by a triple vallum, the diameter in the widest part is three hundred and ten paces, and in the narrowest, two hundred and eleven The river Isis runs through this parish In the parochial register is an entry of the baptism of Bishop Fell, July 16th, 1625, whose father was rector of Longworth

LONGWORTH, a township in the parish of BOLTON, hundred of SALFORD, county palatine of LANCASTER, 5½ miles (N by W) from Great Bolton, containing 238 inhabitants

LOOE (EAST), a sea-port, borough, market town, and chapelry, having separate jurisdiction, in the parish of ST MARTIN, locally in West hundred, county of CORNWALL, 16 miles (W) from Plymouth, and 232 (W S W) from London, containing 770 inhabitants This place was formerly the only sea-port in Cornwall of any importance, excepting Fowey, and hence was derived its name, Lo, in Cornish, signifying a port In the reign of Edward III it furnished twenty ships and three hundred and fifteen mariners towards the

Seal and Arms.

equipment of the English fleet for the siege of Calais
Its situation is beautifully romantic, on the eastern
bank of Looe bay, near the mouth of the river Looe,
over which is a narrow bridge of thirteen stone arches,
one hundred and forty-one yards in length, and only
six feet wide, built about the year 1400 the sea view
is very fine, and the land scenery richly diversified, the
air is salubrious, and the inhabitants are supplied with
excellent water On the beach is a fort mounted with
ten guns, and opposite to the town is Looe island, or
St George s, which is much frequented by flocks of sea-
fowl during the spring The pilchard fishery is carried
on to a considerable extent, the exports consist of tin,
copper, and lead ore, bark, timber, salt, pilchards, and
pilchard oil, and coal, culm, and limestone are imported.
Here is a custom-house, and a collector, a comptroller,
and a surveyor of the customs, are resident Four British vessels entered inwards from foreign parts, and
three cleared outwards, in 1826, three vessels were
built and registered here the same year, and in 1828,
there were two vessels of more than one hundred tons,
and twenty-four of less, burden belonging to the port
This town derives considerable advantages from the
Liskeard and Looe canal, recently completed The market is on Saturday, and fairs are held, February 13th,
July 10th, September 10th, and October 10th

East Looe is a borough by prescription, the charter
of incorporation, granted by Elizabeth in 1587, was confirmed by charters of James I and II The corporation
consists of a mayor, recorder, eight aldermen, and an
indefinite number of burgesses, with a town clerk, four
serjeants at mace, and inferior officers the mayor and
recorder are elected by the aldermen, the aldermen and
free burgesses by the mayor and aldermen, the town clerk
is appointed by the recorder, and the serjeants at mace
are nominated by the mayor the mayor, the late
mayor, the deputy mayor, the recorder, and the deputy recorder, are justices of the peace, within the
borough Sessions for the borough are held once or
twice a year, at which prisoners charged with petty
larceny are tried, but those committed for transportable, or capital, offences, are generally tried at the
assizes or sessions for the county, though there is
a clause in the charter to prohibit the judicial interference of the county magistrates The charter of
James II gives the mayor and aldermen authority to
hold a court of record every three weeks, for the recovery of debts not exceeding £100, but no business
has been transacted in this court for many years
There is a common gaol for felons and debtors A
court leet, with view of frank-pledge, is held for the
manor This borough, conjointly with Fowey, sent
a representative to a great council at Westminster,
in the reign of Edward I, but members were not
sent to parliament until the 13th of Elizabeth since
which two members have been returned, who are elected
by a majority of the corporation the mayor is the returning officer, and the influence of the Buller family is
predominant The living is a perpetual curacy, in the
archdeaconry of Cornwall, and diocese of Exeter, and
in the joint patronage of James Buller, Esq, and the
Rev Sir H Trelawney, Bart The chapel, rebuilt in
1806, is a small but handsome structure There are
places of worship for the Society of Friends and Wes
leyan Methodists

LOOE (WEST), a bo-
rough and chapelry (for-
merly a market town) in
the parish of TALLAND,
WEST hundred, county of
CORNWALL, 16 miles (W)
from Plymouth, and 231
(W S W) from London,
containing 539 inhabitants
This place, also called Port
Pigham, a corruption of Port
Vichan, which signifies in
Cornish the "Little Port,"

Seal and Arms.

is situated on the opposite bank of the river to that
of East Looe, with which it is connected by a bridge
The town is of inconsiderable size, the harbour is
small but commodious, and is defended by a strong battery, the river is navigable for vessels of one hundred
tons burden, and divides itself into two branches, just
above the bridge There is no market, but a cattle
fair is held on the 6th of May A charter of incorporation was granted by Elizabeth, in 1573, whereby the municipal body consists of a mayor and eleven burgesses,
who are empowered to choose a steward, with a town
clerk, and other officers the mayor and steward are
justices of the peace A court leet, with view of frank-
pledge, is held The charter authorises the mayor to
hold a court for the recovery of debts under £5, every
week, but no proceedings have taken place in this court
for several years There is a small prison, called the
Dark house The borough first sent members to parliament in the 6th of Edward VI, since which period it
has returned two representatives, who are elected by a
majority of the corporation the mayor is the returning
officer, and the influence of the Buller family is predominant The chapel, formerly dedicated to St Nicholas,
but now desecrated, has been converted into a guildhall
There is a place of worship for Independents A mathematical free school was founded here, in 1716, by the
trustees under the will of John Specott, Esq, who in
1730 bequeathed the sum of £1000 for charitable uses,
£30 per annum was appropriated by them for the
instruction of poor children in the mathematics, par
ticularly in those branches which relate to navigation, and the appointment of the master, after the
death of the original trustees, was vested in the heirs
of Charles Trelawney, Esq, and the proprietor of Trelawney house In the vicinity of West Looe are the
remains of a mound, supposed to have been on the
line of a Roman road, and some vestiges of military
works

LOOSE, a parish in the hundred of MAIDSTONE
lathe of AYLESFORD, county of KENT, 2½ miles (S)
from Maidstone, containing 882 inhabitants The living
is a perpetual curacy, in the peculiar jurisdiction and
patronage of the Archbishop of Canterbury The
church, dedicated to All Saints, has recently received an
addition of one hundred and thirty-five sittings, of
which seventy nine are free, the Incorporated Society for
enlarging churches and chapels having contributed
£100 towards defraying the expense A stream of
water runs through this parish, which, in the space of
three miles, turns no less than twelve mills Here is
a quarry of rag-stone, and in the vicinity are large
plantations of hops

LOPEN, a parish in the southern division of the hundred of PETHERTON, county of SOMERSET, 3½ miles (N N W) from Crewkerne, containing 425 inhabitants The living is a perpetual curacy, in the archdeaconry of Taunton, and diocese of Bath and Wells, endowed with £200 private benefaction, and £400 royal bounty The church is dedicated to All Saints The manufacture of coarse linen is carried on to a limited extent

LOPHAM (NORTH), a parish in the hundred of GUILT-CROSS, county of NORFOLK, 5 miles (S E) from East Harling, containing 741 inhabitants The living is a rectory, with that of South Lopham, in the archdeaconry of Norfolk, and diocese of Norwich, rated in the king s books at £17 0 5 George H Barrow, Esq was patron in 1822 The church is dedicated to St Andrew There is a place of worship for Wesleyan Methodists In this parish is Lopham ford, where the rivers Waveney and Little Ouse take their rise, about three yards from each other, and, diverging, pursue opposite courses

LOPHAM (SOUTH), a parish in the hundred of GUILT-CROSS, county of NORFOLK, 5½ miles (S E by S) from East Harling, containing 821 inhabitants The living is a rectory not in charge, annexed to that of North Lopham, in the archdeaconry of Norfolk, and diocese of Norwich The church is dedicated to St Nicholas

LOPPINGTON, a parish in the hundred of PIM-HILL, county of SALOP, 3 miles (W) from Wem, containing 622 inhabitants. The living is a discharged vicarage, in the archdeaconry of Salop, and diocese of Lichfield and Coventry, rated in the king s books at £6 12 1 , and in the patronage of the Crown The church is dedicated to St Mary There is a place of worship for Wesleyan Methodists

LORBOTTLE, a township in the parish of WHIT-TINGHAM, northern division of COQUETDALE ward, county of NORTHUMBERLAND, 5½ miles (N N W) from Rothbury, containing 100 inhabitants

LORTON, a parish in ALLERDALE ward above Darwent, county of CUMBERLAND, comprising the chapelry of Wythop, and the townships of Brackenthwaite and Lorton, and containing 593 inhabitants, of which number, 353 are in the township of Lorton, 3½ miles (S E by S) from Cockermouth The living is a perpetual curacy, in the archdeaconry of Richmond, and diocese of Chester, endowed with £200 private benefaction, £1000 royal bounty, and £600 parliamentary grant, and in the patronage of the Earl of Lonsdale The church is dedicated to St Cuthbert. A school is endowed with the interest of £100

LOSCOW, a joint township with Codnor, in the parish of HEANOR, hundred of MORLESTON and LIT-CHURCH, county of DERBY, 6 miles (S by E) from Alfreton The population is returned with Codnor There is a place of worship for Baptists

LOSTOCK, a hamlet in the parish of BOLTON, hundred of SALFORD, county palatine of LANCASTER, 4½ miles (W) from Great Bolton, containing 576 inhabitants An unendowed school was erected by subscription, on an allotment of land given by the commissioners of enclosures for the instruction of poor children of the neighbourhood about thirty children are instructed at a small charge Here are the remains of a very ancient mansion, called Lostock hall, bearing date 1563 the gateway is of stone, and the royal arms, with

the date 1590, are over the highest bay window it is supposed to have been the residence of the Andertons

LOSTOCK GRALAM, a township in that part of the parish of GREAT BUDWORTH which is in the hundred of NORTHWICH, county palatine of CHESTER, 2½ miles (E) from Northwich, containing 525 inhabitants The Grand Trunk canal passes westward of this place

LOSTWITHIEL, a borough, market town, and parish, having separate jurisdiction, though locally in the eastern division of the hundred of Powder, county of CORNWALL, 6 miles (S) from Bodmin, 26 (S W) from Launceston, and 236½ (W S W) from London, containing 933 inhabitants This place is supposed by some to have been the Roman station called Uzella by Ptolemy, but this opinion does not appear to be warranted by the discovery of any certain traces of Roman residence According to tradition, Lostwithiel was so called as having been the residence of Withiel, anciently Earl of Cornwall, who had a palace at Penkneth, now part of the borough, but in the parish of Lanlivery In the reign of Richard I , the town was held under the Earl of Cornwall, by Robert de Cardinham, who procured for it the privilege of a market , and Richard, Earl of Cornwall, the brother of Henry III , made Lostwithiel, including Penkneth, a free borough His son Edmund, Earl of Cornwall, was a great benefactor to the town, in which he erected a shire hall, an exchequer office, and other handsome buildings, and ordered that the coinage and sale of the tin from the Cornish mines should take place at Lostwithiel only, and that all county meetings should be held there. These exclusive privileges were not preserved inviolate, for, in 1314, the burgesses complained to the parliament that the men of Bodmin, Truro, and Helston, had caused tin to be sold at those towns, and that the prior of Bodmin had then recently procured the county meetings to be held at Bodmin , but notwithstanding these grievances were redressed, Lostwithiel was gradually deprived of its exclusive advantages, the only remnant of which is the election of the knights for the county of Cornwall, which still takes place here, though the previous meetings for the nomination of the candidates are held at Bodmin In the summer of 1644, this place was the head-quarters of the parliamentary general, the Earl of Essex , previously to which, a battle had been fought near the town, in which a body of the king s troops, under Sir Richard Grenville, was defeated by Lord Robartes Dugdale asserts that the parish church was profaned by the parliamentarian soldiers, and injured by an explosion of gunpowder

This town is situated in a beautiful vale, on the banks of the river Fawy, on the high road from Plymouth to Falmouth , the river, which is crossed by a bridge, is navigable for small barges as far as the quay, during the spring tides The town consists of two parallel streets, extending from the river to the foot of a steep hill it is lighted and paved, and there is a good supply of water The houses are chiefly built of stone,

Seal and Arms.

and covered with slate, which abounds in the neighbourhood An annual regatta, or boat race, with a ball, takes place in August, and assemblies are held in the winter There is a tan-yard in the town, but its trade chiefly depends upon the importation of timber, coal, and other articles for the miners, and the recent increase of the copper mines in the neighbourhood has been attended with a correspondent advance of commercial prosperity About three miles from the town are the extensive mines of Lanescot and the Fowey Consols, surpassing, in the variety, extent, and power of their machinery, all others in the kingdom, their produce amounting to an eleventh part of all the copper-ore furnished by the mines of Cornwall The market is held on Friday, and the establishment of a corn market, free of toll, was recently attempted, but without success the market-house was erected at the expense of Viscount Mount-Edgcumbe, in 1781 There are fairs for horses, cattle, and sheep, March 31st, July 10th, September 4th, and November 13th The borough includes portions of the adjoining parishes of Lanhvery and St Winnow A charter of incorporation was granted by James I, in 1623, and renewed by George II, in 1738, under which the corporation consists of seven aldermen or capital burgesses, including the mayor, and seventeen assistants, or common council-men The mayor is elected by the aldermen and assistants, on the first Tuesday after Michaelmas, and the assistants are chosen by the aldermen, who likewise fill up vacancies in their own body The mayor, the late mayor, and the recorder, are justices of the peace, and the mayor is also coroner A court leet is held annually by the mayor, when presentments are made concerning matters relating to the borough and the river, and all persons having boats on the river are required to yield suit and service at this court The petty sessions are generally held here on Friday The quarter sessions for the county, formerly held here in the summer, were, a few years since, removed to Bodmin In the old shire hall, erected by the Earl of Cornwall, and in which the stannary parliaments were held, is the original stannary court-room, with a prison adjoining, which is the only one in the county belonging to the stannaries The town hall is a neat building, with a prison underneath, erected, in 1740, at the cost of Lord Mount-Edgcumbe The borough first returned members to parliament in the 33rd of Edward I, and then ceased till the 4th of Edward II, since which the returns have been regular The right of election is vested in the corporation, and the mayor is the returning officer The Earl of Mount-Edgcumbe possesses paramount influence.

The living is a discharged vicarage, in the archdeaconry of Cornwall, and diocese of Exeter, rated in the king's books at £ 2 13 4, endowed with £600 royal bounty, and in the patronage of the Earl of Mount-Edgcumbe. The church, dedicated to St Bartholomew, is a handsome edifice in the early English style, with a lantern tower at the west end, surmounted by a fine octagonal spire, erected in the fourteenth century it contains an ancient stone font, on the sides of which are sculptured grotesque figures and armorial bearings, rudely executed, and now much defaced There are places of worship for Bryanites, Independents, and Wesleyan Methodists A free grammar school was established by the corporation about 1776, the master of which has a sa-

lary of £50 per annum A writing-school is kept in the town hall, the corporation allowing a salary of £10 per annum to the master There is likewise a school with an endowment of £5 per annum, paid out of the proceeds of a fund left for charitable uses, by the Rev St John Eliot A Sunday school, supported by voluntary contributions, affords instruction to about one hundred and twenty children of both sexes About a mile northward of the town, on the edge of a lofty hill, are the magnificent and venerable ruins of Restormel castle, supposed to have been erected by Robert, Earl of Mortaigne, and anciently the residence of the Earls of Cornwall At the commencement of the great civil war, although then ruinous, it was garrisoned for the parliament, and was taken by the royalist general, Sir Richard Grenville, in August, 1644 The remains are comprised within a circular area, one hundred and ten feet in diameter, the walls of which are nine feet thick, and are surrounded by a deep moat, at the southern entrance, where was formerly a draw-bridge, are two arches supporting a square tower, traces of suites of apartments and stone staircases are visible, and the whole, being richly overgrown with ivy, presents a very picturesque appearance. The chapel of the Holy Trinity, anciently appendant to the castle, is also in ruins

LOTHERS, a parish in the liberty of LOTHERS and BOTHENHAMPTON, Bridport division of the county of DORSET, 2 miles (E N E) from Bridport, containing 857 inhabitants The living is a discharged vicarage, in the archdeaconry of Dorset, and diocese of Bristol, rated in the king's books at £14 5 7½, and in the patronage of the Crown The church is dedicated to St Mary Magdalene Here was an Alien priory subordinate to the abbey of Mountsburgh in Normandy at the suppression by Richard II, being then valued at £80 per annum, it was bestowed on the priory of St Anne, near Coventry, but, in the time of Henry IV, it was restored to its ancient owners, and after the dissolution by Henry V, it became part of the endowment of Sion abbey, Middlesex.

LOTHERTON, a township in the parish of SHERBURN, upper division of the wapentake of BARKSTONE-ASH, West riding of the county of YORK, 6 miles (S S W) from Tadcaster, containing, with a part of Aberford, 427 inhabitants

LOUDWATER, a chapelry in the parish of HIGH WYCOMBE, hundred of DESBOROUGH, county of BUCKINGHAM, 3¼ miles (S E) from High Wycombe, with which the population is returned The living is a perpetual curacy, in the archdeaconry of Buckingham, and diocese of Lincoln, endowed with £1200 private benefaction, £400 royal bounty, and £2400 parliamentary grant, and in the patronage of certain Trustees The chapel was built and endowed, in 1788, by W Davis, Esq

LOUGHBOROUGH, a market town and parish in the western division of the hundred of GOSCOTE, county of LEICESTER, comprising the townships of Knight-Thorpe and Wood-Thorpe, and containing 7494 inhabitants, of which number, 7365 are in the town of Loughborough, 11 miles (N) from Leicester, and 109 (N W) from London The name is probably derived from Lough, a lake, or a large extent of meadow occasionally overflowed The noble family of Despenser, anciently possessors of the manor, obtained the grant of a market and fairs for the town In 1564, the assizes for the county were held here, on account of the plague raging at Leicester at that time From its size and population this may be considered the second town in the county, and it was so reckoned three centuries ago it is a great thoroughfare, being situated on the high road from London to Manchester The buildings in general are of brick, and a great proportion of the houses is modern plaster, which is made of alabaster obtained from the quarries of Burton on the Wold, is mostly used for the floors of the lodging rooms The streets are paved and partially lighted by subscription, and the inhabitants are well supplied with water A neat theatre has been recently built there is likewise a subscription library The manufactures comprise hosiery of all kinds, cotton goods, and bobbin net-lace, for which last article a patent was obtained by the manufacturer, and the machinery is worked here under his license, giving employment to nearly five hundred persons the manufacture of what is termed patent fleecy hosiery is confined entirely to this town The Loughborough canal, which communicates with the Union canal, the Leicester navigation, the river Soar, and the lime-works at Barrow hill has been very beneficial to the town, and abundantly profitable to the proprietors the shares, which originally cost but £120 each, are now worth about £4000 There are some quarries of slate in the neighbourhood The market is on Thursday, and fairs are held February 14th, March 28th, April 25th, Holy Thursday, August 12th, and November 13th, for horses, cows, and sheep, March 24th and September 25th, for cheese, and November 14th is a statute fair for hiring servants An ancient cross and the old market house having been removed, the market place is now open The town is under the superintendence of a constable, headborough, meadow-reeves, and street-masters, all of them chosen at the annual court leet of the lord of the manor A court baron is held annually, and the petty sessions for the hundred are held here weekly The living is a rectory, in the archdeaconry of Leicester, and diocese of Lincoln, rated in the king s books at £40 16 3, and in the patronage of the Master and Fellows of Emanuel College, Cambridge The church, which is dedicated to All Saints is a handsome edifice, in the later style of English architecture, and has a fine tower, which was built by subscription towards the close of the sixteenth century There are places of worship for General and Particular Baptists, Independents, the Society of Friends, Wesleyan Methodists, and Unitarians The free grammar school is endowed with rents arising from lands originally bequeathed by Thomas Burton, in 1495, for the maintenance of a chantry in the parish church, but appropriated, at the Reformation, to the endowment of a free grammar school, the repair of certain public bridges in the parish, and in aid of parochial rates, these estates are called "Burton s Trust, and their present rental is about £1500 per annum as a principal object in the expenditure is the repair of the roads and bridges, an officer is annually elected, under the name of bridgemaster, to superintend its execution The school is open to all the children residing in the parish it is entirely under the direction of the trustees, and consists of three establishments, under separate masters, namely, a Latin school, in which

Vol III

there are from fifteen to twenty scholars, a school in which reading, writing, and arithmetic are taught to about twenty-five boys, and a National school for two hundred and fifty more the surplus of the annual income is appropriated by the trustees to charitable uses Two exhibitions, of £30 each, to Emanuel College, Cambridge, are attached to this institution the school-house is a handsome new building, erected near the churchyard A free school for twenty girls was founded, in 1683, by means of a bequest from Bartholomew Hickling, and endowed with land, and, in 1717, Joseph Clark bequeathed land, directing the proceeds to be applied for the instruction of children Various benefactions have been made, at different periods, for apprenticing poor children, and for annual distribution to the poor A public dispensary is supported by voluntary contributions Dr Richard Pulteney, a distinguished physician and writer on botany, was born here in 1730 Loughborough conferred the title of baron on Alexander Wedderburn, an eminent lawyer, who held the office of Lord High Chancellor, and who was subsequently created Earl of Rosslyn

LOUGHRIGG, a joint township with Rydal, in the parish of GRASMERE, KENDAL ward, county of WESTMORLAND, 2¾ miles (W by S) from Ambleside The population is returned with Rydal

LOUGHTON, a parish in the hundred of NEWPORT, county of BUCKINGHAM, 9¼ miles (N W) from Fenny-Stratford containing 293 inhabitants The living is a rectory, in the archdeaconry of Bucks, and diocese of Lincoln, rated in the king s books at £14 5 2½, and in the patronage of the Master and Fellows of Trinity College, Cambridge The church is dedicated to All Saints

LOUGHTON, a parish in the hundred of ONGAR, county of ESSEX, 14 miles (N E by N) from London, containing 979 inhabitants The living is a rectory, in the jurisdiction of the Commissary of London, concurrently with the Consistorial Court of the Bishop of London, rated in the king s books at £18 3 9 Miss Whitaker was patroness in 1805 The church is dedicated to St Nicholas There is a place of worship for Baptists

LOUGHTON, a chapelry in the parish of CHETTON, hundred of STOTTESDEN, county of SALOP, 9 miles (N E by L) from Ludlow, containing 119 inhabitants

LOUND, a joint township with Toft, in the parish of WITHAM on the HILL, wapentake of BELTISLOE, parts of KESTEVEN, county of LINCOLN, 3 miles (S W by W) from Bourne The population is returned with Toft

LOUND, a township in the parish of SUTTON, liberty of SOUTHWELL and SCROOBY, county of NOTTINGHAM, 4 miles (N by W) from East Retford, containing 370 inhabitants There is a place of worship for Wesleyan Methodists

LOUND, a parish in the hundred of MUTFORD and LOTHINGLAND, county of SUFFOLK, 5 miles (N W by N) from Lowestoft, containing 416 inhabitants The living is a discharged rectory, in the archdeaconry of Suffolk, and diocese of Norwich, rated in the king s books at £8 The Rev J Blanchard was patron in 1826 The church is dedicated to St John the Baptist

Z

Corporate Seal.

LOUTH, a market town and parish, having separate jurisdiction, though locally in the Wold division of the hundred of Louth - Eske, parts of LINDSEY, county of LINCOLN, 28 miles (E N E) from Lincoln, and 150 (N by E) from London, containing, with the hamlet of Louth Park, 6055 inhabitants The ancient name of this town was *Luda*, from its vicinity to the Lud, a small stream formed by the junction of two rivulets It was distinguished for the number of its religious houses previously to the Reformation, and the inhabitants were the first to resist the measures enforced by Henry VIII for their suppression In 1536 they took part in an insurrection called the "Pilgrimage of Grace, and the prior of Barlings, their leader, the vicar of Louth, four other priests, and seven laymen, were executed at Tyburn in the following year A destructive plague, which raged here in the year 1631, from April until the end of November, swept away seven hundred and fifty-four persons The town is pleasantly situated in a fertile vale, eastward of the wolds, bounded on the north and south by chalk hills, which command beautiful and varied prospects it is neat and well built, the houses being chiefly of brick covered with tiles, the streets are paved, and lighted with gas, under the authority of an act passed in 1825, and the inhabitants are supplied with excellent water from several springs in the neighbourhood, some of which issuing from the northern hills, form a rapid and overflowing stream during the summer, and in winter are generally dry the air is considered to be highly salubrious The theatre is opened every alternate winter Assemblies and concerts are held in the mansion-house, which contains an elegant suite of apartments, ornamented in the Grecian style, and a public subscription library, billiard, and news rooms, are always open The vicarage house, denominated the hermitage, is especially worthy of notice, from the ingenious and rustic style in which the garden is laid out, the walks are planted with shrubs, interspersed with appropriate buildings, seats, and cloisters, for the use of the supposed hermit, and decorated with obelisks and vases, bearing numerous devices and mottos the principal building contains the study, kitchen, chapel, and dormitory, and is adorned with moss, flints, bark, bones, and other natural productions, the whole producing a picturesque effect The mode of obtaining water for irrigating the land here, or for domestic purposes, is somewhat unusual the stratum of argillaceous soil, which descends to a depth of twenty-seven yards, is perforated, and a hollow tube of tin or copper is inserted into the bed of gravel beneath, through which the water rises, and thus a perpetual fountain is formed, from which a copious supply is readily obtained throughout a district of thirty miles in length, and ten in breadth A carpet and blanket manufactory, established a few years ago, is conducted on an extensive scale, and is in a very flourishing condition and a paper-mill and soap-house furnish employment to a considerable number of persons, there are likewise several worsted manufacturers and wool-staplers In 1761, an act of parliament was obtained for cutting a canal between this town and the Humber, which was completed at an expense of £12,000, by means of this mode of communication, vessels of considerable burden regularly trade with London, Hull, and several parts of Yorkshire, carrying out corn and wool, and bringing back coal, timber, iron, grocery, and other articles of commerce The wool market is a commodious building, opened in June 1825 The general market days are Wednesday and Saturday, there is a market for cattle and sheep every Friday during the spring, and fairs are held on the third Wednesday after Easter, August 5th, and November 22nd The government of the town is vested in a warden and six assistants, who were incorporated by charter of the 5th of Edward VI, and are empowered to choose a high steward, town clerk and bailiff to the corporation Elizabeth gave, by charter, "the manor of Louth and divers lands there, the annual value then being £78 14 4½, their privileges were subsequently confirmed and extended by James I The warden and one of the assistants, called the justice, are elected annually, and are magistrates in and for the town and parish, and an application has lately been made for a charter, for the appointment of two additional magistrates Sessions for the town are held quarterly, usually in January, April, July, and October The general quarter sessions for the southern parts of the division of Lindsey are held here and at Spilsby alternately Petty sessions are held every Wednesday in the guildhall, and there is a court of requests, under an act passed in the 47th of George III, for the recovery of debts not exceeding £5, the jurisdiction of which extends over a considerable portion of the parts of Lindsey The sessions house and prison is a handsome modern pile, with a portico of Roman Doric architecture The tread-mill is used to grind corn for sale

The living of St James is a discharged vicarage, with the perpetual curacy of Louth St Mary, in the peculiar jurisdiction and patronage of the Prebendary of Louth in the Cathedral Church of Lincoln, rated in the king's books at £12, and endowed with £200 royal bounty Here were formerly two churches, dedicated respectively to St Mary and St James, of these, the latter only remains, and it is one of the finest structures in the county, consisting of a nave, aisles, and a chancel, and exhibiting a remarkably good specimen of the later style of English architecture at the east end is a window of seven lights, with very beautiful tracery, and at the western extremity is a lofty tower, with a rich crocketed spire, the building of which was completed about 1516 the spire, having been blown down some years ago, was rebuilt on the original plan The tower consists of three stories, at its summit are four octagonal embattled turrets, with flying buttresses to the spire, the height of which, to the cross by which it is surmounted, is one hundred and forty-one feet, and the total height, from the base of the tower, two hundred and eighty-eight feet The chancel is of later date than the body of the church, and probably coeval with the steeple The burial-ground has not been used for upwards of half a century, the churchyard formerly belonging to the church of St Mary being the general place of interment There are places of worship for Baptists, Independents, Primitive and Wesleyan Methodists, and a Roman Catholic chapel The free grammar school was founded and endowed by Edward VI , with the property of some ancient guilds in this town, consisting of about one hundred and sixty acres of land, with several messuages and tenements, and the tolls of markets and fairs the trustees are the warden and six assistants, with their successors, who are authorised to make laws for the government of the school the present income is about £600 per annum, of which sum half is directed to be given to the head master, a quarter to the usher, and the remainder to be appropriated to the maintenance of twelve poor women, who reside in almshouses under the school-room The school is open for gratuitous classical instruction to the children of all parishioners A fund is raised from the terms of admission on the annual "speech day,' and from a subsequent ball, out of which assistance is afforded to any young man of superior abilities at either of the Universities, who had been previously educated here A free school for poor boys was founded and endowed by the will of Dr Robert Mapletoft, Dean of Ely, in 1677, with a rent-charge upon his estates, for the support of a master to teach reading, writing, arithmetic, and the church catechism the income is about £5 per annum Thomas Espin, F S.A , whose views of the cathedral, churches, and ruins, in this county, are universally admired, was master of this school for thirty years, and on his death, in 1822, was interred in a mausoleum near his late residence in the town A National school, erected in 1818, and enlarged in 1820, is supported by voluntary contributions, and contains about three hundred children A dispensary for the relief of the sick poor is also supported by subscription About a mile from the town is the hamlet of Louth-Park, where are some slight vestiges of an abbey founded by Alexander, Bishop of Lincoln, in 1139, for monks of the Cistercian order, and dedicated to the Virgin Mary it was a cell subordinate to Fountains abbey in Yorkshire, and at the dissolution its revenue was estimated at £169 5 6

LOVEDALE, a township in the parish of PENKRIDGE, eastern division of the hundred of CUTTLESTONE, county of STAFFORD The population is returned with the parish.

LOVERSALL, a parish in the soke of DONCASTER, West riding of the county of YORK, 3½ miles (S) from Doncaster, containing 131 inhabitants The living is a perpetual curacy, in the archdeaconry and diocese of York, endowed with £600 royal bounty, and £200 parliamentary grant, and in the patronage of the Vicar of Doncaster

LOVINGTON, a parish in the hundred of CATSASH, county of SOMERSET, 2¾ miles (W S W) from Castle-Cary, containing 206 inhabitants The living is a perpetual curacy, in the peculiar jurisdiction and patronage of the Dean and Chapter of Wells, endowed with £800 royal bounty The church is dedicated to St Thomas à Becket John Whitehead, in 1715, bequeathed certain land, and James Clarke subsequently gave a house, the income arising from which is £9, and is applied to the instruction of twelve poor children.

LOWDHAM, a parish in the southern division of the wapentake of THURGARTON, county of NOTTINGHAM, 7¾ miles (N E) from Nottingham, comprising the townships of Caythorpe and Gunthorpe, and containing 1334 inhabitants The living is a discharged vicarage,

in the archdeaconry of Nottingham, and diocese of York, rated in the kings books at £4 18 4 , and in the patronage of Earl Manvers The church is dedicated to St Mary There was formerly a chapel of ease at Gunthorpe, where is now a place of worship for Wesleyan Methodists The manufacture of stockings is carried on here

LOWE, a joint township with Ditches, in that part of the parish of WEM which is in the Whitchurch division of the hundred of BRADFORD (North), county of SALOP, 1 mile (N W) from Wem, containing, with Ditches, 93 inhabitants

LOWESBY, a parish in the eastern division of the hundred of GOSCOTE, county of LEICESTER, 9¾ miles (E by N) from Leicester, containing, with the chapelry of Cold Newton, 217 inhabitants The living is a discharged vicarage, in the archdeaconry of Leicester, and diocese of Lincoln, rated in the king s books at £7 1 5½ , endowed with £800 private benefaction, £600 royal bounty, and £600 parliamentary grant Sir F G Fowke, Bart was patron in 1820 The church is dedicated to All Saints

LOWESTOFT, a sea-port, market town, and parish, in the hundred of MUTFORD and LOTHINGLAND, county of SUFFOLK, 44 miles (N E by N) from Ipswich, and 115 (N E by N) from London, containing 3675 inhabitants The name of this town, anciently Lothnwistoft, or I ays toft, is derived, as some suppose, from Lothbroch, a noble Dane, who obtained a part of the kingdom of the East Angles, and resided here , or, according to others, from Lou-toft, a market formerly held beneath the cliffs In 1349, the great plague which devastated the continent of Europe, raged here with such fury, that not more than one-tenth of the inhabitants escaped the contagion, and in 1547 and 1579 the same malady again prevailed in 1605, it suffered severely from fire, and during the usurpation of Cromwell it was exposed to heavy exactions from its attachment to the royal cause in 1643, Cromwell entered the town at the head of one thousand cavalry, and seizing several persons, sent them prisoners to Cambridge In the war with the Dutch, two sanguinary engagements took place off this coast in 1665 and 1666 , two of the British admirals on that occasion were natives of Lowestoft In consequence of the repeated occurrence of shipwreck, two lighthouses were erected by the inhabitants that on the cliff consisted at first of a circular tower of brick and stone, the upper story of which was sashed and glazed, and a coal fire was constantly kept burning, but having become dilapidated, it has been taken down, and replaced by a cylindrical revolving lantern, furnished with powerful reflectors the other, on the beach beneath, is constructed of timber, and is moveable at pleasure By steering in such a direction as to make the upper and lower lighthouses coincide, vessels are guided to a channel of a quarter of a mile in breadth, between the Holme and Barnard sands, the course of this channel, called Stanford, varies so much, from the violence of currents, and the effect of storms, to which this coast is exposed, that a change in the position of the lower lighthouse is frequently necessary the fort at the south end of the beach having become ruinous in 1744, a battery was erected at the north end, and fortified with two pieces of cannon In 1782, a new fort was built at the south end, and furnished with thirteen pieces of cannon, another fort has also been erected at the north end, and a battery near the Ness

The town is situated on a lofty cliff, bordering on the German ocean, and consists principally of one street, nearly a mile in length, which is well paved, and of several small ones, which diverge from it obliquely, the whole being well lighted the houses, chiefly of brick, are neat and modern, and the inhabitants are well supplied with water from springs, the air is considered highly salubrious, especially to invalids, and the shore, gradually descending to the sea, and having a firm pebbly bottom, is commodious for bathing, which circumstances have made Lowestoft a great resort of fashionable visitors during the summer Races have been recently established on the downs northward of the town, which form an admirable course, the cliffs, rising in a gentle slope, make a natural amph theatre, capable of containing in immense number of spectators There is a good theatre, in which performances take place every alternate year, also a spacious and elegant assembly room, where balls are held at Christmas, and concerts twice a week during the bathing season, and a subscription reading-room and library A new bathing-house, fitted up with hot and cold baths, was erected by subscription among some of the inhabitants in 1824 it is a handsome building of pebble stones, with rusticated angles, and is situated at the south end of the High-street The trade principally arises from the herring fishery, in which about forty boats, from twenty five to forty tons burden each, are engaged, and which employs the inhabitants from the end of May till the end of June, after which time great quantities of mackarel and soles are caught, and sent to the Norwich and London markets the herrings are prepared and dried in houses at the base of the cliff, extending the whole length of the town, and the process of curing is entirely devoid of offensive effluvia. There are rope and twine manufactories of considerable extent An act of parliament has been recently granted to a company, for making a navigable communication from Lowestoft to Norwich, they have already erected a lock and swing bridge at Oulton, and are now carrying on the excavation between Lake Lothing and the sea in order to form a harbour of refuge for vessels in distress Facilities for water carriage are also afforded by communication from Lake Lothing to the Yare at Yarmouth, and by the Waveney to Beccles and Bungay The market is on Wednesday, for grain and provisions, and toy fairs are held May 12th and October 10th The county magistrates hold petty sessions weekly at this place, and manorial courts are occasionally held by the steward of the manor By charter of George II, who landed here, the inhabitants are exempted from serving on juries out of the town There are a commodious town hall, and a market cross

The living is a discharged vicarage, in the archdeaconry of Suffolk, and diocese of Norwich, rated in the king's books at £10 1 0½, endowed with £250 private benefaction, and £200 royal bounty, and in the patronage of the Crown The church dedicated to St Margaret, is a large and handsome structure, in the later style of English architecture, with a tower, surmounted by a wooden spire covered with lead, and a south porch, over which was a chamber, said to have been formerly inhabited by two recluse females, who caused wells to be dug between the church and the town, called Basket wells, vulgarly supposed to be a corruption of their names, "Bess and Kate ' The interior consists of a nave, two side aisles, and a chancel, with a fine east window of stained glass, the ceiling is ornamented with a rude painting intended to represent the Holy Trinity, and two antique shields contain a representation of the Crucifixion, there is a large brass eagle, formerly used as a reading-desk, also a very ancient and handsome font, decorated with a double row of saints sculptured upon it, and approached by an ascent of three steps, but now greatly defaced Sir John Holt, Lord Chief Justice of the Court of King's Bench in the reign of George I, was buried here, and a handsome monument, bearing a Latin inscription, was erected to his memory In 1698, a chapel of ease was rebuilt by subscription, near the centre of the town Here are places of worship for Baptists, Independents, and Wesleyan Methodists A free grammar school was founded, in 1571, by Thomas Annot, Esq, whose endowment of it was increased by his heir to £16 per annum, the master is chosen by the vicar and churchwardens, subject to the approval of the chancellor of the diocese, his salary is now £23 per annum, for which he instructs twenty-three boys Another free school, on the east side of the High street, was founded and endowed by Mr John Wilde, in 1735, for the instruction of forty boys in Latin and English the school-house, in which the master resides, was built in 1788, the master receives a salary of £40 per annum, arising from an estate at Worlingham, the surplus produce of which, amounting in the whole to about £154 per annum, is vested in the churchwardens for charitable purposes A National school for boys is supported by voluntary contributions There are various charitable bequests for the relief of the poor In 1758, a skeleton was discovered in a barrow on Bloodmore hill, near this town, round its neck was a chain, with a gold medal bearing an inscription and device, and an onyx set in gold, bearing a device In the centre of the High-street are some vestiges of a religious house, consisting of a curious Norman arch, and cellars with groined arches, evidently part of an ancient crypt The surrounding cliffs abound with organic remains, such as the bones and teeth of the mammoth, the horns and bones of the elk, with *Cornua Ammonis*, and shells and fossils of various kinds The celebrated William Whiston, Professor of Mathematics at Cambridge, and Mr Potter, the learned translator of Æschylus and Euripides, were vicars of this parish

LOWESWATER, a parochial chapelry in ALLERDALE ward above Darwent, county of CUMBERLAND, 7½ miles (8 by E) from Cockermouth, containing, with Mockerkin, 440 inhabitants The living is a perpetual curacy, in the archdeaconry of Richmond, and diocese of Chester, endowed with £200 private benefaction, £800 royal bounty, and £200 parliamentary grant, and in the patronage of the Earl of Lonsdale The church was erected by subscription among the inhabitants, in 1827, on the site of an ancient chapel founded by a prior of St Bees, to which parish this was formerly a chapelry, and it still pays a small annual tribute to the mother church The river Cocker runs through this deep and extensive vale, which is bounded by lofty mountains, and contains the picturesque lake of Loweswater, part of Crummock lake, and Scale force, the last the most stupendous cataract in this celebrated region, the water of which, falling to the depth of one hundred and fifty-six feet, sinks into a great chasm surrounded by rocks overhung with trees, and profusely fringed with a variety of smaller shrubs A lead mine has lately been opened here On a hill near the village of Mockerkin a school-room was erected in 1781, and endowed by Mary Mirehouse with £200

LOWICK, a chapelry in the parish of ULVERSTONE, hundred of LONSDALE, north of the sands, county palatine of LANCASTER, 5½ miles (N by W) from Ulverstone, containing 378 inhabitants The living is a perpetual curacy, in the archdeaconry of Richmond, and diocese of Chester, endowed with £400 private benefaction, £600 royal bounty, and £600 parliamentary grant W F Blencowe, Esq was patron in 1786

LOWICK, a parish in the hundred of HUXLOE, county of NORTHAMPTON, 2¾ miles (N W by N) from Thrapstone, containing 419 inhabitants The living is a rectory, in the archdeaconry of Northampton, and diocese of Peterborough, rated in the king's books at £16 8 11½, and in the patronage of the Duke of Dorset The church, dedicated to St Peter, is a handsome edifice in the later style of English architecture, with a remarkably elegant tower crowned with pinnacles and a large octagonal lantern the windows exhibit some brilliant specimens of ancient stained glass, and near the chancel is a mutilated monument of alabaster, to a knight and his lady, of which there are sufficient remains to give an idea of its original splendour Here was a chantry, or college, of Secular priests, in honour of the Blessed Virgin, founded by an ancestor of Stafford, Earl of Wiltshire, about the time of Edward II, and granted, at the dissolution, to Sir Edward Montague Drayton-house, built by Henry Green, Esq, is a noble specimen of the prevailing style of architecture in the time of Henry VI There is a charity school, founded and endowed by Sir John Germain, for teaching and clothing twelve boys and eight girls

LOWICK, a parish in the eastern division of GLENDALE ward, county of NORTHUMBERLAND, 8 miles (N by E) from Wooler, containing 1799 inhabitants The living is a perpetual curacy, in the archdeaconry of Northumberland, and diocese of Durham, endowed with £400 private benefaction, £400 royal bounty, and £400 parliamentary grant, and in the patronage of the Dean and Chapter of Durham The church was rebuilt in 1794 A more commodious place of worship for Presbyterians was erected in 1821, the former one having stood on the spot now occupied by Barmoor castle Coal and limestone are obtained here

LOW-QUARTER, a township in the parish of KIRKBY IRELETH, hundred of LONSDALE, north of the sands, county palatine of LANCASTER, 5 miles (W) from Ulverstone, containing 572 inhabitants

LOWSIDE, a township in the parish of WHICKHAM, western division of CHESTER ward, county palatine of DURHAM, containing 1150 inhabitants

LOWSIDE QUARTER, a township in the parish of ST BEES, ALLERDALE ward above Darwent, county of CUMBERLAND, containing 353 inhabitants The township lies between the river Ehen on the east, and the Irish sea on the west, and contains the venerable remains of Egremont castle, built soon after the Conquest, by

William de Meschines, the first Baron of Copeland, and still exhibiting evident traces of its ancient strength and grandeur

LOWTHER, a parish in WEST ward, county of WESTMORLAND, 4¾ miles (S) from Penrith, containing 599 inhabitants The living is a rectory, in the archdeaconry and diocese of Carlisle, rated in the king s books at £25 7 3½, and in the patronage of the Earl of Lonsdale The church, dedicated to St Michael, was almost wholly rebuilt in 1686, and the tower underwent considerable repairs and alterations in 1824 The parish is bounded on the west by the river Lowther It formerly contained a village of the same name, which was demolished in 1682, by Sir John Lowther, who soon afterwards built another, called New-Town, in which carpet and linen manufactories were established, but did not succeed Richard Lowther, in 1638, gave £100 in support of a schoolmaster, and subsequently, —— Allgood, Esq, left a rent charge of £10, for a similar purpose, these, with other donations, produce an income of about £19 a year, for teaching poor children, who pay also a small quarterage In 1738, two schools for girls were founded by the Rev Richard Holme, and endowed with £100, which was laid out in land now rented by the Earl of Lonsdale, his lordship paying £10 10 per annum to each school

LOWTHORP, a parish in the wapentake of DICKERING, East riding of the county of YORK, 4½ miles (E N E) from Great Driffield, containing 149 inhabitants The living is a perpetual curacy, in the archdeaconry and diocese of York, endowed with £200 private benefaction, and £600 royal bounty W St Quintin, Esq was patron in 1808 The church is dedicated to St Martin, in it was a college, or chantry, for a rector, six chaplains, and three clerks, founded in the reign of Edward III, by Sir John Haselarton

LOWTON, a chapelry in the parish of WINWICK, hundred of WEST DERBY, county palatine of LANCASTER, 2½ miles (N E by E) from Newton in Mackerfield, containing 1988 inhabitants The living is a perpetual curacy, in the archdeaconry and diocese of Chester, endowed with £400 private benefaction, and £400 royal bounty, and in the patronage of the Rector of Winwick The church is dedicated to St Luke A school-room was erected in 1751, with a dwelling house for the master, it is endowed with three acres of land, for the income arising from which six poor children receive free instruction

LOXBEAR, a parish in the hundred of TIVERTON, county of DEVON, 4¼ miles (N W) from Tiverton, containing 138 inhabitants The living is a discharged rectory, in the archdeaconry and diocese of Exeter rated in the king s books at £6 14 9½, endowed with £200 private benefaction, and £200 royal bounty Sir T D Acland, Bart was patron in 1802 The church has a rich Norman doorway and a Norman font There was formerly a chapel at Leigh in this parish

LOXHORE, a parish in the hundred of SHERWILL, county of DEVON, 6¼ miles (N E) from Barnstaple, containing 241 inhabitants The living is a rectory, in the archdeaconry of Barnstaple, and diocese of Exeter, rated in the king s books at £9 14 4½ J P Bruce Chichester, Esq was patron in 1825 The church is dedicated to St Michael

LOXLEY, a liberty in the parish of UTTOXETER,

southern division of the hundred of TOTMONSLOW, county of STAFFORD, 2¾ miles (S W) from Uttoxeter, with which the population is returned It is in the honour of Tutbury, duchy of Lancaster, and within the jurisdiction of a court of pleas held at Tutbury every third Tuesday, for the recovery of debts under 40s

LOXLEY, a parish in the Snitterfield division of the hundred of BARLICHWAY, county of WARWICK, 4¼ miles (E S E) from Stratford upon Avon, containing 311 inhabitants The living is a discharged vicarage, in the archdeaconry and diocese of Worcester, rated in the king's books at £5 6 8, endowed with £200 private benefaction, and £200 royal bounty, and in the patronage of the Crown The church is dedicated to St Nicholas The parish abounds with limestone British and Roman coins have been frequently found here

LOXTON, a parish in the hundred of WINTERSTOKE, county of SOMERSET, 3¾ miles (W N W) from Axbridge, containing 165 inhabitants The living is a rectory, in the archdeaconry of Wells, and diocese of Bath and Wells, rated in the king's books at £15 15 5 W Moncrieffe, Esq was patron in 1801 The church is dedicated to St Andrew Eight poor children are instructed for a trifling bequest by Ann Gadd, in 1765

LOXWOOD-END, a chapelry in that part of the parish of WISBOROUGH-GREEN which is in the hundred of ROTHERBRIDGE, rape of ARUNDEL, county of SUSSEX, 9½ miles (W bv N) from Horsham The population is returned with the parish The chapel was built about 1540, at the expense of three maiden ladies, who endowed it with £6 5 per annum The Arun and Wey Junction canal passes through the parish, and then enters Surrey

LOYNTON, a township in the parish of HIGH OFFLEY, northern division of the hundred of PIREHILL, county of STAFFORD, containing 40 inhabitants

LUBBESTHORPE, a chapelry in that part of the parish of AYLESTONE which is in the hundred of SPARKENHOE, county of LEICESTER, 3¾ miles (S W by W) from Leicester, containing 81 inhabitants The chapel is demolished

LUBENHAM, a parish in the hundred of GARTREE, county of LEICESTER, 2 miles (W) from Market-Harborough, containing 531 inhabitants The living is a vicarage, in the archdeaconry of Leicester, and diocese of Lincoln, rated in the king's books at £8 5, endowed with £400 royal bounty, and £1200 parliamentary grant, and in the patronage of — Grimes, Esq, by sequestration The church is dedicated to All Saints The Union canal passes along the eastern boundary of the parish

LUCKER, a chapelry in the parish of BAMBROUGH, northern division of BAMBROUGH ward, county of NORTHUMBERLAND, 4 miles (S E by E) from Belford, containing 194 inhabitants The living is a perpetual curacy, with that of Bambrough, in the archdeaconry of Northumberland, and diocese of Durham, endowed with £400 private benefaction, and £600 royal bounty The village is situated on the western bank of the river Warn. There is a school supported by donations amounting to about £5 per annum

LUCKHAM, a parish in the hundred of CARHAMPTON, county of SOMERSET, 4 miles (W by S) from Minehead, containing 481 inhabitants The living is a rectory, in the archdeaconry of Taunton, and

diocese of Bath and Wells, rated in the king's books at £14 3 6½, and in the patronage of Sir Thomas Dyke Acland, Bart The church is dedicated to St Mary The river Horner runs through the parish Iron-ore is found in great abundance, and is said to have been worked here more than a century ago There are several mineral springs in the neighbourhood

LUCKINGTON, a hamlet in the parish and hundred of KILMERSDON, county of SOMERSET The population is returned with the parish

LUCKINGTON, a parish in the hundred of CHIPPENHAM, county of WILTS, 7½ miles (W S W) from Malmesbury, containing 280 inhabitants The living is a rectory, in the archdeaconry of Wilts, and diocese of Salisbury, rated in the king's books at £9 7 8½ The Rev John Turner and others were patrons in 1821 The church is dedicated to St Mary

LUCTON, a parish in the hundred of WOLPHY, county of HEREFORD, 6 miles (N W) from Leominster, containing 181 inhabitants The living is a perpetual curacy, in the archdeaconry and diocese of Hereford, endowed with £200 private benefaction, and £600 royal bounty, and in the patronage of the Governors of Lucton school The church is dedicated to St Peter The school was founded, in 1708, by John Pierrepont, Esq, for three masters to teach fifty children, not paupers, of the five adjoining parishes the endowment consists of land and tithes in Orlton, Yarpole, Luston, Eyton, and Lucton, the annual value of which is now about £800 it is vested in a body corporate, styled "The Governors of Lucton school, viz, the master and preacher of the Charter house, London, the common serjeant, the rectors of St Botolph's Bishopsgate, and St Peter's Cornhill, the preacher of Gray's Inn, master of Merchant-Taylors school, and the president of Sion College The present number on the establishment is sixty four, viz, fifty sons of poor farmers and labourers, and fourteen of more opulent parents, the latter of whom pay £1 5 per annum each they are taught the classics, English, writing, &c, and are allowed £10 as an apprentice fee, and £20 at the termination of their apprenticeship

LUDBOROUGH, a parish in the wapentake of LUDBOROUGH, parts of LINDSEY, county of LINCOLN, 6½ miles (N by W) from Louth, containing 284 inhabitants The living is a rectory, in the archdeaconry and diocese of Lincoln, rated in the king's books at £20 19 4½ Mrs Thorold and others were patrons in 1826 The church is dedicated to St Mary There is a place of worship for Wesleyan Methodists

LUDDENDEN, a chapelry in the parish of HALIFAX, wapentake of MORLEY, West riding of the county of YORK, 3½ miles (W by N) from Halifax, with which the population is returned The living is a perpetual curacy, in the archdeaconry and diocese of York, endowed with £400 private benefaction, £600 royal bounty, and £1800 parliamentary grant, and in the patronage of the Vicar of Halifax There is a place of worship for Wesleyan Methodists

LUDDENHAM, a parish in the hundred of FAVERSHAM, lathe of SCRAY, county of KENT, 2 miles (N W by W) from Faversham, containing 178 inhabitants The living is a rectory, in the archdeaconry and diocese of Canterbury, rated in the king's books at £12 8 4, and in the patronage of the Crown The church, dedicated to St Mary, is in the early style of English architecture

LUDDESDOWN, a parish in the hundred of Toltingtrough, lathe of Aylesford, county of Kent, 5½ miles (W by S) from Rochester, containing 235 inhabitants   The living is a rectory, in the archdeaconry and diocese of Rochester, rated in the king's books at £11 11 3   The Rev Dr R Thomson was patron in 1819   The church is dedicated to St Peter and St Paul

LUDDINGTON, a parish in the western division of the wapentake of Manley, parts of Lindsey, county of Lincoln, 5 miles (N E by E) from Crowle, containing, with the township of Garthorp, 962 inhabitants   The living is a vicarage, in the archdeaconry of Stow, and diocese of Lincoln, rated in the king's books at £9 M J Lister, Esq was patron in 1824   The church is dedicated to St Oswald   There is a place of worship for Wesleyan Methodists

LUDDINGTON, a hamlet in the parish of Old Stratford, Stratford division of the hundred of Barlichway, county of Warwick, 3½ miles (S W by W) from Stratford upon Avon, containing 164 inhabitants Here was formerly a chapel, the ruins of which are still visible   The navigable river Avon runs through the township

LUDDINGTON in the BROOK, a parish partly in the hundred of Leightonstone, county of Huntingdon, but chiefly in the hundred of Polebrook, county of Northampton, 6 miles (S E by E) from Oundle, containing 119 inhabitants   The living is a rectory, in the archdeaconry of Northampton, and diocese of Peterborough, rated in the king's books at £8 8 9, and in the patronage of the Duke of Manchester, and the Earl and Countess of Cardigan   The church is dedicated to St Andrew   There is a trifling bequest by Nicholas Latham, in 1620, for teaching poor children.

LUDFORD, a parish partly in the hundred of Wolphy, county of Hereford, but chiefly in the hundred of Munslow, county of Salop, ½ a mile (S) from Ludlow, containing 280 inhabitants   The living is a perpetual curacy, in the archdeaconry of Salop, and diocese of Hereford, endowed with £400 private benefaction, and £800 royal bounty, and in the patronage of E L Charlton, Esq   An hospital for six poor infirm persons was founded here, in 1672, by Sir Job Charlton, who endowed it with certain messuages and lands now let for £63 per annum   It was incorporated by the style of the "Warden and Poor of the Hospital of Ludford,' who had a common seal, but the distinction of Warden has long ceased to exist.

LUDFORD (MAGNA), a parish in the eastern division of the wapentake of Wraggoe, parts of Lindsey, county of Lincoln, 6½ miles (E) from Market-Rasen, containing 426 inhabitants   The living is a discharged vicarage, in the archdeaconry and diocese of Lincoln, rated in the king's books at £5 18 4, endowed with £200 royal bounty, and in the patronage of G R. Heneage, Esq   The church is dedicated to St Peter There is a place of worship for Wesleyan Methodists Roman coins have been discovered in the neighbourhood

LUDFORD (PARVA), a parish in the eastern division of the wapentake of Wraggoe, parts of Lindsey, county of Lincoln, 6¼ miles (E) from Market Rasen.

The population is returned with Ludford Magna   The living is a rectory, in the archdeaconry and diocese of Lincoln, and in the patronage of Ayscoghe Boucherett, Esq   The church has been demolished

LUDGERSHALL, a joint parish with Tetchworth, in the hundred of Ashendon, county of Buckingham, 6 miles (S E by E) from Bicester, containing, with the hamlet of Kingswood, 576 inhabitants   The living is a rectory, in the archdeaconry of Buckingham, and diocese of Lincoln, rated in the king's books at £17 6 8, and in the patronage of Mrs Martyn   The church is dedicated to St Mary   Here was formerly an Alien priory, a cell to the great hospital of Santingfield in Picardy, which, at the suppression, was given to King's College, Cambridge

LUDGERSHALL, a borough and parish (formerly a market town) in the hundred of Amesbury, county of Wilts, 16½ miles (N N E) from Salisbury, and 71 (W S W) from London, containing 477 inhabitants This place, formerly called Lurgeshall and Lutgashall, was anciently of considerable extent, and is supposed to have been the residence of some of the Anglo-Saxon kings   A castle existed here soon after the Norman Conquest, wherein, about 1141, the Empress Matilda took refuge, in her flight from Winchester towards the castle of Devizes   no mention of this fortress occurring subsequently to the reign of Henry III , it is believed to have been dismantled soon after that period, for the purpose of curtailing the power of the barons   there are still some slight vestiges of it in a farm-yard in the vicinity   The town, which occupies a delightful situation on the verge of the county, is of inconsiderable size, the streets are neither paved nor lighted   The market was formerly held on Wednesday, but it has long been disused   There is a small pleasure fair on the 25th of July   Ludgershall is a borough by prescription, and sent representatives to all the parliaments of Edward I , to three of Edward II , and to three of Edward III , between the 9th of Richard II and the 9th of Henry V no return was made, but since the latter period no returns have been regular   The right of election was declared, by a committee of the House of Commons, to be vested in "the freeholders and copyholders of the borough houses, and in leaseholders for any term not under three years,   the number of voters is about seventy, and the bailiff is the returning officer, the bailiff is appointed at the court leet held annually by the steward of the manor on Michaelmas-day, when two constables are also chosen   The living is a rectory, in the archdeaconry and diocese of Salisbury, rated in the king's books at £11 6 8, and in the patronage of Sir Sandford Graham, Bart   The church, dedicated to St James, is in the early style of English architecture, and contains some very ancient monuments   There is a place of worship for Baptists   A charity school for educating twenty boys and twenty girls, a certain number of them being also clothed, was founded about three years since, and is supported by the members for the borough   Another school, for ten girls, is supported by subscription   There is a small estate at Longstock, near Stockbridge, producing £20 per annum, which is applied for the relief of the poor during winter, and for occasionally apprenticing poor children, it was bequeathed by an individual commonly called " Beggar Smith," who, when in need, had been relieved by the inhabitants of Ludgershall A few years since, the great seal of England in the reign of Stephen was found in the vicinity

LUDGVAN, a parish in the hundred of PENWITH, county of CORNWALL, 2 miles (N N W) from Marazion, containing 1839 inhabitants The living is a rectory, in the archdeaconry of Cornwall, and diocese of Exeter, rated in the king's books at £30 11 0½ The Duke of Bolton was patron in 1791 The church is dedicated to St. Paul in it lie the remains of the learned antiquary, Dr Borlase, fifty two years rector of the parish There are two places of worship for Wesleyan Methodists Amey Hill, in 1745, and Hugh Rogers, in 1763, each left a trifling sum for teaching poor children The parish lies on the margin of Mount's bay Across the road leading to Marazion is an earthwork thrown up in the civil war by the parliamentarians, during the siege of St Michael's Mount

LUDHAM, a parish in the hundred of HAPPING, county of NORFOLK, 7½ miles (N) from Acle, containing 780 inhabitants The living is a discharged vicarage, in the archdeaconry of Norfolk, and diocese of Norwich, rated in the king's books at £5 6 8, and in the patronage of the Bishop of Norwich The church, dedicated to St Catherine, has a richly-carved font, representing various animals and other figures There are places of worship for Baptists and Wesleyan Methodists Here was formerly a Grange belonging to the abbey of St Bene't, the house connected with which, after the reign of Mary, became the residence of the diocesans, who considerably enlarged it In Bishop Jegon's time, the greater part of the house, with many valuable books, manuscripts, and rolls, relating to the see, was destroyed by an accidental fire, which broke out August 10th, 1611 Bishop Harsnet, who afterwards resided here, built a chapel of brick, and Bishop Redman, in the reign of Elizabeth, obtained grants for a market and a fair, which have long been discontinued

Seal and Arms.

LUDLOW, a borough, market town, and parish, having separate jurisdiction, though locally in the hundred of Munslow, county of SALOP, 29 miles (S by E) from Shrewsbury, and 142 (N W by W) from London, containing 4820 inhabitants This place, called by the Britons Dinan, or the palace of princes, and by the Saxons Leadlowe and Ludlowe, which last name, with a slight variation it still retains, appears to have been distinguished for its importance prior to the Norman Conquest, at which time, Robert de Montgomery, kinsman of William the Conqueror, fortified the town with walls, and erected the greater part of its stately castle, which he made his baronial residence till his death, in 1094 On the attainder of his son, Robert de Montgomery, the castle came into the possession of Henry I, who made it a royal residence, and greatly enlarged and embellished it, and having strengthened the fortifications, placed in it a powerful garrison, under the command of Gervase Paganell, who, in the following reign, having embraced the cause of Matilda held it for a considerable time against the forces of Stephen, by whom it was besieged in person, assisted by Henry, son of the king of Scotland, who, being drawn up from his horse by an iron hook, was rescued from incarceration by the courage and address of the English monarch

From its proximity to Wales, Ludlow was always a station of importance, and a strong garrison was constantly kept up in the castle, for the defence of the frontier from the incursions of the Welch In the reign of Henry III, an order was issued from the castle for all the lords marchers to repair to this place, attended by their followers, to assist Roger Mortimer, at that time governor, in restraining the hostilities of the Welch, and, in the 47th of the same reign, Simon de Montfort, Earl of Leicester, who had joined the confederated barons, assisted by Llewellyn, Prince of Wales, attacked the castle with their united forces, and having set fire to it, nearly demolished it In the reign of Edward II, Roger Mortimer, a descendant of the former governor, having joined the discontented barons, was sent prisoner to the Tower of London, from which he contrived to effect his escape, and in commemoration of his success, erected, in the outer ward of Ludlow castle, a chapel, which he dedicated to St Peter, and endowed it for a priest to celebrate mass, but being arraigned for high treason in the reign of Edward III, he was publicly executed at Tyburn In the reign of Henry VI, Richard, Duke of York, who then had possession of the castle, detained John Sutton, Lord Dudley, Reginald, Abbot of Glastonbury, and others, in confinement here, and issued from this place his declaration of allegiance to the king, which he also repeated some years after, on the defeat of Lord Audley at Blore Heath, but, on his subsequent insurrection and attainder, the king laid siege to the castle, and having taken it, he stripped it of all its ornaments, and the town was plundered of every thing valuable by his soldiers, the Duchess of York, with her two younger sons, was taken prisoner, and confined for some time in one of the outer towers of the castle After the death of the Duke of York, at the battle of Wakefield, the castle descended to his son Edward, Earl of March, afterwards Edward IV The young king, Edward V, and his brother, the Duke of York, lived in the castle, under the superintendence and protection of Earl Rivers, till their removal by order of the Duke of Gloucester, afterwards Richard III, to the Tower of London, where they were barbarously murdered Prince Arthur, son of Henry VII, resided here after his nuptials with Catherine of Arragon, in 1501, and kept a splendid court till his decease in the following year In the reign of Henry VIII, a kind of local government, called the "Council in the Marches of Wales," was established at Ludlow, consisting of a lord president, and many counsellors as the prince chose to appoint, a secretary, an attorney, and four justices of the principality, the lord president residing in the castle During the parliamentary war, the castle held out for the king, under the command of the Earl of Bridgewater, but finally surrendered to the parliament, frequent skirmishes took place in the town between the contending forces, in one of which Sir Gilbert Gerrard, brother to the Earl of Macclesfield, was killed

The remains of the castle still exhibit traces of its original grandeur, and, from their elevated situation in the centre of a country abounding with beautiful and picturesque scenery, form an interesting and venerable ruin they are situated on the summit of an eminence of greystone rock, overhanging the river Corve, the north front consists of massive square towers connected by a lofty embattled wall the ancient fosse and part of the rock have been formed into walks, and planted, in 1772, with beech, elm, and lime trees, affording an extensive and delightful promenade on the west is a precipitous ridge of rock parallel with the castle, and richly crowned with wood, intersected by a chasm, through which the river Teme pursues its course, and on the north and west sides is a deep fosse, cut in the solid rock, over which was a draw-bridge, now replaced by one of stone, of two arches, leading to the principal entrance, the portal is of modern erection, and neither remarkable for beauty nor for strength The interior has a strikingly majestic appearance, on the right hand are the ruins of the extensive barracks which were occupied by the troops of the lords presidents of the marches, near the gate are the apartments of the warden and other officers, and on the left is the keep, a large square embattled tower of four stages, one hundred and ten feet high, with square turrets at the angles, the walls of this tower, which is of Norman architecture, are from nine to twelve feet in thickness Opposite to the entrance gateway are the hall and state apartments, in the early and decorated styles of English architecture, now much dilapidated, in this hall was performed, by the children of the Earl of Bridgewater and others, the celebrated Masque of Comus, composed by Milton, and founded upon an incident which occurred to the family of that nobleman, soon after his appointment to the presidency To the left are the ruins of the chapel, of which the nave and the beautiful Norman arch leading to the choir are the principal remains, within the enclosure are several massive towers, among which are Mortimer s tower, and that in which Butler, after the Restoration, composed several cantos of his Hudibras Though irregular in their arrangement, and greatly dilapidated, these ruins, from the breadth of their masses, the bold projection of some portions, and the depth of the numerous recesses, possess striking features of solemnity and magnificence, and the luxuriant ivy by which they are partly concealed, adds materially to the picturesque beauty of these remains, which hold a prominent rank among the numerous and interesting monuments of feudal grandeur, for which the district formerly constituting the Marches is distinguished

The town is pleasantly situated on an eminence near the confluence of the rivers Teme and Corve, by which latter it is bounded on the north-west, and over which a handsome stone bridge of three arches was erected by the corporation, in 1738, over the Teme, which, after being joined by the Corve, describes a semicircle on the west and south sides of the town, is an ancient bridge, the entrance to which is under the arched passage of Broadgate, the only one remaining entire of the ancient town gates of the wall which surrounded the town, begun in the 13th, and completed in the 32nd, of Edward I, part of the foundation only can be traced From its elevated situation the town has a pleasing and cheerful appearance, the streets are spacious, and the houses in general handsome and well built it is paved, and lighted with oil, but arrangements have been made for lighting it with gas, and, from the salubrity of the air,

and the beauty and interest of the surrounding country, it is regarded as a desirable place of residence by numerous opulent and highly respectable families There are a public subscription library, and two circulating libraries assemblies are held in a suite of rooms in the market-house, and a small theatre is opened by the Worester company, during the races, which take place annually in July, and are succeeded by a ball and public breakfast, which is held in the inner court of the castle The principal branch of manufacture is that of gloves, and the chief trade is in malt there are some corn-mills, a paper-mill, and a small manufactory for woollen cloth, flannel, yarn, and blankets, on the banks of the Teme, and the river Corve turns a mill for grinding bark used in a tannery, and gives motion also to some machinery for making cordage and sacking The principal market day is Monday, for grain, and there are smaller markets for provisions on Wednesday, Friday, and Saturday the market cross is a neat modern building, with a handsome cupola, in which is a bell, formerly belonging to the chapel of St Leonard The fairs are the Monday before February 13th, Tuesday before Easter, May 1st, Wednesday in Whitsun week, August 21st, Sept 28th, and Dec 6th the first and last are cattle marts for butter and cheese, and all the others are for hops, horses, cattle, sheep, and pigs

The town appears to have had a charter of incorporation at a very early period, which was confirmed and renewed by Edward IV, from whose reign till that of Charles II it underwent several modifications, but in the reign of William and Mary it was, on the petition of the inhabitants, restored to its original form by this charter the government is vested in a recorder, two bailiffs, two justices, twelve aldermen, and twenty-five common council-men, assisted by a town clerk, coroner, and subordinate officers The high bailiff is chosen from among the aldermen, and the low bailiff from the common council-men, annually on the 18th of October, and the recorder, who holds his office for life, is appointed by the corporation, with the sanction of his Majesty s approbation the recorder, the bailiffs, and the two justices, who are invariably the bailiffs for the preceding year, are justices of the peace within the borough and liberties The freedom of the borough is inherited by all the sons of burgesses, or acquired by marriage with a freeman s daughter, all persons eligible as burgesses must demand that right by petition to the corporation, according to a form prescribed for that purpose by a by-law made in 1663 The corporation hold quarterly courts of session for the borough, for the trial of all offenders, and formerly have passed sentence of death, but the recorders of late not being barristers, the trial of prisoners for capital offences is removed by Habeas Corpus to the assizes for the county A court of record is held every Tuesday, under the charter of Edward IV, for the recovery of debts to any amount, also a court of requests for the recovery of debts under 40s, the jurisdiction of which is confined to the borough The market house, which may rather be regarded as the town hall, is a large plain brick building, containing commodious rooms for transacting the public business of the corporation, and for holding subscription assemblies, and the balls given by the bailiffs on their election to office beneath it is a spacious area for the use of the corn market, and attached to the buildings are two public reservoirs, into one of which water is raised from the river by machinery, and into the other spring water is conveyed from a place under Whitecliffe coppice, called the Fountain The guildhall, in which the quarter sessions and other courts are held for the borough, is a neat and commodious edifice of modern erection The borough gaol was erected by the corporation, in 1764, in lieu of Goalford tower, an ancient prison and gate of the town, which had then become ruinous it is a commodious edifice, containing four wards for the classification of prisoners, but only one airing-yard The borough first exercised the elective franchise in the 12th of Edward IV, since which time it has continued to return two members to parliament the right of election is vested in the corporation and in all the resident common burgesses, and the number of the electors is about seven hundred the bailiffs are the returning officers The patronage of the borough is divided between the families of Clive and Charlton, but the interest of the former generally predominates

The living is a rectory, in the archdeaconry of Salop, and diocese of Hereford, rated in the king's books at £19 12 6, and in the patronage of the Crown. The church, dedicated to St Lawrence, and formerly collegiate, is a spacious and handsome cruciform structure, in the early and decorated styles of English architecture, with a noble square embattled tower, crowned with pinnacles, rising from the centre to the height of one hundred and thirty feet the entrance is through a beautiful hexagonal porch, leading into the nave, which is separated from the aisles by a series of six gracefully-pointed arches, resting on slender clustered columns, which support the roof, and lighted by a range of clerestory windows, and a large west window, of which the mullions and tracery have been destroyed by recent repairs, the four piers and arches which support the tower are massive and lofty, but finely proportioned and of great beauty, the choir is spacious, and lighted by five elegant windows on each side, and by a noble east window of large dimensions, in which is painted the legendary history of St Lawrence the oak stalls are still remaining, and the roof of richly-carved oak is preserved in the several parts of this sumptuous edifice In the north transept is St John's chapel, in which is some ancient stained glass, representing the history of the Apostles, and the legend of the ring presented to Edward the Confessor, as a prognostic of his death, by some pilgrims from Jerusalem Many external and internal ornaments of this church were destroyed by the parliamentary commissioners during the usurpation of Cromwell The visitations and ecclesiastical courts are held in it, in May and October, for proving wills and granting letters of administration Among the monuments are several of great antiquity and interest, and two highly-finished effigies of Judge Bridgeman and his lady There are places of worship for Independents and Wesleyan Methodists

The free grammar school was founded by Edward VI, who vested in the corporation the estate of the guild or fraternity of Palmers in Ludlow, on condition that they should support this and other charities connected with that guild the school-house was rebuilt in the fifteenth century, at the expense of the corporation, with convenient dwelling houses for a first and second master, who are appointed by the corporation, and receive respectively £80 and £60 per annum, having also the privilege of taking boarders the school is open to all boys of the town without limitation of number, who receive gratuitous instruction in Latin and Greek, and pay a quarterage to the master for writing and arithmetic there are two exhibitions, of £30 per annum each, to Balliol College, Oxford, for boys of this school, founded, in 1704, by the Rev Richard Greaves, in the appointment of the Master and Fellows of that college, and four of the poorest children receive an annual benefaction, of £5 6 8 each, from a bequest by Dr Charles Langford, in 1607 A National school was established in 1813, with which a Blue-coat school, previously instituted, has been incorporated from the funds of the latter, a house has been purchased and fitted up, at an expense of £600, for the instruction of girls, the boys are taught in a room over the market cross the number of children is two hundred, of whom a few are clothed annually, and on leaving school receive an apprentice fee of £3 Alms houses adjoining the churchyard were founded, in 1486, by Mr John Hosyer, who endowed them for thirty-three aged people, to each of whom he assigned a weekly payment of fourpence, now increased to two shillings and sixpence the present building, containing thirty-three distinct apartments, was erected by the corporation, in 1758, at an expense of £1211 18 2½ and is kept in good repair The almspeople are appointed by the corporation, and receive, in addition to their payments from the endowment, a portion of other funds bequeathed by various benefactors Four almshouses for aged persons were founded by Mr Charles Foxe, of Bromfield, which, in 1590, he endowed with houses and rent-charges producing at present about £14 per annum, which is divided in weekly payments among the almspeople, of whom two are chosen from this parish, and two from the parish of Bromfield

A workhouse and house of correction was endowed in 1674, by Thomas Lane, of Ludlow, who in early life had been a servant in the family of Sir Job Charlton, with land and tenements producing nearly £100 per annum, for maintaining a master to superintend the employment of the poor, and for the purchase of raw materials for the spinning and knitting of stockings, and for making shoes it is at present in contemplation to erect a house of correction upon a more extended scale in the gaol yard, at the joint expense of the corporation and the trustees of the charity A public dispensary, established in 1780, is liberally supported by subscription, and a society for the relief of lying-in women is under the superintendence of twelve ladies There are also numerous charitable bequests for distribution among the poor Adjoining the castle is Dinham House, a noble mansion of brick, belonging to the family of Clive, in which Lucien Bonaparte, towards the close of the late war with France, resided while in England Among the religious establishments which flourished here in ancient times, was the college of St. John the Evangelist, founded in the reign of Edward the Confessor, and given, after the dissolution, by Elizabeth to the corporation for charitable uses, the remains of which are divided into separate tenements, and let on lease as dwelling houses, and a priory of White friars, founded, about the year 1349, by Sir Lawrence of Ludlow, Knt, of which some vestiges may be traced in the environs without the Corn gate There are several mineral springs in the neighbourhood, of which one, called the boiling well, is supposed to be efficacious in disorders of the eyes At Saltmoor is a saline spring, the water of which contains small portions of carbonate of iron, and sulphate of magnesia, and a considerable portion of muriate of soda it has been found beneficial in scorbutic diseases, and is much frequented by patients affected with such complaints, tor whose accommodation warm and cold baths have been provided. Thomas Johnes, Esq, the translator of the Histories of Froissart, Monstrelet, and other learned works, Richard Payne Knight, Esq, author of an "Analytical Enquiry into the Principles of Taste, "The Progress of Society, and other works, 1 A Knight, Esq, author of various works on Horticulture, and Dr Badham, the translator of Juvenal, were natives of this town

LUDNEY, a hamlet in the parish of GRAIN-THORPE, Marsh division of the hundred of LOUTH-ESKE, parts of LINDSEY, county of LINCOLN, 8 miles (N E) from Louth   The population is returned with the parish

LUDWORTH, a joint township with Chisworth, in the parish of GLOSSOP, hundred of HIGH PEAK, county of DERBY, 9½ miles (N W by N) from Chapel en le Frith, containing, with Chisworth, 1077 inhabitants

LUFFENHAM (NORTH), a parish in the hundred of WRANDIKE, county of RUTLAND, 6 miles (N E by E) from Uppingham, containing 421 inhabitants   The living is a rectory, in the archdeaconry of Northampton, and diocese of Peterborough, rated in the king s books at £17 0 5, and in the patronage of the Master and Fellows of Emanuel College, Cambridge The church is dedicated to St John the Baptist There are day and Sunday schools supported by funds arising from the rent of an estate, called the Town Estate, left by Arch-deacon Johnson, formerly rector of the parish

LUFFENHAM (SOUTH), a parish in the hundred of WRANDIKE, county of RUTLAND, 5½ miles (E N E) from Uppingham, containing 274 inhabitants The living is a rectory, in the archdeaconry of Northampton, and diocese of Peterborough, rated in the king s books at £12 12 6, and in the patronage of James Bush, Esq   The church is dedicated to St Mary A day and Sunday school is supported by subscription

LUFFIELD ABBEY, an extra-parochial liberty, partly in the hundred and county of BUCKINGHAM, and partly in the hundred of GREENS-NORTON, county of NORTHAMPTON, 5½ miles (N N W) from Buckingham The population is returned with Stowe   A Benedictine priory, in honour of the Virgin Mary, was founded here about 1124, by Robert Bossu, Earl of Leicester, which, falling into decay from the inadequacy of its endowment, was suppressed in 1494, and annexed to the collegiate church at Windsor, but in 1500 it was given to the abbot and convent of Westminster by Henry VII, who was then building the chapel still known by his name In the reign of Edward IV its possessions were valued at £19 19 2 per annum A farm-house occupies the site of the conventual buildings, of which no traces remain.

LUFFINCOTT, a parish in the hundred of BLACK TORRINGTON, county of DEVON, 7 miles (S by W) from Holsworthy, containing 90 inhabitants The living is a discharged rectory, in the archdeaconry of Totness, and diocese of Exeter, rated in the king s books at £5 6 8, endowed with £200 royal bounty, and in the patronage of J Venner and J Spettigue, Esqrs The church is dedicated to St James

LUFTON, a parish in the hundred of STONE, county of SOMERSET, 3 miles (W) from Yeovil, containing 21 inhabitants The living is a rectory, in the archdeaconry of Wells, and diocese of Bath and Wells, rated in the king s books at £5 7 8½, and in the patronage of John Phelips, Esq The church is dedicated to St Peter and St Paul

LUGWARDINE, a parish in the hundred of RAD-LOW, county of HEREFORD, 2¼ miles (E by N) from Hereford, containing 618 inhabitants The living is a vicarage, with the perpetual curacies of Ballingham, Little Dewchurch, Hentland, Langarrin, and St Weonard, in the peculiar jurisdiction and patronage of the Dean and Chapter of Hereford, rated in the king s books at £22. 7 1   The church is dedicated to St Peter

LUKE (ST), a chapelry in the hundred of EASE-BOURNE, rape of CHICHESTER, county of SUSSEX, 3 miles (N N W) from Midhurst

LUKE'S (ST), a parish in the Finsbury division of the hundred of OSSULSTONE, county of MIDDLESEX, comprising the liberties of the City-road, East Finsbury, West Finsbury, Golden-lane, Old-street, and Whitecross-street, and containing 40,876 inhabitants The earliest notice of this district occurs in its connexion with the "Eald, or Old street, by which the Saxons designated the Roman military way from the western extremity of the metropolis, without the great fen, which is stated to have given name to Fensbury, now Finsbury, and to Moorfields this road is said to have extended from London Wall to Hoxton, and to have been continued through the churchyard of St Leonard, Shoreditch, and through the parish of Bethnal Green, to the Old Ford near Hackney The southern part of the fen was gradually raised by various deposits, and particularly by many hundred cart-loads of bones removed from the charnel-house of St. Paul s, by order of the Duke of Somerset, when Protector, whence it obtained the name of Bonehill (now Bunhill) Fields a portion of the site was appropriated by the city as a cemetery during the plague in 1665, and is now a burial ground Another portion of the same fields, was formed into a place of exercise for the practice of archery, by the corporation of the City of London, in 1498 it was subsequently let in trust to Sir Paul Pindar, and appropriated in 1641 as a place of exercise for the City train bands, it is now enclosed by buildings, and is the property of the Hon the Artillery Company, who, during the late war, formed a very efficient regiment, equipped at their own expense they continue to muster occasionally, and have an armoury, a mess-room, and other apartments, forming a handsome and substantial building, in front of which is a spacious plot of ground for field exercise, from which circumstance it has obtained the name of the "Artillery Ground In Golden-lane was the original play-house of Alleyn, founder of Dulwich College, of which the front, bearing the royal arms, is still remaining This district was anciently part of the parish of Cripplegate, the church of which being found inadequate to the accommodation of the parishioners, a new church, dedicated to St Luke, was erected in Old-street by the commissioners for building new churches in the reign of Queen Anne, who assigned to it the present district, which, after the completion of the church, was laid out in numerous streets and squares, covered with buildings in every direction, and has become one of the most extensive and populous parishes in the suburbs of the metropolis Peerless Pool, called by Stowe " Perilous ' Pool, and in 1743 converted into one of the largest swimming baths in the kingdom, surrounded with spacious gardens, and fitted up with every accommodation, is now used for bathing alone , the site of the gardens is occupied by ranges of modern buildings Bath street has been erected on the site of the ancient Pesthouse-row, where was one of the lazarettos in the time of the plague To the west of Bunhill-row was the lord mayor s " Dog house," or kennel for the city hounds, the site of which is occupied by part of Featherstone-street , and at Mount Mill, near the upper end of Goswell-street, now levelled and covered with buildings, was one of the bastions erected by the parliamentarians, in 1643, for the greater security of the metropolis

The parish is well paved, lighted with gas, and supplied with water by the New River Company The City of London Gas Company have one of their establishments in Brick-lane, in this parish Since the formation of the Regent s canal, extensive lime, timber, and coal wharfs have been established on its banks , and within the parish are various cooperages, a brewery an indigo manufactory and a rope-walk all on an extensive scale The city basin, communicating with the Regent s canal, crosses the city road, and forms a grand depôt for merchandise forwarded by water to every part of the kingdom , the principal carriers have large wharfs and warehouses on the banks, of which those belonging to Messrs Pickford and Co are the most extensive The living is a rectory not in charge, in the archdeaconry of Middlesex, and diocese of London, and in the patronage of the Dean and Chapter of St Paul s The church, built in 1732, is a plain substantial edifice of stone, in the Grecian style of architecture, with a lofty steeple in the form of a fluted obelisk, the only steeple of the kind in the metropolis the interior is neatly arranged, and the galleries are supported by Ionic pillars separating the nave from the aisles The churchyard is spacious, and behind it is an additional cemetery of considerable extent , in the former are the tombs of the Caslons, eminent type-founders in the parish, and in the latter are numerous gravestones inscribed with crosses St John s church, in King s-square, a neat edifice of brick, with a stone portico of the Ionic order, surmounted by a slender spire, was erected, in 1823, by grant from the parliamentary commissioners, at an expense of £12,853 3 3, and contains one thousand six hundred and eight sittings, of which nine hundred and seventeen are free The living is a perpetual curacy, in the patronage of the Rector There are places of worship for Baptists, Independents, and Wesleyan and Calvinistic Methodists Of these, the Tabernacle was erected by the Rev G Whitefield the founder of the

Calvinistic Methodists, in which he himself for some time preached That belonging to the Wesleyan Methodists was the chapel of the Rev J Wesley, founder of the sect, who was interred behind it in 1791, and by whom it was built, on the site of the City foundry which was used for casting cannon so late as 1715 In front of the latter is Tindal s, or Bunhill-fields, burial-ground The dues for interments are received by the corporation of the City of London, who appoint a sexton resident on the spot The number of persons interred here annually average from one thousand two hundred to one thousand five hundred, chiefly dissenters among the numerous distinguished non-conformist divines, may be enumerated Mr John Bunyan, author of the Pilgrim s Progress, who died in 1688 , Dr Williams, founder of the Dissenters Library, in Red-cross-street, who died in 1716 , Dr Isaac Watts, the poet, logician, and divine, who died in 1748 , the Rev Dr Neale, author of the History of the Puritans, who died in 1765 , Dr Lardner, author of the Credibility of the Gospel History, who died in 1768 , Dr Gill, who died in 1771 , Dr Richard Price, an eminent mathematician, author of Reversionary Payments, &c , who died in 1791 , the Rev Theophilus Lindsey, who died in 1808 , Dr A Rees, editor of the Encyclopædia, who died in 1825 , the Rev John Townsend, founder of the Deaf and Dumb Asylum, who died in 1826 , and various others, distinguished either by their preaching or their writings In Milton-street (formerly Grub-street) so called from having been the residence of that eminent poet, is a building named the Pantheon, formerly known as the City chapel, having belonged to a congregation of Independents, but now used as a theatre for dramatic exhibitions of an inferior description, and for occasional lectures The parochial school for boys was established in 1698, and that for girls in 1761 , the school-house in Golden lane was built in 1780 these schools were erected, and are supported, by subscription, and by a fund of £6,500 three per cent consols , which has arisen from benefactions and savings There are in them one hundred boys and one hundred girls, who are completely clothed, and with the former an apprentice fee of £2 is given on their leaving school John Fuller, in 1723, bequeathed £1600 Bank stock for the instruction and clothing of boys, in consideration of which, twenty boys are admitted into the parochial school The free school, founded by William Warral in 1689, and formerly in Goat-alley, was, in 1808, removed to Baltic-street, Golden-lane it has an endowment producing about £300 per annum, which is appropriated to the clothing and instruction of forty boys in reading, writing, and arithmetic the master, who is appointed by the trustees, has a salary of £80 per annum The Haberdashers Company have a house and premises in Bunhill-row, in which a considerable number of boys are instructed on the Lancasterian system the master resides in the house A Lancasterian school for boys was established in North-street, City-road, in 1813, and another for girls in 1820 in these schools nearly one thousand children are instructed The orphan working-school, in the City-road, was instituted in 1760, at Hoxton, by subscription, chiefly among the Protestant dissenters, and removed to this place in 1773, when the trustees erected the present commodious building, upon a site of land containing six acres, which they purchased for that purpose the funds of the institution, arising from legacies and benefactions, produce a revenue of £718 per annum, which, with the amount of annual subscriptions, is appropriated to the maintenance, clothing, and education, of orphan children, who are taught reading, writing, and arithmetic the boys are also taught the making of nets and shoes, and the girls, needlework, knitting, and household work, and on leaving the school, are placed out apprentices, or in service the building, which is substantial, contains every requisite accommodation for the purposes of the institution, and a neat chapel in which divine service is occasionally performed, it being open to the public on Sunday evenings during Summer there are forty-five boys and forty six girls in the school, which is adapted to the reception of one hundred

St Luke s hospital, for lunatics, was originally built on the north side of Moorfields, as an auxiliary to Bethlehem hospital, and established on a system free from several of the objections to which that institution was then liable The present spacious and elegant building was erected by subscription, at an expense of £55,000 it is of brick, ornamented with stone, and consists of a centre and two wings, four hundred and ninety three feet in length, of proportionate depth, and three stories high, exclusively of the basement story, and an attic in the centre and at the extremity of each wing it contains apartments for the master, matron, and attendants, a spacious committee-room, and galleries in the east and west wings for the reception of three hundred patients of both sexes, who are classed according to the nature and degree of their malady the average number of patients is one hundred and ten males, and one hundred and fifty three females, who are treated with humane and skilful attention, and provided with every comfort consistent with their security and the promotion of their cure Almshouses for eight aged women, who receive each an annual allowance of £16, paid quarterly, and a chaldron of coal, were founded, in 1650, by Mrs Susan Amias, who erected eight distinct dwellings on the north side of Old-street, which, though becoming old, are still in good repair the income arising from the endowment exceeds £220 per annum Edward Allen, founder of Dulwich College, erected ten almshouses, in Pesthouse-row, now Bath-street, for five aged men and five aged women of this parish of whom, as vacancies occurred, one widower and two widows were to be removed to Dulwich, the inmates are, however, solely supported by the income arising from subsequent benefactions, the funds of the college not being legally available in any respect to the maintenance of this charity Six almshouses were founded in the City-road by the Dyers Company, in 1776, and six by the Girdlers Company, which latter were rebuilt in 1741, and there are four almshouses founded by the Ironmongers Company, in Mitchel-court, Old-street, which were rebuilt in 1811, pursuant to the will of Thomas Lewer, Esq, for four aged men, who receive £10 per annum and a chaldron of coal each The French hospital in Bath-street, for the maintenance and support of French Protestants, was incorporated in the reign of George I it is a substantial build ing of brick, occupying three sides of a quadrangular area, the centre of which is laid out in gardens the premises contain apartments for the master, a committee-room, and tenements for the aged of both sexes, who are clothed and supplied with every necessary comfort, a chapel, and a room for the temporary confinement of lunatics the establishment is under the superintendence of a president and committee, chiefly of the descendants of French families The city of London living in hospital, originally instituted in 1771, in Shaftesbury house, Aldersgate street and subsequently removed to its present situation, is a neat building of brick, ornamented with stone, consisting of a centre, surmounted by an open turret and a spire, and two wings, and containing apartments with every accommodation for the patients, in addition to which is a handsome chapel, behind the building are gardens pleasantly laid out this institution, which is supported by subscription, constitutes also a school of midwifery, to which female pupils only are admitted There are numerous charitable bequests for distribution among the poor of this extensive and populous parish

LULLINGSTANE, formerly a parish, but now united to Lullingstone, in the hundred of AXTON, DARTFORD, and WILMINGTON, lathe of SUTTON at HONE, county of KENT The living was a discharged vicarage the church is demolished

LULLINGSTONE, a parish in the hundred of AXTON, DARTFORD, and WILMINGTON, lathe of SUTTON at HONE, county of KENT, 7 miles (S E by E) from Foot s Cray, containing 41 inhabitants The living is a discharged rectory, with the vicarage of Lullingstane, in the archdeaconry and diocese of Rochester, rated in the king s books at £7 16 8, endowed with £200 private benefaction, and £200 royal bounty, and in the patronage of Sir Thomas Dyke, Bart The church, dedicated to St Botolph, is situated in the park it is a small but neat edifice, the nave and chancel being separated by a richly-carved screen supporting the rood-loft, which is yet in good preservation, and the windows exhibiting a series of scriptural representations in beautiful stained glass, it also contains several fine monuments Roman bricks, coins, military weapons, with part of a tesselated pavement, have been ploughed up here

LULLINGTON, a parish in the hundred of REPTON and GRESLEY, county of DERBY, 7½ miles (S) from Burton upon Trent, containing, with the township of Coton in the Elmes, 586 inhabitants The living is a discharged vicarage, in the archdeaconry of Derby, and diocese of Lichfield and Coventry, rated in the king s books at £4 11 10, and in the patronage of the Crown The church is dedicated to All Saints Lullington written in Domesday-book Lullitune, had a priest, a church, and a mill, at the time of the Norman survey It is in the honour of Tutbury, duchy of Lancaster, and within the jurisdiction of a court of pleas held at Tutbury every third Tuesday, for the recovery of debts under 40s

LULLINGTON, a parish in the hundred of FROME county of SOMERSET, 2¾ miles (N by E) from Frome containing 224 inhabitants The living is a perpetual curacy, in the archdeaconry of Taunton, and diocese of Bath and Wells, endowed with £200 private benefaction, £800 royal bounty, and £300 parliamentary grant Richard H Cox, Esq was patron in 1807 The church, dedicated to All Saints, has some Norman portions, and some of later style

LULLINGTON, a parish in the hundred of ALCISTON, rape of PEVENSEY, county of SUSSEX, 4½ miles (N E) from Seaford, containing 39 inhabitants The living is a discharged vicarage, in the archdeaconry and diocese of Chichester, rated in the king's books at £6 12 11, endowed with £1400 royal bounty, and in the patronage of the Bishop of Chichester The parish is bounded on the west by Cuckmere river

LULLWORTH (EAST), a parish in the hundred of WINFRITH, Blandford (South) division of the county of DORSET, 6 miles (S W) from Wareham, containing 353 inhabitants The living is a discharged vicarage, in the archdeaconry of Dorset, and diocese of Bristol, rated in the king's books at £11 14 7, endowed with £200 private benefaction, and £200 royal bounty The King presented by lapse in 1787 The church, dedicated to St Andrew, contains some ancient memorials of the family of Newburgh, descendants of the Earls of Warwick of the Norman line, who, in the reign of Edward I, succeeded the De Lolleworths, possessors of the place from an early period it afterwards came to the Howards, Earls of Suffolk, one of whom, in 1588, on the site of an ancient castle, laid the foundation of the present noble castle of Lullworth, which was completed in 1641, and then purchased by the family of Weld it is a massive structure, forming an exact cube of eighty feet, with a circular embattled tower rising sixteen feet above the battlements of the walls, and the east front decorated with the arms of Weld, several fine statues, and two inscriptions commemorating the visits of George III and his Royal consort in 1789 Near the castle is a circular Roman Catholic chapel, of elegant architecture, erected several years since by Thomas Weld, Esq, and fitted up with much taste and magnificence This stately edifice was appropriated as the temporary residence of Charles X, his family, and suite, on the expulsion of that monarch from the throne of France, and prior to his seeking an abode in some of the continental states Dr Weld, the present proprietor, has been lately raised to the dignity of cardinal in the church of Rome He liberally received many exiles at the period of the first French revolution, who formed a religious fraternity on his estate here, of the order of La Trappe, which returned to the continent at the general peace Within the parish are many vestiges of antiquity, principally barrows found to contain human and other skeletons, rude urns, trinkets, &c, supposed to be British from the coarseness of the urns and the absence of all Roman relics on one of these, a lofty hill termed Flower s Barrow, is a triple intrenchment, called the British Camp, enclosing an area of about five acres, to which there are two entrances, one on the south-east, the other on the south-west

LULLWORTH (WEST), a parish in the liberty of BINDON, though locally in the hundred of Winfrith, Blandford (South) division of the county of DORSET, 8 miles (S W) from Wareham, containing 365 inhabitants The living is a perpetual curacy, annexed to the rectory of Winfred Newburgh, in the archdeaconry of Dorset, and diocese of Bristol The chapel is dedicated to the Holy Trinity Lullworth Cove is a great natural curiosity, into which the sea flows through a wide gap in the cliff, of sufficient depth for vessels of eighty tons' burden The surrounding rocks, rising to an immense height, are singularly undermined and perforated by the constant lashing of the waves, which keep up a continual and terrific roar The "Arched Rock, about a mile from the Cove, has an opening of about twenty feet high,

through which the sea presents a peculiarly grand appearance Among these rocks, which seem to exhibit some awful convulsion of nature, the razor-bill and puffin lay their eggs, the collecting of which forms part of the support of the country people, who trust themselves to the end of a rope, at the hazard of instant destruction

LULSLEY, a chapelry in the parish of SUCKLEY, upper division of the hundred of DODDINGTREE, county of WORCESTER, 7½ miles (W by N) from Worcester, containing 120 inhabitants The chapel is dedicated to St Giles

LUMBY, a joint township with Huddleston, in the parish of SHERBURN, upper division of the wapentake of BARKSTONE-ASH, West riding of the county of YORK, 4½ miles (N) from Ferry-Bridge The population is returned with Huddleston

LUMLEY (GREAT), a chapelry in that part of the parish of CHESTER le STREET which is in the northern division of EASINGTON ward, county palatine of DURHAM, 5½ miles (N by E) from Durham, containing 1240 inhabitants, who are principally employed in the mines, this being the centre of an immense coal district There are two places of worship for Wesleyan Methodists An hospital, forming a quadrangle, was founded in 1685, by Sir John Duck, for twelve poor women, with a weekly allowance of one shilling each, to whom a master reads prayers daily The endowment is about £40 per annum The remains of the ancient hall have been converted into a granary

LUMLEY (LITTLE), a township in that part of the parish of CHESTER le STREET which is in the northern division of EASINGTON ward, county palatine of DURHAM, 6 miles (N N E) from Durham, containing 351 inhabitants On a fine eminence, sloping to the northern bank of the river Wear, stands the stately castle of Lumley, erected in the reign of Edward I, by Robert de Lumley, an ancestor of the Earls of Scarborough it is built of yellow freestone, in a quadrangular form, having at each corner an octangular machicolated turret the eastern part only retains its ancient appearance

LUND, a chapelry in the parish of KIRKHAM, hundred of AMOUNDERNESS, county palatine of LANCASTER, 2½ miles (E by S) from Kirkham, with which the population is returned The living is a perpetual curacy, in the archdeaconry of Richmond, and diocese of Chester, endowed with £1200 private benefaction, £200 royal bounty, and £1500 parliamentary grant, and in the patronage of the Vicar of Kirkham

LUND, a parish in the Bainton-Beacon division of the wapentake of HARTHILL, East riding of the county of YORK, 7 miles (N W by N) from Beverley, containing 357 inhabitants The living is a discharged vicarage, in the archdeaconry of the East riding, and diocese of York, rated in the king s books at £6 6 0½, and endowed with £200 royal bounty J Blanchard, sen, Esq was patron in 1827 The church is dedicated to All Saints

LUND, a joint township with Cliff, in the parish of HEMINGBROUGH, wapentake of OUZE and DERWENT, East riding of the county of YORK, 9¼ miles (E) from Selby The population is returned with Cliff The living is a perpetual curacy, in the archdeaconry of Richmond, and diocese of Chester, endowed with £800 royal bounty, and in the patronage of the Vicar of Aysgarth

LUNDY-ISLAND, in the hundred of BRAUN TON, county of DEVON, 3½ leagues (N W by N) from Hartland Point, and 4 (N) from Clovelly   It is situated in the mouth of the Bristol channel, is upwards of three miles in length, and nearly one in breadth containing about two thousand acres, of which not more than four hundred are in cultivation, and is so defended by lofty and precipitous rocks, as to be inaccessible, except at a small beach on the eastern side, where there is a tolerably good landing-place, secured by the Isle of Rats   The more elevated ground, rising eight hundred feet above the level of the sea, commands extensive prospects of the English and Welch coasts , and at the northern extremity of the island is a high pyramidal rock, called the Constable   Plantations of various trees have been formed here at considerable labour and expense, but the prevalence of strong north-easterly winds has hitherto stunted their growth   A few cattle, goats, and sheep, are fed on the island, but the last have not been known to thrive   Domestic fowls and rabbits are plentiful, though the rats which infest the place destroy great numbers   There are ruins of an ancient chapel, which was dedicated to St Anne   From the quantities of human bones frequently ploughed up, and some remaining vestiges of ancient cultivation, there are evident proofs of its having been formerly much more populous   It is recorded that one Morisco, having been frustrated in a conspiracy to assassinate Henry III , made this his retreat, became the chief of a band of pirates, and for his crimes was executed here by command of the king   and also that Edward II , at one time during his disturbed reign, proposed retiring hither for safety from his rebellious nobles Morisco s castle, situated near the south-eastern point, was originally a strong fortification, with considerable outworks   it is encompassed by a moat, but no ordnance are now mounted upon the battery, though a few dismounted guns occupy the ramparts, beneath which is a remarkable cave   In the parliamentary war, Lord Saye and Sele held it for Charles I , and in the reign of William and Mary, the French seized it by stratagem, and maintained themselves in it a considerable time

LUNE-DALE, a township in the parish of ROMALD-KIRK, western division of the wapentake of GILLING, North riding of the county of YORK, 11 miles (N W by W) from Barnard Castle, containing 265 inhabitants At Laith, in this township, there is a chapel of ease to the parish church   An annuity of £10 is paid by the trustees of the late Earl of Strathmore to a schoolmaster, for teaching twenty five children

LUNT, a township in the parish of SEPHTON, hundred of WEST DERBY, county palatine of LANCASTER, 7½ miles (N) from Liverpool, containing 75 inhabitants

LUPPITT, a parish in the hundred of AXMINSTER, county of DEVON, 4¼ miles (N) from Honiton, containing 789 inhabitants   The living is a discharged vicarage, in the archdeaconry and diocese of Exeter, rated in the king s books at £13 6 10½   John Eyde, Esq and others were patrons in 1809   The church, dedicated to St Mary, has a stone screen and font in the early English style   Here are remains of the ancient residence of the Mohuns , they were succeeded by the

Carews, who added a chapel to the mansion, and endowed it with £3 6 8 a year   On the brow of a hill within the parish is an old fortification, called Dumpton Fort

LUPTON, a township in the parish of KIRKBY-LONSDALE, LONSDALE ward, county of WESTMORLAND 3¼ miles (W by N) from Kirkby Lonsdale, containing with the hamlet of Cowbrow, 221 inhabitants

LURGASALL, a parish in the hundred of ROTHER-BRIDGE, rape of ARUNDEL, county of SUSSEX, 4½ miles (N W by N) from Petworth, containing 664 inhabitants   The living is a rectory, in the archdeaconry and diocese of Chichester, rated in the king s books at £8, and in the patronage of the Earl of Egremont

LUSBY, a parish in the eastern division of the soke of BOLINGBROKE, parts of LINDSEY, county of LINCOLN, 4 miles (W N W) from Spilsby, containing 126 inhabitants   The living is a discharged rectory, in the archdeaconry and diocese of Lincoln, rated in the king s books at £8 14   R C Brackenbury, Esq was patron in 1780   The church is dedicated to St Peter   There is a place of worship for Wesleyan Methodists

LUSTLEIGH, a parish in the hundred of TEING-BRIDGE, county of DEVON, 5¼ miles (W by N) from Chudleigh, containing 325 inhabitants   The living is a rectory, in the archdeaconry of Totness, and diocese of Exeter, rated in the king s books at £16 7 6   The Earl of Ilchester and the Hon P C Wyndham were patrons in 1791   In the church are a wooden screen and three stone stalls, with the effigies of a knight and his lady , and the windows exhibit some remains of ancient stained glass   In a lane near the church is " Bishop s Stone, ' a block of granite, five feet high, the remains of an ancient cross

LUSTON, a township in the parish of EYE, hundred of WOLPHY, county of HEREFORD, 2½ miles (N) from Leominster, containing 400 inhabitants   There are some fine hop and fruit plantations within the township

LUTON, a parish in the hundred of FLITT, county of BEDFORD, comprising the market town of Luton and the hamlets of East and West Hyde, Leegrave, or Light grave, Limbury with Biscott, and Stopsley, and containing 4529 inhabitants, of which number, 2986 are in the town of Luton, 20 miles (S by E) from Bedford, and 31 (N W by N) from London   The name of this place is a corruption either of Lea-town, and thus derived from the river Lea, which takes its rise in the neighbourhood , or of Low-town, and is in that case descriptive of the relative position of the town with regard to the gentle eminences by which it is surrounded.   At the Conquest, Luton was held in royal demesne , and in 1216 it came into the possession of Baron Fulk de Brent, who built a strong castle here   in the reign of Henry VI., the manor belonged to John, Lord Wenlock, a celebrated partizan in the contests between the houses of York and Lancaster, slain in the battle of Tewkesbury, who had erected a handsome sepulchral chapel on the north side of the church, and commenced building a stately mansion, the portico belonging to which is still standing in the park of Luton Hoo   On the 8th of July, 1828, the town suffered extensive injury from an inundation occasioned by heavy and continued torrents of rain, and so rapid was the increase of the flood that many persons with great difficulty escaped with their lives The town is situated between two hills, on the river Lea from the market-house, which stands in the centre, three streets diverge obliquely, which are neither lighted nor paved, the inhabitants are well supplied with water from the river The manufacture of straw plat is carried on to a very great extent, and it is said to produce a greater proportion of that article than any other town in the county, the proprietor of one of these establishments has recently obtained a patent for the manufacture of Tuscan grass plat, which is here wrought into hats and bonnets there are two good malting-houses in the town The market, which is plentifully supplied with corn and straw plat, is on Monday fairs are held April 18th and October 18th, for cattle, and there is a statute fair in September A court leet is held annually, under the Marquis of Bute, as lord of the manor, at which a high constable and two day constables are appointed

The living is a vicarage, in the archdeaconry of Bedford, and diocese of Lincoln rated in the king s books at £35 12 1, and in the patronage of the Marquis of Bute The church, which is dedicated to St Mary, exhibits some fine specimens of the decorated and later styles of English architecture it has at the west end a handsome embattled tower of flint and freestone in chequers, with a hexagonal turret at each corner, and a doorway, the mouldings of which are peculiarly beautiful in the interior are vestiges of much earlier date than its general character indicates, especially in the north aisle, which contains a fine pier in the early style of English architecture the western door is remarkable for some very good panelling, and in the chancel are some stalls in the later style a few of the windows have remains of stained glass, and in the east window is a representation of St George and the dragon There are also some curious monuments, and a monumental chapel, but the chief object of attraction is a baptistry chapel, of decorated character, with pointed arches, terminating in elegant tabernacle-work, and containing a stone font supported on five pillars There are places of worship for Baptists, the Society of Friends, and Wesleyan Methodists Sundry benefactions for the instruction of children, amounting annually to the sum of £31 18 4 are now applied towards the support of a National school, in which three hundred children are educated, it is further supported by voluntary contributions In 1736, the sum of £10 per annum was bequeathed by Thomas Long, for apprenticing poor boys At the principal entrance to the town are twelve almshouses, which were erected in 1808, for the residence of twenty-four poor widows, who receive the weekly sum of four shillings each In the private chapel at Luton Hoo, the seat of the Marquis of Bute, in this parish, there is very fine carved screen-work, in the later style of English architecture, which originally formed the interior decoration of a chapel erected at Tittenhanger, by Sir Thomas Pope, about the middle of the sixteenth century The Rev John Pomfret, author of a poem entitled "The Choice, and other popular pieces, was born here in 1668

LUTTERWORTH, a market town and parish, in the hundred of GUTHLAXTON, county of LEICESTER, 13 miles (8 by W) from Leicester, and 89½ (N W by N) from London, on the high road to Lichfield, Chester, and Liverpool, containing 2102 inhabitants This place was formerly noted for the peculiar vassalage of the tenants of the manor, who were obliged to grind their corn at one particular mill of the lord, and their malt at another, so lately as the year 1758, when they obtained a decision at the Leicester assizes empowering them to erect mills, and to grind where they pleased The town is situated on the small river Swift, which falls into the Avon It is regularly built, and consists principally of one main street, from which some minor ones diverge it is lighted by subscription, and paved by means of the proceeds of an ancient benefaction of land, now producing about £200 per annum, and under the management of two officers called "Town Masters,' who are annually chosen at the manorial court leet The cotton and tammy manufactures were formerly carried on to a considerable extent, but the latter has been discontinued for many years, and the former declined about the year 1816, the present staple manufacture is coarse worsted hose, and a few ribands are also made The market is on Thursday, and fairs are held on the Thursday after February 19th, April 2nd, Holy Thursday, and September 16th, for horses, cattle, and sheep, the last is also for cheese

The living is a rectory, in the archdeaconry of Leicester, and diocese of Lincoln, rated in the king s books at £26, and in the patronage of the Crown The church, dedicated to St Mary, is a spacious and handsome structure, with a nave, aisles, and a chancel separated from the nave by a beautiful screen the tower was originally surmounted by a spire, which fell down about a century ago, when four pinnacles were substituted This edifice was repaired, beautified, and paved with chequered stone, about the year 1740, and the whole interior renovated, with the exception of the pulpit, which is a fine specimen of the early English style, of an hexagonal shape, composed of thick oak planks, with a seam of carved work in the joints, and possesses great interest, being the same in which the great reformer Wickliffe preached, he having been rector of this parish from 1374 to 1387, when he died, and was interred in the church, but, in the year 1428, his bones were disinterred by a mandate from the Pope, and publicly burnt, and the ashes thrown into the river His portrait is preserved in the church, as well as the chair in which he died, and the communion cloth used by him, which is of purple velvet trimmed with gold The Hon and Rt. Rev Henry Ryder, Bishop of Lichfield and Coventry, and formerly rector of this parish, in 1814, appropriated a library for the use of the parishioners, to be deposited in the church, with an allowance to the clerk to keep it in order There are places of worship for Independents and Wesleyan Methodists A free school and almshouse were founded and endowed by means of a bequest of £200 from the Rev Edward Sherrier the master receives a salary, and four almsmen 7s. each per week A charitable benefaction from Robert Boles, for educating and apprenticing six poor boys, amounts to about £57 per annum, and one from Margaret Bent, for educating four boys, to about £14 per annum Richard Elkington, of Shawell, by will dated May 29th, 1607, devised to the mayor, bailiffs, and burgesses of Leicester, as trustees, the sum of £50, to be lent, in sums of £10 each, to five tradesmen of Lutterworth, for the term of one year, at the rate of five per cent, the interest to be divided among certain poor persons, in default of applications, the money was vested in land some years since, which was recently sold, under a decree of the court of Chancery, and produced £1000, that sum being now lent, in sums of £50, for three years, at three per cent. In the reign of John, an hospital for a master and brethren, dedicated to St John the Baptist, was founded and endowed by Roise de Verdon and Nicholas her son at the dissolution it was valued at £26 9 5 per annum. There is a small petrifying spring in the vicinity.

LUTTLEY, a hamlet in that part of the parish of HALES OWEN which is in the lower division of the hundred of HALFSHIRE, county of WORCESTER, 1¼ mile (W) from Hales-Owen, containing 185 inhabitants.

LUTTON, or LUDDINGTON, in the WOLD, a parish partly in the hundred of NORMAN-CROSS, county of HUNTINGDON, and partly in the hundred of WILLYBROOK, county of NORTHAMPTON, 5½ miles (E) from Oundle, containing 189 inhabitants. The living is a rectory, with Washingley, in the archdeaconry of Northampton, and diocese of Peterborough, rated in the king's books at £21 11 5½. Lord Sondes was patron in 1809. The church is dedicated to St Peter. There is a place of worship for Wesleyan Methodists.

LUTTON (EAST and WEST), a township partly in the liberty of ST PETER of YORK, and partly in the parish of WEAVERTHORPE, wapentake of BUCKROSE, East riding of the county of YORK, 11 miles (E by S) from New Malton, containing 311 inhabitants. At West Lutton is a chapel of ease to the vicarage of Weaverthorpe.

LUXBOROUGH, a parish in the hundred of CARHAMPTON, county of SOMERSET, 4¼ miles (S S W) from Dunster, containing 387 inhabitants. The living is a perpetual curacy, annexed to the vicarage of Cutcombe, in the archdeaconry of Taunton, and diocese of Bath and Wells, endowed with £200 royal bounty. The church is dedicated to St Mary. Within the parish there are many tumuli, on opening some of which numerous urns, human bones, ashes, &c., have been found.

LUXULION, a parish in the eastern division of the hundred of POWDER, county of CORNWALL, 3¼ miles (W S W) from Lostwithiel, containing 1276 inhabitants. The living is a vicarage, in the archdeaconry of Cornwall, and diocese of Exeter, rated in the king's books at £10. J C Rashleigh, Esq was patron in 1813. The church is dedicated to St Cyricus and Julieta. A small school is supported by donations averaging about £6 per annum.

LYDBURY (NORTH), a parish in the hundred of PURSLOW, county of SALOP, 2¾ miles (S E) from Bishop's Castle, comprising the townships of Acton, Brockton, Down, Eaton with Choulton, Eyton with Plowden, Lydbury, and Totterton, and containing 892 inhabitants. The living is a vicarage, in the archdeaconry of Salop, and diocese of Hereford, rated in the king's books at £13 6 8, and in the patronage of the Rev John Bright Bright, M A. The church is dedicated to St Michael. John Shipman, in 1661, bequeathed £200 towards the support of a free school. In Lower Down there are the remains of a strong encampment, the trenches of which are still very perfect. The rivers Onny and Kemp run through the parish. An ancient castle stood here, belonging to the bishops of Hereford, one of whom was presented by the jury, in the reign

of Henry III, for suffering the escape of a prisoner thence. Plowden, who was a distinguished lawyer, and author of the Commentaries, resided at Plowden-hall, in this parish.

LYDD, a market town and parish, in the liberty of ROMNEY - MARSH, though locally in the hundred of Langport, lathe of SHEPWAY, county of KENT, 36 miles (S E) from Maidstone, and 70 (S E by E) from London, containing 1437 inhabitants. This town is situated at the extremity of the county, near the point of land which forms the bay of Dengeness the inhabitants are principally employed in fishing. The market is on Thursday, and a fair is held on the last Monday in July. It is a corporation by prescription, being a member of Romney, one of the cinque ports, and is governed by a bailiff, jurats, and commonalty. The bailiff is coroner, and the jurats are justices of the peace, with exclusive jurisdiction, and have power to hold a general court of session, also a court of record for the recovery of debts to any amount. There is a small common gaol and house of correction. The living is a vicarage, in the peculiar jurisdiction and patronage of the Archbishop of Canterbury, rated in the king's books at £55 12 1. The church, which is dedicated to All Saints, is a spacious edifice of different dates, the tower is in the later style of English architecture, with crocketed pinnacles it contains several monuments with brasses. There is a place of worship for Independents. On the point of land called Dengeness, a lighthouse, one hundred and ten feet in height, has been built, in lieu of an ancient one, and partly on the model of the Eddystone lighthouse, under the direction of the late Mr James Wyatt, architect this point is defended by a fort, and barracks were erected in the vicinity during the late war with France while under the control of the revolutionary government.

LYDDEN, a parish in the hundred of BEWSBOROUGH, lathe of ST AUGUSTINE, county of KENT, 4½ miles (N W) from Dover, containing 149 inhabitants. The living is a discharged vicarage, in the archdeaconry and diocese of Canterbury, rated in the king's books at £6 6, endowed with £640 private benefaction, £200 royal bounty, and £600 parliamentary grant, and in the patronage of the Archbishop of Canterbury. The church, which is dedicated to St Mary, is principally in the early style of English architecture. There are some traces of an ancient monastery in the farm-house called Swenton, in this parish, yet discoverable.

LYDE, a township in the parish of PIPE, hundred of GRIMSWORTH, county of HEREFORD, 3¼ miles (N) from Hereford. The population is returned with the parish.

LYDEARD (BISHOP'S), a parish in the western division of the hundred of KINGSBURY, county of SOMERSET, 5¼ miles (N W) from Taunton, containing, with the tythings of Bishop's Lydeard, Coombs-Ash, East Bagborough, East Coomb Hill, Lydeard-Pun-

chardon, and Quantock, 1016 inhabitants The living
is a discharged vicarage, in the archdeaconry of Taunton, and diocese of Bath and Wells, rated in the king s
books at £20 10, endowed with £200 private benefaction, and £200 royal bounty, and in the patronage
of the Dean and Chapter of Wells The church is dedicated to St Mary in the churchyard there is an
elegant cross An almshouse, which was founded here
in the reign of Charles I , by Sir Richard Grobham,
is endowed with lands now producing an annual in
come of £20

LYDEARD (ST LAWRENCE), a parish in the hundred of TAUNTON and TAUNTON-DEAN, county of So-
MERSET, 4¾ miles (N E) from Wiveliscombe, containing
618 inhabitants The living is a rectory, in the archdeaconry of Taunton, and diocese of Bath and Wells,
rated in the king's books at £22 6 8, and in the patronage of Robert Harvey, Esq

LYDFORD, a parish in the hundred of LIFTON,
county of DEVON, 7¾ miles (N by E) from Tavistock,
containing 734 inhabitants This place was anciently
of some consequence, but in 997 it sustained severe
injury from the Danes, who, after their destruction of
Tavistock abbey, burnt forty of the houses in the town
In the reign of Edward the Confessor it is recorded as
a borough, and had eight burgesses within the walls,
and forty-one without at the time of the Conquest,
these had increased to one hundred and forty, the
town was fortified, and considered of such importance
as to be taxed on an equality with London In 1238,
the Forest of Dartmoor, and the castle of Lydford, were
granted by the king to Richard, Earl of Cornwall, and
the manor now belongs to the duchy Situated in the
centre of a mining district, Lydford was the great mart
for tin, then the staple commodity of the county, and
there are still extant a few pieces of money coined at
the mint here, which is said to have existed in the
time of Ethelred II In the reign of Edward I it
twice sent members to parliament, and, in 1267, a
weekly market was granted, also an annual fair for
three days The Stannary courts were held in this
town till the close of the last century, and offenders
against the Stannary laws were tried and imprisoned in
a castle here, the dungeons of which have been consi
dered scarcely less frightful than those of the Spanish
inquisition In 1512, Richard Strode, Esq , one of
the members for Plympton, having asserted the injurious effects of the mine streams upon the harbour of
Plymouth, was prosecuted by the tinners, and eventually confined for more than three weeks in Lydford castle,
tle, heavily ironed, and fed only upon bread and water
it was a common adage, that " Lydford law punished
first and tried afterwards " Until the reign of Edward III., a gaol delivery took place here, but only once
in ten years In the latter part of the seventeenth century, the foundations of the town gates, and vestiges of
the trenches were visible The village now consists merely
of a few dilapidated cottages The living is a rectory, in
the archdeaconry of Totnes, and diocese of Exeter, rated
in the king s books at £15 13 9, and in the patronage of
the Crown, in right of the duchy of Cornwall The church
is dedicated to St Petrock The scenery which surrounds this village is of the most beautiful description
About a quarter of a mile southward is a small bridge of
one arch, near which is a romantic fall of the river Lyd,

the water of which may be seen rushing over the rugged
bed of a narrow chasm of the depth of eighty feet In
a valley to the south-west is a fine cascade, and another
to the east of the village, called Skart's Hole The only
remains of the castle are the shell of the keep, which is
fifty feet square, and forty feet in height it is situated
on a mound at the eastern end of an area formerly sur
rounded by a wall and a ditch , the western side overlooks a narrow dell of considerable depth

Dartmoor, a dreary but interesting waste, is said to
comprise no less than one hundred and thirty thousand acres According to Polwhele, Dartmoor was once
peopled , and there are extant curious accounts of
" winged serpents in the low, and wolves in the high,
lands , ' also " of a set of wild men inhabiting the verge
of this great waste,' who were remarkable for their
swiftness Near Whistman s wood may be found the
roots of very large trees , and in draining the bogs,
huge pieces of old timber have been discovered The
wild boar, bear, wolf, and moose deer, are said to have
once abounded in this forest, when a peculiar species of
hunting dog, called the Slough hound, was employed
On the surface of the moor are numerous clusters of
rock, called tors The granite here found is remarkable for the size of its feld-spar crystals Among the
rocks are observable numerous indications of this
having been once the scene of Druidical sacrifices
On Crockern tor, the ancient Stannary court has been
held within the memory of man , and till some years
back, the president s chair, jurors' seats, and court
table, were to be seen excavated in the moor-stone on
its summit Besides the latter, there are numerous
other tors, crowning the loftier elevations of the moor
they exhibit immense masses of granite, observable at
a great distance, and in many points of view commanding prospects of much variety and beauty The general
surface of this waste is rather undulating than abrupt,
and varies in height from four hundred to two thousand
one hundred feet above the sea the mean height has
been computed at one thousand seven hundred and
eighty-two feet It is twenty miles long, and, in some
parts, eleven miles wide In its numerous furrows are
collected the waters which form the rivers Dart, Teign,
Tavy, Taw, Plym, Cad, Erme, Yealm, and forty-eight
minor streams The soil is far better than that of
mountainous districts generally The higher elevations,
indeed, are covered with an unproductive black earth,
and in some of the lower spots the bogs are numerous ,
but, in many parts, there is good and sufficient soil for
agricultural purposes, requiring only the assistance of
manure, which may be now readily obtained by means
of the rail-road communicating between Plymouth and
the moor The skirts and other portions of this district
appertain to the surrounding manors, the lords of which
claim the right of summer pasturage for as many head
of cattle as they can maintain on their own estates
through the winter they are called Venville tenants
The duchy, however, is entitled to stock the forest by
agistment Those that pasture their cattle on the moor,
not being Venville tenants, pay the lessees from two to
three shillings a score for sheep and cattle Sir Thomas
Tyrwhitt, about the year 1800, erected a mansion at
Tor Royal, in the very heart of the forest, made extensive plantations, and much improved the land in the
vicinity In 1808, at his instigation, a prison was

erected, for the reception of the numerous French captives that had hitherto crowded the prison ships at Plymouth This immense building comprises, besides an hospital and dwellings for the petty officers, five rectangular edifices, each capable of holding nearly one thousand six hundred men The governor's house adjoins the prison, and at the distance of a quarter of a mile are the barracks for the guards For the supply of the prison, numerous tradesmen established themselves in the vicinity, a small town, called Prince Town, was soon formed, and a chapel built At the close of the war, however, this town was deserted, and its present aspect is one of wretchedness It is still thinly inhabited, but most of the houses are in a state of decay, and many in ruins The minister of the chapel retains his appointment, and divine service is performed weekly In 1819, an act of parliament was obtained for making the rail-road before alluded to, and a second and third act have been since granted for the purpose of extending and ramifying the line From the granite works with which it is connected, great quantities of stone are being constantly forwarded to Plymouth, and the rail-wagons coming from that port are chiefly loaded with lime, manure, and coal An inland wharf has been constructed near the end of the rail-road, which, if the immediate vicinity were more populous, would be of the greatest convenience At Two Bridges, to the east of Prince Town, is held an annual cattle fair it takes place on the first Wednesday after the 16th of August, and is well attended

LYDFORD (EAST), a parish in the hundred of Somerton, though locally in that of Catsash, county of Somerset, 4¾ miles (W) from Castle-Cary, containing 137 inhabitants The living is a discharged rectory, in the archdeaconry of Wells, and diocese of Bath and Wells, rated in the king s books at £7 9 7, and in the patronage of Mrs Rhoda Harbin The old Roman Fosse-way skirts the western boundary of this parish

LYDFORD (WEST), a parish in the hundred of Catsash, county of Somerset, 5½ miles (W) from Castle-Cary, containing 437 inhabitants The living is a rectory, in the jurisdiction of the peculiar court of West Lydford at Wells, rated in the king s books at £17 13 4 E F Colston, Esq and others were patrons in 1810. Elizabeth Pope, in 1755, bequeathed £100, directing the interest to be applied for teaching six children, and to the poor The old Roman Fosse-way passes through the parish

LYDGATE, a chapelry in that part of the parish of Rochdale which is in the upper division of the wapentake of Agbrigg, West riding of the county of York, 3 miles (N N E) from Oldham The population is returned with Saddleworth The living is a perpetual curacy, in the archdeaconry and diocese of Chester, endowed with £1000 royal bounty, and £2000 parliamentary grant. The neighbourhood of Lydgate abounds with establishments connected with the manufacture of cloth, for an account of which see Saddleworth

LYDHAM, a parish partly in the hundred and county of Montgomery, but chiefly in the hundred of Purslow, county of Salop, 2 miles (N N E) from Bishop s Castle, containing 225 inhabitants The living is a rectory, in the archdeaconry of Salop, and

diocese of Hereford, rated in the king s books at £10, and in the patronage of the Rev Herbert Oakeley The church is dedicated to the Holy Trinity The river Camlet takes its rise in this parish

LYDIATE, a chapelry in the parish of Halsall, hundred of West Derby, county palatine of Lancaster, 4½ miles (S W by W) from Ormskirk, containing 691 inhabitants There is a place of worship for Roman Catholics In 1763, Philip Buckley conveyed to trustees a messuage and ground for a school-house the master teaches four children for £4 per annum, received from Walker s charity Mr Gore, in 1825, bequeathed estates worth £90 per annum for the benefit of the poor Within the chapelry are the ruins of an unfinished abbey

LYDLINCH, a parish in the hundred of Sherborne, Sherborne division of the county of Dorset, 3 miles (W by S) from Sturminster-Newton, containing 364 inhabitants The living is a rectory, in the archdeaconry of Dorset, and diocese of Bristol, rated in the king's books at £14 5 10 John Fane, Esq, and another were patrons in 1818 The church is dedicated to St Thomas

LYE-WASTE, a chapelry in that part of the parish of Old Swinford which is in the lower division of the hundred of Halfshire, county of Worcester, 1½ mile (E) from Stourbridge The population is returned with the parish The chapel was erected by the late Thomas Hill, Esq, and is licensed, but not consecrated, it is calculated to contain about two thousand persons the appointment of the minister belongs to the Hill family There are places of worship for Independents, Wesleyan Methodists, and Unitarians The village derives its distinguishing name from having been erected on the waste, and consists of numerous cottages, chiefly inhabited by workmen employed in the iron and coal works, &c, with which the district abounds Several of the inhabitants are engaged in making nails, this being a species of manufacture which extends through a wide district, including the towns of Stourbridge and Dudley, and their neighbourhoods, which, abounding to a great extent in coal and iron-ore, afford the necessary materials for this branch of business, the nails being afterwards dispersed over all parts of the kingdom

LYFORD, a chapelry in that part of the parish of West Hanney which is in the hundred of Ock, county of Berks, 4 miles (N) from Wantage, containing 133 inhabitants An almshouse for ten poor aged persons, who are to be elected from Lyford, one of the Hannings, was founded here in 1603, by Oliver Ashcombe, Esq, formerly chief proprietor of Lyford, eight of the inmates receive an allowance of 4s each per week, and the other two 3s 6d. each

LYME-HANDLEY, a township in the parish of Prestbury, hundred of Macclesfield, county palatine of Chester, 7½ miles (N E by N) from Macclesfield, containing 253 inhabitants Lyme Hall, the principal seat of the family of Legh, is a quadrangular building of white grit-stone the more ancient part of it was erected about the end of the reign of Elizabeth, the south and west fronts are of the Ionic order, from a design by Leoni In the park there are deer, the flesh of which is of a superior flavour and quality, produced, probably, by the peculiar nature of the herbage upon which they feed.

2 B 2

Arms.

LYME-REGIS, a borough, market town, and parish, having separate jurisdiction, though locally in the liberty of Lothers and Bothenhampton, Bridport division of the county of DORSET, 22 miles (W) from Dorchester, and 144 (W S W) from London, containing 2269 inhabitants This place derives its name from the river Lyme, on which it is situated In 774, Cynewulf, King of the West Saxons, granted by charter "the land of one mansion near the west bank of the river Lim, not far from the place where it falls into the sea, to the abbey of Sherborne, that salt should be there boiled to supply the wants of the church In Domesday-book Lvme is surveyed in three parcels, one belonging to the Bishop of Salisbury, a second to Glastonbury abbey, and the third to William Belet, one of the king's servants Edward I gave to it the privileges of a borough and port, and assigned it as part of the dower of his sister, Margaret, Queen of Scotland It furnished Edward III with four ships and sixty-two men for the siege of Calais, but afterwards became so impoverished, that, in Camden's time, it was little better than a fishing-town In the early part of the last century it was in a flourishing state, and had all the conveniences of a harbour, by means of an artificial breakwater, called the Cobb During the civil war in the time of Charles I, Lyme was a station of considerable importance to both parties, it was early fortified bv the parliament, and, notwithstanding that it sustained a siege by Prince Maurice, always remained in their possession The first engagement of the English fleet with the Spanish Armada, in 1558, took place off this part of the coast, and, in 1672, another, between the English and Dutch fleets, occurred, when the latter, being beaten, retired to the coast of France Cosmo de Medici, Duke of Tuscany, on his visit to England, in 1669, landed at Lyme, as did also the Duke of Monmouth, in 1685 he erected his standard and read his declaration in the market place, but was soon after defeated at Sedgemore, whereupon twelve or thirteen of his adherents, who were condemned at Dorchester, by Judge Jefferies, were executed here

The town is situated at that extremity of the county which borders on Devonshire, between two rocky hills, and is divided by the river Lvme, which rises about two miles northward One part of it, occupying a steep declivity, has a very striking appearance, the houses rising above each other in succession, whilst the other, near the sea, is so low as to be subject to repeated inundations from the spring-tides the shore is bold and rugged, the streets are well paved and lighted, and the houses, many of which are handsome, are built of a kind of stone called blue lias, and covered with slate Recent improvements induce the expectation that Lyme will become a fashionable bathing-place, the accommodations for visitors are good, and there are handsome assembly, billiard, and card rooms, with a good library the surrounding scenery is remarkably fine It formerly carried on a considerable trade with France, Spain, and the West Indies, which has greatly declined a few vessels are fitted out for the Newfoundland fishery,

and there is some trade with the Mediterranean ports In a return made to the Exchequer in the 31st of Charles II, Lyme is represented to be a member of the port of Poole The vessels belonging to it are chiefly employed in what is termed "the seeking trade A packet sails to Guernsey once a fortnight The harbour, or Cobb, which forms the only safe shelter for vessels between it and the Start point of Portland, is about a quarter of a mile west-south-west from the town, and existed so early as the time of Edward III it was originally composed of vast pieces of rock, rudely piled on each other, but is now a work of regular masonry, consisting of two artificial piers projecting on each side, and enclosing a basin, it is six hundred and eighty feet in length, twelve in breadth at the foundation, and sixteen in height it was partially rebuilt in 1825, at an expense of £17,337 0 9¼ Various acts have been passed for its maintenance, by one of Charles II, £100 per annum out of the customs were allowed for its repair, which grant is still in force two Cobb-wardens are chosen annually by the inhabitants The number of vessels which entered from foreign parts in 1826, was thirty four British, and four foreign, and the number of those which cleared outwards, thirty-two British, and four foreign Sixteen vessels were built and registered here in 1824, six in 1825, and eight in 1826, and in March 1828, there were belonging to the port thirteen vessels of more than one hundred tons burden, and twenty-six of smaller size The dues of the harbour belong to the town, and among the privileges attached to it is the exemption of its vessels from the payment of duties in the harbours of Dovor, Rye, and Ramsgate The custom-house, a modern brick building, supported by columns, is northward of the Cobb-gate, beneath it is the market-place The manufacture of woollen cloth is carried on in the vicinity The markets are on Tuesday and Friday, and fairs are held on February 13th and October 2nd, for cattle, &c

Corporate Seal.

Lyme was originally incorporated by Edward I, and its privileges have been confirmed and augmented by succeeding monarchs, particularly by Henry VIII A court of pie-powder was granted to the mayor and burgesses by Mary, and a new charter by Elizabeth, to which various privileges were added by James I, Charles I, and William III The municipal body consists of a mayor and fifteen capital burgesses, assisted by a recorder, town clerk, and other officers the capital burgesses are chosen from among the freemen The mayor and two burgesses are justices of the peace, the retiring mayor becoming justice for one year, and the year following he is both justice and coroner The magistrates for the borough hold a court of session quarterly, in January, April, July, and October, and there is within their jurisdiction a small gaol, but no trials have occurred for several years They have also power, under the charter of Edward I, to hold a court of hustings weekly, but about forty years have elapsed since the last was held The royalty of the manor is vested in the corporation, and a manorial court is held twice a year Lyme has returned members to parliament, with only three intermissions, since the 23rd of Edward I the right of election has been much litigated, but in 1785 it was decided, by a select committee of the House of Commons, to be "in the freemen only, as well non-resident as resident, an indefinite number of freemen is elected, and admitted to the freedom of the borough, by a majority of the corporation , the present number is about fifty the mayor is the returning officer

The living is a discharged vicarage, in the peculiar jurisdiction of the Prebendary of Lyme-Regis and Halstock in the Cathedral Church of Salisbury, rated in the king s books at £ 10 5 7½, and alternately in the patronage of the Prebendary and of the lessee tenant The church, which is dedicated to St Michael the Archangel, is an ancient structure, with portions in the decorated and later styles, and consisting of a nave, chancel, and two side aisles, both which are embattled on the outside, and at the upper end of each are three or four steps, appearing to have been ascents to an altar , one of these aisles was formerly dedicated to the Virgin Mary At the entrance to the belfry is a large and lofty stone building, like a porch, over which is a room, used for a school, and bearing date 1720 There are places of worship for Baptists, Independents, and Wesleyan Methodists Here are two almshouses, founded in 1548, by John Tudbolt A convent of Carmelite friars formerly existed here , and in the fourteenth century there was likewise an hospital for lepers, dedicated to St Mary and the Holy Ghost Some fine specimens of antediluvian remains have been found in the vicinity, and are deposited in the British Museum they are considered to be the bones of the *Icthyosauri* and *Plesiosauri* Among the natives of this place was Captain Thomas Coram, to whom the "Foundling Hospital owes its origin, who was born about 1668, and died in 1751 , and Sir George Summers, the celebrated admiral, who discovered the Bermuda Islands

LYMINGE, a parish in the hundred of LONINGBOROUGH, lathe of SHEPWAY, county of KENT, 4¼ miles (N) from Hythe, containing, with the extra-parochial liberty of Lyminge, 718 inhabitants The living comprises a rectory and vicarage, in the peculiar jurisdiction of the Archbishop of Canterbury , the rectory, a sinecure, is rated in the king's books at £21 10 , and the vicarage, with the curacies of Paddlesworth and Stanford, at £10 18 9 The Rev Ralph Price was patron in 1811 The church is dedicated to St Mary and St Eadburgh In 1661, Timothy Bedingfield, devised lands and tenements to trustees for the education and maintenance of poor children belonging to the parishes of Lyminge, Dymchurch, and Smeeth, not receiving parochial relief , also to apprentice, or assist them at the Universities, at the discretion of the trustees the annual income is £111 10 from five to nine children have been annually clothed and educated , one is apprenticed every year, and a fund is reserved for such as may be sent to the University, or otherwise require aid In 1817, William Kingsford bequeathed two rent-charges of £5 each for instructing children of the parishes of Lyminge and Paddlesworth in reading and the church catechism the master receives a salary of £10 per annum The ancient Stanestreet traces the western boundary of this parish

LYMINGTON, a borough, market town, parochial chapelry, and liberty, in the New Forest (East) division of the county of SOUTHAMPTON, 18 miles (S W by S) from Southampton, and 95 (S W) from London, containing 3164 inhabitants The earliest notice of this place is in Domesday-book, in which it is called *Lentune*, afterwards *Limintun*, of which its present name is a variation The town is situated on the western bank of a creek, or river, which falls into the Solent channel it consists principally of one spacious street, nearly half a mile in length, and the houses are modern and neatly built the environs abound with picturesque and romantic scenery Its excellent accommodations for sea bathing have rendered it a favourite place of resort for invalids during the summer there are two bathing establishments , those near the town having fallen into decay, it is contemplated to erect more substantial and commodious rooms in their stead , the others, about half a mile distant, are much frequented A neat theatre is occupied, every alternate year, by a respectable company of performers, from August to October , and there is a commodious assembly room at the Angel Inn In the reign of Henry I this town first rose into note, having then been made a port, and French wines and other foreign commodities were imported at that time also it first became celebrated for its salt-works In the time of Edward III , the petty duties were levied by the inhabitants on certain articles of merchandise brought to this port, but the right to such an impost being questioned by the superior port of Southampton, the case was tried in 1329, and decided against the inhabitants of Lymington, who were subsequently often fined for persisting in their claim At length, in 1730, having again taken these duties, and being sued by the mayor and corporation of Southampton, the defendants procured the removal of the cause to the county assize court, in which they obtained a verdict in their favour, and since that time the petty customs have been regularly paid here The commercial advantages of this port were seriously affected, about ninety years ago, by the construction of a dam, or causeway, to the north of the town, the effect of which has been so to contract the channel of the river, and to diminish its depth, by excluding a great body of water, that it is now navigable only for vessels of three hundred tons burden, instead of five hundred, as formerly the trade, which is confined to coasting (no foreign vessels being allowed to land their cargoes here), consists principally in the exportation of salt, bricks, timber, and brooms, and its chief imports are coal, corn, and stone the only duties receivable at the custom-house, which is in Quay-street, are on coal and slate The manufacture of salt, both common, or bay salt, and medicinal, or Epsom salt, which formerly produced an extensive coasting and foreign trade, has greatly declined, Liverpool and other places having become successful rivals in this branch of business, although the superiority of the Lymington salt is generally acknowledged

Corporate Seal.

the works are situated along the sea-shore, at a short distance from the town, opposite to Hurst castle On the quay are a commodious public wharf and store-rooms Near it is a yard for ship-building, in which several fine yachts and other small vessels have been constructed During the winter season, from twenty to forty sail of outward-bound vessels are often anchored here at one time, paying a toll proportioned to their tonnage the harbour at the entrance of the creek is excellent, and affords a favourite and safe shelter for the vessels belonging to the members of the Royal Yacht Club The market is on Saturday, and fairs are held on the 12th of May and the 2nd of October, for cheese, horses, cattle, &c , each continuing two days Lymington, which is a borough by prescription, was incorporated by charter of James I the municipal body consists of a mayor and an unlimited number of burgesses The mayor is chosen annually on the Sunday after St Matthew's day, and sworn into office at the court leet of the lord of the manor, usually held about the end of October, when also the constables, town crier, serjeant at mace, &c , are appointed Petty sessions for the New Forest (East) division are held by the magistrates for that division, every alternate Saturday The elective franchise was conferred by Elizabeth, in the 27th year of her reign the right of election is vested in the corporation, the number of voters being about thirty the mayor is the returning officer, and the influence of Sir Harry Burrard Neale, Bart , is predominant

The living is a perpetual curacy, with the vicarage of Boldre, in the archdeaconry and diocese of Winchester The chapel, dedicated to St Thomas à Becket, has been built at different periods, being irregularly constructed of brick and stone, with a central tower and spire, the interior is neat, and contains several handsome monuments There are places of worship for Baptists and Independents A grammar school was founded and endowed, in 1668, by George Fulford and others, who devised the sum of £326 for that purpose in 1688, a school-house was granted by the corporation, which, becoming dilapidated, was taken down in 1782, and ten boys are instructed on this foundation in reading, writing, and arithmetic, in the private residence of the master, who receives about £20 per annum on account of the charity A bequest of £300 was made, in 1777, by Anne Burrard, to found a school for the education of poor children ten children of both sexes are instructed, and the interest is equally divided between a master and a mistress A National school is supported by subscription, for which a school-room is about to be built, on a piece of ground given by Sir H B Neale, Bart , and a school for eighty boys and eighty girls is supported by a private individual Rear-Admiral Thomas Rogers, who died in 1814, bequeathed £1000, directing the interest to be divided annually between ten poor men and women There are various charitable institutions for the relief of the sick and indigent On a promontory on the coast, south of Lymington, is Hurst castle, a fortress erected by Henry VIII , to defend this part of the channel between the main land and the Isle of Wight, it consists of a circular tower strengthened by semicircular bastions In this castle, Charles I was confined for several days after his removal from Carisbrooke, in 1648, about one month prior to his decapi-

tation it is now an important station, occupied by the men employed in the preventive service Two light-houses and a beacon are supported for the service of vessels navigating the coast

LYMM, a parish in the hundred of Bucklow, county palatine of Chester, 5½ miles (E S E) from Warrington, containing 2090 inhabitants The living is a rectory in medieties, in the archdeaconry and diocese of Chester, the mediety of Lymm with Warburton is rated in the king's books at £11 0 7½, and in the patronage of Rowland Eyles Egerton Warburton, Esq , the other mediety is rated at £11 0 5, and in the patronage of E Leigh, Esq The church, dedicated to the Virgin Mary, is a very ancient structure There is a place of worship for Wesleyan Methodists A free grammar school was endowed, in 1698, by Sir G Warburton, and W Domville, Esq , the income of which is about £80 per annum The Duke of Bridgewater's canal passes through the village

LYMPNE, a parish partly within the liberty of Romney Marsh, but chiefly in the hundred of Street, lathe of Shepway, county of Kent, 2¾ miles (W) from Hythe, containing 467 inhabitants The living is a discharged vicarage, in the archdeaconry and diocese of Canterbury, rated in the king's books at £9 1 4, endowed with £200 private benefaction, and £200 royal bounty, and in the patronage of the Archdeacon of Canterbury The church, dedicated to St Stephen, stands on the edge of a rock near the village, and is principally in the Norman style of architecture, with a tower rising from the centre near it is Stutfall castle, now the residence of the Archdeacon, but formerly a strong hold or fort of the Romans, the walls are constructed of brick and flint The parish takes its name from the ancient river Limene, now the Rother, a branch of which ran below it, and formed the ancient Roman haven called *Portus Limanus* The place itself is generally considered to have been the *Limin* of Ptolemy The great military road called Stane-street, still visibly straight for some miles, ran hither from the station *Durovernum*, or Canterbury At Shepway Cross, about half a mile from the church, the Lemmarcha, or Lord Warden of the cinque-ports, was sworn into office Near the castle several Roman coins have been found About 633, Ethelburga, a daughter of Ethelbert, built a nunnery here in honour of the Virgin Mary, which subsequently became an abbey, and continued till 964, but after the Danish invasion, it came into the possession of the Archbishop of Canterbury Here are a small endowed school, and an almshouse comprising two dwellings A fair for pedlary and toys is held on July 5th The Shorncliffe and Rye canal passes through the parish

LYMPSHAM, a parish in the hundred of Brent with Wrington, county of Somerset, 7 miles (W) from Axbridge, containing 496 inhabitants The living is a rectory, in the archdeaconry of Wells, and diocese of Bath and Wells, rated in the king's books at £38 5 2½, and in the patronage of the Rev J A Stephenson The church, dedicated to St Christopher, has a very elegant tower There is a place of worship for Wesleyan Methodists

LYMPSTON, a parish in the eastern division of the hundred of Budleigh, county of Devon, 2¼ miles (N) from Exmouth, containing 1020 inhabitants The living is a rectory, in the archdeaconry and diocese of Exeter, rated in the king's books at £15 13 4, and in the patronage of T Porter, Esq The church is dedicated to St. Mary There are places of worship for Wesleyan Methodists and Unitarians A small sum, the produce of several trifling bequests, is paid to two schoolmistresses for the instruction of children This parish is situated on the eastern bank of the river Exe

LYNCOMB, a joint parish with Widcomb, in the hundred of BATH-FORUM, county of SOMERSET, adjacent to the city of Bath, containing 5880 inhabitants The living is a vicarage, annexed to the rectory of St. Peter and St Paul, Bath, in the archdeaconry of Bath, and diocese of Bath and Wells, and in the patronage of the Corporation of Bath The parish is separated from the city of Bath by the river Avon, and the Kennet and Avon canal passes through it, the hills in the neighbourhood are very productive of freestone There is an hospital for idiots, dedicated to St Mary Magdalene, with a chapel annexed, which latter has been partly rebuilt by subscription

LYNDHURST, a parish in the northern division of the hundred of NEW FOREST, New Forest (East) division of the county of SOUTHAMPTON, 9½ miles (W by S) from Southampton, containing 1170 inhabitants The living is a perpetual curacy, annexed to the rectory of Minstead, in the archdeaconry and diocese of Winchester The church is dedicated to St Michael There is a place of worship for Baptists A school, in which about sixteen children of both sexes are educated, is endowed with £26 per annum, arising from a bequest by William Phillips, Esq, for charitable uses There is likewise a National school Prior to the time of Charles II, the jurisdiction of the Chief Justice in Eyre for this forest was exercised here, where the forest courts under the authority of the verderers are still held, some on such days as the presiding judges shall appoint, others annually on September 14th Attached to the wardenship is a house, called the King's house, now occupied by a subordinate officer An ancient stirrup, said to have been used by William Rufus, at the time when he was shot by Sir Walter Tyrrel, is preserved here Courts leet and baron for the hundred of Redbridge and manor of Lyndhurst are held Sir John Singleton Copley, the present Lord High Chancellor of England, on being elevated to that high office, was created Baron Lyndhurst, by patent dated April 27th, 1827

LYNDON, a parish in the hundred of MARTINSLEY, county of RUTLAND, 5 miles (S E) from Oakham, containing 106 inhabitants The living is a rectory, in the archdeaconry of Northampton, and diocese of Peterborough, rated in the king's books at £6 17 1, and in the patronage of S Barker, Esq The church is dedicated to St Martin The river Chater bounds this parish on the south

LYNDON, a quarter in the parish of CHURCH-BICKENHILL, Solihull division of the hundred of HEMLINGFORD, county of WARWICK The population is returned with the parish

LYNEHAM, a chapelry in the parish of SHIPTON under WHICHWOOD, hundred of CHADLINGTON, county of OXFORD, 6 miles (N N E) from Burford, containing 260 inhabitants

LYNESACK, a joint township with Softley, in that part of the parish of AUCKLAND ST ANDREW which is in

the north-western division of DARLINGTON ward, county palatine of DURHAM, 7 miles (S by E) from Wolsingham, containing, with Softley, 732 inhabitants This township contains some extensive collieries it is bounded on the south by the river Gaunless, or Wanless, and on the north by the Lin-Burn

LYNFORD, a parish in the hundred of GRIMSHOE, county of NORFOLK, 5 miles (N N E) from Brandon-Ferry, containing 52 inhabitants The living is a perpetual curacy, in the archdeaconry of Norfolk, and diocese of Norwich The church is in ruins Two Roman urns were dug up in this parish in 1720, and one in 1735, containing ashes and bones

LYNG, a parish in the hundred of EYNSFORD, county of NORFOLK, 6 miles (N E by E) from East Dereham, containing 581 inhabitants The living is a rectory, with that of Whitwell, in the archdeaconry of Norfolk, and diocese of Norwich, rated in the king's books at £11 Edward Lombe, Esq was patron in 1827 The church is dedicated to St Michael

LYNN (WEST), a parish in the Marshland division of the hundred of FREEBRIDGE, county of NORFOLK, ¾ of a mile (W) from Lynn-Regis, containing 367 inhabitants The living is a rectory, in the archdeaconry and diocese of Norwich, rated in the king's books at £9 H H Townsend, Esq was patron in 1811 The church is dedicated to St Peter

LYNN-REGIS, a borough, sea-port, and market town, having exclusive jurisdiction, though locally in the Lynn division of the hundred of Freebridge, county of NORFOLK, 44 miles (W by N) from Norwich, and 97 (N by E) from London, containing 12,253 inhabitants This place is by Camden supposed to have been an ancient British town,

Seal and Arms.

and to have derived its name from the expanse of water near which it is situated, and of which the British word *Llyn* was significant, but Spelman is of opinion that the name is of Saxon origin, derived from the word *Lean*, signifying a tenure in fee, or farm It was anciently called *Len Episcopi*, or Bishop's Lynn, from having been under the jurisdiction, both temporal and spiritual, of the Bishops of Norwich, who had a palace where Gaywood hall now stands, but this authority was, in the reign of Henry VIII., surrendered to that monarch, and from that time the town assumed the name of *Lenne-Regis*, or King's Lynn In Domesday-book it is called *Lun* and *Lena*, and described as the property of Agelmare, Bishop of North Elmham, and Stigand, Archbishop of Canterbury It appears to have been a place of considerable importance, and to have enjoyed valuable privileges, among which were certain customs on the arrival of all merchandise by sea and land, of which the bishops claimed a moiety Henry I granted liberty to the prior of Norwich to hold an annual fair on the feast of St Margaret, with other privileges, and in the reign of Richard I it was the residence of numerous Jews, who carried on an extensive trade with most parts of Europe In 1204, during the contest between John and the barons, Lynn continued faithful to the king, who remained there for some time, and on the petition of John Grey, Bishop of Norwich, made the town a free borough, he presented to the inhabitants a silver cup, weighing seventy-three ounces, richly gilt and beautifully enamelled, which is still preserved by the corporation, and he is said to have presented his own sword to be borne before the mayor on public occasions, the sword now used is, however, reported to have been given by Henry VIII, on his assuming the power previously exercised by the bishops John was frequently here during the war, and from this place he departed just before the disaster which befel him in crossing the Wash, and to which is ascribed the illness that caused his death Henry VI also visited the town, and Edward IV, in 1470, retreating before the celebrated Earl of Warwick, came hither, in company with his brother, the Duke of Gloucester In 1498, Henry VII, with his queen and the Prince of Wales, attended by a numerous retinue, spent some time at the Augustine convent in the town In the parliamentary war the inhabitants embraced the royal cause, and the town was besieged by the parliamentarian forces, under the command of the Earl of Manchester, to whom it surrendered, after a vigorous resistance for three weeks, and was garrisoned with parliamentarian troops Numerous plagues and other diseases have raged here, at different periods, with destructive influence, in 1540, an intermittent fever prevailed to such an extent as to occasion a suspension of the mart for that year In 1636 and 1665, the market and fairs were discontinued, owing to the plague, at the former period, temporary habitations were erected without the town for persons afflicted with it In 1741, the spires of the church of St Margaret and the chapel of St Nicholas were blown down, and several other buildings greatly injured, by a violent hurricane and storm

The town is situated on the east bank of the Great Ouse, which is here of considerable breadth, and at a distance of ten miles from the North sea it extends a mile and a quarter in length, and half a mile in breadth, and is intersected by four rivulets, called fleets, over which are numerous bridges, that have lately been widened, and a new road for carriages constructed over Penfleet bridge Many improvements have been effected under acts of parliament, obtained in 1803 and 1806, for paving, cleansing, and lighting the town, the approaches to which are commodious and pleasant It was anciently defended on the east side by a wall, in which were nine bastions, and by a broad and deep fosse, over which were three drawbridges leading to the principal gates a few fragments of the wall are still remaining, and one of the gates, arched and embattled, at the south entrance, the others have been taken down. On the north side is St Anne's fort, a platform battery, constructed in 1627, and formerly mounting twelve pieces of heavy ordnance The town consists of three principal streets, nearly parallel, from which several smaller streets diverge it is well paved and lighted with gas, but indifferently supplied with water conveyed by pipes from a reservoir at Kettle Mills, in the north-eastern suburb application is about to be made to parliament for increasing the supply, by the construction of more effectual works The houses are in general ancient and inconveniently built, though interspersed with several respectable mansions, and in the more modern parts of the town are several ranges of

handsome dwellings The environs are flat, and not very attractive in their scenery, but the public promenades are pleasant the principal is a mall, three hundred and forty yards in length, and eleven yards wide, constructed and kept in order by the corporation The theatre, a handsome building, was erected by subscription on shares in 1814, and is well arranged and elegantly fitted up it is open annually for about six weeks, commencing at the great mart in February Assemblies are held in a suite of commodious rooms in the townhall, in which also concerts take place occasionally The subscription library, established in 1797, contains three thousand two hundred volumes, and is supported by about one hundred and sixty members, and the inhabitants, by means of a written order from the mayor, have access to an excellent parochial library in St Margaret's church, by permission of the corporation A mechanics institution was established in 1827, which is under the direction of a president and committee

In the reign of Edward the Confessor, Lynn was a place of considerable trade, and it had grown into such commercial importance at the beginning of the 13th century, that the revenue paid to the crown was more than two-thirds of that arising from the trade of the port of London In 1374, the inhabitants furnished nineteen vessels towards a naval armament for the invasion of France, a mint was established here, and there were thirty-one incorporated guilds, or trading companies, some of whom had separate halls The limits of the port extend in a northerly direction from the promontory on which Hunstanton lighthouse stands, in a supposed right line, north-north-west, to fourteen fathoms of water, and likewise from this line towards the east, until it falls into fourteen fathoms of water, at a point northward from the eastern end of the sand-hills, commonly called Burnham Meales, southerly to a place in the channel of the harbour of Lynn, called White Friars' Fleet, and to Gibbon's point opposite thereto, thence down the river, on the western side, and round the coast of Marshland, to a point called Sutton corner The harbour is deep, and sufficient to accommodate three hundred sail, but the entrance is somewhat dangerous, from the frequent shifting of the channel, and the numerous sand banks, and the anchorage is rendered difficult from the nature of the soil, and the rapidity of the tide, which rises to the height of twenty feet to counteract a portion of these disadvantages, a company of pilots has been established, whose office is on St Anne's fort, commanding a view of the channel Anciently the course of the Ouse was by Wisbeach its present direction, according to Dugdale, may be referred to the reign of Henry III, and it has been ascribed to the decay of the outfall at Wisbeach, and to some great flood which rendered a fresh line necessary This accession of water into the channel of a small river, which previously flowed past the town, destroyed a considerable part of Old Lynn, and the church at North Lynn is stated to have been completely engulphed After the sluices at Denver and Salter's Lode had been constructed, for the purpose of draining the fenny tract called Bedford Level, the navigation of the river was much impaired, and the harbour obstructed by the accumulation of silt, to remedy which, the Eau-brink cut was commenced in 1818, and completed in 1820, avoiding a considerable bend in the river, and the old channel of the river is gradually filling with soil, so that in a few years a valuable part of more than seven hundred acres of land will be gained for agricultural purposes, but the accumulation of silt in the harbour still continues, so that vessels which formerly lay immediately along side the quays, cannot now approach within several yards To remedy this inconvenience, three jetties, composed of timber, have lately been constructed, at stated distances, with a view to divert the stream to the eastern, or harbour, side, but their effect has scarcely been ascertained Near the north end of this cut, a handsome wooden bridge has been built, over which a new road leads into Marshland, and a bridge over the river Nine, and an embankment at Cross Keys Wash, are now in progress, affording a direct road from Norfolk and Suffolk, through Lynn, into Lincolnshire The Purfleet and Common Staith quays are the principal places for landing merchandise, on the former, where all wines are landed, the custom-house and exchange stands, occupying the site of the hall of the ancient guild of the Holy Trinity it is a handsome building of freestone, ornamented with two tiers of pilasters, the lower of the Doric, and the upper of the Ionic order, and surmounted by a small turret, in a niche in the front is a statue of Charles II In the High-street is the excise office, to which are attached a collector, supervisor, and other officers This port, from its situation, so near the North sea, and enjoying the advantages of inland communication, carries on an extensive foreign and coasting trade the principal imports are, wine from Spain and Portugal, timber, deals, hemp, and tallow, from the Baltic, corn from the northern parts of Europe, oil-cake from Holland, and timber from America The coasting-trade is very considerable, consisting chiefly of imported and agricultural produce, with which it supplies the neighbouring districts, and a fine species of white sand, much used in the manufacture of glass, of which great quantities are sent to Newcastle and Leith, also a considerable number of shrimps, which are found in abundance on the coast, and are sent to London its intercourse with the interior of the country is greatly facilitated by the river Ouse and its several branches, with which various canals have communication, and not less than one hundred and fifty thousand chaldrons of coal are annually brought into the port. In the year ending January 5th, 1827, sixty British, and one hundred and twenty-seven foreign, ships entered inwards from foreign ports, and twenty-one British, and one hundred and ten foreign, vessels cleared outwards the annual amount of dues paid at the custom-house is on an average £90,000 the number of vessels belonging to the port, in 1828, was one hundred and twelve, averaging a burden of one hundred and twenty-one tons Formerly, several ships were annually fitted out for the Greenland whale fishery, but this branch of the business of the port has, of late years, greatly declined. Ship-building has been carried on here from a very early period, but it is not at present of so much note as formerly There are no particular branches of manufacture deserving notice the chief are ropes and sailcloth, the latter on a very confined scale The market days are Tuesday and Saturday, the former, principally for corn, is held in a spacious paved area of about three acres, surrounded by some well-built houses it contains a handsome but dilapidated market-cross of

freestone, erected in 1710, the lower part of the building is surrounded by a peristyle of sixteen Ionic columns, above which is a walk, defended by iron palisades, and in the centre is an octagonal room, on the exterior sides of which are carved figures facing the cardinal points, the whole being surmounted by a cupola It is in contemplation to form a new market place, by pulling down some houses on the western side of the preceding one, and erecting a market-house, to extend towards the common staith, or quay, where the fish-market now is The market on Saturday, formerly held in the High-street, was removed, in 1782, to an area near St Margaret s church, where shambles have been built In 1826, the weekly cattle-market was removed, from its inconvenient site in the environs of the town, to a more central situation, the mayor and burgesses, in consequence of a petition to that effect, granted a piece of land abutting upon one of the streets, to which convenient approaches have been made, so that cattle can reach the market-place without passing through any of the streets The fairs are, February 14th, which is the grand mart for six days, but generally continued for a fortnight, and October 17th, which is a great cheese fair

The town, which under the bishops was governed by a provost appointed by them, was first incorporated by John, and has had no less than fifteen royal charters The parish of All Saints, or South Lynn, was constituted a part of the borough by a license from Henry VIII, in 1546, and confirmed by charter in the 4th of Philip and Mary By the last charter, granted by Charles II, the government is vested in a mayor, high steward, recorder, twelve aldermen, and eighteen common council-men, assisted by a town clerk, chamberlain, two coroners, and other officers The mayor is chosen annually on the 29th of August, from among the aldermen, by the common council, and enters upon his office on the 29th of September All members of the corporation who have passed the chair are justices of the peace for the borough and liberties, exercising exclusive jurisdiction the freedom of the borough is inherited by the eldest sons of freemen, on the death of their fathers, or acquired by servitude or gift The corporation hold courts of admiralty, for determining all pleas arising within the limits of the port, quarterly courts of session, for the trial of all offenders, except for high treason, and a court of record, under the charter of Henry VIII, for the recovery of debts to any amount a court of requests is also held, under an act passed in the 10th of George III, for the recovery of debts under 40s The mayor, aldermen, magistrates, and clergy, used to hold a meeting for determining all controversies in an amicable manner, called the "Feast of Reconciliation," but this custom, which originated in 1558, has long since become obsolete The borough first exercised the elective franchise in the 23rd of Edward I, since which time it has regularly returned two members to parliament the right of election is vested in the freemen generally, the number of whom is about three hundred and thirty the mayor is the returning officer The guildhall is an ancient structure of stone and flint, in the later style of English architecture, containing a spacious hall, courts for the sessions, and a suite of assembly-rooms, and is ornamented with portraits of many public characters, among which are those of Sir Robert Walpole, Bart, who represented the borough in seventeen successive parliaments, Sir Thomas White, Sir Benjamin Keene, and others The prison for the borough is both a common gaol and house of correction, containing separate rooms for debtors, and for male and female felons, but it is not well adapted to the classification of prisoners, having only one airing-yard, for the alternate use of all classes

King's Lynn comprises the parishes of All Saints, Southgate, St Edmund, North End, and St Margaret, all in the archdeaconry and diocese of Norwich The living of All Saints' is a vicarage, rated in the king s books at £18 6 8, and in the patronage of the Bishop of Ely the church is an ancient cruciform structure, the tower, which fell down in 1763, and demolished part of the body of the church, has not been rebuilt The living of St Edmund's, North End, is a sinecure rectory, rated in the king s books at £13 1 8, to which S Thornton, Esq and others presented in 1799 the church is supposed to have been anciently swept away by the river The living of St Margaret's is a perpetual curacy, with the curacy of St Nicholas annexed, endowed with £1000 parliamentary grant, and in the patronage of the Dean and Chapter of Norwich the church is a spacious structure, combining the early, the decorated, and the later styles of English architecture, with two western towers, and an east front of singularly beautiful design, with two octagonal turrets rising from the flanking buttresses, the chancel is in the early English style, with a fine circular east window, the south porch is highly ornamented with canopied niches and shields, and the roof finely groined The chapel of St Nicholas is a large structure, combining the decorated with the later style of English architecture the original roof of beautifully carved oak is carefully preserved, and the interior contains many parts of great beauty There are places of worship for Baptists, the Society of Friends, Independents, Wesleyan Methodists, and Unitarians, and a Roman Catholic chapel There is a burial-ground for the Jews, but they have now no synagogue The free grammar school was founded in the reign of Henry VII, by Thomas Thoresby, alderman of Lynn, who endowed it with lands producing about £60 per annum a spacious school-room, and a dwelling-house for the master, were erected, in 1825, by the corporation, who are trustees under a charter of Edward IV It has two scholarships at Emanuel College, Cambridge, of £5 10 each per annum, and one scholarship of £2 per annum at either University, both founded by the corporation, and tenable for seven years, one scholarship of £2, at either of the Universities for seven years, founded by the owner of the estate near Highbridge-Lynn, one scholarship of £3 8 6, at Trinity College, Cambridge, for five years, in the gift of the Master and Vice-Master of Trinity, and the Mayor of Lynn, and one scholarship of £6, tenable for four years, in St John s College, Cambridge, in the gift of the Corporation Eugene Aram was usher here when he was apprehended, in 1759, on a charge of murder committed fourteen years previously near Knaresborough, in Yorkshire, for which he was tried and executed, having acknowledged the justice of the sentence a short time before it was carried into effect A school on the Lancasterian plan was established in 1792, which has been enlarged for the instruction of fifty girls, it is supported partly by subscription, and partly by the industry of the girls, who

are employed in needle-work A similar school for boys, established in 1808, is supported entirely by subscription, in which two hundred and thirty boys are instructed. There is a National school for girls

Gaywood s almshouses occupy the site of the ancient hospital of St Mary Magdalene, founded in the reign of Stephen, for a master and twelve brethren and sisters, the endowment, lapsing to the crown, was granted by James I to the mayor and aldermen, in trust for the maintenance of a master and eleven aged and infirm persons The hospital was burnt down by the parliamentary troops in the reign of Charles I, and rebuilt by the corporation in 1649 it contains a chapel, and apartments for a master, who receives ten shillings per week, and eleven poor women, who have five shillings per week each, the charity being under the management of the two senior aldermen The Bede house, an establishment of obscure and uncertain foundation, was rebuilt, in 1822, by Mr Benjamin Smith (who has recently proposed to found a new almshouse, the design having been approved of by the corporation), and is endowed for the maintenance of a reader and eleven aged women, who receive each about six shillings per week Valenger s hospital, founded in 1605, and rebuilt in 1806, is inhabited by four aged women, each of whom receives four shillings per week Paradise, or Framingham's hospital, begun in 1676, by Mr John Heathcote, and completed after his decease by Mr Henry Framingham, is endowed for the support of a reader, who receives four shillings and ninepence per week, and eleven aged men, who receive each three shillings and sixpence per week Among the charities held in trust by the corporation is one by Mr Cook, of London, who bequeathed £5000 three per cents, the dividends on £2300 to be paid to the inmates of the Bede house, the dividends on £2000 to the inmates of Framingham s hospital, and those on the remaining £700 to the hospitallers of South Lynn. There are various benevolent institutions for the relief of the necessitous, among which are a Ladies' Society for the relief of lying-in women, established in 1791, another for visiting the sick at their own habitations, formed in 1827, the Strangers Friend Society, a dispensary, established in 1813, and supported by subscription, and a Dorcas Society there are numerous benefit societies, and various charitable bequests for distribution among the poor The corporation are in possession of funds for apprenticing children, for loans to young tradesmen, and other benevolent purposes. The workhouse was originally a chapel, dedicated to St. James, having become ruinous, it was rebuilt by the corporation, in 1581, and used for the manufacture of sacking, &c this undertaking having failed, it was converted, in 1682, into an hospital or workhouse for fifty decayed old men, women, and poor children By an act passed in 1701, its management was entrusted to an Incorporated Society, styled the "Guardians of the poor of the borough of King s Lynn in the county of Norfolk, and within the liberties of the said borough this act was amended in 1808, adding the churchwardens and overseers to the corporation It is now confined to the reception of the poor of St Margaret s parish only the inhabitants of South Lynn maintain their own poor, and are exempt from this act

The monastic institutions and ancient hospitals consisted of a priory of Benedictine monks, in Priory-lane, a convent of White friars, in South Lynn, one of Grey friars, in St James' street, one of Black friars, between Clough lane and Spinner-lane, one of Augustine friars, in St. Austin s street, a college, near the town hall, St. Mary Magdalene s hospital, the site and endowment of which are appropriated to Gaywood's hospital, also a nunnery, a monastery of friars *de Pœnitentiâ Jesu*, St John s hospital, and four lazar-houses, the sites of which are unknown, besides various chapels, all which were involved in the general dissolution of these establishments Vestiges of the houses which belonged to the Grey, White, Black, and Austin, friars still remain, that of the first consists of the tower and lantern of their conventual church it rises from a pointed arch supported by buttresses, to the height of about ninety feet, and within is groined with stone A spiral staircase leads to the summit, whence a complete view is obtained of the town and its environs It stands in a small enclosure opposite and belonging to the free grammar school, on the left of the entrance into the town from London An ancient building, in a state of complete repair, in Queen-street, near the town hall, has been considered that which formerly constituted the college But the most interesting relic of antiquity is an ancient and curious edifice, at the eastern extremity of the town, denominated the Lady s Chapel, or, the Chapel on the Red Mount It is of singular construction within an octagonal wall of red brick, strengthened by buttresses, is a handsome cruciform chapel of very small dimensions, with an elegant stone roof, it formerly contained an image of the Virgin, before which journeying pilgrims, on their way to Walsingham, are supposed to have presented their offerings The whole has lately undergone a thorough reparation, by means of a subscription Nicholas of Lynn, a celebrated mathematician, astrologer, and navigator, was born here, and became one of the Grey friars, he also died and was buried here in 1369 William Browne, M D, afterwards Sir William Browne, resided here, he was President of the Royal College of Physicians, and the author of several works, chiefly on medical subjects The custom of ushering in May-day with the blowing of horns is still observed at this place At Reffley, about two miles distant, in a sequestered spot, stands an obelisk, from which, by means of an aqueduct, a chalybeate spring issues, near it is an octagonal temple, whither subscribers repair for the benefit of the water Lynn gives the interior title of baron to Marquis Townshend.

LYNT, a tything in the parish of Coleshill, hundred of Shrivenham, county of Berks, though locally in the hundred of Highworth, Cricklade, and Staple, county of Wilts, 1½ mile (N E) from Highworth The population is returned with the parish

LYONSHALL, a parish in the hundred of Stretford, county of Hereford, 2½ miles (E S E) from Kington, containing 896 inhabitants The living is a discharged vicarage, in the archdeaconry and diocese of Hereford, rated in the kings books at £6 10 7½, and in the patronage of the Bishop of Hereford The church is dedicated to St Michael Here are the remains of a moated castle, which, in the early part of the reign of Henry III, belonged to Sir Stephen de Ebroicis, then lord of the manor and castle, on the site of which a curious antique ring was found A railway passes through this village, in its course from Brecon, to the lime-

kilns in the parish of Old Radnor A court leet is held here The parish is bounded on the north by the river Avon

LYPEAT, a hamlet in the parish and hundred of Kilmersdon, county of Somerset, 5¾ miles (W N W) from Frome The population is returned with the parish

LYSS-TURNEY, a chapelry in the parish and hundred of Odiham, Basingstoke division of the county of Southampton, 3¾ miles (N N E) from Petersfield, containing 560 inhabitants The living is a perpetual curacy, in the archdeaconry and diocese of Winchester, endowed with £200 private benefaction, and £1700 parliamentary grant, and in the patronage of the Hon W T L P Wellesley The church is dedicated to St Peter Mary Cole, in 1765, gave a rent-charge of £4, and Dorothea Cole bequeathed another of £3, to be applied for teaching poor children

LYTCHETT-MATRAVERS, a parish in the hundred of Cogdean, Shaston (East) division of the county of Dorset, 8 miles (N by E) from Wareham, containing 609 inhabitants The living is a rectory, in the archdeaconry of Dorset, and diocese of Bristol, rated in the kings books at £13 3 4 W Trenchard, Esq was patron in 1810 The church is dedicated to St Mary There is a place of worship for Wesleyan Methodists

LYTCHETT-MINSTER, a chapelry in the parish of Sturminster-Marshall, hundred of Cogdean, Shaston (East) division of the county of Dorset, 5 miles (N E by N) from Wareham, containing 544 inhabitants The living is a perpetual curacy, with the vicarage of Sturminster-Marshall, in the jurisdiction of the peculiar court of Sturminster Marshall The chapel is demolished This chapelry is bounded on the south-east by Poole harbour, and on the south by Rock Lee river, which latter is crossed by a bridge, and falls into Lytchett bay On the south side of the village is a very large tumulus here was formerly a beacon

LYTH, a hamlet in the parish of Heversham, Kendal ward, county of Westmorland, 6½ miles (S W by W) from Kendal The population is returned with Crosthwaite

LYTHAM, a parish in the hundred of Amounderness, county palatine of Lancaster, 8 miles (S W by W) from Kirkham, containing 1292 inhabitants The living is a perpetual curacy, in the archdeaconry of Richmond, and diocese of Chester, endowed with £800 and a rent-charge of £7 private benefaction, £600 royal bounty, and £600 parliamentary grant, and in the patronage of John Clifton, Esq The church is dedicated to St Cuthbert There is a Roman Catholic chapel A free school was established in 1704, with the produce of various benefactions, which, with others of a later date, yield an income of £104 18 per annum, the number of scholars varies from seventy to one hundred and twenty A Sunday school affords instruction to about one hundred children Lytham is situated on the western coast, on the northern shore of the æstuary of the Ribble, and is much resorted to for sea-bathing Some improvement has taken place within the last few years, by pulling down an extensive range of old buildings, and, after leaving an opening from the Clifton s Arms hotel to the beach, erecting several new houses, among which is a billiard-room Part of the beach has also been levelled, and a public walk formed along it, affording a pleasing view of the scenery on the southern side of the æstuary About a mile eastward is Lytham pool, a large natural basin, where vessels bringing corn, &c, to the port of Preston, discharge their cargoes into smaller craft at its northern extremity is a graving-dock, for building or repairing vessels A few of the inhabitants are employed in fishing Lytham Hall comprises, in its kitchens and out-offices, a portion of the buildings of a Benedictine priory, founded, as a cell to the monastery at Durham, by Richard Fitz Roger, in the latter part of the reign of Richard I, and dissolved, with the smaller monasteries, by Henry VIII

LYTHE, or MILLAND, a chapelry in the hundred of EASEBOURNE, rape of CHICHESTER, county of SUSSEX, 6 miles (N W) from Midhurst

LYTHE, a parish in the eastern division of the liberty of LANGBAURGH, North riding of the county of YORK, comprising the townships of Barnby, Borrowby, Ellerby, Hutton-Mulgrave, Lythe, Nickleby, Newton-Mulgrave, and Ugthorpe, and containing 2194 inhabitants, of which number, 1134 are in the township of Lythe, 3½ miles (W N W) from Whitby The living is a discharged vicarage, in the archdeaconry of Cleveland, and diocese of York, rated in the king s books at £10 12 6, endowed with £1400 parliamentary grant, and in the patronage of the Archbishop of York The church is dedicated to St Oswald, and, although of modern appearance, is an ancient structure There is a place of worship for Wesleyan Methodists Peter de Mauley obtained a weekly market to be held here, and a fair on the eve of the festival of St Oswald, in the reign of Henry III, but both have been long disused

M

MABE, a parish in the hundred of KERRIER, county of CORNWALL, 4½ miles (W) from Falmouth, containing 457 inhabitants The living is a vicarage not in charge, with that of Mylor, in the jurisdiction of the Consistorial Court of the Bishop of Exeter The church, dedicated to St Mabe, has a lofty handsome tower crowned with pinnacles There is a place of worship for Wesleyan Methodists An almshouse was erected with the sum of £200, the proceeds of a small legacy left to accumulate for the purpose

MABLETHORPE (ST MARY), a parish in the Marsh division of the hundred of CALCEWORTH, parts of LINDSEY, county of LINCOLN, 7 miles (N E by N) from Alford, containing 200 inhabitants The living is a rectory, with which that of Stane is united, in the archdeaconry and diocese of Lincoln, rated in the king s books at £17 10 2½ Col. Waters and others were patrons in 1824

MABLETHORPE (ST PETER), a parish in the Marsh division of the hundred of CALCEWORTH, parts of LINDSEY, county of LINCOLN, containing 35 inhabitants The living is a discharged rectory, united, in 1745, to that of Thedlethorpe St. Helen, in the archdeaconry and diocese of Lincoln, rated in the king's books at £7 10 2

MABYN (ST), a parish in the hundred of TRIGG, county of CORNWALL, 3¾ miles (E by N) from Wade-Bridge, containing 715 inhabitants The living is a rectory, in the archdeaconry of Cornwall, and diocese of Exeter, rated in the king s books at £36, and in the

patronage of the Earl of Falmouth There is a place of worship for Wesleyan Methodists

MACCLESFIELD, a market town and parochial chapelry, having separate jurisdiction, though locally in the hundred of Macclesfield, county palatine of CHESTER, on the road from London to Manchester, 36 miles (E by N) from Chester, and 167 (N W by N) from London, containing 17,746 inhabitants Previously to the Norman Conquest it constituted a portion of the royal demesne of the Earls of Mercia, who held a court here for the ancient hundred of Hamestan, hence, in the record of Domesday, it is represented to have been one of the seats of Earl Edwin When that survey was made, it was comprised within the earldom of Chester, of which it continued to form part until the abolition of that jurisdiction, when the hundred, manor, and forest of Macclesfield lapsed to the crown The king is now lord of the hundred, about one-third of which, including the township of Macclesfield, and sixteen other townships, constitutes the manor and forest of Macclesfield The forest was anciently protected by the same laws, and entitled to the same rights as other royal forests, some of these laws expired with the disafforestment of the tract to which they applied, but a few of the executive offices under them survive, and retain their privileges, although the duties attached to them, from the abolition of the feudal system, are either no longer requisite, or have been superseded by other offices Of this description, in particular, are the grand serjeancy of the hundred, and the mastership of the forest, of Macclesfield, which have long been hereditary in the family of Davenport, and are now held by Davies Davenport, of Woodford and Capesthorne, Esq, and that of bailiff of the manor and forest, which has long been vested in the noble family of Cholmondeley There were also eight subordinate hereditary foresters, who held office by grant from the Earls of Chester When this territory lapsed to the crown, parcels of the forest were granted away at different times, and the whole is now under cultivation, the last portion of the common and waste land having been enclosed under an act obtained in 1796, when an allotment was assigned to the king, as lord of the manor, which, with the mineral contents of the soil, has since been alienated Prior to this, a swainmote court was held at Macclesfield, and persons found guilty of misdemeanors against the forest laws were committed to the prison within the town, whither also offenders were sent from the court leet for the forest and hundred For some centuries these courts continued to be held before the Chief Justice of Chester, who presided as Justice in Eyre here, or his deputy, or before special commissioners, the king's steward, or his deputy, or the king s bailiff in process of time they were constantly held under the presidency of the king s steward, or his deputy, to whose office many of the duties originally discharged by other functionaries have been annexed This seneschalship, or stewardship, of the hundred and forest was

Seal and Arms.

given, in the reign of Edward IV, to Thomas, Lord Stanley, and heirs' male, in which noble family, with a short intermission during the time of the Commonwealth, it has since continued, and is now enjoyed by the Earl of Derby

An ecclesiastical council was held at Macclesfield in 1332, and another in 1362, by the Archbishop of Canterbury Whilst the town continued the residence of the Earls of Chester, it was surrounded by a rampart, or walled fence, which had three principal gates In 1508, Thomas Savage, a native of the to vn, who became successively Bishop of London and Archbishop of York, founded a college of Secular priests, of which the chapel, previously communicating with the church of St Michael, by a door now blocked up, alone remains, and is the sepulchral chapel of the family The building is an interesting structure, in the later style of English architecture, with a turret of three stages, through the lower of which an elegant arched gateway, highly enriched with shields and other architectural ornaments, leads into the chapel, above the entrance is a beautiful oriel window, the lower part of which is ornamented with the arms of England in the centre, and on one side those of the see of York, and on the other, those of the family of Savage, quartered with the arms of the sees to which the founder had been preferred in the chapel are many family monuments, and deposited in an urn is the heart of the archbishop, whose body was interred at York During the great civil war in the 17th century, the town experienced much injury from the parliamentarians, by whom it was besieged and taken, and who retained possession of it, under Sir William Brereton, Commander in Chief of the parliamentary forces for this county, after an obstinate attempt on the part of Sir Thomas Acton to gain it for the king On a hill to the east of the town are vestiges of an encampment constructed by the parliamentarians, from which, during the siege, the spire of St Michael s church was battered by the cannon of the besiegers After the decapitation of Charles I, a council was held here, at which it was resolved to raise four regiments, of seven hundred men each, for the service of Charles II, who was then at the head of an army in Scotland In 1745, a party of one hundred cavalry took possession of the town for the Pretender, who, on the evening of the same day, arrived with five thousand men and his whole train of artillery, after passing the night here, he held a council of war, and the day following marched towards Derby, but being alarmed at the approach of the forces under the Duke of Cumberland, he fell back upon Macclesfield, to which place he was pursued by the duke, whom the inhabitants received with every demonstration of joy

The town is pleasantly situated near the southern extremity of the forest, the greater part stands on the declivity of an eminence rising gradually from the western bank of the river Bollin, which flows through the lower part, hence denominated "The Waters" these parts are connected by two bridges of stone, and one of wood. The rapid increase of population has created a proportionate augmentation of the number of buildings, and an extension of the town in every direction, within a short period. Considerable improvements have been made, under the provisions of an act obtained in 1814, by the introduction of police regulations, widening the streets, and removing unsightly objects the streets are well paved, and lighted with gas, and the inhabitants are amply supplied with water brought from springs to the east of the town, and conveyed by pipes to their houses A public subscription library has been established for more than half a century, and contains a valuable collection of works, a public news-room is supported by subscription, and there are a neat theatre, and a handsome suite of assembly-rooms The races, which formerly took place here, have been discontinued for many years, but it is at present in contemplation to revive them Macclesfield was formerly noted for the manufacture of twist buttons, which was introduced at a very early period, and for the regulation and promotion of which, several legislative enactments were procured many of these, with other ware, were carried through the country by itinerant chapmen, of mean principles and reputation, denominated "Flash-men, from residing in and around the hamlet of Flash, just beyond the verge of the county, and within that of Stafford, whose name and occupation still remain, although their number has decreased from the decline of the trade To this succeeded the manufacture of silk, which is carried on in all its branches to a considerable extent The first silk-mill in this town was erected by Mr Roe, in 1756, since which period the trade has rapidly increased, and at present there are not less than seventy mills for throwing silk, which is here manufactured into handkerchiefs and broad silks, the weaving of which, with the manufacture of twist, sewing-silk, and buttons, is now the principal source of trade In 1823, there were three thousand looms in the town, which number had increased in 1828 to six thousand, but in 1829 there were only four thousand The cotton manufacture was also introduced about the same time, and the first mill for that purpose was erected in 1758, since that period it has progressively increased, but with less rapidity, and with less fluctuation, than the silk trade there are several extensive dye-houses and other establishments connected with these branches of manufacture The copper and brass works, formerly carried on here, have been discontinued. In the neighbourhood are extensive mines of coal, and quarries of slate, and of stone of a superior quality for building, of which great quantities are sent to Stockport, Manchester, and into Staffordshire, and other parts of the country A canal is at present being constructed, which will pass by the east side of the town, and join the Peak Forest canal at Marple, opening a communication with Manchester, and, by a junction with the Grand Trunk, on the confines of Staffordshire, with the midland and southern counties, and with London The market, formerly held on Monday, is, by act of parliament obtained in 1814, now held on Tuesday, a market for vegetables is also held on Saturday The fairs are, May 6th, June 22d, July 11th, October 4th, and November 11th, for cattle, woollen cloth, hardware, and toys The town, which had been constituted a borough by Ranulph, third Earl of Chester of that name, was first incorporated by Edward, Prince of Wales and Earl of Chester, in the 45th of Henry III, who conveyed additional privileges, but imposed the usual obligation of grinding at the king s mill, and baking at his oven the latter continued in the possession of the crown until 1818, when it was sold, the building exists, but the practice has, though not long since, fallen into disuse. Various other charters have been granted under that of Charles II, the government is vested in a mayor, recorder, and twenty-four capital burgesses, assisted by a town clerk, coroner, serjeant at mace, and other officers the mayor, chosen annually from among the capital burgesses, and three of that body annually elected for the purpose, are justices of the peace within the borough The freedom is inherited by all the sons of a freeman, or acquired by purchase or gift The corporation hold half-yearly courts of session for the trial of misdemeanants, and the mayor and justices hold daily meetings for the despatch of business connected with the police A court of record for debts to any amount, arising within the liberty of the hundred, is held twice a year by the Earl of Derby, as hereditary steward This nobleman appoints a deputy steward, who must be a barrister, a resident deputy steward, and a clerk of the courts the duties of the last are similar to those of a prothonotary A similar court, called a halmote court, for the manor and forest, is held at the same time and place, and before the same officers, yet each of the separate jurisdictions possesses its own bailiff, who nominates a jury within that peculiar liberty The manor chiefly comprises the townships of Bollington, Disley, Hurdsfield, Kettleshulme, Pott-Shrigley, Rainow, Sutton, Wincell, and Yeardsley cum Whaley, being of copyhold tenure These courts are held monthly, or weekly, by adjournment, before the resident deputy-steward, for the convenience of hearing motions in civil causes, and passing surrenders of copyholds Courts leet for these several jurisdictions are held annually, within a month of Michaelmas, in the same manner, at which constables are appointed for the different townships The guildhall was taken down in 1826, and handsomely rebuilt in the Grecian style of architecture, at the expense of the corporation it is a spacious and commodious edifice, containing, in addition to the court-rooms, handsome assembly and concert rooms attached to it is the town gaol, which was rebuilt at the same time

The living is a perpetual curacy, in the archdeaconry and diocese of Chester, endowed with £800 private benefaction, and £1200 parliamentary grant, and in the patronage of the Mayor and Corporation The parochial chapel, dedicated to St Michael, is an ancient structure, founded by Eleanor, Queen of Edward I, about 1278, and made dependent on the mother church at Prestbury the tower was formerly surmounted by a spire, which was battered down in the parliamentary war, the north side of the edifice was rebuilt in 1740, and the whole has, in many respects, undergone considerable alteration and repair, there are some sepulchral chapels, of which that of the family of Savage has been previously noticed, the chapel of the Legh family, and other portions of the structure, contain several altar-tombs and monuments of great antiquity Christchurch, a spacious edifice of brick, with a square tower, was erected in 1775, at the sole expense of Charles Roe, Esq, who endowed it with £100 per annum for the minister, on the south side of the chancel is a handsome marble monument to the memory of the founder, ornamented with devices emblematical of his mechanical genius, and bearing an inscription commemorative of his acquaintance with the mineral strata of the county, of

his having discovered the valuable mine in the Isle of Anglesey, and of having established the copper-works in this neighbourhood the living is a perpetual curacy, in the patronage of William Roe, Esq St George's church, lately erected as a dissenting place of worship, has been purchased by the corporation for the service of the established church There is a place of worship for the Society of Friends, three for Independents, one for Primitive Methodists, one for those of the New Connexion, three for Wesleyan Methodists, two for Socinians, and a Roman Catholic chapel The free grammar school was founded in 1502, by Sir John Percyvale, born near this town, and lord mayor of London, who endowed it with lands at that time worth £10 per annum, which lapsing to the crown, the school was refounded by Edward VI, in 1552, and more amply endowed, under the designation of the "Free Grammar school of King Edward VI' The government was vested in fourteen trustees, inhabitants of Macclesfield and the parish of Prestbury, who appoint the masters The scholars are gratuitously instructed in the classics, but pay for instruction in the French language, writing, and arithmetic, the income arising from the endowment exceeds £800 per annum, of which sum, £200 per annum is paid to the head master, who has a spacious house rent free, £150 to the second master, £100 to the writing-master, and £50 to the French master This school enjoys a high reputation in the list of masters appear the names of Brownswerd, a celebrated grammarian and Latin poet, and Brancker, a philosopher and mathematician, both lie interred within the parochial chapel of St. Michael A National school is supported by subscription, and there are Sunday schools in connexion with the established church, and the dissenting congregations An almshouse was founded, in 1703, by Mrs Stanley, who endowed it with £6 per annum, for three aged widows, it is now under the patronage of the family of Thornycroft A dispensary was established in 1814, and is liberally supported by subscription There are various charitable bequests for clothing and apprenticing poor children, and for distribution among the indigent Near the road to Congleton is a place called the Castle-field, supposed to have been the site of the palace of the Earls of Chester, and there are some slight vestiges of an ancient mansion, said to have been the property and residence of the celebrated Duke of Buckingham Macclesfield gives the title of earl to the family of Parker

MACCLESFIELD - FOREST, a chapelry in the parish of PRESTBURY, hundred of MACCLESFIELD, county palatine of CHESTER, 4 miles (E by S) from Macclesfield, containing 260 inhabitants The living is a perpetual curacy, in the archdeaconry and diocese of Chester, endowed with £200 private benefaction, and £800 royal bounty The Earl of Derby was patron in 1799

MACEFEN, a township in the parish of MALPAS, higher division of the hundred of BROXTON, county palatine of CHESTER, 2 miles (E) from Malpas, containing 48 inhabitants

MACHEN, a parish in the lower division of the hundred of WENTLLOOG, county of MONMOUTH, 5½ miles (W by N) from Newport, containing 1032 inhabitants The living is a rectory, in the archdeaconry and diocese of Llandaff, rated in the king's books at

£10 16 5½, and in the patronage of Sir Charles Morgan, Bart   The church is dedicated to St Michael There is a place of worship for Wesleyan Methodists The rivers Ebba and Rumsey run through the parish, in which are mines of coal, lead, iron, and calamine, also several mineral springs   There are the remains of an old building, called "the Castle, but no record of its history

MACKWORTH, a parish in the hundred of MORLESTON and LITCHURCH, county of DERBY, 2¾ miles (W N W) from Derby, containing, with the township of Mark Eaton, 650 inhabitants   The living is a discharged vicarage, in the archdeaconry of Derby, and diocese of Lichfield and Coventry, rated in the king s books at £9 3, endowed with £200 royal bounty, and in the patronage of Francis Mundy, Esq   The church, dedicated to All Saints, is partly in the decorated style of architecture   Here is remaining the gateway of a castle, anciently the seat of the De Mackworths, and said to have been demolished during the parliamentary war

MADDINGTON, a parish in the hundred of BRANCH and DOLE, county of WILTS, 5¾ miles (W N W) from Amesbury, containing 369 inhabitants   The living is a perpetual curacy, in the archdeaconry and diocese of Salisbury   J and J Matron, Esqrs were patrons in 1813   The church is dedicated to St Mary

MADEHURST, a parish in the hundred of AVISFORD, rape of ARUNDEL, county of SUSSEX, 3¼ miles (N W by N) from Arundel, containing 169 inhabitants The living is a discharged vicarage, in the archdeaconry and diocese of Chichester, rated in the king s books at £6 8 10, endowed with £200 royal bounty, and in the patronage of the Bishop of Chichester   The church is dedicated to St Mary Magdalene

MADELEY, a parish in the northern division of the hundred of PIREHILL, county of STAFFORD, 5½ miles (W by S) from Newcastle under Line, containing 1166 inhabitants   The living is a discharged vicarage, in the archdeaconry of Stafford, and diocese of Lichfield and Coventry, rated in the king s books at £4 16, endowed with £200 private benefaction, £200 royal bounty, and £200 parliamentary grant, and in the patronage of Lord Crewe   The church, dedicated to All Saints, is an ancient stone structure   This parish abounds with mines of coal   The village is situated on the borders of Cheshire and Shropshire, and consists chiefly of cottages and farm-houses in the Elizabethan style   Here are two free schools, one for boys, the other for girls, endowed, in 1645, with a rent-charge of £60, by Sir John Offley, who founded in the same year, almshouses for ten poor persons, each of whom receives one shilling and ninepence per week   Samuel Stretch, noted for his penurious habits, bequeathed, in 1804, a great bell, to be tolled every night at eight o clock, as a guide to passengers, he himself having accidentally fallen into a ditch, which ultimately caused his death   Madeley is in the honour of Tutbury, duchy of Lancaster, and within the jurisdiction of a court of pleas held at Tutbury every third Tuesday, for the recovery of debts under 40s

MADELEY-HOLME, a liberty in the parish of CHECKLEY, southern division of the hundred of TOTMONSLOW, county of STAFFORD, 3½ miles (N N W) from Uttoxeter, containing 479 inhabitants

MADELEY-MARKET, a market town and parish within the liberties of the borough of WENLOCK, county of SALOP, 4½ miles (S W by W) from Shiffnall, 15 (S E) from Shrewsbury, and 148 (N W) from London, containing 5379 inhabitants   The name of this town indicates its situation between two rivers, and its adjunct was founded on the grant of a market, in the time of Henry III, to a community of Cluniac monks at Wenlock, to whom Madeley then belonged   After the disastrous battle of Worcester, in 1651, Charles II obtained a temporary shelter in a house and barn then occupied by Mr Wolfe, and situated near the church, which are still remaining   Madeley occupies a rising ground, and extends to Colebrookdale, which is environed by lofty hills and hanging woods, and in which are the most extensive iron-works in England, with foundries, furnaces, and all the complicated machinery requisite to so vast an establishment   Across the Severn is a cast-iron bridge of one arch, erected in 1779, the span of which is one hundred feet six inches, and the height from the base line to the centre, forty feet, the total weight of iron being three hundred and seventy-eight tons   all the principal parts were erected in three months, without any accident, or the least obstruction to the navigation of the river   this part of the parish derives its name of Iron-Bridge from this stupendous undertaking   About two miles south-eastward from Madeley, at the junction of the Shropshire canal with the Severn, is Coalport, where coal is landed from the extensive mines and numerous works in the neighbourhood, and conveyed thence to different parts of the counties of Gloucester and Worcester, annually to the average extent of fifty thousand tons, here is likewise a porcelain manufactory, which affords employment to nearly five hundred persons, a manufactory of Wedgwood's ware, a rope-yard, timber-yard, and a mill for extracting linseed oil, which is turned by a wheel two hundred and forty feet in circumference   A neat iron bridge was constructed across the river at this point in 1817, instead of a former one of wood, and not far distant a tunnel, about one mile in length, and partially arched with brick, was begun and intended as a more direct conveyance for coal, but was never completed, from the interstices at the sides, tar flows, and falling on the surface of a small stream, which runs in a narrow channel at the entrance, is there deposited, and at convenient periods is collected, and put into barrels, when the tunnel was first formed, the quantity obtained exceeded one barrel per diem, but now it is not more than twenty barrels per annum   The original market having fallen into disuse, it was revived about 1763, when a new market-house was erected, near the foot of the iron bridge in Colebrook-dale, two miles distant from the site of the first structure, and named Madeley-wood market   The market is on Friday, and fairs are held January 26th, May 29th, and October 12th   This place is within the jurisdiction of a court of requests, for the recovery of debts under 40s, which extends over the parishes of Broseley, Benthall, Madeley, Barrow, Linley, Willey, Little Wenlock, and Dawley, and the extra-parochial place called Posnall, held under an act passed in the 22nd of George III

The living is a discharged vicarage, in the archdeaconry of Salop, and diocese of Hereford, rated in the king s books at £4 17 10, and in the patronage of — Kynaston, Esq   The church is dedicated to All

Saints, the ancient structure, which exhibited several specimens of early Norman architecture, was pulled down in 1796, when the present edifice was erected There is a place of worship for Wesleyan Methodists, also a Roman Catholic chapel The house of industry was completed in 1797, at an expense of £1086 14 7½, on a piece of ground belonging to the poor, of this sum, £806 13 6 was raised by subscription, and £235 15 by the sale, for nine hundred and ninety-nine years, subject to nominal rents, of certain property previously held in trust for the benefit of the poor In the different strata of coal, iron-ore, and sand-stone, which abound in this neighbourhood, numerous petrifactions, with impressions of animal and vegetable substances, of various kinds, have been found The Rev John William Fletcher, a native of Switzerland, whose work, entitled "Checks to Antinomianism,' is a standard theological work, and whose character is so universally known and so deservedly admired, was appointed to the vicarage of Madeley in 1760, which preferment he held during the remainder of his life, and at his death, in 1785, was interred in the churchyard

MADINGLEY, a parish in the hundred of NORTH STOW, county of CAMBRIDGE, 3½ miles (W N W) from Cambridge, containing 231 inhabitants The living is a discharged vicarage, in the archdeaconry and diocese of Ely, rated in the king s books at £6 9 7, and in the patronage of the Bishop of Ely The church is dedicated to St Mary

MADLEY, a parish in the hundred of WEBTREE, county of HEREFORD, 7 miles (W by S) from Hereford, containing 938 inhabitants The living is a vicarage, with the perpetual curacy of Tiberton, in the peculiar jurisdiction of the Dean of Hereford, rated in the king s books at £16 1 8, and in the patronage of the Dean and Chapter of Hereford The church, dedicated to St Mary, is a large and handsome edifice, principally in the decorated style, with an embattled tower at the west end There is a place of worship for Baptists The petty sessions for the division are held here on every fourth Monday

MADRESFIELD, a parish in the lower division of the hundred of PERSHORE, county of WORCESTER, 6 miles (N W by N) from Upton upon Severn, containing 202 inhabitants The living is a rectory, in the archdeaconry and diocese of Worcester, rated in the king s books at £3 13 11½ Earl Beauchamp was patron in 1793 The church exhibits some portions of ancient architecture Ann Bull, in 1705, bequeathed £25, for the produce of which six children are taught to read Madresfield Court, a fine ancient mansion, is the seat of Earl Beauchamp

MADRON, a parish in the hundred of PENWITH, county of CORNWALL, 2¼ mile (N W) from Penzance, containing, exclusively of the market town of Penzance, which is within this parish, 2011 inhabitants The living is a vicarage, with the perpetual curacies of Morva and Penzance, in the archdeaconry of Cornwall, and diocese of Exeter, rated in the king s books at £21 5 10 Henry Penneck, Esq was patron in 1812 The church, dedicated to St Madern, is in the early style of English architecture There is a place of worship for Wesleyan Methodists A school for instructing the poor children of the parish was founded, about 1704, by Mr George Daniel, and endowed with lands and premises, now let

for about £120 per annum, besides a house and garden for the master Here is a stone with an ancient British inscription, stating it to be a sepulchral monument to Rialobran, son of Cunoval, also the once celebrated well of St Madern

MAER, a parish in the northern division of the hundred of PIREHILL, county of STAFFORD, comprising the township of Maer, and the hamlet of Maerway-Lane, and containing 451 inhabitants, of which number, 232 are in the township of Maer, 7 miles (N N W) from Eccleshall The living is a perpetual curacy, in the archdeaconry of Stafford, and diocese of Lichfield and Coventry, and in the patronage of J Wedgwood, Esq The river Tern has its source in a small lake here, which covers about twenty-two acres

MAERWAY-LANE, a hamlet in the parish of MAER, northern division of the hundred of PIREHILL, county of STAFFORD, containing 219 inhabitants

MAGHULL, a chapelry in the parish of HALSALL, hundred of WEST DERBY, county palatine of LANCASTER, 5 miles (S W by S) from Ormskirk, containing 720 inhabitants The living is a perpetual curacy, annexed to the rectory of Halsall, in the archdeaconry and diocese of Chester, endowed with £600 private benefaction, £200 royal bounty, and £2100 parliamentary grant William Harpur, by deed in 1815, vested an annuity of £11 18 1 in certain trustees, for the education of children

MAGOR, a parish in the lower division of the hundred of CALDICOTT, county of MONMOUTH, 6 miles (E S E) from Caerleon, containing with the chapelry of Redwick, 622 inhabitants The living is a discharged vicarage, with the perpetual curacy of Redwick, in the archdeaconry and diocese of Llandaff, rated in the king s books at £7 1 0½, endowed with £200 royal bounty, and in the patronage of the Duke of Beaufort The church is dedicated to St Mary There is a place of worship for Baptists

MAIDEN BRADLEY, a parish partly in the hundred of NORTON-FERRIS, county of SOMERSET, but chiefly in that of MERE, county of WILTS, 5¼ miles (N by W) from Mere, containing, with the hamlet of Yarnfield, 620 inhabitants The living is a perpetual curacy, in the archdeaconry and diocese of Salisbury, endowed with £600 private benefaction, £200 royal bounty, and £1200 parliamentary grant, and in the patronage of the Dean and Canons of Christ Church, Oxford The church, dedicated to All Saints, contains some monuments of the Seymour family, particularly a finely-executed one to Sir Edward Seymour, Bart, of political celebrity in the reigns of Charles II, William and Mary, and Anne At the north-eastern extremity of the village are the remains, now forming part of a farmhouse, of an hospital, founded by Manasser Bisset, in the reign of Henry II, and dedicated to the Blessed Virgin, for poor leprous women, under the care of some Secular brethren, but Herbert, Bishop of Sarum, about 1190, substituted for the latter a prior and canons of the Augustine order, whose revenue, at the dissolution, was estimated at £197 18 8 the situation is very romantic, and there are numerous sites of ponds in the vicinity There are two singular knolls of chalk, which appear to have been detached by a convulsion of nature from Mere down, distant three quarters of a mile, the intervening soil having no tendency to chalk

Corporate Seal.

MAIDENHEAD, a market town and chapelry, having separate jurisdiction, though locally in the hundred of Bray and Cookham, county of BERKS, 13 miles (N E by E) from Reading, and 26 (W) from London, it is partly in the parish of Bray, and partly in that of Cookham, with which parishes the population is returned The ancient name of this place was South Allington, or Ealington, to distinguish it from a manor called Allington, a mile north of the town According to Leland, its present appellation was acquired from the great reverence paid here to the head of a British virgin, who was one of the eleven thousand maidens said to have suffered martyrdom with St Ursula. But in ancient records it is called *Mayden hithe*, confirming the more probable opinion, that the name of the place refers to its having been an extensive wharf for timber a bridge was erected over the Thames previously to the year 1297, which consisted of timber, and a tree was allowed annually out of Windsor Forest for its repair Being situated on one of the great western roads, it was the seat of much contention during the troubles of the seventeenth century at the Greyhound Inn in this town, the unfortunate Charles I had his last interview with his family, and in 1688, the bridge was fortified, and a few Irish soldiers were posted upon it, in order to impede the progress of the Prince of Orange to the metropolis, who, however, deserted their post and cannon in the night, on hearing a Dutch march beat by the townsmen This structure was succeeded by the present elegant edifice, consisting of seven semicircular arches of stone, with three smaller arches of brick at each end, built by the corporation, from a design and under the direction of Sir Robert Taylor, in 1772, at an expense of about £20,000, the central arch separating the counties of Berks and Buckingham by an act of parliament passed that year the corporation were authorised to transfer the tolls received from vessels passing under the bridge to the road over it The town, situated on the road to Bath, consists principally of one street, which extends from the bridge to the bottom of Folley hill, separating the two parishes, the north side being in that of Cookham, and the south in that of Bray it is lighted and paved, and is now the great thoroughfare from the metropolis to Bath, Bristol, and the West of England The adjacent country is in a high state of cultivation, and is richly adorned with woodland scenery, interspersed with elegant villas The trade is principally in malt, corn, meal, and timber, which articles are conveyed by water to London, and the interests of the town are further promoted by the daily passage of not less than sixty-eight coaches, and by its proximity to the Thames, which skirts its eastern extremity The market, established by letters patent of Henry VI, is on Wednesday there are three fairs each of which continue for three days, and commence respectively on the Wednesday in Whitsun-week, for horses, horned cattle, and pigs, September 29th, for horses, cattle, and the hiring of servants, and November 30th, for horses and other

cattle The principal inhabitants of this town, with some of the inmates of the priory of Hurley, were constituted a guild, or fraternity, so early as 1352, by letters patent of Edward III, their principal object being to keep the bridge in proper repair and uphold the chantries, for which purpose a toll was granted at the bridge, on the river, and on all commodities sold in the market these privileges were confirmed and extended by Henry VI, suspended at the Reformation, and renewed by Elizabeth, who four years afterwards granted the first charter of incorporation, with the style of warden, bridge-masters, and burgesses, which charter was renewed by James I, and with still farther privileges by Charles II The charter of the present corporate body, which consists of eleven burgesses, out of whom are chosen annually a mayor and two bridge-masters, with power to appoint a high steward, recorder, town clerk, and other officers, was granted by James II The mayor, who is both clerk of the market and coroner, the late mayor, the high steward, and the recorder, are justices of the peace, and hold a session quarterly in the town hall, a handsome and commodious structure, under which the market is held Under the charter of James II the mayor and corporation have power to hold a court of record on Friday, every three weeks, for the recovery of debts not exceeding £20 Petty sessions for the division are held here by the county magistrates, on the second and fourth Monday, in every month There is a small gaol for the temporary confinement of criminals

The chapel, dedicated to St Andrew and St Mary Magdalene, is of modern erection, and presents a good specimen of ancient English architecture it was erected by subscription, aided by a grant of £500 from the Incorporated Society for the enlargement of churches and chapels, on the condition that four hundred of the sittings should be free The present building was erected nearly on the site of the former chapel, which was taken down in consequence of its being too small for the accommodation of the inhabitants, and forming an obstruction in the public road The living is a perpetual curacy, within the archdeaconry of Berks, and diocese of Salisbury, endowed with £490 private benefaction, £400 royal bounty, and a small annual payment from the Exchequer, it has a commodious residence, built by the corporation for the use of the incumbent The chapel is furnished with a very excellent organ, the bequest of Lady Ann Pocock, and ornamented with a very fine altar piece, painted and presented by Isaac Pocock, Esq, of Maidenhead Bridge the incumbent is styled "the Chaplain of the free chapel of Maidenhead, and is presented by the Corporation The establishment dates its origin at a very early period it had originally a chantry, dedicated to St Andrew, built by Margaret of France, sister of Philip the Fair, and second consort of Edward I of England, upon a piece of ground granted by that king out of his manors of Bray and Cookham, the letters patent of which grant were confirmed by her grandson, Richard II, and which still exists, under the great seal of that monarch, with the muniments of the corporation a chantry, dedicated to St Mary Magdalene, was annexed, in the reign of Edward III, with a bequest of one hundred marks, to the priory of Hurley, to provide a priest to say mass in the chapel It is a curious fact that in the protestant reign of Elizabeth, new letters patent were granted by that queen to this religious fraternity, confirming all former privileges, with its ancient Roman Catholic rights, which instrument still exists, but this resuscitation continued only for four years, when the guild was abolished, and a lay corporation substituted There are places of worship for the Society of Friends, those in the late Countess of Huntingdon s Connexion, and Independents An almshouse for eight poor men and their wives was founded, in 1659, by James Smyth, Esq, the original endowment of £40 per annum was augmented with £8 per annum for fuel, by Mrs Smyth the trust of this charity is vested in the Master and Wardens of the Salters Company A National school is well supported, partly by contribution, and partly by an endowment of £30 per annum, from an estate given by Abraham Spoore, for educating and apprenticing poor boys, producing about £60 per annum, and a rent-charge of £5 per annum, the bequest of Elizabeth Merry, in 1686, for educating five boys Sir Isaac and Lady Pocock bequeathed property for supplying poor persons weekly with bread, and one hundred families with bread, meat, and coal, at Christmas, also £50 in small sums to the aged and infirm, at the commencement of every year A Sunday school was established and endowed by Lady Pocock, for thirty girls, and every two years a bounty of £100, in sums of £10 each, is given to ten female servants of good character, who shall have lived in the same family for a period of seven years other bounties are derived from the same source by the county and neighbourhood, which do not immediately apply to the town, viz £30 a year to the parish of Cookham, and £50 per annum to the widows and orphans of poor clergymen of the county of Berks

MAIDEN-NEWTON, a parish in the hundred of TOLLERFORD, Dorchester division of the county of DORSET, 8¼ miles (N W) from Dorchester, containing 520 inhabitants The living is a rectory, in the archdeaconry of Dorset, and diocese of Bristol, rated in the king's books at £30 5, and in the patronage of Lord Ilchester The church, dedicated to St Mary, is an ancient cruciform structure, with a large embattled tower rising from the intersection Near it is the rectory-house, a spacious antique building, the windows exhibiting the arms of Wadham, Wyndham, &c, in stained glass The privilege of holding a market was granted in the 5th of Henry III, and subsequently a fair for cattle on November 22d, the former has been long disused George Browne, in 1774, bequeathed a rent charge of £21 for teaching ten poor children

MAIDEN-WELL, a parish in the Wold division of the hundred of LOUTH ESKE, parts of LINDSEY, county of LINCOLN, 5½ miles (S) from Louth The population is returned with Farforth The living is a discharged vicarage with the rectory of Farforth, united in 1753 to the rectory of Ruckland, in the archdeaconry and diocese of Lincoln

MAIDFORD, a parish in the hundred of GREENS-NORTON, county of NORTHAMPTON, 5¾ miles (N W by W) from Towcester, containing 319 inhabitants The living is a rectory, in the archdeaconry of Northampton, and diocese of Peterborough, rated in the king's books at £8 8 9, and in the patronage of the Rev Sampson Henry White The church is dedicated to St Peter and St Paul

MAIDSTONE, a borough, market town, and parish, having separate jurisdiction, locally in the hundred of Maidstone, lathe of AYLESFORD, county of KENT, of which it is the county town, 8 miles (S) from Rochester, and 34½ (S E by E) from London, containing, according to the last census, 12,508 inhabitants, and now about 14,000

Seal and Arms.

Some writers have supposed this to be the Caer Meguiad, or Megwad, enumerated by Nennius among the principal cities in Britain Camden considers it to be the Vagniacæ mentioned in the second Itinerary of Antoninus modern authors, however, are doubtful relative to the accuracy of this latter opinion, on a supposition that that celebrated antiquary had mistaken the Watling-street road for another Roman road passing this town to London, from the Portus Lemanis, which had become the landing-place for the Romans after the Portus Rutupensis and Dubris had fallen into disuse All, however, allow Maidstone to have been occupied by the Romans, and that it was, at an early period, a place of considerable note Several Roman coins and urns have been found in the neighbourhood The Saxons named it Meduegestun, a town on the Medwege, or middle river, now Medway In Domesday-book it is written Meddestane, and in records of the time of Edward I, Maydenestane, from which the transition to its present appellation is easy Among the historical events which contribute to distinguish this place, may be mentioned the celebrated meeting held on Penenden heath, about a mile north-eastward from the town, for the purpose of adjusting the differences that had arisen between Lanfranc, Archbishop of Canterbury, and Odo, Earl of Kent, brother of the Conqueror, in consequence of the appropriation by the latter of various lands and privileges previously enjoyed by the primate, and which this assembly decided should be restored During the reign of Mary, Maidstone was deprived of its charter, in consequence of the firmness the inhabitants evinced in support of the Protestant cause, by opposing the queen s marriage with Philip of Spain many of them were put to death, and Sir Thomas Wyatt, who had excited them to make a stand in favour of their religious principles, was executed on Hay hill, London, and his estates were confiscated In 1648, the town was stormed by Fairfax, at the head of ten thousand of the parliamentary forces, and taken, after a most obstinate resistance on the part of the royalists

The town, which is well paved and lighted, and consists chiefly of four large streets, stands principally on the eastern bank of the river Medway, over which is a bridge of five arches The inhabitants are plentifully supplied with excellent water, conveyed from a reservoir at Rocky hill, about half a mile from the town, by means of pipes laid across the bed of the Medway The gasworks were constructed by, and at the expense of, an individual named Gosling, and afterwards sold to a number of the inhabitants, who, by an act of parliament, were constituted The Maidstone Gas-light and Coke Company Pleasantly situated on the bank of the Medway are the barracks, used as a depôt for the king s regiments of cavalry serving in the East Indies, and at the Cape of Good Hope, and for drilling recruits previously to embarkation the establishment consists of a commandant, staff-captain, paymaster, surgeon, adjutant, riding-master, and commissioned and non-commissioned officers The building is principally of wood, painted white, and, amidst the trees that ornament the ground, has a very picturesque appearance Opposite the barrack, on the other side of the road, are the county ball rooms, built in 1819 The theatre, a neat small building, is opened every third year, for a limited number of nights In 1824, a philosophical society was established, which has been dissolved The river Medway being navigable up to the town for large hoys, Maidstone enjoys all the advantages of a cheap communication by water with the metropolis A very large quantity of paper, and that of the finest kind, is made here, and many of the inhabitants are employed in the manufacture of blankets, thread, hop-bagging, ropes, linseed-oil, and oil-cakes, and a considerable trade is carried on in corn, timber, grocery, orchard-fruit, and hops, for the production of which two latter, the soil in the neighbourhood is particularly favourable Formerly this town was celebrated for a distillery of gin, which partook of the flavour of Hollands, and was much in demand, but the establishment has been broken up The market for corn and hops is held on Thursday, under part of the Mitre Inn, and at the back of these premises, that for provisions, on Thursday and Saturday the market for cattle is on the second Tuesday in each month, and the fairs are, February 13th, May 12th, June 20th, and October 17th, for cattle and pedlary, and that for hops during the fairs, a court of pie-powder is held for their regulation

This town was incorporated, in 1549, by Edward VI Several charters were granted to it by succeeding monarchs, and under that of George II, in 1748, by which it is now governed, the civil power is vested in a mayor, recorder, twelve jurats, and forty common council-men, assisted by a town clerk and other officers The mayor (who must be elected from amongst the jurats), the recorder, and the three senior jurats, are justices of the peace, and the mayor is also coroner and clerk of the market. The corporation hold quarter sessions for the trial of persons charged with offences not capital, also a court of pleas every alternate Tuesday, which takes cognizance of "all and all manner of actions, personal and mixed, and of granting replevins, the jurisdiction of which includes the parishes of Maidstone, Allington, Barming, Boxley, East Farleigh, Linton, Looze, and Otham, and the hamlets of Mill Hale and New Hythe A court leet is held annually, at which constables for the town are chosen The assizes for the county, and the quarter sessions for the western division, are also held here The shire-hall, near which malefactors are executed, stands on that part of Penenden heath which is in the parish of Boxley it is a neat edifice of stone, rebuilt in 1830, but not larger, nor more commodious, than the former Maidstone returns two members to parliament the right of election is in the freemen not receiving alms, their number, of whom five hundred are resident, is about nine hundred the mayor is the returning officer The freedom is obtained by appren-

ticeship, and is enjoyed by the eldest son of a freeman, by right of primogeniture, and by the younger sons, on paying forty shillings each strangers are admitted, with the consent of the corporation, on the payment of a fine The county elections also take place here The new county gaol, situated at the end of the town, on the road leading to Rochester, and built of rag-stone procured on the spot, was finished in 1818, at an expense of £200,000 it encloses within its walls fourteen acres of ground, and contains thirty-four wards and four hundred and fifty cells for males, and seven wards and eighty-two cells for females, besides a tread-mill, at which eighty persons may work together the average number of prisoners is three hundred and fifty, and the annual expenditure from £4000 to £5000 New courts, in which the assizes are held, have lately been built in front of the gaol

The living is a perpetual curacy, in the peculiar jurisdiction and patronage of the Archbishop of Canterbury The church, situated at the south-western end of the town, is dedicated to All Saints, and is the largest in the county, but when built is not with certainty known Archbishop Courtenay obtained leave of Richard II to convert the parochial church into a collegiate one, for the warden, chaplain, &c, of the college which he had here founded, on which occasion he probably added the chancel The church had formerly two chantries, one founded in 1366, by Robert Vinter, of the parish of Boxley, and the other about 1405, by Thomas Arundel, Archbishop of Canterbury, on the dissolution of the college, the church was again used for its original purpose From the tower formerly rose a spire eighty feet high, covered with lead, which was destroyed by lightning, November 2nd, 1730 The altar-piece, painted by Mr William Jefferys, a native of this town, justly excites admiration In the vestry-room is the parochial library, considerably augmented, in 1735, by a collection of books left by Dr Bray, perpetual curate of St Botolph s, Aldgate, and the founder of parochial libraries, to any corporate town in the south of England, that should pay £50 to his executors, the inhabitants of Maidstone, having raised a subscription for the purpose, availed themselves of this conditional bequest amongst other scarce works, the library contains a copy, given by the corporation, of Bishop Walton's Polyglott Bible, published about 1630 A new church, containing one thousand two hundred free seats, and eight hundred others, has been recently built, at an expense of about £13,000 There are two places of worship for Wesleyan Methodists, and one each for Baptists, the Society of Friends, Independents, and Unitarians

The free grammar school was founded in the reign of Edward VI, by the corporation, who purchased, for £205 4, the house and lands that belonged to the fraternity of Corpus Christi this sum, which was the proceeds of the sale of jewellery, plate, &c, of the college founded by Archbishop Courtenay, in 1396, was given to the corporation by the commissioners appointed, on the dissolution of this college, to superintend the sale of its effects, for the benefit of the crown, on condition of their founding and endowing a school The master, who must be a clergyman of the established church, receives from the corporation an annual stipend of £20, he is likewise entitled to the rent of sixteen

2 D 2

acres of land in Romney-Marsh, pursuant to the will of Dr John Davy, proved in 1649, and £6 a year arising from the purchase of the land tax of the living of Hoo, near Rochester, given by Mr John Rice, in 1805, he has also a house rent-free The school has two scholarships in University College, Oxford, founded agreeably to the will, dated December 15th, 1618, of the Rev Robert Gunsley, rector of Tilsey, Surrey, who bequeathed the rectory and parsonage of Flamstead, Herts, to the master and fellows of the above college, for founding four scholarships of £15 per annum each, with chambers, two in favour of this school, and two for that at Rochester, directing, nevertheless, that preference should be given to the founder's kindred, wherever born, and afterwards limiting the benefit of his bequest to natives of the county of Kent The will further provides, that the master and fellows of this college shall appoint a curate to the church of Flamstead, with a salary of £60 per annum, and that, on a vacancy occurring in the curacy, those who have been appointed to the scholarships shall have the option of refusing it In 1827 was instituted a subscription academy, of which the following are the prominent particulars it consists of one hundred shares of £20 each, transferable on certain conditions shareholders are entitled to nominate a pupil for each share, paying annually ten guineas per share, including books and all expenses the management is vested in a committee of proprietors, a treasurer, and a secretary the masters are nominated by the committee, but elected by proprietors at a general meeting, the head master must be a graduate of the University of Oxford or Cambridge, and in orders, and his fixed salary is £225 a year, that of the second master is £195, and that of the third, £60, but when the number of pupils exceeds fifty, an addition of £3, £2, and £1, for each, is made to the salaries of the masters respectively The education is English, classical, and mathematical lectures are delivered, monthly at least, by the masters, on literature and the arts and sciences, and public examinations of the pupils take place in the week previous to the vacations at Midsummer and Christmas the French language, drawing, dancing, music, and other accomplishments are taught, and paid for extra none are admitted under six years of age, and the masters are allowed to take pupils of the institution as boarders, under certain regulations

The Blue-coat school, founded in 1711, by the Rev Dr Woodward, for clothing and educating fifty-three boys and forty-three girls, has an annual permanent income of £138. 10, under the management of seven trustees, and is further supported by donations and subscriptions The Green-coat school, for clothing and educating twelve boys and twelve girls is supported by subscription Sir Charles Booth s school, endowed by him in 1795, with the interest of £2000 (now augmented to more than £3000) is under the direction of trustees, and affords instruction to thirty-five boys and thirty-five girls, and the Brown-coat school, for clothing and educating twenty-four boys and twenty four girls, and educating, in addition, about two hundred boys and one hundred girls, is supported by contributions among the dissenters A National and a Lancasterian school are also supported by voluntary contributions There are several societies for the relief of the indigent, a savings' bank, and ten benefit societies, composed of nearly one

thousand six hundred members The almshouses founded and endowed are, six by Sir John Banks, Bart., a native of this town, and one of its representatives in several parliaments, who, by will in 1697, bequeathed the clear yearly income of £60, for six aged persons of both sexes, with comfortable habitations, six by Edward Hunter, Esq, in 1748, for three poor men, and the same number of women, with £8 per annum to each, four by John Brenchley, Esq, in 1789, for aged men, with £12 per annum to each, and three by Mrs Duke, for decayed gentlewomen

Maidstone contains but few objects to gratify the researches of the antiquary The palace, which was formerly the residence of the archbishops of Canterbury, was commenced, in 1348, by Archbishop Ufford, and finished by Simon Islip, it now forms two dwelling-houses An hospital for pilgrims, or travellers, was founded in 1244, or, according to some, in 1260, by Boniface of Savoy, Archbishop of Canterbury, and dedicated to St Peter, St Paul, and St Thomas the Martyr Walter Reynolds, a successor of Boniface in that see, appropriated to the hospital the churches of Sutton, Lillington, alias Linton, and East Farleigh the revenue was afterwards transferred to the college founded by Archbishop Courtenay There are some doubts as to the exact situation of this hospital, but the best authorities suppose it to have stood in the West Borough, it was called the hospital of the *New work* of *Prestes Helle* its remains are extensive, including a large building, almost perfect, probably the chapel a dwelling-house erected on part of the site is still known by the name of *Newark* The college, which possessed various lands and advowsons, was dissolved, according to one account, about 1538, but the best evidence is in favour of its dissolution about 1546, when an act was passed for the suppression of all colleges, free chapels, and chantries it is now used as a farm-house, and appears to have been a fine specimen of decorated English architecture The house of the fraternity of Corpus Christi, now used as the free grammar school, was founded by a few of the inhabitants the religious of both sexes of this fraternity professed the rules of St Benedict, and their number was from one hundred and twenty to one hundred and thirty A small part of St Faith's church, considered by some parochial, though the best accounts call it a free chapel, is still remaining it was, at successive periods, used as a place of worship by the Walloons, who settled in this town in the reign of Elizabeth, and by English Presbyterians in digging the foundation for a soap-manufactory, near to the ground on which it stood, several human skeletons were found

The Rev William Newton, some time vicar of Gillingham, in Dorsetshire, who, in 1751, published the History and Antiquities of Maidstone, was born in this town Also William Woollet, whose talents as an artist obtained for him the honourable appointment of engraver to the king, and to whose memory a monument, finely executed by Banks, was erected in the cloisters of Westminster abbey the Niobe, from Wilson s celebrated picture, the Death of Wolfe, and the Fishery, are considered the most masterly of his productions he died in 1785, in his fiftieth year, and was interred in St Pancras' churchyard, London James Jefferys, son of the above-mentioned William, who painted the altar-piece in the church, was also born here , he far excelled his father in the art of painting, and his bold outline pen-drawings are considered equal to those of the celebrated Mortimer In the churchyard of this town are deposited the remains of William Shipley, Esq , who resided here, and was the founder of the Society for the Encouragement of Arts, Manufactures, and Commerce Maidstone gives the title of viscount to the Earl of Winchilsea

MAIDWELL, a parish in the hundred of ROTH WELL, county of NORTHAMPTON, 10 miles (N) from Northampton, containing 279 inhabitants The living is a rectory, in the archdeaconry of Northampton, and diocese of Peterborough, rated in the king s books at £10 8 1½, and in the patronage of Henry Hungerford Holdish Hungerford, Esq The church is dedicated to St Mary There is good lime and building stone in the parish In a place called the Dales is a petrifying spring, and a chalybeate spring near Scotland wood

MAINSFORTH, a township in the parish of BISHOP'S MIDDLEHAM, north-eastern division of STOCKTON ward, county palatine of DURHAM, 8¾ miles (S S.E) from Durham, containing 44 inhabitants The Little Skerne runs through the township this rivulet was anciently diverted from its original course to form a deep fosse round a circular fortification, still called the Mainfort, situated on a commanding eminence, and supposed to have been successively occupied by the Romans and the Danes it comprises an area of about sixteen acres, exclusively of out-works, of which vestiges have frequently been discovered Some years ago a pair of moose deer horns was found in a cave called the Dane s hole, on the summit of the fort On an adjoining hill is an old house, called the Swan house, where certain dues to the convent of Durham, and afterwards to the chapter, were formerly paid Limestone abounds in the parish

MAINSTONE, a parish partly in the hundred of PURSLOW, county of SALOP, and partly in the hundred and county of MONTGOMERY, containing 451 inhabitants, 4¾ miles (W by S) from Bishop s Castle The living is a rectory, in the archdeaconry of Salop, and diocese of Hereford, rated in the king s books at £4 13 4, and in the patronage of the Earl of Powis The church is dedicated to St John the Baptist

MAISEY-HAMPTON, county of GLOUCESTER — See HAMPTON (MAISEY)

MAISMORE, a parish in the lower division of the hundred of DUDSTONE and KING S BARTON, county of GLOUCESTER, 2¾ miles (N N W) from Gloucester, containing 404 inhabitants The living is a perpetual curacy, in the archdeaconry and diocese of Gloucester, endowed with £600 private benefaction, £400 royal bounty, and £300 parliamentary grant, and in the patronage of the Bishop of Gloucester The church, dedicated to St Giles, is partly Norman, but principally in the decorated and later English styles A branch of the navigable river Severn is here crossed by a bridge

MAKER, a parish partly in the southern division of EAST hundred, county of CORNWALL, and partly in the hundred of ROBOROUGH, county of DEVON, 2¼ miles (S by W) from Devonport, containing, with the town of Milbrook, and the tything of Vaultershome, 3018 inhabitants The living is a discharged vicarage, in the archdeaconry of Cornwall, and diocese of Exeter, rated in the king s books at £ 23 11 0½, and in the patronage of the Crown The church, dedicated to St Macra, is in Devonshire, and, occupying a commanding site on a hill between Mount Edgcumbe and Ramhead, its steeple serves as a land-mark, and in time of war is used as a signal house There are some interesting monuments to the Edgcumbe family, whose title of Earl is derived from their noble domain in this parish, which exhibits the grandest and most beautiful scenery, and from which there is an extensive prospect southward, over Cawsand bay and the channel , Eddystone lighthouse, distant twelve miles, being also conspicuous The commander of the Spanish Armada was so captivated by the appearance of the mansion and grounds of Mount-Edgcumbe from the sea, that he determined on appropriating them to himself, as a reward for the victory which he anticipated Mount-Edgcumbe house, built in the reign of Mary, was the last garrison but one (Salcombe) which held out for Charles I The parish is bounded on the south-east by Plymouth sound, for the defence of which there is a formidable battery on the heights above the village of Maker There is a place of worship for Wesleyan Methodists At the populous village of Inceworth, which was formerly a market town, is a fair for cattle on May 1st , and another at Milbrook, also an ancient market town, on September 29th, when courts leet and baron are held for that ancient borough and the manor of Inceworth, at which a portreeve, constables, and other officers, are chosen

MALBOROUGH, a parish in the hundred of STANBOROUGH, county of DEVON, 4 miles (S W by S) from Kingsbridge, containing, with the chapelry of Salcombe, 1552 inhabitants The living is a perpetual curacy, with the vicarage of West Allington, in the archdeaconry of Totnes, and diocese of Exeter The church, which has a spire ninety feet high, stands on a commanding eminence near Bolt head, on the English channel Here is an endowed school for eight children There are slight remains of Ilton castle, erected about 1336 , also of another, called Fort Charles, repaired by Charles I , at an expense of £3000, during the civil war, it was captured by the forces of the parliament in 1645 Lord Viscount Courtenay holds a court of Admiralty here for an extensive line of coast In some parts of the parish lemons, oranges, citrons, and olives, flourish in the open air, having only temporary protection in very severe weather A plant of the Mediterranean aloe having here attained the height of twenty-seven feet, blossomed before it was quite twenty years old, and then withered away, leaving numerous suckers at its root

MALDEN, a parish in the second division of the hundred of KINGSTON, county of SURREY, 2½ miles (N by W) from Ewell, containing 250 inhabitants The living is a vicarage, with the perpetual curacy of Chessington, in the archdeaconry of Surrey, and diocese of Winchester, rated in the king s books at £8 5 , and in the patronage of the Warden and Fellows of Merton College, Oxford. The church is dedicated to St John near it is the site of the original establishment of Merton College, founded in 1264, and removed to Oxford in 1267 A small but rapid stream, called the Hogs-Mill river, rises in this parish, and falls into the Thames at Kingston In the chapelry of Chessington is a powerful chalybeate spring, termed Jessop s well, once much celebrated, but now almost forsaken A free school is maintained by the vicar, and a National school, is supported by annual contributions

Seal and Arms of Maldon

Obverse. Reverse.

MALDON, a borough, port, and market town, having separate jurisdiction, though locally in the hundred of Dengie, county of ESSEX, 10 miles (E) from Chelmsford, and 38 (E N E) from London, containing 1398 inhabitants This place is, by Camden, in which opinion he is supported by Horsley, supposed to have been the *Camalodunum* of the Romans, one of the earliest colonies established by that people in Britain, and which other antiquaries have fixed at Colchester Its name is said to have been derived from an altar dedicated to Mars, under the name of Camulus, by which also that divinity is designated in some coins, still extant, of Cunobeline, King of the Trinobantes, who, prior to the conquest of the Romans, had his royal residence in the town During its occupation by the Romans, in the reign of Nero, it was destroyed by an insurrection of the Britons, who defeated, with great slaughter, the ninth Roman Legion, which had been sent to its assistance From the Roman name *Camalodunum*, it was called by the Saxons *Meal dune*, or *Male dune*, from which its present appellation is evidently derived During the time of the Saxons, it does not appear to have been distinguished by any events of importance previously to its destruction by the Danes, from which it was restored by Edward the Elder, son of Alfred, who, to guard it against future attacks, fortified it with a castle, of which there are at present no visible remains The town is pleasantly situated on an eminence, near the confluence of the rivers Blackwater and Chelmer, and consists principally of one spacious street, extending for more than a mile from west to east, intersected by a smaller street, the houses, which were in general ancient, have been much improved in their appearance, and within the last half-century, many ranges of handsome modern houses have been erected the town is partially paved, and amply supplied with water from several wells lately made. A library was founded by Dr Thomas Plume, who bequeathed all his books and pictures to this town, with £2 per annum for the purchase of additional volumes, and £40 per annum as a salary to a librarian in holy orders, who should reside in the town, and there are some book societies, which together constitute the chief sources of recreation The haven, formed by the bay of the Blackwater river, affords safe anchorage to vessels not drawing more than eight feet of water, ships of heavier burden anchor in the offing, and discharge their cargoes by lighters on the

quay the trade of the port is principally in coal, of which, not less than ninety thousand chaldrons are, on the average, imported annually, also in corn, deals, and iron There is an excellent fishery, extending for more than twenty miles along the coast, and oysters of very superior quality, called the Wall-fleet oysters, are found here in abundance The custom-house is a neat brick building A canal from Haybridge to Chelmsford passes within a mile of the town The market, principally for corn, is on Saturday the fairs are on May 1st, for horses, cattle, and sheep, and on the 13th and 14th of September

Admiralty Seal.

The town was made a free borough by William de Mandeville, Earl of Essex, in the reign of Henry III, and exempted from all foreign service, except finding one ship for the use of the king, for forty days it received its first charter of incorporation from Henry II, and another from Queen Mary, in 1553, which being forfeited in the 4th of George III the town remained for forty-six years without a charter, till in 1810, when the present charter was granted, by which the government is vested in a mayor, recorder, six aldermen, and eighteen capital burgesses, assisted by a town clerk, chamberlain, water bailiff, and other officers The mayor is chosen annually by the aldermen and capital burgesses, the aldermen by the mayor and capital burgesses, and the capital burgesses by the mayor and aldermen the mayor, the recorder, and the two senior aldermen, are justices of the peace within the borough The freedom is inherited by birth, and obtained by marriage with a freeman s daughter, by servitude, by purchase, or by gift The corporation hold quarterly courts of session, on the days before those for the county, for offences not capital, and have power to hold a court of record, for the recovery of debts to any amount, but this privilege has not been exercised under the new charter a court leet, with view of frank-pledge, is also held, at which a headborough and constables are appointed. The borough, besides its jurisdiction on land, extends twenty-five miles to sea, to the eastward of the Knowle sands The petty sessions for the hundred of Dengie are held here every Saturday The town hall is an ancient edifice of brick, built in the reign of Henry VI, called D Arcy's tower, it contains a neat court for the business of the sessions, a council room for the meetings of the corporation, and a banquet-room The custom of borough English prevails here The borough first exercised the elective franchise in the 2nd of Edward III, since which time it has continued to return two members to parliament the right of election is vested in the freemen not receiving alms, of whom, resident and non-resident, the number is about three thousand five hundred the mayor is the returning officer

The borough comprises the parishes of All Saints, St Peter, and St Mary, the two former in the archdeaconry of Essex, and diocese of London, and the last a royal peculiar, in the jurisdiction of the Dean and Chapter of Westminster The living of All Saints is a vicarage, with which that of St Peter is united, rated in the king's books at £10, and in the patronage of the Rev C Matthew   The church is an ancient and spacious structure, in the early Norman and early English styles of architecture, with a triangular tower surmounted by an hexagonal spire, in the south aisle are three chapels, or chantries, founded by Robert D'Arcy, in the reign of Henry VI   there are various ancient monuments, and a tablet of white marble to the memory of John Vernon, a Turkey merchant, who died in 1653, with a Latin inscription attributing to him the discovery, in the ancient city of Smyrna, of some manuscripts and relics which he brought over to his native country Edward Bright, a shopkeeper in the town, who died in 1750, aged twenty-nine, was with much difficulty interred in this church   he had attained the unusual weight of forty-four stone, the body was drawn to the church in a carriage upon rollers, and lowered into the vault by means of a triangle and pulleys   The living of St Peter is a vicarage not in charge, united to that of All Saints   The church has been demolished, the tower only remaining, adjoining to which is the library, erected by Dr Thomas Plume   The living of St Mary's is a perpetual curacy, in the patronage of the Dean and Chapter of Westminster   The church, a spacious and very ancient structure, is said to have been founded prior to the Norman Conquest, by Ingelric, a Saxon nobleman ; part of the tower and church was rebuilt in the reign of Charles I   There are places of worship for the Society of Friends, Independents, and Wesleyan Methodists

Ralph Breder, in 1608, bequeathed £300 for the endowment of a free grammar school, to which a rent-charge of £3 was added by Mrs Anastatia Wentworth, and the farm of Iltney, in the parish of Mun den, by Dr Plume, for the clothing and instruction of six boys of either parish   A National school, in which three hundred children are instructed, is supported by subscription   Dr Plume bequeathed £2000 for charitable uses, and £100 as a marriage portion for five poor maidens of this parish, and five of the parish of Greenwich, in Kent, who had lived for seven years in one service, and were above twenty-four years of age   there are also other charitable bequests for distribution among the poor   Within less than a mile of the town are the remains of the abbey of Beleigh, founded in 1180, by Robert Mantell, for Premonstratensian canons, and dedicated to St. Nicholas, the revenue of which, at the dissolution, was £196 6 5   the chapel, which is the most perfect portion of the ruins, is a small edifice, chiefly in the early style of English architecture, with later insertions   the roof is groined, and supported on slender-shafted columns, and gracefully-pointed arches   Henry Bourchier, Earl of Essex, and his Countess, were interred in this chapel, and in digging for gravel in the ground adjoining, some leaden coffins and skeletons were discovered   A priory for Carmelite friars was founded here, in 1292, by Richard Gravesend, Bishop of London, the revenue of which, at the dissolution, was £26 0 8, but there are no vestiges of it at present, except the garden walls   An hospital for lepers was also founded here by one of the English monarchs, prior to the 16th of Edward II, which, by Edward IV, was annexed to the abbey of Beleigh   the remains, now converted into a barn, exhibit in their structure a mixture of stone and of bricks and tiles, which appear to have been of Roman origin   A gold coin of Nero and Agrippina, and a coin of Vespasian, have been found at this place   To the west of the town are the remains of a camp, through which is the road to Chelmsford   it is of quadrilateral form, including twenty-two acres, three sides of the ramparts are visible, and the fourth is occupied by buildings   on the north is a fine spring, called Cromwell's spring   Dr Thomas Plume, Archdeacon of Rochester, whose public benefactions to this town have been already recorded, and who founded the Plumean Professorship of Astronomy and Experimental Philosophy at Cambridge, was born at Maldon in 1680, and died in 1704   Maldon gives the inferior title of viscount to the Earl of Essex.

MALHAM, a township in that part of the parish of KIRKBY in MALHAM-DALE which is in the western division of the wapentake of STAINCLIFFE and Ewcross, West riding of the county of YORK, 5½ miles (E by S) from Settle, containing 262 inhabitants   There is a place of worship for Wesleyan Methodists   Rowland Brayshaw, in 1717, conveyed land, &c, for the support of a free school, the income arising from which is £49 per annum   The river Aire has its source here, in a fine lake stored with trout and perch ; the vicinity abounds with scenery of a romantic character   Malham Cove is a remarkable natural amphitheatre of limestone rock, rising to the height of two hundred and eighty-six feet, at its base issues a small subterranean brook, the passage for which, when flooded, not being capacious enough to discharge its swollen stream, the waters rise to the summit of the rock, and tumble down in a fine cataract

MALHAM-MOOR, a township in that part of the parish of KIRKBY in MALHAM DALE which is in the western division of the wapentake of STAINCLIFFE and EWCROSS, West riding of the county of YORK, 5½ miles (N E) from Settle, containing 88 inhabitants

MALLERSTANG, a chapelry in the parish of KIRKBY-STEPHEN, EAST ward, county of WESTMORLAND, 3 miles (S by E) from Kirkby-Stephen, containing 243 inhabitants   The living is a perpetual curacy, in the archdeaconry and diocese of Carlisle, endowed with £600 private benefaction, and £600 royal bounty, and in the patronage of the Earl of Thanet   The chapel, having fallen to ruin, was repaired in 1663, by the celebrated Countess of Pembroke, who endowed it with lands near Sedbergh in Yorkshire, then worth £11 a year, on condition that the curate should teach the children of the dale to read and write, in a room over the west end of the chapel, and in compliance therewith about thirty are instructed   At Castlethwaite are the ruins of a square tower, that formed part of Pendragon castle, built by Uter Pendragon, in the time of Vortigern, the walls of which are twelve feet thick   It was at one period the seat of the Lords de Clifford, and was burned by the Scots about the year 1541, but was completely repaired in 1661, by the Countess of Pembroke, who also built the bridge across the Eden, and erected the stone pillar on the hill called Morrill's Seat   The castle was dismantled by the Earl of Thanet in 1681   near it is an ancient fortification, surrounded by a moat and vallum   At the southern extremity of the chapelry rises the lofty mountain called Wild Boar fell

MALLING (EAST), a parish in the hundred of LARKFIELD, lathe of AYLESFORD, county of KENT, 4¾ miles (W N W) from Maidstone, containing 1403 inhabitants The living is a vicarage, in the peculiar jurisdiction of the Archbishop of Canterbury, rated in the king s books at £10 8 4, and in the patronage of Sir J Twisden, Bart The church, dedicated to St James, is a handsome structure, with a square western tower A fair for pedlary is held on August 6th James Tomlyn, in 1752, bequeathed a rent-charge of £5, for teaching poor children, and the Rev Edward Holme in 1781, erected, and endowed with lands, a school, in which about fifty children are educated

MALLING (SOUTH), a parish in the hundred of RINGMER, rape of PEVENSEY, county of SUSSEX, 1 mile (N) from Lewes, containing 620 inhabitants The living is a perpetual curacy, endowed with £200 private benefaction, £600 royal bounty, and £1700 parliamentary grant South Malling constitutes the head of a deanery, the whole of which is within the peculiar jurisdiction of the Archbishop of Canterbury The church, dedicated to St Michael, is described as collegiate in Domesday book, and is said to have been founded by Ceadwalla, King of the West Saxons, who died in 688 it is a small neat edifice, rebuilt on the site of the former, and consecrated May 23rd, 1632 The dean and prebendaries, who, in later times, were under the immediate jurisdiction of the Archbishops of Canterbury, had, at the dissolution, a revenue of £45 12 5 The present mansion forms part of the ancient buildings of the deanery, but the refectory, used as a barn, was pulled down many years ago The Archbishops of Canterbury had formerly a palace here, the chapel has been converted into a cottage

MALLING (WEST), a parish (formerly a market town) in the hundred of LARKFIELD, lathe of AYLESFORD, county of KENT, 5¾ miles (W N W) from Maidstone, and 29 (S E by E) from London, containing 1205 inhabitants In the year 1090, a Benedictine nunnery was founded here, by Gundulph, Bishop of Rochester, in honour of the Blessed Virgin, about a century afterwards, the town and the nunnery were nearly destroyed by fire, but soon restored, the revenue of the latter, at the dissolution, was estimated at £245 10 2½ the west front of the abbey, which is of Norman architecture, with later insertions, still remains, forming an interesting ruin Stone coffins have been dug up here, and rings, with other relics of antiquity, have been discovered The town is neat and clean and the surrounding walks and scenery are pleasing and picturesque The market, granted, together with the fairs, to the abbess, in the reign of Henry III, was held on Saturday fairs are held on August 12th and October 2nd for pedlary, and November 17th for cattle The living is a vicarage, in the archdeaconry and diocese of Rochester, rated in the king s books at £10, and in the patronage of — Bates, Esq The church, dedicated to St Mary, is an ancient structure, with a fine Norman tower at the west end the roof having fallen in 1778, through the decay of the main columns, the whole of the nave was rebuilt In 1693, Francis Tresse bequeathed land on which to build a school house, and £40 towards its erection, he also gave a small rent-charge for repairs it is now conducted on Dr Bell s system

MALMESBURY, a borough and market town, having separate jurisdiction, locally in the hundred of Malmesbury, county of WILTS, 42 miles (N) from Salisbury, and 94 (W) from London, containing, exclusively of the chapelries of Corstone and Rodborne, and the tythings of Burton-Hill, Cole with West Park, and Milbourn, in that part of the parish of St Paul which is without the precincts of the borough, 2514 inhabitants This place is stated by Leland to have been an ancient British town, which he calls Caer Bladon, but its origin may, with more probability, be ascribed to the period of the Saxon Heptarchy A castle, called Ingelburne, existed here before the middle of the seventh century, and about 642, Maidulph, an Irish monk, founded a hermitage, and being joined by Aldhelm, nephew of Ina, King of Wessex, they, with the assistance of Lutherius, Bishop of Winchester, erected a monastery, from the names of its founders styled Mealdelmesbyrigg, which has been gradually altered to the modern appellation of Malmesbury The monastery, which was one of the most considerable in Wiltshire, belonged to the Benedictines it was splendidly endowed by several princes and noblemen its abbot was made a mitred parliamentary baron by Edward III, and its revenue, at the dissolution, amounted to £803 17 7 A part of the nave only of the conventual church remains, which has been long used as the parish church Buildings gradually rose round the abbey, and notwithstanding the town suffered from the incursions of the Danes, who burnt it in the reign of Alfred the Great, it became a place of so much importance as to have obtained a charter from Edward the Elder, which was confirmed by his son Athelstan, who renewed it, and was a munificent benefactor both to the town and the monastery He bestowed an extensive tract of land, called the Common of King s Heath, on the men of Malmesbury, who had assisted him in gaining a victory over the Danes In the reign of Henry I, or Stephen, a strong castle was built here by Roger, Bishop of Salisbury, who was obliged to surrender it to the king, and on the invasion of England by Prince Henry, afterwards Henry II, he laid siege to this fortress, and took it after an obstinate defence During the civil war in the reign of Charles I, Malmesbury was a royal garrison, and that prince lodged in the town one night, in 1643 Shortly after, the town was captured by Sir William Waller, but it was re-taken by the royalists, who did not long retain possession of it, for the parliament having recovered it, their troops were stationed here till June 1646

The town, situated on a pleasant and commanding eminence, is nearly surrounded by two streams, which unite at its southern extremity, and form the Lower Avon The principal street extends southward from the market-place, near which it is crossed by another street, leading to that part of the town called Westport These streets are paved and lighted, under the authority of an act of parliament obtained in 1798, and the inhabitants are abundantly supplied with water from wells In the centre of the market-place is a fine octagonal

Seal and Arms.

market cross, built in the reign of Henry VII, and ornamented with flying buttresses, pinnacles, and an octangular central turret The manufacture of woollen cloth was anciently carried on here very extensively, and, after it had entirely decayed, it was again introduced, in the latter part of the last century, and now constitutes the chief employment of the lower class Some trade is carried on in tanning and brewing, and bone-lace is made by the women and children The market, principally for butchers meat, is on Saturday, and large cattle markets are held on the last Tuesday in every month, except March, April, and May Fairs for horses, cattle, and sheep, take place March 28th, April 28th, and June 5th

The first charter of incorporation was granted by Charles I, but the charter now in force was obtained from William III, in 1696, under which the corporation consists of an alderman, deputy alderman, eleven capital burgesses, and twenty-four assistants, with a high steward and deputy steward The alderman and his deputy are elected annually on Trinity Tuesday, by the capital burgesses, who are thirteen in all, from their own body Besides these members of the corporation, there are fifty-two landholders, and an indefinite number of commoners, or free burgesses the assistant burgesses are chosen from the landholders, and the latter from the commoners, who are the sons, or sons-in-law, of commoners The steward and deputy steward are elected annually by the capital burgesses The alderman and deputy alderman; and the steward and deputy steward, are justices of the peace, and the alderman is coroner and clerk of the market The petty sessions for the hundred of Malmesbury are held here once a month, and a court of requests for the hundred is held every nine weeks, for the recovery of debts under 40s King s Heath, or Malmesbury common, has been enclosed, pursuant to an act of parliament obtained in 1821, when after assigning fifty acres for defraying the expense of the enclosure, and for providing for an increase in the number of free burgesses, or commoners, it was subdivided into two hundred and eighty allotments, averaging about one acre and a half each, and an allotment assigned to each commoner to be used only for tillage, or garden ground To the east of King s Heath are the Acres, so called from their measure, one acre belonging to each of the assistant burgesses and landholders, and near them are other lands, called Burgess Parts, varying in extent from six to fifteen acres, and belonging, one each, to the capital burgesses The borough has sent members to parliament ever since the reign of Edward I By an order of the House of Commons, December 13th, 1722, the right of election was determined to be in the alderman and twelve capital burgesses the alderman is the returning officer, and the patronage of the borough belongs to Joseph Pitt, Esq, M P, the present high steward

The borough comprises the parishes of St. Paul, St Mary Westport, and the Abbey district, in the archdeaconry of Wilts, and diocese of Salisbury The living of St. Paul s is a discharged vicarage, rated in the king s books at £8. 2 1½, and in the patronage of the Crown The church is dilapidated, but the tower, surmounted by a lofty spire, is still standing, and contains the bells used on public festivals, &c The nave of the conventual church, dedicated to the Virgin Mary, was purchased,

at the dissolution of monasteries, by William Stumpe, a clothier of Malmesbury, and presented to the townspeople for a parish church, under the authority of a license from Archbishop Cranmer This edifice is chiefly in the Norman style, and has a noble south porch, consisting of receding arches, with sculptured mouldings, and other ornaments The western porch was of a similar character, but a small portion of it only remains In the interior, at the east end, is a sepulchral chapel, in which is an ancient tomb with a recumbent crowned statue, ascribed to King Athelstan, who was interred near the high altar of this church About six years since, the whole fabric was substantially repaired and the vaulted roof and other parts of the interior restored over the altar has been placed a painting of the Resurrection of Lazarus, presented by the Earl of Suffolk An addition has lately been made of three hundred and forty-one sittings, three hundred of which are free, the Incorporated Society for the enlargement of churches and chapels having contributed £350 towards defraying the expense The living of the parish of Westport is a vicarage, with which the perpetual curacy of Charlton is united, rated in the king s books at £16 17 8½, and in the patronage of the Crown The church is dedicated to St Mary At Brokenborough, in this parish, there is a chapel of ease There are places of worship for Baptists, Independents, Moravians, and Wesleyan Methodists A free school, under the patronage of the corporation, is endowed with £10 per annum, arising from lands belonging to the burgesses, and £10 per annum, the benefaction of Michael Weekes, Esq, in 1695 Another school was founded and endowed, in pursuance of a bequest from Mrs Elizabeth Hodges, in 1725 the master has a salary of £25 per annum The corporation have the patronage of an almshouse, endowed with £20 per annum, and Robert Jenner, in 1644, founded eight almshouses, with an endowment of £40 per annum, which has not been paid for nearly fifty years past There were anciently a convent of the Knights Hospitallers, some small portions of the buildings belonging to which are still standing Among the distinguished persons connected with the monastery were St Aldhelm, the second abbot, who died Bishop of Sherborne in 709 Ælfric, a learned abbot in the tenth century, who was made Bishop of Crediton, and William of Malmesbury, precentor to the monastery, the celebrated English historian in the reign of Stephen Thomas Hobbes, author of the "Leviathan,' and other philosophical works, was born here in 1588, and Mrs Mary Chandler, an ingenious poetess, was also a native of this town Malmesbury confers the titles of earl and baron on the family of Harris

MALPAS, a parish in the higher division of the hundred of BROXTON, county palatine of CHESTER, comprising the townships of Agden, Bickerton, Bickley, Bradley, Broxton, Buckley, or Bulkeley, Chidlow, Cholmondeley, Chorlton, Cuddington, Duckington, Edge, Egerton, Hampton, Larkton, Macefen, Malpas, Newton juxta Malpas, Oldcastle, Overton, Stockton, Tushingham with Grindley, Wichalgh, and Wigland, and containing 3917 inhabitants, of which number, 1127 are in the township of Malpas, (8 S E) from Chester, and 165 (N W) from London The ancient name of this place was Depenbech, and was of similar import with the present appellation, which signifies a bad pass, or

2 E

road This barony, prior to the Conquest, formed part of the possession of Earl Edwin, and was subsequently given by the first Norman Earl of Chester to Robert Fitz Hugh, one of the eight barons of his parliament it was soon afterwards divided into two unequal parts, and still continues so The ancient barons exercised capital jurisdiction within the limits of the barony, and in them was vested (but distinct from their rights as barons of Malpas) the office of serjeant of the peace for the whole palatinate, excepting the hundreds of Macclesfield and Wirrall the punishment for capital offences, designated in some records as ' the custom of Cheshire,' was decapitation, and it was usual to present the heads of felons at the castle of Chester The jurisdictions have undergone considerable alteration, and the remaining portion of the ancient baronial rights has descended with the manor of Malpas The castle, the head of the ancient barony, was built soon after the Conquest, and stood immediately adjoining the church, but the only vestige of it is a circular mound, on which the keep stood In the early part of the sixteenth century the inhabitants suffered severely from the plague, particularly about the year 1625 The town is very pleasantly situated on an eminence on the line of road from Shrewsbury to Chester, and commands an extensive prospect over a great part of North Wales, Staffordshire, and the Vale Royal it consists of four streets, which diverge at right angles from a common centre, and are well paved, the houses are low and irregularly built, the inhabitants are supplied with water from a public well the walks are pleasing and picturesque, and frequent instances of longevity attest the salubrity of the atmosphere The chief occupation of the inhabitants is in agriculture a copper mine has been recently discovered in the township of Bickerton, in this parish, but its extent and quality have not yet been ascertained The market is on Wednesday Fairs are held on April 5th, July 26th, and December 8th, for cattle, linen and woollen goods, toys, and pedlary Courts leet and baron are held annually, at which constables are appointed, and debts under 40s recoverable

The living is a rectory, divided from time immemorial into two portions, in the archdeaconry and diocese of Chester, the first portion is rated in the king's books at £48 8 6½, and the second at £44 19 2, the right of presentation to the higher mediety belongs to the Marquis of Cholmondeley, and T T Drake, Esq, alternately, and that to the lower to T T Drake, Esq, only an excellent parsonage-house and glebe land are attached to each portion The church, which is dedicated to St. Oswald, is a spacious and venerable edifice, in the later style of English architecture, the windows are enriched with elegant tracery, and in the chancel are some ancient oak stalls, niches, and monuments at the end of the north and south aisles are sepulchral chapels belonging to the families of Cholmondeley and Brereton There are two chapels of ease in the parish, viz, Chad and Whitewell A domestic chapel, open for the tenants and neighbours, is attached to Cholmondeley castle, about four miles distant. In the town and parish are places of worship for Baptists, Independents, and Wesleyan Methodists The grammar school was founded early in the seventeenth century by subscription, to which Hugh, first Earl of Cholmondeley, contributed £200, and receiving the entire sum, amounting to £536 11, charged an estate, called the Old Hall, with the annual payment of £25 He likewise gave a school-room and residence for the master in 1795, the school premises were rebuilt and enlarged, at the expense of the present master This institution is free only to the sons of the representatives of the original subscribers, the master, who is at present appointed by the Marquis of Cholmondeley, likewise receives boarders Richard Alport, in 1709, bequeathed £500 for the support of a school, in which twelve boys and twelve girls were educated and clothed, the funds having considerably increased, a National school has been established, and the former incorporated with it, the number of children receiving instruction being ninety boys and fifty girls Dr Townson, archdeacon of Richmond, and rector of Malpas, bequeathed £500 Old South Sea stock, the dividends on which, amounting now to £16 14 annually, are applied in clothing and educating children An almshouse for several poor persons was built by Sir Randle Brereton, in the time of Henry VIII, and endowed by Sir Thomas Brereton, in the reign of Charles I, with a rent-charge in Newton it was rebuilt in 1721, by Hugh, Earl of Cholmondeley, for six poor widows, who are nominated by the present Marquis, and receive a small weekly allowance, a bequest, by Thomas Poyser, Esq, of the interest of £600 makes an addition of £3 per annum to the income of each of the inmates In 1748, Miss Eliz Taylor left £500 for the purpose of clothing poor men in the townships of Malpas and Edge, which sum being invested in the purchase of £771 Old South Sea stock, now produces about £27 per annum there are several minor benefactions for charitable purposes The late learned and pious Dr Heber, Bishop of Calcutta, was a native of this town, his father having been rector of the higher mediety Philip Henry, the nonconformist, resided at the Broad Oak in this parish, where his son, Matthew Henry, the celebrated commentator on the Bible, was born Malpas confers the title of viscount on the Marquis of Cholmondeley

MALPAS, a parish in the upper division of the hundred of WENTLLOOG, county of MONMOUTH, 2 miles (N by W) from Newport, containing 169 inhabitants The living is a perpetual curacy, in the archdeaconry and diocese of Llandaff, endowed with £600 royal bounty, and £200 parliamentary grant, and in the patronage of Sir C Morgan, Bart The church, dedicated to St Mary, is a handsome structure in the later English style, with a tower embattled and crowned with pinnacles it has a lofty ceiling of wood, richly carved, and in the chancel are some ancient oak stalls A small establishment of Cluniac monks, a cell to the priory of Montacute, in Somersetshire, was founded here about the time of Henry I, the revenue of which, at the dissolution, was £15 6 8

MALSWICK, a tything in the parish of NEWENT, hundred of BOTLOE, county of GLOUCESTER, containing 181 inhabitants

MALTBY, a chapelry in the parish of RAITHBY, Wold division of the hundred of LOUTH-ESKE, parts of LINDSEY, county of LINCOLN, 3 miles (S W by S) from Louth. The population is returned with the parish Ann Bolle, in 1705, bequeathed certain land, directing the income, after deducting 40s, a year for the poor, to be applied in teaching children Here was formerly a preceptory of the Knights Templars, to which Ranulph, one of the earls of Chester of that name, was the first benefactor it afterwards belonged to the Hospitallers

MALTBY, a township in the parish of STAINTON, western division of the liberty of LANGBAURGH, North riding of the county of YORK, 3½ miles (E by N) from Yarm, containing 168 inhabitants

MALTBY, a parish in the southern division of the wapentake of STRAFFORTH and TICKHILL, West riding of the county of YORK, comprising the townships of Hooton-Levet and Maltby, and containing 774 inhabitants, of which number, 679 are in the township of Maltby, 4½ miles (W by S) from Tickhill The living is a discharged vicarage, in the archdeaconry and diocese of York, rated in the king's books at £4 13 4, and endowed with £200 royal bounty, and £1400 parliamentary grant The Earl of Scarborough was patron in 1816 The church is dedicated to St Bartholomew Lord Viscount Castleton, in 1714, gave certain waste land for the support of a free school, the income arising from it is £15 a year, for which eight children are instructed

MALTBY le MARSH, a parish in the Wold division of the hundred of CALCEWORTH, parts of LINDSEY, county of LINCOLN, 3 miles (N by E) from Alford, containing 199 inhabitants The living is a discharged rectory, in the archdeaconry and diocese of Lincoln, rated in the king's books at £11 17 8 The Rev George Allot was patron in 1822 The church is dedicated to All Saints

MALTON (NEW), a borough and market town in the wapentake of RYEDALE, North riding of the county of YORK, 18 miles (N E by N) from York, and 213 (N by W) from London, containing 4005 inhabitants This town is of great antiquity the Roman roads that lead to it, the remains of intrenchments yet visible, and the coins and other relics which have been, and are still occasionally, discovered, denote its former importance as a Roman station, though the name by which it was distinguished is not known After the Conquest a castle was built here by one of the family of De Vesci, but it was destroyed by Henry II, and on its site a castellated mansion was erected by Ralph, Lord Eure, in the reign of James I, of this edifice, the lodge and gateway alone remain The town was wholly burnt, in 1138, by Archbishop Thurston, who besieged it for the purpose of dislodging the Scots, who had seized and garrisoned the castle it was rebuilt by Eustace Fitz-John, in the reign of Stephen, and the epithet *New* was then given to it, by way of distinction from Old Malton The town is agreeably situated on rising ground, northward of the Derwent, which flows through the adjacent vale, and forms the boundary between the East and North ridings, it is about half a mile in length, clean, and well built A theatre was erected in 1814, and there is a handsome suite of assembly-rooms, to which a subscription library and news-room are attached The summit of an eminence, called the Brows, at a short distance, affords an agreeable promenade, and commands a fine prospect of the course of the river and the vale, which is terminated by the Wolds The river is crossed by a handsome stone bridge, which connects this place with Norton In the

first year of the reign of Anne, the Derwent was made navigable from New Malton to the Ouse, thus affording every facility for the conveyance of corn, butter, hams, and other kinds of provision, which are here shipped for Hull, Leeds, Halifax, and other places, from the former, articles of grocery are brought back, and coal, woollen cloth, stuffs, &c, from Leeds Here are two iron foundries, and some small manufactories for linen, hats, gloves, and pelts, malt also is made to a limited extent The market is on Tuesday and Saturday, the latter being the principal day, and it is one of the best in the county for all sorts of provisions, horses, black cattle, and tools for husbandry Fairs are held on the Saturdays before Palm Sunday and Whit Sunday, and October 10th and 11th The market place is spacious, and is divided into two parts by the townhall, the shambles, and St Michael's church

The chief officer is the lord's bailiff, who is appointed at a court leet, held for the manor The general quarter sessions for the North riding are held here during the sitting of the court, on January 12th, 1785, the central beam of the sessions-house gave way, whereby upwards of three hundred persons were precipitated into the area below, in consequence of which several died, others being maimed for life The borough sent members to parliament in the 23rd and 26th of Edward I, when the privilege ceased for a time, but it was restored in 1640, by an order of the House of Commons, since which period two members have been regularly returned the right of election is in the householders, in number about five hundred, the bailiff is the returning officer, the influence of Earl Fitzwilliam is predominant The borough comprises the parishes of St Leonard and St Michael, the livings of which are perpetual curacies, with that of Old Malton, in the arch deaconry of Cleveland, and diocese of York The spire of St Leonard's church, which is in the form of a truncated cone, is said to have been left incomplete by the architect, lest any addition to it might overbalance the whole edifice There are places of worship for Baptists, the Society of Friends, Independents, Methodists, and Unitarians A spacious workhouse has been erected, and is conducted on a systematic and profitable plan, the poor are furnished with tools, and are obliged to work at their respective trades, the manufacture of linen is somewhat extensive in it At the foot of the Brows is a mineral spring, the water of which possesses similar properties to that obtained from the wells at Scarborough

MALTON (OLD), a parish in the wapentake of RYEDALE, North riding of the county of YORK, 1 mile (N E) from New Malton, containing 1064 inhabitants The living is a perpetual curacy, with those of St Leonard and St Michael in New Malton, in the archdeaconry of Cleveland, and diocese of York, endowed with £400 private benefaction, £400 royal bounty, and £1000 parliamentary grant, and in the patronage of Earl Fitzwilliam The church, dedicated to St Mary, is a very ancient structure, adjoining which are the remains of a priory, founded in 1150, by Eustace Fitz-John, in honour of the Blessed Virgin, for Gilbertine canons, the revenue of which, at the dissolution, amounted to £257 7 There is a place of worship for Wesleyan Methodists A free grammar school was founded in the 38th of Henry VIII, by the Archbishop of York, for the instruction of youth in Hebrew, Greek, and Latin, with an endowment, now amounting to about £100 per annum, for the maintenance of a master and an usher; the former of whom teaches the classics, and the latter English

MALVERN (GREAT), a parish in the lower division of the hundred of PERSHORE, county of WORCESTER, 8 miles (W) from Worcester, containing, with the chapelry of Newland, 1693 inhabitants This place is romantically situated on the eastern declivity of a range of hills, separating the counties of Worcester and Hereford, and extending from north to south for nearly nine miles, the greatest height being one thousand four hundred and forty feet, and varying from one to two miles in breadth from east to west of these the most prominent are the Worcestershire and Herefordshire beacons, the summits of which command most extensive and interesting views of the surrounding country, comprehending, in the distance, the counties of Monmouth, Radnor, Brecon, Salop, Warwick, and Stafford, and nearer, the counties of Worcester, Hereford, and Gloucester, with their stately cathedrals, together with the fertile and richly-cultivated tract of country watered by the Severn, and finely clothed with wood Around the base of the Herefordshire beacon is a double in trenchment, from six to twelve feet deep, and in some places more than thirty feet broad, dug by Gilbert de Clare, Earl of Gloucester, as a boundary between his portion of Malvern Chase and that belonging to the Bishop of Hereford, and in other parts of these mountains are similar works The more ancient portion of the village is irregularly built, and consists of houses scattered on the declivity of the mountain, but since the celebrity of the springs and the purity of the air have made it a place of fashionable resort, handsome ranges of modern houses have been erected, and, in detached situations and at different degrees of elevation, several beautiful villas have been built as private summer residences There are a chalybeate and a bituminous spring, the water of which is remarkable for its purity, and for its gently aperient and diuretic properties the former is in the eastern part of the village, near the church the latter, called Holywell, is situated two miles to the south of it, and on the eastern ridge of the hill and at St Anne s well, on the north side of the Worcestershire beacon there are some respectable hotels, and every accommodation has been provided for drinking the waters, and for hot and cold bathing the public library is a neat building of the Doric order, and in every direction there are romantic and agreeable walks

The living is a discharged vicarage, in the archdeaconry and diocese of Worcester, rated in the king s books at £6 3 4, endowed with £200 private benefaction, and £400 royal bounty, and in the patronage of Edward Foley, Esq The church, dedicated to St Mary, formerly the church of the Benedictine abbey, was, at the dissolution, purchased by the inhabitants, and made parochial it is a venerable and elegant cruciform structure, partly rebuilt under the direction of Sir Reginald Bray, in the reign of Henry VII, and combining the Norman and the later English styles of architecture, with a fine square embattled tower rising from the centre, the exterior is in the later English style, and, with the exception of the south side,

which, from its having been anciently concealed by the cloisters of the abbey, is of plainer character, exhibits a good specimen of that style, and the north porch is very rich, the interior retains much of the original character the nave is in the Norman style, with low massive piers and circular arches, the chancel is in the later English style, and is lighted by a fine range of clerestory windows, with rich and elegant tracery, the east window and that in the north transept are particularly beautiful, and several portions of the ancient stained glass, and of the original wood work in the roof, the carved seats, and other evidences of its antiquity, are remaining A few years since, the church was repaired and beautified at the expense of the neighbouring gentry, to commemorate which a small window was fitted in, having the arms of the various benefactors superbly emblazoned upon it It has lately received an addition of three hundred and eighty sittings, of which two hundred and eighty are free, the Incorporated Society for the enlargement of churches and chapels having contributed £260 towards defraying the expense There is a place of worship for Methodists A Sunday school, in which about ninety children are instructed, and a school of industry, are supported by subscription Here was a hermitage, endowed by Edward the Confessor, which, after the Conquest, was converted into a Benedictine priory an abbey and conventual buildings having been erected, in 1083, by Aldewine, the hermit, and endowed by Gislebert, abbot of Westminster, with ample possessions, it became, in consequence, subordinate to the abbey of Westminster, and subsisted till the dissolution, when the revenue was estimated at £375 0 6 of this abbey, the parish church, already noticed, the ancient gateway, a beautiful specimen of the later English style, and the abbey barn, a building in the decorated style, are the remains A celt, of a metal apparently between brass and copper, about five inches long, with a beauti ful patina, and a small ring, was found here, at a considerable depth below the surface of the ground, about the middle of the last century

MALVERN (LITTLE), a parish in the lower division of the hundred of OSWALDSLOW, though locally in the lower division of the hundred of PERSHORE, county of WORCESTER, 5¼ miles (W by N) from Upton upon Severn, containing 67 inhabitants The living is a perpetual curacy, in the archdeaconry and diocese of Worcester, endowed with £1200 royal bounty, and in the patronage of Mrs Wallman The church, dedicated to St Giles, has been long in decay, part of it forming a beautiful and interesting ruin, it belonged to a Benedictine priory, a cell to the abbey of Worcester, founded in 1171, in a gloomy cavity near the ancient intrenchment termed the Herefordshire Beacon, by two brothers, Joceline and Edred, who were successively priors here at the dissolution its revenue was valued at £102 10 9 Adjoining the church are some remains of the conventual buildings, converted into a dwelling house, called Malvern Court There is a Roman Catholic chapel in the parish

MAMBLE, a parish in the lower division of the hundred of DODDINGTREE, county of WORCESTER, 6 miles (W S W) from Bewdley, containing 386 inhabitants The living is a discharged vicarage, with that of Bayton, in the archdeaconry of Salop, and diocese of Hereford, rated in the king s books at £9 4 7, and in the patronage of the Crown The church is dedicated to St John. There are extensive coal-works within the parish. Sodington, the ancient seat of the Blounts, was destroyed by fire in the great civil war, by some troops of the parliament What remained of it was taken down in 1807, when several curious Roman relics were discovered beneath the foundations, whence it seems probable that it was anciently the site of a Roman fort

MAMHEAD, a parish in the hundred of EXMINSTER, county of DEVON, 4¾ miles (E by N) from Chudleigh, containing 320 inhabitants The living is a discharged rectory, in the archdeaconry and diocese of Exeter, rated in the king's books at £10 17 6, and in the patronage of the Crown, by reason of lunacy A school here is supported by annual donations, amounting to about £8 On Mamhead point is an obelisk of Portland stone, one hundred feet high, erected by Thomas Balle, Esq, of Mamhead House, in whose grounds are some noble specimens of the Quercus Ilex, and other rare exotics introduced by him from the continent

MAMILAD, a parish in the upper division of the hundred of ABERGAVENNY, county of MONMOUTH, 5 miles (N W by W) from Usk, containing 237 inhabitants The living is a perpetual curacy, united, with that of Trevenith, to the vicarage of Llanover, in the archdeaconry and diocese of Llandaff

MAMHOLE, a hamlet in the parish of BEDWFITY, lower division of the hundred of WENTLOOG, county of MONMOUTH, containing 1764 inhabitants, who are principally employed at the extensive coal and iron works in the neighbourhood.

MAN (ISLE OF), an island annexed to the British dominions, in the Irish sea, and nearly at an equal distance from the English and Irish coasts, in latitude between 54° and 55° (N), and longitude, about 5° (W), in the centre of the island the distance from Douglas to Liverpool (N W buoy) is 60 miles, and to St Bees Light 42, from the Point of Ayre to the Mull of Galloway 21, and to the Copeland islands at the entrance of Belfast Lough 38, and from the Calf of Man to Dublin 60, to Holyhead 45, and to Liverpool (N W buoy) 68 the population, according to the census of 1821, amounted to 40,081 This island, called by Ptolemy Monoeda, or the farther Mona (in contradistinction to the Isle of Anglesea, which also was called Mona), by Pliny Monapia, and by Bede Menavia Secunda, to distinguish it from Anglesea, which he terms Menavia Prima, was, from the rocky, or stony, nature of the soil, called Menang and Manen, from the latter of which its present name is derived The Britons, by whom it was originally inhabited, practised the superstitious rites of their ancestors under the government of the Druids, till they were converted to Christianity by St. Patrick, who, about the year 440, founded here a church and established a see, of which he appointed St Germanus bishop Under St Germanus and his successors the inhabitants continued for many years to maintain undisturbed possession of the island, till, on the irruption of the northern barbarians, it fell under the do-

Seal and Arms.

minion of the Scots, and was subsequently annexed to that kingdom by Aydan, who sent his three grandsons hither to be educated by Conanus, at that time bishop In 610, it was wrested from the Scots by Edwin, King of Northumberland, who annexed it to his own dominions, and from this period, for nearly three hundred years, the British historians are silent with respect to any circumstances connected with its history The Manks' traditions, however, record, during this interval, a succession of twelve petty kings, called Orries, of whom the first was son of the King of Denmark and Norway, an enterprising prince, who, having subdued the Orcades and the Hebrides, took possession of this island also, where he fixed his residence, and enjoyed for many years a reign of uninterrupted tranquillity Guttred, his son and successor, built the castle of Rushen, in repairing which, in 1815, a beam was discovered by the workmen, inscribed with the date 947 Nothing further is recorded of his reign than that he was interred in the castle which he had built, and was succeeded by his son Reginald, on whose assassination, his younger brother Olave assumed the government, but not having obtained a ratification of his title from the King of Norway, to whom the island was tributary, he was invited to that kingdom, and on his arrival was arraigned and put to death Olain, his brother, next took possession of this and some other islands, and, after a reign of twenty-three years, died in Ireland, and was succeeded by Allen, who, being poisoned by his governor, made room for Macon, but he refusing to do homage for his crown to Edgar, King of England, was deprived of it, but was soon afterwards taken prisoner, and made admiral of the great fleet raised by that monarch to protect the English coasts from the repeated assaults of the northern pirates Macon was one of the eight tributary kings whom Edgar, in token of their vassalage, compelled to row his barge on the river Dee

Godred Crowan, son of Harold Halfager, King of Norway, who accompanied his father in his invasion of England on the death of Edward the Confessor, was, after the defeat of his countrymen, hospitably entertained in this island, in which he had taken refuge Returning the following year with a numerous army, after being twice repulsed by the inhabitants, he succeeded in taking possession of it after a sanguinary contest, and established himself in that part of the isle which lies to the south of the mountainous ridge by which it is divided, granting the remainder to the inhabitants on the absolute condition of their holding it under him, as lord of the whole from this time the island became vested in the kings, or lords, of the isles, and continued to be held of them till the commencement of the last century Godred, who also held the sovereignty of the Hebrides, or Western islands of Scotland, maintained a navy of sufficient force to enable him to keep possession of his conquests, and turned his arms against Ireland, at that time divided into petty principalities, and reduced Dublin and a considerable part of the province of Leinster He left three sons, Lagman, Harold, and Olave Lagman, who succeeded to the government, being jealous of his brother Harold, whom he suspected of exciting insubordination among his soldiers, put him to death, but repenting, he resigned the crown to his youngest brother Olave, and died on a pilgrimage to Jerusalem Olave being then a minor, and residing in the court of

Henry I, where he received his education, the island, from its unsettled state, was exposed to the attacks of the neighbouring powers, and the principal inhabitants applied to the King of Ireland to appoint some person of royal descent, who might act as regent during the minority of that prince The king appointed Donald Tade, but his haughtiness and tyranny disgusting the inhabitants, they expelled him from the island, and entrusted the regency to one Mac Marus, a person of great prudence, moderation, and justice, who, in 1098, laid the foundation of the abbey of Rushen, and continued for a time to preserve the peace, and promote the prosperity of the island ; but a conspiracy being formed against him, internal dissensions were created, and the island became an easy prey to Magnus, King of Norway, who, having conquered the Orkneys and the Hebrides, landed in the parish of St Patrick, and possessed himself, almost without resistance, of the Isle of Man, over which he reigned more than six years ; but having gone with sixteen ships to reconnoitre the Irish coast, in 1102, and incautiously landing, with a party of his followers, he was taken by surprise, and slain

Olave, who had been in exile for sixteen years, was now invited to the government, which he enjoyed in undisturbed tranquillity for many years he went over to Norway, to get his title acknowledged, and was honourably received and crowned king Leaving his son Godred to be educated at the Norwegian court, he returned to his dominions, which he found distracted by the pretensions of the three sons of his brother Harold, who, having been educated in Ireland, raised considerable forces in that country, and landing in the Isle of Man, demanded one moiety of the isles to be surrendered to them ; and while attending a meeting at Ramsey, which had been appointed by the king, for taking their demand into consideration, both parties being drawn up in lines opposite to each other, Reginald, one of the brothers, feigning to address the king, by whom he had been called, raised his battle axe, and at one blow struck off his head. This, which was a preconcerted signal for a general attack, was followed by a sanguinary conflict, in which many fell on both sides But such insidious treachery did not long remain unpunished on the return of Prince Godred from Norway, the whole island submitted to his authority, and the three sons of Harold were delivered up to condign punishment, Reginald having been executed, and his two brothers deprived of their eyes In 1158, Summerled, Thane of Argyle, and brother-in-law to Godred, attempted to usurp the government, but the fleets of Godred and the usurper meeting, a desperate battle ensued, and after an obstinate and sanguinary conflict, without the victory inclining to either side, a truce was agreed upon, and afterwards a treaty, by which the kingdom of the isles was divided between them Another attempt was made to deprive Godred of his throne by his bastard brother, Reginald, but without success ; and that prince, having reigned for some years in peace, died in 1187 Godred left three sons, Reginald, Olave, and Ivar, of whom he appointed Olave his successor, because born in wedlock Olave, being at that time a minor, the people made Reginald king, but afterwards, on his attaining maturer age, raised Olave to the throne Reginald, in order to recover his lost dignity, did homage to John, King of England, for his crown, and made submission to the pope ; and having

obtained assistance from Allen, Lord of Galloway, and Thomas, Earl of Athol, landed on the island, while Olave, with his chief officers and soldiers, was in the Western isles, massacred the unprotected inhabitants, plundered their houses of every thing valuable, burnt the churches, and laid waste the southern parts of the island ; and, even after the return of Olave, succeeded in setting fire to. the shipping, then at anchor under Peel castle An intestine warfare raged for some time with great fury, and Reginald was ultimately killed in a battle fought at Tynwald Mount From minutes of council it appears, that Olave received from Henry III an annual payment in silver coin and wine, for defending this part of the coast ; from which it may be inferred that the island possessed a naval force at that time by no means inconsiderable Olave died in 1237, and was succeeded by his son Harold, who having gone over to Norway, was, with his wife, drowned on his return, and his brother Reginald, who assumed the government in 1249, was slain, with all his party, in an insurrection headed by a knight named Ivar On the death of Reginald, who left only an infant daughter, his brother Magnus was chosen king, and, according to the usual custom, went over to Normandy, where, after two years attendance, he was declared King of the Isles, and had his title confirmed to him and his successors Notwithstanding this, Mary, the daughter of Reginald, set up a claim for the kingdom, and did homage for it to Edw I, which circumstance was, four hundred years afterwards, adduced as a plea on which judgment was obtained in favour of the heirs general of Ferdinand, Earl of Derby, against their uncle, Earl William ; but it was afterwards settled by parliament in favour of a male succession

From this time the power of the Norwegian kings began to decline, and that of the Scottish kings, from whom these islands had been wrested, recovered strength Deprived of that support which the inhabitants had received from Norway, and threatened by the Scots, who were preparing to regain possession of the islands by force, which the death of the Scottish monarch alone suspended, Magnus, in 1256, visited England, in order to secure the protection and assistance of Henry III, by whom he was hospitably entertained, and from whom he received the honour of knighthood In 1263, Aquinus, King of Norway, made an attempt to revenge the affront offered to his authority, by the recent attempt of the Scots upon this island, and made a descent upon that kingdom, but he was so powerfully resisted by Alexander, who had succeeded to the throne, that he was forced to take shelter in the Orcades, where he died at Kirkwall Magnus dying without issue, in 1265, was buried in the abbey church in Rushen ; and the King of Scotland having subdued the Orkneys and the Hebrides, attacked the Isle of Man, now unprotected, and, after many battles fought with varied success, at length achieved the conquest of it with a powerful army under the command of Alexander of Paisley and John Comyn, in 1270, when, after a decisive battle at Ronaldsway, in which five hundred of the Manks, with their leader, were slain, the kingdom was entirely subjugated, and annexed to the dominions of Alexander, who, in token of his conquest, substituted for the ancient armorial ensign of the isle, which was a ship in full sail, the device of the three legs, which it

ISLE of MAN

Scale of English Miles

0 1 2 3 4 5

West 70° Longitude

Drawn by R.Creighton.

DRAWN AND ENGRAVED FOR LEWIS' TOPOGRAPHICAL DICTIONARY.

Engraved by J. & C. Walker.

still retains The tyrannical oppression of the lieutenants (by whom it was governed) under the Scottish kings inspired the inhabitants with the resolution of throwing off the Scottish yoke, or of perishing in the attempt, but the bishop, informed of their determination, interfered to prevent the effusion of blood, and obtained their mutual consent to decide the contest by thirty champions selected from each party, and a place was accordingly chosen for the combat The Manks champions were all killed in the contest, and twenty-five of the Scottish warriors shared the same fate, this victory confirmed the conquest of the Scots, and the Manks, finding no resource, submitted to their fate the ancient regal government was abolished, and a military despotism established in its place In 1289, the island was surrendered by the Scottish commissioners to Edward I, who restored it the following year to John Balliol, and, on the death of Edward, in 1307, his successor, Edward II, seized it, and, in the course of one year, bestowed it successively upon his favourites, Piers de Gaveston, Gilbert de Mac Gascall, and Henricus de Bello Monte In the reign of Edward III, a female descendant of Mary, daughter of Reginald, revived the claims of her family to the sovereignty of the island, and solicited the protection of that monarch, who, having ascertained the validity of her title, gave her in marriage to Sir William de Montacute, and granted them such succours in ships and men, that Sir William expelled the Scots, and, to the great joy of the natives, restored the ancient government in the right line In the prosecution of his lady's claim, Sir William had contracted so large a debt, that he was compelled to mortgage the island for seven years, to Anthony Bec, Bishop of Durham, who, in 1377, obtained from Richard II a grant of it for life, but at his decease it reverted to the natural heir, William de Montacute, Earl of Salisbury, who sold it, in 1395, to Sir William Scroop, afterwards Earl of Wiltshire, who was beheaded at the commencement of the war between the houses of York and Lancaster

In the reign of Henry IV it was in the possession of Henry Percy, Earl of Northumberland, upon whose rebellion against that monarch it was seized for the king's use by Sir William and Sir John Stanley, to the latter of whom it was granted, in 1406, for one year only This grant was revoked, and a new patent passed the great seal, in 1407, bestowing island, castle, peel, and lordship of Man, and the isles appertaining thereto, with all the royalties, regalities, and franchises, with the patronage of the see, on him and his heirs, in as full and ample a manner as had been granted to any former lord, or king, to be held of the crown of Great Britain, by liege homage, paying to the king a cast of falcons at his coronation In this family its royalties and revenues descended regularly to William Stanley, sixth Earl of Derby, who obtained from James I a new grant of the isle, which was confirmed by act of parliament. The title of "King of Man was first exchanged for that of "Lord of Man by Thomas second Earl of Derby During the parliamentary war, the island remained steadily attached to the interests of the king, and was among the last places that yielded to the usurped authority of Cromwell General Ireton, on the part of the parliament, offered to James, Earl of Derby, the repossession of all his estates

in England, upon condition of his surrendering the Isle of Man, but the earl, in a most spirited and memorable reply, rejected the offer with the greatest indignation, and declared his determination to hang any future messenger that should be sent with similar proposals On the execution of the earl at Bolton le Moors, in 1651, its defence was undertaken by his lady, who determined to hold Castle Rushen, to which she had retired, to the last extremity, but Receiver-General William Christian, who had the command of the garrison, deeming her cause hopeless, surrendered the castle to Colonels Birch and Duckenfield, who, with ten armed vessels, had invaded the island, which was subsequently granted by the parliament to Lord Fairfax Charles II restored the island to the son of Earl James, and Christian, being tried by the Manks authorities, and found guilty of treason, was shot, in January 1662, but the sentence was afterwards reversed, and the family restored to their estates, by an order from the king

One of the most important occurrences in the civil history of the island was the granting, in 1703, by James, the tenth Earl of Derby, and Lord of Man, of the Act of Settlement, by which the lessees of estates were finally established in possession of them, and their descent assigned in perpetuity, on the payment of certain fines, rents, and duties to the lord. James dying without issue, in 1735, the lordship of Man descended to James Murray, second Duke of Athol, and, in order to put an end to the contraband trade of the island, which, in the beginning of the last century, had become so excessive, as materially to affect the revenue of the country, an act of parliament was passed, in 1726, authorising the earl to sell the royalty and revenue of the island but though many overtures were made for the purchase of them by government, no treaty was concluded till after the death of the duke, whose only daughter Charlotte, Baroness Strange, being married to her cousin James, heir to the dukedom of Athol, conveyed to him the lordship of Man Proposals for the purchase were renewed to this nobleman, in 1765, and measures having been at the same time introduced into the house of parliament for more effectually preventing the illicit trade of the island, the duke and duchess agreed to alienate the sovereignty of it for £70,000, which sum was accordingly paid, they reserved only the manorial rights, the patronage of the see, and some emoluments and perquisites, respecting which a misunderstanding arose, in consequence of the British government claiming more than the duke and duchess intended by the treaty to relinquish, and a further sum of £2000 per annum was granted to them, upon their lives, and the sovereignty of the island was thus transferred to the crown Soon after this an act of parliament was passed, which effectually checked the contraband trade On the ground of inadequate compensation, their son John presented petitions to parliament, but unsuccessfully, until the year 1805, when an act was passed, assigning to him and his heirs one-fourth of the gross revenue of the island In 1825, an act passed both houses of parliament, authorising the Lords of the Treasury to treat with the duke for the purchase of his remaining interest in the royalty and revenues of the island, the patronage of the see, the manorial rights, and other profits and emoluments The duke agreed to sell, and the valuation was left to arbitrators appointed on both sides, who awarded the sum of £416,000, as an indemnity, and the Isle of Man, with all its privileges and immunities, was entirely ceded to the British government

It is about thirty miles in length, extending in a direction from north-north-east to south-south-west, varying from eight to twelve miles in breadth, and about eighty miles] in circumference It is divided into two unequal parts by a mountainous ridge reaching from North Barrule at the northern, to South Barrule at the southern, extremity of the island, and comprehending in the chain Snawfel, Mount Greeba, Pen-y-Pot, and several others Of these the most considerable for their elevation and extent are, Snawfel, and the North and South Barrules, which are nearly of an equal height , Snawfel, the highest of them, being five hundred and eighty yards above the level of the sea The sides, as is the case in most of the other mountains, are covered to the height of several yards from the base with turbary, or turf, and with various kinds of moss, heath, and rushes, to the summit North Barrule is a rock of clay-slate, which is also the prevailing formation in South Barrule, the latter differing chiefly by its being varied, on the north side, with large masses of granite, containing silvery mica, red and white felspar, and grey quartz Mount Greeba is of very rugged and precipitous ascent, especially in that part near the road leading from Douglas to Peel the stratum near the surface is a glossy clay, intersected by many large veins of quartz, alternating in some parts with layers of mica slate Pen-y-Pot, consisting chiefly of clay-slate from the base to the summit, is extremely marshy, and in dry weather, and even in summer, the ascent is difficult and tedious From Ramsey to Derby haven, and round the south and western shores of the island, the land terminates in cliffs, consisting of clay-slate, and varying in elevation from one hundred to more than two hundred and fifty feet , at the southern extremity is the promontory of Spanish head, consisting of bold precipices, rising perpendicularly from the level of the beach to the height of more than three hundred feet, and divided by extensive chasms into pyramidal and conical masses, which overhang the shore In one of these recesses, which penetrate many yards into the solid rock, is a circle of erect stones, appearing to have been a Druidical temple, for which, from the solitude and sublimity of the situation, no place could be more appropriate Detached from this extremity of the island, by a rocky channel, several hundred yards in breadth, in the middle of which is an island, called Kitterland, whereon sheep are fed in the summer, is the Calf of Man, the largest of numerous rocky islets surrounding the coast it is nearly five miles in circumference, and comprises an area of more than six hundred acres , on the western side, the cliffs rise in perpendicular masses, to the height of four hundred feet, and its summit, which commands an extensive view of the Welch, Scotch, and Irish mountains, is five hundred feet above the level of the sea On the south side of the Calf of Man is a very large mass of rock, called the Burrow, or Barrow, in its form resembling a lofty tower, and separated from the other masses by an opening of romantic appearance near it is another, called the Eye, perforated by a natural arch, resembling the eye of a needle, from which circumstance it has its name Two

handsome lighthouses have been erected here, for the protection of vessels navigating the Irish sea , they are distant from each other one hundred and eighty-seven yards, bearing north half east, and south-west half west. The lower is three hundred and five feet, and the upper three hundred and ninety-six feet, above the level of the sea , they are furnished with double revolving lights, which make their revolution in two minutes, and at their greatest splendour may be seen at the distance of seven leagues the bearing of the upper light is north-east half east from the dangerous sunken rocks, called the Chickens, from which it is nearly one mile and a half distant

The harbours are, Douglas, Ramsey, Peel, Port le Mary, and Castletown The natural harbours are, Derby haven, Laxey, and Port-Erin Douglas, Ramsey, Derby haven, and Laxey, are on the eastern coast, Castletown and Port le Mary on the southern coast, and Peel and Port-Erin on the western coast Douglas harbour, which is dry at low water, being considered the best dry harbour in the Irish sea, admits vessels of considerable burden to approach the quay at high water, the depth being then from fifteen to twenty feet. The pier, constructed by government, at an expense of £22,000, is five hundred and twenty feet in length, and forty feet broad for an extent of four hundred and fifty feet from its commencement, when it expands to a breadth of ninety feet, terminating in a circular area of greater elevation than the narrower part, and having in the centre a handsome lighthouse the whole is built of yellow stone brought from Runcorn in Cheshire, and affords great security to the harbour The quay is spacious, and well adapted to the loading and unloading of vessels, of which all having goods or merchandise for bonding are, by act of parliament, compelled to deliver their cargoes exclusively at this port. The whole bay is two miles across, and has good anchorage, except on the north side, being sheltered from all winds except the east and south-east both its points are rocky, precipitous, and dangerous, and in the centre is a large bed of rocks, called St. Mary s rock, or the Connister, which are just covered at high water, being extremely dangerous to mariners In tempestuous weather the harbour itself affords but insecure shelter to vessels, being exposed to a heavy swell , and those in the bay, at such times, are subject to many accidents, numerous shipwrecks happening on this part of the coast To remedy these inconveniences, Sir William Hillary, Bart , in 1826, submitted a plan to the consideration of government, for forming a spacious central harbour, which, by the construction of a breakwater from Douglas Head, and a pier from St Mary s rock, might be accessible at all times to the largest vessels navigating the Irish sea, and within which a squadron of the largest ships of the line, and a numerous fleet of merchantmen, might ride in safety Ramsey harbour, accessible to vessels of one hundred tons burden, has been greatly improved by the construction of an additional pier in 1830, the depth of water being thereby increased more than three feet. The quay, on which a lighthouse has been built, is very commodious This is the principal port from which wheat is exported The bay is spacious, and the anchorage good , and a considerable number of the herring boats are laid up here during the winter Peel harbour, affording shelter to vessels of small burden, is formed by a pier four hundred yards long, and varying from seven to ten yards in breadth, at the extremity of which is a harbour-light A jetty, forty yards in length, was erected in 1830, at an expense of £550 the depth of water at ordinary spring tides is about fifteen feet, and at neap tides eleven feet There are seventy herring boats, from sixteen to thirty tons burden each, belonging to this harbour Derby haven, the principal resort of the herring boats during the latter part of the fishing season, is about a mile and a half from Castletown, on the further side of the isthmus which joins the peninsula of Langness to the main land At its southern extremity is the small island of St Michael, connected with the main land by a stone wall, about one hundred yards in length, and twelve feet thick on this small isle a circular fort was erected by the Earl of Derby, in the early part of the seventeenth century the walls, on which is placed a harbour-light, are eight feet in thickness, and eighteen in height, they are still entire, and enclose an area eighteen yards in diameter, in which are the ruins of two houses, and near them the remains of a church, now used as a place of interment for Roman Catholics, and for persons who may be shipwrecked on that part of the coast the haven, which is a mile and a half from the direct course, is, from its greater security, generally selected as a place of landing by passengers to Castletown from Ireland Port le Mary has a good harbour, protected by a pier of considerable extent, erected a few years since, at the extremity of which is a harbour light Port-Erin has an excellent bay, affording protection from all winds except the west, and much frequented by the fishing fleet at the commencement of the season Laxey bay affords convenient anchorage, and partial shelter from the winds

In the high lands between North Barrule and Mount Greeba rise several streams, which run into the sea at Douglas, Ramsey, Peel, Laxey, and Castletown, and bear the same names as those places Of these the Ramsey river is the largest it rises in the mountainous group around Snawfel, and, from the flat tract of land through which it passes, within two miles of the sea, its shallow channel is frequently diverted by the sea, at spring tides The Douglas river is formed of two branches, of which the southern rises in the west side of Mount Garraghan, and the northern in the group of which Mount Pen-y-Pot is the centre The river Peel rises in the northern side of South Barrule, and receives also another branch issuing from the western side of the mountains of St German and St Michael. The Laxey river descends from the eastern declivity of Snawfel, and pursues a westerly course to Laxey bay, and the Castletown river has two branches, the principal of which rises in the south side of South Barrule, uniting a little below Athol bridge Besides these rivers, which are shallow and inconsiderable, there are numerous streams in various parts of the island, but few of them are of sufficient force to turn a mill. This island, like those of the Hebrides, is destitute of wood, and almost of all trees not artificially planted, a little brushwood and furze is found on the uncultivated hills and low lands, but seldom on the mountains. In various parts, plantations and shrubberies are brought into a luxuriant state, but there is neither park nor forest scenery in

the island The climate is rather milder in winter than that of the neighbouring coasts the frosts, which rarely commence before Christmas, are but of short duration, and generally so slight as very little to impede vegetation, and the snow seldom remains on the ground for any length of time gales of wind and rains are frequent and of long duration in the spring, rendering the seed-time unfavourable, and being greatly prejudicial to the tender shoots of corn the heat in summer is also more moderate, the harvests being consequently later, in general, the grain does not attain its full size, and the straw is less valuable for fodder The soil of the northern portion of the island is a light sand, resting on a bed of common clay, and in some places of clay-marl, but the greatest part consists of a soil resting on grey wacké, and on clay-slate, in general thin and unproductive without good management A small portion of the land around Castletown is composed of transition limestone, of a bluish grey colour, containing veins of calcareous spar, with impressions of shells and other marine exuviæ, the strata of which are generally from one to four feet in thickness, having a dip to the south and south-west of from five to ten degrees, and frequently alternating with the grey wacké slate, on which it lies The boundaries of this limestone district extend along the coast, from the first creek northward from Derby haven to the most western point of Port le Mary, and from the same creek over land to Ballasalla, and thence across the Castletown river again to Port le Mary The clay, and the grey wacké slate, the latter of which in creases in proportion to the distance from the higher mountains, occupy the southern and central portions of the island The soil of the valley, from St John's to Peel, is alluvial, and abounds with marine exuviæ in some parts it consists of loose sand, with a substratum of grey wacké slate, extending northward to Kirk-Michael, and forming a narrow slip of land, one hundred and fifty feet above the level of the sea, bounded on one side by the sea shore, and on the other by mountainous elevations, consisting chiefly of grey wacké slate, in some parts covered with a bed of common clay The sandy soil along the sea-shore to the north expands over the whole of that part of the island which is separated from the south side, by a line extending from Ramsey to Kirk-Michael, in a direction from east to west. Underneath the sand is a bed of very pure common clay, at the depth of from one to three feet below the surface, called by the inhabitants marl, of which they make an advantageous use in giving consistency to the light sandy surface, and near Ramsey is a bed of real clay marl, containing a considerable portion of lime, and dug midway between high and low water marks there are several pits of shell marl in the vicinity of Ballaugh, and in many parts of this flat northern district peat is found in considerable quantities, usually in layers from six to eight feet in thickness, forming an extensive turbary in the centre of the flat, which has been partly drained, and contains great quantities of diluvial timber, among which are trunks of the pine and the oak Much of the land has been greatly improved by draining, and in the northern part of the island a considerable tract has, by that means, been converted from a marsh into good arable and pasture land, the soil of which is peat moss and clay,

The prevailing mode of agriculture comprises a

succession of crops in the following order First, potatoes or turnips, second, barley, third, clover, fourth, oats, or, if good land, wheat, and fifth, peas, or oats if wheat has preceded After two or three rotations, a poor soil is generally laid down to grass, and is afterwards brought again into tillage Wheat is not generally sown except on the best cultivated farms, and in the best districts, the produce is commonly from twenty-four to thirty-six bushels per acre, the bushel weighing sixty-four pounds About one-half of the arable land is appropriated to the growth of barley, of which two kinds are sown, one having two rows of grain in the ear, and the other four, the latter is used only for malt, and the former is made into bread for the islanders the seed time for this grain is from the middle of April to the middle of May, the four-rowed ear requires to be sown earlier, and in general ripens a fortnight sooner, than the other, the average produce of each sort is thirty-six bushels per acre The other half of the arable land is appropriated to the culture of oats, of which also there are two kinds, the white and the Poland, the former is generally preferred the time for sowing is from the beginning of March to the middle of April, the average produce of both is thirty bushels per acre a very little rye is also grown Potatoes are in general a very favourite crop, and there are many sorts, requiring different modes of cultivation the time of planting is generally from the end of March to the middle of May, the produce is from one hundred and sixty to two hundred bushels per acre Turnips, for which the climate and the soil appear to be extremely favourable, are produced in great quantities, and flax is grown in most parts of the island, but not sufficient for the supply of the manufacturers, the time for sowing it is April Most of the artificial grasses thrive well, the white and red clover, ray-grass, and the common grasses, are generally good crops, and great quantities of hay are stacked in most of the agricultural districts The light ploughs are generally preferred, many being procured from England and Scotland In addition to the general manures, sea-weed is extensively used, and with success, by farmers near the coast

The commons, or uncultivated lands, are estimated to form one-third of the island, including the whole of the mountainous chain nearly to the base Into these pastures horses, cattle, and sheep, are turned to graze, particularly by the upland farmers, who take pride in their mountain breed of sheep Their principal food during the winter season is the evergreen furze, of which the sheep eat only the younger sprouts, the horses eat the larger sprays, first clearing them of the prickles by pawing them with their feet The native breed of horses is of a small kind, but hardy and useful, and patient of labour, being somewhat similar to those of North Wales The horned cattle are numerous, but the native breed having been much neglected, have degenerated, the cows are in general good milchers, but are rather more adapted for fattening than for the dairy the farmers have lately been very attentive to the improvement of the breed, by the introduction of the Dunlop and short-horned cattle, but in general they rely more for keeping up their live stock upon importation, than upon rearing The native breed of sheep is very small and hardy, much resembling the South Down breed of England

their wool is not very long, nor of the finest staple, but the flesh is excellent, and when fat they weigh from five to eight pounds per quarter In the low lands a larger breed has been introduced, besides which is another, called Laughton, having wool of a light brown colour, highly esteemed in the manufacture of cloth, which is much preferred to that made of other wool for this purpose the breed is solely preserved, they are much less hardy in their nature, and more difficult to fatten, than any of the other kinds The sheep are subject to a peculiar and fatal distemper, called by the natives *Onw,* supposed to arise from their eating a certain plant that grows in the pastures Pigs are bred in great numbers, every cottager generally keeping one or two, which, when ten or twelve months old, weigh usually about fifty pounds per quarter The herring fishery, employing so many persons during the summer and autumn, is injurious to the agriculture of the island, and interferes greatly with the proper securing of the crops within the last twenty years the Isle of Man was included in the districts occupying the attention of the Cumberland Agricultural Society The land is chiefly divided into farms containing from fifty to two hundred acres, and that in the immediate neighbourhood of the towns is cultivated by the inhabitants, who, after retaining a sufficient portion of the produce for the supply of their own families, send the remainder to market The enclosures are generally from four to ten acres, fenced with sods of earth raised to the height of four or five feet, and planted on the top with furze, uncemented stone fences are also common, and the gate-posts are invariably of stone, and extremely massive. The farm-houses are roofed with slate, and the cottages with thatch, many of the meaner sort are constructed of sods of earth raised up, and thatched, without eaves, consisting only of two rooms on the ground-floor, with an aperture in the roof to let out the smoke, and frequently without a single window Every inhabitant has the right of quarrying stone for his own use, and also, on the annual payment of one halfpenny to the lord, a sum not now demanded, of digging peat upon the mountains The birds that frequent the coasts are the white and grey larus fuscus, gulls, gannets, cormorants, shags, herons, and Royston crows there are not less than eight different species of birds of passage that spend the breeding season in the Calf of Man, among which are the puffin and the razor-bill, the curlew also frequents the Calf, Langness, and other parts of the island. Among those which are accounted game are partridges, woodcocks, snipes, landrails, plovers, teal, widgeons, and wild ducks and geese hares would be very plentiful if not destroyed by snares, the furze and brushwood affording them excellent shelter The streams abound with trout and salmon, generally small, some beautiful species of the molussa, the *actinea rufa* of Linnæus, are found adhering to the rocks, where pools are formed there are no noxious reptiles in the island

The principal minerals are lead and copper ore, of which veins are found in several of the mountains, the chief mines are at Laxey, Foxdale, and Brada-head, near Port Erin The mines at Laxey are situated near the banks of the Laxey river, and about a mile above the village, they are worked in two levels driven from the steep banks of the river in the higher level, which was opened towards the close of the last century, and extends to the depth of one hundred yards, lead and copper ore are found together, with much blende, some zinc, and a kind of mineral earth, called black jack, which generally sells for thirty-six shillings per ton, and of which a great quantity is sent to Bristol, where, after being ground and prepared, it is manufactured into black paint; the lead-ore contains a large quantity of silver, in some instances in the proportion of two hundred ounces, and generally in that of from sixty to eighty ounces to the ton. The new level is situated about a quarter of a mile further down the river, and is twenty-eight yards below the level of the former mine its chief use is to drain off the water from the upper mine the only metallic substances it had produced in 1808 were carbonate of copper and blende, at that period it had been extended two hundred yards in depth, but the produce was not sufficient to pay the expense of working it The Foxdale mines, between Castletown and St John s, of which the chief produce is lead, with a small portion of copper, after having been for some time relinquished, were resumed, and, in 1830, a new vein of lead-ore was discovered within a few feet from the surface, which promises an abundant supply, with little labour and expense these mines are now being worked with great benefit to the proprietors, to whom they are likely to prove an ample source of wealth sulphuret of copper is also found in those of Brada head, which are worked only at intervals, and between Port-Erin and Kirk-Arbory are shafts of lead mines now deserted The mines belong, by prerogative, to the lord proprietor of the soil, who lets them to companies, consisting generally of nine or ten persons, including the lord, who claims, as lessor, one-eighth part of the produce Limestone is found in various parts of the island, that which is quarried on the coast, to the south of Pool-vash bay, becomes highly indurated, and is of a fine grain and black colour; it is susceptible of a high polish, and is much used for tombstones the steps at the entrances of St Paul s cathedral, in London, are from these quarries, and were presented by Bishop Wilson Below high water mark, at Spanish head, there is a quarry of very tough clay-slate, which is raised in blocks ten or twelve feet long, from eight to twelve inches in breadth, and from four to eight inches in thickness; these blocks are substituted for timber, and used for gate-posts, small bridges across streams, and for other purposes The slate generally is easily split into thin laminæ, well adapted for the roofs of houses, and into thicker slabs, used for walls The public roads, which, till within the last half-century, were dangerous for horsemen in winter, and for carriages even in the summer, have been greatly improved since the passing of an act of parliament, in 1776, by which they were ordered to be eight yards in width, with a ditch on each side, and to be well gravelled on the surface; they are now little inferior to those of England, and are kept in repair by a fund arising from a tax upon retailers of ale and spirituous liquors, on lands, houses, dogs, and by some fines

The chief source of employment is agriculture during the intervals of the seasons great numbers are engaged in the herring fishery, for which the season commences about July, and continues till the end of October there are not less than from two to three hundred boats employed in the trade, which is a source of considerable profit to the fishermen, and furnishes a large supply of food for the inhabitants The immense shoal of herrings that makes its appearance on the British coast, generally in June, is divided in its progress southward into two parts, by the Shetland isles, the western branch passes the Hebrides, and is subdivided, by the northern parts of Ireland, into two parts, of which one disappears in the Atlantic Ocean, and the other passes into the Irish sea The boats employed in the fishery are generally of from fifteen to thirty tons' burden, and mostly without decks this little fleet leaves the harbour in the evening, and returns with its cargoes on the following morning It is a prevailing and long-established custom for the fishermen to offer up public prayer before leaving the harbour, and on no account to go out on the Saturday or Sunday evenings The nets, for the throwing of which certain regulations are in force, are buoyed up with bags of dog-skin inflated with air the produce of each boat is divided into eleven shares and a half, of which two and a half are assigned to the owner of the boat, and one to each fisherman, and a net The nets are always cast after sunset, and taken up before sunrise, and on the return of the fleet to the harbour, great numbers of women and children are employed in carrying the fish to the several receiving houses, which are extensive buildings, generally ninety feet long, sixty feet wide, and thirty feet high, where they are immediately salted, those that are to be preserved white are regularly packed in barrels, with a layer of salt between each row, such as are intended for red herrings are first "royled, or rubbed with salt, in which they remain for two or three days, and are then washed and hung up on rods suspended from the ceiling, within eight feet of the floor, on which fires of wood are kept burning till the fish are sufficiently dried and smoked, when they are packed in barrels for exportation The number of herrings generally cured, though subject to great fluctuation, may be averaged at from eight to ten millions A flight of gulls generally hovers over a shoal of herrings, serving as an index to the fishermen, for which reason the shooting of one of these birds during the fishing season subjects the offender to a penalty of £3

The commerce of the island, previously to the act of revestment in 1765, and the subsequent regulations, consisted principally in the importing and exporting of contraband goods, the average returns of which exceeded £350,000, and by some are stated to have amounted to half a million sterling, per annum during that period the Isle of Man was the grand shelter and storehouse for smugglers, who, as occasion offered, shipped their goods hence to England, Scotland, and Ireland, to the great detriment of the British revenue On the act of revestment, the customs of the ports became vested in the British crown, and were placed under the control of a receiver-general, and subsequently, after various modifications, by an act passed in the 50th of George III, the regulation and management were transferred to the board in England, and have since remained under the superintendence of English commissioners In the interpretation of British acts of parliament, it was formerly contended that they did not extend to the Isle of Man, unless specifically mentioned; and it was questioned whether the word "dominions" comprised this island, but the subject has been decided in the affirmative By an act passed in the 6th of George IV, a new code of revenue laws was framed, the principal feature of which is the system of licensing the importation of certain goods charged with high duties; thus confining it to an extent proportionate to the consumption of the inhabitants, and preventing the island from becoming a depôt for smugglers With very trifling exceptions, the exportation is confined to goods that are the produce or manufacture of the island, on which no export duty is paid. Among the imports are corn, meal, flax, seeds, linen yarn, wood-ashes, and flesh of all kinds, which may be imported from any place duty free, agricultural implements, black cattle, horses, sheep, boards, bricks, cordage, and twine for nets, pack thread, hemp, tackle for the fisheries, hoops, linen, utensils for cloth manufacturers, salt, soap-lees, leather, tiles, trees, and timber, which may be imported duty free from all parts of the United Kingdom, balks, barrels, staves, headings for pipes, ebony, hoops, rod and bar iron, oak planks, oars, spars, pipe clay, and naval stores, from the colonies of Great Britain The revenue, in 1829, was £21,143 8. 7½, and in the same year, ending the 5th of January, 1830, eight vessels were built, of the aggregate burden of five hundred and forty tons The number of ships belonging to the island, in 1829, was two hundred and seventeen, of the aggregate burden of five thousand seven hundred and fourteen tons, and four hundred and fourteen vessels entered inwards, and one hundred and fifty-four cleared outwards The manufacture of sheeting, linen, towelling, sail cloth, and sack-cloth, was introduced about the beginning of the present century, when flax-mills were erected about the same period the woollen manufacture was established there are also extensive breweries, paper-mills, tanneries (chiefly for the Manks' hides and skins), candle and soap manufactories, and various others, which the freedom from the excise duties tends greatly to encourage the quantity of leather being insufficient for the supply of the inhabitants, much is imported from England, which is of a very superior quality Distilleries of all kinds are prohibited by the British government, under a penalty of £200, with forfeiture of all implements employed in the process Brandy, rum, geneva, wine, tea, coffee, chocolate, tobacco, wrought and raw silk, glass, and salt, are among the articles imported by license, the exportation of them being absolutely prohibited. The collector is obliged to give one month's notice of the expiration of licenses, and to receive within fourteen days, all petitions for their renewal, the petitions for imports from England are transmitted to the commissioners at London, and from Scotland to those at Edinburgh On granting the licenses, the parties are bound, under a penalty not exceeding twice the amount of the duties, to import the goods therein mentioned, and if the quantity limited by act of parliament be found insufficient for the consumption of the inhabitants, it may be increased by the Lords of the Treasury

The native inhabitants are naturally of an indolent, credulous, and frequently of a superstitious, character, they are strongly attached to their native vales and mountains, and to their ancient laws and customs Pre-

viously to the act of revestment, they considered themselves independent of every other nation, and they were deeply affected by the sale of the island to the British government, which they imagined would blend the countries, and tend to obliterate their original distinction The higher and the middle ranks associating freely with the English residents, retain few traits of their original character, and many of them are highly accomplished and well informed, those of the lower rank are civil, of an hospitable character, and of a charitable disposition Their language is the Erse, a dialect of the Celtic, many of the country people being unable to understand a word of the English language

The government was originally exercised by a council of elders, called, from a Celtic term of that import, Taxiaxi, or, according to the opinion of a very learned and reverend native of the island, derived from Taxi, a corruption of Taisgi, a guardian, and Acci, hereditary property The first institution of this assembly is attributed to the Danish prince Orry, who having added the Hebrides and the Orcades to his conquest of this island, directed the inhabitants to choose sixteen representatives, and those of the out-isles eight, to assist him in the government. Thus assembly, the representatives of the people from time immemorial, consisted of the principal landowners; what powers they exercised, or for what time the institution continued, cannot be distinctly ascertained In the Chronicon Maniæ, which is continued from the year 1066 to the year 1270, no allusion is made to it, nor is there any record of the people's having had any participation in the government of the island During the time that it was under the Norwegian and Scottish dominion, the ancient form of government appears to have been laid aside, and after the grant of it to the Stanleys, that family retained the feudal government, and, as feudatory princes, lords proprietors of the soil, exercised sovereign authority, dependent only on the British crown Since the act of revestment, the functions of the several officers of administration have been more explicitly defined, but the internal policy, laws, and ancient usages remain unchanged, and it preserves its freedom from the imposition of taxes. Lord Chief Justice Coke observes, that although the island is no parcel of the realm of England, yet it forms part of the dominions of the king, and therefore an acknowledgment of allegiance is preserved in all the public oaths.

The civil government is vested in a governor, lieutenant-governor, a council of ten principal officers, and the House of Keys, consisting of twenty-four constitutional representatives of the people, these estates together constituting a court of Tynwald, by which all public laws are enacted and promulgated. The Governor, who, with all the civil and military officers, is appointed by the crown, is chancellor ex-officio, and he, or his deputy, used formerly to hear and determine all appeals from the inferior courts, on matters not relating to landed property, which appellate jurisdiction was transferred to him in 1777, but in 1793 was restored to the House of Keys his consent, or, in his absence, that of his lieutenant, is necessary to the passing of a law The Lieutenant-Governor performs all the functions of the governor in his absence, and, during his presence, such only as he may choose to entrust to him The Council consists of the lord bishop of the diocese, the attorney-general, the receiver-general, the two deemsters, the clerk of the rolls, the water-bailiff, or admiralty judge, the archdeacon, and the two vicars general, who are *ex-officio* members of that body The duty of the council is to advise the governor, and to assist him in the administration of justice in his several courts, and when not acting in a judicial, or legislative capacity, to act for the public good in a summary way, in cases of emergency, such as laying an embargo on vessels, prohibiting the exportation of grain, or other provisions, in times of scarcity, and similar acts requiring promptitude, a majority of the council is necessary to give validity to their measures The *House of Keys*, consisting of twenty-four of the principal landed proprietors, appears to be only a continuation of the ancient assembly called *Taxiaxi* they are supposed to have obtained the name Keys from their being, in all cases, the interpreters of the common law, to whom lies an appeal from the inferior law courts, and in all cases of disputed titles to landed property, and from their decision an appeal lies only to the king in council To constitute a meeting of the House of Keys, when acting as a separate body, thirteen members must be present they fill up vacancies in their own body by a majority of votes, nominating two persons, who must be possessed of landed property, and above the age of twenty one, of whom the governor returns one, who takes his seat for life they elect a speaker, who must be approved by the governor, and holds his office for life, but without any emolument. The House may be assembled at the pleasure of the governor, who may either accept, or refuse, a tender of resignation from any of the members, if any member, however, accept an office entitling him to become a member of the council, he vacates his seat The three estates may enact, abolish, or revive all insular laws, but before they can be put in force, they must be confirmed by the king, and proclaimed in the Manks and English languages, before the people assembled at the Tynwald Hill, and signed by the governor, or his lieutenant, and such members of the council, and of the House of Keys, as are present at the proclamation. The two *Deemsters* are officers of very extensive jurisdiction and of high authority they are chief justices of the island, one, presiding over the northern part, keeps his court at Ramsey, and the other, over the southern division, holds his court at Douglas they have cognizance of all causes exceeding the sum of 40s, not being actions in which damages are to be assessed, or such as properly belong to the court of Chancery A *High Bailiff* is appointed for each of the four towns, by commission from the governor, and holds his office during the governor's pleasure he is conservator of the peace, and superintendent of police, having jurisdiction in all matters of debt under the amount of 40s, he is also empowered to take the acknowledgment of parties, or the testimony of witnesses, for the probate of all deeds, or instruments, brought before him A *Coroner*, with powers analogous in many respects to those of English sheriffs, is appointed by the governor to each of the six sheadings, or great divisions of the island, he is both a ministerial officer and a conservator of the peace, and, according to an ancient statute, holds his office only for one year in addition to the holding of inquests in case of sudden, or violent

death, he is bound to summon juries, to execute processes issued by the governor and by the judges of the courts of justice, and to carry into effect the sentence of the court in criminal matters, and in breaches of the peace, he can arrest without a warrant, and, after the legal forms have been observed, can sell any property he may have previously distrained it is his duty also to assist in the salvage and sale of wrecks, and he has a deputy in each of the parishes within his sheading, who is called a *Lockman* In each parish there is also an ancient officer, called a *Moar*, whose duty it is to collect the rents, fines, escheats, deodands, waifs, and estrays due to the lord, and to execute the orders of the court baron

The laws of the Isle of Man still retain much of their ancient peculiarity of character, though modified by occasional acts of Tynwald, and in some respects rendered more in unison with those of England The common law was hitherto administered by the deemsters and keys, who, under the lord proprietor, governed the island by a *jus non scriptum*, committed to their loyalty and fidelity, as a sacred trust, and by them orally communicated to posterity This custom appears to have been derived from the Druids, who, as is observed by Cæsar, were deeply versed in the laws, which they would by no means publish for the information of the vulgar Hence the Manks, from the remotest period of antiquity, designated their common law by the name of Breast laws, being deposited in the breasts of the deemsters and keys, and only on important occasions divulged to the people By an act of Tynwald, in 1777, and subsequently, in the 57th of George III, the code now in general use was revised, the institution of the grand jury differing from that of England only in the additional benefit of receiving evidence on the part of the accused, which enables them with more certainty to decide upon the finding of a bill

The principal courts are the court of Chancery, the court of Exchequer, the court of Common Law, the court of General Gaol Delivery, the court of Admiralty, the courts of the Deemsters, the courts of the High Bailiffs, and the Ecclesiastical courts. The *court of Chancery*, in matters of civil property, has the most extensive jurisdiction of all the courts in the island, and is both a court of law and of equity The governor, or, in his absence, the lieutenant-governor, who is the representative of the king, presides in this court, and is assisted by the deemsters, the attorney-general, the clerk of the rolls, and the water-bailiff, or admiralty judge who, since the act of revestment, are all appointed by the king, and hold their places during his royal pleasure Like the English court of Chancery, the proceedings are conducted without the intervention of a jury, and, with the exception only of power to imprison for contempt, this court has equal authority the proceedings in equity differ from those at common law more in practice than in principle. In order to prosecute a suit on the law side of the court, a common action is entered at the Rolls' office, and process granted thereon by the governor, three days previously to the meeting of the court, which is generally on the first Thursday in every month, at Castletown, the defendant must be summoned by the coroner, or his deputy, to appear at the next court day, when the action is called in rotation by the coroner. Should he neglect to appear, an attachment against him may be sued for, and renewed at the second, third, and fourth meetings of the court, at the last of which, if it be a matter of debt, and not defended, it may either be heard and determined on the plaintiff's own oath, or it may be, at his option, deferred to the next court Should the cause of action be disputed, or denied, by the defendant, the court may transfer it for trial in the deemster's court by a jury at common law, or to any other court, ecclesiastical or civil, as the nature of the case may require When a common action for debt is taken out, either against a native about to leave the island, or against a stranger, the defendant may not only be arrested and imprisoned, but his effects may be taken possession of by the constable, till he give security for his personal appearance, and after the decree has been issued, the effects must be sold by auction, or so much as will satisfy the creditor, after paying one year s rent, if due, and such servants wages as may be due by the defendant at the time On the equity side of the court, the proceedings are carried on by bill and answer, as in the English court The Manks law compels a native debtor to give up all his present and future effects to his creditors, but exempts him from imprisonment a native cannot be arrested, or held to bail, for debt, unless he is about to leave the island, and has obtained the governor's pass for that purpose The laws relating to bankruptcy, as practised in England, are wholly unknown in the Manks jurisprudence if an insolvent shall have faithfully accounted for, and delivered up, his property on oath for the satisfaction of his creditors, the governor may order him an allowance of sixpence per day for his subsistence, and in default of payment weekly, liberate the prisoner In respect of arbitrations, no proceedings are cognizable without a rule of court entered into by consent of the parties No person paying a lord s rent of an ancient quarterland, or £3 of yearly intack, which is regarded as equivalent, is liable to arrest for debt

The *court of Exchequer* takes cognizance of all matters connected with the revenue proceedings are here carried on for the recovery of penalties and forfeitures due to the crown, incurred by frauds upon the customs the governor, or lieutenant-governor, presides in this court, which is generally held immediately after the court of Chancery, and has power to make, from time to time, such orders and rules for regulating its proceedings as may be found necessary this court also imposes fines, and determines the right of tithes, which, previously to the act of Tynwald, in 1777, had been cognizable only in the ecclesiastical courts The *court of Common Law* is held at Castle Rushen, or at such other place as the governor shall appoint, in Hilary term, on the Tuesday next after the first Thursday in February, in Easter term, on the Tuesday next after the first Thursday in May, in Trinity term, on the Tuesday next after the last Thursday in June, and in Michaelmas term, on the Tuesday next after the 5th of October. This court, in which the governor, or lieutenant governor presides, assisted by the deemster, takes cognizance of all actions real, personal, and mixed, and of all suits at common law that require to be determined by a jury, which practice of trial by jury appears to have obtained in all places wherein the feudal system was adopted, and in this island has continued from

time immemorial The juries consist of six men, summoned by the coroner, from whose verdict an appeal lies to the House of Keys, who may proceed in the matter according to their judgment, the appellant must, within twenty-one days after the recording of the verdict, give a bond of £3 that he will prosecute the appeal. In cases of trespass, a jury of four men, who are a jury of enquiry, are summoned by one of the deemsters from the parish in which the trespass was committed, or any loss sustained, whose province it is to view and estimate the injury, and to endeavour to discover by whom it was committed The court is opened by the coroner of Glanfaba, with an address in the Manks language The *court of General Gaol Delivery* is held at Rushen Castle twice in the year, or at such times as the governor, or, in his absence, the lieutenant-governor, may direct in this court the governor, or lieutenant-governor, presides, assisted by the bishop of the diocese, the archdeacon, the two vicars-general, the deemsters, the attorney-general, the clerk of the rolls, the water-bailiff, or admiralty judge, and other officers, for determining upon all offences which by the laws of the island are deemed capital The proceedings, by statute of 1777 and an act of Tynwald in the 57th of George III, require the bill of indictment to be previously found by the grand jury, who not only hear the evidence in behalf of the prosecution, but also receive depositions on the part of the prisoner, by these means they are enabled to decide with greater certainty on the necessity of putting the prisoner on his trial, for which purpose four men are summoned from each of the seventeen parishes in the island, and when a jury of twelve men is empanelled, they are sworn and charged by the deemster the prosecution is conducted by the attorney-general, and counsel is allowed to the prisoner When the pleadings are concluded, and the jury have agreed on their verdict, if it be a capital offence, the deemster demands of the foreman, in the Manks language, "*Vod fir charree soie?* in English, "May he that ministers at the altar continue to sit? if the foreman answers that he may, a verdict of not guilty is returned, and the prisoner is instantly discharged, but should he answer that he may not, it is understood to be the precursor of a verdict of guilty, and the bishop and his clergy immediately retire, the verdict is returned, and the senior deemster then pronounces sentence of death, but the execution is delayed till his Majesty's pleasure shall be known.

The *court of Admiralty*, in which the water-bailiff presides as sole judge, is held every Saturday, and takes cognizance of all pleas respecting maritime affairs, and of all offences committed on the seas, within the distance of three leagues from the shores of the island, and, according to ancient statutes, has the superintendence of all concerns relating to the herring fishery Suitors in this court must apply verbally, or by petition, stating the cause of complaint a summons is then granted to compel the defendant to appear at the next court, when the witnesses on both sides are examined, and the cause is heard and determined, either with or without the assistance of a jury, at the discretion of the judge Should he deem the cause of sufficient importance to require the attendance of a jury, the judge issues his warrant to the coroner, requiring him to summon four persons out of his sheading, who must give a unanimous verdict, whereupon the judge pronounces his decree, from which in all civil cases an appeal lies to the governor The *Deemsters courts*, which are of great antiquity, are held weekly in the north and south districts into which the island is divided, the former at Ramsey, and the latter at Douglas they take cognizance of slanders, assaults, batteries, debts, contracts, and all causes not involving the inheritance of land, the process is conducted without the intervention of a jury, and is attended with many advantages independently of their celerity and cheapness The deemster, in particular cases, will elicit a discovery of facts in the absence of more direct evidence, will order the production of deeds and papers not before the court, but essential to a right judgment of the case, which frequently precludes the necessity of a bill in equity, and in all disputes between landlord and tenant, with respect to the possession of lands and tenements, the cause is heard in a summary way, and in the latter instance the deemster by his judgment orders immediate possession to be given In all the courts of the island the parties are at liberty to plead their own cause in person, which is generally practised, and till lately there existed very few attorneys, or, as they are here called, advocates but in matters of great importance the pleadings are usually conducted by an advocate, who, by the statute of 1777, must be commissioned by the governor, and take the requisite oaths By the same statute, should any advocate become bail in an action, or carry on a suit by *champarty*, that is, by making any contract either before or during the pleadings, to have part of the lands or profits that may form the object of the suit, he is liable to be fined, or imprisoned, at the discretion of the court, and be rendered incapable of practising in future The *High Bailiffs courts* are held at Castletown, Douglas, Peel, and Ramsey, for the recovery of debts under 40s, the proceedings are similar to those of courts of requests in England The court for insolvent debtors, which is held quarterly at Castletown, is similar to the English court The *Ecclesiastical courts* are, the consistorial court, the court of the vicars-general, and chapter, or circuit court The consistorial court, in which the bishop, or his vicars-general, and registrar preside, takes cognizance of all matters relating to the probates of wills, granting letters of administration, alimony, church assessments, the guardianship of property belonging to minors, and cases of defamation. The court of the vicars-general has cognizance generally of all offences against religion and the interests of the church, and in all cases not cognizable by the common law courts The chapter, or circuit, court takes cognizance of all matters connected with the see, and the general affairs of the diocese The proceedings in all these courts, when not otherwise provided for by local enactments, are regulated conformably to the practice of similar courts in England

Since the grant of the island, by Henry IV, to Sir John Stanley, it has been governed by its own peculiar laws Its most ancient records are the laws and ordinances enacted by the court of Tynwald, in 1417, the first of which was an act passed by commissioners appointed by the lord of the island and the House of Keys, to prevent abuses of the places of sanctuary, at that time appointed for criminals by some of the ecclesiastics of the island The Manks' statute book commences in 1422, and contains a collection of statutes, ordinances, and customs, "presented, reputed, and used for the laws of the island.' The laws enacted in the fifteenth and sixteenth centuries have but little weight as precedents, a more regular system of legislation subsisted in 1764, subsequently to which period very few alterations have been made The feudal tenure, by which the tenants held their lands in villainage, at the absolute will of the King of Man, or lord proprietor of the soil, in process of time gave way to a more liberal tenure, called holding by the straw, similar to the ancient tenure of the verge in England At length the tenants became not only ascriptitious to the soil, but acquired permanent estates in land descendible from ancestor to heir, in the nature of free soccage, but there are no statutes declaratory of the settled mode of descent, or of the alienation of lands, prior to the act of Tynwald passed by James, Earl of Derby, his council, deemsters, and keys, in 1645 It is supposed that, prior to the passing of that act, the lord's officers had prevailed upon many proprietors of lands to surrender their estates, which descended to the eldest son, and, in default of male issue, to the eldest daughter, and to accept from the lord leases for lives in lieu of them, but the House of Keys interfering, obtained from the earl not only the passing of that act, but ultimately the celebrated act of settlement, which is emphatically designated the Manks *Magna Charta*, in the year 1704 By this act, the purchaser of a farm, quarterland, or other real property, may alienate, or devise his estate, which, if not disposed of, remains as assets, in default of personal property, for the payment of all debts, whether of specialty or of simple contract, without any preference. By the Manks common law, such property, after one descent from the purchaser, becomes an absolute estate of inheritance, descending to the eldest son, or, in default of male issue, to the eldest daughter, and, in default of issue, to the next of kin, but subject always to any gift, grant, sale, mortgage, lease, or assignment, executed by deed of the owner, to the payment of arrears of the lord s rent, in default of personal property, and to forfeiture for felony or treason Though lands may be alienated by deed, they cannot by will, except by the first purchaser, neither, after one descent from the purchaser, are they subject to any other than mortgage debts, except property consisting of mills, cottages, or intacks The term of a Manks' purchase cannot be construed in the larger and more extended sense of Lyttleton s *Perquisitio*, which includes every kind of title, except only that of hereditary transmission, for, in this island, it is considered only as a purchase for a valuable consideration The quarterlands, which are analogous to the hides in England, usually comprising about one hundred acres, have, from time immemorial, been considered as property of the highest order in the island, and, though absolute estates of inheritance, are subject by the act of settlement to the payment of a rent to the lord, and a certain fine upon descent or alienation The tenants names are, by the act, to be entered in the office rolls, to the intent that, in the event of the conveyance being destroyed, the title may not be impugned, and the estates are thus absolutely and irrevocably confirmed An estate on which is an unredeemed mortgage of five years standing passes to the mortgagee, who then becomes the lord's tenant, and pays a certain fine, as in cases of alienation, but the mortgagers have the power of redemption within twenty-one years from the date of the mortgage All mortgages are null and void if not recorded within six months from the time of their being executed the most expeditious and easy mode of recovering either the interest or principal due on a mortgage is by application to the court of the deemster, who, after summoning the parties, and hearing the case, will, if the property consist of quarterlands of inheritance, either order the interest to be levied on the personal effects of the mortgager, or give possession of the premises to the mortgagee, who may hold them till payment of the principal, interest, costs, and all other charges be made, according to the conditions of the mortgage deed In this case he must let the premises by public auction to the highest bidder, and apply the rents to the reduction and discharge of the mortgage If the premises be purchased lands, cottages, mills, or intacks, the deemster will, if the mortgage deed be in the usual form of bond and security, order payment to be made out of them Estates consisting of cottages, mills, and intacks, are subject to the payment of debts of the owner, and may be alienated by gift, grant, demise, will, or assignment, but, by the statute of 1777, cannot be deemed personal effects, or chattels, nor made assets in the hands of executors, or be claimed by right or consanguinity, in exclusion of the heir at law No entail on hereditaments within the island can be created beyond the life of the grantor, or the heirs of persons *in esse* The common conveyance of a Manks' freehold is a deed signed by the parties in the presence of two witnesses, not indented, and without seal or stamp, neither of which is necessary for the validity of any deed, except instruments of a public nature, and letters of attorney to be used out of the island, in which cases the government seal is requisite It is usual and adviseable for the parties to any deed to acknowledge it before a magistrate, who verifies it under his own hand to be their act, and it then becomes admissible as evidence in any court of justice within the island, without the necessity of producing witnesses to prove its execution There is no statutable form prescribed for the execution of written wills, except that, in cases of land, it is requisite to have two witnesses, but by the statute of 1777, no nuncupative will is valid unless proved by the oaths of two witnesses, and the words, or the substance of them, committed to writing within ten days after the uttering or publishing thereof If a man marries an heiress and survives her, he shall be entitled to one moiety of her estate, so long as he remains a widower, and also to a moiety of her purchased lands, and during coverture he is solely entitled to the rents and profits, and an heiress after marriage has no power to sell, or lease, her estate, without being joined in a deed to that effect by her husband, neither can the husband sell, or make a lease, of his own estate, without the consent of his wife, so as to prejudice her right in case of survivorship If a man marry a second wife, having issue by the first, the second can claim after his decease only one-fourth part of his estate of inheritance, during her widowhood, but if there be no issue by the first wife, she can claim a moiety If a woman be married to a man who is seized of an absolute freehold of inheritance, and survives him,

she is entitled to one moiety of his estate, and also to a moiety of his purchased lands, and even in the lifetime of her husband may dispose of them by will to such of her children as she shall think proper, or to her husband, but to no other person, but this right of dower may be barred by settlement before marriage

The military establishment of the island consists generally of a company or two of regular troops detached from regiments in England, stationed at Castletown, for manning the garrisons, and for the defence of the coast, under the command of the governor each of the parishes furnishes four men on horseback, armed with a sabre and a pike, under a captain appointed by the governor, and in each there is also an officer appointed by the governor, called the captain of the parish, with powers similar to those of the high bailiffs of the four towns, for the preservation of the peace

The four towns are, Castletown, Douglas, Peel, and Ramsey CASTLETOWN, in the parish of Kirk-Malen, anciently called Rushen, being the seat of government, is considered the capital it is situated at the southern extremity of the island, and on the western shore of Castletown bay, opposite the promontory of Langness point, 9½ miles (S W) from Douglas, the principal port, and contains 2036 inhabitants This, which is the most ancient of the towns, is supposed to have been coeval with the erection of the castle of Rushen, from which it had its name, and which was founded by Guttred, the second Danish sovereign in succession from Orry the present buildings, however, appear to have been mostly erected during the last century, the houses are in general neatly built, the streets are regular and well paved, and the inhabitants are amply supplied with water Near the castle wall is a spacious area, forming the market-place, and a convenient market-house, with an assembly-room over it, was built in 1830 There is a subscription reading-room well supported In the town and vicinity are breweries, corn-mills, and a tannery The town is intersected by a small river, over which are a drawbridge, opposite to the castle, for foot passengers, and higher up a bridge of stone for carriages The castle, which is of great strength, and was originally the principal fortress in the island, is situated on the west side of the river, which is nearly dry at low water, and is considered to bear a striking resemblance to the castle of Elsinore in Denmark it is surrounded by a lofty embattled wall and fosse, and defended by a glacis of stone, said to have been added by Cardinal Wolsey, when he was guardian to Edward, Earl of Derby The building is quadrangular, with square towers on the sides, the largest more than eighty feet high within the area are some commodious and recently modernised apartments, appropriated as the residence of the lieutenant-governor, and a spacious room in which the several courts of law are held, and on the walls are three buildings of small dimensions, where the records are kept, and the business of the Rolls office is transacted The keep, which is built of hard limestone resembling that found in the neighbourhood, is still entire, forming the only prison in the island it was formerly a very dreary dungeon, in which prisoners were crowded together in dark and damp chambers, but, in 1815, the interior of the castle underwent considerable alterations, and the keep was converted into a prison, divided into three classes, for debtors, and for male and female crimmals   In addition to the general law courts, the Tynwald court, the deemsters summary courts, assembled when they think proper, the water-bailiff's court, every Saturday, the court of the high bailiff of the town, the jurisdiction of which extends over the parishes of Kirk-Arbory, Kirk-Malew, Kirk-Christ-Rushen, and Kirk-St Anne, for the recovery of debts under 40s, every Saturday, the court for insolvent debtors, quarterly, and the chapter and circuit courts of the vicars-general, in spring and autumn, are held within the castle walls   From the summit of the tower, now appropriated to the execution of criminals, there is an extensive view of the surrounding country, and of Castletown and Pool-vash bays   Near the castle is a neat building for the meeting of the House of Keys   In the vicinity many handsome edifices have been erected within these few years   in levelling the ground for the erection of Lorn House, and the formation of the pleasure grounds, some stone coffins and bones were found   At the distance of a few hundred yards from the town, on the road to Derby haven, was formerly the place of execution, called Hango Hill, where Receiver-General William Christian was shot, in 1662, for surrendering the island to the parliamentarians   The numerous rocks in the bay render access to the town by sea so difficult, that most of the supplies for the consumption of the inhabitants are landed at Douglas bay, or Derby haven, from which latter place a great quantity of corn is exported   The parochial church, Kirk-Malew, is one mile and a half from the town   the old chapel, erected in 1698 by Bishop Wilson, was taken down in 1826, and the present edifice, handsomely built of limestone cemented, with an octagonal tower, has been erected, at an expense of £1600   the interior is well arranged, and contains one thousand one hundred sittings, of which three hundred are free, the Incorporated Society for building and enlarging churches and chapels having granted £300 towards defraying the expense   There are places of worship for Primitive and Wesleyan Methodists, and Roman Catholics   King William's College was founded, in 1830, by the Hon Cornelius Smelt, lieutenant-governor, Dr Ward, bishop of the diocese, and the other trustees of property granted by Bishop Barrow, in 1668, for the promotion of sound learning, and for the education and support of two young men, to supply the Manks churches, and other charitable and pious uses   The course of studies embraces religious instruction suited to the age of the pupils, the classics, mathematics, oriental literature, the modern languages, navigation, and other sciences, forming a complete and general system of education   The principal, and the other masters, with the exception only of the professors of the oriental and modern languages, must be members of the church of England, and graduates of one of the Universities   the masters, under certain regulations, are allowed to receive pupils of the college, as boarders, the pupils pay a small sum per quarter towards the funds of the college, and a small admission fee towards the establishment of a library   Provision is made, by Bishop Barrow's gift, for the further education at either of the Universities of young men intended for the church, and when the funds of the college will allow it, professors of divinity, law, physic, and surgery, will be added for the benefit of such pupils as, having passed through the ordinary

courses of study in the college, may be unable to complete their professional education elsewhere   The buildings, partly in the early English, and partly in the Elizabethan, style of architecture, form a spacious cruciform structure, two hundred and ten feet in length from east to west, and one hundred and thirty-five feet from north to south   from the intersection rises an embattled tower, one hundred and fifteen feet high, strengthened with buttresses, surmounted by an octagonal lantern turret, intended for an observatory, having in each of its faces an elegant lofty window, and crowned with a parapet and handsome pinnacles, carried up from angular buttresses   they include a handsome church, in the early English style, and were erected partly with the money saved out of the academic fund, and partly by the liberal subscriptions of the inhabitants, the expense of building the church having been defrayed from funds collected in England by Bishop Ward, for the erection of new churches in the island   there are also a public lecture-room, a large hall for a library, four large class rooms, and houses for the masters, containing numerous apartments for the accommodation of pupils, and every requisite arrangement for the purposes of the institution   this extensive and handsome pile of building was erected under the superintendence, and after a design, of Messrs Hansom and Welch, of Liverpool, who are also the architects of the several churches now in progress of erection in the island   A National school, in which two hundred and twenty children are instructed, is supported by subscription, and a parochial charity school for twenty boys is supported by the impropriate funds of the island   Mrs Catherine Halsalls, in 1758, bequeathed £8 per annum to a mistress, to teach poor girls to read, sew, knit, and spin, and £2 per annum for repairing the school-house, and Mr and Mrs Taubman, in 1799, bequeathed £25 per annum for the support of a free school for twenty-five boys, of which sum, £20 is appropriated as a salary to the master, and £5 to the purchase of books   At Derby haven, which has been previously noticed as a place of landing for persons visiting Castletown, is a small village, chiefly consisting of cottages and some large herring warehouses, and in the neighbourhood of the town are several lime-kilns

DOUGLAS, the largest, most populous, and greatest commercial town in the island, containing 6054 inhabitants, is situated near the centre of the eastern coast, and on the south of the large semicircular bay of the same name, in the parish of Kirk-Braddan   The town derives its name from the rivers Dhoo and Glass uniting their streams a little above it, and falling into the harbour   it is of a triangular form, the longest side extending from the bridge at the upper end of the harbour, in a north-easterly direction, towards the coast, and the shortest from the same point in a direction towards the pier   The streets are in many parts inconvenient and narrow, and the houses without order or uniformity of appearance, but, from the relative importance of its commerce, and the advantages of its port, it has undergone considerable improvements, and in the suburbs are several new streets regularly formed, and many houses of handsome appearance   The town is partially paved, and lighted during the winter, and the inhabitants are supplied with water brought from a declivity behind the town in casks, and carried about for sale the pier forms an agreeable promenade, and is much frequented To the south is a range of hills, called the How of Douglas, and on the north-east are seen the cliff of Clay Head, and the mountains of Snawfel and Pen-y-Pot, with the spacious intervening bay, to the right of which is a long extent of the Cumberland coast, crowned with distant mountains, and from the summit of Douglas head, still more to the right, the high lands of Wales are plainly discernible The bay, with the town and country above it, rising from its shores in the form of an amphitheatre, forms a beautiful object as approached from the sea and to the north of the town are extensive and firm sands, much frequented by company in carriages, on horseback, and on foot About half a mile beyond the town is Mona castle, the magnificent mansion erected by the late Duke of Athol, of a fine white sand-stone, brought from the Isle of Arran, at an expense of £40,000 this castle, and about one hundred acres of land surrounding it, are the only property now belonging to that family Near it is the elegant marine villa of Col Stewart, pleasantly situated in the centre of grounds tastefully laid out, and adjoining the lodge is the Marine Terrace, a handsome range of houses recently erected At the entrance of the bay, on the south shore, is a battery of two guns, and on the banks of the river, to the west of the town, are several handsome seats, among which is the Nunnery, a building in the early style of English architecture, so called from the contiguous ruins of an ancient religious establishment, founded, according to Manks tradition, in the sixth century, by St Bridget, of which the prioress was anciently a baroness of the island The salubrity of the air, and the fineness of the beach, have rendered Douglas a place of general resort for sea-bathing, and suitable residences and lodging-houses have been erected at the northern extremity of the bay, and in the town, for the accommodation of the numerous visitors who frequent it during the summer season a large hotel, with bathing machines and every requisite accommodation, has been established on the coast of the bay, and in the town are several hotels and boarding-houses A commodious establishment of hot and cold sea-water baths was erected in 1816 A neat theatre is opened during the season, and assemblies are held in an elegant suite of rooms at the British Hotel there are several libraries, news-rooms, and billiard tables, in various parts of the town, and a United Service club was established in 1829 Considerable trade is carried on at this port with the neighbouring coasts, and ship-building, both for home and for foreign use, consisting chiefly of small vessels and fishing-boats, is greatly encouraged, the shipwrights being much esteemed for their skill in the construction of those vessels there are also several extensive soap-manufactories, tan-yards, breweries, and corn-mills in the town and neighbourhood. The custom-house, a commodious building, formerly the residence of the Duke of Athol, is situated on the quay The intercourse with the neighbouring kingdoms has been greatly facilitated by means of steam-packets the post-office for the whole island is established in this town, to which letters are brought by the steam-packets from Liverpool, three times in the week during the summer, and once during the winter There are two steam-packets from Douglas to Liverpool direct, every other day, and during the summer the voyage,

seventy-two miles long, is performed in eight hours. Scotch steam-vessels running between Liverpool and Glasgow call here daily, and one from Whitehaven to Dublin calls every Saturday, on her way thither, and every Monday on her return, during the summer there are also several traders from this port to Liverpool, Whitehaven, and to the Scotch and Irish ports The Isle of Man district association of the Royal National Institution, for the preservation of life from shipwreck, which institution originated in this island, under the auspices of Sir William Hillary, Bart, is held in this town It was founded in 1824, under the immediate patronage of the king, the princes of the blood royal, and many of the leading men in the state, and, since its establishment, has paid premiums and bestowed honorary medals for the recovery of one thousand four hundred and forty-six lives it provides with food, clothing, medical assistance, and the means of restoring to their homes, the destitute sufferers of all nations, and has life-boats and a complete set of Captain Manby s apparatus in constant readiness at all the principal ports This district association is under the immediate superintendence of the lieutenant-governor, as patron, Sir William Hillary, Bart, president, the Bishop and the Speaker of the House of Keys, vice-presidents, and a general committee of members of the legislature and of the principal inhabitants The market is on Saturday, and is well supplied with provisions of all kinds brought from different parts of the island the town is amply supplied with fresh fish throughout the year, and with a little salmon during the summer months, the fair is on November 12th, for cattle The deemster for the southern division holds his court here as often as may be necessary, and the high bailiff every Saturday, for the recovery of debts under 40s, the jurisdiction of the latter extends over the parishes of Kirk-Braddan, Kirk-Onchan, Kirk-Lonan, and Kirk-Marown the vicars-general hold an ecclesiastical court every alternate Friday, and a chapter, or circuit court, in spring and autumn The court-house, a plain building, is situated near the pier, and has a small lock-up house for the confinement of offenders previously to their being sent to Castletown for trial The parochial church, called Kirk-Braddan, is two miles distant, on the road to Peel. On one side of the market-place is a small chapel, dedicated to St Matthew, containing about three hundred sittings, to which is attached a library established by Bishop Wilson, and augmented by Bishop Hyldersley with a bequest of two hundred volumes, and on an eminence to the west of the town is a neat chapel, dedicated to St George, containing one thousand sittings A new chapel, which will accommodate one thousand five hundred persons, is now being erected in Fort-street, to be dedicated to St Barnabas it is a neat building in the early style of English architecture, with turrets crowned with pinnacles at the angles of the nave, the interior is lighted by a long range of fifteen clerestory windows on each side, at the west end is a handsome tower, surmounted by a spire, a hundred and forty feet high The livings are perpetual curacies, in the patronage of the Bishop There are places of worship for Independents, Primitive and Wesleyan Methodists, and Roman Catholics A National school, established in 1810, for which commodious school-rooms have been erected in Athol-street, at an expense of

£1120, is supported by subscription, for the instruction of one hundred and twenty boys, and one hundred and twenty girls, an infant school, in which are one hundred children, has been recently established. The establishment of a public kitchen, under the superintendence of the high bailiff, to which each inhabitant contributes what he may think proper, has afforded material relief from the importunate visits of the poor, to which other parishes are exposed those poor persons who, from infirmity or illness, cannot attend the public table, are provided with food at their own houses. A medical dispensary has been instituted within the last few years, and is well supported, and there are various benefit and friendly societies in the town.

PEEL, anciently called Holme town, in the parish of Kirk-German, is situated on the western coast, 10½ miles (N W) from Douglas, and 12 from Castletown, and contains 1909 inhabitants. It is chiefly remarkable for the remains of its ancient castle and cathedral church, to which it was indebted for its early importance. it was a place of considerable commerce prior to the suppression of the contraband trade, and was the grand resort of smugglers, but since that period the inhabitants have been principally employed in agriculture and in the fisheries, herrings on this part of the coast being taken in the greatest abundance, and not less than seventy boats belong to the harbour. The remains of the castle are situated on a small rocky island, about one hundred yards west of the town, being separated from it by Peel river, which is scarcely a foot deep at low water, and joined to the main land by a stone wall shelving towards the summit, built many years since to defend the harbour. the entrance was formerly by a flight of steps on the eastern side, now almost worn away by time. the walls, which are from three to four feet thick, and flanked with towers, are built of clay-slate, and are in many places quoined and faced with red sand-stone, they enclose a polygonal area of about five acres, which is almost filled with the ruins of walls, buildings, and dwelling-houses, and in the centre is a pyramidal mound of earth, about seventeen yards at the base, surrounded by a ditch five feet and a half broad, supposed to have been either a tumulus raised over the ashes of some illustrious chief, or from the summit of which harangues were made to the populace. the time of the erection of the castle is not known, but it is by some supposed to have been prior to the foundation of Castle Rushen. Till the act of revestment, this fortress, as well as Rushen castle, was garrisoned by native troops, in the pay of the lord of the isles, but since the island became vested in the British crown, the armoury has been removed, the garrison reduced, and the building suffered to decay within the walls is a two gun battery. Eleanor, wife of Humphrey, Duke of Gloucester, in the reign of Henry VI, and the Earl of Warwick, who for a time was banished to this island, were at different times confined in this castle. Within the area are the ruins of the ancient church of St German, erected about the year 1245, as the cathedral church, which has not been used, except as a burying-place, for many years beneath the eastern part of it is the ancient ecclesiastical prison, a vault eighteen feet deep, of which the

groined roof is supported on low dwarf pillars, and in one corner is a well. Some of the arches in the transept are remaining, but the building is unroofed and hastening to decay. Bishop Wilson was the last prelate who was enthroned in this church. The ruins of St Patrick's church are a little to the westward of it this is supposed to have been the first Christian church in the island, and, though roofless and in a greatly dilapidated state, it retains some characteristics of the Nor man style of architecture. In the rocks along the neighbouring coast are many curious caverns agates and cornelians are found on the sands. The town is paved, and supplied with water from wells. The market is on Friday, chiefly for provisions, with which it is well supplied, and there are fairs on March 28th and July 24th, for horses and cattle. The deemsters hold their courts here occasionally, and the high bailiff every Saturday, for the recovery of debts under 40s, the jurisdiction of the latter extends over the parishes of Kirk Ballaugh, Kirk-St German, Kirk Michael, and Kirk Patrick the vicars-general hold a chapter, or circuit court, in spring and autumn a new court house is at present being erected. The parochial church, dedicated to St Peter, is not distinguished for its architecture, it will accommodate five hundred persons. The free grammar school was founded, in 1746, by Philip Moore, Esq, who endowed it with £500, directing the interest to be paid to a master qualified to teach "the Latin language, and such other learning as may prepare youth for the service of their country in church and state, the bishop and the twenty four keys are trustees. A mathematical school was founded, in 1763, by the Rev James Moore, of Dublin, who bequeathed the ground-rent of three houses in that city, producing then £20 Irish per annum. he also ordered his books to be sold, or exchanged, for mathematical books and instruments for its use. John Stevenson, Esq, of Ashley Park, in the county of Surrey, bequeathed £100 for the instruction of two additional boys, and Cæsar Corris, Esq, in 1826, gave also £100 for the instruction of two boys of his own kindred, or, in default of such, for any other boys of the town the school premises, which were left by Sir George Moore, are in a dilapidated state, no funds having been appropriated for keeping them in repair. Philip Christian, Esq, in 1652, left two houses in Lovel's Inn, Paternoster Row, London, to the Master and Wardens of the Clothworkers Company, in trust for the yearly payment of £20 to two poor boys, natives of the Isle of Man, as apprentice-fees of £10 each, with an order that, if there should not be a free school in the town of Peel, the money should be paid towards the establishment and maintenance of such a school, £18 per annum of which sum to be paid to the master, and £2 per annum to be appropriated to the purchase of books. Bishop Wilson bequeathed £50 for the instruction of poor girls, and Mr William Cain left a small piece of land for teaching children. About three miles from the town is the Tynwald Mount, where all new laws, according to ancient usage, must be promulgated to the people. the ascent to its summit, which is about eighteen feet high, is by a flight of steps cut in the turf on the western side, around it are several terraces diminishing in breadth from the base. When the legislative assembly is collected, a chair under a canopy is placed on the summit for the governor, or his deputy, below whom, on the terraces, the deemsters, the council, and the keys, take their places, according to their respective orders, the surrounding area being occupied by the people The Tynwald court is held annually on the 5th of July, when different officers are chosen for the year The legislative assembly meet at St John s chapel, from which, after divine service has been performed, they move in procession to the mount

RAMSEY is situated on the north-eastern coast, in the parish of Kirk-Maughold, 15½ miles (N N E) from Douglas, and 25 (N E) from Castletown, near the mouth of the river Sulby, the largest in the island, over which is a stone bridge of three arches, one hundred and fifty feet in length, and twelve in width it contains 1523 inhabitants The town is irregularly built, but the streets are wide, clean, and well paved, and the inhabitants are amply supplied with water The surrounding country is remarkably picturesque, and in a high state of cultivation. Several handsome seats and pleasing villas, inhabited chiefly by native families of respectability, have been erected There are many flourishing apple orchards, and the stone fences on most of the estates have given place to quickset hedges The neighbourhood is remarkable as the scene of the numerous battles fought between the Danes and the Scots, when the latter had possession of the island The trade is principally in exporting Manks' produce, especially wheat the amount of exports is about £40,000 per annum there are no imports, except coal, lime, and such commodities, all colonial and foreign produce being, by act of parliament, landed exclusively at Douglas the custom-house and the revenue establishment here are under the control of the receiver-general at that port Seven steam-packets between Liverpool and Glasgow call at this port twice in the week The market, on Saturday, is abundantly supplied with provisions, which are lower in price than at any other town in the island The common law courts are held here quarterly, at which a deemster presides, and the deemster for the northern division of the island holds his court occasionally, and the high bailiff every Saturday, for the recovery of debts under 40s, the jurisdiction of the latter extends over the parishes of Kirk-Andreas, Kirk-Bride, Kirk-Jurby, Kirk-Christ-Lezayre, and Kirk Maughold An ecclesiastical court, in which either the bishop or his vicar-general presides, is held every alternate week, and a chapter, or circuit court, in spring and autumn The court-house, which is the largest in the island, is a neat building ornamented over the entrances with the arms of England and those of the island sculptured in stone The parish church, dedicated to St Bridget, is nearly three miles distant from the town, near Maughold head A chapel, dedicated to St Paul, is situated in the market-place, and was erected in 1819, by subscription, and a grant of £300 from the Incorporated Society for promoting the enlargement of churches and chapels, in consideration of providing free seats for the poor it is a neat edifice, with a tower, and contains sittings for five hundred persons the old chapel, just without the town, is now used only as a burying-place for strangers There are places of worship for Independents, and Primitive, and Wesleyan Methodists The grammar

school was founded, about the year 1760, by Mr Charles Cowell, who gave a piece of land, on which to erect a school-room, which was built by subscription, the master, who is minister of the chapel, receives a small quarterage from the bishop's registrar, and formerly an annual sum of £10, called Salt money, was paid by Lord Cholmeley, which, though it has been discontinued for many years, is not lost, as, in 1828, an agent from Chester called on the high bailiff, and offered to pay the money, on receiving a proper discharge, but the bishop not being at that time in the island, the money was not paid Captain John Kilpatrick left £200 to the poor, and £100 to the parochial school, and Mr Edward Christian left the moiety of an estate, producing nearly £7 per annum, for the same purpose There are two National schools, one for boys, and the other for girls, both supported by subscription

Arms of the Bishoprick.

The ecclesiastical government is vested in a bishop the see, according to Camden, was first established, in the ninth century, by Pope Gregory IV, in the small village of Sodor, in Iona, or St Columb s isle, corruptly called Icolmkill, a small island of the Hebrides In 1098, Magnus, King of Norway, having by conquest obtained possession of those islands and the Isle of Man, united them under one bishop, under whose jurisdiction they continued till the year 1333, when the English possessed themselves of the Isle of Man, and since that period, though the bishop has maintained no claim to the see of Sodor, he has retained the ancient title, being still styled Bishop of Sodor and Man He enjoys all the dignities and spiritual rights of other bishops, with the exception of having a vote in the house of peers, in which, by courtesy only, he has a seat, the see not being a barony The see of Man was annexed to the province of York by Henry VIII, in the 33rd year of his reign Under the bishop, it is governed by an archdeacon, two vicars general, an episcopal registrar, an official, and other officers

The island is divided into six sheadings, each of them containing three parishes, with the exception of the sheading of Garff, which contains only two there are no church-rates or poor-rates, the churches being usually built and repaired by subscription, and the wants of the poor relieved by collections at the doors of the churches, distributed among them by the church, or chapel, wardens Ayre sheading comprises the parishes of Kirk-Andreas, Kirk-Bride, and Kirk-Christ-Lezayre, Garff sheading, the parishes of Kirk-Lonan and Kirk-Maughold, and Michael sheading, the parishes of Kirk-Ballaugh, Kirk-Jurby, and Kirk-Michael these sheadings are included within the northern division of the island In the southern division are Glanfaba sheading, comprising the parishes of Kirk-German, Kirk-Marown, and Kirk-Patrick, Middle sheading, the parishes of Kirk-St Anne, Kirk-Braddan, and Kirk-Onchan, and Rushen sheading, the parishes of Kirk-Arbory, Kirk-Christ Rushen, and Kirk-Malew Kirk-Andreas contains 2229 inhabitants the living is a rectory, in the gift of the Crown the church, which was one of the oldest in the island, was rebuilt in 1802, and contains six hundred and fifty sittings in the interior is a handsome marble font, which formerly belonged to Philip I of France, and being confiscated at the time of the Revolution, was presented to this parish by Mr Corlett, near the entrance gate is an ancient cross with Runic inscriptions There is a parochial school, and at Kerro Garrvoo a school for girls, of which the mistress receives thirty shillings per annum, bequeathed by Mr John Tear Annual fairs are held in the village, on St Andrew s and St John s days, for cattle Near a seat called Ballacurry is a quadrangular encampment, defended by a bastion at each angle, and surrounded by a wide fosse, in good preservation, supposed to have been constructed by the troops of Cromwell during the parliamentary war, the interior of the area is sufficiently sunk to defend the troops from the fire of an enemy Some fine barrows have been opened in this parish, and found to contain urns and other relics of antiquity *Kirk-St Anne*, or *Santan*, contains 800 inhabitants the living is a vicarage, in the gift of the Crown the church is situated on the old road from Douglas to Castletown There is a parochial school, to which Mr William Leece, in 1805, bequeathed £100, and, in the village, a small school of industry for girls A fair is held on the 31st of May, for cattle About a mile to the east of the church is an irregular circle of stones, probably Druidical remains, and on the coast, to the left of Greenock creek, is an oblong tumulus, called Cronk na Myrrhon, or the hill of the dead *Kirk-Arbory* contains 1455 inhabitants the living is a vicarage, in the gift of the Crown the church, which contains three hundred sittings, has no architectural features The village of Colby is in this parish There is a parochial school, and fairs are held June 22nd, October 28th, and December 6th Near Balladoole is a brackish spring, probably issuing from a salt rock On the high grounds between Balladoole house and the sea is Kiel-Vaal, or Kirk-Michael, and behind Colby house is Kiel-Pharrick, or Kirk-Patrick, both good specimens of the ancient Kiels, or Kirks, so common in the island. These Kiels consist of a small enclosed area occupied with graves, in the centre of which are the ruins of the ancient church, generally of a quadrangular form, and of diminutive proportions In the vicinity of the latter are five lofty stones of uncommon dimensions, and some other Druidical remains, and in several parts of the parish barrows are seen *Kirk-Ballaugh* contains 1467 inhabitants the living is a rectory, in the gift of the Crown the old church, dedicated to St. Mary, and containing three hundred and fifty sittings, is about a mile from the village, near which a new church is now being erected, to contain seven hundred sittings it will be a neat edifice in the early style of English architecture, with a lofty embattled tower of three stages, strengthened with buttresses and crowned with pinnacles There is a parochial school in the village, which is well attended. A public brewery has been established, and fairs take place on May 15th and August 26th In this parish are several rabbit-warrens, and near the village are pits of shell-marl, in which heads, horns, and skeletons of gigantic antediluvian elks have been found, of which a complete skeleton, of the largest dimensions, is deposited in the museum of the University of Edin-

burgh. Mr Burman, of Douglas, has in his possession a head, with the horns extending seven feet from tip to tip Beds of common marl, of great extent and depth, are found in the country towards Kirk Jurby, and in the adjoining parish of Kirk-Andreas the road from Ramsey to Kirk-Michael runs through the village *Kirk-Braddan* contains 1754 inhabitants, exclusively of those in the town of Douglas the living is a vicarage, in the patronage of the Bishop The church, which is pleasantly situated in a picturesque spot, about two miles from Douglas, on the road to Peel, contains four hundred sittings, but claims no architectural notice, though beautifully situated in the churchyard are a Runic pillar, with an inscription, and several ancient crosses There is a parochial school, and in the parish are paper and corn mills, and a linen manufactory, employing about four hundred persons, to which are attached a flax-mill and spacious bleaching grounds, in this factory the whole process is conducted, from the preparation of the raw material to its being spun into yarn, and woven into cloth, the old system of bleaching is adopted, which, being free from any chemical process, has no injurious effect upon the cloth, to which circumstance may be attributed the superior durability of the Manks linen, of which considerable quantities are exported to the neighbouring ports of the United Kingdom Near the bleaching green, on that branch of the Douglas river called the Glass, is a fortified hill, named Castle Ward, and in the vicinity are various ruins of Kiels, or Kirks, which are preserved with scrupulous veneration *Kirk-Bride* contains 1001 inhabitants the living is a rectory, in the gift of the Crown the church, containing two hundred and fifty sittings, is dedicated to St Bridget over the chancel door is a stone, about a foot square, on which are rudely carved figures representing Adam and Eve plucking the forbidden fruit There is a parochial school, and fairs are held on April 12th and May 6th, for cattle. In this parish is the point of Ayre, the northern extremity of the island the land is very low and the shoals that extend to a considerable distance from the shore have occasioned many shipwrecks A few years since, a lighthouse near the point was erected, to the height of one hundred and six feet above the level of the sea it is furnished with a revolving light, shewing alternately a red and white colour, which attain their greatest brilliancy every two minutes the white light may be seen at the distance of four or five leagues, but the red light is not visible at so great a distance Maughold head intercepts the view of a navigator to the south, and Rice point to the west, of Ayre point there are several tumuli in the parish *Kirk Christ Lezayre* contains 2209 inhabitants the living is a vicarage, in the gift of the Crown the church, dedicated to the Holy Trinity, and containing two hundred and fifty sittings, is about two miles from Ramsey, and a little way out of the road to Kirk-Michael A new church is now being erected, in the early style of English architecture, with a tower surmounted by a spire, which will contain eight hundred and fifty sittings The parish, which comprises the village of Sulby, is very extensive, and may be considered as the garden of the Isle of Man, abounding with picturesque views, and diversified with beautiful scenery In addition to the parochial school are the Sulby school, founded by Mrs. Christian, who endowed it with property producing £11 per annum, and Mountain school, founded in 1764, by Mr John Kelly, of Coo il-Isischael, who bequeathed £71 for that purpose, and to the support of which Mr Philip Quayle gave his quarterland of Ischeag, and Mr William Kelly a portion of Intack in Kirk-Ballaugh, called Lhiargey-we-howne, producing about £5 per annum Fairs for cattle are held at Sulby on the 8th and 24th of June Turf and bog timber are found in great abundance in this parish *Kirk-Christ Rushen* contains 2568 inhabitants the living is a vicarage, in the gift of the Crown the church, dedicated to the Holy Trinity, contains four hundred sittings Mrs Clague left £3 per annum out of an estate called the Grampiones, and the Rev John Clague bequeathed £2 11 5 to the parochial school, and Miss Qualtrough left £100 for founding a school In this parish are the small villages of Port-Erin and Port-le-Mary Between these villages are the Giants' quoiting stones, two huge masses of unhewn clay-slate, about ten feet high, three feet wide, and two feet thick Within a mile of these is Fairy Hill, a barrow, situated in a low morass, from which two defiles lead to Port-Erin bay, and the creek of Fleswick the hill is a truncated cone forty feet high, and one hundred and fifty yards in circumference, completely surrounded by a deep and wide ditch, on the summit is a circular excavation, ten yards in diameter, with a regular parapet, the sides of the hill facing the defiles are almost perpendicular, and on the north-east side a pathway to the summit is discernible According to the ancient modes of warfare, it must have been an almost impregnable fortress, all access to which might have been prevented by inundating the morass In this parish are Spanish Head, previously noticed, and the Calf of Man, of which a small portion is converted into arable land, but the greater part consists of sheep-walks it is leased to a farmer, who has erected a house in the centre, and whose family and servants, together with those who have the care of the lighthouses, are the only inhabitants The *Calf of Man* is tithe free, having neither church nor minister, and, except in the garden of the farmer, there is neither tree nor shrub in it Rabbits are found in abundance, nearly two thousand being killed annually, and the islet is a great place of resort for sea-fowl and aquatic birds of every description, the copper mines of Brada are also in this parish *Kirk-German* contains 1849 inhabitants, exclusively of those in the town of Peel the living is a vicarage, in the patronage of the Bishop the church, dedicated to St Peter, which is situated in the town of Peel, contains sittings for five hundred persons There is a parochial school Fairs are held at St John's on May 1st and 18th, July 5th, and November 1st and 18th There are several ancient kiels in the parish *Kirk-Jurby* contains 1108 inhabitants the living is a vicarage, in the patronage of the Bishop the church, dedicated to St. Patrick, and containing two hundred and eighty sittings, is about half a mile to the north-east of Point Jurby, occupying an elevated situation, from which the high lands of England, Scotland, and Ireland, may be plainly discerned In the churchyard is a barrow, and in the parish are various others, besides several watch and ward hills There is a parochial school; and fairs are held on April 5th, for hiring female servants, and on November 20th for cattle

Turf and bog-timber are found in this parish in great abundance *Kirk I onan* contains 1846 inhabitants the living is a vicarage, in the gift of the Crown the church, dedicated to St Lomanus, contains three hundred sittings, and is not distinguished by any architectural features A new church, in the early style of English architecture, with a tower surmounted by a spire, and containing five hundred sittings, is now being erected in the parish There is a parochial school, and an annual fair is held at Laxey, on the 5th of August, for cattle About a mile from the church, on the sea-shore, is the small village of Laxey, pleasantly situated at the mouth of a stream of that name, which abounds with trout Upon the banks of the river, a little higher up the village, are a flax-mill and a paper-mill, in the latter of which a considerable quantity of paper is manufactured for home consumption and for exportation, and about a mile further up the glen are the lead and copper mines The glen presents a fine landscape, having Snawfel and other mountains in the back ground the greater part of Snawfel is in this parish, and the summit, from its central situation, commands a more complete view of the surface of the island than can be obtained from any other eminence On the north side of Laxey hill is an imperfect Druidical circle of small diameter, and a little lower down is a terrace three yards wide, leading to a cairn of considerable magnitude, composed of loose stones thrown together without order, and having, at the extremity of the base, a lofty stone pillar, the summit is nearly level. About two miles on the road to Douglas are the Cloven stones, a Druidical tomb, or altar, so called from two lofty stones more conspicuous than the rest, which appear to have been riven asunder Tradition records these stones to have been the grave of a Welch prince, who, having landed at Laxey, on his invasion of the island, was slain by the natives, and buried on the spot where he fell A little further up the river there is a fine specimen of an ancient fortified hill, and in various parts of the parish are several barrows and cairns, of which considerable numbers are found in many parts of the island *Kirk-Malew* contains 2649 inhabitants, exclusively of those in Castletown the living is a vicarage, in the gift of the Crown the church, containing five hundred and thirty sittings, is situated about a mile and a half from Castletown, on the road to Peel About three miles to the north-east of it is St Mark s chapel, erected in 1772, under the auspices of Bishop Hyldersley, who purchased the glebe for it it was repaired, in 1830, at the expense of the Bishop of the diocese Besides Castletown, this parish includes the village of Ballasalla, Derby haven, and Langness point. Independently of the schools in that town, there are parochial schools at Ballasalla and at St Mark s Fairs are held, January 5th and May 12th, at St Mark s, and April 25th, August 12th, and September 29th, at Ballasalla, for cattle Ballasalla is the most extensive and populous village in the island the scenery in its vicinity is richly diversified and picturesque, the venerable remains of Rushen abbey are seen on the banks of the river, and form an interesting feature in the view, the mountain of South Barrule is chiefly in this parish, and on its northern declivities are extensive slate quarries About two miles from St Mark s chapel are the Foxdale lead mines, which are now being worked with great benefit to the proprietors, there are also in the parish several flax and corn mills, and some extensive breweries In various parts of the coast are barrows and several ancient fortifications, among which are the remains of a circular encampment, surrounded with a fosse, and defended by a parapet with gates adjoining the fosse are some large blocks of granite, one of which is called the Stone of Goddard Crovan, and the fortification, most probably of Danish origin, is, by Sir Walter Scott, in his Peveril of the Peak, noticed under the appellation of the Black Fort Kirk-Marown contains 1201 inhabitants the living is a vicarage, in the gift of the Crown the church, which is situated in the western part of the parish, five miles from Douglas, and six from Peel, contains only two hundred and fifty sittings The parochial school is well attended, and there are fairs on February 2nd and May 20th, for cattle A woollen manufacture, the only one in the island, was established in this parish in 1803, and after having been accidentally burnt down, was rebuilt on a more extensive scale in 1828 about one hundred persons are employed in the manufacture of cloth, which is not inferior in quality to the cloth made in England, though it is full twenty per cent less in price, it is not allowed to be exported, and, with a view to encourage this branch of manufacture, a considerable tax is imposed not only upon all cloths, but even upon all clothes made up, which are imported from any other country This is the most inland parish in the island, and is chiefly remarkable for some relics of antiquity, among which are the remains of the ancient chapel of St Trinian, and, on the northern acclivity of Mount Murray, the most perfect remains of a Druidical temple to be found in the island it is formed of stones of moderate size, placed erect and at regular distances, enclosing a circle fourteen yards in diameter, on each side is a stream of water, issuing from fountains about fifty yards higher up the mountain, which by the Druids were held sacred to the east of the enclosure are two walls, or mounds, constructed of stones and earth, bending round the temple, in a semicircular direction, and about five yards distant from each other the spot of ground on which these remains are situated is barren, bleak, and uncultivated, but from the name "Glen Darrah," which in the Manks language signifies the vale of oaks, it would appear that it was originally planted with those trees, which the Druids held in great veneration there are numerous ancient kiels in the parish Kirk-Maughold contains 1514 inhabitants, exclusively of those in the town of Ramsey, from which the village of Maughold is three miles distant the living is a vicarage, in the gift of the Crown the church, dedicated to St Maughold, and containing two hundred and sixty sittings, is situated in the centre of a spacious area, comprising, at least, three acres of consecrated ground, which was formerly a sanctuary for criminals, the ancient font, which is very large, has been removed from the interior of the church, and placed on one side of the entrance In the churchyard are numerous monuments, among which is a very handsome one to the memory of Captain Hugh Crowe, a native, and commander of several merchant-vessels opposite to the church gate is a Danish cross, and near it a column, consisting of a circular shaft, about five feet high, surmounted by a cubic block of stone, on one

side of which is sculptured a representation of our Saviour on the Cross, with the arms of the Isle of Man beneath, on the opposite side, the Virgin and Child, on the third side, a figure in the attitude of supplication, supposed to represent St Bridget, and on the fourth side is supposed to have been a representation of St Maughold, now totally defaced The Society of Friends have a burial-ground in this parish, and formerly a distinct portion of the churchyard was appropriated exclusively to their use The parochial school has received several small bequests, in addition to its original funds A fair is held on the 11th of August, for cattle About half-way between the village and the town of Ramsey is a stone cross, of great antiquity, six feet high, three feet wide, and five inches thick, having on its summit five raised balls, similar to which are some stones in the churchyard, supposed to be of Danish origin Maughold Head is a bold promontory, terminating in a precipitous and lofty cliff, and forming the most easterly point of the island On its summit are tiers of moss clad rocks, and on one of the acclivities is a spring, called St Maughold s well, which was formerly, and is still, much resorted to for its supposed medicinal virtues At Ballaglass is a waterfall, surrounded with woodland scenery, forming the highest and the most picturesque cascade in the island it arises from the obstruction of the course of the rivulet Dhoones, on the coast between the boundaries of Maughold and Lonan The mountain of North Barrule, one of the most lofty and remarkable elevations, adds greatly to the grandeur of the varied and romantic scenery for which this parish is distinguished Kirk Michael contains 1427 inhabitants the living is a vicarage, in the gift of the Crown the church is in the centre of the village, about a quarter of a mile from the sea, and contains sittings for three hundred persons, the chancel was built by Dr Wilson, after the death of his father the churchyard contains many monuments with Runic inscriptions, and the tombs of the venerable Bishop Wilson, who died in the ninety-third year of his age, and the fifty eighth of his prelacy, and his successor, Bishop Hyldersley, in addition to whom, Dr John Philips, Dr George Mason, and Dr C Crigan, also bishops of this see, were buried here Near the church gate is a lofty square Runic pillar of blue stone, curiously sculptured, from the base to the summit, with devices singularly involved with each other, and bearing an inscription representing it to have been erected in honour of Thurulf, a Norwegian chief there are numerous barrows in the neighbourhood. Near the village a neat court-house has been erected within the last few years, in which the consistory court is held, on the last Thursday in every month, except September and December, and at which the bishop presides, either in person or by his vicars-general and registrar the vicars-general hold their chapter, or circuit courts, in spring and autumn Bishop s Court, the episcopal palace, is situated about a mile to the west of the village it is a very ancient structure, and is mentioned in history so early as the thirteenth century the original building was a massive tower, surrounded at some distance by a deep fosse, but various additions have been subsequently made Dr George Murray, the present Bishop of Rochester, when presiding over this diocese, erected the present elegant chapel, added several rooms, and also improved and embellished the demesne, which comprises from three to four hundred acres Bishop Hyldersley, in 1764, purchased a plot of ground, on which he built a school-house with dwellings for the master and the mistress, and gave £30, the interest to be appropriated to keeping them in repair There are fairs on the 10th and 29th of October, for cattle The high road from Ramsey to Peel runs through the village *Kirk-Onchan* contains 1451 inhabitants the living is a vicarage, in the gift of the Crown the church, dedicated to Oncha, the mother of St. Patrick, contains three hundred sittings, but is not entitled to architectural notice A new church, in the early style of English architecture, with a tower surmounted by a spire, is at present being erected, and will contain five hundred sittings There is a parochial school, and the fair is on the 20th of May, for cattle The village is pleasantly situated about two miles from Douglas, on the road to Laxey and Ramsey, and the high grounds command interesting and extensive views of the bay and harbour of Douglas, with the vessels going in and out of that much-frequented port, and of the surrounding country, which abounds in bold and varied scenery The creeks and bays on the coast produce a variety of marine plants and mosses, the latter of which are tinged with various hues, and with the most beautiful shades of red, green, brown, and yellow, and some few with tints of blue there are several barrows in various parts of the parish *Kirk-Patrick* contains 2031 inhabitants the living is a vicarage, in the gift of the Bishop The parish was united to St German's till 1714, when a separation took place, and the present church, containing three hundred and twenty sittings, was erected, chiefly through the exertions of Bishop Wilson, who gave £50 towards the augmentation of the endowment Mr Thomas Radcliffe, of Knockaloe, bequeathed £5 per annum out of an estate called Gobbreek, to the master of the parochial school, for teaching children from the former place A fair for cattle is held annually on May 17th To the south of the church is the beautiful waterfall of Glen Moij, formed by a rivulet, which, descending from the mountains, winds through the vale, and enters the glen, the banks of which, richly clothed with trees and shrubs, are rugged, and, in some places, nearly perpendicular The stream, murmuring gently through the various obstructions in its course, falls down the precipitous banks of the glen with a pleasing effect, the adjacent scenery is strikingly picturesque The glen is surrounded by hills on the north bank is a precipitous and lofty rock, partly concealed by the ivy that overspreads it, and the south bank is richly wooded the vale, winding round the hill, presents a view of the sea, into which the river, after a circuitous course, gently glides In the vicinity is a vein of lead-ore, near which a mountain stream, descending with impetuosity, and falling over an abrupt rock of considerable elevation, forms a cascade In this parish are several quarries of blue slate, little inferior in quality to that of Wales In the several churches, the service is performed alternately in the Manks and English languages The whole number of dissenting places of worship in the island exceeds forty By letters patent, dated 1675, Charles II granted an annuity of £100, payable from his Majesty's Exchequer, out of the excise duties, towards the main-

tenance of poor clergymen of the Isle of Man, out of which £3 per annum was to be paid to the schools of Castletown, Douglas, Ramsey, Kirk-Andreas, Kirk-Ballaugh, and Kirk-Bride the impropriate tithes of the several parishes of Kirk-Arbory, Kirk-Christ-Lezayre, Kirk-Lonan, Kirk-Malew, Kirk-Marown, Kirk-Michael, Kirk-Onchan, Kirk-Christ-Rushen, and Kirk-St Anne's, were also purchased from Charles, Earl of Derby, by Bishop Barrow and Archdeacon Fletcher, on lease for ten thousand years, for the sum of £1000, as appears by indenture, dated November 1st, 1666, for the purpose of augmenting the stipends of the poorer livings, and for the erection of a free school, and the support of a master, in each of the parishes in the island On the death of James, Earl of Derby, in 1735, James, Duke of Athol, as heir-general of the Derby family, took possession of these tithes, for the recovery of which, or for indemnity for the loss, Bishop Wilson and Archdeacon Kippax, in 1742, filed a bill in Chancery, with a view to seize upon the collateral securities, viz, the manors of Bispham and Methop in the county of Lancaster, which, by a decree of the court of Chancery, were assigned to the earl, in consideration of his paying annually, on Easter-Monday, the sum of £219 7 10½, at the town hall in Liverpool this payment having been discontinued in 1809, a bill of reviver was filed by Bishop Crigan and Archdeacon Mylrea, who eventually obtained the payment into the Bank of England of £16,000, in discharge of the obligation the produce of this sum, £600 per annum, is appropriated to the augmentation of all church livings under £90 per annum, which are raised to that sum ; to the payment of £60 per annum to the master of the grammar school at Castletown, and £5 10 per annum to each of the masters of the parochial schools James, Duke of Ormond, in 1676, charged certain of his estates in Ireland with the payment of £60 per annum, for the establishment of a lectureship in philosophy, history, and logic after the duke's death the payment was discontinued, and Bishop Wilson obtained, in commutation, the sum of £600, the produce of which is appropriated to that purpose Bishop Barrow, in 1668, gave two estates in the island, viz, Ballagilley and Hango Hill, then producing £20 per annum, for the education and support of two young men, to supply the Manks' churches, and for such other charitable uses as his trustees should think proper these estates at present produce £500 per annum Lady Elizabeth Hastings, in 1739, bequeathed £40 per annum from lands and tenements in Collingham, Shadwell, and Burton-Salmon, in the West riding of the county of York, to be distributed among the parishes of Kirk-Arbory, Kirk-Braddan, Kirk-German, Kirk-Jurby, Kirk-Christ-Lezayre, Kirk-Lonan, Kirk-Malew, Kirk-Marown, Kirk-Maughold, Kirk-Michael, Kirk-Onchan, Kirk Patrick, Kirk-Rushen, and Kirk-Santan, for the instruction of children Mrs Catharine Halsalls, in 1758, bequeathed houses and lands in the Isle of Man, now producing £111 14 6 per annum, to erect a dwelling-house for the master of the grammar school at Castletown, to erect and endow a free school there for teaching girls only, to augment the four livings in the patronage of the Bishop, and that of Kirk-Christ-Rushen, with £4 per annum each, and the residue to be annually applied to the support of the widows, and apprenticing the orphan children, of clergymen The

Rev Dr Wilson, in conjunction with his father, Bishop Wilson, in 1730, established a fund for the support of widows and children of clergymen, and a sum of money was raised and vested in the English funds for that purpose, producing £12 per annum, which revenue was subsequently augmented by the purchase of one-third of the tithes of Kirk-Michael from the Duke of Athol, which was assigned to trustees   Miss Stevenson, of Ashley Park, in the county of Surrey, also bequeathed £500 South Sea annuities for the use of this charity, which was afterwards exchanged for a mortgage on lands   the whole income arising from these various sources is at present £110 per annum   Bishop Hyldersley left £600 to the Society for the Promotion of Christian Knowledge, to supply the island with tracts

MANACCAN, a parish in the hundred of KERRIER, county of CORNWALL, 6¼ miles (S W by S) from Falmouth, containing 591 inhabitants   The living is a discharged vicarage, in the archdeaconry of Cornwall, and diocese of Exeter, rated in the king's books at £4 16 0½, and in the patronage of the Bishop of Exeter   The church, dedicated to St Menacus and St Dunstan, has lately received an addition of one hundred free sittings, the Incorporated Society for the enlargement of churches and chapels having granted £13 towards defraying the expense   In this parish is the small port of Helford, and at Tregonnell are the ruins of a chapel   In the vale of Manaccan, or Menachan, was discovered, several years since, a mineral substance, which, being analysed, was found to contain a new metal, called *menachanite*, and subsequently *titanium*

MANATON, a parish in the hundred of TEINGBRIDGE, county of DEVON, 8¼ miles (W by N) from Chudley, containing 403 inhabitants   The living is a rectory, in the archdeaconry of Totness, and diocese of Exeter, rated in the king's books at £13 12 9½   The Rev W Carwithen was patron in 1824   The church, dedicated to St Winifred, has a rich screen   At Grimspound, in this parish, is an enclosure of loose stones, containing about three acres, within which are several minor enclosures   some have thought it a Druidical work, and others, with greater probability, a Stannary court

MANBY, a parish in the Marsh division of the hundred of LOUTH-ESKE parts of LINDSEY, county of LINCOLN, 5¼ miles (T by S) from Louth, containing 236 inhabitants   The living is a discharged rectory, in the archdeaconry and diocese of Lincoln, rated in the king's books at £11 10 2   Mrs Wray was patroness in 1806   The church is dedicated to St Mary   There is a place of worship for Wesleyan Methodists

MANBY, a hamlet in the parish of BROUGHTON, eastern division of the wapentake of MANLEY, parts of LINDSEY, county of LINCOLN, 5 miles (W by N) from Glandford-Bridge   The population is returned with the parish

MANCETTER, a parish in the Atherstone division of the hundred of HEMLINGFORD, county of WARWICK, 1¼ mile (S E) from Atherstone, comprising the market town of Atherstone, and the hamlets of Hartshill and Oldbury, and containing 4482 inhabitants   The living is a vicarage, in the archdeaconry of Coventry, and diocese of Lichfield and Coventry, rated in the king's books at £10 13 4, and in the patronage of the

Rev Benjamin Richings   The church, dedicated to St Peter, occupies an eminence supposed to have been the site of a camp, being deeply intrenched   Near it was the Roman station called, by Antoninus, *Manduessuedum*, of an oblong form, with large ramparts enclosing an area of about seven acres, intersected by the Roman Watling-street, the north-western side, called Castle banks, being in Warwickshire, and the south eastern, called Oldfield banks, in Leicestershire   Oval flint axes, or celts, Roman bricks, coins of gold, silver, and brass, with various other relics of antiquity, have been found here   The river Anker, and the Coventry canal, run through the parish   Here are stone quarries, said to be the most extensive in the kingdom, also several very productive mines of manganese, of superior quality   In the village of Mancetter is an hospital, endowed with a bequest of £2000 from James Gramer, in 1724, for six poor men, each of whom receives six shillings a week   there are also a free grammar and two other endowed schools in the parish

MANCHESTER, a parish in the hundred of SALFORD, county palatine of LANCASTER, comprising the manufacturing and market town of Manchester, the chapelries of Ardwick, Blacklev, Cheetham, Chorlton *cum* Hardy, Denton, Didsbury, Gorton, Heaton-Norris, Newton, Salford, and Stretford, and the townships of Beswick, Bradford, Broughton, Burnage, Chorlton-row, Crumpsall, Droylsden, Failsworth, Harpurhey, Houghton, Hulme, Levenshulme, Moss-Side, Moston, Openshaw, Reddish, Rushulme, and Withington, and containing, according to the last census, 186,942 inhabitants, of which number, including Salford, 133,788 are in the town of Manchester, 36 miles (E by N) from Liverpool (but only 31 by the rail-road), 54 (S E by S) from Lancaster, and 186 (N W by N) from London   The origin of this town, which is remarkable for the extent of its trade and the importance of its manufactures, may be traced to a period of remote antiquity   In the time of the Druids, it was distinguished as one of the principal stations of their priests, and celebrated for the privilege of sanctuary attached to its altar, which, in the British language, was called *Meyne*, signifying a stone   Prior to the Christian era, it was one of the principal seats of the Brigantes, who had a castle, or strong hold, called *Mancenion*, or the place of tents, near the confluence of the rivers Medlock and Irwell, the site of which, still called the "Castle Field," was by the Romans, on their conquest of this part of the island under Agricola, about the year 79, selected as the station of the *Cohors Prima Frisiorum*, and, with reference to its original British name, called by them *Mancunium*, hence its Saxon name *Manceastre*, from which its modern appellation is obviously derived   This station was for nearly four centuries occupied by the Romans, and amply provided with every thing requisite for the accommodation and subsistence of the garrison established in it, having also a water-mill on the Medlock, at some distance below the town, the site of which still retains the name of

Seal and Arms.

Knott mill The station included a quadrangular area, five hundred feet in length and four hundred in width, the interior not exactly level, but rising from the centre towards the sides, on which a rampart of earth sloping inwards was raised from the ground surrounding the enclosure, which is consequently lower than the site of the castrum on the summit of this rampart a wall was originally built, which extended round the enclosure, on one side of which was the castle, or fort, but very little of the foundation of the wall is at present discernible, the few remaining portions being under ground, and the greater part of the site covered with modern buildings From this station, as from a common centre, Roman roads branched off to those of *Cambodunum, I boracum, Condate, Rigodunum, Veratinum,* and *Rerigonium* In the vicinity of the aboriginal settlement, which has obtained the name of Aldport, Roman urns and other vessels, stones inscribed to centurions of the cohort, votive altars, coins, fibulæ, and lachrymatories, have been found at various times , and without the vallum, foundations of Roman buildings, and other vestiges of antiquity, have been frequently discovered The Roman road to *Cambodunum,* commenced at the east gate of the castrum, and pursuing a northeastern direction, passed over Newton heath into the county of York , the road leading to *Eboracum* branched off from the former at a distance of less than two miles from *Mancunium,* and passing by the townships of Chadderton and Royton, continued in a north-eastern direction through Littleborough, and over Blackstone Edge, to the city of York , the road to *Condate* passed from the east gate of the castrum, through the village of Stretford, to the ford of Mersey, and thence to Kinderton , the road to *Rigodunum* branched off from the road to *Condate* about a mile from its commencement, and taking a south-westerly direction, crossed the river Irwell at Old Trafford, terminating at Blackrode , the road to *Veratinum* diverged from that to *Rigodunum,* and after passing by Eccles, continued through Barton to Warrington , and the road to the station *Rerigonium* commenced at the north west gate of *Mancunium,* and passing Quay-street, ran nearly parallel with Deans-gate, and after crossing the river Irk passed over Kersall moor to Ribchester there were also several smaller vicinal ways, of which some slight vestiges may be traced

After the departure of the Romans, the fort of *Mancunium* was taken from the Britons, about the year 488, by a party of the Saxons, who had forcibly established themselves in this part of the kingdom they placed a garrison in it, which, however, surrendered to the British, who retained possession whilst Arthur Pendragon was prosecuting his victories over that people In 620, it was captured by Edwin, King of Northumbria, who annexed it to his dominions, and soon afterwards a colony of Angles settled here In 627, the inhabitants were converted to Christianity, by the preaching of Paulinus, a missionary employed by Gregory I, and a Christian church was built, and dedicated to St Michael Manchester having been taken by the Danes, was, about 920, wrested from their possession by Edward the Elder, who repaired and fortified the castle, and rebuilt the town, which had been almost destroyed in the assaults of the invaders, placing in it a strong garrison of his own soldiers, on account of its being a frontier town between the kingdoms of Mercia and

Northumbria It was raised to the distinction of a burgh, with extensive privileges, and for some time continued highly prosperous , but being exposed to repeated attacks, and having suffered so much injury in the wars between the Northumbrians and the Danes, notwithstanding its enlargement by Edward, it appears, at the time of the Conquest, to have been in every respect inferior to Salford, a Saxon settlement on the opposite bank of the Irwell, which, being a royal demesne, had risen into importance, and imparted name to the hundred in the Norman survey we find that Manchester contained two churches, but it is not otherwise mentioned as a place of any note Soon after the Conquest, it came into the possession of Albert de Gresley, whose descendant, Robert, the fourth lord of Manchester, obtained for it, in the reign of Henry III , the grant of an annual fair on the eve and festival of St Matthew In the reign of Edward I , the barons, in order to raise a greater number of men to serve in the army destined for the invasion of Scotland, conferred several privileges on their vassals , and Thomas de Gresley, sixth baron of Manchester, upon that occasion, granted to the inhabitants those rights and immunities which have been emphatically called the "Magna Charta of Manchester This charter, which was granted on the 14th of May, in the year 1301, among other privileges, confers the right of choosing a borough-reeve , of disposing of their lands of inheritance according to their pleasure, reserving only to the heir, in such cases, the prior right of purchase, the power of arresting for debt within the borough the persons of knights, priests, or clerks, and various other privileges The baron of Manchester was thrice summoned to parliament by writ in the reign of this monarch, by whom he was made Knight of the Bath, and was one of the barons who, in the reign of Edward II , conspired against Piers Gaveston About seventy years before this, Salford was made a free borough, by charter from Ranulph de Blundeville, Earl of Chester

In 1352, the manufacture of "Manchester cottons, a kind of woollen cloth made from the fleece in an unprepared state, was introduced, and obtained a high degree of celebrity , and in the course of this reign, numerous Flemish artisans, who had been invited into England by Edward III , settled in the town, where, finding every requisite advantage, they brought the woollen manufacture to a considerable degree of perfection, and laid the foundation of its staple trade , which, though interrupted by the war between the houses of York and Lancaster, and subsequently, in the reign of Edward VI , by a dreadful malady, called the sweating sickness, had, in the reign of Elizabeth, become of such importance, that one of the queen s aulnagers (officers appointed to examine, and affix the seal to, manufactured cloth) was stationed here, in 1565 During the progress of the Reformation, an ecclesiastical commission for the diocese of Chester was established at Manchester, and numbers of popish recusants, from various parts of Lancashire, were imprisoned in the New Fleet, which appears to have been erected about that time, and probably for that purpose The commissioners were Henry Hastings, Earl of Huntingdon , Edwin Sandys, Archbishop of York , the Earl of Derby, and Dr Chadderton, Bishop of Chester, who then resided in the episcopal palace at Manchester, but, in consequence of frequent disputes between his servants and the inhabitants removed to Chester The commissioners, though principally engaged in promoting the re-formed religion, and in the detection and punishment of popish recusants, published, during their sittings at Manchester, a declaration against pipers and minstrels attending bear and bull baitings, against the "superstitious ringing of bells, wakes, festivals, and other amusements," to counteract the influence of which prohibition, James I published his celebrated Book of Sports Among the persons confined in the New Fleet, under the authority of this commission, were, Sir John Southworth, James Layborne, an eminent layman, who was executed at Lancaster in 1583, his head having been sent to Manchester, and placed, with those of others, on the steeple of the collegiate church, James Bell, and John Finch, who were executed in 1584, John Townley, Esq, and the lady of Bartholomew Hesketh, Esq Having been originally a place of sanctuary, it was one of the eight places to which this privilege was confirmed, by a statute in the 32nd of Henry VIII, which, in the following year, was transferred to Chester During the threatened invasion by Philip of Spain, Manchester supplied one hundred and forty four men armed with bills and pikes, thirty-eight archers, and thirty-eight arquebusiers, to assist in repelling the "Invincible Armada"

At the commencement of the parliamentary war, Sir Cecil Trafford, with a view to strengthen the king s cause, supplied the inhabitants of Manchester and the neighbouring towns with arms and ammunition, but the county, anxiously desirous of peace, sent a petition to the king, then at York, requesting him to propose terms of reconciliation with the parliament, the presentation of which was entrusted to a deputation, consisting of the warden of Manchester, and other freeholders of the county, among whom was John Bradshaw, supposed to be the same individual that, six years after, pronounced sentence of death upon the king, as president of the High Court of Justice All hopes of reconciliation having vanished, Manchester became the scene of much obstinate contention The commissioners of array visited it, to demand ammunition for the use of the king, but the town having been previously secured for the parliament, by Ralph Asheton, one of the representatives of the county, the inhabitants refused to surrender, and Lord Strange, with a considerable force, attempting to enter it, they took up arms, and being joined by numbers from the adjacent country, a skirmish took place, in which several men on both sides were killed this event, which was regarded by the House of Commons as the commencement of the war, was, by the Speaker, announced as "terrible news from the north The inhabitants, apprehending a more serious attack, fortified the town, and the king, having set up his standard at Nottingham, sent Lord Strange, with four thousand infantry, seven pieces of cannon, and some cavalry, to reduce it After an obstinate conflict for several days, during which it was defended by Captain Bradshaw, aided by Lieut Col Rosworm, an able German engineer, Lord Strange, being summoned, on the death of the Earl of Derby, to join the king whose head quarters were then at Shrewsbury, withdrew his forces, and raised the siege To guard against future assaults, the

fortifications which had been hastily thrown up, were completed and enlarged, and instructions were given by the parliament to the committee for the defence of the kingdom, to levy a body of dragoons to serve in Manchester, and the neighbourhood, and to indemnify the inhabitants for the loss they had sustained in resisting the commissioners of array, and, to supply them with money to defray the expense of future services, a loan was raised, the interest of which was paid by parliament, and, as an immediate resource, the pay of the officers of the garrison was ordered to be levied on the estates of the royalists Manchester now became the head-quarters of the parliamentary army stationed in Lancashire, and, in 1643, Sir Thomas Fairfax entered the town, whence he despatched expeditions against Preston and Lancaster, both which surrendered to the parliament It was again summoned by the Earl of Newcastle, at the head of ten or twelve thousand men, but being unsuccessful, the earl took the route to Hull, in pursuit of Fairfax it does not appear to have sustained any further attack During the Protectorate of Cromwell, Manchester, in obedience to the Protector s writ to the high sheriff of Lancaster, made two successive returns of a member to serve in parliament, in common with other towns, which have not since exercised the elective franchise In 1652, the walls were thrown down, the fortifications demolished, and the gates carried away and sold, a measure which appears to have originated in its growing commercial importance, and its increase in wealth and population The restoration of Charles II, however, was celebrated in the town with the most splendid pomp and ceremony, the utmost festivity and rejoicings took place, and the public conduits were made to flow with wine in copious streams In 1715, a tumultuous assembly, headed by one Syddall, a barber, demolished the Independent chapel, in Acres Fields, at that time the only dissenting place of worship in the town, and proceeded to commit other depredations, but the insurrection was quelled, and Syddall, with several of his accomplices, were committed to Lancaster gaol Syddall, on his liberation from prison, joined the rebels in Preston, and, being again taken prisoner, was sent to this town and executed.

In 1745, Prince Charles Edward, the young Pretender, who the year before had visited Manchester, where he was hospitably entertained for several weeks at An coat s Hall, the mansion of Sir Edward Moseley, Bart entered the county of Lancaster, at the head of an army of six thousand men, and advanced to this town, with a view to recruit his forces, and to raise supplies of men, arms, and money On the 28th of November, the advanced guard, consisting of about one hundred cavalry, entered the town, and demanded quarters for ten thousand men, and on the following day the main body arrived, in the afternoon the young Pretender took up his quarters in the house of Mr Dickenson, in Market-street, from that circumstance called the palace, and issued a proclamation, requiring all persons who had any duties to pay, or any of the public money in their hands, to pay the same to his secretary at the palace The borough-reeve was compelled to publish the manifestoes of the rebels and on the following day, the whole of the Pretender s army, with its train of artillery, consisting of sixteen pieces of cannon, and the baggage, assembled in the town and neighbourhood the sum of £3000 was levied in money, from two to three hundred men were raised for the service, and placed under the command of Francis Townley, Esq, of Townley Hall, in the county of Lancaster, and many horses were put under requisition for mounting the cavalry and drawing the baggage On the 1st of December, the rebel army quitted Manchester, marching southward in two columns; and having united at Macclesfield, advanced to Derby, which they reached on the 4th, but to avoid the danger of being enclosed by the armies of Marshal Wade and the Duke of Cumberland, retreated northward to Manchester, where they arrived on the 8th, and continuing their retreat to the north, reached Carlisle on the 10th, closely pursued by the Duke of Cumberland, leaving a garrison of four hundred men in that town, consisting of the Manchester regiment and some Scottish troops, the rebels effected their retreat to the Scottish frontier, which they reached on the 20th of December On the subsequent surrender of the garrison of Carlisle to the Duke of Cumberland, the officers of the Manchester regiment were sent prisoners to London, where, being tried for high treason, and found guilty, they were executed on Kennington Common After the execution, the heads of Col Townley and Capt Fletcher were placed on Temple Bar, and those of Capt. Deacon and Adjutant Syddall, son of the barber, were sent down to Manchester and placed on the exchange

In 1759, an act of parliament was passed for discharging the inhabitants from their obligation to grind corn and other grain at the school mill on the river Irk, a custom which had prevailed from a remote period, and had frequently excited a strong spirit of popular discontent By this act the inhabitants were released from every obligation, except that of grinding malt, which is still retained, and though the sum paid to the feoffees of the mill is very moderate, yet the compulsory clause of grinding malt has induced almost all the public brewers to establish themselves in townships which, though adjoining to, and within the immediate vicinity of, the town, are not subject to that obligation Christian, King of Denmark, on his tour through England, in 1768, took up his abode in this town, and lodged, with his suite, at the Bull Inn, during his stay he visited the recently-formed excavations for the Duke of Bridgewater s canal In 1773, the Russian Princess, Czartoriski, arrived here from Birmingham, to inspect the aqueducts and excavations at Worsley, and during her stay visited the principal factories In 1805, the Archdukes John and Lewis of Austria, accompanied by a retinue of scientific men, spent some time here in visiting the various factories, and inspecting the several processes of the manufactures, and, in 1817, the Grand Duke Nicholas, now Emperor of Russia, honoured the town with a visit for the same purpose Manchester, in common with other large manufacturing towns, has, during the fluctuations of trade, and the varying state of its manufactures, experienced a proportionate number of popular commotions, and occasional disturbances, arising from the depression of commerce, and the consequent low wages of the operative manufacturer, have been, in some instances, attended with serious results The improvement in the various branches of its trade

and manufactures has, however, been uniformly progressive, and justly entitles it to be considered one of the most extensive and prosperous commercial and manufacturing towns in the kingdom

Its staple trade is the cotton manufacture, which, in all its various branches, is carried on to an extent almost incredible The town had obtained considerable eminence for its manufacture of what were called Manchester cottons, which was introduced by the Flemings, in the reign of Edward III, and in that of Charles I the linen and cotton trade had made some progress In the "Treasure of Traffic, published by Lewis Roberts, in 1641, Manchester is said to have purchased linen yarn from Ireland, and cotton wool from London, the goods woven from which were sent to those places for sale About the year 1740, the manufacturers residing here employed agents in different parts of the country to procure a supply of raw cotton, which was manufactured, by the spindle and distaff, in the cottages of the workmen, chiefly into fustians, thicksets, dimities, and jeans, to which were added cotton thicksets, goods figured in the loom, and subsequently cotton velvets, velveteens, and strong fancy cords About the year 1760, these goods, which had till then been made only for home consumption, found a market on the continents of Europe and America, and as the quantity of weft produced in the whole county of Lancashire, by about fifty thousand spindles worked by hand, was insufficient to keep the weavers in Manchester constantly employed, and consequently to afford a supply adequate to the increasing demand, recourse was had to the aid of machinery, and Mr John Kay invented the instrument called the puking peg, by the assistance of which the weaver was not only enabled to produce twice the quantity of work, but also to weave cloths of any width. The facility thus given to the weaving department caused a corresponding increase in the demand for yarn, and Mr Thomas Highs, in conjunction with Mr Kay, invented the spinning jenny, the powers of which were greatly increased by the improvements of Mr Hargreaves, whose success exciting the apprehensions of the hand-workmen, caused the destruction of his machinery, and his retreat to Nottingham, where he died in indigence Mr Highs continued to make the spinning jennies for sale, and also invented the water-frame, or throstle, for spinning twist by means of rollers these machines were subsequently improved under Sir Richard Arkwright, whose exclusive patent right was annulled by a decision of the court of King's Bench, in 1785, and the privilege of using such machinery was thrown open to the public The late Sir Robert Peel, Bart, assisted by Mr Hargreaves, first brought the cylindrical carding-engines into use, and made many improvements in the application of machinery to the cotton manufacture, by the adoption of which, aided by the powers of the steam-engine, the quantity of goods of every description manufactured in this town has been prodigiously increased

Every process of that manufacture is carried on to a very considerable extent, but the branch of it for which Manchester is most distinguished is the spinning, in which department alone there are in the town and vicinity one hundred and fourteen steam-engines, worked by one hundred and eighteen steam-engines, the aggregate power of which is equal to that of three thousand nine hundred and eighty-one horses, by this machinery, about two million one hundred and eighty-two thousand three hundred and fifty spindles, and six thousand nine hundred and twenty-six power-looms, are set in motion The power loom is a recent invention, originating with the Rev Mr Cartwright, of Holland House, in the county of Kent, who, after repeated attempts, ultimately succeeded in establishing a factory upon that principle at Doncaster, and was indemnified by parliament for the losses he had sustained in the course of his experiments Mr Grimshaw, of Manchester, adopting Mr Cartwright s plan, established a factory in which were five hundred power-looms, but the building having been destroyed by fire, the design was for a time abandoned The difficulties which had impeded the general adoption of this invention were finally removed by the aid of Mr Johnson s machine for dressing the warps, and, in 1806, the use of the power-loom was again introduced, with complete success The factories, in several of which the whole process of the manufacture, from the introduction of the raw material to its completion, is carried on, are immense ranges of building, from six to eight stories in height , some employing from eighteen hundred to two thousand persons each, and the whole furnishing employment to upwards of thirty thousand persons The making of muslin was first attempted about the year 1780, at which time the machine called the mule was introduced into the spinning factories, and to such a degree of perfection has this branch of manufacture been brought, that the muslins of Manchester are little inferior to those of India. The silk manufacture has, within the last few years, been revived, under very favourable circumstances, and is rapidly improving , the number of mills already established is considerable, and the silks manufactured are not inferior in the beauty of their texture to those of Spitalfields, or of France The principal articles at present manufactured are, velvets, fustians, jeans, ticking, checks, ginghams, nankeens, diaper, quilting, calico, muslins, muslinets, cambric handkerchiefs, small wares, silks, and, in fact, every variety of cotton and silk goods There are also extensive bleaching-grounds, and works for printing and dyeing, and for every other department of the manufactures , and, in addition to what may be considered the staple manufactures of the town, are numerous others dependent on them, such as that of machinery of all kinds, for which there are extensive forges, foundries, &c , employing about ninety steam-engines, of the aggregate power of one thousand seven hundred horses There are also several laboratories for the making of oil of vitriol, and other chemical productions used in the different processes of the trade, for bleaching, dyeing, &c in the vicinity are several mills for the manufacture of paper of all descriptions, from the coarsest kind, for packages, to the finest kinds of writing and printing paper, all which have been brought to a high degree of perfection, and are manufactured on a very large scale There are extensive manufactories for hats, which have flourished for many years , also various other branches of manufacture, which have all improved with the increasing trade of the town, and afford employment to a very great portion of the inhabitants Engraving, as connected with the printing of calico, muslin, and cotton goods, is extensively carried on , and there are saw-mills on a very extended scale.

For the purchase of the various productions of the town, of which large quantities are exported, foreign merchants have either established agents, or one of their partners, resident here, to conduct their commercial transactions, and to purchase not only Manchester goods, but also the produce of all the adjoining manufacturing districts, which are accumulated here as in a central depôt. A chamber of commerce was established in 1820, by which the trading interests of its members, and those of Manchester generally, have been greatly promoted twenty-five directors are annually chosen at a general meeting of the subscribers, held in February, to whom the management of its affairs is entrusted

The exchange and commercial buildings were erected from a design by Mr Harrison, in 1806, at an expense of £20,000, advanced on shares of £50 each, by four hundred proprietary members, who subsequently added £30 each to the original shares, for the purchase of the site it is a spacious, handsome, and well-arranged edifice of Runcorn stone in the Grecian style of architecture the north front, which faces the market-place, is semicircular, and ornamented with lofty fluted columns of the Doric order , the news-room, which occupies the basement story of this part of the building, is elegantly provided with every accommodation, and lighted by a semicircular dome and handsome windows of plate glass at the distance of fifteen feet from the walls is a circular range of pillars of the Ionic order, supporting the ceiling , and over the central fire-place is a full-length portrait of Thomas Stanley, Esq , for many years member for the county, finely painted by the late Sir Thomas Lawrence there are two thousand subscribers belonging to this establishment Above the news-room, and resting on the pillars which support the ceiling, is a circular range of building, fifteen feet in breadth, and two stories high (originally forming part of the extensive establishment of Mr W Ford, bookseller), of which the lower contains the Exchange library, belonging to a proprietary of four hundred members, and comprising more than fifteen thousand volumes the proprietary ticket is £10 10 , and the annual subscription £1 The gallery is lighted by a range of windows immediately above those in the circular part of the news-room, but of smaller dimensions, and is well arranged for the reception of the books , the upper story is divided into apartments for various uses In the south part of the building is the post-office, adapted in every respect to the commercial importance of the town , and the chamber of commerce occupies another part of the building A handsome geometrical staircase leads from the hall to the upper part of the Exchange buildings, in which is an elegant dining-room, ninety-two feet long, and twenty-nine feet wide, with a rich mantelpiece of Abyssinian marble at each end, and an orchestra on the north side this room, which was opened in celebration of the anniversary of the birthday of George III , in 1809, is well adapted for public entertainments there are several ante-rooms, and a variety of offices, connected with the general purposes of the institution

The vast trade and commercial importance of this town have been in a great degree promoted by its proximity to the port of Liverpool, whence its manufactures are exported to every quarter of the globe, and with which it has a facility of communication by means of the Mersey, and Irwell navigation, constructed in 1720, under an act of parliament amended in 1794, when the proprietors were incorporated, and the celebrated Bridgewater canal, of which a description is given in the article on LANCASHIRE, both of them communicating with the river Mersey at Runcorn. The Manchester, Bolton, and Bury canal, constructed by act of parliament in 1791, crossing the Irwell at Clifton, and again at Little Lever, passes for fifteen miles through a district abounding with coal and mineral produce, and unites with the Leeds and Liverpool canal near Blackburn, by a branch formed in 1793. The Ashton under Line canal, constructed in 1792, is carried, by a lofty archway, in an oblique direction over Store-street, and by another aqueduct, of equal strength and beauty of design, it crosses the river Medlock, branching off to Stockport, and at Fairfield, by another branch, communicates with Oldham. The Rochdale canal, constructed in 1794, forms a communication from the Duke of Bridgewater's canal at Manchester to the Calder navigation at Sowerby bridge, beyond which is a cut from Salter Hebble to Halifax. By means of the Grand Trunk canal, a line of communication is here established with London, Bristol, and other principal towns. In 1826, an act was obtained for the construction of an iron rail road between Manchester and Liverpool, adapted to the use of carriages drawn by locomotive engines impelled by steam, for the conveyance of merchandise and passengers. This stupendous undertaking was completed in 1830, at an expense of upwards of £800,000, subscribed in shares of £100 each, by a company of proprietors: the line of road is carried, by a series of arches, commencing at the Company's warehouses, in the Liverpool road, across the roofs of the houses in Water-street, and over the river Irwell, by a handsome stone bridge of two arches, each sixty five feet in span, and thirty feet high from the surface of the water to the central summit. After passing over a level tract of ground beyond the river for nearly four miles and a half, it is, by means of inclined planes, viaducts, and other contrivances, continued through grounds of various elevation, rising, at its greatest altitude, to a height of one hundred and twenty three feet above, and falling, at its greatest depression, to a depth of one hundred and twenty-four feet and a half below the general level. The whole line from Manchester to Liverpool is thirty-one miles in length, which distance, though it may be travelled in little more than an hour, is generally performed in about two hours on its course not less than sixty three bridges have been erected, and two tunnels made. This important work was opened to the public with a grand procession, on which occasion the late Mr Huskisson, member for Liverpool, having alighted from one of the carriages, which had halted for a few minutes, in endeavouring to regain his seat fell in the line of one of the locomotive engines, which was travelling with a velocity of thirty miles an hour, and was so severely injured, that he died in the course of the evening. For a more minutely detailed account of this noble undertaking, see the article on LANCASHIRE. A joint-stock company, for the conveyance of goods by water, called the New Quay Company, was originally established in 1822, with a capital of £30,000: the shareholders are chiefly merchants and traders, and the company has a considerable number of vessels plying between Manchester and Liverpool.

In addition to the various and numerous branches of inland navigation, by which a facility of conveyance by water is obtained to every part of the kingdom, the trade of the town employs more than two hundred conveyances by land, for the more prompt distribution of its merchandise and manufactures, and upwards of one hundred coaches daily, for the accommodation of passengers.

The town is situated on the banks of the river Irwell, which here receives the tributary streams of the Irk and the Medlock; and on the north-west bank of which is situated the township, or district, of Salford, connected, by means of five bridges, with Manchester, of which it forms an integral part. Of these bridges, the most ancient, which had existed from time immemorial, was rebuilt in the reign of Edward III: the Strangeways iron bridge was erected in 1817, and a sixth bridge, in connexion with the Manchester and Liverpool railway, has been built over the same river. Over the Medlock are nine bridges, in various parts of the town, of which that leading from Oxford street crosses the river in an oblique direction. There are also seven bridges over the river Irk, of which six are very low, and subject to be flooded at high water; the seventh is a very lofty structure of three arches, and a great ornament to the town, connecting a new line of road, from the extremity of Miller-street, with what was anciently Strangeways park, and forming an entrance into the town, which avoids the steep ascent of the Red Bank, and the dangerous turn in the old road from Scotland-bridge. Exclusively of these, there are several smaller bridges over the Shooter's brook, and not less than thirty over the numerous branches of the canals which intersect the town. The town is well paved, and lighted with gas under the direction of two hundred and forty commissioners, appointed by an act of parliament passed in the 9th of George IV, for cleansing, paving, lighting, watching, and regulating it, and forming a body corporate, with a common seal: the gas-works are superintended by thirty directors chosen from among the commissioners. The inhabitants are supplied with water by the Manchester and Salford Water Company, established by act of parliament in 1809, which is conveyed by pipes from their reservoirs at Beswick and at Gorton, that at the latter place, covering more than fifty acres of ground, having been excavated in 1825. Salford was formerly included in the same jurisdiction with Manchester, with respect to its police, the same act of parliament being applicable to both, but by an act passed in the 9th of George IV, they were separated, and Salford is now governed by a distinct code of regulations, under an act passed in the 11th of George IV, and in the same session the local act for Manchester was amended. The environs, in many parts, particularly in Broughton, abound with scenery pleasingly diversified, and in the neighbourhood are some handsome ranges of building, and numerous elegant villas among these are Ardwick Green, in the centre of which is a fine sheet of water, surrounded with respectable residences, Salford Crescent, occupying an elevated site, and commanding a beautiful view of the windings of the Irwell, with the fertile valleys on the opposite bank, and sheltered by rising hills. On the bank of the same river are several successive tiers of houses, which rise above each other from the margin of the river, and on the Irk is Gibraltar, an irregular cluster of rural and pictu-resque cottages The older part of the town con-tains several ancient houses (which, however, are fast disappearing), interspersed with modern dwellings, and the streets, with the exception of such as have been im-proved under various acts of parliament, are incon-veniently narrow   the more modern parts contain many spacious streets, in which are numerous hand-some and respectable houses, but the general plan ap-pears to have been more adapted to the accommodation of its extended trade than to the display of elegance and symmetry in its general appearance   Cotton-mills, fac-tories, and warehouses of immense extent, have been erected in those parts of the town previously occupied by the most pleasant dwelling-houses, and every other part of it is crowded with numerous cottages of families employed in the various works

The Literary and Philosophical Society, established in 1781, consists of ordinary, honorary, and correspond-ing members, who pay £2 2s on their admission, and an annual subscription of £1 1s , they hold meetings every alternate Friday, from October till the end of April, in a hall containing suitable apartments, gold and silver medals are awarded for the best dissertations on particular subjects   the society has published seven volumes of transactions, in the English, French, and German languages, which are much circulated on the continent The Philological Society, consisting of thirty resident, and fifty corresponding, members, was instituted in 1803 , and an Agricultural Society, consisting of mem-bers residing within thirty miles of the town, was esta-blished in 1767, and is one of the earliest institutions of that kind in England   its object is to bestow an an-nual premiums for useful discoveries in cultivation, for superior specimens of produce both in cattle and in crops, and for the encouragement of cottagers who, by their labour, have maintained their families without pa-rochial assistance, and of farming servants who have continued for the greatest length of time, and with the best characters, in one situation, all subscribing members and their tenants, in the counties of Lan-caster and Chester, may claim the premiums   The new circulating library, in St Anne's street, containing four thousand volumes, was established in 1792   A part of Cheetham s hospital is also appropriated as a library, to which, under certain regulations, the pub lic enjoy free admission   Mr Cheetham bequeathed £1000, to be vested in land, directing the produce to be applied in the purchase of books, and £100 to provide a place for their reception   this fund, by the management of the trustees, has considerably ac-cumulated, and the library at present contains more than sixteen thousand volumes, some valuable manu-scripts, a collection of prints, and several natural and artificial curiosities   The Portico, an elegant edifice of the Ionic order, was erected by subscription, in 1806, at an expense of £7000   the building, which is of Run-corn stone, contains a library, a committee-room, a news-room lighted by a dome, a reading-room, and other offices   This institution, which belongs to a pro prietary of four hundred members, holding shares originally of the value of £13 13 , afterwards in-creased to £21, and paying an annual subscription of £2 10 per annum, is under the regulation of a com-mittee   The library, which forms a gallery round the

walls of the news-room, is sixty-five feet long, and forty-two feet wide, and the committee-room and reading-room are each thirty feet long, and sixteen feet wide   A library, established in Spear street, in 1802, is at present held in Fountain-street, and contains a very good collection of theological and other works   The law library was instituted by the members of that pro fession, in 1820   the proprietary ticket is £5 5 , and the annual subscription £1 11 6   There is also a li-brary in St Anne s street   The society for promoting the study of natural history was projected in 1821, and rapidly attained its present state of maturity and im-portance   there are at present more than three hun-dred proprietary members , the terms of admission are £10, and the annual subscription £2 2   Its con-cerns are under the direction of a president and coun-cil of ten proprietary members, annually chosen, four vice-presidents, a treasurer, four curators, and two se cretaries   the buildings comprise a museum, in which, in addition to a valuable collection of insects, made by the late J L Phillips, Esq , is an extensive exhibition of the rarest specimens of the animal kingdom, consisting of quadrupeds, birds, and fishes, and of shells, mine-rals, fossils, and other natural curiosities, scientifically arranged, in a suite of apartments well adapted to their preservation   attached to the museum are, a library of works on natural history, a council-room, a curatory, and apartments for the librarian and keeper of the museum

The Royal Institution, embracing a variety of ob-jects connected with the pursuits of literature and science, and the cultivation of the fine arts, originated with a few public spirited individuals (either artists or persons connected with the arts), in 1823, and was soon honoured with the public, and finally with royal, patron-age   this institution is under the direction of a presi-dent, twelve vice-presidents, and a committee, chosen from a body of nearly seven hundred hereditary and life governors, of whom the former are contributors of forty, and the latter of twenty-five, guineas each The building, which has been erected from a design by Mr Barry, of London, and is of a durable and richly-coloured stone, from the vicinity of Colne, forms a splendid addition to the architectural ornaments of the town , it is in the Grecian style of architecture   The principal elevation, towards Mosley-street, has a noble portico of six lofty columns of the Ionic order, supporting a rich entablature and pediment in the centre, on each side of which are columns and pilasters connecting it with the wings, above the doors and windows are panels for bas reliefs symboli-cal of the design of the institution   the attic story of the hall, rising to a considerable elevation above the wings, is to be surmounted by a finely-sculptured figure of Minerva The area round the building is enclosed with a handsome iron palisade on a lofty plinth of masonry, with pedestals at the angles of the steps leading to the portico and side entrances, on which are to be placed groups of figures and statues The centre comprises the hall and the theatre, and one of the wings is appro-priated as an academy of the fine arts, with exhibition rooms, and the other as a museum of natural history The hall, which is wholly lighted from the attic story, is forty feet square, and sixty feet high , it contains a grand staircase of stone, consisting of central and la-teral flights, with pedestals for sculptures, leading to a gallery on three sides of the hall, supported on Doric pillars, and to the theatre which is of a semicircular form On the gallery are entrances on each side, leading through corridors flanked with columns, into the exhibition rooms in each wing of the building, the ceiling of the hall is richly panelled in deeply-recessed compartments, and beneath the attic windows is a rich cornice with a frieze for bas reliefs ancient sculptures and casts from the antique will be ranged in the hall and corridors The theatre, which will hold six hundred persons, has a gallery supported on columns of bronze, and the walls are decorated with engaged columns, and with isolated columns in the angles the ceiling is richly panelled, and the theatre is lighted by a lantern, which, by machinery, may be darkened instantaneously, at the will of the lecturer There are three exhibition rooms in each wing, which may be thrown into one, they are twenty-three feet in height, and lighted from the ceiling, the principal room in each wing is forty-eight feet long, and thirty feet wide, and the others are thirty feet square There are also various rooms for the use of the officers and others connected with the institution, to which access is obtained from the hall and from other parts of the building The whole cost of this elegant pile, when complete, will be about £50,000, and the building will comprehend an ample and complete arrangement for the various purposes contemplated in its erection

A Floral and Horticultural Society was instituted in 1823, and a Botanical and Horticultural Institution in 1828 the garden for the latter, about two miles from the Exchange, on the new Stretford road, comprising about sixteen acres of ground, contains a great variety of green-house, herbaceous, Alpine, American, rock, and medicinal plants, and is under the care of a curator, who resides on the spot The entrance, on one side of which is the curator s house, and on the other the council-room, botanical library, and porter s lodge, is a handsome structure, in the Grecian style and Ionic order, the erection of which cost about £2000 A mechanics institution was established in 1824, and is supported by subscription the building was erected in 1827, at an expense of £7000, and contains a library, in which are two thousand volumes, and a theatre, in which lectures are delivered on those branches of science which are of practical application in the exercise of their trades The theatre royal was erected in 1806, at an expense of £15,000, advanced on shares by a proprietary of forty it is a plain, but commodious, edifice, of which the interior is well arranged and handsomely decorated The amphitheatre, or, as it is called, the minor theatre, was built in 1753, for a principal theatre, but being found too small, was rebuilt by act of parliament in 1775, and having been burnt down in 1789, was again rebuilt and opened for its present use in 1790 The gentlemen s private subscription concerts were established in 1777, when a room, adapted to the accommodation o eight hundred auditors, was built in Fountain-street which being afterwards found too small, a new concert-room was erected, in 1829, for the reception of one thousand two hundred subscribers, in Lower Mosley-street, at an expense of £7000 the entrance is through a handsome lofty portico of six columns of the Corinthian order, supporting a rich entablature and pediment, the concert-room is one hundred and seven feet long

and forty-nine wide there are eight public concerts in the season, at which vocal and instrumental performers of eminent talents are engaged the private concerts, to which the subscribers and their families are admitted, take place every fortnight. The assembly-rooms in Mosley-street were erected in 1792, they form a capacious suite of rooms elegantly fitted up, and superbly decorated, the ball-room is eighty-seven feet long, and forty-four feet wide, the walls and ceiling are beautifully painted in compartments, and lighted with brilliant chandeliers and lustres of cut-glass the tea-room is fifty-four feet long, and fifty-one feet broad, similarly decorated, and over the mantel piece is a full-length portrait of Lord Strange a billiard-room of equal dimensions, and a card-room of smaller size, are also included in the buildings, which were raised by shares of £100 each The first of a series of triennial musical festivals was attempted here, with complete success, in 1828, for the encouragement of which the sum of £20,000 was immediately advanced, on shares of £100 each, as a guarantee for the indemnity of the managers The late Sir Robert Peel, Bart, on accepting the office of patron, presented the stewards with a contribution of £500 Oratorios were performed in the collegiate church, and miscellaneous concerts and dress balls were given in the theatre and assembly-rooms the produce of the performances, which combined the first-rate musical talents in the country, and were brilliantly and numerously attended, exceeded £15,000, and, after paying all expenses, a surplus of more than £5000 was distributed among the various charitable institutions The races, which were established in 1730, commence on the Wednesday in Whitsun-week, and continue to the end of the week the course, which is enclosed by railing, and carefully guarded against accidents, is on Kersal moor, and is about a mile in circuit, a grand stand and numerous booths have been erected on various parts of it, for the accommodation of the spectators, the number of whom is seldom less than two hundred thousand A riding school and gymnasium have been established, for which a building was erected, in 1829, near the concert-rooms, at the lower end of Mosley-street The barracks for the cavalry, in the township of Hulme, are a uniform and handsome range of building, affording accommodation for a squadron of horse, and comprehending an area sufficient for the performance of their evolutions The barracks for infantry, situated in the Regent s road, Salford, are very extensive, and form a compact range of building calculated for the reception of one thousand men, affording, within the enclosure, ample ground for exercise and every requisite accommodation

The market days are Tuesday, Thursday, and Saturday, the first is principally for the sale of merchandise, of which great quantities are brought in carts and wagons from the different factories The markets are plentifully supplied with corn and provisions of all kinds The corn market is held in a building in Hanging-ditch, which was opened as a corn exchange in 1820 The hay market is held in Bridgewater-street, the cattle market in the new Smithfield, at Shude-hill, the markets for butchers meat are held in Brown-street Bridge-street, and the London road, at the back of which is the leather hall, and in other parts of the town　The fish market, which is abundantly supplied with salmon from the river Ribble, with herrings, soles, and flounders, from the north-west coast, and with cod, haddocks, lobsters, and crabs, from the east coast, is held in a suitable building erected on the site of what was formerly called the Old Shambles (which was the only market-place in the town for butchers' meat), at the expense of Sir Oswald Mosley, Bart., near Smithy Door, in 1828, the meal, flour, and cheese market is held in a building on Shude-hill, the fruit, or apple, market is held in Fennel street, and the upper end of Long Millgate, the vegetable market is held in St Mary's gate, and in the upper end of Smithy Door, the middle and lower end of which is the market for butter, poultry, and eggs　Salford, which had been previously supplied from Manchester, has also a separate market, for which accommodation has been provided under the town hall, of which the first stone was laid by Lord Bexley, in 1825　The fairs are Easter Monday and Tuesday, for toys, and October 1st and 2nd, for horses, cattle, and pigs　the latter, for greater convenience, has been removed to Camp field, near St Matthew's church, but the steward of the manor, attended by the borough-reeve and constables, asserts the right of the lord of the manor to hold it in St Anne's square, where, until within the last few years, it was constantly held　there are some other fairs, but of minor importance　At Salford, a fair, commencing on Whit-Monday, is much frequented by the Yorkshire clothiers, blanket manufacturers, button makers, and japanners　the cloth hall, which is a spacious and convenient building, is occupied by numerous tenants during this fair, which lasts for twenty one days, and there is another fair, commencing November 17th, and continuing for the same space of time, the first day of each is for the sale of cattle

The town is within the jurisdiction of the county magistrates, who hold a petty session for the division every Thursday　the municipal regulations are conducted by a borough reeve and two principal constables, chosen annually from among the most respectable of the inhabitants, by a jury impannelled by the stewards of the manor, at the latter of the courts leet, which are held every year after Easter and Michaelmas　The constables appoint a deputy to act for them, who has a salary of £600 per annum, and is assisted by four beadles and two hundred special constables　A court of requests for the parish is held over the butchers' market in Brown-street, under an act passed in the 48th of George III, every alternate Wednesday, for the recovery of debts under £5　The lord of the manor of Manchester holds a court baron every third Wednesday, and a court for the hundred of Salford is held every third Thursday, for the recovery of debts under 40s　the sheriff's county court is also held here monthly, by adjournment from Preston, for the trial of pleas, and the recovery of debts not exceeding £10, in actions in which the parties reside in the hundred of Salford　The quarter sessions are held at Salford by adjournment, at which the business for the whole of the hundred of Salford is transacted, under the superintendence of a chairman, who has a salary of £800 per annum, paid by the hundred, the number of prisoners tried at these sessions is generally about two hundred　A barrister, with a salary of

£1000 per annum, paid out of the police rates of Manchester and Salford, sits daily as a magistrate, under the provisions of an act of parliament, for the despatch of business, in which he is assisted by some of the county magistrates resident in the neighbourhood　The town hall is a noble and elegant edifice, erected under the superintendence and from a design of Mr Francis Goodwin, in the Grecian style of architecture, at an expense of £40,000, after the model of the Temple of Erectheus, at Athens, with a beautiful tower and dome in the centre, resembling the tower of Andronicus, called the "Temple of the Winds"　the principal entrance is by a magnificent colonnade with a rich entablature, in front of which are some sculptured representations of the town of Manchester, and emblems of trade and commerce, in the wings are niches containing statues of Solon and Alfred, in the medallions of the attic are busts in alto rilievo of Pythagoras, Lycurgus, Hale, and Locke　The building contains various departments for transacting the public business of the town, on the principal floor is a splendid public room, one hundred and thirty-two feet long, forty-three feet eight inches wide, and fifty-one feet and a half in height to the centre of the principal dome　the interior of this noble room is divided into three parts by two ranges of eight elegant Ionic pillars, so disposed that each part may form a separate room, the central part is lighted by a magnificent dome, supported on sixteen dwarf columns of Scagliola marble, corresponding with the exterior design of the tower, and the other parts are finished in a very chaste style of classic beauty　The light is elegantly introduced into the extreme sections of the great room by concealed skylights, and through stained glass in the panels of the ceiling and dome, decorated to correspond with those that are not pierced for that purpose　Three staircases lead to this splendid room, with the interior of which the principal staircase will be made to harmonize　The town hall at Salford is a handsome stone edifice, with a noble portico in the Grecian Doric style, after that of the Temple of Theseus, supporting a triangular pediment, it affords in the lower part an area for the use of the market, and contains in the upper an elegant suite of assembly rooms　The large room, which extends the whole length of the building, is elegantly fitted up, and decorated with pilasters supporting a richly-ornamented frieze and cornice, the ceiling is chastely embellished, and the room is appropriated to the use of the Salford courts, which are held here, being also occasionally used for public balls and concerts　The principal entrance to the market-place is from the centre of the town hall, through a Doric colonnade, there are separate markets for meat, vegetables, fish, and poultry, chiefly covered over and well ventilated　this building was erected under the superintendence of Messrs Lane and Goodwin, at an expense of £10,000

The Chorlton-row town hall, dispensary, and constables' dwelling-house, are connected in one building, the front of which is handsome and imposing　In the central part is a boldly-projecting portico of four Doric columns supporting a pediment, of which the frieze is ornamented with wreaths, the wings are decorated with antæ, rising from a rustic basement　The portico leads to the public offices on the ground floor, including a committee-room, principal clerk s office, assembling-room for the poor, and the pay-office, over these is a spacious room for public meetings, well fitted up, and approached by a wide staircase and lobbies On the basement floor are the watchmen s assembling-room, the lamplighters' room, oil-cellar, and three lock-up rooms, and in the attic are ample store-rooms One of the wings is appropriated as a residence for the constable, and the other as a dispensary, which was established and is supported by subscription this building was erected under the superintendence of Mr Richard Lane, at an expense of £4500 The New Bailey, or house of correction for the hundred of Salford, adjoining which is the governor s residence, was erected in 1790, upon the radiating principle, and comprises twenty-four wards, the same number of day-rooms and airing-yards, one hundred and fifty workshops, for the classification and employment of the prisoners, and a tread mill, with eight wheels, for such as are condemned to hard labour the outer walls include an area of twenty-seven thousand square yards over the entrance, which is a large rusticated stone building, is a sessions-room, in which the weekly and quarter sessions are held, adjoining it are the grand jury rooms and withdrawing-rooms for the magistrates and barristers, and in the lower story are the turnkey's lodge, and rooms for the confinement of prisoners prior to examination The discipline observed in this prison, which is capable of receiving nine hundred and twenty-six prisoners, and in which there are generally five hundred, is admirably calculated to reclaim the guilty, and to afford them, on their release, the means of future subsistence by honest industry, those who have learned any trade are regularly employed in the exercise of it, and receive a considerable portion of their earnings, and such as have not, prior to their committal, are taught, during their confinement, some trade by which they may honestly maintain themselves after their discharge

Manchester comprises only one parish, which is in the archdeaconry and diocese of Chester The old collegiate church, which, till after the Reformation, afforded accommodation for all the inhabitants of Manchester and Salford, was founded and dedicated to the Blessed Virgin, by Thomas, Lord de la Warre, in the 9th of Henry V, who endowed it for a warden and eight fellows, this establishment, the revenue of which was £226 12 5, was dissolved in the reign of Edward VI, and re-established in that of Elizabeth, under the designation of the Warden and Fellows of Christ s College, Manchester The dilapidation of the church, and the misappropriation of the collegiate funds, under the wardenship of Richard Murray, induced the inhabitants to petition the throne for a revival of the former charter, in 1635, and Charles I granted them a new charter of foundation, with rules for the government of the college, drawn up by Archbishop Laud. Under this charter, the management is vested in a warden, to be appointed by the crown, who must at least be a bachelor in divinity, or of canon and civil laws, and in four fellows, who must be masters of arts, or bachelors of laws, they are a body corporate, with a common seal, under the designation of the "Warden and Fellows of Christ s College, Manchester" The same charter provides for the appointment of a

sub-warden, treasurer, collector, registrar, a master of the choir, organist, four singing men (either clerks or laymen), and four boys skilled in music, to be chosen by the warden and fellows, and ordains that there shall be continually in the college, two chaplains, or vicars, of the degree of bachelors of arts, and two clerks to administer the sacraments, visit the sick, and perform other religious offices During the usurpation of Cromwell, the Independents established their own form of worship in the college, in 1649, and, in the same year, the chapter-house and the college chest were broken open, and the foundation deeds seized by the soldiers, and sent, with other papers, to London, where they were subsequently destroyed in the great fire of 1666 The college was soon afterwards dissolved by an act of parliament for the sale of dean and chapter lands, and, during the interregnum, the last warden officiated as parochial minister, for an annual stipend After the Restoration, the institution was revived, subject to the statutes of Charles I, and the warden reinstated in his office The church is a spacious and elaborately ornamented structure, in the later style of English architecture, with a handsome square embattled tower, strengthened with buttresses, and crowned with pinnacles, the roof of the nave, which rises to a considerable height above the aisles, is concealed by a rich pierced parapet and decorated with pinnacles, the windows are spacious, and filled with elegant tracery, and the exterior, which is relieved by the projection of some beautiful chapels, has a splendid and truly magnificent appearance The view of the interior is strikingly impressive, the lofty nave is lighted by a noble range of clerestory windows of fine proportion and beautiful design, and the choir is splendidly enriched with tabernacle work of elaborate and delicate execution, the roof is finely groined and ornamented with grotesque figures of angels playing on musical instruments, shields, and other devices, richly carved, considerable portions of the original stained glass are still preserved in several of the windows, and the altar is decorated with a piece of tapestry representing the offerings of the early Christians, and the punishment of Ananias and Sapphira In different parts of the church, and in several chapels, are many ancient and interesting monuments

Trinity church, at Salford, was founded and endowed by Humphrey Booth, Esq, in 1635, but having fallen into decay, it was rebuilt in 1752 it is a neat edifice in the Grecian style of architecture, and of the Doric order, with a steeple, and contains some handsome monuments and mural tablets the living is a perpetual curacy, in the patronage of Sir Robert Gore Booth, Bart St Ann's church, on the south side of St Ann s square, founded in 1709, under the auspices of Lady Ann Bland, is a spacious structure in the Grecian style of architecture, and of the Corinthian order, with a tower formerly surmounted by a spire, which has been taken down, the interior, affording accommodation for one thousand one hundred and seventy-five persons, is a fine specimen of handsome and appropriate decoration the living is a rectory not in charge, in the patronage of the Bishop of Chester St Mary s, between Deans-gate and the river Irwell, erected by the Warden and Fellows of the College, by act of parliament in 1756, is a handsome edifice of the Doric order, with a lofty tower and spire, one hundred and eighty-six feet in height, the interior, which contains nine hundred and ninety-seven sittings, though dark, from the massive proportions of the pillars supporting the galleries, is very elegant the altar piece is embellished with a well executed painting of the Ascension, after Raphael, by Williams, and the window is enriched with stained glass, beneath which are the heads of St Peter and St Paul the living is a rectory not in charge, in the patronage of the Warden and Fellows of the College St Paul's, a neat edifice of brick, was erected in 1765, and contains one thousand one hundred and forty-seven sittings the living is a perpetual curacy, in the patronage of the Warden and Fellows of the College St John s, in Byrom street, was built by Edward Byrom, Esq, under the authority of an act of parliament, in 1769 it is a handsome structure, in the later style of English architecture, with a tower, the interior, which affords accommodation for one thousand and ninety persons, is remarkably neat, and handsomely ornamented the chancel windows are embellished with stained glass, in one of the south windows is a beautiful representation of Christ entering into Bethlehem, in ancient stained glass, brought from a convent in Rouen, and in the corresponding window, on the opposite side, is also some ancient stained glass, brought from the continent the vestry-room is richly ornamented with painted glass, and contains several fine paintings, among which are those of Paul before Felix, the Last Supper, the Holy Family, the Descent from the Cross (a copy of the original in St Peter s church), a perspective view of the church, and other subjects there are some handsome monuments and tablets in the church, and a piece of sculpture, by Flaxman, erected by the congregation, as a tribute of respect for their pastor, the Rev J Clowes the church is entirely vaulted underneath, and is the property of the heirs of the founder the living is a rectory not in charge, in the patronage of the Heirs of Edward Byrom, Esq, with reversion, after the lapse of two presentations from the period of its consecration, to the Warden and Fellows St James, erected by the Rev Cornelius Bayley, D D, in 1787, is a spacious and handsome brick edifice, with a small stone spire, and contains one thousand three hundred and ninety sittings the living is a perpetual curacy, in the patronage of Dr Bayley, with reversion, after sixty years from the date of consecration, to the Warden and Fellows of the College St Michael s, a large edifice of brick, with a foundation for a steeple not yet built, and containing nine hundred sittings, was founded by the late Rev Humphrey Owen, in 1789 the living is a perpetual curacy, in the patronage of the Heirs of the founder, with reversion, after sixty years, to the Warden and Fellows of the College St Mark's was founded by the late Rev E Ethelston, and finished by his son, in 1794 the living is a perpetual curacy, in the patronage of the Heirs of the founder, with reversion, after sixty years, to the Warden and Fellows of the College St Peter s was erected by subscription among the inhabitants, and consecrated in 1794 it is a handsome edifice of Runcorn stone, in the Grecian style of architecture, with a stately tower and a noble portico of the Doric order the interior, which contains five hundred and fifty sittings, is remarkable for the elegance and chasteness of its decoration, the

altar-piece is embellished with a fine painting of the Descent from the Cross, by Annibal Caracci the living is a perpetual curacy, in the patronage of the Trustees for building the church, with reversion, after sixty years, to the Warden and Fellows St Stephen s, Salford, a neat building of brick ornamented with stone, with a handsome tower, was founded, in 1794, by the Rev N M Cheek, to whose memory a neat mural tablet has been erected the living is a perpetual curacy, in the patronage of the Heirs of the founder, with reversion, after sixty years, to the Warden and Fellows of the College St George s, a large building of brick, with a tower of the same material, was opened for divine service in 1798, and consecrated in 1818, when it was purchased by subscription the living is a perpetual curacy, in the patronage of the Bishop of Chester All Saints, in the centre of Grosvenor-square, a large and elegant structure in the Grecian style of architecture, was built at the sole charge of the Rev Charles Burton, L L.B, at an expense of £14,000, and consecrated in 1820 the interior is elegantly ornamented, in the window over the altar is a fine painting of the Passion of Our Saviour in the Garden of Gethsemane the living is a perpetual curacy, in the patronage of the Founder, with reversion to the Warden and Fellows St Matthew s, in Castle field, was erected, in 1825, by grant from the parliamentary commissioners, at an expense of £11,917 it is an elegant structure, in the later style of English architecture, with a tower and spire, and contains one thousand eight hundred and thirty-eight sittings, of which nine hundred and seventy-eight are free the living is a perpetual curacy, in the patronage of the Warden and Fellows of the College St Philip s, in Salford, a handsome edifice in the Grecian style of architecture, with a tower and semicircular portico of the Ionic order, and containing one thousand eight hundred and twenty-eight sittings, of which one thousand three hundred are free, was erected, in 1825, by grant from the parliamentary commissioners, at an expense of £13,423 5 the living is a perpetual curacy, in the patronage of the Warden and Fellows of the College St George s, Hulme, an elegant edifice in the later style of English architecture, with a tower, and containing two thousand and two sittings, of which one thousand two hundred are free, was built in 1828, at an expense of £14,416 19 5, by grant from the parliamentary commissioners the interior is elegantly arranged, and has a grand and imposing effect the roof is elaborately groined, and enriched with bosses and flowers, the columns separating the nave from the aisles are surmounted by a handsome range of clerestory arches, the altar is highly decorated, and the east end is lighted by three beautiful windows enriched with elegant tracery, the tower is one hundred and thirty-five feet high The commissioners have also granted a sum of £9900 for the erection of a church, to be dedicated to St Andrew, in Travis-street, and to contain two thousand sittings, of which seven hundred are to be free, which is at present in progress An episcopal chapel at Ardwick, dedicated to St Thomas, was consecrated in 1741, and enlarged in 1777, it is a neat building of brick the living is a perpetual curacy, in the patronage of the Warden and Fellows of the College St Clement s, in Lever-street, erected in 1793, and St Luke s chapel, in Bedford-street, built in

1804, are open for the performance of divine service, according to the liturgy of the Church of England, but have not been consecrated   There are five places of worship for Baptists, three for a society calling themselves Bible Christians, one for the Society of Friends, nine for Independents, one for Welch Independents, one for Independent Methodists, two for Methodists of the New Connexion, one for Primitive, one for Tent, eleven for Wesleyan, and two for Welch, Methodists, one for Presbyterians, two for Swedenborgians, and two for Unitarians, there are also three Roman Catholic chapels, and a synagogue   Of the dissenting places of worship, several are conspicuous for architectural beauty, among which may be noticed the Roman Catholic chapel of St Augustine, an elegant structure in the later style of English architecture, built in 1820, from a design by Mr Palmer, at an expense of £16,000 under the chapel are school-rooms for one thousand two hundred children   The meeting house for the Society of Friends is a spacious structure, equally conspicuous for the chaste simplicity of its character and the beauty of its Ionic portico, of which the design was taken from that of the Temple of Ceres on the Ilyssus   the interior is divided, near the centre, into two distinct houses by a sliding partition, of which the upper part is by machinery raised above the ceiling, and the lower depressed beneath the floor, when it may be convenient   it was erected under the direction of Mr Lane, at an expense of £12,000   The Wesleyan meeting house in Oxford road has a handsome portico of the Doric order, and that in Irwell-street, Salford, has a handsome Ionic portico and pediment   A general cemetery, for the interment of persons of all religious denominations, according to their several rites, comprising four acres surrounded with a wall, was opened in 1821   the entrance is from Rusholme road, through a handsome iron gate, on the left of which is a chapel for the performance of the funeral service, and on the right a dwelling-house for similar design for the resident registrar

The free grammar school was founded, in the 7th of Henry VIII, by Hugh Oldham, Bishop of Exeter, who endowed it with certain houses, tenements, and corn-mills, in the town of Manchester, and with lands at Ancoats adjoining, producing a revenue exceeding £4000   The establishment consists of a head-master, whose salary, including £30 allowed for a drawing master, is £446 per annum, a second master, with a salary of £218, an assistant to the head-master, with a salary of £160, an assistant to the second master, with a salary of £125, and a master of the lower school, with a salary of £120 per annum   the head and second masters, who are appointed by the President of Corpus Christi College, Oxford, have each a stall in the collegiate church   The number of scholars is in general from one hundred and fifty to two hundred, who receive gratuitously a classical education, but pay for other instruction   There are twelve exhibitions, of £40 per annum each, to either of the Universities, belonging to this school, which also, in turn with the schools of Hereford and Marlborough, has an interest in sixteen scholarships in Brasenose College, Oxford, and in the same number in St John's College, Cambridge, founded by Sarah, Duchess of Somerset, in 1679, and varying in value from £18 to £26 each per annum   there are also in the nomination of the Warden of the Colle-

giate Church, and the Rectors of Prestwich and Bury, as trustees of Hulme's estates, fifteen fellowships, varying from £60 to £120 each, in Brasenose College, for bachelors of arts, who may remain there four years after taking that degree, founded by William Hulme, Esq., of Kearsley, in this county, which are frequently conferred upon scholars from Manchester   The school-house is a plain but spacious building, erected in 1777, on the site of the original edifice, having an owl, the crest of the founder, sculptured on a large stone medallion over the entrance, and containing an upper school-room, ninety-six feet long, and thirty feet wide, at one end of which are the arms of the founder emblazoned, and a lower school room, of smaller dimensions   the property of the school is vested in twelve trustees, and its management is superintended by the Warden of the College

The Blue coat hospital, part of which is appropriated to the use of the Cheetham library, was founded, in 1653, by means of a bequest from Humphrey Cheetham, Esq, of Clayton hall, near Manchester, who left £7000 to trustees, to purchase estates for its endowment, and a sum of money to purchase a house for the reception of forty scholars, of whom, fourteen were to be natives of Manchester, six of Salford, three of Droylsden, two of Crumpsall, ten of Bolton, and five of Turton, which number has, in the same proportion, from the augmentation of the funds, been increased to eighty   the boys, who are nominated by the churchwardens of the several townships, and elected by the trustees, are clothed, maintained, educated, and apprenticed   The buildings of the college founded by Lord de la Warre were, after its dissolution, purchased by the trustees from the Earl of Derby, to whom it had been presented by the Crown, and appropriated to the use of the hospital   The premises occupy the site of the baronial mansion of the Gresleys, on the bank of the river Irk, near its confluence with the Irwell, and comprise an extensive range of building, exhibiting, through all its subsequent repairs, strong features of its collegiate architecture   the lower apartments are assigned to the use of the Blue-coat hospital, and the upper story contains the library and apartments of the governor and librarian   the library extends through a long gallery divided into compartments, adjoining it is a large reading-room, ornamented with antique carvings, and portraits of the founder, of Dr Alexander Nowell, Dean of St Paul's, Dr William Whitaker, successively Master of Trinity, Queen's, and St John's colleges, Cambridge, Robert Bolton, a learned divine, and John Bradford, a native of Manchester, who having received the rudiments of his education in the grammar school, was afterwards Fellow of Pembroke Hall, Cambridge, and was burned as a heretic in the reign of Mary   The ladies' jubilee school, for maintaining, educating, and qualifying as household servants female orphans, was established in 1809, in commemoration of the fiftieth anniversary of the accession of George III   the school-house is a neat and commodious building on the borders of Strangeways park, there are thirty children in the school, which is supported by subscription, and is under the direction of a committee of ladies   Miss Hall, one of the original and most zealous promoters of this institution, bequeathed, at her death in 1828, £44,000, to be equally divided among four charities in the town, viz, this school, the infirmary, the lying-in hospital, and the fever ward   In 1723, Mrs Ann Hinde bequeathed land and messuages, now producing nearly £200 per annum, for the education and clothing of twenty-eight children of Manchester, and twenty-nine of the township of Stretford   St Paul s charity school, with a dwelling-house for the master, was erected in 1777, for the clothing and instruction of poor children, and is partly supported by subscription, it has also a permanent income of £34 5 per annum   this school was suspended in 1823, and the endowment allowed to accumulate   The National schools in Manchester and at Salford were both founded in 1812, and are supported by subscription   in each there are at present three hundred boys and the same number of girls   The Lancasterian school was founded in 1809, and the present building, in Marshall-street, was erected in 1813, at an expense of £5000   the school-room is one hundred and fifty feet long, and sixty-six wide, and will contain more than one thousand children, there are at present six hundred and ninety boys, and two hundred and ninety girls in the school, which is supported by subscription   There are Sunday schools connected with the established church and the various dissenting congregations, in which not less than from twenty to thirty thousand children are instructed   there are also several infant schools, which are numerously attended

The infirmary was established, in 1752, by Joseph Bancroft, Esq, in conjunction with Charles White, Esq, M D, and, in 1755, a building for the purpose was erected by subscription   it has been supported with a liberality commensurate with its importance in a large manufacturing town, and, since it was first opened for the reception of patients, has afforded medical relief to more than half a million of the labouring class   the buildings, which have been progressively enlarged, and to which other establishments have been attached, contain one hundred and eighty beds for the accommodation of in-patients, with apartments for the officers and attendants, and a surgery, library of medical books, committee-rooms, and other offices, also a complete set of baths, for the exclusive use of the patients   The grounds are tastefully laid out in gravel walks, lawns, and parterres, and form a public promenade, to which the fine pool in front of the buildings adds considerable beauty   A complete set of hot, cold, vapour, and medicated baths has been fitted up here, with every accommodation for the public use, the profits arising from which are appropriated to the support of the institution   A lunatic hospital and asylum was founded in 1765, and the building was opened for the reception of patients in the spring of the following year   The dispensary was established in 1792, and an edifice for its use erected by public subscription adjoining the infirmary   it is of brick, and is ample and commodious, adapted more to use than to the display of architectural beauty, in the centre of the front is a clock, the dial of which is illuminated at night   In 1830, his Majesty, on the solicitation of the chairman and committee, graciously became the patron of this institution, which is now styled " The Manchester Royal Infirmary, Dispensary, Lunatic Hospital, and Asylum, ' the buildings for these several uses being already contiguous, it is intended, in the ensuing spring, to give them a uniformity of design, by facing the front

and the north side with stone   The plan comprehends a principal and a side front, of which the elevation is strikingly elegant and imposing   the principal front has in the centre a lofty and boldly-projecting portico of four fluted Ionic columns, thirty-eight feet high, supporting a pediment, of which the frieze and cornice are carried round the building, the angles of which are ornamented with antæ of appropriate character   the side front is of similar design, differing only in the slighter projection of the portico, which has but two columns in the centre, with engaged antæ at the angles   The whole building is three stories high above the basement, and the lower story is channelled in horizontal lines   The fever hospital, in Aytoun-street, is a plain and substantial structure of brick, erected by subscription, at an expense of £5000, in 1805   it is under the superintendence of a Board of Health, contains twenty one wards for the reception of one hundred patients, and is furnished with all requisite offices and every convenience for promoting the restoration of health, and preventing the spread of contagious disorders

The lying-in hospital, in Stanley-street, Salford, was instituted in 1790, for the assistance of poor married women, and for the cure of diseases incident to females, and to children under two years of age   it is supported by subscription, and its benefits are extended by the Ladies Auxiliary Society for visiting the patients, and furnishing supplies of linen and other necessaries   The school for the deaf and dumb, at present held in this building, was established in 1825, for children of both sexes, and consists of three classes of pupils, viz, parlour boarders, general boarders, who pay each £26 per annum to the funds of the institution, and the children of the indigent poor, who are gratuitously maintained and instructed   The governors intend to erect a suitable building for the purposes of this school, as soon as their funds will enable them   it was commenced under the care of Mr Vaughan, with fourteen scholars, and there are now upwards of fifty receiving instruction   no child is admitted under nine years of age, nor above fourteen   An institution, in Faulkner-street   for curing diseases of the eye, was established by subscription in 1815, and, though its annual income does not exceed £200, affords relief to one thousand five hundred patients generally during the year   The Lock hospital, in Bond-street, established in 1819, for the recovery of persons suffering from disease, has, since its institution, administered relief to many thousands, of whom a very large proportion have been received as in-patients, and the female penitentiary, in Rusholme road, instituted in 1822, as a temporary asylum for such as have deviated from the path of virtue, and may be desirous to qualify themselves for reputable situations, both these institutions are supported by subscription.   There are various provident societies, among which is that of the commercial clerks, established in 1802, each member pays an admission fee according to his age, and an annual subscription   from these funds, aided by honorary contributions, support is derived in sickness and old age, and a provision made for widows and children   the number of members amounts to nearly a thousand.   The Manchester Society for the encouragement and improvement of female servants, was established in 1816, at the rooms of the society in Chapel walk, a free register office is opened for supplying members of the institution with servants, and also for gratuitously supplying female servants with situations, and for the distribution of annual premiums to servants, proportioned to the length of their continuance in the same family, and the propriety of their conduct There are also numerous societies, adapted to the state of the manufacturing population, savings banks, associations for clothing the poor, among which the most considerable are, the Manchester and Salford Church Clothing Society, and the Salford Dorcas Society, both instituted in 1822, for the distribution of clothes among the needy and destitute The Strangers Friend Society was instituted in 1791, under the auspices of the Rev Dr Adam Clarke it is under the direction of a committee, and is open to all objects of distress, without any regard to their religious tenets The Samaritan Society, a similar institution, was established in 1824, and various other institutions for the relief and assistance of human misery are liberally supported There are funds at the disposal of the borough-reeve, amounting to more than £4000 per annum, arising from charitable bequests, for distribution in bread, clothes, money, and other necessaries, among the aged, infirm, and indigent poor

Among the distinguished natives of Manchester, or persons who have been otherwise connected with it, may be enumerated, William Crabtree, an astronomical writer, and the inventor of the micrometer, born at Broughton, within the parish, and killed at the battle of Marston Moor, in 1644, John Byrom, an ingenious poet, and the author of a popular system of short hand, born at Kersal Moor, near the town, in 1691, John Ferriar, M D, author of Illustrations of Sterne, &c, and other popular works, Thomas Barritt, a distinguished antiquary and heraldist, whose large and valuable heraldic collections in manuscript have been placed in the library of Cheetham s hospital, Thomas Faulkner, an enterprising traveller, who published the earliest authentic account of Patagonia, and died in 1774, the Rev John Whitaker, the Manchester historian, Thomas Percival, M D, an eminent physician and popular writer, Charles White, M D, F R S, a distinguished surgeon and anatomist, and Joseph Farington, R A, a landscape painter of considerable celebrity Manchester gives the titles of duke and earl to the family of Montagu

MANEA, a chapelry in the parish of COVENEY, southern division of the hundred of WITCHFORD, Isle of ELY, county of CAMBRIDGE, 7¾ miles (S E by S) from March, containing 657 inhabitants There is a place of worship for Wesleyan Methodists

MANEWDEN, a parish in the hundred of CLAVERING, county of ESSEX, 2½ miles (N W) from Stanstead-Mountfitchet, containing 656 inhabitants The living is a discharged vicarage, in the archdeaconry of Colchester, and diocese of London, rated in the king s books at £14 The Rev H Marsh and others were patrons in 1803 The church is dedicated to St Mary A fair is held here on Easter-Monday

MANFIELD, a parish partly in the western, but chiefly in the eastern, division of the wapentake of GILLING, North riding of the county of YORK, 4¾ miles (W by S) from Darlington, containing, with the township of Cliffe, 493 inhabitants The living is a vicarage, in the archdeaconry of Richmond, and diocese of Chester, rated in the king s books at £6 1 3, and in the patronage of the Crown The church, dedicated to All Saints, is a handsome ancient structure, with a fine tower Here is a free school, with an endowment of £10 a year, payable out of the income arising from the charity estate of the parish

MANGERSBURY, a hamlet in the parish of STOW on the WOLD, upper division of the hundred of SLAUGHTER, county of GLOUCESTER, 1¼ mile (S S E) from Stow on the Wold, containing 226 inhabitants The old Roman Fosse-way passes through this place

MANGOTSFIELD, a parish in the hundred of BARTON-REGIS, county of GLOUCESTER, 5¼ miles (N E by E) from Bristol, containing 3179 inhabitants The living is a perpetual curacy, in the jurisdiction of the Consistory Court of the Bishop of Bristol, endowed with £400 private benefaction, £400 royal bounty, and £1000 parliamentary grant, and in the patronage of Thomas Wadham, Esq The church is dedicated to St James There is a place of worship for Independents Here was once a nunnery, of which part of the cloisters was seen by Leland, but there is not now any vestige of it.

MANLEY, a township in the parish of FRODSHAM, second division of the hundred of EDDISBURY, county palatine of CHESTER, 4¾ miles (S by W) from Frodsham, containing 333 inhabitants

MANNINGFORD-ABBOTS, a parish in the hundred of SWANBOROUGH, county of WILTS, 1¾ mile (W S W) from Pewsey, containing 159 inhabitants The living is a rectory, in the archdeaconry of Wilts, and diocese of Salisbury, rated in the king's books at £9 10 2½, and in the patronage of Sir J D Astley, Bart The river Avon runs through the parish

MANNINGFORD-BOHUN, a tything in the parish of WILSFORD, hundred of SWANBOROUGH, county of WILTS, 2¼ miles (S W) from Pewsey, containing 228 inhabitants

MANNINGFORD BRUCE, a parish in the hundred of SWANBOROUGH, county of WILTS, 2 miles (S W) from Pewsey, containing 222 inhabitants The living is a rectory, in the archdeaconry of Wilts, and diocese of Salisbury, rated in the king's books at £10 3 4, and in the patronage of the Rev Mr Wells The church is dedicated to St Peter, over the altar is a tablet inscribed to the memory of Mary Nicholas, who was greatly instrumental in the preservation of Charles II, after his defeat at Worcester

MANNINGHAM, a township in the parish of BRADFORD, wapentake of MORLEY, West riding of the county of YORK, 1¼ mile (N W) from Bradford, containing 2474 inhabitants, who are principally employed in the spinning of worsted yarn and the manufacture of woollen goods

MANNINGTON, a parish in the southern division of the hundred of ERPINGHAM, county of NORFOLK, 4¾ miles (N W by N) from Aylesham, containing 16 inhabitants The living is a discharged rectory, with that of Itteringham, in the archdeaconry and diocese of Norwich, rated in the king's books at £1 16 5½

MANNINGTREE, a market town and parish, in the hundred of TENDRING, county of ESSEX, 36 miles (N E by E) from Chelmsford and 61 (N E by E)

from London, containing 1265 inhabitants The ancient name of this place was *Scidinghoo*, or, as it is called in Domesday-book, *Sciddinchou* , and in the reign of Henry VIII it had received the name of *Many-tree*, of which the present appellation is an obvious corruption Here was formerly a guild, dedicated to the Holy Trinity, the revenue of which was £8 5 4 , and the importance of the place may be inferred from a certificate of the value of chantry lands, in which it is termed " a great town and also a haven town, having in it to the number of seven hundred houseling people It is situated on the southern bank of the river Stour, on the road from London to Harwich, is irregularly built, and the streets are partially paved, but not lighted , the inhabitants are supplied with excellent water The malt trade is carried on to a great extent, and corn, coal, and deals are imported. The Stour was made navigable from this town to Sudbury by act of parliament in the 4th and 5th of the reign of Anne The market is on Thursday, for corn and cattle, and there is a toy fair on the Thursday in Whitsun-week The petty sessions for the division of Tendring are held on Mondays at Mistley, Thorpe, Great Bromley, and Manningtree alternately, when overseers, surveyors, and constables, are appointed A court baron is held here annually by the lords of the manor of Mistley and Manningtree, the court leet formerly held is discontinued The living is a perpetual curacy, in the archdeaconry of Colchester, and diocese of London, and in the patronage of the Rector of Mistley The church has been enlarged by the addition of three hundred and forty-five free sittings, towards defraying the expense of which, the Incorporated Society for the enlargement of churches and chapels contributed £450 There are places of worship for Baptists, Independents, and Wesleyan Methodists A National school for children of both sexes is supported by voluntary contributions

MANSELL-GAMAGE, a parish in the hundred of GRIMSWORTH, county of HEREFORD, 8½ miles (W N W) from Hereford, containing 154 inhabitants The living is a discharged vicarage, in the archdeaconry and diocese of Hereford, rated in the king s books at £5 6 8 , endowed with £200 private benefaction, and £200 royal bounty, and in the patronage of Sir J G Cotterell, Bart The church is dedicated to St Giles

MANSELL-LACY, a parish in the hundred of GRIMSWORTH, county of HEREFORD, 7 miles (N W by W) from Hereford, containing 287 inhabitants The living is a discharged vicarage, in the archdeaconry and diocese of Hereford, rated in the king s books at £5 3 11½, endowed with £800 private benefaction, £400 royal bounty, and £1200 parliamentary grant, and in the patronage of Sir Uvedale Price, Bart. The church is dedicated to St Michael

MANSERGH, a chapelry in the parish of KIRKBY-LONSDALE, LONSDALE ward, county of WESTMORLAND, 3½ miles (N N W) from Kirkby-Lonsdale, containing 157 inhabitants The living is a perpetual curacy, in the archdeaconry of Richmond, and diocese of Chester, endowed with £400 private benefaction, and £600 royal bounty, and in the patronage of the Vicar of Kirkby-Lonsdale The chapel, dedicated to St Peter, was built in 1726, by the subscriptions of Jacob Dawson and others The river Lune runs through the chapelry

MANSFIELD, a market town and parish, comprising the hamlets of Pleasley Hill, Radmansthwaite, and Moor-Haigh, in the northern division of the wapentake of BROXTOW, county of NOTTINGHAM, 14 miles (N by W) from Nottingham, and 138 (N N W) from London, containing 7861 inhabitants The name of this place, anciently written *Maunsfeld*, is derived from its situation on the small river Mann, or Maun, which rises about three miles westward the town is of great antiquity, and is supposed to have been of British or Roman origin During the Saxon Octarchy it was a temporary residence of the Mercian kings, for the convenience of hunting in the Royal forest of Sherwood in the reigns of Edward the Confessor, William the Conqueror, and William Rufus, it was a royal demesne, and so continued till the time of Elizabeth, except that, in the reign of Henry VIII , it was, with other manors, given to the Duke of Norfolk, but afterwards restored to the crown, in exchange for other property it was ultimately granted away, by letters patent, in the 44th of Elizabeth The custom of gavelkind prevails in this manor, within which there is a small manor belonging to the Dean of Lincoln Till the year 1715, the courts for the forest of Sherwood, celebrated in ballad story as the scene of the exploits of the renowned archer, Robin Hood, and his band of freebooters, were held at Mansfield The town is situated on the road from London to Leeds, in a deep vale, in the centre of the ancient Forest of Sherwood it is of considerable size, and consists of three principal streets, besides others branching from them, which are narrow and irregular the houses are principally built of grey stone, and, at the entrance to the town from Southwell, there are several excavated in the sand stone rock Considerable improvement has been made within the last five years, under two acts of parliament obtained in 1823 and 1825, under the authority of one of which the town is lighted with gas, by a joint-stock company, the approach from the London road has been widened, and the market-place considerably enlarged On the north side of the town is a cold bath, supplied by a spring issuing from an adjacent rock. A small theatre is open during the summer months , and races take place at the July fair a subscription library was established in 1825, and there is an excellent news and reading-room The moot-hall was erected in 1752, in the market-place, at the expense of Henrietta Cavendish Holles, Countess of Oxford and Mortimer besides the apartments for the transaction of public business, the building comprises an assembly-room Mansfield has some considerable manufactures in cotton, hosiery, and lace , of the first, one mill contains two thousand four hundred spindles, and affords employment to one hundred and sixty persons , besides this there are six other cotton mills upon the river Maun, within two miles of the town upwards of seven hundred frames are engaged in weaving stockings and gloves, both of silk and cotton , there are iron-foundries for light castings , and a very extensive trade is carried on in malt, also in cutting and working into architectural ornaments the fine freestone obtained from several adjacent quarries, which is afterwards sent to various parts of the kingdom The trading interests of the town have been much benefited by the construction of a double railway, about seven miles in length, from Mansfield to Pinxton basin, there communicating with the Cromford canal, under an act of parliament passed in 1817, at an expense of £33,000 the price of coal obtained from the pits at Pinxton and Kirkby has thus been reduced about one-third In the reign of Henry III the inhabitants obtained a charter for a weekly market on Monday, afterwards altered to Thursday, also the privilege of *housebote* and *haybot*, or timber for repairs, and wood for fences, out of the forest, which they still enjoy The market has been held on Thursday from time immemorial there are two annual meetings (not chartered fairs), on April 5th and July 10th, for the sale of cattle and hogs, and a fair on the second Thursday in October, for horses, cattle, sheep, and cheese

The living is a vicarage, in the peculiar jurisdiction of the court of the Lord of the Manor of Mansfield, rated in the king's books at £7 7 6, and in the patronage of the Duke of Portland, as lessee under the Dean of Lincoln A chaplaincy is attached to the church, for the support of which the vicar and churchwardens were incorporated and invested with lands in the 4th and 5th of Philip and Mary, there is likewise an afternoon lectureship on Sunday, the stipend arising out of certain lands, called the "Eight Men s Intake,' and from a gallery in the church, called the "Vicar s Gallery the chaplain is appointed by the vicar and churchwardens, and the lecturer by the trustees of the endowment The church, which is dedicated to St Peter, exhibits specimens of each style, from the Norman to the later English, the two lower portions of the tower are in the early Norman style, and there is one window in the early English, the arches, piers, and north door, are in good decorated character, the tower is surmounted by a low spire There are places of worship for General Baptists, the Society of Friends, Independents, Primitive and Wesleyan Methodists, and Unitarians The free grammar school was founded by letters patent, dated March 8th, 1561, for the education of youth in grammar, under a master and an under-master the vicar and churchwardens for the time being were incorporated governors, and enabled to acquire and hold lands, and, with eight of the principal inhabitants, who are chosen by the rest of the parishioners, appoint the master and under-master the deed of incorporation having reference to the maintenance of the chaplain, as well as of the school, and the lands belonging to each having become indistinguishable, it was decided in Chancery, about 1680, that two-thirds of the income of the joint estate should be paid to the chaplain, and the remaining third to the master and his assistant, in the proportion of two-thirds to the former, and one-third to the latter Four scholarships, of £10 each per annum, were founded at Corpus Christi College, Cambridge, by Dr Sterne, Archbishop of York, one for natives of Mansfield The school-house was built in 1567, and rebuilt in 1705, when Queen Anne gave twenty tons of timber from the Forest of Sherwood for that purpose the master s house, which adjoins the school, was erected in 1719 A free school, for the clothing and education of thirty-six poor boys, was established in 1702, and was at that period supported by subscriptions amounting to £12 per annum In 1709, Samuel Brunts bequeathed lands, directing the proceeds, which then amounted to £436 15, to be thus applied, £4 per annum in putting poor boys to school, £4 per annum in apprenticing boys, and the

remainder to be distributed, in sums of £4 per annum each, to poor residents in Mansfield not receiving alms In 1725, Faith Clarkson bequeathed the sum of £2000 to trustees, for erecting a school-house, and vesting the remainder in land for charitable uses by a decree in Chancery, in 1743, it was awarded that the rental of these lands should be divided between Mansfield and Mansfield-Woodhouse, in support of a master and mistress, to teach twenty boys and twenty girls in reading, writing, and arithmetic, £8 to be applied in clothing ten boys and ten girls of the school, and £10 in apprenticing two boys the number of children in this school is sixty two, the master and mistress receive together a salary of £40 per annum. In 1784, Charles Thompson bequeathed £1200 in the three per cents to the trustees of Samuel Brunts charity, for the better educating of poor boys, and £400 to the vicar and churchwardens, the interest to be applied in the purchase of coats and petticoats for twenty poor persons a school-house was built in 1786 An infant school was established in 1830 By deed, dated January 15th, 1691, Elizabeth Heath founded and endowed almshouses for twelve poor persons the inmates receive 40s each per month, with clothing and a load of coal at Christmas, and the surplus rents are applied in apprenticing poor children In 1795, Joseph Sales bequeathed £1000 three per cents to the vicar and churchwardens, as trustees, the interest to be divided amongst six poor housekeepers of Mansfield, of the age of fifty and upwards A bequest of £10 per annum, to be divided amongst poor housekeepers, was made by John Bold, in 1726, and there are numerous other benefactions for the relief of the poor In the neighbourhood are traces of several Roman exploratory camps, also two Roman *villæ* one containing nine rooms, and the other thirteen, with hypocausts, baths, and other appendages, in one of them was a tesselated pavement, also various fragments of *pateræ*, earthenware, and other relics of antiquity Remains of two Roman sepulchres, with urns, bones, &c, have been discovered near the same spot Humphrey Ridley, an eminent physician and anatomist, was born here about 1653 Dr Sterne, Archbishop of York, and Dr William Chappel, afterwards Bishop of Cork and Ross, in Ireland, were natives of Mansfield, and Robert Dodsley, author of the "Economy of Human Life," was born in the vicinity, and apprenticed in the town. James Murray, inventor of the patent circular saw, resided here Sir William Murray, on his being appointed Lord Chief Justice of the court of King's Bench, was elevated to the peerage, November 8th, 1756, by the title of Baron Mansfield, of Mansfield, in the county of Nottingham, of which he was created Earl, October 19th, 1776, and obtained a fresh patent, August 1st, 1792, creating him Earl of Mansfield, of Caen Wood, in the county of Middlesex, the original barony expired at his death, but the earldom is now enjoyed by his grand nephew

MANSFIELD-WOODHOUSE, a parish in the northern division of the wapentake of Broxtow, county of Nottingham, 1¼ mile (N) from Mansfield, containing 1598 inhabitants The living is a perpetual curacy, in the peculiar jurisdiction of the court of the Lord of the Manor of Mansfield, endowed with £200 private benefaction, £200 royal bounty, and £1200 parliamentary grant, and in the patronage of the Duke of Portland The church, dedicated to St Edmund, is a large structure, with a spire-steeple one hundred and eight feet high, which was rebuilt in 1304, together with one of the aisles, after having been injured by a fire, which also destroyed part of the village There are places of worship for Independents and Wesleyan Methodists It anciently formed part of the adjoining parish of Mansfield, but it is not known at what period the separation took place The village is large, and contains several very respectable houses The free school was founded by Faith Clarkson, in 1725, and endowed with certain lands for a master and a mistress Charles Thompson also, in 1784, bequeathed £1300, and Richard Radford, by deed dated May 10th, 1827, gave £800, the interest of both to be applied in educating children. There are lime kilns and quarries of excellent freestone in the parish Several hundred acres of land, formerly barren, have lately been converted into rich arable land, by means of irrigation, the Duke of Portland having dug a canal through this and the adjoining parish of Clipstone, communicating with the river Man, the waters of which are used for that purpose In this parish are thirteen hundred acres of land, which, with some in the parish of Mansfield, is the only unenclosed part of the ancient Forest of Sherwood. In 1786, Major Rooke, distinguished for his fondness for antiquarian research, discovered two Roman villæ in the parish, one of which he called Villa Urbana, and the other Villa Rustica the former contained nine rooms and a hypocaust, part of a very elegant mosaic pavement having been found in the centre room, and the latter comprised thirteen rooms, two hypocausts, and a cold bath: the walls of the rooms were plastered and painted, and the floors stuccoed About one hundred yards to the south-east were two Roman sepulchres, in one of which was an urn containing ashes, with fragments of bones lying near it coins and various other Roman relics were also found Major Rooke enclosed the villæ with a stone wall, erected a square building over the room containing the mosaic pavement, and planted a variety of shrubs around them, but the whole, since his death, has suffered from neglect Dr Mason, Bishop of Sodor and Man, was born in this parish

MANSRIGGS, a township in the parish of ULVERSTONE, hundred of LONSDALE, north of the sands, county palatine of LANCASTER, 1½ mile (N) from Ulverstone, containing 62 inhabitants

MANSTON, a parish in the hundred of REDLANE, Sturminster division of the county of DORSET, 6 miles (S W by S) from Shaftesbury, containing 140 inhabitants The living is a rectory, in the archdeaconry of Dorset, and diocese of Bristol, rated in the king s books at £12 5, and in the patronage of Lord Viscount Bolingbroke The church, dedicated to St Nicholas, is very ancient Thomas Dibben, a divine, orator, and Latin poet, was born here, he died in the Poultry Compter, in 1741, having many years previously become insane.

MANTHORP, a joint township with Little Gonerby, in the soke and borough of GRANTHAM, parts of KESTEVEN, county of LINCOLN, 1 mile (N N E) from Grantham The population is returned with Little Gonerby

MANTHORPE, a hamlet in the parish of WITHAM on the HILL, wapentake of BELTISLOE, parts of KES-

VOL III.

TEVEN, county of LINCOLN, 3¾ miles (S W by S) from Bourne, containing 107 inhabitants

MANTON, a parish comprising the township of Cleatham in the wapentake of CORRINGHAM, and the hamlet of Twigmoor in the eastern division of the wapentake of MANLEY, parts of LINDSEY, county of LINCOLN, 5¼ miles (S W by W) from Glandford-Bridge, and containing 198 inhabitants The living is a rectory, in the archdeaconry of Stow, and diocese of Lincoln, rated in the king's books at £13 6 8 W Dalyson, Esq was patron in 1793 The church is dedicated to St Hibald

MANTON, a parish in the hundred of MARTINSLEY, county of RUTLAND, 3¼ miles (N by E) from Uppingham, containing 229 inhabitants The living is a discharged vicarage, in the archdeaconry of Northampton, and diocese of Peterborough, rated in the king s books at £10, endowed with £400 royal bounty, and £200 parliamentary grant G W Smyth, Esq was patron in 1820 The church is dedicated to St. Mary A college or chantry was founded here, in the 25th of Edward III, by William and John Wade, for a master and two brethren, whose revenue at the dissolution was valued at £22 18 6

MAPERTON, a parish in the hundred of CATSASH, county of SOMERSET, 3¼ miles (S W by W) from Wincanton, containing, with the hamlet of Clapton, 165 inhabitants The living is a rectory, in the archdeaconry of Wells, and diocese of Bath and Wells, rated in the king s books at £13 9 7, and in the patronage of the Warden and Fellows of Wadham College, Oxford The church is dedicated to St Peter and St Paul

MAPLEBECK, a parish in the northern division of the wapentake of THURGARTON, county of NOTTINGHAM, 5¾ miles (N by E) from Southwell, containing 193 inhabitants The living is a perpetual curacy, in the archdeaconry of Nottingham, and diocese of York, endowed with £400 royal bounty, and £200 parliamentary grant, and in the patronage of the Duke of Newcastle A hard stone, fit for building, and a durable material for roads, is obtained here Maplebeck is in the honour of Tutbury, duchy of Lancaster, and within the jurisdiction of a court of pleas held at Tutbury every third Tuesday, for the recovery of debts under forty shillings

MAPLEDERWELL, a parish in the hundred of BASINGSTOKE, Basingstoke division of the county of SOUTHAMPTON, 3½ miles (E S E) from Basingstoke, containing 186 inhabitants The living is a perpetual curacy, annexed to the rectory of Newnham, in the archdeaconry and diocese of Winchester The church is dedicated to St Mary

MAPLE-DURHAM, a parish in the hundred of LANGTREE, county of OXFORD, 4 miles (N W by N) from Reading, containing 508 inhabitants The living is a vicarage, in the archdeaconry and diocese of Oxford, rated in the king s books at £12 10, and in the patronage of the Provost and Fellows of Eton College The church, dedicated to St Margaret, has been the burial-place of the ancient family of Blount for many generations. An almshouse for six poor people, each of whom receives one shilling and sixpence weekly, is supported by Michael Blount, Esq

MAPLESCOMBE, formerly a parish, now forming part of that of KINGSDOWN, in the hundred of AXTON,

2 K

MAP 250 MAR

DARTFORD, and WILMINGTON, lathe of SUTTON at Hone, county of KENT, 6 miles (N N E) from Seven-Oaks The church is in ruins, and the living has been annexed to that of Kingsdown

MAPLESTEAD (GREAT), a parish in the hundred of HINCKFORD, county of ESSEX, 2¾ miles (N by W) from Halstead, containing 428 inhabitants The living is a vicarage, in the archdeaconry of Middlesex, and diocese of London, rated in the king's books at £8 3 4 J Judd, Esq was patron in 1797 The church, dedicated to St Giles, has a chapel attached to the south side, belonging to the proprietor of Dynes hall, and containing two costly monuments of the family of Deane, its former possessors

MAPLESTEAD (LITTLE), a parish in the hundred of HINCKFORD, county of ESSEX, 2¼ miles (N by E) from Halstead, containing 313 inhabitants. The living is a donative, within the jurisdiction of the Commissary of Essex and Herts, concurrently with the Consistorial Court of the Bishop of London, endowed with £200 private benefaction, £600 royal bounty, and £200 parliamentary grant, and in the patronage of —— Davis, Esq The church, dedicated to St John of Jerusalem, is ancient, and remarkable as being one of the few remaining models of the Holy Sepulchre, the east end is semicircular, and it is said once to have had the privilege of sanctuary Juliana, wife of Fitz-Aldelm de Burgo, in the time of Henry I, gave the entire parish to the Knights Hospitallers, who had a preceptory here

MAPPERLEY, a township in that part of the parish of KIRK-HALLAM which is in the hundred of APPLETREE, county of DERBY, 7¼ miles (N E by E) from Derby, containing 338 inhabitants Henry Leaper, in 1791, left an annuity of £6 towards the support of a Sunday school, established in 1792 This township is entitled to share in the benefits of West Hallam school, founded by John Scargill.

MAPPERTON, a parish in the hundred of BEA-MINSTER-FORUM and REDHONE, Bridport division of the county of DORSET, 2½ miles (S E by E) from Beaminster, containing 123 inhabitants The living is a rectory, in the peculiar jurisdiction of the Dean of Salisbury, rated in the king's books at £8 3 1½ H C Compton, Esq was patron in 1822. The church, dedicated to St Mary, was, in 1291, styled a chapel to Netherbury it was rebuilt, in 1704, by Richard Broadrep, Esq, and the interior handsomely fitted up in the chancel is a fine monument of the Broadreps, and underneath it the family vault. There is a small churchyard, but the substratum being rock, the inhabitants bury at Netherbury, for which privilege they annually pay a trifling acknowledgment

MAPPERTON, a hamlet in the parish of ALMER, hundred of LOOSEBARROW, Shaston (East) division of the county of DORSET, 6 miles (S by E) from Blandford-Forum The population is returned with the parish

MAPPLETON, a parish in the hundred of WIRKS-WORTH, county of DERBY, 1¾ mile (N W) from Ashbourn, containing 201 inhabitants The living is a perpetual curacy, united to the vicarage of Ashbourn, in the archdeaconry of Derby, and diocese of Lichfield and Coventry The church, dedicated to St Mary, has a dome surmounted by an urn The river Dove is here

crossed by a stone bridge, having a remarkably flat arch, its span being seventy feet, and its semidiameter only eleven Rowland Okeover, Esq, in 1727, vested certain lands in trustees for (amongst other purposes) building almshouses for three clergymen s widows, and providing them with £10 per annum, which sum, in consequence of the increased value of the estates, has been raised to £30 the building comprises a centre and two wings Mappleton is in the honour of Tutbury, duchy of Lancaster, and within the jurisdiction of a court of pleas held at Tutbury every third Tuesday, for the recovery of debts under 40s

MAPPLETON, a parish in the northern division of the wapentake of HOLDERNESS, East riding of the county of YORK, containing, with the townships of Great Hatfield (which is partly in the parish of Sigglesthorne) and Mappleton with Rowlston (which is partly in the liberty of St Peter of York), and exclusively of Great and Little Cowdon, 314 inhabitants, of which number, 187 are in the township of Mappleton, 13½ miles (E by N) from Beverley The living is a discharged vicarage, in the archdeaconry of the East riding, and diocese of York, rated in the king's books at £4 13 4, endowed with £400 private benefaction, £200 royal bounty, and £600 parliamentary grant, and in the patronage of the Archdeacon of the East riding of York The church, dedicated to All Saints, has some portions of ancient architecture remaining A school, for which the building was erected by voluntary subscription, in 1820, is conducted on Dr Bell s system

MAPPOWDER, a parish in the hundred of BUCK-LAND-NEWTON, Cerne subdivision of the county of DORSET, 6 miles (S W by S) from Sturminster-Newton, containing 247 inhabitants The living is a rectory, in the archdeaconry of Dorset, and diocese of Bristol, rated in the king s books at £17 14 7 Earl Spencer was patron in 1814 The church, dedicated to St. Peter and St. Paul, is an embattled structure with a low plain tower, and contains, among other memorials several to the family of Coker, whose ancient mansion, which was a large and handsome building, erected in the reign of Elizabeth, has been converted into a farm house Of this family, Mr Coker, author of a "Survey of Dorset shire,' was a member

MARAZION, an incorporated market town, in the parish of ST HILARY, hundred of PENWITH, county of CORNWALL, 63½ miles (S W by W) from Launceston, and 282 (W S. W) from London, containing 1253 inhabitants The ancient name of this town was Marghasiewe the more recent appellation of Market-jew, still in use

Corporate Seal.

among the common people, is supposed by some to take its origin from a market formerly held here, which was much frequented by Jews, while others deduce it, somewhat fancifully, from Market-die Jou, in reference to its Thursday's market, thus making it a corruption of the Latin name for that day, Dies Jovis In the early part of the reign of Henry VIII., a party of French soldiers, having landed from a fleet then cruising in the channel, took possession of Marazion, but, on the approach of the sheriff of the county with the *posse comitatus*, they set fire to the town, and retreated to their ships it again suffered by conflagration, in the reign of Edward VI The town is very pleasantly situated on the eastern side of Mount s Bay, chiefly at the bottom of a hill, by which it is sheltered on the north the air is particularly mild and salubrious, the streets are not lighted, nor regularly paved, and, on account of its neighbouring mines, the inhabitants are badly supplied with water It is stated to have formerly been a trading town of great note, and to have fallen into decay in consequence of the second conflagration, having continued in a very dilapidated condition till the grant of a charter by Elizabeth The profits of a fair held here were given to the priory of St Michael's Mount, in the reign of Henry I , and in the reign of Henry III , that religious community was empowered, by Richard, Earl of Cornwall, to hold three fairs and three markets, which had been previously granted to them at Marghas-bigan, by charter of the kings of England, on their own land at Marchadyon In the year 1331, a market on Monday, and a fair on the festival of St Andrew, to continue three days, were granted to Ralph de Bleyon The present market is held on Saturday, and there is a fair on Michaelsday for horses and cattle The town was incorporated by charter from Queen Elizabeth, in 1595 the corporation consists of a mayor, eight burgesses, and twelve capital inhabitants, the mayor being chosen from among the burgesses by the corporation, who also appoint the town clerk, the burgesses are elected from the capital inhabitants the mayor is the only justice of the peace within the borough The living is a perpetual curacy, annexed to the vicarage of St Hilary, in the archdeaconry of Cornwall, and diocese of Exeter, endowed with £200 private benefaction, and £1100 parliamentary grant The church is dedicated to St Catherine There are places of worship for the Society of Friends, Independents, and Wesleyan Methodists In 1753, Joseph Hill gave £100 for the instruction of children, and £40 to the poor inhabitants There is also a free school

MARBURY, a township in that part of the parish of GREAT BUDWORTH which is in the hundred of BUCKLOW, county palatine of CHESTER, 2 miles (N by W) from Northwich, containing 35 inhabitants The Grand Trunk canal passes through the township

MARBURY, a parish in the hundred of NANTWICH, county palatine of CHESTER, containing, with the townships of Marbury with Quoisley, and Norbury, 833 inhabitants, of which number, 395 are in the township of Marbury with Quoisley, 3½ miles (N N E) from Whitchurch The living is a perpetual curacy, with the rectory of Whitchurch, in the archdeaconry and diocese of Chester The church, an ancient structure, has an elegant chancel, rebuilt by the late Earl of Bridgewater A branch of the Chester canal passes through the parish A school-house was erected in 1688, by subscription among the inhabitants Courts are held annually for the manors of Marbury and Norbury, at which constables are appointed

MARCH, a market town and chapelry in the parish of DODDINGTON, northern division of the hundred of WITCHFORD, Isle of ELY, county of CAMBRIDGE, 31

miles (N by W) from Cambridge, and 80 (N) from London, containing 3850 inhabitants The town is situated on the banks of the navigable river Nene, by means of which corn, and the local horticultural produce, are conveyed to Cambridge, Lynn, Peterborough, and other places The market, granted to Sir Alexander Peyton, in 1671, is on Friday, chiefly for butchers meat, and there are two fairs, each of which continues three days, commencing on the Monday before Whit suntide, and on the second Tuesday in October at the first of these, horses are sold only on the third day Manorial courts are held in the guildhall, a modern and commodious edifice situated in the High-street, and this place is within the jurisdiction of a court of requests, for the recovery of debts under 40s throughout the Isle of Ely, established by act of parliament passed in the 18th of George III, held here once a month The chapel, which is dedicated to St. Wendreda, is a very ancient structure, with a spire at the west end it was erected about the year 1343, at which period an indulgence was granted by the Pope to all who should contribute to it, in the interior are several ancient monuments A school was founded, in 1696, by William Neale, Esq, for the education of eight boys in Latin and English, and endowed with thirty-three acres and a half of land in Whites Fen, upon the special condition that the land should never be broken up, unless overgrown with rushes, and in that case it was to be once cropped with oats, and again laid down as greensward, a forfeiture of the property to the heirs of the donor to be the penalty of infringing this condition Mr Henry Wade having bequeathed a house and lands for charitable purposes, the rents were appropriated, under a decree obtained in the court of Chancery in 1713, in the following manner £20 per annum to a schoolmaster, for the instruction of twenty poor children of March, £20 per annum for apprentice fees, £5 per annum for decayed housekeepers, and the residue in the purchase of heifers, on Easter Monday, for poor housekeepers the schoolmaster on Neale's foundation receives the above-mentioned salary, and the further sum of £6 15, arising from land devised, in 1653, by Mr James Sheppard, and the interest of £30, the gift of Mr Gabriel Sheppard, for the instruction of children There are some unendowed almshouses for the parochial poor Between this town and Wisbeach, in the year 1730, urns enclosing burnt bones, and a vessel containing one hundred and sixty Roman denarii of different emperors, were discovered

MARCHAM, a parish in the hundred of OCK, county of BERKS, 3 miles (W by S) from Abingdon, containing, with the chapelries of Frilford and Garford, 1173 inhabitants The living is a vicarage, in the archdeaconry of Berks, and diocese of Salisbury, rated in the king s books at £14 15 7½, and in the patronage of the Dean and Canons of Christ Church, Oxford. The church is dedicated to All Saints There is a place of worship for Wesleyan Methodists John Elwes, the eccentric miser, died here in 1789

MARCHINGTON, a chapelry in the parish of HANBURY, northern division of the hundred of OFFLOW, county of STAFFORD, 4 miles (S E. by E) from Uttoxeter, containing 463 inhabitants The living is a perpetual curacy, in the archdeaconry of Stafford, and diocese of Lichfield and Coventry, endowed with £600 private benefaction, £1000 royal bounty, and £300 parliamentary grant, and in the patronage of the Vicar of Hanbury The chapel is dedicated to St Peter This parish is in the honour of Tutbury, duchy of Lancaster, and within the jurisdiction of a court of pleas held at Tutbury every third Tuesday, for the recovery of debts under 40s

MARCHINGTON-WOODLANDS, a township in the parish of HANBURY, northern division of the hundred of OFFLOW, county of STAFFORD, 3¼ miles (S S E) from Uttoxeter, containing 318 inhabitants It is in the honour of Tutbury, duchy of Lancaster, and within the jurisdiction of a court of pleas held at Tutbury every third Tuesday, for the recovery of debts under 40s

MARCLE (LITTLE), a parish in the hundred of RADLOW, county of HEREFORD, 3 miles (W S W) from Ledbury, containing 168 inhabitants The living is a discharged perpetual curacy, in the archdeaconry and diocese of Hereford, rated in the king s books at £7 1 4, and in the patronage of the Bishop of Hereford. The church has long been in ruins, and the inhabitants bury at Ledbury

MARCLE (MUCH), a parish in the hundred of GREYTREE, county of HEREFORD, 5 miles (S W by W) from Ledbury, containing, with the chapelry of Yatton, 1060 inhabitants The living is a vicarage, with Kinnaston, in the archdeaconry and diocese of Hereford, rated in the king s books at £14 0 5, and in the patronage of James Kyrle Money, Esq The church is dedicated to St Bartholomew

MARDALE, a chapelry partly in the parish of BAMPTON, and partly in that of SHAP, WEST ward, county of WESTMORLAND, 11 miles (W N W) from Orton The population is returned with the respective parishes. The living is a perpetual curacy, in the archdeaconry and diocese of Carlisle, endowed with £800 royal bounty, and in the patronage of the Vicar of Shap, in which parish the chapel is situated.

MARDEN, a parish in the hundred of BROXASH, county of HEREFORD, 5½ miles (N N E) from Hereford, containing, with the chapelry of Amberley, 815 inhabitants The living is a discharged vicarage, in the peculiar jurisdiction of the Dean of Hereford, rated in the king s books at £5 13 5 , and in the patronage of the Dean and Chapter of Hereford The church, dedicated to St Ethelbert, stands on the banks of the Lugg, over the spot where King Ethelbert was buried, and where a well, which still exists, is superstitiously said to have miraculously sprung up at the time the edifice was dedicated to his memory

MARDEN, a parish in the hundred of MARDEN, lathe of SCRAY, county of KENT, 4¼ miles (N by E) from Goudhurst, containing 2051 inhabitants The living is a vicarage, in the archdeaconry and diocese of Canterbury, rated in the king's books at £7 18 4., and in the patronage of the Archbishop of Canterbury The church is dedicated to St Michael There is a place of worship for Independents Sir Charles Booth, in 1792, left certain property to be vested in the three per cents , now bearing an annual interest of about £44, for the support of a school, in which two hundred children are educated on the Madras system A fair is held on the 10th of October

MARDEN, a parish in the hundred of SWANBOROUGH, county of WILTS, 5½ miles (N E by E) from

East Lavington, containing 200 inhabitants The living is a discharged vicarage, in the archdeaconry and diocese of Salisbury, rated in the king s books at £8 17 6 , endowed with £200 private benefaction, and £200 royal bounty, and in the patronage of the Dean and Chapter of Bristol The church is dedicated to All Saints

MARDEN (EAST), a parish in the hundred of WESTBOURN and SINGLETON, rape of CHICHESTER, county of SUSSEX, 8 miles (S W) from Midhurst, containing 85 inhabitants The living is a discharged vicarage, in the archdeaconry and diocese of Chichester, rated in the king s books at £4 16 8, and in the patronage of the Prebendary of Marden in the Cathedral Church of Chichester

MARDEN (NORTH), a parish in the hundred of WESTBOURN and SINGLETON, rape of CHICHESTER, county of SUSSEX, 7 miles (S W by W) from Midhurst, containing 20 inhabitants The living is a discharged rectory, in the archdeaconry and diocese of Chichester, rated in the king s books at £6 17 8 T P Phipps, Esq was patron in 1806

MARDEN (UP), a parish in the hundred of WEST BOURN and SINGLETON, rape of CHICHESTER, county of SUSSEX, 9 miles (S W) from Midhurst, containing 306 inhabitants The living is a perpetual curacy, with the vicarage of Compton, in the archdeaconry and diocese of Chichester The church is dedicated to St Michael The Rev Dr Cox, in 1741, left £100 in support of a school for this parish and that of Compton

MAREFIELD, a township in that part of the parish of TILTON which is in the hundred of GARTREE, county of LEICESTER, 8¼ miles (S by W) from Melton Mowbray, containing 32 inhabitants

MAREHAM le FEN, a parish in the soke of HORNCASTLE, parts of LINDSEY, county of LINCOLN, 5½ miles (S by E) from Horncastle, containing 609 inhabitants The living is a vicarage, in the archdeaconry and diocese of Lincoln, rated in the king s books at £13 10 10 , and in the patronage of the Bishop of Carlisle The church is dedicated to St. Helen There is a place of worship for Wesleyan Methodists

MAREHAM on the HILL, a parish in the soke of HORNCASTLE, parts of LINDSEY, county of LINCOLN, 2 miles (E S E) from Horncastle, containing 133 inhabitants The living is a perpetual curacy, in the archdeaconry and diocese of Lincoln, endowed with £1200 royal bounty, and in the patronage of the Bishop of Carlisle The church is dedicated to All Saints

MARESFIELD, a parish in the hundred of RUSHMONDEN, rape of PEVENSEY, county of SUSSEX, 2¼ miles (N by W) from Uckfield, containing 1439 inhabitants The living is a rectory, in the archdeaconry of Lewes, and diocese of Chichester, rated in the king s books at £12 Lord Viscount Gage was patron in 1812 The church, dedicated to St. Bartholomew, has lately received an addition of fifty-seven sittings, of which fifty are free, the Incorporated Society for the enlargement of churches and chapels having granted £35 towards defraying the expense The Rev Richard Bonner, in 1689, devised a messuage and garden, with two small rent-charges, toward the support of a school, which bequest is applied to the support of a National school, wherein from one hundred to one hundred and fifty children are educated, chiefly at the expense of Sir John and Lady Shelley A cattle fair is held on September 4th The greater part of Ashdowne Forest is in this parish

MARFLEET, a parish in the middle division of the wapentake of HOLDERNESS, East riding of the county of YORK, 3 miles (E) from Kingston upon Hull, containing 127 inhabitants The living is a discharged perpetual curacy, in the archdeaconry of the East riding, and diocese of York, endowed with £100 private benefaction, and £800 royal bounty H Grylls, Esq was patron in 1824 There is a place of worship for Wesleyan Methodists

MARGARET (ST), a parish in the hundred and county of HERTFORD, 1½ mile (N by E) from Hoddesdon, containing 97 inhabitants The living is a perpetual curacy, in the archdeaconry of Middlesex, and diocese of London, and in the patronage of the Lord of the Manor A college, or chantry, for a master and four secular priests, was founded here in 1315, by Sir William de Goldington, Knt, in consequence of the impoverishment of the tithes, oblations, and other ecclesiastical rights of the church, but it was dissolved in 1431, for neglect and the misapplication of its revenue This parish is situated between the New River and the Lea

MARGARET'S (ST), a parish in the hundred of EWYASLACY, county of HEREFORD, 13 miles (W S W) from Hereford, containing 317 inhabitants The living is a perpetual curacy, in the archdeaconry and diocese of St David's, endowed with £800 royal bounty, and in the patronage of the Earl of Oxford

MARGARET (ST) at CLIFFE, a parish in the hundred of BEWSBOROUGH, lathe of ST AUGUSTINE, county of KENT, 3½ miles (N E) from Dovor, containing 613 inhabitants The living is a discharged vicarage, in the peculiar jurisdiction and patronage of the Archbishop of Canterbury, rated in the king's books at £6 10 The church is a spacious structure, in the Norman style This place has received the adjunct to its name from its high situation on the chalk cliffs overlooking the English channel In a small bay where there is a pier, or jetty, for protecting the fishing craft, the finest-flavoured lobsters in England are caught.

MARGARET-MARSH, a parish in the hundred of STURMINSTER-NEWTON-CASTLE, Sturminster division of the county of DORSET, 4 miles (S W) from Shaftesbury, containing 84 inhabitants The living is a perpetual curacy, annexed to the vicarage of Iwerne-Minster, in the archdeaconry of Dorset, and diocese of Bristol The church is dedicated to St Margaret

MARGARETTING, a parish in the hundred of CHELMSFORD, county of ESSEX, 1 mile (N E. by E) from Ingatestone, containing 479 inhabitants The living is a discharged vicarage, in the archdeaconry of Essex, and diocese of London, rated in the king's books at £9 2 C Phillips, Esq and others were patrons in 1827 The church, dedicated to St Margaret, has a wooden belfry surmounted by a spire The Rev C F Bond, in 1827, left £100 Bank stock towards the support of a Sunday school, which is attended by about fifty children A house, called Killigrew's farm, is said to have been the frequent resort of Henry VIII it seems to have been a place of great security, being surrounded by a moat, which, within memory, was crossed by a draw-bridge, having two watch towers

MARGATE, a sea-port, market-town, and parish, in the cinque-port liberty of DOVOR, of which it is a member, though locally in the hundred of Ringslow, or Isle of Thanet, lathe of St Augustine, county of KENT, 44 miles (E N E) from Maidstone, and 72½ (E) from London, containing, according to the last census, 7843 resident inhabitants, and, at the present time (1830), 9500 This place, formerly a small fishing village, was distinguished by a mere, or stream, having its influx into the sea, from which circumstance it obtained the name of *Meregate*, and, subsequently, *Margate* About the middle of the last century it became much frequented as a bathing-place, from the fineness of the beach and the purity of the air, and, though originally consisting of one scattered and irregular street, it has, by the erection of new buildings at various times, to meet the wants of the increased number of visitors, attained its present importance A pier of timber was constructed at a very early period, and, for its preservation, two pier-wardens and sub-deputies were appointed by the lord wardens of the cinque-ports, and certain rates on corn, and other imported produce, were granted in the reign of Elizabeth In 1787 an act was passed for the general improvement of the town, and the rebuilding of the pier, when the entire property and management of the latter were vested in the commissioners for paving and lighting the town, and under this act the old wooden pier was cased with stone, but in a violent storm, on the 14th of January, 1808, it was irreparably injured In July, 1812, an act was obtained for "separating the management of the pier and harbour from the concerns of the town, and establishing a joint-stock company of proprietors,' with a court of fifteen directors, who were empowered to raise money for the building of a new pier, and to levy certain tolls on goods and passengers, to be applied to the liquidation of the original capital and the interest thereon, and the surplus to accumulate until it amounts to the sum of £20,000, as a fund for the future repairs of the pier this effected, the company will be dissolved, and the pier again placed under the control of the commissioners of the town, as heretofore Under this act a new pier was projected, on an entirely new site, by the chairman of the directors, Daniel Jarvis, Esq, M D, and carried into execution from a design by Mr Rennie and Mr Jessop, engineers the work, which had been commenced April 6th, 1810, was completed in 1815, at an expense of £100,000 it is a handsome and substantial stone structure, nine hundred feet in length from east to west, in its plan forming a portion of a polygon, and well calculated to afford protection to the vessels in the harbour it is divided into two stages of buildings, the lower forming a quay, and the upper a promenade, defended on the sea side with a stone parapet, and on the land side by iron railing this promenade, which, as a marine walk, is probably unrivalled, was designed by Mr Thomas Edmunds, builder, of Margate To the east of the pier is "Jarvis' landing-place" for passengers, when the depth

*

of water will not allow vessels to reach the pier This important work was executed in the year 1824, without any additional toll, or cost to the public, by the Pier Company, at an expense of £8000 it is constructed entirely of English oak, and extends northward into the sea one thousand one hundred and twenty feet from the shore, forming, at low water, a most delightful promenade An act of parliament has been obtained, by which certain regulations are enforced to preserve order during the landing and embarking of passengers At the extremity of the pier, a stone lighthouse has lately been erected, from a design by Mr William Edmunds, architect, of this town, the shaft of which forms a Grecian Doric column, placed on an octagonal base, serving as a look-out house, the column is surmounted by an ornamental chamber, or lantern of iron A new pier-house has also been built, under the superintendence of the same architect, for the use of the directors and their officers, having a bell-turret, and a clock with four illuminated dials At the entrance of the landing-place, a handsome cast-iron archway has been placed, by the Pier Company, in compliment to their talented and spirited chairman, Daniel Jarvis, Esq , and, as a further mark of respect, a granite column has been erected, on which is inscribed a detailed account of the principal improvements that have been effected in the town chiefly through the exertions of that gentleman The harbour, though, from its situation, much exposed to storms from the north-east, has been greatly improved by the construction of the new pier, and affords good shelter for vessels several trading vessels are constantly sailing between this place and the Dutch coast This being the nearest and most convenient port for the passage to the opposite coast, caused it to be formerly, and again recently, selected as the station for the Ostend mail packets, but this distinction it does not at present enjoy Amongst the distinguished persons who have embarked, or landed, at Margate are, the Elector Palatine and his consort, in the reign of James I , William III , George I , George II and his queen Caroline , the Duke of Marlborough , the late Duke of York, on his expedition to Flanders, in 1793 , Admiral Duncan, after his victory off Camperdown, in 1797 , and the troops on the expedition to Walcheren, in 1809 the wounded from the battle of Waterloo were also landed here, in 1815

The town is pleasantly situated, partly on the acclivities of two hills, and partly in the valley below , it is lighted with gas, well paved, and abundantly supplied with excellent water from wells Considerable improvements have been effected, and others are still in progress, by the commissioners for paving and lighting, under the authority of numerous acts of parliament , sea defences have been erected, new roads formed, streets widened and Macadamised, public pumps erected, the open areas in the squares and other places enclosed with handsome iron railings, and shrubberies planted , insomuch that the town presents, in general, an appearance of neatness and order highly creditable, The London entrance is, in particular, distinguished by an esplanade, equalled only in extent and beauty by the celebrated work of that nature at Weymouth , it is protected by a stone wall, and lighted with gas, presenting, at night, an imposing appearance, and forming an extended crescent, which is terminated by the pier the whole of the sea-defences are constructed of stone, and

exceed a mile in length, having cost upwards of £20,000 The market is held on Wednesday and Saturday, under a grant obtained in 1777 The town hall and market-place were rebuilt in 1821, at an expense of £4000 a prison is attached, for the temporary reception of criminals prior to their removal to Dovor The public subscription library, in Hawley-square, is a handsome building, and there are also three other excellent libraries, affording the usual accommodation The bathing-rooms in High-street, on the New-road, and the more recently-constructed and extensive works of that kind on the Fort, are all of the best description the warm baths have every modern improvement for the comfort and accommodation of those who frequent them , while the cold bathing unites with the most powerful local advantages the best description of machines, drawn by horses The theatre is a neat building, erected in 1787, at an expense of £4000 The subscription and assembly rooms, attached to the Royal Hotel, are very spacious , the ball-room is ninety feet in length by forty-three feet wide, with card, ante, and refreshment, rooms the whole comprise a most splendid suite, and are under the direction of a master of the ceremonies Independently of the various hotels and numerous inns and taverns in the town, there are many public and private boarding-houses of the first class Several handsome bazaars and boulevards have lately been erected by individuals at considerable cost Adjoining the town, the Tivoli Gardens have been recently opened, and possess the advantages of a most delightful situation, of ornamental sheets of water, and thick plantations In 1815 steam-packets were established , the number of passengers in that year was twenty three thousand five hundred, and, in 1830, the number amounted to ninety-five thousand these vessels now ply daily between London and Margate, making the passage in about six hours and a half, and, in the season, two thousand persons frequently arrive in one day The trade of the town is almost entirely connected with the resort of visitors, here are, however, a very extensive brewery, a rope-manufactory, and some establishments for ship-building, &c A large number of sea-faring men obtain their subsistence in winter by rendering aid to vessels in distress, which is locally called " Foying, and in summer by fishing and taking out pleasure parties in open boats

Margate being a member of the port of Dovor, the mayor of that town appoints one of the inhabitants to act as his deputy, and the town is subject in all matters to the jurisdiction of that port, and of its sessions, although, by a late act of parliament, appeals in certain cases are allowed to be tried at the Canterbury quarter sessions In 1811, local magistrates were appointed, two of whom are now resident A court of requests is held, for the recovery of debts under £5, the jurisdiction of which extends over the parishes of St John (Margate), St. Peter the Apostle, Birchington, and the ville of Wood , and a court leet for the manor of Minster, which comprises most of the parishes in the island, is held annually about Michaelmas

The living is a discharged vicarage, in the archdeaconry and diocese of Canterbury, rated in the king's books at £8, and in the patronage of the Archbishop of Canterbury The church, dedicated to St John the Baptist, is a spacious building of flint and stone, with

*

a square tower and low spire, erected at various periods and in different styles it was originally a chapel of ease to Minster, and was made parochial in 1290 there are several monuments of great antiquity, and a fine organ. At the east end of the north aisle is a strong building of stone, which, from 1661, till 1761, was used as a magazine for gunpowder, but is now appropriated as a vestry-room To the taste and influence of the present vicar, the Rev W F Baylav, the town is indebted for much of the improvements which it has undergone during the last twenty years The new church, dedicated to the Holy Trinity, was completed in 1829, from a design and under the superintendence of Mr William Edmunds it is an elegant structure of Bath stone, in the early style of English architecture, and consists of a nave nearly sixty feet high, and two side aisles, elaborately groined the east end is terminated by a recess for the altar, having a noble window filled with stained glass, and at the west end is a deep recess for the organ, which represents a shrine, having, in front, a stone screen, with pierced arches, buttresses, and finials with elaborate carving the organ forms part of the architecture of the church The side windows are adorned with stained glass, representing the armorial bearings of the principal subscribers, which, with the east window, are considered to be splendid specimens of the art, the expense having been defrayed by private subscription The exterior of the building is decorated with buttresses, pinnacles, and carved finials The tower rises to the height of one hundred and thirty-five feet, and, from the commanding site on which it is built, is seen at a very considerable distance, being the first object perceivable on approaching the English coast. The church contains two thousand sittings, of which one thousand two hundred are free, and its total cost was about £28,000, towards which the parliamentary commissioners contributed £10,000, £6000 was raised by private subscription, the Pier Company gave £2000, and the remainder was levied by parish rates The living is a perpetual curacy, in the patronage of the Vicar of St John s, who appointed the Rev F Barrow first incumbent A charity school, established by subscription in 1787, for thirty girls and thirty boys, afterwards extended to forty of each sex, has, since the adoption of the National system of education, afforded instruction to three thousand children Drapers hospital, about half a mile from the parish church, was founded in 1709, by Michael Yoakley, a member of the Society of Friends, for aged women, who are accommodated in nine comfortable dwellings, and are supplied with money, clothes, and fuel in the centre is a chapel for the Society of Friends The Royal sea-bathing infirmary was instituted in 1792, and opened in 1796, under the patronage of his late Majesty, George IV, the building consists of a centre and two wings, capable of accommodating two hundred patients There are likewise numerous charitable bequests for the relief of the poor, an account of which has recently been published by a committee of gentlemen, in order that the intentions of the founders may not be frustrated by neglect, or otherwise

About a mile and a half to the south-west of the town is Dandelion, the fortified mansion of a family of that name in the reign of Edward I, of which a gate-house, flanked with four towers, remains in good preser-vation About a quarter of a mile to the south of the parish church is Salmstone Grange, where are the remains of a chapel, or oratory, formerly belonging to the monastery of St Augustine, and in the middle of a field, about a mile and a half further, at a place called Chapel Bottom, are the ruins of Dene chapel, held under a license from the abbey of St Augustine, in 1230, by Sir Henry de Sandwich It is supposed that a severe battle was fought between the Danes and the Saxons in this neighbourhood, from the number of graves discovered on both the hills contiguous to the town Various coins and other antiquities have, at different times, been found, and, on the excavations being made for Trinity church, two urns, filled with human bones, standing in, and likewise covered with, patera, were found, in a fine state of preservation, having the name of the Roman Emperor Maximilian impressed on the different pieces

MARHAM, a parish in the hundred of CLACK-CLOSE, county of NORFOLK, 7½ miles (W by N) from Swaffham, containing 678 inhabitants The living is a discharged vicarage, in the archdeaconry of Norfolk, and diocese of Norwich, rated in the king s books at £6 13 4, endowed with £200 private benefaction, and £200 royal bounty, and in the patronage of the Master and Fellows of St John s College, Cambridge The church is dedicated to the Holy Trinity A Cistercian nunnery, in honour of the Blessed Virgin Mary, was founded here in 1251, by Isabella de Albini, Countess of Arundel, which at the dissolution had a revenue of £42 4 7

MARHAM CHURCH, a parish in the hundred of STRATTON, county of CORNWALL, 2 miles (S S W) from Stratton, containing 647 inhabitants The living is a rectory, in the archdeaconry of Cornwall, and diocese of Exeter, rated in the king's books at £15 11 0¼ The Rev John Kingdon was patron in 1818 The church is dedicated to St Marvenne The Bude and Holsworthy canal passes to the north of the church

MARHOLM, a parish in the liberty of PETERBOROUGH, county of NORTHAMPTON, 4½ miles (N W by W) from Peterborough, containing 120 inhabitants The living is a rectory, in the archdeaconry of North ampton, and diocese of Peterborough, rated in the king s books at £9 2 3½ Earl Fitzwilliam was patron in 1791 The church, dedicated to St Guthlac has an ancient font, and, amongst other memorials, a magnificent marble monument to William, Earl Fitzwilliam, and Anne his Countess In this parish is Abbey Milton, one of the seats of that noble family, a large irregular structure, the most ancient part of which is of the time of Elizabeth

MARI-ANSLEIGH, a parish in the hundred of WITHERIDGE, county of DEVON, 3½ miles (S E) from South Molton, containing 289 inhabitants The living is a perpetual curacy, in the archdeaconry of Barnstaple, and diocese of Exeter, endowed with £200 royal bounty, and in the patronage of the Mayor and Corporation of Exeter The church is dedicated to St Mary

MARK, a parish in the hundred of BEMPSTONE, county of SOMERSET, 6½ miles (S W by S) from Ax-bridge, containing 1150 inhabitants The living is a perpetual curacy, in the peculiar jurisdiction of the Consistorial Decanal court of Wells, endowed with £30 per annum private benefaction, and £1200 parliamentary grant, and in the patronage of the Earl of

Harrowby There is a place of worship for Wesleyan Methodists

MARK-EATON, a township in the parish of MACK-WORTH, hundred of MORLESTON and LITCHURCH, county of DERBY, 1¾ mile (W N W) from Derby, containing 258 inhabitants

MARKBY, a parish in the Wold division of the hundred of CALCEWORTH, parts of LINDSEY, county of LINCOLN, 2¾ miles (N E by E) from Alford, containing 94 inhabitants The living is a perpetual curacy, in the archdeaconry and diocese of Lincoln, endowed with £300 private benefaction, and £600 royal bounty —— Massingberd, Esq was patron in 1808. The church is dedicated to St Peter

MARKET-RASEN, county of LINCOLN —See RASEN (MARKET)

MARKET-STREET, a chapelry comprised within the parishes of CADDINGTON, FLAMSTEAD, and STUDHAM, partly in the hundred of DACORUM, county of HERTFORD, and partly in the hundreds of FLITT and MANSHEAD, county of BEDFORD, 3½ miles (S W by S) from Luton The population is returned with the respective parishes The ancient name of Merk-gate, or Mark gate, of which the present is a corruption, appears to have been derived from Merk, a boundary, and Yate, or Gate, this place having formerly been the end of the enclosed country, where it is supposed there was a gate on the high road or Watling-street On a hill in the vicinity, where is now an ancient mansion, a nunnery of the Benedictine order, dedicated to the Holy Trinity, formerly stood it was founded about 1145, principally by Geffrey, Abbot of St Alban s, and at the dissolution its revenue was valued at £143 13 8 the monastic buildings were converted into a mansion in the time of Edward VI, which is still called the priory The village is on the great road from London to Birmingham, and consists of one long-street, the manufacture of hats and bonnets of straw-plat is somewhat considerable A fair is held here about Michaelmas, but the day depends upon that of Luton fair The living is a perpetual curacy, in the archdeaconry of Huntingdon, and diocese of Lincoln, endowed with a rent-charge of £20, and with £200 private benefaction, and £600 royal bounty, and in the patronage of Daniel Goodson Adey, Esq, as proprietor of the manor, under the provisions of an act of parliament passed in the 14th of George II. The chapel, which is dedicated to St. John the Baptist, is situated in Cell, or Priory park, and was erected about a century ago, for the accommodation of the three parishes, in lieu of one at the manor-house, which had been burnt down There are places of worship for Baptists and Wesleyan Methodists Here is a grammar school the school-house and close were conveyed to trustees by John Coppin, Esq, January 25th, 1666, the incumbent of the parish is the nominal master

MARKET-STREET, a township in the parish of WYMONDHAM, hundred of FOREHOE, county of NORFOLK, containing 1308 inhabitants

MARKFIELD, a parish in the hundred of SPARKENHOE, county of LEICESTER, 7 miles (N W by W) from Leicester, containing 1078 inhabitants The living is a rectory, in the archdeaconry of Leicester, and diocese of Lincoln, rated in the king s books at £6 1 8 The Marquis of Hastings was patron in 1804 The church, dedicated to St Michael, has lately received an

addition of one hundred and seventy sittings, of which eighty-five are free, the Incorporated Society for the enlargement of churches and chapels having granted £60 towards defraying the expense

MARKHAM, a parish in the South-clay division of the wapentake of BASSETLAW, county of NOTTINGHAM, 1½ mile (N) from Tuxford, containing, with the chapelry of West Drayton, 756 inhabitants The living is a vicarage, in the archdeaconry of Nottingham, and diocese of York, rated in the king s books at £11 18 11½ The Duke of Newcastle was patron in 1811 The church, dedicated to St John the Baptist, is a large ancient structure, with a lofty embattled tower, and contains a monument to the memory of Judge Markham, erected in 1409 There is a place of worship for Wesleyan Methodists James Gunthorpe, in 1706, and William Dunston, in 1713, bequeathed rent-charges of £5 each towards the support of a school, in which twenty children are clothed and educated, the deficiency being supplied by voluntary contributions

MARKHAM (WEST), a parish in the South-clay division of the wapentake of BASSETLAW, county of NOTTINGHAM, 1¾ mile (N W) from Tuxford, containing 209 inhabitants The living is a vicarage, with that of Bevercoates united, in the archdeaconry of Nottingham, and diocese of York, rated in the king's books at £7 12 1, and in the patronage of the Archbishop of York The church is dedicated to All Saints Richard Miller, in 1721, left an annuity of £8 for the instruction of poor children Sir John Markham, Chief Justice of the King's Bench in the reign of Edward IV, and remarkable for his integrity and impartiality in the discharge of his official duties, was born here

MARKINGTON, a joint township with Wallerthwaite, in that part of the parish of RIPON which is within the liberty of RIPON, West riding of the county of YORK, 4¾ miles (S S W) from Ripon, containing, with Wallerthwaite, 457 inhabitants Here is a small endowment, the gift of Mary Reynard, for the education of poor children

MARKSBURY, a parish in the hundred of KEYNSHAM, county of SOMERSET, 3½ miles (E by S) from Pensford, containing, with the tything of Houndstreet, 354 inhabitants The living is a discharged rectory, in the archdeaconry of Wells, and diocese of Bath and Wells, rated in the king's books at £10 4 2, and in the patronage of General Popham The church is dedicated to St. Peter There are slight remains of an ancient chapel on Wingsbury hill A monastery formerly existed within the parish, the site of which is now occupied by a private mansion Here are some productive coal mines

MARSHALL, a parish in the Witham division of the hundred of LEXDEN, county of ESSEX, 2 miles (N W) from Great Coggeshall, containing 59 inhabitants The living is a rectory, in the archdeaconry of Colchester, and diocese of London, rated in the king s books at £14 F Honeywood, Esq was patron in 1800 The church is dedicated to St Margaret

MARLAND (PETER S), a parish in the hundred of SHEBBEAR, county of DEVON, 4½ miles (S by W) from Great Torrington, containing 343 inhabitants The living is a perpetual curacy, in the archdeaconry of Totness, and diocese of Exeter, and in the patronage of T Stevens, Esq The church is dedicated to St Peter

*

Seal and Arms.

MARLBOROUGH, a borough and market town, having separate jurisdiction, though locally in the hundred of Selkley, county of Wilts, 27 miles (N by E) from Salisbury, and 75 (W by S) from London, and containing 3058 inhabitants The name, anciently written *Marleberg*, or *Marlbridge*, is supposed to be derived from the marl, or chalk, hills by which the town is surrounded Camden supposed this to have been the *Cunetio* of Antoninus, but more recent researches induced Sir R C Hoare, Bart to place that station at Folly Farm, about a mile and a half eastward from the town, where that celebrated antiquary discovered a tesselated pavement, and other relics of a Roman settlement At the time of the Norman survey Marlborough had a church, and was held in royal demesne, soon after which period a castle was erected, which seems to have been the cause of the subsequent enlargement of the town In the time of Richard I, and during his imprisonment in Austria, his brother John took possession of this fortress, but on Richard s return from captivity, he seized it, with all the other possessions belonging to his brother, and on their reconciliation he still retained the castle of Marlborough in his own possession During the subsequent reign, King John occasionally kept his court here, and in the civil war of this period, Marlborough was possessed alternately by the king and the barons it seems, indeed, to have been the occasional residence of subsequent sovereigns till the time of Henry VII, and to have formed part of the dowries of several queens The assizes were held here from the time of Henry III to that of Charles I, and in the 52nd of Henry III that parliament assembled here by which were enacted the laws relative to the police of the kingdom, and to the administration of justice, commonly called the "Statutes of Marlbridge The castle, borough, &c, were granted by Henry VIII to Edward, Duke of Somerset, and became forfeited to the crown on the attainder of that nobleman, in the reign of Edward VI, but were subsequently restored to the Somerset family, and have now descended, by intermarriage, to the Marquis of Ailesbury Even in Camden s time, a few fragments only of the castle were remaining a large house now the Castle Inn which occupies its site, is said to have been commenced by the first duke of Somerset of the Seymour family, and was improved by the Earl of Hertford, in the early part of the eighteenth century the old keep has been converted into a spiral walk, in the grotto of which Mrs Rowe wrote the most celebrated of her works, "Friendship in Death, and here also Thompson is said to have composed a great part of his "Seasons, when on a visit to the Earl of Hertford, one of the most distinguished patrons of literature of that age In the civil war between Charles I and the parliament, the latter had a garrison here under the Earl of Essex, but the royal army, commanded by Lieut Gen Wilmot, marching hither from Oxford, in December 1642, captured above one thousand prisoners, besides large stores of arms and ammunition, with all which they returned in safety to

that city Marlborough having suffered repeatedly from fire prior to the year 1690, an act of parliament was passed in that year to prohibit the use of thatch as a covering for houses and other buildings within the borough

The town is delightfully situated on the banks of the Kennet, on the northern verge of the Forest of Savernake, and on the north of it are the open downs it consists principally of one long street, running from east to west, which is paved, and lighted with gas, the older houses are constructed of wood, and ornamented in front with curious carved work, the more modern are of stone and brick On the north side of the principal street is a piazza projecting in front of the houses, serving for a promenade in wet weather, and at its eastern extremity is a market-house, erected on the site of a former one, by the corporation, in 1790 the upper story is divided into a council chamber, an assembly-room, and a court-room The inhabitants are well supplied with water The manufactures are inconsiderable the trade is principally in corn, coal, and malt, and considerable advantages arise from the situation of the town on a great thoroughfare The Kennet and Avon canal passes within five miles of eht town, and in consequence of its not passing through it, the inhabitants have the privilege of a draw back upon the tonnage of goods The market days are Wednesday and Saturday, the former market has much declined, being now only for vegetables, the latter is considerable, and has long been celebrated for its extensive supply of grain, cheese, butchers' meat, &c fairs are held July 11th, for horses and wool, August 22nd, for lambs, horses, and cows, and November 23rd, for sheep, horses, and cows

Marlborough is a borough by prescription, and in a charter granted by Elizabeth, after referring to numerous preceding charters, the corporation is designated under the style of "The Mayor and Burgesses ' they are self-elected, and the present number is thirteen The mayor (who is also coroner, clerk of the market, and escheator) and two of the burgesses are justices of the peace, and, with a town clerk, a chamberlain, two bailiffs, or serjeants at mace, and two high constables, are chosen annually by the corporation the mayor and justices hold quarter sessions for the borough The county bridewell and house of correction was erected in 1787 it comprises four day-rooms and airing-yards, and is chiefly occupied by prisoners previously to trial Courts leet are held by the corporation, at the Lent and Michaelmas sessions, at which five constables (formerly called aldermen) are appointed, one for each ward, and a court, called the King s court, for the recovery of debts to any amount, is held every three weeks, under the charter of the 6th of John The privilege of sending members to parliament has been exercised ever since the 23rd of Edward I, and the right of election is in the mayor and burgesses the mayor is the returning officer the predominant influence is possessed by the Marquis of Ailesbury In the election of 1826 an effort was made to throw open the borough, and the subject was referred to a committee appointed by the House of Commons, who decided that the members returned by the corporation were duly elected another attempt has recently been made, two members having been nominated by the opposing party in the election of 1830, and who have expressed their intention of trying the question a second time

Marlborough comprises the two parishes of St Mary the Virgin and St Peter and St Paul, within the peculiar jurisdiction of the Consistorial Episcopal Court of Salisbury they are divided into five wards, viz, the Green ward and Marsh ward, in St Mary's parish, the High ward and Bailey ward, in the parish of St Peter and St Paul, and Kingsbury ward, in both parishes The living of St Mary's is a discharged vicarage, rated in the king's books at £10 9 4, endowed with £400 private benefaction, £200 royal bounty, and £500 parliamentary grant, and in the patronage of the Dean of Salisbury the church, a neat edifice of brick, with an ancient stone tower, beneath which is a Norman doorway, sustained considerable damage during the civil war, in 1641 The living of the parish of St Peter and St Paul is a discharged rectory, rated in the king's books at £12, endowed with £400 private benefaction, £200 royal bounty, and £300 parliamentary grant, and in the patronage of the Bishop of Salisbury the church, which stands at the western extremity of the main street, has a lofty square tower with battlements and pinnacles, the nave is supported by light pillars There are places of worship for Huntingtonians, Independents, and Wesleyan Methodists The free grammar school was founded and endowed with the revenue of the dissolved hospital of St John, by grant of Edward VI to the mayor and burgesses who were also empowered to make rules for its government the nomination of the schoolmaster, originally given to the Duke of Somerset, is now exercised by the Marquis of Ailesbury, the income is from £200 to £300 per annum the children of parents who have resided seven years in the town are alone eligible according to the rules, and the number of scholars on the foundation is in general about twenty The scholars share, alternately with those of the free schools of Manchester and Hereford, in sixteen exhibitions at Brasenose College, Oxford, and sixteen scholarships at St John's College, Cambridge, founded by Sarah, Duchess of Somerset, in 1679, and Mrs Brown bequeathed a rent-charge of £5 for any poor scholar from this school to the University of Oxford A National school is supported by voluntary contributions the school rooms were erected at the expense of the late Earl of Ailesbury An almshouse was formerly supported from the funds of the corporation, to which several donations and bequests were made for its support in the reign of Charles II, when it was rebuilt at the expense of that body, but, in 1725, they conveyed it to the officers of St. Mary's parish, by whom it is at present used as a workhouse Northward from the town is a common, on which each householder has a right to turn two milch cows, and eastward of it is a close, of about eighty acres of arable ground, of which a certain portion is granted to each member of the corporate body during his own life and the widowhood of his wife, on the payment of a sum by way of fine, and a fixed rent, the cows of the commoners are depastured on the eighty acres after the harvest and the inhabitants have an ancient privilege of turning two horses, from Old May-day to Old Martinmas day, into the adjacent Forest of Savernake The monastic institutions here were, a Gilbertine priory, dedicated to St Margaret, founded in the reign of John,

the revenue of which, at the dissolution, was £38 19 2, a convent of White friars, founded in 1316 by the merchants of this town, St John's hospital, founded in the reign of Henry II, and St Thomas in that of Henry III, and annexed to the priory of St Margaret in the reign of Richard II A chapel and other portions of the priory were standing a few years since Among the distinguished natives of this town the following may be specified Henry of Marlborough, an English historian of the fourteenth century, Sir Michael Foster, an eminent lawyer, and one of the judges of the Court of King's Bench, born in 1689, Walter Harte, poet and historian, who died in 1773, Dr Henry Sacheverell, of political celebrity, born in 1672, during the incumbency of his father in the parish of St Peter and St Paul, and John Hughes, a poet, and one of the writers in the Spectator, born in 1677 Marlborough confers the title of duke on the family of Spencer Churchill

MARLCLIFT, a hamlet in the parish of BIDFORD, Stratford division of the hundred of BARLICHWAY, county of WARWICK, 5 miles (S) from Alcester The population is returned with the parish

MARLDON, a parish in the hundred of HAYTOR, county of DEVON, 5 miles (N E by E) from Totness, containing 384 inhabitants The living is a perpetual curacy, annexed to the vicarage of Paington, in the peculiar jurisdiction of the Bishop of Exeter, and in the patronage of Sir S Northcote, G Templar, Esq, and the Rev J Templar The church has a rich stone screen In the village of Compton are considerable ruins of an ancient castellated mansion, occupied by Sir Maurice de la Pole in the reign of Henry II

MARLESFORD, a parish in the hundred of LOES, county of SUFFOLK, 2 miles (N E by N) from Wickham-Market, containing 436 inhabitants The living is a discharged rectory, in the archdeaconry of Suffolk, and diocese of Norwich, rated in the king's books at £9 6 8 A Arcedeckne, Esq was patron in 1823 The church is dedicated to St Andrew

MARLINGFORD, a parish in the hundred of FOREHOE, county of NORFOLK, 5 miles (N N E) from Wymondham, containing 179 inhabitants The living is a discharged rectory, in the archdeaconry of Norfolk, and diocese of Norwich, rated in the king's books at £7 12 8½, endowed with £200 private benefaction, and £200 royal bounty L Forman, Esq and others were patrons in 1814 The church is dedicated to St Mary The nave and chancel are thatched

MARLOW, a township in the parish of LEINTWARDINE, hundred of WIGMORE, county of HEREFORD, containing 68 inhabitants

MARLOW (GREAT), a borough, market town, and parish, in the hundred of DESBOROUGH, county of BUCKINGHAM, 35½ miles (S by E) from Buckingham, and 31 (W by N) from London, containing 3763 inhabitants, of which number, 2532 are in the borough The ancient name of this place was Merlaw, supposed to be derived from the Saxon word Mere, a marsh, and Law or Low, a hill The town, situated on the banks of the Thames, consists of two principal streets, which cross in the market-place the surrounding scenery is replete with variety and beauty Races are held in July, and there is a good news-room The river is here crossed by a wooden bridge, but an iron suspension bridge is in progress of erection There are some paper mills and copper-works in the neighbourhood, which, with the manufacture of lace and covered wire, and rope-making, furnish considerable employment to the labouring class there is likewise a good trade in corn, timber, and malt The market, held on Saturday, has nearly fallen into disuse, a pleasure fair is held on the 1st of May, and another for cheese, &c, on the 29th of October The principal civil officer is a high constable The borough first sent representatives to parliament in the 28th of Edward I, and continued so to do till the 2nd of Edward II, when the privilege ceased for upwards of four hundred years, but was restored upon petition to the House of Commons in the 21st of James I, and has since been exercised without intermission the right of election is in the inhabitants paying scot and lot, the number of voters is about five hundred, and the high constable is the returning officer The living is a vicarage, in the archdeaconry of Buckingham, and diocese of Lincoln, rated in the king s books at £13 6 8, and in the patronage of the Dean and Chapter of Gloucester The church, dedicated to All Saints, is a venerable structure, and contains several ancient monuments There are places of worship for Independents and Wesleyan Methodists In 1628, Sir William Borlase bequeathed estates for teaching twenty-four poor children, apprenticing six of them annually, and teaching twenty-four women to make bone-lace, and for a man to keep a house of correc tion A National school for children of both sexes is supported by subscription In the 7th of James I, John Brinkhurst devised to trustees almshouses for six poor widows, and 5s per quarter to each inmate The Royal Military College, established at High Wycombe in 1799, was removed to this town in 1802, but, in 1812, it was again removed to Sandhurst in Berkshire

MARLOW (LITTLE), a parish in the hundred of DESBOROUGH, county of BUCKINGHAM, 1½ mile (E N E) from Great Marlow, containing 775 inhabitants The living is a discharged vicarage, in the archdeaconry of Buckingham, and diocese of Lincoln, rated in the king's books at £8 5 10 The Rev G F L Nicolay was patron in 1822 The church, dedicated to St John the Baptist, is principally in the later style of English architecture Here was a small convent of Benedictine nuns, founded, in honour of the Virgin Mary, by Geoffrey, Lord Spencer, before the reign of John, the revenue of which at the dissolution was estimated at £37 6 11

MARLSTON, a joint township with Leach, in that part of the parish of St Mary, Chester, which is in the lower division of the hundred of Broxton, county palatine of Chester, 2¾ miles (S by W) from Chester, containing, with Leach, 108 inhabitants

MARNHAM, a parish in the northern division of the wapentake of Thurgarton, county of Nottingham, 4¾ miles (E by S) from Tuxford, containing, with the township of Grassthorpe, 351 inhabitants The living is a discharged vicarage, in the archdeaconry of Nottingham, and diocese of York, rated in the king s books at £8 19 2, and in the patronage of Earl Brownlow The church is dedicated to St Wilfrid A school was lately erected by Lord Brownlow for the instruction of ten children, £10 10 being allowed to the master out of the rents of a charitable bequest from

Henry Nicholson, in 1677 A fair for horses, cattle, swine, &c, is held on September 12th The river Trent is here crossed by a ferry

MARNHULL, a parish in the hundred of STUR-MINSTER-NEWTON-CASTLE, Sturminster division of the county of Dorset, 6 miles (W S W) from Shaftesbury, containing 1273 inhabitants The living is a rectory, in the archdeaconry of Dorset, and diocese of Bristol, rated in the king s books at £31 6 10½ The Rev H Place was patron in 1778 The church is dedicated to St Gregory There is a place of worship for Wesleyan Methodists

MARPLE, a chapelry in the parish of Stockport, hundred of Macclesfield, county palatine of Chester, 4¾ miles (E S E) from Stockport, containing, in 1821, 2646 inhabitants, since which period the population is supposed to have nearly doubled The village is situated on the road from London to Manchester through Buxton, and was anciently called Mupull, in allusion to an expansion of the waters of the river Goyt in the vale below The scenery is remarkably picturesque the banks of the river, which, from the highest points, may be seen for several miles, are rocky, precipitous, and well wooded, and the view from the churchyard includes the mountains of the peak on one side, and the Welch hills on the other The cotton manufacture, established here by the late Samuel Oldnow, Esq, is considerable and many of the inhabitants are employed in the manufacture of hats This place derives importance from the Peak Forest and Macclesfield canals, which pass through it a direct communication is afforded by the former from the Cromford canal and the Peak Forest railway to the Ashton canal, and thence to Manchester, and the Macclesfield canal (which is now in progress) unites the Peak Forest and the Trent and Mersey canals, and thus forms, not only a direct, but the shortest, water conveyance from London to Manchester Marple forms part of His Majesty's manor and forest of Macclesfield, at the court leet whereof constables and other officers are appointed The living is a perpetual curacy, in the archdeaconry and diocese of Chester, endowed with £400 private benefaction, £600 royal bounty, and £1200 parliamentary grant, and in the patronage of the Rector of Stockport The church, dedicated to All Saints, is a neat edifice, capable of accommodating one thousand persons it was rebuilt and enlarged in 1812, and the tower contains the bells taken from the old church at Stockport Samuel Oldnow, Esq, who projected the Peak Forest canal, and was a great benefactor to this place and neighbourhood, was interred here There are places of worship for Independents and Wesleyan Methodists This is the birthplace of John Bradshaw, who was president of the court that condemned Charles I he bequeathed £700 to purchase an annuity for maintaining a free school at Marple, but the change of property brought about by the Restoration prevented his bequest becoming available His brother Henry founded a small school here, and endowed it with the interest of £100, which has since been augmented with other benefactions

MARR, a parish in the northern division of the wapentake of Strafforth and Tickhill, West riding of the county of York, 4 miles (W N W) from Doncaster, containing 162 inhabitants The living is a discharged perpetual curacy, in the archdeaconry and diocese of York, endowed with £600 royal bounty, and in the patronage of the Earl of Kinnoul   The church, dedicated to St Helen, is principally in the early style of English architecture, the tower is surmounted by a small spire, and has two singular arched recesses, one on the north, the other on the south, side

MARRICK, a parish in the western division of the wapentake of GILLING, North riding of the county of YORK, $7\frac{1}{2}$ miles (W S W) from Richmond, containing 621 inhabitants   The living is a perpetual curacy, in the archdeaconry of Richmond, and diocese of Chester, endowed with a rent-charge of £10, and £200 private benefaction, £400 royal bounty, and £1500 parliamentary grant   W Powlett, Esq was patron in 1815   The church, dedicated to St Andrew, occupies part of the site of a Benedictine nunnery, founded in honour of the Blessed Virgin, by Roger de Asc, about the close of the reign of Stephen, and which at the dissolution had a revenue of £64 16 9   Two poor widows of this parish, not paupers, receive £5 12 per annum from an institution called the Duke of Bolton s charity

MARRISHES, a township in the parish and lythe of PICKERING, North riding of the county of YORK, $3\frac{3}{4}$ miles (S S E) from Pickering, containing 210 inhabitants   This township is divided into East and West Marrish

MARSDEN, a chapelry partly in the parish of HUDDERSFIELD, but chiefly in that of ALMONDBURY, upper division of the wapentake of AGBRICG, West riding of the county of YORK, 7 miles (S W by W) from Huddersfield, containing 2330 inhabitants   The living is a perpetual curacy, in the archdeaconry and diocese of York, endowed with £600 private benefaction, £1100 royal bounty, and £1100 parliamentary grant, and in the patronage of the Vicar of Almondbury   Independents and Wesleyan Methodists have each a place of worship here   At the distance of half a mile, the Huddersfield and Manchester canal passes under a tunnel three miles in length

MARSDEN (GREAT), a chapelry in that part of the parish of WHALLEY which is in the higher division of the hundred of BLACKBURN, county palatine of LANCASTER, $1\frac{1}{2}$ mile (S by W) from Colne, containing 1893 inhabitants   The living is a perpetual curacy, in the archdeaconry and diocese of Chester, endowed with £200 private benefaction, £600 royal bounty, and £1500 parliamentary grant, and in the patronage of the Vicar of Whalley

MARSDEN (LITTLE), a township in that part of the parish of WHALLEY which is in the higher division of the hundred of BLACKBURN, county palatine of LANCASTER, $3\frac{1}{4}$ miles (N N E) from Burnley, containing 2052 inhabitants

MARSH (CHAPEL), a parish in the wapentake of BRADLEY-HAVERSTOE, parts of LINDSEY, county of LINCOLN, 9 miles (N N E) from Louth, containing 411 inhabitants   The living is a perpetual curacy, with the rectory of North Coates, in the archdeaconry and diocese of Lincoln, endowed with £600 royal bounty, and £200 parliamentary grant   The church is dedicated to St Mary   There is a place of worship for Wesleyan Methodists, and several trifling donations have been made for the support and education of the poor

MARSH-GIBBON, a parish in the hundred and county of BUCKINGHAM, $4\frac{1}{2}$ miles (E by N) from

Bicester, containing 738 inhabitants   The living is a rectory, in the archdeaconry of Buckingham, and diocese of Lincoln, rated in the king s books at £21 9 $4\frac{1}{2}$, and in the patronage of the Crown   The church is dedicated to St Mary   There is a place of worship for Wesleyan Methodists   Near the manor-house are some slight vestiges of earth works, said to have been thrown up by the parliamentarians, in their advance to this place in 1645

MARSHAM, a parish in the southern division of the hundred of ERPINGHAM, county of NORFOLK, 2 miles (S) from Aylsham, containing 624 inhabitants   The living is a discharged rectory, in the archdeaconry and diocese of Norwich, rated in the king s books at £10 12 9   Lord Viscount Anson was patron in 1787   The church is dedicated to All Saints   The manufactures of worsted and bombazine are carried on here

MARSHFIELD, a market town and parish in the upper division of the hundred of THORNBURY, county of GLOUCESTER, $11\frac{1}{2}$ miles (E) from Bristol, and 102 (W by S) from London, containing 1569 inhabitants   The town consists chiefly of a single street of old buildings, nearly a mile in length   The trade is principally in malt, a great part of which is the produce of the vicinity   The market is on Tuesday, and fairs are held on the 24th of May and 24th of October, the former chiefly for horned cattle, and the latter for sheep, horses, and cheese   A bailiff is annually elected at the manorial court, and is assisted by a serjeant at mace, his jurisdiction extends to a considerable distance round the town   The living is a discharged vicarage, in the archdeaconry and diocese of Gloucester, rated in the king s books at £29 4 9, endowed with £200 private benefaction, and £200 royal bounty, and in the patronage of the Warden and Fellows of New College, Oxford   The church, which is dedicated to St Mary, is a handsome and spacious fabric, in the later style of English architecture, with a fine square tower at the west end   There is a place of worship for Unitarians   A free school was founded, about 1722, by John Harrington, Esq, who gave the school-house, it was subsequently endowed with messuages and lands for the support of a schoolmaster, in 1751, by Dionysia Long   the annual income, arising from this and other benefactions, is £62 5, and twenty children are instructed   The present school room was built in 1793   Almshouses for eight poor persons were founded and endowed by Nicholas Crispe, in 1625, and there are benefactions for apprenticing poor boys, and other charitable purposes   In this parish are some barrows and intrenchments, supposed to have been raised by the Britons, or Saxons, about 561, when the battle of Dirham took place in this neighbourhood   Leland mentions the existence of a nunnery also, but there are no vestiges of it   In the vicinity are three stones, which mark the limits of the counties of Gloucester, Somerset, and Wilts

MARSHFIELD, a parish in the upper division of the hundred of WENTLLOOG, county of MONMOUTH, 5 miles (S W) from Newport, containing 483 inhabitants   The living is a discharged vicarage, in the archdeaconry and diocese of Llandaff, rated in the king s books at £6 2 6, endowed with £200 royal bounty, and in the patronage of the Dean and Chapter ot Bristol The church is a large and handsome structure in the later English style , in the chancel are several stone stalls

MARSHWOOD, a chapelry in the parish and hundred of WHITCHURCH-CANONICORUM, Bridport division of the county of DORSET, 4¼ miles (W S W) from Beaminster, containing 532 inhabitants The living is a perpetual curacy, with the vicarage of Whitchurch-Canonicorum, in the archdeaconry of Dorset, and diocese of Bristol This place, which takes its name from the marsh), woody vale in which it is situated, was anciently an honour, the only one in the county, and the head of a barony

MARSK a parish in the western division of the wapentake of GILLING, North riding of the county of YORK, 4¾ miles (W) from Richmond, containing 290 inhabitants The living is a rectory, in the archdeaconry of Cleveland, and diocese of York, rated in the king s books at £12 6 5½ J Hutton, Esq was patron in 1808 The church is dedicated to St Cuthbert A school, erected in 1814, by John Hutton, Esq , is endowed with about £20 per annum, arising from land and money given by John Jackson and — Hutchinson, for the education and support of the poor

MARSK, a parish in the eastern division of the liberty of LANGBAURGH, North riding of the county of YORK, comprising the townships of Marsk and Redcar, and containing 1249 inhabitants, of which number, 576 are in the township of Marsk, 5 miles (N N E) from Guilsborough The living is a discharged vicarage, in the archdeaconry of Cleveland, and diocese of York, rated in the king s books at £10 11 10½ , endowed with £200 private benefaction, £200 royal bounty, and £800 parliamentary grant Lord Dundas was patron in 1799 The church, dedicated to St German, stands near the edge of the cliff, its spire serving as an excellent land-mark There is a place of worship for Wesleyan Methodists Marsk hall was built by Sir William Pennyman Bart , in the style which prevailed in the time of Charles I

MARSTON, a township in that part of the parish of GREAT BUDWORTH which is in the hundred of BUCKLOW, county palatine of CHESTER, 2¼ miles (N N E) from Northwich, containing 404 inhabitants The Grand Trunk canal passes through the township

MARSTON, a parish in the wapentake of LOVEDEN, parts of KESTEVEN, county of LINCOLN, 5 miles (N by W) from Grantham, containing 393 inhabitants The living is a rectory, with that of Hougham, in the archdeaconry and diocese of Lincoln, and in the patronage of Sir J H Thorold, Bart The church is dedicated to St Mary Dame Margaret Thorold, in 1718, gave land, the income to be applied in teaching poor children, and apprenticing one yearly, with a premium of £5

MARSTON, a parish in the hundred of BULLINGTON, county of OXFORD, 1¼ mile (N N E) from Oxford, containing 340 inhabitants The living is a discharged vicarage, in the archdeaconry and diocese of Oxford, endowed with £400 private benefaction, £800 royal bounty, and £200 parliamentary grant, and in the patronage of the Rev T H Whorwood The church is dedicated to St Nicholas The river Cherwell forms part of the boundary of this parish

MARSTON, a township in the parish of CHURCH-EATON, western division of the hundred of CUTTLE-

STONE, county of STAFFORD, 6 miles (W) from Penkridge The population is returned with the parish

MARSTON, a chapelry in that part of the parish of ST MARY, LICHFIELD, which is in the southern division of the hundred of PIREHILL, county of STAFFORD, 2¾ miles (N) from Stafford, containing 96 inhabitants The living is a perpetual curacy, in the archdeaconry of Stafford, and diocese of Lichfield and Coventry, endowed with £400 royal bounty and in the patronage of the Mayor and Corporation of Stafford

MARSTON, a quarter in the parish of CHURCH-BICKENHILL, Solihull division of the hundred of HEMLINGFORD, county of WARWICK, 3½ miles (S S W) from Coleshill The population is returned with the parish

MARSTON, a hamlet in that part of the parish of WOLSTON which is in the Rugby division of the hundred of KNIGHTLOW, county of WARWICK, 6 miles (E by S) from Coventry The population is returned with the parish

MARSTON, a tything in the parish of POTTERNE, hundred of POTTERNE and CANNINGS, county of WILTS, 3¾ miles (S W) from Devizes, containing 192 inhabitants

MARSTON, a chapelry in the parish of YARDLEY, lower division of the hundred of PERSHORE, though locally in the upper division of the hundred of Halfshire, county of WORCESTER, 4½ miles (S E) from Birmingham The population is returned with the parish The living is a donative The chapel was erected in 1704, by Job Marston, Esq

MARSTON (BUTLER S), a parish in the Kington division of the hundred of KINGTON, county of WARWICK, 1½ mile (S W by S) from Kington, containing 275 inhabitants The living is a discharged vicarage in the archdeaconry and diocese of Worcester, rated in the king s books at £8 3 4, endowed with £400 private benefaction, and £400 royal bounty, and in the patronage of the Dean and Canons of Christ Church, Oxford The church is dedicated to St Peter and St Paul Near it is an old mansion of stone, now used as a kennel for the hounds of the Warwickshire hunt Upon an artificial mount on the green is a decayed elm, of remarkably large dimensions, capable of containing twelve persons, and formed by nature into the appearance of a grotto

MARSTON upon DOVE, a parish in the hundred of APPLETREE, county of DERBY, 5 miles (N by W) from Burton upon Trent, containing, with the townships of Hilton and Hoon, and the hamlet of Hatton 905 inhabitants The living is a vicarage, in the archdeaconry of Derby, and diocese of Lichfield and Coventry, rated in the king s books at £7 15 2½ , and in the patronage of E S Pole, Esq The church, dedicated to St Mary, is partly in the early and partly in the decorated style of English architecture

MARSTON (ST LAWRENCE), a parish in the hundred of KING'S SUTTON, county of NORTHAMPTON, 5¾ miles (N W) from Brackley, containing 482 inhabitants The living is a vicarage, consolidated with the rectory of Warkworth, in the archdeaconry of Northampton, and diocese of Peterborough, rated in the king s books at £20 S Blencowe, Esq was patron in 1809

MARSTON (LEA), in the county of WARWICK - See LEA-MARSTON

MARSTON (LONG), a chapelry in the parish of TRING, hundred of DACORUM, county of HERTFORD, 3½ miles (N W by N) from Tring, with which the population is returned   The chapel is dedicated to All Saints

MARSTON (LONG), a parish in the ainsty of the city, and East riding of the county, of YORK, comprising the townships of Angram, Hutton, and Long Marston, and containing 579 inhabitants, of which number, 388 are in the township of Long Marston, 6 miles (N by E) from Tadcaster   The living is a rectory, in the archdeaconry and diocese of York, rated in the king's books at £24 3 9   Sir R T Lawley, Bart was patron in 1821   The church, dedicated to All Saints, was erected about 1400   A National school has been established here, and is partly supported by a rent-charge of £10, the bequest of Richard Roundle, and the interest of £150 left by the Rev Marmaduke Buck, in 1757   Within the parish is Marston Moor, the scene of a memorable and most obstinately disputed battle, fought on July 2, 1644, between the royalists under Prince Rupert, and the parliamentarians, commanded by Fairfax, in which fifty thousand British troops were opposed to each other, and which ended in the total defeat of the king's army

MARSTON (MAGNA), a parish in the hundred of HORETHORNE, county of SOMERSET, 5¼ miles (N N E) from Yeovil, containing 324 inhabitants   The living is a discharged vicarage, in the archdeaconry of Wells, and diocese of Bath and Wells, rated in the king's books at £6 10 10, endowed with £200 private benefaction, and £200 royal bounty   Mrs Williams was patroness in 1785   The church, dedicated to St Mary, is a neat stone structure, with a strong tower crowned with an embattled pediment and pinnacles   In the porch, two feet below the surface of the earth, have lately been found several large stones carved with crosses entwined with palm leaves, and covering human skeletons   Sir John St Barbe, in 1736, devised the rectory, parsonage-house, and lands for the education of ten poor boys of this parish and that of Ashington   fourteen children are instructed   On opening a pit in 1798, near the margin of a brook, some fine specimens of a calcareous blue stone, almost filled with Cornua Ammonis, overspread with white pearl, were discovered, and raised in masses sufficiently large to form slabs, which took a beautiful polish, and were much in request for side tables   In the same field irregular heaps of mundic, with large metalliferous Cornua Ammonis, were also found , and the quarries on the hills, from one of which the brook takes its rise, abound in Am montes Nautili, Belamnites, &c

MARSTON (NORTH), a parish in the hundred of ASHENDON, county of BUCKINGHAM, 3 miles (S by E) from Winslow, containing 558 inhabitants   The living is a discharged perpetual curacy, in the archdeaconry of Buckingham, and diocese of Lincoln, endowed with £400 private benefaction, £400 royal bounty, and £400 parliamentary grant, and in the patronage of the Dean and Chapter of Lincoln   The church, dedicated to St Mary, is a neat structure, containing three stone stalls and a piscina, the chancel was built by the offerings of those who frequented a chalybeate spring here, which once was in high rebute, though now scarcely known

MARSTON (POTTER S), a chapelry in the parish of BARWELL, hundred of SPARKENHOE, county of LEICESTER, 5 miles (E N E) from Hinckley, containing 16 inhabitants

MARSTON (PRIORS'), a parish in the Burton-Dassett division of the hundred of KINGTON, county of WARWICK, 5½ miles (S E by E) from Southam, containing 593 inhabitants   The living is a perpetual curacy, with the vicarage of Priors Hardwick, in the archdeaconry of Coventry, and diocese of Lichfield and Coventry   The Oxford canal passes through the parish James West, in 1705, and Josiah Kay, in 1711, bequeathed property now producing £40 a year, for teaching and apprenticing poor children

MARSTON (SOUTH), a chapelry in the parish of HIGHWORTH, hundred of HIGHWORTH, CRICKLADE, and STAPLE, county of WILTS, 2½ miles (S by W) from Highworth, containing 299 inhabitants   It is in the peculiar jurisdiction of the Prebendary of Highworth in the Cathedral Church of Salisbury

MARSTON-BIGOTT, a parish in the hundred of FROME, county of SOMERSET, 2¼ miles (S S W) from Frome, containing 471 inhabitants   The living is a rectory, in the archdeaconry of Wells, and diocese of Bath and Wells, rated in the king's books at £11 19 9½, and in the patronage of the Earl of Cork and Orrery The church, dedicated to St Leonard, was taken down, within the last fifty years, and another erected on a more convenient site

MARSTON FLEET, a parish in the hundred of ASHENDON, county of BUCKINGHAM, 3 miles (N W by W) from Aylesbury, containing 43 inhabitants The living is a rectory in the archdeaconry of Buckingham and diocese of Lincoln, rated in the king's books at £8 2 8½   Lord Viscount Dillon was patron in 1776   The church is dedicated to St Mary

MARSTON JABBETT, a hamlet in the parish of BULKINGTON, Kirby division of the hundred of KNIGHTLOW, county of WARWICK, 3¼ miles (S by E) from Nuneaton, containing 82 inhabitants

MARSTON-MAISEY, a parish in the hundred of HIGHWORTH, CRICKLADE, and STAPLE, county of WILTS, 3½ miles (N E) from Cricklade, containing 184 inhabitants   The living is a perpetual curacy, with the rectory of Maisey-Hampton, in the archdeaconry and diocese of Gloucester, endowed with £200 private benefaction, and £1000 royal bounty

MARSTON-MONTGOMERY, a parish in the hundred of APPLETREE, county of DERBY, 6¼ miles (S W by S) from Ashbourn, containing 469 inhabitants   The living is a perpetual curacy, annexed to the rectory of Cubley, in the archdeaconry of Derby, and diocese of Lichfield and Coventry   The church is dedicated to St Giles   A school is supported by small annual donations

MARSTON MORETAINE, a parish in the hundred of REDBORNSTOKE, county of BEDFORD, 4 miles (N W) from Ampthill, containing 899 inhabitants   The living is a rectory, in the archdeaconry of Bedford, and diocese of Lincoln, rated in the king's books at £23 17 3½, and in the patronage of the Master and Fellows of St John's College, Cambridge   The church, dedicated to St Mary, is in the later style of English architecture the tower is detached   There is a place of worship for Wesleyan Methodists

MARSTON SICCA, a parish in the upper division of the hundred of KIFTSGATE, county of GLOUCESTER, 6½ miles (N) from Chipping Campden, containing 272 inhabitants   The living is a rectory, in the archdeaconry and diocese of Gloucester, rated in the king s books at £17 10   The Rev William Loggin was patron in 1808   The church is dedicated to St James

MARSTON-STANNETT, a chapelry in the parish of PENCOMBE, hundred of BROXASH, county of HERI-FORD, 6½ miles (W by N) from Bromyard   The living is a perpetual curacy, with the rectory of Pencombe, in the archdeaconry and diocese of Hereford, endowed with £410 private benefaction, and £400 royal bounty, and in the patronage of the Rector of Pencomoe

MARSTON TRUSSEL, a parish in the hundred of ROTHWELL, county of NORIHAMPTON, 3¼ miles (W S W) from Market-Harborough, containing, with the township of Thorpe Lubbenham, 217 inhabitants   The living is a rectory, in the archdeaconry of North-ampton, and diocese of Peterborough, rated in the king s books at £15 2 11   Richard H Bullivant, Esq was patron in 1809   The church is dedicated to St Nicholas

MARSTOW, a parish in the lower division of the hundred of WORMELOW, county of HERFFORD, 5 miles (S W) from Ross, containing 132 inhabitants   The living is a perpetual curacy, annexed to the vicarage of Selleck, in the archdeaconry and diocese of Hereford, endowed with £400 royal bounty, and in the patronage of the Vicar of Selleck   The church is dedicated to St Martin

MARSWORTH, a parish in the hundred of COT-TESLOE, county of BUCKINGHAM, 2¼ miles (8 W by W) from Ivinghoe, containing 391 inhabitants   The living is a vicarage, in the archdeaconry of Buckingham, and diocese of Lincoln, rated in the king s books at £9 9 7, and in the patronage of the Master and Fellows of Trinity College, Cambridge   The church, dedicated to All Saints, has the appearance of considerable antiquity, in the windows are some fragments of stained glass, parts of the floor are of Roman brick, and near the altar is a fine tomb, but much mutilated, in memory of some of the family of West   The old Roman Iknield-street bounds the parish on the south-east, and the discovery of swords, urns, coins, and other ancient relics, in forming the Grand Junction canal, affords some reason for considering it the site of a Roman station, though historians have not recorded it as such

MARTALL, a joint township with Little Warford, in that part of the parish of ROSTHERN which is in the hundred of BUCKLOW, county palatine of CHESTER, 3¼ miles (E S E) from Nether Knutsford, containing, with Little Warford, 267 inhabitants

MARTHA (ST), in the county of SURREY —See CHILWORIH

MARTHAM, a parish in the western division of the hundred of FLEGG, county of NORFOLK, 6¾ miles (N W) from Caistor, containing 845 inhabitants   The living is a discharged vicarage, in the peculiar jurisdiction and patronage of the Dean and Chapter of Norwich, rated in the king s books at £6 13 4   The church is dedicated to St Mary   There are places of worship for Baptists and Wesleyan Methodists   Christopher Amys, in 1622, bequeathed £112, which, together with a tri-

fling bequest by Robert Bower, in 1622, is applied in teaching poor children

MARTIN, a parish in the southern division of the wapentake of GARTREE, parts of LINDSEY, county of LINCOLN, 2½ miles (S W by S) from Horncastle, containing 55 inhabitants   The living is a rectory, in the archdeaconry and diocese of Lincoln, rated in the king s books at £6 4 2, endowed with £400 royal bounty, and in the patronage of John Oldham and —Slater, Esqrs   The church is dedicated to St Michael   The Horncastle canal passes through the parish

MARTIN, a hamlet in the parish of TIMBERLAND, first division of the wapentake of LANGOE, parts of KESTEVEN, county of LINCOLN, 10¾ miles (N N E) from Sleaford, containing 589 inhabitants

MARTIN, a parish in the southern division of the hundred of DAMERHAM, county of WILTS, 4½ miles (N N E) from Cranbourne, containing 528 inhabitants   The living is a perpetual curacy, with the vicarage of South Damerham, in the archdeaconry and diocese of Salisbury

MARTIN, a parish in the eastern division of the wapentake of STAINCLIFFE and EWCROSS, West riding of the county of YORK, 5½ miles (W by S) from Skip ton, containing 382 inhabitants   The living is a rectory, in the archdeaconry and diocese of York, rated in the king s books at £14 14 4½   Mrs Heber was patroness in 1816   The church is dedicated to St Peter

MARTIN (ST), a parish in WEST hundred, county of CORNWALL, 1¼ mile (N) from East Looe, containing, with the borough of East Looe, 1181 inhabitants   The living is a rectory, in the archdeaconry of Cornwall, and diocese of Exeter, rated in the king s books at £36 2 3½, and in the patronage of the Dowager Countess of Sandwich and Viscount Barnard   There is a place of worship for Wesleyan Methodists   The parish is bounded on the west by Looe harbour, and on the south by the English channel   Here was formerly a nunnery

MARTIN (ST), a parish in the hundred of OSWESTRY, county of SALOP, 5½ miles (W by N) from Ellesmere, containing, with the townships of Ifton-Rhyn, Weston-Rhyn, and Bron y gath, 1852 inhabitants   The living is a discharged vicarage, in the archdeaconry and diocese of St Asaph, rated in the king s books at £5 2 3½, endowed with £200 private benefaction, and £200 royal bounty, and in the patronage of the Bishop of St Asaph   There is an ancient wood carving in the roof of the church, in allusion to St. Martin, a translation of whose life was made from the Latin by John Trevor in 1488   The Ellesmere canal passes through the parish, and at its termine, crosses the valley of the Ceiriog by means of an aqueduct, near the neat village of Chirk, where it enters Wales   it then immediately passes under a tunnel, and, a little further on, under another, whence it is continued to the beautiful vale of Llangollen, where it is carried over the river Dee by Pont-y-Cyssyltau aqueduct, a stupendous structure of nineteen tall arches by Mr Telford   on the banks of the canal, near the Welch boundary of the parish, are some coal works   The great road from Shrewsbury to Holyhead has here been recently diverted from its original course, whereby a considerable distance has been saved, and the steep acclivity of Chirk hill avoided

MARTIN (ST), a township in that part of the parish of CATTERICK which is in the eastern division of the wapentake of HANG, North riding of the county of YORK, ¾ of a mile (S E) from Richmond, containing 23 inhabitants About the year 1100, Wymar, chief steward to the Earl of Richmond, gave the chapel of St Martin, with certain land adjoining, to the abbey of St Mary, at York, upon which a cell of nine or ten Benedictine monks was established here, and continued till the dissolution, when its revenue was estimated at £43 16 8

MARTIN (ST) in MENEAGE, a parish in the hundred of KERRIER, county of CORNWALL, 6¾ miles (E S E) from Helston, containing 504 inhabitants The living is a rectory not in charge, with that of Mawgan, in the archdeaconry of Cornwall, and diocese of Exeter Helford river is navigable on the north of this parish Tremayne was for some time the residence of the circumnavigator, Captain Wallis

MARTIN S (ST) STAMFORD BARON, a parish in the liberty of PETERBOROUGH, county of NORTHAMPTON, ½ a mile (S F) from Stamford, containing, with the hamlet of Woothorpe, 1226 inhabitants The living is a discharged vicarage, in the archdeaconry of Northampton, and diocese of Peterborough, rated in the king s books at £7 13 9 , endowed with £1200 parliamentary grant, and in the patronage of the Marquis of Exeter Here is a trifling endowment, the gift of Lady Dorothy Cecil, for teaching and apprenticing poor children A Benedictine nunnery, in honour of our Lady St Mary and St Michael, was founded here in the time of Henry II , by William de Waterville, abbot of Peterborough, to which abbey it was subordinate , it had at one period forty nuns, but at the dissolution it possessed a revenue of only £72 18 10

MARTIN (STOWE), a chapelry in the parish of TAMERTON-FOLIATT, hundred of ROBOROUGH, county of DEVON, 7¼ miles (N by W) from Plymouth

MARTIN HUSSINGTREE, a parish in the upper division of the hundred of PERSHORE, though locally in the lower division of the hundred of Oswaldslow, county of WORCESTER, 3 miles (S W) from Droitwich, containing 217 inhabitants The living is a discharged rectory, in the archdeaconry and diocese of Worcester, rated in the king s books at £5 14 4½ , and in the patronage of the Dean and Chapter of Worcester The church is dedicated to St Nicholas

MARTINDALE, a chapelry in the parish of BARTON, WEST ward, county of WESTMORLAND, 9½ miles N N E) from Ambleside, containing 155 inhabitants The living is a perpetual curacy, in the archdeaconry and diocese of Carlisle, endowed with £800 royal bounty, and £200 parliamentary grant, and in the patronage of John de Whelpdale, Esq Here is a free school, with an endowment of £13 a year, arising from the rent of an estate left by the relict of the Rev Richard Birket, a former incumbent

MARTINHOE, a parish in the hundred of SHERWILL, county of DEVON, 12 miles (E by N) from Ilfracombe, containing 204 inhabitants The living is a discharged rectory, in the archdeaconry of Barnstaple, and diocese of Exeter, rated in the king s books at £8 10 10 , and in the patronage of G Courtenay, Esq The church is dedicated to St Martin.

MARTINSCROFI, a joint township with Woolstone, in the parish of WARRINGTON, hundred of WEST DERBY, county palatine of LANCASTER, 3¼ miles (E by N) from Warrington The population is returned with Woolstone

MARTINSTHORPE, a parish in the hundred of MARTINSLEY, county of RUTLAND, 3¼ miles (N) from Uppingham, containing 4 inhabitants The living is a rectory, in the archdeaconry of Northampton, and diocese of Peterborough, rated in the king s books at £6 0 5 The Duke of Devonshire was patron in 1801 The church, which was dedicated to St Martin, is now in ruins

MARTLESHAM, a parish in the hundred of CARLFORD, county of SUFFOLK, 2 miles (S by W) from Woodbridge, containing 413 inhabitants The living is a discharged rectory, in the archdeaconry of Suffolk, and diocese of Norwich rated in the king s books at £10 18 9 Mrs Goodwin was patroness in 1798 The church is dedicated to St Mary The navigable river Deben forms the eastern boundary of the parish

MARTLEY, a parish in the upper division of the hundred of DODDINGTREE, county of WORCESTER, 7 miles (N W by W) from Worcester, containing with the hamlet of Hillhampton, 1264 inhabitants The living is a rectory, in the archdeaconry and diocese of Worcester, rated in the king s books at £22 10 1 B Paget, Fsq was patron in 1795 The church, dedicated to St Peter, has lately received an addition of two hundred and one sittings, of which one hundred and fifty one are free, the Incorporated Society for the enlargement of churches and chapels having granted £100 towards defraying the expense

MARTOCK, a parish (formerly a market town) in the hundred of MARTOCK, county of SOMERSET, 4½ miles (S W by W) from Ilchester, and 130 (W) from London, containing 2560 inhabitants The name of this place is said to be derived from mart and oak, from the fact of the market having been formerly held under an oak-tree in the centre of the town, the site of which is now occupied by an elegant fluted column, in imitation of the pillar of Trajan, at Rome The town consists principally of one street, about a mile and a half in length the river Parret passes through it The manufacture of fine gloves is carried on to a limited extent, but was formerly of greater note There is a fair on the 21st of August A court leet is held in October, by the lord of the manor The living is a discharged vicarage, with the perpetual curacy of Load, in the archdeaconry of Wells, and diocese of Bath and Wells, rated in the king's books at £15 10 , endowed with £230 private benefaction, and £200 royal bounty, and in the patronage of the Treasurer in the Cathedral Church of Wells The church, which is dedicated to All Saints, is an elegant structure, in the ancient style of English architecture, with a fine embattled tower at the west end in the interior is a superb altar-piece in stucco There is a place of worship for Independents A free grammar school was founded, in 1661, by William Strode, who endowed it with a rent charge of £12, but the endowment being insufficient to support a classical master, it has been discontinued , a few poor children are, however, taught to read by the clerk of the parish, who resides in the school-house The old Roman Fosseway skirts the south-east boundary of the parish

MARTON, a township in the parish of WHITE-GATE, or NEW CHURCH, first division of the hundred of EDDISBURY, county palatine of CHESTER, 4¼ miles (S. W by S) from Northwich, containing 582 inhabitants.

MARTON, a chapelry in the parish of PRESTBURY, hundred of MACCLESFIELD, county palatine of CHESTER, 3½ miles (N by W) from Congleton, containing 341 inhabitants. The living is a perpetual curacy, in the archdeaconry and diocese of Chester, endowed with £200 private benefaction, and £400 royal bounty. D Davenport, Esq was patron in 1806. The chapel is a rude building of wood, with a chancel and spire of more modern date. It had formerly a chantry, which is said to have been founded in the reign of Edward III, by Sir J Davenport and his son, of whom there are in the cemetery two recumbent figures in armour.

MARTON, a chapelry in the parish of POULTON, hundred of AMOUNDERNESS, county palatine of LANCASTER, 5¾ miles (W N W) from Kirkham, containing 1397 inhabitants. The living is a perpetual curacy, in the archdeaconry of Richmond, and diocese of Chester, endowed with £800 private benefaction, £400 royal bounty, and £2200 parliamentary grant. J Clifton, Esq and others were patrons in 1814. A free school was founded in 1717, by James Baines, who endowed it with a messuage and lands producing £91 a year; a master and an assistant are elected annually, and the average number of scholars is about one hundred. There is also a Sunday school, attended by about eighty children, towards the support of which Margaret Whittam left an annuity of 40s.

MARTON, a parish in the wapentake of WELL, parts of LINDSEY, county of LINCOLN, 5¾ miles (S by E) from Gainsborough, containing 395 inhabitants. The living is a discharged vicarage, in the archdeaconry of Stow, and diocese of Lincoln, rated in the king's books at £4 13 4, endowed with £600 royal bounty, and in the patronage of the Bishop of Lincoln. The church is dedicated to St Margaret. There is a place of worship for Wesleyan Methodists. The Roman Tilbridge-lane passes through the parish, which is bounded on the west by the river Trent.

MARTON, a parish in the Southam division of the hundred of KNIGHTLOW, county of WARWICK, 4¾ miles (N by W) from Southam, containing 317 inhabitants. The living is a discharged vicarage, in the archdeaconry and diocese of Worcester, rated in the king's books at £7 14 8. T W Knightley, Esq was patron in 1805. The church is dedicated to St Esperit.

MARTON, a joint township with Sewerby, in the parish of BRIDLINGTON, wapentake of DICKERING, East riding of the county of YORK, 2 miles (N E) from Bridlington. The population is returned with Sewerby. Here are vestiges of an ancient ravine, consisting of a double line of defence, with breast-works, extending one mile and a quarter from the southern shore of Flamborough-head; this immense work is ascribed to the Danes, and is therefore termed "Danes Dike."

MARTON, a township in that part of the parish of SWINE which is in the middle division of the wapentake of HOLDERNESS, East riding of the county of YORK, 9½ miles (N E by N) from Kingston upon Hull, containing 129 inhabitants. There is a Roman Catholic chapel.

MARTON, a parish in the western division of the liberty of LANGBAURGH, North riding of the county of YORK, 6 miles (N) from Stokesley, containing 397 inhabitants. The living is a vicarage, in the archdeaconry of Cleveland, and diocese of York, rated in the king's books at £4 18 9, and in the patronage of the Archbishop of York. The church, dedicated to St Cuthbert, is a small ancient edifice, situated on an eminence at the western end of the village. Captain James Cook, the great circumnavigator, was born here, of humble parents, October 27th, 1728; he was killed at Owhyhee on the 14th of February 1779.

MARTON, a township in that part of the parish of SINNINGTON which is in PICKERING lythe, North riding of the county of YORK, 4¼ miles (W by S) from Pickering, containing 255 inhabitants.

MARTON, a joint parish with Grafton, partly within the liberty of ST PETER of YORK, but chiefly in the upper division of the wapentake of CLARO, West riding of the county of YORK, 3 miles (S) from Aldborough, containing 464 inhabitants. The living is a discharged vicarage, with Grafton, in the archdeaconry of Richmond, and diocese of Chester, rated in the king's books at £2 19 4½, endowed with £200 private benefaction and £200 royal bounty, and in the patronage of the Master and Fellows of St John's College, Cambridge. Various small sums, from a bequest by Nicholas Stowell, in 1597, and other subsequent donations, are applied to the instruction of poor children.

MARTON in the FOREST, a parish in the wapentake of BULMER, North riding of the county of YORK, 5¾ miles (E by S) from Easingwould, containing, with the chapelry of Moxby, 164 inhabitants. The living is a perpetual curacy, in the archdeaconry and diocese of York, endowed with £600 royal bounty, and in the patronage of the Archbishop of York. A priory for Augustine canons and nuns, the latter of whom soon after removed to Moxby, was founded here, in honour of St Mary, by Bertram de Bulmer, who lived in the reigns of Stephen and his successor, the revenue of which at the dissolution was £183 2 4. The nunnery at Moxby, which was erected before 1167, by Henry II, in honour of St John, the Apostle and Evangelist, had at the dissolution a revenue of £32 6 2.

MARTON (LONG), a parish in EAST ward, county of WESTMORLAND, 4 miles (N N W) from Appleby, containing 714 inhabitants. The living is a rectory, in the archdeaconry and diocese of Carlisle, rated in the king's books at £21 15 7½, and in the patronage of the Earl of Thanet. The church, dedicated to St Margaret, is a large edifice. A commodious place of worship for Wesleyan Methodists was erected here in 1816. The village of Long Marton, one of the most considerable in the county, having been rebuilt within the last twenty years, presents an appearance of neatness and opulence. Marton House, a handsome stone edifice, situated at its northern extremity, is occupied by the principal agent to the London Lead Company, whose mining office is here. A trifling endowment left by Thomas Machel, and two annual donations by Miss Fearon and Mrs Rippon, are applied in teaching poor children.

MARTON le MOOR, a chapelry in that part of the parish of TOPCLIFFE which is in the wapentake of

HAILIKELD, North riding of the county of YORK, 3½ miles (N W by N) from Boroughbridge, containing 201 inhabitants The living is a perpetual curacy, in the archdeaconry of Cleveland, and diocese of York, endowed with £800 royal bounty, and in the patronage of the Vicar of Topcliffe There is a small endowment, the bequest of the Rev Mr Day, for the education of the poor

MARWELL, or MEREWELL, a hamlet in the parish of CARISBROOKE, liberty of WEST MEDINA, Isle of Wight division of the county of SOUTHAMPTON, 1¼ mile (S) from Newport A college of four priests was founded here, by Henry de Blois, Bishop of Winchester, and augmented by two of his successors

MARWOOD, a parish in the hundred of BRAUNTON, county of DEVON, 3 miles (N by W) from Barnstaple, containing 869 inhabitants The living is a rectory, in the archdeaconry of Barnstaple, and diocese of Exeter, rated in the king's books at £24 8 6½, and in the patronage of the Master and Fellows of St John's College, Cambridge The church, dedicated to St Michael, has an ancient wooden screen There were formerly two chapels within the parish, one at Patsford, now converted into a cow-house, the other at Whitefield, of which only two pillars remain Here is a school, endowed, in 1782, by the Rev R Harding with about £10 per annum, and, in 1814, with £100 three per cents, by William Westacott Judge Littleton is said to have been born at West Marwood

MARWOOD, a township in that part of the parish of GAINFORD which is in the south-western division of DARLINGTON ward, county palatine of DURHAM, 3 miles (N N W) from Barnard-Castle, containing 212 inhabitants Barnard castle and demesne are within this township, and on an eminence adjoining the town of Barnard Castle, some vestiges of the ancient town of Marwood, once a considerable place, have been discovered, near the same spot is an old chapel, but divine service has not been performed in it for a great number of years

MARY S (ST), a parish in the liberty of ROMNEYMARSH, though locally in the hundred of New Church, lathe of SHEPWAY, county of KENT, 2¼ miles (N) from New Romney, containing 103 inhabitants The living is a rectory, in the archdeaconry and diocese of Canterbury, rated in the king's books at £23 3 9, and in the patronage of the Archbishop of Canterbury

MARY (ST) in ARDEN, a parish partly in the hundred of GARTREE, county of LEICESTER, and partly in the hundred of ROTHWELL, county of NORTHAMPTON, 1 mile (E) from Market-Harborough The living is a perpetual curacy, in the archdeaconry and diocese of Leicester, and in the patronage of the Dean and Canons of Christ Church College, Oxford

MARY le BONE (ST), a parish in the Holborn division of the hundred of OSSULSTONE, county of MIDDLESEX, forming an extensive suburb to the metropolis, and containing 96,040 inhabitants This district, now covered with buildings of the first order, and inhabited by families of the highest rank, was formerly an obscure village in the vicinity of London, difficult of access, and containing only a few solitary houses, with a small church, approached by two irregular and inconvenient paths, leading from Vere street and Tottenham Court-road The adjoining

fields were the lurking-place of robbers, and the church, in Bishop Braybrook's license for its removal, is described as being, from its lonely situation, exposed to continual depredation From its situation near a bourne, called Aye brook, or Eve brook, and from its dedication to the Virgin, the parish was called St Mary at Bourne some, however, have deduced its etymology from St Mary la bonne, but no sufficient reason can be adduced for its having been thus pre-eminently distinguished above various other places, the churches of which were dedicated to the Virgin Mary, and others ascribe the affix to the discovery of a prodigious quantity of human bones near the site in 1729, but this period is too recent to render the latter derivation probable Mary le Bone park, now occupied by buildings, was an extensive tract, well stocked with deer, in which Queen Elizabeth entertained the Russian ambassador with the diversion of hunting the ancient manor-house, in which the Harleian library was deposited previously to its removal to the British Museum, has been taken down, with the exception only of that part of the building containing the library, which is now a boarding-school for young ladies Behind the old manor house were Mary le Bone gardens, much frequented as a place of public entertainment in the reign of Queen Anne, the site of which is now occupied by Beaumont and Devonshire streets On Conduit mead, now Stafford-place, was the banquet-hall used by the mayor and aldermen of the city of London, when they visited the conduits in this part of the parish, which supplied the city with water

Among the earlier of the numerous and magnificent ranges of building which have been erected in this parish, are Cavendish-square, in the centre of which is a gilt equestrian statue of William, Duke of Cumberland, surrounded by several noble mansions, Manchester-square, a spacious area, the north side of which is occupied by a mansion formerly the town residence of the Duke of Manchester, afterwards that of the Spanish ambassador, and now the residence of the Marchioness of Hertford, Portman-square, of which the centre is beautifully laid out in plantations and walks, and the area surrounded by stately residences, Portland place, a noble range of lofty and commodious mansions, four hundred and forty feet in length, and one hundred feet wide, opening at the northern extremity into Park crescent, and commanding a beautiful view of the Regent's Park, bounded by the Hampstead and Highgate hills, Stafford-place, Cumberland-place, and various noble ranges of building, with numerous spacious streets leading from Oxford-street and the Edgware-road, and traversing the parish in all directions, among the principal of which may be noticed Upper and Lower Seymour street, Wigmore and Mortimer streets, in one continued line, Berkeley-street (West), and Upper Berkeley-street, Great and Upper Mary le Bone streets, Harley-street, Wimpole-street, High-street, Orchard-street, Gloucester-place, York-place, and Upper Baker-street and place the latter of these have, by a recent construction, been extended to the New road, which crosses the parish from east to west Among the more recent additions are, Montagu and Bryanston squares, ranges of handsome building with gardens in the central part of the area, Blandford and Dorset squares, and the buildings in Lisson Grove and St John's Wood, on the west, Osnaburgh-street and terrace, and Albany-street, on the east, on the south, the continuation of Regent-street, Langham-place, and Park-crescent, in front of which is a noble colonnade of duplicated columns of the Ionic order, divided into two quadrants by Portland-place, and ornamented with a bronze statue of the Duke of Kent, the area also being tastefully laid out as a shrubbery Opposite this, on the other side of the New road, which is bordered by ranges of handsome buildings, are two avenues leading into the park, forming fine ranges of building, decorated with Ionic pillars and cornices, the eastern of which, including the Diorama, is the only range on this side of the park which is within the parish To the west are, Ulster-terrace, a neat range of building, with a basement story of the Ionic order, York-terrace, divided into two corresponding ranges by York-place, forming an avenue into the park from Mary le Bone church, each range consisting of a basement of the Grecian Doric, from which rise six Ionic columns supporting a triangular pediment in the centre, and four Ionic pillars surmounted by a cornice at each extremity, Cornwall-terrace, an elegant pile of the Corinthian order, consisting of a centre and two wings, richly ornamented, Sussex-place, having also a central portico of six Corinthian columns supporting a triangular pediment, and connected with the wings by a range of duplicated columns of the Ionic order, Clarence-terrace, a noble range of building with a colonnade of the Corinthian order, rising from the balustrade of the basement story, and supporting an enriched cornice and balustrade in front of the attic, and connected with the wings by quadrants of the same order, the centre and the wings being surmounted by conical domes terminating in a point, and disposed in pairs, and Hanover-terrace, consisting of a centre with a portico of six, and two wings of four, fluted columns of the Doric order, supporting triangular pediments, of which the tympana are enriched with subjects in alto relievo, and surmounted by statues of the muses, finely sculptured on the apex and at each extremity of the base.

The central area of the park is tastefully laid out in plantations, lawns, and pleasure grounds, interspersed with elegant villas embosomed in trees, and varied with beautiful sheets of water, in which are some islands of picturesque appearance the western side commands a fine view of the Coliseum, which has an imposing grandeur of effect, of the handsome terraces on that side of the park which is without the parish, and of the chapel of St Catherine s hospital, and other interesting objects the inner circle, to which is a handsome entrance from York-place, by a stone bridge over the artificial water, is laid out in nursery grounds, round which is a pleasant circular promenade and drive for carriages the outer circle forms a more extensive ride, including an area of more than four hundred and fifty acres, beautifully planted On the north side are the Zoological gardens, an extensive tract of ground, elegantly laid out and arranged for the reception, classification, and exhibition of animals of every description from various parts of the globe, forming a rapidly-increasing collection of quadrupeds, birds, fishes, reptiles, and insects, classified with a view to promote the study of that important branch of natural history His present Majesty, William IV, immediately after his accession to the throne, presented a considerable number of animals to the Society, which had been the private collection of George IV In the intermediate space are St John s Lodge, the elegant residence of the Marquis of Wellesley, the Holme, the South Villa, and the residence of the master of St Catherine s hospital, Sir Herbert Taylor, which is in the early style of English architecture, corresponding with the adjacent hospital and chapel, and near St John s Wood, the splendid villa of the Marquis of Hertford

The Portman barracks, for the guards, in Portman street, afford accommodation for five hundred men, with sufficient ground for drilling them The bazaar in King-street and Baker-street, for the sale of horses, carriages, furniture, jewellery, and fancy articles by commission, is a most extensive establishment, containing stabling for three hundred horses, and galleries for five hundred carriages, which are constantly on sale the gallery for the sale of fancy articles is four hundred feet in length, and divided into two ranges, on each side of which are the various stalls the subscription-room, which is handsomely fitted up, is one hundred and thirteen feet in length, forty-five feet wide, and forty-five feet high, and, with four ante-rooms of corresponding embellishment, forms a suite for the exhibition of splendid furniture the buildings occupy more than three acres of ground, and attached to them is a commodious riding-school of large dimensions The Oxford-street bazaar, for the sale of fancy articles and the exhibition of panoramic views, is on a smaller scale it has recently been rebuilt, having, not long after its original establishment, been destroyed by fire The infirmary, exclusively for sick and lame horses, in Regent street, near Langham-place, is a neat building, with a colonnade of the Grecian Doric order, and contains arrangements for the reception of from twenty to thirty horses The London carriage repository, in Langham place, is a capacious building, with a handsome stone front, in which upwards of three hundred carriages of all descriptions are constantly on sale The streets are well paved, splendidly lighted with gas, and amply supplied with water by the West Middlesex and other companies This parish is within the jurisdiction of the magistrates appointed under the police act for the metropolis, passed in the reign of George III, some of whom hold sessions every day, except Sundays, at the police-office, High-street, Mary le bone, and also in the jurisdiction of the county court of Middlesex, for the recovery of debts under 40s, under the act of parliament passed in the 23rd of George II

The parish is divided into four separate districts the livings are all rectories, not in charge, in the archdeaconry of Middlesex, and diocese of London, and in the patronage of the Crown The parochial church is a spacious and handsome structure, in the Grecian style of architecture, with a noble portico of the Corinthian order supporting a triangular pediment, and having at the angles of the building groups of Corinthian pillars, surmounted by a cornice and balustrade from the lower part of the tower, which is square, rises a circular turret, surrounded by pillars of the Corinthian order, and surmounted by a dome supported on caryatides The district church of St Mary, Bryanston-square, is a spacious edifice of brick, with a handsome circular portico of the Ionic order, supporting a cornice and close balustrade, from which rises a circular tower, surrounded by pillars of the Composite order, and surmounted by a campanile turret and dome it was erected in 1823, by grant from the parliamentary commissioners, at an expense of £18,746 3, and contains one thousand e ght hundred and twenty-eight sittings, of which one thousand three hundred are free The district church in Langham-place, dedicated to All Souls, and containing one thousand seven hundred and sixty one sittings, of which three hundred and twenty-two are free, was erected in 1823, by grant from the parliamentary commissioners, at an expense of £17,633 6 2 it is a handsome structure, with a circular range of twelve columns, of the Roman Ionic order, surrounding the base of the tower, and supporting a handsome cornice and balustrade, and surmounted by a circular range of Corinthian pillars, from within which rises a spire terminating in a point, of graceful form and beautiful proportion, but of which the effect is destroyed by the concealment of the base and a considerable portion of its elevation The altar piece is ornamented with a fine painting, by Westall, of Christ crowned with thorns The district church of Christchurch, Stafford-street, containing one thousand eight hundred and forty-four sittings, of which nine hundred and thirty are free, was erected in 1824, by grant from the parliamentary commissioners, at an expense of £17,572 12 it is a handsome edifice of brick ornamented with stone, with a portico of four Ionic columns supporting a triangular pediment, above which is a square tower, of which the sides are decorated with four Corinthian pillars supporting an entablature and cornice, surmounted by an open campanile turret and dome The district church dedicated to the Holy Trinity, in Portland-road, was erected in 1827, by grant from the parliamentary commissioners, at an expense of £21,525 4, and contains two thousand and three sittings, of which seven hundred and forty-three are free it is a neat edifice of brick ornamented with stone, having on each side a range of Ionic pillars supporting a cornice and balustrade, and at the west end an Ionic portico of four columns, above which is a square tower with duplicated Ionic pillars at the angles, surmounted by a small campanile turret surrounded by pillars of the Composite order supporting a conical dome The old parish church in High-street is now a chapel of ease, as is also St John s chapel at St John s Wood, a handsome structure of brick, with a stone portico of four Ionic columns, supporting a triangular pediment, and surmounted by an open campanile turret the livings are both perpetual curacies, the former in the patronage of the Rector, the latter in that of the Crown attached to St John s chapel is an extensive cemetery, and, in addition to the burying-ground of the former, are two capacious cemeteries belonging to the parish, in Paddington-street The proprietary episcopal chapels are, Oxford chapel, in Vere-street, Portland street chapel, Bentinck chapel, in Chapel-street, Lisson Grove, Wellbeck chapel, in Westmorland-street, Portman-street chapel, Quebec-street chapel, Margaret-street chapel, Brunswick chapel, in Upper Berkeley-street, Baker-street chapel, and Percy chapel, in Charlotte street There are places of worship for Baptists, Independents, Wesleyan, and Calvinistic Methodists, and for Seceders from the Scottish church, a chapel belonging to the Greek church, and a French, and a Spanish, Roman Catholic chapel

The parochial school in High street, for the maintenance, clothing, and instruction, of one hundred girls, was established in 1750, and is supported by subscription a similar institution for one hundred boys has been recently discontinued The Philological Society s school, in King-street, Bryanston square, was established for the instruction of the children of clergymen, and naval and military officers The central National school, in High-street, is supported by subscription, and is also endowed with a small sum vested in the funds there are in this institution three hundred boys, and one hundred and fifty girls, of whom one hundred and twenty are clothed the western district National school, in St Mary s, Bryanston square, and the eastern district school, near Langham-place, afford each the means of instruction to nearly four hundred children of both sexes, of whom, about seventy in each school are clothed there are other schools, supported by the dissenting congregations in the parish The schools of the Incorporated Society for clothing, maintaining, and educating, poor orphans of clergymen of the established church, were originally founded at Acton, and at Lisson Green, and continued there till 1812, when a spacious and handsome brick building was erected for that purpose at St John s Wood, near the Regent s park, consisting of a centre containing a committee-room and a house for the master and mistress, and two wings, in the lower part of which are two school rooms seventy feet in length, and on the upper story dormitories for the scholars the boys school, which occupies the north wing, is superintended by a master, who is a clergyman of the established church, and an assistant, and the girls school by a mistress to each, which are separate and distinct establishments, there is a matron, or housekeeper There are at present in this institution from one hundred and twenty to one hundred and thirty children of both sexes the boys are taught reading, writing, arithmetic, and Latin, and the girls receive an English education, and are instructed in needle-work, a considerable fund, arising from subscription, is appropriated to the apprenticing of the children on their leaving school The workhouse is a most extensive building, containing every requisite accommodation for one thousand of the poor, and a school of industry, in which the children are taught the earlier parts of the trades to which they are placed out apprentices, with a fee from the parish funds

Middlesex hospital, in Charles-street, is a spacious building of brick, for the reception of invalids and pregnant women it is attended by physicians, surgeons, and other medical practitioners, forming a school of medicine and surgery, where lectures are read on the practice of medicine and surgery, and a gratuitous course of clinical lectures regularly delivered The general lying-in dispensary, in Charlotte-street, Rathbone-place, was established in 1778, for the assistance of married women at their own habitations, and there is a general dispensary in Wellbeck-street. Queen Charlotte's lying-in hospital, Harcourt-street, Bryanston-square, was originally established, in 1752, at Bayswater, and removed to its present situation in 1809 it is under the direction of a committee, of which His Royal Highness the Duke of Sussex is president, and is adapted to the reception of from twenty to thirty patients, who receive every necessary attention, and the best medical assistance The asylum for the recovery of health, in Lisson Grove (North), was originally established in 1821, under the patronage of His present Majesty, whilst Duke of Clarence, and the Princess Augusta, for patients who are in circumstances to contribute towards the expense of their maintenance in the institution the buildings comprise two separate houses, for the reception of male and female invalids, who are admitted on the recommendation of subscribers, receive medical attendance, and are lodged and boarded in the institution, for 17s 6d per week for adult males, 14s for females, and 10s 6d for children it is under the direction of a committee, of which the Duke of Cambridge is president, about twenty adults and ten children may be accommodated in this institution, which is supported by voluntary contributions The western general dispensary, in Lisson Grove (South), was first established in 1830, for the visitation and relief of the sick poor in this part of the parish of Mary-le-bone, and the adjoining parish of Paddington, and for the reception of one or two casualty patients it is supported by subscription, and is gratuitously visited by the most eminent of the faculty

MARY (ST) CHURCH, a parish in the hundred of HAYTOR, county of DEVON, 2 miles (N W) from Torbay, containing 1005 inhabitants The living is a discharged vicarage, in the archdeaconry of Totness, and diocese of Exeter, rated in the king's books at £31 11, and in the patronage of the Dean and Chapter of Exeter Elias Waymouth, in 1755, gave a rent-charge of £2 for teaching poor boys

MARY (ST) EXTRA, otherwise WESTON, a parish in that part of the hundred of BISHOP'S WALTHAM which is in the Portsdown division of the county of SOUTHAMPTON, adjacent to the town of Southampton, containing 983 inhabitants The living is a perpetual curacy, in the peculiar jurisdiction and patronage of the Bishop of Winchester, rated in the king's books at £37 5 5, and endowed with £200 private benefaction, and £800 royal bounty

MARY (ST) in the MARSH, a chapelry in the parish of NEWTON, hundred of WISBEACH, Isle of ELY, county of CAMBRIDGE, 3 miles (W by S) from Wisbeach

MARYPORT, a chapelry, market town, and seaport, in the parish of CROSS-CANNONBY, ALLERDALE ward below Darwent, county of CUMBERLAND, 30 miles (S W by W) from Carlisle, and 309¾ (N W by N) from London, containing 3514 inhabitants This place, situated at the foot of the river Ellen, which intersects the town, was a very inconsiderable fishing-town, called Ellen-foot, and consisting only of a few small huts, previously to 1750, at which period the foundations of the present town and harbour were laid, by Humphrey Senhouse, Esq, the proprietor of the land, who bestowed upon it the present name of Maryport, in compliment to his lady It is irregularly built, partly on the sea-shore, and partly on the cliff, the streets are spacious, and the atmosphere healthy during the bathing season it is resorted to by a few visitors, the adjacent sands affording great convenience for bathing The subterraneous productions of the neighbourhood are coal, limestone, and red freestone, the export of which to Ireland, Scotland, and other places, constitutes the chief trade of the port, which possesses one hundred and thirty-four ships, and is a member of the port of Whitehaven. There are three yards for ship-building, and

a patent slip, and many vessels of considerable burden have been built for the coasting and foreign trade, by means of which timber is imported from America and the West Indies, and iron and flax from the Baltic A railway has been constructed for the more ready conveyance of the coal wagons to the harbour adjoining the town is a large corn-mill. The manufactures consist chiefly of cotton and linen checks, sailcloth, cables, coarse earthenware, leather, nails, and anchors The herring fishery is productive, and considerable quantities of salmon trout are caught in the river The principal market is on Friday, but not for corn, and there is likewise an inferior one on Tuesdays The living is a perpetual curacy, in the archdeaconry and diocese of Carlisle, endowed with £200 private benefaction, £200 royal bounty, and £1600 parliamentary grant, and in the patronage of H Senhouse, Esq The chapel, erected in 1760, and consecrated by Bishop Lyttleton, in 1763, is dedicated to St Mary There are places of worship for Baptists, Burghers, the Society of Friends, Presbyterians, and Wesleyan Methodists A school, in which one hundred and fifty children are educated on the Madras system, is supported by subscription, each scholar paying one penny per week the salary of the master is £40 per annum A school of industry for twenty girls is supported by voluntary contributions There are several other benevolent institutions for the benefit of the indigent poor The remains of an important Roman station, with military roads leading to Moresby, Old Carlisle, and Ambleside, are visible on an eminence northward of the town, at the village of Ellenborough they consist of a square area with double ditches, in which are four entrances the numerous relics of antiquity discovered are altars, inscriptions, vases, and implements of various kinds, several of which are preserved in the adjoining grounds and mansion of Nether-hall From this station a wall, extending to Workington, is said to have been constructed by the Romans, as a protection against the invasions of the Picts and Scots In the southern part of the town is Mote hill, on which is an artificial moated mound, one hundred and sixty yards in circumference

MARY-STOW, a parish in the hundred of LIFTON, county of DEVON, 6½ miles (N N W) from Tavistock, containing 376 inhabitants The living is a vicarage with the curacy of Thrushelton, in the archdeaconry of Totness, and diocese of Exeter, rated in the king's books at £12 16 0½ The Rev H H Tremayne was patron in 1824 The church, dedicated to St Mary, has an ancient stone font and two stone stalls On the manor of Sydenham is an old mansion, erected early in the seventeenth century, by Sir Thomas Wise, and garrisoned by some of the adherents of Charles I, from whom it was taken by Colonel Holbourn, in 1645 it is a large building, occupying three sides of a quadrangle

MASHAM, a parish partly in the liberty of ST PETER of YORK, but chiefly in the eastern division of the wapentake of HANG, North riding of the county of YORK, comprising the market town of Masham, and the townships of Burton upon Ure, Ellingstring, Ellingtons, Fearby, Healey with Sutton, Ilton with Pott, and Swinton with Warthermask, and containing 2767 inhabitants, of which number, 1171 are in the town of Masham, 34 miles

(N W by W) from York, and 223 (N N W) from London The town is very pleasantly situated upon a gentle eminence in a fertile district, on the western bank of the river Ure the houses are well built, and the air is remarkably pure The trade consists principally in the spinning of yarn, for which an extensive manufactory has of late been established, affording employment to about one hundred persons There is a small market on Wednesday, and fairs are held on the 17th and 18th of September, for live stock During the spring, a fair for cattle and sheep is held every alternate Monday A court leet is held annually, at which a constable is chosen, its jurisdiction also extending to the recovery of debts under 40s The living is a vicarage, with that of Kirkby-Malzeard, in the jurisdiction of the peculiar court of Masham, or in that of the Dean and Chapter of York, being claimed by both, and the matter not yet decided, it is rated in the king s books at £30, and is in the patronage of the Master and Fellows of Trinity College, Cambridge Masham was formerly a prebend, and the richest in the cathedral church of York, being rated in the king s books at £136 it was dissolved and made a lay-fee, by Archbishop Holgate, in 1546 The church, dedicated to St Mary, is a small but handsome edifice, in the English style of architecture, with a tower surmounted by a lofty and elegant spire Over the organ gallery is a fine painting representing an angel praying before the cross of Christ There are places of worship for Baptists, the Society of Friends, and Wesleyan Methodists The grammar school, founded by William Danby, Esq, in 1760, is endowed with property producing about £50 per annum, there are about eighty boys, who are all stipendiary pupils the master is also superintendent of a charity school, for thirty-six poor children, under the same foundation, endowed with about £24 per annum, from the benefactions of Oswald Coates, Isabel Beckwith, and Ann Danby Two Sunday schools, in which two hundred and fifty children are instructed, are supported by subscription This place was anciently the residence of the baronial family of Scroop, to which belonged Henry, Lord le Scroop Lord Treasurer, and Archbishop Scroop, both beheaded for high treason in the reign of Henry IV

MASHBURY, a parish in the hundred of DUNMOW, county of ESSEX, 6 miles (N W) from Chelmsford, containing 85 inhabitants The living is a rectory, united to that of Chignal St James, in the archdeaconry of Middlesex, and diocese of London, rated in the king s books at £9 14 7

MASON, a township in the parish of PONTELAND, western division of CASTLE ward, county of NORTHUMBERLAND, 6¼ miles (N N W) from Newcastle upon Tyne, containing 127 inhabitants

MASSINGHAM (GREAT), a parish in the Lynn division of the hundred of FREEBRIDGE, county of NORFOLK, 9½ miles (N by W) from Swaffham, containing 738 inhabitants The living consists of two consolidated rectories, in the archdeaconry and diocese of Norwich, rated jointly in the king s books at £33 6 9 The Marquis of Cholmondeley was patron in 1816 The church is dedicated to St Mary, that of All Saints has been demolished A free school here is endowed with a rent-charge of £20, by Charles Calthorpe A priory of the order of St Augustine, dedicated to St Mary and St Nicholas, was founded here before 1260, by Nicholas le Syre, the

buildings of which having fallen to decay, and the estate wasted, in 1475, it was united to the priory of Westacre, and became a cell to that house

MASSINGHAM (LITTLE), a parish in the Lynn division of the hundred of FREEBRIDGE, county of NORFOLK, 10½ miles (N by W) from Swaffham, containing 125 inhabitants The living is a discharged rectory, in the archdeaconry and diocese of Norwich, rated in the king s books at £9 13 4 Joseph Wilson, Esq was patron in 1820 The church is dedicated to St Andrew

MATCHING, a parish in the hundred of HARLOW, county of ESSEX, 3¼ miles (E by N) from Harlow, containing 599 inhabitants The living is a vicarage, in the jurisdiction of the Commissary of Essex and Herts, concurrently with the Consistorial Court of the Bishop of London, rated in the king's books at £12 10 5, and in the patronage of the Trustees of Felstead school, on the nomination of the Bishop of London The church is dedicated to St Mary

MATFEN (EAST), a township in the parish of STAMFORDHAM, north-eastern division of TINDALE ward, county of NORTHUMBERLAND, 8¾ miles (N E by E) from Hexham, containing 152 inhabitants This, probably, was formerly a place of some importance, foundations of buildings being still discernible

MATFEN (WEST), a township in the parish of STAMFORDHAM, north-eastern division of TINDALE ward, county of NORTHUMBERLAND, 9½ miles (N E) from Hexham, containing 307 inhabitants On opening a tumulus, supposed to have been a Druidical mausoleum, coffins of four stones set edgeways, with stone bottoms and covers, were found, containing human ashes near it was an upright stone pillar, called the Stob stone

MATHERN, a parish in the upper division of the hundred of CALDICOT, county of MONMOUTH, 3¼ miles (S S W) from Chepstow, containing 374 inhabitants The living is a discharged vicarage, with that of Caerwent, in the archdeaconry and diocese of Llandaff, rated in the king s books at £6 3 6½, and in the patronage of the Chapter of Llandaff The church is dedicated to St Theodorick Charles Pratt, in 1724, bequeathed land, directing the income to be applied in teaching poor children to read A house, called Monks Court, is supposed to have been formerly a monastery

MATHON, a parish in the lower division of the hundred of PERSHORE, county of WORCESTER, 7 miles (N by E) from Ledbury, containing 633 inhabitants The living is a discharged vicarage, in the archdeaconry and diocese of Worcester, rated in the king s books at £8, endowed with £1200 parliamentary grant, and in the patronage of the Dean and Chapter of Westminster The church is dedicated to St John the Baptist

MATLASK, a parish in the northern division of the hundred of ERPINGHAM, county of NORFOLK, 6 miles (S E by E) from Holt, containing 184 inhabitants The living is a discharged rectory, in the archdeaconry of Norfolk, and diocese of Norwich, rated in the king s books at £5, endowed with £200 private benefaction, and £200 royal bounty, and in the patronage of the King, as Duke of Lancaster The church is dedicated to St Peter

MATLEY, a township in the parish of MOTTRAM in LONGDEN-DALE, hundred of MACCLESFIELD, county palatine of CHESTER, 8 miles (N E by E) from Stockport, containing 324 inhabitants

MATLOCK, a parish in the hundred of WIRKS-WORTH, county of DERBY, 17½ miles (N by W) from Derby, containing 2920 inhabitants This place, which is equally celebrated for the romantic beauty of its scenery, and the purity of its medicinal springs, was formerly called *Mesterford*, or *Metesford*, and consists at present of the village and baths, nearly a mile and a half distant from each other The waters were first applied to medicinal uses about the end of the seventeenth century, prior to which period, the neighbourhood consisted only of a few rude dwellings inhabited by miners The original bath of wood was rebuilt of stone by the Rev Mr Fern, of Matlock, and Mr Hayward, of Cromford, who erected some small rooms adjoining it, for the accommodation of invalids the lease of the buildings was afterwards purchased by Messrs Smith and Pennell, of Nottingham, who erected two large and commodious houses with stabling, constructed a carriage-road by the side of the river from Cromford, and improved the horse-road from Matlock bridge A second spring was afterwards discovered, at the distance of a quarter of a mile from the former, a new bath was formed, and additional lodging houses built for the reception of visitors, and a third spring was opened, at a still later period, within four hundred yards of the first, which, after some difficulties in levelling the hill, in order to obtain the water, previously to its mixing with those of a cold spring, was rendered available to medicinal uses, and a third bath was constructed, and another hotel erected These springs, which have a mean temperature of sixty-eight degrees of Fahrenheit, issue from an elevation of one hundred feet from the level of the river, at higher or lower points the springs are cold, and possess no medicinal properties The water is found efficacious in glandular affections, rheumatism, biliary obstructions, incipient consumption, and in all complaints arising from relaxation of the muscular fibres The usual time of bathing is before breakfast, and between breakfast and dinner, the water is taken internally, in gradually increased quantities the season commences in April, and ends in November The three principal hotels, which are all handsome stone buildings, and the lodging houses, afford accommodation for about four or five hundred visitors the museum is replete with the natural curiosities of the district, and with urns and vases formed of spar, marble, and alabaster, obtained in the county, and guides are constantly in attendance to conduct visitors through the several caverns in the vicinity

Matlock Dale, in which the baths are situated, presents, in varying combination, the richest features of majestic grandeur and romantic beauty The river Derwent, for nearly three miles, pursues its course through the windings of the vale, in some places expanding into a broad lake, from the surface of which are reflected the luxuriant foliage of the woods, and the towering precipices which overhang its banks, and in others rushing with impetuosity through the rugged masses of projecting rocks which contract its channel, forming a variety of beautiful cascades The High Tor, arising perpendicularly from the river to the height of four hundred feet, is a prominent feature in the scenery of the dale, and on the opposite bank is Masson hill, from the summit of which, called the Heights of Abraham, to which a winding ascent has been recently made, there is an extensive and most interesting view of the magnificent scenery of the dale Walks have been cut through the woods, in various directions, leading to different points of view, from which the dale is seen in all its variety of beauty, and on the summit of the rocks is a natural and lofty terrace, commanding an extensive prospect of the surrounding country The village is romantically situated on the banks of the river Derwent, over which is a neat stone bridge forming the principal entrance the houses, which are of stone, are irregularly built on the steep acclivity of a mountain, rising above each other in gradual succession from the base nearly to the summit. The lead mines were formerly worked to a great extent in the parish, but at present there are only a few in operation. The cotton manufacture was established here by the late Sir Richard Arkwright, who built a factory near the upper end of the dale, in which machinery of a very complicated description is employed with success, in the production of cotton The market, chiefly for provisions, is well supplied the fairs are February 25th, April 2nd, May 9th, and October 24th, for cattle, sheep, and swine The parish is in the honour of Tutbury, duchy of Lancaster, and within the jurisdiction of a court of pleas held at Tutbury every third Tuesday, for the recovery of debts under 40s The living is a rectory, in the archdeaconry of Derby, and diocese of Lichfield and Coventry, rated in the king's books at £11 2 6, and in the patronage of the Dean of Lincoln The church, dedicated to St Giles, and situated on the summit of a rock, is a small edifice, chiefly in the later style of English architecture There is a place of worship for Independents The free school was founded, in 1647, by Mr George Spateman, who endowed it with £80, to which, in 1668, Mr Anthony Wolley added land producing £5 per annum the present income is about £45 per annum, and the school is open to all children of the parish, who are instructed in reading, writing, and accounts There are some charitable bequests for distribution among the poor On Riber hill, near the church, are the Hirst stones, probably the remains of a cromlech, consisting of four rude masses of grit-stone, one of which, supposed to weigh about two tons, is placed on the others, and has in the centre a hole six inches deep and nine inches in diameter, in which was formerly a stone pillar

MATSON, a parish in the middle division of the hundred of DUDSTONE and KINGS BARTON, county of GLOUCESTER, 2 miles (S by E) from Gloucester, containing 35 inhabitants The living is a discharged vicarage, in the archdeaconry and diocese of Gloucester, rated in the king's books at £3 16 5½, endowed with £200 private benefaction, and £200 royal bounty, and in the patronage of the Dean and Chapter of Gloucester The manor-house was built by Sir Ambrose Willoughby, Knt, in the reign of Elizabeth, and during the siege of Gloucester became the head-quarters of Charles I

MATTERDALE, a chapelry in the parish of GREYSTOCK, LEATH ward, county of CUMBERLAND, 10 miles (E by S) from Keswick, containing 299 inhabitants The living is a perpetual curacy, in the archdeaconry and diocese of Carlisle, endowed with £200 private benefaction, and £600 royal bounty, and in the patronage of the Rector of Greystock The chapel was erected in 1685 Robert Grisdale, in 1722, built a school-house, and endowed it with about £12 12 a year towards the education of poor children

MATTERSEY, a parish in the Hatfield division of the wapentake of BASSETLAW, county of NOTTINGHAM, 3½ miles (S E) from Bawtry, containing 426 inhabitants The living is a discharged vicarage, in the archdeaconry of Nottingham, and diocese of York, rated in the king s books at £6 8 9, and in the patronage of the Archbishop of York The church is dedicated to All Saints There is a place of worship for Wesleyan Methodists The river Idle runs through the parish, and is crossed at the village by a handsome stone bridge Edmund Nettleship, in 1742, founded a free school for seven poor boys, and endowed it with £140, since vested in lands, and producing about £9 per annum A priory of Gilbertine canons, dedicated to St Helen, was founded here before 1192, by Roger de Maresay, which at the dissolution had a revenue of £61 17 7

MATTINGLEY, a chapelry in the parish of HECK FIELD, hundred of HOLDSHOTT, Basingstoke division of the county of SOUTHAMPTON, 2¾ miles (W by S) from Hartford-Bridge, containing, with the tything of Hazely Heath, 513 inhabitants

MATTISHALL, a parish in the hundred of MITFORD, county of NORFOLK, 5 miles (E S E) from East Dereham, containing 930 inhabitants The living is a discharged vicarage, with Pattesley, in the archdeaconry of Norfolk, and diocese of Norwich, rated in the king s books at £7 7 3½, endowed with £200 private benefaction, and £200 royal bounty, and in the patronage of the Master and Fellows of Caius College, Cambridge The church is dedicated to All Saints There is a place of worship for Wesleyan Methodists

MATTISHALL (BURGH), county of NORFOLK — See BURGH-MATTISHALL

MAUGHAN S (ST), a parish in the lower division of the hundred of SKENFRETH, county of MONMOUTH, 6 miles (N N W) from Monmouth, containing 141 inhabitants The living is a perpetual curacy, annexed to the vicarage of Llangattock-Vibon-Avell, in the archdeaconry and diocese of Llandaff

MAULDEN, a parish in the hundred of REDBORNESTOKE, county of BEDFORD, 1½ mile (E) from Ampthill, containing 1017 inhabitants The living is a rectory, in the archdeaconry of Bedford, and diocese of Lincoln, rated in the king's books at £15 9 7 , and in the patronage of the Marquis of Ailesbury The church, dedicated to St Mary, is principally in the later style of English architecture, and has lately received an addition of one hundred and ten free sittings, the Incorporated Society for the enlargement of churches and chapels having granted £30 towards defraying the expense There is a place of worship for Baptists Sundry benefactions have been made for the instruction of children, producing £8 10 a year, which is paid to the master of a Sunday school

MAUNBY, a township in that part of the parish of KIRBY-WISK which is in the eastern division of the wapentake of GILLING, North riding of the county of YORK, 6 miles (S. by W) from North-Allerton, containing 206 inhabitants

MAUTBY, a parish in the eastern division of the hundred of FLEGG, county of NORFOLK, 2¾ miles (W by N) from Caistor, containing 78 inhabitants The living is a rectory, in the archdeaconry and diocese of

Norwich, rated in the king s books at £13 6 8, and in the patronage of Robert Fellowes, Esq The church is dedicated to St Peter and St Paul

MAWDESLEY, a township in the parish of CROSTON, hundred of LEYLAND, county palatine of LANCASTER, 7 miles (W S W) from Chorley, containing 833 inhabitants A school, which has been erected on the waste by subscription, is endowed with a trifling sum by Thomas Cook, for a master to teach fifteen children to read

MAWES (ST), a borough, small sea-port, and market town, in the parish of ST JUST in ROSELAND, western division of the hundred of POWDER, county of CORNWALL, 3 miles (E) from Falmouth, 51 (S W) from Launceston, and 265 (S W by W) from London The population is returned with the parish The name of this town, derived from its

Arms.

patron saint, is, by Leland, attributed to Mauduit, or Machutus, a Welchman , but others, with more probability, consider it to be a corruption of St Mary s, and, indeed, the town is called St Mawes, alias St Mary s, in various ancient records, probably as having belonged to the priory of St Mary, at Plympton A castle was erected here, in 1542, by Henry VIII , during the war with France, as a protection to Falmouth harbour at the dissolution, this fortress, with the lands which had belonged to the priory at Plympton, became the property of the Vyvyan family who possessed them for several generations During the civil commotions in the time of Charles I , it fell into the hands of Fairfax, and, at the Restoration, it was sold, with the annexed estate, by Sir Viel Vyvyan to John, Earl of Bath The castle is now in the custody of a governor, appointed by the king , and the estate is held in moieties by the Duke of Buckingham and James Buller, Esq The town consists principally of one street, which fronts the sea, and lies at the foot of a hill rising somewhat abruptly from the vale it is irregularly built, and is chiefly inhabited by fishermen and pilots , it is neither lighted nor regularly paved, but is well supplied with water The castle stands at the north entrance of the harbour, opposite to that of Pendennis , and there is an open battery below, near the blockhouse The only branch of manufacture in the town is that of cables, ropes, &c , for small craft The pilchard fishery, although on the decline, is the principal source of occupation fourteen thousand hogsheads of pilchards have been exported from St Mawes and Falmouth, of which port this is a member, in one season A small market for butchers meat is held on Friday A chief magistrate, commonly called mayor, is presented by a jury at the court leet of the manor, held in October, in the town hall St Mawes first sent members to parliament in 1562 the right of election is vested in the resident freemen, and in the freeholders within the borough and manor, resident and non-resident, who, as well as the freemen, must be presented and admitted at the manor court , the number of voters is about twenty-five, and the portreeve is the return-

ing officer the influence of the Duke of Buckingham is predominant the elections are always held on the quay, which has been recently repaved The borough and manor extends over the whole creek and harbour, the lord is entitled to certain duties for anchorage, bushelage, &c, and to the possession of wrecks A chapel, erected at the expense of the late Marquis of Buckingham, was completed in July, 1812, but has not been endowed or consecrated it was used for divine service a few years only, and is now appropriated as a school for boys of the town, supported by the Duke of Buckingham, who allows the master a salary of £40 per annum another school for boys is supported by voluntary contributions There are places of worship for Independents and Wesleyan Methodists In this parish are the remains of a chapel, attached to the barton of Roscassa, now a farm house

MAWGAN in MENEAGE, a parish in the hundred of KERRIER, county of CORNWALL, 4¼ miles (E S E) from Helston, containing 1050 inhabitants The living is a rectory, with that of St Martin, in the archdeaconry of Cornwall, and diocese of Exeter, rated in the king s books at £35 10 2½ Sir M Blakiston, Bart and others were patrons in 1816 The church is dedicated to St Mogun There is a place of worship for Wesleyan Methodists

MAWGAN in PYDER, a parish in the hundred of PYDER, county of CORNWALL, 4 miles (N W by W) from St Columb-Major, containing 580 inhabitants The living is a rectory, in the archdeaconry of Cornwall, and diocese of Exeter, rated in the king s books at £26 13 4 The Rev Philip Carlyon was patron in 1806 The church is an ancient fabric, containing some curious monumental brasses of the Arundels, and a richly-carved screen, separating the nave from the chancel. In the churchyard is a fine old sculptured cross with a niche, representing in high relief the Crucifixion, with other figures, probably taken from some ancient legend, and bearing the inscription Cnegum fil Enans, in characters of the ninth century Lanherne house, long the principal residence of the Lords Arundel, was fitted up by his late lordship as an asylum for a convent of Carmelite nuns, who emigrated from Antwerp, and by whom it is still occupied it contains a neat chapel, adorned with a few good paintings brought over by the nuns The parish is bounded on the west by the Bristol channel, and has a small harbour, called Mawgan Porth

MAWNAN, a parish in the hundred of KERRIER, county of CORNWALL, 5 miles (S by W) from Falmouth, containing 536 inhabitants The living is a rectory, in the archdeaconry of Cornwall, and diocese of Exeter, rated in the king s books at £14 16 3, and in the patronage of John Rogers, Esq The church is dedicated to St Mawnan There is a place of worship for Wesleyan Methodists The parish is bounded on the south-east by the English channel, where are two small open bays, called Prisk and Bream bays, and on the south is Helford river, an arm of the sea about a mile wide A day school for poor children is principally supported by voluntary contributions

MAWTHORPE, a township in the parish of WELL, Wold division of the hundred of CALCEWORTH, parts of LINDSEY, county of LINCOLN, 2 miles (S by E) from Alford. The population is returned with the parish

MAXEY, a parish in the liberty of PETERBOROUGH, county of NORTHAMPTON, 1¾ mile (S S W) from Market-Deeping, containing, with the hamlet of Deeping-Gate, 544 inhabitants The living is a discharged vicarage, in the archdeaconry of Northampton, and diocese of Peterborough, rated in the king s books at £10, and in the patronage of the Dean and Chapter of Peterborough The church, dedicated to St Mary, is principally Norman, with portions in the decorated and later English styles In this parish are Lolham bridges, which are of great antiquity, having been constructed by the Romans, to conduct the Ermin-street over the low grounds adjoining the river Welland.

MAXSTOKE, a parish in the Atherstone division of the hundred of HEMLINGFORD, county of WARWICK, 2¾ miles (S E by E) from Coleshill, containing 364 inhabitants The living is a discharged vicarage, in the archdeaconry of Coventry, and diocese of Lichfield and Coventry, rated in the king s books at £5 6 8., endowed with £200 private benefaction, £400 royal bounty, and £500 parliamentary grant, and in the patronage of Chandos Leigh, Esq The church is dedicated to St Michael The parish is bounded on the west and south by the river Blythe The castle, formerly belonging to the De Clintons, and then to Humphrey Stafford, Duke of Buckingham, who richly covered the gates with iron, is still in perfect repair, and there are extensive remains of a priory of Augustine canons, founded, in 1336, by Sir William de Clinton, Earl of Huntingdon, which was dedicated to the Holy Trinity, the Blessed Virgin Mary, St Michael, and All Saints, and at the dissolution had a revenue of £129 11 8.

MAYFIELD, a parish in the southern division of the hundred of TOTMONSLOW, county of STAFFORD, comprising the chapelry of Butterton, and part of that of Calton, and the townships of Mayfield and Woodhouses, and containing 1435 inhabitants, of which number, 890 are in the township of Mayfield, 2¼ miles (S W) from Ashbourn The living is a discharged vicarage in the archdeaconry of Stafford, and diocese of Lichfield and Coventry, rated in the king's books at £6 6 8, and in the patronage of William Greaves, Esq The church, dedicated to St John the Baptist, is a handsome structure, having a lofty tower crowned with pinnacles, and bearing the date 1616 There is a place of worship for Wesleyan Methodists On the banks of the Dove is an extensive cotton-factory, affording employment to upwards of two hundred persons The village comprises several handsome houses, cottages, &c, scattered among well wooded and picturesque scenery, the beauty of which, added to the fertility of the soil, induced the Romans to select it for a settlement, a fact fully evinced by the discovery of Roman coins, arms, and other relics in the neighbourhood Within the parish are two barrows, termed Harlow and Rowloo, vestiges of an ancient paved road were discovered in digging in a morass, and traces of an old fortification, at a place called Clines At Hallsteads are observable considerable remains of a large moated residence, approached by an ancient bridge in fine preservation, though much obscured by foliage and overhanging rocks Mayfield is in the honour of Tutbury, duchy of Lancaster, and within the jurisdiction of a court of pleas held at Tutbury every third Tuesday, for the recovery of debts under 40s

MAYFIELD, a parish in the hundred of LOXFIELD-PELHAM, rape of PEVENSEY, county of SUSSEX, 5½ miles (S W) from Wadhurst, containing 2698 inhabitants The living is a vicarage, in the peculiar jurisdiction of the Archbishop of Canterbury, rated in the king s books at £17 13 4, and in the patronage of the Rev John Kirby The church, dedicated to St Dunstan, is a handsome structure in the later English style There is a place of worship for Wesleyan Methodists The river Rother runs through the parish, which contains iron-ore and some chalybeate springs, but the latter are neglected A free school was founded and endowed by subscription among the inhabitants, in 1749, and several bequests having been since made, the annual income amounts to £40, which is paid for the instruction of about forty children in a National school established here, in which are about eighty others Henry III granted a charter for a market and two fairs to be held at Mayfield, the former has been long disused, the latter are on May 30th for pedlary, and November 13th for cattle and pedlary There are fine remains of a mansion belonging to the Archbishops of Canterbury before the Reformation, consisting of the gatehouse, porter's lodge, a considerable portion of its magnificent hall, and a large room in that part of the building still habitable, termed Queen Elizabeth s room, which her Majesty occupied in 1573, during the entertainment given by Sir Thomas Gresham, then proprietor of the house, to the queen and her suite, in her progress through Kent A great fire broke out at Mayfield, in 1389, which burned the church and the greater part of the village

MAYLAND, a parish in the hundred of DENGIE, county of ESSEX, 4¼ miles (N W by N) from Burnham, containing 218 inhabitants The living is a discharged vicarage, in the jurisdiction of the Commissary of Essex and Herts, concurrently with the Consistorial Court of the Bishop of London, rated in the king s books at £13 6 8, endowed with £200 private benefaction, and £200 royal bounty, and in the patronage of the Governors of St Bartholomew's Hospital, London The church is dedicated to St Barnabas Dr John Gauden, successively Bishop of Exeter and Worcester, supposed by some the author of " Eikon Basilike,' was born here in 1605; he died in 1662

MEABURN (KING S), a township in the parish of MORLAND, WEST ward, county of WESTMORLAND, 4¼ miles (W by N) from Appleby, containing 176 inhabitants

MEARE, a parish in the hundred of GLASTON TWELVE-HIDES, county of SOMERSET, 3¼ miles (N W by W) from Glastonbury, containing 1151 inhabitants The living is a discharged vicarage, in the archdeaconry of Wells, and diocese of Bath and Wells, rated in the king s books at £13 2 8, endowed with £400 private benefaction, and £600 parliamentary grant, and in the patronage of W T H Phelps, Esq The church, dedicated to St Mary, is in the early style of English architecture, with an embattled tower Here are remains of encampments, of Danish origin, with a double ditch

MEALRIGG, a joint township with Langrigg, in that part of the parish of BROOMFIELD which is in ALLERDALE ward below Derwent, county of CUMBERLAND, 9½ miles (W by S) from Wigton The population is returned with Langrigg Here is a spa, reputed to be of considerable efficacy

MEARLEY, a township in that part of the parish of WHALLEY which is in the higher division of the hundred of BLACKBURN, county palatine of LANCASTER, 2 miles (S E by E) from Clitheroe, containing 89 inhabitants

MEASAND, a hamlet in the parish of BAMPTON, WEST ward, county of WESTMORLAND, 4 miles (S W) from Bampton The population is returned with the parish A small stream, called Fordingdale beck, runs in the vicinity, and has several waterfalls in its course on the east is Hawes-water lake The free school was endowed, in 1713, by Richard Wright and Richard Lacy, with an estate producing about £40 per annum

MEASHAM, a parish in the hundred of REPTON and GRESLEY, county of DERBY, though locally in the western division of the hundred of Goscote, county of Leicester, 3¾ miles (S S W) from Ashby de la Zouch, containing 1404 inhabitants The living is a perpetual curacy, in the archdeaconry of Derby, and diocese of Lichfield and Coventry, endowed with £1600 parliamentary grant, and in the patronage of the Marquis of Hastings The church is dedicated to St Lawrence There is a place of worship for Wesleyan Methodists The parish is almost surrounded by the river Mease, and the Ashby de la Zouch canal passes through the village

MEAVY, a parish in the hundred of ROBOROUGH, county of DEVON, 6¼ miles (S E) from Tavistock, containing 321 inhabitants The living is a discharged rectory, in the archdeaconry of Totness, and diocese of Exeter, rated in the king s books at £13 5, and in the patronage of the Crown The church is dedicated to St Peter The village is situated on the river Mew, which winds through a valley of considerable beauty Here are the remains of an old mansion, once the residence of the renowned Sir Francis Drake Near the church is a hollow oak of very large dimensions, and adjoining it are the remains of a stone cross The Plymouth railway passes through the parish

MEDBOURNE, a parish in the hundred of GARTREE, county of LEICESTER, 5 miles (W by N) from Rockingham, containing, with the chapelry of Holt, 514 inhabitants The living is a rectory, in the archdeaconry of Leicester, and diocese of Lincoln, rated in the king s books at £35 11 0½, and in the patronage of the Master and Fellows of St John's College, Cambridge The church is dedicated to St Giles There is a place of worship for Wesleyan Methodists Sarah Moyses, in 1761, bequeathed £800; Thomas Hawkes, in 1785, left £200, and Robert Wade gave a rent charge of £2, for teaching poor children, and providing them with books In a field north westward from the village are the remains of intrenchments, with foundations of buildings, covering a piece of ground about half a mile square In 1721, a tesselated pavement was discovered, and other Roman remains have been dug up at different times

MEDLAR, a joint township with Wesham, in the parish of KIRKHAM, hundred of AMOUNDERNESS, county palatine of LANCASTER, 2¾ miles (N by W) from Kirkham, containing, with Wesham, 215 inhabitants

MEDMENHAM, a parish in the hundred of DESBOROUGH, county of BUCKINGHAM, 3 miles (S W by W) from Great Marlow, containing 369 inhabitants The living is a discharged vicarage, in the archdeaconry of Buckingham, and diocese of Lincoln, rated in the king s books at £5 7 1 Robert Scott, Esq was patron in 1801 The church is dedicated to St Peter An abbey for Cistercian monks was founded here by Hugh de Bolebec, as a cell to the monastery at Woburn, the revenue of which was valued at £20 6 2 a very small portion of the conventual buildings remains, the site is partly occupied by a modern erection, in imitation of ruins, nearly overgrown with ivy Above the village are vestiges of a large camp, nearly square, with a single vallum and ditch, the area comprises about seven acres An ancient circular intrenchment in this parish is called Danesfield.

MEDOMSLEY, a chapelry in that part of the parish of LANCHESTER which is in the western division of CHESTER ward, county palatine of DURHAM, 13 miles (N W) from Durham, containing 461 inhabitants The living is a perpetual curacy, in the archdeaconry and diocese of Durham, endowed with £200 private benefaction, £600 royal bounty, and £200 parliamentary grant, and in the patronage of the Bishop of Durham The chapel, dedicated to St Mary Magdalene, is in the early style of English architecture, with lancet windows Christopher Hunter, M D, physician and antiquary, was born here in 1675, and interred in Shotley church, in July 1757

MEDSTED, a parish in the hundred of FAWLEY, Fawley division of the county of SOUTHAMPTON, 3¾ miles (W S W) from Alton, containing 394 inhabitants The living is a perpetual curacy, annexed to the rectory of Old Alresford, in the peculiar jurisdiction of the incumbent, and in the patronage of the Bishop of Winchester The church is dedicated to St Andrew This parish is within the jurisdiction of the Cheyney Court held at Winchester every Thursday, for the recovery of debts to any amount

MEER, a parish in the county of the city of LINCOLN, 4½ miles (S S L) from Lincoln The living is a discharged vicarage, with the rectory of Waddington, not rated in the king s books in the archdeaconry and diocese of Lincoln The church, which was dedicated to St John the Baptist, has fallen into ruins Here was anciently a house for Knights Templars, also an hospital, in, or near, Dunston, founded about 1246, by Simon de Roppele, which, at the suppression of similar establishments, was allowed to continue

MEERBROOK, a chapelry in that part of the parish of LEEK which is in the northern division of the hundred of TOTMONSLOW, county of STAFFORD, 3½ miles (N) from Leek, with which the population is returned The living is a perpetual curacy, in the archdeaconry of Stafford, and diocese of Lichfield and Coventry, endowed with £200 private benefaction, £400 royal bounty, and £800 parliamentary grant, and in the patronage of the Vicar of Leek The chapel, dedicated to St Mary, is a small edifice with a square tower Twenty-eight children are educated for ±12 5 per annum, the proceeds of a bequest by John Stoddard, in 1673, and of another by Roger Morris In the neighbourhood are the Leek rocks, stupendous overhanging masses, two miles in length, with scattered fragments at their bases and in other parts of the valley

MEESDEN, a parish in the hundred of EDWINSTREE, county of HERTFORD, 4½ miles (S E by E) from

Barkway, containing 164 inhabitants The living is a rectory, in the archdeaconry of Middlesex, and diocese of London, rated in the king's books at £12 13 4 The Rev A Gaussen was patron in 1819 The church is dedicated to St Mary

MEESON, a township in the parish of GREAT BOLAS, Newport division of the hundred of BRADFORD (South), county of SALOP, 5 miles (N W by W) from Newport The population is returned with the parish

MEETH, a parish in the hundred of SHEBBEAR, county of DEVON, 3 miles (N by E) from Hatherleigh, containing 270 inhabitants The living is a rectory, in the archdeaconry of Barnstaple, and diocese of Exeter, rated in the king s books at £9 7 6 The Rev F D Lampriere was patron in 1824 The church is dedicated to St John the Baptist

MELAY, a joint township with Hayton, in the parish of ASPATRIA, ALLERDALE ward below Derwent, county of CUMBERLAND, 8 miles (N by W) from Cockermouth The population is returned with Hayton

MELBECKS, a township in that part of the parish of GRINTON which is in the western division of the wapentake of GILLING, North riding of the county of YORK, 14 miles (W by S) from Richmond, containing 1726 inhabitants

MELBOURN, a parish in the hundred of ARMINGFORD, county of CAMBRIDGE, 3¾ miles (N E by N) from Royston, containing 1179 inhabitants The living is a vicarage, in the archdeaconry and diocese of Ely, rated in the king's books at £19 1 10½, and in the patronage of the Dean and Chapter of Ely The church is dedicated to All Saints There are places of worship for Baptists and Independents Here is a school for the instruction of children, with a small endowment, founded by the Rev W Ayloff A fair is held on the first Wednesday in July

MELBOURN, a parish in the hundred of REPTON and GRESLEY, county of DERBY, 7 miles (N N E) from Ashby de la Zouch, containing 2027 inhabitants The living is a vicarage, in the archdeaconry of Derby, and diocese of Lichfield and Coventry, rated in the king's books at £9 13 4, and in the patronage of the Bishop of Carlisle The church, dedicated to St Michael, is a fine specimen of Norman architecture, with round massive piers, circular arches, fine mouldings, and zigzag ornaments There are places of worship for General Baptists, Independents, and Wesleyan Methodists, the Society of Friends had a meeting-house here, which is now occupied as a school for the children of Swedenborgians In 1738, Lady Eliz Hastings bequeathed land, now producing £20 per annum, for the education of twelve poor children, who are taught by the master of the National school, which was erected in 1822, at an expense of more than £500, defrayed by the Rev James Bagge and the National Society Here was anciently a baronial castle, in which John, Duke of Bourbon, who had been taken prisoner at the battle of Agincourt, was confined for several years it is said to have been dismantled, in 1460, by order of Queen Margaret, but it was afterwards repaired, scarcely any vestiges remain. Melbourn hall was formerly a palace belonging to the Bishops of Carlisle The river Trent bounds the parish on the north This parish is in the honour of Tutbury, duchy of Lancaster, and within the jurisdiction of a court of pleas held at Tutbury every third Tuesday, for the recovery of debts under 40s Melbourn gives the title of viscount to the family of Lamb

MELBOURN, a township in that part of the parish of THORNTON which is in the Holme-Beacon division of the wapentake of HARTHILL, East riding of the county of YORK, 5¼ miles (S W) from Pocklington, containing 437 inhabitants There is a place of worship for Wesleyan Methodists

MELBURY ABBAS, a parish in that part of the hundred of SIXPENNY-HANDLEY which is in the Shaston (West) division of the county of DORSET, 2½ miles (S E) from Shaftesbury, containing 345 inhabitants The living is a rectory, in the archdeaconry of Dorset, and diocese of Bristol, rated in the king s books at £9 18 11½ Thomas Grove and W Goodden, Esqrs were patrons in 1794 Walter Blandford, D D , Bishop of Oxford, and afterwards of Worcester, was a native of this place

MELBURY-BUBB, a parish in the hundred of YETMINSTER, Sherborne division of the county of DORSET, 9¼ miles (S S W) from Sherborne, containing, with the chapelry of Woolcombe, 129 inhabitants The living is a rectory, in the archdeaconry of Dorset, and diocese of Bristol, rated in the king's books at £11 10 5, and in the patronage of the Earl of Ilchester The church, dedicated to St. Mary, is built of flint and stone, chiefly in the later style, with a tower on the south side, which forms a porch, there are some remains of ancient stained glass Woolcombe chapel has been demolished. On an eminence, called Bubb down, was formerly a beacon

MELBURY-OSMOND, a parish in the hundred of YETMINSTER, Sherborne division of the county of DORSET, 8¾ miles (S W) from Sherborne, containing 319 inhabitants The living is a discharged rectory, with which that of Melbury-Sampford was united in 1750, in the archdeaconry of Dorset, and diocese of Bristol, rated in the king s books at £8 3 4, and in the patronage of the Earl of Ilchester The church is dedicated to St Osmond A school for the instruction of poor children has an income of £15 per annum, the bequest of Mrs Susannah Strangeways Horner, in 1754

MELBURY-SAMPFORD, a parish in the hundred of TOLLERFORD, Dorchester division of the county of DORSET, 7½ miles (N E by E) from Beaminster, containing 78 inhabitants The living is a discharged rectory, united in 1750 to that of Melbury-Osmond, in the archdeaconry of Dorset, and diocese of Bristol, rated in the king s books at £5 6 5½, endowed with £200 private benefaction, and £200 royal bounty The church is an ancient structure, and contains several monuments to the Strangeways family

MELCHBOURN, a parish in the hundred of STODDEN, county of BEDFORD, 5¼ miles (E S E) from Higham-Ferrers, containing 244 inhabitants The living is a vicarage, in the archdeaconry of Bedford, and diocese of Lincoln, rated in the king s books at £5, and in the patronage of Lord St John The church, dedicated to St Mary, contains several ancient monuments and brasses Here was a preceptory of Knights Hospitallers, the revenue of which was valued at £241 9 10, after the dissolution it was granted by Queen Elizabeth to the first Earl of Bedford to this preceptory a market and a fair were granted, in 1264 Leland, the historian and antiquary, was a native of this place

MELCHET-PARK, an extra-parochial liberty, in the hundred of ALDERBURY, county of WILTS, containing 9 inhabitants

MELCOMBE-HORSEY, a parish in the hundred of WHITEWAY, Cerne subdivision of the county of DORSET, 8½ miles (W S W) from Blandford-Forum, containing 153 inhabitants The living is a rectory, in the archdeaconry of Dorset, and diocese of Bristol, rated in the king s books at £16 Lord Rivers was patron in 1814 The church is dedicated to St Andrew In the vicinity are the remains of the hamlet of Melcombe-Bingham, consisting only of foundations of houses On an eminence, called Nettlecombe Tout, is a square encampment, occupying a space of twenty acres

MELCOMBE-REGIS, county of DORSET — See WEYMOUTH

MELDON, a parish in the western division of CASTLE ward, county of NORTHUMBERLAND, 6½ miles (W S W) from Morpeth, containing 156 inhabitants The living is a discharged vicarage, in the archdeaconry of Northumberland, and diocese of Durham, rated in the king's books at £4 7 11, endowed with £400 private benefaction, £200 royal bounty, and £300 parliamentary grant, and in the patronage of the Dean and Chapter of Durham The church is dedicated to St John the Evangelist

MELDRETH, a parish in the hundred of ARMINGFORD, county of CAMBRIDGE, 5¼ miles (N N E) from Royston, containing 643 inhabitants The living is a discharged vicarage, in the archdeaconry and diocese of Ely, rated in the king's books at £4 15 10, and in the patronage of the Dean and Chapter of Ely The church is dedicated to the Holy Trinity

MELFORD (LONG), a parish (formerly a market town) in the hundred of BABERGH, county of SUFFOLK, 22 miles (W) from Ipswich, and 58¼ (N E by N) from London, containing 2288 inhabitants This village is situated on a branch of the river Stour, in one of the most fertile parts of the county, and is surrounded by very beautiful scenery silk-weaving is carried on to a limited extent. A large fair for cattle is held on the Thursday in Whitsun-week A court baron is held annually by the lord of the manor, and petty sessions every fortnight by the county magistrates The living is a rectory, in the archdeaconry of Sudbury, and diocese of Norwich, rated in the king s books at £28 2 6 The Executors of the Rev J Leroo were patrons in 1819 The church, dedicated to the Holy Trinity, presents a fine specimen of the later style of English architecture, the tower is of more modern date in the interior are several handsome monuments, especially one to the memory of Sir William Cordell, Knt., speaker of the House of Commons, and privy councillor, in the reign of Mary, and Master of the Rolls under Elizabeth There are places of worship for Independents and Wesleyan Methodists A school for twelve boys is endowed with about £12 per annum, from a benefaction by John Hill, in 1495, and £2 8 1 payable out of the Exchequer, under a grant of Edward VI, and a school for ten boys and ten girls is endowed with £9 per annum, arising from a bequest by John Moore, in 1713 An hospital, for a warden, twelve poor men, and two poor women, being decayed housekeepers of Melford, was founded, under the authority of letters patent in 1580, by Sir W Cordell, and endowed with an estate in land, now producing a very considerable income it is subject to the visitation of the Bishop of Norwich

MELKRIDGE, a township in the parish of HALT-WHISTLE, western division of TINDALE ward, county of NORTHUMBERLAND, 2¼ miles (E) from Haltwhistle, containing 288 inhabitants In this township is Whitchester, a Roman military station, the site is defended on three sides by steep glens

MELKSHAM, a market town and parish in the hundred of MELKSHAM, county of WILTS, 28 miles (N W) from Salisbury, and 95 (W by S) from London, containing, with the chapelry of Seend, 5776 inhabitants The name is supposed to be derived from Milch, or Melch, milk, and Haur, a dwelling, the adjacent land being chiefly occupied as dairy farms During the Saxon era this was a place of some importance at the period of the Norman survey, and for several subsequent reigns, it was held in royal demesne, and gave name to an extensive forest in the reign of Henry VIII it had fallen into decay, but during the last century experienced a revival from its cloth manufacture The town, situated on the great road from London through Devizes to Bath, and on the banks of the Avon, consists principally of one street nearly a mile in length, which is paved and lighted with gas the houses are in general good, and built of freestone, and the inhabitants are well supplied with water Two mineral springs, one saline and the other chalybeate, were discovered in the vicinity, some years ago, and, in 1816, a new saline spa was formed, by boring to a depth of more than three hundred and fifty feet, to which a pump-room, and hot and cold baths, with every requisite accommodation, have been added these buildings form the centre of a handsome crescent, with a viranda in front, and near them is an agreeable promenade the surrounding country abounds with diversified and pleasing prospects The chalybeate spring, which is contiguous to the old spa, yields about eight hundred gallons per day, and is in its qualities similar to the waters of Tonbridge and Bath The saline aperient is highly recommended, both for external and internal use, in scrofulous and scorbutic diseases There is a convenient reading-room, also a circulating library The business of the town formerly consisted in the manufacture of broad cloth and kerseymere, of which it was once the principal seat, but this is now on the decline there is some business done in malt and leather The Wilts and Berks canal passes on the east, and about a mile and a half southward joins the Kennet and Avon canal The river Avon passes through the town, and is crossed by a handsome stone bridge of four arches, with light and elegant balustrades adjoining it is one of the largest corn-mills in the county, and contiguous are an extensive factory and dye-houses The market is held every alternate Monday, for cattle, sheep, pigs, &c, and there is a cattle fair on the 27th of July The county magistrates hold here a petty session for the division, on the last Wednesday in every month, a court leet is held half-yearly by the joint lords of the manor, and a court of requests, under an act of the 47th of George III, for the recovery of debts not exceeding £5, is held once in three weeks, on Tuesday, alternately with Bradford and Trowbridge The living is a vicarage, in the archdeaconry and diocese of Salisbury, rated in the king's

books at £38 9 4½, and in the patronage of the Dean and Chapter of Salisbury The church, dedicated to St Michael, is a spacious cruciform structure of freestone, with a handsome tower rising from the intersection part of the building is of the period of the twelfth century, and the whole is crowned with battlements and pinnacles, in the interior, on the south side, are two chantry chapels There are places of worship for Baptists, the Society of Friends, Independents, and Wesleyan Methodists In 1750, the Rev Bohun Fox bequeathed £135 for instructing and partly clothing poor children A Lancasterian school, established in 1829, is supported by voluntary contributions about two hundred and forty children of both sexes are instructed

MELLING, a parish in the hundred of LONSDALE, south of the sands, county palatine of LANCASTER, comprising the chapelries of Arkholme and Hornby, the townships of Farleton, Melling with Wratton, Roburndale, Wennington, and Wray, and the hamlet of Cawood, and containing 2340 inhabitants, of which number, 210 are in the township of Melling with Wratton, 6 miles (S by W) from Kirkby-Lonsdale The living is a discharged vicarage, in the archdeaconry of Richmond, and diocese of Chester, rated in the king's books at £7 1 10½, endowed with £200 private benefaction, £200 royal bounty, and £800 parliamentary grant, and in the patronage of the Crown The church is dedicated to St Peter A school room, in which the children of this township are taught gratuitously, was built by subscription, and has a permanent income of £12 per annum, the proceeds of bequests, in 1759, by Rebecca Bland, and in 1770, by William Gillison, for educating and apprenticing children

MELLING, a chapelry in the parish of HALSALL, hundred of WEST DERBY, county palatine of LANCASTER, 6¼ miles (S S W) from Ormskirk, containing 528 inhabitants The living is a perpetual curacy, in the archdeaconry and diocese of Chester, endowed with £400 private benefaction, £200 royal bounty, and £1400 parliamentary grant The Earl of Lonsdale was patron in 1796 The chapel is dedicated to Holy Rood A school was founded by the lords of Melling, with a residence for the master, about 1700, to which, in 1709, Edward Smith bequeathed the residue of his personal estate, and in 1712, John Tatlock gave £20, there are about twenty-five free scholars, and the master's income is £25 per annum

MELLION (ST), a parish in the middle division of EAST hundred, county of CORNWALL, 3¼ miles (S E by S) from Callington, containing 321 inhabitants The living is a rectory, in the archdeaconry of Cornwall, and diocese of Exeter, rated in the king's books at £11 12 6, and in the patronage of J T Coryton, Esq The river Lynner runs through the parish

MELLIS, a parish in the hundred of HARTISMERE, county of SUFFOLK, 4 miles (W by N) from Eye, containing 447 inhabitants The living is a rectory, in the archdeaconry of Sudbury, diocese of Norwich, rated in the king's books at £9 15, and in the patronage of the Crown The church is dedicated to St Mary There is a place of worship for Wesleyan Methodists

MELLONS (ST), a parish in the upper division of the hundred of WENTLLOOG, county of MONMOUTH,

3½ miles (N E by N) from Cardiff, containing 551 inhabitants The living is a discharged vicarage, in the archdeaconry and diocese of Llandaff, rated in the king's books at £10 1 5, and in the patronage of the Bishop of Llandaff

MELLOR, a chapelry in the parish of GLOSSOP, hundred of HIGH PEAK, county of DERBY, comprising the townships of Mellor and Ludworth, and the hamlet of Whitle, and containing 4872 inhabitants, of which number, 2099 are in the township of Mellor, 8¼ miles (N W by N) from Chapel en le Frith The living is a perpetual curacy, in the archdeaconry of Derby, and diocese of Lichfield and Coventry, endowed with £400 private benefaction and £600 royal bounty, and in the patronage of the Trustees of the late John Thornton, Esq The chapel, dedicated to St Thomas, is very ancient, the pulpit is carved out of an old oak tree, and the font is also rudely carved There is a place of worship for Wesleyan Methodists, and at Marple Bridge one for Independents A free school was built about 1639, and endowed with £160 bequeathed by Thomas Walklate, to which some trifling augmentations have been made by subsequent benefactors the income is £25 per annum, and all the children of the chapelry who apply are educated at a small charge Here are extensive cotton works, which afford employment to a considerable portion of the inhabitants

MELLOR, a chapelry in the parish, and lower division of the hundred, of BLACKBURN, county palatine of LANCASTER, 2¾ miles (N W) from Blackburn, containing 1981 inhabitants On Mellor moor are the remains of a Roman encampment

MELLS, a parish in the hundred of MELLS and LEIGH, county of SOMERSET, 3 miles (W N W) from Frome, containing 1147 inhabitants The living is a rectory, with the perpetual curacy of Leigh upon Mendip, in the archdeaconry of Wells, and diocese of Bath and Wells, rated in the king s books at £33 16 8 T S Horner, Esq was patron in 1824 The church is dedicated to St Andrew There are extensive coal-works, and iron-manufactories, principally for agricultural implements, in this parish Two fairs are held annually, on the Monday after Trinity week, and on Michaelmas day The Frome here flows between rocks that rear their summits to a great height, somewhat resembling St Vincent s rock below Bristol

MELLS, a hamlet in the parish of WENHASTON, hundred of BLYTHING, county of SUFFOLK, 1¾ mile (E S E) from Halesworth The population is returned with the parish In this hamlet there was formerly a chapel, dedicated to St Margaret, but it is now in ruins

MELMERBY, a parish in LEATH ward, county of CUMBERLAND, 8½ miles (N E by E) from Penrith, containing 250 inhabitants The living is a rectory, in the archdeaconry and diocese of Carlisle, rated in the king s books at £12 11 5½, and in the patronage of Mrs Pattenson. The church, built of red freestone, is dedicated to St John the Baptist This place had anciently a market and a fair a feast is held annually on Old Midsummer-day, In the parish are two springs, one sulphureous, and the other chalybeate There are extensive strata of limestone, and some freestone, and a lead-mine has been worked some years, but it is not very productive The Roman road called the Maiden way is visible here, its width is twenty-one feet On the eastern side of the parish is Hartside Fell, a lofty mountain rising one thousand three hundred and twelve feet above the village, over which passes a new road from Alston to Penrith The Helm winds blow here with great violence

MELMERBY, a chapelry in that part of the parish of WATH which is in the wapentake of HALLIKELD, North riding of the county of YORK, 4 miles (N N E) from Ripon, containing 258 inhabitants

MELMERBY, a township in the parish of COVERHAM, western division of the wapentake of HANG, North riding of the county of YORK, 4¼ miles (W S W) from Middleham, containing 112 inhabitants

MELPLASH, a tything in the parish of NETHERBURY, hundred of BEAMINSTER-FORUM and REDHONE, Bridport division of the county of DORSET, 2¼ miles (S S E) from Beaminster The population is returned with the parish

MELSONBY, a parish in the western division of the wapentake of GILLING, North riding of the county of YORK, 5 miles (N N E) from Richmond, containing 440 inhabitants The living is a rectory, in the archdeaconry of Richmond, and diocese of Chester, rated in the king s books at £10 2 11, and in the patronage of the Master and Fellows of University College, Oxford The church is dedicated to St James In 1757, William Cockin bequeathed an estate for the instruction of poor children the annual profits are £26, for which eight children are instructed

MELTHAM, a chapelry in the parish of ALMONDBURY, upper division of the wapentake of AGBRIGG, West riding of the county of YORK, 5½ miles (S W by S) from Huddersfield, containing 2000 inhabitants The chapel is dedicated to St Bartholomew There are places of worship for Baptists and Wesleyan Methodists The manufacture of woollen and cotton goods is carried on here A school-room was built by subscription, about six years ago, the master receives the interest of £20, the bequest of Matthew Lockwood in 1715, there are no free scholars

MELTHWAITE, a joint township with Santon, in the parish of IRTON, ALLERDALE ward above Darwent, county of CUMBERLAND, 3 miles (N by E) from Ravenglass The population is returned with Santon

MELTON, a parish in the hundred of WILFORD, county of SUFFOLK, 2¼ miles (N E) from Woodbridge, containing 607 inhabitants The living is a discharged rectory, in the archdeaconry of Suffolk, and diocese of Norwich, rated in the king s books at £9 6 8, and in the patronage of the Dean and Chapter of Ely The church is dedicated to St Andrew What was formerly the House of Industry for the hundred of Wilford is in this parish, it has been converted into a county lunatic asylum There are a large iron-foundry and an extensive building establishment in the parish The river Deben is navigable on the south-east, where it is crossed by Wilford bridge

MELTON, a chapelry in the parish of WELTON, wapentake of HOWDENSHIRE, East riding of the county of YORK, 4½ miles (S E) from South Cave, containing 107 inhabitants

MELTON (GREAT), a parish in the hundred of HUMBLEYARD, county of NORFOLK, 5¾ miles (W S W) from Norwich, containing 386 inhabitants The living comprises the united rectories of All Saints and St Mary the Virgin, in the archdeaconry of Norfolk, and diocese of Norwich, each rated in the king's books at £6 13 4, and in the patronage of the Master and Fellows of Caius College, Cambridge   The church is dedicated to the Virgin Mary   the tower was built in 1440   The old church of All Saints, which stood in the same churchyard, was taken down in the 12th year of the reign of Queen Anne

MELTON (HIGH), a parish in the northern division of the wapentake of STRAFFORTH and TICKHILL, West riding of the county of YORK, 4¾ miles (W by S) from Doncaster, containing 137 inhabitants   The living is a perpetual curacy, in the archdeaconry and diocese of York, endowed with £600 private benefaction, and £600 royal bounty   R. F Wilson, Esq was patron in 1826   The church is dedicated to St James   There is a place of worship for Independents

MELTON (LITTLE), a parish in the hundred of HUMBLEYARD, county of NORFOLK, 5¼ miles (W by S) from Norwich, containing 210 inhabitants   The living is a discharged vicarage, in the archdeaconry of Norfolk, and diocese of Norwich, rated in the king s books at £5 6 8, endowed with £200 royal bounty, and in the patronage of the Master and Fellows of Emanuel College, Cambridge   The church is dedicated to All Saints

MELTON-CONSTABLE, a parish in the hundred of HOLT, county of NORFOLK, 5½ miles (S W by S) from Holt, containing, with Little Burgh, 111 inhabitants   The living is a rectory, with Little Burgh, in the archdeaconry and diocese of Norwich, rated in the king's books at £6, and in the patronage of Sir Jacob Astley, Bart. The church is dedicated to St Peter   This parish is said to derive its name from the office of constable having been bestowed on the family of De Mealton by the Conqueror

MELTON-MOWBRAY, a market town and parish, in the hundred of FRAMLAND, county of LEICESTER, 15 miles (N E) from Leicester, and 105 (N W) from London, containing, with the chapelry of Freeby and the township of Welby, 2990 inhabitants   The ancient name of this place was Medeltune, which has been gradually contracted to Melton, indicating the situation of the town in the middle of the five hamlets which compose the parish, the adjunct is the name of its ancient lords, which they assumed by command of Henry I   During the civil commotion in the time of Charles I, a severe action took place in this neighbourhood, between the royalists and the parliamentary troops, in February, 1644, when the forces of the latter, consisting of about two thousand men, were routed with great slaughter   The town sustained considerable damage by fire in 1613, and in 1637 the plague raged here with great violence   It is situated on the direct road from London to Leeds, in a valley on the little river Eye, and is small but neatly built   the streets are paved, watched, and lighted, the expense being defrayed out of the rental of the Town Estate, consisting of property in land, anciently the gift of some unknown benefactor, which produces nearly £800 per annum, and is under the management of a committee of twenty-one, and two wardens, chosen annually by the inhabitants   the first fifty lamps were given by Lord Harborough, in the year 1790   There is

a good supply of water   the Eye and the little brook Scalford are crossed by three bridges, one of which, at the extremity of the town, leading to Oakham, was rebuilt in 1820   Here is a building fourteen feet in diameter, called the Manor oven, in which, in the time of Sir Matthew Lambe, an attempt was made, on the plea of feudal right, to compel the inhabitants to bake their bread, but they having resisted the claim, constructed for themselves another oven of larger dimensions   The principal attraction of Melton, and one great cause of its increasing improvement as a town, may be referred to the celebrated hunt to which it gives name   the season commences in November, and continues about five months, during which there is an influx of sportsmen from all parts of the kingdom, and there is stabling for nearly seven hundred horses   Here is a permanent subscription library and news room   The principal article of manufacture is bobbin net-lace, and there is a minor one of worsted hosiery   The general traffic has been facilitated, especially in the supply of coal, by opening a navigable communication with Loughborough, called the Melton-Mowbray and Oakham canal, which was effected in 1790, and which, near the town, is intersected by the river Wreak   The market is on Tuesday, and on every alternate day there is a large shew of cattle   Fairs are held on the Monday and Tuesday after January 17th, March 13th, May 4th, Whit-Tuesday, August 21st, and September 7th, principally for horses, cattle, and sheep A court leet and baron, for the recovery of debts under 40s, is held every three weeks

The living is a vicarage, in the archdeaconry of Leicester, and diocese of Lincoln, rated in the king s books at £16 8 9, and in the patronage of Peter Godfrey, Esq   The church, dedicated to St Mary, is a spacious, lofty, cruciform structure, the tower, which rises from the intersection, is partly in the early style of English architecture, and at the west end is a handsome entrance porch, the nave is separated from the aisles by six high pointed arches on each side, springing from clustered columns   In the reign of Elizabeth, the church was considerably heightened, and a series of elegant windows was put up over the aisles in 1736, the south and north-east pinnacles being struck by lightning, precipitated fragments of five or six hundred weight through the north transept   the edifice is at present undergoing a thorough repair, and the work is executed in perfect accordance with the original style of the building   There are places of worship for Independents and Wesleyan Methodists Schools appear to have been established here at a very early period, and are noticed as existing previously to 1347, when they were taken under the patronage of Edward III, as possessor of the temporalties of the priory of Lewes   Two schools are at present maintained from the town estate, the National, or lower, school, open to all children of the town above six years of age, free of expense, who are removed, at the discretion of a committee, to the upper school, which is limited to forty-four boys, the number in both schools being about three hundred   there are two exhibitions being this school, conjointly with another at Leicester, to Lincoln College, Oxford.   An hospital was founded in 1638, by Robert Hudson, Esq, for six unmarried men, who were to receive £13 per annum each, by quarterly payments   it has been recently rebuilt and enlarged for the additional accommodation of six poor women, who are maintained from a benefaction made by the Rev Henry Storer, of Frisby, in 1620, for the benefit of the poor, and now producing yearly £27 10 In 1756, Mr John Bourne bequeathed £300, directing the interest to be applied to the support of three unmarried poor inhabitants of Melton, and legally settled there, of the age of sixty years John de Kirkeby, Bishop of Ely in 1286, and founder of Ely palace, Holborn, Archbishop William de Melton, who attained the dignity of Lord High Chancellor of England in the reign of Edward III, and the talented, but eccentric, John Henley, who, under the popular appellation of Orator Henley, acquired considerable notoriety about the middle of the last century, were natives of this place Henley was educated at the free school and the Archbishop was buried in the church

MELTON-ROSS, a parish in the southern division of the wapentake of YARBOROUGH, parts of LINDSEY, county of LINCOLN, 5½ miles (N E by E) from Glandford-Bridge, containing 126 inhabitants The living is a perpetual curacy, in the peculiar jurisdiction of the Dean and Chapter of Lincoln, endowed with £200 private benefaction, and £600 royal bounty, and in the patronage of the Prebendary of Melton Ross with Scamblesby in the Cathedral Church of Lincoln

MELTONBY, a township in the parish of POCKLINGTON, Wilton-Beacon division of the wapentake of HARTHILL, East riding of the county of YORK, 2¼ miles (N by W) from Pocklington, containing 78 inhabitants

MELVERLEY, a parish in the hundred of Oswestry, county of SALOP, 11 miles (W N W) from Shrewsbury, containing 225 inhabitants The living is a perpetual curacy, in the archdeaconry and diocese of St Asaph and in the patronage of the Rector of Llandrinio The church is dedicated to St Peter

MEMBURY, a parish in the hundred of Axminster, county of DEVON, 3½ miles (N N W) from Axminster, containing 837 inhabitants The living is a perpetual curacy, annexed to the vicarage of Axminster, in the archdeaconry and diocese of Exeter The church, dedicated to St. John the Baptist, contains a monument to the memory of Sir S Calmady, who was mortally wounded at the siege of Ford House during the great civil war, likewise a monumental effigy of a lady A cattle fair is held on the 10th of August In the neighbourhood is an ancient encampment, formed by a single vallum, enclosing two acres

MENDHAM, a parish partly in the hundred of EARSHAM, county of NORFOLK, but chiefly in the hundred of HOXNE, county of SUFFOLK, 1½ mile (E. by S) from Harleston, containing 835 inhabitants The living is a discharged vicarage, in the archdeaconry of Suffolk, and diocese of Norwich, rated in the king's books at £5 5 2½, endowed with £400 private benefaction, £400 royal bounty, and £400 parliamentary grant. Mrs Whitaker was patroness in 1788 The church is dedicated to All Saints There is a place of worship for Wesleyan Methodists. At Bruninghurst, in this parish, a Cluniac priory, subordinate to Castleacre in Norfolk, was founded by William, son of Roger de Huntingfield, and dedicated to the Virgin Mary there are extensive remains of the conventual buildings

MENDLESHAM, a parish (formerly a market town) in the hundred of HARTISMERE, county of SUFFOLK, 15½ miles (N W) from Ipswich, and 79 (N E) from London, containing 1250 inhabitants The town is situated in a deep miry soil, and consists of two long and irregular streets, the houses are of mean appearance, and the adjacent roads in bad condition A market was granted in the reign of Edward 1, but has been long disused A fair is held on the 2nd of October and the following day, for cattle and toys Two constables are elected at the manorial courts The living is a vicarage, in the archdeaconry of Sudbury, and diocese of Norwich, rated in the king's books at £14 9 2, and in the patronage of the Rev Robert Field The church, dedicated to St Mary, is a handsome structure There is a place of worship for Wesleyan Methodists In 1473, Robert Lake bequeathed, for charitable purposes, property in land, which, with other benefactions, produces about £350 per annum, from which £20 per annum is paid for the support of a charity school for fifteen poor children, £20 per annum for the maintenance of a Sunday school, and nearly £200 per annum is distributed by the trustees in weekly gratuities to the necessitous poor There are six unendowed almshouses About the close of the seventeenth century, an ancient silver crown, weighing sixty ounces, was found here, and, in 1758, a gold ring, bearing an inscription in Runic characters, was turned up by the plough from these and other circumstances, Mendlesham is supposed to have been the residence of Redwald, one of the kings of the East Angles

MENETHORPE, a township in the parish of WESTOW, wapentake of BUCKROSE, East riding of the county of YORK, 3 miles (S S W) from New Malton, containing 131 inhabitants

MENHENIOT, a parish in the middle division of EAST hundred, county of CORNWALL, 2½ miles (E S E) from Liskeard, containing 1170 inhabitants The living is a vicarage, in the archdeaconry of Cornwall, and diocese of Exeter, rated in the king's books at £21 15 5, and in the patronage of the Rector and Fellows of Exeter College, Oxford, on the nomination of the Dean and Chapter of Exeter The church is dedicated to St Neot A school for the instruction of poor children was endowed with the interest of £42, by the Rev Augustus Question, about 1753, with the interest of £25 by Mr Snell, to which the Rev William Holwell Carr, the present vicar, adds £20 per annum for the master's salary Fairs for cattle and sheep are held April 23rd, June 11th, and July 28th Within the parish, and near the town of Liskeard, was anciently an hospital for lepers, dedicated to St Mary Magdalene The scenery of this district is beautifully diversified with rock and wood. William of Wykham was vicar of this parish

MENSTONE, a township in that part of the parish of OTLEY which is in the upper division of the wapentake of SKYRACK, West riding of the county of YORK, 2¾ miles (S W by W) from Otley, containing 257 inhabitants

MENTHORP, a joint township with Bowthorp, in the parish of HEMINGBROUGH, wapentake of OUZE and DERWENT, East riding of the county of YORK, 7½ miles (N W by N) from Howden, containing, with Bowthorp, 49 inhabitants

MENTMORE, a parish in the hundred of COTTES-LOE, county of BUCKINGHAM, comprising the township of Mentmore, and the hamlet of Ledburn, and containing 302 inhabitants, of which number, 137 are in the township of Mentmore, 4 miles (N W) from Ivinghoe. The living is a discharged vicarage, in the archdeaconry of Buckingham, and diocese of Lincoln, rated in the king's books at £6 17 1, endowed with £200 royal bounty, and in the patronage of Charles Harcourt, Esq The church is dedicated to St Mary

MENWITH, a joint township with Darley, in the parish of HAMPSTHWAITE, lower division of the wapentake of CLARO, West riding of the county of YORK, 11½ miles (W by N) from Knaresborough, containing, with Darley, 648 inhabitants This township is within the peculiar ecclesiastical jurisdiction of the court for the Forest division of the honour of Knaresborough In 1748 William Day gave land for the education of six poor children, the income is £47 per annum, and twelve are taught gratuitously

MEOLS (NORTH), a parish in the hundred of WEST DERBY, county palatine of LANCASTER, 9½ miles (N N W) from Ormskirk, containing 2763 inhabitants The living is a rectory, in the archdeaconry and diocese of Chester, rated in the king's books at £8 3 4, and in the patronage of Peter Hesketh, Esq The church is dedicated to St Cuthbert There is a place of worship for Independents An ancient grammar school, endowed with £370, by means of various benefactions, is now consolidated with a National school, erected by subscription in 1827, on the site of the old school room, sixty boys and eighty girls are educated gratuitously

MEOLSE (GREAT), a township in the parish of WEST KIRBY, lower division of the hundred of WIRRALL, county palatine of CHESTER, 10¼ miles (N N W) from Great Neston, containing 159 inhabitants

MEOLSE (LITTLE), a township in the parish of WEST KIRBY, lower division of the hundred of WIRRALL, county palatine of CHESTER, 10 miles (N W by N) from Great Neston, containing 131 inhabitants This has lately risen into repute as a bathing-place In 1690, the Duke of Schomberg encamped with his army at a place called the Mells, near Hyle lake, in this township, previously to his embarkation for Ireland

MEON (EAST), a parish comprising the hamlet of Westbury with Peak, in the hundred of MEON-STOKE, Portsdown division, and the tythings of Bordean, Coombe, East Meon, Langrish, and Riplington, in the hundred of EAST MEON, Alton (South) division, of the county of SOUTHAMPTON, 4½ miles (W by S) from Petersfield, and containing 1336 inhabitants The living is a vicarage, with the perpetual curacies of Froxfield and Steep, in the peculiar jurisdiction and patronage of the Bishop of Winchester, rated in the king's books at £35 1 8 The church, dedicated to All Saints, is a cruciform structure, with a Norman tower and western doorway, and containing a very ancient font, precisely similar to that in Winchester cathedral There is a school with a small endowment A fair for horses is held on the 19th of September This parish is within the jurisdiction of the Cheyney Court held at Winchester every Thursday, for the recovery of debts to any amount

MEON (WEST), a parish in the hundred of FAWLEY, Fawley division of the county of SOUTHAMPTON, 7½ miles (N E) from Bishop's Waltham, containing 747 inhabit-

ants The living is a rectory, with the perpetual curacy of Privett, in the archdeaconry and diocese of Winchester, rated in the king's books at £30 17 11, and in the patronage of the Bishop of Winchester The church is a curious specimen of Norman architecture There is a place of worship for Independents

MEON-STOKE, a parish in the hundred of MEON-STOKE, Portsdown division of the county of SOUTHAMPTON, 4 miles (N E by E) from Bishop's Waltham, containing 368 inhabitants The living is a rectory, with the perpetual curacy of Soberton, in the peculiar jurisdiction of the incumbent, rated in the king's books at £46 2 11, and in the patronage of the Bishop of Winchester The church is dedicated to St Mary

MEOPHAM, a parish in the hundred of TOLTING-TROUGH, lathe of AYLESFORD, county of KENT, 7½ miles (W by S) from Rochester, containing 833 inhabitants The living is a vicarage, in the peculiar jurisdiction and patronage of the Archbishop of Canterbury, rated in the king's books at £16 3 4 The church, dedicated to St John the Baptist, is in the decorated style of English architecture it was built, in 1396, by Archbishop Courtenay, who likewise founded four almshouses near it for the poor

MEPAL, a parish in the southern division of the hundred of WITCHFORD, Isle of ELY, county of CAMBRIDGE, 8 miles (W by N) from Ely, containing 406 inhabitants The living is a rectory, united to the vicarage of Sutton, in the peculiar jurisdiction of the Bishop of Ely, rated in the king's books at £3 6 8 The church is dedicated to St Mary

MEPPERSHALL, a parish in the hundred of CLIFTON, county of BEDFORD, 1¾ mile (S) from Shefford, containing 397 inhabitants The living is a rectory, in the archdeaconry of Bedford, and diocese of Lincoln, rated in the king's books at £22, and in the patronage of the Master and Fellows of St John's College, Cambridge The church is dedicated to St Mary From thirty to forty children are educated by a schoolmistress for £15 per annum, arising from Emery's charity, at Ampthill A small part of this parish is locally in a detached portion of the county of Hertford

MERCASTON, a township in the parish of MUGGINTON, hundred of APPLETREE, county of DERBY, 7½ miles (N W) from Derby, containing 166 inhabitants At the Norman survey there was a church many ancient coins have been found in the village

MERE, a township in that part of the parish of ROSTHERN which is in the hundred of BUCKLOW, county palatine of CHESTER, 2½ miles (N W by N) from Nether Knutsford, containing 566 inhabitants. Here is a small sum for the instruction of children

MERE, a parish in the hundred of MERE, county of WILTS, comprising the market town of Mere, and the tythings of Woodlands with Chaddenwicke, and Zeals, and containing 2422 inhabitants, of which number, 1220 are in the town of Mere, 21½ miles (W by N) from Salisbury, and 102 (W S W) from London. The name of this place is derived from the Saxon word Mœra, signifying bounds, or limits, and indicates its situation on the borders of the counties of Wilts, Somerset, and Dorset In 1253, permission was granted by Henry III to Richard, Earl of Cornwall, to build and fortify a castle on his manor of Mere, which manor has ever since been attached to the duchy of Cornwall

In the 9th of Henry IV, a grant was made to Henry, Prince of Wales, as Duke of Cornwall, of a market and two annual fairs at this place The town, situated on the high road from Salisbury to Wincanton, is small, and the buildings are irregular the inhabitants are well supplied with water The principal branch of manufacture is that of English dowlas and bed-ticking, there is likewise a silk-throwing mill The market is on Tuesday, and fairs are held for corn and cattle on May 17th and October 10th This town formerly sent members to parliament, but was disfranchised on the plea of poverty Courts leet and baron are held, annually in October, for the duchy of Cornwall, and by the Dean of Salisbury, at which constables and tythingmen are chosen for the town and hundred The living is a vicarage, in the peculiar jurisdiction and patronage of the Dean of Salisbury, rated in the king s books at £28 4 2 The church, which is dedicated to St Michael, is spacious and handsome, consisting of a nave, choir, and chancel, with a tower at the west end, surmounted by spires at the angles on each side of the nave are five pointed arches, springing from light pillars, with clustered shafts, the cornice is enriched with sculpture in wood, a screen of open work separates the nave from the choir on each side of the chancel is a sepulchral chapel, and in the belfry is a beautiful carved oak ceiling There is a place of worship for Independents A bequest of £10 per annum was made, about 1755, by Thomas Tatam, for the instruction of poor children To the north-west of the town are vestiges of a Danish encampment, called " White street camp,' from the hill on which it was situated the circumference of the outer ditch is four furlongs and one hundred and fifty-two yards Francis Lord Cottington a celebrated statesman in the reign of Charles I, and the Rev Francis Potter, an ingenious mechanist, born about 1594, were natives of this place

MEREVALE, a parish partly in the hundred of SPARKENHOE, county of LEICESTER, and partly in the Atherstone division of the hundred of HEMLINGFORD, county of WARWICK, 1½ mile (W by S) from Atherstone, containing 208 inhabitants The living is a perpetual curacy, in the peculiar jurisdiction of the manorial court of Merevale, and in the patronage of D S Dugdale, Esq The church is dedicated to St Mary There are coal mines in the parish, which is bounded by the river Anker the Coventry canal passes on the north-east side of it. An abbey for Cistercian monks, founded by Robert, Earl of Ferrars and Nottingham, about 1148, and dedicated to the Virgin Mary, was valued at the dissolution at £303 10

MEREWORTH, a parish in the hundred of LITTLEFIELD, lathe of AYLESFORD, county of KENT, 5 miles (S E) from Wrotham, containing 711 inhabitants The living is a rectory, in the archdeaconry and diocese of Rochester, rated in the king s books at £14 2 6, and in the patronage of Lord le Despencer The church, dedicated to St Lawrence, was rebuilt by John, Earl of Westmorland it is a very handsome structure, with a fine Corinthian portico, and surmounted by a lofty spire the whole edifice is constructed of different sorts of stone, and the eastern window is of painted glass, collected for the purpose by that nobleman. The grazing land in this parish is supposed to breed the largest oxen in England, some of them having exceeded

three hundred stone This parish is bounded on the north by the Hurst woods

MERIDEN, a parish in the Solihull division of the hundred of HEMLINGFORD, county of WARWICK, 6¼ miles (W N W) from Coventry, containing 927 inhabitants The living is a discharged vicarage, in the archdeaconry of Coventry, and diocese of Lichfield and Coventry, rated in the king s books at £5 12 The Earl of Aylesford was patron in 1816 The church, dedicated to St Lawrence, has recently received an addition of two hundred and twenty five sittings, of which one hundred and eighty two are free, the Incorporated Society for the enlargement of churches and chapels having contributed £150 towards defraying the expense

MERING, an extra-parochial liberty, in the northern division of the wapentake of THURGARTON, though locally in the parish of Girton, northern division of the wapentake of Newark, county of NOTTINGHAM, 8 miles (N by E) from Newark, containing 7 inhabitants

MERKSHALL, or MATTISHALL-HEATH, a parish in the hundred of HUMBLEYARD, county of NORFOLK, 3½ miles (S) from Norwich, containing 23 inhabitants The living is a sinecure rectory, united with that of Caistor St Edmund's, in the archdeaconry of Norfolk, and diocese of Norwich The church, which was dedicated to St Edmund, is in ruins

MERRINGTON, a parish in the south-eastern division of DARLINGTON ward, county palatine of DURHAM, comprising the townships of Chilton, Ferry-Hill, Hett, and Merrington, and containing 1279 inhabitants, of which number, 290 are in the township of Merrington, 3¾ miles (E by N) from Bishop Auckland The living is a vicarage, in the archdeaconry and diocese of Durham, rated in the king s books at £14 4 9½, and in the patronage of the Dean and Chapter of Durham The church, dedicated to St John the Evangelist, is principally in the Norman style, the south door being of an enriched character, and the interior contains a wooden screen, the basement of the tower is Norman, and the upper part of later date it stands on elevated ground, and serves as a land-mark On the usurpation of the see of Durham by Comyn, about 1143, this church was seized by his nephew, who partly encompassed it with a ditch and vallum, and occupied it with armed men. There is a coal mine in the parish

MERRINGTON, a township in the parish of PRESTON-GUBBALS, liberties of SHREWSBURY, county of SALOP, 5¾ miles (N by W) from Shrewsbury, containing 203 inhabitants

MERRIOTT, a parish in the hundred of CREWKERNE, county of SOMERSET, 2 miles (N) from Crewkerne, containing 1212 inhabitants The living is a discharged vicarage, in the archdeaconry of Taunton, and diocese of Bath and Wells, rated in the king s books at £11 11 5½, and in the patronage of the Dean and Chapter of Bristol The church is dedicated to All Saints

MERROW, a parish in the second division of the hundred of WOKING, county of SURREY, 2 miles (E N E) from Guildford, containing 240 inhabitants The living is a discharged rectory, in the archdeaconry of Surrey, and diocese of Winchester, rated in the king's books at £9 0 2½ The Earl of Onslow was patron in 1812 The church is dedicated to St John the Evangelist

MERRYN (ST), a parish in the hundred of PYDER, county of CORNWALL, 2¼ miles (W S W) from Padstow, containing 537 inhabitants The living is a vicarage, in the peculiar jurisdiction and patronage of the Bishop of Exeter, rated in the king s books at £15 6 8 A small quay was constructed under Catacleuse cliffs, about 1794, by Mr Peter, of Harlyn, for the reception of coasting vessels and steam-boats belonging to the pilchard fishery in Portleane bay In the vicinity was anciently a village, with a chapel or church dedicated to St Constantine, the ruins of which still remain The Bristol channel bounds this parish on the west and north

MERSEA (EAST), a parish in the hundred of WINSTREE, county of ESSEX, 9 miles (S S E) from Colchester, containing 282 inhabitants The living is a rectory, in the archdeaconry of Colchester, and diocese of London, rated in the king s books at £21, and in the patronage of the Crown The church which is dedicated to St Edmund, has a square stone tower, which formerly served as a land-mark, and supported a beacon This parish is bounded on the north by Pyefleet channel, and on the east and south by the Colne, near its confluence with the Blackwater

MERSEA (WEST), a parish in the hundred of WINSTREE, county of ESSEX, 9 miles (S) from Colchester, containing 772 inhabitants The living is a discharged vicarage, in the archdeaconry of Colchester, and diocese of London, rated in the king s books at £22 Mrs Simpson was patroness in 1797 The church is dedicated to St Peter and St Paul There is a place of worship for Baptists This parish is bounded on the north and west by the Mersea channel, and on the south by the mouth of the Blackwater river, at low-water, every eight hours, there is a passage from the main land into the parish, over the causeway of the Strode, which is kept in order by the rental of an estate of about thirty acres, called the Strode lands In 1730, when some alterations were made at West Mersea hall, a very fine tesselated pavement was discovered twenty-one feet and a half long, and eighteen and a half broad From these and other antique remains, it is probable that the island of Mersea was the residence of the Count of the Saxon shore, or of some other Roman officer Here was anciently a Benedictine convent, dedicated to St Peter, which was a cell to the abbey of St. Audoen, at Rouen, in Normandy

MERSHAM, a parish in the hundred of CHART and LONGBRIDGE, lathe of SCRAY, county of KENT, 3¾ miles (S E) from Ashford, containing 776 inhabitants The living is a rectory, in the archdeaconry and diocese of Canterbury, rated in the king's books at £26 16 10½, and in the patronage of the Archbishop of Canterbury The church is dedicated to St John the Baptist Over the west door of the tower, which stands on the south side of the nave, is a very curious window, in the later style of English architecture There is a place of worship for Wesleyan Methodists In 1698, a rent-charge of £10 was devised by Dame Jane Knatchbull, for the education of poor children, eight boys are instructed for this sum A fair for pedlary and toys is held on the Friday in Whitsun-week

MERSTHAM, a parish in the second division of the hundred of REIGATE, county of SURREY, ¾ of a mile (N E) from Gatton, containing 796 inhabitants The living is

a rectory, in the peculiar jurisdiction and patronage of the Archbishop of Canterbury, rated in the king s books at £22 1 8 The church, dedicated to St Catherine was erected about the time of Henry VI, and is principally in the later style of English architecture, the tower is in the early English style, and is surmounted by a wooden spire Merstham is now the only place where the Reigate stone, called also fire-stone, is dug for use It was formerly obtained from Reigate and other places, and a considerable quantity of it was used in the erection of old Windsor castle, and of Henry the Seventh's chapel in an ancient record in the tower it is stated, that "the labourers, artificers, carriages, and horses, were pressed from this parish and that of Chaldon adjoining, to convey stone from the King s quarry here to Windsor castle" It is found under beds of chalk and chalk marl it is not, however, adapted to the general purposes of architecture, being subject to decay from exposure to the atmosphere, but it will bear being heated without injury, whence the name of fire-stone The Surrey and Croydon railway commences in this parish

MERSTON, a joint parish with Shorne, in the hundred of SHAMWELL, lathe of AYLESFORD, county of KENT, 4¼ miles (E S E) from Gravesend The population is returned with Shorne The living is a rectory, in the archdeaconry and diocese of Canterbury, rated in the king s books at £2 13 4, and in the patronage of the Crown The church, which was dedicated to St Giles, is in ruins, and its site is included in a plantation of about five acres, called Chapel wood there are some traces of ancient fortifications This place is parochial only in its ecclesiastical jurisdiction, in other respects it is part of the parish of Shorne

MERSTON, a parish in the hundred of Box and STOCKBRIDGE, rape of CHICHESTER, county of SUSSEX, 3 miles (S E) from Chichester, containing 107 inhabitants The living is a rectory, in the archdeaconry and diocese of Chichester, rated in the king's books at £7 4 7 and in the patronage of the Crown The church is partly in the early, and partly in the decorated, style of English architecture The Arundel and Portsmouth canal passes through this parish.

MERTHER, a parish in the western division of the hundred of POWDER, county of CORNWALL, 5 miles (W) from Tregony, containing 370 inhabitants The living is a perpetual curacy, with the vicarage of St Probus, in the archdeaconry of Cornwall, and diocese of Exeter, endowed with £600 royal bounty The church is dedicated to St Merther Here is a place of worship for Wesleyan Methodists At Tresilian bridge, in this parish, the treaty between Sir Ralph Hopton and Sir Thomas Fairfax was concluded, in March 1646, by which this county was surrendered to the parliament. There are fairs at Tresilian bridge, on the second Monday in February, and on the Monday before Whit-Sunray, for cattle St Clement s creek, an inlet of the river Mopus, between Falmouth and Truro, is navigable here Mr William Hals, author of the Parochial History of Cornwall, resided at Tresawson in this parish

MERTON, a parish in the hundred of SHEBBEAR, county of DEVON, 5¾ miles (N by W) from Hatherleigh, containing 697 inhabitants The living is a rectory, in the archdeaconry of Barnstaple, and diocese of

Exeter, rated in the king's books at £20 15 7½ Lord Clinton was patron in 1794 The church is dedicated to All Saints Potheridge house, once the residence of the celebrated General Monk, who rebuilt it, was a noble structure, with a chapel attached, and some magnificent stables, which yet remain, the mansion is now occupied as a farm-house Pipe and potters clay exists in this parish

MERTON, a parish in the hundred of WAYLAND, county of NORFOLK, 2¼ miles (S S W) from Watton, containing 162 inhabitants The living is a discharged rectory, in the archdeaconry and diocese of Norwich, rated in the king's books at £6 0 5 Lord Walsingham was patron in 1803 The church, dedicated to St Peter, has a round tower, in the south window are effigies of St. Edmund and of Robert Clifton, in stained glass

MERTON, a parish in the hundred of BULLINGTON, county of OXFORD, 4 miles (S by W) from Bicester, containing 163 inhabitants The living is a discharged vicarage, in the archdeaconry and diocese of Oxford, rated in the king's books at £8, and in the patronage of the Rector and Fellows of Exeter College, Oxford The church is dedicated to St Swithin

MERTON, a parish in the western division of the hundred of BRIXTON, county of SURREY, 9 miles (S W by S) from London, containing 1177 inhabitants The name of this place in Domesday book is Mereton and Meretune, a Saxon compound of mere, a lake, or marsh, and tun, a town, or vill, being exactly descriptive of its situation According to some writers, this place was the scene of the murder of Cynewulf, King of Wessex, in 784, and of a battle between the Danes and the Saxons, in 871, but there exists some doubt as to its identity with the Merton referred to by ancient historians In 1117, a convent of canons regular of the order of St Augustine was founded here by Gilbert Norman, sheriff of Surrey, and Henry I, in 1121, granted to this community the manor of Merton, towards the erection of a church in honour of the Virgin Mary the priory was liberally endowed by subsequent benefactions, and, at the dissolution, the revenue was valued at £1039 5 3 In the reign of Henry III, Walter de Merton, Lord High Chancellor of England, and afterwards Bishop of Rochester, founded here a seminary of learning, which he afterwards removed to Oxford, on the foundation of Merton College A parliament was held at the priory, in 1236, in which those statutes were enacted which take their name from this place on that occasion the prelates attempted to introduce the imperial and canon law, but were met by that memorable reply of the barons, "Nolumus leges Angliæ mutari Here was concluded the peace between Henry III and the Dauphin of France, through the mediation of Gualo, the pope s legate, and here also Hubert de Bourg, Chief Justice of England, found a temporary asylum from the displeasure of the same monarch During the civil war in the reign of Charles I, a considerable part of the conventual buildings was standing and it appears that a garrison had been established here, for, in July 1648, orders were issued by the government for putting the place in such a condition, that no use might be made of it endangering the peace of the kingdom In 1680, Merton priory was advertised to be let, when it was described as containing several large

rooms and a very fine chapel The only vestiges now remaining are the east window of the chapel, apparently built in the fifteenth century, and the outer walls, constructed of flint and rubble, which are nearly entire, and enclose a space of about sixty acres The village, which is situated on the small river Wandle, consists chiefly of one street, which is paved and lighted the houses are modern, and the inhabitants are supplied with water from several springs and from the river, over which a bridge was built, in 1633, uniting this parish with those of Wimbledon and Mitcham Manufactories for calico-printing have been established on the site of the priory, and formerly more than one thousand persons were employed in them, but at present there are not more than three hundred, at the north-east corner of the premises is a copper-mill Hats are also manufactured here, and there is a silk-throwing establishment

The living is a perpetual curacy, in the archdeaconry of Surrey, and diocese of Winchester, endowed with £600 private benefaction, £200 royal bounty, and £1200 parliamentary grant, and in the patronage of E H Bond, Esq The church, dedicated to St Mary, is in the Norman style of architecture, with later insertions, it was erected by the founder of the abbey, in the twelfth century the arms of England and those of the priory, painted on glass, decorate the chancel window There is a place of worship for Independents An almshouse for six poor women was founded, in 1656, by Rowland Wilson, merchant of London, and endowed with £24 per annum, but it has become private property, and the endowment is lost. In 1687, William Rutlish bequeathed an estate, directing the proceeds to be applied in apprenticing poor children of either sex, the present income of this charity is about £96 per annum. Merton place, having been attached to the rectorial estate for more than two centuries, was separated from it some years ago, and became the residence and property of Admiral Lord Nelson Thomas à Becket was educated here under the first prior, and Walter de Merton a native of this place, also and received his education in the priory Merton confers the title of viscount on the family of Nelson.

MESHAW, a parish in the hundred of WITHERIDGE, county of DEVON, 5¼ miles (S E by S) from South Molton, containing 163 inhabitants The living is a discharged rectory, in the archdeaconry of Barnstaple, and diocese of Exeter, rated in the king s books at £7 4, endowed with £200 private benefaction, and £200 royal bounty G H Wollaston, Esq was patron in 1777 The church is dedicated to St John the Baptist

MESSING, a parish in the Witham division of the hundred of LEXDEN, county of ESSEX, 5½ miles (S E) from Great Coggeshall, containing 705 inhabitants The living is a vicarage, in the archdeaconry of Colchester, and diocese of London, rated in the king s books at £8, and in the patronage of the Earl of Verulam The church is dedicated to All Saints the east window is decorated with paintings of the six Christian graces, supposed to have been the gift of the Chibbornes, in the reign of James I Sir William de Messing, the founder, is represented in the north wall by a recumbent wooden figure of a Knight Templar A school for the education of poor children has a small endowment

MESSINGHAM, a parish in the eastern division of the wapentake of MANLEY, parts of LINDSEY, county of LINCOLN, 7½ miles (W by S) from Glandford Bridge, containing, with the township of East Butterwick, 1103 inhabitants   The living is a discharged vicarage, with the vicarage of Bottesford, in the archdeaconry of Stow, and diocese of Lincoln, rated in the king's books at £10, and in the alternate patronage of the Bishop, and Dean and Chapter, of Lincoln   The church is dedicated to the Holy Trinity   There is a place of worship for Wesleyan Methodists

METFIELD, a parish in the hundred of HOXNE, county of SUFFOLK, 3¾ miles (S E by E) from Harleston, containing 682 inhabitants   The living is a perpetual curacy, in the archdeaconry of Suffolk, and diocese of Norwich, and in the patronage of the Parishioners   The church is dedicated to St John the Baptist

METHAM, a township in the parish of HOWDEN, wapentake of HOWDENSHIRE, East riding of the county of YORK, 5 miles (S E by E) from Howden, containing 45 inhabitants   A Roman pottery, including fragments of urns and other vessels, has been discovered here, about a mile from which the ancient Roman military way passes

METHERINGHAM, a parish in the second division of the wapentake of LANGOE, parts of KESTEVEN, county of LINCOLN, 10½ miles (N) from Sleaford, containing 626 inhabitants   The living is a discharged vicarage, in the archdeaconry and diocese of Lincoln, rated in the king's books at £8 0 10, and in the patronage of the Marquis of Bristol   The church is dedicated to St. Wilfrid.   There is a place of worship for Wesleyan Methodists.

METHLEY, a parish in the lower division of the wapentake of AGBRIGG, West riding of the county of YORK, 5½ miles (N E. by N) from Wakefield, containing 1499 inhabitants.   The living is a rectory, in the archdeaconry and diocese of York, rated in the king's books at £25 8 6½, and in the patronage of the King, as Duke of Lancaster   The church, dedicated to St Oswald, is principally in the later English and decorated styles, and contains several ancient and splendid monuments, the most curious is a mutilated statue of the patron saint, over the south door, now, from its great antiquity, in a state of rapid decay   There is a place of worship for Wesleyan Methodists   A small sum has been given for the instruction of children, and there are eight almshouses for widows   The river Calder bounds this parish on the south, and unites with the Aire on the east

METHOP, a joint township with Ulpha, in the parish of BEETHAM, KENDAL ward, county of WESTMORLAND, 5½ miles (E N E) from Cartmel, containing, with Ulpha, 82 inhabitants.   There is a small sum for the instruction of children   The mouth of the Kent bounds this parish on the south-east

METHWOLD, a parish in the hundred of GRIMSHOE, county of NORFOLK, 4 miles (S S E) from Stoke-Ferry, containing 1164 inhabitants   The living is a discharged vicarage, annexed to the rectory of Cranwick, in the archdeaconry of Norfolk, and diocese of Norwich, rated in the king's books at £9 1 3   The church, dedicated to St George, is a handsome structure with an embattled tower   There is a place of worship for Wesleyan Methodists   Here was formerly

a market, and a fair is still held on the 23rd of April   In the neighbourhood is a celebrated warren, which formerly contained a great number of rabbits, the fur of which was in considerable repute

METTINGHAM, a parish in the hundred of WANGFORD, county of SUFFOLK, 2 miles (E) from Bungay, containing 349 inhabitants   The living is a discharged vicarage, in the archdeaconry of Suffolk, and diocese of Norwich, rated in the king's books at £6 17 3½   Mrs Safford was patroness in 1824   The church is dedicated to All Saints   In the reign of Richard II, a master and chaplains were translated, by royal license, from the college of Raveningham, in Norfolk, to Mettingham castle, in 1535, their revenue amounted to £202 7 5   The navigable river Waveney runs on the north of this parish

METTON, a parish in the northern division of the hundred of ERPINGHAM, county of NORFOLK, 3½ miles (S S W) from Cromer, containing 101 inhabitants   The living is a discharged rectory, with that of Felbrigg, in the archdeaconry of Norfolk, and diocese of Norwich, rated in the king's books at £7   The church is dedicated to St Andrew

MEUX, a township in the parish of WAGHEN, or WAWN, middle division of the wapentake of HOLDERNESS, East riding of the county of YORK, 5½ miles (E) from Beverley, containing 74 inhabitants   A Cistercian abbey was founded here, in 1150, by William le Gros, Earl of Albemarle, and dedicated to the Virgin, the establishment consisted of fifty monks, whose revenue, at the dissolution, amounted to £445 10 5

MEVAGISSEY, a parish in the eastern division of the hundred of POWDER, county of CORNWALL, 6 miles (E S. E) from Grampound, containing 2450 inhabitants.   The living is a vicarage, in the archdeaconry of Cornwall, and diocese of Exeter, rated in the king's books at £6 4 2, and in the patronage of the Earl of Mount-Edgcumbe.   The church is dedicated to St Mevan and St Issi, whence the name of the parish   There are places of worship for Independents and Wesleyan Methodists   This parish borders on a bay of the same name in the English channel

MEWAN (ST), a parish in the eastern division of the hundred of POWDER, county of CORNWALL, 1 mile (W by S) from St. Austell, containing 1174 inhabitants   The living is a rectory, in the archdeaconry of Cornwall, and diocese of Exeter, rated in the king's books at £10   The Rev William Hocker was patron in 1801   The church is dedicated to St Mewan   At Polgooth, which is partly in this parish, is a celebrated tin mine

MEXBOROUGH, a parish partly in the liberty of ST PETER of YORK, but chiefly in the southern division of the wapentake of STRAFFORTH and TICKHILL, West riding of the county of YORK, comprising the townships of Dannaby and Mexborough, and containing 1006 inhabitants, of which number, 865 are in the township of Mexborough, 6¼ miles (N E by N) from Rotherham   The living is a perpetual curacy, in the peculiar jurisdiction and patronage of the Archdeacon of York, endowed with £200 private benefaction, £200 royal bounty, and £1500 parliamentary grant   A celebrated battle was anciently fought at this place, then called Maizebel, between Aurelius Ambrosius and the Saxons, in which the latter were defeated

MICHAEL (ST), or MIDSHALL, a borough (formerly a market town) partly in the parish of St Enoder, and partly in that of Newlyn, hundred of Pyder, county of Cornwall, 36 miles (S W by W) from Launceston, and 249 (W S W) from London   The population is returned with the parishes   The ancient name of this place was *Modeshole*, under which appellation John de Arundell, in 1301, certified his right to a market and fair here, which had been previously granted to Walter de Raleigh   The town is very inconsiderable, consisting only of a few houses, several of which are uninhabited ,   the market has been long disused   fairs are held July 28th and October 15th, the latter chiefly for sheep, of which from three thousand to four thousand are generally offered for sale   A portreeve is presented annually by the jury at the court leet of the high lord, who must be one of the five chief tenants, or mesne-lords   The borough first sent members to parliament in the reign of Edward VI   the right of election is in the portreeve and mesne, or deputy, lords of the manor (who are capable of being portreeves), and the inhabitants of the borough paying scot and lot the number of voters is eight , the portreeve is the returning officer   The influence of Viscount Falmouth, and of the representative of Sir Christopher Hawkins, Bart , is predominant

MICHAEL (ST), a parish partly in the borough of St Alban s, but chiefly in the hundred of Cashio, or liberty of St Alban s, county of Hertford, ¾ of a mile (W by N) from St Alban s, containing 1370 inhabitants, of which number, 453 are in the borough of St Alban s   The living is a discharged vicarage, in the archdeaconry of St Alban's, and diocese of London, rated in the king s books at £10 1 3 , and in the patronage of the Earl of Verulam   The church, though situated in the town of St Alban s, and within the walls of the ancient city of Verulam, is without the limits of the borough   it was erected by Ulsinus, the sixth abbot, and has a square embattled tower , the chancel is built principally of Roman tiles, from the ruins of Verulam, and attached to the south side of the nave is a chapel An almshouse for two poor widows was founded, in 1624, by Roger Pemberton, who endowed it with about £10 per annum

MICHAEL (ST), a parish in the hundred of Amounderness, county palatine of Lancaster, 3¾ miles (S W by S) from Garstang, comprising the chapelry of Wood Plumpton, and the townships of Great Eccleston, Elswick, Inskip with Sowerby, Out Rawcliffe and Upper Rawcliffe with Tarnacar, and containing 4553 inhabitants   The living is a discharged vicarage, in the archdeaconry of Richmond, and diocese of Chester, rated in the king s books at £10 17 6 Joseph Hornby, Esq   was patron in 1825   The church, which was superseded by the present small structure, built in the time of Henry VIII , was one of three erected in this district soon after Christianity was introduced into the north of England.   The parish is situated upon the navigable river Wyre, the mouth of which forms a fine harbour, noted for its security Here, in 1651, the Earl of Derby disembarked from the Isle of Man, with three hundred other adherents to the House of Stuart   Joseph Fielding, in 1808, conveyed £60, and Elizabeth Cromleholme, in 1813, £200, towards a school, in which about fifty children are educated

MICHAEL (ST), a parish adjacent to the city, and within the liberty of the soke, of Winchester, Fawley division of the county of Southampton, containing 499 inhabitants   The living is a discharged rectory, united to that of St Swithin, in the archdeaconry and diocese of Winchester, rated in the king's books at £5 17 11 , and endowed with £500 private benefaction, and £800 royal bounty

MICHAEL (ST) BEDWARDINE, a parish in the lower division of the hundred of Oswaldslow, county of Worcester, forming part of the city of Worcester, and containing, with the extra-parochial district of College Precincts, 793 inhabitants   The living is a discharged rectory, in the archdeaconry and diocese of Worcester, rated in the king's books at £7 12 1 , and endowed with £1000 royal bounty   The King, by lapse, presented in 1799

MICHAEL (ST) CARHAISE, a parish in the eastern division of the hundred of Powder, county of Cornwall, 3¾ miles (S E by E) from Tregoney, containing 174 inhabitants   The living is a rectory, with the perpetual curacies of St Denis and St Stephen, in the archdeaconry of Cornwall, and diocese of Exeter, rated in the king s books at £27 10 7½ , and in the patronage of Lord and Lady Grenville   The church is dedicated to St Michael   There are also the ruins of an ancient chapel   The parish is bounded on the south by the English channel, where is Port Luny bay

MICHAEL'S (ST) MOUNT, an extra - parochial liberty, in the hundred of Penwith, county of Cornwall, ¾ of a mile (S) from Marazion, containing 223 inhabitants   This mount, believed in the remote ages of antiquity to have been situated in a wood, consists of a pyramidal mass of granite rocks rising out of the sea, opposite to the town of Marazion, and is connected with the main land by a narrow bank of pebbles, which is overflowed by the tide   Its original name, in the Cornish dialect, signified " the grey or hoary rock in the wood, which was subsequently changed to its present appellation , this, according to monkish legends, being deduced from the appearance of St Michael, its patron saint, to some hermits who resided here, which event led to the foundation of a monastery   It has been supposed that this is the island called *Ixtis*, mentioned by Diodorus Siculus, whither the tin, when refined and cast into cubic ingots by the Britons who dwelt near the promontory of *Belerium*, was carried in carts over an isthmus dry only at low water   The time of its consecration to religious purposes is unknown , but a priory of Benedictine monks, afterwards changed to Gilbertines, was founded here previously to the year 1044, at which period Edward the Confessor gave the mount, with all its buildings and appendages, to that community   by this charter it is evident that there was a castle, as well as a convent, on the mount In 1070, indulgences were granted by Pope Gregory VII to all persons who should visit the church of St Michael at the Mount with alms and oblations , hence it became a great resort for pilgrims   In the reign of Richard I , Henry de Pomeroy, an adherent of John, Earl of Cornwall, afterwards king of England, took possession of the mount by stratagem, during the king s imprisonment in Austria, fortified it, and continued to hold it even after the return of that monarch , but on the approach of the army of Archbishop Hubert Walter, aided by the sheriff and a civil force, he surrendered at discretion : the king then restored the convent to the Gilbertines, and placed a small garrison in the castle. After the battle of Barnet, in 1471, John, Earl of Oxford, having fled into Wales, assembled a party of soldiers, and crossed over with them to the Cornish coast : under the assumed disguise of pilgrims, they gained admission into the castle, and soon overpowered the small garrison which defended it. Sir John Arundel, the sheriff, was first sent against the earl, but was repulsed and slain in a vigorous assault upon the castle : others were then commissioned to conduct the siege, which, having continued from September till February, terminated in the surrender of the fortress, on condition that the lives of the earl and his adherents should be spared. In 1498, Perkin Warbeck landed at Whitsand bay, and having been admitted into the castle by the monks, who favoured his cause, put it into a state of defence, and during his march to Bodmin, left his wife, the Lady Catherine Gordon, at the mount, as a secure asylum.

The priory of St. Michael, being a cell to the abbey of Mont St. Michel, in Normandy, was seized as an Alien priory by Henry V., during the war with France : it was first given to King's College, Cambridge, and afterwards to the nunnery of Sion in Middlesex, to which it continued to be attached till the dissolution, when the revenue was valued at £110. 12. In 1533, it was given, with all its revenue, to Humphrey Arundel, Esq., of Lanherne, but he having headed a rebellion in Cornwall about 1549, it was seized for the king, and subsequently granted on lease to the sheriff of the county. In 1642, it was fortified for the king, and the Duke of Hamilton was subsequently imprisoned within its walls : it was at last surrendered to the parliament in 1646 ; and after the Restoration it became the property of the family of the present proprietor, Sir John St. Aubyn. The mount consists of granite, nearly bare of soil, and is extremely steep and craggy. The occasional residence of Sir John St. Aubyn is on the summit of the rock, and partakes of the character both of a fortress and a monastery, being castellated and embattled : the dining-room was the refectory of the convent ; and the chapel has been recently fitted up in the ancient English style, for the performance of divine service in one of the angles, at the summit of the chapel tower, which crowns the whole mass of building. On this craggy height are the remains of a moor-stone lantern, formerly used as a beacon for mariners, and vulgarly called St. Michael's chair : the ascent is dangerous, but a superstitious notion connected with having sat therein induces occasional visitors to attempt the adventurous path. The entire height of the mount, from the level of the sea to the platform of the chapel tower, is two hundred and thirty-one feet ; the circumference of the island, which comprises about seven acres of land, is about three quarters of a mile : at the foot of the rock is a wharf, and near it a considerable village inhabited chiefly by fishermen. There is likewise a small harbour with a pier, which was rebuilt by Sir John St. Aubyn in 1727, where about forty vessels may find shelter. The principal imports consist of timber from Norway, coal, &c. ; the exports are copper-ore, china-clay, and pilchards.

MICHAEL (ST.) PENKEVIL, a parish in the western division of the hundred of POWDER, county

of CORNWALL, 5 miles (W. S. W.) from Tregoney, containing 167 inhabitants. The living is a rectory, in the archdeaconry of Cornwall, and diocese of Exeter, rated in the king's books at £9. 14. 2., and in the patronage of the Earl of Falmouth. The church, an ancient edifice adjoining the park, contains a handsome monument, by Rysbrach, to the memory of Admiral Boscawen, a distinguished naval commander, who died in 1761.

MICHAEL-CHURCH, a chapelry in the parish of TRETIRE, lower division of the hundred of WORMELOW, county of HEREFORD, 7 miles (W. N. W.) from Ross. The population is returned with the parish.

MICHAEL-CHURCH (ST.), a parish in the northern division of the hundred of PETHERTON, county of SOMERSET, 5¼ miles (S.) from Bridg-water, containing 50 inhabitants. The living is a vicarage, in the archdeaconry of Taunton, and diocese of Bath and Wells, endowed with £800 royal bounty, and in the patronage of Sir J. P. Acland, Bart.

MICHAEL-CHURCH-ESKLEY, a parish in the hundred of EWYASLACY, county of HEREFORD, 10 miles (S. E.) from Hay, containing 424 inhabitants. The living is a perpetual curacy, in the archdeaconry of Brecon, and diocese of St. David's, endowed with £200 private benefaction, and £600 royal bounty, and in the patronage of the Bishop of Hereford. The church is dedicated to St. Michael. The river Eskley runs through the parish. A few of the inhabitants are employed in the manufacture of woollen goods. A free school has been endowed, by Mrs. Thomas, with lands now producing an annual income of £30, for teaching four poor children of this parish, four of Crasswall, four of Llanveynoe, and four of Peterchurch.

MICHAELSTONE-VEDOW, a parish in the upper division of the hundred of WENTLLOOG, county of MONMOUTH, 5¼ miles (W. S. W.) from Newport, containing 197 inhabitants. The living is a rectory, in the archdeaconry and diocese of Llandaff, rated in the king's books at £7. 12. 3½., and in the patronage of Charles Kemys Tynte, Esq. The church is dedicated to St. Michael.

MICHAELSTOW, a parish in the hundred of LESNEWTH, county of CORNWALL, 3¼ miles (S. W. by S.) from Camelford, containing 216 inhabitants. The living is a discharged rectory, in the archdeaconry of Cornwall, and diocese of Exeter, rated in the king's books at £10. 13. 9., and in the patronage of the King, as Duke of Cornwall. The church is dedicated to St. Michael. The parish is bounded on the east by the river Camel. At Helsbury are the mount and other earth-works of an ancient castle, called the Beacon.

MICKFIELD, a parish in the hundred of BOSMERE and CLAYDON, county of SUFFOLK, 2¾ miles (W. S. W.) from Debenham, containing 246 inhabitants. The living is a rectory, in the archdeaconry of Suffolk, and diocese of Norwich, rated in the king's books at £9. 11. 0½., and in the patronage of the Rev. Maltyward Simpson. The church is dedicated to St. Andrew.

MICKLEFIELD, a township in the parish of SHERBURN, upper division of the wapentake of BARKSTONE-ASH, West riding of the county of YORK, 6½ miles (N. N. W.) from Ferry-Bridge, containing 196 inhabitants.

MICKLEHAM, a parish in the second division of the hundred of COPTHORNE, county of SURREY, 2 miles

(S. by E.) from Leatherhead, containing 505 inhabitants. The living is a rectory, in the archdeaconry of Surrey, and diocese of Winchester, rated in the king's books at £13. Henry Burmester, Esq. was patron in 1813. The church, dedicated to St. Michael, is principally in the early style of English architecture, and has lately received an addition of two hundred sittings, of which, one hundred are free, the Incorporated Society for the enlargement of churches and chapels having granted £150 towards defraying the expense.

MICKLEOVER, a parish in the hundred of Mor-LESTON and LITCHURCH, county of DERBY, 3½ miles (W. S. W.) from Derby, containing, with the chapelries of Findern and Littleover, 1373 inhabitants. The living is a vicarage, in the archdeaconry of Derby, and diocese of Lichfield and Coventry, rated in the king's books at £9. 11. 5½., and in the patronage of Lord Scarsdale. The church is dedicated to All Saints. There are places of worship for Wesleyan Methodists and Unitarians. John Alsop, in 1715, founded a free school, and endowed it with lands now let for about £60 per annum. There are also two smaller sums appropriated to the education of the poor, viz., the interest of £200 bequeathed by Robert Newton, in 1784, and £1 a year by John Erpe.

MICKLETHWAITE, a joint township with Bingley, in the parish of BINGLEY, upper division of the wapentake of SKYRACK, West riding of the county of YORK, 3½ miles (E. by S.) from Keighley. The population is returned with Bingley.

MICKLETON, a parish in the upper division of the hundred of KIFTSGATE, county of GLOUCESTER, 2½ miles (N. by E.) from Chipping-Campden, containing, with the hamlets of Lower and Upper Clapton, and Hitcoat-Batrim, 574 inhabitants. The living is a vicarage, consolidated with that of Ebrington, in the archdeaconry and diocese of Gloucester, rated in the king's books at £9. 14. 4½., and in the patronage of the Crown. The church, dedicated to St. Laurence, is partly Norman and partly of later date: attached to it is a school-room, of similar architecture, founded and endowed, in 1513, by Richard Porter, Esq., for teaching poor children. Sunday schools for both sexes have been also established. Richard Graves, a divine, and miscellaneous writer, was born here; he died in 1804.

MICKLETON, a township in the parish of Ro-MALD-KIRK, western division of the wapentake of GIL-LING, North riding of the county of YORK, 8 miles (N. W.) from Barnard-Castle, containing 356 inhabitants.

MICKLEWAITE-GRANGE, an extra-parochial liberty, in the upper division of the wapentake of BARK-STONE-ASH, West riding of the county of YORK, ½ a mile (S. by W.) from Wetherby, containing 83 inhabitants.

MICKLEY, a chapelry in the parish of OVINGHAM, eastern division of TINDALE ward, county of NORTH-UMBERLAND, 11 miles (E. by S.) from Hexham, containing 178 inhabitants. A chapel of ease was erected in 1824, at Hall-yards, near the village, by W. B. Wrightson, Esq., who had three years previously built a school-room and a house for the master.

MIDDLE, a parish partly in the liberties of SHREWS-BURY, but chiefly in the hundred of PIMHILL, county of SALOP, 8 miles (N. by W.) from Shrewsbury, containing, with the chapelry of Hadnall-Ease, 1190 inhabitants. The living is a rectory, in the archdeaconry of Salop,

and diocese of Lichfield and Coventry, rated in the king's books at £12. 7. 3½., and in the patronage of the Trustees of the late Earl of Bridgewater. The church is dedicated to St. Peter. Here are remains of Middle castle, which was built by Lord L'Estrange. Marton Pool, a lake in this parish, covers about ten acres.

MIDDLE-QUARTER, a township in the parish of KIRK-LINTON, or KIRK-LEVINGTON, ESKDALE ward, county of CUMBERLAND, containing 532 inhabitants.

MIDDLE-QUARTER, a township in the parish of KIRKBY-IRELETH, hundred of LONSDALE, north of the sands, county palatine of LANCASTER, 6 miles (N. W.) from Ulverstone, containing 504 inhabitants.

MIDDLEHAM, a parish (formerly a market town) in the western division of the wapentake of HANG, North riding of the county of YORK, 44 miles (N.W. by W) from York, and 234 (N.N.W.) from London, containing 880 inhabitants. The name of this town is said to be derived from its situation in the centre of a number of hamlets. About the year 1190, a splendid castle was built here by Robert Fitz-Ranulph, wherein, according to Stow, Falconbridge, a partisan of Henry VI., was beheaded, in 1471; though Speed says he was executed at Southampton. Edward IV. was confined in this fortress by the Earl of Warwick, but having escaped, he levied an army, and obtained a decisive victory over his opponent, who lost his life at the battle of Barnet. King Edward subsequently gave the castle to his brother Richard, Duke of Gloucester, whose only son Edward, afterwards Prince of Wales, was born here. The remains of this fabric stand upon a rocky eminence near the town; the ancient Norman keep is surrounded by a quadrangular building, measuring two hundred and ten feet by one hundred and seventy-five, and flanked by a square tower at each angle. The constableship, now merely a nominal office, is vested in the Duke of Leeds. The town is situated on a gentle eminence rising from the river Ure: the houses are indifferently built, and the streets are neither lighted nor paved, but the inhabitants are well supplied with water from springs. About half a mile from it is Middleham moor, a noted place for training horses, either for the field or the race-course. Wool-combing affords employment to a few persons, but the majority are employed in agriculture. The market, now disused, was on Monday. Fairs are held on Easter-Monday and Whit-Monday, and November 5th and 6th, for live stock, &c. Two constables are appointed at the court leet, which is held annually. The petty sessions for the western division of the wapentake of Hang are held here. The living forms a deanery of itself, and is a royal peculiar, rated in the king's books at £15. 9. 4½., and in the patronage of the Crown. The church, which is dedicated to St. Mary and St. Alkeld, is a neat edifice, in the ancient style of English architecture. It was made collegiate by Richard III., when Duke of Gloucester, for a dean, six chaplains, four clerks, and six choristers: the incumbent retains the title of dean, and is installed with the usual ceremonies; he possesses the power of proving wills, and some other rights of ecclesiastical jurisdiction, within his parish, together with a court, an official, and a seal of office: but, owing to the peculiarity of his situation, as being exempt from the jurisdiction of both ordinary and metropolitan, he is unable to give a title for holy orders. There are places of worship for Primitive and Wesleyan Methodists. A small sum was given by William Tennant, in 1792, for the instruction of poor children; and it is now in contemplation to erect a National school.

MIDDLEHAM (BISHOP'S), a parish in the north-eastern division of Stockton ward, county palatine of Durham, comprising the townships of Bishop's Middleham, Cornforth, Garmondsway-Moor, Mainsforth, and Thrislington, and containing 827 inhabitants, of which number, 404 are in the township of Bishop's Middleham, 9 miles (S. S. E.) from Durham. The living is a vicarage, in the archdeaconry and diocese of Durham, rated in the king's books at £4. 19. 2., and in the patronage of the Crown. The church is dedicated to St. Michael. The village is built on the sides of two hills ascending from a deep vale, through which the road runs, and abounding in limestone. At Cornforth are paper-mills and tile-kilns. A halmote court for the manor is held once in six months, at Middleham, Cornforth, and Sedgefield, alternately, for the recovery of debts under 40s. There is a school-room, built by subscription in 1770, but it is not endowed. The castle was one of the principal residences of the Bishops of Durham, from the Conquest till the end of the fourteenth century: it stood on a lofty eminence, where its site may still be traced by the foundations and some fragments of masonry; an old barn, on the opposite side of the road, is supposed to have been part of the out-offices.

MIDDLEHOPE, a township in the parish of Diddlebury, hundred of Munslow, county of Salop, containing 180 inhabitants.

MIDDLE-MEAD, a hamlet in the parish of Little Baddow, hundred of Chelmsford, though locally in the hundred of Dengie, county of Essex, 5 miles (E. N. E.) from Chelmsford, containing 202 inhabitants.

MIDDLENEY, a tything in the parish of Drayton, hundred of Abdick and Bulstone, county of Somerset, 2¾ miles (S. by W.) from Langport, containing 25 inhabitants.

MIDDLESBOROUGH, a parish partly within the liberty of St. Peter of York, but chiefly in the western division of the liberty of Langbaurgh, North riding of the county of York, comprising the townships of Linthorp and Middlesborough, and containing 236 inhabitants, of which number, 40 are in the township of Middlesborough, 5½ miles (E. N. E.) from Stockton upon Tees. The living is a perpetual curacy, in the archdeaconry of Cleveland, and diocese of York, endowed with £600 royal bounty, and in the patronage of Thomas Hustler, Esq. An ancient chapel, dedicated to St. Hilda, with certain lands adjacent, were, in the reign of Henry I., given by Robert de Bruse to Whitby abbey, on condition that a cell of Benedictine monks to that house should be founded here, which was valued, in the 26th of Henry VIII., at £21. 3. 8. per annum: of the chapel no vestiges remain, but the cemetery is still used as a burial-ground.

MIDDLESCEUGH, a hamlet in that part of the parish of St. Mary's, Carlisle, which is in Leath ward, county of Cumberland, 6½ miles (E. N. E.) from Hesket-Newmarket, containing, with the hamlet of Braithwaite, 221 inhabitants.

MIDDLESEX, an inland county, bounded on the south by Surrey and a very small part of Kent, from

both which it is separated by the river Thames; on the east by Essex, from which it is separated by the river Lea; on the north by Hertfordshire; and on the west by Buckinghamshire, from which it is separated by the river Coln. It extends from 51° 22′ to 51° 42′ (N. Lat.), and from 2′ (E. Lon.) to 31′ (W. Lon.), and contains about one hundred and eighty thousand four hundred and eighty acres, or two hundred and eighty-two square miles. The population, in 1821, was, including London, 1,144,531. At the time of Cæsar's invasion, this part of the British territory, together with that now forming the county of Essex, was inhabited by the Trinobantes, the first British tribe that submitted to the Romans; and on the final reduction of Britain to the condition of a Roman province, it was included in the division called Flavia Cæsariensis. The name is slightly corrupted from the Anglo-Saxon *Middel-Seaxe*, signifying the country of the Middle Saxons; this portion of the English territory having lain in the centre of the early Saxon sovereignties established in South Britain. It did not, however, form a distinct kingdom, but was included in that of the East Saxons, established in Essex about the year 530 and shortly after extended over this county. The history of Middlesex is little else than the history of the metropolis itself, a summary of which will be found under its proper head. It is only necessary to specify here a few of the most remarkable movements and occurrences which have taken place in it without the limits of the capital. In 879, the Danish army wintered at Fulham; and in 1016, Canute was defeated at Brentford, by Edmund Ironside. In 1217, at Hounslow, a conference was held between four peers and twenty knights, on the part of Louis the Dauphin, and the same number of nobles and knights on the part of the young king Henry III. In 1264, at Isleworth, the palace of Richard, King of the Romans, and Earl of Cornwall, brother to Henry III., was destroyed by the inhabitants of London, under Sir Hugh Spencer. In 1386, the Duke of Gloucester, and the Earls of Arundel, Warwick, and Derby, with other nobles, assembled at Hornsey, to compel Richard II. to dismiss his favourite, Robert de Vere, Duke of Ireland. During the insurrection under Jack Cade, in 1450, the Essex insurgents encamped at Mile-End; and, in 1461, the Kentish insurgents beheaded, at Highgate, Thomas Thorpe, Baron of the Exchequer. May 4th, 1483, the young king, Edward V., accompanied by the Dukes of Gloucester and Buckingham, who had obtained possession of his person, was met at Hornsey by the lord mayor and citizens, and conducted to the episcopal palace in the city. It was at Sion-house, in 1553, that Lady Jane Grey reluctantly accepted the crown, and was thence conducted with great pomp to the tower. In 1586, at Uxendon, near Harrow, Anthony Babington and his fellow conspirators against Queen Elizabeth were arrested. In 1603, on the accession of James I., that sovereign was met, on his way to London, at Stamford-hill by the lord mayor and citizens, and conducted with great pomp to the Charter-house. November 12th, 1642, at the commencement of the great civil war, the parliamentarians were defeated at Brentford, by Charles I., and the eccentric John Lilburne, with four hundred men, was made prisoner. At Uxbridge, in January 1645, the fruitless negociation between the king's and the parliamentary commissioners was set on foot, and carried on for eighteen days. August 4th, 1647, General Fairfax had his head-quarters at Isleworth, and there received the parliamentarian commissioners; and in the same year, the king was kept in confinement at Hampton-Court, from the 24th of August until his escape on the 11th of November. In 1651, on the 21st of September, Oliver Cromwell, returning from the battle of Worcester, was met at Acton with a congratulatory address, and accompanied to London, by the Lord President and Council of State, many members of both houses of parliament, and the Lord Mayor and aldermen of London, forming, altogether, a train of more than three hundred coaches. Lastly, on the 20th of April, 1814, Louis XVIII., accompanied by the Duchess d'Angoulême, from their asylum at Hartwell in Buckinghamshire, was met at Stanmore by the Prince Regent, and conducted in triumph to London, on his restoration to the French throne.

This county is included in the diocese of London, and province of Canterbury, and forms a deanery and archdeaconry, comprising, with the exception of those parishes in the cities of London and Westminster, and their liberties, which are given in a tabular form under the head of London, seventy parishes, of which twenty-five are rectories, thirty-one vicarages, and fourteen perpetual curacies. The civil division is into the hundreds of Edmonton, Elthorne, Gore, Isleworth, Ossulstone (including the divisions of Finsbury, Holborn, and the Tower), and Spelthorne; and the liberties of the cities of London and Westminster. Within the county are, the city of London (locally), the borough (commonly called the city) of Westminster, and the market towns of Brentford, Staines, and Uxbridge. Two knights are returned to parliament for the shire, four citizens for the city of London, and two burgesses for the borough of Westminster. The shrievalty of Middlesex, being united with that of the city of London, is described under the latter head. The assizes are held eight times a year at the Old Bailey, in London; and the quarter sessions, four times originally, and four times by adjournment, at the sessions-house, on Clerkenwell-green. There are two hundred acting magistrates. The rates raised in the county for the year ending March 25th, 1827, amounted to £666,418. 5.; the expenditure to £711,874. 16., of which £612,147. 14. was applied to the relief of the poor.

The gently undulating surface of the greater part of this small county is peculiarly suited to the general purposes of agriculture; and although it contains little scenery that can properly be termed picturesque, yet these inequalities contribute greatly to its healthfulness and beauty. Middlesex is also diversified with plantations and meandering streams, besides innumerable villas with ornamented grounds and lawns. The northern border of the county is high ground, which, by the shelter it affords, adds considerably to the fertility of the other parts. The principal elevations are, Harrow hill, the hills of Highwood, Hendon, and Barnet, one between Barnet and Elstree, Brockley hill, and the Highgate and Hampstead hills: the summits of these are of nearly equal height, being about four hundred feet above the level of high water mark in the Thames. The most extensive prospects are, that from Harrow hill over the valley of the Thames, those from Hampstead and Highgate hills, including distinct views

of the northern side of the metropolis, and those from Muswell hill, over the north-eastern side of London, into Surrey and Kent, and over the valley of the Lea into Essex. One of the most striking nearer views of London is that from Primrose hill over the Regent's Park, with the splendid new ranges of building that skirt its base, and the rest of the north-western side of the metropolis All the land to the south of the road passing from Brentford, through Hounslow, to Longford, is very nearly an entire flat, the greater part of which is less than ten feet above the level of the Thames, which runs along the whole southern side of it. From Staines, by Ashford and Hanworth commons, to Twickenham, a distance of seven miles and a half, is another flat, lying from ten to twenty feet above the surface of the Thames. From Brentford, along the borders of the Thames, to London, is also an extensive level, chiefly employed in the production of vegetables for the London market; as is also another tract on the north-east side of the town. Round the first milestone on the Kingsland road is an extent of upwards of one thousand acres, the surface of which has been lowered from four to ten feet, by the clay having been dug and made into bricks: a great portion of this is now covered with houses. In the western part of the county, stretching chiefly to the north of Hounslow heath, is a considerable tract of arable land, and another in the north-eastern part of it; but by far the greater portion of the land is meadow or pasture. Upon several of the hills, where the soil is naturally barren, particularly those of Hampstead and Highgate, and at Hadley, the ground is, nevertheless, of great value, on account of the fine situations for building.

The climate in general is healthy, owing to the greater part of the soil being naturally dry, and the less elevated tracts well drained, and consequently free from noxious vapours. The fires of London, from their immense number, have a sensible effect upon the surrounding atmosphere, which they heat and rarefy. In London the air, when dry, is always loaded with, and the atmosphere often obscured by, smoke, containing soot arising from the pit coal commonly consumed. With cultivation and the manure procured from London, the soil has every where been ameliorated, so that, in most places, it assumes the appearance of loam, though varying in quality. The summits of most of the highest hills consist of sand and gravel, frequently intermixed with loam. Hampstead hill is composed of eight or ten feet of yellow iron-stained sand, with some loam and round flints, under which is a pure white sand of considerable depth. The soil of all that portion of the county lying between the road from Hounslow to Colnbrook, on the north, and the river Thames on the south, is sandy, or dry turnip and barley land, generally from eighteen inches to two feet deep, resting on a bed of gravel, or small flints, of six, eight, or ten feet in thickness, under which is a leaden-coloured tenacious earth, of great depth, used by tile-makers. On the eastern side of the county also, the soil is of the same light nature, from six inches to two feet deep, the gravel of small flints, underneath which, being used for the repairing of the roads, can only be dug to the depth of from two to five feet, as it then assumes the appearance of a quicksand, so watery as to prevent all deeper digging. All the land between the

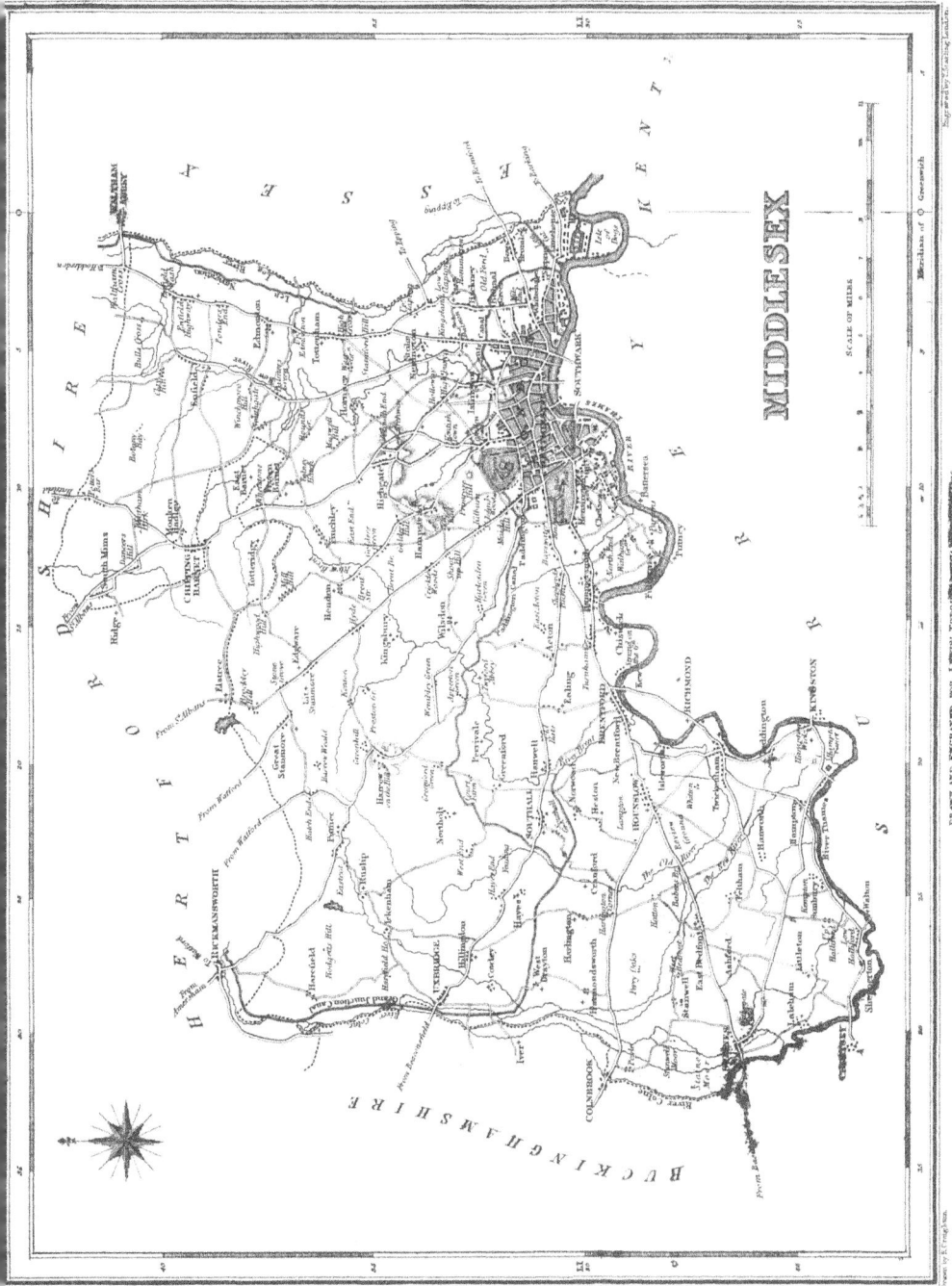

MIDDLESEX

SCALE OF MILES

Meridian of ⊙ Greenwich

DRAWN AND ENGRAVED FOR LEWIS' TOPOGRAPHICAL DICTIONARY.

Colnbrook and Uxbridge roads, from London to the west of Hanwell and Hounslow, and the level tract on the north side of the Thames, from Twickenham down to Westminster, have a good sandy loam, which, in different parts, has been highly enriched by cultivation; the substrata of this are the same as those of the sandy tract first mentioned. The soil around Chiswick varies from a strong to a light sandy loam, and from a rich and fertile to a white and sharp sand and gravel: the district around Fulham consists of a light black and fertile soil. All the land from Ruislip and Ickenham, on the west, to Greenford, Apperton, and Harrow, on the east; and between Pinner, on the north, and Northcote, on the south, together with that about South Mimms, is composed of strong loam. The level between Islington, Hampstead, and Hornsey, is also of the same kind, and very productive. Loamy clay, commonly called clay, is to be found in this county generally on the tops of the lower hills, and on the sides of all, but hardly in any other situation.

The greater part of the arable land is in the common fields; the rest consists of such parts of the said fields as have, at no distant time, been enclosed under various acts of parliament, as at Stanwell, and on Enfield Chase. The total amount is about fourteen thousand acres, or one-thirteenth of the whole county, which does not produce wheat sufficient to supply one-sixtieth of the inhabitants. The corn cultivated is almost wholly wheat and barley; rye and oats being grown only in very small quantities. Beans, peas, turnips, and cabbages, are also commonly cultivated. About ten thousand acres of land are employed in the growth of wheat, the produce varying from ten to upwards of forty bushels per acre; and about four thousand acres are annually sown with barley, the average produce of which is about thirty-two bushels. About three thousand acres are commonly cropped with beans, which are here cultivated with great advantage: the produce, on an average, is about thirty bushels per acre; some of the better sorts are podded when green, and sent to the London market. Peas annually occupy about three thousand acres, being also well cultivated; the average produce of seed per acre is about thirty bushels: About seven-eighteenths of the county, or seventy thousand acres, consist of upland meadows and pastures, which, from previous cultivation, and the constant and abundant supply of manure obtained from London, have been rendered of the first quality: cattle are turned into these meadows immediately after mowing, but to prevent the ground from being trodden, they are removed on the approach of continued wet weather, the rest of the after-grass being eaten by sheep, which remain upon it until the beginning of February. In different parts of this large tract of grass land, and more especially in the more immediate vicinity of the metropolis, it is more constantly every year, and sometimes twice, or even thrice a year. Very little enclosed land of this kind is pastured. Besides the above, there are, on the borders of the river Lea, some excellent grass lands, comprising altogether about two thousand acres; of which one thousand two hundred, lying in the parishes of Enfield and Edmonton, are enclosed, the rest being divided by land-marks among a great number of proprietors. The common meadows are opened for the reception of the cattle of every inha-

bitant of their respective parishes, from the 12th of August until the 5th of April in the following year, when the cattle are taken off, and the ground is soon after prepared for a crop of hay, which it yields in July. This tract is frequently flooded in winter, and sometimes in summer, the water, in consequence of the interruptions which it meets with in the lower part of its course towards the Thames, remaining long on the ground, and doing much damage to the herbage. The Isle of Dogs, now containing, since the formation of the West India docks, only five hundred acres, lies at the south-eastern corner of the county, and would be overflowed by every tide, were it not for the security of its banks: this is considered to be the richest grass land in the county, and is divided and drained by ditches, which communicate with the Thames, at low water, by means of sluices. On the borders of the Thames above London are also different small tracts of meadow land, which are occasionally laid under water, by means of floods in the river, in all amounting to about one hundred acres. And lastly, on the borders of the river Coln, are extensive meadows and pastures, extending from Staines to Harefield, the soil of which is black, peaty, and tender, and but little elevated above the level of the river, in consequence of which it is much subject to floods, which frequently do considerable damage to the crops, and, when they happen during the hay harvest, sometimes carry the whole away. This tract contains about two thousand five hundred acres, and is partly enclosed, but by far the greater portion consists of what are called *Lammas-fields*, in which the occupiers have the entire produce during only four months in the year. The lands of this county have the peculiar advantage of a ready supply of immense quantities of manure from London; whence are also brought large quantities of soot: chalk is brought from the vicinity of Ware, in Hertfordshire, by the Lea navigation, and delivered at Enfield: good marl is found on the borders of the Thames at Shepperton and on Enfield Chase.

Middlesex is not distinguished by any particular breed of cattle, most of the calves that are bred in it being suckled until they are ten weeks old, and then sold to the butcher. The cows kept for the purpose of supplying the metropolis with milk are of a large size, with short horns, known by the name of "Holderness cattle;" they are bred not only in Yorkshire, in which county is the district whence they take their name, but also in nearly all the adjoining counties, where they are bought by dealers, and brought by them to the fairs and markets in this county, more especially to the market in the Liverpool road, Islington. Many are also purchased in the counties where they are bred, by commission, and forwarded to the cow-keepers in and near London, by whom they are preferred, as giving a greater quantity of milk than any other breed, without reference to the quality of it. The number kept for the supply of London, in the county of Middlesex alone, is between seven and eight thousand. There is not, perhaps, a county in England in which less butter is made: the greater part of the butter consumed in London is brought from Ireland, Yorkshire, Buckinghamshire, and Dorsetshire, the remainder from Cambridge, Norfolk, Essex, and other neighbouring counties. The farmers buy their sheep at the fairs in Wiltshire, Berkshire, and Hampshire, and from dealers in the west country sheep at different fairs and markets : the sheep kept on Hounslow heath, and the adjoining common of Sunbury, were originally from the stock of the above-mentioned counties, but they have much degenerated: the practice of folding them is common. Many early house lambs are fed in the county, the stock from which they are bred being sought with great diligence from all parts of Dorsetshire, and the fairs where such stock is usually sold ; and a great number of grass lambs is reared for the Smithfield market. A very large market for the sale of pigs is held on Hadley common, near Barnet, where great numbers are purchased fat by the pork butchers of London, and to which are brought vast quantities of lean stores, from Shropshire and other distant counties, to be fed by the malt-distillers. Very few good horses are bred in the county; the farmers obtaining cart-horses at the different fairs in the neighbouring counties, and at the stables of dealers in the metropolis. Many of the horses used in husbandry, as well as those employed by the carmen in London, are bred in Leicestershire and the adjoining counties, whence they are taken by dealers and sold to the farmers of Wiltshire, Hampshire, and Berkshire, who, having kept them until they are about five years old, and of a proper age for constant work, dispose of them at high prices. The draught horses in the possession of the brewers and distillers, part of which are of Flemish breed, are almost unequalled in strength and beauty.

Passing from Kensington, through Hammersmith, Chiswick, Brentford, Isleworth, and Twickenham, the land on each side of the road, for the distance of seven miles, is in a great measure occupied by fruit gardens, for the supply of London, which produce, in the first place, apples, pears, cherries, plums, walnuts, &c. ; and amongst the trees of these larger kinds of fruit are planted raspberries, gooseberries, currants, strawberries, and all such smaller fruit trees, shrubs, and herbs, as are known to thrive in such situations. The quantity of the richest ground near London employed in the raising of vegetables for its supply is very great ; and at Chelsea, Brompton, Kensington, Hackney, Dalston, Bow, and Mile-End, much land is occupied by nurserymen, who spare no expense in collecting the choicest sorts and greatest variety of fruit-trees, ornamental shrubs, and flowers, from every quarter of the globe, which they cultivate to a high degree of perfection. These grounds occupy about one thousand five hundred acres ; and from them many plants are annually exported to Ireland, Spain, Portugal, Italy, France, and Russia. On the northern slopes of Hampstead and Highgate hills are still a few acres of old woodland, besides one hundred acres on the east side of Finchley common, and two thousand acres to the north-west of Ryslip, in all about three thousand acres, about half of which is wood, tolerably well planted with thriving young oaks, the rest being copse. Many of the hedgerows abound with pollard trees, for the most part elms. In the river Thames are some islands, most of which are planted with osiers for the use of basket-makers, as are also different slips of wet land on the Middlesex border of that river. The common lands of the county which yet remain unenclosed are but of small extent ; viz., Ashford, Littleton, and Laleham commons, Staines and Cowley moors, Hillingdon

heath, Uxbridge and Harefield commons, Clapton marshes, and Hadley, an allotment from Enfield Chase. Besides these are various smaller, containing less than one hundred acres each, such as Hampstead heath, Ealing common, Uxbridge moor, Memsey moor, Gould's green, Peil's heath, Hanwell common, Wormwood-Scrubs, and some others, which altogether contain about five hundred acres. Three-fourths of these commons are covered with heath and furze, while the whole soil but a scanty pasture for the cattle and sheep that are turned upon them. Finchley common, comprising upwards of a thousand acres, has been recently enclosed.

The manufactures of this county are far too numerous and extensive to be here detailed, but they will be found under the names of the places in which they are respectively carried on : the two most important are, that of silk, in the parishes of Spitalfields, Shoreditch, and Bethnal-green, and that of watches in the parish of Clerkenwell. The coach-builders and harness-makers are also very numerous in London and its vicinity, and in their respective labours far excel those of any other city in the world. With regard to the consumption of agricultural produce, the distilleries are of immense importance, and yield a revenue equal to that of all the other distilleries in Great Britain : the breweries, too, are of vast extent. Besides the prodigious amount of the imports and exports of the port of London, innumerable small cargoes of coal and merchandise of various descriptions, including grain, malt, and flour, are conveyed away or received by means of the inland barges on the Thames and the Lea. Tackling, apparel, provisions, and stores, are also supplied for about fourteen thousand vessels which load and unload in the course of the year in the port of London, the commerce of which amounts to three-fifths of that carried on throughout the whole of England. Besides the markets at the country towns, there are in London, Smithfield market, famous for the sale of bullocks, sheep, calves, lambs, and hogs, on every Monday, and again, though to a less extent, on every Thursday, on which latter day is also a market for ordinary horses ; Leadenhall market, the greatest in London for the sale of country-killed meat and poultry, and fresh butter and eggs, and the only skin and leather market within the bills of mortality ; and Newgate market, for the sale of provisions of the same kind as at the last-mentioned, being, like it, held daily. These markets almost entirely supply the butchers round London, to the distance of twelve miles, and, in a less degree, to the distance of twenty miles. The principal market at the Corn-Exchange in Mark-lane, the business of which is almost incalculable, is on Monday, besides which are two of minor importance, on Wednesday and Friday: about one-fourth of the supply is imported coastwise, a great quantity being also foreign corn. At Billingsgate is the great London fish-market every morning ; while the two principal vegetable markets are those of Covent-Garden and Farringdon, at the latter of which other provisions are also sold. There are three public markets for hay and straw in this county, namely, at Whitechapel, in Smithfield, and the Haymarket in St. James' (now about to be removed to "a newly formed area, called Cumberland market, in the parish of St. Pancras"), each of which is held every Tuesday, Thursday, and Saturday. The common fuel of Middlesex is coal, which is brought by vessels from the counties of Northumberland and Durham to the port of London, whence it is forwarded, by land or water carriage, to all parts of the county, and into Buckinghamshire, Berkshire, Surrey, Kent, and Essex. Wood is employed as fuel only in the cottages and small farm-houses on the northern side of the county, the expense of carrying coal to which is considerable.

The principal rivers of Middlesex are the Thames, the Lea, and the Coln, besides which are the smaller streams of the Brent and the Cran. The Thames, so celebrated throughout the world, as connected with the great port of London, constitutes the southern boundary of the county for a distance of forty-three miles, first touching it at Staines, whence it proceeds in a very devious course eastward, by Laleham, Sunbury, Hampton, Teddington, Twickenham, Isleworth, Brentford, Chiswick, Hammersmith, Fulham, and Chelsea, and part of the cities of Westminster and London, to Blackwall, where it quits the county, and continues its progress to the ocean. The largest ships in the service of the East India Company come up this river with safety to the corner of the county at Blackwall; and it is navigable for West India ships to London bridge, and for large barges in the whole of its course on the border of Middlesex, along which the tide flows up it, for the distance of about twenty-three miles, to Richmond bridge. The fish that are occasionally taken in this part of the Thames are sturgeon, salmon, tench, barbel, roach, dace, chub, bream, gudgeon, ruffe, bleak, eels, smelts, and flounders, the three last of which are of particularly good quality. The Lea forms the entire eastern boundary of the county, and is divided, in the greater part of its course, into several natural channels, uniting into one shortly before its influx into the Thames, which takes place near Blackwall. From its mouth upwards the Lea has been made navigable to the distance of about eight miles, where a canal navigation branches from it on the western side, and runs nearly parallel with it through the meadows of Tottenham, Edmonton, and Enfield, whence it is continued to Hertford. The Coln first touches the county at its north-western extremity, being there divided into two or three natural channels, in which manner it flows gently southward, along the western side of the county, to the neighbourhood of Longford and Colnbrook, where it is subdivided into six branches, the three principal of which continue their courses, in the same southerly direction, until they join the Thames at a short distance west of Staines: a fourth branch winds its way from near Longford, by the eastern end of Staines, and through Littleton, to the Thames between Shepperton and Sunbury; a fifth, from the same vicinity, runs south-easterly until it joins the river Cran, near the gunpowder-mills on Hounslow heath; while the sixth, also from the neighbourhood of Longford, passes near Stanwell, over Hounslow heath, and through Hanworth, Bushey, and Hampton-Court parks, to the Thames. The Brent, rising in Hertfordshire, enters this county near Finchley, and making a circuitous course through the middle of it, falls into the Thames at Brentford. The Cran takes its rise between Pinner and Harrow, in this county, and passing under Cranford-bridge, and across Hounslow heath, joins the Thames at Isleworth. The lake called the Serpentine river, in Hyde Park, was formed about the year 1730, and is fed by a small stream which rises near West-end, Hampstead, and passing by Kilburn, enters, just below Bayswater, into that part of the lake which is included in Kensington Gardens, and, quitting the Serpentine again just above Knightsbridge, runs into the Thames at Ranelagh. The Grand Junction canal, which is constructed on a very large and expensive scale, and opens a direct communication by water between London and the great manufacturing towns in Warwickshire, Staffordshire, and Lancashire, commences at the Thames at Brentford, and takes a north-westerly direction, passing near Hanwell, Norwood, Harlington, and West Drayton, to the valley of the Coln, up which it is continued near Cowley, Uxbridge, and Harefield, finally quitting Middlesex for Hertfordshire, near Rickmansworth in the latter county, after a rise from the Thames of a hundred and fourteen feet: the barges that navigate this canal are commonly of sixty tons' burden, and drawn by two horses. From this canal, at Bull bridge, near the place where it crosses the river Cran, commences the important branch of it called the Paddington canal, which passes on one level, through the central part of the county, to Paddington, whence it has been continued, by the Regent's canal, round the whole northern side of London, to the Thames at Limehouse. The basin at Paddington, which formed the termination of this line before the construction of the Regent's canal, is upwards of four hundred yards long, and thirty wide. The Regent's canal, which branches off at a short distance above it, almost immediately enters a tunnel under Maida hill, emerging from which it passes along the northern side of the Regent's Park, to Islington, under which suburb and the bed of the New River it is carried, by means of another tunnel three-quarters of a mile long, and continues its course by Kingsland and Hackney to Limehouse, where it terminates in an extensive basin communicating with the Thames: its length is nearly nine miles, and along its course are twelve locks, of excellent construction, and thirty-seven bridges. Besides the artificial part of the Lea navigation already mentioned, there is an important side cut from that river at Bromley, to a basin at Limehouse communicating with the Thames. A creek from the Thames to Kensington has also been widened within the last few years, and made navigable. Sir Hugh Middleton's canal, for supplying London with water, called the New River, after running a distance of nearly twelve miles from its commencement in Hertfordshire, enters Middlesex at Bull-Cross, and winds in a beautiful and extremely circuitous course of twenty-four miles through the eastern side of the county to Islington, where it is received into a large basin, called the New River Head, from which, by means of engines and pipes, it is conveyed to most parts of London and its northern suburbs. The principal turnpike-roads in Middlesex bear conspicuous marks of their vicinity to a great city: scattered villas and genteel houses, frequently in handsome rows and terraces, are erected on one or both sides of them to the distance of five or six miles out of London; the foot-ways are thronged with passengers, and the carriage-ways with horses, carts, wagons, private carriages, stage coaches, and vehicles of every description. The great roads from London to the north and west of England have the first part of their course in this county. The road to Cambridge and

King's Lynn is a continuation of the line of Bishops-gate-street, through Tottenham and Edmonton, entering Hertfordshire, near Waltham-Cross. The great north road to York, Edinburgh, &c., runs through Highgate, and after passing through a corner of Hertfordshire, at Chipping-Barnet, re-enters Middlesex, which it finally quits just beyond Potter's Bar. The road to Leicester, Leeds, &c., branches from the last-mentioned road at the northern extremity of Chipping-Barnet, about three miles beyond which it enters Hertfordshire in its course to St. Alban's. The road to Oxford is a continuation of the line of Oxford-street, passing through Bayswater, Acton, Hanwell, Southall, &c., to Uxbridge, just beyond which it quits the county for Buckinghamshire. The great western road to Bath, Bristol, Exeter, &c., passes along Piccadilly, through Knightsbridge, Kensington, Hammersmith, Turnham-Green, Brentford, Hounslow, &c., to Staines, where it enters Surrey at the bridge across the Thames.

The only Roman station within the limits of this county, besides *Londinium*, which was the seat of the Roman government of Britain, appears to have been *Sulloniacæ*, the supposed site of which was on Brockley hill, near Elstree, bordering on Hertfordshire, on which spot various Roman remains have been discovered. The ancient Watling-street is supposed to have run from Dowgate, on the northern bank of the Thames, in the city of London, along the line of the modern street called Watling-street, to Aldersgate, where it quitted the city: it is difficult to trace its course through the remainder of London, but it is believed to have been continued north-westerly, and to have fallen into the line of the present road to St. Alban's by Padding-ton, and Edgware. The Ermin-street led northwards through Islington and Highgate, by Stoke-Newington and Hornsey Wood, to Enfield, nearly in the line of the present high road; but turning off near the latter place, it passes Clay Hill, and enters Hertfordshire. A third Roman road led from the metropolis westward into Surrey and Berkshire, in the line of the present great western road, through Brentford, Hounslow, and Staines. A fourth is believed to have led eastward, along Old-street, and over Bethnal-Green, to Old Ford, where it crossed the Lea into Essex; and it is probable that another left the city at Aldgate, and pursued the course of the present high road, through Whitechapel and Stratford le Bow, into Essex. Roman antiquities have been found in different parts of the county, but the account of the more important of them is given in the article on London. Middlesex possesses little that is remarkable in ecclesiastical architecture beyond the limits of the metropolis. The number of religious houses in the county before the Reformation, exclusively of those in the metropolis and its suburbs, was few, and the principal remains are to be found in London and Westminster. Among the most perfect specimens of ancient domestic architecture are, Holland House, Hare-field Place, and Wyer Hall at Tottenham: this class of antiquities also includes various fine old mansions within the ancient limits of the city of London, and the considerable portion still remaining of the royal palace of St. James'. Among the mansions most distinguished for grandeur or elegance may be enumerated, in addition to the great number of magnificent residences which are noticed in the article on London, the royal palaces of Hampton-Court and Kensington; Sion House, the seat of the Duke of Northumberland; Chiswick House, that of the Duke of Devonshire; Osterley Park, that of the Earl of Jersey; Bentley Priory, that of the Marquis of Abercorn; Caen-wood, that of the Earl of Mansfield; Fulham Palace, that of the Bishop of London; Strawberry Hill, formerly that of Horace Walpole, Earl of Orford; and Wrotham Park, the residence of George Byng, Esq. In various parts of the county are springs of mineral water, some of which have been in great repute for their medicinal virtues; but none of them are now much frequented, except Bagnigge Wells, St. Chad's Wells, Islington spa, or New Tonbridge Wells, all which are on the northern side of London.

MIDDLESMOOR, a chapelry in the parish of KIRKBY-MALZEARD, lower division of the wapentake of CLARO, West riding of the county of YORK, 15 miles (W. by N.) from Ripon. The population is returned with Fountains-Earth. The living is a perpetual curacy, annexed to the vicarage of Masham, in the peculiar jurisdiction of the Dean and Chapter of York, though claimed to be in the special jurisdiction of the church, late the prebend of Masham, endowed with £200 private benefaction, £1200 royal bounty, and £800 parliamentary grant. John Lazenby, in 1743, devised lands, now producing about £18 a year, for the establishment and maintenance of a free school for ten boys; also Simon Horner, in 1809, gave a rent-charge of £20, for the education of poor children.

MIDDLESTONE, a township in that part of the parish of ST. ANDREW, AUCKLAND, which is in the south-eastern division of DARLINGTON ward, county palatine of DURHAM, 3½ miles (E. by N.) from Bishop-Auckland, containing 117 inhabitants.

MIDDLETHORPE, a township in that part of the parish of ST. MARY, BISHOPSHILL, SENIOR, which is in the ainsty of the city, and East riding of the county, of YORK, 2¼ miles (S. by W.) from York, containing 44 inhabitants.

MIDDLETON, a joint chapelry with Smerrill, in that part of the parish of YOULGRAVE which is in the hundred of WIRKSWORTH, county of DERBY, 3¾ miles (S. S. W.) from Bakewell, containing, with Smerrill, 280 inhabitants. There are places of worship for Independents and Wesleyan Methodists. Extensive lead mines are now in operation near the village, which is situated on a hill abounding in limestone. Middleton is in the honour of Tutbury, duchy of Lancaster, and within the jurisdiction of a court of pleas held at Tutbury every third Tuesday, for the recovery of debts under 40s.

MIDDLETON, a parish in the hundred of HINCK-FORD, county of ESSEX, 1 mile (S. by W.) from Sudbury, containing 109 inhabitants. The living is a rectory, in the jurisdiction of the Commissary of Essex and Herts, concurrently with the Consistorial Court of the Bishop of London, rated in the king's books at £8, and in the patronage of the Rev. Oliver Raymond. The church has some remains of Norman architecture. The parish is bounded on the east by the river Stour.

MIDDLETON, a township in that part of the parish of LANCASTER which is in the hundred of LONSDALE, south of the sands, county palatine of LANCASTER, 5¼ miles (W. S. W.) from Lancaster, containing 185 inhabitants. It is situated upon the coast of Morecambe bay.

MIDDLETON, a parish in the hundred of SAL-FORD, county palatine of LANCASTER, comprising the market town of Middleton, the chapelry of Ashworth, and the townships of Ainsworth, Birtle *cum* Bamford, Hopwood, Great Lever, Pilsworth, and Thornham, and containing 12,793 inhabitants, of which number, 5809 are in the town of Middleton, 55 miles (S. E. by S.) from Lancaster, and 191½ (N. N. W.) from London. The name of this place is supposed to have originated from its central situation with regard to some neighbouring towns, whence it was called Middle town. The manor was long held by the family of Assheton, to which belonged Sir Richard Assheton, who signalized himself against the Scots, in 1513, at the battle of Flodden, whither he was accompanied by a band of archers from Middleton. In modern times this town has chiefly been distinguished as one of the principal seats of the cotton manufacture, and the weaving of silk is carried on to some extent ; in 1812, when a spirit of discontent and insubordination prevailed among the workmen, Middleton was, for a short time, the scene of riot and bloodshed. It is pleasantly situated on the road from Manchester to Rochdale, and is a considerable thoroughfare. The inhabitants are abundantly supplied with water from springs. Subscription concerts have been established, and are well supported, it being in contemplation to erect a handsome concert-room. The cotton trade, in its various departments of spinning, weaving, bleaching, and printing, is extensively carried on, also the manufacture of nankeens, ginghams, and check-handkerchiefs : there are also a silk-manufactory and extensive dye-works, together with coal mines in the immediate vicinity; in one of the cotton manufactories are two steam-engines, of forty and twenty-four horse power respectively, by which eleven thousand spindles and five hundred power-looms are put in motion. The Rochdale canal from Manchester passes about one mile and a half from the town, and communicates with other canals, affording a navigable conveyance to Hull. To the introduction of the different branches of manufacture Middleton is indebted for its rapid increase of population, and its present prosperity. A royal grant for holding a weekly market was obtained in 1791, since which period a market-house, shambles, and a range of warehouses for general merchandise, have been erected, at the expense of Lord Suffield, to whom the manor belongs. The market was appointed to be held on Friday ; and the fairs on the first Tuesday after the 11th of March, the first Tuesday after the 15th of April, and the second Thursday after the 29th of September, all which, however, are merely nominal, no business being transacted. Manorial courts leet and baron are held in April and October ; at the former of these, the several constables, appointed at a vestry-meeting of the ley-payers, are sworn in for the township.

The living is a rectory, in the archdeaconry and diocese of Chester, rated in the king's books at £36. 3. 11½., and in the patronage of Lord Suffield. The church, dedicated to St. Leonard, is ancient, and appears to be the work of different periods ; the southern side, which is the more modern, was built in 1524, by Sir Richard Assheton and his wife Anne: the tower is low and supports a superstructure of wood, the sandy foundation not being deemed sufficiently firm to sustain an entire erection of stone : the choir is separated from the nave by a screen divided into seven compartments, on which are carved the shields and armorial bearings of several families connected by marriage with the Asshetons ; in both the north and south compartments are several ancient and curious monuments and inscriptions : the windows also are decorated with armorial bearings especially that of the north aisle, on which is depicted a group consisting of a priest and sixteen archers, in a kneeling posture, intended as a representation of the bowmen who accompanied Sir Richard Assheton to Flodden field : the chancel window is decorated with portions of stained glass, removed hither from an ancient apartment in the rectory house, called " the Hall." There are places of worship for the late Countess of Huntingdon's Connexion, Independents, Primitive and Wesleyan Methodists, and Swedenborgians. The grammar school was founded pursuant to royal charter, dated August 11th, 1572, by Alexander Nowell, D.D., Dean of St. Paul's, London : the incorporated governors are the Principal and Fellows of Brasenose College, in which the dean, then Principal, likewise founded and endowed thirteen scholarships for the benefit of this and other schools in the county. It is also entitled to share with others in two scholarships founded in the same college, by Samuel Radcliffe, D.D., in 1648, and endowed with an estate in Bedfordshire. The governors elect the master, whose salary is only £20 per annum, and the usher, who has £10; each of the boys pays for instruction. There is a charity school in the township of Ainsworth, endowed with a cottage for the master, and land producing about £12 per annum, for which from six to eight poor children receive instruction. In 1758, Catherine Hopwood bequeathed £100, directing the interest to be applied to the instruction of poor children, and the school-house was erected at the expense of the inhabitants of the township of Hopwood. Sunday schools belonging to the various religious communities afford instruction to about two thousand children.

MIDDLETON, a joint township with Houghton and Arbury, in the parish of WINWICK, hundred of WEST DERBY, county palatine of LANCASTER, 3 miles (S. E. by E.) from Newton in Mackerfield. The population is returned with Houghton.

MIDDLETON, a parish in the Lynn division of the hundred of FREEBRIDGE, county of NORFOLK, 3½ miles (S. E.) from Lynn-Regis, containing 665 inhabitants. The living is a discharged vicarage, in the archdeaconry and diocese of Norwich, rated in the king's books at £7, and in the patronage of the Rev. P. S. Wood, L.L.D. The church is dedicated to St. Mary. Here are quarries of a rough stone well adapted for buildings of an inferior description. In the village is a high mount, probably the site of an ancient castle ; and in the neighbourhood are the remains of a mansion of the Lords Scales, built in the reign of Henry VI.

MIDDLETON, a township in the parish of COTTINGHAM, hundred of CORBY, county of NORTHAMPTON, 2 miles (S. W. by W.) from Rockingham, containing 377 inhabitants.

MIDDLETON, a township in that part of the parish of BELFORD which is in the northern division of BAMBROUGH ward, county of NORTHUMBERLAND, 1¼ mile (N. N. W.) from Belford, containing 79 inhabitants.

MIDDLETON, a parish in the hundred of BLYTHING, county of SUFFOLK, 2¼ miles (E. S. E.) from Yoxford, containing, with Fordley, 564 inhabitants. The living is a discharged rectory, in the archdeaconry of Suffolk, and diocese of Norwich, rated in the king's books at £5, and in the patronage of — Harrison, Esq. The church is dedicated to the Holy Trinity. There is a place of worship for Wesleyan Methodists.

MIDDLETON, a parish in the hundred of AVIS-FORD, rape of ARUNDEL, county of SUSSEX, 8 miles (S.W. by S.) from Arundel, containing 44 inhabitants. The living is a discharged rectory, in the archdeaconry and diocese of Chichester, rated in the king's books at £5. 10. 10., and in the patronage of the Crown.

MIDDLETON, a parish in the Tamworth division of the hundred of HEMLINGFORD, county of WARWICK, 4½ miles (S.S.W.) from Tamworth, containing 623 inhabitants. The living is a perpetual curacy, in the archdeaconry of Coventry, and diocese of Lichfield and Coventry, and in the patronage of Lord Middleton. The church, dedicated to St. John the Baptist, has portions in the Norman and early English styles, and a tower of later architecture. The Birmingham and Fazeley canal passes through the parish. The several sums arising from bequests by Robert Gorton, in 1640; Francis Willoughby, in 1672; and the Dowager Lady Middleton, in 1782, are applied in teaching poor children, and providing them with bibles. Middleton gives the title of baron to the family of Willoughby.

MIDDLETON, a chapelry in the parish of KIRKBY-LONSDALE, LONSDALE ward, county of WESTMORLAND, 3½ miles (N. by E.) from Kirkby-Lonsdale, containing 252 inhabitants. The living is a perpetual curacy, annexed to the vicarage of Kirkby-Lonsdale, in the archdeaconry of Richmond, and diocese of Chester, endowed with £400 private benefaction, and £600 royal bounty. The chapel, dedicated to the Holy Ghost, was built at the expense of the inhabitants, in 1634, on ground given by Dr. Christopher Bainbridge, a native of this place. A school has been erected by subscription, and is endowed with about £10 per annum for teaching poor children. A battle is stated to have been fought here between the English and the Scots: many human bones have been discovered near the old bridge.

MIDDLETON, a parish in the Bainton-Beacon division of the wapentake of HARTHILL, East riding of the county of YORK, 8¾ miles (N.W.) from Beverley, containing 441 inhabitants. The living is a rectory, in the archdeaconry of the East riding, and diocese of York, rated in the king's books at £15. 3. 4. The Rev. J. Blanchard was patron in 1827. The church is dedicated to St. Andrew. There is a place of worship for Wesleyan Methodists.

MIDDLETON, a parish in PICKERING lythe, North riding of the county of YORK, comprising the townships of Cowthorn, Cropton, Hartoft, Lockton, Middleton, Rosedale (East side), Wretton, and part of Aislaby, and containing 1727 inhabitants, of which number, 247 are in the township of Middleton, 1¾ mile (W. N. W.) from Pickering. The living is a discharged vicarage, in the archdeaconry of Cleveland, and diocese of York, rated in the king's books at £10. 11. 8., endowed with £6 per annum private benefaction, £200 royal bounty, and £400 parliamentary grant, and in the patronage of the Devisees of the Rev. J. Robinson.

MIDDLETON, a township in the parish of ROTHWELL, lower division of the wapentake of AGBRIGG,

West riding of the county of YORK, 5¾ miles (N. N. W.) from Wakefield, containing 1096 inhabitants.

MIDDLETON, a joint township with Stockhill, in that part of the parish of ILKLEY which is in the upper division of the wapentake of Claro, West riding of the county of YORK, 6¼ miles (W. N. W.) from Otley, containing, with Stockhill, 205 inhabitants.

MIDDLETON (ST. GEORGE), a parish in the south-western division of STOCKTON ward, county palatine of DURHAM, 6½ miles (E. S. E.) from Darlington, containing 209 inhabitants. The living is a rectory, in the archdeaconry and diocese of Durham, rated in the king's books at £4, and in the patronage of the Heirs of the late W. Pemberton, Esq. The foundations of Pountney's bridge, thought to have been the first bridge built across the Tees, are still visible : on or near it stood an ancient chapel; within a short distance of it there was a hermitage, and on the brow of the hill immediately above it is an artificial mound, encompassed by a fosse.

MIDDLETON on the HILL, a parish in the hundred of WOLPHY, county of HEREFORD, 6 miles (N. E.) from Leominster, containing 369 inhabitants. The living is a perpetual curacy, in the archdeaconry and diocese of Hereford, endowed with £200 private benefaction, £400 royal bounty, and £200 parliamentary grant, and in the patronage of the Bishop of Hereford. The church is dedicated to St. Mary.

MIDDLETON upon LEVEN, a chapelry in the parish of RUDBY in CLEVELAND, western division of the liberty of LANGBAURGH, North riding of the county of YORK, 3¾ miles (S. E. by E.) from Yarm, containing 111 inhabitants. The living is a perpetual curacy, in the archdeaconry of Cleveland, and diocese of York, endowed with £1000 royal bounty. Lady Amherst was patroness in 1820. The chapel is dedicated to St. Cuthbert.

MIDDLETON (NORTH), a township in the parish of ILDERTON, northern division of COQUETDALE ward, county of NORTHUMBERLAND, 2 miles (S. by E.) from Wooler, containing 128 inhabitants.

MIDDLETON (NORTH), a township in that part of the parish of HARTBURN which is in the western division of MORPETH ward, county of NORTHUMBERLAND, 8¾ miles (W. by S.) from Morpeth, containing 75 inhabitants.

MIDDLETON (SOUTH), a township in the parish of ILDERTON, northern division of COQUETDALE ward, county of NORTHUMBERLAND, 2¾ miles (S.) from Wooler, containing 69 inhabitants.

MIDDLETON (SOUTH), a township in that part of the parish of HARTBURN which is in the western division of MORPETH ward, county of NORTHUMBERLAND, 10 miles (W. by S.) from Morpeth, containing 31 inhabitants.

MIDDLETON (STONEY), a chapelry in the parish of HATHERSAGE, hundred of HIGH PEAK, county of DERBY, 5½ miles (N. by E.) from Bakewell, containing 635 inhabitants. The living is a perpetual curacy, annexed to the vicarage of Hathersage, in the archdeaconry of Derby, and diocese of Lichfield and Coventry, endowed with £200 private benefaction, £800 royal bounty, and £1000 parliamentary grant. The chapel, dedicated to St. Martin, was rebuilt in 1759, in the form of an octagon. There is a place of worship for Unitarians. A considerable quantity of limestone is burned here, and used for manure. This parish is in the honour of Tutbury, duchy of Lancaster, and within the jurisdiction of a court of pleas held at Chapel en le Frith every third Tuesday, for the recovery of debts under 40s.

MIDDLETON (STONEY), a parish in the hundred of PLOUGHLEY, county of OXFORD, 3 miles (W. by N.) from Bicester, containing 340 inhabitants. The living is a rectory, in the archdeaconry and diocese of Oxford, rated in the king's books at £12. 16. 0½., and in the patronage of the Bishop of Lincoln. The church is dedicated to All Saints.

MIDDLETON in TEASDALE, a parish in the southwestern division of DARLINGTON ward, county palatine of DURHAM, comprising the market town of Middleton, the chapelry of Egglestone, and the townships of Forest with Frith, and Newbiggin, and containing 2866 inhabitants, of which number, 1263 are in the town of Middleton, 10 miles (N.W.) from Barnard-Castle, and 253 (N.N.W.) from London. The town is irregularly built, and scattered along the sides of hills which surround, in a somewhat oval form, an extensive green: the environs abound with all the varied scenery of rocks, waterfalls, and chasms of immense depth, with fertile valleys and sloping hills, enriched by the gentle flow of the Tees, in its course through this county to the German Ocean. About two miles above the town is Wynch bridge, seventy feet in length and two in width, thrown from rock to rock across a tremendous chasm sixty feet in depth, and guarded on each side by a hand-rail; and higher up the river are the stupendous cataracts of High Force and Caldron Snout. Several of the inhabitants are occupied in raising and manufacturing the lead-ore produced in the northern part of the parish in immense quantities. The market is held on Saturday, and every alternate market is numerously attended by the miners, who are paid once a fortnight: there are fairs on the third Thursday in April, July 7th, and on the second Thursday in September. The town hall, a neat edifice with a market-place beneath it, was erected at the expense of the Earl of Darlington. Courts leet and baron are held annually for the manor. The living is a rectory, in the archdeaconry and diocese of Durham, rated in the king's books at £25. 17. 1., and in the patronage of the Crown. The church, dedicated to St. Mary, is an ancient but small edifice; the tower is several yards distant from the rest of the building. There are places of worship for Baptists, Independents, and Methodists. Christopher Stephenson and others bequeathed a small estate, now producing £22 per annum, for which eight boys are instructed. A National school, erected and partly supported by the London Lead Company, especially for the children of their own labourers, from six until twelve years of age, who pay 1s. each per quarter, affords instruction to one hundred and thirty children, exclusively of one hundred Sunday scholars; the other children pay two shillings and sixpence quarterage: a small library is attached to the school, for the use of the Company's workmen, to whom the books are lent.

MIDDLETON by WIRKSWORTH, a hamlet in that part of the parish of WIRKSWORTH which is in the hundred of WIRKSWORTH, county of DERBY, 1¼ mile (N.N.W.) from Wirksworth, containing 904 inhabitants. It is in the honour of Tutbury, duchy of Lancaster, and within the jurisdiction of a court of pleas held at Tutbury every third Tuesday, for the recovery of debts under 40s.

MIDDLETON-CHENEY, a parish in the hundred of KING'S SUTTON, county of NORTHAMPTON, 3 miles (E. by N.) from Banbury, containing 1398 inhabitants. The living is a rectory, in the archdeaconry of Northampton, and diocese of Peterborough, rated in the king's books at £31. 11. 3., and in the patronage of the Principal and Fellows of Brasenose College, Oxford. The church, dedicated to All Saints, has a fine tower and spire, and a rich porch. There are places of worship for Baptists and Wesleyan Methodists. The tenure prevailing in this lordship is that, when estates descend in the female line, the eldest sister inherits. In the great civil war a battle was fought here, in which the army of the parliament was defeated.

MIDDLETON-HALL, a township in the parish of ILDERTON, northern division of COQUETDALE ward, county of NORTHUMBERLAND, 1¾ mile (S.) from Wooler, containing 61 inhabitants.

MIDDLETON-QUERNHOW, a chapelry in that part of the parish of WATH which is in the wapentake of HALLIKELD, North riding of the county of YORK, 5 miles (N.N.E.) from Ripon, containing 102 inhabitants.

MIDDLETON-SCRIVEN, a parish in the hundred of STOTTESDEN, county of SALOP, 5½ miles (S.S.W.) from Bridgenorth, containing 86 inhabitants. The living is a discharged rectory, in the archdeaconry of Salop, and diocese of Hereford, rated in the king's books at £4. 6. 8. T. Rowley, Esq. was patron in 1812. The church is dedicated to St. John the Baptist.

MIDDLETON-TYAS, a parish in the eastern division of the wapentake of GILLING, North riding of the county of YORK, comprising the townships of Middleton-Tyas with Kneeton, and Moulton, and containing 805 inhabitants, of which number, 569 are in the township of Middleton-Tyas with Kneeton, 5½ miles (N.E.) from Richmond. The living is a vicarage, in the archdeaconry of Richmond, and diocese of Chester, rated in the king's books at £15. 10., and in the patronage of the Crown. The church is a handsome uniform structure.

MIDDLEWICH, a parish comprising the township of Weever in the first division of the hundred of Eddisbury, the market town of Middlewich, and the townships of Byley with Yatehouse, Clive, Croxton, Kinderton with Hulme, Minshull-Vernon, Mooresbarrow with Parme, Newton, Occlestone, Ravenscroft, Sproston, Stublach, Sutton, and Wimboldsley, in the hundred of NORTHWICH, county palatine of CHESTER; and containing 4450 inhabitants, of which number, 1212 are in the town of Middlewich, 20 miles (E.) from Chester, and 167 (N.W.) from London. The name of this town is derived from its central situation with respect to the Wiches, or salt towns; and it is probable that the Romans had an establishment here, or in the vicinity, as there are traces of a Roman road, and in the township of Kinderton is an intrenched camp, supposed to be the site of the Roman station called Condate. The earliest notice of it is in the reign of Edward the Confessor, when it appears to have been held by the Earl of Mercia under the king: after the Conquest it was annexed to the earldom of Chester, and subsequently to the crown, under which it is held by the present

lessee. It was formerly one of the burghs of the palatinate, and the burgesses received grants of various privileges from some of the baronial proprietors, which they
pleaded in reply to a writ of *Quo Warranto* issued against
them in the 15th of Henry VII. On the occasion of a
contest here between the royalists and the parliamentary forces, March 13th, 1642, the former experienced a
signal defeat ; but in a second engagement, about nine
months afterwards, the parliamentarians were vanquished in consequence of a reinforcement of their opponents by troops from Ireland. The town, which is
neat and well built, and extends into the townships of
Kinderton and Newton, is divided by the Grand Trunk,
or Trent and Mersey, canal, here crossed by the river
Dane ; and the rivers Croco, Weever, and Wheelock,
also run through the parish : upon the two latter are
several corn-mills. A branch from the Chester canal
is now in progress from Wardle to Middlewich, from
which considerable benefit to the trade of this town
is anticipated. The trade consists principally in salt,
which is obtained from powerful brine springs : there
are likewise some silk manufactories. The market
is on Tuesday ; and fairs are held on Holy Thursday,
August 25th, and October 29th. Constables are appointed at the court leet of the lessee of the manor.
The living is a discharged vicarage, in the archdeaconry and diocese of Chester, rated in the king's
books at £14, endowed with £200 private benefaction, £200 royal bounty, and £1000 parliamentary
grant, and in the patronage of the Rev. Isaac Wood.
The church, dedicated to St. Michael and all Angels,
presents indications of various styles of architecture,
having been the work of different periods ; it has a
handsome tower ; at the eastern end of each of the
aisles is a chapel, or chancel, separated by a screen.
There are places of worship for the Society of Friends,
Independents, and Wesleyan Methodists. A free
school was founded in the sixteenth century, for a
few poor boys, custom having limited the number to
eight, who are taught reading only ; the master is
nominated by Lord de Tabley : it is endowed with £160,
and a house and school-room in the township of Newton, the inhabitants of which have added a small portion
of land, to entitle them to send a proportionate number
of boys for instruction. The Rev. Theophilus Lindsey,
a Unitarian divine, and theological writer, was born here
in 1723 ; he died in London, in 1808.

MIDDLEZOY, a parish in the hundred of WHITLEY,
county of SOMERSET, 5½ miles (N.W. by N.) from
Langport, containing, with a part of Boroughbridge,
605 inhabitants. The living is a discharged vicarage,
in the jurisdiction of Glastonbury, and diocese of Bath
and Wells, rated in the king's books at £12, and in the
patronage of the Bishop of Bath and Wells. The
church is dedicated to the Holy Cross. The river Parret
is navigable on the south-west.

MIDDOP, a township in the parish of GISBURN,
western division of the wapentake of STAINCLIFFE and
EWCROSS, West riding of the county of YORK, 5½ miles
(N.W. by W.) from Colne, containing 100 inhabitants.
A school, erected by subscription on the waste, was
endowed, in 1819, by the Rev. Thomas Bland, with
money now producing about £10 per annum.

MIDGHAM, a chapelry in that part of the parish of
THATCHAM which is in the hundred of FAIRCROSS,

county of BERKS, 6¼ miles (E.) from Speenhamland, con-
taining 329 inhabitants. The chapel, dedicated to St.
Margaret, was rebuilt by John Hillersdon, Esq., in 1714.
There are almshouses erected by the late William Poyntz,
Esq. The Kennet and Avon canal passes in the vicinity.

MIDGLEY, a township in the parish of HALIFAX,
wapentake of MORLEY, West riding of the county of
YORK, 4½ miles (W. by N.) from Halifax, containing
2207 inhabitants.

MIDHOPE, a chapelry in the parish of ECCLES-
FIELD, northern division of the wapentake of STRAF-
FORTH and TICKHILL, West riding of the county of
YORK, 3¼ miles (S. S. W.) from Penistone. The population is returned with the parish. The living is a perpetual curacy, in the archdeaconry and diocese of York, endowed with £800 royal bounty, and £200 parliamentary grant, and in the patronage of Major-General
Bawille.

MIDHURST, a borough, market town, and parish,
in the hundred of EASEBOURNE, rape of CHICHESTER,
county of SUSSEX, 11½ miles (N. by E.) from Chichester,
and 49½ (S. W.) from London, containing 1335 inhabitants. This is evidently a place of great antiquity, having
been a large town prior to the Conquest, and having enjoyed its privilege of parliamentary representation ever
since the reign of Edward II. The town is agreeably
situated upon a gentle eminence surrounded by hills, and
on the banks of the river Rother : the streets are clean
and the houses well built ; and the inhabitants are remarkable for longevity, which is attributed to the great
salubrity of the atmosphere. The market is on Thursday : fairs are held on April 8th and October 27th.
The Rother, or Arundel, navigation commences at this
town. A bailiff is chosen annually at the court leet
of the lord of the manor : the petty sessions for the
hundred are held at the Angel Inn. The borough
comprises a plot of ground without the boundaries of
the present town, probably the site of some more ancient place : there is not a single house upon it, but the
situation of the burgage tenements is accurately marked
by large stones set up for that purpose. Midhurst is a
borough by prescription, and has sent members to
parliament ever since the 4th of Edward II. : the right
of election is vested in about one hundred and twenty
burgage-holders, and the bailiff is the returning officer.
The living is a perpetual curacy, in the archdeaconry
and diocese of Chichester, endowed with £400 private
benefaction, £600 royal bounty, and in the patronage of William Stephen Poyntz, Esq. The church,
which is dedicated to St. Denis, has a south chapel
at its east end, which contains some handsome monuments of the family of Browne, Viscounts Montague,
the most remarkable being that of Anthony, first Lord
Montague, and his two wives : he is represented in his
robes of the garter, with armour and ruff, kneeling at a
square pedestal or altar, on which his helmet is placed.
This church has received an addition of one hundred
and thirty-three free sittings, for which the Incorporated
Society for enlarging churches and chapels contributed
£50. The free grammar school was founded by Gilbert
Hannam, of Midhurst, in 1672, who during his life
granted a rent-charge of £20 for ever, for the education of twelve boys in Latin, Greek, and arithmetic, and
at his decease, in 1677, bequeathed a moiety of his
estate for the further support of the master : it is

open to the sons of inhabitants who have resided seven years in Midhurst, and the late head-master, Dr. Bailey, having made large additions to the school-house, it has now become a classical school of considerable importance : the total annual income arising from the above-mentioned benefaction is £32. 18. A National school is°supported by subscription. At a short distance from the town are the picturesque ruins of Cowdray House, once the magnificent seat of the Montague family, which was accidentally destroyed by fire in 1793.

MIDLEY, a parish in the liberty of ROMNEY-MARSH, though locally in the hundred of Martin-Pountney, lathe of SHEPWAY, county of KENT, 3 miles (W.S.W.) from New Romney, containing 33 inhabitants. The living is a rectory, in the archdeaconry and diocese of Canterbury, rated in the king's books at £30, and in the patronage of — Eve, Esq. The church has been demolished.

MIDLOE, an extra-parochial liberty, in the hundred of TOSELAND, county of HUNTINGDON, containing 43 inhabitants.

MIDRIDGE, a township in the parish of HEIGHINGTON, south-eastern division of DARLINGTON ward, county palatine of DURHAM, 4¾ miles (S. E. by S.) from Bishop-Auckland, containing 201 inhabitants. The school-room, built in 1817, was enlarged in 1821, and is used as a chapel of ease, the curacy having been endowed with £27. 6. a year, by the late Bishop of Durham, who also endowed the school with £10 per annum, which is further supported by the subscriptions of the Earl of Eldon and others.

MIDRIDGE-GRANGE, a township in that part of the parish of AUCKLAND ST. ANDREW which is in the south-eastern division of DARLINGTON ward, county palatine of DURHAM, 4½ miles (S.E.) from Bishop-Auckland, containing 58 inhabitants.

MID-VILLE, a township in the eastern division of the soke of BOLINGBROKE, parts of LINDSEY, county of LINCOLN, containing 139 inhabitants. This township is independent of any parish, it having been so created by act of parliament, in 1812, on occasion of an extensive drainage of fen-lands.

MILBORNE- PORT, a borough and parish (formerly a market town) in the hundred of HORE-THORNE, county of SOMERSET, 2¼ miles (N.E. by E.) from Sherborne, and 115 (W.) from London, containing 1440 inhabitants. This town, which is irregularly built, and consists chiefly of detached houses, is situated at the bottom of a hill, adjoining the river Ivel, on the high road from Yeovil to Shaftesbury. The manufacture of sail-cloth, dowlas, lindsey-woolsey, and stockings, has been superseded by glove-making and leather-dressing. Fairs are held on June 5th and October 28th, for cattle and pedlary. There are nine pieces of borough land, or burgage tenements, and the persons to whom they are conveyed by the proprietors are called capital bailiffs; two of them in rotation preside annually, being called reigning bailiffs, who, at a court leet held

Seal and Arms.

in October, appoint two deputies, or sub-bailiffs; and there are two stewards of the commonalty lands, or public property, belonging to the parish, which is divided into three tythings, Milborne-Port, Milborne-Wick, and Kingsbury-Regis. At the last a court baron is held annually, when a constable, tythingman, and hayward, are appointed. Milborne-Port is a borough by prescription, and returned members to parliament from the 26th to the 35th of Edward I., from which time, until the reign of Charles I., it ceased to exercise the privilege, but in 1628 the franchise was restored : the right of election is in the nine capital bailiffs, their two deputies, the two commonalty stewards, and the inhabitants paying scot and lot ; the number of voters is about eighty : the two sub-bailiffs are the returning officers, and the predominant influence is in the Marquis of Anglesey and Sir William Coles Medlycott. The living is a vicarage, in the archdeaconry of Wells, and diocese of Bath and Wells, rated in the king's books at £14. 1. 3., and in the patronage of the Marquis of Anglesey. The church, dedicated to St. John the Evangelist, is an ancient cruciform structure, with a large quadrangular tower, and has recently received an addition of four hundred sittings, of which three hundred and fifty are free, the Incorporated Society for the enlargement of churches and chapels having contributed £200 towards defraying the expense. There is a place of worship for Independents.

MILBOURN, a tything in the parish and hundred of MALMESBURY, county of WILTS, 1 mile (E. N. E.) from Malmesbury, containing 115 inhabitants.

MILBOURNE (ST. ANDREW), a parish in the liberty of DEWLISH, Blandford (North) division, though locally in the Dorchester division, of the county of DORSET, 8 miles (S. W.) from Blandford-Forum, containing, with Milbourne-Churchstone, 244 inhabitants. The living is a discharged vicarage, with that of Dewlish, in the archdeaconry of Dorset, and diocese of Bristol, rated in the king's books at £13. 6. 8. T. Gundry, Esq. was patron in 1800. In this parish is an oblong double-intrenched camp, the area of which is about seven acres. Cardinal Morton, Archbishop of Canterbury in the reign of Henry VII., was born here.

MILBOURNE-CHURCHSTONE, a tything in the parish of MILBOURNE ST. ANDREW, liberty of DEWLISH, Blandford (North) division of the county of DORSET. The population is returned with the parish.

MILBOURNE - STYLEHAM, a parish in the hundred of BEER-REGIS, Blandford (South) division of the county of DORSET, adjacent to Milbourne St. Andrew's, containing 264 inhabitants.

MILBROOK, a chapelry (formerly a market townin that part of the parish of MAKER which is in the southern division of EAST hundred, county of CORNWALL, 7½ miles (S.) from Saltash. The population is returned with the parish. The inhabitants are chiefly occupied in an extensive fishery. Fairs are held on May 1st and September 29th. Milbrook is said to have anciently sent members to parliament. Courts leet and baron are still held, annually about Michaelmas, for what is called the borough of Milbrook, and the manor of Inswork, at which, by a jury appointed and sworn, a portreeve, clerk of the market, and other officers, are chosen, but their powers are become obsolete from disuse. The living is a perpetual curacy, in the archdeaconry of Cornwall, and diocese of Exeter, and in the patronage of the Vicar of Maker. The chapel, which contains six hundred sittings, of which three hundred and fifty-seven are free, was erected at the expense of £300, contributed by the Incorporated Society for the enlargement of churches and chapels. There is a place of worship for Wesleyan Methodists.

MILBURN, a township in the parish of PONTELAND, western division of CASTLE ward, county of NORTHUMBERLAND, 11 miles (N.W.) from Newcastle upon Tyne, containing 82 inhabitants. Coal and limestone are obtained in the parish.

MILBURN, a chapelry in the parish of KIRKBY-THORE, EAST ward, county of WESTMORLAND, 7 miles (N. by W.) from Appleby, containing, with Milburn-Grange, 303 inhabitants. The living is a perpetual curacy, in the archdeaconry and diocese of Carlisle, endowed with £500 private benefaction, and £400 royal bounty, and in the patronage of the Earl of Thanet. The chapel, dedicated to St. Cuthbert, was founded by William de Lancaster, about 1355. Sarah Atkinson, in 1790, left £100 for the education of poor children, the interest of which is about £4. 10. a year. There are some inferior veins of coal and lead-ore in the neighbourhood, but neither of them is worked. On the southern end of Greenfell there are vestiges of a circular fort, deeply moated, called Green Castle, near which was found an altar inscribed " DEO SILVANO."

MILBURN-GRANGE, a township in the parish of PONTELAND, western division of CASTLE ward, county of NORTHUMBERLAND, 11¼ miles (N.W.) from Newcastle upon Tyne, containing 32 inhabitants.

MILBURN-GRANGE, a hamlet in the parish of KIRKBY-THORE, EAST ward, county of WESTMORLAND, 5¼ miles (N. by W.) from Appleby. The population is returned with the chapelry of Milburn.

MILBY, a joint township with Humberton, partly in the parish of KIRBY on the MOOR, wapentake of HALLIKELD, North riding, and partly in that part of the parish of ALDBOROUGH which is in the lower division of the wapentake of CLARO, West riding, of the county of YORK, 1 mile (N. by E.) from Boroughbridge. The population is returned with Humberton. The river Ure, which separates this place from Boroughbridge, was, before the Conquest, crossed by a wooden bridge, on the line of the great north road; some remains of it are still visible when the water is low.

MILCOMBE, a chapelry in the parish and hundred of BLOXHAM, county of OXFORD, 6 miles (N.W. by W.) from Deddington, containing 220 inhabitants.

MILCOTT, a hamlet in that part of the parish of WESTON upon AVON which is in the Alcester division of the hundred of BARLICHWAY, county of WARWICK, 2¾ miles (S.W.) from Stratford upon Avon, containing 14 inhabitants.

MILDEN, a parish in the hundred of BABERGH, county of SUFFOLK, 3 miles (S.W. by W.) from Bildeston, containing 167 inhabitants. The living is a rectory, in the archdeaconry of Sudbury, and diocese of Norwich, rated in the king's books at £10. 13. 4. Mrs. M. Hallward was patroness in 1827. The church is dedicated to St. Peter. A trifling rent-charge, the gift of the Rev. William Burkitt, in 1700, is applied in teaching poor children.

MILDENHALL, a parish in the hundred of SELKLEY, county of WILTS, 1½ mile (E.N.E.) from Marlborough, containing 414 inhabitants. The living is a rectory, in the archdeaconry of Wilts, and diocese of Salisbury, rated in the king's books at £17. 8. 9., and in the patronage of the Executors of the late Rev. Richard Pococke. The church, dedicated to St. John the Baptist, was repaired by the Rev. Charles Francis, late rector, at a considerable expense; he also built and endowed a " Protestant " free school, for the education of poor children. There is a place of worship for Wesleyan Methodists. On the right of the London road leading from the forest to Marlborough are slight traces of the ancient Roman station *Cunetio;* where many Roman coins, tesselated pavements, &c., have been discovered.

MILDENHALL (ST. ANDREW'S), a market town and parish in the hundred of LACKFORD, county of SUFFOLK, 38½ miles (N.W.) from Ipswich, and 70 (N.N.E.) from London, containing 2974 inhabitants. The town is situated on a tributary of the river Ouse, called the Lark, which is navigable along the south and west boundaries of the parish, on the high road from Norwich to London through Newmarket. It is large, including, besides one principal and several smaller streets, others of considerable extent, forming detached portions, reaching towards the fens on the east. The streets are neither lighted nor paved, but the inhabitants are plentifully supplied with water from wells and springs. There is a small spinning-mill for raw silk, which affords employment chiefly for children; but the principal branch of commerce is the exportation of grain and other commodities. A market is held on Friday, which is well supplied with fish, wild fowl, and provisions in general; and there is a fair on the 10th of October, for toys, pedlary, &c. A manorial court is held twice or thrice a year, as occasion requires. A high constable is annually appointed; but the town is within the jurisdiction of the county magistrates, who meet occasionally for the despatch of business. The living is a vicarage, in the archdeaconry of Sudbury, and diocese of Norwich, rated in the king's books at £22. 8. 1½., and in the patronage of Sir Henry Edward Bunbury, Bart. The church, which is dedicated to St. Mary, a large handsome structure with a lofty tower; the ceiling is of wood-work, richly carved, and the entrance is through a highly-finished old English porch; in the interior are several ancient monuments. There are places of worship in the parish for Baptists, those in the late Countess of Huntingdon's Connexion, and Wesleyan Methodists. A National school for children of both sexes is supported by subscription. An almshouse for four widows was founded, in 1722, by Sir Thomas Hanner; the inmates have 2s. 6d. a week, and an allowance for coal, clothes, &c.

MILE-END, a district in the parish of STEPNEY, Tower division of the hundred of OSSULSTONE, county of MIDDLESEX, 1 mile (E.) from London, comprising Mile-End Old Town, containing 22,876 inhabitants, and Mile-End New Town, containing 7091. In the rebellion under Jack Cade, in the reign of Henry VI., the insurgents who attacked the metropolis encamped for some time at Mile-End; and in 1642, at the commencement of the civil war, fortifications were raised here, by order of the parliament, for the defence of the city. The Old and the New Towns form one of the most extensive suburbs of London, extending, in a line from west to east, along the principal road to Essex, and comprising many handsome ranges of buildings, and detached houses, and two recently-erected squares, *viz.*, Tredegar-square, on the north side of the road, and Beaumont-square, on the south. The streets are partially paved, and lighted with gas, and the inhabitants are supplied with water chiefly from the West Ham water-works, the reservoir belonging to which is situated to the north of the high road. Here are some extensive breweries, a large distillery, floor-cloth manufactories, and a tobacco-pipe manufactory, also a considerable nursery-ground. The Regent's canal crosses the turnpike-road here, under a stone bridge, and on its banks are several coal and timber wharfs. This district is within the magisterial jurisdiction of the police office at Lambeth-street, Whitechapel; and here is one of the stations of the new police. It is also within the jurisdiction of the Tower Hamlets court of requests, for debts under 40*s.*, established by act of parliament in the 23rd of George II. The only episcopal places of worship here are the chapels belonging to certain almshouses. The principal places of worship for Dissenters are, one for Calvinistic Methodists, built in 1780, and Brunswick chapel, for Independents.

The charity school at Mile-End Old Town was established, by voluntary contributions, in 1714, and has been subsequently endowed with various benefactions, producing £143. 16. per annum; the surplus of the annual expenditure, about £470, arising from subscriptions: one hundred and sixty boys and one hundred and five girls are educated on the Madras system; a school-room for the girls and other apartments were erected at Stepney-green, in 1786, and the school for boys is situated in Mile-End-road. The Stepney Meeting charity school, for Mile-End Old Town, was founded, by voluntary contributions, in 1783, and afterwards endowed with various benefactions producing £188 per annum: the annual expense is about £400, which is defrayed principally by subscriptions, for which one hundred and thirty boys and sixty girls are instructed, partly on Dr. Bell's, and partly on Lancaster's plan. The charity school for Mile-End New Town was established by voluntary contributions, in 1785, for thirty boys and thirty girls: the permanent income arises from £715 four per cents., and the annual expense, about £230, is chiefly defrayed by subscriptions. Here are almshouses in the patronage of the Vintners' Company, originally founded in 1357, in Thames-street; but having been destroyed by the fire in 1666, they were rebuilt at Mile-End, but taken down and rebuilt a second time, in 1802, in consequence of the bequest of £2250 from Mr. Benjamin Kenton, for that purpose: they consist of twelve sets of apartments, with a chapel, and they are appropriated to the benefit of widows of freemen of the Vintners' Company, who receive about £36 per annum each; and there is a chaplain who performs weekly service, and has a salary of £52. 10. per annum. The almshouses erected by the Brethren of the Trinity-house, consist of twelve sets of apartments, with a handsome chapel in the centre, in the front windows of which are some armorial bearings in stained glass. Francis Bancroft gave, by will, in 1727, in trust to the Drapers' Company, property then valued at £28,000, to found and endow twenty-four almshouses, and a school for one hundred boys: the buildings, which

were completed in 1736, consist of two parallel rows of houses, and a central range containing a chapel, a school-room, and other apartments. The present income of this charity, arising from landed property, from £40,800 three per cent. consols., and from £33,400 three per cent. reduced annuities, is more than £4000 per annum; the almsmen have £20 per annum each, and there is a chaplain whose salary is £31. 10. per annum. Twelve almshouses were founded, in 1592, by John Fuller, with an endowment of £50 per annum, for twelve poor single men; and there are almshouses for four poor women, founded in 1698, by John Pemer. At Mile-End Old Town is the Jews' hospital for aged poor, and the education and employment of youth, founded in 1806, and enlarged in 1818: the building, which is handsome and spacious, is adorned in front with a central pediment and Ionic pilasters: it is situated on the south side of the road, and nearly opposite to it is the Spanish and Portuguese Jews' hospital, instituted in 1747, for sick poor, lying-in women, and as an asylum for the aged, and supported by voluntary contribution. On the north side of the high road are two large cemeteries belonging to the Portuguese Jews, and a third belonging to the German, or Dutch Jews, in which are interred several of the rabbins and other distinguished Jews. At Mile-End is the East London lying-in institution, supported by voluntary contribution.

MILE-END (ST. MICHAEL), a parish within the liberty of the borough of COLCHESTER, county of ESSEX, 1 mile (N.) from Colchester, containing 447 inhabitants. The living is a rectory, in the archdeaconry of Colchester, and diocese of London, rated in the king's books at £7. 10. The Countess de Grey was patroness in 1817.

MILEHAM, a parish in the hundred of LAUNDITCH, county of NORFOLK, 6¾ miles (N. W.) from East Dereham, containing 516 inhabitants. The living is a rectory, in the archdeaconry and diocese of Norwich, rated in the king's books at £11. 1. 10½. The Rev. C. B. Barnwell was patron in 1825. The church is dedicated to St. John the Baptist. The river Nar rises in the parish. Charles Ward, in 1743, bequeathed £200 for teaching children, and clothing the poor. A strong castle was erected here, soon after the Conquest, by Alan, son of Flaald, ancestor of the Fitz-Alans, Earls of Arundel, vestiges of which may be traced within a double intrenchment enclosing an area of twelve acres, and the site of the keep encompassed by an inner trench. Sir Edward Coke, Lord Chief Justice of the King's Bench, was born here; he died September 3rd, 1634.

MILFIELD, a township in the parish of KIRK-NEWTON, western division of GLENDALE ward, county of NORTHUMBERLAND, 5¾ miles (N. W.) from Wooler, containing 259 inhabitants. This was the residence of the Saxon kings of Bernicia, after the death of Edwin. South of the village is a fine plain, the scene of a battle fought, before that of Flodden, between the English and the Scots, in which the former were defeated. Under an immense heap of stones, supposed by some to have been raised by the Britons, a Roman urn, containing ashes and burnt bones, was discovered in 1823.

MILFORD, a village partly in the township of BELPER, and partly in the hamlet of MAKENY, in the parish of DUFFIELD, hundred of APPLETREE, county of DERBY, 1 mile (S.) from Belper. The population is returned with the parish. This flourishing little place, which is situated on the road from Derby to Chesterfield, Matlock, &c., prior to 1781, consisted only of eight houses, and had a small iron-forge : at that period Messrs. Strutt built a cotton-mill, and subsequently a handsome stone bridge over the river Derwent, which is now a county bridge. An extensive trade is carried on in spinning, dyeing, and bleaching cotton goods, which affords employment to about seven hundred persons. There are places of worship for Primitive and Wesleyan Methodists. A school has been built, and is supported by the proprietors of the different works, for the education of poor children.

MILFORD, a parish partly in that part of the hundred of RINGWOOD which is in the New Forest (East) division, but chiefly in the hundred of CHRISTCHURCH, New Forest (West) division, of the county of SOUTHAMPTON, 3 miles (S. W.) from Lymington, containing, with the tythings of Keyhaven and Pennington, 1332 inhabitants. The living is a vicarage, with the perpetual curacy of Hordle, in the archdeaconry and diocese of Winchester, rated in the king's books at £20. 13. 1½., and in the patronage of the Provost and Fellows of Queen's College, Oxford. The parish is bounded on the south-east by the Isle of Wight channel.

MILFORD, a tything in that part of the parish of LAVERSTOCK which is in the hundred of UNDERDITCH, county of WILTS, ½ a mile (E.) from Salisbury, contain ing 489 inhabitants.

MILFORD, a joint township with Kirkby-Wharf, in that part of the parish of KIRKBY-WHARF which is in the upper division of the wapentake of BARKSTONE-ASH, West riding of the county of YORK, 3½ miles (S. S. E.) from Tadcaster. The population is returned with Kirkby-Wharf.

MILFORD (SOUTH), a township in the parish of SHERBURN, partly within the liberty of ST. PETER of YORK, but chiefly in the upper division of the wapentake of BARKSTONE-ASH, West riding of the county of YORK, 4¾ miles (N. by E.) from Ferry-Bridge, containing 631 inhabitants. There is a place of worship for Wesleyan Methodists.

MILKHOUSE-STREET, a hamlet in the parish and hundred of CRANBROOKE, lathe of SCRAY, county of KENT, 1¼ mile (N.E.) from Cranbrooke. Here are the interesting remains of a chapel, dedicated to the Holy Trinity. There is a place of worship for Wesleyan Methodists. A small manufacture for hop-bagging is carried on.

MILLAND, a chapelry in that part of the parish of TROTTON which is in the hundred of EASEBOURNE, rape of CHICHESTER, county of SUSSEX, 6 miles (N.W.) from Midhurst. The population is returned with the parish.

MILLAND-VILLE, an extra-parochial liberty, adjacent to the city, and within the liberty of the soke, of WINCHESTER, Fawley division of the county of SOUTHAMPTON, containing 101 inhabitants.

MILLBROOK, a parish in the hundred of RED-BORNESTOKE, county of BEDFORD, 1¼ mile (W. by N.) from Ampthill, containing 405 inhabitants. The living is a rectory, in the archdeaconry of Bedford, and diocese of Lincoln, rated in the king's books at £9. 16. 3., and in the patronage of Lord Holland. The church is dedicated to St. Michael. Here was anciently a small cell of

Benedictine monks, subordinate to the abbey of St. Alban's, who were afterwards removed to the Hermitage of Moddry, belonging also to St. Alban's.

MILLBROOK, a parish in the hundred of BUDDLES-GATE, Fawley division of the county of SOUTHAMPTON, 2 miles (W.N.W.) from Southampton, containing, with the village of Redbridge, 2124 inhabitants. The living is a rectory, in the archdeaconry and diocese of Winchester, rated in the king's books at £10. 6. 3., and in the patronage of the Bishop of Winchester. The church, dedicated to St. Nicholas, and lately rebuilt, has received an addition of four hundred sittings, of which two hundred are free, the Incorporated Society for the enlargement of churches and chapels having granted £200 toward defraying the expense, the remainder having been defrayed, partly by subscription and partly by a rate levied on the parishioners. There was formerly a chapel at Shirley, in this parish. A commodious school-house has been recently erected, in which about one hundred and twenty children are taught upon the National system. Here is an iron-foundry, also a manufactory for agricultural implements, at which about sixty persons are employed; and at Shirley are iron-works for the manufacture of spades, shovels, and various descriptions of edge-tools. At Redbridge, where the river Test is crossed by an ancient bridge of five arches, and discharges itself into Southampton water, there was formerly a considerable trade in timber, coal, corn, malt, &c., for which its situation is peculiarly well adapted, but of late years it has much decreased, though by means of the Andover canal, which commences here, there is still some traffic in those articles with the interior of the county. Ship-building, both for the naval and merchant service, was, till within the last few years, carried on to a greater extent than it is at present; sloops of war, mounting from twenty-eight to thirty-two guns, and schooners of a particular construction, having been built here about the close of the last century. A court is held annually by the lord of the manor. This parish is within the jurisdiction of the Cheyney Court held at Winchester every Thursday, for the recovery of debts to any amount.

MILLFORD, a hamlet in the parish of DUFFIELD, hundred of APPLETREE, county of DERBY, 6 miles (N.) from Derby. The population is returned with the parish : about seven hundred persons are employed in the spinning and bleaching of cotton. There are places of worship for Wesleyan Methodists and Unitarians. There is also a Lancasterian school, in which about four hundred children are taught.

MILLINGTON, a township in that part of the parish of ROSTHERN which is in the hundred of BUCK-LOW, county palatine of CHESTER, 4½ miles (N. N. W.) from Nether Knutsford, containing 334 inhabitants.

MILLINGTON, a parish partly within the liberty of ST. PETER of YORK, but chiefly in the Wilton-Beacon division of the wapentake of HARTHILL, East riding of the county of YORK, 3 miles (N. E.) from Pocklington, containing 282 inhabitants. The living is a perpetual curacy, annexed to the vicarage of Great Givendale, in the peculiar jurisdiction of the Dean of York. There is a place of worship for Wesleyan Methodists. John Wilkinson, in 1801, bequeathed £200 for the education of ten children, and William Flint, in 1804, gave £100 for teaching four others. Four ancient roads meet at this place, which is supposed to be the Roman *Del-*

govicia, where are traces of a strong camp defended by immense earth-works, from sixty to ninety feet in height, carried indiscriminately over hills and vallies, and encompassed with four, and in some places six, ditches, enclosing altogether an area of four thousand one hundred and eighty-five acres, within which are several tumuli. About half a mile north-east from the village foundations of a circular temple and two oblong buildings, Roman pavements, tiles, coins, and various other relics of antiquity, have been discovered.

MILLO, a hamlet in the parish of DUNTON, hundred of BIGGLESWADE, county of BEDFORD, 3 miles (E. S. E.) from Biggleswade. The population is returned with the parish. The chapel has been demolished.

MILLOM, a parish (formerly a market town) in ALLERDALE ward above Darwent, county of CUMBERLAND, comprising the chapelries of Thwaits and Ulpha, and the townships of Birker with Austhwaite, Chapel-Sucken, Lower Millom, and Upper Millom, and containing 1815 inhabitants, of which number, 460 are in the township of Lower Millom, and 320 in that of Upper Millom, 12 miles (S. E.) by S.) from Ravenglass. This parish is bounded on the west and south by the Irish sea, and on the east by the river Duddon, which forms a bay famous for cockles and muscles, and abounding with salmon and sand-eels. The mineral productions are limestone, slate, and iron and copper ore; the limestone alone is found in quantities sufficient to be worked with advantage. A market and a fair were granted in the reign of Henry III., but have been long disused. The living is a discharged vicarage, in the archdeaconry of Richmond, and diocese of Chester, rated in the king's books at £8. 5. 8., endowed with £610 private benefaction, and £200 royal bounty, and in the patronage of the King, as Duke of Lancaster. The church, which is dedicated to the Holy Trinity, is an ancient structure, and contains a mural tablet, with effigies to the memory of the Huddlestone family. A school was endowed by this family with £200, which has long been lost, but the children of the parish are entitled to instruction in a grammar school at Whicham, and there are charity schools at Millom, with small endowments from a benefaction by William Atkinson, in 1809. Here are the remains of Millom castle, the ancient seat of the Lords of Millom. In Upper Millom are several springs, called Holy wells, impregnated with a purgative salt. In 1824, a curious battle-axe and other relics were found at Lowscales.

MILLSHIELDS, a joint township with Espershields, in the parish of BYWELL ST. PETER, eastern division of TINDALE ward, county of NORTHUMBERLAND, 10½ miles (S. E. by S.) from Hexham. The population is returned with Espershields.

MILNROW, a chapelry in that part of the parish of ROCHDALE which is in the hundred of SALFORD, county palatine of LANCASTER, 2 miles (E. by S.) from Rochdale. The living is a perpetual curacy, in the archdeaconry and diocese of Chester, endowed with £400 private benefaction, £600 royal bounty, and £1200 parliamentary grant, and in the patronage of the Vicar of Rochdale. John Collier, otherwise "Tim Bobbin," the popular author of "The Lancashire Dialect," an eccentric caricaturist, poet, and musician, resided fifty-seven years at this place, as the village school-master.

MILNTHORPE, a market town, and joint township with Heversham, in the parish of HEVERSHAM, KENDAL ward, county of WESTMORLAND, 32 miles (S. W. by S.) from Appleby, and 256 (N. W. by N.) from London, containing, with the township of Heversham, 1401 inhabitants. This town is situated on the northern bank of the river Belo, near the mouth of the Kent, and consists chiefly of one long street; the houses are in general of neat appearance, and some of them are handsome. Flax and paper mills, with the spinning of twine, the manufacture of sheeting, bed-ticks, sacking, sails, &c., and some carding and spinning of wool, furnish employment to the working class: there is also some tanning, and in the vicinity are quarries of marble and limestone. This is the only sea-port in the county, being a member of the port of Lancaster, and is accessible by none but very small vessels. The market is on Friday, but not for corn; and fairs are held on May 12th and October 17th, for cattle, sheep, and horses: the former is of ancient institution, and is proclaimed by the steward of the lord of the manor and a procession of gentlemen: during its continuance tolls are collected. Courts leet and baron are held annually, and petty sessions every alternate Wednesday. The parochial church is at Heversham, one mile north of the town. There is a place of worship for Independents, built in 1820. A National school was established in 1819, and is supported by voluntary contributions, George Wilson, Esq. contributing about one-third of the expense: one hundred children, exclusively of Sunday scholars, are educated. A workhouse, for the use of sixteen incorporated townships, was erected at a short distance north-east of the town, in 1813, at an expense of £4,990: the premises occupy two acres of ground; the paupers are employed in weaving; and a meeting of visitors and guardians is held monthly. Detached from the house, on an eminence, is a fever ward in connexion with it.

MILSON, a parish in the hundred of OVERS, county of SALOP, 3¼ miles (S. W.) from Cleobury-Mortimer, containing 125 inhabitants. The living is a perpetual curacy, annexed to the rectory of Neen-Sollars, in the archdeaconry of Salop, and diocese of Hereford. The church is dedicated to St. George.

MILSTEAD, a parish in the hundred of MILTON, lathe of SCRAY, county of KENT, 3 miles (S. by W.) from Sittingbourne, containing 191 inhabitants. The living is a discharged rectory, in the archdeaconry and diocese of Canterbury, rated in the king's books at £8. 15. Sarah T. Patterson was patroness in 1819. The church, dedicated to St. Mary and the Holy Cross, is in the early style of English architecture. There are almshouses for five poor persons. John Wyatt, in 1722, gave land now let for £20 a year, for the education of eight poor children of this parish, and the same number of that of Frinsted.

MILSTON, a parish in the hundred of AMESBURY, county of WILTS, 2¾ miles (N.) from Amesbury, containing, with Brigmis, 98 inhabitants. The living is a rectory, in the archdeaconry and diocese of Salisbury, rated in the king's books at £12. 15. 2½. P. Templeman, Esq. was patron in 1802. The church is dedicated to St. Mary. Joseph Addison, the distinguished essayist and poet, was born at the parsonage-house, in 1672, his father being then rector.

MILTHORPE, a hamlet in the parish of As-LACKBY, wapentake of AVELAND, parts of KESTEVEN, county of LINCOLN, containing 86 inhabitants.

MILTON, a parish in the hundred of OCK, county of BERKS, 3½ miles (S. by W.) from Abingdon, containing 421 inhabitants. The living is a rectory, in the archdeaconry of Berks, and diocese of Salisbury, rated in the king's books at £17. 9. 7., and in the patronage of the Dean and Canons of Christ Church, Oxford, on the demise of the present incumbent, and another individual named in the will of the late Rev. J. G. Warner. The church is dedicated to St. Blaise. The Rev. J. G. Warner, late rector, gave the dividends on certain property in the public funds, for the education of poor children of the parish; the income is about £67 per annum, for which twenty of each sex are taught on the National system. The manor-house was erected by Inigo Jones.

MILTON, a parish in the hundred of NORTHSTOW, county of CAMBRIDGE, 3½ miles (N.E. by N.) from Cambridge, containing 341 inhabitants. The living is a discharged vicarage, in the archdeaconry and diocese of Ely, rated in the king's books at £4. 16. 0½., endowed with £400 royal bounty, and in the patronage of the Rector: the rectory is a sinecure, rated at £4. 7. 1., and in the patronage of the Provost and Fellows of King's College, Cambridge. The church is dedicated to All Saints.

MILTON, a joint township with Weaverham, in the parish of WEAVERHAM, second division of the hundred of EDDISBURY, county palatine of CHESTER, 4 miles (W. by N.) from Northwich. The population is returned with Weaverham.

MILTON, a hamlet in the parish of PRITTLEWELL, hundred of ROCHFORD, county of ESSEX, ¾ of a mile (S. by E.) from Prittlewell, with which the population are returned. This hamlet is situated on the coast, and was once a distinct parish, which has been encroached on by the sea; at low water some remains of the church were visible not long since. Here are fine beds of oysters.

MILTON, a parish in the hundred of WESTGATE, lathe of ST. AUGUSTINE, county of KENT, 2½ miles (S.W. by W.) from Canterbury. The living is a discharged rectory, in the archdeaconry and diocese of Canterbury, rated in the king's books at £4. 14. 4., and in the patronage of W. P. Honeywood, Esq. The church is dedicated to St. Nicholas. This parish contains only one house and two hundred acres of land.

MILTON, a chapelry in the parish of EAST ADDERBURY, hundred of BLOXHAM, county of OXFORD, 2¼ miles (N.N.W.) from Deddington, containing 190 inhabitants. The chapel has been demolished.

MILTON, a chapelry in the parish of SHIPTON under WHICHWOOD, hundred of CHADLINGTON, county of OXFORD, 3¼ miles (N. by E.) from Burford, containing 567 inhabitants.

MILTON, a parish in the hundred of CHRISTCHURCH, New Forest (West) division of the county of SOUTHAMPTON, 4¾ miles (E. by N.) from Christchurch, containing 702 inhabitants. The living is a perpetual curacy, in the archdeaconry and diocese of Winchester, endowed with £200 private benefaction, £600 royal bounty, and £1200 parliamentary grant, and in the patronage of the Provost and Fellows of Queen's College,

Oxford. The church is dedicated to St. Mary Magdalene. There is a place of worship for Independents. The parish is bounded on the south by Christchurch bay, where there is a preventive station.

MILTON next GRAVESEND, a parish in the hundred of TOLTINGTROUGH, lathe of AYLESFORD, county of KENT, comprising part of the town of Gravesend, and containing 2769 inhabitants. The living is a rectory, in the archdeaconry and diocese of Rochester, rated in the king's books at £16. 5. 10., endowed with £200 royal bounty, and in the alternate patronage of the Crown and the Bishop of Rochester. The church is dedicated to St. Peter and St. Paul. Over the porch is a curious dial, constructed by Mr. Giles, master of Gravesend school, and within the church are painted the crests of the kings of England, from Edward III. to James I. The parish is bounded on the north by the Thames, and the Thames and Medway canal passes through it. Milton is incorporated with the town of Gravesend, the corporation being styled "The Mayor, Jurats, and Inhabitants of the parishes of Gravesend and Milton." It has a fair, commencing on the festival of the Conversion of St. Paul, and continuing a week. Here was formerly a free chapel, or hospital, under the government of some Regular friars. For an account of the school, &c., See GRAVESEND.

MILTON (GREAT), a parish partly in the hundred of BULLINGTON, but chiefly in that of THAME, county of OXFORD, 4 miles (W. by N.) from Tetsworth, containing, with the hamlets of Ascott and Chilworth, 701 inhabitants. The living is a vicarage, in the peculiar jurisdiction of the Prebendary of Great Milton in the Cathedral Church of Lincoln, rated in the king's books at £15. The Rev. O. Manning was patron in 1800. The church is dedicated to St. Mary. Here was formerly a monastery, a cell to that at Abingdon.

MILTON (LITTLE), a chapelry in the parish of ADDERBURY, hundred of THAME, county of OXFORD, 5 miles (W.) from Tetsworth, containing 442 inhabitants. The chapel, dedicated to St. John, has been demolished.

MILTON next SITTINGBOURNE, a market town and parish in the hundred of MILTON, lathe of SCRAY, county of KENT, 12 miles (N. E. by E.) from Maidstone, and 40 (E. by S.) from London, containing 2012 inhabitants. This town was anciently called Middletun, a Saxon appellation, indicative of its central position in the county, and also "the king's town of Milton," having probably been, in early ages, the place of residence of the kings of Kent, as well as a part of the demesne of the crown. Its proximity to the Swale, which separates the Isle of Sheppy from the main land, rendered it easily accessible to the invading Danes, by whom it was frequently plundered in the ninth century. Here their veteran chief, Hastings, attempted to establish himself in the time of Alfred; and the remains of his encampment, or fortress, in the marshes of Kemsley, between Milton church and the north end of the creek, are still visible. The ancient town, together with the palace of the Kentish kings, was burnt by Earl Godwin, about the year 1052. Milton appears to have been rebuilt, and to have become a place of importance in the time of the Conqueror, who, according to Domesday-book, held the manor, which, for a long while afterwards, was vested in the crown, and frequently granted in dower to the queens of England.

From Isabella, the consort of Edward II., the grant of a market and an annual fair for four days was obtained. In the reign of John the right of the fishery in the manor and hundred of Milton was granted to Faversham abbey, but at the dissolution, becoming again vested in the crown, the manor continued to be royal property till it was finally alienated by Charles I. The town is situated about half a mile from the high road from London to Dovor, on a hill sloping down to a small creek, or channel, which separates it from the Isle of Sheppy; the streets are narrow and badly paved. The commercial business consists chiefly in shipping, for the London market, the agricultural produce of the neighbourhood, and in bringing goods in return. The oyster fishery affords employment to a great number of the inhabitants; the right of this fishery is now held on lease by a company of free dredgers, about one hundred and forty in number, who are governed by laws made in the court baron of the manor : the oysters, under the name of native Milton oysters, are very fine and in great request. There are extensive yards for making bricks of a very superior quality, which, together with flints dug in the neighbourhood, and wild fowl, of which there is a decoy in the marshes, are sent to London. The market is on Saturday; and a fair for cattle is held on the 24th of July: the market-house and shambles are near the centre of the town. A portreeve for the hundreds of Milton and Marden, who is supervisor of weights and measures, is chosen, with a warden, on the 25th of July, at a court baron held before the steward of the manor, by such of the inhabitants as pay church and poor rates. The manor courts and public meetings are held at the market-house, under which is the town gaol.

The living is a vicarage, in the archdeaconry and diocese of Canterbury, rated in the king's books at £13. 2. 6., and in the patronage of the Dean and Chapter of Canterbury. The church, which is dedicated to the Holy Trinity, is large and handsome, with portions in the decorated style of English architecture: it consists of a nave, south aisle, and two chancels, with a heavy embattled tower at the west end, built of square flints; in the south chancel, or chapel, which belonged to the ancient family of Northwood, are a piscina and two stone seats : it also contains several ancient monuments. There are places of worship for Independents and Wesleyan Methodists. A free school is endowed with £10 per annum from benefactions by Elizabeth Morley, in 1714, and John Knotts, in 1718, for which ten children are educated; both the master and the children are appointed by the minister and church-wardens. National schools, for more than two hundred children of both sexes, are supported by voluntary contributions. In the western part of the parish is a coppice of several hundred acres, and one adjoining it extends five miles southward : these woods are noted for chesnut trees, many of which are very ancient, and serve as "termini," or boundaries, as well for private property as for parishes. The remains of the Danish fortress at Kemsley-down form a square, surrounded by a high vallum and a broad ditch; and being overgrown by trees and underwood, it has received the appellation of Castle-rough : a raised causeway, leading from it to the sea-shore, may be distinctly traced.

MILTON (SOUTH), a parish in the hundred of STANBOROUGH, county of DEVON, 2¾ miles (W. S. W.)

from Kingsbridge, containing 356 inhabitants. The living is a perpetual curacy, annexed to the vicarage of West Allington, in the archdeaconry of Totness, and diocese of Exeter.

MILTON upon STOUR, a hamlet in the parish and liberty of GILLINGHAM, Shaston (West) division of the county of DORSET, 5½ miles (N. W.) from Shaftesbury. Here was formerly a free chapel.

MILTON (WEST), a chapelry in the parish and liberty of POORSTOCK, though locally in the hundred of Eggerton, Bridport division of the county of DORSET, 3¾ miles (N. E.) from Bridport. The population is returned with the parish.

MILTON-ABBAS, a parish (formerly a market town) in the hundred of WHITEWAY, Cerne subdivision of the county of DORSET, 7 miles (S. W. by W.) from Blandford-Forum, containing 767 inhabitants. The present appellation of this place is a contraction of its ancient name of Middleton, implying its central situation within the county; the adjunct being given from its ancient lords, the abbots : it was formerly much larger than it is at present. In 1658, the upper part of the town was destroyed by fire, and a brief was granted for rebuilding it in 1661. A Benedictine monastery was founded here, in the year 933, by King Athelstan, and dedicated to the honour of St. Mary, St. Michael, St. Sampson, and St. Branwalader, the revenue of which, at the dissolution, was valued at £720. 4. 1. The church, which stood northward of the abbey, was destroyed by lightning, on September 2nd, 1309 : it was handsomely rebuilt, with the exception of the nave, in the reign of Edward II., and is now used as the private chapel of the Damer family : it consists of the choir, transepts, and tower of the abbey church; the former is in the decorated, and the two latter in the later English, style of architecture. The conventual buildings, with the exception of the ancient hall, were taken down in 1771, and replaced by the present splendid mansion, called Milton Abbey, erected from a design by Sir William Chambers, in imitation of the later style of English architecture. An ancient chapel, dedicated to St. Catherine, has long been desecrated. A market was granted by King Athelstan and confirmed by Edward I., who also granted a fair, to be held on the 27th and 28th of July: the market was originally held on Monday, and afterwards on Tuesday, but has wholly declined. In the 22nd of Charles II., a fair was granted to John Tregonwell, Esq., which was held at Windmill-Ash, on the 5th of June, and lasted a week, until its removal to Milton-Abbas, when it fell to decay. The living is a discharged vicarage, in the jurisdiction of the peculiar court of Milton-Abbas, rated in the king's books at £10, endowed with £200 private benefaction, £200 royal bounty, and £1200 parliamentary grant, and in the patronage of Lady Caroline Damer. The church, dedicated to St. Mary and St. Sampson, was built at the expense of the first earl of Dorchester. Here is a free school, with a considerable endowment : the school-room was burnt in 1658, and rebuilt four years afterwards. An almshouse for six poor persons was founded and endowed by John Tregonwell, Esq., in 1674 : the inmates receive a pecuniary allowance weekly, and some articles of clothing and money annually on St. Thomas' day.

MILTON-ABBOT, a parish in the hundred of TAVISTOCK, county of DEVON, 5½ miles (N. W. by W.) from Tavistock, containing 1151 inhabitants. The living is a vicarage, in the archdeaconry of Totness, and diocese of Exeter, rated in the king's books at £19. 13. 6½., and in the patronage of the Duke of Bedford. The church is dedicated to St. Constantine. In this parish, which is watered by the river Tamar, is the Anglo-Swiss domain of the Duke of Bedford, distinguished for its beautiful scenery and landscape gardening.

MILTON-BRYANT, a parish in the hundred of MANSHEAD, county of BEDFORD, 2¾ miles (S. E.) from Woburn, containing 346 inhabitants. The living is a rectory, in the archdeaconry of Bedford, and diocese of Lincoln, rated in the king's books at £11. 16. 3., and in the patronage of the Crown. The church is dedicated to St. Peter.

MILTON-CLEVEDON, county of SOMERSET.—See CLEVEDON (MILTON).

MILTON-DAMERELL, a parish in the hundred of BLACK TORRINGTON, county of DEVON, 5½ miles (N.E.) by N.) from Holsworthy, containing 661 inhabitants. The living is a rectory, with the perpetual curacy of Cookbury, in the archdeaconry of Totness, and diocese of Exeter, rated in the king's books at £26. 13. 6½. Lord Viscount Courtenay was patron in 1799. The church is dedicated to the Holy Trinity.

MILTON - ERNEST, a parish forming, with the parishes of Clapham and Oakley, a detached portion of the hundred of STODDEN, county of BEDFORD, 5 miles (N. W. by N.) from Bedford, containing 364 inhabitants. The living is a vicarage, in the archdeaconry of Bedford, and diocese of Lincoln, rated in the king's books at £7. 6. 8. Edmund Turnor, Esq. was patron in 1825. The church is dedicated to All Saints. An almshouse for six poor persons was founded, in 1693, by Sir Edmund Turnor, who endowed it with lands now producing about £40 per annum.

MILTON-KEYNES, a parish in the hundred of NEWPORT, county of BUCKINGHAM, 3½ miles (S. by E.) from Newport-Pagnell, containing 338 inhabitants. The living is a rectory, in the archdeaconry of Buckingham, and diocese of Lincoln, rated in the king's books at £20, and in the patronage of the Earl of Winchilsea. The church is dedicated to All Saints : the southern porch has an ancient open-work screen on each side. Dr. Francis Atterbury, Bishop of Rochester, was born here in 1662 ; he died an exile in France, in 1731 ; and Dr. William Wotton, a learned divine, critic, and historian, the author of " Reflections on Ancient and Modern Learning," was rector of this parish from 1693 till his death in 1726.

MILTON-LILBORNE, a parish in the hundred of KINWARDSTONE, county of WILTS, 1½ mile (E. by N.) from Pewsey, containing 632 inhabitants. The living is a discharged vicarage, in the archdeaconry of Wilts, and diocese of Salisbury, rated in the king's books at £7. 13. 6., endowed with £600 parliamentary grant. P. Pulse, Esq. was patron in 1800. The church, dedicated to St. Peter, has lately received an addition of sixty-nine free sittings, the Incorporated Society for the enlargement of churches and chapels having granted £25 towards defraying the expense.

MILTON, or MIDDLETON-MALZOR, a parish in the hundred of WYMERSLEY, county of NORTHAMPTON, 3½ miles (S. by W.) from Northampton, containing 492 inhabitants. The living is a rectory, in the archdeaconry of Northampton, and diocese of Peterborough, rated in the king's books at £16. 15. 10., and in the patronage of the Rev. J. C. Miller. The church is dedicated to the Holy Cross. There is a place of worship for Baptists. The Northampton canal crosses the northwestern part of the parish. Six poor children are instructed for a trifling rent-charge bequeathed, in 1756, by Elizabeth Gaffield.

MILTON-PODIMORE, county of SOMERSET. — See PODIMORE (MILTON).

MILVERTON, a market town and parish in the hundred of MILVERTON, county of SOMERSET, 26 miles (W. by S.) from Somerton, and 151 (W. by S.) from London, containing 1930 inhabitants. The present name of this town, which is a place of very great antiquity, is considered to be a corruption of Mill-fordtown : it was formerly a royal borough, and the king, as superior lord, still receives certain chief rents and fines. Milverton is delightfully situated, amidst woodland scenery, upon an eminence just above the western extremity of the vale of Taunton- Dean, over the whole of which it commands an uninterrupted view : it consists of three irregular streets, which are neither paved nor lighted ; but the inhabitants are well supplied with water. Here was formerly an extensive manufacture of serges, druggets, and flannels; at present the chief employment is silk-throwing, and this has much declined of late years. The market is on Friday : a fair, chartered by Queen Anne, formerly held on Easter Tuesday, is now disused ; but one is held on the 10th of October, for broad cloth and pedlary. A portreeve and subordinate officers are appointed annually ; but the town is under the jurisdiction of the county magistrates, who hold petty sessions here. The living is a vicarage, with the perpetual curacy of Langford-Budville, in the peculiar jurisdiction and patronage of the Archdeacon of Taunton, as Prebendary of Milverton in the Cathedral Church of Wells, rated in the king's books at £21. 19. 2. The church, which is dedicated to St. Michael, is a spacious edifice, supposed to have been one of the numerous churches in this county which were built in the reign of Henry VII. There are places of worship for the Society of Friends and Independents. In 1721, Mary Lamb devised £300 for the education of children, and the funds having accumulated for several years, the present income is £54. 2. per annum ; twenty boys and twenty girls are instructed by a master, whose salary is £40 per annum. An old house, called the parsonage-house, is said to have been erected by Cardinal Wolsey, whose arms are visible over the door : he had considerable property in this town. John de Milverton, a Carmelite friar in the fifteenth century, who distinguished himself by writing against Wickliff, was a native of this place.

MILVERTON, a parish in the Kenilworth division of the hundred of KNIGHTLOW, county of WARWICK, 1¾ mile (N.N E.) from Warwick, containing, with Edmonscott, 193 inhabitants. The living is a perpetual curacy, in the archdeaconry of Coventry, and diocese of Lichfield and Coventry, endowed with £200 royal bounty, and £200 parliamentary grant. The Earl of Warwick was patron in 1792. The church is dedicated to St. James. Six children are instructed for a rent-charge of £3, left by John Ayeares in 1775.

MILWICH, a parish in the southern division of the hundred of PIREHILL, county of STAFFORD, 5 miles (E.S.E.) from Stone, containing 567 inhabitants. The living is a discharged vicarage, in the archdeaconry of Stafford, and diocese of Lichfield and Coventry, rated in the king's books at £4. 3. 4. Lewis G. Dyve, Esq. was patron in 1803. The church is dedicated to All Saints. Ten children are instructed for £5 a year, the gift of Elizabeth Harrison.

MIMMS (NORTH), a parish in the hundred of DA-CORUM, though locally in that of Cashio, or liberty of St. Alban's, county of HERTFORD, 4 miles (S.S.W.) from Bishop's Hatfield, containing 1007 inhabitants. The living is a discharged vicarage, in the archdeacon-ry of Huntingdon, and diocese of Lincoln, rated in the king's books at £10, endowed with £200 private bene-faction, and £200 royal bounty, and in the patronage of Mrs. Gaussen. The church, dedicated to St. Mary, is built of flints, with a square tower embattled, and sur-mounted by a lofty spire; it contains many effigies, and brasses with inscriptions in black letter, and other an-cient memorials of the dead. On the north side of the chancel is the chantry chapel of St. Catherine, founded in 1328, by Simon de Swonlond, the windows of which exhibit, in stained glass, various shields and coats of arms, principally of the Coningsby family.

MIMMS (SOUTH), a parish in the hundred of EDMONTON, county of MIDDLESEX, 3½ miles (N.N.W.) from Chipping-Barnet, containing 1906 inhabitants. The living is a discharged vicarage, in the archdea-conry of Middlesex, and diocese of London, rated in the king's books at £12. 3. 4. W. P. Hammond, Esq. was patron in 1812. The church is dedicated to St. Giles.

MINCHINHAMPTON, county of GLOUCESTER.—See HAMPTON (MINCHIN).

MINCHINTON, a tything in the parish of HANDLEY, in that part of the hundred of SIXPENNY-HANDLEY which is in the Shaston (East) division of the county of DORSET, 7 miles (W. by N.) from Cranborne. The population is returned with the parish.

MINDTOWN, a parish in the hundred of PURSLOW, county of SALOP, 5 miles (E.N.E.) from Bishop's Castle, containing 31 inhabitants. The living is a discharged rectory, in the archdeaconry of Salop, and diocese of Hereford, rated in the king's books at £4. 13. 4., en-dowed with £200 private benefaction, and £200 royal bounty. The Earl of Powis was patron in 1820. The church is dedicated to St. John the Baptist.

MINEHEAD, a borough, market town, and parish, in the hundred of CARHAMPTON, county of SOMERSET, 38½ miles (W.N.W.) from Somerton, and 160 (W. by S.) from London, containing 1239 inhabitants. At the Conquest this town, then called *Manheved*, was given by the Conqueror to William de Mohun : between the years 1550 and 1654 it was repeatedly visited by the plague, and has also at various periods suffered from fires : it is situated on the shore of the Bristol channel, and consists of the Church town, which is composed of mean irregular streets, on a sloping eminence called " Greenleigh ;" the Lower town, which is the principal part, comprising some respectable streets, and the town hall, lately erected at the expense of John Fownes Lut-trell, Esq.; and the Quay town, near the water's edge, including the custom-house : the quay is a solid piece of masonry, with a parapet towards the sea, into which

it extends about a quarter of a mile, affording a tolerable shelter for small vessels. The climate here is so mild that myrtles and geraniums flourish in the open air during the whole winter, and vegetation is supposed to commence earlier than in any other part of England. Minehead is occasionally visited by invalids from Bris-tol, Bath, &c., for the purpose of sea-bathing, but its reputation as yet is not sufficient to give it the title of a bathing-place. The inhabitants were formerly engaged in foreign commerce to a great extent, and even at the commencement of the last century, forty vessels from this harbour were in constant communication with Ireland alone : at present five or six vessels only belong to the port, two of which trade with Bristol in grain, malt, bark, timber, flour, and leather, and are freighted back with grocery, iron, &c.; the rest convey similar commodities to Wales, and return with coal, culm, and limestone. A considerable number of herrings is taken on the coast; and there is an annual importation of cattle, sheep, and pigs, but the vessels return with ballast. By an act of parliament, granted in the 13th of William III., and subsequently extended, the harbour and quay are supported and kept in repair, by eleven trustees, including the lord of the manor, from certain duties chargeable upon goods entering the port. There is a custom-house, with a collector and other officers. The market, for fish and provisions, is held on Wed-nesday; and there is a chartered fair, for pedlary, &c., on the Wednesday in Whitsun-week. Under a charter granted by Elizabeth, the town was governed by a port-reeve; but now only by two constables, who are annu-ally elected at the court leet of the lord of the manor. The borough first sent members to parliament in the reign of Elizabeth : the elective franchise is vested in all the parishioners of Minehead, and the inhabitants of that part of the parish of Dunster which is within the manor of Minehead, who are housekeepers not receiving alms : the constables are the returning officers, and the influence of John Fownes Luttrell, Esq. is predomi-nant. The living is a vicarage, in the archdeaconry of Taunton, and diocese of Bath and Wells, rated in the king's books at £18. 9. 7., and in the patronage of John Fownes Luttrell, Esq. The church, which is dedicated to St. Michael, is spacious and handsome, with an em-battled tower at the west end. In the chancel is an an-cient monument, supposed to be that of Judge Bracton, Chief Justice of England in the reign of Henry III., and author of the earliest treatise on the Laws of England extant; likewise a handsome statue of Queen Anne, the gift of Sir Jacob Bankes, once a representative of the borough. There is a place of worship for Baptists. A free school for thirty boys is supported by the lord of the manor. An almshouse for eleven poor and impotent persons was built and endowed by Robert Quirke, about 1648 : it has been used as a parish workhouse, but is about to be restored to its original purpose. By an act of parliament passed in the 18th of Charles II. it was enacted, that the importation of cattle into Mine-head should be considered a nuisance after February 1st, 1666, and that they should be forfeited, half the value to be applied for the use of the poor, and the other half given to the captors : a certain capture having been made, the moiety was laid out in the purchase of an estate the rental of which, amounting to about £30 per annum, together with the interest of £1197. 5. 7.

three per cent. consols., arising from unappropriated accumulation of income, is distributed annually to the poor in money and clothing; this charity is called the "Cow charity." A species of shell fish is found, at low water, on the rocks off Minehead, which affords a peculiar fluid, having the property of communicating to linen a purple tint, supposed to be similar to the *murex*, which produced the Tyrian purple mentioned by Pliny. The celebrated lawyer above mentioned, Henry de Bracton, is said to have been born at Bratton Court, an old English mansion here: over the principal gateway which remains is a room called the Judge's Chamber, traditionally reported to have been his study; but the building is of a later period than the age in which he lived. Dr. Brocklesby, the friend of Johnson and Burke, distinguished as a physician and medical writer, was likewise a native of Minehead.

MINETY, a parish chiefly in the hundred of CROW-THORNE and MINETY, county of GLOUCESTER, though partly in the hundred of MALMESBURY, county of WILTS, 5½ miles (N. E. by E.) from Malmesbury, containing 562 inhabitants. The living is a discharged vicarage, in the archdeaconry of Wilts, and diocese of Salisbury, rated in the king's books at £7. 7. 6., endowed with £12 per annum private benefaction, and £200 royal bounty, and in the patronage of the Archdeacon of Wilts. The church, dedicated to St. Leonard, with the parsonage-house and some other houses, and about forty acres of land, is in Wiltshire, and surrounded by that part of the parish which is in Gloucestershire, though the entire parish is bounded on every side by the former county. There is a spring in the parish, the water of which is impregnated with iron.

MININGSBY, a parish in the western division of the soke of BOLINGBROKE, parts of LINDSEY, county of LINCOLN, 6 miles (W. by S.) from Spilsby, containing 134 inhabitants. The living is a discharged rectory, in the archdeaconry and diocese of Lincoln, rated in the king's books at £9. 8. 6½., endowed with £200 private benefaction, and £200 royal bounty, and in the patronage of the King, as Duke of Lancaster. The church is dedicated to St. Andrew.

MINLEY, a tything in the parish of YATELY, hundred of CRONDALL, Basingstoke division of the county of SOUTHAMPTON, 3 miles (E. by N.) from Hartford-Bridge, containing 33 inhabitants.

MINSHULL (CHURCH), a parish in the hundred of NANTWICH, county palatine of CHESTER, 5½ miles (N. by E.) from Nantwich, containing 528 inhabitants. The living is a perpetual curacy, in the archdeaconry and diocese of Chester, endowed with £200 private benefaction, and £200 royal bounty, and in the patronage of J. Brooke, Esq. The church is dedicated to St. Bartholomew. There is a place of worship for Independents. A school, erected by subscription in 1785, is endowed with about £15 per annum.

MINSHULL-VERNON, a township in that part of the parish of MIDDLEWICH which is in the hundred of NORTHWICH, county palatine of CHESTER, 4 miles (S. S. W.) from Middlewich, containing 349 inhabitants.

MINSKEP, a township in that part of the parish of ALDBOROUGH which is in the lower division of the wapentake of CLARO, West riding of the county of YORK, 1½ mile (S. by W.) from Boroughbridge, containing 243 inhabitants.

MINSTEAD, a parish in the northern division of the hundred of NEW FOREST, New Forest (East) division of the county of SOUTHAMPTON, 2¾ miles (N. N. W.) from Lyndhurst, containing, with a part of Cadnam, 1007 inhabitants. The living is a rectory, in the archdeaconry and diocese of Winchester, rated in the king's books at £7. 12. 6., and in the patronage of H. C. Compton, Esq. The church is dedicated to All Saints. Near Malwood Castle lodge, and within this parish, stands a triangular stone about five feet in height, erected in 1745, by John, Lord De la Warre, commemorating the site of the tree from which Tyrrell's arrow glanced and killed William II., in the year 1100: the place was visited by George III. and his Royal consort, June 27th, 1789.

MINSTER, a parish in the hundred of LESNEWTH, county of CORNWALL, 3½ miles (E. N. E.) from Bossiney, containing, with a part of the small sea-port of Boscastle, 425 inhabitants. The living is a discharged rectory, in the archdeaconry of Cornwall, and diocese of Exeter, rated in the king's books at £22. 17. 11, and in the patronage of Thomas John Phillips, Esq. The church is dedicated to St. Metherian: near it are some slight remains of a priory of Black monks, founded by William de Bottreaux, as a cell to the priory of Tywardreth.

MINSTER, a parish in the hundred of RINGSLOW, or Isle of THANET, lathe of ST. AUGUSTINE, county of KENT, 4½ miles (W. by S.) from Ramsgate, containing 920 inhabitants. The living is a vicarage, in the archdeaconry and diocese of Canterbury, rated in the king's books at £33. 3. 4., and in the patronage of the Archbishop of Canterbury. The church, dedicated to St. Mary, is a handsome cruciform structure, in the early style of English architecture, with a lofty spire steeple; in the choir are eighteen stalls. There is a place of worship for Wesleyan Methodists. The river Stour runs along the southern boundary of the parish, and its navigation to Sandwich is materially shortened by a canal called Stonar Cut. Minster once possessed a charter for a market and a fair: the former is disused, but the latter, for pedlary and toys, is still kept on Good Friday. Courts leet and baron are held here. About half a mile south-east from the church is Ebbsfleet, where Hengist and Horsa first landed in 449, St. Augustine in 596, and subsequently, from France, St. Mildred, the first abbess of a convent of seventy nuns, founded here about 670, in honour of the Virgin Mary, by her mother Domneva, a niece of King Egbert. In 980, and 1011, this convent was pillaged and burned, and its inmates murdered, by the Danes; after which only a few Secular priests occupied the remains, its possessions having been given to the monks of St. Augustine's abbey, Canterbury, who removed the body of St. Mildred to their own church. About a mile to the eastward of St. Mary's, St. Eadburgha, in 740, built another convent, in honour of St. Peter and St. Paul.

MINSTER in SHEPPY, a parish in the liberty of the Isle of SHEPPY, lathe of SCRAY, county of KENT, 3 miles (E. by N.) from Queenborough, containing, with Sheerness, 8414 inhabitants. The living is a perpetual curacy, in the archdeaconry and diocese of Canterbury, endowed with £1400 parliamentary grant, and in the patronage of Robert Mitchell, Esq. The church, dedicated to St. Mary and St. Sexburg, has a large square tower crowned with a turret. There is a place of worship for Independents. A convent was founded here, in 675, by Sexburg, the mother of Egbert, King of Kent, for seventy-seven nuns, who suffered much during the invasions of the Danes, by whom their house was finally destroyed; but in 1130 it was rebuilt and dedicated to St. Mary and St. Sexburg, by William, Archbishop of Canterbury, for Benedictine nuns, whose revenue, at the dissolution, was estimated at £122. 14. 6: the ruins are still visible near the church. The port of Sheerness, at the western extremity of the parish, and formerly within its limits, has been made a separate vill, with an independent civil jurisdiction.

MINSTER (SOUTH), a parish in the hundred of Dengie, county of Essex, 3 miles (N. by E.) from Burnham, containing 1445 inhabitants. The living is a vicarage, in the archdeaconry of Essex, and diocese of London, rated in the king's books at £21, and in the patronage of the Governors of the Charter-house, London. The church, dedicated to St. Leonard, is a cruciform structure, and has lately received an addition of three hundred and sixty sittings, of which two hundred and fifty are free, the Incorporated Society for the enlargement of churches and chapels having granted £400 towards defraying the expense. There are slight remains of a chapel at Southminster hall. The Independents have a place of worship here. A National school was established by the late vicar. The parish is bounded on the south-east by Crouch river, and on the east by the North sea.

MINSTER-LOVELL, a parish in the hundred of Chadlington, county of Oxford, 2¾ miles (W. N.W.) from Witney, containing 326 inhabitants. The living is a discharged vicarage, in the archdeaconry and diocese of Oxford, rated in the king's books at £8. 9. 7., endowed with £200 private benefaction, and £200 royal bounty, and in the patronage of the Provost and Fellows of Eton College. The church, dedicated to St. Kenelm, is a large ancient structure, with a tower rising from the centre; in the chancel is a splendid monument, encircled with military trophies, to the memory of Henry Heylyn, Esq., a distinguished officer in the service of Charles I. Minster-Lovell is situated on the declivity of two opposite hills, between which runs the river Windrush, dividing the parish into what is termed Great and Little Minster. An Alien priory of Benedictine monks, a cell to the abbey of St. Mary de Ibreio, was founded here in the reign of John, and at the suppression granted to Eton College.

MINSTERLEY, a chapelry in the parish of Westbury, hundred of Ford, county of Salop, 9¼ miles (S. W.) from Shrewsbury, containing 758 inhabitants. The living is a perpetual curacy, annexed to the rectory of Westbury, in the archdeaconry of Salop, and diocese of Hereford, endowed with £800 parliamentary grant. The chapel is dedicated to the Holy Trinity. There is a place of worship for Baptists, and another for Independents.

MINSTERWORTH, a parish in the duchy of Lancaster, county of Gloucester, 4½ miles (W. by S.) from Gloucester, containing 462 inhabitants. The living is a discharged vicarage, in the archdeaconry and diocese of Gloucester, rated in the king's books at £10. 13. 4., endowed with £800 private benefaction, £600 royal bounty, and £500 parliamentary grant, and in the patronage of the Bishop of Bristol. The

church is dedicated to St. George. The parish is bounded on the east and south by the navigable river Severn, in which is a considerable salmon fishery. A great quantity of cider is made in the neighbourhood. Daniel Ellis, in 1784, bequeathed £100 for the erection of a school, which was built, in 1808, on land given by Jeremiah Hawkins: there is an endowment of £4 per annum, left by Susannah Crump in 1763, and paid to this charity for teaching ten children.

MINTERN (MAGNA), a parish partly in the liberty of Fordington, Dorchester division, partly in the hundred of Cerne, Totcombe, and Modbury, but chiefly in the liberty of Piddletrenthide, Cerne subdivision of the county of Dorset, 10 miles (N. by W.) from Dorchester, containing, with the tything of Hartly, 311 inhabitants. The living is a discharged rectory, in the archdeaconry of Dorset, and diocese of Bristol, rated in the king's books at £12. 14. 2. Mrs. Sturt and another were patrons in 1798. The church is dedicated to St. Andrew: round the north aisle, which is the burial-place of the Napiers, are coats of arms, and inscriptions to the memory of several members of that ancient family.

MINTERN (PARVA), a tything in the parish and hundred of Buckland-Newton, Cerne subdivision of the county of Dorset, 9½ miles (N. by W.) from Dorchester, containing 105 inhabitants.

MINTING, a parish in the southern division of the wapentake of Gartree, parts of Lindsey, county of Lincoln, 5¾ miles (N. W. by W.) from Horncastle, containing 270 inhabitants. The living is a vicarage, in the archdeaconry and diocese of Lincoln, rated in the king's books at £5. 7. 11., and in the patronage of the Master and Fellows of St. John's College, Cambridge. The church, dedicated to St. Andrew, was given, before 1129, to the abbey of Leyr in France, upon which an Alien priory of Benedictine monks was established and continued here till its suppression by Henry V., who granted it to the Carthusian priory of Mountgrace, and, as parcel of its possessions, it was given in exchange to the Dean and Chapter of Westminster.

MINTLYN, a parish in the Lynn division of the hundred of Freebridge, county of Norfolk, 2¾ miles (E. S. E.) from Lynn-Regis, containing 30 inhabitants. The church, which was dedicated to St. Michael, has been demolished.

MINVER (ST.) HIGHLANDS, a parish in the hundred of Trigg, county of Cornwall, 3½ miles (E.N.E.) from Padstow, containing, with St. Minver Lowlands, 1028 inhabitants. The living is a vicarage, in the archdeaconry of Cornwall, and diocese of Exeter, rated in the king's books at £13. 10. 2½., and in the patronage of William Sandys, Esq., who, in 1810, presented the beautiful window of stained glass erected in the chancel of the church. There is a place of worship for Wesleyan Methodists, also a disused meeting-house, with a cemetery, belonging to the Society of Friends. Trewornan bridge was built, through the exertions of Mr. Sandys, about 1721, across a dangerous and frequently impassable ford at high tides, on the road between St. Minver and Egloshayle, and has since been made a county bridge. The stream separates these two parishes, and, by the flowing of the tide, it is rendered navigable up to Amblebridge in the parish of St. Kew.

MINVER (ST.) LOWLANDS, a chapelry in the parish of St. Minver Highlands, hundred of Trigg, county of CORNWALL, 1½ mile (E.) from Padstow, containing 315 inhabitants. The chapel, dedicated to St. Michael, and commonly called Porthilly church, is situated on the margin of Padstow river. The village of that name has long been deserted, owing to the drifting of the sands.

MINWORTH, a township in the parish of CURD-WORTH, Birmingham division of the hundred of HEM-LINGFORD, county of WARWICK, 4 miles (N. W. by W.) from Coleshill, containing 287 inhabitants.

MIRFIELD, a parish in the lower division of the wapentake of AGBRIGG, West riding of the county of YORK, 2¾ miles (W. by S.) from Dewsbury, containing 5041 inhabitants. The living is a discharged vicarage, in the archdeaconry and diocese of York, rated in the king's books at £6. 1. 0½., endowed with £400 private benefaction, and £400 royal bounty, and in the patronage of Sir G. Armytage, Bart. The church, dedicated to St. Mary, has lately received an addition of four hundred and ninety-eight sittings, of which two hundred and eighty are free, the Incorporated Society for the enlargement of churches and chapels having granted £250 towards defraying the expense. There is a place of worship for Wesleyan Methodists. Richard Thorpe, in 1667, conveyed to trustees certain houses and lands, now producing about £53 a year, for teaching fifteen poor children. This income, with the sum of £2. 10. a year, given by Joseph Lidgard and Thomas Holdsworth, are applied to the free instruction of twenty children, in a school-room erected by the inhabitants. The river Calder runs through the parish, in which the woollen manufacture is carried on to a great extent. Up to 1261, Mirfield formed a part of the Saxon parish of Dewsbury; but the lady of Sir John Heton, on her way to Dewsbury church, before dawn on Christmas-day, was attacked by robbers, and her attendant murdered, in consequence of which, at the intercession of her husband, then at Rome, the Pope granted permission to build a chapel here, which became parochial, and is the present parish church. Near it is a conical mount, thrown up by the Saxons for the defence of the ancient mansion, still called Castle-hall. The plague raged here with great fury in 1631, and swept off a great number of persons.

MISERDEN, a parish in the hundred of BISLEY, county of GLOUCESTER, 5 miles (E. S. E.) from Painswick, containing 514 inhabitants. The living is a rectory, in the archdeaconry and diocese of Gloucester, rated in the king's books at £8. 13. 4., and in the patronage of Sir Edwin Sandys, Bart. The church is dedicated to St. Andrew. There are quarries of limestone and some tile-kilns in the parish. Of Miserden castle little more remains than loose fragments of stone strewed about its ancient site.

MISSENDEN, a hamlet in the parish of HITCHIN, hundred of HITCHIN and PIRTON, county of HERTFORD, 3 miles (S. by E.) from Hitchin, with which the population is returned.

MISSENDEN (GREAT), a parish in the hundred of AYLESBURY, county of BUCKINGHAM, 26 miles (S. E. by S.) from Buckingham, containing 1735 inhabitants. The living is a discharged vicarage, in the archdeaconry of Buckingham, and diocese of Lincoln. William Astle, Esq. and others were patrons in 1820. The church is dedicated to St. Peter and St. Paul.

There is a place of worship for Baptists. A free school on the British system was established here on the 1st of January, 1827, by Mr. John Hull, and is attended by about one hundred and fifty pupils. An abbey for Black canons, in honour of the Virgin Mary, was founded here, in 1133, by Sir William de Missenden, the revenue of which, at the dissolution, was £285. 15. 9. John Randall, an eminent divine in the reign of James I., was born here.

MISSENDEN (LITTLE), a parish in the hundred of AYLESBURY, county of BUCKINGHAM, 2½ miles (W. N. W.) from Amersham, containing 814 inhabitants. The living is a discharged vicarage, in the archdeaconry of Buckingham, and diocese of Lincoln, rated in the king's books at £13. 3. 9., and in the patronage of Earl Howe. The church is dedicated to St. John the Baptist.

MISSON, a parish in the Hatfield division of the wapentake of BASSETLAW, county of NOTTINGHAM, 2¾ miles (E. N. E.) from Bawtry, containing 720 inhabitants. The living is a discharged vicarage, in the archdeaconry of Nottingham, and diocese of York, rated in the king's books at £6. 4. 4½., and in the patronage of the Crown. There is a place of worship for Wesleyan Methodists. A free school, erected here in 1693, by Thomas Mowbray and John Pinder, is endowed with land, &c., now producing an annual income of about £65, for teaching poor children.

MISTERTON, a parish in the hundred of GUTH-LAXTON, county of LEICESTER, 1 mile (E. by S.) from Lutterworth, containing, with the chapelry of Walcote, and the hamlet of Poultney, 539 inhabitants. The living is a rectory, in the archdeaconry of Leicester, and diocese of Lincoln, rated in the king's books at £16. 13. 4., and in the patronage of Jacob Henry Franks, Esq. The church is dedicated to St. Leonard. The river Swift, which at times rises and falls very rapidly, runs through the parish. James Blick, in 1730, left a trifling sum to provide books for poor children.

MISTERTON, a parish in the North-clay division of the wapentake of BASSETLAW, county of NOTTINGHAM, 4¾ miles (N. W.) from Gainsborough, containing, with the chapelry of West Stockwith, 1429 inhabitants. The living is a discharged vicarage, in the peculiar jurisdiction of the lord of the manor of Gringley on the Hill, rated in the king's books at £10. 5., endowed with £10 per annum, and £200 private benefaction, £400 royal bounty, and £1100 parliamentary grant, and in the patronage of the Dean and Chapter of York. The church is dedicated to All Saints. There are places of worship for Calvinistic and Wesleyan Methodists, and a Roman Catholic chapel. The Chesterfield and Trent canal, also Bycar Dyke, from the stop of the river Idle, passes through the parish.

MISTERTON, a parish in the hundred of CREW-KERNE, county of SOMERSET, 1¼ mile (S. E. by S.) from Crewkerne, containing 362 inhabitants. The living is a discharged vicarage, in the archdeaconry of Taunton, and diocese of Bath and Wells, endowed with £500 private benefaction, and £400 royal bounty, and in the patronage of the Dean and Chapter of Winchester. The church is dedicated to St. Leonard.

MISTLEY, a parish in the hundred of TENDRING, county of ESSEX, ½ a mile (E.) from Manningtree, containing 778 inhabitants. The living is a discharged rectory, with the curacy of Manningtree, and the vicarage of Bradfield, in the archdeaconry of Colchester, and diocese of London, rated in the king's books at £16. 13. 4. F. H. Rigby, Esq. was patron in 1811. The church, dedicated to St. Mary, stands about a mile north-west from the site of the former structure, and was consecrated in 1735, having been rebuilt, principally at the expense of Edward Rigby, Esq. The river Stour is navigable at the village, where are good quays and commodious warehouses for corn, malt, and coal, in which articles much business is carried on : the quay, port, and warehouses, at Mistley, belong to the proprietor of Mistley hall. The petty sessions for the division of Tendring are held here on Mondays, once in five weeks, alternately with Thorpe, Manningtree, and Great Bromley.

MITCHAM, a parish in the second division of the hundred of WALLINGTON, county of SURREY, 9 miles (S.S.W.) from London, containing 4453 inhabitants. This place, anciently *Michelham*, or the great dwelling, is beautifully situated on the river Wandle, a stream abounding with excellent trout, and remarkable for the transparency of its waters, and in the centre of extensive grounds appropriated to the culture of aromatic and medicinal plants. Sir Walter Raleigh resided here in an old mansion, of which the remains are at present occupied as a private dwelling-house ; and Sir Julius Cæsar, Master of the Rolls to Queen Elizabeth, had the honour of entertaining Her Majesty at his seat in this parish. The village is irregularly built, and sheltered by surrounding eminences, among which, Box Hill, so called from the trees planted on its southern declivity by the Earl of Arundel, in the reign of Charles I., having its northern side shaded with yew trees of venerable appearance, forms an interesting and picturesque object. The houses are in general respectable; and the inhabitants are amply supplied with water from the river. The environs afford delightful promenades, and abound with elegant villas, inhabited by opulent individuals, who, from the retirement of its situation, the beauty of its scenery, and its proximity to the metropolis, have been induced to select it as a place of residence. The trade is principally in calico-printing, for which there are extensive and convenient grounds, and on the banks of the Wandle are numerous mills, for corn, logwood, and tobacco. Rhubarb, liquorice, peppermint, and lavender, are extensively cultivated here for sale. The rail-road from Croydon passes through the parish. The annual fair commences on the 12th of August, and continues for three days. Mitcham is within the jurisdiction of the court of requests for the hundred of Blackheath, established by an act passed in the 6th of George III., for the recovery of debts under 40s., which was extended to the hundred of Wallington, and its powers to the recovery of debts not exceeding £5, by an act passed in the 47th of the same reign.

The living is a discharged vicarage, in the archdeaconry of Surrey, and diocese of Winchester, rated in the king's books at £10, endowed with £200 private benefaction, and £200 royal bounty, and in the patronage of Mrs. Simpson. The church, dedicated to St. Peter and St. Paul, an ancient structure of flint and stone, having become greatly dilapidated, was taken down, and the present beautiful edifice, in the later style of English architecture, with a square embattled tower,

was erected in 1821 : five hundred and fifty-five additional sittings, of which five hundred and twenty-one are free, have been lately provided, at an expense of £600, granted by the Incorporated Society for the enlargement of churches and chapels. There are places of worship for Independents and Wesleyan Methodists. The Sunday school has an endowment of £62. 11. 10. per annum, arising from accumulated savings, amounting to £1600, vested in the three per cent. consols., and from donations : the school-room was built by subscription, in 1788. There are various charitable bequests for distribution among the poor.

MITCHELDEVER, a parish in the hundred of MITCHELDEVER, Basingstoke division of the county of SOUTHAMPTON, 6¼ miles (N. by E.) from Winchester, containing, with the tythings of Northbrook, West Stratton, and Weston-Colley, 828 inhabitants. The living is a vicarage, with the perpetual curacies of Northington, Popham, and Stratton, in the archdeaconry and diocese of Winchester, rated in the king's books at £26. 13. 4., and in the patronage of Sir Thomas Baring, Bart. The church is dedicated to St. Mary.

MITCHELMERSH, a parish in the hundred of BUDDLESGATE, Fawley division of the county of SOUTHAMPTON, comprising the hamlets of Awbridge, Brushfield, and Mitchelmersh, and containing 908 inhabitants, of which number, 374 are in the hamlet of Mitchelmersh, 3½ miles (N.) from Romsey. The living is a rectory, in the peculiar jurisdiction of the Incumbent, rated in the king's books at £26. 12. 8½., and in the patronage of the Bishop of Winchester. The church is dedicated to St. Mary. The Andover canal runs through the parish. A Sunday school is endowed with about £8. 10. per annum, arising from some small bequests. Mitchelmersh is within the jurisdiction of the Cheyney Court held at Winchester every Thursday, for the recovery of debts to any amount.

MITCHEL-TROY, a parish in the upper division of the hundred of RAGLAND, county of MONMOUTH, 2¼ miles (S.W.) from Monmouth, containing 305 inhabitants. The living is a rectory, with the perpetual curacy of Cwmcarvan, in the archdeaconry and diocese of Llandaff, rated in the king's books at £12. 8. 1½., and in the patronage of the Duke of Beaufort. The church is dedicated to St. Michael.

MITFORD, a parish comprising the townships of Edington and Molesden in the western division of CASTLE ward, and the townships of Benridge, High and Low Heighley, Mitford, Newton-Park, Newton-Underwood, Nunridge, Pigdon, Spittle-hill, and Thropple in the western division of MORPETH ward, county of NORTHUMBERLAND, and containing 625 inhabitants, of which number, 178 are in the township of Mitford, 1¾ mile (W. by S.) from Morpeth. The living is a discharged vicarage, in the archdeaconry of Northumberland, and diocese of Durham, rated in the king's books at £10. 6. 8., endowed with £400 private benefaction, £200 royal bounty, and £1100 parliamentary grant, and in the patronage of the Bishop of Durham. The rivers Wansbeck and Font run through the parish. Here are the remains of a castle formerly belonging to Sir Gilbert Middleton, for whose treasonable practices it was demolished by order of Edward II.

MITMEECE, a township in the parish of ECCLESHALL, northern division of the hundred of PIREHILL, county of STAFFORD, containing 131 inhabitants. It is within the peculiar jurisdiction of the Prebendal Court of Eccleshall.

MITTON, a parish comprising the township of Old Laund-Booth in the higher division, and the township of Aighton with Bailey and Chaigley in the lower division, of the hundred of BLACKBURN, county palatine of LANCASTER; the chapelries of Grindleton and Waddington, and the townships of Bashall-Eaves, West Bradford, and Mitton, in the western division of the wapentake of STAINCLIFFE and EWCROSS, West riding of the county of YORK; and containing 4925 inhabitants, of which number, 324 are in the township of Mitton, 3 miles (W.S.W.) from Clitheroe. The living is a discharged vicarage, in the archdeaconry and diocese of York, rated in the king's books at £14. 7. 8½., and in the patronage of the Rev. John Wilson. The church, dedicated to St. Michael, was erected in the reign of Edward III. The chapel of St. Nicholas, on the north side of the choir, is the burial-place of the Sherburnes, and contains numerous memorials to that knightly family. It stands near the confluence of the rivers Calder, Holder, and Ribble, the neighbourhood of which was the scene of a great slaughter committed by the Scots, in one of their irruptions into England, during the existence of the plague, in 1319. Helen Heighton, in 1795, devised a school-house and certain messuages, the annual income arising from which, viz., £38. 10., is applied to the free instruction of about twenty children. There is also a rent-charge of £4. 10. bequeathed by William Parkinson, towards the support of a Sunday school.

MITTON, a township in that part of the parish of PENKRIDGE which is in the eastern division of the hundred of CUTTLESTONE, county of STAFFORD, 2¾ miles (W.N.W.) from Penkridge. The population is returned with the parish.

MITTON (LITTLE), a township in that part of the parish of WHALLEY which is in the higher division of the hundred of BLACKBURN, county palatine of LANCASTER, 3¼ miles (S.W.) from Clitheroe, containing, with Coalcoates and Hewthorn, 99 inhabitants.

MITTON (LOWER), a chapelry in the parish of KIDDERMINSTER, lower division of the hundred of HALFSHIRE, county of WORCESTER, and containing, with the town of Stourport, 2544 inhabitants. The living is a perpetual curacy, in the archdeaconry and diocese of Worcester, and in the patronage of the Vicar of Kidderminster. The chapel, dedicated to St. Michael, is· a small unadorned edifice of brick, erected in 1790, the chancel at the expense of John Folliott, Esq., as lord of the manor of Lickhill. In Leland's time, Mitton was distinguished for the number of its corn-mills, for the establishment of which, the river Stour, branching here in various directions, afforded great convenience. There are now a manufactory for worsted-yarn, an iron-foundry, a tannery, and a vinegar-yard. The Staffordshire and Worcestershire canal joins the Severn at this place, and, by uniting that river with the Trent, affords an extended line of inland navigation for the conveyance of goods; whence the origin and growth of the adjoining town of Stourport, now a depôt for the manufactures and agricultural produce of the surrounding counties, and described under its proper-head.

MITTON (UPPER), a hamlet in the parish of HAR-

TLEBURY, lower division of the hundred of HALFSHIRE, county of WORCESTER, ¾ of a mile (N.E.) from Stourport, containing 181 inhabitants.

MITTONS, a hamlet in the parish of BREDON, middle division of the hundred of OSWALDSLOW, county of WORCESTER, 1 mile (N.E.) from Tewkesbury. The population is returned with the parish.

MIXBURY, a parish in the hundred of PLOUGHLEY, county of OXFORD, 8 miles (N. by E.) from Bicester, containing, with the hamlet of Fulwell and the township of Willason, 336 inhabitants. The living is a rectory, in the archdeaconry and diocese of Oxford, rated in the king's books at £15. 9. 4½., and in the patronage of the Bishop of Rochester. The church is dedicated to All Saints. The river Ouse runs through the parish.

MOAT, a township in the parish of KIRK-ANDREWS upon ESK, ESKDALE ward, county of CUMBERLAND, 4½ miles (N.N.E.) from Longtown, containing 300 inhabitants. On the banks of the Liddel are the ruins of a strong square tower, called Liddel Strength, surrounded by a double moat. It more than once fell into the power of the Scots, and on one occasion was the scene of a barbarous act of David, King of Scotland, who, after making himself master of the place, caused the two sons of the Governor, Sir Walter Selby, to be strangled.

MOBBERLEY, a parish in the hundred of BUCKLOW, county palatine of CHESTER, 3 miles (E.N.E.) from Nether Knutsford, containing 1198 inhabitants. The living is a rectory, in the archdeaconry and diocese of Chester, rated in the king's books at £23. 3. 4., and in the patronage of the Rev. J. H. Mallory. The church, dedicated to St.Wilfrid, has a rich screen, the remains of a rood loft, and some stalls in the chancel: it was thoroughly repaired and the tower rebuilt with stone in 1533, at the expense of Sir John Talbot. There are places of worship for Independents and Wesleyan Methodists. A free grammar school was founded, in 1569, by the Rev. William Griffith, who endowed it with the interest of £200. The manufacture of cotton is carried on at this place, a large factory affording employment to about one hundred persons. Three distinct courts baron are annually held for the several manors within the parish. A priory of Black canons, in honour of the Blessed Virgin Mary and St. Wilfrid, was founded here, in 1206, by Patrick de Modberley, who having only a life interest in the property with which he endowed it, the establishment existed but a short time.

MOCCAS, a parish in the hundred of WEBTREE, county of HEREFORD, 9½ miles (W.N.W.) from Hereford, containing 185 inhabitants. The living is a discharged rectory, in the archdeaconry and diocese of Hereford, rated in the king's books at £6. 4. 4., endowed with £200 private benefaction, and £200 royal bounty, and in the patronage of Sir G. Cornewall, Bart. The church is dedicated to St. Michael.

MOCKERKIN, a hamlet in the parochial chapelry of LOWESWATER, ALLERDALE ward above Darwent, county of CUMBERLAND, 5 miles (S.S.W.) from Cockermouth. The population is returned with Loweswater. This hamlet forms a constablewick with Sosgill.

MODBURY, a market town and parish in the hundred of ERMINGTON, county of DEVON, 35 miles (S.W. by S.) from Exeter, and 208 (W.S.W.) from London, containing 2194 inhabitants. This place, called in Latin records "Motberia," was in the possession of

Wado at the time of the Confessor; it subsequently became the property of the Valletorts, Okestons, and Champernownes. In 1334, Richard Champernowne obtained permission to fortify his manorial residence at Modbury. During the contest between Charles and the parliament, this fortress was taken by the garrison at Plymouth; and, in February 1643, Sir N. Stanning, when intrenched here with two thousand soldiers, was defeated by the Devonshire clubmen. The town is situated at the junction of the roads leading to Plymouth, Kingsbridge, and Dartmouth, and occupies the bottom and declivities of a valley: it consists of four streets, which meet at right angles, the point of junction being in the lowest part of the town : the inhabitants are supplied with water from two conduits, which are connected by pipes with a neighbouring spring. A new line of turnpike-road is in progress, from Dartmouth, Kingsbridge, and Salcombe, through this town to Plymouth : the new London mail road from Plymouth to Exeter passes about a mile from Modbury. The manufacture of woollen goods, which was formerly considerable, has decayed : there is still some weaving of long ells for the East India Company, also a tolerable trade in corn and malt. A creek, navigable for barges, extends from the æstuary of the river Erme, which bounds this parish on the west, to within two miles of the town, and thus facilitates the importation of coal, and the export of the produce of the soil. The principal general market is on Thursday, and there is another on Saturday for butchers' meat; also a great cattle market on the second Tuesday in every month, to which the navy contractors and others resort. Of the two fairs once held on St. George's and St. James' days, only the former is retained; it takes place on the 4th of May, unless that day fall later in the week than Thursday, in which case the fair is postponed till the following Tuesday. The town is governed by a portreeve (usually styled mayor), constables, and other subordinate officers, who are annually appointed at one of the courts leet, which are held at Michaelmas and Ladyday, the mayor being returned by a jury of twelve householders. This borough sent two members to parliament in the 34th of Edward I., but was afterwards relieved from making returns, on the plea of poverty.

The living is a vicarage, in the archdeaconry of Totness, and diocese of Exeter, rated in the king's books at £19. 11. 0½., and in the patronage of the Provost and Fellows of Eton College. The church, which is dedicated to St. George, and stands upon an eminence south-westward of the town, is an ancient embattled structure, with modern additions ; the tower, which was rebuilt in 1622, is surmounted by a spire : the interior is very neat and spacious, and contains some mutilated monuments of the Champernowne family. There are places of worship for Baptists, the Society of Friends, Independents, and Wesleyan Methodists. A free school was established, in 1730, by subscription: the permanent income is £12 per annum, and twelve poor boys are instructed in reading, writing, and arithmetic. Sunday and infant schools are supported by voluntary contributions. There are some remains of a Benedictine priory, founded here in the reign of Stephen, and dedicated to St. Gregory, as a cell to the abbey of St. Peter sur Dive, in Normandy : its possessions, valued at £70 per annum, were given by

Henry VI. to Eton College, afterwards bestowed by Edward IV. upon the abbey of Tavistock, but eventually restored to Eton, to which foundation it still belongs. Sir John Fortescue, a celebrated lawyer, Lord Chief Justice in the reign of Henry VI., was a native of this place ; and Sir George Baker, M.D., President of the Royal College of Physicians, and author of some valuable medical works, was born here in 1722.

MOGGERHANGER, a hamlet in the parish of BLUNHAM, hundred of WIXAMTREE, county of BEDFORD, 4½ miles (N. W. by N.) from Biggleswade, containing 405 inhabitants.

MOLDASH, a parish in the hundred of FELBOROUGH, lathe of SCRAY, county of KENT, 5˜ miles (E. N. E.) from Charing, containing 378 inhabitants. The living is a perpetual curacy, annexed to the vicarage of Chilham, in the archdeaconry and diocese of Canterbury. The church is dedicated to St. Peter.

MOLESDEN, a township in that part of the parish of MITFORD which is in the western division of CASTLE ward, county of NORTHUMBERLAND, 3½ miles (W. by S.) from Morpeth, containing 21 inhabitants.

MOLESWORTH, a parish in the hundred of LEIGHTONSTONE, county of HUNTINGDON, 4½ miles (E. by S.) from Thrapston, containing 191 inhabitants. The living is a rectory, in the archdeaconry of Huntingdon, and diocese of Lincoln, rated in the king's books at £11. 10., and in the patronage of the Archbishop of York. The church is dedicated to St. Peter.

MOLLAND, a parish in the hundred of SOUTH MOLTON, county of DEVON, 7 miles (E. N. E.) from South Molton, containing 456 inhabitants. The living is a vicarage not in charge, united to that of Knowstone, in the archdeaconry of Barnstaple, and diocese of Exeter. The church is dedicated to St. Mary. Eight poor children are educated by a schoolmistress for £4 a year, the gift of Thomas Clarke, in 1776. There are vestiges of an ancient earth-work within the parish.

MOLLINGTON, a chapelry in that part of the parish of CROPREDY which is in the hundred of BLOXHAM, county of OXFORD, and the Burton-Dassett division of the hundred of KINGTON, county of WARWICK, 4¾ miles (N. by W.) from Banbury, containing 310 inhabitants. The chapel is dedicated to All Saints. The chapelry is within the jurisdiction of the peculiar court of Banbury in the Cathedral Church of Lincoln.

MOLLINGTON (GREAT), a township in that part of the parish of BACKFORD which is in the higher division of the hundred of WIRRALL, county palatine of CHESTER, 2¾ miles (N. W. by N.) from Chester, containing 122 inhabitants.

MOLLINGTON (LITTLE), a township in that part of the parish of St. MARY, CHESTER, which is in the higher division of the hundred of WIRRALL, county palatine of CHESTER, 2¼ miles (N. W. by N.) from Chester, containing 28 inhabitants.

MOLSCROFT, a township in that part of the parish of ST. JOHN which is within the liberties of the borough of BEVERLEY, East riding of the county of YORK, 1¼ mile (W. N. W.) from Beverley, containing 111 inhabitants.

MOLTON (NORTH), a parish in the hundred of SOUTH MOLTON, county of DEVON, 3 miles (N. N. E.) from South Molton, containing 1847 inhabitants. The living is a discharged vicarage, with the perpetual cu-

2 S

racy of Twitchen annexed, in the archdeaconry of Barnstaple, and diocese of Exeter, rated in the king's books at £16. 16. 1., endowed with £600 private benefaction, £400 royal bounty, and £1100 parliamentary grant. The Earl of Morley was patron in 1820. The church, dedicated to All Saints, is furnished with a rich pulpit: there were formerly three chapels of ease in the parish. There is a place of worship for Wesleyan Methodists. Almshouses for six poor families were founded and endowed by an ancestor of George Parker: there is also a small sum, the gift of William Mourman, for teaching six boys. A weekly market, formerly held at this place, has been long disused.

MOLTON (SOUTH), an incorporated market town and parish, having separate jurisdiction, though locally in the hundred of South Molton, county of DEVON, 28 miles (N. W. by N.) from Exeter, and 181 (W. by S.) from London, containing 3314 inhabitants. This town derives its name from the river Mole, on the western bank of which it is situated,

Corporate Seal.

having Exmoor on the north, and Dartmoor faintly perceptible on its southern boundary: over the river, which falls into the Taw about four miles hence, is a bridge of three arches: the streets are well paved and lighted, and the inhabitants are supplied with water from wells. Monthly assemblies are held in the town hall, which stands in the market-place; and there is a subscription reading-room. The principal branch of manufacture is that of woollen goods, considerable supplies of which are occasionally furnished to the East Indies; shalloons, serges, and coarse woollen cloth, are the articles chiefly made. The general market is on Saturday; others are held on Tuesday and Thursday: there are cattle fairs on the Wednesday before the 22nd of June, and on the Wednesday after August 26th: great markets also are held on the Saturday after February 13th, which is noted for its fine show of North Devon cattle, March 25th, August 1st, October 10th, and December 12th. For several successive weeks in the spring, there are large markets for sheep, one year old. The sale for cattle is almost constant, the landholders here being chiefly breeders. On the river are several flour-mills and a fulling-mill. The charter of incorporation was granted by Elizabeth, and confirmed by Charles II. The municipal government is vested in a mayor, recorder, three capital burgesses, and thirteen common council-men, with a town clerk, serjeants at mace, and other officers: the mayor is elected annually by a majority of the corporation. The mayor, recorder, and two capital burgesses, are justices of the peace, and hold quarter sessions, with power to transport; also a court of record, called the three weeks' court, for the recovery of debts under £40, by charter of Elizabeth; but this court is seldom resorted to, on account of the expense of the proceedings. The county magistrates hold petty sessions for the hundred in a building over the corn market. The freedom of the borough is obtained by birth, every son of a freeman being entitled to it, whether born in or out of the parish; it is also conferred by gift of the corporation:

every freeman is exempt from serving on county juries, and the inhabitants do not pay county rates. The town sent representatives to parliament once in the reign of Edward I. The town hall is a handsome building of Portland stone; and a new prison is in progress of erection, to comprise four cells, two dwelling-houses for the serjeants, and a place of confinement for less criminal offenders.

The living is a perpetual curacy, in the archdeaconry of Barnstaple, and diocese of Exeter, endowed with £400, and a stipend of £30 per annum, private benefaction, £400 royal bounty, and £600 parliamentary grant, and in the patronage of the Dean and Canons of Windsor. The church, dedicated to St. Mary Magdalene, is a very spacious structure, in the ancient style of English architecture; it has been considerably enlarged by bringing out the walls of the north and south aisles almost to the angles of the transepts, whereby its ancient form of a cross has been destroyed: in the interior is a richly-carved pulpit of stone: from the summit of the tower, Hartland point and Lundy island are discernible. There are places of worship for Independents and Wesleyan Methodists. The free school was founded, in 1686, by Hugh Squier, who also endowed it with lands for the education of twenty poor children: the annual income is £57. 9., and twenty boys are instructed. The Blue school was established by subscription, in 1711, since which period many augmentations have been made to its funds: the present income is about £112. 13. 3. per annum, out of which a salary of £26.17.6. is paid to the master and mistress: forty-five boys and twenty girls, appointed by the corporation from the poor of this and the neighbouring parishes, are instructed and clothed annually. There are numerous benefactions for the relief of the poor. A Sunday school, in which one hundred and fifty children of both sexes are instructed, is supported by voluntary contributions. Iron-ore is found in the neighbourhood, which also abounds in a species of slate, or flag-stone, enclosing within its bed a considerable portion of limestone. Fragments of *encrinites* and *corallimes* have been discovered. Some vestiges of an ancient encampment are visible at Cadbury, near this place. The late Mr. Justice Buller received the early part of his education at the grammar school here; and the Rev. Samuel Badcock, who distinguished himself in a controversy with Dr. Priestley, and assisted Dr. White in writing his celebrated Bampton Lectures, was born here in 1747; he died in London in 1788.

MONCKTON (BISHOP'S), a chapelry in that part of the parish of RIPON which is in the liberty of RIPON, West riding of the county of YORK, 4 miles (S. S. E.) from Ripon, containing 479 inhabitants. The living is a perpetual curacy, in the jurisdiction of the peculiar court of Ripon, belonging to the Archbishop of York; endowed with £800 royal bounty, and £800 parliamentary grant, and in the patronage of the Dean and Chapter of Ripon. There is a place of worship for Wesleyan Methodists.

MONCKTON (TARRANT), a parish in the hundred of MONCKTON up WIMBORNE, Shaston (East) division of the county of DORSET, 4¼ miles (E.N.E.) from Blandford-Forum, containing 236 inhabitants. The living is a discharged vicarage, with the perpetual curacy of Tarrant-Launceston, in the archdeaconry of Dorset, and diocese of Bristol, rated in the king's books at £17. 16. 8., endowed with £200 private benefaction, £200 royal bounty, and £300 parliamentary grant. J. Farquharson, Esq. was patron in 1822. The church is dedicated to All Saints. The river Tarrant runs through the parish, in which there was formerly a monastic establishment, whence the derivation of the name Monckton.

MONCKTON up WIMBORNE, a tything in the parish and hundred of CRANBORNE, though locally in the hundred of Monckton up Wimborne, Shaston (East) division of the county of DORSET, 2 miles (W.) from Cranborne, with which the population is returned. The river Allen has its source here.

MONEWDEN, a parish in the hundred of LOES, county of SUFFOLK, 5 miles (W. N. W.) from Wickham-Market, containing 188 inhabitants. The living is a rectory, in the archdeaconry of Suffolk, and diocese of Norwich, rated in the king's books at £8. 13. 4. C. Archdeckne, Esq. was patron in 1803. The church is dedicated to St. Mary.

MONGEHAM (GREAT), a parish in the hundred of CORNILO, lathe of ST. AUGUSTINE, county of KENT, 2 miles (W.S.W.) from Deal, containing 281 inhabitants. The living is a rectory, in the archdeaconry and diocese of Canterbury, rated in the king's books at £18. 5., and in the patronage of the Archbishop of Canterbury. The church, dedicated to St. Martin, is a large handsome structure, in the early English style. A market on Thursday, granted by Henry III., has been long disused, but a fair for cattle and pedlary is held on October 29th.

MONGEHAM (LITTLE), a parish in the hundred of CORNILO, lathe of ST. AUGUSTINE, county of KENT, 2½ miles (W.S.W.) from Deal, containing 113 inhabitants. The living is a discharged rectory, in the archdeaconry and diocese of Canterbury, rated in the king's books at £5. 15., endowed with £200 private benefaction, and £200 royal bounty, and in the patronage of the Archbishop of Canterbury. The church has fallen into ruins.

MONGEWELL, a parish in the hundred of LANG-TREE, county of OXFORD, 1½ mile (S.) from Wallingford, containing 142 inhabitants. The living is a rectory, in the archdeaconry and diocese of Oxford, rated in the king's books at £9. 9. 4½. Uvedale Price, Esq. was patron in 1792. The church, dedicated to St. John the Baptist, has some portions in the Norman style remaining.

MONINGTON, a township in the parish of Vow-CHURCH, hundred of WEBTREE, county of HEREFORD, 10 miles (W. by S.) from Hereford. The population is returned with the parish.

MONKHILL, a township in the parish of PONTE-FRACT, upper division of the wapentake of OSGOLD-CROSS, West riding of the county of YORK, containing 40 inhabitants.

MONKLAND, a parish in the hundred of STRET-FORD, county of HEREFORD, 2½ miles (W. S. W.) from Leominster, containing 187 inhabitants. The living is a discharged vicarage, in the archdeaconry and diocese of Hereford, rated in the king's books at £11. 0. 9., and in the patronage of the Dean and Canons of Windsor. The church, dedicated to All Saints, with the manor, was, in the time of William Rufus, given by Ralph Tony to the abbey of Conches in Normandy, upon which a cell of Benedictine monks was established

here, the possessions of which, at the suppression, were granted to the Dean and Canons of Windsor. Courts leet are occasionally held here.

MONKLEIGH, a parish in the hundred of SHEB-BEAR, county of DEVON, 2¾ miles (W. N. W.) from Great Torrington, containing 509 inhabitants. The living is a vicarage, in the archdeaconry of Barnstaple, and diocese of Exeter, rated in the king's books at £12. 14. 7. Mrs. Saltern was patroness in 1815. The church, dedicated to St. George, contains a wooden screen, an altar-tomb under an arch in the later English style, and some interesting monuments, among which is one to the memory of Sir William Hankford, Chief Justice of the King's Bench, who died here in 1424, or, as tradition relates, was accidentally killed by his park-keeper, near a tree still called Hankford's oak.

MONKRIDGE-WARD, a township in the parish of ELSDON, southern division of COQUETDALE ward, county of NORTHUMBERLAND, 8 miles (N. E.) from Bellingham, containing 109 inhabitants.

MONKSEATON, a township in the parish of TYNE-MOUTH, eastern division of CASTLE ward, county of NORTHUMBERLAND, 2½ miles (N.) from North Shields, containing 537 inhabitants, many of whom are employed in the neighbouring collieries. There is a place of worship for Wesleyan Methodists. Within the township is a large brewery. On Monkhouse farm are the remains of an old cross, called the Monks' stone, with this inscription, "O horror, to kill a man for a pig's head;" concerning which a curious tradition prevails of a monk of Tynemouth having been scourged on the spot by a Mr. Delaval, for having cut off a pig's head whilst roasting in the kitchen of the latter, and, dying within a year and a day, his brethren charged Mr. Delaval with his murder, who, in order to obtain absolution, assigned to the monastery the manor of Elswick and other estates, and erected an obelisk on the spot where he chastised the monk.

MONKS-ELEIGH, a parish in the hundred of BABERGH, county of SUFFOLK, 2¼ miles (W. S. W.) from Bildeston, containing 713 inhabitants. The living is a rectory, in the peculiar jurisdiction and patronage of the Archbishop of Canterbury, rated in the king's books at £14. 18. 11½. The church is dedicated to St. Peter. There is a place of worship for Wesleyan Methodists.

MONKSILVER, a parish in the hundred of WIL-LITON and FREEMANNERS, county of SOMERSET, 7 miles (N. by W.) from Wiveliscombe, containing 306 inhabitants. The living is a rectory, in the archdeaconry of Taunton, and diocese of Bath and Wells, rated in the king's books at £9. 8. 1½., and in the patronage of the Dean and Canons of Windsor. The church is dedicated to All Saints.

MONKSTON, a parish in the hundred of ANDOVER, Andover division of the county of SOUTHAMPTON, 3¼ miles (W.) from Andover, containing 257 inhabitants. The living is a rectory, in the archdeaconry and diocese of Winchester, rated in the king's books at £14. 12. 11., and in the patronage of the Provost and Fellows of King's College, Cambridge.

MONKSWOOD, an extra-parochial liberty, in the lower division of the hundred of USK, county of MON-MOUTH, 2¾ miles (N. W. by W.) from Usk, containing 156 inhabitants. The living is a perpetual curacy, in

2 S 2

the archdeaconry and diocese of Llandaff, endowed with £1000 royal bounty. The Duke of Beaufort was patron in 1788.

MONKTON, a parish in the hundred of COLYTON, county of DEVON, 2 miles (N. E. by N.) from Honiton, containing 136 inhabitants. The living is a perpetual curacy, annexed to the vicarage of Colyton, in the peculiar jurisdiction of the Dean and Chapter of Exeter. The church is dedicated to St. Mary Magdalene.

MONKTON, a joint township with Jarrow, in the parish of JARROW, eastern division of CHESTER ward, county palatine of DURHAM, 5 miles (E.) from Gateshead. The population is returned with Jarrow : the inhabitants are chiefly employed at the adjacent coal works. This is said to be the birthplace of Venerable Bede: a well, lately used as a bath for weakly or diseased children, and the spot where the rustics celebrated the eve of Midsummer-day, still retain his name.

MONKTON, formerly a distinct parish, but now in the parish of OTTERDEN, hundred of EYHORNE, lathe of AYLESFORD, county of KENT. The church has been long since demolished.

MONKTON, a parish in the hundred of RINGSLOW, or Isle of THANET, lathe of St. AUGUSTINE, county of KENT, 7 miles (W.) from Ramsgate, containing 348 inhabitants. The living is a vicarage, with the perpetual curacy of Birchington, in the peculiar jurisdiction and patronage of the Archbishop of Canterbury, rated in the king's books at £13. 8. 4. The church is dedicated to St. Mary. The river Stour runs along the southern boundary of the parish. A market, formerly held here, is now disused; but fairs are still kept on July 22nd for hogs, and October 11th for toys, &c.

MONKTON (MOOR), a parish in the ainsty of the city, and East riding of the county, of YORK, comprising the townships of Hessey and Moor-Monkton, and containing 430 inhabitants, of which number, 269 are in the township of Moor-Monkton, 7¾ miles (N.W. by W.) from York. The living is a rectory, in the archdeaconry and diocese of York, rated in the king's books at £16. 19. 7., and in the patronage of the Crown. The church, dedicated to All Saints, is an ancient structure, situated half a mile from the village. A free school has been endowed by Sir Saville and Lady Sarah Slingsby, for twelve poor children. Red House, built in the reign of Charles I. by Sir Henry Slingsby, commands a noble and extensive view, including the city and cathedral of York.

MONKTON (NUN), a parish in the upper division of the wapentake of CLARO, West riding of the county of YORK, 8¼ miles (N.W.) from York, containing 344 inhabitants. The living is a perpetual curacy, in the archdeaconry of Richmond, and diocese of Chester, endowed with £400 private benefaction, £600 royal bounty, and £300 parliamentary grant. S. J. Tuffnell, Esq. was patron in 1815. The church, dedicated to St. Mary, formerly belonged to a priory of Benedictine nuns, founded in the reign of Stephen, by William de Arches and Ivetta his wife, which, before the dissolution, possessed a revenue of £85. 14. 8. There is a place of worship for Wesleyan Methodists. A school for twelve poor boys was founded and endowed by Thomas and Leonard Wilson, about 1716; and another, for the like number of girls, by Mary and Dorothy Wilson; the annual income is £30.

MONKTON (WEST), a parish forming a detached portion of the hundred of WHITLEY, county of SOMERSET, 3½ miles (N.E. by N.) from Taunton, containing 1004 inhabitants. The living is a rectory, in the archdeaconry of Taunton, and diocese of Bath and Wells, rated in the king's books at £26, and in the patronage of the Rev. J. F. Maddison. The church, dedicated to St. Augustine, has lately received an addition of sixty-two sittings, of which fifty are free, the Incorporated Society for the enlargement of churches and chapels having granted £34 towards defraying the expense. There are places of worship for Baptists and Wesleyan Methodists. The navigable river Tone, and the Taunton and Bridg-water canal, run through the parish. Nearly adjoining the town of Taunton is the Spital almshouse, founded, in 1270, by Thomas Lambret, destroyed by fire in the reign of Henry VIII., and rebuilt soon afterwards by an abbot of Glastonbury : it is endowed with several parcels of land, producing an annual income of about £44. 10., and at present affords an asylum to eleven poor widows. John Claymond gave £15 per annum to establish an exhibition at Brasenose College, Oxford, for boys from this school.

MONKTON-FARLEY, a parish in the hundred of BRADFORD, county of WILTS, 4 miles (N. N. W.) from Bradford, containing 347 inhabitants. The living is a discharged rectory, in the archdeaconry and diocese of Salisbury, rated in the king's books at £7. 15. 2½., and in the patronage of the Bishop of Salisbury. The church is dedicated to St. Peter. Here are some remains of a convent of Cluniac monks, founded, about 1125, as a cell to the priory of Lewes : it was dedicated to St. Mary Magdalene, and at the dissolution had a revenue of £217. 0. 4.

MONMOUTH, a borough, market town, and parish, having separate jurisdiction, though locally in the lower division of the hundred of Skenfreth, county of MONMOUTH, of which it is the chief town, 130 miles (W. N. W.) from London, containing 4164 inhabitants. This place, which derives its name from being situated at the mouth of

Arms.

the river Monnow, is by some antiquaries supposed to have been the Blestium of Antoninus, but no Roman antiquities have been discovered to confirm that opinion. It was a place of considerable importance during the time of the Saxons, who, to secure their conquests between the Severn and the Wye, and to repel the frequent incursions of the Britons, erected a stately castle, and fortified the town with walls of immense strength; of the former, a small portion is still remaining, and of the latter, one of the gateway towers, at the entrance from the Ross road, is almost entire, and several other vestiges may be traced in various parts of the town. At the time of the Norman Conquest, it was bestowed upon William Fitz-Baderon, one of the Conqueror's followers, who, from that circumstance, assumed the name of William de Monmouth. The celebrated John of Gaunt, Duke of Lancaster, resided for some time in the castle; which was also the birthplace of Henry V., who passed his infancy here, and whose cradle, and the sword which he used at the battle of Agincourt, are deposited in Troy House, belonging to the Duke of Beaufort, at a short distance on the road to Chepstow.

The town is beautifully situated on the banks of the river Wye, near its confluence with the Monnow, in a luxuriant vale, environed by hills of various elevation, some of them being richly crowned with wood, and consists of one spacious street extending from the market-place to the river Monnow, over which is an ancient stone bridge with an arched gateway, erected in 1272, forming an entrance from the Abergavenny road, and of several other streets diverging in different directions to the river Wye, over which is also a handsome stone bridge. The houses are in general well built; many of those in the principal street have gardens and orchards attached to them, and in various parts of the town are ancient buildings interspersed with handsome modern houses; the streets on the side towards the Wye contain several ranges of respectable buildings: the town is well paved and lighted, and amply supplied with water from springs, and with soft water, for culinary purposes, by carts which convey it to the houses of the inhabitants at a moderate charge. The public library is well furnished with modern works; and assemblies are held occasionally at the Beaufort Arms and at the town hall. Chippenham meadow, an extensive plot of ground, forms a delightful promenade on the bank of the Wye, and is intersected by the river Monnow, which empties itself into that river: races are annually held in October, and are well attended. On the opposite side of the river, and on the acclivities of the hills which rise from its banks, numerous picturesque and beautiful villas are irregularly scattered at different elevations: on the Kymin, a lofty hill commanding an extensive view of the windings of the river through a finely varied tract of country, and of the town lying at its base, a marine pavilion has been erected in honour of the distinguished Lord Nelson, and other naval heroes, whose achievements are recorded by paintings and inscriptions. Beaulieu Grove is a rich wood, through which many pleasing walks have been made, commanding in different points of view agreeable prospects of the scenery in the neighbourhood. The steep banks of the Wye, clothed in many places with the most luxuriant verdure, are rich in every variety of beauty; and the windings of the river lead through a succession of scenes not surpassed by any of like character in the country. The beauty of the landscape, the mildness of the air, and its peculiar adaptation as a place of retirement, have made it the retreat of many respectable families, who have erected on the shores of the river, and on the heights which crown its banks, numerous handsome villas. The trade principally arises from the navigation of the river Wye, in the traffic carried on with Hereford and Bristol; and the preparation of bark from the forests of the Upper Wye, of which a great quantity is sent to Chepstow for exportation to the south of England and different parts of Ireland, and in which a considerable number of men, women, and children, are employed. The iron and tin manufactures were introduced into this kingdom, and established at Monmouth, by a native of Switzerland, and are now carried on to a considerable extent: the town is well supplied

with coal from the neighbouring Forest of Dean, from which a rail-road has been constructed, passing through Coleford and Newland. Paper is largely manufactured at mills situated on streams near the town, and there are also several corn-mills. The market, which is well supplied, is on Saturday, and a market is held on the first Wednesday in each month, for the sale of cattle, sheep, and pigs: the fairs are on Whit-Tuesday, for toys; the Wednesday before the 20th of June, for wool and cheese; and September 4th, and November 22d, for cattle, hops, and cheese.

The inhabitants were first incorporated by Edward VI., who confirmed the preceding privileges granted by Henry VIII., which were afterwards extended by Charles II., by whose charter the government is vested in a mayor, recorder, two bailiffs, and fifteen common council-men, assisted by a town clerk, chamberlain, coroner, two serjeants at mace, and subordinate officers. The corporation hold quarterly courts of session for the trial of misdemeanants within the borough. The assizes for the county, and the petty sessions for the upper division of the hundred of Usk, are held here. The town is within the duchy of Lancaster, and subject to the jurisdiction of the duchy courts. The town hall is a substantial stone structure on piazzas, and ornamented with a statue of Henry V.: the lower part is appropriated to the use of the market, and the upper part contains the court-rooms for the assizes and the sessions, and a spacious assembly-room. The county gaol and house of correction is a spacious stone building in the form of a castle, on the road to Hereford, and contains forty-one cells, ten day-rooms, and seven airing-yards, in one of which is a tread-wheel, for the classification of prisoners. The borough first exercised the elective franchise in the 27th of Henry VIII., in conjunction with those of Usk and Newport: it returns one member to parliament. The right of election is vested in the resident burgesses of these several boroughs, the number of whom is about eight hundred, chiefly in the interest of the Duke of Beaufort: the mayor and bailiffs are the returning officers. The election of knights for the shire also takes place in Monmouth, as the county town.

The living is a discharged vicarage, in the archdeaconry and diocese of Hereford, rated in the king's books at £9. 2. 3., endowed with £200 private benefaction, £200 royal bounty, and £200 parliamentary grant, and in the patronage of the Duke of Beaufort. The church, dedicated to St. Mary, was anciently the conventual church of a Benedictine priory, founded here in the reign of Henry II., the revenue of which at the dissolution was £56. 1. 11. The body of the church has been rebuilt in the modern style, and the only part remaining of the original building is the tower, surmounted by an elegant and finely-proportioned spire, in the early style of English architecture, two hundred and ten feet high, and forming an interesting feature in the view of the town. St. Thomas, a chapel of ease to the vicarage, is an ancient edifice with a low

Corporate Seal.

tower, exhibiting good specimens of the early English and the Norman styles, with some portions of an earlier period; it is supposed to have been founded prior to the Conquest, and is now undergoing repair, on the completion of which it is proposed to assign to it a district, under the authority of the commissioners for building new churches. There are places of worship for Baptists, Independents, and Wesleyan Methodists, and a Roman Catholic chapel. The free grammar school was founded in the reign of James I., by William Jones, a native of Newland in this vicinity, and citizen and haberdasher of London, who bequeathed £9000 for the endowment of a school and almshouse, and for the establishment of a lectureship in the church: the school is open to all children of the neighbourhood, with preference to those of this parish, for instruction in the Latin and Greek languages: the premises, near Wye bridge, are handsomely built, comprising houses for the master, who has a salary of £120 per annum, the usher, who has £60, and the lecturer, whose stipend is £140 per annum. The English language, writing, arithmetic, and the mathematics, are taught by an additional master, recently appointed, with a salary of £60 per annum. The almshouses consist of twenty separate tenements, with a garden to each, for twenty aged men and women, who have a weekly allowance of six shillings each, with a supply of coal and clothing: the school and almshouses are under the direction of the corporation and the Haberdashers' Company. A National school, supported by subscription, and in which nearly one hundred boys and upwards of ninety girls are instructed, is kept in an ancient room, with a fine oriel window, part of the priory of Benedictine monks, said to have been the study of the celebrated Geoffrey of Monmouth, a native of this town, who resided many years in this neighbourhood. Of the hospitals of the Holy Trinity and St. John, founded here, in the early part of the thirteenth century, by Wihenoc de Monemue, there are no remains. At the distance of a mile from the town, on the road to Staunton, is a rocking-stone of very large dimensions, called the Buck stone: it is twenty-four feet high, fifty-seven feet in circumference at the upper surface, and three inches and one-sixth at the base; and near it is a flight of nine steps, above which is a large stone, having the appearance of a baptismal font, with a cavity for holding water; they are supposed to be Druidical remains. Monmouth formerly gave the title of duke to James, natural son of Charles II.

MONMOUTHSHIRE, a maritime county, bounded on the west by the counties of Glamorgan and Brecknock, in South Wales; on the north by part of Brecknockshire and by Herefordshire; on the east by Gloucestershire, from which it is separated by the river Wye; and on the south-east and south by the river Severn and the Bristol channel. It extends from 51° 28' to 51° 54' (N. Lat.), and from 2° 42' to 3° 19' (W. Lon.), and comprises an area of four hundred and ninety-eight square miles, or three hundred and eighteen thousand seven hundred and twenty acres. The population in 1821 amounted to 71,833. At the time of the second Roman invasion of Britain, Monmouthshire formed part of the territory of the Silures. In the reign of the Emperor Claudius, when Ostorius Scapula had succeeded to the chief command, that general, leaving gar-

risons in the chain of forts which his predecessor Aulus Plautius had established upon the rivers Avon and Severn, crossed the latter with his army, and landed, according to some authors, at a place called Aust-ferry, but, according to others, and with greater probability, at Caldecot-pill. The conquest of the Silurian territory, however, owing to the difficulties of the ground and the spirited and persevering resistance of the British inhabitants, proved to be a task much more arduous than the Romans, so accustomed to triumph over hordes of barbarians, had anticipated: their commander fell a victim to the fatigue, anxiety, and chagrin, which he experienced in this expedition, and it was left for Julius Frontinus, in the reign of Vespasian, to achieve the final conquest of this portion of Britain. That part of it which now constitutes the county of Monmouth then became a portion of the Roman division called Britannia Secunda. From the many stations and camps which those conquerors here established, and from the numerous fragments of their buildings and sculptures that have been discovered, it appears that the fine climate and great natural beauty of this pleasant county rendered it a favourite resort of the Romans, in the elegant and luxurious, though declining, age of Rome.

At a period not long subsequent to the Saxon conquests, Monmouthshire, together with the rest of the country west of the Severn, continued free from the Anglo-Saxon dominion; and Caerleon, at that time its capital, was one of the most flourishing cities of the Britons. Wales, which name was given to this part of the country by the Anglo-Saxons, then included three regions or principalities, viz., Groynnedd, containing the greater part of the present North Wales; Powysland, comprising part of North Wales and parts of Shropshire and Worcestershire; and Dehenbarth, including the present South Wales, parts of Herefordshire and Gloucestershire, and the whole of Monmouthshire. In those remote and obscure times it is difficult to trace the particular history of this county, which sometimes formed a separate territory under the name of Gwent, and at others was comprehended in Morgannoe, which included Glamorganshire and part of Carmarthenshire. The petty chieftains of this latter province were professedly tributary to the Prince of South Wales. The attempts of the Anglo-Saxon sovereigns to subjugate Wales were opposed by the Gwentians with extraordinary courage; nor does it appear that they were ever completely conquered during the Anglo-Saxon period. Canute entered Gwent, in the year 1034, with a powerful army, on which occasion he defeated Rytherch Ap Jestin, Prince of South Wales; but his conquest seems not to have been permanent. In the reign of Edward the Confessor, when Harold, afterwards king of England, penetrated into the interior of the country, defeated Gryffidd, Prince of North Wales, placed a prince upon the throne of South Wales, forced the inhabitants to swear fealty to the English crown, and took hostages for the payment of the customary tribute, the Anglo-Saxons, or English, appear to have occupied Monmouth, Chepstow, Caerwent, and Caerleon, and Harold is said to have erected a palace at Portscutt. After the Norman Conquest, when various Norman adventurers received permission to make incursions into Wales, and endeavour to establish themselves upon the Welch territory, several of those petty feudal sovereignties were here established. These

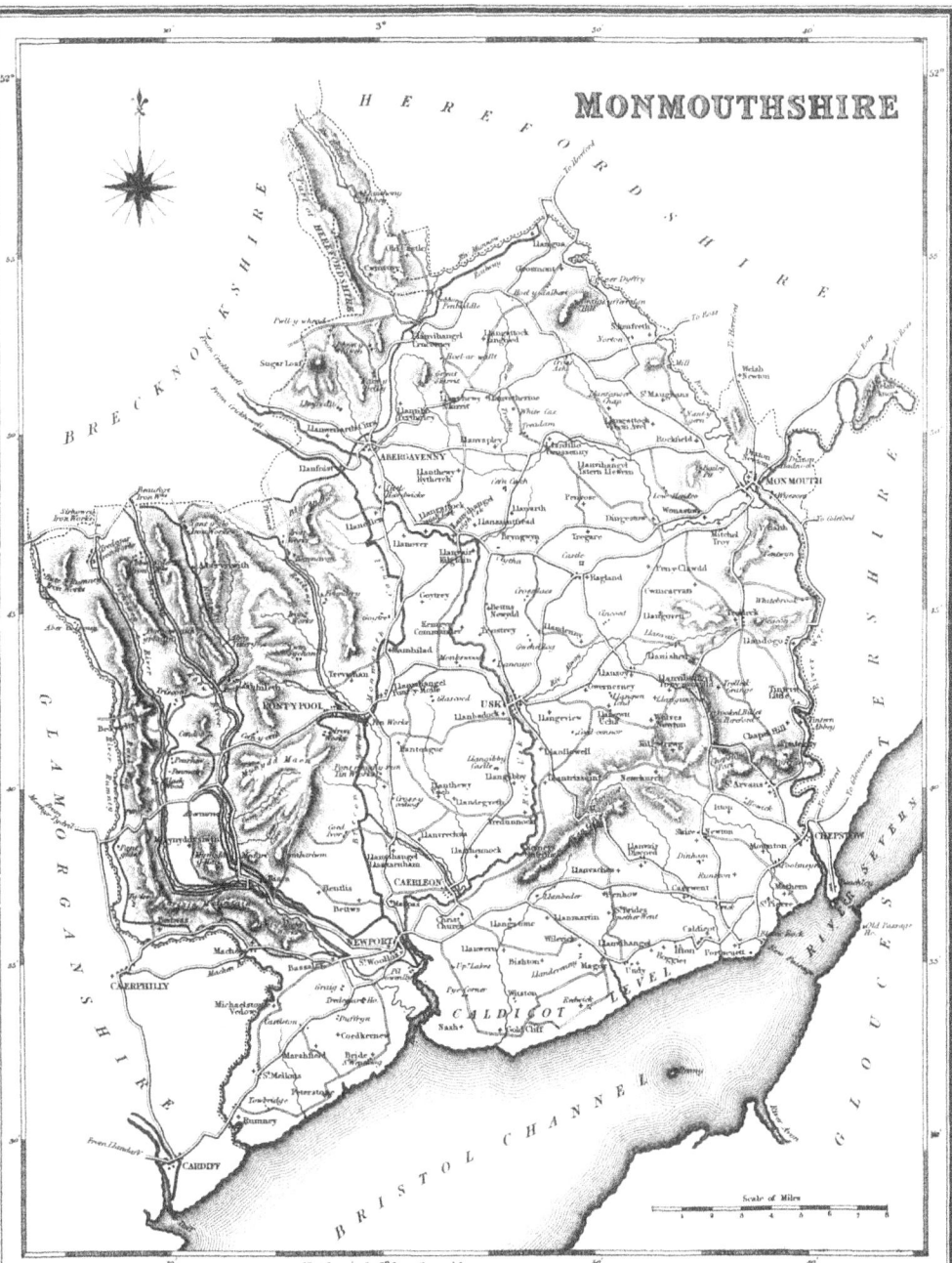

MONMOUTHSHIRE

Drawn by R. Creighton.

DRAWN AND ENGRAVED FOR LEWIS' TOPOGRAPHICAL DICTIONARY.

Engraved by J. & C. Walker.

Scale of Miles

West Longitude 3° from Greenwich

lands, having been holden *per baroniam*, with full power to administer justice to the tenants, were invested with *jura regalia*, so that the king's writs did not run in them. But in case of a contest between two lords marchers (as these territorial proprietors were denominated), concerning the limits of their respective territories, they had recourse to the king as their supreme lord, and justice was administered to them in the superior courts of the realm. This system of feudal jurisprudence was continued here, as in the other Welch marches, until Henry VIII., in 1535, abolished the government of the lords marchers, divided Wales into twelve shires, and included Monmouthshire among the counties of England. As regards the administration of justice, however, Monmouthshire appears to have been considered a Welch county until the reign of Charles II., when it was first included in the Oxford circuit : and even since that time it seems to have been affected in some degree by the ancient border law, as the jurisdiction of the supreme court of the lords marchers, usually held at Ludlow, in Shropshire, was not absolutely and finally abolished until the first year of William and Mary, when it was suppressed by act of parliament, on petition of the gentlemen and inhabitants within the principality of Wales. Reverting to the course of national events which occurred within the limits of this county subsequently to the Norman Conquest, the following appear to be the most remarkable :—In 1171, Caerleon was taken by Henry II. in his progress to Ireland. In 1215, Abergavenny castle was taken from the forces of King John, by Llewellyn, Prince of Wales. In 1233, November 12th, at Grosmont, Henry III. was surprised in the night, and defeated by Richard Marshal, Earl of Pembroke. In 1405, at Usk, Owen Glyndwr was defeated and driven to the mountains by the forces of Henry IV. In 1645, Chepstow castle, which had been garrisoned for the king, surrendered to the parliamentarians. In 1648, the royalists, under Sir William Kemeys, re-possessed themselves of it, but on the 25th of May of that year, the parliamentarians, under Colonel Ewer, retook it. On the 19th of August, 1648, Ragland castle, under the celebrated Henry Somerset, first Marquis of Worcester, after a most vigorous and protracted defence, was surrendered to Sir Thomas Fairfax.

Monmouthshire is included in the archdeaconry and diocese of Llandaff, with the exception, however, of six parishes, three of which, Welch-Bicknor, Newton-Dixon, and St. Mary's in Monmouth, are comprised in the diocese of Hereford, and the other three, those of Old-Castle, Llantony, and Cwmyoy, in the diocese of St. David's : it is within the province of Canterbury, and is divided into the deaneries of Abergavenny, Netherwent, Newport, and Usk, containing one hundred and twenty-three parishes, of which forty-four are rectories, thirty-nine vicarages, and forty perpetual curacies. For civil purposes it is divided into the six hundreds of Abergavenny (Lower and Upper), Caldicott (Lower and Upper), Ragland (Lower and Upper), Skenfreth (Lower and Upper), Usk (Lower and Upper), and Wentlloog (Lower and Upper). It contains the borough, market, and sea-port, town of Newport, the borough and market towns of Monmouth and Usk, the market and sea-port town of Chepstow, and the market towns of Abergavenny, Caerleon, and Pontypool. Two knights are returned to parliament for the

county, and one representative for the boroughs of Monmouth, Newport, and Usk conjointly. This county is included in the Oxford circuit : the assizes are held at Monmouth, and the quarter sessions at Usk. The county gaol is at Monmouth. There are thirty-nine acting magistrates. The rates raised in the county, for the year ending March 25th, 1827, amounted to £32,144. 5. ; the expenditure to £31,851. 7. ; of which £23,734. 1. was applied to the relief of the poor.

The general aspect of the county is pleasingly diversified : much of it is mountainous and rocky, and those parts abutting upon the mountain-ridges are sterile, and afford but a scanty subsistence for the flocks which feed upon them ; but the rich land in the valleys, and on the slopes of the hills, is finely chequered with woods and pastures, intermingled with spots of tillage. The beautiful scenery on the banks of the Wye has often afforded subjects for the pencil and the pen : the course of that river is particularly sinuous, and its banks generally lofty, and much diversified with woods and projecting rocks. In the hundreds of Wentlloog and Caldicott, sea-walls have been raised for a considerable extent, and at a vast expense, to keep off the sea at high tides and in stormy weather, particularly during the prevalence of such winds as blow from the south-west, from overflowing the spacious marshes in this district, which would otherwise be subject to continual damage by frequent inundations. Some of these walls are of the height of twelve or fourteen feet, falling back from the sea by a gradual slope, the stone-work in front being supported by a large embankment of earth : in other parts, particularly in the level of Wentlloog, where they are not required to be so high nor so strong, they are wholly constructed of earth. The walls of Caldicott extend from that village almost the whole distance to Goldcliff : the length of those of Wentlloog is upwards of fifteen miles and a half. These expensive works are kept in repair by the contributions of the several proprietors, assessed according to the value of their estates in the respective levels ; they being under the control of a court of sewers, and subject to the same laws and regulations as Romney Marsh in Kent. This land is divided by parallel ditches, in some of which the water is stagnant, while in others it runs in constant streams, called *rheens*, which at ebb tides fall through flood-gates, or *gouts*, into the sea. The general humidity of the western districts of the kingdom is felt in this county : the rains are frequently of long continuance, more particularly towards the sea-coast ; the great æstuary of the Severn attracting the clouds that rise from the western ocean, and causing torrents of rain to fall on its northern and southern shores much more frequently than on the inland parts of Wales and the West of England. Of the general salubrity of the atmosphere the longevity of the inhabitants affords numerous proofs.

In an agricultural point of view Monmouthshire may be divided into three districts. The first, comprising the southern part of the county, consists partly of large tracts of moor or marsh land, having in some parts a rich loamy soil of great depth, and in others a vast body of black peaty matter : other portions, again, consist of a light loamy soil, which produces fine timber of various kinds, while in another part there is a mixture of clay and loam, forming fertile meadows, and above them an excellent reddish soil, well adapted to the growth of corn, turnips, or potatoes. The second division includes the eastern part of the county, and extends for a considerable distance along the banks of the river Usk : the soil is of a light red colour, and such are its natural advantages and fertility that the whole district has the appearance of a garden. The third division comprises the western and more hilly portion of the county, the soil of which, upon the hills, is generally thin, of a peaty nature, and covering strata of stone lying upon beds of coal, or iron-ore. The low or marshy lands are chiefly in a state of meadow and pasture; the uplands are partly pasture, and partly arable.

The corn chiefly cultivated is wheat, barley, and oats; and a few peas, or beans, are sometimes sown: the common artificial grasses, such as clover, ray-grass, and trefoil, are also cultivated. Notwithstanding that much of the county is mountainous and rocky, and that it contains numerous wastes and commons in comparatively an unproductive state, yet the amount of agricultural produce is considerably greater than is required for the consumption of its inhabitants: much of this surplus is conveyed to Bristol and other markets. Lime forms the principal manure; and the system of summer fallowing is very general. The oxen are principally bred in the northern parts of the county, and fed in the southern: they are, for the most part, of a large useful kind, of a deep red and brindled colour, rather short in the leg and compact in the body, being evidently a cross between the breeds of the two adjacent districts to the north-east and south-west, the Hereford and Glamorgan: some, indeed, are the pure breed of each. They generally grow to a large size, weighing, when fattened, from seven to nine hundred weight: when young they are in great demand for the graziers, who purchase them at the great cattle fairs when about three years old, and sell them again for the labours of the field: after they have been worked for a certain period, they are also frequently purchased in store condition, and then fed for the market. The sheep are in general particularly small, and partake of the properties so conspicuous in the mountain breed of South Wales: the wool is of a coarse and rather short staple, but the flesh is fine in grain and of delicate flavour: many of these characteristic qualities are owing to their migratory mode of feeding, and continual exposure to the vicissitudes of the weather. This breed is now chiefly prevalent in the mountainous parts of the county: in the middle and lower districts are found some of the true Ryeland breed; and numerous crosses have been tried with the Cotswold, South Down, and Dorset breeds. The horses are of an inferior kind, being meagre, light, and not well adapted either for the business of the road, or the labours of the field. Numbers of mules, and those among the finest in the kingdom, are bred and worked in this county : they are strong in bone, and of exquisite symmetry, selling at very high prices; and are chiefly employed in carrying coal in the mountainous districts, and heavy articles from the navigable rivers and canals, iron-ore from the mines, and manufactured iron to the respective depôts, whence it is forwarded to the different markets. A considerable portion of the land is in sheep-walks; the quantity lying in commons is very considerable : Greenmore common is supposed to contain about five thousand acres, and

that of Caldicott about eight hundred, besides those of Devandon, Chepstow, and various others of smaller extent; much ground is occupied by the extensive mines and quarries. The woods and coppices are numerous, and contain a great quantity of various kinds of timber, particularly beech and oak.

The most important mineral productions are iron, coal, limestone, and various other kinds of stone, valuable for building, and other purposes. The iron-ore is found in such a quantity as to form, in consequence of the district abounding with coal also, its principal branch of manufacture. Although the mines had been partially worked in very remote times, the works in this and the neighbouring county of Glamorgan were carried on with little spirit until the latter part of the eighteenth century, since which time great facilities have been obtained by the application of the steam-engine, by improvements in hydraulic machinery, and by the adoption of rollers instead of forge hammers. The present works on the Welch border are of considerable extent and importance, producing both pig and bar iron: attached to some are wire-works. Lead-ore is also found; and the coal obtained furnishes more than sufficient fuel for the supply of the inhabitants. Limestone of the finest kind is found in almost every part of the county, and, besides innumerable quarries of it, there are some of *brescia*, for millstones, and of other valuable kinds of stone. In addition to the manufacture of iron, there are, at Caerleon and Rogerstone, some tin-works. The manufacture of flannel has been long established, but is of very limited extent. Some few coarse cloths, woollen stockings, and coarse caps, are made by the inhabitants among the mountains, and brought to the great fairs for sale. The caps, which are much in demand for seafaring men, were formerly manufactured in much larger quantities than at present, the principal part of this trade having been removed to Bewdley, in Worcestershire, the few caps still manufactured there being called "Monmouth caps." A manufactory of japanned goods, celebrated under the name of " Pontypool ware," from its having been first invented in that town, in the reign of Charles II., was formerly carried on both there and at Usk, but has nearly declined, that trade having been transferred to the towns of Birmingham, Wolverhampton, &c. Hats are manufactured at Abergavenny, Monmouth, and Newport; and in the vicinity of Monmouth are several paper mills. The commerce, though considerable, yet being chiefly carried on through the medium of Chepstow and Newport, is identified with the imports and exports of those places.

The principal rivers are the Severn, the Wye, the Usk, the Rumney, the Monnow, and the Ebwy; besides which are numerous smaller rivers and streams, flowing through different parts of the county. When the Severn first touches this county, which it does at the angle where it receives the waters of the Wye, it is a river of great magnitude, with a strong tide, and in its progress, which is in a south-westerly direction, it widens rapidly, and forms the Bristol channel. The Wye first reaches Monmouthshire, from Herefordshire, at Newton-Dixon, and then forms a long line of separation between this county and Gloucestershire, falling into the Severn below Chepstow : the course of this river is peculiarly winding: it is navigable for large vessels only to Chepstow bridge, but for barges, with some difficulty, as high as Hereford. The Usk, rising in the Hatterell, or Black mountains of Brecknockshire, enters Monmouthshire at Llangrunny, and takes its course nearly through the centre of the county to the Severn, in a southerly direction, and through a most beautiful valley, between lofty hills : this river, when swollen by floods, is particularly impetuous : it is navigable for coasting vessels up to Newport, and for barges as high as Tredunnock bridge. The Rumney rises in the lower part of Brecknockshire, and flowing through Duffin-Rumney, forms the line of division between this county and that of Glamorgan throughout the rest of its course, falling into the Bristol channel below the village of Rumney. The Monnow, rising in the Black mountains, takes a southerly course, and after forming for a considerable distance the north-eastern border of the county, which it separates from Herefordshire, it falls into the Wye at the town of Monmouth. The Ebwy also rises in Brecknockshire, and passing under the Beacon mountain, flows through the wild valley of Ebwy, and, having been joined by a stream similar to its own from the Sorwy valley, falls into the æstuary of the Usk below Newport. This county has some lines of valuable canal navigation. The Monmouthshire canal, which was begun in 1792, and finished in 1798, commences on the western side of the town of Newport, having there a basin connected with the river Usk, and passing between the town and the river, crosses the Chepstow road, and proceeds to Malpas, where it divides into two branches : one of these pursues a route, parallel to the river Avon and by Pontypool, to Pontnewyndd, a distance of nearly eleven miles, in which it has a rise of four hundred and forty-seven feet : the other runs parallel to the river Ebwy, in the direction of Crumlin bridge, and forms a line of upwards of eleven miles in length, having a rise of three hundred and fifty-eight feet : the average depth of the water is three feet and a half, the boats which navigate it carrying from twenty-five to twenty-eight tons. By virtue of an act obtained in the year 1797, the proprietors were authorised to extend the line eastward one mile and a half; and by another, passed in 1802, various further powers were obtained, for making collateral tram-roads. In the 33rd of George III., an act was obtained for the formation of the Brecknockshire canal, which was designed to form a communication between Brecknock and Newport, by way of Abergavenny and Pontypool, in this county, forming a junction with the Monmouthshire canal eight miles and a half from Newport, and one from Pontypool : from that canal it proceeds across the river Avon and, having been carried through a tunnel one hundred and eighty yards in length, it passes by Mamhilad, Llanover, &c. The commodities chiefly conveyed on the Monmouthshire canal, of which the Brecknockshire canal may be considered a branch, are coal, timber, pig-iron, and iron in different stages of manufacture, also various kinds of shop goods, together with furniture, deals, &c., for the supply of the interior. On the banks of the canal, at Pontnewyndd, commences an iron rail-road, which runs along the side of the river Avon to the Blaenavon iron-works, a distance of five miles and a quarter, in which it has a rise from the canal of six hundred and ten feet. One of the principal modern roads passes across the southern part of the

VOL. III.

county, entering it at Chepstow; and, proceeding past Caerleon and through Newport, it leaves at Rumney. Another mail-coach road runs across the northern part of the county, from Monmouth, in a circuitous line through Abergavenny, to a little north-west of that town, where it enters Brecknockshire.

There were five principal Roman stations in that part of the territory of the Silures which is included within the present county of Monmouth : viz., *Venta Silurum*, fixed by the general consent of antiquaries at Caerwent; *Isca Silurum*, at Caerleon; and *Gobannium*, at Abergavenny : *Burrium* and *Blestium*, according to the opinion of Horsley, which is the most probable one, were at Usk and Monmouth respectively. Although it is supposed that most of the great roads connecting the southern part of Britannia Secunda with the Roman-British territory east of the Severn, must have passed through Monmouthshire, yet the only one that can be distinctly traced is one which passed south-westward from Abergavenny to Neath, or to some station in Glamorganshire, and which is called by the natives *Sarn-hir*, signifying the long paved causeway. The miscellaneous Roman antiquities discovered in this county at different times are numerous and various ; comprising aqueducts, baths, sudatories, tesselated pavements, columns, statues, bas-reliefs, hypocausts, altars, votive and sepulchral stones, sarcophagi, urns, medals, coins, fibulæ, &c. Remains of numerous ancient encampments are still visible in various parts of the county, the construction of which, as this part of the British territory was never permanently occupied either by the Saxons or the Danes, it seems reasonable to attribute almost exclusively to the Britons and the Romans. The ancient castles, from its contiguity to the border of Wales, were also very numerous, the sites of no fewer than twenty-five being still distinguishable, most of which were of Norman erection, and of several of them considerable portions yet remain, though for the most part ruinous : those of Caerleon, Usk, and Skenfreth, have the most decided claim to antiquity ; that of Ragland, though presenting the most magnificent extent of ruins, is the most modern of all the ancient fortresses. Many of the churches have a remarkably picturesque appearance : they generally stand isolated, in the midst of fields, on the banks of rivers or streams, and are often embosomed among trees. Their styles of architecture are very various : many of them, especially in the mountainous parts, are very ancient : a few may be referred to the British period, and several to the early Norman ; but the greater number are of a date subsequent to the introduction of the pointed arch. The most ancient of all have somewhat the appearance of barns, being of small dimensions, without lateral aisles, or any distinction in height or breadth between the nave and the chancel, and without a steeple. Those of the second period have the chancel narrower and lower than the nave; and a small belfry, consisting of two arches, is fixed over the roof, at the western end. The third class have a tower, which in some instances is placed in the centre, in some at the side, and in others at the west end : some in the eastern part of the county have spires, and seem to have been erected in the thirteenth century. Few of the Monmouthshire churches having undergone much alteration since the Reformation,

2 T

they still exhibit many vestiges of the Roman Catholic worship and discipline, such as rood-lofts, niches, auricular recesses, and confessional chairs. The custom of whitewashing the outside of these edifices prevails in this part of the kingdom, its origin being attributed to the churches having been, in many instances, constructed of pebbles and ragstone intermixed, which producing an extremely rough surface, it was thought requisite to cover them both internally and externally with plaster; the external whitewashing, though usually confined to the body of the church, sometimes includes the tower also. The number of religious houses, including two hospitals, was seventeen : the most interesting remains are those of Llanthony priory church, and of the Cistercian abbey of Tintern, both which exhibit large masses of beautiful ruins, in picturesque situations.

The customs of the inhabitants much resemble those which prevail in the adjacent parts of Wales. One, which is peculiarly striking to the eye of the English traveller, is that of whitewashing the outsides of the houses, which is usually done once a year, and gives an appearance of remarkable neatness and cheerfulness even to the humblest dwellings, considerably heightening the picturesque effect of the diversified landscapes with which the county abounds. The custom of not only scattering flowers, but planting them and evergreens upon the graves of deceased friends, a usage of great antiquity, prevails here as in South Wales. Among the poorest classes of the inhabitants, Protestant as well as Roman Catholic, a superstitious custom is observed, of begging bread for the souls of the departed, on All Souls' day, the bread so given being termed *bara ran*, that is, dole-bread. In the north-eastern and south-eastern parts of the county, the English language is in common use; but in the north-western and south-western districts, the Welch is generally spoken, excepting in the towns. The natives of the midland parts are accustomed to both languages: in several places divine service is performed wholly in Welch, in others in English, and in some alternately in both. The same tenacity shews itself in the lower orders of the inhabitants of this county that distinguishes those of the principality itself, with respect to the original language, customs, and manners; and, though continual attempts have been made to efface them, by establishing English schools, yet the antipathy of the people to the introduction of the language and manners of the English is still inveterately strong. The natives of the western and north-western parts, which are mountainous and sequestered, retain their ancient national prejudices with little abatement, and continue to stigmatize every thing assimilating to what is English with the epithet, opprobrious in their estimation, of *Saxon*. The provincial language, as in the adjoining county of Glamorgan, is the *Gwentian*, one of the three dialects of Wales, in which many of the Welch odes were composed, and which was considered the next in purity to that of the *Gwynedd*.

MONNINGTON upon WYE, a parish in the hundred of GRIMSWORTH, county of HEREFORD, 9 miles (W.N.W.) from Hereford, containing 116 inhabitants. The living is a discharged rectory, in the archdeaconry and diocese of Hereford, rated in the king's books at £7. 12. 10., and in the patronage of Sir G. Cornewall, Bart. The church is dedicated to St. Mary.

MONTACUTE, a parish in the hundred of TINTINHULL, county of SOMERSET, 4½ miles (W. by N.) from Yeovil, containing 973 inhabitants. The living is a discharged vicarage, in the archdeaconry of Wells, and diocese of Bath and Wells, rated in the king's books at £8. 10., endowed with £200 private benefaction, and £200 royal bounty, and in the patronage of Henry Phelips, Esq. The church is dedicated to St. Catherine. There are places of worship for Baptists and Wesleyan Methodists. This place, in the time of the Saxons, was called *Logaresburch*, which is said to have been changed for its present name by William, Earl of Moreton, who, soon after the Conquest, built a strong castle here, on the sharp point of a hill. On the same ridge is a double-moated Roman camp, called Hampden Hill, about three miles in circuit, the north-west part of which is further defended by a high rampart, partly of stone, enclosing twenty acres, within which many Roman coins have been found. Several large cisterns have been discovered in a morass below; and in the neighbourhood are extensive quarries of freestone, where materials have been furnished for building many of the churches in this and the adjoining counties. A priory, in honour of St. Peter and St. Paul, founded here by William the Conqueror, was, in the reign of Henry I., amply endowed, and granted to the monks of Cluny, by the Earl of Moreton; its revenue, at the dissolution, was estimated at £524. 11. 8.

MONTFORD, a parish in the hundred of PIMHILL, county of SALOP, 5 miles (W.N.W.) from Shrewsbury, containing 517 inhabitants. The living is a discharged vicarage, in the archdeaconry of Salop, and diocese of Lichfield and Coventry, rated in the king's books at £4. 18. 6., and in the patronage of the Earl of Powis. The church is dedicated to St. Chad. The parish is bounded on the south by the river Severn, across which there is a bridge.

MONYASH, a chapelry in the parish of BAKEWELL, hundred of HIGH PEAK, county of DERBY, 4¾ miles (W.S.W.) from Bakewell, containing 381 inhabitants. The living is a perpetual curacy, annexed to the vicarage of Bakewell, in the peculiar jurisdiction of the Dean and Chapter of Lichfield and Coventry, endowed with £200 private benefaction, and £1200 royal bounty. The chapel, dedicated to St. Leonard, has a low tower and spire. There is a meeting-house for the Society of Friends. A court of miners, for the hundred of High Peak, is held here once in six months, at which all pleas of debt, and disputes as to title, relating to the lead mines within the hundred, are determined by the steward and barmasters, assisted by a jury of twenty-four persons. Monyash is in the honour of Tutbury, duchy of Lancaster, and within the jurisdiction of a court of pleas held at Chapel en le Frith every third Tuesday, for the recovery of debts under 40s. A school-house was built by subscription, in 1750, towards the endowment of which, the commissioners for enclosing waste lands subsequently awarded fourteen acres, now producing an annual income of about £17, for which sixteen poor children are educated free. At Rucklow-Dales are extensive rocks of grey marble, much admired for its variegated surface, of which a large quantity is quarried; and near them rises the river Lathkill, noted for the beautiful scenery on its banks.

MOOR, a joint township with Batchcott, in that part of the parish of RICHARD'S CASTLE which is in the hundred of MUNSLOW, county of SALOP. The population is returned with the parish.

MOOR, a joint township with Hill, in the parish of FLADBURY, middle division of the hundred of OSWALD-SLOW, county of WORCESTER, 3 miles (E. by N.) from Pershore. The population is returned with Hill.

MOOR-TOWN, a township in the parish of BRANDS-BURTON, northern division of the wapentake of HOLDER-NESS, East riding of the county of YORK, 10 miles (N. E.) from Beverley, containing 29 inhabitants.

MOORBY, a parish in the soke of HORNCASTLE, parts of LINDSEY, county of LINCOLN, 4½ miles (S. E. by S.) from Horncastle, containing 118 inhabitants. The living is a discharged rectory, in the archdeaconry and diocese of Lincoln, rated in the king's books at £7. 11. 8., and in the patronage of the Bishop of Carlisle. The church is dedicated to All Saints. There is a place of worship for Wesleyan Methodists.

MOORE, a township in the parish of RUNCORN, hundred of BUCKLOW, county palatine of CHESTER, 4 miles (S. W. by S.) from Warrington, containing 243 inhabitants. The Mersey and Irwell canal and the Duke of Bridgewater's canal pass through the township.

MOORESBARROW, a joint township with Parme, in that part of the parish of MIDDLEWICH which is in the hundred of NORTHWICH, county palatine of CHES-TER, 2¾ miles (E. by S.) from Middlewich, containing, with Parme, 25 inhabitants.

MOORHOUSE, a township in the parish of BURGH upon the SANDS, ward and county of CUMBERLAND, 4½ miles (W. by N.) from Carlisle, containing 254 inhabitants. There is a meeting-house for the Society of Friends, in which Thomas Stordy, who died in 1684, after suffering many persecutions; and Jonathan Ostell, who died in 1755, distinguished themselves as pious and unyielding preachers.

MOORHOUSE, a township in the parish of HOUGH-TON le SPRING, northern division of EASINGTON ward, county palatine of DURHAM, 3¼ miles (N. E.) from Durham, containing 29 inhabitants.

MOORHOUSE, a chapelry in the parish of LAXTON, or LEXINGTON, South-clay division of the wapentake of BASSETLAW, county of NOTTINGHAM, 3¼ miles (S. S. E.) from Tuxford. The population is returned with the parish.

MOORLINCH, a parish in the hundred of WHIT-LEY, county of SOMERSET, 7 miles (E.) from Bridgwater, containing, with the chapelries of Catcott, Chilton upon Poldon, Edington, and Stawell, and the hamlet of Sutton-Mallet, 1887 inhabitants. The living is a discharged vicarage, with the chapel of Chilton upon Poldon, in the archdeaconry of Wells, and diocese of Bath and Wells, rated in the king's books at £10. H. Bradridge, Esq. was patron in 1818. The church is dedicated to St. Mary. Here was a cell to the abbey of Glastonbury.

MOORSHAM (GREAT), a township in the parish of SKELTON, eastern division of the liberty of LANG-BAURGH, North riding of the county of YORK, 6 miles (E. by S.) from Guilsbrough, containing 353 inhabitants.

MOORSLEY, a township in the parish of HOUGH-TON le SPRING, northern division of EASINGTON ward, county palatine of DURHAM, 4½ miles (E. N. E.) from Durham, containing 48 inhabitants.

MOORTHWAITE, a joint township with North-sceugh, in the parish of CUMWHITTON, ESKDALE ward, county of CUMBERLAND, 10 miles (S. E. by S.) from Carlisle, containing, with Northsceugh, 259 inhabitants.

MOORTON, a tything in the parish, and lower division of the hundred, of THORNBURY, county of GLOUCESTER, 2 miles (N. by E.) from Thornbury. The population is returned with the chapelry of Falfield.

MOORWINSTOW, a parish in the hundred of STRATTON, county of CORNWALL, 7¼ miles (N. N. W.) from Stratton, containing 1091 inhabitants. The living is a vicarage, in the archdeaconry of Cornwall, and diocese of Exeter, rated in the king's books at £13. 10. 10., and in the patronage of the Bishop of Exeter. The church, dedicated to St. Morvenna, is principally Norman, with an enriched south porch and a large font of the same character; it has some portions in the later English style. The parish, situated at the most northern extremity of Cornwall, extends across that portion of the county, having on the west the Bristol channel, and on the east the river Tamar, which here takes its rise.

MORBORN, a parish in the hundred of NORMAN-CROSS, county of HUNTINGDON, 2½ miles (N. W.) from Stilton, containing 95 inhabitants. The living is a rectory, in the archdeaconry of Huntingdon, and diocese of Lincoln, rated in the king's books at £10. 6. 10½., and in the patronage of R. E. Duncombe, Esq. The church is dedicated to All Saints.

MORCHARD (BISHOP'S), a parish in the hundred of CREDITON, county of DEVON, 6½ miles (N. W. by N.) from Crediton, containing 1935 inhabitants. The living is a rectory, in the peculiar jurisdiction of the Bishop of Exeter, rated in the king's books at £36. R. H. Tuckfield, Esq. was patron in 1827. The church is dedicated to St. Mary. Thomasine Tucker, in 1733, gave a rent-charge of £16 for teaching and clothing eight boys and eight girls. There is a fair for cattle on the Monday after September 8th.

MORCOTT, a parish in the hundred of WRANDIKE, county of RUTLAND, 4¼ miles (E. by N.) from Upping-ham, containing 443 inhabitants. The living is a rectory, in the archdeaconry of Northampton, and diocese of Peterborough, rated in the king's books at £10. 19. 7. The Rev. E. Thorold was patron in 1825. The church is dedicated to St. Mary.

MORDEN, a parish in the hundred of LOOSEBAR-ROW, Shaston (East) division of the county of DORSET, 6 miles (N.) from Wareham, containing 650 inhabitants. The living is a vicarage, in the archdeaconry of Dorset, and diocese of Bristol, rated in the king's books at £8. 4. 7., and in the patronage of Richard Erle Drax, Esq. The church is an ancient building, with an embattled tower crowned with pinnacles. Among other sepulchral memorials of the Erle family, there are in the chancel an altar-tomb, and a monument of freestone, having the figure of a man in complete armour, in the attitude of prayer, with three children behind him. There is a place of worship for Wesleyan Methodists.

MORDEN (GUILDEN), a parish in the hundred of ARMINGFORD, county of CAMBRIDGE, 5½ miles (E.) from Biggleswade, containing 570 inhabitants. The living is a discharged vicarage, in the archdeaconry and diocese of Ely, rated in the king's books at £7. 3. 6., and in the patronage of the Master and Fellows of Jesus College, Cambridge. The church is dedicated to St. Mary.

MORDEN (STEEPLE), a parish in the hundred of ARMINGFORD, county of CAMBRIDGE, 5 miles (W. by N.) from Royston, containing 614 inhabitants. The living is a discharged vicarage, in the archdeaconry and diocese of Ely, rated in the king's books at £6. 18. 6., endowed with £600 private benefaction, and £600 royal bounty, and in the patronage of the Warden and Fellows of New College, Oxford. The church is dedicated to St. Peter and St. Paul : the steeple fell to the ground about seventy years since.

MORDIFORD, a parish in the hundred of GREY-TREE, county of HEREFORD, 5 miles (E. S. E.) from Hereford, containing 638 inhabitants. The living is a rectory, in the archdeaconry and diocese of Hereford, rated in the king's books at £10. 6. 5½., and in the patronage of E. T. Foley, Esq. The church, dedicated to the Holy Rood, had formerly a wooden spire rising from the centre, (which was taken down in 1814, when a tower was erected at the west end,) whereon had been emblazoned for several previous centuries, a dragon, probably the bearing of Uter Pendragon, anciently of note in this vicinity. A school-house, lately erected on the east side of the churchyard, at an expense of £400, raised by subscription, is endowed with about £5 per annum. The parish, which is situated at the confluence of the rivers Frome, Lug, and Wye, abounds with limestone, in which is found a great variety of fossils ; and within its limits is a small portion of St. Ethelbert's camp, on Blackbury hill.

MORDON, a township in the parish of SEDGEFIELD, north-eastern division of STOCKTON ward, county palatine of DURHAM, 8½ miles (E. by S.) from Bishop-Auckland, containing 124 inhabitants.

MORDON, a parish in the second division of the hundred of WALLINGTON, county of SURREY, 10 miles (S. W. by S.) from London, containing 638 inhabitants. The living is a rectory, in the archdeaconry of Surrey, and diocese of Winchester, rated in the king's books at £7. 12. 11., and in the patronage of Mrs. Lowndes Stone, as lady of the manor. The church, dedicated to St. Lawrence, is a small brick edifice, erected about 1636 ; it has a large window of stained glass. Elizabeth Gardiner, in 1718, gave £300, and Elizabeth Garth, in 1776, £100, which together produce an annual income of about £30, applied to the instruction of twenty poor children. There is also a Sunday school supported by voluntary contributions. The small river Wandle runs through the parish, and the Croydon railway passes near it. Here is a tobacco and snuff manufactory.

MORE, a parish in the hundred of PURSLOW, county of SALOP, 3 miles (N. E. by N.) from Bishop's Castle, containing 277 inhabitants. The living is a discharged rectory, in the archdeaconry of Salop, and diocese of Hereford, rated in the king's books at £8. 6. 2. R. Moore, Esq. was patron in 1776.

MOREBATH, a parish in the hundred of BAMPTON, county of DEVON, 2¼ miles (N. by W.) from Bampton, containing 415 inhabitants. The living is a discharged vicarage, in the archdeaconry and diocese of Exeter, rated in the king's books at £7. 8. 9. Thomas E. Clarke, Esq. was patron in 1813. The church is dedicated to St. George. Here is an almshouse for two poor persons. A charity school was endowed, in 1688, by Mr. John Brook, with £10 a year, for the instruction of poor children of the parish.

MOREBY, a joint township with Stillingfleet, in that part of the parish of STILLINGFLEET which is in the wapentake of OUZE and DERWENT, East riding of the county of YORK, 5¼ miles (S.) from York. The population is returned with Stillingfleet.

MORELEIGH, or MORLEY, a parish in the hundred of STANBOROUGH, county of DEVON, 5½ miles (S. W. by S.) from Totnes, containing 202 inhabitants. The living is a discharged rectory, in the archdeaconry of Totness, and diocese of Exeter, rated in the king's books at £9. 8. 1., and in the patronage of the Earl of Morley. The church is dedicated to All Saints. A weekly market and an annual fair were formerly held here. Within the parish is Stanborough, the site of an ancient fort, which gives name to the hundred. Morley gives the title of earl to the family of Parker.

MORESBY, a parish in ALLERDALE ward above Darwent, county of CUMBERLAND, containing, with the townships of Moresby and Parton, 934 inhabitants, of which number, 438 are in the township of Moresby, 2 miles (N. by E.) from Whitehaven. The living is a discharged rectory, in the archdeaconry of Richmond, and diocese of Chester, rated in the king's books at £6. 2. 3½., endowed with £200 private benefaction, and £200 royal bounty, and in the patronage of the Earl of Lonsdale. The church, dedicated to St. Bridget, has lately received an addition of three hundred and sixty-two sittings, of which two hundred and twelve are free, the Incorporated Society for the enlargement of churches and chapels having granted £150 toward defraying the expense. A school was founded and endowed by Joseph Williamson, Esq., of which the Bishops of Chester and Carlisle are the governors. There is an iron-foundry within this parish, which is bounded on the west by the Irish sea. It is evident that this was the site of a Roman station, from the numerous foundations of buildings, caverns, and Roman inscriptions, which have been discovered. Horsley thinks that it was *Arbeia*, where, according to the *Notitia*, the *Numerus Barcariorum Tigritensium* was in garrison.

MORESTEAD, a parish in the hundred of FAWLEY, Fawley division of the county of SOUTHAMPTON, 3¼ miles (S.E. by S.) from Winchester, containing 80 inhabitants. The living is a discharged rectory, in the peculiar jurisdiction of the Incumbent, rated in the king's books at £6, endowed with £300 private benefaction, and £200 royal bounty, and in the patronage of the Bishop of Winchester. Morestead is within the jurisdiction of the Cheyney Court held at Winchester every Thursday, for the recovery of debts to any amount.

MORETON, a liberty in that part of the parish of DINTON which is in the hundred of DESBOROUGH, county of BUCKINGHAM, 4 miles (S. W. by S.) from Aylesbury, containing 14 inhabitants.

MORETON, a joint township with Alcumlow, in that part of the parish of ASTBURY which is in the hundred of NORTHWICH, county palatine of CHESTER, 3 miles (S. W. by S.) from Congleton, containing, with Alcumlow, 129 inhabitants.

MORETON, a township in the parish of BIDSTONE, lower division of the hundred of WIRRALL, county palatine of CHESTER, 9½ miles (N. by W.) from Great Neston, containing 273 inhabitants.

MORETON, a parish in the hundred of WINFRITH, Blandford (South) division of the county of DORSET 8 miles (E. by S.) from Dorchester, containing 256 inhabitants. The living is a rectory, in the archdeaconry of Dorset, and diocese of Bristol, rated in the king's books at £9. 19. 2. James Frampton, Esq. was patron in 1827. The church, dedicated to St. Magnus the Martyr, is a small but very ancient edifice, with a tower rising from the centre: the south aisle, formerly styled the chapel of the Holy Trinity, has been the burial-place of the Framptons, and was rebuilt by James Frampton, Esq., in 1733.

MORETON, a parish in the hundred of ONGAR, county of ESSEX, 3 miles (N. by W.) from Chipping-Ongar, containing 408 inhabitants. The living is a rectory, in the archdeaconry of Essex, and diocese of London, rated in the king's books at £20, and in the patronage of the Master and Fellows of St. John's College, Cambridge. The church is dedicated to St. Mary.

MORETON, a chapelry in the parish of LLANY-BLODWELL, hundred of OSWESTRY, county of SALOP, 3¼ miles (S.) from Oswestry. The population is returned with the parish. The living is a perpetual curacy, in the archdeaconry and diocese of St. Asaph, endowed with £32 per annum private benefaction, and £200 royal bounty. The chapel is dedicated to St. Michael. Here is a mineral spring.

MORETON, a hamlet in the parish of GNOSALL, western division of the hundred of CUTTLESTONE, county of STAFFORD, 4 miles (E.S.E.) from Newport, containing 754 inhabitants. It is in the honour of Tutbury, duchy of Lancaster, and within the jurisdiction of a court of pleas held at Tutbury every third Tuesday, for the recovery of debts under 40s.

MORETON (MAIDS'), a parish in the hundred and county of BUCKINGHAM, 1½ mile (N. E.) from Buckingham, containing 407 inhabitants. The living is a rectory, in the archdeaconry of Buckingham, and diocese of Lincoln, rated in the king's books at £18. 2. 11., and in the patronage of the Rev. J. L. Long. The church, dedicated to St. Edmund, is a handsome structure in the later English style, containing some stalls highly enriched; the porch and belfry have groined roofs. It was built in 1450, by two maiden sisters, daughters of the last male heir of the family of Pegore. The river Ouse, and a branch of the Grand Junction canal, pass through the parish.

MORETON in the MARSH, a market town and parish in the upper division of the hundred of WEST-MINSTER, county of GLOUCESTER, 28½ miles (E. N. E.) from Gloucester, and 83 (W. N. W.) from London, containing 1015 inhabitants. This town is situated in a pleasant valley, on the high road from London to Worcester, which is here crossed by the Roman Fosse-way: it is an inconsiderable place, and is neither lighted nor paved. A public library is supported by subscription. The only branch of manufacture is that of linen-cloth, which furnishes employment to about fifty persons. A railway passes hence to Stratford upon Avon, being chiefly used for the conveyance of coal. In the reign of Henry III., the abbot of Westminster, lord of the manor, procured a charter for a weekly market, which, though on the decline, is still held on Tuesday. There are fairs on the 25th of March, and the 1st of November, but they are very little resorted to. Constables are appointed at the court held for the manor. The living is a perpetual curacy, annexed to the rectory of Bourton on the Hill, in the archdeaconry and diocese of Gloucester. The church is dedicated to St. David. There is a place of worship for Independents. A National school was endowed in 1813, with £4000, by Lord Redesdale and Dr. Winford; the present income is about £140 per annum, and about one hundred children of both sexes are educated: there is likewise a free school for the children of dissenters, having about thirty boys on the foundation. On the heath is a stone, marking the junction of four counties, near which a memorable battle was fought between the English and the Danes.

MORETON (NORTH), a parish in the hundred of MORETON, county of BERKS, 4¼ miles (W.) from Wallingford, containing 348 inhabitants. The living is a discharged vicarage, in the archdeaconry of Berks, and diocese of Salisbury, rated in the king's books at £7. 17. 8., endowed with £200 private benefaction, and £200 royal bounty, and in the patronage of the Archdeacon of Berks. The church is dedicated to All Saints. In Stapleton's chantry chapel, founded before 1467, are two old tombs of dignified ecclesiastics, with processional crosses, but without dates: there are also two ancient mutilated tombs, with Saxon inscriptions.

MORETON (SOUTH), a parish in the hundred of MORETON, county of BERKS, 3 miles (W. S. W.) from Wallingford, containing 364 inhabitants. The living is a rectory, in the archdeaconry of Berks, and diocese of Salisbury, rated in the king's books at £12. 15. 5., and in the patronage of the University of Oxford, in trust for the Principal and Fellows of Magdalene Hall. The church is dedicated to St. John. A small stream runs through the village, and upon it there are three paper-mills.

MORETON-CORBET, a parish in the Whitchurch division of the hundred of BRADFORD (North), county of SALOP, 5¼ miles (S. E.) from Wem, containing, with the township of Preston-Brockhurst, 235 inhabitants. The living is a discharged rectory, in the archdeaconry of Salop, and diocese of Lichfield and Coventry, rated in the king's books at £5. 3. 6., and in the patronage of Sir A. Corbett, Bart. The church, dedicated to St. Bartholomew, is a neat structure, containing some fine ancient monuments of the Corbet family, whose magnificent mansion, built in the time of Elizabeth, was burned in the civil war, by a detachment from Cromwell's army, which was stationed at Wem; the remains have been converted into workshops, &c.

MORETON-HAMPSTEAD, a market town and parish in the hundred of TEINGBRIDGE, county of DEVON, 11 miles (W.S.W.) from Exeter, and 184 (W. S. W.) from London, containing 1932 inhabitants. This town is romantically situated on the verge of Dartmoor Forest, and occupies a gentle eminence environed by lofty hills. It consists of several streets, which are indifferently paved: the houses in general are ancient, and built in the cottage style, with thatched roofs: the appearance of the surrounding district is somewhat peculiar, the surface being strewn with fragments of rock, while the barren heights of Dartmoor on the west are strikingly contrasted with the cultivated slopes of land more immediately adjacent to the town. The woollen trade here was formerly extensive, but only a few blankets and stockings are now made: there are some tan-yards, and a rope manufactory, the produce of the former being sent chiefly to Bristol and Exeter: in the vicinity there are quarries of excellent granite. A market is held on Saturday, and there are two great cattle markets, on Whitsun-eve and the first Saturday in October. Fairs are held on the third Thursday in July and the last Thursday in November, principally for cattle. A new market-house and shambles were built, at the expense of Lord Courtenay, in 1827. A portreeve is annually elected at a court leet and baron for the manor, held early in November: four constables are chosen at the same court, by a jury; also a bailiff, to examine weights and measures, and two officers, called jurors, to superintend the internal affairs of the town.

The living is a rectory, in the archdeaconry of Totness, and diocese of Exeter, rated in the king's books at £49. 19. 7., and in the patronage of the Lord of the Manor. The church, dedicated to St. Andrew, occupies the summit of the elevation on which the town is situated; it is an ancient edifice, with nave, aisles, transeptal porch, and chancel, the last being separated from the body by a carved wooden screen. There are places of worship for Independents, Wesleyan Methodists, and Unitarians. The sum of £10 per annum is paid by the governors of St. John's hospital, in the city of Exeter, agreeably to the directions of Eliza Hele, for the maintenance of a free school in this parish; ten poor children are instructed gratuitously. Some Druidical remains and Roman antiquities have been found in the immediate vicinity of the town.

MORETON-SEA or SAY, a parish in the Drayton division of the hundred of BRADFORD (North), county of SALOP, 3¼ miles (W.) from Drayton in Hales, containing 762 inhabitants. The living is a perpetual curacy, annexed to the rectory of Hodnet, in the archdeaconry of Salop, and diocese of Lichfield and Coventry. The church is dedicated to St. Margaret.

MORETON-VALENCE, a parish in the upper division of the hundred of WHITSTONE, county of GLOUCESTER, 7¼ miles (N. W. by W.) from Stroud, containing 348 inhabitants. The living is a perpetual curacy, in the archdeaconry and diocese of Gloucester, endowed with £400 private benefaction, £800 royal bounty, and £300 parliamentary grant, and in the patronage of—Pitt, Esq. The church is dedicated to St. Stephen. The navigable river Severn bounds the parish on the north-west, and the Gloucester and Berkeley canal passes through it. Here are considerable iron-works.

MORLAND, a parish in West ward, county of WESTMORLAND, comprising the chapelries of Bolton and Thrimby, and the townships of Kings-Meaburn, Morland, Newby, Sleagill, Great Strickland, and Little Strickland, and containing 1911 inhabitants, of which number, 372 are in the township of Morland, 6¼ miles (W.N.W.) from Appleby. The living is a discharged vicarage, in the archdeaconry and diocese of Carlisle, rated in the king's books at £11. 18., and in the patronage of the Dean and Chapter of Carlisle. The church, dedicated to St. Lawrence, is a large ancient edifice. There is a place of worship for Wesleyan Methodists, also a meeting-house, with a burial-ground attached, belonging to the Society of Friends. The river Lyvennet runs through the parish, the northern and western boundaries of which are formed by the river Leeth, and the eastern by the Eden. An abundance of limestone and some coal are obtained here. A free school, erected and partly supported by subscription, has been endowed, by the Dean and Chapter of Carlisle, with £16 a year and thirty acres of waste land, enclosed before 1800: the master's annual stipend is upwards of £30, for which about forty children are instructed. At Chapelgarth there formerly stood a chapel, dedicated to St. Mary. Bewley castle, of which there are still some vestiges, often afforded security to the Bishops of Carlisle, during the border warfare, when driven from their usual residence, Rose castle, by the Scots. Within the parish are the remains of a monastic building, and several old halls, now converted into farm-houses.

MORLEY, a parish in the hundred of MORLESTON and LITCHURCH, county of DERBY, containing the chapelry of Smalley, and the township of Morley, 1000 inhabitants, of which number, 273 are in the township of Morley, 4½ miles (N. E.) from Derby. The living is a rectory, in the archdeaconry of Derby, and diocese of Lichfield and Coventry, rated in the king's books at £13. 6. 8., and in the patronage of E. S. Pole, H. S. Bateman, and T. S. Sitwell, Esqrs., alternately. The church, dedicated to St. Matthew, is a large structure with a lofty spire, in part built by Ralph Statham, Esq., who died in 1380, and completed by his widow Goditha: it contains several monuments of the ancient families of Statham and Sacheverell; and in the north aisle are four windows of stained glass, curiously designed, said to have been brought from Dale abbey at the dissolution. There is an almshouse, founded about 1657, by Jacinth Sacheverell, for six poor men, each receiving £5 per annum. At Smalley is a schoolhouse, built by John and Samuel Richardson, who, in 1721, endowed it for the instruction of twelve poor boys, with lands now let for £88 per annum; the number of scholars has been increased to twenty-eight. The latter also gave £400 to purchase lands, now let for £40 per annum, directing the rental to be applied towards the support of fourteen infirm colliers of Smalley, Heanor, and Horsley-Woodhouse.

MORLEY, a chapelry in that part of the parish of BATLEY which is in the lower division of the wapentake of AGBRIGG, West riding of the county of YORK, 4½ miles (S. W. by S.) from Leeds, containing 3031 inhabitants, who are principally employed in the manufacture of woollen cloth. A chapel is now being erected by the commissioners appointed under the late act for building additional churches. Morley, previously to the Conquest, had a parochial church, which subsequently became dependent on that of Batley; but in the time of Charles I. it was conveyed by the Earl of Sussex to trustees of the Presbyterian church, and was never afterwards restored to the establishment: it retains much of its ancient appearance, and now belongs to the Independents, who, besides this, have a place of worship recently erected: there is another belonging to the Wesleyan Methodists.

MORLEY (ST. BOTOLPH), a parish in the hundred of FOREHOE, county of NORFOLK, 3 miles (W. S. W.) from Wymondham, containing 269 inhabitants. The living is a rectory, with the perpetual curacy of

Morley St. Peter annexed, in the archdeaconry of Norfolk, and diocese of Norwich, rated in the king's books at £14. 11. 5¼. B. N. Cooper, Esq. was patron in 1800. The church is an ancient structure, with a large square tower : the chancel was repaired and beautified about 1480, by Thomas Warde, the then rector, of whom it contains several painted representations, particularly in the east window. Elizabeth Brown, in 1732, bequeathed £150, directing the income to be applied in teaching and clothing six children, and providing them with books.

MORLEY (ST. PETER), a parish in the hundred of FOREHOE, county of NORFOLK, 4 miles (S. W. by W.) from Wymondham, containing 201 inhabitants. The living is a perpetual curacy, annexed to the rectory of Morley St. Botolph, in the archdeaconry of Norfolk, and diocese of Norwich. Elizabeth Brown, in 1732, left £90 for teaching poor children, and supplying them with books and clothes.

MORNING-THORPE, a parish in the hundred of DEPWADE, county of NORFOLK, 2 miles (E.) from St. Mary Stratton, containing 160 inhabitants. The living is a discharged rectory, in the archdeaconry of Norfolk, and diocese of Norwich, rated in the king's books at £7, and in the patronage of the Crown. The church is dedicated to St. John the Baptist.

Arms.

MORPETH, a parish, comprising the townships of Catchburn and Hepscot in the eastern, and Newminster-Abbey, Shilvington, Tranwell with High Church, and Twizell, in the western, division of CASTLE ward ; and Buller's Green, and the borough and market town of Morpeth, in the western division of MORPETH ward, county of NORTHUMBERLAND, and containing 4292 inhabitants, of which number, 3415 are in the town of Morpeth, 15 miles (N.) from Newcastle upon Tyne, and 289 (N.) from London. This town, which is stated to derive its name from "Moor-path," or the road across the moor, was an inconsiderable village prior to the Conquest, when it became the head of a barony, and, in 1358, a castle was erected by William, Lord Greystock. In 1215, the town was set on fire by the barons, in order to obstruct the military operations of King John ; and in 1689, it was again nearly destroyed by an accidental conflagration. Morpeth is agreeably situated in a valley on the northern bank of the river Wansbeck, which is crossed by a stone bridge of two arches, and on the great road from London to Edinburgh, in the centre of a richly-cultivated district : an elegant bridge of three arches, from a design by Mr. Telford, is now being erected a little below the old bridge. The town consists chiefly of one long street, which is not lighted, and but indifferently paved with pebbles; the houses are of an inferior description : an abundant supply of water is conveyed into the town, through pipes, from a spring at Stobhill, the works having been constructed in 1820 ; and there is a large well at the end of Manchester-lane, called St. Thomas' well. Races are held annually in September, on Cottingwood, immediately northward of the town. A subscription library, established in 1817, is well supported; and in 1825 a mechanics' and scientific institution was founded, which at present consists of about two hundred members, and is furnished with a good library and lecture-room. The trade principally arises from a colliery in the neighbourhood, two manufactories for flannel, and one for carpets, and there is considerable business in tanning and brewing. The market cross, built in 1699, and rebuilt in 1783, at the expense of the corporation, stands in the centre of the town, and is a small edifice supported by eight stone pillars and arches. The market, which is on Wednesday, is one of the principal markets in the North of England for live cattle, and is generally well supplied with corn and provisions ; fairs are held on Wednesday week before Whitsuntide, and the Wednesday before July 22nd, for sheep and cattle ; and there is a statute fair for hiring servants, on the Wednesday before Martinmas-day.

Corporate Seal.

Morpeth is a borough by prescription, and received a charter of confirmation from Charles II. The officers of the corporation are two bailiffs, a serjeant at mace, two ale-tasters and breadweighers, two fish and flesh lookers, four constables, and an indefinite number of free burgesses, seldom exceeding two hundred and twenty in the whole. The Earl of Carlisle, as lord of the manor, holds two courts leet annually, one on the Monday next after Easter week, and the other on the first Monday after Michaelmas-day, at which latter the officers of the corporation are annually elected. The corporation is composed of, and contains within itself, seven inferior companies, or fraternities, each governed by an alderman, and consisting of freemen who are members of the general body corporate, and of persons who are members only of their respective companies, and called free brothers. The freemen are appointed by the seven companies, who elect, from among their own free brothers, the full number of twenty-four ; viz., the Merchant-Taylors four, the Tanners six, the Fullers and Dyers three, the Smiths three, the Cordwainers three, the Weavers three, and the Butchers two : the whole being sworn and admitted freemen at the ensuing court leet, after which the companies may elect twenty-four more : the free brothers become such by servitude, or by being sons of freemen who are brothers of some particular company. The borough is within the jurisdiction of the county magistrates, who hold a petty session on the first Wednesday in every month. Quarter sessions for the county are held here alternately with Alnwick, Newcastle, and Hexham. On the south side of the town are about four hundred acres of common land, on which each of the freemen and free brothers is entitled to turn two head of cattle. The borough first returned representatives to parliament in 1553 : the two members are elected by the bailiffs and the free burgesses : the bailiffs are the returning officers, and the parliamentary influence is enjoyed by the Earl of Carlisle and the Ord family. The town hall is a plain structure of hewn stone, with a piazza and turrets, erected in 1714, by the family of Howard: it is generally appropriated to meetings for public business, and the lower part is occasionally used as a theatre. A large and commodious gaol for the county, with a magnificent sessions-house and offices, has been lately erected, at the south entrance to the town: the first stone was laid on the 24th of July, 1822, by his Grace the Duke of Northumberland: the estimated expense of erection was £80,000. The prison wards are arranged in the form of a radiated octagon, with the houses of the governor and turnkeys in the centre, and a chapel on the east side; the sessions-house and a turreted gateway form the grand western entrance: the area consists of about three acres of ground, and the height of the outer wall is twenty-one feet.

The living is a rectory, with Ulgham annexed, in the archdeaconry of Northumberland, and diocese of Durham, rated in the king's books at £32. 16. 8., and in the patronage of the Earl of Carlisle. The church, dedicated to St. Mary, is situated upon an eminence called "Kirk Hill," at a considerable distance from the town: it is a plain structure, in the ancient style of English architecture, with a low square western tower: in the chancel is a fine east window, which was formerly of painted glass throughout. An old square tower of hewn freestone, called the 'Clock House,' standing near the market-place, contains a clock and a ring of six bells. On the north of the bridge is a small but handsome chapel of ease, built of freestone. There are places of worship for Independents, Presbyterians, and Primitive and Wesleyan Methodists, also a Roman Catholic chapel. The free grammar school was founded by Edward VI., in 1552, for the sons of freemen, and endowed with the lands of dissolved chantries here and at Nether Witton, the proceeds of which amount to about £240 per annum, of which sum, the master receives two-thirds, and the usher the remainder. An English free school, supported by the corporation, was erected in 1792: the master receives a salary of £70 per annum, and about sixty children of burgesses are educated. A dispensary, established in 1817, is liberally supported by voluntary contributions; and a savings bank has lately been erected. The remains of the ancient baronial castle consist of the old gateway tower, with part of two exploratory turrets, together with the outer wall: near the gateway tower, towards the north, is a large mound of earth on a natural elevation, the height of which appears to have been greatly increased by art: this was probably part of the outworks. William Turner, M.D., the first English writer on botany, who died in 1568, was born here; and Dr. Robert Morrison, the celebrated Chinese linguist and missionary, and author of a Chinese dictionary, is also a native of this place. Morpeth gives the title of viscount to the family of Howard, Earls of Carlisle.

MORRAGE, a joint township with Foxt, in that part of the parish of IPSTONES which is in the southern division of the hundred of TOTMONSLOW, county of STAFFORD, containing, with Foxt, 415 inhabitants.

MORRICK, a township in that part of the parish of WARKWORTH which is in the eastern division of MORPETH ward, county of NORTHUMBERLAND, 9 miles (S. E. by S.) from Alnwick, containing 72 inhabitants.

MORROWE, a hamlet in the parish and hundred of WISBEACH, Isle of ELY, county of CAMBRIDGE, 6 miles (W. S. W.) from Wisbeach, with which the population is returned. Here was anciently a chapel, or oratory, in which, by reason of the distance of the parish church, the inhabitants obtained license from the bishop, in 1388, to attend divine service for one year.

MORSTON, a parish in the hundred of HOLT, county of NORFOLK, 3¼ miles (W. by N.) from Clay, containing 139 inhabitants. The living is a rectory, with that of Stiffkey St. John, in the archdeaconry and diocese of Norwich, rated in the king's books at £18. The church is dedicated to All Saints.

MORTHOE, a parish in the hundred of BRAUNTON, county of DEVON, 4 miles (S. W. by W.) from Ilfracombe, containing 280 inhabitants. The living is a discharged vicarage, in the archdeaconry and diocese of Exeter, rated in the king's books at £9. 19. 3., endowed with £200 private benefaction, and £200 royal bounty, and in the patronage of the Dean and Chapter of Exeter. The church, dedicated to St. Mary, contains an altar-tomb to the memory of Sir William de Tracey, who, in 1308, founded a chantry, and, after the murder of Thomas à Becket, ended his days in a hermitage at this place. A school, conducted on the Madras system, has been established here. Within the parish is a Druidical monument, termed Mortstone.

MORTIMER (WEST), a tything in that part of the parish of STRATFIELD-MORTIMER which is in the hundred of HOLDSHOTT, Basingstoke division of the county of SOUTHAMPTON, 8 miles (N.) from Basingstoke, containing 340 inhabitants.

MORTLAKE, a parish in the western division of the hundred of BRIXTON, county of SURREY, 6½ miles (S. W. by W.) from London, containing, with East Sheen, 2484 inhabitants. In this parish, about the year 1616, a manufactory of tapestry was established, but it was destroyed in the time of the civil war; there is at present one for earthenware. The cultivation of asparagus and lavender was formerly extensive, but not more than thirty acres are now applied to this use. A farm, comprising eighty acres, on the Richmond side of the parish, was formerly the private property of George III. The river Thames flows on the north side of the parish. The living is a perpetual curacy, in the peculiar jurisdiction of the Archbishop of Canterbury, being in the exempt deanery of Croydon, and in the patronage of the Dean and Chapter of Worcester. The church, which was founded in the fourteenth, and rebuilt in the sixteenth, century, has undergone many modern repairs; the tower, which is very ancient, is of stone and flint, square and embattled: in the interior is an ancient font, ornamented with rich tracery, the gift of Archbishop Bourchier. There is a place of worship for Independents. A free school, for the education of poor children in the principles of the established church, founded in 1700, and endowed by the will of Dorothy, Lady Capel, in 1719, was enlarged by subscription in 1815, when the National system was introduced; about ninety boys and fifty girls are instructed. An ancient house in this parish, said to have belonged to Oliver Cromwell, was subsequently the residence of Edward Colston, Esq., the great benefactor to the city of Bristol, who, during his lifetime, expended more than £70,000 in the support of various charitable institutions. The only remaining vestige of Mortlake House, anciently the residence of the Archbishops of Canterbury, is the foundation of a single wall.

MORTON, a parish in the hundred of SCARSDALE, county of DERBY, 3½ miles (N.) from Alfreton, containing, with the chapelry of Brackenfield, 502 inhabitants. The living is a rectory, in the archdeaconry of Derby, and diocese of Lichfield and Coventry, rated in the king's books at £11. 10., endowed with £200 private benefaction, and £800 royal bounty, and in the alternate patronage of the Master and Fellows of St. John's College, Cambridge, and the Turbutt family. The church is dedicated to the Holy Cross.

MORTON, a parish in the wapentake of AVELAND, parts of KESTEVEN, county of LINCOLN, 2½ miles (N.) from Bourne, containing, with the chapelry of Hanthorpe, or Harmthorpe, 765 inhabitants. The living is a discharged vicarage, united, in 1732, to that of Haconby, in the archdeaconry and diocese of Lincoln, rated in the king's books at £9. 1. 10½., and in the patronage of the Bishop of Lincoln. The church, dedicated to St. John the Baptist, is a handsome cruciform structure, with a lofty and finely-groined tower rising from the intersection: it has portions in the Norman, and in the early, decorated, and later English styles of architecture. Rebecca Leaband, in 1717, bequeathed land producing a trifling income, for the education of poor children.

MORTON, an extra-parochial liberty, in the higher division of the wapentake of BOOTHBY-GRAFFO, parts of KESTEVEN, county of LINCOLN, 8 miles (S. W. by W.) from Lincoln, containing 9 inhabitants.

MORTON, a hamlet in the parish of GAINSBOROUGH, wapentake of CORRINGHAM, parts of LINDSEY, county of LINCOLN, 1¾ mile (N. by W.) from Gainsborough, containing 580 inhabitants. There are places of worship for Independents and Wesleyan Methodists. A school for twenty poor children was endowed with land, in 1708, by Joshua Teeler.

MORTON, a parish in that part of the liberty of SOUTHWELL and SCROOBY which separates the northern and southern divisions of the wapentake of THURGARTON, county of NOTTINGHAM, 2½ miles (S. E.) from Southwell, containing 150 inhabitants. The living is a perpetual curacy, in the peculiar jurisdiction of the Chapter of the Collegiate Church of Southwell, endowed with £400 royal bounty, and in the patronage of the Prebendary of Dunham in the Collegiate Church of Southwell. The church, dedicated to St. Denis, is a small brick edifice. Here is a trifling endowment in land, bequeathed by John Dabile, for teaching four poor children of Morton, and four of Fisherton.

MORTON, an extra-parochial liberty, in the wapentake of BIRDFORTH, North riding of the county of YORK, 5½ miles (N. W. by W.) from Helmsley. The population is returned with the township of Newborough.

MORTON, a township in the parish of AINDERBY-STEEPLE, eastern division of the wapentake of GILLING, North riding of the county of YORK, 3½ miles (W. S. W.) from North Allerton, containing 240 inhabitants. There is a place of worship for Wesleyan Methodists.

MORTON, a township in that part of the parish of ORMSBY which is in the eastern division of the liberty of LANGBAURGH, North riding of the county of YORK,

4¼ miles (N. N. E.) from Stokesley, containing 26 inhabitants.

MORTON (ABBOT'S) a parish in the lower division of the hundred of BLACKENHURST, county of WORCESTER, 5½ miles (W. S. W.) from Alcester, containing 236 inhabitants. The living is a rectory, in the archdeaconry and diocese of Worcester, rated in the king's books at £8. T. B. Eades, Esq. was patron in 1796. The church is dedicated to St. Peter.

MORTON (EAST), a township in the parish of DALTON le DALE, northern division of EASINGTON ward, county palatine of DURHAM, 8½ miles (E. N. E.) from Durham, containing 72 inhabitants.

MORTON (EAST and WEST), a township in the parish of BINGLEY, upper division of the wapentake of SKYRACK, West riding of the county of YORK, 3 miles (E. N. E.) from Keighley, containing 1199 inhabitants. There is a place of worship for Wesleyan Methodists.

MORTON on the HILL, a parish in the hundred of EYNSFORD, county of NORFOLK, 5¾ miles (S. by E.) from Reepham, containing 153 inhabitants. The living is a discharged rectory, in the archdeaconry of Norfolk, and diocese of Norwich, rated in the king's books at £3. 14. 7. Mrs. Le Grys was patroness in 1804. The church is dedicated to St. Margaret: under an arch in the north wall is an ancient monument, with a cross, cut in wood, but without any inscription.

MORTON upon LUGG, a parish in the hundred of GRIMSWORTH, county of HEREFORD, 4¼ miles (N.) from Hereford, containing 110 inhabitants. The living is a rectory, not in charge, in the peculiar jurisdiction of the Dean of Hereford, and in the patronage of the Prebendary of Moreton Magna in the Cathedral Church of Hereford. The church is dedicated to St. Andrew.

MORTON-BAGGOTT, a parish in the Alcester division of the hundred of BARLICHWAY, county of WARWICK, 3½ miles (W. S. W.) from Henley in Arden, containing 168 inhabitants. The living is a rectory, in the archdeaconry and diocese of Worcester, rated in the king's books at £6, and in the patronage of the Countess of Warwick. The church is dedicated to the Holy Trinity.

MORTON-GRANGE, a township in the parish of HOUGHTON le SPRING, northern division of EASINGTON ward, county palatine of DURHAM, 6 miles (N. E. by N.) from Durham, containing 308 inhabitants.

MORTON-JEFFRIES, a parish in the hundred of RADLOW, county of HEREFORD, 5½ miles (S. W.) from Bromyard, containing 64 inhabitants. The living is a perpetual curacy, in the archdeaconry and diocese of Hereford, endowed with £800 royal bounty, and in the patronage of the Dean and Chapter of Hereford.

MORTON-MORRELL, a parish in the Warwick division of the hundred of KINGTON, county of WARWICK, 3¾ miles (N. N. W.) from Kington, containing 257 inhabitants. The living is a perpetual curacy, in the archdeaconry and diocese of Worcester, endowed with £200 private benefaction, and £200 royal bounty, and in the patronage of the Crown. The church is dedicated to the Holy Cross. There is a small endowment, the gift of the Rev. Thomas Harbridge, for the instruction of six children.

MORTON-PINKNEY, a parish in the hundred of GREENS-NORTON, county of NORTHAMPTON, 8 miles

(W. by N.) from Towcester, containing 540 inhabitants. The living is a perpetual curacy, in the archdeaconry of Northampton, and diocese of Peterborough, endowed with £186. 15. private benefaction, £400 royal bounty, and in the patronage of the Provost and Fellows of Oriel College, Oxford. The church is dedicated to St. Mary. A school-house has been recently built, in which the children are taught upon the National system. There is a mineral spring, the water of which is said to be efficacious in healing diseases of the eye.

MORTON-TYNEMOUTH, a township in that part of the parish of GAINFORD which is in the south-western division of DARLINGTON ward, county palatine of DURHAM, 8½ miles (N. W. by W.) from Darlington, containing 31 inhabitants.

MORVAH, a parish in the hundred of PENWITH, county of CORNWALL, 6 miles (N. W.) from Penzance, containing 325 inhabitants. The living is a perpetual curacy, annexed to the vicarage of Madron, in the archdeaconry of Cornwall, and diocese of Exeter. The church has lately received an addition of two hundred and ninety-two free sittings, the Incorporated Society for the enlargement of churches and chapels having granted £250 towards defraying the expense. There is a place of worship for Wesleyan Methodists. The parish is bounded on the north by St. George's channel. At Tregaminian are the remains of an ancient chapel; and Castle Clum, in the neighbourhood, is the most regular Danish fortification in the county.

MORVAL, a parish in WEST hundred, county of CORNWALL, 2¾ miles (N.) from East Looe, containing 615 inhabitants. The living is a vicarage, in the archdeaconry of Cornwall, and diocese of Exeter, rated in the king's books at £6. 14. 9½., and in the patronage of the Crown. The church is dedicated to St. Wenn. The river Love bounds the parish on the west. John Buller, Esq., in 1714, founded a free school, and endowed it with £8 per annum, for teaching poor children.

MORVILL, a parish in the hundred of STOTTESDEN, county of SALOP, 3 miles (W. by N.) from Bridgenorth, containing, with the chapelry of Aston-Eyre, 430 inhabitants. The living is a perpetual curacy, in the archdeaconry of Salop, and diocese of Hereford, endowed with £200 private benefaction, and £200 royal bounty. — Weaver, Esq. was patron in 1797. The church is dedicated to St. George: in it was originally a society of Secular canons, and subsequently one of Benedictine monks, a cell to the abbey of Shrewsbury: it was founded by Earl Roger, and at the dissolution had a revenue of £15.

MORWICK, a joint township with Scholes, in the parish of BARWICK in ELMETT, lower division of the wapentake of SKYRACK, West riding of the county of YORK, 6 miles (N. E. by E.) from Leeds, containing, with Scholes, 491 inhabitants.

MOSBOROUGH, a township in the parish of ECKINGTON, hundred of SCARSDALE, county of DERBY, 8 miles (N. N. E.) from Chesterfield, containing 818 inhabitants. Joseph Stones, in 1680, devised a dwelling-house, croft, and garden, for the use of a schoolmaster, also land now producing an annual income of about £18, for the free education of fifteen children.

MOSELEY, a hamlet in that part of the parish of BUSHBURY which is in the northern division of the hundred of SEISDON, county of STAFFORD, 4 miles

(N. by E.) from Wolverhampton, containing 55 inhabitants.

MOSELEY, a chapelry in the parish of KING'S NORTON, upper division of the hundred of HALFSHIRE, county of WORCESTER, 2 miles (S.) from Birmingham. The population is returned with the parish. The living is a perpetual curacy, in the archdeaconry and diocese of Worcester, endowed with £100 private benefaction, £400 royal bounty, and £600 parliamentary grant, and in the patronage of the Vicar of Bromsgrove. The chapel, dedicated to St. Mary, has lately received an addition of three hundred and sixty-two sittings, of which two hundred and forty-seven are free, the Incorporated Society for the enlargement of churches and chapels having granted £250 towards defraying the expense.

MOSS, a township in the parish of CAMPSALL, upper division of the wapentake of OSGOLDCROSS, West riding of the county of YORK, 6¾ miles (W. by N.) from Thorne, containing 242 inhabitants.

MOSSER, a chapelry in the parish of BRIGHAM, ALLERDALE ward above Darwent, county of CUMBERLAND, 4½ miles (S.) from Cockermouth, containing 102 inhabitants. The living is a perpetual curacy, in the archdeaconry of Richmond, and diocese of Chester, endowed with £1200 royal bounty, and in the patronage of the Earl of Lonsdale. The chapel is dedicated to St. Philip. There are a few trifling donations for the education of children.

MOSSLEY, a chapelry in the parish of ASHTON under LINE, hundred of SALFORD, county palatine of LANCASTER, 9½ miles (E.) from Manchester. The population is returned with the parish. The living is a perpetual curacy, in the archdeaconry and diocese of Chester, endowed with £1000 royal bounty, and £1600 parliamentary grant, and in the patronage of the Rector of Ashton under Line. The chapel was built in 1755, and enlarged in 1786. There is a place of worship for Methodists of the New Connexion, who support a school in which there are nearly six hundred children. There is a charity school, affording instruction to about two hundred and twenty children in connexion with the establishment. Mossley is a neat village, the houses being principally built with stone. The manufacture of cotton and woollen goods is extensively carried on, but the former prevails. There are two fairs for cattle, on June 21st and the last Monday in October. On an eminence in the vicinity is Hartshead Pike, a lofty and circular tower surmounted by a spire: it was rebuilt of stone in 1758, and has been used as a beacon.

MOSS-SIDE, a township in the parish of MANCHESTER, hundred of SALFORD, county palatine of LANCASTER, 2 miles (S.) from Manchester, containing 172 inhabitants.

MOSTERTON, a parish in the hundred of BEAMINSTER-FORUM and REDHONE, Bridport division of the county of DORSET, 4 miles (N. N. W.) from Beaminster, containing 284 inhabitants. The living is a perpetual curacy, annexed to the rectory of South Perrot, in the archdeaconry of Dorset, and diocese of Bristol. The church has lately received an addition of one hundred and fifty-six sittings, of which eighty are free, the Incorporated Society for the enlargement of churches and chapels having granted £50 towards defraying the expense.

MOSTON, a township in that part of the parish of St. MARY, CHESTER, which is in the lower division of the hundred of BROXTON, county palatine of CHESTER, 3 miles (N. by W.) from Chester, containing 18 inhabitants.

MOSTON, a township in the parish of WARMING-HAM, hundred of NORTHWICH, county palatine of CHESTER, 2¼ miles (W. by N.) from Sandbach, containing 143 inhabitants. The Grand Trunk canal passes through the township.

MOSTON, a township in the parish of MANCHESTER, hundred of SALFORD, county palatine of LANCASTER, 4 miles (N. E.) from Manchester,, containing 593 inhabitants.

MOSTON, a township in the parish of STANTON upon HINE-HEATH, Whitchurch division of the hundred of BRADFORD (North), county of SALOP, containing 66 inhabitants.

MOTCOMB, a parish in the liberty of GILLINGHAM, Shaston (West) division of the county of DORSET, 1½ mile (N. N. W.) from Shaftesbury, containing 1184 inhabitants. The living is a perpetual curacy, annexed to the vicarage of Gillingham, in the jurisdiction of the royal peculiar court of the manor of Gillingham. The church is an ancient structure. There is a place of worship for Wesleyan Methodists.

MOTHERBY, a joint township with Gill, in the parish of GREYSTOCK, LEATH ward, county of CUMBERLAND, 6½ miles (W. by S.) from Penrith, containing, with Gill, 112 inhabitants.

MOTTINGHAM, a hamlet partly in the parish of CHISELHURST, hundred of RUXLEY, but chiefly in the parish of ELTHAM, hundred of BLACKHEATH, lathe of SUTTON at HONE, county of KENT, 8 miles (S. E.) from London, containing 94 inhabitants.

MOTTISFONT, a parish in the hundred of THORNGATE, Andover division of the county of SOUTHAMPTON, 4¾ miles (N. N. W.) from Romsey, containing 501 inhabitants. The living is a rectory, with the perpetual curacy of Lockerley, in the archdeaconry and diocese of Winchester, rated in the king's books at £14. 18. 11½., and in the patronage of Sir Charles Mill, Bart. The church is dedicated to St. Andrew. Mottisfont House, a spacious and venerable edifice, occupies a portion of the site of a priory of canons Regular of the order of St. Augustine, founded in the beginning of the reign of King John, by William Briwere, and dedicated to the Holy Trinity. In 1494, the establishment being reduced from eleven, its original number of religious, to three, Henry VII. procured a bull from Pope Alexander for its suppression, but it continued till the dissolution, at which period its revenue was valued at £167. 15. 8.

MOTTISTON, a parish in the liberty of WEST MEDINA, Isle of Wight division of the county of SOUTHAMPTON, 5¼ miles (S.E.) from Yarmouth, containing 149 inhabitants. The living is a rectory, united to the vicarage of Shorewell, in the archdeaconry and diocese of Winchester, rated in the king's books at £11. 16. 3. The church, dedicated to St. Peter and St. Paul, is principally in the later English style.

MOTTRAM (ST. ANDREW), a township in the parish of PRESTBURY, hundred of MACCLESFIELD, county palatine of CHESTER, 4¾ miles (N.N.W.) from Macclesfield, containing 382 inhabitants.

MOTTRAM in LONGDEN-DALE, a parish in the hundred of MACCLESFIELD, county palatine of CHESTER, comprising the townships of Godley, Hattersley, Hollingworth, Matley, Mottram in Longden-Dale, Newton, Stayley-Bridge, and Tintwisle, and containing 10,086 inhabitants, of which number, 1944 are in the township of Mottram in Longden-Dale, 7 miles (E. N. E.) from Stockport. The living comprises a rectory and a vicarage, in the archdeaconry and diocese of Chester, rated in the king's books at £32. 3. 9., the former an impropriation belonging to the Bishop of Chester, the latter endowed with £200 private benefaction, and £200 royal bounty, and in the patronage of the Bishop. The church, dedicated to St. Michael, is in the later style of English architecture, with a handsome tower : it stands upon an eminence called War-hill ; the vicarage-house, near it, is surrounded by intrenchments similar to those of a Roman station. In the churchyard lie the remains of Lawrence Earnshaw, an eminent self-taught genius in mechanics and the fine arts ; he died in 1767. There is a place of worship for Independents, and another, with a school attached, belonging to the Wesleyan Methodists. A free grammar school was founded, in 1612, by Robert Garside, and is endowed with about £53 per annum. There are also a parochial school, in which about four hundred children are taught, and a small subscription library. The river Mersey, rising at the north-eastern extremity of the parish, separates it from Derbyshire on the south ; and the Tame, from Lancashire on the north. At the village of Mottram, which consists of one long and spacious street, the Mersey expands into a broad stream, upon which are the extensive mills of Messrs. Marshland, occupying a large space excavated in the rock, and reaching to the middle of the river, which, lower down, is crossed by a stone bridge of one immense arch. Here are extensive manufactories for cotton and woollen goods, paper, and machinery; works for printing calico, and an establishment for smelting iron-ore, which abounds in the south-west part of the parish, and has the advantage of large collieries in the neighbourhood. A court leet is held annually on Michaelmas-day, at which a constable is elected. There are fairs for cattle on April 27th and October 31st. The Car Tor, rising above the village, is a precipitous elevation, eighty feet in perpendicular height, its face exhibiting various strata of rock, coal, slate, and freestone, disposed with great regularity ; and the sides being partly clothed with foliage, it has a picturesque effect. Mottram hill rises above this to the height of four hundred and fifty feet, and even this, with the village, lies far beneath the adjacent immense heights of Charleworth Neck, Wernoth-Loe, &c., the summits of which command most extensive prospects of the surrounding country. In this parish are the remains of Bucton castle, supposed to be of British origin.

MOULDSWORTH, a township in that part of the parish of TARVIN which is in the second division of the hundred of EDDISBURY, county palatine of CHESTER, 9 miles (N.E. by E.) from Chester, containing 138 inhabitants.

MOULSEY (EAST), a parish in the first division of the hundred of ELMBRIDGE, county of SURREY, 3 miles (E.N.E.) from Walton upon Thames, containing 526 inhabitants. The living is a perpetual curacy, in the archdeaconry of Surrey, and diocese of Winchester, and in the patronage of the Provost and Fellows of King's College, Cambridge. The parish is bounded on the north by the Thames, and on the west by the river Mole. John Winkins, in 1779, founded a school, and endowed it with £400, for teaching twelve poor children. Here are three almshouses, the origin of which is unknown.

MOULSEY (WEST), a parish in the first division of the hundred of ELMBRIDGE, county of SURREY, 2½ miles (N.E. by E.) from Walton upon Thames, containing 430 inhabitants. The living is a perpetual curacy, in the archdeaconry of Surrey, and diocese of Winchester, endowed with £200 private benefaction, £600 royal bounty, and £500 parliamentary grant. The Rev. Hibbert Binney, D.D., was patron in 1824. The parish is bounded on the north by the Thames, and on the east by the river Mole.

MOULSFORD, a parish in the hundred of MORETON, county of BERKS, 4 miles (S.S.W.) from Wallingford, containing 176 inhabitants. The living is a perpetual curacy, united to the vicarage of Cholsey, in the archdeaconry of Berks, and diocese of Salisbury. The church is dedicated to St. John the Baptist.

MOULSOE, a parish in the hundred of NEWPORT, county of BUCKINGHAM, 3 miles (S.E. by E.) from Newport-Pagnell, containing 260 inhabitants. The living is a rectory, in the archdeaconry of Buckingham, and diocese of Lincoln, rated in the king's books at £16. 16. 3., and in the patronage of Lord Carrington. The church is dedicated to St. Mary. The river Lovet runs through the parish. There is a free school for poor children, founded, in 1719, by the Countess of Northampton, and endowed with about £10 per annum.

MOULTON, a township in the parish of DAVENHAM hundred of NORTHWICH, county palatine of CHESTER, containing 196 inhabitants.

MOULTON, a parish in the wapentake of ELLOE, parts of HOLLAND, county of LINCOLN, 4 miles (W.) from Holbeach, containing 1629 inhabitants. The living is a vicarage, with the perpetual curacy of Chapel-Moulton, in the archdeaconry and diocese of Lincoln, rated in the king's books at £28. 13. 4. The Rev. M. Johnson was patron in 1780. The church is dedicated to All Saints. There is a place of worship for Wesleyan Methodists. A free school was founded and liberally endowed with lands, by John Harrox, in 1561.

MOULTON, a parish in the hundred of WALSHAM, county of NORFOLK, 3 miles (S.) from Acle, containing 185 inhabitants. The living is a discharged vicarage, with the perpetual curacy of Tunstall, in the archdeaconry and diocese of Norwich, rated in the king's books at £5. 6. 3., endowed with £200 royal bounty. The Rev. George Anguish was patron in 1813. The church is dedicated to St. Mary.

MOULTON, a parish in the hundred of SPELHOE, county of NORTHAMPTON, 4½ miles (N.N.E.) from Northampton, containing, with the extra-parochial liberty of Moulton Park, 1072 inhabitants. The living is a vicarage, in the archdeaconry of Northampton, and diocese of Peterborough, rated in the king's books at £14. 3. 9., and in the patronage of the Rev. W. Stanton. The church, dedicated to St. Peter and St. Paul, is partly in the Norman style of architecture. There are places of worship for Baptists and Wesleyan Methodists.

MOULTON, a parish in the hundred of RISBRIDGE, county of SUFFOLK, 3¼ miles (E. by N.) from Newmarket, containing 312 inhabitants. The living comprises a rectory and a vicarage, in the peculiar jurisdiction of the Archbishop of Canterbury, the former rated in the king's books at £13. 6. 8., and the latter at £4. 7. 8½., and in the patronage of the Master and Fellows of Christ's College, Cambridge. The church is dedicated to St. Peter.

MOULTON, a township in the parish of MIDDLETON-TYAS, eastern division of the wapentake of GILLING, North riding of the county of YORK, 5 miles (E.N.E.) from Richmond, containing 236 inhabitants.

MOULTON (CHAPEL), a chapelry in the parish of MOULTON, wapentake of ELLOE, parts of HOLLAND, county of LINCOLN, 7½ miles (N.E. by N.) from Crowland. The population is returned with the parish. The living is a perpetual curacy, united to the vicarage of Moulton, in the archdeaconry and diocese of Lincoln, endowed with £8 per annum private benefaction, and £800 royal bounty.

MOULTON (LITTLE), a parish in the hundred of DEPWADE, county of NORFOLK, 3 miles (W.S.W.) from St. Mary Stratton. The living is a discharged rectory, in the archdeaconry of Norfolk, and diocese of Norwich, rated in the king's books at £4. 3. 1½., and in the patronage of S. Webster, Esq. The church, which was dedicated to All Saints, was demolished in 1570.

MOULTON (ST. MICHAEL), a parish in the hundred of DEPWADE, county of NORFOLK, 3 miles (W.S.W.) from St. Mary Stratton, containing 417 inhabitants. The living is a discharged rectory, in the archdeaconry of Norfolk, and diocese of Norwich, rated in the king's books at £6. 13. 4., and in the patronage of W. Chute, Esq. The church formerly contained a chapel, in which a light was constantly kept burning before the altar and image of the Virgin Mary: the tower is circular at the base, and octangular above. The pious, learned, and eloquent preacher, John Moulton, a Carmelite friar, who flourished about 1400, was born here.

MOULTON-PARK, an extra-parochial liberty, in the hundred of SPELHOE, county of NORTHAMPTON, 2¾ miles (N.N.E.) from Northampton. The population is returned with Moulton.

MOUNTFIELD, a parish in the hundred of NETHERFIELD, rape of HASTINGS, county of SUSSEX, 2½ miles (S.) from Robert's Bridge, containing 683 inhabitants. The living is a discharged vicarage, in the archdeaconry of Lewes, and diocese of Chichester, rated in the king's books at £5. 13. 4. The Duke of Dorset was patron in 1795. The church is dedicated to All Saints.

MOUNT-GRACE, in the parish of EAST HARSLEY, wapentake of BIRDFORTH, North riding of the county of YORK, 5½ miles (N.E. by E.) from North Allerton. A Carthusian priory, dedicated to the Blessed Virgin and St. Nicholas, was founded here, about 1396, by Thomas de Holland, Duke of Surrey, who endowed it with extensive possessions; but dying in rebellion against Henry IV., before the completion of his design, its progress was interrupted, but again renewed in 1440, by Henry VI., who confirmed in parliament the former grants: its revenue at the dissolution was valued at £382. 5. 11.: there are considerable remains of the monastic buildings, and of the church, which was cruciform, with a tower rising from the intersection.

MOUNTHEALY, a township in the parish of ROTHBURY, western division of COQUETDALE ward, county of NORTHUMBERLAND, 2½ miles (E. S. E.) from Rothbury, containing 38 inhabitants.

MOUNTNESSING, a parish in the hundred of CHELMSFORD, county of ESSEX, 2 miles (S. W.) from Ingatestone, containing 728 inhabitants. The living is a discharged vicarage, in the archdeaconry of Essex, and diocese of London, rated in the king's books at £11, endowed with £400 private benefaction, and £400 royal bounty. F. B. Bramston, Esq. was patron in 1802. The church is dedicated to St. Giles. Richard Beyley, in 1743, bequeathed a house and land in support of a school for teaching poor children. A priory of Augustine canons was founded, in the reign of Stephen, at Thoby in this parish, by Michael Capra, Roise his wife, and William their son: it was dedicated to St. Mary and St. Leonard, and, at the dissolution, had a revenue of £75. 6. 10.

MOUNTON, a parish in the upper division of the hundred of CALDICOTT, county of MONMOUTH, 2¾ miles (W. S. W.) from Chepstow, containing 52 inhabitants. The living is a perpetual curacy, in the archdeaconry and diocese of Llandaff, endowed with £1000 royal bounty, and £200 parliamentary grant, and in the patronage of ——Lloyd, Esq. There is a place of worship for Wesleyan Methodists.

MOUNTSORREL, a market town and chapelry, partly in the parish of ROTHLEY, but chiefly in that of BARROW upon SOAR, western division of the hundred of GOSCOTE, county of LEICESTER, 7½ miles (N.) from Leicester, and 104½ (N. N. W.) from London, containing 1422 inhabitants. The name of this place, prior to the Conquest, appears to have been Soar-hill, which with its present appellation, is evidently derived from its situation on a mount or hill near the river Soar. On the highest of a range of hills, impending above the town, and called Castle hill, a fortress once stood, which is mentioned in the reign of Stephen, when it was assigned to Robert le Bossu, Earl of Leicester, and his heirs, on condition that Ralph, Earl of Chester, who also laid claim to it, should, with his family, be amicably received within the borough, bailiwick, and castle, whenever they might choose to reside there. In 1167, Robert Blanchmains, Earl of Leicester, on his rebellion against Henry II., was dispossessed of it with his other estates; the latter were subsequently restored to him, but the king retained the castle, and governors were appointed to hold it during this and succeeding reigns. In 1215, it was garrisoned by Saer de Quincey, its governor, for the Dauphin of France, whom the barons had invited to their assistance; and when the royal cause became triumphant, in the beginning of the reign of Henry III., was taken and razed to the ground. This small town is rather romantically situated, amidst rocky and variegated scenery, and consists principally of one street, which extends about three-quarters of a mile along the high road, and is paved with red granite from the adjacent cliffs; the houses in general are constructed of the same material. Worsted-hose and net-lace are manufactured here; and the Soar canal affords facility for the conveyance of stone for the repair of roads throughout the neighbourhood. The market, which is almost disused, is on Monday; and there is a fair on the 29th of July, during which a court of pie-powder is held. There

is a small stone bridge over the Soar. The market-house, a small building in the centre of the town, was erected in 1793, at the expense of Sir John Danvers, Bart., who at the same time removed a curious and ancient cross, which occupied a portion of the site, into his own ground. In addition to the usual manorial courts, a court of pleas is held every three weeks, for the recovery of small debts within the eastern and western divisions of the hundred of Goscote, having the same jurisdiction over that district as a county court has over the county at large. The chapel, dedicated to St. Peter, is a chapel of ease to the vicarage of Barrow. There are places of worship for Baptists, Presbyterians, Unitarians, and Wesleyan Methodists. A free school, for educating twelve boys, was founded in 1742, by Sir John Danvers; the endowment is about £12 per annum. There are several considerable benefactions for the relief of the poor.

MOUSON, a township in the parish and northern division of BAMBROUGH ward, county of NORTHUMBERLAND, 2¼ miles (S. S. E.) from Belford, containing 73 inhabitants. Here are vestiges of a Roman camp.

MOWSLEY, a chapelry in that part of the parish of KNAPTOFT which is in the hundred of GARTREE, county of LEICESTER, 6½ miles (W. by N.) from Market-Harborough, containing 263 inhabitants. The Grand Union canal passes on the south of this place.

MOXHALL, a hamlet in the parish of WHISHAW, Birmingham division of the hundred of HEMLINGFORD, county of WARWICK, 4¼ miles (N. by W.) from Coleshill. The population is returned with the parish.

MOZE, a parish in the hundred of TENDRING, county of ESSEX, 7½ miles (S. E.) from Manningtree. The population is returned with the parish of Beaumont. The living is a rectory not in charge, united in 1678 to that of Beaumont, in the archdeaconry of Colchester, and diocese of London. The church, which was dedicated to St. Mary, has been demolished.

MUCHELNEY, a parish in the hundred of PITNEY, county of SOMERSET, 2½ miles (S. S. E.) from Langport, containing 329 inhabitants. The living is a vicarage, in the archdeaconry of Wells, and diocese of Bath and Wells, rated in the king's books at £10, endowed with £600 private benefaction, £800 royal bounty, and £300 parliamentary grant. Henry Tripp, Esq. was patron in 1822. The church is dedicated to St. Peter and St. Paul. The navigable river Yeo bounds the parish on the north-east. A Benedictine abbey, in honour of St. Peter and St. Paul, was founded here, in 939, by King Athelstan, the revenue of which, at the dissolution, was valued at £498. 16. 3.

MUCKING, a parish in the hundred of BARSTABLE, county of ESSEX, 2 miles (S. E. by S.) from Horndon on the Hill, containing 189 inhabitants. The living is a vicarage, in the archdeaconry of Essex, and diocese of London, rated in the king's books at £10, and in the patronage of the Dean and Chapter of St. Paul's, London. The church is dedicated to St. John the Baptist. The parish is bounded on the east by the river Thames.

MUCKLEFORD, a tything in the parish of BRADFORD-PEVERELL, hundred of GEORGE, Dorchester division of the county of DORSET, 5¼ miles (W. N. W.) from

Dorchester. The population is returned with the parish.

MUCKLESTON, a hamlet in that part of the parish of SHAWBURY which is in the Whitchurch division of the hundred of BRADFORD (North), county of SALOP, 9¾ miles (N. E. by E.) from Shrewsbury. The population is returned with the township of Edgbolton.

MUCKLESTON, otherwise MUXON, a parish comprising the townships of Bearston, Dorrington, Gravenhanger, and Woore, in the Drayton division of the hundred of BRADFORD (North), county of SALOP, and the townships of Aston, Kneighton, Muckleston, Oakley, and Winnington, in the northern division of the hundred of PIREHILL, county of STAFFORD, and containing 1753 inhabitants, of which number, 179 are in the township of Muckleston, 4 miles (N. E.) from Drayton in Hales. The living is a rectory, in the archdeaconry of Stafford, and diocese of Lichfield and Coventry, rated in the king's books at £20. 3. 9., and in the patronage of Lord Crewe. The church is dedicated to St. Mary. Several small sums have been bequeathed by different individuals for the education of children.

MUCKLEWICK, a township in that part of the parish of HYSSINGTON which is in the hundred of CHIRBURY, county of SALOP, containing 53 inhabitants.

MUCKTON, a parish in the Wold division of the hundred of LOUTH-ESKE, parts of LINDSEY, county of LINCOLN, 5½ miles (S. E.) from Louth, containing 131 inhabitants. The living is a discharged rectory, in the archdeaconry and diocese of Lincoln, rated in the king's books at £6 3. 6½., endowed with £200 royal bounty. M. B. Lister, Esq. was patron in 1817.

MUDFORD, a parish in the hundred of STONE, county of SOMERSET, 3 miles (N. N. E.) from Yeovil, containing 375 inhabitants. The living is a discharged vicarage, in the archdeaconry of Wells, and diocese of Bath and Wells, rated in the king's books at £9. 4. 9½., and in the patronage of the Dean and Chapter of Wells. The church is dedicated to St. Mary.

MUGGINTON, a parish in the hundred of APPLE-TREE, county of DERBY, 7 miles (N. W.) from Derby, containing, with the township of Mercaston, and the hamlet of Ravensdale Park, 525 inhabitants. The living is a rectory, in the archdeaconry of Derby, and diocese of Lichfield and Coventry, rated in the king's books at £9. 12. 8½., and in the patronage of E. S. Pole, Esq. The church is dedicated to All Saints. The Rev. Samuel Pole, rector, in 1746, and Mrs. Frances Pole, in 1751, gave land now producing about £21. 5. a year, which, with the profits of a lime-kiln, let for upwards of £100 per annum, is applied to the free education of thirty-six children.

MUGGLESWICK, a parish in the western division of CHESTER ward, county palatine of DURHAM, 10 miles (N. by W.) from Walsingham, containing 278 inhabitants. The living is a perpetual curacy, in the archdeaconry and diocese of Durham, endowed with £200 private benefaction, £200 royal bounty, and £200 parliamentary grant, and in the patronage of the Dean and Chapter of Durham. The church is small, though vrey ancient. There are places of worship for Baptists and Wesleyan Methodists. The parish is bounded on the north by the river Derwent, along the bank of which is a range of hills, abounding in very productive mines of lead-ore, containing some silver, for smelting which there is a mill in the neighbourhood.

MUKER, a chapelry in that part of the parish of GRINTON which is in the western division of the wapentake of GILLING, North riding of the county of YORK, 6 miles (N. W. by N.) from Askrigg, containing 1425 inhabitants. The living is a perpetual curacy, annexed to the vicarage of Grinton, in the archdeaconry of Richmond, and diocese of Chester, endowed with £800 royal bounty, and £1000 parliamentary grant. The chapel, dedicated to St. Mary, was consecrated in 1580. The river Swale runs through the parish, and forms a romantic cataract, called Keasden Force. Anthony Metcalfe, in 1678, bequeathed a messuage for the foundation of a free school, the income arising from which is about £20. 10. a year. A subscription library was formed here in 1819. A customary market is held on Wednesday, and a fair for sheep, &c., on the Wednesday preceding Christmas - day. The parish abounds with lead and iron ore, coal, and limestone.

MULBARTON, a parish in the hundred of HUMBLEYARD, county of NORFOLK, 5½ miles (S. S. W.) from Norwich, containing 417 inhabitants. The living is a rectory, with Keningham, in the archdeaconry of Norfolk, and diocese of Norwich, rated in the king's books at £14. John Steward, Esq. was patron in 1812. The church, dedicated to St. Mary Magdalene, was erected by Thomas de St. Omer, justice itinerant for Cambridgeshire, who obtained from Henry III. the privileges of a fair and free warren for this place, and subsequently view of frankpledge, with other liberties attached to a court leet. Sir Thomas Richardson, an eminent lawyer, who was raised to the office of Chief Justice of the Common Pleas, was born here, in 1626 ; he died about 1634.

MULLION, a parish in the hundred of KERRIER, county of CORNWALL, 6¼ miles (S. by E.) from Helston, containing 692 inhabitants. The living is a discharged vicarage, in the archdeaconry of Cornwall, and diocese of Exeter, rated in the king's books at £9. 4. 4., and in the patronage of the Bishop of Exeter. The church is dedicated to St. Melan : its tower forms the most conspicuous object in this part of Cornwall. There is a place of worship for Wesleyan Methodists. The parish is bounded by the English channel on the west, where there is a small cove, convenient for fishing, which is the principal employment of the inhabitants.

MULWITH, a joint township with Newby, in that part of the parish of RIPON which is within the liberty of RIPON, West riding of the county of YORK, 4½ miles (S. E.) from Ripon. The population is returned with Newby.

MUMBY, a parish in the Marsh division of the hundred of CALCEWORTH, parts of LINDSEY, county of LINCOLN, 4 miles (E. S. E.) from Alford, containing, with Chapel-Mumby, 582 inhabitants. The living is a discharged vicarage, in the archdeaconry and diocese of Lincoln, rated in the king's books at £9. 12. 3., endowed with £200 royal bounty, and in the patronage of the Bishop of Lincoln. The church is dedicated to St. Peter.

MUMBY (CHAPEL), a chapelry in the parish of MUMBY, Marsh division of the hundred of CALCEWORTH, parts of LINDSEY, county of LINCOLN, 7 miles (E. S. E.) from Alford. The population is returned with the parish.

MUNCASTER, a parish in ALLERDALE ward above Darwent, county of CUMBERLAND, 1½ mile (E. by N.) from Ravenglass, containing, with the township of Birkby, 555 inhabitants. The living is a perpetual curacy, in the archdeaconry of Richmond, and diocese of Chester, endowed with £1000 royal bounty, and £1200 parliamentary grant, and in the patronage of Lord Muncaster. The church is dedicated to St. Michael. This place, anciently written *Meol-castre*, derives its name from a castle, the ancient residence of the Penningtons, lords of the manor, situated at Esk-meol, near the mouth of the river Esk, the principal tower of which is retained in the modern mansion, which was neatly built by the late Lord Muncaster. Richard Brockbank, in 1696, left £160 towards the establishment of a school for the children of those who should contribute to the building of a school-room, which has been further endowed with £100, by Sir William Pennington, Bart., and some smaller sums by others : the annual income, about £12, is paid to the master, who receives also trifling quarterages from the children, of whom from forty to fifty are instructed. This parish includes the market town of Ravenglass, which See. Muncaster gives the title of baron to the ancient and noble family of Pennington, an Irish peerage, without a seat in the House of Lords.

MUNDEN (GREAT), a parish in the hundred of BROADWATER, county of HERTFORD, 2 miles (W. by N.) from Puckeridge, containing 515 inhabitants. The living is a rectory, in the archdeaconry of Huntingdon, and diocese of Lincoln, rated in the king's books at £21. 9. 7., and in the patronage of the Crown. The church is dedicated to St. Nicholas. At Rownay are slight remains of a Benedictine nunnery, founded in honour of St. John the Baptist, by Conan, Duke of Britain and Earl of Richmond, in the reign of Henry II., which falling into decay, through mismanagement, was surrendered in the time of Henry VI., and its possessions appropriated to the maintenance of a chantry priest till the dissolution, when they were valued at £13. 10. 9. per annum.

MUNDEN (LITTLE), a parish in the hundred of BROADWATER, county of HERTFORD, 4 miles (W. by S.) from Puckeridge, containing 464 inhabitants. The living is a rectory, in the archdeaconry of Huntingdon, and diocese of Lincoln, rated in the king's books at £15, and in the patronage of Robert Thornton Heysham, Esq. The church is dedicated to All Saints. There is a place of worship for Wesleyan Methodists. A National school is supported by subscription : the school-house was erected in 1822.

MUNDFORD, a parish in the hundred of GRIMSHOE, county of NORFOLK, 5 miles (N. N. E.) from Brandon-Ferry, containing 397 inhabitants. The living is a discharged rectory, in the archdeaconry of Norfolk, and diocese of Norwich, rated in the king's books at £7. 17. 6. Mrs. Newcome was patroness in 1815. The church, dedicated to St. Leonard, is built of flint, having an embattled tower at the west end, with freestone coping and coins : the chancel is separated from the body of the building by a wooden screen, which is surmounted by the royal arms sculptured in stone. This parish is bounded on the north by the river Wissey, which is crossed by a bridge at a short distance from the village.

MUNDHAM, a parish in the hundred of LODDON, county of NORFOLK, 5¾ miles (N. by W.) from Bungay, containing 304 inhabitants. The living is a perpetual curacy, in the archdeaconry of Norfolk, and diocese of Norwich, and in the patronage of the Mayor and Corporation of Norwich. The church is dedicated to St. Peter.

MUNDHAM (NORTH), a parish in the hundred of Box and STOCKBRIDGE, rape of CHICHESTER, county of SUSSEX, 2½ miles (S. E. by S.) from Chichester, containing 422 inhabitants. The living is a discharged vicarage, in the archdeaconry and diocese of Chichester, rated in the king's books at £9. 0. 10. W. Brereton, Esq. was patron in 1803. The church has lately received an addition of sixty free sittings, the Incorporated Society for the enlargement of churches and chapels having granted £50 towards defraying the expense. The Arundel and Portsmouth canal passes through the parish.

MUNDON, a parish in the hundred of DENGIE, county of ESSEX, 3¼ miles (S. E. by S.) from Maldon, containing 309 inhabitants. The living is a vicarage, in the archdeaconry of Essex, and diocese of London, rated in the king's books at £13, and in the patronage of the King, as Duke of Lancaster. The church is dedicated to St. Mary. The parish is bounded on the north by Blackwater river, which is navigable.

MUNDSLEY, a parish in the northern division of the hundred of ERPINGHAM, county of NORFOLK, 5 miles (N. N. E.) from North Walsham, containing 333 inhabitants. The living is a discharged rectory, in the archdeaconry of Norfolk, and diocese of Norwich, rated in the king's books at £8. 9. 9., endowed with £200 royal bounty, and in the patronage of the King, as Duke of Lancaster. The church is dedicated to All Saints. The parish lies on the coast of the North sea, in a cliff near which were found, some years ago, large petrified bones of the elephant, also horns of the moose deer, and other bones of an immense size, supposed to be diluvial remains.

MUNGRISDALE, a chapelry in the parish of GREYSTOCK, LEATH ward, county of CUMBERLAND, 8½ miles (N. E. by E.) from Keswick, containing 236 inhabitants. The living is a perpetual curacy, in the archdeaconry and diocese of Carlisle, endowed with £200 private benefaction, and £800 royal bounty, and in the patronage of the Rector of Greystock. The chapel was rebuilt in 1754. There are quarries of blue slate and flag-stone within the chapelry. John Slee, a member of the Society of Friends, and a distinguished mathematician, was born here ; he died at Terril in 1828.

MUNSLEY, a parish in the hundred of RADLOW, county of HEREFORD, 4 miles (N. W.) from Ledbury, containing 182 inhabitants. The living is a rectory, in the archdeaconry and diocese of Hereford, rated in the king's books at £8. 7. 6., and in the patronage of Miss Ann Jones. The church is dedicated to St. Bartholomew.

MUNSLOW, a parish in the hundred of MUNSLOW, county of SALOP, 11 miles (N.) from Ludlow, containing 708 inhabitants. The living is a rectory, in the archdeaconry of Salop, and diocese of Hereford, rated in the king's books at £21. 15. 2½. The Rev. R. Powell was patron in 1806. The church is dedicated to St.

Michael. Munslow gave birth, in 1589, and the title of baron, in 1640, to Edward Littleton, Lord Chief Justice of the Common Pleas, and Keeper of the Great Seal; he died in 1645.

MURCOT, a hamlet in the parish of CHARLTON upon OTMORE, hundred of PLOUGHLEY, county of OXFORD, 4½ miles (S.) from Bicester. The population is returned with Fencot.

MURCOTT, a hamlet in the parish of LONG BUCK-BY, hundred of GUILSBOROUGH, county of NORTH-AMPTON, 5 miles (N. E. by N.) from Daventry, containing 46 inhabitants.

MURRAH, a township in the parish of GREYSTOCK, LEATH ward, county of CUMBERLAND, 9½ miles (N. E. by E.) from Keswick. The population is returned with the township of Berrier.

MURRELL-GREEN, a tything in the parish and hundred of ODIHAM, Basingstoke division of the county of SOUTHAMPTON, 2¾ miles (S. W.) from Hartford-Bridge. The population is returned with the parish.

MURSLEY, a parish in the hundred of COTTESLOE, county of BUCKINGHAM, 3¾ miles (E. by N.) from Winslow, containing, with the hamlet of Salden, 473 inhabitants. The living is a rectory, in the archdeaconry of Buckingham, and diocese of Lincoln, rated in the king's books at £11. Lord Say and Sele was patron in 1790. The church is dedicated to St. Mary. Mursley had formerly the privilege of a market on Thursday; also two fairs on Assumption day, and on the festival of the Nativity of the Blessed Virgin, but they have been long disused.

MURSTON, a parish in the hundred of MILTON, lathe of SCRAY, county of KENT, 1 mile (E. S. E.) from Milton, containing 141 inhabitants. The living is a rectory, in the archdeaconry and diocese of Canterbury, rated in the king's books at £10. 14. 2., and in the patronage of the Rev. Dr. Poore. The church, dedicated to All Saints, is a spacious edifice, with a square western tower and wooden turret. The parish is bounded on the north by the Swale, which separates the Isle of Sheppy from the main land. William Houssin, in 1783, bequeathed £200, directing the interest to be applied in teaching poor children of Bapchild, Murston, and Tonge.

MURTON, otherwise MOOR-TOWN, a township in the parish of LAMPLUGH, ALLERDALE ward above Darwent, county of CUMBERLAND, 8 miles (E. by N.) from Whitehaven. The population is returned with the parish. The manufacture of spades, shovels, and edge-tools is carried on here, and there are several lime-works in the township. A charity school is supported by donations amounting to about £8. 8. per annum.

MURTON, otherwise MOOR-TOWN, a township in the parish of TYNEMOUTH, eastern division of CASTLE ward, county of NORTHUMBERLAND, 2½ miles (N. W.) from North Shields, containing 556 inhabitants, who are chiefly employed in the coal mines with which the district abounds. There is a place of worship for Wesleyan Methodists. Freestone is obtained here, and in raising it, a stone coffin, containing a perfect skeleton, was found in one of the quarries, in 1790.

MURTON, a township in the parish of BONGATE, or ST. MICHAEL, APPLEBY, EAST ward, county of WEST-MORLAND, 3 miles (E. N. E.) from Appleby, containing 204 inhabitants. There is a place of worship for

Wesleyan Methodists. A school is endowed with about £8 per annum. Some veins of lead-ore are now in operation.

MURTON, a township in the parish of OSBALDWICK, liberty of ST. PETER of YORK, East riding, though locally in the wapentake of Bulmer, North riding, of the county of YORK, 3 miles (E. by N.) from York, containing 134 inhabitants: it is within the peculiar jurisdiction of the Prebendary of Strensall in the Cathedral Church of York.

MUSBURY, a parish in the hundred of AXMINSTER, county of DEVON, 2 miles (E. by N.) from Colyton, containing 375 inhabitants. The living is a rectory, in the archdeaconry and diocese of Exeter, rated in the king's books at £19. 11. 8., and in the patronage of George Tucker, Esq. The church is dedicated to St. Michael. The river Axe passes between this parish and Colyton. Ash House, now occupied as a farm-house, derives interest from having been the birthplace, in 1650, of the renowned Duke of Marlborough, whose mother was then on a visit to her father, Sir John Drake. Within the parish is an ancient fortress, of an elliptical form, having a double intrenchment enclosing an area of twenty acres.

MUSBURY, a township in that part of the parish of BURY which is in the higher division of the hundred of BLACKBURN, county palatine of LANCASTER, 3 miles (S. W.) from Haslingden, containing 728 inhabitants.

MUSCOATES, a township in that part of the parish of KIRKDALE which is in the wapentake of RYEDALE, North riding of the county of YORK, 5¼ miles (E. S. E.) from Helmsley, containing 65 inhabitants.

MUSCOTT, a hamlet in the parish of NORTON, hundred of FAWSLEY, county of NORTHAMPTON, 4½ miles (E. by N.) from Daventry. The population is returned with the parish.

MUSGRAVE (GREAT), a parish in EAST ward, county of WESTMORLAND, 2 miles (W. S. W.) from Brough, containing 188 inhabitants. The living is a discharged rectory, in the archdeaconry and diocese of Carlisle, rated in the king's books at £16. 1. 11½., endowed with £200 private benefaction, and £200 royal bounty, and in the patronage of the Bishop of Carlisle. The church is dedicated to St. Theobald. The parish is bounded on the south-east by the river Belo, and on the south-west by the Eden, which is crossed by a bridge of two arches, erected in 1826. The late Rev. Septimus Collinson, D.D., in 1827, left £1500 three per cent. consols., for the endowment of a free school on the Madras system: the school-room and residence for the master were built by subscription.

MUSGRAVE (LITTLE), a township in the parish of CROSBY-GARRETT, EAST ward, county of WESTMORLAND, 3 miles (W. S. W.) from Brough, containing 80 inhabitants.

MUSKHAM (NORTH), a parish in the northern division of the wapentake of THURGARTON, county of NOTTINGHAM, 3 miles (N.) from Newark, containing, with the township of Bathley, 617 inhabitants. The living is a discharged vicarage in medieties, in the peculiar jurisdiction of the Chapter of the Collegiate Church of Southwell: the first mediety is rated in the king's books at £5. 6. 8., endowed with £200 royal bounty, and in the patronage of the Prebendary of North Muskham in the Collegiate Church of Southwell; the second is rated at £8. 19. 7., endowed with £400 royal bounty, and in the patronage of the Duke of Portland. The church is dedicated to St. Wilfrid. There is a place of worship for Wesleyan Methodists. The parish is bounded on the east by the Trent, which is crossed by a ferry to Holme. A free grammar school was founded in 1727, by Mrs. Woolhouse, who endowed it with land producing upwards of £50 per annum. There are two almshouses, founded by a Mr. Kemp; also a bequest of £10 per annum, with clothing, for ten poor persons, by John Smith, who also left £1. 6. 8. each to six poor scholars in Pembroke Hall, Cambridge.

MUSKHAM (SOUTH), a parish in the northern division of the wapentake of THURGARTON, county of NOTTINGHAM, 2¼ miles (N.) from Newark, containing, with the hamlet of South Carlton, 278 inhabitants. The living is a discharged vicarage, in the peculiar jurisdiction of the Chapter of the Collegiate Church of Southwell, rated in the king's books at £4, and in the patronage of the Prebendary of South Muskham in the Collegiate Church of Southwell. The church is dedicated to St. Wilfrid. The parish is bounded on the east and south by the river Trent, which is crossed by a bridge leading towards Newark.

MUSTON, a parish in the hundred of FRAMLAND, county of LEICESTER, 5¼ miles (W. by N.) from Grantham, containing 242 inhabitants. The living is a rectory, in the archdeaconry of Leicester, and diocese of Lincoln, rated in the king's books at £15. 13. 1½., and in the patronage of the Crown. The church is dedicated to St. John the Baptist. There is a place of worship for Wesleyan Methodists. The Grantham canal passes through the parish.

MUSTON, a parish in the wapentake of DICKERING, East riding of the county of YORK, 6¼ miles (S. E. by S.) from Scarborough, containing 350 inhabitants. The living is a discharged vicarage, in the archdeaconry of the East riding, and diocese of York, rated in the king's books at £6. 10., and in the patronage of H. Osbaldeston, Esq. The church is dedicated to All Saints. There is a place of worship for Independents.

MUTFORD, a parish in the hundred of MUTFORD and LOTHINGLAND, county of SUFFOLK, 3½ miles (E. S. E.) from Beccles, containing 387 inhabitants. The living is a discharged vicarage, with the rectories of Barnby and Wheatacre All Saints, in the archdeaconry of Suffolk, and diocese of Norwich, rated in the king's books at £7. 17. 1. The church is dedicated to St. Andrew.

MYERSCOUGH, a township in that part of the parish of LANCASTER which is in the hundred of AMOUNDERNESS, county palatine of LANCASTER, 4 miles (S.) from Garstang, containing 557 inhabitants. A free school is endowed with land producing a considerable annual income, the gift of an unknown benefactor.

MYLOR, a parish in the hundred of KERRIER, county of CORNWALL, 3 miles (E. by N.) from Penryn, containing 2193 inhabitants. The living is a vicarage, with that of Mabe, in the peculiar jurisdiction and patronage of the Bishop of Exeter, rated in the king's books at £16. 15. The church is dedicated to St. Melor. There are places of worship for Independents and Wesleyan Methodists. This parish is bounded on the southeast by Falmouth harbour, and includes the small seaport of Flushing, which has considerably increased in population since the improvements made, in the early part of the last century, by Samuel Trefusis, Esq., who

at great expense levelled the ground, constructed quays, erected numerous buildings, and endeavoured, but unsuccessfully, to establish the packets there. This place has of late years been much resorted to by invalids, on account of the mildness of the climate; there is a ferry to Falmouth, at the distance of half a mile. Within the parish is part of Perran wharf, also a large iron-foundry.

MYNYDDMAEN, a hamlet in the parish of MYNYDDYSLWYN, lower division of the hundred of WENTLLOOG, county of MONMOUTH, containing 511 inhabitants.

MYNYDDYSLWYN, a parish in the lower division of the hundred of WENTLLOOG, county of MONMOUTH, 9½ miles (N. W. by W.) from Newport, containing, with the hamlets of Clawrplwyf, Mynyddmaen, and Penmain, 3186 inhabitants. The living is a perpetual curacy, in the archdeaconry and diocese of Llandaff, endowed with £600 royal bounty, and £1800 parliamentary grant, and in the patronage of the Bishop of Llandaff. The church is dedicated to St. Tyder.

MYTHE, an extra-parochial liberty, in the hundred of SPARKENHOE, county of LEICESTER, containing 14 inhabitants.

MYTON upon SWALE, a parish in the wapentake of BULMER, North riding of the county of YORK, 3¾ miles (E.) from Boroughbridge, containing 185 inhabitants. The living is a discharged vicarage, in the archdeaconry of Cleveland, and diocese of York, rated in the king's books at £6, endowed with £200 private benefaction, and £300 parliamentary grant, and in the patronage of the Archbishop of York. The church is dedicated to St. Mary. There is a ferry over the Swale at this place. A battle was fought here, in 1319, between the Scots and about ten thousand undisciplined Yorkshiremen, headed by Melton, Archbishop of York, amongst whom was a great number of priests, in which the latter were defeated with immense slaughter.

MYTTON (UPPER), a hamlet in that part of the parish of HARTLEBURY which is in the lower division of the hundred of HALFSHIRE, county of WORCESTER, containing 181 inhabitants.

N.

NABURN, a chapelry in that part of the parish of ACASTER-MALBIS which is in the wapentake of OUZE and DERWENT, East riding of the county of YORK, 4¼ miles (S.) from York, containing 366 inhabitants. The living is a perpetual curacy, annexed to the rectory of St. Denis in York, in the archdeaconry and diocese of York. There is a place of worship for Wesleyan Methodists. A school is endowed with £10 per annum, £5 having been left by Edward Loftus, in 1784, and £5 by Lady Hewley. The river Ouse bounds this chapelry on the west.

NACKINGTON, a parish in the hundred of BRIDGE and PETHAM, lathe of St. AUGUSTINE, county of KENT, 2¼ miles (S.) from Canterbury, containing 165 inhabitants. The living is a perpetual curacy, in the archdeaconry and diocese of York, endowed with £400 royal bounty, and in the patronage of the Archbishop of Canterbury. The church is dedicated to St. Mary. The ancient Stane-street passes through the parish.

NACTON, a parish in the hundred of COLNEIS, county of SUFFOLK, 4 miles (S. E.) from Ipswich, containing 527 inhabitants. The living is a discharged rectory, united to that of Levington, in the archdeaconry of Suffolk, and diocese of Norwich, rated in the king's books at £8. 7. 1. The church is dedicated to St. Martin. The navigable river Orwell runs along the southern boundary of the parish.

NAFFERTON, a township in the parish of OVING-HAM, eastern division of TINDALE ward, county of NORTHUMBERLAND, 9 miles (E.) from Hexham, containing 39 inhabitants. Coal is obtained within the township. There are vestiges of an old monastic building, said to have been occupied by banditti in the times of Henry VI. and his successor.

NAFFERTON, a parish in the wapentake of DICK-ERING, East riding of the county of YORK, comprising the townships of Nafferton and Wansford, and containing 1261 inhabitants, of which number, 917 are in the township of Nafferton, 2¼ miles (E. N. E.) from Great Driffield. The living is a discharged vicarage, in the archdeaconry of the East riding, and diocese of York, rated in the king's books at £13. 15. 4., endowed with £400 royal bounty, and £1200 parliamentary grant, and in the patronage of the Archbishop of York. The church is dedicated to All Saints. There are places of worship for Independents and Wesleyan Methodists. Rope, twine, and linen-cloth, are manufactured here. John Baron, in 1709, gave a rent-charge of £5, for teaching children.

NAFFORD, formerly a parish, but now in the parish of ECKINGTON, upper division of the hundred of PERSHORE, county of WORCESTER. The church, which was dedicated to St. James, has been demolished, and the living consolidated with that of Eckington.

NAILSEA, a parish in the hundred of PORTBURY, county of SOMERSET, 8½ miles (N. by W.) from Bristol, containing 1678 inhabitants. The living is a perpetual curacy, in the archdeaconry of Bath, and diocese of Bath and Wells, and in the patronage of Adam Gordon, Esq. The church is dedicated to the Holy Trinity. There is a place of worship for Wesleyan Methodists. In this parish are extensive coal-works, and a manufactory for crown glass upon a very large scale, which together give employment to a great portion of the inhabitants.

NAILSTONE, a parish in the hundred of SPARK-ENHOE, county of LEICESTER, 3½ miles (N.N.E.) from Market Bosworth, containing, with the chapelry of Normanton le Heath, 574 inhabitants. The living is a rectory, in the archdeaconry of Leicester, and diocese of Lincoln, rated in the king's books at £24. 9. 9½., and in the patronage of the Crown. The church is dedicated to All Saints. Nailstone is in the honour of Tutbury, duchy of Lancaster, and within the jurisdiction of a court of pleas held at Tutbury every third Tuesday, for the recovery of debts under 40s.

NAILSWORTH, a chapelry partly in the parishes of HORSLEY and MINCHIN-HAMPTON, but chiefly in that of AVENING, hundred of LONGTREE, county of GLOU-CESTER, 2 miles (S.W. by W.) from Minchin-Hampton, containing 898 inhabitants. This place is situated in the centre of a district in which the manufacture of woollen cloth is carried on to a considerable extent, and for which the numerous brooks and rivulets that abound are extremely favourable. There are places of worship for Baptists, the Society of Friends, Independents, and Wesleyan Methodists. A small customary market is held on Saturday.

NANTWICH, a parish in the hundred of NANT-WICH, county palatine of CHESTER, comprising the market town of Nantwich, and the townships of Alvaston, Leighton, and Woolstanwood, and containing 5333 inhabitants, of which number, 4661 are in the town of Nantwich, 20 miles (S. E. by E.) from Chester, and 164 (N. W.) from London, on the road to Chester. The origin of this town, which is of uncertain date, has been attributed to the Britons prior to the Roman invasion, when it is said to have been called Halen Gwyn, the white salt town: its modern appellation is probably a compound of the British term Nant, a brook, or marsh, and the Saxon Vic, by corruption Wich, a vill, or settlement, which latter term appears indefinably to be appropriated to towns where salt is made. Previously to the Conquest, the importance of this place consisted in its numerous brine springs, which became an ample source of revenue to the King and Earl Edwin, between whom, according to the record of Domesday, the district was at that period unequally divided: it was soon after erected into a barony by Hugh Lupus, the first Norman Earl of Chester, who conferred it, together with the whole hundred, on William Malbedeng, or Malbank, and in consequence thereof the town was for some time denominated Wich Malbank. At the time of the Norman invasion, Nantwich was defended by a line of earth-works constructed along the bank of the river, but the opposition made to the progress of the invaders was terminated by a battle fought here in 1069: the inhabitants then became subject to the incursions of the Welch, who are said to have destroyed the town in 1133. In 1146, a predatory band of that people was routed here, on returning from one of their plundering inroads; and in 1282 Edward I. came hither, to concert measures of protection for the inhabitants from similar annoyance. On the return of James I. from Scotland, in 1617, he was received here with demonstrations of joy; but during the subsequent disastrous reign, the town was remarkable for its firm adherence to the cause of the parliament, and was garrisoned in its behalf: in 1642 it was captured by the royalists, but soon after was retaken by Sir W. Brereton, who fortified and made it his headquarters. Sir Thomas Aston made an effort to dislodge him, but this attempt, as well as a regular investment and vigorous assault of the town by Lord Byron, about the close of the year 1643, proved unsuccessful; and Sir Thomas Fairfax having defeated the royalists in the neighbourhood of Nantwich, the siege was raised, and the parliamentarians held the town during the remainder of the war. The anniversary of this victory, the 25th of January, was for many years afterwards esteemed a kind of festival, and the event was commemorated by the inhabitants wearing sprigs of holly in their hats. On the defeat of the Scottish army in 1646, the Duke of Hamilton, with three thousand and fifty cavalry, found a temporary refuge here. In 1438 and 1583, the town suffered severely from fire; the injury sustained in the latter year was estimated at upwards of £30,000, and a royal license was granted for a general collection for its renovation. Other calamities have at different periods befallen the inhabitants, such as the ague in 1587, the flux in 1596, and the plague in 1604, which severally produced considerable mortality: on the cessation of the last disease, the court of assize was removed hither from Chester, where that infectious malady still prevailed.

The town is situated on the banks of the river Weever, in a level and fertile tract of country: it is irregularly built, and consists of three principal streets, which are very indifferently paved; most of the houses are of timber and brick, covered with plaster, having large bay windows and projecting stories, but some, of modern erection, are of respectable appearance: the inhabitants enjoy a plentiful supply of water. There is a small theatre, also an assembly-room. Throughout a long period, the brine springs were a source of extensive commerce: during the conflicts between Henry III. and the Welch, that sovereign imposed a temporary restraint on the manufacture, in order to harrass his opponents, who carried on an extensive traffic in salt, but on the restoration of peace it was resumed. In the time of Henry VIII. there were three hundred salt-works, but this number, from the destruction of several by fire, and the discovery of springs and mines of superior quality elsewhere, where the facility of communication by water was greater, has been gradually reduced, until only one spring remains. In the time of Elizabeth and James, the tanning business, and the manufacture of bone-lace and stockings, prevailed somewhat extensively, but they have been long superseded by that of shoes, chiefly for the London and Manchester markets, gloves, and cotton goods, which afford employment to about two thousand persons. Cheese is the principal article of agricultural produce. A canal from Chester, terminating about a quarter of a mile from the town, was completed in 1778, at an expense of about £80,000; and the construction of another, to be called the Liverpool and Birmingham junction canal, is in progress. In 1734, an act was obtained for making the Weever navigable, but the design has never been carried into effect : the first stone bridge across the river here, in lieu of the original one of timber, was built in 1663. The market is on Saturday, and fairs, chiefly for cattle, sheep, and pigs, are held on March 26th, the second Tuesday in June, September 4th, and December 4th; a market for cattle also is held once a fortnight, from Candlemas until the fair in March. The civil government of the town was anciently vested in a guild, whose common hall was the present school-house : during its existence, a bailiff and various other officers were regularly appointed : the fraternity was suppressed in the time of Edward VI.; the nomination of the bailiff, however, at the court leet of the lord of the manor, continued to be observed for a few years, but has long since been abandoned. A manorial court, and a court for the hundred, are held by the Marquis of Cholmondeley; at the former constables are chosen. Petty sessions for the hundred are also held here: the general quarter sessions, formerly held at Nantwich, were removed to Knutsford about 1760. Lord Crewe, as proprietor of certain fees of the ancient barony, holds a manorial court, at which a few of the inhabitants render suit and service; and a similar court is annexed to the fee granted by Hugh Malbanck to the abbot of Combermere, and now in the possession of Lord Dysart. A court of requests, for the recovery of debts under 40s., is held under the presidency of an officer appointed by the joint lords of the manor: the inhabitants are exempted from being impannelled on juries beyond the jurisdiction of the town. The town hall was built in 1720, by George, Prince of Wales and Earl of Chester, afterwards George II., at an expense of £600; but, in 1737, a por-

tion of it fell down, and a few persons were killed : it was rebuilt, but not many years afterwards, a similar accident being apprehended from a sudden crash heard during the holding of the sessions, it was taken down, and a modern edifice, used as a market-house and town hall, has been erected on its site.

The living is a rectory, in the archdeaconry and diocese of Chester, endowed with £200 private benefaction, £200 royal bounty, and £800 parliamentary grant, and in the patronage of Lord Crewe. The church, dedicated to St. Mary and St. Nicholas, is a spacious and venerable cruciform structure, principally in the decorated and later styles of English architecture, and comprising a nave, with lateral aisles, a chancel, transepts, and an ornamented octagonal tower rising from the intersection : the chancel has a groined roof, and contains stalls with carved subsellia, and enriched with tabernacle work : under the north-eastern angle of the arches which support the tower is a stone pulpit projecting from the piers, neatly carved in the ancient style of English architecture : the church contains several ancient monuments. There are places of worship for Baptists, the Society of Friends, Independents, Primitive and Wesleyan Methodists, and Unitarians. The grammar school, an ancient edifice in the churchyard, was vested in the crown at the suppression of the ancient guild to which it belonged, and subsequently purchased for its present purpose : it was endowed, in 1611, with a small sum, the joint benefactions of John and Thomas Thrush, natives of this town, and woolpackers in the city of London, for which a limited number of boys are educated. The Blue-cap school has been endowed with various benefactions, principally by the family of Wilbraham, of Townsend, for the education and clothing of forty boys. An almshouse for six poor men was founded, in 1613, by Sir Roger Wilbraham, and endowed by Lady Wilbraham with £12 per annum; another for the same number, by Sir Edmund Wright, in 1638: an almshouse for four poor men and their wives was founded, in 1722, by Mrs. Ermine Delves ; one by Roger Wilbraham, Esq., in 1676 ; and one for seven poor persons, in 1767, by John Crewe, Esq. (afterwards Lord Crewe), in accordance with the will of Sir Thomas and Sir John Crewe : the inmates of these respective hospitals receive stipends proportioned to the endowments. The ancient castle, erected here by the first Norman baron, was in ruins prior to the reign of Henry VII., and its site alone is now visible. Thomas Harrison, a major-general in the parliamentarian army, and one of the judges at the trial of Charles I.; John Gerarde, the herbalist, born in 1545; and Geoffrey Witney, a minor poet in the reign of Elizabeth, were natives of this town. The widow of the poet Milton was born in the vicinity, where she spent the latter period of her life, and died, at an advanced age, in the year 1726. The Marquis of Cholmondeley enjoys the inferior title of Baron Cholmondeley of Namptwich.

NAPPA, a township in the parish of GISBURN, western division of the wapentake of STAINCLIFFE and EWCROSS, West riding of the county of YORK, 8½ miles (S.S.E.) from Settle, containing 44 inhabitants.

NAPTON on the HILL, a parish in the Southam division of the hundred of KNIGHTLOW, county of WARWICK, 3½ miles (E. by S.) from Southam, containing 892 inhabitants. The living is a discharged vicar-

2 X 2

age, in the archdeaconry of Coventry, and diocese of Lichfield and Coventry, rated in the king's books at £9. 14., and in the patronage of the Crown. The church is dedicated to All Saints. There is a place of worship for Baptists. The Oxford canal and the Warwick and Napton canal form a junction in this parish.

NARBOROUGH, a parish in the hundred of Sparkenhoe, county of Leicester, 5¼ miles (S. W. by S.) from Leicester, containing, with the hamlet of Huncote, 1064 inhabitants. The living is a rectory, in the archdeaconry of Leicester, and diocese of Lincoln, rated in the king's books at £26. 14. 4½., and in the patronage of John Pares, Esq. The church is dedicated to All Saints. There is a place of worship for Independents. The river Soar runs through the parish, and is crossed by a bridge on the line of the old Fosse-road.

NARBURGH, a parish in the southern division of the hundred of Greenhoe, county of Norfolk, 5½ miles (N.W. by W.) from Swaffham, containing 294 inhabitants. The living is a vicarage, with which that of Narford is united, in the archdeaconry of Norfolk, and diocese of Norwich, rated in the king's books at £9. 10. The Rev. H. Spelman was patron in 1799. The church, dedicated to All Saints, originally an ancient structure, has at various times received more modern additions and improvements : it contains some ancient monuments to the family of Spelman. Narburgh, so called by the Saxons, from the river Nar, was a British city in the fifth century, and subsequently, when governed by Earl Okenard, it endured a long siege by Waldy, a neighbouring chieftain, who took it and razed it to the ground. There are several earth-works and intrenchments denoting its antiquity, with an artificial large fosse and rampart running hence, from an artificial eminence called the Burgh, to Eastmore Fen, which completely defended the western boundary of the hundred : human bones, pieces of armour, &c., have been found here.

NARFORD, a parish in the southern division of the hundred of Greenhoe, county of Norfolk, 4¾ miles (N. W.) from Swaffham, containing 129 inhabitants. The living is a discharged vicarage, with that of Narburgh, in the archdeaconry of Norfolk, and diocese of Norwich, rated in the king's books at £6. 13. 4. The church is dedicated to St. Mary. This seems to have been a Roman station, from the bricks, urns, and other relics that have been discovered.

NASEBY, a parish in the hundred of Guilsborough, county of Northampton, 11¾ miles (N. N. W.) from Northampton, containing 697 inhabitants. The living is a discharged vicarage, in the archdeaconry of Northampton, and diocese of Peterborough, rated in the king's books at £8, endowed with £32. 12. per annum private benefaction, £800 royal bounty, and £200 parliamentary grant. The King, by lapse, presented in 1783. The church is dedicated to All Saints. The river Avon has its source in the village, where a market-cross is still standing, this having been formerly a market town. In the vicinity was fought, June 14th, 1645, the decisive battle between the royalists and the army of the parliament, in which the former were irretrievably defeated.

NASH, a hamlet in the parish of Whaddon, hundred of Cottesloe, county of Buckingham, 5 miles (S. by W.) from Stony-Stratford, containing 375 inhabitants. Here are two endowed almshouses.

NASH, a joint township with Rod and Little Brampton, in that part of the parish of Presteigne which is in the hundred of Wigmore, county of Hereford, 2 miles (S. by W.) from Presteigne. The population is returned with Rod.

NASH, a parish in the lower division of the hundred of Caldicott, county of Monmouth, 3½ miles (S. E. by S.) from Newport, containing 233 inhabitants. The living is a discharged vicarage, united with that of Goldcliff, in the archdeaconry and diocese of Llandaff, rated in the king's books at £9. 15., and endowed with £1200 royal bounty. The church is dedicated to St. Mary. There is a place of worship for Baptists.

NASH, a joint township with Tilsop and Weston, in the parish of Burford, hundred of Overs, county of Salop, 2½ miles (N. by E.) from Tenbury, containing, with Tilsop and Weston, 377 inhabitants.

NASSINGTON, a parish in the hundred of Willybrook, county of Northampton, 2¼ miles (S. S. W.) from Wandsford, containing 555 inhabitants. The living is a discharged vicarage, in the peculiar jurisdiction and patronage of the Prebendary of Nassington in the Cathedral Church of Lincoln, rated in the king's books at £7. 13. 4. The church is dedicated to St. Mary. There is a place of worship for Wesleyan Methodists.

NATEBY, a township in the parish of Garstang, hundred of Amounderness, county palatine of Lancaster, 1½ mile (N. N. W.) from Garstang, containing 406 inhabitants.

NATEBY, a township in the parish of Kirkby-Stephen, East ward, county of Westmorland, 1¼ mile (S.) from Kirkby-Stephen, containing 140 inhabitants. — Clayton, in 1786, gave a sum of money, now producing about £6 per annum, which, with some smaller benefactions, is applied in teaching poor children. The township is bounded on the west by the river Eden, which here forms a tremendous cataract, dashing with great violence and noise from rock to rock. There is a lofty fell, about two miles and a half east of the village, called the Nine Standards, from some stones erected there to mark the boundary of the counties of York and Westmorland.

NATELEY (UP), a parish in the hundred of Basingstoke, Basingstoke division of the county of Southampton, 2½ miles (W. by N.) from Odiham, containing 143 inhabitants. The living is a perpetual curacy, annexed to the vicarage of Basingstoke, in the archdeaconry and diocese of Winchester. The church is dedicated to St. Stephen.

NATELEY-SCURES, a parish in the hundred of Basingstoke, Basingstoke division of the county of Southampton, 4½ miles (E.) from Basingstoke, containing 245 inhabitants. The living is a discharged rectory, in the archdeaconry and diocese of Winchester, rated in the king's books at £5. 10. 10. Lord Dorchester was patron in 1819. The church is dedicated to St. Swithin.

NATLAND, a chapelry in that part of the parish of Kendal which is in Kendal ward, county of Westmorland, 2¼ miles (S.) from Kendal, containing 244 inhabitants. The living is a perpetual curacy, in the archdeaconry of Richmond, and diocese of Chester, endowed with £400 private benefaction, and £800 royal bounty, and in the patronage of the Vicar of Kendal. The chapel was rebuilt about 1735, but taken down in 1825, and the present edifice built near its site, at an expense of £550, defrayed by contributions, aided by a grant of £100 from the Incorporated Society for the enlargement of churches and chapels. The river Kent, and the Lancaster canal, run through the parish. Water Crook, a place so called from a bend in the river, was the site of the Roman station *Concangium*, a square fort, the ramparts of which are still discernible, where foundations of buildings, coins, seals, fragments of altars, statues, and urns, with other relics, have been found. A school is endowed with £40 a year, the income arising from Crow Park estate, given by Charles Shippards, in 1779, for the education of children.

NATTON, a joint tything with Fiddington, in the parish of ASHCHURCH, lower division of the hundred of TEWKESBURY, county of GLOUCESTER, 2¾ miles (E.) from Tewkesbury. The population is returned with Fiddington.

NAUGHTON, a parish in the hundred of COSFORD, county of SUFFOLK, 2¼ miles (E.) from Bildeston, containing 155 inhabitants. The living is a discharged rectory, in the archdeaconry of Sudbury, and diocese of Norwich, rated in the king's books at £10. 15. The Rev. W. Edge was patron in 1810. The church is dedicated to St. Mary.

NAUNTON, a hamlet in the parish of WINCHCOMBE, lower division of the hundred of KIFTSGATE, county of GLOUCESTER. The population is returned with the parish.

NAUNTON, a parish partly in the hundred of BRADLEY, but chiefly in the lower division of the hundred of SLAUGHTER, county of GLOUCESTER, 5 miles (W. S. W.) from Stow on the Wold, containing, with the chapelry of Eastington, and the hamlets of Aylworth and Harford, 691 inhabitants. The living is a rectory, in the archdeaconry and diocese of Gloucester, rated in the king's books at £16. 13. 4., and in the patronage of the Bishop of Worcester. The church is dedicated to St. Andrew. There is a place of worship for Baptists.

NAUNTON-BEAUCHAMP, a parish in the upper division of the hundred of PERSHORE, county of WORCESTER, 4¾ miles (N. N. E.) from Pershore, containing 149 inhabitants. The living is a rectory, in the archdeaconry and diocese of Worcester, rated in the king's books at £15, and in the patronage of the Crown. The church is dedicated to St. Bartholomew.

NAVENBY, a parish (formerly a market town) in the higher division of the wapentake of BOOTHBY-GRAFFO, parts of KESTEVEN, county of LINCOLN, 9½ miles (N. W.) from Sleaford, and 120 (N. by W.) from London, containing 625 inhabitants. The living is a rectory, in the archdeaconry and diocese of Lincoln, rated in the king's books at £17. 10., and in the patronage of the Master and Fellows of Christ's College, Cambridge. The church, dedicated to St. Peter, is partly in the early English, and partly in the decorated, style of architecture. There is a place of worship for Wesleyan Methodists. The market, which was held on Thursday, has fallen into disuse. There is a trifling endowment for teaching nine poor children.

NAVESTOCK, a parish in the hundred of ONGAR, county of ESSEX, 4¼ miles (S. S. W.) from Chipping-Ongar, containing 840 inhabitants. The living is a vicarage, in the peculiar jurisdiction of the Dean and Chapter of St. Paul's, London, rated in the king's books

at £13. 3. 9., and in the patronage of the President and Fellows of Trinity College, Oxford. The church is dedicated to St. Thomas the Apostle.

NAWORTH, a township in the parish of BRAMPTON, ESKDALE ward, county of CUMBERLAND, 2¼ miles (N. E. by E.) from Brampton, containing 377 inhabitants. Within this township is Naworth castle, anciently the head of the great barony of Gilsland. It is situated in a fine park, overlooking the river Irthing, which bounds it on the north, and is a spacious quadrangular structure, with two lofty towers. The hall is a noble room, containing paintings of some of the kings of Scotland; in another apartment is a full-length likeness of Mary I.; and in the chapel, a profusion of ancient armour, with portraits of the Patriarchs and some of the Kings of Israel, &c.

NAWTON, a township in that part of the parish of KIRKDALE which is in the wapentake of RYEDALE, North riding of the county of YORK, 2¾ miles (E.) from Helmsley, containing 333 inhabitants. There is a place of worship for Wesleyan Methodists.

NAYLAND, a parish (formerly a market town) in the hundred of BABERGH, county of SUFFOLK, 17 miles (S. W. by W.) from Ipswich, and 57 (N. E.) from London, containing 1019 inhabitants. The town is situated on the river Stour, over which is a bridge of brick, in a fertile valley surrounded by hills, on the high road to Hadleigh : it consists of several streets, the principal of which contains some good dwelling-houses, and has three large flour-mills in the centre: the inhabitants are supplied with water from springs : the adjacent eminences command a fine view of the harbour of Harwich and the surrounding country. The woollen manufacture flourished here for many years, but is now extinct, and, at present, the trade of the town is chiefly in flour. The river is navigable from Sudbury to Harwich, by which means a considerable quantity of corn and flour is conveyed to Mistley, for the port of London, and coal is brought back. The market, now discontinued, was on Friday : a fair is held on the first Wednesday in October, for horses, cattle, and toys. A court leet is held twice a year, at which the steward of the manor presides. The living is a perpetual curacy, in the archdeaconry of Sudbury, and diocese of Norwich, endowed with £400 private benefaction, and £400 royal bounty, and in the patronage of the Parishioners. The church, dedicated to St. James, is situated in the centre of the town, and is a fine structure in the later style of English architecture : in the interior is a good painting of our Saviour, and several ancient marble monuments inlaid with brass. There is a place of worship for Independents. A small fund, arising from the rent of certain lands, is appropriated to the instruction of about fourteen poor children : it is under the management of feoffees. A National school, for all poor children residing in the parish, is supported by annual subscriptions ; as is also a Sunday school in connexion with the established church. There are several houses belonging to the parish, in which poor families live rent-free.

NAZEING, a parish in the hundred of WALTHAM, county of ESSEX, 5¼ miles (N. W.) from Epping, containing 744 inhabitants. The living is a discharged vicarage, in the jurisdiction of the Commissary of London, concurrently with the Consistorial Court of the

Bishop of London, rated in the king's books at £14. 5. 5., endowed with £200 private benefaction, and £200 royal bounty, and in the patronage of the Crown. The church is dedicated to All Saints. At the eastern extremity of the parish are vestiges of an ancient fortification, supposed to be British, called Ambersbank. The learned Dr. Joseph Hall, Bishop of Norwich, was at one time vicar of this parish; as was subsequently Dr. Thomas Fuller, the church historian.

NEASHAM, or NYSAM, a township in the parish of HURWORTH, south-western division of STOCKTON ward, county palatine of DURHAM, 4½ miles (S. E.) from Darlington, containing 313 inhabitants, who are chiefly employed in the linen manufacture. The village consists of one street, extending some distance along the northern bank of the Tees, over which, at this point, there are a ferry and a ford: the latter is noted as the spot selected for the performance of a long-accustomed ceremony, in which, when the river is fordable, the lord of Sockburn, or his agent, meeting the Bishop of Durham, on his first entering the county, and presenting him with a falchion, as an emblem of his temporal power, repeats as follows; "My Lord Bishop, I here present you with the falchion wherewith the champion Conyers slew the worm dragon, or fiery serpent, which destroyed man, woman, and child; in memory of which, the king then reigning gave him the manor of Sockburn, to hold by this tenure, that upon the first entrance of every bishop into the county, this falchion should be presented." The bishop, taking the falchion in his hand, immediately returns it, wishing the lord of Sockburn health and long enjoyment of the manor. A Benedictine nunnery, founded in honour of the Blessed Virgin, formerly existed here, which at the dissolution had a revenue of £26. 9. 9.

NEATESHEAD, a parish in the hundred of TUN-STEAD, county of NORFOLK, 5¼ miles (E. by S.) from Coltishall, containing 576 inhabitants. The living is a discharged vicarage, in the archdeaconry of Norfolk, and diocese of Norwich, rated in the king's books at £3. 13. 1½., and in the patronage of the Bishop of Norwich. The church, dedicated to St. Peter, has been long without a steeple. There is a place of worship for Baptists.

NEATHAM, an extra-parochial liberty, in the hundred of ALTON, Alton (North) division of the county of SOUTHAMPTON, 2 miles (E.) from Alton, containing 92 inhabitants.

NECTON, a parish in the southern division of the hundred of GREENHOE, county of NORFOLK, 3¾ miles (E.) from Swaffham, containing 867 inhabitants. The living comprises a rectory and a vicarage, which are consolidated, and annexed to the rectory of Holme-Hale, in the archdeaconry of Norfolk, and diocese of Norwich, the former rated in the king's books at £8. 6. 8., and the latter at £8. 1. 8. The church is dedicated to All Saints. A free chapel formerly stood at Sparham Hall. There is a place of worship for Baptists.

NEDGING, a parish in the hundred of COSFORD, county of SUFFOLK, 1 mile (S. E.) from Bildeston, containing 203 inhabitants. The living is a discharged rectory, in the archdeaconry of Sudbury, and diocese of Norwich, rated in the king's books at £8. 12. 11., endowed with £200 private benefaction, and £300 par-

liamentary grant, and in the patronage of the Rev. William Edge. The river Brent passes through the parish.

NEEDHAM, a parish in the hundred of EARSHAM, county of NORFOLK, 1¼ mile (S. W.) from Harleston, containing 351 inhabitants. The living is a perpetual curacy, in the archdeaconry of Norfolk, and diocese of Norwich, endowed with £200 private benefaction, and £1000 royal bounty, and in the patronage of — Freston, Esq. The church, dedicated to St. Peter, was originally a chapel to Mendham.

NEEDHAM-MARKET, a chapelry (formerly a market town) in the parish of BARKING, hundred of BOSMERE and CLAYDON, county of SUFFOLK, 8½ miles (N. W. by N.) from Ipswich, and 74 (N. E.) from London, containing 1300 inhabitants. The town is situated on low ground near the river Stour, and on the high road to Ipswich and Bury St. Edmund's: it is tolerably well built, and the houses are neat, and many of them handsome: the inhabitants are supplied with water from springs: the surrounding country is pleasant, and abounds in agreeable walks. Near the town is a lake, between thirty and forty acres in extent, called Bosmere, which gives name to the hundred. The trade formerly consisted in wool-combing, and weaving calimancoes, which has long since ceased; the manufacture of paper and glue is of considerable extent. The Stow-Market and Ipswich navigation passes along the north-east boundary of the parish, and is crossed by a bridge leading from the town; and the Stour is navigable to Ipswich, being used chiefly for the conveyance of corn and coal. The market, formerly held on Wednesday, was removed to Stow-Market, in consequence of the plague having raged here for three years: a fair for toys is held on the 28th of October. Constables are appointed at the court leet and baron of the lord of the manor, held annually, and oftener as occasion may require. The living is a perpetual curacy, in the archdeaconry of Suffolk, and diocese of Norwich, endowed with £600 royal bounty, and £800 parliamentary grant, and in the patronage of the Rector of Barking: the inhabitants, from time immemorial, have had the right of electing a lecturer. The chapel, dedicated to St. John the Baptist, is an ancient edifice, with a belfry of wood. There are places of worship for the Society of Friends and Independents. The free grammar school was founded pursuant to the will of Francis Theobald, Esq., dated January 10th, 1632, and endowed by him with estates subsequently conveyed to trustees, and now producing a rental of £55 per annum: the master's salary is £50, with a dwelling-house; twenty-one poor children from Needham-Market, Barking, and Darmsden, are instructed. An almshouse, comprising two tenements, was founded, by some person unknown, for the benefit of poor widows and widowers, and endowed with land now producing about £20 per annum: eight poor women reside in it.

NEEDINGWORTH, a chapelry in the parish of HOLYWELL, hundred of HURSTINGSTONE, county of HUNTINGDON, 2¼ miles (E. by N.) from St. Ives. The population is returned with the parish. The chapel, which was dedicated to St. James, has been demolished. There is a place of worship for Baptists.

NEEDWOOD-FOREST, a district in the northern division of the hundred of OFFLOW, county of STAF-

FORD, formerly extra-parochial, but now included in the several parishes to which it was allotted for enclosure, viz. Hanbury, Tatenhill, Tutbury, and Yoxhall. This forest, in its ancient state, was divided into five districts, called Barton Ward, Marchington Ward, Tutbury Ward, Yoxhall Ward, and Uttoxeter Ward, and included thirteen parks, which were given to the earls of Mercia. It was about twenty three miles and a half in compass, and the nearest part of it was one mile from the castle of Tutbury. The kings of England often enjoyed the diversion of hunting here, down to the time of Charles I., who disafforested a great portion of the district, by selling and granting away various parts of it. In 1797, it consisted of the four first-named wards only, each having its separate lodge and keeper, and then comprised nearly ten thousand acres; but it was subsequently enclosed by act of parliament, the bill for that purpose having received the royal assent in 1801: up to that period, it having been extra-parochial, no less than twenty-two neighbouring townships had right of pasturage upon it, independently of a numerous herd of deer belonging to the king. At the enclosure, an allotment of land was made to each of the above-mentioned parishes, and, from that reserved to the crown, timber valued at £60,000 was sold; and upwards of sixty miles of road were formed in various directions throughout its extent. The crown still possesses a considerable portion of it, chiefly woodland, for the preservation of deer, &c. It is under the superintendence of a lieutenant, chief ranger, and other officers, viz., a surveyor, or axe-bearer, four keepers, &c. The king's steward of the honour of Tutbury holds an annual court for the forest, called the woodmote, at which these officers attend, and a jury of twenty-four men, residing within the jurisdiction, present and amerce for all encroachments and offences committed therein. This fine tract now contains many elegant mansions, with extensive parks, &c., the property of individuals vying with each other in efforts to render their possessions at once beautiful and of public utility. A church, called Christchurch in Needwood, was erected from funds left by Isaac Hawkins, Esq., and consecrated in 1809: it is a handsome structure, situated at an equal distance from each of the parish churches, of which the living is independent, being a perpetual curacy, in the archdeaconry of Stafford, and diocese of Lichfield and Coventry, endowed, by his late Majesty, George III., with one hundred and sixty acres of the forest land, and in the patronage of the Crown.

NEEN-SAVAGE, a parish in the hundred of STOTTESDEN, county of SALOP, 1¼ mile (N. by E.) from Cleobury Mortimer, containing 485 inhabitants. The living is a vicarage, in the archdeaconry of Salop, and diocese of Hereford, rated in the king's books at £6, and in the patronage of the Crown. A school is endowed with upwards of £39. 4. per annum, arising from a bequest by Richard Edwards.

NEEN-SOLLARS, a parish in the hundred of OVERS, county of SALOP, 3¼ miles (S. by W.) from Cleobury-Mortimer, containing 231 inhabitants. The living is a rectory, with the curacy of Milson, in the archdeaconry of Salop, and diocese of Hereford, rated in the king's books at £13. 9. 9½., and in the patronage of the Provost and Fellows of Worcester College, Oxford. The church, dedicated to All Saints, contains a monument to the memory of Humphrey Conyngsby, Esq., who was born about 1567, an accomplished scholar, and great traveller. The small river Rea, and the Kington canal, run through the parish.

NEENTON, a parish in the hundred of STOTTESDEN, county of SALOP, 6½ miles (S. W. by W.) from Bridgenorth, containing 119 inhabitants. The living is a discharged rectory, in the archdeaconry of Salop, and diocese of Hereford, rated in the king's books at £5. 3. 6½., and in the patronage of the Inhabitants. The church is dedicated to All Saints.

NEITHROP, a hamlet in the parish and hundred of BANBURY, county of OXFORD, ¼ of a mile (W. N. W.) from Banbury, containing 1851 inhabitants: it is within the jurisdiction of the peculiar court of Banbury, belonging to the Dean and Chapter of Lincoln.

NEMPNETT-THRUBWELL, a parish in the hundred of KEYNSHAM, county of SOMERSET, 9 miles (N. E. by E.) from Axbridge, containing 264 inhabitants. The living is a perpetual curacy, annexed to the rectory of Compton-Martin, in the archdeaconry of Bath, and diocese of Bath and Wells. The church is dedicated to St. Mary. Within the parish is a large tumulus, of an oval form, the finest in the kingdom, on opening which in 1789, it was found to contain two rows of cells, running from south to north, formed by immense stones set edgeways, and covered with others of still larger dimensions. Sculls, a vast heap of bones, and other relics, having been discovered, it is conjectured to have been a work of the Druids, and to be the cemetery belonging to their great temple at Stanton-Drew, three miles off. An old mansion, in this parish, called Reghillbury, where Sir William Wyndham spent the period of his retirement from public life, is supposed to have been once a royal palace.

NEOT (ST.), a parish in WEST hundred, county of CORNWALL, 5 miles (N. W. by W.) from Liskeard, containing 1255 inhabitants. The living is a vicarage, in the archdeaconry of Cornwall, and diocese of Exeter, rated in the king's books at £9. 1. 0½. The Rev. R. G. Grylls was patron in 1793. The church is an elegant structure, and the windows exhibit some remains of the legend of St. Neot and other saints, in ancient stained glass. Here are the ruins of a chapel, dedicated to St. Luke; also the site of a monastery, or college, founded in honour of St. Neotus, brother to King Alfred, who was buried here. John Austis, Esq., a distinguished herald and antiquary, was born in this parish, in 1699.

NEOTS (ST.), a market town and parish in the hundred of TOSELAND, county of HUNTINGDON, 9 miles (S. S. W.) from Huntingdon, and 56 (N. N. W.) from London, containing 2272 inhabitants. The name of this place is derived from St. Neot, a learned Christian missionary, whose body was transferred hither from Neot stock in Cornwall, and in honour of whom a monastery was founded here, which was subsequently endowed, by Earl Leofric, as a priory of monks subordinate to Ely: about 1113, it became a cell to the abbey of Bec in Normandy, but, being afterwards made independent, it existed till the time of Henry VIII., when its revenue was £256. 1. 3¼. After the death of Charles I., the Earl of Holland took up arms here in favour of the royal cause, but was eventually defeated, in July 1648, and, being subsequently taken prisoner at St. Ives, he suffered on the scaffold. The town is situated on the east bank of the river Ouse, over which is a stone bridge of one central arch, with two smaller ones over the stream, and six others forming a causeway over the low lands adjoining: it consists of three principal streets, and, from its low situation, is exposed to occasional inundations, which have sometimes rendered it necessary to navigate the streets; the back streets are usually flooded every year to the depth of from one to two feet. The manufacture of paper is carried on to a considerable extent, by means of patent machinery introduced by Mons. Fourdrinier, in a mill upon the river Ouse, which is navigable from Bedford to Lynn, and furnishes the means of conveyance for corn, coal, wine, iron, timber, and grocery: the market, held under a grant from Henry I./ is on Thursday, for corn; and there are fairs on Holy Thursday, that day three weeks, and December 17th, and a statute fair for hiring servants on the 1st of August: the market-place is very spacious and convenient. A manorial court is held annually. The living is a discharged vicarage, in the archdeaconry of Huntingdon, and diocese of Lincoln, rated in the king's books at £10, endowed with £200 royal bounty, and in the patronage of the Crown. The church, dedicated to St. Mary, is a remarkably fine specimen of the later style of English architecture, with an elegant tower; in the interior is a fine timber roof, also some ancient screen-work. There are places of worship for Baptists and Wesleyan Methodists. A free school was founded and endowed with the interest of £100, bequeathed by Loftus Hatley, in 1736, which was augmented by Alderman Newton, of Leicester, and others, for the clothing and educating of thirty-five poor boys.

NEPICAR, a township in the parish and hundred of WROTHAM, lathe of AYLESFORD, county of KENT, 1 mile (E. by S.) from Wrotham, with which the population is returned.

NESBIT, a township in the parish of MONK-HESLETON, southern division of EASINGTON ward, county palatine of DURHAM, 12 miles (N.) from Stockton upon Tees, containing 9 inhabitants.

NESBIT, a township in the parish of STAMFORD-HAM, north-eastern division of TINDALE ward, county of NORTHUMBERLAND, 11 miles (W.N.W.) from Newcastle upon Tyne, containing 38 inhabitants.

NESBITT, a township in the parish of DODDINGTON, eastern division of GLENDALE ward, county of NORTHUMBERLAND, 3½ miles (N.) from Wooler, containing 52 inhabitants.

NESFIELD, a joint township with Langbar, in that part of the parish of ILKLEY which is in the upper division of the wapentake of CLARO, West riding of the county of YORK, 7¼ miles (W.N.W.) from Otley, containing, with Langbar, 210 inhabitants.

NESS, a township in the parish of GREAT NESTON, higher division of the hundred of WIRRALL, county palatine of CHESTER, 1¼ mile (S. S. E.) from Great Neston, containing 394 inhabitants.

NESS (EAST), a township in the parish of STONE-GRAVE, wapentake of RYEDALE, North riding of the county of YORK, 6¼ miles (S. E. by E.) from Helmsley, containing 59 inhabitants.

NESS (GREAT), a parish in the hundred of PIM-HILL, county of SALOP, 7½ miles (N.W. by W.) from Shrewsbury, containing, with the chapelry of Little

Ness, 833 inhabitants. The living is a discharged vicarage, in the archdeaconry of Salop, and diocese of Lichfield and Coventry, rated in the king's books at £9, and in the patronage of the Crown. The church is dedicated to St. Andrew. At Nesscliff there was formerly a chapel, dedicated to St. Mary, the site of which is now occupied by the parish school, which was founded by William Parry, in 1767, and is supported by several small bequests subsequently made. Near it is a remarkable cave, the ascent to which is by a very steep flight of steps. The interior is divided into two apartments by a massive pillar of the rock, upon which is carved the date 1564, and H. K., the initials of the name of the celebrated outlaw, Humphrey Kynaston, son of Sir Roger Kynaston, of Hordley, who, having contracted enormous debts, and suffered his mansion, Middle castle, to fall into decay, is stated to have sheltered himself in this cave, leading an eccentric life, and committing various depredations in the neighbourhood. The parish contains fine red freestone, of which it is said the castle, abbey, walls, and other buildings, in Shrewsbury were composed.

NESS (LITTLE), a chapelry in the parish of GREAT NESS, hundred of PIMHILL, county of SALOP, 8 miles (N. W.) from Shrewsbury, containing 253 inhabitants.

NESS (WEST), a township in the parish of STONE-GRAVE, wapentake of RYEDALE, North riding of the county of YORK, 6 miles (S. E. by E.) from Helmsley, containing 65 inhabitants.

NESTON (GREAT), a parish in the higher division of the hundred of WIRRALL, county palatine of CHESTER, comprising the market town of Great Neston, and the townships of Ledsham, Leighton, Ness, Little Neston, Raby, Thornton-Mayow, and Willaston, and containing 3216 inhabitants, of which number, 1418 are in the market town of Great Neston, 11 miles (N. W.) from Chester, and 191¼ (N.W.) from London. The town is pleasantly situated on the south-west side of a peninsula, formed by the æstuaries of the rivers Dee and Mersey, and derives its chief support from visitors, during the summer months, for the benefit of bathing: races are held on Whit-Monday and the two following days. The canal between the Mersey and the Dee passes near this town. The market is on Friday; and fairs are held, February 2nd, May 29th, and September 29th, for cattle. A court leet and baron is held annually; a court for the recovery of debts throughout the hundred of Wirrall, every month; and petty sessions. The living is a vicarage, in the archdeaconry and diocese of Chester, rated in the king's books at £11. 5., and in the patronage of the Dean and Chapter of Chester. The church is dedicated to St. Mary and St. Helen. There are places of worship for Independents and Wesleyan Methodists. A National school is supported by voluntary contributions; and there is a savings bank.

NESTON (LITTLE), a township in the parish of GREAT NESTON, higher division of the hundred of WIRRALL, county palatine of CHESTER, 1 mile (S. E.) from Great Neston, containing 316 inhabitants.

NESWICK, a township in the parish of NORTH DALTON, Bainton-Beacon division of the wapentake of HARTHILL, East riding of the county of YORK, 5½ miles (S.W.) from Great Driffield, containing 55 inhabitants.

NETHERAVON, a parish in the hundred of EL-STUB and EVERLEY, county of WILTS, 5¼ miles (N. by W.) from Amesbury, containing, with the tything of Chisenbury, 464 inhabitants. The living is a discharged vicarage, in the peculiar jurisdiction and patronage of the Prebendary of Netheravon in the Cathedral Church of Salisbury, rated in the king's books at £13. 6. 8. The church is dedicated to All Saints.

NETHERBURY, a parish in the hundred of BEA-MINSTER-FORUM and REDHONE, Bridport division of the county of DORSET, 2 miles (S.S.W.) from Beaminster, comprising the tythings of Aish, Bowood, Melplash, and Netherbury, and containing 1954 inhabitants. The living is a vicarage with Beaminster, in the peculiar jurisdiction and patronage of the Prebendary of Netherbury in the Cathedral Church of Salisbury, rated in the king's books at £41. 15. The church, dedicated to St. Mary, is in the later style of English architecture. There was formerly a chapel of ease at Mangerton, in this parish, which has long been desecrated and in ruins. A great quantity of cider is made in the parish. There is an endowment for a free grammar school, left by an unknown benefactor.

NETHERBY, a township in the parish of ARTHU-RET, ESKDALE ward, county of CUMBERLAND, 2½ miles (N.N.E.) from Longtown, containing 490 inhabitants. There are some trifling donations for the support of a charity school. Here was a Roman station of considerable importance, connected with the Picts' wall by a direct road, but its name has not been clearly ascertained : foundations of streets extending to the river Esk denote its site, and a large collection of Roman coins, altars, fragments of domestic utensils, &c., there discovered, is deposited in Netherby Hall.

NETHERBY, a joint township with Kirkby, in the parish of KIRKBY-OVERBLOWS, upper division of the wapentake of CLARO, West riding of the county of YORK, 4¾ miles (W. by S.) from Wetherby. The population is returned with Kirkby.

NETHERCOTE, a hamlet in the parish of WARK-WORTH, hundred of KING'S SUTTON, county of NORTH-AMPTON, 2 miles (E.) from Banbury. The population is returned with the parish.

NETHER-EXE, a parish in the hundred of HAY-RIDGE, county of DEVON, 5 miles (N. by E.) from Exeter, containing 103 inhabitants. The living is a perpetual curacy, in the archdeaconry and diocese of Exeter, endowed with £200 private benefaction, £600 royal bounty, and £500 parliamentary grant, and in the patronage of the Earl of Ilchester and the Hon. Percy Wyndham. The river Exe bounds the parish on the west.

NETHERMORE, a joint tything with Tytherton-Stanley, in the parish and hundred of CHIPPENHAM, county of WILTS, 2 miles (E. by S.) from Chippenham. The population is returned with Tytherton-Stanley.

NETHERTON, a township in the parish of BED-LINGTON, eastern division of CHESTER ward, county palatine of DURHAM, though locally on the east side of the county of Northumberland, 4 miles (S. E.) from Morpeth. The population is returned with the parish. Coal is obtained here.

NETHERTON, a township in the parish of SEPH-TON, hundred of WEST DERBY, county palatine of LAN-CASTER, 6½ miles (N. by E.) from Liverpool, containing 186 inhabitants.

NETHERTON, a chapelry in the parish of CROP-THORN, middle division of the hundred of OSWALDSLOW, county of WORCESTER, 4 miles (W.S.W.) from Evesham, containing 106 inhabitants. A chapel is now being erected, the former one having gone to ruin. There is a place of worship for Baptists.

NETHERTON-NORTH-SIDE, a township in the parish of ALLENTON, western division of COQUETDALE ward, county of NORTHUMBERLAND, 6¼ miles (N. W.) from Rothbury, containing 54 inhabitants.

NETHERTON-SOUTH-SIDE, a township in the parish of ALLENTON, western division of COQUETDALE ward, county of NORTHUMBERLAND, containing 71 inhabitants.

NETHER-WASDALE, county of CUMBERLAND.— See WASDALE (NETHER).

NETSWELL, or NETTESWELL, a parish in the hundred of HARLOW, county of ESSEX, 2¼ miles (S.W.) from Harlow, containing 306 inhabitants. The living is a rectory, in the jurisdiction of the Commissary of Essex and Herts, concurrently with the Consistorial Court of the Bishop of London, rated in the king's books at £13. 6. 8. The King, by reason of lunacy, presented in 1821. William Martin, in 1710, left certain bank stock, producing about £40 per annum, for erecting and endowing a school for ten boys and ten girls.

NETTLEBED, a parish in the hundred of EWELME, county of OXFORD, 4¾ miles (N.W. by W.) from Henley upon Thames, containing 545 inhabitants. The living is a perpetual curacy, with that of Pishill, in the jurisdiction of the peculiar court of Dorchester, and in the patronage of — Stoner, Esq. The church is dedicated to St. Bartholomew.

NETTLECOMBE, a tything in the parish and liberty of POORSTOCK, though locally in the hundred of Eggerton, Bridport division of the county of DORSET, 4¼ miles (N.E. by E.) from Bridport. The population is returned with the parish.

NETTLECOMBE, a parish in the hundred of WIL-LITON and FREEMANNERS, county of SOMERSET, 7 miles (N. by W.) from Wiveliscombe, containing 372 inhabitants. The living is a rectory, in the archdeaconry of Taunton, and diocese of Bath and Wells, rated in the king's books at £16. 16. 3., and in the patronage of Sir J. Trevelyan, Bart. The church, dedicated to St. Mary, is a small but handsome edifice. A school-house was erected at the expense of the late Sir John Trevelyan, in which the poor children of the parish are taught.

NETTLEDEN, a chapelry in the parish of PIGLES-THORNE, hundred of COTTESLOE, county of BUCKING-HAM, 3 miles (N.N.E.) from Berkhampstead, containing, with the hamlet of Friesden, 108 inhabitants. The living is a perpetual curacy, in the archdeaconry of Buckingham, and diocese of Lincoln, endowed with £8 per annum private benefaction, £1000 royal bounty, and £200 parliamentary grant, and in the patronage of the Trustees of the late Earl of Bridgewater. The chapel, which is dedicated to St. Lawrence, was consecrated in the year 1470.

NETTLEHAM, a parish in the wapentake of LAWRESS, parts of LINDSEY, county of LINCOLN, 3 miles (N.E. by N.) from Lincoln, containing 572 inhabitants. The living is a perpetual curacy, in the arch-

2 Y

deaconry of Stow, and diocese of Lincoln, and in the patronage of the Chancellor of the Cathedral Church of Lincoln. The church is dedicated to All Saints. There is a place of worship for Wesleyan Methodists. A school for poor children is supported by subscription. A court leet and a court baron are held here annually, about Lady-day. The bishops of Lincoln had formerly a palace here, the foundations of which are still discernible.

NETTLESTEAD, a parish in the hundred of TWY-FORD, lathe of AYLESFORD, county of KENT, 5¼ miles (W.S.W.) from Maidstone, containing 255 inhabitants. The living is a rectory, united to that of West Barming, in the archdeaconry and diocese of Rochester, rated in the king's books at £12. 10. 10. Mrs. Bouverie was patroness in 1820. The church, dedicated to St. Mary, is in the later style of English architecture, and the windows exhibit some fine specimens of stained glass of the time of Edward I. The navigable river Medway is crossed by Brand bridge on the south of the parish.

NETTLESTEAD, a parish in the hundred of Bos-MERE and CLAYDON, county of SUFFOLK, 4¾ miles (S.) from Needham, containing 85 inhabitants. The living is a discharged rectory, in the archdeaconry of Suffolk, and diocese of Norwich, rated in the king's books at £8. 11. 10½., endowed with £200 royal bounty. L. H. Moore, Esq. was patron in 1815. The church, which is dedicated to St. Mary, contains several handsome mural monuments. There are some remains of the splendid mansion of the Wentworths, who were Barons of Nettlestead.

NETTLETON, a parish in the southern division of the wapentake of YARBOROUGH, parts of LINDSEY, county of LINCOLN, 1 mile (S. by W.) from Caistor, containing 353 inhabitants. The living is a rectory, in the archdeaconry and diocese of Lincoln, rated in the king's books at £19. 10. 10. The Rev. William Jackson was patron in 1823. The church is dedicated to St. John the Baptist. There is a place of worship for Wesleyan Methodists.

NETTLETON, a parish in the northern division of the hundred of DAMERHAM, county of WILTS, 8½ miles (N.W. by W.) from Chippenham, containing 423 inhabitants. The living is a rectory, in the archdeaconry of Wilts, and diocese of Salisbury, rated in the king's books at £18. 12. 1., and in the patronage of Dr. Carrick. The church is dedicated to St. Mary. There are places of worship for Baptists and Wesleyan Methodists. The old Roman Fosse-road passes through the parish.

NEVENDON, a parish in the hundred of BARSTA-BLE, county of ESSEX, 5¼ miles (S.E. by E.) from Billericay, containing 186 inhabitants. The living is a discharged rectory, in the archdeaconry of Essex, and diocese of London, rated in the king's books at £10. 13. 4. The Rev. V. Edwards was patron in 1814. The church is dedicated to St. Peter.

NEWARK, a chapelry in that part of the parish of ST. JOHN the BAPTIST, PETERBOROUGH, which is in the liberty of PETERBOROUGH, county of NORTHAMPTON, 1¾ mile (N.E. by N.) from Peterborough. The population is returned with Eastfield. The chapel, which was dedicated to St. Mary Magdalene, has fallen to ruins.

NEWARK upon TRENT, a borough, market town, and parish, having exclusive jurisdiction, though locally in the southern division of the wapentake of Newark, county of NOTTINGHAM, 20 miles (N. E.) from Nottingham, and 124 (N. N. W.) from London, containing 8034 inhabitants. The origin of this town has been ascribed to the *Ceritani*, a tribe of ancient Britons; and it is supposed to have been subsequently a station of the Romans: it was the *Sidnacester* of the Saxons, and the old town having been destroyed by the Danes, the name of *New wark* was given to that erected on its site. Here was a castle, probably erected by Egbert, the first King of England, which has been emphatically designated "the Key of the North:" it was repaired by Leofric, Earl of Mercia, who was governor and lord of this district in the reign of Edward the Confessor: Leofric and Godiva his wife gave the town to the monastery of Stow, near Lincoln. In 1125 the castle was almost entirely rebuilt and enlarged by Alexander, Bishop of Lincoln, who obtained a royal charter for establishing a mint here. In 1139, that prelate having engaged in an insurrection against Stephen, was taken prisoner, and sent captive to his own castle at Newark, and was compelled to purchase his liberty by the surrender of this and other fortresses to the crown. During the baronial wars in the reign of John, it was a royal garrison; and, in order to put an end to the depredations of the troops, the Dauphin of France, whose interposition had been sought by the barons, ordered Gilbert de Gaunt, Earl of Lincoln, to proceed against the garrison with considerable force, but on intimation of the approach of John at the head of a large body of troops, the earl returned to London; and that sovereign, having in his march sustained great loss in men, carriages, and baggage, owing to a rapid flood-tide in crossing the Washes, and harrassed by disease of body and distress of mind, was seized with a fever; and having been carried on a litter to Sleaford, and thence to Newark castle, he there expired, on the 19th of October, 1216. The fortress was then given up to the barons, who retained possession till it was besieged by the Earl of Pembroke, and after eight days resistance, having surrendered, it was restored to the Bishop of Lincoln. In the last year of the reign of Edward III. it was used as a state prison. In 1530, Cardinal Wolsey and his splendid retinue were accommodated here, on their way to Southwell. In April, 1603, on the arrival of James I. at Newark, in his journey to London after his accession, he was addressed, by Alderman John Twentyman, in a Latin speech, and being much pleased therewith, he conferred upon him the office of purveyor of wax to the royal household in the counties of York, Nottingham, Lincoln, and Derby: it was in this town that James is said to have ordered a cut-purse to be hanged without legal process. In the reign of Charles I., Newark was garrisoned for the king, and held in subjection the whole of this county, excepting the town of Nottingham; and a great part of Lincolnshire was laid under contribution: here that unfortunate sovereign

Seal and Arms.

established a mint, and issued various pieces of money, consisting of half-crowns, shillings, ninepences, and six-pences, some of which were of diagonal shape, bearing the impress of a castle, and others the royal arms and crown, with the dates 1645 and 1646. During this con-test, the town sustained three sieges : in the first, all Northgate was burnt by order of the governor, Sir John Henderson ; in the second, when under the government of Sir John, afterwards Lord Byron, the town was re-lieved by the arrival from Chester of Prince Rupert, who, according to Clarendon, in an action between his forces and the parliamentarians under Sir John Meldrum, on Beacon hill, half a mile eastward of the town, took four thousand prisoners and thirteen pieces of artillery; in the third siege, after the display of much prowess and several vigorous sallies, the fortress remained unim-paired ; afterwards Lord Bellasis, then governor, sur-rendered the town to the Scottish army, by the king's order, on the 8th of May, 1646. At the close of this siege, the works and circumvallations were demolished by the country people, with the exception of two con-siderable earth-works, which are now nearly perfect, and are called the King's sconce and the Queen's sconce : about this time the castle also was destroyed.

The town is neatly built, and consists of several streets, which are well paved and lighted : the inha-bitants are well supplied with water. The town is situated in a level tract on the eastern branch of the Trent, which joins the main river about a mile below it ; a lateral stream, uniting the two rivers above the town, forms rather an extensive island on the north-west, which is remarkably fertile; over this the London road passes, the river being crossed by a handsome bridge. About three hundred and fifty yards from the site of the old castle is the ancient bed of the Trent, the current of which was diverted, partly by a cut formerly made from it to the brook at Kelham, and partly by obstructions occasioned by the Newark mills. The town is approached from the north by an excellent turnpike-road, constructed about the year 1770, over the Trent vale, from Newark bridge to Muskham bridge, and no longer inconvenienced, as formerly, by inundations of the river, owing to the erection of fourteen bridges of different sizes, and ninety-six arches, at irregular dis-tances : this road is carried on a level over the Trent vale from Newark bridge to Muskham bridge, a dis-tance of one mile and a half : the execution of this useful project was completed by Mr. Smeaton, at an expense of £12,000. The bridge, which crosses the river in the vicinity of the castle, was originally of wood, but, in 1775, it was rebuilt of brick, faced with stone, by Henry, Duke of Newcastle. Under the sanction of an act of parliament, obtained in 1793, great improvement has taken place in the town, the expense of which has been defrayed from funds vest-ed in the corporation for its general benefit. One side of a narrow and dangerous street, called Dry bridge, has recently been taken down, and new houses erected, thereby rendering the approach to the market-place wide and commodious. The "Newark Stock Library" was established in 1825, and a new building has been recently erected in the market-place by Lord Middle-ton, and presented by him, as a library and news-room, to the shareholders, of whom there are two hundred and fifty, at £4.4. each ; the annual subscription is £1. 1.

Concerts and assemblies are held in the town hall ; and there is a theatre occasionally opened for dramatic per-formances. The prominent commercial feature of this town is its very extensive trade in malt and flour : of the former fifty thousand quarters are annually sent to Man-chester, Liverpool, and London, exclusively of supplies to the midland counties, and upwards of eighty thousand sacks of the latter commodity are disposed of annually, by two mercantile houses alone, and the revenue receiv-ed from this town is about £92,000 : upwards of three hundred persons are employed in an extensive weaving and bleaching establishment at the southern extremity of the town. In consequence of the Trent navigation, there is a flourishing trade in corn, coal, cattle, wool, and other commodities, and the corn market here is one of the largest in this part of the kingdom. An extensive iron and brass foundry affords employment to several per-sons, in the various departments of fancy castings, ar-chitectural ornaments, fac-similes of medallions, coins, seals, &c., which are so exquisitely finished as to sur-prise the most experienced virtuoso. Among the different branches of business is the preparation of *terra alba*, for paper-mills ; and in the town is a depôt for sheet copper, brass, iron, and tin plates. Large quan-tities of gypsum and limestone are obtained in the neighbourhood : the former is calcined and pulverised for the use of sculptors and plasterers, and sent by sea to London. During the summer season many persons are employed in making bricks and tiles : the manu-facture of tambour lace and stockings employs a few females. The market is on Wednesday ; and fairs, principally for cattle, are held on the Friday after Mid-Lent Sunday, May 14th, Whit-Tuesday, August 2d, November 1st, and on the Monday before December 11th. In the year 1800, an annual cheese market was estab-lished, to be held on the Wednesday before October 2nd. The market-place, formerly much more spacious than at present, still forms a handsome square.

The first charter of incorporation was granted by Edward VI., and it was renewed, with extended privileges, by Charles II., in consideration of the loyalty of the inhabitants during the preceding reign. The corporation consists of a mayor and twelve aldermen, with a re-corder, town clerk, chamberlain, and other officers : the members of the corporation are self-elected. The mayor and his predecessor, with the recorder and four senior aldermen, exercise exclusive magisterial authority within the borough, which comprises the whole parish of New-ark, together with the castle precincts and water-mills, which lie in the adjoining parish of East Stoke. A court of record is held weekly, on Thursday, for the cognizance of pleas to the amount of £300 ; its juris-diction is co-extensive with the borough : sessions are held quarterly. The sessions for the hundreds of Newark and Thurgarton are held quarterly at the county hall in Cartergate. The county magistrates also hold a petty ses-sion every alternate Wednesday. The town hall, which stands in the market-place, is an elegant stone build-ing, erected by the corporation, under the superinten-dence of Mr. Carr, out of the produce of testamentary estates for the improvement of the town, which they were empowered to sell under an act of parliament passed in the 13th year of George III. ; the total ex-pense of its erection was £1790 : two wings have since been added, and the building is considered equal to any in this part of the county: the front is light and airy; it is three stories high, having seven windows in each story: the room used for assemblies is elegantly finished with Corinthian columns and pilasters, and a richly-carved ceiling: at one end of this edifice the sessions are held, and at the other the corporation transact public business; in the rear are very extensive shambles. It is uncertain when the borough was first represented in parliament, but there was a contested election in 1592, when only one member appears to have been returned; and two members were first sent in the 29th of Charles II. The right of election is vested in the corporation, and all the inhabitants who have paid scot and lot for at least six months previously to the election: the mayor is the returning officer. The Duke of Newcastle, in consequence of the extensive property which he possesses in the borough, has very considerable political influence, together with Lord Middleton and others.

The living is a vicarage, in the archdeaconry of Nottingham, and diocese of York, rated in the king's books at £21. 5. 2½., and in the patronage of the Crown. The church, dedicated to St. Mary Magdalene, is one of the largest and most elegant parochial churches in the kingdom: it exhibits portions in all the styles of English architecture, and is a cruciform structure, consisting of a nave, aisles, transepts, choir, and sepulchral chapels, with a lofty western tower, surmounted by a fine octagonal spire; the base of the tower is Norman, and in the nave are two Norman piers: the choir is of exquisite workmanship: it is separated from the nave by a richly-carved oak screen, some parts of which becoming decayed, have been successfully imitated by iron castings, the work of a resident artist; in this part of the edifice is one of the largest engraved brasses in the kingdom, elaborately ornamented, to the memory of Allan Flemyng, who died in 1361; a portion of this has also been restored by the same artist. The large east window is in the later style of English architecture, and the corresponding piers and arches of the nave and choir are unusually rich: there are some excellent specimens of stained glass in the windows. The altar-piece, an admirable painting of the "Resurrection of Lazarus," by Hilton, was presented by the artist, whose father was a native of the town. There are places of worship for General and Particular Baptists, Independents, Calvinistic, Primitive, and Wesleyan Methodists, and Roman Catholics. The free grammar school was founded, in 1530, by Dr. Thomas Magnus, Archdeacon of the East riding of Yorkshire, and a native of Newark, who, by will in 1550, bequeathed certain lands in the counties of Lincoln, Nottingham, and York, for the support of a "school of grammar and a school of song." The vicar, mayor, senior alderman, and three churchwardens are the trustees of the charity, and the present annual income, amounting to nearly £2,400, is thus appropriated: namely, to the master of the grammar school £220 per annum; to the usher, £50; to the master of the song school, £105; to ten singing boys, £37. 16; to the National schools for boys and girls, £150; to the dispensary, £150; to the commissioners for lighting, paving, and improving the town, £290; to the church-wardens for the repair of the church, clerk's and sexton's salaries, &c., £750; besides incidental disbursements.

The school is open to all boys of the town and neighbourhood: the present number of scholars on the foundation is sixty-five; the master, who is allowed to receive a limited number of boarders, resides on the premises, which are admirably adapted to the purpose: the house was erected by the master, at an expense of £2500, in consequence of which the corporation agreed to pay him £30 per annum towards the insurance of his life for fifteen years: there are at present no exhibitions connected with this school, but the trustees contemplate this desirable addition to the institution. The National school was erected in 1829, which affords instruction to about one hundred and ten boys and eighty girls. Henry Stone, in 1688, bequeathed to the corporation £700, directing the produce to be appropriated to the foundation and support of a Jersey, or working school, the master of which has a salary of £28 per annum. Almshouses, for fourteen decayed tradesmen and ten widows, were respectively founded and endowed under the wills of William Phillipott, merchant, dated March 18th, 1556, and George Lawrence, dated December 1st, 1797; the present amount of income is £789. 13. St. Leonard's hospital was founded by Alexander, Bishop of Lincoln, about 1125, and endowed with lands now producing a rental of more than £1000: the present building contains three small rooms, occupied by as many poor men, who receive five shillings each per week; the master, who is appointed by the Bishop of Lincoln, receives the surplus income: various other charitable benefactions, amounting to about £500 per annum, are applied under the direction and management of the corporation. The ruins of the ancient castle consist of the outer walls, which enclose a spacious area, now used as a bowling-green; and the elegant crypt, with its light groined arches nearly perfect, is used as a coal wharf and stables: at the north-east angle of the western front is a square tower, and another in the centre of the elevation; the remains of an ancient portal are visible in the north front. Of the conventual buildings there are no vestiges, except the walls of the Augustine friary, which has been converted into a dwelling-house: the site of the house of the chantry priests is now occupied by a small but elegant mansion, finished throughout in the most splendid style, principally in imitation of the antique, and containing many rare and valuable cabinets, vases, busts, armour, fossils, and coins. Amongst other curious Roman relics are six entire urns of baked earth, found in digging for the foundation of a house in 1826, filled with calcined bones and ashes. The great Roman road from London to Lincoln passed through Newark: in a straight line near the church are the remains of ancient military works. Amongst the eminent natives of this town may be enumerated, in addition to Dr. Magnus, its munificent benefactor, John Ardern, a learned writer on medicine and surgery in the fifteenth century; Dr. Thomas White, Bishop of Peterborough; Dr. Lightfoot, the celebrated Hebraist; and Dr. William Warburton, Bishop of Gloucester, born in 1698. Newark confers the inferior title of viscount upon Earl Manvers.

NEWBALD, a parish within the liberty of St. Peter of York, though locally in the Hunsley-Beacon division of the wapentake of Harthill, East riding of the county of York, containing 722 inhabitants, of which number, 543 are in the township of North Newbald, 4 miles (S. E.), and 179 in that of South Newbald, 4½ miles (S.E. by S.), from Market-Weighton. The living is a discharged vicarage, in the peculiar jurisdiction and patronage of the Prebendary of North Newbald in the Cathedral Church of York, rated in the king's books at £4, endowed with £200 private benefaction, £400 royal bounty, and £600 parliamentary grant. The church, dedicated to St. Nicholas, is a cruciform structure, principally in the Norman style, with a tower rising from the intersection, and several enriched doors and arches; the font is early English, curiously formed and ornamented. There is a place of worship for Wesleyan Methodists. Six poor children are educated for a small sum paid from the poor's estate.

NEWBALL, a hamlet in the parish of STAINTON by LANGWORTH, western division of the wapentake of WRAGGOE, parts of LINDSEY, county of LINCOLN, 4½ miles (W. S. W.) from Wragby. The population is returned with the parish.

NEWBIGGIN, a township in the parish of DACRE, LEATH ward, county of CUMBERLAND, 3¾ miles (W. by S. from Penrith. The population is returned with the parish.

NEWBIGGIN, a township in the parish of MIDDLETON in TEASDALE, south-western division of DARLINGTON ward, county palatine of DURHAM, 12½ miles (N. W.) from Barnard-Castle, containing 416 inhabitants. There is a place of worship for Wesleyan Methodists. A charity school is supported by annual donations. There is a smelting-mill for refining lead-ore found in the neighbourhood.

NEWBIGGIN, a chapelry in that part of the parish of NEWBURN which is in the western division of CASTLE ward, county of NORTHUMBERLAND, 4 miles (N. W.) from Newcastle, containing 47 inhabitants. There are twenty-four acres of land within the chapelry, extra-parochial.

NEWBIGGIN, a chapelry in the parish of WOODHORN, eastern division of MORPETH ward, county of NORTHUMBERLAND, 8¼ miles (E. by N.) from Morpeth, containing 434 inhabitants, who are principally fishermen for the Carlisle, Hexham, and Newcastle markets. The chapel, dedicated to St. Bartholomew, is an ancient edifice with a spire steeple, situated near the sea-shore, a fine smooth beach about a mile in length, which is much resorted to for bathing. There is a suite of warm, cold, and shower baths at the chief inn, which contains excellent accommodations for visitors, who may also provide themselves with private lodgings at several well-built houses in the village. The bay affording tolerable security and anchorage for small vessels, much corn is shipped from the granaries erected for its reception from the interior. Five boats and nineteen men were lost in a violent tempest which happened here, in January 1805, upon which upwards of £1700 was subscribed at Newcastle and the neighbourhood, for the relief of the families of the sufferers. A branch Bible Society was established at this place in 1826.

NEWBIGGIN, a township in the parish of SHOTLEY, eastern division of TINDALE ward, county of NORTHUMBERLAND, 9¼ miles (S.) from Hexham, containing 69 inhabitants.

NEWBIGGIN, a parish in EAST ward, county of WESTMORLAND, 7¼ miles (N. W. by N.) from Appleby, containing 152 inhabitants. The living is a discharged rectory, in the archdeaconry and diocese of Carlisle,

rated in the king's books at £4. 14. 2., endowed with £200 private benefaction, and £200 royal bounty, and in the patronage of W. Crackenthorpe, Esq. The church, dedicated to St. Edmund, is an ancient building, repewed in 1804. Newbiggin Hall is a fine old castellated mansion, erected in 1533, upon the site of the previous manor-house. Some rocks near it are represented to have formerly borne various Roman inscriptions.

NEWBIGGIN, a hamlet in the parish of KIRKBY-LONSDALE, LONSDALE ward, county of WESTMORLAND, 1½ mile (S. W. by W.) from Kirkby-Lonsdale. The population is returned with Hutton-Roof.

NEWBIGGIN, a township in the parish of AYSGARTH, western division of the wapentake of HANG, North riding of the county of YORK, 8½ miles (W. by S.) from Middleham, containing 128 inhabitants.

NEWBIGGIN (EAST and WEST), a township in the parish of BISHOPTON, south-western division of STOCKTON ward, county palatine of DURHAM, 4¾ miles (W.) from Stockton upon Tees, containing 26 inhabitants.

NEWBOLD, a hamlet in the parish of CHESTER-FIELD, hundred of SCARSDALE, county of DERBY, 1¼ mile (N. W.) from Chesterfield, containing, with Dunstan, 962 inhabitants. A school-house was erected by the Executors of George Milnes, Esq., who endowed it with land producing an annual income of £23. 8., for which about fifteen children are instructed. An almshouse was founded, in 1781, by Mrs. Elizabeth Tomlinson, who endowed it with £400 four per cents., for the maintenance of three poor women.

NEWBOLD, a hamlet in the parish of OUSTON, hundred of GARTREE, county of LEICESTER, 7 miles (S. by E.) from Melton-Mowbray. The population is returned with the parish.

NEWBOLD, a liberty in the parish of BREEDON, western division of the hundred of GOSCOTE, county of LEICESTER, 4 miles (N. E. by E.) from Ashby de la Zouch. The population is returned with the chapelry of Worthington.

NEWBOLD, a hamlet in the parish of TREDINGTON, upper division of the hundred of OSWALDSLOW, county of WORCESTER, though locally in the Kington division of the hundred of Kington, county of Warwick, 4 miles (N. by W.) from Shipston upon Stour, containing 258 inhabitants.

NEWBOLD upon AVON, a parish in the Rugby division of the hundred of KNIGHTLOW, county of WARWICK, 2½ miles (N. W. by N.) from Rugby, containing, with the hamlets of Cosford, Little Harborough, Little Lawford, and Long Lawford, 968 inhabitants. The living is a vicarage, in the archdeaconry of Coventry, and diocese of Lichfield and Coventry, rated in the king's books at £14. 12. 1., and in the patronage of the Rev. Mr. Parker. The church is dedicated to St. Botolph. The rivers Avon and Swift, and the Oxford canal, run through the parish, in which are very extensive lime-works.

NEWBOLD (LEA), county palatine of CHESTER.— See LEA-NEWBOLD.

NEWBOLD-GROUNDS, a hamlet in the parish of CATESBY-ABBEY, hundred of FAWSLEY, county of NORTHAMPTON, 3¾ miles (W. S. W.) from Daventry. The population is returned with the parish.

NEWBOLD-PACEY, a parish in the Warwick division of the hundred of KINGTON, county of WAR-

WICK, 5¾ miles (N. W. by N.) from Kington, containing, with Ashorn, 331 inhabitants. The living is a discharged vicarage, in the archdeaconry and diocese of Worcester, rated in the king's books at £8. 3. 9., endowed with £200 private benefaction, and £200 royal bounty, and in the patronage of the Provost and Fellows of Queen's College, Oxford. The church is dedicated to St. George.

NEWBOLD-REVEL, a hamlet in the parish of MONKS-KIRBY, Kirby division of the hundred of KNIGHTLOW, county of WARWICK, 5½ miles (N. W. by N.) from Rugby. The population is returned with Stretton under Foss.

NEWBOLD-VERDON, a parish in the hundred of SPARKENHOE, county of LEICESTER, 2¾ miles (E. by N.) from Market-Bosworth, containing 576 inhabitants. The living is a rectory, in the archdeaconry of Leicester, and diocese of Lincoln, rated in the king's books at £6. 8. 11½. G. Greenaway, Esq. was patron in 1823. The church is dedicated to St. James. Nathaniel, Lord Crewe, in 1720, bequeathed a rent-charge of £20, for teaching poor children.

NEWBOROUGH, a parish in the liberty of PETER-BOROUGH, county of NORTHAMPTON, 5 miles (N. E. by N.) from Peterborough, containing 129 inhabitants. This place, formerly a common, called Borough-Fen, has lately been elevated into a parish. A church, of which the Bishop of Peterborough is the patron, has been erected, but it has not yet been consecrated or endowed.

NEWBOROUGH, a chapelry in the parish of HANBURY, northern division of the hundred of OFFLOW, county of STAFFORD, 3½ miles (E.) from Abbot's Bromley, containing 744 inhabitants. The living is a perpetual curacy, in the archdeaconry of Stafford, and diocese of Lichfield and Coventry, endowed with £200 private benefaction, £400 royal bounty, and £800 parliamentary grant, and in the patronage of the Vicar of Hanbury. The chapel is dedicated to All Saints. There are several small bequests, producing about £8 a year, for the instruction of children. Newborough is in the honour of Tutbury, duchy of Lancaster, and within the jurisdiction of a court of pleas held at Tutbury every third Tuesday, for the recovery of debts under forty shillings.

NEWBOROUGH, a township in the parish of COXWOLD, wapentake of BIRDFORTH, North riding of the county of YORK, 8 miles (S. W.) from Helmsley, containing, with the extra-parochial district of Morton, 162 inhabitants. A priory of Black canons, in honour of St. Mary, was founded here, in 1145, by Roger de Mowbray, which, at the dissolution, had a revenue of £457. 13. 5. William de Newburgh, the celebrated monkish historian, was a member of this establishment.

NEWBOTTLE, a township in the parish of HOUGHTON le SPRING, northern division of EASINGTON ward, county palatine of DURHAM, 8 miles (N. E. by N.) from Durham, containing 2306 inhabitants, who are principally employed in the various collieries and potteries in the vicinity. There is a place of worship for Wesleyan Methodists. Fifty-seven individuals lost their lives by an explosion in one of the coal mines in 1815.

NEWBOTTLE, a parish in the hundred of KING's SUTTON, county of NORTHAMPTON, 4½ miles (W.) from Brackley, containing, with Charleton, 352 inhabitants.

The living is a discharged vicarage with Charleton, in the archdeaconry of Northampton, and diocese of Peterborough, rated in the king's books at £10. 0. 10. W. R. Cartwright, Esq. was patron in 1809. The church is dedicated to St. James. At Charlton in this parish is an ancient fortification, called Ruinsborough Hill.

NEWBOURN, a parish in the hundred of CARLFORD, county of SUFFOLK, 4 miles (S. by E.) from Woodbridge, containing 181 inhabitants. The living is a discharged rectory, in the archdeaconry of Suffolk, and diocese of Norwich, rated in the king's books at £7. 4. 2., endowed with £200 royal bounty, and in the patronage of Sir W. Rowley, Bart. The church is dedicated to St. Mary. The navigable river Deben runs on the east of this parish.

NEWBROUGH, a parochial chapelry in the north-western division of TINDALE ward, county of NORTHUMBERLAND, 4¾ miles (N. W. by W.) from Hexham, containing 451 inhabitants. The chapel is dedicated to St. Peter. A school-room has been erected by subscription, in which twelve children are instructed for £10 per annum, the gift of the Rev. H. Wastell, who also built a house for the master.

NEWBURN, a parish comprising the chapelry of Newbiggin, and the townships of Black Callerton, Butterlaw, East Denton, West Denton, North Dissington, South Dissington, Newburn, Newburn-Hall, Sugley, Throckley, Wallbottle, East and West Whorlton, and Woolsington, in the western division of CASTLE ward, and the township of Dalton in the eastern division of TINDALE ward, county of NORTHUMBERLAND, and containing 4202 inhabitants, of which number, 918 are in the township of Newburn, 5¼ miles (W. by N.) from Newcastle upon Tyne. The living is a discharged vicarage, in the archdeaconry of Northumberland, and diocese of Durham, rated in the king's books at £16, and in the patronage of the Bishop of Carlisle. The church, dedicated to St. Michael, was partly rebuilt and considerably enlarged in 1827, at an expense of about £1200 : it is a neat cruciform structure of stone, containing some ancient monuments to the Delavals, and the east window exhibits, in stained glass, the figure of St. James, and the arms of those who contributed to the renovation of the building. The parish, which abounds with coal, stretches along the northern bank of the Tyne, where are some coal-staiths, iron-foundries, crown glass, and brick and tile manufactories, chemical works, and a paper-mill. A school-room was erected, in 1822, by the Duke of Northumberland, who endowed it with £15. 15. per annum, for teaching fifteen children : the number has been lately increased to thirty, in consequence of the members of the Glass Company and the lessees of Walbottle colliery having subscribed £10. 10. a year, in augmentation of the master's salary. In the reign of John, Newburn was styled a borough town. Severus' Wall passed through the parish, but its course is no longer traceable. Here Lord Conway, in 1640, at the head of the royalists, disputed the passage of the Tyne with the Scots under General Leslie, but the latter, after a violent conflict, at length succeeded.

NEWBURN-HALL, a township in that part of the parish of NEWBURN which is in the western division of CASTLE ward, county of NORTHUMBERLAND, containing 629 inhabitants.

Corporate Seal.

NEWBURY, a market town and parish, having separate jurisdiction, though locally in the hundred of Faircross, county of BERKS, 17 miles (W. by S.) from Reading, and 56 (W. by S.) from London, on the road to Bath, containing, with Sandleford Priory, 5364 inhabitants. This place, which is said to have risen from the ruins of the ancient *Spinæ*, a Roman station, the site of which is occupied by the village of Speen, was, in contradistinction to the old town, called *Newbyrig*, of which its present name is only a slight modification. It is a town of considerable antiquity, having been of some importance at the time of the Conquest, and bestowed by the Conqueror on Ernulph de Hesdin, whose grandson was killed in the battle of Lincoln, in the reign of Stephen. In the reign of Edward I. Newbury returned two members to parliament, and in the 11th of Edward III. it sent three deputies to a grand council of trade held at Westminster. In the reign of Henry VIII. it was one of the most flourishing towns in the kingdom, and was particularly distinguished for its extensive manufacture of woollen clothes. At this period lived the celebrated John Winchcombe, commonly called Jack of Newbury, said to have been the most eminent clothier in England, and to have sumptuously entertained Henry VIII. and his queen Catherine, on their visit to the town. When the Earl of Surrey marched against James IV., King of Scotland, who was ravaging the borders of the kingdom, this spirited individual, at his own expense, armed and clothed one hundred of his workmen; and, at the head of this little band, accompanied the earl to Flodden Field, where he greatly signalised himself by his intrepid conduct. On the termination of the war, he returned to his native place, and at his own charge built the greater part of the parish church, in which he was interred in 1519. His descendants possessed large estates for many years, and the last of them was united in marriage to Lord Bolingbroke. Part of the house in which he lived, was, about a century since, converted into an inn, bearing the sign of Jack of Newbury. During the parliamentary war, two battles took place in the vicinity, in both which the king commanded in person: the first was fought on the 18th of September, 1643, on the common called the Wash; the second on the 27th of October, 1644, in the fields between Newbury, Speen, and Shaw. In this battle, the king, though he kept possession of the field, suffered the Earl of Essex to march with his army to London, and the royal cause sustained an irreparable loss in the deaths of many distinguished officers, among whom were the Earls of Sunderland and Caernarvon, and the celebrated Lord Falkland. The parliamentarians in the following year obtained possession of the town, which they fortified, and retained till the close of the war.

The town is pleasantly situated on a fertile plain, on the banks of the river Kennet, over which was an ancient wooden bridge of one arch, rebuilt of stone, at the expense of the corporation, in 1770: it is one of the largest towns in the county: the houses are mostly of brick, generally well built and of modern appearance; the streets, diverging obliquely from the market-place, are spacious, well paved under the powers of an act recently obtained, and lighted with gas by a company, whose works being neatly and scientifically constructed, are much admired: the inhabitants are amply supplied with water from springs in the neighbourhood. In the hamlet of Speenhamland, adjoining the borough, is a small theatre, which is open for about two months during the season. The environs are pleasant, and afford many agreeable walks on the banks of the Kennet, and in the vicinity of the village of Speen. The trade is principally in malt and flour, for the latter of which are many large mills on the banks of the river: there are also a small paper-mill, and a mill for throwing silk; and in the parish of Speen, about a mile from the town, is a manufactory for ribands and galloons. The river Kennet, which in 1723 was made navigable to Reading; and the Kennet and Avon canal, which passing through the town, in a line parallel with the river, joins the Thames at Reading, afford great facilities to the trade. The market is on Thursday, and is one of the largest in the country for corn, which is pitched in the market-place for sale: for nearly a century the corporation took toll of all grain brought into the town for consumption, or merely passing through it, and that whether bought and tolled in any other market, or not; they also took toll of corn exposed in the market-place for sale, which practice continued until the year 1818, when proceedings at law were commenced, and a verdict given against the corporation, as regarded " toll-thorough and toll-traverse," leaving the question of market-toll undecided : the corporation, however, discontinued the taking of toll altogether, with the exception of some members of their own body allowing their corn to be tolled for about two years after the decision, and since then no toll has been demanded, although the corporation have recently issued notice of their intention to resume the practice. The fairs are on Holy Thursday, for horses and cattle; July 5th for horses, cows, and hogs; September 4th and November 8th, for horses and cheese; and on the first Thursday after October 11th is a statute fair for hiring servants.

The inhabitants were first incorporated by Queen Elizabeth, in 1596, in whose charter Newbury is styled "an ancient and populous borough, which had enjoyed divers liberties, franchises and privileges by the charters of many of her ancestors and predecessors, kings of England." Under this charter the government is vested in a mayor, high steward, recorder, six aldermen, and twenty-four burgesses, assisted by a town clerk and other officers: the mayor is chosen annually on St. Matthew's day, and, with one of the aldermen appointed for that purpose, is justice of the peace within the borough; the other officers and the burgesses, as vacancies occur, are chosen by the corporation: the freedom of the borough has become obsolete, persons being admitted indiscriminately to the privilege of carrying on trade. The corporation hold quarterly courts of session for the trial of misdemeanants within the borough, and have power to hold a court of record, under the charter of Elizabeth, every week, for the recovery of debts not exceeding twenty marks, now fallen into disuse. The Easter quarter session for the county is held here, and the petty sessions for the division every Thursday. The town hall, called the mansion house, is a substantial modern brick building, erected in 1740, and supported on piers and arches: the lower part affords an area for the market, and the upper part consists of a handsome suite of rooms, in the largest of which the courts are held, and assemblies during the season : it is a spacious and very handsome room, ornamented with two beautiful copies, by Cosino Fioravante, from Rubens' Choice of Hercules, and the Dire Effects of War ; adjoining it are refreshment and card rooms. Part of the workhouse has recently been converted into a borough gaol, containing nine wards for the classification of prisoners, and used also as a bridewell, or house of correction ; but the inhabitants having been deemed liable to the payment of the county rate, all prisoners committed by the magistrates for the borough are sent to the county gaol at Reading.

The living is a rectory, in the archdeaconry of Berks, and diocese of Salisbury, rated in the king's books at £38. 16. 10½., and in the patronage of the Crown. The church, dedicated to St. Nicholas, is a spacious edifice in the later style of English architecture, with a lofty square embattled tower crowned with pinnacles : the tower and the western part of the nave were the portions built by John Winchcombe, whose effigy, on a brass plate removed from over his tomb, is placed against the east wall of the north aisle, and above the altar is some beautiful screen - work. A handsome chapel of ease, in the later style of English architecture, is now in process of erection in Speenhamland. There are places of worship for Baptists, the Society of Friends, Independents, Wesleyan Methodists, and Unitarians. A Blue-coat school was founded, in 1706, by the corporation, to whom, in 1624, John Kendrick gave the sum of £4000, for the purchase of a house and garden for the employment of the poor, and for other charitable uses, of which £350 was laid out in the purchase of an estate, called the Hospital Estate, let on lease, at £106 per annum, to the Kennet Navigation Company, at the expiration of which it is expected to produce £400 per annum, the rental being appropriated to the clothing and instruction of twenty poor boys. To this several augmentations were made for the clothing and instruction of additional scholars, by Mr. Richard Cowslade, in 1715 ; Mr. Nicholas Clement, in 1722; Mr. Thomas Stockwell, in 1736; and by Mr. John Kimber, who in 1790 gave funds for the instruction of ten more scholars, to be clothed in green, and on their leaving school to be apprenticed, with premiums of £10 each. There are forty boys on the foundation, who are now instructed by the master of a National school, established by subscription in 1811, in which are educated about one hundred and fifty boys, and one hundred and sixty girls, in addition to the charity boys. There are also Lancasterian schools for boys and girls, supported by voluntary contributions. The parish has, under the will of Mr. John West and Frances his wife, the privilege of sending several children to Christ's Hospital, London, who are elected by the vestry. St. Bartholomew's hospital, supposed to have been founded by King John, and comprising fourteen houses for the reception of men and women, was, by charter of Elizabeth, vested in the corporation ; the inmates receive a weekly allowance of five shillings each, with an annual supply of

fuel and clothes ; ten other houses have been added to the original establishment, the endowment of which exceeds £700 per annum. Opposite to St. Bartholomew's are twelve almshouses, erected and endowed in 1670, by Jemmit Raymond, Esq., for six aged men and six aged women, who have a weekly allowance of five shillings each, with coats and gowns annually ; the number of houses has been augmented for the reception of ten aged persons of each sex. Thomas Pearce, in 1690, and Mr. Francis Coxhead, each built two almshouses, which have been consolidated for the maintenance and support of aged persons, who have each three shillings and sixpence per week, with an allowance of clothes and fuel; after defraying these charges, the residue of the endowment, which is about £112 per annum, is appropriated to the instruction of poor children in reading and writing. In 1727, Mr. Thomas Hunt bequeathed lands at Greenham, which have been exchanged for an estate at Ashmoor Green, producing a rental of £70 ; and £270 in money, for the support of three aged widows, who have four shillings each per week, with an annual allowance of clothes and fuel : the residue of the income is appropriated to the instruction of fourteen poor children in the Lancasterian school. In Cheap-street are twelve more almshouses, erected in 1793, and endowed by Mr. John Kimber, in the centre of which is a neat brick building, with a stone recording the date of their erection and the name of the founder. Twelve almshouses, which formerly stood near the church, have been rebuilt near St. Bartholomew's hospital ; they are endowed by Mr. Henshaw, for six aged men and six aged women of the parish, who are nominated by the corporation : there are also two for poor weavers, founded by Mr. Robinson, and six for aged women, at St. Mary's Hill.

Extending sixteen miles in length, on both sides of the Kennet, are strata of peat half a mile in breadth, and varying in depth from one foot to eight feet, which being dug sells for ten shillings per load : in digging for it have been found oaks, alders, willows, and firs, indiscriminately mixed, which appear to have been torn up by the roots ; the horns, skulls, and bones of several kinds of deer ; the horns of the antelope, the heads and tusks of boars, and the heads of beavers. In rebuilding the bridge, in 1770, a leaden seal of Pope Boniface IX., a pix, some knives of singular construction, and several coins from the time of Henry I. to William III., were discovered. Some years since, an urn of a light brown colour, of the size of a gallon, was found in the peat-moss, at the distance of from eight to ten feet from the river, but being broken by the workmen, the contents were lost. The present rector of Newbury, the Rev. James Roe, possesses a private collection of specimens in natural history, unequalled in the county for the rarity of the subjects and their suitable arrangement. Within a mile and a quarter of the town is Sandleford, a hamlet in the parish, where a small Augustine priory was founded, about the year 1200, by Geoffrey, Earl of Perche, and dedicated to St. John the Baptist, which was given by Edward IV. to the Collegiate Church of Windsor, and the revenue of which, in the reign of Henry VIII., was valued at £10. Newbury gives the inferior title of baron to the Marquis of Cholmondeley.

NEWBY, a township in the parish of IRTHINGTON, ESKDALE ward, county of CUMBERLAND, 6 miles (E. N.E.) from Carlisle, containing 97 inhabitants.

NEWBY, a township in the parish of MORLAND, WEST ward, county of WESTMORLAND, 7 miles (W. by N.) from Appleby, containing 338 inhabitants. Coal and limestone are obtained here, and there are lime-kilns at Towcett, within the township.

NEWBY, a joint township with Rainton, in that part of the parish of TOPCLIFFE which is in the wapentake of HALLIKELD, North riding of the county of YORK, 6 miles (N. by W.) from Boroughbridge. The population is returned with Rainton. Christopher Coulson, in 1640, bequeathed certain land, directing the income to be applied in teaching and clothing poor children.

NEWBY, a township in the parish of STOKESLEY, western division of the liberty of LANGBAURGH, North riding of the county of YORK, 3 miles (N.N.W.) from Stokesley, containing 152 inhabitants. A small free school was founded here in 1640.

NEWBY, a township in the parish of SCALBY, PICKERING lythe, North riding of the county of YORK, 3 miles (N.W. by W.) from Scarborough, containing 40 inhabitants.

NEWBY, a joint township with Clapham, in the parish of CLAPHAM, western division of the wapentake of STAINCLIFFE and EWCROSS, West riding of the county of YORK, 7¼ miles (N.W.) from Settle. The population is returned with Clapham.

NEWBY, a joint township with Mulwith, in that part of the parish of RIPON which is in the liberty of RIPON, West riding of the county of YORK, 3¼ miles (S.E.) from Ripon, containing, with Mulwith, 52 inhabitants. It is situated on the river Ure, which occasionally inundates and enriches the adjacent lands. Newby Hall was built by Sir Edward Blacket, from a design by Sir Christopher Wren.

NEWBY-WISK, a township in that part of the parish of KIRBY-WISK which is in the eastern division of the wapentake of GILLING, North riding of the county of YORK, 4½ miles (S.) from North Allerton, containing 265 inhabitants. There is a stone bridge of five arches over the river Wiske. The Wesleyan Methodists have a place of worship here. A Sunday school has been established, and is supported by the Rev. Christopher Bethel, D.D. There is a trifling bequest by William Crank, for teaching and apprenticing poor children.

NEWCASTLE, a township in the parish of CLUN, hundred of PURSLOW, county of SALOP, containing 315 inhabitants.

Seal and Arms.

NEWCASTLE under LYNE, a borough, market town, and parish, having separate jurisdiction, though locally in the northern division of the hundred of Pirehill, county of STAFFORD, 16 miles (N.N.W.) from Stafford, and 149 (N. W. by N.) from London, containing 7031 inhabitants. This was a place of some note before the Conquest, though known by a different name; its present appellation being derived from a castle built here by Edmund, Earl of Lancaster, in the reign of Henry III., a former edifice, called Chesterton castle, having fallen into decay; and the descriptive affix, "under Lyne, or

Lyme," denotes its proximity to a forest of that name, serving also to distinguish it from Newcastle in Northumberland. The town is situated on a small branch of the river Trent, on the great road from Birmingham and London to Liverpool and Manchester, and consists of two principal and several smaller streets, which are paved (the foot-paths with brick), and lighted with gas, under the provisions of an act passed in 1819: the inhabitants are supplied with water by means of pipes leading from water-works in the town, which is raised by an engine; the houses are mostly ancient. There is a small theatre, also a concert and assembly room; and the races, held annually in the first week in August, on a course near the town, are well attended. The manufacture of hats is very extensive, and is conducted under an incorporated company of Felt-makers; and silk-throwing, cotton-spinning, tanning, malting, the manufacture of copperas, white lead, and paper, are also carried on: considerable business is done in the corn trade, and in the vicinity are some iron-works. Its commercial prosperity is much promoted by the neighbouring potteries, which occupy a district nearly eight miles in extent. A branch canal from this town, about four miles in length, joins the Trent and Mersey canal at Stoke; and another to Apedale is used chiefly for the conveyance of coal hither. The markets are on Monday and Saturday, and on every alternate Monday is a great cattle market: fairs are held on Shrove-Monday, for cattle; Easter-Monday, Whit-Monday, and July 14th, for wool; Monday after September 13th, and the first Monday in November.

The first charter of incorporation was granted in the 19th of Henry III., and was confirmed by subsequent monarchs: that now in force is dated in the 32nd of Elizabeth, and is a confirmation of all former grants, with several additions. Under it the corporation consists of a mayor, two bailiffs, and twenty-four capital burgesses, who form a common council, by which body the mayor and bailiffs are annually elected on the Tuesday next after Michaelmas-day; assisted by a recorder, town clerk, and two serjeants at mace; the two former enjoy the office for life. By a confirmation of this charter, in the fifteenth of Charles II., the members of the common council are empowered to elect annually from among themselves two justices of the peace, who, with the mayor, hold general sessions for the borough quarterly, but have no power to try capital offenders. A court of record is held every three weeks, for the recovery of debts not exceeding £50; the mayor and bailiffs are the presiding officers. Courts leet and baron are likewise held every three weeks. This borough has returned members to parliament from the 27th of Edward III.: the right of election is in the resident freemen, in number about eight hundred; the mayor is the returning officer. The freedom is obtained by birth (being extended to all the sons of resident sworn burgesses), by apprenticeship within the borough, by gift of the common council, and by purchase.

Newcastle was formerly a chapelry in the parish of Stoke upon Trent. The living is a rectory not in charge, in the archdeaconry of Stafford, and diocese of Lichfield and Coventry, and in the patronage of the Society for purchasing livings. The church, dedicated to St. Giles, was rebuilt in 1720: it is a modern edifice of brick, with a very ancient tower of red sandstone. A new church, or chapel, containing six hundred and seventy-one free sittings, was completed in 1828, the parliamentary commissioners having granted £4400 towards defraying the expense, the remainder being raised by subscription : it is intended as a chapel of ease during the incumbency of the present rector, after which the right of presentation will belong to the Society for purchasing livings. There are places of worship for Baptists, Independents, Methodists of the New Connexion, and Primitive and Wesleyan Methodists. The free grammar school originated in a benefaction from Richard Cleyton, Esq., in 1602, augmented by a bequest from John Cotton, and various other charitable contributions ; the entire annual income is about £90 : it is free for all the sons of burgesses, and poor inhabitants of the borough : the school-house has been rebuilt. An English school was founded, in 1704, by means of a bequest from the Rev. Edward Orme, for the instruction of the children of the poor in reading, writing, and arithmetic ; the income is about £160 per annum, and there is a residence for the master, who instructs fifty children. About fifteen or twenty children are taught by a schoolmistress, for a salary of £8 per annum, paid by the corporation : there is likewise a National school. Almshouses for twenty poor aged widows were erected and endowed under the will of Christopher Monk, Duke of Albemarle, dated July 4th, 1687. John Goodwin, an eminent Nonconformist divine and controversialist, was born here about 1593 ; and Elijah Fenton, the coadjutor of Pope in his translation of Homer's Odyssey, was also a native of the town. Newcastle confers the title of duke on the family of Clinton.

NEWCASTLE upon TYNE, an ancient borough, port, and market town, and a county of itself, locally in Castle ward, county of NORTHUMBERLAND, 276 miles (N. N. W.) from London, and 117 (S. E.) from Edinburgh, containing, exclusively of the townships of Byker, Cramlington, Heaton, and Jesmond, in the eastern division, and of Benwell, Elswick, Fenham, and Westgate, in the western division, of CASTLE ward, 35,181 inhabitants, and, including the environs, about 60,000. This place was anciently called *Pons Ælii*, from a bridge erected by the Emperor Adrian, on his return from an expedition against the Picts and Scots, to whose incursions this part of the island was particularly exposed, and as a barrier against which, the Emperor Severus afterwards constructed the wall called after his name, which, reaching from the mouth of the Tyne to Solway Frith, passed through this town, and was defended by numerous forts and exploratory towers, of which one at Pandon gate was remaining till the year 1796, when it was removed for the purpose of widening the passage. During the Octarchy the kings of Northumbria held their court here ; and, in 653, Peada, King of Mercia, on a visit to Osweo, whose daughter he obtained in marriage, was converted, with all his retinue, to the Christian faith, and baptized by Finan, Bishop of Lindisfarn. From being a fortified

Seal and Arms.

place, and from having afforded protection to numerous ecclesiastics from the neighbouring convents of Tynemouth, Jarrow, Lindisfarn, and Wearmouth, which had been ravaged by the Danes, it obtained the name of *Monkchester ;* but, in turn, it experienced the devastations of those barbarians, who destroyed its sacred edifices, and massacred the monks and nuns who had found an asylum within their walls. From the union of the several kingdoms of the Octarchy under Egbert till the Conquest, it was the residence of the Earls of Westmorland and Northumberland ; and on the partition of the kingdom between Edmund Ironside and Canute, it fell, together with the rest of Northumbria, East Anglia, and Mercia, into the possession of the latter. In 1068, Edgar Atheling, and Malcolm, King of Scotland, with a numerous retinue of native insurgents and foreign auxiliaries, marched from this town to oppose the sovereignty of William the Conqueror, who, hastening to crush the conspiracy formed against him, met the insurgents at Gateshead Fell, and, entering the town after the defeat of his opponents, levelled it nearly with the ground. Robert Curthose, eldest son of the Conqueror, built a fortress here in 1080, which, in contradistinction to the old Roman *castrum* of Pons *Ælii*, was called the *New castle,* and hence the present name of the town. The barons, who under the conduct of Earl Mowbray had conspired to dethrone William Rufus, took possession of this castle, which was besieged by that monarch and taken by storm, in 1095. After the death of Henry I., the town was seized by David, King of Scotland, in support of the claims of Matilda, and continued in the possession of the Scots till 1157, when it was restored by treaty to Henry II. ; against whom, in 1173, William of Scotland, surnamed the Lion, marched into England, with an army of eighty thousand men, but was made prisoner by a small number of troops under the command of Ralph de Glanville, sheriff of Yorkshire, and brought into this place.

Newcastle, from its situation as a frontier station, has participated largely in all the border feuds, and has been frequently selected as the place of rendezvous for troops destined for the invasion of Scotland, and of interview between the contending monarchs. Balliol, King of Scotland, in 1292, did homage for that crown to Edward I. in the hall of the castle, before a numerous assembly of the nobles of both countries. To arrest the progress of the Scots under Wallace, who had pillaged the neighbourhood, the parliament assembled at York, in 1298, summoned the military force of the country, and collected here in eight days an army of one hundred thousand men, which, marching into Scotland, defeated the enemy at Falkirk. During this reign the town was erected into a borough, and fortified with strong walls, which were begun by an inhabitant who had been carried off by an incursion of the Scots, and completed by his fellow townsmen, who, stimulated by his efforts, joined with him in the work. Edward II., in 1311, retired hither with his favourite Gaveston, from the pursuit of the exasperated barons, where they remained till the arrival of the baronial troops headed by the Earl of Lancaster. In 1322, the town was besieged by the Scots, who, renewing their attempts a few years afterwards, were vanquished by Edward III., who, marching hence, obtained a signal victory over them in their own territory. It was again attempted by David II., King of

Scotland, during the absence of Edward in France ; but his queen Philippa, assembling at Newcastle a body of sixteen thousand forces, marched against the assailants, and defeated them at Neville's Cross, with the loss of fifteen thousand of their men, and the capture of their king. In the reign of Richard II., a grand rendezvous of the military was appointed here, in 1388 ; and in the same year, the Scots having advanced to Durham, encamped on their return before this town, from which, after several skirmishes, they were compelled to retreat. In the reign of Henry IV., an army of thirty-seven thousand men was assembled at this place, in 1405, to oppose an insurrection under the Earl of Northumberland ; and, in that of Henry VI., commissioners met in the vestry-room of St. Nicholas' church, to arrange the terms of a treaty of cessation from hostilities between the English and the Scots, which was signed in August 1451. Margaret, eldest daughter of Henry VII., was sumptuously entertained here, in 1503, on her way to Scotland, to celebrate her nuptials with James IV., to whom she had been affianced ; and, in 1513, the Earl of Surrey passed through the town, with an army of twenty-six thousand men, on his way to Flodden Field, where a sanguinary contest took place, in which the Scottish king and the chief of his nobility were slain ; the royal corpse having been embalmed at Berwick, was brought through Newcastle on its way for interment at Richmond, in Surrey.

The town continued to maintain its importance as a frontier, till the union of the two kingdoms in 1603, by the accession of James of Scotland to the English throne. In the insurrection of the Covenanters, during the reign of Charles I., it was surprised and taken possession of by the Scottish army, under Leslie, Montrose, and other disaffected leaders, who are said to have destroyed most of the public documents. When the war broke out between the king and the parliament, the inhabitants declared for the former ; and the town, having been put into a state of defence, was besieged by the Earl of Leven, and after a gallant resistance was taken, in October 1644, and continued in the possession of the parliamentarians till the conclusion of hostilities. In the beginning of 1646, King Charles having surrendered himself to the Scots at Newark, was conveyed to Newcastle, where he continued till the arrival of the parliamentary commissioners, to whose custody he was transferred in 1647, on the departure of the Scots, and by whose directions he was conducted to London. Tedcastle, which occupied a lofty eminence, was a building of great strength and, with its several wards, comprised an area of more than three acres : the walls were of a thickness varying from fourteen and a half to seventeen feet. After being dismantled it was used as a prison, and for holding the assizes for the county and, though the town had been made a county of itself, the castle and its precincts still formed part of the county of Northumberland : the site and remains of this ancient building were purchased by the corporation in 1812, since which time considerable alterations and additions have been made, but not in harmony with its original character, which was in the early Norman style of architecture. In the rebellion of 1745, Newcastle was the head-quarters of the king's forces under General Wade, prior to their advance into Scotland, where the insurgents were defeated at Culloden, in April 1746.

The town is situated on the summit and declivities of three lofty eminences, rising abruptly from the northern bank of the river Tyne, over which is an elegant stone bridge, finished in 1781, of nine elliptic arches, built at an expense, with subsequent alterations, of £60,000, and connecting Newcastle with the suburb of Gateshead : it extends nearly two miles along the banks of the river, from east to west. The streets in the more ancient part are inconveniently narrow, and the houses irregularly built in the Elizabethan style ; in the modern parts are spacious streets and squares, containing handsome and uniform ranges of elegant building, among which, Eldon and Charlotte squares, and Mosley-street, Dean-street, Blackett-street, the Leazes Terrace, and others, have been recently erected, and other plans are now in progress for the enlargement and improvement of the town : it is well paved, and lighted with gas. The inhabitants are amply supplied with water, by aqueducts from Spring gardens, Coxlodge, the town moor, and other places in the vicinity. A Literary and Philosophical Society was instituted in 1793 ; a part of the funds is appropriated to the maintenance of a lectureship, commenced in 1802, under the title of the New Institution, and a course of lectures is periodically delivered on subjects of natural and experimental philosophy : the buildings, erected in 1825, at an expense of £13,885, and forming a handsome structure of the Doric order, comprise a museum, a library, and a room for an extensive philosophical apparatus, with other apartments and offices : the library contains nine thousand volumes, and is ornamented with a marble bust of the late Dr. Charles Hutton, by Chantrey ; a bust of Mr. Thomas Bewick, by Bailey ; and a cast from the bust of the late Mr. James Watt, presented by his son. The Antiquarian Society was established in 1813, and the members hold their meetings in a part of the buildings of the Philosophical Society ; they have a museum of coins, Roman altars, funereal inscriptions, &c., and a library of works on philosophical and antiquarian subjects ; and a volume of Transactions is annually published, under the title " Archaelogia Æliana." An institution for the promotion of the fine arts, formed in 1822, is under the direction of a president and a committee, and exhibition rooms, of elegant proportions, have lately been erected. A Botanic and Horticultural Society was established in 1824, a Law Society in 1826, and a Natural History Society in 1829. In addition to the New library, already noticed, are various others containing valuable collections, among which are those of St. Nicholas, the Trinity House, Hanover-square chapel, besides numerous congregational libraries, and a medical library : there are several subscription news-rooms, billiard-rooms, a racquet-court, and similar sources of amusement. The theatre royal, a handsome building, erected at an expense of £6281, was opened in 1788, and is generally open four months in the year, there being performances during the assizes and races : the interior is well arranged and appropriately decorated, and is capable of accommodating one thousand three hundred and fifty persons. A circus also, for equestrian exercises and the performance of pantomimes, was opened in 1789. The assembly-rooms, an elegant edifice in the Grecian style of architecture, with a lofty Ionic portico rising in the centre of the front to a considerable height above the wings, and supporting a triangular pediment, form a handsome suite of apartments, of which, the principal is ninety-four feet long, thirty-six feet in width, and thirty-two feet high : it is lighted by brilliant chandeliers of cut glass ; the card and refreshment rooms are of corresponding character, and are ornamented with a good painting, by Downman, of Sir John Falstaff and the Merry Wives of Windsor : the building, with its furniture, cost about £6700, of which sum, the corporation subscribed £200. A Philharmonic and Choral Society hold occasional meetings. Races take place annually in July : the course is well adapted to the purpose, and the grand stand, a handsome building of stone, erected by subscription in 1800, affords good accommodation to the numerous visitors. Public baths of every kind were erected in 1781, near the West gate, and are provided with every requisite accommodation. The artillery barracks and depôt form an extensive range of building, enclosed within a stone wall : they were erected in 1807, at an expense of £40,000, and are chiefly occupied by cavalry. The environs are pleasant, and contain much diversified and romantic scenery, particularly the vales called Pandon, Jesmond, and Heaton deans. Bridges have been constructed across the deep dells in several parts, which have a picturesque appearance : the bridge over Pandon dean was erected in 1812, at an expense of £7448. 12. 10.

Newcastle has been one of the principal seats of trade from a very early period : the extensive mineral districts abounding with coal, of which prodigious quantities are exported, not only to London and every part of Great Britain, but also to France, Holland, and Germany, and the numerous foundries and manufactories, for the establishment of which the abundance of that mineral has afforded the greatest facility, have contributed materially to the increase of the trade. The harbour, which is deep, and affords secure shelter, is accessible to ships of four hundred tons' burden : the quay, which is commodious and well adapted to the loading and unloading of merchandise, is five hundred and forty yards in length, and is, with the exception of that of Yarmouth, the largest in the kingdom. The principal exports are coal and the produce of the various manufactories in the town and neighbourhood, namely, tin, brass, and other metals, lead, cast and wrought iron, glass, pottery, chemical productions, copperas, soap, colours, grindstones, salt, and salmon from the fisheries : the annual produce of the lead mines is estimated at twenty thousand tons, at the least ; the value of glass manufactured, in its different varieties, is about £500,000 annually, and the quantity of coal sent from the port in 1826, was eight hundred and sixty-three thousand and fifty-seven Newcastle chaldrons, containing each sixty-eight Winchester bushels ; of which, eight hundred thousand four hundred and thirty-seven chaldrons were sent coastwise, and sixty-two thousand six hundred and twenty were exported. This branch of trade affords employment to about seventy-five thousand persons ; its weekly produce has been estimated at £60,000, and the annual duty at £600,000. The chief imports are wine, spirituous liquors, and fruit from the southern parts of Europe ; corn, timber, flax, tallow, and hides from the Baltic, and various other commodities from the opposite coasts : there is also a considerable trade with North America. A few vessels sail annually to Davis' Straits, on account of the whale fishery. The number

of vessels which cleared out, in 1819, was, coastwise, eight thousand eight hundred and twenty-eight ; and to foreign ports, nine hundred and ninety-five : the number which entered inwards from foreign ports, in 1826, was three hundred British, and two hundred and twenty-six foreign ; and of those which cleared outwards, eight hundred and eighty-five British, and four hundred and forty-five foreign. The number of vessels belonging to the port, in 1830, was nine hundred and eighty-seven ships, and fifty-nine steam-boats ; and the amount of tonnage was two hundred and two thousand three hundred and seventy-nine. The jurisdiction of the port extends over the river Tyne, from Sparhawk in the sea to Hedwin streams, and its extent is navigated annually by the corporation, who are conservators of the river, and in whom the jurisdiction was vested on the abolition of the admiralty court, by Lord Howard of Effingham, Lord High Admiral of England, and admiral of the port. A plan for the improvement of the navigation of the Tyne has been produced by Mr. Rennie, the engineer, the probable expense of which is estimated at £519,320, but it has not yet been carried into execution. The Newcastle Association, in connexion with the "Royal National Institution for the Preservation of Life from Shipwreck," have ten stations along the coast, extending from South Shields to Berwick upon Tweed, at each of which life boats and apparatus are placed, in constant readiness to render assistance to vessels in distress. Ship-building is carried on to a considerable extent : there are large manufactories for ropes and sail-cloth : fire-bricks, coal-tar, and brown paper, are made in large quantities ; and there are numerous tanneries, breweries, iron-foundries, and various other works. The salmon fishery, for which the town was distinguished, has materially declined, which is attributed to the construction of locks at Bywell and Winlaton mills, whereby the fish are prevented ascending the smaller streams during the spawning season ; to the pollution of the Tyne, by the discharge of fœtid mineral and other deleterious water from the great number of manufactories upon its banks ; and to the agitation of the river, by the steam-boats which daily ply between this town and Shields. On the banks of the river are numerous mills for grinding corn. The custom-house, built in 1765, having become insufficient for the increased trade of the port, it is now being enlarged, and improved in its external appearance : it is situated nearly in the centre of the quay. The duties paid in 1772 were £56,000, and in 1824 they had increased to nearly half a million sterling per annum. A chamber of commerce was established in 1815. The inland trade is also very considerable, and is likely to be greatly extended by the construction of a rail-road from Newcastle to Carlisle, which is now in progress. The market days are Tuesday and Saturday : the market for wheat and rye is held in St. Nicholas' square, for oats in the Bigg market ; the grain is pitched in sacks : the fish-market is held in a handsome and commodious building, supported on a circular range of Doric columns, at the east end of the exchange, and general markets for provisions of every kind are held daily. The fairs commence on August 1st and October 29th, for woollen cloth, hardware, and toys, and continue nine days, on the first of which horses and cattle are sold ; August 13th and October 30th, for leather ; and

November 22nd, which is called the Stone's fair, and is chiefly for fat cattle. Among the numerous improvements in contemplation is the formation of a spacious corn-exchange, this being one of the greatest corn markets in the kingdom.

Newcastle, which is a borough by prescription, was first incorporated by Henry II., separated from the county of Northumberland and made a county of itself by Henry IV., under the designation of " The Town and County of the Town of Newcastle upon Tyne," and was exempted by Henry VI. from the jurisdiction of the high constable, marshal, and admiral of England: these several privileges were confirmed and extended by Queen Elizabeth, who granted them, in 1589, a new charter, ratified by succeeding sovereigns, under which the government is vested in a mayor, recorder, ten aldermen, a sheriff, twenty-four common councilmen, assisted by a town clerk, under-sheriff, sword bearer, eight chamberlains, two coroners, water-bailiff, quay-master, eight serjeants at mace, and other officers. The mayor and other officers are chosen annually, by a body of twenty-four electors, who are themselves appointed annually, under the regulations of the charter. The mayor, recorder, and aldermen, are justices of the peace within the town and county of the town. The borough is divided into twenty-four wards, for each of which two constables are appointed. The incorporated fraternities, several of which have separate halls, exercise important privileges; of these the twelve principal send two deputies, and the fifteen by-trades one each, to the election of the officers of the corporation. The freedom of the borough is inherited by all the sons of freemen, and is obtained by servitude to a resident freeman, or by gift of the corporation, but the power of conferring the franchise by gift is rarely exercised: among the privileges are exemption from toll and quay-dues, and the liberty of depasturing cattle on the town moor is secured by act of parliament to resident burgesses, and resident widows of deceased burgesses. Courts of assize and quarter session for the town and county of the town are held, for the trial of all offenders; two courts of record, for the recovery of debts and the determination of pleas to any amount; one held every Monday, at which the mayor presides, in causes relating to free burgesses or their widows; and the other on the Wednesday and Friday in every week, at which the sheriff presides, in causes relating to such inhabitants of the town or county of the town as are not free burgesses: in both these courts the recorder sits as judge, or assessor. A court of requests is held, on the first Wednesday in every month, by commissioners, under an act passed in the 1st of William and Mary, for the recovery of debts under 40s., the jurisdiction of which extends over the town and liberties. A guild is held thrice a year, for the purpose of proclaiming the names and titles of persons seeking admission to the freedom of the borough. The court of pie-powder has fallen into disuse. The borough first exercised the elective franchise in the 23rd of Edward I., since which time it has returned two members to parliament: the right of election is vested in the free burgesses, whether resident or not, the number of whom is about three thousand five hundred: the sheriff is the returning officer.

The guildhall, in which the assizes, sessions, and other courts for the town and county of the town are held, forms part of an extensive range of buildings, which include also an exchange, merchants' court, and various other offices: they were erected in 1658, at an expense of £10,700; and, in 1809, underwent considerable alteration and enlargement. The hall is a spacious room ninety-two feet long and thirty feet wide; the ceiling is ornamented with paintings, and the floor laid with chequered marble; at the foot of the grand staircase is a statue of Charles II., in Roman costume; above the bench are full-length portraits of Charles II. and James II., between which is that of George III.; on one side of the hall is the portrait of Lord Chancellor Eldon, and on the other that of Lord Stowell, Judge of the Admiralty court; and at the east end, above the entrance to the merchants' hall, is a portrait of Admiral Lord Collingwood. The grand staircase leading to the merchants' court is in a handsome style, and lighted by a dome; the court is thirty feet square, with a richly groined roof, twenty-two feet high; above these are offices for the town clerk and other officers of the corporation, and an apartment fire-proof, in which the town records are deposited. The mansion-house, erected in 1691, at an expense of £6000, is a handsome edifice of brick, with quoins and cornices of stone, and has a pleasant terrace overlooking the river on the south: the grand saloon is ornamented with various kinds of armour tastefully displayed; the principal staircase, of black oak, leads into a room forty-two feet in length, handsomely decorated, and used as a ball-room on public occasions; the banqueting-room is fifty feet long, and ornamented with two views of the town, painted by Richardson, and with engraved portraits of several distinguished characters; the mayor's parlour contains the regalia; the drawing-room is splendidly furnished, and the other apartments are of corresponding style. The mayor resides in the mansion-house during his mayoralty, and has an allowance of £2100 per annum, a state coach and barge, and an elegant service of plate. The common gaol and house of correction for the town and county of the town is a spacious building of stone, commenced in 1823, and completed in 1828: the exterior has a characteristic appearance of massive strength; the entrance in the centre is through a square gateway tower leading to the keeper's house and other offices, from which diverge six radiating wards, with day-rooms and airing-yards, for the classification of prisoners: the expense of the building, which is in every respect well adapted to its purpose, was £35,000. The new courts for the county of Northumberland, erected on that part of the precincts of the castle which is included within that county, were commenced in 1810, and form a handsome range of building, one hundred and forty-four feet in length and seventy-two in breadth, having on the south front a noble portico of six lofty fluted columns of the Doric order, supporting a handsome frieze, cornice, and architrave, and on the north, a similar portico of four columns, leading into the grand entrance hall, on the right of which is the Crown court, and on the left the Nisi Prius court, commodiously arranged, and having large galleries for the admission of the public: beyond these are the grand jury room, with which both the courts have communication; in the wings are rooms for the judge, petty juries, and witnesses, above which are apartments for the gaoler and other officers connected with the courts ; under the courts are ranges of cells for prisoners, from which is a communication with the Crown bar. These buildings, which are in the purest style of architecture, were erected at an expense of £52,000, of which the Duke of Northumberland, whose portrait is in the grand jury room, contributed £3000. In digging for the foundation, two Roman altars, some coins, and other relics of antiquity were found.

The town, originally comprising but one parish, is now divided into four parochial districts, St. Nicholas', the original parish, All Saints', St. Andrew's, and St. John's, in the archdeaconry of Northumberland, and diocese of Durham. The living of St. Nicholas' is a vicarage, rated in the king's books at £50, and in the patronage of the Bishop of Carlisle. The church, originally built in 1091, was burnt down in 1216, and the present structure was rebuilt in 1359. It is a spacious cruciform structure, two hundred and forty feet long, and seventy-three broad, principally in the decorated style of English architecture, with a steeple one hundred and ninety-five feet high, of singular beauty, in the later style : from the battlements of the tower rise octagonal turrets, crowned with crocketed pinnacles, of which the central are lower than those at the angles ; from these spring four flying buttresses of graceful curve, meeting in a point, and supporting an elegant lantern turret, unequalled in beauty, and surmounted by a small crocketed spire, terminating in a vane : the interior retains many vestiges of its former antiquity, among which are the carved oak roofs, the font, and other relics; in the east window is a painting of our Saviour bearing his cross, presented, at the cost of £50, by the corporation : over the communion table is a fine painting of the Last Supper, by J. Tintoretti, presented by Sir M. W. Ridley, Bart. During the occupation of the town by the Scottish army, many of the ancient monuments were destroyed, and others were removed in the repairs and modernizations which have taken place; of those that remain, the principal are to the memory of Sir Matthew White Ridley, M.P., Vice-Admiral Collingwood, the Rev. Hugh Moises, A.M., Calverley Bewicke, Esq., and several others. On the southern side of the church is a building erected by the late Sir Walter Blackett, Bart., who bequeathed a salary for a librarian, for the preservation of a very ancient collection of books, the ancient library of works on Divinity, bequeathed by Dr. Thomlinson : the lower part is used as a vestry-room, and the upper for Thomlinson's library. The church, dedicated to All Saints, situated on the summit of an eminence rising abruptly from the river, was founded prior to 1286, and rebuilt in 1786: it is a handsome edifice in the Grecian style of architecture, with a lofty tower, surmounted by a light and elegant spire ; the south entrance is through a noble portico of four Doric columns, on one side of which is a chapel for the performance of the funeral service, and on the other a large vestry-room, forming two handsome wings ; the body of the church is of an elliptic form, with a circular portico at the west end, corresponding with the projection of the chancel at the east ; the interior is beautifully arranged, and derives peculiar advantage from its elliptic form ; the galleries and pews are of mahogany : the living is a perpetual curacy, endowed with £600 royal bounty, and £1600 parliamentary grant, and in the

patronage of the Vicar. St. Andrew's is a very ancient structure, with a low square embattled tower of large dimensions, the date of which is not known ; it displays portions in various styles of architecture, from the early Norman to the later English ; it suffered much in the siege of the town, in 1644, and has undergone repeated alterations and repairs ; the interior contains numerous ancient monuments : the living is a perpetual curacy, endowed with £600 royal bounty, and £2200 parliamentary grant, and in the patronage of the Vicar. The church of St. John the Baptist is a spacious and ancient cruciform structure, founded prior to 1286, in the early style of English architecture, with a square embattled tower; the windows, which are of large dimensions, were formerly ornamented with painted glass, of which there is scarcely any vestige : there are several ancient monuments, and an ancient font, in this church : the churchyard contains the remains of John Cunningham, the pastoral poet, who died here in 1773 : the living is a perpetual curacy, endowed with £600 royal bounty, and £1800 parliamentary grant, and in the patronage of the Vicar. The pious Robert Rhodes, who died about 1490, was a liberal benefactor to this, as well as to most of the other churches in the town. St. Anne's chapel was built in 1768, by the corporation, who endowed a lectureship in it, and also make an annual voluntary payment to the minister, who is appointed by the vicar, but the payment being at the will of the corporation, their nomination of a candidate is always attended to. The ancient chapel near the bridge, dedicated to St. Thomas à Becket, and annexed to the hospital of St. Mary Magdalene, after being repeatedly curtailed in its dimensions, was taken down, and a handsome edifice, in the decorated style of English architecture, erected in the Magdalene meadows : it is a beautiful structure, with a lofty tower of elegant design and proportion, having slender octagonal buttresses at the angles, carried above the battlements, terminating in canopies, and surmounted by pinnacles : the belfry windows are lofty, and ornamented with tracery; over the western entrance, which is through a stately arch, with deeply receding mouldings, is an elegant triple shrine, finely sculptured ; the sides of the church are strengthened with panelled buttresses of two stages, ornamented with canopies, of which those at the angles rise considerably above the roof: the interior is lighted on each side by a noble and lofty range of windows of two lights, enriched with tracery, and corresponds in every respect with the general beauty of style for which the exterior is distinguished : the master of the hospital, who is appointed by the corporation, is the incumbent. There are two places of worship for Baptists, one for the Society of Friends, three for Independents, two for Wesleyan and one each for Independent and Primitive Methodists, and those of the New Connexion, five for members of the Scottish Kirk, and one each for the Scots relief congregation, the Seceders, and Separatists from them, one each for Burghers, Antiburghers, Sandemanians, Swedenborgians, and Unitarians, and a Roman Catholic chapel.

The free grammar school was founded by Thomas Horsley, who was mayor in 1525 and 1533, and made a royal foundation in the 42nd of Elizabeth ; and a part of the buildings of St. Mary's hospital was appropriated to its use by the corporation, who added four marks per annum to the original endowment; they have the appointment of the master, who has a salary of £120 per annum: it is open for the gratuitous instruction of all boys of the town, and has, in common with other schools in the diocese, an interest in twelve exhibitions, of £20 per annum each, to Lincoln College, Oxford, founded by Lord Crewe; two exhibitions to either of the Universities, of £10 per annum each, founded by Dr. Hartwell, for boys from this town and Durham; and a scholarship in Emanuel College, Cambridge, founded for boys from the same schools by Dr. Michael Smith. Bishop Ridley, the Protestant martyr, is stated to have received the rudiments of his education in this school, though more probably in some similar establishment in the town, prior to its foundation; since which period Lords Eldon and Stowell, Vice-Admiral Lord Collingwood, Sir Robert Chambers, William Elstob, an antiquary and divine; the poet Akenside; the Rev. George Hall, Bishop of Dromore; and the Rev. John Brand, author of a history of Newcastle, and Secretary to the Antiquarian Society of London, received the early part of their education in this school. The Trinity House school was established in 1712, and rebuilt in 1753, for the instruction of the children of members of that fraternity, in writing, arithmetic, and the mathematics: the master has a salary of £80 per annum, with a house, and the privilege of taking twenty boarders, or of instructing twenty scholars in addition to those on the foundation. A charity school was founded in the parish of St. Nicholas, in 1705, by Mrs. Eleanor Allen, who endowed it with a certain sum, which, being augmented by subsequent benefactions, is appropriated the clothing and instruction of forty boys and forty girls: this school was incorporated with the Clergy Jubilee school, founded in 1819, in commemoration of the attainment of the fiftieth year of his prelacy by the late Bishop of Durham, for an indefinite number of children, who are instructed on Dr. Bell's system. There are about four hundred and eighty-five boys and one hundred and fifty girls in the school; the boys on the foundation, at fourteen years of age, are put to some trade or sent to sea: the revenue, including a penny a week paid by scholars not on the foundation, is about £425 per annum: the building is substantial, handsome, and commodious. St. Andrew's school was founded, in 1705, by Sir William Blackett, Bart., for the education of thirty boys, clothed from a fund appropriated by his son in 1728; the number has been augmented to thirty-four by subsequent endowment. A similar establishment, for fifteen girls, was instituted in this part of the parish, in 1772. St. John's charity school was founded, in 1705, by Mr. John Ord, who endowed it with property producing about £54 per annum, for the clothing and instruction of twenty boys, each of whom receives an apprentice-fee of forty shillings on leaving the school. All Saints' charity school, established in 1709, and supported by subscription, affords clothing and instruction to forty boys and forty girls; the boys receive an apprentice-fee of forty shillings, and the girls a donation of twenty shillings, on leaving the school. St. Ann's chapel school was built, in 1682, by the corporation, by whom it is supported. Hanover-square school, in which fifteen boys are educated and clothed, is chiefly supported by subscriptions. The Royal Ju-

bilee school was established in 1810, to commemorate the fiftieth anniversary of the accession of George III., and a handsome building erected for the purpose, at an expense of £2195; a good library was annexed to it in 1822: the master's salary is £120 per annum; the scholars are instructed on the Lancasterian plan, and the school is supported by subscription. The Improved school for girls was established in 1812, and is supported by subscription; the building, erected in 1814, is neat and commodious. The Carpenter's Tower school, instituted in 1822, is chiefly supported by the Wesleyan Methodists: the Union day school affords instruction to one hundred girls; and there are numerous similar establishments and Sunday schools (the latter under the superintendence of a Sunday-school Union, formed in 1815), supported by the members of the established church, and the various congregations of dissenters. Infant schools have been established in various parts of the town since the year 1825, and are liberally supported and numerously attended.

The infirmary was instituted in 1751, and a commodious and handsome building was erected (on a piece of ground presented by the corporation, who also subscribe £100 a year), in 1752, at an expense of £3700, and a chapel, dedicated to St. Luke, was consecrated in 1754: in 1801, a plan for enlarging the buildings was adopted by the governors, and £5329 was subscribed for the purpose. The building, which is situated at a short distance from the town, is a plain but neat edifice of stone, four stories in height, with a wing of brick two stories high: it contains warm baths on an improved principle, and every accommodation requisite for the patients and the recovery of their health: in the governors' room are portraits of Sir Walter Blackett, Bart., by Reynolds; Matthew Ridley, Esq.; Dr. Joseph Butler, Bishop of Durham; Dr. Benson, Bishop of Gloucester, and other benefactors to the institution: it is principally supported by subscription, and a fund arising from benefactions, among which is a sum bequeathed by Mrs. E. Davison, of Durham, for the relief of patients dismissed as incurable: the average number of in-patients is about one hundred and twenty, and the annual expenditure about £3000. The dispensary was established in 1777, and an appropriate building was purchased and adapted to its use in 1790; a department for the recovery of persons apparently drowned was, in 1789, added to the original institution; it is supported by subscription, and gratuitously visited by members of the medical profession resident in the town and neighbourhood. The lying-in hospital was founded in 1760, and the present building erected, at an expense of £1550, in 1826: it is supported by subscription, and, under good regulations, is open to the poor married women of the town and neighbourhood. The society for the relief of pregnant women at their own houses was instituted in 1760, and is liberally supported. The house of recovery from fever, and other contagious diseases not admissible into the infirmary, was erected in 1804, at an expense of £1800, on a site of land granted for that purpose by the corporation: it is well regulated and amply supported by subscription, and is open to persons not objects of charity, on payment of a moderate remuneration. The Lock hospital, instituted in 1814, and the infirmary for diseases of the eye, established in 1822, are supported by subscription. The lunatic asylum was erected, by subscription, upon a part of the Warden Close, granted by the corporation, in 1767, and was greatly enlarged and improved by that body in 1824: it contains a complete suite of wards for the classification of the patients, who are provided with every accommodation requisite for their health and consistent with their condition; the establishment comprises warm, cold, and shower baths, and is conducted on a system combining humanity and skill in the treatment of that malady.

Jesus' hospital was founded by the corporation, in 1681, for the maintenance of freemen, their widows, and children: the premises are neatly built of brick, three stories high; in front is a piazza, forming a pleasant walk ninety-one feet in length, and in front of the upper stories are galleries extending the whole length of the building: it contains forty-two apartments, for the reception of as many inmates, who receive each £13 per annum from the corporation, with an allowance of coal and other necessaries. Mrs. Davison's hospital was founded in 1719, and endowed by her with £940, in consideration of which an annuity of £55 per annum is paid by the corporation, who erected the present buildings, in 1754, for the accommodation of a governess and five sisters, widows of Protestant clergymen, merchants, or freemen of the town, who are appointed by the corporation, and have an annual income of £13, with a supply of coal. An hospital was also founded, in 1754, by Thomas Davison and his sisters, who gave £1200 in trust for that purpose to the corporation, who erected apartments, adjoining the two former hospitals, for six unmarried women, daughters or widows of burgesses, who have an allowance of £13 per annum, with a supply of coal and other necessaries. Sir Walter Blackett's hospital was founded in 1754, for six unmarried burgesses, and endowed by him with £1200, given in trust to the corporation, by whom the building was erected, and by whom the inmates are appointed; they have the same allowance as the inmates of Jesus' hospital. The Westgate hospital, containing twenty apartments, arranged in a quadrangular building of stone, in the ancient style of English architecture, was founded by the corporation, to celebrate the peace with France, in 1814, and in 1817 it was augmented by twenty additional rooms, for a governor and twenty brethren and sisters, who receive each five shillings per week, paid monthly, and a supply of coal, the governor having £2 per annum extra. The Trinity almshouses were founded by the guild, or fraternity, of the Blessed Trinity, originally incorporated in 1492, and refounded in the reign of Elizabeth, in 1584, for the regulation of the pilotage of the harbour, and the erection of lighthouses on the coast: the buildings comprise a hall for the transaction of business, a chapel, and two ranges of dwellings for thirteen agèd men and thirteen aged widows, who receive each £1. 8. per month, with other necessary supplies: connected with this institution are two classes of out-pensioners, the first of which receives £7, and the second £5, per annum each, with an extra allowance of £1 per annum for every child under fourteen years of age: the total number of brethren is about three hundred and forty. The association for the preservation of life from shipwreck was instituted, under the patronage of this society, in 1825.

The Keelmen's hospital was founded in 1788, and is under the management of twenty-one guardians, who are empowered to levy one penny per chaldron on the freight of all keels laden with coal at the port; these funds are augmented by the payment of one farthing per chaldron on all coal exported from the Tyne, by the owners or lessees of the mines, according to agreement, confirmed by act of parliament in 1820: the buildings, which were erected in 1701, on ground granted by the corporation, at an expense of £2000, comprise an office, a club-room, and sixty dwellings for the reception of poor keelmen, whose weekly allowance varies, according to circumstances, from one to five shillings. The Society of the Sons of the Clergy of the diocese of Durham and Hexhamshire was instituted in 1709, and, in 1725, united with a similar institution for the deaneries of Alnwick and Bambrough; the anniversary meetings are held alternately at Durham and at Newcastle. A fund for the widows of Protestant dissenting ministers was established in 1764; the society hold their meetings in this town, at Alnwick, and at Morpeth, in rotation. There are numerous societies for the relief of the poor and indigent of every class, among which are the Friendless Poor Society, formed in 1797; the Benevolent Society, in 1811; the Society for clothing distressed females, in 1815; the Strangers' Friend Society, in 1821; the Repository for the sale of the work of industrious females, opened in 1825; the Society for the relief of the indigent sick, instituted in 1827, and various others. Among the provident societies are, the Association of Protestant schoolmasters of the North of England, established in 1774; the Liberal Society of Tradesmen, in 1791; the Clerks' Society, in 1807; the Roman Catholics' Friendly Society, in 1823; and numerous benefit societies, consisting in the aggregate of about sixteen thousand members.

Of the various monastic establishments existing here at a very remote period of antiquity there are scarcely any vestiges; and of several the memorial is preserved only in the names which they have given to different parts of the town: among these was a small Benedictine nunnery, founded in the reign of William the Conqueror, and dedicated to St. Bartholomew, the revenue of which, at the dissolution, was £37. 4. 2.; a convent of Dominican friars, founded in 1260, by Sir Peter Scot and his son, of which there are some remains; a convent of Franciscans, founded in the reign of Henry III.; a priory of brethren of the order De Pœnitentiâ Jesu Christi, of which the first notice occurs in the year 1268; a priory of Carmelites, supposed to have been founded here in the reign of Henry III.; an establishment of Augustine friars, said to have been founded, in 1290, by Lord Ros, Baron of Wark upon Tweed; and the priory of St. Michael, founded in 1360, for brethren of the order of the Holy Trinity, associated for the redemption of captives. There still exist two hospitals, one founded by Henry I., and dedicated to St. Mary Magdalene, for a master and three brethren, to which was annexed the hospital of St. Thomas, near the bridge; and the other, called the hospital of St. Mary the Virgin, in Westgate, for a master and six brethren, the remains of which are still apparent, and the ancient chapel is now appropriated to the use of the free grammar school.

Newcastle has been distinguished as the birthplace of many eminent characters, among whom are the celebrated Dr. John Scot, usually called "Duns Scotus," who received his education in the Franciscan convent in this town; and his disciple and panegyrist, Hugh of Newcastle, a native of the town, and a friar of the same convent; Dr. Nicholas Durham, a resident in the convent of the White friars, in 1360, and a zealous opponent of Wickliff; William Elstob, a learned antiquary and divine, who was born in 1673; and his sister Elizabeth Elstob, born in 1683, and eminent for her knowledge of Saxon literature; Dr. Richard Grey, author of the *Memoria Technica*, who was born in 1694; Mark Akenside, poet and physician, born in 1721; the Rev. Henry Bourne, historian of the town, who died in 1733; the Rev. John Brand, a subsequent historian, born in 1743; Sir Robert Chambers, Judge of the Supreme Court of Judicature at Calcutta, born in 1737; Dr. Charles Hutton, born in the same year, an eminent mathematician, author of the Mathematical and Philosophical Dictionary, Tables of Logarithms, a Course of Mathematics, and numerous other works, and one of the compilers employed in the abridgment of the philosophical transactions of the Royal Society; John Scott, Earl of Eldon, and late Lord High Chancellor of England, born in 1751; and his brother, William Scott, Baron Stowell, born in 1745; and Cuthbert, late Baron Collingwood, Vice-Admiral of the Red, born in 1748: Mr. Thomas Bewick, the celebrated engraver on wood, a native of Cherryburn, fourteen miles from Newcastle, resided in this town from 1767 till his decease.

NEWCHURCH, or WHITEGATE, county palatine of Chester.—See WHITEGATE.

NEWCHURCH, a township in that part of the parish of Kinnersley which is in the hundred of Wolphy, county of Hereford. The population is returned with the parish.

NEWCHURCH, a parish in the liberty of Romney-Marsh, though locally in the hundred of Newchurch, lathe of Shepway, county of Kent, 5 miles (N.) from New Romney, containing 281 inhabitants. The living comprises a rectory and a vicarage, in the peculiar jurisdiction and patronage of the Archbishop of Canterbury; the rectory is rated in the king's books at £8. 4. 2., and the vicarage at £19. 16. 0½. The church is dedicated to St. Peter and St. Paul.

NEWCHURCH, a chapelry in the parish of Winwick, hundred of West Derby, county palatine of Lancaster, 6 miles (E. by S.) from Newton in Mackerfield. The population is returned with the parish. The living is a perpetual curacy, annexed to the rectory of Winwick, in the archdeaconry and diocese of Chester.

NEWCHURCH, a parish in the upper division of the hundred of Caldicott, county of Monmouth, 6 miles (N. W. by W.) from Chepstow, containing 562 inhabitants, of which number, 422 are in the East, and 140 in the West, division. The living is a perpetual curacy, in the archdeaconry and diocese of Llandaff, endowed with £800 royal bounty, and £1400 parliamentary grant, and in the patronage of the Duke of Beaufort.

NEWCHURCH, a parish in the liberty of East Medina, Isle of Wight division of the county of Southampton, 4½ miles (S. E. by E.) from Newport, containing, with the north and south divisions and the town of Ryde, 3945 inhabitants. The living is a discharged vicarage, in the archdeaconry and diocese of Winchester,

Vol. III.

rated in the king's books at £12. 6. 8., and in the patronage of the Bishop of Bristol. The church is dedicated to All Saints. Maurice Bockland, in 1755, gave land whereon to build a school-house, and William Bowles bequeathed £500 for its erection and endowment: the annual income, including other bequests, is £7.

NEWCHURCH in PENDLE-FOREST, a chapelry in that part of the parish of Whalley which is in the higher division of the hundred of Blackburn, county palatine of Lancaster, 4½ miles (W.) from Colne. The living is a perpetual curacy, in the archdeaconry and diocese of Chester, endowed with £10 per annum private benefaction, and £800 royal bounty, and in the patronage of Earl Howe. The chapel is dedicated to St. Mary. There is a place of worship for Wesleyan Methodists, also an endowed free school.

NEWCHURCH in ROSSENDALE-FOREST, a chapelry in that part of the parish of Whalley which is in the higher division of the hundred of Blackburn, county palatine of Lancaster, 3½ miles (E. S. E.) from Haslingden, containing, with Bacup, Deadwin-Clough, Tunstead, and Wolfenden, 8557 inhabitants. The living is a perpetual curacy, in the archdeaconry and diocese of Chester, and in the patronage of the Vicar of Whalley. The church is dedicated to the Holy Trinity. The Wesleyan Methodists and Unitarians have each a place of worship here, and the former a Sunday school. A free grammar school was founded, in 1701, by Edward Ashworth and John Hoyle, who surrendered an estate, now producing an annual income of £60, in support of the master, for teaching about thirty-five children. The river Irwell passes through the parish, in which cotton and woollen goods are manufactured to a considerable extent, in their various branches. Coal mines and quarries of freestone, slate, &c., abound here. A fair for cattle is held on April 29th, and one for cattle, clothing, and pedlary, on June 29th.

NEWDIGATE, a parish comprising the hamlet of Newdigate, in the first division of the hundred of Reigate, but chiefly in the second division of the hundred of Copthorne, county of Surrey, 5¾ miles (S.S.E.) from Dorking, containing 579 inhabitants. The living is a rectory, in the archdeaconry of Surrey, and diocese of Winchester, rated in the king's books at £8. 18. 4., and in the patronage of the Crown. The church, dedicated to St. Peter, is principally in the early style of English architecture. George Steer, in 1661, gave a school-house, and endowed it with a rent-charge of £6. 13. 4. a year, to which George Booth, in 1681, added £100; the present annual income amounts to upwards of £20, and is applied to the education of about eighteen poor children.

NEWENDEN-LIBERTY, a parish in the hundred of Selbrittenden, lathe of Scray, county of Kent, 5½ miles (S. W. by S.) from Tenterden, containing 151 inhabitants. The living is a rectory, in the archdeaconry and diocese of Canterbury, rated in the king's books at £7. 13. 4., and in the patronage of the Archbishop of Canterbury. The church is dedicated to St. Peter. This place, now an inconsiderable village, but still governed by a bailiff and under-bailiff, independent of the hundred, was formerly a large city and sea-port, and is said to have contained fifty-two taverns. The Roman station *Anderidæ* has by some been fixed near this spot, where large remains of earthworks, many Roman coins, foundations, and other antiquities have been from time to time discovered. The river Rother, which is crossed by a modern brick bridge of three arches, on the high road from Kent to Sussex, runs through the parish. A fair, principally for pedlary, is held on July 1st. At Losenden are the remains of a Carmelite friary, founded in 1241, by Sir Thomas Fitz-Aucher, Knt., in honour of the Blessed Virgin. Here is a powerful chalybeate spring.

NEWENT, a parish in the hundred of BOTLOE, county of Gloucester, comprising the liberty and market town of Newent, and the tythings of Boulsdon with Killcot, Compton, Cugley, and Malswick, and containing 2660 inhabitants, of which number, 1287 are in the town of Newent, 8½ miles (N. W.) from Gloucester, and 112 (W. N. W.) from London. The name of this place is supposed to have been derived from a new inn erected for the accommodation of travellers, on the site of a dilapidated mansion, now called the Boothall. A Benedictine priory, a cell to the abbey of Cormeile in Normandy, was founded here soon after the Conquest; and on the suppression of Alien priories it was given to the college of Fotheringhay. The town, which is situated westward of the river Severn, in the Forest of Dean, is small and irregularly built, and owes its present importance to some springs near it, which possess the same qualities as the Cheltenham water. Some coal mines were opened in the parish, but the working of them has been discontinued: the Hereford and Gloucester canal passes through the parish, and communicates by a short branch with the town. The market is on Friday; and fairs are held on the Wednesday before Easter, the Wednesday before Whitsuntide, and August 12th, and a statute fair on the 19th of September. The town, which was formerly more extensive than it is at present, was governed by a bailiff, whose office became obsolete about the end of the seventeenth century. The living is a discharged vicarage, in the archdeaconry and diocese of Gloucester, rated in the king's books at £23, and in the patronage of the Rev. William Andrew Foley. The church, which is dedicated to the Virgin Mary, is a spacious fabric, the work of different periods; over the porch is a tower with a lofty spire, built in 1679, as was also the roof of the nave, which is supported without pillars. There are two places of worship for Dissenters. Here are two free schools, and an unendowed almshouse for twenty poor persons of either sex; and other purposes.

NEWFIELD, a township in that part of the parish of St. Andrew Auckland which is in the northwestern division of Darlington ward, county palatine of Durham, 3½ miles (N.) from Bishop Auckland, containing 11 inhabitants.

NEW-FOREST, a township in the parish of Kirkby-Ravensworth, western division of the wapentake of Gilling, North riding of the county of York, 11 miles (W. N. W.) from Richmond, containing 73 inhabitants. An individual, whose name is unknown, left a rent-charge of £12 for teaching poor children.

NEWHALL, a township in the parish of Acton, hundred of Nantwich, county palatine of Chester, 5½ miles (S. W. by S.) from Nantwich, containing 854 inhabitants. The site of the ancient castle, which suffered greatly from the incursions of the Welch, can no longer be traced.

NEWHALL, a township in the parish of Daven-ham, hundred of Northwich, county palatine of Chester, 3½ miles (E. S. E.) from Northwich, containing 17 inhabitants.

NEWHALL, a joint township with Stanton, in the parish of Stapenhill, hundred of Repton and Gresley, county of Derby, 2¾ miles (S. E. by E.) from Burton upon Trent. The population is returned with Stanton. There is a place of worship for Wesleyan Methodists. Newhall is in the honour of Tutbury, duchy of Lancaster, and within the jurisdiction of a court of pleas held at Tutbury every third Tuesday, for the recovery of debts under 40s.

NEWHALL, a joint township with Clifton, in that part of the parish of Otley which is in the upper division of the wapentake of Claro, West riding of the county of York, ¾ of a mile (N. N. W.) from Otley, containing, with Clifton, 208 inhabitants. This was the residence of Edward Fairfax, Esq., a celebrated poet in the reigns of Elizabeth and James I.

NEWHAM, a township in the parish of Bambrough, northern division of Bambrough ward, county of Northumberland, 7 miles (S. E.) from Belford, containing 298 inhabitants.

NEWHAM, a township in the parish of Whalton, western division of Castle ward, county of Northumberland, 11¼ miles (N. W.) from Newcastle upon Tyne, containing 76 inhabitants.

NEWHAVEN, otherwise MEECHING, a parish and sea-port, in the hundred of Holmstrow, rape of Lewes, county of Sussex, 7 miles (S.) from Lewes, 9 (E.S.E.) from Brighton, and 58 (S.) from London, containing 927 inhabitants. The ancient name of this place was Meeching, and its present appellation was probably given about 1713, on the formation of the harbour, on which its importance chiefly depends. In 1731, an act of parliament was obtained to empower commissioners to repair the piers, and to cleanse and enlarge the harbour, which during the last thirty years has been progressively improving, the frequent dredging of boulders, or large stones driven upon the beach by the tide, having essentially contributed to that effect. It is one of the best tide harbours in the channel between the Downs and the Isle of Wight, and the bay forms one of the finest roadsteads on the southern coast: with the wind from north-north-west to east by south, facility of entrance to it is afforded, when a similar attempt at other places would be perilous. The piers are one hundred and twenty feet distant from each other; the west pier is seven hundred feet in length, and the east six hundred: at low water of spring tides the depth is five feet; at high water, during the neap tides, it stands at fourteen feet; and during spring tides, from twenty to twenty-two feet. Skilful pilots are constantly stationed on the piers; and in the day-time a flag is hoisted, as soon as the depth of water in the harbour reaches ten feet, and whilst it continues so long on the ebb as it is safe for vessels to enter. Ships of three hundred and three hundred and fifty tons' burden have found shelter here during tempestuous weather. At the mouth of the harbour is a small fort, and here also is moored H. M. frigate Hyperion, with three attendant cutters, to prevent smuggling along the coast: two steam-packets sail hence to Dieppe twice a week. It is worthy of observation, that Newhaven is the nearest sea-port to the metropolis of England, and the nearest English port to that of France.

The town, which is about half a mile distant from the sea, is situated near the mouth of the Ouse, over which, about thirty-five years since, a drawbridge was erected, leading towards Sleaford, in lieu of the ferry: the streets are of neat and clean appearance, and are lighted by subscription; the houses are respectable, many of them being of modern erection: the inhabitants are supplied with water by means of wells. A new and more commodious turnpike-road to Brighton has been formed, which has proved highly advantageous to the interests of the town. In the early part of the last century the inhabitants were extensively engaged in trade, which afterwards declined, owing to the decay of the old wooden piers that protected the harbour; but from the improvement in it, and its having been constituted, under a license from the Lords of the Treasury, a bonding port for all kinds of timber, as it was previously for wine and spirits, the commercial interests of the inhabitants have considerably improved; commodious bonding warehouses have been constructed on the quay, on a principle similar to those at the West India docks. The importation of coal has been extensive and progressive for several years: it is conveyed by the navigable river Ouse to Lewes and other parts, the navigation extending twenty miles inland. There is likewise a considerable trade in the importation of foreign timber, and the exportation of English oak for the dock-yards: the coasting trade in flour, butter, and corn, is also considerable. Many of the poor are employed in collecting boulders, which are shipped for the potteries in Staffordshire, and otherwise used in building walls. Ship-building formerly constituted a considerable source of employment, and at one period several were built for the West India trade; but this branch of occupation has greatly declined, only two vessels having been built and registered here in 1825. There are two extensive breweries, and the town is noted for the excellence of its beer. The number of vessels which entered from foreign parts in 1826 was forty-three British, and five foreign; and the number of those which cleared outwards, four British, and four foreign. The number of vessels belonging to Newhaven, in March 1828, was sixteen, averaging sixty-four tons each. Here is a custom-house; and a collector, comptroller, and harbour-master, are stationed at the port. A fair for pedlary is held on the 10th of October. The living is a discharged rectory, in the archdeaconry of Lewes, and diocese of Chichester, rated in the king's books at £8. 3. 4., and in the patronage of the Crown. The church, which is dedicated to St. Michael, and originally consisted of but one aisle and a tower, in the Norman style, has undergone enlargement; one hundred and seventy-five new sittings have been added, of which one hundred and twenty are free, and towards defraying the expense of which, the Incorporated Society for the enlargement of churches and chapels contributed £50: some windows, in the early style of English architecture, have been inserted on the south side. Near to and on the northern side of the churchyard is an obelisk, erected to commemorate the wreck of the Brazen sloop of war on the Ave rocks, near this town, during a violent storm on the morning of January 26th, 1800, when Captain Hancock and one hundred and three men were drowned, and only one was saved. A charity school, for children of both sexes, is supported by voluntary contributions. On Castle hill, about a mile from the town, westward of the mouth of the Ouse, are the remains of a military encampment; and the strata of the sub-soil of this eminence contains some curious minerals and fossils.

NEWHOLM, a joint township with Dunsley, in the parish of WHITBY, liberty of WHITBY-STRAND, North riding of the county of YORK, 2¼ miles (W.) from Whitby, containing, with Dunsley, 259 inhabitants.

NEWICK, a parish in the hundred of BARCOMB, rape of LEWES, county of SUSSEX, 4¾ miles (W.) from Uckfield, containing 540 inhabitants. The living is a rectory, in the archdeaconry of Lewes, and diocese of Chichester, rated in the king's books at £7. 17. 8½., and in the patronage of the Rev. T. B. Powell. The church, dedicated to St. Mary, is principally in the early English and decorated styles of architecture. George Venables Vernon and Louisa Barbara his wife, in 1771, founded and endowed, with a rent-charge of £50, a school for the education and clothing of twelve poor girls.

NEWINGTON, a parish in the hundred of MILTON, lathe of SCRAY, county of KENT, 3½ miles (W.) from Milton, containing 629 inhabitants. The living is a vicarage, in the archdeaconry and diocese of Canterbury, rated in the king's books at £14, and in the patronage of the Provost and Fellows of Eton College. The church, dedicated to St. Mary, is a handsome structure, principally in the early English style, with some windows in the decorated. There is a place of worship for Wesleyan Methodists. The village, which had formerly a market, is supposed to occupy the site of a town inhabited by the Britons, and after them by the Romans: the ancient Watling-street crosses the parish. In a field, called Crockfield, an abundance of Roman urns and other vessels has been found, lying in various positions, and frequently empty, which has induced an opinion that this was only the site of a Roman pottery, though eminent antiquaries have here fixed the station Durolevum, and suppose this field to have been a burial-place for the Romans stationed at the adjacent military works, numerous vestiges of which may still be traced, such as Julius Cæsar's-hill, Standard-hill, Key-street, anciently Caii Stratum, &c. There is a traditional account of a nunnery, and afterwards of a college of Secular canons, having existed here.

NEWINGTON, a parish in the hundred of EWELME, county of OXFORD, 4¾ miles (N. by E.) from Wallingford, containing, with the chapelry of Brightwell-Prior, the tythings of Brockhampton and Holcomb, and the liberty of Berrick-Prior, 445 inhabitants. The living is a vicarage, with Brightwell-Prior, in the peculiar jurisdiction and patronage of the Archbishop of Canterbury, rated in the king's books at £18. 13. 4. A small rent-charge was bequeathed by Mary White, in 1729, for teaching three children of the hamlet of Berwick.

NEWINGTON next HYTHE, a parish in the hundred of FOLKESTONE, lathe of SHEPWAY, county of KENT, 2½ miles (N. E. by N.) from Hythe, containing 498 inhabitants. The living is a vicarage, united to the rectory of Cheriton, in the archdeaconry and diocese of Canterbury, rated in the king's books at £7. 12. 6. The church, dedicated to St. Nicholas, is an embattled structure, partly in the decorated style of architecture. The ancient chapel of St. Nicholas, every vestige of which has disappeared, was once famous for the resort of fishermen to make offerings at the shrine of their patron saint, on escaping imminent dangers at sea. The Grand Military canal passes through a detached portion of the parish. From an eminence near the fine mansion of Beachborough is a noble prospect over the country, and across the channel to the coast of France. Roman coins have been dug up in the village, and in 1760, three human skeletons, with beads of agate, pebbles, glass, coral, and red earth, were discovered in levelling a fence.

NEWINGTON (ST. MARY), or NEWINGTON-BUTTS, a parish in the eastern division of the hundred of BRIXTON, county of SURREY, 1¾ mile (S.) from London, containing, with the hamlet of Walworth, 33,047 inhabitants. This parish obtained the adjunct by which it is distinguished from other parishes of the same name from the shooting butts anciently erected in it. It has, by the recent addition of numerous ranges of building in various parts, become one of the most populous parishes in the suburbs of the metropolis, and is inhabited by numerous families, whose residences are in general respectable, and in some instances distinguished by the pleasantness of their situation, and the style of their architecture. Among the more ancient of the buildings are a few which still preserve considerable vestiges of their original character; but by far the greater part of the parish consists of wide and extended ranges, of modern erection and appearance: the principal roads leading through the village, from the metropolis to Camberwell and Clapham, and the streets which generally diverge from them at right angles, are partially paved, and well lighted with gas, and the inhabitants are amply supplied with water by the New Lambeth water-works. Among the more recent improvements which have contributed to extend the parish, are the handsome ranges of houses on the north and east sides of Kennington-common, Doddington-grove, Surrey-square, and several lines of houses on the Kent road, together with those which have been erected in the vicinity of Trinity-square, in the centre of which a new district church has been built. The Dover and the Brighton roads diverge from a point in this parish, at the Elephant and Castle, where the number of coaches stopping and passing is estimated at about five hundred daily. The village is not distinguished by any particular branch of manufacture, or by any other trade than what it derives from its situation as a great thoroughfare, and its proximity to London. There is a manufactory for oil of vitriol on the east side of Kennington-common, which occupies three acres of ground, and between that and the Kent road are a smelting-house for lead and antimony, a tannery, a manufactory for glue, another for tobacco pipes, with manufactories for floor-cloth and carriages, and several nursery grounds. The parish is within the jurisdiction of the court of requests for the borough of Southwark, the authority of which was extended, by an act passed in the 46th of George III., to the recovery of debts under £5: it is also within the limits of the new police establishment. The sessions-house, in which the

quarter sessions for the county of Surrey are held regularly, is situated in that part of the parish which adjoins the borough of Southwark: it is a neat building of brick, containing a convenient court-room for the trial of prisoners, to which is a private communication from the adjoining prison, and rooms for the accommodation of the grand jury, the clerk of the peace, and other officers. The common gaol in Horsemonger-lane is a spacious building of brick ornamented with stone, containing nine wards for the classification of prisoners, with airing-yards, &c., and affording room for the reception of one hundred and fifty-six prisoners in separate cells. The Surrey asylum, for the reception, clothing, maintenance, and instruction of discharged prisoners, was instituted in 1824, under the patronage of His Royal Highness the Duke of Gloucester, and His Grace the Archbishop of Canterbury, and is supported by subscription: the building is handsomely constructed of brick, and is capable of receiving sixty inmates; there are at present twenty males and seven females in this institution; the former, after a due time, are apprenticed to different trades, with a small premium, and the latter placed out as servants.

The living is a rectory, in the exempt deanery of Croydon, which is within the peculiar jurisdiction of the Archbishop of Canterbury, rated in the king's books at £16, and in the patronage of the Bishop of Worcester. The church, dedicated to St. Mary, is a neat modern edifice of brick, with a small cupola and campanile turret surmounted by a dome; the interior is well arranged, and there are several handsome mural tablets: the churchyard, which is spacious, contains some ancient tombs and several good monuments. Two district churches were erected in this parish, in 1824 and 1825, by aid of the parliamentary commissioners, who granted one moiety of the expense, and lent the other moiety for eight years without interest, to be repaid by a rate on the inhabitants. The church dedicated to the Holy Trinity, in Trinity-square, is a handsome edifice in the Grecian style of architecture, with a portico of six fluted Corinthian columns, supporting a triangular pediment, and having a square tower ornamented with pillars of the Doric order, and surmounted by a campanile turret surrounded with pillars of the Corinthian order; the interior is appropriately ornamented, and contains two thousand and forty-eight sittings, of which seven hundred and seventy-one are free: the expense of its erection was £13,316. 4. The church dedicated to St. Peter, in the hamlet of Walworth, containing two thousand sittings, of which five hundred are free, was erected at an expense of £19,126. 13.: it is a spacious and handsome edifice of brick, ornamented with stone, having at the western entrance a receding portico of four Ionic columns, supporting a cornice and central balustrade, with a slender square tower, ornamented at the quoins with pilasters of the Corinthian order, and surmounted by an open campanile turret of graceful elevation, surrounded with Corinthian pillars, and crowned with a conical dome. The livings are perpetual curacies, in the patronage of the Vicar of Newington. There are two places of worship for Baptists, two for Independents, one for Wesleyan Methodists, and one for the followers of Johanna Southcote. The parochial charity, National, and Sunday schools, supported partly by endowment and partly by subscription, were united in 1820, and a handsome and commodious building erected for their use, containing, on the basement story, a school-room seventy-five feet in length and forty-five feet wide for boys, and on the upper story a room of similar dimensions for girls : in this establishment, which is calculated for the admission of one thousand children, there are at present four hundred boys and two hundred girls; of the former sixty-five, and of the latter fifty-five, are annually clothed. The female charity school, established in 1793, and a school of industry, opened in 1796, previously separate institutions, were united in 1818, and a neat and commodious school-house erected in Mount-street, by subscription; there are one hundred girls, who are clothed, and instructed in reading, writing, arithmetic, and in household work; and, when qualified to become useful servants, are placed in respectable families, and encouraged to good conduct by annual presents : this institution, which is under the direction of a president and a committee of ladies, is supported by subscription among the different dissenting congregations. The female school in South-street, established in 1810, is supported by subscription, and conducted by a committee of ladies : there are one hundred girls in this establishment, who are instructed on the plan of the British and Foreign Society. The school for boys, in Flint-street, conducted on the same system, was established in 1816, and a spacious school-room, capable of receiving four hundred boys, with a dwelling-house for the master, was erected by subscription : there are at present three hundred and twenty boys in this institution. The York-street female charity school, founded in 1810, chiefly by the congregation of Independents, is conducted under the superintendence of a committee of ladies, with a view to qualify the scholars for service in respectable families : there are fifty girls, who are instructed in reading, writing, arithmetic, and needlework, and of whom thirty are annually clothed. In the parish work-house forty-three boys and twenty-five girls are clothed, maintained, and instructed in reading, writing, and arithmetic, and, at a suitable age, placed out apprentices with a premium of £7 each: in connexion with the work-house, and within the walls, is a manufactory for ropes, twine, and door-mats. The southern quadrangle of the Fishmongers' almshouses, consisting of twenty additional tenements, founded in 1721, by James Hulbert, whose statue is placed on a pedestal in the centre of the area, is within the parish; the older portion of the almshouses, erected by that company about a century before, is in the parish of St. George the Martyr : the more ancient part consists of an outer and an inner quadrangle, comprising twenty-three tenements, of two rooms each, for the residence of decayed members of the company, who receive twelve shillings per week, if married, and eight shillings, if single: the buildings, of brick ornamented with stone, are of the Elizabethan style : the entrance of the outer quadrangle is a chapel, with a window over the archway, in the early English style, and a small belfry turret, and on one side of the inner quadrangle is a hall, with some painted glass, in which the wardens of the company hold their meetings for the business of the charity; behind are extensive gardens pleasantly laid out, and communicating with those of the additional buildings, which are of somewhat more modern appearance. There are also some almshouses in

Cross-street, under the superintendence of the Drapers' Company. Of the hospital of our Lady and St. Katherine, which existed here till the middle of the sixteenth century, there are no vestiges.

NEWINGTON (NORTH), a hamlet in the parish of BROUGHTON, hundred of BLOXHAM, county of OXFORD, 2¾ miles (W. by S.) from Banbury, containing 291 inhabitants.

NEWINGTON (SOUTH), a parish in the hundred of WOOTTON, county of OXFORD, 5 miles (W. N. W.) from Deddington, containing 428 inhabitants. The living is a discharged vicarage, in the archdeaconry and diocese of Oxford, rated in the king's books at £8, endowed with £600 private benefaction, £400 royal bounty, and £900 parliamentary grant, and in the patronage of the Rector and Fellows of Exeter College, Oxford. The church, dedicated to St. Peter, has lately received an addition of two hundred and twenty-four sittings, of which one hundred and forty-six are free, the Incorporated Society for the enlargement of churches and chapels having granted £100 towards the expense. The small river Swere separates this parish from those of Milcombe and Wigginton.

NEWINGTON (STOKE), a parish in the Finsbury division of the hundred of OSSULSTONE, county of MIDDLESEX, 3 miles (N. by E.) from London, containing 2670 inhabitants. The village consists principally of a long street, extending from Kingsland road to Stamford-hill, and on the high road from the metropolis to Cambridge. The eastern side of this street is within the parish of Hackney; and from the western side, near the centre, branches off a street leading to the parish church. These streets are paved and lighted with gas, and the inhabitants are supplied with water from the New River, which pursues a serpentine course through the parish, in which are a continuous line of respectable private houses, and several detached handsome residences, among the latter the ancient manor-house is particularly worthy of notice, as also a modern mansion near the church; the grounds around which are laid out with much taste, and the New River winding through them gives to the whole an agreeable and pleasing effect. Here are several extensive nursery gardens, but no distinguishing manufacture, the trade of the place depending on the resident population, and on its situation as a thoroughfare on a great public road. The New River Company are constructing a large reservoir, and erecting a steam engine in the parish. Courts leet and baron for the manor are held annually. The living is a rectory, in the peculiar jurisdiction of the Dean and Chapter of St. Paul's, rated in the king's books at £10, and in the patronage of the Prebendary of Newington in the Cathedral Church of St. Paul. The church, dedicated to St. Mary, is a low building, re-erected by William Patten, Esq., lessee of the manor, in 1563, and since repeatedly enlarged. Considerable alterations have recently been made, and a new gallery erected, a steeple has also been added to the tower : it contains several handsome monuments. There are places of worship for the Society of Friends, Independents, and Unitarians. A charity school, with an endowment arising from the benefactions of Thomas Stock and others, was founded in the early part of the last century, which, having fallen into decay, was revived in 1790, with the aid of subscriptions and charity sermons; and since that time an additional fund has been formed of £1100 three per cent. consols., from legacies, donations, and savings of income. Thirty boys and twenty-five girls are educated and clothed, and some of them apprenticed with a premium of £8. The joint salaries of the master and mistress amount to £100 per annum. A school for the education and clothing of fourteen poor girls is supported by dissenters. There is also an infant school. A brick gateway, with a pointed arch, on the north side of Church-street, is the only part now standing of the buildings belonging to the old manor-house. Near the church is a walk between trees, called Queen Elizabeth's walk: and at Newington resided her favourite, Robert Dudley, Earl of Leicester, and his contemporary, Edward Vere, Earl of Oxford. Dr. Isaac Watts, an eminent dissenting divine and poet, after having passed the last thirty years of his life at the mansion of Sir Thomas Abney, died here November 25th, 1748. Among the other distinguished residents in this parish, were the republican general, Fleetwood; Daniel Defoe, author of Robinson Crusoe; Adam Anderson, who wrote a valuable "History of Commerce;" Thomas Day, the author of the History of Sandford and Merton, and other popular productions; Howard, the philanthropist; Dr. John Aikin, compiler of the "General Biography;" and his sister, the celebrated Mrs. Barbauld.

NEWINGTON-BAGPATH, a parish in the upper division of the hundred of BERKELEY, county of GLOUCESTER, 4¾ miles (W. N. W.) from Tetbury, containing 247 inhabitants. The living is a rectory, with the perpetual curacy of Owlpen, in the archdeaconry and diocese of Gloucester, rated in the king's books at £14, and in the patronage of Robert Kingscote, Esq. The church is dedicated to St. Bartholomew.

NEWLAND, a liberty in that part of the parish of HURST which is in the hundred of SONNING, county of BERKS, 3¾ miles (W. by S.) from Wokingham, containing 264 inhabitants.

NEWLAND, a parish in the hundred of ST. BRIAVELLS, county of GLOUCESTER, comprising the chapelries of Breem and Coleford, and the tythings of Clearwell, Lee-Bailey, and Newland, and containing 3383 inhabitants, of which number, 486 are in the tything of Newland, 4 miles (S. E. by S.) from Monmouth. The living is a discharged vicarage, in the archdeaconry and diocese of Gloucester, rated in the king's books at £18. 6. 10½., and in the patronage of the Bishop of Llandaff. The church, dedicated to All Saints, is a large structure, with a handsome western tower ornamented with pinnacles and open-worked battlements: adjoining the churchyard is a free school, also an almshouse for four poor persons of each sex, both founded by Edward Bell, who, in 1651, endowed them with an annuity of £20: the annual income, with subsequent donations, has been raised to upwards of £180, of which £40 is paid for teaching fifteen children, the schoolmaster having also apartments in the school-house: £104 a year is received by the eight alms-people, 5s. per week being paid to each, and the residue expended in fuel and clothing for them, and in repairing the premises of both establishments. There are also two charity schools, conducted on the National system. The navigable river Wye forms the western boundary of the parish, through which run several rapid rivulets, and the rail-road from

Colford to Monmouth. Iron and coal mines abound, and limestone may be obtained, in the neighbourhood. Redbrook, where there is now a considerable manufactory for tin plates, was formerly the site of the earliest copper-smelting furnaces in England. The remains of High Meadow House, which was garrisoned by the troops of Charles I., when the parliament had possession of Gloucester, are still visible. There is a spring of water in Birchamp, which in purity is not inferior to St. Ann's well at Malvern.

NEWLAND, a township in the parish of ULVERSTONE, hundred of LONSDALE, county palatine of LANCASTER, 2¾ miles (N. N. E.) from Ulverstone, containing 440 inhabitants.

NEWLAND, a chapelry in the parish of GREAT MALVERN, lower division of the hundred of PERSHORE, county of WORCESTER, 5¾ miles (S. W.) from Worcester, containing 125 inhabitants. The living is a perpetual curacy, in the archdeaconry and diocese of Worcester, endowed with £10 per annum private benefaction, and £400 royal bounty, and in the patronage of the Vicar of Malvern. The chapel is dedicated to St. Michael. Courts leet and baron are occasionally held here.

NEWLAND, an extra-parochial liberty, in the lower division of the wapentake of AGBRIGG, West riding of the county of YORK, 3 miles (N. E.) from Wakefield, containing 46 inhabitants. There was formerly an old chapel near the mansion house, but it was taken down about fifty years ago. Courts leet and baron are annually held here, under the styles of " the Court Leet of our Sovereign Lord the King," and "the Great Court Baron of the Manor of Newland cum Woodhouse Moor," which was parcel ·of the possessions of the Knights Hospitallers, who, in the reign of John, established here a preceptory of their order, valued at the dissolution at £202. 3. 8. per annum.

NEWLAND, a township in the parish of DRAX, lower division of the wapentake of BARKSTONE-ASH, West riding of the county of YORK, 4½ miles (N. E. by E.) from Snaith, containing 269 inhabitants. Charles Read, in 1669, bequeathed land and £2000, directing the income to be applied for teaching all the poor children of the parish, and for the clothing and maintenance of six poor people and six boys of the parish of Drax.

NEWLANDS, a chapelry in that part of the parish of CROSTHWAITE which is in ALLERDALE ward above Darwent, county of CUMBERLAND, 5 miles (S. W. by W.) from Keswick, containing 115 inhabitants. The living is a perpetual curacy, in the archdeaconry and diocese of Carlisle, endowed with £1200 royal bounty, and in the patronage of the Vicar of Crosthwaite. The chapel is situated near the small village of Little Town, which, lying under a mountain knot, does not receive the rays of the sun from Martinmas to Candlemas. There is a place of worship for Wesleyan Methodists. A fair for sheep is held at Little Town on the first Friday in September. Rich copper-mines were formerly in operation here, from which so much gold and silver was extracted as to entitle them to be considered royal property; upon which a law suit was instituted, in the reign of Elizabeth, against the Earl of Northumberland, in whose lordship the mines were discovered, which terminated in favour of the crown, but since the parliamentary war, in which the original works were destroyed, and most of the miners slain, they have been worked on a much smaller scale. The ruins of smelting-houses and other buildings may still be traced on the banks of the Bure. Immense quantities of lead-ore have also been raised in the neighbourhood, but the mines are now comparatively unproductive. A quarry of fine slate for roofing has lately been opened, and at Stairs there is a mill for carding wool.

NEWLANDS, a township in the parish of BYWELL ST. PETER, eastern division of TINDALE ward, county of NORTHUMBERLAND, 12½ miles (S. E. by E.) from Hexham, containing 154 inhabitants.

NEWLAND-SIDE, a township in the parish of STANHOPE, north-western division of DARLINGTON ward, county palatine of DURHAM, 1½ mile (S. W.) from Stanhope, containing 763 inhabitants. There is a smelting mill for lead-ore at Bollihope.

NEWLYN, a parish in the hundred of PYDER, county of CORNWALL, 2¼ miles (W. N. W.) from St. Michael, containing, with part of the borough of St. Michael, or Midshall, 1045 inhabitants. The living is a vicarage, in the archdeaconry of Cornwall, and diocese of Exeter, rated in the king's books at £16. 13. 4., and in the patronage of the Bishop of Exeter. The Independents and Wesleyan Methodists have each a place of worship here, and there is a small endowed school. Several rapid streams run through the parish, in which are some chalybeate springs, and a valuable lead mine. The petty sessions for the division are held here, on the last Monday in every month. At Cargol there was formerly a palace belonging to the bishops of Exeter, to one of whom a market and a fair were granted in 1312 : fairs are held on the first Tuesday in October and November 8th. In this parish is the fine old mansion of Trerice, built in 1572, and once the seat of a branch of the Arundel family.

NEWMARKET, a market town, comprising the parish of St. Mary, in the hundred of LACKFORD, county of SUFFOLK, and the parish of All Saints, in the hundred of CHEVELEY, county of CAMBRIDGE, 13 miles (N. E. by E.) from Cambridge, and 61 (N. N. E.) from London, on the road to Norwich, containing 2514 inhabitants. The earliest account of this town has reference to the year 1227, when it is supposed to have derived its name from a market then recently established, which is said to have been removed hither, on account of the plague raging at Exning, a village about two miles distant, where was, probably, the parochial church : and in the time of Edward III. it gave name to Thomas Merks, or de Novo Mercatu, Bishop of Carlisle, who was probably a native of the place. A house, called the King's house, was originally built here by James I., for the purpose of enjoying the diversion of hunting, and the subsequent reputation of this town for horse-racing seems to have arisen from the spirit and swiftness of some Spanish horses, which having been wrecked with the vessels of the Armada, were thrown ashore on the coast of Galloway and brought hither. Its celebrity greatly increased in the reign of Charles II., the grand patron of the turf, who rebuilt the King's house, which had fallen into decay during the civil war, and frequently honoured the races with his presence. On the 22nd of March, 1683, being the time of the races, the King, Queen, and Duke of York were present, but a sudden

conflagration compelled them to return hastily to London, to which event some writers have attributed the defeat of the Rye-house plot : by this disaster a great part of the town was destroyed, and the damage was estimated at £20,000. A second conflagration happened about the beginning of the last century. At the close of the civil war, Charles I. was removed from the house of Lady Cutts, of Childerley, to Newmarket, on the 9th of June, 1647, and remained here about ten days.

The town consists principally of one street, the north side of which is in the county of Suffolk, and the south in that of Cambridge : it is neither lighted nor paved ; the houses are modern and well built, and some, erected for the occasional residence of visitors, are handsome : the inhabitants are supplied with water from springs. Coffee-houses, billiard-rooms, and others, furnish appropriate accommodation for all meetings, preliminary to the races. The race-course and training-grounds are the finest in the kingdom ; the former is on a grassy heath near the town, and in the county of Cambridge, extending in length four miles : the training-ground is more than a mile and a half long, on a very gentle acclivity, admirably adapted to keep the horses in wind. The races are held seven times in the year, and are distinguished as the Craven meeting, commencing on the Monday in Easter week ; the first and second spring meetings, the former on the Monday fortnight following, and the latter a fortnight afterwards ; the July meeting ; the first and second October meetings, and the third October, or Houghton meeting, the first of these commencing on the Monday preceding the first Thursday in that month : the king gives two plates annually. The palace erected by King James has been sold, and converted into shops : the one added to the original structure by King Charles is standing, and was the residence of the late Duke of York during the meetings ; belonging to it are extensive stables for the king's horses. The training of race-horses is a source of extensive profit, several of them, among which are some of the finest horses in the world, being constantly exported, at exceedingly high prices : about four hundred are here during the greater part of the year ; and it is computed, that the weekly consumption of oats in the town alone, amounts to the amazing quantity of five hundred quarters. The market, which was granted or confirmed in 1227, is held on Tuesday ; and there are fairs on Whit-Tuesday and November 8th, the latter being extensively supplied with cattle, horses, corn, butter, cheese, hops, &c. The county magistrates hold petty sessions here every Tuesday ; and a court leet is held occasionally.

The parishes of St. Mary and All Saints are in the archdeaconry of Sudbury, and diocese of Norwich ; the former is a discharged rectory, consolidated with the vicarage of Wood-Ditton, rated in the king's books at £4. 15. 2½., and in the patronage of the Duke of Rutland : the church is a handsome structure with a fine tower and spire. The latter is a perpetual curacy, endowed with £400 royal bounty, and in the patronage of the Bishop of Norwich. There is a place of worship for Independents. Free schools are supported by a donation of £50 per annum from Queen Anne, which is equally divided, after the deduction of fees of the Exchequer, between the master and the mistress, for which they are required to teach twenty-one boys and twenty-one girls : a National school having been recently established, the twenty-one boys on Queen Anne's foundation are instructed there as free scholars; the remainder, being about one hundred and ten, are paid for by the subscribers; the girls, instructed by the schoolmistress, are provided with cloaks and bonnets. About a mile and a half from the town is a remarkable excavation, called the "Devil's Dyke," extending nearly in a straight line for seven miles, and being in some places above one hundred feet in width: this work, unquestionably of very remote antiquity, has been attributed to the Britons anterior to the time of Cæsar, and by some to Uffa, the first king of the East Angles; but, notwithstanding that much pains have been taken in the research, no authentic account has ever yet appeared of this remarkable monument of human industry and perseverance: it serves for the boundary between the dioceses of Norwich and Ely. Several Roman coins were found near Newmarket heath, in the year 1750.

NEW-MILLS, a manufacturing district in the parish of GLOSSOP, hundred of HIGH PEAK, county of DERBY, 21 miles (N. W.) from Derby, and 170 (N. W. by N.) from London, containing about 5000 inhabitants. Its original name was Bowden-Middle-Cale. Situated along the north bank of the Guyt, and reaching from Kinder-Scout to Mellor, it formerly comprised seven hamlets; but about a century ago it was subdivided, three of the hamlets remaining attached to Hayfield, and the other four, Beard, Ollerset, Whitle, and Thornset, being formed into a township: formerly the whole of the inhabitants of the hamlets included in Bowden-Middle-Cale were accustomed to grind their corn at a common mill in Hayfield, but upon their subdivision, a new mill was erected upon the river Kinder, in the hamlet of Ollerset, and the name of New Mills was, in consequence, conferred on the four above-mentioned hamlets, the inhabitants of which ground their corn here. The Kinder derives its source from the mountain of Kinder-Scout, and, separating the county of Derby from that of Chester, falls into the river Guyt at a place called the Tor. The appellation of New Mills is yet more definitely applied to a cluster of factories and houses, which rise one above another from the brink of the river to the summit of the Crags, a height of several hundred feet, and also extend along the turnpike-road, as far as London Place. The original branches of manufacture in this district were those of paper and cloth, which have been superseded by cotton, calico-printing, and bleaching works, &c.: coal mines abound in the neighbourhood, and contain some veins of lead-ore. In the year 1821, Mr. John Potts conceived the idea of adapting the method used by engravers in the potteries to the purposes of calico-printing, with the view of producing a more durable and brilliant effect than had hitherto been obtained in that branch of the art; his experiment was crowned with complete success, and proved the origin of a style of engraving which has been adopted by every calico engraver in that branch, not only in Great Britain and Ireland, but throughout the whole of Europe and the United States: the engraving establishment, belonging to the firm of Potts, Oliver, and Potts, is a neat and spacious fabric of red brick, tastefully decorated with various statues and vases, and affords employment to about one hundred artists; in the grounds at the back of the works is an extensive picture gallery, containing specimens of painting in oil and water colours, by Mr. John Potts: this repository promises, at no very distant period, to become an object of considerable interest to the scientific traveller. A local subscription, amounting to £1000, has been raised towards the erection of a new church; the sum of £2500 has been granted by the parliamentary commissioners, in aid of the work; and a piece of ground has been given by Lord George Cavendish, for the site of the edifice, which will contain five hundred free sittings. The living will be a perpetual curacy, in the archdeaconry of Derby, and diocese of Lichfield and Coventry, and in the patronage of the Vicar of Glossop. There are places of worship for Independents, and Primitive and Wesleyan Methodists. A charity school in the hamlet of Whitle, erected by subscription, affords gratuitous instruction to nine poor children, and the master receives about £10. 10. per annum, arising from bequests by Mary Trickett, in 1712, and Ralph Bowden, in 1730; besides which, on a division of the common lands of Whitle, an extensive allotment was assigned towards the support of the school.

NEWMINSTER-ABBEY, a township in that part of the parish of MORPETH which is in the western division of CASTLE ward, county of NORTHUMBERLAND, containing 79 inhabitants. An abbey of Cistercian monks from Fountains, in honour of the Blessed Virgin Mary, was founded here, in 1198, by Ranulph de Merlay, and Julian his wife, which at the dissolution had a revenue valued at £140. 10. 4.: of this once magnificent structure only a part of the gateway remains.

NEWNHAM, a market town and parish in the hundred of WESTBURY, county of GLOUCESTER, 11½ miles (W. S. W.) from Gloucester, and 116 (W. by N.) from London, containing 1012 inhabitants. This town appears to have originated in a ford over the river Severn, formed by a ridge of rocks and a sand-bank, the shifting of which latter, in 1802, rendered the river no longer fordable. Here was anciently a castle, which constituted one of the fortresses on the Welch frontier, in the times of our Norman kings, but there are no traces of it. The town is situated on the western bank of the river, which is navigable, and across which there is a ferry to Arlingham. A harbour for vessels of one hundred and fifty tons' burden was constructed about eighty years ago, and some coasting trade is carried on, though the difficult navigation of the river near the town has contributed to lessen its commerce, much of which has been transferred to a port, a few miles to the south, called Gatcombe. A verdegris manufactory, and ship-building, afford employment to some of the inhabitants; and at Aylesford, in this parish, are large forges for working iron and making iron-wire. There being in the neighbourhood extensive iron and coal mines, and the carriage of their produce is facilitated by the Bullo Pill railway, which passes from the marble works on the Severn southward of the town, into the Forest of Dean, through a tunnel one thousand and sixty yards in extent, and also by the Berkeley canal. The market, now very inconsiderable, is on Friday; and fairs are held on the 11th of June and 18th of October. The government was vested in a mayor and burgesses in the reign of Edward I., but there are now few relics of its former importance, except a sword of state, said to have been the gift of King John : two constables, locally termed *Beams*, are appointed ; but, until the beginning of the present century, the inhabitants annually celebrated the election of a mayor and six aldermen. The lord of the manor holds a court leet yearly ; and petty sessions for the Forest of Dean are held here and at Woolaston alternately. Newnham was returned as one of the five boroughs in Gloucestershire, on a mandate from the Crown, in the ninth of Edward I., and is said formerly to have sent two members to parliament. The living is a perpetual curacy, in the archdeaconry and diocese of Gloucester, and in the patronage of the Mayor and Corporation of that city. The church, which is dedicated to St. Peter, and stands on a cliff near the river, contains some portions of Norman architecture, especially the arched entrance into the chancel, ornamented with zig-zag mouldings, and supposed to have belonged to a more ancient edifice. There is a place of worship for Independents. Fifteen poor boys are annually clothed from the funds of a charity, called "Jocham's charity;" James Jocham having, by will, dated December 21st, 1764, given the interest of £1000 for ever, for this and other benevolent purposes. There is also a savings bank.

NEWNHAM, a parish in the hundred of CASHIO, or liberty of ST. ALBAN'S, county of HERTFORD, 3 miles (N.) from Baldock, containing 112 inhabitants. The living is a discharged vicarage, in the archdeaconry of St. Alban's, and diocese of London, rated in the king's books at £5, endowed with £400 royal bounty. P. Yorke, Esq. was patron in 1796. The church is dedicated to St. Vincent.

NEWNHAM, a parish in the hundred of FAVERSHAM, lathe of SCRAY, county of KENT, 4½ miles (S. W. by W.) from Faversham, containing 356 inhabitants. The living is a discharged vicarage, in the archdeaconry and diocese of Canterbury, rated in the king's books at £5. 12. 6., endowed with £200 private benefaction, and £400 royal bounty, and in the patronage of Miss Thorncroft and Mrs. Hill. The church, dedicated to St. Peter and St. Paul, is principally in the early English style of architecture. A fair is held on the festival of St. Peter. There is a small charity school in the parish.

NEWNHAM, a parish in the hundred of FAWSLEY, county of NORTHAMPTON, 2½ miles (S. S. E.) from Daventry, containing 574 inhabitants. The living is a perpetual curacy, with the vicarage of Badby, in the archdeaconry of Northampton, and diocese of Peterborough. The church, dedicated to St. Michael, exhibits portions in the various styles of English architecture. The business of lace-making has been introduced into this parish. Thomas Randolph, the poet and dramatist, was born here, in 1605.

NEWNHAM, a parish in the hundred of BASINGSTOKE, Basingstoke division of the county of SOUTHAMPTON, 4½ miles (E. by N.) from Basingstoke, containing 266 inhabitants. The living is a rectory, with the perpetual curacy of Maplederwell, in the archdeaconry and diocese of Winchester, rated in the king's books at £17. 17. 1., and in the patronage of the Provost and Fellows of Queen's College, Oxford. The church is dedicated to St. Nicholas.

NEWNHAM, a hamlet in the parish of LINDRIDGE, lower division of the hundred of OSWALDSLOW, though locally in the upper division of the hundred of Doddingtree, county of WORCESTER, 4 miles (E.) from Tenbury. The population is returned with the chapelry of Knighton upon Teame.

NEWNHAM (KING'S), a parish in the Rugby division of the hundred of KNIGHTLOW, county of WARWICK, 4¼ miles (N. W. by W.) from Rugby, containing 134 inhabitants. The living is a vicarage, united to the rectory of Church-Lawford, in the archdeaconry of Coventry, and diocese of Lichfield and Coventry, rated in the king's books at £5. The Oxford canal crosses the north-eastern angle of the parish ; and on the bank of the river Avon is a once celebrated bath, to which the water is conveyed from a chalybeate spring, about a mile distant ; it is impregnated with alum, and said to be efficacious in scorbutic complaints, and in healing fresh wounds.

NEWNHAM-MURREN, a parish in the hundred of LANGTREE, county of OXFORD, 1 mile (S.) from Wallingford, containing 260 inhabitants. The living is a perpetual curacy, annexed to the vicarage of North Stoke, in the archdeaconry and diocese of Oxford. The church is dedicated to St. Mary.

NEWNTON (LONG), a parish in the hundred of MALMESBURY, county of WILTS, 3¼ miles (N. N. W.) from Malmesbury, containing 306 inhabitants. The living is a discharged rectory, in the archdeaconry of Wilts, and diocese of Salisbury, rated in the king's books at £8. 5. Thomas Estcourt, Esq. was patron in 1808. The church is dedicated to the Holy Trinity. Elizabeth Hodges, in 1723, and Amy Haddon, subsequently, bequeathed each a trifling rent-charge towards the support of a school.

NEWPARKS, a liberty in the parish of THURLASTON, hundred of SPARKENHOE, county of LEICESTER, 6½ miles (S. W. by W.) from Leicester, containing 17 inhabitants.

NEWPORT, a borough in the parish of ST. STEPHENS, northern division of EAST hundred, county of CORNWALL, adjoining the town of Launceston, and 214 miles (W. S. W.) from London. The population is returned with the parish. This place is separated from Launceston only by a small rivulet, and it appears to have been joined with it in the parliamentary representation, under the name of Dunheved. Two representatives have been separately returned from it since the time of Edward VI : the right of election is in the burgageholders, and inhabitants paying scot and lot : the number of voters is about sixty ; and two vianders, appointed at the court leet held for the manor, are the returning officers : the influence of the Duke of Northumberland is predominant.

NEWPORT, a parish (formerly a market town) in the hundred of UTTLESFORD, county of ESSEX, 3½ miles (S. S. W.) from Saffron-Walden, containing 852 inhabitants. The living is a discharged vicarage, in the jurisdiction of the Commissary of Essex and Herts, concurrently with the Consistorial Court of the Bishop of London, rated in the king's books at £9. 10., endowed with £200 private benefaction, and £200 royal bounty, and in the patronage of the Crown. The church, dedicated to St. Mary, is a fine structure in the later English style, having a lofty western tower, crowned with embattled turrets. There is a place of worship for Independents. A free grammar school was founded in

1586, by Joyce Frankland and William Saxie, her son, who endowed it with a rent-charge and other property, now producing together an annual income of about £200. At the northern end of the village are slight remains of an hospital, founded, in the reign of John, by Richard de Newport, the revenue of which, at the dissolution, was £23. 10. 8. Two fairs are held, on Easter-Tuesday and November 17th, but the market has been long disused.

NEWPORT, a sea-port and incorporated market town, in the parish of St. Woollos, upper division of the hundred of Wentlloog, county of Monmouth, 25 miles (S.W.) from Monmouth, and 146 (W.) from London. The population is returned with the parish. This place, called by Giraldus *Novus Burgus*, or *New Town*, in contradistinction to the ancient city of Caerleon, arose out of the declining greatness of that celebrated station. Here Robert, Earl of Gloucester, natural son of Henry I., erected a castle for the defence of his possessions, whence it was denominated *Castell Newydd*, or *New Castle*: from him it descended through several noble families, till, on the execution of Edward, Duke of Buckingham, it was, together with the lordship, seized by Henry VIII. The town is pleasantly situated on the river Usk, which is navigable for vessels of large size, and crossed by an elegant stone bridge, about four miles from its junction with the Severn: it consists principally of a long narrow street, which extends from an eminence, on which is the parish church, to the river, and forms part of the mail road from Bristol to Milford-Haven; the streets are paved, and brilliantly lighted with gas; and the inhabitants are supplied with water under an act of parliament obtained in the 7th of George IV. Several new and handsome buildings in progress evince the rapid improvement of the town. Book-clubs and a reading-room have been established; and races are held in the first week in July. Newport possesses a good haven, and, by means of its river and a canal which communicates with it, has become a place of great trade. The chief articles of export are, iron and coal from the counties of Monmouth and Brecknock, and tin-plate from the neighbouring districts, which, with other commodities, are shipped here for Bristol and the adjacent counties, also for Ireland, France, the Mediterranean, and America: the exports for 1829 were, of iron, one hundred and eight thousand seven hundred and twenty-six tons; of coal, four hundred and seventy-one thousand six hundred and seventy-five tons: the imports consist of provisions and other articles of general consumption. The number of vessels which entered inwards from foreign ports in 1826, was fifteen British and twelve foreign; and the number which cleared outwards, fifty-two British and twenty-two foreign; and the number of vessels belonging to the port in 1828, was twelve of one hundred tons', and thirty-nine below that burden. Ship-building is extensively carried on; nine ships were built and registered here in 1825, and ten in 1826. Two branches diverge from the main ca-

nal, which passes through the town, one of which unites with the Brecon and Abergavenny canal: a rail-road, consisting of three lines, leads hence to the iron-works, which are about twenty-four miles distant. Here is a custom-house, and a collector and a comptroller of the customs are stationed at the port. The markets are on Wednesday and Saturday; and fairs are held on Ascension-day, April 30th, September 19th, and November 6th, for cattle of all kinds; during their continuance courts of pie-powder are held. The first charter appears to have been granted by Edward II., but that under which the town is now governed is dated in the 21st of James I. The corporation consists of a mayor and twelve aldermen, with a recorder and steward: the mayor is elected by the steward of the manor, and on his election nominates two water-bailiffs for the port, two for the town, constables, clerk of the market, and other officers: vacancies in the court of aldermen, and the offices of recorder and town clerk, are filled up by the corporation. The mayor, two senior aldermen, and the steward of the manor, are justices of the peace, with power to hold courts of session for offences committed within the borough, which has not been exercised for the last twenty years, all offenders being committed for trial to the house of correction for the county. A court of requests, for the recovery of debts to any amount, formerly held by the mayor, is also disused. The sheriffs' county court is held here, alternately with Monmouth, every month. Newport returns one member to parliament, conjointly with Monmouth and Usk: the right of election is in the resident burgage inhabitants: the number of voters is about one hundred, and the mayor is the returning officer. The freedom is obtained by birth, marriage, apprenticeship within the borough, gift, and purchase.

The parish church of St. Woollos is situated at the outskirts of this town; the tower is said to have been built by Henry III., as a reward for the successful resistance of the inhabitants to Simon Montfort, Earl of Leicester, and was formerly ornamented with the statue of that monarch, part of which is still preserved: the church exhibits specimens of various styles of architecture; the nave is Norman, and is entered by a fine arch of that style; the aisles are Anglo-Norman. A mariners' church, for the accommodation of seamen entering this port, has been recently constructed between Newport and Pillgwenlly, on the Caerdiff road. There are two places of worship for Baptists, four for Independents, two for Wesleyan Methodists, and a Roman Catholic chapel. A Lancasterian school for boys, and a National school for girls, together capable of accommodating about three hundred children, are supported by voluntary contributions: in 1824, another school for boys, on the National system, was erected by Rowley Lascelles, Esq., for the instruction of the children of Pillgwenlly; it is under the superintendence and management of the directors of the Tredegar Iron Company and is supported by means of subscription. The only vestiges of an ancient castle, now converted into a large brewery, are the external walls and three strong towers: this fortress was evidently intended as a protection to the inhabitants of the surrounding country, from the incursions of the Normans and the English, when Monmouthshire formed a part of the principality of Wales.

Corporate Seal.

NEWPORT, an incorporated market town and parish, in the Newport division of the hundred of BRADFORD (South), county of SALOP, 19 miles (E. N. E.) from Shrewsbury, and 139 (N. W. by N.) from London, containing 2343 inhabitants. This town is situated near the line of the Roman Watling-street, on the north-east border of the county, and contains some respectable dwelling-houses: it sustained a loss, estimated at £30,000, from a fire in the year 1665. The inhabitants are supplied with water from large cisterns, which are filled from a neighbouring spring, by means of a watercourse and pipes, kept in repair from the proceeds of some property vested in the corporation: in the vicinity are mines of coal and iron, and quarries of limestone. A branch canal, which connects the Birmingham and Liverpool with the Shrewsbury canal, passes a little to the north of this town. The market is on Saturday; and fairs are held on the first Tuesday in February, the Saturday before Palm-Sunday, May 28th, July 27th, Sept. 25th and December 10th, principally for live stock. The earliest municipal privileges were granted by Henry I., and confirmed by charters of succeeding sovereigns, until the time of Edward VI.: the corporation consists of a high steward, deputy steward, two bailiffs, and about twenty-five burgesses. Courts leet are held by the joint lords of the manor, as are also petty sessions for the Newport division of the hundred. Under the provisions of an act passed in the 4th of George III., a trust was formed, for the purpose of enclosing a tract of waste land, one hundred and twelve acres in extent, on which each householder had the right of pasturage for one milch cow, directing the rental to be appropriated to the repairs of the streets, market-hall (which was erected at the expense of William Adams, Esq.), and the market cross. A bridge trust was formed in 1750, having the control of funds arising from enclosures, which are applied to general improvements.

The living is a perpetual curacy, in the archdeaconry of Salop, and diocese of Lichfield and Coventry, and in the patronage of the Crown. The church, which is dedicated to St. Nicholas, anciently belonged to the abbey of St. Peter and St. Paul, in Shrewsbury, and was alienated, by permission of Henry VI., to Thomas Draper and his heirs, by whom it was made collegiate, for a warden and four lay chaplains: the structure is principally in the ancient style of English architecture, with a square tower, but the aisles have been rebuilt with brick. There is a place of worship for Independents. The free grammar school was built at the expense of William Adams, Esq., a native of this place, who, by indenture, dated November 27th, 1656, assigned certain lands for the support of a master and an usher, for the endowment of four exhibitions at any of the colleges in Oxford or Cambridge, for the erection and endowment of four almshouses for as many poor persons, for annually apprenticing three poor children, and for other purposes: this grant was confirmed by two acts of parliament, obtained in 1660 and 1661, by which the master and four wardens of the Company of Haberdashers were incorporated governors; and the property thus appropriated was exempted from the payment of all taxes and assessments, parochial and parliamentary. The land belonging to the charity, in 1820, comprised about eight hundred and eighty-three acres, yielding an annual income of £957. 3. 6., which, by the dividends on stock,

was increased to £1330 per annum. In consequence of applications made to the court of Chancery, in 1797 and 1808, for an extension of the plan of this charity, a decree was issued, pursuant to which the master receives an increased salary of £150 per annum, the usher one of £75, each of the four exhibitioners £22. 10., the resident minister £60, each of the four alms-people £19. 10., each of the three apprentices £18, twenty poor persons free of the Company of Haberdashers £3. 15. each, a writing-master £45, the receiver £21, various incidental charges increasing the expenditure to about £815 per annum. By the statutes of the founder, the number of boys was limited to eighty, to be chosen from the boys in the town and its vicinity; these being inadequate to supply the number, boys are admitted indiscriminately from other parts, and are instructed in the usual course of classical and English literature, preparatory to entering the University. The master and usher are respectively appointed by the governors, each possessing a rent-free residence. This school also enjoys the benefit of four exhibitions founded by Mr. Careswell for an account of which, see BRIDGENORTH. An English school, originating in a free grammar school founded prior to the time of Edward VI., was endowed by subsequent benefactions, producing an annual income of £49. 1.; from fifty to sixty children are educated. Almshouses for the residence of four poor aged persons, who receive weekly allowances, were also founded by Mr. Adams, who gave a sum for annually apprenticing three poor children. The Town's almshouses, for four poor females, were built in 1446, at the expense of William Glover of this town, and are endowed with £70 per annum. Various other charitable benefactions, amounting to nearly £200 per annum, are distributed amongst the poor. Tom Brown, a witty, but licentious, poet of the seventeenth century, was educated at the free school, and born here, or at Shiffnall.

NEWPORT, a borough, market town, and parish, having separate jurisdiction, though locally in the parish of Carisbrooke, liberty of WEST MEDINA, Isle of Wight division of the county of SOUTHAMPTON, 18 miles (S. S. E.) from Southampton, and 84 (S. W.) from London, containing 4059 inhabitants. The situation of Newport on the principal branch of the Medina river being considered more advantageous for commercial purposes than that of Carisbrooke, which was formerly a market town, has caused it to supersede the latter as the capital of the island. The town is situated on a gentle ascent, and is bounded on the east by the chief branch of the river, and on the west by a small stream which unites with the latter at the quay, where it becomes navigable hence to the Isle of Wight channel at West Cowes: it consists of five parallel streets, crossed by three others at right angles, which are well paved, lighted with gas under an act of parliament, and kept in excellent order; the inhabitants are abundantly supplied with water, by means of pumps which have been recently

Seal and Arms.

3 B 2

erected. Here is a small theatre; and assemblies are held occasionally: a public library and news-room, called the "Isle of Wight Institution," was established in 1810: monthly meetings are held, during the winter, by a Philosophical Society, in a room adjoining the library, which also contains a museum of natural and artificial curiosities: a mechanics' institution also has been recently established, to which is annexed a library. The town has been much improved of late years, and some new sewers are now in progress. The manufacture of thread-lace occupies a considerable number of persons, chiefly children, and furnishes an article for exportation: some commerce is carried on in timber, iron, and malt, and large quantities of wheat and flour are exported. The market for corn and provisions is on Saturday; there is likewise a cattle market every alternate Wednesday: fairs are held on Whit-Monday and the two following days; and there is a statute fair at Michaelmas.

The first charter was granted, about 1193, by Richard de Redvers, second Earl of Devon; and a more important grant was made by the Countess Isabella de Fortibus, in which the town is styled "The New Borough of Medina," and its burgesses invested with all the market tolls and other privileges: Henry VII. granted the petty customs within all ports and creeks of the island, which charter was confirmed and extended by Edward VI. and Elizabeth. The borough was first incorporated by James I., and is at present governed by the confirmatory charter of the 13th of Charles II.: the corporation consists of a mayor, eleven aldermen, and twelve burgesses, assisted by a recorder, deputy recorder, town clerk, two serjeants at mace, eight water-bailiffs, and other officers, all of them chosen by the corporation, the burgesses from among the principal inhabitants, and the aldermen from the burgesses: the mayor, the preceding mayor, the recorder, and his deputy, and the two aldermen, are all justices of the peace, with exclusive jurisdiction. A court of record is held before the mayor, recorder, and aldermen, every Tuesday and Friday, for the trial of actions to any amount. A court of requests for the Isle of Wight, for the recovery of debts not exceeding £5, is held before the commissioners appointed by act of parliament passed in the 46th of George III. A Knighton court (Curia Militum), of unknown origin, the jurisdiction of which extends over the whole island, excepting the borough of Newport, is seldom used, except on occasion of the annual appointment of constables; it is held under the presidency of the governor's steward, or his deputy. A court of pie-powder is held annually. Sessions for the borough are held quarterly, and a petty session of magistrates weekly. The guildhall, a very handsome edifice of the Ionic order, with corresponding pillars on the west front, was erected, about fourteen years ago, from a design by Mr. Nash, at an expense to the corporation of more than £10,000: the upper part comprises the town hall, council-chamber, and other offices, and the base forms an excellent market-place; in the interior is a fine portrait of the late Sir L. T. W. Holmes, Bart., by Owen, presented to the corporation by the inhabitants. There is a common gaol and house of correction for the borough, under the jurisdiction of its magistrates, which is also used as a bridewell for the whole island: it is divided into

four departments, and will contain thirty prisoners. This borough first returned members to parliament in the 23rd of Edward I.; its privileges then ceased until the 27th of Elizabeth: the right of election is vested in the corporation, the number of voters being twenty-four: the mayor is the returning officer; and the influence of the trustees of the late Sir L. T. W. Holmes, Bart., is predominant.

The living is a perpetual curacy, annexed to the vicarage of Carisbrooke, in the archdeaconry and diocese of Winchester. The church, dedicated to St. Thomas à Becket, is a spacious building, of different styles of architecture, with an embattled tower at the west end: in the interior were interred the remains of the Princess Elizabeth, second daughter of Charles I., who died a prisoner in Carisbrooke castle, at the early age of fifteen. The burial-ground was first appropriated to this church in the reign of Elizabeth, in consequence of a plague, the ravages of which were so great, that the churchyard at Carisbrooke was too small to receive the dead. There are places of worship for Baptists, Independents, Wesleyan Methodists, and Unitarians, and a Roman Catholic chapel. The free grammar school was founded originally by subscription, in 1619, and endowed with a grant of land to the extent of thirty-four acres, by the bailiffs and burgesses; also with land given by Sir Thomas Fleming, and augmented by several subsequent benefactors: the income is about £78 per annum; the schoolmaster is appointed by the corporation, and there are fifteen boys on the foundation, some of whom are instructed in classical literature: in the school-room the negociations between Charles I. and the parliamentary commissioners were conducted, in 1648. A girls' charity school was founded by subscription, in 1761, for the clothing and instruction of a number of poor girls, to which, in 1764, Benjamin Cooke devised land; it is otherwise supported by voluntary contributions: the annual income is £84. 8. 2., and twenty girls are educated and clothed, some of them being also boarded. National and Lancasterian schools, for children of both sexes, and an infant school, are supported by voluntary contributions: the children educated in these institutions amount to nearly six hundred. An almshouse was founded, pursuant to the will of Giles Kent, by Sir Richard Worsley, Bart., in 1618, for five or more poor aged persons; and another, of unknown foundation, is inhabited by four poor families, each of which receives a small sum annually. About a mile southward of the town is the house of industry, erected under an act of parliament obtained about the year 1770, the management of which is vested in a corporation, styled "The Guardians of the Poor in the Isle of Wight:" the requisite officers for the internal government of the house include a governor, treasurer, chaplain, steward, schoolmaster, matron, two surgeons, and a secretary, all of whom, excepting the treasurer, have regular salaries. The house consists of several ranges of building, of sufficient magnitude for the reception and employment of about seven hundred and fifty persons: attached to the edifice are extensive workshops, a chapel, and a pest-house for persons affected with contagious disorders: the sum borrowed for the erection was £20,000. The principal articles manufactured in it are, sacks, clothing, dowlas-sheeting, mops, shoes, &c.; and the number of inmates varies from seven hundred to seven hundred and fifty. A little towards the south-west are the Parkhurst barracks and military hospital, erected in the year 1798, and capable of receiving upwards of three thousand soldiers: they consist of parallel ranges of building, the principal of which is one hundred and sixty-three feet and a half in length : the hospital comprises a centre and two wings, with fumigating rooms, baths, &c.: the whole enclosure occupies an extent of twenty acres: water for domestic purposes is procured from four wells of different depths, from two hundred and sixty-two to two hundred and eighty-six feet.

NEWPORT-PAGNELL, a market-town and parish in the hundred of NEWPORT, county of BUCKINGHAM, 15 miles (N.E. by E.) from Buckingham, and 51 (N.W.) from London, containing 3103 inhabitants. The distinguishing addition to its name is derivable from the family of Paganell, or Pagnell, to whom the manor descended from William Fitzansculf, a powerful baron, who held it at the time of the Conquest. Their castle had fallen to decay previously to the time when Camden wrote : it was a place of great strength, but probably suffered in the great civil war, in the early part of which Newport was garrisoned by Prince Rupert : this garrison was withdrawn after the first battle of Newbury, in 1643, when the parliamentary troops, under the Earl of Essex, entered the town. Sir Samuel Luke, supposed to have been the Hudibras of Butler, was the governor in 1645. The town, one of the largest in the county, is pleasantly situated on a gentle eminence ; it is well built, particularly the principal street, but badly paved, and not lighted. Water is supplied from wells, and, by means of an hydraulic machine, from the small river Levet, which runs through the town, and falls into the Ouse. Coal is brought from Staffordshire by a branch of the Grand Junction canal. Over the Levet, at its junction with the Ouse, in 1810, an elegant bridge of cast-iron, having one arch fifty-eight feet in the span, was constructed ; and, about the same time, a very handsome stone bridge was erected over the Ouse ; the expense of both was about £12,000. The races, which had been discontinued for forty years, were revived in 1827, and are held regularly in the month of August. The assizes for the county were occasionally held here, from the reign of Henry III. to that of Henry VI.: the petty sessions for the three hundreds of Newport are still held here ; and a manorial court is held once in two years, at which constables are appointed. The manufacture of bone-lace here and in the neighbourhood was formerly carried on to a very considerable extent, the market for its sale being on Wednesday ; but of late years the trade has very much declined. There are a few wool-sorters ; and a paper manufactory affords employment to a considerable number of individuals. A grant of a market and a fair was made, or confirmed, to Roger de Somery, in 1270, and a renewal of the charter for the market, which is held on Saturday, was obtained by John de Botetort, in 1333. Six fairs are now held, viz., February 22nd, April 22nd, June 22nd, August 29th, October 22nd, and December 22nd.

The living is a discharged vicarage, in the archdeaconry of Buckingham, and diocese of Lincoln, rated in the king's books at £10, endowed with £200 private benefaction, and £200 royal bounty, and in the patron-age of the Crown. The church, dedicated to St. Peter and St. Paul, is an ancient and spacious edifice, with a square tower, standing on an eminence which affords a fine view of the surrounding country. The sum of £6000 has been recently expended in repairing it ; and two hundred new sittings have been added, one hundred of which are free, the Incorporated Society for the enlargement of churches and chapels having contributed £40 towards defraying the expense. In 1619, in the north aisle of this church, the body of a man was disinterred, whose scull and other hollow bones had been filled with lead : that taken from the scull is preserved in the library of St. John's College, Cambridge. In the churchyard is a fine epitaph, written by Cowper, on Thomas Abbott Hamilton, who died in 1788. There are places of worship for Baptists, Independents, and Wesleyan Methodists. Here is a school for twenty girls, founded and endowed with £10 per annum, from a bequest by Dr. Lewis Atterbury, brother of the celebrated Bishop of Rochester. A Lancasterian school, supported by voluntary contributions, was built in 1824 ; and a National school, supported in a similar manner, was erected two years afterwards. In 1280, John de Somery founded an hospital, dedicated to St. John the Baptist and St. John the Evangelist, which was refounded by Anne of Denmark, queen of James I., and, in consequence, called Queen's hospital ; the vicar of the parish is always the master : its revenue is about £70 a year, which is divided amongst three poor men and three poor women, for whose maintenance it was endowed. Two other hospitals, called St. Margaret's and the New hospital, were founded so early as 1240, but they have fallen to decay. Dr. Lewis Atterbury, brother of the Bishop of Rochester, gave £10 a year for a schoolmistress to instruct twenty girls. Mr. John Revis, citizen and draper of London, founded and endowed an almshouse, in 1763, for four poor men and three women, each of whom now receives six shillings a week. A close in North Crawley was given, by a person unknown, to the widow of any vicar of this parish ; when there is no widow, the rental is applied to the apprenticing of poor children. Fulk Paganell, in the reign of William Rufus, founded a convent of Cluniac monks at Teckford, adjoining this town, which was a cell to the abbey of Marmontier in Normandy, and the monastery and lands, valued at £126. 17., were given, in the 17th of Henry VIII., to Cardinal Wolsey.

NEWPORT-WALLINGFEN, a township in the parish of EASTRINGTON, wapentake of HOWDENSHIRE, East riding of the county of YORK, 6 miles (W. by S.) from South Cave, containing 339 inhabitants. There is a place of worship, erected in 1814, for Wesleyan Methodists, in connexion with which is a large Sunday school. About half a century ago, this was an uncultivated morass, called Walling Fen ; but a bed of clay, of very superior quality, having been discovered, which is dug to the depth of thirty-feet from the surface, it became noted for the manufacture of bricks, tiles, and coarse earthenware, to a very great extent, whereby the value of the land was amazingly increased, and a thriving village sprang up. The Market-Weighton canal is in the vicinity.

NEWSHAM, a township in the parish of EAGLES-CLIFFE, south-western division of STOCKTON ward, county palatine of DURHAM, 3 miles (W.) from Yarm, containing 44 inhabitants. Here was anciently a chapel, dedicated to St. James.

NEWSHAM, a township in the parish of KIRKHAM, hundred of AMOUNDERNESS, county palatine of LANCASTER, 5 miles (N.N.W.) from Preston. The population is returned with the chapelry of Goosnargh.

NEWSHAM, a joint township with Brind, in the parish of WRESSEL, Holme-Beacon division of the wapentake of HARTHILL, East riding of the county of YORK, 2¼ miles (W. N. W.) from Howden, containing, with Brind, 177 inhabitants.

NEWSHAM, a joint township with Breckenbrough, in that part of the parish of KIRBY-WISK which is in the wapentake of BIRDFORTH, North riding of the county of YORK, 4¼ miles (W.N.W.) from Thirsk, containing, with Breckenbrough, 173 inhabitants. Dr. George Hicks, a learned divine, was born here in 1642 ; he died in 1715.

NEWSHAM, a township in the parish of KIRKBY-RAVENSWORTH, western division of the wapentake of GILLING, North riding of the county of YORK, 2¾ miles (S. E.) from Greta-Bridge, containing 511 inhabitants.

NEWSHOLME, a township in the parish of GISBURN, western division of the wapentake of STAINCLIFFE and EWCROSS, West riding of the county of YORK, 9¼ miles (S. by E.) from Settle, containing 75 inhabitants.

NEWSTEAD, a township in the parish of BAMBROUGH, northern division of BAMBROUGH ward, county of NORTHUMBERLAND, 5¼ miles (S.E. by S.) from Belford, containing 90 inhabitants.

NEWSTEAD, a liberty in the parish of PAPPLEWICK, northern division of the wapentake of BROXTOW, county of NOTTINGHAM, 5¼ miles (S.) from Mansfield, containing 174 inhabitants. A priory of Black canons, in honour of the Blessed Virgin Mary, was founded here in 1170, by Henry II. : at the dissolution its revenue was valued at £219. 18. 8., and the site granted to the then lieutenant of Sherwood Forest, Sir John Byron, in whose family the estate continued until it was sold by the late Lord Byron, the poet. The present mansion, in which his lordship resided but for a short period, exhibits considerable remains of the venerable monastic buildings ; the cloisters and the west end of the abbey church are elegant specimens of the early English style of architecture, and in excellent preservation.

NEWSTEAD on ANCOLM, an extra-parochial liberty, in the southern division of the wapentake of YARBOROUGH, parts of LINDSEY, county of LINCOLN, 1½ mile (S.) from Glandford-Bridge. It was given by Henry II. to St. Gilbert and the canons of Sempringham, who here founded a priory of their order, in honour of the Holy Trinity, the revenue of which, at the dissolution, was valued at £55. 1. 8.

NEWTHORP, a township in the parish of SHERBURN, partly in the liberty of ST. PETER of YORK, East riding, and partly in the upper division of the wapentake of BARKSTONE-ASH, West riding, of the county of YORK, 6½ miles (N. N. W.) from Ferry-Bridge, containing 83 inhabitants.

NEW-TIMBER, a parish in the hundred of POYNINGS, rape of LEWES, county of SUSSEX, 3 miles (S.S.W.) from Hurst-Pierrepoint, containing 161 inhabitants. The living is a rectory, in the archdeaconry of Lewes, and diocese of Chichester, rated in the king's books at £8. 8. 4. Charles Gordon, Esq. was patron

in 1774. The church is dedicated to St. John the Evangelist.

NEWTON, a parish in the hundred of THRIPLOW, county of CAMBRIDGE, 6¼ miles (S.) from Cambridge, containing 146 inhabitants. The living is a discharged vicarage, annexed to that of Hauxton, in the archdeaconry and diocese of Ely. The church is dedicated to St. Margaret.

NEWTON, a parish in the hundred of WISBEACH, Isle of ELY, county of CAMBRIDGE, 3¾ miles (N. N. W.) from Wisbeach, containing 368 inhabitants. The living is a rectory, with the vicarage of St. Mary in the Marsh, in the peculiar jurisdiction and patronage of the Bishop of Ely, rated in the king's books at £18. 14. 9. The church is dedicated to St. James. A college, or chantry, in honour of St. Mary, was founded here, in the reign of Henry IV., by Sir John Colville, Knt., consisting of a warden, four chaplains, four clerks, and ten poor brethren, whose lands at the dissolution were annexed to the rectory of Newton.

NEWTON, a township in the parish of MOTTRAM in LONGDEN-DALE, hundred of MACCLESFIELD, county palatine of CHESTER, 6¼ miles (N. E. by E.) from Stockport, containing 2159 inhabitants, about two-thirds of whom are employed in the manufacture of cotton and hats, and in the printing of calico. The Peak Forest canal passes through the township, which abounds with stone of a good quality. There are also salt, coal, and iron works ; and for smelting the ore of the latter, a large furnace has lately been erected.

NEWTON, a township in the parish of PRESTBURY, hundred of MACCLESFIELD, county palatine of CHESTER, 5¼ miles (N. N. W.) from Macclesfield, containing 95 inhabitants.

NEWTON, a township in that part of the parish of MIDDLEWICH which is in the hundred of NORTHWICH, county palatine of CHESTER, ¼ of a mile (W.) from Middlewich, containing 1520 inhabitants.

NEWTON, a joint township with Larton, in the parish of WEST KIRBY, lower division of the hundred of WIRRALL, county palatine of CHESTER, 8¼ miles (N. N. W.) from Great Neston, containing, with Larton, 48 inhabitants.

NEWTON, a hamlet in the parish of PONSONBY, ALLERDALE ward above Darwent, county of CUMBERLAND, 7 miles (S. E. by S.) from Egremont. The population is returned with the parish.

NEWTON, a joint tything with Northway, in the parish of ASHCHURCH, lower division of the hundred of TEWKESBURY, county of GLOUCESTER. The population is returned with Northway.

NEWTON, a township in the parish of CLODOCK, hundred of EWYASLACY, county of HEREFORD, containing 257 inhabitants.

NEWTON, a joint township with Letton and Walford, in the parish of LEINTWARDINE, hundred of WIGMORE, county of HEREFORD, 5¾ miles (E. S. E.) from Knighton. The population is returned with Walford.

NEWTON, a township in the parish of CROFT, hundred of WOLPHY, county of HEREFORD, 5½ miles (N. W. by N.) from Leominster, containing 106 inhabitants.

NEWTON, a joint township with Scales, in the parish of KIRKHAM, hundred of AMOUNDERNESS, county palatine of LANCASTER, 2 miles (S. E. by E.) from Kirkham, containing, with Scales, 380 inhabitants. The Bluecoat school here was founded and liberally endowed, in 1707, by John Hornby; and James Boys, in 1809, bequeathed £800 in furtherance of this charity, the annual income of which now amounts to £670, and the number of scholars averages about forty, viz., twenty-seven boys and thirteen girls, who are clothed, boarded, and educated.

NEWTON, a joint township with Hardhorn, in the parish of POULTON, hundred of AMOUNDERNESS, county palatine of LANCASTER, 2 miles (S.) from Poulton. The population is returned with Hardhorn.

NEWTON, a chapelry in the parish of MANCHESTER, hundred of SALFORD, county palatine of LANCASTER, comprising the townships of Bradford, Droylsden, Failsworth, Moston, and Newton, and containing 9478 inhabitants, of which number, 2577 are in the township of Newton, 2 miles (N. E. by E.) from Manchester. The living is a perpetual curacy, in the archdeaconry and diocese of Chester, endowed with £500 private benefaction, £200 royal bounty, and £1000 parliamentary grant, and in the patronage of the Warden and Fellows of the Collegiate Church of Manchester. The chapel, dedicated to All Saints, is a handsome edifice in the later style of English architecture, erected, at an expense of £8000, defrayed by a rate on the inhabitants, on the site of an old chapel, which fell down on the 2nd of May, 1808. There are places of worship for Wesleyan Methodists and Unitarians; and at Fairfield is an establishment of Moravians. The manufacture of cotton and silk, and the printing of calico, are carried on to a considerable extent, and silk-weaving on a smaller scale. A school has been erected by subscription, in which twenty children are instructed for about £10 per annum, the united bequests of William Purnall, in 1766, and Elizabeth Chetham.

NEWTON, a township in the parish of SWEEPSTONE, western division of the hundred of GOSCOTE, county of LEICESTER, 5½ miles (S. by E.) from Ashby de la Zouch. The population is returned with the parish.

NEWTON, a joint township with Botcheston, in the parish of RATBY, hundred of SPARKENHOE, county of LEICESTER, 6¼ miles (E. by N.) from Market-Bosworth. The population is returned with Botcheston.

NEWTON, a parish in the wapentake of AVELAND, parts of KESTEVEN, county of LINCOLN, 2¼ miles (N. W. by W.) from Falkingham, containing 162 inhabitants. The living is a rectory, in the archdeaconry and diocese of Lincoln, rated in the king's books at £10. Sir W. E. Welby, Bart. was patron in 1802. The church is dedicated to St. Botolph.

NEWTON, a hamlet in the parish of TROWSE, hundred of HENSTEAD, county of NORFOLK, 1½ mile (S. E. by S.) from Norwich. The population is returned with the parish.

NEWTON, a parish in the hundred of CORBY, county of NORTHAMPTON, 3¾ miles (N. by E.) from Kettering, containing 94 inhabitants. The living is a donative. The church is dedicated to St. Faith. This parish was anciently divided into two townships, Great and Little Newton, each of which had a chapel, subordinate to the church of Geddington, and part of the possessions of Pippewell abbey.

NEWTON, a township in the parish of EMBLETON, southern division of BAMBROUGH ward, county of NORTHUMBERLAND, 10 miles (N. N. E.) from Alnwick, containing 247 inhabitants, most of whom are employed in a very productive fishery. There are coal mines in the neighbourhood, and on sinking a pit, a few years ago, cockle shells were discovered, eighteen fathoms below the surface of the earth.

NEWTON, a township in the parish of CHILLINGHAM, eastern division of GLENDALE ward, county of NORTHUMBERLAND, 3½ miles (E. S. E.) from Wooler, containing 117 inhabitants. Near the village is an ancient cross, twelve feet high, called the Hurl Stone.

NEWTON, a township in the parish of BYWELL St. PETER, eastern division of TINDALE ward, county of NORTHUMBERLAND, 7¾ miles (E. by N.) from Hexham, containing 105 inhabitants.

NEWTON, a township partly in the parish of BINGHAM, northern division, and partly in the parish of SHELFORD, southern division, of the wapentake of BINGHAM, county of NOTTINGHAM, 2 miles (N. N. W.) from Bingham. The population is returned with the parishes. Newton is in the honour of Tutbury, duchy of Lancaster, and within the jurisdiction of a court of pleas held at Tutbury every third Tuesday, for the recovery of debts under 40s.

NEWTON, or NEWTOWN, a borough in the parish of CALBOURN, liberty of WEST MEDINA, Isle of Wight division of the county of SOUTHAMPTON, 5¼ miles (W. by N.) from Newport, and 92 (S. W.) from London. The population is returned with the parish. This place was formerly called *Francheville*, which name occurs in a charter granted by Oymer, Bishop of Winchester, who bestowed such liberties and franchises on the burgesses of Newton as were enjoyed by those of Taunton, Alresford, and Farnham. This charter was confirmed by Edward II., by Edward IV., and by Queen Elizabeth. The town, which is situated at the mouth of the river Newton, was anciently of much greater moment than it is at present: it was burned by the Danes in 1001, and by the French in the reign of Richard II., and is now reduced to a very few cottages. The town hall contains some oaken chairs curiously carved, and supposed to be of the time of Elizabeth: it stands on an eminence overlooking one of the creeks of Newton harbour, which is formed by the junction of the river with the sea; at high water it will admit vessels of five hundred tons' burden. It is one of the stations of the preventive service. This borough has a titular mayor, chosen by the burgageholders: courts leet are held, at which constables are appointed. It first sent representatives to parliament in the 27th year of the reign of Elizabeth. The right of election is vested in the titular mayor and the burgesses, or proprietors of burgage tenements: the number of voters is thirty-three: the titular mayor is the returning officer. The parliamentary influence is enjoyed by Sir Fitzwilliam Barrington, Lord Yarborough, and the trustees of Sir Leonard T. W. Holmes. Twelve

Corporate Seal.

poor children are instructed by a schoolmistress for £10 per annum, the gift of Lady Constance Lucy, in 1771.

NEWTON, a liberty in the parish of BLITHFIELD, southern division of the hundred of PIREHILL, county of STAFFORD, 3 miles (W. by N.) from Abbot's Bromley, containing 263 inhabitants.

NEWTON, a parish in the hundred of THINGOE, county of SUFFOLK, 2¾ miles (S. S. E.) from Bury-St. Edmund's, containing 171 inhabitants. The living is a rectory, in the archdeaconry of Sudbury, and diocese of Norwich, rated in the king's books at £5. 19. 4½. Sir Charles Davers, Bart. was patron in 1802. The church is dedicated to St. Peter.

NEWTON, a joint hamlet with Biggin, in the parish of CLIFTON upon DUNSMOOR, Rugby division of the hundred of KNIGHTLOW, county of WARWICK, 3½ miles (N. E.) from Rugby, containing, with Biggin, 240 inhabitants. Edward Cave, the original editor of the Gentleman's Magazine, was born here in 1691; he died in 1754.

NEWTON, a township in the parish of BURNESTON, wapentake of HALLIKELD, North riding of the county of YORK, 3¼ miles (E. by S.) from Bedale. The population is returned with Exelby.

NEWTON, a parish in the western division of the liberty of LANGBAURGH, North riding of the county of YORK, 4 miles (S. W. by W.) from Guilsbrough, containing 119 inhabitants. The living is a perpetual curacy, in the peculiar jurisdiction of the Dean of York, endowed with £600 royal bounty, and £200 parliamentary grant, and in the patronage of the Vicar of Rudby in Cleveland.

NEWTON, a township in the parish and lythe of PICKERING, North riding of the county of YORK, 5 miles (N. by E.) from Pickering, containing 212 inhabitants. There is a place of worship for Independents. Richard Poad, in 1726, bequeathed £178, directing the income to be applied to teaching poor children.

NEWTON, a township in the parish of SLAIDBURN, western division of the wapentake of STAINCLIFFE and EWCROSS, West riding of the county of YORK, 7 miles (N. N. W.) from Clitheroe, containing 581 inhabitants.

NEWTON (ARCHDEACON), a township in the parish of DARLINGTON, south-eastern division of DARLINGTON ward, county palatine of DURHAM, 3 miles (N. W.) from Darlington, containing 64 inhabitants.

NEWTON (BANK), a township in the parish of GARGRAVE, eastern division of the wapentake of STAINCLIFFE and EWCROSS, West riding of the county of YORK, 6 miles (W. by N.) from Skipton, containing 139 inhabitants.

NEWTON by CASTLEACRE, a parish in the southern division of the hundred of GREENHOE, county of NORFOLK, 4¼ miles (N. by E.) from Swaffham, containing 68 inhabitants. The living is a discharged vicarage, in the archdeaconry of Norfolk, and diocese of Norwich, rated in the king's books at £2. 15., endowed with £200 royal bounty, and in the patronage of the Bishop of Ely. The church, dedicated to All Saints, is an ancient structure, with a low square tower rising from the centre, and surmounted by a wooden turret.

NEWTON by CHESTER, a township in that part of the parish of ST. OSWALD, CHESTER, which is in the lower division of the hundred of BROXTON, county pala-

tine of CHESTER, 1¾ mile (N. N. E.) from Chester, containing 192 inhabitants. There is a tan-yard at Hookersbrook, in this township.

NEWTON (COLD), a chapelry in the parish of LOWESBY, eastern division of the hundred of GOSCOTE, county of LEICESTER, 9 miles (E. by N.) from Leicester, containing 104 inhabitants.

NEWTON (ST. CYRES), a parish in the hundred of CREDITON, county of DEVON, 3½ miles (S. E. by E.) from Crediton, containing 1083 inhabitants. The living is a vicarage, in the archdeaconry and diocese of Exeter, rated in the king's books at £16. 15. 5. J. Quicke, Esq. was patron in 1824. A fair for cattle is held on the Monday following Midsummer-day. Lead-ore and manganese are obtained in the parish.

NEWTON by DARESBURY, a township in the parish of RUNCORN, hundred of BUCKLOW, county palatine of CHESTER, 5 miles (N. E. by E.) from Frodsham, containing 124 inhabitants.

NEWTON upon DERWENT, a township in the parish of WILBERFOSS, Wilton-Beacon division of the wapentake of HARTHILL, East riding of the county of YORK, 5½ miles (W.) from Pocklington, containing 205 inhabitants. There is a place of worship for Wesleyan Methodists.

NEWTON (EAST), a township in the parish of ALDBROUGH, middle division of the wapentake of HOLDERNESS, East riding of the county of YORK, 12½ miles (N. E. by E.) from Kingston upon Hull, containing 38 inhabitants. An hospital, in honour of St. Mary Magdalene, was founded here by William, Earl of Albemarle, who died in 1179, which, at the dissolution, possessed a revenue of about £40.

NEWTON (EAST), a joint township with Laysthorpe, in the parish of STONEGRAVE, wapentake of RYEDALE, North riding of the county of YORK, 3¾ miles (S. E. by S.) from Helmsley, containing, with Laysthorpe, 72 inhabitants.

NEWTON (ST. FAITH), a hamlet in the parish of HORSHAM ST. FAITH, hundred of TAVERHAM, county of NORFOLK, 5 miles (N.) from Norwich, containing 394 inhabitants.

NEWTON by FRODSHAM, a township in the parish of FRODSHAM, second division of the hundred of EDDISBURY, county palatine of CHESTER, 2¼ miles (S. E. by S.) from Frodsham, containing 109 inhabitants. There is a place of worship for the Society of Friends.

NEWTON (KIRK), a parish in the western division of GLENDALE ward, county of NORTHUMBERLAND, comprising the townships of Akeld, Couldsnouth with Thompson's Walls, Coupland, Crookhouse, Grey's Forest, Heathpool, Howtell, Kilham, Kirk-Newton, Lanton, Milfield, West Newton, Paston, Selby's Forest, and Yeavering, and containing 1701 inhabitants, of which number, 83 are in the township of Kirk-Newton, 5¼ miles (W. by N.) from Wooler. The living is a vicarage, in the archdeaconry of Northumberland, and diocese of Durham, rated in the king's books at £3. 13. 4, and in the patronage of the Heirs of William Lowes, Esq. The church is dedicated to St. Gregory.

NEWTON (ST. LOE), a parish in the hundred of WELLOW, county of SOMERSET, 3½ miles (W.) from Bath, containing 431 inhabitants. The living is a rectory, in the archdeaconry of Bath, and diocese of Bath and Wells, rated in the king's books at £17. 18. 4., and in the patronage of W. G. Langton, Esq. The church is dedicated to the Holy Trinity. The river Avon is here crossed by a bridge. A school-house was erected in 1698, in pursuance of the will of Richard Jocis, who endowed it with about £60 per annum, for which twenty children are instructed.

NEWTON (LONG), a parish in the south-western division of STOCKTON ward, county palatine of DUR-HAM, 4½ miles (S. W. by W.) from Stockton upon Tees, containing 338 inhabitants. The living is a rectory, in the archdeaconry and diocese of Durham, rated in the king's books at £20, and in the patronage of the Bishop of Durham. The church, dedicated to St. Mary, was rebuilt in 1806, but has no tower: the churchyard is tastefully ornamented with shrubs. There are places of worship for Primitive and Wesleyan Methodists.

Seal and Arms.

NEWTON in MACKER-FIELD, a borough (for-merly a market town) and chapelry, in the parish of WINWICK, hundred of WEST DERBY, county palatine of LANCASTER, 47 miles (S. by E.) from Lancaster, and 192½ (N. W. by N.) from London, containing 1643 inhabitants. During the parliamentary war, and about the month of August, 1648, some High-landers having been defeated and made prisoners by the parliamentary forces, at Red Bank, near this place, were hanged in an adjacent field, which still retains the appellation of Gallows Cross. The town consists chiefly of one broad street; and there are an ancient court-house, and a handsome assembly-room. The manu-facture of fustians is the principal branch of business, and spinning and dyeing cotton is also carried on. The market has long been discontinued, but the cross is standing. Fairs are held on May 17th and August 11th, for horned cattle; and on May 18th and August 12th, for horses. Newton, anciently the head of a ba-rony, is a borough by prescription, and has returned two members to parliament ever since the first year of the reign of Elizabeth: the right of election is in the free-holders to the value of forty shillings and upwards: the number of voters is about sixty: the steward of the borough, and the bailiff of the manor, are the returning officers; and the influence of Thomas Legh, Esq., is predominant. Courts leet and baron are held three times a year, at which small debts are recoverable. The living is a perpetual curacy, in the archdeaconry and diocese of Chester, endowed with £200 private benefaction, £400 royal bounty, and £600 parliamentary grant, and in the patronage of Thomas Legh, Esq. The chapel, which is parochial, and dedicated to St. Peter, was built in 1682, by Richard Legh, Esq.: the burial-ground has been recently enlarged, and enclosed with a stone wall and palisades, by the patron. A free school is kept in the court-house for the instruction of poor children; the average number is from seventy to one hundred: the master receives about £55 per annum, arising from the proceeds of certain enclosures of Leyland common, and the rental of a messuage called Dean school. Upwards of four hundred children are instructed in the Sunday schools, which were established in 1823. About half a mile northward of the town are the remains of an ancient barrow, called Castle Hill, the sides and summit of which are crowned with venerable oaks; it is from eight to nine yards high, and twenty-five in diameter. A whetstone, encased in wood, was discovered in sinking a coal-pit in this neighbourhood, in 1822, about thirty yards below the surface of the earth.

NEWTON juxta MALPAS, a township in the parish of MALPAS, higher division of the hundred of BROXTON, county palatine of CHESTER, 1½ mile (S. W.) from Malpas, containing 18 inhabitants.

NEWTON on the MOOR, a township in the parish of SHILBOTTLE, eastern division of COQUETDALE ward, county of NORTHUMBERLAND, 5½ miles (S. by W.) from Alnwick, containing 244 inhabitants. A considerable quantity of limestone is obtained here for burning. There is a powerful chalybeate spring near the village; and in the neighbourhood are vestiges of an ancient for-tification. Frances and Jane Strother, about 1770, left £300, the interest of which is applied to the education of poor children.

NEWTON (NORTH), a chapelry in the parish of NORTH PETHERTON, northern division of the hundred of PETHERTON, county of SOMERSET, 4¾ miles (S.) from Bridg-water. The population is returned with the parish. The living is a perpetual curacy, in the archdeaconry of Taunton, and diocese of Bath and Wells, endowed with £200 private benefaction, and £600 royal bounty, and in the patronage of Sir Thomas D. Acland, Bart.

NEWTON (NORTH), a parish in the hundred of SWANBOROUGH, county of WILTS, 3¼ miles (S. W. by W.) from Pewsey, containing, with the tything of Hilcott, 288 inhabitants. The living is a vicarage, in the archdeaconry of Wilts, and diocese of Salisbury, rated in the king's books at £7. 1. 3., and in the pa-tronage of the Prebendary of Beaminster-Secunda in the Cathedral Church of Salisbury. The church is de-dicated to St. James.

NEWTON (OLD), a parish in the hundred of STOW, county of SUFFOLK, 3 miles (N. by E.) from Stow-Market, containing, with the hamlet of Dag-worth, 577 inhabitants. The living is a discharged vicarage, in the archdeaconry of Sudbury, and diocese of Norwich, rated in the king's books at £7. 15. 5., endowed with £600 private benefaction, and £900 par-liamentary grant. Mrs. Torless was patroness in 1823. The church is dedicated to St. Mary.

NEWTON (OUT), a township in the parish of EASINGTON, southern division of the wapentake of HOLDERNESS, East riding of the county of YORK, 4 miles (E.) from Patrington, containing 69 inhabitants.

NEWTON upon OUZE, a parish in the wapentake of BULMER, North riding of the county of YORK, com-prising the townships of Benningbrough, Linton upon Ouze, and Newton upon Ouze, and containing 862 in-habitants, of which number, 495 are in the township of Newton upon Ouze, 8½ miles (N. W.) from York. The living is a perpetual curacy, in the peculiar jurisdic-tion of the Lord of the Manor of Newton, endowed with £200 parliamentary grant, and in the patronage of Mrs. Earle. The church is a very handsome structure. There are places of worship for Primitive and Wes-leyan Methodists.

NEWTON (ST. PETROCK), a parish in the hundred of SHEBBEAR, county of DEVON, 7½ miles (S. W.) from Great Torrington, containing 278 inhabitants. The living is a rectory, in the archdeaconry of Barnstable, and diocese of Exeter, rated in the king's books at £8. 5. 7½. The Rev. F. D. Lempriere was patron in 1824.

NEWTON (POTTER), a township in the parish of ST. PETER, within the liberty of the town of LEEDS, West riding of the county of YORK, 2 miles (N. by E.) from Leeds, containing 664 inhabitants.

NEWTON (SOUTH), a parish in the hundred of BRANCH and DOLE, county of WILTS, 2½ miles (N. by W.) from Wilton, containing, with the chapelries of Chilhampton and Ugford, and the tythings of Burdens-Ball, Stoford, and Wishford, 579 inhabitants. The living is a discharged vicarage, in the archdeaconry and diocese of Salisbury, rated in the king's books at £12. 18. 4., and in the patronage of the Earl of Pembroke. The church, dedicated to St. Andrew, has lately received an addition of fifty-four sittings, of which forty-eight are free, the Incorporated Society for the enlargement of churches and chapels having granted £50 towards defraying the expense.

NEWTON near SUDBURY, a parish in the hundred of BABERGH, county of SUFFOLK, 3¾ miles (E.) from Sudbury, containing 343 inhabitants. The living is a rectory, in the archdeaconry of Sudbury, and diocese of Norwich, rated in the king's books at £17. 3. 9., and in the patronage of the Master and Fellows of St. Peter's College, Cambridge. The church is dedicated to All Saints.

NEWTON by TATTENHALL, a township in the parish of TATTENHALL, lower division of the hundred of BROXTON, county palatine of CHESTER, 5¼ miles (S. W. by W.) from Tarporley, containing 75 inhabitants.

NEWTON in the THISTLES, or NEWTON-REGIS, a parish in the Tamworth division of the hundred of HEMLINGFORD, county of WARWICK, 5¾ miles (N. E. by E.) from Tamworth, containing 410 inhabitants. The living is a rectory, in the archdeaconry of Coventry, and diocese of Lichfield and Coventry, rated in the king's books at £14. 1. 5½., and in the patronage of Sir F. Burdett, Bart. The church is dedicated to St. Mary.

NEWTON by TOFT, a parish in the northern division of the wapentake of WALSHCROFT, parts of LINDSEY, county of LINCOLN, 4¼ miles (W. S. W.) from Market-Rasen, containing 70 inhabitants. The living is a discharged rectory, in the archdeaconry and diocese of Lincoln, rated in the king's books at £4. 10. 10., and endowed with £200 royal bounty. Tyrwhit Smith Esq. and others were patrons in 1809. The church is dedicated to St. Michael. John Holdsworth, in 1748, bequeathed £200 for teaching poor children.

NEWTON upon TRENT, a parish in the wapentake of WELL, parts of LINDSEY, county of LINCOLN, 10 miles (W. N. W.) from Lincoln, containing 295 inhabitants. The living is a discharged vicarage, in the archdeaconry of Stow, and diocese of Lincoln, rated in the king's books at £4, endowed with £400 private benefaction, £800 royal bounty, and £300 parliamentary grant. Miss Stowe and others were patrons in 1807. The church is dedicated to St. Peter. There is a place of worship for Wesleyan Methodists.

NEWTON (WATER), a parish in the hundred of NORMAN-CROSS, county of HUNTINGDON, 6 miles (N. N. W.) from Stilton, containing 138 inhabitants. The living is a rectory, in the archdeaconry of Huntingdon, and diocese of Lincoln, rated in the king's books at £6. 9. 2., and in the patronage of the Rev. Randolph Richard Knipe. The church is dedicated to St. Remigius. The river New runs through the parish.

NEWTON (WELCH), a parish in the lower division of the hundred of WORMELOW, county of HEREFORD, 4 miles (N. by W.) from Monmouth, containing 220 inhabitants. The living is a perpetual curacy, in the archdeaconry and diocese of Hereford, rated in the king's books at £4. 10., endowed with £800 royal bounty, and in the patronage of W. H. Jenkins, Esq. The church is dedicated to St. Mary.

NEWTON (WEST), a township in that part of the parish of BROOMFIELD which is in ALLERDALE ward below Darwent, county of CUMBERLAND, 9½ miles (N.) from Cockermouth, containing 309 inhabitants. Here are the remains of a tower, which formed part of an ancient castle or hall. In the neighbourhood is a quarry of red freestone.

NEWTON (WEST), a parish in the Lynn division of the hundred of FREEBRIDGE, county of NORFOLK, 3 miles (N. E. by E.) from Castle-Rising, containing 211 inhabitants. The living is a discharged rectory, in the archdeaconry and diocese of Norwich, rated in the king's books at £5. 6. 8., and in the patronage of the Crown. The church is dedicated to St. Peter.

NEWTON (WEST), a township in the parish of KIRK-NEWTON, western division of GLENDALE ward, county of NORTHUMBERLAND, 5¾ miles (W. by N.) from Wooler, containing 95 inhabitants.

NEWTON (WEST), a township in the parish of ALDBROUGH, middle division of the wapentake of HOLDERNESS, East riding of the county of YORK, 9¾ miles (N. E.) from Kingston upon Hull, containing 158 inhabitants.

NEWTON le WILLOWS, a township in that part of the parish of BROMPTON PATRICK which is in the eastern division of the wapentake of HANG, North riding of the county of YORK, 4 miles (W. N. W.) from Bedale, containing 250 inhabitants. There is a place of worship for Wesleyan Methodists. Two children are educated for a trifling sum, the bequest of Samuel Atkinson, in 1707.

NEWTON (WOLD), or NEWTON upon the WOLDS, a parish in the wapentake of BRADLEY-HAVERSTOE, parts of LINDSEY, county of LINCOLN, 9¼ miles (S. by W.) from Great Grimsby, containing 125 inhabitants. The living is a discharged rectory, in the archdeaconry and diocese of Lincoln, rated in the king's books at £7. 10. 10., and in the patronage of the Bishop of Durham. The church is dedicated to All Saints.

NEWTON (WOLD), a parish in the wapentake of DICKERING, East riding of the county of YORK, 11½ miles (N. by E.) from Great Driffield, containing, with the chapelry of Fordon, 225 inhabitants. The living is a discharged vicarage, in the archdeaconry of the East riding, and diocese of York, rated in the king's books at £6. 19. 9½., and in the patronage of the Hon. D. Langley. This was anciently a chapelry within the parish of Hunmanby, and is remarkable for one of those clear and copious springs, called the Gipsey springs, which issues out of the ground with great force, and is thought to be one of the Wold streams emerging from its subterraneous channel.

NEWTON (WOOD), a parish in the hundred of WILLYBROOK, county of NORTHAMPTON, 4½ miles (N.) from Oundle, containing 362 inhabitants. The living is a perpetual curacy, in the peculiar jurisdiction and patronage of the Prebendary of Nassington in the Cathedral Church of Lincoln, endowed with £400 royal bounty, and £200 parliamentary grant. The church is dedicated to St. Mary.

NEWTON-ABBOTS, a market town and chapelry, in the parish of WOOLBOROUGH, hundred of HAYTOR, county of DEVON, 14½ miles (S.S.W.) from Exeter, and 187 (S.W. by W.) from London. The population is returned with the parish. It is probable that Newton-Abbots and Newton-Bushell were formerly included under the name of Nuietone, and retained this common appellation till their separate manors became the property of different possessors. Newton-Abbots was so denominated from its being held by the abbot of Tor, to whom it was given by William, Lord Brewer, founder of that monastery. The town appears to have possessed a market and a fair in the time of Edward I. In 1625, Charles I. and his suite, when on their way to and from Plymouth, were entertained at Ford House, near this town, on which occasion the king attended divine service in the parish church. In 1688, the same mansion was occupied by William, Prince of Orange, after his landing at Torbay; and from the pedestal of the market cross, on which is an inscription commemorative of the fact, his declaration to the people of England was first read. The town is situated on the river Teign, on the high road between Exeter and Plymouth, and consists of two large, and several minor, streets, which are roughly paved: the inhabitants are supplied with water from pumps and adjacent springs. Here was formerly an extensive woollen manufactory, but the principal business now is that connected with the tan-yards: small quantities of shoes are exported to Newfoundland, with which island the inhabitants formerly carried on a very extensive trade, which having declined during the war in the beginning of the present century, has not since been revived. The river Teign is navigable to its junction with the Teigngrace canal, about three quarters of a mile from the town: lighters and boats come up by the Stover canal from Teignmouth with coal, and return with granite and potters' clay. The markets are on Wednesday and Saturday, and on the last Wednesday in February is a great annual market for cattle: the market-place is new, spacious, and commodiously arranged. Fairs are held on June 24th, September 11th, and November 6th, unless these fall on Wednesday, in which case the fairs take place on that day week. A portreeve, reeve, and inferior officers, are annually elected by a jury, at the borough court; the office of portreeve being always filled by the reeve for the preceding year. A court leet is held annually, and a petty session monthly. The chapel, dedicated to St. Leonard, is used only for baptisms and occasional service. There are places of worship for Baptists and Independents: the latter, with a free school, was founded and liberally endowed, pursuant to the will of Mr. Bearne, in 1787. A National school for children of both sexes

is supported by subscription. The Widows' hospital, founded by Lucy, Lady Reynell, in 1638, and situated beyond the precincts of the town, was originally intended for four, but is now occupied by two, clergymen's widows, who receive £10 per annum, and have a pew allotted to them in the parish church; there are likewise some smaller almshouses. At Milberdown, near this place, are the vestiges of an ancient elliptical encampment, with a triple intrenchment, where the Prince of Orange stationed his artillery, when on his way from Brixham to Exeter. Hacknield ford, in this neighbourhood, is supposed to have derived its name from its situation on the line of the ancient Roman road, called the Iknield-way.

NEWTON-ARLOSH, a hamlet in the parish of HOLME-CULTRAM, ALLERDALE ward below Darwent, county of CUMBERLAND, 6¾ miles (N.W.) from Wigton. In consequence of the destruction of Skinburness by an irruption of the sea, in 1404, the abbot of Holme-Cultram was licensed to build a small church at this place, and hold here the market and fair, now disused, which had previously been granted him at Skinburness. The church, which has long been desecrated, was constructed so as to serve the purpose of a fortress, and its thick rugged walls remain in the cemetery, which is still used by the parishioners.

NEWTON-BEWLEY, a township in the parish of BILLINGHAM, north-eastern division of STOCKTON ward, county palatine of DURHAM, 5½ miles (N.N.E.) from Stockton upon Tees, containing 86 inhabitants. It anciently belonged to the prior of Durham, who resided and had his court-house here.

NEWTON-BLOSSOMVILLE, a parish in the hundred of NEWPORT, county of BUCKINGHAM, 3 miles (E.) from Olney, containing 243 inhabitants. The living is a rectory, in the archdeaconry of Buckingham, and diocese of Lincoln, rated in the king's books at £8. 8. 1½., and in the patronage of F. G. S. Farrer, Esq. The church is dedicated to St. Nicholas.

NEWTON-BROMSHOLD, a parish in the hundred of HIGHAM-FERRERS, county of NORTHAMPTON, 3¼ miles (S.E.) from Higham-Ferrers, containing 115 inhabitants. The living is a rectory, in the archdeaconry of Northampton, and diocese of Peterborough, rated in the king's books at £8. 3. 4. The Rev. E. Tanqueray was patron in 1788. The church is dedicated to St. Peter.

NEWTON-BUSHELL, a chapelry (formerly a market town) in the parish of HIGHWEEK, hundred of TEINGBRIDGE, county of DEVON, 14½ miles (S.S.W.) from Exeter, and 187 (W. S. W.) from London. The population is returned with the parish. This town received its distinguishing appellation from Robert Bussell, or Bushell, the foster-child and kinsman of Theobald de English Ville, made lord of the manor by Henry III., in 1246, and who granted to the inhabitants a charter for a market. This town is separated from Newton-Abbots by the river Lemon. A port-reeve and two constables are annually chosen at the court held by the lord of the manor. The chapel is a large edifice, in the ancient style of English architecture, and has received an addition of two hundred and seventy sittings, of which one hundred and seventy are free, the Incorporated Society for the enlargement of churches and chapels having contributed £250 towards defraying

3 C 2

the expense. There is a place of worship for Wesleyan Methodists. Limestone, with argillaceous slate, and organic remains, are found in the vicinity of the town.

NEWTON-CAPP, a township in that part of the parish of St. Andrew Auckland which is in the north-western division of Darlington ward, county palatine of Durham, ½ a mile (N.W.) from Bishop-Auckland, containing 145 inhabitants. It is situated on the Wear, which is here crossed by a bridge. On the north bank of the river are the ruins of an unfinished mansion, erected by the Bacon family, who were long proprietors of this place.

NEWTON-FERRERS, a parish in the hundred of Ermington, county of Devon, 6 miles (S. by E.) from Earl's Plympton, containing 719 inhabitants. The living is a rectory, in the archdeaconry of Totness, and diocese of Exeter, rated in the king's books at £41.12.1. The Rev. John Yonge was patron in 1821. The church, dedicated to the Holy Cross, contains three stone stalls. Here is an almshouse. The parish is bounded on the west by the æstuary of the Yealm, and the vicinity is remarkable for scenery of great beauty.

NEWTON-FLOTMAN, a parish in the hundred of Humbleyard, county of Norfolk, 3½ miles (N. by E.) from St. Mary Stratton, containing 390 inhabitants. The living is a rectory in medieties, in the archdeaconry of Norfolk, and diocese of Norwich, rated in the king's books at £10. Miss Long was patroness in 1790. The church, dedicated to St. Mary, contains memorials of several of the Blundeville family, and an arched monument with a representation of Noah's Ark. This place received the adjunct to its name from the ancient flote, or ferry, over the river Taus, which is now passed by a bridge of brick.

NEWTON-GRANGE, a liberty in that part of the parish of Ashbourn which is in the hundred of Wirksworth, county of Derby, 4½ miles (N. by W.) from Ashbourn, containing 38 inhabitants.

NEWTON-HALL, a township in the parish of Bywell St. Peter, eastern division of Tindale ward, county of Northumberland, 7¾ miles (E. by N.) from Hexham, containing 89 inhabitants.

NEWTON-HARCOURT, a chapelry in the parish of Wistow, hundred of Gartree, county of Leicester, 6¾ miles (S.E. by S.) from Leicester, containing 298 inhabitants. The Union canal passes through the chapelry.

NEWTON-KYME, a parish in the upper division of the wapentake of Barkstone-Ash, West riding of the county of York, 2¼ miles (N. W. by W.) from Tadcaster, containing, with Toulston, 184 inhabitants. The living is a rectory, in the archdeaconry and diocese of York, rated in the king's books at £14, and in the patronage of T. L. Fairfax, Esq. The church is dedicated to St. Andrew.

NEWTON-LONGVILLE, a parish in the hundred of Newport, county of Buckingham, 3 miles (S. W. by W.) from Fenny-Stratford, containing 486 inhabitants. The living is a rectory, in the archdeaconry of Buckingham, and diocese of Lincoln, rated in the king's books at £20. 9. 7., and in the patronage of the Warden and Fellows of New College, Oxford, by whose predecessors the church, dedicated to St. Faith, was erected about 1415. In the chancel are two piscinæ, one of them bearing the arms of William of Wykeham, and of others. An Alien priory of Cluniac monks, subordinate to the abbey of St. Faith, at Longueville in Normandy, was founded here in the reign of Henry I., and suppressed in 1415, when it was granted to New College, Oxford. The learned Grocyn, tutor to Erasmus, and one of the revivers of classical literature in the sixteenth century, was rector of this parish.

NEWTON-MORRELL, a township in the parish of Barton, eastern division of the wapentake of Gilling, North riding of the county of York, 6¾ miles (S. W.) from Darlington, containing 31 inhabitants.

NEWTON-MULGRAVE, a township in the parish of Lythe, eastern division of the liberty of Langbaurgh, North riding of the county of York, 9 miles (N. W. by W.) from Whitby, containing 134 inhabitants.

NEWTON-PARK, a township in that part of the parish of Mitford which is in the western division of Morpeth ward, county of Northumberland, 3 miles (W. by N.) from Morpeth, containing 18 inhabitants.

NEWTON-POPPLEFORD, a chapelry in the parish of Aylesbear, eastern division of the hundred of Budleigh, county of Devon, 3¾ miles (N. W. by W.) from Sidmouth, containing 481 inhabitants. The living is a perpetual curacy, annexed to the vicarage of Aylesbear, in the archdeaconry and diocese of Exeter, endowed with £600 royal bounty. The chapel, dedicated to St. Luke, was originally founded as a chantry by Edward III., about 1330; it has lately received an addition of one hundred and twenty free sittings, the Incorporated Society for the enlargement of churches and chapels having granted £75 towards defraying the expense. In the neighbourhood is Woodbury castle, occupying the brow of a considerable eminence: it is deeply intrenched, and within its enclosure are the remains of a building from which visitors could enjoy a magnificent view over the Ex, and the vale, to Exeter, Honiton, &c., and the sea.

NEWTON-PURCELL, a parish in the hundred of Ploughley, county of Oxford, 5 miles (N.N.E.) from Bicester, containing 143 inhabitants. The living is a rectory, with that of Shelswell, in the archdeaconry and diocese of Oxford, rated in the king's books at £3. 15. 5. J. Harrison, Esq. was patron in 1805. The church is dedicated to St. Michael.

NEWTON-RIGNY, a parish in Leath ward, county of Cumberland, 3 miles (W. N. W.) from Penrith, containing, with the townships of Catterlen and Newton-Rigny, 250 inhabitants, of which number, 126 are in the township of Newton-Rigny. The living is a perpetual curacy, in the archdeaconry and diocese of Carlisle, endowed with £400 private benefaction, £200 royal bounty, and £300 parliamentary grant, and in the patronage of the Bishop of Carlisle. The river Petteril runs through the parish.

NEWTON-SOLNEY, a parish in the hundred of Repton and Gresley, county of Derby, 2¼ miles (N. E.) from Burton upon Trent, containing 261 inhabitants. The living is a perpetual curacy, in the archdeaconry of Derby, and diocese of Lichfield and Coventry, and in the patronage of Sir Henry Every, Bart. The church is dedicated to St. Mary. The parish is bounded on the west by the river Trent. On a commanding eminence is a large castellated building, called "Hoskins' Folly." This place is in the honour of Tutbury, duchy of Lancaster, and within the jurisdiction of a court of pleas held at Tutbury every third Tuesday, for the recovery of debts under 40s.

NEWTON-STACEY, a tything in the parish and hundred of BARTON-STACEY, Andover division of the county of SOUTHAMPTON, 6 miles (S. W. by S.) from Whitchurch. The population is returned with the parish.

NEWTON-TONEY, a parish in the hundred of AMESBURY, county of WILTS, 4½ miles (E. by S.) from Amesbury, containing 282 inhabitants. The living is a rectory, in the archdeaconry and diocese of Salisbury, rated in the king's books at £19. 13. 9., and in the patronage of the President and Fellows of Queen's College, Cambridge.

NEWTON-TRACEY, a parish in the hundred of FREMINGTON, county of DEVON, 5½ miles (E.) from Bideford, containing 84 inhabitants. The living is a discharged rectory, in the archdeaconry of Barnstaple, and diocese of Exeter, rated in the king's books at £5. 8. 1½., endowed with £200 royal bounty, and in the patronage of the Crown. The church is dedicated to St. Thomas à Becket.

NEWTON-UNDERWOOD, a township in that part of the parish of MITFORD which is in the western division of MORPETH ward, county of NORTHUMBER-LAND, 3 miles (W.) from Morpeth, containing 75 inhabitants. Here are the ruins of an ancient tower.

NEWTON-VALENCE, a parish in the hundred of SELBORNE, Alton (North) division of the county of SOUTHAMPTON, 4 miles (S.) from Alton, containing 280 inhabitants. The living is a vicarage, in the archdeaconry and diocese of Winchester, rated in the king's books at £13. 10. 2¼. The Rev. E. White was patron in 1795.

NEWTOWN, a township in the parish of IRTHING-TON, ESKDALE ward, county of CUMBERLAND, 2¾ miles (N. W. by W.) from Brampton, containing 222 inhabitants.

NEWTOWN, a hamlet in the parish of LEO-MINSTER, hundred of WOLPHY, county of HEREFORD, 4 miles (S. by E.) from Leominster. The population is returned with Ivington.

NEWTOWN, a township in the parish of ROTH-BURY, western division of COQUETDALE ward, county of NORTHUMBERLAND, 1½ mile (W. S. W.) from Roth-bury, containing 56 inhabitants.

NEWTOWN, a chapelry in that part of the parish of WEM which is in the Whitchurch division of the hundred of BRADFORD (North), county of SALOP, 4 miles (N.W.) from Wem, containing 72 inhabitants. The living is a perpetual curacy, in the archdeaconry of Salop, and diocese of Lichfield and Coventry, endowed with £600 royal bounty, and £200 parliamentary grant, and in the patronage of the Inhabitants. The chapel was consecrated in 1663, and dedicated to King Charles the Martyr.

NEWTOWN near NEWBURY, a parish in the hundred of EVINGAR, Kingsclere division of the county of SOUTHAMPTON, 2 miles (S. by E.) from Newbury, containing 268 inhabitants. The living is a perpetual curacy, annexed to the rectory of Burghclere, in the archdeaconry and diocese of Winchester. The church is dedicated to St. Mary and St. John the Baptist. Lady Lucy Berkeley, in 1626, bequeathed a rent-charge of £10 for teaching poor children.

NEWTOWN-LINFORD, a parish in the western division of the hundred of GOSCOTE, county of LEI-CESTER, 5½ miles (N. W.) from Leicester, containing 549 inhabitants. The living is a perpetual curacy, in the peculiar jurisdiction of the Lord of the Manor of Groby.

NEW-VILLAGE, an extra-parochial liberty, in the Hunsley-Beacon division of the wapentake of HARTHILL, East riding of the county of YORK, 2½ miles (S.W.) from North Cave, containing 149 inhabitants.

NEYLAND, formerly a parish, now a hamlet in that of ASHWELLTHORPE, hundred of HUMBLEYARD, county of NORFOLK, 4½ miles (S. E.) from Wymond-ham. The population is returned with the parish. The church, which was dedicated to St. Peter, has long since been demolished, and the living consolidated with that of Ashwellthorpe.

NIBLEY (NORTH), a parish in the upper division of the hundred of BERKELEY, county of GLOUCESTER, 2½ miles (N. W.) from Wotton under Edge, containing 1553 inhabitants. The living is a perpetual curacy, in the archdeaconry and diocese of Gloucester, endowed with £400 private benefaction, £400 royal bounty, and £800 parliamentary grant, and in the patronage of the Dean and Canons of Christ Church, Oxford. The church, dedicated to St. Martin, has lately received an addition of fifty free sittings, the Incorporated Society for the enlargement of churches and chapels having granted £50 towards defraying the expense. There is a place of worship for Wesleyan Methodists. William Purnell, in 1763, bequeathed £300 to purchase an annuity for teaching five boys of the parish, also an estate for apprenticing the sons of parishioners, with each of whom a premium of about £20 is given, the total annual income being £57. 2. 6. There is a bequest of £4. 10. per annum by Matthew Tyndall, for teaching poor children to read.

NIBTHWAITE, a township in the parish of COUL-TON, hundred of LONSDALE, north of the sands, county palatine of LANCASTER, 8 miles (N.) from Ulverstone. The population is returned with the parish.

NICHOL-FOREST, a chapelry in the parish of KIRK-ANDREWS upon ESK, ESKDALE ward, county of CUMBERLAND, 10½ miles (N. E. by N.) from Longtown, containing 795 inhabitants. The living is a perpetual curacy, in the archdeaconry and diocese of Carlisle, endowed with £1000 royal bounty, and in the patronage of the Rector of Kirk-Andrews upon Esk. The chapel, situated at Kingfield, was rebuilt in 1812. There is a small charity school. The Liddel and Kershope rivers, which separate the chapelry from Scotland, form here some beautiful cascades, and from the bed of the former rises a chalybeate spring, called Hert-fell Spa, the water of which is strongly impregnated with alum. Arm-strong, the poet, was born in this neighbourhood.

NICHOLAS (ST.), a parish in the hundred of WON-FORD, county of DEVON, 5½ miles (E. by S.) from New-ton-Abbots, containing 969 inhabitants. The living is a discharged vicarage, in the archdeaconry and diocese of Exeter, endowed with £200 private benefaction, £800 royal bounty, and £500 parliamentary grant, and in the patronage of Lord Clifford. The parish is bounded on the east by the river Teign, and lies opposite to Teign-mouth, a pleasant and much improved bathing-place.

NICHOLAS (ST.), a chapelry in the parish of STANFORD le HOPE, hundred of BARSTAPLE, county of

ESSEX. Four almshouses were endowed, with about £6 per annum, by Ralph Finch.

NICHOLAS (ST.) CASTLE-HOLD, a parish in the liberty of WEST MEDINA, Isle of Wight division of the county of SOUTHAMPTON, adjacent to the town of Newport, containing 281 inhabitants. The living is a discharged vicarage, in the archdeaconry and diocese of Winchester, rated in the king's books at £7, and in the patronage of the Governor of the Isle of Wight.

NICHOLAS (ST.) at WADE, a parish in the hundred of RINGSLOW, or Isle of THANET, lathe of ST. AUGUSTINE, county of KENT, 6½ miles (W. S. W.) from Margate, containing 590 inhabitants. The living is a vicarage, in the peculiar jurisdiction and patronage of the Archbishop of Canterbury, rated in the king's books at £15. 19. 7., and endowed with £200 parliamentary grant. Thomas Paramore, in 1636, gave a house and land, also a rent-charge of £6, in support of a schoolmaster, who, by the further aid of the parishioners, instructs about forty-two children.

NICKLEBY, a township in the parish of LYTHE, eastern division of the liberty of LANGBAURGH, North riding of the county of YORK, 6½ miles (W. by N.) from Whitby, containing 147 inhabitants. There is a place of worship for Independents.

NIDD, a parish in the liberty of RIPON, West riding of the county of YORK, 1½ mile (E.) from Ripley, containing, with Killinghall, 86 inhabitants. The living is a discharged vicarage, in the archdeaconry of Richmond, and diocese of Chester, rated in the king's books at £3. 6. 10½., endowed with £200 royal bounty, and in the patronage of the King, as Duke of Lancaster.

NIGHTON, a chapelry in the parish of ST. WINNOW, WEST hundred, county of CORNWALL, 2 miles (E. by N.) from Lostwithiel. The population is returned with the parish. The chapel, dedicated to St. Necton, has lately received an addition of one hundred and twenty free sittings, the Incorporated Society for the enlargement of churches and chapels having granted £60 towards defraying the expense.

NINEBANKS, a chapelry in the parish of ALLENDALE, southern division of TINDALE ward, county of NORTHUMBERLAND, 6½ miles (N. E.) from Alston-Moor. The population is returned with the parish. The living is a perpetual curacy, annexed to that of Allendale, in the peculiar jurisdiction of the Archbishop of York, endowed with £400 private benefaction, £1000 royal bounty, and £600 parliamentary grant, The chapel was rebuilt and the cemetery enlarged about 1813.

NINEHEAD, a parish in the hundred of TAUNTON and TAUNTON-DEAN, county of SOMERSET, 1½ mile (N. by W.) from Wellington, containing 308 inhabitants. The living is a discharged vicarage, in the archdeaconry of Taunton, and diocese of Bath and Wells, rated in the king's books at £8. 7. 11., endowed with £200 private benefaction, and £200 royal bounty, and in the patronage of the Crown. The church is dedicated to All Saints. The river Tone, which runs through the parish, was wont frequently to overflow its banks, till the spirited proprietor of the parish, W. A. Sanford, Esq., caused its bed to be widened to the extent of about forty yards, at which work and in building a bridge of three arches, one hundred and seventy

feet in length, forming several picturesque cascades, &c., he employed from five hundred to six hundred men during the greater part of the years 1815 and 1816. A school also has been erected and is supported by his son, E. A. Sanford, Esq., for the education of from sixty to seventy children upon the National system. Limestone is obtained in the parish.

NINFIELD, a parish in the hundred of NINFIELD, rape of HASTINGS, county of SUSSEX, 5¼ miles (S. W. by W.) from Battle, containing 618 inhabitants. The living is a vicarage, in the archdeaconry of Lewes, and diocese of Chichester, rated in the king's books. at £8, and in the patronage of the Earl of Ashburnham. The church is dedicated to St. Mary.

NITON, a parish in the liberty of EAST MEDINA, Isle of Wight division of the county of SOUTHAMPTON, 8 miles (E.) from Newport, containing 443 inhabitants. The living is a rectory, united to the vicarage of Godshill, in the archdeaconry and diocese of Winchester, rated in the king's books at £20. 7. 1. The church, dedicated to St. John the Baptist, is a very ancient structure: on the south side of it, without the wall of the cemetery, is a cross raised upon steps with a basin on the top, supposed to have been used anciently as a baptismal font. Richard Weecks, in 1784, bequeathed £150, which, with subsequent gifts, produces an annual income of £10, for teaching the children of the parish to read.

NIXONS, a township in the parish of BEWCASTLE, ESKDALE ward, county of CUMBERLAND, 13 miles (E. N. E.) from Longtown, containing 224 inhabitants. Several trout streams bound and intersect the township.

NOCKHOLT, a parish in the hundred of RUXLEY, lathe of SUTTON at HONE, county of KENT, 5 miles (N. W.) from Seven-Oaks, containing 407 inhabitants. The living is a perpetual curacy, in the exempt deanery of Shoreham, which is in the peculiar jurisdiction of the Archbishop of Canterbury, endowed with £400 private benefaction, and £600 parliamentary grant, and in the patronage of the Rector of Orpington. There is a place of worship for Wesleyan Methodists.

NOCTON, a parish in the second division of the wapentake of LANGOE, parts of KESTEVEN, county of LINCOLN, 7 miles (S. E.) from Lincoln, containing 376 inhabitants. The living is a vicarage, in the archdeaconry and diocese of Lincoln, rated in the king's books at £7. 17. 11., and in the patronage of the Crown. The church is dedicated to St. Peter. A priory of Black canons, in honour of St. Mary Magdalene, was founded here, in the reign of Stephen, by Robert D'Arcy, which at the dissolution had a revenue of £52. 19. 2.

NOCTORUM, a township in the parish of WOODCHURCH, lower division of the hundred of WIRRALL, county palatine of CHESTER, 7½ miles (N.) from Great Neston, containing 30 inhabitants.

NOKE, a parish in the hundred of PLOUGHLEY, county of OXFORD, 5¼ miles (N. N. E.) from Oxford, containing 168 inhabitants. The living is a discharged rectory, in the archdeaconry and diocese of Oxford, rated in the king's books at £7. 19. 7. The Duke of Marlborough was patron in 1804. The church is dedicated to St. Giles.

NONINGTON, a parish in the hundred of WINGHAM, lathe of ST. AUGUSTINE, county of KENT, 4½ miles (S. by E.) from Wingham, containing 730 inhabitants.

The living is a perpetual curacy, with that of Womenswold, in the archdeaconry and diocese of Canterbury, and in the patronage of the Archbishop of Canterbury. The church, dedicated to St. Mary, is principally in the early style of English architecture.

NOOK (THE), a township in the parish of BELLINGHAM, north-western division of TINDALE ward, county of NORTHUMBERLAND, ½ a mile (E.) from Bellingham, containing 113 inhabitants. It is bounded on the south by the North Tyne river.

NORBRECK, a joint township with Bispham, in the parish of BISPHAM, hundred of AMOUNDERNESS, county palatine of LANCASTER, 3 miles (W. N. W.) from Poulton. The population is returned with Bispham.

NORBURY, a chapelry in the parish of STOCKPORT, hundred of MACCLESFIELD, county palatine of CHESTER, 4¼ miles (S. S. E.) from Stockport, containing 680 inhabitants. The living is a perpetual curacy, in the archdeaconry and diocese of Chester, endowed with £600 royal bounty. Thomas Leigh, Esq. was patron in 1795. A school-house was erected about 1760, by Peter Leigh, Esq.

NORBURY, a township in the parish of MARBURY, hundred of NANTWICH, county palatine of CHESTER, 4¼ miles (N. by E.) from Whitchurch, containing 438 inhabitants. A branch of the Chester canal passes through the township.

NORBURY, a parish in the hundred of APPLETREE, county of DERBY, 4 miles (S. W.) from Ashbourn, containing, with the township of Roston, 498 inhabitants. The living is a rectory, with the perpetual curacy of Snelstone, in the archdeaconry of Derby, and diocese of Lichfield and Coventry, rated in the king's books at £15. 16. 0½., and in the patronage of Thomas Fitzherbert, Esq. The church is dedicated to St. Mary: the chancel is a fine specimen of the decorated style, with large windows exhibiting the original stained glass, which is strikingly beautiful. Here, amongst many ancient monuments of the Fitzherberts, is one to the memory of Sir Anthony, a celebrated writer on the law, who was born at this place, and died in 1538. A free school was founded in 1678, by a bequest from Mr. Thomas Williams, and endowed with land now let for £18 per annum, for which about twenty poor children are instructed.

NORBURY, a parish in the hundred of PURSLOW, county of SALOP, 4½ miles (N. E.) from Bishop's Castle, containing 377 inhabitants. The living is a perpetual curacy, with the vicarage of North Lydbury, in the archdeaconry of Salop, and diocese of Hereford, and in the patronage of the Rev. John Bright Bright. The church is dedicated to All Saints.

NORBURY, a parish in the western division of the hundred of CUTTLESTONE, county of STAFFORD, 4 miles (N. E.) from Newport, containing, with the township of Weston-Jones, 309 inhabitants. The living is a rectory, in the archdeaconry of Stafford, and diocese of Lichfield and Coventry, rated in the king's books at £10. 2. 6., and in the patronage of Lord Anson. The church is dedicated to St. Peter.

NORCOTT, a township in that part of the parish of ST. HELEN, ABINGDON, which is in the hundred of HORMER, county of BERKS, 1 mile (N.) from Abingdon, containing 85 inhabitants.

NORDLEY (KING'S), a township in that part of the parish of ALVELEY which is in the hundred of STOTTESDEN, county of SALOP, 5¾ miles (S. E.) from Bridgenorth. The population is returned with the parish.

NORFOLK, a maritime county, bounded on the north and east by the German Ocean, or North Sea; on the south by the county of Suffolk, from which it is separated by the river Waveney, and the Lesser Ouse; and on the west by Cambridgeshire and a small part of Lincolnshire, from which it is separated by the Greater Ouse and Nene rivers. It extends from 52° 22′ to 52° 58′ (N. Lat.), and from 10′ to 1° 43′ (E. Lon.); and includes an area of two thousand and ninety-two square miles, or one million three hundred and thirty-eight thousand eight hundred and eighty statute acres. The population, in 1821, was 344,368. The name is but slightly altered in orthography and pronunciation from the Saxon compound, North-folc, signifying "the northern people," which term was used in the early Saxon kingdom of East Anglia, to distinguish the inhabitants of the northern part of it from those of the southern, who were called Suth-folc, for the like reason. At the period of the Roman Conquest this county was inhabited by the Cenomanni, or Cenimagni, a tribe of the Iceni, who, according to Whitaker, were descended from the Cenomanni of Gaul, and had their chief city at Caistor, near Norwich. Within the limits of the county, or contiguous to it, were established five principal, besides several subordinate, Roman stations. These and other fortifications were placed under the command of an officer, whose title, according to some authors, was Comes tractus maritimi, Count of the maritime district; and, according to others, Comes litoris Saxonici, Count of the Saxon shore; the Saxons at that period greatly harassing the Roman possessors of Britain by their piratical attacks on this part of the coast. After the disastrous events which succeeded the retirement of the Roman forces from Britain, in the year 575, Uffa, the first Saxon leader that established himself in this part of the island, assumed dominion over the territory now comprised in the counties of Norfolk, Suffolk, and Cambridge, which then took the name of East Anglia, of which Norfolk continued to form a very important part until all the kingdoms of the octarchy were united under the dominion of Egbert, about four hundred years after the first landing of the Saxons. Norfolk shared largely in the general calamity produced by the hostile and piratical incursions of the Danes, who at first chiefly directed their attacks upon East Anglia, landing, in 870, within the mouth of the river Yare. Prior to the death of Egbert they obtained possession of the whole of East Anglia; and although, during the reigns of several of his successors, they were masters of almost every part of the kingdom, yet, having been totally defeated by the Saxon forces under Alfred, that prince limited their residence to the province of East Anglia, and Norwich became their chief city. In revenge for the general massacre of the Danes by King Ethelred II., Sweyn, King of Denmark, invaded England with a numerous army and a powerful fleet, and landing on the coast of Norfolk, burned the cities of Norwich and Thetford; but in this desolating career his army was opposed by the Saxons under Earl Ulfketel, who defeated the Danes in successive battles, and at last compelled them to re-embark. In the year 1010 they returned, and having landed at Ipswich, and defeated Ulfketel, once more possessed themselves of East Anglia; and this province was afterwards included in that portion of the country allotted to Canute, the son of Sweyn, when the kingdom was divided between him and Edmund Ironside, and which was in consequence called *Denelege*, or the Danish jurisdiction.

After the Norman Conquest, and in the reign of William Rufus, Roger Bigod, Earl of Norfolk, taking part with Robert, Duke of Normandy, against William, Norfolk sustained considerable devastation in the conflicts that ensued. It also greatly participated in the disasters caused by the attempt of Prince Henry to deprive his father, King Henry II., of the crown, his cause having been espoused by the Earl of Norfolk. In the reign of John, Roger Bigod, Earl of Norfolk, took part with the refractory barons, and that monarch, laying waste the baronial possessions in this part of his dominions, came to Lynn, and thence crossed the washes into Lincolnshire, but, in consequence of the advance of the tide, lost his baggage in the passage. This county was afterwards over-run by the forces of Louis the Dauphin, who exacted heavy contributions from the inhabitants. In the reign of Richard II., during the rebellion headed by Jack Straw and Wat Tyler, the standards of those leaders were joined by several of the lower orders in this county; and Norwich was invested by the insurgents, led on by an individual named Letester : these, however, were so dispirited by the seizure and condemnation of their captain, that they forthwith dispersed. Henry VII., when Lambert Simnel was counterfeiting the person of Edward Plantagenet, and as such had been crowned in Dublin, doubtful of the loyalty of the eastern counties, or apprehensive that the Pretender would attempt a landing on this coast, went in person through the counties of Suffolk and Norfolk, and kept his Christmas at Norwich, whence he proceeded on a pilgrimage to the chapel of Our Lady at Walsingham, to offer his devotions at the holy shrine; and when all fear of danger had been dissipated, he sent his banner to the chapel in acknowledgment of his deliverance, and returned to the capital. In the reign of Edward VI., owing to a system of enclosing adopted by the nobility and gentry who had become possessed of the abbey lands, a rebellion broke out in this county; and the insurgents, being actuated by the same spirit as the levellers in the reign of Richard II., proceeded to abolish all distinctions of rank or title, and to execute their designs under the direction of two ringleaders named Ket. Their chief place of rendezvous was Mousehold heath, near Norwich, where the elder of the leaders, Robert Ket, with assistant deputies from every hundred, held his councils under a large tree, hence called "The Oak of Reformation." After the county had long been harassed by exactions and other outrages, committed by these rebels, and all previous attempts to quell the insurrection had failed, a large army, which had been raised for the king's service in Scotland, was despatched against them, under the command of the Earl of Warwick, by which Robert Ket was taken, and the rebels dispersed, though, it appears, with considerable loss to the king's troops. At the commencement of the dis-

sensions between Charles I. and his subjects, the county of Norfolk took an active part; and when the parliament had voted the necessity of taking up arms, the inhabitants generally approved of the determination. This was one of the associated eastern counties placed under the command of the Earl of Manchester, and at an early period of the contest, Norwich was fortified against the royalists. At no period of the struggle do the king's forces appear to have gained much advantage in this county; Lynn was at first in their possession, but was quickly besieged and taken by the Earl of Manchester's troops.

Norfolk is in the diocese of Norwich, and province of Canterbury, and comprises the two archdeaconries of Norfolk and Norwich, in the former of which are included the deaneries of Brooke, Burnham, Cranwick, Depwade, Fincham, Hingham, Hitcham, Humbleyard, Reddenhall, Repps, Rockland, and Wacton, and in the latter those of Blofield, Breckles, Brisley, Flegg, Holt, Ingworth, Lynn, Norwich, Sparham, Taverham, Toft-Trees, and Walsingham, and part of that of Thetford, which together contain seven hundred and fifty parishes, of which four hundred and forty-one are rectories, one hundred and seventy-one vicarages, and seventy-eight perpetual curacies. For the purposes of civil government it is divided into the thirty-three hundreds of Blofield, Brothercross, Clackclose, Clavering, Depwade, Diss, Earsham, Erpingham (North and South), Eynsford, Flegg (East and West), Forehoe, Freebridge (Lynn and Marshland divisions), Gallow, Greenhoe (North and South), Grimshoe, Guilt-Cross, Happing, Henstead, Holt, Humbleyard, Launditch, Loddon, Mitford, Shropham, Smithdon, Taverham, Tunstead, Walsham, and Wayland. It contains the city of Norwich, the borough, market, and sea-port towns of Lynn-Regis and Yarmouth; the small sea-port and market town of Cley; the borough and market town of Thetford; the borough of Castle-Rising; the market towns of Aylsham, East Dereham, Diss, Downham-Market, Fakenham, Foulsham, Harleston, East Harling, Holt, Loddon, Reepham, Swaffham, North Walsham, Watton, and Wymondham; and the little sea-port towns of Blakeney and Wells, which have no market. Two knights are returned to parliament for the shire, two representatives for the city of Norwich, and two for each of the boroughs. This county is included in the Norfolk circuit : the assizes and quarter-sessions are held at Norwich and Thetford, alternately. There are one hundred and fifty-four acting magistrates. The rates raised in the county for the year ending March 25th, 1827, amounted to £343,970. 17., and the expenditure to £344,950. 1., of which £297,156. 3. was applied to the relief of the poor.

The marine department of the civil government is vested in the Vice-Admiral of Norfolk, an officer appointed under a commission from the Board of Admiralty. He has power to hold a court of admiralty for the county, with judges, marshals, and other proper officers, subordinate to him, for the purpose of exercising jurisdiction in all maritime affairs. From the sentence of this court an appeal lies to the High Court of Admiralty, from the Lords Commissioners of which he regularly receives his instructions. This county, besides containing several places having separate jurisdiction, has various courts possessing peculiar privileges ;

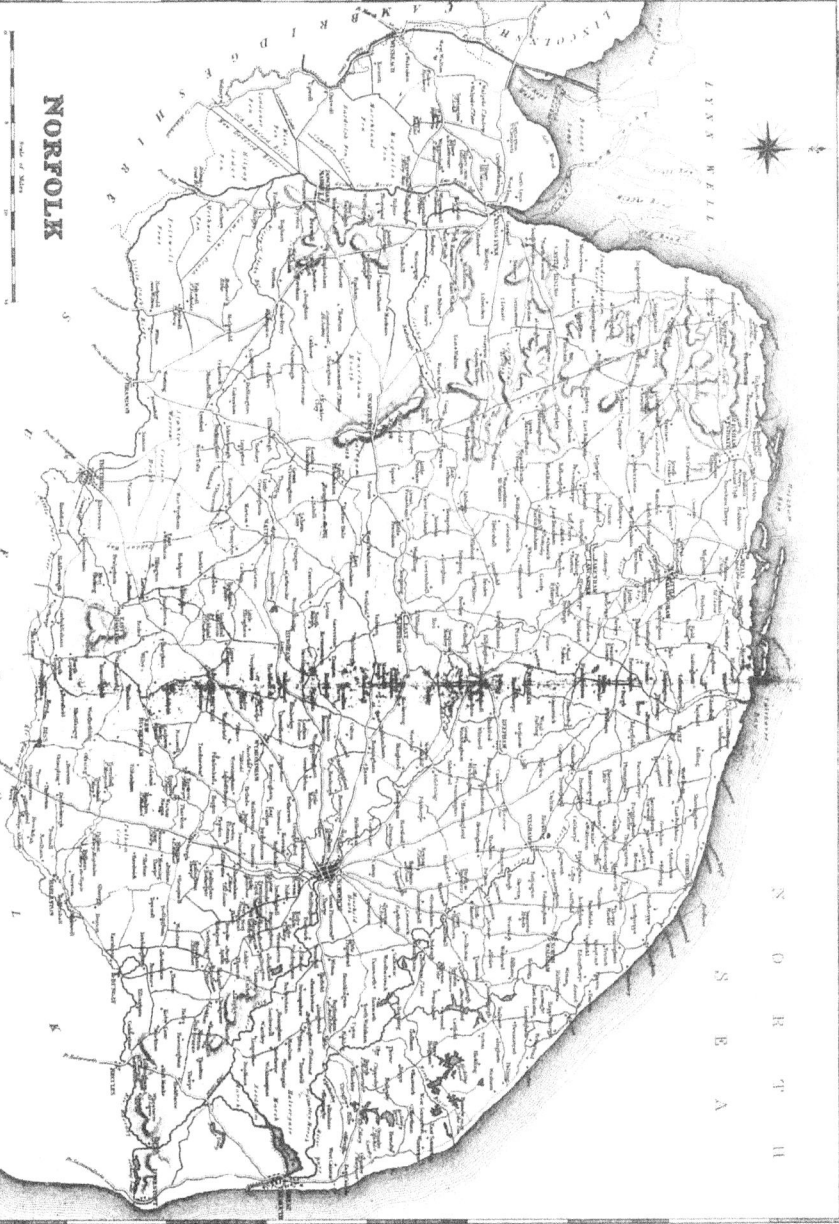

NORFOLK

of which the principal are the Court of the Liberty of the Duchy of Lancaster, held at Aylsham, and the Court of the Liberty of the Duchy of Norfolk, which is held at Lopham, or elsewhere within the liberty, at the discretion of the Duke of Norfolk. This latter liberty is of great extent within the county, comprising the whole hundred of Earsham, and the half-hundred of Guilt-Cross, besides the manors of Forncett, Framlingham Parva, Ditchingham, Ditchingham Parva, Loddon, Sisland, Halvergate, South Walsham, Cantley, Strumpshaw, Caistor, Winterton, Dickleburgh, Beighton, and Byfield; it also includes some small portions of the counties of Essex, Suffolk, Surrey, and Sussex. It was granted by Edward IV., by patent dated at Westminster, December 7th, 1468, to John, Duke of Norfolk, and Elizabeth, his wife, and their heirs for ever; the duke to have within the said manors, lordships, and jurisdictions, the return of all writs, bills, summonses, precepts, and mandates of the king, so that no sheriff, or any other officer, shall enter the said liberty: to this privilege were added all fines, amercements, profits, penalties, and other royalties; and with these was conveyed to the duke full power to have his own coroners, clerks of the markets, and other officers, and to appoint a steward of the liberty, who should have power to determine all actions under the value of 40s., and that persons residing within the said liberty should not be liable to answer for debts of such amount in any other court. The present Duke of Norfolk is lord of this liberty, and appoints a steward, coroner, &c., having also a prison for debtors. Formerly one sheriff served for the counties of Norfolk and Suffolk, but they were placed under distinct shrievalties in the reign of Queen Elizabeth, in the year 1576, and have continued so ever since.

The shape of the county is nearly elliptical; and it is so surrounded by the sea and by rivers that it may almost be considered an island, being actually connected with the main land only by a narrow causeway, raised across the marshes near Lopham. The surface is less varied in feature than perhaps that of any tract in the kingdom of equal extent, being for the most part flat; yet this uniformity of appearance is sometimes interrupted, particularly in the northern parts, where the ground is broken by gentle elevations, the hills and valleys being diversified by woods, coppices, hedge-rows, and plantations. On the south side of the county is a fine rich tract, extending towards the north and north-east; and these parts being enclosed, well cultivated, and abounding in timber more than most maritime districts, exhibit a variety of pleasing and cheerful prospects. In some parts the hedge-rows abound with trees, which at a distance have the appearance of extensive woods; but in others the great expanse of heath and bare unenclosed land has a dreary aspect: some of the most uninteresting parts lie on the south-western side of it. The most extensive prospects are those from Ashill, near Swaffham; Holkham; Docking, near Burnham; Melton, near Holt; Poringland; and Thorpe, near Norwich. The road from Warham is picturesque, overlooking Stiffkey vale, across which the hills rise in a bold manner, though bare of wood; near Blakeney also is another pleasing valley. Most of the rivers rise in marshy lands, and running through a comparatively level country, the fall is con-

sequently small, and their current slow; so that they contribute to keep the adjacent grounds in a swampy state, and to fill the atmosphere with dense and noxious vapours. When swelled by land-floods, their æstuaries being for the most part choked with silt driven up by the violence of the tide, they often overflow the low lands, and in their course form numerous small shallow lakes, or pools, provincially termed broads, or meres, which are plentifully stocked with fish, and much frequented by aquatic birds. The principal of these are in the districts through which the Bure, the Wensum, and the Waveney pursue their courses. Breedon, or Breydon broad, at the mouth of the Waveney, and immediately to the west of Yarmouth, is three miles in length and one and a half in breadth; Hickling-broad is nearly three miles in length, and one in breadth; and that at Rockland is a mile and a half long, and half a mile wide. There are a few in other parts of the county, as at Quiddenham, Diss, and Hingham; and in the fenny districts many temporary ones are formed during the winter season, in the vicinity of which are numerous decoys for wild fowl.

The coast has no indentations of magnitude, and although it terminates that great bed of chalk which, commencing in the high cliffs of Dorsetshire, passes across the kingdom to this county, yet it is for the most part flat, and, exclusively of some bold headlands in the vicinity of Cromer, and some wooded hills in the neighbourhood of Sherringham, the only remarkable promontory throughout its whole extent is Hunstanton cliff, commonly called St. Edmund's Point. The other eminences on the east consist of clay, and are continually being undermined by the violence of the waves. Much of the coast consists of a low sandy beach, covered with gravel and loose pebbles, called shingles, which, by the force of the waves, are frequently thrown up in vast heaps: these, by the constant accumulation of sand, are formed into banks, and are held together by the matted roots of what is called "sea-reed grass." Numerous banks of the same kind have been raised off the coast, far out at sea, and, being only discoverable at ebb or quarter tides, are frequently fatal to coasting vessels: the most remarkable is the large bank running parallel with the coast near Yarmouth, between which and the shore is a deep channel, known by the name of Yarmouth Roads, where ships ride safely in all states of the weather. The ranges of sand-hills on this, as on the opposite coast of Holland, tend to preserve a valuable portion of the county from inundation: a line of them, called the Meals, or Marum Hills, commences at Caistor, two miles north of Yarmouth, and extends, with occasional interruptions, to Happisburgh point, and thence to Cromer bay, where what are called "Mud Cliffs" begin, and line the northern shore to Lynn-Regis: these sand-banks are not all permanent, sometimes shifting their station suddenly by a submarine movement. Large portions of the county being exposed to the winds from the ocean, and other tracts to winds that blow over an immense extent of marsh land, the air is there extremely cold in winter and during the early part of the spring. Winds from the north and north-east are more prevalent here than in any other part of the kingdom, and are severely felt, so as considerably to retard the growth of vegetation.

3 D

With regard to soil, Norfolk may be divided into five districts. The first, lying to the north and east of Norwich, and comprising the eastern and western divisions of the hundred of Flegg, the hundreds of Walsham, Blofield, Happing, Tunstead, and the greater part of the northern and southern divisions of the hundred of Erpingham, consists of a deep, mellow, putrid sandy loam, similar to that of the most fertile part of the Austrian Netherlands; but unfortunately much of this tract is occupied by meres and marshes. The second, lying to the south and south-east of Norwich, includes the hundreds of Loddon, Clavering, Henstead, Earsham, Diss, Depwade, and Humbleyard, and some portions of those of Forehoe and Mitford, and consists of stiff wet land, composed of a mixture of sand and clay abounding in springs. The third includes the northern division of the hundred of Greenhoe, the hundreds of Taverham, Eynsford, Gallow, Launditch, Brothercross, Smithdon, Freebridge, and Clackclose: this is generally called " West Norfolk," and consists principally of light sandy land. Part of it in the north-western angle of the county, contains large tracts of excellent land, with a good deal of inferior quality; and here is practised the system of agriculture to which the general epithet of "Norfolk husbandry" is applied. Along the Ouse is a line of rich marshes. All the more central portion of the county has considerable natural fertility: marl is found in almost every part of it, and extensively employed as manure. The fourth tract, lying in the south-western part of the county, comprises the southern division of the hundred of Greenhoe, the hundreds of Shropham, Guilt-Cross, Wayland, and Grimshoe, and is composed of a light sand, so light indeed, in the last-mentioned hundred, that it frequently drifts with the wind, and is bare of vegetation. The whole of the westernmost part of the county, which is cut off from the rest of it by the Ouse, consists of the rich tract of Marshland, forming a fifth district, consisting of ooze, or silt, as it is provincially called, a marine deposit resting on clay at various depths: in some parts the clay mixes with the silt to the surface, and forms the richer grazing lands. Of this kind also is a narrow tract of land on the easternmost part of the coast, near the mouth of the united rivers Yare and Waveney, which extends a considerable distance inland towards Norwich; the whole in winter being commonly under water, so that in the spring it is necessary to drain it in order to convert it into pasture. There are also large tracts of swampy ground in the vicinity of Lodham, frequently inundated by land-floods, and producing little, except sedge and reeds. In the south-westernmost part of the county is an extensive tract of level land, forming part of the great fenny district, which also includes large portions of the counties of Suffolk, Cambridge, Huntingdon, Northampton, and Lincoln. The district called Marshland is one of the richest in the kingdom; it extends also into Lincolnshire, and forms an immense salt-marsh. The soil is strongly impregnated with salt, and is of so argillaceous a quality as to be generally regarded as a strong clay. It is intersected by ranges of banks, raised at different periods, to secure the fresh tracts which had been abandoned by the ocean: one of these is called the Roman bank. Other tracts have at various later times been regained from the sea: at Titchwell, three hundred acres were embanked in the

year 1786; and in 1790, eight hundred and sixty-eight acres were embanked and enclosed in the parishes of Terrington St. Clement and Terrington St. John. A still greater improvement was also accomplished by the family of Bentinck, in Marshland, where one thousand acres were reclaimed by an embankment about four miles in length; and in 1797, an act passed for the drainage and allotment of the immense tract of land situated in Marshland, Smeeth, and Fenn, besides much private property. According to the table of the soils furnished by the late secretary to the Board of Agriculture, Mr. Arthur Young, there are, of light sand, two hundred and twenty square miles; of more valuable sand, four hundred and twenty; of marshland clay, sixty; of various loams, nine hundred; of rich loam, one hundred and forty-eight; and of peat-earth, eighty-two. The substrata of the county, as far as research has discovered, consist of clunch, or indurated chalk; chalk in which flints are imbedded; gault, gravel, sand, silt, and peat-earth. On Mousehold heath, and in some other places, are extensive beds of clunch, which is used in building, and burned for lime: the chalk-pits in the vicinity of Norwich abound with those large black flints which compose the walls of many buildings in that city. In the gault, or argillaceous strata, has been found a sort of clay which is manufactured into an excellent species of earthenware: good brick-clay abounds in various places. The silt, or sea-sand, finely pulverised, is found at various depths, and is used in repairing the roads; and throughout the fen lands the peat-earth furnishes the poor with an abundant supply of fuel. On the shore near Thornham, at low water, is the appearance of a large forest having been, at some period, swallowed up by the waves, the stools of many large timber trees and many trunks being distinguishable, but in a state of great decay; these lie in a black mass of vegetable fibres, consisting of decayed branches, leaves, rushes, flags, &c.: a great extent of this matter is discoverable at low water.

Although by nature sterile, superior cultivation has rendered Norfolk one of the most productive counties in the kingdom. The arable lands form about two-thirds of the county; and the usual course of crops is, first year, turnips; second, barley; third, seeds for hay; fourth, seeds; fifth, wheat or rye; and sixth, barley: the next most frequently practised is the old four-shift system of turnips, barley, seeds, and wheat, in succession. Wheat is a general crop, but thrives best on the stiff loamy soils: the produce varies, according to the soil, from two to six quarters per acre; the general average is computed at three quarters. A vast quantity of barley is raised on the lighter soils, made into malt, and then shipped off; malt, indeed, may be considered the staple commodity of the county: the general average produce of barley is stated at four quarters per acre. Oats are sown only as a shifting crop, more than is consumed in the county being seldom grown: the rich lands in Flegg and Marshland usually produce ten quarters per acre. Rye is a common crop upon the light arenaceous lands of the south-western district. Other crops frequently cultivated are, buck-wheat, peas, beans, potatoes, vetches, or tares, cole-seed, clover, and other artificial grasses; and, but less frequently, cabbages. A considerable quantity of mustard is cultivated between March and Wisbeach, and around the latter place. Saffron is grown in the south-western district, and in the parts adjacent to Cambridgeshire. Flax is cultivated in the vicinities of Wisbeach, Downham, and Outwell; and hemp near Downham, Old Buckenham, Diss, Harleston, &c. Some of the marshes are peculiarly favourable to the growth of corn; but their liability to inundations has induced the inhabitants to prefer the dairy system, and in these parts large quantities of butter are made and exported, under the name of "Cambridge butter." On the whole, the grass lands of Norfolk, from the prevailing system being arable, have been too generally neglected, though some have been greatly improved by the practise of marling and by under-draining. The quantity of upland meadow and pasture has been estimated at nearly one hundred and twenty-seven thousand acres; and that of the marsh lands at upwards of sixty-three thousand. From Norwich to Yarmouth is an extensive range of meadow and marsh land; at Dawling and Guestwick is a considerable extent of pasture; and at Tasburgh, between Wymondham and Stratton, are many excellent meadows. One of the richest tracts of grazing land in Norfolk is the marshy district lying to the south of Lynn, and on the eastern side of the Ouse: these marshes, like all others in the county, are in general hired by the upland farmers, and not stocked regularly, but only when convenience requires it. Besides the marl, there are several peculiar kinds of manure employed, one of which is the little fish called stickleback, which is sometimes taken in immense quantities in the Lynn rivers. In East Winch and West Bilney, and scattered for ten miles thence to Wallington, is a remarkable bed of oyster shells lying in sea mud, from which the farmers obtain a great quantity to apply to their lands. Lime, sea-ooze, pond-weed, oil-cake, and river mud, are also used for the same purpose.

Of the cattle, the native cow is of small size, with middle-sized horns turned up, resembling those of the Alderney breed, generally of a red colour, and not profitable for the dairy, but hardy, and well calculated for barren pastures. Few of this kind are now kept by the large farmers, the Suffolk, polled, dun-coloured cow, having been generally substituted, and being deemed more profitable, though less hardy. The greater part of the cattle fed for the market are brought from Scotland, and purchased by the graziers, at a large fair held at St. Faith's, a small village near Norwich: several are also imported from Ireland. The average number of fat cattle annually sent from this county to the markets at Smithfield, Islington, St. Ives, and other places, is estimated at not less than twenty-thousand. The open sheep-walks were formerly very extensive: the native breed, and that which prevails in the county, carries a fleece of about two pounds in weight, and, when fattened, weighs about eighteen pounds per quarter. The wool was formerly classed for fineness as a third-rate among the native breeds; but it has been discovered that the neck wool of the Norfolk sheep is equal to the fleece of the Spanish breed. Although this was considered the breed best adapted to the soil, situation, and system of management of the county, yet the South Down is now to be found in almost entire possession of all the district from Swaffham to Holkham, and also in some other parts, together with a few of the Leicester breed. The num-

ber of sheep annually fattened for distant markets, in the same manner as the cattle, is supposed to be not less than thirty thousand. Some persons keep flocks of ewes solely for breeding; and at weaning time sell off the wether lambs to other counties. The hog is comparatively small, and of a thin bristly breed, very prolific, and the flesh is esteemed of good flavour: the number has been diminished by the decline of dairy farms, and the enclosure of waste lands. The horses, whether native or a cross with the Suffolk breed, are a hardy, and active race, from fourteen to fifteen hands high, and well adapted for the purposes of husbandry and the road. Poultry of all kinds is very plentiful; and in the sandy and loamy districts, owing to the dryness of the soil, and the range afforded by the unenclosed parts, the turkies are extremely numerous, and esteemed of excellent quality and flavour; besides affording a supply to several of the neighbouring counties, numerous large flocks are annually driven out of the county to London, and other distant places. Large supplies of geese are also bred in the fenny parts, and annually driven on foot to London, from the neighbourhoods of Downham, Wisbeach, and Lynn: turkey-poults, goslings, chickens, &c., are sent hence to the same market by light cara-vans, or stage-coaches. Rabbits are extremely numerous on the light sandy soils, being a considerable object of trade: numbers are bred about Castle-Rising, Thetford, Winterton, and Sherringham; but Methwold heath is the most celebrated, as producing the finest and best flavoured: this spot was noticed as a rabbit-warren so early as the reign of Canute. Woodcocks, snipes, widgeons, ducks, and other aquatic fowl, in consequence of the numerous marshes and meres, are very abundant: the heath-lands are frequented by the great bustard, the largest of British land-fowl.

A great part of this county was, within a century and a half, comparatively wild, bleak, and unproductive, more than half of it being rabbit-warrens and sheep-walks; and notwithstanding that so much has been effected towards bringing the whole of the land into a state of cultivation, and although the commons have been very much diminished during the latter part of the last century, and the early part of the present, yet the open and waste lands are still of great extent. Of the former, a great quantity lies in the northern division of the hundred of Greenhoe, the Lynn division of the hundred of Freebridge, and the hundreds of Brothercross, Smithdon, Grimshoe, Loddon, &c.; and large wastes and commons still exist at Attleborough, Turnmoor, Westear, Broad Moor, Fen and Row, Lyng, Beaconthorpe, Decoy, Borough, South Creake, Holt, and Flegg. From either Brandon or Thetford to Swaffham, the road lies for eighteen miles across a tract consisting of warrens or sheep-walks, with but few cultivated patches. Eccles common comprises four hundred acres of thick fern. A peculiar custom exists in Norfolk respecting the grazing of sheep on commonable lands; which is, that the lord, as he is called, of every township, orders how many and what sort of sheep the people shall have, where the walks shall be fixed both in summer and winter, on what spots they shall be folded, and how they shall be driven from place to place. Norfolk contains numerous woods, though they are partially scattered through the county: the principal are

3 D 2

those of Foxley, in the hundred of Eynsford; some to the westward of Wymondham, in that of Forehoe; Shottesham, in Henstead; Ashwellthorpe, Hempnall, and Bunwell, in Depwade; and Hethel, Hethersett, and Ketteringham, in Humbleyard; besides smaller woods in Erpingham, Clavering, Earsham, &c. There are also some large woods at Billingford and Thorpe-Abbots, where hurdles and hoops are the principal articles of profit; and in several parts of the county, particularly in those to the north-west, are extensive woods of timber: these woods and plantations have been computed to occupy not less than ten thousand acres.

The manufactures, excepting for home consumption, consist chiefly of woven goods, which, in a variety of branches, still constitute the staple trade. The small village of Worsted, in this county, is remarkable as having given name to a kind of cloths made of wool differently dressed from that of which woollen goods are made; the yarn of the former being spun from combed, and that of the latter from carded, wool. Dormics, cambrics, calicoes, &c., which in like manner took their names from the places where they were first made, formerly constituted the principal articles of manufacture; and these were followed by druggets, serges, shalloons, duffields, &c.; which, in their turn, have been superseded by bombazines, worsted damasks, flowered satins, camblets, crapes, stuffs, tabinets, poplins, shawls, and a great variety of fancy articles, most of which are formed of wool, mohair, and silk, by different intermixtures and curious combinations. In this trade Norwich takes the lead; but the articles which have usually been considered as having been made in that city only, have been produced by the joint labour of several towns and villages of the county. Since the introduction of machinery, however, the trade has been more concentrated, and is now almost exclusively confined to Norwich, in which city are several silk-mills; the silk after being prepared, passes through other hands for the purpose of being manufactured into crape: there are establishments at North Walsham and Yarmouth, connected with the manufacturers at Norwich in this branch of trade: the Lincolnshire and Leicestershire wools are chiefly used, while that of Norfolk is for the most part exported for the use of the Yorkshire clothiers. At Norwich the making of cotton thread-lace has been introduced of late years.

Possessing a great extent of sea-coast, and abounding in rivers and streams, accompanied by numerous broads, or meres, Norfolk is well supplied both with fresh and salt-water fish: the latter are of all species, and in great plenty. The two chief fisheries are those of the herring and the mackarel. The herring fishery is by far the most important, and Yarmouth is the grand place of rendezvous for the boats engaged in it. The large shoal of herrings, which appears from the north of the Shetland Islands, is there separated into two divisions, one of which takes its course along the western shores of Britain, while the other, proceeding southward in the German Ocean, appears off the eastern coast of England in the month of September, when the grand fishing season commences. The merchants fit out large decked boats, of from forty to fifty tons' burden, each of which is manned with a master, mate, hawseman, waleman, net-rope man, and net-stower man, besides five or six labourers, called capstan-men: these

all engage to serve for the season at stipulated wages besides which the master, mate, hawseman, and waleman, have an allowance of a certain sum per last. The vessels, being victualled, and having some tons of salt on board, proceed four, six, or even twelve leagues from shore. Numerous boats from other parts of the eastern coast of England, and many from Holland, also fish on this coast, selling their cargoes at the free Michaelmas mart at Yarmouth. In prosperous years, as many as seventy thousand barrels have been exported, exclusively of the home consumption, which may be estimated at fifteen thousand more. A summer fishing for herrings was formerly practised, and numerous French and Dutch vessels repaired to the coast for that purpose; but the herrings have ceased to frequent it during the warm season. In the course of the summer months, therefore, the boats are employed in the mackarel fishery, which is very considerable, and, though of minor importance in a commercial point of view, yet, during the spring and summer season, when this fish, which is gregarious and migratory, appears off the coast in vast shoals, it furnishes an abundant supply of food, at a very moderate expense, to the inhabitants of Norfolk and the neighbouring counties. This county also participates in the Greenland fishery.

Norfolk, by means of its rivers, &c., has a most extensive internal communication with the northern and midland counties; but, having only two grand outlets to the sea, its foreign and coasting trade are almost wholly engrossed by the ports of Lynn and Yarmouth; Wells, Blakeney, Burnham-Market, and Cley, although they share in the corn trade, being chiefly fishing towns. By means of the Greater Ouse, and the rivers and canals with which it is connected, Norfolk supplies the central parts of the kingdom with coal, wine, timber, grocery, and other articles, previously imported into the ports above mentioned; and in return receives large quantities of cheese, corn, and malt. Its foreign trade, though now comparatively small, was formerly very considerable, especially to the Baltic, Norway, Holland, Portugal, and Spain. The agricultural produce of Norfolk amounting to twice as much as is consumed by its inhabitants, the exports are consequently great; and in a good corn year, when the exportation is free, it has been stated that the ports of this county, including that brought down the rivers, which forms about one-tenth of the whole, export as much corn as all the other ports of England collectively.

The principal rivers are the Greater Ouse, the Lesser Ouse, the Waveney, the Bure, the Wensum, the Yare, and the Nar. The Greater Ouse, rising in Northamptonshire, and having previously received the waters of the Lark, the Cam, and the Lesser Ouse, enters this county on its western border, to the south-west of Downham-Market, and having passed under Stow, Magdalen, and German bridges, is then joined by the Nar from the eastward, and empties its waters, after a course of nearly sixty miles, into the large arm of the German Ocean called the Wash, two miles below the harbour of Lynn-Regis, which is formed by it, the large æstuary at its mouth being called Lynn Deeps. The tide flows up this river to the vicinity of Denver, where it is checked by sluices erected for the purposes of drainage and navigation: at the period of the equinoxes this tide rushes up with great fury, and is called by the inhabitants "the Eagre." Besides admitting merchant-vessels of considerable burden as high as Lynn, it is navigable for barges above that port for the whole of its course through this county. The Lesser Ouse, or Brandon river, rises in a swampy meadow near the village of Lopham, in the southern part of the county, and almost immediately becomes its boundary, which it thenceforward continues to be; it takes a course, at first westward, but afterwards gradually inclines towards the north: at Thetford, where it becomes navigable, it is joined by the little river Thet, and thence, meandering through a sandy soil, it passes under Brandon bridge, and afterwards flows sluggishly through the fens until it joins the Greater Ouse at Littleport, on the borders of Cambridgeshire. The Waveney has its source in the same tract as the Lesser Ouse, but it pursues an opposite direction, immediately becoming the boundary of the county, which it continues to be throughout the rest of its course, and running eastward by Diss, Billingford, and Harleston to Bungay in Suffolk, it there makes an extensive curvature, in the form of a horse-shoe, and then proceeds to Beccles, in the same county, where it continues nearly north to Burgh, being there joined by the Yare, or Wensum, at the head of Breedon water, an expansion formed by these united rivers, which, contracting again, joins the sea below Yarmouth: the Waveney is navigable for barges as high as Bungay bridge. The Bure rises near Hindolveston, on the northern side of the county, and, running by Blickling, becomes navigable at Aylsham, whence its general course is in a south-easterly direction: after receiving several tributary streams, among which is the Thone, which flows from a lake near North Walsham, it passes under Acle bridge, and after being increased by the superfluous waters of the marshes, it joins the Yare on the northern side of Yarmouth. The Bure and its attendant broads abound with various kinds of fish, such as pike, tench, trout, and perch, the last being particularly plentiful. The Wensum rises near West Rudham, in this county, and being joined by numerous smaller streams in its course, which is in a south-easterly direction, it passes the city of Norwich, where it begins to be navigable; at Trowse it receives the Tass, or Tase, and near Burgh it is joined by the Waveney, and proceeds towards Yarmouth. The Yare is considered to rise near Attleborough, and, taking a north-easterly course, it joins the Wensum to the east of Norwich, and in this latter river its name is lost until the Wensum has been joined by the Waveney at the head of Breedon water, between which place and Yarmouth the united waters again assume the name of Yare, flowing past that town to the sea, to which it opens in a south-easterly direction. In the Yare, or Wensum, is found a singular species of perch, called a *ruffe*, which is smaller and of a more slender form than the common perch. The Nar, called also Sechy and Seechy river, has its source at Litcham, whence it flows westward by Castle-Acre to Narburgh, and thence under Sechy bridge, shortly below which it assumes a northerly course, and finally falls into the Greater Ouse, near Lynn-Regis, whence it is navigable up to Narburgh, a distance of about fifteen miles. The navigable river Nene forms part of the western boundary of the county, which it separates from Lincolnshire. This county has little artificial

navigation in the form of canals; the principal exertions of that kind having been directed towards extending and improving the navigation of the rivers. There is a canal from Wisbeach in Cambridgeshire to Outwell creek and Salter's Load in Norfolk, an extent of about six miles, for the purpose of improving the navigation of the river Nene. With a view to the more effectual drainage of the fens, as well as to facilitate the carriage of heavy goods, an act was obtained in the year 1795, for making a navigable canal, called the Eau-brink cut, to Lynn-Regis: in the year 1805, another act was passed to amend the former; but the work was not begun till 1818, and completed in 1820. Different private estates have small cuts to the navigable rivers for the conveyance of corn, &c. A navigable communication with the sea at Lowestoft, in the county of Suffolk, is now in progress, under the superintendence of an incorporated body of shareholders. All the principal modern roads crossing the county concentrate at Norwich: the mail-coach road from London, through Newmarket, enters the county near Thetford, and that from Ipswich, near Scole, or Osmondiston, both passing on to Norwich. The road from London, through Cam bridge, enters near Outwell, and passes through Downham-Market, Swaffham, and East Dereham, to Norwich: parallel with this, more northerly, a line of road from Lynn-Regis leads through Fakenham, Foulsham, and Reepham, to the same city. From Norwich, northward, a road leads through Aylsham, and terminates at Cromer, on the coast of the North sea; another extends north-eastward to the coast; and a third eastward, through Castle-Thorpe, Acle, &c., to Caistor, with a bend southerly to Yarmouth.

Five principal Roman stations were established in, and contiguous to, this county, viz.: *Branodonum, Garianonum, Venta-Icenorum, Sitomagus,* and *Ad-Tuam,* besides various encampments, where different remains of that people, such as coins, urns, &c., have been discovered, particularly at Brompton, Buckenham, and Thetford. Of the Roman roads that traversed this county there are few distinct vestiges. The great road which crossed the island from east to west, from the Norfolk coast to St. David's Head in Pembrokeshire, is supposed to have commenced at Burgh, near Yarmouth, whence it passed by Caistor, and is now conspicuous near Downham-Market, whence, crossing the river Ouse, it passes through the fens into Cambridgeshire. Some traces of vicinal ways are also still discernible. What is called Pedder's way, running from Thetford, by Ickborough, Swaffham, Castle-Acre, and Tring, to the sea near Brancaster, appears to be one of these. The road leading by Long Stratton to Tasburgh was probably another, whilst a third branched off from this to the north-west, passing through Marshland, Upwell, and Elm, to Wisbeach. What is called the *Milky Way* has been considered Roman; but is more likely of later date, and was probably made for the convenience of the pilgrims to the chapel of our Lady of Walsingham: it is traceable in several places, and is tolerably perfect in the vicinity of the tumuli called Grimes Graves. Other tumuli may be seen in different parts of the county, but they are not very numerous. On Mousehold heath, near Norwich, are many excavations in the earth, which King and other antiquaries have considered hiding-pits, or British.

caves. The number of parishes in this county being greater than that in any other county in England, the ecclesiastical edifices are numerous in a corresponding degree, though few of them possess grandeur of architecture. Many of them are in great part of Saxon, or Danish construction, and several have circular towers. There are also a few fine specimens of the Norman period, the principal of which is Norwich cathedral. Other examples of nearly the same style and age may be found in the ruinous churches of Wymondham, Attleborough, Binham, Castle-Acre, and St. Margaret's, in the town of Lynn. Many of the parishes have also been united, and, either as a cause or consequence thereof, several churches have fallen into ruins. Of ancient fonts, particularly fine specimens are contained in the churches of Binham, Norwich, Walsingham, and Wymondham. This county producing scarcely any stone, the greater number of the churches, as well as many of the other public buildings, are constructed almost wholly with flints, which are found in great abundance, and in many edifices are faced and squared, and laid in regular courses. The religious houses were extremely numerous, amounting, at the time of the general dissolution, to no fewer than one hundred and twenty-three, of all orders. The principal remains of monastic buildings are those of the abbeys of Creake, Dereham, and St. Bene't at Holme; and of the priories of Binham, Bromeholme, Old Buckenham, Castle-Acre, Flitcham, Thetford, and Walsingham. Of ancient castles, chiefly Norman, there are considerable remains at Norwich, Castle-Acre, and Castle-Rising. The most remarkable ancient mansions are Caistor Hall, near Yarmouth; Oxborough Hall, near Stoke; Winwal House, near Stoke; Stiffkey Hall, near Walsingham; and Beaconsthorpe Hall.

NORHAM, otherwise NORHAMSHIRE, a parish forming a detached portion of the county palatine of DURHAM, comprising the chapelry of Cornhill, and the townships of Duddo, Felkington, Grindon, Horncliffe, Loan-End, Longridge, Norham, Norham-Mains, Shoreswood, Thornton, and Twizel, and containing 3906 inhabitants, of which number, 901 are in the township of Norham, 7 miles (S. W. by W.) from Berwick upon Tweed. The living is a vicarage, in the archdeaconry of Northumberland, and diocese of Durham, rated in the king's books at £15. 6. 8., and in the patronage of the Dean and Chapter of Durham. The church, dedicated to St. Cuthbert, and built about 840, is principally in the Norman style of architecture, but it comprises only a part of the original edifice, the chancel and the east end having been demolished. It had anciently three chantries, in honour of St. Cuthbert, the Blessed Virgin Mary, and St. Nicholas, and had the privilege of sanctuary for thirty-seven days. The remains of Ceolwulph, a lineal descendant of Ida, and King of Northumberland, were brought from Lindisfarne and buried here, where also Gospatric, Earl of Northumberland, was interred. There is a place of worship for Independents. A free school, with a house for the master, was erected by subscription in 1809, and is endowed with about twenty acres of land allotted on enclosing the common, and producing an annual income of £36. The doctrine of Christianity is stated to have been first preached to the Northumbrians, by the Scottish missionaries, at Norham On the establishment of a see

for Northumbria, this place was given to Aidan, the first bishop, and continued in the possession of his successors until the time of Bishop Barnes, who alienated his rights to the crown : the bishops exercised a special jurisdiction throughout the district, having their sheriff, coroner, justices, and other civil officers, their court of exchequer, gallows, &c. By charter of Bishop Pudsey, the inhabitants enjoyed very extensive privileges.

Being situated on a pass, or ford, on the river Tweed, called Ubbanford, on the borders of England and Scotland, Norham was frequently the scene of rapine and bloodshed, and the place of meeting between the nobility and principal individuals of the two kingdoms for settling the affairs relative to the border. Bishop Flambard, in 1121, probably erected the first regular fortress, which, having been enlarged and strengthened by succeeding prelates, was, when well garrisoned, deemed almost impregnable. David I., King of Scotland, however, in 1138, took and destroyed the town and castle, after a spirited resistance ; but they were restored, in 1154, by Bishop Pudsey, who built the present great tower of the castle. Various treaties between the Scots and King John were arranged here, and, in 1215, that monarch, in consequence of the defection of the Northumbrian barons, and their having sworn homage to the Scottish king, Alexander II., laid siege to the castle, which held out successfully for forty days, when he was obliged to withdraw his forces. In 1318, it was unsuccessfully besieged by the Scots, who, however, were more fortunate in an attack in 1322, when they obtained possession of it, but were soon afterwards obliged to abandon it, having for ten days resisted an assault of Edward II. Soon after the accession of Edward III., they stormed the castle with success, but did not long retain it. The town was plundered and burnt, in 1355, by a party of Scottish troops, under the command of Sir William Ramsay ; and the castle, in 1498, was besieged by the Scottish monarch, but the Earl of Surrey advancing to the relief of the garrison, the assailants were compelled to retire. A short time prior to the battle of Flodden Field they again invested the fortress, which fell into their possession through information given by a deserter from the garrison. The remains of this strong edifice occupy the summit of a steep rocky eminence impending over the bed of the river, and so near that portions have been washed away by the stream : the keep, or main tower, with its vaults and prisons entire, is the principal part, and is constructed of a soft red freestone. About two miles below Norham, on the banks of the river, two urns, containing human bones, were found in a gravel pit, called the Crooks, near which are the pedestals of two ancient crosses, also an artificial eminence, probably a barrow, surrounded by stone steps. At New Waterford the Tweed is crossed by a chain bridge, the first of the kind erected in England : it was commenced in August 1819, and opened July 26th, 1820, having been completed at an expense of not more than £5000, to which the trustees added £1050 above the estimate of the engineer : the extreme length of the suspension chains, from the point of junction on each side of the river, is five hundred and ninety feet, and from the abutments four hundred and thirty-two; the height of the bridge from the surface of the river, twenty-seven feet ; and its width sufficient to allow two carriages to pass between the foot-paths : the weight of the chains, platform, &c., is about one hundred and sixty tons. Here is a considerable salmon fishery ; and two annual fairs are held on the second Thursday in May, and the third Thursday in October : a market was formerly held at Norham, but it has been long discontinued. The learned Dr. George Carlton, successively Bishop of Llandaff and Chichester, was born here.

NORHAM-MAINS, a township in the parish of NORHAM, otherwise Norhamshire, county palatine of DURHAM, though locally to the northward of Northumberland, 6½ miles (S. W. by W.) from Berwick upon Tweed, containing 122 inhabitants.

NORLAND, a township in the parish of HALIFAX, wapentake of MORLEY, West riding of the county of YORK, 2½ miles (S. W.) from Halifax, containing 1665 inhabitants. On Norland moor is an immense rock, called the Lad Stone: a name supposed to be derived from the British word *Llad*, to slay, and to have been in some way connected with the sacrifices of the Druids.

NORLEY, a township in the parish of FRODSHAM, second division of the hundred of EDDISBURY, county palatine of CHESTER, 5 miles (S. E.) from Frodsham, containing 434 inhabitants. There is a place of worship for Wesleyan Methodists.

NORMANBY, a parish in the eastern division of the wapentake of ASLACOE, parts of LINDSEY, county of LINCOLN, 7 miles (W. by S.) from Market-Rasen, containing 328 inhabitants. The living is a discharged vicarage, in the archdeaconry of Stow, and diocese of Lincoln, rated in the king's books at £5, endowed with £600 royal bounty, and in the patronage of the Dean and Chapter of Lincoln. The church is dedicated to St. Peter and St. Paul. There is a place of worship for Wesleyan Methodists. Mrs. Dunn, in 1767, gave a small endowment for the instruction of children. The parish is bounded on the east by the river Ancholme.

NORMANBY, a township in the parish of STOW, wapentake of WELL, parts of LINDSEY, county of LINCOLN, 7¾ miles (S. E.) from Gainsborough, containing 21 inhabitants.

NORMANBY, a tything in that part of the parish of ASH which is in the first division of the hundred of WOKING, county of SURREY, 5¼ miles (W. N. W.) from Guildford. The population is returned with the parish.

NORMANBY, a township in that part of the parish of ORMSBY which is in the eastern division of the liberty of LANGBAURGH, North riding of the county of YORK, 5¾ miles (W. N. W.) from Guilsbrough, containing 122 inhabitants.

NORMANBY, a parish in the wapentake of RYEDALE, North riding of the county of YORK, comprising the townships of Normanby and Thornton-Risebrough, and containing 223 inhabitants, of which number, 191 are in the township of Normanby, 5¼ miles (W. S. W.) from Pickering. The living is a discharged rectory, in the archdeaconry of Cleveland, and diocese of York, rated in the king's books at £9. 12. 6., and in the patronage of Arthur Cayley, Esq. Five poor children are educated for £6 a year, arising from a rent-charge left by Judith Boynton, in 1700. Here is a sulphureous mineral spring, the water of which contains carbonic acid and a small portion of neutral salt, and is taken as an alterative and purgative. Normanby gives the title of viscount to the family of Phipps, Earls of Mulgrave.

NORMANBY on the WOLD, a parish in the northern division of the wapentake of WALSHCROFT, parts of LINDSEY, county of LINCOLN, 4 miles (N. by E.) from Market-Rasen, containing 96 inhabitants. The living is a discharged rectory, united to that of Claxby in 1740, in the archdeaconry and diocese of Lincoln, rated in the king's books at £9. 10. 10. The church is dedicated to St. Peter.

NORMANTON, a parish in the hundred of REPTON and GRESLEY, county of DERBY, 2 miles (S.) from Derby, containing 294 inhabitants. The living is a perpetual curacy, annexed to the vicarage of St. Peter in Derby, in the archdeaconry of Derby, and diocese of Lichfield and Coventry. Normanton is in the honour of Tutbury, duchy of Lancaster, and within the jurisdiction of a court of pleas held at Tutbury every third Tuesday, for the recovery of debts under 40s. The Derby canal crosses the north-east part of the parish.

NORMANTON, a hamlet (formerly à chapelry) in the parish of BOTTESFORD, hundred of FRAMLAND, county of LEICESTER, 8 miles (N. W. by W.) from Grantham. The population is returned with the parish. The chapel is demolished.

NORMANTON, a parish in the wapentake of LOVEDEN, parts of KESTEVEN, county of LINCOLN, 7¼ miles (N. N. E.) from Grantham, containing 189 inhabitants. The living is a discharged rectory, in the archdeaconry and diocese of Lincoln, rated in the king's books at £10. 2. 6., and in the patronage of the Marquis of Bristol. The church, dedicated to St. Nicholas, is partly Norman, and partly in the early style of English architecture, with a curious tower, and a large stone font.

NORMANTON, a hamlet in the parish of SOUTHWELL, liberty of SOUTHWELL and SCROOBY, county of NOTTINGHAM, 1 mile (N. E. by N.) from Southwell. Here was formerly a chapel, which, after its desecration, was converted into a barn.

NORMANTON, a parish in the hundred of MARTINSLEY, county of RUTLAND, 5 miles (E. S. E.) from Oakham, containing 26 inhabitants. The living is a discharged rectory, in the archdeaconry of Northampton, and diocese of Peterborough, rated in the king's books at £5. 4. 7., and in the patronage of Sir Gilbert Heathcote, Bart. The church is dedicated to St. Matthew. The river Gwash runs through the parish, in which there is a chalybeate spring strongly impregnated with steel.

NORMANTON, a parish in the lower division of the wapentake of AGBRIGG, West riding of the county of YORK, comprising the townships of Altofts, Normanton, and Snydale, and containing 773 inhabitants, of which number, 250 are in the township of Normanton, 4½ miles (E. N. E.) from Wakefield. The living is a discharged vicarage, in the archdeaconry and diocese of York, rated in the king's books at £7, and in the patronage of the Master and Fellows of Trinity College, Cambridge. The church is dedicated to All Saints. A free school was founded here about 1592, by John Freeston, who endowed it with £10 a year, besides two hundred marks for the building of a house for the master and usher : twenty children are taught upon this foundation, and eight poor girls are instructed for about £5 per annum, the bequest of Elizabeth Levitt.

NORMANTON le HEATH, a chapelry in the parish of NAILSTONE, hundred of SPARKENHOE, county of LEICESTER, 3½ miles (S. S. E.) from Ashby de la Zouch, containing 215 inhabitants. There is a place of worship for Wesleyan Methodists.

NORMANTON upon SOAR, a parish in the southern division of the wapentake of RUSHCLIFFE, county of NOTTINGHAM, 4½ miles (N. N. W.) from Loughborough, containing 326 inhabitants. The living is a rectory, in the archdeaconry of Nottingham, and diocese of York, rated in the king's books at £7. 11. 0½., and in the alternate patronage of — Richards, and — Buckley, Esqrs. The church is dedicated to St. John. There is a place of worship for Wesleyan Methodists.

NORMANTON (SOUTH), a parish in the hundred of SCARSDALE, county of DERBY, 2¾ miles (E.N.E.) from Alfreton, containing 1056 inhabitants. The living is a rectory, in the archdeaconry of Derby, and diocese of Lichfield and Coventry, rated in the king's books at £9. 15. 5., and in the patronage of Sir E. Wilmot, Bart. The church is dedicated to St. Mary. There is a place of worship for Wesleyan Methodists. A charity school is supported by voluntary contributions. Some collieries are in operation in the neighbourhood, but the inhabitants are principally employed in frame-knitting. Jedediah Strutt, Esq., the ingenious inventor of the machine for manufacturing ribbed stockings, was born here.

NORMANTON (TEMPLE), a chapelry in the parish of CHESTERFIELD, hundred of SCARSDALE, county of DERBY, 3¼ miles (S.E.) from Chesterfield, containing 141 inhabitants. The living is a perpetual curacy, in the archdeaconry of Derby, and diocese of Lichfield and Coventry, endowed with £1400 royal bounty, and in the patronage of Miss Lord. A school is supported by small annual donations.

NORMANTON upon TRENT, a parish in the northern division of the wapentake of THURGARTON, county of NOTTINGHAM, 3¾ miles (E.S.E.) from Tuxford, containing 297 inhabitants. The living is a discharged vicarage, in the archdeaconry of Nottingham, and diocese of York, rated in the king's books at £4. 5., endowed with £400 private benefaction, and £400 royal bounty, and in the patronage of the Duke of Devonshire. The church is dedicated to St. Matthew. There is a place of worship for Wesleyan Methodists. Peter Moreau, in 1725, left a trifling sum for teaching poor children and providing each a bible : ten are instructed in a schoolhouse erected by Henry Jackson, whose daughter, Elizabeth Hall, in 1781, conveyed certain land, producing about £10 per annum, in further support of the master.

NORMANTON on the WOLDS, a township in that part of the parish of PLUMTREE which is in the northern division of the wapentake of RUSHCLIFFE, county of NOTTINGHAM, 6 miles (S.E. by S.) from Nottingham, containing 194 inhabitants. It is in the honour of Tutbury, duchy of Lancaster, and within the jurisdiction of a court of pleas held at Tutbury every third Tuesday, for the recovery of debts under 40s.

NORMANTON-TURVILLE, a hamlet in the parish of THURLASTON, hundred of SPARKENHOE, county of LEICESTER, 5¾ miles (N.E. by E.) from Hinckley, containing 19 inhabitants.

NORMICOTT, a liberty in the parish of STONE, southern division of the hundred of PIREHILL, county of STAFFORD, containing 878 inhabitants.

NORTHALL, a hamlet in the parish of EDDLESBOROUGH, hundred of COTTESLOE, county of BUCKINGHAM, 3½ miles (N. by E.) from Ivinghoe, containing 482 inhabitants.

NORTHALLERTON, North riding of the county of YORK.—See ALLERTON (NORTH).

NORTHAM, a parish in the hundred of SHEBBEAR, county of DEVON, 1½ mile (N. by W.) from Bideford, containing 2550 inhabitants. The living is a discharged vicarage, in the archdeaconry of Barnstaple, and diocese of Exeter, rated in the king's books at £10. 10., endowed with £200 private benefaction, £200 royal bounty, and £400 parliamentary grant, and in the patronage of the Dean and Canons of Windsor. The church is dedicated to St. Margaret. A place of worship for Independents was erected in 1829. Here are almshouses for four widows, and several small endowments for teaching poor children, of which some are applied in support of a school conducted on the Madras system. The parish is bounded by the Bristol channel on the west, and by the navigable river Torridge on the east.

NORTHAMPTON, a borough and market town, having separate jurisdiction, locally in the hundred of Spelhoe, county of NORTHAMPTON, of which it is the chief town, 66 miles (N. W. by N.) from London, on the road to Leicester, containing 10,793 inhabitants. This place, from its situation to the north of the river Nine, or Nene, (called by Camden the Avon)

Seal and Arms.

formerly the *Aufona*, is by some antiquaries supposed to have been called *North Aufonton*, of which this present name is probably a contraction ; by others it is said to have been called, by the Saxons, *Hamtune*, and to have had the word *North* prefixed by way of distinguishing it from other towns of the same name. It is unquestionably a place of antiquity, and must have attained a considerable degree of importance prior to the division of the kingdom into shires, from its having given name to that in which it is situated. In the reign of Edward the Elder it was in the possession of the Danes, who, in 921, made it the principal station of their forces, who marched thence to the siege of Towcester. In 1010, it was again attacked by the Danes, who burnt the town and laid waste the adjacent country. During the insurrection of the Northumbrians, in 1064, against Tosti, son of Earl Godwin, the insurgents, under Earl Morcar, whom they had chosen for their leader, marched to this place, where they committed excessive outrages, burning the houses of the inhabitants, whom they massacred, and carrying off great quantities of cattle, and several hundred prisoners. Harold, afterwards king, being sent against the insurgents, encountered them near the town, but listening to their just representations of the tyranny and oppression of Tosti, he entered into an accommodation with them, and procured for Morcar a confirmation of his assumed authority. The town, which had scarcely recovered from the depredation it suffered upon this occasion, was, at the time of the Conquest, given to Earl Waltheof, who had married the Countess Judith, niece of the Conqueror; but the earl having entered into a conspiracy against the king, was executed as a traitor, and his confiscated possessions were bestowed on Simon de St. Liz, Earl of Huntingdon and Northampton, who repaired and beautified the town, erected a strong castle for its defence, and surrounded it with massive walls, in which were four gates. From this period it rapidly improved, and from its central situation and the security of its fortifications, became the occasional residence of several of the kings, of whom Henry I., in the twenty-third year of his reign, celebrated the festival of Easter here with great pomp, and, in 1131, assembled a parliament, in which the English barons swore homage to his daughter, the Empress Matilda, whom he appointed his successor. In the 11th of Henry II., a council was convened here, at which Archbishop Becket was summoned to appear for his refusal to submit to the constitutions of Clarendon; and on the rebellion of Prince Henry, Anketil Mallore, one of his partizans, advancing to Northampton with a body of forces, defeated the king's troops, aided by a party of the inhabitants, and took two hundred of the latter prisoners. William, King of Scotland, being taken prisoner at the battle of Alnwick, was brought to Northampton, where Henry was then residing, and the Bishop of Durham, Roger de Mowbray, Earl Ferrers, with Anketil Mallore, and William de Dive, constables of the Earl of Leicester, waited upon him, to surrender the several castles which they had held against him. In 1180 a convention of barons and prelates was held here, to take into consideration the laws of the realm, and to amend and enforce the constitutions of Clarendon, by which the kingdom was first divided into six circuits, and three itinerant justices were assigned to each, for the administration of the laws and the punishment of offenders; and in the following year the king held a council previously to his visiting his dominions on the continent.

Richard I., soon after his return from captivity, kept the festival of Easter in this town, where he entertained William of Scotland, who came to solicit a grant of the county of Northumberland. During this reign a mint existed here, and on the death of Richard, the barons assembled in council at this place, and took the oath of allegiance to his brother John, at that time in Normandy. John, in the tenth year of his reign, being displeased with the citizens of London, removed his court of Exchequer to Northampton, and three years afterwards assembled a council of temporal lords, at which Pandulph and Durand, legates from the pope, attended on behalf of the exiled clergy, whom the king allowed to return to their country; but refusing to restore their confiscated property, he was excommunicated by the legates. Previous to the commencement of the war between the king and the barons, the latter transmitted to him their memorial of grievances, which the king having indignantly refused to redress, they laid siege to the castle of Northampton, but, being unable to reduce it, they withdrew their forces, after remaining before it fourteen days : it was, however, on the signing of Magna Charta, among other castles, placed in their custody, as security for the fulfilment of the conditions; but, on the renewal of the war, it was entrusted to Fulke

de Brente, a determined loyalist. In 1216, the townsmen attacked and killed many of the garrison under the command of that officer, in retaliation for which the soldiers burnt a considerable portion of the town. Henry III., attended by his court, celebrated the festival of Christmas at the castle, where he was splendidly entertained by the governor; and in the thirtieth year of his reign, the king gave the inhabitants ten marks to purchase books for a public library, a sacramental chalice for the church of All Saints, and smaller vessels of silver for the other churches. The castle was, in 1264, occupied by the insurgent barons under the Earl of Leicester, from whose son, Simon de Montfort, it was taken by stratagem, after many fruitless attempts to reduce it; but the following year it was retaken by the Montforts, who celebrated a tournament there, which was numerously and brilliantly attended; soon after which the elder Montfort was defeated and slain at the battle of Evesham. In 1268, a parliament was held here, in which the rebellious barons were deprived of their estates, and Simon de Montfort was banished the realm; and a council of prelates was assembled at the same time, at which the pope's legate excommunicated those bishops who had joined their party. During this reign, repeated attempts were made to establish a university in the town, in consequence of dissensions between the students and the citizens of Oxford; in 1258, a large party of students removed to this place, and a royal license was obtained for erecting public schools for teaching the arts and sciences : subsequent disputes between the students and the townsmen, both of Oxford and Cambridge, occasioned fresh accessions to Northampton, but, in 1265, the establishments were dissolved by order of the king, and the professors returned with their pupils to their ancient seats. In the reign of Edward II., John Poydras, the son of a tanner of Exeter, who pretended to be the son and heir of Edward I., was convicted and executed as an impostor in the town; and in the second year of the reign of Edward III., a treaty was concluded with the Scots, by which the king resigned his pretensions to the sovereignty of Scotland, in consideration of thirty thousand marks paid by Robert Bruce, whose infant son David was affianced to Jane, the king's sister, also an infant : in the same parliament was enacted the statute of Northampton, specifying in what cases pardon should be granted for felony, and regulating the appointment of judges of assize. The last parliament held here, was summoned in the fourth year of the reign of Richard II., to grant supplies for the troops, destined to serve in a war against France, when a poll-tax was ordered, the levying of which excited the rebellion headed by Wat Tyler : this parliament, together with the convocation of Canterbury, sat in the chancel of All Hallows' church, now All Saints', the castle having fallen into a ruinous state. During the war between the houses of York and Lancaster, a sanguinary and decisive battle took place on the 9th of July, 1460, in which Henry VI. was defeated and taken prisoner. The treacherous desertion of Lord Grey of Ruthin, who commanded the vanguard of the king's army, contributed to the defeat of the royal forces, on whose side fell the Duke of Buckingham, the Earl of Shrewsbury, Viscount Beaumont, Lord Egremont, and other nobles, who were buried in the town; the duke was interred in the church of the Grey friars, and several of the others in St. John's hospital, where their bones have been recently discovered. In the 9th of Edward IV., Earl Rivers and his son, who had been taken by the rebels under Sir Henry Nevil and Sir John Coniers, who headed the insurrection in Yorkshire, were beheaded in this town. Queen Elizabeth, in her progress through the country, visited Northampton, where she was hospitably received, and presented by the magistrates with a valuable purse containing £20 : a similar mark of respect was also paid to Charles I. and his consort, who, on passing through the town, were presented by the mayor and corporation with two bowls of silver gilt, containing one hundred marks. In 1637, the court of Eyre for the forests was held here, under the Earl of Holland, Chief Justice, as head of the commission, assisted by five of the judges and many of the nobility and gentry. During the parliamentary war, Lord Brooke took possession of the town, which he fortified for the parliament; and in 1675 it was nearly destroyed by a fire, which consumed six hundred houses, chiefly built of wood and roofed with thatch. From this severe calamity, of which the damage was estimated at £150,000, it recovered, under the auspices of the Earl of Northampton, who procured an act of parliament for its restoration.

The town is pleasantly situated on the acclivity of an eminence rising gradually from the north bank of the river Nene, over which are two bridges of stone, of which that to the south is a handsome structure of three elliptic arches : it consists principally of two spacious and regular streets, nearly a mile in length, which, intersecting each other at right angles, divide it into four nearly equal parts ; the houses are handsomely built of stone, and the town, which is well paved, and lighted with gas, under an act of parliament recently obtained, has a clean, respectable, and cheerful appearance : the central part is supplied with water from a reservoir near the market-place, into which it is conveyed by pipes from a spring, called the Conduit Head, in a field to the east of the town. The theatre, a handsome modern building, conveniently arranged and well fitted up, was opened in 1806, and the performances are well conducted by a provincial company : races take place annually in September, and are in general well attended ; and within these few years a spring meeting has been held, about the last week in March ; the race-course comprises about one hundred and seventeen acres, at a short distance from the town. At the end of Derngate-street is a fine promenade, made at the expense of the corporation : it is shaded by a range of lofty trees, and commands a pleasing view of the adjoining meadows. The environs are pleasant, and abound with handsome villas and thriving plantations : at the northern extremity of the town are the barracks, erected in 1796, forming a handsome range of building, consisting of a centre and two wings. The principal articles of manufacture are, boots and shoes, of which great quantities are made for the supply of the army; and stockings and lace, the latter of which, since the introduction of machinery, has materially declined : a considerable trade is carried on in the currying of leather. A branch canal was constructed, in 1815, from the river Nene to the Grand Junction canal, by means of which a facility of communication is obtained with almost every part of the kingdom. The market days are Wednesday, Friday, and

Saturday ; the last, a very large cattle market : the fairs are on the second Tuesday in January, February 20th, the third Monday in March, April 5th, May 4th, June 19th, August 5th and 26th, September 19th (for cheese), the first Thursday in November, the 28th of the same month, and December 19th, principally for horses, cattle, sheep, and pigs : the fairs for horses and cattle are numerously attended by dealers. The market-place is a spacious and commodious area, in the centre of which is a column with a powerful gas-light, and on the south side the conduit from which the town is supplied with water.

The borough received a charter of incorporation in the 31st of Henry II., which was confirmed in several succeeding reigns, and modified and enlarged in the 36th of George III., by which the government is vested in a mayor, an indefinite number of bailiffs who have served that office, a recorder, deputy recorder, an indefinite number of aldermen, and forty-eight common councilmen, assisted by a town clerk, chamberlain, two coroners, four serjeants at mace, and subordinate officers. The mayor, who is annually chosen, becomes an alderman on the expiration of his office ; the bailiffs are chosen from the common council, in which vacancies are filled up by the mayor and aldermen from the general body of freemen. The mayor, the late mayor, the recorder, deputy recorder, and three aldermen annually appointed, are justices of the peace within the borough. The freedom of the borough is inherited by birth, acquired by servitude, or obtained by marriage with a freeman's widow or daughter, or by purchase. The corporation hold quarterly courts of session, and have power to try for capital offences, which, however, they transfer to the assizes for the county : they also hold a court of record, at which the mayor and bailiffs preside, every third week, for the recovery of debts and determining pleas to any amount. The town hall is an ancient edifice commodiously arranged, and decorated with portraits of Sir Thomas White, the founder of St. John's College, Oxford, and a munificent benefactor to Northampton and other towns, and of the late Rt. Hon. Spencer Perceval, Chancellor of the Exchequer, and first lord of the Treasury. The borough gaol and house of correction is a small modern building adapted to the classification of prisoners. The borough has returned two members to parliament from the early part of the reign of Edward I. : the right of election is vested in the inhabitant householders not receiving alms, of whom the number is about two thousand : the mayor and bailiffs are the returning officers. The assizes for the county and the election of knights of the shire are held here. The county hall is a spacious and elegant structure, in the Grecian style of architecture, and contains courts for the assizes and quarter sessions, and a suite of rooms well adapted to the transaction of the general business of the county; in the hall, the ceiling of which is splendidly decorated, are portraits of King William III. and Queen Mary, Queen Anne, George I., and George II. : this edifice is deservedly admired as a handsome specimen of the Corinthian order. Adjoining the shire-hall is the common gaol and house of correction for the county, erected in 1794, at an expense of £16,000 : it is a spacious building, and contains eleven wards, four work-rooms, twelve day-rooms, and eleven airing-yards, for the classification of prisoners; an additional piece of ground has been enclosed within the area of the prison, for the erection of a tread-mill; the prisoners are employed in grinding and dressing corn, splitting beans, and drawing wire, and receive one-half of their earnings: the old county gaol has been converted into a lodge for the turnkey, and a prison for debtors.

The town comprises the parishes of All Saints, St. Giles, St. Peter, and St. Sepulchre, all in the archdeaconry of Northampton, and diocese of Peterborough, and formerly had seven parochial churches within the walls, and two without, of which only four are remaining. The living of All Saints' is a vicarage, rated in the king's books at £22, and in the patronage of such members of the Corporation as are Parishioners: the church, rebuilt soon after the fire in 1675, is a spacious edifice, in the Grecian style of architecture, having in the centre a cupola supported on columns of the Ionic order, and at the west end the original square embattled tower, which escaped the conflagration, and in which is a dial illuminated with gas, and a portico of twelve lofty Ionic columns supporting a cornice and balustrade, in the centre of which is a statue of Charles II.; on the pedestal is recorded his donation of one thousand tons of timber for the rebuilding of the church; the interior is appropriately ornamented; the altar-piece is decorated with paintings of Moses and Aaron, by Sir Godfrey Kneller; the chancel is separated by a richly-carved oak screen, and among the monuments are, one to the memory of the learned Dr. Conant, Prebendary of Worcester, and vicar of this parish, and a handsome marble monument, by Chantrey, to the Rt. Hon. Spencer Perceval, many years member for the borough, who was assassinated in the lobby of the House of Commons; his statue, elevated on a pedestal, is admirably sculptured, and exhibits gracefulness of form and dignity of expression: the old stone wall which enclosed the churchyard has been taken down, and a handsome iron palisade substituted in its place. The living of St. Giles' is a discharged vicarage, rated in the king's books at £7. 19., endowed with £200 parliamentary grant, and in the patronage of the Rev. Edward Watkins: the church is a large cruciform structure, with a lofty square embattled tower rising from the intersection; it displays good portions in various styles of English architecture, with a fine western Norman entrance; the chancel is in the early English, with an east window of the decorated, style, and in the nave and transepts the windows and other portions are of the later English; in a chapel in the south aisle is a beautiful altar-tomb of alabaster, with a recumbent figure of a female, supposed to represent some individual of the family of Gobion, and an octagonal font, richly panelled in the later English style. The living of St. Peter's is a rectory, with the perpetual curacies of Kingsthorpe and Upton, rated in the king's books at £34. 2. 11., and in the patronage of the Governors of St. Katherine's hospital, London: the church, supposed to have been erected about the same time as the castle, is a beautiful and perfect specimen of the enriched Norman style of architecture, with a highly-ornamented tower, communicating with the church by a richly-moulded arch; the details are exquisitely wrought, and, having been cleared from the plaster and whitewash which concealed their beauty, exhibit some of the finest models in that style

of architecture; to the east of the chancel is a vaulted crypt; the roof of the church is supported on circular arches, and a series of alternately clustered and single-shafted columns; the font is richly ornamented in the later English style: there are various ancient and some modern monuments, among which latter is one to the memory of John Smith, an eminent mezzotinto engraver, who died in 1742. The living of St. Sepulchre's is a discharged vicarage, rated in the king's books at £6. 1., endowed with £200 royal bounty, and £1000 parliamentary grant, and in the patronage of Thomas Butcher, Esq: the church is supposed to have been built by the Knights Templars, after the model of the church of the Holy Sepulchre at Jerusalem, and is one of four buildings of that kind remaining in the kingdom; it is of a circular form, and has a cupola in the centre of the roof, which is supported on eight round Norman columns, and plain pointed arches, with a western tower surmounted by a spire, and a chancel, in which are many curious figures and ancient inscriptions. There are two places of worship for Baptists, one for the Society of Friends, one for Huntingtonians, three for Independents, one for Wesleyan Methodists, and a Roman Catholic chapel.

The free grammar school was founded, in 1542, by Mr. Thomas Chipsey, who endowed it with lands, which, together with subsequent benefactions, produce an income of about £120 per annum; in 1557, Cardinal Pole granted for its use the remains of the dilapidated church of St. Gregory: the master is appointed by the mayor and corporation, and the usher by the master, the mayor, deputy recorder, the vicar of all Saints, and the lord of the manor of Lillingston-Lovell. The corporation charity school was founded by the corporation, who appropriated to that purpose an unrestricted gift of £1000 by the Earl of Northampton, with which sum and other benefactions an estate was purchased, producing an income of £310 per annum, of which a part is appropriated to the clothing of twenty aged freemen, to each of whom ten shillings per annum is also paid. The Blue-coat school was founded, in 1710, by Mr. John Dryden of Chesterton, who endowed it with a house, to which Mr. Zachariah Herbert added a farm, the rents of which are applied to clothing, instructing, and apprenticing twenty boys, who, on the expiration of their indentures, receive each a gratuity of £10. The Green school was founded, in 1761, by Mr. Gabriel Newton of Leicester, who endowed it with a rent-charge of £26 per annum. In 1738, Mrs. Dorothy Becket, and her sister, Mrs. Ann Sargeant, established a school for the clothing and education of thirty poor girls; the number has been increased, and a more convenient school-room and house for the mistress were erected in 1813. A National and a British and Foreign school are supported by subscription. St. John's hospital, said to have been founded, in 1090, by William, Archdeacon of Northampton, for the reception of aged and infirm persons, is governed by a master, appointed by the Bishop of Lincoln, and two brothers, nominated by the master, who must be in holy orders, and officiate as chaplains: there are also eight aged women, who receive a small weekly allowance in money, and a supply of coal. To the south of St. John's is the hospital of St. Thomas à Becket, founded by the burgesses, about the year 1450, and endowed for the support of twelve aged widows:

the endowment was augmented, in 1654, by Sir John Langham, for six additional widows, and has been increased by subsequent benefactions: the present income is about £780 per annum ; the inmates receive each 4s. per week, besides clothes, fuel, &c., and fifty out-pensioners £8 per annum each : the establishment is governed by a warden, who is one of the aldermen; the vicar of All Saints' is chaplain. The general infirmary, tq the east of the town, erected and fitted up by subscription in 1793, at an expense of near £25,000, is a handsome building of white stone, three stories high, and well adapted to its various uses : it is under the management of a committee, and is gratuitously attended by the physicians and surgeons resident in the town : it is supported by the income arising from benefactions, and by annual subscription : there are numerous and extensive bequests for benevolent purposes, among which may be noticed Sir Thomas White's fund, amounting to upwards of £13,000, for loans, in sums of £100 each, for nine years without interest, to young tradesmen on their commencing business, and various charitable donations for distribution among the indigent and necessitous poor.

Among the monastic institutions formerly established here, were the priory of St. Andrew, founded about 1076, for Cluniac monks, the revenue of which, at the dissolution, was £344. 13. 7.; an abbey of Black canons, founded about 1112, by William Peverill, natural son of William the Conqueror, and dedicated to St. James, the revenue of which was £213. 17. 2.; the abbey de la Pré, or de Pratis, for nuns of the Cluniac order, founded in the reign of Stephen, by Simon de St. Liz, second Earl of Northampton, and dedicated to St. Mary, the revenue of which was £119. 9. 7¼.; a house of Friars minors, built about the year 1217, on ground to the north of the market-place, given to them by the inhabitants, who were consequently regarded as the founders, of which the revenue was £6. 13. 4.; an hospital, on the south side of the town, for a master and leprous brethren, founded in 1240, by Henry III., and dedicated to St. Leonard, of which the revenue was £12. 4. 8., now consolidated with the hospital of St. Thomas à Becket ; a Carmelite priory, founded in 1271, by Simon de Montfort, the revenue of which was £10. 10.; a priory and chapel for Augustine friars, founded in 1322, by John Longville, near the South gate; and the college of All Saints, founded in 1459, for a master and two fellows, of which the revenue was £2. 13. 4. Of the ancient castle only a few vestiges, consisting of mounds of earth, are to be traced ; and of the embattled walls and the four gates, which were demolished by order of the king, in 1662, there are no remains. Robert Brown, founder of the religious sect called Brownists, was a native of this town ; and Dr. Samuel Parker, Bishop of Oxford under James II., and author of some curious historical memoirs, was born here in 1640. Dr. Philip Doddridge, author of the "Family Expositor," was tutor in a dissenting academy at Northampton, until a short time previous to his death in 1749. Northampton gives the titles of earl and marquis to the family of Compton.

NORTHAMPTONSHIRE, an inland county, bounded on the north by the counties of Leicester, Rutland, and Lincoln ; on the east by those of Cambridge, Huntingdon, and Bedford; on the south by Buckinghamshire and Oxfordshire ; and on the west by Oxfordshire and Warwickshire : it extends obliquely from 52° to 52° 42' (N. Lat.), and from 8' to 1° 19' (W. Lon.), and includes an area of one thousand and seventeen square miles, or six hundred and fifty thousand eight hundred and eighty statute acres. The population, in 1821, was 162,483. This county, which in the ancient British times was the most southern part of the territory of the Coritani, was included by the Romans in the division of Flavia Cæsariensis, and by the Saxons in the kingdom of Mercia. It suffered repeatedly and severely from the ravages of the Danes, to which its situation particularly exposed it. Hamtune, now Northampton, was in the possession of those invaders for nearly forty years: Towcester appears to have been burned by them, and King Edward the Elder ordered it to be rebuilt. In the year 921, the same sovereign marched with his army to Passenham, in order to expel the Danes from this part of the country. The central situation of the county, and that of its capital, the ancient town of Northampton, have occasioned the former, in the earlier periods of English history, to become a scene of action in almost every civil war that has agitated the nation ; and the latter, where the royal court was often held, to be frequently chosen as a military rallying-point, or for holding important national councils. Any details of these transactions, anterior to the reign of Charles I., belong more properly to the histories of particular places within the county, and some mention of the most important of them will be found in the preceding article on the town of Northampton. In February 1642, a petition of the knights, gentlemen, and freeholders of the county was presented to the parliament, commending its exertions, and entreating a continuance of them. On the commencement of hostilities, several skirmishes took place in Northamptonshire, and on the 6th of May, 1643, the parliamentarians were defeated by the Earl of Northampton, at Middleton-Cheney. In this county also, on the 14th of June, 1645, was fought the memorable battle of Naseby, between Sir Thomas Fairfax and the king in person, which gave the final blow to the power of the latter. When the king had been placed in the hands of the parliamentary commissioners, he was brought to Holdenby, or Holmby House, on the 16th of February, 1647, and remained there until the 4th of June, when he was seized by Cornet Joyce. General Monk, in his march to the south, reached Northampton about the 24th of January, 1660, on which day an address was presented to him by the gentlemen, ministers, and freeholders of this county, requesting him to use his power to restore the freedom of parliament, and procure the adoption of other salutary measures ; and on the 15th of March following, a letter, subscribed by above fifty of the most considerable Northamptonshire gentlemen, was presented to the same general at Whitehall, thanking him for having procured the restoration of the excluded members to their seats in the house.

Northamptonshire is contained in the diocese of Peterborough, and province of Canterbury, excepting the parishes of Gretton and Nassington, which are in the diocese of Lincoln, and that of King's Sutton, which is a peculiar belonging to the Dean and Chapter of Lincoln, in the diocese of Peterborough. It forms an archdeaconry, comprising the ten deaneries of Brack-

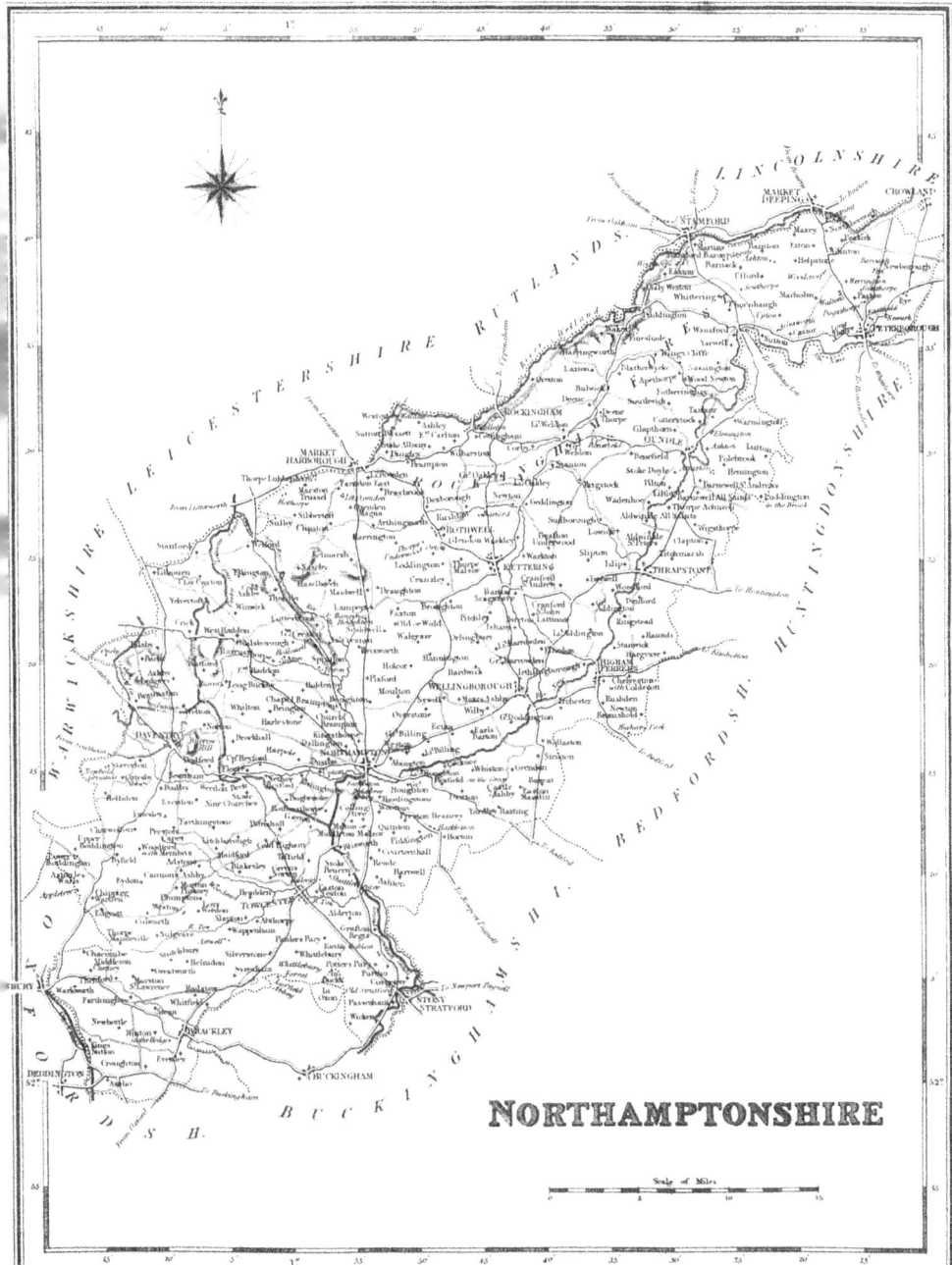

NORTHAMPTONSHIRE

Scale of Miles

ley, Daventry, Haddon, Higham-Ferrers, Northampton, Oundle, Peterborough, Preston, Rothwell, and Weldon, containing two hundred and ninety-three parishes, of which one hundred and seventy-two are rectories, ninety-three vicarages, and twenty-nine perpetual curacies. For purposes of civil government it is divided into the nineteen hundreds of Chipping-Warden, Cleley, Corby, Fawsley, Greens-Norton, Guilsborough, Hamfordshoe, Higham-Ferrers, Huxloe, Navisford, Nobottle-Grove, Orlingbury, Polebrooke, Rothwell, Spelhoe, King's Sutton, Towcester, Willybrook, and Wymersley, and the liberty of Nassaburgh, or Peterborough. Of these, the hundreds of Corby, Hamfordshoe, Higham-Ferrers, Huxloe, Navisford, Orlingbury, Polebrooke, Rothwell, and Willybrooke, and the liberty of Nassaburgh, or Peterborough, are in the eastern division of the county, and the rest in the western. It contains the city of Peterborough, the borough of Higham-Ferrers, the borough and market towns of Brackley and Northampton, and the market towns of Daventry, Kettering, Oundle, Thrapston, Towcester, and Wellingborough. Two knights are returned to parliament for the shire; two representatives for the city of Peterborough; two for each of the boroughs of Brackley and Northampton; and one for that of Higham-Ferrers. Northamptonshire is included in the Midland circuit: the assizes are held at Northampton, where is the county gaol: the quarter sessions are held at Northampton on January 14th, April 22d, July 15th, and October 21st; and at Peterborough on January 13th, April 21st, July 14th, and October 20th. There are seventy-nine acting magistrates. The rates raised in the county for the year ending March 25th, 1827, amounted to £168,068. 1., the expenditure to £167,352, of which, £148,175. 13. was applied to the relief of the poor.

The general aspect of the county exhibits great beauty and variety; extensive flats being of rare occurrence. The greater part of it is agreeably diversified by gentle undulations, the valleys being watered by numerous rivulets, and the whole forming an interesting scene of vale and upland. The entire surface is available for agricultural purposes; the trees and hedge-rows flourish luxuriantly, and the county is in numerous places adorned with woods and ornamented grounds. The higher and middle parts are more particularly ornamented with extensive woods, which are intersected by numerous vistas and beautiful lawns. The summits of the hills around Daventry, which are supposed to be the highest land in the county, are only about eight hundred feet above the level of the tide in the Thames, at the mouth of the Grand Junction canal at Brentford. The county contains no land that can properly be called bog: the lowest is Peterborough fen. The climate is favourable both to health and vegetation; the county being seldom visited by deep falls of snow, or long-continued rains. These advantages it derives from its inland situation and moderate degree of elevation; the aqueous vapours from the distant ocean being in some measure exhausted before their arrival here, and even when they reach the county, overcharged with snow, there are no mountains to precipitate an immediate and heavy fall.

The fertility of the soil renders it equally well adapted either for corn or pasturage; and although numerous instances of light soils occur, yet by much

the greater portion is of a strong heavy staple, which is applied to the culture of beans and wheat, while in a state of open common; but when enclosed is generally laid down to permanent grass: the lighter enclosed lands are kept more in tillage. The land varies considerably in nature and quality, but seldom changes abruptly: the general excellency of the Northamptonshire soils seems owing partly to their sufficient depth, and partly to the looseness and porous nature of the stony substratum. They may be classed as follows: first, the black, or dark-coloured soils, being generally a deep strong loam, on a strong gravelly or clay-loam substratum: of these the county has a greater proportion than any other; as they extend over the whole of the western part of it, from Market-Harborough, on the Leicestershire border, to its most southern extremity, and include the whole of its rich upland feeding-pastures, and a part of its cultivated common fields and enclosures. Daventry field and its neighbourhood consist, however, generally of brownish or greyish loam, on a rubble stone bottom: a considerable tract north and east of this has also a similar soil, resting on a clay, marl, or sandy bottom, but sometimes on a stony substratum. Second, the red land, as it is called, which includes the brown and snuff-coloured loams, is tolerably extensive, comprising a portion of the common fields, as well as enclosures, and extends over a large tract of country, to the north-west of Northampton, and through various other parts of the county, in divers shades of colour and consistence. Third, the white or grey loams, which are inferior in fertility to the above; they are found to the south of the Nen, from which river, in an extensive district lying south of Northampton, they extend to the borders of Buckinghamshire. Fourth, the miscellaneous upland district, including the light thin soils near Stamford, and those dispersed in other parts of the county, not classing with the above descriptions, such as the sands of Harlestone, &c.: this, with some exceptions, includes the whole north-eastern portion of the county, beyond Rothwell, Kettering, and Wellingborough. Fifth the soil of the natural meadows and pasture-lands of the vales, and of the fen land north of Peterborough, consisting of the decomposed matter of decayed grasses and aquatic vegetables, combined with the sediment of the streams, which, being drained and consolidated, forms the basis of meadow soil. The red soils are of the lightest quality, the grey or black soils more tenacious; the latter having less of sand, and more of calcareous earth in their composition, with a loose substratum of a kind of stone, generally either half or wholly calcareous.

Of the superficies of the county about one hundred and fifty thousand acres are in common fields, by much the greater part being under tillage; and there are one hundred and fifty thousand acres of modern enclosures, in alternate grass and tillage, besides occasional, though rare, instances of tillage in the ancient enclosures. On the arable land of the open fields the following course of crops is practised: first year, fallow or turnips; second, wheat and some barley; and third, beans, with a few acres of oats, and occasionally a few peas, vetches, or a little barley. The newly-enclosed lands are cropped thus: first year, fallow or turnips; second, wheat, or barley after the turnips; third, beans or peas; fourth, barley, with red clover; fifth and sixth, clover; seventh, part beans, and part oats. Wheat is cultivated in large quantities in both the open fields and the enclosures, on the red friable soils, and is supposed annually to occupy sixty thousand acres, the general average produce being estimated at twenty-five and one-third bushels per acre. About thirty-three thousand acres are annually sown with barley, the average produce being thirty-one bushels per acre: this is the favourite crop on the red and light sand soils. Oats are grown on twenty-four thousand acres annually, the average produce per acre being forty-two bushels, and the quantity thus raised is not only sufficient to supply the consumption of this county, but also contributes to meet the demands of the neighbouring counties of Leicester, Warwick, Buckingham, Hertford, and Bedford. Rye is cultivated to a considerable extent, particularly in the vicinity of Northampton, and upon the light lands in other quarters: it occupies about three thousand acres, which produce, on an average, thirty-two bushels each: this grain is also frequently sown immediately after harvest, to form spring food for sheep. The quantity of beans cultivated is very considerable, as they annually occupy an extent of thirty thousand acres: the average is twenty-one and two-thirds bushels per acre, and notwithstanding the great consumption within the county, by horses employed on the thoroughfares to London, a considerable surplus remains to be exported to other districts. Peas are grown in a much less quantity than beans: vetches are extensively cultivated in most parts of the county, and considerable quantities are kept for seed: these two crops annually occupy about fifteen thousand acres, and green crops thirty thousand acres, while thirty thousand more remain in fallow. Turnips are cultivated, in considerable quantities, upon all the red light soils; the Swedish turnip is grown in most parts of the county. Rape or cole-seed is cultivated, but not generally: cabbages are grown in the field in several parts of the county; clover is not only sown for hay and pasture, but much is also kept for seed. Sainfoin is cultivated on the soils that have a stony substratum. Hemp is grown to a considerable extent in the fenny district on the borders of Lincolnshire and Cambridgeshire; of flax there is but very little. Lentils are produced on the poor common fields of Easton and Collyweston, near Stamford. Woad is cultivated and prepared for the dyers by persons whose sole occupation it is; the crop is gathered three times during each season. Onions are grown about Northampton, to a great extent and in high perfection: the same neighbourhood is also famous for carrots.

The grass land, including not only all pleasure grounds, but also clover and other artificial and temporary grasses, is computed to amount to three hundred and seventy-five thousand acres. The extent of meadow land is not less than forty thousand acres; the most considerable tract being that on both sides of the river Nen, which, commencing in different branches many miles above Northampton, extends down to Peterborough, and, in consequence of its sinuousness, is upwards of sixty miles in length. The meadow land is generally rich, owing to the frequent inundations; but it frequently sustains great damage from floods, particularly upon mowing-grass. The upland pasture occupies a much greater extent, the strong deep loams having been found naturally disposed to turf, and affording herbage on which cattle and sheep fatten with great rapidity. About one-half of the enclosed land has long been laid down, and principally occupied as grazing or dairy farms. From Northampton, westward, a great quantity of cheese is made, and in that part of the county south of the Coventry and London road are numerous dairies, the produce of which is chiefly butter: some of the fresh butter from this county is sold in London as "Epping butter." In the parishes of Grafton-Regis, Yardley-Gobion, Potters-Pury, and a large district in that neighbourhood, there are considerable dairies, the chief produce of which is butter for the London market, as also about Charwelton and between Daventry and Banbury, from which much butter and pork is sent to London: dairies are also kept in several other districts. As manure, lime is extensively used; marl, but little; woollen rags are employed to a considerable extent; and, besides what are procured in the county, considerable quantities are purchased in Leicestershire and other neighbouring counties.

Numerous sheep and cattle are fattened on the pastures: of the sheep many are bred within the county, and the rest brought from other districts. Most of the cattle are brought from other parts of the island: those bred in the county are almost wholly an improved variety of the long-horned breed: of the sorts brought in from distant places, the short-horned Holderness cows, which are supplied from Yorkshire, are generally preferred for the dairy, particularly in the south-western part of the county, in consequence of the greater quantity of milk which they afford: there are, however, numerous dairies of the long-horned breed. The calves are seldom reared, being sold when a few days old to dealers, who carry them to the markets of Buckinghamshire and other counties, where they are purchased by dairy-farmers from Essex, to be fattened for the London market. The oxen fattened, by far the greater part of which are brought from distant parts of the kingdom, include almost all sorts; they are principally fattened at grass, and great numbers are sold from the pastures, but some are kept through the winter: those chiefly in the graziers' hands are of the long-horned Hereford, and of the Devon, Scotch, and Welch breeds, with a few of a mixed kind bred in the county, and others of a particularly small kind from Monmouthshire, called Pontypools, from the fair at which they are generally purchased: cattle from Staffordshire, Shropshire, and Ireland are also introduced: a great many half-fed cattle are brought from Staffordshire and other counties, early in the spring, to be fattened in the early feeding-pastures of this county. A few black cattle are grazed in the open field lordships: very few oxen are worked. It is computed that, besides what are consumed in the county, or sold in the neighbouring districts, fifteen thousand head of fat cattle are annually sent to London from Northamptonshire. The sheep of the common fields are considered the original breed of the county, but are much inferior to those of the ancient pastures, having longer legs, smaller and less compact bodies, and sometimes horns, and well adapted for folding, which is constantly practised with them: their wool is of a combing quality. A great portion of the county, particularly the middle and northern tracts, has an improved breed, which is a cross between the old stock and the new Leicester sheep, being extremely handsome, well-made, and much disposed to fatten; they will also thrive on comparatively bare pastures: the wool is less in quantity, but of better quality than that of the old breed; their pelts are lighter; and they are considered altogether much more profitable, and are ready for the butcher at an earlier age: the weight of the full-grown wether varies from twenty-five to forty pounds per quarter. London is annually supplied with about one hundred thousand sheep and lambs from this county. The beef and mutton produced annually are supposed to be nearly equal in weight, amounting each to about twenty-seven millions of pounds: the number of sheep is estimated at two hundred and fifty thousand, that of cattle at about thirty-three thousand seven hundred and fifty. The most approved hogs are a cross between the Berkshire and Tonquin breeds; they have fine bones, thin hides, thick bodies, short legs, and a disposition to fatten rapidly. The horses bred in the county are chiefly for draught or other purposes of husbandry; they are mostly of the strong black breed; but the number being insufficient for its supply, many are brought from the counties of Derby, Lincoln, and York, generally when about two or three years old: the number kept is estimated at twenty thousand.

Northamptonshire does not abound in fruit trees, though there are a few productive orchards in different parts of it. There is much excellent garden-ground around Northampton, besides some very good orchards of different kinds of fruit for domestic use. A considerable portion of the county, supposed to be about one-fourth, remains unenclosed; yet the waste lands are of comparatively trifling extent. Some of the hilly land near Daventry is confined to sheep-walks, and of the same description are, the common of Stoke-Bruerne, and a few others; the whole amount of unproductive land, with the exception of Peterborough fen, being less than one thousand acres. The great Peterborough fen is a perfectly level tract, originally formed, like the adjoining fen-lands of the counties of Cambridge and Lincoln, by the deposits of the neighbouring rivers Ouse, Nen, and Welland, containing between six and seven thousand acres, and having a fine soil susceptible of the highest cultivation. It is situated between Peterborough and Crowland, forming the north-eastern extremity of the county, and is subject to the depasturage of the cattle, horses, and sheep of the thirty-two parishes and townships which are comprised in the soke of Peterborough: the right of common, however, is considered by its possessors to be of very little value, the drainage of this extensive tract being in a very imperfect state. The woodlands are very extensive; so much so, when the excellence of their soil is considered, as to form objects of considerable national importance: they may be arranged into the four distinct classes of forests, chases, purlieu woods, and woods and plantations on freehold property. The forests are held by the same tenure as the other crown lands: the most considerable is that of Rockingham, situated towards the north-west side of the county. This was anciently one of the largest forests in the kingdom, extending for about thirty miles in length, from Northampton to Stamford, and about eight in breadth, from the river Nen to the Welland and the Maidwell: it now reaches from the

vicinity of Wansford, on the great north road, towards Weldon and Rockingham, and still further to the south-west, forming an almost continued chain of woodland for a distance of nearly twenty miles: its boundaries are not very exactly defined, but it is supposed to contain from eight to ten thousand acres. It consists of three divisions, called the bailiwicks of Rockingham, Brigstock, and Clive or Cliffe, each of which is divided into several walks: the three bailiwicks were formerly under the superintendence of one warden, or master-forester; but that office was abolished by Charles I., who appointed a master-forester to each, since which period the bailiwicks have been wholly distinct, with respect to their government and management. The election of verderers is still continued, although, since the abolition of the office of warden, and the discontinuance of the forest courts, their office has been little more than nominal. The next in extent is Whittlebury, or Whittlewood Forest, which reaches along the southern border of the county to the south of Towcester, for a distance of upwards of eleven miles, and contains about seven thousand acres. This forest, which is part of the honour of Grafton, is under the superintendence of a lord-warden, a lieutenant or deputy warden, two verderers, a woodward, a purlieu-ranger, five keepers, and six page-keepers: the Duke of Grafton is hereditary lord-warden: the number of deer kept in the forest is about eighteen hundred, of all sorts. If to these two be added the remaining one, Salcey Forest, between Northampton and Newport-Pagnell, to the south of the road, the whole will amount to about twenty thousand acres. The forest of Salcey was likewise made part of the honour of Grafton, by act of parliament, in the 33d of Henry VIII., and, by a grant in reversion made in the 25th of Charles II., the Duke of Grafton has now the property of the underwood in the several coppices. This forest is under the government of a warden, a lieutenant, or deputy-warden, two verderers, a woodward, three yeomen-keepers of the three walks into which it is divided, and one page-keeper: no courts are now held for the forest. The chases of Geddington and Yardley are of considerable extent; the former having been anciently a part of the forest of Rockingham, and the latter of that of Salcey: the purlieu woods are numerous, and cover large breadths of land; and these, together with the extensive woods and plantations that abound on freehold property, amount to twenty thousand acres more.

The whole of what are now considered forest woods are subject to the depasturing of deer, and, at a stated time of the year, to that also of the cattle belonging to the inhabitants of the neighbouring townships, who claim commonage. The underwood in the forests and chases chiefly consists of black and white thorn, ash, sallow, maple, and a small proportion of hazel: it is generally cut at from twelve to eighteen years' growth; and the different woods are divided into as many parts, or sales, as the number of years' growth of the underwood may amount to, so that a regular rotation in cutting takes place every year: those parts which had been last cut, the proprietors of the underwood are empowered, by the ancient laws and customs of the forests, to fence in for four years against the deer, and for seven years against the cattle. A considerable portion is made into hurdles for folding sheep; the remainder is chiefly used as fuel. The principal trees are oak, ash, elm, and poplar : besides which are considerable quantities of other white wood, as beech, chesnut, lime, &c. A fall of oak timber is generally made in that part, or sale, in which the underwood has been last cut. In some parts of Whittlebury Forest the timber is not very thick upon the ground, but in most parts the spaces which are thus left are occupied by thick masses of underwood : this part of the produce belongs, by a grant of the crown in the time of Charles II., to the Duke of Grafton and his heirs male for ever, with the right of fencing out the deer and all commonable cattle during nine years after cutting : the timber is reserved for the crown : the number of parishes having right of common for such cattle and horses as they can support through the winter is fourteen. Salcey Forest contains some large oaks, but they are thin upon the ground. Geddington Chase is supposed to contain about fourteen thousand acres, of which about twelve thousand are woodland, the remainder consisting of lawns, ridings, and vistas: it once formed part of Rockingham Forest, but permission was given by the crown to the ancestors of the Montagu family to disafforest it, and convert it to its present state : deer are kept in it, and it is subject to a commonage, from May-day to about Martinmas, for the adjoining townships : it is in every respect managed like the forest-woods in fencing out the deer and cattle from the recently felled portions : it also contains a valuable stock of large oak timber. Yardley Chase once formed part of Salcey Forest, but has likewise been disafforested. Purlieu woods are those which are situated immediately in the vicinity of the forests, and which have at some time formed part of it : but the respective owners having obtained grants and permissions from the crown to disafforest them, and appropriate them to their own use, they are not now subject to any of the laws and regulations that regard the forest-woods. From the extensive woods above enumerated a considerable supply is procured for the navy. The common fuel is wood and coal : of the former the county itself produces abundance ; and though of coal it used to have but a scanty supply, which was obtained at a very dear rate, yet great quantities are now brought into it from the Staffordshire collieries, by means of the Grand Junction canal : some are also brought up the river Nen from the north. Several societies have been formed for the promotion of improvements in agriculture, one of which holds its meetings at Wellingborough, another at Lamport, and a third at Peterborough.

The mineral productions include neither coal nor any of the metals ; but limestone in great plenty is found in almost every part of the county, and is used in some instances to form enclosures, but is more extensively burned into lime, or used in the making and repairing of roads. Freestone for building is raised at Brackley, at Kingsthorpe, near Northampton, and at various other places : it is often of a calcareous nature. A whitish kind of slate, used for roofing, is dug in considerable quantities at Collyweston, near Stamford ; the laminæ are generally of a good size, but rather thick and heavy ; most of the buildings in that and the neighbouring townships are covered with it : it is customary to raise large blocks of it in the autumn, which being placed in a position different from what they had in the

quarry, the rain insinuates itself between the layers, and, in frosty weather, the water expanding, splits the block into plates of a proper thickness. Good clay for making bricks and tiles is found in different parts of the county.

The principal articles of manufacture are shoes, bone-lace, and woollen stuffs, the latter confined chiefly to moreens, tammies, and calimancoes. In Northampton, Wellingborough, and some other towns, many persons are employed in making shoes for the supply of the army and navy, and the shops in London, and some for exportation to different foreign countries, about seven or eight thousand pair being manufactured weekly : the leather is purchased partly in this and the neighbouring counties, but is obtained chiefly from the London market. In Wellingborough and its neighbourhood, and towards the south-western corner of the county, lace-making affords employment to a great proportion of the population, chiefly young women and boys. The manufacture of silk stockings is carried on at Towcester and at Kettering, and at Towcester wool-stapling constitutes the principal branch of trade: the material is, in the first instance, purchased of the growers, or farmers, in the neighbourhood, and, after having undergone a very minute assortment, the finest is sent into Yorkshire, for the clothiers, or into Leicestershire for the hosiers, and the other qualities disposed of to other markets, while some of the longest staple only is reserved to be worked at home. At Daventry there is a considerable manufactory for whips. The produce of the soil exported from the county consists of wheat, wheat-flour, oats, beans, timber, oak-bark, fat cattle and sheep, wool, butter, and cheese: the manufactured exports are chiefly shoes, lace, and woollen stuffs, which are sent to London, and various other parts of Great Britain ; also to Ireland, America, and the West Indies ; the stuffs are sold to the London and Yorkshire markets, to persons who dress and dye them. The imports are chiefly lean cattle, store sheep, coal, iron, deals, and leather.

All the principal rivers of the county rise within its limits : they are the Nene, the Welland, the Ouse, the Charwell, the Avon, and the Leam. The Nene is the most considerable : it takes its rise near Catesby and Hellidon, in the hundred of Fawsley, near the borders of Warwickshire, and being quickly joined by a number of other small streams in the vicinity of Daventry, it runs directly eastward to Northampton, where it becomes navigable : from that town its course is for the most part in a north-easterly direction, which it pursues through the county for nearly the whole length of its south-eastern side, and at a short distance from its borders, passing the towns of Wellingborough, Thrapstone, Oundle, and Peterborough : at the distance of a few miles above Wansford bridge, however, it begins to form the southern boundary of the county, which it separates from Huntingdonshire, and so continues as far as the last-mentioned town, where it wholly quits it. The Welland rises near Hothorpe, in the hundred of Rothwell, and immediately becoming the northern boundary of the county, winds by Rockingham and Stamford, at which latter place it becomes navigable, and finally quits it at its north-eastern extremity. The Ouse has its rise in a spring, called Ousewell, near Brackley, in the hundred of King's Sutton, in the southernmost part of the county, which it soon quits; but, after taking a circuitous course through a part of Buckinghamshire, it touches upon it again at Stony-Stratford, soon however diverging from it towards Newport-Pagnell. The Charwell, rising near the source of the Nene, and running southwards through a small portion of Oxfordshire, afterwards forms the boundary between that county and Northamptonshire for a few miles, finally quitting it at its south-western extremity, in its course to the Thames. The Avon, rising on the borders of this county and Leicestershire, and taking a westerly course, forms the boundary line between them for the distance of a few miles, and then enters the county of Warwick. The Leam, rising near the sources of the Nene and the Charwell, almost immediately enters Warwickshire. The county abounds, almost in every part of it, with fine springs and numerous smaller streams; and derives considerable benefit from its canal navigation, more especially in the conveyance of coal. The Oxford canal runs for a considerable distance along its western confines, through a small projecting portion of which it passes, in the vicinity of Barby and Braunston, and through another at its south-western extremity, near the river Charwell. The Grand Junction canal commences at the Oxford canal, at Braunston, and is continued, after having passed through a tunnel about a mile in length, in a devious south-easterly course, to Weedon, where, having crossed the great London road, it is carried over a valley, by means of an embankment of earth nearly half a mile in length and about thirty feet high, under which pass one small river and two carriage roads: it soon after again crosses the London road, and is continued in a south-easterly direction by Lower Heyford, Bugbrooke, Gayton, Blisworth (where it passes under another tunnel), Stoke-Bruerne, Grafton-Regis, and Cosgrove, at which latter place it quits the county for Buckinghamshire: it is navigable for barges of sixty tons' burden. It was intended to make a collateral cut from this canal at Gayton to the river Nene at Northampton; but this communication has been effected by means of a railway. The only other artificial navigation is that of the Union canal, so called because it was designed to unite the navigation of the Trent and Soar with that of the Grand Junction canal and the Nene: commencing from the navigable channel of the river Soar above Leicester, it was intended to enter this county near Market-Harborough, and be continued to Northampton, where it was to communicate with the Nene, and the Grand Junction canal.

The road from London to Holyhead, through Buckingham and Shrewsbury, or through Birmingham, enters this county from Mixbury in Oxfordshire, and passing through Barley-Mow, Croughton, and Aynho, re-enters the latter county. The road from London to Holyhead, through Chester, enters from Stony-Stratford in Buckinghamshire, passes through Towcester, Daventry, and Braunston, and quits for Willoughby in Warwickshire: this is also the road from London to Warrington, Lancaster, and Carlisle. The road from London to Manchester and Preston, through Derby, enters from Stoke-Goldington in Buckinghamshire, and passing through Horton, Northampton, Kingsthorpe, Brixworth, and Kelmarsh, quits the county for Market-Harborough in Leicestershire: this is also the road from London to

Sheffield, Settle, Kirkby-Lonsdale, and Whitehaven, through Derby. The road from London to Halifax and Clitheroe, through Bedford, Nottingham, and Rotherham, enters the county from Bletsoe in Bedfordshire, and passing through Higham-Ferrers, Kettering, and Rockingham, quits it for Uppingham in Rutlandshire. The road from London to Manchester and Clitheroe, through Leek, branches from the former Manchester road at Northampton, and passing through Welford, quits the county for Kegworth in Leicestershire. The road from London to Scarborough, through Huntingdon and Lincoln, enters from Yaxley in Huntingdonshire, and passes through Peterborough and Glinton to Market-Deeping in Lincolnshire. The great mail-roads are for the most part level, wide, and good: some of the collateral turnpike-roads are likewise kept in good repair; but the cross roads are much neglected. Few counties, however, possess a greater number of handsome, well-built stone bridges; not only the larger streams, but every brook and rivulet being crossed by a stone arch.

Of the four consular or military ways made by the Romans in Britain, two are still visible in different parts of this county. The Watling-street, having crossed the Ouse, enters Northamptonshire at Old Stratford, and running towards its western border, passes the Lesser Avon at Dow bridge, and proceeds into Leicestershire: its course may very easily be traced. The Ermin-street enters the county from Cambridgeshire at Castor, on the eastern side, and subsequently divides into two branches, which direct their courses into Lincolnshire by two different points on the Welland. Most of the Roman fortresses and garrisons were erected either upon these ways or in their vicinity. Stations and forts are also thought to have been erected on the southern banks of the Nene, to guard the passages and fords, and prevent the inroads of the Britons inhabiting the woods on the other side, which extended from the Nene to the Welland. On the course of the Watling-street there are supposed to have been three principal stations within the limits of this county, viz. Lactodorum, which is placed at Towcester; Benaventa, or Bennavennum, which has been variously placed, at Weedon-Beck, at Castle-Dykes, and near Daventry; which latter supposition seems to be the most probable; and Tripontium, usually placed at Lilbourn, though Horsley supposes it to have been at Rugby in Warwickshire. Parts of the Ermin-street are still lofty and conspicuous between Castor and Upton, and again in the parish of Barnack: the only station in the county on this line was Durobrivæ, at or near Castor. Remains of tesselated pavements, coins, &c., have been found in various places, especially at Weldon, and at Cotterstock near Oundle. Besides the intrenchments already mentioned as either decidedly Roman, or supposed to be such, there are several other ancient encampments of considerable magnitude, such as Arbury Banks, Raynsbury Camp, and " the Boroughs," at Guilsborough.

Of ancient church architecture this county affords numerous interesting specimens. Peterborough cathedral and the contiguous buildings display some fine and varied examples, from the early Norman down to the latest English. St. Sepulchre's church, at Northampton, is one of the remaining few built by the Templars on the model of the Holy Sepulchre at Jerusalem: St. Peter's, in the same town, and the churches of Castor,

Barnack, Earls-Barton, Barnwell, Twywell, and Spratton, also furnish specimens of the Anglo-Saxon or the early Norman style. Among large churches displaying fine examples of enriched and florid architecture may be enumerated those of Fotheringhay, Oundle, Lowick, Kettering, Higham-Ferrers, Wellingborough, and Finedon. The elegant crosses at Geddington and near Northampton are two of the only three now remaining of the monuments erected by Edward I. to the memory of his queen, Eleanor. In sepulchral monuments of marble, brass, &c., Northamptonshire is considered to be richer than any part of the kingdom, of equal or smaller extent, Middlesex alone excepted; which circumstance seems to be in some degree accounted for by the number of noble families that have been settled here from an early period. The number of religious houses of all denominations, including colleges, hospitals, &c., was about fifty-five : the remains of monastic buildings are inconsiderable, excepting Peterborough cathedral, which was the conventual church of the ancient abbey of Medeshamsted, or Peterborough; to which may be added the anciently collegiate churches of Fotheringhay, Higham-Ferrers, and Irthlingborough. Of ancient mansion-houses the county affords a few interesting specimens, particularly in those of Burleigh, Kirby, Castle-Ashby, Fawsley, Rushton, and Drayton. Burleigh House, the seat of the Marquis of Exeter, is the finest among the great number of modern seats which adorn this highly ornamented county; amongst which Althorp, the property and residence of Earl Spencer, is also one of the most distinguished. There are mineral springs at Astrop, Northampton, and Wellingborough ; and at Rothwell, a petrifying well and a bone well.

NORTHAW, a parish in the hundred of CASHIO, or liberty of ST. ALBAN'S, county of HERTFORD, 4½ miles (N. E. by N.) from Chipping-Barnet, containing 566 inhabitants. The living is a perpetual curacy, in the archdeaconry of St. Alban's, and diocese of London, and in the patronage of the Rev. A. Trenchard, D.D. The church, dedicated to St. Thomas à Becket, was rebuilt in 1810, at an expense of £1600, defrayed by W. Strode, Esq., the late patron. There is a free school for eight boys, endowed with £20 per annum. Within the parish is a fine saline spring, formerly much resorted to, but now almost neglected.

NORTHBOROUGH, a parish in the liberty of PETERBOROUGH, county of NORTHAMPTON, 1¾ mile (S. E. by S.) from Market-Deeping, containing 232 inhabitants. The living is a rectory, in the archdeaconry of Northampton, and diocese of Peterborough, rated in the king's books at £10. 19. 7., and in the patronage of the Dean and Chapter of Peterborough. The church, dedicated to St. Andrew, has a fine admixture of the Norman and the various later styles of English architecture, and contains a monument, with other memorials, to the family of Claypole, of whom John married Elizabeth, daughter of Oliver Cromwell, who created him a baronet in 1657, and made him Master of the Horse, and a Lord of the Bedchamber. Their ancient mansion, a beautiful specimen of the decorated style, has been converted into a farm-house.

NORTHBOURNE, a parish in the hundred of CORNILO, lathe of ST. AUGUSTINE, county of KENT, 2¾ miles (W.) from Deal, containing 757 inhabitants. The

living is a vicarage, with the perpetual curacy of Sholden, in the archdeaconry and diocese of Canterbury, rated in the king's books at £12. 11. 8., and in the patronage of the Archbishop of Canterbury. The church is dedicated to St. Augustine. Here are the remains of an ancient chapel.

NORTHBROOK, a tything in the parish and hundred of MITCHELDEVER, Basingstoke division of the county of SOUTHAMPTON, 5 miles (S. E.) from Whitchurch. The population is returned with the parish.

NORTHCHAPEL, a parish in the hundred of ROTHERBRIDGE, rape of ARUNDEL, county of SUSSEX, 5 miles (N. by W.) from Petworth, containing 749 inhabitants. The living is a rectory not in charge, in the archdeaconry and diocese of Chichester, and in the patronage of the Earl of Egremont. The church is dedicated to St. Michael. This was formerly part of the parish of Petworth.

NORTHCHURCH, county of HERTFORD. — See BERKHAMPSTEAD (ST. MARY).

NORTHCOTT, a hamlet in that part of the parish of BOYTON which is in the hundred of BLACK TORRINGTON, county of DEVON, 5¼ miles (N. by E.) from Launceston, containing 83 inhabitants.

NORTHEN, or NORTHENDEN, a parish in the hundred of MACCLESFIELD, county palatine of CHESTER, containing, with the township of Northen, and part of that of Etchells, 1406 inhabitants, of which number, 630 are in the township of Northen, 4½ miles (W.) from Stockport. The living is a rectory, in the archdeaconry and diocese of Chester, rated in the king's books at £10. 7. 6., and in the patronage of the Dean and Chapter of Chester. The church, dedicated to St. Wilfrid, is principally in the later style of English architecture, with an enriched wooden screen. A part of the hall, the seat of the Tattons, is very ancient; it was garrisoned by Charles I., and besieged and taken by the parliamentarians.

NORTHFIELD, a parish in the upper division of the hundred of HALFSHIRE, county of WORCESTER, 6 miles (S. W. by S.) from Birmingham, containing 1567 inhabitants. The living is a rectory, with the curacy of Coston-Hacket, in the archdeaconry and diocese of Worcester, rated in the king's books at £14. 15. 2½., and in the patronage of the Rev. John Thomas Fenwick. The church, dedicated to St. Lawrence, is partly in the early English, and partly in the decorated, style, with a Norman door. The small river Rea, also the Birmingham and Worcester, and the Netherton canals, run through the parish, in which there are quarries of freestone. Here are some remains of Weoley castle, formerly belonging to the Jervoise family. A charity school is supported with the income arising from a bequest of £150 by William Worth, and another of £100, in 1779, by the Rev. Mr. Soley.

NORTHFLEET, a parish in the hundred of TOLTINGTROUGH, lathe of AYLESFORD, county of KENT, 1½ mile (W.) from Gravesend, and 20 miles (E.) from London, containing 1964 inhabitants. This place is mentioned in Domesday-book, and is supposed to have been more anciently a Roman and a Danish station. The river Thames bounds the parish on the north. At a distance from the river the face of the country is diversified with gently rising hills and small vallies ; but to the north-west the land lies so low as to be overflowed at high tides, and the flood would extend even beyond the London road, if not prevented by a raised causeway and bridge, to which flood-gates are affixed as a barrier against the tides, and an outlet for the fresh water. The bridge was erected at an early period, and rebuilt of brick in 1634, which being found inconvenient, another has been constructed in a line with the direction of the road. Large chalk and lime works extend from the north side of the village to the Thames. Lime is sent in very considerable quantities for the use of the builders in London, and is also exported to Holland and Flanders, the refuse being used for manuring the land in Essex, Suffolk, and Norfolk. The chalk pits are very extensive, and strata of flint stones abound, which are frequently wrought into flints for guns. Embedded in the chalk are found many curious fossils, chiefly *echinites* and *glossopetræ* (or sharks' teeth); and some of the flints enclose cockle-shells filled with chalk, forming singular natural curiosities. Here is a large yard for ship-building, near which is a spacious dock excavated in the solid chalk, and capable of containing six or seven large ships : the first vessel built here was the Royal Charlotte, East Indiaman, in 1789. At this place is an establishment for the manufacture of Parker's Roman cement. Fairs are held on Easter and Whit Tuesdays, and on the 24th of March. The living is a vicarage, within the exempt deanery of Shoreham, in the peculiar jurisdiction of the Archbishop of Canterbury, rated in the king's books at £21, and in the patronage of the Crown. The church, which is dedicated to St. Botolph, is one of the largest in the diocese : it displays various styles of English architecture, with some good decorated windows : in the chancel are the remains of some ancient oak stalls ; in the south wall are three stone seats, and on a slab in the pavement a full-length brass figure of a priest standing beneath a richly-ornamented canopy, with an imperfect Latin inscription around the verge of the slab ; the grave beneath being opened about forty years ago, the body of Peter de Lucy was found enveloped in leather. Among the monuments of more modern date is a fine alabaster tomb to the memory of Dr. Edward Browne, physician to Charles II., and author of Travels in Hungary. There is a place of worship for Wesleyan Methodists.

NORTH-FORTY-FOOT-BANK, or FEN-CORNER, an extra-parochial liberty, in the wapentake of KIRTON, parts of HOLLAND, county of LINCOLN, 9 miles (N.W. by W.) from Boston, containing 136 inhabitants.

NORTH-FORTY-FOOT-BANK near FOSDYKE, an extra-parochial liberty, in the wapentake of KIRTON, parts of HOLLAND, county of LINCOLN, containing 179 inhabitants.

NORTH-FORTY-FOOT-BANK near PELHAM'S LANDS, an extra-parochial liberty, in the wapentake of KIRTON, parts of HOLLAND, county of LINCOLN, containing 27 inhabitants.

NORTH-HALES, otherwise COVEHITHE, a parish in the hundred of BLYTHING, county of SUFFOLK, 4¼ miles (N. by E.) from Southwold, containing 169 inhabitants. The living is a discharged vicarage, with the rectory of Binacre, in the archdeaconry of Suffolk, and diocese of Norwich, rated in the king's books at £5. 6. 8., and endowed with £200 royal bounty. The church is dedicated to St. Andrew.

NORTH-HILL, a parish in the northern division of EAST hundred, county of CORNWALL, 6¾ miles (S.W. by S.) from Launceston, containing 1089 inhabitants. The living is a rectory, in the archdeaconry of Cornwall, and diocese of Exeter, rated in the king's books at £36. 6. 8., and in the patronage of Mrs. Darley. The church is dedicated to St. Torney. There is a place of worship for Wesleyan Methodists.

NORTH-HOLME, a parish in the Marsh division of the wapentake of CANDLESHOE, parts of LINDSEY, county of LINCOLN, 8 miles (S. E. by E.) from Spilsby, containing 155 inhabitants. The living is a rectory with Wainfleet, not rated in the king's books, in the archdeaconry and diocese of Lincoln. The church has long since been destroyed : the cemetery is also used by the inhabitants of Wainfleet.

NORTHIAM, a parish in the hundred of STAPLE, rape of HASTINGS, county of SUSSEX, 7¾ miles (N. W. by W.) from Rye, containing 1358 inhabitants. The living is a rectory, in the archdeaconry of Lewes, and diocese of Chichester, rated in the king's books at £15. 10. 2½., and in the patronage of Miss Lord. The church, dedicated to St. Mary, is partly in the early English and partly in the decorated style. The river Rother bounds the parish on the north, and separates it from the county of Kent. Robert Iden, in 1614, conveyed a house and certain land upon which a school-house was subsequently erected, at an expense of £700, defrayed by Frewin Turner : the annual income, including the proceeds of £500 left, in 1723, by George Bainsley, is applied to the education of poor children.

NORTHILL, a parish in the hundred of WIXAMTREE, county of BEDFORD, 3 miles (W. N. W.) from Biggleswade, containing, with the hamlets of Brookend, Budnor, Upper and Lower Caldicotts, Hatch, Ickwell, Thorncote, and part of Beeston, 1001 inhabitants. The living is a perpetual curacy, in the archdeaconry of Bedford, and diocese of Lincoln, and in the patronage of the Master and Wardens of the Grocers' Company, London. The church, dedicated to St. Mary, is a handsome structure, in the ancient English style, the east window exhibiting beautiful specimens of stained glass, by Oliver : it was endowed by Sir John Traylly, Knt., and made collegiate in the reign of Henry IV., for a master, warden, and fellows, whose revenue at the dissolution was estimated at £61. 5. 5. Elizabeth Hutchinson, in 1728, gave £200 for the education of poor fatherless girls ; the annual income is now about £16, for which four are taught. The navigable river Ivel bounds the parish on the east.

NORTHINGTON, a parish in the hundred of MITCHELDEVER, Basingstoke division of the county of SOUTHAMPTON, 3¾ miles (N. N. W.) from New Alresford, containing 277 inhabitants. The living is a perpetual curacy, annexed to the vicarage of Mitcheldever, in the archdeaconry and diocese of Winchester. The church is dedicated to St. John. Northington is within the jurisdiction of the Cheyney Court held at Winchester every Thursday, for the recovery of debts to any amount.

NORTHLEACH, a market town and parish, in the hundred of BRADLEY, county of GLOUCESTER, 20 miles (E. by S.) from Gloucester, and 82 (W. N. W.) from London, containing 773 inhabitants. This is a small town, consisting principally of a long irregular street, situated in a vale at the base of the Cotswold hills, near the source of the little river Leche, from which it derives its name, and on the road from Cheltenham to Oxford. The ancient British road, called the Lower Salt-way, leading from Droitwich to the eastern parts of the island, is here crossed by the Roman Fosse-way, which forms the north-western boundary of the parish. About the beginning of the sixteenth century it was one of the most considerable clothing towns in the county, and a principal mart for the sale of wool; but the deficiency of water occasioned a gradual decay of the manufacture, and the trade is no longer carried on. The market is held on Wednesday; and there are fairs on the Wednesdays before May 4th and June 1st, August 3rd, the first Wednesday in September, and the Wednesdays before and after October 10th. A bailiff and two constables are chosen annually at the manorial court leet; and petty sessions for the district are held here. Near the town is a house of correction for the county, capable of containing thirty-eight prisoners. The living is a vicarage, with Eastington, in the archdeaconry and diocese of Gloucester, rated in the king's books at £11, and in the patronage of the Bishop of Gloucester. The church, dedicated to St. Peter and St. Paul, is a handsome and extensive edifice, in the decorated style of English architecture, with a lofty tower at the west end: the south porch is ornamented with elegant tracery; the lateral buttresses have sculptured niches; and two niches with statues are placed over the arch, the cornice bordering which is decorated with various figures, in oval compartments: the tower has open-worked battlements; and the whole building is adorned with an embattled parapet and pinnacles: there are several sepulchral brasses, one of which is to the memory of John Fortey, a rich clothier of the town, who rebuilt the nave, in 1458. Hugh Westwood, Esq. founded a free grammar school, in the first year of the reign of Elizabeth, and endowed it with the impropriate tithes of Chedworth, and a messuage and tenement, now producing about £600 per annum, vested, by an act of incorporation passed in the fourth of James I., in the patronage of the Provost and Scholars of Queen's College, Oxford, who appoint a master, and pay him two-thirds of the annual income, and an usher the remainder. The scholars on the foundation are usually very few; but they are entitled to share with the schools of Gloucester, Cheltenham, and Chipping-Campden, in the exhibitions at Pembroke College, Oxford, instituted by George Townsend, Esq., who also gave property producing £10 per annum, for the instruction of twelve poor boys, a similar sum for poor girls, and an annual sum for apprenticing a poor boy. An hospital, or almshouse, for six poor women was founded by Thomas Dutton, Esq., in 1615, and endowed with about £30 per annum. In 1816, Mrs. Mary Harritts Allen bequeathed £2649. 17. 6. for charitable purposes, including £93. 12. per annum, for the endowment of an almshouse for six poor men; and a small sum in augmentation of the stipends of the women in Mr. Dutton's almshouse. Adjoining the Fosse-way is an intrenched camp, with a double vallum, called Norbury, and supposed to be of Roman origin.

NORTHMOOR, a parish in the hundred of CHADLINGTON, county of OXFORD, 6¼ miles (W. S. W.) from Oxford, containing 366 inhabitants. The living is a perpetual curacy, in the archdeaconry and diocese of Oxford, endowed with £1100 private benefaction, £400 royal bounty, and £900 parliamentary grant, and in the patronage of the President and Fellows of St. John's College, Oxford. The church is dedicated to St. Denis.

NORTHOLT, a parish in the hundred of ELTHORNE, county of MIDDLESEX, 2¾ miles (S.W. by S.) from Harrow on the Hill, containing 455 inhabitants. The living is a vicarage, in the archdeaconry of Middlesex, and diocese of London, rated in the king's books at £15, and in the patronage of the Bishop of London. The church is dedicated to St. Mary.

NORTHORPE, a hamlet in the parish of THURLBY, wapentake of NESS, parts of KESTEVEN, county of LINCOLN, containing 136 inhabitants.

NORTHORPE, a parish in the wapentake of CORRINGHAM, parts of LINDSEY, county of LINCOLN, 8 miles (N.E.) from Gainsborough, containing 127 inhabitants. The living is a discharged vicarage, in the archdeaconry of Stow, and diocese of Lincoln, rated in the king's books at £4, endowed with £400 Bank annuities and £119 private benefaction, and £800 royal bounty, and in the patronage of the Bishop of Lincoln. The church is dedicated to St. John the Baptist. The river Eau runs through the parish and falls into the Trent.

NORTHOVER, a parish in the hundred of TINTINHULL, county of SOMERSET, ¼ of a mile (N.) from Ilchester, containing 121 inhabitants. The living is a discharged vicarage, in the archdeaconry of Wells, and diocese of Bath and Wells, rated in the king's books at £6. 12. 11., and in the patronage of J. H. Chichester, Esq. The church is dedicated to St. Andrew. The navigable river Yeo, and the old Fosse-way, pass through the parish.

NORTHSCEUGH, a joint township with Moorthwaite, in the parish of CUMWHITTON, ESKDALE ward, county of CUMBERLAND, 6½ miles (N. N. W.) from Kirk-Oswald. The population is returned with Moorthwaite.

NORTHUMBERLAND, a maritime county, and, excepting a detached part of the county of Durham, the most northern of England; bounded on the east by the North sea, or German Ocean, and by a small detached portion of the county of Durham, called Bedlingtonshire, which is situated on the coast, between the mouths of the rivers Blyth and Wansbeck; on the south, by the county of Durham; on the west, by Cumberland, and by Roxburghshire in Scotland; and on the north, by the Scottish county of Berwick, from which it is separated by the Tweed; and by the larger detached part of Durham (divided into Norhamshire and Islandshire), which includes Holy Island, and a large triangular space, the two other sides of which are bounded by the river Tweed and the North sea. It extends from 54° 51' to 55° 41' (N. Lat.), and from 1° 9' to 2° 28' (W. Lon.), and includes an area of one thousand eight hundred and seventy-one square miles, or one million one hundred and ninety-seven thousand four hundred and forty statute acres. The population, in 1821, was 198,965. The historical notices respecting the aboriginal inhabitants of Northumberland are extremely scanty. According to Ptolemy, the people inhabiting the tract of sea-coast which extends from the river Tyne to the Frith of Forth, were called the Otodini; to the west of whom, in the mountainous districts, and in Tiviotdale, were seated

NORTHUMBERLAND

the Gadeni; both which tribes appear to have been either dependent on, or confederated with, the Brigantes, whose extensive territory lying southward, included some portion of the south-western part of this county. The Romans did not penetrate into this part of Britain until the year 79, when Agricola led his legions into the north, and partly by the terror of his arms, and partly by the fame of his clemency, subjugated the country; to secure which he erected a chain of forts extending from the Solway Frith to Tynemouth. This barrier, however, being soon broken through by the British refugees, in conjunction with the Britons of Caledonia, the Emperor Adrian constructed a rampart of earth, which, connecting the forts of Agricola, likewise extended across the county from sea to sea. The Brigantes who settled north of this wall appear to have assumed the name of *Meatæ*, supposed to be derived from the British word *meath*, a plain. In the reign of Antoninus Pius, about the year 140, the Meatæ fought several severe battles with the Romans under Lollius Urbicus, who at length re-conquered the whole country as far as the isthmus, between the Friths of Forth and Clyde, where the Roman commander, by the emperor's order, constructed a second rampart, after the manner of Adrian's, and upon the same line along which Agricola had also previously built a second chain of forts. The country between the two ramparts being, however, again devastated by the barbarians, the Emperor Severus, about the year 207, took the field against them in person; and entering Caledonia at the head of a large army, compelled the inhabitants to purchase peace by the surrender of a large portion of territory : on his return he repaired and strengthened Adrian's rampart. During his subsequent indisposition at York, the Meatæ and Caledonians recommenced hostilities, which so much exasperated him, that he resolved upon their utter extermination : his son Caracalla led the army to the north; but, on the death of his father, which soon afterwards ensued, he hastily concluded a dishonourable peace, and returned to the southern provinces of Britain, the more effectually to prosecute his claims to the empire. A chasm of more than seventy years now occurs in the Roman history of Britain; and we find nothing on record regarding this particular district, until the year 306, about which time Constantine the Great, having allayed the disturbances on the northern frontiers, entrusted their defence to an officer, styled Duke of Britain, who had under him fourteen thousand foot, and nine hundred horse, being more than two-thirds of the whole Roman force in the island. In the reigns of the succeeding emperors, the rampart was frequently broken through by the northern tribes, denominated *Scots, Picts*, and *Attacotes*, and the contiguous districts on the south depopulated in the most savage and unrelenting manner. At length the Emperor Valentinian having sent over Theodosius with a formidable body of troops, that commander repelled the barbarians, and recovered all the country between the wall of Severus and the rampart of Antoninus, which tract now received the name of *Valentia*, and was added, as a fifth province, to the four into which the more southern parts of the island were divided. About the year 380, Maximus having withdrawn the Roman forces from Britain, to support him in aspiring to the government of the eastern provinces

of the empire, the Scots and Picts renewed their incursions with dreadful success, until the arrival of the legion under the command of Stilicho, which was sent over to expel the northern invaders and to guard the rampart, but which, on the death of Theodosius in 402, was recalled to Italy to repel the Gothic invaders under Alaric. It is believed to have been during the stay of this legion in Britain that the *wall* was added to the former line of defensive works across this part of the country: this was a massive bulwark of stone, defended by an outer ditch, and guarded by an interior chain of forts and military stations, many vestiges of it still being visible : it extended in a line nearly parallel with Adrian's barrier, and at a very short distance from it. The Britons being left without the safeguard of a Roman force, and the extinction of the Roman authority in the island speedily following, a number of petty states sprang up, which were continually involved in sanguinary dissensions, whereby the barbarians of the north were more easily able to carry their devastations into the very heart of South Britain. The district north of the Tyne, under the name of Bernicia, formed at this period one of the numerous independent sovereignties.

The establishment of the Saxon dominion in this part of the country took place about the year 547, when the Saxon chief, Ida, landed at Flamborough, and after many obstinate conflicts, drove the Northumbrian Britons from the vicinity of the coast, and subsequently obtained sole dominion in the province of Bernicia, which appears to have comprised all the country between the Tyne and the Frith of Forth. Having assumed the title of King of Bernicia, he erected the strong fortress of Bambrough, on the coast opposite the Farn isles, in a remarkably eligible situation, and made it his principal residence : his reign was one of almost incessant warfare with the Scots and the fugitive Britons, and he was at length slain in battle by Owen, in 560, being succeeded by his son Adda. At the same period, Ælla, one of the chieftains who had come over with Ida, made himself master of the province or kingdom of Deïra, being the whole of the country between the Tyne and the Humber. The two sovereignties were united by Ethelfrith, grandson of Ida, who having ascended the Bernician throne in 593, invaded Deïra, then under the government of Edwin, son of Ælla, who had succeeded at the age of three years, and by expelling this infant monarch and espousing his sister Ethelfrith, became the first king of *Northan-hymbra-land*, as it is called in the ancient Saxon, signifying the land, or country, north of the Humber; which name was contracted by the Anglo-Saxons into *Northymbraland*, and has since been slightly corrupted into *Northumberland*, being in modern times confined to that portion of country only which lies on the eastern side of the island, between the rivers Tyne and Tweed, which was but a small part of the ancient Northumberland, or *Northumbria*, as it is called according to the Latin orthography. The young Edwin having found a protector in Redwald, King of East-Anglia, Ethelfrith waged war against the latter, and was slain in a battle fought on the banks of the Idle, in Nottinghamshire; upon which event Edwin, supported by the arms of Redwald, entered the capital of Northumbria, and in 617 was restored to the throne. Cwichelm, King of Wessex, having employed an assassin to murder Edwin in his palace, and the attempt failing, Edwin marched a powerful army against Cwichelm, and after devastating the kingdom of Wessex, returned to Northumberland in triumph. The reign of this prince was distinguished by the introduction of Christianity into the North of England, at the instance of his queen, a daughter of the Christian king of Kent, under whose influence the Roman missionary Paulinus succeeded in converting the Northumbrian sovereign and his people. Edwin was now the greatest prince of the Heptarchy, distinguished both by his influence over the other kingdoms, and by his strict and impartial administration of justice in his own dominions. He subdued a considerable part of Wales, including the isle of Anglesey, and for some time all the British princes paid him tribute ; but the latter forming an alliance with Penda, King of Mercia, their united forces defeated those of Edwin on Hatfield Chase, in Yorkshire, who, with his son Osfrid, perished in the battle : Edwin's widow and his other children, together with the Archbishop Paulinus, were now compelled to take refuge in Kent, and Northumbria was again divided into two kingdoms, and reverted to paganism ; Bernicia being taken possession of by Eanfrid, the son of Ethelfrid, who now returned from his exile in Scotland ; and Deïra by Osric, a cousin of Edwin. The former of these princes having perished by treachery, and the latter in battle against Cadwallon the Briton, Oswald, brother of Eanfrid, in 634, again united the two provinces : this prince surprised the camp of Cadwallon near Hexham, where, after a sanguinary conflict, he gained a complete victory over the Britons, who could never after successfully make head against the Saxons. In this reign the see of Lindisfarne was founded, and in a few years the church of Northumbria was fixed on a solid and permanent basis. Oswald being slain in battle against Penda, the pagan king of Mercia, at Oswestry in Shropshire, the latter ravaged Northumberland, but, being unable to make himself master of the royal city of Bambrough, he marched back to oppose the East Anglians, and the ancient division of Northumbria was once more revived ; Oswy, the brother of Oswald, being elected king of Bernicia, while Oswin, son of Osric, the last king of Deïra, assumed the sceptre of the latter province. Penda, King of Mercia, still exhibiting the most inveterate malignity against the Northumbrians of Bernicia, again marched against Oswy, who met, defeated, and slew him near Leeds.

In 664, on the death of Adelwald, who had succeeded his father Oswin on the throne of Deïra, Oswy assumed the latter sovereignty. In the same year a council was held in Whitby abbey, to determine the proper time for the celebration of Easter. The dispute was conducted with great acrimony, and terminated against the opinion of the Scottish clergy ; which circumstance is thought to have had some influence in protracting the subsequent wars between the Northumbrians and their northern neighbours. Oswy died in 670, and was succeeded by his son Egfrid, who, after repelling an incursion of the Picts, waged a violent war against the Mercians, which was terminated by the mediation of Theodore, Archbishop of York, after a sanguinary battle had been fought on the banks of the Trent. By the unsuccessful wars of this prince, the limits of the Northumbrian kingdom were afterwards

greatly diminished ; the Welch made encroachments on the western side, and the Picts on the northern, as far as the Solway and the Tweed. Alefrid, or Alfred, the natural son of Oswy, was raised to the throne on the demise of his brother : he was a meritorious prince, attentive to the welfare of his subjects, and reigned in peace over Northumbria for seventeen years. But from the time of this sovereign's death, in 705, until the kingdom became tributary to Egbert, King of Wessex, in 828, excepting only the vigorous reign of Eadbert, from 737 to 759, Northumberland seems to have been little else than a scene of the most frightful anarchy ; one tyrannical usurper succeeding another on the throne, and one after another falling by open rebellion, or treacherous assassination ; insomuch that the Emperor Charlemagne declared that the Northumbrians were more perfidious than pagans. It was under King Eardulf, who had been liberated from confinement through the intervention of that powerful potentate, by a bull from Pope Leo III., that Northumberland first became tributary to Wessex, being the last kingdom of the Octarchy which acknowledged that subjection.

The short period of tranquillity it now enjoyed was interrupted by the descents of the Danes, to which its situation particularly exposed it, who inflicted upon it a devastation still more horrible than it had ever before experienced. Northumbria ceased to be an Anglo-Saxon kingdom in 867, when Ivar, the Dane, assumed the government of all the country between the Humber and the Tyne ; the people north of the Tyne then chose Egbert as their sovereign ; but ten years afterwards Halfden completed the conquest of their country, which he parcelled out amongst his Danish officers, and in which the Danes became permanently settled, this being a part of the territory which, by treaty with Alfred, they were allowed peaceably to occupy. After Alfred's death, the Northumbrian Danes soon threw off their subjection ; and when Athelstan ascended the English throne, in 925, Sygtryg, the Dane, enjoyed the title of King of Northumbria. To secure the attachment of the Anglo-Danes, Athelstan gave one of his sisters in marriage to the Northumbrian prince, who at the same time embraced Christianity, but he afterwards returned to paganism, and repudiated his wife ; upon which Athelstan led his army through the whole extent of the Northumbrian territory, and annexed it to his paternal dominions. This conquest was finally completed by the great battle of Brunanburh, in which Athelstan and his son so signally overthrew the combined forces of the Scotch, Welch, Irish, and Danes, and which, among the various parts of the country where, by different antiquaries, it has been thought to have taken place, has been supposed by some to have been fought within the limits of the present Northumberland. But the Northumbrian Danes again revolted against Athelstan's successor, Edmund, and subsequently against Edred, who desolated their country, and under whom it ceased to be a nominal kingdom, being reduced to an earldom. It was soon after involved in the Danish conquest of all the North of England, which ensued upon the impolitic massacre of the Danes of the South, by command of Ethelred II. In the reign of Edward the Confessor, an army of Northumbrians, under Malcolm, son of the murdered Duncan, King of Scotland, and Siward, Earl of Northumberland, entered Scotland, destroyed the usurper Macbeth, and seated Malcolm on the throne. The rapacity of Tostig, brother to Harold, afterwards King of England, who was appointed Earl of Northumberland on the death of Siward, provoked the people to revolt, and elect Morcar for their earl, which election was confirmed by King Edward. After the death of the latter, Harold espoused the sister of Morcar, and defeated his brother Tostig, who attempted to resume his authority in Northumberland. It was also at the instigation of Tostig that Harfagar, King of Norway, undertook the formidable invasion of England, which terminated in Harold's memorable victory at Stamford-bridge, when the expelled earl and the Norwegian king were both slain.

In this part of England, the resistance to the Norman conquerors was the most obstinate, and the revolts against their power the most frequent and formidable. The unsparing devastation which this persevering resistance of the northern English brought upon them from the vengeance of the Conqueror was such, that this county, in common with the remainder of that district, lay uncultivated and unpeopled for a century after. To this desolation is attributed the omission in the Norman survey of the northern counties of Northumberland, Durham, Cumberland, and Westmorland. Nearly a century later, however, about the year 1170, it was included in the survey made by order of Hugh Pudsey, Bishop of Durham, of all the ancient demesne lands and possessions of his bishoprick, which is recorded in a small folio volume, called "Boldon Buke," still existing in the office of the bishop's auditor, at Durham. The succession of the earls of Northumberland after the Conquest may be thus briefly summed up, nearly in the words of Camden:— Copsi, being made earl by William the Conqueror, expelled Osulf, the former earl, who soon after slew him at Newburn, but did not long survive this revenge, being killed by a javelin from the hands of a robber. Gospatric then purchased the earldom of the Conqueror, but was soon deposed. Waltheof, the son of Siward, succeeded him, but was soon after beheaded on a charge of treason brought against him by his wife, niece to the Conqueror. Walcher, Bishop of Durham, next enjoyed the earldom, but was slain in a riotous assemblage of the people. Robert Mowbray then attained this honour, which he forfeited by attempting to depose William Rufus in favour of Stephen, Earl of Albemarle. King Stephen gave the earldom to Henry, son of David, King of Scots; and his son William afterwards assumed the title in right of his mother, as one of the family of the Earls of Warren. Some time afterwards, Richard I. sold it to Hugh Pudsey, Bishop of Durham, for life; but when that king had been made prisoner in his return from the Holy Land, the same bishop having contributed what Richard considered too small a sum towards his ransom, the king divested him of his earldom, and the title lay dormant for about one hundred and eighty years, until it was revived in the ancient family of Percy, in which it still continues.

The period of the Norman Conquest may be regarded as the commencement of that long era of rivalry between the English and the Scottish crowns, which occasioned an almost uninterrupted series of hostilities upon the common border of the two kingdoms, until the accession of James VI. of Scotland to the English crown. The military movements which took place in this county during these five centuries are far too numerous to be here detailed: the following are some of the most remarkable. In 1043, Alnwick was successfully defended against Malcolm, King of Scots, and his eldest son Edward, both of whom were surprised and slain by Robert de Mowbray, Earl of Northumberland. In 1095, Tynemouth castle, under Earl Robert de Mowbray (who had revolted in consequence of his having received no reward for his victory at Alnwick), after a siege of two months, was taken by William Rufus; but the earl escaped to Bambrough castle, which the king immediately invested, but being unable to take it by siege, he commenced a blockade, by building a castle, called Malvoisin, to interrupt supplies from the surrounding country, when the earl, endeavouring to escape, was taken prisoner at Tynemouth, and his wife surrendered Bambrough castle to the king, on his threatening to put out her husband's eyes if she refused; the earl was carried to Windsor castle, where he suffered a long imprisonment. In 1073, Harbottle castle was taken by William, King of Scotland, who shortly after, at the siege of Alnwick, was defeated and made prisoner. In 1215 and 1216 Northumberland was ravaged by an army of Flemings, under King John, in consequence of the barons of the county having done homage to Alexander of Scotland, at Felton-hall. In 1244, at Ponteland, peace was concluded between England and Scotland, through the medium of the prior of Tynemouth. In 1295, Carham was burned by Sir William Wallace. In 1302, on Red Rigs, near Yeavering, ten thousand Scots, under Earl Douglas, were defeated by Henry, Lord Percy, and George, Earl of March. In July 1314, after the battle of Bannockburn, Harbottle castle was taken by the Scots. In 1316, Tynemouth priory was plundered by the insurgents under Sir William Middleton and Walter de Serlby, who were shortly after taken prisoners, sent to London, and hanged. In 1318, Harbottle, Milford, and Werk castles were demolished by the Scots; and, in 1333, Bambrough castle, in which was Philippa, Queen of Edward III., was ineffectually besieged by them. In 1341, Newcastle was successfully defended by Sir John Nevill, against David, King of Scotland. In 1346, Hexham priory was pillaged, and the surrounding country devastated, by David, King of Scotland. In 1388, at Otterburn, on the 9th of August, the English were defeated, having two thousand five hundred men killed and wounded, and one thousand, with their commander, Sir Ralph Percy, taken prisoners, by the Scots, whose general, Earl Douglas, was slain; which battle furnished the subject of the celebrated ballad of Chevy Chase, in which, however, there are material deviations from truth. In 1414, the Scots were defeated at Yeavering, by Sir Robert Umfraville, Lord Warden of the Marches; and in 1419, Werk castle was taken by them, but retaken by the English. In 1463, Margaret, Queen of Henry VI., having landed from France at Berwick, advanced to Bambrough castle, which she took, and proceeded to Hexham, near which town was fought, on Lyvel's plain, on the 24th of June, the celebrated battle in which she was defeated by John Nevill, Lord Montague, brother of the great Earl of Warwick, when her general, the Duke of Somerset, with Lords Ros and Hungerford, were taken prisoners, and she herself, with her son, Prince Edward, after falling into the hands of banditti, at length escaped into Scotland, and thence to Flanders. After this victory, Bambrough and Dunstonbrough castles were taken from the Lancastrians by the Earl of Warwick, who also besieged the French garrison in that of Alnwick, which, however, was rescued by the arrival of a Scottish army under the Earl of Angus. A few days before the battle of Hexham, a body of Lancastrians, on their march to join the queen, had been defeated by Lord Montague, on Hedgeley moor. James IV. of Scotland, in his invasion of the north of England in 1513, took Etal castle; but a division of his army was routed on Millfield plain, by the men of Durham, under Sir William Bulmer; and on the 9th of September, on Branxton-Westfield, near Flodden Hill, the Scotch sustained that signal defeat from the English forces under the Earl of Surrey, in which their king, with the flower of his nobility, and about ten thousand men, was slain. In 1523, Werk castle was successfully defended against the Scots and their French auxiliaries, under the Scottish Regent, the Duke of Albany. In 1640, the army of the Scottish covenanters, under General Leslie, having crossed the border, defeated the king's forces under Lord Conway at Newburn.

On the breaking out of the parliamentary war, this was one of the four northern counties which, together with the town of Newcastle, were placed by the king under the command of the Earl of Newcastle, who levied a considerable army in this part of England at his own expense. In 1644, General Leslie again entered Northumberland, and after capturing the castle of Tynemouth, besieged Newcastle unsuccessfully; but after a second siege, which continued from August 14th to October 22nd, it surrendered to the Earl of Callender and General Leven. At the time of the unsuccessful movement in the year 1648, in favour of the captive king, Charles I., the garrison of Tynemouth castle having declared for the king, it was taken by assault by the parliamentarians, and its governor beheaded. In the ill-concerted rebellion of 1715, the friends of the Stuart family assembled on the 6th of October at Greenrigs, under the conduct of Mr. Thomas Foster, member of parliament for the county, and on Waterfalls-hill were joined by the Earl of Derwentwater, after which they proceeded to Rothbury. The next day they marched to Warkworth, and on the 10th they passed through Alnwick to Morpeth, where their number was about three hundred horse. Finding the gates of Newcastle shut against them, they marched to Hexham, where they proclaimed James III., and on the 19th returned to Rothbury, where they formed a junction with the Scots under Viscount Kenmure. On the 20th they marched to Wooler, and thence proceeded to Kelso in Scotland. Of the three marches into which the northern borders were anciently divided, the Middle march, comprising Tyndale and Reedsdale, was within the present limits of this county, the greater part of the Western march being included in that of Cumberland, and of the eastern in the detached portion of the county of Durham, which extends to the mouth of the Tweed. Each of these marches was governed by a lord-warden, with almost unlimited authority. These border jurisdictions, and their laws, were abolished in the early part of the seventeenth century, on the accession of James VI. of Scotland to the English throne. Many of the moss-troopers,

however, as the border plunderers were commonly called, still continued their depredations, until they were checked by an edict which prohibited all borderers, except gentlemen of rank, from wearing weapons. The civil war in the reign of Charles I., however, afforded some of them an opportunity of resuming their ancient practices; and in the reign of Charles II., several fresh statutes were enacted against the moss-troopers, who are stated in the preambles to have been very numerous. So lately as the year 1701, the police of Tyndale and of Reedsdale was maintained by officers called country-keepers, who, for a certain sum, ensured their respective districts against theft and robbery. Many of the borderers were engaged in the rebellion of 1715; but in the course of the last century, their ancient peculiarities have entirely disappeared, and their habits, manners, and customs, have become assimilated to those of their countrymen in general.

Northumberland is contained in the diocese of Durham, excepting the parishes of Allendale, Hexham, St. John Lee, and Throckington, which are included in that of York: it is in the province of York, and forms an archdeaconry, which includes the five deaneries of Alnwick, Bambrough, Corbridge, Morpeth, and Newcastle, and comprises eighty-seven parishes, of which eighteen are rectories, forty-one vicarages, and the remainder perpetual curacies. For purposes of civil government it is divided into six wards, viz., those of Bambrough (North and South), Castle (East and West), Coquetdale (East, North, South, and West), Glendale (East and West), Morpeth (East and West), and Tindale (East, North-East, North-West, South, and West). It contains the borough, market, and sea-port town of Newcastle; the borough and market town of Morpeth; the market and sea-port town of North Shields; the market towns of Allendale, Alnwick, Belford, Bellingham, Haltwhistle, Hexham, Rothbury, and Wooler; and the small sea-port towns of Alnmouth, Bamborough, Blyth, Hartley, Seaton, and Warkworth. Two knights are returned to parliament for the shire, and two representatives for each of the boroughs: the county members are elected at Alnwick. This county is included in the northern circuit: the assizes are held at Newcastle, and the quarter sessions alternately at Newcastle, Morpeth, Hexham, and Alnwick; the county goal is at Morpeth: there are forty-three acting magistrates. The rates raised in the county for the year ending March 25th, 1827, amounted to £78.923.17, the expenditure to £79,117. 17., of which £69.290.7. was applied to the relief of the poor.

The surface of the county is very various; along the sea-coast it is nearly level, but nearer the middle it is more diversified, and rises into large swelling ridges, which are separated by the principal rivers: these districts are well enclosed, and in some parts are adorned with woods and plantations, which, however, are but thinly scattered. The whole western side of the county is an open, mountainous, and uncultivated tract. Of these mountainous districts, the parts around Cheviot are the most valuable, being in general fine green hills, in an endless variety of form, and enclosing numerous deep, narrow, and sequestered glens: they extend from the source of the Coquet down to Allenton, and thence northward to Prendick, Branton, Ilderton, Wooler, Kirknewton, and Mindrim, and óccupy an area of at least ninety thousand acres. The other mountainous tracts are not marked by any striking irregularities of surface, being in general open, extensive, elevated, solitary wastes, having little vegetation besides heath, and affording an extremely scanty subsistence to the flocks that are depastured upon them: the greatest expanse of these reaches from the Roman wall to the borders of the Coquet, and beyond that river includes the moors to the north of Rothbury. The whole of the mountainous tracts are included in the three wards of Tindale, Coquetdale, and Glendale; and comprise about four hundred and fifty thousand acres of land, which is unfit for any kind of cultivation. These three wards, however, contain also a considerable portion of enclosed and cultivated country; and the three others, namely Bambrough ward, Morpeth ward, and Castle ward, all which adjoin the sea-coast, being without any mountainous tracts, have long been under cultivation: the vast beds of coal, also, which these three possess, and the increased population which the coal trade has occasioned in them, give them a decided pre-eminence in wealth, although in magnitude they are far inferior, occupying less than one-fourth of the whole county. At the distance of a mile from the main land, opposite the mouth of the river Coquet, is Coquet island, which is about a mile in circumference. The Farn islands, situated off the coast, to the south of Coquet Island, form two groups of islets and rocks, seventeen in number, several other rocky points appearing above the surface of the sea at low water: the one nearest to the shore, from which it is distant a mile and sixty-eight chains, is called House island.

The climate, with regard to temperature, is very variable, and generally changes to extremes. Upon the mountains snow often continues for several months, and frequently to a considerable depth, when none is to be seen in the lower districts. In the spring months, cold, piercing, easterly winds are the most prevalent; and the longest droughts experienced are always accompanied by them: in some parts of Northumberland, in consequence of the slow progress of vegetation whenever they continue for a few weeks, they have received the provincial name of sea pines; and so great is the cold attending them, that hardly any benefit is experienced from rain which falls during their prevalence. Mild breezes from the west and south are rarely experienced earlier in the year than the month of June: they are the certain harbingers of rain and vigorous vegetation, and are the most prevailing winds during the summer and autumn: in the latter season they often blow with tempestuous fury, and frequently do great damage by shaking out the grain from the ears of corn.

The various soils are disposed as follows: a strong fertile clayey loam occupies the level tract of country along the sea-coast, and, in its whole length, almost every where extends as far inland as the great north road from London to Edinburgh: it is well adapted to the culture of wheat, pulse, and clover, and to the purposes of grazing. Sandy, gravelly, and dry loam, or what is generally called a turnip soil, is found on the banks of the Tyne, from Newburn to Haltwhistle; on those of the Coquet about and above Rothbury; on those of the Aln, from its mouth to Alnwick; and on the borders of the Tweed: but a still

greater extent of this kind of soil is found in the vales of Breamish, Beaumont, and the river Till. The hills surrounding the Cheviot mountains are mostly of a dry, sharp-pointed, gravelly loam. Moist loams on a cold, wet, and clayey bottom occupy a large portion of the county, prevailing most in the middle and south-eastern parts of it: the soil which is composed of them is unsafe for sheep, and unfit for turnips, and is principally employed in the production of grain, the rearing of young cattle, and the feeding of ewes and lambs. Black peat-earth is the prevailing soil in most of the mountainous districts, and is found in many places in the lower parts of the county.

On the arable lands the following rotations of crops are commonly practised, viz.: on the clayey soils, first, fallow; second, wheat; third, clover for one or two years, pastured by sheep; fourth, beans or peas: on dry strong loams, first, turnips; second, barley; third and fourth, clover or grass seeds, pastured for two or three years by sheep, and a small number of cattle; fifth oats; sixth, beans or peas; seventh, wheat; and lastly, on the sandy and dry loams, after having been ploughed from grass, first, oats; second, turnips; third, barley or wheat, with clover, which is pastured for three or more years by sheep and a small number of cattle. Wheat is extensively cultivated, the produce varying considerably, but aver aging from twenty-four to thirty bushels per acre. Rye was formerly the principal grain grown upon all the light dry soils, but it is now only grown on very sandy land: the produce is from twenty to thirty bushels per acre: the chief part of the rye grown here, and considerable quantities which are imported from abroad, are consumed in the southern parts of the county, where it forms the common bread of the labouring class: after being leavened until it gains a considerable degree of acidity, it is made into loaves and baked in a large brick oven, or made into cakes of one and a half or two inches thick, called "sour cakes," and baked on the girdle: this is very firm, solid, and dark-coloured, and retains its moistness longer than any other kind of bread. Wheat and rye mixed, provincially called maslin, is sown in some parts of the county, and bread made from the grain thus raised, which is of finer quality than when the two species are grown separately, is esteemed by many as much superior to that made from wheat alone. Barley is grown to a considerable extent, being generally sown after turnips: the produce is from thirty to sixty bushels per acre: great quantities of this grain are made into pearl or shelled barley, or pot-barley, as it is here called, not only for home consumption, but also, for exportation, very few corn-mills in the northern part of the county being found witho ut the appendage of a barley-mill: the common bread of the labouring people in the northern parts is made from this grain, with the addition of grey peas or beans, in the proportion of one-third: the meal is kneaded with water, made into unleavened cakes, and immediately baked on a girdle; very little being ever leavened, or baked in loaves. Oats are grown in every part of the county; the varieties cultivated are numerous: the produce of common oats is from twenty to forty bushels per acre, that of the Poland and the Dutch kind from forty to sixty: those grown in Glendale are of remarkably fine quality and appearance, being known in the

London market by the name of Berwick oats: oatmeal, both for home-consumption and for exportation, is prepared to a considerable extent: it is a principal article of food with the great mass of the inhabitants, not only in the form of bread, but in crowdies, or hasty-pudding, provincially called "*meal kail*," which is taken for breakfast and supper, with butter, or, more commonly, skimmed milk, being with the latter an agreeable, nutritive, and healthy food. The wheat is invariably cut with sickles: oats and barley are sometimes, though very seldom, mown. Beans have, from time immemorial, been a prevailing crop on all the strong lands, especially along the southern part of the sea-coast: twenty bushels per acre are considered a fair average produce. Peas were formerly a more general crop than at present; from twenty-five to thirty bushels per acre are considered a good crop. Turnips and tares are of common cultivation: the former are chiefly applied to the feeding and rearing of cattle and sheep, but small quantities are reserved for seed; the average produce being about twenty bushels, or half a ton, per acre; the latter are principally consumed as green food for horses. Potatoes are also much grown, and are frequently given raw as spring food to horses: cabbages are of less frequent cultivation. Rape, together with a little rye, is often sown for early spring food for sheep. The artificial grasses most commonly cultivated are red clover, white clover, and ray-grass, with which are sometimes mixed rib-grass and hop-medic: few of these are ever grown alone, except the red clover. Woad is cultivated at Newburn, on the banks of the Tyne. Of natural meadows, which term is generally understood to mean such lands as are occasionally overflowed by rivers, and receive no other manure than what is deposited by such inundations, this county has very few; what are here called meadows being such old grass lands as are employed for growing hay almost every year, the greatest part of which are upland, and generally produce from one ton to a ton and a half per acre: the aftermath, or fog, as it is herecalled, is mostly consumed in fattening oxen and cows. Natural pastures, or old grass lands, are most prevalent along the sea-coast, and are frequently pastured with both sheep and oxen.

The greatest number of oxen is grazed in the eastern part of the county, and a few in the vicinity of Whittingham: they are bought in May or June, and sold, as they become ready, to supply the large fleets of colliers and other trading vessels belonging to the ports of Newcastle, Shields, Sunderland, Hartley, and Blyth. A great number of sheep is fattened on grass in the same manner, and many for the same purpose; but a large portion of the lands being liable to give them the rot, the occupiers only venture to have ewes for one year: the lambs are sold fat in the months of May, June, and July, and the ewes are then fattened and sold in October and November. It was formerly a general practice to milk ewes after the lambs had been weaned, for six, eight, or ten weeks, and from this milk a great quantity of cheese was made; but it has almost wholly been discontinued. In the vicinity of Wooler, a large tract of low flat ground, called *haughs*, adjoining the rivers Till and Glen, being subject to frequent inundation, both that and haughs of

a similar kind at Turvilaws, Doddington, Ewart, &c., have been successfully protected by means of embankments of from three to five feet high. Lime is very extensively applied as a manure, and has superseded the use of stone-marl, which was employed in considerable quantities on the borders of the Tweed; shell-marl is used with great advantage in some small tracts. Marine plants, thrown on shore by the tide, and here called sea-wrack, or sea-ware, are also applied with great effect for the same purpose, whenever they can be obtained: coal-ashes are much used in the vicinity of the principal towns, as a dressing for grass land.

Almost the only kind of cattle bred is the short-horned breed, which has been long established in every part of the county. In Chillingham park is a peculiar race of wild cattle, their colour being invariably white, with black about the mouths: the whole of the inside of the ear and about one-third of the outside, from the tip downwards, being red: the horns, which are very fine and are bent upwards, are white, with black tips: some of the bulls have a thin upright mane of about an inch and a half, or two inches long: their disposition, which is ferocious, has many singularities: the weight of the oxen is from thirty-five to forty five stones per quarter, that of the cows from twenty-five to thirty-five; and their flesh is finely marbled and of excellent flavour. Some of the graziers purchase, for the purpose of fattening, an excellent breed of small cattle, called *Kyloes*, which are brought from the Highlands of Scotland, and sold at Falkirk *trysts*, or meetings, or at Newcastle October fair. The few dairies which the county contains are chiefly for the supply of Newcastle and the other populous towns with milk and fresh butter: but the breeding of young cattle is practised in almost every part of it, and upon the large farms many cows are kept, much more for this purpose than for the profit of the dairy. Oxen are sometimes, but not generally, worked. Of sheep, Northumberland contains three distinct breeds, the Cheviot, the heath, and the long woolled. The Cheviot are a very hardy and valuable mountain sheep, without horns, and their faces and legs generally white: when fat they weigh from twelve to eighteen pounds per quarter: they are bred only on the hilly districts in the north-western part of the county, and are seldom found much farther south than Preedwater: none of them are bred on the mountain of Cheviot itself, the higher districts being pastured with old sheep. The heath sheep have a fierce wild-looking eye, and short firm bodies, covered with fleeces of long, coarse, shaggy wool: they are an exceedingly active and hardy race, the best adapted for high, exposed, heathy districts, like that which they occupy, from the western parts of the county of Durham to the North Tyne. The old breed of long-woolled sheep, which formerly occupied the lower districts of the county, were called *mugs*, probably from their faces being covered with a muff of wool close up to the eyes; these, however, have been much improved in consequence of the introduction of the New Leicester sheep among them; the weight of the carcass in general is from eighteen to twenty six pounds per quarter; the fleece, upon an average, weighs seven pounds and a half: many of this kind are bred to be sold to the graziers to fatten. Scarcely any are bred in Castle ward, or the south-eastern part of Morpeth ward. Goats are kept in small numbers on many parts of the Cheviot hills, where the shepherds assert that the sheep are healthier in consequence: the chief profit obtained from them is by the sale of their milk to invalids, who resort to Wooler during the summer season. The Berkshire hogs and the large white breed of swine were formerly the most prevalent in this county; but they have been in a great measure superseded by the small, black, Chinese breed, besides which there is a small white breed of still more modern introduction. The horses are of various sorts, amongst which are excellent hunters, and road and carriage horses, besides the draught horses, which are in general middle-sized and active, well adapted to the husbandry of the country: the best draught-horses are obtained from Clydesdale, in Scotland; they are strong and hardy, being about fifteen and a half or sixteen hands high. Rabbits are found in considerable numbers among the sand hills on the sea-coast: foxes are also very numerous, and are very destructive to the young lambs. The nocturnal frosts, and the north-east winds, which are here so prevalent in the spring, are very hurtful to fruit crops; so that orchards are but rarely seen, at least nine-tenths of the apples consumed in the county being imported from Kent, Essex, and other southern counties. The commons capable of being converted into profitable tillage land are now very trifling; but the extent of the open mountainous districts incapable of affording profit by cultivation with the plough, is very great. Woods growing in a natural state are found chiefly on the banks of the rivers, those of the greatest extent being on those of the North and South Tyne, the Wansbeck, the Coquet, and their tributary streams; they comprise much valuable oak timber. The demand for small wood at the collieries and lead-mines has induced the proprietors of woods on the Derwent, Tyne, &c., to cut the oak, ash, and elm, which they contain, at from twenty-five to thirty years' growth; birch, willow, and alder, at a somewhat shorter growth; and hazel, for corf-rods, once in three or four years; these corves are a kind of large wicker baskets used for drawing up the coal from the pits. Flourishing plantations, on an extensive scale, are scattered over the county. among the great variety of the trees of which they are composed, the larch is one of the most prevalent and conspicuous. On the edges of the moors towards the western parts of the county a few peats are burned, but in every other part of it coal is generally used as fuel.

Of the rarer birds, the golden eagle is sometimes to be seen on the highest summits of the Cheviot hills, and the osprey breeds annually near Greenley lake. The common and the moor-buzzard are frequently seen; several species of owls, and the butcher-bird, inhabit the woods and mountainous wilds; the heron frequents the waters in Glendale; and the moors about Wallington, Elsdon, &c., abound with red grouse. The cormorant breeds in the cliffs of the Farn islands; and wild geese and ducks, with a variety of other aquatic birds, are often found on Prestwick Car and other waters. Among the fish on this coast are the lump-fish and the porpoise. Vast quantities of cod are taken weekly, and furnish a cheap food to the labouring poor. Ling, haddock, sole, plaice, flounders, turbot, herrings, skate, and thornbacks, are very plentiful. Mackarel, basse, gar, sturgeon, and halibut, are very scarce. The

lamprey is frequently taken near the mouths of the large rivers, and the conger-eel abounds in the sea sands. A great variety of flat fish is found in the Tyne and other rivers. Crustaceous and testaceous fishes are taken in great diversity on the sea-coast, of which the most valuable is the lobster: it is said that between £12,000 and £15,000 worth of lobsters were caught in one year between Newbiggin and Newton. Cockles are very plentiful along the coast, the best and largest being found at Budle: oysters of an excellent quality are sometimes taken among the sea rocks. Every variety of trout abounds in the rivers, rivulets, and other waters of this county.

The most important mineral productions are coal and lead. The great coal field of the north-eastern extremity of England, which extends over the greater part of this county, and the neighbouring one of Durham, forms a most important object in the national economy. This district is included within an irregular triangle, having its apex at Berwick upon Tweed, and its base upon the river Tees: it consists of a series of beds, which, including several smaller ones of nearly the same material, amount to two hundred and twenty-nine: they consist of five different substances, some of which alternate with each other several times, viz., coal, sandstone, slate-clay or shale, limestone, and basalt. All the beds of coal dip towards the east, so that the lowest of them, which rises to the surface at Cross Fell, in Cumberland, is calculated to lie three hundred and eighty-seven fathoms below the lowest of the Newcastle beds, a little eastward of that town. The whole district has been divided into two separate formations, which are distinguished as the "Independent Coal Formation," and the "Newcastle Coal Formation," and familiarly into "lead measures" and "coal measures." The tract termed the lead measures, from the veins of lead which abound in a particular part of it, extends from Berwick on the north, to the Tees on the south; its northern part being bounded, on the east by the sea, and on the west by the Cheviot hills; and its southern part, on the east by the coal measures, and on the west by a range of high land, of which Cross Fell is the apex. The coal measures extend from the river Coquet on the north, nearly to the Tees on the south, the length of this tract being about fifty-eight miles, and its greatest breadth about twenty-four. The leading distinction between the two formations appears to be this; that of the numerous and various organic remains which have been found in the course of the mining operations in both of them, those discovered in the strata constituting the coal measures are exclusively vegetable, or belonging to fresh water; while in the strata of the lead measures are found both sandstone and limestone, containing marine shells, or impressions of them. The beds of coal, and of the other strata composing the coal measures, are not every where of uniform thickness, but, from the best information, their thickness is calculated at one thousand six hundred and twenty feet; and the lead measures, which pass beneath them, and are tolerably regular, are estimated at two thousand seven hundred and forty-nine feet. The beds of coal rise to the surface one after the other, each to the eastward of that which immediately precedes it in point of age; they are sometimes visible, but are more frequently covered by alluvial soil. The latter contains masses of the different rocks composing the whole district, and among them portions of hard black basalt are found every where in abundance: of this stone the ancient Britons formed the heads of their battle-axes, which are usually denominated *celts*. Barbed arrow-heads of pale-coloured flint, neatly finished, are frequently found on the moors, and are provincially called *elf-bolts*. This alluvium also contains portions of the trap rocks of the Cheviot range; and masses of fine granite are scattered over the surface of the whole county. In the coal measures, potters' clay of a blueish, and sometimes of a yellow, colour, is found immediately below the vegetable soil, and is used for making coarse earthenware, bricks, and tiles. The number of beds of coal in the lead measures has not been precisely ascertained; seven have been enumerated, of which only four exceed three or four feet in thickness, and consist of a slate coal, similar to the Scotch, Welch, or Staffordshire, and which does not cake; it is used only for home consumption, and for burning lime, for which latter purpose it is peculiarly adapted, being also generally found together with limestone: the mines are very numerous between Berwick and the river Coquet, south of which there are but few in the tract termed the lead measures, and the coal is very inferior in quality to that of the mines north of that river; these mines are very shallow, and it is remarkable that the beds of coal and the strata between which they lie undulate with the surface of the country, which is not the case with the coal measures. The whole surface of the coal measures has been calculated at one hundred and eighty square miles: the majority of the numerous mines are situated on both sides of the river Tyne, and not far distant from its banks. In these measures forty beds of coal have been seen, but of that number many are of inconsiderable thickness: the two most important are those distinguished by the names of the *high main* and the *low main*; the thickness of the former being six feet, and that of the latter six feet six inches. The high main coal is about sixty fathoms above the low main, which, at St. Anthon's colliery near Newcastle, is a hundred and thirty-five fathoms from the surface: between them occur eight beds of coal, one of which is four feet thick, and another three: seven beds have been found under the low main, but the quality is inferior. Thus the quantity of coal in the district termed the lead measures is far less considerable than that in the coal measures, besides which, the superiority of the latter over every other is well known.

The quantity of coal raised annually in this district, and exported from Shields and Sunderland to London, and the whole eastern and southern coasts of Great Britain, is immense; and there is a curious distribution of the trade consequent upon the relative magnitudes of the rivers Tyne and Wear. The Tyne vessels, being large, are chiefly destined for the London market; the Wear vessels, on the contrary, are so small that they can make their way into all the small rivers and harbours, so that they supply the whole eastern coasts, and the southern as far westward as Plymouth. Besides the coal exported to different parts of England, a large quantity is consumed in the two counties, which cannot easily be calculated. About forty years ago a practise was adopted at the pits, where the coal was of a fragile nature, of erecting screens to separate the small from the larger coal. This system is now become universal, and immense

heaps of coal are thus raised at the mouths of the pits: these soon take fire from the heat of the decomposing pyrites, and continue to burn for several years. Not less than one hundred thousand chaldrons are thus annually destroyed on the Tyne, and nearly an equal quantity on the Wear. The choak damp, the fire-damp, and the after-damp, or stythe, are the mining terms for the gases with which the coal mines are affected, and of these the second, both from its immediate violence and as occasioning the other kinds of damp, is the most to be dreaded; the accidents arising from it have become more frequent of late years, although every possible precaution is taken in examining and in ventilating the mines. The beds of sandstone in the lead measures, when coarse-grained, are called grit, which is quarried for mill-stones, whence the beds are termed mill-stone grit. In the coal measures, sandstone is termed *post* by the miners: but when the bed is very hard it is termed *whin*. A hard bituminous shale often forms the floor of the coal beds, and is used by the manufacturers of firebricks. No beds of limestone occur in the coal measures; but in the lead measures there are about twenty, varying in thickness from three feet to sixty or seventy, making an aggregate thickness of five hundred and sixty-seven feet: they are generally hard, of a blue colour, not crystalline, and are without petrifactions, except two of the beds, one of which is full of madrepores, and hard enough to receive a polish; the other is full of shells, and is called the cockle-shell limestone.

The lead veins, which occupy but a small part of the large district named from them, are chiefly situated in a space of about fifteen miles from north to south, and twenty from east to west, the southern boundary of which, lying partly in this county and partly in that of Durham, may be defined to be a line extending about twenty miles eastward from Cross Fell. In this district there are two descriptions of nearly vertical veins: those which run north and south, or nearly so, are without lead, and are frequently filled with quartz; those running east and west contain it in great abundance: the latter are the most numerous, and have been wrought for at least two hundred years; some are only a few inches wide, while others are several fathoms: they also vary in width in the different veins through which they pass. The only lead-ore procured in abundance from these mines is galena: it contains silver, the proportion of which varies from two to forty-two ounces in the fother of twenty-one hundred-weight: the average is twelve ounces; but eight are considered to be worth extracting. When it is of good quality, thirty-two hundred-weight of clean ore yield twenty hundred-weight of lead. Basalt is found both in the lead and coal measures: in the first it occurs in the form of beds, interstratified with beds of sandstone, limestone, &c., in veins, and in masses lying on the surface, termed *over-lying masses:* in the latter situation it occurs in the general form of a long range, crossing the country from south-west to north-east, north of the lead-mines. Further north other masses are visible, and still further basaltic eminences form a striking feature in the country between Alnwick and Berwick, and have frequently been chosen for the sites of castles, as at Dunstanbrough, Bambrough, and Holy Island. Some of the small islands near the coast are also composed of this rock. The number of basaltic veins, or dykes, traversing the coal measures is very considerable; the largest, in the immediate neighbourhood of Newcastle, is that which passes through Coley-hill, about four miles west of the town, which is twenty-four feet wide, and in which a long range of quarries has been opened, in some places to the depth of fifty feet.

The richest fields of lead-ore are at Allenhead and Coalcleugh, which, with the other five mines in the parish of Allendale, furnish an annual produce of about two thousand five hundred tons of lead. Lead-ore is also found in some of the northern parts of the county: a strong vein is now worked near Fallow field; and strings of ore have been discovered on the coast at Elwick, and on the eastern side of Holy Island. Arsenic is found in the lead mines. The washing of the ore and the other operations at these mines have been much facilitated during the last thirty years by the introduction of improved machinery. The ore is wrought by a measure containing eight hundred-weight of clear ore, called a bing; most of the proprietors have smelting-mills of their own, where they smelt the ore, take out the silver it contains by refining, and then cast the lead into pigs, of one hundred-weight and a half each. Ore of zinc is found in great abundance in most of the veins producing lead-ore; but its distance from any brass-works and the want of water-carriage render it of little value: in these mines is also found a great variety of the different kinds of spar. Iron-ore is found both in the coal and lead districts. Immense quantities of iron pyrites lie imbedded in the strata of indurated clay through all the coal-field. The iron-works at Lemington are chiefly supplied with this metal from the neighbouring collieries. Iron-stone is still more abundant in the shale of the lead-mines; but owing to the high price of fuel, and the great distance from any water-carriage, it cannot be manufactured to advantage. There were formerly furnaces at Lee-hall, near Bellingham, and at Bebside: iron-ore was got about four miles west of Blyth; and the Carron Company were once accustomed to collect on Holy Island a part of the ore smelted at their furnaces. The remains of some ancient blomeries are found in different parts of Northumberland, seeming to indicate that the Romans were acquainted with these iron mines, which is further evinced by a Roman altar, found at Benwell, inscribed to Jupiter Dolichenus, the deity who presided over iron.

The great coal trade of this district has been flourishing for the last five centuries, and has been constantly increasing with the increasing population of the country. Of the quantity raised it is not easy to form an exact estimate; but it is supposed to be about equal in extent to the exports of this article from the river Tyne, in which a considerable quantity from the county of Durham is included, the latter being reckoned equal to the quantity consumed within this county. The average annual export of coal from Newcastle, Sunderland, Hartley, and Blyth, for five years, ending with 1826, was one million three hundred and thirty-three thousand seven hundred and seventy Newcastle chaldrons; which, added to the home consumption and waste, estimated at three hundred and forty thousand chaldrons, makes the aggregate amount of coal raised annually from the mines in the counties of Durham and Northumberland, one million six hundred and seventy-

three thousand seven hundred and seventy chaldrons, equal to four millions four hundred and thirty-five thousand four hundred and ninety tons and a half, nearly two-thirds of which was shipped at the different ports. The facilities derived from the introduction of steam machinery at these collieries has been immense; for, besides working the hydraulic machinery and drawing up the coal from the pits, it is now employed at nearly all the collieries in propelling the coal wagons along the rail-ways to the different staiths, or loading-places on the Tyne.

Limestone abounds through the whole of Bambrough ward, and that part of Glendale ward lying east of the river Till; and thence it stretches, in a south-westerly direction, through the central parts of the county, being found at Shilbottle, Long Framlington, Hartburn, Ryall, Corbridge, &c., and at numerous other places to the westward of these. Freestone, of various kinds, abounds in almost every part of the county, and is applied to all the purposes of building: many of the quarries afford tolerably good slate for roofing, and flag-stones for floors; and at some of them are obtained excellent grind-stones, of which many are exported. Whinstone, of the blue kind, is found in many parts of the county, particularly in that called Bambrough-shire; and the district on the western side of the river Till, including all the Cheviot mountains, produces scarcely any other mineral substance than brown, red, or grey whinstone, which is a superior material for making roads, and is sometimes carried several miles for that purpose. Stone-marl abounds in many places near the Tweed; and shell-marl is found in a few places in Glendale ward: clay-marl is also found in small quantities, but in situations unfavourable to its being used as manure.

The staple manufactures of the county are principally derived from, or connected with, the coal trade and mines, such as ship-building, rope-making, and the production of the several articles made at the forges; foundries, copperas-works, soda, or marine alkali manufactories; white-lead works, potteries, glassworks, &c. Hexham has long been known for its manufacture of gloves, called "Hexham Tan." A manufacture of straw-plat is carried on to a considerable extent in the county; and in some of its branches much ingenuity is displayed. The coal trade is the chief basis of the commerce of the county, and the principal source of its wealth, as well as a nursery for some of the best seamen in the world. The principal exports from the Tyne, besides coal, are lead, shot, cast and wrought iron, grind-stones, bricks, earthenware, and glass. The exports through the medium of the port of Berwick are chiefly corn, flour, oatmeal, shelled barley, potatoes, eggs, pork, and wool, which are conveyed coastwise. The foreign trade is chiefly to the north of Europe. The port of Alnmouth also employs a few vessels in exporting corn, flour, &c.; and during the summer season a few are engaged in carrying lime from the neighbourhood of Bambrough to different parts of Scotland. Among the chief imports are corn, flax, hemp, linen, yarn, timber, and iron.

The principal rivers are the Tyne, the Tweed, the Coquet, the Aln, the Blyth, the Wansbeck, and the Till. The Tyne is formed by the confluence, a little above Hexham, of two streams of nearly equal magnitude, called the North Tyne and the South Tyne : the former has its sources in the mountainous heaths, on the extreme western confines of the county, and runs in a south-easterly direction towards Hexham. The South Tyne, rising behind Cross Fell in the county of Cumberland, enters the south-western extremity of the county, and runs directly east to its junction with the North Tyne, their united waters pursuing the same direction by Hexham to Newcastle, and thence to Shields, immediately below which the Tyne falls into the North sea : the tide flows up this river to a short distance above Newburn; it is navigable up to Newcastle for vessels of three or four hundred tons' burden, the larger vessels loading at Shields; about forty steam-boats now ply upon it between Newcastle and Shields. The conservancy of the Tyne belongs to the corporation of Newcastle, by grant of Edward II.; and their jurisdiction extends to high-water mark on both sides of the river, from Spar-Hawk, a rock at the mouth of the haven, to Hedwin streams, above Newburn, a distance of nineteen miles. The Tweed forms the northern boundary of the county for a few miles in the vicinity of Wark. The Tyne and Tweed have been long famous for their salmon fisheries, more especially the latter, in which the fish taken are the salmon, bull-trout, whitling, and large common trout, nearly the whole of which are sent to London, in pounded ice, by means of fast-sailing vessels, called smacks, constructed for the purpose: they are from seventy to one hundred and twenty tons' burden; twelve men on an average being employed in each. The Coquet, rising among the Cheviot hills, pursues an easterly course by Allenton, Rothbury, and Felton, to Warkworth, immediately below which it falls into the sea. The Aln has a source similar to that of the last-mentioned river, but its course is much shorter, although in the same direction, and only a few miles to the north of it: it passes by Whittingham and Alnwick, and falls into the sea at Alemouth, or Alnmouth. The Blyth rises to the east of the course of the North Tyne, and discharges itself into the sea at Blyth, the small harbour of which it constitutes. The Wansbeck, which runs a few miles to the northward of the last-mentioned, is formed by different small streams, which, descending from the mountain wastes, unite before they reach Morpeth, their combined waters continuing an easterly course to the sea, which they join at Cambois, a few miles below that town. The Till, which is the largest stream that joins the Tweed from this county, rises among the Cheviot hills, where it is called the Brennich, and has upon it the cataract called Linhope-spout, a fall of fifty-six feet: this name it retains until it has passed Wooler, at first running eastward; but it afterwards assumes a northerly course, receiving from the same mountainous tract the waters of different smaller streams, the principal of which is the Glen, and passing by Chillingham, Doddington, and Ford, below the latter village it soon enters the detached part of the county of Durham. The river Derwent forms the southern boundary of the county for the distance of some miles, both to the east and west of Allensford; and afterwards running through a small part of the county of Durham, it joins the Tyne above Newcastle. The road from London to Berwick, through York, enters this county from Chester le Street, in Durham, and runs the whole length of it, passing through Newcastle,

Morpeth, Alnwick, and Belford, to Berwick. A railroad from Newcastle to Carlisle has been long projected, which it is thought will be of great convenience to those two commercial towns, and to all the intermediate country: contractors to commence and complete this great undertaking were advertised for about the year 1828.

The principal Roman remains, which, indeed, are among the most interesting in the island, are those of the great barrier constructed as a security against the incursions of the North Britons. Of the eighteen stations along its line, the sites of eleven are in this county, viz., *Segedunum, Pons Ælii, Condercum, Vindobala, Hunnum, Cilurnum, Procolitia, Borcovicus, Vindolana, Æsica,* and *Magna,* which are here enumerated as they occur in succession, from the mouth of the Tyne, westward, and which were at Wallsend, Newcastle, Benwell, Rutchester, Halton-Chesters, Walwick-Chesters, Carrawbrugh, House-Steads, Little Chesters, Great Chesters, and Caervoran, respectively. Of all these there are traces, more or less distinct; and numerous remains of Roman buildings, utensils, coins, &c., of almost every description, have been discovered among their foundations, and deposited in various antiquarian repositories. The most extensive remains of a Roman, or Roman-British, town, are those at House-Steads, where they occupy a space of two miles and a half in length. The most conspicuous fragments of the wall itself are at Dentonburn, Heddon on the Wall, Harlowhill, and near Chollerford bridge, on the Tyne. In addition to the stations along the wall, there were others in this county, at Old Town, Bellingham, Corchester, Hexham, Tynemouth, Elsdon, and Rochester; which have also furnished various and interesting remains. Besides the paved way which ran from turret to turret, immediately within the wall, another was carried by the most direct course from one station to another, and is still distinguishable in different places. The Watling-street traversed the county from south to north, entering it at Corbridge on the Tyne, and crossing the great wall at Portgate, a mile and a half beyond which it separates into two branches, the one running north-north-east, and entering Scotland, near Berwick, the other north-north-west, crossing the border at Black Halls: the former branch, commonly called the Devil's causeway, passes on the east side of Kirk-Heaton, and crossing the Wansbeck, proceeds by the west of Hartburn church, in a straight line between Netherwitton and Wittonshiels, to Brinkburn Abbey: it may be distinctly traced across Rimside Moor, whence it proceeds by Glanton, Horton castle, Lowick, and Ancroft, to Cornmills, where it crosses the Tweed. The other line runs by Swinburn castle, Corsenside, Elishaw, Rochester, and over the head of the Coquet, between Chewgreen and Thirlmoor, to Black-Halls. The vicinal road called the Maiden Way, supposed to be a corruption of Made-way, runs from Caervoran, on the western side of the county, to Whitley castle, and thence to Whellop castle in Westmorland. The ecclesiastical architecture of Northumberland has little that is especially remarkable: the number of churches, in proportion to the size of the county, is but small, some of the parishes being very extensive, particularly in the more barren and mountainous portions of it. The religious houses, too, owing, it is probable;

partly to the unfruitfulness of a great part of the county, and to the great insecurity of its border situation, during the whole period of the existence of those establishments, were not numerous, amounting only to about forty-nine, including hospitals and colleges. There are some remains of the abbeys of Alnwick, Blanchland, and Hulne; but the chief monastic ruins are those of the priories of Brinkburn, Hexham, and Tynemouth; the anciently conventual church of Hexham is one of the finest ecclesiastical buildings in the county. There are medicinal springs at Eglingham, Halliwell, Snowhope, and Thurston, but none of them are much frequented. There are numerous ancient castles remaining, either wholly or in part; amongst which that of Bambrough is of the highest antiquity, while that of Alnwick is the most extensive, and one of the greatest historical celebrity: in this class of remains are several of the ancient border towers, of comparatively small dimensions, but of strong though simple construction. Alnwick Castle, so long the seat of the noble family of Percy, with its modern additions, also takes the lead amongst the present mansion-houses of Northumberland. On the mountain streams there are several falls of considerable height, but owing to the very great barrenness of the tracts in which they are situated, they are less picturesque than those of the adjoining county of Durham. The lawless and predatory habits of the ancient borderers, so large a portion of whom inhabited this county, are well known; they were finally suppressed about the commencement of the last century; and the numerous ballads in which the achievements of these half-licensed brigands were celebrated, have, like the ballad of Robin Hood, ceased to engage the public mind, but have assumed a less changeable form in the volumes of Percy and of Scott, as lasting memorials of a state of manners which, at least in Britain, has probably disappeared for ever.

NORTHWAY, a joint tything with Newton, in the parish of ASHCHURCH, lower division of the hundred of TEWKESBURY, county of GLOUCESTER, 2¼ miles (E. N.E.) from Tewkesbury, containing, with Newton, 185 inhabitants.

NORTHWICH, a market town in the parochial chapelry of WITTON, which is included in that part of the parish of GREAT BUDWORTH which is in the hundred of NORTHWICH, county palatine of CHESTER, 17½ miles (E.N.E.) from Chester, and 173 (N.W.) from London, containing 1490 inhabitants. The name of this place is intended to point out its situation with regard to the other *wiches*, or salt towns. Camden states that it was called by the Britons *Hellath*, or *Hellah Du*, meaning the Black Salt Town: it is situated on the line of the northern Watling-street, and the same author is of opinion that its brine springs were used by the Romans. At the Norman survey it constituted part of the demesne belonging to the earldom of Chester, and eventually passed to the crown: in the reign of Richard III., the manor was, with many others, granted to the Derby family, but it has since been alienated. During the civil commotions in 1643, the town was fortified, and the parliamentary forces had a garrison here; the first attack of the royalists was unsuccessful, but, on the arrival of a reinforcement, they took the town and garrisoned it; it was, however, subsequently retaken by the parliamentarians, and retained by them during the remainder of the war. What is usually considered, from the contiguity of the streets, to constitute the town, lies on the verges of the adjoining townships of Witton, Castle-Northwich, Winnington, Leftwich, Marston, and Anderton, at the confluence of the rivers Dane and Weaver, and at the intersection of the high road from Chester to Manchester, with that from London to Liverpool: it is irregularly built, the streets are paved and lighted, many of the houses are ancient, and the inhabitants are supplied with water conveyed by pipes from a reservoir.

The commercial prosperity of Northwich is entirely dependent on its numerous brine springs and extensive mines of rock-salt, in which article the trade is so great as to produce an annual export of one hundred thousand tons from the springs alone: they were discovered at a very early period, and are usually from twenty to forty yards in depth; the water is so intensely impregnated as to be fit for immediate evaporation. The brine being raised by pumps set in motion by steam-engines, is conveyed directly, by means of pipes, into pans from thirty to forty feet square; these are fixed over furnaces, the heat arising from which causes the water to evaporate, when the salt chrystallizes on the surface, and ultimately sinks to the bottom. The evaporation being completed, the salt is put into moulds perforated at the bottom to drain off the moisture, and afterwards dried in rooms heated by hot air pipes, or in stoves, when it is ready for sale. The grain of salt differs in size according to the degree of heat that is applied: a period of from twenty to twenty-four hours is required to dry a pan of coarse-grained salt, whilst two pans of salt having a fine grain may be worked off in that time; hence the latter is considerably cheaper than the former. The mines of rock-salt were discovered in 1670; the upper stratum, lying about sixty yards below the surface of the earth, is ten yards thick: about 1773, a second stratum, of superior quality and ten feet in thickness, was discovered, at the depth of one hundred and ten yards, the intermediate space being occupied by a solid mass of stone. This alone is worked, and by the following process: a shaft is sunk, and on reaching the mine, a roof is left, which is supported by pillars of the same material; as the excavation proceeds the fragments are raised in buckets, by means of steam-engines. The pits include an area of two, three, or four acres, and when greatly illuminated, present a singularly magnificent appearance, the light being reflected from all points in every variety of hue, as from a promiscuous assemblage of mirrors and prisms. The rock-salt is conveyed down the Weaver: one-third undergoes a refining process at Frodsham, and at the works on the Lancashire side of the Mersey, and the remainder is sent to Liverpool, whence it is exported to Ireland and the ports of the Baltic. From an account published in 1818, it appears that two hundred thousand tons of manufactured salt, and upwards of forty thousand tons of rock-salt, were landed at Liverpool during the preceding year, and that upwards of two hundred and eighty thousand bushels are annually sold for internal consumption, by far the greater portion having been obtained in this neighbourhood; since that period the business has materially increased. The number of vessels thus employed, and which return with coal, is about three hundred, of from ninety to one hundred tons' burden each. Many others are engaged exclusively in the importation from Liverpool of timber, grain, wine, spirituous liquors, raw cotton, grocery, &c., and these frequently return with oak timber. Some vessels of small burden are built here in the docks and ship-yards. Facilities of water-carriage are supplied by the Weaver, which flows through the town, and the Grand Trunk canal, which passes in a semicircular direction through the salt-works, about one mile to the northward. The market, which is held by prescription, is on Friday; and there are fairs on April 10th, for cattle only, on August 2nd, and December 6th, which are numerously attended by the manufacturers from Manchester, York-shire, Birmingham, and Sheffield, with their respective goods, and by venders of Irish linen; a commodious range of booths for their use was erected about a quarter of a mile from the town by Mr. Mort, a late lord of the manor of Northwich. Courts leet and baron are held, at which constables and other officers are appointed. The general quarter sessions, formerly held here once in the year, were removed to Knutsford in 1784. There are places of worship for Independents and Wesleyan Methodists. Here is a charity school for twelve poor children, with a small endowment given by Thomas Key, in 1735.

NORTHWICH, a hamlet in the parish of BLOCK-LEY, upper division of the hundred of OSWALDSLOW, county of WORCESTER, though locally in the upper division of the hundred of Kiftsgate, county of Glou-cester, 1¾ mile (S.) from Chipping-Campden, contain-ing 37 inhabitants.

NORTHWICK, a chapelry in that part of the parish of HENBURY which is in the lower division of the hun-dred of HENBURY, county of GLOUCESTER, 6½ miles (S. W. by W.) from Tewkesbury: the population is re-turned with Redwick. It is within the peculiar juris-diction of the Bishop of Bristol. The navigable river Severn runs through the chapelry.

NORTHWOLD, a parish in the hundred of GRIMS-HOE, county of NORFOLK, 4¼ miles (S. E. by E.) from Stoke-Ferry, containing 981 inhabitants. The living is a rectory, in the archdeaconry of Norfolk, and diocese of Norwich, rated in the king's books at £29. 14. 9½., and in the patronage of the Bishop of Ely. The church, built in the reign of Edward IV., and dedicated to St. Andrew, has a stately quadrangular tower of flint, em-battled and quoined with freestone, and crowned with eight richly-carved pinnacles. The river Wissy runs through the parish. Bridget Holder, in 1736, gave cer-tain land, and John Carter, in 1782, bequeathed £200, the income to be applied for teaching sixteen children.

NORTHWOOD, a township in that part of the parish of WEM which is in the Whitchurch division of the hundred of BRADFORD (North), county of SALOP, containing 182 inhabitants.

NORTHWOOD, a parish in the liberty of WEST MEDINA, Isle of Wight division of the county of SOUTH-AMPTON, 1¾ mile (S.) from West Cowes, containing, with the town of West Cowes, 3579 inhabitants. The living is a perpetual curacy, with the vicarage of Caris-brooke, in the archdeaconry and diocese of Winchester. The parish is bounded on the east by the navigable river Medina. There is a small endowment for a school,

the gift of Thomas Cole, in 1725. A rent-charge of about £15 was bequeathed by John Mann, in 1687, for the maintenance of poor orphans.

NORTON, a township in the parish of RUNCORN, hundred of BUCKLOW, county palatine of CHESTER, 4½ miles (N. E.) from Frodsham, containing 294 inhabit-ants. A priory of Augustine canons, originally founded in 1133, at Runcorn, by William Fitz-Nigell, was removed hither by his son William, constable of Chester: this house was dedicated to the Blessed Virgin Mary, and at the dissolution had a revenue of £258. 11. 8.: it was subsequently a private mansion, and was besieged by the royalists in the early part of 1643. The Mersey and Irwell and the Duke of Bridgewater's canal pass through the township.

NORTON, a parish in the hundred of SCARSDALE, county of DERBY, 3 miles (N. by E.) from Dronfield, con-taining 1697 inhabitants. The living is a discharged vicarage, in the archdeaconry of Derby, and diocese of Lichfield and Coventry, rated in the king's books at £6. 13. 4., endowed with £200 private benefaction, and £200 royal bounty, and in the patronage of the Rev. Henry Pearson. The church, dedicated to St. James, contains several monuments, among which is an altar-tomb to the memory of the parents of John Blythe, Bishop of Salisbury, and Geffrey Blythe, Bishop of Lich-field, both which prelates were born here. There is a place of worship for Unitarians. A free grammar school was founded and endowed, in 1654, by Edward Gill, in pursuance of the will of his father: the annual in-come, including several subsequent gifts, is £80, which is applied to the education of about sixty children, in a school-room rebuilt upwards of forty years ago.

NORTON, a parish in the south-western division of Stockton ward, county palatine of DURHAM, 2 miles (N.) from Stockton upon Tees, containing 1186 inha-bitants. The living is a vicarage, in the archdeaconry and diocese of Durham, rated in the king's books at £31. 11. 5½., and in the patronage of the Bishop of Durham. The church, dedicated to St. Mary, was formerly collegiate: it is partly Norman, and partly in the early English style, with various windows of later date, and a tower rising from the centre, and has lately received an addition of four hundred and forty-five sittings, of which three hundred and thirty-nine are free, the Incorporated Society for the enlargement of churches and chapels having granted £350 towards defraying the expense. There is a place of worship for Wesleyan Methodists. Henry II. granted permis-sion for a market to be held here weekly, on Sunday. Norton enjoys the privilege of one of the six scholar-ships founded in the University of Oxford, in 1536, by the Rev. John Claymund, then vicar of this parish, and master of Corpus Christi College. The Rev. John Wallis, author of the history and antiquities of North-umberland, died here in 1793.

NORTON, a parish in the upper division of the hundred of DUDSTONE and KING'S BARTON, county of GLOUCESTER, 4 miles (N. E. by N.) from Gloucester, containing 349 inhabitants. The living is a perpetual curacy, in the archdeaconry and diocese of Gloucester, endowed with £400 royal bounty, and £400 parliament-ary grant, and in the patronage of the Dean and Chap-ter of Bristol. The church, dedicated to St. Mary, is a small structure, principally in the later English style.

NORTON, a township in the parish of BROMYARD, hundred of BROXASH, county of HEREFORD, 3 miles (N. E. by E.) from Bromyard, containing 574 inhabitants.

NORTON, a parish in the hundred of CASHIO, or liberty of ST. ALBAN'S, county of HERTFORD, 1 mile (W. N. W.) from Baldock, containing 313 inhabitants. The living is a discharged vicarage, in the archdeaconry of St. Alban's, and diocese of London, rated in the king's books at £5. 6. 8., endowed with £200 royal bounty, and in the patronage of the Rev. R. W. Sutton. The church is dedicated to St. Nicholas.

NORTON, a parish in the hundred of FAVERSHAM, lathe of SCRAY, county of KENT, 3¼ miles (W.) from Faversham, containing 98 inhabitants. The living is a rectory, in the archdeaconry and diocese of Canterbury, rated in the king's books at £10. 18. 4., and in the patronage of the Bishop of Rochester. The church, dedicated to St. Mary, is principally in the early English style of architecture.

NORTON, a parish in the hundred of FAWSLEY, county of NORTHAMPTON, 2¼ miles (E. N. E.) from Daventry, containing, with the hamlets of Muscott and Thorpe, 474 inhabitants. The living is a vicarage, in the archdeaconry of Northampton, and diocese of Peterborough, and in the patronage of Beriah Botfield, Esq. The church is dedicated to All Saints. There is a place of worship for Wesleyan Methodists. The Grand Junction canal crosses the parish on the east and north.

NORTON, a township in the parish of CUCKNEY, Hatfield division of the wapentake of BASSETLAW, county of NOTTINGHAM, 4¾ miles (S. by W.) from Worksop, containing 391 inhabitants.

NORTON, a parish in the hundred of BLACKBOURN, county of SUFFOLK, 3½ miles (S. E. by S.) from Ixworth, containing 691 inhabitants. The living is a rectory, in the archdeaconry of Suffolk, and diocese of Norwich, rated in the king's books at £14. 3. 9., and in the patronage of the Master and Fellows of St. Peter's College, Cambridge. The church is dedicated to St. Andrew.

NORTON, a parish in the lower division of the hundred of BLACKENHURST, county of WORCESTER, 3 miles (N. by E.) from Evesham, containing, with the chapelry of Lench-Wick, 386 inhabitants. The living is a vicarage, in the archdeaconry and diocese of Worcester, rated in the king's books at £5. 17. 8½., and in the patronage of the Dean and Chapter of Worcester. The church, dedicated to St. Egwin, was a small cruciform structure, principally in the later English style, but the nave having fallen down, the tower is now distinct from the rest of the building. There is a trifling endowment, the gift of Anne Walter, for teaching poor children.

NORTON, a parish in the wapentake of BUCK-ROSE, East riding of the county of YORK, comprising the townships of Norton, Sutton, and Welham, and containing 1168 inhabitants, of which number, 1017 are in the township of Norton, ¾ of a mile (E. S. E.) from New Malton. The living is a perpetual curacy, in the archdeaconry of the East riding, and diocese of York, endowed with £200 private benefaction, £400 royal bounty, and £1100 parliamentary grant, and in the patronage of — Ewbank, Esq. Norton is separated from Malton by the river Derwent, which is here crossed by a stone bridge, at the foot of which there was formerly an hospital, founded early in the reign of Henry II., by Roger de Flamville, and made subordinate to the priory of Malton. From the great number of Roman coins discovered, this is supposed to have been anciently a place of more consequence than it is now.

NORTON, a township in the parish of CAMPSALL, upper division of the wapentake of OSGOLDCROSS, West riding of the county of YORK, 8½ miles (N. by W.) from Doncaster, containing 668 inhabitants. There is a place of worship for Wesleyan Methodists.

NORTON (BISHOP'S), a parish in the eastern division of the wapentake of ASLACOE, parts of LINDSEY, county of LINCOLN, 10 miles (W. N. W.) from Market-Rasen, containing, with the township of Atterby, 413 inhabitants. The living is a discharged vicarage, in the peculiar jurisdiction and patronage of the Prebendary of Bishop's Norton in the Cathedral Church of Lincoln, rated in the king's books at £9. The church is dedicated to St. Peter. There is a place of worship for Wesleyan Methodists.

NORTON by BREDON, a chapelry in the parish of BREDON, middle division of the hundred of OSWALDSLOW, county of WORCESTER, 4½ miles (N.E. by N.) from Tewkesbury, containing 199 inhabitants.

NORTON (BRIZE), a parish in the hundred of BAMPTON, county of OXFORD, 5 miles (S. E.) from Burford, containing 528 inhabitants. The living is a discharged vicarage, in the archdeaconry and diocese of Oxford, rated in the king's books at £9. 7. 11., and in the patronage of the Dean and Canons of Christ Church, Oxford. The church is dedicated to St. Brise. Ten poor children are educated for an annuity of £10, the gift of Goddard Carter, in 1723.

NORTON under CANNOCK, a parish in the southern division of the hundred of OFFLOW, county of STAFFORD, 8¼ miles (W. by S.) from Lichfield, containing, with the township of Little Wyrley, 669 inhabitants. The living is a perpetual curacy, in the peculiar jurisdiction of the Prebendary of Hansacre and Harmitage in the Cathedral Church of Lichfield, endowed with £200 royal bounty, and £1400 parliamentary grant, and in the patronage of the Prebendary of Alrewas in the Cathedral Church of Lichfield. The church, dedicated to St. Margaret, is an ancient structure, much dilapidated. The Essington and Wyrley canal passes through the parish, which abounds with excellent coal. Richard Gildart and Phineas Hussey, in 1776, founded a school, and endowed it with an estate now producing £20 a year, for teaching poor children. There is also a Sunday school for children, who are clothed and educated by voluntary contributions.

NORTON (CHIPPING), a market town and parish, having exclusive jurisdiction, though locally in the hundred of Chadlington, county of OXFORD, 18 miles (N. W.) from Oxford, and 73 (N. W. by W.) from London, containing, with the hamlet of Over Norton, 2640 inhabitants. The prefix Chipping is a corruption of *Ceapan*, a market, or place of trade, *Norton* implying the north town, from which it appears to have been a place of some note during the Saxon era. The streets are partially paved and lighted, and there is a plentiful supply of water. A woollen manufactory, which has existed here for some time, is now on the decline. The market is on Wednesday: fairs are held on March 7th, May 6th, the last Friday in May, July 18th, September 4th, the last Wednesday in September, November 8th, and the last Friday in November; there are also three statute fairs in October. The following large markets are for cattle; the last Wednesday in January, the second in April, June, and August, and the Wednesday next after December 11th. The civil government is vested in two bailiffs and ten burgesses, who are chosen at the court baron held at Michaelmas; the bailiffs are justices of the peace, exercising exclusive jurisdiction within the borough; they hold a court of session for the trial and punishment of offenders. The petty sessions are held here; and there was formerly a court of record, held under a charter of James I., for the recovery of debts under £4, now disused. The borough returned two representatives to parliament, once in the reign of Edward I., and twice in that of Edward III. The living is a discharged vicarage, in the archdeaconry and diocese of Oxford, rated in the king's books at £10. 6. 8., endowed with £200 parliamentary grant, and in the patronage of the Dean and Chapter of Gloucester. The church, which is dedicated to St. Mary, stands a little below the town, and exhibits specimens of exquisite workmanship, particularly in the middle aisle and the windows. There are places of worship for Baptists, the Society of Friends, and Methodists. On the dissolution of the Trinity guild, in the 1st of Edward VI., the grammar school was re-founded, its former endowment of £6 per annum, which had long been paid out of the revenue of the guild, having been continued, and since paid at the Salt office, out of the land revenue belonging to the crown. A bequest of £300 was left by Francis Barnes, by will, dated May 21st, 1762, the income arising from which is about £17 per annum: out of this sum the master is bound to keep his residence (which is rent-free) and school in repair: he receives boarders: two boys, appointed by the corporation, are gratuitously instructed in the elements of English and classical literature, the rest pay seven shillings and sixpence each per quarter. The Lancasterian school for girls is supported by voluntary subscription. Eight almshouses for poor widows, who are appointed by the bailiffs and burgesses, were built about 1649, by Henry Cornish, who, amongst other charities, also devised twelve cottages, on condition that they should always be let at the same moderate rent, for the residences of poor persons of good repute. In a part of the parish, called Cock's Town End, there are four almshouses for persons appointed by the corporation, which are repaired at the expense of the parishioners; but the origin of this charity is unknown. An ancient monument, called Rowldrich, or Rollrich stones, is situated about two miles from the town: it originally consisted of sixty stones, now reduced to twenty-two, forming a circle thirty-five yards in diameter from north to south, and thirty-three from east to west. Few of them exceed four feet in height, and sixteen inches in thickness, except one at the northern point, which is seven feet high, and five and a half broad. Eighty-four yards northeast is a large one, called the King stone, which is eight feet high, and seven broad, and about twelve inches in thickness. There are various conjectures as to the origin of this monument. Camden considers it to be a

memorial of some victory, erected probably by Rollo, the Dane, who invaded England in 876; but Dr. Stukeley ascribes the work to the Druids, *Rholdrwg* signifying the circle, or church of the Druids. He assigns the same origin to the several barrows near this spot, one of which is sixty feet long and twenty broad. Near this monument are four stones contiguous to each other, each of which is the boundary of a county, the several counties of Oxford, Gloucester, Worcester, and Warwick, terminating at this point. At Cold Norton, in this parish, an Augustine priory was founded by William Fitz-Alan, in the reign of Henry II., and dedicated to the Virgin, St. John the Evangelist, and St. Giles, which having escheated to the crown in the reign of Henry VII., was purchased by Dr. William Smith, Bishop of Lincoln, and given to Brasenose College, Oxford.

NORTON le CLAY, a township in the parish of CUNDALL, wapentake of HALLIKELD, North riding of the county of YORK, 3 miles (N.) from Boroughbridge, containing 142 inhabitants.

NORTON (COLD), a parish in the hundred of DENGIE, county of ESSEX, 5 miles (S.) from Maldon, containing 226 inhabitants. The living is a rectory, in the archdeaconry of Essex, and diocese of London, rated in the king's books at £16. 13. 4., and in the patronage of the Governors of the Charter-house, London. The church, dedicated to St. Stephen, stands on a hill.

NORTON (COLD), a township in the parish of CHEBSEY, southern division of the hundred of PIREHILL, county of STAFFORD, 2¾ miles (N. E. by E.) from Eccleshall, containing 44 inhabitants.

NORTON (EAST), a parish in the eastern division of the hundred of GOSCOTE, county of LEICESTER, 6 miles (W. by N.) from Uppingham, containing 120 inhabitants. The living is a perpetual curacy, with the vicarage of Tugby, in the archdeaconry of Leicester, and diocese of Lincoln. The church is dedicated to All Saints. A small sum, the bequest of Catharine Parker in 1747, is applied to teaching poor children.

NORTON (GREENS), county of NORTHAMPTON.—See GREENS-NORTON.

NORTON in HALES, a parish in the Drayton division of the hundred of BRADFORD (North), county of SALOP, 3½ miles (N. E. by N.) from Drayton in Hales, containing 241 inhabitants. The living is a discharged rectory, in the archdeaconry of Salop, and diocese of Lichfield and Coventry, rated in the king's books at £5. 9. 4. The King presented for that turn in 1786. The church is dedicated to St. Chad. The learned Dr. Lightfoot, Master of Clare Hall, Cambridge, was rector of this parish.

NORTON under HAMBDON, a parish in the hundred of HOUNDSBOROUGH, BERWICK, and COKER, county of SOMERSET, 4½ miles (N. N. E.) from Crewkerne, containing 482 inhabitants. The living is a rectory, in the archdeaconry of Wells, and diocese of Bath and Wells, rated in the king's books at £9. 16. 3., and in the patronage of W. Locke, Esq. The church is dedicated to St. Mary.

NORTON (HOOK), a parish in the hundred of CHADLINGTON, county of OXFORD, 5¼ miles (N. E. by N.) from Chipping-Norton, containing, with the township of Southrope, 1351 inhabitants. The living is a perpetual curacy, in the archdeaconry and diocese of Oxford, and in the patronage of the Bishop of Oxford. The church is dedicated to St. Peter. There are places of worship for Baptists and Wesleyan Methodists. William Hobbs, in 1810, bequeathed £5 towards the support of a Sunday school, which is further aided by subscriptions, and an annuity of £2. 2. from the lessees under the Bishop of Oxford.

NORTON by KEMPSEY, a parish in the lower division of the hundred of OSWALDSLOW, county of WORCESTER, 3½ miles (S. S. E.) from Worcester, containing 517 inhabitants. The living is a perpetual curacy, in the peculiar jurisdiction and patronage of the Dean and Chapter of Worcester, rated in the king's books at £2. 12. 6., endowed with £600 royal bounty, and £200 parliamentary grant. The church is dedicated to St. James. There are extensive quarries of limestone within the parish.

NORTON (KING'S), a parish comprising the chapelry of Stretton Parva and part of that of Illston on the Hill, and the township of King's Norton, in the hundred of GARTREE, county of LEICESTER, and containing 199 inhabitants, of which number, 71 are in the township of King's Norton, 7½ miles (E.S.E.) from Leicester. The living is a discharged vicarage, in the archdeaconry of Leicester, and diocese of Lincoln, rated in the king's books at £7, and in the patronage of Henry Greene, Esq. The church is dedicated to St. John the Baptist.

NORTON (KING'S), a parish (formerly a market town) in the upper division of the hundred of HALFSHIRE, county of WORCESTER, 6 miles (S. S. W.) from Birmingham, containing, with Headley, Moseley, Moundsley, and Rednal, 3651 inhabitants. The living is a perpetual curacy, annexed to the vicarage of Bromsgrove, in the archdeaconry and diocese of Worcester. The church, which is dedicated to St. Nicholas, is spacious, and principally in the decorated style of English architecture, with later insertions; the tower and spire are very fine. A free grammar school was endowed by Edward VI. This town received the grant of a market from James I.; and during the succeeding reign, in the year 1645, Hawkesley house, then belonging to the Middlemores, was burnt down by the royalists. The market is disused; but fairs are held April 25th and September 5th. The Birmingham and Worcester canal, in passing through this parish, forms a junction with that of Stratford on Avon, and is conveyed through a tunnel into the parish of Alvechurch.

NORTON (MIDSOMER), a parish in the hundred of CHEWTON, county of SOMERSET, comprising the tythings of Clapton, Downside, Midsummer-Norton, and Wilton, and containing 2326 inhabitants, of which number, 893 are in the tything of Midsummer-Norton, 9½ miles (S. W. by S.) from Bath. The living is a discharged vicarage, in the archdeaconry of Wells, and diocese of Bath and Wells, rated in the king's books at £10. 3. 4., and in the patronage of the Dean and Canons of Christ Church, Oxford. The church, dedicated to St. John the Baptist, is a large and handsome structure, with a modern tower, having on the south side a recess containing a statue of Charles II. There is a place of worship for Wesleyan Methodists. At the southern extremity of the parish is a modern Roman Catholic establishment, from Douay in French Flanders, called

Downside College, where young men are prepared for ordination for the priesthood, and a number of boys educated : connected with the institution is a very elegant chapel, completed about eight years ago, also a good library. The parish is bounded on the east by the old Roman Fosse-way, and abounds with coal of a superior quality, of which there are extensive mines, affording employment to a great portion of the inhabitants. A fair for cattle, pigs, &c., is held annually on April 25th. Ann Harris, in 1719, gave the residue of her personal estate, now producing about £45, for teaching poor children ; forty are instructed.

NORTON on the MOORS, a parish in the northern division of the hundred of PIREHILL, county of STAFFORD, containing, with the townships of Bermersley and Norton on the Moors, 1983 inhabitants, of which number, 1793 are in the township of Norton on the Moors, 2½ miles (N. by E.) from Hanley. The living is a perpetual curacy, in the archdeaconry of Stafford, and diocese of Lichfield and Coventry, endowed with £200 royal bounty, and in the patronage of the Rev. J. Wildig. The church is dedicated to St. James. The Caldon canal passes through the parish. Five poor children are educated for a trifling bequest by Hugh Ford, in 1730.

NORTON (OVER), a hamlet in the parish of CHIPPING-NORTON, hundred of CHADLINGTON, county of OXFORD, ¾ of a mile (N. by E.) from Chipping-Norton, containing 374 inhabitants.

NORTON (ST. PHILIP), a parish in the hundred of WELLOW, county of SOMERSET, 6½ miles (S. by E.) from Bath, containing 669 inhabitants. The living is a vicarage, with the perpetual curacy of Hinton-Charterhouse annexed, in the archdeaconry of Wells, and diocese of Bath and Wells, rated in the king's books at £5. 11. 3., and in the patronage of the Bishop of Bath and Wells. The church, dedicated to St. Philip and All Saints, is partly in the later style of English architecture. There is a place of worship for Baptists. Rachael Coles, in 1756, bequeathed £10 per annum towards the foundation of a school for twenty poor children.

NORTON (PUDDING), a parish in the hundred of GALLOW, county of NORFOLK, 1½ mile (S.) from Fakenham, containing 14 inhabitants. The living is a discharged rectory, in the archdeaconry and diocese of Norwich, rated in the king's books at £6, and in the patronage of Thomas Wright, Esq. Of the church, which was dedicated to St. Margaret, there are no remains, except a small square tower.

NORTON juxta TWYCROSS, a parish in the hundred of SPARKENHOE, county of LEICESTER, 6¼ miles (W. N. W.) from Market-Bosworth, containing, with the chapelry of Bilstone, 502 inhabitants. The living is a rectory, in the archdeaconry of Leicester, and diocese of Lincoln, rated in the king's books at £14, and in the patronage of the Crown. The church is dedicated to the Holy Trinity. William Whiston, the celebrated divine, was born here in 1667, during the incumbency of his father.

NORTON-BAVANT, a parish in the hundred of WARMINSTER, county of WILTS, 2¾ miles (S. E. by E.) from Warminster, containing 268 inhabitants. The living is a discharged vicarage, in the archdeaconry and diocese of Salisbury, rated in the king's books at £6. 0. 10., and in the patronage of the Crown. The church is dedicated to All Saints. Ann Jacob, in 1709, bequeathed £100, directing the interest to be applied for teaching poor children.

NORTON-CANON, a parish in the hundred of GRIMSWORTH, county of HEREFORD, 3¼ miles (S. S. W.) from Weobley, containing 347 inhabitants. The living is a discharged vicarage, in the peculiar jurisdiction of the Dean of Hereford, rated in the king's books at £5, and in the patronage of the Dean and Chapter of Hereford. The church is dedicated to St. Nicholas. A court leet is annually held here. There is a small school, endowed by a Mr. Barnett with about £8 a year.

NORTON-COLEPARLE, a parish in the hundred of MALMESBURY, county of WILTS, 3¾ miles (S. W. by W.) from Malmesbury, containing 110 inhabitants. The living is a discharged vicarage, in the archdeaconry of Wilts, and diocese of Salisbury, rated in the king's books at £2. 19. 9½., endowed with £200 royal bounty, and in the patronage of E. T. Gould, Esq. The church is dedicated to All Saints.

NORTON-CONYERS, a chapelry in that part of the parish of WATH which is in the wapentake of AL-LERTONSHIRE, North riding of the county of YORK, 3½ miles (N. by E.) from Ripon, containing 87 inhabitants. This was the seat of Richard Norton, Lord Chief Justice of England in the early part of the reign of Henry IV.; and subsequently of the gallant royalist, Sir Richard Graham, who, having received numerous wounds in the battle of Marston Moor, and finding it lost, fled to his house here, and died the same night.

NORTON-DISNEY, a parish in the lower division of the wapentake of BOOTHBY-GRAFFO, parts of KES-TEVEN, county of LINCOLN, 7 miles (N. E. by E.) from Newark, containing 214 inhabitants. The living is a discharged vicarage, in the archdeaconry and diocese of Lincoln, rated in the king's books at £6. 6. 10., endowed with £400 private benefaction, and £600 parliamentary grant, and in the patronage of Sir Thomas Clarges, Bart. The church is dedicated to All Saints. The parish is bounded on the east by the river Witham.

NORTON-FALGATE, an extra-parochial liberty, locally in the Tower division of the hundred of Ossul-stone, county of MIDDLESEX, adjoining the ward of Bishopsgate (Without) in the city of London, containing 1896 inhabitants. Norton-Falgate, or Folgate, called also Norton-Folley, derives its name from its situation north of Bishopsgate, and probably the adjunct from the Saxon *Foldweg*, a highway, the Roman Ir-min-street having passed through the place. It is a precinct exempt from archidiaconal jurisdiction, being subject to the Dean and Chapter of St. Paul's, to whom the manor belongs, and who are stated in Domesday-book to have held ten cottages and nine acres of land here in the reign of Edward the Confessor. According to some authorities, this place belongs to the parish of St. Faith under St. Paul's, but the inhabitants consider it an extra-parochial liberty, marrying and burying where they please, and maintaining their own poor, except in that part of the liberty which includes part of Long-alley, Hog-lane, and Blossom-street, the inhabitants of which pay poor rates to the parish of Shoreditch, but as to watch and ward they pay to this liberty. It is within the jurisdiction of the court of requests held for the Tower Hamlets, for the recovery of debts under 40s. A court-

house formerly stood in the High-street, which was long used as a free school for boys, founded in 1691; but the school has been removed to Primrose-street, in the parish of St. Botolph, Bishopsgate, where a school-house was erected in 1775, in which sixty boys are educated, and thirty of them clothed. The endowment consists of £7000 three per cent. consols., arising from the benefactions of Mr. Richard Turner and others, which, with a house in Lombard-street, produces £228 per annum. A school for girls was established in this liberty in 1703, by voluntary subscription; it is now endowed with £1720 stock in the three per cents., with the dividends on which, aided by subscriptions, thirty-six girls are clothed and educated. In Elder-street are alms-houses for six poor members of the Weavers' Company, founded and endowed, in 1729, by Nicholas Garrat, Esq., and adjoining them are others for the poor of Norton-Falgate, erected in 1728. St. Mary Spital, a priory for canons and brethren of the order of St. Augustine, was founded by William Brune, a citizen of London, in 1197: its revenue, at the dissolution, was £557. 14. 10.

NORTON-FITZWARREN, a parish in the hundred of TAUNTON and TAUNTON-DEAN, county of SOMERSET, 2¾ miles (W. N. W.) from Taunton, containing 475 inhabitants. The living is a rectory, in the archdeaconry of Taunton, and diocese of Bath and Wells, rated in the king's books at £20. 10. 10. William Peachey, Esq. was patron in 1797. The church is dedicated to All Saints.

NORTON-HAWFIELD, a ville in the hundred of CHEW, county of SOMERSET, containing 43 inhabitants.

NORTON-LINDSEY, a parish in the Snitterfield division of the hundred of BARLICHWAY, county of WARWICK, 3¾ miles (W. S. W.) from Warwick, containing 149 inhabitants. The living is a perpetual curacy, annexed to the vicarage of Claverdon, in the archdeaconry and diocese of Worcester, endowed with £200 royal bounty. The church is dedicated to the Holy Trinity.

NORTON-MALEREWARD, a parish in the hundred of CHEW, county of SOMERSET, 2¼ miles (N. W.) from Pensford, containing 118 inhabitants. The living is a rectory, in the archdeaconry of Bath, and diocese of Bath and Wells, rated in the king's books at £9. 2. 6., and in the patronage of the Rev. W. P. Wait.

NORTON-MANDEVILLE, a parish in the hundred of ONGAR, county of ESSEX, 3 miles (N. E. by E.) from Chipping-Ongar, containing 141 inhabitants. The living is a perpetual curacy, in the archdeaconry of Essex, and diocese of London, endowed with £200 private benefaction, and £800 royal bounty, and in the patronage of C. Cure, Esq. The church is dedicated to All Saints.

NORTON-SUBCOURSE, a parish in the hundred of CLAVERING, county of NORFOLK, 6 miles (N. by W.) from Beccles, containing 367 inhabitants. The living is a perpetual curacy, in the archdeaconry of Norfolk, and diocese of Norwich, endowed with £400 private benefaction, and £600 parliamentary grant, and in the patronage of Sir Edmund Bacon, Bart. The church is dedicated to St. Margaret. A chantry, or college of eight Secular priests, was removed hither from Raveningham, in the reign of Edward III.; in 1387 the number was increased to thirteen, and in 1393 the society was translated to Castle-Mettingham in Suffolk.

NORWELL, a parish in the northern division of the wapentake of THURGARTON, county of NOTTINGHAM, 6 miles (N. by W.) from Newark, containing, with the chapelry of Carlton upon Trent, and the township of Norwell-Woodhouse, 874 inhabitants. The living is a discharged vicarage divided into three portions, denominated respectively Norwell-Secunda, Norwell-Tertia, and Norwell-Overhall, in the peculiar jurisdiction of the Chapter of the Collegiate Church of Southwell; Norwell-Secunda is rated in the king's books at £4. 12. 11., and in the patronage of the Prebendary of Norwell-Tertia; Norwell-Overhall is rated in the king's books at £4. 12. 11., endowed with £200 royal bounty, and in the patronage of the Prebendary thereof. The church is dedicated to St. Lawrence.

NORWELL - WOODHOUSE, a township in the parish of NORWELL, northern division of the wapentake of THURGARTON, county of NOTTINGHAM, 7¼ miles (N. N. W.) from Newark, containing 111 inhabitants.

NORWICH, a city and county of itself, locally in the hundred of Humble-yard, county of NORFOLK, of which it is the capital, 108 miles (N.E. by N.) from London, containing, exclusively of that part of the parish of Hellesdon which is in the hundred of Taverham, and of that part of the parish of Thorpe St. Andrew which is in the hundred of Blofield, 50,288 inhabitants. This ancient city, which rose from the ruins of the *Venta Icenorum* of the Romans, so named from the river Wentsum, or Wensum, the site of which is now occupied by the village of Caistor, was by the Britons, in allusion to that circumstance, called *Caer Gwent*; and by the Saxons, in reference to its situation with respect to the Roman station, *North wic*, or the northern castle, of which its present name is an evident contraction. Uffa, first king of the East Angles, is stated to have built a castle here in 575, and to have made it his residence: Henry I. granted to Harvey, first Bishop of Ely, exemption for the lands of his church from the service of castle guard to Norwich, by which tenure they were held previously to the erection of the monastery of Ely by Ethelreda, daughter of Anna, King of the East Angles, and wife of Egfrid, King of Northumbria, in the year 673. According to Spelman, it was a residence of the kings of East Anglia, who established a mint here, from which issued coins of Alfred and several succeeding kings. Being an object of frequent contention between the Saxons and the Danes, it was alternately in the possession of each party, and was repaired and fortified by Alfred the Great against the latter, to whom, after a treaty of peace, that monarch finally conceded it. The Danes being subsequently driven out, it remained in the possession of the Saxons till 1004, when those invaders, stimulated by the weakness of Ethelred II. and the treachery of Alfric, Earl of Mercia, landed on the coast of Essex under Sweyn their king, plundered and burnt the city, and left it in a state of desolation till

Arms.

their return in 1018, when they again took possession of it under Canute, by whom it was rebuilt and the fortifications of the castle were restored. From this time it rapidly increased in extent and importance till the Norman conquest, when it was inferior only to the city of York. It was bestowed by the Conqueror on Ralph Guader, who, with the Earls of Hereford and Northumberland, entered into a conspiracy against the king; but, being frustrated in his design by the vigilance of the Bishop of Worcester, the sheriff for that county, and Walter Lucy, Baron of Hereford, he withdrew into Brittany, leaving in the castle a garrison of Britons under the command of his wife, who heroically sustained a protracted siege, till, being reduced by famine, she surrendered to the king, on condition of being suffered to leave the kingdom with all her forces in perfect security. During this siege the city sustained material injury, and was so much reduced that, from one thousand three hundred and twenty burgesses who inhabited it in the reign of Edward the Confessor, there were only five hundred and sixty remaining. It gradually recovered from this severe calamity, and in 1094, Herbert de Lozinga, who accompanied William Rufus from Normandy, being made bishop of East Anglia, removed that see from Thetford to Norwich, where he erected a cathedral, an episcopal palace, and a monastery, in which he placed sixty monks.

From this time the city rapidly improved, and, according to William of Malmesbury, soon became famous for the number of its inhabitants, and the extent of its trade. It was rebuilt in the reign of Stephen, who incorporated the inhabitants, and gave the town as an appanage to his third son William, from whom it was afterwards taken by Henry II.; whose son gave it to Hugh Bigod, Earl of Norfolk, in order to secure his interest in his rebellion against his father. The earl having repaired the fortifications, and placed a strong garrison of French and Flemings in the castle, held it for some time against the king, but, after a vigorous defence, he was compelled to surrender it, and to purchase peace by the payment of one thousand marks. In the reign of John, the Dauphin of France, whom the confederated barons had invited to their assistance, besieged and took possession of the castle, plundered the citizens, and committed numerous depredations. In the reign of Edward I., having recovered from the injury it had sustained, and grown into importance, it abounded with opulent citizens, who environed it with walls of great strength; and in the reign of Henry IV., in 1403, they obtained permission to elect a mayor and sheriffs, in lieu of their ancient bailiffs, whereby Norwich was constituted a county of itself. In the reign of Richard II. an insurrection was excited by John Listher, a dyer in the town, which was quelled by the exertions of the Bishop of Norwich, by whom he was defeated, and, being taken prisoner, was executed in 1381. The city suffered severely by continued discord between the monks and the citizens; the latter assaulted and set fire to the monastery, which, with the exception of the chapel, was burnt down. The king, having been informed of this outrage, visited Norwich, and, after due examination, caused thirty young men of the city to be executed. In 1446, another assault on the monks was restrained by the activity of the Duke of Norfolk, who seized and punished the ringleaders, displacing the mayor from his office, and appointing Sir John Clifton governor of the city, till the king might be pleased to restore its forfeited privileges. Soon after the suppression of these tumults, the city, which had repeatedly suffered from a similar calamity, was nearly consumed by a fire, which broke out in a house in the parish of St. George. In the reign of Edward VI., Robert Kett, a tanner, and his brother William, both of Wymondham, under the pretence of resisting the enclosure of waste lands, excited a formidable rebellion; and, having seized on the palace of the Earl of Surrey, plundered and converted it into a prison, in which they confined many noblemen and gentlemen : they then encamped on Mousehold heath, where they were at length defeated by the Earl of Warwick with a numerous army, and the two brothers being taken prisoners, Robert was hanged on Norwich castle, and William on the steeple of Wymondham church. In the reign of Elizabeth, the manufacture of bombazine and other articles, for which the city has been since noted, was introduced by the Dutch and Walloons, who, fleeing from the Netherlands, found in this country an asylum from the persecution of the Duke of Alva : that queen, who, by the encouragement she gave to the emigrants, laid the foundation of the commercial and manufacturing prosperity of this and other towns, visited Norwich, where she was received with great demonstration of respect, and pompously entertained for several days. During the civil war in the reign of Charles I., the city was held by the parliamentarian forces, who defaced the cathedral, stripped it of all its plate and ornaments, and greatly damaged the episcopal palace. After the Restoration, Norwich was visited by Charles II. and his consort, and subsequently by Queen Anne, who were hospitably entertained by the corporation.

The city is pleasantly situated on the summit and acclivities of an eminence rising gently from the river Wensum, which, after pursuing a winding course through the town, joins the river Yare, thus affording a line of navigation from the sea at Yarmouth. The houses are in general of antique appearance, and the city, from being thickly interspersed with orchards and garden-grounds, presents a rural aspect, almost unparalleled in towns of such extent : the principal streets are well paved, the others only partially. There are not less than nine bridges over the river, connecting the various parts of the town, which has recently been lighted wholly with gas : the streets are in many places narrow, and diverge from one common centre. The town, extending a mile and a half in length, and one mile and a quarter in breadth, was formerly surrounded on all sides, except where it was defended by the river, with embattled walls, in which were forty towers and twelve principal gates; the former are in a dilapidated state, and the latter have been taken down. Various parts of it are supplied with water by means of public water-works. The environs, which are in the highest state of cultivation, have, from the salubrity of the air, and the pleasantness of their situation, become the residence of numerous opulent families. A public subscription library, established in 1784, contains more than fourteen thousand volumes : the admission ticket is £5. 5., and the annual subscription £1. 1. The Norwich and Norfolk Literary Institution, under the direction of a committee of twenty-one members, was formed by a proprietary, who also subscribe annually £1. 11. 6.: it

is open to subscribers not being shareholders at £2. 2. per annum. The Norwich and Norfolk United Medical Book Society was established in 1824, and is supported by professional members in the city and county. A society of artists was instituted in 1803, for promoting the study of painting, sculpture, and architecture ; and, in 1816, some of the original members instituted the Norwich and Norfolk society of artists and amateurs, who hold their meetings in a room built for that purpose near the corn exchange. The Friars' Society, for the dissemination of useful knowledge, was established in 1785 ; and a mechanics' institution in 1825. The theatre royal, a handsome building tastefully fitted up, is a newly-erected edifice opened in 1826, under the direction of the Norwich company. Near it is an extensive suite of assembly-rooms, consisting of a larger ball-room, sixty-six feet long, and twenty-three wide ; a smaller, fifty feet long, and twenty-seven wide; and a tea-room, twenty-seven feet square, which, by the removal of partitions, form one room one hundred and forty-three feet in length ; they are lighted with gas, and furnished in an elegant style ; there are also two appropriate card-rooms. The new concert-room, in the parish of St. Andrew, erected by subscription in 1816, is fifty feet in length, and thirty-five wide ; it is handsomely ornamented, and well adapted to its purpose ; the orchestra contains an excellent organ. The public gardens, in which is a handsome edifice called the Pantheon, are tastefully laid out for the reception and entertainment of visitors. The cavalry barracks, in Pockthorpe, form an extensive and handsome range of building of red brick, consisting of a centre and two wings : the walls enclose an area of ten acres, for the exercise of the troops.

The principal articles of manufacture are bombazines, crapes, camlets, shawls, plaids, worsted stuffs, fabrics in which silk, wool, and mohair are interwoven (called Norwich shawls), and various others; to prevent fraud in the manufacture of which, eight wardens, of whom four are chosen from the citizens, and four from the neighbourhood, are annually appointed, with full powers of inspection : the number of looms in these several factories is about fourteen thousand, affording employment to more than fifteen thousand persons. There are several silk-mills, in the principal of which from three to four hundred persons are employed; it is worked by steam-engines of various degrees of power : the silk, after being properly prepared, is distributed to the weavers to be manufactured into crape. The towns of Yarmouth, Bungay, and North Walsham, participate in the benefit of this manufacture, of which branch establishments have been opened in those several places. There are extensive iron-foundries, breweries, establishments for making vinegar, snuff-manufactories, and numerous corn-mills : a considerable trade in agricultural produce arises from the situation of the town in the centre of an extensive district remarkable for its fertility and the improved state of its agriculture. The trade between Norwich and Yarmouth is carried on by keels and wherries of very light construction, varying from fifteen to forty tons' burden, by which coal, timber, grain, and various other articles of merchandise, are brought from that port by the river, on which is a regular establishment of steam-packets; and great facility will be also afforded to the trade of the city by a navigable communication with the sea at Lowestoft, in the county of Suffolk, now in progress under the superintendence of the Norwich and Lowestoft Navigation Company, incorporated in the 8th of George IV. Besides the British products just mentioned, considerable quantities of wine and oil are imported from the continent of Europe, and yarn from Ireland; and the manufactures of Norwich are exported from London and Yarmouth to Russia, the Baltic, Germany, the Netherlands, France, Spain, Portugal, and Italy, as well as the East and West Indies and to America. The market days are Wednesday and Saturday, the latter being a very considerable market for corn : the corn exchange is a commodious building, erected in 1828, the front of which is ornamented with a noble Ionic portico of four columns, and the interior constitutes one of the most spacious rooms in the kingdom. A very extensive market is held on the same day, on the Castle Ditches, for horses and cattle ; and there is a market for fish daily. The fairs are on the day before Good Friday, and on the Monday and Tuesday in Easter and Whitsun weeks.

Corporate Seal.

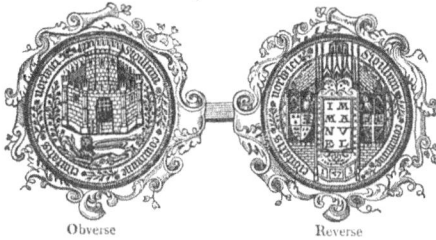

Obverse   Reverse

The government of the city, by charter of Charles II., is vested in a mayor, recorder, steward, two sheriffs, twenty-four aldermen, and sixty common council-men, assisted by a town clerk, chamberlain, two coroners, water-bailiff, sword-bearer, serjeants at mace, and subordinate officers. The mayor is nominated annually by the resident freemen, who appoint two of the aldermen, the latter choosing one to be mayor ; the other officers of the corporation are also appointed by the aldermen. The mayor, recorder, steward, and such of the aldermen as have filled the office of mayor, are justices of the peace within the city and county of the city. The freedom is inherited by birth, acquired by servitude, or obtained by purchase. A court of assize is held annually under the judges travelling the Norfolk circuit, which is opened by a commission distinct from that for the county of Norfolk ; courts of general quarter session, for the trial of all but capital offenders ; and, under a grant from Richard I. and other charters, a court of record for the recovery of debts to any amount, called the " Court of Guildhall of the City of Norwich," is held on Wednesdays and Saturdays, the judges of which are the sheriffs, assisted by the steward, who is a barrister. A court of requests is held every Monday, under an act passed in the 12th and 13th of William and Mary, before an alderman and two common council-men, for the recovery of debts under 40s. The guildhall, situated on the north of the market-place, is an ancient structure of black flint, containing convenient and well-arranged courts for the assizes and quarter sessions for the city and county of the city, with the requisite offices for the town clerk, chamberlain, and other officers of the corporation: the mayor's council-chamber is a noble room, splendidly fitted up, and ornamented with a series of historical paintings and with numerous portraits of eminent persons; at the east end is a fine window of stained glass : in this chamber is deposited the sword of Don Xavier Francisco Winthuysen, the Spanish admiral, presented to the corporation by Admiral Lord Nelson, and accompanied with a letter in his lordship's own hand-writing. St. Andrew's Hall, formerly the church of the monastery of the Black friars, and now converted into a banqueting-hall, and used occasionally for public meetings, is an ancient structure, of which the front has been carefully restored : the choir is used as a church for the inmates of the city workhouse, which stands near it, having been formerly appropriated to the use of a Dutch congregation, and thence called the Dutch church : the nave, one hundred and twenty-four feet long, is elegantly fitted up, and decorated with paintings ; the roof is supported on twelve lofty pillars, and the windows, which are of large dimensions and ornamented with rich tracery, were formerly embellished with painted glass : among other decorations in the hall is the ensign of the French ship Le Genereux, captured in the Mediterranean by the squadron under the command of Admiral Lord Nelson, in 1800, and presented to the corporation by Captain Sir Edward Berry, Knt.; and at the east end is a fine portrait, by Sir William Beechy, of Admiral Lord Nelson, presented to the corporation in 1804 : in this hall are held the grand musical festivals. The new city gaol erected in 1829, at an expense of £24,000, is a massive and appropriate building, containing requisite wards, airing-yards, and other offices adapted to the classification of prisoners, and amply supplied with water by means of pumps worked by the tread-mill. The city first exercised the elective franchise in the 23rd of Edward I., since which time it has regularly returned two members to parliament: the right of election is vested in the freeholders, and in the freemen generally not receiving alms, the number of whom is about four thousand : the sheriffs are the returning officers. The assizes and quarter sessions for the county of Norfolk are held in the shire-hall, a spacious edifice, erected in 1822 ; and, this being the county town, the election of knights of the shire regularly takes place in it. The castle, which, though situated in the centre of the city, belongs to the county of Norfolk, has been converted into a prison for that county, and a new gaol and shire-hall have lately been erected in connexion with it. The principal remains of the ancient building are, the shell of the keep, a massive structure on the summit of an artificial eminence, and Bigod's tower, a fine specimen of the Norman style of architecture ; over the fosse, an ancient stone bridge of one circular arch, of forty feet span, is still entire, and, from the supposed date of its erection, is considered to be of Saxon architecture. The outer walls, of which only some small portions are remaining, formerly enclosed an area of twenty-three acres, on part of which the new buildings have been erected. The county gaol and house of correction is a commodious building, comprising fifteen wards, fifteen day-rooms, and the same number of airing-yards, in one of which is a tread-mill, applied to the grinding of corn, for the employment of the prisoners.

Norwich was raised into an episcopal see by Herbert de Lozinga, who having been made Bishop of Thetford (which had become the head of the diocese of East Anglia, founded by Segebert, King of the East Angles, in 630), whither the episcopal chair had been removed from North Elmham in 1091, transferred the seat of the diocese to this city

Arms of the Bishoprick.

in 1094, where, having purchased a large plot of ground near the castle, he erected a cathedral, an episcopal palace, and a monastery for sixty Benedictine monks, the revenue of which, at the dissolution, was £1050. 17. 6. The diocese comprehends the counties of Norfolk and Suffolk, and eleven parishes in the county of Cambridge: the ecclesiastical establishment consists of a bishop, dean, four archdeacons, six prebendaries, six minor canons, of whom one is precentor, an epistoler, a gospeller, eight lay clerks, ten choristers, an organist, and other officers. The bishop is a suffragan of the Archbishop of Canterbury; and, besides being entitled by his episcopal dignity, he sits in the House of Peers as titular abbot of St. Bene't at Holme, being the only abbot in England. The cathedral church, dedicated to the Holy Trinity, after being destroyed by fire, was rebuilt by John of Oxford, the fourth bishop; and having suffered materially from frequent accidents, and from repeated assaults arising from the dissensions between the monks and the citizens, it has undergone numerous repairs and alterations, especially in 1806, when a thorough reparation took place. In its present state it displays much of its original Norman architecture, of which it affords some

of the finest specimens in the kingdom: it is a spacious cruciform structure, with a tower of the most finished and highly ornamented Norman style rising from the centre, and surmounted by an octagonal spire in the later decorated style, crocketed at the angles; the west front of Norman character, has a central entrance, with a large window above it in the later English style; the east, end has several circular chapels, and the lady chapel, now destroyed, was in the early English style of architecture: there are some vestiges of a part resembling that portion of Canterbury cathedral which is called Becket's Crown, and, amidst all the alterations and insertions which have been made, there are still numerous remains of its ancient character. The interior is finely arranged, and has an impressive grandeur of effect; the nave, of which and of the aisles the roof is finely vaulted, is purely Norman; the triforium is large, and surmounted by a fine range of clerestory windows; the choir is richly ornamented with tracery in the later English style, of excellent design, and is decorated with screen and tabernacle-work of elaborate execution: the font, in St. Luke's chapel, is remarkably beautiful, and there are some ancient monuments of great beauty and interest. The cloisters are peculiarly fine, displaying a continued series of the purest specimens, from the early decorated to the later style of English architecture. In the chapel of St. Mary the Less, within the cathedral, are held the consistorial episcopal courts. The chapter-house has been demolished: of the bishop's palace the entrance gate and hall are remaining; and St. Ethelbert's and Erpingham gates, both beautiful structures, are in good preservation. The precincts of the cathedral are under the special jurisdiction of the dean and other members of the establishment, who exercise magisterial powers within them.

PARISHES IN THE CITY OF NORWICH.

PARISHES.	LIVINGS.	Value in King's Books. £ s. d.	Private Benefaction £	Royal Bounty. £	Parliamentary Grant. £	PATRONS.	Population in 1831.
All Saints St. Julian	United Rectory	3 14 7	700	600		S. Thornton, Esq.	934 743
St. Andrew	Vicarage	5 0 0		800	600	Parishioners	1513
St. Augustine	Discharged Rectory	6 17 8½			1400	Dean and Chapter	1625
St. Benedict	Perpetual Curacy			1000	800	Parishioners	1125
St. Clement	Discharged Rectory	7 9 2	200	200		Caius College, Cambridge	2364
St. Edmund	Discharged Rectory	4 6 3	600	400	600	Rev. C. D. Brereton	677
St. Etheldred	Perpetual Curacy			800		Mayor and Corporation	273
St. George Colegate	Perpetual Curacy			1000		Dean and Chapter	1610
St. George Tombland	Perpetual Curacy		800	1000	900	Bishop of Ely	797
St. Giles	Perpetual Curacy			100		Dean and Chapter	1422
St. Gregory	Perpetual Curacy		600	600		Dean and Chapter	1244
St. Helen	Perpetual Curacy			200		Mayor and Corporation	345
St. John Maddermarket	Discharged Rectory	7 10 2		1000	800	New College, Oxford	957
St. John Sepulchre	Perpetual Curacy		400	800		Dean and Chapter	1599
St. John Timberhill	Perpetual Curacy			800	600	Dean and Chapter	1103
St. James St. Paul } United	Perpetual Curacy Rectory	Not in charge.		600 600		} Dean and Chapter. {	1268 2160
St. Lawrence	Discharged Rectory	4 13 9		400	1000	The Crown	1092
St. Margaret de Westwick	Discharged Rectory	5 4 9½	200	800	200	Bishop of Norwich	938

PARISHES.	LIVINGS.	Value in King's Books. £ s. d.	Endowments under act of 13th of Anne.			PATRONS.	Population in 1831.
			Private Benefaction £	Royal Bounty. £	Parliament-ary Grant. £		
St. Martin at Palace	Perpetual Curacy			1000	800	Dean and Chapter	1262
St. Martin at Oak	Perpetual Curacy ...		200	800	600	Dean and Chapter	2477
St. Mary Coslany	Perpetual Curacy		200	800	1400	Marquis Townshend	1521
St. Mary	Discharged Rectory, now held as a Perpetual Curacy	5 0 10		600		Dean and Chapter ..., ...	
St. Michael Coslany	Discharged Rectory ..	13 6 8	400	400	1000	Caius College, Cambridge	1340
St. Michael at Plea	Discharged Rectory ..	6 10 0		600	1000	Sir T. B. Lennard, Bart.	389
St. Michael at Thorn........	Perpetual Curacy			1000	1000	Dowager Lady Suffield	1750
St. Peter Hungate	Discharged Rectory ..	3 1 5½		400	200	The Crown, by lapse..........	511
St. Peter Mancroft..........	Perpetual Curacy		200	200	600	Parishioners	2671
St. Peter Mountergate	Perpetual Curacy			200	800	Dean and Chapter	1789
St. Peter Southgate	Discharged Rectory ..	2 17 3½		1000		Bishop of Norwich	529
St. Saviour	Perpetual Curacy			1000	800	Dean and Chapter	1266
St. Simon and St. Jude	Discharged Rectory ..	3 10 0		1000		Bishop of Norwich	447
St. Stephen	Discharged Vicarage ..	9 0 0		600	400	Dean and Chapter	2927
St. Swithin	Discharged Rectory ..	6 3 4	200	800	800	Bishop of Norwich	750

PARISHES IN THE LIBERTY OF THE CITY OF NORWICH.

PARISHES.	LIVINGS.	Value in King's Books. £ s. d.	Endowments under act of 13th of Anne.			PATRONS.	Population in 1831.
			Private Benefaction £	Royal Bounty. £	Parliament-ary Grant. £		
Eaton (St. Andrew)	Vicarage	Not in charge.	200	200		Dean and Chapter..	1313
Heigham..................	Rectory	6 13 4				Bishop of Norwich	1503
Pockthorpe...............	Perpetual Curacy					Dean and Chapter	1313
Lakenham	V. united with that of Trouse, in the county of Norfolk					Dean and Chapter	1875

All the above parishes, with the exception of those of St. Andrew, St. Helen, St. James, St. Paul, and Lakenham, which are within the peculiar jurisdiction of the Dean and Chapter, are in the archdeaconry and diocese of Norwich.

Many of the churches, of which the prevailing style is that of the later English, with portions of an earlier date, and some Norman remains, are deserving of architectural notice: among these are the church of St. Peter Mancroft, a spacious structure in the later style of English architecture, with a lofty square embattled tower highly enriched; the interior is remarkably light and elegant; the intervals between the arches of the nave are ornamented with niches of exquisite design, and the windows are large and filled with excellent tracery; the east window is ornamented with stained glass, and in the vestry are some ancient portraits of the saints, and a painting of the Resurrection; there are numerous ancient monuments, of several of which the inscriptions are obliterated. The church of St. Michael Coslany is a handsome structure of flint and stone, and affords a fine specimen of that mode of building; the prevailing character is the later English, intermixed with the decorated and early styles; the details are elaborately wrought, and the chancel in particular is beautifully ornamented. The churches of St.

Benedict, St. Etheldred, and St. Julian, have round towers, in which, though greatly obscured by alterations and repairs, many remains of Norman architecture are discernible. The church of St. Lawrence is a handsome edifice, with a tower of flint and stone one hundred and twelve feet high; over the western entrance are sculptured representations of the martyrdom of St. Lawrence, and of St. Edmund, King of East Anglia. The churches of St. Andrew, St. George Colegate, St. Giles, St. Saviour, and various others, are handsome structures in the later style of English architecture, with lofty and elegant towers of flint and stone, and contain numerous interesting portions in earlier styles, together with valuable specimens of architectural skill. There are four places of worship for Baptists; two for the Society of Friends, two each for Independents and Wesleyan Methodists, and one each for those in the late Countess of Huntingdon's Connexion, and Unitarians, a synagogue, and two chapels belonging to the Roman Catholics, one of which is an elegant edifice lately erected.

The free grammar school, originally built by Bishop Salmon, was established by Edward VI., and is endowed by the corporation, who have the appointment of the master, and the nomination of the scholars; the master's salary is £50 per annum, with a house and the privilege of taking boarders; the under-master's salary is £30: gratuitous instruction in the classics is afforded to a certain number of boys of the city. Belonging to this school and that at Aylsham are three scholarships, of £2. 13. 4. each per annum, founded at Corpus Christi College, Cambridge, by Archbishop Parker; and two scholarships for boys educated at Norwich, Aylsham, or Wymondham; four scholarships, of £5 each per annum, founded at Emanuel College, Cambridge, by William Braithwaite, in 1618; and two of three scholarships, of £5 per annum each, founded at Caius College, for natives of Norfolk. Edward Coleman also, in 1659, bequeathed £20 per annum to Corpus Christi College, for the maintenance of four scholars from this school, or from the school of Wymondham. The boys' hospital, founded in 1618 by Mr. Thomas Anguish, mayor, for the maintenance and education of forty boys; and the girls' hospital, endowed in 1649, for thirty-two girls, are both conducted under good regulations, and provide for an increased number of children. There are twelve charity schools supported by subscription, for the clothing and education of children, in which are two hundred and ten boys, and one hundred and thirty girls. In 1775, Mr. Moy, of this city, bequeathed £1000 Bank stock, directing the interest to be appropriated to apprenticing children educated in the schools; and Mr. Elmy left £400 for the same purpose. The National schools afford instruction to nearly one thousand eight hundred children; and in the county of Norfolk there are not less than ten thousand children instructed in these institutions, which are supported by subscription. The Norwich British and Foreign school was instituted in 1811, and is supported by subscription; there are nearly four hundred children in this establishment.

St. Giles' hospital was founded, in 1249, by Bishop Suffield, who endowed it for the maintenance and support of aged persons of both sexes, who are nominated by the corporation: the ancient collegiate church of St. Helen has been appropriated to its use; the choir is fitted up for the residence of fifty women, part of the nave has been prepared for the reception of fifty men, and the remainder is used as a chapel: this edifice, notwithstanding the alterations it has undergone, still displays many interesting portions of its ancient architecture. Doughty's hospital was founded, in 1687, by Mr. William Doughty, who bequeathed £6000 for its erection and endowment; there are forty aged persons of both sexes, who have a weekly sum of money, clothes, firing, and other necessaries; according to the directions of the founder, no person can be admitted who is under sixty years of age. Cook's hospital was founded prior to the year 1701, by Robert and Thomas Cook, who endowed it for the residence and support of ten poor women of the city, who receive each a weekly allowance of money. The Norfolk and Norwich hospital, a handsome building of red brick, erected in 1771, at an expense of £13,323. 8. 11., contains spacious accommodation for the reception of all classes of patients: the institution is under the direction of a president and

a committee, and is gratuitously attended by the principal medical practitioners of the city: as a school of medicine and surgery it is distinguished by its successful operations in cases of lithotomy. The Magdalen asylum is under the management of a committee of ladies; there are now twenty females in it, the greatest number which it can accommodate. Bethel hospital, for the reception of lunatics, was erected by Mrs. Mary Chapman, in 1713, and is supported by funds arising from donations, and by annual subscription; and at Thorpe, about two miles from the city, is the Norfolk and Norwich lunatic asylum, established in 1814, under the statute of the 48th of George III., "for the better care and maintenance of lunatics, being criminals or paupers." The Norwich dispensary, established in 1804, is chiefly supported by subscription. An infirmary for the cure of diseases of the eye was established in 1822, since which period nearly two thousand five hundred persons have been cured or relieved. The institution for the relief of the indigent blind, established chiefly by the exertions of Thomas Tawell, Esq., one of its greatest benefactors, embraces also a school for the instruction of blind children, in which there are thirty pupils, in addition to eight aged persons now in the asylum: it is under the direction of a president, three vice-presidents, and a committee of subscribers, by whom a matron and an instructor of the blind are appointed. Among the charitable associations are, a society for the relief of clergymen's widows; a benevolent medical society, for the widows and children of surgeons and apothecaries, and indigent members of that profession, in the city and county, and a similar society for the widows and children of attornies; a society for the relief of decayed tradesmen, their widows, and orphans; the Friendly Society, for the relief of poor women in sickness and old age; the society of universal good will, for the relief of strangers; the Humane Society, for the recovery of persons apparently drowned, and various others; and there are also considerable charitable bequests for distribution among the poor.

Of the monastic establishments formerly existing in the town and neighbourhood, numerous vestiges of which are still visible, were the priory and church of St. Leonard at Thorpe-wood, near the city, in which Herbert de Lozinga placed several monks, while he was erecting the cathedral; also an hospital for lepers, endowed by him, the revenue of which, at the dissolution, was £10: the hospital of St. Paul, founded in 1121, by the prior and convent of Norwich; a nunnery, dedicated to St. Mary and St. John, and endowed by King Stephen, for sisters of the Benedictine order, who in 1146 founded a new convent at Carrow, the revenue of which, at the dissolution, was £84. 12. 1¾.; St. Edward's hospital, founded in 1200, by Hildebrand de Mercer, citizen of Norwich, which had so far decayed, that at the dissolution its revenue was only 14s. 6d.; the monastery of the Black friars, founded in the reign of Edward II., of which the ancient church is now St. Andrew's Hall; the monastery of the Grey friars, founded in 1226, by John de Hastingford, the site of which is now occupied by Cook's hospital; the monastery of White friars, founded in 1256, by Philip Congate, merchant, which remained till the dissolution; the convent of Augustine friars, founded in the reign of Edward I., by one of the bishops; a convent of friars of the order "de pœnitentiâ Jesu," founded in 1266, and which, after the suppression of that order, was annexed to the convent of the Black friars; the college of St. Mary, originally a chapel, founded in 1250, by Sir John Broun, or Brom, and at the time of the dissolution consisting of a dean, four prebendaries, and others, with a revenue of £86. 16.; also various hospitals, vestiges of which may be traced in several parts of the city.

William Bateman, Bishop of Norwich in the fourteenth century, and founder of Trinity Hall, Cambridge; Matthew Parker, second Protestant Archbishop of Canterbury, chaplain to Queen Anne Boleyn, whom he attended to the scaffold; Dr. John Kaye, or Caius, founder of Gonville and Caius College, Cambridge, author of a treatise on the antiquities of that university, and other works; Robert Green, a popular writer in the reign of Elizabeth; Dr. John Cosin, Bishop of Durham in the reign of Charles II.; the learned Dr. Samuel Clarke, the son of an alderman of this city, born in 1675; Edward King, F.R.S. and F.S.A., a most erudite antiquary, and author of a work on ancient architecture, entitled " *Munimenta Antiqua*," born in 1734; the Rev. William Beloe, the translator of Herodotus; and Sir James Edward Smith, M.D., founder and first president of the Linnæan Society, and author of the "*Flora Britannica*," were natives of this city. Among the distinguished residents were Sir Thomas Erpingham, Knight of the Garter, and chamberlain to Henry IV.; he distinguished himself at the battle of Agincourt, and built the beautiful gate facing the western end of the cathedral, which is still called Erpingham gate; he died in 1428, and was interred in the cathedral: Sir John Fastolf, a renowned warrior, who signalized himself in the wars with France in the reigns of Henry IV., V., and VI.; he died in 1459, and was interred in a chapel which he had founded in the abbey of Holme; and various others.

NORWOOD, a precinct and parochial chapelry in the hundred of ELTHORNE, county of MIDDLESEX, 2½ miles (N. by W.) from Hounslow, containing 1124 inhabitants. The living is a perpetual curacy, annexed to the vicarage of Hayes, in the exempt deanery of Croydon, which is in the peculiar jurisdiction of the Archbishop of Canterbury, endowed with £210 private benefaction, and £200 royal bounty. The chapel has received an addition of three hundred and sixty free sittings, towards defraying the expense of which the Incorporated Society for the enlargement of churches and chapels contributed £300.

NORWOOD, a district partly in the parish of LAMBETH, eastern division of the hundred of BRIXTON, partly in that of BATTERSEA, western division of the same hundred, and partly in that of CROYDON, first division of the hundred of WALLINGTON, county of SURREY, 6½ miles (S.) from London. The population is returned with the respective parishes. The village derives its name from an adjacent wood, which borders on a common formerly a noted resort for numerous camps of gypsies. Its elevated situation, the beauty of the surrounding scenery, and the salubrity of the atmosphere, have of late years caused the erection of many elegant seats in the vicinity. The only manufactory is a pottery, where coarse earthenware is made. Norwood is within the limits of the new police act. There are two new churches in this district. The church dedicated to St. Luke, in the parish of Lambeth, is a large and handsome edifice in the Grecian style, with a Corinthian portico, and a steeple tower, containing one thousand four hundred and twelve sittings, of which six hundred and eighty-eight are free: it was commenced in 1823, and completed in 1825, at an expense of £12,897. 13. 10., of which the commissioners gave one moiety, and lent without interest the other, together with the sum of £49. 6. 9. for extra expenses; they also lent on interest the further sum of £4325. 6. 11., expended in making a cemetery, furnishing the church, &c. The living is a district incumbency, in the patronage of the Rector of Lambeth. The church situated at Beaulieu Hill, in the parish of Croydon, is in the English style of architecture, with four turrets, containing one thousand and five sittings, of which six hundred and thirty-two are free: it was completed in 1829, by a grant of £3000 from the commissioners. The living is a perpetual curacy, in the patronage of the Vicar of Croydon. There is a place of worship for Independents. A school of industry for poor children of the parish of Lambeth has been founded here; also a charity school for the instruction of children of both sexes.

NORWOOD, a joint township with Clifton, in the parish of FEWSTON, lower division of the wapentake of CLARO, West riding of the county of YORK, 6 miles (N. by E.) from Otley. The population is returned with Clifton.

NOSLEY, an extra-parochial liberty, in the hundred of GARTREE, county of LEICESTER, 8½ miles (N. by E.) from Market-Harborough, containing 18 inhabitants. A chantry, or college, was founded here about 1274, by Sir Anketine de Martival; it was dedicated to the Ascension of our Lord and the Assumption of the Blessed Virgin, and in the reign of Henry VI. was valued at £6. 13. 4. per annum.

NOSTAL, a joint township with Hurstwick, in that part of the parish of WRAGBY which is in the upper division of the wapentake of OSGOLDCROSS, West riding of the county of YORK, 4¾ miles (S. W. by W.) from Pontefract. The population is returned with Hurstwick. A priory of Augustine canons, in honour of St. Owald, king and martyr, was founded here in the time of William Rufus, by Ilbert de Lacy, the revenue of which at the dissolution was valued at £606. 9. 3.

NOTGROVE, a parish in the hundred of BRADLEY, county of GLOUCESTER, 4¾ miles (N.) from North Leach, containing 198 inhabitants. The living is a rectory, in the archdeaconry and diocese of Gloucester, rated in the king's books at £15. 6. 8., and in the patronage of the Crown. The church is dedicated to St. Bartholomew.

NOTLEY (BLACK), a parish in the hundred of WITHAM, county of ESSEX, 1½ mile (S. by E.) from Braintree, containing 418 inhabitants. The living is a rectory, in the archdeaconry of Colchester, and diocese of London, rated in the king's books at £15, and in the patronage of Marmaduke Wyvill, Esq. The church is dedicated to St. Peter and St. Paul. There is a school for fifteen poor children, endowed by James Coker in 1702. On raising gravel, in 1752, some curious relics of antiquity were discovered, consisting of fragments of a fluted column and a vessel, both of copper, also an

3 I 2

oblong blue glass vessel, with pieces of another, and of several glazed earthen urns. The learned William Bedell, Bishop of Kilmore, was born in this parish, in 1570, as was also John Ray, A.M., author of some works on Natural history.

NOTLEY (WHITE), a parish in the hundred of WITHAM, county of ESSEX, 3½ miles (N. W.) from Witham, containing 397 inhabitants. The living is a vicarage, in the archdeaconry of Colchester, and diocese of London, rated in the king's books at £10. D. Pennell, Esq. was patron in 1804.

NOTTINGHAM, a borough, market town, and county of itself, locally in the county of Nottingham, of which it is the chief town, 124 miles (N. N. W.) from London, containing the extra-parochial liberty of Standard Hill, and the limits of the castle, which are in the south division of the wapentake of Broxtow, 40,415 inhabitants. This place, from the numerous caverns and subterraneous dwellings excavated in the sandy rock on which it is situated, was by the Saxons called *Snottinga ham*, or place of caverns, of which its present name is only a slight modification. According to the Saxon Chronicle, the Danes, having in one of their numerous predatory incursions made themselves masters of the town, in 868, were attacked by Burrhed, King of Mercia, who, having obtained the assistance of King Ethelred I. and his brother Alfred, afterwards Alfred the Great, compelled the invaders to conclude a treaty of peace, and to retire to York. The town having subsequently suffered material injury from their renewed attempts to take possession of it, in which they were frequently successful, was fortified with a wall by Edward the Elder, who in 910 built a bridge over the river Trent. In 924, the town was repaired on the south side, towards the river, but soon after fell again into the hands of the Danes, who retained it till they were finally subdued by Edmund, in 940. In the reign of Edward the Confessor, Tosti, brother of Harold, had considerable possessions in Nottingham, which at that time contained one hundred and ninety-two burgesses ; but this number, at the time of the Conquest, had decreased to one hundred and twenty. The Conqueror, in order to keep his new subjects in awe, erected on the site of the ancient fort a formidable castle, the government of which he conferred on William Peverel, his natural son : this castle, from its situation on the summit of a bold eminence, rising perpendicularly from the river Leen, and from the strength of its fortifications, was regarded as impregnable, and the town was at the same time strongly fortified. During the war between Stephen and Matilda, Nottingham was besieged by the Earl of Gloucester, who having gained possession of it, plundered and burnt it, and in a few years after it experienced a similar calamity from the partisans of the young prince Henry, in his rebellion against his father, Henry II. On the death of the prince, and the consequent pacification of the kingdom, the king greatly contributed to the rebuilding of the town ; and to

reward the fidelity and loyalty of the inhabitants, granted them a charter, by which he confirmed all the privileges they enjoyed under Henry I. Richard I., previously to his embarking in the crusades, assembled a parliament here, to deliberate upon the requisite measures for the administration of the government during his absence, which was entrusted to his younger brother John, in whose attempts to usurp the dominion, the castle was alternately in the possession of his partisans and of those of his absent brother, by whom, on returning from his captivity in Germany, it was finally reduced. Richard, on taking possession of the throne, held another parliament in this town, in which he demanded justice against the unnatural usurpation of his brother John, whom, however, he ultimately pardoned. In the reign of John the town and castle were unsuccessfully assaulted by the confederate barons, who had invited the Dauphin of France to accept the English crown. In the early part of the reign of Edward III., Mortimer, Earl of March, and the queen dowager Isabel, resided in the castle, which was strongly fortified ; but a party of noblemen in the interest of the king, having obtained entrance through a subterranean passage which led to the keep, surprised that nobleman in an apartment adjoining the queen's, and having seized him, conveyed him to London, when, being convicted of high treason, he was hanged at Elmes. In the same reign a parliament was held here, which passed the first enactments for prohibiting the exportation of English wool, and for encouraging foreign manufacturers to settle in the kingdom. David Bruce, who had been made prisoner at the battle of Durham, was for some time confined in the castle, previously to his removal to London ; and in 1386, Richard II. held a council here, the members of which having declared the proceedings of the parliament which had impeached his ministers to be illegal, were afterwards accused of treason by the House of Commons, and many of them executed. In 1461, Edward IV., after landing at Ravenspur in Yorkshire, assembled his forces in this town, where he caused himself to be proclaimed king, and made extensive additions to the castle, which were completed by Richard III., who marched hence with his forces to Bosworth Field. Henry VII. held a council of war here previously to the battle of Stoke, in which the rebels who had espoused the pretensions of Lambert Simnel were defeated, with the loss of four thousand men.

Previously to the commencement of the parliamentarian war, Charles I., having retired to York, received the answer of the parliament to his various propositions for an accommodation ; but the conditions proposed by that body being so humiliating and unreasonable, the monarch resolved upon war as the milder alternative, and collecting what forces he could in those parts of the country that still adhered to his cause, advanced to Nottingham, where he set up his standard on a hill within the limits of the castle, which is still distinguished by the appellation of Standard Hill ; but, wishing to avoid extremities, he again made overtures for a treaty, which were still refused. Very early in the war, Prince Rupert, commanding a body of cavalry which had been stationed at Worcester, to observe the movements of the Earl of Essex, defeated a party under the command of Colonel Sandys, who was killed in the encounter, a short time prior to the battle

NOTTINGHAMSHIRE

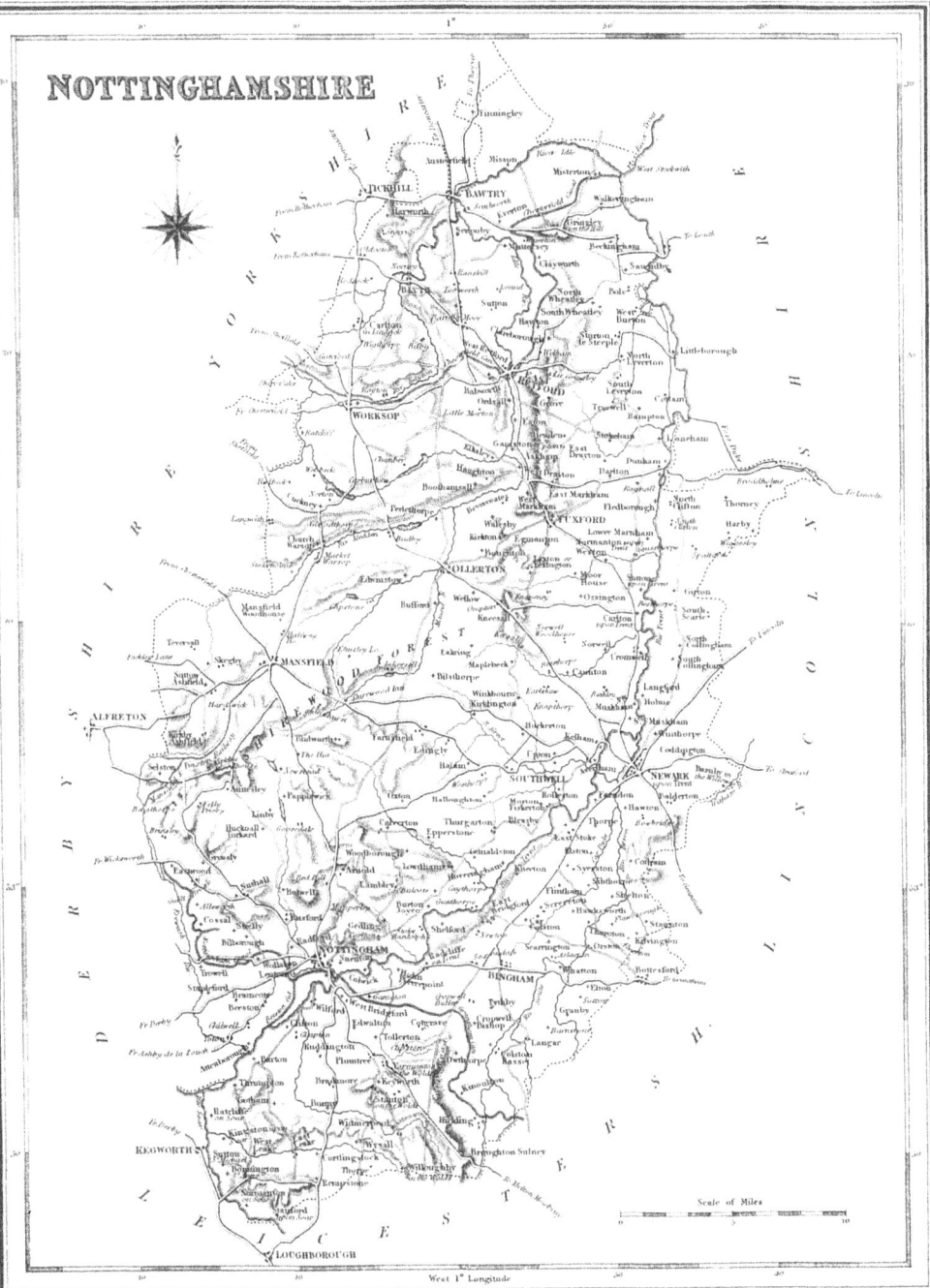

YORKSHIRE

DERBYSHIRE

LINCOLNSHIRE

LEICESTERSHIRE

WORKSOP

MANSFIELD

ALFRETON

TUXFORD

OLLERTON

BAWTRY

BLYTH

RETFORD

SOUTHWELL

NEWARK

NOTTINGHAM

BINGHAM

KEGWORTH

LOUGHBOROUGH

Scale of Miles

West 1° Longitude

Drawn by R. Creighton.   DRAWN AND ENGRAVED FOR LEWIS' TOPOGRAPHICAL DICTIONARY.   Engraved by J. & C. Walker.

of Edge Hill. The town and castle were soon afterwards besieged and taken by the parliamentarians, who stationed Colonel Hutchinson, with a powerful body, as a check on the garrison at Newark, which still held out for the king. During the usurpation of Cromwell, the castle was dismantled, and so far demolished as to render it unserviceable. After the Restoration, it became the property of the Duke of Buckingham, who sold it to the Duke of Newcastle, by whom it was pulled down, and a mansion commenced on a part of the site, which was completed in a few years after his death. At the time of the revolution in 1688, the Earl of Devonshire and other noblemen who had declared for a free parliament, held a meeting here on the landing of William, Prince of Orange, whom they assisted with all their influence in establishing his claims to the crown. During the French revolution of 1798, there existed a considerable degree of political excitement in the town; and in the years 1811 and 1812, the workmen, ascribing their distresses to the introduction of the improved machinery, were excited to the destruction of property to a considerable amount, by the party called "Luddites;" since which time some disturbances, originating with the frame-work knitters, occasioned the passing of the act of the 57th of George III.

The town is situated nearly in the centre of the kingdom, and at the south-western extremity of the Forest of Sherwood, and occupies the acclivity of a sandy rock, commanding an extensive view of the beautiful vale of Trent, the fertile meadows watered by that river, and the Leen, from the bank of which rises the precipitous rock on which its castle is built, and skirted by the pleasant village of Sneinton on the east: it is sheltered from the winds by a chain of hills on the north, and on the south is open to the vale of Belvoir, the Nottinghamshire wolds, and the Leicestershire hills. The streets in the central and more ancient part of the town are narrow, but, since the increase of the manufactures, it has experienced considerable improvement, and several spacious streets have been formed, and handsome ranges of building erected: it is well paved, lighted with gas, and supplied with water by two companies, incorporated by act of parliament in 1827, and with spring water of great purity by pumps in various parts; the general appearance of the town is interesting, and, from its elevated situation, the streets are always clean. At the distance of a mile, on the London road, is an ancient stone bridge of twenty arches over the river Trent, which is here of considerable breadth, being increased by the waters of the Derwent, the Soar, the Dove, and the Erwash: this bridge, for the repairs of which ample funds are vested in the corporation, having been repeatedly damaged by floods, exhibits a great diversity of style, corresponding with the several times at which it has been repaired: from the frequency of the rapid floods to which the river is exposed in rainy seasons, a flood-road, or causeway, over the meadows has been constructed, by act of parliament, and a strong embankment raised for the protection of the lower part of the town, which are maintained by a toll granted under the act: the approaches have been widened and greatly improved, and a considerable improvement has been effected in the entrance from Mansfield. The environs abound with pleasant walks, and with interesting and diver-

sified scenery. A public subscription library and news-room was established in 1816; and, in 1821, a spacious mansion at the west end of the market-place was purchased by the subscribers (of whom there are about two hundred and thirty-five), and appropriated to the use of the institution: it contains a commodious suite of rooms, comprising the library, in which there are eight thousand volumes (a valuable library of old books, given by the Rev. Mr. Standfast, in 1744, is also deposited here, but kept distinct from the other works), a news-room, lecture-room, law library, and a billiard-room: a mineralogical cabinet has been recently added to the establishment: the price of a proprietor's share is £20, and the annual subscription £2; the admission to the news-room is £1. 5. per annum. A Literary Society, consisting of one hundred members, established in 1824, meets every alternate Monday, during the winter, in the lecture-room of the library, for the discussion of literary and scientific subjects. A mechanics' institution, formed in 1824, has a library of two thousand volumes, and a reading-room; the members hold their meetings in one of the upper apartments of the Exchange buildings, where is also a commodious suite of assembly-rooms, in which concerts and balls are held; there are also other assembly-rooms, in that part of the town called the Low Pavement, where the assize and race balls are held. The theatre, a small plain building in Marygate, is open generally for about three months in the year. Races formerly took place on the second Tuesday in August, but have lately varied; they are well attended: the course, which is situated to the north-east of the town, is one of the finest in the kingdom, and is two miles in circumference; the grand stand, a handsome brick building, was erected by subscription, in 1777: adjoining the course is a spacious cricket ground. The cavalry barracks, an extensive range of building at the upper extremity of the Castle park, were erected in 1793, on land leased to the crown by the Duke of Newcastle. Near the Castle-gate is a spacious brick building, erected in 1798, as a riding-house, by the Nottingham yeomanry cavalry, which is occasionally used as a circus, and for other public amusements.

The staple manufactures are cotton and silk stockings, bobbin-net and lace, which afford employment to nearly forty thousand persons in the town and environs; and so much has the trade of the town increased, that the manufacturers have agents, or factors, in most parts of the world with which commercial intercourse is carried on. For its present prosperity Nottingham is greatly indebted to science for the improvements lately made in the machinery employed in these branches of national industry, which have given to the manufactures of the town a decided superiority. The machines for making the bobbin-net and lace are exceedingly expensive, and being therefore beyond the purchase of the poor, are let out to them at a weekly rent by the proprietors, who invest large capitals in this species of property, which has lately so much decreased in value; that a machine which, about four years since, would have cost from £1000 to £1200, may now be purchased for about £200. The improved lace machines have been latterly worked by steam, but the recent depression of the lace trade has compelled the manufacturers to limit the hours of employment, and, in some instances, to suspend their operation for a time: the machines for stockings and lace are principally made in the town, and afford employment to a considerable number of persons, who, till the depression in the lace trade, were receiving very high wages. There are several mills for spinning and twisting silk, and for spinning cotton and woollen yarn. In addition to the staple branches of manufacture, pin-making, wire-drawing, and the manufacture ¡ of brass fenders, are carried on to a considerable extent; there are also white lead-works, an iron-foundry, and several breweries; the trade in malt is very extensive; and the ale brewed here is in high repute. The town derives great facility of trade from its situation on the river Trent, which is navigable to the Humber; from the Grantham canal, affording communication with Lincolnshire and part of Leicestershire; and from the Nottingham, Cromford, and Erwash canals, with those of Staffordshire, Leicestershire, and Derbyshire, and opening a communication with the extensive mines of coal, lead, and iron, in those counties, and affording a medium of intercourse with the metropolis and the principal manufacturing towns. The market days are Wednesday and Saturday; the latter, which is principally for corn and cattle, is the most considerable in the midland district: the fairs are on the Friday after January 13th, for cattle; March 7th and 8th, for cheese, cloth, and cattle; Thursday before Easter, for horses; October 2nd, called Goose fair, which is very considerable for geese, cheese, cloth, and cattle, and continues nine days. The market-place, including an area of more than five acres and a half, is one of the most extensive and commodious in the kingdom: it is surrounded with lofty buildings, the first stories of which, projecting over the pavement, form a piazza. At the east end is the New Exchange, a handsome building of brick, erected by the corporation in the early part of the last century, and in 1814 repaired and faced with Roman cement; the ground-floor has been converted into shops, behind which are the shambles; the upper stories contain a suite of noble rooms for the transaction of public business; of these the principal is seventy-five feet long, thirty feet wide, and thirty feet high, with an arched ceiling; two other rooms communicate with the principal hall by folding doors, forming a suite one hundred and twenty-three feet in length.

The town, with the exception of the castle and the county gaol, was separated from the county of Nottingham, and constituted a distinct county, under the designation of "the Town and County of the Town of Nottingham," in the 27th of Henry VI., by which title it is recognised in an act of the 3rd of George I. The inhabitants have been

Corporate Seal.

incorporated by various charters ·from time immemorial; under the last of which, granted by Henry VI., the government is vested in a mayor, recorder, deputy recorder, two sheriffs, six aldermen, eighteen senior and six junior common council-men, assisted by a town clerk, two chamberlains, two coroners, two bridge-masters, and subordinate officers. The mayor is elected from among the aldermen by the corporation at large, by whom also vacancies in that body are filled up: the common council-men are chosen by the burgesses at large; the senior members from those who have filled the office of chamberlain, after which they are chosen sheriffs, and the junior members from the burgesses generally. The mayor and aldermen are justices of the peace, with whom the county magistrates have concurrent jurisdiction, by an act passed in the 43rd of George III., called the Nottingham election and police bill, in consequence of the tumultuous proceedings which took place at the election in 1802. The freedom of the borough is inherited by the eldest sons of freemen, born in the town, and by the younger sons after the expiration of their indentures of apprenticeship in any place; by others it is obtained by servitude to a resident freeman, by gift from the corporation, or by purchase: among the privileges of the freemen is the right of depasturing three head of cattle, or forty-five sheep, in the common fields and meadows, which comprise nearly sixteen hundred acres. The corporation hold courts of quarter session for the borough for the trial of all but capital offenders; a court of record, under the mayor and sheriffs, every alternate Wednesday, for the recovery of debts to any amount, the power of which extends to the recovery of freehold property by ejectment; the sheriffs hold their monthly county court for the recovery of debts under 40s., and courts leet and baron are held twice in the year. The town hall, rebuilt in the reign of George I., is a spacious and commodious edifice, two stories in height, containing on the ground-floor the town prison or common gaol, comprising cells and rooms for the classification of prisoners, and on the first story the court-room for the sessions, appropriately fitted up, and other apartments. The town bridewell, or house of correction, is an extensive edifice, well adapted to the classification and employment of the prisoners, to whom one-half of their earnings is given on their discharge. The borough has returned two members to parliament from the reign of Edward I.: the right of election is vested in the freemen generally, and in freeholders to the amount of 40s. per annum, the number of whom is about five thousand; the sheriffs are the returning officers. This being the county town, the election of knights of the shire, and the assizes and quarter sessions for the county are held in it. The county hall, rebuilt in 1770, is a handsome edifice with a stone front, containing two well-arranged courts for the Crown and Nisi Prius bar, with the requisite rooms for the grand jury, and offices for transacting the business of the county: behind it is the common gaol for the county, comprising one ward for debtors, one for prisoners convicted of misdemeanor, three for felons, and five airing-yards, for the classification of prisoners.

The town comprises the parishes of St. Mary, St. Nicholas, and St. Peter, in the archdeaconry of Nottingham, and diocese of York, and the liberty of St. James, which is extra-parochial. The living of St. Mary's is a vicarage, rated in the king's books at £10. 5., and in the patronage of Earl Manvers: the church is a spacious and elegant cruciform structure, in the later style of English architecture, with a beautiful tower rising from the centre to the height of two stages, and

crowned with battlements and pinnacles: the west front, which has been modernized, presents a striking contrast to the rest of the building, which is of beautiful design and of elaborate execution; the south porch is highly enriched with panels and fan tracery, depending from the roof, which is finely groined; the interior is lighted by ranges of noble windows of exquisite tracery, and under the end windows of the north and south transepts are two monuments of elegant design. It has received an addition of three hundred free sittings, in consequence of a grant of £500 from the Incorporated Society for the enlargement of churches and chapels. The archbishop holds his triennial, and the archdeacon, his annual, visitation in this church. The living of St. Nicholas' is a discharged rectory, rated in the king's books at £2. 16. 8., endowed with £600 royal bounty, and in the patronage of the Crown: the church was rebuilt in 1678, the former structure having been taken down during the parliamentary war: it is a neat edifice of brick, with quoins and cornices of stone, and was enlarged in 1756 and in 1783, by subscription, and the churchyard enclosed with neat iron palisades in 1824. The living of St. Peter's is a discharged rectory, rated in the king's books at £8. 7. 6., endowed with £400 private benefaction, and £600 royal bounty, and in the patronage of the Crown: the church is a spacious edifice, in the later style of English architecture, of which it retains some few good portions, though the greater part of it has been modernized; it has a lofty spire, and has lately received three hundred and eighty additional sittings, of which two hundred and sixty-four are free, at the expense of the Incorporated Society for the enlargement of churches and chapels, who granted £800 for that purpose: the spiritual courts are held in this church. St. James' church, or chapel, was erected in 1808, on Standard Hill, which is extra-parochial, and within the county of Nottingham: it is a neat edifice in the later style of English architecture, with a low square embattled tower: the living is a perpetual curacy, in the patronage of the subscribers, for a certain number of years, with reversion to the Crown. St. Paul's, a chapel of ease to the vicarage of St. Mary's, was erected in 1822: it is a handsome edifice in the Grecian style of architecture, with a portico of the Doric order. There are four places of worship each for Baptists, Independents, and Wesleyan Methodists, one each for the Society of Friends, Huntingtonians, Sabellians, Sandemanians, and Unitarians, a synagogue, and a Roman Catholic chapel, which last is a handsome edifice in the Grecian style of architecture. The free grammar school was founded, in 1513, by Agnes Mellors, but had nearly fallen into disuse prior to 1807, when the corporation made some regulations for its better government; the property with which it is endowed produces about £500 per annum: there are nearly one hundred scholars instructed in the classics gratuitously, and in writing and arithmetic, on payment of ten shillings per annum. The Blue-coat school, for the clothing and instruction of children, is supported by an income arising from property in land, and by subscription; there are sixty boys and twenty girls in this establishment: the school-house, a neat building, was erected on land given for that purpose by Mr. William Thorpe. A National school, established about twenty years since, is supported by subscription; and

in 1815 a Lancasterian school was opened, which is supported by subscription, chiefly among the dissenting congregations, who maintain a similar institution for girls: there are Sunday schools in connexion with the established church and the dissenting congregations, in which more than three thousand children are instructed: an infant school has also been established.

Plumtree hospital was founded, in 1392, by John de Plumtree, who endowed it for two chaplains, of whom one was master, and thirteen aged widows; in 1751, a descendant of the founder built four new tenements, to which two more were added by his son, who also repaired the old buildings: in 1823, John Plumtree, Esq., the late trustee, obtained an act of parliament to dispose of part of the trust property, and rebuilt the hospital. Exclusively of the widows who reside in the hospital, and receive each a weekly allowance of six shillings, a ton of coal, and a gown annually, there are thirty out-pensioners, who receive each £10 per annum: the premises are neatly built of brick, coated with cement, and in the ancient style of English architecture. Collins' hospital was founded, in 1704, by Mr. Abel Collin, who bequeathed an estate for its erection and endowment: there are in this institution twenty-four aged widowers and widows, who have each a tenement consisting of three rooms, a weekly allowance of four shillings, and two tons and a half of coal annually. Willoughby's hospital, in Fishergate, founded in 1525, and comprising nineteen tenements, has at present but a very trifling endowment, which is expected to be considerably augmented on the expiration of the present leases in 1831. Handley's hospital, in Stoney-street, comprising twelve ancient tenements for aged persons, who receive at present a quarterly sum of sixteen shillings and eightpence, is endowed with some estates, of which the produce is likely to be augmented. Bilby's almshouses, in Coal Pit lane, founded in 1709, comprise eight tenements for aged persons, who have each a sixpenny loaf weekly, and two tons of coal yearly, with a gratuity at Christmas. Labray's hospital was founded, in 1700, for six poor frame-work knitters, who have a weekly allowance of four shillings each. The Lambley hospital, a neat building, consisting of a centre and two wings, with a grass-plot in the front, comprises twenty-two tenements for decayed burgesses, or their widows, who are nominated by the corporation. Wartnaby's hospital was founded, in 1665, for six aged persons, who have a weekly allowance of one shilling, and an annual supply of clothes and coal. Warser-gate hospital, Wooley's almshouses, and St. Nicholas' White rents, comprise each six tenements: there are also the Charitable Society, patronised by the Society of Friends, and several similar establishments, together with numerous charitable bequests for apprenticing poor children, and for distribution among the infirm and indigent. The general hospital, a spacious and commodious building, consisting of a centre and two projecting wings, was erected in 1781, on the highest part of Standard Hill, on a site given by the corporation and the Duke of Newcastle: it is supported by funds arising from liberal donations, and by annual subscription, and is under the direction of a president and committee, being open to invalids from any part of the country: near it is a house of recovery from fever, under the same management. The lunatic asylum, a large and well-arranged building, erected in 1812, at an expense of nearly £20,000, in an airy situation in the parish of Sneinton, about a quarter of a mile to the north-east of the town, is under the inspection of the town and county magistrates : it is adapted to the reception of three classes of patients ; namely, such as are in circumstances to pay a full remuneration, the poor who are admitted on very moderate terms, and paupers who are paid for by the county : it comprises distinct wards and separate airing-grounds for the classification of patients, according to their rank and degree of malady, and is partly supported by donations and subscription.

Some fragments of the town walls are visible on the side of the hill above Narrow Marsh; and of the ancient castle, the gateway, repaired some years since, and some portions of the outworks, are still remaining: a subterraneous passage, called Mortimer's Hole, is still an object of interest; and there are numerous caverns and galleries excavated in the rock, which are of great antiquity, and attract much notice. The mansion erected by the Duke of Newcastle in the seventeenth century, on the castle hill, a noble edifice in the Grecian style of architecture, with a handsome façade of the Corinthian order, in front of which is an equestrian statue of the founder, has been for many years divided into separate dwellings. Thurland Hall, formerly called Clare Hall, an ancient brick mansion faced with stone, of which the great room is still used as a dining-room on public occasions, was the temporary residence of James I., during his frequent visits to Nottingham. In the northern part of the town was an ancient hospital, dedicated to St. John the Baptist, founded about the reign of John, for a master, warden, two chaplains, and several sick persons, the revenue of which, at the dissolution, was £5. 6. 8. In the reign of Henry III., there was a cell for two monks in the chapel of St. Mary, in the rock under the castle, in which latter there were also a house of brethren of the Holy Sepulchre, and a college of Secular priests. To the west of the town was a convent of Grey friars, founded by Henry III., in 1250 ; and in the parish of St. Nicholas was a convent of Carmelite friars, founded in 1276, by Reginald, Lord Grey de Wilton, and Sir John Shirley, Knt. At Babbington colliery, near Nottingham, a saline chalybeate spring has been recently discovered, the properties of which, according to an analysis by a medical gentleman in the town, are such as to render it one of the most valuable mineral springs in this country. Near the Forest of Sherwood, on the spot formerly used for the execution of criminals, a great quantity of human bones was lately discovered. Among the eminent natives of this town were, the Rev. Dr. Andrew Kippis, a celebrated biographer, who was born in 1725 ; the Rev. Gilbert Wakefield, distinguished for his acquaintance with classical literature, born in 1756; and the poet, Henry Kirke White, who was born in 1785, and died whilst pursuing his studies at Cambridge, in 1806. Nottingham gives the title of earl to the family of Finch-Hatton.

NOTTINGHAMSHIRE, an inland county, bounded on the north by Yorkshire, on the east by Lincolnshire, on the south by Leicestershire, and on the west by Derbyshire. It extends from 52° 51′ to 53° 34′ (N. Lat.), and from 44′ to 1° 23′ (W. Lon.) ; including an area of eight hundred and thirty-seven

square miles, or five hundred and thirty-five thousand six hundred and eighty statute acres. The population, in 1821, was 186,873. This county, having formed part of the territory of the *Coritani*, was included in the Roman district called *Flavia Cæsariensis*. On the establishment of the Anglo-Saxon kingdom of Mercia, which took place about the year 560, the greater part of Nottinghamshire, viz., that on the north-western bank of the river Trent, became part of the country of the North Mercians, the portion on the other side of that river being in South Mercia. The first memorable event in the history of the octarchy, recorded as having occurred within its limits, is the defeat of Ethelfrith, King of Northumbria, by Redwald, King of East Anglia, who had espoused the cause of Edwin of Northumbria, expelled by Ethelfrith ; the battle, in which the latter perished, having been fought on the eastern bank of the river Idel, or Idle. When Egfrid of Northumbria invaded Mercia in 679, the Mercians met him on the banks of the Trent, and in the first conflict his brother Ælfuin was slain; but the further effusion of blood was prevented by the mediation of Theodore, Archbishop of York. The Danes first visited this county in 868, when they crossed the Humber into Mercia, and possessed themselves of Nottingham, where they wintered, and where they were besieged by Burrhed, King of Mercia, and Ethelred, King of Wessex, with the whole force of their dominions, when a treaty was entered into, by virtue of which they evacuated Mercia, and retired with their plunder to York. The entire subjection of this shire to the Danish power was involved in the final overthrow of the Anglo-Saxon sovereignty of Mercia, which took place in 874. When Alfred had delivered the Mercian territory from its subjection to the Danes, he did not avowedly incorporate it with Wessex, but constituted Ethelred its military commander, to whom he afterwards gave his daughter Ethelfleda in marriage. In the early part of the following century, Nottinghamshire again fell under the Danish dominion, and so continued until 941, when it was again rescued by Edward the Elder. At the period of the Norman Conquest, a great portion of the territorial property of the county was given by the Conqueror to his illegitimate son, William Peverel, whose principal fortified residence was the castle of Nottingham. In almost all the English civil wars of the middle ages, the central situation of the county, and the circumstance of its being intersected by the large river Trent, which in those ages was an important barrier, defended by the two strong fortresses of Nottingham and Newark, made it the scene of numerous important military movements, and consequently of many ravages, which are detailed in the account of the places in which they respectively occurred. In 1216, King John died at Newark, after his disastrous march across the Washes of Lincolnshire; and in the neighbourhood of the same town, in 1487, Lambert Simnel, the pretended Earl of Warwick, assisted by John de la Pole, Earl of Lincoln, and Fitzgerald, Earl of Kildare, with a body of Irish, and two thousand Germans, was defeated and taken prisoner, with the loss of four thousand men, including the Earls of Lincoln and Kildare, and Lord Lovel.

In the course of the parliamentary war, this county was the scene of several of the most remarkable transactions. It was at Nottingham that the king first solemnly erected his standard, in August 1642. In 1643, Newark was successfully defended against the parliamentarians under Lord Willoughby of Parham, and Sir John Meldrum, whose forces, on the arrival of the troops under Prince Rupert, sent to raise the siege, were totally defeated, with the loss of their ordnance and ammunition. The castle of Nottingham being held for the parliament, several skirmishes occurred during the war between the garrison and detachments from the royalist garrison at Newark. In this county also, at Southwell, on the 6th of May, 1646, Charles I. surrendered himself to the commissioners from the Scottish army then lying before Newark, the garrison of which, under Lord Bellasis, surrendered to the Scots, on the 19th of the same month, by the king's special command. In the year 1812, the manufacturing district, of which Nottingham is the centre, was much agitated by the disturbances among the framework knitters, owing to the very low rate of wages ; and by the operations of the *Luddites*, as they were called, being parties of the working manufacturers, who, with masks on their faces and otherwise disguised, broke into many houses and workshops in the night, and destroyed several stocking-frames ; and in June 1817, the south-western part of the county was thrown into some alarm, by the insurrection of a number of misguided men in the vicinity of South Winfield, in Derbyshire, on the Nottinghamshire border, who attempted to march upon Nottingham, but were dispersed by a party of the military within a few miles of that town, when many of them were taken and committed to the prisons of Nottingham and Derby; several of whom being tried by special commission at Derby, in the following October, for high treason, three of those who were convicted were executed on the 7th of November.

Nottinghamshire is included in the diocese and province of York, and forms an archdeaconry, comprising the deaneries of Bingham, Newark, Nottingham, and Retford, which contain two hundred and five parishes, of which seventy-five are rectories, eighty-nine vicarages, and the remainder perpetual curacies. Two synods of the clergy of this county are held annually at Southwell. For purposes of civil government it is divided into six wapentakes, or hundreds, *viz.*, Bassetlaw, which is subdivided into North Clay, South Clay, and Hatfield divisions ; Bingham (North and South), Broxtow (North and South), Newark (North and South), Rushcliffe (North and South), and Thurgarton (North and South), and the liberty of Southwell and Scrooby. It contains the borough and market towns of Nottingham, Newark, and East Retford ; and the market towns of Bingham, Mansfield, Ollerton, Southwell, Tuxford, and Worksop. Two knights are returned to parliament for the shire, two representatives for each of the boroughs of Nottingham and Newark, and two by the burgesses of East Retford, conjointly with the freeholders of the hundred of Bassetlaw : the county members are elected at Nottingham. This county is included in the midland circuit ; the assizes are held at Nottingham ; the quarter sessions at Nottingham, on January 11th, April 19th, July 12th, and October 18th ; at Newark, on January 15th, April 23d, July 16th, and October 22d ; and at East Retford, on January 18th, April 26th, July 19th, and October 25th.

The county gaol is at Nottingham, and the county house of correction, or bridewell, at Southwell. Nottinghamshire was under the same shrievalty with Derbyshire, until the 10th year of the reign of Queen Elizabeth. There are fifty-eight acting magistrates. The rates raised in the county for the year ending March 25th, 1827, amounted to £99,085.18., the expenditure to £99,685.9., of which £71,935.13. was applied to the relief of the poor.

The shape of this county is elliptical. Its surface is for the most part uneven, but none of the hills are of great elevation : those of the sandy district, which anciently formed a considerable part of the celebrated Forest of Sherwood, are chiefly long ridges of gentle acclivity, running from west to east, and forming narrow valleys, through the principal of which run fine streams of water. The tract formed by these ridges would, on the whole, be dreary and monotonous, as the view from one generally extends only to the summit of the next, were it not that it is adorned by numerous noblemen's and gentlemen's seats, surrounded by very extensive parks and plantations, several of them having magnificent artificial sheets of water : the view from its southern extremity at Nottingham, over the vale of the Trent and into Leicestershire, is rich and extensive. The noble river Trent is bordered, in the whole of its course through Nottinghamshire, by a fine rich tract of level land, varying in breadth from about a mile and a half to upwards of five miles, many parts of which are bounded by high woody cliffs ; below Newark, however, its borders are flatter : it is for the most part enclosed, and the greater proportion, particularly in the immediate vicinity of the river, is rich grass land. The part of the county lying south of the Trent, and forming the three hundreds of Bingham, Rushcliffe, and Newark, comprises, besides the lower and more extensive part of the vale of Belvoir, and the fertile levels in the vicinity of the Soar, at the south-western extremity of the county, the range of high bleak country, called the Nottinghamshire Wolds, lying to the south and south-east of Bunny, and including the townships of Clipston, Normanton on the Wolds, Broughton-Sulney, Plumtree, Stanton on the Wolds, Widmerpool, Willoughby on the Wolds, and Wysall, most of which are enclosed. The view from Beacon Hill, in the hundred and near the town of Newark, is remarkably extensive. The hundred of Bassetlaw comprises the whole northern part of the county, from the vicinity of Mansfield, and includes the towns of Ollerton and Tuxford : from Gringley on the Hill, near its north-eastern extremity, are obtained some remarkably fine and extensive views, over the broad vale of the Trent, the Isle of Axholme, and a great extent of the counties of Nottingham, Lincoln, and York : the other two hundreds occupy the space between the southern border of the last-mentioned and the river Trent, that of Broxtow on the west, and Thurgarton on the east : they include a considerable part of those tracts of the forest which still remain unenclosed, and which are of comparatively small extent.

The soils may be divided into the three classes of sand or gravel, clay, and limestone and coal land. The forest district, the soil of which is for the most part a deep light sand, extends northward, from Nottingham to the northern boundary of the county at

Tickhill, Bawtry, Finningley, and West Stockwith, in length about thirty miles, and in breadth from seven to ten, including the towns of Mansfield, Ollerton, Worksop, Retford, and Blyth. The tract of level country on the eastern bank of the Soar, and that on the borders of the Trent, from its entrance into the county to the vicinity of Sutton, where the clay soil reaches down to the river on the western side, have in general a mellow vegetable mould, resting on sand or gravel, which in some places rise to the surface: nearly similar is also the ground lying between the wolds and the level of the Soar, on an elevation between the two, and contained in the townships of East and West Leake, Cortlingstock, and Rempstone; as well as the strip of higher land on the borders of the Trent vale, comprising the townships of East Bridgford, Kneeton, Flintham, and Stoke, both of which have a good mellow mixed soil of easy tillage. At the north-eastern extremity of the Trent vale district of light land just described, is a tongue of land on the eastern bank of the Trent, projecting into Lincolnshire, of a sandy soil, which is in general very poor. The clay lands north of the Trent include the North and South clay division of the hundred of Bassetlaw, and almost the whole of the hundred of Thurgarton: they are in general not of the most tenacious quality, being rendered more friable by the intermixture of a portion of sand, particularly the red clay, of which there is a great extent in the country round Tuxford, and in the hundred of Thurgarton, and the black clay soil, commonly called a "woodland soil." The whole of the vale of Belvoir, with the exception of those parts included in the districts of the lighter soils before described, consists of clay, or very strong loam; the soil of the wolds is a cold clay. The limestone and coal district is a narrow tract lying on the western side of the county, to the west of a line drawn from the little river at Shireoaks, in the north, nearly south by west to the river Lene near Wollaton and Radford, no limestone being found east of the Lene; the limestone, running from Shireoaks, begins to abut upon the coal near Teversall, to the west of Mansfield, and afterwards runs between it and the sand; the line of coal, which in this county is scarcely more than a mile broad, commencing a little to the north of Teversall, runs nearly south by west to Brookhill, then south to Eastwood, and thence, in nearly a south-easterly direction to Bilborough, Wollaton, and the river Lene: the soil upon the limestone is of a hungry quality; that upon the coal a cold blue or yellow clay.

Nearly all the enclosed part of the forest district which is not occupied by woods, most of the coal and lime district, and a considerable portion of the other parts of the county, are under tillage. It has been besides an immemorial custom for the inhabitants of townships to take up "breaks," or temporary enclosures, and keep them in tillage for five or six years: for this the permission of the lord of the manor is necessary, and two verderers of the forest must inspect, who report to the lord chief justice in Eyre that it is not to the prejudice of the king or subject; they are also to see that the fences are not such as to exclude the deer: the increased number of enclosures, and the consequent decrease in the waste lands, have rendered this custom almost ob-

solete. The crops usually cultivated are, wheat, rye, barley, oats, beans, and peas. The produce of wheat varies from two to four quarters per acre. Rye is chiefly grown in the Trent vale, in the vicinity of Markham, &c., and on the forest; the produce is generally from three to four quarters per acre. Barley is very extensively cultivated, the produce varying from three to six and sometimes seven quarters per acre. Oats of various kinds are grown: the produce is generally from four to seven quarters per acre, but sometimes as much as ten quarters: the Trent vale produces remarkably fine oats: there, is also cultivated an inferior species of oats, almost peculiar to this county, called *skegs*, which will grow on the forest land, and although seldom brought to market, they are much esteemed by those who grow them, and are frequently given as fodder in the straw. The produce of beans varies from three to five quarters per acre; that of peas, from four to six quarters: in the clay district north of the Trent, crops of peas and beans mixed are not unfrequent. Buck-wheat is cultivated in small quantities. Turnips are most cultivated on the sandy and lighter soils; and on the limestone tract the Swedish turnip is also frequently grown: rape is sometimes sown instead of turnips in the clayey districts, as food for sheep and oxen; and when reserved for seed, it is generally found to produce four or five quarters per acre. Winter tares are common in several parts, as green food for horses and cattle. Potatoes in small quantities are grown in every part of the county: the common artificial grasses, red and white clover, trefoil, ray-grass, and rib-grass, are cultivated, as is also lucerne: burnet grows naturally and plentifully in the Trent meadows. Hops form a considerable article in the produce of the clay districts north of the Trent, more particularly in the part about Retford, and, in a minor degree, in the vicinity of Southwell: they are generally known by the name of North Clay hops, and are much stronger than the Kentish, but those who are accustomed to the latter object to their flavour as rank; they are also cultivated to a small extent at Rufford, Ollerton, and Elksley, situated on the sand: the quantity grown fluctuates, some grounds being laid down and others taken up every year: the extent of land occupied in this manner is upwards of one thousand acres. The crops in the best seasons are small compared with those of the Kentish plantations, and do not in the very best years average eight hundred-weight per acre. Woad is cultivated at the northern extremity of the county, on the light soils in the vicinity of Scrooby, Ranskill, and Torworth, but the quantity varies greatly, according to the demand; it is sown with barley and clover, and is pulled up from among the clover the next year, when the latter is coming into blossom, and then tied in bundles and dried: about six hundred-weight per acre is an average crop.

On the banks of the Trent and the Soar is much excellent grass land, which is employed more for feeding than for the dairy, except along the course of the Soar, and in the vale of the Trent above Nottingham, where there are large dairies, the chief produce of which is cheese. The large island formed by the two branches of the Trent near Newark is remarkably fine feeding land. In the clay district north of the Trent, most of the farmers keep cows for the dairy; but it is not their principal object, except in the vicinity of Fledborough; and thence also along the Trent, as far as Gainsborough, a good many young cattle are reared, and in some parts, particularly in the North Clay, many cattle are fed. In the forest district very little land remains permanently in grass, except the bottoms near brooks and rivers, as meadow. A considerable quantity of meadow land has been improved by irrigation in various parts of the county, the most considerable tract being in the valley of the Maun, between Mansfield and Edwinstow, the property of the Duke of Portland. Lime to a greater or less extent is used as a manure in every part of Nottinghamshire, and in various quarters of it bone-dust, malt-combs, and soot are commonly used for the same purpose. The cattle on the borders of the Soar are of the long-horned breed; almost all the cow-calves are reared, and at three years old are taken into the dairy, and the old cows fed off. The cattle reared in the clay district north of the Trent are of a poor coarse kind, commonly called " woodland beasts : " those reared in the vale of Belvoir are a mixture between the long-horned and the short-horned breed. The lime and coal district has a mixture of long-horned and short-horned woodland cattle : few are reared in either the forest district, or in the Trent vale; those fed in the latter tract are generally of the short-horned, Lincolnshire, and the Holderness breeds.

The old forest sheep are a small polled breed (though some few have horns), with grey faces and legs, and a fleece of fine wool, the average weight of which is nearly two pounds; when fat they weigh from seven to nine pounds per quarter : this breed has of late years been much improved by crossing with the Leicestershire sheep, and the new sort thus produced are a round compact kind, carrying a fleece of about four pounds weight, and weighing generally from seventeen to twenty-two pounds per quarter. In the Trent vale, and the vale of Belvoir, the breed has also been much improved by the introduction of Leicester sheep, and they are now of a good size, and carry a fleece upwards of seven pounds' weight. In the clay district north of the Trent they are of a mixed kind, generally between the forest and the Lincolnshire pasture sheep, with an intermixture of the New Leicester breed. In the lime and coal district also the Leicester sheep now prevail : of late years many of the South Down breed have been introduced. The breed of hogs for bacon is the old lop-eared; that for pork the Chinese, or swing-tailed; a mixture with the old sort is very prevalent. In the Trent vale some horses are bred, chiefly tolerably good, middle-sized, black cart-horses; in the clay district north of the Trent, some of the same kind also are reared, though of a rather inferior sort; in the lime and coal district the breed of black horses is much attended to, and many of them are sold to the · southern dealers, who come down to purchase them. The rabbit warrens were formerly very numerous and extensive in the forest district, and they are still very considerable : in the clay district north of the Trent more pigeons are kept than in any other district of equal size in the kingdom. In several parts of the county are considerable market-gardens and nursery-grounds, particularly in the vicinity of Newark; and in the clay district are many orchards of apples and pears, among the most considerable of which are those about the villages of Halam

and Edingly, and in the vicinity of Southwell; a very ready sale for this fruit is found at Mansfield market, whence it is forwarded for the supply of the Peak of Derbyshire : some of it is also sent to Sheffield. Little waste land is now left in the county, by far the greater part of the forest being enclosed : the parts which remain are chiefly about the centre of the forest district, in the space between the towns of Mansfield, Southwell, and Ollerton, and consists in great part of rabbit warrens. On the tongue of sandy land east of the Trent, between Newark and Gainsborough, before mentioned, are some low, flat, barren commons, almost always under water in the winter. The Nottinghamshire Wolds, properly so called, are wastes in the open parishes, which afford a stinted pasture for young cattle and horses.

The ancient royal Forest of Sherwood extends from Nottingham to the vicinity of Worksop, in length about twenty-five miles, and varies in breadth from seven to upwards of nine miles. Several smaller tracts of land, particularly in the northern part of the county, as far as Rossington bridge, have been usually called forest; but, from the survey made in the year 1609, they appear either not to have belonged to the forest, or to have been disafforested before that period. In Sherwood Forest are included several large parks, which have been taken in at different times, as those of Welbeck, Clumber, Thoresby, Beskwood, Newstead, Clipstone, and several villages, or lands, belonging to them. The whole soil of the forest is understood to have been granted from the crown to different lords of manors, reserving only what is called in forest language the " vert and venison,"or trees and deer : the latter, which were all of the red kind, though formerly very numerous, are now, in consequence of the advance of cultivation over their sylvan haunts, entirely extirpated. The forest is the only one that remains under the superintendence of the lord chief justice in Eyre, north of the Trent, or which now belongs to the crown in that portion of England. The officers are, the lord-warden, at present the Duke of Newcastle, who holds his office by letters patent from the crown during pleasure; the bow-bearer and ranger, who is appointed by the lord warden, and holds his office also during pleasure; four verderers, elected by the freeholders of the county for life, who have each a tree out of the king's hays of Birkland and Bilhagh, and a fee of £2. 2. on attending the enclosure of a break; a steward; nine keepers, appointed by the verderers during pleasure, who have so many different walks, and receive a salary of £1 per annum from the Duke of Newcastle, paid out of a fee-farm rent from Nottingham castle; and two sworn woodwards for Sutton and Carlton. Thorneywood Chase comprises a great part of the southern division of the forest lying on the eastern side : the Earl of Chesterfield is hereditary keeper of it, by grant of the 42nd of Queen Elizabeth to J. Stanhope, Esq.

The principal remains of the ancient woods are the hays of Birkland and Bilhagh, situated to the north of Ollerton and Edwinstow, which form an open wood of large old oaks, most of them in decay, and stag-headed, as it is called; that is, the tops have decayed, and the highest branches now forming the top, being sapless, have somewhat the appearance of a stag's horns: this wood is about three miles in length, and one and a half in breadth, occupying an extent of about one thousand four hundred acres, and is without underwood, except some birch in one part, which has given name to one of its divisions. From a survey made in the year 1790, it appears that there were then, in both, ten thousand one hundred and seventeen trees, valued at £17,147. 15. 4.: during the late war with France, however, nearly all the valuable timber was felled for the use of the royal navy: a part of this tract has been taken by grant into Thoresby park. Harlow wood, Thieves' wood, and the scattered remains of Mansfield woods, are of small extent, containing timber of an inferior size: in Clumber park are also some remains of ancient woods. The effects of a disposition for planting which has prevailed among the noblemen and gentlemen of this county since the middle of the last century, are amazing, the Duke of Newcastle, in Clumber park alone, having one thousand eight hundred and forty-eight acres of plantation. Extensive tracts of plantations, consisting chiefly of firs of various kinds, occupy many miles of country to the south and south-east of Mansfield; and there is an immense extent of the same kind of woods in a similar direction from Worksop, chiefly on the large estates of the Duke of Norfolk, the Duke of Portland, the Duke of Newcastle, and Earl Manvers. There are besides numerous large plantations still further north in the county, and some close upon its western border. In the clay districts, north of the Trent, are considerable tracts of wood, which are chiefly sprung, their principal value, in common with that of all other spring woods in the county, arising from the ash hop-poles and the stakes and bindings, &c. for the farmers' use, which they produce: in the limestone and coal district are also considerable woods, and in the sandy tongue of land east of the Trent, are extensive plantations: but in the rest of the county they are comparatively few, and of small extent. Besides the various kinds of fir, including Weymouth pine, the woods contain much fine oak, ash, beech, chesnut, and elm, besides inferior kinds of timber: numerous plantations of willow, sallow, and owler, are made in the low bottoms. The fuel almost universally used is coal, much of which is raised in the lime and coal district, and a great deal brought from Derbyshire, by the Erwash, Cromford, and Chesterfield canals.

The chief minerals are coal, gypsum, and stone of various kinds. Coal is got in the line before described, on the western border of the county, whence it is conveyed by the Erwash and Nottingham canals, or distributed over the country by land-carriage. Gypsum of an excellent quality is dug on Beacon Hill, near Newark, and is much used for plastering floors: a considerable quantity is also sent in lumps to the colourmen of London; and some of the white kind, ground and packed in hogsheads, is likewise sent to the metropolis. At Red Hill, at the junction of the Trent and the Soar, is a quarry of the same mineral: it is also found at Great Markham, the Wheatleys, and many other places in the red clay district. Lime is burned at various places in the limestone tract, as also on Beacon Hill, near Newark, from a blue stone. At Mansfield a very good yellowish freestone is quarried, for the purpose of building, paving, &c., and a courser red kind for cisterns and troughs.

At Maplebeck is a blueish stone used for building, which, with continued exposure to the air, bleaches to nearly a clear white. At Beacon Hill, near Newark, is obtained a blue stone for hearths, approaching to a marble in texture, and which also burns to lime. At Linby, a few miles to the south-west of Mansfield, a coarse paving stone is raised, much used at Nottingham.

The manufacture of stockings from cotton and silk is that most anciently established in the county, and is carried on to a great extent, affording employment to a large number of persons at Nottingham, and the villages for some miles round it, as also in Mansfield and its neighbourhood. The very high state of improvement to which the machinery for manufacturing British lace was here brought, about twelve years ago, and the great demand for the superior article thus produced, have rendered the manufacture of "bobbin net," and the embroidering of machine lace, a source of employment to a great portion of the inhabitants of the same district, the dense population of which it has also materially contributed to collect. The cotton-mills and silk-mills for the supply of these manufactures are very numerous. The bleaching trade in the vicinity of Nottingham is very extensive; there are several large starch-mills and some paper-mills in different parts of the county. The malting business is carried on to a great extent, particularly at Nottingham, Newark, Mansfield, Worksop, and Retford: a great deal of malt is sent up the Trent and the canals into Derbyshire, Cheshire, and Lancashire. At Newark are large breweries, which rival those of Burton in their trade to the Baltic and other quarters: Nottingham also has extensive breweries. The exports are chiefly lace and stockings, much of which is sent to London by the stage coaches and light vans, coal, oak timber and bark, and malt and hops; the principal imports are coal, into the northern part of the county, from Derbyshire, foreign timber, and iron.

The principal river, the Trent, ranks the first in England after the Thames and the Severn; after forming, for about two miles, the boundary between Derbyshire and this county, it enters it near Thrumpton, and runs in a north-easterly direction, by the Trent bridge, south of Nottingham, to the vicinity of Newark, where it forms a large island; a small branch of it passing by that town, while the main stream flows two miles to the northward of it, and then almost immediately assumes a direction nearly north, which it continues throughout the rest of its course, beginning, a little above Dunholm ferry, to form the eastern boundary of the county, which it separates from Lincolnshire, and so continuing until just below Stockwith, where it wholly quits Nottinghamshire, and enters Lincolnshire. The tide in this river, which flows for a distance of some miles above Gainsborough, more particularly at spring tides, rushes up with great violence, bearing a breast of water several feet in perpendicular height, provincially called the *agar*, supposed to be a corrupt pronunciation of the word *eager*. The Trent is navigable for merchant ships of considerable burden up to Gainsborough, and for barges during the rest of its course in this county: to facilitate this navigation, there is a side-cut of ten miles in length, in order to avoid the numerous shallows which occur in about thirteen miles of its course, between the Trent bridge, at the commencement of the Nottingham canal, and Sawley ferry in Derbyshire, at the commencement of the Trent and Mersey canal: this side-cut, sometimes called the Trent canal, has a rise of twenty-eight feet, and not only crosses and communicates with the Erwash canal near Sawley, but has also a short cut and lock into the Trent at Beeston. The Soar forms the south-western boundary of the county, which it separates from Leicestershire for the distance of between seven and eight miles, above its junction with the Trent near Thrumpton; this river is navigable for the Trent barges. The Erwash forms the boundary between this county and that of Derby, for the distance of ten or twelve miles, down to its junction with the Trent, a little below Thrumpton. No less than five fine streams cross the sandy forest district, from west to east: the junction of two of these, the Maun from Mansfield, and the Meaden, forms the river Idle, which, receiving the other streams at irregular distances, flows northward by Retford and Bawtry, and thence eastward to the Trent at Stockwith, having below Bawtry formed the northern boundary of the county for a few miles. From Bawtry to the Trent it has been rendered navigable, and has gates at its mouth sixteen feet high, for the purpose of preventing the tide from overflowing the low lands which border the latter part of its course: this channel in one part has the name of Bycar Dyke, and about half a mile from Stockwith assumes that of Misterton Sluice. Numerous smaller streams pursue a more direct course from the higher parts of the county to the Trent; the principal being the Lene, which falls into it at Nottingham; the Dover, or Darebeck, which joins it near Caythorpe; the Greet, from Southwell; and the Smite and Devon, united, from the vale of Belvoir, which have their confluence with it at Newark.

The commerce of this county is materially facilitated by its great extent of canal navigation. The Nottingham canal, commencing in the Trent near that town, passes along the southern side of it, and then proceeds in a devious north-westerly course of about fifteen miles to its termination in the Cromford canal, near Langley bridge, and not far from the termination of the Erwash canal, the rise being comparatively small: the Trent canal, before mentioned, forms a junction with this a little to the westward of Nottingham: the Nottingham canal was completed in 1802: the articles brought down it are chiefly coal from the Derbyshire and Nottinghamshire pits, and lime from Crich, in the former county; those conveyed up it are for the most part corn and malt, for the supply of the populous district in the central parts of Derbyshire. A small part of the course of the Erwash canal is within the county of Nottingham. The Grantham canal commences from the Trent near Holme-Pierrepoint, and takes a course nearly east towards the head of the vale of Belvoir, where it enters the north-eastern extremity of Leicestershire: it has a branch of upwards of three miles in length to the town of Bingham; in the ascent from the Trent to the Wolds, this canal has a rise of eighty-two feet in a space of only six miles and a half. The proprietors of the Trent river navigation, having been at considerable expense in deepening the river near the entrance of this canal, are entitled to certain toll on all goods passing along that river, from this to the Nottingham canal. The Chesterfield canal enters Nottinghamshire near Shire-Oaks, on the north-western

border of the county, and proceeds to Worksop, at a little distance below which it crosses the small river Ryton, by an aqueduct, and continues its course in an irregular easterly direction to Retford: here, having crossed the Idle, it takes a northerly direction to Drakelow, where it passes through a tunnel of two hundred and fifty yards in length, and then runs, in a north-easterly direction, near Gringley on the Hill, across Misson Car to Misterton, and across Walkeringham moor to West Stockwith, terminating in a large basin which communicates with the Trent: the whole line of this canal is about forty miles in length, and from the summit level, at Norwood in Derbyshire, it has a fall to the Trent of three hundred and thirty-five feet. [For an account of the Pinxton railway, see the article on MANSFIELD.]

The great north road from London to Edinburgh enters Nottinghamshire about three miles to the south of Newark, passing through which town it crosses the Trent, and continues by Tuxford and Retford, quitting the county as it enters Bawtry in Yorkshire. The great road from London to Sheffield and Leeds enters it from Leicestershire immediately to the south of Rempstone, and passing through Nottingham and Mansfield, quits it for Derbyshire at Pleaseley, about three miles beyond the latter town. The Leeds mail road enters from Leicestershire between Nether Broughton and Over Broughton, whence it crosses the Nottinghamshire Wolds, and falls into the last-mentioned road at the southern extremity of the Trent bridge, near Nottingham. An excellent turnpike-road branches from the great Leeds road at Mansfield, and passing through Worksop quits the county for Yorkshire at South Carlton, in its way to Doncaster, where it falls into the great north road. A branch of the great north road also diverges from it at Newark, and passing through Ollerton, falls into the last-mentioned road at Worksop.

Nottinghamshire possesses comparatively few monuments of remote antiquity: the most remarkable British remains are the caves in the sand-rock near Nottingham. At Barton, four miles to the south-west of Nottingham, is Brent's Hill, considered by Aubrey to have been a fortified place of the Britons; and at Oxton are three large tumuli, supposed by Major Rooke to be of equal antiquity: brass celts have also been found, particularly between Hexgrove and the little stream called Rainworth-water. Of Roman antiquities, the camp on Holly-hill, near Arnold, is considered by Dr. Gale to have been the important Roman station *Causennis*; and about two miles from Mansfield are still the remains of a Roman villa, while in various other parts of the county have been found spears, fibulæ, and brass keys, of Roman workmanship. The principal remains of Roman roads are those of the Fosse-way, which, coming from Leicestershire, enters this county near Willoughby on the Wolds, proceeds to Newark, and crossing the line of the Ermin-street, enters Lincolnshire. This may be traced for many miles across the Wolds, being literally a fosse, dug to a great depth, so as to form a spacious covered way. Another ancient road, formerly called "the Street," commences at Newark and proceeds through part of Southwell to Mansfield: it is still discernible between the two former towns. The most various and interesting examples of ancient ecclesiastical architecture are conspicuous in the collegiate church of

Southwell; fine specimens may also be seen in the churches of Worksop, Newark, and Nottingham: in those of Southwell and Worksop in particular, the Anglo-Saxon, or early Norman style, is strikingly exhibited. The religious houses, including colleges and hospitals, were about thirty-nine: the chief remains of monastic buildings are those of the abbeys of Newstead and Worksop, and of the college at Southwell. There are considerable remains of the once important castle of Newark, and some interesting relics of that of Nottingham. Bunny Park, the seat of Viscount Rancliffe, and Thurland Hall, in Nottingham, are among the most curious specimens of ancient mansion houses. Among the most distinguished of the numerous modern seats which adorn the county, more especially the northern part of its once dreary forest district, may be enumerated Worksop manor, the property of the Duke of Norfolk, and the residence of the Earl of Surrey; Welbeck abbey, the property and residence of the Duke of Portland; Clumber park, that of the Duke of Newcastle; Thoresby park, that of Earl Manvers; Wollaton Hall, that of Lord Middleton; and Newstead abbey, recently that of the late Lord Byron, but now of Lieut. Col. Wildman. The ordinary houses, except on the borders of Derbyshire, where stone is more plentiful, are generally of brick and tiled, though sometimes thatched: some of the poor cottages and barns in the clay country are of lath and plaster, but all new buildings are there of brick and tiled: in the southern part of the county, many of the better class of houses are slated. The traditions respecting Robin Hood and the Sherwood outlaws of the twelfth and thirteenth centuries, which, in the form of popular ballads, were current for ages among the lower orders, seem to have fallen into oblivion in the latter part of the last century, and are now scarcely preserved, except in the libraries of the curious.

NOTTON, a township in the parish of ROYSTON, wapentake of STAINCROSS, West riding of the county of YORK, 5 miles (N.) from Barnesley, containing 339 inhabitants.

NUFFIELD, a parish in the hundred of EWELME, county of OXFORD, 4¼ miles (E. by S.) from Wallingford, containing 198 inhabitants. The living is a rectory, in the archdeaconry and diocese of Oxford, rated in the king's books at £7. 16. 10½. The Rev. B. R. Fisher, and the Rev. W. Hopkins, were patrons in 1826. The church is dedicated to the Holy Trinity. A house of friars, of the order of the Holy Trinity, existed here before the 33rd of Edward III.

NUN-BURNHOLME, a parish comprising the township of Thorpe in the Street in the Holme Beacon, and the township of Nun-Burnholme in the Wilton-Beacon, division of the wapentake of HARTHILL, East riding of the county of YORK, and containing 240 inhabitants, of which number, 203 are in the township of Nun-Burnholme, 3½ miles (E. by S.) from Pocklington. The living is a rectory, in the archdeaconry of the East riding, and diocese of York, rated in the king's books at £9. 12. 6., and in the patronage of the Archbishop of York. The church is dedicated to St. James. Here was a small Benedictine nunnery, founded by an ancestor of Roger de Morley, Lord of Morpeth, who lived in the time of Henry III; wherein a short time previous to the dissolution were eight religious, it had a revenue of £10. 3. 3.

NUNEATON, a market town and parish, in the Atherstone division of the hundred of HEMLINGFORD, county of WARWICK, 18 miles (N. N. E.) from Warwick, and 100 (N. W. by W.) from London, containing, with the hamlets of Attleborough and Stockingford, 6610 inhabitants. The name of this place is derived from the river in its neighbourhood, Ea in Saxon signifying water, and from a priory established here, in the reign of Stephen, by Robert, Earl of Leicester, for nuns of the order of Fontevrault, in whose convents abroad there were sometimes nuns and monks in one establishment, but here there were only a prior, a prioress, and nuns, the prioress having supreme authority. In the reign of Henry III., a weekly market was granted to the prioress, and at the dissolution the revenue of the nunnery was £290. 15. 0½. The town is pleasantly situated on the river Anka, over which are two bridges, and consists principally of one long street, from which a cross street leads to the market-place; the houses are in general of mean appearance, though interspersed with some handsome modern buildings: it is neither paved nor lighted, but is well supplied with water. The principal source of occupation is riband-weaving for the London market, in which branch of manufacture French looms and machinery have been recently introduced, especially in the figured gauze riband. The Birmingham and Coventry canal passes by the north-west extremity of the town, and about two miles distant are coal mines: fine clay for pottery, and also manganese, are dug here, and there are quarries of freestone in the parish. The market is on Saturday; and fairs are held on May 14th, 15th, and 16th, for cattle and hardware; on February 18th, and October 31st, for horses and cattle; and a statute fair is held fourteen days before Michaelmas. Three constables are annually elected, and sworn in at the court leet for the town and hamlets; there is also a permanent constable: the town hall is a neat modern edifice of brick, containing in the upper story several apartments, of which one is used as a subscription news-room, and two others for a Sunday school.

The living is a vicarage, in the archdeaconry of Coventry, and diocese of Lichfield and Coventry, rated in the king's books at £24. 14. 7., and in the patronage of the Crown. The church, dedicated to St. Nicholas, is a fine structure, exhibiting portions in the various styles of English architecture, with a square embattled tower having pinnacles at the angles: the interior consists of a nave, chancel, and aisles separated by clustered columns and pointed arches; the roof is of oak, divided into panels, and richly ornamented with ribs and foliage. A proprietary chapel has been recently erected, and elegantly fitted up in the cathedral style, but it is not yet used. There are places of worship for Independents and Wesleyan Methodists. The free grammar school was founded in the 6th of Edward VI., and endowed with one hundred and three acres of land at Coventry for the management is vested in twelve trustees, who appoint the masters; the classical master has a salary of £50 per annum, with a house and garden; and the under master, who teaches reading, writing, and arithmetic, £45 per annum. An English free school, for forty boys and thirty girls, under the management of seven trustees, was founded in 1712, by the will of Mr. Richard Smith, of St. Ann's, Westminster, and endowed with ninety-four acres of land at Hartshill: the salary of the master is £15 per annum, and that of the mistress £7 per annum, with houses and gardens : a great augmentation of the endowment having taken place, from the discovery of mines of manganese on the estate, an additional annual gratuity of £10 is given to the master, and one of £8 to the mistress. In the churchyard is an almshouse for four aged persons, who receive each a small annual stipend : there is likewise a fund arising from land, for putting out poor apprentices. The site and ground-plan of the ancient monastery, with fragments of columns, and richly-moulded arches, together with a considerable portion of the walls of the main building, are yet visible ; the outer walls, which enclosed a spacious quadrangular area, are still standing on the east and north sides ; a considerable portion of the materials was used in repairing or rebuilding the church.

NUNEHAM-COURTNEY, a parish in the hundred of BULLINGTON, county of OXFORD, 6¼ miles (S. S. E.) from Oxford, containing 312 inhabitants. The living is a rectory, in the archdeaconry and diocese of Oxford, rated in the king's books at £15..6. 0½., and in the patronage of the Archbishop of York. The church, dedicated to All Saints, is an elegant building of the Ionic order, erected in 1764, at the expense of Simon, Earl of Harcourt. The parish is bounded on the west by the river Isis. Nuneham gives the inferior title of viscount to the Earl of Harcourt, who has a splendid mansion and park here.

NUNKEELING, a parish in the northern division of the wapentake of HOLDERNESS, East riding of the county of YORK, 10¾ miles (N. E.) from Beverley, containing, with the hamlet of Bewholme, 243 inhabitants. The living is a perpetual curacy, in the archdeaconry of the East riding, and diocese of York, endowed with £600 royal bounty, and £200 parliamentary grant, and in the patronage of R. R. Dixon and H. Hudson, Esqrs. A priory of Benedictine nuns, in honour of St. Mary Magdalene and St. Helen, was founded here in the reign of Stephen, by Agnes de Archis, the revenue of which, at the dissolution, was £50. 17. 2.

NUNNEY, a parish in the hundred of FROME, county of SOMERSET, 2¾ miles (S. W. by W.) from Frome, containing, with the hamlet of Trudox-hill, 1120 inhabitants. The living is a rectory, in the archdeaconry of Wells, and diocese of Bath and Wells, rated in the king's books at £15. 9. 4½. C. Theobald, Esq. was patron in 1817. The church, dedicated to St. Peter, is a handsome structure, and has lately received an addition of four hundred sittings, of which three hundred and fifty are free, the Incorporated Society for the enlargement of churches and chapels having granted £250 towards defraying the expense. There is a place of worship for Wesleyan Methodists. The Rev. Samuel Whitchurch, in 1797, left an annuity of £2. 10. in support of a Sunday school for both sexes. On the banks of the Frome is a small manufactory for agricultural implements. Here are the remains of a castle, erected by the family of De la Mere, and subsequently garrisoned for Charles I., during which it was besieged and taken, after a stout resistance, by the parliamentary forces, in September 1643. Near the site is an old decayed mansion, now occupied as a farm-house ; and on a steep hill in the neighbourhood are vestiges of a single intrenched Roman camp.

NUNNIKIRK, a township in the parish of NETHER-WITTON, western division of MORPETH ward, county of NORTHUMBERLAND, 9¾ miles (W.N.W.) from Morpeth, containing 13 inhabitants.

NUNNINGTON, a parish in the wapentake of RYE-DALE, North riding of the county of YORK, 4½ miles (S. E. by E.) from Helmsley, containing 418 inhabitants. The living is a discharged rectory, in the archdeaconry of Cleveland, and diocese of York, rated in the king's books at £13. 6. 8., and in the patronage of the Crown. The church is dedicated to All Saints. There is a place of worship for Wesleyan Methodists.

NUNRIDGE, a township in that part of the parish of MITFORD which is in the western division of MORPETH ward, county of NORTHUMBERLAND, 4¼ miles (W. by N.) from Morpeth, containing 39 inhabitants.

NUNTHORPE, a chapelry in the parish of AYTON, western division of the liberty of LANGBAURGH, North riding of the county of YORK, 4 miles (N. N. E.) from Stokesley, containing 110 inhabitants. The living is a perpetual curacy, in the archdeaconry of Cleveland, and diocese of York, endowed with £1000 royal bounty, and in the patronage of T. Simpson and T. Masterman, Esqrs. The chapel, dedicated to St. Mary, is much dilapidated. This place, anciently called Thorpe, received its distinguishing appellation about 1162, from a Cistercian nunnery, then removed hither from Hutton.

NUNTON, a chapelry in the parish and hundred of DOWNTON, county of WILTS, 3 miles (S. S. E.) from Salisbury. The population is returned with Bodenham.

NUNWICK, a joint township with Howgrave, in that part of the parish of RIPON which is in the liberty of RIPON, West riding of the county of YORK, 2½ miles (N. N. E.) from Ripon, containing, with Howgrave, 28 inhabitants. Here were formerly five stones, each eight feet high, and twenty in girt, enclosing a circular area.

NURSLING, otherwise NUTSHALLING, a parish in the hundred of BUDDLESGATE, Fawley division of county of SOUTHAMPTON, 3 miles (S.) from Romsey, containing 637 inhabitants. The living is a rectory, in the archdeaconry and diocese of Winchester, rated in the king's books at £13. 11. 10½., and in the patronage of the Bishop of Winchester. The church has a tower surmounted by a wooden spire. There is a place of worship for Wesleyan Methodists. The Andover canal runs through the parish. A Sunday school is partly supported with £1. 10. per annum, the bequest of the Rev. Robert Cramer. Nursling is within the jurisdiction of the Cheyney Court held at Winchester every Thursday, for the recovery of debts to any amount. Grove House, formerly a hunting-seat which belonged to Queen Elizabeth, has been converted into a private asylum for lunatics.

NURSTED, a parish in the hundred of TOLTING-TROUGH, lathe of AYLESFORD, county of KENT, 4¼ miles (S. by W.) from Gravesend, containing 33 inhabitants. The living is a discharged rectory, in the archdeaconry and diocese of Rochester, rated in the king's books at £4. 15., endowed with £200 private benefaction, and £200 royal bounty, and in the patronage of H. Edmeads, Esq. The church, dedicated to St. Mildred, is a small decayed building with a square western tower.

NURSTED, a tything in the parish of BURITON, hundred of FINCH-DEAN, Alton (South) division of the county of SOUTHAMPTON, 1½ mile (S.) from Petersfield, The population is returned with the parish.

NUTFIELD, a parish in the second division of the hundred of REIGATE, county of SURREY, 1¼ mile (W.) from Bletchingley, containing 707 inhabitants. The living is a rectory, in the archdeaconry of Surrey, and diocese of Winchester, rated in the king's books at £14. 14. 7., and in the patronage of the Principal and Fellows of Jesus College, Oxford. The church, dedicated to St. Peter and St. Paul, is partly in the early, and partly in the later, style of English architecture. Fullers' earth is found here in great quantities and of superior quality. In 1755, an earthen vessel was discovered, containing nine hundred coins of the Lower Empire.

NUTHALL, a parish in the southern division of the wapentake of BROXTOW, county of NOTTINGHAM, 4½ miles (N.W.) from Nottingham, containing, with the chapelry of Awsworth, 465 inhabitants. The living is a discharged rectory, in the archdeaconry of Nottingham, and diocese of York, rated in the king's books at £3. 14. 9½., and in the patronage of Robert Holden, Esq., whose elegant mansion, Nuthall-Temple, occupying a commanding site near the village, is built in imitation of the Villa Capra, at Vicenza in Italy, one of the most celebrated works of Palladio. The church is dedicated to St. Patrick. Richard Smedley, in 1744, gave certain land, directing the income to be applied in teaching twenty children.

NUTHAMPSTEAD, a hamlet in the parish of BARKWAY, hundred of EDWINSTREE, county of HERTFORD, 2½ miles (E. by S.) from Barkway, containing 222 inhabitants. Here was formerly a chapel, which has been long since demolished.

NUTHILL, formerly a parish in the southern division of the wapentake of HOLDERNESS, East riding of the county of YORK, 8½ miles (E. by N.) from Kingston upon Hull. The living is rated in the king's books at £2, as a rectory, in the archdeaconry of the East riding, and diocese, of York: but the church is in ruins, and there is now only one farm-house, which is assessed with the parish of Burstwick.

NUTHURST, a parish in the hundred of SINGLE-CROSS, rape of BRAMBER, county of SUSSEX, 3¾ miles (S. S.E.) from Horsham, containing 628 inhabitants. The living is a rectory, in the archdeaconry and diocese of Chichester, rated in the king's books at £10, and in the patronage of the Bishop of Chichester. The church, dedicated to St. Andrew, is in the decorated style of architecture.

NUTHURST, a hamlet in the parish of HAMPTON in ARDEN, Solihull division of the hundred of HEMLINGFORD, county of WARWICK, containing 76 inhabitants. The chapel is demolished.

NUTLEY, a parish in the hundred of BERMONDSPIT, Basingstoke division of the county of SOUTHAMPTON, 5 miles (S. S. W.) from Basingstoke, containing 130 inhabitants. The living is a perpetual curacy, annexed to the vicarage of Preston-Candover, in the archdeaconry and diocese of Winchester.

NYLAND, formerly a parish in the hundred of GLASTON-TWELVE-HIDES, county of SOMERSET, 6¼ miles (N. W. by W.) from Wells, containing, with the tything of Batcombe, 38 inhabitants. Here was anciently a church, dedicated to St. Andrew, which, in

670, was given by Kenewalch, King of the West Saxons, to the abbot of Glastonbury, to which parish Nyland is now considered to belong.

NYMETT (BROAD), a parish in the hundred of NORTH TAWTON with WINKLEY, county of DEVON, 1½ mile (W. S. W.) from Bow. The living is a rectory, in the archdeaconry of Barnstaple, and diocese of Exeter, rated in the king's books at £2. 4. 2., and in the patronage of Sir T. B. Lethbridge, Bart. This parish is very small, containing only fifty acres.

NYMETT-ROWLAND, a parish in the hundred of NORTH TAWTON with WINKLEY, county of DEVON, 4¾ miles (S.S.E.) from Chulmleigh, containing 102 inhabitants. The living is a discharged rectory, in the archdeaconry of Barnstaple, and diocese of Exeter, rated in the king's books at £6. 1. 3., endowed with £400 private benefaction, £400 royal bounty, and £300 parliamentary grant, and in the patronage of the Rev. H. Radford. The church is dedicated to St. Bartholomew.

NYMPSFIELD, a parish in the upper division of the hundred of BERKELEY, county of GLOUCESTER, 5¼ miles (E. by N.) from Dursley, containing 462 inhabitants. The living is a discharged rectory, in the archdeaconry and diocese of Gloucester, rated in the king's books at £11. 5. 0½., and in the patronage of the Crown. The church is dedicated to St. Margaret.

NYMPTON (BISHOP'S), a parish in the hundred of WITHERIDGE, county of DEVON, 3 miles (E. S. E.) from South Molton, containing 1096 inhabitants. The living is a vicarage, in the archdeaconry and diocese of Exeter, rated in the king's books at £20. 7. 3½., and in the patronage of the Bishop of Exeter. The church contains some elegant screen-work, and a rich monument to one of the Pollard family. Cattle fairs are held here on April 14th and October 20th.

NYMPTON (ST. GEORGE), a parish in the hundred of SOUTH MOLTON, county of DEVON, 2½ miles (S.S.W.) from South Molton, containing 259 inhabitants. The living is a rectory, in the archdeaconry of Barnstaple, and diocese of Exeter, rated in the king's books at £9. 19. 2., and in the patronage of Sir T. D. Acland, Bart.

NYMPTON (KING'S), a parish in the hundred of WITHERIDGE, county of DEVON, 3½ miles (N.) from Chulmleigh, containing 623 inhabitants. The living is a rectory, in the archdeaconry of Barnstaple, and diocese of Exeter, rated in the king's books at £28. 6. 8. The Rev. J. Southcombe was patron in 1820. The church, dedicated to St. James, has a handsome wooden screen. A considerable number of poor children are supported and educated at the expense of — Buller, Esq., of Nympton-park.

O.

OADBY, a parish in the hundred of GUTHLAXTON, county of LEICESTER, 3½ miles (S. E.) from Leicester, containing 856 inhabitants. The living is a discharged vicarage, in the archdeaconry of Leicester, and diocese of Lincoln, rated in the king's books at £8, endowed with £240 private benefaction, and £400 royal bounty; and in the patronage of Miss Wright. The church, dedicated to St. Peter, contains some fine specimens of ancient sculpture. There is a place of worship for Baptists.

OAKE, a parish in the hundred of TAUNTON and TAUNTON-DEAN, county of SOMERSET, 5¾ miles (W.) from Taunton, containing 189 inhabitants. The living is a rectory, in the archdeaconry of Taunton, and diocese of Bath and Wells, rated in the king's books at £11. 0. 5., and in the patronage of the Rev. Bowse Ford. The church is dedicated to St. Bartholomew. Six poor children are educated for a trifling rent-charge, the gift of the Rev. Francis Prowde.

OAKEN, a hamlet in that part of the parish of TETTENHALL which is in the northern division of the hundred of SEISDON, county of STAFFORD, 4¾ miles (N. W. by W.) from Wolverhampton, containing 244 inhabitants. It is within the jurisdiction of the royal peculiar court of Tettenhall.

OAKENGALE, a hamlet in the parish of SHIFF-NALL, Shiffnall division of the hundred of BRIMSTREE, county of SALOP. The population is returned with the chapelry of Priors-Lee.

OAKENSHAW, a hamlet in the parish of BIR-STALL, wapentake of MORLEY, West riding of the county of YORK, 3¾ miles (S. by E.) from Bradford. The population is returned with Clackheaton. The printing of muslins and calicoes is carried on here to a great extent.

OAKFORD, a parish in the hundred of WITHE-RIDGE, county of DEVON, 3¾ miles (W. by S.) from Bampton, containing 474 inhabitants. The living is a rectory, in the archdeaconry of Barnstaple, and diocese of Exeter, rated in the king's books at £24. The Bishop of Exeter, by lapse, presented in 1813. The church is dedicated to St. Peter. Gertrude Pyncombe, in 1730, left an annuity of £5 for teaching poor children of the parish.

OAKHAM, or OAKHAM-LORDSHOLD, a parish and market town, in the soke of OAKHAM, county of RUTLAND, of which it is the chief town, 95 miles (N. N. W.) from London, containing, with Oakham-Deanshold, which includes the chapelry of Barley-thorpe, 2160 inhabitants. This place is situated in the luxuriant vale of Catmose, so called from the woods with which it abounded (*Coet-maes* signifying, in the British language, a woody plain), and is supposed to have derived its name from the oaks which formerly grew in the vicinity. A castle, of which there are still some remains, was erected here soon after the Norman Conquest, by Walkelin de Ferrars, in relation to which a singular custom still prevails; but whether originating with the family of Ferrars, whose arms are three horse-shoes, or of later origin, has not been distinctly ascertained. Every peer of the realm, on first passing through the town, is compelled to give a shoe from the foot of one of his horses, which, upon his refusal, the bailiff of the lordship may take by force, or, in commutation, a sum of money for the purchase of a horse-shoe, to be nailed upon the castle gate, or placed in some part of the building. Among many of different sizes, in proportion to the sum paid for the purchase, and of which some are gilt and stamped with the donor's name, with which various parts of the castle are decorated, are those of Queen Elizabeth, the late Duke of York, and the late king, George IV., when Prince Regent. Richard II. having advanced Edward,

son of the Duke of York, to the earldom of Rutland, assigned to him the castle, which, in the reign of Henry VIII., was the baronial seat of Thomas, Lord Cromwell. Of the ancient building the hall only is remaining, in which the assizes are held, and the public business of the town and county is transacted; the other parts are in ruins. The houses are neatly built, and the inhabitants are amply supplied with water. The town formerly enjoyed the staple of wool, and many French merchants settled in it, of whose descendants several may still be traced among the present inhabitants. A silk-manufactory was established here about three years since, chiefly for weaving silk shag for covering hats; but the town is not at present distinguished for trade, though it possesses the advantage of a canal to Melton-Mowbray in Leicestershire, by which coal is brought from Derbyshire, and corn sent to Manchester and Liverpool. The market, which is well supplied with corn, is on Saturday; the fairs are on March 15th, May 6th, September 9th, under the original charters, and on February 4th, April 9th, June 2nd, July 16th, August 13th, October 15th, November 19th, and December 15th, which have been established within the last thirty years, and are principally for the sale of cattle. The town is within the jurisdiction of the county magistrates; and courts leet are held annually by the lord of the manor of Lordshold, and triennially by the Dean of Westminster, who is lord of the manor of Deanshold, for the election of parochial and other officers. The assizes and quarter sessions for the county, and the election of knights of the shire, take place in this town. The common gaol and house of correction for the county is a commodious edifice, containing seven wards, seven work-rooms, and the same number of day-rooms and airing-yards, for the classification of prisoners.

The living is a vicarage, with the perpetual curacies of Brooke and Langham, in the archdeaconry of Northampton, and diocese of Peterborough, rated in the king's books at £28. 3. 1½., and in the patronage of George Finch, Esq. The church, dedicated to All Saints, is a spacious structure, chiefly in the later style of English architecture, with a fine tower, surmounted by a lofty spire. There are places of worship for Baptists, the Society of Friends, Independents, and Wesleyan Methodists. The free grammar school was founded, about 1584, by the Rev. Robert Johnson, Archdeacon of Leicester, who also founded a similar school at Uppingham; these schools, to each of which an hospital for the relief and support of poor persons is annexed, were incorporated by Queen Elizabeth, who endowed them with certain alienated ecclesiastical property, producing an income of more than £3000 per annum, and placed them under the control of twenty-four governors, including the Bishops of London and Peterborough, the Deans of Westminster and Peterborough, the Archdeacon of Northampton, and the Masters of Trinity and St. John's Colleges, in Cambridge: these schools, the masters of which receive a salary of £150, and the ushers one of £120 each, are open gratuitously to all boys of the towns of Oakham and Uppingham, whose parents cannot afford to pay, and, upon moderate terms regulated by the governors, to others of those towns. There are belonging to them twenty exhibitions, of £40 per annum each, tenable for seven years, to any of the colleges of Oxford or Cambridge; four scholarships of £24 per annum each, in Emanuel College; four of £20 per annum each, in Sidney Sussex College; four of £13 per annum each, in Clare Hall; and four in St. John's College, Cambridge, founded by Archdeacon Johnson, in the gift of the master and senior fellows, with preference to boys from Oakham and Uppingham schools; and two exhibitions, of £40 per annum each, founded by W. Lovett, for the sons of graduated clergymen, who have been for three years in the schools of Oakham or Grantham. In the hospitals annexed to them were originally twenty-eight aged men, the number of whom has been augmented to one hundred, who receive each £10 per annum at their own dwellings, the buildings of the hospitals being occupied by the schoolmasters for the accommodation of boarders. The hospital of St. John and St. Anne, originally founded about the 22nd of Richard II., by Walter Dalby, for two chaplains and twelve aged men, and of which at the dissolution the revenue was £12. 12. 11., was refounded in the reign of Elizabeth, by Archdeacon Johnson, who enlarged the endowment: there are at present twenty aged men on this foundation, who receive each £6 per annum at their own dwellings, the buildings of the hospital, with the exception of a house for the warden, who has a salary of £15 per annum, and in which the sub-warden, whose salary is £10 per annum, at present resides, a chapel, and four separate tenements under one roof, having fallen to decay. A National school, established in 1816, is supported by subscription. There are also several charitable bequests for distribution among the poor. Geoffrey Hudson, a dwarf only three feet nine inches in height, was a native of Oakham; he was of mean parentage, but became page to Henrietta Maria, consort of Charles I., and during the civil war he was a captain of cavalry in the king's service; after which he went to France with his mistress, and there fought a duel and killed his antagonist; in the reign of Charles II., he suffered imprisonment as a Roman Catholic, on account of the pretended Popish plot; and being discharged, died in poverty about 1682.

Seal and Arms.

OAKHAMPTON, a borough, market town, and parish, having separate jurisdiction, though locally partly in the hundred of Black Torrington, but chiefly in that of Lifton, county of DEVON, 22 miles (W. by N.) from Exeter, and 198 (W. by S.) from London, containing with the hamlet of Kigbear, 2023 inhabitants. This place is interesting as having been the head of the earldom of Devon, and the seat of the hereditary county sheriffs, keepers of the castle of Exeter. This great barony was given by the Conqueror to Baldwin de Brioniis, one of his most faithful followers, who distinguished himself for courage and generalship at the battle of Hastings. The castle erected by this nobleman, was remarkable for its grandeur, of which there is abundant evidence in the venerable remains. The power and possessions of the barons were co-extensive: they exercised the right of capital punishment over eight manors; besides these, they held a great number in demesne, no less than one hundred and

sixty-four having been at one time occupied by inferior tenants. They acted as stewards at the installation of the bishops of the diocese, claiming on the occasion perquisites to a very great amount. They possessed also numerous advowsons, and were the patrons of several priories; holding three fees of the see of Exeter, and ninety-two by knights' service. In the reign of Henry II. this barony came, by marriage, to the Courtenay family, in which it continued till the reign of Edward IV., when Thomas, Earl of Devon, was beheaded at Pontefract, for taking part with Henry VI. at the battle of Towton Field, in 1461. From this period until the accession of Henry VII. it passed through divers hands, but in that reign it was restored to the Courtenays, of whom Henry having forfeited his life under a charge of treasonable correspondence, the park of Oakhampton was laid waste, and its noble castle reduced to ruins. During the great civil war, this town was twice visited by King Charles, and as often by his victorious enemy, Sir Thomas Fairfax. Oakhampton is situated in the lowest part of a valley, watered by a rapid stream, called the Ock, or Oke, over which there is a bridge, leading into the market-place. The forest of Dartmoor lies on the south and south-east, and the town is on all sides surrounded by hills. It is of mean appearance, but is a great thoroughfare between Exeter and Cornwall: there is a plentiful supply of water from pumps. The roads in the vicinity have been lately improved, a new road having been made to Plymouth about eight years since. The forest of Dartmoor affords pasturage to numerous flocks of sheep, the flesh of which, from the sweetness of the herbage, is esteemed for its superior flavour, in consequence of which, great numbers are sent hence to the London market. At the weekly market, which is held on Saturday, by prescription, there is an excellent supply of every necessary commodity, including fish and corn. Six annual fairs are held by charter, viz., second Tuesday after March 11th, May 14th, first Wednesday after July 6th, August 5th, first Tuesday after September 11th, and first Wednesday after October 11th: there are also great markets on the Saturday before Christmas, and on the Saturday after "Giglet's market," where the rustic swain, weary of his bachelorship, enjoys the privilege of self-introduction to any disengaged female who may attract his particular notice.

Oakhampton is governed by a mayor, recorder, justice, five principal burgesses, and eight assistants, aided by a town clerk and other officers. The mayor is chosen on the first Monday after Michaelmas-day, by the entire body, from two principal burgesses nominated by the late mayor: the principal burgesses are in all eight, the mayor, the late mayor, who is styled justice, and the town clerk, being included: the mayor, the late mayor, and the recorder, are justices of the peace: there is also a portreeve, who is appointed annually. The county magistrates have concurrent jurisdiction only as regards regulations for the poor: quarter sessions are held for the borough, but there are seldom any prisoners. A court of record formerly held for the recovery of debts not exceeding £30, has become obsolete. The freedom is acquired by birth and servitude; the eldest son alone becomes free at his father's death, though not unless born within the borough. The first return of members to parliament was in the reign of Edward I., and the next in the 7th of Edward II., after which there was an intermission till 1640, but from that period the returns have been regular. The right of election is vested in the freemen and proprietors of freeholds within the borough, about two hundred in number: the mayor is the returning officer. The living is a vicarage, in the archdeaconry of Totness, and diocese of Exeter, rated in the king's books at £20, and in the patronage of Albany Saville, Esq., as lord of the manor. The church, dedicated to All Saints, is an ancient edifice, about half a mile from the town, with a handsome square tower, surmounted with pinnacles, and having north and south porches. St. James' chapel, a small structure, was originally founded as a chantry, and now belongs to the corporation, divine service being performed in it during the sessions, and occasionally in Lent. There is a place of worship for Independents. Some small endowments have been left for the education of poor children; a school for boys, and another for girls, are principally supported by subscription. Two almshouses were founded, in 1586, by Mr. Richard Brock; and there is another, called the Wester almshouse. Several sums have been given for apprenticing poor boys and other purposes. The castle, situated about half a mile from the town, is a most interesting ruin, and is particularly striking when first observed on approaching from the south: it occupies the summit and declivity of a conoidal mount, so thickly clothed with trees that, although the ruins are of considerable extent and magnitude, the keep and a smaller fragment northward are alone visible from the road. This road is cut along the western side of a valley, from the bed of which the mount rises; the latter is close to the road, and its summit nearly on the same level.

OAKHAMPTON (MONK), a parish in the hundred of BLACK TORRINGTON, county of DEVON, 2¾ miles (E. N. E.) from Hatherleigh, containing 229 inhabitants. The living is a rectory, in the archdeaconry of Totness, and diocese of Exeter, rated in the king's books at £6. 14. 7., and in the patronage of Sir S. Northcote, Bart.

OAKINGHAM, county of BERKS.—See WOKINGHAM.

OAKINGTON, a parish partly in the hundred of CHESTERTON, but chiefly in that of NORTHSTOW, county of CAMBRIDGE, 5 miles (N. N. W.) from Cambridge, containing, with the hamlet of Westwick, 440 inhabitants. The living is a vicarage, in the archdeaconry and diocese of Ely, rated in the king's books at £4. 13. 1½., and in the patronage of the President and Fellows of Queen's College, Cambridge. The church is dedicated to St. Andrew. There is a place of worship for Baptists.

OAKLEY, a parish forming, with the parishes of Clapham and Milton-Ernest, a detached portion of the hundred of STODDEN, county of BEDFORD, 4 miles (N. W.) from Bedford, containing 486 inhabitants. The living is a discharged vicarage, in the archdeaconry of Bedford, and diocese of Lincoln, rated in the king's books at £8. 14. 9., endowed with £200 royal bounty, and in the patronage of the Provost and Fellows of Eton College. The church, dedicated to St. Mary, contains an ancient altar-tomb, and effigy in robes, of the family of Reynes.

OAKLEY, a parish in the hundred of ASHENDON, county of BUCKINGHAM, 6 miles (N. W. by N.) from Thame, containing 382 inhabitants. The living is a discharged vicarage, in the archdeaconry of Buckingham, and diocese of Lincoln, rated in the king's books at £5. 17. 1. Sir J. Aubrey, Bart. was patron in 1810. The church, dedicated to St. Mary, was formerly the mother church of Brill, Borstall, and Addingrave; the two first have been made distinct parishes; the last had a chapel of ease, which has gone to decay. A rentcharge of £25, upon the parish charity estate, is applied to the education of poor children.

OAKLEY, a township in that part of the parish of CROXALL which is in the northern division of the hundred of OFFLOW, county of STAFFORD, 6¼ miles (N. by W.) from Tamworth, containing 31 inhabitants.

OAKLEY, a township in that part of the parish of MUCKLESTON which is in the northern division of the hundred of PIREHILL, county of STAFFORD, 3¼ miles (N. E. by N.) from Drayton in Hales, containing 94 inhabitants.

OAKLEY, a parish in the hundred of HARTISMERE, county of SUFFOLK, 3 miles (N.N.E.) from Eye, containing 403 inhabitants. The living is a rectory, annexed to that of Broome, in the archdeaconry of Sudbury, and diocese of Norwich, rated in the king's books at £9. 4. 9½. The church is dedicated to St. Nicholas.

OAKLEY (CHURCH), a parish in the hundred of CHUTELY, Kingsclere division of the county of SOUTHAMPTON, 4½ miles (W. by S.) from Basingstoke, containing 246 inhabitants. The living is a rectory, in the archdeaconry and diocese of Winchester, rated in the king's books at £11. 13. 11½., and in the patronage of the Provost and Fellows of Queen's College, Oxford. The church is dedicated to St. Leonard. George Wither, in 1666, gave certain lands and tenements, also a rentcharge of £8, in support of a school for the education of eight poor boys; and Gilbert Wither, in 1676, gave a rent-charge of 40s., to be applied in apprenticing boys. William Warham, successively Bishop of London, and Archbishop of Canterbury, and an eminent statesman, was born here; he died in 1532.

OAKLEY (GREAT), a parish in the hundred of TENDRING, county of ESSEX, 7 miles (S. E. by E.) from Manningtree, containing 990 inhabitants. The living is a rectory, in the archdeaconry of Colchester, and diocese of London, rated in the king's books at £23, and in the patronage of the Master and Fellows of St. John's College, Cambridge. The church is dedicated to All Saints. There is a place of worship for Wesleyan Methodists. This parish, with the other Oakleys, lies contiguous to an inlet of the North sea, opposite Pewit island, and is celebrated as the scene of a bloody battle fought between King Ethelwolf and the Danes. It had formerly a castle, the remains of the keep and moat of which are still visible.

OAKLEY (GREAT), a parish in the hundred of CORBY, county of NORTHAMPTON, 5 miles (N.) from Kettering, containing 183 inhabitants. The living is a perpetual curacy, in the archdeaconry of Northampton, and diocese of Peterborough, and in the patronage of Sir Richard Brooke, Bart. The church is dedicated to St. Michael.

OAKLEY (LITTLE), a parish in the hundred of TENDRING, county of ESSEX, 4½ miles (S. W. by W.)

from Harwich, containing 262 inhabitants. The living is a rectory, in the archdeaconry of Colchester, and diocese of London, rated in the king's books at £13. 11. 0½. Thomas Scott, Esq. was patron in 1800. The church is dedicated to St. Mary.

OAKLEY (LITTLE), a parish in the hundred of CORBY, county of NORTHAMPTON, 5½ miles (N. N. E.) from Kettering, containing 121 inhabitants. The living is a rectory, in the archdeaconry of Northampton, and diocese of Peterborough, rated in the king's books at £7. 7. 6., and in the patronage of the Duke of Buccleuch. The church is dedicated to St. Peter.

OAKLEY (PARVA), in the hundred of HARTISMERE, county of SUFFOLK, 2¾ miles (N. N. E.) from Eye. This was formerly a distinct parish, which was consolidated with Oakley Magna in 1449. The church, now in ruins, was dedicated to St. Peter.

OAKMERE, a township in the parish of DELAMERE, first division of the hundred of EDDISBURY, county palatine of CHESTER, containing 90 inhabitants.

OAKOVER, a parish in the northern division of the hundred of TOTMONSLOW, county of STAFFORD, 2½ miles (N. W. by W.) from Ashbourn, containing 69 inhabitants. The living is a perpetual curacy, in the diocese of Lichfield and Coventry, and in the patronage of H. F. Okeover, Esq.: it is exempt from the jurisdiction of the Archdeacon, but there is no official. The church, dedicated to All Saints, is a small ancient structure, completely overgrown with ivy, eglantine, and roses. The river Dove runs through the parish. In the park are several tumuli, and in the neighbourhood a square intrenchment, all of them supposed to be of Roman origin. This parish is entitled to partake in the benefit of a bequest by Rowland Okeover, in 1727, now applied for clothing and apprenticing poor children. Oakover is in the honour of Tutbury, duchy of Lancaster, and within the jurisdiction of a court of pleas held at Tutbury every third Tuesday, for the recovery of debts under 40*s*.

OAKSEY, a parish in the hundred of MALMESBURY, county of WILTS, 5½ miles (N. E.) from Malmesbury, containing 385 inhabitants. The living is a rectory, in the archdeaconry of Wilts, and diocese of Salisbury, rated in the king's books at £6. 8. 4. Thomas Ryder, Esq. was patron in 1808. The church is dedicated to All Saints.

OAKSHOT, a hamlet in the parish of STOKE D'ABERNON, second division of the hundred of ELMBRIDGE, county of SURREY, 2¼ miles (N. N. W.) from Leatherhead. The population is returned with the parish.

OAKTHORPE, a hamlet partly in the parish of MEASHAM, partly in that of STRETTON en le FIELDS, but chiefly in that of CHURCH-GRESLEY, hundred of REPTON and GRESLEY, county of DERBY, 3¾ miles (S. W. by S.) from Ashby de la Zouch, containing, with the hamlet of Donisthorpe, 732 inhabitants. There are places of worship for Baptists and Wesleyan Methodists. Oakthorpe is in the honour of Tutbury, duchy of Lancaster, and within the jurisdiction of a court of pleas held at Tutbury every third Tuesday, for the recovery of debts under 40*s*.

OAKWOOD, a chapelry in the parish, and first division of the hundred, of WOTTON, county of SURREY, 9 miles (S. S. W.) from Dorking. The population is returned with the parish. The living is a perpetual curacy, in the archdeaconry of Surrey, and diocese of Winchester, endowed with £400 private benefaction, and £400 royal bounty, and in the patronage of Sir J. Evelyn, Bart. The chapel is dedicated to St. John the Baptist.

OARE, a chapelry in the parish of CHIEVELEY, hundred of FAIRCROSS, county of BERKS, 5½ miles (N. N. E.) from Speenhamland. The population is returned with the parish.

OARE, a parish in the hundred of FAVERSHAM, lathe of SCRAY, county of KENT, 1½ mile (N. W. by N.) from Faversham, containing 197 inhabitants. The living is a discharged perpetual curacy, in the archdeaconry and diocese of Canterbury, endowed with £400 private benefaction, and £800 royal bounty, and in the patronage of the Archbishop of Canterbury. The church is dedicated to St. Peter. The parish is bounded on the north-east by the Swale, over which there is a ferry to Harty Island.

OARE, a parish in the hundred of CARHAMPTON, county of SOMERSET, 12 miles (W.) from Minehead, containing 66 inhabitants. The living is a discharged rectory, in the archdeaconry of Taunton, and diocese of Bath and Wells, rated in the king's books at £4. 17. 6., endowed with £400 private benefaction, £400 royal bounty, and £300 parliamentary grant. Mrs. Oliver and others were patrons in 1809. The church is dedicated to St. Mary.

OATHILL, a tything in the parish of WAYFORD, hundred of CREWKERNE, county of SOMERSET, 3 miles (S. W.) from Crewkerne. The population is returned with the parish.

OBLEY, a joint township with Clunbury, in the parish of CLUNBURY, hundred of PURSLOW, county of SALOP, 9 miles (S.) from Bishop's Castle. The population is returned with Clunbury.

OBORNE, a parish in the hundred of SHERBORNE, Sherborne division of the county of DORSET, 1¼ mile (N. E. by E.) from Sherborne, containing 123 inhabitants. The living is a discharged vicarage, in the peculiar jurisdiction of the Dean of Salisbury, rated in the king's books at £6. 5. 10., and in the patronage of Earl Digby. The church is dedicated to St. Cuthbert.

OBTHORPE, a hamlet in the parish of THURLBY, wapentake of NESS, parts of KESTEVEN, county of LINCOLN, containing 12 inhabitants.

OBY, a parish in the western division of the hundred of FLEGG, county of NORFOLK, 3½ miles (N. by E.) from Acle. The population is returned with Ashby. The living is a rectory, with that of Ashby, in the archdeaconry and diocese of Norwich.

OCCANEY, an extra-parochial district, in the upper division of the wapentake of CLARO, West riding of the county of YORK, 3½ miles (N.) from Knaresborough. The population is returned with Walkingham Hill.

OCCLESTONE, a township in that part of the parish of MIDDLEWICH which is in the hundred of NORTHWICH, county palatine of CHESTER, 3½ miles (S. S. W.) from Middlewich, containing 94 inhabitants.

OCCOLD, a parish in the hundred of HARTISMERE, county of SUFFOLK, 2½ miles (S. by E.) from Eye, containing 461 inhabitants. The living is a rectory, in the archdeaconry of Sudbury, and diocese of Norwich, rated in the king's books at £19. 1. 5½., and in the patronage of George Thomas, Esq. The church is dedicated to St. Nicholas.

OCKBROOK, a parish in the hundred of MORLESTON and LITCHURCH, county of DERBY, 5½ miles (E. by S.) from Derby, containing 1203 inhabitants. The living is a perpetual curacy, in the archdeaconry of Derby, and diocese of Lichfield and Coventry, endowed with £800 private benefaction, £600 royal bounty, and £300 parliamentary grant, and in the patronage of John Pares, Esq. The church, dedicated to All Saints, has portions in the Norman style of architecture, and some of later date. There is a place of worship for Wesleyan Methodists. A National school, erected in 1816, is attended by about two hundred and fifty children. The rivers Derwent and Trent, and the Derby canal, run through the parish. On the banks of the former are extensive cotton-mills, affording employment to upwards of three hundred of the poor in the manufacture of bobbin and lace thread for the Buckingham, Nottingham, and Loughborough markets. At a short distance from the village is a considerable establishment of the Moravians, founded in 1750 : the principal buildings stand in a regular line, and consist of the single sisters' house, containing thirty or forty females, who are employed in fine muslin work, a smaller house for about the same number of single men, and between them a commodious chapel, and a boarding-school for fifty boys and thirty girls.

OCKENDON (NORTH), a parish in the hundred of CHAFFORD, county of ESSEX, 4½ miles (E.S.E.) from Hornchurch, containing 325 inhabitants. The living is a rectory, in the archdeaconry of Essex, and diocese of London, rated in the king's books at £16. 13. 4, and in the patronage of Sir Charles Hulse, Bart. The church is dedicated to St. Mary Magdalene.

OCKENDON (SOUTH), a parish in the hundred of CHAFFORD, county of ESSEX, 4¼ miles (N.N.W.) from Grays-Thurrock, containing 777 inhabitants. The living is a rectory, in the archdeaconry of Essex, and diocese of London, rated in the king's books at £33. 6. 8. G. Leith, Esq. was patron in 1819. The church, dedicated to St. Nicholas, has a circular embattled tower. There is a place of worship for Wesleyan Methodists. Some Saxon silver coins have been found in the parish, and vestiges of a Roman road may be traced. There is a building, called Furnace House, where iron was formerly smelted.

OCKHAM, a parish in the second division of the hundred of WOKING, county of SURREY, 1 mile (E.) from Ripley, containing 565 inhabitants. The living is a rectory, in the archdeaconry of Surrey, and diocese of Winchester, rated in the king's books at £11. 2. 1, and in the patronage of Lord King. The church, dedicated to All Saints, has portions in the decorated, and some in the later English, style.

OCKLEY, a parish in the first division of the hundred of WOTTON, county of SURREY, 6¼ miles (S. by W.) from Dorking, containing 642 inhabitants. The living is a rectory, in the archdeaconry of Surrey, and diocese of Winchester, rated in the king's books at £16. 5. 2½., and in the patronage of the Master and Fellows of Clare Hall, Cambridge. The church, dedicated to St. Margaret, has lately received an addition of one hundred and fifty-four free sittings, the Incorpo-

rated Society for the enlargement of churches and chapels having granted £100 towards defraying the expense. Eight children are taught for £8. 8. a year, the produce of £100, bequeathed by Elizabeth Eversted in 1721. On Holmbury Hill are vestiges of a Roman encampment ; and a battle is stated to have taken place here, in 851, between the Saxons and the Danes, which terminated in the defeat of the former, with great slaughter.

OCLE-LIVERS, an extra-parochial liberty, in the hundred of BROXASH, county of HEREFORD, 6½ miles (N.E.) from Hereford. Here was a priory of Benedictine monks, a cell to that of Lira, in Normandy, founded about 1160.

OCLE - PITCHARD, a parish in the hundred of BROXASH, county of HEREFORD, 7½ miles (N. E. by E.) from Hereford, containing 224 inhabitants. The living is a discharged vicarage, in the archdeaconry and diocese of Hereford, rated in the king's books at £4. 19., endowed with £200 private benefaction, and £200 royal bounty, and in the patronage of the Representatives of the Rev. J. Lilly. The church is dedicated to St. James.

OCTON, a township in the parish of THWING, wapentake of DICKERING, East riding of the county of YORK, 8 miles (W.) from Bridlington. The population is returned with the parish.

OCTON - GRANGE, a township in the parish of THWING, wapentake of DICKERING, East riding of the county of YORK, 9 miles (W. N. W.) from Bridlington. The population is returned with the parish.

ODCOMBE, a parish in the hundred of HOUNDSBOROUGH, BERWICK, and COKER, county of SOMERSET, 3¼ miles (W. by S.) from Yeovil, containing 540 inhabitants. The living is a rectory, in the archdeaconry of Wells, and diocese of Bath and Wells, rated in the king's books at £15. 9. 9½., and in the patronage of the Dean and Canons of Christ Church, Oxford. The church is dedicated to St. Peter and St. Paul. Humphrey Hody, an eminent divine, was born here in 1659; he died in 1706.

ODDINGLEY, a parish in the lower division of the hundred of OSWALDSLOW, county of WORCESTER, 3 miles (S.) from Droitwich, containing 168 inhabitants. The living is a discharged rectory, in the archdeaconry and diocese of Worcester, rated in the king's books at £4. 19. 4½., and in the patronage of J. H. Galton, Esq. The church is dedicated to St. James. A charity school is supported by voluntary subscription.

ODDINGTON, a parish in the upper division of the hundred of SLAUGHTER, county of GLOUCESTER, 2½ miles (E.) from Stow on the Wold, containing 458 inhabitants. The living is a rectory, in the archdeaconry and diocese of Gloucester, rated in the king's books at £21. 7. 1., and in the patronage of the Precentor of the Cathedral Church of York. The church has a Norman door, but the rest of the building is of later date ; it has recently received an addition of sixty free sittings, the Incorporated Society for the enlargement of churches and chapels having granted £50 towards defraying the expense. Edward Chamberlayne, an English historian, was born here in 1616 ; he died in 1703.

ODDINGTON, a parish in the hundred of PLOUGHLEY, county of OXFORD, 7 miles (S. W. by S.) from

Bicester, containing 166 inhabitants. The living is a rectory, in the archdeaconry and diocese of Oxford, rated in the king's books at £12. 16. 0½., and in the patronage of the President and Fellows of Trinity College, Oxford. The church is dedicated to St. Andrew. The river Ray runs through the parish.

ODELL, a parish in the hundred of WILLEY, county of BEDFORD, 1¼ mile (N. E by N.) from Harrold, containing 439 inhabitants. The living is a rectory, in the archdeaconry of Bedford, and diocese of Lincoln, rated in the king's books at £19. T. Alston, Esq. was patron in 1798. The church is dedicated to All Saints. This place formerly possessed a market, granted to William Fitzwarren, in 1222, which has been long disused; but a fair is held on the Thursday and Friday in Whitsun-week. Odell castle, the seat of the Alston family, a small part of which constitutes the remains of the ancient building of the same name, stands conspicuously on an eminence, commanding a fine view of the river Ouse.

ODESTONE, a hamlet in the parish of SHACKERSTONE, hundred of SPARKENHOE, county of LEICESTER, 3½ miles (N. by W.) from Market-Bosworth, containing 216 inhabitants.

ODIHAM, a market-town and parish in the hundred of ODIHAM, Basingstoke division of the county of SOUTHAMPTON, 26 miles (N. E.) from Winchester, 37 (N. E.) from Southampton, and 40 (W. S. W.) from London, containing, with the chapelry of Lyss-Turney, and the tythings of Hillside, Murrell-Green, Rye with Stapeley, and North Warnborough, 2983 inhabitants. This place was formerly a free borough belonging to the Bishops of Winchester; and the castle, which stood about a mile north-west of the town, was built before the time of King John, in whose reign it became celebrated for its resistance to the army of Louis, the Dauphin of France, having sustained a siege for fifteen days, though garrisoned only by three officers and ten private soldiers. That monarch was here a few days before the signing of Magna Charta, attended by a retinue of not more than seven knights. In the 27th of Edward I., the town, park, and hundred, were granted to the queen, as part of her dower. In the reign of Edward III., David Bruce, King of Scotland, having been made prisoner at the battle of Neville's Cross, was confined in this fortress for eleven years. The town is pleasantly situated on the side of a chalk hill, and from the neighbouring chalk-pits the adjacent country is supplied with manure, the means of conveying which is afforded by the Basingstoke canal, which passes about a mile north-east of the town. A book-club has been established about forty years, and races were formerly held here. The manufacture of cotton stockings was carried on a few years since, but at present there is no trade deserving particular notice. In some parts of the parish hops are cultivated. The market is on Tuesday; and fairs are held on the Saturday preceding Mid-Lent Sunday, and July 31st, for horses and cattle. The county magistrates hold a meeting every fortnight; and constables are annually chosen at the court leet of the manor, held at Easter: a court for the recovery of small debts has fallen into disuse. Odiham was summoned to send members to parliament in the reigns of Edward I. and Edward II., but never made any return.

The living is a vicarage, with the perpetual curacy of Grewell, in the archdeaconry and diocese of Winchester, rated in the king's books at £23. 11. 5½., and in the patronage of the Chancellor of the Cathedral Church of Salisbury. The church, which is dedicated to All Saints, is a large ancient building of brick, coated with stucco. There are places of worship for those in the Connexion of the late Countess of Huntingdon, and Independents. A free school, for the education of twenty boys, was founded in 1694, by Robert May, and endowed with £600 for its support, and £200 for apprenticing the children; the funds were subsequently augmented by a rent-charge of £10 for five additional children, and an addition of £20 per annum to the apprentice fund, the bequest of James Zouch, Esq., but this benefaction has become much reduced in value from losses: about twenty-three children are educated, and three on an average are annually apprenticed. A National school is supported by subscription, and another school, in which the children are partly clothed, is supported by dissenters. Near the church is an almshouse, founded and endowed by Sir Edward More, in 1623, with property producing about £80 per annum, for the support of eight poor widowers and widows; and there are apartments for two more poor persons, with stipends from other benefactions. Vestiges of the keep of the ancient castle are visible about a mile north-west of the town; and the remains of a royal residence have been converted into a farm-house, still called Palace Gate. William Lilly, the grammarian and astrologer, was born here about 1468.

ODSTOCK, a parish in the hundred of CAWDEN and CADWORTH, county of WILTS, 3 miles (S.) from Salisbury, containing 133 inhabitants. The living is a rectory, in the archdeaconry and diocese of Salisbury, rated in the king's books at £11. 17. 11., and in the patronage of the Earl of Radnor. The church is dedicated to St. Mary.

ODSTONE, a tything in the parish of ASHBURY, hundred of SHRIVENHAM, county of BERKS, containing 31 inhabitants.

OFFCHURCH, a parish in the Kenilworth division of the hundred of KNIGHTLOW, county of WARWICK, 5 miles (E. by N.) from Warwick, containing 337 inhabitants. The living is a discharged vicarage, in the archdeaconry of Coventry, and diocese of Lichfield and Coventry, rated in the king's books at £7. 7. 6., endowed with £200 private benefaction, and £200 royal bounty. T. W. Knightley, Esq. was patron in 1805. The church is dedicated to St. Gregory. The Warwick and Napton canal intersects the old Roman Fosse-way on the southern boundary of the parish. In the Anglo-Saxon times this was a place of some importance, and during the Octarchy, Offa, King of Mercia, made it his residence.

OFFCOAT, a joint liberty with Underwood, in that part of the parish of ASHBOURN which is in the hundred of WIRKSWORTH, county of DERBY, containing, with Underwood, 341 inhabitants. It is in the honour of Tutbury, duchy of Lancaster, and within the jurisdiction of a court of pleas held at Tutbury every third Tuesday, for the recovery of debts under 40s.

OFFENHAM, a parish in the upper division of the hundred of BLACKENHURST, county of WORCESTER, 2½ miles (N.E. by N.) from Evesham, containing 342 inhabitants. The living is a discharged perpetual curacy, annexed to that of Littleton, in the archdeaconry and diocese of Worcester, rated in the king's books at £6. 11. 5½. The church is dedicated to St. Milburgh. Offenham took its name from the Saxon King, Offa, who had a palace here; it was afterwards possessed by the abbots of Evesham, and became their favourite residence, some remains of the boundary walls being still discernible. The navigable river Avon is here crossed by a ferry. A small school is supported by the income arising from £110, left by Mr. Brent.

OFFERTON, a township in the parish of Stockport, hundred of Macclesfield, county palatine of Chester, 2½ miles (S.E. by E.) from Stockport, containing 401 inhabitants. There is a trifling sum, left by Richard Dodge in 1765, for teaching two poor children whose parents do not receive parochial relief.

OFFERTON, a hamlet in the parish of Hope, hundred of High Peak, county of Derby, 5½ miles (N.E.) from Tideswell, containing 40 inhabitants.

OFFERTON, a township in the parish of Houghton le Spring, northern division of Easington ward, county palatine of Durham, 4 miles (W.S.W.) from Sunderland, containing 198 inhabitants. The ancient manor-house has been converted into a public-house.

OFFHAM, a parish in the hundred of Larkfield, lathe of Aylesford, county of Kent, 3¼ miles (E.S.E.) from Wrotham, containing 274 inhabitants. The living is a discharged rectory, in the archdeaconry and diocese of Rochester, rated in the king's books at £6, endowed with £200 private benefaction, and £200 royal bounty, and in the patronage of the Crown. The church, dedicated to St. Michael, is principally in the early style of English architecture, with a tower steeple. The great Roman military way, from the Weald to London, crosses this parish. Jack Straw, the rebel in the reign of Richard II., is said to have been born at Pepingstraw in this parish. Offham-green is remarkable for having on it the ancient instrument of amusement called a quintin, which the lord of the manor is obliged to preserve.

OFFHAM, a tything in the parish of Southstoke, hundred of Avisford, rape of Arundel, county of Sussex, 1¾ mile (N.E.) from Arundel. The population is returned with the parish.

OFFLEY, a parish in the hundred of Hitchin and Pirton, county of Hertford, 3¼ miles (W.S.W.) from Hitchin, containing 873 inhabitants. The living is a discharged vicarage, in the archdeaconry of Huntingdon, and diocese of Lincoln, rated in the king's books at £9, and in the patronage of the Marquis of Salisbury. The church, dedicated to St. Mary Magdalene, has a very handsome chancel, erected, in 1777, by Dame Sarah Salusbury, who also left £1000, which has been applied to the foundation and support of a charity school; the children, seventy in number, are partly clothed. Mrs. Alice Pigott, in 1724, endowed the living with a rent-charge of £20 in aid of the vicarial tithes, and bequeathed another of £10 for apprenticing two poor children. Offley received its name from King Offa, who resided, and is said to have died, here. In a wood at Highdowns are several barrows and dikes, supposed to be of British origin.

OFFLEY (HIGH), a parish in the northern division of the hundred of Pirehill, county of Stafford, comprising the townships of Loynton and High Offley, and containing 609 inhabitants, of which number, 569 are in the township of High Offley, 4¼ miles (S.W.) from Eccleshall. The living is a vicarage, in the peculiar jurisdiction of the Prebendary of Offley and Flixton in the Cathedral Church of Lichfield, rated in the king's books at £6. 6. 0½., and in the patronage of the Bishop of Lichfield and Coventry. The church is dedicated to St. Mary. The Birmingham and Liverpool canal passes through the parish.

OFFLOW (BISHOP'S), a township in the parish of Abdaston, northern division of the hundred of Pirehill, county of Stafford, 3 miles (W.) from Eccleshall, containing 210 inhabitants. Eight poor children are taught for £4 a year, the bequest of John Wright, in 1724.

OFFORD-CLUNY, a parish in the hundred of Toseland, county of Huntingdon, 5 miles (N.N.E.) from St. Neots, containing 237 inhabitants. The living is a rectory, in the archdeaconry of Huntingdon, and diocese of Lincoln, rated in the king's books at £19. 2. 1., and in the patronage of the Bishop of London. The church is dedicated to All Saints. A charity school is endowed with £30, the bequest of Dr. Newcome, in 1763.

OFFORD-DARCY, a parish in the hundred of Toseland, county of Huntingdon, 4½ miles (N.N.E.) from St. Neots, containing 214 inhabitants. The living is a rectory, in the archdeaconry of Huntingdon, and diocese of Lincoln, rated in the king's books at £15. 2. 8½., and in the patronage of G. Thornhill, Esq. The church is dedicated to St. Peter.

OFFTON, a parish in the hundred of Bosmere and Claydon, county of Suffolk, 5 miles (E.) from Bildeston, containing 328 inhabitants. The living is a discharged rectory, with that of Little Bricett, in the archdeaconry of Suffolk, and diocese of Norwich, rated in the king's books at £7. 16. 0½. J. G. Sparrow, Esq. was patron in 1796. The church is dedicated to St. Mary.

OFFWELL, a parish in the hundred of Colyton, county of Devon, 2½ miles (E.S.E) from Honiton, containing 379 inhabitants. The living is a rectory, in the archdeaconry and diocese of Exeter, rated in the king's books at £14. 3. 6½., and in the patronage of the Rev. G. B. Coplestone.

OGBOURN (ST. ANDREW), a parish in the hundred of Selkley, county of Wilts, 2 miles (N.) from Marlborough, containing 415 inhabitants. The living is a vicarage, with Temple Rockley, in the peculiar jurisdiction and patronage of the Dean and Canons of Windsor, rated in the king's books at £15. 2. 11. At Rockley the knights of St. John of Jerusalem had formerly a preceptory: there was also a chapel of ease, dedicated to St. Leonard, but it has been long demolished. In the neighbourhood are several mineral springs. The remains of Barberry Castle, a large British encampment, may still be traced; they are partly in this parish, but chiefly in that of Wroughton.

OGBOURN (ST. GEORGE), a parish in the hundred of Selkley, county of Wilts, 3¼ miles (N.) from Marlborough, containing 493 inhabitants. The living is a vicarage, in the archdeaconry of Wilts, and diocese of Salisbury, rated in the king's books at £14. 5. 10., and in the patronage of the Dean and Canons of Windsor.

A priory of Benedictine monks, subordinate to the abbey of Bec-Herlowyn in Normandy, was founded here about 1149, and became the richest and principal cell to that house in England. In 556, a most sanguinary battle between the Britons and the West Saxons was fought here, which lasted a whole day, and ended in the total rout of the Britons, and the capture of their neighbouring fortress, Barberry Castle, in the vicinity of which numerous barrows are still visible.

OGLE, or OCLE, a township in the parish of WHALTON, western division of CASTLE ward, county of NORTHUMBERLAND, 7¾ miles (S. W.) from Morpeth, containing 148 inhabitants. There are slight remains of the once strong fortress of Ogle castle, in which David, King of Scotland, was confined after the battle of Nevill's Cross.

OGLY-HAY, an extra-parochial district, in the southern division of the hundred of OFFLOW, county of STAFFORD, containing 23 inhabitants. The Essington and Wyrley canal passes through this place.

OGWELL (EAST), a parish forming, with the parish of West Ogwell, a distinct portion of the hundred of WONFORD, county of DEVON, 1½ mile (W. S. W.) from Newton-Abbots, containing 295 inhabitants. The living is a rectory, in the archdeaconry and diocese of Exeter, rated in the king's books at £19. 3. 9., and in the patronage of P. J. Taylor, Esq. The church is dedicated to St. Bartholomew. Richard Reynell, in 1735, gave certain land, the income arising from which, about £10 a year, is applied in teaching twenty-eight children. Here are two almshouses, founded by Lady Lucy Reynell.

OGWELL (WEST), a parish forming, with the parish of East Ogwell, a distinct portion of the hundred of WONFORD, county of DEVON, 2½ miles (W. S. W.) from Newton-Abbots, containing 42 inhabitants. The living is a discharged rectory, in the archdeaconry and diocese of Exeter, rated in the king's books at £7. 2. 11., and in the patronage of P. J. Taylor, Esq. The church contains three ancient stone stalls.

OKEFORD (CHILD), a parish in the hundred of REDLANE, Sturminster division of the county of DORSET, 6½ miles (N. W. by N.) from Blandford-Forum, containing 694 inhabitants. The living consists of two rectories, Superior and Inferior, in the archdeaconry of Dorset, and diocese of Bristol, the former rated in the king's books at £6. 13. 4., and the latter at £7, and in the patronage of the Rev. Charles Edward North. The church is dedicated to St. Nicholas. The navigable river Stour runs through the parish. On Hameldon Hill are traces of an extensive intrenchment, in which Roman coins have been found.

OKEFORD-FITZPAINE, a parish in the hundred of STURMINSTER-NEWTON-CASTLE, Sturminster division of the county of DORSET, 7½ miles (N. W. by W.) from Blandford-Forum, containing 499 inhabitants. The living is a rectory, in the archdeaconry of Dorset, and diocese of Bristol, rated in the king's books at £21. 12. 8½., and in the patronage of Lord Rivers. The church is dedicated to St. Andrew. The navigable river Stour runs through the parish. Okeford was anciently possessed by the family of Nichole, one of whom obtained the privilege of a market to be held here; from them it came to the Fitz-Paynes, and, by a corruption of that name, is vulgarly called Fipenny-Okeford. Several British silver coins were found here in 1753. In the

neighbourhood is Banbury Hill, a circular camp with a single trench.

OKENEY cum PETSOE, a parish in the hundred of NEWPORT, county of BUCKINGHAM, 2 miles (S. S. E.) from Olney. The population is returned with Emberton. The living is a discharged rectory, with that of Petsoe, in the archdeaconry of Buckingham, and diocese of Lincoln, rated in the king's books at £2. 17. 6. The church, which was dedicated to St. Martin, has been long since demolished. The parish is assessed with the adjoining parish of Emberton.

OLAVE (ST.) MARY-GATE, a parish partly in the liberty of ST. PETER of YORK, East riding, and partly in the wapentake of BULMER, North riding, of the county of YORK, comprising the township of St. Olave Mary-Gate, and part of those of Clifton and Rawcliffe, and containing 992 inhabitants, of which number, 666 are in the township of St. Olave Mary-Gate, adjacent to the north-western side of the city of York. The living is a perpetual curacy, in the archdeaconry and diocese of York.

OLD, or WOLD, a parish in the hundred of ORLINGBURY, county of NORTHAMPTON, 6½ miles (S. W. by W.) from Kettering, containing 450 inhabitants. The living is a rectory, in the archdeaconry of Northampton, and diocese of Peterborough, rated in the king's books at £18. 12. 8½., and in the patronage of the Principal and Fellows of Brasenose College, Oxford. The church is dedicated to St. Andrew. There is a place of worship for Independents.

OLDBERROW, a parish forming a detached portion of the lower division of the hundred of BLACKENHURST, county of WORCESTER, 2¼ miles (W.) from Henley in Arden, containing 102 inhabitants. The living is a discharged rectory, in the archdeaconry and diocese of Worcester, rated in the king's books at £4, and in the patronage of the Rev. John Peachell. The church is dedicated to St. Mary.

OLDBURY, a parish in the hundred of STOTTESDEN, county of SALOP, 1 mile (S. by W.) from Bridgenorth, containing 110 inhabitants. The living is a discharged rectory, in the archdeaconry of Salop, and diocese of Hereford, rated in the king's books at £5, endowed with £200 private benefaction, and in the patronage of the Crown. The church is dedicated to St. Nicholas. His Majesty's Commissioners have proposed a grant for the erection of a new church. There are places of worship for Baptists, Independents, and Wesleyan Methodists. The iron trade is here carried on to a considerable extent: there are also steel-works; and an abundance of iron-stone and coal is obtained. The Birmingham canal nearly surrounds the village. Fairs are on June 6th and October 3rd. A court of requests is held, once a fortnight, for the recovery of debts under £5, also courts leet and baron annually: here is a spacious prison for debtors. Edmund Darby, in 1659, gave land, among other purposes, for the erection and endowment of a school, in which twenty children are educated.

OLDBURY, a hamlet in the parish of MANCETTER, Atherstone division of the hundred of HEMLINGFORD, county of WARWICK, 4¼ miles (N. W. by W.) from Nuneaton, containing 79 inhabitants. Here was a small nunnery of the Dominican order, dedicated to St. Lawrence, and subordinate to Pollesworth; it is said to have been founded by Walter de Hastings and Athawis his wife, and at the dissolution possessed a revenue of £6. 0. 10.

OLDBURY on the HILL, a parish in the upper division of the hundred of GRUMBALD'S ASH, county of GLOUCESTER, 5¼ miles (S. W. by W.) from Tetbury, containing 371 inhabitants. The living is a rectory, united to that of Didmarton, in the archdeaconry and diocese of Gloucester, rated in the king's books at £16. The Duke of Beaufort was patron in 1803. The church is dedicated to St. Arila.

OLDBURY upon SEVERN, a chapelry in the parish of THORNBURY, lower division of the hundred of THORNBURY, county of GLOUCESTER, 2¾ miles (N. W. by W.) from Thornbury, containing 528 inhabitants. The navigable river Severn passes in the vicinity.

OLDCASTLE, a township in the parish of MALPAS, higher division of the hundred of BROXTON, county palatine of CHESTER, 1½ mile (S. W.) from Malpas, containing 93 inhabitants. This place took its name from an ancient castle, which was destroyed before 1585. A battle was fought here in 1644, between the parliamentarian forces from Nantwich and some of the king's cavalry, in which the latter were defeated, and Colonels Vane and Conyers killed.

OLDCASTLE, a parish in the lower division of the hundred of ABERGAVENNY, county of MONMOUTH, 8¼ miles (N. by E.) from Abergavenny, containing 67 inhabitants. The living is a perpetual curacy, in the archdeaconry of Brecon, and diocese of St. David's, endowed with £400 private benefaction, and £600 royal bounty, and in the patronage of the Earl of Oxford. The church is dedicated to St. John the Baptist.

OLDCOTT, a township in the parish of WOLSTANTON, northern division of the hundred of PIREHILL, county of STAFFORD, containing 615 inhabitants.

OLDFIELD, a joint township with Heswall, in the parish of HESWALL, lower division of the hundred of WIRRALL, county palatine of CHESTER, 4¼ miles (N. N. W.) from Parkgate. The population is returned with Heswall.

OLDHAM cum PRESTWICH, a parochial chapelry in the hundred of SALFORD, county palatine of LANCASTER, comprising the chapelries of Chadderton and Royton, and the townships of Crompton and Oldham, and containing 38,201 inhabitants, of which number, 21,662 are in the township of Oldham, 7 miles (N. E. by E.) from Manchester. This place, the name of which appears to indicate some degree either of absolute or of relative antiquity, is not connected with any event of historical importance, and has only within the last fifty years risen into notice from the rapid progress of its manufactures, for which it is indebted to its vicinity to Manchester, and to the mines of excellent coal which abound in the neighbourhood. The town is situated on elevated ground, near the source of the river Irk, and is bounded on the east by a branch of the Medlock. The houses are irregularly built, but, since the extension of its manufactures, the town has been very much enlarged, and is undergoing considerable improvement. It was first lighted with gas on March 1st, 1827, the works, situated at the bottom of Greaves-street, having been erected by a company incorporated in 1825, at an expense, including the laying of the mains, &c., of £20,000: it is supplied with water conveyed by iron pipes

from a reservoir covering about twelve acres of ground, in Strines-dale, about two miles and a half east of the town, partly in Lancashire and partly in Yorkshire, the whole having been constructed at an expense of £28,000: it is only partially paved. The affairs of the town are regulated by commissioners appointed under a police act obtained in 1828, which also provides for the erection of a town hall and other offices. A subscription library has been established. Oldham has for a long period been celebrated for the manufacture of hats, which was established so early as the fifteenth century, and is still carried on to a considerable extent; but the principal manufactures are fustians, velveteens, cotton and woollen corduroys, and the spinning of cotton, for which there are now about seventy-five mills in full operation, for the most part worked by steam, and not less than one hundred and fifty steam-engines employed in the other different factories and in the mines. A great quantity of the coal obtained in the neighbourhood is sent to Manchester, where it obtains a ready market, at a superior price; the mines are exceedingly productive, and afford employment to a considerable number of persons. The trade of the town is greatly facilitated by the Oldham canal, constructed in pursuance of an act of parliament obtained in 1792, which commences at Hollinwood, and forms a direct communication with Manchester, the grand mart for the sale of its manufactures, and with Ashton under Line and Stockport, and the Rochdale canal, which passes through the township of Chadderton. A railway has been projected from Oldham to Manchester, but not yet carried into effect. A customary market for provisions is held on Saturday; and fairs are held on the first Thursday after Candlemas-day, May 2nd, July 8th, and the first Wednesday after October 12th, for horses, cattle, sheep, and pedlary. Petty sessions for the Middleton division of the hundred of Salford are held here once a fortnight.

The living is a perpetual curacy, in the archdeaconry and diocese of Chester, endowed with £400 royal bounty, and £1200 parliamentary grant, and in the patronage of the Rector of Prestwich. The ancient chapel, dedicated to St. Mary, erected in 1476, by "Sir Ralph Langley, priest of Prestwich," and third warden of Manchester college, was taken down and rebuilt on a larger scale, the first stone having been laid on the 16th of October, 1827, and the expense estimated at upwards of £12,000 : the present edifice, dedicated to St. Paul, is in the later style of English architecture, with a handsome embattled tower surmounted by angular turrets and pinnacles. St. Peter's chapel was built by subscription in 1765, and enlarged in 1804 : the living is a perpetual curacy, endowed with £2200 parliamentary grant, and in the patronage of the Rector of Prestwich. The church dedicated to St. James, erected in 1829, by grant from the parliamentary commissioners, at an expense of £8905. 16. 6., is a neat edifice in the later style of English architecture, with a tower and campanile turret, and contains two thousand and eighty-one sittings, of which one thousand two hundred and eighty-five are free : the living is a perpetual curacy, in the patronage of the Incumbent of Oldham : this church is situated about a quarter of a mile east of the town, where a subscription library and news-room has been established. Near Chadderton Hall, within the township of

3 M

Oldham, is an episcopal chapel, built in 1765; and there are two other chapels of ease at Crompton and Royton. There are places of worship for Baptists, the Society of Friends, Independents, Kilhamites, Moravians; Primitive, Wesleyan, and Independent, Methodists; and Unitarians. The free grammar school was founded, in 1611, by James Assheton, Esq., of Chadderton Hall, who endowed it with an acre of land in the town, which has been let for building, and the endowment was augmented by the bequest of £3 per annum from Mr. Thomas Nuttall, in 1726; the whole income is about £35 per annum, and the school is free to all boys of the town for instruction in the classics, a quarterly sum being paid for writing and arithmetic, and six boys are taught English on Mr. Nuttall's foundation. In 1747, Samuel Scoles gave £16 per annum, for which thirty-nine poor children of the township of Oldham are instructed at three different schools. A school was founded by subscription in the hamlet of Hollingwood, in this parish, in 1786, with an endowment of £8 per annum, chiefly from a bequest by the Rev. John Darbey in 1808, and £7 per annum from another benefaction, for which twenty children are instructed. Thomas Henshaw, Esq., by will dated the 14th November 1807, gave the sum of £20,000 for the endowment of a Blue coat school at Oldham, and a like sum for an asylum for the blind at Manchester, and subsequently added a codicil by which he gave the farther sum of £20,000, for the endowment of the school, with liberty to his trustees to establish it either at Oldham or Manchester on condition that persons at either place would provide a site and suitable buildings for the institution in this town, the trustees determined, upon establishing the school here. The testator having died in 1810, a bill was filed in the Court of Chancery by his heirs, praying that the will might be set aside, but a decree was ultimately obtained by the trustees in favour of the charity. In consequence of the delay occasioned by this suit, on the part of the inhabitants of Oldham and Manchester, on providing land and building, the sum bequeathed has accumulated to nearly £100,000; and three acres of land having been given for that purpose by R. Radcliffe and Joseph Jones, Esquires, the first stone of a commodious and substantial edifice in the English style of architecture, for the use of this school, was laid at Oldham-Edge, in April 1829, and the building completed at an expense of about £8000, defrayed by subscription. There are other benefactions for the education of boys and girls. A benevolent, or medical charity, for the relief of the poor, was established in 1814; and there is also a humane society. Hugh Oldham, Bishop of Exeter, and Mr. Thomas Henshaw, an opulent hat-manufacturer, whose munificent charitable endowments are noticed here and in Manchester, were both natives of this town.

OLDLAND, a chapelry in the parish of BITTON, upper division of the hundred of LANGLEY and SWINEHEAD, county of GLOUCESTER, 5 miles (E. S. E.) from Bristol, containing 4297 inhabitants. The chapel has lately received an addition of three hundred and eighty-five free sittings, the Incorporated Society for the enlargement of churches and chapels having granted £408 towards defraying the expense. An additional chapel, dedicated to the Holy Trinity, has been built, under the provisions of a late act, towards defraying the expense of which the same society contributed

£700; it contains one thousand and nineteen sittings, of which eight hundred and eighty-eight are free. The navigable river Avon, and the Julian way, pass in the vicinity.

OLDMOOR, a township in that part of the parish of BOTHALL which is in the eastern division of MORPETH ward, county of NORTHUMBERLAND, 4 miles (N. E. by E.) from Morpeth, containing 79 inhabitants.

OLD-PARK, a township in that part of the parish of AUCKLAND ST. ANDREW which is in the south-eastern division of DARLINGTON ward, county palatine of DURHAM, 3¾ miles (N. E. by N.) from Bishop-Auckland, containing 30 inhabitants.

OLDRIDGE, a chapelry in the parish of ST. THOMAS the APOSTLE, hundred of WONFORD, county of DEVON, 3 miles (S. by W.) from Crediton. The population is returned with the parish. The living is a perpetual curacy, in the archdeaconry and diocese of Exeter, endowed with £200 private benefaction, £800 royal bounty, and £200 parliamentary grant, and in the patronage of the Vicar of Tavistock. The chapel was erected at the expense of James Buller and the late Giles Yarde, Esqrs.

OLERSET, a hamlet in the parish of GLOSSOP, hundred of HIGH PEAK, county of DERBY, containing 293 inhabitants.

OLLERTON, a township in the parish of KNUTSFORD, hundred of BUCKLOW, county palatine of CHESTER, 2½ miles (S. E.) from Nether Knutsford, containing 246 inhabitants.

OLLERTON, a market town and chapelry in the parish of EDWINSTOW, Hatfield division of the wapentake of BASSETLAW, county of NOTTINGHAM, 18½ miles (N. N. E.) from Nottingham, and 138¼ (N. N. W.) from London, containing 576 inhabitants. This is a small town in the Forest of Sherwood, situated on the banks of the little river Mann. In the neighbourhood a considerable quantity of hops is produced. The market, which is but of trifling importance, is held on Friday; and there is a fair for cattle and sheep on the 1st of May. The chapel is a modern edifice in the English style of architecture. There is a place of worship for Wesleyan Methodists. A small bequest for the education of poor children was left by Francis Thompson.

OLLERTON, a township in the parish of STOKE upon TERN, Drayton division of the hundred of BRADFORD (North), county of SALOP, 7¼ miles (N. W. by W.) from Newport, containing 133 inhabitants.

OLNEY, a market town and parish, in the hundred of NEWPORT, county of BUCKINGHAM, 19 miles (N. E.) from Buckingham, and 57 (N. W. by N.) from London, containing 2339 inhabitants. The town is situated on the northern bank of the Ouse, and consists of one long street, paved, but not lighted: most of the houses were thatched previously to the occurrence of a destructive fire in 1786, and those erected since are covered with tiles; they are in general built of stone, and some of them are of very respectable appearance: the inhabitants enjoy an abundant supply of water. Over the Ouse is a bridge, with four large arches, and a considerable number of smaller ones, the latter extending across the adjoining low meadow lands, which are frequently overflowed during heavy rains. For keeping in repair this causeway and the foot-paths around the town there is an especial fund, arising from a public benefaction. The principal branch of manufacture was that of bone-lace, which has declined, in consequence of the general use of machinery ; and a few persons are now employed in making worsted hose, and in silk-weaving, both of recent introduction. The market is held on Thursday ; and there are fairs on Easter-Monday, June 29th, and October 21st. Courts leet and baron for the manor are held annually. The living is a vicarage, in the archdeaconry of Buckingham, and diocese of Lincoln, rated in the king's books at £13. 6. 8., endowed with £200 private benefaction, and £500 parliamentary grant, and in the patronage of the Earl of Dartmouth. The church, dedicated to St. Peter and St. Paul, is a large ancient edifice, in the English style, with a handsome tower and a spire, which was partially rebuilt in 1807. In the churchyard was formerly a chapel, dedicated to the Virgin Mary, with a chantry, founded by Lord Basset. There are places of worship for Baptists, the Society of Friends, Independents, and Wesleyan Methodists. National and Lancasterian schools are supported by subscription. Almshouses for twelve single women have been erected and endowed by the Misses Smith. Moses Browne, author of "Piscatory Eclogues," and other works, was vicar of Olney ; and John Newton, afterwards minister of the parish of St. Mary Woolnoth, Lombard-street, London, and a popular preacher and writer, was once curate ; at which time Cowper, the poet, resided here, his house and garden, with his favourite seat, being still shewn.

OLVESTON, a parish in the lower division of the hundred of LANGLEY and SWINEHEAD, county of GLOUCESTER, comprising the tythings of Olveston and Upper Tockington, and containing 1351 inhabitants, of which number, 681 are in the tything of Olveston, 3¼ miles (S. W.) from Thornbury. The living is a vicarage, to which that of Elberton was united, in 1767, in the peculiar jurisdiction of the Bishop of Bristol, rated in the king's books at £24, and in the patronage of the Dean and Chapter of Bristol. The church is dedicated to St. Mary. There is a place of worship for Wesleyan Methodists. The parish is partly bounded by the river Severn, and contains extensive strata of limestone.

OMBERSLEY, a parish in the lower division of the hundred of OSWALDSLOW, county of WORCESTER, 4¼ miles (W.) from Droitwich, containing, with the townships of Borley, Hadley with Hay-Elms, Mayeux with Chatley, Northampton-Parsonage with Powers, Ombersley, Sychampton with Brookhampton and Comhampton, Uphampton, Winnall with Acton and Dunhampton, 1814 inhabitants. The living is a discharged vicarage, in the archdeaconry and diocese of Worcester, rated in the king's books at £15. 7. 3½., and in the patronage of the Marchioness of Downshire. The church, dedicated to St. Andrew, has lately been rebuilt, in the later style of English architecture, and is now one of the most elegant in the county : in the churchyard are the remains of an ancient cross, supported on steps. The river Severn passes through the parish. Here was formerly a market, granted by Edward III., but it has been long disused. A charity school was founded, in 1701, by Thomas Tolley, to which Thomas Baker, in 1722, bequeathed £100, and Richard Lloyd, in 1723, liberally endowed it with land and houses.

OMPTON, a township in that part of the parish of KNEESALL which is in the South-clay division of the wapentake of BASSETLAW, county of NOTTINGHAM, 2¾ miles (S. E. by E.) from Ollerton, containing 106 inhabitants.

ONECOTE, a chapelry in that part of the parish of LEEK which is in the northern division of the hundred of TOTMONSLOW, county of STAFFORD, 5 miles (E. by S.) from Leek, containing 585 inhabitants. The living is a perpetual curacy, in the archdeaconry of Stafford, and diocese of Lichfield and Coventry, endowed with £800 royal bounty, and £1400 parliamentary grant, and in the patronage of the Vicar of Leek. The chapel is a small stone structure. There are copper-mines at Mixen, and small portions of copper and lead are found imbedded among limestone in most of the hills in the neighbourhood. Within the chapelry is a deep valley surrounded by rocks, called Narrowdale, in which the inhabitants, during several months in the year, cannot behold the sun.

ONE-HOUSE, a parish in the hundred of STOW, county of SUFFOLK, 2 miles (W.) from Stow-Market, containing 185 inhabitants, exclusively of the house of industry for the hundred of Stow, which is in this parish, and contains 235 inmates. The living is a rectory, in the archdeaconry of Sudbury, and diocese of Norwich, rated in the king's books at £7. 2. 6, and in the patronage of R. Pettiward, Esq. The church is dedicated to St. John the Baptist. Two streams, which run through the parish, are formed into ornamental pieces of water below the park. There is also a mineral spring. The chapel of Stow and the Hundred-House are situated within this parish.

ONELY, a hamlet in the parish of BARBY, hundred of FAWSLEY, county of NORTHAMPTON, 7 miles (N. W. by N.) from Daventry. The population is returned with the parish.

ONGAR (CHIPPING), a market town and parish in the hundred of ONGAR, county of ESSEX, 12 miles (W. by S.) from Chelmsford, and 21 (N. E.) from London, containing 768 inhabitants. Its name is derived from the Saxon aungre, i.e. the place, or, as Morant supposes, from the old word hangre, a hill, the addition of chipping, or cheaping, signifying a market. It was anciently denominated Ongar ad Castrum, on account of its castle, and to distinguish it from High Ongar, a village in the vicinity. The town is of considerable antiquity, having probably been founded by the Saxons soon after their settlement in England. At the time of the Norman survey, the manor was held in demesne by Eustace, Earl of Boulogne, and after passing through several families, came into the possession of Richard de Lucy, Chief Justice of England under Henry II., who procured for the town, as the head of the barony, a market and fairs, and built the castle on a high circular eminence to the east of it, surrounded by a moat and some earthworks, of which there are still traces ; the castle itself was destroyed in the reign of Elizabeth. The town occupies an eminence on the bank of the river Roden, and consists principally of one long street, within the area of an extensive intrenchment, which may be distinctly traced : it is neither paved nor lighted, but amply supplied with water from wells and springs. A new road has been recently made through it from London to Clare, in Suffolk. A market for corn and cattle is held on Saturday ; and there is a fair on the 12th of October, for hiring servants. The magistrates hold a petty session on the market day. The living is a discharged rectory, in the archdeaconry of Essex, and diocese of London, rated in the king's books at £6, endowed with £200 private benefaction, and £200 royal bounty, and in the patronage of Mrs. Bennett. The church, dedicated to St. Martin, is a small neat structure, partly built with Roman bricks, and is remarkable for the castellated loop-hole appearance of its windows. There is a place of worship for Independents. A free school was founded, in 1678, pursuant to the will of Joseph King, a native of this town, who bequeathed to trustees five houses, the rents of which, amounting to £70 per annum, are applied to the education and apprenticing of six poor boys, for teaching poor girls to read, and for other charitable purposes ; any one of the scholars that may be eligible for the University is entitled annually to £5 for four years from this fund.

ONGAR (HIGH), a parish in the hundred of ONGAR, county of ESSEX, ¾ of a mile (N. E.) from Chipping-Ongar, containing 1126 inhabitants. The living is a rectory, in the archdeaconry of Essex, and diocese of London, rated in the king's books at £39. 10. 5. The Executors of the Rev. E. Earle were patrons in 1823. The church, dedicated to St. Mary, is lofty and spacious, with an arched roof, having clouds, stars, and a rising sun, painted on it.

ONIBURY, a parish in the hundred of Munslow, county of SALOP, 5½ miles (N. W.) from Ludlow, containing 445 inhabitants. The living is a rectory, in the archdeaconry of Salop, and diocese of Hereford, rated in the king's books at £8. 17. 8½, and in the patronage of the Bishop of Hereford. The church is dedicated to St. Michael. A court baron is occasionally held here. William Norton, in 1593, left a rent-charge of £6. 6. 8. for teaching poor children.

ONN (HIGH), a township in the parish of CHURCH-EATON, western division of the hundred of CUTTLESTONE, county of STAFFORD, 7¼ miles (W. by N.) from Penkridge. The population is returned with the parish.

ONN (LITTLE), a township in the parish of CHURCH-EATON, western division of the hundred of CUTTLESTONE, county of STAFFORD, 6¼ miles (W. by N.) from Penkridge. The population is returned with the parish.

ONSTON, a township in the parish of WEAVERHAM, second division of the hundred of EDDISBURY, county palatine of CHESTER, 5 miles (W. by N.) from Northwich, containing 71 inhabitants.

OPENSHAW, a township in the parish of MANCHESTER, hundred of SALFORD, county palatine of LANCASTER, 3½ miles (E. by S.) from Manchester, containing 497 inhabitants.

ORBY, a parish in the Marsh division of the wapentake of CANDLESHOE, parts of LINDSEY, county of LINCOLN, 6½ miles (E. by N.) from Spilsby, containing 282 inhabitants. The living is a discharged vicarage, in the archdeaconry and diocese of Lincoln, rated in the king's books at £9. 19. 4., and in the patronage of the Bishop of Lincoln. The church is dedicated to All Saints. There is a place of worship for Baptists.

ORCHARD (EAST), a parish in that part of the hundred of SIXPENNY-HANDLEY which is in the Shaston (West) division of the county of DORSET, 4 miles (S. S. W.) from Shaftesbury, containing 193 inhabitants. The living is a perpetual curacy, annexed to the vicarage of Iwerne-Minster, in the archdeaconry of Dorset, and diocese of Bristol.

ORCHARD (WEST), a parish in that part of the hundred of SIXPENNY-HANDLEY which is in the Shaston (West) division of the county of DORSET, 5 miles (S. S. W.) from Shaftesbury, containing 173 inhabitants. The living is a perpetual curacy, annexed to the vicarage of Fontmell-Magna, in the archdeaconry of Dorset, and diocese of Bristol.

ORCHARD-PORTMAN, a parish in the hundred of TAUNTON and TAUNTON-DEAN, county of SOMERSET, 2 miles (S. S. E.) from Taunton, containing 100 inhabitants. The living is a discharged rectory, in the archdeaconry of Taunton, and diocese of Bath and Wells, rated in the king's books at £7. 11. 5, and in the patronage of E. B. Portman, Esq. The church is dedicated to St. Michael.

ORCHARDLEIGH, a parish in the hundred of FROME, county of SOMERSET, 2 miles (N.) from Frome, containing 27 inhabitants. The living is a discharged rectory, in the archdeaconry of Wells, and diocese of Bath and Wells, rated in the king's books at £2, and endowed with £600 royal bounty. T. S. Champneys, Esq. was patron in 1818.

ORCHESTON (ST. GEORGE), a parish in the hundred of HEYTESBURY, county of WILTS, 6½ miles (W. N. W.) from Amesbury, containing, with the tything of Elston, 177 inhabitants. The living is a rectory, in the archdeaconry and diocese of Salisbury, rated in the king's books at £19. 7. 6. The Rev. Francis Gibbs was patron in 1802.

ORCHESTON (ST. MARY), a parish in the hundred of BRANCH and DOLE, county of WILTS, 7 miles (N. W. by W.) from Amesbury, containing 110 inhabitants. The living is a rectory, in the archdeaconry and diocese of Salisbury, rated in the king's books at £13. 13. 9., and in the patronage of the Master and Fellows of Clare Hall, Cambridge.

ORCOP, a parish in the upper division of the hundred of WORMELOW, county of HEREFORD, 9½ miles (W. N. W.) from Ross, containing 491 inhabitants. The living is a perpetual curacy, in the peculiar jurisdiction of the Chancellor of the diocese of Hereford, and in the patronage of William Palmer, Esq. Limestone is obtained here.

ORDSALL, a parish in the Hatfield division of the wapentake of BASSETLAW, county of NOTTINGHAM, 1½ mile (S.) from East Retford, containing 632 inhabitants. The living is a rectory, in the archdeaconry of Nottingham, and diocese of York, rated in the king's books at £19. 10. 7½., and in the patronage of Lord Wharncliffe. The church, dedicated to All Saints, exhibits various styles of architecture. On the river Idle, in this parish, are some paper-mills. The Chesterfield canal passes through the parish.

ORE, a parish in the hundred of BALDSLOW, rape of HASTINGS, county of SUSSEX, 2½ miles (N. N. W.) from Hastings, containing 546 inhabitants. The living is a discharged rectory, in the archdeaconry of Lewes, and diocese of Chichester, rated in the king's books at £3. 0. 2½. Miss Palmer was patroness in 1815. The church, dedicated to St. Helen, is principally in the later style of English architecture.

'Corporate Seal.

ORFORD, a borough and parish, formerly a market town, having separate jurisdiction, though locally in the hundred of Plomesgate, county of SUFFOLK, 20 miles (E. by N.) from Ipswich, and 89 (N. E. by E.) from London, containing,with the hamlet of Gedgrave, 1119 inhabitants. This was formerly a place of trade and importance, but has been reduced to an inconsiderable hamlet. The town is situated on the river Alde, and consists of houses irregularly scattered and indifferently built : the streets are neither lighted nor paved, but the inhabitants are well supplied with water. Its decline is attributable to the loss of the harbour by the retiring of the sea, which, on its retreat, threw up a barrier that rendered the navigation dangerous. The oyster fishery is carried on here, under license from the corporation. Coal is imported, and corn exported to London and other places. The river Alde is navigable up to Aldborough quay, for vessels of three hundred tons' burden. The market, which was on Monday, is disused: a toy fair is held on June 24th.

The inhabitants received a charter of incorporation prior to the reign of Richard III., by which monarch, by Elizabeth, and by James I., their privileges were confirmed. Under the charter granted by King James, the corporation consists of a mayor, eight portmen, and twelve capital burgesses, assisted by a recorder, coroner, chamberlain, town clerk, two serjeants at mace, two water-bailiffs, and a harbour-master. The mayor and two portmen are justices of the peace. The corporation are empowered to hold sessions twice a year, or as often as may be requisite, and a court of record for the recovery of debts under 40s., at which the mayor, two portmen, the recorder, and the town clerk, preside. The freedom is obtained by gift or purchase for £5. The elective franchise was granted in the 23rd of Edward I., but the exercise of it was discontinued till the reign of Henry VIII., since which period two members have been regularly returned to parliament : the right of election is vested in the mayor, portmen, capital burgesses, and freemen not receiving alms : the number of voters is about one hundred : the mayor is the returning officer, and the patronage of the borough belongs to the Marquis of Hertford.

The living is a perpetual curacy, with the rectory of Sudbourne, in the archdeaconry of Suffolk, and diocese of Norwich. The church, which is dedicated to St. Bartholomew, was, when entire, a spacious and magnificent structure of great antiquity, with a square embattled tower : the chancel, now in ruins, appears to be more ancient than the rest of the building, and is separated from the church by a wall built across the east end of the nave; the ruins are in the Norman style, and consist of a single row of massive columns, supporting semicircular arches decorated with zigzag mouldings and other highly finished carvings; the columns are cased with hewn freestone, and display great diversity of style in their embellishments. In the church is a font of exquisite workmanship and great

antiquity, and, amongst several others, a monument to the memory of the Rev. Francis Mason, who died in 1621, at the advanced age of one hundred and ten years, eighty of which he was rector of Sudbourne. The porch, which is curious, was formerly adorned with eleven heads of kings, and is still decorated with escutcheons : the windows contain rich tracery, and there is an elegant cross of exquisite workmanship. At the west end of the town are the ruins of an ancient castle, supposed to have been built about the time of the Conquest, and evidently of Norman architecture ; the keep only remains, a polygonal building of eighteen sides, flanked by three square embattled towers, equidistant from each other, on the north, north-east, and south-east; the lower part of the walls is solid, the upper parts contain chambers : the whole was formerly surrounded by a double fosse, with a bridge and gateway tower. This structure was anciently in the centre of the town, as the names of fields taken from streets formerly existing, and the frequent discovery of the foundations of buildings sufficiently prove. In the interior of the castle a room has been elegantly fitted up by the Marquis of Hertford, which commands two extensive views of the North sea, and one of the interior of the country for many miles. An hospital for a master and brethren was founded in the time of Edward II., and dedicated to St. Leonard, which continued until after 1586 ; and a priory of Augustine friars was founded in the 23rd of Edward I.: part of the walls of a monastery, and the burial-ground, yet remain ; in the latter a quantity of bones and of Saxon and Roman coins has been found. On the south-east of this parish, towards the North sea, is a lighthouse; and in the parish of Sudbourne, a little north of the Ness, is another, together being designated "The Orford Ness Lights." Orford confers the title of earl upon the Walpole family.

ORFORTH, an extra-parochial district, in the southern division of the wapentake of WALSHCROFT, parts of LINDSEY, county of LINCOLN. The population is returned with the parish of Binbrooke St. Mary.

ORGARSWICK, a parish in the liberty of ROMNEY-MARSH, though locally in the hundred of Worth, lathe of SHEPWAY, county of KENT, 5 miles (N. N. E.) from New Romney, containing 10 inhabitants. The living is a rectory, in the archdeaconry and diocese of Canterbury, rated in the king's books at £3, and in the patronage of the Dean and Chapter of Canterbury. The church has been demolished.

ORGREAVE, a hamlet in the parish of ALREWAS, northern division of the hundred of OFFLOW, county of STAFFORD, 4¾ miles (N. N. E.) from Lichfield, containing 87 inhabitants.

ORGREAVE, a township in that part of the parish of ROTHERHAM which is in the southern division of the wapentake of STRAFFORTH and TICKHILL, West riding of the county of YORK, 4¼ miles (S. by W.) from Rotherham, containing 47 inhabitants.

ORLESTONE, a parish partly in the liberty of ROMNEY-MARSH, and partly in the hundred of HAM, lathe of SHEPWAY, county of KENT, 5½ miles (S. by W.) from Ashford, containing 453 inhabitants. The living is a discharged rectory, in the archdeaconry and diocese of Canterbury, rated in the king's books at £4. 15. 9., endowed with £200 private benefaction, and £200 royal bounty, and in the patronage of J. Thornhill, Esq.

The church is dedicated to St. Mary. The Royal Military canal passes through the parish, in which there are some chalybeate springs, but of no great efficacy.

ORLETON, a parish in the hundred of WOLPHY, county of HEREFORD, 6 miles (N. by E.) from Leominster, containing 574 inhabitants. The living is a perpetual curacy, in the archdeaconry and diocese of Hereford, endowed with £400 private benefaction, and £400 royal bounty, and in the patronage of the Governors of Lucton school. The Leominster canal passes through the parish. Courts leet and baron are held in March and October; and the petty sessions for the division take place here. There is a great fair for cattle annually on the 23rd and 24th of April. Blount, the celebrated antiquary, was a native of the parish, and lies buried in the chancel of the church.

ORLETON, a chapelry in the parish of EASTHAM, upper division of the hundred of DODDINGTREE, county of WORCESTER, 7½ miles (E. by S.) from Tenbury, containing 135 inhabitants.

ORLINGBURY, a parish in the hundred of ORLINGBURY, county of NORTHAMPTON, 3¾ miles (N. W. by N.) from Wellingborough, containing 343 inhabitants. The living is a rectory, in the archdeaconry of Northampton, and diocese of Peterborough, rated in the king's books at £20. 7. 3½., and in the patronage of Sir B. W. Bridges, Bart. The church is dedicated to St. Mary. The Rev. Owen Manning, the editor of Lye's Saxon Dictionary, was born here in 1721.

ORMSBY, a parish partly in the eastern and partly in the western division of the hundred of LANGBAURGH, North riding of the county of YORK, 5¼ miles (W. by N.) from Guisbrough, containing, with the chapelry of Eston, and the townships of Morton, Normanby, and Upsall, 785 inhabitants. The living is a vicarage, in the archdeaconry of Cleveland, and diocese of York, rated in the king's books at £6. 18. 6½., and in the patronage of the Archbishop of York. The church is dedicated to St. Cuthbert. A rent-charge of £10, from an unknown benefactor, is paid for teaching poor children.

ORMSBY (ST. MARGARET), a parish in the eastern division of the hundred of FLEGG, county of NORFOLK, 3 miles (N. W.) from Caistor, containing, with Scratby, 687 inhabitants. The living is a discharged vicarage, with the perpetual curacy of Ormsby St. Michael, and with which was united, in 1548, the vicarage of Scrowtby, in the archdeaconry and diocese of Norwich, rated in the king's books at £10. 0. 10., endowed with £210 private benefaction, and £200 royal bounty, and in the patronage of the Dean and Chapter of Norwich.

ORMSBY (ST. MICHAEL), a parish in the eastern division of the hundred of FLEGG, county of NORFOLK, 2¼ miles (N. W. by N.) from Caistor, containing 261 inhabitants. The living is a perpetual curacy, united to the vicarage of Ormsby St. Margaret, in the archdeaconry and diocese of Norwich.

ORMSBY (NORTH), a parish in the wapentake of LUDBOROUGH, parts of LINDSEY, county of LINCOLN, 6¾ miles (N. W. by N.) from Louth, containing 111 inhabitants. The living is a discharged vicarage, in the archdeaconry and diocese of Lincoln, rated in the king's books at £3, endowed with £600 royal bounty. The Misses E. and S. Ansell were patronesses in 1813. The church is dedicated to St. Helen. A monastery, for

nuns and brethren of the Sempringham order, was founded here in the time of Stephen, by William, Earl of Albemarle, and Gilbert, son of Robert de Ormesby: it was dedicated to the Blessed Virgin Mary, and its revenue was valued at the dissolution at £80.

ORMSBY (SOUTH), a parish in the hundred of HILL, parts of LINDSEY, county of LINCOLN, 7¼ miles (N. N. W.) from Spilsby, containing, with Ketsby, 261 inhabitants. The living is a rectory, with that of Ketsby, with which the vicarage of Calceby, and the rectory of Driby, were united in 1774: it is in the archdeaconry and diocese of Lincoln, rated in the king's books at £14. 13. 11½., and in the patronage of C. B. Massingberd, Esq. The church is dedicated to St. Leonard. Within the parish are the remains of a Roman exploratory camp.

ORMSIDE, a parish in EAST ward, county of WESTMORLAND, 3¼ miles (S. E. by S.) from Appleby, containing 202 inhabitants. The living is a discharged rectory, in the archdeaconry and diocese of Carlisle, rated in the king's books at £17. 17. 3½., and in the patronage of the Bishop of Carlisle. The church, dedicated to St. James, is a small ancient structure, situated on a commanding eminence. In the bed of the river Eden, which runs through the parish, several brazen vessels were discovered in 1689, which probably were placed there during the parliamentary war.

ORMSKIRK, a parish in the hundred of WEST DERBY, county palatine of LANCASTER, comprising the market town of Ormskirk, the chapelry of Skelmersdale, and the townships of Bickerstaffe, Birkdale, Burscough, Lathom, and Scarisbrick, and containing 12,422 inhabitants, of which number, 3838 are in the town of Ormskirk, 13 miles (N. N. E.) from Liverpool, 40 (S. by W.) from Lancaster, and 209 (N. W. by N.) from London. This place is supposed to derive its name from a church built here by two sisters of the name of Orm; and it constituted part of the possessions with which Robert Fitz-Henry, lord of Latham, endowed Burscough priory, an establishment founded by him for Black canons, in the reign of Richard I. The town, which is situated on the road from Liverpool to Preston, is clean and well built: it consists chiefly of four streets, diverging at right angles from a central area used as the market-place: it is not lighted, but paved under the direction of the surveyors of highways. Its trade and manufactures are on a limited scale; the principal establishments are hat-manufactories and roperies. The manufacture of cotton and silk has also been introduced, but the produce has hitherto been inconsiderable: there is also a small trade in balance-making. The loamy soil in this parish produces a great quantity of carrots, which are sent to the market at Liverpool; and the farmers in the neighbourhood are noted for the culture of early potatoes of a superior quality. The inhabitants have also long been famous for making gingerbread, which meets with a rapid sale in the surrounding towns, and is even exported. The disposal of local produce, and the importation of articles of consumption, are greatly facilitated by the Leeds and Liverpool canal and the Douglas navigation, which are about three miles distant from the town. There are considerable coal mines within the parish. The market, granted in the 14th of Edward I. to the prior of Burscough, is on Thursday; and fairs are held on Whit-Monday and

Whit-Tuesday, and on the 8th of September. The petty sessions for the division are held here; and a court leet is held annually in October, at which a constable and other officers are appointed for the town. Quarter sessions, formerly held here, have been removed to Kirkdale.

The living is a discharged vicarage, in the archdeaconry and diocese of Chester, rated in the king's books at £10, endowed with £200 private benefaction, and £200 royal bounty, and in the patronage of the Earl of Derby. The church, dedicated to St. Peter and St. Paul, is of ancient, but obscure, foundation. It is stated to have been built at the expense of the two sisters above named, to a disagreement between whom, regarding the completion of the design, tradition ascribes the peculiarity of its possessing a tower and a steeple detached from each other : but it is more probable that the tower was erected for the express purpose of receiving eight bells, removed hither from Burscough priory, on the dissolution of that monastery. Within the building are a chapel and vault, constructed pursuant to the will, dated in 1572, of Edward, the third Earl of Derby, for a cemetery for that noble family, the deceased members of which have been interred here since the dissolution of the priory, when such bodies as were not already reduced to ashes, were removed hither. An episcopal chapel at Skelmersdale was erected by subscription in 1776, and greatly enlarged in 1823 : it is presented to by the Vicar. That at Latham is a donative, belonging to Lord Skelmersdale. There are places of worship for Independents, Methodists of the New Connexion, and Unitarians. The free grammar school was founded about 1614, and is endowed with various benefactions, producing £138. 15. per annum: the salary of the master is £60 per annum, with permission to receive small gratuities : the school is open to all boys of the parish, and about forty free scholars are instructed in classical and general literature. A school-room, in Church-street, was built in 1724, at the expense of James, Earl of Derby, for a Blue-coat school, now called the United charity school, in which seventy boys and fifty girls receive gratuitous instruction on Dr. Bell's plan : it is supported partly from permanent funds, amounting to about £32 per annum, and partly by subscriptions. There is also an infant school. A dispensary was established in 1705; and a bank for savings in 1822.

ORPINGTON, a parish in the hundred of RUXLEY, lathe of SUTTON at HONE, county of KENT, 3 miles (S. by W.) from Foot's Cray, containing 754 inhabitants. The living comprises a sinecure rectory and a discharged vicarage, with the perpetual curacy of St. Mary Cray, the rectory rated in the king's books at £30. 14. 4½., and in the peculiar jurisdiction and patronage of the Archbishop of Canterbury, and the vicarage at £11. 10. 5., and in the patronage of the Rector. The church is dedicated to All Saints. There is a place of worship for Independents. The river Cray, which has its source in this parish, gives name to several places in the neighbourhood. Queen Elizabeth was splendidly entertained at the manor-house in 1573. Orpington is entitled to participate in the advantages of a school at St. Mary Cray.

ORRELL, a joint township with Ford, in the parish of SEPHTON, hundred of WEST DERBY, county palatine of LANCASTER, 4½ miles (N.) from Liverpool, containing, with Ford, 217 inhabitants.

ORRELL, a township in that part of the parish of WIGAN which is in the hundred of WEST DERBY, county palatine of LANCASTER, 3¼ miles (W.) from Wigan, containing 2106 inhabitants. There is a place of worship for Independents. At Orrell Mount is an establishment of French Benedictine nuns, who, driven by the Revolution from their native country, first settled at Heath in Yorkshire, and in 1821 removed hither. There are mines of coal in the neighbourhood.

ORSETT, a parish in the hundred of BARSTABLE, county of ESSEX, 18½ miles (S. S. W.) from Chelmsford, containing 1130 inhabitants. The living is a rectory, in the jurisdiction of the Commissary of Essex and Herts, concurrently with the Consistorial Court of the Bishop of London, rated in the king's books at £29. 6. 8., and in the patronage of the Bishop. The church is dedicated to St. Giles and All Saints. There is an endowed school for educating and clothing fourteen boys, founded by Edward Anson, Esq. Orsett Hall, the manor-house, was erected upwards of three hundred and fifty years ago. In the neighbourhood are vestiges of ancient intrenchments, enclosing four or five acres.

ORSTON, a parish in the northern division of the wapentake of BINGHAM, county of NOTTINGHAM, 6¼ miles (E. by N.) from Bingham, containing, with a part of Flawborough chapelry, 391 inhabitants. The living is a discharged vicarage, to which is annexed the perpetual curacies of Scanington and Thoroton, in the archdeaconry of Nottingham, and diocese of York, rated in the king's books at £12. 4. 7., and in the patronage of the Dean of Lincoln. The church is dedicated to St. Mary. There is a place of worship for Wesleyan Methodists. The small river Smite runs through the parish ; and here is a powerful chalybeate spring impregnated with sulphur. Limestone abounds here. Orston is in the honour of Tutbury, duchy of Lancaster, and within the jurisdiction of a court of pleas held at Tutbury every third Tuesday, for the recovery of debts under 40s.

ORTON, a parish in the ward and county of CUMBERLAND, comprising the townships of Baldwin-Holme and Orton, and containing 442 inhabitants, of which number, 208 are in the township of Orton, 5¼ miles (W. by S.) from Carlisle. The living is a rectory, in the archdeaconry and diocese of Carlisle, rated in the king's books at £9, and in the patronage of Sir Wastell Brisco, Bart. Near the church is the schoolhouse, endowed, in 1785, by Thomas Pattinson, with the interest of £100, for teaching ten children. A market, once held here, has been long disused. Orton was anciently of greater importance than it is now, many Roman remains having been discovered in the neighbourhood. The whole parish was formerly encompassed by a rampart and ditch, and at each extremity of two lanes, running northward and eastward from the village, is an intrenchment for the defence of the road, across which an iron chain was fixed, to guard against sudden attacks from the moss-troopers during the border warfare. A remarkably neat sandal was found some years since in digging peat. Coal is found in the parish. William Nicholson, a learned divine and antiquary, was born here in 1655; he died in 1727.

ORTON, a chapelry in the parish and hundred of ROTHWELL, county of NORTHAMPTON, 4¼ miles (W. by N.) from Kettering, containing 91 inhabitants.

ORTON, a liberty in the parish of WOMBOURNE, southern division of the hundred of SEISDON, county of STAFFORD, containing 170 inhabitants.

ORTON, a market town and parish, in EAST ward, county of WESTMORLAND, 9 miles (S.W. by S.) from Appleby, and 275 (N.W. by N.) from London, containing, with part of Birbeck Fells and Fawcet Forest, 1525 inhabitants. The town is pleasantly situated near the river Lune, and consists chiefly of one irregular street, which is neither paved nor lighted : it is supplied with water by two small rivulets, which unite at its extremity. The knitting of hose was formerly carried on to a considerable extent, but has now fallen into decay. There is a copper mine in the neighbourhood, which also abounds with limestone : at Coalflat, about a mile from the town, is a small mill for spinning flax. A small market is held on Friday, the grant of which was confirmed by Cromwell, in 1653; and there are fairs on May 3rd, Friday before Whit-Sunday, and on the second Friday after Old Michaelmas, for horned cattle and sheep. The land is freehold, the manorial rights being vested in the landowners ; the freeholders elect four nominal lords, who hold a court occasionally for the enrollment of the names of purchasers of land, and for other matters. The living is a vicarage, in the archdeaconry and diocese of Carlisle, rated in the king's books at £16. 17. 3½., and in the patronage of the Landowners. The church, which is dedicated to All Saints, stands upon rising ground on the north side of the town ; it is a neat edifice, in the ancient style of English architecture, with a low embattled tower : in the interior is a monument in memory of Dr. Richard Burn, vicar of Orton, chancellor of the diocese, author of treatises on "The Office of a Justice of the Peace," and on "Ecclesiastical Law," and, conjointly with Joseph Nicholson, of the History of Westmorland and Cumberland. The free school, which was founded by subscription, about 1730, was rebuilt on a different spot in 1809 ; Mrs. Frances Wardale, in 1781, bequeathed the sum of £400, which with other benefactions produces annually £21. 15. ; from seventy to eighty children are instructed, those who can afford it paying a small quarterage. At Tebay, within this parish, is a free grammar school, endowed by Robert Adamson, in 1672, with land in Kendal parish, producing £45 per annum ; about sixty children are instructed gratuitously : another, at Greenholme, was endowed by George Gibson, Esq., in 1733, with £400 original Bank stock : the master receives a small quarterly payment from some of the children. On the highest part of Orton Scar there was formerly a beacon, communicating with those of Penrith, Stanmore, and Whinfell, in Kendale ; and behind the Scar, to the east, is Castle-Folds, a place of safety for cattle, in case of incursions from the Scottish borderers, before the union of the two kingdoms. Near Raisgill hall is a circular tumulus of loose stones, one hundred yards in circumference, on digging beneath which, a human skeleton and several bones were found. In a field, called "Gamelanes," is a number of large granite stones, considered to be the remains of a Druidical temple. Near the church is Our Lady's Well, with a small chapel,

formerly appropriated to the reception of offerings made by pilgrims. Dr. Thomas Barlow, Bishop of Lincoln, and a writer of some eminence, was born in this parish in 1607 ; he died in 1691.

ORTON on the HILL, a parish in the hundred of SPARKENHOE, county of LEICESTER, 4¾ miles (N.) from Atherstone, containing 370 inhabitants. The living is a discharged vicarage, in the archdeaconry of Leicester, and diocese of Lincoln, rated in the king's books at £6. 12. 8., and in the patronage of the Bishop of Oxford. The church is dedicated to St. Edith. This parish is in the honour of Tutbury, duchy of Lancaster, and within the jurisdiction of a court of pleas held at Tutbury every third Tuesday, for the recovery of debts under 40s.

ORTON-LONGVILLE, a parish in the hundred of NORMAN-CROSS, county of HUNTINGDON, 2¼ miles (S.W. by W.) from Peterborough, containing 213 inhabitants. The living is a rectory, to which that of Botolph-Bridge was united in 1721, in the archdeaconry of Huntingdon, and diocese of Lincoln, rated in the king's books at £12. 6. 5½., and in the patronage of the Earl of Aboyne. The church is dedicated to the Holy Trinity.

ORTON-WATERVILLE, a parish in the hundred of NORMAN-CROSS, county of HUNTINGDON, 3 miles (S.W. by W.) from Peterborough, containing 282 inhabitants. The living is a rectory, in the archdeaconry of Huntingdon, and diocese of Lincoln, rated in the king's books at £12. 11. 5½., and in the patronage of the Master and Fellows of Pembroke Hall, Cambridge. The church is dedicated to St. Mary.

ORWELL, a parish in the hundred of WETHERLEY, county of CAMBRIDGE, 7½ miles (N.N.W.) from Royston, containing 475 inhabitants. The living comprises a sinecure rectory and a discharged vicarage, in the archdeaconry and diocese of Ely, the rectory rated in the king's books at £19. 19. 4½., and the vicarage at £7. 10. 10., the former in the patronage of the Master and Fellows of Trinity College, Cambridge, and the latter in that of the Rector. The church is dedicated to St. Andrew. At Malton, anciently a distinct parish, is a desecrated church, now used as a barn. A school for poor children was founded and liberally endowed, in 1750, by the Rev. John Colbatch, D.D., some time rector.

OSBALDESTON, a township in the parish, and lower division of the hundred, of BLACKBURN, county palatine of LANCASTER, 4½ miles (N.W. by N.) from Blackburn, containing 319 inhabitants.

OSBALDWICK, a parish in the liberty of ST. PETER of YORK, East riding, though locally in the wapentake of Bulmer, North riding, of the county of YORK, comprising the townships of Murton and Osbaldwick, and containing 310 inhabitants, of which number, 176 are in the township of Osbaldwick 2¼ miles (E.) from York. The living is a discharged vicarage, in the peculiar jurisdiction and patronage of the Prebendary of Strensall in the Cathedral Church of York, rated in the king's books at £4, and endowed with £600 royal bounty. The church is dedicated to St. Thomas.

OSBASTON, a township partly in the parish of MARKET-BOSWORTH, but chiefly in that of CADEBY, hundred of SPARKENHOE, county of LEICESTER, 2 miles (N.E.) from Market-Bosworth, containing 176 inhabitants.

OSBOURNBY, a parish in the wapentake of AVE-LAND, parts of KESTEVEN, county of LINCOLN, 2¾ miles (N.) from Falkingham, containing 428 inhabitants. The living is a discharged vicarage, in the archdeaconry and diocese of Lincoln, rated in the king's books at £7. 0. 5., endowed with £200 private benefaction, and £200 royal bounty, and in the patronage of the Duke of Devonshire. The church, dedicated to St. Peter and St. Paul, is principally in the decorated style of archi-tecture : it contains some stalls, the remains of a rood-loft, screen, and a large ancient font.

OSGARTHORPE, a parish in the western division of the hundred of GOSCOTE, county of LEICESTER, 5¼ miles (E. N. E.) from Ashby de la Zouch, containing 352 inhabitants. The living is a rectory, in the archdeaconry of Leicester, and diocese of Lincoln, rated in the king's books at £7, and in the patronage of the Marquis of Hastings. The church is dedicated to St. Mary. A free school was erected by Thomas Hardy, Esq., who, in 1670, vested in trustees so much money as would pur-chase lands to the value of £100 a year, for the main-tenance of a schoolmaster and six clergymen's widows. A canal passes from Barrow Hill, in this parish, crosses the parish of Sheepshead, and terminates in that of Loughborough.

OSGODBY, a township in the parish of LAVING-TON, or LINTON, wapentake of BELTISLOE, parts of KESTEVEN, county of LINCOLN, 4¼ miles (N. E.) from Corby, containing 95 inhabitants.

OSGODBY, a joint parish with Kirkby, in the north-ern division of the wapentake of WALSHCROFT, parts of LINDSEY, county of LINCOLN, 4 miles (N. W.) from Market-Rasen. The population is returned with Kirkby. There is a place of worship for Wesleyan Methodists.

OSGODBY, a township in the parish of HEMING-BROUGH, wapentake of OUZE and DERWENT, East riding of the county of YORK, 2½ miles (E. N. E.) from Selby, containing 185 inhabitants.

OSGODBY, a township in the parish of CAYTON, PICKERING lythe, North riding of the county of YORK, 2¾ miles (S. by E.) from Scarborough, containing 72 inhabitants.

OSGOODBY-GRANGE, a hamlet in that part of the parish of KILBURN which is in the liberty of RIPON, West riding of the county of YORK, 4¾ miles (E. by S.) from Thirsk. The population is returned with the township of Hood.

OSLESTON, a joint township with Thurvaston, in the parish of SUTTON on the HILL, hundred of APPLE-TREE, county of DERBY, 7½ miles (W. by N.) from Derby, containing, with Thurvaston, 440 inhabitants.

OSLOW, a township in the parish of CHURCH-EATON, western division of the hundred of CUTTLE-STONE, county of STAFFORD. The population is returned with the parish.

OSMASTON, a parish in the hundred of APPLE-TREE, county of DERBY, 2¼ miles (S.E. by S.) from Ashbourn, containing 296 inhabitants. The living is a perpetual curacy, in the archdeaconry of Derby, and diocese of Lichfield and Coventry, and in the patronage of the Rector of Brailsford. The church, dedicated to St. Martin, has lately received an addition of forty-eight free sittings, the Incorporated Society for the en-largement of churches and chapels having granted £50 towards defraying the expense.

VOL. III.

OSMASTON, a parish in the hundred of REPTON and GRESLEY, county of DERBY, 2¼ miles (S.E.) from Derby, containing 159 inhabitants. The living is a perpetual curacy, in the archdeaconry of Derby, and diocese of Lichfield and Coventry, endowed with £200 private benefaction, and £400 royal bounty, and in the patronage of Sir Robert Wilmot, Bart. The church is dedicated to All Saints. The river Derwent and the Derby canal pass through the parish.

OSMINGTON, a parish in the hundred of CULLI-FORD-TREE, Dorchester division of the county of DOR-SET, 4½ miles (N.E.) from Melcombe-Regis, containing 318 inhabitants. The living is a vicarage, in the arch-deaconry of Dorset, and diocese of Bristol, rated in the king's books at £11. 0. 2½., and in the patronage of the Bishop of Salisbury. The church is dedicated to St. Osmond. The parish is bounded on the south by the English channel.

OSMOTHERLEY, a township in the parish of ULVERSTONE, hundred of LONSDALE, north of the sands, county palatine of LANCASTER, 3 miles (N. by W.) from Ulverstone, containing 264 inhabitants. There is a place of worship for Wesleyan Methodists. A school has been erected by subscription ; the income is about £10. 10. per annum, for which twenty children are educated.

OSMOTHERLEY, a parish in the wapentake of ALLERTONSHIRE, North riding of the county of YORK, comprising the townships of Ellerbeck, West Harsley, Osmotherley, and Thimbleby, and containing 1087 in-habitants, of which number, 755 are in the township of Osmotherley, 7½ miles (E.N.E.) from North Allerton. The living is a discharged vicarage, in the peculiar juris-diction of the Court of the Bishop of Durham for Al-lerton and Allertonshire, rated in the king's books at £8. 10., endowed with £600 royal bounty, and £1000 parliamentary grant, and in the patronage of the Bishop of Durham. The church is dedicated to St. Peter. Here are places of worship for the Society of Friends, Wesleyan Methodists, and Roman Catholics. There are extensive quarries of freestone in the parish, and mills for spinning small cordage. Two small endowments were bequeathed by the Rev. Mr. Nicholson, in 1757, and by Daniel Tyerman, in 1786, for teaching poor children. A Carthusian priory was founded here, about 1396, by Thomas, Duke of Surrey, the revenue of which, at the dissolution, was valued at £323. At West Harley are the remains of a castle, the tower of which having been much damaged by a thunder-storm, was, a few years since, taken down.

OSPRINGE-LIBERTY, a parish in the hundred of FAVERSHAM, lathe of SCRAY, county of KENT, ¾ of a mile (W.S.W.) from Faversham, containing 912 inha-bitants. The living is a vicarage, in the archdeaconry and diocese of Canterbury, rated in the king's books at £10, and in the patronage of the Master and Fellows of St. John's College, Cambridge. The church, dedi-cated to St. Peter and St. Paul, is principally in the early style of English architecture. This was doubtless the site of the ancient *Durolevum*, though some have fixed that station at Newington. A Roman fortifica-tion and burial-place have been discovered here, be-sides numerous Roman antiquities of various kinds. Ospringe is an independent franchise, governed by its own constable, and has a fair annually on May 25th.

3 N

Here is a neat range of infantry barracks, erected during the late war. On a stream which flows through the village are extensive gunpowder-mills, belonging to government, and on its northern bank are some remains of a Maison Dieu, founded by Henry III., about 1235, and dedicated to the Blessed Virgin Mary; it was formerly of great repute, and consisted of a master and three brethren of the order of the Holy Cross, and two Secular clerks; but falling into decay, at the close of the reign of Edward IV., it escheated to the crown, and its remains have since been converted into dwelling-houses.

OSSETT, a chapelry in that part of the parish of DEWSBURY which is in the lower division of the wapentake of AGBRIGG, West riding of the county of YORK, 4¼ miles (W.) from Wakefield, containing 4775 inhabitants. The living is a perpetual curacy, in the archdeaconry and diocese of York, endowed with £800 private benefaction, £800 royal bounty, and £600 parliamentary grant, and in the patronage of the Vicar of Dewsbury. The chapel, dedicated to the Holy Trinity, has lately received an addition of three hundred free sittings, the Incorporated Society for the enlargement of churches and chapels having granted £300 towards defraying the expense. There are places of worship for Independents and Wesleyan Methodists. A school was established by subscription in 1745; part of the money was applied for the erection of a schoolroom and a house for the master, and the remaining portion was invested in the purchase of certain premises, producing about £20 per annum; for several years the income has been allowed to accumulate for the repair of the school-house, and establishing a Sunday school.

OSSINGTON, a parish in the northern division of the wapentake of THURGARTON, county of NOTTINGHAM, 4¼ miles (S. S. E.) from Tuxford, containing 301 inhabitants. The living is a donative, in the patronage of J. E. Denison, Esq. The church is dedicated to the Holy Rood.

OSWALD (KIRK), county of CUMBERLAND.—See KIRK-OSWALD.

OSWALD (ST.), county of NORTHUMBERLAND.—See WALL.

OSWALD-KIRK, a parish in the wapentake of RYEDALE, North riding of the county of YORK, 3½ miles (S.) from Helmsley, containing 212 inhabitants. The living is a rectory, in the archdeaconry of Cleveland, and diocese of York, rated in the king's books at £10. 1. 8., and in the patronage of William Gray, Esq. The church, dedicated to St. Oswald, is principally in the Norman style. Here are the remains of an old monastic edifice. Eight poor children are instructed for £4 a year, the gift of Mary Fyshe, and the charity school has an endowment of £5 per annum, by Thomas Carter. Roger Dodsworth, the antiquary, was born at Newton-Grange, in 1585; he died in 1654.

OSWALDTWISTLE, a township in that part of the parish of WHALLEY which is in the lower division of the hundred of BLACKBURN, county palatine of LANCASTER, 3¾ miles (E. by S.) from Blackburn, containing 4960 inhabitants. Here are print-works on a large scale, and other establishments for the manufacture of cotton goods. Coal is obtained in the township.

OSWESTRY, a borough, market town, and parish, having separate jurisdiction, though locally in the hundred of Oswestry, county of SALOP, comprising the townships of Llanforda with Trefarclawdd, Pontregaer, and Lynymon; Maesbury with Morton and Crickheath; Middleton with Aston, Hisland, and Wooton; Weston with Sweeney, Treflach, and Trefonnen; and containing 7523 inhabitants, of which number, 3910 are in the town of Oswestry, 17 miles (N. W.) from Shrewsbury, and 180 (N. W.) from London. This town is supposed to have been founded, in the fourth century, by the Britons, and having been given by Cunetha Wledic, Prince of North Wales, to his son Ussa, in the sixth century, was named *Maes Usswalt*, and subsequently *Maserfield*. Its present appellation is a corruption of the Saxon *Oswaldstre*, Oswald's tree, or town, and originated in a battle fought here, August 5th, 642, between Oswald, the Christian King of Northumberland, and Penda, the Pagan King of Mercia, in which the former was slain; and the members of his body were severally affixed to three crosses, in token of conquest, and in derision of his religious tenets: on this account also the Welch called it *Croes Oswald*, which name they still retain. The esteem in which Oswald had been held by the monks led to his canonization; the scene of his death became hallowed, miraculous virtues were attributed to his relics, and a monastery was soon afterwards raised to his memory, from which institution this place received the appellation of *Blanc minster*, with other names of similar import. Oswestry continued in the possession of the Britons, and constituted a portion of the kingdom termed Powysland, until the year 777, when it was annexed to the kingdom of Mercia, by conquest, and an earthen mound, called *Clawdd Offa*, Offa's dyke, and vulgarly the Devil's ditch, was raised, as a line of demarcation between that kingdom and the principality of Wales. This dyke extends from the river Wye, along the counties of Hereford, Radnor, Montgomery, and Denbigh, and terminates near the Clwydian hills; near this town it crosses the race-course on Cefn-y-bwch. Parallel with it, but at unequal distances, is a similar rampart, called Watt's Dyke, or perhaps originally Watch Dyke, from the number of Watch forts on its course: the Welch call it Clawdd Wat, from Cadwalader, King of Wales. The formation of this work is of much earlier date, and is ascribed to the Britons, as a means of defence against Roman invasion: the intervening space was esteemed neutral ground, whereon the Britons, Danes, &c., were accustomed to meet for the purpose of traffic, without molestation. On the line of Watt's Dyke, about a mile northward of the town, is another work of the ancient Britons, denominated by their descendants *Llys Ogran*, or *Ogyrvan*, or *Caer Ogran*, Ogran's palace, or strong hold; and also *Hên Dinas*, old camp or city: its present name is *Old Fort*, or, by corruption, *Old Port*, and it is occasionally called Old Oswestry, there being a vulgar tradition that it was anciently the site of the town: it was a famous military post, being a lofty natural eminence, of an oblong shape, and surrounded by

Corporate Seal.

a deep triple intrenchment on the summit and sides, the area comprising nearly sixteen acres, and the fortifications, which are covered with timber and brushwood, upwards of forty.

Oswestry is not mentioned in the Norman survey: according to Dugdale, it was given by the Conqueror to Alan, ancestor of the Fitz-Alans, Earls of Arundel, in which noble family the barony continued upwards of five hundred years; but another authority states that the Fitz-Alans became lords of it by marriage of one of the lords of Clun with Maud, widow of Madog ap Meredydd, who, on partition of Powysland by his father, succeeded to the division termed Powys Vadog, of which Oswestry formed part. This was Madog's chief residence, and, according to the Welch records, he built the castle about 1149, though the English historians mention it to have existed before the Conquest : it stood on an artificial mound on the north-west side of the town, but there are scarcely any remains. When Henry II. attempted to subjugate the principality, in the year 1164, he assembled his army and encamped here for a considerable time, prior to the sanguinary conflict beneath Castell Crogen, now Chirk castle, the scene of which is yet marked by a heap of stones, called *Adw'yr Bedhan*, or the Passage of the Graves. During the contest between John and the barons, about 1216, the castle was destroyed by fire, and, in 1233, the town experienced a similar fate from Llewellyn ap Jorwerth, Prince of Wales. In 1277, Edward I., still meditating the subjugation of Wales, began to surround this town with walls, for the completion of which he imposed a murage tax upon the county for six years : they were about a mile in circumference, had four gates, and were flanked by a foss. Soon after the dissolution of the parliament held at Shrewsbury, in which the Duke of Hereford, afterwards Henry IV., accused the Duke of Norfolk of treasonable expressions, those illustrious persons were cited to appear before the king, and the commissioners appointed by that parliament, in this town. During an insurrection of the Welch, under Owen Glyndwr, in 1400, Oswestry was again nearly destroyed by fire; and in 1403; that renowned leader, having caused himself to be proclaimed Prince of Wales, assembled a force of twelve thousand men here, with a view to join Lord Percy against the king; but this union was not effected; and, on the issue of that celebrated battle, Glyndwr retreated precipitately into Wales. At the commencement of the parliamentary war, Oswestry was garrisoned in support of the royal cause; but on June 22nd, 1644, the forces were compelled to surrender to a detachment of the parliamentary army, under the command of the Earl of Denbigh and General Mytton : an ineffectual attempt was made to retake the town, and a few years afterwards the castle was demolished. A great part of the town was destroyed by casual fires, which occurred in 1542, 1544, and 1567 : the western suburb is yet called *Pentre poedd*, the burnt town. In 1559, the plague swept off more than five hundred of its inhabitants, on which occasion the market was removed to a place on the road to Welchpool, about half a mile distant, where is the base of an old cross, called *Croes Willin*, which is supposed to have been erected at the time; in 1585, a similar visitation took place, and during its continuance, the flannel market, for which Oswestry was then noted, was held at Knockin.

The town, situated on the road from London to Holyhead, occupies the declivity of a range of hills which skirt it on the western side, and commands an extensive view over the fertile plain of Salop : the streets are paved and lighted, under the provisions of an act obtained in 1810, gas having been introduced in 1825; the old buildings, of timber and brick, have been succeeded by respectable modern edifices, and the town, which has long since stretched beyond its ancient boundaries, is still progressively increasing in size, and improving in appearance. A neat theatre, in Willow-street, is occupied by a respectable company in the autumn; races are held annually in September; and accommodation for occasional assemblies is provided at the Wynnstay Arms. The sale of Welch flannel and of cotton goods, which was formerly carried on to a great extent, was removed to Shrewsbury about 1625 : at present the chief business of the town is in malting, and there is some trade in flannel. Coal abounds in the neighbourhood. The markets are on Wednesday and Saturday, the former being the principal. A fair on the eve, day, and morrow of St. Andrew was granted by Henry III.; fairs are also held on the third Wednesday in January, March 15th, May 12th, Wednesday before Midsummer-day, August 15th, Friday before September 29th, and December 10th. The first charter was granted to the inhabitants by William Fitz-Alan, their feudal lord, in the reign of Henry II., and the first royal charter by Richard II., confirmations having been received from subsequent sovereigns : the borough is now governed by the charter of Charles II., under which the corporate body consists of a mayor, high steward, twelve aldermen, and fifteen common council-men, assisted by a recorder, coroner, town clerk, murenger, and other officers. The mayor, recorder, and murenger, are elected by the aldermen and members of the common council; the high-steward and town clerk are appointed by the lord of the manor : the mayor for the preceding year acts as coroner. Courts for the borough, and petty sessions for the hundred, are held here. The guildhall is a plain stone edifice, with a small turret, comprising apartments for holding quarter sessions and other public meetings, and a jury-room; it is private property, and forms one side of the square denominated Bailey-head : near it is the town clerk's office, a lofty edifice built with the stone which formerly belonged to the town gates; behind it is a small prison. The living is a discharged vicarage, in the archdeaconry and diocese of St. Asaph, rated in the king's books at £23. 15. 7½., and in the patronage of Lord Clive. The church, dedicated to St. Oswald, was originally the conventual church of the ancient monastery, and was greatly damaged during the commotions of 1616 and 1644, at which latter period the tower was taken down by the royalists, lest, as it stood without the town walls, their opponents should annoy them from its summit. On the north side of the churchyard is a pleasant walk, shaded by a double row of lime trees, and terminated by an alcove. A chapel of ease was erected, in 1810, at Trefonnen, in this parish, by subscription, for the accommodation of the Welch inhabitants, the service being performed in the Welch language. There are places of worship for Baptists, Independents, and Wesleyan Methodists.

The free grammar school was founded, about the time

of Henry IV., by Davy Holbecke, and endowed with land then worth £10; in 1776, the sum of £780 was raised by subscription, for the erection of a new school-room and a residence for the master; at the same time a field, called *Cae Groes*, from having contained the cross, or pole, on which the mangled remains of Oswald were exposed, was given to the school by Sir W. W. Wynn, Bart., having been regularly conveyed to it, by deed dated September 22nd, 1815, at a small rental, by the present baronet of that name : the premises then begun were completed by the present master, who also recovered about twenty-six acres of land for the institution, which had been considered lost. The annual rental arising from the original endowment is about £260 : the master's salary, including the value of the house, &c., is about £300 per annum, and he receives a considerable number of boarders : the school is free to all the sons of parishioners for instruction in English and classical literature. Thomas Bray, D.D., a learned divine, the principal promoter of the "Society for the Propagation of the Gospel in Foreign Parts," and the founder of parochial and lending libraries, received the early part of his education at this school. A National school for boys and girls is held in apartments above the town clerk's office and town hall, and is supported by voluntary contributions, the National Society having contributed £200 towards its establishment; here also schoolmasters are prepared for Wales. The house of industry, a spacious and handsome edifice of brick, about a mile from the town, was erected for the poor of this town and parish, and those of ten neighbouring parishes, with the township of Llwyntedman, in the parish of Llanymynech, at the joint expense of the respective places, pursuant to an act passed in 1791. There is a society for ameliorating the condition of the poor. A little westward from the town is Oswald's well, a small basin under an arch in the recess of a stone wall, with a crowned head of Oswald, near the spot where that monarch is supposed to have fallen; a chapel formerly stood near it. On the ancient walls which surrounded the town were several towers, and the entrance was through four gates, called respectively, New gate, Beatrice gate, Willow, or, more properly, Wallia gate, and Black gate, the last-named having been taken down in 1766, and the others in 1782. Oswestry confers the inferior title of baron on the Duke of Norfolk.

OSYTH (ST.) CHICH, a parish in the hundred of TENDRING, county of ESSEX, 11 miles (S. E.) from Colchester, containing 1414 inhabitants. The living is a perpetual curacy, in the archdeaconry of Colchester, and diocese of London, and in the patronage of F. Nassau, Esq. The church is a large, irregular building, some parts being of considerable antiquity, and others of the time of Henry VI. : in the chancel are two handsome monuments in alabaster, erected to the memory of the two first Lords D'Arcy, and their wives. A creek, or arm of the river Colm, dividing into two branches, leads to two wharfs in this parish, and is navigable for barges and sloops. At the south-eastern boundary are a martello tower, for the defence of the coast, and a signal station. A school is endowed with land producing about £7 per annum. This place, remarkable for the remains of its noble monastery, derives its name from St. Osyth, daughter of Redwald, King of East Anglia, who, having made a vow of virginity, retired hither, where she founded a church and a nunnery : these were afterwards plundered by the Danes, who beheaded the foundress near an adjacent fountain. About the year 1118, Belmeis, Bishop of London, established a priory for Augustine canons on the supposed site of the nunnery, which, at the dissolution, had a revenue of £758. 5. 8. The quadrangle of this building is almost entire, excepting part of the north side, where are some modern apartments : the entrance is by a beautiful gateway of hewn stone, mixed with flints, having two towers and posterns : to the east are three towers, one larger and loftier than the rest.

OTFORD, a parish in the hundred of CODSHEATH, lathe of SUTTON at HONE, county of KENT, 3 miles (N.) from Seven - Oaks, containing 630 inhabitants. The living is a perpetual curacy, in the peculiar jurisdiction of the Archbishop of Canterbury, endowed with £400 private benefaction, £200 royal bounty, and £900 parliamentary grant, and in the patronage of the Dean and Chapter of Westminster. The church, dedicated to St. Bartholomew, is principally in the decorated style of architecture. There is a place of worship for Wesleyan Methodists. An hospital for lepers existed here in the reign of Henry III. The river Darent runs through the parish. In the village are the extensive ruins of an ancient palace of the Archbishops of Canterbury, once the residence of the celebrated Thomas à Becket, the square tower of which is still in good preservation : some idea may be formed of its extent and grandeur from the repairs, in Warham's time, having cost upwards of £33,000. Near it is a well, thirty feet deep and fifteen in diameter, enclosed by a wall, which is called Thomas à Becket's well, and said to have been used by him as a bath. Archbishop Winchelsea died here in 1313. At this place, in 773, Offa, King of Mercia, gained a great victory over Ealhmund, King of Kent; and here Edmund Ironside, in 1016, defeated the Danes with great slaughter : many skeletons and bones of the slain have been discovered in the neighbourhood.

OTHAM, a parish in the hundred of EYHORNE, lathe of AYLESFORD, county of KENT, 2¾ miles (S. E. by E.) from Maidstone, containing 337 inhabitants. The living is a rectory, in the archdeaconry and diocese of Canterbury, rated in the king's books at £9. 17. 3½., and in the patronage of the Rev. W. Horne. The church is dedicated to St. Nicholas. The small river Lenham forms the northern boundary of the parish, in which there is an abundance of what is called Kentish ragstone. An abbey of Premonstratensian canons was founded here, and dedicated to the Blessed Virgin and St. Lawrence, about the time of Henry II.; but, in the reign of John, they removed to a more convenient situation at Beaulieu, in the parish of Frant. Bishop Horne was born in this parish in 1730; he died in 1792.

OTHERTON, a township in that part of the parish of PENKRIDGE which is in the eastern division of the hundred of CUTTLESTONE, county of STAFFORD, 1 mile (S. S. E.) from Penkridge, with which the population is returned.

OTHERY, a parish in the hundred of WHITLEY, county of SOMERSET, 4½ miles (N. W. by N.) from Langport, containing, with a part of Boroughbridge, 509 inhabitants. The living is a discharged vicarage, within the jurisdiction of Glastonbury, and diocese of

Bath and Wells, rated in the king's books at £12, endowed with £200 royal bounty, and in the patronage of the Bishop of Bath and Wells. The church, dedicated to St. Michael, is a large cruciform structure, with a handsome tower, seventy-five feet in height. The navigable river Parret forms the western and southern boundaries of the parish, in which there is a quarry of good building stone.

OTLEY, a parish in the hundred of CARLFORD, county of SUFFOLK, 5¾ miles (N.W. by N.) from Woodbridge, containing 629 inhabitants. The living is a rectory, in the archdeaconry of Suffolk, and diocese of Norwich, rated in the king's books at £16. 6. 5½., and in the patronage of the Earl of Abergavenny. The church is dedicated to St. Mary. There is a place of worship for Baptists.

OTLEY, a parish comprising the market town of Otley, the chapelries of Baildon, Bramhope, Burley, and Poole, and the townships of Esholt, Hawksworth, and Menstone, in the upper division of the wapentake of SKYRACK, and the chapelry of Denton in the lower, and the townships of Farnley, Lindley, Newhall with Clifton, and Little Timble in the upper, division of the wapentake of CLARO, West riding of the county of YORK, and containing 9358 inhabitants, of which number, 3065 are in the market town of Otley, 28 miles (W. by S.) from York, and 206 (N.N.W.) from London. The name has been considered a contraction of *Oat-lea*, from the quantity of oats formerly cultivated in the neighbourhood; but, with more probability, and on better evidence, it is believed to be a corruption of *Othelai*, as spelt in Domesday-book, meaning the field of *Othe*, or *Otho*. The town, which is pleasantly situated on the banks of the river Wharf, is small, and neatly built. A few persons are employed in the worsted manufacture. Considerable quantities of smelts, eels, and trout, are taken in the river, near Otley, and occasionally salmon. The market, which is amply supplied with corn, cattle, sheep, and calves, is on Friday; and fairs are held, on the first Monday after August 2nd, for horses and cattle; on the Friday between New and Old Martinmas day, for hiring servants; and on every second Monday, for cattle and sheep.

The living is a discharged vicarage, in the archdeaconry and diocese of York, rated in the king's books at £13. 1. 8., and in the patronage of the Crown. The church, which is dedicated to All Saints, was originally of Norman architecture, but of the ancient building the north door alone remains: it is a spacious edifice, and contains several monuments of the families of Fairfax, Fawkes, Vavasour, &c. There are places of worship for the Society of Friends, Independents, and Wesleyan Methodists. The free grammar school, founded by means of a bequest of £250 from Thomas Cave, in the year 1602, was established by letters patent of James I., and named, in honour of the then Prince of Wales, "The Free Grammar School of Prince Henry;" the above bequest having been augmented by subscription, a school-room, and other apartments, were erected about 1611, under the direction of the governors; the master receives £20 per annum: the school is open for gratuitous classical instruction to the sons of parishioners, but three boys only are taught on the foundation, and about forty are instructed by the usher, in English grammar, writing, and arithmetic, on paying quarterage. Here was anciently an hospital for lepers. Sir Thomas, afterwards

Lord Fairfax, the celebrated parliamentary general, was born at Denton Park, in this parish, in the year 1611, and died in the same house, on the 12th of November, 1671.

OTTERBOURNE, a parish in the hundred of BUDDLESGATE, Fawley division of the county of SOUTHAMPTON, 4¼ miles (S. S. W.) from Winchester, containing 565 inhabitants. The living is a perpetual curacy, annexed to the vicarage of Hursley, in the peculiar jurisdiction of the Vicar of Hursley. The church is dedicated to St. Matthew. The Itchen navigation passes through the parish, which is within the jurisdiction of the Cheyney Court held at Winchester every Thursday, for the recovery of debts to any amount.

OTTERBURN, a township in that part of the parish of KIRKBY in MALHAM-DALE which is in the western division of the wapentake of STAINCLIFFE and EWCROSS, West riding of the county of YORK, 8½ miles (S. E.) from Settle, containing 40 inhabitants.

OTTERBURN-WARD, a township in the parish of ELSDON, southern division of COQUETDALE ward, county of NORTHUMBERLAND, 11 miles (N. E. by N.) from Bellingham, containing 388 inhabitants, who are principally employed in the manufacture of woollen cloth, including carding, dyeing, and fulling. Otterburn castle was a strong fortress well adapted for sustaining the frequent attacks of the Scottish borderers. Here was fought, in 1388, the famous battle between the English, under Henry Percy, surnamed Hotspur, and the Scots, commanded by Earl Douglas, in which the latter fell by the sword of the former, who, with many of his knights, was afterwards taken prisoner. The ancient and popular ballad of "Chevy Chase," in which, however, there are material deviations from historical facts, was founded upon this sanguinary contest. On the spot where the battle was fought are several tumuli, also remains of intrenchments, and a cross erected where Douglas is said to have fallen.

OTTERDEN, a parish partly in the hundred of FAVERSHAM, lathe of SCRAY, but chiefly in the hundred of EYHORNE, lathe of AYLESFORD, county of KENT, 3½ miles (N.) from Charing, containing 172 inhabitants. The living is a rectory, in the archdeaconry and diocese of Canterbury, rated in the king's books at £6. 14. 2., and in the patronage of W. G. Paxton, Esq. The church, dedicated to St. Lawrence, was erected in 1753, near the ruins of a more ancient edifice, which are still discernible.

OTTERFORD, a parish in the hundred of TAUNTON and TAUNTON-DEAN, county of SOMERSET, 7 miles (S.) from Taunton, containing 366 inhabitants. The living is a perpetual curacy, in the archdeaconry and diocese of Taunton, and diocese of Bath and Wells, endowed with £200 private benefaction, £600 royal bounty, and £300 parliamentary grant, and in the patronage of R. Buncombe, Esq. The church is dedicated to St. Leonard. John Boles, in 1769, bequeathed £50 in support of a school for six poor children.

OTTERHAM, a parish in the hundred of LESNEWTH, county of CORNWALL, 6 miles (N. E. by N.) from Camelford, containing 212 inhabitants. The living is a discharged rectory, in the archdeaconry of Cornwall, and diocese of Exeter, rated in the king's books at £6. 14. 2., and in the patronage of W. Chilcott, Esq. The church is dedicated to St. Denis.

OTTERHAMPTON, a parish in the hundred of CANNINGTON, county of SOMERSET, 5¾ miles (N. W.) from Bridg-water, containing 221 inhabitants. The living is a discharged rectory, in the archdeaconry of Taunton, and diocese of Bath and Wells, rated in the king's books at £13. 6., and in the patronage of J. Evered, Esq. The navigable river Parret bounds the parish on the east.

OTTERINGTON (NORTH), a parish comprising the townships of North Otterington and Thornton le Beans, in the wapentake of ALLERTONSHIRE, and the township of Thornton le Moor, in that of BIRDFORTH, North riding of the county of YORK, and containing 585 inhabitants, of which number, 44 are in the township of North Otterington, 3½ miles (S.) from North Allerton. The living is a discharged vicarage, in the jurisdiction of the peculiar court of Allertonshire, belonging to the Bishop of Durham, rated in the king's books at £4, and in the patronage of the Dean and Canons of Christ Church, Oxford. The church is dedicated to St. Michael.

OTTERINGTON (SOUTH), a parish in the wapentake of BIRDFORTH, North riding of the county of YORK, 4½ miles (S. by E.) from North Allerton, containing 201 inhabitants. The living is a discharged rectory in two portions, called Gamwell House, and Weatherel House, in the archdeaconry of Cleveland, and diocese of York, the former endowed with £200 royal bounty, each rated in the king's books at £7. 14. 4½., and in the patronage of the Rev. J. Sampson. The church is dedicated to St. Andrew.

OTTERTON, a parish in the eastern division of the hundred of BUDLEIGH, county of DEVON, 4 miles (S. W. by W.) from Sidmouth, containing 1297 inhabitants. The living is a vicarage, in the archdeaconry and diocese of Exeter, rated in the king's books at £22, and in the patronage of Lord Rolle. The church is dedicated to St. Michael. There was formerly a chapel at Hederland. The river Otter runs through the parish. Fairs are held on the Wednesday in Easter week and October 11th. Here was an Alien priory of Black monks, founded in the reign of the Conqueror, and subordinate to the abbey of St. Michael in Pericula Maris, in Normandy; at the suppression, in the 1st of Edward IV., its revenue was estimated at £87. 10. 4., and its possessions were given to the monastery of Sion. The prior enjoyed the singular rights of first choice in the fish-market, of appropriating to himself the half of every dolphin brought thither, and of claiming every porpoise at the price of "twelve pence, and a loaf to each sailor, and two to the master."

OTTERY (ST. MARY), a parish, market town, and hundred, in the county of DEVON, 12 miles (E. by N.) from Exeter, and 156 (W.S.W.) from London, containing 3522 inhabitants. The town is agreeably situated on the eastern bank of the river Otter, from which it receives its name, the adjunct having originated either from the foundation of a collegiate church, in honour of the Virgin Mary, by John Grandisson, Bishop of Exeter, in 1337; or, from the manor having been given by Edward the Confessor to the church of St. Mary at Rouen, in Normandy. During the civil war between Charles I. and the parliament, this town was alternately occupied by both parties; and in 1645, a detachment of the parliamentary army being quartered here, under Sir Thomas Fairfax, on the refusal of the inhabitants to furnish the contribu-

tions required by that commander, his troops are reported to have defaced the church, and destroyed two organs in it. The town is situated a little to the south of the high road from Honiton to Exeter: it is irregularly built on very uneven ground, and, exclusively of a few respectable houses in the higher part of it, near the church, it is composed chiefly of cottages. There is a good supply of water from wells and springs, and the surrounding country is pleasant and fertile. The manufacture of serge, which once flourished here, has been superseded by extensive silk-works, the machinery belonging to which is very ingeniously constructed, and is put in motion by a water-wheel of large dimensions. Handkerchiefs and ribands are among the chief articles now made, and the factory furnishes employment to between three and four hundred persons. Here are also a tan-yard and a rope-walk, and some lace is made in the town. The market is on Thursday; and fairs are held on the Tuesday before Palm-Sunday, Whit-Tuesday, and August 15th, for cattle, and at the last a considerable quantity of cheese also is sold: there is a great market on the Thursday before the second Friday in every month. Courts leet and baron are held annually for the manor, at which two constables are appointed for the parish, and two for the town, and there is likewise a constable for the hundred, whose office is permanent.

The living is a discharged vicarage, in the archdeaconry and diocese of Exeter, rated in the king's books at £20, endowed with £1400 parliamentary grant, and in the patronage of the Crown. After the suppression of the college founded by Bishop Grandisson, the church, the cemetery, the school-house, and other collegiate buildings and premises, were granted in trust to four inhabitants of the town, who were incorporated as "Governors of the Church of St. Mary Ottery," who collect the small tithes, and have the exclusive possession of the choir of the church: they also nominate a chaplain, sexton, and church-keeper. The church, dedicated to St. Mary, a large and curious edifice, has been called "a cathedral in miniature," being constructed, like that of Exeter, with towers in the transepts, besides which it comprises a nave, choir, aisles, and Lady chapel. The principal part of the body of the church exhibits the early English style of architecture, having been erected about 1260. The groined roof of the whole of the interior is of a later date than the structure itself, and the north aisle of the nave, which is in the latest style, has a very rich ceiling, with pendant ornaments. The Lady chapel has, at the east end, some fine tabernacled niches, of a more modern date than the chapel itself. In the nave is a plain altar-tomb, with a recumbent statue of an armed knight, under a monumental arch, embellished with fine mouldings and pendant tracery, having an ogee canopy, with crockets and a handsome finial: the pulpit is decorated with carved wood-work. There are places of worship for Independents and Unitarians. A free grammar school was founded by Henry VIII., and endowed with £10 per annum from the church corporation trust, and with various subsequent benefactions, amounting in the whole to about £60 per annum, but no boys have been instructed on this foundation for many years; two or three free scholars only receive classical education, in consideration of a donation of land, in 1666, by Mr. Edward Salter.

who also assigned from the proceeds an exhibition of £6 per annum to any one of the colleges or halls of Oxford, for four years, for a scholar from this school; and in default of which, the sum thus appropriated was to be divided between two children of the school for their maintenance and education. A charity school is supported by subscription, also a Sunday school. Two sets of almshouses have been founded here; and there are considerable benefactions for distribution among the poor, and for other purposes. Races are held occasionally at Caddy Lawn, about half a mile from the town. In the neighbourhood is a spring, called "Hawkins' Well," said to be efficacious as a remedy for diseases of the eye.

OTTRINGHAM, a parish in the southern division of the wapentake of HOLDERNESS, East riding of the county of YORK, 6¼ miles (S. E. by E.) from Hedon, containing 637 inhabitants. The living is a perpetual curacy, in the archdeaconry of the East riding, and diocese of York, endowed with £400 royal bounty, and £1200 parliamentary grant, and in the patronage of the Chancellor of the University of Oxford. The church, dedicated to St. Wilfrid, is principally in the decorated style of architecture, with a tower surmounted by a spire. There is a place of worship for Wesleyan Methodists. Four poor children are instructed for the interest arising from £100 stock, the gift of Mary Fox, in 1792.

OUGHTERBY, a township in the parish of KIRK-BAMPTON, ward and county of CUMBERLAND, 7¼ miles (W.) from Carlisle, containing 105 inhabitants.

OULSTON, a township in the parish of COXWOLD, wapentake of BIRDFORTH, North riding of the county of YORK, 4 miles (N. N. E.) from Easingwould, containing 225 inhabitants.

OULSWICK, a chapelry in the parish of MONKS-RISBOROUGH, hundred of AYLESBURY, county of BUCKINGHAM, 5½ miles (W. by S.) from Wendover. The population is returned with the parish. The chapel, now demolished, was dedicated to St. Peter. Oulswick is within the peculiar and exempt jurisdiction of the Archbishop of Canterbury.

OULTON, a township in the parish of WIGTON, ward and county of CUMBERLAND, 2 miles (N. N. W.) from Wigton, containing 336 inhabitants. There is a place of worship for Baptists, with a cemetery attached. A workhouse was erected in 1828, the expense of which was defrayed by the sale of an allotment of common land.

OULTON, a parish in the southern division of the hundred of ERPINGHAM, county of NORFOLK, 4 miles (W. N. W.) from Aylsham, containing 382 inhabitants. The living is a discharged vicarage, in the archdeaconry and diocese of Norwich, rated in the king's books at £8. 5., and in the patronage of R. Bell, Esq. The church is dedicated to St. Paul. There is a place of worship for Independents. A workhouse has been erected here for several united parishes.

OULTON, a parish in the hundred of MUTFORD and LOTHINGLAND, county of SUFFOLK, 3 miles (W.) from Lowestoft, containing 471 inhabitants, exclusively of the house of industry for the hundred, which is in this parish, and contains two hundred and thirty-three inmates. The living is a rectory, in the archdeaconry of Suffolk, and diocese of Norwich, rated in the king's books at £14. 13. 4., and in the patronage of the Exe-

cutors of J. Marston, Esq. The church is dedicated to St. Michael. The river Waveney bounds the parish on the west, and receives the surplus water of Lake Lothing on the south.

OULTON (LOW), a township in the parish of OVER, first division of the hundred of EDDISBURY, county palatine of CHESTER, 3¾ miles (E. by N.) from Tarporley, containing 60 inhabitants.

OUNDLE, a market town and parish, in the hundred of POLEBROOKE, county of NORTHAMPTON, 30 miles (N.E.) from Northampton, and 77 (N. by W.) from London, containing, with the chapelry of Ashton, and the hamlets of Biggin, Churchfield, and Elmington, 2279 inhabitants. A monastery was established here before the year 711, when Wilfrid, Archbishop of York, died in it: by some it is thought to have been founded by that primate, whilst others consider it to have been a cell to the abbey of Peterborough, and part of its possessions. The town is situated on a gentle declivity on the northern bank of the river Nene, by which it is nearly surrounded, and over which are two bridges, leading respectively to the Thrapston and Peterborough roads: North bridge is remarkable for its length and the number of its arches, which support an elevated causeway. The streets are well paved and lighted, and, in consequence of recent improvements made under the provisions of a local act of parliament, the general appearance of the town has been entirely modernised: two or three houses yet remain, which were built with the stones of Fotheringhay castle. Several of the inhabitants are employed in making bobbin-lace. The market is on Thursday; and fairs are held on February 25th, Whit-Monday, and August 21st, for horses, cattle, and sheep, and on October 12th, for cheese, cattle, &c.: a commodious market-house and shambles have been recently erected. Manorial courts leet and baron, and a court for the hundred, are held annually: a court is likewise held for the rectorial manor of Oundle, once in two or three years. The petty sessions for the division take place here once a fortnight. A court for the recovery of debts under 40s. was attached to the hundred court, but it has been disused for several years.

The living is a discharged vicarage, in the archdeaconry of Northampton, and diocese of Peterborough, rated in the king's books at £13. 6. 8., and in the patronage of the Crown. The church, which is dedicated to St. Peter, is a spacious and very handsome cruciform structure, combining the different styles of English architecture, with a lofty tower, terminated at the angles by octagonal turrets, and surmounted by an hexagonal crocketed spire, erected in 1634: in the chancel are some rich stalls, good screenwork, and a portion of ancient stained glass. There are places of worship for Baptists, Independents, and Wesleyan Methodists. The free grammar school was founded, in 1556, by Sir William Laxton, a native of this town, and lord mayor of London in 1544, the amount of endowment is about £400 per annum, and the management is vested in the Master and Wardens of the Grocers' Company, who appoint the master, with a stipend of £40 per annum, for himself and usher, and a gratuity of £60: the school is open to boys of the town for free instruction. A school, for the education of thirty poor men's sons, was built and endowed, in 1620, by the Rev. Nicholas Latham, with £10 per annum, for a master to teach reading and writing : the master at present receives a salary of £20 per annum, with a house for his residence, and the writing-master about £16. A Blue-coat school is supported by voluntary contributions. An almshouse, founded and endowed by Sir William Laxton, for seven poor men, is also under the superintendence of the Grocers' Company. An hospital for sixteen poor women, who must each exceed the age of fifty years, with two nurses for the sick, and a weekly allowance to each inmate, was also founded by the Rev. N. Latham. There are two contingent exhibitions to the University of Cambridge, of £4 per annum each, for poor scholars of the parishes of Oundle, Glapthorne, Cotterstock, and Tansor. In the vicinity of this town are some chalybeate springs.

OUSBY, a parish in LEATH ward, county of CUMBERLAND, 9¼ miles (E. N. E.) from Penrith, containing 276 inhabitants. The living is a rectory, in the archdeaconry and diocese of Carlisle, rated in the king's books at £13. 13. 4., and in the patronage of the Bishop of Carlisle. The church is dedicated to St. Luke : it contains in a niche a wooden effigy of a man in armour, probably of a knight who had fought under the banners of the cross, though, according to a vulgar tradition, it is said to represent a wild man killed in an attempt to repel an invasion of the Scots. Limestone and red sandstone abound here, and there are veins of lead-ore, also some small seams of coal. Ousby, properly *Ulfsby*, the seat of Ulff, a Dane, is situated to the west of that chain of mountains which runs in a south-east direction from the borders of Scotland, through Northumberland, Cumberland, Westmorland, and Yorkshire, and terminates in Derbyshire. Here are the remains of a British fortification, consisting of an outer and an inner rampart, within the area of which Roman urns and other antiquities have been found. The Maiden Way traverses the mountainous part of this parish, which, from its elevated position, is subject to great damage from the "Helm Winds" that occur frequently from September to May, and do great injury to the corn.

OUSDEN, a parish in the hundred of RISBRIDGE, county of SUFFOLK, 6¼ miles (E. S. E.) from Newmarket, containing 331 inhabitants. The living is a rectory, in the archdeaconry of Sudbury, and diocese of Norwich, rated in the king's books at £10. 3. 9., and in the patronage of the Rev. J. T. Hand. The church is dedicated to St. Peter. Richard Moseley, in 1743, gave £10 a year as a salary to a master for teaching twenty children.

OUSEBURN (GREAT), a parish in the lower division of the wapentake of CLARO, West riding of the county of YORK, 4¼ miles (S. E.) from Aldborough, containing 437 inhabitants. The living is a discharged vicarage, in the peculiar jurisdiction of the court of the honour of Knaresborough, rated in the king's books at £3. 10., and in the patronage of the Crown. The church, dedicated to St. Mary, has lately received an addition of one hundred and twenty sittings, of which sixty are free, the Incorporated Society for the enlargement of churches and chapels having granted £60 towards defraying the expense. There is a place of worship for Independents. Six poor children are instructed for £3 a year, the produce of sundry trifling bequests for that purpose.

OUSEBURN (LITTLE), a parish comprising the townships of Kirkby-Hall and Thorp-Underwoods, in the lower, and those of Little Ouseburn and Widdington, in the upper, division of the wapentake of CLARO, West riding of the county of YORK, and containing 558 inhabitants, of which number, 293 are in the township of Little Ouseburn, 5 miles (S. E. by S.) from Aldborough. The living is a vicarage, in the archdeaconry of Richmond, and diocese of Chester, rated in the king's books at £3. 8. 4., endowed with £100 and £3 per annum private benefaction, and £600 royal bounty, and in the patronage of the Precentor in the Cathedral Church of York. The church is dedicated to the Holy Trinity. There is a place of worship for Wesleyan Methodists. Five poor children are educated for a trifling annuity, the gift of Elizabeth Colston in 1756.

OUSEFLEET, a township in the parish of WHITGIFT, lower division of the wapentake of OSGOLDCROSS, West riding of the county of YORK, 7 miles (S. E. by E.) from Howden, containing 253 inhabitants : it is within the jurisdiction of the peculiar court of Snaith.

OUSTON, a township in that part of the parish of CHESTER le STREET which is in the middle division of CHESTER ward, county palatine of DURHAM, 9 miles (N.) from Durham, containing 304 inhabitants.

OUSTON, a parish in the hundred of GARTREE, county of LEICESTER, 8 miles (S. by E.) from Melton-Mowbray, containing, with the hamlet of Newbold, 212 inhabitants. The living is a perpetual curacy, in the archdeaconry of Leicester, and diocese of Lincoln, endowed with £200 private benefaction, and £200 royal bounty, and in the patronage of the Rev. Henry Palmer. The church, dedicated to St. Andrew, formerly belonged to a small priory of canons regular of the order of St. Augustine, which was founded here, in the time of Henry II., by Sir Robert Grimbald, and possessed, at the dissolution, a revenue of £173. 18. 9.

OUSTON, a township in the parish of STAMFORDHAM, north-eastern division of TINDALE ward, county of NORTHUMBERLAND, 12½ miles (W. N. W.) from Newcastle upon Tyne, containing 32 inhabitants.

OUTCHESTER, a township in the parish of BAMBROUGH, northern division of BAMBROUGH ward, county of NORTHUMBERLAND, 2½ miles (E. by S.) from Belford, containing 109 inhabitants. This place, situated on the western bank of the river Warn, near its outlet into Budle bay, was the site of the *Castrum Ulterius* of the ancient port of Warnmouth. The camp is of a square form, and there are vestiges of a Roman road extending from it towards Alnwick. The bay affords secure anchorage for small vessels, which are principally employed in the exportation of corn and flour, and in importing coal and wood.

OUTERSIDE, a joint township with Allerby, in the parish of ASPATRIA, ALLERDALE ward below Darwent, county of CUMBERLAND, 6½ miles (N.) from Cockermouth, containing, with Allerby, 347 inhabitants. Coal is obtained in the township, which is bounded on the south by the river Ellen.

OUTSEATS, a hamlet in the parish of HATHERSAGE, hundred of HIGH PEAK, county of DERBY, containing 177 inhabitants. Benjamin Ashton left a rent-charge of £5 for teaching ten poor boys.

OUTTON, a township in the parish of ROTHWELL, lower division of the wapentake of AGBRIGG, West riding of the county of YORK, containing 936 inhabitants.

OUTWELL, a parish, partly in the hundred of WISBEACH, Isle of ELY, county of CAMBRIDGE, and partly in the hundred of CLACKCLOSE, county of NORFOLK, 5½ miles (S. E.) from Wisbeach, containing 954 inhabitants. The living is a discharged rectory, in the archdeaconry of Norfolk, and diocese of Norwich, rated in the king's books at £16, and in the patronage of the Bishop of Ely. The church, dedicated to St. Clement, is a very handsome structure. This parish is remarkable for its extensive market-gardens, the produce of which is conveyed by the Nene, which runs through the village, to many of the towns situated on that river. A school is supported by annual subscriptions. Molycourt priory, or the chapel of St. Mary de Bello Loco, which was situated in this parish, was founded before the Conquest, for Benedictine monks; but its revenue having considerably diminished, Henry VI. appropriated it to the priory of Ely, and it continues parcel of the possessions of that see.

OVENDEN, a township in the parish of HALIFAX, wapentake of MORLEY, West riding of the county of YORK, 1¼ mile (N. W.) from Halifax, containing 6360 inhabitants. There is a place of worship for Wesleyan Methodists.

OVER, a parish in the hundred of PAPWORTH, county of CAMBRIDGE, 4¼ miles (E. by S.) from St. Ives, containing 802 inhabitants. The living is a discharged vicarage, in the archdeaconry and diocese of Ely, rated in the king's books at £19. 0. 10., and in the patronage of the Master and Fellows of Trinity College, Cambridge : the rectory, an impropriation belonging to the college, is rated at £51. 13. 11½. The church is dedicated to St. Mary. There is a place of worship for Baptists. Alice Walpole, in 1709, left a trifling sum for the education of children; and the late Mrs. Kirkby gave £300, since laid out in land, for the endowment of a charity school, and the relief of poor widows.

OVER, a parish having separate jurisdiction, locally in the first division of the hundred of Eddisbury, county palatine of CHESTER, comprising the town of Over (formerly a market town), the chapelry of Wettenhall, and the township of Little Oulton, and containing 2514 inhabitants, of which number, 2157 are in the town of Over, 16¼ miles (E.) from Chester, and 168 (N. W. by N.) from London. The town is situated on the road from Middlewich to Chester, and consists chiefly of one long and irregular street, in which are remains of several crosses: over the river Weever, between the parishes of Over and Davenham, is Winsford bridge, on each side of which houses have been built, in consequence of the extension of the salt manufacture in this neighbourhood; on both sides of the river, which bounds this parish on the east, and is navigable to Winsford, are brine pits, and by means of it salt is conveyed in flats to Liverpool. The market, formerly held on Wednesday, under the authority of a charter of Edward I., has been disused for about a century: fairs are held on May 15th and September 25th. The town, called in ancient records the borough of Over, has been from time immemorial under the government of a mayor, who is chosen annually at the court leet and baron of the lord of the manor, held in October; two juries are then empannelled, one for the borough, called the

Grand Jury, the other for the subordinate townships, called the County Jury: the former return six inhabitants of the lordship of Over to the lord of the manor, by whom, at an adjourned court held fourteen days afterward, one of them is nominated mayor for the year ensuing, and, during his mayoralty, acts as justice of the peace within the borough and lordship, including the parishes of Over and Whitegate, and has a sworn serjeant who executes all processes within his jurisdiction : on quitting office he takes the title of alderman, but is no longer invested with any authority. The living is a discharged vicarage, in the archdeaconry and diocese of Chester, rated in the king's books at £7. 4., endowed with £1000 private benefaction, £600 royal bounty, and £600 parliamentary grant, and in the patronage of the Bishop of Chester. The church, dedicated to St. Chad, was rebuilt in 1543, by Hugh Starkey, gentleman usher to Henry VIII.; it is in the later style of English architecture : in the interior is a font with a decorated niche over a water basin, some good stained glass, tabernacle-work, and an altar-tomb, supporting an effigy in brass to the memory of Hugh Starkey. There is a place of worship for Independents. The free grammar school, near the church, was founded in 1689, by Mrs. Elizabeth Venables, and her son, Thomas Lee, Esq., at Darnhall, in the adjoining parish of Whitegate, endowed with lands, the present value of which is £53 per annum : the school is open to children of Over and Whitegate, also to those of the township of Weever; it was removed to its present situation in 1803.

OVER, a hamlet in that part of the parish of CHURCHAM, which is in the lower division of the hundred of DUDSTONE and KING'S BARTON, county of GLOUCESTER. The population is returned with Highnam and Linton.

OVER, a tything in that part of the parish of ALMONDSBURY which is in the lower division of the hundred of LANGLEY and SWINEHEAD, county of GLOUCESTER, 6½ miles (N. by W.) from Bristol, containing 133 inhabitants.

OVER (CHURCH), county palatine of CHESTER.—See UPTON.

OVERBURY, a parish in the middle division of the hundred of OSWALDSLOW, county of WORCESTER, 5½ miles (N. E. by E.) from Tewkesbury, containing, with the chapelries of Alstone, Teddington, and Little Washbourn, and the hamlet of Conderton, 764 inhabitants. The living is a discharged vicarage, in the archdeaconry and diocese of Worcester, rated in the king's books at £9. 10., and in the patronage of the Dean and Chapter of Worcester. The church is dedicated to St. Faith. Here are some malt-kilns and a paper-mill.

OVERSLEY, a hamlet in that part of the parish of ARROW which is in the Stratford division of the hundred of BARLICHWAY, county of WARWICK, ¼ a mile (S. E.) from Alcester, containing 211 inhabitants.

OVERSTONE, a parish in the hundred of SPELHOE, county of NORTHAMPTON, 5 miles (N. E.) from Northampton, containing 192 inhabitants. The living is a rectory, in the archdeaconry of Northampton, and diocese of Peterborough, rated in the king's books at £12. 16. 3., and in the patronage of Earl Brownlow. The church is dedicated to St. Nicholas.

OVERSTRAND, a parish in the northern division of the hundred of ERPINGHAM, county of NORFOLK,

1¾ mile (S. E. by E.) from Cromer, containing 154 inhabitants. The living is a discharged rectory, in the archdeaconry of Norfolk, and diocese of Norwich, rated in the king's books at £2. 1. 5½., endowed with £200 royal bounty, and in the patronage of Lord Suffield. The church, dedicated to St. Martin, which was formerly in a very dilapidated state, has lately received an addition of sixty sittings, of which fifty are free, the Incorporated Society for the enlargement of churches and chapels having granted £10 towards defraying the expense.

OVERTON, a township in the parish of MALPAS, higher division of the hundred of BROXTON, county palatine of CHESTER, 1½ mile (N. W.) from Malpas, containing 101 inhabitants. There is a place of worship for Wesleyan Methodists.

OVERTON, a chapelry in that part of the parish of LANCASTER which is in the hundred of LONSDALE, south of the sands, county palatine of LANCASTER, 4½ miles (S. W.) from Lancaster, containing 344 inhabitants. The living is a perpetual curacy, in the archdeaconry of Richmond, and diocese of Chester, endowed with £400 private benefaction, and £400 royal bounty, and in the patronage of the Vicar of Lancaster. The chapel is a very ancient building. Overton occupies a peninsula formed by the river Lune and Morecambe bay.

OVERTON, a township in that part of the parish of RICHARD's CASTLE which is in the hundred of MUNSLOW, county of SALOP, 1¾ mile (S. by W.) from Ludlow. The population is returned with the parish.

OVERTON, a parish (formerly a borough) in the hundred of OVERTON, Kingsclere division of the county of SOUTHAMPTON, 3 miles (E. N. E.) from Whitchurch, and 54 (W. S. W.) from London, containing 1341 inhabitants. This village is situated on the great western road: a manufactory for throwing-silk affords employment to the greater part of the female inhabitants. The river Test, which has its source about a mile distant, passes through the village. Fairs are held on May 4th, Whit-Monday, and July 18th, and on October 22nd is a considerable fair for sheep. This place formerly sent two members to parliament. The living is a vicarage, with the perpetual curacy of Tadley, in the peculiar jurisdiction and patronage of the Rector, rated in the king's books at £14. 12. 3½.; the rectory is a sinecure, rated in the king's books at £29. 19. 7., and in the patronage of the Bishop of Winchester. The church is dedicated to St. Mary. There is a place of worship for Independents.

OVERTON, a parish partly in the hundred of ELSTUB and EVERLEY, but chiefly in that of SELKLEY, county of WILTS, 2½ miles (S. by W.) from Marlborough, containing, with the chapelry of Alton-Priors, the township of Lockeridge, and the tything of Stowell, 900 inhabitants. The living is a vicarage, in the archdeaconry of Wilts, and diocese of Salisbury, rated in the king's books at £23. 0. 5., and in the patronage of the Duke of Marlborough. The church is dedicated to St. Michael.

OVERTON, a parish partly in the liberty of ST. PETER of YORK, East riding, but chiefly in the wapentake of BULMER, North riding, of the county of YORK, comprising the townships of Overton, Shipton, and Skelton, and containing 709 inhabitants, of which number,

59 are in the township of Overton, 4¾ miles (N. W.) from York. The living is a discharged vicarage, in the archdeaconry of Cleveland, and diocese of York, rated in the king's books at £4. 8. 11½., endowed with £200 royal bounty, and in the patronage of Mrs. Earle. The church is dedicated to St. Cuthbert. A free school was founded, in 1655, under the will of Ann Middleton, who bequeathed £1000 for its erection and maintenance: the income is £40 a year, for which fifty boys are instructed.

OVERTON (COLD), a parish forming, with the parishes of Somerby and Withcote, a detached portion of the hundred of FRAMLAND, county of LEICESTER, 7 miles (S. E. by S.) from Melton-Mowbray, containing 123 inhabitants. The living is a rectory, in the archdeaconry of Leicester, and diocese of Lincoln, rated in the king's books at £19. 12. 3½., and in the patronage of E. H. Wigley, Esq. The church is dedicated to St. John the Baptist.

OVERTON (MARKET), a parish in the hundred of ALSTOE, county of RUTLAND, 6 miles (N. by E.) from Oakham, containing 468 inhabitants. The living is a rectory, in the archdeaconry of Northampton, and diocese of Peterborough, rated in the king's books at £14. 11. 3., and in the patronage of John Wingfield, Esq. The church is dedicated to St. Peter and St. Paul. A market, formerly held on Tuesday, has been long disused.

OVING, a parish in the hundred of ASHENDON, county of BUCKINGHAM, 6 miles (N. N. W.) from Aylesbury, containing 372 inhabitants. The living is a rectory, in the archdeaconry of Buckingham, and diocese of Lincoln, rated in the king's books at £7. 17. 11., and in the patronage of the Crown. The church is dedicated to All Saints.

OVING, a parish in the hundred of Box and STOCKBRIDGE, rape of CHICHESTER, county of SUSSEX, 2¾ miles (E.) from Chichester, containing 637 inhabitants. The living is a vicarage, in the archdeaconry and diocese of Chichester, rated in the king's books at £10. 11. 10½., and in the patronage of the Precentor in the Cathedral Church of Chichester. The church is principally in the early style of English architecture. Stephen Challen, in 1731, left a small sum for teaching poor children.

OVINGDEAN, a parish in the hundred of YOUNSMERE, rape of LEWES, county of SUSSEX, 2¼ miles (E. by S.) from Brighton, containing 79 inhabitants. The living is a discharged rectory, in the archdeaconry and diocese of Chichester, rated in the king's books at £9. 5. 6., and in the patronage of the Rev. John Marshall. The church is in the early style of English architecture. In this parish, not far from the church, is an ancient farm-house, recently modernised, in which Charles II. sought refuge, and was entertained for a few days, by the then occupant, Mr. Maunsell, prior to his escape to the continent. The village is situated in a pleasant valley, about a mile from the coast.

OVINGHAM, a parish in the eastern division of TINDALE ward, county of NORTHUMBERLAND, comprising the chapelry of Mickley, and the townships of Dukeshagg, Eltringham, Harlowhill, Hedley, Hedley-Woodside, Horsley, Nafferton, Ovingham, Ovington, Prudhoe, Prudhoe-Castle, Rouchester, Spittle, Welton, Whittle, and Wylam, and containing 2742 inhabitants, of which number, 265 are in the township of Ovingham, 11 miles (W.) from Newcastle upon Tyne. The living is a vicarage, in the archdeaconry of Northumberland, and diocese of Durham rated in the king's books at £5. 8. 4., endowed with £200 private benefaction, £400 royal bounty, and £1200 parliamentary grant, and in the patronage of C. W. Bigge, Esq. The church is dedicated to St. Mary. There is a place of worship for Independents. The river Tyne passes through the parish, which abounds with mines of coal. Here are a brewery, a dye-house, and bleaching-grounds. Courts leet and baron are occasionally held; and there are two fairs, on April 26th and October 26th. The vicarage-house occupies the site of a cell of Black canons, founded by one of the Umfravilles, the revenue of which, at the dissolution, was valued at £13. 4. 8.

OVINGTON, a parish in the hundred of HINCKFORD, county of ESSEX, 2¼ miles (S. by W.) from Clare, containing 149 inhabitants. The living is a rectory, consolidated with that of Tilbury, in the archdeaconry of Middlesex, and diocese of London, rated in the king's books at £7, and in the patronage of John Fisher, Esq. A small charity school is supported by annual donations.

OVINGTON, a parish in the hundred of WAYLAND, county of NORFOLK, 1½ mile (N. N. E.) from Watton, containing 219 inhabitants. The living is a discharged rectory, in the archdeaconry and diocese of Norwich, rated in the king's books at £7. 3. 6½., and in the patronage of the Chancellor, Masters, and Scholars of the University of Cambridge. The church is dedicated to St. John the Evangelist.

OVINGTON, a township in the parish of OVINGHAM, eastern division of TINDALE ward, county of NORTHUMBERLAND, 12 miles (W.) from Newcastle upon Tyne, containing 362 inhabitants. An extensive coal mine is now in operation, and there are a large malthouse, and a brewery, within the township.

OVINGTON, a parish in the hundred of FAWLEY, Fawley division of the county of SOUTHAMPTON, 2 miles (W. by S.) from New Alresford, containing 180 inhabitants. The living is a rectory, in the peculiar jurisdiction of the Incumbent, rated in the king's books at £9. 10., and in the patronage of the Bishop of Winchester. Ovington is within the jurisdiction of the Cheyney Court held at Winchester every Thursday, for the recovery of debts to any amount.

OVINGTON, a township in the parish of FORCETT, western division of the wapentake of GILLING, North riding of the county of YORK, 4 miles (E. N. E.) from Greta-Bridge, containing 166 inhabitants. A priory of Gilbertine canons, subordinate to that of Sempringham, was founded here about the reign of John, by Alan de Wilton, which, at the dissolution, was valued at £11. 2. 8.

OWERMOIGNE, a parish and liberty in the Blandford (South) division of the county of DORSET, 7¼ miles (S. E.) from Dorchester, containing 377 inhabitants. The living is a rectory, in the archdeaconry of Dorset, and diocese of Bristol, rated in the king's books at £23. 4. 7., and in the patronage of the Hon. William Damer. The church is dedicated to St. Michael. The parish is bounded on the south by the English channel. A charity school is supported by donations amounting to about £8 per annum.

OWERSBY, a parish in the northern division of the wapentake of WALSHCROFT, parts of LINDSEY, county of LINCOLN, 5½ miles (N.W. by N.) from Market-Rasen, containing 408 inhabitants, of which number 272 are in North, and 136 in South, Owersby. The living is a discharged vicarage, with those of Kirby and Osgodby, in the archdeaconry and diocese of Lincoln, rated in the king's books at £8. 18. 4., and in the patronage of Lord Monson. The church is dedicated to St. Martin. There is a school with a trifling endowment by Dunn Rawvy.

OWLPEN, a parish in the upper division of the hundred of BERKELEY, county of GLOUCESTER, 3¾ miles (E.) from Dursley, containing 232 inhabitants. The living is a perpetual curacy, annexed to the rectory of Newington-Bagpath, in the archdeaconry and diocese of Gloucester. The church has lately received an addition of sixty sittings, of which forty are free, the Incorporated Society for the enlargement of churches and chapels having granted £50 towards defraying the expense.

OWMBY, a parish in the eastern division of the wapentake of ASLACOE, parts of LINDSEY, county of LINCOLN, 7½ miles (W. by S.) from Market-Rasen, containing 196 inhabitants. The living is a rectory, in the archdeaconry of Stow, and diocese of Lincoln, rated in the king's books at £9. 3. 4., and in the patronage of the King, as Duke of Lancaster. The church is dedicated to St. Peter and St. Paul.

OWMBY, a joint parish with Searby, in the southern division of the wapentake of YARBOROUGH, parts of LINDSEY, county of LINCOLN, 4½ miles (N. W.) from Caistor. The population is returned with Searby. The living is a discharged vicarage, with the rectory of Searby, in the archdeaconry and diocese of Lincoln.

OWRAM (NORTH), a township in the parish of HALIFAX, wapentake of MORLEY, West riding of the county of YORK, 2¼ miles (N. E.) from Halifax, containing 6841 inhabitants. A free school was erected here, about 1711, by Joseph Crowther, who endowed it with a dwelling-house and croft for the master, and certain lands let for £21 per annum, for which twelve poor children are instructed. Jeremiah Hall, in 1687, bequeathed land, directing the income to be applied towards the maintenance of two men and two women, each of them receiving an annuity of £5, and £5 per annum is paid for teaching five boys and five girls.

OWRAM (SOUTH), a township in the parish of HALIFAX, wapentake of MORLEY, West riding of the county of YORK, 1¾ mile (S. E.) from Halifax, containing 4256 inhabitants.

OWRE, county of KENT.—See OARE.

OWSLEBURY, a parish in the hundred of FAWLEY, Fawley division of the county of SOUTHAMPTON, 5 miles (S. S. E.) from Winchester, containing 603 inhabitants. The living is a perpetual curacy, annexed to the vicarage of Twyford, and in the peculiar jurisdiction of the Vicar. The church is dedicated to St. Andrew. The parish is within the jurisdiction of the Cheyney Court held at Winchester every Thursday, for the recovery of debts to any amount.

OWSTHORPE, a township in the parish of POCKLINGTON, Wilton-Beacon division of the wapentake of HARTHILL, East riding of the county of YORK, 1¼ mile (N. by E.) from Pocklington, containing 9 inhabitants.

OWSTON, a parish in the western division of the wapentake of MANLEY, parts of LINDSEY, county of LINCOLN, 7¼ miles (N.) from Gainsborough, containing, with the chapelry of West Butterwick, and the township of Kelfield, 1969 inhabitants. The living is a discharged vicarage, in the archdeaconry of Stow, and diocese of Lincoln, rated in the king's books at £19. 10., endowed with £400 private benefaction, and £1600 parliamentary grant, and in the patronage of the Archbishop of York. The church is dedicated to St. Martin. Near Millwood park a Carthusian monastery was founded, about 1395, by Thomas Moubray, Earl of Nottingham, afterwards Duke of Norfolk: it was dedicated to St. Mary, St. John the Evangelist, and St. Edward the Confessor, and at the dissolution had a revenue of £290. 11. 7.

OWSTON, a parish in the upper division of the wapentake of OSGOLDCROSS, West riding of the county of YORK, comprising the townships of Owston and Skellow, and containing 452 inhabitants, of which number, 306 are in the township of Owston, 5¼ miles (N. by W.) from Doncaster. The living is a discharged vicarage, in the archdeaconry and diocese of York, rated in the king's books at £7. 0. 2½., and in the patronage of P. D. Cooke, Esq. The church is dedicated to All Saints. Four poor children are instructed for a trifling annuity left by Ann Jackson, in 1675.

OWSTWICK, a township partly in the parish of GARTON, and partly in that of Rooss, middle division of the wapentake of HOLDERNESS, East riding of the county of YORK, 12½ miles (E. by N.) from Kingston upon Hull, containing 139 inhabitants.

OWTHORNE, a parish comprising the township of Waxholme, in the middle division, and the townships of South Frodingham, Owthorne, and Rimswell, in the southern division, of the wapentake of HOLDERNESS, East riding of the county of YORK, and containing 415 inhabitants, of which number, 143 are in the township of Owthorne, 18½ miles (E.) from Kingston upon Hull. The living is a vicarage, in the archdeaconry of the East riding, and diocese of York, rated in the king's books at £11. 6. 3., and in the patronage of the Crown. The church, which was dedicated to St. Peter, fell into the sea on February 16th, 1816, and, in consequence of the continual encroachments of that element, the village has also sustained considerable damage.

OWTHORPE, a parish in the southern division of the wapentake of BINGHAM, county of NOTTINGHAM, 8½ miles (S. E. by E.) from Nottingham, containing 138 inhabitants. The living is a perpetual curacy, in the archdeaconry of Nottingham, and diocese of York, endowed with £1000 royal bounty, and in the patronage of Sir R. H. Bromley, Bart. The church, dedicated to St. Margaret, was built by Colonel Julius Hutchinson, an active parliamentary officer during the great civil war, and for some time governor of Nottingham castle: he died a prisoner at Landown castle, in 1664, and lies interred in the family vault here; a monument having been erected to his memory, among others of the family. The Grantham canal passes through the parish, and the Foss road forms its western boundary.

OXBOROUGH, a parish in the southern division of the hundred of GREENHOE, county of NORFOLK, 3 miles (E. N. E.) from Stoke-Ferry, containing 320 inhabitants. The living is a discharged rectory, with the vicarage of Foulden united, in the archdeaconry of

Norfolk, and diocese of Norwich, rated in the king's books at £18. 6. 8., and in the patronage of the Master and Fellows of Gonville and Caius College, Cambridge. The church, dedicated to St. John the Evangelist, is a spacious structure of flint and stone, with a square tower embattled, and surmounted by a lofty spire. The east window exhibits the most striking portions of our Saviour's history, the Virgin Mary, &c., in richly-stained glass, and the roof, composed of oak panels, is curiously carved with various emblems. Attached to the south aisle is a chantry, built in 1573, having a stone screen of the earliest revived Grecian architecture. The small river Wissey runs through the parish, in which are many tumuli, and some pits called Danes' graves. Roman and Saxon coins have been found here, from which, and the remains of a considerable vallum to the north-west of the village, it seems to have been anciently a place of importance. Edward I. granted a market, several fairs, and various other privileges, long since disused. The mansion-house, which much resembles Queen's College, Cambridge, was erected in the same year, and is a fine specimen of the style of architecture that prevailed in the time of Edward IV.; the outer walls stand in a moat supplied by a stream from an adjoining rivulet.

OXCLIFFE, a joint township with Heaton, in that part of the parish of LANCASTER which is in the hundred of LONSDALE, south of the sands, county palatine of LANCASTER, 2 miles (W.) from Lancaster. The population is returned with Heaton.

OXCOMB, a parish in the hundred of HILL, parts of LINDSEY, county of LINCOLN, 7 miles (N. E. by N.) from Horncastle, containing 28 inhabitants. The living is a discharged rectory, in the archdeaconry and diocese of Lincoln, rated in the king's books at £6. 15. 7½., and endowed with £200 royal bounty. B. Grant, Esq. was patron in 1821. The church is dedicated to All Saints.

OXENDEN (GREAT), a parish in the hundred of ROTHWELL, county of NORTHAMPTON, 3 miles (S. by E.) from Market-Harborough, containing 277 inhabitants. The living is a rectory, in the archdeaconry of Northampton, and diocese of Peterborough, rated in the king's books at £13. 8. 4. Henry Boulton, Esq. was patron in 1786. The church is dedicated to St. Helen. Sir George Buswell, in 1667, founded and liberally endowed a free school and hospital here, for the benefit of the inhabitants of Clipston, East Farndon, Haselbeech, Kelmarsh, Marston, Oxenden, and Trussell, to which Francis Horton subsequently bequeathed £200.

OXENDEN (LITTLE), a hamlet in the parish of LITTLE BOWDEN, hundred of ROTHWELL, county of NORTHAMPTON, 2 miles (S. S. W.) from Market-Harborough, containing 6 inhabitants. The chapel has been demolished.

OXENHALL, a hamlet in the parish of DARLINGTON, south-eastern division of DARLINGTON ward, county palatine of DURHAM, 2¾ miles (S.) from Darlington, with which the population is returned. In the neighbourhood are three remarkable pools, termed Hell Kettles.

OXENHALL, a parish in the hundred of BOTLOE, county of GLOUCESTER, 1 mile (N. N. W.) from Newent, containing 323 inhabitants. The living is a discharged vicarage, in the archdeaconry of Hereford, and diocese

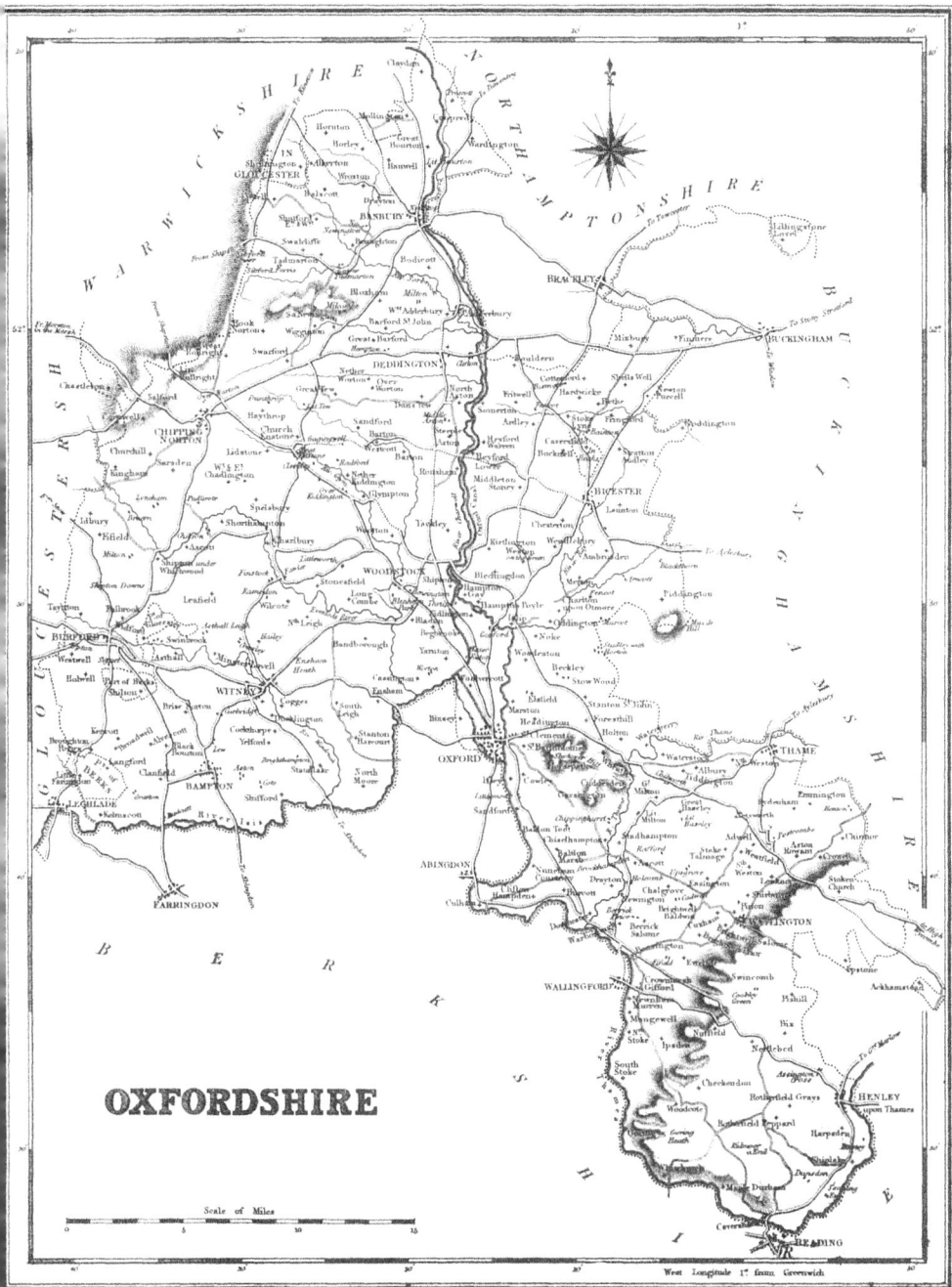

OXFORDSHIRE

Scale of Miles

Drawn by R. Creighton.

DRAWN AND ENGRAVED FOR LEWIS' TOPOGRAPHICAL DICTIONARY.

Engraved by J. & C. Walker.

West Longitude 1° from Greenwich

of Gloucester, rated in the king's books at £9. 12. 6., endowed with £400 royal bounty, and £200 parliamentary grant, and in the patronage of the Bishop of Gloucester. The church is dedicated to St. Anne. The Herefordshire and Gloucestershire canal passes through a tunnel, extending two thousand one hundred and ninety-two yards, in this parish.

OXENTON, a parish in the lower division of the hundred of TEWKESBURY, county of GLOUCESTER, 5½ miles (E. by S.) from Tewkesbury, containing 178 inhabitants. The living is a perpetual curacy, with that of Tewkesbury, in the archdeaconry and diocese of Gloucester, endowed with £600 royal bounty, and in the patronage of the Earl of Coventry. The church is dedicated to St. John the Baptist.

Seal and Arms.

OXFORD, a university and city, having separate jurisdiction, locally in the hundred of Wootton, county of OXFORD, of which it is the capital, 55 miles (N. N. W.) from London, containing 16,364 inhabitants. This place, which, from a very remote period of antiquity, has been celebrated as a seat of learning, is supposed by some to have derived its Saxon name, *Oxenford*, from its ford over the river for the passage of oxen. By others that name is said to be a corruption of *Ouseford*, from the river Ouse, now the Isis, from which source an island in that river, whereon the wealthy abbey was erected, was also named Ouseney, or Osney. To the establishment of schools in this place, supposed to have been originally by Alfred the Great, the origin of the city is by some historians attributed; but though Alfred unquestionably restored, and more liberally endowed, the university, its original foundation is demonstrated to have been many years prior to the reign of that monarch, in an act of confirmation by Pope Martin II., 802, in which it is described as an ancient academy of learning. During the earlier times of the Saxons, a monastery, dedicated to St. Mary and All Saints, was founded here, about the year 730, by Didanus, one of the Saxon princes, for twelve sisters of noble birth, of which Frideswide, his daughter, was first abbess, who, being canonized after her death, the abbey, in which she was interred, was dedicated to St. Frideswide, in honour of her memory: this monastery having been plundered during the Danish wars, and the nuns dispersing, was restored for Secular canons. In the interval between the destruction of the abbey and its restoration, Alfred, with his three sons, resided here, where he founded three public schools, established a royal mint, and contributed greatly to the rebuilding of the city. In the reign of Ethelred, the Danes burnt the city, in retaliation for the general massacre of their countrymen by order of that monarch; and, in 1013, another party of those rapacious invaders, under the command of King Sweyn, landed in England, and having laid waste the adjoining country, compelled the inhabitants of Oxford to surrender, and to give hostages for their fulfilment of the terms of capitulation. The city was again burnt by the Danes, in 1032; and, in 1036,

Harold Harefoot was crowned at Oxford, on which, in revenge for the slaughter of some of his men, he inflicted considerable injury. At the time of the Norman Conquest, Oxford, refusing to submit to the Conqueror, was, in 1067, taken by storm, and given to Robert D'Oily, who erected a strong castle on the west side of it, for the purpose of keeping the inhabitants in subjection, and fortified it with strong earthworks, within which he built a collegiate church, dedicated to St. George, and settled in it Secular canons of the order of St. Augustine. William Rufus held a council in the town, under Lanfranc, Archbishop of Canterbury, at which several bishops assisted, for the purpose of defeating a conspiracy formed against him by Odo, Bishop of Bayeux, his uncle, in favour of Robert, Duke of Normandy. Robert D'Oily, nephew of the former, and chamberlain to Henry I., founded the abbey of Osney, which was situated a little below the castle. Henry I. built a new hall, or palace, at Oxford, called Beaumont, where he celebrated the festival of Easter, in 1133, with great pomp, and in which Richard I. was born. Stephen, in the early part of his reign, assembled a council of the principal nobility here, to whom, in order to attach them to his interests, and to strengthen his party in the kingdom, he promised to abolish the tax called Dane Gelt, and to restore the laws of Edward the Confessor. Matilda, having obtained possession of the castle, was besieged by Stephen, but, previously to surrendering it, she contrived to escape by night over the river, which was at that time frozen. During this siege, the inhabitants being excluded from the church of St. George, within the castle, the chapel of St. Thomas was erected for their accommodation, and Stephen is reported to have repaired the city walls, which had fallen into decay : these walls are supposed to have been built in the seventh century, but by whom is uncertain.

During the contest between Henry II. and Thomas à Becket, that monarch held a parliament at Oxford, for the purpose of counteracting the authority of the pope, who had threatened to lay the kingdom under an interdict, and in 1167, another parliament, in which the partitioning of Ireland among those of his subjects who had at different times achieved the conquest of it, was deliberated upon. Richard I. invested Oxford, his native city, with many privileges, in gratitude for which, the citizens contributed largely to his ransom when detained prisoner in Austria, on his return from the Holy Land. King John held a parliament here in 1204, in order to raise supplies, which were liberally granted. In the reign of Henry III., who kept the festival of Christmas in this city, in 1222, Stephen Langton, Archbishop of Canterbury, held here a synod for reforming abuses in the ecclesiastical polity of the kingdom, by a decree of which two men were crucified, each pretending that he was Christ, and two women starved to death, for pretending to be the Virgin Mary, and Mary Magdalene. The same king, in 1227, when he became of age, assembled a parliament here, in which he assumed the government, and revoked the grant of Magna Charta, and the charter of Forests, alledging that they were signed by him when a minor. Towards the end of this reign, an adjourned parliament was held at Oxford, in which all Poictevins and other foreigners were ordered to leave the kingdom. In 1319, a man named Pondras, son of a tanner at Exeter, came to

Oxford, affirming that he was the rightful heir of Edward I., and had been stolen from his cradle and exchanged for Edward II., the reigning prince; but the imposture was soon detected, and Pondras was executed at Northampton. Queen Isabel, on her return from France, remained for some time in this city, while prosecuting the war against the two Spensers. In the reign of Henry IV., a conspiracy was formed by the Earls of Huntingdon, Kent, Salisbury, and Rutland, for assassinating the king at a tournament to be held here, and restoring the deposed monarch, Richard II., to the throne; but their plot was discovered, and the Earls of Kent and Salisbury, Sir Thomas Blount, and others, were hung at Greenditch, near Oxford. Henry VIII. erected Oxford into a see, separating it, with the county, from the diocese of Lincoln, in which it had previously been included. Soon after the accession of Mary, Cranmer, Archbishop of Canterbury, Ridley, Bishop of London, and Latimer, Bishop of Worcester, were conveyed from the Tower, where they had been imprisoned, to hold a disputation with the learned men of the University, at a convocation held in St. Mary's church; and in the following year, the Bishops of London, Gloucester, and Bristol, were sent commissioners to Oxford, to examine Ridley and Latimer, whom they condemned to the stake. This sentence was executed in a place called Canditch, on the 16th of October, 1555, in presence of the chief magistrates of the university and city; and on the 21st of the following March, Cranmer, who had witnessed the spectacle from the prison Bocardo, in which he was confined, suffered martyrdom in the same place. In 1625, the parliament having adjourned from London, on account of the plague, assembled at Oxford; but, on symptoms of the infection appearing in the city, the king hastily dissolved it, after repeated and unavailing attempts to procure supplies.

Oxford was intimately connected with many of the principal events during the parliamentary war. In the earlier part of it, Sir John Byron, with a party of the royal forces, attempted to garrison the city for the king; but Lord Say, then lieutenant of the county, advancing against him with a superior force, the former retired, leaving Oxford in possession of the latter. Sir John Byron, on his retreat from Oxford, advanced to Worcester, of which he gained possession, and garrisoned it for the king, who, reinforced by numbers whom his victory at Edgehill had drawn over to his party, marched to Oxford, took possession of it, and there fixed his headquarters. During the king's occupation of the town, a treaty of negociation was opened, and the Earl of Northumberland, and four members of the lower house, were appointed commissioners by the parliament: the conferences continued for several weeks, and after various propositions for a mutual accommodation, terminated without their differences being adjusted. A deputation from the citizens of London afterwards waited upon the king, who had resolved to pass the winter at Oxford, with proposals for peace, which, through the agency of the parliament, were also rendered ineffectual. The king invited the members who had either retired or had been expelled from the Westminster parliament, to meet him at Oxford, and assembled a parliament in the great hall of Christ Church College. Sir Thomas Fairfax, advancing with his army to besiege the city, was for a time diverted from his purpose by Prince Rupert, who attacked his castle at Leicester, but Fairfax returning to the siege, and the garrison being reduced by famine, it surrendered to the parliament, and the king escaping to Newcastle, placed himself under the protection of the Scottish army. In 1665, the plague raging in London, the parliament adjourned to Oxford, and continued their deliberations in the schools of the university. In this parliament, supplies were granted for carrying on the war against the Dutch, and statutes were enacted against the non-conforming clergy, who were prohibited approaching within five miles of any corporate town. During the continuance of the plague, the courts of law, at Michaelmas term, were held in this city; in which also Charles II., having dissolved the parliament at Westminster in 1681, assembled a new parliament, which, after sitting only a few days, was dissolved by the king, for the apparent purpose of preventing the differences that threatened to arise between the lords and the commons, the former having rejected a vote of impeachment decreed by the latter.

Oxford, for the splendour of its public buildings, among which the colleges and halls of the university are conspicuous, for the grandeur of their elevation, and, in many instances, for the beauty of their architecture, is not surpassed by any city in the kingdom; and, from the antiquity and importance of its venerable institutions, possesses an intense degree of interest. It is pleasantly situated on a gentle acclivity, at the confluence of the rivers Cherwell and Isis, by which it is nearly surrounded: over these rivers are several bridges, handsomely built of stone, of which, Magdalene bridge over the river Cherwell, and a new bridge over the Isis, on the Abingdon road, lately erected at an expense of £11,000, are the principal. The approaches are spacious, and afford striking and finely varied prospects of the city, and of its sumptuous edifices and stately towers. The entrance from the London road, over Magdalene bridge, is exquisitely beautiful; on the right is the small but pleasing vale of the Cherwell, in which the newly-erected church of St. Clement's forms an interesting feature, together with the grounds, the water-walk, and the noble towers of Magdalene College; and on the left are seen Christchurch meadows, watered by the Isis and the Cherwell, with the spire of the Cathedral Church, and the tower of Merton College in the distance. The entrance from Woodstock is remarkably fine, leading into the town through the broad street of St. Giles', on each side of which is a row of stately trees, and on the east side the college of St. John, and part of Balliol College. The entrance from Abingdon, over Folly, or the New bridge, leads through St. Aldate's-street, on the east side of which is the magnificent front of Christchurch College, and the town hall. The city, which is more than a mile in length, from east to west, and, including the suburbs, more than three miles in circumference, is divided into four parts by two principal streets, which intersect each other nearly at right angles in the centre, where was formerly a handsome conduit, erected in the seventeenth century, by Otho Nicholson, one of the examiners in Chancery, but removed in 1787, and presented by the university to the late Earl of Harcourt, who placed it in Nuneham - Courtney park. The High-street is one of the noblest streets in Europe, presenting in pleasing succession, from its great length and easy and graceful curvature, many of the stately and venerable public edifices for which this city is so eminently distinguished: on the north side, after crossing Magdalene bridge, and passing the college of St. Mary Magdalene on the right, and the Physic Garden on the left, are Queen's and All Souls' colleges, beyond which are the churches of St. Mary and All Saints, and at its upper extremity, that of St. Martin, or Carfax; and on the south side are University College, and some handsome private houses. Near Magdalene bridge are the warm and cold baths, in St. Clement's parish, a handsome establishment recently constructed, comprising a saloon, reading-room, and other appendages, and a very superior arrangement of warm and cold baths, with dressing-rooms, and every requisite accommodation. Races are annually held on Port-meadow, near the city, and are well attended. The city is well paved, lighted with gas, and amply supplied with water. The gardens of the colleges afford delightful promenades, and in the environs, which contain many handsome residences, are varied rides and agreeable walks, of which latter, that to Headington Hill, commanding a fine view of the city and its vicinity, may be considered the principal. The rivers Cherwell and Isis, branching into several streams, and pursuing a winding course, contribute greatly to adorn the city, and their united streams afford the means of aquatic excursions. The trade is principally in corn and other agricultural produce of the surrounding district, which is extremely fertile. Coal is brought from Staffordshire by the Oxford canal, which communicates with those of Birmingham, Warwick, and Coventry; and a considerable traffic is carried on with the metropolis and the intermediate towns, by the Thames, which is navigable to London. Convenient wharfs and quays have been constructed at considerable expense, and every facility has been obtained for the promotion of the inland trade. Oxford has been long celebrated for the superior quality of its brawn, of which a considerable quantity is forwarded to London. The market days are Wednesday and Saturday, which are abundantly supplied, the latter being also for corn, which is sold by sample at the upper extremity of the High-street, near a spot called the Butter Bench, the farmers preferring to transact their business in the open air, though the corporation have offered them the use of a convenient area under the town hall. The market-place is a suitable area, arranged into various sections for the different kinds of produce, on the northern side of the High-street, from which there are entrances by means of iron gates, the houses in front being appropriated as shops. The fairs are on May 3rd, on Gloucester Green; another in St. Giles', on the Monday after the festival of St. Giles, which is a pleasure fair; and the Thursday before New Michaelmas-day, for cattle.

The city received a regular charter of incorporation from Henry II., confirming all preceding grants, and extending to the inhabitants all the rights and privileges enjoyed by the citizens of London, besides conferring upon the mayor the distinction of assisting, with the lord mayor of London, in the king's buttery at the coronation festivals, upon which occasion he is attended by the recorder, four aldermen, the town clerk, bailiffs, and mace-bearer, and receives a silver cup and cover richly gilt, from the king. This charter was confirmed by Henry III., who vested the government of the city in a mayor, four aldermen, eight assistants, two bailiffs, and twenty-four common council-men. Many other charters were granted by succeeding sovereigns, but that by which the city is at present more especially governed was granted by James I., in 1605; by this an addition was made of the offices of high steward (usually a nobleman of high rank), recorder, town clerk, two chamberlains, mace bearer, and subordinate officers. The mayor is chosen annually, from among the aldermen or assistants, by the freemen generally, and, previously to entering upon his office, takes an oath to observe the lawful customs and privileges of the university, as does also the sheriff for the county. The bailiffs must have served the office of chamberlain. The mayor, recorder, aldermen, and assistants, are justices of the peace within the city and liberties, which office they hold, not by their charter of incorporation, but by commission under the great seal, renewed from time to time, under which authority also they hold a commission of gaol delivery. The freedom of the city is inherited by birth, and acquired by apprenticeship to a freeman for seven years, by gift of the corporation, or by purchase: among the privileges is the right of depasturing cattle on Port-meadow, a tract of about four hundred and forty acres near the city. The corporation hold quarterly courts of session, which take cognizance of all capital offences except high treason; and two courts of record, for the trial of pleas and the recovery of debts to any amount, one called the mayor's court (styled also a Hustings' court), and in which actions of ejectment are tried, and the other the court of the mayor and bailiffs: the practice, which is similar in both, is nearly the same as in the common law courts at Westminster; the town clerk sits as judge, or assessor.

The town hall is a spacious stone building, one hundred and thirty-five feet in length, and thirty-two feet broad, with a basement story of rustic work, forming an open corridor, and surmounted in the centre by a handsome pediment. George IV., when Prince Regent, the late Emperor of Russia, the King of Prussia, the late Duke of York, the Prince of Orange, the Prince of Mecklenburgh, Prince Metternich, General Blucher, and other illustrious persons repaired to the town hall, and received the honorary freedom of the city, in 1814, during their visit at the university: the council-chamber is decorated with portraits of Queen Anne, John the first Duke, and George the third Duke, of Marlborough, and several distinguished members of the corporation and benefactors to the city. The city gaol was erected in 1789, prior to which delinquents were confined in the prison of Bocardo, over one of the city gates, which was taken down in 1771: the door of the cell in which Cranmer was confined has been preserved, and fixed up in the present gaol, with an appropriate inscription: this prison contains four wards for the classification of prisoners, and thirty-two cells, and has a neat chapel. The city has regularly sent two members to parliament from the earliest returns extant of the reign of Edward I.: the right of election is vested in the mayor and corporation, and in the freemen generally, the number of whom is about one thousand eight hundred: the mayor is the returning officer. The assizes for the county and the election of knights of the shire are held here, as the county town. The county gaol and house of correction is an extensive building, erected on part of the site of the ancient castle, the remains of which consist of the original tower and a vaulted magazine for the use of the garrison, the principal entrance is through a large gateway, flanked by embattled towers : it comprises eleven wards, the same number of day-rooms and airing-yards, for the classification of prisoners, and two tread-mills, on which they are employed in grinding corn and raising water for the use of the prison : the prisoners receive a portion of their earnings on their discharge.

The origin of the university is by different historians attributed to various eras and to different founders: by some, Oxford is supposed to have been selected as a place of resort for students at a very early period of British history, and to have attained considerable eminence as a seat of learning during the Saxon Octarchy; and it is stated

Arms of the University.

that Alfred, during his residence in the city, founded and endowed three halls, or additional colleges, which, involved in its fate, were destroyed by the Danes, whose frequent incursions and devastation of this part of the country materially retarded the progress of the university. Amidst a mass of conflicting testimony its origin may, perhaps, be attributed to the monastic institutions established in the city and neighbourhood, which, by the encouragement they afforded to the pursuit of literature, drew around them a number of students, who, not being able to find admission as residents in these establishments, may have taken up their residence in the city and suburbs with the view of obtaining that assistance in their studies which the learned members of those institutions were capable of affording them. At the time of the Conquest, Robert D'Oily, to whom the Conqueror gave the government of the city, founded, within the precincts of the castle, the collegiate church of St. George, for Secular canons, which, being subsequently annexed to the abbey of Osney, founded by his descendant, the buildings were occupied by students, and the society existed for some time under the style of the Warden and Scholars of St. George within the Castle. Soon after the foundation of Osney abbey, Robert Pullein, a learned member of that institution, first began to read lectures on the sacred scriptures at Oxford, which had been much neglected, and revived the divinity lectures, which had fallen into disuse, and, under the patronage of Henry I. and his successors, greatly promoted the interests of literature. In the reign of Stephen, Roger Vacarius introduced the study of the Roman or civil law, which, being regarded as an innovation, was vehemently opposed by other professors. At this time the students are said to have amounted to nearly thirty thousand, and to have lived at their own expense in inns, or hostels, of which not less than three hundred were rented by them for their accommodation ; for their supply, the country for twenty miles round Oxford was appropriated by the king, whose purveyor was not permitted within that distance to purchase provisions for the king's household : exclusively of such as lived in these hostels, and who were under the control of a governor, or principal,

who presided over the literary and moral discipline of the seminaries, were several who were resident in St. Frideswide's priory, and Osney abbey. In 1209, a scholar having accidentally killed a woman of the city, while amusing himself with athletic sports, made his escape, and the exasperated citizens seized upon three scholars of the same hall, whom, upon receiving a mandate from the king (then at Woodstock) to that effect, they hanged, which so exasperated the students, that three thousand of them left the university for some time ; but the citizens having obtained pardon from the pope's legate, then in England, and having done penance in the churches at Oxford, the scholars returned. Repeated disturbances arose between the citizens and the students, some of which were attended with very serious consequences. In 1229, disputes having arisen in Paris, on account of the high price of wine, Henry III. invited the students of that city to Oxford, where more than one thousand of them soon afterwards settled. Cardinal Otho, legate from the pope in 1236, on his arrival in England, took up his residence at Osney abbey, and the scholars having sent him presents, in token of their respect, waited upon him in great numbers to pay him their congratulations, when a dispute arising between the scholars, who pressed for admission, and the legate's servants, in which the legate's brother, who, from fear of treachery by poison, officiated as principal cook, was killed, thirty of the scholars were put under confinement, and, to compromise the affair, the principals of the schools were compelled to implore pardon of the legate.

In 1248, Henry III. granted the university a charter, to defend it more effectually against the attacks of the citizens, who had wantonly assassinated a young nobleman, a student in one of the schools. In 1274, Walter de Merton founded Merton College, which appears to have been the first regular establishment in the university, and the foundation of that system by which, under certain trifling modifications, it was afterwards organized, and is still governed. About this time the number of scholars in the various hostels was about fifteen thousand, but by what regulations they were controuled does not distinctly appear. The statutes of Merton College, which with little alteration are still observed, appear to be the result of experience, and to have been adapted, in an extraordinary degree, to the diffusion of learning and to the establishment of moral discipline. Henry III., who visited the shrine of St. Frideswide, and held a parliament in the city, to settle his disputes with the barons, conferred many privileges upon the university, renewing all previous charters ; and in 1286, Edward I. invested the chancellor with authority to take cognizance of offences committed by the Jews resident at Oxford, and subsequently gave him power to summon any of the burgesses before him, to answer any plea originating in personal action with any of the scholars. Edward II. ratified all the rights and privileges of the university, and, by letters patent, took that institution under his immediate protection. Prior to this the pope had formally conferred upon Oxford, which was considered the next great school to Paris, the rank of university, a distinction then only enjoyed by Paris, Bologna, and Salamanca ; and in the reign of Edward II., schools for the Hebrew, Arabic, and Chaldee languages were founded, by order of the council of Vienna, in 1311. In the reign of Edward III., a dispute having arisen between a scholar and an inn-keeper, the latter, by an appeal to the citizens, incited them to an insurrection against the scholars, and both parties having recourse to arms, a violent conflict ensued for two days, when, after repeated skirmishes, a party of two thousand rustics, whom the citizens had invited to their assistance, entered the city, which the scholars had barricadoed, and attacking the halls, to several of which they set fire, killed sixty-three of the scholars, and plundered their halls. After the suppression of this tumult, the sheriff of the county, and the mayor of the city, being called to a severe account, were compelled to pay a very heavy fine, and to take an oath, on entering upon their office, to protect the interests and privileges of the university : the fine was afterwards commuted for the payment of one penny each by the mayor and principal citizens, annually in St. Mary's church, at the festival of St. Scholastica ; but in the year 1825 the university relinquished all claim to the payment. On the breaking out of the war with France, in 1369, all the French students were ordered to quit the kingdom. The privileges of the university appear to have been an object of particular regard with all succeeding sovereigns ; Henry VI., in 1444, gave power to the chancellor to banish any refractory person to the distance of twelve miles from the city, which, with all other privileges, was confirmed by Edward IV., in the first year of his reign. The wars between the houses of York and Lancaster appear to have had an unfavourable influence upon its interests, and, during their continuance, to have considerably diminished the number of students. Richard III. visited Oxford, and was met, on his way from Windsor, by the whole body, by whom he was escorted to Magdalene College, where he passed the night, and the following day attended the public exercises and disputations ; and in 1501, Prince Arthur, son of Henry VII., came hither, where he was sumptuously entertained, and lodged in Magdalene College. In the reign of Henry VIII., the public chest of the university was robbed, and the registers stolen ; and in 1518, the king and the queen, attended by Cardinal Wolsey and a large retinue of the nobility, having arrived at Abingdon, a deputation from the university waited on them to offer their respects, and escorted the queen to St. Frideswide's shrine, after having visited which, her majesty returned to Merton College, where she was sumptuously entertained. Queen Elizabeth paid visits to the university in 1566, 1571, and in 1592.

The members of the University of Oxford are a body corporate, possessing important privileges, which have been confirmed and extended by a long succession of royal charters, from the earliest period to the reign of Charles I.; and, under various munificent and royal patrons, its ancient halls have been endowed, and new colleges founded, which, taken collectively, form one of the most comprehensive and magnificent seats of learning in Europe. The university was incorporated in the 13th year of the reign of Elizabeth, by the style and title of the Chancellor, Masters, and Scholars of the University of Oxford ; it comprises nineteen colleges, the members of which are all distinct corporate bodies, and five halls, which are not incorporated, associated for the acquirement of learning requisite to qualify their members for the learned professions, and the high offices of the state : these several colleges and halls have their own statutes,

though subject to the paramount authority of the university. Every member of the university must be matriculated, and on appearing before the chancellor, or vice-chancellor, must declare his rank in life, whether the son of a nobleman, baronet, gentleman, or plebeian, and pay a matriculation fee accordingly, subscribe to the thirty-nine articles of the church of England, and, if sixteen years of age, take the oaths of allegiance and supremacy, and swear to observe all the statutes, privileges, and customs of the university, and neither to sue before the mayor or bailiffs of the city, nor answer before them as justices, so long as he continues to enjoy its privileges. The laws by which the university is at present governed were compiled by its members in the reign of James I., and confirmed in the 14th of the reign of Charles I., since which they have been modified or ratified by subsequent parliaments.

The principal officers are a chancellor, vice-chancellor, high steward, two proctors, a public orator, a keeper of the archives, a registrar of the university, a registrar of the university courts, two curators of the theatre, a librarian, keeper of the Ashmolean museum, two clerks of the market, three esquire bedels, three yeoman bedels, and other officers. The *Chancellor*, who is the highest officer in the university, and is generally a distinguished nobleman, is elected by the members of the house of convocation ; his office was anciently for one, two, or three years, but was made perpetual in 1484, when Dr. John Russel, Bishop of London, was first elected for life : he does not attend the meetings of the university, except at his installation, and upon the occasion of royal visits. The *Vice-chancellor*, who is the highest resident officer, is always the head of a college, and is nominated by the chancellor, but must be approved by the house of convocation : he appoints four pro-vice-chancellors, also heads of houses, to assist him in his office, which is annual, though generally continued for four years, by renewed nominations : to him is assigned the superintendence of the university ; he enforces the observance of every regulation, convenes the houses of congregation and convocation, and the courts ; he is a magistrate for the university, the county and city of Oxford, and the county of Berks, and is preceded in all academic processions by the esquire and yeoman bedels ; he grants wine licenses to taverns and vintners, and expels offenders from the city ; at all meetings of convocation, and at the annual commemoration in the theatre, he remains covered during the whole ceremony. The *High Steward*, who is always a nobleman, is appointed by the chancellor, subject to approval by the house of convocation, and holds his office for life : his province is to assist the chancellor, vice-chancellor, and proctors, in the execution of their respective duties, and to defend the rights and privileges of the university ; to hear and determine on capital causes in which either scholars or privileged persons are parties, and either personally, or by deputy, to hold the university court leet. The *Proctors*, who must be masters of arts of four years' standing at least, and of not more than ten, are appointed annually, and are taken from the various colleges in rotation : they each nominate two pro-proctors, also masters of arts, of any college or hall, as their deputies : the office of proctor is to inspect the conduct of all members of the university, and to take coguizance of, and punish for, all offences committed by them without the walls of their respective colleges, to see that the members of the several colleges appear in public in their proper dresses, that just weights and measures are used, and to preserve the public peace. The *Public Orator*, who must be at least master of arts, or bachelor of civil law, is chosen by the members of the house of convocation : his office is to write letters and addresses upon public occasions, and to pronounce harangues to princes and other illustrious persons visiting the university, to present the honorary degrees conferred by the university, and, alternately with the professor of poetry, to deliver the annual Creweian oration. The *Keeper of the Archives* (an officer established in 1634), who must be at least master of arts, is appointed by convocation : his duty is to take charge of, and to arrange, all charters, records, and documents, relating to the rights, privileges, and possessions of the university. The *Registrar of the University*, who must be at least master of arts, or a bachelor in civil law, and a notary public, is chosen by the house of convocation : his office is to attend all meetings, to register graces, dispensations, elections, and degrees ; to copy all letters, leases, indentures, and grants, that pass the seal of the university, or the chancellor, and to receive the rents. The *Registrar of the University Court* is appointed by patent from the chancellor : his office is to make probates of wills, and grant letters of administration to the effects of persons dying intestate within the university, as well as to record all the transactions of the court. The *Clerks of the Market*, who must be principals of halls, masters of arts, or bachelors of divinity, law, or medicine, are appointed annually, one by the chancellor, and the other by the vice-chancellor : their office is to take cognizance of the quality of bread, and of all provisions, and to inspect the weights and measures.

The public business is transacted by two principal assemblies, called respectively the houses of congregation and convocation, in both which the chancellor, the vice-chancellor, or, in his absence, one of his deputies, and the proctors, or their deputies, preside. The house of congregation consists exclusively of *Regents*, who are either *necessary* regents, or regents *ad placitum*; the former are doctors of every faculty, and masters of arts during the first year of their regency ; the latter are doctors of every faculty, resident in the university, heads of colleges and halls (and, in their absence, their deputies), professors, and public lecturers, the masters of the schools, the public examiners, the deans and censors of colleges, and all other masters of arts during the second year of their regency. The house of convocation, or, as it is sometimes called, the great congregation, consists both of regents and non-regents : the right of voting in this house is, by the statutes, restricted to the chancellor, vice-chancellor, the two proctors and their deputies, doctors in divinity, medicine, or civil law, who are necessary regents, masters of arts during the first year of their necessary regency, heads of colleges and halls, or their deputies ; members on the foundation or any college, who have at any time been regents ; doctors of divinity, medicine, or law, living with their families within the precincts of the university : professors, and public lecturers, who have at any time been regents, and have performed the exercises required by the statutes, and paid all fees due to

the university ; and *convictores*, or persons not on the foundation of any college or hall, who have at any time been regents, and whose names have been constantly on the books, from the time of their admission to the degree of master of arts, or to that of doctor in either of the three faculties. The business of the house of congregation is principally confined to the passing of graces and dispensations, and to the granting of degrees. All suffrages in cases of graces and dispensations are to be whispered in the ear of the proctors, by a majority of which, given in the words *"placet,"* or *"non placet,"* the fate of the measure is decided. The business of the house of convocation embraces all subjects affecting the credit, interest, or welfare of the university. Nine regents, exclusively of the vice-chancellor and the proctors, are necessary to form a congregation ; the number requisite for a convocation is not defined. In both houses, the chancellor, or vice-chancellor singly, and the two proctors jointly, have an absolute negative upon all proceedings, except in elections. All elections, except for members of parliament, are made in writing by private scrutiny, at which the vice-chancellor presides, and the proctors act as scrutators, and, previously to their proceeding to elect, the act of the 31st of Elizabeth, and the statute *de Electionibus* are read, and the vice-chancellor administers an oath to the proctors that they will make a faithful scrutiny, and to each of the electors that he will vote only once, and for a person whom he firmly believes to be duly qualified : the election is decided by a majority ; should two candidates have an equal number of votes, the senior is elected, if they are graduates, if not, the chancellor, or vice-chancellor, decides by a casting vote. For the better government of the university, a meeting takes place every Monday, and at other times when convened by the vice-chancellor ; in these the vice-chancellor, heads of houses, and the proctors, deliberate upon all matters relating to the privileges and liberties of the university, previously to their being proposed in congregation, or decreed in convocation. The chancellor holds a court of record every week during term, at which his assessor presides, for the recovery of debts to any amount, the jurisdiction of which is confined to members of the university. The university received the elective franchise by charter of James I., in 1603, since which time it has regularly returned two members to parliament : the right of election is vested in the doctors and regent masters of arts in convocation : the vice-chancellor is the returning officer.

There are seven Regius Professorships, namely, Divinity, Civil Law, Medicine, Hebrew, Greek, Modern Languages and History, and Botany : the first five were founded by Henry VIII., who endowed each of them with a yearly stipend of £40, payable, those of Divinity, Hebrew, and Greek, by the Dean and Canons of Christ Church ; the others out of the Royal Exchequer. The *Regius Professorship of Modern Languages and History* was founded by George I., in 1724, and confirmed by George II., in 1728 ; and the *Regius Professorship of Botany* by George III., in 1793. The original endowment of these professorships has been subsequently augmented ; to that of *Divinity* have been annexed a canonry in Christ Church and the rectory of Ewelme, in this county ; to that of *Civil Law*, a lay prebend in the Cathedral Church of Salisbury ; to that of *Medicine*, the mastership of the hospital of Ewelme, with Tomlins' prelectorship of Anatomy, founded in 1623, by Richard Tomlins, Esq., of Westminster, and to that of *Hebrew*, a canonry in Christ Church. *The Margaret Professorship of Divinity* was founded by Margaret, Countess of Richmond, mother of Henry VII., who endowed it with an annual stipend of twenty marks, to which Charles I., in 1627, added a prebend in the Cathedral Church of Worcester: the election is vested in the graduates of divinity; the appointment is for two years from the 8th of September following the election, but the professor is usually continued, by re-election, for life. *The Professorship of Natural Philosophy* was founded, in 1618, by Sir William Sedley, of Aylesford in Kent, who bequeathed to the university £2000 for its endowment, which sum was invested in the purchase of an estate producing £120 per annum: the appointment is vested in the vice-chancellor, the president of Magdalene College, and the warden of All Souls. *The Savilian Professorships of Geometry and Astronomy* were founded and endowed, in 1619, by Sir Henry Savile, Knt; they are open to eminent mathematicians of all countries, who, if Englishmen, must have taken the degree of master of arts: the professors are admitted in congregation on the nomination of the Archbishop of Canterbury, the Lord Chancellor, the Chancellor of the university, the Bishop of London, the principal secretary of state, the chief justices, the chief baron of the Exchequer, and the dean of the Arches. *The Camden Professorship of Ancient History* was founded, in 1622, by William Camden, Clarencieux King at Arms, the celebrated antiquary, who endowed it with the manor of Bexley in Kent. *The Professorship of Music*, the appointment to which is annual, and vested in the proctors, was founded in 1626, by William Heather, doctor in music, who also established a fund for the payment of a *Choragus*, or *Præfectus Musicæ Exercitationis*, who is nominated by the vice-chancellor, the dean of Christ Church, the warden of New College, the president of Magdalene, and the president of St. John's. *The Laudian Professorship of Arabic* was founded, in 1636, by William Laud, Archbishop of Canterbury, who endowed it with lands in the parish of Bray, in the county of Berks: the appointment is vested in the presidents of St. John's and Magdalene Colleges, and in the wardens of New College, All Souls', and Merton. *The Professorship of Botany* was founded, in 1728, by William Sherrard, D.C.L., &c., some time fellow of St. John's, and afterwards consul at Smyrna, who bequeathed to the university £3000 for its endowment, and his valuable library and herbarium: the appointment is in the gift of the Royal College of Physicians. *The Professorship of Poetry* was founded and endowed by Henry Birkhead, Esq., barrister of the Inner Temple, and D.C.L., some time of Trinity, and afterwards fellow of All Souls': the appointment is in the members of convocation, being tenable for five years, and may be retained for five years more by re-election.

The Anglo-Saxon Professorship was founded, in 1750, by Richard Rawlinson, Esq., D.C.L., of St. John's College, who endowed it with rent-charges on lands in Lancashire: the appointment, which is tenable for five years, is in the members of convocation, and is open to candidates from all the colleges in rotation, reserving every fifth turn to St. John's: the candidate must be unmarried, and remain so while he holds the profes-

sorship; he must not be a member of the Royal or Antiquarian Societies, nor a native of Scotland, Ireland, the Colonies, or the son of any native of those places.

The *Vinerian Professorship of Common Law* was founded, in 1755, by Charles Viner, Esq., who bequeathed £12000 to the university for its endowment, and also for the endowment of as many fellowships of £50 per annum, and scholarships of £30 per annum, of the common law, as those funds would permit; the appointment is in the members of convocation. Sir William Blackstone was the first professor on this foundation, and the substance of his lectures forms the subject of his celebrated Commentaries. *The Clinical Professorship for reading Clinical lectures to the students in the Radcliffe Infirmary* was founded, in 1772, by the Earl of Lichfield, Chancellor of the university: the appointment, which is vested in the members of convocation, is tenable only by a person who has taken a doctor's degree in medicine five years before the time of election. *The Aldrichian Professorships of Anatomy, of the practice of Medicine, and of Chemistry*, were founded and endowed, in 1803, by George Aldrich, of the county of Nottingham, M.D.: the endowment of the professorship of Chemistry, which, with that of Medicine, is in the nomination of the members of convocation, has been augmented by a grant from the crown: the professorship of Anatomy is annexed to the prelectorship founded by Richard Tomlins, Esq., and both held with the regius professorship of medicine: one course of lectures in chemistry is annually delivered at the museum. *The Professorship of Political Economy* was founded, in 1825, by Henry Drummond, Esq., of Albury park, in the county of Surrey, who endowed it with a rent-charge of £100 on his estates in that county: the appointment is in the members of convocation, and is tenable for five years by a master of arts, or bachelor of civil law, who has regularly graduated at Oxford. *The Lord Almoner's Reader in Arabic* is appointed by the Lord Almoner, and has an annual stipend out of the Almonry bounty. *The Readership in Experimental Philosophy* was founded by grant from the crown, in 1810: two courses of lectures are read in the museum, comprising the principal experiments in mechanics, hydrostatics, optics, electricity, and magnetism. *The Readership in Mineralogy*, established in 1813, and *the Readership in Geology*, in 1818, were also founded by grants from the crown. *The Anatomical Lectureship* was founded, in 1750, by the late Matthew Lee, M.D., of Christ Church: two courses of lectures are delivered in the Anatomical school at Christ Church, one in Lent, and the other at Michaelmas term. *The Bampton Lectures* were founded, about the year 1780, by John Bampton, M.A., canon of Salisbury, who bequeathed funds for the annual preaching of eight divinity lecture sermons on the leading articles of the Christian faith; of which thirty copies are to be printed for distribution among the heads of houses: the preachers, who are appointed by the heads of colleges only, must have taken the degree of master of arts in either of the universities, and no person can be appointed to preach the divinity lecture sermons twice. *The Whitehall Preacherships* were founded by George I., in 1724: the preachers were appointed by the Bishop of London, as Dean of His Majesty's chapel, and were resident fellows of colleges during the time they held the office; there were twenty-four preachers, of whom twelve were chosen from each of the universities, but in 1829 the establishment was broken up by the Bishop of London. The *University Sermons* are, with certain exceptions, preached in St. Mary's church every Sunday morning during term, by the heads of colleges, the dean and canons of Christ Church, the two professors of divinity, and the professor of Hebrew: the dean and canons of Christ Church, when it comes to their turn, preach these sermons in their own cathedral church. Ten select preachers, who must be doctors, or bachelors in divinity, or in civil law, or masters of arts, are nominated by the vice-chancellor and proctors, and the Regius and Margaret professors of divinity; of these, five go out of office annually, but may be re-appointed after one year.

Dr. Radcliffe founded two fellowships in the university, which he endowed with £600 per annum, for the maintenance of two fellows for ten years, one-half at least to be spent in travelling in foreign parts for their improvement, and to whom, while in the university, he assigned chambers in New College; the *Travelling Fellows* are appointed by the electors of the Radcliffe librarian. *The Vinerian fellowships* of £50 each, and *scholarships* of £30 each, per annum, tenable for ten years only after the date of election, vary in number, according to the state of the revenue of the endowment: the election is made by the members of convocation: the fellows must have taken the degree of master of arts, or bachelor in civil law, at the time of their appointment; and if the candidate be not a barrister at the time, he must become one within a year after his election; the fellowships are given in preference to such as have been scholars on this foundation: the scholars must have completed twenty-four months from the time of their matriculation, and take the degree of bachelor in civil law as soon as possible after the appointment, and within one year after the taking that degree become barristers. *The Craven Scholarships* were founded, in 1647, by John, Lord Craven, who bequeathed lands for the endowment of two scholarships, tenable for fourteen years, in this university, and two in the university of Cambridge: the nomination is vested in the vice-chancellor, the regius professors, and the public orator: three additional scholarships, tenable for seven years only, supported by the same funds, were established by a decree of the Court of Chancery, in 1819; in the appointment to these scholarships, preference is given to candidates of the name or family of the founder, and no one is eligible who is a graduate in the university, or a fellow or scholar of any college, or whose parents are able to maintain him otherwise. *The Ireland Scholarships* were founded, in 1825, by John Ireland, D.D., Dean of Westminster, who transferred to the university £4000 in the three per cent. consols., for the endowment of four scholarships of £30 per annum each, for undergraduates, who shall not have exceeded their sixteenth term from the date of matriculation: the candidate must produce in writing the consent of the head of his college, and the certificate of his standing: the election is made by three examiners appointed by the trustees. A circular has recently been sent round to the respective colleges by the managers of the "Eldonian Testimonial Fund," stating that the *Law scholarship*, to be founded from that source, will be filled up in May or June, 1831; candidates to be persons who have gained distinguished honours at this university.

The four terms in the year are, Michaelmas, which commences on the 10th of October, and ends on the 17th of December; Hilary term, which commences on the 14th of January, and ends on the Saturday before Palm-Sunday, or, if that day be a festival, on the Monday after; Easter term, which commences on the 10th day after Easter-Sunday, and ends on the day before Whit-Sunday; and Trinity term, which commences on the Wednesday after Whit-Sunday, and ends on the Saturday after the first Tuesday in July: the full term begins on the first day of the week after the first congregation is held. Michaelmas and Hilary terms are kept, by six weeks' residence, by such as have not taken any degree in arts, and Easter and Trinity terms, by a residence of three weeks each. Sixteen terms are requisite to qualify for the degree of bachelor of arts, except the sons of English, Scotch, or Irish peers, matriculated as such, and not on the foundation of any college, who are admitted candidates for that degree after three years' residence. Twelve terms, exclusively of the term of matriculation, are requisite for bachelors of arts keeping terms for a master's degree, and for students in civil law, who, having resided three weeks in each term, assume the civilian's gown. For the degree of bachelor in civil law, without proceeding through arts, twenty-eight terms are requisite; but of these, two are considered as being kept by matriculation in term, and by taking the degree, and, as in the case of a master's degree, three others are dispensed with by congregation, and six more by the chancellor's letter. For the degree of doctor in civil law, five years are requisite, to be computed from the time of taking the bachelor's degree; but, upon making oath in convocation of intention to practise in Doctors' Commons, one year is remitted. For the degree of bachelor in medicine, one year is requisite from the regency, and for that of doctor, four years' residence from the time of matriculation. For the degree of bachelor in divinity, seven years are required from the time of matriculation, and for that of doctor, four years more. Candidates for all degrees, who possess certain property, must go out, according to the local phrase, as grand compounders; the property requisite for this purpose may arise either from civil or ecclesiastical property if the former, it must amount to 300 per annum: if the latter, the preferment must be rated in the king's books at £40: candidates who do not possess property to that amount are termed petty compounders, and must at least have ecclesiastical property of the annual value of five shillings, or property of any other description to the amount of £5 per annum. The exercises for the degree of bachelor of arts are, responsions held in Michaelmas, Hilary, and Trinity terms, to which candidates who have entered on their sixth term and not completed their ninth are admitted, on giving their names for that purpose to the junior proctor, at least three days previously to the commencement of the exercises, which consist of examination in the classics, the rudiments of logic, and in Euclid's elements of Geometry; and public examinations, held twice a year, in Michaelmas and Easter terms, to which candidates who have entered on their fourth year of matriculation, and have previously responded before the masters of the schools, are admitted, by giving their names for that purpose three days before the examination commences: the public examination comprehends the rudiments of religion, under which is included a sufficient knowledge of the Gospels in the original Greek, of the thirty-nine articles of the church of England, and of the evidences of natural and revealed religion; the *literæ humaniores*, including a competent knowledge of the Latin and Greek languages, rhetoric and moral philosophy, as derived from the Greek and Roman writers, logic, and Latin composition; and the elements of the mathematical sciences and of physics. In the *literæ humaniores*, and in the elements of the mathematical sciences and physics, the examiners have a certain discretionary power, but they have none with respect to the rudiments of religion, any failure in which inevitably excludes the candidate from his degree, without regard to his other attainments. The examinations, both in the responsions and in the public examinations, may be conducted either in the Latin or English language. The public examiners, who are nine in number, are chosen from those who have taken the degree of master of arts, or doctor of civil law; they are nominated by the vice-chancellor and proctors, but must be approved by the houses of congregation and convocation; six of them examine *in literis humanioribus*, and four must be present at each examination; the other four examine *in Disciplinis Mathematicis et Physicis*, and three at least must be present at each examination: there cannot be two examiners of either class from the same college or hall, neither can any of them examine a candidate belonging to his own college or hall. Three masters, who have been admitted regents in arts, preside over the schools, of whom one is nominated by the vice-chancellor, and one by each of the proctors, annually on the first day of Trinity term: two masters must always be present at the responsions, and when the proctors are absent during the performance of the exercises, the masters are invested with procuratorial power.

The exercises requisite for a bachelor's degree in divinity, law, or medicine, are disputations on two distinct days, before the professors of those respective faculties; in divinity, the preaching of a Latin sermon at St. Mary's, before the vice-chancellor, is also required. For a doctor's degree in either of the faculties, three distinct lectures are to be read in the schools, on three several days, which, by a dispensation from the houses of congregation or convocation, are permitted to be read at three different hours on the same day. Three prizes of £20 each are given annually by the chancellor for the best compositions in Latin verse, Latin prose, and English prose; for the first, candidates only who have not exceeded four years from their matriculation can contend; for the other two, all such as have exceeded four years, but not completed seven, and have not taken the degree of M.A., or B.C.L., may be competitors. Sir Roger Newdigate, in 1806, bequeathed to the university funds for an annual prize for English verses on ancient sculpture, painting, or architecture. Dr. Ellerton, fellow of Magdalene College, gave a rent-charge of £21, on an estate at Horspath, in the county of Oxford, for an annual prize for the best English essay on some doctrine or duty of the Christian religion, or on some subject in theology. The subjects of all these compositions are given out by the vice-chancellor, and the compositions are sent, under a sealed cover, without the author's name, but distinguished by a motto, a duplicate of which, signed with the author's name, is also sent to the registrar of the university, on a day fixed by the vice-chancellor, who, with the two proctors, the public orator, and the professor of poetry, decide on their merits in the theatre, where the compositions are publicly recited at the commemoration. The university enjoys the right of presentation to the rectory of South Moreton, in the county of Berks, held in trust for Magdalene Hall; the vicarage of South Petherwin *cum* Trewen, in the county of Cornwall; the vicarage of Holme-Cultram, in the county of Cumberland; the rectory of Gatcomb, in trust for the Principal of St. Edmund Hall, in the county of Southampton; the vicarage of Syston, in the county of Leicester; the rectory of Stutchbury, in the county of Northampton; the lectureship of St. Giles', in the city of Oxford; and the perpetual curacy of Kirkdale, in the county of York.

Arms.

University College is supposed by some to have been founded so early as 872, by Alfred the Great, and to have constituted the largest of his three halls, but, with far greater probability, its foundation is ascribed to William, Archdeacon of Durham, who, in 1249, left three hundred and ten marks to the chancellor and university, in order to purchase certain annual rents for the support of ten, twelve, or more masters, at that time the highest academical title, the first purchase having been made in 1253. The funds left by him were appropriated to the support of a limited number of individuals, chosen by the various halls of the university, and who at first did not form an independent society, but were subordinate to the several schools in which they had been educated: in 1280, the institution of a society was determined upon, and the statutes eventually settled by the university bear the date 1292. The situation of the original house, or hall, is generally considered to be the site now occupied by Brasenose College, and historians assert that the society removed to the present college about 1343, under the style of "the Master and Scholars of the Hall of the University of Oxford," giving to their house the name of "University Hall;" at what period it was first denominated a college is unknown. The style at present in use, namely, "the Master and Fellows of the College of the Great Hall of the University, commonly called University College in Oxford," was fixed by Queen Elizabeth, in 1572. A common seal was used so early as 1320, and the statutes now in force were enacted in 1726. The foundation consists of a master, twelve fellows, and twenty-four scholars and exhibitioners: two of the fellowships were founded by William of Durham, for that county; three by Henry IV., for the dioceses of York and Durham; three, in 1442, by the Earl of Northumberland, for the dioceses of Durham, Carlisle, and York; and four, in 1631, by Sir Simon Bennet, for any part of England, except these three dioceses. The King became visitor in the beginning of the reign of George II., in consequence of a decree in the court of King's Bench, assigning the foundation to Alfred; the House of Convocation had previously exercised that power, as trustees under the will of William of Durham. The livings in the patronage of the Master and Fellows are, the rectory of Tarrant-Gunville, in the county of Dorset; the rectory of North Cerney, in the county of Gloucester; the rectory of Headbourn-Worthy, in the county of Southampton; the perpetual curacy of Flamstead, in the county of Hertford; the rectory of Elton, in the county of Huntingdon; the rectory of Checkendon, in the county of Oxford; the rectory of Kingsdon, in the county of Somerset; the rectory of Beckley, in the county of Sussex; the vicarage of Arncliffe, and the rectory of Melsonby, in the county of York. The college, which is on the south side of the High-street, is in the ancient style of English architecture, with portions in the Italian style, and comprises two parallel quadrangles: one, built at various periods, with a chapel and hall on the south side, is one hundred feet square; the other, built principally by Dr. Radcliffe, has only three sides, each being about eighty feet in length; on the south is the master's garden: the two constitute a front of about two hundred and forty feet in extent, from the High-street, which it faces, presenting a magnificent appearance; each quadrangle is entered by a gateway surmounted by a tower; over one entrance, in front, is the statue of Queen Anne, and within, that of James II.; over the other, in front, that of Mary II., and within, that of Dr. Radcliffe. The chapel, built in 1665, displays a profusion of painted glass, and contains a fine cenotaph, by Flaxman, to the memory of Sir William Jones. In the library, which was completed in 1660, is a very valuable collection of books and manuscripts. Amongst the most eminent members formerly belonging to this society may be enumerated Ridley, Bishop of London, who was burnt at the stake in this city; Bingham, author of *Origines Ecclesiasticæ*; Sir William Jones; Dr. Radcliffe; Edward, Lord Herbert of Cherbury; Dr. John Hudson, a learned critic; Carte, the historian; Richard Jago, an ingenious poet; Sir Robert Chambers, Vinerian Professor, afterwards a Judge in India; two archbishops, and nine bishops. The members on the books are two hundred and eighteen, of whom one hundred and ten are members of convocation.

Balliol College appears to have been founded, about 1260, by John Balliol, of Bernard Castle, father of John Balliol, King of Scotland: he gave to each of his scholars 8d. per week for their commons, and settled yearly exhibitions upon them, with the intention of providing a house and appropriate accommodation, which was carried into effect after his decease, in 1269, by his wife Devorguilla, who, in 1281, purchased a tenement in Horsemonger-street, now called Broad-street, and prescribed statutes for their government: in 1284, she likewise purchased the adjoining hall of St. Mary, and having repaired it, established the society there by charter of incorporation, which, being confirmed by the king, her son, and Oliver, Bishop of Lincoln, the name of New Balliol College was given to it: the code of statutes at present in force was enacted in 1507. The number of scholars has varied at different times, according to the state of the finances: in 1610 the society included not less than one hundred and twenty-seven persons; at present it consists of a master, twelve fellows, and fourteen scholars, of whom nine fellows and ten scholars are on the old foundation. In 1620, Lady Eliz. Periam, widow of the Lord Chief Baron, Sir William Periam, Knt., added one fellowship, which, as well as those on the old foundation, is open to candidates indiscriminately: in 1615, and 1676, the trustees of Mr. Peter Blundell founded two fellowships for persons to be elected from his grammar school at Tiverton, in the county of Devon: there are also thirty-three scholarships and exhibitions; and, in 1522, lands were given by Thomas Harrope to increase the number of scholarships: among the exhibitions are four founded by John Warner, Bishop of Rochester, in 1666 or 1667, for natives of Scotland, to support the cause of episcopacy in that country; they are endowed with £20 per annum each, and are now held by four of the exhibitioners of John Snell, Esq. This college alone has the privilege of electing its own visitor, who at present is the Archbishop of Canterbury. The livings in the patronage of the Master and Fellows are the rectory and vicarage of Duloe, in the county of Cornwall; the vicarage of Beer-Regis, in the county of Dorset; the rectories of All Saints', St. Leonard, St. Nicholas, Holy Trinity, and the perpetual curacy of St. Botolph's, in the town of Colchester; the vicarage of Marks-Tey, and the rectory of Tendring, in the county of Essex; the vicarage of Abbotsley, in the county of Huntingdon; the rectories of Brattleby, Fillingham, and Riseholme, in the county of Lincoln; the consolidated vicarages of St. Lawrence Jewry and St. Mary Magdalene, Milk-street, London; the vicarage of Long Benton, in the county of Northumberland; and the rectories of Kilve *cum* Stringston, Huntspill, and Timsbury, in the county of Somerset. The buildings of this college chiefly form a quadrangle of one hundred and twenty feet by eighty, in addition to which is an area on the north-west side: in the centre of the front is a fine square embattled tower, surmounted by a turret, and ornamented with a highly enriched canopied niche, and the arms of the founder: on the west side of the quadrangle are the hall and master's residence; on the north the chapel and library, which latter, originally completed in 1477, was repaired and embellished under the direction of Mr. James Wyatt, architect, and contains a valuable collection of illuminated manuscripts, several rare English Bibles, and other works: the other sides consist of rooms for the fellows and scholars. The buildings to the north-east of the quadrangle were the gift of Archbishop Abbot; those to the south-west of it, fronting the street, and containing twelve sets of rooms, were erected at the expense of Mr. Fisher, formerly a fellow of this college; to which was added, in 1827, a building on the north, fronting the church of St. Mary Magdalene, containing twenty-two sets of rooms. Among the more eminent members may be enumerated John Wickliff, the Reformer, who was master; Humphrey, Duke of Gloucester; Tiptoft, Earl of Worcester; John Ross and Robert Parsons; Sir John Popham, Chief Justice of the King's Bench; Sir Robert Atkyns, Chief Baron of the Exchequer; Sir John Evelyn; Dr. Bradley, Astronomer Royal; Rev. John Hutchins, author of the History of Dorsetshire; three archbishops, and eight bishops. The members on the books are two hundred and forty-eight, of whom one hundred are members of convocation.

Arms.

Arms.

Merton College was founded by Walter de Merton, Bishop of Rochester, and Lord High Chancellor of England, who having previously founded one at Merton, in the county of Surrey, removed the society hither in 1274, under the name of *Domus Scholarum de Merton*, and the statutes bear that date : this college, in point of legal establishment, is the oldest in the university, and was so well endowed, that in the 26th of Henry VIII. its revenue was valued at £354. The society consists of a warden, twenty-four fellows, fourteen postmasters, four scholars, two chaplains, and two clerks. The natives of the following dioceses are ineligible to fellowships, *viz.*, St. Asaph, Bangor, St. David's, Llandaff, Hereford, Chichester, Exeter, Rochester, Lichfield and Coventry, Chester, and Carlisle. Exhibitions for the twelve portionists, called postmasters, were given in 1380, by John Willyott, D.D., Chancellor of Exeter; these were increased to fourteen by John Chamber, fellow of Eton, and canon of Windsor, who directed his exhibitioners to be elected from Eton College: the four scholarships were founded, in 1753, by Henry Jackson, M.A., of this college, and afterwards a minor canon of St. Paul's, London: the sum of £20 per annum is vested in the Warden and Fellows, for general distribution among poor scholars. The Archbishop of Canterbury is visitor. The livings in the patronage of the Warden and Fellows are, the rectory of Gamlingay, in the county of Cambridge; the vicarage of Diddington, in the county of Huntingdon ; the vicarage of Elham, in the county of Kent, on the nomination of the Archbishop of Canterbury ; the rectory of Kibworth-Beauchamp, in the county of Leicester ; the vicarages of Embleton and Ponteland, in the county of Northumberland ; the rectories of Cuxham and Ibstone, with the perpetual curacies of Holywell and Wolvercott, in the county of Oxford ; the perpetual curacies of St. John the Baptist, and St. Peter in the East, in the city of Oxford ; the rectory of Farley, and the vicarage of Malden, with the perpetual curacy of Chessington, in the county of Surrey ; the rectory of Lapworth, and the vicarage of Great Wolford, in the county of Warwick ; and the vicarage of Stratton St. Margaret, in the county of Wilts : the Archbishop of Canterbury must also collate one of the fellows, or one who has been a fellow, of this college, to the rectory of Denton, in the county of Norfolk. The college is situated on the south side of the city, in St. John's street, and its buildings form three quadrangles ; the first, which opens by a noble arch into the inner quadrangle, is one hundred and ten feet by one hundred feet, and was rebuilt in 1589, with the exception of the tower and gatehouse, which were constructed in the early part of the fifteenth century, during the wardenship of the celebrated mathematician, Thomas Redburn, Bishop of St David's : it contains the warden's apartments, some portions of which are supposed to be coeval with the original edifice. The second, or grand court, is of modern date, and exhibits a mixed style of architecture , the centre elevation is adorned with tiers of columns of the Tuscan, Doric, Ionic, and Corinthian orders. The third, or small court, is ancient, and supposed to have been built, as it now stands, about the

same time as the library, which forms its south and west sides, and was founded in 1376, by Rede, Bishop of Chichester: this is thought to be the most ancient structure of the kind in existence. At the western end of the outer court is the chapel, which is considered one of the finest in the university, and consists of a choir in the decorated style, and transepts, with a low massive tower at the intersection, in the later style of English architecture ; the windows are of painted glass, and the east window of seven lights is ornamented with a rich wheel, crocketed canopies and pinnacles, being considered a remarkable specimen of fine taste, and is called the Catharine Wheel window : the tower is embattled and pinnacled. It is the parish church of St. John the Baptist, being used only as the college chapel, and the parochial duties are discharged by one of the chaplains of the college, a small portion of the interior being allotted as a burial-place for the inhabitants. Among the eminent members of this society may be classed Dr. Harvey, who discovered the circulation of the blood, warden of the college; the celebrated Duns Scotus; Archbishop Bradwardyn; John Wickliff; Sir Henry Savile; John Greaves; John Hales; Francis Cheynell; Hugh Cressy; Samuel Clarke; Anthony à Wood; the Oxford historian; Sir Richard Steele; the Earl of Essex; the parliamentary general; Thomas Farnaby, a learned critic; Dr. Edmund Dickenson; Thomas Tyrwhitt, editor of Chaucer's Tales; thirteen bishops, and five archbishops: Savile and Wood were buried here. The members on the books are one hundred and twenty seven, of whom sixty-four are members of convocation.

Arms.

Exeter College was founded, in 1314, by Walter de Stapledon, Bishop of Exeter, and called Stapledon Hall: on the removal of his scholars to this spot from Hart Hall the foundation comprised a rector and twelve fellows, eight of the thirteen to be elected from the archdeaconries of Exeter, Totness, and Barnstaple, four from the archdeaconry of Cornwall, and one, to be nominated by the Dean and Chapter of Exeter, from any other place, provided the candidate should be in priest's orders. Two additional fellowships were founded, in 1404, by Edmund Stafford, Bishop of Exeter (who obtained leave to bestow on the college its present name), to be chosen from the diocese of Salisbury; eight, in 1565, by Sir William Petre, Knt., for natives of the counties of Devon, Somerset, Dorset, Oxford, and Essex, and any others in which his descendants might have lands of inheritance, or other possessions, who also procured a new body of statutes, and a regular deed of incorporation for this college ; one by Charles I., in 1636, for a native of Jersey or Guernsey ; and two, about 1700, by Lady Elizabeth Shiers, for natives of the counties of Hertford and Surrey, which are exclusively in the gift of the rector and five senior fellows : the society at present includes a rector and twenty-five fellows; there are also sixteen scholarships and exhibitions. The Bishop of Exeter is visitor. The livings in the patronage of the Rector and Fellows are, the vicarage of Long Wittenham, in the county of Berks ; the vicarage of Menheniot, in the county of Cornwall, on the nomination, by the Dean and Chapter of Exeter, of one who is or has been a fellow of the college; the rectory of Bushey, in the county of Hertford; the rectory of Wootton, in the county of Northampton; the vicarages of Merton and South Newington, in the county of Oxford; the rectories of Ripe and Waldron, in the county of Sussex; and the rectories of Baverstock and Somerford Magna, in the county of Wilts: the vicarage of Kidlington, in the county of Oxford, is annexed, without institution, to the rectorship. The front of this college is on the eastern side of the Turle, and is two hundred and twenty feet in length; a gateway of rustic work, surmounted by a tower, with Ionic pilasters, which support a semicircular pediment, ornamented with the arms of the founder, leads into the first quadrangle, in which are the hall, a handsome building in the later style of English architecture, erected about 1610, by Sir John Ackland; the chapel, in similar style, towards the erection of which, about 1623, Dr. George Hakewill contributed £1200, and which possesses the peculiarity of having two aisles; and the rector's lodgings: there is an inner court, of similar construction, one hundred and thirty-five feet square; behind it is a garden laid out with great taste. The library was erected, about 1778, and contains, with other valuable works, a fine collection of the Aldine classics, also a portrait of Mr. Sandford, a learned but eccentric divine, who included in his valuable bequest to this college, the extremely rare and valuable Hebrew Bible, printed at Soncino in Italy, in 1488. Among the eminent members may be enumerated the following writers: Trevisa; Grocyn; Sir John Dodderidge; Digory Whear; George Hakewill; Joseph Caryll; Browne, the poet; the celebrated lawyer, Sir John Fortescue; and Anthony Astley Cooper, Earl of Shaftesbury; Maundrell, the oriental traveller; Dr. William Borlase, the Cornish antiquary; Jonathan Toup, an eminent critic; Nicholas Tindal, the continuator of Rapin; Sir Michael Foster, a learned lawyer; Dr. Benjamin Kennicott; also two archbishops, and eleven bishops. The members on the books are two hundred and eighty-eight, of whom one hundred and twenty-three are members of convocation.

Arms.

Oriel College was founded, in 1326, by license of Edward II. to his almoner, Adam de Brome, to build and endow a college to the honour of the Virgin Mary, towards which project that sovereign had, in 1325, given the advowson of St. Mary's, and the parsonage-house of that rectory: of this institution Brome became the first provost. In 1333, the parsonage-house was converted into an academical hall, called St. Mary's Hall, and Edward III. gave to the society a tenement, called *L'Oriele*, on which this college was founded, and whence its name is derived. The original foundation included a provost and ten fellows; four fellowships were added about 1441, by John Frank, Master of the Rolls, for the counties of Somerset, Dorset, Wilts, and Devon; one by John Carpenter, Bishop of Worcester, about 1476; one by William Smyth, Bishop of Lincoln, in 1507; and two by Richard Dudley, chancellor of the church of Salisbury, in 1529. A prebend in Rochester cathedral was annexed to the office of provost for ever, by Queen Anne. There are fifteen exhibitions.

The King is visitor. The livings in the patronage of the Provost and Fellows are, the rectory of Ufton, in the county of Berks; the rectory of Purleigh, in the county of Essex; the rectories of Abbot's Cromhall and Tortworth, in the county of Gloucester; the vicarage of Coleby, in the county of Lincoln; the perpetual curacy of Morton-Pinkney, in the county of Northampton; the vicarage of St. Mary the Virgin, in the city of Oxford; the rectory of Swainswick, and the vicarage of Twiverton, in the county of Somerset; the rectory of Cholderton, in the county of Wilts; and the vicarage of Aberford, in the county of York; the rectory of Plymptree, in the county of Devon; and the rectory of Saltfleet by St. Peter's, in the county of Lincoln; are in the gift of the Provost. The buildings consist of a spacious and handsome quadrangle, and two lateral ranges of chambers on the east and west sides of the garden; the eastern wing, erected by Robinson, Bishop of London, in 1719; the western, by Dr. George Carter, provost, in 1729; and in 1817 a modern stone building, comprising fifteen sets of rooms, was erected to the southward of Bishop Robinson's wing. The entrance to the quadrangle from the street is through a towergateway, the roof of which is decorated with the royal arms of Charles I., and the tower with a bay window, or oriel. The hall, immediately opposite, is approached by a flight of steps, under a portico, surmounted by statues of Edward II. and Edward III., in niches, and above these, in another niche, are sculptured representations of the Virgin and Child. The Provost's house is on the north side of the quadrangle; the south and west sides are occupied by the members' apartments: on the east side is the entrance to the chapel, which edifice was completed in 1642, and, with the hall, presents specimens of the later style of English architecture: the library was designed and constructed under the direction of Mr. James Wyatt. Among the eminent members are Dr. Joseph Butler, the learned Bishop of Durham; Sir Walter Raleigh; William Prynne; Sir John Holt, an eminent lawyer; and Dr. Joseph Warton. The members on the books are two hundred and ninety-eight, of whom one hundred and fifty-nine are members of convocation.

Arms.

Queen's College was founded, in 1340, by Robert de Egglesfield, rector of Brough, in the county of Westmorland, and Confessor to Philippa, Queen of Edward III., and it has, in consequence, received the especial patronage of the Queens of England. The original foundation consisted of a provost and twelve fellows, afterwards increased to sixteen, to be elected exclusively from the counties of Cumberland and Westmorland; to these, eight fellowships were added, on the foundation of John Michel, Esq., of Richmond in Surrey, for natives of any county: there are also forty-eight scholarships and exhibitions: the Archbishop of York is visitor. The livings in the patronage of the Provost and Fellows are, the vicarage of Sparsholt, and the rectories of Sulhampstead-Abbas, and Sulhampstead Bannister, in the county of Berks; the rectory of Holwell, in the county of Somerset; the vicarage of Chedworth, in the county of Gloucester; the vicarages of Bramley, Carisbrooke, Godshill with the rectory of Niton,

Milford with the perpetual curacy of Hordle, Monks' Sherborne, Holy Rood (Southampton), the rectories of Bramshot, Knight's Enham, Headley, Newnham with the perpetual curacy of Maplederwell, Church-Oakley, and Weyhill, and the chapels of Pamber and Upton-Grey, in the county of Southampton; the rectories of Blechingdon, Charlton upon Otmore, Hampton-Poyle, and South Weston, in the county of Oxford; the vicarage of Newbold-Pacey, in the county of Warwick; and the vicarage of Brough, in the county of Westmorland. The livings on Mr. Michel's, or the New, foundation are, the vicarage of Wendron with Helston, in the county of Cornwall; the rectory of English-Bicknor, in the county of Gloucester; the second portion of the rectory of Pontesbury, in the county of Salop; and the rectory of Upton-Scudamore, in the county of Wilts. The whole of this magnificent edifice was erected in the last century: the entire area forms an oblong square of three hundred feet by two hundred and twenty, and is divided into two spacious courts by the chapel and hall; the principal front is on the north side of the High-street, and the grand entrance is under a large central gateway, which is surmounted by an open cupola, supported on pillars, and containing a statue of Queen Caroline, consort of George II., by whose munificence it was erected: this gateway leads into the first quadrangle, which was erected in 1710, by Hawksmore, at the expense of Provost Lancaster, and is one hundred and forty feet by one hundred and thirty, being thought to bear a resemblance to the Luxembourgh palace in Paris: on three of its sides are lofty cloisters, supported by square pillars, leading to the lodgings of the provost, and the rooms of the different members of the society; the north side, at the extremities of which are the chapel and hall, consists of a grand Doric elevation, with an enriched central pediment, supported on four lofty columns, terminating in a circle, with intervening pilasters; and crowned with a balustrade and fine Ionic cupola: the south front is ornamented with six figures, of which, the two placed on pediments are Jupiter and Apollo: the chapel windows contain several exquisite specimens of ancient stained glass, and the ceiling is decorated with a painting of the Ascension by Sir James Thornhill. The inner court is one hundred and thirty feet by ninety: on its western side is the library, which was completed in 1690: it is one of the largest in the university, and contains, besides a valuable collection of books amounting to more than eighteen thousand volumes, some fine busts and paintings, two very ancient paintings in glass of Henry V., who was educated at this college, and a most magnificent cast of a Florentine boar. In the buttery is an ancient and curious drinking horn, capable of containing two quarts, and presented to the college by Queen Philippa; the ornamental engravings are rich and curious, and it bears several inscriptions of the Saxon word *Wacceyl*. Among the more eminent members may be enumerated, Dr. Holyoake, Wycheley, Halley, Addison, Tickell, and Burn, author of the "Justice of the Peace;" Henry V., said to have been a student here; Bernard Gilpin, called "the Apostle of the North;" Dr. John Mill, the learned editor of the New Testament; Sir John Davies, a learned lawyer and poet; Dr. Thomas Hyde, Professor of Arabic; Sir John Floyer, a learned physician; Dr. Thomas Shaw,
Vol. III.

the traveller; Collins, the poet; as clerical dignitaries, one archbishop, and fourteen bishops, including Cardinal Beaufort, and Bishops Gibson, Nicholson, and Tanner. The members on the books are three hundred and fifty-one, of whom one hundred and sixty-four are members of convocation.

Arms.

New College was founded, in 1386, by William of Wykeham, Bishop of Winchester, and Lord High Chancellor of England, for a warden, seventy fellows and scholars, ten chaplains, an organist, three clerks, and sixteen choristers. In the original charter it is called the College of St. Mary of Winchester: the present popular appellation was acquired at the time of its erection, and has continued to the present time. Wykeham's school, at Winchester, was instituted as a nursery to supply scholars by election to this college, and is annually subject to the visitation of the warden; for which reason the fellows enjoy the privilege of admission to degrees, without obtaining a grace from the house of congregation, or being examined in the public schools, provided they have undergone examinations in their own college, according to the forms of the university: the fellows and scholars must be elected from the college, or school, at Winchester, at a regular meeting held annually for that purpose, and attended by the wardens of both colleges, two fellows of New College, and the subwarden and head master of that at Winchester. The founder's kin are fellows on admission; others are probationary scholars until the expiration of two years. The statutes of the founder, the counterpart of those at Winchester, were deemed so complete that they have served as a model in framing regulations for most of the succeeding colleges. The Bishop of Winchester is visitor. The livings in the patronage of the Warden and Fellows are, the rectories of Akely, Hardwick, Great Horwood, Newton-Longville, Radclive, and Tingewick, and the vicarage of Whaddon, in the county of Buckingham; the vicarage of Steeple-Morden, in the county of Cambridge; the rectory of Abbot's Stoke, in the county of Dorset; the rectories of Birchanger and Little Sampford, the vicarages of Hornchurch, and Writtle with Roxwell chapel, and the perpetual curacy of Romford, in the county of Essex; the vicarage of Marshfield, in the county of Gloucester; the vicarage of Heckfield with Mattingley chapel, in the county of Southampton; the rectories of Saham-Toney, Stratton St. Michael, St. John Madder-Market (in the city of Norwich), Weston, and Witchingham St. Faith consolidated with the vicarage of Witchingham St. Mary, in the county of Norfolk; the rectory of Paulers-Pury, in the county of Northampton; the vicarages of East Adderbury, Chesterton, and Swalcliffe with the chapelry of Epwell, and the rectories of Bucknell, Heyford-Warren, Stanton St. John, and Wootton, in the county of Oxford; the rectory of Worthen, in the county of Salop; the rectory of Long Ditton, in the county of Surrey; the rectory of Stockton, in the county of Warwick; the rectories of Alton-Barnes, Berwick St. John, and Donhead St. Mary, in the county of Wilts; the sinecure rectory of Colerne, in the county of Wilts, is annexed to the Wardenship, and the Warden is patron of the vicarage. This college is situated in New College
3 Q

lane, and consists of a principal quadrangle, measuring one hundred and sixty-eight feet by one hundred and twenty-nine, which includes the chapel, hall, and library; and a smaller quadrangle, called the Cloisters, adjacent to which is a lofty and substantial square tower: the other buildings, which form the garden-court, are an addition to the original design, and were built in imitation of the palace of Versailles, or, according to some, of the king's house at Winchester, but with battlements to correspond with the old quadrangle and city wall, by which the more ancient part of the buildings is surrounded: this part of the college was finished in 1684, and is separated from the garden, which is spacious and tastefully arranged, by an iron palisade; the approach to the great quadrangle is by a portal, surmounted by a tower, the front of which still retains, in one of its ornamented niches, the sculptured effigy of the founder. The chapel and hall, on the north side of the great court, present a magnificent elevation; the former was remarkable for its splendour prior to the Reformation, and still retains a primary rank among the sacred structures of the university: it is in the later style of English architecture, with a very rich interior, and consists of an ante-chapel, eighty feet by thirty-six, leading at right angles into a choir of one hundred feet by thirty-five: in the former division is a splendid display of painted glass, in four different styles of execution, but these are surpassed by the great west window, which is divided into two parts, the higher representing the Nativity, and the lower seven figures emblematical of the Christian and cardinal virtues, executed by Jarvis, from the designs of Sir Joshua Reynolds: on the north and south sides of the choir are other paintings; those on the south side were originally Flemish, and are said to have been done from designs by some of the scholars of Rubens; they were purchased by the college, and repaired in 1740: over the altar are some beautiful specimens of sculpture, by Westmacott. The costly and beautiful crosier of the founder, seven feet in height, of silver gilt, and richly decorated, is preserved in the chapel. Among the eminent literary persons educated here were Somerville, the poet; and Wood, author of the "Institutes;" amongst its clerical dignitaries, two archbishops, and twenty-nine bishops, including Archbishop Warham, and Dr. Lowth. The members on the books are one hundred and fifty-three, of whom sixty-six are members of convocation.

Lincoln College was founded, in 1427, by Richard Fleming, Bishop of Lincoln, from which see it takes its name, under permission, obtained from Henry VI., to make the church of All Saints collegiate, and establish a college for a rector and seven scholars: it was completed by Rotheram, Archbishop of York, who added five fellowships, and, by a new body of statutes, enacted in 1479, limited the election of all the fellows to the old dioceses of York and Lincoln, with one exception to the diocese of Wells: there are thirteen exhibitions, eight scholarships, and one bible clerkship. The Bishop of Lincoln is visitor. The livings in the patronage of the Rector and Fellows are, the rectory of Cublington, in the county of Buckingham; the rectory

of Winterborne-Abbas united with that of Winterborne-Steepleton, in the county of Dorset; the rectories of Hadleigh and Great Leighs, in the county of Essex; the rectory of Waddington, in the county of Lincoln; the perpetual curacies of All Saints' and St. Michael's, in the city, and Long Combe, and Forest-Hill, in the county, of Oxford: the rectory of Twyford, in the county of Buckingham, is annexed to the Rectorship. The college, which is situated between All Saints' church and Exeter College, consists of two quadrangles, one eighty feet, and the other seventy feet square; the larger, begun soon after the founder's death, and finished by Bishop Rotheram, is entered by a tower gateway, and contains the hall, library, rector's lodgings, and rooms for members; the inner quadrangle was erected about 1612, and six sets of rooms were added, in 1759, from the funds of the college: the chief ornament of this court is the chapel, on its south side, erected by Bishop Williams; the windows, which present splendid specimens of painted glass and emblazonry, were procured from Italy, by that prelate, in 1629; the large east window is divided into six compartments, and exhibits a variety of scriptural subjects: in the twelve side windows are representations of the Prophets and Apostles: on the south side of the college is a handsome garden. Among the eminent members may be enumerated Sir William D'Avenant; James Hervey, author of the "Meditations;" John Wesley, the celebrated founder of Methodism, who, though a student of Christchurch, was elected a fellow of this college; Dr. Robert Sanderson, Bishop of Lincoln, a learned divine and casuist; Sir William Davenant; Dr. George Hickes; Sir George Wheler; Dr. Matthew Tindal; Archbishop Potter, and nine bishops. The members on the books are one hundred and forty-two, of whom sixty-seven are members of convocation.

All Souls' College was founded, in 1437, by Henry Chichele, Archbishop of Canterbury, who induced Henry VI. to assume the title of co-founder; it was chiefly endowed with the lands of Alien priories dissolved by that monarch. A code of statutes, on the model of Wykeham's, were drawn up by the archbishop, by which, in conformity with the charter, the society consists of a warden, forty fellows, two chaplains, and clerks; the fellowships are open to the descendants of the founder's family, or to others born within the province of Canterbury: there are also six scholarships. The Archbishop of Canterbury is visitor. The livings in the patronage of the Warden and Fellows are, the rectory of Weston-Turville, in the county of Buckingham; the vicarage of Barking, in the county of Essex; the perpetual curacy of Walton-Cardiff, in the county of Gloucester; the rectory of Welwyn, in the county of Hertford; the rectories of Chelsfield with Farnborough, Elmly, and Harrietsham, and the vicarages of New Romney and Upchurch, in the county of Kent; the rectory of Harpsden, and the vicarage of Lewknor, in the county of Oxford; the vicarage of Alberbury, or Abberbury, in the county of Salop; the rectory of Buckland, in the county of Surrey; the rectory of Barford St. Martin, in the county of Wilts; and the vicarages of Llangennith and Pen-arth, in the county of

Glamorgan : the rectory of East Lockinge, in the county of Berks, is annexed to the Wardenship. The college buildings consist of two quadrangles; that erected by the founder is about one hundred and twenty-four feet by seventy-two, and still retains many of its ancient features : it is entered from the High-street, through two gateways, the western surmounted by a tower beautifully-ornamented with large and well-sculptured effigies of Henry VI. and Chichele : it contains a curious dial, designed by Sir Christopher Wren : the whole line of building is adorned with battlements. The other quadrangle is comparatively modern, and measures, with the court, one hundred and seventy-three feet by one hundred and fifty - five : it contains the grand entrance from Radcliffe square, and the cloister, on the west ; the common and other rooms, with two magnificent towers, on the east ; the chapel and hall on the south ; and the library on the north : the whole of this square is in the later style of English architecture, with some admixtures. The chapel is very generally admired, and is separated from the ante-chapel by an elegant screen, constructed by Sir Christopher Wren ; the windows are in *chiaro oscuro*, and among the interior decorations, immediately over the altar, is the beautiful *Noli me tangere* of Raphaello Mengs, purchased of the artist for £315 ; above it is a remarkably fine *al fresco* painting, intended to represent the assumption of the founder, by Sir James Thornhill : the respective dimensions of the chapel and ante-chapel are seventy feet by thirty. The hall contains a fine marble bust of Chichele, and paintings. The splendid library, consisting of about forty thousand volumes, was the gift of Colonel Codrington, a member of the college, who, in addition to his own library, bequeathed £4000 for the purchase of books, and £6000 to defray the expense of the building : it was completed in 1756, and its principal room, exclusively of a central recess, containing a statue of the colonel, is one hundred and ninety-eight feet by thirty-three and a half ; the foundation stone was laid by Dr. Young, author of the " Night Thoughts." Among the eminent members are, Leland, the antiquary ; Linacre ; Caius ; Sir Christopher Wren, who removed hither from Wadham College ; Sir William Blackstone ; Dr. Thomas Sydenham ; Robert Heyrick, the poet ; and Marchmont Nedham, a political writer in the reign of Charles I. ; with one archbishop, and twelve bishops. The members on the books are one hundred, of whom sixty-eight are members of convocation.

Magdalene College was founded, in 1456, by William of Waynfleet, Bishop of Winchester, and Lord High Chancellor of England, on or near the site of the ancient hospital of St. John the Baptist, which, with all the estates belonging to it, was given to him by Henry VI., for a president, forty fellows, thirty scholars (called demies, because formerly they were entitled only to half-commons), a schoolmaster, usher, four chaplains, an organist, eight clerks, and sixteen choristers. The fellows are eligible alone from the following dioceses and counties :—five from the diocese of Winchester, four from Norwich, two from York and Durham, two from Chichester, seven from the county of Lincoln, four from Oxford, three from Berks, one from

Arms.

York, two from Gloucester, two from Warwick, one each from the counties of Buckingham, Kent, Nottingham, Essex, Somerset, Northampton, and Wilts, and one from the city of London. Demies are eligible from any of the above-mentioned dioceses or counties, excepting those of York and Durham. There are nine exhibitions, exclusively of some founded by John Hygden, D.D. The Bishop of Winchester is visitor. The livings in the patronage of the President and Fellows are, the rectories of Appleton, Aston-Tirrold, East-Ilsley and Tubney, and the vicarage of Ashbury, in the county of Berks ; the rectories of Beaconsfield and Saunderton, in the county of Buckingham ; the rectory of Stanway, in the county of Essex ; the rectory of Slimbridge, in the county of Gloucester ; the vicarages of Basingstoke, Selborne, and East Worldham, and the perpetual curacy of West Tisted, in the county of Southampton ; the rectories of Candlesby, Horsington, Saltfleet by All Saints, and Swaby, in the county of Lincoln ; the rectory of Brandistone, in the county of Norfolk ; the vicarage of Evenley and the rectory of Great Houghton, in the county of Northampton ; the rectory of East Bridgford, in the county of Nottingham ; the rectories of Ducklington, Standlake, Swerford with the chapel of Showell, and the perpetual curacy of Horsepath, in the county of Oxford ; the rectories of Ashurst and Bramber, and the vicarages of Findon, Beeding, New Shoreham, Old Shoreham, and Washington, in the county of Sussex ; the vicarage of Willoughby, in the county of Warwick ; and the rectories of Boyton, Fittleton, Winterbourne-Bassett, and the vicarage of Dinton, in the county of Wilts. The college is situated at the bottom of the High-street, on the western bank of the river Cherwell, near the bridge to which it gives name, and from the unaltered state of the buildings, it presents the most venerable appearance : it consists chiefly of two ancient quadrangles built by Waynfleet, one side of a third, called the New Buildings, a lofty tower, and the chaplain's court. The principal entrance is from the gravel walk, through a modern Doric gateway, ornamented with a statue of the founder, which leads into the first quadrangle, on the north side of which are the president's lodgings, and near them an ancient gateway, now disused, surmounted by a tower (in which is an apartment called the founder's chamber), with battlements and pinnacles, and adorned with small statues of the founder, Henry VI., St. Mary Magdalene, and St. John the Baptist, under canopies of exquisite workmanship : in the south-east angle of this court is a stone pulpit, from which an annual sermon was formerly preached on the festival of St. John the Baptist : a passage leads from this court into the second quadrangle, which is surrounded by covered cloisters, and from which are the entrances to the chapel, library, hall, common rooms, and apartments for the fellows and demies : the interior of this court is adorned by a series of hieroglyphics, the solution of which has been given by William Reeks, fellow of the college, in a manuscript preserved in the library. The chapel, which occupies its south-western angle, was erected by the founder, but has undergone several modern alterations, and is now under a course of considerable embellishment : near the west door, which opens into the first quadrangle, is a light detached stone arch : this elegant structure is adorned with beautiful stained windows, and the ante-chapel contains several interesting monu-

ments; the western window, painted in *chiaro oscuro*, and executed after a design by Christopher Swartz, exhibits a representation of the Last Judgment; underneath the altar-piece, by Isaac Fuller, which was placed here about 1680, is the celebrated picture of Christ bearing his Cross, now generally attributed to Moralez, a Spanish artist of the sixteenth century, and presented to the college by William Freeman, Esq., of Hamels, in the county of Hereford: the inner chapel is paved with black and white marble, and separated from the ante-chapel by a handsome screen, over which is a fine organ. The library, which occupies the western side of the cloisters, is spacious. The hall, at the south-eastern angle, is decorated with various devices in wainscot, principally from scripture history, and with portraits of different dimensions; the windows exhibit some curious specimens of old painting in glass: the remainder of the quadrangle is occupied by the fellows' and demies' common rooms, the kitchen, and the rooms of members of the society; a passage on the north side leads to the New Buildings, the first stone of which was laid in 1733: the structure is three hundred feet in length, and consists of three stories, divided into their respective ranges of apartments: in front is a handsome covered cloister. Eastward of this quadrangle are the water walks, which, bordered with trees, and extending along the side of a branch of the Cherwell, surrounding a spacious meadow, afford a delightful and retired promenade: part of these is called Addison's Walk, from having been the favourite retreat of the poet, whilst a student at this college: on the north is the College Grove, adorned with more private walks, and enlivened by a number of deer. In the centre of a range of buildings, on the south side of the chaplain's court, is the lofty and elegant tower, crowned with eight rich pinnacles, which was completed in 1498; in the belfry story are two fine windows, and a rich open battlement, and it contains a ring of ten musical bells. On the summit of this tower, mass was performed every May-day, previously to the Reformation, for the repose of the soul of Henry VII., and some pieces of choral music are now annually performed there, by the choristers, at five o'clock in the morning of that day. Magdalene college is required by its statutes to maintain the Kings of England, and their eldest sons, on the occasions of their visiting the university of Oxford; the hall has, in consequence, been honoured at various times with the presence of several royal guests, amongst whom were Edward IV., Richard III., Prince Arthur, in 1496, James I., and Prince Henry, who was admitted a member in 1605. During the parliamentary war, Generals Cromwell and Fairfax, with their officers, were also entertained here in 1647, and after dinner amused themselves at bowls on the college green. Among the former eminent members were Lilly, the grammarian and astrologer; Fox, the martyrologist; Hampden, the patriot; Heylin, the controversial writer; the poets Addison, Collins, and Holdsworth; Cardinals Wolsey and Pole; Dean Colet, founder of St. Paul's school; Theophilus Gale, author of "The Court of the Gentiles;" Dr. Henry Hammond; Dr. Sacheverell; Gibbon, the historian, who took no degree; Dr. Richard Chandler, a learned traveller and antiquary; one archbishop, and twenty-seven bishops. The members on the books are one hundred and sixty-seven, of whom one hundred and thirty-one are members of convocation.

Arms.

Brasenose College was founded, in 1509, by William Smyth, Bishop of Lincoln, and Sir Richard Sutton, of Prestbury, in Cheshire, the latter of whom revised its statutes. The society originally consisted of a principal and twelve fellows, who must be natives of the old diocese of Lichfield and Coventry, with preference to persons born in the county of Chester, and in those parts of Lancashire which were then in that diocese, especially in the parishes of Prescot and Prestbury; in default of eligible candidates, the society may elect from the diocese of Lincoln, or, if none be there found, from the university itself: eight additional fellowships have been founded, *viz.*, two by the will of J. Williamson, rector of St. George's, Canterbury, in 1522, confined to his kindred, or those of John Port, serjeant at law, who are natives of the city, or county palatine, of Chester; one by John Elton, alias Baker, canon of Salisbury, in 1528, with preference to his kindred, born in the diocese of Hereford, or in that of Worcester, or, in default thereof, from the diocese of Salisbury, or elsewhere; one by William Porter, clerk, in 1531, for the county, or diocese, of Hereford, or, in default of a qualified person, then for a native of any diocese next adjacent to Oxford; one by Edward Darbie, Archdeacon of Stow, in the county of Lincoln, in 1538, for a graduate born in the said archdeaconry, or, in case of successive defects of graduates from the counties of Leicester, Northampton, Oxford, and Lincoln, then an under-graduate, to be elected under similar restrictions; one by William Clyfton, subdean of York, in 1538, for a priest and graduate of the counties of York and Lincoln alternately, or else of the county of Nottingham, or university of Oxford; one by Brian Higden, Dean of York, in 1549, alternately for the counties of York and Lincoln; and one, in 1586, by Joyce Frankland, of London, widow, for her kindred, especially those of the Trapps and Saxies, or, in defect of such, then for any county in England. There are also thirty-two scholarships, and fifteen exhibitions. The Bishop of Lincoln is visitor. The livings in the patronage of the Principal and Fellows are, the rectories of Dudcote and West Shefford, in the county of Berks; the lectureship of Rodborough, in the parish of Minchinhampton, county of Gloucester; the rectory of Tedstone-Delamere, in the county of Hereford; the rectory of Great Catworth, in the county of Huntingdon; the vicarage of Gillingham, in the county of Kent; the vicarage of Preston, and the perpetual curacies of Downham, Longridge, Newchurch in Pendle, Church Kirk in Whalley, in the county of Lancaster; the vicarage of Osburnby, in the county of Lincoln; the rectories of St. Matthew, Bethnal-Green, Stratford le Bow, St. Anne Limehouse, Christ Church Spitalfields, Stepney, St. George in the East, St. John Wapping, Poplar, St. Mary Whitechapel, and the perpetual curacies of St. John Bethnal Green, and Stepney chapel, in the county of Middlesex; the rectories of Great Billing, Cottingham, Middleton-Cheney, Old or Wold, and Stoke-Bruerne, in the county of Northampton; the rectories of Great Rollright, and Steeple-Aston, in the county of Oxford; the rectories of Clayton and Selham, in the county of Sussex; and the rectory of Wootton-Rivers, in the county of Wilts, alternately with the President and Fellows of St. John's College; the rectory of Begbrooke, in the county of Oxford, is in the patronage of Sir George Dashwood, Bart., for three turns, and of the Principal of this college for the fourth. The college is situated on the west side of Radcliffe-square : the buildings consist of a spacious quadrangle, which contains the hall and rooms for members, and, in the centre, statues called "Cain and Abel," which were presented by Dr. Clarke; and a small court towards the south, in which are the chapel and library, and an elegant house for the principal, which fronts the High-street : over the gateway entrance to the great quadrangle is a square tower, ornamented with architectural designs : the small court was built in the seventeenth century, from the plan, as is believed, of Sir Christopher Wren; its style is of the mixed kind, windows with pointed arches being occasionally opposed by Grecian pilasters and capitals. Amongst the eminent members of this college may be reckoned, John Fox, the martyrologist, prior to his removal to Magdalene College; Prince, author of the "Worthies of Devon;" Sampson Erdeswick; John Gwillim, author of "the Heraldry;" James, Lord Ley; William and Robert Burton, of Leicester; Sir Elias Ashmole, founder of the museum called after his name; Sir Peter Leicester; John Watson, author of "the History of the Earls of Warren and Surrey;" Dr. Whitaker, the late learned Manchester historian, Reginald Heber, late bishop of Calcutta, and nine other bishops. The members on the books are four hundred and three, of whom two hundred and twenty-five are members of convocation.

Arms.

Corpus Christi College was founded, in 1516, by Richard Fox, Bishop of Winchester, and Lord Privy Seal to Henry VII. and Henry VIII., for a president, twenty fellows, twenty scholars, two chaplains, two clerks, and two choristers : Hugh Oldham, Bishop of Exeter, gave six thousand marks towards the building, and land towards the endowment. The fellows are elected from the scholars, and these from the following dioceses and counties; four from the diocese of Winchester, of which two must be of the county of Southampton, and two of Surrey; two from the diocese of Bath and Wells, two from the diocese of Exeter, two from the county of Gloucester, two from the county of Lincoln, one from the county of Wilts, two from the county of Kent, one from the county of Lancaster, one each from the counties of Bedford and Oxford, one from the diocese of Durham, and one founded by William Frost, of Yavington, Hants, in 1529, for his kindred; in failure of which, election to be made from that county. The Bishop of Winchester is visitor. The livings in the patronage of the President and Fellows are, the rectory of Little Staughton, in the county of Bedford; the rectories of Childrey and Letcomb-Bassett, and the vicarage of West Hendred, in the county of Berks; the rectory of Ruan-Lanyhorne, in the county of Cornwall; the rectory of Skelton, in the county of Cumberland; the rectory of Great Holland, in the county of Essex; the rectories of Duntsbourn-Rouse and Maisey-Hampton, in the county of Gloucester; the rectory of Stoke-Charity, in the county of Southampton; the rectory of Pembridge, in the county of Hereford; the rectory of Bassingham, in the county of

Lincoln; the rectories of Church-Brampton, Byfield, and Helmdon, in the county of Northampton; the rectories of Goddington and Lower Heyford, and the perpetual curacy of Warborough, in the county of Oxford; the rectory of Trent, in the county of Somerset; the rectory of Fenny-Compton, in the county of Warwick; and the rectories of Steeple-Langford and Stratford St. Anthony, in the county of Wilts. The entrance to this college is opposite to the south wall of Oriel college, through a gateway, above which is a square tower, ornamented in front with three vacant canopied niches : it leads to the quadrangle, which is one hundred and one feet by eighty, and contains in the centre a curious cylindrical dial, constructed by Charles Turnbull, fellow of the college, and described in a manuscript in the library, written by Robert Pegge : on the eastern side of the college are apartments for the gentlemen commoners; and in 1700, the fellows' building was erected, at the expense of Dr. Turner, president, on the site of the old cloisters, facing the broad walk in Christ Church meadow. In the chapel, which was built by the founder, is a very fine altarpiece of the Adoration, by Rubens, presented to the college, in 1804, by the late Sir R. Worsley, Bart.; there are also monuments to the memory of distinguished members. In the hall are three full-length portraits, admirably painted by Owen, of the Rt. Hon. Lord Tenterden, Lord Chief Justice of England; the Rt. Rev. Dr. Burgess, Bishop of Salisbury; and the Rt. Rev. Dr. Copleston, Bishop of Llandaff; formerly fellows on this foundation : in the college are still preserved the crosier of the founder, which is upwards of three hundred years old, of silver gilt, richly ornamented, and about six feet in length; his gold sacramental plate, salt cellar of silver gilt, rings, and other valuable relics. On the visit of the sovereigns to the university, the King of Prussia resided in the president's lodgings. Amongst its eminent members have been, Basil Kennett, author of the "Antiquities of Rome," and president of the college; Hooker, the celebrated author of "Ecclesiastical Polity;" Hales, commonly called 'the ever-memorable;' and Fiddes, the biographer of Cardinal Wolsey. The members on the books are one hundred and thirty-two, of whom eighty-one are members of convocation.

Arms.

Christ Church College was founded, about 1525, by Cardinal Wolsey, on the site of the monastery of St. Frideswide, and intended to comprise a dean, subdean, one hundred canons, ten public readers, thirteen chaplains, an organist, twelve clerks, and sixteen choristers; but, on the disgrace of that dignitary, the establishment was suspended for a short time : in 1532 it was completed, under the name of Henry the Eighth's college, for a dean and twelve canons, again suppressed in 1545, and in the following year, on the removal of the episcopal see from Osney to this college, the church of St. Frideswide was constituted a cathedral, under the name of Christ's Church; the society to consist of a dean, eight canons, and one hundred students, eight chaplains, a schoolmaster, an organist, eight clerks, and eight choristers; an addition of one student was made, in 1664, on the foundation of William Thurstone, Esq.: many of the studentships are filled up from Westminster school, the rest open to all parts of the kingdom.

The deanery and canonries are in the gift of the Crown; one is annexed to the Regius Professorship of Divinity, and one to the Regius Professorship of Hebrew : there are thirty scholarships and exhibitions. The King is visitor. The livings in the patronage of the Dean and Canons are, the vicarages of Cople, and Flitton with the curacy of Silsoe, in the county of Bedford ; the vicarages of Ardington, East Garston, and Marcham, and the rectory of East Hampstead, in the county of Berks ; the perpetual curacies of Ashendon, Dorton, Hillersdon, Lathbury, the rectory of Slapton, and the vicarage of Willen, in the county of Buckingham ; the vicarages of Great Budworth, Frodsham, Runcorn, and the perpetual curacy of Daresbury, in the county of Chester; the rectory of St. Tudy, in the county of Cornwall ; the vicarage of Great Torrington, in the county of Devon ; the vicarage of Tolpuddle, in the county of Dorset ; the rectory of Sheering, in the county of Essex ; the rectory of Batsford and Iron-Acton, the vicarages of Bledington, Ampney-Downe, Lower Swell, Thornbury, Turkdean, Twining, Wotton under Edge, and the perpetual curacies of Little Compton, North Nibley, and Temple Guyting, in the county of Gloucester ; the rectory of Staunton upon Wye, in the county of Hereford ; the perpetual curacies of Tring and Wigginton, in the county of Hertford ; the vicarage of Hawkhurst, in the county of Kent ; the vicarage of Kirkham, in the county of Lancaster ; the perpetual curacies of Great Bowden and Market-Harborough, in the county of Leicester ; the united rectories of Swanton-Novers and Wood-Norton, in the county of Norfolk ; the vicarages of Badbey with that of Newnham, Easton-Maudit, Floore, Harringworth, Ravensthorpe, Staverton, and the perpetual curacy of Daventry, in the county of Northampton ; the perpetual curacies of Bensington, alias Benson, Binsey, Caversham, Cowley, Drayton, and Stratton-Audley, the vicarages of Black-Bourton, Brize-Norton, Cassington, Chalgrove with the chapel of Berrick-Salome, Pirton, South Stoke, and Spelsbury, and the rectories of Wendlebury and Westwell, in the county of Oxford; the vicarage of St. Mary Magdalene, and the perpetual curacy of St. Thomas, in the city of Oxford ; the rectory of Wentnor, in the county of Salop ; the vicarages of Bath-Easton, Midsummer-Norton, and the rectory of Odcombe, in the county of Somerset ; the vicarages of Charlton, Chippenham, East Lavington, the perpetual curacy of Maiden-Bradley, and the rectory of Semley, in the county of Wilts; the perpetual curacies of Badsey, Great Hampton, South Littleton with that of North Littleton, Offenham, and Wickhamford, in the county of Worcester; the vicarages of Bramham, Broughton, Carleton, Featherstone, Kildwick, North Otterington, Long Preston, Skipton, Thornton le Street, and Wath upon Dearn, in the county of York. The extensive buildings of this college occupy the site of the ancient monastery, and form three quadrangles : the grand front is in St. Aldate's-street, and extends to a length of four hundred feet, presenting a very grand elevation, though its effect is much weakened by the declivity of the ground on which it stands, the narrowness of the approach to it, and the proximity of other buildings. The principal entrance is through a gateway, begun by Wolsey, and finished by Sir Christopher Wren, over which is a most magnificent circular tower, surmounted by an ogee dome, and containing the huge bell, called " Great Tom of Oxford,"

which weighs nearly seventeen thousand pounds, is seven feet one inch in diameter, and five feet nine inches from the crown to the brim ; the weight of the clapper is three hundred and forty-two pounds . it formerly belonged to Oseney abbey, and was recast in 1680 : this bell tolls every night at a quarter after nine o'clock, as a signal for students to repair to their respective colleges, before the gates are closed, agreeably to the statutes of the university. The court to which this gateway leads is called the Great quadrangle, and measures two hundred and sixty-four feet by two hundred and sixty : it contains the hall, the dean's lodgings, those of some of the canons, and rooms for members of the society ; in the centre is a small fountain, supplied with water from the Isis and from the spring at Hincksey ; over the passage at the north-east corner is a statue of Bishop Fell, and over the opposite one leading to the hall and chapel is one of Cardinal Wolsey : the ascent to the hall, which is in the south-eastern angle, is by a stately staircase, with a vaulted roof supported by a single central pillar : the interior of this magnificent refectory, which was erected by Wolsey, is one hundred and fifteen feet by forty, and fifty feet in height ; the roof, which is lofty, presents a fine specimen of open work in wood highly ornamented, and at the upper end of the south side is a large window, having a fine carved canopy in the ancient style of English architecture : in this hall many of the kings and queens of England have been entertained. The second quadrangle, called Peckwater square, derives its name from an ancient hall which stood at the south-west corner, and was the property of Richard Peckwater ; but having been given to the ancient monastery, in the reign of Henry III., and having received, in that of Henry VIII., the addition of another, called Vine-hall, eventually formed the present quadrangle, which was rebuilt in 1705, and towards defraying the expense £3000 were bequeathed by Anthony Radcliffe, canon, an inscription on the north side of the court, which was built with his money, recording the munificence of the benefactor : the south side is formed by the library, which contains an ample collection of books, manuscripts, prints, and coins, also several paintings, statues, and busts ; the upper room is one hundred and forty-one feet by thirty, and thirty-seven feet in height, having a richly-decorated ceiling, with wainscot and pillars of the best Norway oak. Eastward of Peckwater is Canterbury quadrangle, the smallest of the three, which consists of modern buildings; its principal ornament is a magnificent Doric gateway, erected, in 1778, under the superintendence of Mr. James Wyatt : the chapel is also the cathedral of the diocese, in the account of which it is described. Attached to this college, and situated southward of the great quadrangle, are a grammar school for choristers and other boys, and a theatre, which contains many anatomical preparations, and some very elegant and beautiful wax models : lectures are delivered here by Dr. Lees, Reader in Anatomy, who is appointed by the Dean and Canons. Here also are the chapter-house, common room, chaplains' quadrangle, Fell's buildings, and east cloisters, with a portal and passage leading to Christ Church meadow, which is bounded on the south and west by the Isis, on the east by the Cherwell, and on the north by a wide walk overshadowed by lofty elms, and leading to narrower walks on the margin of the rivers, forming a circumference of one mile and a quarter, and, being kept in excellent order, they constitute the most frequented promenade in the city. Some of the most illustrious names of which this or any other country can boast have been enrolled on the books of this college, amongst which are those of Littleton, Bolingbroke, Ben Jonson, Philip Sydney, Otway, Colman, Locke, Browne Willis, and Canning. The members at present on the books are nine hundred and twenty-two, of whom four hundred and forty-two are members of convocation.

Arms.

Trinity College was originally founded and endowed by Edward III., Richard II., and the Priors and Bishops of Durham, and dedicated to the Holy Trinity, St. Mary, and St. Cuthbert; it was also called Durham College: at the dissolution the site and buildings were purchased by Sir Thomas Pope, Knt., of Tittenhanger, in the county of Hereford, and the present college was refounded by him, in 1554, for a president, twelve fellows, and twelve scholars: only two natives of the same county can be fellows at one time, excepting those from the county of Oxford, from which five are admissible as cotemporaries; the scholars to be chosen from the founder's manors, or, in default of candidates on Trinity Monday, which is the day of election, from any county in England: four scholarships and exhibitions have since been added. The Bishop of Winchester is visitor. The livings in the patronage of the President and Fellows are, the lectureship of St. Nicholas', Abingdon, in the county of Berks; the rectory of Farnham, and the vicarages of Navestock and Great Waltham, in the county of Essex; the rectories of Oddington and Rotherfield-Grays, in the county of Oxford; the perpetual curacy of Hill-Farrance, in the county of Somerset; and the rectory of Barton on the Heath, in the county of Warwick: the rectory of Garsington, in the county of Oxford, is annexed to the Presidentship. The college is situated opposite the Turl, in Broad-street, from which it is separated by an iron palisade, enclosing a spacious area. The chapel, as seen from the street, is a light and elegant edifice, with columns supporting a rich cornice, and surmounted by a balustrade, and is terminated at its western end by a tower of similar construction, beneath which is the principal entrance to the first quadrangle, which contains the hall, library, and lodgings of the president: in the chapel, which opens into this court, is a monument to the memory of the founder and his lady, whose remains were removed hither, in 1567, from the church of St. Stephen, Walbrook, London: the effigy in marble represents him in complete armour, with a helmet and crest at the head, and a griffin at the feet. The second court consists of three sides, with an opening on the east into a spacious garden, which is partly enclosed by yew hedges, in the formal Dutch style, and partly arranged in devious walks, interspersed with shrubs and evergreens. Among the more eminent names of former members enrolled here are those of Archbishop Sheldon, Chillingworth, Sir John Denham, Merrick, and Warton. The members at present on the books are two hundred and sixty, of whom one hundred and five are members of convocation.

Arms.

St. John's College was founded, in 1557, by Sir Thomas White, a citizen and merchant of London, on the site of a college dedicated to St. Bernard, for student monks of the Cistercian order: the society comprises a president, fifty fellows, or scholars, one chaplain, an organist, six singing men, six choristers, and two sextons; six of the fellows are elected from the founder's kin, two from Coventry, two from Bristol, two from Reading, and one from Tunbridge grammar schools, and the rest from Merchant Taylors' school. Twelve of the fellows must enter on the law, and one may proceed in medicine, retaining his fellowship under the title of College Physician. The founder's kin are actual fellows on admission, others are scholars, or probationary fellows, until the expiration of three years: there are also eighteen scholarships and exhibitions. The Bishop of Winchester is visitor. The livings in the patronage of the President and Fellows are, the rectory of Sutton, in the county of Bedford; the rectory of Kingston-Bagpuze, and the vicarages of Fyfield and Reading St. Lawrence, in the county of Berks; the vicarage of Chalfont St. Peter, in the county of Buckingham; the rectory of Cranham, in the county of Essex; the rectory of Winterbourne, in the county of Gloucester; the sinecure rectory of Leckford, and the rectory of South Warnborough, in the county of Southampton; the vicarage of Linton, in the county of Hereford; the vicarage of Great Staughton, in the county of Huntingdon; the rectory of Barfreston, in the county of Kent; the vicarage of St. Sepulchre's, London; the rectories of Aston le Walls, Crick (to one from Merchant Taylors' school), and East Farndon, in the county of Northampton; the vicarages of Charlbury and Kirtlington, the rectories of Handborough and Tackley, and the perpetual curacy of Northmoor, in the county of Oxford; the vicarage of St. Giles', in the city of Oxford; the rectory of Bardwell, in the county of Suffolk; the rectory of Cheam, in the county of Surrey; the rectory of Codford St. Mary, in the county of Wilts; the rectory of Belbroughton, in the county of Worcester; and the rectory of Bainton, in the county of York. The buildings contain an outer and an inner quadrangle: in the former are the hall, chapel, and president's lodgings; a passage leads from this to the inner quadrangle, on the east and west sides of which are cloisters, supported by eight pillars, over which are busts, representing the four cardinal virtues, the three Christian graces, and the arts and sciences, with emblematical cornices: each cloister is divided by a Doric gateway, surmounted by a semicircular pediment of the Ionic and Corinthian orders. This quadrangle leads to the spacious and picturesque gardens of the college: a range of buildings to the north-east includes two very handsome common rooms, and other apartments. The chapel belonged to the original monastery of St. Bernard; the altar is ornamented with a representation in tapestry of our Saviour and his two disciples at Emmaus, and on the north wall is a black marble urn, containing the heart of Dr. Richard Rawlinson, a distinguished benefactor to the college: the remains of the founder, of Archbishop Laud (once president), of Archbishop Juxon, and of Dr. Bailie, repose in vaults beneath the altar: in a small inner chapel, called Bailie's chapel, are various monuments to subsequent presidents. The library is on the south and east sides of the inner quadrangle, and consists of two spacious and handsome rooms: amongst its many curious and valuable contents are, a picture of Charles I., comprising the whole book of Psalms written in the lines of the face and on the hairs of the head ; and an ancient crosier of dark wood beaded with silver, recently discovered in a garret of the president's lodgings; also many old missals, manuscripts, and coins. Amongst eminent members were, Archbishops Laud, Juxon, and Dawes ; Bishops Meaux and Buckeridge ; Shirley, the dramatic poet ; William Louth and Charles Wheatley, learned divines and commentators ; and Sherard, the botanist. The members on the books are two hundred and nineteen, of whom one hundred and twenty-nine are members of convocation.

Arms.

Jesus' College was founded, in 1571, by Queen Elizabeth, on petition of Hugh ap Price, D. C. L., a native of Brecknock, and Treasurer of St. David's, for a principal, eight fellows, and eight scholars: in consequence of various benefactions, the society now consists of a principal, and nineteen fellows (among whom is one from Jersey or Guernsey, on the foundation of Charles I., in 1636), and there are eighteen scholarships and several exhibitions. The Earl of Pembroke is visitor. The livings in the patronage of the Principal and Fellows are, the rectories of Longworth and Remenham, in the county of Berks ; the rectory of Aston-Clinton, in the county of Buckingham ; the sinecure rectory of Badgeworth, the rectory of Badgington, and the perpetual curacy of King's Charlton, in the county of Gloucester ; the rectory of Scartho, in the county of Lincoln ; the perpetual curacy of Llanthewy-Vach, in the county of Monmouth ; the rectories of Braunston and Furtho, in the county of Northampton ; the rectories of Rotherfield-Peppard and Wigginton, in the county of Oxford ; the rectory of Nutfield, in the county of Surrey ; the vicarage of Shipston upon Stour *cum* Tidmington, and the rectory of Tredington, in the county of Worcester ; the perpetual curacy of Holyhead, in the Isle of Anglesea ; the vicarage of Holywell, in the county of Flint ; and the rectory of Llandow, in the county of Glamorgan : the rectory of Llandyssul, in the county of Cardigan, and the rectory of Clynnog and the vicarage of Llanwnda, in the county of Carnarvon, are annexed to the Headship. The buildings consist chiefly of two quadrangles : the first contains the chapel and hall, and the second the library : the altar-piece in the chapel is a fine copy of Guido's painting of St. Michael overcoming the Devil : in the library are many scarce and curious books and manuscripts ; the statutes of the society, written on vellum, beautifully illuminated ; a curious metal watch, given by Charles I. ; one of Queen Elizabeth's stirrups ; and a capacious silver gilt bowl, containing ten gallons, and weighing two hundred and seventy-eight ounces, the gift of Sir Watkin Williams Wynn, in 1732. Amongst its eminent members were, David Powell, the celebrated antiquary ; and John Davis, lexicographer and antiquary. The members on the books are one hundred and eighty-one, of whom fifty-seven are members of convocation.

Wadham College was founded, in 1613, on the site of an ancient and magnificent priory of Augustine friars, by Nicholas Wadham, Esq., of Edge and Merrifield, and Dorothy his wife, for a warden, fifteen fellows, fifteen scholars, two chaplains, and two clerks. The fellows

Arms.

are superannuated on the completion of eighteen years from the expiration of their regency ; they are elected from the scholars, of whom, three are chosen from the county of Somerset, three from that of Essex, and the remainder from any county in Great Britain. There are also several other scholarships and exhibitions, among which are four for the study of Hebrew, six for Greek, and one for botany : the most eminent benefactor was the Rev. John Wills, D.D., Warden of the College, who died in 1806, and bequeathed, subject to legacy duty, £400 per annum to the office of warden, £1000 to improve the warden's lodgings, £100 a year for a law exhibition to a fellow, £20 a year for a law exhibition to a scholar, £100 for a medical exhibition to a fellow, and £20 for a medical exhibition to a scholar ; also £31. 10. per annum to a divinity lecturer and preacher, £75 a year to one superannuated fellow, and £50 a year to a second ; he also appointed the society his residuary legatees. The Bishop of Bath and Wells is visitor. The livings in the patronage of the Warden and Fellows are, the rectory of Fryerning, and the vicarage of Hockley, in the county of Essex ; the vicarage of Southrop, in the county of Gloucester ; the rectories of Maperton and Limington, in the county of Somerset ; the rectory of Esher, in the county of Surrey ; and the vicarage of Wadhurst, in the county of Sussex. The buildings form an extensive quadrangle of one hundred and thirty feet square : in the centre of the eastern side is a portico, ornamented with statues of James I., in his robes, and of Nicholas and Dorothy Wadham, with a Latin inscription commemorative of the foundation : in an adjoining court are two buildings of three stories, one erected in 1694, the other in 1829, and inhabited by members. The front of this college was greatly improved in 1822, by the removal of some heavy iron and stone work, and substituting light iron palisades. The chapel contains a fine east window, the work of Bernard Van Linge, exhibiting typical paintings and historical subjects, and presented by Sir John Strangeways : the subject of the altar-piece is the Lord's Supper, in brown and white crayons, on cloth, by Isaac Fuller, accompanied with other subjects. At right angles with the choir is a noble ante-chapel, containing monuments of several distinguished members of the society : on the north side of the chancel is a handsome marble monument to the memory of Sir John Portman, Bart., who died in 1624 : there is also a well-executed brass eagle. The hall is one of the largest in the university, and adorned with handsome modern painted windows : the gardens are extremely neat. The Royal Society of London originated in this college. Amongst its eminent and scientific members may be classed, Walsh, the poet ; Sir E. Sedley ; Admiral Blake ; Sir Christopher Wren ; and Lord Chief Justice Pratt. The members on the books are two hundred and fourteen, of whom eighty-three are members of convocation.

Arms.

Pembroke College, formerly *Broadgate Hall*, was founded, in 1624, by means of a bequest from Thomas Tesdale, Esq., of Glympton, in the county of Oxford, aided by a donation of Richard Wightwick, B. D., rector of East Ilsley, in the county of Berks, under letters patent of James I., and during the chancellorship of the Earl of Pembroke, from whom it received its name : the original foundation included a master, ten fellows, and ten scholars, now extended to fourteen fellows, and thirty-one scholars and exhibitioners; four fellows to be chosen from the kindred of Thomas Tesdale, Esq., and two from those of Richard Wightwick ; the rest from the free school at Abingdon. In 1636, a fellowship was founded by Charles I., for a native of Guernsey or Jersey ; and, about 1672, two fellowships were added by Sir John Bennet, afterwards Lord Ossulstone ; also one, in 1749, by Sir John Phillips, Bart. The Chancellor of the university is visitor. The livings in the patronage of the Master and Fellows are, the rectory of Coln St. Denis, in the county of Gloucester ; the rectory of Sibson, in the county of Leicester ; the rectory of St. Aldate's, in the city of Oxford ; the perpetual curacies of West Harroldston and Lambston, in the county of Pembroke ; the rectory of Ringshall, in the county of Suffolk ; the rectories of Brinkworth, Codford St. Peter, and Liddiard-Millicent, in the county of Wilts ; the perpetual curacy of Colnbrook, in the county of Buckingham ; and the perpetual curacy of Uxbridge, in the county of Middlesex ; the two last intended for the exhibitioners on Townshend's foundation. This college, which is situated nearly opposite to the grand front of Christ Church College, consists chiefly of a quadrangle, erected at different periods, and regularly built. The interior has within the last two years been newly faced with Bath stone, and altered from the Palladian to a later style of English architecture, the whole presenting a neat appearance. The northern front and the master's lodgings have been very neatly decorated (these buildings likewise being originally Palladian) after a design by Mr. Daniel Evans of Oxford, in the later style of English architecture. The oriel windows may be mentioned as well worthy of attention, particularly that over the gateway, constructed on the model of the remains of one in John of Gaunt's palace at Lincoln. The battlement of the tower and the chimnies is executed in a style corresponding with the other parts of the building. The hall, which has been considerably enlarged and improved, contains a bust of Dr. Johnson, by Bacon, presented to the college by the late Samuel Whitbread, Esq. The chapel is a small building of the Ionic order ; the altar-piece is a copy from a picture of Rubens, at Antwerp, of our Saviour after his Resurrection, presented by Archdeacon Corbett. Among the eminent residents may be enumerated, the laborious Camden, who studied at the original hall, after he left Magdalene College ; Judge Blackstone, previously to his removal to All Souls'; Dr. Johnson, whose rooms were upon the second floor, over the gateway ; George Whitefield, founder of the Calvinistic Methodists ; Shenstone, the poet ; Sir Thomas Brown, author of the " Medici ;" Richard Graves, author of the " Spiritual Quixote ;" and Dr.

Newman, Primate of Ireland, and author of the " Harmony of the Gospels." The members on the books are one hundred and ninety-five, of whom eighty-four are members of convocation.

Arms.

Worcester College was founded, in 1714, by the trustees of Sir Thomas Cookes, Bart., of Bently Pauncefort, in the county of Worcester, by elevating Gloucester Hall, also named St. John the Baptist's Hall, to the rank of a college: the original foundation was for a provost, six fellows, and six scholars, the last eligible only from the grammar schools of Bromsgrove, Feckenham, Worcester, Hartlebury, and Kidderminster, or, in default of candidates, from any endowed school in the county of Worcester, such schools to have a priority of claim in the order in which they stand, and the candidates to have been at the schools for at least two years previously to the election, the founder's kin always to be preferred : the right of election is vested in the provost and three senior fellows of the foundation. In 1727, two fellowships and two scholarships were added, by James Finney, D.D., prebendary of Durham, for natives of Staffordshire ; six fellowships and three scholarships were founded, in 1734, by George Clark, D.C.L., the scholars to be of English parents, born in the provinces of Canterbury and York, with preference to the orphans of clergymen : the election is vested in the provost and six senior fellows on this and Sir Thomas Cookes' foundation. In 1731, seven fellowships and five scholarships were founded by Sarah Eaton : candidates for the latter must produce testimonials that they are sons of clergymen, requiring assistance to support them at the university : the election is in the provost and five senior fellows of this foundation and that of Sir T. Cookes. The fellows are invariably elected from the scholars, and must take holy orders, except in cases specifically provided for. The society at present includes a provost, twenty-one fellows, sixteen scholars, and three exhibitioners. The Bishops of Oxford and Worcester, and the Vice-Chancellor of the university, are visitors. The livings in the patronage of the Provost and Fellows are, the vicarage of Denchworth, in the county of Berks ; the rectory of Hogston, in the county of Buckingham ; the rectory of Dinedor, in the county of Hereford ; the rectory of Whitfield, in the county of Northampton ; the rectory of Tadmarton, in the county of Oxford ; the rectory of Neen-Sollars, in the county of Salop ; and the rectories of High-Ham and Windford, in the county of Somerset. The college is pleasantly situated on an eminence, at the western extremity of the university, near the Isis : the buildings form three sides of a quadrangle, the eastern elevation being occupied by the library, hall, and chapel ; on the north is an elegant pile, containing the provost's lodgings, and rooms for fellows and scholars, and on the south, the old buildings of Gloucester Hall. The chapel has a richly-ornamented stucco roof ; the altar-piece is a fine old painting of a Magdalene. In the library is the large and curious collection of books bequeathed by Dr. Clarke, who also left £1000 towards the building : the room is one hundred and twenty feet in length, with an extensive gallery. The gardens, which are laid out with great taste, occupy three acres of ground, and are ornamented with a fine sheet of water. Thomas Allen, the mathematician, and Sir Kenelm Digby, studied here, previously to the conversion of Gloucester Hall into a college. The members on the books are two hundred and twenty-two, of whom ninety-one are members of convocation.

Besides the above colleges are five halls, enjoying the same privileges, and requiring the same terms and exercises for taking degrees in them as the colleges, but not incorporated, the estates and other property belonging to them being held in trust by the university. The Chancellor of the university is visitor, and appoints the principals, with the exception of St. Edmund Hall, the headship of which is vested in the Provost and Fellows of Queen's College. *St. Alban Hall* derives its name and foundation from Robert de Sancto Albano, a burgess of Oxford, who lived in the time of John: it now belongs to the Warden and Fellows of Merton College, to which it was united June 15th, 1549: the buildings are situated eastward of Merton College. The members on the books, including the principal and vice-principal, are forty-three, of whom eight are members of convocation. *St. Edmund Hall* is situated in Queen's-lane, and derives its name from St. Edmund, Archbishop of Canterbury in the reign of Henry III.: it is the most ancient of the halls now remaining, having been devoted to the purposes of academical instruction so early as the thirteenth century; in 1537 it had come into the possession of Queen's College, which society soon afterwards obtained from the university the right of nominating the principal. Sir William Jones, the celebrated lawyer; Oldham, the poet; and Hearne, the indefatigable antiquary, were educated here. The members on the books are one hundred and five, of whom fifty-two are members of convocation. *St. Mary Hall*, formerly the parsonage-house of the rectors of St. Mary's, was given to the Provost and Fellows of Oriel College, in 1325, and made academical in 1333. Four scholarships for natives of the county of Somerset, were founded by Thomas Dyke, M.D., in 1677. The buildings, which are near Oriel College, are comprised in a quadrangle, in which are the hall, the chapel, the principal's lodgings, and rooms for members. Sir Thomas More, and Sandys, the poet, were educated here. The members on the books are eighty-six, of whom forty-one are members of convocation. *New Inn Hall*, formerly Trilleck's Inn, was originally inhabited by Bernardine monks, and subsequently by students of canon and civil law: it came into the possession of the Warden and Fellows of New College in 1392. During the civil war, from 1642 to 1646, it was used as a mint by Charles I., where the plate, sent by different colleges for his Majesty's use, was melted: after the Restoration it again became a place of study, but of late years has had no members; the only part of its buildings now remaining is a house for the principal, who is a member of convocation. The celebrated Blackstone was one of its principals. *Magdalene Hall*, originally erected by Waynfleet, for students previously to admission into his college, became an independent hall in 1602. The society was removed by act of parliament from its former house, adjoining Magdalene College, to Hertford College, in 1822, which, having lapsed to the crown and become decayed, was repaired and fitted up for their reception: there are twenty-three scholarships and exhibitions. The rectory of South Moreton, in the county of Berks, is in the pa-

tronage of the society. Among eminent persons educated here were, Warner the poet, Lord Clarendon, Sir Matthew Hale, and Dr. Plot. The members on the books are one hundred and eighty-four, of whom fifty-nine are members of convocation.

The principal public buildings connected with the university are, the Theatre, Schools (comprising the Bodleian Library and Picture Gallery), Clarendon Printing-House, New Printing-House, Ashmolean Museum, Radcliffe Library, Physic Garden, Astronomical Observatory, and Music Room. The *Theatre* is situated northward of Radcliffe-square, on the south side of Broad-street, and is appropriated to holding the acts denominated *Comitia et Encænia*, Lord Crewe's annual commemoration of benefactors, the recitation of prize compositions, the ceremony of conferring degrees on illustrious personages, and other public meetings of the university: it was constructed in 1664, by Sir Christopher Wren, at an expense of £12,470, which was defrayed by Archbishop Sheldon, who also gave £2000 towards keeping it in repair, directing the surplus to be applied in the erection of a printing-house: the plan of the building is that of the Theatre of Marcellus, at Rome, and it is capable of containing nearly four thousand persons: the first stone was laid in 1664; a new roof was constructed in 1802, the ceiling exhibiting a magnificent allegorical painting, by Streater, serjeant painter to Charles II., divided into compartments: the room is adorned with portraits of the founder, of George IV., by Sir Thomas Lawrence, and of the late Emperor of Russia, and the King of Prussia, presented by those respective sovereigns; the latter of whom, with other illustrious personages, received honorary degrees in this noble edifice, on their visit to the university in 1814. The *Schools* form a handsome quadrangle on the north side of Radcliffe-square, and were founded early in the fifteenth century, by Thomas Huskenorton, abbot of Oseney, and completed in the commencement of the seventeenth century: this range of building comprises schools for divinity, logic, moral philosophy, music, sculpture, &c., in which lectures are read by the professors of the different sciences, and candidates for degrees pass their respective examinations; the Bodleian Library is on the western side, and the Picture Gallery in the upper story of the other three sides: on the north is the Clarendon printing-office. The principal front, in Cat-street, is one hundred and seventy-five feet in length, and is divided by a tower gateway, adorned with pinnacles and mullioned windows, and exhibiting all the five orders of architecture: this part of the building is the repository for the muniments and registers of the university, and is surmounted by a statue of James I., enthroned, and presenting a copy of his works, with his right hand, to Fame, and with the left to the university; over the throne are the emblems of Justice, Peace, and Plenty: these devices were once doubly gilt, and presented a magnificent appearance. In the logic and moral philosophy school, at the southeast angle of the court, are the Pomfret statues, given to the university, in 1755, by the Countess Dowager of Pomfret. The Divinity school, which is opposite the principal gateway, and devoted to the exercises for the degrees of Bachelor and Doctor in Divinity, exhibits a beautiful specimen of later English architecture, with a roof consisting of bold four-centered arches, with fan tracery, in delicate workmanship of elegant design. The *Bodleian Library* was founded by Sir Thomas Bodley, of Dunscombe, near Crediton, in the county of Devon, Knt., on the remains of one by Humphrey, Duke of Gloucester, and opened to the public, November 8th, 1602 : it is entered at the south-west angle of the court, and consists of three principal, and several smaller rooms ; one is devoted to topographical works and manuscripts, bequeathed to the university by Mr. Gough, the antiquary, in 1799 ; a second to foreign, and a third to domestic, literature : on the entrance staircase is the *Auctarium*, for the reception of the choicest and most valuable books and manuscripts : the several rooms are decorated with many valuable portraits. In addition to the continual increase of books by donations and purchase, this institution claims, as a matter of right, in common with the British Museum and other national establishments, a copy of every book printed in this country. The library is open from nine o'clock till four in the afternoon, between Lady-day and Michaelmas, and from ten till three during the other half year, and, next to that of the Vatican, is considered to have the richest collection of books and manuscripts in Europe : the officers are a librarian, two sub-librarians, and two assistants. The *Picture Gallery* contains, in addition to numerous portraits, landscapes, and historical pieces, some fine busts, especially one near the entrance of John, Duke of Marlborough ; casts of Apollo and Venus de Medicis ; a superb brass statue of William, Earl of Pembroke, Chancellor of the university from 1616 to 1630, designed by Rubens, and executed by Hubert le Sœur ; and many elegant models of ancient buildings. In an apartment on the north side of the quadrangle are the famous Arundelian marbles, collected by the Earl of Arundel, and presented to the university by his grandson, the Duke of Norfolk ; here also are the antique marbles, presented by the executors of the learned Selden. The *Clarendon printing-office* was erected, in 1711, by Sir John Vanburgh, out of the profits arising from the sale of Lord Clarendon's History of the Rebellion, the copyright of which was bequeathed by his son to the university ; over the south entrance is a fine statue of Lord Clarendon, and the north entrance is by a flight of steps from Broad-street ; the summit is ornamented with the statues of the nine Muses. A New Printing-House has been recently erected westward of the Observatory, at the expense of the university, and under the direction of Mr. Daniel Robertson, architect, with a press-room of two hundred and one feet by twenty-eight, and other apartments and conveniences, which render it the most complete, and, with the exception of the royal printing-house at Paris, the largest, establishment of the kind in Europe : the buildings occupy an area of two acres and a half, and form a square, two sides of which are devoted to the Bible department, and the other two are appropriated to that of the classics, with their respective accommodations. This edifice is constructed of stone, procured in the neighbourhood, and faced with Bath stone : the principal front is decorated with a splendid entrance gateway into the quadrangle, designed after the model of the arch of Constantine at Rome. Nearly adjoining the theatre, on the western side, is the *Ashmolean Museum*, which was founded, in 1682, by Elias Ashmole, from whom it is named, and who gave to the university his own collection of coins, medals, and

manuscripts, together with a valuable and curious collection made by the Tradescants, two eminent gardeners and botanists at Lambeth, on condition that the university should erect a building for their reception : at his death the museum was enlarged, by the addition of his valuable antiquarian library, and has been since greatly increased by various donations. On the first floor of this building the lectures on experimental philosophy and mineralogy are delivered, and in the lower one, those on chemistry, for which the apparatus is kept here.

The *Radcliffe Library*, esteemed one of the most splendid architectural ornaments of the university, and situated in the centre of Radcliffe-square, was completed by Gibbs, in 1749, at the expense of the celebrated and eccentric Dr. Radcliffe, who bequeathed £40,000 for the building, £150 per annum for the librarian, £100 per annum for the purchase of books, and legacies, to a great amount, for other purposes connected with this public establishment : this superb structure is circular in form, and consists of a rustic basement, in which are several arched entrances into an area, from which a flight of steps affords an ascent to the principal room, which contains a variety of casts and busts, and, by a recent determination of the trustees, is to become the repository of books in natural history and medicine ; above the basement rises a series of duplicated columns of the Corinthian order, supporting an enriched frieze, entablature, and cornice, and surmounted by an open balustrade ornamented with urns ; the building is crowned with a spacious and well-proportioned dome, which rises to the height of eighty feet from the floor. Over the door of the entrance from the principal staircase is a portrait of the founder, by Sir Godfrey Kneller, and within the library is his statue finely sculptured by Rysbrach. On the visit of the allied sovereigns, a magnificent dinner was provided by the university for the imperial, royal, and illustrious guests, of which they partook in this library, on the 14th of June, 1814.

The *Botanic Garden*, said to be the site of an ancient burial-ground belonging to the Jews, is situated opposite to the tower of Magdalene College, near the bridge, and was founded, in 1622, by Henry, Lord D'Anvers, Earl of Danby : it consists of about five acres of ground, divided into four parts, and containing a great variety of plants, arranged according to their respective classes : on the right and left of the entrance are green-houses, and eastward of the garden, without the walls, is an excellent hot-house : the entrance is by an elegant arched gateway, said to have been designed by Inigo Jones, the centre of which is ornamented by a bust of the founder, and the sides by statues of Charles I. and II. : it is fronted by a broad area next the High-street, and encompassed by a parapet surmounted with iron pallisades : the library attached to it was built, and furnished with a valuable collection of botanical works, by Dr. Sherard, Fellow of St. John's College : there is a handsome residence for the professor at a small distance from the garden. The *Astronomical Observatory* is situated at the northern extremity of Oxford, on the road to Woodstock, and was erected by trustees under the will of Dr. Radcliffe, who bequeathed £7000 for this object, the Duke of Marlborough having given ten acres of ground for the site : this beautiful pile of building comprises an excellent library, apartments for observation and lectures,

3 R 2

a valuable apparatus of astronomical instruments, and a residence for the professor : the tower, which exhibits a general representation of the Temple of the Winds, at Athens, is surmounted by figures of Hercules and Atlas supporting the globe. In Holywell-street is the *Music-room*, built at an expense of £1263, and opened in 1748, the funds having been principally raised by means of subscription oratorios : concerts, under the direction of stewards from different colleges, are performed during term.

Oxford, on the removal of the see of Dorchester to Lincoln, was included within that diocese, from which it was separated in 1542, and erected into a see, by Henry VIII., who appointed the conventual chapel of the abbey of Osney the cathedral church, which distinction was subsequently transferred to the monastery of St. Frideswide, on the site of

Arms of the Bishoprick.

which Cardinal Wolsey had commenced the foundation of a splendid college, afterwards completed, but upon a scale of less magnificence, by the king ; who having dedicated the chapel of the college to Christ, assigned it as the cathedral church of the diocese. The jurisdiction of the see comprehends the whole of the county, except seven parishes : the ecclesiastical establishment consists of a bishop, dean, archdeacon, eight canons, eight chaplains, one hundred and one students, eight clerks, eight choristers, and twenty-four almsmen. The cathedral is a spacious cruciform structure, in the Norman style of architecture, and of singular character, with a central tower surmounted by a spire of early English architecture : the exterior is concealed by the college buildings, with which it is surrounded ; the interior contains many interesting portions of singular and beautiful design ; the arches of the nave, part of which has been demolished, are in a double series, the tower springing from corbels on the piers ; the roof of the choir is richly groined, and decorated with pendants : on the north of the choir are some chapels of later character than the rest of the building, and the Latin chapel has several windows in the decorated style ; in the Dean's chapel are altar-tombs of considerable antiquity, a monument in the decorated style, with three canopied niches of great beauty, and the shrine of St. Frideswide, an elaborate and magnificent design, in the later style of English architecture, consisting of three tiers of tabernacle work, the upper tier of which is richly ornamented with canopied niches. Many of the windows were destroyed during the parliamentary war : in those that remain are several devices in painted glass ; in the east window is a painting of the Nativity, from a design by Sir James Thornhill : the central west window is embellished with ancient painted glass, representing St. Frideswide, St. Catherine, and other saints ; in the central part of the great window in the north transept is a representation of the murder of Becket, which appears to be of great antiquity : the pulpit is very antique and richly carved. There are numerous ancient and interesting monuments, among which are those of Lady Elizabeth Montacute ; of

Robert Burton, author of the Anatomy of Melancholy ; and of several distinguished members of the university, and of other eminent persons who died at Oxford while Charles I. held his court at Christ Church ; also a very fine statue of Dr. Cyril Jackson, by Chantrey, from his portrait in the hall. Part of the cloisters, in the later style of English architecture, is remaining ; and the chapter-house is a beautiful and valuable specimen of the early English style.

The city comprises the parishes of St. Aldate, All Saints, Holywell, or St. Cross, St. Ebbe, St. Giles, St. John the Baptist, St. Martin, St. Mary Magdalene, St. Mary the Virgin, St. Michael, St. Peter le Bailey, St. Peter in the East, and St. Thomas. The living of St. Aldate's is a discharged rectory, rated in the king's books at £8. 13. 4., endowed with £200 private benefaction, and in the patronage of the Master and Fellows of Pembroke College : the church is a very ancient structure, with a tower, surmounted by an octagonal spire, and is said to have been restored in 1004. The living of All Saints' is a discharged perpetual curacy, rated in the king's books at £5. 6. 8., and in the patronage of the Rector and Fellows of Lincoln College : the church is a handsome modern structure, in the Grecian style of architecture, with a tower, crowned with a circlet of Corinthian pillars, from within which rises an elegant spire : it was erected by subscription in 1708, on the site of the former edifice : the walls are ornamented by a handsome balustrade, the floors laid with variegated marble, and the ceiling adorned with curious fret-work, and with the arms of benefactors, painted in compartments. The living of the parish of St. Cross, or Holywell, is a perpetual curacy, endowed with £200 private benefaction, and £400 royal bounty, and in the patronage of the Warden and Fellows of Merton College : the church is an ancient edifice, in the early style of English architecture, with some later insertions, having a tower, which was added to it in 1664. The living of St. Ebbe's is a discharged rectory, rated in the king's books at £3. 5., endowed with £400 private benefaction, £600 royal bounty, and £1200 parliamentary grant, and in the patronage of the Crown : the church is said to have been founded by Athelmer, Earl of Cornwall, and annexed to the monastery of Eynesham, on the destruction of which by the Danes it was given to the monastery of Stow, which grant was confirmed by Henry I. ; the ancient edifice was taken down in 1814, and the present, a plain neat building of English architecture, was erected in 1816. The living of St. Giles' is a discharged vicarage, rated in the king's books at £14. 12. 3½., endowed with £600 private benefaction, £400 royal bounty, and £800 parliamentary grant, and in the patronage of the President and Fellows of St. John's College : the church, an ancient structure in the early style of English architecture, with lancet-shaped windows, and having a square embattled tower, is said to have been built in 1120. The living of St. John the Baptist is a perpetual curacy, in the patronage of the Warden and Fellows of Merton College. The living of St. Martin's is a discharged rectory, rated in the king's books at £8. 1. 5½., endowed with £800 royal bounty, and in the patronage of the Crown : the church is an ancient structure, with a tower, which, in the reign of Edward III., was considerably lowered, on complaint of the scholars that the townsmen used to retire into it and annoy them with arrows, stones, and other missiles. The living of St. Mary Magdalene's is a discharged vicarage, rated in the king's books at £6, endowed with £600 private benefaction, £600 royal bounty, and £200 parliamentary grant, and in the patronage of the Dean and Canons of Christ Church: the church, an ancient structure, founded long prior to the Conquest, was given, by Robert D'Oilly, and annexed, to the college of St. George, within the castle, and, after the annexation of that college to Osney abbey, was, with that monastery, given to Christ Church by Henry VIII. The living of St. Mary's the Virgin is a discharged vicarage, rated in the king's books at £5. 4. 2., endowed with £200 private benefaction, and £200 royal bounty, and in the patronage of the Provost and Fellows of Oriel College: the church, which is the University church, though used by the parishioners at other times, is a spacious and elegant structure, in the later style of English architecture, with a tower on the north side, surmounted by a beautiful spire, rising to the height of one hundred and eighty feet, in the decorated style; the front of the church is in the best style of the period of Henry VII., but is rather disfigured by a porch of heavy twisted pillars, over which is a statue of the Virgin: the interior is very beautiful; the piers and arches are richly moulded, and above each pier are elegant niches, from which spring corbels, carrying the wooden arches of the finely-carved ceiling; the windows are enriched with good tracery: on the north of the chancel is the sepulchral chapel of Adam de Brome, founder of Oriel College: there are several ancient and interesting monuments. The living of St. Michael's is a perpetual curacy, in the patronage of the Rector and Fellows of Lincoln College: the church is an ancient edifice, in the early style of English architecture, with a square embattled tower, and a handsome porch in the later style; the windows are in general of large dimensions and finely pointed. The living of St. Peter's le Bailey is a discharged rectory, rated in the king's books at £3. 14. 2., endowed with £800 royal bounty, and £1600 parliamentary grant, and in the patronage of the Crown: the church is a neat modern edifice, erected in 1740, on the site of the old structure, which fell down in 1726. The living of St. Peter's in the East is a discharged vicarage, rated in the king's books at £13. 2. 1., endowed with £200 private benefaction, £400 royal bounty, and £600 parliamentary grant, and in the patronage of the Warden and Fellows of Merton College: the church is a very ancient structure, said to have been originally built in the ninth century; the prevailing character, however, is decidedly Norman, and the details are very rich and elaborately wrought: it has undergone many alterations and repairs, and received several additions, in the later style of English architecture, which have materially altered its external appearance: at the west end of the north aisle is a square tower, which has vestiges of great antiquity; underneath the chancel is a fine Norman crypt, of which the roof is vaulted, and supported on four ranges of low massive pillars; several of the windows have remains of ancient painted glass, and there are many ancient monuments. Hearn, the antiquary, was interred in the churchyard, and, in 1754, Dr. Rawlinson repaired the monument erected to his memory. This was formerly the university church, and

the university sermons preached there on the Sunday afternoons during Lent, and on Easter-Sunday, were discontinued about two years ago. The living of St. Thomas' is a perpetual curacy, endowed with £600 private benefaction, £600 royal bounty, and £1200 parliamentary grant, and in the patronage of the Dean and Canons of Christ Church: the church was founded by the canons of Osney priory, in 1141; it is a neat and ancient structure, with a square embattled tower, and has recently undergone an extensive repair: the churchyard is tastefully laid out, and planted with trees, flowering shrubs, and evergreens. There are places of worship for Baptists, and Wesleyan Methodists, and a Roman Catholic chapel.

A charity school was founded, in 1658, by John Nixon, alderman, who bequeathed £600 for its endowment; and, in 1685, Mrs. Joan Nixon left eighteen acres of land, producing £35 per annum, for apprenticing two boys every year from the school; which funds have been consolidated. Christian Smith, in 1718, gave a rent-charge of £2 for teaching poor girls of the parish of St. Mary Magdalene. The Blue-coat school, supported by subscription, was instituted in 1710; thirty-five boys are clothed and educated in it, and a certain number of them apprenticed, with a premium of £10 each, and £2 for clothing: there are also thirty-five other boys, who are educated only. Mrs. Ann Alworth, in 1721, gave £400, to be laid out in lands, for the education of twenty children belonging to St. Michael's parish. Mr. John Coombe, in 1702, gave a house for a schoolmaster to teach ten boys gratuitously, in St. Thomas' parish. Mrs. Elizabeth Rowney gave the interest of £50 for teaching poor children of the parish of St. Giles. A school for thirty-six girls, who are instructed, clothed, and placed out to service, is supported by subscription among the ladies. A National school is supported by the university, in which three hundred and thirty boys are educated, including forty, called the Grey-coat boys, who are also clothed, and eight of them apprenticed annually, with a premium of £20 each. A Lancasterian school, for one hundred boys and fifty girls, is supported by voluntary contributions; and a charity school for two hundred girls, wholly by the lady of J. D. Macbride, D.C.L., Principal of Magdalene Hall. Considerable sums have been left by several individuals for apprenticing poor children, for distribution in loans without interest to young tradesmen, and for clothing and annual payments to aged and indigent persons: others have also been appropriated, by will, for the repair of the several churches, with the remainder for distribution among the poor, and for various other charitable uses. Edmund Boulter, Jun., of Hasely-Court, Esq., built and endowed an almshouse for an aged man from each of the parishes of Wimple in Cambridgeshire, Harwood in the county of York, Wherwell in Hampshire, Hasely in the county of Oxford, Barlings in Lincolnshire, and Deptford with Brockley, in Kent; the inmates receive an allowance of eight shillings each per week. The infirmary, an elegant and commodious building of stone, was erected and completely furnished by the trustees of Dr. Radcliffe, and was opened for the reception of patients in 1770: the buildings, to which are attached five acres of land given by Thomas Rowney, Esq., comprise a chapel, to which the late Duke of Marlborough presented a communion service of gilt plate : the institution is under the direction of a president and a committee of governors, and is attended by four physicians, who divide between them the interest of £2000, bequeathed to them by the late Dr. Frewin, of Christ Church; four surgeons, who officiate gratuitously ; a chaplain, resident apothecary, secretary, matron, and assistants. The lunatic asylum at Headington, in the vicinity of the city, a spacious and handsome building of stone, was erected in 1813, at an expense of £20,000 raised by subscription, towards which the trustees of the Radcliffe Infirmary, with whom the design originated, contributed £2700 : the institution, the interest of which was greatly promoted by the Rev. John Cooke, D.D., President of Corpus Christi College, is adapted to the reception of various classes of patients, who are admitted on terms varying according to their accommodations, from 12s. to £2. 2. per week and upwards, according to the rank and circumstances of the patient. The house of industry, a neat stone building, two hundred and thirty-seven feet in length, and two stories in height, was erected for the accommodation of eleven of the parishes, incorporated by act of parliament, in 1771, for the maintenance of their poor : it is under the direction of a governor, two deputy governors, weekly visitors, and a committee, who afford their services gratuitously : the parishes of St. Giles and St. John separately maintain their own poor.

Of the numerous monastic establishments which formerly flourished here, some have been incorporated in the buildings of the various colleges, in which only a few small memorials have been preserved, and of others there are still some remains in various parts of the city and neighbourhood. About a quarter of a mile from the church of St. Thomas are some trifling remains of Osney abbey, already noticed, consisting chiefly of an arched window and a small portion of a wall now belonging to a corn-mill, which occupies the site ; the bells are now in the steeple of Christ Church. About half a mile to the east of the city was the hospital of St. Bartholomew, founded by Henry I., when he built the palace of Beaumont, and which was annexed to Oriel College by Edward III., in 1328. There are some slight remains of the convent for Benedictine nuns, founded at Godstow, in 1138, by Editha, and dedicated to the Virgin Mary and St. John the Baptist, in which Rosamond Clifford was interred, and to which Henry II. was a great benefactor ; the revenue at the dissolution was £319. 18. 8. The hospital of St. John the Baptist, without the east gate, was founded previously to the reign of John, who was a great benefactor to the institution, and was rebuilt by Henry III. : in the reign of Henry VI. it was given to Waynfleet, Bishop of Winchester, who founded on its site his magnificent college of Magdalene, in the walls of which some vestiges of the ancient building may be traced. The house of Dominican friars was founded, in 1221, by Isabel de Bulbec, widow of Robert, Earl of Oxford, and subsequently removed to a small island near the Watergate, in the parish of St. Ebbe, given to that fraternity by Henry III., where it continued till the dissolution. The Franciscan priory was originally founded, in 1224, by Richard Le Mercier and others, and was afterwards refounded by Henry III. : the fine chapel and extensive enclosures of this establishment were alienated in the reign of Henry VI. The priory of Carmelite or White friars was founded in 1254, to whom King Edward II. assigned the palace of Beaumont, built by Henry I. : there are scarcely any vestiges of the buildings. The monastery of Augustine friars was founded by Henry III., in 1268, and continued till the foundation of Wadham College, which was built on part of the site. Rewley abbey, for monks of the Cistercian order, was founded in 1280, by Edmund, Earl of Cornwall, in pursuance of the will of his father, Richard, King of the Romans, on an island called North Osney, and dedicated to the Virgin Mary ; at the dissolution, the revenue was estimated at £174. 3.: some arched windows and door-ways in an out-building remain, and some stones on which are inscriptions and armorial bearings. Oxford confers the title of earl on the family of Harley.

OXFORDSHIRE, an inland county, bounded on the south-west, south, and south-east by Berkshire; on the east by Buckinghamshire ; on the north-east by Northamptonshire ; on the north and north-west by Warwickshire ; and on the west by Gloucestershire. It extends from 51° 28′ to 52° 9′ (N. Lat.), and, in its greatest breadth, which is a little north of the centre of the county, from 1° 2′ to 1° 38′ (W. Lon.), and comprises an area of seven hundred and fifty-two square miles, or about four hundred and eighty-one thousand two hundred and eighty acres. The population, in 1821, was 136,971. At the period of the Roman invasion, this county formed part of the territory of the Dobuni, who, desirous of releasing themselves from subjection to their eastern neighbours, the Cattieuchlani, offered no resistance to the Romans, who, on their first division of the island, included it in *Britannia Prima*. Its central situation retarded its final subjection to the Saxon dominion, until the latter part of the sixth century. It had been the scene of several sanguinary conflicts between the Saxons and the retiring Britons, and became that of several others between the sovereigns of Wessex and Mercia. In the year 778, this county, being ceded by Cynewulf, King of Wessex, to Offa, King of Mercia, the latter made a wide and deep trench, as a boundary between the two kingdoms, which may still be traced at Ardley, Middleton-Stoney, Northbrook, Heyford, and Kirtlington. In 917, the Anglo-Saxons were defeated with great slaughter by the Danes, at Hook-Norton, who burned the town of Oxford three several times, in the years 979, 1003, and 1009, and plundered that of Thame, in 1010. In the early progress of the Norman Conquest, Oxford was stormed and burned by the Conqueror. In 1142, the Empress Matilda was besieged in the castle of that place by King Stephen, for three months, until the river being frozen, and the ground covered with snow, she, accompanied by three knights, all dressed in white, passed the sentinels unobserved, crossed the river, and proceeded on foot to Abingdon, whence she took horse, and arrived safely at Wallingford. In 1264, Oxford was taken from the barons by Henry III. In 1387, at Radford bridge, between this county and Berkshire, Thomas de Vere, Marquis of Dublin and Earl of Oxford, was defeated by Thomas of Woodstock, Duke of Gloucester, and Henry, Earl of Derby, afterwards Henry IV., when the marquis with difficulty saved his life by swimming across the Isis. In 1469, at Danesmoor, near Banbury, on July 26th, the Yorkists, under the Earl of Pembroke, were defeated by Sir John Conyers, when six thousand five hundred men were slain, and the earl made prisoner.

One of the earliest transactions relating to the great civil war occurred on Chalgrove Field, in this county, on the 15th of August, 1642, when the celebrated John Hampden appeared in arms, to enforce the ordinance of the militia. Such of the other events connected with that memorable contest as relate especially to this county may be thus briefly recounted. On the 14th of September, 1642, Sir John Byron, having taken possession of Oxford for the king, was driven from it by Lord Say and Sele. On the 27th of October, four days after the battle of Edge-Hill, Banbury castle, in which was a garrison of eight hundred foot and a troop of horse, and Broughton castle, surrendered to the king, who the next day entered Oxford, whence he marched to Brentford, and after the battle there, returned with his prisoners to Oxford, on the 28th of November. At Oxford, in April 1643, the twelve commissioners from the parliament waited on the king with proposals of peace, which negociation was broken off on the 15th of the same month; and on the 25th, at Caversham bridge, between this county and Berkshire, Ruthven, Earl of Forth, with the van of the king's army, was repulsed by Lord Robarts, in an attempt to relieve Reading, which surrendered on the following day to the Earl of Essex. In the night of June 17th, detachments from the army under the Earl of Essex were attacked at Wycombe and Postcombe, by Prince Rupert, who, on his return, with many prisoners and much booty, was overtaken the following morning on Chalgrove Field, but after a smart skirmish, the parliamentarians were repulsed, Colonel John Hampden was mortally wounded, and the prince returned in triumph to Oxford. On the 1st of August the king left Oxford for Bristol, but returned on the 16th; on the 18th he proceeded to the unsuccessful siege of Gloucester; and on September 23rd, three days after the battle of Newbury, he again returned to Oxford. That city having been now for some time the head-quarters of the royalists, to supply its garrison with provisions became a heavy burden upon the county: on the 15th of April, 1644, a royal proclamation was issued to the inhabitants of the counties of Oxford and Berks, requiring them to bring in supplies for the garrison, on pain of being visited with fire and sword: this produced a declaration from both houses of parliament, dated the 22nd of the same month, expressing their horror at the proclamation, and their determination to hazard their lives and fortunes to prevent its being carried into effect. Vigorous operations were accordingly commenced, with a view to the reduction of Oxford, and that city being nearly surrounded by two numerous detachments of the parliamentarian army, under the Earl of Essex and Sir William Waller, the king, in the night of June 3rd, effected his escape, and proceeded to Worcester, upon which the enemy relinquished their intention of besieging Oxford. At Cropredy bridge, on the 30th of June, an indecisive action took place beween the king and Sir William Waller. The garrison of Banbury, commanded by Sir William Compton, was besieged by the parliament's troops, under Colonel Fiennes, who, on October 25th, was compelled, by the Earl of Northampton, to raise the siege. November 27th, the king returned to Oxford. On the 24th of April, 1645, near Islip bridge, four regiments of the royal horse were routed by Cromwell, who on the same day took Blechingdon house without resistance, for which surrender its governor, Colonel Windebank, was shot at Oxford on the 3rd of May. The king left Oxford on May 7th, and Fairfax laid siege to it on the 22nd; but the siege was raised on the 7th of June, and the king again returned thither, on the 27th of August. On the 30th he departed for Hereford, and on November 6th he once more came to Oxford, where he passed the winter. April 26th, 1646, Woodstock manor-house, after a vigorous defence, surrendered to the parliamentarian forces; and the next day the king left Oxford to surrender himself to the Scottish army besieging Newark. May 8th, the garrison in Banbury castle, after an heroic defence for ten weeks, capitulated on honourable terms to Colonel Whalley; and on the 24th of June, Oxford, which had been besieged by Fairfax since May 2nd, surrendered at the king's command. At the time of the rebellion of 1715, several partizans of the Stuart family were seized at Oxford.

This county lies in the diocese of Oxford, and in the province of Canterbury, and forms an archdeaconry, comprising, exclusively of Oxford, the deaneries of Aston, Burcester, Chipping-Norton, Cuddesden, Dedding-ton, Henley, Witney, and Woodstock; and containing two hundred and twelve parishes, of which ninety-nine are rectories, seventy-two vicarages, and the remainder perpetual curacies. For purposes of civil government it is divided into the fourteen hundreds of Bampton, Banbury, Binfield, Bloxham, Bullington, Chadlington, Dorchester, Ewelme, Langtree, Lewknor, Pirton, Ploughley, Thame, and Wootton. It contains the city and university of Oxford, the borough and market towns of Banbury and Woodstock, and the market towns of Bampton, Bicester, Burford, Chipping-Norton, Henley upon Thames, Thame, Watlington, and Witney. Two knights are returned to parliament for the shire; two representatives for the city, and two for the university, of Oxford; two for the borough of Woodstock; and one for that of Banbury: the county members are elected at Oxford. This county is in the Oxford circuit: the assizes are held at Oxford, where is the county gaol; and the quarter sessions at the same city, on January 11th, April 19th, July 12th, and October 18th: there are fifty-nine acting magistrates. The rates raised in the county for the year ending March 25th, 1827, amounted to £139,005; the expenditure to £135,886, of which, £119,738. 19. was applied to the relief of the poor.

The shape of the county is extremely irregular: near the middle of it, at Oxford, it is not more than seven miles across, and though the northern part spreads out to the breadth of about thirty-eight miles, yet that lying to the south of Oxford is not in any part more than twelve miles broad: the latter is computed to contain one hundred and forty-one thousand acres; the former, three hundred and nine thousand. The southernmost part has a fine alternation of hill and dale, which produces much pleasing scenery; and the Chiltern elevations, more particularly, which are partly clothed with fine woods of beech, partly arable, and partly in open sheep downs, are beautifully varied. The more central district has little inequality of surface, but is adorned with numerous woods, which present a rich and pleasing aspect. In the northern and western districts of that portion of the county lying north of Oxford, the scenery is for the most part less agreeable, in consequence of the enclosures being formed by bare stone walls : in Whichwood Forest, however, are many grassy vales and woody glens, which afford much charming scenery. But the rivers of Oxfordshire are among its chief natural beauties, flowing through almost every part of it, and being always accompanied by luxuriant meadows, and varying prospects. In the vicinity of Oxford, the vale of the Isis expands into a spacious amphitheatre, bounded by some striking hills, in the centre of which rise the majestic towers, domes, and spires of that city, from behind the thick shade of venerable groves. Shillingford bridge occupies a romantic situation on the same river, soon after it has been joined by the Thame ; and after having passed Wallingford, in Berkshire, the scenery upon its banks assumes an immense variety of fresh beauties, and forms an indented valley through the range of the Chiltern hills, which, gradually losing the appearance of downs, exhibited by some of their more naked summits in the distance, become adorned by numerous varied beauties of art and nature : thick woods clothe their sides and summits, while the slopes, in the more immediate vicinity of the river, consist of rich meadows. Towns and villages lie scattered along its banks, and magnificent seats adorn the declivities on each side. Having been joined by the Kennet and the Loddon, which it receives from the south, the Thames swells into a majestic river, navigated by numerous small craft, and glides onward through the plain, until it becomes engulphed amidst the fine hills around Henley, the scenery of which is among the most interesting on its banks. The climate of Oxfordshire, its situation and latitude considered, is cold, particularly in the western part of the northern division of the county, where the fences consist chiefly of stone walls, affording but little shelter. In the Chiltern district, at the southern extremity of the county, it is moist : it is also cold upon the Chiltern hills, and in their vicinity, more especially upon the poor white lands at the foot of them, where it is observed that the frosts always take effect sooner, and are of longer continuance, than on the other soils.

With regard to soil, this county comprises three different tracts, the limits of which are pretty clearly defined, and which may be distinguished as the red-land district, the stonebrash land, and the Chiltern hills. The red-land occupies the whole northern part, and may be separated from the rest of it by an irregular line drawn from Little Rollright, on the borders of Warwickshire, by Westcott-Barton and Somerton, to the vicinity of Mixbury, near the confines of Northamptonshire and Buckinghamshire : this district, which much exceeds in fertility any other of equal extent in Oxfordshire, and contains about seventy-nine thousand six hundred and thirty-five acres, consists of a rich sandy loam of a reddish colour, which is deep, sound, and friable, being well adapted to the production of every crop: the substratum is red grit-stone rock. The stonebrash district adjoins the former, and extends from the borders of Gloucestershire, on the west, nearly to those of Buckinghamshire, on the east, the southern border of it running from the boundary of the county, near Broughton-Poggs, in a north-easterly direction by Brize-Norton, Witney, North Leigh, Bladon, Kirtling-

ton and Bicester, to Stratton-Audley, and thence northward, at a short distance from the borders of Buckinghamshire, to Mixbury : in so extensive a tract as this, which is computed to comprise one hundred and sixty-four thousand and twenty-three acres, a great variety is found, from poor loose sandy slopes, to deep and more heavy soils, approaching to clay ; but that which predominates is a loose, dry, friable sand, or loam, apparently formed in a great measure of abraded limestone, of which it contains many fragments : in the vales various loams are found. The Chiltern district comprises the south-eastern extremity of Oxfordshire ; its boundary from the rest of the county extending from Chinnor, in a south-westerly direction, near Watlington, to the vicinity of the Thames at Gatehampton : the basis of this tract, which contains sixty-four thousand seven hundred and seventy-eight acres, is chalk, in some places very white and pure, in others imperfect, which is covered to various depths with a clayey loam, generally sound and dry, and containing a considerable quantity of flints, mostly brown, rough, and honey-combed, frequently to perforation : many of these flints have also a sparry incrustation, and the best soils are often the most covered with them : on the banks of the Thames, and in some other places where the hills recede, the soil is an excellent sandy loam, which, as well as the flinty hills, forms a good turnip soil. The remaining large portion of the county, extending from this to the stonebrash district, and calculated to comprise one hundred and sixty-six thousand four hundred acres, includes all sorts of soils, from a loose sand to a heavy clay, and these are so intermixed, and the respective tracts of each so small, as to render it difficult to give a distinct account of them. Peat-earth is occasionally found; and it is considered as a mark of the general fertility of the county, that good crops of wheat grow on all its soils. Quarries of freestone are numerous ; limestone is very plentiful ; and slate, fit for roofing common buildings, is obtained in several parts : the ochre found at Shotover is esteemed of the very best quality.

On the arable lands, which occupy by far the greater part of the county, the courses of cropping are very irregular, even on soils that are alike. The corn crops commonly cultivated are wheat, barley, and oats : the general average produce of wheat is estimated at three quarters per acre ; that of barley, at four quarters ; and that of oats, at five quarters. Peas are occasionally cultivated ; beans are sown on the heavier soils ; and there exists likewise a practice of sowing what is here called *poulse*, namely beans and peas mixed, of which good crops are produced on the lighter lands. The common turnip and the Swedish turnip are both extensively cultivated. Tares are commonly grown ; lentils to a small extent ; rape, but little ; cabbages, carrots, and potatoes occasionally as agricultural crops. Clover and trefoil are frequently cultivated ; and sainfoin is grown to a great extent upon all the soils that are proper for it. Of the grass lands, the chief part is situated in the narrow flat tracts on the borders of the rivers, containing most of the open field meadows, which are extensive, and situated so low as to be frequently overflowed by sudden rains, and sometimes even during the hay-harvest, insomuch, that the crops are either spoiled or entirely swept away : this flooding, however, improves the soil, when the waters do not remain out long enough to injure the grass, which seldom receives any other manure than the sediment thus deposited. At Water-Eaton is the best grass land in the county, which is occupied for dairies ; but it is very liable to summer floods : at North Weston, in the rich district near Thame, the meadows are mown twice a year. The enclosed pasture, or meadow land, is chiefly confined to the central part of the county, near Oxford, where there is a considerable tract of deep rich soil : besides the quantity of butter made here, which is considerable, numerous calves are suckled, to supply the London market with veal ; in various parts of this district some cattle and sheep are also fattened : many of the pasture grounds, however, are full of ant-hills, and a great part of the herbage is consequently coarse. Much butter is sent to the London market from some other parts of Oxfordshire, particularly from the vicinity of Bicester ; and in the district around Thame many calves are also fattened, to be sent as veal to the same market : little cheese is made : the produce of hay per acre is calculated to average nearly two tons. The best feeding-land lies on the banks of the rivers Thame, Isis, and Cherwell, but the lowest meadows are subject to floods, which sometimes do much damage to the herbage, when they occur late in the spring. Lime is extensively used as a manure, as are also peat and coal ashes ; and great quantities of rags, purchased in London, are brought for the same purpose. Oxfordshire has no peculiar breed of cattle, nor does any particular sort prevail ; those most frequently seen are the short-horned Yorkshire, the·long-horned Leicestershire, the Devon, and the Alderney breeds : oxen are frequently employed in agricultural labours, for which the Herefordshire breed is preferred. It is well stocked with sheep, of which the most common are the South Down, the Berkshire, the New Leicester, a cross between the Berkshire and the Leicester, a Spanish breed, which is sometimes found mingled with the South Down, and a mixed breed between the New Leicester and the Cotswold sheep. Of hogs, the Berkshire breed is the most common throughout the county : many boars are fed for the purpose of making brawn and sausages, which form considerable articles of trade at Oxford, and some other places in the county.

Oxfordshire may be considered a well-wooded county, excepting the northernmost part of it, but there is comparatively but very little oak. The woodlands may be classed as follows ; first, groves on spring-woods ; secondly, woods consisting of timber trees and underwood ; and thirdly, coppices consisting of underwood only. Of the first class, the extensive natural beech-woods confined to the Chiltern district are the principal, consisting of large trees, among which is a succession of younger ones that have been produced by the falling of the beech mast : these woods are never all felled at once, except for the purpose of bringing the land under tillage, but are drawn occasionally. Of the second kind are the woods in the vicinity of Stanton St. John, called "the Quarters," the soil of which is a strong clay : there are also numerous spots of woodland of this description dispersed in various other parts of the county. Coppices are not very numerous, there being hardly any extensive ones, except those tracts of Whichwood Forest that are thus called, but which, containing timber trees, are ·more properly

woods. There are extensive artificial plantations in several places, particularly at Blenheim. The waste lands, excepting the large tract of Whichwood Forest, is inconsiderable. This forest, situated towards the western confines of the county, and having a soil, in some places of reddish loam, and in others of the common stonebrash of the extensive district in which it is included, contains six thousand seven hundred and twenty acres, and is subject to a right of commonage for horses and sheep only. It comprises thirty-four coppices, eighteen of which belong to the king, twelve to the Duke of Marlborough, and four to different individuals; and contains some thriving young oak timber : next to oak, ash is the most abundant, and after that beech, with some elm. The coppices occupy three thousand and thirty-seven acres, the keepers' lodges and lawns one hundred and thirty-four, and the open forest (which produces nothing but brushwood and pasturage for the numerous deer and the cattle) two thousand four hundred and twenty-one acres. After having been cut, the coppices are fenced off for seven years against the cattle and sheep, but the deer are never excluded. Comprised within the forest are also the chase woods, occupying four hundred and eighty-eight acres; and Blandford park, containing six hundred and forty acres. Otmoor, near Islip, six miles north of Oxford, contains about four thousand acres, and, prior to its enclosure, under an act obtained in 1815, was commonable to eight adjoining townships: the soil is generally a good loam, but the whole tract is so extremely flat, and situated so low, that in wet seasons much of it lies under water for a long time, the consequence of which is that the cattle and sheep upon it become diseased. Formerly the number of cattle turned upon the moor by each householder was subject to no limitation : some large flocks of geese were also kept upon it. What are called·flits upon this moor are the holes from which peat has been dug ; pills are hills of quaking bog. The poor inhabitants of these townships, who had been deprived of their customary right of common by the enclosure bill, destroyed the fences repeatedly, and, in September 1830, assembled in a numerous body, and proceeded, in a riotous manner, to effect the removal of what they considered to be an encroachment on their ancient rights, insomuch that the military were called in, and some of the ringleaders taken into custody, but subsequently liberated by their companions on their way to prison, under a small escort. Most of the unenclosed parishes, which are rather numerous, have larger or smaller tracts of waste, or down land, which is appropriated chiefly to the pasturage of sheep : the range of the Chiltern hills, which crosses the southern end of the county, has much land of this description, being in many places too steep to admit of cultivation. In the more northern parts too are considerable tracts of downs, which are in many instances overrun with ant-hills and coarse herbage, and of little value, being chiefly appropriated to the pasturage of young cattle, and sometimes of oxen that are employed in the plough. At Kidlington is a large common, which feeds three hundred cows, from May 16th until Michaelmas ; and at Campsfield, in the same parish, is an extensive common pastured by sheep.

The principal manufactures are, that of blankets, at

Witney; and those of gloves and articles of polished steel, at Woodstock: the glove manufacture was established about the middle of the last century, and now furnishes employment to the poor for many miles around that town. A coarse kind of velvet, called Shag, is made at Banbury: the female poor in the southern part of the county are chiefly employed in lace-making.

The principal rivers are the Thames (or Isis), the Cherwell, the Thame, the Evenlode, and the Windrush. The first-mentioned river, which forms the entire southern boundary of the county, separating it from Berkshire, rises in Gloucestershire, and having been joined by different small streams near Lechlade, first touches this county at its south-western extremity, being then imperfectly navigable, and bearing the name of Isis: hence it pursues its course, for a considerable distance, through an undiversified plain, and in an easterly direction, until it has received the waters of the Windrush, when it takes a north-easterly course, and having been joined by the Evenlode, soon after suddenly turns southward to Oxford, a little above which city it divides into small channels, which traverse the meadows of Witham, and, leaving Oxford immediately on the left, pass under several stone bridges, connected by a grand causeway, which forms the principal approach to that city on the west: these streams soon re-uniting, the river winds round the city towards the north-east, and having been crossed by an ancient stone bridge, and joined by the Cherwell, becomes navigable, and pursues a very devious course, for the most part in a south-easterly direction, through an extensive tract of rich low meadows, to a short distance below Dorchester, where it is joined by the Thame: at this junction the river loses its assumed poetical name of Isis, and is first popularly called Thames, although in various old grants and charters, both of the period of the Saxon sway in England, and since the Norman Conquest, it is always denominated by the latter title in the higher parts of its course also. The Thames immediately passes under Shillingford bridge, and shortly after under that of Wallingford, below which the river continues a protracted southerly course, until it begins to make an extensive sweep round by the east to the north, enclosing the southern extremity of the county, which it wholly quits at a short distance below Henley, when it takes an easterly direction, and begins to form the boundary between Berkshire and Buckinghamshire. Though by no means a rapid river, it is far from being sluggish in its course, and has been poetically described as "without o'erflowing full :" its waters are here clear and silvery, except when disturbed by floods. The principal fish which it contains, in that part of its course bordering on Oxfordshire, are pike, chub, barbel, perch, eels, roach, dace, and gudgeons: salmon are also sometimes taken. The Cherwell, rising in Northamptonshire, enters this county at its northernmost extremity, and almost immediately, in the vicinity of Banbury, becomes its eastern boundary, separating it from Northamptonshire for the distance of seven or eight miles; it then finally enters Oxfordshire, and, receiving numerous smaller streams, continues its irregular southerly course through an extensive tract to the eastern side of Oxford, where it runs under Magdalene bridge, and soon after joins the Thames. The Thame, rising on the borders of Buckinghamshire and Oxfordshire, near Chinnor, takes a north-westerly course, forming the eastern boundary of the county, and passing by the town of Thame, until, in the vicinity of Waterstock, it enters it, and pursues a south-westerly, and afterwards a southerly, course, passing under the bridges of Wheatley and Dorchester, to the Isis, a little below the latter place, the united waters then taking the name of Thames. The Evenlode, rising on the north-western borders of the county, and descending by Whichwood Forest, pursues a very irregular south-easterly course by Charlbury, and having been augmented by the smaller stream of the Glyme, which flows past Woodstock, and forms the magnificent sheet of water in Blenheim park, joins the Thames a few miles above Oxford. The Windrush, rising at a short distance within the borders of Gloucestershire, soon enters this county, and pursues a nearly eastern course by Burford to Witney, to the manufactures of which latter town it is of great service, and whence it takes a direction about south-south-east, falling into the Thames near Northmoor. The smaller streams, all of which fall into some of the larger rivers before mentioned, are extremely numerous. The Oxford canal, which is of immense advantage to the county, by opening a communication, through other canals, with Birmingham, Liverpool, Manchester, and the Wednesbury collieries, enters at its northern extremity, and soon approaching the Cherwell, runs nearly parallel with the course of that river, which it crosses, near Banbury, and a few miles to the east of Deddington and Woodstock, to the city of Oxford, where it communicates with the navigation of the Thames.

The turnpike roads are generally very good, especially in situations where gravel can be obtained: in the northern part of the county, the red grit-stone is used, but is not so good for the purpose. The road from London to Cheltenham, Gloucester, and Hereford, enters the county from Maidenhead, in Berkshire, and, passing through Henley, Nettlebed, Dorchester, Oxford, Witney, and Burford, leaves it a little beyond that town. The upper road from London to Oxford, Worcester, and Aberystwith, enters from High Wycombe in Buckinghamshire, and passes through Stokenchurch, Tetsworth, Wheatley, Oxford, Woolvercott, Woodstock, Over Kiddington, Chapel-House, and Little Rollright, and enters Gloucestershire at the Four Shire Stone: this is also the road from London to Holyhead, through Worcester. The road from London to Holyhead, through Buckingham and Shrewsbury, enters the county from Tingewick in Buckinghamshire, passes through Finmere and Mixbury, and, after crossing a part of Northamptonshire, re-enters it at Nell bridge, and passes through Adderbury, Banbury, Drayton, and Wroxton, to Upton in Warwickshire: this is also the road from London to Holyhead, through Birmingham, and from London to Chester, through the same town. The road from London to Aylesbury, Bicester, and Oxford, enters from Fleet-Marston in Buckinghamshire, and passes through Bicester to Oxford.

Several very curious British coins have been found in the county; and one of the most interesting remains of antiquity which it contains is the circle of high stones, called *Rollrich stones*, in the vicinity of Chipping-Norton. Few considerable remnants of Roman military works exist in Oxfordshire: at Alcester, or Aldchester, in the eastern part of the county, are the traces of a Roman station, the *Alauna* of the Itinerary, and it is probable that there was another at Dorchester. Various Roman coins and pavements have been discovered, at different periods, in almost every quarter of the county; and, in addition to these, may be noticed several sepulchral mounds, formed of rude grassy squares of turf, which, says Dr. Plot, the Roman soldiers were accustomed to raise over the ashes of any eminent warrior, and the most remarkable of which is termed Astal Barrow, in the vicinity of the Akeman-street: numerous urns and other funereal relics of the same people have also been dug up, at various periods, in different parts of the county. Only one of the four consular, or prætorian ways passed through Oxfordshire: this was the Iknield-street, which crossed the southern part of it, from north-east to south-west; and though its remains are not very conspicuous, in consequence of the dry soil over which it passes not having required it to be formed into a paved ridge, or with deep trenches, yet its course may be pretty accurately described: entering from Buckinghamshire, at the parish of Chinnor, it proceeds along the base of the Chiltern hills; leaves Lewknor, Shirburn, and Watlington to the north-west; crosses the vallum, or ridged bank, called Grime's Dyke; and, passing Ipsden, may be traced to an enclosure about three miles distant from the village of Goring, whence its course out of the county cannot be followed; but it is asserted by Dr. Plot, that it quitted it at Goring, and the name of the hamlet on the opposite bank of the Thames, *viz.*, *Streatley*, seems to corroborate this opinion. Of the vicinal ways, the principal was the Akeman-street, which in different parts of its course seems to have been constructed either with or without a raised bank, according to the nature of the soil over which it passed: it enters from Buckinghamshire, in the parish of Ambrosden, whence it proceeds to the north of Gravenel, or Gravenhill, Wood, and Alchester, to Chesterton and Kirtlington, and, crossing the river Cherwell, near Tackley, passes through Blenheim park towards the village of Stonesfield, where it crosses the Evenlode, and then passes near Wilcote and Ramsden, to Asthall-Leigh and Asthall, and thence to Broadwell Grove, where its form is bold and perfect, and whence it proceeds nearly in a straight line towards Gloucestershire. Several minor roads, traces of which are still visible, diverged from this, or crossed it in different parts of its course through the county. Between Mongewell and Nuffield, towards the southern extremity of the county, is a vallum, or long earthwork, called Grime's Dyke: it is very high, and only single until it approaches the vicinity of Nuffield, where it is double, with a deep trench between the ramparts: it has been conjectured that the other part of it was once likewise double-banked, but that the trench was filled up by one of the banks being thrown into it in the progress of agricultural improvements. Marks of the sanguinary contests between the Saxons and the Danes are distinguishable in many parts of the county, consisting chiefly of military intrenchments, and sepulchral mounds, or barrows.

At the period of the general dissolution, the number of religious houses in the county, exclusively of the colleges at Oxford, was about forty, including hospitals, &c. The principal relic of the monastic buildings is St.

Frideswide's abbey church, now the cathedral church of Oxford. Amongst the parochial churches are some interesting specimens of Saxon, or early Norman, especially in that of Iffley, and many fine examples of English, architecture. In number, beauty, and magnificence of its public and private buildings, Oxfordshire at least rivals any other county in England. Blenheim House is well known as one of the most magnificent residences in the kingdom; and many other of the mansions of the resident nobility and gentry possess considerable beauty and grandeur, both of exterior appearance and interior decoration: among the principal are, Ditchley Park, the property and residence of Lord Viscount Dillon; Nuneham-Courtney, that of the late Earl of Harcourt; and Wroxton Priory, that of the Earl of Guildford. The facility with which building materials are procured causes the habitations of the middle and lower classes to be commodious, substantial, and neat in appearance: nearly every cottage has a good garden. The medicinal springs are very numerous, the greater number being of the various kinds of chalybeate. In the extensive bed of gravel on which Oxford stands, and which forms one of the geological features of England, are found many remarkable fossils, such as fragments of teeth, tusks, and bones of elephants; bones of the hippopotamus; horses' teeth; and horns of a species of stag; sometimes in a complete state of preservation.

OXHEY, a hamlet in the parish of WATFORD, hundred of CASHIO, or liberty of ST. ALBAN'S, county of HERTFORD, containing 560 inhabitants. An earthen vessel, containing some Roman seals, was, a few years since, turned up here by the plough.

OXHILL, a parish in the Kington division of the hundred of KINGTON, county of WARWICK, 4 miles (S. S. W.) from Kington, containing 307 inhabitants. The living is a rectory, in the archdeaconry and diocese of Worcester, rated in the king's books at £14. 10., and in the patronage of the Rev. Devenport Bromley. The church is dedicated to St. Lawrence. There is a place of worship for Wesleyan Methodists.

OXNEAD, a parish in the southern division of the hundred of ERPINGHAM, county of NORFOLK, 4 miles (S.E.) from Aylsham, containing 53 inhabitants. The living is a discharged rectory, united to that of Skeyton, and the vicarage of Buxton, in the archdeaconry and diocese of Norwich, rated in the king's books at £9. 1. 5. The church is dedicated to St. Nicholas.

OXNEY, formerly a parish, now annexed to that of St. Margaret at Cliffe, hundred of CORNILO, lathe of St. AUGUSTINE, county of KENT, 5½ miles (N. E.) from Dovor, containing 11 inhabitants. The church has long been demolished.

OXSPRING, a township in the parish of PENISTONE, wapentake of STAINCROSS, West riding of the county of York, 2½ miles (E.) from Penistone, containing 247 inhabitants.

OXTED, a parish in the first division of the hundred of TANDRIDGE, county of SURREY, 2 miles (E. by N.) from Godstone, containing 777 inhabitants. The living is a rectory, in the archdeaconry of Surrey, and diocese of Winchester, rated in the king's books at £24. 6. 0½., and in the patronage of C. L. H. Master, Esq. The church is dedicated to St. Mary. A fair is held here on the 1st of May.

OXTON, a township in the parish of WOODCHURCH, lower division of the hundred of WIRRALL, county palatine of CHESTER, 7¼ miles (N. E.) from Great Neston, containing 169 inhabitants.

OXTON, a parish in the southern division of the wapentake of THURGARTON, county of NOTTINGHAM, 5 miles (W. by S.) from Southwell, containing 798 inhabitants. The living is a discharged vicarage, in the peculiar jurisdiction and patronage of the Chapter of the Collegiate Church of Southwell, rated in the king's books at £6, endowed with £200 royal bounty. The church is dedicated to St. Peter. There is a place of worship for Wesleyan Methodists. Oxton constitutes the endowment of two prebends, *Prima et Secunda*, in the Collegiate Church of Southwell. The small river Dove runs through the parish, which lies in the centre of the ancient Forest of Sherwood, though it is said never to have formed part of that district. In the village is a free school, founded by Mrs. Sherbrooke, and endowed with a rent-charge of £20, for teaching all the poor children of the parish. In 1789, a barrow was opened in the neighbourhood, and found to contain a curious urn of iron, a sword in a wooden scabbard, a dagger much corroded, and several glass beads.

OXTON, a township in that part of the parish of TADCASTER which is in the ainsty of the city, and East riding of the county, of YORK, 1½ mile (E.) from Tadcaster, containing 66 inhabitants.

OXWICK, a parish in the hundred of LAUNDITCH, county of NORFOLK, 3¼ miles (S. by W.) from Fakenham, containing, with Pattesley, 79 inhabitants. The living is a discharged rectory, in the archdeaconry and diocese of Norwich, rated in the king's books at £6. 9. 2., and in the patronage of the Rev. Joseph Alderson. The church is dedicated to All Saints.

OZELWORTH, a parish in the upper division of the hundred of BERKELEY, county of GLOUCESTER, 3½ miles (E. by S.) from Wotton under Edge, containing 134 inhabitants. The living is a discharged rectory, in the archdeaconry and diocese of Gloucester, rated in the king's books at £6. 10. 5., and in the patronage of Mrs. Fisher. The church, dedicated to St. Nicholas, has an octagonal central tower, rising from enriched Norman arches.

OZENDIKE, a parish in that part of the parish of RYTHER which is in the lower division of the wapentake of BARKSTONE-ASH, West riding of the county of YORK, 8 miles (N. W.) from Selby. The population is returned with the parish.

P.

PACKINGTON, a parish partly in the hundred of REPTON and GRESLEY, county of DERBY, but chiefly in the western division of the hundred of GOSCOTE, county of LEICESTER, 1¾ mile (S. by E.) from Ashby de la Zouch, containing, with the hamlet of Snibston, 702 inhabitants. The living is a vicarage, in the archdeaconry of Leicester, and diocese of Lincoln, rated in the king's books at £5. 15. 10., and in the patronage of Sir Charles Abney Hastings, Bart. The church is dedicated to the Holy Rood.

PACKINGTON, a liberty in the parish of WEEFORD, southern division of the hundred of OFFLOW, county

of STAFFORD, 3¾ miles (W. N. W.) from Tamworth, containing 53 inhabitants.

PACKINGTON (GREAT), a parish in the Solihull division of the hundred of HEMLINGFORD, county of WARWICK, 4¾ miles (S. E. by S.) from Coleshill, containing 351 inhabitants. The living is a discharged vicarage, in the archdeaconry of Coventry, and diocese of Lichfield and Coventry, rated in the king's books at £7. 10. 2½., and in the patronage of the Earl of Aylesford. The church is dedicated to St. James.

PACKINGTON (LITTLE), a parish in the Solihull division of the hundred of HEMLINGFORD, county of WARWICK, 3½ miles (S. S. E.) from Coleshill, containing 150 inhabitants. The living is a discharged rectory, in the archdeaconry of Coventry, and diocese of Lichfield and Coventry, rated in the king's books at £3, and in the patronage of the Earl of Aylesford. The church is dedicated to St. Bartholomew.

PACKWOOD, a parish in the Warwick division of the hundred of KINGTON, county of WARWICK, 4½ miles (N. N. E.) from Henley in Arden, containing 279 inhabitants. The living is a perpetual curacy, in the peculiar jurisdiction of the Manorial Court of Packwood, endowed with £400 private benefaction, and £800 royal bounty, and in the patronage of Earl Cornwallis. The church is dedicated to St. Giles. The Stratford on Avon canal passes through the parish.

PADBURY, a parish in the hundred and county of BUCKINGHAM, 2¾ miles (S. E. by S.) from Buckingham, containing 618 inhabitants. The living is a discharged vicarage, in the archdeaconry of Buckingham, and diocese of Lincoln, rated in the king's books at £6. 13. 4., endowed with £400 parliamentary grant, and in the patronage of the Crown. The church is dedicated to St. Mary. There is a place of worship for Wesleyan Methodists. Padbury is situated on the river Ouse, over which is a substantial stone bridge, erected in 1742. In July 1643, a skirmish took place here between the king's troops under Sir Charles Lucas, and a detachment of the parliamentarians commanded by Colonel Middleton, in which the latter were defeated.

PADDINGTON, a parish in the Holborn division of the hundred of OSSULSTONE, county of MIDDLESEX, a suburb of the metropolis, containing 6476 inhabitants. The manor was given by King Edgar to the abbey of Westminster, and at the dissolution it was appropriated to the endowment of the then newly-founded bishoprick of Westminster, since the abolition of which, in the reign of Edward VI., it has belonged to the see of London. The hamlet consists principally of several modern streets and handsome detached houses: it is partially paved, and lighted with gas, under a local act; and the inhabitants are supplied with water from the West Middlesex water-works: the reservoir, originally constructed for the supply of Kensington palace, and now belonging to the Grand Junction water-works, is situated in this parish. It is within the jurisdiction of the magistrates acting for the metropolis, and under the superintendence of the New Police, established under Sir Robert Peel's act: debts under 40s. are recoverable at the county court held in Kingsgate-street, Holborn. A customary market is held on Friday, for poultry, butter, eggs, &c. The living is a perpetual curacy, or donative, in the jurisdiction of the Commissary of London, concurrently with the Consistorial

Court of the Bishop, and in the patronage of the Bishop of London. The church, which is dedicated to St. James, and was anciently a chapel of ease to St. Margaret's Westminster, was originally founded by Sir Joseph Sheldon, lessee of the manor, about the year 1700. The present edifice was begun in 1788, and consecrated April 27th, 1791: it stands on a piece of ground adjoining the old churchyard, and is a neat building, with a Doric portico on the south side, and a handsome cupola. In the church and adjacent cemetery lie the remains of John Bushnell, an eminent statuary, who died in 1701; Sir John Elliot, M.D., a popular writer, who became deranged in consequence of a disappointed attachment to a lady, whose life he attempted, by shooting at her in the public street, and shortly after destroyed himself, while in confinement, in 1787; Dr. Alexander Geddes, a very learned but eccentric Roman Catholic divine, interred in 1802; Thomas Banks, an ingenious sculptor; Lewis Schiavonetti, engraver; and John Henry Petty, late Marquis of Lansdowne. A handsome chapel of ease is now being erected, partly by means of a grant from the parliamentary commissioners, and partly by subscription. There are places of worship for Baptists and Wesleyan Methodists. The Paddington canal, which communicates with all the principal canals in the kingdom, and on the banks of which are extensive wharfs and warehouses, was constructed in consequence of an act of parliament passed in 1795: it is joined by the Regent's canal, which unites it with the Thames at Limehouse. A National school, in which upwards of three hundred children are instructed, and fifty of them clothed, is supported by voluntary contributions: the school premises were built by subscription in 1822. There are some unendowed almshouses, built by Peps Cockerill, Esq., and others by the inhabitants, for the use of the aged poor, for whose relief funds amounting to about £250 per annum, arising from lands and tenements assigned for that purpose, are appropriated.

PADDLESWORTH, a joint parish with Snodland, in the hundred of LARKFIELD, lathe of AYLESFORD, county of KENT, 6¼ miles (S.W.) from Rochester. The population is returned with Snodland. The living is a rectory, united at an early period to that of Snodland, in the archdeaconry and diocese of Rochester, rated in the king's books at £3. 6. 8. The church has been destroyed, and the inhabitants have married, baptized, and buried at Snodland since the reign of Elizabeth.

PADDLESWORTH, a parish in the hundred of LONINGBOROUGH, lathe of SHEPWAY, county of KENT, 3¾ miles (N.W.) from Folkestone, containing 44 inhabitants. The living is a perpetual curacy, with that of Stamford, annexed to the vicarage of Lyminge, in the peculiar jurisdiction of the Archbishop of Canterbury. The church, dedicated to St. Oswald, is in the early style of English architecture.

PADDOCKS, an extra-parochial district, in the wapentake of CORRINGHAM, parts of LINDSEY, county of LINCOLN, containing 3 inhabitants.

PADFIELD, a township in the parish of GLOSSOP, hundred of HIGH PEAK, county of DERBY, 10½ miles (N. by W.) from Chapel en le Frith, containing 499 inhabitants.

PADIHAM, a chapelry in that part of the parish of WHALLEY which is in the higher division of the hundred of BLACKBURN, county palatine of LANCASTER, 3½ miles (W. by N.) from Burnley, containing 3060 inhabitants. The living is a perpetual curacy, in the archdeaconry and diocese of Chester, endowed with £400 private benefaction, £200 royal bounty, and £900 parliamentary grant, and in the patronage of Le Gendre Pierce Starkie, Esq. The chapel, dedicated to St. Leonard, has lately received an addition of two hundred and twenty-nine free sittings, the Incorporated Society for the enlargement of churches and chapels having granted £150 towards defraying the expense. There are places of worship for Wesleyan Methodists and Unitarians. The Leeds and Liverpool canal passes in the vicinity. Coal and stone abound here; and the cotton manufacture is carried on to a considerable extent. A fair is held on August 12th, chiefly for pedlary. A school was erected and endowed by subscription in 1698, in which from seventy to eighty children are instructed, each paying a trifling quarterage.

PADLEY (NETHER), a hamlet in the parish of HOPE, hundred of HIGH PEAK, county of DERBY, 2¾ miles (N.E. by N.) from Stony-Middleton, containing 36 inhabitants.

PADSIDE, a township in the parish of HAMPSTHWAITE, lower division of the wapentake of CLARO, West riding of the county of YORK, 7½ miles (W.) from Ripley. The population is returned with the chapelry of Thornthwaite.

PADSTOW, a sea-port, market town, and parish, in the hundred of PYDER, county of CORNWALL, 14 miles (W. N. W.) from Bodmin, and 249 (W. S. W.) from London, containing, according to the last census, 1700 inhabitants, which number is estimated to have since increased to 2000. The town is of great antiquity, and was known, under the name of Lodenek at Heglemith, in the earliest annals of Cornish history. According to Borlase and others, the first religious house, called Laffenack, was established here in 432, by St. Patrick; about a century afterwards, he was succeeded by St. Petroc, and under the auspices of this popular saint a monastery was founded, in 513, which, having progressively increased in extent and holy reputation, was visited by Athelstan, on the occasion of his triumphant excursion into Cornwall, in 926. This sovereign conferred important privileges on both the monastery and the town, the latter of which he named after himself, Adelstow, or Aldestow. Whitaker has satisfactorily proved that at this time the localities of Bodmin presented little more than the solitary cell of St. Guron: the same authority, however, rejects the visit of St. Patrick in favour of his successor. In ancient records Patrickstowe and Petrocstowe are equally common; from the former of these Padestowe, or Padstow, is more naturally derived, and perhaps the continued influx of Irish at this port from the earliest times may have had some influence on the change of name. It was in the year 981, when the monastery was in the plenitude of its prosperity, that it was ravaged by Danish pirates, and burnt to the ground.

Seal formerly used by the Corporation.

On this event it became necessary to find a situation less exposed for the new foundation, which was fixed at Bodmin, and the sacred ashes of St. Petroc were transferred to its sanctuary. It has been a subject of antiquarian dissertation, whether Padstow is described as Elhil or Lancuhoc in Domesday-book. In 1344, this place was one of the few ports in Devonshire and Cornwall that furnished ships for the siege of Calais. In 1645, the Prince, afterwards Charles II., was for some time resident here: the inhabitants were at that time zealous in their support of royalty; but about five years after, a singular change appears to have taken place in their political feelings. A vessel from Ireland, with troops and dispatches, having arrived, with the certainty of a favourable reception, was boarded by the townspeople, assisted by some parliamentary dragoons, and after a contest, in which many lives were lost, she was captured, and the troops made prisoners. As the only port on the coast for the exportation of large quantities of grain, Padstow was, in the last century, repeatedly exposed to the inroads of large parties of miners, from the districts in the west: they assembled to the number of upwards of one thousand men, armed with bludgeons. The high price of bread was the grievance complained of, and they generally returned home after having broken open the granaries, and distributed the corn. The interference of the military on these occasions was usually found necessary.

The town is beautifully situated on an æstuary, formed by the confluence of the river Camel and other subordinate streams, and opening into St. George's channel: it is embosomed in a richly cultivated vale, the eastern side of which opens on the harbour, a sheet of water which, being apparently enclosed by a bold range of hills, and singularly retaining its clear azure hue, presents the attractive beauties of lake scenery. The high land to the north and west of the town is occupied by the grounds of Place, an ancient seat of the Prideaux family. On the southern eminences and along the vale are the fine plantations of Saunders Hill, which command a varied and luxuriant prospect. In the immediate vicinity, however, nature assumes a severity and boldness of character seldom equalled: the cliffs of black granite on the coast, which are alike remarkable for their stupendous height and grotesque form, are frequently visited by the scientific traveller; they present curious specimens of geological strata peculiar to this part of the kingdom. The streets are roughly paved, but not lighted, and the town is plentifully supplied with water. The houses are all covered with the fine blue slate raised in the neighbourhood. Previously to the sixteenth century the harbour of Padstow was considered one of the finest on the western coast of England, but from the accumulation of sand, the driving of which was so violent as, in the course of one night, to cover several houses on the coast, it became of less importance: the trade was very considerable at the commencement of the present century, and it now carries on a large coasting trade, corn, malt, and other merchandise being sent to Liverpool, Bristol, London, Wales, and Ireland. The port was formerly noted for valuable importations of Russian produce, much of which was re-shipped to Bristol; and the exportation of pilchards; but the little foreign trade which it at present enjoys is chiefly with Norway and America.

The number of vessels that entered inwards from foreign ports in 1826, was five British and five foreign, and the number that cleared outwards, eighteen British and five foreign. In 1826 seven vessels were built and registered; and the number which belonged to the port in March, 1828, was three of more than one hundred tons' burthen, and sixty-nine of smaller size. One hundred and seventy-five vessels have been wrecked and stranded, and upwards of two hundred lives lost, in the last thirty-three years, within the limits of the port. Several important works have been constructed, for the assistance of ships entering the harbour, by a benevolent association, established in November 1829, which having been liberally supported by gentlemen of influence in the county, has already been attended with the most beneficial results. A life boat is attached to the apparatus. The Trinity House has recently brought the port under the regulation of branch pilots. Several persons are employed in ship-building, and sail and rope making. The market is held on Saturday, by prescription, for meat and provisions; but the fairs, on April 18th and September 31st, which were formerly well supplied with cattle and staple produce, are no longer continued.

In the 25th of Elizabeth the town was incorporated by royal charter, under the title of the "Mayor and Burgesses of the Borough of Padstow," when the executive government was vested in the mayor, steward, five aldermen, and two serjeants at mace, annually elected by the burgesses; a market was established on Friday, of which the mayor was constituted clerk; and two fairs were granted. The corporation were empowered to hold a weekly court, for the recovery of debts to the amount of £40: the charter likewise contained a clause reserving to the lord of the manor several important rights and privileges. About the middle of the seventeenth century, the municipal rights having been allowed to lapse by desuetude, the town was placed under the jurisdiction of the county magistrates, one of whom, Thomas Rawlings, Esq., was for a long period resident, but on his decease the magisterial business was transferred to the petty sessions at St. Columb. A portreeve, who formerly had the control of the harbour, and other officers, are still chosen at the manorial court leet, but their duties are little more than nominal.

The living is a discharged vicarage, in the peculiar jurisdiction of the Bishop of Exeter, rated in the king's books at £11. 3. 4., endowed with £200 private benefaction, and in the patronage of the Rev. C. Prideaux Brune. The church is a spacious light structure, in the decorated and later styles of English architecture, built at different periods, the earliest in the fourteenth century: the richly-sculptured font and curious piscina have attracted much attention. A commodious place of worship has been recently built for the Wesleyan Methodists. A National school for children of both sexes was established in 1819; the school-room was erected by the contributions of the resident gentry, assisted by the National Society. In 1640, £200 was laid out in land for the benefit of the poor, and vested in trustees by enfeoffment, called "Stock Money;" £10 per annum for a free school for ten boys, and £5 per annum from the Rev. St. John Eliot, are also similarly secured. The learned Dr. Humphrey Prideaux, Dean of Norwich, was born here in 1648.

With some slight exceptions, the remains of nine religious edifices in the town and its immediate vicinity have entirely disappeared. The old provincial festivities of Christmas and May-day are attended with many singular customs, traditionally connected with the early history of the place.

PADWORTH, a parish in the hundred of THEALE, county of BERKS, 9 miles (S. W. by W.) from Reading, containing 271 inhabitants. The living is a rectory, in the archdeaconry of Berks, and diocese of Salisbury, rated in the king's books at £6. 6. 8., and in the patronage of the Crown. The church, dedicated to St. John the Baptist, is an ancient structure with a semi-circular chancel, the roof of which is supported by a well-proportioned Norman arch. The Kennet and Avon canal, and the old Roman vallum, or earthwork, called Grime's Dyke, pass through the parish. Elizabeth Brightwell, in 1750, gave £200 South Sea Annuities, for teaching poor children of both sexes.

PAGHAM, a parish in the hundred of ALDWICK, rape of CHICHESTER, county of SUSSEX, 6 miles (S. S. E.) from Chichester, containing 1009 inhabitants. The living is a vicarage, in the peculiar jurisdiction and patronage of the Archbishop of Canterbury, rated in the king's books at £9. 18. 9. The church, dedicated to St.Thomas à Becket, is in the early style of English architecture. The parish is bounded on the south by the English channel.

PAGLESHAM, a parish in the hundred of ROCHFORD, county of ESSEX, 4 miles (N. E. by E.) from Rochford, containing 396 inhabitants. The living is a rectory, in the archdeaconry of Essex, and diocese of London, rated in the king's books at £26, and in the patronage of the Bishop of London. The church is dedicated to St. Peter. This parish includes the western part of Wallisea island: on the north runs the navigable river Crouch, and on the south the Bromhill river.

PAINGTON, a parish in the hundred of HAYTOR, county of DEVON, 5¾ miles (E.) from Totness, containing 1796 inhabitants. The living is a vicarage, to which the perpetual curacy of Marldon is annexed, in the peculiar jurisdiction of the Bishop of Exeter, rated in the king's books at £52. 1. 0½., and in the patronage of the Rev. John Templar. The church, dedicated to St. John the Baptist, has an enriched Norman door, the upper part of the tower and the transept being in the later English style; there are also a screen of elegant tabernacle-work, and a stone pulpit, richly ornamented with foliage. There is a place of worship for Independents. Paington was anciently held in demesne by the Bishops of Exeter, who had here a palace, of which some fragments still remain. It is situated on Torbay, at its western extremity, and carries on a considerable trade in cider, for shipping which and discharging coal, &c., vessels come close up to the village. A small fair is held on Whit-Tuesday. John Kellond, in 1692, gave £100 for teaching, and Charles Kellond, in 1690, £50 for apprenticing, poor children. In 1800, Allan Balfield bequeathed £1000 three per cents. for the education of twenty poor children.

PAINSFORD, a chapelry in the parish of ASHPRINGTON, hundred of COLERIDGE, county of DEVON. The chapel, which was dedicated to St. David, is in ruins. Here is a mineral spring, the water of which is occasionally used for medicinal purposes.

PAINSHAW, a chapelry in the parish of HOUGHTON le SPRING, northern division of EASINGTON ward, county palatine of DURHAM, 3 miles (N. by E.) from Houghton le Spring, containing 2090 inhabitants. The living is a perpetual curacy, in the archdeaconry and diocese of Durham, endowed with £400 private benefaction, and £600 royal bounty, and in the patronage of the Rector of Houghton. The chapel was built in 1746. There is a place of worship for Wesleyan Methodists. Freestone, limestone, and firestone abound here, a considerable quantity of the latter being exported. At Low Lambton, within the township, are some coal-staiths.

PAINSWICK, a market town and parish, in the hundred of BISLEY, county of GLOUCESTER, 7 miles (S. S. E.) from Gloucester, and 100 (W. by N.) from London, comprising the tythings of Edge, Shepscomb, Spoonbed, and Stroudend, and containing 4044 inhabitants. The manor is noticed in Domesday-book under the name of Wiche, among the possessions of Roger de Lacy; its prefix is derived from one of its subsequent proprietors, Pain Fitz-John. The town is situated on the declivity of Spoonbed hill, at the foot of which runs a branch of the Stroud river, and the turnpike roads from Stroud to Gloucester, and from Cheltenham to Bath, pass through it. The streets are neither lighted nor paved; the inhabitants are supplied with water from wells. The manufacture of cloth is extensively carried on in the town and neighbourhood, although, by comparison with its former state, it may be considered on the decline: there are quarries of freestone and weather-stone in the vicinity. The market is on Tuesday, but it is very inconsiderable; there is a large market for sheep on the first Tuesday after All Saints' day (O. S.). Fairs are held, principally for cattle and sheep, on Whit-Tuesday and September 19th. A court leet for the manor is held annually, at which constables and tythingmen are chosen. The living is a vicarage, in the archdeaconry and diocese of Gloucester, rated in the king's books at £14. 15. 2½., and in the patronage of J. Gardener, Esq., and others, as trustees for the inhabitants who pay poor rates. The church, which is dedicated to St. Mary, is a spacious edifice, with a very lofty spire, and a fine ring of twelve bells : it was erected at different periods, and is somewhat remarkable for the incongruous combination of the Grecian and English styles of architecture : the entrance is under a portico of the Ionic order ; Doric columns appear in another part of the building, and, under the battlements on the north side, the spouts represent singularly grotesque heads of demons. In the chancel are monuments of the Jerningham family, to which the manor belonged in the reign of Elizabeth ; and there is a handsome altar-piece, erected in 1743. There are places of worship for Independents and Wesleyan Methodists. A free school was founded, in 1707, for the education of ten boys, by Giles Smith, who bequeathed £200 for this purpose; and £200 more having been raised by voluntary contributions, lands were purchased, now producing about £30 per annum, for which twenty-six boys are educated : other benefactions have since been made, the most considerable of which is the sum of £500, the bequest of John Hillman, in 1808. A benevolent school was established here in 1809, and there is a National school, both supported by subscription. On the summit of Spoonbed hill is an ancient camp, with a double intrenchment, called Kimsbury Castle, King's barrow, or Castle Godwin: it comprehends a space of about three acres, is nearly quadrangular, and is supposed to have been a British fortress, afterwards occupied by the Romans, as many Roman coins, with a sword, and spear-heads greatly corroded, have been found at different periods. In the reign of Edward the Confessor, this camp was occupied by Earl Godwin, who headed an insurrection against the king,'in 1052. During the siege of Gloucester by Charles I., his forces encamped on this hill, and it is related, that after raising the siege, the king being seated on a stone near the camp, with his two elder sons, one of them asked him when they should return home, "Alas! my Son," replied the unfortunate monarch, "I have no home to go to." During the insurrections in the west and other parts of the kingdom, in the reign of Edward VI., Sir Anthony Kingston, then Knight Marshall, being lord of the manor of Painswick, caused a gallows to be erected on Shepscombe Green, in this parish, for the execution of insurgents, and gave three plots of land in his lordship, since called *Gallows' lands*, for the purpose of keeping in readiness a gallows, two ladders, and halters; he likewise appointed the tythingman of Shepscombe to the office of executioner, with an acre of land in the tything, as a reward for his services; a field at Shepscombe, held by the tythingman for the time being, is still known by the appellation of Hangman's Acre.

PAITTON, a hamlet in the parish of MONKS' KIRBY, Kirby division of the hundred of KNIGHTLOW, county of WARWICK, 5¼ miles (N. N. W.) from Rugby, containing 552 inhabitants.

PAKEFIELD, a parish in the hundred of MUTFORD and LOTHINGLAND, county of SUFFOLK, 2¼ miles (S. S. W.) from Lowestoft, containing 349 inhabitants. The living is a discharged rectory, in medieties, in the archdeaconry of Suffolk, and diocese of Norwich, both rated in the king's books at £14, and in the patronage of the Earl of Gosford. The church is dedicated to All Saints. Pakefield is a small fishing-village, lying on the coast of the North sea. The Rev. Francis Cunningham, rector, supports schools for the education of children.

PAKENHAM, a parish in the hundred of THEDWESTRY, county of SUFFOLK, 5 miles (E. N. E.) from Bury St. Edmund's, containing 928 inhabitants. The living is a discharged vicarage, in the archdeaconry of Sudbury, and diocese of Norwich, rated in the king's books at £10. 3. 9., and in the patronage of Lord Calthorpe. The church is dedicated to St. Mary.

PALGRAVE, a hamlet in the parish of SPORLE, southern division of the hundred of GREENHOE, county of NORFOLK, 4 miles (N. N. E.) from Swaffham. The population is returned with the parish. Here was formerly a chapel, which has been demolished.

PALGRAVE, a parish in the hundred of HARTISMERE, county of SUFFOLK, 1¼ mile (S.) from Diss, containing 654 inhabitants. The living is a rectory, annexed to the vicarage of Sporle, in the archdeaconry of Sudbury, and diocese of Norwich, rated in the king's books at £19. 11. 3. The church, which was dedicated to St. Peter, has been destroyed. There is a place of worship for Unitarians.

PALLING, a parish in the hundred of HAPPING, county of NORFOLK, 11¼ miles (E. S. E.) from North

Walsham, containing 300 inhabitants. The living is a discharged vicarage, annexed to the rectory of Waxham, in the archdeaconry of Norfolk, and diocese of Norwich, rated in the king's books at £2. 6. 8., and endowed with £800 royal bounty. The church is dedicated to St. Margaret.

PAMBER, a parish in the hundred of BARTON-STACEY, Andover division, though locally in that of Basingstoke, Basingstoke division, of the county of SOUTHAMPTON, 4¼ miles (N. N. W.) from Basingstoke, containing 409 inhabitants. The living is a perpetual curacy, in the archdeaconry and diocese of Winchester, and in the patronage of the Provost and Fellows of Queen's College, Oxford.

PAMINGTON, a tything in the parish of ASHCHURCH, hundred of TEWKESBURY, county of GLOUCESTER, 3 miles (E.) from Tewkesbury, containing 126 inhabitants.

PAMPISFORD, a parish in the hundred of CHILFORD, county of CAMBRIDGE, 4½ miles (W. by N.) from Linton, containing 285 inhabitants. The living is a discharged vicarage, in the archdeaconry and diocese of Ely, rated in the king's books at £8, endowed with £200 royal bounty, and in the patronage of the Trustees of J. Mortlock, Esq. The church, dedicated to St. John the Baptist, is principally in the Norman style of architecture.

PANBOROUGH, a hamlet in the parish of WEDMORE, hundred of BEMPSTONE, though locally in the hundred of Glaston-Twelve-Hides, county of SOMERSET, 5 miles (W.) from Wells. The population is returned with the parish.

PANCRAS (ST.), a parish in the Holborn division of the hundred of OSSULSTONE, county of MIDDLESEX, a suburb to London, containing 71,838 inhabitants. This parish exhibits, in an extraordinary degree, the vast increase which within the last half century, and particularly within the last ten years, has taken place in the numerous districts bordering upon the metropolis. In the year 1765, it was a remote and isolated spot, consisting of a few scattered dwellings, and containing only sixty inhabitants, and its ancient church, of diminutive size, suited to the smallness of the population, formed a romantic feature in the landscape. Since that period, large tracts of meadow land have been covered with buildings, and it is now one of the most extensive and populous parishes in the vicinity of London; Kentish-Town, Camden - Town, Somers-Town, and Battle-Bridge, each a thickly-inhabited district, forming only chapelries and hamlets within its limits. Among the principal additions are, the numerous spacious and regularly formed streets, leading from the north side of Holborn to the New-road, intersected by various handsome streets from Gray's-Inn-lane, and Regent, Mecklenburgh, Brunswick, Tavistock, Gordon, and Fitzroy squares, handsome ranges of modern houses, the areas of which are tastefully laid out; the numerous continuous lines of respectable buildings on both sides of the New-road, extending from Battle-Bridge to Albany-street; Cumberland market, an extensive quadrangular area, surrounded with neat brick houses, of which the centre will be appropriated to the hay market now about to be removed from St. James'; Clarence market, the continuation of Tottenham Court-road to Primrose-hill, Chalk-farm, and Haverstoke-hill, on the Hampstead road, comprising Mornington-crescent, and numerous handsome villas and pleasant cottages; and the eastern ranges of building in the Regent's Park, including part of the Zoological gardens. The streets are well paved, and lighted with gas, and the inhabitants are supplied with water by the West Middlesex and New River companies, the latter of which has a large reservoir in the Hampstead-road. Of the principal buildings on the south side of the New-road, the London University is the most conspicuous: it occupies an area of seven acres at the upper end of Gower-street, and was founded in 1827, for the purpose of affording to the youth of the metropolis, and to such as might object to the religious conformity required at the Universities of Oxford and Cambridge, a liberal course of instruction, calculated to qualify them for professional pursuits. The institution is governed by a council of twenty-four, who appoint a warden, and the several professors in the various departments of literature, to whom a regular stipend is paid till the fees of the students form an income sufficient for their remuneration. According to the statutes, the funds of the institution are not to be less than £150,000, nor more than £300,000, advanced on shares of £100 each, every proprietor receiving a dividend of £4 per cent., and having the privilege of appointing one pupil. The course of studies comprehends the ancient, modern, and oriental languages and literature, the mathematics, natural, moral, and experimental philosophy, mechanics, astronomy, ancient and modern history, logic, political economy, botany, chemistry, medicine, and surgery. The buildings, of which the first stone was laid by the Duke of Sussex, in 1827, are not yet completed: the principal range has, in the centre, a lofty portico of ten Corinthian pillars, supporting a cornice and triangular pediment, surmounted by a handsome elliptical dome, and on each side a noble façade of the Doric order: it contains the lecture-rooms, libraries, the museum, and offices for the present use of the professors and students, projecting behind which are the different theatres, laboratory, &c.: the entire plan is intended to include two projecting wings in front also, of corresponding character with the central range, having in the centre of each a tetrastyle portico of the Corinthian order, surmounted by a pediment and dome, facing the interior of the quadrangle, and having the end fronts decorated with four Doric pilasters, supporting a cornice and triangular pediment.

The Colosseum, in the Regent's Park, erected in 1824, for the exhibition of the grand panoramic view of London, and of the environs for ten miles round, taken by Mr. Horner, from the cross of St. Paul's Cathedral, is a structure very much resembling the Pantheon at Rome, a stately polygonal building of stone, four hundred feet in circumference, with a massive and boldly projecting portico of six columns, of the Grecian Doric style, supporting a cornice and triangular pediment; from the main building rises a spacious and well-proportioned dome, crowned with a parapet, forming a circular gallery, from which an extensive and pleasing view of the surrounding country is obtained. A flight of steps leading from the entrance affords a descent to the saloon on the right hand, a circular apartment, fitted up as a tent, with festooned and flowing draperies, and containing a beautiful assemblage of statuary, sculptures, alto relievos, bronzes, verds antique, and numerous specimens

of beautiful design and exquisite art: in this interesting collection of marbles are full-length statues and busts of the principal public characters, the muses, personifications of the passions and virtues, and some composition pieces of striking beauty, several subjects from the pagan mythology, a fine sculpture in marble of Christ on the Cross, in alto relievo, by Sievier, various models of buildings, and many objects of interest and attraction; among which is preserved the only perfect copy of the only three in Europe of the sacred code of the Burmese laws, from the collection of Lieut. Brand, R.N., taken from a niche in a pagoda by the brother of that gentleman, at the storming of Syriam, in 1825, only a few minutes before the destruction of the fort. In the central part of the saloon, exclusively of a spiral staircase on the outside, is a circular enclosure, containing a coved chamber, capable of holding twenty persons, which by machinery is raised to the platform of the gallery from which the panorama is viewed. The view of London is arranged in the interior of the dome, well lighted by a circular sky-light, which surrounds the upper section, and by which also the interior of the building is lighted: the view, extending over so wide a field, embraces an almost inconceivable multitude of objects, represented with complete effect, and with the utmost accuracy and precision, and which, from the truth of their relative proportions, the accuracy of the linear and aërial perspective, and the just distribution of light and shade, are powerfully delusive in their effect upon the sight; and those in the distance, which are almost undistinguishable by the eye, are, with the aid of the prospect-glass, brought into view in all the fulness of minute and faithful detail. The conservatories, abounding with choice specimens of exotic plants, and ornamented with jets d'eau, fountains, and grotto-work, afford a delightful promenade; and the Swiss cottage, containing several apartments, with windows in recesses, affording miniature views of the beautiful and romantic scenery peculiar to that country, are objects of high interest; a veranda surrounds the front of the building, which appears to be on an island in a lake, in which fish of various kinds are seen gliding in every direction, and numerous waterfowls sailing along the surface, or seated on the points of rock which rise above it; the distant view is a mass of rugged rocks, in the fissures of which are various waterfalls, and on the higher crags, which are interspersed with trees and mountain plants, are seen the eagle and other birds of prey. The whole of the apartments, promenades, galleries, and conservatories, are warmed to the temperature of summer, by hot water, conveyed in tubes by means of an excellent apparatus. The exterior of the building forms a grand and interesting object in the scenery of the Regent's Park, from many parts of which it is seen with beautiful effect, and the noble dome appears with striking grandeur from many of the higher grounds in various parts of the town.

Beyond the Colosseum, on that side of the Regent's Park which is in this parish are Cambridge-place, a range of plain substantial houses, undistinguished by any architectural features; Chester-terrace, an elegant pile of buildings, consisting of a centre decorated with a range of eight Corinthian pillars supporting an entablature and cornice, with similar arrangements of four columns at each extremity, and two handsome wings projecting at right angles, and connected by lofty arched portals with the main building; Cumberland-terrace, consisting of a centre and two continuous wings of the Ionic order, connected by arched portals; the tympana of the central pediment and of those in each wing being enriched with alto relievos, and surmounted on the apex and at each end with finely-sculptured statues; and Gloucester-terrace, a handsome range of building, having in the centre six Ionic pillars supporting a cornice surmounted by an open balustrade, and a similar arrangement of four pillars at each end.

At the north-western extremity of the park, are the gardens of the Zoological Society, recently laid out in walks and shrubberies, and divided into compartments, in which various buildings have been erected, for the reception and classification of animals of every description, from every part of the globe, of which there is a beautiful and extensive collection, consisting of more than six hundred species of mammalia, including feræ and pecora, four hundred birds, one thousand reptiles, one thousand testacea and crustacea, and thirty thousand insects, classed according to their respective genera, and secured within enclosures accommodated to their several habits, and well adapted to their complete exhibition. The entrance to the south garden is through a rustic lodge, leading to a broad terrace, at the extremity of which, on the right hand, is the bear pit, containing six varieties of that animal, with a rugged pole in the centre, on which they climb for exercise. Below the terrace, on the north side, is an enclosed lawn, with a piece of water for aquatic birds, among which are, the cormorant, the sea-pheasant, the gull, several black swans, and other varieties of water-fowl: nearly opposite is an aviary, in which are the Balearic, or crowned, the Numidian, or Demoiselle, and the African, or gigantic, crane; white and black storks; the tiger bittern; two white spoon-bills; and several varieties of the curassow, and the heron: to the west is an enclosure, in which are two pair of white pelicans. At the foot of the terrace is an octagonal cage, containing beautiful specimens of the red and yellow, blue and yellow, and red and blue, maccaw, and of the sulphur-crested cockatoo; and opposite to this is the lama-house and paddock, in which are several red and black specimens of that beautiful animal: in the roof of this building is a collection of pigeons. To the south, is a court-yard, in which are mastiffs from Cuba, wolf-dogs from Italy and Hungary; in a shed is a fine dromedary; in others are several varieties of deer; and in a den, a large sloth bear. On one side is a building, containing dens for feline quadrupeds, among which are, an African lion, a lioness, tigers, panthers, leopards, a jaguar, a puma, and chittahs, or hunting leopards; and on the opposite side, a range of building, in which are, American fallow deer, a gnu, zebras, two American tapirs, antelopes, nylghaus, two gazelles, a nine-banded armadillo, and some of the more delicate birds, among which is the scarlet ibis. In the adjoining grounds are aviaries, containing elegant varieties of the hybrid, gold, silver, and ring-necked Chinese pheasants; and near them is an enclosure with a pond, for the white, or polar bear. In this part of the gardens are aviaries for eagles, vultures, falcons, kites, and other birds of prey, with a variety of owls of every species; and enclosures for seals, otters, beavers, and land tortoises. To the north of

these is a house for monkeys and baboons, of which there is an extensive variety from every part of the world. In the western division of the cattle sheds are two zebras, the zebus, the Brahmin bull, the bison, or American buffaloe, and several other buffaloes. An archway, ornamented on the south side of the entrance, with a greyhound and a buffaloe, well sculptured in stone, and surmounted by a balustrade, behind which is a handsome range of four Doric pillars, supporting a triangular pediment, leads under the road surrounding the park, from the south into the north garden, which has more recently been added, and is similarly laid out; and in which are various ranges of building, the principal of them containing several striped and spotted hyænas, leopards, a jaguar, several ocelets, civet cats, racoons, jackalls, coati mondi, agoutis, a harpy eagle, eagles from Africa and Chili, vultures, condors, and other birds. Adjoining this building is a kennel, in which are several dogs from different countries, and an Esquimaux dog of great beauty, brought over by Capt. Sir Edward Parry; and to the west of it are a shed and paddock, in which are four specimens of the ostrich, of remarkably fine growth. Nearly adjoining is the kangaroo hut, beyond which is a large building, not yet completed, for the reception of the Wapiti deer, from North America, given by the king, who has also presented to the society the collection of birds and beasts of his late Majesty, George IV. At the farthest extremity of the garden are some sties, in which are a wild boar, and several species of the peccary. The cavalry barracks in Albany-road are neatly built of brick, and occupy an area of eight acres and a half: the buildings comprise accommodation for four hundred men, with stabling for their horses, a riding-school, infirmary, magazine, and requisite offices for the establishment, and include an extensive ground for exercise. The city light-horse barracks, in Gray's-Inn-lane, are a neat range of substantial brick building, with a gateway entrance ornamented with sculpture. King's Cross, at Battle-Bridge, is a handsome pile of freestone building, having a square basement, and at each angle a projecting group of two Doric pillars, designed to support pedestals, on which it is intended to erect the statues of George I., II., III., and IV.; above this stage are to be four illuminated dials surmounted by a pedestal, on which is to be placed a statue of his present Majesty, King William IV. The Tottenham-street theatre is a plain building: the interior comprises a pit, two tiers of boxes, and a gallery, and is well arranged for the reception of about eight hundred persons: performances take place regularly during the season. The Panarmonion is a handsome small theatre, opened by Signior Lanza as a dramatic school: the exterior consists of a plain and neat façade, with a niche over the entrance, containing a statue; the interior is elegantly decorated and conveniently arranged. The bazaar, in Liverpool-street, to which the principal entrance is from Gray's-Inn-lane, is a handsome quadrangular building of stone, originally intended solely as a repository for horses, but lately adapted also to the purposes of a general bazaar; around the quadrangle are stabling and boxes for horses, above which are extensive galleries for carriages; the public room, of large dimensions, is appropriated to the sale of trinkets, millinery, perfumery, toys, and other similar wares. Bagnigge wells, noted for its chalybeate water, and still a place of resort as a tea-garden, St. Chadd's wells, and Pancras wells, are in this parish. Brookes' menagerie, in the New-road, has long been celebrated for an extensive collection of foreign birds, constantly on sale. Croggon's manufactory and shew-rooms of artificial stone, which, by a process of fire, is rendered proof against the injuries of the atmosphere, contains an elegant assortment of fonts, shrines, and statuary, with many beautiful devices in bas and alto relievo, Scagliola marbles, and busts. On the line of the New-road are numerous statuaries and masons, and shew-rooms for ornamental marble chimney-pieces; there are also several organ-builders and piano-forte manufacturers, but there is no particular branch of trade peculiar to the parish: the Regent's canal passes through it, and there are several wharfs in various parts. In addition to the newly-formed Cumberland market, which is intended for hay, there is an extensive general market for butchers' meat and provisions, in a part of Somers-Town, called the Brill. The parish is within the jurisdiction of the stipendiary magistrates of the metropolis, and within the limits of the new police act: the jurisdiction of the county court, in Kingsgate - street, Holborn, for the recovery of debts under 40s., also extends to this parish.

The living is a vicarage, in the peculiar jurisdiction and patronage of the Dean and Chapter of St. Paul's, rated in the king's books at £9. 5. The old parish church, now a chapel of ease, has undergone so many alterations and repairs, that it retains few vestiges of its original character: it is of great antiquity, and the churchyard has been long the burial-place of Roman Catholics; of many eminent foreigners, among whom were the Archbishop of Narbonne, and seven bishops expelled from France; General Paoli; several of the French marshals; the Chevalier D'Eon; and of the following distinguished persons; viz., Mary Wollstonecroft Godwin: John Walker, author of a treatise on Elocution, and compiler of the Pronouncing Dictionary; Tiberius Cavallo, a philosophical writer; Woollet, an eminent engraver; Webbe, the glee composer; Dr. J. E. Grabe, a learned divine; and Jeremiah Collier, a celebrated nonconformist preacher. The new parochial church in Euston-square is a splendid structure, begun in May 1819, and consecrated May 7th, 1822, having been built and furnished at an expense of upwards of £76,600: it is after the model of the temple of Erectheus at Athens, with a lofty tower of three stages, resembling the Temple of the Winds; at the west entrance is a stately portico of six fluted Ionic columns, supporting an entablature and cornice, surmounted by a triangular pediment; at the east end are two projecting wings forming the vestry and registry, the roofs of which, on the facia, are supported on caryatides: the interior is chastely decorated, and the altar-piece is ornamented with six verd antique columns of Scagliola marble. A new church, in Regent-square, was erected by grant of the parliamentary commissioners in 1824, at an expense of £16,025. 10. 2., and contains one thousand eight hundred and thirty-two sittings, of which seven hundred and seventy-four are free: it is a handsome edifice, in the Grecian style of architecture, with a portico of the Ionic order, and an octagonal tower of two stages. The living is a district incumbency, in the patronage of the Vicar. Churches have been built also

at Camden-Town and Somers-Town, by parliamentary grant, and a chapel by subscription at Kentish-Town, in this parish, which are severally described in the account of those places. Fitzroy proprietary episcopal chapel is a neat building of brick. A chapel to the church of St. James', Piccadilly, with an extensive cemetery in Hampstead-road; the chapel and cemetery belonging to St. Giles' in the Fields; the burial-grounds of St. Andrew's, Holborn, St. George's, Bloomsbury, St. George's the Martyr, and St. Martin's in the Fields, are in this parish. There are places of worship for Baptists, Huntingtonians, Independents, and Calvinistic, Wesleyan, and other Methodists, a Scottish church, and a Roman Catholic chapel. Of these the Scotch church in Regent-square is an elegant structure in the later style of English architecture, with two lofty towers at the western entrance. The St. Pancras female charity school, in Hampstead-road, is supported by funds arising from donations, and by annual subscriptions: the premises are neatly built of brick, and accommodated to the reception of sixty-five girls, who are maintained, clothed, and instructed till fourteen years of age, when they are placed out to service. A National school, in which are more than four hundred children, is supported by subscription; and there is a school in connexion with the Roman Catholic chapel, for the maintenance, clothing, and instruction of Catholic children.

The Foundling hospital, situated on the north side of Guildford-street, between Brunswick and Mecklenburgh squares, was founded by charter of George II. in 1739, "for the maintenance and instruction of deserted infants, who are put under the care of nurses in the country till of a proper age to receive instruction: there are generally about four hundred children in the institution, who, after having received a suitable education, are placed out apprentices, or put to service, and, at the discretion of the committee, are supplied with money, clothes, or other necessaries, to the amount of £10 each. The income is about £14,000 per annum, arising from funded property, the produce of sums given for admission to the chapel, the children's work, and subscriptions. The premises consist of a spacious and elegant chapel, which occupies the centre, and two wings for the dormitories, schools, offices, and apartments for the conductors of the establishment. The chapel is decorated with a fine altar-piece, painted by West, and the organ was presented by Handel, who devoted to the use of the charity the profits arising from the performance of his oratorio of the Messiah. The Welch charity school, in Gray's-Inn-lane, was established in 1714, for the maintenance, clothing, and education of children, born of Welch parents resident in or near London. The premises, occupying three sides of a quadrangle, are handsomely built of brick, and contain school-rooms and dormitories for the children, and apartments for the master and mistress: in this institution are several interesting manuscripts illustrative of the history of the ancient Britons. St. Katherine's hospital was originally founded by Matilda, wife of Stephen, in 1148, and the endowment was augmented by Eleanor, queen dowager of Henry III., for a master, three clerical brethren, three sisters, ten bedeswomen, and six poor clerks: the institution was subsequently patronised by succeeding queens of England, and takes its name from

Katherine, consort of Henry VIII. On the construction of St. Katherine's docks, near the Tower, the old buildings were taken down, in 1826, and the establishment removed to the Regent's Park, where the present buildings were erected. The premises, handsomely built of white brick, comprise two ranges, consisting of three separate houses, in the Elizabethan style, with an oriel window at the end front, for the residence of the brethren and sisters, between which is the chapel, an elegant structure in the later style of English architecture, with two angular turrets at the west end, crowned with bold pinnacles; the west front is ornamented with sculptures, and the entrance doorway and window above it are of elegant design; the windows of the chapel are of lofty dimensions and enriched with tracery, and the large east window is embellished with painted glass: adjoining the chapel is the school, in which twenty-five boys and twelve girls are instructed and clothed from the funds of the establishment. Opposite to the hospital, in the area of the park, is the elegant villa of Sir Herbert Taylor, who is master of the hospital. The small-pox hospital at Battle-Bridge was instituted by subscription, in 1746, and the present building erected in 1767; it consists of a centre and two wings, handsomely built of brick, and surmounted by a central cupola and dome: since the introduction of vaccination, the practice of inoculation has been abandoned, and not less than one hundred thousand patients have been vaccinated in this institution. Near the building is a fever hospital, of later erection, for the reception of patients afflicted with typhus and scarlet fever, and other contagious diseases.

PANCRASSWEEK, a parish in the hundred of BLACK TORRINGTON, county of DEVON, 4 miles (W. N. W.) from Holsworthy, containing 529 inhabitants. The living is a perpetual curacy, with the vicarage of Bradworthy, in the archdeaconry of Totness, and diocese of Exeter, endowed with £400 royal bounty. The church is dedicated to St. Pancras. The river Tamar, and the Bude and Launceston canal, pass through the parish. At Lana is the site of an ancient chapel.

PANFIELD, a parish in the hundred of HINCKFORD, county of ESSEX, 2½ miles (N. W. by N.) from Braintree, containing 263 inhabitants. The living is a rectory, in the archdeaconry of Middlesex, and diocese of London, rated in the king's books at £10. 10. The Rev. R. L. Page was patron in 1809. The church is dedicated to St. Mary and St. Christopher. Panfield hall, built in 1546, is a curious specimen of the domestic architecture of that period. An Alien priory of Benedictine monks, subordinate to the abbey of St. Stephen, at Caen in Normandy, was founded here in the reign of William the Conqueror; but in that of Henry V. it became parcel of the possessions of the prior and convent of Canterbury, and at the dissolution was granted to Sir Giles Capel.

PANGBOURN, a parish in the hundred of READING, county of BERKS, 5½ miles (W. N. W.) from Reading, containing 703 inhabitants. The living is a rectory, in the archdeaconry of Berks, and diocese of Salisbury, rated in the king's books at £10, and in the patronage of J. S. Breedon, Esq. The church is dedicated to St. James. There is a place of worship for Independents. A fine trout stream, called the Pang, runs through the parish, and flows into the Thames,

which separates this from the parish of Whitchurch in Oxfordshire. A school for twelve boys was founded in 1685, by John Breedon, Esq., who endowed it with a rent-charge of £40, payable by the lord of the manor; the master's salary is £25 a year, and the remainder is applied in apprenticing the boys. Mrs. Dibble, in 1800, bequeathed £100 three per cents. towards repairing the school premises.

PANNALL, a parish in the lower division of the wapentake of CLARO, West riding of the county of YORK, 7 miles (W. N. W.) from Wetherby, containing, with a part of the township of Swindon, 1314 inhabitants. The living is a discharged vicarage, in the peculiar jurisdiction of the Court of the Honour of Knaresborough, rated in the king's books at £5. 5., endowed with £323 private benefaction, and £200 royal bounty. The Rev. R. B. Hunter was patron in 1816. The church is dedicated to St. Robert of Knaresborough. There is a place of worship for Wesleyan Methodists. Five poor children are educated for a trifling annuity, the gift of Richard Wright, in 1813.

PANTEAGUE, a parish in the lower division of the hundred of USK, county of MONMOUTH, 4 miles (W. S. W.) from Usk, containing 1478 inhabitants. The living is a discharged rectory, in the archdeaconry and diocese of Llandaff, rated in the king's books at £7. 10. 2½., and in the patronage of Capel Hanbury Leigh, Esq. The church is dedicated to St. Mary.

PANTON, a parish in the eastern division of the wapentake of WRAGGOE, parts of LINDSEY, county of LINCOLN, 3¼ miles (E. by N.) from Wragby, containing 83 inhabitants. The living is a rectory, in the archdeaconry and diocese of Lincoln, rated in the king's books at £12. Edmund Turnor, Esq. was patron in 1825. The church is dedicated to St. Andrew.

PANXWORTH, a parish in the hundred of WALSHAM, county of NORFOLK, 4½ miles (N. W. by W.) from Acle. The population is returned with Ranworth. The living is a discharged rectory, with the vicarage of Woodbastwick annexed, in the archdeaconry and diocese of Norwich.

PAPCASTLE, a joint township with Goat, in the parish of BRIDEKIRK, ALLERDALE ward below Darwent, county of CUMBERLAND, 1 mile (N. W.) from Cockermouth, containing 384 inhabitants. It is finely situated on an eminence above the river Darwent, and occupies the site of a Roman castrum, where a great number of urns and coins, remains of baths, &c., have been discovered. After the Conquest, the castle becoming the property of Waldeof, Lord of Allerdale, he caused it to be demolished, and the materials to be used in the erection of Cockermouth castle, the seat of his descendants.

PAPERHAUGH, a township in the parish of ROTHBURY, western division of COQUETDALE ward, county of NORTHUMBERLAND, 3½ miles (E. S. E.) from Rothbury, containing 80 inhabitants. The river Coquet runs through the township, parallel to which a fine road has been recently made from Rothbury to Weldon, at the expense of about £1400..

PAPPLEWICK, a parish in the northern division of the wapentake of BROXTOW, county of NOTTINGHAM, 7½ miles (N. by W.) from Nottingham, containing, with Newstead Priory, 767 inhabitants. The living is a perpetual curacy, in the archdeaconry of Nottingham, and diocese of York, endowed with £400 royal bounty, and £1200 parliamentary grant, and in the patronage of Fontayne Wilson, Esq. The church, dedicated to St. James, was rebuilt in 1797, in the later style of English architecture. Here are extensive cotton-mills, affording employment to a great number of persons. In the side of a hill in the neighbourhood is a curious ancient excavation, with passages and doorways, traditionally called Robin Hood's Stable.

PAPWORTH (ST. AGNES), a parish partly in the hundred of Toseland, county of Huntingdon, but chiefly in the hundred of Papworth, county of Cambridge, 5 miles (N. N. W.) from Caxton, containing 74 inhabitants. The living is a rectory, in the archdeaconry and diocese of Ely, rated in the king's books at £9. 16. 3., and in the patronage of Henry Piper Sperling, Esq. The church, dedicated to St. John the Baptist, is in Cambridgeshire. From the extensive ruins scattered throughout the parish, Papworth appears to have been formerly a place of considerable importance, and the remains of the old manor-house, now a farm-house, still exhibit vestiges of decayed magnificence. There is a saline chalybeate spring in the parish, which at one time was in great repute.

PAPWORTH (ST. EVERARD), a parish in the hundred of Papworth, county of Cambridge, 4 miles (N. N. W.) from Caxton, containing 117 inhabitants. The living is a discharged rectory, in the archdeaconry and diocese of Ely, rated in the king's books at £9. 15. 10., and in the patronage of the Master and Fellows of Trinity College, Cambridge. The church is dedicated to St. Peter.

PARACOMBE, a parish in the hundred of Sherwill, county of Devon, 11 miles (E. by S.) from Ilfracombe, containing 364 inhabitants. The living is a rectory, in the archdeaconry of Barnstable, and diocese of Exeter, rated in the king's books at £13. 10. 10., and in the patronage of L. St. Albyn, Esq. There are vestiges of an ancient fortification in the neighbourhood.

PARBOLD, a township in the parish of Eccleston, hundred of Leyland, county palatine of Lancaster, 5¾ miles (N. W.) from Wigan, containing 339 inhabitants.

PARDSEY, a joint township with Ullock and Dean-Scales, in the parish of Dean, Allerdale ward above Darwent, county of Cumberland, 4 miles (S. S. W.) from Cockermouth. The population is returned with Ullock.

PARHAM, a parish in the hundred of Plomesgate, county of Suffolk, 3½ miles (N. by E.) from Wickham-Market, containing 448 inhabitants. The living is a discharged vicarage, consolidated with that of Hacheston, in the archdeaconry of Suffolk, and diocese of Norwich, endowed with £200 private benefaction, and £200 royal bounty. Mrs. White was patroness in 1818. The church is dedicated to St. Mary. Parham Hall is one of the curious remaining specimens of domestic architecture prevalent in the reign of Elizabeth. Richard Porter bequeathed a cottage for a school-house, and a rent-charge of £12 for teaching twelve poor boys of Parham and Hacheston.

PARHAM, a parish in the hundred of West Easwrith, rape of Arundel, county of Sussex, 6 miles (N. E. by N.) from Arundel, containing 77 inhabitants.

The living is a discharged rectory, in the archdeaconry and diocese of Chichester, rated in the king's books at £10, and in the patronage of Lord de la Zouche. The church, dedicated to St. Peter, is in the later style of English architecture: it was repaired and the tower added in 1800, and has an ancient leaden font in good preservation. Here was formerly a cell to the abbey of Glastonbury.

PARK, a ward in the parish of St. Stephen, hundred of Cashio, or liberty of St. Alban's, county of Hertford, 2½ miles (S.) from St. Alban's. The population is returned with the parish.

PARK-END, a township in the parish of Audley, northern division of the hundred of Pirehill, county of Stafford, containing 88 inhabitants.

PARKGATE, a hamlet in the township of Leighton, parish of Neston, higher division of the hundred of Wirrall, county palatine of Chester, 12 miles (N. W.) from Chester, and 192 (N. W.) from London. The importance of this place is derived from its being the resort of visitors during the bathing-season: it consists principally of one long and irregular range of houses built of brick, which front the æstuary of the Dee, over which is a commodious ferry to Flint: here is a custom-house for vessels loading from the contiguous collieries: formerly this place was a sea-port of considerable importance, and packets and other vessels were employed, especially in the trade with Ireland; but at present it is neglected as a packet station, vessels of burden being prevented from approaching the quay, owing to the formation of a large sand-bank, which greatly impedes the navigation of the channel.

PARKHAM, a parish in the hundred of Shebbear, county of Devon, 6½ miles (S.W.) from Bideford, containing 967 inhabitants. The living is a rectory, in the archdeaconry of Barnstable, and diocese of Exeter, rated in the king's books at £20. 6. 8. The Rev. Dr. Woodcock was patron in 1824. The church, dedicated to St. James, has an enriched Norman door. A school is supported by the united bequests of John Lovering, in 1671, and Wear Giffard. Bableigh, in this parish, was long held by the family of Risdon, of which the county historian was a member.

PARKHOLD, a township in the parish of Ledbury, hundred of Radlow, county of Hereford, 2 miles (S. by E.) from Ledbury, containing 55 inhabitants.

PARK-LEYS, an extra-parochial district, in the northern division of the wapentake of Thurgarton, county of Nottingham, containing 10 inhabitants.

PARK-QUARTER, a township in the parish of Stanhope, north-western division of Darlington ward, county palatine of Durham, 3 miles (W.) from Stanhope, containing 1259 inhabitants.

PARKSTON, a chapelry in the parish of Canford Magna, hundred of Cogdean, Shaston (East) division of the county of Dorset, 2 miles (E. by N.) from Poole, containing 385 inhabitants. The chapel contains four hundred free sittings, towards defraying the expense of which the Incorporated Society for building and enlarging churches and chapels contributed £500.

PARLEY (WEST), a parish in that part of the hundred of Cranborne which is in the Shaston (East) division of the county of Dorset, 6¾ miles (E. S. E.) from Wimborne Minster, containing 204 inhabitants. The living is a rectory, in the archdeaconry of Dorset, and diocese of Bristol, rated in the king's books at £6. 17. 6. Thomas Deverell, Esq. and others were patrons in 1798. There is a place of worship for Independents. The navigable river Stour flows past the village.

PARLINGTON, a township in the parish of ABER-FORD, lower division of the wapentake of SKYRACK, West riding of the county of YORK, 7 miles (S. W.) from Tadcaster, containing 229 inhabitants.

PARLY, a joint tything with Hurn, in the parish and hundred of CHRISTCHURCH, New Forest (West) division of the county of SOUTHAMPTON. The population is returned with the parish.

PARME, a joint township with Mooresbarrow, in that part of the parish of MIDDLEWICH which is in the hundred of NORTHWICH, county palatine of CHESTER, 2¼ miles (E. by S.) from Middlewich. The population is returned with Mooresbarrow.

PARNDON (GREAT), a parish in the hundred of HARLOW, county of ESSEX, 3½ miles (S. W. by W.) from Harlow, containing 396 inhabitants. The living is a rectory, in the jurisdiction of the Commissary of Essex and Herts, concurrently with the Consistorial Court of the Bishop of London, rated in the king's books at £16. 10. 7½., and in the patronage of the Hon. W. T. L. P. Wellesley.

PARNDON (LITTLE), a parish in the hundred of HARLOW, county of ESSEX, 2¼ miles (W. by S.) from Harlow, containing 103 inhabitants. The living is a discharged rectory, in the jurisdiction of the Commissary of Essex and Herts, concurrently with the Consistorial Court of the Bishop of London, rated in the king's books at £6. William Smith, Esq. was patron in 1812. The church is dedicated to St. Mary.

PARR, a township in the parish of PRESCOT, hundred of WEST DERBY, county palatine of LANCASTER, 3½ miles (W. by S.) from Newton in Mackerfield, containing 1523 inhabitants. It adjoins the eastern part of the town of St. Helen's.

PARSON-DROVE, a chapelry in the parish of LEVERINGTON, hundred of WISBEACH, Isle of ELY, county of CAMBRIDGE, 4¾ miles (W. by S.) from Wisbeach, containing 675 inhabitants. The living is a perpetual curacy, with the rectory of Leverington, in the peculiar jurisdiction of the Bishop of Ely. The chapel is dedicated to St. John the Baptist. A school is supported by annual subscriptions amounting to about £15.

PARTINGTON, a township in the parish of BOW-DON, hundred of BUCKLOW, county palatine of CHESTER, 5 miles (N. W.) from Altrincham, containing 434 inhabitants. There is a place of worship for Independents. The village is situated on the navigable river Mersey, where are extensive paper-mills, a mill-board manufactory, a large corn-mill, and two tan-yards.

PARTNEY, a parish in the Wold division of the wapentake of CANDLESHOE, parts of LINDSEY, county of LINCOLN, 1½ mile (N. by E.) from Spilsby, containing 293 inhabitants. The living is a discharged rectory, in the archdeaconry and diocese of Lincoln, rated in the king's books at £11. 10. 2½., and in the patronage of Lord Gwydir. The church is dedicated to St. Nicholas. There is a place of worship for Baptists. So early as the seventh century, a monastery is said to have existed at Partney; and it is certain that, in the time of Henry I., there was an hospital dedicated to St. Mary Magda-

lene: Bede also mentions another religious establishment here, over which the abbess Edelhild presided.

PARTON, a township in the parish of MORESBY, ALLERDALE ward above Darwent, county of CUMBER-LAND, 1¾ mile (N.) from Whitehaven, containing 496 inhabitants. There is a place of worship for Independents. Several vessels were employed here in the coal trade until 1795, when the pier was washed away by an unusually high tide, since which the harbour has been resorted to by only a few fishing-boats: north of the village is an extensive iron-foundry. Some years ago a tunnel was constructed through Rednees point, in continuation of a railway from the neighbouring coalworks to Whitehaven. A free school was erected, in 1818, by Joseph Williamson, Esq., with an endowment of £42 per annum, to which Chilwell Williamson, Esq. has since bequeathed a house for the master, who teaches sixty children.

PARTON, a township in the parish of THURSBY, ward and county of CUMBERLAND, 2¼ miles (N. E.) from Wigton, containing 95 inhabitants.

PARWICK, a parish in the hundred of WIRKS-WORTH, county of DERBY, 6 miles (N. by E.) from Ashbourn, containing 551 inhabitants. The living is a perpetual curacy, in the archdeaconry of Derby, and diocese of Lichfield and Coventry, endowed with £400 private benefaction, £400 royal bounty, and £600 parliamentary grant, and in the patronage of William Evans, Esq. The church, dedicated to St. Peter, has some portions of Norman architecture. A railway from the Peak Forest canal to the Cromford canal crosses the northern part of the parish. William Beresford, in 1695, granted certain land, now producing about £8 per annum, for which ten poor children are instructed. Parwick is in the honour of Tutbury, duchy of Lancaster, and within the jurisdiction of a court of pleas held at Tutbury every third Tuesday, for the recovery of debts under 40s.

PASSENHAM, a parish in the hundred of CLELEY, county of NORTHAMPTON, 1¼ mile (S. by W.) from Stony-Stratford, containing, with the hamlet of Denshanger and part of that of Old Stratford, 753 inhabitants. The living is a rectory, in the archdeaconry of Northampton, and diocese of Peterborough, rated in the king's books at £20, and in the patronage of Lord Viscount Maynard. The church is dedicated to St. Guthlake. The Buckingham canal passes through the parish. Six poor children are educated for £2. 10. a year, arising from a rent-charge bequeathed by John Swannell, in 1707. This is mentioned in the Saxon Chronicle as the place where the army of Edward the Elder lay whilst he was fortifying Towcester against the Danes. Shrob Lodge, in this parish, was the seat of the learned and industrious antiquary, Browne Willis, Esq.

PASTON, a parish in the hundred of TUNSTEAD, county of NORFOLK, 4 miles (N. E.) from North Walsham, containing 238 inhabitants. The living is a discharged vicarage, in the archdeaconry of Norfolk, and diocese of Norwich, rated in the king's books at £6. 13. 4., endowed with £400 royal bounty, and in the patronage of Lord Viscount Anson. The church is dedicated to St. Margaret. Near it are the ruins of the old hall and chapel belonging to the Paston family.

PASTON, a parish in the liberty of PETERBOROUGH, county of NORTHAMPTON, 2¼ miles (N. by W.) from

Peterborough, containing, with the hamlets of Gunthorpe, Walton, and Werrington, 764 inhabitants. The living is a rectory, in the archdeaconry of Northampton, and diocese of Peterborough, rated in the king's books at £13. 7. 11., and in the patronage of the Bishop of Peterborough. The church is dedicated to All Saints.

PASTON, a township in the parish of KIRK-NEWTON, western division of GLENDALE ward, county of NORTHUMBERLAND, 9½ miles (W. N. W.) from Wooler, containing 209 inhabitants. It is bounded on the north by the Beaumont river, and about a mile to the southward of the village is Pawston Tarn, a large lake of a circular form.

PATCHAM, a parish in the hundred of DEAN, rape of LEWES, county of SUSSEX, 3¼ miles (N. by W.) from Brighton, containing 403 inhabitants. The living is a discharged vicarage, in the archdeaconry of Lewes, and diocese of Chichester, rated in the king's books at £7. 1. 5½., and in the patronage of the Crown. The church, dedicated to All Saints, is partly in the early English, and partly in the decorated, style of architecture.

PATCHING, a parish and hundred in the rape of BRAMBER, county of SUSSEX, 4¾ miles (E. by S.) from Arundel, containing 222 inhabitants. The living is a rectory, in the peculiar jurisdiction and patronage of the Archbishop of Canterbury, rated in the king's books at £11. 13. 4.

PATCHWAY, a joint tything with Hempton, in that part of the parish of ALMONDSBURY which is in the lower division of the hundred of LANGLEY and SWINEHEAD, county of GLOUCESTER, 5¾ miles (N. by E.) from Bristol. The population is returned with Hempton.

PATELEY-BRIDGE, a market town and parochial chapelry in the lower division of the wapentake of CLARO, West riding of the county of YORK, 8 miles (W. N. W.) from Ripley, and 224 (N. N. W.) from London. The population is returned with the township of High and Low Bishopside, parish of Ripon, in which it is situated. This town is situated on the northern bank of the river Nidd, and is indebted for its importance to the adjacent lead mines. A weekly market, granted by Edward II., in 1324, is held on Saturday : fairs are on Easter and Whitsun eves, May 11th, September 17th (if on a Saturday, otherwise on the following Saturday), Monday after October 10th, and on Christmas-eve. The living is a perpetual curacy, in the peculiar jurisdiction of the Archbishop of York, in the deanery of Ripon, endowed with £400 private benefaction, £200 royal bounty, and £1900 parliamentary grant, and in the patronage of the Dean and Chapter of the Collegiate Church of Ripon. The chapel, dedicated to St. Mary, has received three hundred and sixty-five additional sittings, of which two hundred are free, the Incorporated Society for the enlargement of churches and chapels having contributed £500 towards defraying the expense. A new church, in the English style of architecture, was commenced in October, 1825, and completed in 1827, the parliamentary commissioners having granted £2000 towards its erection; it contains eight hundred and three sittings, of which four hundred and thirty-two are free. There is a place of worship for Independents. An ancient foundation, called Rake's school, from the site of ground on which it stands, was augmented, in 1806,

with a bequest of £1800 stock by Mrs. Alice Shepherd, the dividends to be applied to the education and clothing of twenty poor children.

PATMER, a hamlet partly in the parish of ALBURY, hundred of EDWINSTREE, and partly in the parish of BISHOP'S STORTFORD, hundred of BRAUGHIN, county of HERTFORD, adjacent to the town of Bishop's Stortford. It belongs to the Bishops of London, who here hold courts leet and baron, at which a constable and other officers are annually chosen, and misdemeanants punished.

PATNEY, a parish forming a distinct portion of the hundred of ELSTUB and EVERLEY, county of WILTS, 4¾ miles (E. S. E.) from Devizes, containing 141 inhabitants. The living is a rectory, in the archdeaconry and diocese of Salisbury, rated in the king's books at £19. 8. 4., and in the patronage of the Bishop of Winchester. The church is dedicated to St. Swithin.

PATRINGTON, a market town and parish in the southern division of the wapentake of HOLDERNESS, East riding of the county of YORK, 56 miles (E. S. E.) from York, and 189 (N. by E.) from London, containing 1244 inhabitants. This place, which is of great antiquity, is supposed by some antiquaries to be the Prætorium of Antoninus, and the point where the Roman road leading from the great Picts' wall terminates: about seventy years ago, a stone, which had formed part of a Roman altar, was dug up here. The town is pleasantly situated near a small river, which empties itself into the æstuary of the Humber, and although in a flat country, different points in the vicinity afford commanding views of the Humber and its fertile shores, as far as Spurn Point, about seven miles south-eastward, and also of the opposite coast of Lincolnshire : the houses are but indifferently built. The haven, about a mile distant, according to tradition, was formerly capable of admitting large vessels, but it has become so obstructed by the accumulation of silt, as only to afford access to small craft, which convey corn to Hull and London, and import lime and coal from the West riding. The market is on Saturday, principally for corn, the trade in which is considerable ; and fairs are held on March 28th, July 18th, and December 6th, for shoes, linen-drapery, woollen cloth, copper and tin ware, toys, &c. The living is a rectory, in the archdeaconry of the East riding, and diocese of York, rated in the king's books at £22, and in the patronage of the Master and Fellows of Clare Hall, Cambridge. The church, dedicated to St. Patrick, is a spacious and handsome cruciform edifice, combining the decorated and later styles of English architecture : it is surmounted by a fine lofty spire, visible at a great distance, and forming a land-mark for mariners approaching the mouth of the Humber. There are places of worship for Independents, and Primitive and Wesleyan Methodists.

PATRIXBOURNE, a parish in the hundred of BRIDGE and PETHAM, lathe of ST. AUGUSTINE, county of KENT 3¼ miles (S. E. by E.) from Canterbury, containing 268 inhabitants. The living is a vicarage, with the curacy of Bridge annexed, in the archdeaconry and diocese of Canterbury, rated in the king's books at £5. 7. 3½., and in the patronage of E. Taylor, Esq. The church, dedicated to St. Mary, is principally in the Norman style, but there are some portions of later date. A priory of Augustine canons, a cell to the abbey of Beaulieu in Normandy, was founded here about 1200, and in 1399, or the year following, was made subject to the priory of Merton, in Surrey.

PATSHULL, a parish in the southern division of the hundred of SEISDON, county of STAFFORD, 5¾ miles (S. E.) from Shiffnall, containing 144 inhabitants. The living is a perpetual curacy, in the archdeaconry of Stafford, and diocese of Lichfield and Coventry, endowed with £200 private benefaction, and £400 royal bounty, and in the patronage of Sir George Pigot, Bart. The church is dedicated to St. Mary. Within the parish are two fine lakes, called Patshull-pool and Snowdon-pool.

PATTERDALE, a joint chapelry with Hartsop, in the parish of BARTON, WEST ward, county of WESTMORLAND, 7¼ miles (N. by E.) from Ambleside. The population is returned with Hartsop. The living is a perpetual curacy, in the archdeaconry and diocese of Carlisle, endowed with £200 private benefaction, £600 royal bounty, and £500 parliamentary grant, and in the patronage of the Earl of Lonsdale. The church is dedicated to St. Patrick. There is a small school endowed with £6 per annum. Patterdale lies along the upper reach of Ullswater, amidst scenery of a most sublime character, the view being bounded by a vast amphitheatre of mountains, which surrounds the lake. It is intersected by numerous rills from the mountains, and by others flowing from the three tarns, Brotherwater, Hayswater, and Angle tarn, emptying themselves into lake Ullswater : at the head of the latter is an inn for the convenience of tourists, near which a large fair for sheep is held in October. There are several very productive quarries of fine blue slate in the neighbourhood.

PATTESLEY, a parish in the hundred of LAUNDITCH, county of NORFOLK, 4 miles (S. S. W.) from Fakenham. The population is returned with Oxwick. The living is a sinecure rectory, annexed to the vicarage of Mattishall, in the archdeaconry and diocese of Norwich, rated in the king's books at £8. 18. 9., endowed with £200 private benefaction, and £400 royal bounty. The church, which has fallen into ruins, was dedicated to St. John the Baptist.

PATTINGHAM, a parish partly in the hundred of STOTTESDEN, county of SALOP, but chiefly in the southern division of the hundred of SEISDON, county of STAFFORD, 6½ miles (W.) from Wolverhampton, containing, with the township of Rudge, 935 inhabitants. The living is a discharged vicarage, in the archdeaconry of Stafford, and diocese of Lichfield and Coventry, rated in the king's books at £8, and in the patronage of Sir George Pigot, Bart. The church is dedicated to St. Chad : in the cemetery is an old Roman cross. A school is endowed with £12 per annum.

PATTISHALL, a parish in the hundred of TOWCESTER, county of NORTHAMPTON, 4 miles (N. N. W.) from Towcester, containing 695 inhabitants. The living is a vicarage in two portions, in the archdeaconry of Northampton, and diocese of Peterborough, respectively rated in the king's books at £6. 11. 10½., and in the patronage of the Crown and the Rev. T. C. Welch, alternately. The church is dedicated to the Holy Trinity. Thomas Young, in 1684, bequeathed houses and land, now producing an income of about £14 a year, for which six boys receive instruction, and four others are taught for an annuity of £5, paid from the funds of Foxley charity. The Roman Watling-street passes through the parish.

PATTISWICK, a parish in the Witham division of the hundred of LEXDEN, county of ESSEX, 2¾ miles (W. N. W.) from Great Coggeshall, containing 320 inhabitants. The living is a perpetual curacy, in the archdeaconry of Colchester, and diocese of London, and in the patronage of the Bishop of London. The church is dedicated to St. Mary Magdalene.

PATTON, a township in that part of the parish of KENDAL which is in KENDAL ward, county of WESTMORLAND, 3½ miles (N. E. by N.) from Kendal, containing 89 inhabitants.

PAUL, a parish in the hundred of PENWITH, county of CORNWALL, 2¾ miles (S. by W.) from Penzance, containing 3790 inhabitants. The living is a vicarage, in the archdeaconry of Cornwall, and diocese of Exeter, rated in the king's books at £13. 11. 0½., and in the patronage of the Crown. In this parish are the villages of Mousehole and Newlyn, both situated on the coast of Mount's bay, and numerously inhabited by fishermen. The pilchard and mackarel fisheries are carried on to a great extent. The various kinds of fish that frequent this part of the channel are sent in abundance to Penzance and several of the other Cornish towns ; and the London market, in the early part of the season, is chiefly supplied with mackarel from this place, by way of Portsmouth. Mousehole, otherwise called Port Enys, was anciently a port of considerable importance, a new quay having been constructed so early as 1392 : it was also a market town, but the market has been discontinued since that place and Newlyn were burned by the Spaniards in 1595 : it is still defended by a battery. There is an almshouse for six poor men, founded in 1709, by Captain Stephen Hitchens, and endowed with land now producing about £70 per annum.

PAUL, a parish in the southern division of the wapentake of HOLDERNESS, East riding of the county of YORK, comprising the chapelry of Thorn-Grumbald, and the township of Paul, and containing 745 inhabitants, of which number, 486 are in the township of Paul, 2¼ miles (S.W.) from Hedon. The living is a discharged vicarage, in the archdeaconry of the East riding, and diocese of York, rated in the king's books at £10. 0. 5., and in the patronage of the Archbishop of York. The church, dedicated to St. Andrew and St. Mary, is a small cruciform structure in the later English style. There is a place of worship for Wesleyan Methodists, with a Sunday school attached. Here is an extensive dock-yard, in which several ships of the line were built during the late war.

PAULERS-PURY, a parish in the hundred of CLELEY, county of NORTHAMPTON, 3 miles (S.E. by S.) from Towcester, containing 1069 inhabitants. The living is a rectory, in the archdeaconry of Northampton, and diocese of Peterborough, rated in the king's books at £24. 4. 2., and in the patronage of the Warden and Fellows of New College, Oxford. The church, dedicated to St. James, contains a curious ancient font. There is a place of worship for Wesleyan Methodists. William Marriott, in 1721, bequeathed certain land, directing the income to be applied in teaching six poor boys. The ancient Watling-street passes through the parish, in which coins of Constantine, Maximian, and other emperors have been found. Dr. Edward Bernard, a learned astronomer and Savilian professor at Oxford, was born here in 1638 ; he died in 1697.

PAULTON, a parish in the hundred of CHEWTON, county of SOMERSET, 9½ miles (S.W.) from Bath, containing 1380 inhabitants. The living is a perpetual curacy, annexed to the vicarage of Chewton-Mendip, in the archdeaconry of Wells, and diocese of Bath and Wells. The church is dedicated to the Holy Trinity. There are places of worship for Baptists and Wesleyan Methodists.

PAUNTLEY, a parish in the hundred of BOTLOE, county of GLOUCESTER, 2¾ miles (N.E. by N.) from Newent, containing 280 inhabitants. The living is a perpetual curacy, in the archdeaconry of Hereford, and diocese of Gloucester, endowed with £600 royal bounty, and £200 parliamentary grant, and in the patronage of the Bishop of Gloucester. The church, dedicated to St. John the Evangelist, has an enriched Norman door. The river Leddon runs through the parish. Here are springs, the water of which is similar in quality to the Cheltenham waters.

PAVENHAM, a parish in the hundred of WILLEY, county of BEDFORD, 7 miles (N.W.) from Bedford, containing 455 inhabitants. The living is a perpetual curacy, annexed to the vicarage of Felmersham, in the archdeaconry of Bedford, and diocese of Lincoln. The church is dedicated to St. Peter.

PAWLETT, a parish in the northern division of the hundred of PETHERTON, county of SOMERSET, 5 miles (N.) from Bridg-water, containing 529 inhabitants. The living is a discharged vicarage, in the archdeaconry of Wells, and diocese of Bath and Wells, rated in the king's books at £10. 17. 11., and in the patronage of the Crown. The church is dedicated to St. John the Baptist. There is a place of worship for Wesleyan Methodists. The navigable river Parret bounds the parish on the east and south.

PAXFORD, a hamlet in the parish of BLOCKLEY, upper division of the hundred of OSWALDSLOW, county of WORCESTER, though locally in the upper division of the hundred of Kiftsgate, county of Gloucester, 4 miles (N. by W.) from Moreton in the Marsh, containing 153 inhabitants.

PAXTON (GREAT), a parish in the hundred of TOSELAND, county of HUNTINGDON, 3 miles (N.E. by N.) from St. Neot's, containing 250 inhabitants. The living is a vicarage, with the perpetual curacies of Little Paxton and Toseland, in the archdeaconry of Huntingdon, and diocese of Lincoln, rated in the king's books at £16. 2. 11., and in the patronage of the Dean and Chapter of Lincoln. The church is dedicated to the Holy Trinity. The river Ouse bounds the parish on the west.

PAXTON (LITTLE), a parish in the hundred of TOSELAND, county of HUNTINGDON, 2 miles (N.) from St. Neot's, containing 301 inhabitants. The living is a perpetual curacy, annexed to the vicarage of Great Paxton, in the archdeaconry of Huntingdon, and diocese of Lincoln. The church is dedicated to St. James. The river Ouse runs through the parish.

PAYHEMBURY, a parish in the hundred of HAYRIDGE, county of DEVON, 5¼ miles (W.N.W.) from Honiton, containing 507 inhabitants. The living is a vicarage, in the archdeaconry and diocese of Exeter, rated in the king's books at £18. 4. 2. The Rev. T. T. Jackson was patron in 1810. The church, dedicated to St. Mary, is a handsome structure, and has a fine wooden
VOL. III.

screen. At Leyhill is an old mansion, with a chapel; and at Hembury is an ancient intrenchment.

PAYTHORNE, a township in the parish of GISBURN, western division of the wapentake of STAINCLIFFE and EWCROSS, West riding of the county of YORK, 9 miles (S.) from Settle, containing 242 inhabitants.

PAYTON, a township in the parish of LEINTWARDINE, hundred of WIGMORE, county of HEREFORD, containing, with the townships of Adforton and Grange, 212 inhabitants.

PEAK, a joint hamlet with Westbury, in that part of the parish of EAST MEON which is in the hundred of MEON-STOKE, Portsdown division of the county of SOUTHAMPTON, 10 miles (W. by S.) from Petersfield. The population is returned with Westbury.

PEAK-FOREST, an extra-parochial liberty, in the hundred of HIGH PEAK, county of DERBY, 3½ miles (N.W.) from Tideswell, containing 680 inhabitants. Here is a chapel, dedicated to King Charles the Martyr: the living is a perpetual curacy, in the peculiar jurisdiction of the Dean and Chapter of Lichfield, and in the patronage of the Duke of Devonshire. A free school is endowed with about £10 per annum, for the education of ten poor children. This district is in the honour of Tutbury, duchy of Lancaster, and within the jurisdiction of a court of pleas held at Tutbury every third Tuesday, for the recovery of debts under 40s.

PEAKIRK, a parish in the liberty of PETERBOROUGH, county of NORTHAMPTON, 3¼ miles (S.E.) from Market-Deeping, containing 180 inhabitants. The living is a rectory, with the perpetual curacy of Glinton, in the archdeaconry of Northampton, and diocese of Peterborough, rated in the king's books at £18. 3. 11½., and in the patronage of the Dean and Chapter of Peterborough. The church is dedicated to St. Pega, who, in 714, settled here in a cell which Edmund Atheling afterwards converted into a monastery, which, though twice destroyed by the Danes, existed till 1048. A charity school for five poor girls of Peakirk, and ten of Glinton, is supported with the interest of a sum of money bequeathed by Ann Ireland in 1712.

PEALS, a township in the parish of ALLENTON, western division of COQUETDALE ward, county of NORTHUMBERLAND, 8¼ miles (W. by N.) from Rothbury, containing 76 inhabitants. It is situated on the river Coquet.

PEASEMORE, a parish in the hundred of FAIRCROSS, county of BERKS, 4¼ miles (W. S. W.) from East Ilsley, containing 284 inhabitants. The living is a rectory, in the archdeaconry of Berks, and diocese of Salisbury, rated in the king's books at £12. 12. 1., and in the patronage of J.A. Houblon, Esq. In the church is a memorial of William Coward, lord of the manor, who, though his income did not exceed £110 per annum, built at his own expense the tower of the church, and gave the great bell and communion plate, besides performing various other acts of charity; he died in 1739. The Wesleyan Methodists have a place of worship here.

PEASENHALL, a parish in the hundred of BLYTHING, county of SUFFOLK, 2¾ miles (W. by N.) from Yoxford, containing 746 inhabitants. The living is a perpetual curacy, annexed to the vicarage of Sibton, in the archdeaconry of Suffolk, and diocese of Norwich, endowed with £400 royal bounty. The church is dedi-
3 U

cated to St. Michael. There is a place of worship for Wesleyan Methodists.

PEASMARSH, a parish in the hundred of GOLD-SPUR, rape of HASTINGS, county of SUSSEX, 3¼ miles (N. W. by W.) from Rye, containing 913 inhabitants. The living is a discharged vicarage, in the archdeaconry of Lewes, and diocese of Chichester, rated in the king's books at £5. 9. 2., and in the patronage of the Master and Fellows of Sidney Sussex College, Cambridge. The church, dedicated to St. Peter and St. Paul, is in the early style of English architecture. There is a place of worship for Wesleyan Methodists.

PEATLING (MAGNA), a parish in the hundred of GUTHLAXTON, county of LEICESTER, 6½ miles (N. E. by N.) from Lutterworth, containing 228 inhabitants. The living is a discharged vicarage, united in 1729 to the rectory of Willoughby-Waterless, in the archdeaconry of Leicester, and diocese of Lincoln, rated in the king's books at £5. 9. 2. The church is dedicated to All Saints.

PEATLING (PARVA), a parish in the hundred of GUTHLAXTON, county of LEICESTER, 4¾ miles (N. E. by N.) from Lutterworth, containing 173 inhabitants. The living is a rectory, in the archdeaconry of Leicester, and diocese of Lincoln, rated in the king's books at £9. 14. 7., and in the patronage of the Crown. The church is dedicated to St. Andrew. There are some mild chalybeate springs in the parish.

PEATON, a township in the parish of DIDDLEBURY, hundred of MUNSLOW, county of SALOP, containing 193 inhabitants.

PEBMARSH, a parish in the hundred of HINCK-FORD, county of ESSEX, 3½ miles (N. E. by E.) from Halsted, containing 601 inhabitants. The living is a rectory, in the archdeaconry of Middlesex, and diocese of London, rated in the king's books at £10, and in the patronage of the Earl of Verulam. The church is dedicated to St. John the Baptist.

PEBWORTH, a parish in the upper division of the hundred of KIFTSGATE, county of GLOUCESTER, 6¼ miles (N. by W.) from Chipping-Campden, containing 620 inhabitants. The living is a discharged vicarage, in the archdeaconry and diocese of Gloucester, rated in the king's books at £10. 1. 2., endowed with £400 royal bounty, and £1200 parliamentary grant, and in the joint patronage of Messrs. Shekell and Millard. The church is dedicated to St. Peter. There is a place of worship for Wesleyan Methodists. Two small schools are endowed to a trifling extent. Several mineral springs rise in this parish, which are said to resemble the Cheltenham waters, but they are not generally known.

PECKFORTON, a township in that part of the parish of BUNBURY which is in the first division of the hundred of EDDISBURY, county palatine of CHESTER, 4½ miles (S. S. W.) from Tarporley, containing 294 inhabitants. Horseley bath, a mineral spring formerly in considerable esteem, is in this township. A school is supported by small annual subscriptions.

PECKHAM, a hamlet in the parish of CAMBER-WELL, eastern division of the hundred of BRIXTON, county of SURREY, 4 miles (S. E. by S.) from London. The population is returned with the parish. This pleasant village contains many spacious and excellent houses, forming one principal street, which is lighted with gas: a branch of the Surrey canal approaches within a short distance of it, Peckham Rye, was formerly the scene of a popular fair annually in August, which has been suppressed: a little beyond this point is Forest Hill, commanding many varied and beautiful prospects. A silk-factory has been recently established. There are two proprietary episcopal chapels, one in Hill-street, which is in the later style of English architecture, and is surmounted by a spire; the other has been recently erected, and is in the same style, with a tower. There are places of worship for Baptists and Independents. A National school, for children of both sexes, amounting to two hundred and eighty in number; a Lancasterian school, for one hundred and forty children; and an infant school, are severally supported by voluntary contributions. In that part of the hamlet called Peckham New Town is the asylum for decayed victuallers, instituted in 1827, under the patronage of His Royal Highness the Duke of Sussex, who laid the first stone of the building, which, when completed, will consist of a spacious range, occupying three sides of a quadrangular area enclosed with a handsome palisade, and tastefully laid out in parterres of flowers and shrubs; the north and south wings are not yet above the foundation, but the centre forms a noble range of building, comprising the committee-room and other offices, fronted with a handsome portico of six pillars of the Ionic order, supporting an entablature and triangular pediment, in the tympanum of which is a clock, and surmounted by a handsome cupola, surrounded with Ionic pillars supporting a dome; the whole number of tenements will be one hundred and one, of which forty-three are at present occupied: the grounds surrounding the asylum comprise more than six acres, commanding a pleasing view of the Surrey hills on the south, and of the metropolis to the north.

PECKHAM (EAST), a parish in the hundred of TWY-FORD, lathe of AYLESFORD, county of KENT, 6 miles (N. E. by E.) from Tunbridge, containing 1724 inhabitants. The living is a vicarage, in the peculiar jurisdiction of the Archbishop of Canterbury, rated in the king's books at £14, and in the patronage of the Dean and Chapter of Canterbury: the impropriate rectory is rated at £23. The church, dedicated to St. Michael, has lately received an addition of one hundred and five sittings, of which eighty-five are free, the Incorporated Society for the enlargement of churches and chapels having granted £40 towards defraying the expense.

PECKHAM (WEST), a parish in the hundred of LITTLEFIELD, lathe of AYLESFORD, county of KENT, 6 miles (N.E.) from Tunbridge, containing, with Oxenoath, 498 inhabitants. The living is a discharged vicarage, in the archdeaconry and diocese of Rochester, rated in the king's books at £7. 5. 10., endowed with £200 private benefaction, and £200 royal bounty, and in the patronage of the Dean and Chapter of Rochester. The church, dedicated to St. Dunstan, is a small building, with a tower surmounted by a spire, situated on an eminence nearly in the centre of the parish. There is a place of worship for Wesleyan Methodists. Hops and fruit are cultivated to a considerable extent, and a fair is held on Whit-Thursday. A preceptory of Knights Hospitallers was founded here, in 1408, by John Colepepper, one of the Justices of the Common Pleas.

PECKLETON, a parish in the hundred of SPARK-ENHOE, county of LEICESTER, 5½ miles (N. E. by N.)

from Hinckley, containing, with the hamlet of Tooley, 359 inhabitants. The living is a rectory, in the archdeaconry of Leicester, and diocese of Lincoln, rated in the king's books at £8, and in the patronage of the Rev. Mr. Cooper. The church is dedicated to St. Mary. There is a place of worship for Wesleyan Methodists. Peckleton is in the honour of Tutbury, duchy of Lancaster, and within the jurisdiction of a court of pleas held at Tutbury every third Tuesday, for the recovery of debts under 40s.

PEDMORE, a parish in the lower division of the hundred of HALFSHIRE, county of WORCESTER, 1½ mile (S. by E.) from Stourbridge, containing 307 inhabitants. The living is a rectory, in the archdeaconry and diocese of Worcester, rated in the king's books at £9. 10., and in the patronage of Lord Foley. The church, dedicated to St. Peter, is a very ancient structure, with some remains of Norman architecture. About 1699, a free school was founded and endowed with £6 per annum, by Thomas Foley, Esq.

PEDWARDINE, a joint township with Boresford, in that part of the parish of BRAMPTON-BRYAN which is in the hundred of WIGMORE, county of HEREFORD, 4¾ miles (N. E.) from Presteigne. The population is returned with Boresford. Here was formerly a castle belonging to the family of Hay, Barons of Penwardine, and now Earls of Kinnoul.

PEEL, county palatine of LANCASTER.—See HULTON (LITTLE).

PEELE, a joint township with Horton, in that part of the parish of TARVIN which is in the second division of the hundred of EDDISBURY, county palatine of CHESTER, 7½ miles (E.N.E.) from Chester. The population is returned with Horton.

PEERSTON-JAGLIN, a township in that part of the parish of FEATHERSTONE which is in the upper division of the wapentake of OSGOLDCROSS, West riding of the county of YORK, 2¼ miles (S.W.) from Pontefract, containing 244 inhabitants. There is a place of worship for Wesleyan Methodists.

PEGSWORTH, a township in that part of the parish of BOTHALL which is in the eastern division of MORPETH ward, county of NORTHUMBERLAND, 1½ mile (E. N.E.) from Morpeth, containing 155 inhabitants. Here are some collieries.

PELDON, a parish in the hundred of WINSTREE, county of ESSEX, 5½ miles (S. by W.) from Colchester, containing 438 inhabitants. The living is a rectory, in the archdeaconry of Colchester, and diocese of London, rated in the king's books at £16. 15. 10., and in the patronage of Earl Waldegrave. The church is dedicated to St. Mary. The parish is bounded on the south-east by Mersea channel.

PELHAM (BRENT), a parish in the hundred of EDWINSTREE, county of HERTFORD, 5¾ miles (E. by N.) from Buntingford, containing 280 inhabitants. The living is a discharged vicarage, consolidated, in 1771, with that of Furneux-Pelham, in the peculiar jurisdiction of the Dean and Chapter of St. Paul's, London, rated in the king's books at £7. 6. 8., endowed with £210 private benefaction, and £200 royal bounty, and in the patronage of the Bishop of London. The church, dedicated to the Virgin Mary, has a square embattled tower; the chancel is less than it formerly was, the south side having fallen down some years ago.

PELHAM (FURNEUX), a parish in the hundred of EDWINSTREE, county of HERTFORD, 5½ miles (E. by S.) from Buntingford, containing 566 inhabitants. The living is a discharged vicarage, consolidated, in 1771, with that of Brent-Pelham, in the peculiar jurisdiction of the Dean and Chapter of St. Paul's, London, rated in the king's books at £9, endowed with £250 private benefaction, and £200 royal bounty, and in the patronage of the Bishop of London. The church, dedicated to St. Mary, has a chapel, the burial-place of the Calvert family, on the south side of the chancel; and at the west end a square tower, embattled, and surmounted by a short spire. Mrs. Wheatley, in 1754, founded a school, and endowed it with a house and land, for teaching poor children.

PELHAM (STOCKING), a parish in the hundred of EDWINSTREE, county of HERTFORD, 6½ miles (E.) from Buntingford, containing 150 inhabitants. The living is a rectory, in the archdeaconry of Middlesex, and diocese of London, rated in the king's books at £7. 10. 7½., and in the patronage of — Calvert, Esq. The church, dedicated to St. Mary, has a small wooden tower with a low spire.

PELSALL, a chapelry in that part of the parish of WOLVERHAMPTON which is in the southern division of the hundred of OFFLOW, county of STAFFORD, 3¼ miles (N.) from Walsall, containing 579 inhabitants. The living is a perpetual curacy, in the jurisdiction of the royal peculiar court of Wolverhampton, endowed with £200 private benefaction, and £400 royal bounty, and in the patronage of the Dean of Windsor. The chapel is dedicated to St. Michael. The Essington and Wyrley canal passes through the parish.

PELTON, a township in that part of the parish of CHESTER le STREET which is in the middle division of CHESTER ward, county palatine of DURHAM, 8 miles (N. by W.) from Durham, containing 522 inhabitants.

PELYNT, a parish in WEST hundred, county of CORNWALL, 4 miles (W. N.W.) from West Looe, containing 750 inhabitants. The living is a vicarage, in the archdeaconry of Cornwall, and diocese of Exeter, rated in the king's books at £17. 18. 6½., and in the patronage of J. Buller, Esq. The church, dedicated to St. Nunn, contains a curious monument to the memory of Francis Buller, Esq., who died in 1615. At Trelawny, in this parish, there remains a portion of a castellated mansion, erected by Lord Bonville, in the fifteenth century.

PEMBERTON, a chapelry in that part of the parish of WIGAN which is in the hundred of WEST DERBY, county palatine of LANCASTER, 2¼ miles (W. S. W.) from Wigan, containing 3679 inhabitants, who are chiefly employed in the coal mines, which are worked here to a considerable extent. The parliamentary commissioners for building new churches and chapels have given directions for the erection of a new chapel at this place. In the neighbourhood is Hawkley Hall, a very ancient building, the original proprietors of which came over with the Conqueror.

PEMBRIDGE, a parish and borough (formerly a market town), in the hundred of STRETFORD, county of HEREFORD, 15½ miles (N.W. by N.) from Hereford, containing 1203 inhabitants. The living is a rectory, in the archdeaconry and diocese of Hereford,

3 U 2

rated in the king's books at £36. 10. 2½., and in the patronage of the President and Fellows of Corpus Christi College, Oxford. The church, dedicated to St. Peter, is a large and lofty structure, with a detached steeple of singular construction, its wooden frame-work being particularly curious. The Wesleyan Methodists have places of worship here; and there is also a chapel belonging to the Home Missionary Society. The river Arrow passes through the town, which is governed by a high bailiff, chosen every two years by a majority of the householders. Courts leet and baron are held annually; and there are fairs, on May 13th for hiring servants, &c., and November 22nd for the sale of cattle; but the market, granted by Henry I., has long since declined. A free school, endowed by William Carpenter in 1650, is at present conducted on Dr. Bell's system. Here are almshouses, erected and endowed, in 1661, by Jeffry and Bishop Duppa, for six poor persons, each to receive £5 per annum.

PEMBURY, a parish in the hundred of WASHLINGSTONE, lathe of AYLESFORD, county of KENT, 3½ miles (S. E.) from Tunbridge, containing 891 inhabitants. The living is a discharged vicarage, in the archdeaconry and diocese of Rochester, rated in the king's books at £6. 8. 8., endowed with £200 private benefaction, and £200 royal bounty, and in the patronage of the Rev. S. S. Woodgate. The church, dedicated to St. Peter, has lately received an addition of sixty free sittings, the Incorporated Society for the enlargement of churches and chapels having granted £30 towards defraying the expense. Several small streams, tributary to the Medway, run through the parish. An almshouse for six poor blind persons was erected, in 1716, by Charles Selby, in pursuance of the will of Charles Amherst, who previously, in 1702, bequeathed a rent-charge of £213 for its maintenance.

PENALTH, a parish in the upper division of the hundred of RAGLAND, county of MONMOUTH, 1¾ mile (S. E. by S.) from Monmouth, containing 464 inhabitants. The living is a perpetual curacy, annexed to the vicarage of Trellack, in the archdeaconry and diocese of Llandaff.

PENCOMBE, a parish in the hundred of BROXASH, county of HEREFORD, 4¼ miles (W. by S.) from Bromyard, containing, with the townships of Grendon-Warren and Marstone-Stannett, 453 inhabitants. The living is a rectory, in the archdeaconry and diocese of Hereford, rated in the king's books at £13. 6. 8., and in the patronage of Richard Arkright, Esq. A court leet is held here once in three years; and, by ancient custom, the lord of the manor claims a pair of gilt spurs whenever a mayor of Hereford dies while in office.

PENCOYD, a parish in the upper division of the hundred of WORMELOW, county of HEREFORD, 6 miles (W. N. W.) from Ross, containing 161 inhabitants. The living is a perpetual curacy, united with that of Marstow, in the archdeaconry and diocese of Hereford, endowed with £800 royal bounty, and in the patronage of the Rev. Francis Coke.

PENDEFORD, a township in that part of the parish of TETTENHALL which is in the southern division of the hundred of SEISDON, county of STAFFORD, 4¼ miles (N. N. W.) from Wolverhampton, containing 253 inhabitants.

PENDLEBURY, a township in the parish of Ec

cles, hundred of SALFORD, county palatine of LANCASTER, 4¼ miles (N. W. by W.) from Manchester, containing 1047 inhabitants, who are chiefly employed in the manufacture and printing of cotton. There is a place of worship for Independents. The Bolton and Bury canal runs through the township. Agecroft Hall is a fine ancient fabric, supposed to have been built before the time of Richard II.: it was the birthplace of Cardinal Langley, and a staining of the royal arms, still remaining in the window of its chapel, was presented by John of Gaunt to that family.

PENDLETON, a chapelry in that part of the parish of WHALLEY which is in the higher division of the hundred of BLACKBURN, county palatine of LANCASTER, 2¼ miles (S. S. E.) from Clitheroe, containing 1319 inhabitants, of whom about one thousand are employed at the extensive calico-printing establishment here.

PENDLETON, a chapelry in the parish of ECCLES, hundred of SALFORD, county palatine of LANCASTER, 2½ miles (W. by N.) from Manchester, containing 5948 inhabitants. The living is a perpetual curacy, annexed to the vicarage of Eccles, in the archdeaconry and diocese of Chester, endowed with £200 royal bounty, and £1800 parliamentary grant. The chapel, dedicated to St. Thomas, was built by Messrs. S. Brierly and John Fletcher, in 1777, and was purchased by subscription among the inhabitants shortly afterwards: it was originally used as a place of worship for Methodists, the celebrated John Wesley having first officiated in it. The first stone of a new church was laid in July 1829, in which it is intended to accommodate one thousand six hundred persons, the commissioners for building additional churches having granted £600, and the inhabitants having subscribed £1000, towards defraying the expense. The Independents, Wesleyans, and Methodists of the New Connexion, have each a place of worship here. The Liverpool and Edinburgh road, the Bolton and Bury canal, and the Manchester and Liverpool railroad, pass through the chapelry. There are several cotton-mills, with dyeing, printing, and bleaching establishments, also a flax-mill upon an improved principle, together affording employment to about two thousand five hundred persons, the remainder of the inhabitants being chiefly occupied in the manufacture of silk and cotton, in handicraft trades, and at the neighbouring collieries. A small library of useful works was established in 1829 at the village, adjacent to which are many pleasant genteel villas. A school is supported by subscription, in which about two hundred children are instructed.

PENDOCK, a parish in the lower division of the hundred of OSWALDSLOW, though locally in the lower division of that of Pershore, county of WORCESTER, 5¼ miles (S. S. W.) from Upton upon Severn, containing 276 inhabitants. The living is a rectory, in the archdeaconry and diocese of Worcester, rated in the king's books at £11. 2. 11. There is a place of worship for Wesleyan Methodists.

PENDOMER, a parish in the hundred of HOUNDSBOROUGH, BERWICK, and COKER, county of SOMERSET, 4¼ miles (S. W. by S.) from Yeovil, containing 70 inhabitants. The living is a rectory, in the archdeaconry of Wells, and diocese of Bath and Wells, rated in the king's books at £3. 4. 4½. William Helyar, Esq. was patron in 1810.

PENGE, a hamlet in that part of the parish of BATTERSEA which is in the eastern division of the hundred of BRIXTON, county of SURREY, 3¾ miles (N. N. E.) from Croydon, containing 228 inhabitants.

PENHOW, a parish in the lower division of the hundred of CALDICOTT, county of MONMOUTH, 5½ miles (E. by S.) from Caerleon, containing 220 inhabitants. The living is a discharged rectory, in the archdeaconry and diocese of Llandaff, rated in the king's books at £5. 4. 9½., and in the patronage of John Cave, Esq. The church is dedicated to St. John the Baptist. There are still some remains of Penhow castle.

PENHURST, a parish in the hundred of NETHER-FIELD, rape of HASTINGS, county of SUSSEX, 3¾ miles (W. by N.) from Battle, containing 106 inhabitants. The living is a discharged rectory, with the vicarage of Ash-burnham, in the archdeaconry of Lewes, and diocese of Chichester, rated in the king's books at £3. 18. 4., endowed with £200 private benefaction, and £200 royal bounty. The church is principally in the later style of English architecture.

PENISTONE, a parish in the wapentake of STAIN-CROSS, West riding of the county of YORK, comprising the market town of Penistone, the chapelry of Denby, and the townships of Gunthwaite, Hunshelf, Ingbirchworth, Langsett, Oxspring, and Thurlestone, and containing 5042 inhabitants, of which number, 645 are in the town of Penistone, 8 miles (W. S. W.) from Barnesley, and 177 (N. N. W.) from London. The town is situated on the southern bank of the river Don, and consists of four streets, which intersect each other at right angles: it is in general well built. The only branch of manufacture is that of linen, which is not very extensive. The market is on Thursday, principally for cattle. The living is a discharged vicarage, in the archdeaconry and diocese of York, rated in the king's books at £16. 14. 2. Major-General G. Bosville was patron in 1809. The church is dedicated to St. John the Baptist. There are places of worship for the Society of Friends, Independents, and Wesleyan Methodists. A free grammar school was founded in 1604, and endowed by sundry persons with houses, lands, and rent-charges, now producing an income of about £110 per annum, which till lately was applied for teaching the classics, but at present the children are only taught English. There is also a free school for girls, erected in 1821 by subscription, to which the National School Society also contributed: it is endowed with £420 four per cents., producing £16. 16. per annum; one hundred and twenty are instructed: the mistress also receives £10 per annum, the bequest of Josias Wordsworth, for which twenty additional girls are taught. Dr. Nicholas Sanderson, the celebrated blind Professor of Mathematics in the University of Cambridge, was a native of this parish.

PENKETH, a township in the parish of PRESCOT, hundred of WEST DERBY, county palatine of LANCASTER, 3¾ miles (W.) from Warrington, containing 477 inhabitants. There is a place of worship for Wesleyan Methodists.

PENKHUL, a joint township with Boothen, in the parish of STOKE upon TRENT, northern division of the hundred of PIREHILL, county of STAFFORD, 1 mile (S. E. by E.) from Newcastle under Lyne, containing, with Boothen, 4915 inhabitants. It is in the honour of Tutbury, duchy of Lancaster, and within the jurisdic-

tion of a court of pleas held at Tutbury every third Tuesday, for the recovery of debts under 40s.

PENKRIDGE, a parish partly in the western, but chiefly in the eastern, division of the hundred of CUT-TLESTONE, county of STAFFORD, comprising the town of Penkridge, the chapelries of Coppenhall and Dunston, and the townships of Lovedale with Drayton, Mitton, Otherton, Pileton, Water-Eaton, Rodbaston, and Whiston with Bickford, and containing 2641 inhabitants, of which number, 2299 are in the town of Penkridge, 6 miles (S.) from Stafford, and 128 (N. W.) from London. This place is of great antiquity, and is supposed by Camden to have been the Roman *Pennocrucium*; part of its modern name is evidently deduced from the river *Penk*, on which it stands, but whether the remainder denotes the bank of this stream, or is a corruption of *bridge*, is a matter of conjecture: there is a stone bridge over the river. This small town, from its low situation, is subject to frequent inundations: it consists principally of two streets. Here are some iron works; and the Staffordshire and Worcestershire canal passes eastward of the town. The market, formerly held on Tuesday, is now disused; fairs are held April 30th, the first Monday in September, and the 10th of October, the first of which is said to be one of the greatest marts for cattle in the kingdom, and the second a noted horse fair. The petty sessions for the east and west divisions of the hundred are occasionally held here. The living is a perpetual curacy, in the jurisdiction of the royal peculiar court of Penkridge, endowed with £400 private benefaction, £400 royal bounty, and in the patronage of E. J. Littleton, Esq. The church, dedicated to St. Michael, is principally in the later style of English architecture, but the east window is of the decorated character, with elegant tracery: it was made collegiate by King John, and given by him to the see of Dublin, the archbishop of which was dean, and under him were thirteen prebendaries, whose prebends, at the Reformation, were valued at £106. 15. 1. A school-house was erected by subscription in 1695; and in 1731, Francis Sherratt endowed it with land for the education of eight poor boys; the income, arising from this and other bequests, amounts to £36. 3. per annum; twelve boys and eight girls are now educated. In 1819, two school-rooms, and a residence for the master and mistress, were built by E. J. Littleton, Esq., in which two hundred children are instructed on Dr. Bell's system, at his sole expense. Congreve, a hamlet in this parish, was long the seat of an ancient family of the same name, and it is stated by some writers to have been the native place of Congreve, the poet, but it is most probable that he was born in Ireland: this hamlet is, however, the birthplace of the learned divine and critic, Dr. Richard Hurd, Bishop of Worcester, who died in 1808.

PENMAIN, a hamlet in the parish of MYNYDDYS LWYN, lower division of the hundred of WENTLLOOG, county of MONMOUTH, 12 miles (N. W.) from Newport, containing 1425 inhabitants. There is a place of worship for Independents, established upwards of a century, in which service is performed in the Welch language.

PENN, a parish in the hundred of BURNHAM, county of BUCKINGHAM, 3 miles (N. W. by N.) from Beaconsfield, containing 1054 inhabitants. The living is a discharged vicarage, in the archdeaconry of Buckingham, and diocese of Lincoln, rated in the king's books at £9. 13. 4., and in the patronage of Earl Howe. The church is dedicated to the Holy Trinity. There are places of worship for Baptists and Wesleyan Methodists. A school was founded, in 1750, by Sir Nathaniel and Elinor Curzon, for teaching poor children.

PENN, a parish in the northern division of the hundred of SEISDON, county of STAFFORD, comprising the township of Lower Penn, and the liberty of Upper Penn, and containing 769 inhabitants, of which number, 539 are in the liberty of Upper Penn, 2 miles (S.W. by S.) from Wolverhampton. The living is a discharged vicarage, in the archdeaconry of Stafford, and diocese of Lichfield and Coventry, rated in the king's books at £4. 5. 10., endowed with £200 private benefaction, and £200 royal bounty, and in the patronage of the Bishop of Lichfield and Coventry. The church is dedicated to St. Bartholomew. A manorial court is annually held by the Marquis of Stafford's agent, to decide upon encroachments on Penn-Wood common. Here are several small manufactories for locks, keys, coffee-mills, &c., from which the warehouses in Wolverhampton and Sedgeley are supplied : there is also a small nail-manufactory. The Rev. Charles Wynn, in 1669, gave a messuage, &c., and a rent-charge of £6, in support of a free school, in aid of which Dr. Sedgewick, in 1747, gave an annuity of £10; the total income is nearly £105 and the average number of children about fifty. An almshouse was founded, in 1761, by Ann Sedgewick, for five aged women.

PENN (LOWER), a township in the parish of PENN, northern division of the hundred of SEISDON, county of STAFFORD, 3 miles (W. S. W.) from Wolverhampton, containing 230 inhabitants.

PENNARD (EAST), a parish in the hundred of WHITESTONE, county of SOMERSET, 5¾ miles (S. S. W.) from Shepton-Mallet, containing 755 inhabitants. The living is a discharged vicarage, with the perpetual curacy of West Bradley annexed, in the archdeaconry of Wells, and diocese of Bath and Wells, rated in the king's books at £7. 4. 9½., endowed with £200 private benefaction, and £200 royal bounty, and in the patronage of the Bishop of Bath and Wells. The church is dedicated to All Saints. The old Roman Fosse-way bounds the parish on the south-east.

PENNARD (WEST), a parish in the hundred of GLASTON-TWELVE-HIDES, county of SOMERSET, 3½ miles (E. by S.) from Glastonbury, containing 890 inhabitants. The living is a perpetual curacy, annexed to that of St. John the Baptist in Glastonbury, and in the peculiar jurisdiction of Glastonbury, endowed with £1400 parliamentary grant. The church is dedicated to St. Nicholas. There is a place of worship for Wesleyan Methodists.

PENNINGTON, a parish in the hundred of LONS-DALE, north of the sands, county palatine of LANCAS-TER, 2 miles (W. S. W.) from Ulverstone, containing 284 inhabitants. The living is a perpetual curacy, in the archdeaconry of Richmond, and diocese of Chester, endowed with £200 private benefaction, and £600 royal bounty, and in the patronage of the King, as Duke of Lancaster. The church, dedicated to St. Michael, has lately received an addition of one hundred and ten sittings, of which seventy-five are free, the Incorporated Society for the enlargement of churches and chapels having granted £100 towards defraying the expense. James Fell, in 1733, gave £60, now producing £3 per annum, for teaching poor children. Iron-ore and blue slate abound in the parish.

PENNINGTON, a township in the parish of LEIGH, hundred of WEST DERBY, county palatine of LANCAS-TER, 1 mile (S. by W.) from Leigh, containing 2782 inhabitants. This township includes part of the market town of Leigh. The manufacture of cotton is extensively carried on; and the neighbourhood produces coal, and lime of a very superior quality. At Pennington Hall is a small chapel for Swedenborgians.

PENRITH, a parish in LEATH ward, county of CUMBERLAND, 18 miles (S. E. by S.) from Carlisle, and 283 (N. N. W.) from London, comprising the market town of Penrith, and the townships of Burrowgate, Dock-ray, Middlegate with Sandgate, Netherend-Bridge with Carleton, and Town with Plumpton-Head, and containing 5385 inhabitants. This is a place of considerable antiquity: its name is evidently of British origin, and, signifying "the red hill or summit," has reference either to the nature of the adjacent soil, or to the red free stone of which the town is built. Old Penrith, the Breme-tenracum of the Romans, is situated about five miles north-by-west of the town. At the Conquest, the honour of Penrith was a royal franchise, which, after repeated changes, was assigned to Alexander III., King of Scotland, in consideration of his ceding all claim to the counties of Cumberland, Northumberland, and Westmorland, at that time subjects of frequent contests between the sovereigns of England and Scotland; from him it descended to John Balliol, on whose defection it was seized by Edward I., and given to Anthony Beck, Bishop of Durham: having repeatedly lapsed to the crown, in 1696 it was granted to William Bentinck, Earl of Portland, and was sold by the late duke, in 1783, to the Duke of Devonshire, its present proprietor. During the reigns of Edward III. and Richard II., this town suffered greatly from the incursions of the Scots, who, in the latter, having ravaged the country, fired towns and villages, and enslaved many of the inhabitants; but becoming infected by the plague, which then raged here, and conveying the contagion into Scotland, on their return, nearly one-third of the inhabitants of that country fell a sacrifice: a second visitation of this disease, in the years 1597 and 1598, swept away upwards of two thousand inhabitants of this town and parish.

The town is pleasantly situated in a fine fertile vale, which is enclosed by eminences of varied cultivation, and watered by three small rivers, the Eamont, the Lowther, and the Petteril, and on the west are the ruins of an ancient castle : it consists principally of one long street, situated at the junction of the main roads from Lancashire and London to Glasgow, and is well paved, and lighted with oil; the houses, many of which are modern, are built chiefly of red freestone, covered with plaster and whitewashed, and roofed with slate. About the year 1400, a water course was cut through the town from the river Petteril to the Eamont, at the expense of Wm. Strickland, Bishop of Carlisle. On Beacon Hill, so called from having been anciently crowned with a beacon, is a square stone edifice, erected in 1719, the windows of which command an extensive and diversified prospect, combining nearly all the varieties of landscape scenery; the principal objects being Lowther and Greystoke castles, with their magnificent parks; the ancient castles of Brougham and Penrith; a beautiful, though limited, view of Ullswater lake, with the finely-wooded hill of Dunmallet; the mountain scenery of the lakes, viz., Helvelyn, Saddleback, Skiddaw, &c.; also the Penine Alps, viz., Crossfell, &c.; and the river and vale of Eden, including Eden Hall, with the park and forest scenery. Towards the north is an excellent enclosed race-course, with a handsome grand stand, where, on the four last days of the first week in October, horse races and stag hunts are numerously and respectably attended. An assembly-room, occasionally used as a theatre, a bowling-green, news-room, subscription and circulating libraries, in the town, and many picturesque and beautiful walks in its neighbourhood, contribute to furnish amusement and recreation to the inhabitants. The manufacture of checks, gingham, calico, and other cotton goods, was formerly carried on to a considerable extent, but is now on the decline: the mineral produce of the neighbourhood consists of red freestone, slate, and limestone. The principal market is held on Tuesday, at which a considerable quantity of corn is pitched, and there is a smaller one for butchers' meat on Saturday: fairs for cattle are held on the 1st of March, 24th and 25th of April, and the third Tuesday in October; two fairs for hiring servants are held annually on the Tuesdays at Whitsuntide and Martinmas. New shambles were erected, and the old market cross, shambles, and moot-hall, were removed from the market-place, in 1807. The market and fairs are under the regulation of the bailiff appointed by the Duke of Devonshire, whose steward presides at a court baron, every third Monday, the powers of which extend to the recovery of debts under 40s.: the county court is held here four or five times a year, and petty sessions every alternate Tuesday; also a quarter session for the county, on the Tuesday in the first week after October 11th. A house of correction was built in 1826, at an expense of £400, which was defrayed out of the county rate.

The living is a vicarage, in the archdeaconry and diocese of Carlisle, rated in the king's books at £12. 6. 3., and in the patronage of the Bishop of Carlisle. The church, which is dedicated to St. Andrew, was given by Henry I. to the see of Carlisle, then newly founded: it was rebuilt, with the exception of the tower, in 1722, and is a plain, neat, and spacious edifice, consisting of a centre and two side aisles; the choir and centre aisle are open, and from the lofty ceiling depend two gilt chandeliers, the gift of the Duke of Portland; the side aisles are covered with galleries uniting at the western end, and supported by twenty pillars of the Ionic order, each consisting of one entire stone, which, from its colour and high polish, looks like mahogany; the upper range of pillars from the gallery to the roof are of wood painted white, with gilt mouldings. The altar is placed in a semicircular recess adorned with appropriate paintings in very good style: the church contains many monuments preserved from the former building, and, among other inscriptions, a record of the devastation caused here by the plague. In the churchyard are two stone monuments, called the Giant's Grave, or more commonly the Giant's legs; they are about twelve feet high, and fifteen feet distant from each other, and are traditionally said to have been raised

to commemorate the exploits of Sir Ewen Cæsarius, an ancient hero, against the robbers and wild boars that infested Inglewood Forest. There are places of worship for the Society of Friends, Independents, Primitive and Wesleyan Methodists, and Scottish Seceders. The free grammar school was founded, in 1340, by Bishop Strickland, who, having established a chantry here, required his chantry priest to teach music and grammar, at a salary of £6 per annum: it was refounded by Queen Elizabeth, at the request of her secretary, Sir Thomas Smith, Dean of Carlisle, and endowed with the above salary, which was augmented, in 1661, with a rent-charge of £10, by Mr. William Robinson, and, in 1782, with another of £6, by Mr. William Bleamire; the whole endowment at present is nearly £30 per annum, and the school is on the decline: it is entitled to share, with other schools in the counties of Westmorland and Yorkshire, in five exhibitions of £50 per annum each at Queen's College, Oxford, the bequest of Lady Elizabeth Hastings, in 1739; and the above-mentioned Mr. William Bleamire gave an additional rent-charge for providing a silver medal for the best composition in Latin verse, a silver pen for the best writer, and a book on arithmetic for the best arithmetician, with the remainder, if any, to the master: there are thirty-four scholars, each of whom pays 10s. 6d. per quarter. Mr. William Robinson built a school for the education of girls, and in 1661 endowed it with £20 a year, to which the sum of £5 per annum was added by the Executors of Mrs. Joan Lascelles, for the instruction of the girls in knitting; these, with subsequent benefactions, yield an income of about £30 per annum, for which sixty poor girls are instructed in reading, writing, needlework, &c., and several of them in knitting. A school of industry for fifty poor girls was established in 1813; and there is a National school, erected in 1816, a commodious stone building, situated in Benson's Row: it is supported by voluntary contributions, and one hundred and seventy boys are instructed, exclusively of more than one hundred girls, who attend on Sundays.

The remains of the ancient castle are westward of the town: this fabric is supposed to have been erected as a protection from the incursions of the Scots; it was repaired and enlarged by Richard, Duke of Gloucester, who resided here, and was sheriff of Cumberland for five years in succession: the site favours the opinion of its having been a Roman encampment, being irregularly quadrilateral. It exhibits no indication of very ancient date, being built of red stone; and the ruins are remarkable, more for their extent than their magnificence: the chief objects of interest are the projecting corbels in the eastern front, which appear to have supported an open corridor; there are some large vaults, which were probably prisons: the walls, broken in many places, and intersected with remaining windows, assume, from different points of view, many striking varieties of perspective scenery. After the great civil war, the edifice was dismantled, and part of the materials was sold. About half a mile north of Penrith is a square mount, measuring twenty yards on each side, which is generally supposed to have been used, during the rebellion, as a place of execution for the Scotch rebels. Three miles east by south of the town, on the north side of the river Eamont, are two remarkable excavations in a perpendicular rock, called Giant's Caves, according to fabulous tradition, the residence of Isis, a giant. On the south bank of the same river is a circular intrenchment, called King Arthur's Round Table.

PENROSE, a parish in the lower division of the hundred of RAGLAND, county of MONMOUTH, 2 miles (N.) from Ragland, containing 385 inhabitants. The living is a perpetual curacy, annexed to the vicarage of Lantillio-Grossenny, in the archdeaconry and diocese of Llandaff. The church is dedicated to St. Cadocus. There is a place of worship for Baptists.

PENRUDDOCK, a hamlet in the parish of GREYSTOCK, LEATH ward, county of CUMBERLAND, 6¼ miles (W. by S.) from Penrith. The population is returned with the parish. The Independents have a place of worship here, which is endowed with land producing £11 per annum.

Corporate Seal.

PENRYN, a borough, market town, and chapelry, having separate jurisdiction, though locally in the parish of Gluvias, hundred of KERRIER, county of CORNWALL, 2 miles (N.W.) from Falmouth, and 266 (W. S. W.) from London, containing 2933 inhabitants. The manors of Penryn-Borough and Penryn-Foreign have belonged from time immemorial to the Bishops of Exeter, who had formerly a country-house at or near this place. In the thirteenth century, Bishop Stapleden founded a college here for twelve prebendaries, the revenue of which, at the dissolution, was valued at £205. 10. 6.: the building is said to have occupied an area of three acres, and to have been surrounded by embattled walls. During the great civil war, Penryn was garrisoned for the king, but was surrendered to Sir Thomas Fairfax, in March 1646. The town is large, and pleasantly situated on the declivity of a hill, at the head of an inlet communicating with Falmouth harbour, of which it commands a fine view. It consists principally of one street, from which others diverge at right angles, not lighted, and roughly paved; the inhabitants are supplied with water from streams which issue from the adjacent eminences, one of which forms a cascade, and the scene, diversified with mills and cottages, presents a scene of picturesque beauty. The adjacent country is highly cultivated, and interspersed with elegant mansions. In addition to the general trade of the town, great quantities of granite, supplied by the neighbouring quarries, are shipped here, for London and elsewhere. The manufactures consist of paper, woollen cloth, gunpowder, and arsenic, and paint is made in great quantities by the "Cornish Colour Company:" corn-mills and breweries afford employment to several persons; and there are spacious warehouses, generally well filled with flour and grain from the Isle of Wight and Hampshire, this being considered the granary for the south-eastern part of the county. A market and fair were granted, in 1258, by the Bishop of Exeter, and a fair on the festival of St. Vitalis, in 1312: the present market is on Saturday, for meat, fish, poultry, and vegetables; and cattle fairs are held on Wednesday after

March 6th, May 12th, July 7th, October 8th, and December 21st.

Penryn is a borough by prescription, and was incorporated in the 18th of James I.: it is governed by a mayor, eleven more aldermen, and twelve common council-men, with a recorder, steward, town clerk, and inferior officers. The mayor, commonly styled portreeve, is chosen at the manorial court; the town clerk is appointed by the recorder; and the remaining officers are elected by a majority of that body. The mayor, recorder, deputy recorder, and justice (who is the mayor for the preceding year), are magistrates for the borough, exercising concurrent jurisdiction with the county magistrates, and holding a court of session quarterly. A court of record for the manor of Penryn-Foreign is held for pleas to any amount, at which the steward of the manor presides. The borough first regularly sent representatives to parliament in the reign of Mary, but is said to have returned once in the reign of Edward VI.: the right of election is in the inhabitants paying scot and lot, in number about one hundred and forty: the mayor is the returning officer; and the influence of Lord de Dunstanville is predominant. The living is a perpetual curacy, with the vicarage of Gluvias, within the peculiar jurisdiction of the Bishop of Exeter. The chapel, dedicated to St. Mary Magdalene, has received an addition of one hundred and forty free sittings, to which the Incorporated Society for the enlargement of churches and chapels contributed £85. There are places of worship for Bryanites, Independents, and Calvinistic and Wesleyan Methodists. A grammar school was founded by Elizabeth for the education of three boys, and endowed with a rent-charge of £6. 13. 4., which is for the present discontinued. In 1758, John Verran bequeathed £1000, which sum was laid out in the three per cents., for the support of eight poor men, or women, who have never received public relief, and other purposes. James Humphry, Esq., in 1823, bequeathed £3000, directing the sum to be invested also in the three per cent. consols., and the dividends to be appropriated, first, to the payment of certain annuities, and, on the death of the annuitants, the whole to be given, in sums of £10 per annum each, to inhabitants in reduced circumstances, not receiving any other charitable relief.

PENSAX, a chapelry in the parish of LINDRIDGE, lower division of the hundred of OSWALDSLOW, but locally in the upper division of the hundred of Doddingtree, county of WORCESTER, 6 miles (S. W.) from Bewdley, containing 574 inhabitants. Coal is obtained in the neighbourhood.

PENSBY, a township in the parish of WOODCHURCH, lower division of the hundred of WIRRALL, county palatine of CHESTER, 4½ miles (N. N. W.) from Great Neston, containing 22 inhabitants.

PENSCELLWOOD, a parish in the hundred of NORTON-FERRIS, county of SOMERSET, 3¾ miles (N. E.) from Wincanton, containing 332 inhabitants. The living is a discharged rectory, in the archdeaconry of Wells, and diocese of Bath and Wells, rated in the king's books at £6. 14. 9½., and in the patronage of the Earl of Ilchester. The church is dedicated to St. Michael. On the site of an ancient Danish camp, in this parish, a tower, one hundred and twenty feet in height, was erected, by an ancestor of Sir R. C. Hoare, Bart., to commemorate the celebrated visit of Alfred the

Great, in the disguise of a minstrel, to the tent of Guthrum, whom he afterwards defeated and converted to Christianity, himself being sponsor at the font.

PENSFORD (ST. THOMAS), a parish in the hundred of KEYNSHAM, county of SOMERSET, 27 miles (N. N. E.) from Somerton, containing 319 inhabitants. The living is a perpetual curacy, annexed to the vicarage of Stanton-Drew, in the archdeaconry of Bath, and diocese of Bath and Wells. The church is dedicated to St. Thomas à Becket. There are places of worship for Independents and Wesleyan Methodists. The river Chew runs through the parish, and turns several considerable copper-mills, which, with the adjacent coal mines, afford employment to the greater portion of the inhabitants. A market, formerly held by charter at this place, has been disused for some years past; but there are still two fairs, on May 6th and November 8th.

PENSHAM, a hamlet in the parish of ST. ANDREW, PERSHORE, upper division of the hundred of PERSHORE, county of WORCESTER, 1½ mile (S. by W.) from Pershore, containing 95 inhabitants.

PENSHURST, a parish in the hundred of SOMERDEN, lathe of SUTTON at HONE, county of KENT, 4¼ miles (W. S. W.) from Tunbridge, containing 1392 inhabitants. The living is a rectory, in the peculiar jurisdiction of the Archbishop of Canterbury, rated in the king's books at £30. 6. 0½., and in the patronage of Sir J. S. Sidney Bart. The church, dedicated to St. John the Baptist, has a spire steeple and three chancels, and is rich in ancient monuments. There is a place of worship for Independents. The river Eden here meanders in divided streams, and unites with the Medway in its course to Tunbridge. Penshurst castle, adjoining the village, is a noble pile erected in the reign of Henry VIII., on the site of an ancient mansion, which, in the time of William the Conqueror, belonged to the Penchester family; but, since that of Edward IV., to the Sydneys, from whom Sir Philip Sydney was descended. A fair is held here on June 25th and 26th : on the evening of the latter day, as soon as it is dusk, the young peasants in the vicinity, and sometimes the gentry, have been accustomed, time immemorially, to resort to a flat wooden bridge over the river Medway, about a quarter of a mile off, and there dance all night; a public house, two or three cottages near the bridge, and the bridge itself, being illuminated. In the neighbourhood are remains of a Roman fortification. Penshurst gives the inferior title of baron to the family of Smythe, Viscounts Strangford.

PENSTHORPE, a parish in the hundred of GALLOW, county of NORFOLK, 2 miles (E. S. E.) from Fakenham, containing 26 inhabitants. The living is a rectory, in the archdeaconry of Norfolk, and diocese of Norwich, rated in the king's books at £10. A. Hamond, Esq. was patron in 1818. The church has been demolished.

PENTERRY, a parish in the upper division of the hundred of CALDICOTT, county of MONMOUTH, 3¼ miles (N. by W.) from Chepstow, containing 60 inhabitants. The living is a perpetual curacy, in the archdeaconry and diocese of Llandaff, endowed with £1000 royal bounty, and in the patronage of the Prebendary of Caire in the Cathedral Church of Llandaff.

PENTLOW, a parish in the hundred of HINCKFORD, county of ESSEX, 2¾ miles (E. by N.) from Clare, containing 310 inhabitants. The living is a rectory, in the jurisdiction of the Commissary of Essex and Herts, con-

currently with the Consistorial Court of the Bishop of London, rated in the king's books at £12. The Rev. John Bull was patron in 1816. The church is dedicated to St. George.

PENTNEY, a parish in the Lynn division of the hundred of FREEBRIDGE, county of NORFOLK, 7½ miles (N. W. by W.) from Swaffham, containing 418 inhabitants. The living is a perpetual curacy, in the archdeaconry and diocese of Norwich, endowed with £800 royal bounty, and held by sequestration. The church is dedicated to St. Mary Magdalene. About a mile to the westward is the remaining gate-house of a priory of Black canons, founded in honour of the Holy Trinity, the Blessed Virgin Mary, and St. Mary Magdalene, by Robert de Vallibus, a follower of the Conqueror; at the dissolution here were twelve canons, whose revenue was estimated at £215. 18. 8.

PENTON-GRAFTON, a hamlet (formerly a parish) in the parish of WEYHILL, hundred of ANDOVER, Andover division of the county of SOUTHAMPTON, 3 miles (W. by N.) from Andover. The population is returned with Weyhill. An annuity of £9, the gift of John Read, in 1651, is applied for teaching poor children, and other charitable uses.

PENTON-MEWSEY, a parish in the hundred of ANDOVER, Andover division of the county of SOUTHAMPTON, 2¾ miles (N. W. by W.) from Andover, containing 202 inhabitants. The living is a rectory, in the archdeaconry and diocese of Winchester, rated in the king's books at £9. 12. 8½., and in the patronage of the Rev. E. Fulham. The church is dedicated to the Holy Trinity. A school-room was erected in 1815, by subscription, to which £6 a year, the bequest of John Read, in 1651, has been added, in support of a schoolmistress, who instructs about forty children.

PENTONVILLE, a chapelry in the parish of ST. JAMES, CLERKENWELL, Finsbury division of the hundred of OSSULSTONE, county of MIDDLESEX. The population is returned with the parish. The chapel, a neat edifice, was erected in 1791, since which period a considerable number of streets has been formed, and it now constitutes one of the most populous and respectable suburbs of the metropolis; a further description of which is given in the article on CLERKENWELL.

PENTRICH, a parish in the hundred of MORLESTON and LITCHURCH, county of DERBY, comprising the townships of Pentrich and Ripley, and containing 2143 inhabitants, of which number, 508 are in the township of Pentrich, 2¾ miles (S. W. by S.) from Alfreton. The living is a discharged vicarage, in the archdeaconry of Derby, and diocese of Lichfield and Coventry, rated in the king's books at £6, endowed with £600 royal bounty, and £1000 parliamentary grant, and in the patronage of the Duke of Devonshire. The church is dedicated to St. Matthew. There are places of worship for Independents and Unitarians. The parish is bounded on the west by the river Amber. The population of the township of Pentrich has decreased one-third since the disturbances which broke out there in 1817, when the agents of the Duke of Devonshire razed many of the houses to the ground. It had anciently a market and two fairs; the latter are still held on the Wednesday in Easter-week and October 23rd. At Butterley are iron-works, established about 1793, underneath which the Cromford canal is conducted through a tunnel two thousand nine hundred and sixty-six yards in length; and in the neighbourhood is the reservoir of the Nottingham canal, covering an extent of many acres. There are also considerable coal and iron-stone works in the parish. A National school, erected by the Duke of Devonshire in 1819, is supported by voluntary contributions. The Romans had a camp on the adjoining common, near which passed the Iknield-street.

PENTRIDGE, a parish in that part of the hundred of CRANBORNE which is in the Shaston (East) division of the county of DORSET, 3½ miles (N.W. by N.) from Cranborne, containing 272 inhabitants. The living is a rectory, in the archdeaconry of Dorset, and diocese of Bristol, rated in the king's books at £6. 15. 10., and in the patronage of the Crown. The church is dedicated to St. Rumbold. On Penbury hill, which commands an extensive prospect, there was formerly a beacon.

PENWORTHAM, a parish in the hundred of LEYLAND, county palatine of LANCASTER, comprising the chapelry of Longton, and the townships of Farrington, Howick, Hutton, and Penwortham, and containing 4554 inhabitants, of which number, 1501 are in the township of Penwortham, 1¾ mile (S.W.) from Preston. The living is a perpetual curacy, in the archdeaconry and diocese of Chester, endowed with £1600 parliamentary grant, and in the patronage of L. Rawstorne, Esq. The church is dedicated to St. Mary. A free grammar school was founded at Hutton, in 1552, by Christopher Walton, who endowed it with houses and lands now producing an annual income of about £675, for which a few boys are instructed in the rudiments of Latin, and about one hundred and forty children of both sexes are educated on the National system. The petty sessions for the hundred of Leyland are held here on Mondays, once in five weeks, alternately with Chorley, Cuerdon, Leyland, and Rufford. A Benedictine priory, in honour of the Virgin Mary, was founded here, on lands granted by Warine Bussel to the abbey of Evesham, in the time of the Conqueror, and several monks of that establishment placed therein, whose revenue at the dissolution was valued at £114. 16. 9.

PEN-Y-CLAWDD, a parish in the lower division of the hundred of RAGLAND, county of MONMOUTH, 4¾ miles (S.W.) from Monmouth, containing 41 inhabitants. The living is a perpetual curacy, annexed to that of Llangoven, in the archdeaconry and diocese of Llandaff, endowed with £800 royal bounty, and £200 parliamentary grant, and in the patronage of the Chapter of Llandaff.

Corporate Seal.

PENZANCE, a sea-port, market town, and chapelry, in the parish of MADRON, having exclusive jurisdiction, though locally in the hundred of Penwith, county of CORNWALL, 67 miles (S. W. by W.) from Launceston, and 282 (W. S. W.) from London, containing 5224 inhabitants. The former appellation of this town was *Burriton*; its present name, signifying "the head of the bay," is indicative of its situation, which is at the north-west side of Mount's bay. In the year 1595, it was set on fire by a small party of Spaniards, who landed near Mousehole, a mile and a half distant, on the 23rd of July, and who, as observed by historians, were the only Spaniards that ever landed in the kingdom as enemies: on this occasion, Sir Francis Godolphin summoned the county to his assistance, and attempted to save Penzance from the threatened danger, but his followers being seized with a sudden panic, he was obliged to abandon it to its fate; the Cornish men having rallied the next day in greater numbers and better courage, the Spaniards, who had already set fire to Newlyn, Mousehole, and Penryn, quitted the coast without attempting further hostilities. During the great civil commotions, the town is said to have been plundered by the army of Sir Thomas Fairfax, in 1646, as a punishment for the kindness which the inhabitants had shewn to the troops under Lord Goring and Lord Hopton.

The town, which has of late years considerably increased in size and population, is situated on the north-west side and nearly at the bottom of Mount's bay, opposite to St. Michael's Mount, and Marazion on the east: the streets are lighted and paved; the houses in general modern, neat, and commodious; and the inhabitants are supplied with water from a reservoir. The fine situation of the town, its salubrious atmosphere, and the picturesque beauties of the vicinity, through which the walks and rides are particularly pleasant, have rendered it a place of resort for valetudinarians, and gained for it the well-deserved epithet of the Montpellier of England; the great variety of boats and shipping constantly lying in Mount's bay contributes much to the interest of the scenery, which, in its diversity and combinations, is considered to be unsurpassed by that of any other place in Great Britain. A battery pier, constructed in 1766, extended in 1782, and again in 1812, is now more than six hundred feet in length; and in 1816, a lighthouse was erected at its extremity, which is illuminated only when there are nine feet of water in the harbour. Among the scientific and literary institutions is "The Royal Geological Society of Cornwall," which was established here in 1814, under the patronage of his late Majesty, George IV., and has published three volumes of transactions, which were received in the most flattering manner by the various scientific institutions of Europe and America; attached to it is a most splendid museum of minerals, illustrative of geology and mineralogy: there is also a public library, established about ten years since, and now containing nearly three thousand volumes of standard works; besides which, several book clubs, subscription and commercial news-rooms, and commodious apartments for public assemblies, contribute to the instruction and recreation of the inhabitants. Here is a considerable export trade in tin, copper, china, clay, pilchards, and other fish: the imports are timber, iron, hemp, tallow, and groceries, with various other articles of merchandise. The pilchard fishery is chiefly carried on by the inhabitants of Newlyn and Mousehole, on the west side of the bay, and the fish are brought hither for exportation. About the period of the Restoration, Penzance was added as a fifth stannary town, and all the Cornish tin is now coined here and at Truro, and about two-thirds of it shipped at this port. A dry dock has been constructed, and the port regulations are efficient and well conducted. A packet sails weekly to the Scilly islands. The manufacture of yarn and coarse woollen cloth affords employment to several persons. A market and an annual fair for seven days were granted in 1332, and under the charter of incorporation, two markets and seven fairs, most of which have fallen into disuse. The present markets are on Thursday and Saturday; the former is well supplied with corn: fairs are held on May 28th, Thursday after Trinity-Sunday, and Thursday before Advent-Sunday. The annual income from the tolls of the market is about £600, and that from the pier dues about £1200, both being under the control of the corporation. A grant of anchorage, keelage, and bushellage, was made to the inhabitants by Henry VIII., which was confirmed in the charter of incorporation granted by James I., bearing date May 9th, 1614, under which the corporation consists of a mayor, eight aldermen, and twelve assistants, with a recorder, town clerk, and other officers: the mayor is elected from among the aldermen, by the corporation at large, on the Friday after Michaelmas; the retiring mayor is justice of the peace for the ensuing year: the aldermen are elected from among the assistants, and these from the inhabitants: the aldermen and assistants have an equal vote on all corporation affairs. The mayor, recorder, and justice, are magistrates for the borough, with exclusive jurisdiction, but have no power to appoint deputies (excepting the mayor in the court of record): the aldermen and assistants hold their situation for life, but the recorder and town clerk only during the pleasure of the corporation. A court of record is held every alternate Friday by the mayor and town clerk, who is steward of the court, for the recovery of debts under £50: after having been disused seventy years, this court was revived in 1826. Sessions for the borough are held quarterly, on the Friday following those for the county, by the officers of the corporation, whose power extends to transportation for seven years, and has been recently exercised for the first time. Petty sessions for the west division of the hundred are held here, on the first. Friday in every month. A court for the hundred is held by the steward, as occasion requires.

The living is a perpetual curacy, annexed to the vicarage of Madron, in the archdeaconry of Cornwall, and diocese of Exeter, endowed with £800 parliamentary grant. The chapel, dedicated to St. Mary, was erected prior to 1612, enlarged in 1671, and at its consecration, in 1680, was endowed with land which now lets for £20 per annum, by John Tremenhere, Esq.; a cemetery was then enclosed, and the limits of the town were defined to be those of the chapelry. There are places of worship for Baptists, the Society of Friends, Independents, and Wesleyan Methodists, also a synagogue. The free school was endowed, in 1714, by John Buller, Esq., with £15 per annum: the poor children of the chapelry also receive instruction in a school at Madron, founded in 1704, by Mr. George Daniel. Northward of this town there are considerable earthworks, with a treble intrenchment, called *Leseaddock*, or *Leseudjack*, supposed to be of remote antiquity. An annual custom, the origin of which is unknown, prevails here on Midsummer-eve, when a great quantity and variety of fire-works, accompanied with bonfires, ignited tar barrels, and torches, are exhibited, and attended by young persons of both sexes; and on Midsummer-day, a fair is held on the pier, and a number of persons from the town and neighbourhood enjoy the gratification of water excursions: similar customs are observed on the 28th and 29th of June. Sir Humphrey Davy, the celebrated natural philosopher and chemist, and late President of the Royal Society, was a native of this town, and bequeathed £100 four per cents. to the master of the grammar school, to allow the boys a holiday annually on his birthday, the 17th of December.

PEOPLETON, a parish in the upper division of the hundred of PERSHORE, county of WORCESTER, 3½ miles (N.) from Pershore, containing 264 inhabitants. The living is a rectory, in the archdeaconry and diocese of Worcester, rated in the king's books at £11. 10., and in the patronage of —— Dineley, Esq. The church is dedicated to St. Michael.

PEOVER (LITTLE), a township in that part of the parish of GREAT BUDWORTH which is in the hundred of BUCKLOW, county palatine of CHESTER, 3 miles (S. by W.) from Nether Knutsford, containing 88 inhabitants. A school is supported by considerable donations for the education of poor children.

PEOVER (NETHER), a chapelry in that part of the parish of GREAT BUDWORTH which is in the hundred of NORTHWICH, county palatine of CHESTER, 3 miles (S. by W.) from Nether Knutsford, containing 250 inhabitants. The living is a perpetual curacy, in the archdeaconry and diocese of Chester, endowed with £400 parliamentary grant, and in the patronage of Lord de Tabley. The chapel is dedicated to St. Oswald.

PEOVER (SUPERIOR), a chapelry in that part of the parish of ROSTHERN which is in the hundred of BUCKLOW, county palatine of CHESTER, 4 miles (S. S. E.) from Nether Knutsford, containing 543 inhabitants. The living is a perpetual curacy, in the archdeaconry and diocese of Chester, and in the patronage of Sir H. Mainwaring, Bart. The church is dedicated to St. Lawrence. A school-house was built about 1730, in which four boys and four girls are taught and clothed for £10 a year, the proceeds of certain property bequeathed for the purpose by Charlotte Mainwaring, in 1728.

PEPPER-HARROW, a parish in the first division of the hundred of GODALMING, county of SURREY, 3 miles (W.) from Godalming, containing 130 inhabitants. The living is a discharged rectory, in the archdeaconry of Surrey, and diocese of Winchester, rated in the king's books at £6.7.6., and in the patronage of Viscount Midleton. The church is dedicated to St. Nicholas. The river Wey passes through the parish.

PERLETHORPE, a chapelry in the parish of EDWINSTOW, Hatfield division of the wapentake of BASSETLAW, county of NOTTINGHAM, 2¼ miles (N. by W.) from Ollerton, containing 93 inhabitants. The chapel, though small, is a very handsome structure, erected by one of the Pierrepoint family, upon the site of a former one: the windows exhibit both ancient and modern specimens of stained glass, and over the altar is a painting, by West, of Peter denying Christ.

PERRAN-ARWORTHAL, a parish in the hundred of KERRIER, county of CORNWALL, 4 miles (N.) from Penryn, containing 1362 inhabitants. The living is a perpetual curacy, annexed to the vicarage of Stithians, in the archdeaconry of Cornwall, and diocese of Exeter. The church is dedicated to St. Piran. There is a place

3 X 2

of worship for Wesleyan Methodists. This parish includes part of Perran-Wharf, or Perran-Cove, in Falmouth harbour, to which there is a rail-road communicating with the Redruth and Gwennap mines. Here is a manufactory for arsenic.

PERRAN-UTHNOE, a parish in the hundred of PENWITH, county of CORNWALL, 1¼ mile (S. E.) from Marazion, containing 786 inhabitants. The living is a rectory, in the archdeaconry of Cornwall, and diocese of Exeter, rated in the king's books at £17. 11. 5½., and in the patronage of Sir J. Trevelyan, Bart. The parish, which lies near the entrance to Mount's bay, is bounded on the south by the English channel. At Gold-Sithney is a large fair for cattle, coarse cloths, hardware, &c.

PERRANZABULOE, a parish in the hundred of PYDER, county of CORNWALL, 7 miles (W. N. W.) from St. Michael, containing 1702 inhabitants. The living is a discharged vicarage, to which is annexed the perpetual curacy of St. Agnes, in the peculiar jurisdiction and patronage of the Dean and Chapter of Exeter, rated in the king's books at £24. The ancient church was collegiate, for a dean and canons, in the time of Edward the Confessor, and had the privilege of sanctuary, but having been overwhelmed with the sand, another church has been erected, near the village of Lambourn, which was consecrated in 1805. There are tin, copper, and lead mines in full operation within the parish. At Perran Porth is a fine sandy beach, frequented as a bathing-place, the visitors procuring lodgings in the cottages by the sea-side. The western part of the parish is very populous, being inhabited by miners, who live in detached cottages, thickly scattered over the commons. A fair is held on Easter - Tuesday, sometimes at Millingy, and at other times at Penhallow. St. Perran's well, near Lambourn, which is enclosed by an ancient stone building, is one of those to which the power of working miraculous cures was formerly ascribed. On the downs, about a mile and a half from the same place, is St. Perran's Round, one of the ancient Cornish amphitheatres : there are several other old earth-works within the parish.

PERRIVALE, a parish in the hundred of ELTHORNE, county of MIDDLESEX, 3¼ miles (S. by E.) from Harrow on the Hill, containing 25 inhabitants. The living is a discharged rectory, in the archdeaconry of Middlesex, and diocese of London, rated in the king's books at £6. 13. 4. John Lateward, Esq. was patron in 1812.

PERROT (NORTH), a parish in the hundred of HOUNDSBOROUGH, BERWICK, and COKER, county of SOMERSET, 3¼ miles (E.) from Crewkerne, containing 387 inhabitants. The living is a rectory, in the archdeaconry of Wells, and diocese of Bath and Wells, rated in the king's books at £9. 18. 1½. Henry Hoskins, Esq. was patron in 1814. The church is dedicated to St. Martin.

PERROT (SOUTH), a parish in the hundred of BEAMINSTER-FORUM and REDHONE, Bridport division of the county of DORSET, 4¼ miles (N. by W.) from Beaminster, containing 317 inhabitants. The living is a rectory, with the perpetual curacy of Mosterton annexed, in the archdeaconry of Dorset, and diocese of Bristol, rated in the king's books at £17. 14. 2. Samuel Wills, Esq. was patron in 1809. The church is dedicated to St. Mary.

PERRY (EAST), a hamlet in the parish of GRAFFHAM, hundred of LEIGHTONSTONE, county of HUNTINGDON, 3¼ miles (E. by S.) from Kimbolton. The population is returned with the parish.

PERRY-HILL, a tything in the parish of WORPLESDON, first division of the hundred of WOKING, county of SURREY. The population is returned with the parish. The parish church stands in this tything.

PERSHALL, a township in the parish of ECCLESHALL, northern division of the hundred of PIREHILL, county of STAFFORD, 1 mile from Eccleshall, containing 80 inhabitants. It is within the peculiar jurisdiction of the Prebendary of Eccleshall in the Cathedral Church of Lincoln.

PERSHORE, a market town, partly in the parish of St. ANDREW, and partly in that of HOLY CROSS, upper division of the hundred of PERSHORE, county of WORCESTER, 9 miles (S. E.) from Worcester, and 102 (N.W. by W.) from London, containing, exclusively of those portions of the parishes which are without the town, 2328 inhabitants. The name of this place, variously spelt Persore, Pearshore, and Pershore, is supposed by Camden to be derived from Periscoran, in allusion to the numerous pear-trees which grew in the vicinity : a convent was founded here, according to William of Malmesbury, by Egelward, Duke of Dorset, or, according to others, by Oswald, nephew of Etheldred, King of Mercia, about 689, for Secular clerks. It was remodelled by Edgar, as a monastery for Benedictine monks, about 984, and dedicated to the Virgin Mary, St. Peter, and St. Paul, and afterwards to Edburga, eighth daughter of Edward the Elder. The buildings suffered repeatedly from fire, especially in 1287, when a considerable part of the town was also destroyed: at the dissolution its revenue was valued at £666. 13. The only remains are the church of the Holy Cross, and the Abbey house, the latter having undergone such alterations that every vestige of its ancient character has been removed. The town is pleasantly situated on the lower road from Worcester to London, and on the western bank of the river Avon, which is here navigable, and is crossed by a bridge on the south. The principal street is about three quarters of a mile in length; it is well paved, and the houses are of respectable appearance. There is a manufactory for stockings, and two for watch mainsprings. The market is on Tuesday : fairs are held on Easter-Tuesday, June 26th, first Monday in August, and on the Tuesday before November 1st. This town returned two burgesses to parliament in the reign of Edward I., since which period the privilege has been discontinued. As to all civil jurisdiction the parishes of St. Andrew and Holy Cross are absolutely distinct, each having its own officers : the former includes the chapelries of Bricklehampton, Defford, Penvin, and Wick, and the hamlet of Pensham ; and the latter the hamlets of Wadborough and Walcott.

The living of St. Andrew's is a discharged vicarage, in the archdeaconry and diocese of Worcester, rated in the king's books at £8. 19. 2., and in the patronage of the Dean and Chapter of Westminster. The church consists of a choir and south transept, the remains of a noble cruciform church, and is partly in the Norman, but principally in the early English, style of architecture. The church of the Holy Cross is in the later English style, and was formerly conventual, having belonged to the abbey: the living is held as a curacy, with the vicarage of St. Andrew's: both are subject to the jurisdiction of the Archdeacon of Worcester. There is a place of worship for Baptists.

PERTENHALL, a parish in the hundred of STODDEN, county of BEDFORD, 2 miles (S. W. by S.) from Kimbolton, containing 324 inhabitants. The living is a rectory, in the archdeaconry of Bedford, and diocese of Lincoln, rated in the king's books at £18, and in the patronage of the Rev. J. R. Martyn. The church is dedicated to St. Peter and St. Paul. Here was formerly a preceptory of the Knights Templars, of which only the site, surrounded with a moat, is now remaining. There is a chalybeate spring, called Chad-well.

PERTHOLEY, a parochial chapelry in the lower division of the hundred of USK, county of MONMOUTH, 4¼ miles (S. by E.) from Usk. The population is returned with the parish of Llantrissent. The living is a perpetual curacy, annexed to the vicarage of Llantrissent, in the archdeaconry and diocese of Llandaff, endowed with £200 royal bounty. The chapel is dedicated to St. Bartholomew.

PERTWOOD (UPPER), a parish forming a distinct portion of the hundred of WARMINSTER, though locally in that of Dunworth, county of WILTS, 2 miles (N. W.) from Hindon, containing 23 inhabitants. The living is a discharged rectory, in the archdeaconry and diocese of Salisbury, rated in the king's books at £3. 1. 5½., endowed with £200 royal bounty. R. Rickwood, Esq. was patron in 1815. The church is dedicated to St. Peter.

PETER (ST.), a parish and a member of the cinque-port liberty of DOVOR, though locally in the hundred of Ringslow, or Isle of Thanet, lathe of ST. AUGUSTINE, county of KENT, 2½ miles (N.) from Ramsgate, containing, with the hamlets of Broadstairs, Kingsgate, &c., 2101 inhabitants. The living is a vicarage, in the archdeaconry and diocese of Canterbury, rated in the king's books at £9, and in the patronage of the Archbishop of Canterbury. The church, though small, is remarkable for its neatness. There is a place of worship for Wesleyan Methodists. At Broadstairs, in this parish, a chapel of ease was erected by subscription in 1828. The village is much frequented by visitors from Margate; and there are public gardens, called Ranelagh Gardens, disposed with much taste, and at a considerable expense, and placed under the superintendence of the master of the ceremonies at Margate, during the season, when it is not unusal for seven hundred persons to assemble at one time, to partake of the amusements of the place. Elizabeth Lovejoy, in 1694, bequeathed her interest in certain tithes for the support of a schoolmaster to teach twenty boys; the income is £20 a year, and is applied as directed by the donor.

PETER (ST.) CHEESEHILL, a parish within the liberty of the soke, and adjacent to the city, of WINCHESTER, Fawley division of the county of SOUTHAMPTON, containing 581 inhabitants. The living is a discharged rectory, in the archdeaconry and diocese of Winchester, rated in the king's books at £14. 9. 9½., endowed with £600 private benefaction, £400 royal bounty, and £600 parliamentary grant, and in the patronage of the Crown.

PETER-CHURCH, a parish in the hundred of WEBTREE, county of HEREFORD, 11½ miles (W.) from Hereford, containing 686 inhabitants. The living is a discharged vicarage, in the archdeaconry and diocese of Hereford, rated in the king's books at £5. 6. 8., and in the patronage of the Governors of Guy's Hospital, London. The church is dedicated to St. Peter. There is a place of worship for Baptists.

PETERBOROUGH, a city, and the seat of a diocese, having separate jurisdiction, and the head of the liberty of Nassaburgh, or Peterborough, county of NORTHAMPTON, 42 miles (N. E. by E.) from Northampton, and 79 (N. by W.) from London, containing, with the precinct of the Minster-close, and exclusively of the chapelries of Dogsthorpe, Eastfield with Newark, and Longthorpe, in that part of the parish which is within the liberty, 4598 inhabitants. The original name of this place, according to ancient records, was Medeswelhamsted, or Medeshamsted, from a whirlpool in that part of the river Aufona, now the Nene, near which the town was built. During the Saxon Octarchy, Peada, fifth king of Mercia, having embraced the Christian faith, laid the foundation of a monastery, about 655, which was completed by his brother Wulfhere, in atonement for having murdered his own sons, for their attachment to the Christian doctrine, prior to his own conversion to Christianity. From this monastery, which was dedicated to St. Peter, and soon became celebrated for the magnificence of its buildings and the richness of its endowments, the town derived the name Petriburgus, whence its present appellation. The monastery continued to flourish until about the middle of the ninth century, when the Danes having laid waste the neighbouring country, plundered the town, massacred the monks, and burnt the monastic buildings. In this state of desolation it remained for more than a century, till it was restored by Ethelwold, Bishop of Winchester, with the assistance of King Edgar, and of Adulph, the king's chancellor, who appropriated all his wealth to the rebuilding of the monastery, of which, after its restoration, he was made abbot. In the reign of William the Conqueror, Hereward, the last of the Anglo-Saxon warriors who distinguished themselves by their exploits, having heard that the Conqueror had given away his paternal lands to a Norman, set sail from Flanders, whither he had retired, and having landed in Lincolnshire, made an incursion into this city, and setting fire to the gates and outbuildings of the monastery, which he was unable to storm, opened for himself a passage through the flames, plundered the treasury, and having committed various outrages, retired to his ships with an immense booty. Against this invader, and for the protection of the abbey from similar attacks, Abbot Turold erected a fort, or castle, which, from his name, is called Mont Turold: this mound, or hill, is on the outside of the deanery garden, and is now called Tot-hill, or Toot-hill. In 1116, the monastery and town were greatly injured by fire, and to this accident may be attributed the existence of the present cathedral church, the building of which was commenced two years afterwards by Abbot Salisbury; and at this period the town, which had previously stood on the eastern side of the monastery, was re-erected on the situation it now occupies. The town suffered materially in the war between John and the confederate barons, many of whom took refuge in the monastery here and in Croyland abbey, from which sanctuaries they were forced by the king's soldiers, who plundered the religious houses and carried off a rich booty. This was a mitred abbey of the Benedictine order, the abbots having been summoned to parliament in the reign of Henry III.: at the dissolution, its revenue was estimated at £1972. 7. 0¾., and the conventual church, on the establishment of the see, became the cathedral of the diocese. During the civil war in the reign of Charles I., the parliamentary forces under the command of Cromwell, destined for the siege of Croyland, were stationed in this town, where they committed numerous depredations, defacing the cathedral, which they stripped of its plate and ornaments, and pulling down part of the cloisters, the chapter-house, and the episcopal palace, which were sold by order of the parliament.

The city is pleasantly situated on the north side of the river Nene, over which is a wooden bridge: it consists of several regular and well-formed streets; the houses are in general neatly built, and many of them have been modernised in the recent improvements of the city, which have been effected under the provisions of an act of parliament in 1790: the town is well paved, lighted with gas, and amply supplied with water. The environs are pleasant, and afford much agreeable and diversified scenery. A book society was established in 1730: there is a small theatre, which is opened generally in June, for six weeks; and assemblies are held at stated times, generally for the benefit of the dispensary and the National school. The trade is principally in corn, coal, timber, coke, lime, bricks, and stone, the produce of the neighbourhood. The river Nene is not navigable for shipping, but boats pass to Northampton, where it communicates with the Grand Junction canal; and in the opposite direction vessels proceed through Wisbeach to Lynn, to the former of which packets sail twice a week. The market is on Saturday: the fairs commence July 9th and October 1st, each for three days, for cattle, timber, and various kinds of merchandise: the former only is held in the city, and the latter, called "Bridge Fair," on the opposite side of the river, in the adjoining part of the county of Huntingdon. The liberty, or soke, of Peterborough, is co-extensive with the hundred, and comprises thirty-two townships and hamlets: the civil government is vested in the lord of the hundred, a custos rotulorum, and magistrates appointed by the crown, with powers equal to that of judges of assize, and in a high bailiff of the city, who is appointed by the dean and chapter, who are lords of the manor; constables and other officers are appointed at the court leet held annually. Courts of quarter session, for all offences committed within the soke, are held here, on the day preceding those for the county; also a court of record, for the recovery of debts to any amount, but in which debts above £5 are seldom sued for. The town hall, erected in 1671, is a neat building, under which is a covered area for the use of the market. There are two gaols; that for the liberty is a small building, containing three cells, being calculated to receive only seven prisoners: it is under the superintendence of the Marquis of Exeter, as lord of the hundred: the other, usually called the house of correction, is adapted to the reception of eleven prisoners. The city first sent members to parliament in the 1st of Edward VI., since which time it has regularly returned two: the right of election is vested, by a decision of the House of Commons, May 13th, 1728, in the inhabitants within the precincts of the Minster, being householders not receiving alms, and in the other inhabitants of the city paying scot and lot; the high bailiff is the returning officer, and the patronage belongs to Earl Fitzwilliam. The great borough fen between Peterborough and Crowland, containing nearly seven thousand acres, was, until the year 1815, subject to the pasturage of the cattle belonging to the inhabitants of the thirty-two townships which comprize the soke, it has since been enclosed, and a new parish, called Newborough, formed.

Arms of the Bishoprick.

This city was anciently included in the diocese of Lincoln, from which, with the counties of Northampton and Rutland, it was separated by Henry VIII., in 1541, and erected into an episcopal see, of which the last abbot of Peterborough was made the first bishop, the conventual church of that monastery appropriated as the cathedral, and the abbot's house as the episcopal palace. The ecclesiastical establishment consists of a bishop, dean, sub-dean, six prebendaries, four minor canons, a master and eight choristers, six singers, an organist, two schoolmasters, twenty scholars, a steward, and six almsmen. The cathedral is a spacious and venerable structure, partly in the Norman, and partly in the early English, style of architecture, with a low lantern tower rising from the centre. An ancient gateway entrance of the Norman style, which has received some additions in the later English, leads into a small quadrangle, on one side of which are the conventual buildings, which retain much of their original character; and opposite the entrance is the magnificent west front of the cathedral, consisting of three lofty arches in the early English style, of unparalleled beauty, but the effect greatly diminished by a small porch (over which is the chapel of St. Thomas à Becket), which, though of elegant design, is not in accordance with the general character of this part of the building. Each of the three magnificent arches is surmounted by a decorated gable, pierced with Catherine-wheel windows: on each side is a highly-enriched turret, surmounted by a spire, and at the north-west angle of the nave is a square tower with angular turrets crowned with pinnacles, with which a similar tower at the south-west angle formerly corresponded. The nave, which is in the Norman style, is separated from the aisles by finely-clustered piers and arches, of lighter character than generally prevails in that style, and is a fine specimen of just proportion and elegant arrangement: the roof, which is of wood, is divided into compartments, panelled, and ornamented with paintings and with gilt fillets and mouldings: the choir has a groined roof of wood; on the south side is the shrine of St. Tibba, generally mistaken for the cenotaph of Mary, Queen of Scots, who was buried near the spot, but whose remains were afterwards removed to Westminster; and on the north was the tomb of Queen Catherine of Arragon, destroyed by the parliamentarian troops under Cromwell, which has been replaced by a marble slab to the memory of that queen.

The east end is circular, and there are several chapels in the later English style, with fan tracery of elegant design; the windows generally appear to have been enriched with tracery, subsequently to their original formation, and many of them have been enlarged. To the south of the south transept are the remains of what was probably the refectory, and the infirmary of the convent, exhibiting a beautiful specimen of the early English style: the cloisters, of which part only remains, appear to have been singularly beautiful, and to have combined various styles of architecture, from the early Norman to the later English. The length of the cathedral, from east to west, is four hundred and seventy-one feet, and the breadth, along the transepts, one hundred and eighty feet: among the monuments are three for abbots of the twelfth century, and one for the abbot, and eighty-four of the monks, who were massacred by the Danes, in the year 870, of black and blue marble, formed like a shrine, and sculptured with figures of Christ and the Apostles, which is placed behind the altar. The Cathedral Close exhibits several interesting remains of English architecture, and it has a gateway communicating with the town, another leading to the Bishop's palace, and a third, of considerable beauty, to the deanery.

The city comprises only the parish of St. John the Baptist. The living is a discharged vicarage, in the archdeaconry of Northampton, and diocese of Peterborough, endowed with £200 private benefaction, and £200 royal bounty, and in the patronage of the Bishop of Peterborough. The church of St. John, a spacious structure, recently repaired and partly rebuilt, has a handsome altar-piece, painted by Sir Robert Ker Porter. There are places of worship for Baptists, Independents, and Wesleyan and other Methodists. The free grammar school was founded by Henry VIII., on the dissolution of the monastery, and placed under the control of the Dean and Chapter, being endowed for twenty scholars, nominated by them, who receive each £2. 13. 4. annually, and are instructed in the classics and in English literature: there are belonging to this school three exhibitions, of £6 per annum each, to St. John's College, Cambridge, founded by Edmund Munsteven, Esq., in the patronage of the Bishop and Dean of Peterborough, which, on failure of candidates from this school, are open to Oundle, or any other school in the county of Northampton; in the same college are one fellowship and two scholarships, founded by Francis Dee, Bishop of Peterborough, for boys of his kindred and name, who have been educated at this school, or at Merchant Taylors', London, also three exhibitions of seven shillings per week, with preference to boys educated here. A charity school was founded, in 1721, by Mr. Thomas Deacon, who endowed it with land for clothing, educating, and apprenticing poor children, for which purpose also Mr. Lowry, in 1707, had bequeathed £20, and Mrs. Ann Ireland, in 1712, £100. A National school for children of both sexes, upon an extensive plan, and a dispensary, with an infirmary, are supported by subscription; and there are various charitable bequests for distribution among the poor. — Wortley, Esq., formerly one of the representatives of the city, bequeathed a commodious dwelling and premises, as a workhouse for the parish. An ancient hospital, dedicated to St. Leonard, for lepers, dependent on St.

Peter's abbey, was founded in the reign of Stephen; and an hospital near the abbey gate was founded, in 1180, by Benedict, Abbot of Peterborough, to the honour of Thomas à Becket, whose life he wrote. Among the eminent natives of this place were, Abbot Benedict, just mentioned; and John of Peterborough, an English historian in the beginning of the fourteenth century, also abbot of the monastery; Archdeacon Paley, celebrated as a divine and moralist, who was born in 1743, and died in 1805; to whom may be added Sir John Hill, a popular writer, supposed to have been born in 1716. The title of Earl of Peterborough, now extinct, was bestowed on the family of Mordaunt by Charles I., and was held by Charles, Earl of Peterborough and Monmouth, a distinguished military officer and statesman, in the reigns of Anne and George I.

PETERSFIELD, a parish in the hundred of Finch-Dean, Alton (South) division of the county of Southampton, comprising the borough town of Petersfield, and the tything of Sheet, and containing 1752 inhabitants, of which number, 1446 are in the borough of Petersfield, 24 miles (E. N. E.) from Southampton, and 54 (S. W.) from London. This small town is situated on the road from London to Portsmouth; the streets are partly lighted by subscription, tolerably paved, and well supplied with water. In the centre of the market-place is a fine equestrian statue of William III., erected at the expense of the late William Jolliffe, Esq., one of the representatives for this borough; it was formerly gilt, but has been lately coloured to resemble stone. Great improvements have been recently made in the roads in the neighbourhood, and others are in progress. The market, which is also for corn and cattle, is every alternate Wednesday; and fairs are on July 10th, for toys, &c.; October 6th, established within the last ten years, for lean cattle; and December 11th, for sheep. The town, which was incorporated by charter of Elizabeth, is governed by a mayor and commonalty: the mayor, whose office is become merely titular, is appointed annually at the court leet of the lord of the manor, held in January, in the town hall, at which a constable and two tythingmen are also chosen. A court of requests, for the recovery of debts under 40s., formerly held here, has been disused for the last forty years. The town hall was rebuilt, about three years since, at the expense of Hylton Jolliffe, Esq. This borough made one return to parliament in the 35th of Edward I., and then discontinued until the reign of Edward VI., since which it has returned two members: the right of election was originally vested in the proprietors of houses, or shambles, built on ancient foundations, but is now in the freeholders generally: the number of voters is not precisely known; the mayor is the returning officer, and the influence of Hylton Jolliffe, Esq. is predominant.

The living is a perpetual curacy, annexed to the rectory of Buriton, in the archdeaconry and diocese of Winchester. The chapel is dedicated to St. Peter. There are places of worship for Independents and Wes-

Arms.

leyan Methodists. Churcher's college was founded and endowed with £3000 by Richard Churcher, in 1722, for boarding, clothing, and educating from ten to twelve boys, who should be subsequently apprenticed to masters of ships voyaging to the East Indies : this institution was further regulated by act of parliament, obtained in 1744 ; the annual income is £568. 8. 8.; the master receives a salary of £40 per annum, and is allowed to take boarders and day scholars : there are twelve boys on the foundation. One poor child is eligible for apprenticeship from this town, every alternate year, by means of a benefaction from Bishop Lanney to the parish of Buriton. There is an unendowed almshouse, consisting of four tenements, for poor and aged persons, founded by Thomas Antrobus, in 1622.

PETERSHAM, a parish in the first division of the hundred of KINGSTON, county of SURREY, 7 miles (S. W. by W.) from London, containing 516 inhabitants. The living is a perpetual curacy, annexed to the vicarage of Kew, in the archdeaconry of Surrey, and diocese of Winchester. The church is dedicated to St. Peter. Petersham gives the title of viscount to the family of Stanhope, Earls of Harrington.

PETERSTONE, a parish in the upper division of the hundred of WENTLLOOG, county of MONMOUTH, 6½ miles (S. S. W.) from Newport, containing 122 inhabitants. The living is a perpetual curacy, in the archdeaconry and diocese of Llandaff, endowed with £600 royal bounty, and £200 parliamentary grant, and in the patronage of William Jones, Esq. The church is dedicated to St. Peter.

PETERSTOW, a parish in the lower division of the hundred of WORMELOW, county of HEREFORD, 3 miles (W. by N.) from Ross, containing 277 inhabitants. The living is a rectory, in the archdeaconry and diocese of Hereford, rated in the king's books at £7. 10. 10., and in the patronage of the Governors of Guy's Hospital, London. The church is dedicated to St. Peter. There is a place of worship for Wesleyan Methodists.

PETHAM, a parish in the hundred of BRIDGE and PETHAM, lathe of ST. AUGUSTINE, county of KENT, 6 miles (S. S. W.) from Canterbury, containing 536 inhabitants. The living is a vicarage, with that of Waltham annexed, in the archdeaconry and diocese of Canterbury, rated in the king's books at £8. 0. 2½., and in the alternate patronage of the Archbishop of Canterbury, and Sir J. C. Honywood, Bart. The church, dedicated to All Saints, is principally in the early style of English architecture. The parish is bounded on the east by the ancient Stane-street.

PETHERICK (LITTLE), a parish in the hundred of PYDER, county of CORNWALL, 2 miles (S.) from Padstow, containing 217 inhabitants. The living is a rectory, in the peculiar jurisdiction of the Bishop of Exeter, rated in the king's books at £6. 6. 8., and in the patronage of Sir W. Molesworth, Bart. The church is dedicated to St. Petrock. A noble bridge has been built by subscription across a small river that flows through the parish and into the Camel. A small hospital is endowed with funds under the superintendence of the rector.

PETHERTON (NORTH), a parish in the northern division of the hundred of PETHERTON, county of SOMERSET, 3¼ miles (S. by W.) from Bridg-water, containing 3091 inhabitants. The living is a vicarage, in the archdeaconry of Taunton, and diocese of Bath and Wells, rated in the king's books at £27. 7. 11., and in the patronage of the Rev. W. George. The church, dedicated to St. Mary, is a fine structure with a lofty tower, in the later English style. The navigable river Parret, and the Bridg-water and Taunton canal, pass through the parish, which is one of the most extensive in the county. The village, which consists of one well-built street on the turnpike-road from Bridg-water to Taunton, had formerly a large market, principally for corn, which has long been disused; but two considerable fairs are still held for cattle and pedlary, on May 1st and the Monday before November 13th. The principal bequests for the education of children are a house and land, the gift of Dorothy Cheek, in 1687, for teaching six or more; the sum of £500, by Sir Thomas Wroth, in 1721, and a rent-charge of £2, by Thomas Bacon; the two latter produce an income of about £41 a year, for which twenty boys are clothed and instructed in a school-room erected by the late John Slade, Esq.

PETHERTON (SOUTH), a market town and parish in the southern division of the hundred of PETHERTON, county of SOMERSET, 5½ miles (N. by W.) from Crewkerne, and 130 (W. S. W.) from London, containing 2090 inhabitants. This town is ancient, and derives its name from the river Peder, or Parret, which passes it on the east, over which, on the old Roman Fosse-way, is a stone bridge of three arches; it was formerly of wood, but rebuilt in its present state by the parents of two children who were drowned in the river, and whose effigies are placed upon it to commemorate the event. It comprises three principal streets, which, by uniting, form a triangle. A few of the inhabitants are engaged in the manufacture of dowlas and sail-cloth; and on the river are several corn-mills. The markets, formerly considerable, but now on the decline, are on Thursday and Saturday; and a fair, principally for lambs, is held on the 6th of July. Courts leet for the manor and hundred are held annually in October. The living is a vicarage, in the archdeaconry of Taunton, and diocese of Bath and Wells, rated in the king's books at £24, and in the patronage of the Dean and Chapter of Bristol. The church, which is dedicated to St. Peter and St. Paul, is a spacious cruciform edifice, with an octangular tower surmounted by a spire. There are two places of worship for Independents, and one each for Baptists and Wesleyan Methodists. The free school was founded, about 1732, by William Glandfield, who bequeathed £60, augmented, in 1739, by Mary Prowse, who bequeathed £100, and by a further bequest from Thomas Musgrave, commuted for £100 in the four per cents., for educating and clothing poor children: twenty boys are instructed, and occasionally clothed by subscription : the salary of the master is £30 per annum. In 1720, a large earthen vessel, full of Roman coins, was dug up in a field near the bridge; and other Roman antiquities have at different times been discovered in the vicinity.

PETHERWIN (NORTH), a parish in the hundred of BLACK TORRINGTON, county of DEVON, 4½ miles (N. W.) from Launceston, containing 955 inhabitants. The living is a vicarage, in the archdeaconry of Cornwall, and diocese of Exeter, rated in the king's books at £9. 10. 10., and in the patronage of the Duke of Bedford. The church is dedicated to St. Paternus.

PETHERWIN (SOUTH), a parish in the northern division of the hundred of EAST, county of CORNWALL, 3 miles (S. W. by S.) from Launceston, containing 914 inhabitants. The living is a vicarage, with the curacy of Trewin annexed, in the peculiar jurisdiction of the Bishop of Exeter, rated in the king's books at £9. 2. 6., and in the patronage of the Chancellor and Fellows of the University of Oxford. The church is dedicated to St. Paternus. There is a place of worship for Wesleyan Methodists. Fairs are held on the second Tuesdays in May and October.

PETROCKSTOW, a parish in the hundred of SHEBBEAR, county of DEVON, 4 miles (N. N. W.) from Hatherleigh, containing 571 inhabitants. The living is a rectory, in the archdeaconry of Barnstaple, and diocese of Exeter, rated in the king's books at £17. 0. 2½., and in the patronage of Lord Clinton.

PETSOE, a hamlet in the parish of OKENEY, hundred of NEWPORT, county of BUCKINGHAM, 2½ miles (S. E. by S.) from Olney. The population is returned with Emberton, to the church of which parish the inhabitants resort. This was formerly a parish, but the church, dedicated to St. James, having been demolished, the living, a discharged rectory, was annexed to that of Okeney. Petsoe still maintains its own poor, excepting those of Petsoe-End, who are supported by the parishioners of Emberton.

PETT, a parish in the hundred of GUESTLING, rape of HASTINGS, county of SUSSEX, 3½ miles (S. W.) from Winchelsea, containing 300 inhabitants. The living is a rectory, in the archdeaconry of Lewes, and diocese of Chichester, rated in the king's books at £4. 15. 10., and in the patronage of Mrs. Wynch. The church is dedicated to St. Mary and St. Peter. The Royal Military canal passes through the parish.

PETTAUGH, a parish in the hundred of THREDLING, county of SUFFOLK, 2¼ miles (S.) from Debenham, containing 254 inhabitants. The living is a discharged rectory, in the archdeaconry of Suffolk, and diocese of Norwich, rated in the king's books at £9. 12. 1., and in the patronage of the Countess of Dysart. The church is dedicated to St. Catherine.

PETTERELL-CROOKS, a township in the parish of HESKET in the FOREST, LEATH ward, county of CUMBERLAND, 9 miles (N. N. W.) from Penrith, containing 513 inhabitants.

PETTISTREE, a parish in the hundred of WILFORD, county of SUFFOLK, ¾ of a mile (S. by W.) from Wickham-Market, containing 260 inhabitants. The living is a discharged vicarage, to which that of Lowdham has been annexed, the church of that parish having been demolished; it is in the archdeaconry of Suffolk, and diocese of Norwich, and in the patronage of the Crown. The church is dedicated to St. Peter and St. Paul.

PETTON, a parish in the hundred of PIMHILL, county of SALOP, 6¼ miles (S. S. E.) from Ellesmere, containing 48 inhabitants. The living is a discharged vicarage, in the archdeaconry of Salop, and diocese of Lichfield and Coventry, rated in the king's books at £3. 4. 2., endowed with £200 royal bounty, and in the patronage of the Crown.

PETWORTH, a market town and parish, in the hundred of ROTHERBRIDGE, rape of ARUNDEL, county of SUSSEX, 14 miles (N. E. by N.) from Chichester, and 49 (S. W. by S.) from London, containing 2781 inhabitants.

This ancient town, called in Domesday-book *Peteorde*, is situated on a small branch of the Arun, near the navigable river Rother, and on the high road from London to Arundel and Chichester. It is in general well built, and consists of several irregular streets: the inhabitants are supplied with water from a spring in the Earl of Egremont's park, and from wells, but principally from the Rother, by means of an engine at Coultershallmill, whence it is conveyed through pipes: the Rother is navigable about a mile and a half south of the town, and joins the river Arun at Stopham, about five miles south-east, being crossed by a bridge at Coultershall in this parish. The market is on Saturday, for corn; and fairs are on Holy Thursday and November 20th, for cattle and corn. In the centre of the town is the market-house, a handsome edifice adorned at one end with a bust of William III.; the lower part consists of piazzas, with an open space for holding the market, and above is the court-room for transacting public business. A capital court baron for the honour and manor is holden annually, under the Earl of Egremont: formerly there was a court baron for pleas under 40s., but it has long since fallen into disuse. A court leet under the Duke of Norfolk, for the hundred of Rotherbridge, is held annually; the Epiphany and Easter quarter sessions for the western division of the county are held in the court-room; as is also a petty session of magistrates, every alternate Saturday. The bridewell, or house of correction, a brick building, was erected in 1787, on Howard's plan; it stands in a healthy situation, and contains a tread-mill: the prisoners are employed in manufacturing rugs, horsecloths, and other coarse woollen articles.

The living is a rectory, in the archdeaconry and diocese of Chichester, rated in the king's books at £41. 10. 5., and in the patronage of the Earl of Egremont. The church, which is dedicated to St. Mary, and was erected apparently about the time of Henry VII., is in the decorated style, and has recently undergone reparation, having also received two hundred additional sittings, of which one hundred and twenty-six are free, and towards defraying the expense, the Incorporated Society for the enlargement of churches contributed £70: the greater part of the tower has been rebuilt, with the addition of a beautiful spire, one hundred and eighty feet high, the whole having been executed, in a superior manner, under the direction of Mr. C. Barry, architect, and at the sole expense of the Earl of Egremont. There are places of worship for Independents and Wesleyan Methodists. The free school, called Taylor's charity, which was founded in 1753, by the Rev. John Taylor, who bequeathed the sum of £2400, for instructing and apprenticing twenty poor children, and for other purposes, and a further sum of £800 for clothing them, has merged into a large school on the National system, for children of both sexes, which is supported by voluntary contribution. Thompson's hospital, for twelve poor men and women, was founded in 1618, by Thomas Thompson, Gent., and originally endowed with land for the payment of £5 a year to each of the inmates; which sum, from the accumulation of the funds, has been increased to £20. Almshouses were founded, in 1746, by Charles, Duke of Somerset, for twenty-two widows, each of whom receives £20 per annum; in addition to which, several widows, as out-pensioners, receive annual sums varying from £5 to £20. Donations of £12 each per annum to two clergymen's widows of the neighbourhood, and of £6 each to two poor tradesmen, to assist them in business, were included in the bequests of the above-mentioned Rev. John Taylor, founder of the free school.

PEVENSEY, a parish and a member of the town and port of Hastings, locally in the lowey and rape of Pevensey, county of SUSSEX, 6 miles (S.E. by E.) from Hailsham, and 60 (S.E. by S.) from London, containing 292 inhabitants. The living is a vicarage, in the archdeaconry of Lewes, and diocese of Chichester, rated in the king's books at £18. 7. 8½., and in the patronage of the Chancellor of the Cathedral Church of Chichester. The church, dedicated to St. Nicholas, is in the early style of English architecture. The manor of Pevensey is in ancient records styled the honour of Aquila, or the Eagle. Somner considers this to have been the *Anderida* of the Romans; it was by the Saxons called *Peowensea*, by the Normans *Pevensel*, and is now vulgarly pronounced Pemsey. It is known to have been anciently much resorted to as a sea-port, and various historical circumstances connected with it occur so early as the invasion of England by Sweyn, King of Denmark, and again, in the reign of Edward the Confessor, when Godwin, Earl of Kent, is stated to have taken several ships from it. It is distinguished as the place of landing of William the Conqueror, in 1066; who thence proceeded to, and fortified, Hastings castle, previously to the conflict which took place at Battle, eight miles distant. On ascending the throne, William gave Pevensey to his half-brother, Earl Robert, who fortified it with a noble castle, now in ruins. It subsequently reverted to the crown, and was, by Henry I., bestowed on Gilbert de Aquila, from whom it afterwards assumed the name of the Honour of the Eagle, the castle being esteemed the head of that honour. The lordship afterwards passed through several hands: John of Gaunt had a grant, in tail general, of the castle and leucata of Pevensey, from whom it descended to the king, in the person of his son and heir, Henry IV. It was, by the latter, given to Sir John Pelham, and continued in that family till disposed of by the late Lord Pelham to its present proprietor. It lies in the parishes of Pevensey, Halysham, Westham, and Boxhill. Pevensey is at present a small village, standing on a rivulet which runs into Pevensey bay. Its decline from the importance it once possessed has been, like several other places in this neighbourhood, principally owing to the receding of the sea, from which it is now a considerable distance, being only accessible to small boats, which crowd up the stream on which it is situated: it has still a corporation, consisting of a bailiff, jurats, and commonalty. A fair for live stock is held on the 5th of July. Here is a National school for children of both sexes. The remains of Pevensey castle, an interesting relic of antiquity, are situated on a craggy steep, commanding a beautiful view of the adjacent country. The external walls are circular, and enclose an area of seven acres, being, together with the towers, tolerably entire for the height of twenty-five feet: they display throughout abundance of Roman bricks, affording the strongest presumption of there having originally been a Roman fortress on the spot. Tradition informs us, that the rock on which the castle is built

was once on a level with the sea; and, from fossils and shells of various sorts, occasionally met with about the base, the account is most probably true. The Duke of York, in the reign of Henry IV., was for some time confined within the walls of this castle. Andrew Borde, in Latin *Perforatus*, physician to Henry VIII., and, from his jocularities, thought to have given origin to the appellation of "Merry Andrew," was a native of this village.

PEVINGTON, a parish in the hundred of CALEHILL, lathe of SCRAY, county of KENT, 4 miles (S.W. by W.) from Charing. The population is returned with the parish of Pluckley. The living is a rectory, united to that of Pluckley, in the archdeaconry and diocese of Canterbury, rated in the king's books at £5. 13. 4. The church, now in ruins, was dedicated to St. Mary.

PEWSEY, or PUSEY, a parish in the hundred of GANFIELD, county of BERKS, 4½ miles (E. by N.) from Great Farringdon, containing 122 inhabitants. The living is a rectory, in the archdeaconry of Berks, and diocese of Salisbury, rated in the king's books at £8. 12. 11., endowed with £200 private benefaction, £200 royal bounty, and £300 parliamentary grant, and in the patronage of the Bishop of Salisbury. The church, dedicated to All Saints, was rebuilt at the expense of Mr. Allen Pusey, who died in 1789, and to whose memory it contains a handsome marble monument. The Antiquarian Society has caused an engraving to be made of the celebrated Pusey Horn, by which the manor is held by the Pusey family. According to Dr. Hickes, the manor was possessed in his time by Charles Pusey, Esq., who had recovered it in Chancery before Lord Chancellor Jefferies, when the horn being produced in court, was proved to be the identical horn by which, under a charter, Canute the Great granted the manor to his ancestor, seven hundred years before. The horn is that of an ox, of a dark brown colour, and may have been used either as a hunting or a drinking horn, but more particularly the former.

PEWSEY, a parish in the hundred of KINWARDSTONE, county of WILTS, 6 miles (S.W.) from Great Bedwin, containing 1337 inhabitants. The living is a rectory, in the archdeaconry of Wilts, and diocese of Salisbury, rated in the king's books at £26. 16. 8., and in the patronage of the Earl of Radnor. The church, dedicated to St. John the Baptist, has lately received an addition of one hundred and five sittings, of which ninety are free, the Incorporated Society for the enlargement of churches and chapels having granted £25 towards defraying the expense. The petty sessions for the division are held here.

PEWSHAM, an extra-parochial liberty, in the hundred of CHIPPENHAM, county of WILTS, 1½ mile (S.E. by S.) from Chippenham, containing 322 inhabitants.

PEXALL, a joint township with Henbury, in the parish of PRESTBURY, hundred of MACCLESFIELD, county palatine of CHESTER, 3 miles (W.S.W.) from Macclesfield. The population is returned with Henbury.

PEYTON, a chapelry in the parish and hundred of BAMPTON, county of DEVON, 4 miles (N.E.) from Bampton, with which the population is returned.

PHILLACK, a parish in the hundred of PENWITH, county of CORNWALL, 7½ miles (N.E. by N.) from Marazion, containing 2529 inhabitants. The living is a rectory, with that of Gwithian annexed, in the archdeaconry of Cornwall, and diocese of Exeter, rated in the king's books at £45. 10. 10., and in the patronage of the Rev. William Hockin. The church is dedicated to St. Felix. This parish includes the port of Hayle, also several villages, the principal of which, Hayle Copper House, carries on a considerable trade in coal, timber, iron, and limestone, imported from Wales; and earthenware, groceries, &c., from Bristol : the chief exports are copper-ore, in considerable quantities, from the western mines. Extensive improvements have been recently made in the harbour by canals, flood-gates, wharfs, &c.; and a grand causeway, one thousand and forty feet in length, across an arm of the sea, was finished in 1826, at the expense of £7200 : a weekly market has been established, and a market-house erected. Here is the largest and most complete iron-foundry and factory in Cornwall, where apparatus for steam-engines of the greatest dimensions are made. The smelting and refining of copper were formerly carried on to a great extent, but within these last few years the works have ceased, owing to the great expense, and the arsenic smoke having been found destructive to the health of the workmen, and to vegetation in general. There is a smelting-house for tin at Argarrack. The great wheal Alfred, which formerly produced one thousand tons of copper-ore per month, and several other mines, are within this parish, though none are at present in operation. The north side of the parish is overwhelmed with sand, blown up from the coast of St. Ive's bay. There was once a castle at Hayle Bar Riviere, and another at Castle Hayle, of which the moat still remains.

PHILLEIGH, or FILLEY, a parish in the western division of the hundred of POWDER, county of CORNWALL, 6 miles (S.W.) from Tregoney, containing 395 inhabitants. The living is a rectory, in the archdeaconry of Cornwall, and diocese of Exeter, rated in the king's books at £15. 6. 0½. The Trustees of T. Bedford, Esq. were patrons in 1804. The church is dedicated to St. Felix. The navigable river Mopus bounds the parish on the west, and Tregoney river runs on the north.

PHILLYHOLME, a tything in that part of the parish of HAWKCHURCH which is in the hundred of UGGSCOMBE, Dorchester division of the county of DORSET, containing 558 inhabitants.

PHOSIDE, a liberty in the parish of GLOSSOP, hundred of HIGH PEAK, county of DERBY, 4 miles (N. by W.) from Chapel en le Frith, containing 504 inhabitants. Mary Trickett, in 1712, and John Hague, in 1782, each bequeathed a small sum for teaching poor children.

PICKBURN, a joint township with Brodsworth, in the parish of BRODSWORTH, northern division of the wapentake of STRAFFORTH and TICKHILL, West riding of the county of YORK, 4½ miles (N.W.) from Doncaster. The population is returned with Brodsworth.

PICKENHAM (NORTH), a parish in the southern division of the hundred of GREENHOE, county of NORFOLK, 3½ miles (S.E. by E.) from Swaffham, containing 218 inhabitants. The living is a discharged rectory, with that of Houghton on the Hill annexed, in the archdeaconry of Norfolk, and diocese of Norwich, rated in the king's books at £5. 14. 2., and in the patronage of the Rev. Henry Say. The church is dedicated to St. Andrew.

PICKENHAM (SOUTH), a parish in the southern division of the hundred of GREENHOE, county of NORFOLK, 4¼ miles (S. E. by S.) from Swaffham, containing 146 inhabitants. The living is a discharged rectory, in the archdeaconry of Norfolk, and diocese of Norwich, rated in the king's books at £8. 1. 5½., and in the patronage of C. W. Chute, Esq. The church is dedicated to All Saints. The north window of the chancel exhibits some fragments of ancient stained glass, which, when perfect, represented the Salutation. Attached to the north side was a chapel, erected by Henry, younger son of Sir Henry Hobart, Knt., Lord Chief Justice of the Common Pleas, whose remains lie buried there; it has long been dilapidated and is overgrown with ivy.

PICKERING, a parish in PICKERING lythe, North riding of the county of YORK, comprising the market town of Pickering, the chapelry of Goadland, or Goathland, and the townships of Kingthorp, Marrishes, and Newton, and containing 3555 inhabitants, of which number, 2746 are in the town of Pickering, 26 miles (N.N.E.) from York, and 222 (N. by W.) from London. The origin of this town is of very remote antiquity, being dated two hundred and seventy years before the commencement of the Christian era, and ascribed to Peridurus, a British king, who was interred here, on the brow of a hill called Rawcliff. According to local tradition, its name is derived from the circumstance of a *ring* lost by the founder whilst washing in the river Costa, and subsequently found in the belly of a *pike*. An ancient castle, of great strength and extent, which occupied an eminence near the western extremity of the town, where some vestiges are still visible, was the prison of Richard II., after his deposition, and previously to his removal to Pontefract, where he was murdered : in one of the towers still remaining Queen Elizabeth is supposed to have been imprisoned, during the reign of Mary; and it still retains the name of Queen Elizabeth's tower. During the great civil war this fortress was besieged by the parliamentary forces, and sustained considerable injury. The town, which is long and straggling, is situated on a declivity, at the bottom of which, and through a part of the town, flows a small stream, called Pickering-beck : the castle hill commands a fine view of the fertile vale of Pickering, and on one side is a barren mountainous district, called Black, or Blake moor, which extends to a considerable distance, and furnishes materials for making brooms : on the river Costa, which rises at Kildhead, and upon the old Beck stream, are several flour-mills. The market is on Monday ; and fairs are held on the Mondays before February 14th and May 13th, on September 25th, and on the Monday before November 23rd. Pickering was formerly of more importance than it is at present, having been the principal town in this district ; in the 23rd of Edward I. it sent members to parliament. It is the head of an honour in the duchy of Lancaster, having jurisdiction throughout the lythe and wapentake, which are co-extensive, including two market towns and forty-six townships. A manorial court, for all actions under 40s. arising within the honour, is held on the second and third Mondays after Easter, and on the first and second Mondays after Michaelmas, in Queen Elizabeth's tower in the castle. The living is a discharged vicarage, in the peculiar jurisdiction and patronage of the Dean of York, rated in the king's books at £8. 3. 9. The church, which is dedicated to

3 Y 2

St. Peter, is an ancient and spacious edifice, with a lofty spire. There are places of worship for the Society of Friends, Independents, and Wesleyan Methodists. The free school is supported by the interest of various endowments, and rent-charges, of unknown origin, amounting to about £80, with some subsequent small legacies, vested in trustees, and applied, under their direction, for the instruction of the children of poor inhabitants : the average number is one hundred and fifty. On Pickering moor are vestiges of two Roman encampments of great strength, and several others between the barrows and the town, as well as on the western moors.

PICKHILL, a parish comprising the township of Holme with Howgrave, in the wapentake of ALLERTON-SHIRE, and the townships of Ainderby-Quernhow, Howe, Pickhill with Roxby, Sinderby, and Swainby with Allarthorp, in the wapentake of HALLIKELD, North riding of the county of YORK, and containing 686 inhabitants, of which number, 334 are in the township of Pickhill with Roxby, 7 miles (W. by N.) from Thirsk. The living is a discharged vicarage, in the archdeaconry and diocese of York, rated in the king's books at £5. 13. 4., endowed with £400 private benefaction, £400 royal bounty, and £600 parliamentary grant, and in the patronage of the Master and Fellows of Trinity College, Cambridge. The church is dedicated to All Saints. There is a place of worship for Wesleyan Methodists. Sarah Eden, in 1742, bequeathed £200 for teaching twenty poor children. The river Swale forms the eastern boundary of the parish. Here was once a castle, and there are still some fields called the Roman fields.

PICKMERE, a township in that part of the parish of GREAT BUDWORTH which is in the hundred of BUCKLOW, county palatine of CHESTER, 3½ miles (N.E.) from Northwich, containing 217 inhabitants.

PICKTON, a township in that part of the parish of PLEMONSTALL which is in the lower division of the hundred of BROXTON, county palatine of CHESTER, 4¾ miles (N. N. E.) from Chester, containing 93 inhabitants.

PICKTON, a township in the parish of KIRK-LEAVINGTON, western division of the liberty of LANGBAURGH, North riding of the county of YORK, 4 miles (S.) from Yarm, containing 94 inhabitants.

PICKWELL, a parish forming a detached portion of the hundred of GARTREE, being locally in that of Guthlaxton, county of LEICESTER, 5¼ miles (S. S. E.) from Melton-Mowbray, containing, with the hamlet of Leesthorpe, 167 inhabitants. The living is a rectory, in the archdeaconry of Leicester, and diocese of Lincoln, rated in the king's books at £16, and in the patronage of Sir G. Noel, Bart. The church is dedicated to All Saints. Dr. William Cave, an eminent church historian, was born here in 1637.

PICKWORTH, a parish in the wapentake of AVELAND, parts of KESTEVEN, county of LINCOLN, 2¼ miles (W.) from Falkingham, containing 186 inhabitants. The living is a rectory, in the archdeaconry and diocese of Lincoln, rated in the king's books at £11. 12. 3½., and in the patronage of the Duke of St. Albans. The church is dedicated to St. Andrew.

PICKWORTH, a parish in EAST hundred, county of RUTLAND, 4¾ miles (N. W. by N.) from Stamford, containing 140 inhabitants. The living is a rec-

tory, annexed to that of Great Casterton, in the archdeaconry of Northampton, and diocese of Peterborough, rated in the king's books at £4. Of the church, which was dedicated to All Saints, only the steeple is remaining.

PIDDINGHOE, a parish in the hundred of HOLMSTROW, rape of LEWES, county of SUSSEX, 5½ miles (S. by E.) from Lewes, containing 251 inhabitants. The living is a discharged vicarage, in the archdeaconry of Lewes, and diocese of Chichester, rated in the king's books at £7. 14. 2. Thomas Crewe, and J. Philpot, Esqrs., were patrons in 1825. The church, which is principally of flint, with a circular tower, is in the early style of English architecture. The parish is bounded on the east by the Ouse, or Lewes river, and on the south by the English channel.

PIDDINGTON, a parish in the hundred of WYMERSLEY, county of NORTHAMPTON, 5¾ miles (S. E. by S.) from Northampton, containing, with the hamlet of Hackleton, 871 inhabitants. The living is a perpetual curacy, united to the vicarage of Horton, in the archdeaconry of Northampton, and diocese of Peterborough. The church is dedicated to St. Mary. Limestone is obtained in the parish.

PIDDINGTON, a parish in the hundred of BULLINGTON, though locally in that of Ploughley, county of OXFORD, 5½ miles (S. E.) from Bicester, containing 359 inhabitants. The living is a perpetual curacy, in the archdeaconry and diocese of Oxford, and in the patronage of the Parishioners. The church is dedicated to St. Nicholas.

PIDDLE (NORTH), a parish in the upper division of the hundred of PERSHORE, county of WORCESTER, 8¼ miles (E. by S.) from Worcester, containing 133 inhabitants. The living is a rectory, in the archdeaconry and diocese of Worcester, rated in the king's books at £9. 1. 3., and in the patronage of Earl Somers. The church is dedicated to St. Michael.

PIDDLEHINTON, a parish in the liberty of PIDDLEHINTON, Dorchester division of the county of DORSET, 5¼ miles (N. N. E.) from Dorchester, containing 853 inhabitants. The living is a rectory, in the archdeaconry of Dorset, and diocese of Bristol, rated in the king's books at £17. 3. 9., and in the patronage of the Provost and Fellows of Eton College. The church is dedicated to St. Mary. The small river Piddle runs through the parish. A school is supported by annual donations averaging about £16.

PIDDLETOWN, a parish in the hundred of PIDDLETOWN, Dorchester division of the county of DORSET, 5 miles (N. E. by E.) from Dorchester, containing 961 inhabitants. The living is a vicarage, in the archdeaconry of Dorset, and diocese of Bristol, rated in the king's books at £31. 2. 11. The Rev. G. H. Templer was patron in 1822. The church, dedicated to St. Mary, is a large structure with an embattled tower, partly in the decorated, and partly in the later English style : the font is curiously carved with trellice-work and foliage. This extensive parish is bounded on the north by the river Piddle, and had formerly a market, long since disused, and two fairs, which are still held on April 8th and October 29th, for horses, bullocks, hogs, and sheep.

PIDDLETRENTHIDE, a parish in the liberty of PIDDLETRENTHIDE, Cerne subdivision of the county of DORSET, 7½ miles (N. by E.) from Dorchester, containing 590 inhabitants. The living is a vicarage, in the archdeaconry of Dorset, and diocese of Bristol, rated in the king's books at £19. 10. 5., and in the patronage of the Dean and Chapter of Winchester. The church is dedicated to All Saints. John Harding, in 1750, left the sum of £431. 13., the interest to be applied for teaching poor children.

PIDLEY, a parish in the hundred of HURSTINGSTONE, county of HUNTINGDON, 2 miles (W. N. W.) from Somersham, containing, with the hamlet of Fenton, 374 inhabitants. The living is a perpetual curacy, united to the rectory of Somersham, in the archdeaconry of Huntingdon, and diocese of Lincoln. The church is dedicated to All Saints. A school here is endowed with about £20 per annum, arising from the bequests of unknown benefactors.

PIECOMBE, a parish in the hundred of POYNINGS, rape of LEWES, county of SUSSEX, 3 miles (S.) from Hurst-Pierrepoint, containing 218 inhabitants. The living is a rectory, in the archdeaconry of Lewes, and diocese of Chichester, rated in the king's books at £15. 8. 9., and in the patronage of the Crown. The church is in the later style of English architecture.

PIERRE (ST.), a parish in the upper division of the hundred of CALDICOTT, county of MONMOUTH, 3 miles (S. W. by S.) from Chepstow, containing, with the hamlet of Runston, 81 inhabitants. The living is a discharged rectory, annexed to that of Portscuett, in the archdeaconry and diocese of Llandaff, rated in the king's books at £3. 12. 3½., and endowed with £200 royal bounty.

PIERSE-BRIDGE, a township in that part of the parish of GAINFORD which is in the south-western division of DARLINGTON ward, county palatine of DURHAM, 5½ miles (W. by N.) from Darlington, containing 236 inhabitants. This place occupies the site of a considerable Roman station, the north and west sides of the vallum, and part of the south side, being still conspicuous. The Roman road, called Watling-street, passes a few yards to the east of it, and many coins and other antiquities, particularly a fine altar and several urns, have been found. There is a stone bridge over the river Tees at this place, said to have been built by two priests, who erected near it a chapel, of which there are still some remains. About two hundred yards below the present bridge, foundations of a more ancient one were visible a few years ago, but every vestige has been since swept away by the floods.

PIGDON, a township in that part of the parish of MITFORD which is in the western division of MORPETH ward, county of NORTHUMBERLAND, 3¾ miles (W. N. W.) from Morpeth, containing 36 inhabitants.

PIGLESTHORNE, a parish in the hundred of COTTESLOE, county of BUCKINGHAM, 1 mile (S. by W.) from Ivinghoe, containing, with the chapelry of Nettleden with Friesden, 461 inhabitants. The living is a perpetual curacy, in the archdeaconry of Buckingham, and diocese of Lincoln, endowed with £600 royal bounty, and £400 parliamentary grant, and in the patronage of the Trustees of the late Earl of Bridgewater. The church is dedicated to St. Mary. The Grand Junction canal passes through the parish.

PILETON, a township in that part of the parish of PENKRIDGE which is in the eastern division of the hundred of CUTTLESTONE, county of STAFFORD, 1¾ mile (E. S. E.) from Penkridge, with which the population is returned.

PILHAM, a parish in the wapentake of CORRINGHAM, parts of LINDSEY, county of LINCOLN, 4¾ miles (N. E. by E.) from Gainsborough, containing 102 inhabitants. The living is a discharged rectory, in the archdeaconry of Stow, and diocese of Lincoln, rated in the king's books at £6. 3. 4., and in the patronage of the Crown. The church is dedicated to All Saints.

PILKINGTON, a township in the parish of OLDHAM cum PRESTWICH, hundred of SALFORD, county palatine of LANCASTER, 4½ miles (S. by W.) from Bury, containing 8976 inhabitants. The manufacture of silk and cotton is here carried on to a great extent. Henry Siddall, in 1688, devised a messuage and land towards the endowment of a free grammar school; the income is £30 a year, but the boys are not educated gratuitously, there being eleven day scholars, who pay £5. 5. per annum each.

PILL (ST. GEORGE'S), a chapelry in the parish of EASTON in GORDANO, hundred of PORTBURY, county of SOMERSET, 6 miles from Bristol, containing nearly 2000 inhabitants. The chapel contains six hundred free sittings, the Incorporated Society for the enlargement of churches and chapels having contributed £450 for that purpose. There are places of worship for Baptists, Independents, and Wesleyan Methodists. This is a pilot station for the port of Bristol, being situated at the mouth of the river Avon. The Roman Fosseway passes through it, and Roman coins, urns, and fibulæ, have been found here.

PILLATON, a parish in the middle division of EAST hundred, county of CORNWALL, 3½ miles (S.) from Callington, containing 452 inhabitants. The living is a rectory, in the archdeaconry of Cornwall, and diocese of Exeter, rated in the king's books at £16. 15. 7½., and in the patronage of Edward Helyar, Esq. The parish is bounded on the west by the small river Lyner, and on the east by the river Tamar, which separates it from Devonshire. There is a mine of antimony, but not at present in operation. A fair is held on Whit-Tuesday.

PILLERTON - HERSEY, a parish in the Brails division of the hundred of KINGTON, county of WARWICK, 3¼ miles (S. W. by W.) from Kington, containing 268 inhabitants. The living is a vicarage, with the perpetual curacy of Pillerton-Priors, in the archdeaconry and diocese of Worcester, rated in the king's books at £8, endowed with £643 private benefaction, and £1200 royal bounty, and in the patronage of the Rev. Francis Mills. The church, dedicated to St. Mary, bears the architectural character of Queen Mary's time. The parish is situated to the westward of a lofty range of hills, called Edge Hills, of historical celebrity. Limestone exists here.

PILLERTON-PRIORS, a parish in the Brails division of the hundred of KINGTON, county of WARWICK, 4 miles (S. W. by W.) from Kington, containing 211 inhabitants. The living is a perpetual curacy, annexed to the vicarage of Pillerton-Hersey, in the archdeaconry and diocese of Worcester. The church, which was dedicated to St. Mary Magdalene, was burnt down in 1666. This place received the adjunct to its name from having formerly belonged to Kenilworth priory.

PILLING, a chapelry in the parish of GARSTANG, hundred of AMOUNDERNESS, county palatine of LANCASTER, 6½ miles (W. by N.) from Garstang, containing 1043 inhabitants. The living is a perpetual curacy, in the archdeaconry of Richmond, and diocese of Chester, endowed with £400 private benefaction, £400 royal bounty, and £1100 parliamentary grant. G. Hornby, Esq., was patron in 1802. The chapel, consecrated in 1721, is dedicated to St. John the Baptist. There is a place of worship for Wesleyan Methodists. Robert Carter, in 1710, gave a house, land, and £60, towards the support of a school; the income is about £40 a year, for which sum from fifteen to thirty children are instructed.

PILSDON, a parish in the hundred of WHITCHURCH - CANONICORUM, Bridport division of the county of DORSET, 4½ miles (W. by S) from Beaminster, containing 100 inhabitants. The living is a discharged rectory, in the archdeaconry of Dorset, and diocese of Bristol, rated in the king's books at £7. The Hon. Lady Damer was patroness in 1802. The church is small and very ancient.

PILSGATE, a hamlet in the parish of BARNACK, liberty of PETERBOROUGH, county of NORTHAMPTON, 2¾ miles (E. S. E.) from Stamford, containing 153 inhabitants.

PILSLEY, a hamlet in the parish of EDENSOR, hundred of HIGH PEAK, county of DERBY, 2½ miles (N. E.) from Bakewell, containing 243 inhabitants. Pilsley is in the honour of Tutbury, duchy of Lancaster, and within the jurisdiction of a court of pleas held at Chapel en le Frith every third Tuesday, for the recovery of debts under 40s.

PILSLEY, a hamlet in the parish of CHESTERFIELD, hundred of SCARSDALE, county of DERBY, 6 miles (S. S. E.) from Chesterfield, containing 284 inhabitants.

PILSWORTH, a township in the parish of MIDDLETON, hundred of SALFORD, county palatine of LANCASTER, 3 miles (S. E.) from Bury, containing 499 inhabitants.

PILTON, a parish in the hundred of BRAUNTON, county of DEVON, ½ a mile (N.) from Barnstaple, containing 1230 inhabitants. The living is a perpetual curacy, in the jurisdiction of the Precentor of the Cathedral Church of Wells, endowed with £8 per annum and £200 private benefaction, £400 royal bounty, and £600 parliamentary grant, and in the patronage of — Basset, Esq. The church, dedicated to St. Margaret, contains a wooden screen and a stone pulpit, also a handsome monument to Sir John Chichester, dated 1569. A Benedictine priory, a cell to the abbey of Malmesbury, was founded here by King Athelstan; it was dedicated to the Blessed Virgin Mary, and at the dissolution had a revenue of £56. 12. 8. The prior, in 1345, obtained for Pilton the grant of a weekly market and an annual fair. An ancient hermitage is said to have been established here; and an hospital, founded in honour of St. Margaret, before 1191, is still in existence; the inmates are a prior, brother, and sister. Pilton communicates with Barnstaple by a bridge over the river Yeo.

PILTON, a parish in the hundred of NAVISFORD, county of NORTHAMPTON, 2¾ miles (S. S. W.) from Oundle, containing 116 inhabitants. The living is a discharged rectory, in the archdeaconry of Northampton, and diocese of Peterborough, rated in the king's books at £11, and in the patronage of Sir G. Robinson, Bart. The church, dedicated to St. Mary, is principally in the early style of English architecture, with a tower and spire.

PILTON, a parish in the hundred of WRANDIKE, county of RUTLAND, 4¾ miles (N. E. by E.) from Uppingham, containing 66 inhabitants. The living is a discharged rectory, in the archdeaconry of Northampton, and diocese of Peterborough, rated in the king's books at £4. 17. 3½., and in the patronage of Sir Gilbert Heathcote, Bart. The church is dedicated to St. Nicholas. The small river Charter bounds the parish on the north : and limestone is obtained in the southern part of it.

PILTON, a parish in the hundred of WHITESTONE, county of SOMERSET, 2¾ miles (S. W.) from Shepton-Mallet, containing, with the chapelry of North Wotton, and the hamlet of West Holm, which is in the hundred of Glaston-Twelve-Hides, 1100 inhabitants. The living is a discharged vicarage, in the peculiar jurisdiction and patronage of the Precentor of the Cathedral Church of Wells, rated in the king's books at £7, endowed with £200 private benefaction, and £200 royal bounty. The church, dedicated to St. Mary, has lately received an addition of one hundred and twelve sittings, of which seventy-six are free, the Incorporated Society for the enlargement of churches and chapels having granted £40 towards defraying the expense. There is a place of worship for Wesleyan Methodists. The Roman Fosse-way passes through the parish. An old building, now used as a barn, formerly belonged to Glastonbury abbey.

PIMLICO, a parochial district, formerly a chapelry in the parish of ST. GEORGE, HANOVER-SQUARE, liberty of the city of WESTMINSTER, county of MIDDLESEX, 3 miles (S. W. by W.) from St. Paul's. The population is returned with the parish. The origin of this place is comparatively modern, but the name is of earlier date, though at what period, or on what occasion, it was appropriated to the suburb of the metropolis westward of St. James' and the Green Park, is uncertain. Most, if not all the present buildings are of a date subsequent to the erection of Buckingham House, in the beginning of the last century. The eastern part of Pimlico contains a range of handsome houses, called Grosvenor-place, extending southward from Hyde Park corner, and fronting the Green Park and the Royal gardens ; and the ground to the west, between Knightsbridge and Chelsea, is partly occupied by many well-executed and several truly magnificent buildings, both public and private, which, when completed, will form various streets and squares, that may vie with the contemporary erections in the Regent's Park. To the north is Wilton-crescent, a semicircular range of buildings, with another along the diameter, the latter ornamented in front with Corinthian pilasters. Eaton-place and Wilton-place contain some handsome and much embellished mansions, especially the former. Belgrave-square, which perhaps may be fairly termed the finest square in the metropolis, includes in its plan four detached lines of buildings, respectively fronting the east, west, north, and south, with four isolated structures at the angles, of which last one only is yet completed, a mansion, with low wings and a good Ionic portico in the centre. The four lateral lines of houses are embellished with various architectural ornaments : the fronts of those on the eastern and western sides have corresponding decorations, and the central houses on each of the four sides are ornamented with columns and sculpture, as also in a less degree are those near the extremities ; but the central edifice on the south side is the most remarkable, having in the lower story a colonnade with highly enriched capitals, and in the principal story Corinthian columns, the windows of the attic story, as well as the parapet, having sculptured ornaments : this edifice is from the design of G. Bassevi, architect. The opposite house, on the north side of the square, has a similar front, exclusively of the colonnade ; and the corresponding edifices in general, being uniform in plan and decorations, afford a display of much architectural taste and elegance. From this square, Belgrave-street forms a noble avenue to Eaton-square, of which only the eastern part, including the new church of St. Peter, and some detached portions, is yet erected.

The royal palace, now almost completed, stands on the site of Buckingham House, so called, because it was erected, in 1703, by John Sheffield, Duke of Buckingham, on a piece of ground which had been a place of public entertainment, called the Mulberry Gardens. Buckingham House was purchased as a residence for the Queen, in 1761, by a grant from parliament of £21,000. The entrance to the new palace is through a triumphal arch, said to be the largest work of the kind executed in modern times, and equalling, in its dimensions and general effect, the Arch of Constantine at Rome. It consists of three gateways, that in the centre rising to the architrave ; over those on the sides are tablets, containing on one side female representatives of England, Scotland, and Ireland ; and on the other the Genius of England inciting youth : between the arches are columns twenty feet high, which will support groups of trophies and figures ; and behind is a representation in bold relief of the battle of Waterloo. On the opposite side, fronting the palace, is a representation of the battle of Trafalgar ; and this structure, which is about sixty feet high, will be adorned above with several figures, and surmounted by a bronze equestrian statue of His Majesty. The gates will be of Mosaic gold, and a handsome palisade will connect this building with the wings of the palace, enclosing a quadrangle, surrounded by a peristyle of Grecian Doric columns. The principal order of the palace is the Roman Corinthian, raised on a Doric basement. The central portion of the front is a *porte cochere*, superior portico of eight coupled columns, and corresponding towers, with four columns each at both extremities. The tympanum of the central portico is filled with sculpture, and the pediment crowned with statues. The projecting wings, or sides, of the quadrangle are less embellished, the centre compartments only (forming the entrances respectively to the Lord Steward's and Lord Chamberlain's apartments) are decorated with pilasters, and adorned, the one with a clock tower, and the other with a wind tower, both enriched with appropriate groups of sculpture : the ends of the wings towards the park display Corinthian porticos, with statues, and other sculptured ornaments. In the centre of the edifice is a cupola yet unfinished, which will be adorned with ribs and other decorations. The entrance

under the portico leads into a handsome hall, beyond which is the guard-chamber ; and from the hall the grand staircase, which is of white marble, and consists of a centre, with two returning flights, conducts to the state apartments, consisting of the saloon, throne chamber, picture gallery, state bed-chamber, and drawing-rooms, all which are of noble dimensions, and, when finished, will display the utmost splendour and magnificence of style and embellishment. To make room for the enlargement of this magnificent edifice, and for the arrangement of the grounds belonging to it, a considerable number of dwelling-houses will be taken down in its vicinity, and the entire neighbourhood laid out on an improved plan. The architect of the new palace is Mr. Nash, whose taste and professional skill are said to have been assisted by the suggestions of the late royal proprietor, George IV. The principal streets and squares of Pimlico are well paved and lighted with gas, under the direction of commissioners appointed by act of parliament ; and water is supplied chiefly from the Chelsea water-works, which were constructed in 1724, when the proprietors were incorporated by act of parliament, and a canal was made from the Thames, near Ranelagh, to Pimlico, whence the water is conveyed by pipes to the reservoirs in Hyde Park and the Green Park. Here are saw-mills, a Roman cement manufactory, white lead works, and a distillery ; and on the banks of the Grosvenor canal, extending from the Thames, and those of the basin in which it terminates, are coal, stone, and timber wharfs. In Grosvenor-place are Tattersall's well-known betting and auction rooms, and the large establishment connected with them for the sale of horses, and the arrangement of affairs belonging to the turf ; and in Halkin-street is Fozard's riding-school.

Pimlico was constituted a district, by order of the king in council, in July 1830. The church, dedicated to St. Peter, is a Grecian edifice, with a grand Ionic portico of six fluted columns, supporting a plain pediment, behind which is a square tower, surmounted by a dome and cross. The building was commenced in September, 1824, and completed in 1827, at an expense of £5555. 11. l., granted by the parliamentary commissioners ; and it contains one thousand six hundred and fifty-seven sittings, of which six hundred and forty-one are free. The incumbency is in the patronage of the Rector of St. George's, Hanover-square. The episcopal chapels are Belgrave chapel, in Halkin-street, the front of which has a noble Ionic portico of four plain columns ; Charlotte chapel, in Charlotte-street, erected as a chapel of ease to St. George's, Hanover-square ; Ebury chapel, near Chelsea ; and the Lock chapel, Grosvenor-place. In Palace-street, near the border of St. George's parish, is Buckingham chapel, a place of worship for Independents. The new grammar school, in Ebury-street, erected in 1830, is a handsome structure, in front of which is a well-executed portico of two Doric columns between pilasters, supporting a pediment decorated with triglyphs and dentils : this institution is supported by a proprietary subscription, for the classical education of youth on moderate terms. St. George's hospital, for the sick and wounded poor, was originally established in 1733, when an edifice, which had been the residence of a nobleman, was enlarged and appropriated to the purposes of the charity. A new and handsome structure in Grosvenor-place, on the site of the old hospital, has been recently erected, consisting of a central compartment and projecting wings. The hospital is supported by the interest of property in the funds and by annual subscriptions; and attached to it is a charity for convalescents. The Lock hospital, in Grosvenor-place, was instituted in 1746, for the relief of persons suffering under syphilitic diseases; the name is said to be derived from an old French term, *les Loques*, signifying a house for lepers. It is supported by subscription, and the interest of funded property; and connected with it is the Lock asylum, for the reception of indigent females who have been discharged from the hospital. Near Buckingham gate stood a building called Tart Hall, erected in 1638, by Nicholas Stone, an eminent architect, for the Countess Alathea, wife of Thomas Howard, Earl of Arundel, who formed the celebrated collection of Arundelian marbles, a part of which was placed in it. After the death of the countess the mansion became the property of her second son, Lord Stafford, who fell a victim to the popular rage against Roman Catholics, in the reign of Charles II., and at that period the statues and sculptured marbles were buried, to preserve them from the mob, who, says Pennant, "would have mistaken the statues for Popish saints." They were sold in 1720, and the house pulled down.

PIMPERNE, a parish in the hundred of PIMPERNE, Blandford (North) division of the county of DORSET, 2½ miles (N.E.) from Blandford-Forum, containing 426 inhabitants. The living is a rectory, in the archdeaconry of Dorset, and diocese of Bristol, rated in the king's books at £19. 2. 6., and in the patronage of E. B. Portman, Esq. The church, dedicated to St. Peter, has several Norman portions, particularly an enriched doorway and an arch between the nave and chancel; the font is very ancient, and in the churchyard are several coffin-shaped stones, each having a cross carved on it. There is a trifling endowment for teaching six poor children. In this parish are some irregular earth-works, anciently forming a maze, which covered about an acre of ground, but, in 1730, it was almost obliterated by the plough.

PINCHBECK, a parish in the wapentake of ELLOE, parts of HOLLAND, county of LINCOLN, 2¼ miles (N. by W.) from Spalding, containing 2099 inhabitants. The living is a vicarage, in the archdeaconry and diocese of Lincoln, rated in the king's books at £40. 6. 5½. The Rev. John Caparn was patron in 1821. The church, dedicated to St. Mary, is principally in the later style of English architecture. There is a place of worship for Independents. Fourteen children are instructed for a trifling rent-charge, bequeathed by James Rawlett, aided by the gifts of other charitable persons, whose names are unknown. In the garden of the mansion-house, which is an ancient moated building, was found, in 1742, a large commodus of brass; on the reverse, a female sitting on a globe, the right hand extended, and in the left a victory: several pipes of baked earth were also met with in 1743.

PINCHINGTHORPE, a township in the parish of GUILSBROUGH, eastern division of the liberty of LANGBAURGH, North riding of the county of YORK, 2¼ miles (W. S. W.) from Guilsbrough, containing 80 inhabitants.

PINDLEY, a hamlet in the parish of CLAVERDON, Henley division of the hundred of BARLICHWAY, county of WARWICK, 4½ miles (E.) from Henley in Arden, con-

taining 26 inhabitants. A Cistercian nunnery, in honour of the Blessed Virgin Mary, was founded here, in the time of Henry I., by Robert de Pilardinton, which, at the dissolution, had a revenue valued at £27. 14. 7.

PINHOE, a parish in the hundred of WONFORD, county of DEVON, 3 miles (N. E. by E.) from Exeter, containing 477 inhabitants. The living is a vicarage, in the archdeaconry and diocese of Exeter, rated in the king's books at £14. 13. 4., and in the patronage of the Bishop of Exeter. The church, dedicated to St. Michael, is furnished with a screen and pulpit of wood highly enriched. Twelve poor children are instructed for about £3 a year, the united bequests of Sir Edmond Elwill and John Sanders. Pinhoe is said to have been the scene of a bloody conflict between Ethelred and the Danes, in 1001.

PINNALS, an extra-parochial liberty, in the hundred of SPARKENHOE, county of LEICESTER, 1½ mile (N.) from Atherstone. The population is returned with Merevale.

PINNER, a parish in the hundred of GORE, county of MIDDLESEX, 2½ miles (N.W. by W.) from Harrow on the Hill, containing 1076 inhabitants. The living is a perpetual curacy, in the peculiar jurisdiction of the Archbishop of Canterbury, endowed with £1000 private benefaction, £400 royal bounty, and £900 parliamentary grant, and in the patronage of the Vicar of Harrow. The church, dedicated to St. John the Baptist, is a large edifice, chiefly of flints, erected in 1321; in it lies interred Sir Bartholomew Shower, an eminent lawyer in the time of James II. Pinner received a grant of a weekly market from Edward III., and two fairs, one on the nativity of John the Baptist, and the other on the decollation of the same saint. At this place died, in 1798, John Zephaniah Holwell, who had been Governor of Bengal, and who published a curious and interesting account of his confinement, with many other persons, in the Black Hole at Calcutta.

PINNOCK, a parish in the lower division of the hundred of KIFTSGATE, county of GLOUCESTER, 3¾ miles (E.) from Winchcombe, containing 33 inhabitants. The living is a discharged rectory, annexed to the vicarage of Didbrook, in the archdeaconry and diocese of Gloucester, rated in the king's books at £3. 13. 4. The church is demolished.

PINNOCK (ST.), a parish in WEST hundred, county of CORNWALL, 4 miles (W. S. W.) from Liskeard, containing 431 inhabitants. The living is a rectory, in the archdeaconry of Cornwall, and diocese of Exeter, rated in the king's books at £17. 13. 6½., and in the patronage of the Rev. Joseph Pomeroy, Tilly Corington, Esq., and Joseph Austen, Esq., alternately. A stream, called Herod's Foot, runs through the parish, and there is a lead mine of the same name. A school is supported here by subscription amounting to about £10 per annum.

PINVIN, a chapelry in the parish of ST. ANDREW, PERSHORE, upper division of the hundred of PERSHORE, county of WORCESTER, 2 miles (N. N. E.) from Pershore, containing 199 inhabitants.

PINXTON, a parish in the hundred of SCARSDALE, county of DERBY, 4 miles (E. by S.) from Alfreton, containing 681 inhabitants. The living is a rectory, in the archdeaconry of Derby, and diocese of Lichfield and Coventry, rated in the king's books at £6. 0. 10., and in the patronage of D. Ewes Coke, Esq. The church is dedicated to St. Helena. There is a place of worship for Wesleyan Methodists. The Erewash canal passes through the parish, and a railway leads hence to Mansfield.

PION (CANON), county of HEREFORD. — See CANON-PION.

PION (KING'S), a parish in the hundred of STRETFORD, county of HEREFORD, 3 miles (E. S. E.) from Weobley, containing 376 inhabitants. The living is a discharged vicarage, with that of Birley, in the archdeaconry and diocese of Hereford, rated in the king's books at £5. 11. 8., endowed with £200 royal bounty, and in the patronage of S. Peploe, Esq. The church is dedicated to St. Mary. A court leet is occasionally held here. A charity school is supported by subscription.

PIPE, a parish in the hundred of GRIMSWORTH, county of HEREFORD, 3 miles (N.) from Hereford, containing, with the township of Lyde, 141 inhabitants. The living is a discharged vicarage, in the peculiar jurisdiction of the Dean of Hereford, rated in the king's books at £7. 1½., endowed with £200 private benefaction, and £400 royal bounty, and in the patronage of the Dean and Chapter of Hereford. The church is dedicated to St. Peter.

PIPE-HILL, a hamlet in that part of the parish of ST. MICHAEL, LICHFIELD, which is in the southern division of the hundred of OFFLOW, county of STAFFORD, 1¾ mile (S. W.) from Lichfield, containing 92 inhabitants.

PIPEWELL, a hamlet partly in the parishes of GREAT OAKLEY and WILBARSTON, hundred of CORBY, and partly in the parish of RUSHTON, hundred of ROTHWELL, county of NORTHAMPTON, 6¼ miles (N. N. W.) from Kettering. An abbey for Cistercian monks, in honour of the Blessed Virgin, was founded here, in 1143, by William de Boutevylein, which, at the dissolution, had a revenue of £347. 8.

PIRBRIGHT, county of SURREY. — See PURBRIGHT.

PIRTON, a parish in the hundred of HITCHIN and PIRTON, county of HERTFORD, 3½ miles (N. W.) from Hitchin, containing 630 inhabitants. The living is a vicarage, united with the rectory of Ickleford, in the archdeaconry of Huntingdon, and diocese of Lincoln. The church is dedicated to St. Mary.

PIRTON, a parish in the hundred of PIRTON, county of OXFORD, 5 miles (S.) from Tetsworth, containing, with the hamlets of Assendon, Clare, Golder, and Standhill, and the liberty of Christmas-Common, 622 inhabitants. The living is a vicarage, in the archdeaconry and diocese of Oxford, rated in the king's books at £17. 9. 4½., and in the patronage of the Dean and Canons of Christ Church, Oxford. The church is dedicated to St. Mary.

PIRTON, a joint hamlet with Trescott, in that part of the parish of TETTENHALL which is in the northern division of the hundred of SEISDON, county of STAFFORD, 3 miles (W.) from Wolverhampton, containing, with Trescott, 259 inhabitants. It is within the jurisdiction of the royal peculiar court of Tettenhall.

PIRTON, a parish in the upper division of the hundred of PERSHORE, county of WORCESTER, 4½ miles (N. N. W.) from Pershore, containing 214 inhabitants.

The living is a rectory, united to that of Croom-D'Abitot, in the archdeaconry and diocese of Worcester, rated in the king's books at £8. 3., and in the patronage of the Earl of Coventry. The church is dedicated to St. Peter.

PISFORD, a parish in the hundred of SPELHOE, county of NORTHAMPTON, 5 miles (N.) from Northampton, containing 506 inhabitants. The living is a rectory, in the archdeaconry of Northampton, and diocese of Peterborough, rated in the king's books at £17. 19. 7., and in the patronage of Colonel Vyse. The church, dedicated to St. Mary, has a mixture of various styles; the south doorway is a fine specimen of the Norman, and the font is very curious and ancient. There is a place of worship for Wesleyan Methodists. A branch of the river Nene, and numerous smaller streams, run through the parish. Limestone and a peculiar white soft sand abound here. Near the London road is a sepulchral tumulus, called Lyman Hill; and on a neighbouring heath is a small ancient encampment, called Barrow, or Borough Dykes, nearly obliterated by the plough.

PISHILL, a parish in the hundred of PIRTON, county of OXFORD, 5½ miles (N. N. W.) from Henley, upon Thames, containing 155 inhabitants. The living is a perpetual curacy, united with that of Nettlebed, in the jurisdiction of the peculiar court of Dorchester.

PITCHCOMB, a parish in the middle division of the hundred of DUNSTONE and KING'S BARTON, county of GLOUCESTER, 1¾ mile (S. W. by W.) from Painswick, containing 187 inhabitants. The living is a discharged rectory, united with that of Harescomb, in the archdeaconry and diocese of Gloucester. The church was erected about 1819, on the site of a more ancient structure, and exhibits a chaste specimen of the decorated style of English architecture. There is a place of worship for Independents.

PITCHCOTT, a parish in the hundred of ASHENDON, county of BUCKINGHAM, 5¾ miles (N. W. by N.) from Aylesbury, containing 44 inhabitants. The living is a rectory, in the archdeaconry of Buckingham, and diocese of Lincoln, rated in the king's books at £10, and in the patronage of Thomas Saunders, Esq. The church is dedicated to St. Giles.

PITCHFORD, a parish in the hundred of CONDOVER, county of SALOP, 6½ miles (S. S. E.) from Shrewsbury, containing 226 inhabitants. The living is a discharged rectory, in the archdeaconry of Salop, and diocese of Lichfield and Coventry, rated in the king's books at £6. 5. 5., and in the patronage of the Earl of Liverpool. The church, dedicated to St. Michael, is a very ancient fabric, and much admired for its neat appearance: in it are four curious and handsome alabaster monuments of the Otley family, also a very fine oaken figure of a Knight Templar, supposed to represent a Baron de Pitchford, a crusader, who was buried here. Pitchford derives its name from a stream issuing out of a rock, and forming a well near a brook or ford adjoining the village; the surface of the water being frequently covered with an oily substance, called *Petroleum*, and having a strong pitchy smell, from which has been extracted a medicinal preparation, called British oil, for which a patent was a few years since obtained: it is considered efficacious for burns, bruises, &c. The petty sessions for the division are held here.

PITCHLEY, a parish in the hundred of ORLINGBURY, county of NORTHAMPTON, 2¾ miles (S. by W.)

from Kettering, containing 452 inhabitants. The living is a vicarage, in the archdeaconry of Northampton, diocese of Peterborough, endowed with £200 private benefaction, and £200 royal bounty, and in the patronage of the Bishop of Lichfield and Coventry. The church is dedicated to All Saints. There is a place of worship for Wesleyan Methodists. William Aylworth, in 1661, bequeathed a rent-charge of £18 for the support of a free school : there is also a small endowment in land, with a house for the master, by a person unknown, for a similar purpose.

PITCOMB, a parish in the hundred of BRUTON, county of SOMERSET, 1¾ mile (S. W.) from Bruton, containing, with the tythings of Cole and Hadspen, 431 inhabitants. The living is a perpetual curacy, in the archdeaconry of Bath, and diocese of Bath and Wells, endowed with £600 royal bounty, and £200 parliamentary grant, and in the patronage of Sir R. C. Hoare, Bart. The church is dedicated to St. Leonard : in the churchyard is an ancient stone cross, the top of which is a cross patée perfect. In the neighbouring meadows, the banks of the fish ponds formerly belonging to Glastonbury abbey may still be traced.

PITMINSTER, a parish in the hundred of TAUNTON and TAUNTON-DEAN, county of SOMERSET, 4½ miles (S. by W.) from Taunton, containing, with the tythings of Blagdon, Duddlestone, Fulford, Leigh, Poundisford, and Trendle, 1416 inhabitants. The living is a discharged vicarage, in the archdeaconry of Taunton, and diocese of Bath and Wells, rated in the king's books at £15. 10. 5., and in the patronage of F. Grey Cooper, Esq. The church is dedicated to St. Andrew and St. Mary. There is a place of worship for Independents.

PITNEY, a parish in the hundred of PITNEY, county of SOMERSET, 2½ miles (W.) from Somerton, containing 301 inhabitants. The living is a discharged rectory, in the archdeaconry of Wells, and diocese of Bath and Wells, rated in the king's books at £9. 14. 9½. Wm. Pyne, and J. Williams, Esqrs. were patrons in 1825. The church is dedicated to St. John the Baptist.

PITSEA, a parish in the hundred of BARSTABLE, county of ESSEX, 4½ miles (W. S. W.) from Rayleigh, containing 289 inhabitants. The living is a rectory, in the archdeaconry of Essex, and diocese of London, rated in the king's books at £16. 13. 4., and in the patronage of Mrs. Heathcote and others. The church is dedicated to St. Michael.

PITTINGTON, a parish in the southern division of EASINGTON ward, county palatine of DURHAM, 3½ miles (E. N. E.) from Durham, comprising the townships of Hall-Garth, Shadforth, and Sherburn, and containing 808 inhabitants. The living is a discharged vicarage, in the archdeaconry and diocese of Durham, rated in the king's books at £14. 14. 2., endowed with £200 private benefaction, and £200 royal bounty, and in the patronage of the Dean and Chapter of Durham. The church, dedicated to St. Lawrence, is an ancient structure, principally in the Norman style, and had formerly two chantries, in honour of St. Mary and St. Katherine. In the churchyard, among other memorials, are the effigy of a cross-legged knight, and a stone in the shape of a coffin, with a Saxon inscription. Limestone and coal abound here ; and a rail-road, eight miles long, extends from Hall-Garth colliery to the river Wear at Painshaw.

PITTLEWORTH, an extra-parochial district, consisting of only one farm, in the hundred of THORNGATE, Andover division of the county of SOUTHAMPTON. The population is returned with the parish of Broughton. There was formerly a chapel, now in ruins.

PITTON, a chapelry in the parish and hundred of ALDERBURY, county of WILTS, 4½ miles (E. by N.) from Salisbury, containing 308 inhabitants. This chapelry is in the peculiar jurisdiction of the Treasurer in the Cathedral Church of Salisbury. The chapel is dedicated to St. Peter. Sir Stephen Fox, in 1711, gave £188 in support of an hospital for twelve poor persons, and for clothing and teaching twenty poor children.

PIXLEY, a parish in the hundred of RADLOW, county of HEREFORD, 3¾ miles (W. by N.) from Ledbury, containing 132 inhabitants. The living is a discharged rectory, in the archdeaconry and diocese of Hereford, rated in the king's books at £4. 0. 2½., endowed with £200 private benefaction, and £200 royal bounty, and in the patronage of Earl Somers. The church is dedicated to St. Andrew.

PLAINMELLOR, a township in the parish of HALTWHISTLE, western division of TINDALE ward, county of NORTHUMBERLAND, 3½ miles (S. by E.) from Haltwhistle, containing 184 inhabitants. It is so named from a mountain within its limits, and is bounded on the north by the South Tyne, across which there is a wooden bridge.

PLAISTOW, a ward in the parish of WEST HAM, hundred of BEACONTREE, county of ESSEX, 5 miles (E. by N.) from London. The population is returned with the parish. It is bounded on the south by the Thames, and on the west by Bow creek. The living is a district incumbency, in the archdeaconry of Essex, and diocese of London, and in the patronage of the Vicar of West Ham. The church, dedicated to St. Mary, was completed in 1830, at an expense of £4800, towards which the parliamentary commissioners contributed £2300 : it is a neat edifice, in the later style of English architecture. There are places of worship for Independents and Wesleyan Methodists.

PLAITFORD, a parish forming a distinct portion of the hundred of ALDERBURY, locally in that of Frustfield, county of WILTS, 4½ miles (W. by S.) from Romsey, containing 276 inhabitants. The living is a perpetual curacy, annexed to the vicarage of West Grimstead, in the archdeaconry of Wilts, and diocese of Salisbury.

PLASHETS, a township in the parish of FALSTONE, north-western division of TINDALE ward, county of NORTHUMBERLAND, 12½ miles (W. N. W.) from Bellingham, containing 234 inhabitants. Coal is obtained here.

PLAWSWORTH, a township in that part of the parish of CHESTER le STREET which is in the middle division of CHESTER ward, county palatine of DURHAM, 4 miles (N.) from Durham, containing 227 inhabitants.

PLAXTOL, a chapelry in the parish and hundred of WROTHAM, lathe of AYLESFORD, county of KENT, 5 miles (S. by W.) from Wrotham. The population is returned with the parish. The living is a perpetual curacy, in the peculiar jurisdiction of the Archbishop of Canterbury, endowed with £400 private benefaction, and £800 parliamentary grant, and in the patronage of the Rector of Wrotham.

PLAYDEN, a parish in the hundred of GOLDSPUR, rape of HASTINGS, county of SUSSEX, ¾ of a mile (N.) from Rye, containing 317 inhabitants. The living is a dfscharged rectory, annexed to that of East Guildford, in the archdeaconry of Lewes, and diocese of Chichester, rated in the king's books at £12. Thomas P. Lamb, Esq. was patron in 1807. The church, dedicated to St. Michael, is in the early style of English architecture. The river Rother and the Royal Military canal pass through the parish. Foundations of old buildings are frequently met with, denoting the population to have been formerly greater than it is now. Here was also an hospital, founded in honour of St. Bartholomew, and placed under the government of the abbey of Westminster.

PLAYFORD, a parish in the hundred of CARLFORD, county of SUFFOLK, 4¼ miles (N. E. by E.) from Ipswich, containing 264 inhabitants. The living is a perpetual curacy, in the archdeaconry of Suffolk, and diocese of Norwich, endowed with £800 royal bounty, and £200 parliamentary grant, and in the patronage of the Marquis of Bristol. The chapel is dedicated to St. Mary.

PLEASELEY, a parish in the hundred of SCARSDALE, county of DERBY, 3¼ miles (N. W. by N.) from Mansfield, containing 529 inhabitants. The living is a rectory, in the archdeaconry of Derby, and diocese of Lichfield and Coventry, rated in the king's books at £11. 4. 7., and in the patronage of Bache Thornhill, Esq. The church, dedicated to St. Michael, is an ancient stone edifice, remarkably long and narrow; there is a large chasm in the steeple, caused by the shock of an earthquake, which was felt over a great part of the midland counties, on March 17th, 1816. Limestone abounds in the parish, and there are some considerable manufactories for cotton thread, hosiery, &c., principally for the Nottingham market. Pleaseley had anciently a market on Monday, granted, in 1284, to Thomas Bec, Bishop of St. David's, with a fair for three days; the former has been long disused, but fairs are now held on May 6th and October 29th, for cattle, horses, and sheep. Seven children are instructed for £9 a year, the bequest of William Pearse, in 1818, by a schoolmistress, who also superintends a Sunday school, according to the will of the donor. In the park adjoining the cotton-mills is a large enclosure, with a double vallum and intrenchments, two sides of which are secured by natural precipices: it is two hundred and fifty feet in length, by one hundred and ninety-five in breadth, and is evidently a Saxon work, though not hitherto noticed by antiquaries.

PLEASINGTON, a township in the parish, and lower division of the hundred, of BLACKBURN, county palatine of LANCASTER, 3 miles (W. by S.) from Blackburn, containing 625 inhabitants. A handsome Roman Catholic chapel, called Pleasington Priory, was erected by the late J. F. Butler Esq.

PLEDGON, a hamlet in that part of the parish of HENHAM which is in the hundred of CLAVERING, county of ESSEX, 3½ miles (N. E. by E.) from Stansted-Mountfitchet, containing 160 inhabitants.

PLEMONSTALL, a parish comprising the townships of Hoole, Pickton, and Mickle-Trafford, in the lower division of the hundred of BROXTON, and the township of Bridge-Trafford, in the second division of the hundred of EDDISBURY, county palatine of CHESTER, 4¼ miles (N.E.) from Chester, and containing 710 inhabitants. The living is a vicarage, in the archdeaconry and diocese of Chester, rated in the king's books at £6. 13. 4., and in the patronage of the Earl of Bradford. The church, dedicated to St. Peter, stands in the township of Mickle-Trafford, a mile and a half north-east of the village of that name. There is a small endowed school, erected by subscription, more than a century ago. At Trafford, in this parish, a garrison was placed for the king, by Sir William Brereton, during the siege of Chester in the parliamentary war.

PLESHEY, a parish in the hundred of DUNMOW, county of ESSEX, 6¼ miles (N. N. W.) from Chelmsford, containing 289 inhabitants. The living is a perpetual curacy, in the jurisdiction of the Commissary of Essex and Herts, concurrently with the Consistorial Court of the Bishop of London, endowed with £200 private benefaction, and £400 royal bounty. W. Tuffnell, Esq. was patron in 1811. The church, dedicated to the Holy Trinity, was rebuilt of brick in 1708, chiefly by the munificence of Bishop Compton; the tower, which rose from the intersection of the ancient cruciform structure, still remaining in decay, until renovated by the late Samuel Tuffnel, Esq., who also added a handsome chancel. To the southward of the church a college was founded, about 1394, in honour of the Holy Trinity, by Thomas of Woodstock, Duke of Gloucester, sixth son of Edward III., for a master, warden, eight chaplains, two clerks, and two choristers, whose revenue, at the dissolution, was estimated at £143. 12. 7. Pleshey, though now an obscure village, was once a place of considerable importance, having been the seat of the high constables of England, from the first institution of their office till nearly four centuries after the Norman Conquest. From discoveries made here it seems to have been the site either of a Roman station, or a villa. The village is surrounded by an intrenchment, enclosing also the keep mount of the Norman fortress, of which there only remains the stone bridge, of singular construction, across the moat to the keep. The treacherous arrest of the Duke of Gloucester by Richard II. was planned while the former lay at this castle, to which the king himself came, and decoyed him from it under the pretence of a friendly invitation to London.

PLESSEY, a joint township with Shotton, in the southern division of the parish of STANNINGTON, western division of CASTLE ward, county of NORTHUMBERLAND, 6 miles (S. by E.) from Morpeth, containing, with Shotton, 395 inhabitants.

PLOMPTON, a township in the parish of SPOFFORTH, upper division of the wapentake of CLARO, West riding of the county of YORK, 2½ miles (S. S. E.) from Knaresborough, containing 208 inhabitants. It is within the jurisdiction of the peculiar court of the honour of Knaresborough.

PLUCKLEY, a parish in the hundred of CALEHILL, lathe of SCRAY, county of KENT, 3 miles (S. W.) from Charing, containing, with Pevington, 663 inhabitants. The living is a rectory, with that of Pevington united, in the archdeaconry and diocese of Canterbury, rated in the king's books at £20. 1. 5½., and in the patronage of the Archbishop of Canterbury. The church is dedicated to St. Nicholas. A fair is held on Whit-Tuesday, for toys, and another on December 6th, for cattle and hogs, which are brought in great numbers, the prices they bear here generally regulating those at the neighbouring markets. A school is supported by voluntary subscriptions.

PLUMBLAND, a parish in ALLERDALE ward below Darwent, county of CUMBERLAND, 6½ miles (N. by E.) from Cockermouth, containing 396 inhabitants. The living is a rectory, in the archdeaconry and diocese of Carlisle, rated in the king's books at £20. 14. 9½., and in the patronage of C. Curwen, Esq. The church is dedicated to St. Cuthbert. Coal and limestone abound here, and much of the latter is burned into lime. Freestone of an inferior quality is also obtained. There is an excellent free school, founded in 1759, by Captain John Sibson, who endowed it with lands now producing an annual income of £87: the school-house was erected of freestone in 1800, and contains two very spacious rooms, one for teaching the classics, the other for English and the mathematics; also an entrance porch and clock tower.

PLUMLEY, a township in that part of the parish of GREAT BUDWORTH which is in the hundred of BUCKLOW, county palatine of CHESTER, 3 miles (S. W. by S.) from Nether Knutsford, containing 366 inhabitants. A school is supported by subscription amounting to about £10 per annum.

PLUMPTON, a joint township with Westby, in the parish of KIRKHAM, hundred of AMOUNDERNESS, county palatine of LANCASTER, 3 miles (W. by N.) from Kirkham. The population is returned with Westby. There is a place of worship for Wesleyan Methodists. This place was celebrated, no less than five centuries ago, for its mines of iron, and a considerable quantity of ore is still obtained at Whitrigs, in the neighbourhood.

PLUMPTON, a parish in the hundred of GREENS-NORTON, county of NORTHAMPTON, 6½ miles (W.) from Towcester, containing 63 inhabitants. The living is a discharged rectory, in the archdeaconry of Northampton, and diocese of Peterborough, rated in the king's books at £10, and in the patronage of the Rev. Benjamin Hill. The church is dedicated to St. John the Baptist.

PLUMPTON, a parish in the hundred of STREET, rape of LEWES, county of SUSSEX, 4¾ miles (N. W. by W.) from Lewes, containing 272 inhabitants. The living is a rectory, in the archdeaconry of Lewes, and diocese of Chichester, rated in the king's books at £10, and in the patronage of Mrs. Woodward. The church is a small mean building. There is a trifling sum, the bequest of Anthony Springet, in 1735, for teaching poor children and supplying them with books. On Plumpton plain, a considerable eminence between Ditchling and Lewes, Sir Simon de Montford drew up his army, previously to the battle of Lewes.

PLUMPTON (WOOD), a chapelry in the parish of ST. MICHAEL, hundred of AMOUNDERNESS, county palatine of LANCASTER, 4½ miles (N. W. by N.) from Preston, containing 1635 inhabitants. The living is a perpetual curacy, in the archdeaconry of Richmond, and diocese of Chester, endowed with £400 private benefaction, and £600 royal bounty, and in the patronage of the Vicar of St. Michael's.

PLUMPTON-STREET, a township in the parish of HESKET in the FOREST, LEATH ward, county of CUMBERLAND, 6½ miles (N. by W.) from Penrith, containing 128 inhabitants.

PLUMPTON-WALL, a chapelry in the parish of LAZONBY, LEATH ward, county of CUMBERLAND, 5¼ miles (N. by W.) from Penrith, containing 268 inhabitants. The living is a perpetual curacy, in the archdeaconry and diocese of Carlisle, endowed with £200 royal bounty, and in the patronage of the Bishop of Carlisle. The chapel, dedicated to St. John the Baptist, was built by subscription among the inhabitants. This was the ancient Voreda, where a Roman altar has been found; and at Castle Steads, in the neighbourhood, an inscribed stone, with a bust, was discovered.

PLUMSTEAD, a parish in the hundred of LESS-NESS, lathe of SUTTON at HONE, county of KENT, 10 miles (S. by E.) from London, containing 2386 inhabitants. The living is a vicarage, in the archdeaconry and diocese of Rochester, rated in the king's books at £6. 18. 4., and in the patronage of B. Bowell, Esq. The church is dedicated to St. Nicholas. The river Thames bounds the parish to the northward. Plumstead was formerly a market town, and possessed also a charter for fairs, now disused. John Budgen, Esq., in 1807, granted land whereon to build a schoolroom, which was afterwards erected by private subscription; in the same year William Cole bequeathed £1000, now producing upwards of £46 per annum, for the support of a day and a Sunday school, in which fifty-seven boys and fifty girls are educated, the additional expense being defrayed by contributions.

PLUMSTEAD, a parish in the northern division of the hundred of ERPINGHAM, county of NORFOLK, 5 miles (S. E. by E.) from Holt, containing 159 inhabitants. The living is a discharged rectory, in the archdeaconry and diocese of Norwich, rated in the king's books at £5. 3. 4., and in the patronage of the King, as Duke of Lancaster. The church is dedicated to St. Michael.

PLUMSTEAD (GREAT), a parish in the hundred of BLOFIELD, county of NORFOLK, 5¼ miles (E.) from Norwich, containing 288 inhabitants. The living is a perpetual curacy, in the peculiar jurisdiction and patronage of the Dean and Chapter of Norwich, endowed with £600 royal bounty, and £200 parliamentary grant. The church is dedicated to St. Mary.

PLUMSTEAD (LITTLE), a parish in the hundred of BLOFIELD, county of NORFOLK, 5¾ miles (E. by N.) from Norwich, containing 247 inhabitants. The living is a discharged rectory, consolidated with those of Brundall and Witton, in the archdeaconry and diocese of Norwich, rated in the king's books at £7. 12. 6., and in the patronage of the Rev. Charles Penrice. The church is dedicated to St. Gervase and St. Protasius.

PLUMTREE, a parish comprising the township of Clipston, in the southern division of the wapentake of BINGHAM, and the township of Normanton on the Wolds, in the northern division of the wapentake of RUSHCLIFFE, county of NOTTINGHAM, 5¼ miles (S. S. E.) from Nottingham, and containing 579 inhabitants. The living is a rectory, in the archdeaconry of Nottingham, and diocese of York, rated in the king's books at £19. 19. 7. W. Elliott, Esq. and others were patrons in 1817. The church, dedicated to St. Mary, is principally in the Norman style of architecture. The villages of Plumtree and Normanton adjoin each other; at the latter the Wesleyan Methodists have a place of worship, erected in 1827. A school is supported by voluntary contributions. There are considerable rocks of limestone in the parish. Courts leet are annually held here. Plumtree is in the honour of Tutbury, duchy of Lancaster, and within the jurisdiction of a court of pleas held at Tutbury every third Tuesday, for the recovery of debts under 40s.

PLUNGAR, a parish in the hundred of FRAMLAND, county of LEICESTER, 10½ miles (N. by E.) from Melton-Mowbray, containing 203 inhabitants. The living is a discharged vicarage, in the archdeaconry of Leicester, and diocese of Lincoln, endowed with £600 royal bounty, and in the patronage of the Duke of Rutland. The church is dedicated to St. Helen. There is a place of worship for Wesleyan Methodists. The Grantham and Nottingham canal passes through the parish.

PLUSH, a tything in the parish and hundred of BUCKLAND-NEWTON, Cerne subdivision of the county of DORSET, 3 miles (S. E.) from Buckland, containing 167 inhabitants. Here is a chapel of ease to the vicarage of Buckland.

PLYMOUTH, a sea-port, oorough, and market town, having separate jurisdiction, locally in the hundred of Roborough, county of DEVON, 44 miles (S.W.) from Exeter, and 215 (W. S. W.) from London, containing, exclusively of parts of the parishes of St. Andrew and Charles the Martyr, but including the towns of Devonport and Stonehouse, 61,212 inhabitants, of which about 35,000 are in Plymouth. This place, which is one of the principal naval and military stations in the kingdom, and, during war, the most important, as commanding the entrance of the English channel, and being the grand rendezvous of the channel fleet, is by some supposed to have been the *Tameorwerthe* of the Saxons. At the time of the Conquest, however, it was known only as a small fishing-town, which, under the appellation of Sutton, or South Town, was dependent on the abbey of Plympton, and which some time afterwards obtained the name of Plymouth, descriptive of its situation on the river Plym, near its influx into the bay called Plymouth Sound. Henry III., in the 37th of his reign, granted to the prior of Plympton a market and a fair, with the right of holding weekly courts, assize of bread and beer, and view of frankpledge. This port became at an early period the occasional rendezvous of the British navy; and here, in 1355, Edward the Black Prince embarked, on his expedition to France, and landed, on his return, with his royal prisoners. From the convenience of its harbour the town appears to have obtained a considerable degree of importance, and to have become extremely populous. The French effected a landing here in the course of this reign, and attempted to burn it, but were repulsed by the intrepidity of Courtenay, Earl of Devonshire, who, with the neighbouring gentry and their vassals, drove them back to their ships, with the loss of five hundred men. They made various other attempts, and, in the reign of Henry IV., landed with a party of troops from Bretagne, under the command of the Marshal of Bretagne and Monsieur De Castell, and, before any effectual resistance could be opposed to them, burnt six hundred houses in the town; but failing in their design to reduce the castle, and take possession of the higher part of the town, they retreated to their ships, and proceeded to Dartmouth, where De Castell and several hundred of his men were made prisoners. From this time the town declined into a mere fishing-village again, till the reign of Henry VI., during which it was improved greatly by the prior of Plympton, who rebuilt many of the houses, and, by granting liberal leases, encouraged persons to reside there, thus considerably promoting the increase of its population; its port became once more frequented by merchants, its trade revived, and its importance as a naval and military station became apparent. On a petition from the inhabitants, urging the necessity of fortifying the town and port against the future assaults of the enemy, the king granted them a toll on all merchandise entering the port. To these fortifications Leland alludes, in his description of the town, with which a chart, taken in the reign of Henry VIII., and now in the British Museum, exactly coincides. In 1439 the town was incorporated, under the designation of Plymouth; and the manor of Sutton-Prior, with all its rights and appurtenances, was settled on the corporation, with a reserved annual rent of £40 payable to the prior of Plympton, and an annuity of ten marks to the abbot of Bath. In 1512, an act was passed for enlarging and strengthening the fortifications, a grant of indulgences being issued by Bishop Lacy to all who contributed to that work; and, to prevent the accumulation of sand at the mouth of the harbour, the tin miners were prohibited working in the neighbourhood of any river communicating with the sea at Plymouth. In the 27th of Elizabeth, Sir Francis Drake obtained an act of parliament for supplying the town with fresh water, which he brought by a rivulet, called a leat, from the confines of Dartmoor, which, after a circuitous course of twenty-four miles, discharges itself into a reservoir in the town.

In 1588, the British fleet of one hundred and twenty sail, to which this port contributed seven ships, assembled in Plymouth Sound, under the command of Sir Francis Drake, Lord Howard, and Sir John Hawkins, to oppose the Spanish Armada, the admiral of which, confident of success, and delighted with the beauty of the place, had selected Mount-Edgecumbe as his place of residence in England. The Armada, after appearing off Penlee point, the Hoe, and adjacent coast, advanced to the east, where it was attacked by the British fleet, which had sailed to Torbay, to join the Exeter squadron, and after having suffered severely from a storm, this formidable armament was annihilated. In 1595, a body of Spaniards effected a landing on the coast of Cornwall, but their progress was checked by the activity of Sir Francis Godolphin, and twenty-two chests, full of Papal bulls, dispensations, and pardons, which had been taken in that county, were brought into Plymouth and burnt in the market-place. In 1596, this port was the place of rendezvous for the British fleet destined for the expedition against Cadiz, under the command of the Earls of Essex and Nottingham, in which Lord Howard was Vice-Admiral, and Sir Walter Raleigh Rear-Admiral; and from it also the Earl of Essex embarked on his unfortunate expedition to Ireland. In 1625, Charles I., with one hundred and twenty ships, and six thousand troops, arrived from Portsmouth, and remained in this town for ten days, during which time he was, with his whole court, sumptuously entertained by the mayor and commonalty. At the commencement of the parliamentary war, the inhabitants, embracing the cause of the parliament, seized the town during the absence of the king's delegate; and, in 1643, the royalists under Prince Maurice and Colonel Digby, after having besieged it for more than three months without success, were compelled to withdraw their forces. After repeated attempts to obtain possession of the town, Sir R. Grenville endeavoured to blockade it, but was repulsed by the arrival of the Earl of Essex. Sir Robert, however, commenced a second blockade, which, after a continuance of nearly a year and a half, was found unavailing, and notwithstanding repeated assaults, the parliamentarians remained in quiet possession of the town : many of the fortifications and military works which were raised on this occasion are still perceptible on the heights in the vicinity. After the Restoration, the present citadel was erected, and the fortifications rendered more complete. On the appearance of the combined fleets in the channel, in 1779, the French prisoners of war were removed from this place to Exeter; and in 1814, the Bellerophon anchored in the Sound, on her voyage to St. Helena with the Emperor Napoleon. In 1828, the Russian fleet remained for some time in this harbour, while waiting for tidings of the Admiral's ship, which had parted from it in a storm ; and in 1829, Don Miguel, Regent of Portugal, visited Plymouth, which subsequently afforded an hospitable asylum for several months to three thousand of the adherents of Don Pedro of Brazil.

The town is pleasantly situated at the mouth of the river Plym, on the north shore of the Sound : the eastern portion exhibits several irregularly-formed streets, which in some parts are inconveniently narrow ; but the western part is more regularly built, and contains many ranges of handsome and substantial houses, among which are several fine specimens of architecture : it is lighted with gas, and amply supplied with excellent water. The surrounding scenery abounds with objects of intense interest and striking magnificence. From the summit of the Hoe, an eminence near the town, are seen on the south the spacious Sound, containing within the Breakwater an area of nearly five square miles, affording safe anchorage to ships of the largest burden, and bounded on the west by the richly-wooded heights of Mount-Edgecumbe, and on the east by Mount-Batten and the Wembury cliffs ; the fortified summit of Drake island, near the shore, and the Breakwater, in the distance. The inland view is bounded by the lofty elevations of Cornwall, and the barren heights of Dartmoor; and in the foreground are seen the towns of Plymouth, Stonehouse, and Devonport, extending in a continued line. This place is chiefly distinguished for the capaciousness of its harbours, and for the importance of its maritime commerce; the naval arsenal, and yards for building ships of war, are noticed under the head of Devonport (which see). The principal harbours are the

Sound, Sutton Pool, the Hamoaze, Stonehouse Pool, Barn Pool, the Catwater, and several smaller ones. The Sound, which is capable of holding two thousand vessels, has been rendered much more secure by the construction of the Breakwater, which may be regarded as the most gigantic work ever effected in England. It was commenced on the 12th of August, 1812, and has, during its progress, experienced two most severe trials, effectually proving its strength and utility. In January 1817, and November 1824, the southern coast of England was strewed with wrecks. The Breakwater, presenting an uneven and unfinished surface, was the more liable to be disturbed by the violence of the waters ; but it was by no means seriously injured, and evidently served as a very great protection to the town of Plymouth. This immense barrier is composed of granite blocks of several tons' weight. It is in length at the base one thousand seven hundred and sixty yards ; in breadth, one hundred and twenty. The slope facing the sea is much more gradual than the inclination toward the land. The flat surface on the top forms a fine promenade, approached by three flights of steps, leading to one common landing, near the centre of the work. On the eastern side of the Sound, at Staddon Point, is a quay for the accommodation of vessels taking in fresh water. Near it, in a hollow between two hills, a reservoir has been constructed, capable of containing twelve thousand tons of fresh water, for the use of the navy, which is constantly supplied by an excellent stream : the water is thence conveyed to the quay in iron pipes. Near the reservoir is the residence of the superintendent of the Breakwater establishment, and in the vicinity are numerous cottages for the convenience of those who visit this interesting spot.

The Eddystone Lighthouse, as a successful effort of art, is scarcely less extraordinary than the gigantic structure just described. It is built on a rock in the channel, about fifteen miles south-south-west from the citadel of Plymouth. In 1696, a wooden lighthouse was first erected on this rock by Mr. Winstanley, who was so convinced of its security, that he desired to be within it during "the greatest storm that might ever blow under the heavens." His wish was fatally fulfilled: in November 1703, he perished with the structure itself. A second lighthouse of stone and timber was completed by Mr. Rudyerd, in 1709, which was destroyed by an accidental fire, in December 1755. The present building was begun on the 1st of June, 1757, and completed in October 1759, according to the masterly design of Mr. Smeaton : it is one hundred feet high, and twenty-six feet in diameter. The outside and basement are formed of granite, the lantern on the summit being composed of cast-iron and copper : it is octagonal in plan. The Citadel is a most noble fortification, consisting of three regular and two irregular bastions, the curtains of the former being strengthened by ravelins, &c. This extensive building includes houses for the governor and officers, barracks, an hospital, chapel, magazine, and armoury. The ramparts are three quarters of a mile in circuit. Here are in general from four to five hundred men, a portion of whom relieve the garrison on St. Nicholas' Island every month. The Victualling-Office below the citadel, on the east, is a vast range of buildings, including the Navy cooperage, &c. The ovens are large and of remarkable construction : they are eight in number; and it is said, that in time of war a sufficient quantity of bread has been baked in one day for sixteen thousand men. The Mill Bay Prisons of War are capable of holding three thousand men; the building stands on an eminence near the sea, whereby it is rendered, not only more healthy, but more convenient for the landing of prisoners.

The Union Sea Baths, lately erected, comprise shower, vapour, private, plunging, and swimming baths, a reading-room, and another for refreshments, with all necessary appendages. The greatest architectural ornament in the town is the Royal hotel, assembly-room, and theatre, comprised in one design, covering nearly an acre of ground. The north-west front is nearly three hundred feet in length, the centre being decorated with a noble Ionic portico of eight columns, under which is the entrance to the assembly-room and the theatre; the former is a most elegant apartment, eighty feet in length, and forty feet wide, decorated with Corinthian columns. The theatre is sufficiently spacious, and appropriately decorated: it contains a good pit, and two tiers of boxes, with gallery and slips above: the proscenium is ornamented with Ionic columns, and the scenery is superior to what might be expected in a provincial town. The entrance to the inn is under a smaller portico at the eastern side of the building, which is in every respect a noble structure: it was commenced in September 1811, and completed at an expense of £60,000, defrayed by the corporation. Near this is the Athenæum, a structure of inferior magnitude, though of equal architectural merit: its front exhibits a Grecian Doric portico, and in the interior is a spacious lecture-room, decorated with casts from the Elgin marbles, &c. The foundation stone was laid in 1818, by the president of the Plymouth Institution for the promotion of the Arts, Science, and Literature, and the institution was opened February 4th, 1819: the society meet once a week during the season, when a paper is read, and the subject subsequently discussed; a volume of transactions is also published from time to time. The public library is another ornament to the town; simple, but classical: adjoining the library, which is a handsome vaulted apartment, are reading and committee rooms. The Freemasons' Hall is a well-designed edifice, including, besides the hall used by the brethren, an auction-room, &c. A mechanics' institute was opened in December 1827, when a most excellent introductory paper was read by Dr. Cookworthy: its members are numerous and respectable.

Plymouth Regatta usually takes place in the Sound, in July, when thousands assemble on the Hoe to witness the splendid exhibition. The races are held on Chelson meadow, containing one hundred and seventy-five acres, which have been recovered from the sea by an embankment two thousand nine hundred and ten feet in length: this great improvement was executed under the directions of the Earl of Morley, who received, in consequence, a gold medal from the Society of Arts. To this nobleman the inhabitants are also indebted for a magnificent iron bridge over the Lara, opened to the public on the 16th of July, 1827. It consists of five elliptical arches of cast-iron, the central arch being one hundred feet in span. As a design it is highly worthy of encomium; and its convenience is equally unquestionable; for, by following the new line

of road to which it leads, the hills in the old route to Totness are avoided. Near this bridge is Saltram, the noble residence of the Earl of Morley.

A considerable trade in timber is now carried on with North America, the Baltic, the Mediterranean, &c.; and a direct intercourse has been established with the West Indies, highly advantageous to the port, inasmuch as the imports, coming immediately from the colonies, escape the agencies, duties, and port-charges of London and Bristol. The coasting trade is chiefly with London, Newcastle, Newport (in Wales), and Bristol. Great quantities of manganese are shipped to Scotland, wool to Hull, and lead to Bristol and the metropolis. In the foreign trade there are employed, besides numerous chartered vessels, thirty sail belonging to the port of Sutton, their burden varying from sixty to five hundred tons. Upwards of fifty coasting vessels also belong to Sutton Pool, which, in the year 1828, received within its piers one thousand one hundred and ninety-four ships, the cargoes of which amounted to seventy-five thousand and sixty-seven tons. Besides the Sutton harbour, there are others, viz., Hamoaze (see Devonport), Stonehouse Pool, Barn Pool, Catwater, with several smaller harbours. To the entire port of Plymouth it may be said, that three hundred merchant-vessels belong, the combined burden of which amounts to twenty-one thousand tons. The fishery is accounted excellent, whiting and hake being among the fish which more particularly abound. Fifty trolling, and twelve hooking, boats, employed in this fishery, belong to Sutton Pool. The harbour is held on lease under the duchy of Cornwall. The piers, through which it is entered, were erected by means of parliamentary grants, in 1791 and 1799. The quays surrounding it are numerous and convenient: here are also several yards for building and repairing merchant-ships. Catwater harbour, into which the river Plym falls, is capable of receiving a thousand sail of large merchant-vessels. The Custom House is a commodious and substantial structure, with a handsome granite front, and a well-designed long room. The exchange has no pretensions to elegance, though fully serving its intended purpose: it includes a Chamber of Commerce, Marine Insurance Office, Steam-Packet Office, &c.

The manufacture of serge is carried on to a small extent. The neighbourhood abounds with quarries of granite and slate, and the traffic in these articles has been greatly facilitated by a rail-road, the projection of which is mainly attributable to Sir Thomas Tyrwhitt: it is in length twenty-four miles, reaching from King's Tor on Dartmoor, to Jory-street, and communicating with Sutton Pool. Among its advantages may be enumerated the means it affords for conveying coal, lime, and, in particular, manure, from Plymouth into the interior. The Plymouth marble is justly esteemed, on account of its veining and susceptibility of polish. The principal quarry is at Oreston, near the Lara bridge, from which is obtained the material for the breakwater. It was opened in 1812, and in the progress of the work a cavity was discovered in the marble rock, about twenty-five feet long, and twelve feet square. Here were found, imbedded in clay, numerous bones of the rhinoceros, wolf, deer, cow, horse, &c., containing less animal matter in them than any fossil bones hitherto discovered, and unusually perfect. The market days are Monday, Thursday, and Saturday; the market-place, a spacious area comprising three acres, is enclosed with a wall, in which are three principal entrances. The fairs, in April and November, are not fixed to any particular day, but are regulated by those of Plympton; the latter, which is called the great market, is well attended.

The government, by successive charters of incorporation, is vested in a mayor, twelve aldermen, and twenty-four common council-men, assisted by a recorder, town clerk, chamberlain, coroner, serjeants at mace, and subordinate officers. The mayor is annually elected by the corporation on the 17th, and sworn into office on the 29th, of September, and, with the late mayor, recorder, and two senior aldermen, is a justice of the peace within the borough. The corporation hold courts of quarter session after the festivals of Lady-day, Midsummer, Michaelmas, and Christmas, for all offences not capital. A court of record, formerly held by prescription under the prior of Plympton, and confirmed by an act of the 18th of Henry VI., for the recovery of debts to an unlimited amount, is held every Monday, under the presidency of the mayor, assisted by the town clerk, who must be a barrister of three years' standing; and the mayor, chamberlain, and other officers, sit every Monday and Thursday at the guildhall, for determining minor offences. The borough exercised the elective franchise in the 26th and 33rd of Edward I., and in the 4th and 7th of Edward II., since which time it omitted till the 20th of Henry IV.; it has since regularly returned two members to parliament, the right of election being vested in the freemen generally: the mayor is the returning officer. The guildhall is an irregular structure, in a mixed style of architecture, comprising a hall for the transaction of the public business, jury and committee rooms, the central watch-house, and the town prison.

The town is included within the parishes of St. Andrew and King Charles the Martyr. The living of St. Andrew's is a vicarage, in the archdeaconry of Totness, and diocese of Exeter, rated in the king's books at £12. 15. 5., endowed with £600 private benefaction, and £3000 parliamentary grant, and in the patronage of the Mayor and Corporation: the church is a spacious structure of very ancient foundation, and has been recently repaired and improved, at an expense of £3000: it has a lofty square embattled tower; the interior is finely arranged, and coloured in imitation of granite, and has a handsome altar-piece. The living of the parish of King Charles the Martyr is a vicarage, in the archdeaconry of Totness, and diocese of Exeter, rated in the king's books at £12. 15. 5., and in the patronage of the Mayor and Corporation: the church, begun a little before, and completed soon after, the parliamentary war, is a neat edifice in the later style of English architecture, with a square tower surmounted by a well-proportioned spire. St. Andrew's and St. Charles' chapels are neat edifices, of which the former, built at the expense of the Rev. Robert Lampen, and

Corporate Seal.

Messrs. Woollcombe, Gill, and Pridham, was consecrated in 1823, and the latter in 1829. There are places of worship for Baptists, the Society of Friends, Independents, Wesleyan Methodists, Presbyterians, and Unitarians, and a synagogue.

The grammar school, a substantial stone building, with a residence for the master, was founded, in 1572, by Queen Elizabeth, who granted to the corporation the arrears of a rent-charge upon the vicarage, on condition that they should find a curate, and pay £20 a year to a schoolmaster. The Red boys' school was established in pursuance of the will of E. Hele, Esq., of Wembury, dated 1632: eight poor boys are clothed, educated, and apprenticed. The Blue boys' school was founded by means of a bequest by Mr. J. Lanyon: it has the same advantages as the Red boys' school, and there are generally twelve children on the foundation. In 1625, Messrs. T. and N. Sherwill founded a school and asylum for orphans: this charity is managed by a committee, including four aldermen and two common council-men: there are now twelve boys on the foundation. In Vennel-street is the Household of Faith, in which near two hundred children are educated: it is supported by contributions. The Grey school was founded in 1713: it is supported by subscription, and affords instruction to one hundred boys, of whom forty are clothed; and sixty girls, of whom twenty are clothed. The public school, conducted on the plans of Mr. Lancaster and Dr. Bell, is supported by subscription, and affords instruction to three hundred boys and girls: the master has a salary of £70 per annum: the committee of management assemble monthly, and the school is open to public inspection twice a week. In Princes-square is the subscription classical school, a neat Doric building. In Dame Rogers' school forty-five girls are clothed, maintained, and educated. Here are also a school of industry, chiefly supported by the Society of Friends, and a Presbyterian school for fifty girls. A Misericordia Society was established in 1794. The Merchantmen's hospital is for the relief of maimed or disabled seamen, and for the widows and orphans of such as are killed or drowned in the merchants' service. St. Andrew's almshouses are for the reception of twelve poor widows, who receive two shillings and sixpence per week each: behind these are others belonging to the workhouse. Charles' almshouses, built in 1679, are capable of containing forty persons, who receive a weekly allowance from the parish. In 1703, Col. Jory erected a building for twelve sailors' widows, each of whom now receives a monthly allowance of twenty-five shillings. The public dispensary was erected, in 1807, in consequence of a bequest of £1000 by C. Yonge, Esq.: it is gratuitously attended by two physicians, surgeons, &c. Here is also an eye infirmary, supported by voluntary contributions. The workhouse was established by act of parliament in 1708: it is under the management of a body corporate, entitled "the Governor and Guardians of the poor's portion in Plymouth." The guardians are fifty-two in number, the mayor and recorder being among them; the remainder are chosen annually, six from the aldermen, six from the common council, twenty from the parish of St. Andrew, and eighteen from the parish of King Charles the Martyr. The right of voting is obtained by paying at the rate of sixpence per month to the poor, and the election takes place in May; the

establishment includes, besides the wards for the paupers, school-rooms for boys and girls, a bridewell, infirmary, &c: the principal governor has the right of committing offenders to the bridewell for a period not exceeding seven days. The remaining charitable societies are, for lying-in women, for reclaiming dissolute females, and for the relief of the sick poor generally. This is the birthplace of Sir Thomas Edmondes, a distinguished statesman and political writer, born in 1563; of the gallant admiral, Sir John Hawkins, who died in 1590; and of Jacob Bryant, a learned antiquary, who was born in 1715, and died in 1804. Plymouth gives the title of earl to the family of Windsor.

PLYMOUTH-DOCK, county of DEVON.—See DEVONPORT.

Corporate Seal.

PLYMPTON (EARL'S), a borough, market town, and parish, having separate jurisdiction, though locally in the hundred of Plympton, county of DEVON, 39 miles (S. W.) from Exeter, and 210 (W. S. W.) from London, containing 762 inhabitants. This place was the head of an ancient barony, and had a magnificent castle, supposed to have been erected by Rivers, Earl of Devon, to whom the barony was given by Henry I., about the year 1100, and delivered up to Stephen by certain knights who held it during the absence of Earl Baldwin, who had rebelled against that monarch: the lords of the barony were invested with the power of inflicting capital punishment.

The town is beautifully situated on an elevation rising out of a vale, south-eastward of the river Plym: it is small, but of respectable appearance, and the surrounding scenery is rich and picturesque. The market is on Friday; and fairs are held on February 25th, August 12th, eve of the Ascension, eve of the Annunciation (O. S.), and October 28th. The charter of incorporation, and for permission to hold a market, is said to have been obtained by Earl Baldwin, and subsequently confirmed by Edward III. and other sovereigns. The town is governed by a mayor, eight aldermen, and a recorder, who constitute the common council: the mayor, recorder, and the senior alderman, are magistrates. A court of record, for the recovery of debts to any amount, is occasionally held, under a charter of William and Mary, but it is used only to a trifling extent. The guildhall, which bears date 1696, is a neat and substantial edifice, supported on pillars and arches, and in the dining-room are some ancestral portraits of the Treby family, also one of Sir Joshua Reynolds, by himself. The borough first sent members to parliament in the 23rd of Edward I., and was constituted a stannary town in 1328; the right of election is vested in the mayor and freemen: the freedom is elective, and dependent on the common council; the number of voters is about forty: the mayor is the returning officer, and the influence of the Earl of Mount-Edgecumbe, and of Paul Treby Treby, Esq., is predominant. The living is a perpetual curacy, in the archdeaconry of Totness, and diocese of Exeter, endowed with £400 royal bounty, and £600 parliamentary grant, and in the patronage of the

Dean and Canons of Windsor. The church, which contains some interesting monuments, was anciently the chantry chapel of St. Maurice. There are places of worship for Independents and Wesleyan Methodists. A grammar school was founded and endowed, in 1658, by the trustees of Eliza Hele: the school-house, a spacious building in the ancient English style, with large antique windows, and a piazza of nine arches, supported on stone pillars, was erected in 1664: the master is appointed by the trustees, but there are no scholars on the foundation. Sir Joshua Reynolds, the celebrated portrait painter, who was born here in 1723, received the rudiments of his education at this school, under the tuition of his father, at that time master. Some of his earliest sketches were inscribed upon the walls, and preserved for many years, but were at length obliterated. A few vestiges of the ancient castle are still visible: the artificial mount on which it was erected is considered one of the most perfect specimens of the kind now in existence.

PLYMPTON (ST. MARY), a parish in the hundred of PLYMPTON, county of DEVON, 1 mile (N. W. by W.) from Earl's Plympton, containing 2044 inhabitants. The living is a perpetual curacy, in the archdeaconry of Totness, and diocese of Exeter, endowed with £15 per annum private benefaction, and £1300 parliamentary grant, and in the patronage of the Dean and Canons of Windsor. The church is principally in the later style of English architecture, with a handsome tower: it contains three stone stalls, and, among various other monuments, an altar-tomb, much mutilated, with a recumbent figure of a knight in armour. The village is chiefly remarkable as having been the site of a priory, accounted the richest in the county. A college is said to have been founded here by one of the Saxon kings, for a dean and four prebendaries. This was suppressed by Bishop Warlewast, in 1121, in consequence of the obstinacy of the monks, who, notwithstanding the injunction of celibacy, passed twenty years before, still entertained their connubial inclinations. The bishop's newly-founded priory was for Black canons, and dedicated either to the Virgin Mary, or to St. Peter and St. Paul. The families of Baldwin and Valletort were considerable benefactors to it; and in 1534 the society consisted of a prior and twenty monks: at this time its yearly revenue was stated to be £912. 11. 8. The prior's pension, after the monastery was dissolved, amounted to £120 per annum. St. Anthony's abbey in Cornwall, and that of St. Mary de Marisco near Exeter, were subject to it. Among its possessions were included Plymouth and the Isle of St. Nicholas: it was also distinguished for the extent of its church patronage. The site was granted to James Coffin and Thomas Goodwin. The parish workhouse occupies the site of an ancient hospital, and is endowed with land yielding £50 per annum.

PLYMSTOCK, a parish in the hundred of PLYMPTON, county of DEVON, 3 miles (S. W. by S.) from Earl's Plympton, containing 2735 inhabitants. The living is a perpetual curacy, in the archdeaconry of Totness, and diocese of Exeter, endowed with £15 per annum private benefaction, and £1500 parliamentary grant, and in the patronage of the Dean and Canons of Windsor. The church, dedicated to St. Mary and All Saints, was formerly attached to Plympton priory, and has lately received an addition of one hundred and forty sittings, of which one hundred and ten are free, the Incorporated Society for the enlargement of churches and chapels having granted £120 for that purpose. At Hooe was formerly a chapel, dedicated to St. Catherine. There is a place of worship for Wesleyan Methodists. A free school was endowed, in 1790, with £2000 three per cents., by the Rev. Vincent Warren, the interest of which is applied for teaching thirty children on the National system, and clothing twenty of them, viz., ten of each sex. An almshouse was founded, in 1600, by Sir Christopher Harris, for four poor persons. At Oreston, in this parish, is the great marble quarry from which the material was obtained for the construction of the Breakwater. There are wet docks at Turnchapel, belonging to the Earl of Morley, sufficiently capacious for the reception of frigates, and a yard adjoining, in which seventy-four gun ships have been built. Plymstock was an important post during the civil war between Charles and his parliament. Radford, in this parish, is said to have been the residence of Sir Walter Raleigh, after his arrival at Plymouth, in 1618; and Stoddescombe was the birthplace of Dr. Forster, the editor of Plato.

PLYMTREE, a parish in the hundred of HAYRIDGE, county of DEVON, 3¾ miles (S. E. by S.) from Cullompton, containing 381 inhabitants. The living is a rectory, in the archdeaconry and diocese of Exeter, rated in the king's books at £21. 18. 1½., and in the patronage of the Provost and Fellows of Oriel College, Oxford. The church, dedicated to St. John the Baptist, has an elegant gilt wooden screen and an octagonal stone font.

POCKLEY, a township in the parish of HELMSLEY, wapentake of RYEDALE, North riding of the county of YORK, 2¼ miles (N. E. by E.) from Helmsley, containing 227 inhabitants. A neat chapel of ease was erected in 1822, by C. Duncombe, Esq.

POCKLINGTON, a parish in the Wilton-Beacon division of the wapentake of HARTHILL, East riding of the county of YORK, comprising the market town of Pocklington, the chapelry of Yapham, and the townships of Meltonby and Owsthorpe, and containing 2163 inhabitants, of which number, 1962 are in the town of Pocklington, 13 miles (E. by S.) from York, and 195 (N. by W.) from London. This town is small, and pleasantly situated in a level country, about two miles from the western edge of the Wolds, on a small stream which falls into the river Derwent: it consists principally of two streets. Races are held annually on the 2nd of May. About a mile distant is a navigable canal, recently completed, which communicates with the river, and furnishes the means of supplying the town and neighbourhood with coal, lime, manure, and merchandise, and of conveying to different places corn, flour, timber, and other articles. The market is on Saturday; and fairs are held March 7th, May 6th, August 5th, and November 8th: on the 9th of November is a statute fair for hiring servants. Petty sessions for the Wilton-Beacon division are held here. The living is a discharged vicarage, in the peculiar jurisdiction and patronage of the Dean of York, rated in the king's books at £10. 1. 10½., endowed with £1400 private benefaction, £400 royal bounty, and £300 parliamentary grant. The church is dedicated to All Saints. There are places of worship for Independents, Primitive and Wesleyan Methodists, and Roman Catholics. The free grammar school was founded,

in the 6th of Henry VIII., by John Dowman, L.L.D. under writ of the privy seal, for the instruction in classical literature of all children resorting to this town, the government being vested in an ancient guild, established by the founder, in the parochial church here. In the 5th of Edward VI., the appointment of the master was vested in the Master and Fellows of St. John's College, Cambridge, and that of the usher, in the churchwardens of Pocklington; and the master and usher were incorporated, and authorised to receive all endowments of the said school, and also, with the vicar, curate, or churchwardens, to nominate to the vacancies in any of the five exhibitions established and endowed in St. John's College, Cambridge, by the founder, for scholars from this school: the endowments were augmented, in the 5th of Mary, by the conveyance of messuages, lands, and hereditaments from Thomas Dowman, the founder's nephew, and still further by a similar grant from the Rev. Thomas Mountfrith: the annual income is £1020. 9. 8., which sum the master retains for his own use, after deducting £200 for the salary of the usher: about seventeen boys are instructed on the foundation. The old school apartments and master's house were taken down in 1819, and new premises erected on the site by the master. A National school, in which about seventy-five boys and sixty girls are educated, was erected at the sole expense of Robert Dennison, Esq., and is supported by voluntary contributions. In 1763, four human skeletons, one of which was enclosed in a coffin, with an urn at the head, were dug up in Barnsley field, near this town: several ancient characters were inscribed on the urn.

PODEN, a hamlet in the parish of CHURCH-HONEY-BOURNE, upper division of the hundred of BLACKEN-HURST, county of WORCESTER, 2¾ miles (N. N. W.) from Chipping-Campden. The population is returned with the parish.

PODIMORE (MILTON), a parish forming one of five unconnected portions of the hundred of WHITLEY, being locally in that of Somerton, county of SOMERSET, 2 miles (N. E. by N.) from Ilchester, containing 176 inhabitants. The living is a rectory, in the archdeaconry of Wells, and diocese of Bath and Wells, rated in the king's books at £12. 6. 5½., and in the patronage of T. S. Horner, Esq. The church is dedicated to St. Peter.

PODMORE, a township in the parish of ECCLES-HALL, northern division of the hundred of PIREHILL, county of STAFFORD, 3 miles from Eccleshall, containing 75 inhabitants: it is within the peculiar jurisdiction of the Prebendary of Eccleshall in the Cathedral Church of Lichfield.

POINTINGTON, a parish in the hundred of HORE-THORNE, county of SOMERSET, 2¼ miles (N. by E.) from Sherborne, containing 162 inhabitants. The living is a rectory, in the archdeaconry of Wells, and diocese of Bath and Wells, rated in the king's books at £13. 8. 4., and in the patronage of Lord Willoughby de Broke. The church is dedicated to All Saints.

POINTON, a chapelry in the parish of SEMPERING-HAM, wapentake of AVELAND, parts of KESTEVEN county of LINCOLN, 3¼ miles (E. S. E.) from Falkingham, containing 363 inhabitants.

POLEBROOK, a parish in the hundred of POLE-BROOK, county of NORTHAMPTON, 2¼ miles (E. S. E.) from Oundle, containing, with the hamlet of Armston,

339 inhabitants. The living is a rectory, in the archdeaconry of Northampton, and diocese of Peterborough, rated in the king's books at £29. 3. 6½., and in the patronage of the Bishop of Peterborough. The church, dedicated to All Saints, is partly Norman, but principally in the early English style, with a beautiful tower and spire at the western extremity of the south aisle: the font has a cylindrical base, and an octagonal top with trefoil panelling. There is a trifling endowment, the bequest of William Tawyer, in 1721, for teaching children.

POLESWORTH, a parish in the Tamworth division of the hundred of HEMLINGFORD, county of WARWICK, 4¾ miles (E. S. E.) from Tamworth, containing 1834 inhabitants. The living is a discharged vicarage, in the archdeaconry of Coventry, and diocese of Lichfield and Coventry, rated in the king's books at £10, and in the patronage of the Crown. The church is dedicated to St. Edith. The Independents have recently erected a place of worship here. A Benedictine nunnery, in honour of our Lady, was founded here about the beginning of the ninth century, by King Egbert, of which his daughter Editha was abbess, to whom, on her canonization, it was afterwards dedicated. Soon after the Conquest, the nuns were dispossessed of their lands, and retired to their cell at Oldbury; but, in the time of Stephen, they returned hither, and from Henry III. had the grant of a weekly market and an annual fair: at the dissolution this house possessed a revenue of £109. 6. 6.: there are still considerable remains of the conventual buildings. The Coventry canal passes through the parish. Francis Nethersole, in 1656, founded and liberally endowed a free school: the income is applied for teaching and apprenticing children of both sexes.

POLING, a parish in the hundred of POLING, rape of ARUNDEL, county of SUSSEX, 3 miles (S. E.) from Arundel, containing 191 inhabitants. The living is a discharged vicarage, in the archdeaconry and diocese of Chichester, rated in the king's books at £10, and in the patronage of the Provost and Fellows of Eton College, on the nomination of the Bishop of Chichester. The church is principally in the later style of English architecture. John Tilly, in 1785, bequeathed a rent-charge of £3 for teaching poor children. The knights of St. John of Jerusalem had a preceptory here, which, at the dissolution, was granted to the college of Arundel.

POLLARDS-LANDS, a township in that part of the parish of ST. ANDREW AUCKLAND which is in the north-western division of DARLINGTON ward, county palatine of DURHAM, containing 117 inhabitants.

POLLECOT, a hamlet in the parish and hundred of ASHENDON, county of BUCKINGHAM, 6 miles (N.) from Thame. The population is returned with the parish.

POLLINGTON, a township in that part of the parish of SNAITH which is in the lower division of the wapentake of OSGOLDCROSS, West riding of the county of YORK, 2¾ miles (S. W.) from Snaith, containing 483 inhabitants. It is within the jurisdiction of the peculiar court of Snaith. There is a place of worship for Independents.

POLPERRO, a sea-port and market town partly in the parish of LANSALLOES, and partly in that of TALLAND, hundred of WEST, county of CORNWALL,

5 miles (E.) from Fowey, and 3 (W. S. W.) from West Looe. The population is returned with the parishes. This is a small fishing-town, romantically situated, the houses being built on the sides of two steep rocky hills, and between them, through a very narrow valley, flows a small river which separates the parishes. Here is a harbour for vessels of one hundred and fifty tons' burden: the imports are chiefly coal, culm, and limestone, and grain is occasionally exported. A pilchard fishery and an extensive hook and line fishery are carried on, the latter of which supplies Bath, Plymouth, &c., with large quantities of fine whiting, pipers, dace, plaice, and turbot. A small market is held on Friday; and a pleasure fair on July 10th, which continues for several days, on which occasion a nominal mayor is elected by a mock council of aldermen. There was formerly a chapel at Polperro, dedicated to St. Peter, some remains of which, called the Chapel house, are on the brow of the western hill above the town. There are places of worship for Independents and Wesleyan Methodists, in that part of the town which is in the parish of Talland. The interest of £200, the benefaction of Captain Charles Kendall, and of £100, the gift of Mrs. Mary Kendall, is paid to a master and a mistress, for the education of children of both sexes.

POLSTEAD, a parish in the hundred of BABERGH, county of SUFFOLK, 3¼ miles (N. N. E.) from Nayland, containing 900 inhabitants. The living is a rectory, in the archdeaconry of Sudbury, and diocese of Norwich, rated in the king's books at £22, and in the patronage of F. R. Reynolds, Esq. The church is dedicated to St. Mary.

POLTIMORE, a parish in the hundred of WONFORD, county of DEVON, 4 miles (N. E.) from Exeter, containing 270 inhabitants. The living is a rectory, annexed to that of Huxham, in the archdeaconry and diocese of Exeter, rated in the king's books at £15. 15. 5., and in the patronage of Sir G. W. Bampfylde, Bart. The church, dedicated to St. Mary, is principally in the decorated style of English architecture, with an elegant wooden screen: it was built by John Bampfylde, who died in 1390, and to whose memory it contains a slab. Near it is an almshouse for four poor persons, founded by Mrs. Bampfylde about 1595, and endowed at different times by Sir Amias Bampfylde and several of his descendants. Poltimore is situated on the river Clist, and there are mines of manganese within the parish.

PONDERS-END, a hamlet in the parish of ENFIELD, hundred of EDMONTON, county of MIDDLESEX, 9 miles (N. N. E.) from London. The population is returned with the parish. Here is an establishment for finishing crape, at which about one hundred and fifty persons are employed. The Lea navigation passes within a mile of the village. The Independents have a place of worship; and an infant school has recently been established.

PONSONBY, a parish in ALLERDALE ward above Darwent, county of CUMBERLAND, 4¾ miles (S. E. by S.) from Egremont, containing, with the hamlet of Newton, 150 inhabitants. The living is a perpetual curacy, in the archdeaconry of Richmond, and diocese of Chester, endowed with £800 private benefaction, £1000 royal bounty, and £600 parliamentary grant, and in the patronage of E. Stanley, Esq. The church is a neat structure, exhibiting in the windows some ancient stained glass brought from Dalegarth Hall. The river Calder bounds the parish on the north. Freestone is obtained here ; and on an eminence at Infell are some remains of a Roman camp.

PONTEFRACT, a parish in the upper division of the wapentake of Os-GOLDCROSS, West riding of the county of YORK, comprising the borough of Pontefract, which has a separate jurisdiction, the chapelry of Knottingly, and the townships of Carleton, East Hardwick, Monkhill, and Tanshelf, and containing 8824 inhabitants, of which number, 4447 are in the borough of Pontefract, 23 miles (S. S. W.) from York, and 177½ (N. N. W.) from London. This place, which appears to have risen from the ruins of the ancient *Legeolium*, a Roman station in the vicinity, now Castleford, was by the Saxons called *Kirkby*, and after the Conquest obtained the name of *Pontfract*, from the breaking of a bridge over the river Aire, while William, Archbishop of York, and son of the sister of King Stephen, was passing over it, attended by an immense crowd, who escorted him on his return from Rome. Though not itself a Roman station, it was probably a place of inferior importance connected with *Legeolium*, as the Watling-street passed through the park, near the town, and vestiges of a Roman camp were distinctly traceable previously to the recent enclosure of waste lands. During the time of the Saxons, to whom some historians attribute the building of the town, Alric, a Saxon chief, erected a castle here, which having been demolished, or suffered to fall into decay, was repaired, or more probably rebuilt, by Hildebert de Lacy, to whom, at the time of the Conquest, William granted the honour and manor of Pontefract. In the reign of Edward II., the castle being then in the possession of Thomas, Earl of Lancaster, who had revolted against the king, on account of his partiality to Piers Gaveston, was besieged and taken ; and the earl being soon after made prisoner, by Andrew de Hercla, at Boroughbridge, was brought to Pontefract, where, being condemned by the king, he was beheaded, and several of the barons who had joined his party were hanged. Having been canonized, a chapel was erected on the spot of his decapitation, and, in honour of his memory, dedicated to St. Thomas. His descendant, the renowned John of Gaunt, retired to this castle in the reign of Richard II., and fortified it against the king, but a reconciliation taking place, through the medium of Joan, the king's mother, no further hostilities ensued. Henry de Bolingbroke, Duke of Hereford, then an exile in France, exasperated by the king's attempt to deprive him of the duchy of Lancaster and honour of Pontefract, to which he had succeeded by the death of his father, and having received an invitation from some of the principal nobility, landed at Ravenspur in this county, and being joined by the Lords Willoughby, Ross, D'Arcy, Beaumont, and other persons of distinction, with an army of sixty thousand men, a battle ensued, which terminated in the deposition and imprisonment of the king, and the exaltation

Arms.

of the duke to the throne, by the title of Henry IV. Richard, after his deposition, was for some time confined in this castle, where he was inhumanly put to death. Henry frequently resided in it, where he held a parliament, after the battle of Shrewsbury, and, in 1404, signed the truce between England and Scotland. Scroop, Archbishop of York, having raised an insurrection, in which he was joined by the Earl of Northumberland, for the dethronement of the king, was by treachery made prisoner, and being brought hither, where Henry at that time resided, was sentenced to death and executed. Queen Margaret, during the absence of the king in Scotland, resided in this castle, and was delivered of her fifth son at Brotherton, in the immediate vicinity, having been taken ill while on a hunting excursion. After the battle of Agincourt, in the reign of Henry V., the Duke of Orleans and several French noblemen of the highest rank, whom that monarch had taken prisoners, were confined in the castle ; and in the year following, the young king of Scotland, who had been taken prisoner on his voyage to France, was confined here till the commencement of the following reign. During the war between the houses of York and Lancaster, this castle was the prison of numerous noblemen, of whom several were put to death within its walls. Earl Rivers, who had been kept a prisoner here by the Duke of Gloucester, whose designs he had ineffectually attempted to oppose, was put to death in the castle, together with Sir Richard Grey and Sir Thomas Vaughan. In 1461, Edward IV., with an army of forty thousand men, fixed his head-quarters here, whence he marched against the Lancastrians ; the two armies met at Towton, where the battle took place, and nearly thirty-seven thousand men were left dead on the field. After the union of the houses of York and Lancaster, in the person of Henry VII., that monarch visited the castle, in the second year of his reign : it was honoured also by a visit from Henry VIII., in 1540 ; from James I., in 1603 and 1617, on his progress to Scotland ; and from Charles I., in 1625. In the rebellion called the Pilgrimage of Grace, the castle was surrendered by Thomas, Lord D'Arcy, to the troops under the command of Aske. At the commencement of the parliamentary war, it was garrisoned for the king, and, in 1644, it was closely invested by Sir Thomas Fairfax, who had taken possession of the town for the parliament. The royalists maintained a spirited defence under a heavy cannonade, which continued several days, and held out till the arrival of Sir Marmaduke Langdale, with a detachment of two thousand men, who after a severe conflict with the parliamentarians in Chequer field, in which he was assisted by sallies from the castle, at length obliged them to raise the siege. On the departure of Sir Marmaduke, the parliamentarians again obtained possession of the town, and throwing up intrenchments for a blockade, renewed their efforts to reduce the castle. The garrison under Governor Lowther fought with obstinate intrepidity, and did considerable execution by frequent sallies, but being in want of provisions, and, owing to the blockade of the town, unable to obtain supplies, they capitulated on honourable terms, and surrendered the castle to the parliamentary forces. After it had been for a short time in their possession, it was retaken by Col. Morrice, and a small band of determined royalists, disguised as peasants carrying in provisions, who entered it without being suspected, and having a reinforcement at hand, secured Col. Cotterell, the governor, and his men in the dungeons, and kept possession of it till it was afterwards invested by Cromwell in person. The garrison, however, maintained their post, and it was not till after the execution of the king that they surrendered this fortress, which the parliament soon afterwards ordered to be dismantled, and the materials to be sold. Of this castle, so memorable for its connexion with the most interesting periods of English history, and which consisted of numerous massive towers, connected by walls of prodigious strength, and fortified by its situation on the summit of an isolated rock, only a small circular tower remains.

The town is pleasantly situated on dry and elevated ground, near the confluence of the rivers Aire and Calder: the streets are spacious and clean: the houses, mostly of brick, are commodious and well built: the town is paved, and lighted with oil, under an act of parliament for its general improvement, and abundantly supplied with excellent water from springs. Two subscription reading rooms have been established. The theatre, a small neat building, erected by subscription, is opened at Easter, and at the time of the races. The races, which commence in the first week of September, and continue three days, are well attended, and are annually growing into repute: the course, which is in the park, is one of the finest in the country, and the rising ground on the south-west side affords a commanding view of the whole: a grand stand was built in 1802, and is well adapted to the accommodation of the visitors. At a short distance from the town a neat monument was erected, in 1818, in commemoration of the battle of Waterloo. In the environs, which are pleasant, and abound with interesting and diversified scenery, are several noblemen's seats. The gardens and nursery grounds produce abundance of excellent fruit and vegetables for the supply of the neighbouring markets, and are famous for the superior quality of the liquorice, which is cultivated extensively; and the making of it into cakes forms the only article of manufacture carried on to any extent. The town has an excellent local trade, arising from the populousness and respectability of the surrounding neighbourhood. The market, which is well supplied with corn and provisions of every kind, is on Saturday: the market-place is a spacious area; in the centre of it was formerly a cross, dedicated to St. Oswald, around which, for a certain space, extended the privilege of freedom from arrest, which was for a considerable time kept unpaved, as a memorial of that right: the cross was removed in 1734, and a neat market-house, ornamented with pillars of the Doric order, erected in pursuance of the will of Mr. Solomon Dupier, by his widow. The fairs are, St. Andrew's, on the first Saturday in December; the twenty days' fair, on the first Saturday after the twentieth from Christmas; Candlemas fair, on the first Saturday after the 13th of February; St. Giles,' on the first Saturday after the 12th of September; April 8th, and May 4th, for cattle and sheep, with the moveable fairs on the Saturdays preceding Palm-Sunday, Low Sunday, and Trinity Sunday: there are also fairs every fortnight, on the Saturday next after those of York. The Aire and Calder canal affords a conveyance by water

from the ports of Hull and Goole, to Ferrybridge, from which place there is a direct land-carriage to Pontefract.

Corporate Seal.

The town, which had enjoyed various and extensive privileges under the charters of the lords of the honour and manor, was first incorporated by royal charter in the reign of Richard III., which was confirmed by James I., in the 4th year of his reign: the government is vested in a mayor and twelve aldermen, assisted by a recorder, town clerk, and subordinate officers. The mayor is elected by ballot of the burgesses, from the body of aldermen, and appoints the recorder and town clerk, subject to approval by the king. The mayor and aldermen are justices of the peace within the borough, and hold quarter sessions in the town hall, where all the business of the corporation is transacted; a court of record for the borough, every three weeks, for the recovery of debts to any amount; and a court baron for the honour, of which the power was extended, in the 17th of George III., to the recovery of debts not exceeding £5: the general quarter sessions for the West riding of the county are held here at Easter. The town hall is a neat building, erected at the joint expense of the county and the corporation: the lower part, surrounded by an open corridor, is used as a prison, and above is the hall, which is conveniently arranged for the borough courts, and occasionally used as an assembly-room: the front of the building is ornamented with pilasters of the Doric order, surmounted by a cornice. The court-house, erected at the expense of the county, is a handsome structure of freestone, in the Grecian style of architecture, and of the Ionic order, and is in every respect adapted to the business of the county. The borough exercised the elective franchise in the 23rd and 26th of Edward I., from which period it was discontinued till the privilege was revived by James I., in 1621, since which time it has regularly returned two members to parliament: the right of election is vested in the resident householders: the mayor is the returning officer.

The living is a discharged vicarage, with the curacy of St. Giles', in the archdeaconry and diocese of York, rated in the king's books at £13. 6. 8., endowed with £200 private benefaction, and £200 royal bounty, and in the patronage of the King, as Duke of Lancaster. The church, dedicated to All Saints, formerly the parish church, was nearly demolished in the parliamentary war, and is in ruins; and the church of St. Giles was, by an act of parliament passed in the 29th of George III., rendered parochial: it is a neat edifice, of which the old tower was taken down and rebuilt, in 1707, at the charge of Sir John Bland, of Kippax Park, Bart. The collegiate chapel, dedicated to St. Clement, within the precincts of the castle, and the free chapel of St. Thomas, erected on the spot where the Earl of Lancaster was beheaded, have long since disappeared. There are places of worship for the Society of Friends, Independents, Primitive and Wesleyan Methodists, and Roman Catholics. The free grammar school was founded and endowed in the second year of the reign of Edward VI., and the endowment was augmented in the reign of Elizabeth ; but the institution having fallen into decay, was refounded, on petition of the inhabitants, in the 32nd of George III., and is open to all boys of the town. An exhibition of £10 per annum, with rooms, and one of £5 per annum, to two scholars from this school, were founded in University College, Oxford, by John Frieston, of Altofts, who also founded two scholarships in Emanuel College, Cambridge, for boys from Normanton school, and in failure of such, for boys from the schools of Pontefract, Leeds, Rotherham, and Wakefield. There are fourteen boys on the foundation, who are nominated by the mayor, recorder, aldermen, and the vicar : the master and usher are appointed by the Chancellor of the duchy of Lancaster. A charity school, which had an endowment of £95 per annum, including a share in Lady Elizabeth Hastings' charity, and was further supported by subscription, for the clothing and instruction of children of both sexes, has been incorporated with a National school, recently built, on an extensive scale, for children of both sexes; and there are Sunday schools in connexion with the established church and the dissenting congregations. The college and hospital of St. Nicholas was originally founded by an abbot of the monastery of St. Oswald, in the county of York, for a reader and thirteen poor persons, and endowed with an income of £23. 13. 4., payable out of the revenue of the duchy of Lancaster : it was vested in the corporation of the borough by James I., and was rebuilt, or materially repaired, by a legacy of £100, bequeathed for that purpose by Mr. Thomas Sayle, of Pontefract : the endowment, by subsequent donations, has been increased to £36 per annum : the premises comprise two separate houses, with a common room to each, and separate lodging-rooms for thirteen aged persons, who receive one shilling each per week, with a supply of coal. Knolles, or the Trinity, almshouse, was founded in the reign of Richard II., by Sir Robert Knolles, and endowed with an annual sum, payable from the revenue of the duchy of Lancaster, the moiety of an estate in Whitechapel, London, devised by Mr. John Mercer, and other property, producing an income of more than £108 per annum : the premises comprise a large common room, and sixteen lodging-rooms for seven aged men and nine women, between whom the revenue of the hospital is divided in equal weekly payments. Perfect's hospital was built at the joint expense of the corporation and the town, and endowed by Mr. William Perfect with land, which, with other donations, produces an income of £40 per annum : the premises comprise three separate dwellings, each for an aged man and his wife, who receive each five shillings per week. The Bede house, of which the origin is unknown, is maintained by the overseers, for the residence of the parish poor. Thwaite's hospital, comprising two cottages with gardens, was bequeathed for the residence of four aged unmarried women, by Mr. Richard Thwaites, in 1620 : the inmates divide among them the rents of the gardens, producing, together with subsequent benefactions, about £7 per annum. Cowper's hospital was founded, in 1668, by Mr. Robert Cowper, who bequeathed two cottages, which have been rebuilt at the expense of the parish, and contain a kitchen and four sleeping-rooms, for four aged widows, who receive twenty shillings each per annum, and the interest of

£100, bequeathed to them by Mr. Matthew Swinney, in 1765. Two hospitals, or almshouses, built respectively by Mr. Matthew and Mr. Robert Franks, in 1737, and containing each apartments for two aged widows, have an endowment of £11. 10., and £17. 10., per annum, which sums are divided among them, in equal shares weekly. Watkinson's hospital was founded, in 1765, by Edward Watkinson, M.D., who endowed it with personal estates producing £87. 14. 6.: the premises contain apartments for four aged men and four aged women, from the parishes of Pontefract and Ackworth, among whom the income, after paying the necessary repairs, is equally divided. George Talbot, Earl of Shrewsbury, gave in trust to the mayor and corporation £200 per annum, to be distributed in loans to poor tradesmen; and there are numerous charitable bequests for distribution among the poor. Among the numerous monastic institutions formerly existing here, was a Cluniac priory, founded in the reign of William Rufus, by Robert de Lacy, and dedicated to St. John the Evangelist, the revenue of which, at the dissolution, was £472. 16. 1.: there are not any remains. During the erection of this priory, the monks inhabited a building which afterwards became the hospital of St. Nicholas, before noticed. A convent of Carmelites was founded, in 1257, by Edmund Lacey, Earl of Lincoln, of which not even the site can be traced. A convent of Dominican, or Black friars, was founded, in 1266, by Symon Pyper, in a place now called Friar-Wood, which at the dissolution consisted of a prior, seven brethren, and a novice. There was also an hospital for Lazars, dedicated to St. Mary Magdalene, of uncertain foundation, to which, in 1286, Archbishop Romain was a benefactor ; and an hospital for a chaplain and eight poor brethren was founded, in the reign of Edward III., by William la Tabourere, which is supposed to be identified with the Bede-house. On the 25th of March, 1822, as two labourers were trenching the land for liquorice, in a field, called Paper Mill Field, near St. Thomas' Hill, one of them struck his spade against a stone coffin, which weighed about a ton and a half, and, on examination, was found to contain the skeleton of a man, with the head between the legs, in good preservation, supposed to be the decapitated remains of Thomas, Earl of Lancaster, who suffered on the 22nd of March, 1322, exactly five hundred years previously: the coffin and its contents were removed into the grounds of Frystone Hall, where they now remain. Dr. Bramhall, who after the Restoration was made Primate of Ireland, was a native of this place. Thomas de Castleford, a monkish historian, was a brother of the Dominican convent ; and Dr. Johnson, a physician and eminent antiquary, resided in the town. Pontefract gives the title of earl to the family of Fermor, who are styled Earls of Pomfret.

PONTEFRACT-PARK, an extra-parochial liberty, in the upper division of the wapentake of Osgoldcross, West riding of the county of York, ½ a mile (N. W. by N.) from Pontefract, containing 47 inhabitants.

PONTELAND, a parish in the western division of Castle ward, county of Northumberland, comprising the townships of Berwick-Hill, Brenkley, High Callerton, Little Callerton, Coldcoats, Darras-Hall, Dinnington, Higham-Dykes, Horton-Grange, Kirkley(including Benridge and Cartermoor), Mason, Milburn, Milburn-Grange, Ponteland, and Prestwick, and containing 1524 inhabitants, of which number, 358 are in the township of Ponteland, 7½ miles (N. W. by N.) from Newcastle upon Tyne. The living is a vicarage, in the archdeaconry of Northumberland, and diocese of Durham, rated in the king's books at £13. 6. 8., and in the patronage of the Warden and Fellows of Merton College, Oxford. The church, dedicated to St. Mary, is partly in the Norman style of architecture, with a square tower surmounted by a low spire. It was formerly collegiate, and had a chantry, and was repaired in 1810, when the north wall was rebuilt. There is a place of worship for Scotch Presbyterians. A free school was founded, in 1719, by Richard Coates, Esq., who bequeathed property in Newcastle upon Tyne, producing, in 1828, about £70 a year for its support: the school-house was erected at the expense of his widow, in 1727; about twenty-five children are instructed in it. The rivers Blyth and Pont run through the parish: coal is obtained here; and there are some slight remains of a castle in the village of Ponteland. This place was built by Elius Hadrianus, and was garrisoned by the first cohort of the Cornavii. In 1244, Henry III. and the king of Scots concluded a peace here.

PONTESBURY, a parish in the hundred of Ford, county of Salop, comprising the chapelry of Longdon, and the townships of Cruckton, Edge, and Pontesbury, and containing, with Little Hanwood, 2458 inhabitants, of which number, 1322 are in the township of Pontesbury, 7¾ miles (S. W. by W.) from Shrewsbury. The living is a rectory, in three portions: the first is rated in the king's books at £17. 13. 4., and in the patronage of the Rev. Ham. Harrison; the second also at £17. 13. 4., and in the patronage of the Provost and Fellows of Queen's College, Oxford; and the third at £8. 10., and in the patronage of W. E. Owen, Esq. The church, dedicated to St. George, was formerly collegiate, including a dean and three prebendaries: it has lately received an addition of three hundred and twenty sittings, of which three hundred are free, the Incorporated Society for the enlargement of churches and chapels having granted £200 for that purpose. There is a place of worship for Baptists. Lead mines are worked here to a considerable extent.

PONTISBRIGHT, or CHAPEL, a parish in the Witham division of the hundred of Lexden, county of Essex, 5½ miles (N. E.) from Great Coggeshall, containing 331 inhabitants. The living is a perpetual curacy, in the archdeaconry of Colchester, and diocese of London, and in the patronage of the Parishioners.

PONTON (GREAT), a parish in the soke of Grantham, parts of Kesteven, county of Lincoln, 4 miles (N.) from Colsterworth, containing 418 inhabitants. The living is a rectory, in the archdeaconry and diocese of Lincoln, rated in the king's books at £11. 9. 7., and in the patronage of the Prebendary of North Grantham in the Cathedral Church of Salisbury. The church, dedicated to the Holy Cross, has a tower and spire, erected in 1519, at the expense of Anthony Ellys, Esq., and much admired for their beauty. W. Archer, in 1713, liberally endowed with land and houses a free school for poor children. The river Witham runs through the village, which was the *Ad Ponem* of Antoninus. Here, and in the immediate vicinity, Ro-

man coins, arched vaults, tessellated pavements, bricks, &c., have been discovered at different periods.

PONTON (LITTLE), a parish in the wapentake of Winnibriggs and Threo, parts of Kesteven, county of Lincoln, 2⅔ miles (S. S. E.) from Grantham, containing 180 inhabitants. The living is a discharged rectory, in the archdeaconry and diocese of Lincoln, rated in the king's books at £7. 10., and in the patronage of the Rev. Dr. Dewdeswell. The church is dedicated to St. Guthlake. A silver Trajan was found in digging near the high dyke in this parish.

PONTOP, a hamlet in that part of the parish of Lanchester which is in the western division of Chester ward, county palatine of Durham, 12 miles (N. W.) from Durham. The population is returned with the township of Colliery.

PONT-Y-POOL, a market town and chapelry in the parish of Trevethan, upper division of the hundred of Abergavenny, county of Monmouth, 20 miles (S. W. by W.) from Monmouth, and 146 (W. by N.) from London. The population is returned with the parish. This town, the name of which is a corruption of Pont ap Howel, is situated on a declivity between the river Avon and the canal to Newport, near the base of the bold elevation of Mynydd-Maen. It appears to have arisen out of the village of Trevethin, and to have owed its present importance to the inventive genius of Thomas Allgood, a native of Northamptonshire, who made some discoveries here of considerable advantage to the manufactures of the country, in the art of imitating japan varnish, from which the articles were denominated Japan ware: in addition to which his son introduced and carried on here for a considerable time, a branch of art in cleansing and polishing iron, which produced articles of such excellent workmanship, as eventually to obtain for them the name of Pont-y-pool ware. The prosperity of the town was completed, about the close of the sixteenth century, by the establishment of iron-works, under the auspices of Capel Hanbury, to which the mineral productions of the county, with the numerous forges and furnaces, and the more modern accommodations of conveyance, both by land and water, have essentially contributed. The surrounding scenery is of a rugged character, the prospect from some points being exceedingly extensive. The town is situated on the great basin of coal and iron stone which extends westward through Wales to Pembrokeshire; it is irregularly built, and consists chiefly of two streets, which contain many neat, but detached, houses: the streets are partially Macadamized, lighted with gas, and well supplied with water from the small river Avon, and the adjacent springs: many good houses are in progress of erection, and the town is in a state of moderate improvement. In the vicinity is a great number of new buildings for the accommodation of agents to the different companies, also numerous cottages for workmen, the walls of which are invariably whitewashed. The extensive iron-works were begun in 1565, and enlarged by John Hanbury, Esq., who, in addition to various improvements in machinery, discovered the method of making sheet-iron by the compression of rollers, and of casting iron with tin. Numerous forges and iron-mills, for making tin plate, are continually at work. The furnaces of the British Mining Company are situated at the Varteage, about three miles distant from the town. A great part of the soil in this district is upon limestone, and the sheep fed here yield excellent mutton. About a mile south-west of the town, at the base of the mountain called Mynydd-Maen, a level and colliery have been lately open-ed, which drain ten veins of coal forty-two feet in thick-ness, with an equal number of iron-stone, one hundred feet thick, whence issues a stream of chalybeate water. The manufacture of the Japan and Pont-y-pool ware is still carried on, though it is now rivalled by that of Birmingham. The chief articles of trade are, iron of every description and quality, of which this parish is capable of sending thirty thousand tons annually to market; and coal, in which the neighbouring hills abound: these works, with the lime-kilns, afford em-ployment to many thousand persons. There is also some business in the leather trade, and a good brewery. Facility of conveyance is supplied by several tram-roads, and, to the port of Newport, by the Monmouthshire and Brecon canals, which pass through Pont-y-pool, and form a junction at the village of Pent-y-Moil. The market is on Saturday, and, during the summer, there is an additional market on Wednesday: fairs are on April 2nd and 22nd, July 5th, and October 10th, for horses, cattle, sheep, cheese, &c. The government of the town is under the jurisdiction of the county magis-trates, of whom one is resident; and petty sessions for the upper division of the hundred of Abergavenny are held here; as also an annual court leet for the lords of the manors of Wensland and Brynwyn, at which the stewards preside.

The living is a perpetual curacy, united to that of Trevethan, in the archdeaconry and diocese of Llandaff, endowed with £2200 parliamentary grant, and in the patronage of the Chapter of Llandaff. The chapel, dedicated to St. James, is a very ancient building, but it has recently undergone such considerable repairs as to make it a neat and commodious structure: it contains four hundred and fifty free sittings, the Incor-porated Society for building and enlarging churches and chapels having contributed £350 towards defraying the expense. There are four places of worship for Baptists, four for Wesleyan Methodists, three for Independents, and one each for the Society of Friends, and Roman Catholics; some of these are situated on the adjacent hills.

POOL, a joint township with Byrome, in the parish of BROTHERTON, partly within the liberty of ST. PETER of York, East riding, and partly in the lower division of the wapentake of BARKSTONE-ASH, West riding, of the county of York, 1¾ mile (N. N. E.) from Ferry-Bridge, containing 61 inhabitants.

POOL (NETHER), a township in the parish of EAST-HAM, higher division of the hundred of WIRRALL, county palatine of CHESTER, 7½ miles (N. by W.) from Chester, containing 24 inhabitants.

POOL (OVER), a township in the parish of EAST-HAM, higher division of the hundred of WIRRALL, county palatine of CHESTER, 8 miles (N. by W.) from Chester, containing 74 inhabitants.

POOL (SOUTH), a parish in the hundred of COLE-RIDGE, county of DEVON, 4¾ miles (S. E.) from Kings-bridge, containing 493 inhabitants. The living is a rectory, in the archdeaconry and diocese of Exeter, rated in the king's books at £22. 16. 5½. T. H. Hayes,

Esq. was patron in 1826. The church is dedicated to St. Cyriac.

POOLE, a township in the parish of ACTON, hun-dred of NANTWICH, county palatine of CHESTER, 2¼ miles (N. W. by N.) from Nantwich, containing 185 in-habitants. The Chester canal passes within its western boundary.

POOLE, a borough, sea-port, and market town, being a distinct county of itself, styled "the Town and County of the Town of Poole," though locally in the hundred of Cogdean, Shaston (East) division of the county of DORSET, 28 miles (E.) from Dorchester, and 104 (S.W. by W.) from London, containing 6390 inhabitants. This town ap-

Seal and Arms.

pears to have risen from insignificance as a fishing hamlet, about the time of Edward III., at which period the port was much frequented; and it furnished that sovereign with four ships and ninety-four men in aid of the siege of Calais: after much fluctuation in its pros-perity during the succeeding reigns, about the time of Henry VI. the population had considerably increased, and the immediate successors of that monarch granted various privileges to the inhabitants. Becoming the resort and residence of Spanish merchants, the trade improved greatly, until the commencement of the reign of Elizabeth, and the breaking out of the war with Spain, when a temporary failure in its commercial interests succeeded their departure; but various addi-tional privileges and immunities having been granted, its rising importance was established on a solid and permanent basis. During the great civil war, Poole was fortified and garrisoned for the parliament, and became the scene of severe contests and extensive slaughter, and in the succeeding reign its fortifications, though inconsiderable, were destroyed.

The town is situated on a peninsula, which is con-nected by an isthmus with the main land, on the north side of the harbour, from which it derives its name, and consists of several good streets, paved under the general highway act, and lighted and watched, ac-cording to the provisions of a local act obtained in the 29th of George II.: the houses in general are of a re-spectable appearance, several of them being of a superior order: the inhabitants are supplied with water brought from a well at Tatnam, about a mile distant, and there are wells of good water belonging to most of the dwell-ing-houses. Different reading societies have been form-ed, and a public library has recently been established, for which a building is about to be erected in the High-street, at the expense of the Hon. W. F. S. Pon-sonby, one of the representatives for the borough, on ground given by the other, B. L. Lester, Esq. The town-house, a neat structure on the quay, has been recently erected by subscription, and is used by the subscribers, who are chiefly merchants, as a news-room. The trade of the port is principally with Newfound-land, and was formerly more extensive than it is at present: the exports consist of provisions, wearing ap-parel, and commodities of all kinds useful for the residents there, which are exchanged for cod and salmon, the greater part of which is sent to foreign markets; and oil, seal skins, furs, and cranberries, for home consumption. Considerable quantities of corn are imported and exported. The manufactures of the town and neighbourhood consist principally of rope, twine, and sail-cloth; and in the yards for ship-building many workmen are engaged. The oyster-fishery employs a great number of boats; and, with the abundance of other fish taken in the harbour, especially plaice and herrings, which are remarkably fine, furnishes a large supply for the London market. By charter of Henry VI., who transferred the privileges of the port of Melcombe-Regis hither, a market and two fairs were granted; the former is held on Thursday, there being also another on Monday: one fair is held on the feast of St. Philip and St. James, the other on All Souls' day, each continuing seven days. The butchers' market is held under the guildhall, and there are two adjacent market-places for vegetables and poultry, one of them recently erected by the corporation.

The municipal government is vested in a mayor, recorder, sheriff, four justices of the peace, and an indefinite number of aldermen, with a town clerk, and other officers. The first charter, which is without date, is supposed to have been granted between the 1st and 9th of Richard I., by which William Longespee, lord of the manor of Canford, of which Poole then formed a part, granted to his burgesses of Poole certain privileges, and prescribed the form of government for the borough. This charter was confirmed by William de Montacute, in the 45th of Edward III., and subsequently by Thomas de Montacute, in the 12th of Henry IV., both Earls of Salisbury, and lords of the manor of Canford: these, with all former charters, were confirmed by Elizabeth, by charter dated February 18th, 1559: that sovereign also granted a new one, in the 10th of her reign, which is the governing charter, and re-incorporated the burgesses and inhabitants, by the style of "the Mayor, Bailiffs, Burgesses, and Commonalty of the Town of Poole," erecting it into a county of itself, entirely independent of the county of Dorset. Other charters, with an extension of former privileges, were granted by Charles II., in the 19th of his reign, and James II., in the 4th. The burgesses are chosen by the corporation at large, and the mayor is elected by the burgesses from their own body, on the Friday before St. Matthew's day; he is a justice of the peace, and the ensuing year is elected senior bailiff and a justice: the number of aldermen is unlimited, as every person who has served the office of mayor becomes an alderman: the recorder and town clerk are chosen by the corporation, subject to the approval of the king. On the day of election for mayor, the burgesses appoint from among their own number, a senior bailiff, four justices of the peace, a sheriff, water-bailiff, and two coroners: the two serjeants at mace are elected by the corporation. The county magistrates have no jurisdiction within the town. A weekly court of record is held under the charter of Elizabeth, in which the mayor and the senior bailiff preside as judges: the jurisdiction embraces pleas of any amount within the town and county of the town, with the same power of personal arrest and attachment of goods as that exercised by the superior courts.

Admiralty Seal.

A court of admiralty, formerly annual, is now occasionally held by the mayor, as admiral within the liberties; a jury is empannelled, and a perambulation of the boundaries of the port made, and all nuisances and encroachments are presented. The sheriff holds his *Tourn* annually, at which presentments of illegal weights and measures are made. Quarter sessions are held before the recorder, mayor, and justices. The guildhall, in which the sessions and public meetings of the corporation are held, was erected, in 1761, at the joint expense of Joseph Gulston, jun., Esq., and Lieut. Col. Calcraft: the chandeliers and sconces with which it is ornamented were given by William Morton Pitt, Esq., formerly one of the representatives for Poole, and late member for the county of Dorset, who also gave a pair of handsome silver gilt maces, now in use. The first return made by this borough was to a council in the 14th of Edward III., and to two of his parliaments, there having been an intermission from that time until the 31st of Henry VI., since which it has regularly returned two members. The elective franchise is prescriptive: the right is vested in the corporation, the number of voters being two hundred and nine, of whom one hundred and forty-seven are resident, and sixty-two non-resident; thirty-two of the residents, however, are minors: the sheriff is the returning officer, and the interest of the Garland family predominates. The number of the electors having considerably decreased, and several being non-resident, the corporation, pursuant to a notice given by William Jolliffe, Esq., then mayor, held a special meeting on the 16th of September, 1830, at which, on the nomination of forty-eight burgesses, ninety-six inhabitants were admitted to the freedom, each burgess being allowed to nominate two.

The living is a perpetual curacy, in the jurisdiction of the peculiar court of Great Canford and Poole, and in the patronage of the Mayor and Corporation. The church, dedicated to St. James, is a new and elegant edifice of Purbeck stone, the old church having become dilapidated. There are places of worship for Baptists, the Society of Friends, Independents, Wesleyan Methodists, and Unitarians. A free school, on the National system, for poor children of both sexes, is conducted by a master, who receives £24 per annum, arising from a bequest of £300 by a Mr. Harbin, in trust to the corporation, and invested in the purchase of land at Corfe-Castle, now producing £60 a year, the residue being distributed among the poor at Christmas. Almshouses in West-street, for twelve poor persons, were founded and endowed, early in the seventeenth century, with an annuity of £18, chargeable on an estate near Longham, by Mr. Robert Rogers, of London. Other almshouses, for a similar number, situated at Hungerhill, were founded in 1812, by George Garland, Esq., who endowed them with £200 and the rent of property in Poole, amounting at present to £26 per annum, appointing the corporation trustees. There are also some almshouses in Church-street, of unknown foundation. Sir Peter Thompson, a Hamburgh merchant, and many years fel-

4 B

low of the Royal and Antiquarian Societies, collected all the known ancient records relating to this his native place, where he almost constantly resided, and where, at his death, he was buried. This was also the birthplace of John Lewis, a divine and antiquary.

POOLE, a chapelry in that part of the parish of OTLEY which is in the upper division of the wapentake of SKYRACK, West riding of the county of YORK, 2½ miles (E.) from Otley, containing 294 inhabitants. The living is a perpetual curacy, in the archdeaconry and diocese of York, endowed with £200 private benefaction, and £1000 royal bounty, and in the patronage of the Vicar of Otley. There is a trifling annuity, the gift of Mr. Fleetham, for teaching six children.

POOLE-KEYNES, a parish in the hundred of MALMESBURY, county of WILTS, 7 miles (N. E. by N.) from Malmesbury, containing 146 inhabitants. The living is a rectory, in the archdeaconry of Wilts, and diocese of Salisbury, rated in the king's books at £7. 12. 6., and in the patronage of the King, as Duke of Lancaster. The church is dedicated to St. Michael.

POORSTOCK, a parish partly in the hundred of EGGERTON, but chiefly in the liberty of POORSTOCK, Bridport division of the county of DORSET, 4 miles (N. E. by E.) from Bridport, containing, with the tythings of West Milton, Nettlecombe, and South Poorton, 1010 inhabitants. The living is a discharged vicarage, in the archdeaconry of Dorset, and diocese of Bristol, rated in the king's books at £16. 16. 8., and in the patronage of the Dean and Chapter of Salisbury. The church is dedicated to St. Mary. In the 7th of Ed ward III., a market on Thursdays, and a fair on the eve, day, and morrow, of St. Philip and James, and two days afterwards, were granted to John Wroxhale, to be held here. At Mappercombe are the remains of an ancient chapel.

POORTON (NORTH), a parish in the hundred of BEAMINSTER-FORUM and REDHONE, Bridport division of the county of DORSET, 5 miles (S. E.) from Beaminster, containing 89 inhabitants. The living is a discharged rectory, in the archdeaconry of Dorset, and diocese of Bristol, rated in the king's books at £5. 11. 5½. T. Banger, Esq. was patron in 1820. The church is dedicated to St. Mary.

POORTON (SOUTH), a tything in that part of the parish of POORSTOCK which is in the hundred of EGGERTON, Bridport division of the county of DORSET. The population is returned with the parish.

POPHAM, a parish in the hundred of MITCHEL-DEVER, Basingstoke division of the county of SOUTHAMPTON, 7 miles (S. W.) from Basingstoke, containing 98 inhabitants. The living is a perpetual curacy, in the archdeaconry and diocese of Winchester, and in the patronage of Sir Thomas Baring, Bart. The church is dedicated to St. Catherine.

POPLAR, formerly a joint hamlet with Blackwall, in the parish of STEPNEY, now a parish, in the Tower division of the hundred of OSSULSTONE, county of MIDDLESEX, 3 miles (E. by S.) from London, containing, at the time of the last census, 12,223 inhabitants, and at present (1830) nearly 16,000. This place, which was separated from Stepney, and erected into a parish, by act of parliament, in 1817, derived its name from the number of poplar trees with which it abounded, and for the growth of which its situation near the river was ex-

tremely favourable. It is situated at the south-east extremity of the county, and is bounded on the east, west, and south, by the river Thames, and on the north by the parishes of Bromley and Limehouse. It is inhabited chiefly by persons engaged in the shipping interest, by numerous artizans employed in the various yards for building and repairing ships, and by a multitude of labourers, who find employment in the docks. The West India docks, an extensive establishment for the accommodation of the homeward and outward bound fleets, were constructed in this parish, in 1802; and, from the peculiar advantages of its situation, the East India docks were also established here, in 1804: these magnificent undertakings, which are honourable to the commercial enterprise of the country, have been described under the head of BLACKWALL. The parish is partially paved, well lighted with gas, and amply supplied with water by the East London water-works. It is within the jurisdiction of the court of requests, for the Tower Hamlets, for the recovery of debts under the amount of 40s., and within the limits of the new police establishment. The town hall was erected in 1770, on the removal of an ancient edifice, which stood in the highway, and which was taken down in the preceding year. The management of the poor, and the superintendence of the watching, paving, and lighting of the parish, were, by act of parliament in 1813, vested in certain of the parishioners, who were subsequently appointed a vestry to regulate the parochial concerns.

The living is a rectory not in charge, in the jurisdiction of the Commissary of London, concurrently with the Consistorial Episcopal Court: the present incumbent was appointed by the inhabitants, but at his decease, the right of presentation will lapse to the Principal and Fellows of Brasenose College, Oxford. The church, dedicated to All Saints, was erected by the parishioners, at an expense of £37,000: it is a handsome structure in the Grecian style of architecture, with a lofty steeple of the Composite order: the interior, of which the central part is appropriated to the use of the poor, is conveniently arranged, and chastely ornamented, and ample accommodation is provided for the children of the numerous schools in the parish. It is situated on the south side of the East India road, in the centre of a spacious cemetery, on the west of which is a handsome house for the rector. A chapel of ease, dedicated to St. Mary, was built by subscription in 1654, at an expense of £2000, on a piece of ground given for that purpose by the East India Company, by whom it was almost entirely rebuilt in 1776; it is a neat building, and has a spacious burial-ground : the living is a perpetual curacy, in the patronage of the Hon. the East India Company, being attached to the hospital supported by them here. There are places of worship for Baptists, Independents, and Wesleyan Methodists. The boys' school, established in 1711, in union with the parish of Limehouse, for thirty children, but now a separate institution, affords instruction on the National system to two hundred and thirty boys, of whom seventy are annually clothed. The free school, instituted in 1816 by subscription, for children of Poplar, Blackwall, and the neighbourhood, is liberally supported, and affords instruction to three hundred boys and two hundred girls, of whom, one hundred and fifty of each are clothed : a school-room for boys, and another for girls, with houses for the master and mistress, have been erected, at an expense of £3,037. 1. 11½., on a piece of ground given by the East India Company. This institution has an income of £240, arising from benefactions : the master's salary is £100 per annum, and that of the mistress £70, with an allowance of coal and candles : it is open to children of all religious denominations. A Roman Catholic school, for the children of the numerous Irish labourers employed in the docks, affords the means of instruction to upwards of one hundred and fifty; and in the Ladies' charity school, in union with the National Society, one hundred girls are taught and annually clothed, under the superintendence of a committee of ladies. An infant school has recently been erected, and is solely maintained by George Green, Esq., ship-builder, who has been a munificent benefactor to the parish, and a zealous promoter of the schools, to the establishment and support of which, and to other charitable uses, he has appropriated more than £10,000.

The East India hospital, in connexion with the chapel, which the inmates attend for divine service, was established for the maintenance of widows of officers and seamen in the Company's service : it is a spacious and substantial quadrangular structure, comprising twenty-two tenements, having been entirely rebuilt by the Company in 1802: the south front contains the chaplain's residence in the centre, and on each side dwellings for the hospitallers; and to the north of the chapel are superior dwellings for the widows of superior officers: the institution is maintained partly by contribution from the pay of seamen employed in the East India service, and by funds appropriated by the Company. Sir Henry Johnson, in 1683, bequeathed £300 for the purpose of building six almshouses for poor ship-carpenters, which design was not accomplished till 1756, when they were erected chiefly through the exertions of Dr. Glo'ster Ridley. Mrs. Esther Hawes founded an almshouse for six aged widows, and endowed it with £9 per annum; and Mr. John Till, by will, gave four almshouses at Blackwall for poor watermen. The workhouse is a substantial brick building, with a handsome front elevation, and is in every respect well adapted to the comforts of the poor. There are various charitable bequests for distribution among the necessitous and aged parishioners. George Stevens, the celebrated commentator and editor of Shakspeare's plays, was born here in 1736, and buried in the chapel in 1800, where is a monument to his memory, with a fine bas relief, in which he is represented contemplating the bust of his favourite author. In the cemetery are the tombs of Dr. Glo'ster Ridley, minister of Poplar, who died in 1774, and of his son, the Rev. James Ridley, author of the "Tales of the Genii :" he died in 1765. Among the eminent men who occasionally resided here were, Ainsworth, the compiler of the Latin Dictionary, who kept a school in the neighbourhood; and Sir Richard Steele, coadjutor with Addison in the Tatler and Spectator; he is said to have had a laboratory here, and to have expended large sums of money in the study of alchymy.

POPPLETON (NETHER), a parish in the ainsty of the city, and east riding of the county, of YORK, 4 miles (N.W.) from York, containing 254 inhabitants. The living is a vicarage, in the archdeaconry and diocese of York, and in the patronage of the Archbishop of York. The church, dedicated to All Saints, is a very ancient structure. A school was established, in 1799, by John Dodsworth, who endowed it with £10 per annum : it is conducted upon the National system, and is aided by voluntary subscriptions. The parish is situated on the river Ouse.

POPPLETON (UPPER), a chapelry in that part of the parish of ST. MARY BISHOPSHILL, JUNIOR, which is in the ainsty of the city, and East riding of the county, of YORK, 4½ miles (N. W. by W.) from York, containing 346 inhabitants. The living is a perpetual curacy, in the peculiar jurisdiction and patronage of the Dean and Chapter of York. The chapel is a small edifice. There is a place of worship for Wesleyan Methodists.

PORCHESTER, or PORTCHESTER, a parish in the hundred of PORTSDOWN, Portsdown division of the county of SOUTHAMPTON, 2½ miles (E.S.E.) from Fareham, containing 757 inhabitants. This place, the ancient Caer Peris of the Britons, and the Portus Magnus of the Romans, was by the Saxons called Port ceastre, either from the castle which defended its spacious harbour, or from Port, a Saxon chief, who landed here with his two sons, Bieda and Maegla, and having obtained a settlement in this part of the island, assisted Cerdic in establishing the kingdom of the West Saxons. A castle of great strength was erected on the old Roman works, which was greatly enlarged, or more probably rebuilt, soon after the Conquest; and previously to the destruction of the harbour, on the retiring of the sea, this place was the principal station of the British navy, subsequently removed to Portsmouth. Porchester castle is situated on a neck of land projecting for a considerable way into the sea: the walls, which are from eight to twelve feet in thickness, and eighteen feet high, enclose a quadrangular area of nearly five acres, and are defended by numerous towers, and surrounded by a broad and deep moat: the keep is a strong square building, one hundred and fifteen feet in length, and sixty-five feet in breadth, with four towers, the largest of which forms the north-west angle; it contains many spacious rooms, of which some are vaulted with stone, and one appears to have been the chapel: the entrance to the outer area is through massive Norman towers on the east and west sides. The ancient parish church of St. Mary is within the outer area of the castle, of which several of the towers and a considerable portion of the walls are now in ruins: the castle, during the late war, was appropriated as a place of confinement for prisoners of war. The village of Porchester, called by way of distinction Porchester-street, extends for about a mile on the road to Fareham, and contains several neat houses: the publicans, by charter of Elizabeth, enjoy exemption from having soldiers billeted in their houses. The living is a discharged vicarage, in the archdeaconry and diocese of Winchester, rated in the king's books at £6, endowed with £200 royal bounty, and in the patronage of the Crown. The church, dedicated to St. Mary, is an ancient and venerable cruciform structure, in the Norman style of architecture, with a low central tower; the south transept has been destroyed, and the chancel, which is small, is of later date, and has an east window of three lights, in the later style of English architecture; the west front is in good preservation, and exhibits a fine specimen of the Norman style.

PORINGLAND (GREAT, or EAST), a parish in the hundred of HENSTEAD, county of NORFOLK, 5 miles (S.S.E.) from Norwich, containing, with Little Poringland, 407 inhabitants. The living is a discharged rectory, in the archdeaconry of Norfolk, and diocese of Norwich, rated in the king's books at £6. 13. 2½., and in the patronage of the Duke of Norfolk. The church, dedicated to All Saints, was founded before the Conquest, and the body of it rebuilt about 1432; the windows are decorated with stained glass, particularly one in the chancel, which is in fine preservation, and represents the Salutation.

PORINGLAND (LITTLE, or WEST), a parish in the hundred of HENSTEAD, county of NORFOLK, 5¾ miles (S.S.E.) from Norwich. The population is returned with Great Poringland. The living is a perpetual curacy, united, in 1728, to the rectory of Howe, in the archdeaconry of Norfolk, and diocese of Norwich. The church is dedicated to St. Michael.

PORLOCK, a parish (formerly a market town) and small port, in the hundred of CARHAMPTON, county of SOMERSET, 6 miles (W.) from Minehead, containing 769 inhabitants. The name is derived from the Saxon Portlocan, an enclosed harbour. The place is of considerable antiquity, having been a residence of the West Saxon kings, who also had an extensive chase here. About the year 918, a band of pirates entered this harbour, but the greater number were slain by the inhabitants, and the rest having escaped to the island of Steep-holmes, died of hunger. In 1052, Harold, the son of Earl Godwin, having sailed from Ireland with nine ships, entered Porlock bay, and having been unsuccessfully opposed by the inhabitants, he slew great numbers, set fire to the town, and carried off much booty. The town is romantically situated near the sea, being surrounded on all sides, except the sea, by lofty hills, winding valleys, and deep glens: it consists of two streets, composed of straggling houses of the meanest order. At the western corner of Porlock bay is a small harbour, to which three sloops and several fishing-boats belong, but they have little employment: the inhabitants were formerly occupied in spinning yarn of excellent quality, and which was carried to Dunster market, at that time the resort of dealers in that commodity: the trade at present consists in the importation of coal and lime from Wales. The market, which was held on Thursday, has been discontinued. Fairs are held on the Thursday before the 13th of September, October 11th, and November 12th, for cattle, and a small breed of sheep, called Porlocks. A manorial court is held annually. The living is a rectory, in the archdeaconry of Taunton, and diocese of Bath and Wells, rated in the king's books at £18. 11. 8., and in the patronage of the Crown. The church, dedicated to St. Dubritius, is a fine structure in the ancient English style, and contains some old monumental effigies, supposed to be in memory of the early feudal lords. Eight poor persons living within the manor are maintained from the rents and profits of lands purchased with a bequest assigned, for the benefit of this and other places, by Henry Rogers, Esq., about 1672, who also bequeathed £600 towards a workhouse and a fund, for the maintenance of those poor in-

habitants of the parish whose ancestors were born in it. In an adjacent wood are the remains of an imperfect oval encampment, supposed to have been constructed at the time of Harold's invasion, within the area of which swords and other warlike implements have been dug up. John Bridgewater, a controversial divine, and Matthew Hales, D.D., the companion and friend of Dr. Stukeley, and author of "Vegetable Statics," were once rectors of this parish; the former subsequently resigned all his preferment, and embraced the tenets of the church of Rome.

PORTBURY, a parish in the hundred of PORTBURY, county of SOMERSET, 6 miles (W. by N.) from Bristol, containing 594 inhabitants. The living is a discharged vicarage, with that of Tickenham annexed, in the archdeaconry of Bath, and diocese of Bath and Wells, rated in the king's books at £10. 11. 3., and in the patronage of the Bishop of Bristol. The church is dedicated to St. Mary. Portbury is a very ancient place, and gives name to the hundred. It was occupied by the Romans, as is evident from the coins and foundations discovered here, as well as from traces of the Roman road being still visible through the parish to the sea at Portshead, whence there was a passage to Caerleon, anciently Isca Silurum. Here was formerly a cell to the Augustine priory of Breamore, Hants.

PORTCASSEGG, a hamlet in that part of the parish of ST. ARVANS which is in the upper division of the hundred of RAGLAND, county of MONMOUTH, containing 18 inhabitants.

PORTGATE, a township in the parish of ST. JOHN-LEE, southern division of TINDALE ward, county of NORTHUMBERLAND, 5 miles (N.E. by E.) from Hexham; containing 33 inhabitants. It was so called from a passage through the great Roman wall, the site of which at this place has been levelled by the plough. Here is an old border tower, near which the Devil's Causeway branches from Watling-street.

PORTINGSCALE, a joint township with Coledale, in that part of the parish of CROSTHWAITE which is in ALLERDALE ward above Darwent, county of CUMBERLAND, 1¼ mile (W. by N.) from Keswick. The population is returned with Coledale. There is a place of worship for Wesleyan Methodists. The village is situated on the margin of Derwentwater, of which and the lake Bassenthwaite, with the beautifully romantic tract from Swineshead to Skiddaw, there are fine prospects from the adjacent heights.

PORTINGTEN, a joint township with Cavil, in the parish of EASTRINGTON, wapentake of HOWDENSHIRE, East riding of the county of YORK, 3¼ miles (N.E.) from Howden, containing, with Cavil, 98 inhabitants.

PORTISHAM, a parish in the hundred of UGGSCOMBE, Dorchester division of the county of DORSET, 7¾ miles (S.W. by W.) from Dorchester, containing 600 inhabitants. The living is a vicarage, in the archdeaconry of Dorset, and diocese of Bristol, rated in the king's books at £8. 14. 2., endowed with £1000 parliamentary grant. Joseph Hardy, Esq. was patron in 1814. The church, dedicated to St. Peter, is a large ancient structure, having a lofty embattled tower crowned with pinnacles. Charles Masterman, in 1771, left £100 for teaching poor children. In this parish is the largest cromlech in the county; it consists of a flat stone, ten feet by six, resting horizontally on nine upright ones, and stands on a tumulus, having on the north-west an avenue leading to it: there is a small barrow to the eastward of this ancient monument.

PORTISHEAD, a parish in the hundred of PORT-BURY, county of SOMERSET, 8½ miles (W. N. W.) from Bristol, containing 506 inhabitants. The living is a rectory, in the archdeaconry of Bath, and diocese of Bath and Wells, rated in the king's books at £32. 15. 7½, and in the patronage of the Mayor and Corporation of Bristol. There is a place of worship for Wesleyan Methodists. The parish is bounded on the north by the Bristol channel; and there is a battery at Portishead point for the defence of King Road, where ships of war on this station usually anchor. The Britons, Romans, and Danes, successively occupied this spot: the form of the camp approaches that of an irregular rhomboid, its longer diameter being four hundred, and its shorter about two hundred, yards; it was converted to similar purposes during the great civil war, for, according to the parliamentary records of that period, the royalists posted here surrendered to Sir Thomas Fairfax, who had been sent against them. The ancient boundary called Wansdyke terminates here. It is in contemplation to form a landing pier at this place, for the delivery of the Irish mails, to communicate with a suspension bridge, now about to be constructed over the Avon, at St. Vincent's rock.

PORTLAND, a parish, forming the liberty of the Isle of PORTLAND, in the Dorchester division of the county of DORSET, 4 miles (S.) from Weymouth, containing 2254 inhabitants. Though called an island, this parish is in reality a peninsula, connected with the main land by an extremely narrow isthmus, called Chesil Bank, a line of shingles thrown up by the sea, and extending for more than eight miles from Portland to Abbotsbury. The parish, which contains seven villages is bounded on the north by Portland road and Smallmouth, leading into the waters called the Fleets, behind Chesil Bank, across which is a ferry to Weymouth; on the east by Portland Race, the passage of which, even in the calmest weather, is rendered dangerous by an eddy of two opposing currents; and on the south and west by the channel. The island is about four miles and a half in length, and two miles in breadth, of an elliptical form, and nearly ten miles in circumference; the shores are steep and rugged, but the summit is smooth, and the soil produces wheat, peas, oats, and barley. At the southern extremity, called Portland Bill, are the higher and lower lighthouses, and a signal station called the "Lowes:" near the former is a remarkable cavern, from which the water rises as from a fountain. On the eastern side are Rufus and Pennsylvania castles; and on the northern side are Portland castle, and a signal station called Veru. The whole island is one vast rock of stone, of very superior quality, much esteemed, and generally used in the most magnificent buildings; it was first brought into repute in the reign of James I., and the digging of it constitutes the principal employment of the inhabitants. The quarries are in the western part of the island, and have proved an inexhaustible source of wealth to the proprietors. The village of Easton is nearly in the centre of the island, and, with the various other hamlets, is chiefly inhabited by the families of the men employed in the quarries. This is a royal manor, the lands being ancient demesne, and

the king's steward holds two courts yearly, viz., at Lady-day and Michaelmas. The custom of gavelkind prevails in it; and the inhabitants have a curious practice of passing lands by sale, viz., by church gift: the seller and buyer go into the church, taking with them three or four persons, tenants of the island, and there make the church gift, which is very concise. The living is a rectory, in the archdeaconry of Dorset, and diocese of Bristol, rated in the king's books at £18. 2. 1., and in the patronage of the Bishop of Winchester. The church is dedicated to St. George. There is a place of worship for Wesleyan Methodists. In the southern part of the island are the remains of an ancient castle, and the ruins of the old church, which formerly was in the centre; and behind the Portland Arms Inn are traces of what is supposed to have been a Roman encampment. This place gives the title of duke to the family of Bentinck.

PORTLEMOUTH (EAST), a parish in the hundred of COLERIDGE, county of DEVON, 6 miles (S. by E.) from Kingsbridge, containing 391 inhabitants. The living is a rectory, in the archdeaconry of Totness, and diocese of Exeter, rated in the king's books at £29. 18. 4., and in the patronage of the Duke of Bolton. The church, dedicated to St. Onolaus, has a handsome wooden screen. Portlemouth commands one of the most beautiful sea-views in the county, including Kingsbridge, the æstuaries, and Salcombe harbour. Walter Jago and others, in 1679, left small sums towards the support of a schoolmaster for teaching Latin and arithmetic.

PORTON, a tything in the parish of IDMISTON, hundred of ALDERBURY, county of WILTS, 5¼ miles (N. E. by N.) from Salisbury, containing 140 inhabitants.

PORTSCUETT, a parish in the upper division of the hundred of CALDICOTT, county of MONMOUTH, 5 miles (S. W. by S.) from Chepstow, containing 168 inhabitants. The living is a discharged rectory with that of St. Pierre, in the archdeaconry and diocese of Llandaff, rated in the king's books at £7. 2. 1., and in the patronage of Charles Lewis, Esq. Near the bank of the Severn are vestiges of a Roman camp, part of which has been swept away by the river. The ancient road from this station to the great camp at Caerwent passes through the parish. From Black Rock there is a ferry over the Severn, called the New Passage, connecting the great road from London into South Wales.

PORTSEA, a parish, divided into the liberty part, which is within the jurisdiction of the borough of PORTSMOUTH, and the Guildable part, which is in the hundred of PORTSDOWN, Portsdown division of the county of SOUTHAMPTON, 17 miles (S. E. by E.) from Southampton, and 71½ (S. W.) from London, and containing 38,379 inhabitants. This place, which is now the principal naval arsenal of Great Britain, takes its name from the island of Portsea, to which, on the retiring of the sea from the ancient Portchester, the inhabitants removed, and at the mouth of the harbour built the town of Portsmouth, to which it was originally a small suburb. The island is nearly sixteen miles in circumference, and is bounded on the south by Spithead, on the east by Langston harbour, on the west by Portsmouth harbour, and on the north by a channel uniting them, over which is a bridge, connecting it with the main land. It abounds with a great variety of animal and vegetable productions, but has nothing peculiar in its geological formation. Widgeons, wild ducks, teal, and curlew, are found in abundance ; larks congregate in numerous flocks, and the snow-bunting, the cross-bill, and other scarce birds, are occasionally seen. More than two hundred different species of insects have been collected in the course of one summer, and a great variety of shells is found on the beach. The town, which is situated on the waste ground formerly called Portsmouth common, has rapidly increased within the last century, and its population is at present more than five times as great as that of Portsmouth, though the houses were originally permitted to be built on condition of their demolition in the event of an enemy landing. It contains many good and regularly-formed streets, several terraces, crescents, and handsome ranges of respectable houses, inhabited by the more opulent families connected with Portsmouth, and has very extensive suburbs, chiefly inhabited by artizans employed in the dock yards : it is well paved, lighted with gas, by a company incorporated by act of parliament in 1821, and amply supplied with water by the Portsea Island water-works. The Hampshire subscription library is well supported, and contains a valuable collection of volumes in the various departments of literature.

The fortifications, which were begun in 1770, are very complete, and are unrivalled for strength and beauty : the lines extend from north to south, presenting to the eastward several strong bastions and outworks, crowned with batteries of heavy ordnance ; and the trenches, which are broad and deep, can be instantaneously filled with water up to the bridges, which connect it with Portsmouth, on the south. The Royal Dock-yard occupies an area of one hundred and ten acres, and comprises, on the grandest scale, and on the most scientific principles, the numerous arrangements for supplying the necessary equipments, and extensive depôts of naval and military stores. The entrance into the yard, which forms a town of itself, is through a lofty handsome gateway ; and among the numerous buildings within the walls, the residence of the commissioner is conspicuous for its stateliness : in the centre of the building is a noble portico, and on each side are the various offices connected with the establishment. The great basin comprehends an area of thirty-three thousand square yards, communicating with four dry docks ; and there is also a double dock for frigates. Ships of the line may at any time enter from the harbour into the dock-yard, where twelve men of war can be fitted up at the same time. The covered building-docks are very capacious : the rope house is of vast extent, being one thousand and ninety-four yards long, and four stories high ; on the lower story, the floor of which is laid with iron and tin, is the immense machinery for making cables, of which some are thirty inches in circumference ; the three upper stories are appropriated to the manufacture of twine and cordage. The anchor forge is an immense building, in which anchors weighing more than ninety hundred weight are made for the navy. Near the forge are the copper-foundry, and the admirable machinery for making blocks, invented by Mr. Brunel, who for many years superintended its operation: it is impelled by a steam-engine of extraordinary power, and the various processes,

from the sawing of the wood to the completion of the block, are conducted by the aid of machinery alone, with a degree of precision and celerity difficult to describe. The rigging and the mast houses are upon the largest scale ; and every department in this extensive and ably-conducted establishment exhibits a combination of skill, efficiency, and grandeur, in every respect characteristic of the arsenal of a great maritime state. The Dock chapel, appropriated to the officers of the dock-yard, the crews of the ships in ordinary, and the various classes of artizans, is a neat modern structure, with a cupola, in which hangs the bell originally belonging to the Royal George, which was sunk off Spithead. The principal officers are, a commissioner, clerk of the checque, storekeeper, master-wright, chaplain, surgeon, and purveyor. During the war, nearly four thousand men were employed.

Within the walls are the Royal Naval College, founded, in 1720, for one hundred students in time of war, and for seventy during peace ; of these, thirty, the sons of commissioned naval officers, pay £ 60 per annum, for board, clothing, and education ; and the remainder, sons of noblemen, military, or civil officers, pay £ 100 per annum : the term of continuance in the college is two years, and no one can remain in it more than three, at the end of which, if qualified, the students are appointed midshipmen in the navy, from which if they retire before the expiration of the term requisite for obtaining a lieutenancy, a fine of £ 200 is imposed on those of the first class, and of £ 100 on those of the second. This institution is under the superintendence of a governor, who is first lord of the Admiralty, a lieutenant-governor, a post-captain, and professor, each of whom has a salary of £ 800 per annum, with apartments ; four lieutenants, who have each £ 250 per annum, with board and lodging ; a mathematical assistant, with a salary of £ 250 ; two other assistants, with £ 200 per annum, who have apartments rent-free ; and French, drawing, and fencing masters, who have each a salary of £ 100 per annum. The buildings are extensive, and contain many noble apartments ; over them is an Observatory, in which is a beautiful model of H. M. S. the Victory, of one hundred guns, which was wrecked off the French coast on her first voyage: a new Observatory has been recently erected over the central arch of the western storehouses, commanding a view of the whole coast, from the Needles to the coast of Sussex. A school of naval architecture was projected, in 1809, by Mr. Robinson, in the House of Commons, and, in 1816, incorporated with the Naval College, in which provision is made for the maintenance and education of twenty-four shipwrights' apprentices, who are required, previously to their admission, to write English grammatically, to speak French, and to be acquainted with the first six, and the eleventh and twelfth, books of Euclid, and with quadratic equations in Algebra. Their admission is dependent on examination before the commissioners, the professor, and the lieutenant-governor ; they remain for seven years in the establishment, and, at the expiration of that term, they are appointed to some situation in the Royal Dock-yard : during their apprenticeship they are under the superintendence of a professional shipwright, and receive an annual salary, which increases gradually from £ 25 to £ 60. The Gun wharf, without the dock-yard, includes an area of fourteen acres, and consists of a spacious building of brick, ornamented with stone, occupying three sides of a quadrangle, with an arched entrance in the centre of the fourth side, surmounted by a lofty tower and cupola; it contains a vast number of guns and gun-carriages, and an immense quantity of ordnance stores: on the right of the entrance is the armoury, containing twenty-five thousand stand of small arms, arranged in the most exact order, a laboratory, and an extensive ordnance department, with residences for the principal officers; on the opposite side are the offices of the Royal Engineers, with stores adjoining, and a large depôt of ammunition. The dock-yard has suffered from several destructive fires, the last of which occurred in 1776; the incendiary, John Aitkin, more commonly known as Jack the Painter, was gibbeted on Block House heath. No other trade is carried on except what arises from, or is connected with, the dock-yard. In that part of the parish called the Guildable is a considerable number of market gardens, from which the towns of Portsea and Portsmouth are principally supplied with vegetables. The Portsmouth and Arun canal passes through the town: it was opened in 1823, and joins Langston harbour, across which barges are towed by steam-boats constructed for the purpose. The market days are Tuesday, Thursday, and Saturday. That part of the parish which is not within the limits of the borough of Portsmouth, is within the jurisdiction of the county magistrates.

The living is a vicarage, in the archdeaconry and diocese of Winchester, rated in the king's books at £12, and in the patronage of the Warden and Fellows of Winchester College. The church, dedicated to St. Mary, was erected in the reign of Edward III., and is surrounded by one of the largest cemeteries in the kingdom. St. George's church, a commodious brick structure, was erected for the additional accommodation of the increasing population in 1753: the living is a perpetual curacy, endowed with £200 private benefaction, and £900 parliamentary grant, and in the patronage of the Vicar of Portsea. St. John's church, a neat commodious edifice, of which the internal decorations are extremely rich, was consecrated in 1789: the living is a perpetual curacy, endowed with £800 parliamentary grant, and in the patronage of the Vicar. The church dedicated to St. Paul, in the suburb of Southsea, was erected in 1822, at an expense of £15,229. 18. 8., of which £600 was raised by subscription, and the rest by grant from the parliamentary commissioners; it is a handsome structure in the later style of English architecture, with four turrets at the angles, and contains one thousand eight hundred and twenty-one sittings, of which nine hundred and three are free: the living is a perpetual curacy, in the patronage of the Vicar. In this suburb is an excellent bathing establishment, which has contributed greatly to the attractions of Portsea, as a watering-place. The church dedicated to All Saints, in the suburb of Mile-End (including the Half-Way houses, Newtown, and several spacious streets, forming an extensive district, now called Southport), was erected, in 1827, by grant from the parliamentary commissioners, at an expense of £12,064: it is an elegant edifice, in the later style of English architecture, with a splendid western front, surmounted by a campanile turret, and contains one

thousand seven hundred and thirty-nine sittings, of which one thousand one hundred and six are free; the interior is neatly arranged, and over the altar is a window of beautiful design. In Portsea and its suburbs are six places of worship for Baptists, and one each for Independents and Wesleyan Methodists. St. Paul's school, a commodious building, near the church of that name, has been recently established by one hundred subscribers, for the education of their children. The National school, in which two hundred children are educated, is supported partly by subscription, and with funds arising from various benefactions. Mr. Edward Crafts bequeathed a house and premises, in 1780, which produced £28 per annum; Mr. Richard Wilmot, in 1805, bequeathed £500; and Major Ebenezer Vavasour, in 1808, left £100, towards the support of this institution. A dispensary, and an infirmary for diseases of the eye, are supported by subscription. Thomas Fitzherbert, Esq., in 1821, left £10,000 in the four per cents., in trust to the vicar and ministers of the chapels, for the maintenance of five aged men, ten aged widows, and five single women, of this parish: there are also various charitable bequests for distribution among the poor. The eastern part of the island, not included in the boundaries of Portsmouth and Portsea, is extra-parochial, and belongs chiefly to government; in this part are numerous salt-works.

PORTSLADE, a parish in the hundred of FISHERGATE, rape of LEWES, county of SUSSEX, 2½ miles (E. by N.) from New Shoreham, containing 421 inhabitants. The living is a discharged vicarage, in the archdeaconry of Lewes, and diocese of Chichester, rated in the king's books at £8. 18. 8., and in the patronage of the Crown. The church, dedicated to St. Nicholas, is principally in the early style of English architecture.

PORTSMOUTH, a seaport, borough, market town, and parish, having separate jurisdiction, locally in the hundred of Portsdown, Portsdown division of the county of SOUTHAMPTON, 18 miles (S. E. by E.) from Southampton, and 72 (S.W.) from London, containing, exclusively of that part of the parish of Portsea which is within its jurisdiction, 7269 inhabitants. This place, which is one of the principal naval and military stations of the British empire, derives its name from its situation at the mouth of a capacious harbour on the southern coast. In 501, a body of Saxons, under the command of Port, a German chieftain, and his two sons Biedda and Maegla, landed on this part of the coast, and, after a severe conflict with the Britons, succeeded in gaining possession of the surrounding country. They are supposed to have founded the ancient town of Portchester, so called from the name of their leader, about three miles to the north-west, from which, on the contraction of the harbour by the retiring of the sea, the inhabitants removed to Portsea island, on the south-west side of which they erected the present town. Alfred having fitted out a fleet of nine ships at this port, after an obstinate engagement, defeated the Danes, who infested the coasts of

Arms.

Hampshire and Dorsetshire, and caused many of them to be hanged along the coast, in order to deter their countrymen. Harold equipped a large fleet at this port, with a view of intercepting the armament of William, on its way from Normandy, for the conquest of the country; and after the death of William Rufus, Robert, Duke of Normandy, landed here with his forces, to take possession of the throne. Henry, who had raised an army to support his own claim to the crown, also assembled his forces here, where, after the two armies had lain for some time, an accommodation took place, and Robert returned to Normandy. At this place Henry III. collected a numerous army for the invasion of France, but the enterprize was abandoned, in consequence of the treachery of his ally, the Duke of Bretagne: the same monarch established a guild merchant here, in 1256. In 1377, the French attacked and burnt a considerable part of the town, but were compelled to retire to their ships with considerable loss. Edward IV., for the greater security of the harbour, erected two towers commanding the entrance, and made additions to the fortifications of the town, which consisted only of a single wall, strengthened at the angles with bastions. According to Leland, Henry VII. established seven extensive breweries for supplying the troops in the time of war; and Henry VIII. erected Southsea castle, at the south-west extremity of the Isle of Portsea. In 1544, a powerful French fleet anchored off St. Helen's, having on board a large military force for the invasion of England. The English army, under the command of the Duke of Suffolk, assembled at Portsmouth, and the British fleet, commanded by Viscount Lisle, the Lord High Admiral, after an obstinate engagement, repulsed the enemy with considerable loss: at the commencement of the action, the Mary Rose, the largest British ship next to the admiral's, by some unknown accident, foundered between the fleets, and sunk, when the commander, and his crew of six hundred men, perished. Edward VI. passed a night at Southsea castle, and reviewed the fortifications, ordering, for the greater security of the harbour, two towers to be erected, with an immense iron chain extending from one to the other, across the mouth of the harbour, which, on the French fleet in the American war appearing off Plymouth, was raised, so as to prevent the vessels entering. During the reign of Elizabeth the fortifications were greatly strengthened, and the signals now used on the approach of any vessels were established. In the reign of Charles I., John Villiers, Duke of Buckingham, who had arrived at Portsmouth to superintend the movements of the fleet and army assembled there for the invasion of France, was assassinated by Felton, a disappointed officer, who had served under him at the Isle of Rhé, and the spot, in the High-street, then an inn called the Spotted Dog, is still pointed out. Felton was soon after hanged at Tyburn, and gibbeted on Southsea common. Soon after the commencement of the parliamentary war, a party of Cromwell's soldiers surprised Southsea castle, of which they took possession, and the town itself subsequently fell into the hands of the parliamentarians. After the Restoration, the nuptials of Charles II. with Catherine of Portugal were solemnized in the chapel of the garrison; and James II., while Lord High Admiral, frequently visited Portsmouth, but previously to his abdication of the government, he imprisoned the officers of the garrison for

refusing to admit his Irish troops. In 1782, the Royal George, of one hundred and ten guns, and one thousand two hundred men, commanded by Admiral Kempenfelt, while under the process of careening at Spithead, unfortunately sank, and the admiral, and more than two-thirds of the crew, perished: many of her guns, and a considerable portion of her stores, have, by the use of the diving-bell, been recovered, but all attempts to raise her have hitherto failed; the spot where she lies is marked by a red buoy attached to the wreck. George III. frequently visited this port, and, in 1814, the Prince Regent, afterwards George IV., remained here for several days with the allied sovereigns.

The town, which is about a mile and a half in circuit, is divided into two nearly equal parts, by the principal street, and intersected by numerous others in every direction: it is well paved, lighted with gas by a company established in 1821, and supplied by two companies, incorporated by act of parliament, with excellent water from Portsea isle, and from springs at the foot of Portsdown Hill. The house of the governor, at the upper end of the grand parade, originally the *Domus Dei* founded by Peter de Rupibus, Bishop of Winchester, retains but few vestiges of its monastic character; it has undergone repeated alterations, for adaptation to its present use, and is become a splendid modern mansion, having been the residence of his late Majesty, on his visit to the town. The residences of the port-admiral, and of the lieutenant-governor, are elegant and commodious buildings; the former, situated in the High-street, has been recently improved at the expense of government. A Philosophical Society was established in 1818: it has a convenient theatre, in which lectures are delivered weekly, from October till March, and a good museum, containing more than nine thousand specimens in natural history: a handsome building is now being erected for its use in St. Mary-street. A mechanics' institution was founded in 1825, and is, under good regulations, numerously attended. The theatre, a handsome and well-arranged building, is opened during the season; and concerts and assemblies are held in a suite of rooms elegantly fitted up, and well adapted to the purpose. The various gateways leading into the town, through its gigantic fortifications, which surround it in a semicircular form, are remarkable for the justness and variety of their architectural character; that erected by James II. is an elegant specimen of the Corinthian order, that of St. Thomas is Doric, and that of George III. in the rustic character. The ramparts, which are in parts ornamented with timber, afford extensive and beautiful prospects; and the view of the town from Portsdown hill, combining an infinite variety of objects of the deepest interest and stately grandeur, is strikingly magnificent. The fortifications, which are the most complete in Europe, combine beauty with strength, and, exclusively of those which immediately surround the town, consist of numerous and extensive outworks: the entrance to the harbour is defended by Brockhurst fort, on the one side, and the fortifications of the town on the other. Southsea castle having suffered considerable damage from an accidental explosion, was rebuilt in 1814, and contains a garrison of two hundred men, with well-mounted batteries of heavy ordnance. Fort Monkton is a regular fort, of prodigious strength, defended with thirty-two pieces of heavy ordnance, and numerous re-doubts: these two forts, built by Edward VI., also serve to defend the mouth of the harbour; on the east and west sides of which, along the coast, are various strong fortifications, of which Cumberland fort, erected in 1820, and commanding the approach to Langston harbour, is mounted with one hundred pieces of heavy ordnance, and contains accommodations for four thousand troops. At Hilsea, about four miles on the London road, is a strong military fortress, with extensive outworks, and a double draw-bridge. Within the town are four guard-houses; and near the principal entrance gate are Cole-worth barracks, being numerous extensive ranges of buildings, with a parade ground: the garrison includes three regiments of infantry, a division of the royal marines, with detachments of artillery and engineers: over the magazine a semaphore was erected, in 1823, by means of which signals may be transmitted to the Admiralty in London, in the space of three minutes. The naval department is under the control of the port-admiral, and the garrison is under the command of a lieutenant-governor.

The port extends from the opening of Southampton water, on the west, to the town of Emsworth on the east, including Langston, St. Helen's, and Portsmouth harbours, and Spithead. The custom-house, a neat and commodious building, was erected in 1785, and is under the direction of a collector, comptroller, surveyor, or searcher, and warehouse-keeper for bonded goods. In the port watchhouse are kept the boats of the revenue officers, and from this place all vessels entering the harbour are hailed: the preventive stations are at Southsea castle, Cumberland fort, Hay-ling island, Stokes bay, and Hill head. The harbour is unrivalled for capaciousness, security, and depth of water: it is about two hundred and fifty yards broad at the mouth, and expanding into an open and broad lake, extends for several miles to the north, affording secure and capacious shelter to ships of the largest burden: its security is greatly increased by the Isle of Wight, which forms a natural breakwater, and by the inland elevations, which afford additional protection. From the western side of the entrance is the sand bank called the Spit, at the head of which a ship of war is always stationed: this bank is about three miles in length, but is not perceptible above water; the roadstead, called from this circumstance Spithead, is marked out by buoys fixed at regular intervals. The foreign trade consists chiefly in the importation of timber from the Baltic, and eggs from France: the coasting trade is very extensive, and in time of war the influx of merchant ships is very great: the principal branch of manufacture carried on is rope-making. The port is the general rendezvous where all ships either homeward or outward bound take convoy, and frequently seven hundred merchant-men have sailed at one time from Spithead. Packet-boats sail daily for the Isle of Wight and Southampton, and steam-vessels ply regularly between this port and Plymouth and Havre. The ferry to Gosport is under the regulations of an act of parliament, the fares differing according to the state of the weather. The market days are Tuesday, Thursday, and Saturday: the fairs are, July 10th, which, by charter of Richard I., continues fourteen days, and July 26th, a well-frequented fair on Portsdown Hill, which continues three days.

Corporate Seal.

Obverse. Reverse.

The civil government, by a succession of charters, of which the last was conferred by Charles I., is vested in a mayor, twelve aldermen, and an indefinite number of burgesses, assisted by a recorder, town clerk, chamberlain, harbour-master, serjeants at mace, and subordinate officers. The mayor is elected by the aldermen and burgesses; the former fill up vacancies in their own body, and elect the burgesses. The mayor, the late mayor, and three aldermen chosen for that purpose, are justices of the peace. The corporation hold courts of quarter-session for all offences not capital; a court of record, on Tuesday in every week, for the recovery of debts to any amount; and a court leet, at which the constables and other officers are appointed. The town hall is a large and commodious building in the centre of the High-street, with an open area underneath for the use of the market, the space for holding which, within the last five years, has been considerably curtailed: it was repaired and considerably enlarged in 1796. The borough gaol, completed in 1809, at an expense of £18,000, is a large range of building, including court-rooms for the business of the sessions, a council-chamber, and a bridewell, well arranged for the classification of prisoners: the prison is about to be enlarged. The borough first exercised the elective franchise in the 23rd of Edward I., since which time it has regularly returned two members to parliament: the right of election is vested in the mayor, aldermen, and burgesses, of whom the number is about forty-five, thirteen only being resident: the mayor is the returning officer; and the principal parliamentary influence belongs to the family of Carter.

The living is a vicarage, in the archdeaconry and diocese of Winchester, rated in the king's books at £6. 13. 4., and in the patronage of the Warden and Fellows of Winchester College. The church, dedicated to St. Thomas à Becket, is a venerable and spacious cruciform structure in the early English style of architecture, with a tower surmounted by a cupola, one hundred and twenty feet high, forming an excellent land-mark: the interior is handsomely arranged; the cenotaph of the Duke of Buckingham, in which his heart is enshrined, forms the principal ornament of the altar-piece. The garrison chapel, once appertaining to the monastery of Domus Dei, has been thoroughly repaired, for the use of the officers and soldiers of the garrison: the communion cloth exhibits a view of Lisbon, and the plate was presented by Queen Anne. There are places of worship for Baptists, Independents, Wesleyan Methodists, and Unitarians, a Roman Catholic chapel, and a synagogue. The free grammar school was founded, in 1732, by Dr. Smith, a physician of the town, who bequeathed for its support the farm of East Standon, in the Isle of Wight: there are fifty boys, natives of Portsmouth, who receive a gratuitous education in the classics: the head master, who is allowed to take boarders, is appointed by the Dean and Canons of Christ Church, Oxford. The National and Lancasterian schools, in which, in conjunction with Portsea, not less than seven thousand children are instructed, are supported by subscription; and there are Sunday schools in connexion with the established church and the dissenting congregations. There are various charitable bequests for distribution among the poor. On the summit of Portsdown Hill, and fronting the harbour, is a beautiful stone pillar, erected to the memory of Lord Nelson, by those who fought under his command in the memorable battle of Trafalgar, which forms a most interesting object, whether viewed from the sea or the land. Jonas Hanway, the philanthropist, was born here in 1712; he died in 1786. Portsmouth gives the title of earl to the family of Wallop.

PORTSWOOD, a tything in that part of the parish of SOUTH STONEHAM which is within the jurisdiction of the borough of SOUTHAMPTON, 2 miles (N. by E.) from Southampton, containing 440 inhabitants.

POSENHALL, an extra-parochial district, within the liberties of the borough of WENLOCK, county of SALOP, 1¼ mile (W.) from Broseley, containing 14 inhabitants.

POSLINFORD, a parish in the hundred of RISBRIDGE, county of SUFFOLK, 1¾ mile (N.) from Clare, containing, with Chipley, 295 inhabitants. The living is a discharged vicarage, in the archdeaconry of Sudbury, and diocese of Norwich, rated in the king's books at £6. 10. The Rev. G. G. Golding was patron in 1804.

POSTCOMBE, a chapelry in that part of the parish of LEWKNOR which is in the hundred of LEWKNOR, county of OXFORD, 2 miles (S.E.) from Tetsworth. The population is returned with the parish.

POSTERN, a joint township with Shottle, in the parish of DUFFIELD, hundred of APPLETREE, county of DERBY. The population is returned with Shottle. It is in the honour of Tutbury, duchy of Lancaster, and within the jurisdiction of a court of pleas held at Tutbury every third Tuesday, for the recovery of debts under 40s.

POSTLING, a parish in the hundred of HAYNE, lathe of SHEPWAY, county of KENT, 3¾ miles (N. by W.) from Hythe, containing 175 inhabitants. The living is a vicarage, in the archdeaconry and diocese of Canterbury, rated in the king's books at £6. 8. 1½., and in the patronage of the Archbishop of Canterbury. The church is in the early style of English architecture; in it is a stone bearing an inscription stating that it was consecrated to the Virgin Mary, 19th Kal. Sept., St. Eusebius' day. White Kennett, Bishop of Peterborough, tutor to the Duke of Gloucester, and author of the Roman Antiquities, &c., was vicar of this parish; he died in 1714.

POSTLIP, a hamlet in the parish of WINCHCOMBE, lower division of the hundred of KIFTSGATE, county of GLOUCESTER, 2½ miles (S.W. by W.) from Winchcombe, with which the population is returned.

POSTWICK, a parish in the hundred of BLOFIELD, county of NORFOLK, 4¼ miles (E. by S.) from Norwich,

containing 254 inhabitants. The living is a rectory, in the archdeaconry and diocese of Norwich, rated in the king's books at £10, and in the patronage of the Earl of Rosebery. The church is dedicated to All Saints.

POTSGROVE, a parish in the hundred of MANSHEAD, county of BEDFORD, 3¼ miles (S. by E.) from Woburn, containing 183 inhabitants. The living is a rectory, united to that of Battlesden, in the archdeaconry of Bedford, and diocese of Lincoln, rated in the king's books at £10. 19. 4½. The church is dedicated to St. Mary.

POTT, a joint township with Ilton, in the parish of MASHAM, eastern division of the wapentake of HANG, North riding of the county of YORK, 5¼ miles (W.S.W.) from Masham. The population is returned with Ilton.

POTT-SHRIGLEY, a chapelry in the parish of PRESTBURY, hundred of MACCLESFIELD, county palatine of CHESTER, 4½ miles (N.N.E.) from Macclesfield, containing 331 inhabitants. The living is a perpetual curacy, in the archdeaconry and diocese of Chester, endowed with £1200 private benefaction, £600 royal bounty, and £1200 parliamentary grant, and in the patronage of William Turner, Esq. The chapel is a neat building of stone, with an embattled tower. The Macclesfield and Congleton canal passes through the parish. Freestone and coal abound in the neighbourhood. John Barlow, in 1684, founded a school for ten poor children, with an endowment of about £6 per annum, and £2 for apprenticing one every third year. There is another smaller sum, the bequest of William Lunt, in 1688, for teaching two children.

POTTER-HANWORTH, a parish in the second division of the wapentake of LANGOE, parts of KESTEVEN, county of LINCOLN, 6¼ miles (S. E. by E.) from Lincoln, containing 374 inhabitants. The living is a rectory, in the archdeaconry and diocese of Lincoln, rated in the king's books at £13. 16. 8., and in the patronage of the Crown. The church is dedicated to St. Andrew.

POTTERNE, a parish in the hundred of POTTERNE and CANNINGS, county of WILTS, 1¾ mile (S. by W.) from Devizes, comprising the tythings of Marston and Worton, and containing 1609 inhabitants. The living is a vicarage, in the peculiar jurisdiction of the Bishop of Salisbury, rated in the king's books at £20. 6. 8., and in the patronage of the Bishop of Salisbury, as Prebendary of Potterne. The church, dedicated to St. Mary, is an ancient cruciform structure: a new gallery has been lately erected in the north transept, at the expense of the present vicar, who has in other respects contributed to the embellishment of this venerable edifice. The Bishops of Salisbury had formerly a residence here, of which there are no traces, excepting a garden wall.

POTTERS-BAR, a hamlet in the parish of MONKENHADLEY, hundred of EDMONTON, county of MIDDLESEX, 3 miles (N.N.E.) from Chipping-Barnet. The population is returned with the parish. There is a place of worship for Baptists.

POTTERS-PURY, a parish in the hundred of CLELEY, county of NORTHAMPTON, 2½ miles (N.W.) from Stony-Stratford, comprising the hamlet of Yardley-Gobion, and part of that of Old Stratford, and containing 1410 inhabitants. The living is a discharged vicarage, in the archdeaconry of Northampton, and diocese of Peterborough, rated in the king's books at £8. 6., endowed with £200 private benefaction, £200 royal bounty, and £600 parliamentary grant, and in the patronage of Earl Bathurst. The church is dedicated to St. Nicholas. There is a place of worship for Independents. The old Roman Watling-street, and the Grand Junction canal, pass through the parish, in which there is a large manufactory for coarse earthenware.

POTTERTON, a joint township with Kiddal, in the parish of BARWICK in ELMETT, lower division of the wapentake of SKYRACK, West riding of the county of YORK, 7½ miles (S. W. by W.) from Tadcaster. The population is returned with Kiddal.

POTTO, a township in the parish of WHORLTON, western division of the liberty of LANGBAURGH, North riding of the county of YORK, 5¼ miles (S. W.) from Stokesley, containing 207 inhabitants.

POTTON, a market town and parish in the hundred of BIGGLESWADE, county of BEDFORD, 11½ miles (E.) from Bedford, and 48 (N. by W.) from London, containing 1498 inhabitants. A great part of this town was destroyed by fire in 1783, on which occasion the damages were estimated at £25,000, exclusively of the expense of temporary erections in the adjacent fields, for the accommodation of the inhabitants, until their houses could be rebuilt. It is pleasantly situated at the foot of a hill, on the high road from London to Cambridge, and consists principally of one long street : the inhabitants are supplied with water by means of several small rivulets, and the adjacent neighbourhood is highly respectable, and contains some genteel and handsome mansions. The market is on Saturday, chiefly for corn and straw-plat, but the business done is very inconsiderable. In 1227, a fair was granted by charter of Henry III.: at present, fairs are held on the third Tuesday in January, the last Tuesday in April, first Tuesday in July, and the Tuesday before the 29th of October, all which are noted for the sale of horses and sheep. The living is a discharged vicarage, in the archdeaconry of Bedford, and diocese of Lincoln, rated in the king's books at £13. 6. 8., and in the patronage of the Crown. The church is dedicated to St. Mary. There is a place of worship for Baptists. Three several bequests have been made for the instruction of children ; in 1711, of £50, by Dame Constance Burgoyne ; in 1712, of £30, by Alexander Atkinson ; and in 1770, of £400, by John Caryer; which are vested in land, and, with the sum of £3. 16. 8. per annum, a proportion of the town land receipts, are applied to the instruction of about thirty of both sexes.

POUGHILL, a parish in the hundred of STRATTON, county of CORNWALL, 1¼ mile (N. W.) from Stratton, containing 378 inhabitants. The living is a discharged vicarage, in the archdeaconry of Cornwall, and diocese of Exeter, rated in the king's books at £6. 12. 1., and in the patronage of the Crown. The church is dedicated to St. Olave. The Bude and Holsworthy canal passes through the parish. Here was fought, on May 16th, 1643, the celebrated battle of Stratton, in which the parliamentarian troops, under the Earl of Stamford, were signally defeated by the Cornish forces, under Sir Beville Granville.

POUGHILL, a parish in the western division of the hundred of BUDLEIGH, county of DEVON, 6¼ miles

(N. by E.) from Crediton, containing 321 inhabitants. The living is a rectory, in the archdeaconry and diocese of Exeter, rated in the king's books at £8. 17. 8½., and in the patronage of the Crown. The church is dedicated to St. Mary. Here was formerly a chantry chapel, dedicated to St. John the Baptist. Gertrude Pyncombe, in 1730, bequeathed £5 a year, and, in 1725, Robert Gay gave £1 a year, for teaching poor children.

POULSHOT, a parish in the hundred of MELKSHAM, county of WILTS, 3¾ miles (S. W. by W.) from Devizes, containing 323 inhabitants. The living is a rectory, in the archdeaconry and diocese of Salisbury, rated in the king's books at £6. 5., and in the patronage of the Bishop of Salisbury. The church, dedicated to St. Peter, has lately received an addition of forty free sittings, the Incorporated Society for the enlargement of churches and chapels having granted £20 towards defraying the expense.

POULTNEY, a hamlet in the parish of MISTERTON, hundred of GUTHLAXTON, county of LEICESTER, 2¾ miles (E. by N.) from Lutterworth. The population is returned with the parish.

POULTON, a township in the parish of PULFORD, lower division of the hundred of BROXTOW, county palatine of CHESTER, 5½ miles (S. by W.) from Chester, containing 132 inhabitants. A Cistercian abbey was founded here, in 1153, by Robert, who was butler to Ranulph, second Earl of Chester ; but the monks, having suffered greatly from the frequent incursions of the Welch, were translated, in 1214, to Dieulacres in Staffordshire, and thenceforth, till the dissolution, Poulton continued parcel of the possessions of that monastery.

POULTON, a joint township with Spittle, in the parish of BEBBINGTON, lower division of the hundred of WIRRALL, county palatine of CHESTER, containing, with Spittle, 101 inhabitants.

POULTON, a joint township with Seacomb, in the parish of WALLAZEY, lower division of the hundred of WIRRALL, county palatine of CHESTER, 11 miles (N. by E.) from Great Neston, containing, with Seacomb, 380 inhabitants.

POULTON, a parish in the hundred of BEWSBOROUGH, lathe of ST. AUGUSTINE, county of KENT, 3½ miles (W.) from Dovor, containing 29 inhabitants. This parish comprises only three houses, and has no church. Here are the venerable ruins of Bradsole, or St. Radegund's abbey, said to have been founded, in 1191, by Richard I., for monks of the Premonstratensian order, the abbots of which were afterwards summoned to parliament, to sit as peers. It was dedicated to St. Mary and St. Radegund, and at the dissolution possessed a revenue of £142. 8.

POULTON, a chapelry in that part of the parish of LANCASTER which is in the hundred of LONSDALE, south of the sands, county palatine of LANCASTER, 3¼ miles (N. W.) from Lancaster, containing 363 inhabitants. The living is a perpetual curacy, in the archdeaconry of Richmond, and diocese of Chester, endowed with £400 private benefaction, £200 royal bounty, and £600 parliamentary grant. The chapel was consecrated in 1745. Poulton has of late years become a favourite bathing-place : it commands fine views of Morecambe bay and the Westmorland, Cumberland, and Yorkshire mountains. Francis Bowes, in 1732, demised, for the foundation of a free school, lands now producing an annual income of about £35, for which sixty children are instructed: the school-room was erected in 1745.

POULTON, a joint township with Fearnhead, in the parish of WARRINGTON, hundred of WEST DERBY, county palatine of LANCASTER, 2 miles (N. E. by E.) from Warrington, containing 631 inhabitants.

POULTON, a parish in the hundred of HIGH-WORTH, CRICKLADE, and STAPLE, county of WILTS, 4 miles (W. by S.) from Fairford, containing 309 inhabitants. The living is a perpetual curacy, in the archdeaconry of Wilts, and diocese of Salisbury, endowed with £200 royal bounty, and £200 parliamentary grant, and in the patronage of T. Ingram, Esq. The church is dedicated to St. Michael. A Gilbertine priory, in honour of the Blessed Virgin Mary, was founded here, about 1347, by Sir Thomas de Sancto Mauro, or Seymor, which, at the dissolution, was valued at £20. 3. 2. per annum.

POULTON in the FYLDE, a parish in the hundred of AMOUNDERNESS, county palatine of LANCASTER, comprising the market town of Poulton, the chapelry of Marton, and the townships of Carleton, Hardhorn with Newton, and Thornton, and containing 4031 inhabitants, of which number, 1011 are in the town of Poulton, 21 miles (S. W. by S.) from Lancaster, and 235 (N. W. by N.) from London. This is a small and very ancient port under Preston, situated near the mouth of the Wyre, in an extensive district called the Fylde, and much frequented in the bathing season. The inhabitants are chiefly employed in agriculture. The market is on Monday; and fairs for cattle, cloth, and other commodities, are held on February 6th, April 13th, and November 3rd. The living is a discharged vicarage, in the archdeaconry of Richmond, and diocese of Chester, rated in the king's books at £7. 16. 8., endowed with £400 private benefaction, and £600 royal bounty, and in the patronage of Peter Hesketh, Esq. The church, which is dedicated to St. Chad, occupies the site of an ancient structure, which, having stood for nearly seven centuries, was taken down in 1751, with the exception of the tower, which was rebuilt in the time of Charles I., and remains attached to the modern edifice. There are places of worship for the Society of Friends, Independents, Wesleyan Methodists, and Roman Catholics. A free school was founded, in 1717, by James Baines, who endowed it with land now producing an income of £69 per annum: a master and an usher are elected annually, and the number of children instructed varies from eighty to one hundred and twenty. The founder likewise bequeathed land, of the present value of £100 a year, for apprenticing poor children of this parish.

POUNDEN, a hamlet in the parish of TWYFORD, hundred and county of BUCKINGHAM, 6¼ miles (S. W. by S.) from Buckingham, containing 91 inhabitants.

POUNDISFORD, a tything in the parish of PIT-MINSTER, hundred of TAUNTON and TAUNTON-DEAN, county of SOMERSET, 4 miles (S. by W.) from Taunton. The population is returned with the parish.

POUNDSTOCK, a parish in the hundred of LES-NEWTH, county of CORNWALL, 4¼ miles (S. S. W.) from Stratton, containing 744 inhabitants. The living is a discharged vicarage, in the archdeaconry of Cornwall, and diocese of Exeter, rated in the king's books

at £13. 6. 8., and in the patronage of John Dayman, Esq. The church is dedicated to St. Neot. The parish is bounded on the west by Widemouth bay, in the Bristol channel. A fair is held on the Monday before Ascension-day.

POWDERHAM, a parish in the hundred of Ex-MINSTER, county of DEVON, 8¼ miles (S. E. by S.) from Exeter, containing 216 inhabitants. The living is a rectory, in the archdeaconry and diocese of Exeter, rated in the king's books at £27. 3. 6½., and in the patronage of Viscount Courtenay. The church, dedicated to St. Clement, has a wooden screen, and in a window of the north aisle is the stone effigy of a lady, probably one of the Courtenays. Powderham castle and grounds are delightfully situated on an acclivity rising from the western bank of the navigable river Exe. The former, now merely retaining its castellated appearance, was, in Leland's time, a strong fort, with a barbican for the protection of Exe haven. During the parliamentary war it was fortified with eighteen pieces of ordnance, and garrisoned with three hundred men: the present drawing-room was formerly a chapel. The Belvidere tower, occupying an elevated site above the castle, commands a noble terra-marine view. The Exeter canal joins the river near this place.

POWICK, a parish in the lower division of the hundred of PERSHORE, county of WORCESTER, 2¼ miles (S. S. W.) from Worcester, comprising the chapelry of Clieveload, and the hamlet of Woodsfield, and containing, exclusively of a part of the chapelry of Bransford, which is in this parish, 1452 inhabitants. The living is a discharged vicarage, with the curacy of Mordeford annexed, in the archdeaconry and diocese of Worcester, rated in the king's books at £10. 2. 7., and in the patronage of the Earl of Coventry. The church is dedicated to St. Peter and St. Lawrence. The river Teme is here crossed by an ancient bridge, a short distance below which it falls into the Severn. In December 1642, an action was fought near this place, between the parliamentarian troops under Colonel Sandes, and the royalists under Prince Rupert and Prince Maurice, in which the former were defeated, and the colonel was mortally wounded.

POWNAL-FEE, a township in the parish of WILMSLOW, hundred of MACCLESFIELD, county palatine of CHESTER, 3¾ miles (S. by W.) from Stockport, containing 1432 inhabitants.

POXWELL, a parish in the hundred of WINFRITH, Blandford (South) division of the county of DORSET, 6 miles (S. E. by S.) from Dorchester, containing 73 inhabitants. The living is a rectory, united, in 1749, to that of Warmwell, in the archdeaconry of Dorset, and diocese of Bristol, rated in the king's books at £9. 5. 5. J. Trenchard, Esq. was patron in 1781.

POYNINGS, a parish in the hundred of POYNINGS, rape of Lewes, county of SUSSEX, 3½ miles (S. W. by S.) from Hurst - Pierrepoint, containing 232 inhabitants. The living is a rectory, in the archdeaconry of Lewes, and diocese of Chichester, rated in the king's books at £10, and in the patronage of the Crown. The church, dedicated to the Holy Trinity, is partly in the decorated, and partly in the later English, style of architecture. The Rev. George Beard, in 1786, gave £100, directing the interest to be applied for teaching eight poor children.

POYNTON, a chapelry in the parish of PRESTBURY, hundred of MACCLESFIELD, county palatine of CHESTER, 5¼ miles (S. S. E.) from Stockport, containing 540 inhabitants. The living is a perpetual curacy, in the archdeaconry and diocese of Chester, endowed with £200 private benefaction, and £800 royal bounty, and in the patronage of Sir George Warren, Bart. The chapel, dedicated to St. Mary, was rebuilt, in 1789, by the late Sir George Warren, Bart., K.B., and some of the windows exhibit the arms of the Warren and Bulkeley families, in stained glass. A school-house was built by subscription in 1703. There are several collieries in the neighbourhood. A court baron is held twice a year.

PREEN (CHURCH), a parish in the hundred of CONDOVER, county of SALOP, 6¼ miles (W. by S.) from Much Wenlock, containing 73 inhabitants. The living is a perpetual curacy, with that of Longnor, in the archdeaconry of Salop, and diocese of Hereford, endowed with £800 royal bounty, and £200 parliamentary grant, and in the patronage of W. Webster, Esq. The church is dedicated to St. John the Baptist. Here was a small Cluniac priory, a cell to that of Wenlock.

PREES, a parish in the Whitchurch division of the hundred of BRADFORD (North), county of SALOP, comprising the chapelries of Calverhall and Whixhall, and the townships of Prees with Steel, and Sandford, and containing 3190 inhabitants, of which number, 1525 are in the township of Prees with Steel, 4¾ miles (N. E.) from Wem. The living is a vicarage, with the perpetual curacy of Preston-Gubbals, in the peculiar jurisdiction of the Prebendary of Prees, otherwise Pipa Minor, in the Cathedral Church of Lichfield, rated in the king's books at £10, and in the patronage of the Bishop of Lichfield and Coventry. The church, dedicated to St. Chad, is an ancient cruciform structure, with a tower of modern erection: it contains two old figures of Moses and Aaron, and some pieces of tesselated pavement, also several monuments to the ancestors of General Lord Hill, who was born here in 1772. There is a place of worship for Independents. Prees had formerly a weekly market and an annual fair, the former of which has been long disused; two fairs are now held on the 2nd Mondays in April and October. Here are charity schools for about one hundred and sixty children, towards the support of which there are several small endowments. A considerable traffic in coal, lime, and slate, is carried on by means of Quise Brook canal, which runs through the parish.

PREESALL, a joint township with Hackersall, in that part of the parish of LANCASTER which is in the hundred of AMOUNDERNESS, county palatine of LANCASTER, 6 miles (N. by E.) from Poulton, containing 700 inhabitants. Richard Fleetwood, Esq., in 1687, built a school-house, and endowed it with an annuity of £13. 6. 8., for which the children of parishioners are taught to read.

PRENDICK, a township in the parish of ALNHAM, northern division of COQUETDALE ward, county of NORTHUMBERLAND, 10 miles (N. N. W.) from Rothbury, containing 68 inhabitants.

PRENTON, a township in the parish of WOODCHURCH, lower division of the hundred of WIRRALL, county palatine of CHESTER, 6 miles (N. by E.) from Great Neston, containing 99 inhabitants.

PRESCOT, an extra-parochial liberty, in the upper division of the hundred of TEWKESBURY, county of GLOUCESTER, 5¼ miles (N. N. E.) from Cheltenham, containing 56 inhabitants.

PRESCOT, a parish in the hundred of WEST DERBY, county palatine of LANCASTER, comprising the market town of Prescot, the chapelries of Rainford and Great Sankey, and the townships of Bold, Cronton, Cuerdley, Ditton, Eccleston, Parr, Penketh, Rainhill, Sutton, Whiston, Widness with Appleton, and Windle, and containing 22,811 inhabitants, of which number, 4468 are in the town of Prescot, 51 miles (S.) from Lancaster, and 197 (N. W.) from London. This town, consisting chiefly of one long straggling street, on the high road from Liverpool to Manchester, lies principally on a substratum of coal, several mines of which are excavated to its very edge, and which not only furnish abundant employment to the labouring class, but supply fuel at a cheap rate to the inhabitants, and essentially promote the manufacturing interests of the district, which has long been noted for the superior construction of watch tools, and the more minute parts of that beautiful piece of mechanism comprised in what is termed motion-work. The drawing of pinion wire, extending to fifty different sizes, and remarkable for its exquisite adaptation to the requisite purposes, originated here; and small files, considered to be of unparalleled excellence, are made, and exported in large quantities. The manufacture of coarse earthenware, especially sugar moulds, has been established here for a very long period, the clay of the neighbourhood being peculiarly adapted to that purpose; and a few persons are employed in the cotton business. The Liverpool and Manchester railway passes about one mile south of the town. A charter for a market and a fair was granted in the 7th of Edward III.: there are now two markets, on Tuesday and Saturday; a fortnight fair for cattle, from Shrove-Tuesday to the first Tuesday in May, and annual fairs on Ash-Wednesday, the Wednesday after Corpus Christi, August 24th and 25th, October 21st, and November 1st. The inhabitants have, since the time of Henry VII., claimed exemption from serving on juries, except within the manor, also from the payment of all tolls to public markets, with divers other privileges. A court baron is held six times a year; a court leet annually, on the festival of Corpus Christi, when a coroner for the manor and liberty is appointed; and a court of requests, for the recovery of debts to any amount, at which last, the steward of the manor presides: petty sessions for the Prescot division of the hundred also are held once a month. The living is a vicarage, in the archdeaconry and diocese of Chester, rated in the king's books at £24. 10., and in the patronage of the Provost and Fellows of King's College, Cambridge. The church, dedicated to St. Mary, is an ancient edifice: in 1789, the old steeple was taken down, and replaced by an elegant tower and spire, one hundred and fifty-six feet high: in the interior are some modern monuments, particularly one of great elegance, by Chantrey, to the memory of William Atherton, Esq. There are places of worship for Independents, Wesleyan Methodists, and Unitarians. The free grammar school is of somewhat uncertain foundation: it has been endowed by various benefactors, and, in 1759, the present school-house was built by subscription: the entire income is estimated at £159. 17. 4.; the stipend of the master is £90 per annum : nearly fifty boys are instructed, but classical education has not of late been required. This school has a preference to seven fellowships in Brasenose College, Oxford, and two exhibitions to the same college, for boys being natives of Prescot, and educated in it ; several children not on the foundation are instructed for pay. In 1824, Mrs. Jane Chorley bequeathed to trustees the sum of £2000, for establishing and supporting a schoolmistress to educate poor girls. Almshouses were founded and endowed originally by Oliver Lyme, to which several additions have been made ; nineteen almspeople are eligible under the direction of the trustees, preference being given to inhabitants not receiving relief in Prescot and Whiston, and to widows. Among the numerous benefactions to the parish are funds for apprenticing poor children. The celebrated tragedian, John Philip Kemble, was born here, in 1757.

PRESCOTT, a hamlet in that part of the parish of CROPREDY which is in the hundred of BANBURY, county of OXFORD, 5 miles (N. N. E.) from Banbury, containing 19 inhabitants.

PRESHUTE, a parish in the hundred of SELKLEY, county of WILTS, 1¼ mile (S. W. by W.) from Marlborough, containing, with the tything of Clatford, 693 inhabitants. The living is a vicarage, in the peculiar jurisdiction of the Bishop of Salisbury, rated in the king's books at £8, and in the patronage of the Choristers in the Cathedral Church of Salisbury, on the nomination of the Bishop. The church, dedicated to St. George, is partly in the Norman style, and has a plain ancient font of dark grey marble.

PRESTBURY, a parish in the hundred of MACCLESFIELD, county palatine of CHESTER, comprising the market town of Macclesfield, the chapelries of Bosley, Capesthorne, Chelford, Macclesfield - Forest, Marton, Poynton, Pott-Shrigley, Rainow, Siddington, and Wincell, and the townships of Adlington, Birtles, Bollington, Butley, Eaton, Fallybroom, Henbury with Pexall, Hurdsfield, Kettleshulme, Lyme-Handley, Mottram St. Andrew, Newton, Prestbury, North Rode, Sutton, Tytherington, Upton, Wildboar-Clough, Lower Withington, Old Withington, Woodford, and Worth, and containing 34,976 inhabitants, of which number, 440 are in the township of Prestbury, 2¾ miles (N. N. W.) from Macclesfield. The living is a vicarage, in the archdeaconry and diocese of Chester, rated in the king's books at £10, and in the patronage of Thomas Legh, Esq. The church, dedicated to St. Peter, is of great antiquity, and has portions in various styles : on the south side is an ancient low building of stone, now used as a parochial school-house, which is considered to be an ancient Norman church, and consists of a nave and chancel, with an enriched west entrance : in a private chapel, which terminates the south aisle of the church, is a piscina, together with a portion of a carved oak screen. There is a place of worship for Wesleyan Methodists. A school-house was built in 1720, principally at the expense of John Legh, Esq., and endowed by Mrs. Ann Whittacres, with the interest of £100, for the instruction of ten of the poorest children in the township. In the parochial school belonging to the church, one hundred children are taught. Fairs for cattle are held on April 28th and October 22nd. A court leet and baron for the township is held in May and December, the

jurisdiction of which comprehends all pleas under 40s. In the township of Butley, in this parish, several ancient tumuli, containing urns and other relics of antiquity, were discovered some years since ; in these vessels it is said that oak leaves, and shells of acorns, were found, retaining a freshness of appearance as if recently gathered : stones from several of the tumuli have been used for the repair of the roads in the neighbourhood.

PRESTBURY, a parish in the lower division of the hundred of DEERHURST, county of GLOUCESTER, 1½ mile (N. E.) from Cheltenham, containing 906 inhabitants. The living is a vicarage, in the archdeaconry and diocese of Gloucester, rated in the king's books at £11, and in the patronage of W. J. Agg, Esq. The church is dedicated to St. Mary.

PRESTON, a parish in the liberty of SUTTON-POINTZ, Dorchester division of the county of DORSET, 3½ miles (N. E. by N.) from Melcombe-Regis, containing, with the tything of Sutton-Pointz, 508 inhabitants. The living is a discharged vicarage, in the peculiar jurisdiction and patronage of the Prebendary of Preston in the Cathedral Church of Salisbury, rated in the king's books at £8. 18. The church, dedicated to St. Andrew, is very ancient, and had formerly ten pensionary chapels belonging to it. There is a place of worship for Wesleyan Methodists.

PRESTON, a parish in the hundred of CROWTHORNE and MINETY, county of GLOUCESTER, 1½ mile (E. S. E.) from Cirencester, containing 160 inhabitants. The living is a vicarage, in the archdeaconry and diocese of Gloucester, rated in the king's books at £9. 10. 7½., and in the patronage of Miss Master. The church, dedicated to All Saints, is an ancient and singular structure in the early style of English architecture. The river Churn runs through the parish.

PRESTON, a parish in the lower division of the hundred of DUDSTONE and KING'S BARTON, county of GLOUCESTER, 3¾ miles (W. by S.) from Ledbury, containing 87 inhabitants. The living is a discharged vicarage, in the archdeaconry of Hereford, and diocese of Gloucester, rated in the king's books at £7. 6. 8., and in the patronage of the Bishop of Gloucester.

PRESTON, a hamlet in the parish of HITCHIN, hundred of HITCHIN and PIRTON, county of HERTFORD, 3 miles (S. by W.) from Hitchin. The population is returned with the parish.

PRESTON, a parish in the hundred of FAVERSHAM, lathe of SCRAY, county of KENT, ½ a mile (S.) from Faversham, containing 351 inhabitants. The living is a vicarage, in the archdeaconry and diocese of Canterbury, rated in the king's books at £8. 12. 6., and in the patronage of the Archbishop of Canterbury. The church, dedicated to St. Catherine, is principally in the early style of English architecture, with a tower and spire at the east end of the south aisle : on the north side of the chancel is a sumptuous altar-tomb of black and white marble, in memory of Roger Boyle, Esq., and his wife Joan, ancestors of the Earls of Cork ; there are also some sepulchral brasses of the fifteenth century. In a school, founded by Thomas Smith, in 1730, thirteen children are taught to read for about £10 per annum, arising from various bequests.

PRESTON, a parish in the hundred of PRESTON, lathe of St. AUGUSTINE, county of KENT, 2 miles (N.) from Wingham, containing 504 inhabitants. The living is a discharged vicarage, in the archdeaconry and diocese of Canterbury, rated in the king's books at £9. 15., and in the patronage of the Dean and Chapter of Canterbury. The church is dedicated to St. Mildred.

Seal and Arms.

PRESTON, a parish in the hundred of AMOUN-DERNESS, county palatine of LANCASTER, comprising the borough of Preston, which has a separate jurisdiction, the chapelries of Broughton, and Grimsargh with Brockholes, and the townships of Barton, Elston, Fishwick, Haighton, Lea (with Ashton, Ingol, and Cottam), and Ribbleton, and containing 27,300 inhabitants, of which number, 24,575 are in the borough of Preston, 21¾ miles (S. by E.) from Lancaster, and 217 (N. W. by N.) from London. This place, which is supposed to have grown out of the ruins of the ancient *Rerigonium*, a Roman station, of which the site is now occupied by the village of Ribchester, is supposed, from its having belonged to the monks, to have obtained the appellation of Priest's town, of which its present name is a contraction. Though it may be difficult to ascertain its precise origin, it was unquestionably a place of considerable importance prior to the Conquest, soon after which it was granted to Tosti, fourth son of Godwin, Earl of Kent. In 1307, the town was burnt and nearly levelled with the ground by the Scottish army under Robert Bruce, and, in 1333, Edward III. passed through it, on his way to Halidown Hill, where he defeated the Scots, with the loss of twenty thousand men, and took Baliol, their king, prisoner. The same monarch, in recompense for the assistance he derived from the inhabitants, gave the corporation a common seal, and invested them with several valuable privileges. During the war between the houses of York and Lancaster, the Earl of Derby raised considerable supplies of troops in the town for the service of the Lancastrian cause. Soon after the commencement of the parliamentary war, a battle was fought on Ribbleton common, to the east of the town, in which the parliamentarians were commanded by General Fairfax; and in 1645, another battle took place, in which the mayor, and several of the principal inhabitants became the victims of their attachment to the royal cause. In 1648, a fierce engagement took place at the pass of Walton bridge, between the English and Scottish allied forces, commanded by the Duke of Hamilton and Sir Marmaduke Langdale, and a detachment of the parliamentarian troops under the command of General Lambert, in which the former were defeated, and the duke and his officers, who had retired into the town, were compelled to effect their escape by crossing the river at the ford below Walton bridge. Throughout the whole of this contest the town of Preston suffered materially for its adherence to the royal cause, and the inhabitants were treated by the parliamentarians with the utmost severity. In 1715, the party in the interest of the Pretender obtained possession of the town, which they endeavoured to fortify against the assault of the king's forces; but being attacked suddenly by General Wills, aided by the subsequent arrival of General Carpenter, with a party of dragoons, they were compelled, after an obstinate resistance, to surrender at discretion. The town suffered severely also during this contest, a considerable part of it being burnt by the inhabitants, who were in the interest of the king, to assist the movements of the besiegers, and many of the houses of those who assisted the rebels having been given up to plunder after the town was taken. The Lords Widdrington, Derwentwater, and Nairn, were taken in the town, and sent prisoners to London, where they were condemned and executed; and sixteen of the rebels were hanged on Gallows' Hill for high treason. The rebels again made their appearance, in 1745, and attempted to intrench themselves in the town; but on the approach of the royal forces under the Duke of Cumberland, made their escape from Preston, only a few hours before the duke's arrival.

The town is pleasantly situated on an eminence rising from the north bank of the river Ribble, over which are Walton and Penwortham bridges: the former, a neat structure of three arches, leading from the London road, was erected in 1782; and the latter, a handsome bridge of five arches, leading from the Liverpool road, was built by act of parliament in 1759. The streets are spacious and well paved; the houses are neatly and substantially built of brick, and many of them are handsome and of large dimensions; the inhabitants are partially supplied with water conveyed by cast-iron pipes from a large reservoir, called the Folly, at the bottom of Mid Spit Wiend, into which it is raised by an engine constructed in 1729; and with spring-water by carts, at a moderate price. A company was established for lighting the town with gas in 1816, and considerable improvements are daily taking place. The environs, in which are many handsome villas, inhabited by opulent families, abound with richly-diversified scenery, and the high grounds afford extensive and interesting prospects. There are several pleasant and extensive promenades, of which the principal are, Avenham Walk, belonging to the corporation, by whom it is kept in order; Common Bank, from which are extensive views; and the Marsh, along the margin of the river, by which an ancestor of Sir Walter Scott, with his comrades, escaped to Liverpool, during the siege of Preston in 1715. The library was founded by R. Shepherd, Esq., M.D., twice mayor for the borough, who, in 1761, endowed it with £50 per annum for its augmentation, and with the interest of £200, as a salary to the librarian; it is open to the inhabitants under certain regulations. A botanical society was established in 1804, from which a smaller establishment has branched; and a Literary and Philosophical Society was instituted in 1810, of which the members hold their meetings in the town hall. A society for promoting the study of natural history was established in 1823, to which is annexed an appropriate library, and a museum is about to be added to it. There are also a law society, consisting principally of attorneys' clerks, a mechanics' institution, two principal news-rooms and several on a smaller scale, and various book societies. The theatre, a neat and well-arranged building, erected by a proprietary in 1802, is opened occasionally; and assemblies are held in a handsome suite of rooms, built at the sole expense of the Earl of Derby. A choral society was established in 1819, and a musical academy has been instituted, which is well supported, and ably conducted. Warm and cold baths have been constructed, which are arranged with every attention to the convenience of the visitors, and fitted up with the requisite accommodation; and races are annually held in July on Fulwood moor, which are well attended.

The trade of the town, till within the last half century, principally consisted of the manufacture and sale of linen cloth, which, from a petition of the mayor and corporation to parliament, for preventing the exportation of Irish linen to the colonies, and of Scotch linen into Ireland, appears to have been for ages the staple trade of the town and neighbourhood for twenty miles round. The manufacture of cotton goods was introduced, in 1791, by John Horrocks, Esq., to whose public-spirited enterprise the town is indebted for its present prosperity. There are at present numerous factories, many of which are upon a very large scale; that in the township of Fishwick is said to be the largest in England. Machinery impelled by steam has been introduced with great success into the factories, in which the raw material, supplied from Liverpool, is conducted, through every process, to the printing and dyeing of the manufactured article. The greater portion of the goods is sold to the Manchester merchants, and the remainder is sent to London, or into foreign markets: in connexion with the machinery employed in the factories, several iron-foundries have been established in the town. At spring tides, vessels of one hundred and fifty tons' burden can navigate the Ribble to Preston Marsh, where convenient quays have been constructed, and, by an act of parliament passed in the 46th of George III., commissioners were appointed for improving the navigation of the river; buoys have been placed to mark out these parts, which have been deepened by excavation. The river is supposed, by Dr. Whitaker, to have been formerly navigable to Ribchester, and the discovery in that neighbourhood of anchors, and of the hull of a larger vessel than could now be floated so far up the river, seems to confirm that opinion. The port of Preston includes Lytham, Freckleton, Hesketh, and Poulton; a few vessels sail annually to foreign parts, and a coasting trade is carried on to a moderate extent: there are forty-five vessels belonging to it, averaging a burden of seventy-one tons. The custom-house, a neat and commodious building in Fox-street, is under the management of the usual officers. The fishery on the river is of very ancient establishment, and forms part of the revenue of the borough: salmon, plaice, eels, and smelts, are found in abundance, and of good quality. In the years 1715 and 1774, the river is said to have ceased to flow, in the latter year for five hours, and for a length of three miles to have been dry, except in the deeper places; at the expiration of that time the water returned with a strong current. Common and cannel coal are brought to the town by the river Douglas, which, by an act of parliament obtained in 1727, was made navigable from the mouth of the Ribble to within one mile of Ormskirk, whence a short line, parallel with its course, by which the navigation is continued to Wigan, has been since constructed by the proprietors of the Leeds and Liverpool canal, who have purchased the right of the Douglas navigation. The Lancaster canal passes by the west side

of the town, and, after being conducted through a tunnel about two miles in length, which crosses the river Ribble, joins the Leeds and Liverpool canal one mile north of Chorley, affording a communication with the principal navigable rivers in England. The market days are Wednesday, Friday, and Saturday, the last being principally for corn. The market-place is a spacious well-paved area, in the centre of which is an obelisk, supporting a gas-light; and the sides of the quadrangle contain several good buildings, and shops well stored with wares of every kind: the cattle market is held in the north road, and that for vegetables in Cheapside. The fairs are the week before the first Sunday after Epiphany, which is a great horse fair; the spring fair, March 27th, which continues for three days; the summer fair, August 26th, which continues for eight days; and the winter fair, November 7th, which continues for five days: to all these fairs is attached a court of pie-powder.

The borough has received numerous charters from successive sovereigns, of which the first was granted by Henry II., and the last by George IV. The government is vested in a mayor, recorder, two bailiffs, seven aldermen, and seventeen common council-men, assisted by a town clerk, serjeants at mace, and subordinate officers. The mayor and other officers are elected by a jury of twenty-four guild burgesses, empannelled by two elisors, who are appointed for that purpose, on the Friday before the festival of St. Wilfred. The mayor, recorder, and aldermen, are justices of the peace, and have power to hold quarterly courts of session for all offences, but the prisoners are generally referred to the quarter sessions for the county. A court of record is held every third Friday, before the mayor and two or more of the aldermen, for the recovery of debts to any amount; and a court leet, twice in the year, for the examination of weights and measures, and for the presentation of nuisances. The Preston guild, or *Guilda Mercatoria*, a jubilee celebrated every twentieth year, is the tenure by which the freemen retain their privileges: it was originally granted by Henry II., and confirmed by the charters of Charles II. It commences in the last week of August, and is proclaimed to continue twenty-eight days; the festivities, however, have been limited to a fortnight: the last guild was held in 1822. The celebration of this jubilee is conducted under the superintendence of the mayor and three aldermen, appointed as stewards, who, with the other officers of the corporation, dressed in their robes of ceremony, and preceded by their insignia of office and the regalia of the borough, walk from the guildhall, attended by the several trading companies, with their banners and bands of music, and by the principal gentry resident in the neighbourhood, to the ancient cross, or obelisk, in the market-place, where a proclamation is read, calling upon all the burgesses, resident and non-resident, to appear before the stewards of the guild and three senior aldermen, in open court, and renew their freedom. During this festival, various processions of the municipal bodies take place; balls, concerts, dramatic representations, public banquets, and every species of amusement, are provided, and attract an immense concourse from the surrounding districts, to assist at the ceremony, and partake of the festivities. The quarter sessions for the hundreds of Amounderness, Blackburn, and Leyland, are held here, by adjournment from Lancaster; the hundred court for Amounderness, for the recovery of debts under 40s., is held every third Wednesday; and the county court, every fourth Tuesday, for the recovery of debts under the same sum, of which the jurisdiction extends through the whole county, with the exception only of Salford hundred: the quarter sessions for the county, the meetings of the deputy lieutenants, and other county meetings, are held here; and, from its central situation, the offices of the courts of chancery, common pleas, and other courts of the duchy of Lancaster, unless when the officers attend the assizes at Lancaster, are also held at Preston. The principal officers of the duchy court are, the vice-chancellor, the registrar, the cursitor, the clerk of the crown, the clerk of the peace, and the deputy protho-notary of the common pleas. The offices of the under sheriff and treasurer for the county are also in this town. The town hall is a neat brick building with quoins and cornices of stone, surmounted by a turret and dome; the interior comprises a court-room, in which the borough sessions are held, a council chamber, a news-room, and various offices: it was rebuilt on the site of the ancient moot-hall, which fell down in 1780, within a few hours after a party that had assembled there for a ball had departed. The sessions-house and house of correction is a capacious building, enclosed within a lofty boundary wall, including every requisite accommodation for the county sessions, the meeting of the county magistrates, a house for the governor, two hos-pitals, a chapel, and extensive workshops: the prison is on the radiating principle, and is well adapted to the classification of prisoners, including day-rooms, airing-yards, a tread-mill, and other things requisite for the employment of the prisoners. The borough, which made returns to parliament in the 23rd, 26th, 33rd, and 35th of the reign of Edward I., and in the 1st of Edward II., intermitted till the reign of Edward VI., since which time it has regularly returned two members: the right of election is vested in all the inhabitants having resided six months, and not receiving parochial relief within twelve months prior to the election, of whom the num-ber is about five thousand: the mayor and bailiffs are the returning officers.

The living is a vicarage, in the archdeaconry of Rich-mond, and diocese of Chester, rated in the king's books at £15. 3. 11½., and in the patronage of the Trustees of the late Mr. Hulme, Manchester. The church, formerly dedicated to St. Wilfred, was a very ancient structure, repaired by Wilfred, Archbishop of York, in 700: it has been rebuilt, and dedicated to St. John, and has a hand-some square embattled tower crowned with clustered pinnacles, which was erected in 1814; the whole style is a mixture of the later Norman and the early En-glish: the interior contains some good stucco-work and some ancient monuments. St. George's church, built in 1723, is a cruciform structure of brick, with a square embattled tower crowned with pinnacles, and chiefly in a style resembling the Norman: the living is a perpetual curacy, endowed with £800 private benefaction, £800 royal bounty, and £1300 parliament-ary grant, and in the patronage of the Vicar of Pres-ton. The church of the Holy Trinity, a neat stone edifice in the later style of English architecture, with a square embattled tower crowned with pinnacles, was erected in 1814, at an expense of £9080. 9. 3., of which

£4000 were donations, and the remainder was raised by subscription: the living is a perpetual curacy, endowed with £400 private benefaction, and £2200 parliament-ary grant, and in the patronage of the Trustees and the Vicar alternately. St. Paul's, a handsome structure in the later style of English architecture, with four turrets, and containing one thousand two hundred and fifty-nine sittings, of which eight hundred and thirteen are free, was erected in 1825, by grant from the parliamentary commissioners, at an expense of £6063. 17. 10.; and St. Peter's in the Fylde road, a handsome edifice in the same style of architecture, with a small campanile turret, and containing one thousand two hundred and fifty sittings, of which eight hundred and sixty-one are free, was erected by the same means, at an expense of £6638. 10. 2.: the livings are both perpetual curacies, in the patronage of the Vicar. There are two places of worship for Independents, and one each for Baptists, the Society of Friends, Primitive and Wesleyan Methodists, and Unitarians, also two Roman Catholic chapels, one of which, dedicated to St. Wilfred, is a stately and elegant structure.

The free grammar school is of uncertain founda-tion: it is under the direction of the officers of the corporation, who appoint the master and usher, each having a salary of £45 per annum, arising from ground given by Mr. R. Worthington: it is open to all boys of the town. A National school, for children of both sexes, is supported by subscription; the school-house, a handsome and capacious brick building, was erect-ed in 1814: the Blue-coat charity schools, founded in 1701, by Mr. Roger Sudell, have been incorporated with this institution. The Roman Catholic school was esta-blished in 1814; and a large day school is supported by the Wesleyan Methodists. The dispensary was in-stituted in 1809, and is well supported: a room in the building is appropriated to the use of a committee of ladies, who superintend the lying-in charity con-nected with this establishment; and a house of reco-very from fever and other contagious diseases was opened in 1813. The corporation almshouses, built in 1790, in lieu of sixteen others, the site of which is now occupied by the house of correction, have no endow-ment, and afford only a rent-free residence to the in-mates. Adjoining these are others rebuilt by the cor-poration, in lieu of some originally founded, in 1663, by Mr. Worthington, which, having neither endowment nor funds for their maintenance, fell into decay. There are also numerous benevolent and benefit societies, and various charitable bequests for distribution among the poor. There were anciently a convent of Grey friars on the north-west of the town, founded by Ed-ward, Earl of Lancaster, son of Henry III., and an hos-pital, dedicated to St. Mary Magdalene, of which there are no remains.

PRESTON, a township in the parish of Elling-ham, southern division of Bambrough ward, county of Northumberland, 8½ miles (N.) from Alnwick, containing 63 inhabitants. Here is an ancient lofty tower.

PRESTON, a township in the parish of Tyne-mouth, eastern division of Castle ward, county of Northumberland, ¾ of a mile (N.) from North Shields, containing 627 inhabitants. Here were formerly barracks, which have been converted into dwelling-houses. There are two breweries and a linen manufactory.

PRESTON, a parish in the hundred of MARTINSLEY, county of RUTLAND, 1¼ mile (N.) from Uppingham, containing 295 inhabitants. The living is a rectory, in the archdeaconry of Northampton, and diocese of Peterborough, rated in the king's books at £9. 17. 6. The Rev. H. Shield was patron in 1802. The church is dedicated to St. Peter and St. Paul.

PRESTON, a parish in the hundred of STONE, county of SOMERSET, 1¼ mile (W.) from Yeovil, containing 317 inhabitants. The living is a perpetual curacy, annexed to the vicarage of Yeovil, in the archdeaconry of Bath, and diocese of Bath and Wells. This parish has the privilege of sending a certain number of boys to the Yeovil charity school.

PRESTON, a parish in the hundred of BABERGH, county of SUFFOLK, 2½ miles (E. N. E.) from Lavenham, containing 320 inhabitants. The living is a rectory, in the archdeaconry of Sudbury, and diocese of Norwich, rated in the king's books at £5. 6. 0½., and in the patronage of the Master and Fellows of Emanuel College, Cambridge. The church is dedicated to St. Mary.

PRESTON, a parish in the hundred of PRESTON, rape of LEWES, county of SUSSEX, 1¾ mile (N. N. W.) from Brighton, containing 319 inhabitants. The living is a discharged vicarage, with that of Hove, in the archdeaconry and diocese of Chichester, rated in the king's books at £20. 2. 11., and in the patronage of the Prebendary of Hova Villa in the Cathedral Church of Chichester. The church, dedicated to St. Peter, is in the early style of English architecture.* Anne of Cleves, the divorced queen of Henry VIII., resided at Preston House, which contains her portrait, a good original painting: from this place she retired to a convent at Falmer, about three miles distant, where she died and was buried.

PRESTON, a parish partly in the liberty of ST. PETER of YORK, and partly in the middle division of the wapentake of HOLDERNESS, East riding of the county of YORK, comprising the townships of Lelley and Preston, and containing 947 inhabitants, of which number, 828 are in the township of Preston, 7 miles (E. by N.) from Kingston upon Hull. The living is a discharged vicarage, with the perpetual curacy of Hedon, in the peculiar jurisdiction and patronage of the Sub-Dean of York, rated in the king's books at £12, and endowed with £200 private benefaction, £400 royal bounty, and £200 parliamentary grant. The church, dedicated to All Saints, is in the later style of English architecture. There are places of worship for Primitive and Wesleyan Methodists. Thomas Holmes, in 1718, gave £200 to support of a school, which sum was laid out in land, now producing an annual income of about £27, for which twenty-seven children are educated.

PRESTON (EAST), a parish in the hundred of POLING, rape of ARUNDEL, county of SUSSEX, 3½ miles (E.) from Little Hampton, containing 259 inhabitants. The living is a vicarage not in charge, in the archdeaconry and diocese of Chichester, and in the patronage of the Prebendary of Ferring in the Cathedral Church of Chichester.

PRESTON (GREAT and LITTLE), a township in the parish of KIPPAX, lower division of the wapentake of SKYRACK, West riding of the county of YORK, 6¼ miles (N. W.) from Pontefract, containing 478 inhabitants.

PRESTON on the HILL, a township in the parish of RUNCORN, hundred of BUCKLOW, county palatine of CHESTER, 4 miles (N. E. by E.) from Frodsham, containing 391 inhabitants. The Grand Trunk canal passes through the township, and forms a junction with the Duke of Bridgewater's canal, along both which the transmission of goods is very considerable. There is a place of worship for Wesleyan Methodists.

PRESTON (LONG), a parish in the western division of the wapentake of STAINCLIFFE and EWCROSS, West riding of the county of YORK, comprising the townships of Hellifield, Long Preston, and Wigglesworth, and containing 1491 inhabitants, of which number, 733 are in the township of Long Preston, 4½ miles (S. by E.) from Settle. The living is a vicarage, in the archdeaconry and diocese of York, rated in the king's books at £10. 18. 11½., and in the patronage of the Dean and Canons of Christ Church, Oxford. The church is dedicated to St. Mary. There is a place of worship for Wesleyan Methodists.

PRESTON under SCAR, a township in the parish of WENSLEY, western division of the wapentake of HANG, North riding of the county of YORK, 5 miles (N. W. by W.) from Middleham, containing 378 inhabitants. There is a place of worship for Wesleyan Methodists.

PRESTON le SKERNE, a township in the parish of AYCLIFFE, south-eastern division of DARLINGTON ward, county palatine of DURHAM, 7 miles (N. by E.) from Darlington, containing 126 inhabitants.

PRESTON upon STOUR, a parish in the upper division of the hundred of DEERHURST, county of GLOUCESTER, 4½ miles (S.) from Stratford upon Avon, containing, with Alscote, 334 inhabitants. The living is a perpetual curacy, in the archdeaconry and diocese of Gloucester, rated in the king's books at £8. 13. 4., endowed with £1200 royal bounty, and £200 parliamentary grant, and in the patronage of James Roberts West, Esq. The river Stour runs through the parish.

PRESTON (TARRANT), a tything in the parish of CRAWFORD-TARRANT, hundred of BADBURY, Shaston (East) division of the county of DORSET. The population is returned with the parish.

PRESTON upon TEES, a township in the parish of STOCKTON upon TEES, south-western division of STOCKTON ward, county palatine of DURHAM, 2 miles (S. S. W.) from Stockton upon Tees, containing 57 inhabitants. It is bounded on the south by the navigable river Tees, and is intersected by the Stockton and Darlington railway.

PRESTON upon the WILD MOORS, a parish in the Wellington division of the hundred of BRADFORD (South), county of SALOP, 3½ miles (N. E. by N.) from Wellington, containing 209 inhabitants. The living is a discharged rectory, in the archdeaconry of Salop, and diocese of Lichfield and Coventry, rated in the king's books at £3, and in the patronage of the Trustees of Preston Hospital. The church is dedicated to St. Lawrence. The Shrewsbury canal passes within the south-west boundary of the parish. Here is a large hospital for decayed widows and their children, with ample funds for its support: the Earl of Bradford is the trustee.

PRESTON upon WYE, a parish in the hundred of WEBTREE, county of HEREFORD, 8¼ miles (W. by N.) from Hereford, containing 272 inhabitants. The living is a discharged vicarage, united to that of Blakemere, in the peculiar jurisdiction of the Dean of Hereford, rated in the king's books at £3. 16. 9., endowed with £400 private benefaction, and £400 royal bounty. The church is dedicated to St. Lawrence.

PRESTON-BAGGOTT, a parish in the Henley division of the hundred of BARLICHWAY, county of WARWICK, 2¼ miles (E. by S.) from Henley in Arden, containing 219 inhabitants. The living is a rectory, in the archdeaconry and diocese of Worcester, rated in the king's books at £4, and in the patronage of Mrs. Elizabeth Cartwright. The church is dedicated to All Saints. The Stratford and Avon canal passes through the parish. A school has been established here on the British system.

PRESTON-BISSETT, a parish in the hundred and county of BUCKINGHAM, 4½ miles (S. W.) from Buckingham, containing, with the hamlet of Cowley, 396 inhabitants. The living is a rectory, in the archdeaconry of Buckingham, and diocese of Lincoln, rated in the king's books at £11. 9. 4½., and in the patronage of T. W. Coke, Esq. The church is dedicated to St. John the Baptist.

PRESTON-BROCKHURST, a township partly in the parish of SHAWBURY, hundred of PIMHILL, and partly in the parish of MORETON-CORBET, Whitchurch division of the hundred of BRADFORD (North), county of SALOP, 3¼ miles (S. E. by S.) from Wem. The population is returned with Moreton-Corbet.

PRESTON-CAPES, a parish in the hundred of FAWSLEY, county of NORTHAMPTON, 5¾ miles (S.) from Daventry, containing 441 inhabitants. The living comprises a rectory and a vicarage, in the archdeaconry of Northampton, and diocese of Peterborough, rated in the king's books at £8. 0. 5., and in the patronage of Sir C. Knightley, Bart. The church is dedicated to St. Peter and St. Paul. Richard Knightley, in 1667, bequeathed a rent-charge of £24 for a charity school, which is further supported with a voluntary gift of £20 a year by Sir Charles Knightley. A Cluniac priory formerly here was transferred to Daventry.

PRESTON-DEANERY, a parish in the hundred of WYMERSLEY, county of NORTHAMPTON, 4¼ miles (S. E. by S.) from Northampton, containing 67 inhabitants. The living is a vicarage, in the archdeaconry of Northampton, and diocese of Peterborough, rated in the king's books at £7, and in the patronage of Langham Christie, Esq. The church is dedicated to St. Peter and St. Paul.

PRESTON-GUBBALS, a parish in the liberties of the town of SHREWSBURY, county of SALOP, 4¾ miles (N.) from Shrewsbury, containing, with the township of Merrington, 369 inhabitants. The living is a perpetual curacy, united to the vicarage of Prees, in the archdeaconry of Salop, and diocese of Lichfield and Coventry, endowed with £400 private benefaction, and £600 royal bounty. The church is dedicated to St. Martin.

PRESTON-PATRICK, a chapelry in that part of the parish of BURTON in KENDAL which is in KENDAL ward, county of WESTMORLAND, 6 miles (N. W. by W.) from Kirkby-Lonsdale, containing 398 inhabitants.

The living is a perpetual curacy, in the archdeaconry of Richmond, and diocese of Chester, endowed with £400 private benefaction, and £600 royal bounty, and in the patronage of the Inhabitants. The chapel, dedicated to St. Patrick, is a neat building, situated on the acclivity of a hill rising from the eastern bank of the Belo, which is here crossed by the Lancaster canal, in its course through the parish. A school, founded by subscription in 1780, is endowed with an allotment of land, awarded under the enclosure act, and now let for £12. 12. a year, for which ten children receive free instruction. There are marble works in the neighbourhood, where large blocks, raised at Dent in Yorkshire, and conveyed hither, are cut and polished for the trade. Challen, or Chanon hall, stands on the site of an abbey which existed here for a short time, but was ultimately removed to Shap.

PRESTON-QUARTER, a township in the parish of ST. BEES, ALLERDALE ward above Darwent, county of CUMBERLAND, on the south side of the town of Whitehaven, containing 4256 inhabitants. Here are very extensive collieries, the produce of which is shipped at Whitehaven. There is an endowed free school.

PRESTON-RICHARD, a township in the parish of HEVERSHAM, KENDAL ward, county of WESTMORLAND, 6 miles (W. N. W.) from Kirkby-Lonsdale, containing 348 inhabitants. The Kendal canal passes through the township, and on its banks are several coke ovens, and a large coal wharf. At Birkrigg is a burial-ground, termed "the Sepulchre," formerly belonging to the Society of Friends, but now disused. A school is supported by subscription, amounting to about £15 per annum. At End-Moor an antique hammer-head of stone was found in 1770.

PRESTON-WYNNE, a chapelry in the parish of WITHINGTON, hundred of BROXASH, county of HEREFORD, 6½ miles (N. E. by N.) from Hereford, containing 167 inhabitants. The living is a perpetual curacy, in the peculiar jurisdiction and patronage of the Dean of Hereford, endowed with £200 private benefaction, and £200 royal bounty. The chapel is dedicated to the Holy Trinity.

PRESTWICH, a parish with Oldham, in the hundred of SALFORD, county palatine of LANCASTER, 4¾ miles (N. W. by N.) from Manchester, containing 2724 inhabitants. The living is a rectory, in the archdeaconry and diocese of Chester, rated in the king's books at £46. 4. 9½., and in the patronage of Earl Grosvenor. The church, dedicated to St. Mary, has a lofty tower, forming a fine object in the general landscape. Here are manufactories to a very considerable extent. (See OLDHAM.)

PRESTWICK, a township in the parish of PONTELAND, western division of CASTLE ward, county of NORTHUMBERLAND, 6½ miles (N. W. by N.) from Newcastle upon Tyne, containing 155 inhabitants. Prestwick Carr, an extensive marsh, is, in wet seasons, so completely inundated by the river Pont, as to form one vast lake; but in summer, when the waters retire, it affords excellent pasturage common to the neighbouring townships.

PRESTWOOD, a township in the parish of ELLASTONE, southern division of the hundred of TOTMONSLOW, county of STAFFORD, 7 miles (N.) from Uttoxeter, containing 88 inhabitants. It is in the honour of Tutbury, duchy of Lancaster, and within the jurisdiction of a court of pleas held at Tutbury every third Tuesday, for the recovery of debts under 40s.

PRESTWOULD, a parish in the eastern division of the hundred of Goscote, county of Leicester, 3 miles (E.N.E.) from Loughborough, containing, with the chapelry of Hoton, and the townships of Burton on the Wolds, and Coates, 974 inhabitants. The living is a perpetual curacy, in the archdeaconry of Leicester, and diocese of Lincoln, and in the patronage of C. Packe, Esq. The church is dedicated to St. Andrew.

PRIDDY, a parish in the hundred of Wells-Forum, county of Somerset, 4¼ miles (N.N.W.) from Wells, containing 141 inhabitants. The living is a perpetual curacy, annexed to the vicarage of Westbury, in the peculiar jurisdiction of the Archidiaconal Court of Wells. One of the largest cattle fairs in the county is held here annually, on August 21st. In the neighbourhood are vestiges of a Roman encampment and nine barrows.

PRIESTCLIFFE, a township in the parish of Bakewell, hundred of High Peak, county of Derby, 3 miles (S.S.W.) from Tideswell. The population is returned with the chapelry of Taddington. The Rev. Roger Wilkinson, late of this place, gave £400 for the endowment of a charity school, which, having been invested in land, produces £80 per annum.

PRIME-THORP, a township in the parish of Broughton-Astley, hundred of Guthlaxton, county of Leicester, 5½ miles (N. by W.) from Lutterworth, containing 270 inhabitants.

PRINCETHORPE, a hamlet in the parish of Stretton upon Dunsmoor, Rugby division of the hundred of Knightlow, county of Warwick, 6¼ miles (N. by W.) from Southam. The population is returned with the parish.

PRINKNASH-PARK, an extra-parochial district, in the middle division of the hundred of Dudstone and King's Barton, county of Gloucester, 3¼ miles (N. by E.) from Painswick, containing 9 inhabitants.

PRIORS-ASH, county of Somerset.—See ASH (PRIORS).

PRIORS-DEAN, county of Southampton.—See DEAN (PRIORS).

PRIORS-LEE, a chapelry in the parish of Shiffnall, Shiffnall division of the hundred of Brimstree, county of Salop, 3 miles (W. N. W.) from Shiffnall, containing, with Oakengale, 1851 inhabitants. The living is a perpetual curacy, in the archdeaconry of Salop, and diocese of Lichfield and Coventry, endowed with £600 private benefaction, £600 royal bounty, and £1400 parliamentary grant, and in the patronage of the Vicar of Shiffnall.

PRISTON, a parish in the hundred of Keynsham, county of Somerset, 5¼ miles (S. W. by W.) from Bath, containing 286 inhabitants. The living is a rectory, in the archdeaconry of Bath, and diocese of Bath and Wells, rated in the king's books at £12. 18. 4., and in the patronage of the Heir of the late William Vaughan, Esq., a minor. The church is dedicated to St. Luke. Six poor children are taught by a schoolmistress for £20 a year, paid out of the poor's estate.

PRITTLEWELL, a parish in the hundred of Rochford, county of Essex, 19 miles (S. E.) from Chelmsford, containing, with Milton, 1922 inhabitants. The living is a vicarage, in the archdeaconry of Essex, and diocese of London, rated in the king's books at £18.13.4., and in the patronage of the Bishop of London. The church, dedicated to St. Mary, is a handsome structure in the later English style of architecture, with a fine pinnacled tower, which serves as an excellent sea-mark. The parish borders on the Thames, and includes Southend, a noted bathing-place, a short distance above which is Crow Stone, marking the extreme eastern boundary of the jurisdiction of the lord mayor of London, as conservator of the river. A Cluniac priory, in honour of St. Mary, and subordinate to the abbey of Lewes in Sussex, was founded here, in the reign of Henry II., by Robert Fitz-Swaine, which at the dissolution had a revenue of £194. 14. 3. Mrs. Scrattons and others gave a house and land in support of a free school for sixteen poor children.

PRIVETT, a parish in the hundred of Fawley, Fawley division of the county of Southampton, 5¾ miles (N. W. by W.) from Petersfield, containing 229 inhabitants. The living is a perpetual curacy, annexed to the rectory of West Meon, in the peculiar jurisdiction of the Incumbent. This parish is within the jurisdiction of an ancient court, called the Cheyney Court, held at Winchester every Thursday, for the recovery of debts to any amount.

PROBUS, a parish in the western division of the hundred of Powder, county of Cornwall, 2¼ miles (W. by S.) from Grampound, containing, with part of the borough of Grampound, 1353 inhabitants. The living is a vicarage, with the perpetual curacies of Cornelly and Merther, in the archdeaconry of Cornwall, and diocese of Exeter, rated in the king's books at £13. 16. 8., and in the patronage of the Bishop of Exeter. The church is remarkable for the beautiful simplicity of its architecture, and its stately tower, a fine specimen of the later English style, which, rising to the height of one hundred and eight feet, forms a striking contrast with the low thatched dwellings around. There is a place of worship for Wesleyan Methodists. A market was formerly held weekly; and large fairs for horses and cattle are now held, on April 5th and 23rd, July 5th, and September 17th. A free school was founded, in 1688, by Mr. John Williams, who endowed it with about £10 per annum. There is also a trifling endowment in land by William Williams, in augmentation of the master's salary.

PRUDHOE, a township in the parish of Ovingham, eastern division of Tindale ward, county of Northumberland, 12½ miles (W. by S.) from Newcastle upon Tyne, containing 293 inhabitants. There is a place of worship for Wesleyan Methodists, with a Sunday school attached: a school-room was erected in 1823.

PRUDHOE-CASTLE, a township in the parish of Ovingham, eastern division of Tindale ward, county of Northumberland, 12¾ miles (W.) from Newcastle upon Tyne, containing 79 inhabitants. Here was formerly a chapel, dedicated to St. Thomas. On an eminence sloping to the southern bank of the Tyne stood the castle, once the chief baronial seat of the Umfravilles: it has been long in ruins, but its ivy-mantled towers and lofty keep still remain, venerable monuments of its ancient grandeur and importance. Its present possessors are the Percy family, of whom Algernon, the only brother of the Duke of Northumberland, was created Lord Prudhoe, Baron of Prudhoe castle, in 1816.

PUBLOW, a parish in the hundred of KEYNSHAM, county of SOMERSET, ¼ of a mile (N. E.) from Pensford, containing 836 inhabitants. The living is a perpetual curacy, in the archdeaconry of Bath, and diocese of Bath and Wells, and in the patronage of — Cox, Esq.

PUCKINGTON, a parish in the hundred of ABDICK and BULSTONE, county of SOMERSET, 2¾ miles (N.N.E.) from Ilminster, containing 220 inhabitants. The living is a rectory, in the archdeaconry of Taunton, and diocese of Bath and Wells, rated in the king's books at £7. 13. 3½. The Bishop of Bath and Wells presented by lapse in 1787.

PUCKLE-CHURCH, a parish in the hundred of PUCKLE-CHURCH, county of GLOUCESTER, 5¼ miles (S.W. by S.) from Chipping-Sodbury, containing 612 inhabitants. The living is a vicarage, with the perpetual curacies of Abston and Westerleigh, in the archdeaconry and diocese of Gloucester, rated in the king's books at £14. 13. 4., and in the patronage of the Dean and Chapter of Wells. The church, dedicated to St.Thomas à Becket, is partly Norman and partly of later date. The Rev. Henry Berrow, in 1718, founded a free school for ten boys and ten girls : the annual income is £52. 10., of which one-fifth is paid towards the education of the poor of Abston and Wick. This was the site of a royal palace of the Saxon kings of England, in which Edmund received a stab from one Leof, that caused his death. A market was formerly held here, but it has been long disused.

PUDDINGTON, a parish in the hundred of WILLEY, county of BEDFORD, 5 miles (N. by W.) from Harrold, containing 581 inhabitants. The living is a discharged vicarage, in the archdeaconry of Bedford, and diocese of Lincoln, rated in the king's books at £7. 6. 8., endowed with £200 parliamentary grant. R. Orlebar, Esq. was patron in 1801. The church, dedicated to St.Mary, contains several ancient monuments, the principal of which is erected to the memory of General Livesay. The manufacture of thread-lace is carried on here. There is a petrifying spring in the parish; and small shells of the ostroites, belemnitæ, and turbinitæ species are found imbedded in the clay and gravel pits. Canary birds in a wild state are frequently met with in the neighbourhood.

PUDDINGTON, a township in the parish of BURTON, higher division of the hundred of WIRRALL, county palatine of CHESTER, 8 miles (N. W.) from Chester, containing 155 inhabitants.

PUDDINGTON, a parish in the hundred of WITHERIDGE, county of DEVON, 8 miles (W. by S.) from Tiverton, containing 176 inhabitants. The living is a rectory, in the archdeaconry of Barnstaple, and diocese of Exeter, rated in the king's books at £6. 8. 1½. Thomas Welman, Esq. was patron in 1826. Here is a Presbyterian place of worship, with an endowment in land yielding about £35 per annum. A charity school is partly supported by some small benefactions.

PUDDLESTONE, a parish in the hundred of WOLPHY, county of HEREFORD, 5¾ miles (E. by N.) from Leominster, containing, with While and the township of Brockmanton, 316 inhabitants. The living is a discharged vicarage, with While, in the archdeaconry and diocese of Hereford, rated in the king's books at £7. 17. 8½. Thomas Rose, Esq. was patron in 1819. The church is dedicated to St. Peter.

PUDLICOTT, a tything in that part of the parish of CHARLBURY which is in the hundred of CHADLINGTON, county of OXFORD, 4½ miles (S. by W.) from Chipping-Norton. The population is returned with the chapelry of Chilson.

PUDSEY, a chapelry in the parish of CALVERLEY, wapentake of MORLEY, West riding of the county of YORK, 4¼ miles (E.) from Bradford, containing 6229 inhabitants. The living is a perpetual curacy, in the peculiar jurisdiction of the manorial court of Crossley, Bingley, and Pudsey, endowed with £200 private benefaction, and £200 royal bounty, and in the patronage of the Vicar of Calverley. The chapel is dedicated to St. Lawrence. A new church, in the later style of English architecture, was erected in 1823, under the sanction of " His Majesty's Commissioners for building churches;" the amount of contract, including incidental expenses, was £13,362. 1. 10. There are places of worship for Independents and Wesleyan Methodists. The manufacture of woollen cloth is here carried on to a considerable extent. Jacob Simpson, in 1737, bequeathed £100 for the relief of decayed housekeepers, and for teaching poor children.

PULBOROUGH, a parish in the hundred of WEST EASWRITH, rape of ARUNDEL, county of SUSSEX, 9 miles (N. N. E.) from Arundel, containing 1901 inhabitants. The living is a rectory, in the archdeaconry and diocese of Chichester, rated in the king's books at £19. 0. 7½., and in the patronage of the Earl of Egremont. The church, dedicated to St. Mary, is principally in the early style of English architecture. The river Arun, and the Arun canal, pass through the parish.

PULFORD, a parish in the lower division of the hundred of BROXTON, county palatine of CHESTER, comprising the townships of Poulton and Pulford, and containing 318 inhabitants, of which number, 186 are in the township of Pulford, 5¼ miles (S. S. W.) from Chester. The living is a rectory, in the archdeaconry and diocese of Chester, rated in the king's books at £6. 15. 10., and in the patronage of Earl Grosvenor. The church is dedicated to St. Mary. Earl and Countess Grosvenor support two schools in the parish, one for boys, and the other for girls. A Cistercian monastery, a cell to the abbey of Combermere, was founded in 1153, by Robert, the Earl of Chester's baker, the monks being placed in it to pray for the earl while a prisoner in the hands of King Stephen. This establishment, on account of the frequent incursions of the Welch, was removed, in 1214, to Dieulacres in Staffordshire. In a field, called the Castle Hill, are traces of a foss and other remains of an ancient fortification.

PULHAM (EAST), a parish in the hundred of BUCKLAND-NEWTON, Cerne subdivision of the county of DORSET, 7½ miles (S. E.) from Sherborne, containing, with the manor of West Pulham, 272 inhabitants. The living is a rectory, in the archdeaconry of Dorset, and diocese of Bristol, rated in the king's books at £18. 17. 11. Joseph Haseley, Esq. was patron in 1813. The church is dedicated to St. Thomas à Becket. A school is partly supported by some trifling donations.

PULHAM (ST. MARY MAGDALENE), a parish in the hundred of EARSHAM, county of NORFOLK, 3¼ miles (N. W.) from Harleston, containing 1009 inhabitants. The living is a perpetual curacy, annexed to the rectory of Pulham St. Mary the Virgin, in the archdeaconry of Norfolk, and diocese of Norwich. The church, called Pulham Market church, is a neat building with a large square tower, and a handsome north porch. Pulham Market hall, formerly the seat of a junior branch of the Percies, is an ancient edifice, surrounded by an embattled brick wall; the greater part of it was built by William Brampton, a staunch royalist during Kett's rebellion.

PULHAM (ST. MARY the VIRGIN), a parish in the hundred of EARSHAM, county of NORFOLK, 2½ miles (N. W.) from Harleston, containing 797 inhabitants. The living is a rectory, with the perpetual curacy of Pulham St. Mary Magdalene, in the archdeaconry of Norfolk, and diocese of Norwich, rated in the king's books at £33. 6. 8., and in the patronage of the Crown. The church is adorned with numerous shields, also a great quantity of imagery of stone; and the east window exhibits emblems of the Trinity, &c., in stained glass. A rent-charge of £5, the bequest of William Pennóyer, in 1670, is applied for teaching poor children.

PULHAM (WEST), a manor in the parish of EAST PULHAM, hundred of BUCKLAND-NEWTON, Cerne subdivision of the county of DORSET, 9¼ miles (S.E. by S.) from Sherborne. The population is returned with the parish.

PULLOXHILL, a parish in the hundred of FLITT, county of BEDFORD, 2¼ miles (S.W.) from Silsoe, containing 475 inhabitants. The living is a discharged vicarage, in the archdeaconry of Bedford, and diocese of Lincoln, rated in the king's books at £9. 10., and in the patronage of the Countess de Grey. The church is dedicated to St. James. A vein of gold has been discovered here, but the produce is not sufficient to defray the expense of working it.

PULVERBATCH (CHURCH), a parish in the hundred of CONDOVER, county of SALOP, 8 miles (S. W. by S.) from Shrewsbury, containing 539 inhabitants. The living is a rectory, in the archdeaconry of Salop, and diocese of Hereford, rated in the king's books at £10. 13. 4., and in the patronage of Lord Kenyon. The church is dedicated to St. Edith. This parish was distinguished in ancient times for its extensive castle, which had within it a chapel, called the royal free chapel of Pullerbache. It had a charter for a weekly market and an annual fair, granted by Henry III. Courts leet and baron are held twice a year for the manor.

PUNCKNOWLE, a parish in the hundred of UGGSCOMBE, Dorchester division of the county of DORSET, 6½ miles (S.E. by E.) from Bridport, containing 300 inhabitants. The living is a rectory, with West Bexington, in the archdeaconry of Dorset, and diocese of Bristol, rated in the king's books at £14. The Rev. Robert Frome was patron in 1825. The church is dedicated to St. Mary. This parish is bounded on the south by the English channel. A school is supported by subscription.

PURBRIGHT, a parish in the first division of the hundred of WOKING, county of SURREY, 6½ miles (N. W. by N.) from Guildford, containing 472 inhabitants. The living is a perpetual curacy, in the archdeaconry of Surrey, and diocese of Winchester, endowed with £600 royal bounty, and £400 parliamentary grant, and in the patronage of Henry Halsey, Esq. The church is dedicated to St. Michael. The Basingstoke canal passes through the parish.

PURFLEET, a township in the parish of WEST THURROCK, hundred of CHAFFORD, county of ESSEX, 16½ miles (E. by S.) from London. The population is returned with the parish. It is situated at the mouth of a rivulet, which empties itself into the Thames. The village is chiefly inhabited by people employed in the extensive lime-works and chalk-pits. The walks among the vast caverns which have been excavated in the neighbourhood are romantic, and the views from the elevations remarkably fine. Here are considerable bomb-proof magazines for gunpowder, belonging to government.

PURITON, a parish in the hundred of HUNTSPILL and PURITON, county of SOMERSET, 4 miles (N. N. E.) from Bridg-water, containing, with Woollavington, 350 inhabitants. The living is a discharged vicarage, united with that of Woollavington, in the archdeaconry of Wells, and diocese of Bath and Wells, rated in the king's books at £6. 15. 10. The church is dedicated to St. Michael. The navigable river Parret runs on the south-west of this parish. A small school is supported from the poor's estate.

PURLEIGH, a parish in the hundred of DENGIE, county of ESSEX, 4 miles (S. by W.) from Maldon, containing 967 inhabitants. The living is a rectory, annexed to the Provostship of Oriel College, Oxford, and holden without institution, in the archdeaconry of Essex, and diocese of London, rated in the king's books at £25. The church, dedicated to All Saints, is large and handsome, with an embattled tower of flint and stone. The parish school is supported by subscription.

PURLEY, a parish in the hundred of THEALE, county of BERKS, 4 miles (N. W. by W.) from Reading, containing 196 inhabitants. The living is a rectory, in the archdeaconry of Berks, and diocese of Salisbury, rated in the king's books at £12. 17. 3½., and in the patronage of the Crown. The church, dedicated to St. Mary, is a very neat structure.

PURSON, a hamlet in the parish and hundred of KING'S SUTTON, county of NORTHAMPTON, 4¾ miles (W. N. W.) from Brackley. The population is returned with the parish.

PURTON, a parish in the hundred of HIGHWORTH, CRICKLADE, and STAPLE, county of WILTS, 3¾ miles (N. N. E.) from Wootton-Bassett, containing, with the hamlet of Braydon, 1766 inhabitants. The living is a vicarage, in the archdeaconry of Wilts, and diocese of Salisbury, rated in the king's books at £22. 17. 6., and in the patronage of the Earl of Shaftesbury. The church, dedicated to St. Mary, is a handsome structure, with a lofty tower and spire. There is a place of worship for Wesleyan Methodists. Fairs are held for cattle, on the Tuesday before May 6th, and the Friday after September 19th. Miriam Stevens, in 1723, bequeathed a rent-charge of £17. 10. for the support of a free school.

PUSEY, county of BERKS.—See PEWSEY.

PUTFORD (EAST), a parish in the hundred of SHEBBEAR, county of DEVON, 8½ miles (W. by S.) from Great Torrington, containing 194 inhabitants. The living is a perpetual curacy, annexed to the vicarage of Buckland-Brewer, in the archdeaconry of Barnstaple, and diocese of Exeter.

PUTFORD (WEST), a parish in the hundred of BLACK TORRINGTON, county of DEVON, 9 miles (W. S. W.)

from Great Torrington, containing 425 inhabitants. The living is a rectory, in the archdeaconry of Totness, and diocese of Exeter, rated in the king's books at £9. 11. 0½., and in the patronage of Lord Clinton.

PUTLEY, a parish in the hundred of GREYTREE, county of HEREFORD, 5¾ miles (W.) from Ledbury, containing 163 inhabitants. The living is a discharged rectory, in the peculiar jurisdiction of the Dean of Hereford, rated in the king's books at £3. 18. 4., and in the patronage of the Dean and Chapter of Hereford. There are hop plantations in the neighbourhood.

PUTNEY, a parish in the western division of the hundred of BRIXTON, county of SURREY, 4 miles (S. W.) from London, containing 3394 inhabitants. In Domesday-book this place is styled *Putelei*, and it was subsequently called *Puttenheath*, or *Pottenheath*, since contracted into its present name. The village is situated on the southern bank of the Thames, opposite to Fulham, with which it is connected by a wooden bridge. Queen Elizabeth was a frequent visitor here at the house of Mr. Lacy, who also had the honour to entertain James I., a short time before his coronation. During the civil war in the reign of Charles I., a bridge of boats was constructed across the Thames, and forts were built on each side of the river, by order of the Earl of Essex, on the retreat of the royalists to Kingston, after the battle of Brentford; and in 1647, the head-quarters of the army under Cromwell were fixed at Putney, while the king was a prisoner at Hampton Court. An ancient ferry over the Thames at this place is mentioned in Domesday-book, as yielding to the lord of the manor of Wimbledon a toll of twenty shillings per annum. In 1729, the bridge was erected in pursuance of an act of parliament, at the expense of £23,975, subscribed by thirty shareholders, who purchased the ferry for £8000. Here was a fishery at the time of the Norman Conquest, and smelts are now caught in great abundance. Putney is within the jurisdiction of the court of requests for the western division of the hundred of Brixton, for the recovery of debts under £5. The living is a perpetual curacy, in the deanery of Croydon, which is within the peculiar jurisdiction of the Archbishop of Canterbury, endowed with £600 parliamentary grant, and in the patronage of the Dean and Chapter of Worcester. The church, dedicated to St. Mary, was founded as a chapel of ease to Wimbledon, and was rebuilt about the reign of Henry VII.: it has a handsome stone tower at the west end, and at the east end of the south aisle is a small chantry chapel, erected by Nicholas West, Bishop of Ely, and having the roof adorned with rich tracery, interspersed with the arms of the founder, who was a native of Putney, and became a favourite of Henry VIII., by whom he was employed in various embassies. In 1684, Thomas Martyn bequeathed lands for the foundation and support of a charity school for twenty boys; and by a decree of the court of Chancery, in 1715, the property was vested in trustees: it produces about £270 per annum, from which the master receives £80 per annum, and the boys are boarded, clothed, and educated. An alms-house for twelve poor women, dedicated to the Holy Trinity, was erected by Sir Abraham Dawes, who, by will in 1639, endowed it with a rent-charge of £40, which, with subsequent benefactions, produces an income of £110 per annum. On Putney heath, to the

south of the village, is an obelisk, erected by the corporation of London, with an inscription commemorating an experiment made, in 1776, by David Hartley, Esq., to prove the efficacy of a method of building houses fire-proof, which he had invented, and for which he obtained a grant from parliament of £2500. On the heath also is a semaphore station, forming part of the line of communication between the Admiralty office and Portsmouth. Putney was the birthplace of Bishop West, already mentioned; of Thomas Cromwell, who was made Earl of Essex by Henry VIII., but perished on the scaffold; and of Edward Gibbon, the celebrated author of the "Decline and Fall of the Roman Empire," born in 1737, and died in London, in 1794. John Toland, a noted freethinking writer, died at Putney in 1722, and was interred in the churchyard; and Robert Wood, Under Secretary of State, who published "The Ruins of Palmyra," and other curious archaeological works, was interred in the new burial-ground, in 1771.

PUTTENHAM, a parish in the hundred of DACORUM, county of HERTFORD, 3¾ miles (N. W.) from Tring, containing 112 inhabitants. The living is a rectory, in the archdeaconry of Huntingdon, and diocese of Lincoln, rated in the king's books at £10. 1. 0½., and in the patronage of the Bishop of Lincoln. The church is dedicated to St. Mary: the tower is built of flint and stone in square compartments, and the ceiling of the nave, which is of carved oak, is supported by figures representing some of the Apostles: there are on the cross beams other figures habited as ecclesiastics.

PUTTENHAM, a parish in the first division of the hundred of GODALMING, county of SURREY, 4¼ miles (W. by S.) from Guildford, containing 389 inhabitants. The living is a rectory, with the perpetual curacy of Wanborough, in the archdeaconry of Surrey, and diocese of Winchester, rated in the king's books at £11. 17. 11., and in the patronage of the Crown. The church is dedicated to St. John the Baptist.

PUXTON, a parish in the hundred of WINTERSTOKE, county of SOMERSET, 6 miles (N. by W.) from Axbridge, containing 137 inhabitants. The living is a perpetual curacy, in the jurisdiction of the peculiar court of Banwell in the Cathedral Church of Wells, endowed with £200 private benefaction, and £600 royal bounty, and in the patronage of the Dean and Chapter of Bristol.

PYLLE, a parish in the hundred of WHITESTONE, county of SOMERSET, 3½ miles (S. by W.) from Shepton-Mallet, containing 176 inhabitants. The living is a discharged rectory, in the archdeaconry of Wells, and diocese of Bath and Wells, rated in the king's books at £8. 19. 9½., and in the patronage of E. B. Portman, Esq. The church is dedicated to St. Thomas à Becket. The old Roman Fosse-way passes through the parish.

PYRFORD, a parish in the first division of the hundred of GODLEY, county of SURREY, 1¼ mile (N. N. W.) from Ripley, containing 294 inhabitants. The living is a discharged vicarage, annexed to the rectory of Wisley, in the archdeaconry of Surrey, and diocese of Winchester. The Wey and Arun canal passes through the parish.

PYWORTHY, a parish in the hundred of BLACK TORRINGTON, county of DEVON, 2¼ miles (W. S. W.) from Holsworthy, containing 630 inhabitants. The living is a rectory, in the archdeaconry of Totness, and diocese of Exeter, rated in the king's books at £27. 8. 4. The Rev. T. H. Kingdon was patron in 1826. The church is dedicated to St. Swithin. The Bude and Launceston canal passes through the parish.

Q.

QUADRING, a parish in the wapentake of KIRTON, parts of HOLLAND, county of LINCOLN, 8½ miles (N. by W.) from Spalding, containing 704 inhabitants. The living is a discharged vicarage, united to that of Wigtoft, in the archdeaconry and diocese of Lincoln, rated in the king's books at £10. 1. 3. The church is dedicated to St. Margaret. There are several endowments for the education of children, the principal of which is a rent-charge of £10, the gift of Thomas Cowling, in 1701.

QUAINTON, a parish in the hundred of ASHENDON, county of BUCKINGHAM, 6 miles (N. W.) from Aylesbury, containing, with the hamlets of Denham, Doddershall, and Shipton-Lee, 1017 inhabitants. The living is a rectory, in the archdeaconry of Buckingham, and diocese of Lincoln, rated in the king's books at £30. 12. 1., and in the patronage of the Rev. F. Ekins. The church, dedicated to St. Mary, has lately received an addition of one hundred and thirty free sittings, the Incorporated Society for the enlargement of churches and chapels having granted £15 towards defraying the expense: it contains, among other interesting monuments, a memorial to the learned orientalist, Richard Brett, one of the translators of the Bible, and a Fellow of Chelsea College. There is a place of worship for Baptists. An almshouse was founded here, about 1688, for eight poor persons, pursuant to the will of Richard Winwood, Esq., who bequeathed £200 for its erection, and endowed it with lands which afford a weekly allowance of two shillings, and some clothing, to each inmate. There is a school with a small annual income.

QUANTOXHEAD (EAST), a parish in the hundred of WILLITON and FREEMANNERS, county of SOMERSET, 15½ miles (N. W. by W.) from Bridg-water, containing 276 inhabitants. The living is a rectory, in the archdeaconry of Taunton, and diocese of Bath and Wells, rated in the king's books at £9. 8. 4. J. F. Luttrell, Esq. and others were patrons in 1818. The church is dedicated to St. Mary.

QUANTOXHEAD (WEST), a parish in the hundred of WILLITON and FREEMANNERS, county of SOMERSET, 15½ miles (W. N. W.) from Bridg-water, containing 225 inhabitants. The living is a discharged rectory, in the archdeaconry of Taunton, and diocese of Bath and Wells, rated in the king's books at £11. 8. 8. Miss Balch was patroness in 1814. The church is dedicated to St. Ethelred.

QUARLES, an extra-parochial district, in the northern division of the hundred of GREENHOE, county of NORFOLK, 3¾ miles (W. N. W.) from New Walsingham, containing 23 inhabitants.

QUARLEY, a parish in the hundred of ANDOVER, Andover division of the county of SOUTHAMPTON, 7 miles (W. by S.) from Andover, containing 213 inhabitants. The living is a rectory, in the archdeaconry and diocese of Winchester, rated in the king's books at £15. 12. 1., and in the patronage of the Master and

Brethren of St. Katherine's Hospital, London. The church is dedicated to St. Michael. The Rev. Thomas Sheppard, D.D., and Richard Cox, Esq., in 1802, endowed a free school for poor children; the income is about £16 a year ; the school-house was erected by Mrs. Sheppard. On the summit of Quarley Mount, five miles north-west from Danebury Hill, is a considerable ancient camp with quadruple intrenchments still visible, on the south side ; those on the east have been nearly obliterated by the plough : various tumuli are scattered over the adjacent downs.

QUARLTON, a township in the parish of BOLTON, hundred of SALFORD, county palatine of LANCASTER, 4¾ miles (N. N. E.) from Bolton, containing 320 inhabitants.

QUARNDON, a parish in the hundred of MORLESTON and LITCHURCH, county of DERBY, 3 miles (N. N. W.) from Derby, containing 438 inhabitants. The living is a perpetual curacy, in the archdeaconry of Derby, and diocese of Lichfield and Coventry, endowed with £200 private benefaction, and £800 royal bounty, and in the patronage of Lord Scarsdale. Sir John Curzon, in 1725, bequeathed an annuity of £20 for the support of a free school for twenty poor children of Kedleston, Quarndon, Weston, and Ravensdale park. Near this place is a chalybeate spring, which was considerably resorted to upwards of a century ago, and is still visited in the summer, the water being highly beneficial in cases of debility.

QUARNFORD, a chapelry in the parish of ALLSTONEFIELD, northern division of the hundred of TOTMONSLOW, county of STAFFORD, 8 miles (N. by E.) from Leek, containing 695 inhabitants. The living is a perpetual curacy, in the archdeaconry of Stafford, and diocese of Lichfield and Coventry, endowed with £400 royal bounty, and £1200 parliamentary grant, and in the patronage of the Freeholders.

QUARRENDON, a parish in the hundred of ASHENDON, county of BUCKINGHAM, 2¼ miles (N. N. W.) from Aylesbury, containing 68 inhabitants. The living is a perpetual curacy, annexed to the vicarage of Bierton, in the peculiar jurisdiction of the Dean and Chapter of Lincoln. The church, dedicated to St. Peter, is fast hastening to decay ; it was founded by John Farnham, about 1392, and rebuilt in the reign of Elizabeth, by Sir Henry Lee, to some of the deceased members of whose family it contains some handsome monuments. A great storm happened here in 1570, which did considerable damage to property of different kinds.

QUARRINGTON, a township in the parish of KELLOE, southern division of EASINGTON ward, county palatine of DURHAM, 4½ miles (S. E.) from Durham, containing 177 inhabitants. It was anciently the chief town of a district called Queringdonshire. There are two collieries in the neighbourhood.

QUARRINGTON, a parish in the wapentake of ASWARDHURN, parts of KESTEVEN, county of LINCOLN, 1½ mile (S. W. by S.) from Sleaford, containing 132 inhabitants. The living is a rectory, in the archdeaconry and diocese of Lincoln, rated in the king's books at £7. 2. 3½., and in the patronage of the Marquis of Bristol. The church, dedicated to St. Botolph, is partly in the early, and partly in the decorated, style of English architecture : the font is of later date and curiously shaped.

QUATFORD, a parish partly in the borough of BRIDGENORTH, but chiefly in the hundred of STOTTES-DEN, county of SALOP, 2 miles (S. E.) from Bridgenorth, containing, with the township of Eardington, 411 inhabitants. The living is a perpetual curacy, in the jurisdiction of the royal peculiar court of Bridgenorth, endowed with £14 per annum private benefaction, £800 royal bounty, and £1000 parliamentary grant, and in the patronage of W. Whitmore, Esq. The church is dedicated to St. Mary Magdalene.

QUATT-MALVERN, a parish partly within the liberties of the borough of BRIDGENORTH, but chiefly in the hundred of STOTTESDEN, county of SALOP, 4½ miles (S. E.) from Bridgenorth, containing 342 inhabitants. The living is a rectory, in the archdeaconry of Salop, and diocese of Lichfield and Coventry, rated in the king's books at £14. 5., and in the patronage of W. Whitmore, Esq. The church, dedicated to St. Andrew, was rebuilt in 1763, when representations of the Seven Charities, the Day of Judgment, &c., were discovered painted on the walls.

QUEDGLEY, a parish partly in the middle division of the hundred of DUDSTONE and KING'S BARTON, but chiefly in the upper division of the hundred of WHITSTONE, county of GLOUCESTER, 3¼ miles (S. W.) from Gloucester, containing, with the hamlet of Woolstrop, 263 inhabitants. The living is a perpetual curacy, in the archdeaconry and diocese of Gloucester, and in the patronage of the Duke of Manchester. The church is dedicated to St. James. The navigable river Severn runs on the north, and the Gloucester and Berkeley canal passes through the parish.

QUEENBOROUGH, a borough and parish (formerly a market town) having exclusive jurisdiction, though locally in the liberty of the Isle of Sheppy, lathe of SCRAY, county of KENT, 15 miles (N. E.) from Maidstone, and 45 (E. by S.) from London, containing 881 inhabitants. This place, then called Cyning-burgh, was a residence of the Anglo-Saxon kings; their castle was near the entrance of the Swale, and afterwards received the name of the castle of Sheppy: in the reign of Edward III., it was entirely rebuilt, on a magnificent scale, from a plan by William of Wykeham, afterwards Bishop of Winchester. That king, on visiting it for a few days, made the place a free borough, and, in honour of his Queen Philippa, conferred its present name : in 1366, he incorporated it by charter, and three years afterwards gave it the staple of wool. The castle was repaired by Henry VIII., in 1536, at which time he erected several others for the defence of the coasts ; but, on a survey made by order of parliament, in 1650, being found unserviceable as a fortress in modern warfare, it was soon afterwards demolished. The town is situated near the West Swale, which is here navigable, and consists principally of one wide street; the houses in general are modern ; and the inhabitants are supplied with water from the Castle well. The chief source of employment is fishing and oyster-dredging, and the lobster trade,

Seal and Arms.

large supplies being brought from Norway and Sweden and sent to the London market : there is also a copperas manufactory. Two weekly markets and two annual fairs were granted by Edward III., but at present only one fair is held, on the 5th of August. The first charter of incorporation was granted by the same monarch, and that now in force by Charles I., under which the corporation consists of a mayor, four jurats, and two bailiffs, with a recorder, chamberlain, town clerk, and other officers. The mayor and senior jurat are justices of the peace, and have exclusive jurisdiction within the borough : a court of session, half-yearly, is held before the recorder and magistrates. The mayor and the steward, who are elected by the select body of mayor, jurats, and bailiffs, are empowered under their charter to hold a court of record "on Monday, from three weeks to three weeks," for pleas to an unlimited amount, but it has fallen into disuse. The guildhall is a neat edifice near the centre of the town. The freedom is obtained by the eldest son of a freeman, being a native of the borough, and by servitude under freemen residing within it. This borough first sent representatives to parliament in the 13th of Elizabeth, since which it has continued to return two: the right of election is vested in the mayor, jurats, bailiffs, and burgesses : the number of voters is about four hundred : the mayor is the returning officer.

The living is a perpetual curacy, in the archdeaconry and diocese of Canterbury, endowed with £600 private benefaction, £200 royal bounty, and £1600 parliamentary grant, and in the patronage of the Mayor and Corporation. The church, dedicated to the Holy Trinity, has an ancient tower at the west end. There is a place of worship for Independents. A school for the education of one hundred children of freemen is principally supported by the voluntary contributions of the corporation and the representatives of the borough: the schoolmaster receives £2 per annum, out of the dividends of £1000 three per cent. consols., bequeathed to the corporation for this and other purposes, in 1813, by Mr. Richard Webb. The only remains of the old castle are the moat and a very deep well, which latter was cleared out by order of the commissioners of the Navy, on account of the want of water at Sheerness. Here was anciently an hospital, dedicated to St. John.

QUEENHILL, a chapelry in that part of the parish of RIPPLE which is in the lower division of the hundred of PERSHORE, county of WORCESTER, 3 miles (S. S. E.) from Upton upon Severn, containing 94 inhabitants.

QUENIBOROUGH, a parish in the eastern division of the hundred of GOSCOTE, county of LEICESTER, 6¼ miles (N. E. by N.) from Leicester, containing 469 inhabitants. The living is a discharged vicarage, in the archdeaconry of Leicester, and diocese of Lincoln, rated in the king's books at £8, endowed with £200 private benefaction, and £200 royal bounty. E. L. Loveden, Esq. was patron in 1802. The church is dedicated to St. Mary.

QUENBY, a hamlet in that part of the parish of HUNGERTON which is in the eastern division of the hundred of GOSCOTE, county of LEICESTER, 7 miles (E. by N.) from Leicester, containing 30 inhabitants. The manor-house is a large and curious specimen of ancient domestic architecture.

4 E

QUENDON, a parish in the hundred of UTTLES-FORD, county of ESSEX, 4½ miles (N.) from Stansted-Mountfitchet, containing 156 inhabitants. The living is a discharged rectory, in the jurisdiction of the Commissary of Essex and Herts, concurrently with the Consistorial Court of the Bishop of London, rated in the king's books at £9, and in the patronage of Henry Cranmer, Esq.

QUENNINGTON, a parish in the hundred of BRIGHTWELLS-BARROW, county of GLOUCESTER, 2 miles (N.) from Fairford, containing 345 inhabitants. The living is a rectory, in the archdeaconry and diocese of Gloucester, rated in the king's books at £7. 18. 4. M. H. Beach, Esq. was patron in 1822. The church, dedicated to St. Swithin, has enriched Norman doors, and has lately received an addition of sixty-four free sittings, the Incorporated Society for the enlargement of churches and chapels having granted £60 towards defraying the expense. Here was formerly a preceptory of Knights Hospitallers of St. John of Jerusalem, founded before the reign of John, the revenue of which, at the dissolution, was valued at £137. 7. 1.

QUERNMOOR, a township in that part of the parish of LANCASTER which is in the hundred of LONSDALE, south of the sands, county palatine of LANCASTER, 3¼ miles (E.) from Lancaster, containing 672 inhabitants.

QUETHIOCK, a parish in the middle division of the hundred of EAST, county of CORNWALL, 4 miles (E.) from Liskeard, containing 684 inhabitants. The living is a vicarage, in the archdeaconry of Cornwall, and diocese of Exeter, rated in the king's books at £15. 11. 0½., and in the patronage of the Bishop of Exeter. The church is a building of the eleventh century. The parish is bounded on the east by the river Lynher, and on the west by the Tide.

QUIDDENHAM, a parish in the hundred of GUILT-CROSS, county of NORFOLK, 2 miles (E. by N.) from East Harling, containing 121 inhabitants. The living is a discharged rectory, in the archdeaconry of Norfolk, and diocese of Norwich, rated in the king's books at £8. 4. 6½., and in the patronage of the Earl of Albemarle. The church is dedicated to St. Andrew.

QUINTON, a parish in the upper division of the hundred of KIFTSGATE, county of GLOUCESTER, 7 miles (N.N.E.) from Chipping-Campden, containing, with the hamlet of Admington, 598 inhabitants. The living is a vicarage, in the archdeaconry and diocese of Gloucester, rated in the king's books at £18. 13. 4., and in the patronage of the Dean and Chapter of Worcester. The church, dedicated to St. Swithin, is a large handsome structure, in the Norman style, supposed to have been erected by the Laceys, soon after the Conquest.

QUINTON, a parish in the hundred of WY-MERSLEY, county of NORTHAMPTON, 4½ miles (S.S.E.) from Northampton, containing 115 inhabitants. The living is a rectory, in the archdeaconry of Northampton, and diocese of Peterborough, rated in the king's books at £11. 3. 9., and in the patronage of the Crown. The church is dedicated to St. John the Baptist.

QUOISLEY, a joint township with Marbury, in the parish of MARBURY, hundred of NANTWICH, county palatine of CHESTER, 3¼ miles (N. by E.) from Whitchurch. The population is returned with Marbury.

QUORNDON, a chapelry in the parish of BARROW upon SOAR, western division of the hundred of Gos-COTE, county of LEICESTER, 1½ mile (N.W.) from Mountsorrel, containing 1503 inhabitants. The living is a perpetual curacy, in the archdeaconry of Leicester, and diocese of Lincoln, endowed with £200 private benefaction, and £400 royal bounty, and in the patronage of the Vicar of Barrow. The church is dedicated to St. Bartholomew. Baptists and Primitive and Wesleyan Methodists have each a place of worship here. Stocking weaving and the manufacture of warp and bobbin twist lace afford employment to a great portion of the inhabitants. The Loughborough canal passes through the northern part of the parish, and joins the river Soar. Thomas Rawlins, in 1691, gave a rent-charge of £45. 10. for apprenticing poor boys, and to a schoolmaster for teaching six boys.

QUY, a chapelry in the parish of STOW, hundred of STAINE, county of CAMBRIDGE, 4¾ miles (E. by N.) from Cambridge. The population is returned with the parish.

R.

RABY, a township in the parish of NESTON, higher division of the hundred of WIRRALL, county palatine of CHESTER, 2 miles (N.E.) from Great Neston, containing 145 inhabitants.

RABY, a joint township with Keverstone, in the parish of STAINDROP, south-western division of DARLINGTON ward, county palatine of DURHAM, 6½ miles (N.E. by E.) from Barnard-Castle, containing 203 inhabitants. Raby castle, situated on an eminence commanding a vast prospect, is a noble and extensive pile, surrounded with ramparts and a deep fosse, enclosing an area of two acres; from its stately exterior, which retains most of its original appearance, a good idea may be formed of the grandeur of a baronial mansion in ancient times; the style of the south front, with the elegant symmetry of its windows, have at once a pleasing and sublime effect; the interior has been much modernised, and comprises numerous convenient apartments, furnished with great elegance. A carriage-road now passes over the site of the great hall, or ancient place of rendezvous, which was a truly magnificent apartment, having two rows of octagonal piers and a beautiful groined roof.

RACKENFORD, a parish in the hundred of WITHE-RIDGE, county of DEVON, 8¼ miles (N.W. by W.) from Tiverton, containing 395 inhabitants. The living is a rectory, in the archdeaconry of Barnstaple, and diocese of Exeter, rated in the king's books at £19. 17. 3½. Thomas Comins, Esq. was patron in 1822. The church is dedicated to All Saints. A weekly market and an annual fair were granted in 1235; the former has been long disused, but a small cattle fair is still held on the Wednesday before September 19th. Courts leet and baron are held here. Charles Kempe, a blacksmith, gave £13 a year, which Mary Ayre, in 1695, augmented to £15, for the education of poor children.

RACKHEATH, a parish in the hundred of TAVER-HAM, county of NORFOLK, 5 miles (N.E. by N.) from Norwich, containing 260 inhabitants. The living is a discharged rectory, in the archdeaconry and diocese of Norwich, rated in the king's books at £6. 13. 4., and in the patronage of Edward Stracey, Esq. The church is dedicated to All Saints. Rackheath formerly comprised two villages and parishes, Rackheath Magna and Rackheath Parva, but the church of the latter, which was dedicated to the Holy Trinity, no longer exists, and the livings have been consolidated. Here was anciently a small priory, the revenue of which was valued, in 1428, at £2. 1. 3.

RACTON, a parish in the hundred of WESTBOURN and SINGLETON, rape of CHICHESTER, county of SUSSEX, 6½ miles (N. W. by W.) from Chichester, containing 100 inhabitants. The living is a rectory, with Lordington, in the archdeaconry and diocese of Chichester, rated in the king's books at £5. 19. 2., and in the patronage of the Dean and Chapter of Chichester. The church is principally in the early style of English architecture.

RADBOURN, a parish in the hundred of APPLETREE, county of DERBY, 4½ miles (W.) from Derby, containing 260 inhabitants. The living is a rectory, in the archdeaconry of Derby, and diocese of Lichfield and Coventry, rated in the king's books at £8. 3. 4., and in the patronage of E. J. Chandos Pole, Esq. The church is dedicated to St. Andrew: near it are slight remains of the ancient hall. A school was founded, in 1683, by German Pole, Esq., the present annual income of which is £15. 10., besides a moiety of the profits of a lime-kiln, lately let for upwards of £100 per annum. Radbourn is in the honour of Tutbury, duchy of Lancaster, and within the jurisdiction of a court of pleas held at Tutbury every third Tuesday, for the recovery of debts under 40s.

RADBOURN (LOWER), an extra-parochial district, in the Southam division of the hundred of KNIGHTLOW, county of WARWICK, 3¾ miles (S.S.E.) from Southam, containing 30 inhabitants.

RADBOURN (UPPER), an extra-parochial district, in the Southam division of the hundred of KNIGHTLOW, county of WARWICK, 3½ miles (S. S.E.) from Southam, containing 14 inhabitants.

RADCLIFFE, a parish in the hundred of SALFORD, county palatine of LANCASTER, 2½ miles (S. S. W.) from Bury, containing 3089 inhabitants. The living is a rectory, in the archdeaconry and diocese of Chester, rated in the king's books at £21. 0. 5., endowed with £200 private benefaction, and £1900 parliamentary grant, and in the patronage of the Earl of Wilton. Besides the parish church, a neat chapel of ease has been recently erected, at the expense of £5000, defrayed by Countess Grosvenor. The cotton manufacture is here carried on to a considerable extent; and several coal mines are worked in the neighbourhood. The Bolton and Bury canal passes near the village.

RADCLIFFE upon SOAR, county of NOTTINGHAM.—See RATCLIFFE upon SOAR.

RADCLIFFE on TRENT, county of NOTTINGHAM.— See RATCLIFFE on TRENT.

RADCLIVE, a parish in the hundred and county of BUCKINGHAM, 1¾ mile (W.) from Buckingham, containing, with the hamlet of Chackmore, 296 inhabitants. The living is a rectory, in the archdeaconry of Buckingham, and diocese of Lincoln, rated in the king's books at £8. 1. 3., and in the patronage of the Warden and Fellows of New College, Oxford. The church is dedicated to St. John the Evangelist. The river Ouse

runs through the parish. Here was formerly a chantry, but there are no remains of it. The old manor-house has been converted into a farm-house.

RADCUTT, a hamlet in that part of the parish of LANGFORD which is in the hundred of BAMPTON, county of OXFORD, 4½ miles (E. by N.) from Lechlade, containing 30 inhabitants.

RADDINGTON, a parish in the hundred of WILLITON and FREEMANNERS, county of SOMERSET, 4¾ miles (W. S. W.) from Wiveliscombe, containing 101 inhabitants. The living is a discharged rectory, in the archdeaconry of Taunton, and diocese of Bath and Wells, rated in the king's books at £8. 7. 8½. Richard Darch, Esq. was patron in 1807. The church is dedicated to St. Michael.

RADFORD, a hamlet in that part of the parish of ST. MICHAEL which is in the county of the city of COVENTRY, 1¾ mile (N. N. W.) from Coventry, containing 206 inhabitants.

RADFORD, a parish in the southern division of the wapentake of BROXTOW, county of NOTTINGHAM, 1 mile (W. by N.) from Nottingham, containing 4806 inhabitants. The living is a discharged vicarage, in the archdeaconry of Nottingham, and diocese of York, rated in the king's books at £3. 9. 4½., endowed with £200 royal bounty, and in the patronage of the Crown. The church, dedicated to St. Peter, has lately received an addition of one hundred sittings, of which fifty are free, the Incorporated Society for the enlargement of churches and chapels having granted £100 towards defraying the expense. Various branches of manufacture, similar to those at Nottingham, are carried on here to a considerable extent. A priory of Black canons, was founded here, about 1102, by William de Luvitot, which, at the dissolution, had a revenue of £302. 6. 10.

RADFORD, a hamlet in the parish of CHURCH-ENSTONE, hundred of CHADLINGTON, county of OXFORD, containing 74 inhabitants.

RADFORD-SEMELE, a parish in the Kenilworth division of the hundred of KNIGHTLOW, county of WARWICK, 4 miles (E.) from Warwick, containing 472 inhabitants. The living is a discharged vicarage, in the archdeaconry of Coventry, and diocese of Lichfield and Coventry, rated in the king's books at £5. 16. 0½., endowed with £200 royal bounty, and in the patronage of H. G. Lewis, Esq. The church is dedicated to St. Nicholas. The Warwick and Napton canal passes through the parish.

RADIPOLE, a parish in the hundred of CULLIFORD-TREE, Dorchester division of the county of DORSET, 2½ miles (N. N.W.) from Melcombe-Regis, containing 226 inhabitants. The living was formerly a discharged rectory, in the archdeaconry of Dorset, and diocese of Bristol, rated in the king's books at £11. 5. 5., but the church at Melcombe-Regis having been made parochial, in the 1st of James I., this church was declared to be the chapel of ease: it is dedicated to St. Mary. The parish is situated at the upper end of Weymouth harbour.

RADLEY, a parish in the hundred of HORMER, county of BERKS, 2½ miles (N. E. by E.) from Abingdon, containing, with part of the chapelry of Kennington, and the liberty of Thruppwick, 500 inhabitants. The living is a donative, in the patronage of Sir George Bower, Bart. The church is dedicated to St. James.

4 E 2

RADNAGE, a parish in the hundred of DESBO-ROUGH, county of BUCKINGHAM, 6 miles (N. W. by W.) from High Wycombe, containing 366 inhabitants. The living is a rectory, in the archdeaconry of Buckingham, and diocese of Lincoln, rated in the king's books at £6. 13. 11½., and in the patronage of the Crown. The church is dedicated to St. Mary. There is a place of worship for Wesleyan Methodists.

RADNOR, a township in that part of the parish of ASTBURY which is in the hundred of NORTHWICH, county palatine of CHESTER, 1¾ mile (N. W.) from Congleton, containing 14 inhabitants.

RADSTOCK, a parish in the hundred of KILMERS-DON, county of SOMERSET, 7½ miles (N.W.) from Frome, containing 902 inhabitants. The living is a rectory, in the archdeaconry of Wells, and diocese of Bath and Wells, rated in the king's books at £6. 11. 0½., and in the patronage of Earl Waldegrave. The church is dedicated to St. Nicholas. There is a place of worship for Wesleyan Methodists. Coal mines are in operation in the vicinity. A railway runs through the village, and the old Fosse-road passes through the parish. Radstock gives title of baron to a branch of the family of Waldegrave.

RADSTON, a parish in the hundred of KING'S SUT-TON, county of NORTHAMPTON, 2½ miles (N.) from Brackley, containing 212 inhabitants. The living is a perpetual curacy, in the archdeaconry of Northampton, and diocese of Peterborough, endowed with £200 private benefaction, and £800 royal bounty. W. Holbech, Esq. was patron in 1812. The church is dedicated to St. Lawrence.

RADWAY, a parish in the Kington division of the hundred of KINGTON, county of WARWICK, 3¼ miles (S. E. by E.) from Kington, containing 346 inhabitants. The living is a discharged vicarage, in the archdeacon-ry of Coventry, and diocese of Lichfield and Coventry, rated in the king's books at £5. 12., and in the pa-tronage of the Crown. The church is dedicated to St. Peter.

RADWELL, a hamlet in the parish of FELMERS-HAM, hundred of WILLEY, county of BEDFORD, 7 miles (N. W. by N.) from Bedford, containing 168 inha-bitants. There is a place of worship for Wesleyan Methodists.

RADWELL, a parish in the hundred of ODSEY, county of HERTFORD, 1½ mile (N.W. by N.) from Baldock, containing 91 inhabitants. The living is a rectory, in the archdeaconry of Huntingdon, and dio-cese of Lincoln, rated in the king's books at £13. 6. 8., and in the patronage of Francis Pym, Esq. The church is dedicated to All Saints.

RADWINTER, a parish in the hundred of FRESH-WELL, county of ESSEX, 4½ miles (N.) from Thaxted, containing 773 inhabitants. The living is a rectory, in the jurisdiction of the Commissary of Essex and Herts, concurrently with the Consistorial Court of the Bishop of London, rated in the king's books at £21. 12. 11. John Bullock, Esq. was patron in 1806. The church is dedicated to St. Mary.

RAGDALE, a parish in the eastern division of the hundred of GOSCOTE, county of LEICESTER, 7 miles (W. by N.) from Melton-Mowbray, containing 98 inha-bitants. The living is a perpetual curacy, annexed to the vicarage of Queeniborough, in the archdeaconry of Leicester, and diocese of Lincoln. The church is dedi-cated to All Saints.

RAGLAND, a parish in the lower division of the hundred of RAGLAND, county of MONMOUTH, 7½ miles (S. W. by W.) from Monmouth, containing 633 inha-bitants. The living is a discharged vicarage, annexed to Llandenny, in the archdeaconry and diocese of Llan-daff, rated in the king's books at £4. 6. 8., endowed with £200 royal bounty, and in the patronage of the Duke of Beaufort. The church is dedicated to St. Cadocus. There is a place of worship for Baptists. Ragland Castle, said to have been mostly built by one of the Lords Herbert, is one of the finest remains of the kind in this part of the kingdom. It was gallantly defended for three months by the Earl of Worcester, against General Fairfax, after the entire reduction of Wales, and until the king's imprisonment at Holmby, when he surrendered, upon conditions honourable to the garrison. Charles I. was entertained here by the earl with great magnificence for three weeks, in 1645.

RAGLEY, a hamlet in that part of the parish of ARROW which is in the Alcester division of the hun-dred of BARLICHWAY, county of WARWICK, 1¾ mile (S. W. by S.) from Alcester. The population is returned with the parish.

RAGNALL, a chapelry in the parish of DUNHAM, South-clay division of the wapentake of BASSETLAW, county of NOTTINGHAM, 4¾ miles (E. N. E.) from Tux-ford, containing 146 inhabitants. This chapelry is within the peculiar jurisdiction of the Chapter of the Collegiate Church of Southwell.

RAINFORD, a chapelry in the parish of PRESCOT, hundred of WEST DERBY, county palatine of LAN-CASTER, 5¼ miles (N. by E.) from Prescot, containing 1375 inhabitants. The living is a perpetual curacy, in the archdeaconry of Richmond, and diocese of Chester, endowed with £400 private benefaction, £400 royal bounty, and £400 parliamentary grant, and in the patronage of the Vicar of Prescot. There is a place of worship for Independents.

RAINHAM, county of ESSEX.—See RAYNHAM.

RAINHAM, a parish in the hundred of MILTON, lathe of SCRAY, county of KENT, 4 miles (E. S. E.) from Chatham, containing 1030 inhabitants. The living is a vicarage, in the archdeaconry and diocese of Canter-bury, rated in the king's books at £14. 4. 7., and in the patronage of the Archbishop of Canterbury. The church, dedicated to St. Margaret, is in the early style of English architecture : it has a lofty beacon tower, and contains several costly monuments to the Tuftons, Earls of Thanet. The parish is bounded on the north by the Medway ; and the village, situated on the great London and Dovor road, contained, in the reign of Elizabeth, eight houses, and there were then three quays, with thirteen small vessels, the largest not exceeding thirty-five tons, belonging to the place. Cherries and apples formerly abounded here, but at present they are not cultivated to any great extent.

RAINHAM (EAST), a parish in the hundred of GALLOW, county of NORFOLK, 4 miles (S. W.) from Fakenham, containing 130 inhabitants. The living is a rectory, with West Rainham, in the archdeaconry and diocese of Norwich, rated in the king's books at £18. 13. 4., and in the patronage of William Ainge, Esq. The church is dedicated to St. Mary.

RAINHAM (SOUTH), a parish in the hundred of GALLOW, county of NORFOLK, 5¼ miles (S. W. by S.) from Fakenham, containing 101 inhabitants. The living is a discharged vicarage, with Helloughton, in the archdeaconry and diocese of Norwich, rated in the king's books at £6, endowed with £200 royal bounty, and in the patronage of William Ainge, Esq. The church is dedicated to St. Martin. A Cluniac priory, in honour of St. Mary and St. John, a cell to that of Castle-Acre, was founded here, about 1160, by William de Lisewis.

RAINHAM (WEST), a parish in the hundred of GALLOW, county of NORFOLK, 5½ miles (S. W. by W.) from Fakenham, containing 341 inhabitants. The living is a rectory, with East Rainham, in the archdeaconry and diocese of Norwich, rated in the king's books at £13. 6. 8. The church is dedicated to St. Margaret.

RAINHILL, a township in the parish of PRESCOT, hundred of WEST DERBY, county palatine of LANCASTER, 3 miles (S. E. by E.) from Prescot, containing 640 inhabitants.

RAINOW, a chapelry in the parish of PRESTBURY, hundred of MACCLESFIELD, county palatine of CHESTER, 2½ miles (N. E. by E.) from Macclesfield, containing 1530 inhabitants. The living is a perpetual curacy, in the archdeaconry and diocese of Chester, endowed with £200 private benefaction, £800 royal bounty, and £1800 parliamentary grant, and in the patronage of the Vicar of Prestbury. The chapel, called Jenkin, or Saltersford chapel, was built by the inhabitants, in 1739. There is a place of worship for Wesleyan Methodists, with a Sunday school attached ; and there are several trifling endowments for the education of children. The Roman road from Buxton to Manchester crossed the township, within the limits of which it is supposed there was once a Roman station. The manufacture of silk and cotton is carried on here, though the former has been in a declining state for some time. Near Kerridge hill are extensive quarries of flag-stone and slate.

RAINSCLIFF, a township in the parish of WOLSTANTON, northern division of the hundred of PIREHILL, county of STAFFORD, containing 679 inhabitants.

RAINSTHORPE, county of NORFOLK.—See TASEBURGH.

RAINTON, a joint township with Newby, in that part of the parish of TOPCLIFFE which is in the wapentake of HALLIKELD, North riding of the county of YORK, 5½ miles (N. N.W.) from Boroughbridge, containing, with Newby, 347 inhabitants. The Wesleyan Methodists have a place of worship here. There are various small endowments, producing about £3. 10. per annum, for the instruction of poor children.

RAINTON (EAST), a township in the parish of HOUGHTON le SPRING, northern division of EASINGTON ward, county palatine of DURHAM, 5½ miles (N.E.) from Durham, containing 671 inhabitants, many of whom are employed in the neighbouring coal mines, of which, Plain pit, in 1817, and again in 1823, exploded, and destroyed about eighty human beings. There is a place of worship for Wesleyan Methodists.

RAINTON (WEST), a chapelry in the parish of HOUGHTON le SPRING, northern division of EASINGTON ward, county palatine of DURHAM, 4¼ miles (N.E.)

from Durham, containing 1160 inhabitants. A chapel, dedicated to the Blessed Virgin, formerly existed here, but there are now no traces of it : a chapel of ease, however, was erected in 1825, and contains four hundred sittings, of which three hundred are free, the Incorporated Society for the enlargement of churches and chapels having granted £200 towards defraying the expense. There is a place of worship for Wesleyan Methodists. Two Sunday schools are attended by about three hundred children. The population of this place has increased of late years, in proportion to the great extension of the neighbouring collieries.

RAISTHORPE, a joint township with Birdall, in the parish of WHARRAM-PERCY, wapentake of BUCKROSE, East riding of the county of YORK, 9 miles (S. E. by S.) from New Malton, containing 47 inhabitants.

RAITHBY, a parish in the eastern division of the soke of BOLINGBROKE, parts of LINDSEY, county of LINCOLN, 2½ miles (W. N.W.) from Spilsby, containing 180 inhabitants. The living is a discharged rectory, in the archdeaconry and diocese of Lincoln, rated in the king's books at £6. 14. 7., and in the alternate patronage of the Crown, and Charles Chaplin, Esq. The church is dedicated to the Holy Trinity. There is a place of worship for Wesleyan Methodists.

RAITHBY, a parish in the Wold division of the hundred of LOUTH-ESKE, parts of LINDSEY, county of LINCOLN, 2 miles (S. W.) from Louth, containing, with Maltby, 120 inhabitants. The living is a rectory, united to Hallington, in the archdeaconry and diocese of Lincoln. The church is dedicated to St. Peter.

RAMBOTTOM, a hamlet in the chapelry of LOWER TOTTINGTON, in that part of the parish of BURY which is in the hundred of SALFORD, county palatine of LANCASTER, 4½ miles (N.) from Bury. The population is returned with Tottington. There is a place of worship for Wesleyan Methodists. At this place are very extensive cotton-spinning and printing establishments, affording employment to about three thousand persons.

RAME, a parish in the southern division of the hundred of EAST, county of CORNWALL, 4½ miles (S. S. W.) from Devonport, containing 807 inhabitants. The living is a rectory, in the archdeaconry of Cornwall, and diocese of Exeter, rated in the king's books at £12. 7. 6., and in the patronage of the Earl of Mount-Edgecumbe. The church is dedicated to St. German. In this parish is the noted promontory on the shore of the English channel, called Rame Head, the nearest point of land to the Eddystone lighthouse, and on which are slight remains of the ancient chapel of St. Michael. Cawsand bay is partly in this parish, at the entrance of which is a beacon, on Penlee point.

RAMPISHAM, a parish in the hundred of TOLLERFORD, Dorchester division of the county of DORSET, 6½ miles (E.) from Beaminster, containing 368 inhabitants. The living is a rectory, with that of Wraxhall united, in the archdeaconry of Dorset, and diocese of Bristol, rated in the king's books at £11. 17. 8½., and in the patronage of W. White, Esq. The church is dedicated to St. Mary.

RAMPSIDE, county palatine of LANCASTER.—See RAMSYDE.

RAMPTON, a parish in the hundred of NORTHSTOW, county of CAMBRIDGE, 6½ miles (N. by W.) from Cambridge, containing 217 inhabitants. The living is a rectory, in the archdeaconry and diocese of Ely, rated in the king's books at £9. 10., and in the patronage of the Heirs of William Strode, Esq. The church is dedicated to All Saints.

RAMPTON, a parish in the South-clay division of the wapentake of BASSETLAW, county of NOTTINGHAM, 6¾ miles (E.S.E.) from East Retford, containing 391 inhabitants. The living is a discharged vicarage, in the peculiar jurisdiction and patronage of the Prebendary of Rampton in the Collegiate Church of Southwell, rated in the king's books at £10. 0. 3., endowed with £200 private benefaction, and £200 royal bounty. The church is dedicated to All Saints. Thirteen children are educated free for £6. 5., and the occupation of land worth £1. 10., per annum, given by some persons unknown. Here is a curious ancient gateway, which formerly belonged to a mansion-house erected in the reign of Henry VIII., and taken down about a century ago.

RAMSBURY, a parish in the hundred of RAMSBURY, county of WILTS, comprising the tythings of Axford, Eastridge, and the Town tything, and containing 2335 inhabitants, of which number, 1653 are in the town of Ramsbury, 5½ miles (N. W. by W.) from Hungerford. The living is a vicarage, in the peculiar jurisdiction of the Dean of Salisbury, rated in the king's books at £9. 13. 1½., and in the patronage of the Crown. The church, dedicated to the Holy Cross, is a large ancient structure, with a massive tower supported by strong buttresses, and is considered the mother church to Salisbury cathedral; for, when Pleymund, Archbishop of Canterbury, about 909, constituted Wiltshire a distinct bishoprick, the two first bishops of that see fixed their seats here, but the third removed it to Wilton. Ramsbury church, however, is thought to have continued to be the cathedral of the diocese after the Conquest, and until the union of the bishopricks of Wiltshire and Sherborne, and the establishment of the seat of the new diocese at Sarum. The Wesleyan Methodists have a place of worship here.

RAMSDEN, a chapelry in the parish of SHIPTON under WHICHWOOD, hundred of CHADLINGTON, county of OXFORD, 3½ miles (N.) from Witney, containing 391 inhabitants.

RAMSDON-BELLHOUSE, a parish in the hundred of BARSTABLE, county of ESSEX, 4 miles (E.) from Billericay, containing 415 inhabitants. The living is a rectory, with Stock, in the archdeaconry of Essex, and diocese of London, rated in the king's books at £14. The church is dedicated to St. Mary.

RAMSDON-CRAYS, a parish in the hundred of BARSTABLE, county of ESSEX, 3 miles (E.S.E.) from Billericay, containing 276 inhabitants. The living is a rectory, in the archdeaconry of Essex, and diocese of London, rated in the king's books at £20, and in the patronage of Vicesimus Knox, Esq. The church is dedicated to St. Mary. The navigable river Crouch runs through the parish.

RAMSEY, a parish in the hundred of TENDRING, county of ESSEX, 3 miles (W.S.W.) from Harwich, containing 676 inhabitants. The living is a discharged vicarage, in the archdeaconry of Colchester, and diocese of London, rated in the king's books at £15, and in the patronage of the Crown. The church is dedicated to St. Michael. There is a place of worship for Wesleyan Methodists. The river Stour is navigable here

for vessels of two hundred and fifty tons' burden. At the lower part of Ramsey creek, which is crossed by a bridge on the London and Harwich road, an embankment has been made, to check the encroachments of the tide, upon five hundred acres of marsh land, gained from the sea within the last twenty years. Thomas Darall, in 1771, founded a free school, the annual income of which is about £14.

RAMSEY, a market town and parish in the hundred of HURSTINGSTONE, county of HUNTINGDON, 11 miles (N.N.E.) from Huntingdon, and 68½ (N. by W.) from London, containing 2814 inhabitants. The only feature of importance in the ancient history of this place is a mitred abbey of Benedictine monks, of great wealth and magnificence, founded here, in 969, by Ailwine, Alderman of all England, and Duke or Earl of the East Angles, and dedicated to St. Mary and St. Benedict, the revenue of which, at the dissolution, was valued at £1983. 15. 3.: the site is now occupied by a private residence, partially consisting of the remains of the ancient fabric, and still exhibiting the gateway in a fine state of preservation. The town is situated at the bottom of a hill on Bury brook, and on the verge of the fens. The market is on Wednesday; and a fair is held on July 22nd, for cattle and toys. A manorial court leet, at which a constable is appointed, is held annually in May or June. The living is a perpetual curacy, in the archdeaconry of Huntingdon, and diocese of Lincoln, and in the patronage of William Henry Fellowes, Esq. The church, which is dedicated to St. Thomas à Becket, is partly Norman, and partly in the early style of English architecture. There is a place of worship for Independents. Various benefactions in land have been made for the support of a free school and a spinning school, but, owing to frequent inundations, the school-house became ruinous, and the institution declined.

RAMSGATE, a sea-port, market town, and parish, in the cinque-port liberty of SANDWICH, of which it is a member, though locally in the hundred of Ringslow, or Isle of Thanet, lathe of St. Augustine, county of KENT, 4 miles (S.) from Margate, 17 (E. N. E.) from Canterbury, and 72 (E.) from London, containing 6031 inhabitants. It was originally a small fishing hamlet in the parish of St. Lawrence, until the 21st of June, 1827, at which period it was constituted a distinct parish, by an act passed in the 7th and 8th of George IV. It is stated, in the maritime survey of Kent in the reign of Elizabeth, to have contained only twenty-five houses, and when Leland wrote his itinerary, was only protected from the sea by a small wooden pier : in this state of obscurity it remained until 1688, when the inhabitants commenced trading with Russia, which trade has long since been discontinued: from this period its buildings increased, and it is now a town of importance, celebrated as a watering-place of considerable resort, and particularly distinguished for its harbour, which

Seal of the Trustees of the Harbour.

was commenced in 1749, under an act passed in the 22nd of George II., being designed to afford protection on the east coast to shipping in distress, especially those driven by gales from the Downs. Mr. Smeaton was the engineer first employed on this work, and after his death, the late Mr. Rennie, and subsequently his son and successor. The pier, which forms the harbour on the sea side, is built principally of Purbeck and Portland stone, and latterly of Cornish granite, and for extent is unequalled by any in the kingdom. It projects eight hundred feet into the sea, before making an angle, and, including the parapet, is twenty-six feet broad at the top; the front presents a polygon, each side of which is four hundred and fifty feet long. The eastern pier extends two thousand feet, and the western one thousand five hundred and fifty. The harbour covers an area of forty-eight acres, and is two hundred feet wide at the mouth, across which the tide was found to run so rapidly in tempestuous weather, as to render it dangerous for vessels entering the harbour, and the eastern pier was in consequence lengthened four hundred feet to the south-west. In the upper part of the harbour a basin has been constructed, capable of containing two hundred vessels, the gates of which being shut at high and opened at low water, the stream carries away any drifted mud or sand, and keeps open a channel under the curve of the eastern pier, sufficiently wide to admit two vessels abreast, with a depth of water of from fifteen to sixteen feet at neap tides, and from twenty to twenty-two feet at spring tides, enabling vessels of three hundred tons' burden to enter at all times, and much larger ones at spring tides; and vessels of six hundred tons can ride safely in the harbour, which affords shelter on an average to one thousand one hundred vessels annually, the greater part of which are blown, or run, from the Downs in bad weather: the continued ravages of the sea have hitherto prevented the works from being completely finished, and a considerable expense is annually incurred in repairing the damages occasioned by its inroads. On the western pier-head is a stone lighthouse, with argand lamps and red reflectors, which, when lighted at night, denote that there is ten feet of water at the entrance, the same intimation being conveyed in the day time by a red flag hoisted on the cliff. On the eastern pier-head, in time of war, are four sixty-eight pound carronades, for the defence of the town and harbour; and on the inner pier is a neat stone building, in which the trustees and directors transact their business. There is also a dwelling-house for the harbour-master, and several watch-houses, and other buildings connected with this great work. A life-boat is suspended from the parapet, about the middle of the eastern pier, which has often been effectually employed in saving life. To defray the expenses of this establishment, certain dues are collected from British vessels passing the harbour to or from foreign parts, and coasters, which do not contribute to similar establishments in the ports to which they belong, viz., Dovor, Lyme-Regis, Melcombe-Regis, Weymouth, and Great Yarmouth, pay an annual rate; foreign vessels also, if entering or passing the harbour, and bound to, or touching at, an English port, are liable to the payment of dues. All legal proceedings are carried on in the name of the Deputy Master of the Trinity House. A handsome stone staircase has been constructed up the side of the cliffs

contiguous to the harbour, at each end of the town, by the trustees; that on the western side is particularly beautiful, as cending at right angles in a treble range of steps to the summit, and is named "Curtis' stairs" The harbour affords great convenience to the different steam-packets which arrive at this port in the summer, the inner landing being accessible to them at all times of the tide. There is also a dry dock, which is public property.

The town is beautifully situated on the declivity of a hill, opening south to the sea, and commands from many points very extensive marine and land views, the former embracing in clear weather the French coast. The recent buildings are generally handsome edifices, and amongst those which add more particularly to the beauty of the town may be mentioned, Albion Place, three crescents, and numerous detached villas. The streets are Macadamized and lighted with gas: the town is very indifferently supplied with water. Ramsgate, being a member of the port of Sandwich, the mayor of that place appoints his deputy, who acts here as constable, but the town is under the jurisdiction of magistrates appointed, under an act obtained in 1812, to act for the liberties of the cinque-ports; two of them are resident, but prisoners are committed to Sandwich gaol. A court of requests is held for the recovery of debts not exceeding £5, the jurisdiction of which extends over the parish of St. Lawrence. To the eastward of the harbour, in front of a range of chalk cliffs, and on a beach of soft reddish sand, are the bathing machines, every convenience being provided for sea-bathing. At the bath-house are four warm salt-water baths, and a plunging and shower bath, for either warm or cold water. The Isabella warm sea-water baths, which stand on the west cliff, one hundred and ten feet above the level of the sea, the water for which is raised through an aperture in the rock, by pumps worked by horses, are constructed of white marble; the vapour baths are upon the plan of the Hon. Mr. Cochrane, being heated by steam, which is conducted from the outside of the building, into a handsome vase in each dressing-room, and the temperature of which is varied at pleasure: there are well-conducted assemblies, and two good public libraries, and the boarding and lodging houses are generally of a superior character.

The rides and walks in the vicinity are pleasant and diversified, but the principal and most attractive promenade is the pier, which is not surpassed by any thing of the kind in the country. Pegwell bay, which abounds with shell and flat fish, is about one mile and a half west of the town. On the 25th of September, 1821, his late Majesty, George IV., embarked here for Calais, in his progress to Hanover, having been entertained the previous night at the residence of the late Sir William Curtis; and he also landed here on the following 8th of November, on his return, to commemorate which event the inhabitants, trustees of the harbour, and visitors, erected an obelisk at the entrance of the pier on the land side, on which is an appropriate inscription. The trade, which has been greatly improved by the erection of the harbour, consists of a large coasting trade, particularly in coal. Timber from the Baltic was formerly imported, but this branch of commerce has been discontinued. A considerable fishery is carried on off this coast, by large vessels from the westward, the choice fish being principally sent to the London market. Several small vessels belonging to the port are also similarly engaged, and are often efficaciously employed in rendering assistance to vessels in distress, particularly to those wrecked on the Goodwin sands, which lie about three miles and a half south-east by east from this place. Here are two spacious yards for ship-building, rope-walks, and warehouses furnishing every description of stores for the shipping. The market is on Wednesday and Saturday, and is frequently attended by French people bringing over eggs, fruit, and other articles. The living is a vicarage not in charge, in the archdeaconry and diocese of Canterbury, and in the patronage of the Archbishop of Canterbury. The church, dedicated to St. George, is a handsome edifice, lately built, at an expense of £27,000, towards defraying which the parliamentary commissioners granted £9000. There is also a chapel of ease. Baptists, Independents, and Wesleyan Methodists, have each a place of worship.

RAMSGRAVE, a township in the parish of BLACK-BURN, lower division of the hundred of BLACKBURN, county palatine of LANCASTER, 2¼ miles (N. W. by N.) from Blackburn, containing 534 inhabitants.

RAMSHOLT, a parish in the hundred of WILFORD, county of SUFFOLK, 7 miles (S. S. E.) from Woodbridge, containing 174 inhabitants. The living is a perpetual curacy, in the archdeaconry of Suffolk, and diocese of Norwich, endowed with a rent-charge of £16 per ann. private benefaction, and £600 royal bounty. J. Pennington, Esq. was patron in 1813. The church is dedicated to All Saints. The navigable river Deben runs on the west, where there is a dock.

RAMSHOPE, an extra-parochial district, in the southern division of COQUETDALE ward, county of NORTHUMBERLAND, 16¼ miles (N. N. W.) from Bellingham, containing 7 inhabitants. This wild region is separated from Scotland by Carter-fell, a mountainous ridge rising one thousand six hundred and two feet above the level of the sea. The Reedswire, a less stupendous barrier, extending from the former to Hound-law, was, in 1575, the scene of a warm conflict between the English and the Scottish wardens, in which the former, who was the aggressor, being defeated and taken prisoner, was conveyed, with several of the border chieftains, to Dalkeith: the old ballad, called "The Battle of Reid Squair," was founded upon this affray.

RAMSHORN, a township in the parish of ELLA-STONE, southern division of the hundred of TOTMONS-LOW, county of STAFFORD, 5¾ miles (E. N. E.) from Cheadle, containing 152 inhabitants.

RAMSYDE, or RAMPSIDE, a chapelry in the parish of DALTON in FURNESS, hundred of LONSDALE, north of the sands, county palatine of LANCASTER, 5¼ miles (S. by E.) from Dalton, with which the population is returned. The living is a perpetual curacy, in the archdeaconry of Richmond, and diocese of Chester, endowed with £800 royal bounty, and £1400 parliamentary grant, and in the patronage of the Vicar of Dalton.

RANBY, a parish in the northern division of the wapentake of GARTREE, parts of LINDSEY, county of LINCOLN, 6½ miles (E. by N.) from Wragby, containing 121 inhabitants. The living is a vicarage, in the archdeaconry and diocese of Lincoln, rated in the king's books at £4. 13. 4., endowed with £200 private bene-

faction, £1000 royal bounty, and £300 parliamentary grant, and in the patronage of Miss A. Otter. The church is dedicated to St. German.

RAND, a parish in the western division of the wapentake of WRAGGOE, parts of LINDSEY, county of LINCOLN, 2¼ miles (W. N. W.) from Wragby, containing 102 inhabitants. The living is a rectory, with Fulnetby, in the archdeaconry and diocese of Lincoln, rated in the king's books at £8. 5., and in the patronage of H. Hudson, Esq. The church is dedicated to St. Oswald.

RANDS-GRANGE, a hamlet in that part of the parish of BEDALE which is in the eastern division of the wapentake of HANG, North riding of the county of YORK, 1 mile (N. W.) from Bedale. The population is returned with the township of Crakehall.

RANDWICK, a parish in the upper division of the hundred of WHITSTONE, county of GLOUCESTER, 2 miles (N. W. by W.) from Stroud, containing 984 inhabitants. The living is a perpetual curacy, in the archdeaconry and diocese of Gloucester, endowed with £200 private benefaction, £400 royal bounty, and £800 parliamentary grant, and in the patronage of the Vicar of Standish. The church, dedicated to St. John, has recently undergone considerable improvement, a new chancel having been built by Lord Sherborne, and one hundred and seventy-nine sittings, of which one hundred and thirty-four are free, added to the original number, the Incorporated Society for the enlargement of churches and chapels having contributed £125 towards defraying the expense. There are places of worship for Wesleyan Methodists, and those in the connexion of the late Countess of Huntingdon. The Thames and Severn canal passes through the parish, in which the manufacture of woollen cloth is carried on. A school is endowed for forty poor children, who are taught by the parish clerk, to which a National school has been lately appended. There are also a school of industry for poor girls, and a small parochial library for the use of the poor. On a hill called "The Castles" are traces of an ancient settlement, supposed, from the discovery of a burial vault of stone, containing human remains, to be of Saxon origin; and in many parts of the parish have been found small balls of stone, rudely turned, indicative of some battle having been fought in the neighbourhood. A petrifaction, termed by geologists "calcareous tuphur," abounds here; of this stone the ancient porch of the church is constructed. An annual festival is kept on Low-Monday: it is attended with a ridiculous custom, and is said to have originated in the dedication of the church.

RANGEWORTHY, a chapelry in the parish of THORNBURY, lower division of the hundred of THORN-BURY, county of GLOUCESTER, 3¾ miles (S. W. by W.) from Wickwar, containing 296 inhabitants. The living is a perpetual curacy, in the archdeaconry and diocese of Gloucester, endowed with £800 royal bounty, and in the patronage of the Vicar of Thornbury. The chapel, dedicated to the Holy Trinity, is a small edifice, with a Norman south door. There is a place of worship for Wesleyan Methodists.

RANSKILL, a township in that part of the parish of BLYTH which is in the liberty of SOUTHWELL and SCROOBY, county of NOTTINGHAM, 3¾ miles (S.) from Bawtry, containing 317 inhabitants. There is a place of worship for Independents.

RANWORTH, a parish in the hundred of WALS-HAM, county of NORFOLK, 4 miles (N. W.) from Acle, containing, with Panxworth, 352 inhabitants. The living is a discharged vicarage, with that of Upton united, in the archdeaconry and diocese of Norwich, rated in the king's books at £4, endowed with £400 royal bounty, and in the patronage of the Bishop of Ely. The church is dedicated to St. Helen.

RASEN (MARKET), a market town and parish in the southern division of the hundred of WALSHCROFT, parts of LINDSEY, county of LINCOLN, 12 miles (N. E.) from Lincoln, and 144 (N.) from London, containing 1166 inhabitants. This town is situated near the source of the river Ancholme, on a small stream, called the *Rase*, whence it derives its name, and has a very neat appearance: the surrounding country is beautiful and fertile. The market is on Tuesday; and a fair is held on the 25th of September. The living is a discharged vicarage, in the archdeaconry and diocese of Lincoln, rated in the king's books at £10, and in the patronage of the Crown: the incumbent is entitled to the tythe on ale brewed in this parish. The church, dedicated to St. Thomas, is a commodious edifice, with an embattled tower, the upper windows of which are of a curious form, having a pointed arch, divided into two pointed lights, and a quatrefoil head; a strong mullion runs up the centre, crossed by a transom, terminating at the imposts. On the south side of the tower is a representation of Adam and Eve under a fruit tree, on the trunk of which is the dart of death. There are places of worship for Independents and Wesleyan Methodists, also a Roman Catholic chapel. A National school was erected in 1822, at which period the revenue of the free grammar school, of unknown foundation, amounting to £25 per annum, was appropriated towards its support. Sir George St. Paul, of Snarford, having bequeathed £40 per annum, arising out of lands, for the support of eight poor bachelors or widowers, three of whom must be of this parish, and £100 towards the erection of an almshouse for them, the design was carried into effect by his widow, afterwards Countess of Warwick, who, at her own cost, furnished eight apartments, besides a chamber for the sick.

RASEN (MIDDLE), a parish in the southern division of the wapentake of WALSHCROFT, parts of LINDSEY, county of LINCOLN, 1½ mile (W. by N.) from Market-Rasen, containing, with Drakes, 508 inhabitants. The living is a discharged vicarage, in the archdeaconry and diocese of Lincoln, rated in the king's books at £7. 10. 10., endowed with £400 royal bounty, and in the patronage of Earl Brownlow. The church is dedicated to St. Peter and St. Paul. There is a place of worship for Wesleyan Methodists.

RASEN (WEST), a parish in the northern division of the wapentake of WALSHCROFT, parts of LINDSEY, county of LINCOLN, 3¼ miles (W.) from Market-Rasen, containing 210 inhabitants. The living is a rectory, in the archdeaconry and diocese of Lincoln, rated in the king's books at £19. 10. 10. The Rev. W. Cooper was patron in 1809. The church is dedicated to All Saints.

RASKELF, a chapelry in the parish of EASINGWOULD, wapentake of BULMER, North riding of the county of YORK, 2 miles (W. N. W.) from Easingwould, containing 440 inhabitants. The living is a perpetual curacy, in the

archdeaconry of Cleveland, and diocese of York, endowed with £400 royal bounty, and in the patronage of the Bishop of Chester. The chapel is dedicated to St. Mary. There are two trifling endowments, applied for teaching six poor children.

RASTRICK, a chapelry in the parish of HALIFAX, wapentake of MORLEY, West riding of the county of YORK, 4½ miles (N.) from Huddersfield, containing 2796 inhabitants. The living is a perpetual curacy, in the archdeaconry and diocese of York, endowed with £800 private benefaction, £800 royal bounty, and £200 parliamentary grant, and in the patronage of the Vicar of Halifax. The ancient chapel was taken down about forty years ago, and the present one, a handsome structure, erected upon its site. There is a place of worship for Independents. The manufacture of woollen cord and fancy goods is extensive. A free school, founded in 1741, by Mary Bedford, has been endowed by her and subsequent donors, with about £50 per annum.

RATBY, a parish in the hundred of SPARKENHOE, county of LEICESTER, 5 miles (W. by N.) from Leicester, containing, with the township of Botcheston with Newton, and the hamlet of Grooby, 1025 inhabitants. The living is a discharged vicarage, in the peculiar jurisdiction of the Lord of the Manor of Grooby, rated in the king's books at £5. 5. 10., endowed with £400 parliamentary grant, and in the patronage of the Earl of Stamford. The church is dedicated to St. Philip. On an eminence near the village are the remains of a large Roman encampment.

RATCHWOOD, a township in the parish of BAMBROUGH, northern division of BAMBROUGH ward, county of NORTHUMBERLAND, 4½ miles (S. E. by S.) from Belford, containing 10 inhabitants.

RATCLIFFE, a hamlet in the parish of STEPNEY, Tower division of the hundred of OSSULSTONE, county of MIDDLESEX, 1 mile (E.) from London, containing 6973 inhabitants. The present name appears to be a corruption of *Redcliff*, an appellation derived from the red cliff, or bank of the river Thames, which flows southward of the parish. In Camden's time this was a village inhabited principally by seafaring men, but it is now much increased in size and population. "The Highway," a broad street formerly planted on each side with elm-trees, now consists of lines of houses, and extends to Limehouse. For a particular account of this place see the article on STEPNEY.

RATCLIFFE upon SOAR, a parish in the northern division of the wapentake of RUSHCLIFFE, county of NOTTINGHAM, 1½ mile (N. by E.) from Kegworth, containing 168 inhabitants. The living is a discharged vicarage, in the archdeaconry of Nottingham, and diocese of York, rated in the king's books at £10. 11. 3., endowed with £400 private benefaction, £400 royal bounty, and £300 parliamentary grant, and in the patronage of Earl Howe. The church is dedicated to the Holy Trinity. The navigable river Soar runs through the parish, in which there is a mine of alabaster. Ratcliffe is in the honour of Tutbury, duchy of Lancaster, and within the jurisdiction of a court of pleas held at Tutbury every third Tuesday, for the recovery of debts under 40s.

RATCLIFFE on TRENT, a parish in the southern division of the wapentake of BINGHAM, county of NOTTINGHAM, 5½ miles (E. by S.) from Nottingham, containing 993 inhabitants. The living is a vicarage, in the archdeaconry of Nottingham, and diocese of York, rated in the king's books at £4. 12. 6., endowed with £200 private benefaction, and £600 royal bounty, and in the patronage of Earl Manvers. The church, dedicated to St. Mary, was rebuilt about 1793, prior to which the spire that surmounted the tower fell down, and has not been replaced. There is a place of worship for Wesleyan Methodists. The river Trent runs through the parish, and is fordable in two places. There is a wharf belonging to Earl Manvers, chiefly used for coal, at which the freeholders of Ratcliffe are allowed to land their goods wharfage free : the manufacture of hosiery is carried on here. Near the village is a perpendicular cliff of red clay, from which the parish took its name.

RATCLIFFE on the WREAK, a parish in the eastern division of the hundred of GOSCOTE, county of LEICESTER, 6¾ miles (N. N. E.) from Leicester, containing 124 inhabitants. The living is a vicarage, in the archdeaconry of Leicester, and diocese of Lincoln, rated in the king's books at £7. 16. 8., and in the patronage of the Crown. The church is dedicated to St. Botolph. The Fosse-road passes through the parish, and the Leicester and Melton-Mowbray canal touches upon its eastern boundary.

RATCLIFFE-CULEY, a chapelry in the parish of SHEEPY MAGNA, hundred of SPARKENHOE, county of LEICESTER, 1½ mile (N. E.) from Atherstone, containing 211 inhabitants.

RATHMILL, a township in the parish of GIGGLESWICK, western division of the wapentake of STAINCLIFFE and EWCROSS, West riding of the county of YORK, 4 miles (S. W. by S.) from Settle, containing 328 inhabitants. George Clarke, in 1716, devised the profits of an estate in support of a school, and, in 1725, Stephen Carr bequeathed £80 in augmentation of the master's salary : the annual income is about £23, for which all children who apply are taught to read, but pay for further instruction.

RATLEY, a parish in the Burton-Dassett division of the hundred of KINGTON, county of WARWICK, 4¼ miles (S. E.) from Kington, containing, with Upton, 402 inhabitants. The living is a discharged vicarage, in the archdeaconry of Coventry, and diocese of Lichfield and Coventry, rated in the king's books at £6. 12., endowed with £400 royal bounty, and in the patronage of the Crown. The church is dedicated to St. Peter. There is a place of worship for Wesleyan Methodists. About sixty poor children are educated at the vicarage-house, which is occupied by a schoolmaster rent-free, who receives £15 a year from the revenue of the poor's land. On the brow of Edge Hill, within this parish, is a large triangular fortification, called Nadbury Camp, supposed to be of Roman construction. This hill commands a delightful prospect of a fertile country in a high state of cultivation, including the Vale of Red Horse, which skirts its base: it is further celebrated, in the annals of history, as the scene of a sanguinary battle, between the royalists and the parliamentary forces, September 2nd, 1642, in which, though several hundreds were slain on both sides, and among them many of the nobility, both armies kept the field : numerous fragments of skeletons have been found in the vicinity.

RATLINGHOPE, a parish in the hundred of PURSLOW, county of SALOP, 4½ miles (N. W. by W.) from Church-Stretton, comprising the townships of Gatton and Ratlinghope, and containing 277 inhabitants. The living is a rectory, in the archdeaconry of Salop, and diocese of Hereford, rated in the king's books at £3. 6. 8., endowed with £800 royal bounty, and £200 parliamentary grant, and in the patronage of the Rev. J. Hawkins. The church is dedicated to St. Margaret. A priory of Augustine canons was founded here, under the auspices of Llewellyn, Prince of North Wales, by his kinsman, Walter Corbet, one of that order.

RATTERY, a parish in the hundred of STANBOROUGH, county of DEVON, 4¼ miles (W. N. W.) from Totness, containing 559 inhabitants. The living is a vicarage, in the archdeaconry of Totness, and diocese of Exeter, rated in the king's books at £14. 10., and in the patronage of Sir H. Carew, Bart. The church has an elegant wooden screen, and a Norman font. A vein of lead-ore has been discovered in this parish.

RATTLESDEN, a parish in the hundred of THEDWESTRY, county of SUFFOLK, 4¾ miles (W.) from Stow-Market, containing 1032 inhabitants. The living is a rectory, in the archdeaconry of Sudbury, and diocese of Norwich, rated in the king's books at £20. 0. 2¼. James Oakes, Esq. was patron in 1808. The church is dedicated to St. Nicholas. There is a place of worship for Baptists.

RAUCEBY (NORTH), a parish in the wapentake of FLAXWELL, parts of KESTEVEN, county of LINCOLN, 4 miles (W.) from Sleaford, containing 252 inhabitants. The living is a discharged vicarage, in the archdeaconry and diocese of Lincoln, rated in the king's books at £5. 1. 0½., endowed with £400 private benefaction, and £400 royal bounty, and in the patronage of Sir J. H. Thorold, Bart. The church is dedicated to St. Peter.

RAUCEBY (SOUTH), a joint parish with North Rauceby, in the wapentake of FLAXWELL, parts of KESTEVEN, county of LINCOLN, 4 miles (W. by S.) from Sleaford, containing 255 inhabitants.

RAUGHTON, a joint township with Gatesgill, in the parish of DALSTON, ward and county of CUMBERLAND, 5½ miles (S. by W.) from Carlisle, containing 294 inhabitants.

RAUGHTON-HEAD, a chapelry in the parish of CASTLE-SOWERBY, LEATH ward, county of CUMBERLAND, 7½ miles (S. by W.) from Carlisle. The population is returned with the parish. The living is a perpetual curacy, in the archdeaconry and diocese of Carlisle, endowed with £200 private benefaction, and £600 royal bounty, and in the patronage of the Vicar of Castle-Sowerby and twelve Trustees. The chapel was rebuilt in 1678, and enlarged in 1760. A school-house was erected, in 1744, by John Head, and rebuilt in 1806, but it is not endowed.

RAUNDS, a parish in the hundred of HIGHAM-FERRERS, county of NORTHAMPTON, 4¼ miles (N. E.) from Higham-Ferrers, containing 1301 inhabitants. The living is a vicarage, in the archdeaconry of Northampton, and diocese of Peterborough, rated in the king's books at £11. 9. 7., endowed with £200 private benefaction, and £200 royal bounty, and in the patronage of the Crown. The church, dedicated to St. Peter, is a large and handsome edifice, with a lofty tower and spire, considered the finest specimen of the early English style in the county ; similar characteristics predominate in the rest of the building, though there are some decorated windows and others of later date: in the churchyard is the base of an ancient cross. There are places of worship for Baptists and Wesleyan Methodists.

RAVELEY (GREAT), a parish in the hundred of HURSTINGSTONE, county of HUNTINGDON, 3¾ miles (S. W.) from Ramsey, containing 222 inhabitants. The living is a perpetual curacy, with Upwood, in the archdeaconry of Huntingdon, and diocese of Lincoln, and in the patronage of Earl Sandwich. The church is demolished. There is a place of worship for Wesleyan Methodists.

RAVELEY (LITTLE), a parish in the hundred of HURSTINGSTONE, county of HUNTINGDON, 4¼ miles (S. W. by S.) from Ramsey, containing 68 inhabitants. The living is a perpetual curacy, in the archdeaconry of Huntingdon, and diocese of Lincoln, endowed with £1200 royal bounty, and in the patronage of the Earl of Sandwich. The church is dedicated to St. James. Within the last few years several skeletons were dug up here in a gravel pit, and a Roman urn of blue earth.

RAVENDALE (EAST), a parish in the wapentake of BRADLEY-HAVERSTOE, parts of LINDSEY, county of LINCOLN, 7 miles (S. S. W.) from Great Grimsby, containing, with the chapelry of West Ravendale, 95 inhabitants. The living is a discharged vicarage, in the archdeaconry and diocese of Lincoln, rated in the king's books at £5, endowed with £1000 royal bounty, and £200 parliamentary grant, and in the patronage of the Master and Fellows of Trinity College, Cambridge. The church is dedicated to St. Martin.

RAVENDALE (WEST), a chapelry in the parish of EAST RAVENDALE, wapentake of BRADLEY-HAVERSTOE, parts of LINDSEY, county of LINCOLN, 7½ miles (S. W. by S.) from Great Grimsby, containing 32 inhabitants. The living is a perpetual curacy, in the archdeaconry and diocese of Lincoln, endowed with £400 royal bounty, and in the patronage of the Chapter of the Collegiate Church of Southwell.

RAVENFIELD, a parish in the southern division of the wapentake of STRAFFORTH and TICKHILL, West riding of the county of YORK, 4 miles (N. E. by E.) from Rotherham, containing 187 inhabitants. The living is a perpetual curacy, in the peculiar jurisdiction and patronage of the Archdeacon of York, endowed with £31 per annum and £900 private benefaction, £800 royal bounty, and £900 parliamentary grant. The church is dedicated to St. James.

RAVENGLASS, a small sea-port and market town, in the parish of MUNCASTER, ALLERDALE ward above Darwent, county of CUMBERLAND, 54 miles (S. S. W.) from Carlisle, and 282 (N. W. by N.) from London. The population is returned with the parish. This town is pleasantly situated along the sea-shore, near the confluence of the rivers Eske, Mite, and Irt, which form a commodious and safe harbour for shipping, particularly in tempestuous weather. It consists of a long range of irregularly, though well, built houses, and is sheltered in the back ground by the mountains of Black Combe, between which and the town are some fine meadow lands; the Eske has its source near the foot of a rugged eminence, called Hard Knot. The trade of the place is inconsiderable, a few vessels being engaged in bringing coal from Whitehaven, for the lime-kilns, and in taking back oysters, which abound here, and are considered to be the finest found upon this part of the coast; a little

corn and timber is also exported: some small vessels are constructed here. The market was formerly on Wednesday and Friday, but it is now held only on the former day, and is in very little repute: a fair for cattle is held on the 6th of May, and others of ancient date, for horses and cattle, on June 8th and August 5th; the latter, which terminates with horse races and other diversions, is proclaimed by the steward and tenantry of the Earl of Egremont, attended by a band of music and some halberdiers, in memory, probably, of the armed retinue which in former times attended to preserve from theft the goods exposed for sale. A small free school for poor children was endowed by Sir William Pennington, and Richard Brooksbank, his cook, with £12 per annum. Near the ruins of Walls castle, about one mile distant, where is now the mansion-house and residence of Lord Muncaster, a lineal descendant of the Penningtons, who have held this manor since the Conquest, many relics of antiquity, consisting of battle-axes made of flint, heads of arrows, and Roman and Saxon coins, have been discovered. About a mile and a half eastward from Muncaster House, on the opposite side of the river Eske, may be traced the ruins of an ancient city, called "the city of Barnscar," the origin of which is traditionally ascribed to the Danes, but of its history no records have been found. The site is an oblong square, about three hundred yards long from east to west, and one hundred long from north to south; it was intersected by one long street, and several transverse ones: the city was defended by a wall, except at the east end, and, with its suburbs, was nearly three miles in circumference: an ancient road led through it from Ulpha to Ravenglass. About 1730, a great quantity of silver coins was found in the ruins of one of the houses. On an eminence called Hard Knot are the ruins of an ancient church and castle, also the remains of a round tower on one of the adjacent mounts.

RAVENINGHAM, a parish in the hundred of CLAVERING, county of NORFOLK, 4¼ miles (N.N.W.) from Beccles, containing 261 inhabitants. The living is a perpetual curacy, in the archdeaconry of Norfolk, and diocese of Norwich, endowed with £200 royal bounty, and £200 parliamentary grant, and in the patronage of Sir Edmund Bacon, Bart. The church is dedicated to St. Andrew. A college of eight Secular priests was founded here, in 1343, by Sir John de Norwich, which was afterwards removed to Norton-Subcourse, and, in 1393, to Castle-Mettingham in Suffolk.

RAVENSCROFT, a township in that part of the parish of MIDDLEWICH which is in the hundred of NORTHWICH, county palatine of CHESTER, 1¼ mile (N. by W.) from Middlewich, containing 26 inhabitants.

RAVENSDALE-PARK, a hamlet in the parish of MUGGINTON, hundred of APPLETREE, county of DERBY, containing 51 inhabitants.

RAVENSDEN, a parish in the hundred of BARFORD, county of BEDFORD, 4 miles (N.N.E.) from Bedford, containing 263 inhabitants. The living is a discharged vicarage, in the archdeaconry of Bedford, and diocese of Lincoln, rated in the king's books at £7, and in the patronage of the Duke of Bedford. The church is dedicated to All Saints.

RAVENSTHORPE, a parish partly in the hundred of GUILSBOROUGH, but chiefly in that of NOBOTTLE-GROVE, county of NORTHAMPTON, 9½ miles (N.W.)

4 F 2

by N.) from Northampton, containing, with the hamlets of Coaton and Teeton, 710 inhabitants. The living is a vicarage, in the archdeaconry of Northampton, and diocese of Peterborough, rated in the king's books at £11. 13. 4., and in the patronage of the Dean and Canons of Christ Church, Oxford. The church is dedicated to St. Denis. There is a place of worship for Baptists.

RAVENSTONE, a parish in the hundred of NEWPORT, county of BUCKINGHAM, 3¼ miles (W. by S.) from Olney, containing 418 inhabitants. The living is a vicarage, in the archdeaconry of Buckingham, and diocese of Lincoln, endowed with the fee-farm rent of the manor of Ravenstone, amounting to about £84 per annum, rated in the king's books at £6. 13. 4., and in the patronage of the Earl of Winchilsea and Nottingham. The church, dedicated to All Saints, contains a splendid monument to the memory of Heneage Finch, Earl of Nottingham, and Lord High Chancellor of England, who died in 1682. Besides the gift of the above endowment, and another of £10 per annum towards ornamenting the church, his lordship founded an hospital for six men and six women, with a weekly allowance of three shillings and sixpence each, and a gown every year. A charity school was founded by the Rev. Mr. Chapman, a former vicar, for all the poor children of the parish: the income is £12 per annum. A small monastery of Black canons, in honour of the Blessed Virgin Mary, was founded here by Henry III., about the thirty-ninth year of his reign, which, in the 16th of Henry VIII., was valued at £66. 13. 4., and given to Cardinal Wolsey, towards the endowment of his intended colleges.

RAVENSTONE, a parish partly in the hundred of REPTON and GRESLEY, county of DERBY, but chiefly in the western division of the hundred of GOSCOTE, county of LEICESTER, 4 miles (S. E. by E.) from Ashby de la Zouch, containing 444 inhabitants. The living is a rectory, in the archdeaconry of Derby, and diocese of Lichfield and Coventry, rated in the king's books at £5. 1. 0½., and in the patronage of the Crown. The church, dedicated to St. Michael, is a very ancient structure. There is a place of worship for Wesleyan Methodists. An hospital for thirty-two aged widows of the parishes of Ravenstone, Swannington, and Cole-Orton, was built and endowed by John Wilkins, Esq. and Rebecca his wife, in 1712: the endowment consists of about eight hundred acres of land, producing an annual income of £940: each of the inmates receives four shillings and sixpence per week, besides a liberal allowance of coal; the master, or chaplain, has a salary of £60, and a good house, built in 1784, when the present chapel was erected, the expense having been defrayed from the accumulated funds of the charity. A National school is supported by voluntary contributions.

RAVENSTONEDALE, a parish in EAST ward, county of WESTMORLAND, 4½ miles (S. W.) from Kirkby-Stephen, containing 1059 inhabitants. The living is a perpetual curacy, in the peculiar jurisdiction and patronage of the Earl of Lonsdale, as lord of the manor; it is endowed with £600 private benefaction, £400 royal bounty, and £500 parliamentary grant. The church, dedicated to St. Oswald, was rebuilt in 1744. There is a place of worship for Independents. This manor formerly belonged to the priory of Watton in York-

shire, and, in common with the other possessions of that monastery, afforded the privilege of sanctuary. The lord of the manor, by his steward, administers the oath of office to the churchwardens of the parish. The steward and jury of the manor anciently held their court, for the trial of felons and other offenders, in the church, near which there was an arched vault, in which malefactors were confined: Gallow Hill, a short distance hence, appears to have been the spot where capital punishment was inflicted. The parish is composed of numerous vallies and fells, among which rise several streams, forming the source of the river Lune. The town appears to have been formerly much larger than at present: a small market is held on Tuesdays, and a fair on the Thursday after Whit-Sunday. The free grammar school was founded, about 1688, by Thomas Fothergill, B. D., Master of St. John's College, Cambridge, aided by other members of his family, all natives of the parish: a good school-house was built by contribution in 1758. The salary and emoluments of the master amount to about £70 per annum: he has a commodious dwelling-house, and is allowed to receive boarders. Boys whose parents reside in the parish are instructed gratuitously in Latin and Greek, but pay a small quarterage for tuition in other branches. At a place called Rasate there are two tumuli, in which, on being opened, human bones were found; and near Rother bridge there is a circle of stones, supposed to have been a place of Druidical worship. The family of Fothergill has produced several distinguished members, among whom were, George Fothergill, D. D., principal of St. Edmund Hall, and Thomas Fothergill, D. D., Provost of Queen's College, Oxford.

RAVENSWORTH, a township in that part of the parish of CHESTER le STREET which is in the middle division of CHESTER ward, county palatine of DURHAM, 4¼ miles (S. S. W.) from Gateshead, containing 161 inhabitants, who are chiefly employed in the adjacent coal mines. The total rebuilding of the castle commenced in 1808, after a design by Nash; the work is constructed of excellent white freestone, raised near the spot, and when finished will be a most imposing edifice in the ancient baronial style. In the neighbourhood is a cross, to which, during the prevalence of the plague at Newcastle, in 1645, the country people brought their market goods for sale. Ravensworth gives the title of baron to the family of Liddel.

RAVENSWORTH, a township in the parish of KIRKBY-RAVENSWORTH, western division of the wapentake of GILLING, North riding of the county of YORK, 4¼ miles (N. N. W.) from Richmond, containing 317 inhabitants. There is a place of worship for Wesleyan Methodists.

RAVENSWORTH (KIRKBY), North riding of the county of YORK.—See KIRKBY-RAVENSWORTH.

RAW, a township in the parish of ROTHBURY, western division of COQUETDALE ward, county of NORTHUMBERLAND, 2½ miles (S. E. by E.) from Rothbury, containing 51 inhabitants.

RAWCLIFF, a chapelry in that part of the parish of SNAITH which is in the lower division of the wapentake of OSGOLDCROSS, West riding of the county of YORK, 3¼ miles (E. by N.) from Snaith, containing 1496 inhabitants. The living is a perpetual curacy, with that of Snaith, in the jurisdiction of the peculiar court of Snaith, endowed with £600 parliamentary grant. The chapel is dedicated to St. James. There is a place of worship for Wesleyan Methodists. The free school here is supposed to have been founded by a Mr. Boynton, for the education of eight children; the master's income is £27 a year, with a house and garden.

RAWCLIFFE, a township partly in the parish of St. Michael le Belfrey, city of York, and partly in the parish of St. Olave, Mary-Gate, wapentake of Bulmer, North riding of the county of York, 3 miles (N. W. by N.) from York. That part which is in the parish of St. Olave contains 57 inhabitants, the remainder being returned with the parish of St. Michael.

RAWCLIFFE (OUT), a township in the parish of St. Michael, hundred of Amounderness, county palatine of Lancaster, 4½ miles (N. E. by E.) from Poulton, containing 598 inhabitants.

RAWCLIFFE (UPPER), a joint township with Tarnicar, in the parish of St. Michael, hundred of Amounderness, county palatine of Lancaster, 6 miles (S. W. by W.) from Garstang, containing, with Tarnicar, 643 inhabitants.

RAWDEN, or RAWDON, a chapelry in the parish of Guisley, upper division of the wapentake of Skyrack, West riding of the county of York, 7 miles (N. E. by N.) from Bradford, containing 1759 inhabitants. The living is a perpetual curacy, in the archdeaconry and diocese of York, endowed with £400 private benefaction, £400 royal bounty, and £600 parliamentary grant, and in the patronage of the Lord of the Manor. The chapel, erected in 1721, has lately received an addition of three hundred and fifty sittings, of which one hundred and seventy-five are free, the Incorporated Society for the enlargement of churches and chapels having granted £500 towards defraying the expense. There are places of worship for Baptists and Wesleyan Methodists; the latter have a seminary at Woodhouse Grove. The manufacture of woollen goods is carried on to a considerable extent. A school-house was built, in 1746, by Thomas Layton, Esq., at which period £200, raised by subscription for its support, was invested in land, now producing an annual income of £10, which is paid to a master for teaching sixteen children. Rawdon gives the inferior title of baron to the Marquis of Hastings.

RAWLEIGH, a tything partly in the parishes of Bicton and Rockbear, eastern division of the hundred of Budleigh, and partly in the parish of Whimple, hundred of Cliston, county of Devon. The population is returned with the parishes.

RAWLEIGH (COLYTON), county of Devon. — See COLYTON-RAWLEIGH.

RAWMARSH, a parish in the northern division of the wapentake of Strafforth and Tickhill, West riding of the county of York, 2½ miles (N. by E.) from Rotherham, containing 1259 inhabitants. The living is a rectory, in the archdeaconry and diocese of York, rated in the king's books at £8. 7..3½., and in the patronage of the Crown. The church is dedicated to St. Mary. There are places of worship for Independents and Wesleyan Methodists. Here is a manufacture of coarse earthenware. Thomas Wilson, in 1653, enfeoffed a school-house, messuage, and land, for the free education of poor children; the annual income, arising from

this and various other gifts and bequests, is now about £62, for which from forty to fifty receive instruction.

RAWRETH, a parish in the hundred of Rochford, county of Essex, 3 miles (N. W.) from Rayleigh, containing 327 inhabitants. The living is a rectory, in the archdeaconry of Essex, and diocese of London, rated in the king's books at £20. 13. 4., and in the patronage of the Master and Fellows of Pembroke College, Cambridge. The church, dedicated to St. Nicholas, has lately received an addition of sixty free sittings, the Incorporated Society for the enlargement of churches and chapels having granted £50 towards defraying the expense. A charity school is partly supported by contributions, averaging about £10 per annum.

RAYDON, a parish in the hundred of Samford, county of Suffolk, 3¼ miles (S. E. by S.) from Hadleigh, containing 501 inhabitants. The living is a rectory, in the archdeaconry of Suffolk, and diocese of Norwich, rated in the king's books at £'14. The Rev. Thomas Reeve was patron in 1817. The church is dedicated to St. Mary.

RAYLEIGH, a parish (formerly a market town) in the hundred of Rochford, county of Essex, 14 miles (S. E. by S.) from Chelmsford, and 34 (E. by N.) from London, containing 1203 inhabitants. This place, formerly the head of an honour, or barony, was at the Conquest in the possession of a Dane, named Sweyn, or Swene, who built a stupendous and magnificent castle, some ruins of which, with earth-works and ditches, yet remain, and from the eminence which they occupy is an extensive prospect of the surrounding country. The town is situated upon the shore of Hadley bay, and had formerly a market on Saturday: a cattle fair is held on Trinity-Monday. At King's hill is occasionally held what is termed the "Lawless Court." On the Wednesday morning next after Michaelmas-day, the tenants, or their agents, are bound to appear at the first cock-crowing, and, kneeling, offer their homage of suit and service. The steward of the court, at this dark hour of the night, in a low tone of voice, and without any previous notice, calls over the names of all who are bound to appear, and he who answers not, forfeits to the lord of the manor double his rent for every hour of his absence. All the business is transacted in whispers, and the use of pens and ink not being allowed, the deficiency is supplied by a coal. Some years ago, a tenant forfeited his land from non-attendance, but it was restored to him in consideration of a reasonable amercement. The penalties are said to have been originally imposed upon certain tenants of the adjacent manors, for having conspired in this place to raise a commotion. The living is a rectory, in the archdeaconry of Essex, and diocese of London, rated in the king's books at £17. 17. 6., and in the patronage of R. Bristow, Esq. The church, dedicated to the Holy Trinity, has a tower with a low spire, and is principally in the later style of English architecture. There is a place of worship for Baptists. A small sum, arising from land bequeathed, in 1640, by Isaac Gilbert, and from £200 South Sea stock, left by Dr. Sykes, in 1756, is applied, according to the directions of the respective testators, to the instruction of twenty poor children.

RAYNE, a parish in the hundred of Hinckford, county of Essex, 1¼ mile (W.) from Braintree, containing 343 inhabitants. The living is a rectory, in the archdeaconry of Middlesex, and diocese of London, rated in the king's books at £14. 13. 4., and in the patronage of the Earl of Essex. The church is dedicated to All Saints; the nave is extremely ancient.

RAYNHAM, a parish in the hundred of CHAFFORD, county of ESSEX, 3¼ miles (N. W. by N.) from Purfleet, containing 573 inhabitants. The living is a vicarage, in the archdeaconry of Essex, and diocese of London, rated in the king's books at £10. J. C. G. Crosse, Esq. was patron in 1826. The church, dedicated to St. Helen and St. Giles, has some Norman remains, particularly the arch between the nave and the chancel, and an enriched semicircular doorway. The parish is bounded on the west and south by extensive marshes and the Thames. The Rev. Lewis Bruce, D.D., in 1779, left £2. 10. per annum for teaching poor children to read.

REACH, a joint chapelry with Heath, in the parish of LEIGHTON-BUZZARD, hundred of MANSHEAD, county of BEDFORD, 2½ miles (N. by E.) from Leighton-Buzzard. The population is returned with Heath. It is within the peculiar ecclesiastical jurisdiction of the Prebendary of Leighton-Buzzard in the Cathedral Church of Lincoln.

REACH, a hamlet partly in the parish of BURWELL, hundred of STAPLOE, and partly in that of SWAFFHAM-PRIOR, hundred of STAINE, county of CAMBRIDGE, 5½ miles (W. N. W.) from Newmarket. The population is returned with the parishes. This was anciently a market town, to which ships of considerable burden had access before the draining of the fens: it had a church, which has long been demolished. A large fair for horses, granted to the corporation of Cambridge by charter of King John, is still held here on Rogation Monday.

READ, a township in that part of the parish of WHALLEY which is in the higher division of the hundred of BLACKBURN, county palatine of LANCASTER, 5 miles (S. S. E.) from Clitheroe, containing 510 inhabitants. Edmund Dickenson, in 1743, bequeathed £60 towards the support of a schoolmaster; and in 1798, James Hilton demised land, and a house to be used as a school; the income is about £6 a year, for which five poor children are taught free.

Arms.

READING, a borough and market town, having separate jurisdiction, locally in the hundred of Reading, county of BERKS, 26 miles (S. E. by S.) from Abingdon, and 39 (W. by S.) from London, on the road to Bath, containing, according to the last census, 13,264 inhabitants, since which period the population has increased to upwards of 16,000. This place, which is unquestionably one of very great antiquity, is supposed to have derived its name either from the British word *Redin*, signifying fern, with which the soil abounded, or from *Rhyd*, a ford, and *Ing*, a meadow, which, from its situation on a tract of land intersected by the river Kennet, appears to be the more probable. It is noticed, in 871, by Asser, the biographer of Alfred, as a fortified town taken from the Saxons by the Danes, to which, after their defeat at Englefield, by Earl Ethelwolf, they retired, and were

pursued by that Saxon nobleman, who was killed in attempting to take the town, in a sally of the besieged inhabitants. During the reign of Alfred, and occasionally in that of his successors, the Danes appear to have held possession of the town, which, on the invasion of Sweyn, King of Denmark, to revenge the massacre of his countrymen, in the reign of Ethelred, was burnt to the ground, in 1006, together with the nunnery founded there by Elfrida, in expiation of the murder of her step-son, Edward the Martyr. From this calamity it appears to have recovered prior to the Conquest, for in the Norman survey it is noticed as forming part of the royal demesne. In 1121, Henry I. founded a magnificent monastery, for monks of the Benedictine order, which he endowed with an ample revenue, and dedicated to the Holy Trinity, the Virgin Mary, and St. John the Evangelist. He invested it with the dignity of a mitred abbey, bestowed on the abbots the privilege of coining money, of conferring the honour of knighthood, and many other important privileges. Henry was a frequent visitor at the abbey during his life, and after his death was interred in the abbey church, as was also his consort, Adeliza. Stephen, his successor, erected a strong castle here, which, after having been one of his garrisons during his contest with Matilda, was, in 1153, given up to her son Henry, who, on his accession to the throne, ordered it, together with several other fortresses which had been erected in the preceding reign, to be demolished. This monarch, in 1163, presided at a judicial combat which took place here, on an island to the east of Caversham bridge, between Henry de Essex, the royal standard-bearer, and Robert de Montfort, who accused his antagonist of treasonable cowardice in a battle with the Welch near Chester. Essex being vanquished, his estates were forfeited to the crown, but his life being spared, he became a monk in this abbey. Henry II. visited the town on several other occasions, and in 1185 had an interview here with Herodius, patriarch of Jerusalem, who presented to him the keys of the holy sepulchre, and the royal banner of Jerusalem, and endeavoured, but without success, to induce him to undertake an expedition to recover Palestine from the Saracens. In 1209, the professors and students of Oxford, disgusted with the severity with which they had been treated by the king's officer, in a dispute with the townspeople, retired hither, where they continued to prosecute their studies, till, on expiation being made, they returned to their ancient seats. In 1212, a council was held by the legate of the Pope, for the purpose of effecting a reconciliation between King John and the bishops, whom he had driven into exile; and various civil and ecclesiastical councils were also held here in this and the following reign. Edward III. held a grand tournament here in 1346, and in 1359, his son, John of Gaunt, was married, in the abbey church, to Blanche, daughter and co-heiress of Henry Plantagenet, Duke of Lancaster. In 1389, a reconciliation was effected between Richard II. and his barons, through the mediation of John of Gaunt, who assembled here a great council for that purpose: in 1440, and 1451, parliaments were held in this town; and in 1452, and 1466, the grand parliament adjourned to this place from Westminster, on account of the plague. Henry VIII. frequently visited Reading, and in 1541 took up his residence for some time at the abbey. Edward VI., and the queens Mary and Elizabeth, were frequent visitors, and the latter had a canopied pew appropriated to her use in the parish church of St. Lawrence. In the beginning of the reign of Charles I., the courts of Chancery, King's Bench, and Common Pleas, with the court of Exchequer, and the courts of Wards and Liveries, were held at Reading, in Michaelmas term, in the year 1625, and again in 1635, in consequence of the prevalence of the plague, which was then raging in the metropolis, and a commission under the great seal, for putting in force the laws against the Popish recusants, was read in the courts here. At the commencement of the parliamentary war in this reign, the town was garrisoned for the parliament, but was abandoned by the governor on the approach of the royal forces in 1642; after which it was held by the king's troops, till taken for the parliament by the Earl of Essex, in the following year, after a siege of eight days. After the battle of Newbury, Essex marched to Reading, where he remained for two days; on his departure, it was again garrisoned for the king, who, on his visit in 1644, ordered the military works which had been erected, to be demolished: there are still many extensive remains of the outworks in the Forbury. The inhabitants suffered severely from the contributions levied by both parties, who had alternate possession of the town. In 1688, some Irish and Scottish troops belonging to the army of James II. were posted at Reading, from which they fled on the approach of the Dutch troops under the Prince of Orange; but returning soon after, a skirmish took place in the town, in which the only officer in the prince's army who lost his life in the expedition, was killed: the anniversary of this battle, which was called "Reading Fight," was annually commemorated till about the year 1788, when it was discontinued.

The town is pleasantly situated on the banks of the river Kennet, which, after passing through it, divides into two branches, uniting again previously to its confluence with the Thames. It is in the form of an equilateral triangle, and consists of four principal streets intersected by several smaller: the houses are in general well built of brick, and many of them are spacious and handsome; but there are several constructed of lath and plaster, with high gables, most of which are of the date of the fifteenth century, and were formerly roofed with thatch. The town is well paved, and lighted with gas by a company established by an act obtained in 1825, and amply supplied with water by a joint stock company, originally established in 1694, for the distribution of the water from the Kennet, by machinery, which has been greatly improved since the beginning of the present century, when a lofty brick tower was erected on the bank of the Kennet, and a large reservoir constructed at the upper end of Castle-street, for supplying that part of the town. In addition to the bridges over the different branches of the river, a handsome stone bridge of one arch, ornamented with balustrades, has been erected over the main stream in Duke-street, at the expense of the corporation; and at a small distance to the north-east of the town is another, called Blake's bridge. A public library is supported by subscription among the inhabitants of the town and neighbourhood, under the designation of the Reading Institution, comprising a library, reading-rooms, and a residence for the librarian: there is also a subscription news-room in High-street; and a Philosophical Institution is about to be established: there are commodious baths in London-street. The theatre, a small inconvenient building, erected a few years since, is open for a month or six weeks, annually, but is not well supported.

From its situation near the confluence of two navigable rivers, Reading has from an early period been a place of commercial importance. The manufacture of woollen cloth was introduced in the reign of Edward I.; and in the legendary history of the town, Thomas Cole, called Thomas of Reading, a rich clothier, is said to have obtained from that monarch a standard measure for cloth, the yard being fixed to the precise length of his Majesty's arm. Mr. John Kendrick, alias John à Larder, another eminent clothier in the town, to which he was a great benefactor, in 1624, bequeathed £7500 in trust to the mayor and burgesses, for building a house for the employment of the poor, which was soon afterwards carried into effect, at an expense of £2000: it forms a quadrangle, with a handsome gateway entrance, and the whole edifice, which was a great ornament to the town, obtained from some unknown cause the appellation of the "Oracle." In this establishment the woollen manufacture was carried on, for a considerable period, with success; but during the parliamentary war the building was converted into a depôt for military stores, and the property was lost, with the exception of £500, which Mr. Kendrick had appropriated to be distributed in loans, without interest, to young tradesmen beginning business. After the manufacture of woollen cloth had declined, various other branches were carried on at the Oracle; among these were pin-making, the weaving of sheeting, sail-cloth, and sacking, and the manufacture of floor-cloth. The weaving of coarse linen is carried on here to a small extent; and there are manufactories for silk ribands and galloons, which afford employment to from two to three hundred persons, and for floor and sail-cloth: there are also iron-foundries, breweries, and several yards for building boats. The trade of the town, however, is principally in flour, of which twenty thousand sacks are annually sent to London; wheat, oats, beans, peas, and various kinds of seeds; malt, the business in which has been for some time declining; and oak-bark, timber, hoops, wool, cheese, and beer, &c. The river is navigable for barges of one hundred and twenty tons' burden, and on its banks are wharfs for landing goods, &c. A new wharf and dock were constructed in 1828, on the bank of the Kennet; over which river, in 1830, an iron bridge was completed, on the line of the great western road. The river Kennet, and the Kennet and Avon canal, open a navigable communication with the principal parts of the kingdom. In 1800, a canal was designed by Mr. Rennie, in consequence of the difficult navigation of the Kennet, in part of its course, to the west of the town; but it has not been yet so far completed as to afford all the advantages anticipated. The market days are Wednesday and Saturday, the former for fruit, vegetables, butter, and poultry, and the latter for corn and provisions, which is very numerously attended. The corn market is held in the market-place, a convenient area, of which three sides are occupied by shops, and the fourth by the church of St. Lawrence: these shops are kept in repair by the corporation, who are entitled to the toll of one pint out of each sack of corn sold in the market. The market for provisions is held in a quadrangular building, with a portico, including shambles, shops, and stalls, and a residence for the clerk of the market, who is generally one of the serjeants at mace : there is also, on Saturday, a market for cattle and store pigs ; and a market every Monday for fat cattle, at Loddon bridge, about four miles distant, on the road to Wokingham. The fairs are on February 2nd, May 1st, July 25th, and September 21st ; the three first, principally for horses and cows, and the last, which is also a statute fair, for cattle and cheese, the latter chiefly from Gloucestershire and North Wiltshire, of which, at the fair in 1830, seven hundred tons were pitched for sale ; the cheese fair is held in that part of the Forbury which faces the grammar school.

The town, which is a borough by prescription, has received a succession of charters, from the reign of Henry III. to that of Charles I., the whole of which are in excellent preservation, and the seals nearly perfect: the charter of Henry VII. is splendidly illuminated and emblazoned, the initial letter containing a portrait of that monarch. Under the last of these charters, as modified in the last year of the reign of George IV., the government is vested in a mayor, high steward, recorder, and thirteen aldermen, including the mayor and common council, consisting of nine capital and sixteen inferior burgesses, assisted by a town clerk, two chamberlains, three serjeants at mace, and subordinate officers. The mayor is elected annually, on the first Monday after St. Bartholomew's day, by the aldermen and burgesses, from three candidates nominated by the former body : the mayor, his deputy, the senior alderman, the Bishop of Salisbury, and his chancellor, are justices of the peace for the borough. The corporation formerly held quarterly courts of session for the trial of all but capital offenders ; they at present hold a court of record every Wednesday, under the charter of Charles I., for the recovery of debts under £ 10. The inhabitants are exempt from serving on juries at the assizes and sessions for the county, and from the payment of county rates. The borough has continued to return two members to parliament from the 23rd of Edward I. to the present time : the right of election is vested in the freemen paying scot and lot, and in the inhabitants not receiving alms, of whom the number is about one thousand two hundred and fifty : the mayor is the returning officer. The old town hall was taken down in 1786, and a handsome building erected over part of the free grammar school : adjoining it is the council-chamber, a handsome room in which the borough courts are held, and which is decorated with a portrait of Queen Elizabeth, a bust of Archbishop Laud, finely painted, and portraits of Sir Thomas White and Mr. Kendrick. The portrait of Elizabeth is considered, by Mr. Hanshall, who is now preparing a History of Reading for the press, to be by Hans Holbein, and the painting of Laud is esteemed an admirable production ; but these, and indeed all the por-

Corporate Seal.

traits, are in a very dirty state. The petty sessions for the division are held here every Saturday; the spring assizes and the Epiphany sessions for the county are regularly held in the town ; and the Michaelmas sessions are held alternately here and at Abingdon, at the discretion of the magistrates. The gaol and house of correction for the county, adapted to the reception of one hundred and sixty prisoners, contains a good house for the keeper, a room for the meeting of the magistrates, a chapel, and an infirmary, and comprises five day-rooms and airing-yards for male prisoners in the gaol and bridewell, and five day-rooms and airing-yards for females ; a tread-mill with four wheels, and a large shop for employing prisoners not committed to hard labour, who receive on their discharge one-fifth of their earnings : prisoners committed for offences within the borough are now confined in this gaol.

The town comprises the parishes of St. Giles, St. Lawrence, and St. Mary, in the archdeaconry of Berks, and diocese of Salisbury. The living of St. Giles' is a vicarage, rated in the king's books at £ 14. 17. 3½., and in the patronage of the Crown : the church, an ancient structure, having been much damaged during the parliamentary war, was subsequently repaired, and the tower, which had been destroyed, was rebuilt, with the addition of a slender spire of wood cased with copper : in 1829 it underwent a thorough repair, and received an addition of six hundred and eighty-five sittings, of which four hundred and twenty-four are free, the Incorporated Society for the enlargement of churches and chapels having granted £ 500 towards defraying the expense. The living of St. Lawrence's is a vicarage, rated in the king's books at £ 10, and in the patronage of the President and Fellows of St. John's College, Oxford : the church, which was rebuilt in the fifteenth century, is a spacious structure, in the later style of English architecture, with a beautiful tower of chequered flints : the interior, which is well arranged, contains a mural monument with a bust of John Blagrave, an eminent mathematician, who died in 1611. The living of St. Mary's is a vicarage, rated in the king's books at £ 11. 12. 3½., and in the patronage of the Crown : the church was rebuilt about the year 1550, chiefly with the materials of the abbey, which was demolished about that time ; it is a plain massive structure, in the later style of English architecture, with a square tesselated tower of flint and stone : two hundred and ten additional sittings have been erected, of which one hundred are free, the Incorporated Society for the enlargement of churches and chapels having contributed £ 60 towards defraying the expense. In the parish of St. Lawrence was formerly a chapel, founded and endowed, in 1284, by Lawrence Burgess, bailiff of the borough, and dedicated to St. Edmund ; having been desecrated previously to the year 1479, it was used as a barn, and during the parliamentary war turned into a fort ; in 1750, it was taken down, and rebuilt at Battle farm, but was destroyed by fire within about twenty years since. A chapel of ease to the vicarage of St. Mary's has been erected, by the Rev. George Hulme, on the north side of the road to Oxford. There are three places of worship for Baptists, two for Independents, and one each for the Society of Friends and Wesleyan Methodists, also a Roman Catholic chapel; and in Castle-street is a chapel, erected, in 1798, by the congregation formerly

under the pastoral care of the Hon. and Rev. Bromley Cadogan, now supplied by a minister in the Connexion of the late Countess of Huntingdon. The free grammar school was founded by Abbot Thorne, in the reign of Henry VII., and endowed with the revenue of the decayed hospital of St. John, from which, at the dissolution, a grant of £10 per annum was given for the support of the school, which, since the charter of Elizabeth, has been paid by the corporation. Archbishop Laud gave £20 per annum for augmenting the master's salary, and a house for his residence was, in 1785, purchased by subscription: two fellowships in St. John's College, Oxford, were founded and endowed by Sir Thomas White, for persons educated in this school. The Blue-coat school, for the maintenance, clothing, and education of boys, was founded, in 1646, by Richard Aldworth, Esq., who endowed it with £4000; in addition to which, Sir Thomas Rich, Bart. gave £1000, in 1666, for six additional boys, of which three were to be from the parish of Sonning. Mr. John Hall gave lands for the instruction of three boys; John West, Esq. gave £1000, in 1720, for educating and apprenticing two boys; W. Malthus, Esq., a rent-charge of £91, for eleven boys; and Mr. John Pottenger, £15 per annum, for two boys: the whole income at present exceeds £1000 per annum: there are forty-seven boys on the foundation, who, with the exception of the three under Sir Thomas Rich's endowment, who are appointed by the landholders in the parish of Sonning, are nominated by the corporation, who appoint the master, with a salary of £50 per annum, and maintenance for himself, his wife, and one servant, for whose wages he is allowed £6 more. The girls' green school, in the parish of St. Lawrence, was founded, and is supported, by subscription, for the maintenance, clothing, and education of girls, of whom twenty-one are now in the school: this establishment has an income of £132 per annum, arising from property in the funds: the mistress has a salary of £63. 10. per annum. A school for teaching very young children to read was founded, in 1714, by Mr. Joseph Neale, who endowed it with £11 per annum. A Sunday school, founded in 1810, by Edward Simeon, Esq., who endowed it with £2500, is under the control of the corporation: in this establishment one hundred and fifty-one boys and one hundred and ninety-seven girls are instructed, and partly clothed every alternate year. A school of industry was instituted under the patronage of Mrs. Cadogan; a National school, held in what was formerly the great hall of the abbey, in which is preserved part of a sarcophagus, supposed to be that of the founder, Henry I.; and a Lancasterian school, in Southampton-street, are supported by subscription: in the former, three hundred and eighty boys and one hundred and eighty girls; and in the latter, one hundred and sixty boys and one hundred and twenty girls, receive instruction.

Almshouses in St. Mary's Butts were founded, in 1477, by John à Larder, by whom they were endowed for eight aged persons, who receive each one shilling and eight-pence per week: they were rebuilt by the corporation in 1775. The almshouses in St. Giles' parish, founded in 1617, by Mr. Barnard Harrison, and lately rebuilt by the corporation, have a trifling endowment. An almshouse was founded, in 1634, by Mr. William Kendrick, for four aged men and one woman, of the parishes

of St. Lawrence and St. Giles; the former have an allowance of one shilling and sixpence, and the latter of one shilling, per week, with some gratuities. Almshouses founded in the same year, by Sir Thomas Vachell, for six aged unmarried men, have an endowment of £40 per annum: those in St. Mary's parish were founded, in 1647, by Mr. Richard Jeys, who endowed them, for four aged women, with lands producing about £5 per annum: an almshouse for four aged widows of the parish of St. Lawrence was founded, in 1653, by Mr. John Webb, who endowed it with funds producing a small weekly stipend: almshouses founded by Mr. John Hall, in 1696, for five aged and unmarried women, are endowed with a rent-charge of £25; and, in 1624, Mr. Griffith Jenkins gave five houses, as rent-free dwellings, for poor persons of the parishes of St. Lawrence and St. Mary. Archbishop Laud bequeathed £100 per annum to be appropriated for two successive years to the apprenticing of ten poor boys, and every third year to be divided in marriage portions among five poor maidens, natives of Reading: there are various other bequests of a similar nature, and for other charitable uses. The dispensary was established in 1802, and is liberally supported by subscription. Of the ancient castle erected by Henry I. there is not the slightest vestige, nor can the site of it be traced; the only memorial is preserved in the name of Castle-street, near which it is supposed to have stood. Of the magnificent abbey, erected by the same founder, and which, with the conventual buildings, extended nearly half a mile in circuit, there remain only the abbey gate, a fine specimen of the early Norman style of architecture, and in tolerable preservation, and some vestiges in the abbey mill; the walls, which were eight feet in thickness, have been stripped of their casings, and present only a mass of ruins, with the exception of that part of the hall in which the National school is held: a considerable portion of the materials of the conventual church was used in building the parish church of St. Mary; the principal ornaments were removed for the decoration of Field Marshal Conway's seat, Park Place, near Henley; and a great part of the remaining materials was employed in constructing the great arch over which the Walgrave road is carried. A convent of Franciscan friars was anciently established here, of which there are no remains; and, previously to the year 1400, a convent of Grey friars was founded, on the north side of Castle-street, of which part of the church, with its beautiful west window, is still remaining, and the lavatory is preserved in the pleasure grounds of a house erected on the conventual lands, by Mr. Austwick, the late mayor. An hospital, dedicated to St. Mary Magdalene, for twelve leprous persons and a chaplain, was founded here, in 1134, by Aucherius, second abbot of Reading; and in 1190, Hugh, the eighth abbot, founded an hospital for twenty-six poor brethren, and for the entertainment of pilgrims and travellers, for the maintenance of which he appropriated the church of St. Lawrence. Among the eminent natives of this town were, William of Reading, Archbishop of Bourdeaux in the reign of Henry III.; and Archbishop Laud, the principal minister of Charles I., and one of the earliest victims of that period: he was beheaded on Tower Hill, in 1644.

REAGILL, a hamlet (formerly a chapelry) in the

parish of CROSBY-RAVENSWORTH, WEST ward, county of WESTMORLAND, 3 miles (N. E.) from Shap. The population is returned with the parish. There are no vestiges of the chapel, except in the names of certain enclosures, such as Chapel-Garth, Chapel-Lands, &c. The Rev. Randal Sanderson, in 1733, left £120 for the erection of a free school here, to which the commissioners, on the enclosure of waste lands in 1803, awarded an allotment now let for £25 per annum, for the support of the master, who also receives an annuity of £5, the donation of William Twaytes, Esq.: thirty children are instructed.

REARSBY, a parish in the eastern division of the hundred of GOSCOTE, county of LEICESTER, 7¼ miles (N. E. by N.) from Leicester, containing 451 inhabitants. The living is a rectory, in the archdeaconry of Leicester, and diocese of Lincoln, rated in the king's books at £17. 9. 7., and in the patronage of the Rev. N. Morgan. The church is dedicated to St. Michael. There is a place of worship for Wesleyan Methodists. Two trifling bequests by the Rev. John Orton and Mrs. Faunt are applied for teaching poor children.

REAVELEY, a township in the parish of INGRAM, northern division of COQUETDALE ward, county of NORTHUMBERLAND, 7¼ miles (S. by E.) from Wooler, containing 74 inhabitants.

RECULVER, a parish in the hundred of BLEANGATE, lathe of ST. AUGUSTINE, county of KENT, 10 miles (N. E.) from Canterbury, containing 266 inhabitants. The living is a vicarage, with the perpetual curacy of Hoath annexed, in the peculiar jurisdiction and patronage of the Archbishop of Canterbury, rated in the king's books at £9. 12. 3½. The church, dedicated to St. Mary, is a handsome structure in the early style of English architecture, with two towers at the west end, each surmounted by a spire; it has received considerable damage from encroachments of the sea: it was founded some time in the seventh century, together with a monastery for Black canons, by one Basse, upon land granted to him by Egbert, King of Kent; in 949, King Eadred annexed it to Christ Church in Canterbury; yet it seems to have been afterwards of some note, being under the government of a dean, in 1030. There are considerable remains of *Regulbium*, a Roman fort, within the walls of which the royal palace of Ethelbert and the monastery before mentioned were erected. Roman coins, tesselated pavements, cellars, cisterns, fibulæ, and a variety of trinkets, with some British and Saxon coins, have been discovered. By the fall of the cliff at different times, lumps of metal have been met with, seeming to indicate the destruction of the place by fire.

REDBOURN, a parish in the hundred of CASHIO, or liberty of ST. ALBAN's, county of HERTFORD, 17 miles (W.) from Hertford, containing 1784 inhabitants. The living is a discharged vicarage, in the archdeaconry of St. Alban's, and diocese of London, rated in the king's books at £16. 5., and in the patronage of the Earl of Verulam. The church, dedicated to St. Mary, stands about a mile west from the village, and is approached by a fine avenue of elms. There are places of worship for Baptists, Independents, and Wesleyan Methodists. Here was a cell of Benedictine monks from St. Alban's, dedicated to St. Amphibalus the Martyr and his companions. Fairs are held on the Wednesday after New

Year's day, Wednesday in Easter-week, and Wednesday at Whitsuntide.

REDBOURN, a parish in the eastern division of the wapentake of MANLEY, parts of LINDSEY, county of LINCOLN, 2½ miles (E. N. E.) from Kirton, containing 270 inhabitants. The living is a discharged vicarage, in the archdeaconry of Stow, and diocese of Lincoln, rated in the king's books at £5. 10., endowed with £200 private benefaction, and £200 royal bounty, and in the patronage of the Duke of St. Albans. The church is dedicated to St. Andrew; part of the tower is ancient, and the rest of the building modern.

REDBRIDGE, a hamlet in the parish of MILLBROOK, hundred of BUDDLESGATE, Fawley division of the county of SOUTHAMPTON, 3½ miles (N. W. by W.) from Southampton. The population is returned with the parish. This is an extensive and populous village of very remote origin; according to Bede's ecclesiastical history, its original name was *Reodford*, afterwards changed to *Rodbridge*, now by corruption Redbridge, probably from an ancient bridge which here crosses the Test. Here was a monastery in the infancy of the Saxon church; and, in 687, Cynbreth, at that time abbot, converted and baptized the two brothers of Arvandus, Prince of the Isle of Wight, preparatory to their execution by command of Ceadwalla, King of Essex. The village is situated at the head of the Southampton water, and the Andover canal terminates at it. There is a considerable trade in the importation of coal, and in exporting timber and corn. Ship-building affords employment to several persons, and there is a large brewery.

REDCAR, a chapelry in the parish of MARSK, eastern division of the liberty of LANGBAURGH, North riding of the county of YORK, 6¼ miles (N.) from Guisbrough, containing 673 inhabitants. The chapel, which has been recently erected, contains seven hundred sittings, of which three hundred and fifty are free, the Incorporated Society for promoting the building of additional churches, &c., having granted £500 towards defraying the expense. There is a place of worship for Wesleyan Methodists. Redcar is bounded on the northeast by the North sea, the coast of which is extremely rocky and dangerous to mariners, but the number of lives lost by shipwreck has greatly diminished since the establishment of a life-boat here in 1802. Formerly the place contained only a few fishermen's huts, but of late years it has become the resort of many genteel families, for the purpose of sea-bathing, and the fisheries are now prosecuted with ardour and success. The village contains some excellent inns, and good private lodging-houses, for the accommodation of visitors during the summer months, but in winter it exhibits a somewhat dreary aspect, from the vast quantity of sand which the wind drifts from the beach into the streets.

REDDENHALL, a parish in the hundred of EARSHAM, county of NORFOLK, 1½ mile (E. N. E.) from Harleston, containing, with Harleston, 1641 inhabitants. The living is a rectory, in the archdeaconry of Norfolk, and diocese of Norwich, rated in the king's books at £20, and in the patronage of the Duke of Norfolk, on the nomination of the Bishop of Norwich. The church, dedicated to St. Mary, is in the later style of English architecture: at the end of the north aisle is a sepulchral chapel of the family of Gawdy, dedicated to the Assumption of the Virgin Mary, and containing many ancient monuments. Wm. Sancroft, in 1688, gave £900 for founding a public school, to which John Dove, in 1712, bequeathed £200.

REDDISH, a township in the parish of MANCHESTER, hundred of SALFORD, county palatine of LANCASTER, 5½ miles (S. E. by S.) from Manchester, containing 574 inhabitants.

REDDITCH, a chapelry in that part of the parish of TARDEBIGG which is in the upper division of the hundred of HALFSHIRE, county of WORCESTER, 5¾ miles (E. S. E.) from Bromsgrove. The population is returned with the parish. This flourishing village, which has the appearance of a small market town, is pleasantly situated on a commanding eminence near the Warwickshire border, on the new line of road from London to Birmingham, and contains, besides a neat modern chapel of ease, places of worship for Independents and Wesleyan Methodists. The principal articles of manufacture, for which it has long been famous, are needles and fish-hooks, which have been brought to perfection, and afford employment to about four thousand persons in the village and neighbourhood. There are fairs for cattle, on the first Monday in August, and third Monday in September, and it is in contemplation to petition the legislature for the privilege of holding a weekly market. A National school is attended by about ninety boys, and supported by the Earl of Plymouth, who has an elegant mansion in the vicinity, and holds a court leet annually in October, as lord of the manor, at which a constable and other officers are appointed. A Cistercian abbey of considerable note formerly existed at Bordesley, near this place, some slight remains of which may be traced : it was founded, in 1138, by the Empress Matilda, in honour of the Blessed Virgin, and was valued at the dissolution at £392. 8. 6., when it was granted to Lord Windsor, one of the ancestors of the present Earl of Plymouth.

REDGRAVE, a parish in the hundred of HARTISMERE, county of SUFFOLK, 2 miles (N. E. by N.) from Botesdale, containing 713 inhabitants. The living is a discharged rectory, with Botesdale, in the archdeaconry of Sudbury, and diocese of Norwich, rated in the king's books at £25. 7. 1. G. St. Vincent Wilson, Esq. was patron in 1802. The church, dedicated to St. Botolph, has a steeple of white brick, recently erected, and is adorned with several fine monuments of considerable beauty of design and execution, particularly that of the celebrated Lord Keeper, Sir Nicholas Bacon, and another to the eminent Lord Chief Justice, Sir John Holt, both of whom resided here. A free grammar school for six boys was founded, in 1651, by Sir Nicholas Bacon, who endowed it with a rent-charge of £30, and a dwelling-house for the master, whose salary is £20, and the usher's £8; the residue being appropriated for repairs. There is also a trifling sum for the education of children, left by Mary Foster in 1686. Cardinal Wolsey was rector of this parish.

REDISHAM, a parish in the hundred of WANGFORD, county of SUFFOLK, 5 miles (N. N. E.) from Halesworth, containing 156 inhabitants. The living is a perpetual curacy, in the archdeaconry of Suffolk, and diocese of Norwich, endowed with £1000 royal bounty, and in the patronage of the Earl of Gosford. The church is dedicated to St. Peter.

REDISHAM (LITTLE), county of SUFFOLK.—See RINGFIELD.

REDLINGFIELD, a parish in the hundred of HARTISMERE, county of SUFFOLK, 3½ miles (S. E.) from Eye, containing 222 inhabitants. The living is a perpetual curacy, in the archdeaconry of Sudbury, and diocese of Norwich, endowed with £400 private benefaction, and £800 royal bounty. A. Adair, Esq. was patron in 1825. A Benedictine nunnery, in honour of St. Andrew, was founded here, in 1120, by Manasses, Earl of Ghisness, and Emma his wife, the revenue of which, at the dissolution, was valued at £81. 2. 5.

REDLYNCH, a chapelry in the parish and hundred of BRUTON, county of SOMERSET, 2 miles (S. E. by S.) from Bruton, containing 93 inhabitants. The living is a perpetual curacy, annexed to that of Bruton, in the archdeaconry of Wells, and diocese of Bath and Wells, endowed with £600 royal bounty, and £200 parliamentary grant. The chapel is dedicated to St. Peter. Redlynch gives the inferior title of baron to the Earl of Ilchester.

REDMAIN, a joint township with Blindcrake and Isall, in the parish of ISALL, ALLERDALE ward below Darwent, county of CUMBERLAND, 3¼ miles (N. N. E.) from Cockermouth. The population is returned with Isall.

REDMARLEY-D'ABITOT, a parish in a detached portion of the lower division of the hundred of OSWALDSLOW, county of WORCESTER, 5½ miles (S. E. by S.) from Ledbury, containing 955 inhabitants. The living is a rectory, in the archdeaconry and diocese of Worcester, rated in the king's books at £10. 7½., and in the patronage of Mrs. Nillet. The church, dedicated to St. Bartholomew, has been much modernised; the font is circular and very ancient. There is a trifling sum, the bequest of William Church, in 1727, for teaching poor children.

RED-MARSHALL, a parish in the south-western division of STOCKTON ward, county palatine of DURHAM, comprising the chapelries of Carleton and Stillington, and the township of Red-Marshall, and containing 264 inhabitants, of which number, 75 are in the township of Red-Marshall, 4¾ miles (W. N. W.) from Stockton upon Tees. The living is a rectory, in the archdeaconry and diocese of Durham, rated in the king's books at £17. 18. 1½., and in the patronage of the Bishop of Durham. The church, dedicated to St. Cuthbert, has a massive western tower, a Norman arch leading into the chancel, and on the south side of it three stone stalls, opposite to which is an arched recess. The rectory-house appears to have been once fortified, an embattled tower still remaining.

REDMILE, a parish in the hundred of FRAMLAND, county of LEICESTER, 12¼ miles (N. by E.) from Melton-Mowbray, containing 411 inhabitants. The living is a rectory, in the archdeaconry of Leicester, and diocese of Lincoln, rated in the king's books at £12. 9. 2., and in the patronage of the Duke of Rutland. The church is dedicated to St. Peter. The Grantham canal crosses the parish on the north-west side.

REDMIRE, a chapelry in the parish of WENSLEY, western division of the wapentake of HANG, North riding of the county of YORK, 6¼ miles (W. N. W.) from Middleham, containing 399 inhabitants. The living is a perpetual curacy, annexed to that of Bolton, in the archdeaconry of Richmond, and diocese of Chester, endowed with

£600 royal bounty, and £400 parliamentary grant, and in the patronage of the Rector of Wensley. The chapel is dedicated to St. Mary. There is a place of worship for Wesleyan Methodists. The Rev. Thomas Baynes, in 1725, founded a free school and endowed it with lands and tenements now producing an annual income of about £19, for which fourteen children are instructed. The lead mines formerly in operation here have been almost exhausted, but calamine is got in abundance. Coal also is obtained in the neighbourhood; and there is a fine spring strongly impregnated with sulphur, with convenient well for bathing, the water having been found efficacious in the cure of rheumatism, scurvy, and weakness of sight.

REDRUTH, a market town and parish in the hundred of PENWITH, county of CORNWALL, 49 miles (S. W. by W.) from Launceston, and 262¾ (W. S. W.) from London, containing 6607 inhabitants. This ancient town, originally called *Uny*, subsequently received the appellation of *Dre druth*, or "Druids' town," of which its present name is evidently an abbreviation. It appears to have existed previously to the division of the kingdom into parishes, and to have been a central point for the exercise of the religious rites of the ancient Britons, of which the adjacent rocks, basins, circles, and erect stones, with numerous remains of cromlechs, cairns, and other objects of superstitious veneration, are standing memorials; especially one rock, formerly the scene of human sacrifices, and therefore called "the Sacrificing Rock." The town is situated on the brow of a hill in the midst of the mining district, and consists chiefly of one long street, which is indifferently paved, lighted with gas, and supplied with water from a spring near Trefula. A small theatre is open occasionally, and there is a subscription reading-room. A savings bank has been recently erected; it is a handsome edifice, with a colonnade in front. The prosperity of this place, and the rapid increase of its population, have been eminently promoted by the discovery of extensive tin and copper mines in its neighbourhood, the produce of which is said to realize nearly a million sterling per annum. Sales of copper-ore are held weekly by ticket, and there are several very extensive stores of gun-powder, tools, and other articles, for the use of the miners; some hats are manufactured here. A railroad, about nine miles in length, recently constructed, under the provisions of an act obtained in 1824, from Point quay, in Restrongeth creek, to this town, and also communicating with a branch of the river Fal, facilitates the exportation of ore, and the conveyance of timber and coal, for the supply of the mines, and for general purposes. A market and two annual fairs were granted by charter of Charles II., and a third fair by Henry VII. Markets are now held on Tuesday and Friday, the latter of which is a great corn market, especially for oats. Fairs are on Easter-Tuesday, May 2nd, August 3rd, and October 12th, chiefly for cattle; the tolls and dues of the markets, and of the fairs in May and August, also those of a fair commonly called Roast Goose fair, belong to Lord De Dunstanville, who, as lord of the manor, appoints examiners of weights and measures. A market-house, shambles, and other buildings, have been recently erected, at the expense of his lordship. At the entrance to the market-place is a handsome square stone tower, built on arches, and ornamented with a clock, having four dial plates, which is lighted with gas, on the east and west sides.

The living is a rectory, in the archdeaconry of Cornwall, and diocese of Exeter, rated in the king's books at £20, and in the patronage of Lord De Dunstanville. The church, which is dedicated to St. Uny, and situated about half a mile from the town, near the foot of Carn-Brea Hill, was rebuilt about 1770, and consists of a nave, with a flat ceiling supported by pillars. A chapel of ease, in the ancient style of English architecture, has been erected by subscription, aided by a grant from the commissioners for building churches and chapels; but is yet in an unfinished state. There are places of worship for Baptists, the Society of Friends, and Primitive and Wesleyan Methodists. A free grammar school was built by subscription in 1803, and supported for some time by voluntary contributions, but is now used only for pay-scholars. On the eastern side of Carn-Brea Hill are the ruins of a castle, parts of which are of great antiquity. At the village of Plain an Quarry, in this parish, are the remains of one of those circles in which the ancient plays were performed. The application of gas to the purposes of domestic light, as a substitute for candles and oil, was first made here, by Mr. Murdock, and afterwards successfully introduced by him into the Soho foundry at Birmingham.

REDWICK, a tything in that part of the parish of HENBURY which is in the lower division of the hundred of HENBURY, county of GLOUCESTER, 6 miles (S. W. by W.) from Thornbury, containing, with the chapelry of Northwick, 257 inhabitants. It is within the peculiar jurisdiction of the Bishop of Bristol.

REDWICK, a chapelry in the parish of MAGOR, lower division of the hundred of CALDICOTT, county of MONMOUTH, 8 miles (E. by S.) from Newport, containing 238 inhabitants. The living is a perpetual curacy, annexed to the vicarage of Magor, in the archdeaconry and diocese of Llandaff, endowed with £400 royal bounty. The chapel is dedicated to St. Thomas.

REDWORTH, a township in the parish of HEIGHINGTON, south-eastern division of DARLINGTON ward, county palatine of DURHAM, 7 miles (N. N. W.) from Darlington, containing 307 inhabitants. Here are the remains of a Danish fortification, called Shackleton, surrounded with triple embankments.

REED, a parish in the hundred of ODSEY, county of HERTFORD, 1¾ mile (W. by N.) from Barkway, containing 214 inhabitants. The living is a rectory, consolidated, in 1800, with the vicarage of Barkway, in the archdeaconry of Middlesex, and diocese of London, rated in the king's books at £13. 6. 8. The church, dedicated to St. Mary, has a square embattled tower of flint.

REED, a parish in the hundred of THINGOE, county of SUFFOLK, 6½ miles (S.W. by S.) from Bury-St.Edmunds, containing 239 inhabitants. The living is a discharged rectory, in the archdeaconry of Sudbury, and diocese of Norwich, rated in the king's books at £2. 18. 1½., and in the patronage of the Crown. The church is dedicated to All Saints. A National school, recently established here, is supported by a bequest from Thomas Sparke, in 1721, producing an annual income of £12, with some other smaller benefactions: about twenty-six children are instructed by a schoolmistress, who also superintends a Sunday school.

REEDHAM, a parish in the hundred of WALSHAM, county of NORFOLK, 6 miles (S. by E.) from Acle, containing 437 inhabitants. The living is a rectory, with the vicarage of Freethorpe annexed, in the archdeaconry and diocese of Norwich, rated in the king's books at £18. The Rev. John Love was patron in 1801. The church is dedicated to St. John the Baptist. The Danish king Lothbroc, when driven by stress of weather upon the coast of East Anglia, landed at this place.

REEDLY-HALLOWS, a joint township with Filly-Close and New Laund-Booth, in that part of the parish of WHALLEY which is in the higher division of the hundred of BLACKBURN, county palatine of LANCASTER, 2 miles (N. N. E.) from Burnley, containing, with Filly-Close and New Laund-Booth, 422 inhabitants.

REEDNESS, a township in the parish of WHITGIFT, lower division of the wapentake of OSGOLDCROSS, West riding of the county of YORK, 6 miles (S.E. by S.) from Howden, containing 683 inhabitants. John Wressel, in 1795, bequeathed a rent-charge of £15, for teaching twelve children of this and the neighbouring townships. Reedness is within the jurisdiction of the peculiar court of Snaith.

REEPHAM, a parish in the wapentake of LAWRESS, parts of LINDSEY, county of LINCOLN, 4¼ miles (E. N. E.) from Lincoln, containing 247 inhabitants. The living is a discharged vicarage, in the archdeaconry of Stow, and diocese of Lincoln, rated in the king's books at £6. 13. 4., endowed with £200 royal bounty, and in the patronage of the Master and Wardens of the Mercers' Company, London. The church is dedicated to St. Peter and St. Paul.

REEPHAM, a market town and parish in the hundred of EYNSFORD, county of NORFOLK, 12 miles (N. W. by N.) from Norwich, and 116 (N. E. by N.) from London, containing 345 inhabitants. This town is situated on an elevation near the small river Eyne, and is neat and well built; in the market-place are several good houses, which are fronted by a row of evergreens. The chief trade is in malt, and there is an extensive brewery. The market, obtained by charter of Edward I., is on Wednesday; and there is a fair for horses and toys on June 29th; both, for the sake of convenience, are held at Hackford. The living is a discharged rectory, with Kerdeston, in the archdeaconry of Norfolk, and diocese of Norwich, rated in the king's books at £18. 1. 0½., and in the patronage of the Rev. John Mathew. The church, dedicated to St. Mary, contains some ancient monuments, and, formerly, a celebrated image of the Virgin, which became an object of general attraction, and was much enriched by the offerings of religious votaries; there were formerly three fine churches within one enclosure, one for the town, and two for the lordships of Whitwell and Hackford; that belonging to Hackford was burnt down in 1600, the steeple only remaining, which was taken down about thirty-two years ago. The living of Whitwell is a vicarage, in the archdeaconry and diocese of Norwich, and in the patronage of George Hunt Holley, Esq. The church contains a few marble tablets to the memory of the Bircham family. There are places of worship for Baptists and Wesleyan Methodists. A National school for girls is supported by voluntary contributions.

REETH, a market town in that part of the parish of GRINTON which is in the western division of the wapentake of GILLING, North riding of the county of YORK, 9¼ miles (W. by S.) from Richmond, containing 1460 inhabitants. This town is situated on an elevated spot of ground, at a short distance from the confluence of the rivers Arkle and Swale, and commands a beautiful and picturesque view of the adjacent country. It is nearly quadrangular, and is irregularly built. The knitting of stockings is extensively carried on, and in the neighbourhood are lead mines in operation. A market, granted by charter in the 6th of William and Mary, is held on Friday; and fairs are on the Friday before Good Friday, Old May-day, Old Midsummer-day, the festival of St. Bartholomew, Old Martinmas-day, and St. Thomas' day. There are places of worship for Independents and Wesleyan Methodists. The Friends' school was erected at the expense of George and John Raw, the former of whom, in 1814, bequeathed £1500 for its support, and the latter, in 1815, left £500 for a similar purpose; the interest of these benefactions, amounting to £72 per annum, is paid in support of a master, who educates thirty-three poor children. Opposite to Healaugh, in this township, on Harker-hill, are the remains of an intrenchment, one hundred feet square, called Maiden's Castle; on the east side of the hill and in the dale are others, in one of which some pieces of armour have been found: they are supposed to be of Roman origin.

REIGATE, a borough, market town, and parish, in the first division of the hundred of REIGATE, county of SURREY, 19 miles (E.) from Guildford, and 21 (S. by W.) from London, containing 2961 inhabitants : the parish is divided into two precincts, each of which supports its own poor, viz., the borough, which contains 1328 inhabitants, and the foreign, including the districts of Santon, Woodhatch, Howleigh, Linkfield, and Colley, in which are 1633. This place, which is of considerable antiquity, was called in Domesday-book Cherche felle, and afterwards Church-field, in Reigate, by which name the church was given by Hamelin, Earl of Surrey, to the priory of St. Mary Overy, Southwark, in the reign of King John. The origin of its present name is uncertain : Camden says that, if borrowed from the ancient language, it signifies the course of the stream ; while Mr. Bray and others consider it to be derived, and with great probability, from the Saxon words rige, or ridge, and gate, from a gate, or bar, placed across the road which runs by the high ridge of hill, now called Reigate hill. He is also inclined to think that the gate existed so early as the formation of the Saxon Stane-street ; and there are many other places in the vicinity the names of which terminate in a similar way, all seemingly derived from a like circumstance. The inhabitants are recorded to have routed the Danes, when they were ravaging the kingdom, on more than one occasion ; and Camden has preserved a distich commemorating their courageous conduct in these conflicts. The next historical circumstance connected with Reigate is the assault and capture of its castle by Louis the Dauphin, in the reign of John, in revenge for the adherence of its then owner, William de Warren, to the cause of that monarch, in his quarrel with the barons. The manor of Reigate was originally of great extent : it belonged in the Confessor's time to his Queen Edith, at which period it was rated at three thousand seven hundred and fifty-six acres, and is thought to have included, besides the parish of that name, the present parishes also of Leigh, Newdigate, Churchwell, Horley, and Brostow. The town is beautifully situated on a branch of the river Mole, in the valley of Holmesdale, on the high road from London to Brighton, and stands upon a rock of white sand, which, for purity and colour, is said to be unequalled by any in the kingdom: it consists of two principal streets and several smaller ones, which are only partially paved, and indifferently lighted: water of very good quality is procured from the rock on which it stands. The High-street, which is the main street, extends in a direction nearly from east to west, having at its eastern extremity the church: the other chief street, called Bell-street, runs north and south, containing some respectable houses, and is terminated at its southern extremity by the priory. A considerable quantity of oatmeal was formerly made here, nearly twenty mills having been employed, but the number is now reduced to one; some pits of fullers' earth have been opened of late years. A weekly market on Tuesday was granted by Edward III., and, in 1679, Charles II. granted a second market, on the first Wednesday in every month, which afterwards fell into disuse, but has lately been revived, and is held for cattle, the market on Tuesday being for corn and provisions: the market-house, built by Sir Joseph Jekyll, is an appropriate and convenient edifice. The fairs are on Whit-Monday and Tuesday, September 14th, and December 9th, chiefly for horses, cattle, &c. A court leet and baron is held here, at which a bailiff and subordinate officers are elected, by whom the local affairs of the town are managed. The town hall is in the market-place, and was built as a prison for felons brought to be tried at the sessions, which were formerly held here. This borough sent two members to parliament so early as the reign of Edward I., and has continued to do so since that period : the right of election is vested in the freeholders of messuages, or burgage tenements, within the borough precincts, in number about two hundred : the bailiff is the returning officer, and the parliamentary influence is possessed by Lord Hardwick and Lord Somers.

The living is a discharged vicarage, in the archdeaconry of Surrey, and diocese of Winchester, rated in the king's books at £20. 5. 5., and in the patronage of Miss Snelson. The church, dedicated to St. Mary Magdalene, is a substantial stone building, with an embattled tower of hewn stone at the west end, and with double buttresses : it contains some handsome monuments, amongst which is one to the memory of the Earl of Nottingham, Lord High Admiral in the reign of Queen Elizabeth, who commanded the naval equipment against the Invincible Armada. The Society of Friends and Independents have each a place of worship here. The free school was founded, in 1675, by the inhabitants, and ten boys, selected by the trustees from the parish, are instructed in reading, writing, and arithmetic, a house having been built for the master, who receives about £23 per ann. from endowments by Robert Bishopp and John Parker. There is also a National school, supported by voluntary contributions, in which about one hundred boys and girls are educated. The origin of Reigate castle, which stood on the north side of the town, within the precincts of the borough, is generally ascribed to the ancient Earls of Warren and Surrey,

although some writers consider it to be of Saxon foundation, with subsequent erections : it is spoken of by Lambarde, in the reign of Elizabeth, as a ruin, although enough of it remained at the time of the parliamentary war to induce a committee sitting at Derby House to take notice of it; it appears to have been soon afterwards completely demolished, and little now remains to point out even its site. In the castle court is an entrance to a cavern, called the Barons' Cave, in which it is said that the barons met and settled the articles of Magna Charta, prior to meeting King John at Runymede. The priory was founded by William, Earl Warren, for canons regular of the order of St. Augustine, about the same period as the presumed erection of the castle : it was dedicated to the Virgin Mary and the Holy Cross, and, at the period of its dissolution by Henry VIII., was valued at £78. 16. 8.: a manor was attached to this foundation, for which courts are still held, many of the burgage tenements are of borough being holden of it : the noble mansion erected on its site retains the name of Reigate Priory. The walls and roof of an ancient chapel, dedicated to St. Lawrence, are still standing in the town, the building having been converted into a dwelling-house : another chapel, dedicated to the Holy Cross, supposed to have belonged to the priory, and which stood in the town, has been demolished, having been previously occupied as a barn; and a third, dedicated to St. Thomas the Apostle, and standing in the market-place, was used as a court-house and market-house until 1708, when it was taken down. John Fox, the martyrologist, resided in this town, in the family of the Duchess of Richmond, as tutor to her son, the Earl of Surrey, when expelled from New College, Oxford, on a charge of heresy, and continued under the protection of the family during the latter part of the reign of Henry VIII., that of Edward VI., and part of that of Mary, when his pupil, then Duke of Norfolk, sent him abroad, to avoid the malice of Gardiner.

REIGHTON, a parish in the wapentake of DICKERING, East riding of the county of YORK, 6¼ miles (N. W. by N.) from Bridlington, containing 217 inhabitants. The living is a discharged vicarage, in the archdeaconry of the East riding, and diocese of York, rated in king's books at £9. 10., endowed with £200 royal bounty, and in the patronage of Sir W. Strickland, Bart.

REMENHAM, a parish in the hundred of BEYNHURST, county of BERKS, 1½ mile (N. by E.) from Henley upon Thames, containing 380 inhabitants. The living is a rectory, in the archdeaconry of Berks, and diocese of Salisbury, rated in the king's books at £20. 1. 0½., and in the patronage of the Principal and Fellows of Jesus College, Oxford. The church is dedicated to St. Nicholas. The river Thames flows through the parish. Park Place, in this parish, was formerly the residence of General Lord Conway, and subsequently of the Prince of Wales, grandfather to his present Majesty ; the former established the growth and distillery of lavender in this neighbourhood, which are still carried on.

REMPSTONE, a parish in the southern division of the wapentake of RUSHCLIFFE, county of NOTTINGHAM, 4¼ miles (N. E. by N.) from Loughborough, containing 368 inhabitants. The living is a rectory, in the archdeaconry of Nottingham, and diocese of York, rated in the king's books at £13. 2. 6., and in the patronage of the Master of Sidney Sussex College, Cambridge. The church, dedicated to All Saints, which was consecrated in 1773, was erected with the materials of the former edifice of St. Peter in the Rushes, and of a chapel long before in disuse.

RENDCOMBE, a parish in the hundred of Raps-gate, county of Gloucester, 5½ miles (N.) from Cirencester, containing 190 inhabitants. The living is a rectory, in the archdeaconry and diocese of Gloucester, rated in the king's books at £13. 6. 8., and' in the patronage of Joseph Pitt, Esq. The church is dedicated to St. Peter.

RENDHAM, a parish in the hundred of Plomes-gate, county of Suffolk, 2½ miles (N. W. by W.) from Saxmundham, containing 452 inhabitants. The living is a vicarage, in the archdeaconry of Suffolk, and diocese of Norwich, endowed with £400 private benefaction, and £600 parliamentary grant, and in the patronage of certain Trustees. The church is dedicated to St. Michael. There is a place of worship for Independents. Thomas Neale, in 1722, bequeathed land, producing a small income, in support of a free school.

RENDLESHAM, a parish in the hundred of Loes, county of Suffolk, 3 miles (S. E. by S.) from Wickham-Market, containing 249 inhabitants. The living is a rectory, in the archdeaconry of Suffolk, and diocese of Norwich, rated in the king's books at £24. 13. 4., and in the patronage of the Crown. The church is dedicated to St. Gregory. Here Suidhelm, King of the East Angles, was baptized by Cedda. Rendlesham gives the title of baron to the family of Thelusson, in the Irish peerage.

RENHOLD, a parish in the hundred of Barford, county of Bedford, 3¾ miles (N. E.) from Bedford, containing 340 inhabitants. The living is a discharged vicarage, in the archdeaconry of Bedford, and diocese of Lincoln, rated in the king's books at £8. 3. 4., endowed with £200 private benefaction, and £200 royal bounty, and in the patronage of John Polhill, Esq. The church is dedicated to All Saints. The river Ouse runs through the parish. William Belcher, in 1723, gave £600 for the support of a school, in which from twenty to thirty children are educated; the annual income is about £20. In the neighbourhood are several ancient mounds, called " the Amphitheatre."

RENISHAW, a township in the parish of Ecking-ton, hundred of Scarsdale, county of Derby, 7¼ miles (N. E.) from Chesterfield, containing 551 inhabitants, who are principally employed in the extensive iron-foundry established on the Chesterfield canal, which passes through the township. Thomas Camm, in 1702, bequeathed land and premises yielding about £46 per annum, which sum, and two subsequent bequests by Lady Frecheville and Peter Cadman, amounting to £10 a year, are applied for the instruction of about twenty-seven children.

RENNINGTON, a chapelry in the parish of Emble-ton, southern division of Bambrough ward, county of Northumberland, 3¾ miles (N. E. by N.) from Alnwick, containing 272 inhabitants. The living is a perpetual curacy, united with that of Rock, in the archdeaconry of Northumberland, and diocese of Durham, endowed with £400 private benefaction, and £800 royal bounty. The chapel, dedicated to All Saints, is very ancient.

RENWICK, a parish in Leath ward, county of Cumberland, 3¾ miles (E. N. E.) from Kirk-Oswald, con-taining 364 inhabitants. The living is a perpetual cura-cy, in the archdeaconry and diocese of Carlisle, endowed with £200 private benefaction, and £800 royal bounty, and in the patronage of the Bishop of Carlisle. The church, dedicated to All Saints, was rebuilt in 1733, at the expense of the parishioners. There is a place of worship for Wesleyan Methodists, with a Sunday school attached.

REPPS, a parish in the western division of the hundred of Flegg, county of Norfolk, 5¼ miles (N. N. E.) from Acle, containing, with the hamlet of Bastwick, 219 inhabitants. The living is a perpetual curacy, in the archdeaconry and diocese of Norwich, endowed with £200 royal bounty, and in the patronage of the Dean and Chapter of Norwich. The church is dedicated to St. Peter.

REPPS (NORTH), a parish in the northern division of the hundred of Erpingham, county of Norfolk, 3 miles (S. S. E.) from Cromer, containing 529 inhabitants. The living is a rectory, in the archdeaconry and diocese of Norwich, rated in the king's books at £18, and in the patronage of the King, as Duke of Lancaster. The church is dedicated to St. Mary. On Tolls Hill, near a neat marine cottage called the Hermitage, is a remark-ably distinct echo.

REPPS (SOUTH), a parish in the northern division of the hundred of Erpingham, county of Norfolk, 4¾ miles (N. N. W.) from North Walsham, containing 656 inhabitants. The living is a rectory, in the arch-deaconry and diocese of Norwich, rated in the king's books at £16, and in the patronage of the King, as Duke of Lancaster. The church is dedicated to St. James. On a lofty eminence about a mile from the vil-lage are the remains of an ancient beacon, whence Nor-wich and Yarmouth are discernible on a clear day.

REPTON, a parish in the hundred of Repton and Gresley, county of Derby, 4¼ miles (N. E. by E.) from Burton upon Trent, containing, with the chapelry of Bradby, 2104 inhabitants. The living is a perpetual cu-racy, in the archdeaconry of Derby, and diocese of Lich-field and Coventry, endowed with £200 royal bounty, and in the patronage of Sir George Crewe, Bart. The church, dedicated to St. Wyston, is principally Norman, but ex-hibits portions in the several later styles of English ar-chitecture : under it is a curious ancient crypt, believed to have been part of the conventual church, which was destroyed by the Danes. There are places of worship for Independents and Wesleyan Methodists. The navigable river Trent bounds the parish on the north, and on its banks are vestiges of a small Roman camp, near which is an immense rock of freestone. Here were anciently a market and a fair ; there is now a statute fair at Michaelmas for hiring servants, and an annual court leet is held by the lord of the manor. Repton, anciently called Repington, is supposed to have been the Roman station *Repandunum*. Under the Saxon dominion it was called *Repandum*, and was the capital of the kingdom of Mercia. Before the year 660, here was a nunnery under the government of an abbess, in which Ethelbald and others of the Mercian kings were interred. The Danes having expelled Burrhred, viceroy of Mercia, from his throne, wintered at Repandum in 874, at which period it is supposed that the nunnery was destroyed. The manor being possessed soon after the Conquest by the Earls of Chester, a priory of Black canons was removed hither, in 1172, from Caulk in this county, by Matilda, widow of Ranulph de Blundeville, Earl of Chester : its revenue at the dissolution was estimated at £118. The remains of the conventual buildings, which are principally in the Norman style, have been converted into the school-room and offices belonging to Repton grammar school; and the mansion-house, to which is attached a brick tower in the later English style, is rented by the governors, and occupied by the head master. In 1556, Sir John Port devised all his estates in Lancashire and Derbyshire, in trust, for the foundation and endowment of this school, and an hospital at Etwall. The Harpur family had the direction of these institutions until the year 1621, when Sir John Harpur assigned the superintendence of them to the Earl of Huntingdon, Lord Stanhope, and Sir Thomas Gerard, Bart., as heirs of the founder : the present hereditary governors are, the Marquis of Hastings, the Earl of Chesterfield, and Sir William Gerard, Bart. In 1621, the master of Etwall hospital, the schoolmaster of Repton, the poor men, and the poor scholars, were made a body corporate. The establishment consists of a head master, two ushers, and twenty scholars on the foundation : the master has a salary of £200, the first usher £100, and the second £80, and the scholars have an allowance of £20 per annum each, for seven years. The improved rental of the estates, which is now about £2500 per annum, has long ..ince enabled the governors to increase the number of pensioners in the hospital, to augment the establishment of the school, and to give larger salaries to the masters. They elect the master of the hospital and the master and ushers of the school; the Harpur family have, by the original charter, a fourth term with them in the appointment of the pensioners of the hospital, and of the foundation scholars. The learned divine and Hebraist, John Lightfoot, was appointed first usher, on the original establishment of the school. Amongst eminent persons educated here may be noticed, Samuel Shaw, a learned nonconformist divine ; Stebbing Shaw, the historian of Staffordshire ; Jonathan Scott, translator of the Arabian Tales ; W. L. Lewis, the translator of Statius ; and F. N. C. Mundy, Esq., author of the poems of Needwood Forest and the Fall of Needwood. The sum of £200 was given by Mrs Mary Burdett, in 1701, and the like sum by Mrs. Dorothy Burdett, in 1718, for buying bread for the poor, and clothing and teaching poor children of Repton, Ingleby, and Foremark.

RESTON (NORTH), a parish in the Marsh division of the hundred of LOUTH-ESKE, parts of LINDSEY, county of LINCOLN, 4¾ miles (S. E.) from Louth, containing 46 inhabitants. The living is a discharged vicarage, in the archdeaconry and diocese of Lincoln, rated in the king's books at £4. 11. 10½., endowed with £200 royal bounty. Mrs. Jackson was patroness in 1827. The church is dedicated to St. Edith. There is a place of worship for Wesleyan Methodists.

RESTON (SOUTH), a parish in the Marsh division of the hundred of CALCEWORTH, parts of LINDSEY, county of LINCOLN, 6¼ miles (N. W. by N.) from Alford, containing 111 inhabitants. The living is a discharged rectory, in the archdeaconry and diocese of Lincoln, rated in the king's books at £5. 10. 2½., endowed with £200 royal bounty, and in the patronage of the King, as Duke of Lancaster. The church is dedicated to St. Edith.

RETFORD (EAST), a borough, market town, and parish, having exclusive jurisdiction, though locally in the North-clay division of the wapentake of Bassetlaw, county of NOTTINGHAM, 32 miles (E. N. E.) from Nottingham, and 144 (N. by W.) from London, containing 2465 inhabitants. This place is supposed to have derived its

Seal and Arms.

name from an ancient ford over the river Idle (on the eastern bank of which it is situated), at a place where the soil was a reddish clay, which abounds here ; in Domesday-book it is written *Redeford*, and early in the thirteenth century *Este Reddfurthe*. The town is pleasantly situated, and is connected with West Retford by a bridge across the Idle : it is well built and paved, and the open square, or market-place, is surrounded by good houses : its situation on the great north road to York and Edinburgh gives it many advantages as a place of residence. There is a small but neat theatre, usually open for the six weeks preceding Christmas ; and a news-room was erected by the corporation a few years since, to which Lord Galway presented portraits of George II. and his queen : there are about forty members, who subscribe £1. 11. 6. each annually. A considerable trade was formerly carried on in malt, but it is much reduced : hats and shoes are the principal articles manufactured, and a paper-mill is now in operation. The Chesterfield canal, which was opened in 1777, is conveyed by an aqueduct over the river Idle, to the south-west of the town ; and the corporation paid £500 to the proprietors for making the canal from Retford to Stockwith, on a scale to admit the passage of vessels of greater burden than was otherwise intended : the company have here a spacious warehouse for the reception of corn, &c. The market is on Saturday, and is well supplied with all kinds of provisions, with the addition, in Autumn, of great quantities of hops ; it has been much improved by the corporation having relinquished the tolls : there is also a large market for cheese and hops on the first Saturday in November. The fairs are on the 23rd of March, for horses and black cattle, and the 2nd of October for horses, cattle, cheese, and hops, which are brought in great quantities.

East Retford is an ancient borough by prescription, and a royal demesne. It was granted by Edward I., in 1279, to the burgesses at a fee-farm rent of £10 per annum, with the privilege, amongst others, of choosing a bailiff from among themselves : in 1336, Edward III. confirmed their privileges, and in 1424, Henry VI. granted them a charter, empowering the bailiff to hold courts of record, and to execute the duties of escheator and clerk of the market. These immunities were subsequently confirmed, and others added, by the charter of James I., under which the town is now governed by two bailiffs, the senior bailiff being chosen from among the aldermen, and the junior bailiff from such of the freemen as have served the office of chamberlain, and eleven aldermen (exclusively of the bailiff), who compose a common council ; they are empowered to choose a high steward, a recorder, with two chamberlains, a town clerk, and two serjeants at mace : the two bailiffs and the recorder are justices of the peace, and have exclusive jurisdiction within the borough. A court of record, for the recovery of debts to any amount, is held every third Monday, or oftener, if the bailiffs require it, at which one or both of the bailiffs, assisted by the steward, or his deputy, preside ; this court having fallen into disuse, was revived in 1827. General quarter sessions of the peace for the borough, and also for the northern division of the county, are held in the town hall, which was erected in 1755, and is a handsome and commodious edifice, surmounted by a neat cupola, the principal room being sixty feet long, twenty-six wide, and twenty feet high, with good shambles underneath. The petty sessions for the division are held here every alternate Saturday.

Retford first sent members to parliament in the 9th of Edward II.; but in the year 1330, the burgesses petitioned for a suspension of this privilege, on account of their poverty, and it consequently lay dormant until the year 1571, when it was again exercised. The borough has frequently been, since that period, the scene of electioneering dissensions ; and it appears that within the last century, committees of the House of Commons have been engaged no less than seven times in determining the freedom : in 1705, it was decided by that house, " That the right of electing burgesses to serve in parliament for this borough is in such freemen only as have a right to their freedom by birth, as eldest sons of freemen, or by serving seven years apprenticeship, or have it by redemption, whether inhabiting or not inhabiting the said borough at the time of their being made free :" the two bailiffs are the returning officers. At the election in 1826, Sir H. W. Wilson, the unsuccessful candidate, protested against the whole of the proceedings, in consequence of the riotous transactions which occurred, and the intervention of the military ; and on the assembling of parliament, in February 1827, he brought the matter before the House of Commons, a committee of which, after declaring the election void, directed the attention of the House to the very corrupt state of the borough ; and after various motions had been made, with a view to transfer the elective franchise to Birmingham, Manchester, and other large places, it was settled, in 1829, that the franchise should be thrown open to the whole of the hundred of Bassetlaw, the freeholders of which, in common with the freemen of the borough, now exercise the right.

The living is a discharged vicarage, in the archdeaconry of Nottingham, and diocese of York, rated in the king's books at £5. 5., endowed with £400 private benefaction, £400 royal bounty, and £1000 parliamentary grant, and in the patronage of Sir Richard Sutton, Bart. The church, which is dedicated to St. Swithin, is a large and handsome structure, with a lofty square tower ; it is composed of several styles of architecture, a portion being very old. It was formerly a very large church, and, in 1258, was presented by Roger, Archbishop of York, to his chapel of St. Mary and the Holy Angels, near York Minster ; in 1392 it contained two altars (in a chapel at the back), dedicated to St. Trinity and St. Mary, endowed by the bailiffs of East Retford, who appointed two cantuarists to minister daily ; in 1528, the chapel was pulled down to repair the church, both being in a ruinous condition ; and in October 1651, the

building was demolished by the fall of the steeple and tower, and a brief was granted by Richard Cromwell, during his short protectorate, for rebuilding it, which was done by the corporation, in 1658, at an expense of £1500. A handsome chapel of ease, in the later style of English architecture, has been erected at Moorgate, chiefly by subscription ; the site and chapel-yard were given by H. C. Hutchinson, Esq., with a donation of £500, and the Incorporated Society for building and enlarging churches and chapels contributed £800 ; the whole cost was £4000 : it contains sittings for one thousand and forty persons, six hundred of which are free. There are places of worship for General Baptists, Independents, and Wesleyan Methodists, the two latter with Sunday schools attached to them. The free grammar school was founded by Edward VI., who endowed it with the possessions of the dissolved chantries of Sutton in Loundale, Tuxford, and Annesley, and placed it under the government of the bailiffs and burgesses, who appoint the master and under-master : the present school-house was built, in 1779, by the corporation, who, in 1797, built a house for the master, and in 1810, one for the second master : the present income is about £400 per annum, and there are at this time two boys only in the school. The corporation have been long in possession of considerable property in their own right, and as trustees for the grammar school, almshouses, &c., which, from the loss of some old deeds, has become so mixed, as to occasion a Chancery suit, at this time pending. A National school for boys was erected in 1813, to be supported by voluntary subscription, but it has been closed for want of sufficient support. Sloswicke's hospital was founded by Richard Sloswicke, in 1657, who gave his dwelling-house to be converted into a Maison de Dieu, and endowed it with property from which six poor men were to receive £3. 6. 8. each annually. It was rebuilt by the corporation in 1806, and is inhabited by aged burgesses, who receive 2s. each weekly : the estate now lets for £84. 10. a year. There are also nine other almshouses. The workhouse was built, in 1818, by the corporation, who receive five per cent. for the money expended on it : it is on a large scale, being intended for the poor of twenty-six incorporated parishes, which pay an annual rent of £3 each, and three shillings a week for each pauper they send ; in the square is a relic of antiquity, called the Broad stone, supposed to be part of an ancient cross, which formerly stood near the town : the corn market is held round it.

RETFORD (WEST), a parish in the Hatfield division of the wapentake of Bassetlaw, county of Nottingham, ¼ of a mile (W.) from East Retford, containing 571 inhabitants. The living is a discharged rectory, in the archdeaconry of Nottingham, and diocese of York, rated in the king's books at £9. 13. 4., and in the patronage of the Mayor and Corporation of East Retford. The church, dedicated to St. Michael, is a small edifice, with a tower and an elegant crocketed spire. The Chesterfield canal passes through the parish, which is separated from the borough and parish of East Retford by the river Idle. Richard Brownlow, in 1691, bequeathed £300 for the endowment of a free school, but the money has not been applied to that purpose. Stephen Johnson, in 1725, gave a house and land for the use of a schoolmaster, with a rent-charge of £10, which he receives for teaching poor children to read.

An hospital, dedicated to the Holy Trinity, was founded, in 1664, by Dr. John Darrell, and endowed with lands for the maintenance of a master and sixteen brethren : part of the original building remains, and, with some modern additions, is occupied as an almshouse by poor men. Dr. Darrell also founded a scholarship in Exeter College, Oxford, and endowed it with an estate in this parish, now producing £52 a year ; the scholar to be chosen from the counties of Nottingham and Lincoln alternately, by the archdeacon of the former and the subdean of the latter. The old hall was formerly the residence of the family of Denman, from whom, by intermarriage, descended two queens of England, viz., Anne, consort of James II., and Anne her daughter, who succeeded William III.

RETTENDON, a parish in the hundred of CHELMS-FORD, county of ESSEX, 4½ miles (N. N. W.) from Rayleigh, containing 580 inhabitants. The living is a rectory, in the archdeaconry of Essex, and diocese of London, rated in the king's books at £32. 6. 3., and in the patronage of the Bishop of Ely. The church is dedicated to All Saints. The river Crouch is here navigable for barges. A school for twenty poor children was endowed by James Humphrey, Esq. Here is an ancient farm-house, formerly the residence of the Bishops of Ely.

REVELSTOKE, a parish in the hundred of PLYMP-TON, county of DEVON, 7½ miles (S. by E.) from Earl's Plympton, containing 484 inhabitants. The living is a perpetual curacy, annexed to the vicarage of Yealmpton, in the archdeaconry of Totness, and diocese of Exeter. The parish is bounded on the south by the English channel, and on the north and west by the rive Yealm.

REVESBY, a parish in the western division of the soke of BOLINGBROKE, parts of LINDSEY, county of LINCOLN, 2½ miles (N. by W.) from Bolingbroke, containing 572 inhabitants. The living is a perpetual curacy, in the archdeaconry and diocese of Lincoln. The church is dedicated to St. Lawrence. There is a place of worship for Wesleyan Methodists. An abbey of Cistercian monks, in honour of the Virgin Mary and St. Lawrence, was founded here, in 1142, by William de Romara, Earl of Lincoln, which, at the dissolution, had a revenue of £349. 4. 10.

REWE, a parish partly in the hundred of HAY-RIDGE, but chiefly in that of WONFORD, county of DEVON, 4¼ miles (N. N. E.) from Exeter, containing, with the tything of Up-Exe, 280 inhabitants. The living is a rectory, in the archdeaconry and diocese of Exeter, rated in the king's books at £22. 4. 2., and in the joint patronage of the Earl of Ilchester and the Hon. P. Wyndham. The church is dedicated to St. Mary. At Up-Exe, in this parish, are the ruins of an ancient chapel.

REYDON, a parish in the hundred of BLYTHING, county of SUFFOLK, 1¾ mile (N. W. by N.) from South-wold, containing 325 inhabitants. The living is a discharged vicarage, with the perpetual curacy of South-wold, in the archdeaconry of Suffolk, and diocese of Norwich, rated in the king's books at £13. 6. 8., and in the patronage of the Earl of Stradbroke. The church is dedicated to St. Margaret. The navigable river Blyth runs on the south of the parish.

REYMERSTON, a parish in the hundred of MIT-FORD, county of NORFOLK, 6 miles (S. S. E.) from East Dereham, containing 285 inhabitants. The living is a discharged rectory, in the archdeaconry of Norfolk, and diocese of Norwich, rated in the king's books at £11. 3. 6., and in the patronage of T. T. Gurdon, Esq. The church is dedicated to St. Peter.

RIBBESFORD, a parish in the lower division of the hundred of DODDINGTREE, county of WORCESTER, ¾ of a mile (S.) from Bewdley, containing, with the borough of Bewdley, 3798 inhabitants. The living is a rectory, in the archdeaconry and diocese of Worcester, rated in the king's books at £27. 19. 2., and in the patronage of the Rev. Edward Winnington Ingram. The church, dedicated to St. Leonard, is an ancient and curious structure, in a retired situation, surrounded by wooded heights, which environ the windings of the Severn. Coal exists in the parish, but it is not worked. A weekly market, and a fair on St. Margaret's day, were granted by Edward I.

RIBBY, a chapelry in the parish of KIRKHAM, hundred of AMOUNDERNESS, county palatine of LAN-CASTER, 1½ mile (W. by N.) from Kirkham, containing, with Wrea, 500 inhabitants. The living is a perpetual curacy, in the archdeaconry of Richmond, and diocese of Chester, endowed with £600 private benefaction, £800 royal bounty, and £300 parliamentary grant, and in the patronage of the Vicar of Kirkham. The chapel was consecrated in 1775. James Thistleton, in 1693, bequeathed £180 towards the establishment of a free school, to which Nicholas Sharples, in 1716, left the residue of his estate, amounting to £850 ; these bequests now produce an annual income of about £220, which is applied for the support of a school of forty boys, another of forty girls, erected in 1818, and for clothing the children of both once a year.

RIBBLETON, a township in the parish of PRES-TON, hundred of AMOUNDERNESS, county palatine of LANCASTER, 1½ mile (N. E.) from Preston, containing 151 inhabitants.

RIBCHESTER, a parish comprising the township of Alston with Hatherall, in the hundred of AMOUN-DERNESS, and the townships of Dilworth, Dutton, and Ribchester, in the lower division of the hundred of BLACKBURN, county palatine of LANCASTER, and containing 4198 inhabitants, of which number, 1760 are in the township of Ribchester, 6 miles (N. N. W.) from Blackburn. The living is a discharged vicarage, with the perpetual curacy of Stidd annexed, in the archdeaconry of Richmond, and diocese of Chester, and in the patronage of the Bishop of Chester. The church is dedicated to St. Wilfrid. This was a place of consequence in the time of the Romans, the Coccium of Antoninus, ranking as one of their first cities in Britain ; in proof of which, numerous relics of antiquity have been and are still met with, such as ruins of temples, statues, coins, altars, and inscriptions. There are several cotton manufactories, also quarries of slate and stone, and the streams of the rivers Calder, Holder, and Ribble, wind through the parish. John Dewhurst, in 1771, founded a free school for poor children of the townships of Ribchester, Dutton, and Hathersall ; the income is £19 a year.

RIBSTON (GREAT), a joint township with Walshford, in the parish of HUNSINGORE, upper division of the wapentake of CLARO, West riding of the county of YORK, 3¼ miles (N.) from Wetherby, containing, with Walshford, 155 inhabitants. It is almost surrounded by the river Nidd. There is a place of worship for Wesleyan Methodists. The fine apples, known by the name of Ribston Pippins, were first cultivated here, the original tree having been raised from a pippin brought from France. Here was a preceptory of Knights Templars, founded by Robert, Lord Ross, and afterwards granted to the Knights Hospitallers: at the dissolution it was valued at £265. 9. 6. per annum, and is now a private mansion, the chapel of which contains some memorials to the family of Goodriche; and in the cemetery is the sepulchral monument of the Roman standard-bearer to the ninth legion, which was found at York, in 1638. This township is within the peculiar jurisdiction of the Manorial Court of Hunsingore.

RIBSTON (LITTLE), a township in the parish of SPOFFORTH, upper division of the wapentake of CLARO, West riding of the county of YORK, 3½ miles (N. by W.) from Wetherby, containing 195 inhabitants. It is within the peculiar jurisdiction of the court of the honour of Knaresborough.

RIBTON, a township in the parish of BRIDEKIRK, ALLERDALE ward below Darwent, county of CUMBERLAND, 4½ miles (W.) from Cockermouth, containing 36 inhabitants. Here are the remains of an ancient chapel, which was dedicated to St. Lawrence.

RIBY, a parish in the eastern division of the wapentake of YARBOROUGH, parts of LINDSEY, county of LINCOLN, 7 miles (W. by S.) from Great Grimsby, containing 168 inhabitants. The living is a discharged vicarage, in the archdeaconry and diocese of Lincoln, rated in the king's books at £4. 18. 4., endowed with £200 private benefaction, and £200 royal bounty, and in the patronage of W. E. Tomline, Esq. The church is dedicated to St. Edmund.

RICCALL, a parish partly within the liberty of ST. PETER of YORK, and partly in the wapentake of OUZE and DERWENT, East riding of the county of YORK, 4½ miles (N. by E.) from Selby, containing 599 inhabitants. The living is a discharged vicarage, in the peculiar jurisdiction and patronage of the Prebendary of Riccall in the Cathedral Church of York, rated in the king's books at £6, and endowed with £1000 parliamentary grant. The church is dedicated to St. Mary. There is a place of worship for Wesleyan Methodists. Twelve poor children are taught to read in a school erected by subscription in 1791, and supported by voluntary contributions, in addition to several trifling bequests amounting to about £6 per annum. The village, situated on the banks of the Ouse, is noted as the landing-place of the Danes under Harfager their king, in 1066, from a fleet of six hundred sail. Here are the remains of a once magnificent palace of the diocesan, encompassed by a triple moat. Seven human skulls and a rough flag-stone, with a sculptured cross, were discovered here several years ago.

RICHARD'S CASTLE, a parish partly in the hundred of WOLPHY, county of HEREFORD, and partly in the hundred of MUNSLOW, county of SALOP, 4¼ miles (S. S. W.) from Ludlow, containing, with the townships of Moor with Batchcott, Overton, and Woolferton, 490 inhabitants. The living is a rectory, in the archdeaconry of Salop, and diocese of Hereford, rated in the king's books at £15. 1. 3., and in the patronage of the Bishop

of Worcester. The church, dedicated to St. Bartholomew, is situated in the county of Hereford : it is a fine old structure, exhibiting some beautiful remains of stained glass, and had formerly a spire, which several years ago was burned down. The Kington canal passes to the south-east of the parish, and coal is obtained in the neighbourhood. A charter for a market and a fair was granted by King John, but both have been long disused. A National school, established about eight years since, is supported, and the children occasionally clothed, by voluntary subscriptions. There are some remains of the keep and walls of the castle, built by Richard Scrope, in the reign of Edward the Confessor, but they are so embosomed in wood as to be scarcely perceptible : on the declivity of its mount, two thousand royalists under Sir Thomas Dundesford were defeated in the civil war, by an inferior force headed by Colonel Birch. A spring in this parish, called Boney well, is remarkable for casting up small fish or frog bones in spring and autumn.

RICHMOND, a parish in the first division of the hundred of KINGSTON, county of SURREY, 8 miles (W. S. W.) from London, containing 5994 inhabitants. This place, although not mentioned in Domesday-book, is noticed in a record of nearly the same date, under the name of Syenes, and it was afterwards called Shene, or Sheen : the manor became the property of the crown in the latter part of the reign of Edward I., who resided here, as also did his successors Edward II. and III., and the latter monarch either built a palace, or made very considerable additions to one already in existence, in which he ended his days ; since this period it has belonged either to the crown or to some branch of the royal family, and has very frequently been the residence of the Sovereign. Queen Anne, wife of Richard II., dying here, it so affected that king, that he abandoned the palace, and allowed it to become ruinous : it was restored to its former splendour by Henry V., and, in 1492, was the scene of a grand tournament held by Henry VII.; and having been destroyed by fire in 1498, it was rebuilt by that monarch, when he changed the name of the place to Richmond, after the town of that name in Yorkshire, from which he had received his title of earl. Philip I., King of Spain, having been driven on the English coast by a storm, was entertained here, in 1506, with great magnificence ; and Henry VII. expired in this palace in 1509. Henry VIII. also held a tournament here; and the Emperor Charles V., of Germany, was lodged in the castle, on his visit to England, in 1523. The Princess Elizabeth was confined at Richmond by her sister Mary, and it became her favourite residence after her accession to the throne ; she died here in 1603, in which year, and in 1625, the courts of justice were removed hither, on account of the plague. In 1605, Henry, Prince of Wales, resided here ; and it was the occasional residence of Charles I., who here formed a large collection of pictures, and of his queen, on whom it was settled : in 1649 it was surveyed by order of parliament, and sold in 1650; but shortly after the Restoration it was delivered to the queen mother, though in a very dilapidated state : it was shortly afterwards pulled down, and private houses erected on the site, the owners of which hold on lease from the crown. A park appears to have been formed in the reign of Edward I., and in the time of Henry VIII. there were two parks, distinguished as the Great and the Little Park, the second being probably formed on the rebuilding of the palace by Henry V. or VII. These parks were afterwards united, and called the Old, or Little, Park, by way of distinction from the New, or Great, Park, formed by Charles I., which was made one of the articles of his impeachment. The Old Park, commencing near Kew bridge, extends along the banks of the Thames to Richmond, and comprises the beautiful and extensive royal gardens, and a dairy and grazing farm, which was cultivated under the immediate direction of George III., who occasionally resided here, and who directed the old lodge to be demolished, with a view to the erection of a palace in its place, for which the foundation was prepared, but the building was never executed. It was given to the lord mayor and citizens of London, during the Protectorate, but after the Restoration, it reverted to the crown. The Observatory is also in this park, and was built in 1769, by Sir William Chambers : it is furnished with excellent astronomical instruments, apparatus for philosophical experiments, and some models, and until lately contained a collection of ores from the mines in the forest of Hartz, in Germany, which have been removed to the British Museum : on its summit is a moveable dome, containing an equatorial instrument. The New, or Great, Park, enclosed by Charles I., is situated to the southward of Richmond, extending from the hill to the road from London to Kingston : it is eight miles in circumference, being encompassed with a brick wall, and comprises about two thousand two hundred and fifty-three acres.

The village of Richmond, from the beauty of its situation and of the surrounding country, possesses attractions of a very rare character. The view from the summit of the hill, though not extensive, embraces every thing required to constitute a picturesque landscape, consisting of a fertile and richly-wooded plain, through which the Thames flows in a winding course, with its banks ornamented by numerous mansions and villas, and bounded by hills in the distance. Its proximity to the metropolis, combined with the attractions of scenery which it possesses, and the facility of conveyance both by land and water, causes it to be much resorted to. It in all respects resembles a town, and has a neat and genteel appearance, containing some very good houses, with several inns of a superior description; also a neat theatre, which is opened three or four nights in the week during the summer season : the repair of the highways, paving, and watching, is, by act of parliament, under the control of thirty-one select vestry-men. The Thames, which is here nearly three hundred feet wide, is crossed by a handsome bridge of five arches, the centre one being twenty-five feet high from low water mark, and sixty wide; the first stone was laid on the 23rd of August, 1774, and the structure was completed in December, 1777, at an expense of about £26,000.

The living is a vicarage, consolidated with that of Kingston, by act of parliament, in 1760, in the archdeaconry of Surrey, and diocese of Winchester. The church, dedicated to St. Mary Magdalene, is a neat brick edifice, with a low square embattled tower, ornamented with buttresses, at its western end. Amongst other monuments is a brass tablet, erected by the Earl of Buchan, in 1792, to the memory of James

Thomson, author of the Seasons, who died at Richmond, in 1748. The school was founded, in 1713, by contribution among several noblemen and gentlemen, and it was, in 1719, endowed by Lady Dorothy Capel, with part of the rental of an estate, from which it now receives £37. 10. : there are also £3700 New South Sea Annuities, and £100 four per cents., in the possession of the trustees, being the produce of benefactions and contributions, the dividends of which are applied to the use of the school, which is supported, in addition to the above, by an annuity of £30, originally given by George I., and continued by his successors, by an annual subscription, and by a collection made after a sermon preached for its benefit. The school-house, in which the master and the mistress reside, is a neat building in good repair, and all the poor children of the parish may here be educated in reading, writing, and arithmetic, about sixty of them being also clothed. The charitable institutions for the relief of the poor are on a very liberal scale ; they consist of almshouses, called Queen Elizabeth's, supposed to have been founded, in the year 1600, by Sir George Wright, and originally situated under Richmond hill; but the present building was erected by private subscription, in 1767, at a place called the Vineyard, on a piece of ground given by William Turner, Esq. : the present income is about £132 per annum, arising principally from the dividends on £3800 three per cent. reduced annuities, which was purchased with money given, or bequeathed, by different persons to the charity, and from a fee-farm rent of £8 per annum, assigned by John Michell : it affords lodging and maintenance to eight poor women. On the hill is an almshouse, founded and endowed by Bishop Duppa, in 1661, the present income of which, with some small additional benefactions, is £206 per annum, and in which ten poor widows of Richmond are lodged and supported. Michell's almshouses were founded, in 1696, by Humphry Michell, for ten poor old men, and augmented by John Michell and William Smither, Esqrs. : the tenements were rebuilt, in 1810, in the Vineyard, at an expense of £3014, derived from savings from the income, which is at present about £420 per annum. The income of almshouses founded, in 1757, by Rebecca Houblon, is now about £280 per annum ; nine poor women are supported in them. In addition to these charities, William Hickey, in 1727, bequeathed estates, which, with the interest of the accumulation of savings, now produces upwards of £700 per annum, and from which twenty pensioners receive £12 per annum each; and, from the excess of income beyond the expenditure, the trustees contemplate an application to the court of Chancery, for leave to erect almshouses for the pensioners, and such further extension of the charity, as may be deemed expedient. There is also another valuable charity, called the Church Estate, under the management of trustees, for repairing the church, the present income of which is about £600 per annum ; of this, £250 is appropriated to the support of deserving poor, at the discretion of the trustees, who have applied also to the court of Chancery, for permission to build ten almshouses, for five poor men and five poor women, to which number they now allow weekly 5s. each, the surplus of the £250 being allowed to accumulate for building the almshouses. Lands in the manor of Richmond are holden by copy of court roll, and descend to the youngest son, or, in default of male issue, to the youngest daughter. A convent of Carthusians, called the House of Jesus of Bethlehem, was founded and richly endowed by Henry V., in 1414, at the hamlet of West Sheen, about a quarter of a mile from the palace; and, in 1416, a hermitage for a recluse was founded within this monastery: in the reign of Henry VII., Perkin Warbeck sought an asylum within its walls, when defeated by that monarch, and the body of James IV., King of Scotland, was brought hither, after his defeat and death at Flodden Field: at the time of its suppression, its revenue was estimated at £777. 12. 1. It was revived by Queen Mary, but finally suppressed at her death, a few months afterwards: an ancient gateway, the last remains of this priory, was taken down about sixty years since, and the hamlet of West Sheen was at the same time demolished, the site now forming a part of the royal enclosure. A convent of Carmelites had been previously founded here by Edward II., but it was removed to Oxford, at the expiration of two years from its foundation. Henry VII. is said to have founded a convent of Observant friars near the palace, in 1499, the suppression of which, in 1534, is recorded by Hollinshed. A mineral well, discovered here about 1680, appears to have attracted a great deal of company; it was in considerable repute for about half a century, but afterwards rapidly declined.

Arms.

RICHMOND, a borough, market town, and parish, having separate jurisdiction, though locally in the western division of the wapentake of Gilling, North riding of the county of YORK, 44 miles (N.W.) from York, and 234 (N.N.W.) from London, containing 3546 inhabitants. This place appears to have been founded in the reign of William the Conqueror, by his nephew Alan Rufus, to whom he granted the whole district called Richmondshire, with the title of Earl of Richmond, and who built the castle, and gave the place the name of "Rich Mount," indicating, it is presumed, the value he attached to it. The castle appears to have been inaccessible, from its situation and immense artificial strength, but was suffered to fall into decay at an early period, as, when Leland wrote his itinerary, in the reign of Henry VIII., it was in ruins: the town at the same period retained its walls, but the three gates, called French, Finkel, and Bar gates, were destroyed. The discovery of a great number of Roman silver coins near the castle, in 1720, led to the conjecture that the town was of Roman origin, but there is no farther confirmation of this opinion. Richmond is beautifully situated on the declivity of a hill, at the foot of which the river Swale winds in a semicircular course, and the vale to which it gives name, and the other parts of the country surrounding the town, are celebrated for their romantic and diversified beauties. It is a neat well-built town, chiefly of stone, and the society consists in a great degree of persons of independent property; the beauty of the town and surrounding country, and the moderate rate at which the necessary articles of consump-

tion can be procured, attracting many of this class. The principal streets contain some good houses; the town is lighted with gas, and a handsome stone bridge of three arches, crossing the river Swale, was erected in 1789, at the joint expense of the corporation and the inhabitants of the North riding. In the market-place, where are some very good houses and handsome shops, is a column, under which a reservoir has been constructed, capable of containing about twelve thousand gallons of water, brought by pipes from Aislabeck spring, and conveyed in the same manner to the different parts of the town: there is also another reservoir, containing about three thousand gallons, at the spring head. From the period of its foundation, during several successive reigns, Richmond appears to have been a place of very considerable trade; but the grant of charters for markets to some of the neighbouring towns, and other causes, interrupted its prosperity, and the want of a water communication (the Swale from its rocky bed not being navigable) is a great bar to the increase of its trade, which is now principally in corn and lead, the latter being brought from the mines about fourteen miles westward; there are also some quarries of good stone. A very considerable trade in knitted yarn stockings, and woollen caps for sailors, was formerly carried on; they were manufactured here, and exported to Holland and the Netherlands, but it has nearly ceased. The market is on Saturday, and great quantities of corn are sold at it to the corn-factors and millers of the adjacent grazing and mining districts: there are three fairs, on the Saturday before Palm-Sunday, granted by Queen Elizabeth; on the Saturday before the feast of St. Thomas à Becket, and on the feast of the Holy Rood, granted by Edward I.; the first and last are for cattle, woollen goods, and various kinds of merchandise, and are numerously attended.

Corporate Seal.

The town, which is a borough by prescription, as well as by divers royal grants and charters, was fully incorporated by Queen Elizabeth, in the 19th year of her reign: and in the 27th of the same reign it first sent members to parliament. By a charter granted by Charles II., in 1668, the government is vested in a mayor, recorder, twelve aldermen, a town clerk, twenty-four common council-men, and subordinate officers: the mayor and late mayor are justices of the peace. A court of record is held every alternate Tuesday before the mayor, recorder, and three aldermen, at which actions under £100 may be tried. A meeting of magistrates is held every Monday, and a court leet at Easter and Michaelmas. The general quarter sessions for the borough are held in the town hall, which is a handsome building, erected by the corporation. The gaol for debtors, arrested by warrant from the sheriff of the county, directed to the chief bailiff, formerly belonged to the Earls of Richmond, and is now the property of Lord Dundas, and rented by the Duke of Leeds, as high steward and chief bailiff of the liberty and franchise of Richmond and Richmondshire, in which capacity His Grace has peculiar jurisdiction, with power of appointing courts and holding pleas of civil action under 40s. There is also a borough gaol. The borough first sent members to parliament in the reign of Elizabeth : the right of election is vested in the owners of ancient burgages in the borough, who have a right of common on Whitcliffe pasture ; the number of voters is about two hundred and seventy: the mayor is the returning officer, and the preponderating influence is possessed by Lord Dundas.

The living is a rectory, in the archdeaconry of Richmond, and diocese of Chester, rated in the king's books at £15. 5. 7½., and in the patronage of the Crown. The church, which is dedicated to St. Mary, is conjectured, from the style of part of the building, to have been erected about the time of Henry III. : it presents some portions in the Norman style, but the variety of additions and alterations it has undergone has left little trace of its original architecture : it contains a few handsome monuments and armorial bearings, a beautiful font, and an excellent organ. The chapel of the Holy Trinity, in the centre of the town, is supposed to have been the original parish church : it formerly belonged to the abbey of St. Mary at York, but was suffered to become ruinous, and no service was performed in it from the year 1712 until 1740, at which period it was repaired by the corporation: the living is a perpetual curacy, endowed with £200 private benefaction, £600 royal bounty, and £1200 parliamentary grant, and in the patronage of the Mayor and Corporation : in part of the ancient church, adjoining to this chapel, the Archdeacon of Richmond holds his consistorial court. There are places of worship for Baptists, Wesleyan Methodists, and Roman Catholics : in a window of the Roman Catholic chapel is a very fine painting of the Crucifixion. The Society of Friends had a meeting-house, but in consequence of there being none of that sect in the town it was disposed of, and has been converted to other purposes. The free grammar school, which enjoys considerable repute, was founded and endowed by the burgesses in the reign of Queen Elizabeth, who granted letters patent, authorising its institution, and vesting the government of it in the bailiffs of the borough, which power is now exercised by the mayor and aldermen, who appoint the master : the children entitled to be taught free are those who " are natives of the borough, or children of persons exercising any trade or occupation therein ;" the average number of free children instructed is about eighteen, and the present produce of the endowment amounts to about £335 per annum. A rent-charge of £8 was bequeathed by Dr. Bathurst, in 1659, towards the maintenance of scholars going from this school to the University of Cambridge ; the candidates are elected by the trustees, and may hold the exhibitions until they take the degree of M.A. In 1730, Dr. William Allen left his estate at Bures St. Mary, in Suffolk, for founding two scholarships at Trinity Hall, Cambridge, with preference to his next of kin, and afterwards to this school ; they are now worth £17 per annum, with a prospect of considerable increase when the present leases expire. A National Sunday school was built in 1825 ; and the corporation have also a school for which they provide a master to instruct forty poor boys in reading, writing, and arithmetic. The Rev. Matthew Hutchinson's charity, bequeathed in 1704, and now producing about £68 per annum, is appro-

priated to the education of twelve poor boys, for which £10 per annum is paid ; to the payment of £4 each to poor boys as apprentice fees, and £3. 3. per annum each to sixteen poor widows having a settlement in Richmond : there is also a rent-charge of £4, bequeathed by Dr. Bathurst, for apprenticing a poor boy, besides several other small charities distributed in various ways.

Bowes' hospital was founded, in 1607, by Eleanor Bowes, for three poor widows, two of Richmond, and one of Easby, with an endowment of £10 per annum : the management is vested in the aldermen, recorder, rector, and master of the free grammar school. Thompson's hospital was founded, in 1781, by William Thompson, and endowed with property now producing about £13 per annum, for four widows of tailors, who had been residents of Richmond ; they are lodged, and receive £3 per annum each : the management is vested in four trustees, with power to fill up vacancies, the rector of Richmond being always one. Pinkney's hospital was founded, in 1699, by Mr. George Pinkney, for three poor widows, who receive £6. 10. a year between them : the management is vested in the mayor, recorder, rector, foreman of the common council, and two head churchwardens. The ruins and relics of antiquity possess extreme interest ; of these, the principal is the castle, the site of which comprises nearly six acres : the remains shew the great strength of the building whilst entire, and the great square tower, or keep, which was supposed to have been built at a rather more recent period than the other parts, and which was repaired, in 1761, by the Duke of Richmond, is in good preservation. To the northward of the town are the ruins of a house of Grey friars, of which the tower is almost the only part remaining : it is a most beautiful structure, in the richest style of English architecture, ornamented with buttresses and pinnacles, and was erected shortly before the dissolution in 1538, at which time the society consisted of a master and fourteen brethren : the establishment was founded, in 1258, by Ralph Fitz-Randal, Lord of Middleham. St. Nicholas' hospital, for sick and infirm people, and pilgrims, a short distance from the town, is of uncertain origin, but is mentioned so early as the 18th of Henry II.: the present building is supposed to have been erected soon after the dissolution of the religious establishments, and contains little of the original edifice. Nearly opposite the castle, on the other side of the river Swale, are the ruins of the priory of St. Martin, which was granted to the abbey of St. Mary, York, and richly endowed by Whyomar, Lord of Aske, chief steward to the Earl of Richmond, and founded in 1100, under John de Poppleton, the first prior ; some fine Norman arches are nearly the only remains of this edifice. Richmond gives the title of duke to the family of Lennox.

RICKERBY, a township in that part of the parish of Stanwix which is in Eskdale ward, county of Cumberland, 1½ mile (N.E. by E.) from Carlisle, containing 108 inhabitants.

RICKERSCOTE, a township in the parish of Castle-Church, eastern division of the hundred of Cuttlestone, county of Stafford, 1¾ mile (S.S.E.) from Stafford. The population is returned with the parish. It is situated on the banks of the river Peak, near its confluence with the Sow, amid scenery highly picturesque and beautiful, and is distinguished by its valuable spa, recently discovered, and found to be efficacious in the cure of various disorders, internal and external.

RICKINGHALL (INFERIOR), a parish in the hundred of BLACKBOURN, county of SUFFOLK, ¼ of a mile (S. W. by W.) from Botesdale, containing 428 inhabitants. The living is a discharged rectory, consolidated with that of Rickinghall Superior, in the archdeaconry of Suffolk, and diocese of Norwich, rated in the king's books at £16. 5. 2½. The church is dedicated to St. Mary.

RICKINGHALL (SUPERIOR), a parish in the hundred of HARTISMERE, county of SUFFOLK, ¾ of a mile (S. by W.) from Botesdale, containing 705 inhabitants. The living is a discharged rectory, with Rickinghall Inferior, in the archdeaconry of Sudbury, and diocese of Norwich, rated in the king's books at £9. 13. 11½., and in the patronage of George St. Vincent Wilson, Esq. The church is dedicated to St. Mary.

RICKLING, a parish in the hundred of UTTLESFORD, county of ESSEX, 5¾ miles (N. by W.) from Stansted-Mountfitchet, containing 419 inhabitants. The living is a discharged vicarage, in the jurisdiction of the Commissary of Essex and Herts, concurrently with the Consistorial Court of the Bishop of London, rated in the king's books at £10, endowed with £200 private benefaction, and £200 royal bounty, and is in the patronage of the Bishop of London. The church is dedicated to All Saints.

RICKMANSWORTH, a market town and parish in the hundred of CASHIO, or liberty of ST. ALBANS, county of HERTFORD, 24 miles (S. W. by W.) from Hertford, and 18 (N. W. by W.) from London, containing 3940 inhabitants. In the earliest records in which this town is named, it is written *Rykemereswearth* and *Richmeresweard*, signifying the rich moor meadow. The manor, which, with four others, constituted the lordship of Pynesfield, formed a part of the demesne of the Saxon kings, and was bestowed by Offa of Mercia on the abbot and monks of St. Alban's, to whom it was confirmed by succeeding kings, and who retained it until their dissolution, when it reverted to the crown, and was given by Edward VI. to Ridley, Bishop of London, after whose martyrdom, it was granted by Mary to his successor, Bonner, and in the reign of Elizabeth again became the property of the crown, and ultimately passed into private hands. The town is pleasantly situated in a valley, near the confluence of the rivers Colne and Gade with the Chess: these rivers are much frequented by anglers, being noted for trout, and the last, which rises in Buckinghamshire, turns several mills in its course. It is irregularly built, but its distance from London, combined with an agreeable adjacent country, renders it a desirable place of residence. Two constables and one headborough are appointed annually. Within the parish are several flour-mills, and six paper-mills, affording employment to nearly six hundred persons; there is also an extensive brewery; the manufacture of horse-hair seating for chairs, and straw plat, is carried on to a considerable extent; and the cultivation of water-cresses for the London market gives employment to many individuals. The Grand Junction canal passes through the town, and affords a communication with the metropolis and various parts of the kingdom. The market, formerly held on

Wednesday, was granted by Henry III. for the benefit of the monastery of St. Alban's, during the abbacy of John of Hertford, but it has been discontinued of late years: there are fairs for cattle on the 20th of July and the 24th of November, and a statute fair on Saturday before the third Monday in September.

The living is a vicarage, in the archdeaconry of St. Alban's, and diocese of London, rated in the king's books at £16, and in the patronage of the Bishop of London. The church, which is dedicated to St. Mary, has an embattled tower of hewn flints at its western end; the body has lately been rebuilt of brick, coloured in imitation of weather-stained stone, to defray part of the expense of which, £700 was granted by the Incorporated Society for building and enlarging churches: some ancient ecclesiastical coins, and leaden and stone coffins, were discovered in digging for the foundation: over the altar is a beautiful window of painted glass, representing the Crucifixion; it was brought originally from St. Peter's at Rome, and purchased in Paris, in 1800, for £200. There are places of worship for Baptists and Independents. A National school for boys and girls is supported by donations and subscription; and there is also a British school for boys at Mill-End, within the parish; another for girls being about to be opened in the town. There are two sets of almshouses, one belonging to the parish, and one endowed with £10 per annum by John Fotherley, Esq., in 1674. More Park, a splendid mansion in the vicinity, has been the residence of several distinguished characters, having been occupied at different times by Neville, Archbishop of York in the reign of Henry VI.; by Cardinal Wolsey; by the unfortunate Duke of Monmouth, son of Charles II.; and by Lord Anson. Rickmansworth was the birth-place, in 1553, of Sir Thomas White, a merchant-tailor, and lord mayor of London, who is honourably distinguished as the founder of Gloucester Hall (now Worcester College), and of St. John's College, Oxford; also of Merchant-Tailors' school, London; and for his extensive charitable benefactions.

RIDDINGS, a market town and chapelry in the parish of ALFRETON, hundred of SCARSDALE, county of DERBY, 3 miles (S.) from Alfreton, with which the population is returned. The living is a perpetual curacy, in the archdeaconry of Derby, and diocese of Lichfield and Coventry, and in the patronage of W. P. Morewood, Esq. The chapel having long been demolished, a new one is now being erected in the early English style, for the completion of which, £1000 has been subscribed, and the remaining expense is to be defrayed by the commissioners, appointed under the late act, for promoting the building of additional churches and chapels. There are places of worship for Baptists, Independents, and Wesleyan Methodists. The new line of road from Manchester to Nottingham, and a branch of the Cromford canal, connected with Mansfield by a rail-road, pass through this place, which has recently obtained the grant of a market: there are extensive iron-works, and furnaces for smelting iron-ore, immense quantities of which and of coal are obtained in the immediate neighbourhood, and give employment to a large proportion of the inhabitants, of whom some are also employed in the adjacent mines, forges, &c., of Birch-wood and Codnor Park. These establishments, formed about 1801, have been the cause of greatly increasing the population of Riddings, which, prior to that period, was but small; although in early ages it was a place of considerable consequence.

RIDDLES-QUARTER, a township in the parish of LONG HORSLEY, western division of MORPETH ward, county of NORTHUMBERLAND, containing 206 inhabitants, who are chiefly employed at the neighbouring coal and lime works.

RIDDLESWORTH, a parish in the hundred of GUILT-CROSS, county of NORFOLK, 4¼ miles (S. W. by S.) from East Harling, containing 83 inhabitants. The living is a discharged rectory, with that of Gasthorpe, in the archdeaconry of Norfolk, and diocese of Norwich, rated in the king's books at £11. 2. 8½. T. Thornhill, Esq. was patron in 1815. The church is dedicated to St. Peter.

RIDGE, a parish in the hundred of CASHIO, or liberty of ST. ALBANS, county of HERTFORD, 3½ miles (N. W. by N.) from Chipping-Barnet, containing 390 inhabitants. The living is a discharged vicarage, in the archdeaconry of St. Albans, and diocese of London, rated in the king's books at £6. 13. 4., and in the patronage of the Earl of Hardwicke. The church, dedicated to St. Margaret, is principally in the later style of English architecture. The river Colne runs through the parish. Here was a religious house, formerly an appendage to the abbey of St. Albans, but now a private residence.

RIDGE, a tything in the parish of CHILMARK, hundred of DUNWORTH, county of WILTS. The population is returned with the parish.

RIDGMONT, a parish in the hundred of REDBORNESTOKE, county of BEDFORD, 3¼ miles (N. E.) from Woburn, containing 810 inhabitants. The living is a discharged vicarage, with Segenhoe, in the archdeaconry of Bedford, and diocese of Lincoln, rated in the king's books at £9, endowed with £200 private benefaction, £400 royal bounty, and £1200 parliamentary grant, and is held by sequestration. The church, dedicated to All Saints, has lately received an addition of ninety-one free sittings, the Incorporated Society for the enlargement of churches and chapels having granted £100 towards defraying the expense. The church at Segenhoe has been long since demolished. There is a place of worship for Baptists.

RIDGWELL, a parish in the hundred of HINCKFORD, county of ESSEX, 5 miles (N. W.) from Castle-Hedingham, containing 551 inhabitants. The living is a discharged vicarage, in the jurisdiction of the Commissary of Essex and Herts, concurrently with the Consistorial Court of the Bishop of London, rated in the king's books at £10, endowed with £1400 private benefaction, £1000 royal bounty, and £600 parliamentary grant, and in the patronage of the Master and Fellows of Catherine Hall, Cambridge. The church is dedicated to St. Lawrence. There are places of worship for Baptists and Independents.

RIDING, a township in the parish of BYWELL ST. ANDREW, eastern division of TINDALE ward, county of NORTHUMBERLAND, 6 miles (E. S. E.) from Hexham, containing 135 inhabitants. A bridge was erected, in 1822, across a dangerous ford of Dipton Burn. The Roman Watling-street passes through the township.

RIDLEY, a township in that part of the parish of BUNBURY which is in the first division of the hundred of EDDISBURY, county palatine of CHESTER, 6¼ miles (W. by N.) from Nantwich, containing 123 inhabitants. Sir Thomas Egerton, an eminent lawyer, Lord Chancellor under James I., by whom he was created Viscount Brackley, was born here in 1540; he died in 1617.

RIDLEY, a parish in the hundred of AXTON, DARTFORD, and WILMINGTON, lathe of SUTTON at HONE, county of KENT, 3¼ miles (N.) from Wrotham, containing 74 inhabitants. The living is a rectory, in the archdeaconry and diocese of Rochester, rated in the king's books at £3. 14. 9½., and in the patronage of M. Lambard, Esq. The church is dedicated to St. Peter.

RIDLEY, a township in the parish of HALTWHISTLE, western division of TINDALE ward, county of NORTHUMBERLAND, 5½ miles (E. by S.) from Haltwhistle, containing 231 inhabitants. It is environed by the rivers Allen and South Tyne, which afterwards form a junction.

RIDLINGTON, a parish in the hundred of TUNSTEAD, county of NORFOLK, 4¼ miles (E.) from North Walsham, containing 203 inhabitants. The living is a discharged rectory, with East Ruston, in the archdeaconry of Norfolk, and diocese of Norwich, rated in king's books at £4. 6. 8., and in the patronage of — Norris, Esq. The church is dedicated to St. Peter.

RIDLINGTON, a parish in the hundred of MARTINSLEY, county of RUTLAND, 2¼ miles (N. W. by N.) from Uppingham, containing 247 inhabitants. The living is a rectory, in the archdeaconry of Northampton, and diocese of Peterborough, rated in the king's books at £10. 1. 3., and in the patronage of Sir G. N. Noel, Bart. The church is dedicated to St. Mary and St. Andrew.

RIDWARE (HAMSTALL), county of STAFFORD, — See HAMSTALL-RIDWARE.

RIDWARE (MAVESYN), a parish in the northern division of the hundred of OFFLOW, county of STAFFORD, 4¾ miles (E. by S.) from Rudgeley, containing 598 inhabitants. The living is a rectory, in the peculiar jurisdiction of the Dean of Lichfield, rated in the king's books at £7. 2. 11., and in the patronage of Charles Chadwick and J. N. Lane, Esqrs. The church is dedicated to St. Nicholas. The parish is bounded by the Trent, and intersected by the river Blythe and the Grand Trunk canal. A court leet is held annually for the Ridwares, at Hamstall-Ridware and Aldridge alternately. A free school is supported by subscription. About three miles north of the church are slight remains of Blythbury priory.

RIDWARE (PIPE), a parish in the northern division of the hundred of OFFLOW, county of STAFFORD, 4¾ miles (E.) from Rudgeley, containing 114 inhabitants. The living is a perpetual curacy, in the peculiar jurisdiction of the Dean of Lichfield, endowed with £600 royal bounty, and in the patronage of the Prebendary of Alrewas in the Cathedral Church of Lichfield. The church is dedicated to St. James. The river Trent and the Grand Junction canal pass through the parish.

RIGSBY, a parish in the Wold division of the hundred of CALCEWORTH, parts of LINDSEY, county of LINCOLN, 1½ mile (W. by S.) from Alford, containing, with Ailsby, 107 inhabitants. The living is a perpetual curacy, annexed to the vicarage of Alford, in the archdeaconry and diocese of Lincoln. The church is dedicated to St. James.

RIGTON, a township in the parish of KIRKBY-OVERBLOWS, upper division of the wapentake of CLARO, West riding of the county of YORK, 6¼ miles (N. E.) from Otley, containing 429 inhabitants. It is within the peculiar jurisdiction of the Court of the Honour of Knaresborough. There is a place of worship for Wesleyan Methodists.

RIGTON, a joint township with Bardsey, in the parish of BARDSEY, lower division of the wapentake of SKYRACK, West riding of the county of YORK, 4 miles (S. W. by S.) from Wetherby. The population is returned with Bardsey.

RILLINGTON, a parish in the wapentake of BUCK-ROSE, East riding of the county of YORK, comprising the chapelry of Scampston, and the township of Rillington, and containing 883 inhabitants, of which number, 683 are in the township of Rillington, 3¾ miles (E. N. E.) from New Malton. The living is a discharged vicarage, in the archdeaconry of the East riding, and diocese of York, rated in the king's books at £8. 14. 9½., endowed with £400 royal bounty, and in the patronage of the Crown. The church is dedicated to St. Andrew. There are places of worship for Independents and Wesleyan Methodists.

RILSDON, a chapelry in the parish of BURNSALL, eastern division of the wapentake of STAINCLIFFE and EWCROSS, West riding of the county of YORK, 5½ miles (N. by W.) from Skipton, containing 145 inhabitants.

RIMMINGTON, a township in the parish of GIS-BURN, western division of the wapentake of STAIN-CLIFFE and EWCROSS, West riding of the county of YORK, 5 miles (N. E.) from Clitheroe, containing 698 inhabitants.

RIMPTON, a parish forming a distinct portion of the hundred of TAUNTON and TAUNTON-DEAN, county of SOMERSET, 6¼ miles (N. E. by N.) from Yeovil, containing 219 inhabitants. The living is a rectory, in the archdeaconry of Wells, and diocese of Bath and Wells, rated in the king's books at £9. 19. 9½., and in the patronage of the Bishop of Winchester. The church is dedicated to St. Mary.

RIMSWELL, a township in that part of the parish of OWTHORNE which is in the southern division of the wapentake of HOLDERNESS, East riding of the county of YORK, 16½ miles (E.) from Kingston upon Hull, containing 129 inhabitants.

RINGEY, a chapelry in the parish of BOWDON, hundred of BUCKLOW, county palatine of CHESTER, 3½ miles (S. E.) from Altrincham. The population is returned with the parish. The living is a perpetual curacy, in the archdeaconry and diocese of Chester, endowed with £800 private benefaction, £1000 royal bounty, and £600 parliamentary grant, and in the patronage of W. Egerton, Esq.

RINGLAND, a parish in the hundred of EYNSFORD, county of NORFOLK, 7½ miles (N. W. by W.) from Norwich, containing 286 inhabitants. The living is a discharged vicarage, in the archdeaconry of Norfolk, diocese of Norwich, rated in the king's books at and £3. 6. 0½., endowed with £200 royal bounty, and in the patronage of the Bishop of Ely. The church is dedicated to St. Peter; the east window exhibits some ancient stained glass, representing several persons kneeling before a crucifix, and underneath them labels with Latin inscriptions.

RINGLEY, a chapelry in the parish of OLDHAM cum PRESTWICH, hundred of SALFORD, county palatine of LANCASTER, 7 miles (N. W.) from Manchester. The population is returned with the parish. The living is a perpetual curacy, in the archdeaconry and diocese of Chester, endowed with £200 private benefaction, and £200 royal bounty, and in the patronage of the Rector of Prestwich. The chapel is dedicated to the Holy Trinity. A school-house was erected, in 1640, by Nathan Walworth, who endowed it with land now producing an annual income of about £50, for which from forty to fifty children are taught to read; four others from Kearsley are taught here, for a trifling bequest by William Baguley.

RINGMER, a parish in the hundred of RINGMER, rape of PEVENSEY, county of SUSSEX, 2¾ miles (N. E. by E.) from Lewes, containing 1271 inhabitants. The living is a vicarage, in the peculiar jurisdiction and patronage of the Archbishop of Canterbury, rated in the king's books at £13. The church, dedicated to St. Mary, is in the later style of English architecture. The river Ouse separates this parish from that of Barcombe. On the Broyle road, about three quarters of a mile from Ringmer, are commodious barracks for a detachment of the royal artillery usually stationed there. Lady Barbara, Thomas, and Sybilla Stapley, in 1699, gave each £100, for teaching sixteen poor children; the annual income, amounting to £10, is applied in support of a National school, and upwards of one hundred children are instructed in a school-house, which has been lately enlarged by subscription.

RINGMORE, a parish in the hundred of ERMING-TON, county of DEVON, 4 miles (S. by W.) from Modbury, containing 328 inhabitants. The living is a rectory, in the archdeaconry of Totness, and diocese of Exeter, rated in the king's books at £19. 10. 7½., and in the patronage of the Rev. R. Butland. The parish is bounded on the north by the river Teign, across which a bridge has lately been erected, affording a direct communication between Teignmouth, Torquay, and the places adjacent.

RINGSFIELD, a parish in the hundred of WANG-FORD, county of SUFFOLK, 2 miles (S. W. by W.) from Beccles, containing 280 inhabitants. The living is a rectory, consolidated with Little Redisham, in the archdeaconry of Suffolk, and diocese of Norwich, rated in the king's books at £12, and in the patronage of the Rev. Gunton Postle. The church, dedicated to All Saints, is a small ancient building, covered with thatch. There are some remains of the chapel of Little Redisham. This parish enjoys the right of sending two children to the free school at Beccles.

RINGSHALL, a parish in the hundred of Bos-MERE and CLAYDON, county of SUFFOLK, 3¾ miles (W. S.W.) from Needham, containing 304 inhabitants. The living is a rectory, in the archdeaconry of Suffolk, and diocese of Norwich, rated in the king's books at £11. 18. 1½., and in the patronage of the Master and Fellows of Pembroke College, Oxford.

RINGSTEAD, a parish in the hundred of HIGHAM-FERRERS, county of NORTHAMPTON, 2¾ miles (S. by W.) from Thrapston, containing 583 inhabitants. The living is a perpetual curacy, with Denford, in the archdeaconry of Northampton, and diocese of Peterborough. Thomas Burton, Esq. was patron in 1822. The church, dedicated to St. Mary, is principally in the early style of English architecture, with a tower and spire; it contains a plain ancient font on moulded shafts. There are places of worship for Baptists and Wesleyan Methodists. At the hamlet of Mill Cotton are the remains of a square Roman camp, consisting of lofty ramparts, defended by a deep moat; and near it is the site of an ancient town, where fragments and foundations of walls, with a few coins, have been turned up by the plough.

RINGSTEAD (GREAT), a parish in the hundred of SMITHDON, county of NORFOLK, 7¾ miles (W. by S.) from Burnham-Westgate, containing, with the hamlet of Chosell, 453 inhabitants. It comprises the consolidated parishes of St. Andrew and St. Peter, in the archdeaconry of Norfolk, and diocese of Norwich, the former of which is a discharged rectory, rated in the king's books at £9, and the latter a rectory, rated at £11. 6. 8. H. Styleman, Esq. was patron in 1811.

RINGSTEAD (LITTLE), a parish in the hundred of SMITHDON, county of NORFOLK, 8 miles (W. by S.) from Burnham-Westgate. The living is a rectory, in the archdeaconry and diocese of Norwich, rated in the king's books at £3. 6. 8., but the church dedicated to St. Andrew being demolished, it has been united to the vicarage of Great Ringstead. There is only a farmhouse remaining.

RINGSWOULD, a parish in the cinque-port liberty of DOVOR, though locally in the hundred of Cornilo, lathe of St. Augustine, county of KENT, 3 miles (S. S. W.) from Deal, containing 495 inhabitants. The living is a rectory, in the archdeaconry and diocese of Canterbury, rated in the king's books at £13. 12. 6., and in the patronage of the Rev. John Monins. The church is dedicated to St. Nicholas. A market and a fair were formerly held here, but both have been disused. Kingsdown, in this parish, lies adjacent to the sea-shore, and from its being noticed in ancient charters, appears to have been a place of considerable importance, though it is at present only a small fishing village : by means of a capstan, the fishermen wind on shore their boats, commonly called Kingsdown boats. In a valley between two downs in the vicinity are vestiges of an encampment supposed to be of Roman construction.

RINGWOOD, a parish partly in the northern division of the hundred of NEW FOREST, New Forest (East) division, but chiefly in that part of the hundred of RINGWOOD which is in the New Forest (West) division, of the county of SOUTHAMPTON, comprising the market town of Ringwood, the tything of Burley with the Ville of Bistern Closes, and the extra-parochial liberty of Burley Lodge, and containing, exclusively of the extra-parochial liberty of Woodgreen, 3804 inhabitants, of which number, 3471 are in the town of Ringwood, 20 miles (W. S. W.) from Southampton, and 91 (S. W. by W.) from London. This place is of great antiquity, having been of considerable importance during the Saxon times, and was originally named *Regnum*, or "the town of the Regni," mentioned by Antoninus; and afterwards *Rinovid*, and *Regnewood*, which, by a Saxon termination, denotes "the wood of the Regni." The town is situated on the eastern bank of the navigable river Avon, which, dividing eastward into three branches, over each of which is a stone bridge, afterwards collects its waters into a broad expanse, with an island in the middle, crossed by a causeway : it

is well built, and consists principally of four streets ; the inhabitants are supplied with good water, and the atmosphere is considered to be very salubrious. The manufacture of woollen cloth and stockings was formerly carried on to a considerable extent, but it has declined : here is a large brewery for ale. The market is on Wednesday, and fairs are held on July 10th and December 11th, principally for cattle and forest colts. Manorial courts are held twice a year, at one of which a constable is annually appointed ; and petty sessions for the New Forest (West) division are holden here. The living is a vicarage, with the chapel of Harbridge, in the peculiar jurisdiction of the Incumbent, rated in the king's books at £75. 5. 5., and in the patronage of the Provost and Fellows of King's College, Cambridge. The church, which is dedicated to St. Peter and St. Paul, is an ancient and spacious structure, but has undergone much modern alteration. There are places of worship for Independents and Unitarians. The free grammar school was founded, in 1586, by Richard Lyne, who bequeathed a house and rent-charge of £13. 6. 8. for that purpose; this endowment having been subsequently increased by various bequests, the present annual income is upwards of £30 : about sixteen children are instructed, but classical tuition has not been required for several years. An exhibition of £6 per annum to either of the Universities was founded by Thomas Lyne, by will dated 1621, for a poor scholar from this school.

RIPE, a parish in the hundred of SHIPLAKE, rape of PEVENSEY, county of SUSSEX, 6 miles (W. by N.) from Haylsham, containing 364 inhabitants. The living is a rectory, in the archdeaconry of Lewes, and diocese of Chichester, rated in the king's books at £11. 10., and in the patronage of the Rector and Fellows of Exeter College, Oxford. The church, dedicated to St. John the Baptist, is a handsome structure, partly in the decorated, and partly in the early English, style ; the windows were formerly filled with stained glass, of which there are now but slight remains. Here is a powerful chalybeate spring.

RIPLEY, a chapelry in the parish of PENTRICH, hundred of MORLESTON and LITCHURCH, county of DERBY, 3¾ miles (S. by W.) from Alfreton, containing 1635 inhabitants. The living is a perpetual curacy, in the archdeaconry of Derby, and diocese of Lichfield and Coventry, endowed with £2200 parliamentary grant, and in the patronage of the Duke of Devonshire, by whose liberality, and that of others, aided by a grant of £375 from the Incorporated Society for building and enlarging churches, &c., the present commodious chapel was erected in 1820, and consecrated in 1821. There are places of worship for Wesleyan Methodists and Unitarians. A free school, built in 1819, is supported by voluntary contributions, and attended by about thirty-five children. At Hartshay, in this township, are extensive collieries. Ripley was anciently a market town, chartered about the reign of Henry III., and is still a flourishing place. An urn, containing a number of coins of Gallienus, Carausius, Victorinus, and others, was discovered here in 1730.

RIPLEY, a chapelry in the parish of SEND, second division of the hundred of WOKING, county of SURREY, 6 miles (N. E.) from Guildford. The population is returned with the parish. The chapel has lately received an addition of one hundred and sixty sittings, of which one hundred are free, the Incorporated Society for the enlargement of churches and chapels having granted £100 towards defraying the expense. There is a place of worship for Baptists. George Ripley, the famous alchymist, and Carmelite friar, whose works were printed at Cassel, in 1549, is stated to have been born here.

RIPLEY, a parish (formerly a market town) partly in the upper, but chiefly in the lower, division of the wapentake of CLARO, West riding of the county of YORK, 23 miles (W. by N.) from York, and 208 (N.N.W.) from London, containing, with the townships of Clint and Killinghall, 1182 inhabitants. This place is situated on rising ground, about half a mile north from the river Nidd, and consists of one broad street, the old houses in which having been recently taken down, and replaced by others of stone, in the English style of architecture, at the expense of Sir W. A. Ingilby, Bart., it presents a very pleasing appearance, and the country surrounding it is highly cultivated, and beautifully picturesque. The market was held on Wednesday, but it has fallen into disuse. The fairs are on Easter-Monday and Tuesday, and the 26th of August, principally for horses, sheep, and cattle.

The living is a rectory, in the archdeaconry of Richmond, and diocese of Chester, rated in the king's books at £23. 8. 9., and in the patronage of Sir William Amcotts Ingilby, Bart. The church, dedicated to All Saints, contains some handsome monuments of the Ingilby family, among which is one to the memory of Sir Thomas de Ingilby, Justice of the Common Pleas in the time of Edward III., and in the churchyard there is a curious pedestal of an ancient cross, with eight niches, apparently intended for kneeling. A free school was founded and endowed, in 1702, by Mary and Catherine Ingilby; the present income is about £40 a year, and from fifty to sixty children are instructed in reading, writing, and arithmetic: this school is free for the children of the whole parish. A school at Burnt Yates was founded by Admiral Long, in 1760, and endowed with property, which, with some small additions subsequently made to it, now produces £200 per annum; of this sum £70 a year is paid to the master and mistress, £50 a year to a superannuated master, the remainder being applied to paying off a debt, and sundry expenses connected with the establishment. Children from the townships of Clint and Winsley are admitted, and instructed in reading, writing, and arithmetic; the average number is about twenty-two boys, and as many girls. There are charitable endowments to the amount of about £40 per annum in the town of Ripley, the principal of which are Lord Craven's and Mrs. Hardy's. Ripley castle, the seat of the Ingilby family, was erected in 1555, though so much modernised, as to retain few traces of the original structure. Oliver Cromwell passed the night succeeding the battle of Marston Moor in this castle.

RIPLINGTON, a township in the parish of WHALTON, western division of CASTLE ward, county of NORTHUMBERLAND, 7½ miles (W. S. W.) from Morpeth, containing 25 inhabitants.

RIPLINGTON, a tything in that part of the parish of EAST MEON which is in the hundred of EAST MEON, Alton (South) division of the county of SOUTHAMPTON,

6 miles (W. by N.) from Petersfield. The population is returned with the parish. It is within the jurisdiction of the Cheyney Court held at Winchester every Thursday, for the recovery of debts to any amount.

RIPON, a parish comprising the borough and market town of Ripon, the chapelries of Bishop-Monckton, Bishop-Thornton, Pateley - Bridge, Sawley, and Skelton, and the townships of Aismunderby with Bondgate, High and Low Bishopside, Bishopton, Clotherholme, Eavestone, Givendale, Grantley with Skeldin, Hewick - Bridge, Hewick-Copt, Ingerthorpe, Markington with Wallerthwaite, Marston with Moseby, Newby with Mulwith, Nunwick with Howgrave, Sharrow, North Stainley with Leningford, Sutton-Grange, Warsill, Westwick, and Whitcliff with Thorpe, within the liberty of RIPON, and the chapelries of Aldfield and Winksley, and the townships of Beverley, Dacre, Shelding, Studley-Roger, and Studley-Royal, in the lower division of the wapentake of CLARO, West riding of the county of YORK, and containing 14,115 inhabitants, of which number, 4563 are in the town of Ripon, which possesses separate jurisdiction, though locally in the liberty of Ripon, 23 miles (N. W. by W.) from York, and 212 (N. N. W.) from London. This town, which is of considerable antiquity, is supposed to derive its name from the Latin *Ripa*, from its situation on the bank of the river Ure. The earliest record we find respecting it is about the middle of the seventh century, when a monastery was founded here by Eata, abbot of Melrose in Scotland (the town at that time consisting of only thirty houses), which was subsequently given by Alfred, King of Northumbria, to Wilfred, Archbishop of York, who not only improved the monastery, but by his patronage of the town very much increased its wealth and consequence. In the ninth century it was plundered and burnt by the Danes, and so complete was the devastation, that only the remaining ruins denoted its former existence; it, however, recovered so quickly as to be incorporated a royal borough by Alfred the Great, in 886, but it shared in the destruction which Edred, in suppressing the insurrections of the Northumbrian Danes, carried through that province; and it had scarcely recovered from this devastation when it suffered from the unrelenting vengeance of William the Conqueror, who, after defeating the Northumbrian rebels, in 1069, laid waste the country, and so effectually demolished this town that it remained for some time in ruins, and at the period of the Norman survey it lay waste and uncultivated. The monastery, after its destruction by Edred, was rebuilt, chiefly by Oswald and his successors, Archbishops of York, and was endowed and made collegiate by Archbishop Aldred, about the time of the Conquest. Profiting by a period of comparative tranquillity, Ripon had again begun to revive, when it was once more exposed to the ravages of war by the progress of the Scots, under Robert Bruce, in the reign of Edward II., who, after exacting from the wretched inhabitants all that could be wrung from them, destroyed the town by

Seal and Arms.

4 I 2

fire. Aided by donations from the Archbishop of York and the neighbouring gentry, and by the industry of the remaining inhabitants, it so rapidly recovered as to be selected by Henry IV. for the residence of himself and his court, when driven from London by the plague; and the same calamity induced the Lord President of York to remove his court hither in 1604. In 1617, James I. passed a night here, on his route from Scotland to London; and was presented by the mayor with a gilt bowl and a pair of Ripon spurs; and it was also visited by his unfortunate successor, Charles I., in 1633. In the great civil war it was taken possession of, and held for the parliament, by the troops under the command of Sir Thomas Mauleverer, who defaced and injured many of the monuments and ornamental parts of the church, and were at length defeated and driven from the town by a detachment of the king's cavalry, under Sir John Mallory of Studley.

Ripon is situated between the rivers Ure and Skell, and although the streets are narrow and irregular, the houses, which are chiefly of brick, are, with few exceptions, well built: it is well paved, and was first lighted with gas in November 1830: the inhabitants are plen·tifully supplied with water from the Skell, by an engine erected by Alderman Askwith. The theatre, built in 1792, has been converted into a riding-school. The river Ure, which is crossed, at a short distance from the town, by a handsome stone bridge of seventeen arches, two hundred and fifty-six yards in length, was made navigable as far as Ripon by an act passed in 1767, and a second act, obtained in 1820, incorporated the proprietors, by the style of "The Company of Proprietors of the River Ure Navigation to Ripon:" barges of from twenty-five to thirty tons' burden are employed in bringing coal and merchandise of various kinds from Hull, York, and other places to the town, and are laden in return with lead, butter, and other produce. This place was formerly celebrated for its manufacture of spurs and woollen cloths, both which have, however, ceased to exist, and its present trade is somewhat limited: linen is manufactured to an inconsiderable extent, and during the season there is a weekly market for wool, which is much resorted to by the manufacturers from Leeds, Halifax, &c. The market, which is on Thursday, is well supplied with provisions: in the market-place, a spacious and well-built square, is an obelisk, ninety feet in height, erected in 1781, by William Aislabie, Esq., on the top of which are a bugle-horn and a spur-rowel, the arms of Ripon. Fairs are held on the first Thursday after the 20th day after Old Christmas-day, May 13th and 14th, first Thursday and Friday in June, Thursday after August 2nd, first Thursday in November, and November 23rd, for cattle and various kinds of merchandise. By charter of James I., in 1604, and confirmed by James II., in 1687, the officers of the corporation consist of a mayor, twelve aldermen, and twenty-four common council-men, assisted by a recorder and town clerk: the mayor and his two immediate predecessors are magistrates for the borough and liberty. A court military, for the recovery of debts to any amount, the officers of which are appointed by the Archbishop of York, whose authority for their appointment existed by prescription before the Conquest, and has been subsequently confirmed by several charters of inspeximus; the last granted in the reign of George II., has jurisdiction

within the borough and liberty; the latter of which, exclusively of the parish of Ripon, comprises the townships of Felix-Kirk and Sutton under Whitestone Cliffe in the parish of Felix-Kirk, the township of Kilburn, in the parish of Kilburn, the parish of Nidd with Killinghall, and the township of Marton *cum* Moxby, in the parish of Marton. Justices of the peace for the liberty are appointed by the Archbishop of York, and, in conjunction with the mayor and the recorder, hold sessions for the borough and liberty; and petty sessions are held in the town hall every Friday, by the magistrates for the borough and liberty, occasionally for the North and West ridings of the county. The town hall, built in 1801, at the expense of Mrs. Allanson of Studley, is a lofty, spacious, and handsome structure of freestone, comprising assembly-rooms, and a committee-room for magisterial business and public meetings. The Archbishop of York has a criminal court and a prison here. This borough first sent members to parliament in the 23rd of Edward I.; in the reign of Edward II. the privilege was discontinued, but was revived in the time of Edward VI., and has been since exercised without interruption. The right of election is vested in burgage tenants, the number of voters being one hundred and seventy-seven; the mayor is the returning officer, and the principal influence is possessed by Mrs. Lawrence of Studley.

Ripon was formerly the see of a bishop, and is now the head of a deanery, in the patronage of the Crown: at the period of the dissolution of the monastic establishments, it possessed seven prebends and nine chantries, with subordinate officers; it was refounded by James I., in 1604, who added a dean to the seven prebendaries, and endowed it with £247 per annum: its present establishment consists of a dean, subdean, and six prebendaries, with inferior officers, and it sends a proctor to the convocation of the province of York. The dean and chapter have a prison, and are authorised, by charter of James I., to hold a court of pleas, called the Canon Fee Court, in which they appoint their own officers, the charter stating that such authority had long appertained to them, but this court has fallen into disuse. The living is a perpetual curacy, in the peculiar jurisdiction of the Archbishop of York, and in the patronage of the Dean and Chapter of Ripon. The church, dedicated to St. Peter and St. Wilfred, is a large cruciform building, with two square towers at the western end, each one hundred and ten feet high, embattled and surmounted with pinnacles; and, in the centre, another square tower standing upon four pillars with arches, and ornamented with a cupola on its north-western angle: on each of these towers there was formerly a spire, those on the towers at the western end being each one hundred and twenty feet in height, and that on the central tower still higher; but the latter having been blown down in 1660, causing considerable damage to the roof, the others were taken down. The length of the side aisles is one hundred and ten feet, and that of the transverse aisle, one hundred and twenty-nine. The choir is ninety-two feet in length, and thirty-four in breadth; on its southern side is the chapter-house, over which is the library, containing a good collection of ancient works, and portraits of many of the kings and queens of England. Under the nave of the church is a chapel, in which is a place called St. Wilfred's Needle, which tradition says was used for the trial of female chastity. The bishop's throne and the stalls are ornamented with carved work; the east window, which is fifty-one feet by twenty-five, and in which are the arms of James I., of England and France, of the ecclesiastical society, and of the town, is very magnificent, the painted glass having been lately renovated: there are many beautiful and curious monuments in the church. A new church, dedicated to the Holy Trinity, erected at an expense of about £13,000, by the Rev. Edward Kilvington, was built in 1826: it is a handsome structure of freestone, in the later style of English architecture, with a tower seventy-one feet in height, upon which is a beautiful spire sixty-five feet high: the interior is neatly fitted up, and contains one thousand sittings, two hundred of which are free. There are two places of worship for Wesleyan Methodists, and one each for Independents and Primitive Methodists.

The free grammar school was founded and liberally endowed by Philip and Mary, in 1553: the management is vested in trustees, by whom the master and usher are appointed, the former of whom has a rent-free residence, and a salary of £180 per annum, and the latter £63 per annum: the school is open to the sons of resident inhabitants, and the number of scholars on the foundation varies from fourteen to nineteen. Jepson's hospital was founded and endowed by Zacharias Jepson, in 1672, for boarding, clothing, and educating twenty sons of poor freemen, or orphans: the number now in the establishment is only ten, who are admitted at seven years of age, and at fifteen are apprenticed, with a premium of £5 each: the present income is about £217 per annum. National schools for children of both sexes are supported by donations and subscription. The hospital of St. Mary Magdalene, situated in Stammergate, was founded and endowed by Thurstan, Archbishop of York, early in the twelfth century, and rebuilt by Dr. Hooke, Prebendary of Ripon, and master of the hospital, in 1674; it affords an asylum to six poor widows, who have a yearly allowance: the Dean of Ripon is usually the master, the appointment being in the gift of the Archbishop of York. A chapel adjoins the hospital, in which, on certain days, divine service is performed. The hospital of St. John the Baptist was founded by an archbishop of York, probably so early as the reign of King John: it is a small building, in which two poor women, who are named by the master, are lodged, and have a small annual allowance. The dean is also master of this hospital, under the appointment of the archbishop. The hospital of St. Anne, in Agnes' Gate, under the management of the mayor and aldermen, was founded, in the reign of Edward IV., by one of the family of Neville, in which eight poor women are lodged, and receive a yearly allowance. At the eastern end of the town is a curious relic of antiquity, called Alla, or Ailo's, Hill: it is a tumulus in the form of a cone, composed of sand, gravel, and human bones, and is supposed to derive its name from Ælla, King of Northumberland, who was slain in 867, fighting against the Danes. The circumference of this hill, at the base, is about three hundred yards, and the height of the slope about seventy-four yards. In Studley park, about three miles from Ripon, are the magnificent remains of Founntai's abbey, supposed to be the most perfect and splendid in the kingdom; the ruins occupy a space of about two acres, and this noble institution, at the period of its dissolution, covered nearly twelve acres of ground, and was valued at £1173 per annum. The ancient custom of blowing a horn three times at the mayor's door, and at the market cross, at nine o'clock every evening, continues, though that part of it which imposed a tax of fourpence upon every housekeeper, if any house or shop was robbed between that hour and sunrise the next morning, has ceased. Ripon was the birthplace of Dr. Beilby Porteus, a recent Bishop of London.

RIPPINGALE, a parish in the wapentake of AVELAND, parts of KESTEVEN, county of LINCOLN, 4¼ miles (N.) from Bourne, containing 611 inhabitants. The living is a rectory in three parts, consolidated in 1725, in the archdeaconry and diocese of Lincoln; two parts are rated in the king's books at £14. 7. 1., and the third at £7. 3. 9.; it is in the patronage of the Governors of the Charter-house, London. The church, dedicated to St. Andrew, is a large structure, partly in the decorated and partly in the later English style, containing several fine tombs, the principal of which being in a portion of the building used as a school, are much mutilated.

RIPPLE, a ward in the parish of BARKING, hundred of BECONTREE, county of ESSEX, 10 miles (E. by N.) from London, containing 361 inhabitants.

RIPPLE, a parish in the hundred of CORNILO, lathe of ST. AUGUSTINE, county of KENT, 2¼ miles (S. W. by W.) from Deal, containing 171 inhabitants. The living is a rectory, in the archdeaconry and diocese of Canterbury, rated in the king's books at £5. 19. 4½., and in the patronage of the Rev. R. Mesham, and C. F. Palmer, and Thomas Huddleston, Esqrs. The church, dedicated to St. Mary, is in the early style of English architecture: near it is a military work, thrown up by Cæsar in his route from the sea to his principal camp on Barham Down. There is also, in another part of the parish, a small oblong intrenchment, enclosing several small mounds.

RIPPLE, a parish partly in the lower division of the hundred of PERSHORE, but chiefly in the lower division of the hundred of OSWALDSLOW, county of WORCESTER, 3 miles (S. E. by E.) from Upton upon Severn, containing, with the chapelry of Queenhill, and the hamlet of Holdfast, 963 inhabitants. The living is a rectory, in the peculiar jurisdiction of the Incumbent, rated in the king's books at £42. 6. 4., and in the patronage of the Bishop of Worcester. The church is dedicated to St. Mary. The river Severn passes through the parish, which abounds with good limestone. A court leet is occasionally held here. A monastery existed at Ripple so early as the year 770, in Bishop Mildred's time, and was granted to the church of Worcester, by Duke Ælfred, about the commencement of the ninth century.

RIPPONDEN, a chapelry in the parish of HALIFAX, wapentake of MORLEY, West riding of the county of YORK, 5¾ miles (S. W.) from Halifax, with which the population is returned. The living is a perpetual curacy, in the archdeaconry and diocese of York, endowed with £200 private benefaction, and £200 royal bounty, and in the patronage of the Vicar of Halifax. The chapel, dedicated to St. Bartholomew, was rebuilt in the Tuscan order soon after the great flood that happened here in 1722, which not only did considerable injury to the ancient structure, but laid open many graves, and carried away bridges, mills, houses, and every other impediment to its progress. The cemetery is surrounded with ancient yew-trees cut in the form of Saxon arches. There is a place of worship for Wesleyan Methodists.

RIPTON (ABBOTT'S), a parish in the hundred of HURSTINGSTONE, county of HUNTINGDON, 4 miles (N.) from Huntingdon, containing, with Wennington, 379 inhabitants. The living is a rectory, in the archdeaconry of Huntingdon, and diocese of Lincoln, rated in the king's books at £21. 7. 6. Mr. and Mrs. Rooper were patrons in 1806. The church is dedicated to St. Andrew. There is a chapel of ease at Wennington, in this parish.

RIPTON (KING'S), a parish in the hundred of HURSTINGSTONE, county of HUNTINGDON, 3½ miles (N. E. by N.) from Huntingdon, containing, with the hamlet of Sapley, 260 inhabitants. The living is a rectory, in the archdeaconry of Huntingdon, and diocese of Lincoln, rated in the king's books at £11. 19. 7., and in the patronage of the Crown. The church is dedicated to St. Peter.

RISBOROUGH (MONKS'), a parish in the hundred of AYLESBURY, county of BUCKINGHAM, 6¼ miles (W. N. W.) from Great Missenden, containing 934 inhabitants. The living is a rectory, in the peculiar jurisdiction and patronage of the Archbishop of Canterbury, rated in the king's books at £30. The church is dedicated to St. Dunstan. There is a place of worship for Wesleyan Methodists. William Quarby, in 1727, bequeathed £2 per annum for teaching poor boys. The great cross, called White Leaf Cross, cut on the side of the chalk hills near the village, is supposed to be a memorial of some victory obtained by the Saxons over the Danes.

RISBOROUGH (PRINCE'S), a market town and parish in the hundred of AYLESBURY, county of BUCKINGHAM, 6 miles (W. by N.) from Great Missenden, and 37 (W. N. W.) from London, containing 1958 inhabitants. This place, which is situated at the foot of the Chiltern hills, derives its distinguishing appellation from having been the residence of Edward the Black Prince, whose palace is supposed to have stood within the site of a spacious moat, now dry, in a field adjoining the churchyard. The manor had at an early period been granted by the crown to Richard, Earl of Cornwall and King of the Romans, who died in 1272; and at a later date it was assigned to Katherine, queen of Henry V., for her dower; it was sold by Charles I., in 1637, to certain citizens of London. The town, though greatly improved of late, is still badly paved and not lighted; it is abundantly supplied with water from wells. The market was established by charter of Henry III., who also granted the inhabitants other privileges, including exemption from toll, and from attendance at assizes, sessions, &c.; it was formerly on Saturday, but was changed to Thursday, on which day it is now held; it is a pitched market for corn, and pigs and sheep are also brought to it; there is an annual fair for cattle on the 6th of May: the market-house, a small brick building, was rebuilt in 1824: there is a small theatre.

The living is a perpetual curacy, in the archdeaconry of Buckingham, and diocese of Lincoln, endowed with £8 per annum, and £1100 private benefaction, £200 royal bounty, and £2300 parliamentary grant, and in the patronage of John Grubb, Esq. The church, which is dedicated to St. Mary, is an ancient structure, with a neat spire: it contains some monuments of crusaders, or Knights Templars, stone stalls, and other interesting relics of antiquity: an addition of two hundred and sixty-seven sittings, of which two hundred and forty-two are free, have been recently made, towards defraying the expense of which, the Incorporated Society for building and enlarging churches and chapels contributed £150. There are places of worship for Baptists and Wesleyan Methodists. Mrs. Chibnall, who formerly owned the manor, gave a sum of money to provide clothing for twenty-four poor women annually.

RISBRIDGE (MONKS'), an extra-parochial liberty, in the hundred of RISBRIDGE, county of SUFFOLK, 4¾ miles (N. W.) from Clare, containing 11 inhabitants.

RISBURY, a township partly in the parish of HUMBER, and partly in that of STOKE-PRIOR, hundred of WOLPHY, county of HEREFORD, 4¾ miles (S. E. by E.) from Leominster, containing 150 inhabitants. Here are the remains of a Danish camp, with triple intrenchments, enclosing an area of about thirty acres.

RISBY, a joint parish with Roxby, in the northern division of the wapentake of MANLEY, parts of LINDSEY, county of LINCOLN, 8 miles (N. W. by N.) from Glandford-Bridge. The population is returned with Roxby. The living is a vicarage, united in 1717 to that of Roxby, in the archdeaconry of Stow, and diocese of Lincoln, rated in the king's books at £5. 6. 8. The church is dedicated to St. Bartholomew.

RISBY, a parish in the hundred of THINGOE, county of SUFFOLK, 3¾ miles (N. W. by W.) from Bury-St. Edmund's, containing 293 inhabitants. The living is a rectory, with that of Fornham St. Genevève, in the archdeaconry of Sudbury, and diocese of Norwich, rated in the king's books at £19. 10. 5. The church is dedicated to St. Giles.

RISCA, a parish in the upper division of the hundred of WENTLLOOG, county of MONMOUTH, 5 miles (N. W. by W.) from Newport, containing 358 inhabitants. The living is a perpetual curacy, in the archdeaconry and diocese of Llandaff, endowed with £800 royal bounty, and £1200 parliamentary grant, and in the patronage of the Vicar of Bassaleg. The church is dedicated to St. Michael. There is a place of worship for Wesleyan Methodists.

RISE, a parish in the northern division of the wapentake of HOLDERNESS, East riding of the county of YORK, 8¼ miles (E. by N.) from Beverley, containing 221 inhabitants. The living is a rectory, in the archdeaconry of the East riding, and diocese of York, rated in the king's books at £10. 0. 5., and in the patronage of the Crown. The church is an ancient structure, in a very dilapidated state, containing several marble monuments to the Bethell family.

RISEBROUGH (THORNTON), a township in the parish of NORMANBY, wapentake of RYEDALE, North riding of the county of YORK, 3¼ miles (W. by S.) from Pickering, containing 32 inhabitants.

RISEHOLME, a parish in the wapentake of LAWRESS, parts of LINDSEY, county of LINCOLN, 2½ miles (N. by E.) from Lincoln, containing, with the extra-parochial district of Grainge de Ligne, 73 inhabitants. The living is a discharged rectory, in the archdeaconry of Stow, and diocese of Lincoln, rated in the king's books at £4, and in the patronage of the Master and Fellows of Balliol College, Oxford. The church is dedicated to St. Mary.

RISHANGLES, a parish in the hundred of HARTISMERE, county of SUFFOLK, 4 miles (S.) from Eye, containing 208 inhabitants. The living is a rectory, in the archdeaconry of Sudbury, and diocese of Norwich, rated in the king's books at £7. 13. 1½. John Vernon, Esq. was patron in 1821. The church is dedicated to St. Margaret.

RISHTON, a township in the parish of BLACKBURN, lower division of the hundred of BLACKBURN, county palatine of LANCASTER, 3½ miles (N. E. by E.) from Blackburn, containing 1170 inhabitants.

RISHWORTH, a township in the parish of HALIFAX, wapentake of MORLEY, West riding of the county of YORK, 4 miles (S. W.) from Halifax, containing 1588 inhabitants. The Baptists have a place of worship here. A free grammar school, founded by John Wheelwright in 1724, for the poorest of his tenants' children, is liberally endowed.

RISLEY, a parish in the hundred of STODDEN, county of BEDFORD, 5¼ miles (S. W. by W.) from Kimbolton, containing 790 inhabitants. The living is a vicarage, in the archdeaconry of Bedford, and diocese of Lincoln, rated in the king's books at £8. 7. 6., and in the patronage of Lord St. John. The church is dedicated to All Saints. There is a place of worship for Wesleyan Methodists, and a Moravian establishment. A fair is held on Shrove Tuesday. Near Melchburne House, the seat of Lord St. John, are the remains of the old castle, from which the family derive their title.

RISLEY, a chapelry partly in the parish of SANDIACRE, and partly in that of SAWLEY, hundred of MORLESTON and LITCHURCH, county of DERBY, 7½ miles (E. by S.) from Derby, containing 288 inhabitants. The living is a perpetual curacy, in the peculiar jurisdiction of the Prebendary of Sawley in the Cathedral Church of Lichfield, endowed with £200 private benefaction, £400 royal bounty, and £200 parliamentary grant, and in the patronage of the Earl of Stamford and Warrington. A school-house was erected, in 1718, by Elizabeth Gray, who endowed it with certain lands, now producing, with a rent-charge of £13. 6. 8. previously bequeathed by Catharine Willon, an annual income of about £380, for which from fifty to seventy boys, and about fifty girls, receive gratuitous instruction. The poor are entitled to be admitted into Smedley's almshouse at Ilkeston. Sir Hugh Willoughby, a native of this place, was employed to discover the north-west passage in the reign of Edward VI., but was frozen to death with his crew on the coast of Lapland, in 1554.

RISSINGTON (GREAT), a parish in the lower division of the hundred of SLAUGHTER, county of GLOUCESTER, 5¼ miles (S.) from Stow on the Wold, containing 446 inhabitants. The living is a rectory, in the archdeaconry and diocese of Gloucester, rated in the king's books at £22. 0. 5., and in the patronage of Lord Dynevor. The church is dedicated to St. John the Baptist. The parish is bounded on the west by the river Windrush, and on the east by Oxfordshire.

RISSINGTON (LITTLE), a parish in the lower division of the hundred of SLAUGHTER, county of GLOUCES-

TER, 3¾ miles (S.) from Stow on the Wold, containing 229 inhabitants. The living is a rectory, in the archdeaconry and diocese of Gloucester, rated in the king's books at £10. 3. 1½., and in the patronage of the Crown. The church is dedicated to St. Peter.

RISSINGTON (WICK), a parish in the lower division of the hundred of SLAUGHTER, county of GLOUCESTER, 3 miles (S.) from Stow on the Wold, containing 231 inhabitants. The living is a rectory, in the archdeaconry and diocese of Gloucester, rated in the king's books at £16. 2. 6., and in the patronage of the Crown. The church, dedicated to St. Peter, has lately received an addition of fifty-five sittings, thirty of which are free, the Incorporated Society for the enlargement of churches and chapels having granted £50 towards defraying the expense. The old Fosse-way bounds the parish on the north-east.

RISTON, county of NORFOLK.—See RYSTON.

RISTON, a joint township with Brompton, in that part of the parish of CHURCH-STOKE which is in the hundred of CHIRBURY, county of SALOP, 7 miles (N.W.) from Bishop's Castle. The population is returned with Brompton.

RISTON (LONG), a parish in the northern division of the wapentake of HOLDERNESS, East riding of the county of YORK, 6¼ miles (E. N. E.) from Beverley, containing, with part of the township of Arnold, 361 inhabitants. The living is a rectory, united to the vicarage of Hornsea, in the archdeaconry of the East riding, and diocese of York. The church is dedicated to St. Margaret. There is a place of worship for Independents.

RITTON-COLTPARK, a township in the parish of NETHERWITTON, western division of MORPETH ward, county of NORTHUMBERLAND, 6 miles (S. by E.) from Rothbury, containing 64 inhabitants.

RITTON-WHITEHOUSE, a township in the parish of NETHERWITTON, western division of MORPETH ward, county of NORTHUMBERLAND, 5¾ miles (S.) from Rothbury, containing 23 inhabitants.

RIVAULX, a township in the parish of HELMSLEY, wapentake of RYEDALE, North riding of the county of YORK, 2¾ miles (W. by N.) from Helmsley, containing 212 inhabitants. An abbey, the first of the Cistercian order in Yorkshire, was founded here in 1131, by Walter L'Espec, in honour of the Blessed Virgin Mary, and at the dissolution possessed a revenue of £351. 14. 6. The venerable ruins of this once sumptuous monastery are situated near the rural village of Rivaulx, in a sequestered valley, through which winds the river Rye, on every side encompassed by heights crowned with majestic woods. The principal remains, which are those of the church and the refectory, exhibit a mixture of Norman and early English architecture; the choir, in particular, is a beautiful composition still in good preservation; it is one hundred and forty-four feet long, by sixty-three feet wide, the transept one hundred and eighteen feet by thirty-three, and the probable length of the nave one hundred and fifty feet, dimensions which entitled it to rank amongst the largest, as it did with the most magnificent, abbey churches in the kingdom.

RIVENHALL, a parish in the hundred of WITHAM, county of ESSEX, 2¾ miles (N. by E.) from Witham, containing 591 inhabitants. The living is a rectory, in the archdeaconry of Colchester, and diocese of London, rated in the king's books at £21. 5. 5. C. W. Western, Esq. was patron in 1824. The church is dedicated to St. Mary and All Saints. Thomas Tusser, author of a popular work, entitled "Five Hundred Points of good Husbandry," was born here about the beginning of the sixteenth century.

RIVER, a parish in the hundred of BEWSBOROUGH, lathe of ST. AUGUSTINE, county of KENT, 2½ miles (N. W.) from Dovor, containing 701 inhabitants. The living is a discharged vicarage, in the archdeaconry and diocese of Canterbury, rated in the king's books at £7. 1. 0½., endowed with £200 private benefaction, and £600 royal bounty, and in the patronage of the Archbishop of Canterbury. The church, dedicated to St. Peter and St. Paul, is principally in the early style of English architecture, and has lately received an addition of one hundred and seventy-five sittings, of which one hundred and thirty-five are free, the Incorporated Society for the enlargement of churches and chapels having granted £120 towards defraying the expense. Upon a hill on the north side of the parish several tumuli have been opened, each of which contained a skeleton, the head of a spear, and a sword about three feet long and two inches broad.

RIVER-GREEN, an extra-parochial liberty in the western division of CASTLE ward, county of NORTHUMBERLAND, 5 miles (W. S. W.) from Morpeth, containing 51 inhabitants.

RIVERHEAD, a chapelry in the parish of SEVEN-OAKS, hundred of CODSHEATH, lathe of SUTTON at HONE, county of KENT, 1½ mile (N. W. by N.) from Seven-Oaks, containing 1216 inhabitants. An episcopal chapel is now being erected by Lord Amherst and M. Lambard, Esq., by whom it will be endowed: the living will be a district incumbency, in the patronage of the founders, at whose decease the right of presentation will lapse to the Vicar of Seven-Oaks. There is a small endowment for instructing ten poor children in reading, writing, and arithmetic.

RIVINGTON, a chapelry in the parish of BOLTON, hundred of SALFORD, county palatine of LANCASTER, 4½ miles (E. S. E.) from Chorley, containing 583 inhabitants. The living is a perpetual curacy, in the archdeaconry and diocese of Chester, endowed with £400 private benefaction, £400 royal bounty, and £200 parliamentary grant, and in the patronage of the Inhabitants. The Unitarians have a place of worship here. A free grammar school was founded, about 1586, by the inhabitants, pursuant to letters patent granted by Queen Elizabeth, on petition of James, Bishop of Durham. The original endowment amounted to only £15 per annum, but, in 1823, the governors obtained the permission of his late Majesty, to hold lands not exceeding the annual value of £400; the present income is upwards of £300: there are three masters, who instruct about one hundred and fifty children, many of whom receive a classical education. Veins of lead and calamine have been worked in the neighbourhood. On a lofty hill in this chapelry is an old building, called the Pike.

RIXTON, a township in the parish of WARRINGTON, hundred of WEST DERBY, county palatine of LANCASTER, 5½ miles (E. by N.) from Warrington, containing 990 inhabitants.

ROACH, or ROCHE, a parish in the eastern division of the hundred of POWDER, county of CORNWALL, 5¼ miles (E. S. E.) from St. Columb Major, containing 1425 inhabitants. The living is a rectory, in the archdeaconry of Cornwall, and diocese of Exeter, rated in the king's books at £20. Samuel Thornton, Esq. was patron in 1819. The church, dedicated to St. Gomonda, has lately received an addition of one hundred free sittings, the Incorporated Society for the enlargement of churches and chapels having granted £70 towards defraying the expense. There is a place of worship for Wesleyan Methodists. This place is believed to have derived its name from some remarkable rocks, commonly called Roche rocks, on the principal of which are the ruins of a small chapel and cell of a celebrated hermit, dedicated to St. Michael. Hainsborough, or Hensborough, one of the loftiest elevations in Cornwall, commanding a most extensive prospect, is partly in this parish.

ROAD, a parish in the hundred of FROME, county of SOMERSET, 4½ miles (N. E. by N.) from Frome, containing 1217 inhabitants. The living is a discharged rectory, with that of Wolverton, in the archdeaconry of Wells, and diocese of Bath and Wells, rated in the king's books at £11. 9. 4. Sir A. Baynton, Bart. was patron in 1812. The church is dedicated to St. Lawrence. There are places of worship for Baptists and Wesleyan Methodists. A considerable manufacture of cloth is carried on here; and a fair for cattle and cheese is held on the Monday after August 29th. In the neighbourhood is a chalybeate spring.

ROADE, a parish in the hundred of CLELEY, county of NORTHAMPTON, 5 miles (S.) from Northampton, containing 480 inhabitants. The living is a perpetual curacy, annexed to the rectory of Collingtree, in the archdeaconry of Northampton, and diocese of Peterborough, endowed with £200 private benefaction, £600 royal bounty, and £200 parliamentary grant. The church is dedicated to St. Mary. There is a place of worship for Baptists.

ROBOROUGH, a parish in the hundred of FREMINGTON, county of DEVON, 5½ miles (E. by S.) from Great Torrington, containing 523 inhabitants. The living is a rectory, in the archdeaconry of Barnstaple, and diocese of Exeter, rated in the king's books at £10. 8. 9., and in the patronage of the Rev. Thomas May. The church is dedicated to St. Peter.

ROBURNDALE, a township in the parish of MELLING, hundred of LONSDALE, south of the sands, county palatine of LANCASTER, 8½ miles (E.N.E.) from Lancaster, containing 237 inhabitants.

ROBY, a township in the parish of HUYTON, hundred of WEST DERBY, county palatine of LANCASTER, 2½ miles (S. W. by W.) from Prescot, containing 310 inhabitants.

ROCESTER, a parish in the southern division of the hundred of TOTMONSLOW, county of STAFFORD, 4¼ miles (N. by E.) from Uttoxeter, containing 1037 inhabitants. The living is a discharged vicarage, in the archdeaconry of Stafford, and diocese of Lichfield and Coventry, rated in the king's books at £4, endowed with £400 private benefaction, £600 royal bounty, and £600 parliamentary grant, and in the patronage of Mrs. Alsop. The church, dedicated to St. Michael, has lately received an addition of three hundred and thirty sittings, of which two hundred and seventy are free, the Incorporated Society for the enlargement of churches and chapels having granted £250 towards defraying the expense. The rivers Churnet and Dove run through the parish, and unite a little below the village. A canal passes from Uttoxeter to the Potteries, by which coal and lime are brought for the supply of the neighbourhood, as also goods from Liverpool and Manchester. A large cotton-mill, built by the late Sir Richard Arkwright, is in active operation. Two poor children are taught for a trifling annuity, the gift of Mary Biddulph. An abbey for Black canons, in honour of the Blessed Virgin Mary, was founded here, in 1146, by Richard Bacoun, the revenue of which, at the dissolution, was valued at £111. 11. 7.

ROCHDALE, a parish comprising the chapelries of Blatchinworth and Todmorden, and the townships of Butterworth Castleton, Spotland (Further Side), Spotland (Nearer Side), Walsden, Wardleworth, and Wuerdale with Wardle, in the hundred of SALFORD, county palatine of LANCASTER, and the chapelry of Saddleworth with Quick, in the upper division of the wapentake of AGBRIGG, West riding of the county of YORK, and containing 61,011 inhabitants ; the market town of Rochdale being situated partly in the townships of Castleton, Spotland, and Wardleworth, 50 miles (S. E.) from Lancaster, and 198 (N. N. W.) from London. This place takes its name from the river Roche, on which it is situated, and appears, from the name of a part of the vale below Castle Hill, which is called Killer Dane, or Deyne, to have been celebrated for the slaughter of the Danes, who having, in their predatory incursions, penetrated into this part of the county, met with a signal overthrow. The castle, from which the township of Castleton has its name, and of which the keep still remains, was one of the twelve Saxon'forts which, probably, were destroyed in the frequent conflicts that took place between the Saxons and Danes in the tenth and eleventh centuries. The Roman Watling-street, leading from *Mancunium* to *Cambodunum*, traversed this parish ; and in the neighbourhood have been found various Roman antiquities, among which were some brass coins of the reign of Claudius, and the right arm of a silver statue of Victory, ten inches in length, and weighing nearly six ounces, having about the wrist a loose armilla, and another united to it above the elbow ; attached to the former was a plate of silver, inscribed Victoriæ Leg. VI. Vic. Val. Rufus. V. S. L. M.; and near Rochdale, in 1820, was found a small iron box, containing a rouleau of brass coins of the Lower Empire in good preservation. Rochdale is not distinguished by any events of historical interest, but owes its importance to the extent of its manufactures, which are comparatively of recent introduction, and to the produce of the mines of coal, and quarries of slate and stone, with which the district abounds. The town is pleasantly situated in a valley on the banks of the river Roche, and consists of several streets, which, though formerly narrow and inconvenient, have been widened, and in other respects greatly improved, under the provisions of an act obtained in the 50th year of the reign of George III. In 1824, a company was formed for the purpose of widening the principal street, and the road from Yorkshire to Lancashire ; in which, and in erecting a market-house and town hall, and other public improvements, they have expended more than £40,000. The stone bridge of three arches over the river Roche has

been widened and greatly improved. Within a few paces to the east of it a handsome iron bridge has been constructed, for the accommodation of foot passengers ; and about a quarter of a mile to the west is a stone bridge of one arch, connecting the town meadows with Pinfold, by a new line diverging from the old Bury road. The houses are chiefly built of brick, but several of the most substantial and respectable in the town and its vicinity are built of the fine freestone from the neighbouring quarries : the town is well paved, lighted with gas by a company established in 1824, whose works were erected at an expense of £12,000, and amply supplied with water brought from small rivulets near Moor-End, into four large reservoirs in Castleton, by a company established under an act of George III. The environs are pleasant, abounding with fertile vales sheltered by a range of high hills, called Blackstone Edge, and containing many handsome villas, and agreeable walks. From Summer Castle, an ancient mansion, the late residence of Charles Smith, Esq., a celebrated sporting character, an extensive view is obtained of the town, and the surrounding hills and dales. The public subscription library and news-rooms are well supported ; a Horticultural Society has been established, and is extensively patronised ; there are several billiard-rooms ; and a small neat theatre is occasionally opened : concerts take place in the public assembly-rooms, and races are held annually during the first week in July, which are well attended. A cricket club has been recently established, and there are various other sources of recreation. The principal branches of manufacture are those of baize, flannel, coating, kerseys, and woollen broad cloth ; calicoes and strong cotton goods are made to a very considerable extent, and, within the also last few years, the spinning of cotton has been introduced with success, and is making rapid progress ; the making of hats also constitutes an important part of the trade of this place. The factories are very extensive, and are increasing in number, and the town is gradually assuming a due share of importance as regards others in the manufacturing districts of Yorkshire and Lancashire. Since the American Tariff took place, the flannel trade has considerably declined, but the other branches of manufacture are prosperous : the woollen trade employs twelve thousand persons, and produces about eight thousand pieces weekly ; and the cotton trade furnishes employment to about six thousand persons. The number of steam-engines in the town and neighbourhood amounts to fifty-seven, being equal in power to nine hundred and forty-eight horses. The Rochdale canal, communicating with the Duke of Bridgewater's canal at Manchester, and the Aire and Calder canal, afford a facility of intercourse with the ports of Liverpool and Hull, and with the whole line of inland navigation : convenient quays and wharfs, for the loading and unloading of goods, have been constructed on the banks of the canal, and the basin is very capacious. The market days are Monday and Saturday, the former for corn, wool, and manufactured articles of flannel ; the latter for provisions of all kinds. The fairs are, May 14th, Whit-Tuesday, and November 7th, for horses, cattle, and pedlary ; there is also a fair, or rather a great mart, for wares, on the first Monday in every month, which is generally well attended. The parish is within the jurisdiction of the county magistrates, of whom some reside near the town; and the lord of the manor holds a court leet twice a year, and a court baron every third week, at which latter debts under 40s. are recoverable. The town hall is a neat and substantial building of brick, and contains an elegant saloon, in which the merchants and traders meet for the transaction of business, and for reading the news-papers. The gaol for the town, called the New Bailey, is a convenient building, adjoining the workhouse.

The living is a vicarage, in the archdeaconry and diocese of Chester, rated in the king's books at £11.4.9½., and in the patronage of the Archbishop of Canterbury. The church, dedicated to St. Chad, is a spacious and venerable structure, in the early style of English architecture, with a square embattled tower, crowned with pinnacles; the interior has some few remains of Norman character, and contains many ancient monuments, and an antique font: the churchyard is extensive, and a new cemetery has been added to it, which is peculiar for the neatness of its arrangement. The building stands on a lofty eminence, to which there is an ascent of one hundred and twenty-four steps from the lower part of the town. St. Mary's chapel, a neat brick building, was erected in 1744, as a chapel of ease to the vicarage. The chapel dedicated to St. James, a handsome edifice of stone, in the later style of English architecture, with a square embattled tower, was erected in 1820: the living is a perpetual curacy, in the patronage of the Vicar. There are several places of worship for Baptists, the Society of Friends, Independents, Primitive and Wesleyan Methodists, and Unitarians, and a Roman Catholic chapel. The free grammar school was founded, in 1565, by Archbishop Parker, and the school premises were erected, on a piece of ground given for that purpose, by the Rev. Richard Midgley, then vicar of the parish: the original endowment, £17 per annum for the master, and £2 for the usher, payable out of the archbishop's tithes, has been augmented by subsequent benefactions: the institution is open to all boys of the parish for gratuitous instruction in the classics only, and there are forty-five on the foundation, who pay £6.6.per annum to the master for the other branches of their education. The school has an interest, in turn with the schools of Middleton, in this county, and of Steeple-Aston, in the county of Oxford, in two scholarships founded at Brasenose College, Oxford, by Dr. Radcliffe, Principal of that college. The Moss school, so called from its situation on Vicar's Moss was founded, in 1769, by Mrs. Jane Hardman, who endowed it with two small estates, for the instruction of thirty boys and girls: the master's salary, originally £40, has, from the improvement in the funds, been increased to £100, and forty boys and twenty girls are instructed in reading, writing, and accompts; the latter are also taught sewing and knitting. A National school was erected in 1814, and is supported by subscription: there are nearly two hundred children instructed in this establishment, and there are Sunday schools in connexion with the established church and the dissenting congregations, in which more than three thousand children receive instruction. Numerous bequests have been made for the relief of the poor. About a mile and a half from the town, on the banks of the river Roach, is a romantic spot, called "Tyrone's bed," where, according to generally received tradition, the Earl of Tyrone was concealed, when he fled from Ireland, in 1603, after his unsuccessful efforts to release his countrymen from the English yoke: the whole transaction, with a sketch of his life, has been interestingly narrated by Mr. Roby, of this town, in his "Traditions of Lancashire." The eccentric Mr. John Collier, a schoolmaster, painter, poet, and caricaturist, better known by the appellation of Tim Bobbin, resided here for many years. Rochdale gives the title of baron to the family of Byron.

ROCHESTER, an ancient city and port, having separate jurisdiction, locally in the lathe of Aylesford, county of KENT, 8½ miles (N.) from Maidstone, and 29 (E. S. E.) from London, on the road to Dovor, containing, with the precinct of the Cathedral Church, part of Chatham, and Stroud Intra, 9309 inhabitants. This place, the

Arms.

Durobrivæ of the Romans, and one of their stipendiary towns, was by the Saxons called "*Hrove ceaster*," from which by contraction its present name is derived. The Roman Watling-street from Canterbury passed through the city, which was defended by walls built, according to the Roman custom, in the direction of the Cardinal points, and extending for half a mile from east to west, and about a quarter of a mile from north to south. Little of its history has been recorded previously to the Saxon era, in the early period of which, Ethelbert, King of Kent, having been converted to Christianity by the preaching of St. Augustine, to whom he gave large possessions at Canterbury, founded a church in this city, which he erected into a see, and thus laid the foundation of its subsequent importance. In 676, Etheldred King of Mercia, having made an irruption into Kent, plundered and nearly destroyed the city, which also suffered severely from repeated attacks of the Danes, who committed the most barbarous outrages. In 839, these ferocious invaders having landed at Romney, and defeated the troops sent to oppose them, plundered the city, and massacred the inhabitants; and, in 885, another party of them, under their leader Hasting, sailed up the Medway, and laid siege to Rochester, before which they threw up a strong intrenchment; the inhabitants opposed a vigorous resistance, and defended their city till Alfred coming to their assistance obliged the enemy to raise the siege, and retire to their ships with considerable loss. Athelstan, about the year 930, established three mints at Rochester, which at that time was one of the chief ports in the island, of which two were for the use of the king, and one for the bishop. On another invasion of the Danes, who in 999 appeared in the Medway, with a large fleet, the inhabitants, struck with terror at their approach, abandoned the city to their fury, and fled into the interior of the county. At the time of the Conquest, Rochester was given by William to his half-brother, Odo, Bishop of Bayeux, whom he created Earl of Kent, and who, in the reign of William Rufus, having headed a conspiracy against that monarch, in favour of Robert, Duke of Normandy, was besieged in the castle, and deprived of his possessions, which reverted to the crown. In 1130,

Henry I., with several of his nobles, attended at the consecration of the church of St. Andrew, in this city, by Lanfranc, Archbishop of Canterbury; during the ceremony a dreadful fire broke out, which raged with such fury that the city was nearly reduced to ashes: in 1137, it was again burnt, and it had scarcely recovered from that calamity, when a third destructive fire spread with such rapidity and to such an extent, that traces of its devastation were visible for ages. In 1141, Robert, Earl of Gloucester, chief general and counsellor of Matilda, after having effected that queen's escape, was himself taken prisoner at Winchester, and confined in the castle of this city, but was exchanged for King Stephen, who was soon afterwards made prisoner by Matilda's party. In 1215, the barons seized Rochester castle, which they held against King John, who having invested it with his troops, obtained possession after an obstinate defence, and ordered many of the garrison to be hanged. In the reign of Henry III., the castle was considerably repaired, and the walls strengthened, and the city was, by that monarch's liberality, greatly restored from the dilapidation it had previously suffered; Henry held a grand tournament here in 1251, in which the English knights entered the lists against all foreigners, without exception. In 1254, the castle was besieged by Simon de Montfort, on the part of the confederate barons, and successfully defended for the king by Edward, Earl Warren; during this siege, the bridge, with the tower upon it, which were both constructed of wood, were burnt. On the insurrection of Wat Tyler, in the reign of Richard II., a party of the rebels assaulted the castle, and took away by force one of their comrades, who had been placed there in confinement. Edward IV. repaired the castle and the walls of the city, and bestowed several privileges upon the inhabitants. In 1522, Henry VIII., accompanied by the Emperor Charles V., visited Rochester; and, in 1573, Queen Elizabeth, during her tour in Kent, remained here for five days, and conferred many marks of her favour on the citizens, by whom she was hospitably entertained. On the restoration of Charles II., that monarch, on his arrival from the continent, passed through the city on his route to the metropolis, and was joyfully received by the mayor and corporation, who presented him with a silver basin and ewer; and, in 1688, James II., on his retreat from the capital, embarked privately at this port on board a tender lying in the Medway, which conveyed him to France.

The city is pleasantly situated on rather a low point of land, bounded on the west by the river Medway, which, pursuing a northerly course till it has passed the city, suddenly bends to the south-east, thus environing it nearly on three sides. On the river is a handsome stone bridge of eleven arches, connecting the city with Stroud, which was built on piles, chiefly at the expense of Sir Robert Knolles and Sir John de Cobham, who, with several other gentlemen, bequeathed estates now fully adequate for keeping it in repair. They are vested in two wardens and twelve assistants, chosen annually from the commonalty, and incorporated by patent of Richard II., their powers having been afterwards enlarged by charter of Elizabeth; it is a handsome building, five hundred and sixty feet long, and is defended by a stone parapet and balustrade. The bridge chamber, in which the records of the Bridge

Company are kept, and the business of that trust transacted, is a neat building of Portland stone, with a handsome portico, occupying the site of an ancient chapel, erected near the east end of the bridge, by Sir John de Cobham. The approach from the bridge is peculiarly striking; the magnificent remains of the stately castle, on an eminence rising abruptly from the Medway, and the view of that noble river, which expands to a considerable breadth, immediately beyond the bridge, with Chatham lines, and the martello towers ranged along the shores, contribute to heighten the effect.

The town, within the ancient walls, consists principally of one spacious street, intersected by several smaller, and is bounded by the bridge on the west, and on the east by St. Margaret's bank, connecting it with Chatham; the houses are in general respectable and of ancient appearance, interspersed with several timber and brick buildings; the city is well paved, lighted with gas, and amply supplied with water, conveyed to the houses by pipes from an excellent spring near a field called the Vines. The environs are extremely pleasant, and contain several handsome villas; and on the north-west, on an easy ascent, are several streets of neat modern houses, called, from the owner of the estate, Troy Town: the air is salubrious, and the scenery pleasing, and on the banks of the Medway are extensive and beautiful promenades. The city is strongly fortified on the south side, and most of the works are of modern construction, having been erected since the peace of Amiens. Fort Pitt, partly in the parish of St. Margaret, and partly in Chatham, now used as a military hospital, and Fort Clarence, to the west of St. Margaret's church, now appropriated as a naval lunatic asylum, in conjunction with Chatham Lines, form a regular series of defensive works, commanding the river Medway from Gillingham fort to Rochester bridge. The theatre, a small neat building, is open occasionally; assemblies are held in a suite of rooms well fitted up, and there are floating baths, supplied with every requisite accommodation. The Rochester and Chatham Literary and Philosophical Institution is of recent establishment, and in concert with it, exertions are being made to erect a public library and museum. As regards mercantile pursuits, Rochester enjoys a favourable situation on the river Medway, and possesses a considerable share of commerce, but is not distinguished by any particular branch of manufacture. The number of registered vessels belonging to the port, in 1828, amounted to about two hundred and forty-three, averaging a burden of forty-two tons, most of them are colliers, or coasting vessels, which bring supplies for the dock-yards at Chatham. The average number of vessels entering the port annually is about three hundred and twenty foreign, and one hundred and twenty British. The trade of the town principally arises from the great number of persons employed in the dock-yards and victualling-office, and temporary residents connected with the army and navy, in addition to a small degree of ship-building. The oyster fishery is carried on to a considerable extent, and is a great source of profit to the inhabitants; large quantities of oysters are sent to London, Holland, and Westphalia. The market, on Friday, is well supplied with fish and provisions of every kind; a corn market, recently established, is held on Tuesday: the fairs, formerly on May 30th and December 11th, have nearly fallen into disuse, but there is a cattle market monthly on Wednesday.

Corporate Seal.

Obverse.   Reverse.

The city received its first charter of incorporation from Henry II., in 1165, and its privileges have been ratified and extended by succeeding monarchs to the time of Charles I., by whose charter the government is vested in a mayor, eleven aldermen, and twelve common council-men, assisted by a recorder, town clerk, two chamberlains, a water-bailiff, a principal serjeant at mace, and two under-serjeants, with subordinate officers. The mayor is annually elected by the citizens, from among the aldermen, who, with the common council-men, fill up vacancies in their bodies as they occur; the recorder is chosen by the mayor and aldermen. The mayor, recorder, late mayor, and senior alderman, are justices of the peace within the borough and liberties; the freedom is inherited by birth, and obtained by servitude, purchase, or gift. The corporation hold quarterly courts of session for all offences within the city and liberties, which include part of Chatham; and a court of portmote, every fifteen days, for the determination of all pleas, and for the recovery of debts to any amount. A court of requests is held for the recovery of debts not exceeding £5, the jurisdiction of which extends over the parishes of Stroud, Frindsbury, Cobham, Shorne, Higham, Cliffe, Cooling, High Halstow, Chalk, Hoo, Burham, Wouldham, Halling, Cuxton, Chatham, Gillingham, and the ville of Sheerness, in the county of Kent.

The corporation have jurisdiction over the oyster fisheries in the creeks and branches of the Medway; and the mayor and aldermen, assisted by a jury of free dredgers, hold a court of admiralty, in which they make regulations for the opening, stocking, and shutting of the oyster beds: the free dredgers are governed by an act

Admiralty Seal.

passed in the 9th of George II., and no one can be free who has not served an apprenticeship of seven years to one of that body. The town hall, erected in 1687, is a handsome brick building, supported on duplicated columns of the Doric order; the hall is commodiously fitted up for holding the several courts, and for the transaction of the public business of the city, and is forty-seven feet long, and twenty-eight feet wide: the ceiling is enriched with trophies, and with the city arms, together with those of Sir Cloudesley Shovel, at whose expense it was embellished; at the upper end are full-length portraits of King William and Queen Anne, by Sir Godfrey Kneller; there are also portraits of Sir Cloudesley Shovel, Sir John Jennings, Sir Thomas Colby, Sir Joseph Williamson, Richard Watts, Esq., and various other benefactors to the city: the area underneath is paved with Purbeck stone, and is appropriated to the use of the market; behind it is the gaol for the city, containing six wards, and adapted to the reception of sixteen prisoners. The clock-house was erected on the site of the ancient guildhall (in which the assizes for the county were formerly held), at the sole expense of Sir Cloudesley Shovel, in 1706; it is a neat brick building, and over the dial of the clock are the arms of the founder. The city first exercised the elective franchise in the 23rd of Edward I., since which time it has regularly returned two members to parliament: the right of election is vested in the freemen generally not receiving alms, whether resident or non-resident, of whom the number is about one thousand two hundred: the mayor is the returning officer.

Arms of the Bishoprick.

The see of Rochester, which is the smallest in the kingdom, and the most ancient, except Canterbury, was established in 600, by Ethelbert, King of Kent, who, at the persuasion of St. Augustine, erected a church in this city, which he dedicated to St. Andrew, and establishing a monastery for Secular priests, appointed for their bishop, Justus, who had accompanied St. Augustine into Britain. The diocese comprehends the western division of the county, and includes ninety-one parishes, in the deaneries of Rochester, Malling, and Dartford, separated from the see of Canterbury by the river Medway. The ecclesiastical establishment consists of a bishop, dean, an archdeacon, six prebendaries, six minor canons, a chancellor, eight choristers, a grammar master, twenty scholars, six poor bedesmen, and subordinate officers. The cathedral church, dedicated to St. Andrew, and rebuilt by Bishop Gundulph, in 1080, is a spacious and venerable structure, in the form of a double cross, with a central tower surmounted by a spire; the west front is a fine specimen of Norman architecture, elaborately enriched with sculpture, but the great window over the entrance is an insertion in the later style of English architecture, as are many of the windows in the nave and other parts of the building. On each side of the west door is a square tower; that on the north side has been lately rebuilt, and has a niche in which is a statue supposed to be that of Gundulph: a descent of several steps leads into the nave, which, with the exception of the windows, and a part near the transepts, is in the Norman style; the roof is supported on massive piers and circular arches, and, though now flat, has evidently been much loftier, and is finely groined. From the nave an ascent of ten steps leads through the arch of the stone screen into the choir, which is in the early English style of architecture, the roof finely groined, and the columns of marble from the quarries near Petworth in Sussex: the altar-piece is decorated with a painting, by West, of the Angel appearing to the Shepherds, and on the north of the altar, within the railing, are two very ancient tombs, supposed to have been erected for Bishop Lawrence de St. Martin, and Bishop Gilbert de Glanville. There are several chapels, among which are the Lady chapel, where the bishop holds his consistory court; St. Edmund's, a square chapel, from which a door, now closed up, formerly led to the chapter-house; a small chapel in the south aisle of the choir, in which is a beautiful window in the decorated style; and at the north end of the eastern transept, the chapel of St. William, whose shrine is still preserved in it. On the east side of the north transept is a building, called Gundulph's Tower, but the style scarcely warrants the supposition of its having been built by him. The crypt, under the eastern part of the cathedral, is a fine specimen of the early English style; the roof is plainly groined, and in that part of it which extends under the north aisle, the architecture is scarcely to be distinguished from the Norman style. The length of the cathedral from east to west is three hundred and six feet, and the breadth along the greater transepts is one hundred and twenty-two feet, and along the smaller ninety feet. There are numerous ancient monuments, but they are much mutilated, and the inscriptions for the most part obliterated; among them is a statue in red-veined marble of Walter de Merton, founder of Merton College, Oxford: there are also monuments to Lord Henniker and his lady, by Bacon, Jun. This was anciently a priory of Secular priests, who were removed in 1087, by Bishop Gundulph, who placed in their stead Benedictine monks, whose revenue, at the dissolution, amounted to £486. 11. 5. The ancient chapter-house, now in ruins, has been a magnificent structure, and still displays the remains of several fine Norman arches; and the prebendal houses contain many relics of the monastic buildings.

The city comprises the parishes of St. Margaret and St. Nicholas, in the archdeaconry and diocese of Rochester. The living of St. Margaret's is a vicarage, rated in the king's books at £10, and in the patronage of the Dean and Chapter: the church is an ancient structure with a tower, and contains several ancient monuments and an antique font: five hundred and seventy additional sittings, of which three hundred are free, have been erected, at an expense of £600, defrayed by grant from the Incorporated Society for the enlargement of churches and chapels. The living of St. Nicholas' is a vicarage, with that of St. Clement's, rated in the king's books at £20. 8. 9., and in the patronage of the Bishop: the church, which has been extensively repaired at different times, is a substantial and commodious edifice, principally in the later style of English architecture, with a square embattled tower at the north-west angle: the roof of the nave is supported by a range of lofty columns and finely-pointed arches: there are some monuments of no great antiquity, and a very ancient stone font. The churches of St. Clement and St. Mary the Virgin have been demolished. There are places of worship for the Society of Friends, Independents, Wesleyan Methodists, and Unitarians.

The Royal free grammar school, founded by Henry VIII., for the education of twenty boys, forms part of the establishment of the cathedral church, and is under the superintendence of the Dean and Chapter: there are four exhibitions of £5 per annum each, two to each of the Universities, which, on taking the degree of master of arts, are augmented to £6, and subsequently to £6. 13. 4. per annum: this school has also, with that of Maidstone, two of four exhibitions of £15 per ann. each, with chambers, in University College, Oxford, founded by the Rev. Robert Gunsley. A free school was founded, in 1701, by Sir Joseph Williamson, who bequeathed £5000 for its erection and endowment; the present income is about £600 per annum, and about one hundred boys are instructed in the ancient and modern languages, the mathematics, astronomy, and navigation: the head master receives a salary of £100 per annum, with a gratuity of £200; and the second master £40 per annum, with a gratuity of £110. Several distinguished naval characters have been educated in this establishment. Sir John Hayward having, in 1635, devised estates for charitable uses, his trustee, Mr. Francis Barrel, in 1718, appropriated £33 per annum to the payment of £12 annually to a master for teaching twenty poor boys, and £8 per annum to a mistress for teaching twelve poor girls, of the parish of St. Nicholas, and £10 per annum to a mistress for teaching thirty children of the parishes of Stroud and Frindsbury. Mr. Henry Barrel, in 1764, bequeathed funded property producing £4 per annum, for the support of a charity school; and Mr. John Baynard left £300 for the support of a Sunday school in the parish of St. Margaret. There are also a National school, and several Sunday schools, supported by subscription. Near the site of the ancient market cross are the custom-house, and a house for the reception of poor travellers, founded by Richard Watts, Esq.: in this establishment six travellers, not being "rogues nor proctors," may claim a lodging for one night, and fourpence each: the term "proctor" was applied to concealed itinerant popish missionaries, who at that time were in the habit of wandering about the country to absolve the people from their allegiance: the funds originally left for the support of this institution, then amounting only to £36 per annum, now produce £1000 per annum; the surplus is, by a decree of the court of Chancery, appropriated to the support of the parochial poor. St. Catherine's hospital, founded in 1316, by Symond Potyn, for the support of lepers and other diseased persons, is now appropriated as an almshouse for the reception of twelve aged persons, among whom the sum arising from the endowment is divided. Dr. Lamplugh, Dean of Rochester, and Bishop of Exeter, bequeathed £50 in trust to the corporation, to be lent, without interest, in sums varying from £5 to £10, to young tradesmen for four years; and there are various other bequests for distribution among the poor, and for other charitable uses.

The remains of the castle, which was erected after the Conquest, on the site of the ancient Roman fortress, consist principally of the keep, or great tower, in the south-west angle of an enclosed quadrangular area, three hundred feet in length: it was built by Bishop Gundulph, and is considered one of the most entire and curious specimens of Norman military architecture now remaining; it is a square tower with angular turrets, one hundred and four feet high, and seventy feet in breadth at the base ; the walls are twelve feet in thickness, and a winding staircase in the east angle, communicating with every story, leads to the summit, from which a most extensive view of the surrounding country is obtained : the state apartments are on the second story, communicating with which is an arched gallery in the thick wall, extending round the whole tower : the walls of the castle and of the keep are of Kentish rag-stone, cemented with mortar, which by time has been rendered harder than the stone itself, and the whole fabric has acquired such a degree of solidity, as to have baffled an interested attempt to demolish it, for the value of the materials, which was made about the beginning of the last century. Several estates in Kent being held by the ancient tenure of Castle guard, on St. Andrew's day, O. S., a banner is displayed on the castle, when every tenant who does not attend and discharge his arrears, is liable to have his rent doubled on every return of the tide, till payment is made. Some parts of the city walls remain entire, and the north-east angle in particular displays its height, form, and embrasures. Near Minor Canon-row is a small embattled tower, through which was the entrance into the cloisters of the priory, of which some parts are still remaining. At Boley Hill, to the south of the city, the Romans are supposed to have had a cemetery, and sepulchral urns and lachrymatories have been found there in great numbers : a part of the hill is, however, supposed to have been thrown up by the Danes, when they besieged the city, in 885. Under an elm-tree on this hill the corporation hold a separate court leet for this small district, in which the recorder presides as steward, and appoints an officer, called the Baron of Boley, to whom it is supposed the custody of this place was entrusted by the governor of the castle : a court of piepowder is also held here, under the mayor and two "discreet" citizens. Rochester gave the title of earl to the facetious John Wilmot, in the reign of Charles II.

ROCHESTER-WARD, a township in the parish of ELSDON, southern division of COQUETDALE ward, county of NORTHUMBERLAND, 12 miles (N.) from Bellingham, containing 491 inhabitants. A small village, called High Rochester, situated on the brow of a rugged eminence, occupies the site of the ancient *Bremenium*, the strongest of the Roman stations in the north, and previously the chief fortification of the Ottodini. Portions of the walls on the west and south-west sides still remain ; they were seven feet in thickness, chequered with ashlar-work, and defended by triple ramparts of earth. The hypocaust was in the north-eastern part of the walls, and the conduits leading to it were, a few years since, in a tolerably perfect state. Numerous altars, urns, and other relics, have been found here ; and in the neighbourhood are several rude sepulchral monuments of the ancient Britons, which prove that it must have been the scene of many sanguinary conflicts between the Ottodini and the Romans, before the conquest of the former.

ROCHFORD, a market town and parish in the hundred of ROCHFORD, county of ESSEX, 19¼ miles (S. E.) from Chelmsford, and 40 (E. by N.) from London, containing 1382 inhabitants. It is situated on the small river Roche, from which it is supposed to derive its name, and is an irregularly built town, neither lighted nor paved, supplied with water from a spring, by a pump erected in the market-place. The trade is principally in corn. The river Crouch is navigable to Broomhills, within about a mile of the town. The market is on Thursday ; and the fairs are on Tuesday and Wednesday in Easter week, and on the Wednesday and Thursday after the 29th of September, chiefly for toys : there is a market-house, built of wood, but not used as such, being occupied only as a store-room for wool. The magistrates for the hundred hold their sittings here on Thursday, once a fortnight, and occasionally weekly, for general business. The living is a rectory, in the archdeaconry of Essex, and diocese of London, rated in the king's books at £20, and in the patronage of the Hon. W. T. L. P. Wellesley. The church, situated about a quarter of a mile west from the town, is dedicated to St. Andrew ; it is a plain edifice, consisting of a nave, chancel, and two aisles, with a lofty tower of very fine ancient brickwork. A new gallery, the seats in which are free, was erected in 1827, at the expense of £40, by the Incorporated Society for building and enlarging churches and chapels, and the church was repaired and beautified in 1828. There is a place of worship for Independents. A National school, for an unlimited number of children of both sexes, is supported chiefly by subscription. Almshouses, in which six poor persons are lodged, and receive a weekly allowance, were founded and endowed by Lord Riche, about the middle of the sixteenth century. Rochford Hall, the greater part of which was destroyed by fire, about sixty years since, was the birthplace of the unfortunate Anne Boleyn, queen of Henry VIII. : it stands a short distance west of the town. Rochford gave the title of earl to the family of Nassau, which, on the death of the late earl, Sept. 3rd, 1830, became extinct.

ROCHFORD, a parish in the hundred of WOLPHY, county of HEREFORD, 2½ miles (E. by N.) from Tenbury, containing 264 inhabitants. The living is a perpetual curacy, annexed to the vicarage of Tenbury, in the archdeaconry of Salop, and diocese of Hereford. The church is dedicated to St. Michael.

ROCK, a chapelry in the parish of EMBLETON, southern division of BAMBROUGH ward, county of NORTHUMBERLAND, 4½ miles (N.N.E.) from Alnwick, containing 185 inhabitants. The living is a perpetual curacy, in the archdeaconry of Northumberland, and diocese of Durham, endowed with £400 private benefaction, and £800 royal bounty, and in the patronage of the Vicar of Embleton. The chapel is dedicated to St. Philip and St. James. Here is an endowed free school, with an income of about £7 per annum, for which and small quarterages from the parents, twenty children receive instruction.

ROCK, a parish in the lower division of the hundred of DODDINGTREE, county of WORCESTER, 4¾ miles (S. W. by W.) from Bewdley, containing, with the hamlets of Alton, Hightington, Lindons, and Snead, 1266 inhabitants. The living is a rectory, in the archdeaconry of Salop, and diocese of Hereford, rated in the king's books at £17. 11. 8. Mr. Woodhull and others were patrons in 1812. The church, dedicated to St. Peter and St. Paul, is very ancient. There is a charity school, the salary of the master being paid out of the crown rent.

ROCK-SAVAGE, county palatine of CHESTER.—See CLIFTON.

ROCKBEAR, a parish in the eastern division of the hundred of BUDLEIGH, county of DEVON, 5¼ miles (W.) from Ottery St. Mary, containing, with part of the tything of Rawleigh, 443 inhabitants. The living is a discharged vicarage, in the archdeaconry and diocese of Exeter, rated in the king's books at £9, and in the patronage of the Bishop of Exeter. The church is dedicated to St. Mary. Lawrence Colesworthy, in 1702, bequeathed £4 per annum for teaching poor children.

ROCKBURNE, a parish in the hundred of FORD-INGBRIDGE, New Forest (West) division of the county of SOUTHAMPTON, 3½ miles (N. W. by N.) from Fording-bridge, containing 464 inhabitants. The living is a donative, in the patronage of Lady Coote. The church is dedicated to St. Andrew.

ROCKCLIFF, a parish in the ward and county of CUMBERLAND, comprising the townships of Castle-Rock-cliff and Church-Rockcliff, and containing 722 inhabitants, of which number, 362 are in the township of Church-Rockcliff, 4¾ miles (N. W.) from Carlisle. The living is a perpetual curacy, in the archdeaconry and diocese of Carlisle, endowed with £200 royal bounty, and £1600 parliamentary grant, and in the patronage of the Dean and Chapter of Carlisle. The parish is bounded on the north by the river Esk, on the north-west by the Solway firth, and on the south-west by the river Eden, the latter of which is navigable to the village of Rockcliff, which is situated opposite to Port Carlisle. Within reach of the tide is a remarkable spring, with a scum floating on its surface, which turns paper to a complete golden hue; and the banks of the river produce a medicinal plant, termed Mother of Thyme.

ROCKCLIFF (CASTLE), a township in the parish of ROCKCLIFF, ward and county of CUMBERLAND, 5¾ miles (N. W.) from Carlisle, containing 360 inhabitants. The river Eden is here crossed by an iron bridge of three arches, on the road to Gretna-Green, three miles distant. Some remains of a small castle, built by the Lords Dacre, are still visible : it was gar-risoned by Leonard Dacre, when in rebellion against Queen Elizabeth, in 1570, and was taken possession of by Lord Hunsdon, for the queen, in February of the same year.

ROCKFIELD, a parish in the lower division of the hundred of SKENFRETH, county of MONMOUTH, 2 miles (N. W.) from Monmouth, containing 335 inha-bitants. The living is a discharged vicarage, in the archdeaconry and diocese of Llandaff, rated in the king's books at £4. 3. 1½., endowed with £800 royal bounty, and £200 parliamentary grant. Robert Wil-liams, Esq. was patron in 1807. The church is dedi-cated to St. Kenelm.

ROCKHAM, a hamlet in the parish of AMBERLEY, hundred of WEST EASWRITH, rape of ARUNDEL, county of SUSSEX, 6 miles (N. E. by N.) from Arundel. The population is returned with the parish. The chapel is demolished.

ROCKHAMPTON, a parish in the lower division of the hundred of LANGLEY and SWINEHEAD, county of GLOUCESTER, 2½ miles (N. E. by N.) from Thorn-bury, containing 159 inhabitants. The living is a rectory, in the archdeaconry and diocese of Gloucester, rated in the king's books at £15, and in the patronage of Danvers Ward, Esq. The church is dedicated to St.

Oswald. The parish is partly bounded by the navigable river Severn.

ROCKINGHAM, a parish in the hundred of COR-BY, county of NORTHAMPTON, 25 miles (N. N. E.) from Northampton, containing 278 inhabitants. The living is a rectory, in the archdeaconry of Northampton, and diocese of Peterborough, rated in the king's books at £10. 2. 3½., endowed with £200 private benefaction, and £200 royal bounty, and in the patronage of Lord Sondes. The church is dedicated to St. Leonard. The river Wel-land runs through the parish. This place, formerly a market town, is situated in the midst of Rockingham Forest. On the top of a hill, the declivity of which is occupied by the village, a castle was erected by William the Conqueror, for the defence of the extensive iron-works then existing in the adjacent woodlands. Here was convened, in 1094, the council of barons, bishops, and clergy, which sat for the purpose of determining the dispute between William Rufus and Anselm, Arch-bishop of Canterbury, respecting the right of episcopal investiture. Of the castle, the two massive bastions which flanked the gateway are the only remains. The tower and part of the body of the church were destroyed in the great civil war during the siege of the castle, which was garrisoned for the king by its proprietor, Sir Lewis Watson, afterwards created Lord Rockingham.

ROCKLAND, a parish in the hundred of HENSTEAD, county of NORFOLK, 6½ miles (S. E. by E.) from Nor-wich, containing 318 inhabitants. The living is a rec-tory, consolidated with that of St. Margaret, and a me-diety of Holverstone, in the archdeaconry of Norfolk, and diocese of Norwich, rated in the king's books at £6. 13. 4., and in the patronage of the President and Fellows of Queen's College, Cambridge. The church-yard formerly contained two churches ; that now in use is dedicated to St. Mary, but that of St. Margaret has been demolished.

ROCKLAND (ALL SAINTS), a parish in the hundred of SHROPHAM, county of NORFOLK, 3¾ miles (W. by N.) from Attleburgh, containing 267 inhabitants. The living is a discharged rectory, with Rockland St. Andrew, annexed to the rectory of Caston, in the arch-deaconry of Norfolk, and diocese of Norwich, rated in the king's books at £10. 19. 4½.

ROCKLAND (ST. ANDREW), a parish in the hun-dred of SHROPHAM, county of NORFOLK, 3½ miles (W.) from Attleburgh, containing 143 inhabitants. The liv-ing is a discharged rectory, with Rockland All Saints, annexed to the rectory of Caston, in the archdeaconry of Norfolk, and diocese of Norwich.

ROCKLAND (ST. PETER), a parish in the hundred of WAYLAND, county of NORFOLK, 4¼ miles (W.N.W.) from Attleburgh, containing 349 inhabitants. The liv-ing is a discharged rectory, in the archdeaconry of Norfolk, and diocese of Norwich, rated in the king's books at £4. 16. 5½., and in the patronage of the Rev. J. T. Bird.

ROCLIFFE, a township in that part of the parish of ALDBOROUGH which is in the lower division of the wapentake of CLARO, West riding of the county of YORK, 1¾ mile (W.S.W.) from Boroughbridge, containing 248 inhabitants. A school for children of both sexes is supported by voluntary contributions.

ROD, a joint township with Little Brampton and Nash, in that part of the parish of PRESTEIGNE which is in the hundred of WIGMORE, county of HEREFORD, 2 miles (S. S. E.) from Presteigne, containing, with Little Brampton and Nash, 148 inhabitants.

RODBASTON, a township in that part of the parish of PENKRIDGE which is in the eastern division of the hundred of CUTTLESTONE, county of STAFFORD, 1¾ mile (S. by E.) from Penkridge. The population is returned with the township of Penkridge.

RODBORNE, a chapelry in the parish and hundred of MALMESBURY, county of WILTS, 3 miles (S. by E.) from Malmesbury, containing 139 inhabitants.

RODBORNE-CHENEY, a parish in the hundred of HIGHWORTH, CRICKLADE, and STAPLE, county of WILTS, 3 miles (N. W. by N.) from Swindon, containing 544 inhabitants. The living is a vicarage, in the archdeaconry of Wilts, and diocese of Salisbury, rated in the king's books at £17, and in the patronage of Mrs. Evans. The church is dedicated to St. Mary.

RODBOROUGH, a chapelry in the parish of MINCHINHAMPTON, hundred of LONGTREE, county of GLOUCESTER, 1 mile (S.W. by W.) from Stroud, containing 2038 inhabitants. The living is a perpetual curacy, annexed to the rectory of Minchinhampton, in the archdeaconry and diocese of Gloucester, and in the patronage of the Principal and Fellows of Brasenose College, Oxford. The chapel, dedicated to the Holy Trinity, was a chantry to the priory of Minchinhampton, whence it had formerly a subterranean passage. There is a place of worship for Independents. The river Stroud, and the Thames and Severn canal, pass through the parish. Henry King, in 1699, bequeathed the residue of his personal estate, in equal moieties, to the parish of Minchinhampton and to this chapelry, the proportion to each being about £25 a year: the parochial school, to which these sums have hitherto been paid, has been recently enlarged out of the funds of this charity. There is also a bequest of £100 three per cents., by Samuel Horrill, for teaching three girls, and another of £100 for teaching three boys, which, with accumulations from the sale of timber, &c., produce about £16 per annum. Here was born, in 1638, Richard Clutterbuck, who, though blind, was an extraordinary mechanical and musical genius; he also had the faculty of hearing in a remarkably acute manner.

RODDAM, a township in the parish of ILDERTON, northern division of COQUETDALE ward, county of NORTHUMBERLAND, 5½ miles (S. S. E.) from Wooler, containing 90 inhabitants.

RODDEN, a parish in the hundred of FROME, county of SOMERSET, 2 miles (E. by S.) from Frome, containing 272 inhabitants. The living is a perpetual curacy, in the archdeaconry of Wells, and diocese of Bath and Wells, endowed with £400 private benefaction, £600 royal bounty, and £200 parliamentary grant, and in the patronage of Lord Heytesbury. The church was built at the expense of the parishioners, about 1640.

RODDINGTON, a parish in the Wellington division of the hundred of BRADFORD (South), county of SALOP, 5 miles (N. W. by W.) from Wellington, containing 445 inhabitants. The living is a discharged rectory, in the archdeaconry of Salop, and diocese of Lichfield and Coventry, rated in the king's books at £6. 13. 4., and in the patronage of the Crown. The church is dedicated to St. George. The river Rode and the Shrewsbury canal pass through the village.

RODE (NORTH), a township in the parish of PRESTBURY, hundred of MACCLESFIELD, county palatine of CHESTER, 3½ miles (N. E.) from Congleton, containing 262 inhabitants. A school is supported by small annual donations.

RODE (ODD), a township in that part of the parish of ASTBURY which is in the hundred of NORTHWICH, county palatine of CHESTER, 4 miles (S. W. by S.) from Congleton, containing 1143 inhabitants. The Grand Trunk canal passes through the parish. A school is supported by annual subscriptions averaging about £25.

RODE - HUISH, a chapelry in the parish and hundred of CARHAMPTON, county of SOMERSET, 3 miles (S. S. E.) from Dunster. The population is returned with the parish.

RODLEY, a township in the parish of WESTBURY upon SEVERN, hundred of WESTBURY, though locally in the duchy of Lancaster, county of GLOUCESTER, 5 miles (E. by N.) from Newnham. The population is returned with the parish.

RODMARTON, a parish in the hundred of LONGTREE, county of GLOUCESTER, 6 miles (W. S. W.) from Cirencester, containing 357 inhabitants. The living is a rectory, in the archdeaconry and diocese of Gloucester, rated in the king's books at £18. 1. 3., and in the patronage of the Rev. Daniel Lysons. The church is dedicated to St. Peter. The old Akeman-street passes near the south-eastern boundary of the parish. In a field called Hocbery, a tesselated pavement, with coins of Antoninus and Valentinian, was discovered, in 1636. A farm-house at Hasleden, in this parish, is supposed to have been at one time a monastery; and attached to the old manor-house at Tarlton are the remains of a chapel. Samuel Lysons, F. R. S., and F. S. A., author of the "Environs of London," and joint author of the "Magna Britannia," was born here, in 1763.

RODMELL, a parish in the hundred of HOLMS-TROW, rape of LEWES, county of SUSSEX, 3¾ miles (S. by E.) from Lewes, containing 336 inhabitants. The living is a rectory, in the archdeaconry of Lewes, and diocese of Chichester, rated in the king's books at £15. 6. 0½., and in the patronage of the Bishop of Chichester. The church, dedicated to St. Peter, is principally in the early style of English architecture. There was formerly a chapel at Northese. The river Ouse runs through the parish, also a branch of the ancient Ermin-street, in a direction towards Newhaven. A school is supported by subscription, in which about sixty children are educated.

RODMERSHAM, a parish in the hundred of MILTON, lathe of SCRAY, county of KENT, 2 miles (S. E. by S.) from Sittingbourne, containing 307 inhabitants. The living is a discharged vicarage, in the archdeaconry and diocese of Canterbury, rated in the king's books at £8. 6. 8., endowed with £200 private benefaction, and £200 royal bounty, and in the patronage of Wm. Lushington, Esq. The church, dedicated to St. Nicholas, is in the early style of English architecture, and has in the chancel four elegant canopied stalls, thought to have been intended for the knights of St. John of Jerusalem, to whom the church belonged, when they came to visit their estate.

RODSLEY, a hamlet in the parish of LONGFORD, hundred of APPLETREE, county of DERBY, 4½ miles (S. S. E.) from Ashbourn, containing 208 inhabitants.

It is in the honour of Tutbury, duchy of Lancaster, and within the jurisdiction of a court of pleas held at Tutbury every third Tuesday, for the recovery of debts under 40s. There is a place of worship for Wesleyan Methodists. A school is supported by a trifling bequest from Lady Coke, and some small annual subscriptions.

ROEHAMPTON, a hamlet in the parish of PUTNEY, western division of the hundred of BRIXTON, county of SURREY, 5½ miles (S. W. by W.) from London. This place is pleasantly situated at the western extremity of Putney Heath, bordering on which are several handsome villas of the nobility and gentry, including that of the Earl of Besborough, built by Sir William Chambers, and containing some antique sculptures and paintings by Flemish and Italian artists. Here also is Roehampton House, formerly called Putney Park, which, in the reign of Charles I., belonged to the Earl of Portland, and was subsequently the property of Christiana, Countess of Devonshire, a lady distinguished for her talents, who is said to have had some share in the restoration of Charles II. A chapel attached to this mansion, erected by Lord Portland, was consecrated in 1632, and dedicated to the Holy Trinity: it was taken down in 1777, by Thomas Parker, Esq., then proprietor of Roehampton House, who built a new chapel at a short distance. This place suffered great injury from a violent hurricane which occurred October 15th, 1780, and extended from Lord Besborough's mansion to Hammersmith, tearing up trees in its course, and driving them to a considerable distance; some buildings were unroofed, and a windmill was thrown down.

ROFFORD, a liberty in the parish of CHALGROVE, hundred of EWELME, county of OXFORD, 4¾ miles (W. S. W.) from Tetsworth, containing 31 inhabitants.

ROGATE, a parish in the hundred of DUMPFORD, rape of CHICHESTER, county of SUSSEX, 6 miles (W. N. W.) from Midhurst, containing 724 inhabitants. The living is a discharged vicarage, in the archdeaconry and diocese of Chichester, rated in the king's books at £10. 5., and in the patronage of the Crown. The church, dedicated to St. Bartholomew, is in the early style of English architecture. There is a place of worship for Independents.

ROGERSTONE, a hamlet in that part of the parish of BASSALEG which is in the upper division of the hundred of WENTLLOOG, county of MONMOUTH, 2¾ miles (W.) from Newport, containing 662 inhabitants.

ROGGIET, a parish in the lower division of the hundred of CALDICOTT, county of MONMOUTH, 6½ miles (S. W.) from Chepstow, containing 42 inhabitants. The living is a discharged rectory, with that of Ifton united, in the archdeaconry and diocese of Llandaff, rated in the king's books at £12. 6. 0½., and in the patronage of J. Morgan, Esq.

ROKEBY, a parish in the western division of the wapentake of GILLING, North riding of the county of YORK, 1¼ mile (N. W. by W.) from Greta-Bridge, containing, with Eggleston Abbey, 222 inhabitants. The living is a discharged vicarage, in the archdeaconry of Richmond, and diocese of Chester, rated in the king's books at £4. 3. 9., and in the patronage of the Crown. The church, dedicated to St. Mary, was formerly situated near the manor-house, and its site is now marked by heaps of rubbish and a few grave-stones; it was de-

VOL. III.

molished about the middle of the last century, and the present small structure erected by Sir Thomas Robinson. Rokeby is situated on the rivers Tees and Greta, and the vicinity is replete with beautiful scenery, which has been celebrated by the poetry of Sir Walter Scott and Mr. Mason, the latter of whom made it his favourite retreat. A Roman road led through the parish, and here are vestiges of an ancient encampment, near which various inscribed stones and other Roman relics have been found. In a close adjoining the embattled keep of Mortham, the ancient residence of the Rokebys, is a large tomb, removed thither from Eggleston abbey, the sides of which are ornamented with shields.

ROLLESBY, a parish in the western division of the hundred of FLEGG, county of NORFOLK, 5¼ miles (N. E.) from Acle, containing, with the inmates of the house of industry for the eastern and western divisions of the hundred of Flegg, 619 inhabitants. The living is a discharged rectory, in the archdeaconry and diocese of Norwich, rated in the king's books at £17, and in the patronage of—Fielding, Esq. The church is dedicated to St. George.

ROLLESTON, a chapelry in the parish of BILLESDON, hundred of GARTREE, county of LEICESTER, 10 miles (E. by S.) from Leicester, containing 31 inhabitants. The chapel is dedicated to St. John.

ROLLESTON, a parish in the northern division of the wapentake of THURGARTON, county of NOTTINGHAM, 4½ miles (W. by S.) from Newark, containing 306 inhabitants. The living is a vicarage, in the archdeaconry of Nottingham, and diocese of York, rated in the king's books at £10. 1. 3., and in the patronage of the Chapter of the Collegiate Church of Southwell. The church is dedicated to the Holy Trinity. The village is situated on the river Trent, which receives a smaller stream that bounds the parish on the west.

ROLLESTON, a parish in the northern division of the hundred of OFFLOW, county of STAFFORD, 3¼ miles (N. N. W.) from Burton upon Trent, containing, with the township of Anslow, or Annesley, 869 inhabitants. The living is a rectory, in the archdeaconry of Stafford, and diocese of Lichfield and Coventry, rated in the king's books at £13. 19. 7., and in the patronage of Sir Oswald Mosley, Bart. The church is dedicated to St. Mary. There is a place of worship for Wesleyan Methodists. The river Dove runs through the parish. A free school was founded, about 1520, by Robert Sherbourne, Bishop of Winchester, who endowed it with an annuity of £10, to which subsequent benefactions have been added, producing together an income of £37 a year, which is applied to the instruction of forty-five children. Near the school are ten almshouses, called the hospital, for aged people of both sexes, endowed in 1672, by Mr. Rolleston; six of the inmates have an allowance of coal and four shillings a week each, and the remaining four have three and sixpence each. Rolleston is in the honour of Tutbury, duchy of Lancaster, and within the jurisdiction of a court of pleas held at Tutbury every third Tuesday, for the recovery of debts under 40s.

ROLLRIGHT (GREAT), a parish in the hundred of CHADLINGTON, county of OXFORD, 3 miles (N. by E.) from Chipping-Norton, containing 419 inhabitants. The living is a rectory, in the archdeaconry and diocese of Oxford, rated in the king's books at £16. 9. 4½., and

4 L

in the patronage of the Principal and Fellows of Brasenose College, Oxford. The church is dedicated to St. Andrew. The Rev. James Parker, in 1780, bequeathed £100 towards the support of a school for teaching poor children to read. This parish was noted among agriculturists for a peculiar species of cattle, called the Rollright breed.

ROLLRIGHT (LITTLE), a parish in the hundred of CHADLINGTON, county of OXFORD, 2¼ miles (N. W. by N.) from Chipping-Norton, containing 28 inhabitants. The living is a discharged rectory, in the archdeaconry and diocese of Oxford, rated in the king's books at £5. 6. 8., endowed with £200 private benefaction, and £200 royal bounty, and in the patronage of Sir John Chandos Reade, Bart. There are in this parish some stones set up in the form of a circle, the diameter of which is twenty yards, termed the King's Stones, and supposed to be remains of a Druidical temple.

ROLLSTONE, a parish forming a detached portion of the hundred of ELSTUB and EVERLEY, county of WILTS, 5¼ miles (W. by N.) from Amesbury, containing 41 inhabitants. The living is a discharged rectory, in the archdeaconry and diocese of Salisbury, rated in the king's books at £7. 19. 5½., and in the patronage of the Crown. The church is dedicated to St. Andrew.

ROLVENDEN, a parish in the hundred of ROLVENDEN, lathe of SCRAY, county of KENT, 2½ miles (S. W. by W.) from Tenterden, containing 1403 inhabitants. The living is a discharged vicarage, in the archdeaconry and diocese of Canterbury, rated in the king's books at £10, endowed with £200 private benefaction, and £500 parliamentary grant, and in the patronage of the Dean and Chapter of Rochester. The church, dedicated to St. Mary, is principally in the later style of English architecture, and has lately received an addition of two hundred and twenty sittings, of which one hundred and forty are free, the Incorporated Society for the enlargement of churches and chapels having granted £200 towards defraying the expense. There is a place of worship for Wesleyan Methodists. Major John Gibbon, in 1707, bequeathed property amounting to £921. 4. three per cent. consols., producing £27. 2. 9., for teaching and apprenticing poor children of both sexes.

ROMALD-KIRK, a parish in the western division of the wapentake of GILLING, North riding of the county of YORK, comprising the townships of Cotherston, Holwick, Hunderthwaite, Lartington, Lune-Dale, Mickleton, and Romald-Kirk, and containing 2461 inhabitants, of which number, 377 are in the township of Romald-Kirk, 6 miles (N. W.) from Barnard-Castle. The living is a rectory, in the archdeaconry of Richmond, and diocese of Chester, rated in the king's books at £58. 14. 2., and in the patronage of the Earl of Strathmore. The church, dedicated to St. Romald, is an ancient cruciform structure, with a large square tower crowned with pinnacles: it contains several handsome monuments. John Parkin, in 1632, bequeathed £300, now producing about £20 per annum, for which all the poor children of the parish are entitled to free instruction.

ROMANBY, a township in the parish of NORTHALLERTON, wapentake of ALLERTONSHIRE, North riding of the county of YORK, ¾ of a mile (S. W.) from North Allerton, containing 294 inhabitants. It derived its name from the Roman road passing by it.

ROMANSLEIGH, a parish in the hundred of WITHERIDGE, county of DEVON, 3¼ miles (S. by E.) from South Molton, containing 214 inhabitants. The living is a rectory, in the archdeaconry of Barnstaple, and diocese of Exeter, rated in the king's books at £10. 14. 9½., and in the patronage of Sir T. D. Acland, Bart. The church is dedicated to St. Rumon.

ROMFORD, a market town and parish in the liberty of HAVERING atte BOWER, county of ESSEX, 18 miles (S. W.) from Chelmsford, and 12 (E.N.E.) from London, containing 3777 inhabitants. This town is supposed by Dr. Stukeley to occupy the site of the Roman station *Durolitum*, and he considers its name to be a contraction of Roman-ford, in which opinion he is supported by the eminent antiquary Smart Lethellier, Esq.; others, however, derive it from a ford over a small stream running into the Thames, called the Rom, which intersects the town, and is crossed by a bridge. It is situated on the high road from London to Bury, Colchester, Ipswich, Harwich, Norwich, and Yarmouth, and is consequently a great thoroughfare, consisting chiefly of one long and wide street, which is well paved, and lighted with gas, according to the provisions of an act of parliament passed in the year 1819; the houses are tolerably good, and the inhabitants are well supplied with water. The market, held on Wednesday, was granted so early as 1247; it is the general market for all kinds of agricultural produce, cattle &c., and is numerously attended; another is held on Monday for hogs, and one on Tuesday for calves: there is an annual fair on Midsummer-day for horses and cattle, and a statute fair for hiring servants, on the market days next before and after the 29th of September: the market-place and tolls have been recently purchased of the crown by Hugh Macintosh, Esq. This town, which, with Hornchurch and Havering, constitutes "the liberty of Havering atte Bower," was formerly considered one of the wards of Hornchurch, but by an act of parliament passed for the regulation of the poor, in 1786, it is recognized, so far as relates to civil jurisdiction, as a separate parish, and comprises the wards of Collier Row, Harold's Wood, Noke Hill, and the Town; as regards ecclesiastical affairs it is still partly dependent on the parish of Hornchurch. The earliest charter was granted by Edward the Confessor, which has received several confirmations and additions: the government is vested in the high steward, the deputy steward, and one justice elected by the inhabitants of the liberty, all of whom exercise magisterial authority: they are a corporation, and have a patent authorising them at their own quarter sessions, which are held on the Friday after the county quarter sessions, to try for all manner of offences, high treason not excepted, upon payment of a trifling fee, but no commission of this kind has been applied for of late years; and also to hear and determine, every three weeks, all actions for debt, trespasses, ejectments, and replevins, in a court of ancient demesne. The tenants of this liberty claim exemption from toll every

Corporate Seal.

where throughout the realm, both for goods and cattle sold, and provisions purchased; from payment towards the county expenses, and also a personal exemption from being empannelled on juries and inquests, save within their own liberty, with various other privileges: the county magistrates have no jurisdiction within the liberty. The court-house is in the market-place, and beneath it is a small gaol for the liberty. During the war there were cavalry barracks, built of wood, but they have since been pulled down.

The living is in the nature of a vicarage, in the peculiar jurisdiction and patronage of the Warden and Fellows of New College, Oxford, who appoint a commissary. The great and small tithes of the whole liberty, were given by William of Wykeham to the Warden and Fellows of New College, Oxford, founded by him; the great tithes being now demised to two laymen, and the small tithes of Romford to the chaplain of Romford, and those of Hornchurch to the chaplain of Hornchurch. The church, dedicated to St. Edward the Confessor, was erected in 1407, and consists of a nave, north aisle, and chancel, with a tower at the west end; in the east window is the figure of the patron saint, in fine old painted glass: there are several ancient monumental tablets and effigies, of which the most remarkable are, one to Sir Anthony Coke, Ambassador to Queen Elizabeth, who died in 1576, and was interred here; and two others to the memory of Sir George Hervey, Knt., and his daughter. There are places of worship for Independents and Wesleyan Methodists, the first having a small endowment of £20 per annum, and a house for the minister. A free school, for children of both sexes, was erected in 1728, and has been endowed with various benefactions, amounting to more than £1300; it is further supported by voluntary contributions, and contains sixty boys and thirty girls. An almshouse was founded by Roger Reed, in 1483, for the support of five poor men, whose widows are allowed £20 a year for life, with clothes and coal; the present value of the endowment is £280 per annum: the almshouse was rebuilt in 1784. The workhouse is a commodious building, erected in 1787, at an expense of £4000, under the provisions of an act of parliament, whereby the management of the poor is confided to thirty guardians, exclusively of the two churchwardens. Here were anciently a guild and a chantry; the revenue of the former was valued, at the dissolution, at £4. 10. 2., and that of the latter at £13; also an hospital, a cell to that of Mount St. Bernard, in the Savoy, London, founded at an early period, and dedicated to St. Nicholas and St. Bernard. Francis Quarles, the poet, and author of "The Divine Emblems," cup-bearer to the Queen of Bohemia, and afterwards secretary to Archbishop Usher, whom he accompanied to Ireland, was a native of this place; he died in 1644.

ROMILY, or CHAD-KIRK, a chapelry in the parish of Stockport, hundred of Macclesfield, county palatine of Chester, 4 miles (E.) from Stockport, containing 1181 inhabitants. The living is a perpetual curacy, in the archdeaconry and diocese of Chester, endowed with £400 private benefaction, £600 royal bounty, and £200 parliamentary grant, and in the patronage of the Rector of Stockport. The chapel, dedicated to St. Chad, was rebuilt by subscription in 1746. The Peak Forest canal passes through the parish.

ROMNEY (NEW), a cinque-port, market town, and parish, having separate jurisdiction, in the cinque-port liberty of Romney, county of Kent, 34 miles (S. E.) from Maidstone, and 68 (S. E. by E.) from London, containing 962 inhabitants. The name is probably derived from the Saxon *Rumen-ea*, "a large watery expanse, or marsh." It arose from the decay of

Arms.

the haven at Old Romney, by the retiring of the sea, and, in contradistinction to that town, obtained the appellation of New Romney. At the time of the Conquest it was a place of considerable importance, divided into twelve wards, and containing five parish churches, of which that of St. Nicholas is now the only one remaining. It was soon after that period given by William the Conqueror to his brother Odo, Bishop of Bayeux, whom that monarch created Earl of Kent; subsequently to which it was made a cinque-port, and the towns of Old Romney and Lydd were included within its jurisdiction. In return for such privileges, it was charged with the duty of supplying five ships of war for the service of the king. In the 15th of Edward I. an irruption of the sea inundated an extensive tract of land, destroyed the populous village of Bromhill, and a considerable part of the town, diverted the course of the river Rother, and ruined its fine haven on the western shore; since which time it has shared the fate of its predecessor, and though still inhabited as a market town, has as a port fallen into comparative insignificance and decay. On several occasions, Romney, as a cinque-port, furnished a complement of five ships, duly manned and equipped for naval engagements, especially in the reigns of John, Edward III., Henry VII., and Henry VIII. The town is situated on rising ground near the centre of Romney-Marsh, and consists of one broad well-paved street, with a smaller one intersecting it almost at right angles. The chief trade arises from the grazing of cattle on Romney-Marsh. The market, on Saturday, is held under the guildhall; and there is a considerable fair for live stock on the 21st of August.

Corporate Seal.

Romney is a borough by prescription; the inhabitants received the first charter of incorporation from Edward III., under the style of "Barons of the Town and Port of Romney;" a new charter was granted by Elizabeth, under which the town is now governed: the corporation consists of a mayor, twelve jurats, and common council-men, with a recorder, chamberlain, town clerk, and other officers, under the style of "Mayor, Jurats, and Commonalty:" the mayor is chosen annually upon Lady-day, from among the jurats. A court, called a Brotherhood and Guestling, connected with the business of the various cinque-ports and their members, is, held, when necessary, on the Tuesday next after St. Margaret's day. A court of record for pleas to an unlimited extent was granted by Charles II., to be held by the mayor and jurats: no writs have been issued of late years, but the court is still used for levying fines. Sessions are held quarterly, and by adjournment every six weeks, in the guildhall, a neat structure of brick, cemented so as to resemble stone, recently erected. Two representatives, under the title of Barons, are returned to parliament: the right of election is in the corporation: the mayor is the returning officer, and the influence of the Deering family is predominant. This place enjoys all the exclusive privileges of the cinque-ports, and its barons are second in rank to bear the canopies over the king and queen at the coronation.

The living is a vicarage, in the peculiar jurisdiction of the Archbishop of Canterbury, rated in the king's books at £6. 16. 3., and in the patronage of the Warden and Fellows of All Souls' College, Oxford. The church, dedicated to St. Nicholas, is a spacious edifice, consisting of three aisles and three chancels, and a square tower at the west end, with several portions of Norman architecture, and some in the later styles, and contains a variety of monuments and brasses. An hospital was founded in 1610, and endowed with land by John Southland, for the maintenance of a governor, who must be a scholar of Oxford or Cambridge, four poor persons, and two poor children, the latter to be instructed by the governor in the English language and arithmetic, until they are fourteen years old: the children are appointed by the mayor as vacancies arise. Here was formerly a cell, subordinate to the abbey of Pountney, or Pontiniac, in France, also an hospital for lepers, founded in the reign of Henry II., and afterwards converted into a chantry; of both which there are some trifling vestiges.

ROMNEY (OLD), a parish partly in the cinque-port liberty of NEW ROMNEY, and partly in the liberty of ROMNEY-MARSH, lathe of SHEPWAY, county of KENT, 1¾ mile (W. by N.) from New Romney, containing 153 inhabitants. The living is a rectory, in the peculiar jurisdiction and patronage of the Archbishop of Canterbury, rated in the king's books at £15. 19. 2. The church is dedicated to St. Clement. This town had a good and much-frequented haven prior to the Conquest; but in the reign of Edward III. it sustained considerable damage from violent tempests, and its harbour being choked up and obstructed, and the river Rye having changed its course, it was superseded in its maritime privileges and prosperity by New Romney. An hospital for lepers, founded here by Adam de Cherring, and dedicated to St. Stephen and St. Thomas à Becket, was, in the fourteenth century, converted into a chantry, and in 1481 became annexed to the college of St. Mary Magdalene, in Oxford.

ROMNEY-MARSH, a liberty in the lathe of SHEPWAY, county of KENT, comprising the parishes of Broomhill, Burmarsh, Dymchurch with Blackmanstone, East-Bridge, Hope (All Saints), Ivy-Church, Lydd, St. Mary's, Midley, Newchurch, Orgarswick, New Romney, Old Romney, Snargate, and Snave; and parts of those of Aldington, Bilsington, Bonnington, Brenzett, Hurst, Lympne, and Orlestone. For a further account, see article on the county of KENT.

ROMSEY, a market town and parish having separate jurisdiction, though locally in the hundred of King's Sombourn, Andover division of the county of SOUTHAMPTON, 8 miles (N. W. by N.) from Southampton, and 75 (S. W. by S.) from London, containing 5128 inhabitants. This town is of great antiquity, and its name is of Saxon

Seal and Arms.

origin. An abbey for nuns of the Benedictine order was founded by Edward the Elder, whose daughter Elfleda was the first abbess: the foundation was augmented by Edgar in 967, and his son Edmund was interred in the abbey church. All the first abbesses were of royal birth, and eminent for their sanctity. About the year 992 it was plundered by the Danes, but the nuns, with the relics, and other articles of the greatest value, had been previously removed to Winchester, through the precaution of Elwina the abbess. An enumeration of some of the possessions of this monastery appears in Domesday-book, in which it is called the abbey de Romesyg. In 1085, Christina, cousin to Edward the Confessor, took the veil here, and to her was entrusted the education of Matilda, daughter of Malcolm, King of Scotland, and subsequently wife of Henry I. In the next reign, Mary, daughter of King Stephen, became abbess, and was induced to quit her charge by Matthew, younger son of Theodore, Earl of Flanders, to whom she was married, which step so excited the indignation of the Papal see, that she was compelled to return to her conventual duties after having borne two children. The benefactors to the abbey were numerous, and its revenue, at the dissolution, was valued at £528. 8. 10¼.: in the 35th of Henry VIII., the site was granted to the inhabitants of the town, and three years afterwards to John Bellew and R. Bigot.

The town is situated on the river Test, which falls into the Southampton water, in a flat country, on the road from Southampton to Bath, and is surrounded by an amphitheatre of hills and fertile and pleasant meadows, which are rendered more productive by the occasional overflowing of the river: it consists of several good streets, which are lighted and paved under the provisions of an act of parliament: the inhabitants are well supplied with water: there are a news-room and some book clubs: concerts are held annually, and musical festivals occasionally. The clothing trade was formerly carried on to a considerable extent, but has long declined; employment is given to nearly three hundred persons in three paper-mills, one flax-mill, and three sacking manufactories; there are also some tanneries, malting establishments, and several corn-mills upon the river Test. The town is supplied with coal and other commodities by means of the canal from Redbridge to Andover, which passes through it. The market, which was formerly on Saturday, has been recently changed to Thursday, by letters patent granted to the lord of the manor; it is chiefly for corn, and on alternate Thursdays is also supplied with cattle: the fairs are on Easter-Monday and Tuesday, August 26th, and November 8th, for horses, cattle, cheese, cloth, and other articles of mer-

chandise. The inhabitants were first incorporated by charter of James I., which was confirmed by William III.: the government is vested in a mayor, lord high steward, recorder, six aldermen, and twelve burgesses, assisted by a town-clerk, two serjeants at mace, and two ale-tasters. The mayor, late mayor, the recorder, and three senior aldermen, are justices of the peace, and are empowered to hold quarter sessions for the trial of felons and misdemeanants: the mayor, recorder, and aldermen, hold a court of record every Thursday, for the recovery of debts not exceeding £40, the jurisdiction of which is confined to the borough: the county magistrates cannot preside at either of these courts. Romsey Extra is within the jurisdiction of the Cheyney Court held at Winchester every Thursday, for the recovery of debts to any amount. The new court-house, or town hall, in which the quarter sessions and assemblies are held, is situated in the abbey precinct, and was built by the corporation in 1820: near it is a gaol.

The living, which comprises the two parishes of Romsey Infra and Romsey Extra, is a discharged vicarage, in the archdeaconry and diocese of Winchester, rated in the king's books at £20. 18. 1½., and in the patronage of the Dean and Chapter of Winchester. The church, dedicated to St. Mary, and formerly belonging to the abbey, is a very magnificent cruciform structure, with a low tower rising from the intersection: the principal portion was erected in the middle of the tenth century, and exhibits some fine specimens of the Norman style of architecture; within are various admixtures of round and pointed arches, with zigzag and other ornaments; the more modern parts of the edifice are in the early English style. The interior contains several ancient memorials of the abbesses who were interred here; an elegant sepulchral inscription to Frances, Viscountess Palmerston, who died in childbed, in 1769; and a neat tablet to the memory of Sir William Petty, a native of this town, and ancestor to the present Marquis of Lansdowne: there is also a remarkable monument, with effigies and a curious inscription, to the family of John St. Barbe, Esq., a representative of this county in parliament in 1654. An apple-tree, supposed to be at least two hundred years old, grew on the roof until lately, but it is now dead. This venerable edifice has lately received an addition of eight hundred sittings, of which seven hundred and twenty-seven are free, the Incorporated Society for enlarging and building churches and chapels having contributed £450. At the east end of the building several stone coffins were discovered some years ago; at the angle of the southern transept are the remains of a fine Norman doorway, and in its western wall is a very ancient image of Christ on the Cross, in basso relievo: the west end is separated from that part of the building appropriated to divine service by a curious and ancient oak screen: about fourteen years since, some curious old paintings were found behind the altar-piece. There are places of worship for Baptists, Independents, Wesleyan Methodists, and Sandemanians. A free school, in which thirty boys are educated and annually clothed, and some apprenticed every year, having been founded, probably, by subscription, was, in 1718, endowed from the estate of John Nowes, Esq., with an income of £30 per annum, for the instruction of twenty poor boys, and £60 per annum to clothe them: this endowment was augmented, in 1723, by a rent-charge of £25, for clothing and teaching ten boys, under the will of Sir John St. Barbe. The National school for three hundred boys is a neat building, erected in 1827, the site, and £150 towards the erection, having been given by Lord Palmerston: it is supported by voluntary contributions. The Union school for eighty boys, on the Lancasterian system, is supported by subscription. Almshouses for six widows were founded, in 1692, by John Hunt, Esq.; and six others for single women, in 1809, by John Bartlett, Esq. The only vestiges of the ancient abbey, exclusively of the church, are a few fragments of the old walls. Mr. Giles Jacob, author of the Law Dictionary, was born here, in 1686.

ROMSLEY, a liberty in that part of the parish of ALVELEY which is in the borough of BRIDGENORTH, county of SALOP, 8 miles (S. E.) from Bridgenorth, containing 144 inhabitants.

RONTON, a parish in the southern division of the hundred of PIREHILL, county of STAFFORD, 4 miles (S. by E.) from Eccleshall, containing 334 inhabitants. The living is a perpetual curacy, in the archdeaconry of Stafford, and diocese of Lichfield and Coventry, and in the patronage of the Earl of Aboyne. The church is dedicated to All Saints.

RONTON-ABBEY, an extra-parochial liberty, in the southern division of the hundred of PIREHILL, county of STAFFORD, 3½ miles (S. by E.) from Eccleshall, containing 11 inhabitants. A priory of Black canons, subordinate to the abbey of Haughmond in Shropshire, was founded, in the reign of Henry II., by Robert Noel, in honour of the Blessed Virgin Mary, and at the dissolution was valued at £102. 11. per annum: the tower and a small portion of the cloisters still remain, with the moat that enclosed the grounds, comprising thirty acres.

ROOKWITH, a township in the parish of THORNTON-WATLASS, eastern division of the wapentake of HANG, North riding of the county of YORK, 4¼ miles (W. S. W.) from Bedale, containing 76 inhabitants.

ROOSDOWN, an extra-parochial liberty, though locally in the parish of Axminster, hundred of AXMINSTER, county of DEVON, 3¼ miles (W. S. W.) from Lyme-Regis, containing 14 inhabitants.

ROOSS, a parish in the middle division of the wapentake of HOLDERNESS, East riding of the county of YORK, 14 miles (E.) from Kingston upon Hull, containing 442 inhabitants. The living is a rectory, in the archdeaconry of the East riding, and diocese of York, rated in the king's books at £19, and in the patronage of the Rev. C. Sykes. The church, dedicated to All Saints, is partly in the decorated and partly in the later style of English architecture. There is a place of worship for Wesleyan Methodists. Jane Hogg, in 1754, bequeathed a rent-charge of £6 for teaching poor children.

ROOTHING (ABBOT'S), a parish partly in the hundred of DUNMOW, but chiefly in that of ONGAR, county of ESSEX, 5¾ miles (N. by E.) from Chipping-Ongar, containing, with the hamlet of Barwick, 236 inhabitants. The living is a rectory, in the archdeaconry of Middlesex, and diocese of London, rated in the king's books at £14. 10., and in the patronage of the Rev. Thomas Dyer. The church is dedicated to St. Edmund.

ROOTHING (AYTHORPE), a parish in the hundred of DUNMOW, county of ESSEX, 5½ miles (S. W. by S.) from Great Dunmow, containing 234 inhabitants. The living is a rectory, in the jurisdiction of the Commissary of Essex and Herts, concurrently with the Consistorial Court of the Bishop of London, rated in the king's books at £12, and in the patronage of the Rev. J. Oldham. The church is dedicated to St. Mary.

ROOTHING (BEAUCHAMP), a parish in the hundred of ONGAR, county of ESSEX, 4¼ miles (N. N. E.) from Chipping-Ongar, containing 211 inhabitants. The living is a rectory, in the archdeaconry of Middlesex, and diocese of London, rated in the king's books at £16. 13. 4., and in the patronage of Mrs. Jane Foxcroft. The church is dedicated to St. Botolph.

ROOTHING (BERNERS), a parish in the hundred of DUNMOW, county of ESSEX, 5¾ miles (N. E. by N.) from Chipping-Ongar, containing 93 inhabitants. The living is a perpetual curacy, in the archdeaconry of Middlesex, and diocese of London, endowed with £200 private benefaction, £400 royal bounty, and £500 parliamentary grant, and in the patronage of T. G. Bramston, Esq.

ROOTHING (HIGH), a parish in the hundred of DUNMOW, connty of ESSEX, 4½ miles (S. W. by S.) from Great Dunmow, containing 388 inhabitants. The living is a rectory, in the archdeaconry of Middlesex, and diocese of London, rated in the king's books at £20, and in the patronage of Lord Rodney. The church is dedicated to All Saints.

ROOTHING (LEADEN), a parish in the hundred of DUNMOW, county of ESSEX, 6½ miles (S. S. W.) from Great Dunmow, containing 157 inhabitants. The living is a rectory, in the jurisdiction of the Commissary of Essex and Herts, concurrently with the Consistorial Court of the Bishop of London, rated in the king's books at £12. 13. 4., and in the patronage of the Crown. Five pounds per annum, the gift of an unknown benefactor, is applied for teaching poor children.

ROOTHING (MARGARET), a parish in the hundred of DUNMOW, county of ESSEX, 7¼ miles (N.N.E.) from Chipping-Ongar, containing 209 inhabitants. The living is a rectory, in the archdeaconry of Middlesex, and diocese of London, rated in the king's books at £10. 12. 6., and in the patronage of Mrs. Harding. The church is dedicated to St. Margaret.

ROOTHING (MORRELL), a hamlet in the parish of WHITE ROOTHING, hundred of DUNMOW, though locally in the hundred of Ongar, county of ESSEX, 6¼ miles (S. W.) from Great Dunmow. The population is returned with the parish.

ROOTHING (WHITE), a parish in the hundred of DUNMOW, county of ESSEX, 6¾ miles (S. W.) from Great Dunmow, containing, with Morrell-Roothing, 439 inhabitants. The living is a rectory, in the archdeaconry of Middlesex, and diocese of London, rated in the king's books at £26. The Rev. Henry Budd was patron in 1808. The church is dedicated to St. Martin.

ROPE, a township in the parish of WYBUNBURY, hundred of NANTWICH, county palatine of CHESTER, 2¾ miles (E. by N.) from Nantwich, containing 95 inhabitants.

ROPLEY, a parish in the hundred of BISHOP'S SUTTON, Alton (North) division of the county of SOUTHAMPTON, 4 miles (E.) from New Alresford, containing 730 inhabitants. The living is a perpetual curacy, annexed to the vicarage of Bishop's Sutton, in the archdeaconry and diocese of Winchester. The church is dedicated to St. Peter. Ropley is within the jurisdiction of the Cheyney Court held at Winchester every Thursday, for the recovery of debts to any amount.

ROPSLEY, a parish in the wapentake of WINNIBRIGGS and THREO, parts of KESTEVEN, county of LINCOLN, 6¼ miles (W.) from Falkingham, containing, with the hamlet of Little Humby, 554 inhabitants. The living is a rectory, in the archdeaconry and diocese of Lincoln, rated in the king's books at £11. 14. 2., and in the patronage of the Duke of Rutland. The church is dedicated to St. Peter. James Thompson, in 1719, bequeathed a rent-charge of £6 for teaching six poor children.

ROSEACRE, a joint township with Treales and Wharles, in the parish of KIRKHAM, hundred of AMOUNDERNESS, county palatine of LANCASTER, 4 miles (N. by E.) from Kirkham. The population is returned with Treales.

ROSE-ASH, a parish in the hundred of WITHERIDGE, county of DEVON, 5¾ miles (E. S. E.) from South Molton, containing 436 inhabitants. The living is a rectory, in the archdeaconry of Barnstaple, and diocese of Exeter, rated in the king's books at £18. 19. 7., and in the patronage of the Representatives of the families of Esse and Giffard. A charity school is partly supported with two small endowments, by Ann Vicary in 1753, and John Bray in 1764.

ROSEDALE (EAST SIDE), a township in the parish of MIDDLETON, PICKERING lythe, North riding of the county of YORK, 10 miles (N. N. W.) from Pickering, containing 339 inhabitants. Thomas Pierson, in 1720, gave a rent-charge of £5 for teaching five children.

ROSEDALE (WEST SIDE), a chapelry in the parish of LASTINGHAM, wapentake of RYEDALE, North riding of the county of YORK, 11 miles (N.W. by N.) from Pickering, containing 179 inhabitants. The living is a perpetual curacy, in the archdeaconry of Cleveland, and diocese of York, endowed with £200 private benefaction, £600 royal bounty, and £200 parliamentary grant, and in the patronage of the Vicar of Middleton. The chapel is dedicated to St. Lawrence. A convent of Benedictine, or Cistercian, nuns, in honour of St. Mary and St. Lawrence, was founded here in the reign of Richard I., by Robert, son of Nicholas de Stutevil, which at the dissolution possessed a revenue of £41. 13. 8.

ROSEDON, a township in the parish of ILDERTON, northern division of COQUETDALE ward, county of NORTHUMBERLAND, 5 miles (S. E. by S.) from Wooler, containing 74 inhabitants. On Rosedon Edge are the remains of a semicircular intrenchment of earth, with an inner wall of loose stones, supposed to be of British origin, and subsequently improved by the Romans.

ROSLEY, a township in the parish of WESTWARD, ALLERDALE ward, below Darwent, county of CUMBERLAND, 5¼ miles (E. S. E.) from Wigton, containing 302 inhabitants. A great fair for horses, cattle, sheep, cloth &c., is held on Whit-Monday and every alternate Monday following till All Saints' day, at which it is computed that two thousand head of cattle, and five hundred horses, are exhibited for sale; forty acres of land on Rosley Hill were allotted for holding this fair under the enclosure act of 1811.

ROSLISTON, a parish in the hundred of REPTON and GRESLEY, county of DERBY, 4½ miles (S. by W.) from Burton upon Trent, containing 359 inhabitants. The living is a perpetual curacy, with the rectory of Walton upon Trent, in the archdeaconry of Derby, and diocese of Lichfield and Coventry. The church, dedicated to St. Mary, which was rebuilt by subscription in 1827, has received an addition of two hundred free sittings, the Incorporated Society for the enlargement of churches and chapels having granted £150 towards defraying the expense.

ROSS, a township in that part of the parish of BELFORD which is in ISLANDSHIRE, a detached portion of the county palatine of DURHAM, 3 miles (N. E.) from Belford, containing 55 inhabitants.

ROSS, a market town and parish in the hundred of GREYTREE, county of HEREFORD, 14 miles (S. E.) from Hereford, and 120 (W. N. W.) from London, containing 2957 inhabitants. Tradition reports this place to have been founded from the ruins of the Roman town *Ariconium*, which stood at a short distance. It was formerly a free borough, having been made so by Henry III. In the thirty-third year of the reign of Edward I. it sent members to parliament, but this privilege was relinquished, on the petition of the inhabitants, the following year, and has never been resumed. Henry IV. passed a night here, on his way to Monmouth to see his queen, at the time his son and successor was born; and the unfortunate Charles I. slept here, in 1645, on his way from Ragland Castle. The town is situated on an eminence, at the foot of which the river Wye runs, in a meandering course, in the midst of a richly-cultivated, beautiful, and picturesque country: it consists chiefly of two streets, crossing each other, which are narrow and badly paved; and the houses generally are old and ill-constructed, though the town has of late years been much improved, and some good houses have been built: the inhabitants are well supplied with water, raised by an engine from the Wye. A Horticultural Society has been established, by which three hundred prizes and thirty silver medals are annually distributed, with flowers and fruit; and there is an annual display of the works of artists; besides a mechanics' institution, and four reading societies. Ross had formerly a considerable trade in iron, which has long declined, cider and wool being the principal articles of produce at present. A weekly market was granted by King Stephen to Bishop Betren, to be held on Thursday; it is well supplied with cattle and provisions: there are fairs on Thursday after March 10th, Ascension-day, June 21st, July 20th, Thursday after October 10th, and December 11th. The town is divided into two parts, called the Borough and the Foreign; and a serjeant at mace, four constables, and some other subordinate officers, are chosen at a court leet and baron, which is held about Michaelmas, by the nominal mayor, for the former, and two constables for the latter: the petty sessions for the hundred are holden here.

The living is a rectory and a vicarage united, in the archdeaconry and diocese of Hereford, rated in the king's books at £38. 16. 3., and in the patronage of the Bishop of Hereford. The church, dedicated to St. Mary, is an irregularly built, though handsome, edifice, with a lofty well-proportioned spire, in an extremely beautiful situation: the east window is ornamented with stained glass, and contains a figure of Thomas de Cantelupe, Bishop of Hereford, in the act of giving benediction. There are places of worship for Baptists, the Society of Friends, and Independents. In the churchyard is a free school, called St. Mary's, founded and endowed with £10 per annum by Lord Weymouth, in 1709: it has lately been rebuilt, and two sons of poor tradesmen of the borough are instructed here. The Blue-coat school was founded, in 1709, by Dr. Whiting, Lord Scudamore, and others, and endowed, in 1786, with £200 per annum, by Walter Scott, who had been educated in it; sixty boys and girls are clothed and instructed. Two National schools for boys and girls are supported by voluntary contributions, as well as a dispensary, and an infant school recently established. There is an hospital for seven poor parishioners, who receive a weekly allowance, founded by Mr. Webbe, a native of the town. The Bishops of Hereford, who were lords of the manor, had formerly a palace here, but it has been long since demolished; and the prison belonging to them was pulled down about ninety years since: an old stone cross, called Cob's Cross, a corruption of Corpus Christi Cross, is still standing, supposed to be commemorative of the ravages of the plague in 1635, and the two subsequent years. Ross was the birthplace of John de Ross, a celebrated Doctor of Law, who was established by the pope in the bishoprick of Carlisle, without any election, in 1318, and died in 1331. The benevolent John Kyrle, " Pope's man of Ross," died here in 1724, aged eighty-eight, and lies buried in the church, where a rich monument, with a medallion, was erected to his memory, in 1776, from a bequest by Lady Betty Duplin for that purpose. At the castellated mansion of L. Merrick, Esq., near Ross, is a celebrated collection of ancient armour, and other antiquities, which attracts numerous visitors.

ROSSINGTON, a parish in the soke of DONCASTER, West riding of the county of YORK, 4½ miles (N. W. by N.) from Bawtry, containing 383 inhabitants. The living is a rectory, in the archdeaconry of Nottingham, and diocese of York, rated in the king's books at £11. 1. 5½., and in the patronage of R. Bower, Esq. The church is dedicated to St. Michael. In the churchyard are several good monuments, and near the entrance to the choir, under a stone, lie the remains of James Boswell, the King of the Gipsies, who died in January 1708. Annual visits were formerly made to his grave by gipsies, who, amongst other ceremonies, used to pour a flagon of ale on it. A free school, founded here in 1650, by William Plaxton, is supported by a rent-charge of £6. 13. 4., left by him, and £10 per annum allowed by the corporation of Doncaster, for which twenty children are taught free.

ROSTHERN, a parish comprising the chapelries of High Leigh and Peover (Superior), and the townships of Agden, Bollington, Martall with Little Warford, Mere, Millington, Rosthern, Tabley (Superior), and Tatton, in the hundred of BUCKLOW, and the township of Snelson, in that of MACCLESFIELD, county palatine of CHESTER, and containing 3791 inhabitants, of which number, 373 are in the township of Rosthern, 3½ miles (N. by W.) from Nether Knutsford. The living is a vicarage, in the archdeaconry and diocese of Chester, rated

ROT 632 ROT

Henley, containing 717 inhabitants. The living is a rectory, in the archdeaconry and diocese of Oxford, rated in the king's books at £10. 12. 8½., and in the patronage of the President and Fellows of Trinity College, Oxford. The church contains a font of singular shape: in the chancel is a brass effigy of a warrior, in good preservation, under a tabernacle, with a Latin inscription in old letter, to the memory of Robert de Grey, Lord of Rotherfield, who died in 1387; and in one of the aisles a splendid monument, of the period of James I., to Sir Francis Knollys, his lady, and their numerous progeny., Here are the remains of a castellated mansion of the de Greys, erected in the reign of Edward I.

ROTHERFIELD-PEPPARD, a parish in the hundred of BINFIELD, county of OXFORD, 3¾ miles (W. by S.) from Henley upon Thames, containing 401 inhabitants. The living is a rectory, in the archdeaconry and diocese of Oxford, rated in the king's books at £9. 9. 4½., and in the patronage of the Principal and Fellows of Jesus College, Oxford. The church is dedicated to All Saints. The river Thames runs through the parish.

ROTHERHAM, a parish, comprising the market town of Rotherham, the chapelry of Tinsley, and the townships of Brinsworth, Catcliffe, Dalton, and Orgreave, in the southern, and the chapelry of Greasbrough, and the township of Kimberworth in the northern, division of the wapentake of STRAFFORTH and TICKHILL, West riding of the county of YORK, and containing 9623 inhabitants, of which number, 3548 are in the town of Rotherham, 49 miles (S. S. W.) from York, and 159 (N. N. W.) from London. The town is situated in the midst of a district abounding in mineral wealth : it is built partly on the declivity of an eminence, and partly in a vale, near the confluence of the rivers Don and Rother; from the latter, which forms its western boundary, the town derives its name, and it is bounded on the north-west by the former, over which a handsome stone bridge connects it with the village of Masborough, which is of nearly equal extent with the town. The houses are in general built of stone, and most of them are low and of mean appearance, though occasionally intermixed with some of more modern erection; in the immediate neighbourhood of the church, several substantial and respectable dwellings have been recently erected, and at the east end of the town are two elegant mansions, called Cliffton and Eastwood. The streets are narrow, and irregularly formed; and though from its situation the town is capable of very great improvement, comparatively little has been effected. It is well paved, lighted with oil, and amply supplied with water. The environs are pleasant, and abound with varied scenery, and coal and iron-ore exist in great profusion. Within a short distance, on the road to Barnesley, is Wentworth House, the magnificent seat of Earl Fitz-William. The public subscription library contains several thousand volumes in the general departments of literature, and is liberally supported by a proprietary, and by annual subscribers of £1. 1. each. The extensive iron-foundries belonging to Messrs. Walker were celebrated for the casting of cannon of the largest calibre for government, and of works of great magnitude; the iron bridges of Sunderland, Yarm, Staines, and the Southwark bridge over the river Thames, were cast in these foundries, in which at present the principal branches are the manufacture and

rolling of iron. The manufacture of sail-cloth was formerly carried on, but it has been discontinued. The spinning of flax affords employment to about sixty persons; there are also roperies, a manufactory for starch, a large malting establishment, two extensive ale and porter breweries, several oil and chemical works, and a small glass-house. The river Don, which is navigable to Sheffield, communicates with the river Aire on the north-east, with the Stainforth and Keadby canal on the east, with the Dearn and Dove, and Barnesley canals on the north-west, and consequently with the river Calder, by which means Rotherham obtains a facility of intercourse with all the principal towns in the great manufacturing districts of Yorkshire and Lancashire. The market is on Monday, for corn, cattle, and provisions; and on every alternate Monday there is a celebrated market for fat cattle, sheep, and hogs, which is numerously attended by graziers from distant parts of the country. Fairs are held on Whit-Monday and December 1st, for cattle. A court leet is held annually, at which constables and other officers for the internal regulation of the town are appointed. The Midsummer sessions for the West riding are held here in the court-house, a handsome stone building recently erected, at an expense of £4000, in which also the justices of the peace hold their sittings, and all public business relating to the town is transacted. On the bridge leading to Masborough is an old structure, in the English style of architecture, now used as the town prison, but supposed to have been formerly a chapel of ease to the church.

The living is a discharged vicarage, in the archdeaconry and diocese of York, rated in the king's books at £16. 8. 6., endowed with £200 royal bounty, and in the patronage of Lord Howard, of Effingham. The church, dedicated to All Saints, is situated on an elevated knoll near the centre of the town, and is a spacious and venerable cruciform structure, in the later style of English architecture, with a central tower and spire highly enriched with panels, canopies, and crockets : the exterior is profusely, but tastefully and correctly, ornamented with sculptures of beautiful design, the doorways richly moulded, and the sides strengthened with panelled and crocketed buttresses : the south porch, of appropriate character, is highly enriched. The interior is lofty and finely arranged ; the roof of the nave, which is of oak elaborately carved, is supported on piers of graceful elevation, and the windows, with a very few exceptions, are enriched with tracery of elegant design : the chancel is separated from the nave by a screen of elaborate workmanship, and there are some excellent monuments in the transepts, and near the altar a beautiful monument of marble to the memory of Samuel Buck, Esq., a native of the town, and late recorder of Leeds, who died in 1806. There are places of worship for Baptists, Independents, Wesleyan Methodists, and Unitarians. The free grammar school was founded, in 1584, by Lawrence Woodnett and Anthony Collins, of London, Esqrs., who endowed it with a small portion of land in and near the town : the endowment was subsequently augmented by a grant of £10. 15. 4. per annum, from the revenue of the crown lands, the government being in the feoffees of the common land. The school is kept in a room under the court-house, and is open, for gratuitous instruction in the classics only, to all boys of the town ; the master's salary is £22. 19. 6. per annum, and his house was rebuilt in 1810: this school, in conjunction with those of Pontefract, Leeds, and Wakefield, is entitled to two scholarships, founded in Emanuel College, Cambridge, by John Frieston of Altofts, in the county of York, in failure of candidates from Normanton school. A charity school was founded by Mr. Scott, and the funds for its support, now under the superintendence of the feoffees of the common lands, were originally vested in separate trustees: the premises, comprising a school-room and apartments for the master, were erected by the feoffees, on a site of land given for that purpose by Lord Howard of Effingham: the income, arising from the original endowment, increased by subsequent benefactions, among which is a bequest of £20 per annum by Mr. Ellis, is about £80 per ann.: there are twenty-eight boys and twenty girls instructed and clothed with these funds, the deficiency being made up out of the rents of the common lands.

The Rotherham Independent College, at Masborough in this parish, for the education of young men intended for the ministry among that denomination of Protestant dissenters, was removed from Heckmondwicke, where it had subsisted for nearly forty years, and established here, in 1795, under the superintendence of the late Edward Williams, D.D.: the students are instructed in the classics, mathematics, rhetoric, and composition, and attend regular lectures in theology, to which all their studies are subservient. The premises, which are handsomely built, and occupy a healthy and pleasant eminence, were originally intended for the reception of sixteen students, but have been since adapted to the accommodation of twenty-five: the funds for the support of the institution arise solely from donations and annual subscription. A school for the instruction of thirty poor children of dissenters was founded by Thomas Hollis, Esq., whose trustees appoint the master, with a salary of £20 per annum, for teaching reading, writing, and arithmetic, to the children on the foundation, for which he also receives quarterly payments. The new dispensary, a handsome stone building, erected by subscription, at an expense of £2000, contains on the ground-floor, in addition to the offices requisite for the institution, a spacious room for the grammar school, which it is intended to remove from the court-house, and on the upper story an elegant room for the reception of the library, and a commodious news-room. Almshouses for four aged widows, or unmarried women, were founded in 1780, by Mrs. Mary Bellamy, who bequeathed £250, to be vested in the purchase of land for their endowment. She also left £200 in trust to the feoffees of the common lands, directing the interest to be applied to the apprenticing of two poor boys, and £200 for the use of the poor of the parish. Mr. Edward Bellamy, in 1776, bequeathed £200, the interest to be divided among four poor housekeepers in reduced circumstances and not receiving alms.

In 1480, Thomas Scott, usually called Thomas of Rotherham, who was then Bishop of Lincoln, founded a college in this town, for a provost, five priests, six choristers, and three schoolmasters, which he dedicated to the Holy Jesus: of the buildings, which subsisted for nearly a century, there remain the inn in Jesus' gate, and the opposite buildings now used as stables. This prelate was master of Pembroke Hall, chaplain to Edward IV., and, in 1475, made Lord Chancellor of England; he was soon after Bishop of Lincoln, and subsequently Archbishop of York; after the death of Edward, he was committed to the Tower by the Duke of Gloucester, who, on his ascent to the throne, released him; he died in 1500. Dr. Saunderson, Bishop of Lincoln, and a very eloquent preacher, in the time of Charles II., by whom he was particularly distinguished, was also a native of this town. On the summit of a hill, called Wincobank, about four miles from the town, and commanding a variety of extensive prospects, is the site of a military encampment, of nearly circular form, the mound and vallum of which may be distinctly traced; and at the foot of this hill, near the village of Grimesthorpe, is a quarry of stone, in which are imbedded various vegetable remains, chiefly calamites.

ROTHERHITHE, a parish in the eastern division of the hundred of BRIXTON, county of SURREY, 1 mile (S. E.) from London, containing 12,523 inhabitants. This place, corruptly called Redriff, was anciently a village and marsh south-eastward of London, to which it now forms an extensive suburb, on the opposite side of the river. The trench cut by Canute, in order to besiege the metropolis, commenced in this parish, and reached to Vauxhall; and the channel through which the river was turned, in 1173, for the rebuilding of London bridge, is supposed to have taken a similar course. In the reign of Edward III., a large naval armament was fitted out here, preparatory to an invasion of France, by Edward the Black Prince and the Duke of Lancaster; and during the commotions in the reign of Richard II., respecting the poll-tax, that monarch came hither in his barge, in order to pacify the malcontents; but his refusal to land so enraged the rioters, that, with their leaders, John Tyler, alias Jack Straw, and Wat, his brother, they broke open the Marshalsea and King's Bench prisons, liberated the inmates, and having proceeded to the house of the Duke of Lancaster, in the Savoy, destroyed it and all the valuable furniture and jewels by fire. In 1785, a dreadful fire broke out here, which in a few hours consumed two hundred and six houses, and did other extensive damage; but since the period of rebuilding them the population of the parish has nearly doubled its former amount, and is still on the increase. The situation of Rotherhithe, on the southern bank of the Thames, has induced numbers of seafaring men, watermen, and others, to reside here, and its inhabitants are now almost exclusively engaged in pursuits of this nature: in that part of the parish which forms the bank of the Thames are eleven dock-yards, for the building of East India ships and small merchant vessels; boat and lighter builders' wharfs; seven timber wharfs; three deal-yards, and a mast-yard; besides anchor-wharfs, shipbreakers' wharfs, and numerous warehouses for rigging and victualling the navy: the rest is occupied by the residences of masters of ships, seafaring people, and the tradesmen whose interests are dependent on navigation. The principal of the docks on this side of the river are, the Commercial dock, the several basins of which are capable of containing upwards of two hundred ships of burden; and the East Country dock, adjoining, appropriated to vessels for those parts and for America: the business connected with this place in general has been much circumscribed since the opening of the London, the East and West India, and St. Katherine's docks, on the opposite side of the river. The manufactures comprise the works carried on in the ordnance department at the three government wharfs, employed in making gun-carriages, &c. ; extensive iron-works, chiefly for the construction of iron bolts out of old iron hoops and other materials ; and the king's mills for grinding corn, some years ago occupied by the London Flour Company. A canal, leading from the Thames by the Gun wharf through Deptford to Mitcham, and begun in 1801, pursuant to act of parliament, now communicates with the Croydon canal at Deptford; and by the same act authority was given to make a collateral cut thence to Greenland dock. The Thames Tunnel, a passage attempted to be formed beneath the bed of the river, intended to facilitate the communication with the opposite shore, having been projected and begun on a small scale in 1809, was again commenced here, from a design and under the direction of Mr. Brunel, in 1825, and carried on so far, that the archwork reaches within two hundred and thirty feet of the opposite shore, but this ingenious project is for the present discontinued : for a more detailed account of it, see article on London. The inhabitants possess a charter for two weekly markets and two annual fairs, but both have been long disused. A court of requests, for the recovery of debts not exceeding £5, the jurisdiction of which comprises the town and borough of Southwark, and the eastern division of the hundred of Brixton, is held here.

The living is a rectory, in the archdeaconry of Surrey, and diocese of Winchester, rated in the king's books at £18, and in the patronage of the Master and Fellows of Clare Hall, Cambridge. The church is dedicated to St. Mary : in the churchyard is the tombstone of Prince Lee Boo, son of Abba Thule, King of one of the Pelew islands, who died of the small pox, in 1784, and whose memoirs have been transmitted to posterity, in the interesting narrative of Mr. Keate. There are places of worship for Baptists, Independents, and Wesleyan Methodists. A free school, originally founded by Peter Hills, and Robert Bell, Esqrs., for the education and clothing of eight sons of seamen, and afterwards united with another, which was refounded in 1745, affords instruction to one hundred and fifty boys and fifty girls : it has a permanent income of £32 per annum, and is further supported by subscription. The Amicable school, founded in 1739, educates forty-five boys ; and in the United Society school, established in 1755, are thirty-one ; both these institutions are supported by voluntary contributions : there is likewise a school of industry for twenty girls.

ROTHERSTHORPE, a parish in the hundred of WYMERSLEY, county of NORTHAMPTON, 4 miles (S. W.) from Northampton, containing 272 inhabitants. The living is a discharged vicarage, in the archdeaconry of Northampton, and diocese of Peterborough, rated in the king's books at £5. 9. 4¼., endowed with £400 royal bounty, and in the patronage of T. S. W. Samwell, Esq. The church is dedicated to St. Peter and St. Paul. The Northampton canal passes through the parish.

ROTHERWICK, a parish in the hundred of ODIHAM, Basingstoke division of the county of SOUTHAMPTON, 5 miles (W. by S.) from Hartford-Bridge, containing 402 inhabitants. The living is a perpetual curacy, in the archdeaconry and diocese of Winchester, endowed with £200 royal bounty, and in the patronage of the Chancellor of the Cathedral Church of Salisbury. A

school-house was erected, in 1713, by Frederick Tylney, who in 1716 endowed it with a rent-charge of £10, for teaching ten children of each sex.

ROTHLEY, a parish comprising the chapelries of Keyham, Wartnaby, and Wycomb with Chadwell, in the eastern, and the chapelry of Mountsorrel, and the extra-parochial liberty of Rothley-Temple, in the western division of the hundred of GOSCOTE, county of LEICESTER, 1½ mile (S. by E.) from Mountsorrel, and containing 1349 inhabitants. The living is a vicarage, rated in the king's books at £11. 0. 5., and in the peculiar jurisdiction and patronage of Thomas Babington, Esq., as lord of the manor and soke of Rothley. The church, dedicated to St. Mary, is large and ancient, and contains some curious old monuments : it was given, with the manor, by Henry III. to the Knights Templars, who settled a commandery at Rothley Temple, which mansion is remarkable as being one of the few founded by that order, now remaining in the kingdom : it subsequently came to the Knights Hospitallers, and at the dissolution, was valued at £87. 13. 4. per annum. In the churchyard is the shaft of an ancient stone cross ; and, in 1722, a Roman pavement, with foundations of walls, was discovered in the village. There is a place of worship for Wesleyan Methodists. The official of the lord of the manor holds visitations and a spiritual court twice a year, both for ecclesiastical and civil matters ; its jurisdiction not only extending over the parish, but to several other parts of the county, in which it is the most extensive manor, enjoying the privileges of court leet, court baron, &c., oyer, terminer, and gaol delivery, independent of the rest of the county. The custom of gavelkind is still observed throughout the soke. The river Soar forms a boundary of the parish. Bartholomew Hickling, in 1691, founded and endowed a school for fourteen boys ; and, in 1736, Elizabeth Daniel bequeathed a small sum, to be applied for teaching six girls.

ROTHLEY, a township in that part of the parish of HARTBURN which is in the western division of MORPETH ward, county of NORTHUMBERLAND, 11 miles (W. by N.) from Morpeth, containing 150 inhabitants. On a rocky eminence to the northward of the village is Rothley castle, which, though erected by the late Sir W. C. Blackett, has all the appearance of an ancient baronial residence. In the park are two large lakes, in one of which the river Font has its source. A depôt for cattle formerly here was attacked, during the border warfare, by the Scots, who were defeated with great loss, and the slain buried at a place called Scots' Gap.

ROTHLEY-TEMPLE, an extra-parochial liberty, in the western division of the hundred of GOSCOTE, county of LEICESTER, 1½ mile (S.) from Mountsorrel. The population is returned with the parish of Rothley, which see.

ROTHWELL, a parish in the wapentake of BRADLEY-HAVERSTOE, parts of LINDSEY, county of LINCOLN, 2¾ miles (E. S. E.) from Caistor, containing 197 inhabitants. The living is a discharged rectory, in the archdeaconry and diocese of Lincoln, rated in the king's books at £7. 10. 10., and in the patronage of Lord Viscount Midleton. The church is dedicated to St. Mary Magdalene.

ROTHWELL, a parish (formerly a market town) in the hundred of ROTHWELL, county of NORTHAMPTON,

19 miles (N.N.E.) from Northampton, and 79 (N.W. by N.) from London, containing, with the chapelry of Orton, and the hamlet of Thorpe-Underwood, 1845 inhabitants. This town is supposed to have been much more extensive in former days than it is at present, and to have been surrounded with a wall and gates: it is situated on the southern side of a rocky hill. A small priory of nuns of the order of St. Augustine was founded here, probably by some of the Clare family; at the dissolution its revenue was estimated at £10. 10. 4. The market, which was considerable, has fallen into disuse, but one of the largest fairs in the county for cattle is held on Trinity-Monday: the ancient market-house, begun by Sir Thomas Tresham, but left in an unfinished state, is a curious ruin. The living is a discharged vicarage, in the archdeaconry of Northampton, and diocese of Peterborough, rated in the king's books at £7. 18. 11., endowed with £800 parliamentary grant, and in the patronage of the Rev. W. Smythe, and W. T. Smythe, Esq. The church, dedicated to Holy Trinity, has an embattled tower at the west end; the door is a fine specimen of the early style of English architecture. In a vault beneath is a remarkably curious collection of sculls and other bones, discovered about two hundred years ago by some workmen, whilst examining the lower part of the church. Here are two springs, one of a strong petrifying quality, and in the other are found numerous small bones.

ROTHWELL, a parish in the lower division of the wapentake of AGBRIGG, West riding of the county of YORK, comprising the townships of Carlton, Lofthouse, Middleton, Outton, Rhodes-Green, Rothwell, Rothwell-Haigh, Thorp, and Woodlesford, and containing 6253 inhabitants, of which number, 2155 are in the township of Rothwell, 6 miles (N. by E.) from Wakefield. The living is a discharged vicarage, in the archdeaconry and diocese of York, rated in the king's books at £19. 12. 11. The Rev. R. H. Brandling was patron in 1804. The church, dedicated to the Holy Trinity, is in the later style of English architecture, and has lately received an addition of eight hundred and four sittings, of which six hundred and forty-four are free, the Incorporated Society for the enlargement of churches and chapels having granted £800 towards defraying the expense. There is a place of worship for Wesleyan Methodists. This ancient parish derived its name from a well near the church, adjacent to which are the remains of a castle, or mansion-house. Here are manufactures of woollen cloth, stuff, and hair sieves, and there are extensive coal mines in the neighbourhood.

ROTHWELL-HAIGH, a township in the parish of ROTHWELL, lower division of the wapentake of AGBRIGG, West riding of the county of YORK, 5½ miles (N.) from Wakefield. The population is returned with the township of Rothwell.

ROTSEA, a township in the parish of HUTTON-CRANSWICK, Bainton-Beacon division of the wapentake of HARTHILL, East riding of the county of YORK, 6½ miles (S. E. by S.) from Great Driffield, containing 23 inhabitants.

ROTTINGDEAN, a parish in the hundred of YOUNSMERE, rape of LEWES, county of SUSSEX, 4 miles (E. S. E.) from Brighton, containing 772 inhabitants. The living is a vicarage, in the archdeaconry of Lewes, and diocese of Chichester, rated in the king's books at £9. 10., and in the patronage of the Earl of Thanet. The church, dedicated to St. Margaret, is in the early style of English architecture, with a low massy tower in the centre: it was originally a larger structure than at present, and has lately undergone a thorough repair. This place, in ancient records termed Rottington, was, in the reign of Richard II., the landing-place of the French, who, in revenge for their loss of the battle of Cressy, burned Rye and Hastings, and would have also destroyed Lewes, but for the gallant resistance made by the prior of Lewes, Sir Thomas Cheney, and Sir John Falseley, at the head of the armed peasantry, who attacked and compelled them to retreat to their ships. The village is pleasantly situated near the coast of the English channel, on the Newhaven road, and is celebrated for its wells, which are nearly empty at high water, but rise as the tide ebbs, and which, from their salubrious qualities, are in considerable repute. It has within the last few years become a bathing-place, frequented by such families as prefer the privacy of a secluded village to the more open beach and gaiety of Brighton. The old road hence to Brighton approached so close to the edge of the cliff, which is here two hundred feet high, as frequently to cause the most lamentable accidents to travellers; which circumstance has occasioned the formation of a new one considerably to the northward, and by a more circuitous, though pleasant, route. From Rottingdean the cliffs gradually become more elevated, as far as Beachy Head; those called the Three Charles's, or Cheorls, the highest on the Sussex coast, rising about five hundred feet above the level of the sea. Two apartments cut in the chalk rock under the cliff bear the name of " Parson Danby's Holes," from his having formed and occupied them, till he fell a victim to the dampness of the situation. Semi-translucent pebbles of agate and chalcedony, of a blueish grey colour, abound on the sea-shore, which, when cut and polished, are used as ornaments in bracelets, &c., under the name of Rottingdean Pebbles. In 1757, on opening a tumulus in the neighbourhood, a Roman dagger was discovered.

ROTTINGTON, a township in the parish of St. BEES, ALLERDALE ward above Darwent, county of CUMBERLAND, 3½ miles (S. by W.) from Whitehaven, containing 56 inhabitants. Here was formerly a small nunnery, subordinate to that of St. Bees.

ROUDHAM, a parish in the hundred of SHROPHAM, county of NORFOLK, 2¼ miles (W.) from East Harling, containing 72 inhabitants. The living is a discharged vicarage, in the archdeaconry and diocese of Norwich, rated in the king's books at £4. 16. 5½., and in the patronage of Sir J. S. Sebright, Bart. The church is dedicated to St. Andrew.

ROUGHAM, a parish in the hundred of LAUNDITCH, county of NORFOLK, 7¼ miles (N. by E.) from Swaffham, containing 330 inhabitants. The living is a discharged vicarage, in the archdeaconry of Norfolk, and diocese of Norwich, rated in the king's books at £1. 8. 6½., endowed with £400 royal bounty, and in the patronage of the Crown. The church is dedicated to St. Mary: attached to the south side is a library, built by Mr. North, and containing several volumes presented by that individual and others.

ROUGHAM, a parish in the hundred of THEDWESTRY, county of SUFFOLK, 4½ miles (E. S. E.) from Bury-St. Edmunds, containing 778 inhabitants. The living is a rectory, in the archdeaconry of Sudbury, and diocese of Norwich, rated in the king's books at £23. 18. 6½. Philip Bennett, Esq. was patron in 1815. The church is dedicated to St. Mary. Edward Sparke, in 1720, bequeathed land now producing about £40 a year, to be applied in support of a school for eight children of Rougham, and four of Thurston; and Thomas Sparke, in 1721, gave a rent-charge of £4 for a similar purpose. There are several other bequests, the principal of which is that of Roger Kerrington, in 1702, for apprenticing poor children, with a premium of £30 each.

ROUGH-LEE-BOOTH, a township in that part of the parish of WHALLEY which is in the higher division of the hundred of BLACKBURN, county palatine of LANCASTER, 3¼ miles (W.) from Colne, containing 958 inhabitants. The Wesleyan Methodists have a place of worship here.

ROUGHTON, a parish in the soke of HORNCASTLE, parts of LINDSEY, county of LINCOLN, 4 miles (S. S. W.) from Horncastle, containing 110 inhabitants. The living is a discharged rectory, united in 1741 to Haltham upon Bain, in the archdeaconry and diocese of Lincoln, rated in the king's books at £6. 15. 2. The church is dedicated to St. Margaret. The river Bain and the Horncastle and Witham canal run through the parish.

ROUGHTON, a parish in the northern division of the hundred of ERPINGHAM, county of NORFOLK, 3¾ miles (S.) from Cromer, containing 337 inhabitants. The living is a discharged vicarage, in the archdeaconry of Norfolk, and diocese of Norwich, rated in the king's books at £6, and in the patronage of the Bishop of Ely. The church is dedicated to St. Mary.

ROUGHWAY, a township in the parish and hundred of WROTHAM, lathe of AYLESFORD, county of KENT, 5 miles (S. by E.) from Wrotham, with which the population is returned.

ROULSTON, a parish in the wapentake of FLAXWELL, parts of KESTEVEN, county of LINCOLN, 7 miles (N. by E.) from Sleaford, containing 123 inhabitants. The living is a discharged vicarage, in the archdeaconry and diocese of Lincoln, rated in the king's books at £6. 6. 2½., and in the patronage of Samuel Thorold, Esq. The church is dedicated to St. Clement.

ROUNCTON (EAST), a chapelry in the parish of RUDBY in CLEVELAND, western division of the liberty of LANGBAURGH, North riding of the county of YORK, 6½ miles (S. by W.) from Yarm, containing 135 inhabitants. The living is a perpetual curacy, in the archdeaconry of Cleveland, and diocese of York, endowed with £800 royal bounty, and £200 parliamentary grant, and in the patronage of Lady Amherst.

ROUNCTON (WEST), a parish in the wapentake of ALLERTONSHIRE, North riding of the county of YORK, 7½ miles (S. by W.) from Yarm, containing 217 inhabitants. The living is a rectory, in the peculiar jurisdiction of the Dean and Chapter of Durham, rated in the king's books at £6, and in the patronage of the King, as Duke of Lancaster. The church is dedicated to St. James. There is a place of worship for Wesleyan Methodists.

ROUNDHAY, a chapelry in the parish of BARWICK in ELMETT, lower division of the wapentake of SKYRACK, West riding of the county of YORK, 3 miles (N. E.) from Leeds, containing 186 inhabitants.

ROUSHAM, a parish in the hundred of WOOTTON, county of OXFORD, 6¼ miles (N. E. by N.) from Woodstock, containing 160 inhabitants. The living is a rectory, in the archdeaconry and diocese of Oxford, rated in the king's books at £11. 9. 4½. Sir C. C. Dormer, Knt. was patron in 1804. The church is dedicated to St. Mary.

ROUTH, a parish in the northern division of the wapentake of HOLDERNESS, East riding of the county of YORK, 4¼ miles (N. E. by E.) from Beverley, containing 124 inhabitants. The living is a rectory, in the archdeaconry of the East riding, and diocese of York, rated in the king's books at £8. 17. 1., and in the patronage of the Misses Ellerkers. The church, dedicated to All Saints, has a Norman door and three stone stalls.

ROWBERROW, a parish in the hundred of WINTERSTOKE, county of SOMERSET, 4 miles (N. E. by N.) from Axbridge, containing 334 inhabitants. The living is a discharged rectory, in the archdeaconry of Wells, and diocese of Bath and Wells, rated in the king's books at £7. 10., endowed with £600 private benefaction, and £600 royal bounty, and in the patronage of the Bishop of Bristol. The church is dedicated to St. Michael. There is a place of worship for Baptists. The parish abounds with lapis calaminaris, the working of which affords employment to many of the inhabitants.

ROW-BOUND, a township in the parish of CASTLE-SOWERBY, LEATH ward, county of CUMBERLAND, containing 112 inhabitants.

ROWDE, a parish in the hundred of POTTERNE and CANNINGS, county of WILTS, 2 miles (W. by N.) from Devizes, containing 961 inhabitants. The living is a discharged vicarage, in the archdeaconry of Wilts, and diocese of Salisbury, rated in the king's books at £6.10., and in the patronage of the Rev. Dr. Starkey. The church is dedicated to St. Mary.

ROWELL, a hamlet in the parish of HAWLING, lower division of the hundred of KIFTSGATE, county of GLOUCESTER, 4¼ miles (S. E. by E.) from Winchcombe, containing 32 inhabitants. The Independents have a place of worship here.

ROWINGTON, a parish in the Henley division of the hundred of BARLICHWAY, county of WARWICK, 6 miles (N. W. by W.) from Warwick, containing 888 inhabitants. The living is a discharged vicarage, in the archdeaconry and diocese of Worcester, rated in the king's books at £7. 11. 8., and in the patronage of the Crown. The church, dedicated to St. Lawrence, is a cruciform structure, principally in the Norman style. The Warwick and Birmingham canal passes through the parish. National schools, for about ninety children of both sexes, are supported out of the annual income arising from the poor's estate.

ROWLAND, a township in the parish of BAKEWELL, hundred of HIGH PEAK, county of DERBY, 2¼ miles (S. W. by W.) from Stony-Middleton, containing 109 inhabitants. It is in the honour of Tutbury, duchy of Lancaster, and within the jurisdiction of a court of pleas held at Chapel en le Frith every third Tuesday, for the recovery of debts under 40s.

ROWLEY, a hamlet in the parish of LANCHESTER, western division of CHESTER ward, county palatine of DURHAM, 8½ miles (N. by E.) from Walsingham. The population is returned with the parish. Here was formerly a chapel, which has been long since demolished.

ROWLEY, a parish in the Hunsley-Beacon division of the wapentake of HARTHILL, East riding of the county of YORK, comprising the townships of Rowley and Wauldby, and containing 469 inhabitants, of which number, 425 are in the township of Rowley, 4 miles (E. N. E.) from South Cave. The living is a rectory, in the archdeaconry of the East riding, and diocese of York, rated in the king's books at £20. 1. 8., and in the patronage of Col. Hildyard. The church is dedicated to St. Peter.

ROWLEY-REGIS, a parish in the northern division of the hundred of SEISDON, county of STAFFORD, 3 miles (S. E.) from Dudley, containing 6062 inhabitants. The living is a perpetual curacy, annexed to the vicarage of Clent, in the archdeaconry of Stafford, and diocese of Worcester. The church is dedicated to St. Giles. There is a place of worship for Baptists. Lady Elizabeth Monnins, in 1703, founded a free school, with an endowment of £15 a year, for the education of twenty-four children; and in 1790, George Macklinnan gave a rent-charge of £21, which is applied to teaching thirty children. Coal is obtained in the vicinity.

ROWLSTON, a joint township with Mappleton, in the parish of MAPPLETON, partly in the liberty of St. PETER of YORK, and partly in the northern division of the wapentake of HOLDERNESS, East riding of the county of YORK, 14 miles (E. N. E.) from Beverley. The population is returned with Mappleton.

ROWLSTONE, a parish in the hundred of EWYAS-LACY, county of HEREFORD, 13 miles (S. W. by W.) from Hereford, containing 145 inhabitants. The living is a perpetual curacy, in the archdeaconry of Brecon, and diocese of St. David, endowed with £800 royal bounty. Mrs. Price was patroness in 1803. The church is dedicated to St. Peter. A court leet is occasionally held here. Limestone is obtained in the neighbourhood, and the soil in general is well adapted for the cultivation of apples, of which cider is made. Six boys of the parish are entitled to be taught free in Grosmont school.

ROWNER, a parish in the hundred of TITCHFIELD, Portsdown division of the county of SOUTHAMPTON, 3 miles (S.) from Fareham, containing 158 inhabitants. The living is a rectory, in the archdeaconry and diocese of Winchester, rated in the king's books at £6. 0. 2½. The Rev. C. P. Brune was patron in 1805. The parish is bounded on the east by Portsmouth harbour.

ROWSLEY (GREAT), a township in the parish of BAKEWELL, hundred of HIGH PEAK, county of DERBY, 3½ miles (S. E. by E.) from Bakewell, containing, with part of the township of Aport, 238 inhabitants. The village is situated near the confluence of the rivers Derwent and Wye. The township is entitled to partake in the benefit of Lady Manners' school at Bakewell.

ROWTON, a township in the parish of CHRISTLE-TON, lower division of the hundred of BROXTON, county palatine of CHESTER, 3¼ miles (E. S. E.) from Chester, containing 108 inhabitants. The Chester canal passes by this township. Here was fought the battle which terminated so fatally for the cause of Charles I.; and on Rowton Heath the Cheshire gentry assembled, and declared for a free parliament, on the attempt of Sir George Booth to restore Charles II., in 1659.

ROWTON, a township in that part of the parish of ABBERBURY which is in the hundred of FORD, county of SALOP, 7 miles (W.) from Shrewsbury, containing, with the township of Amaston, 227 inhabitants.

ROWTON, a joint township with North Skirlaugh, in that part of the parish of SWINE which is in the northern division of the wapentake of HOLDERNESS, East riding of the county of YORK, 9 miles (E. by N.) from Beverley. The population is returned with North Skirlaugh.

ROXBY, a joint parish with Risby, in the northern division of the wapentake of MANLEY, parts of LINDSEY, county of LINCOLN, 9 miles (W. S. W.) from Barton upon Humber, containing, with Risby, 350 inhabitants. The living is a vicarage, with that of Risby, in the archdeaconry of Stow, and diocese of Lincoln, rated in the king's books at £6. 3. 4. R. C. Elwes, Esq. was patron in 1816. The church is dedicated to St. Mary. Near it was found, some years ago, a tesselated pavement, about seven yards square, also fragments of red and yellow plaster, bones of oxen, &c.

ROXBY, a joint township with Pickhill, in that part of the parish of PICKHILL which is in the wapentake of HALLIKELD, North riding of the county of YORK, 7 miles (W. by N.) from Thirsk. The population is returned with Pickhill.

ROXBY, a township in the parish of HINDERWELL, eastern division of the liberty of LANGBAURGH, North riding of the county of YORK, 11½ miles (W. N. W.) from Whitby, containing 236 inhabitants. Here is a small chapel of ease.

ROXHAM, a parish in the hundred of CLACKCLOSE, county of NORFOLK, 3¾ miles (S. E. by S.) from Downham-Market, containing 40 inhabitants. The living is a perpetual curacy, annexed to that of West Ryston, in the archdeaconry of Norfolk, and diocese of Norwich.

ROXHOLME, a hamlet in the parish of LEASINGHAM, wapentake of FLAXWELL, parts of KESTEVEN, county of LINCOLN, 2¾ miles (N. by W.) from Sleaford, containing 87 inhabitants.

ROXTON, a parish in the hundred of BARFORD, county of BEDFORD, 4¼ miles (S. W. by S.) from St. Neot's, containing 537 inhabitants. The living is a discharged vicarage, united to that of Great Barford, in the archdeaconry of Bedford, and diocese of Lincoln, rated in the king's books at £10, and in the patronage of the Master and Fellows of Trinity College, Cambridge. The church is dedicated to St. Mary. There is a place of worship for Independents. The river Ouse bounds the parish on the east.

ROXWELL, a parish in the hundred of CHELMSFORD, county of ESSEX, 4½ miles (W. N. W.) from Chelmsford, containing 817 inhabitants. The living is a donative, annexed to the perpetual curacy of Writtle, in the jurisdiction of the peculiar court of Writtle with Roxwell. John Blencowe, in 1774, founded a school for teaching poor children of Roxwell and Writtle.

ROYDON, a parish partly in the hundred of WALTHAM, but chiefly in that of HARLOW, county of ESSEX, 4½ miles (W. by S.) from Harlow, containing 796 inhabitants. The living is a discharged vicarage, in the archdeaconry of Middlesex, and diocese of London, rated in the king's books at £12, endowed with £200 private benefaction, and £200 parliamentary grant, and in the patronage of the Hon. W. T. L. P. Wellesley. The church is dedicated to St. Peter. John Manning, in 1768, founded a free school, and endowed it with a house and lands for teaching the children of the parish. Here is still standing the curious ancient gateway of the mansion of Nether Hall, demolished about 1773.

ROYDON, a parish in the hundred of DISS, county of NORFOLK, 1¼ mile (W.) from Diss, containing 601 inhabitants. The living is a rectory, in the archdeaconry of Norfolk, and diocese of Norwich, rated in the king's books at £9, and in the patronage of the Rt. Hon. J. H. Frere. The church is dedicated to St. Remigius.

ROYDON, a parish in the Lynn division of the hundred of FREEBRIDGE, county of NORFOLK, 2½ miles (S.E. by E.) from Castle-Rising, containing 205 inhabitants. The living is a discharged rectory, consolidated with that of Castle-Rising, in the peculiar jurisdiction of the Rector of Castle-Rising, rated in the king's books at £5. The church is dedicated to All Saints.

ROYSTON, a market town and parish, partly in the hundred of ARMINGFORD, county of CAMBRIDGE, but chiefly in the hundred of ODSEY, county of HERTFORD, 20 miles (N. by E.) from Hertford, and 38 (N.) from London, (parts of the town, exclusively of its own parish, extending into the parishes of Barkway and Therfield, county of Hertford, and into those of Melbourne, Bassingbourn, and Kneesworth, county of Cambridge,) containing 1474 inhabitants. This place is supposed to have had its origin in the reign of William the Conqueror, and to derive its name from a cross having been erected at that period in the highway here, by the Lady Roysia, Countess of Norfolk, which was called Royse's Cross; and a monastery having been established shortly afterwards, by Eustachius de Mere and others, which led to the erection of houses, it acquired the appellation of Royse's town, whence its present name. It had become a considerable town in the reign of Henry IV., when it was nearly consumed by fire; and again, in 1747, it was subjected to the same calamity. A house was built here by James I., who made it his occasional residence, for the enjoyment of hunting and hawking; and it was here that his favourite, the Earl of Somerset, was arrested in his presence, for the murder of Sir Thomas Overbury. At the commencement of the civil war, Charles I. removed to this house from Hampton Court, previously to setting up his standard at Nottingham; and here this unfortunate monarch passed two nights, in June 1647, when a prisoner to the army, which had its head-quarters at this place. The survey of this palace, made during the Commonwealth, describes it as in good repair, but it has since gone to ruin, and but few vestiges of it can be traced. Royston is situated at the intersection of the Iknield-way and the Ermin-street, in a very bleak open country, near a chain of high hills, and, though improved of late, is very irregularly built: it consists of one long and narrow street, crossed by two shorter ones, and neither lighted nor paved; there is a very scanty supply of water, which the inhabitants generally are obliged to purchase. A public walk, planted with trees, has been lately opened, at the expense of Lord Dacre. The malting business is carried on to a considerable extent, and there is a large corn trade. The market, which was granted by Richard I., who also granted a fair, is on Wednesday, for corn, sheep, and pigs, and also for straw-plat; and there are fairs on Whit-Wednesday,

attached to which is a pie-powder court; on Shrove Wednesday; the feast of St. Thomas à Becket, and the Wednesday in Easter week, pleasure fairs; and one for hiring servants, on the first Wednesday after the 10th of October: a market-house was built in 1830, at the expense of Lord Dacre. A petty session is held every alternate Wednesday.

The living is a vicarage, in the jurisdiction of the Commissary of Essex and Herts, concurrently with the Consistorial Court of the Bishop of London, rated in the king's books at £10, endowed with £200 private benefaction, and £700 parliamentary grant, and in the patronage of Lord Dacre. The church was originally that of the priory, and dedicated to St. Thomas à Becket, but was purchased by the inhabitants at the dissolution of the monastery, and, by an act passed in the 32nd of Henry VIII., is called the parish church of St. John the Baptist in Royston.: it is a rude, though venerable, structure, with a low square massive tower at its western end, and contains some very ancient monuments; in the vestry-room is a library, comprising about one hundred and fifty volumes, chiefly theological. There is a place of worship for the Society of Friends, and two for Independents. A grammar school was erected by subscription in 1716, but it possesses no endowment, and a house has been recently erected for a free school. In 1769, Mrs. Glover bequeathed £3500 for building and endowing a charity school, but it was never received. An infant school is supported by subscription; and there are Sunday schools in connexion with the different places of worship, in which nearly three hundred children of both sexes are educated. The monastery, at the period of its dissolution, was valued at £89. 16. per annum, and, with the exception of the church, has been entirely demolished. Here was also an hospital, dedicated to St. John and St. James, but there are no vestiges. Many relics of antiquity have been discovered in and about Royston, among which is an ancient chapel, or cave, found near the site of the present market-house by some workmen, in 1742, which had been dug out of the chalk rock, and had an opening from the top: it has been conjectured to have been the oratory and burial-place of the Lady Roysia, although this opinion has been strongly controverted. Tumuli, or barrows, are found on the summits of the adjacent hills, and the discovery of a number of bones and corroded spear heads near the town, renders it probable that it was the scene of an engagement with the Danes. A species of crow, with a whitish head, denominated the "Royston Crow," is found on the neighbouring hills, and is peculiar to this part of the kingdom; it emigrates to Sweden in the spring, where it breeds, and returns to pass the winter here. Henry Andrews, many years a resident in this town, was employed by the Board of Admiralty in assisting to compute the celestial observations for the Nautical Almanac; and he was longer and more extensively engaged in making the calculations for Moore's Almanac: he died in 1820, and is buried here.

ROYSTON, a parish in the wapentake of STAINCROSS, West riding of the county of YORK, comprising the chapelries of Monk-Bretton, and Woolley with Emley, and the townships of Carlton, Chevett, Cudworth, Notton, and Royston, and containing 3126 inhabitants, of which number, 549 are in the township of Royston,

4¼ miles (N. N. E.) from Barnesley. The living is a discharged vicarage, in the archdeaconry and diocese of York, rated in the king's books at £17. 3. 4., endowed with £1000 parliamentary grant, and in the patronage of the Archbishop of York. The church is dedicated to St. John the Baptist. There is a place of worship for Wesleyan Methodists. The free grammar school is endowed with an annuity of £4. 6. 11. from the revenue of the duchy of Lancaster, also with a house and land granted by the crown in 1605; the total annual income is £82. 15. 1., for which the master is bound to teach the classics and writing, but for arithmetic he receives a quarterage from the children, whose average number is about thirty-five. At Monk-Bretton are the remains of an ancient monastery.

ROYTON, a chapelry in the parish of OLDHAM cum PRESTWICH, hundred of SALFORD, county palatine of LANCASTER, 3½ miles (E. N. E.) from Middleton, containing 4933 inhabitants. The living is a perpetual curacy, in the archdeaconry and diocese of Chester, endowed with £200 private benefaction, £400 royal bounty, and £1400 parliamentary grant, and in the patronage of the Rector of Prestwich. The chapel, dedicated to St. Paul, was built by subscription in 1754. There are places of worship for the Society of Friends, and Calvinistic and Wesleyan Methodists, with a Sunday school attached to the last; the Friends' meeting-house is said to be coeval with the foundation of that sect. The cotton and fustian manufactures are extensively carried on, and there are considerable coal mines in the parish. The village, forty years ago, contained only a few straggling cottages, but within the last twenty years it has assumed the appearance of a considerable town, by the erection of several regular streets and large manufactories. There is a school in connexion with the established church, attended by about five hundred children.

RUAN (MAJOR), a parish in the hundred of KERRIER, county of CORNWALL, 8 miles (S. S. E.) from Helston, containing 187 inhabitants. The living is a rectory, in the archdeaconry of Cornwall, and diocese of Exeter, rated in the king's books at £10. 10. 2½., and in the patronage of Philip Vivian Robinson, Esq. The church is dedicated to St. Rumon.

RUAN (MINOR), a parish in the hundred of KERRIER, county of CORNWALL, 9½ miles (S. E. by S.) from Helston, containing 293 inhabitants. The living is a discharged rectory, in the archdeaconry of Cornwall, and diocese of Exeter, rated in the king's books at £4. 4. 4½., and endowed with £200 royal bounty. The Rev. W. Robinson was patron in 1814. The church is dedicated to St. Rumon. There is a place of worship for Wesleyan Methodists. The parish is bounded on the east by the English channel, upon which is situated Cadgwith Cove, the resort of fishermen.

RUAN-LANYHORNE, a parish in the western division of the hundred of POWDER, county of CORNWALL, 2½ miles (S. W.) from Tregoney, containing 376 inhabitants. The living is a rectory, in the archdeaconry of Cornwall, and diocese of Exeter, rated in the king's books at £12, and in the patronage of the President and Fellows of Corpus Christi College, Oxford. The church is dedicated to St. Rumon. There is a place of worship for Wesleyan Methodists. The Tregoney river is navigable on the north-west. The petty

sessions for the division are held here, on the first Monday in every month. John Whitaker, B. D., the learned historian and antiquary, was for thirty years rector of this parish; he died in 1808, and was buried in the church.

RUARDEAN, a parish in the hundred of ST. BRIAVELLS, county of GLOUCESTER, 6¼ miles (N. W.) from Newnham, containing 729 inhabitants. The living is a perpetual curacy, annexed to the vicarage of Walford, in the archdeaconry of Hereford, and diocese of Gloucester. The church, dedicated to St. John the Baptist, is partly Norman, but principally of later date, and the west window is finely enriched with tracery. There is a place of worship for Independents. The navigable river Wye forms the eastern boundary, and the Severn and Wye railway passes through the parish. A small school is endowed with about £5 per annum, the united bequests of the Rev. Richard Greenaway, in 1744, and Thomas Richards, in 1763. There are a few remaining fragments of an ancient castle.

RUCKINGE, a parish in the hundred of NEWCHURCH, lathe of SHEPWAY, county of KENT, 6½ miles (S. by E.) from Ashford, containing 331 inhabitants. The living is a rectory, in the archdeaconry and diocese of Canterbury, rated in the king's books at £14. 13. 4., and in the patronage of the Archbishop of Canterbury. The church, dedicated to St. Mary Magdalene, is principally in the early style of English architecture. There is a place of worship for Wesleyan Methodists. The Grand Military canal passes through the parish.

RUCKLAND, a parish in the Wold division of the hundred of LOUTH-ESKE, parts of LINDSEY, county of LINCOLN, 6¼ miles (S. by E.) from Louth, containing 33 inhabitants. The living is a discharged rectory, with that of Farforth and the vicarage of Maiden Well, in the archdeaconry and diocese of Lincoln, rated in the king's books at £6. 3. 9., and in the patronage of Lord Yarborough. The church is dedicated to St. Olave.

RUCKLEY, a township in the parish of ACTON-BURNELL, hundred of CONDOVER, county of SALOP, 7 miles (W.) from Much-Wenlock, containing, with the chapelry of Langley, 75 inhabitants.

RUDBY in CLEVELAND, a parish in the western division of the liberty of LANGBAURGH, North riding of the county of YORK, comprising the chapelry of Middleton upon Leven, and the townships of Hutton, East Rouncton, Rudby in Cleveland, Skutterskelfe, and Sexhow, and containing 1311 inhabitants, of which number, 76 are in the township of Rudby in Cleveland, 3¾ miles (W. S. W.) from Stokesley. The living is a vicarage, in the archdeaconry of Cleveland, and diocese of York, rated in the king's books at £30, endowed with £1200 parliamentary grant, and in the patronage of Lady Amherst. The church is dedicated to All Saints. The river Leven runs through the parish. Five poor children are educated for £5 a year, in a school built by subscription.

RUDDINGTON, a parish in the northern division of the wapentake of RUSHCLIFFE, county of NOTTINGHAM, 5 miles (S.) from Nottingham, containing 1138 inhabitants. The living is a discharged vicarage, in the archdeaconry of Nottingham, and diocese of York, rated in the king's books at £6. 13. 4., endowed with £200 private benefaction, and £400 royal bounty, and in the patronage of the Rev. C. Simeon. The church, dedicated to St. Peter, has lately received an addition of three hundred and ninety-four sittings, of which three hundred and fifty are free, the Incorporated Society for the enlargement of churches and chapels having granted £500 towards defraying the expense. About one mile from this structure is an extensive churchyard, and the site of an ancient church, called Flawford, thought by some to have been originally the parish church. There are places of worship for Baptists and Wesleyan Methodists. Frame-work knitting and the weaving of lace is carried on in the village, which is of considerable size. A free school was founded, in 1641, by James Peacock, citizen of London, who endowed it with lands in the parish, now producing an annual income of £75, for teaching all the children of parishioners. There is also an infant school, supported by Lady Parkyns. Ruddington is in the honour of Tutbury, duchy of Lancaster, and within the jurisdiction of a court of pleas held at Tutbury every third Tuesday, for the recovery of debts under 40s. A college was founded here, in the reign of Henry VI., by William Babington, Esq., who endowed it with a revenue which was valued, in the 26th year of the reign of Henry VIII., at £30.

RUDFORD, a parish partly in the hundred of BOTLOE, and partly in the lower division of the hundred of DUDSTONE and KING'S BARTON, county of GLOUCESTER, 3½ miles (N. W. by W.) from Gloucester, containing, with the hamlet of High Leadon, 189 inhabitants. The living is a rectory, in the archdeaconry of Hereford, and diocese of Gloucester, rated in the king's books at £10, and in the patronage of the Dean and Chapter of Gloucester. The church is dedicated to St. Mary. The river Leadon separates this parish from that of Hartpury, and the Gloucester and Ledbury canal passes through it.

RUDGE, a township in that part of the parish of PATTINGHAM which is in the hundred of STOTTESDEN, county of SALOP, 7¼ miles (E. N. E.) from Bridgenorth, containing 69 inhabitants.

RUDGWICK, a parish in the hundred of WEST EASWRITH, rape of ARUNDEL, county of SUSSEX, 7 miles (N. W. by W.) from Horsham, containing 974 inhabitants. The living is a vicarage, in the archdeaconry and diocese of Chichester, rated in the king's books at £7. 10., and in the patronage of the Bishop of Chichester. The church is dedicated to the Holy Trinity. The river Wanford runs through the parish.

RUDHAM (EAST), a parish in the hundred of GALLOW, county of NORFOLK, 6¾ miles (W. by S.) from Fakenham, containing 807 inhabitants. The living is a discharged rectory, with the vicarage of West Rudham, in the archdeaconry of Norfolk, and diocese of Norwich, rated in the king's books at £6. 6. 8., and in the patronage of Marquis Townshend. The church is dedicated to St. Mary. There is a place of worship for Wesleyan Methodists.

RUDHAM (WEST), a parish in the hundred of GALLOW, county of NORFOLK, 7¼ miles (W. by S.) from Fakenham, containing 376 inhabitants. The living is a discharged vicarage, united with the rectory of East Rudham, in the archdeaconry of Norfolk, and diocese of Norwich, rated in the king's books at £7. 6. 8. The church is dedicated to St. Peter.

RUDHEATH, a township partly in the parishes of GREAT BUDWORTH and SANDBACH, but chiefly in that of DAVENHAM, hundred of NORTHWICH, county palatine of CHESTER, 4 miles (N.E.) from Middlewich, containing 363 inhabitants.

RUDSTON, a parish in the wapentake of DICKERING, East riding of the county of YORK, 5 miles (W.) from Bridlington, containing 417 inhabitants. The living is a discharged vicarage, in the archdeaconry of the East riding, and diocese of York, rated in the king's books at £9. 13. 6½., and in the patronage of the Archbishop of York. The church is dedicated to All Saints. In the churchyard is a lofty pyramidal stone, which probably gave name to the place, Rod, in Saxon, signifying a cross.

RUDYARD, a joint township with Caudery, in that part of the parish of LEEK which is in the southern division of the hundred of TOTMONSLOW, county of STAFFORD, 2¾ miles (N. N. W.) from Leek, containing 112 inhabitants.

RUFFORD, a parish in the hundred of LEYLAND, county palatine of LANCASTER, 5½ miles (N. E. by N.) from Ormskirk, containing 1073 inhabitants. The living is a rectory not in charge, in the archdeaconry and diocese of Chester, and in the patronage of Pierce Starkie, Esq. The church is dedicated to St. Mary. This parish was formerly a chapelry in the parish of Croston, but was made parochial by act of parliament. The Leeds and Liverpool canal passes through it. Sir Thomas Hesketh, Bart., in 1816, erected a school, which is supported at his own expense, for the education of all the poor children of the parish. The petty sessions for the division are held here once in five weeks, alternately with Chorley, Cuerdon, Leyland, and Penwortham.

RUFFORD, an extra-parochial liberty, in the Hatfield division of the wapentake of BASSETLAW, county of NOTTINGHAM, 2 miles (S. S. W.) from Ollerton, containing 323 inhabitants. An abbey for Cistercian monks, in honour of the Blessed Virgin Mary, was founded in 1148, by Gilbert, Earl of Lincoln, which, at the dissolution, possessed a revenue of £254. 6. 8.

RUFFORTH, a parish in the ainsty of the city, and East riding of the county, of YORK, 5½ miles (W.) from York, containing 295 inhabitants. The living is a discharged vicarage, in the archdeaconry and diocese of York, rated in the king's books at £4. 13. 4., endowed with £400 private benefaction, and £600 royal bounty, and in the patronage of Mrs. Thompson. Eight children are taught for £4 a year, the gift of Lady Hewley.

RUGBY, a market town and parish in the Rugby division of the hundred of KNIGHTLOW, county of WARWICK, 16½ miles (E. N. E.) from Warwick, and 83 (N. W. by N.) from London, containing 2300 inhabitants. At this place, anciently called Rocheberie, is supposed to have been one of those fortresses which Stephen, expecting Matilda's invasion, permitted his nobles to erect upon their estates; it obtained also the name of Rokeby from its owner, Henry de Rokeby, in the reign of Henry III., and from this, its present appellation is derived. The town is pleasantly situated upon rising ground, on the south side of the Avon: it consists of one street leading to the market-place, parallel with which, on the one side, is a narrower street, in which the shambles are placed, and on the other a handsome and spacious street leading to the church. The houses are in general well built of brick, and of modern appearance, though occasionally intermixed with some of ancient character, with plastered walls and thatched roofs. The Oxford canal passes in the vicinity. The market, which is well attended, and abundantly supplied with corn, and provisions of every kind, is on Saturday : thirteen fairs are held annually, but the greater number are only cattle markets ; these are held on the second Tuesday after Twelfth day, February 17th, March 31st, the last Monday in April, May 5th (which is chiefly a pleasure fair), the second Monday in June, July 7th, the ninth Monday before New Michaelmas-day, August 21st, the Monday before Michaelmas-day, the Monday preceding the 22nd of October, November 22nd (which is a very great horse fair), the Tuesday before St. Thomas' day, and the Monday after Christmas-day. A constable and headborough are appointed at the court leet of the lord of the manor.

The living is a rectory, in the archdeaconry of Coventry, and diocese of Lichfield and Coventry, rated in the king's books at £17. 19. 2., and in the patronage of Earl Craven. The church, dedicated to St. Andrew, is an ancient structure, in the early style of English architecture, with a massive square embattled tower, strengthened by buttresses, and a turret at the south-east angle, to which there is no entrance but from within the church, and which appears to have been erected as a place of security, after the demolition of the castle; the roof of the nave is supported on massive octagonal pillars and sharply - pointed arches, of which those nearer to the chancel are much more lofty than the others : the building is at present undergoing considerable enlargement, from a plan by Mr. Rickman. There are places of worship for Baptists and Wesleyan Methodists. The grammar school, which is the distinguishing feature in Rugby, is a noble and magnificent establishment, and has for many years maintained a high degree of reputation. It was founded in the 9th of Elizabeth, by Lawrence Sheriff, of London, grocer, a native of Brownsover, a neighbouring hamlet, in the parish of Clifton, who endowed it with a house and land in that parish, and with about eight acres of land, called the Conduit close, near the Foundling Hospital, London. At that time the income was inconsiderable, and in the year 1780, the rental did not exceed £116 per annum; but from the subsequent improvement of the estate, by the erection of numerous dwelling-houses, and the laying out of several streets upon the site, the revenue has been augmented to more than £5000 per annum. The school is under the superintendence of twelve trustees, who appoint the head master, with a fixed salary of £113. 6. 8., a house and some land, and an annual payment of £16. 5. 6. for every boy on the foundation, of which latter sum he pays £6. 6. to the six assistant classical masters, £2. 2. to the master of modern languages, and £1. 11. 6. to the mathematical master ; instruction in these two last branches of literature forming a part of the regular course of education pursued at the school. The assistant classical masters also receive severally from the trustees a permanent salary of £120 per annum, and salaries are also given to a writing-master and a drawing-master. By a late regulation of

the trustees, the number of boys not on the foundation is never to exceed two hundred and sixty ; the actual number at present (November 1830) is about two hundred and thirty, besides about forty foundationers. Belonging to this noble establishment are twenty-one exhibitions of £60 per annum, tenable for seven years, in either of the Universities ; and several fellowships, varying in value from £100 to £300 per annum, but not exceeding £1000 per annum in the aggregate amount, which are given exclusively to the head master and ushers, who may choose to retire after having been ten years in the establishment. The school premises were taken down and rebuilt in 1808 ; they form a splendid range of building, in the Elizabethan style of architecture; the principal entrance is under a square gateway tower, with octagonal turrets at the angles, through a richly-groined archway, above which is a beautiful oriel window embellished with stained glass, into a spacious quadrangle, of which two sides are cloistered. The school-rooms are lofty, and the great school, as it is called, in which the annual Prize Compositions are recited, on the Wednesday in Easter-week, is of large dimensions and of stately elevation. The room in the gateway tower, over the principal entrance, is appropriated to the school library. Through an archway diagonally opposite to the principal entrance is the approach to the chapel, a detached and elegant edifice, in the later style of English architecture, to which there is also an entrance from the public road : the sides of the building are strengthened with ornamented buttresses, and relieved by three elegant windows with dripstones resting on antique heads ; and the east and west ends are decorated with crocketed pinnacles at the angles, and a cross on the apex of the gable. The interior is fitted up like the choir of a cathedral ; the roof, which is flat and painted to resemble oak, is panelled, and ribbed with diagonal intersections ; the east window is enriched with tracery, and at the west end are two canopied seats for the head master and the chaplain, over which is a gallery, with an organ of appropriate design. On the south side, near the altar, is a white monument of marble, by Chantrey, erected to the memory of the late Dr. James, head master, in which he is represented in a sitting posture, reading, with several volumes at his feet. The entrance to the head master's apartments is through a large octangular turret forming the hall and staircase, and the whole range of buildings is relieved with turrets at various intervals. From the funds of this institution are supported twelve almshouses, lately rebuilt in a corresponding style of architecture, for twelve aged men, who have each two apartments and a garden, a gown, two tons of coal annually, and a weekly allowance of seven shillings and sixpence. Boys are eligible to the school, and men to the almshouses, who live within ten miles of the town, if in the county of Warwick, or within five miles, if in any other county. A charity school was founded, in 1707, by Mr. Elborough, who endowed it with a house and fifty acres of land for the instruction of thirty boys and girls : it is under the direction of six trustees, who appoint the master, with a salary of £20 per annum, a house, and two acres of land. Adjoining the school, and supported out of the same funds, are six almshouses for six aged widows, who receive half a ton of coal annually, a stuff gown every two years, and an allowance of three shillings per week. There are various charitable bequests for distribution among the poor. At Lawford, one mile west from Rugby, are large quarries of blue lias, covered with a thick bed of gravel, in which elephants' bones, and the remains of other animals, have been found in considerable quantities. On the road to Lawford is a Roman tumulus; and at Brownsover, one mile north-west of Rugby, is an earthwork, supposed to be a British camp, surrounded by the rivers Swift and Avon; skeletons buried in the ancient British manner, with the limbs contracted, have been discovered here.

RUGELEY, a market town and parish in the eastern division of the hundred of CUTTLESTONE, county of STAFFORD, 9 miles (E.S.E.) from Stafford, and 127 (N.W. by N.) from London, containing 2677 inhabitants. This town is agreeably situated near the south bank of the river Trent, on the road from Stafford to Lichfield; it is of remarkably clean and respectable appearance, and consists of several good streets, two of them recently formed, called Albion-street and Church-street; many of the houses in the latter are of a very superior order. Cannock heath is within a mile of the town, on the south. The trade of the place is greatly promoted by the proximity of the Grand Trunk canal, which connects the navigation of the rivers Trent and Mersey, and passing northward of the town, between it and the river, communicates with Brereton collieries by a rail-road, and not far distant is carried over the Trent by a fine aqueduct. Here are an iron-foundry, and mills for rolling sheet-iron, also a small manufactory for sugar of lead and verdegris; hats were formerly made to a considerable extent, but this branch of trade has very much declined. At Brereton, in this parish, are extensive coal-works belonging to Earl Talbot and the Marquis of Anglesey: the depth of the shaft is one hundred and twenty-seven yards; the strata of coal is five yards in thickness, and generally good, exclusively of some thin veins not yet worked: about four hundred persons are employed in these works, most of whom reside in cottages on the estate. In sinking, good iron-ore is found in detached pieces, but not in sufficient quantity to pay the expense of working it. The market is on Thursday: fairs are held on April 15th; June 6th, a very large horse fair, which continues eight or nine days; and October 21st, for cattle, sheep, and horses. A court leet is held annually in October, by the lord of the manor, at which two constables are appointed. The living is a discharged vicarage, in the peculiar jurisdiction and patronage of the Dean and Chapter of Lichfield, rated in the king's books at £5. 2., and endowed with £200 private benefaction, and £200 royal bounty. The church, dedicated to St. Augustine, has been lately but indifferently rebuilt, with stone given by the Marquis of Anglesey; it contains eight hundred sittings, of which four hundred and thirty-two are free, the Incorporated Society for the building and enlargement of churches, &c., having contributed £800 towards defraying the expense. Of the old church, the tower and chancel remain entire, the latter being used as a school-room; the arches are in ruins. There is a place of worship for Independents, and one for Wesleyan Methodists at Brereton. The free grammar school was founded, in the 8th of James I., by Walter Wolsley, and endowed by him with estates now producing about £320 per annum, which is paid to the master, who has also a good residence: there are twenty boys on the foundation, besides which the master is allowed by the trustees to take boarders, and eleven day scholars, who pay for their education. Bamford's school was founded by John Bamford, who by will dated Feb. 11th, 1733, gave £400 for the education of sixteen poor boys: this benefaction having been augmented by £50 left by Mrs. Mary Jenks, and further, in 1802, by a gift of £500 from John Riley, the income is now £35 per annum, and thirty-five boys are on the foundation, all of them appointed by the minister and church-wardens. A National school for girls was founded by the Hon. Mrs. Curzon; another at Brereton, by Mrs. Sneyd; and an almshouse here, for four old women, by Mrs. Hopkins.

RUISHTON, a parish in the hundred of TAUNTON and TAUNTON-DEAN, county of SOMERSET, 2½ miles (E.) from Taunton, containing 329 inhabitants. The living is a perpetual curacy, in the archdeaconry of Taunton, and diocese of Bath and Wells, endowed with £250 private benefaction, and £400 royal bounty. John Guy, Esq. was patron in 1800. The church is dedicated to St. George. The navigable river Tone passes on the northern side of the village. Nine poor children are educated for about £4 per annum, arising from £100, the gift of Elizabeth Strong, in 1742.

RUISLIP, a parish in the hundred of ELTHORNE, county of MIDDLESEX, 3½ miles (N.E.) from Uxbridge, containing 1343 inhabitants. The living is a vicarage, in the archdeaconry of Middlesex, and diocese of London, rated in the king's books at £12, and in the patronage of the Dean and Canons of Windsor. The church is dedicated to St. Martin. Here was formerly a cell to the abbey of Bec in Normandy, the revenue of which at the suppression was valued at £18.

RUMBOLD'S WYKE, a parish in the hundred of Box and STOCKBRIDGE, rape of CHICHESTER, county of SUSSEX, ¾ of a mile (S.E.) from Chichester, containing 303 inhabitants. The living is a discharged vicarage, in the archdeaconry and diocese of Chichester, rated in the king's books at £4, and in the patronage of the Dean and Chapter of Chichester. The church is dedicated to St. Rumbald. A branch of the Arundel and Portsmouth canal passes near the parish.

RUMBURGH, a parish in the hundred of BLYTHING, county of SUFFOLK, 4 miles (N.W. by N.) from Halesworth, containing 445 inhabitants. The living is a perpetual curacy, with the rectory of South Elmham St. Michael, in the archdeaconry of Suffolk, and diocese of Norwich, endowed with £10 per annum and £400 private benefaction, £400 royal bounty, and £1200 parliamentary grant. The church is dedicated to St. Michael. Here was a cell to the abbey of St. Ben'et at Holme; it was dedicated to St. Michael, and was one of those suppressed in 1528, and granted to Wolsey, towards the endowment of his college at Ipswich.

RUMNEY, a parish in the upper division of the hundred of WENTLLOOG, county of MONMOUTH, 3 miles (N.E.) from Cardiff, containing 255 inhabitants. The living is a discharged vicarage, in the archdeaconry and diocese of Llandaff, rated in the king's books at £5. 10. 7½., endowed with £600 royal bounty, and in the patronage of the Dean and Chapter of Bristol. The church is dedicated to St. Augustine.

RUMWORTH, a township in the parish of DEAN, hundred of SALFORD, county palatine of LANCASTER, 3 miles (W. S. W.) from Great Bolton, containing 847 inhabitants. James Crompton, in 1636, bequeathed £100 towards the support of a school, to which subsequent bequests have been added, producing an annual income of £36. 17., for which about fifty children are taught to read only, in a school-room rebuilt in 1820, at an expense of £750.

RUNCORN, a parish in the hundred of BUCKLOW, county palatine of CHESTER, comprising the chapelries of Aston by Sutton, Daresbury, Halton, and Thelwall, and the townships of Acton-Grange, Aston-Grange, Clifton, alias Rock-Savage, Hatton, Keckwick, Moore, Newton by Daresbury, Norton, Preston on the Hill, Runcorn, Stockham, Sutton, Walton (Inferior), Walton (Superior), and Weston, and containing 7738 inhabitants, of which number, 3103 are in the township of Runcorn, 4½ miles (N. by W.) from Frodsham. The living is a vicarage, in the archdeaconry and diocese of Chester, rated in the king's books at £10. 4. 2., and in the patronage of the Dean and Canons of Christ Church, Oxford. The church, dedicated to St. Bartholomew, is partly in the early, and partly in the later, style of English architecture; of the north door and the piers in the nave, the design is very uncommon, yet good in execution. There is a place of worship for Wesleyan Methodists. In 915, Ethelfleda, sister to King Edward the Elder, and widow of Ethelred, Earl of Mercia, built a town and castle near the river Mersey, at this place, then called *Romicofan*, some traces of which are visible at a place called Castle-Rock, by the river side, about three hundred yards below the church: this part of the Mersey is called Runcorn Gap, and at high water is about four hundred yards broad. This ancient fortress commanded the passage from the kingdom of Mercia to that of Northumberland. In 1133, William Fitz-Nigel founded here a monastery of canons Regular, which, about the reign of Stephen, was removed to Norton. The Duke of Bridgewater's canal passes through a great part of this parish: at Runcorn it is sixty feet above the level of the Mersey, with which it communicates by a chain of ten locks. Runcorn, which had previously been a very poor village, has, in consequence of the trade on the canal, and its having become a place of considerable resort for bathing, grown very populous, and been improved in its appearance by the erection of many handsome buildings. The township abounds in fine stone quarries, from which considerable quantities of hewn stone are sent by water to Chester, Liverpool, Manchester, &c. The chapel at Aston was rebuilt on an enlarged scale in 1737.

RUNCTON (NORTH), a parish in the Lynn division of the hundred of FREEBRIDGE, county of NORFOLK, 3 miles (S. S. E.) from Lynn-Regis, containing, with the hamlet of Hardwick, 314 inhabitants. The living is a rectory, with that of Hardwick and Setchy, in the archdeaconry and diocese of Norwich, rated in the king's books at £8. 10., and in the patronage of the Master and Fellows of Trinity College, Cambridge. The church, dedicated to All Saints, was rebuilt about 1710, its ancient structure having been injured by the fall of its steeple.

RUNCTON (SOUTH), a parish in the hundred of CLACKCLOSE, county of NORFOLK, 4¼ miles (N. N. E.)

from Downham - Market, containing 123 inhabitants The living is a rectory, with Holme and Wallington, in the archdeaconry of Norfolk, and diocese of Norwich, rated in the king's books at £12. The church is dedicated to St. Andrew.

RUNFOLD, a tything in the parish and hundred of FARNHAM, county of SURREY. The population is returned with Badshot.

RUNHALL, a parish in the hundred of FOREHOE, county of NORFOLK, 5¼ miles (N. W. by N.) from Wymondham, containing 160 inhabitants. The living is a discharged vicarage, in the archdeaconry of Norfolk, and diocese of Norwich, rated in the king's books at £6. 18. 1½., endowed with £1200 royal bounty, and in the patronage of Lord Wodehouse. The church is dedicated to All Saints.

RUNHAM, a parish in the eastern division of the hundred of FLEGG, county of NORFOLK, 4¾ miles (W. by S.) from Caistor, containing 211 inhabitants. The living is a discharged vicarage, in the archdeaconry and diocese of Norwich, rated in the king's books at £4, endowed with £200 royal bounty, and in the patronage of the Bishop of Ely. The church is dedicated to St. Peter and St. Paul: a sum of money was bequeathed, in 1501, by Rose Dook, for erecting the steeple. A market, and a fair on the vigil and festival of St. Peter ad Vincula, were granted by King John to Robert de Evermere.

RUNNINGTON, a parish in the hundred of MILVERTON, county of SOMERSET, 2 miles (W. N. W.) from Wellington, containing 90 inhabitants. The living is a discharged rectory, in the archdeaconry of Taunton, and diocese of Bath and Wells, rated in the king's books at £5. 1. 5½., and in the patronage of the Crown.

RUNSTON, a hamlet in the parish of ST. PIERRE, upper division of the hundred of CALDICOTT, county of MONMOUTH, 3¼ miles (S. W. by W.) from Chepstow. The population is returned with the parish. The chapel has been demolished.

RUNTON, a parish in the northern division of the hundred of ERPINGHAM, county of NORFOLK, 2½ miles (W. by N.) from Cromer, containing 417 inhabitants. The living is a discharged rectory, with that of Aylmerton, in the archdeaconry of Norfolk, and diocese of Norwich, rated in the king's books at £10. The church is dedicated to the Holy Trinity.

RUNWELL, a parish in the hundred of CHELMSFORD, county of ESSEX, 5 miles (N. W.) from Rayleigh, containing 307 inhabitants. The living is a rectory, in the archdeaconry of Essex, and diocese of London, rated in the king's books at £13, and in the patronage of Vicesimus Knox, Esq. The church is dedicated to St. Mary. The Crouch river is navigable from the sea to this place.

RUNWICK, a tything in the parish and hundred of FARNHAM, county of SURREY, containing 197 inhabitants.

RUSCOMB, a parish in the hundred of SONNING, county of BERKS, 5½ miles (E. N. E.) from Reading, containing 208 inhabitants. The living is a perpetual curacy, in the peculiar jurisdiction of the Dean of Salisbury, and in the patronage of the Prebendary of Combe and Harnham in the Cathedral Church of Salisbury. The church is dedicated to St. James. In the chancel lie buried the remains of Lord Chief Justice Eyre, who occasionally resided here. There is a place of worship for Independents.

RUSHALL, a parish in the hundred of EARSHAM, county of NORFOLK, 3 miles (W.) from Harleston, containing 279 inhabitants. The living is a discharged vicarage, in the archdeaconry of Norfolk, and diocese of Norwich, rated in the king's books at £4, endowed with £200 royal bounty, and in the patronage of Joseph Sewell, Esq. The church is dedicated to St. Mary. A farm-house here is called the Priory, from having once belonged to the priory of Buckenham.

RUSHALL, a parish in the southern division of the hundred of OFFLOW, county of STAFFORD, 1 mile (N. E. by N.) from Walsall, containing 670 inhabitants. The living is a discharged vicarage, in the archdeaconry of Stafford, and diocese of Lichfield and Coventry, rated in the king's books at £4. 5., endowed with £400 private benefaction, and £400 royal bounty, and in the patronage of the Rev. Edward Mellish. The church is dedicated to St. Michael. The Wyrley and Essington canal passes through the parish, in which there are considerable quarries of limestone, and the ruined walls of an ancient castellated mansion.

RUSHALL, a parish in the hundred of SWAN-BOROUGH, county of WILTS, 3½ miles (S. W.) from Pewsey, containing 248 inhabitants. The living is a rectory, in the archdeaconry and diocese of Salisbury, rated in the king's books at £12. 11. 8., and in the patronage of the Wardens of New and Merton Colleges, and of the Principal of Brasenose College, Oxford, for a scholar on Jackson's foundation at Merton College. The church is dedicated to St. Matthew.

RUSHBROOK, a parish in the hundred of THED-WESTRY, county of SUFFOLK, 3 miles (S. E. by E.) from Bury-St. Edmunds, containing 194 inhabitants. The living is a discharged rectory, with that of Bradfield St. George, in the archdeaconry of Sudbury, and diocese of Norwich, rated in the king's books at £8. 1. 5½., and in the patronage of the Marquis of Bristol. The church is dedicated to St. Nicholas. Lord Jermyn, in 1700, founded and endowed with property, now producing £32 a year, almshouses for one man and three women. Other almshouses were erected, in 1724, by Sir Jermyn Davers, for four poor persons, which, not being endowed, are kept in repair by the proprietor of the Rushbrook estate.

RUSHBURY, a parish in the hundred of MUNS-LOW, county of SALOP, 4¾ miles (E. S. E.) from Church-Stretton, containing, with the townships of East-Wall, Gretton, Lutwytch with Stanway, Rushbury, Stone-Acton, and Wall under Haywood, 478 inhabitants. The living is a rectory, in the archdeaconry of Salop, and diocese of Hereford, rated in the king's books at £19. 7. 8½., and in the patronage of the Bishop of Worcester. The church is dedicated to St. Peter. This is presumed to be the site of the Roman station *Bravinium*, situated between Old Radnor and Worcester. A market and a fair, granted by Edward I., were formerly held here.

RUSHDEN, a parish in the hundred of ODSEY, county of HERTFORD, 4¾ miles (W. N. W.) from Buntingford, containing 333 inhabitants. The living is a discharged vicarage, in the archdeaconry of Huntingdon, and diocese of Lincoln, rated in the king's books at £8. 1. 10½., and in the patronage of the Dean and Chapter of Lincoln. The church, dedicated to St. Mary, contains the handsome monument of Sir Adolphus Meetkerke, which was removed hither, in 1754, from the church of St. Botolph, Aldersgate : there is also a memorial to William Love, late a servant in the Meetkerke family, who in 1819 left £233. 6. 8. three per cents. towards the support of a Sunday school. The late Rev. James Ford, vicar of the parish, bequeathed £300 three per cents. for the benefit of future incumbents.

RUSHDEN, a parish in the hundred of HIGHAM-FERRERS, county of NORTHAMPTON, 1½ mile (S.) from Higham-Ferrers, containing 1077 inhabitants. The living is a rectory, in the archdeaconry of Northampton, and diocese of Peterborough, rated in the king's books at £12. 16. 3., and in the patronage of the Crown. The church, dedicated to St. Mary, is large and handsome, partaking of the different styles of English architecture ; the tower, a fine specimen of the later style, is surmounted by an elegant crocketed spire ; the transepts are in the decorated style ; and in the chancel are three early English stalls : there are also some remains of screen-work, and ancient stained glass. There are two places of worship for Baptists. Daniel Whitby, a learned scripture commentator, and writer on controversial divinity, was born here in 1638; he died in 1726.

RUSHFORD, a parish in the hundred of GUILT-CROSS, county of NORFOLK, 4 miles (E. S. E.) from Thetford, containing, with Snarehill, 168 inhabitants. The living is a donative. The church is dedicated to St. John the Evangelist. A chapel and college for a master and six priests was founded upon the site of the parsonage-house, about 1342, by Sir Edmund de Gonville, the rector and founder of Gonville Hall, Cambridge ; it was dedicated to St. John the Evangelist, and at the dissolution was valued at £85. 15. per annum.

RUSHMERE, a parish in the hundred of CARLFORD, county of SUFFOLK, 2 miles (N. E. by E.) from Ipswich, containing 437 inhabitants. The living is a discharged vicarage, in the archdeaconry of Suffolk, and diocese of Norwich, rated in the king's books at £4. 6. 8., and in the patronage of the Marquis of Bristol. The church is dedicated to St. Andrew.

RUSHMERE, a parish in the hundred of MUTFORD and LOTHINGLAND, county of SUFFOLK, 5 miles (S. W.) from Lowestoft, containing 114 inhabitants. The living is a discharged rectory, in the archdeaconry of Suffolk, and diocese of Norwich, rated in the king's books at £7. 6. 8., and in the patronage of Charles Gurney, Esq. The church is dedicated to All Saints.

RUSHOCK, a parish in the lower division of the hundred of HALFSHIRE, county of WORCESTER, 5½ miles (W. by N.) from Bromsgrove, containing 181 inhabitants. The living is a rectory, in the archdeaconry and diocese of Worcester, rated in the king's books at £10. 6. 8., and in the patronage of the Crown. The church is dedicated to St. Michael. William Norris, in 1702, bequeathed a house and land in support of a school for teaching fifteen children of this parish, and the same number of that of Elmbridge.

RUSHROFT, a hamlet in the parish of AINSTA-BLE, LEATH ward, county of CUMBERLAND, 3 miles (N. W. by N.) from Kirk-Oswald. The population is returned with the parish.

RUSHTON, a township in the parish of TARPORLEY, first division of the hundred of EDDISBURY, county palatine of CHESTER, 2½ miles (E. N. E.) from Tarporley, containing 315 inhabitants.

RUSHTON, a village in the hundred of ROTHWELL, county of NORTHAMPTON, 2¾ miles (N. E.) from Rothwell, containing 366 inhabitants, and comprising the parishes of All Saints and St. Peter, in the archdeaconry of Northampton, and diocese of Peterborough ; the former, a rectory, rated in the king's books at £10. 12. 1., and the latter, also a rectory, rated at £11. 13. 4., both in the patronage of W. Haggitt, Esq.

RUSHTON-JAMES, a township in that part of the parish of LEEK which is in the northern division of the hundred of TOTMONSLOW, county of STAFFORD, 5¾ miles (N. W.) from Leek, containing 354 inhabitants.

RUSHTON-SPENCER, a chapelry in that part of the parish of LEEK which is in the northern division of the hundred of TOTMONSLOW, county of STAFFORD, 5 miles (N. W. by N.) from Leek, containing 359 inhabitants. The living is a perpetual curacy, in the archdeaconry of Stafford, and diocese of Lichfield and Coventry, endowed with £1200 private benefaction, £200 royal bounty, and £1200 parliamentary grant, and in the patronage of the Vicar of Leek. The chapel, dedicated to St. Lawrence, is a small stone building fast falling to decay. Cotton-spinning affords employment to a few of the inhabitants.

RUSHULME, a township in the parish of MANCHESTER, hundred of SALFORD, county palatine of LANCASTER, 2¼ miles (S. S. E.) from Manchester, containing 913 inhabitants.

RUSKINGTON, a parish in the wapentake of FLAXWELL, parts of KESTEVEN, county of LINCOLN, 3¼ miles (N. N. E.) from Sleaford, containing 678 inhabitants. The living is a discharged vicarage, in the archdeaconry and diocese of Lincoln, rated in the king's books at £3. 17. 3½., endowed with £600 royal bounty, and £200 parliamentary grant, and in the patronage of the Crown. The church is dedicated to All Saints. Lady Hodgson, in 1719, bequeathed a rent-charge of £42. 16., in support of three aged women, and a school for ten children, with a fund for apprenticing them. There is also a trifling annuity left by Martha Chamberlain, in 1702, for educating children.

RUSLAND, a chapelry in the parish of COULTON, hundred of LONSDALE, north of the sands, county palatine of LANCASTER, 8½ miles (N.N.E.) from Ulverstone. The population is returned with the parish. The living is a perpetual curacy, in the archdeaconry of Richmond, and diocese of Chester, endowed with £400 private benefaction, £400 royal bounty, and £200 parliamentary grant, and in the patronage of Trustees. The chapel, dedicated to St. Paul, was consecrated in 1745.

RUSPER, a parish in the hundred of SINGLECROSS, rape of BRAMBER, county of SUSSEX, 5¼ miles (N.N.E.) from Horsham, containing 487 inhabitants. The living is a rectory, in the archdeaconry and diocese of Chichester, rated in the king's books at £9. 10. 10., and in the patronage of the Rev. Peter Wood. The church, dedicated to St. Mary, is in the early style of English architecture, and has lately received an addition of one hundred and seven sittings, of which ninety-nine are free, the Incorporated Society for the enlargement of churches and chapels having granted £70 towards de-fraying the expense. There are slight remains of a priory of Black nuns, founded by Gervase of Canterbury, who flourished in the reign of Richard I. ; it was dedicated to St. Mary Magdalene, and at the dissolution possessed a revenue of £39. 13. 7.

RUSSELS, a hamlet in the parish of DANBURY, hundred of CHELMSFORD, though locally in that of Dengie, county of ESSEX, 1 mile (E.) from Danbury. The population is returned with the parish.

RUSTINGTON, a parish in the hundred of POLING, rape of ARUNDEL, county of SUSSEX, 2 miles (E.N.E.) from Little Hampton, containing 327 inhabitants. The living is a discharged vicarage, in the archdeaconry and diocese of Chichester, rated in the king's books at £6, endowed with £400 private benefaction, and £400 royal bounty, and in the patronage of the Bishop of Chichester. The church is in the early style of English architecture.

RUSTON (EAST), a parish in the hundred of HAPPING, county of NORFOLK, 5¾ miles (E. by S.) from North Walsham, containing 613 inhabitants. The living is a discharged vicarage, with the rectory of Ridlington, in the archdeaconry of Norfolk, and diocese of Norwich, rated in the king's books at £11. 11. 10., endowed with £200 royal bounty. The church is dedicated to St. Mary. Professor Porson, celebrated as a critic and classical scholar, was born here in 1759.

RUSTON (PARVA), a parish in the wapentake of DICKERING, East riding of the county of YORK, 3¾ miles (N. E.) from Great Driffield, containing 140 inhabitants. The living is a perpetual curacy, in the archdeaconry of the East riding, and diocese of York, endowed with £800 royal bounty, and £200 parliamentary grant, and in the patronage of W. T. St. Quintin, Esq.

RUSTON (SOUTH), a parish in the hundred of TUNSTEAD, county of NORFOLK, 1½ mile (N. E.) from Coltishall, containing 103 inhabitants. The living is a perpetual curacy, annexed to the vicarage of Tunstead, in the archdeaconry of Norfolk, and diocese of Norwich. The church is dedicated to St. Michael.

RUSWARP, a township in the parish of WHITBY, liberty of WHITBY-STRAND, North riding of the county of YORK, 1¾ mile (S. W. by S.) from Whitby, containing 1918 inhabitants. There is a handsome suspension bridge across the river Esk.

RUTCHESTER, a township in the parish of OVINGHAM, eastern division of TINDALE ward, county of NORTHUMBERLAND, 8½ miles (W. by N.) from Newcastle upon Tyne, containing 31 inhabitants. In the reign of Edward I., Rutchester tower was occupied by a family of the same name. This was the site of the Roman station Vindobala, which was garrisoned by the Cohors Prima Frixagorum. A broken statue of Hercules, coins of the Lower Empire, silver fibulæ, and numerous other relics, have been found here; and, in 1766, an urn full of gold and silver coins, among which was an almost complete series of those of the Higher Empire, was discovered at Castlestead, in the neighbourhood. Adrian's wall, the remains of which are still visible, passed from its east and west ramparts, which, towards the enemy's frontier, were defended by strong towers.

RUTHALE, a joint township with Ashfield, in that part of the parish of PRIOR'S DITTON which is in the hundred of MUNSLOW, county of SALOP, 8½ miles

(w. by S.) from Bridgenorth, containing, with Ashfield, 40 inhabitants.

RUTLANDSHIRE, an inland county, bounded on the north - west and south-west by Leicestershire, on the south and south-east by Northamptonshire, and on the east and north-east by Lincolnshire. It extends from 51° 31′ 28″ to 51° 45′ 34″ (N. Lat.), and from 25′ to 48′ (W. Lon.) This is the smallest county in England, its extreme length being only eighteen miles, its greatest breadth fifteen miles, and its circumference fifty-eight miles, containing, according to Parkinson's Agricultural Survey, drawn up for the consideration of the Board of Agriculture, ninety-one thousand and two acres and twenty-nine perches, or about one hundred and forty-two square miles. The population, in 1821, was 18,487. This district, at the period of the Roman invasion, formed part of the territory of the Coritani; and, under the Roman dominion, was included in the division called *Flavia Cæsariensis:* on the complete establishment of the Saxon Octarchy, Rutlandshire was comprised in the kingdom of Mercia. For the name Rutland, in Saxon *Roteland*, no probable derivation has been assigned. In Domesday-book *Roteland* is spoken of as comprising the two wapentakes of Alstoe and Martinsley, which, according to the same record, belonged to the sheriffdom of Nottingham, so far as the king's tax was concerned. The rest of the county was, at that period, included in Northamptonshire. Rutland is first mentioned as a distinct county in the 5th of King John, at the coronation of whose queen, Isabel, it was amongst other lands, assigned in parliament for her dower. Owing to its inferior size, and its containing no important military post, few memorable events have occurred within its limits. In 1016, however, near Essendine, the invading Danes were repulsed by the inhabitants of Rutlandshire, and the men of Stamford, under the command of the baron of Essenden; but the Saxons, abandoning order in the pursuit, were finally routed. In 1311, at Burley, Henry Spencer, the warlike Bishop of Norwich, assembled the troops with which he afterwards defeated the Norfolk insurgents under John Letester, who had taken up arms at the time of the formidable insurrection headed by Wat Tyler. In 1470, on April 27th, an army of Lancastrians, consisting chiefly of Lincolnshire men, was defeated by Edward IV., at Horn, with a loss of thirteen thousand men, when their commander, Sir Thomas Wells, and Sir Thomas de Launde, were taken prisoners and shortly after beheaded: this engagement has been jocularly styled "the battle of Lose-coat field," from the fugitives having cast off their coats, in order to be less incumbered.

Rutlandshire lies within the diocese of Peterborough (excepting the parishes of Empringham, Ketton *cum* Tixover, and Liddington *cum* Caldecott, which are included in that of Lincoln), and in the province of Canterbury: it forms a deanery, in the archdeaconry of Northampton, and contains fifty parishes, of which thirty are rectories, thirteen vicarages, and the remainder perpetual curacies. For civil purposes it is divided into the four hundreds of Alstoe, East, Martinsley, and Wrandike, and the soke of Oakham. It contains the market towns of Oakham and Uppingham. Two knights are returned to parliament for the shire, and are elected

at Oakham. This county is included in the Midland circuit: the assizes and quarter sessions are held at Oakham, where is the county gaol; there are seven acting magistrates. The rates raised in the county for the year ending March 25th, 1827, amounted to £14,029. 7., the expenditure to £13,873. 14., of which £9,479. 18. was applied to the relief of the poor.

The general appearance of the county is of an interesting character, more especially where it has abundance of timber, being greatly diversified by gently rising hills, running in the direction of east and west, between which are vallies about half a mile in width, so that the prospects, which are always agreeable and lively, are also pleasingly varied. Some of the finest views may be obtained from Manton, which is the highest ground in the county; Beaumont Chase, Burley House, Rakesborough Hill, the village of Teigh, the Whissendine Hills, and Witchley common. The soils are for the most part fertile, but in their nature vary greatly, and sometimes abruptly. The eastern and south-eastern parts have in general a clay soil of shallow staple, resting upon limestone rock, with a small mixture of cold woodland; the rest of the county has a strong red loamy soil, amongst which ironstone is found; some of this is provincially termed *keal*: there are also some small tracts of rich clay, and others of a blueish clay. The substratum of the greater part of it is a very strong blue clay. The thin-stapled soils are well adapted for the production of turnips, barley, clover, wheat, and all other green crops, though they make but poor meadow land: abundant crops of grass are produced upon the red keal. Upwards of forty-two thousand five hundred acres are under tillage: the course of crops observed on the thin limestone soil is, first, turnips; second, barley; third, clover; fourth, wheat: on the other soils it is various. The crops commonly grown are, wheat, barley, oats, peas, beans, turnips, cabbages, tares, and lentils. The average crop of wheat is twenty-two bushels and three quarters per acre; that of barley thirty-two; the latter grain is here of a very superior quality. The average produce of oats per acre is forty-two bushels and a quarter; that of peas, twenty-four and three quarters; and that of beans, twenty-three and three quarters. The turnips are for the most part eaten on the land by sheep: the greater part of the tares is consumed as green food for horses in the stable: the lentils are greatly esteemed as winter food for sheep. The artificial grasses are clover, trefoil, ray-grass, and sainfoin. The quantity of grass land rather exceeds that under tillage, being almost forty-five thousand acres: the meadows are chiefly upland, the only tracts ever flooded being those on the margins of the rivers Welland, Guash, and Chater. In this case the waters of the two latter streams quickly subside; but the river Welland having very little fall, and the meadows in its vicinity being very flat, the water retires but slowly, frequently continuing so long upon the land, that the pasturage is rendered unwholesome, and produces the rot amongst sheep that are put upon it: the average produce of hay is from a ton to a ton and a half per acre. Much of what is called Stilton cheese is made in the district of Leafield Forest, and in the Vale of Catmose. About one half of the grass land is good feeding land; the rest is of an inferior quality, and is used to feed store cattle:

in general the ground is healthy for sheep and cattle, and the management of the grazing lands is considered to be well understood. The cattle reared are of no particular breed, and in general of rather an inferior kind; many of the calves are sold fat to the butcher; the dairies are few, grazing being the chief object. The cattle most in request are the Irish and small Scotch, which, after one summer's grass, are in general sent to the London market. Some long-horned and a few short-horned heifers of the Durham breed are brought in at two years old, and when three years old, are sold out to jobbers, who take them to the dairy counties, or to London. Some of the cattle grazed here obtained are from Wales, and others from Lancashire. The sheep are nearly all of the polled, long-woolled kind, and in the open fields of a very poor sort, little care being taken of them; in the enclosures, however, they are better attended to, but are for the most part very inferior, being small in size and light in flesh: their wool also is light, short, and mossy. The breeds are the Old and the New Leicester; but in that part of the county bordering on Lincolnshire, the breed of that county, with a cross of the New Leicester, prevails. The horses are of an inferior kind, being strong, but very ill shaped. The county contains several very large orchards. There are nearly three thousand acres of native wood and of plantations, containing very little oak timber: the coppice wood is felled at from ten to fifteen years' growth. The woodlands were formerly much more extensive, the forest of Leafield, or Lyfield, having once occupied the greater part of the soke of Oakham; and Beaumont Chase, forming a part of the same forest, having extended over much of Martinsley hundred: several townships in its vicinity, as well as those within its limits, still claim certain forest rights; and the whole tract is now a particularly rich and beautiful scene of woodland and high cultivation. The forestership of Leafield, together with the property of the manor of Leigh, from which it is supposed to take its name, became vested, in the reign of James I., by purchase, in the family of Noel, and are now possessed by its present representative, Sir Gerard Noel, Bart. Limestone of two kinds, softer and harder, is obtained in many parts of the county; and at Ketton, an excellent stone for building is procured. Coal is brought by the Milton canal to Oakham, and forms the chief fuel of the county, but is mostly used in conjunction with wood, while in some few parishes wood is still the principal article of fuel.

The river Welland forms the south-eastern boundary of the county, separating it from Northamptonshire: the small river Eye, which rises in Leicestershire, and takes a south-easterly course to the Welland, is its south-western boundary for some miles in the latter part of its course. The two principal streams which run through it are the Guash, or Wash, and the Chater, both which have their sources beyond its western boundary, in Leicestershire, and take an easterly course to the Welland. The Melton-Mowbray canal, from the river Soar to Melton-Mowbray, was extended to Oakham, in the centre of the county, by virtue of an act of parliament obtained in the year 1793. This is the only line of navigation that Rutlandshire possesses: from Leicestershire it enters it near Teigh, and proceeds by Market-Overton, Barrow, Cottesmore, and Burley, to

the northern side of Oakham, in the level of the vale of Catmose: that part of its course contained within its limits is about six miles and a half in length, and on one level: it has a reservoir for its supply with water, near Langham, in this county: the expense of the whole was £86,000: the principal articles of traffic upon it are coal, timber, and agricultural produce. The great north road from London to Edinburgh passes through the easternmost portion of the county, which it enters a little to the north of Stamford. The Leeds mail-road enters the county from Kettering in Northamptonshire, and passes through Uppingham and Oakham to Melton-Mowbray in Leicestershire.

At Great Casterton was a Roman station, but antiquaries disagree concerning its name. The castle, church, county-hall, and hospital, of Oakham, present some interesting relics of antiquity. There were not more than four or five religious houses and hospitals in the county. Of ancient church architecture, the chancel of Tickencote church is a fine specimen of the early Norman: the following are also worthy of notice, viz., Essendine church, more particularly its southern doorway; that of Exton, considered the handsomest in the county; that of Ketton, which is remarkable for its fine lofty spire; and those of Empingham, Stretton, and Tinwell: there are some ancient and handsome monuments in the churches of Ashwell, Drystoke, and Exton. Liddington hospital, originally a palace of the Bishops of Lincoln, and Preston manor-house, are also remarkable for their antiquity. Among the seats of the nobility and gentry, Burley, that of the Earl of Winchilsea and Nottingham, is the most distinguished. Chalybeate springs are numerous in almost every part of the county; but the strongest, which has long been noted, and some years ago was much resorted to, is situated between Teigh and Market-Overton. Numerous marine exuviæ are found in the limestone. Rutland gives the titles of duke and earl to the family of Manners.

RUYTON in the ELEVEN TOWNS, a parish in the hundred of OSWESTRY, county of SALOP, 10½ miles (N. W.) from Shrewsbury, containing 862 inhabitants. The living is a discharged vicarage, in the archdeaconry of Salop, and diocese of Lichfield and Coventry, rated in the king's books at £5. 18., and in the patronage of the Crown. The church is dedicated to St. John the Baptist. The river Perry runs on the eastern side of the parish.

RYALL, a chapelry in the parish of STAMFORD-HAM, north-eastern division of TINDALE ward, county of NORTHUMBERLAND, 9½ miles (N. E.) from Hexham, containing 118 inhabitants. The chapel, an ancient structure, has undergone frequent repairs.

RYALL, a parish in the hundred of EAST, county of RUTLAND, 2½ miles (N. by E.) from Stamford, containing, with the hamlet of Belmisthorp, 439 inhabitants. The living is a discharged vicarage, with the perpetual curacy of Essendine, in the archdeaconry of Northampton, and diocese of Peterborough, rated in the king's books at £13. 17., and in the patronage of the Marquis of Exeter. The church is dedicated to St. John the Evangelist.

RYARSH, a parish in the hundred of LARKFIELD, lathe of AYLESFORD, county of KENT, 6¾ miles (N. W. by W.) from Maidstone, containing 359 inhabitants.

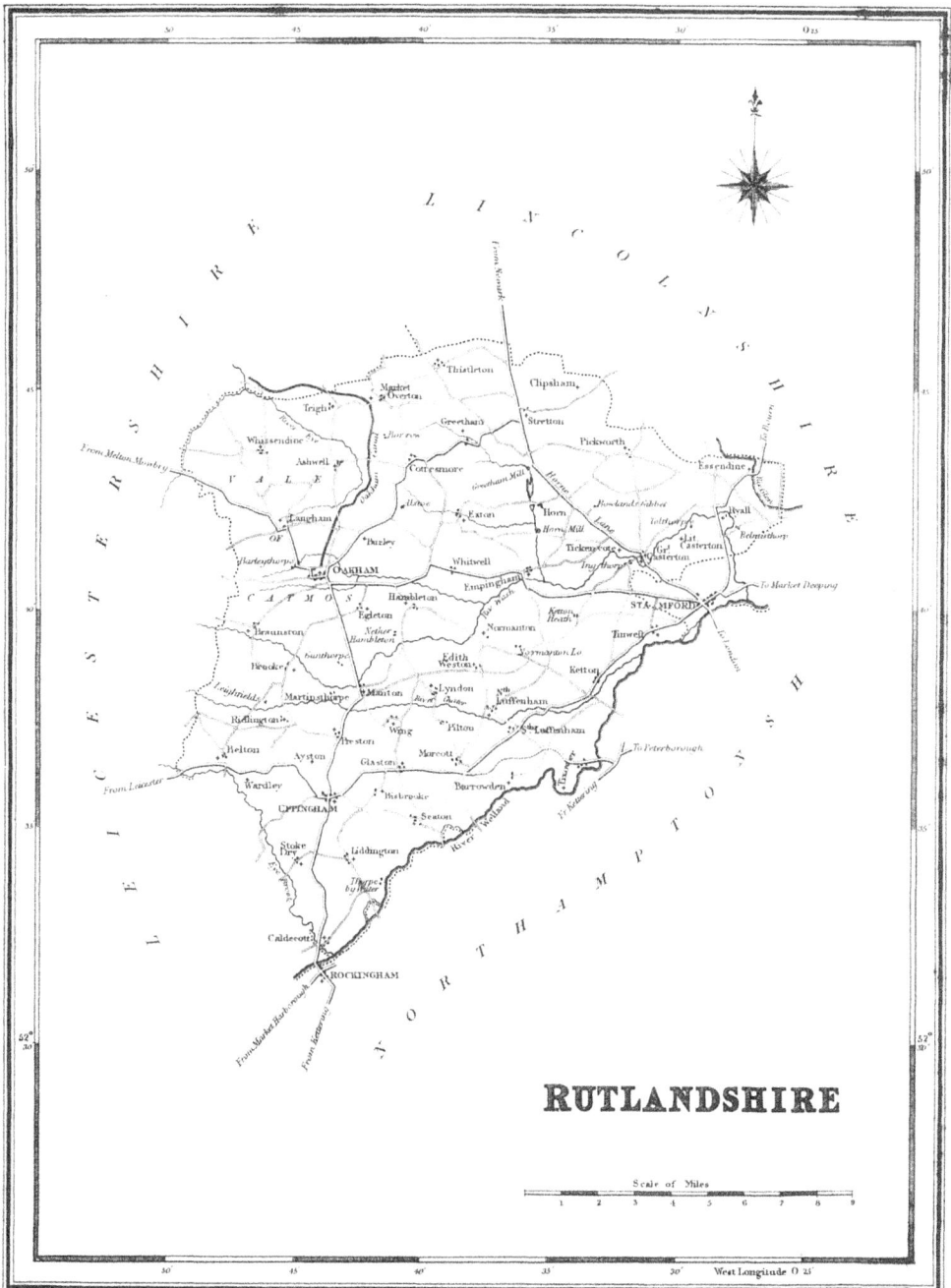

RUTLANDSHIRE

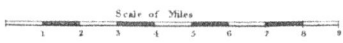

L I N C O L N S H I R E

L E I C E S T E R S H I R E

N O R T H A M P T O N S H I R E

Thistleton
Clipsham
Market Overton
Greetham
Stretton
Pickworth
Essendine
Trigh
Whissendine
Ashwell
Cottesmore
Ryall
Langham
Hove
Eaton
Horn
Gt. Casterton
Lit. Casterton
Barley
Tickencote
OAKHAM
Whitwell
Empingham
STAMFORD
CATMOS
Hambleton
Egleton
Normanton
Ketton Heath
Tinwell
Braunston
Nether Hambleton
Edith Weston
Normanton Lo.
Ketton
Brooke
Martinsthorpe
Manton
Lyndon
Luffenham
Redington
Preston
Wing
Pilton
North Luffenham
Belton
Ayston
Glaston
Morcott
Wardley
Bisbrooke
Barrowden
UPPINGHAM
Seaton
Stoke Dry
Liddington
Thorpe by Water
Caldecott
ROCKINGHAM

VALE

From Melton Mowbray
From Leicester
From Market Harborough
From Kettering
To Peterborough
To Market Deeping

Scale of Miles

1 2 3 4 5 6 7 8 9

Drawn by R. Creighton.

DRAWN AND ENGRAVED FOR LEWIS' TOPOGRAPHICAL DICTIONARY.

Engraved by J. & C. Walker

The living is a discharged vicarage, in the archdeaconry and diocese of Rochester, rated in the king's books at £8. 10., and in the patronage of the Crown. The church is dedicated to St. Martin.

RYBURGH (GREAT), a parish in the hundred of GALLOW, county of NORFOLK, 4 miles (S. E. by E.) from Fakenham, containing 525 inhabitants. The living is a discharged rectory, with the vicarage of Little Ryburgh, in the archdeaconry of Norfolk, and diocese of Norwich, rated in the king's books at £14. 16. 10¼. S. Clayton, Esq. was patron in 1820. The church, dedicated to St. Andrew, contains an altar-tomb, with several armorial bearings, but no inscription.

RYBURGH (LITTLE), a parish in the hundred of GALLOW, county of NORFOLK, 3¾ miles (E. S. E.) from Fakenham, containing 111 inhabitants. The living is a discharged vicarage, united to the rectory of Great Ryburgh, in the archdeaconry of Norfolk, and diocese of Norwich, rated in the king's books at £7. 13. 4., endowed with £200 private benefaction, and £400 royal bounty. The church is dedicated to All Saints.

RYCOTE, a chapelry in the parish of GREAT HASELEY, hundred of EWELME, county of OXFORD, 2½ miles (W. by S.) from Thame. The population is returned with the parish. The chapel is dedicated to St. Michael and All Angels.

RYDAL, a chapelry and joint township with Loughrigg, in the parish of GRASMERE, KENDAL ward, county of WESTMORLAND, 1½ mile (N. W.) from Ambleside, containing, with Loughrigg, 299 inhabitants. The living is a perpetual curacy, in the archdeaconry of Richmond, and diocese of Chester, endowed by Lady le Fleming with land and money, and with £1000 royal bounty, and in the patronage of Lady le Fleming, who, at the expense of £1500, erected the chapel, which is a small but handsome edifice, with an octagonal spire, consecrated in 1825, and dedicated to the Virgin Mary. Day and Sunday schools are supported by her ladyship, for the instruction of the poor children of the township. Rydal water, which winds through the valley for nearly a mile, and in its course forms two beautiful cascades, is surrounded by fine romantic scenery of wood and mountain, and is remarkable for the beauty of its small circular islands. Rydal Hall, the seat of the Le Flemings, was plundered in the great civil war by Sir Wilfrid Lawson, one of Cromwell's partisans.

RYDE, a market town and chapelry in the parish of NEWCHURCH, liberty of EAST MEDINA, Isle of Wight division of the county of SOUTHAMPTON, 6¼ miles (E. N. E.) from Newport, and 77 (S. W.) from London. The population is returned with the parish. This place, anciently denominated La Rye, was at that period a post for sentinels who guarded this part of the island, and in the reign of Richard II. was burnt and laid waste by the French. It is situated on the shores of the Solent, opposite to Stokes bay, and commands a fine view of Spithead and the Motherbank, with a more distant prospect of Haslar hospital and the town of Portsmouth; from an insignificant fishing hamlet it has, within the last thirty years, assumed the appearance of a neat, improving, and populous town; the original distinction into Upper and Lower Ryde is still preserved, but they are now united, the former comprising the more elevated buildings, the latter those near the sea-shore. The town consists chiefly of three streets, the

VOL. III.

principal of which is spacious and well paved; the houses are irregularly built, and are in general either in clusters or detached marine cottages; several handsome lodging-houses have been recently erected, and near the chapel is a fine range of well-built houses, called the Terrace: the facility and accommodation for sea-bathing, and the delightful walks and rides in its vicinity, the constant communication with Portsmouth by means of steamboats, and the rapid increase of residences on its eastern and western sides, afford every indication of its increase and prosperity. Assembly-rooms, libraries, and a small theatre, erected by the late Mr. Thornton, which is open during the season, add to its attractions. A fine pier, erected under the provisions of an act granted in 1814, at the expense of £12,000, is an object of general admiration: the entrance is through an arched gateway to a fine promenade one thousand seven hundred and forty feet in length, and from twelve to twenty feet in width, which is protected on each side by a neat iron railing; the admission to it is by periodical subscriptions, or a demand of twopence is made upon the visitors each time they enter the gateway, to which a neat porter's lodge is annexed: certain regulations have been established to secure the convenience of passengers, and all impositions are punishable by a fine to be levied by the acting magistrate for this division. The herring fishery affords employment to several persons. The markets are on Tuesday and Friday; and there is an annual fair on the 5th of July, for pedlary. Constables and other officers are chosen annually at a court leet for the manor, held at Ashey farm, and designated Ashey Court. The chapel, dedicated to St. Thomas, was originally built, in 1719, by Thomas Player, Esq.; a new one, erected in 1827, by George Player, Esq., is a neat edifice in the ancient style of English architecture, with a lofty tower and spire. A little to the westward is an episcopal chapel, erected in the same year, and licensed by the Bishop of Winchester: it is of modern architecture, and surmounted by a small cupola. There are places of worship for Independents and Wesleyan Methodists. A free school, recently erected by subscription among the inhabitants, is supported by voluntary contributions.

RYE, a joint tything with Stapeley, in the parish and hundred of ODIHAM, Basingstoke division of the county of SOUTHAMPTON, 2¼ miles (E. by S.) from Odiham, with which the population is returned.

RYE, a cinque-port, borough, market town, and parish, having separate jurisdiction, locally in the hundred of Gostrow, rape of HASTINGS, county of SUSSEX, 76 miles (E. by N.) from Chichester, and 63 (S. E. by E.) from London, containing 3599 inhabitants. This place belonged originally to the monastery of Feschamp in Normandy,

Arms.

from which it was separated, and, together with Winchelsea, annexed to the cinque-ports of England in the reign of Henry III., in all the charters granted to which, these towns are invariably styled "ancient towns." In the reign of Edward III., Rye was sur-

4 O

rounded by a strong wall defended by several towers, erected by William of Ypres, Earl of Kent, the only one now remaining being called Ypres' tower. An inundation of the sea having formed a natural harbour, which was subsequently much improved by a similar recurrence, the town began to flourish, and soon became so considerable a port, that it furnished nine ships of war towards the invasion of France in the reign of Edward III., and was the place at which that monarch landed on his return from the conquest of that country. In the following reign it was burnt and plundered by the French, and from that calamity and others which it subsequently experienced it suffered so much, that in 1464, Henry VI., to indemnify the corporation for their losses, annexed to it Tenterden, which he separated from the county of Kent. From this time the town began to revive, and in the reign of Elizabeth it was a place of considerable importance; it has since been invested with several additional privileges, and a confirmation of all preceding charters. The town occupies the declivity of a hill, on a peninsula bounded on the south and west by the sea, and on the east by the river Rother, and consists of several regular and well-formed streets: the houses are in general well built of brick, but mostly old-fashioned, and command fine views of the channel, and the surrounding country, which abounds with interesting scenery: the town is well paved, lighted, and supplied with water by pipes from a reservoir under Playden heights, and there are a public subscription library and a small theatre. It is in contemplation to make a road to the sea-side along the banks of the harbour, and to drain the marshes in the neighbourhood of the town, which improvement, combined with the natural advantages of its situation, will contribute greatly to its eligibility as a watering-place. The harbour, which flows up to the town, receives the rivers Rother, Tillingham, and Brede, and under proper management might be rendered safe for vessels of any burden; and the rivers, in their course through the interior of the country, afford valuable commercial advantages. The old harbour having been choked up with sand, a large canal was cut to communicate with the sea, and vessels of two hundred tons' burden can now come up to the quay. On the north side of the town, about a mile from the original entrance, a great improvement was effected by throwing across the old channel a dam of peculiar construction, the invention of the Rev. Daniel Pope; but the harbour is still incomplete, and the water rises to such a height at spring tides, as materially to annoy the inhabitants. The trade is principally in hops, corn, coal, bark, wool, and timber, and several sloops are constantly employed in conveying chalk from the cliffs at Eastbourne, for the purpose of being burnt into lime. The herring and mackarel fisheries are carried on to a considerable extent, and the fish, which are sent to the London market, are in great estimation; flat fish are also taken in abundance. This port comprises within its jurisdiction the port of Hastings, and there are seventy-one vessels, averaging a burden of fifty-eight tons, belonging to it. The market days are Wednesday and Saturday, the former for corn, of which there is a good supply, and the latter for provisions of all kinds; there is also a large cattle market every alternate Wednesday: the fairs are on Whit-Monday and August 10th.

Corporate Seal.

Obverse.   Reverse.

The borough has received a succession of charters: the earliest that can be traced is that of Richard I., which recites and confirms some previous privileges, that have been further ratified and extended in successive reigns to that of Charles II. The government is vested in a mayor, twelve jurats, and an indefinite number of freemen. The mayor is chosen annually from the jurats by a majority of the freemen, and the jurats are nominated by the mayor immediately after he has been sworn into office: the freedom is inherited by the eldest son of a freeman, or acquired by election of the corporation, and by nomination of the mayor, who has the privilege of appointing one freeman during his mayoralty. The mayor and jurats are justices of the peace, and hold regularly courts of session and general gaol delivery for all offences not capital; and, every alternate Wednesday, a court of record, for the recovery of debts to any amount. The town hall is a convenient building in the centre of the town, in which the sessions and other courts for the borough are held, and the public business of the corporation is transacted; the area underneath it is appropriated to the use of the market. Ypres' tower is now the borough gaol, a small building comprising two wards, and adapted to the reception of about twelve prisoners. The borough has exercised the elective franchise from the earliest period of parliamentary representation, and has regularly returned two barons to parliament, as well as canopy bearers, to assist in supporting the royal canopy at coronations—two to each canopy. The right of election is vested in the mayor, jurats, and freemen, of whom the number qualified to vote is nearly fifty, and will probably be much increased: the mayor is the returning officer.

The living is a discharged vicarage, in the archdeaconry of Lewes, and diocese of Chichester, rated in the king's books at £42. 13. 4., and in the patronage of Lord G. H. Cavendish. The church, dedicated to St. Mary, is a spacious and ancient cruciform structure, partly in the Norman, and partly in the early, style of English architecture, with a central tower, in which is a clock of peculiar mechanical construction: the interior is lofty, and lighted with windows, of which many are of modern insertion; the aisles of the chancel have narrow lancet-shaped windows, and in several parts are some portions in that style; the east window, in the later English style, is of large dimensions and elegant design. There are places of worship for Baptists, Independents, and Wesleyan Methodists. A school was founded, in 1644, by Mr. Thomas Pecock, who endowed it with a rent-charge of £32, the interest of £50, and a school-house, which is still remaining in the principal street; and in 1702, another school was founded by Mr. James Saunders, who endowed it with estates producing £116 per annum; these schools, according to a decree of the court of Chancery, in 1818, are to be both conducted under one master in the school-house built by Mr. Pecock; seventy boys upon the latter foundation, and fifty on the former, who are nominated by the corporation, will be instructed in reading, writing, arithmetic, the mathematics, and navigation, as soon as the funds are released from the expenses of the Chancery suit, with the payment of which they are at present charged. A monastery of friars of the order of St. Augustine was founded near the town, prior to the reign of Edward III., of which the principal remains have been converted into a store-house. An arched gateway, leading into the town from the London road, is in tolerable preservation; and some portions of the ancient walls are also remaining.

RYE-HILL, a township in the parish of ROTHBURY, western division of COQUETDALE ward, county of NORTHUMBERLAND, 3 miles (W.) from Rothbury, containing 49 inhabitants.

RYHILL, a hamlet in the parish of EPPING, hundred of WALTHAM, though locally in the hundred of Harlow, county of ESSEX, 2¾ miles (N. by W.) from Epping. The population is returned with the chapelry of Epping-Upland.

RYHILL, a joint township with Camerton, in the parish of BURSTWICK, southern division of the wapentake of HOLDERNESS, East riding of the county of YORK, 3 miles (S. E. by E.) from Hedon, containing, with Camerton, 315 inhabitants. There is a place of worship for Wesleyan Methodists.

RYHILL, a township in that part of the parish of WRAGBY which is in the wapentake of STAINCROSS, West riding of the county of YORK, 7 miles (S. E.) from Wakefield, containing 147 inhabitants.

RYHOPE, a township in the parish of BISHOP-WEARMOUTH, northern division of EASINGTON ward, county palatine of DURHAM, 3 miles (S.) from Sunderland, containing 368 inhabitants. A chapel of ease was erected in 1826. Ryhope bay has a smooth sandy beach convenient for bathing; and the village, which is a considerable place, containing some good inns, affords excellent accommodation for those who frequent it for that purpose.

RYLE (GREAT), a township in the parish of WHITTINGHAM, northern division of COQUETDALE ward, county of NORTHUMBERLAND, 9 miles (N. N. W.) from Rothbury, containing 99 inhabitants.

RYLE (LITTLE), a township in the parish of WHITTINGHAM, northern division of COQUETDALE ward, county of NORTHUMBERLAND, 8½ miles (W. by S.) from Alnwick, containing 48 inhabitants.

RYME-INTRINSICA, a parish and liberty in the Sherborne division of the county of DORSET, 6¼ miles (S. W.) from Sherborne, containing 159 inhabitants. The living is a discharged rectory, united with the vicarage of Hermitage, in the peculiar jurisdiction of the Dean of Salisbury, rated in the king's books at £6. 5. 8. The church is dedicated to St. Hyppolite. A market and fair were granted to be held here in the 26th of Edward I., both which have been long disused. Within this liberty there was anciently a royal mansion and park; the site of the former, which was standing in the reign of James I.,

is still called Court Hill, and commands a fine view over the park, of which the boundary or terrace is yet distinguishable, being called the Keeper's walk. It borders upon Somersetshire, and was termed White Hart Forest, from a white deer, celebrated for its size and beauty, chased in it by Henry III. Buckshead, Bucksland, Buckshaw, Stagford, and several other places in the neighbourhood, derive their names from this deer, which was hunted and slain, contrary to the king's command, by Thomas de Linde and other gentlemen of Dorset, whose lands for this were laid under a pecuniary mulct, paid into the Exchequer by the name of White Hart Silver.

RYSTON, a parish in the hundred of CLACKCLOSE, county of NORFOLK, 1¾ mile (S. S. E.) from Downham-Market, containing 25 inhabitants. The living is a perpetual curacy, with that of Roxham, in the archdeaconry of Norfolk, and diocese of Norwich, endowed with £800 royal bounty, and in the patronage of the Dean and Chapter of Norwich. The church is dedicated to St. Michael.

RYTHER, a parish partly in the upper, but chiefly in the lower, division of the wapentake of BARKSTONE-ASH, West riding of the county of YORK, 6¼ miles (N. W. by N.) from Selby, containing, with the townships of Lead-Hall and Ozendike, 385 inhabitants. The living is a rectory, in the archdeaconry and diocese of York, rated in the king's books at £6. 11. 10½., and in the patronage of the Crown. The church is dedicated to All Saints.

RYTON, a parish in the western division of CHESTER ward, county palatine of DURHAM, comprising the townships of Chopwell, Crawcrook, Ryton, Ryton-Woodside, Stella, and Winlaton, and containing 5763 inhabitants, of which number, 445 are in the township of Ryton, 8¾ miles (W. by N.) from Gateshead. The living is a rectory, in the archdeaconry and diocese of Durham, rated in the king's books at £42. 10. 10., and in the patronage of the Bishop of Durham. The church, dedicated to the Holy Cross, is principally in the early style of English architecture, with a tower surmounted by a lofty spire; in the chancel are some ancient oaken stalls and screen-work, carved in open tracery. Near the northern wall of the churchyard is a large barrow planted with trees, which does not appear to have been opened; but in a similar one at Bradley Hall the remains of a human body were discovered a few years ago. There are two places of worship for Methodists. This parish, which is bounded on the north by the Tyne, and on the east and south by the river Derwent, contains some very extensive works for the preparation of iron and steel, coal and ironstone being obtained here in abundance: there are also quarries of limestone. The village is well built, and in the neighbourhood are many neat villas. The petty sessions for the division are held here on the first Monday in every month; and a statute fair for hiring servants takes place twice a year, in May and November. Ryton savings bank was the first established in England. The school, built in 1791, is supported by subscriptions, and an endowment of £5 per annum by Lord Crewe's trustees. Ryton has frequently suffered from the incursions of the Scots, particularly in 1297, when the village was reduced to ashes by Wallace, who at that time occupied Hexham.

Here is a spring, the water of which is impregnated with sulphur.

RYTON, a parish in the Shiffnall division of the hundred of BRIMSTREE, county of SALOP, 4 miles (S. by E.) from Shiffnall, containing 131 inhabitants. The living is a rectory, in the archdeaconry of Salop, and diocese of Lichfield and Coventry, rated in the king's books at £5. 12. 1., and in the patronage of G. Molineux, Esq. This place had anciently a weekly market, and an annual fair for four days, both which have been long disused. Ryton gave the title of baron to John, second son of Sir William Craven, Knt., and brother to William, Earl of Craven, but it is now extinct.

RYTON, a hamlet in the parish of BULKINGTON, Kirby division of the hundred of KNIGHTLOW, county of WARWICK, containing 345 inhabitants.

RYTON, a township in the parish of KIRKBY-MISPERTON, PICKERING lythe, North riding of the county of YORK, 3 miles (N. by E.) from New Malton, containing 212 inhabitants.

RYTON upon DUNSMOOR, a parish in the Rugby division of the hundred of KNIGHTLOW, county of WARWICK, 4½ miles (S. E.) from Coventry, containing 498 inhabitants. The living is a perpetual curacy, in the archdeaconry of Coventry, and diocese of Lichfield and Coventry, rated in the king's books at £11. 6. 8., endowed with £800 private benefaction, and £1400 parliamentary grant, and in the patronage of the Prebendary of Ryton in the Cathedral Church of Lichfield. The church, dedicated to St. Leonard, is partly in the early style of English architecture.

RYTON-WOODSIDE, a township in the parish of RYTON, western division of CHESTER ward, county palatine of DURHAM, 8¼ miles (W.) from Gateshead, containing 1057 inhabitants. Coal is obtained within the township.

THE END OF VOLUME III.

www.ingramcontent.com/pod-product-compliance
Lightning Source LLC
Chambersburg PA
CBHW072037020426
42334CB00017B/1298